THE UNION ARMY
1861-1865

☆ ☆ ☆ ☆

Organization And Operations

VOLUME I: THE EASTERN THEATER

THE UNION ARMY

1861-1865

★★★★

Organization and Operations

VOLUME I: THE EASTERN THEATER

By Frank J. Welcher

INDIANA UNIVERSITY PRESS

BLOOMINGTON AND INDIANAPOLIS

Manufactured in the United States of America

Library of Congress Cataloging-in-Publication Data
Welcher, Frank Johnson
The Union Army, 1861–1865 : organizations and operations / by Frank J. Welcher.
p. cm.
Contents: v. 1. The Eastern theater.
ISBN 0–253–36453–1 (v. 1)
1. United States. Army—History—Civil War, 1861–1865.
2. United States. Army—Organization—History—19th century.
3. United States—History—Civil War, 1861–1865—Campaigns. I. Title.
E491.W43 1989
973.7'41—dc19   88–45749
CIP

2 3 4 5 6 04 03 02 01 00 99

For
Helen Beasley Welcher
with love and respect

VOLUME I: THE EASTERN THEATER

CONTENTS

☆☆☆☆

FIELD ARMIES

ARMY CORPS

MISCELLANEOUS ORGANIZATIONS

BATTLES AND CAMPAIGNS

x CONTENTS

ACKNOWLEDGMENTS

During the years this book has been in preparation, many people have contributed in one way or another to its completion. To all of these I am very grateful. To one group, I am especially indebted. On my numerous trips to the battlefields of the war, many people have served as guides, provided me with information, or otherwise aided me in locating points of interest or significance in the study of battles and campaigns. Those who have been particularly helpful are Darrell K. Young at Perryville, Kentucky; Chris Calkins at Petersburg, Virginia; Paul Branch, Jr., at Fort Macon and New Berne, North Carolina; Edward Tinney at Chickamauga, Georgia and Chattanooga, Tennessee; and Mr. and Mrs. Michael K. Smith at Droop Mountain, West Virginia. In addition, there are many local people whom I sought out or encountered by chance who have offered welcome information about events of the war that took place in their communities. Major General Richard D. Chegar, Brigadier General Thomas P. Jones, and Claude R. Johnson accompanied me on visits to many battlefields, and contributed materially to my understanding of battles and the problems of command and leadership.

There is one person particularly whom I would like to recognize because of his influence on my interest in the Civil War, and therefore his indirect contribution to the preparation of this book: Edwin C. Bearss, National Park Service Chief Historian at Washington, D.C. His clear and detailed explanations of events on many battlefields of the Civil War, his incredible knowledge of battles and campaigns, and his great enthusiasm for Civil War military history have greatly influenced my decision to write this book.

Others too have helped in many ways. At Indiana University-Purdue University at Indianapolis, Barbara K. Fischler, Director of University Libraries, and William F. Mayles, Science, Engineering, and Technology Librarian, have offered all possible assistance in securing requested information, and have made available all library facilities. Much of my work has been done at the university, and Robert N. Keck, Acting Dean of the School of Science, kindly arranged for my use of their facilities and strongly encouraged me to avail myself of them. Elizabeth Ileana Hogan of the School of Liberal Arts read the manuscript for the book and made many helpful suggestions for improving its quality. Thanks are also due to Katy Kroupa for typing a part of the manuscript.

I also wish to thank my son, Robert B. Welcher, who devoted much time to setting up and instructing me in the use of the computer, and for his continued interest and advice in preparing a better manuscript. In addition, I have appreciated his constant encouragement as the work has progressed.

Above all others, I am indebted to my wife Helen for her strong support through all the years that I have been preoccupied with writing. During that time, she has aided me in almost every phase of my undertaking. She has been a patient and helpful companion on numerous visits to battlefields throughout the South; she has read parts of the manuscript and offered many suggestions for its improvement; she has been a constant advisor, and I have made few major decisions without her counsel and approval; and she has assumed numerous responsibilities that normally would have been mine so that I would have more time for writing. Above all, she has been patient, tolerant, and strongly supportive of my work, and for all of this I am deeply grateful.

INTRODUCTION

The Civil War had scarcely ended when numerous publications began to appear relating to almost all aspects of the war. Since that time there has been a constant flow of new volumes and the reissue of earlier works, until today the literature on the war includes thousands of publications. These include many general histories covering the entire war; detailed descriptions of campaigns, battles, and expeditions; histories of armies, army corps, divisions, brigades, and regiments; biographies and autobiographies of numerous generals, the presidents of the United States and of the Confederacy, cabinet members, and other important personages; diaries, letters, and personal reminiscences of the common soldier; causes of the war; Reconstruction; and many, many other subjects.

Despite this vast literature, no single volume, or set of volumes, has been written that has been devoted in its entirety to a detailed description of the organization and operation of all Union armies that were in existence during the war, and to the many military divisions and geographical departments that were created for administrative purposes during the same period. It is true that much information of this type is to be found in the *The War of the Rebellion: A Compilation of the Official Records of the Union and Confederate Armies*, but it is usually deeply buried in the pages of the 128 volumes of this monumental work. Consequently, the process of locating specific information is often difficult and time-consuming.

Throughout the war, there were frequent reorganizations in the various armies and in the military departments, with the result that the roster for a particular organization on a given date might well be quite different for the same organization at a later time. Also, for many reasons, there were changes in the commanders of the armies, army corps, divisions, and brigades. These resulted from casual-

ties in battle, sickness, leaves of absence, transfer to other commands, incompetence, muster out, problems of seniority, and assignment to special services. These reorganizations and changes in commanders frequently make it difficult to trace the history of the divisions and brigades of an army when they are listed only periodically in the literature, as in the orders of battle that are commonly given only for the major battles of the war.

Most of the writings from which we derive information on the organization and command of the armies during the war have been largely episodic. This is simply because most of these sources are histories of the major battles of the war, and these occurred generally only at rather infrequent intervals. As a result, we are left with comparatively little detailed information about affairs in the army during the periods of inactivity, and this has resulted generally in the lack of ready material for the professional historian and general reader alike to obtain a continuous history of the armies, army corps, and departments of the army during the periods of their existence. Thus, for example, the many excellent accounts of the battles of Fredericksburg, fought in mid-December 1862, and Chancellorsville, in early May 1863, give very detailed information about the organization and command of the Army of the Potomac at the time of the battles; but generally there is only limited readily available detailed information about the changes in organization and command of the army during the period from December 1862 to May 1863. The problem of finding such information, moreover, is even greater when studying the less well-known campaigns and battles, and this is especially true for those periods of relative inactivity in the army. Thus, for example, some time is required for the Civil War historian to obtain detailed information about the organization, positions, and commanders of the troops of the Army of the Potomac while in the trenches at Petersburg, or in the Army of the James while it was more or less idle in the defenses at Bermuda Hundred.

There is also another type of problem that arises from the frequent transfer of troops and officers from one theater of the war or from one command to another. For example, if we study the operations of the Army of the James near Richmond, Virginia at the end of December 1864, we find that Alfred H. Terry was in command of Twenty-Fourth Corps, Army of the James. Later, however, if we become interested in the operations in North Carolina during the closing days of the war in the East, we find that Terry was in command of Tenth Corps, Department of North Carolina, and that this corps was present with William T. Sherman's Army of the Military Division of the Mississippi at the time of the surrender of Joseph E. Johnston's army in April 1865. Again, some search might be required to determine what had happened in the meantime that resulted in the transfer of Terry, and also troops of the Army of the James, to North Carolina, and the details of their transfer to Tenth Corps.

It was problems such as those mentioned above that prompted me, some fifteen years ago, to undertake a detailed study of the organization, command, and operations of all Union armies that were organized during the Civil War, and this has led to the present work, *The Union Army, 1861–1865: Organization and Operations*. From the outset, this work was planned as a special kind of history, and it is different in content from any other book that has been written on the subject. Its single aim has been to give in detail a complete and continuous account of the organization of all Union military divisions, departments, armies, army corps, divisions, and brigades, and the numerous special commands that were in existence during the war. The descriptions include such information as the date of creation and the composition of each army, army corps, division, and brigade, all changes in organization, commanders, and dates when each was discontinued. Also described are all military departments of the army, including for each the dates created and discontinued, geographical boundaries, changes in the boundaries, districts in each department, organization of the troops in each department, military operations within each department, and the commanders of each department.

As the work on the manuscript progressed, the magnitude of the undertaking became apparent, and it was clearly recognized that, because of limitations of space and time, there must be some restrictions on exactly what types of information were to be included. As a general working rule, therefore, in the sections on organization, only the basic facts relating to how the armies were organized into corps, divisions, and brigades, and the names of the commanders of these units, particularly during the active campaigns, battles, and expeditions, are included. Not included, for example, are such subjects as the legal and political aspects of organization; recruitment; the draft; equipment, supply, and training of troops; and the many other aspects of creating and maintaining an army.

In the sections on the operations of the Union armies during the war, all campaigns, all major battles, and all significant engagements, expeditions, raids, and reconnaissances have been included, but the descriptions are generally quite different from the usual complete accounts found in most Civil War literature. In the accounts of the operations given in this volume, largely because of limitations of space, the details are mostly confined to simple descriptions of, as nearly as can be determined, exactly what happened at a given time and place. The activities of each division, brigade, and regiment during the periods of combat are generally not minutely detailed, and usually the description of the part played by each unit is confined to noting its position, or positions, on the battlefield, when and where it attacked, or was attacked, and the outcome of the action. For the most part, the activities of the regiments are not included except in some of the lesser engagements.

As a rule, there is only a brief discussion of the political, economic, and broad military considerations that influenced the decisions of the administration and the generals as how best to employ the armies in resolving the issues of the Civil War, and there is no attempt to discuss in detail, or to evaluate the decisions on strategic and tactical matters, relating to each campaign, battle, or expedition. Nothing is included that describes the personal experiences of the common soldier in combat, nor is there any attempt to evaluate the quality of leadership of the officers commanding the armies, corps, divisions, and brigades.

In describing all major Union troop movements during the campaigns of the war, the itineraries of all major units are given, usually on a day-by-day basis, and when the troops were formed for offensive or defensive operations, the position of each corps, division, and brigade is given, if known. In addition, all changes in troop positions are described.

Numbers and losses in the armies are generally not given in this book. The values that appear in the literature often vary significantly, depending on the sources in which they are reported, and without a careful analysis of the existing data, the use of such information could result in serious inaccuracies. I simply have not had the time for a thorough study of the numbers and losses in the Union Army.

As the title of this book indicates, this is a history of the Union Army, and the emphasis throughout is centered on the description of its organization and operations. For this reason, there is little attempt to describe in detail the organization and operations of the Confederate armies. Generally, only sufficient information about enemy troop organizations, movements, and positions is given to provide for a better understanding of the operations of the Federal forces during the war.

No maps have been included in this book because the scope of the material covered extends to every theater of the war and covers the entire period from 1861 to 1865, and to have done so would have required another volume. Happily, this is not a serious problem because most books written on Civil War military history contain maps adequate for most purposes, and, in addition, there is the *Atlas* to accompany the *Official Records (The Official Military Atlas of the Civil War)*, which has been the principal source of the geographical information used by the author.

As with maps, the inclusion of a complete bibliography to accompany this history of the Union Army, covering, as it does, the entire war, would not be feasible because of the space that would be required. The reader is referred to the many bibliographies that have been published, generally to cover the different campaigns. Similarly, because of the extent of the information contained in the work, citation of the sources of all such information has not been attempted. The author's principal source of information used in preparing this history has been the *Official Records,* but numerous other primary and secondary sources have been consulted. Attempts have been made in most cases to verify information from the latter sources.

This book provides a continuous history of all the various units during the periods of their existence. The organization of the Union armies during the war was exceedingly complex, and because of this there is no practicable way that a complete description of a single unit, such as a brigade or division, could be given without interruption. Thus, the history of a brigade cannot be well understood unless it is included in the history of the division to which it belonged and, in turn, the corps to which the division belonged. The history of an army corps would be seriously impaired if it were interrupted frequently to describe in detail the part played by the corps, and consequently the divisions and brigades of the corps, in each campaign or battle in which it was involved. To eliminate such interruptions in the narrative, the method adopted in this work has been to present a continuous history of each corps, with emphasis on the activities of the corps during the periods between the major campaigns and battles, to indicate briefly the campaigns and battles in which it took part, and then to refer, by suitable cross-references, to other sections of the book where additional detailed information about each can be found.

My background for undertaking this work has been a life-long interest in the campaigns and battles of the Civil War. This interest had led to numerous visits to all the major battlefields of the war, and to those of almost all of the lesser engagements, even those as remote as Picacho Pass in Arizona, Valverde in New Mexico, Pea Ridge in Arkansas, Olustee in Florida, and Carthage and Boonville in Missouri. I not only have examined the areas where the battles were fought, but in addition have followed the roads traveled by the armies in all of the major campaigns of the war. This same interest has resulted in the accumulation of an extensive library on the military history of the Civil War, which has been my principal source of reading matter for many years.

THE UNION ARMY
1861-1865

☆☆☆☆

Organization And Operations

VOLUME I: THE EASTERN THEATER

COMMAND OF THE ARMIES
OF THE UNITED STATES

According to Article 2, Section 2 of the Constitution of the United States, the president of the United States is the commander in chief of the army and navy. The three presidents who were in office during the Civil War period, and therefore exercised this responsibility, were:

James Buchanan	March 4, 1857 to March 4, 1861
Abraham Lincoln	March 4, 1861 to April 15, 1865
Andrew Johnson	April 15, 1865 to March 4, 1869

THE WAR DEPARTMENT

The War Department was originally created by the Continental Congress February 7, 1781, to provide a continuity to the congressional administration of the army. Later, under the Constitution, Congress legislated for a War Department, but with the important difference that the secretary of war was made responsible to the president instead of to Congress. One important omission in this legislation, and one that was to cause difficulties in the administration of military affairs for a long time, was that it did not clearly define the respective functions of the secretary of war and the commander in chief of the army. During the Civil War the particular responsibilities of the secretary of war were the business management and maintenance of the armies through the Staff and War Department Bureaus.

The secretaries of war prior to and during the Civil War were as follows:

John B. Floyd	March 6, 1857 to December 29, 1860, resigned
Joseph B. Holt	December 31, 1860 to March 5, 1861
Simon Cameron	March 5, 1861 to January 14, 1862
Edwin M. Stanton	January 15, 1862 to May 28, 1868

A number of assistant secretaries of war also served during this period. These were:

Thomas A. Scott	August 3, 1861 to (not known)
Peter H. Watson	January 24, 1862 to January 21, 1863
	February 3, 1863 to July 31, 1864
John Tucker	January 29, 1862 to January 21, 1863
Christopher P. Wolcott	June 12, 1862 to January 23, 1863 (resigned, and died in January 1863)
Charles A. Dana	January 28, 1864 to July 31, 1865

At the time of his appointment Scott was vice-president of the Pennsylvania Railroad, and he later returned to the railroad, but the date of his resignation is not known. Wolcott, who replaced him, assumed his duties June 12, 1862.

Chiefs of Bureaus, or Staff Corps of the Army

During most of the war there were ten staff departments in Washington, collectively known as general staff departments. The heads of these general staff departments, however, functioned as heads of War Department bureaus and not as members of a general staff.

Adjutant General's Department. The adjutant general was an important figure in the control of military affairs. Among his duties were handling the correspondence of the secretary of war; receiving reports for the secretary of war and the keeping of records; conducting recruiting service under the secretary of war; handling the assignment of officers and other personnel matters; and issuing orders, including those of the president and the secretary of war. There were two adjutant generals who served during the Civil War period. These were:

Samuel Cooper	July 15, 1852 to March 1861
Lorenzo Thomas	March 7, 1861 to February 22, 1869

Thomas was absent on special duty inspecting the armies, military posts, and military operations from March 23, 1863 to the latter part of December 1863 (he left the Southwest for Washington December 17, 1863), and his duties in the office in Washington during his absence were performed by Edward O. Townsend. Thomas was on detached service again in 1865, and Townsend was once more left in charge of the office.

Inspector General's Department. The inquiries conducted by the Inspector General's Department included almost every aspect of military affairs. The inspectors general during the war were:

Sylvester Churchill	June 25, 1841 to September 25, 1861, retired
Randolph B. Marcy	September 25, 1861 to January 2, 1881

Judge-Advocate General's Department. The head of the Judge-Advocate General's Department was primarily concerned with matters relating to the proceedings of courts-martial, courts of inquiry, and military commissions. Those who served as judge-advocate general during the war were as follows:

John F. Lee	March 2, 1849 to September 3, 1862
Joseph Holt	September 3, 1862 to December 1, 1875

Ordnance Department. The duties of the chief of the Ordnance Department were the procurement, by purchase or manufacture, and the distribution of the necessary ordnance and ordnance stores for the army, and the establishment and maintenance of arsenals and depots for their manufacture and safekeeping. The chiefs of ordnance during the war were:

Henry K. Craig	July 10, 1851 to April 23, 1861, relieved
James W. Ripley	April 23, 1861 to September 15, 1863, retired
George D. Ramsay	September 15, 1863 to September 12, 1864, retired
Alexander B. Dyer	September 12, 1864 to May 20, 1874

Subsistence Department. The head of the Subsistence Department, the commissary general, was primarily concerned with the purchase and distribution of food supplies for the army. Those who served as commissary general during the war were:

George Gibson	April 18, 1818 to September 29, 1861, died
Joseph T. Taylor	September 29, 1861 to June 29, 1864, died
Amos B. Eaton	June 29, 1864 to May 1, 1874

Quartermaster's Department. The head of the Quartermaster's Department, the quartermaster general, was responsible for obtaining all supplies not provided by the Ordnance Department and the Subsistence Department. These included uniforms, equipment, tentage, barracks, horses, and fodder. This department also had charge of the transportation of all types of supplies by rail, water, and road. Three men served as quartermaster general during the war period. These were:

Joseph E. Johnston	June 20, 1860 to April 22, 1861, resigned
Ebenezer Sibley (acting)	April 22, 1861 to May 15, 1861
Montgomery C. Meigs	May 15, 1861 to February 6, 1882

Meigs was on inspection duty from August 1863 to January 1864, and Charles Thomas served as acting quartermaster general during this period.

Medical Department. The head of the Medical Department, the surgeon general, was charged with the duty of investigating the sanitary conditions of the army, and of making recommendations relating to their improvement. He was also responsible for caring for the sick and wounded and administering military hospitals. He also provided all medical and hospital supplies except those for animals. There were four men who served as surgeon general during the war. These were:

Thomas Lawson	November 30, 1836 to May 15, 1861, died
Clement A. Finley	May 15, 1861 to April 14, 1862, retired
William A. Hammond	April 14, 1862 to August 18, 1864, relieved
Joseph K. Barnes	August 18, 1864 to June 30, 1882

Hammond was on a tour of inspection from September 3, 1863 to August 18, 1864, and during this time Barnes was acting surgeon general.

Pay Department. The head of the Pay Department, the paymaster general, had charge of the supply and distribution of, and accounting for, funds for the payment of the army. Those who served as paymaster general during the war were:

Benjamin F. Larned	July 20, 1854 to July 15, 1862
Cary H. Fry (acting)	July 15, 1862 to December 10, 1862
Timothy P. Andrews	December 11, 1862 to November 29, 1864
Benjamin W. Brice	November 29, 1864 to January 1, 1872

Larned died September 6, 1862.

Corps of Engineers. The duties of the Corps of Engineers consisted of reconnoitering and surveying for military purposes; planning for defensive and offensive works in the field; and constructing and repairing military roads, railroads, and bridges. The title of the head of the Corps of Engineers was chief engineer until March 1863, and then was changed to chief of engineers. The officers holding these positions were:

Joseph G. Totten *(Chief Engineer)*	December 7, 1838 to March 3, 1863
Joseph G. Totten *(Chief of Engineers)*	March 3, 1863 to April 22, 1864
Richard Delafield *(Chief of Engineers)*	April 22, 1864 to August 8, 1866

Corps of Topographical Engineers. Topographical engineers were primarily concerned with the minute description of places, with special reference to their adaptability to military purposes. The commanders of the Corps of Topographical Engineers were:

John J. Abert	July 7, 1838 to September 9, 1861, retired
Stephen H. Long	September 9, 1861 to March 3, 1863

The corps was abolished by an act of March 3, 1863, and it was merged into the Corps of Engineers.

Signal Corps. June 21, 1860, Congress authorized the addition to the staff of the army of one signal officer. Albert J. Myer served as signal officer from June 21, 1860 to March 3, 1863. The Signal Corps was then organized by an act of Congress March 3, 1863, and the head of the Signal Corps was known as chief signal officer. This officer had charge, under the secretary of war, of all military signal duties. The chief signal officers were:

Albert J. Myer	March 3, 1863 to November 15, 1863
Benjamin F. Fisher	December 3, 1864 to July 28, 1866

William J. L. Nicodemus served as acting chief signal officer in Washington from November 15, 1863 until Fisher assumed charge of the office.

Provost Marshal General's Bureau. The Provost Marshal General's Bureau was established in the War Department by an order dated September 24, 1862. The provost marshal general was charged with the arrest of all deserters and disloyal persons, and other similar duties, and later he supervised the entire draft, which was conducted under the Enrollment Act of March 3, 1863. Simon Draper was appointed to head the bureau October 1, 1862, and he was succeeded by James B. Fry March 17, 1863. The office was discontinued August 28, 1866.

****

There were other staff officers not associated with the War Department. Two of these were:

Cavalry Bureau. A Cavalry Bureau was created July 28, 1863 by an order of the War Department. The chief of the Cavalry Bureau was to have charge of the organizing and equipping of the cavalry forces of the army, and the provision of mounts and remounts. A Cavalry Depot was established at Giesboro Point on the Potomac River, southeast of Washington. George Stoneman was announced as chief of the Cavalry Bureau, with headquarters in Washington. Stoneman was replaced by Kenner Garrard January 2, 1864, and he in turn was relieved by James H. Wilson January 26, 1864. April 7, 1864, Wilson was ordered to report to Ulysses S. Grant for assignment to a cavalry division in the Army of the Potomac, and the Cavalry Bureau was placed under the direction of Henry W. Halleck, chief of staff of the army.

Chief and/or Inspector of Artillery. There was no chief of artillery on the bureau level, but in August 1862, William F. Barry was assigned to the chief of ordnance as inspector of artillery.

COMMANDING GENERALS OF THE ARMY

There were three commanding generals of the army during the Civil War. Winfield Scott held this position from July 5, 1841 to November 1, 1861. He left for Mexico November 24, 1846, and from that date until May 11, 1849 exercised no control over the army that was not included in his own command. When he returned to the United States after the war with Mexico, he was, for political reasons, assigned to command only the Eastern Division of the army August 31, 1848. On May 11, 1849, however, he was restored to the command of the army. George B. McClellan relieved Scott November 1, 1861 and remained in command until March 11, 1862. Lincoln and Stanton then directed operations of the army from March 11, 1862 until July 23, 1862, when Henry W. Halleck assumed command.

By an act approved February 29, 1864, Congress revived the grade of lieutenant general and authorized the president to assign the officer of that grade to the command of the Armies of the United States. Ulysses S. Grant received the commission March 9, 1864 and was assigned general in chief of the armies by an executive order dated March 10, 1864. Stanton's General Order No. 98, dated March 12, 1864, formally assigned Grant to this command, which he retained until March 4, 1869. Halleck was relieved from duty as commanding general and was assigned as chief of staff of the army. His principal duty was to convert the decisions of Grant and Stanton into detailed orders. His headquarters was in Washington.

During the early part of the army's existence there was no clear-cut answer to the question as to who actually commanded the Army—the commanding general or the secretary of war, and this question remained generally unresolved during the Civil War. There were uncertainties in the constitutional position of the commanding general, and, although his office was in existence for a long time, there was no statutory authority that defined his role. This problem was not satisfactorily resolved until 1903, when the Office of Chief of Staff replaced Headquarters of the Army.

For a long period of time army regulations assigned to the commanding general of the army the control of matters that related to discipline and military affairs, but left to the secretary of war the conduct of fiscal affairs through the staff departments given above. It was further generally accepted that the command exercised by the commanding general of the army was composed of the various territorial military divisions and departments established by the president.

At the beginning of the Civil War, Secretary of War Simon Cameron and General Winfield Scott attempted to divide their responsibilities as follows: Cameron directed the organization and administration of the new armies, and Scott concerned himself with matters of strategy. This division of responsibilities was generally followed by Stanton and the succeeding commanders in chief.

When McClellan replaced Scott as commanding general November 1, 1861, the former attempted to exercise control over the War Department. He was relieved as commanding general March 11, 1862, but he assumed that he would be responsible for military control. Actually, however, the president submitted his own plans to McClellan and expected him to put them into suitable form for military operations, and then to oversee their execution. Under this system the control of the army remained with Lincoln and Stanton until Grant was appointed to the command of the Armies of the United States in the spring of 1864. From that time, Lincoln exercised only a loose control over the army, and left largely to Grant matters relating to military affairs.

MILITARY DIVISIONS OF THE ARMY

★ ★ ★ ★

MILITARY DIVISION
OF THE ATLANTIC

In an order dated June 27, 1865 reorganizing the military divisions and departments of the army, the Military Division of the Atlantic was created to consist of the departments of the East, Virginia, North Carolina, and South Carolina, and the Middle Department. The territory included within its boundaries consisted of the New England states and the states of New York, New Jersey, Pennsylvania, Delaware, West Virginia, Virginia (except Alexandria and Fairfax counties), North Carolina, South Carolina, and Maryland (except Montgomery County and that part of Anne Arundel County south of the Annapolis and Elk Ridge Railroad, including the city of Annapolis and the counties of Prince George's, Calvert, Charles, and Saint Mary's). George G. Meade was assigned command (assumed command July 1, 1865), with headquarters at Philadelphia, Pennsylvania.

Joseph Hooker commanded the Department of the East, with headquarters at New York; Winfield S. Hancock commanded the Middle Department, with headquarters at Baltimore; Alfred H. Terry commanded the Department of Virginia, with headquarters at Richmond; John M. Schofield commanded the Department of North Carolina, with headquarters at Raleigh; and Quincy A. Gillmore commanded the Department of South Carolina, with headquarters at Hilton Head.

May 19, 1866, the departments of North Carolina and South Carolina were consolidated, and the division then consisted of the Middle Department and the departments of the East, of Virginia, and of the Carolinas.

The Military Division of the Atlantic was discontinued August 6, 1866.

MILITARY DIVISION
OF THE JAMES

Following Robert E. Lee's surrender of the Army of Northern Virginia at Appomattox Court House April 9, 1865, there were in Virginia and northeastern North Carolina several organizations under separate commanders, and to provide a unified control of these forces the Military Division of the James was constituted April 19, 1865. This included the Department of Virginia and that part of North Carolina not occupied by troops under William T. Sherman. It also included George G. Meade's Army of the Potomac and Philip H. Sheridan's cavalry for as long as they remained in the Department of Virginia. Henry W. Halleck assumed command April 22, 1865 (assigned April 19, 1865), with headquarters at Richmond, Virginia.

On May 4, 1865, after Joseph E. Johnston's surrender at Durham's Station, North Carolina, Sherman's army of the Military Division of the Mississippi departed for Washington. Sherman then relinquished command of the state of North Carolina, and the entire state came under the jurisdiction of the Military Division of the James.

The Army of the Potomac and Sheridan's cavalry were soon ordered to Washington, and they remained only briefly in the Department of Virginia. In fact, the Ninth Corps, the first of Meade's troops to leave, began its march northward April 20, 1865, two days before Halleck assumed command of the Division of the James. Sheridan's cavalry left Petersburg May 10, 1865, and Sixth Corps, the last of the Army of the Potomac remaining in the Department of Virginia, departed May 16, 1865.

During the early part of May 1865, Sherman's army, consisting of Oliver O. Howard's Army of the Tennessee and Henry W. Slocum's Army of Georgia, was briefly within the limits of the Division of the James. April 30, 1865, the Army of Georgia left Raleigh, North Carolina for Alexandria, Virginia, and the Army of the Tennessee followed the next day from its camps on the Neuse River. These troops arrived at Manchester, Virginia, opposite Richmond, during the period May 7–10, 1865. Sherman, who had been absent on business at Hilton Head and Savannah in the Department of the South, rejoined his army at Manchester May 9, 1865 and reported to Halleck. Sherman's marching orders, however, were received directly from Ulysses S. Grant.

The Military Division of the James was discontinued June 30, 1865, the date on which Halleck was relieved from command. The commanding officers of the Department of Virginia and the Department of North Carolina were ordered to report directly to the Adjutant General's Office in Washington.

MIDDLE MILITARY DIVISION

Throughout the war Confederate forces in the Shenandoah Valley were a constant threat to the Baltimore and Ohio Railroad and to Washington, D.C., and on several occasions their activities had forced the administration to retain relatively large forces for the defense of the area when they could have been used to better advantage elsewhere. This was particularly true during Thomas J. (Stonewall) Jackson's Shenandoah Valley Campaign of 1862, and Jubal A. Early's Washington Raid in July 1864.

Attempts to contain or destroy enemy troops in the valley usually ended in failure, and this was attributed, at least in part, to a lack of coordination among the troops of the different departments that bordered this region. Finally, in order to secure the desired cooperation, the Middle Military Division was constituted August 7, 1864, to consist of the Middle Department and the departments of Washington, West Virginia, and the Susquehanna. Included within the limits of the division were the states of West Virginia, Pennsylvania, Maryland, Delaware (except Fort Delaware), and that part of Virginia lying east and north of a line beginning at the confluence of Goose Creek and the Potomac River and running south along the creek and the Bull Run Mountains and to the mouth of the Occoquan River. It also included that part of Virginia in the vicinity of Harper's Ferry. Philip H. Sheridan was assigned temporary command August 7, 1864, and he assumed command that day with headquarters at Harper's Ferry. On September 21, 1864, two days after his victory at Opequon Creek, Sheridan was assigned permanent command of the Middle Military Division.

At Harper's Ferry, Sheridan assumed command of a field army that had been assembled there early in August 1864 by David Hunter, and this force was strongly reinforced later in the month. With this Army of the Middle Military Division, which later became the Army of the Shenandoah, Sheridan carried out his successful Shenandoah Valley Campaign of August 7–November 28, 1864. For details, see Shenandoah Valley Campaign (Sheridan).

December 1, 1864, the designation of the Department of the Susquehanna was changed to the Department of Pennsylvania, and the Middle Military Division then consisted of the Middle Department and the departments of Washington, West Virginia, and Pennsylvania.

February 27, 1865, Sheridan left Winchester, Virginia with Wesley Merritt's First Cavalry Division (then commanded by Thomas C. Devin) and George A. Custer's Third Cavalry Division on an expedition to destroy the Virginia Central Railroad and the James River Canal. During his absence, Winfield S. Hancock was left in command of the Department of West Virginia and of all troops in the Middle Military Division not under the immediate command of Sheridan. Sheridan did not return to the valley, however, but moved on and joined Grant's army near Petersburg March 28, 1865.

Some confusion may result from a study of the orders and correspondence for the period February 27–March 28, 1865, relating to Sheridan's expedition and to affairs in the Shenandoah Valley and West Virginia. During this period both Sheridan and Hancock issued orders and communications under the heading "Headquarters Middle Military Division." This is explained by the fact that Hancock's assignment was temporary during the absence of Sheridan, and both were issuing orders in different areas and were, therefore, not likely to be in conflict. Sheridan was, however, the proper commander of the Middle Military Division.

April 22, 1865, Hancock moved headquarters of the Middle Military Division from Winchester to Washington, D.C. Sheridan was officially relieved from command of the division May 17, 1865, and he was succeeded by Hancock.

The Middle Military Division was discontinued June 27, 1865.

MILITARY DIVISION OF THE POTOMAC

Following the disastrous defeat of Irvin McDowell's Army of Northeastern Virginia at the Battle of Bull Run July 21, 1861, George B. McClellan was called to Washington from Western Virginia and July 25, 1861 was assigned command of the newly constituted Military Division of the Potomac. McClellan assumed command July 27, 1861, with headquarters at Washington. The division consisted of the departments of Washington and Northeastern Virginia. Included within its boundaries were the District of Columbia; Fort Washington and the adjacent country; the state of Maryland as far as Bladensburg, inclusive, and the counties of Prince George's, Montgomery, and Frederick in Maryland; and that part of Virginia east of the Allegheny Mountains, except Fort Monroe and the country around for a radius of sixty miles.

The Military Division of the Potomac was in existence for only a short time when on August 17, 1861 (ordered August 15, 1861), the departments of Washington, Northeastern Virginia, and the Shenandoah were merged into the newly created Department of the Potomac.

McClellan's principal task when he assumed command was to restore order in the capital and reorganize the army. He appointed Andrew Porter

provost marshal, and the latter, with the aid of regular troops, proceeded to establish order in Washington.

When McClellan arrived in Washington the brigade organization created by McDowell still existed, and these troops were on the Virginia side of the Potomac River. The army, however, was in a seriously disorganized state. Much of McClellan's command consisted of three-month regiments, whose terms of service were about to expire, or had expired, and in addition many organizations had been wrecked during the recent battle at, and retreat from, Bull Run. McClellan promptly began the reorganization. As new regiments arrived in the city they were formed into provisional brigades and were placed in camps in the suburbs of the city for equipment, instruction, and discipline. When these troops were in suitable condition for transfer to the forces across the Potomac, they were assigned to the brigades encamped there. Fitz John Porter was first assigned to command the provisional brigades, but he was soon replaced by Ambrose E. Burnside. Burnside was relieved by Silas Casey, who remained in command until the army left for the Peninsula in March 1862. The newly arrived artillery units reported to William F. Barry, chief of artillery of the army, and the cavalry reported to George Stoneman, chief of cavalry.

On August 4, 1861, McClellan announced the following brigade organization of the Military Division of the Potomac.

Hunter's Brigade, David Hunter
Heintzelman's Brigade, Samuel P. Heintzelman
Sherman's Brigade, William T. Sherman
Kearny's Brigade, Philip Kearny
Hooker's Brigade, Joseph Hooker
Keyes' Brigade, Erasmus D. Keyes
Franklin's Brigade, William B. Franklin
Blenker's Brigade, Louis Blenker
Richardson's Brigade, Israel B. Richardson
Stone's Brigade, Charles P. Stone
Smith's Brigade, William F. Smith
Couch's Brigade (temporary), Darius N. Couch

Three additional brigades were also constituted as follows:

McCall's Brigade of Pennsylvania Reserves, George A. McCall, August 2, 1861

Sickles' Brigade, Daniel E. Sickles, August 5, 1861
Provisional Brigade, Rufus King, August 9, 1861

There was also a special command in the Division of the Potomac. August 11, 1861, Charles P. Stone, commanding the Third Brigade of Nathaniel P. Banks' Department of the Shenandoah, was ordered to Poolesville, Maryland, where he was assigned command of six infantry regiments, a battery of artillery, and one company of cavalry. This command was designated as Corps of Observation, Military Division of the Potomac. Stone assumed command August 12, 1861. His mission was to observe the Potomac River from Point of Rocks to Seneca Mills (Banks was in command beyond that point), and to oppose, until help could arrive, any attempt by the enemy to cross the river and advance into Maryland. When the Department of the Potomac was constituted August 17, 1861, the designation of Stone's command was changed to Corps of Observation, Department of the Potomac. For additional information, see Army of the Potomac, Period of Organization.

DEPARTMENTS OF THE ARMY

★★★★

DEPARTMENT OF ANNAPOLIS

One of the most critical problems of the administration at the outbreak of hostilities was the transfer of troops and supplies from the North and East to Washington, D.C., which was situated in a dangerously exposed position. Any delay in assembling there a sizeable Union army would have seriously jeopardized the safety of the capital. The city of Baltimore, Maryland, which had a large pro-Southern population, was a vital communications center between Washington and the Northern states. It was connected with Philadelphia and the East by the Philadelphia, Wilmington, and Baltimore Railroad, and with Harrisburg by the Northern Central Railroad. The Baltimore and Ohio Railroad ran west from Baltimore to Relay, a distance of about eight miles, and there it branched. The main line ran on through Harper's Ferry and Western Virginia to the Midwest, and a branch line ran down to Washington.

April 19, 1861, Edward F. Jones' 6th Massachusetts Infantry, the leading regiment of Benjamin F. Butler's Massachusetts State Militia, was attacked by a mob while passing through Baltimore on its way to Washington. Largely because of political reasons, this action effectively closed all rail traffic between Washington and Pennsylvania, New Jersey, New York, and the New England states. The next day Butler, recognizing the urgency of moving his troops to the capital, sent Timothy Munroe's 8th Massachusetts Infantry by rail from Philadelphia to Perryville on the Chesapeake Bay, and then on by boat to Annapolis, Maryland. Marshall Lefferts' 7th New York Regiment also moved to Annapolis, and

arrived at the Naval Academy April 22, 1861. Annapolis was connected with Washington by the Elk River Railroad, which ran to Annapolis Junction, eighteen miles south southwest of Baltimore, and from there by the Baltimore and Ohio branch line to Washington. April 25, 1861, Butler was assigned command at Annapolis, and from there he sent the 8th Massachusetts and 7th New York on to Washington.

To secure Annapolis as a base, and to keep open the rail communications between that place and Washington, the Department of Annapolis was constituted April 27, 1861. It included the line of the railroad, and the country for a distance of twenty miles on each side, and extended toward Washington as far as Bladensburg, Maryland. This territory was taken from the Department of Washington (see). Butler was assigned command, with headquarters at Annapolis.

It was informally agreed that Baltimore was within the limits of the Department of Annapolis, and Winfield Scott, the commander in chief, ordered Butler to occupy Relay with the 6th Massachusetts. This was done May 5, 1861, and six days later the 8th Massachusetts was also sent to Relay. May 13, 1861, Butler, acting without orders, occupied Federal Hill overlooking the city of Baltimore, and from that time Baltimore remained under Union control, and rail communications with Washington were secure. Butler, however, was relieved from command of the Department of Annapolis May 15, 1861, and he was succeeded by George Cadwalader. Headquarters was established at Baltimore. June 11, 1861, Nathaniel P. Banks relieved Cadwalader. July 23, 1861 (ordered July 19, 1861), John A. Dix relieved Banks, and on that date the Department of

Annapolis was discontinued by a change of designation to the Department of Maryland (see).

The posts in the department were Annapolis, Annapolis Junction, Baltimore, Bladensburg, Federal Hill, Fort McHenry, and Relay (Relay's House).

DEPARTMENT OF THE EAST OCTOBER 31, 1853– OCTOBER 26, 1861

The Department of the East was created October 31, 1853 and was in existence at the beginning of the Civil War. It consisted of all territory of the United States east of the Mississippi River. In April 1861, John E. Wool was in command of the department, with headquarters at Troy, New York.

Beginning April 9, 1861, the department was steadily reduced in size by the formation of new departments from its former territory until it was discontinued October 26, 1861. At that time, the loyal territory within its boundaries included only the states of Michigan, New Jersey, and Wisconsin. The transfers of territory from the Department of the East were as follows:

The first reduction in size occurred when the Southern states seceded, but the commander of the department continued to exercise theoretical jurisdiction over the entire original area until April 9, 1861. That day the Department of Washington was created to consist of the District of Columbia and the state of Maryland. April 13, 1861, the state of Florida was transferred to the Department of Florida. April 19, 1861, the states of Delaware and Pennsylvania were transferred to the Department of Washington. April 27, 1861, the post of Fort Adams, Rhode Island was transferred to the control of the Navy Department. May 3, 1861 the states of Illinois, Indiana, and Ohio were transferred to the Department of the Ohio. May 22, 1861, Fort Monroe, Virginia and the country for a distance of sixty miles around it was transferred to the Department of Virginia. May 27, 1861, that part of Virginia east of the Allegheny Mountains, north of the James River, and west of the Department of Virginia was transferred to the Department of Northeastern Virginia. May 28, 1861, that part of Kentucky lying within

100 miles of the Ohio River was transferred to the Department of Kentucky. July 19, 1861, the Shenandoah Valley of Virginia was transferred to the Department of the Shenandoah. August 15, 1861, the states of Kentucky and Tennessee were transferred to the Department of the Cumberland. September 19, 1861, all of the present state of West Virginia was transferred to the Department of Western Virginia. October 1, 1861, the New England states were transferred to the Department of New England. October 26, 1861, the state of New York was transferred to the Department of New York.

The Department of the East was officially discontinued October 26, 1861, but there appears to have been no department commander after August 17, 1861, when Wool assumed command of the Department of Virginia.

DEPARTMENT OF THE EAST JANUARY 3, 1863–JUNE 27, 1865

The Department of the East was re-created January 3, 1863 to consist of the New England states and the state of New York. It was formed from the Department of New York and the territory of the discontinued Department of New England. John E. Wool assumed command January 12, 1863 (assigned January 3, 1863), with headquarters at New York City. The state of New Jersey was transferred from the Middle Department to the Department of the East February 6, 1863, but there were no further changes in its boundaries during the war.

June 27, 1865, the Department of the East was included in the Military Division of the Atlantic. The department was not discontinued until October 31, 1873, and then its territory was included in the Military Division of the Atlantic.

COMMANDERS OF THE DEPARTMENT OF THE EAST (DURING THE CIVIL WAR PERIOD)

John E. Wool	January 12, 1863 to July 18, 1863
John A. Dix	July 18, 1863 to April 10, 1865
John J. Peck	April 10, 1865 to April 19, 1865

John A. Dix   April 19, 1865 to July 15, 1865
Joseph Hooker   July 15, 1865 to August 13, 1866

Note. Dix relieved Wool in command of the department during the Draft Riots in New York (see below).

TROOPS, POSTS, AND DISTRICTS IN THE DEPARTMENT

When the Department of the East was re-created January 3, 1863, the troops of the department were on garrision duty at the following posts:

Fort Hamilton, New York Harbor
Fort La Fayette, New York Harbor
Fort Schuyler, New York Harbor
Fort Richmond, New York Harbor
Camp Washington, Staten Island, New York
Fort Ontario, Oswego, New York
Fort Independence, Boston, Massachusetts
Fort Warren, Boston, Massachusetts
Fort Preble, Portland, Maine
Fort Trumbull, New London, Connecticut
Fort Adams, Newport, Rhode Island

During the next few months posts were added as follows: Fort at Sandy Hook, New York; Portland, Maine; Portsmouth Grove, Rhode Island; and Clark's Point, New Bedford, Massachusetts. The garrisons of the posts in the department consisted of troops of 1st United States Artillery; 5th United States Artillery; 11th, 12th, 14th, 15th, 16th, and 17th United States Infantry; New York cavalry and artillery; and three companies of Massachusetts Heavy Artillery. Later, New Hampshire and Rhode Island troops were used to garrison some of these posts.

The posts in New York Harbor reported separately to department headquarters until July 17, 1863. On that date Edward R. S. Canby was assigned command of the City and Harbor of New York during the Draft Riots (see below). The posts included in Canby's command were: David's Island, Fort Hamilton, Fort Schuyler, Fort at Sandy Hook, Fort Columbus, Fort Richmond, Fort La Fayette, Fort Wood, and Riker's Island. September 9, 1863, George J. Stannard was assigned command of the district on the west side of the Narrows, including the Fort at Sandy Hook. Headquarters was at Fort Richmond. November 9, 1863, Canby was assigned to the War Department as assistant adjutant general, and was succeeded in command of the City and Harbor of New York by Stannard. Stannard was transferred to Benjamin F. Butler's Army of the James May 6, 1864, and he was succeeded by P. Regis De Trobriand. Lewis C. Hunt relieved De Trobriand June 24, 1864 and remained in command of the City and Harbor of New York until the end of the war.

During the Draft Riots in July 1863, and also during the November elections of 1864, many troops were sent to New York to restore and preserve order, but when the emergencies were ended they returned to their proper commands. For more information, see sections on the Draft Riots in New York, 1863; and the November Election of 1864 in New York, below.

In December 1863, the Department of the East was organized as follows:

DEPARTMENT OF THE EAST, John A. Dix

City and Harbor of New York, George J. Stannard
    David's Island, Isaac H. Baker
    Fort Hamilton, Hannibal Day
    Fort Schuyler, Harvey Brown
    Fort at Sandy Hook, Enoch Steen
    Fort Columbus, Gustavus Loomis
    Fort Richmond, Clarence H. Corning
    Fort La Fayette, Martin Burke
    Fort Wood, Clarence S. Merchant

Independent Posts
    Fort Adams, Rhode Island, Oliver L. Shepherd
    Fort Constitution, New Hampshire, Charles H. Long
    Fort Independence, Boston, De Lancey Floyd-Jones
    Fort McClary, Kittery Point, Maine, Ira McL. Barton
    Forts Preble and Scammel, Portland, Maine, George L. Andrews
    Fort Warren, Boston, Stephen Cabot
    Riker's Island, New York, Nathaniel J. Jackson
    Fort at Clark's Point, New Bedford, John A. P. Allen
    Fort at Eastern Point, Gloucester, Thomas Herbert
    Fort Knox, near Buckport, Maine, Thomas H. Palmer
    Fort Ontario, Oswego, New York, Charles H. Lewis
    Fort Trumbull, New London, Connecticut, William Gates
    Plymouth Grove, Rhode Island, Christopher Blanding
    Winter Island, Salem, Massachusetts, James M. Richardson

There was no further change in the organization

of the department until July 1864. Then Floyd-Jones was assigned command of Boston Harbor and the Massachusetts Seacoast Defenses, and Samuel K. Dawson was assigned command of the Maine Seacoast Defenses. Dawson's command was later designated as Defenses of Portsmouth Harbor and the Maine Seacoast. The Boston Harbor and Massachusetts Seacoast Defenses consisted of the following: Clark's Point, New Bedford; Eastern Point, Fort Gloucester; Long Point Batteries, Provincetown; Forts Pickering and Lee, Salem; Fort Sewall, Marblehead; Fort Warren, Boston Harbor; Fort Independence (Floyd-Jones' headquarters), Boston. The Defenses of Portsmouth Harbor and the Maine Seacoast consisted of the following: Fort Constitution, Portsmouth; and Forts Knox, McClary, and Sullivan.

Two districts were organized in the Department of the East in September 1864. These were:

District of Northern New York. The Military District of Northern New York was constituted September 14, 1864 (ordered by the secretary of war September 12, 1864) to consist of congressional districts No. 11 through No. 20. John C. Robinson was assigned command, with headquarters at Albany, New York. The principal posts in the district were Albany, Champlain, Ogdensburg, Sacket's Harbor, and Malone. The troops at Albany belonged to the Veteran Reserve Corps, and for the defense of the frontier there were three companies of the First Battalion, Massachusetts Cavalry, two companies of New York Cavalry, and one independent company of New York Cavalry. In addition, there was one company of 17th United States Infantry and a detachment of First Battalion, Massachusetts Heavy Artillery.

District of Western New York. The Military District of Western New York was constituted September 14, 1864 (ordered by the secretary of war September 12, 1864) to consist of congressional districts No. 21 through No. 31. Alexander S. Diven was assigned command, with headquarters at Elmira, New York. The principal posts in the district were Elmira, Fort Ontario, Fort Niagara, Fort Porter, and the General Hospital at Rochester. The post of Elmira consisted of the Draft Rendezvous and the Depot Prisoners of War, both under the command of

Benjamin F. Tracy. Initially, at Elmira there were eight regiments of the New York National Guard, but these were replaced by regulars and units of the Veteran Reserve Corps. Troops at the other posts were recruits and units of the Veteran Reserve Corps.

****

At the end of September 1864 the Department of the East was organized as follows:

City and Harbor of New York, Lewis C. Hunt
Boston Harbor and Massachusetts Seacoast Defenses, De Lancey Floyd-Jones
Defenses of Portsmouth Harbor and the Maine Seacoast, Samuel K. Dawson
Military District of Northern New York, John C. Robinson
Military District of Western New York, Alexander S. Diven

Note. In April 1865 John C. Robinson was in command of both the districts of Northern and Western New York.

Other commands

Fort Adams, Rhode Island, Oliver L. Shepherd
Portsmouth Grove, Rhode Island, Christopher Blanding
Forts Preble and Scammel, Maine, George L. Andrews
Fort Trumbull, Connecticut, John D. O'Connell

This organization remained essentially unchanged to the end of the war.

DRAFT RIOTS IN NEW YORK, JULY 1863

On July 11, 1863, the first names of the new Federal draft, which had been signed into law March 3, 1863, were drawn in New York City. These names were published in the newspapers the next day, and immediately crowds began gathering in the streets. For some time there had been unrest in the city because of the draft, and particularly because of the provisions that allowed substitutions and the purchase of exemptions. The situation was further complicated by the fact that some state politicians were not giving their full support to the war.

When the drawing was resumed on the morning of July 13, 1863, mobs gathered, and soon they were engaged in widespread rioting. Draft headquarters was stormed, dwellings were entered, and business establishments were looted. Numerous fires were started, and many people were killed or injured. Major General Charles W. Sandford of the New York National Guard was assigned command of all troops called in for the protection of the city. Robert Nugent, colonel of the 69th New York Infantry and acting provost marshal general, was assigned command of all regular troops in the city, and Brevet Brigadier General Harvey Brown, United States Army, was assigned to command under Sandford. Brown was not cooperative and was relieved from his command in the City and Harbor of New York by Edward R. S. Canby July 17, 1863 (assigned July 15, 1863). Judson Kilpatrick, who at the time was in the city on leave, reported July 17, 1863 and offered his services for a few days. He was placed in charge of Wool's cavalry, which was commanded by Thaddeus P. Mott and Henry E. Davies. John A. Dix arrived in New York from the Department of Virginia, and July 18, 1863 relieved Wool in command of the Department of the East.

As soon as trouble started in New York, troops were sent into the city from outside the Department of the East. The 8th United States Infantry, 7th New York State Militia, and a regular battery were sent immediately from the Army of the Potomac. During the period July 15–16, 1863, eleven New York National Guard Regiments were ordered to New York from William F. Smith's First Division, Department of the Susquehanna (for details, see Department of the Susquehanna). The terms of enlistment of most of these regiments expired shortly their arrival. Also from the Department of the Susquehanna were the 5th and 12th New York Regiments under Charles Yates, which arrived July 18, 1863. Later, 26th Michigan and six companies of 152nd New York arrived from First Brigade, First Division, Seventh Corps, Department of Virginia.

July 30, 1863, the following regiments from the Army of the Potomac were ordered to report to Canby in New York. From Third Corps: 1st Massachusetts of First Brigade, Second Division; and 20th Indiana of First Brigade, First Division. From Sixth Corps: 37th Massachusetts of Second Brigade, Third Division; and 5th Wisconsin of Third Brigade, First Division. In mid-August 1863, an additional 9,600 men were sent to New York from the Army of the Potomac as follows: August 14, 1863 about 4,000 men consisting of the regulars of Romeyn B. Ayres' Second Division, Fifth Corps; and Lewis A. Grant's Second Brigade, Second Division, Sixth Corps (the Vermont Brigade). August 15, 1863, 1,800 men from Second Corps and Third Corps followed, and August 16, 1863 an additional 3,800 men, largely from Twelfth Corps, but also including regiments from Second Corps and Third Corps.

In New York August 23, 1863, the above troops were organized into two brigades under the command of Canby. First Brigade was commanded by Ayres and consisted of the regulars of Ayres' Second Division, Fifth Corps; Grant's Vermont Brigade; and 152nd New York Regiment. Second Brigade was commanded by Thomas H. Ruger, commander of Third Brigade, First Division, Twelfth Corps, and it consisted of nine Ohio regiments, two Indiana regiments, two Michigan regiments, and one regiment each from Wisconsin, Minnesota, Massachusetts, and Connecticut.

Early in September 1863, troops were sent to the various districts where the draft was to take place, and where additional protection was required. They were stationed at Elmira, Watervliet Arsenal, Buffalo, Poughkeepsie, Kingston, Ulster County, Brooklyn, Jamaica, Long Island, Albany, and Schenectady.

September 5, 1863, 6,000 men were ordered to return to the Army of the Potomac, and September 9, 1863, Ruger was ordered to embark his troops and return to Virginia. At the end of the month fewer than 5,000 men remained of Canby's command of the City and Harbor of New York.

ELECTION OF 1864 IN NEW YORK

As the date for the November elections of 1864 drew near, the administration became increasingly concerned about affairs in New York. There was the possibility of fresh outbreaks in the state, and also illegal voting, and in addition there was the threat of invasion from Canada by Confederates led by Jacob Thompson. To deal with these problems if they should arise, preparations were made to send additional troops into the state. October 31, 1864, Ulysses S. Grant ordered Frederick Winthrop with the regulars of his First Brigade, Second Division, Fifth Corps, Army of the Potomac to New York City, and

Winthrop's command departed the next day. November 2, 1864, he also ordered Benjamin F. Butler, commander of the Army of the James and the Department of Virginia and North Carolina, to go to New York and assume command of the troops that would arrive there during the emergency. Butler arrived in New York November 3, 1864, and two days later assumed command as directed.

November 2, 1864, Joseph R. Hawley was ordered to move with his Second Brigade, First Division, Tenth Corps of the Army of the James to Deep Bottom, Virginia, and there he was also to assume command of four regiments of Eighteenth Corps that would meet him there. He was then to proceed to New York with his command and report to Butler. Other troops of Tenth Corps were also sent to New York. These were the 10th Connecticut and 11th Maine of Third Brigade, First Division, 112th New York of First Brigade, Second Division, and 13th Indiana of Third Brigade, Second Division. Other troops of Eighteenth Corps sent to New York were 81st New York and 98th New York of First Brigade, First Division; 92nd New York, 96th New York, and 118th New York of Second Brigade, First Division; 148th New York of First Brigade, Second Division; and 9th Vermont of Second Brigade, Second Division.

The troops taken to New York by Hawley were organized as Provisional Division, Army of the James, which was under his command. First Brigade was commanded by Joseph C. Abbott, and Second Brigade by John B. Raulston, commander of First Brigade, First Division, Eighteenth Corps. Shortly after arriving in New York, Raulston was sent with two regiments to Watervliet Arsenal, and Alfred P. Rockwell assumed command of Second Brigade, Provisional Division.

November 11, 1864, Hawley was ordered to return with his command to the Army of the James. Embarkation began November 14, 1864, and by the next day all troops had departed for Virginia.

DEPARTMENT OF FLORIDA
APRIL 11, 1861–MARCH 15, 1862

The Department of Florida was constituted April 11, 1861 to consist of the state of Florida and the contiguous islands in the Gulf of Mexico. This territory was taken from the Department of the East. Harvey Brown was assigned command, with headquarters at Key West. Brown assumed command April 13, 1861, and April 18, 1861 moved his headquarters to Fort Pickens, near Pensacola.

The department was reduced in size January 11, 1862, when the Department of Key West was formed from a part of its territory. The department then consisted of the state of Florida, except Key West, the Tortugas, and also the mainland on the west coast north of Apalachicola and the east coast north of Cape Canaveral. Lewis G. Arnold assumed command of the department February 22, 1862.

March 15, 1862, the Department of the South was created to include the states of Florida, Georgia, and South Carolina, and the expedition and forces then under the command of Thomas W. Sherman. The Department of Florida was thus merged into the Department of the South.

In January 1861, Adam Slemmer was in command of Company G, 1st United States Artillery at Barrancas Barracks. Slemmer was in command of Barrancas Barracks and Fort Barrancas on Pensacola Harbor. To avoid capture by Florida state forces, and also to secure Fort Pickens on Santa Rosa Island, which was then unmanned, Slemmer transferred his command to Fort Pickens January 10, 1861. Two days later Barrancas Barracks, Fort Barrancas, Fort McRee, and the Navy Yard were seized by Florida state troops.

January 14, 1861, Fort Taylor at Key West was garrisoned by troops of the 1st United States Artillery from Key West Barracks under John M. Brannan. In March 1861, William H. French assumed command at Key West. January 18, 1861, Fort Jefferson, Tortugas was occupied by United States troops under Lewis G. Arnold from Boston, Massachusetts. January 24, 1861, Israel Vogdes sailed from Fort Monroe, Virginia with his Company A, 1st United States Artillery and some men of 1st, 2nd, 3rd, and 4th United States Artillery to reinforce Fort Pickens. Vogdes arrived at Fort Pickens and assumed command February 6, 1861. The above were the troops in the Department of Florida at the beginning of the war.

March 11, 1861, Braxton Bragg assumed command of the Confederate forces at Pensacola, and they occupied the mainland area until they were withdrawn May 9, 1861.

April 1, 1861, Harvey Brown, of the 2nd United States Artillery, was ordered to New York to command an expedition to reinforce Fort Pickens. This force consisted of Company M, 2nd United States Artillery, an engineer company, and Companies C and E of the 3rd United States Infantry. Brown was ordered to assume command of all United States land forces within the limits of the state of Florida upon his arrival. He assumed command April 13, 1861.

The 6th New York Infantry left New York for Florida, and during the period June 15–23, 1861 moved to Santa Rosa Island. October 9, 1861, Confederate forces attempted to capture Fort Pickens by advancing along Santa Rosa Island. They partially destroyed the camp of the 6th New York, but were finally repulsed when the regulars arrived from the fort. The 75th New York Regiment left New York December 6, 1861, and arrived on Santa Rosa Island December 15, 1861.

DEPARTMENT OF FLORIDA
JUNE 27, 1865–AUGUST 6, 1866

In the reorganization of the military divisions and geographical departments of the army June 27, 1865, the Department of Florida was constituted to include the state of Florida. The department was assigned to the Military Division of the Gulf. John G. Foster was assigned command, with headquarters at Tallahassee. John Newton assumed command of the District of Florida June 19, 1865, and some of his orders were issued under the heading of "Headquarters Department of Florida," but he never officially announced his assumption of command of the department.

General Order No. 1, Military Division of the Tennessee, dated June 20, 1865, included the Department of Florida in the Military Division of the Tennessee, but this was done in error and the order was revoked June 30, 1865.

The Department of Florida was merged into the Department of the South August 6, 1866.

DEPARTMENT OF GEORGIA

In the reorganization of the military divisions and geographical departments of the army June 27, 1865, the Department of Georgia was created to consist of the state of Georgia. It was formed from parts of the Department of the Cumberland and the Department of the South. James B. Steedman was assigned command, with headquarters at Augusta, Georgia. The Department of Georgia was included in the newly created Military Division of the Tennessee. James H. Wilson relieved Steedman in command of the department December 10, 1865, and he in turn was succeeded by John M. Brannan December 19, 1865.

The Department of Georgia was merged into the Department of the South May 19, 1866.

DEPARTMENT OF HARPER'S FERRY AND CUMBERLAND

In October 1861, the War Department created the Department of Harper's Ferry and Cumberland for better administration of the troops guarding the Baltimore and Ohio Railroad. It consisted of the line of the railroad from Harper's Ferry, Virginia to Cumberland, Maryland, and a strip of contiguous territory thirty miles wide, extending along the Virginia side of the Potomac River. Frederick W. Lander was assigned command.

Lander was wounded in a skirmish at Edwards Ferry October 22, 1861, and that day Benjamin F. Kelley, who was in command along the railroad, was ordered to Romney, Virginia to assume command of the department until Lander returned. Lander was again in command in December 1861, but at the end of February 1862 he became ill, and he died March 2, 1862. Meantime, Lander's troops, under the command of James Shields, had marched from the railroad to join Nathaniel P. Banks and Alpheus S. Williams, whose combined forces occupied Winchester, Virginia March 12, 1862. With the departure of Shields from the line of the railroad, the department was discontinued.

DEPARTMENT OF KEY WEST

The Department of Key West was constituted January 11, 1862 to consist of Key West, Florida, the Tortugas, and the mainland of Florida on the west coast as far north as Apalachicola, and on the east coast up to Cape Canaveral. The department was formed from a part of the territory of the Department of Florida. John M. Brannan was assigned command, with headquarters at Key West. Brannan assumed command February 21, 1862. The department was merged into the Department of the South March 31, 1862 (ordered March 15, 1862). For information about the troops in the department, see Department of the South.

DEPARTMENT OF MARYLAND

July 19, 1861, John A Dix was ordered to relieve Nathaniel P. Banks in command of the Department of Annapolis. Banks' department consisted of the railroad running from Annapolis, Maryland to Washington, D.C., as far as Bladensburg, Maryland; and also the country for a distance of twenty miles on each side. The same order assigning Dix to command, also changed the name of the Department of Annapolis to the Department of Maryland. Dix assumed command July 23, 1861, with headquarters at Baltimore. Two days later, however, the Department of Maryland was merged into the departments of Washington and Pennsylvania. Prince George's County, through which the railroad passed, was attached to the Department of Washington.

MIDDLE DEPARTMENT

The Middle Department was created March 22, 1862 to consist of the states of Delaware, New Jersey, and Pennsylvania; the Eastern Shore of Maryland (counties of Kent, Queen Anne's, Talbot, Caroline, Dorchester, Somerset, and Worcester), and the counties of Cecil, Harford, Baltimore, and Anne Arundel in Maryland; and the Eastern Shore of Virginia (counties of Accomac and Northampton). The department was formed from a part of the Department of the Potomac. John A. Dix was assigned command, with headquarters at Baltimore, Maryland.

There were numerous changes in the limits of the department, and also some changes affecting the responsibilities of the commander of the department during the period of its existence. Listed in chronological order, these were as follows:

June 17, 1862, the defenses of the Baltimore and Ohio Railroad east from Cumberland, Maryland to Baltimore, and the railroad between Harper's Ferry and Winchester, Virginia was placed under John E. Wool, commander of the Middle Department. This order did not change the geographical limits of the department, but only the troops under Wool's command.

July 22, 1862, Eighth Corps was constituted to include all troops serving in the Middle Department.

September 2, 1862, the limits of the department were extended to include the entire state of Maryland, except that part bounded by a line from Fort Washington on the Potomac River to Annapolis Junction, and from there to the mouth of Seneca Creek, about eleven miles west of Rockville, Maryland. The excepted territory was included in the Defenses of Washington.

December 22, 1862, Robert C. Schenck assumed command of the Middle Department, and that same day he was informed that his command covered the Baltimore and Ohio Railroad from Baltimore west to the Ohio River. This extended his control to include the lower Shenandoah Valley as far south as Winchester, the upper Potomac region as far north as Hancock, Maryland, and all of northwestern Virginia north of the Great Kanawha River. This applied to the command of troops only, and did not redefine departmental boundaries.

The Department of Washington was created February 2, 1863, and included within its limits, in addition to some territory in Virginia, was that part of Maryland within a line extending from Piscataway Creek to Annapolis Junction and thence to the mouth of the Monocacy River.

February 6, 1863, the state of New Jersey was transferred to the Department of the East.

March 16, 1863, all of Western Virginia (at that time this was the District of Western Virginia,

Department of the Ohio) was included in the Middle Department.

June 9, 1863, the state of Pennsylvania was transferred to the departments of the Susquehanna and the Monongahela, and also the counties of Hancock, Brooke, and Ohio in Western Virginia (near Wheeling) were assigned to the Department of the Monongahela. It should be noted here that Western Virginia became the state of West Virginia June 20, 1863.

June 22, 1863, Henry W. Halleck directed that all of Eighth Corps and the Middle Department east of Cumberland, Maryland be placed under the immediate control of the commander of the Army of the Potomac. By this order, issued during the Gettysburg Campaign, the Middle Department and Eighth Corps were subject to the orders first of Joseph Hooker, and then of George G. Meade. During the Gettysburg Campaign, the Army of the Potomac operated in the counties of Montgomery, Frederick, Carroll, and Washington in Maryland.

June 24, 1863, that part of West Virginia west of a north-south line through Hancock, Maryland was included in the newly created Department of West Virginia.

By an order of July 23, 1863 from the Adjutant General's Office, the county of Saint Mary's in Maryland was detached from the Middle Department and organized as a separate District of Saint Mary's, which reported directly to the War Department. Despite this order, however, it has also been stated that Saint Mary's County was a part of the Department of the Potomac at that time and not of the Middle Department. The largest northern prison camp was established August 1, 1863 in Saint Mary's County, on a peninsula where the Potomac River flows into the Chesapeake Bay. Headquarters was at Point Lookout during the latter part of the war. For additional information, see Miscellaneous Organizations, District of Saint Mary's.

August 3, 1863 (announced by Benjamin F. Kelley August 10, 1863), all of the state of Maryland west of the Monocacy River, and that part of Virginia in the vicinity of Harper's Ferry were transferred to the Department of West Virginia.

December 21, 1863, the Eastern Shore of Virginia was transferred to the Department of Virginia and North Carolina.

March 12, 1864, Fort Delaware, which was then a prisoner-of-war camp on an island in the Delaware River, was detached from the Middle Department and was ordered to report directly to the War Department.

June 21, 1864, the boundaries of the Department of Washington were redefined (see Department of Washington), and as a result the Middle Department was again reduced in size. It then consisted only of the state of Delaware and that part of Maryland bounded on the west and south as follows: south along the Monocacy River to its mouth, then from that point east along a line to the Patuxent River, and finally south along the river to the Chesapeake Bay.

The boundaries of the department then remained unchanged to the end of the war.

To secure better cooperation among the commanders of the various departments involved with Jubal A. Early's invasion of Maryland and threats against Baltimore and Washington in July 1864, Henry W. Halleck, chief of staff of the United States Army, was assigned July 27, 1864 to exercise control over the Middle Department and the departments of Washington, West Virginia, and the Susquehanna. Then, on August 7, 1864, Philip H. Sheridan was assigned command of the Middle Military Division, which consisted of the above-mentioned departments.

In the reorganization of the military divisions and the geographical departments of the army June 27, 1865, the Middle Department was defined as follows: the states of Delaware, Pennsylvania, West Virginia, and Maryland (except the counties of Anne Arundel, Prince George's, Calvert, Charles, and Saint Mary's), and the line of the Baltimore and Ohio Railroad in Virginia. Winfield S. Hancock was assigned command, with headquarters at Baltimore.

The department was discontinued August 6, 1866, and was merged into the departments of Washington, of the East, and of the Potomac.

COMMANDERS OF THE MIDDLE DEPARTMENT

Middle Department
John A. Dix	March 22, 1862 to June 9, 1862
John E. Wool	June 9, 1862 to July 22, 1862

Middle Department, Eighth Corps
John E. Wool	July 22, 1862 to December 22, 1862
Robert C. Schenck	December 22, 1862 to March 12, 1863

William W. Morris	March 12, 1863 to March 20, 1863
Robert C. Schenck	March 20, 1863 to August 10, 1863
William W. Morris	August 10, 1863 to August 31, 1863
Robert C. Schenck	August 31, 1863 to September 22, 1863
William W. Morris	September 22, 1863 to September 28, 1863
Erastus B. Tyler	September 28, 1863 to October 10, 1863
Robert C. Schenck	October 10, 1863 to December 5, 1863
Henry H. Lockwood	December 5, 1863 to March 22, 1864
Lewis Wallace	March 22, 1864 to February 1, 1865
William W. Morris	February 1, 1865 to April 19, 1865
Lewis Wallace	April 19, 1865 to July 18, 1865
Winfield S. Hancock	July 18, 1865

Note. Schenck resigned from the army December 5, 1863 to take his seat in Congress.

July 11, 1864, Edward O. C. Ord was assigned command of Eighth Corps during Early's Washington Raid. Wallace was ordered to report to Ord, but remained in charge of the administration of the department. The active command of the Middle Department reverted to Wallace July 28, 1864, when Ord was relieved.

POSTS AND DISTRICTS IN THE MIDDLE DEPARTMENT

District of Annapolis. Annapolis, Maryland was an important post in the Middle Department during the war. It was organized into the District of Annapolis in April 1865, to consist of City and Camp Parole. Frederick D. Sewall was assigned command.

Defenses of Baltimore. John A. Dix was in command at Baltimore, Maryland when the Middle Department was created March 22, 1862. Prior to that time his command was known as Dix's Command at Baltimore, Department of the Potomac. When Dix was assigned command of the Middle Department, William W. Morris was given the post of Baltimore. In September 1862, Morris' command was called the Defenses of Baltimore.

In September and October 1862 William H. Emory, who had commanded First Brigade, Second Division, Fourth Corps during the Peninsular Campaign, was in command of the troops designated as Forces Guarding Baltimore, or the Defenses of Baltimore, and also Emory's Brigade, Defenses of Baltimore. In November 1862, Emory was assigned command of a brigade composed of five regiments of his command at Baltimore, and was ordered to Fort Monroe to join Nathaniel P. Banks' Southern Expedition to New Orleans in the Department of the Gulf.

January 5, 1863, the Defenses of Baltimore was organized into a separate brigade, and February 14, 1863, this brigade was designated as Second Separate Brigade, with Morris in command. The Defenses of Baltimore was re-created June 29, 1863 during the Gettysburg Campaign and was assigned to Erastus B. Tyler. October 21, 1863, the Defenses of Baltimore was organized into Third Separate Brigade (see below), with Tyler in command. In December 1863 and January 1864, the troops in Baltimore, exclusive of the separate brigades, were Frederic W. Alexander's Artillery Reserve and Charles C. Tevis' Cavalry Reserve. From this time on, Baltimore was protected largely by Morris' Second Separate Brigade.

District of Delaware. July 3, 1863, Daniel Tyler was assigned as military governor, and also as commander of a district consisting of the state of Delaware and the troops within the state. He was also given the responsibility of protecting the Philadelphia, Wilmington, and Baltimore Railroad within the state of Delaware. He established his headquarters at Wilmington. After assuming command, Tyler used as the heading for his communications "Department of Delaware" until November 1863. He then changed the heading to "District of Delaware."

March 12, 1864, Fort Delaware, which was a prisoner-of-war camp on an island in the Delaware River, was detached from the District of Delaware and the Middle Department, and the commander was ordered to report directly to the War Department.

John R. Kenly assumed command of the district April 4, 1864, and May 16, 1864 was assigned command of Third Separate Brigade, in addition to the District of Delaware. His headquarters was at Baltimore. The District of Delaware was reorganized August 20, 1864, and was then no longer included in the Third Separate Brigade (see below). Samuel M. Bowman was assigned command of the District of Delaware, and Henry H. Lockwood was assigned command of Third Separate Brigade. The District of Delaware was again included in the command of Third Separate Brigade November 18, 1864, but this order was revoked November 29, 1864.

March 24, 1865 the District of the Eastern Shore of Maryland (see below) was included in the command of the District of Delaware, and the combined districts were designated as the District of Delaware and the Eastern Shore (see below).

The commanders of the District of Delaware were as follows:

Daniel Tyler	July 3, 1863 to January 19, 1864
Henry B. Judd	January 19, 1864 to April 4, 1864
John R. Kenly	April 4, 1864 to July 20, 1864
Henry H. Lockwood	July 20, 1864 to August 20, 1864
Samuel M. Bowman	August 20, 1864 to March 24, 1865

Note 1. Judd commanded the post of Wilmington and the District of Delaware while Tyler was on detached service.
Note 2. Kenly and Lockwood commanded Third Separate Brigade in addition to the District of Delaware.

District of Delaware and the Eastern Shore of Maryland. The District of the Eastern Shore of Maryland (see below) and the District of Delaware were consolidated March 24, 1865 to form the District of Delaware and the Eastern Shore of Maryland. John R. Kenly was assigned command, with headquarters at Wilmington, Delaware. John M. Wilson relieved Kenly June 5, 1865, and remained in command until August 1, 1865. Kenly was assigned command of First Separate Brigade.

A provisional brigade of Ninth Corps under Francis Wister arrived at Dover, Delaware May 3, 1865, and was assigned to the District of Delaware and the Eastern Shore of Maryland May 6, 1865.

District of the Eastern Shore. When the Middle

Department was created July 22, 1862, troops of John A. Dix's command at Baltimore, Army of the Potomac occupied the Eastern Shore of Maryland and the Eastern Shore of Virginia (counties of Accomac and Northampton). This command was variously referred to as the Eastern Shore of Maryland, the Eastern Shore, and the Eastern Shore of Maryland and Virginia. After January 1863, this area was a part of the command of First Separate Brigade, and later of Third Separate Brigade until December 13, 1864. On that date the counties of the Eastern Shore of Maryland were removed from the command of Third Separate Brigade, and were designated as the District of the Eastern Shore of Maryland. John R. Kenly was assigned command, with headquarters at Salisbury, Maryland. March 24, 1865, the district was included in the command of the District of Delaware, and the combined districts were designated as the District of Delaware and the Eastern Shore of Maryland (see above).

TROOPS IN THE MIDDLE DEPARTMENT
MARCH 22, 1862–JULY 22, 1862

The Middle Department was created March 22, 1862 to provide better administrative control of the troops guarding the railroads connecting Washington with the northeastern, northern, and western parts of the country, and also to ensure better military supervision of the country immediately to the north and east of the capital.

When the department was first organized, the troops were largely unbrigaded and were engaged in guarding the Baltimore and Ohio; the Philadelphia, Wilmington, and Baltimore; and the Northern Central railroads. They were also serving as garrison troops at Baltimore, Philadelphia, Wilmington, Annapolis, and Fort Delaware, and on the Eastern Shore of Maryland and Virginia. The only brigade organizations during this period were the following:

The Railroad Brigade. The Railroad Brigade, Army of the Potomac was organized in November 1861. On March 17, 1862, Dixon S. Miles, commanding the brigade, was ordered to report to Dix, of the Department of the Potomac, at Baltimore. March 29, 1862, Miles was assigned the duty of protecting the line of the Baltimore and Ohio Railroad to the western limits of the Department of the Potomac, with headquarters at Harper's Ferry.

The Middle Department was created March 22, 1862, and when the Army of the Potomac was transferred from Washington to the Peninsula in March 1862, the Railroad Brigade became a part of the forces of the Middle Department under Dix. The designation was changed July 22, 1862 to Railroad Brigade, Middle Department, Eighth Corps. As finally organized, the brigade consisted of troops from Dix's division at Baltimore, the Defenses of Washington, and Nathaniel Banks' command in the Shenandoah Valley. Brigade headquarters was at Harper's Ferry.

In September 1862, the regiments of the Railroad Brigade formed a part of the force under Miles that was captured at Harper's Ferry by Thomas J. (Stonewall) Jackson during the Maryland Campaign. For additional information, see Maryland Campaign (South Mountain and Antietam), Capture of Harper's Ferry.

Lockwood's Brigade (Peninsula Brigade). March 16, 1862, George B. McClellan directed Dix to organize a brigade in the vicinity of Baltimore for active service. This brigade was formed from regiments not needed on the Eastern Shore, which were stationed at Drummondtown (present-day Accomac) and Eastville in Virginia and at Salisbury in Maryland. Henry H. Lockwood was assigned command.

Cooper's Brigade. This brigade was organized in April 1862 under James Cooper, and the troops were stationed at Cockeysville, Havre de Grace, Mount Clare, and McKims' Mansion. The brigade was disbanded May 25, 1862, and Cooper with three regiments was ordered to Harper's Ferry. There he was assigned command of a new brigade, also called Cooper's Brigade. For further information, see Shenandoah Valley Campaign (Jackson),1862.

Amory's Brigade. March 27, 1862 Thomas J. C. Amory was ordered with a brigade of three regiments from Dix's Division at Baltimore to Hatteras Inlet, North Carolina to report to Ambrose E. Burnside. For further information, see Department of North Carolina, January 7, 1862–July 15, 1863.

* * * * * * * * * * * * * * *

There were no other significant changes in the organization of the troops of the Middle Department until July 22, 1862.

TROOPS IN THE MIDDLE DEPARTMENT, EIGHTH CORPS JULY 22, 1862–AUGUST 1, 1865

Eighth Corps was constituted July 22, 1862 to include all troops serving in the Middle Department under John E. Wool. This corps was not created as a combat force, and was not organized in the usual manner into brigades and divisions as, for example, in the Army of the Potomac. At no time did Eighth Corps take the field as a unit, and with few exceptions, its brigades were not seriously engaged in battle during the war. To avoid confusion, it should be noted that the Army of West Virginia under George Crook, which served in the Shenandoah Valley with Philip H. Sheridan in the fall and summer of 1864, was sometimes erroneously called Eighth Corps. Crook's command consisted in part of troops formerly belonging to the Middle Department, Eighth Corps, but its official designation was, by an order of August 8, 1864, Army of West Virginia.

The forces constituting Eighth Corps might generally be regarded as belonging to two separate groups. One consisted of those troops occupying the country included within the geographical limits of the Middle Department, and serving as more or less permanent garrisons of the posts and defenses of the department. The other consisted of those troops assigned to guard the line of the upper Potomac and the Baltimore and Ohio Railroad westward from Baltimore. The former were generally organized into districts and separate brigades. These brigades did not, as a rule, serve as units, but rather their troops were scattered by regiments and companies along the railroads and at the posts and in districts of the department. The latter consisted of troops from the Middle Department, and also from other departments, which, for the purpose of better administration of the defenses of the railroad, were placed under the jurisdiction of the commander of the Middle Department. The two groups are not to be regarded as unrelated, however, because both were under the same command, and transfers from one to the other occurred frequently.

For a few months during the spring of 1863, the troops on the railroad and the upper Potomac were organized into divisions, but these were discontinued in June of that year at the beginning of the Gettysburg Campaign (see below).

June 17, 1862, the defense of the Baltimore and Ohio Railroad between Baltimore and Cumberland, Maryland, and the railroad between Harper's Ferry and Winchester, Virginia was assigned as the responsibility of John E. Wool, commander of the Middle Department; and December 22, 1862, the defense of the railroads was extended under Robert C. Schenck westward to the Ohio River. At the same time, however, the geographical limits of the Middle Department were not similarly extended. Thus, for administrative reasons there were times when the commanders of the Middle Department had under their supervision troops that were outside the limits of their department.

There were also several occasions when troops of the Army of the Potomac were temporarily within the limits of the Middle Department. During the Maryland Campaign of 1862, and thereafter until December 1862, and again during the Gettysburg Campaign of late June and early July 1863, the Army of the Potomac operated within the limits of the Middle Department. George B. McClellan did not assume direct control of the department during the Maryland Campaign, but on June 22, at the beginning of the Gettysburg Campaign, the troops of the Middle Department and Eighth Corps east of Cumberland were placed under the immediate orders of Joseph Hooker, commander of the Army of the Potomac, and later under George G. Meade. Again, during Jubal A. Early's Washington Raid in July 1864, James B. Ricketts' Third Division, Sixth Corps, Army of the Potomac arrived at Baltimore from the Petersburg front, and June 9, 1864 was engaged under Lewis Wallace at the Battle of the Monocacy. Ricketts' division then returned to Baltimore, and remained in the Middle Department until it left to join the other two divisions of Sixth Corps at Leesburg, Virginia during the pursuit of Early from Washington.

Because of the diverse and changing nature of the organization of the troops of Eighth Corps, and of those under the control of the commander of the Middle Department, it is not presented in the usual manner, but is described below under the following headings: Posts and Districts in the Middle Department, Defenses of the Upper Potomac and the Baltimore and Ohio Railroad, Divisional Organization, Separate Brigades, and Military Operations in the Middle Department.

Posts and Districts in the Middle Department

The troops in the various posts and districts of the Middle Department are described in the section on Troops in the Middle Department, above.

Defenses of the Upper Potomac and the Baltimore and Ohio Railroad

One of the principal responsibilities of the troops of Eighth Corps was the protection of the Baltimore and Ohio Railroad westward from Baltimore, and especially the vulnerable part of the line beyond Harper's Ferry. At different times various organizations were engaged in this duty, and they are described in the following sections.

Railroad Brigade at Harper's Ferry. Shortly after the order creating the Middle Department was issued, George B. McClellan, commander of the Army of the Potomac, assigned Dixon S. Miles with the Railroad Brigade the duty of protecting the railroad from Baltimore to the western limits of the department. This order was dated March 29, 1862. When John E. Wool assumed command of the Middle Department June 17, 1862, he was given the responsibility of defending the Baltimore and Ohio Railroad east of Cumberland, and also the railroad between Harper's Ferry and Winchester, Virginia, and this placed Miles' brigade under his control.

The Railroad Brigade remained along the railroad during the summer of 1862, with headquarters at Harper's Ferry. As a result of Confederate troop movements following the Second Battle of Bull Run, a brigade under Julius White (formerly A. Sanders Piatt's brigade) retired from its exposed position at Winchester, Virginia and September 3, 1862 joined Miles at Harper's Ferry. The next day

White was assigned command of the troops at Martinsburg, Virginia. September 5, 1862, Miles organized his forces at Harper's Ferry into a division of four brigades as follows:

Miles' Division, Dixon S. Miles
First Brigade, Frederick G. D'Utassy
Second Brigade, William H. Trimble
Third Brigade, Thomas H. Ford
Fourth Brigade, William G. Ward
Artillery
15th Indiana Light Artillery, John C. H. Von Sehlen
Rigby's (Wilder's) Indiana Battery, Silas F. Rigby
26th Battery, Ohio Light Artillery, Benjamin F. Potts
Battery M, 2nd Illinois Light Artillery, John C. Phillips
Company A, 5th New York Heavy Artillery, John H. Graham
Company F, 5th New York Heavy Artillery, Eugene McGrath

Note. Fourth Brigade was composed largely of troops of the former Railroad Brigade.

Miles was further reinforced September 12, 1862 by White's troops from Martinsburg. Upon the approach of Thomas J. (Stonewall) Jackson's corps, Army of Northern Virginia during the Maryland Campaign, these troops evacuated the town and retired to Harper's Ferry.

By September 14, 1862, enemy forces completely invested Harper's Ferry, and Miles' position had become untenable. That night Benjamin F. Davis and Hasbrouck Davis escaped with about 1,300 cavalry, but the next day, after an enemy bombardment of the town, White, at Miles' direction, surrendered the entire garrison. For additional information, see Maryland Campaign (South Mountain and Antietam), Capture of Harper's Ferry.

Army of the Potomac. After the Battle of Antietam the Army of the Potomac remained at Harper's Ferry and in Maryland along the Potomac River until October 26, 1862, and then it began its advance into Virginia toward Warrenton. McClellan left behind to guard the Potomac River and the Baltimore and Ohio Railroad Henry W. Slocum's Twelfth Corps at Harper's Ferry, and John R. Kenly's Maryland Brigade at Williamsport, Maryland. For additional information, see Army of the Potomac, Antietam to Warrenton, Virginia.

Morell's Defenses of the Upper Potomac, Army of the Potomac. October 30, 1862, as the Army of the Potomac was marching southward in Virginia, George W. Morell, formerly commander of First Division, Fifth Corps, was assigned command of the troops left by McClellan on the upper Potomac between the mouth of Antietam Creek and Cumberland, Maryland. This command was designated as Defenses of the Upper Potomac, and Morell was assigned command November 1, 1862. For details of the organization of Morell's command, see Army of the Potomac, Defenses of the Upper Potomac. Morell continued under McClellan's orders until December 1862, and then jurisdiction was transferred to the commander of the Middle Department, Eighth Corps. For further information, see following section.

Kelley's Defenses of the Upper Potomac, Eighth Corps. December 16, 1862, Benjamin F. Kelley was ordered to relieve Morell in command of the forces on the upper Potomac (Kelley assumed command about December 20, 1862), and he was charged with defense of the Baltimore and Ohio Railroad. At that time, Kelley commanded the Railroad Division of the District of Western Virginia, Department of the Ohio. The Railroad Division consisted of four brigades as follows: James A. Mulligan's First Brigade, Nathan Wilkinson's Second Brigade, Robert Bruce's Third Brigade, and John R. Kenly's Maryland Brigade. Slocum's Twelfth Corps at Harper's Ferry had left in the early part of December 1862 to rejoin the Army of the Potomac. Kelley's troops were stationed in Western Virginia and in the Defenses of the Upper Potomac, including Point of Rocks, Williamsport, and Cumberland in Maryland, and Harper's Ferry and Martinsburg in Virginia.

Robert C. Schenck relieved Wool in command of the Middle Department December 22, 1862 (assigned December 17, 1862), with orders to cover the Baltimore and Ohio Railroad from Baltimore west to the Ohio River. The Defenses of the Upper Potomac were thus transferred from the Army of the Potomac to Eighth Corps, and Kelley was placed under Schenck's orders.

On the same day that Schenck assumed command of the Middle Department and Eighth Corps, Jacob D. Cox, commander of the District of Western Virginia, Department of the Ohio, ordered all forces of the district east of Rich Mountain and Cheat Mountain, consisting of those at New Creek, Petersburg, Moorefield, and Cumberland, to report directly to Kelley. These troops belonged to Kelley's Railroad Division and Robert H. Milroy's Cheat Mountain Division. Prior to this order, Milroy was at New Creek, where he reorganized his division into a First Brigade under Gustave P. Cluseret, and a Second Brigade under James Washburn.

Milroy occupied Petersburg and Moorefield in Hardy County, Virginia, but Washburn's brigade was detained at Burlington, Virginia, and was later sent to Romney. December 25, 1862, Cluseret occupied Winchester with his brigade. The next day Schenck decided to occupy Winchester permanently, and Milroy joined Cluseret with two regiments of Washburn's brigade under J. Warren Keifer. Washburn with the other two regiments of his brigade remained at Romney. Milroy's command at Winchester then consisted of Cluseret's brigade and Keifer's brigade.

In February 1863, the forces in the Defenses of the Upper Potomac were reorganized, and the Defenses, as an organization, was discontinued. It was at this time that the only divisions organized in Eighth Corps were formed, and these were composed of troops guarding the Baltimore and Ohio Railroad.

Divisional Organization of Eighth Corps

As noted above, the first divisions in Eighth Corps were Kelley's Railroad Division and Milroy's Cheat Mountain Division, and these were transferred from the District of Western Virginia, Department of the Ohio. In February 1863, Kelley's division was designated as First Division, Eighth Corps, and Milroy's division as Second Division, Eighth Corps. It also appears that in late February or early March 1863, a Third Division was organized under Benjamin S. Roberts, who was assigned to duty in the Middle Department January 24, 1863. There is, however, some uncertainty as to the divisional organization at this time. In early March 1863, Kelley was in command of the troops in and around Harper's Ferry, in the Defenses of the Upper

Potomac, and on the line of the Baltimore and Ohio Railroad. March 11, 1863, he was relieved of this command and was assigned command of Roberts' Third Division, with headquarters at Cumberland, Maryland. It seems that Third Division consisted of three brigades commanded by John M. Campbell, James A. Mulligan, and Nathan Wilkinson, and First Division consisted of brigades commanded by John R. Kenly, William H. Morris, and Benjamin F. Smith. Milroy's Second Division was at Winchester. March 16, 1863, the same day that the District of Western Virginia was transferred to the Middle Department, Kelley assumed command of Third Division and relieved Roberts. Troops of Third Division were then assigned to First Division under Kelley, and a new First Division of six brigades was organized March 27, 1863. Roberts was assigned command of a new Fourth Separate Brigade that was formed from troops just transferred to Eighth Corps from the District of Western Virginia (see below).

A description of the divisions of Eighth Corps as finally organized in March 1863 follows.

First Division, Eighth Corps. This division was constituted March 27, 1863, and was charged with the protection of the Baltimore and Ohio Railroad from Monocacy Bridge, Maryland to the Ohio River. Kelley was assigned command, with headquarters at Harper's Ferry. The division was organized as follows:

First Division, Benjamin F. Kelley
    First Brigade, John R. Kenly
    Second Brigade, William H. Morris
    Third Brigade, Benjamin F. Smith
    Fourth Brigade, John M. Campbell
    Fifth Brigade, James A. Mulligan
    Sixth Brigade, Nathan Wilkinson

Note 1. First Brigade was organized from the Maryland Brigade, Defenses of the Upper Potomac, Eighth Corps.

Note 2. Second Brigade was organized from troops at Point of Rocks, Defenses of the Upper Potomac, Eighth Corps.

Note 3. Third Brigade was composed largely from troops at Martinsburg, Grafton, and Sir John's Run.

Note 4. Fourth Brigade was formed from troops at North Mountain and Romney.

Note 5. Fifth Brigade was formed from troops at New Creek and Cumberland.

Note 6. Sixth Brigade was formed from troops at Clarksburg and Parkersburg.

The brigades of First Division were posted as follows: First Brigade at Harper's Ferry and Winchester; Second Brigade at Maryland Heights and Point of Rocks; Third Brigade at Charlestown, Kearneysville, Martinsburg, North Mountain, and Sir John's Run; Fourth Brigade near Romney; Fifth Brigade at Cumberland and New Creek; and Sixth Brigade at Grafton and Parkersburg.

June 24, 1863, during the advance of the armies toward Gettysburg, First Division was discontinued and the brigades were assigned as follows: Fourth, Fifth, and Sixth brigades were transferred to the newly created Department of West Virginia as separate commands. Fourth Brigade became Campbell's Brigade, Department of West Virginia; Fifth Brigade became Mulligan's Brigade, Department of West Virginia; and Sixth Brigade became Wilkinson's Brigade, Department of West Virginia. First, Second, and Third brigades became a part of Daniel Tyler's (and later William H. French's) command at Harper's Ferry. For further information about the latter, see Middle Department, Troops in the Middle Department, Gettysburg Campaign, below.

Second Division, Eighth Corps. In December 1862, Robert H. Milroy, commander of the Cheat Mountain Division, District of Western Virginia, Department of the Ohio, was ordered to report to Benjamin F. Kelley, commanding the Defenses of the Upper Potomac, Eighth Corps. Kelley then directed him to occupy Winchester, which he did later that month. March 5, 1863, Milroy's command at Winchester was designated as Second Division, Eighth Corps. It consisted largely of regiments from the Railroad Division and from the District of Western Virginia, and was organized into a First Brigade commanded by Washington L. Elliott, and a Second Brigade commanded by George Hay. William G. Ely succeeded Hay May 25, 1863. A Third Brigade was formed later under John F. Staunton, but he was soon relieved by Andrew T. Mc-Reynolds. First and Second brigades were stationed at Winchester, and Third Brigade was sent to Berryville, Virginia.

When Richard S. Ewell's Confederate corps moved down the Shenandoah Valley at the beginning of the Gettysburg Campaign, McReynolds' Third Brigade moved back to Winchester, and the division attempted to halt the enemy advance. It was overwhelmed and virtually destroyed in the fighting at Winchester and Stephenson's Depot June 13–15, 1863. A part of the division reached Harper's Ferry in safety, and some troops moved to the north and crossed the Potomac at Hancock, Maryland. The latter then continued on and assembled at Bloody Run (present-day Everett) in Pennsylvania.

Second Division was not reorganized, but what remained of First and Third brigades was assigned to Washington L. Elliott's command at Harper's Ferry, and Second Brigade was broken up. Elliott's brigade became a part of William H. French's division. For additional information, see Gettysburg Campaign, and also see below, Military Operations in the Middle Department, Gettysburg Campaign.

Third Division, Eighth Corps. In early March 1863, Benjamin S. Roberts was in command of Third Division, Eighth Corps, which was on the Baltimore and Ohio Railroad. March 11, 1863 Benjamin F. Kelley was assigned command of this division. March 16, 1863, the District of Western Virginia was transferred to the Middle Department, and Kelley assumed command of the division, relieving Roberts. Later, the troops of Third Division were assigned to First Division, Eighth Corps, which was organized under Kelley. Also on March 16, 1863, Roberts was assigned command of a new Fourth Separate Brigade, which consisted of a part of the troops of Western Virginia that were transferred to the Middle Department. This brigade was organized March 28, 1863. See Fourth Separate Brigade, below. The remainder of the troops in Western Virginia belonged to Eliakim P. Scammon's Kanawha Division, and these were organized in April 1863 into Third Division, Eighth Corps. Rutherford B. Hayes commanded First Brigade, Third Division, and Carr B. White commanded Second Brigade. Scammon was assigned command, with headquarters at Charleston, Western Virginia. First Brigade was posted at Barboursville, Camp White, and Hurricane Bridge. Second Brigade was at Cannelton, Fayetteville, and Gauley Bridge. Third Division was transferred to the newly created Department of West Virginia June 24, 1863 as Scammon's Division, Department of West Virginia.

Roberts' Independent Division. March 28, 1863, Benjamin S. Roberts was assigned command of Fourth Separate Brigade, and was ordered to Clarksburg in Western Virginia to assume command. April 20, 1863, John D. Imboden with a Confederate force started on a raid in Western Virginia, and the next day William E. Jones began a raid on the Baltimore and Ohio Railroad in cooperation with Imboden. The purpose of these raids, known as the Jones-Imboden Raid, was to destroy all bridges and trestles on the railroad from Oakland, Maryland to Grafton in Western Virginia, and to capture the Union forces at Beverly, Philippi, and Buckhannon. Strong reinforcements were sent to Western Virginia, and Roberts, at Clarksburg, was assigned command of a temporary independent division during the emergency. His force consisted of his own Fourth Separate Brigade under Augustus Moor, and three brigades (or parts of brigades) of First Division, Eighth Corps. These were John R. Kenly's First Brigade, James A. Mulligan's Fifth Brigade, and Nathan Wilkinson's Sixth Brigade.

The enemy threat ended in mid-May 1863, when Confederate forces withdrew from the area. Roberts was ordered to report to John Pope, commander of the Department of the Northwest, May 19, 1863, and he was succeeded in command by William W. Averell. May 23, 1863, Kenly's brigade was ordered to return to Harper's Ferry.

On August 3, 1863, the responsibility for the defense of the Baltimore and Ohio Railroad (except for that part east of the Monocacy River) and the upper Potomac by troops of the Middle Department was largely at an end. On that date, all of Maryland west of the Monocacy River was transferred to the Department of West Virginia.

Separate Brigades

Early in 1863, three separate brigades were organized in the Middle Department, and these were continued, although with some changes, until the end of the war. This was done to provide for better administration of the forces in the department, and also to give legal authority for such functions as courts martial. A Fourth Separate Brigade was organized in March 1863, from troops transferred from Western Virginia.

First Separate Brigade. In the latter part of 1862, Henry H. Lockwood was in command of the Eastern Shore of Maryland and Virginia with one regiment of infantry and one company of cavalry. This command was known as Lockwood's Brigade, Eastern Shore of Maryland and Virginia. January 26, 1863, it was designated as a separate brigade, and was defined generally to include the following: the forces then in, and later to be added to, the counties of the Eastern Shore of Maryland, and the counties of Accomac and Northampton in Virginia; those forces on the Western Shore of Maryland between the Potomac River and the Patuxent River as far up as the Piscataway River and Upper Marlboro in the county of Calvert; and in the state of Delaware, except the guards on the Philadelphia, Wilmington, and Baltimore Railroad. Lockwood was assigned command. February 14, 1863, this brigade was designated as First Separate Brigade, Eighth Corps, and in May 1863, its troops were posted as follows: Prince George's County, Cambridge, Leonardtown, Port Tobacco, Point Lookout, and Townfield in Maryland, and Wilmington, Delaware.

During the Gettysburg Campaign First Separate Brigade was discontinued, and Lockwood with a provisional brigade (consisting in part of troops of First Separate Brigade) was ordered June 25, 1863 to Monocacy Bridge to report to Joseph Hooker, commanding the Army of the Potomac. At Monocacy Bridge, Lockwood was ordered on to Gettysburg, where he arrived July 2, 1863. His brigade was then attached to Henry W. Slocum's Twelfth Corps as Second Brigade, First Division (see Lockwood's Provisional Brigade, below). It was engaged with Twelfth Corps during the Battle of Gettysburg.

First Separate Brigade was reorganized October 21, 1863, when Lockwood was assigned command of a district consisting of the counties of the Eastern Shore of Maryland as far north as, and including, Kent County; the counties of Accomac and Northampton in Virginia; the county of Calvert in Maryland; and all of the Western Shore of Maryland lying between the Potomac River and the Patuxent River as far north as the Piscataway River and Upper Marlboro, excepting Saint Mary's County. The troops of this district were designated as First Separate Brigade. Headquarters of the brigade was at Drummondtown (present-day Accomac), Virginia.

December 18, 1863, First Separate Brigade (as constituted October 12, 1863) was discontinued, but it was reorganized the same day largely from troops of Third Separate Brigade, and it was also to include troops that might be assigned to duty in a district of the department that was west of the Chesapeake Bay and south of, and adjacent to, the line of the Baltimore and Ohio Railroad. Excepted were the command of Carlos A. Waite at Annapolis, Maryland and the hospitals at Annapolis Junction. Erastus B. Tyler was assigned command, with headquarters at Relay's House, Maryland. The troops of the new First Separate Brigade were stationed at Relay's House on the Baltimore and Ohio Railroad, Chapel Point, and Ellicott's Mills (now Ellicott City) in Maryland. Later posts occupied by this command were: Monrovia, Monocacy Junction, Mount Airy, Annapolis Junction, Buckeystown, Elysville, Hood's Mills, Urbana, and Barnesville in Maryland.

During Jubal A. Early's invasion of Maryland in 1864, First Separate Brigade was engaged at the Battle of the Monocacy as a part of Lewis Wallace's command. For details, see Early's Washington Raid (and Operations in the Shenandoah Valley, Maryland, and Pennsylvania).

First Separate Brigade was redefined June 6, 1865 to include the Baltimore and Ohio Railroad to point of Rocks, Maryland; the counties of Anne Arundel and Calvert; and parts of the counties of Baltimore, Carroll, Frederick, Howard, and Montogomery in Maryland. John R. Kenly was assigned command.

Commanders of First Separate Brigade were as follows:

Henry H. Lockwood	February 14, 1863 to June 25, 1863
Henry H. Lockwood	October 21, 1863 to December 18, 1863
Erastus B. Tyler	December 18, 1863 to November 17, 1864
John R. Kenly	November 17, 1864 to December 13, 1864
Erastus B. Tyler	December 13, 1864 to June 5, 1865
John R. Kenly	June 5, 1865 to June 12, 1865
Erastus B. Tyler (temporarily)	June 12, 1865

Second Separate Brigade. January 5, 1863, William W. Morris was assigned command of a brigade that was formed from regiments of the Defenses of Baltimore and troops at Cockeysville, Maryland; troops on the line of the Philadelphia, Wilmington, and Baltimore Railroad as far as Perryville; and all troops on the line of the Northern Central Railroad, including York, Pennsylvania. Included also were Forts McHenry, Federal Hill, and Marshall at Baltimore. This brigade was designated as Second Separate Brigade, Eighth Corps February 14, 1863, with headquarters at Fort McHenry. This brigade continued in existence during the rest of the war. Commanders were as follows:

William W. Morris	January 5, 1863 to January 20, 1864
Peter A. Porter	January 20, 1864 to May 10, 1864
William W. Morris	May 10, 1864 to January 31, 1865
Daniel Macauley	January 31, 1865 to April 19, 1865
William W. Morris	April 19, 1865 to July 29, 1865

Third Separate Brigade. Third Separate Brigade, Eighth Corps was organized February 14, 1863, under the command of Henry S. Briggs. It was assigned to guard duty in and around Baltimore, guarding the Baltimore and Ohio Railroad from Baltimore to Monocacy Junction, and to Frederick, Maryland; and the Washington Branch of the Baltimore and Ohio Railroad to Annapolis Junction. In late June 1863, during the Gettysburg Campaign, this brigade was broken up and the troops were assigned largely to the Army of the Potomac.

Third Separate Brigade was reorganized July 16, 1863 and assigned to Samuel A. Graham. It was then again discontinued August 10, 1863, and once more reorganized October 21, 1863, this time under Erastus B. Tyler. The brigade consisted of all troops of Eighth Corps stationed in Baltimore City and County, including all defensive works therein, excepting the following: Second Separate Brigade, and Forts McHenry, Marshall, Federal Hill, and Dix. December 18, 1863, Third Separate Brigade was discontinued by a change of designation to First Separate Brigade (see above).

March 24, 1864, Third Separate Brigade was again reorganized to include troops of Eighth Corps within the counties of Frederick, Carroll, and Harford; the counties of the Eastern Shore of Maryland; and the city and county of Baltimore, excepting Forts McHenry, Federal Hill, Carroll, and Marshall, which were within the limits of Second Separate

Brigade. Henry H. Lockwood was assigned command, with headquarters at Baltimore. May 16, 1864, John R. Kenly was assigned command of Third Separate Brigade and also of the District of Delaware, with headquarters at Baltimore.

July 11, 1864, Lockwood was assigned command of all the defenses of Baltimore, except the above-mentioned forts and the areas not a part of the territories held by First Separate Brigade and Second Separate Brigade. This order was amended July 20, 1864 as follows: Lockwood was assigned command of Third Separate Brigade and the district included therein as described in the order of March 24, 1864 (see above).

December 13, 1864, the counties of the Eastern Shore were removed from the control of Third Separate Brigade, and designated as the District of the Eastern Shore of Maryland. Kenly, who had been in temporary command of First Separate Brigade during the absence of Erastus B. Tyler, was relieved and assigned command of the District of the Eastern Shore of Maryland.

June 9, 1865, Lockwood's Third Separate Brigade was defined as consisting of the city and county of Baltimore; the counties of Harford and Cecil; Havre de Grace; and the bridges at Gunpowder, Bush, and Black rivers on the Philadelphia, Wilmington, and Baltimore Railroad.

The commanders of Third Separate Brigade were:

Henry S. Briggs	February 14, 1863 to June 25, 1863
Samuel A. Graham	July 16, 1863 to August 10, 1863
Erastus B. Tyler	October 21, 1863 to December 18, 1863
Henry H. Lockwood	March 24, 1864 to May 16, 1864
John R. Kenly	May 16, 1864 to July 20, 1864
Henry H. Lockwood	July 20, 1864 to July 31, 1865

Note. The order of July 20, 1864 assigning Lockwood to the command of Third Separate Brigade says that Kenly's relief was to take effect July 14, 1864.

Fourth Separate Brigade. Fourth Separate Brigade was constituted March 28, 1863 (by an order of March 16, 1863) to consist of troops transferred from Western Virginia. These were stationed along the Baltimore and Ohio Railroad at Beverly, Buckhannon, Clarksburg, Parkersburg, and Weston. Benjamin S. Roberts was assigned command, with headquarters at Clarksburg. During the Jones-Imboden Raid in Western Virginia April 21, 1863–May 21, 1863, Fourth Separate Brigade, under the temporary command of Augustus Moor, formed a part of Roberts' Independent Division (see above). Roberts was ordered to report to John Pope, commander of the Department of the Northwest, and was relieved in command of Fourth Separate Brigade May 20, 1863 by William W. Averell. The brigade was transferred to the Department of West Virginia June 24, 1863.

MILITARY OPERATIONS IN THE MIDDLE DEPARTMENT

On three occasions during the war there were major invasions of the state of Maryland by troops of the Army of Northern Virginia, and these resulted in the battles of South Mountain, Antietam, and the Monocacy in Maryland, and Gettysburg, a short distance north of the border in Pennsylvania. These operations resulted in some changes in the organization of the troops in the Middle Department, and also in the troops present in the department. These are described in the following sections.

The Maryland Campaign (South Mountain and Antietam)

During Robert E. Lee's invasion of Maryland in September 1862, George B. McClellan's Army of the Potomac operated in the counties of Montgomery, Washington, and Frederick in Maryland. During this time, the army was under McClellan's orders, and not those of the commander of the Middle Department. After the Battle of Antietam, the Army of the Potomac remained along the Potomac River in Maryland, from Poolesville to Williamsport, until October 26, 1862, and then it crossed the river into Virginia. When the army departed, McClellan left Henry W. Slocum's Twelfth Corps at Harper's Ferry and John R. Kenly's Maryland Brigade at Williamsport to guard the Potomac River. Kenly's Maryland Brigade was formed September 12, 1862 from troops of the Defenses of Baltimore; and September 17, 1862, the day of the Battle of Antietam, Kenly was ordered to Hagerstown to report to McClellan. Kenly arrived at Hagerstown two days later, and was then ordered to Williamsport to join the Army of the Potomac in guarding the river.

The Gettysburg Campaign

When Lee invaded Maryland and Pennsylvania in 1863, the Army of the Potomac followed, and during the period June 25, 1863–July 19, 1863 operated in the counties of Montgomery, Frederick, Carroll, and Washington in Maryland. Joseph Hooker commanded the army until June 28, 1863, and then was relieved by George G. Meade. June 22, 1863, Henry W. Halleck directed that all of Eighth Corps and the Middle Department be placed under the immediate orders of the commander of the Army of the Potomac, and this arrangement continued until the army left the department July 19, 1863. For additional information, see Gettysburg Campaign.

During the Gettysburg Campaign several new commands were formed in the Middle Department and in the Army of the Potomac, and in addition some organizations in the Middle Department were discontinued or transferred from the department. These changes are described in the following sections.

Milroy's Second Division, Eighth Corps. When Lee's army began its advance northward in the Shenandoah Valley at the beginning of the Gettysburg Campaign, Robert H. Milroy's Second Division, Eighth Corps was in an isolated position at Winchester and Berryville, and despite all efforts by Halleck to have Milroy withdraw, he remained to confront the advance of Richard S. Ewell's Corps of the Army of Northern Virginia. In the ensuing battle at Winchester and at Stephenson's Depot, on the Martinsburg Road, June 13–15, 1863, the division was virtually destroyed, losing about 4,400 men. Milroy led one group of about 1,200 men to Harper's Ferry, where it arrived on the evening of June 15, 1863. The remainder of the division went generally in the direction of Bath, Virginia, crossed the Potomac River at Hancock, Maryland, and finally assembled at Bloody Run (present-day Everett), Pennsylvania with about 2,700 men present. Milroy assumed command of the troops at Bloody Run, and June 23, 1863 was ordered by Robert C. Schenck to

bring these troops to Baltimore. Milroy's command, however, was then in Darius N. Couch's Department of the Susquehanna, and was retained there by Couch during the emergency. Lewis B. Pierce relieved Milroy June 26, 1863. For additional information, see Gettysburg Campaign, From the Rappahannock to Gettysburg, Withdrawal of the Army to the Orange and Alexandria Railroad, Engagement at Winchester, Virginia, and Engagement at Stephenson's Depot (or Station), Virginia.

Tyler's Command at Harper's Ferry. June 13, 1863, Robert C. Schenck ordered Daniel Tyler to Harper's Ferry to assume command of all troops there, including Benjamin F. Smith's Third Brigade, First Division, Eighth Corps at Martinsburg, Virginia. Tyler arrived at Martinsburg in time to order the evacuation of the town June 14, 1863, the day of Milroy's battle at Winchester. Tyler, with Smith's brigade, retired the next day to Harper's Ferry, and there he assumed command of the troops of the garrison. That same day, June 15, 1863, Benjamin F. Kelley was directed to assume command of all troops west of Martinsburg, including William W. Averell's Fourth Separate Brigade, and to concentrate them as far as possible at New Creek. June 16, 1863, Tyler crossed the Potomac with his command and occupied Maryland Heights. He assembled there about 3,300 men and organized them into three brigades, which were commanded by John R. Kenly, Washington L. Elliott, and William H. Morris. Kenly's Maryland Brigade was formerly First Brigade, First Division, Eighth Corps; Elliott's Brigade was formed from regiments of Milroy's Second Division, Eighth Corps, and Elliott was assigned command June 19, 1863; and Morris' Brigade was composed largely of regiments of Second Separate Brigade and Third Separate Brigade of Eighth Corps. Morris' Brigade was designated as Third Provisional Brigade. Andrew T. McReynolds was assigned command of the cavalry at Harper's Ferry.

During the next ten days about 3,400 men were sent to reinforce Tyler, and in addition about 1,500 survivors of Milroy's division came in. Milroy was given no further command at that time. Among the reinforcements was Albert B. Jewett's Brigade, Defenses of Washington, which arrived from Poolesville, Maryland. This brigade was broken up and its regiments were reassigned.

Department of West Virginia Created. In mid-June 1863, at the beginning of the Gettysburg Campaign, the Middle Department consisted of the state of Delaware, most of the state of Maryland, and all of Western Virginia except the counties of Hancock, Brooke, and Ohio, which were near Wheeling. June 24, 1863, four days after the new state of West Virginia was admitted to the Union, the Middle Department, Eighth Corps was divided, and all of the state of West Virginia, except the above-mentioned counties, and all of Maryland west of a north-south line through Hancock was assigned to the newly constituted Department of West Virginia. This caused a significant reduction in the number of troops in the Middle Department, and the divisional organization of Eighth Corps was discontinued. Kelley's First Division, Eighth Corps was broken up, and the First, Second, and Third brigades became a part of Daniel Tyler's (and later William H. French's) command at Harper's Ferry. For details, see below, French's Division. The Fourth, Fifth, and Sixth brigades of Kelley's division were transferred to the Department of West Virginia as Campbell's Brigade, Mulligan's Brigade, and Wilkinson's Brigade, and October 21, 1863, these three brigades were organized into Second Division, Department of West Virginia. Milroy's Second Division, Eighth Corps had been destroyed at Winchester and Stephenson's Depot June 13–15, 1863. Eliakim P. Scammon's Third Division, Eighth Corps was transferred intact to the Department of West Virginia as Scammon's Division, Department of West Virginia. William W. Averell's Fourth Separate Brigade, Eighth Corps was also transferred to the Department of West Virginia as Averell's Brigade, Department of West Virginia.

French's Division. June 23, 1863, William H. French, commanding Third Division, Second Corps, Army of the Potomac, was ordered by Joseph Hooker to relieve Daniel Tyler in command at Harper's Ferry. Alexander Hays from the Department of Washington assumed command of French's division of Second Corps. French assumed command June 26, 1863 and organized the approximately 11,000 men at Harper's Ferry into a division of four brigades as follows:

French's Division, William H. French
   Elliott's Brigade, Washington L. Elliott

   Kenly's Brigade, John R. Kenly
   Third Provisional Brigade, William H. Morris
   Smith's Brigade, Benjamin F. Smith

Note. Smith's Brigade was composed of regiments from Third Brigade, First Division, Eighth Corps. For information about the other three brigades, see Tyler's Command at Harper's Ferry, above.

June 29, 1863, George G. Meade, then commander of the Army of the Potomac, ordered the evacuation of Harper's Ferry. The brigades of Elliott and Smith, designated as Elliott's command, were left at Harper's Ferry to complete the removal of the government property and to escort it to Washington, D.C. French, with Kenly's and Morris' brigades, marched to Frederick, Maryland, where he arrived June 30, 1863, and remained during the Battle of Gettysburg. Elliott with his command moved from Harper's Ferry by way of the Chesapeake and Ohio Canal, and arrived in Washington July 4, 1863. He then moved to Tennallytown, D.C. That day Morris' Brigade of French's Division was sent from Frederick to Turner's Gap in South Mountain.

July 6, 1863, Elliott with his two brigades was ordered to Frederick to join French. He arrived the next day, and then French with the brigades of Elliott and Smith moved by way of Middletown to Antietam Creek, and there he was joined by Morris' Brigade from Turner's Gap. Kenly's Brigade was sent to reoccupy Harper's Ferry July 6, 1863. French's Division then joined Third Corps, Army of the Potomac July 9, 1863, and the next day it was organized and assigned as Third Division, Third Corps. French assumed command of Third Corps, and Elliott assumed command of Third Division. First Brigade was then commanded by William H. Morris, Second Brigade by J. Warren Keifer, and Third Brigade by Benjamin F. Smith.

Lockwood's Provisional Brigade, Eighth Corps. In late June 1863, Henry H. Lockwood's First Separate Brigade, Eighth Corps was discontinued, and Lockwood was assigned command of a new provisional brigade, consisting, in part, of troops from his former First Separate Brigade. June 25, 1863, Lockwood was ordered from Baltimore to Monocacy Bridge to report to Joseph Hooker. Lockwood was then ordered on to Gettysburg, where he arrived July 2, 1863, during the battle. His brigade was engaged during the battle, although not assigned, but later it was assigned to Henry W. Slocum's Twelfth Corps as Second Brigade, First Division. July 17, 1863 Lockwood was sent to Harper's Ferry with the Maryland regiments of his brigade, and there he was assigned command of Maryland Heights, relieving Henry M. Naglee.

First Provisional Brigade, Eighth Corps. This brigade was organized in Baltimore June 27, 1863, and assigned to Daniel Tyler. The troops were generally disposed on the northern and northwestern approaches to the city. Daniel Tyler was relieved from command of First Provisional Brigade, and was assigned command of the District of Delaware. Erastus B. Tyler was assigned command of all forces at Baltimore except those of Second Separate Brigade and the troops on the Northern Central Railroad.

Second Provisional Brigade, Eighth Corps. June 30, 1863, Erastus B. Tyler was assigned command of Second Provisional Brigade, which consisted of all armed citizens who had volunteered for the defense of Baltimore, and also of other troops that might later be assigned.

Third Provisional Brigade, Eighth Corps. As noted above this brigade was organized at Harper's Ferry in the latter part of June 1863, as a part of Daniel Tyler's (and later William H. French's) division. It was commanded by William H. Morris.

Briggs' Brigade, Eighth Corps. July 5, 1863, Henry S. Briggs, whose Third Separate Brigade was discontinued, was assigned command of a new brigade at Baltimore. This brigade was formed from new regiments and some regiments recently arrived from Eighteenth Corps, Department of North Carolina, and was ordered to report to William H. French at Frederick, Maryland. The brigade was then sent off to Harper's Ferry, where it became a part of Henry M. Naglee's command (see below).

Occupation of Harper's Ferry. July 6, 1863, French was ordered to reoccupy Harper's Ferry, and Kenly's Brigade arrived on Maryland Heights the next day. He was joined there by Briggs with his brigade. July 8, 1863, George G. Meade ordered

Henry M. Naglee to go with Francis B. Spinola's brigade (Keystone Brigade), just arrived from the Department of Virginia, to Harper's Ferry and assume command. Naglee's command there consisted of the brigades of Kenly, Briggs, and Spinola. Kenly's Brigade left July 10, 1863 to join the Army of the Potomac. It was then assigned to First Corps as Third Brigade, Third Division under Nathan T. Dushane. Kenly was assigned command of Third Division, First Corps. Henry H. Lockwood relieved Naglee of command at Harper's Ferry July 17, 1863. July 19, 1863, as the Army of the Potomac was leaving the line of the Potomac River on its advance into Virginia, Meade placed Lockwood's command on Maryland Heights under the orders of Darius N. Couch, commander of the Department of the Susquehanna.

Early's Washington Raid

July 5, 1864, Lewis Wallace, commanding the Middle Department, learned that Jubal A. Early had crossed the Potomac River with his corps of the Army of Northern Virginia, and was advancing eastward across Maryland toward Frederick. Wallace immediately collected all available troops of Eighth Corps and marched out to the Monocacy River near Frederick. His command consisted of Erastus B. Tyler's First Separate Brigade and some cavalry under David R. Clendenin. July 8, 1864, James B. Ricketts arrived in Baltimore from the Army of the Potomac at Petersburg with his Third Division, Sixth Corps, and he then marched out to join Wallace at Monocacy Junction. The next day Early attacked the combined forces under Wallace and drove them from the field. Ricketts retreated to Ellicott's Mills (now Ellicott City) July 10, 1864, and the next day moved on to Baltimore. Tyler's brigade and the cavalry also fell back to Baltimore. Early moved on and reached the northern outskirts of Washington about noon July 11, 1864. For additional information, see Early's Washington Raid (and Operations in the Shenandoah Valley, Maryland, and Pennsylvania).

July 11, 1864, Edward O. C. Ord was assigned command of Eighth Corps and all troops in the Middle Department, and assumed command the same day. By this arrangement Wallace reported to

Ord, but remained in charge of the administration of the department.

John R. Kenly, commander of Third Separate Brigade, was relieved from command of that brigade July 13, 1864, and the next day was assigned by Ord to command a new brigade formed from Erastus B. Tyler's First Separate Brigade. Tyler was assigned command of Kenly's Third Separate Brigade. July 14, 1864, Ord was ordered to Washington with Kenly's brigade and Ricketts' division to join Horatio G. Wright's command that was formed for the pursuit of Early toward the Shenandoah Valley. When Kenly's brigade reached Washington, it continued on to Leesburg, Virginia by way of Edwards Ferry, and there it was attached to Detachment Nineteenth Corps July 17, 1864. Ricketts' division rejoined the other two divisions of Sixth Corps near Leesburg the same day. When Ord departed for Washington July 14, 1864, Wallace resumed command of Eighth Corps. Ord was assigned command of Eighteenth Corps July 22, 1864.

DEPARTMENT OF THE MONONGAHELA

Early in June 1863, reports indicated that some Confederate movement was imminent in Virginia, and both Governor Andrew G. Curtin of Pennsylvania and Secretary of War Edwin M. Stanton believed that Pennsylvania was the objective. Specifically, one report gave Pittsburgh as the most likely target. To ensure better control of military affairs in the state, it was decided June 9, 1863 to establish two new departments, and the next day orders were issued constituting the Department of the Monongahela and the Department of the Susquehanna (see).

The Department of the Monongahela was formed from a part of the Middle Department and a part of the Department of the Ohio. It consisted of that part of the state of Pennsylvania west of Johnstown and the Laurel Hill range of mountains; the counties of Hancock, Brooke, and Ohio in the northern tip of Western Virginia; and the counties of Columbiana, Jefferson, and Belmont in Ohio. The eastern border

ran from the southern state line of Pennsylvania, at the point of intersection with the western boundary of Maryland, northeast to Johnstown, and then north to the northern state line of Pennsylvania at a point near where the Allegheny River crosses from New York into Pennsylvania. William T. H. Brooks assumed command of the department June 11, 1863, with headquarters at Pittsburgh.

October 12, 1863, the counties of Hancock, Brooke, and Ohio in West Virginia were transferred to the Department of West Virginia.

January 12, 1864, the counties of Columbiana, Jefferson, and Belmont in Ohio were transferred to the Northern Department.

April 6, 1864, the Department of the Monongahela was merged into the Department of the Susquehanna.

The posts in the Department of the Monongahela were as follows: Barnesville, Hendrysburg, New Wilmington, and Somerton in Ohio; Camp Howe, Connellsville, Fort Herron, Pittsburgh, Pulaski, Somerset, West Alexander, and West Finley in Pennsylvania; and Wheeling, West Virginia. Charles C. Churchill commanded at Pittsburgh until August 1863, and he was succeeded by Samuel T. Griffith. Joseph Darr, Jr. commanded at Wheeling until the end of June 1863, and he was succeeded by Wesley Thorpe. Thorpe continued in command until the post was transferred to the Department of West Virginia October 12, 1863. Joseph B. Kiddoo commanded at Camp Howe from June 18, 1863 to July 21, 1863. On the latter date the camp was occupied as a rendezvous for drafted men.

On June 9, 1863, the day before the department was constituted, the War Department authorized the formation of a departmental army corps, which was to be designated as the Army Corps of the Monongahela, and directed that it be enrolled and organized. There was, however, a poor response to the call for troops, which were to be enrolled for three months and six months, and by the end of June 1863, there were only 784 men reported in the department. These were stationed at Wheeling and Pittsburgh, and at Camp Howe, near Pittsburgh.

In July 1863, during Lee's invasion of Pennsylvania, the number of troops in the department increased to a high of about 1,800 men, but the number was generally between 700 and 800. These were, for the most part, emergency militia, and they served at the various posts in the department as companies and battalions. That month a number of militia units were transferred to West Virginia to report to Benjamin F. Kelley at Hancock, Maryland for service on the Baltimore and Ohio Railroad. Also in July 1863, three regiments of Pennsylvania Militia were sent to Ohio to aid in the capture of John H. Morgan and his raiders, who surrendered July 16, 1863.

MOUNTAIN DEPARTMENT

The Mountain Department was created March 11, 1862. It consisted of those parts of the states of Michigan, Ohio, Kentucky, and Tennessee that were east of a north-south line passing through Knoxville, Tennessee; and all of Maryland and Virginia west of a line beginning on the north on Flintstone Creek in Maryland and running southward in Virginia, from the Potomac River at a point opposite the mouth of Flintstone Creek, along South Branch Mountain, Town Hill Mountain, Branch Mountain or Big Ridge, North or Shenandoah Mountain, Purgatory Mountain, and the Blue Ridge and Allegheny mountains to the North Carolina border. The department was bounded on the east by the Department of the Potomac, and on the west by the Department of the Mississippi, and its territory was taken from the Department of Western Virginia and a part of the Department of the Ohio. John C. Fremont was assigned command March 11, 1862, but William S. Rosecrans assumed command March 14, 1862 pending Fremont's arrival. Fremont assumed command at Wheeling, in Western Virginia, March 29, 1862.

As the Mountain Department was first defined, its organization involved little more than a change in designation from the Department of Western Virginia to the Mountain Department. Although the eastern parts of Michigan, Ohio, Kentucky, and Tennessee were included within the limits of the Mountain Department, neither Rosecrans nor his successor, Fremont, exercised any significant control over this territory. The only Federal troops operating in eastern Tennessee were in the vicinity of Cumberland Gap, and these belonged to Don Carlos Buell's Army of the Ohio, Department of the

Mississippi. The troops in eastern Kentucky under James A. Garfield also belonged to the Army of the Ohio. From the outset, it was clear that the Federal troops in eastern Kentucky and eastern Tennessee were to remain under Buell's control. March 13, 1862, Henry W. Halleck, commander of the Department of the Mississippi, informed Buell that the formation of the Mountain Department and the Department of the Mississippi would not interfere with his command, and that he would command the same army and the same district of the country as before. March 23, 1862, Edwin M. Stanton, secretary of war, informed Buell that he did not intend to place Garfield under Fremont's orders, and the next day he directed Rosecrans not to interfere with Garfield's movements.

The order of March 11, 1862 placed the greater part of the state of Ohio in the Mountain Department, and the smaller western part of the state in the Department of the Mississippi, but there is no evidence that the commander of either department exercised control over any Union forces in the state. On the contrary, the governor of Ohio appears to have held a semi-military jurisdiction over the troops at Johnson's Island and at other posts. Thus, in fact, the eastern parts of Ohio, Kentucky, and Tennessee were never a part of the Mountain Department.

During Thomas J. (Stonewall) Jackson's Shenandoah Valley Campaign of March 22, 1862–June 17, 1862, Fremont moved with his army of the Mountain Department into the Shenandoah Valley to cooperate with troops of Nathaniel P. Banks' Department of the Shenandoah and Irvin McDowell's Department of the Rappahannock in an attempt to cut off and destroy Jackson's army, which had advanced to the Potomac River. Jackson eluded the converging troops of Fremont and McDowell, however, and retreated up the valley. After the battles at Cross Keys and Port Republic, Jackson left the valley to join Robert E. Lee at Richmond. McDowell's troops were then shifted eastward toward Fredericksburg to be in position to cooperate with George B. McClellan's Army of the Potomac on the Peninsula. As a result, it became necessary for Fremont to remain with his command in the Shenandoah Valley, which at that time was a part of the Department of the Shenandoah. In order that Fremont be in the territory of the Mountain Department, which he commanded, the department was extended eastward June 8, 1862 to include that part of Maryland west of Flintstone Creek, and all of Virginia west of the road running south from Williamsport, Maryland, through Martinsburg, Winchester, Strasburg, and Harrisonburg to Staunton (including that place), and then along a line running in the same direction until it reached the Blue Ridge Mountains, and then along the Blue Ridge to the southern border of Virginia.

The western limits of the department were also changed. That part of Michigan and Ohio east of the north-south line through Knoxville remained in the Mountain Department, but the eastern limits of the Department of the Mississippi were moved eastward so as to include all of the states of Kentucky and Tennessee.

The Mountain Department was discontinued June 26, 1862, and the troops of the department were organized into the First Corps of John Pope's newly created Army of Virginia. Fremont was assigned command of First Corps, but he refused to serve under Pope, who was his junior in rank. Rufus King was assigned temporary command June 27, 1862, and two days later Franz Sigel assumed command of the corps.

DISTRICTS IN THE MOUNTAIN DEPARTMENT

When the Mountain Department was created, there were within its limits three districts that had been transferred from the Department of Western Virginia. These were the Cheat Mountain District, the District of the Kanawha, and the Railroad District. A short time later the District of Cumberland, District of the Gap, and District of the Valley of the Big Sandy were added.

District of Cumberland. The District of Cumberland was constituted to include all the territory of the department east of the Allegheny Mountains and west of the Department of the Potomac. Robert C. Schenck had been assigned command at Cumberland, Maryland March 3, 1862, and when the district was constituted, Schenck was assigned command, with headquarters at Cumberland. The principal posts were Moorefield and Romney in Virginia, and

Cumberland in Maryland. These posts were held by three regiments of infantry and one company of cavalry. The district was discontinued April 7, 1862.

Cheat Mountain District. When the Cheat Mountain District was transferred to the Mountain Department, it was defined as including all the territory west of the Allegheny Mountains, south of the Baltimore and Ohio Railroad, east of the Weston-Summerville Road, and north of the Gauley River. Robert H. Milroy was assigned command. Milroy was assigned command of troops in the field during Thomas J. (Stonewall) Jackson's operations in the Shenandoah Valley in late March 1862, and April 19, 1862, Thomas M. Harris was assigned command of the district. The district was then redefined to consist of the counties of Braxton, Webster, Upsher, and Randolph in Western Virginia. The principal posts were Cheat Mountain Summit, Huttonsville, Elkwater, Beverly, Weston, and Buckhannon.

Railroad District. When the Railroad District was transferred to the Mountain Department, it was commanded by Benjamin F. Kelley and consisted of the lines of the Baltimore and Ohio Railroad and the Northwestern Railroad. March 29, 1862, the district was redefined to consist of all of Western Virginia north and east of the counties of Jackson, Roane, Calhoun, Braxton, Lewis, Barbour, and Tucker, inclusive, and west of the Allegheny Mountains, Maryland, and Pennsylvania. Kelley remained in command. The district was extended May 5, 1862 to include that part of Hampshire and Hardy counties in Virginia lying within the Mountain Department. Kelley's command then included the line of the Baltimore and Ohio Railroad west of Allegany County, Maryland. The principal posts in the district were Grafton, Clarksburg, Parkersburg, and Wheeling.

District of the Kanawha. When the District of the Kanawha was transferred to the Mountain Department, it consisted of the valleys of the Kanawha, Gauley, New, and Guyandotte rivers, and the mouth of the Big Sandy River. Jacob D. Cox commanded the district. The principal posts were Point Pleasant, Charleston, Gauley Bridge, Summersville, Fayetteville, Ceredo, and Guyandotte.

District of the Valley of the Big Sandy River. The Valley of the Big Sandy River was, by definition, a part of the Mountain Department from March 11, 1862 to June 8, 1862. This territory was designated as a military district, but this was a paper organization only, because neither Rosecrans nor Fremont exercised any control over the troops in the area. These consisted of three regiments of infantry, a company of cavalry, and some artillery at Piketon, Kentucky, and two infantry regiments below Piketon. James A. Garfield was in command in the valley until late March 1862, and then he was ordered with his troops from eastern Kentucky.

District of the Gap. Rosecrans referred to the District of the Gap as consisting of all troops of the Mountain Department west of the valley of the Big Sandy River. Like the District of the Valley of the Big Sandy, the District of the Gap was only a paper organization. The only Federal troops in the area belonged to Samuel P. Carter's Twelfth Brigade of Don Carlos Buell's Army of the Ohio, Department of the Mississippi; and these were near Cumberland Gap. Neither Rosecrans nor Fremont exercised any control over the troops in the district, which was discontinued June 8, 1862, when eastern Kentucky and eastern Tennessee were transferred from the Mountain Department to the Department of the Mississippi.

TROOPS AND OPERATIONS IN THE MOUNTAIN DEPARTMENT

When first organized in March 1862, the troops of the Mountain Department were reported by Rosecrans as as follows: Robert C. Schenck's command at Cumberland, Maryland; Robert H. Milroy's Cheat Mountain District; Benjamin F. Kelley's Railroad District; Jacob D. Cox's District of the Kanawha; James A. Garfield's District of the Valley of the Big Sandy; and Samuel P. Carter's District of the Gap. This report, however, was misleading because, as explained above, the troops under Garfield and Carter belonged to the Army of the Ohio, Department of the Mississippi, and were in fact never a part of the Mountain Department.

Important events were soon to cause significant changes in the organization, distribution, and operations of the Union forces in the Mountain Department. Most important of these were the Battle of Kernstown, Virginia March 23, 1862; the Engagement at McDowell, Virginia May 8, 1862; and Jackson's Shenandoah Valley Campaign in May and June 1862.

March 22, 1862, Thomas J. (Stonewall) Jackson moved down the Shenandoah Valley with his division of the Confederate Valley District, and the next day was engaged at Kernstown with troops of Nathaniel P. Banks' Fifth Corps, Army of the Potomac. Jackson was defeated and retired up the valley, but thereafter the organization and operations of Fremont's forces of the Mountain Department were closely related to affairs in the Shenandoah Valley. For details of the Battle of Kernstown, see Shenandoah Valley Campaign (Jackson), 1862.

Early in April 1862, Milroy was directed to leave sufficient troops to hold the Cheat Mountain area, and to advance with the remainder of his command to Allegheny Mountain and Monterey, in the direction of Staunton, Virginia. Thomas M. Harris was left in charge of troops near Cheat Mountain, and Milroy's force was designated as Milroy's Brigade, Mountain Department.

April 7, 1862, Schenck was ordered to turn over the task of protecting the Baltimore and Ohio Railroad in the vicinity of Cumberland, Maryland to Kelley, and with that part of his command (District of Cumberland) at Romney and Moorefield to advance on the road running to Elkhorn and Franklin, Virginia. The troops that were to accompany Schenck were designated as Schenck's Brigade, Mountain Department. The movements of Milroy and Schenck were to correspond as closely as possible with Banks' advance up the Shenandoah Valley, as he pursued Jackson after the latter's withdrawal from Kernstown.

As one result of Jackson's appearance at Kernstown, Louis Blenker's division of Edwin V. Sumner's Second Corps, Army of the Potomac was detached April 1, 1862, and ordered to proceed from Washington to the Shenandoah Valley. Later, Blenker's destination was changed, and he was sent on to the Mountain Department to report to Fremont. Progress of the division was very slow, and it did not arrive at Petersburg, Virginia until May 4–11, 1862, and it was then in poor condition.

Milroy advanced with his brigade from Cheat Mountain through Hightown and Monterey, and arrived at McDowell, Virginia May 6, 1862. The next day his advance encountered Confederate troops beyond McDowell at Shenandoah Mountain, on the Staunton-Parkersburg Turnpike. These belonged to Edward Johnson's Army of the Northwest. Johnson had joined Stonewall Jackson, who was marching westward with his division from Staunton toward McDowell. Milroy returned to McDowell with his brigade, and the next day Jackson followed to Bull Pasture Mountain, a short distance east of the village. Meantime, Schenck had advanced with his brigade through Petersburg, Franklin, and Monterey, and he joined Milroy at McDowell June 8, 1862. As senior officer, Schenck assumed command of both brigades. He then unsuccessfully attacked Jackson's position at Bull Pasture Mountain, and that night withdrew with both brigades toward Franklin, where he arrived May 11, 1862. Jackson followed to Franklin, but then withdrew and returned to the Shenandoah Valley. For details of the Engagement at McDowell, see Shenandoah Valley Campaign (Jackson), 1862.

May 7, 1862, Fremont established headquarters of the Mountain Department at Petersburg, where Blenker's division was then arriving. He left there May 12, 1862, with Blenker's division and a new brigade commanded by Gustave P. Cluseret, and two days later joined Schenck and Milroy at Franklin. Fremont's command that was then organized for field duty consisted of the following:

Blenker's Division, Louis Blenker
   First Brigade, Julius Stahel
   Second Brigade, Adolph Von Steinwehr
   Third Brigade, Henry Bohlen

Note 1. At this time, John A. Koltes commanded Second Brigade.
Note 2. The artillery with Blenker's Division was as follows: Louis Schirmer's 2nd Battery, New York Light Artillery and Frank Buell's Battery C, West Virginia Light Artillery were assigned to First Brigade; Julius Dieckmann's 13th Battery, New York Light Artillery was assigned to Second Brigade; and Michael Wiedrich's Battery I, 1st New York Light Artillery was assigned to Third Brigade.

Advance Brigade, Gustave A. Cluseret
   60th Ohio, William H. Trimble
   8th West Virginia, John H. Oley

Milroy's Brigade, Robert H. Milroy

Note. Chatham T. Ewing commanded the artillery of Milroy's Brigade, which consisted of his own Battery G, West Virginia Light Artillery; Henry F. Hyman's Battery I, 1st Ohio Light Artillery; and Aaron C. Johnson's 12th Battery, Ohio Light Artillery

Schenck's Brigade, Robert C. Schenck

Note. William L. De Beck's Battery K, 1st Ohio Light Artillery and Silas F. Rigby's Battery of Indiana Light Artillery were attached to Schenck's Brigade

George D. Bayard's Cavalry Brigade later joined Fremont from the Department of the Rappahannock, and June 7, 1862 was temporarily attached to his command. James A. Hall's 2nd Battery (B), Maine Light Artillery was attached to Bayard's brigade.

May 23, 1862, after Jackson had returned to the Shenandoah Valley from Franklin, Virginia, he advanced in the Luray Valley, and the next day surprised a Federal outpost at Front Royal and drove it back in disorder. Banks, who was then at Strasburg with Williams' First Division, Department of the Shenandoah, hastily withdrew northward to Winchester, where he was attacked by Jackson May 25, 1862 and driven from the town. Banks then retreated to Williamsport, Maryland, and Jackson followed to the Potomac River.

May 24, 1862, while Jackson was advancing toward Winchester, Fremont was ordered to march with his command from Franklin to the Shenandoah Valley. There he was to join Irvin McDowell, commanding the Department of the Rappahannock, in an attempt to cut off and capture Jackson's army before it could escape up the valley. Fremont began his march May 25, 1862, and moved back to Petersburg, and he then marched eastward through Moorefield and Wardensville toward Strasburg. He arrived at Strasburg too late to accomplish his mission, but he followed Jackson up the valley and was engaged with Richard S. Ewell's division at Cross Keys June 8, 1862. For details of the operations of Fremont's field force during the period March–June 1862, see Shenandoah Valley Campaign (Jackson), 1862.

June 26, 1862, the troops under Fremont's immediate command were merged into John Pope's newly created Army of Virginia as First Corps. Fremont's troops were reassigned as follows: First Brigade, Blenker's Division as First Brigade, First

Division, First Corps; Schenck's Brigade as Second Brigade, First Division, First Corps; Second Brigade, Blenker's Division as First Brigade, Second Division, First Corps; Third Brigade, Blenker's Division as Second Brigade, Third Division, First Corps; and Milroy's Brigade was designated as Independent Brigade, First Corps. Second Brigade, Second Division, First Corps was formed from unattached regiments of the Mountain Department, and First Brigade, Third Division, First Corps was formed from one regiment from Cluseret's Advance Brigade, one regiment from Blenker's Brigade, and one new regiment.

Cox's Advance from the Kanawha Valley to East River and Lewisburg, West Virginia, May 1862.

After assuming command of the Mountain Department, Fremont formulated a plan for the capture of Knoxville, Tennessee. According to this plan, which was never carried out, Fremont was to advance with Blenker's Division from Romney, up the valley of the South Branch of the Potomac River, and pick up, in turn, Schenck's Brigade and Milroy's Brigade, the latter to join at Monterey. Fremont intended to continue on to Staunton, and then to follow the valleys southwestward to the New River, and to the Virginia and Tennessee Railroad near Christiansburg. Upon arriving there, Fremont was to open communications with a force commanded by Jacob D. Cox. The latter was to have advanced from Gauley Bridge with the troops of his Kanawha Division (see below) by two roads: the main column by Fayetteville (Fayette, or Fayette Court House) and Raleigh Court House (Beckley), over Flat Top Mountain, and then on to Princeton and the narrows of New River; and a secondary column was to march on the turnpike to Lewisburg. After destroying the Virginia and Tennessee Railroad, the combined forces of Fremont and Cox were to advance along the railroad to the southwest toward Knoxville.

As noted above, Fremont's command became involved in Jackson's Shenandoah Valley Campaign, and was unable to carry out its part of the plan, but Cox advanced on schedule. On May 2, 1862, Cox organized the troops of his District of the Kanawha into a division of four brigades. This division was known as the Kanawha Division, and was organized as follows:

Kanawha Division, Jacob D. Cox

First Provisional Brigade, Eliakim P. Scammon
Second Provisional Brigade, Augustus Moor
Third Provisional Brigade, George Crook
Fourth Provisional Brigade, Joseph A. J. Lightburn

Note 1. Lightburn's brigade included all troops on the Kanawha and Guyandotte rivers below the mouth of the Gauley.

Note 2. James R. McMullin's 1st Battery, Ohio Light Artillery was attached to Scammon's brigade, and Seth J. Simmonds' battery of Kentucky Light Artillery was assigned to Moor's brigade.

Cox left Lightburn's brigade to garrison the lower Kanawha Valley, and marched with the brigades of Scammon and Moor on the road to Princeton. Crook's brigade took the turnpike toward Lewisburg. Scammon's brigade arrived at Princeton May 6, 1862, and his advance troops occupied Giles Court House (Pearisburg) the next day. On May 16, 1862, the rest of Scammon's brigade and Moor's brigade were at East River, seven or eight miles southeast of Princeton, and Crook's brigade was at Lewisburg. At this point Cox was ready to join Fremont, but, as already noted, Fremont's advance ended when Schenck and Milroy retreated to Franklin after their defeat at McDowell by Jackson May 8, 1862. Cox was thus left on his own in his advanced position.

Meantime, the Confederates were attempting to concentrate the brigades of Humphrey Marshall, Henry Heth, and John S. Williams to oppose Cox's advance. All three brigades were under the command of Marshall, the senior officer present. May 16, 1862, Marshall advanced on Princeton, and drove out the small Federal detachment left there, but during the night Moor's brigade marched back from East River and reoccupied the town. Scammon's brigade also returned the next day. Cox then retired with Moor's and Scammon's brigades to Flat Top Mountain, about midway between Raleigh Court House and Princeton. Crook moved to Lewisburg, on the other side of New River, within supporting distance. May 23, 1862, Crook was attacked at Lewisburg by Heth's brigade, but after a sharp engagement, Heth was driven off with considerable loss.

There was little change in the positions occupied by Cox's troops until the Mountain Department was discontinued June 26, 1862.

For further information relating to the troops belonging to the Mountain Department after the latter was discontinued, see Pope's Northern Virginia Campaign.

DEPARTMENT OF NEW ENGLAND

Benjamin F. Butler was relieved from command at Fort Monroe, Virginia in August 1861, and he then requested permission to recruit 5,000 volunteers from the New England states for a Special Service Force. The War Department granted Butler's request August 17, 1861, and September 10, 1861 authorized him to raise and organize a force that was not to exceed six regiments of volunteers.

October 1, 1863, a temporary Department of New England was constituted to consist of the six New England states. The department was formed from a part of the territory of the Department of the East. Butler, while engaged in recruiting service, was to command the department, with headquarters at Boston, Massachusetts.

From the beginning, there was some uncertainty as to the destination of Butler's force. Several plans were considered. The first was for an expedition to advance toward the Virginia shore along the Eastern Shore of Maryland. This was to move by rail from Wilmington, Delaware to Salisbury, Maryland, and from there to Cape Charles, Maryland. When this idea was abandoned, Butler gave some thought to an attack on Mobile, Alabama. Then, on December 2, 1862, he submitted a plan for the invasion of the coast of Texas, which could possibly lead to the capture of New Orleans. Because of the overriding importance of opening the Mississippi River, however, Butler's troops were finally organized into Butler's Gulf Expedition and sent to capture New Orleans in the Department of the Gulf.

The Department of New England was created to facilitate Butler's recruiting program, and when this was essentially completed, the department was discontinued. Its territory was merged into the re-created Department of the East January 12, 1863 (ordered January 3, 1863), but the official records indicate that the Department of New England was discontinued February 20, 1863.

DEPARTMENT OF NEW YORK

The Department of the East was discontinued August 17, 1861, and Governor Edwin D. Morgan of New York was appointed by the president as major general of volunteers to assume control of military affairs within the state. These matters were primarily concerned with recruitment and organization of state troops. October 19, 1861, Morgan urged the organization of the state as a military department, and October 26, 1861, the Department of New York was created. Morgan was assigned command, with headquarters at Albany. The department was discontinued January 12, 1863 (ordered January 3, 1863), when John E. Wool assumed command of the re-created Department of the East, which consisted of the New England states and the state of New York.

DEPARTMENT OF NORTH CAROLINA
JANUARY 7, 1862–JULY 15, 1863

In October 1861, Ambrose E. Burnside was given permission to organize a special division to operate along the Atlantic Coast. The troops that he raised were assembled at Annapolis, Maryland, and were organized into three brigades, which were commanded by John G. Foster, Jesse L. Reno, and John G. Parke. On January 7, 1862, Burnside was ordered to take his division to North Carolina, and by the same order, the Department of North Carolina was constituted to consist of the state of North Carolina. Burnside was assigned command of the department, and he assumed command January 13, 1862, when his expedition arrived at Hatteras Inlet.

The department was defined as consisting of the entire state of North Carolina, but at the time that it was organized, only the post of Hatteras Inlet was occupied by United States troops. These belonged to Thomas Williams' brigade from the Department of Virginia. For additional information, see Department of Virginia, May 22, 1861–July 15, 1863, Troops and Operations in the Department of Virginia, Expedition to Hatteras Inlet. Actually, during the first period of the department's existence, that part of North Carolina that was under Federal control was limited to the eastern part of the state in the vicinity of the posts of Hatteras Inlet, Roanoke Island, New Berne (also Newbern, and present-day New Bern), Fort Macon, Beaufort, Carolina City, Morehead City, Newport, Plymouth, Washington, and Portsmouth.

There were no changes in departmental boundaries during the period January 7, 1862–July 15, 1863. Ambrose E. Burnside commanded the department from January 13, 1862 to July 6, 1862, and John G. Foster commanded from July 6, 1862 to July 18, 1863. Innis N. Palmer was in temporary command from March 29, 1863 to April 16, 1863, while Foster was at Washington, North Carolina during the enemy siege of that place (see below).

DISTRICTS IN THE DEPARTMENT OF NORTH CAROLINA

In order to achieve better supervision of the posts in the Department of North Carolina, Foster issued an order April 23, 1863 that constituted the District of the Neuse, the District of the Albemarle, and the District of the Pamlico. In an amended order of April 27, 1863, the name of the District of the Neuse was changed to the District of Beaufort. A brief description of these districts follows:

District of the Neuse. The District of the Neuse was constituted April 23, 1863 to include that part of the Department of North Carolina lying beyond the outside limits of the post of New Berne, the Atlantic and North Carolina Railroad, and all stations on the line—Morehead City, Carolina City, Beaufort, and Fort Macon. Henry M. Naglee was assigned command, with headquarters at Beaufort, North Carolina.

The name of the district was changed to the District of Beaufort April 27, 1863 (see below).

District of the Pamlico. The District of the Pamlico was constituted April 23, 1863 to include the post of Washington, North Carolina; Hatteras Inlet; and such other posts as might be established within the limits of the district. Henry Prince was assigned

command, with headquarters at Washington. The district was redefined April 27, 1863 to include all posts that were already in, or might be established in, that part of Craven County north of the Neuse River, excepting the post of Fort Anderson; and in the counties of Pitt, Beaufort, and Hyde; and also the post of Portsmouth, North Carolina.

The district was organized from Prince's Fifth Division, which at that time consisted of Francis B. Spinola's First Brigade (the Keystone Brigade) and James Jourdan's Second Brigade (see below, Troops and Operations in the Department of North Carolina; Department of North Carolina, Eighteenth Corps). In May 1863, Jourdan's brigade was transferred to New Berne, and it was attached to First Division, Eighteenth Corps as Jourdan's Independent Brigade. Spinola was assigned command of the District of Beaufort May 29, 1863, and David B. McKibbin assumed command of the Keystone Brigade. In June 1863, this brigade was at Washington under the command of Everard Bierer, and at the end of the month it was sent to the Department of Virginia. It remained there only a short time, and was then sent north and assigned to duty at Harper's Ferry, in the Middle Department, Eighth Corps.

In early July 1863, the only troops in the district were the 1st North Carolina (Union) Regiment, the 58th Pennsylvania, and artillery. At that time, Joseph M. McChesney was in command of the district. August 1, 1863, the designation of the district was changed to Sub-District of the Pamlico, District of North Carolina, Eighteenth Corps, Department of Virginia and North Carolina.

District of Beaufort. On April 27, 1863, the name of the District of the Neuse was changed to the District of Beaufort. At the same time, the district was redefined to include all posts which were in, or might be established in, that part of Craven County lying south of a line drawn from Evans' Mill due east to the Neuse River, including Evans' Mill; and also in the counties of Jones and Carteret, excepting the post of Portsmouth. Henry M. Naglee was assigned command.

The district was organized May 2, 1863 from Second Division, Eighteenth Corps, which at that time consisted of only Charles A. Heckman's First Brigade. William W. H. Davis' Second Brigade was detached and was serving in the Department of the South.

Naglee was sent north May 29, 1863, and later assumed command at Harper's Ferry. Francis B. Spinola was assigned command of the District of Beaufort. Jacob J. DeForest was assigned command of Heckman's brigade, and in June 1863, Heckman assumed command of the district. August 1, 1863, the designation of the district was changed to the Sub-District of Beaufort, District of North Carolina, Department of Virginia and North Carolina, Eighteenth Corps.

District of the Albemarle. The District of the Albemarle was constituted April 23, 1863 to include the posts of Plymouth and Roanoke Island, and such other posts as might be established in the district. Henry W. Wessells was assigned command, with headquarters at Plymouth, North Carolina. The district was redefined April 27, 1863, to include all posts that were, or might be established, in the counties of Washington and Tyrrell, and in all the counties in the state of North Carolina northwest of those counties whose waters flowed into Albemarle Sound.

The district was organized May 3, 1863 from Wessells' Fourth Division, Eighteenth Corps, which consisted of only Lewis C. Hunt's First Brigade. Thomas G. Stevenson's Second Brigade had left the division March 26, 1863 for service in the Department of the South.

August 1, 1863, the district was designated as the Sub-District of the Albemarle, District of North Carolina, Department of Virginia and North Carolina, Eighteenth Corps.

Post of New Berne. This post was organized April 22, 1863 from James Jourdan's Second Brigade, Fifth Division, Eighteenth Corps. On July 21, 1863, the post was transferred to the Defenses of New Berne, Eighteenth Corps, Department of Virginia and North Carolina.

TROOPS AND OPERATIONS IN THE DEPARTMENT OF NORTH CAROLINA

It is convenient to describe the organization and

operations of the troops in the Department of North Carolina in three parts, based on organizational changes occurring in the department. The first Union troops in the department, except those at the post of Hatteras Inlet, belonged to Ambrose E. Burnside's expedition to North Carolina, and these took part in the capture of Roanoke Island and New Berne and the siege of Fort Macon. On April 2, 1862, Burnside's Expedition was discontinued as an organization, and the troops were reorganized into three divisions of the Department of North Carolina. Then on December 24, 1862, the troops of the department were organized into Eighteenth Corps. A description of the troops and operations in the department during these three periods of organization is given in the following sections:

Burnside's Expedition to North Carolina January 7, 1862–April 2, 1862

September 12, 1861, Ambrose E. Burnside was ordered to New England to raise and organize a force of two brigades of five regiments each. These brigades were to be used for coastal service, in cooperation with the Army of the Potomac, in the bays and inlets of the Chesapeake Bay and the Potomac River. In October 1861, a plan to organize a "Coast Division" of 12,000–15,000 men was approved, but the destination of this force was changed. It was to be transported to the South Atlantic coast to establish lodgments there, and it was then to move into the interior and secure possession of the inland waters. Burnside was ordered to New York to prepare for the expedition, and October 23, 1861 he was directed to establish headquarters at Annapolis, Maryland for the assembly of the Coast Division. This division was organized as follows:

Coast Division, Ambrose E. Burnside
    First Brigade, John G. Foster
    Second Brigade, Jesse L. Reno
    Third Brigade, John G. Parke

Transports for the expedition had arrived at Annapolis by January 4, 1862, and embarkation began the next day. The nature and direction of the expedition were changed somewhat January 7, 1862, when

Burnside was ordered to North Carolina. On that date, George B. McClellan, commander in chief of the army, directed Burnside to sail with his division to Fort Monroe. There he was to join with Flag Officer Louis M. Goldsborough, who was to command the naval forces that were to accompany the expedition. Together they were to proceed to Hatteras Inlet, and from there pass into Pamlico Sound. Burnside was to assume command of the garrison at Hatteras Inlet, which consisted of Thomas Williams' brigade of the Department of Virginia; and then, with the aid of the fleet, he was to attack and capture Roanoke Island. After that was accomplished, Burnside was to move on New Berne, Beaufort, and Fort Macon and, if possible, to penetrate inland as far as Raleigh, North Carolina. Also on January 7, 1862, as noted above, the Department of North Carolina was created to consist of the state of North Carolina, and Burnside was assigned command.

The transports sailed from Annapolis for Fort Monroe January 9, 1862, and the combined land and naval forces left Fort Monroe on the night of January 11, 1862. They arrived off Hatteras Inlet two days later, and there, on January 13, 1862, Burnside assumed command of the Department of North Carolina. Because of bad weather and shallow water in the inlet, the fleet was not safely anchored in Pamlico Sound until February 4, 1862.

The complete organization of Burnside's Expedition is given below. Because many of the regimental commanders later exercised higher command, they too are listed, together with their regiments.

Burnside's Expedition (Coast Division), Ambrose E. Burnside

First Brigade, John G. Foster
    10th Connecticut, Charles L. Russell, to February 8, 1862, killed
        Albert W. Drake
    23rd Massachusetts, John Kurz
    24th Massachusetts, Thomas G. Stevenson
    25th Massachusetts, Edwin Upton
    27th Massachusetts, Horace C. Lee

Second Brigade, Jesse L. Reno
    21st Massachusetts, Albert C. Maggi
        William S. Clark
    9th New Jersey, Charles A. Heckman
    51st New York, Edward Ferrero
    51st Pennsylvania, John F. Hartranft

Note. Maggi commanded the 21st Massachusetts at Roanoke Island, and Clark at New Berne.

Third Brigade, John G. Parke
    8th Connecticut, Edward Harland
    11th Connecticut, Charles Mathewson
    9th New York, Rush C. Hawkins
    4th Rhode Island, Isaac P. Rodman
    5th Rhode Island (one battalion), John Wright

Unassigned Troops
    Detachment 1st New York Marine Artillery, William A. Howard
    Company B, 99th New York (Union Coast Guard), Charles W. Tillotson
    Battery F, 1st Rhode Island Light Artillery, James Belger

Note. Tillotson was captured at New Berne.

When Burnside arrived at Hatteras Inlet with his expedition, he assumed command of Thomas Williams' brigade, which already occupied the post. This brigade was organized as follows:

Williams' Brigade, Thomas Williams
    6th New Hampshire, Nelson Converse
    89th New York, Harrison S. Fairchild
    48th Pennsylvania, James Nagle
    Battery F, 1st Rhode Island Artillery, James Belger
    Battery C, 1st United States Artillery, Lewis O. Morris

Battle of Roanoke Island, February 8, 1862. On February 5, 1862, Burnside's command, accompanied by the fleet, sailed for Roanoke Island; and two days later it arrived at Ashby's Harbor, about midway up the western side of the island. At about 4:00 P.M. February 7, 1862, Foster's brigade began to land, and when it was ashore, Reno's brigade followed. Parke's brigade disembarked last. Williams' brigade was left behind at Hatteras Inlet.

The next morning, February 8, 1862, Burnside left the 10th Connecticut to guard the landing, and the battalion of 5th Rhode Island to hold the Ashby house and grounds, and with the rest of his command advanced toward the enemy positions on the northern part of the island. With Foster's brigade in the lead, Burnside moved inland about a half mile to a road that ran northward up the center of the island, and he then advanced up that road toward the enemy lines.

The Confederate commander on the island was Henry A. Wise, whose troops consisted of his own

Fourth Brigade (Chowan District) of Benjamin Huger's Confederate Department of Norfolk. Wise was ill on the day of the battle, and Henry M. Shaw commanded the troops on the field. Wise had established a defensive position across the road on which Burnside was advancing, a short distance north of the center of the island. This consisted of a three-gun battery, placed on the road, with infantry lines extending to the right and to the left. A reserve was in position to the rear of this work. The battery was located in the middle of a swamp, and could be approached only with great difficulty except by the road, which ran along a narrow causeway.

Foster's brigade, with 25th Massachusetts in the lead, moved up the road to a point about 350 yards in front of the battery, and then Foster prepared for an attack. Fighting began about 8:00 A.M., but Foster made little progress until Reno arrived and was sent to the left of the road to strike the enemy right flank. With 51st New York in the lead, and followed by 21st Massachusetts and then 9th New Jersey, Reno finally reached the enemy right and opened fire on the troops inside the works. The enemy quickly returned the fire, but failed to drive Reno back.

While Reno's attack was in progress, Foster demonstrated with 25th Massachusetts and 10th Connecticut on Shaw's front, and attempted to penetrate the swamp on the right of the road with the 23rd Massachusetts and 27th Massachusetts, so as to move against his left. At about 11:00 A.M., Parke arrived in rear of Foster with that part of his brigade that had not been left at the landing. He then ordered the 4th Rhode Island to follow the 23rd Massachusetts and 27th Massachusetts on the right of the road, and later the 51st Pennsylvania of Reno's brigade was sent in support of these three regiments. Parke then ordered Rush C. Hawkins to advance with his 9th New York, and Hawkins charged along the causeway and around noon entered the enemy works and drove out the defenders. At about the same time, the 21st Massachusetts and 51st New York of Reno's brigade came into the works from the Federal left. The enemy forces rapidly retreated northward up the island, and Foster and Reno pursued them four or five miles to their camps in rear of Weir's Point Battery. There, further resistance being useless, Shaw surrendered his command.

Battle of New Berne, March 14, 1862. After the Battle of Roanoke Island, Burnside remained on the island for about a month while he prepared for the next phase of his operation, which was the capture of New Berne and the occupation of the mainland of North Carolina. During this period, the Union fleet under Commodore Stephen C. Rowan destroyed William F. Lynch's Confederate navy in the Sounds (the so-called "Mosquito Fleet"), and for a time occupied Elizabeth City and Edenton, North Carolina. Also during this period, Burnside sent the prisoners captured on Roanoke Island to Elizabeth City for exchange.

In March 1862, Thomas Williams, commanding the Federal brigade at Hatteras Inlet, was relieved from command there, and was assigned command of a brigade in Benjamin F. Butler's expedition against New Orleans in the Department of the Gulf. Then, on March 10, 1862, just two days before Burnside's command embarked for New Berne, Burnside formed a new Fourth Brigade under Rush C. Hawkins for garrison duty on Roanoke Island. The brigade was organized as follows:

Fourth Brigade, Department of North Carolina, Rush C. Hawkins
6th New Hampshire, Nelson Converse
89th New York, Harrison S. Fairchild
9th New York, Rush C. Hawkins

Note. 6th New Hampshire and 89th New York were from Williams' Brigade, and 9th New York was from John G. Parke's Third Brigade, Burnside's Expedition.

On the morning of March 11, 1862, Burnside embarked his command for Hatteras Inlet and a rendezvous with the rest of the fleet before proceeding toward New Berne. Goldsborough, commanding the North Atlantic Blockading Squadron, was ordered to Hampton Roads when the Confederate ironclad *Merrimac* (formerly *Virginia*) attacked the Union fleet there March 9, 1862, and he turned over the command of the United States Naval Forces on Pamlico and Albemarle sounds to Stephen C. Rowan.

Early on the morning of March 12, 1862, the expedition left Hatteras Inlet, and at 2:00 P.M. entered the Neuse River. At 9:00 that evening the fleet anchored off the mouth of Slocum's Creek, about eighteen miles below New Berne. At daylight the next morning, the navy bombarded the shore at Slocum's Creek, and then the infantry disembarked and marched toward New Berne.

Lawrence O'B. Branch commanded the Confederate forces at New Berne, and these occupied a defensive line about six miles below the town. The line began on the Confederate left at Fort Thompson, a thirteen-gun earthwork (only three guns were bearing on the land front) on the Neuse River. From there it extended westward a little over a mile to the Atlantic and North Carolina Railroad. Originally, it was intended that the line be continued across the railroad to a dense swamp near Brice's Creek, but Branch's force was too small to extend that far, and it was necessary to shorten the line. To do this, Branch moved back that part of his line west of the railroad about 150 yards, and then from the railroad westward he constructed a series of redans and rifle pits to a point just behind Bullin's Branch, which flowed into Brice's Creek on the right. This arrangement left a gap of 150 yards in the defenses along the railroad at Wood's Brickyard. Four North Carolina regiments occupied the line between Fort Thompson and the railroad at the brickyard. Zebulon B. Vance, later governor of North Carolina, commanded the 26th North Carolina, which was the only enemy force west of the railroad. Some local militia were at the brickyard to occupy the gap in the line, and Clark G. Avery's 33rd North Carolina was held in reserve.

During March 13, 1863, after disembarking his troops, Burnside advanced toward New Berne, and that night bivouacked near the Fort Thompson line. At 7:00 the next morning, the Federal troops moved up toward the enemy position in three columns. Foster's brigade was on the right between the river and the railroad; Reno's brigade was on the left, west of the railroad; and Parke's brigade was in reserve along the railroad, where it was in position to help either column as needed.

Foster advanced along a country road (the Old Beaufort Road), with 24th and 25th Massachusetts on the right of the road, and 27th and 23rd Massachusetts on the left. Without waiting for Reno to get in position, Foster attacked, but was unable to make any progress. He then ordered up the 10th Connecticut to the left of 23rd Massachusetts, next

to the railroad, and the 11th Connecticut of Parke's brigade replaced 27th Massachusetts, whose ammunition was exhausted. Reno's brigade then came up and formed on the left of the railroad, with 21st Massachusetts on the right next to the railroad, the 51st New York in the center, and the 9th New Jersey on the left. The 51st Pennsylvania was held in reserve to support the left of the line.

As the 21st Massachusetts was moving into position, Colonel William S. Clark discovered the gap in the enemy line at the brickyard, and he immediately changed front to the right, and with four companies of his regiment charged the North Carolina militia holding that part of the line, and drove them from the field. At that time, however, enemy troops on, and to the west of, the railroad opened with a destructive fire and prevented the movement of more Federal troops across the railroad, and also forced Clark's companies to withdraw. By that time it was about 11:00 A.M., and after three hours of fighting the enemy line was still intact. Parke then learned of the gap at the railroad, and ordered Isaac P. Rodman to advance with his 4th Rhode Island and pass through this opening into the rear of the enemy line east of the railroad. The 4th Rhode Island, supported by the battalion of the 5th Rhode Island, then moved to the right across the railroad and past the brickyard and into the rear of the Fort Thompson line. At the same time, Foster advanced with his brigade against the enemy front. As a result of these combined attacks, the Federals carried the whole line of works between the river and the railroad, and drove the enemy in disorder from that part of the field. West of the railroad, Vance and Avery, who were engaged with Reno, were unaware of the disaster on their left, and for a time they continued fighting, but then they too were forced to flee to avoid capture.

Following the battle, Branch's command withdrew across the Trent River into New Berne, and then continued on to Kinston. During the afternoon of March 14, 1862, Burnside's army, aided by Rowan's gunboats, occupied New Berne.

Siege of Fort Macon, March 23, 1862–April 26, 1862. After the occupation of New Berne, Burnside decided to move against Fort Macon before attempting any further advance in the direction of

Goldsboro and the interior of North Carolina. Fort Macon was in rear of the Union position at New Berne, and it guarded Beaufort Inlet, the only entrance through the outer banks not then under control of United States forces. The fort was situated on the eastern extremity of Bogue Banks, a narrow sandy island that extended westward about twenty-five miles from a point opposite Beaufort, and it was separated from the mainland by Bogue Sound.

As a preliminary to the operations against Fort Macon, Burnside ordered Parke, with his Third Brigade, to move down the Atlantic and North Carolina Railroad and occupy Morehead City and Beaufort. During the period March 20–24, 1862, Parke occupied, with detachments of his brigade, Havelock Station, Newport, Carolina City, Morehead City, and finally, on the night of March 24, 1862, moved into Beaufort. From Beaufort, Parke made contact with the Union blockading vessels patrolling off the harbor entrance to arrange for their cooperation with the land operations, and he then began preparations for the investment of Fort Macon. Parke established his headquarters at Carolina City because this village was opposite the nearest landing place on Bogue Banks.

On March 29, 1862, a small reconnaissance party, covered by the guns of a Union warship, secured a beachhead on Bogue Banks, and two days later two companies of the 8th Connecticut established a permanent camp about eight miles from Fort Macon. During the period March 29, 1862–April 10, 1862, a siege train and supplies were transported across the five-mile stretch of water between Carolina City and the landing place on Bogue Banks. By April 10, 1862, eight companies of 4th Rhode Island; seven companies of 8th Connecticut; the 5th Rhode Island Battalion; one company of 1st United States Artillery; and Company I, 3rd New York Artillery had crossed Bogue Sound. There were clashes between Confederate pickets and Union troops April 8–10, 1862, and April 11, 1862 Parke made a reconnaissance in force to within a mile of the fort. The next day he began work on approaches, batteries, and rifle pits; this was continued day and night with all of his available forces, and by the middle of April 1862, Fort Macon was completely invested.

On the afternoon of April 23, 1862, Parke demanded the surrender of the fort, but this was refused by Moses J. White, the commander. At dawn April 25, 1862, Federal land batteries opened fire, and about 8:45 A.M. the naval force under Samuel Lockwood joined in the bombardment. The enemy artillery in the fort returned the fire, and after about an hour the navy was forced to withdraw. Parke's land batteries, however, continued throughout the morning and into the afternoon to shell the fort with deadly accuracy, and finally, later in the afternoon, a white flag appeared over the fort. After discussing terms, the Confederate commander surrendered the fort and garrison the next morning, April 26, 1862.

Department of North Carolina
April 2, 1862–December 24, 1862

On April 2, 1862, while operations were proceeding against Fort Macon, Burnside reorganized the troops of the Department of North Carolina into three divisions. By this reorganization, Burnside's Expedition (Coast Division) was merged into the Department of North Carolina and was discontinued as a separate command. The divisional organization of the department was as follows:

DEPARTMENT OF NORTH CAROLINA, Ambrose E. Burnside

First Division, John G. Foster
    First Brigade, Thomas J. C. Amory
    Second Brigade, Thomas G. Stevenson
    Artillery
        3rd New York Light Artillery, James H. Ledlie
        Battery F, 1st Rhode Island Light Artillery, Charles H. Pope

Note. The two brigades were organized from the former First Brigade, Burnside's Expedition.

Second Division, Jesse L. Reno
    First Brigade, James Nagle
    Second Brigade, Edward Ferrero

Note 1. First Brigade was organized from unbrigaded regiments.
Note 2. Second Brigade was organized from Second Brigade, Burnside's Expedition.

Third Division, John G. Parke
    8th Connecticut, Edward Harland
    9th New Jersey, Charles A. Heckman
    4th Rhode Island, Isaac P. Rodman
    5th Rhode Island (one battalion), John Wright

Battery C, 1st United States Artillery, Lewis O. Morris

Note. Third Division was organized from Parke's former Third Brigade, Burnside's Expedition, and at the time of the reorganization no brigade organization was announced.

Fourth Brigade, Rush C. Hawkins

Note 1. Fourth Brigade was formerly Fourth Brigade, Burnside's Expedition.
Note 2. In addition to Fourth Brigade, Hawkins also commanded the post of Roanoke Island, where it was stationed.

Engagement at South Mills, Camden County, April 19, 1862.

During the first week of April 1862, Burnside learned of rumors that the Confederates were building two small ironclad gunboats at Norfolk, Virginia, and that they intended to transfer them to Albemarle Sound through the Dismal Swamp Canal and that part of the Albemarle and Chesapeake Canal that connected Currituck Sound with the North River (Burnside called the latter canal the Currituck Canal). To prevent the possible destruction of the United States fleet on the sounds by these two vessels, Burnside decided to send a force under Reno to block the two canals at their southern exits. He directed Reno to proceed to South Mills on the Dismal Swamp Canal, and destroy the locks near the junction of the canal with the Pasquotank River, and then to move to North River and block the head of the "Currituck Canal" by blowing in the banks.

Reno left New Berne April 17, 1862, with the 21st Massachusetts and 51st Pennsylvania regiments, which belonged to Edward Ferrero's Second Brigade of Reno's Second Division, and the next day arrived at Roanoke Island. He was joined there by Hawkins' Fourth Brigade, and the combined forces then sailed for Elizabeth City. The transports carrying Reno, in person, and Hawkins' brigade arrived during the night of April 18, 1862, and the troops began disembarking about midnight. They went ashore about three miles below the town, on the east side of the Pasquotank River, and at 3:00 A.M. marched northward toward South Mills. Reno waited at the landing for the two regiments of Ferrero's brigade, which were then assigned to Thomas S. Bell, colonel of the 51st Pennsylvania. Bell's command had been delayed at the mouth of the river and did not arrive until until 7:00 A.M.

Reno then set out on the direct road to South Mills. About twelve miles from the landing he met Hawkins' brigade, which had been misled by its guide and had marched ten miles out of its way after leaving the landing. Because of the exhaustion of Hawkins' troops, Bell's brigade took the lead and Hawkins was directed to follow.

The enemy forces ahead of Reno's column belonged to Benjamin Huger's Confederate Department of Norfolk. These consisted of Ambrose R. Wright's 3rd Georgia Regiment of Albert G. Blanchard's Third Brigade, William W. McComas' Light Battery, a part of Dennis D. Ferebee's First Brigade of North Carolina Militia, and one company of cavalry. About three miles below South Mills, the road running south to Camden Court House and Elizabeth City emerged from a woods, and then ran on southward through cleared land that was bordered on the east and west by thick woods and swamps. The wooded swamp on the west was situated between the field and the Pasquotank River. Wright placed two pieces of artillery on the road at the point where it left the woods at the northern end of the field, and he formed a part of his infantry on both the right and left of the guns, along the edge of the woods. He placed a part of his infantry to the rear as a reserve.

About noon April 19, 1862, Reno's leading regiment, the 51st Pennsylvania, came under fire from McComas' artillery and halted. It was then ordered to move across the field to the woods on the right and gain the left of the enemy battery and of the troops supporting it. The 21st Massachusetts followed the 51st Pennsylvania to the woods. Then, after advancing with considerable difficulty, these regiments moved toward the left of Wright's line. About 3:00 P.M. Hawkins' brigade came up from the rear, and a short time later the 9th New York of this brigade charged across the open field on its front, but was repulsed with considerable loss. The 51st Pennsylvania and 21st Massachusetts under Bell charged on the right. At the same time, 6th New Hampshire advanced on the left of the road, and the 9th New York and 89th New York of Hawkins' brigade moved forward on the center, and at 5:00 P.M. the enemy retired to Joy's Creek, about two miles in rear of their original position. Because it was late, Reno did not pursue. His troops bivouacked on the field that night, but at 9:00 P.M. he gave the order for his command to return to the transports near Elizabeth City. Hawkins arrived at the embarkation point at 4:00 A.M. and then returned to Roanoke Island. Reno, with his two regiments, sailed back to New Berne, where he arrived April 22, 1862.

The organization of Reno's command at South Mills was as follows:

Second Brigade, Second Division, Department of North Carolina, Thomas S. Bell
21st Massachusetts. William S. Clark
51st Pennsylvania, Edwin Schall

Fourth Brigade, Department of North Carolina, Rush C. Hawkins
9th New York, Edward A. Kimball
89th New York, Harrison S. Fairchild
6th New Hampshire, Simon G. Griffin

1st New York Marine Artillery, William A. Howard

* * * * * * * * * *

After the reorganization of April 2, 1862, there were no further significant changes in the organization of the forces in the Department of North Carolina until July 1862. On June 28, 1862, during the Seven Days' Battles on the Peninsula, the secretary of war directed Burnside to send such troops as could be spared from the department to reinforce George B. McClellan's Army of the Potomac. July 6, 1862, Burnside began the transfer of Reno's and Parke's divisions, a total of about 7,500 men, to Newport News, Virginia. In mid-July, Isaac I. Stevens joined Burnside with a division from the Department of the South, and July 22, 1862, the three divisions at Newport News were organized into a new Ninth Corps, and Burnside was assigned command. Later, Burnside with Ninth Corps moved to northern Virginia, and neither Burnside nor his two divisions returned to North Carolina. On July 6, 1862, when Burnside left the Department of North Carolina, John G. Foster assumed command and established his headquarters at New Berne.

At the end of July 1862, the troops remaining in the department were as follows:

New Berne
First Division, Department of North Carolina, John G. Foster
First Brigade, Thomas J. C. Amory
Second Brigade, Thomas G. Stevenson

New York Rocket Battery A
Battery F, 1st Rhode Island Light Artillery, James Belger
3rd New York Artillery, James H. Ledlie
3rd New York Cavalry, Simon H. Mix
Beaufort, Battalion of 5th Rhode Island Infantry
Fort Macon, Battery C, 1st United States Artillery
Hatteras Inlet, three companies of 103rd New York
Plymouth, Company F, 9th New York
Newport Barracks, 9th New Jersey and New York Rocket Battery B
Roanoke Island, Part of the Marine Artillery, William A. Howard
Washington, 1st North Carolina (Union) Infantry and one company of 3rd New York Cavalry, Edward E. Potter

Note. Foster's division was at New Berne.

In October 1862, a number of nine-month Massachusetts regiments arrived in the department, and Foster's division was reorganized to consist of three brigades, including a new Third Brigade, which was commanded by Horace C. Lee. At the end of November 1862, the following troops were present in North Carolina:

Foster's Division
First Brigade, Thomas J. C. Amory
Second Brigade, Thomas G. Stevenson
Third Brigade, Horace C. Lee

Unassigned Troops
25th Massachusetts Infantry, Josiah Pickett
3rd New York Cavalry, Simon H. Mix
3rd New York Light Artillery, James H. Ledlie
23rd Battery, New York Light Artillery, Alfred Ransom
24th Battery, New York Light Artillery, Jay E. Lee
Battery F, 1st Rhode Island Light Artillery, James Belger
Battery C, 1st United States Artillery, Cornelius Hook, Jr.

December 5, 1862, Henry W. Wessells' brigade of Fourth Corps, then serving with John J. Peck's command at Suffolk, Virginia, was detached and ordered to report to Foster in the Department of North Carolina. The brigade arrived at New Berne December 9, 1862, and then participated in Foster's expedition to Goldsboro, North Carolina (see below).

In addition to Reno's expedition to South Mills in April 1862, the troops of the Department of North

Carolina carried out numerous reconnaissances and expeditions during the period April–December 1862, but most of these involved only small units. There were, however, two expeditions that were of divisional strength. A brief description of these expeditions follows.

Expedition to the Eastern Counties of North Carolina (Washington and Hyde), October 31, 1862–November 12, 1862. In November 1862, Foster led an expedition into Eastern North Carolina in an attempt to capture three Confederate regiments that were foraging and obtaining conscripts in the area. The expedition consisted of the three brigades of Foster's Division, James Belger's Battery F, 1st Rhode Island Light Artillery, four batteries of James H. Ledlie's 3rd New York Light Artillery, and Simon H. Mix's 3rd New York Cavalry.

Foster left New Berne October 31, 1862 and arrived at Washington the next day. He left there for Williamston November 2, 1862, but that evening he found the enemy in position at Little Creek. Stevenson's brigade, aided by Belger's battery, drove this force back to Rawle's Creek, where it made another stand. This time, the way was cleared by fire of Belger's battery and two batteries of Ledlie's 3rd New York Artillery. Foster pursued the enemy through Williamston and arrived at Hamilton November 4, 1862. He continued on toward Tarboro November 6, 1862, and arrived within ten miles of the town that day. At this point Foster decided to return to New Berne, because his supplies were exhausted and the men were in poor physical condition. The next day he turned back and marched through Williamston toward Plymouth, where he arrived November 10, 1862. He reembarked his troops the next day and reached New Berne November 12, 1862.

Expedition from New Berne to Goldsboro, December 11–20, 1862. In December 1862, John G. Foster led an expedition from New Berne to Goldsboro, North Carolina to interrupt communications between Richmond and the southeastern Atlantic states. He planned to do this by destroying track, bridges, and culverts on the Wilmington and Weldon Railroad, including the bridge over the Neuse River at Goldsboro. Foster's command consisted of the following:

FOSTER'S EXPEDITION, John G. Foster

First Division, Department of North Carolina, John G. Foster
  First Brigade, Thomas J. C. Amory
  Second Brigade, Thomas G. Stevenson
  Third Brigade, Horace C. Lee
  Wessells' Brigade, Henry W. Wessells

Note. Wessells' Brigade of John J. Peck's command at Suffolk, in the Department of Virginia, joined Foster for this expedition at New Berne December 6, 1862.

Artillery Brigade, James H. Ledlie
  3rd New York Light Artillery (Batteries B, E, F, H, I, and K), James H. Ledlie
  Battery F, 1st Rhode Island Light Artillery, James Belger
  23rd Battery, New York Light Artillery (one section), Alfred Ransom
  24th Battery, New York Light Artillery (one section), Jay E. Lee

3rd New York Cavalry (640 men), Simon H. Mix

Foster left New Berne December 11, 1862, and marched on the Trent Road, which ran a few miles west of the Trent River, and almost parallel to it. On the morning of December 13, 1862, the head of the column reached a crossroad that led back in a northerly direction toward Kinston. Foster moved forward on this road to Southwest Creek, about six miles from Kinston, and there he found Nathan G. Evans' brigade of Samuel G. French's Confederate Department of North Carolina posted on the opposite side of the creek. The enemy had burned the bridge, but Charles A. Heckman's 9th New Jersey of Lee's brigade and Joshua B. Howell's 85th Pennsylvania of Wessells' Brigade succeeded in crossing the creek to the left of Evans and forced him to retire.

December 14, 1862, Foster continued his advance and at 9:00 A.M. again encountered Evans in position about two miles from the Kinston Bridge. Wessells moved forward on the right and left of the road and, aided by the 3rd New York Light Artillery, drove the enemy back toward the bridge. Amory's brigade also moved up and became engaged, and then when Stevenson's and Lee's brigades arrived, Evans retreated across the Neuse River. Heckman's 9th New Jersey and John F. Fellows' 17th Massachusetts followed and occupied Kinston. Evans once more formed in line of battle about two miles from the town, but he withdrew when Amory's and Stevenson's brigades crossed the river.

The next morning, Foster recrossed his troops to the south side of the Neuse and took the River Road toward Goldsboro. That night he halted three and a half to four miles from White Hall (also Whitehall), a small village on the south side of the Neuse about eighteen miles from Goldsboro.

On the morning of December 16, 1862, Foster sent Jeptha Garrard with three companies of the 3rd New York Cavalry and a section of artillery to Mount Olive, a station on the Wilmington and Weldon Railroad, about fourteen miles from Goldsboro. Garrard destroyed some track and a number of bridges in the vicinity and returned to camp. Foster's main column reached White Hall that morning and found Beverly H. Robertson's brigade holding the other side of the Neuse. Foster advanced Amory's brigade and the 9th New Jersey as if to cross, and then opened fire with the artillery on the enemy position. Amory's and Stevenson's brigades demonstrated for a time from their positions on the river bank, but they made no effort to cross. Meantime, Lee's brigade marched on toward the railroad, and about an hour later the rest of Foster's command followed. The entire force bivouacked that night about eight miles from Goldsboro.

On the morning of December 17, 1862, Foster reached the railroad near Everettsville, and from that point he sent Charles Fitz Simmons with a detachment of the 3rd New York Cavalry to destroy the track at Dudley Station, about five miles from Goldsboro. He then moved the main column, with Lee's brigade in the lead, up the railroad to burn the bridge over the Neuse. Thomas L. Clingman's Confederate brigade held the crossing at the bridge, and Evans' brigade was at Goldsboro. The 9th New Jersey and 17th Massachusetts, supported by the rest of Lee's brigade, moved steadily up the railroad, and after two hours reached the bridge and succeeded in burning it. When the bridge was destroyed, Foster's mission was completed, and he ordered his troops back to New Berne. They arrived there December 20, 1862.

Department of North Carolina, Eighteenth Corps
December 24, 1862–July 15, 1863

On December 24, 1862, the troops in the Depart-

ment of North Carolina were designated as Eighteenth Corps. John G. Foster was assigned command, with headquarters at New Berne. The corps was organized by an order of December 28, 1862, as follows:

EIGHTEENTH CORPS, John G. Foster

First Division, Henry W. Wessells
    First Brigade, Lewis C. Hunt
    Second Brigade, Thomas G. Stevenson

Note 1. First Brigade was organized from Wessells' Brigade, which was transferred December 6, 1862 from John J. Peck's command at Suffolk in the Department of Virginia.
Note 2. The designation of First Division, Eighteenth Corps was changed to Fourth Division, Eighteenth Corps in the reorganization of January 2, 1863.

Unattached Brigades
    Amory's Brigade, Thomas J. C. Amory
    Lee's Brigade, Horace C. Lee
    Heckman's Brigade, Charles A. Heckman
    Artillery Brigade, James H. Ledlie

Note. Heckman's Brigade was formed from regiments of the other brigades.

3rd New York Cavalry, Simon H. Mix

Early in January 1863, Eighteenth Corps was strongly reinforced by the transfer of troops from the Department of Virginia, Seventh Corps. Henry M. Naglee's First Brigade of John J. Peck's Division, Fourth Corps had arrived at New Berne from Yorktown by January 5, 1863, and Orris S. Ferry's brigade also began arriving from Suffolk on the same date. Francis B. Spinola's brigade also arrived from Suffolk early in January 1863.

By an order of January 2, 1863, Eighteenth Corps was reorganized into five divisions as follows:

EIGHTEENTH CORPS, John G. Foster

First Division, Innis N. Palmer
    First Brigade, Thomas J. C. Amory
    Second Brigade, Horace C. Lee

Note 1. First Brigade was organized from Amory's Unattached Brigade, Department of North Carolina.
Note 2. Second Brigade was organized from Lee's Unattached Brigade, Department of North Carolina.

Second Division, Henry M. Naglee

First Brigade, Charles A. Heckman
Second Brigade, William W. H. Davis

Note 1. First Brigade was formed from regiments of Naglee's Brigade, Fourth Corps, and Heckman's Unattached Brigade, Department of North Carolina.
Note 2. Second Brigade was organized from Naglee's Brigade, Fourth Corps.

Third Division, Orris S. Ferry
  First Brigade, Thomas O. Osborn
  Second Brigade, Joshua B. Howell

Note 1. First Brigade was organized from Ferry's Brigade, Division at Suffolk, Seventh Corps.
Note 2. Second Brigade was organized from regiments of the Department of North Carolina.

Fourth Division, Henry W. Wessells
  First Brigade, Lewis C. Hunt
  Second Brigade, Thomas G. Stevenson

Note. Fourth Division was formerly First Division, Department of North Carolina, Eighteenth Corps.

Fifth Division, Henry Prince
  First Brigade, Francis B. Spinola
  Second Brigade, James Jourdan

Note 1. First Brigade was organized from Spinola's Brigade, Division at Suffolk, Seventh Corps.
Note 2. Second Brigade was formed from regiments of Heckman's Unattached Brigade, and also from Spinola's Brigade, Division at Suffolk, Seventh Corps.

Artillery Brigade, James H. Ledlie
3rd New York Cavalry, Simon H. Mix

Not all of these troops remained very long in North Carolina. In January 1863, Foster was ordered to take two divisions of Eighteenth Corps to Charleston Harbor to take part in operations against Fort Sumter and Charleston. Foster sailed from Beaufort, North Carolina about January 24, 1863, with Naglee's Second Division and Ferry's Third Division, and arrived at Beaufort, South Carolina February 1, 1863. The two divisions were then moved to Saint Helena Island February 7, 1863, and while there Foster learned that operations would not begin for several weeks. He turned over the command of Detachment Eighteenth Corps to Naglee, and March 10, 1863 returned to North Carolina to look after affairs in his department. May 26, 1863, Stevenson's Second Brigade, Fourth Division,

Eighteenth Corps embarked for duty in the Department of the South, and it later joined Detachment Eighteenth Corps.

Originally it was intended that Detachment Eighteenth Corps was to serve as a distinct unit during the operations at Charleston Harbor, and was to serve under the direction of the commander of the Department of the South. This arrangement later led to a controversy between David Hunter, commander of the Department of the South, and Naglee, commander of Detachment Eighteenth Corps; and as a result the latter was relieved of command March 5, 1863, and March 10, 1863, he left the Department of the South. Heckman was assigned command of Naglee's division, and Stevenson assumed command of Heckman's brigade. Second Division and Third Division were carried on the roster of Eighteenth Corps as detached, but April 16, 1863, they were broken up and the regiments were assigned to various organizations in Tenth Corps, Department of the South.

On March 30, 1863, Confederate forces laid siege to Washington, North Carolina, and April 12, 1863, Heckman was ordered back from the Department of the South with his First Brigade, Second Division to New Berne. Naglee was also ordered back to New Berne to resume command of Second Division, which at that time consisted only of Heckman's brigade. Naglee arrived at New Berne and assumed command of Second Division April 16, 1863. For additional information relating to Second Division and Third Division in the Department of the South, see Tenth Corps, Department of the South, and also Department of the South, Part III, Department of the South, Tenth Corps. See also Siege of Washington, North Carolina, below.

Following the departure of Second Division and Third Division for the Department of the South, the organization of the troops remaining in Eighteenth Corps in February 1863 was as follows:

DEPARTMENT OF NORTH CAROLINA, EIGHTEENTH CORPS, John G. Foster

First Division, Innis N. Palmer
  First Brigade, Thomas J. C. Amory
  Second Brigade, Horace C. Lee

Fourth Division, Henry W. Wessells
  First Brigade, Lewis C. Hunt
  Second Brigade, Thomas G. Stevenson

Note. Stevenson's brigade was sent to the Department of the South March 26, 1863.

Fifth Division, Henry Prince
  First Brigade, Francis B. Spinola
  Second Brigade, James Jourdan

Artillery Brigade, James H. Ledlie
3rd New York Cavalry, Simon H. Mix
Washington, North Carolina, Edward E. Potter
  1st North Carolina (Union)

There were few organizational changes in the Department of North Carolina until the reorganization of April 23, 1863, and these have already been noted; namely, the transfer of Stevenson's Second Brigade, Fourth Division to the Department of the South March 26, 1863; the return of Heckman's First Brigade, Second Division from the Department of the South April 12, 1863, during the siege of Washington, North Carolina; and the reorganization of Second Division under Naglee.

During the siege of Washington March 30, 1863–April 20, 1863, Innis N. Palmer was in temporary command of Eighteenth Corps while Foster was in personal command at Washington.

By an order of April 23, 1863 (and amended April 27, 1863), the Department of North Carolina was divided into three districts. The District of the Pamlico was organized from Fifth Division, Eighteenth Corps, and Henry Prince was assigned command; the District of Beaufort was organized May 2, 1863 from Second Division, Eighteenth Corps, and Henry M. Naglee was assigned command; and the District of the Albemarle was organized May 3, 1863 from Fourth Division, Eighteenth Corps, and Henry W. Wessells was assigned command. For additional information, see above, Districts in the Department of North Carolina.

The organization of the Department of North Carolina, Eighteenth Corps in May 1863 was as follows:

EIGHTEENTH CORPS, John G. Foster

First Division, Innis N. Palmer
  First Brigade, Thomas J. C. Amory
  Second Brigade, Horace C. Lee

Note 1. First Division was at New Berne, North Carolina.
Note 2. The division return for May 1863 reported

Amory in command of the division, Charles L. Holbrook in command of First Brigade, and George H. Pierson in command of Second Brigade.

Independent Brigades
  Jourdan's Brigade, James Jourdan
  Lee's Brigade, Francis L. Lee
  Cavalry Brigade, Simon H. Mix
  Outpost (132nd New York Regiment), Peter J. Claassen
  Artillery
    3rd New York Light Artillery, Terance J. Kennedy
    Battery F, 1st Rhode Island Light Artillery, James Belger

Note 1. The independent brigades were at New Berne.
Note 2. Jourdan's Brigade was organized April 22, 1863 from Second Brigade, Fourth Division, Eighteenth Corps. The brigade was broken up in June 1863.
Note 3. Lee's Brigade was organized in May 1863, largely from Second Brigade, Fourth Division, Eighteenth Corps. The brigade was broken up in June 1863.
Note 4. Mix's Cavalry Brigade was organized in May 1863.

District of the Albemarle, Henry W. Wessells
District of Beaufort, Henry M. Naglee
District of the Pamlico, Henry Prince

Note 1. Francis B. Spinola was assigned command of the District of Beaufort May 29, 1863.
Note 2. Edward A. Wild arrived in the department May 19, 1863, for the purpose of raising a brigade of colored troops.

For a description of the troops present in the districts, see above, Districts in the Department of North Carolina.

In June 1863, the number of troops in the department was greatly reduced by transfer and muster out. When Robert E. Lee invaded Pennsylvania during the Gettysburg Campaign, Spinola's brigade of Pennsylvania regiments (the Keystone Brigade) was ordered north. It went first to Fort Monroe, and remained temporarily in the Department of Virginia at White House until July 7, 1863, and it then embarked for Washington, D.C. Also, during the period June 6–24, 1863, eight Massachusetts regiments of nine-month men returned home for muster out.

Henry Prince went north with a brigade of Massachusetts militia, and later was assigned command of Second Division, Third Corps, Army of the Potomac. Prince assumed command of the division at South Mountain July 10, 1863. Henry M. Naglee also went north under orders to report to Third

Corps, Army of the Potomac, but July 8, 1863, he was assigned command at Harper's Ferry, Middle Department. Spinola's brigade was sent to Harper's Ferry, and was mustered out in late July and early August 1863.

At the end of June 1863, the Department of North Carolina, Eighteenth Corps was organized as follows:

New Berne, North Carolina
First Division, Eighteenth Corps, Thomas J. C. Amory
First Brigade, Luther Day
Second Brigade, Horace C. Lee

Note 1. First Brigade consisted only of Day's 17th Massachusetts Regiment.
Note 2. Second Brigade consisted only of 25th and 27th Massachusetts regiments.
Note 3. Eight Massachusetts regiments left the division June 6–24, 1863 for muster out.

Jourdan's Brigade, James Jourdan
Unbrigaded infantry (four regiments)
Cavalry Brigade, George W. Lewis
Artillery
3rd New York Light Artillery, Terance J. Kennedy
Battery F, 1st Rhode Island Light Artillery, James Belger

District of Beaufort, Charles A. Heckman
District of the Albemarle, Henry W. Wessells
Infantry Brigade, Theodore F. Lehmann
District of the Pamlico, Joseph M. McChesney

On July 10, 1863, just before the department was discontinued, the troops present were organized as follows:

New Berne
First Division, Thomas J. C. Amory
Jourdan's Brigade, James Jourdan
United States Colored Troops, Edward A. Wild

District of Beaufort, Charles A. Heckman
District of the Albemarle, Henry W. Wessells
District of the Pamlico, Joseph M. McChesney

July 15, 1863, the Department of North Carolina was consolidated with the Department of Virginia to form the Department of Virginia and North Carolina.

Daniel H. Hill's Expedition against New Berne, March 8–16, 1863.

After the Battle of Fredericksburg in December 1862, James Longstreet was detached from the Army of Northern Virginia and was sent to the south side of the James River. Then, on February 25, 1863, Longstreet replaced Gustavus W. Smith as commander of the Confederate Department of Virginia and North Carolina, and established his headquarters at Petersburg, Virginia.

Eastern North Carolina was a fertile region and an important source of supplies for the armies of the Confederacy, and Longstreet, with Robert E. Lee's approval, decided on a plan to protect the supply lines and also to collect provisions in that region, especially east of the Chowan River. An important part of Longstreet's plan was to hold the United States forces near their bases in Tidewater Virginia and eastern North Carolina, and to accomplish this, he directed Daniel H. Hill, commander of the Confederate forces in North Carolina, to demonstrate against New Berne and Washington, North Carolina while Longstreet moved against Suffolk, Virginia.

Hill, whose forces were at Kinston, North Carolina, decided to move on New Berne first, and issued orders for his command to advance on three roads. Junius Daniel's brigade marched toward New Berne on the Lower Trent Road; Beverly H. Robertson's cavalry brigade moved along the south side of the Trent River; and James J. Pettigrew, with his brigade and the artillery, approached the town near Barrington's Ferry. Robertson was ordered to destroy the Atlantic and North Carolina Railroad, and Pettigrew was directed to shell Fort Anderson and the gunboats on the river.

On the evening of March 13, 1863, Daniel's scouts encountered Union pickets about ten miles from New Berne, and pushed them back about two miles to a line of works at Deep Gully on the Trent Road. The Federal outpost was held by four companies of Josiah Pickett's 25th Massachusetts of Horace C. Lee's 2nd Brigade, Palmer's First Division, Eighteenth Corps, and a part of the 3rd New York Cavalry. When Daniel began his attack, the rest of 25th Massachusetts moved up, and the regiment was reinforced that evening by the 14th and 46th Massachusetts regiments, also of Lee's brigade. It was then dark, and the troops bivouacked for the night.

At daybreak the next morning, Pickett sent forward a company of skirmishers and they immediately became engaged. Palmer then took charge at Deep Gully and ordered forward the 25th Massachusetts. He also sent up in support the 5th and 46th Massachusetts; a section of William J. Riggs' Battery H, 3rd New York Light Artillery; and one gun of James Belger's Battery F, First Rhode Island Light Artillery. There was skirmishing on this front for about three hours, but no heavy fighting developed.

Meantime, Pettigrew arrived with his command in front of Fort Anderson, an earthwork on the north bank of the Neuse River, directly opposite New Berne, and he opened with his artillery. He did not advance the infantry, however, but held it in reserve ready for an assault. The Federal troops in Fort Anderson consisted of the 92nd New York, commanded by Hiram Anderson, Jr. This regiment belonged to Jonathan S. Belknap's First Brigade of Theodore F. Lehmann's Fourth Division, Eighteenth Corps.

When Pettigrew began his attack on Fort Anderson, the regiments supporting Pickett's 25th Massachusetts were withdrawn for the defense of New Berne, leaving only the 25th Massachusetts and two guns to confront Daniel. Pickett then fell back to a better position at the Jackson house, and there he awaited the enemy advance. Daniel did not attack, however, and at 4:30 P.M. Pickett discovered that he was falling back. Meantime, on the south side of the Trent River, Robertson advanced to within six miles of New Berne, and then he too withdrew without making any effort to enter the town.

Pettigrew continued his fire on Fort Anderson until Federal gunboats arrived on the scene, and they then opened on the enemy artillery. This fire, combined with that from a battery on the New Berne side of the river, soon caused Pettigrew to withdraw without delivering an infantry assault. With the failure of Pettigrew and Robertson, Hill ended the attack and moved back with his command to Kinston. Prince's Fifth Division, Eighteenth Corps followed Robertson March 15–16, 1863, as far as Pollocksville, and then returned to New Berne.

Siege of Washington, North Carolina, March 30, 1863–April 20, 1863. A short time after Hill's unsuccessful attack on New Berne, he marched with his command toward Washington, North Carolina, and by March 30, 1863 had arrived there and placed the town under siege. He erected batteries along the Pamlico River east of Washington to engage the Federal gunboats, and to turn back any attempt to reinforce the garrison by water. Hill also placed the brigades of Daniel and Pettigrew between Chockowinity Cross Roads and Blount's Creek to stop any Federal relief column moving overland from New Berne. Richard B. Garnett's brigade took position across the river (the Tar River joined the Pamlico River at Washington) and invested Washington from that direction.

When John G. Foster, commanding the department, learned that Hill planned to attack Washington, he left New Berne with several members of his staff and arrived at the town only a short time before the enemy troops arrived. At Washington at that time were about 1,200 men belonging to the 27th and 44th Massachusetts regiments; the 1st North Carolina (Union) Regiment; 3rd New York Cavalry; and Battery G, 3rd New York Light Artillery. Later, these troops were reinforced by the 5th Rhode Island and 43rd Massachusetts. Almost all of the fighting at Washington during the siege consisted of artillery fire, and there was very little infantry action.

When Foster left New Berne for Washington, he placed Innis N. Palmer in charge, and Palmer assigned Henry Prince to command a force composed of regiments of Eighteenth Corps to go to the relief of Washington. Prince left New Berne by steamer April 4, 1863 and moved to the mouth of the Pamlico River near Fort Hill. After looking over the ground, Prince decided not to continue on, and he returned to New Berne April 6, 1863. Two days later, Francis B. Spinola left New Berne with a second relief column, and marched toward Washington. He organized the regiments of his expedition into a provisional division of three brigades as follows:

Provisional Division, Francis B. Spinola
  First Brigade, Frederic J. Coffin
  Second Brigade, Horace C. Lee
  Third Brigade, Everard Bierer

Note. Coffin was in command of the regiments of James Jourdan's Second Brigade, Fifth Division during Jourdan's absence from the department.

Spinola arrived at Blount's Creek April 9, 1863, and there he found the enemy strongly entrenched. There was some skirmishing and artillery fire, and then Spinola returned to New Berne without making any serious effort to continue the march. Foster then decided to run the Confederate blockade, return to New Berne, and personally organize a new relief column. Foster assigned Edward E. Potter, his chief of staff, to command at Washington, and April 15, 1863 left for New Berne.

On April 12, 1863, Charles A. Heckman was ordered to return to North Carolina from the Department of the South with his brigade of Second Division, Eighteenth Corps. At the same time, Henry M. Naglee, formerly commander of Second Division, and who was also in the Department of the South, was ordered to resume command of his division in North Carolina. When Heckman arrived, he relieved Spinola, who was then in command along the Pamlico River.

Foster then sent Spinola to attack the enemy at Swift Creek, and ordered Prince, with Jourdan's Brigade, to move up the Atlantic and North Carolina Railroad toward Kinston. Foster left New Berne April 18, 1863 with Naglee's Division—which consisted of Heckman's brigade, a detachment of 3rd New York Cavalry, and some artillery—and marched toward Washington. When he arrived near the town, he routed a Confederate rear guard and found that Hill's main force had withdrawn April 15, 1863. The arrival of reinforcements and supplies had made the capture of Washington unlikely, and Longstreet had decided that he could no longer afford to keep a large force watching Washington; accordingly, he had directed Hill to abandon the siege.

COMMANDERS OF THE DEPARTMENT OF NORTH CAROLINA

Ambrose E. Burnside	January 13, 1862 to July 6, 1862
John G. Foster	July 6, 1862 to March 29, 1863
Innis N. Palmer	March 29, 1863 to April 16, 1863, temporarily
John G. Foster	April 16, 1863 to July 18, 1863

DEPARTMENT OF NORTH CAROLINA
JANUARY 31, 1865–MAY 19, 1866

November 15, 1864, William T. Sherman with his Army of the Military Division of the Mississippi set out from Atlanta on his march across Georgia. He arrived near the coast December 10, 1864, and occupied Savannah eleven days later. He then began preparations for further operations. For details of his march, see Savannah Campaign (Sherman's March through Georgia).

Ulysses S. Grant, general in chief of the armies, originally intended that when Sherman arrived on the coast, he would bring his army north by sea to cooperate with Union forces in Virginia in a final campaign to end the war. Sherman, however, proposed that he march northward through the interior of the Carolinas to join Grant and, while on the march, destroy the railroads and all public property that contributed to the Confederate war effort. On January 2, 1865, Sherman received authorization from Grant to begin his march through the Carolinas as soon as practicable.

The success of Sherman's operation would depend in part upon his ability to open communications with Union forces on the Atlantic coast at Wilmington or Beaufort, North Carolina, from which ports his army could be supplied when it reached the vicinity of Goldsboro, North Carolina.

Because North Carolina was the immediate objective of Sherman's march, it became necessary to make such organizational changes in the state as would ensure the necessary cooperation of the United States forces operating in that area. The state of North Carolina had been a part of the Union Department of Virginia and North Carolina since mid-July 1863, but January 12, 1865 it was detached and made a part of John G. Foster's Department of the South, through which Sherman's army was then preparing to march. January 16, 1865, the state was designated as the District of North Carolina, Department of the South. This arrangement, however, presented some difficulties, because Foster's headquarters was at Hilton Head, South Carolina, and more time was required for his orders to reach North Carolina than those from Grant at City Point, Virginia. For this reason, on January 31, 1865, the Department of North Carolina was constituted to consist of the state of North Carolina, which was then detached from the Department of the South. John M. Schofield, commander of Twenty-Third Corps, Army of the Ohio, which had been transferred to North Carolina from Tennessee, was assigned command of the new department. To secure the necessary cooperation with Sherman's army as it advanced toward Goldsboro, Schofield was placed under Sherman's orders, and the department was thus attached to the Military Division of the Mississippi. The Department of North Carolina was organized February 9, 1865, when Schofield assumed command. His headquarters was in the field.

There were no changes in the limits of the Department of North Carolina during the period of its existence, but a greater part of the state came under Federal control as a result of Schofield's operations during March and April 1865.

April 19, 1865, that part of the department not occupied by Sherman's troops was attached to the Military Division of the James. Also in April 1865, headquarters was established at Raleigh, North Carolina.

After the surrender of Joseph E. Johnston's Confederate army at Durham Station, North Carolina April 26, 1865, the Army of the Tennessee and the Army of Georgia immediately marched northward toward Washington, D.C. On May 4, 1865, with the departure of his troops from the state, Sherman relinquished command of the Department of North Carolina. The department then became a part of Henry W. Halleck's Military Division of the James, and remained under Halleck's control until his military division was discontinued June 30, 1865. The commander of the Department of North Carolina was then ordered to report directly to the adjutant general in Washington. In June 1865, Schofield relinquished command of the department, and Jacob D. Cox assumed command June 21, 1865. Schofield departed on a one-year leave of absence to assume control of the measures to be adopted for the purpose of causing the French army to evacuate Mexico.

In the general reorganization of the military divisions and departments of the army June 27, 1865, the Department of North Carolina was again organized to consist of the state of North Carolina. The order of June 27, 1865 also assigned the Department of North Carolina to George G. Meade's Military Division of the Atlantic. Thomas H. Ruger assumed command of the department June 28, 1865, relieving Cox. Two days later, Cox was ordered to report to Edward O. C. Ord, commander of the Department of the Ohio, for assignment to command the District of Ohio, with headquarters at Columbus.

The Department of North Carolina was merged into the Department of the Carolinas May 19, 1866.

DISTRICTS IN THE DEPARTMENT OF NORTH CAROLINA

District of North Carolina. On January 31, 1865, the date when the Department of North Carolina was reconstituted, Innis N. Palmer was in command of the District of North Carolina, Department of the South. Palmer's command consisted of Edward Harland's Sub-District of New Berne, Theodore F. Lehmann's post of Roanoke Island, James Stewart's Sub-District of Beaufort, and Jones Frankle's post of Plymouth. When John M. Schofield assumed command of the Department of North Carolina February 9, 1985, Palmer was still in command of the District of North Carolina, and he remained in command until March 1, 1865, when Jacob D. Cox assumed command of the newly constituted District of Beaufort (see next section).

District of Beaufort. February 25, 1865, Cox, then commanding Third Division, Twenty-Third Corps at Wilmington, North Carolina, was ordered to New Berne to assume command of the District of Beaufort, which was to include all posts and United States forces in the Department of North Carolina north of Fort Macon. Cox's assignment to the district was temporary, and his instructions were to gain possession of the railroad from New Berne to Goldsboro so that it might be put in running order for the use of the army. Innis N. Palmer, who was then in command of the District of North Carolina, which was discontinued by the creation of the District of Beaufort, was ordered to report to Cox for duty.

Cox assumed command of the District of Beaufort March 1, 1865, and that day ordered the reorganization of the troops in the district into two divisions. These were to be commanded by Palmer and Samuel P. Carter, and they were, together with Thomas H. Ruger's First Division, Twenty-Third Corps, organized into a provisional corps under the command of Cox.

Cox advanced with the Provisional Corps along the railroad toward Goldsboro and, after defeating a Confederate force under Braxton Bragg at Wise's

Forks March 8–10, 1865, occupied Kinston, North Carolina March 14, 1865.

Cox was relieved from the command of the District of Beaufort March 18, 1865, but he retained command of the forces remaining in the field. Palmer was assigned command of the District of Beaufort, and retained control of Edward Harland's Brigade of his, Palmer's, First Division, District of Beaufort, which remained to garrison Kinston when Cox moved on with his Provisional Corps to Goldsboro. For details of the organization of the troops of the District of Beaufort, and their operations, see below, Troops in the Department of North Carolina, Cox's Provisional Corps, Army of the Ohio; and Operations in the Department of North Carolina, Advance of Schofield's Army to Goldsboro (Battle of Kinston or Wise's Forks).

Palmer remained in command of the District of Beaufort until early June 1865. June 1, 1865, Charles J. Paine, commanding Third Division, Tenth Corps, was ordered with two of his brigades to relieve all white troops serving in the district. Palmer was instructed to encamp his troops, when relieved, near New Berne; and to prepare for muster out those that had been so ordered, and to put the remainder in serviceable condition. June 4, 1865, Delevan Bates' First Brigade and Samuel A. Duncan's Second Brigade of Paine's division moved from Goldsboro to New Berne, and Bates' brigade was sent on to Morehead City. Nathan Goff's Third Brigade was sent to Wilmington, North Carolina.

The District of Beaufort was discontinued July 6, 1865 by the same order that created the District of New Berne (see District of New Berne, below).

District of Wilmington. The District of Wilmington was constituted March 1, 1865 to consist of all territory under Union military control in rear of Schofield's forces then operating from the Cape Fear River as a base. Joseph R. Hawley was assigned command of the district, and was given the responsibility of protecting the depot at Wilmington, the harbor on the Cape Fear River, and the line of the Wilmington and Weldon Railroad in rear of the army. Joseph C. Abbott, with his Second Brigade, First Division, Twenty-Fourth Corps of Alfred H. Terry's Provisional Corps (after April 2, 1865, designated as Second Brigade, First Division, Tenth

Corps), was assigned to Hawley's command. Abbott was assigned command of the post of Wilmington March 5, 1865, and his brigade performed guard duty in the city of Wilmington and garrison duty at Forts Fisher, Caswell, and Anderson, as well as at the other defenses of the Cape Fear River and Smithfield. It also picketed the railroad between Wilmington and Magnolia Station.

Also present in the district at the time of its organization were Nathaniel C. McLean's Second Division and James W. Reilly's Third Division of Twenty-Third Corps, both under the command of Darius N. Couch; and Alfred H. Terry's Provisional Corps, which consisted of Adelbert Ames' Second Division, Twenty-Fourth Corps and Charles J. Paine's Third Division, Twenty-Fifth Corps. These troops, however, remained in the district for only a short time. March 6, 1865, Couch's two divisions left Wilmington to join Jacob D. Cox's force near Kinston, North Carolina, and March 15, 1865, Terry's Provisional Corps departed to join Schofield near Goldsboro.

June 9, 1865, Abbott was ordered with his brigade to Goldsboro, and he was relieved in command of the post of Wilmington by Nathan Goff. Goff's Third Brigade, Third Division, Tenth Corps, which had been ordered from Goldsboro to Wilmington June 2, 1865, relieved Abbott's brigade in the district.

Hawley remained in command of the District of Wilmington until June 23, 1865, and he then left for Richmond to report to Alfred H. Terry, commanding the Department of Virginia. John W. Ames succeeded Hawley in command of the District of Wilmington. Hawley was appointed as Terry's chief of staff July 5, 1865.

In the general reorganization of the districts in the Department of North Carolina July 6, 1865, the District of Wilmington was reconstituted to consist of the counties of New Hanover, Duplin, Sampson, Cumberland, Robeson, Bladen, Columbus, and Brunswick. John W. Ames was assigned command, with headquarters at Wilmington.

District of Raleigh. The District of Raleigh was constituted April 14, 1865 to include the posts of Raleigh and Goldsboro, the railroad running between the two cities, and all of the surrounding country then under Federal military control. Henry

W. Birge was assigned command of the district. The order creating the district, however, was suspended the next day.

In the general reorganization of the districts in the Department of North Carolina July 6, 1865, the District of Raleigh was reconstituted to consist of the counties of Person, Orange, Chatham, Moore, Granville, Wake, Harnett, Warren, Franklin, Johnson, Halifax, Nash, Edgecombe, Wilson, and Wayne. Adelbert Ames was assigned command, with headquarters at Raleigh.

District of New Berne. In the general reorganization of the districts of the Department of North Carolina July 6, 1865, the District of New Berne was constituted to consist of the counties of Hertford, Bertie, Martin, Pitt, Greene, Lenoir, Jones, and Onslow, and all counties to the east of those named above. Charles J. Paine was assigned command, with headquarters at New Berne.

District of West North Carolina. July 4, 1865, Samuel P. Carter was assigned command of the District of West North Carolina, and also of First Division, Twenty-Third Corps (*note*. Second Division and Third Division, Twenty-Third Corps were broken up July 4, 1865) during the temporary absence of Thomas H. Ruger. Headquarters was to be at Greensboro. July 6, 1865, however, in the order reorganizing the districts of the Department of North Carolina, Carter was assigned command of the District of Greensboro (see below). By the same order, the District of West North Carolina was reconstituted to consist of the counties of Ashe, Wilkes, Caldwell, Burke, and Rutherford, and all other counties to the west of those named above. Thomas T. Heath was assigned command, with headquarters at or near Morganton, North Carolina.

District of Greensboro. In the general reorganization of the districts in the Department of North Carolina July 6, 1865, the District of Greensboro was constituted to consist of the counties between the District of West North Carolina and the District of Raleigh as follows: Caswell, Rockingham, Stokes, Surry, Yadkin, Forsyth, Guilford, Alamance, Randolph, Davidson, Davie, Catawba, Cleveland, Lincoln, Gaston, Mecklenburg, Union, Anson, Richmond, Stanley, Cabarrus, and

Montgomery. Samuel P. Carter was assigned command, with headquarters at Greensboro. Carter assumed command July 12, 1865.

TROOPS IN THE DEPARTMENT OF NORTH CAROLINA

When the Department of North Carolina was constituted January 31, 1865, Union troops serving in the state consisted of Alfred H. Terry's command of the Army of the James, which had captured Fort Fisher on Confederate Point (later, Federal Point) January 15, 1865; and the troops of Innis N. Palmer's District of North Carolina, which were largely on garrison duty at New Berne, Morehead City, Roanoke Island, Fort Macon, and Plymouth. There were several additions to this force before hostilities ended in April 1865.

During February 1865, John M. Schofield's Twenty-Third Corps, Army of the Ohio, and a provisional division under Thomas F. Meagher, consisting of troops en route to join Sherman's army, which was then advancing in the Carolinas, arrived at Fort Fisher, Morehead City, and New Berne from Tennessee. When Schofield assumed command of the Department of North Carolina February 9, 1865, he was in command of the Army of the Ohio, which consisted of Twenty-Third Corps. Thereafter, he used for the designation of his command Department of North Carolina, Army of the Ohio, and the troops of the department constituted the Army of the Ohio. In addition to the above reinforcements, two brigades of Henry W. Birge's Second Division, Nineteenth Corps arrived from Savannah, Georgia, and two more provisional divisions of troops for Sherman's army arrived, one from Tennessee and one from Hilton Head, during March and April 1865.

A number of new organizations were formed from the above-mentioned troops during the period February–April 1865. A provisional corps commanded by Alfred H. Terry was organized February 21, 1865 from Terry's United States Forces at Fort Fisher; and a provisional corps commanded by Jacob D. Cox was organized March 1, 1865 from troops of Innis N. Palmer's District of North Carolina and Thomas H. Ruger's First Division, Twenty-Third Corps. The other two divisions of

Twenty-Third Corps formed a separate command at Wilmington under Darius N. Couch.

Cox's Provisional Corps was discontinued April 2, 1865, and the three divisions of Twenty-Third Corps were united at Goldsboro under Cox. Also on April 2, 1865, Tenth Corps, Department of North Carolina was organized from Terry's Provisional Corps and the two brigades of Nineteenth Corps.

In addition to the troops belonging to the Department of North Carolina, William T. Sherman's Army of the Military Division of the Mississippi arrived in North Carolina from Savannah, Georgia about March 8, 1865, and remained in the state until after the surrender of Joseph E. Johnston's army April 26, 1865. Then, Judson Kilpatrick's Cavalry Division of Sherman's army was transferred to the Department of North Carolina, and the rest of the army departed for Washington, D.C.

By an order of April 1, 1865, Sherman designated Schofield's Tenth Corps and Twenty-Third Corps as the "Center" while it was operating with his Army of the Military Division of the Mississippi. Prior to that date, Sherman's army had consisted of a Right Wing and a Left Wing.

A more detailed description of the above-mentioned organizations is given in the following sections.

United States Forces at Fort Fisher (Alfred H. Terry). For details of this organization, see the following section, Terry's Provisional Corps, Department of North Carolina.

Terry's Provisional Corps, Department of North Carolina. In January 1865, Alfred H. Terry was assigned command of a force, taken from Benjamin F. Butler's Army of the James, which consisted of Adelbert Ames' Second Division, Twenty-Fourth Corps, Charles J. Paine's Third Division, Twenty-Fifth Corps, and Joseph C. Abbott's Second Brigade, First Division, Twenty-Fourth Corps. Terry was ordered with this force on an expedition to attempt the capture of Fort Fisher, North Carolina. Terry's command landed near the fort January 13, 1865, and two days later gained possession of the works. For details, see Army of the James, Terry's Expedition to Fort Fisher, North Carolina.

Terry remained on Federal Point (formerly Confederate Point), garrisoning Smithville and the forts

at the mouth of the Cape Fear River, until the arrival of John M. Schofield February 8–9, 1865 with Jacob D. Cox's Third Division, Twenty-Third Corps. During this period, Terry's command was known as United States Forces at Fort Fisher, and also as United States Forces at Federal Point.

Under the command of Schofield, Terry's troops joined Cox's division in an advance on Wilmington, North Carolina, which ended with the occupation of the city February 22, 1865. For details of the campaign, see below, Operations in the Department of North Carolina, Capture of Wilmington, North Carolina.

On February 21, 1865, while the movement on Wilmington was in progress, the designation of Terry's command was changed to Provisional Corps, Department of North Carolina, or simply Terry's Provisional Corps. The United States Forces at Fort Fisher, and also Terry's Provisional Corps, was organized as follows:

TERRY'S PROVISIONAL CORPS, Alfred H. Terry

First Division, Twenty-Fourth Corps
  Second Brigade, Joseph C. Abbott

Second Division, Twenty-Fourth Corps, Adelbert Ames
  First Brigade, Rufus Daggett
  Second Brigade, James A. Colvin
  Third Brigade, G. Frederick Granger

Third Division, Twenty-Fifth Corps, Charles J. Paine
  First Brigade, Delevan Bates
  Second Brigade, John W. Ames, to February 27, 1865
    Samuel A. Duncan
  Third Brigade, Elias Wright, to February 27, 1865, wounded
    John H. Holman

Artillery
  Companies B, G, and L, 1st Connecticut Heavy Artillery, William G. Pride
  Company A, 2nd Pennsylvania Heavy Artillery, Benjamin F. Everett
  16th Battery, New York Light Artillery, Richard H. Lee
  Battery E, 3rd United States Artillery, John R. Myrick

The enemy evacuated Wilmington on the night of February 21, 1865, and early the next morning, troops of the Provisional Corps entered the city. They only passed through Wilmington, however, and then pursued the Confederate troops to the Northeast River (Northeast Station on the Wilmington and Weldon Railroad) before halting, about ten miles to the north.

February 24, 1865, Abbott's brigade was attached to Paine's division, and it remainded as a part of this command until March 1, 1865. That day Joseph R. Hawley was assigned command of the District of Wilmington (see above, Districts in the Department of North Carolina), and Abbott's brigade was ordered to report to Hawley to garrison the city of Wilmington. March 5, 1865, Abbott was assigned command of the post of Wilmington.

Schofield maintained his Headquarters Department of North Carolina at Wilmington until March 5, 1865, and then departed to join Cox's Provisional Corps, Department of North Carolina, which was beginning its advance from New Berne toward Goldsboro. During Schofield's absence, Hawley was directed to report to Terry.

March 14, 1865, Terry left Wilmington with the divisions of Ames and Paine to join Schofield's forces near Goldsboro. Terry's command arrived at Cox's Ferry on the Neuse River near Goldsboro March 21, 1865, and waited there for Sherman's army to cross the river March 23–24, 1865. It then moved to Faison's Station on the Wilmington and Weldon Railroad, and remained there until April 10, 1865. While there, on April 2, 1865, Terry's Provisional Corps was discontinued as an organization, and its troops were included in Terry's newly created Tenth Corps, Department of North Carolina. For additional information, see the following sections: Troops in the Department of North Carolina, Tenth Corps, Department of North Carolina; and Operations in the Department of North Carolina, Advance of Schofield's Army to Goldsboro (Battle of Kinston or Wise's Forks).

Twenty-Third Corps, Army of the Ohio. Early in January 1865, John M. Schofield was ordered to take his Twenty-Third Corps, Army of the Ohio, which was then in Tennessee, to North Carolina to reinforce the Union troops serving in the state under Innis N. Palmer. The corps left Clifton, Tennessee, on the Tennessee River, January 15–19, 1865, and then moved by way of Louisville, Kentucky, Cincinnati, Ohio, and Washington, D.C. to Alexandria, Virginia, where it embarked for Fort Fisher.

The organization of Twenty-Third Corps at that time was as follows:

TWENTY-THIRD CORPS, John M. Schofield

First Division, Thomas H. Ruger
  First Brigade, John M. Orr
  Second Brigade, John C. McQuiston
  Third Brigade, Minor T. Thomas
  Artillery
    22nd Battery, Indiana Light Artillery, Edward W. Nicholson
    Battery F, 1st Michigan Light Artillery, Byron D. Paddock

Second Division, Darius N. Couch
  First Brigade, Joseph A. Cooper
  Second Brigade, Orlando H. Moore
  Third Brigade, Nathaniel C. McLean
  Artillery
    15th Battery, Indiana Light Artillery, Alonzo D. Harvey
    19th Battery, Ohio Light Artillery, Frank Wilson

Third Division, Jacob D. Cox
  First Brigade, Oscar W. Sterl
  Second Brigade, John S. Casement
  Third Brigade, Thomas J. Henderson
  Artillery
    23rd Battery, Indiana Light Artillery, James H. Myers
    Battery D, 1st Ohio Light Artillery, Cecil C. Reed

Schofield arrived on Federal Point (formerly Confederate Point) February 8, 1865, and that day and the next, Jacob D. Cox's Third Division arrived and disembarked. Orlando H. Moore's Second Brigade of Darius N. Couch's Second Division arrived at Fort Fisher February 14, 1865. Cox's division and Moore's brigade took part in Schofield's operations, which resulted in the capture of Fort Anderson on the Cape Fear River February 19, 1865, and the occupation of Wilmington, North Carolina February 22, 1865. For details, see below, Operations in the Department of North Carolina, Capture of Wilmington, North Carolina.

Couch with his other two brigades landed at Smithville, at the mouth of the Cape Fear River, February 22–23, 1865, and by February 26, 1865, the three brigades of Second Division were assembled at Wilmington. Thomas H. Ruger's First Division arrived at Fort Fisher February 22–23, 1865, but it was ordered on to New Berne, where it arrived February 25, 1865–March 1, 1865. On February 25, 1865, Cox left Wilmington to take command of the District of Beaufort, and James W. Reilly assumed command of Cox's Third Division.

On March 1, 1865, Cox assumed command of the District of Beaufort at New Berne, and that day he organized a provisional corps for the purpose of opening the railroad from New Berne to Goldsboro. For details, see below, Cox's Provisional Corps, Army of the Ohio. Ruger's division was included in Cox's command, and advanced with it to Wise's Forks, near Kinston, North Carolina, where it was engaged March 10, 1865. For details, see below, Operations in the Department of North Carolina, Advance of Schofield's Army to Goldsboro (Battle of Kinston or Wise's Forks). Cox occupied Kinston March 14, 1865, and remained there until March 20, 1865. He then marched on and arrived at Goldsboro the next day.

Meantime, on February 28, 1865, Couch assumed command of his own Second Division and Reilly's Third Division, Twenty-Third Corps, which were still at Wilmington, and March 6, 1865, marched with them to join Cox's Provisional Corps at Kinston. Couch arrived near the town March 13–14, 1865, and then marched with Cox's command to Goldsboro March 20–21, 1865.

March 24, 1865, Reilly's Third Division was transferred to Cox's Provisional Corps, and was assigned as the garrison of Goldsboro. Ruger's First Division took the place of Third Division in Couch's command, and Couch was then sent back to the vicinity of Moseley Hall, about halfway to Kinston, to guard the railroad.

March 27, 1865, Cox was assigned by the president to the permanent command of Twenty-Third Corps. Cox received the order March 31, 1865 and assumed command that day, but the official order announcing his assumption of command was dated April 2, 1865. Cox's Provisional Corps was discontinued March 31, 1865, and the regiments of Samuel P. Carter's division of the District of Beaufort were assigned to the divisions of Twenty-Third Corps, and Reilly's division rejoined Twenty-Third Corps. For additional information, see below, Cox's Provisional Corps, Army of the Ohio.

April 1, 1865, Sherman reorganized his Army of the Military Division of the Mississippi to consist of a right wing, a left wing, and a center. The latter was assigned to Schofield, and consisted of Cox's Twenty-Third Corps and Terry's newly organized Tenth Corps. The center organization was in effect while Schofield's troops operated with Sherman's army against Joseph E. Johnston's Confederate army in North Carolina. April 11–13, 1865, Twenty-Third Corps marched with the rest of the army from Goldsboro to Raleigh, where it was encamped at the time of Johnston's surrender April 26, 1865. For more detailed information about the organization of Schofield's center, and its movements in North Carolina, see Carolinas Campaign, Goldsboro to Raleigh, North Carolina (Surrender of Joseph E. Johnston's Army).

Ruger's First Division, Twenty-Third Corps remained near Raleigh until May 3, 1865, and it then moved by way of Greensboro to Charlotte, where it arrived May 11–16, 1865. It was there when the corps was discontinued August 1, 1865. Joseph A. Cooper's Second Division moved by way of Greensboro to Salisbury, North Carolina May 3–19, 1865, and it remained there until the division was broken up July 4, 1865. Third Division, then commanded by Carter, remained at Raleigh until May 5, 1865, and it then marched to Greensboro, and was still there when the division was broken up July 4, 1865. Carter was assigned command of the newly constituted District of Greensboro July 6, 1865.

Provisional Divisions (Army of the Cumberland and Army of the Tennessee). When Sherman's army left Atlanta in November 1864 on its march through Georgia, thousands of men who were absent from their commands because of wounds, sickness, and furloughs, and for other reasons, were left behind. When these troops arrived at Chattanooga on their way to rejoin their proper commands, they were unable to do so, and they were then organized into temporary provisional divisions of the District of the Etowah, Department of the Cumberland, until such time as communications could be opened with Sherman's marching columns.

When Sherman was authorized to march northward from Savannah, through the Carolinas, beginning in January 1865, the men in the District of the Etowah belonging to the Army of the Tennessee and the Army of the Cumberland (then called the Army of Georgia) were organized into provisional divisions and sent to North Carolina to await Sherman's arrival there. These divisions were as follows:

Meagher's Provisional Division. In January 1865, approximately 6,000 men belonging to the Army of the Tennessee and the Army of the Cumberland were in the District of the Etowah, and these were organized into a provisional division under Thomas F. Meagher. This division consisted of three brigades, which were commanded by Horace Boughton, Joshua B. Culver, and Adam G. Malloy. This organization was for administrative purposes only, while moving the men to North Carolina. It was composed of squads or detachments belonging to most of the regiments of Sherman's army. About half of the division consisted of recruits, substitutes, and drafted men, and the remainder was largely convalescents and furloughed men.

Meagher's command left Tullahoma, Tennessee January 14, 1865, and proceeded to Annapolis, Maryland, where it began to embark for North Carolina February 4, 1865. Meagher arrived at Morehead City February 9, 1865 with 5,000 men; and Samuel P. Carter, who had been ordered to report to Meagher at Annapolis, arrived with an additional 800 men of the division February 19, 1865. Meagher was ordered to report to Schofield until he could join Sherman with his division, and he was then sent to New Berne to report to Innis N. Palmer, commanding the District of North Carolina.

Grant had been dissatisfied with Meagher's performance while bringing his troops east, and February 24, 1865 relieved him from duty in the Department of North Carolina, and ordered him home to report to the adjutant general of the army.

March 1, Jacob D. Cox, commanding the newly constituted District of Beaufort, organized at New Berne a provisional corps, to which Meagher's division was assigned. The division was not transferred intact, but was broken up and the troops were assigned by battalions to the various brigades of the corps. They served under this arrangement during Cox's advance to Kinston, North Carolina, and then on March 18, 1865, they were again assembled as a division under the command of George S. Greene.

Greene's Provisional Division. While at Kinston, Cox's Provisional Corps was reorganized, and the troops of Meagher's former Provisional Division were organized into a new provisional division under the command of George S. Greene. Greene had joined Cox before the Battle of Wise's Forks, while on his way to report to the Army of the

Cumberland (Army of Georgia). Greene's Provisional Division, then a part of Cox's reorganized Provisional Corps, marched with Cox to Goldsboro, where it arrived March 21, 1865. Sherman's army marched into Goldsboro March 23–24, 1865, and Greene's troops rejoined their proper commands. Greene's division was discontinued March 24, 1865, and Greene was assigned command of Third Brigade, Third Division, Fourteenth Corps.

Cruft's Provisional Division. February 23, 1865, James B. Steedman, commander of the District of the Etowah, ordered all officers and men belonging to Fourteenth Corps, Fifteenth Corps, Seventeenth Corps, Twentieth Corps, and Twenty-Third Corps, and also to the cavalry and artillery then serving with Sherman in the Carolinas, to report to Charles Cruft at Chattanooga. By March 9, 1865, about 5,000 men had assembled there and had been organized into a Provisional Division, Army of the Cumberland under Cruft. The division consisted of two brigades commanded by Isaac McManus and William O'Brien.

Cruft's division left Chattanooga March 14, 1865, under orders to proceed to New Berne, North Carolina. It passed through Nashville, Tennessee the next day and then continued on through Louisville, Kentucky and Cincinnati, Ohio to Washington, D.C. It then embarked for Morehead City March 27, 1865. Cruft's command arrived in North Carolina April 1–4, 1865, and then moved to Goldsboro. There the troops joined their proper commands in Sherman's army, and Cruft's division was discontinued. Cruft returned to the District of the Etowah May 9, 1865.

Prince's Provisional Division, Sherman's Army. February 4, 1865, Henry Prince was ordered to take charge of all officers and men arriving in the Department of the South at Hilton Head en route to join Sherman's army. He was directed to place these troops in camp at Blair's Landing, which was located between Beaufort, South Carolina and Pocotaligo. At first, this command consisted of only several hundred men, but eventually numbered about 2,400 men. These troops were organized by Prince into the Provisional Division, Sherman's Army.

March 22, 1865, Prince was directed to have his

division ready to move to North Carolina when ordered, and embarkation began April 10, 1865. The division arrived at Wilmington, North Carolina April 20–21, 1865, and then marched to Raleigh to join Sherman's army. April 27, 1865, after the men of the Provisional Division had rejoined their commands, Prince was relieved from duty in the Military Division of the Mississippi, and was ordered to report to the adjutant general in Washington.

Cox's Provisional Corps, Army of the Ohio. When John M. Schofield was assigned to the newly constituted Department of North Carolina, he was given the primary task of gaining possession of the Atlantic and North Carolina Railroad from New Berne to Goldsboro, putting it in running order, and establishing a depot of supplies for Sherman's advancing army as near Goldsboro as possible.

On February 10, 1865, the day after he assumed command of the department, Schofield ordered Innis N. Palmer, commander of the District of North Carolina, to advance along the railroad from New Berne to fulfill the first part of his mission. Palmer had not moved by February 25, 1865, and Schofield ordered Jacob D. Cox, then commanding Third Division, Twenty-Third Corps at Wilmington, North Carolina, to go to New Berne, and there assume command of the newly constituted District of Beaufort. He was to organize a force, and then advance with it and open the railroad toward Kinston and Goldsboro. By this order, the District of North Carolina was discontinued, and Palmer was directed to report to Cox for duty.

Cox arrived at New Berne on the last day of February 1865, and the next day assumed command of the District of Beaufort. That same day, March 1, 1865, Cox ordered the reorganization of the troops serving in the district into divisions, which were to be commanded by Palmer and Samuel P. Carter. The troops at his disposal consisted of the garrisons at New Berne, Morehead City, Fort Macon, Roanoke Island, and Plymouth, all formerly of Palmer's District of North Carolina, and also the troops of Thomas F. Meagher's Provisional Division, recently arrived from Tennessee. This division was composed largely of convalescents and recruits belonging to Sherman's army, and was not organized for combat. For additional information, see Provisional Divisions (Army of the Cumberland and Army of the Tennessee), above. Cox organized

these troops into temporary battalions, and distributed these among the brigades of organized troops of the district. Meagher was relieved from command of the Provisional Division February 24, 1865.

Also on March 1, 1865, Cox organized his troops into a provisional corps, consisting of the divisions of Palmer and Carter, and also Thomas F. Ruger's First Division, Twenty-Third Corps, which had just arrived at New Berne from Tennessee. This command was commonly called Cox's Provisional Corps. It should be noted, however, that until March 18, 1865, Cox signed his official papers under the heading Headquarters District of Beaufort; but after the reorganization of his command March 18, 1865 (see below), at which time Cox relinquished command of the District of Beaufort, he referred to his force as Provisional Corps, Army of the Ohio.

Cox's Provisional Corps was organized as follows:

PROVISIONAL CORPS, Jacob D. Cox

First Division, Twenty-Third Corps, Thomas H. Ruger
  First Brigade, John M. Orr
  Second Brigade, John C. McQuiston
  Third Brigade, Minor T. Thomas
  Artillery
    Battery F, 1st Michigan Light Artillery, Byron D. Paddock
    Elgin Battery, Illinois Light Artillery, Andrew M. Wood

First Division, District of Beaufort, Innis N. Palmer
  First Brigade, Edward Harland
  Second Brigade, Peter J. Claassen
  Third Brigade, Horace Boughton
  Artillery
    Battery C, 3rd New York Artillery, William E. Mercer
    Battery D, 3rd New York Light Artillery, Stephen Van Heusen

Note 1. First Brigade was formed from three regiments of Harland's Sub-District of New Berne, District of North Carolina, plus a battery of artillery.

Note 2. Second Brigade was formed from Claassen's own 132nd New York Regiment and a brigade of Meagher's former Provisional Division, plus a battery of artillery. Claassen was assigned command March 2, 1865.

Note 3. Third Brigade was formed from 18th Wisconsin and two battalions of the provisional division formerly commanded by Meagher.

Note 4. About 2,000 men were left to garrison the posts of the District of Beaufort, and these were regarded as a part of Palmer's division.

Second Division, District of Beaufort, Samuel P. Carter
First Brigade, Adam G. Malloy
Second Brigade, Charles L. Upham
Third Brigade, Henry Splaine
Artillery
Battery A, 3rd New York Light Artillery, Samuel P. Russell
Battery G, 3rd New York Light Artillery, William A. Kelsey
Battery I, 3rd New York Light Artillery, William Richardson

Note 1. First Brigade was formed from troops of the provisional division formerly commanded by Meagher.
Note 2. Second Brigade was formed from two regiments from the Sub-District of New Berne, District of North Carolina.
Note 3. Third Brigade was formed from a regiment from the Sub-District of New Berne, District of North Carolina, one regiment from the Sub-District of Beaufort, District of North Carolina, and a battery of artillery.

Cox left New Berne with his command March 2, 1865 and advanced to Wise's Forks, near Kinston. He was engaged there March 8–10, 1865, and then crossed the Neuse River and occupied Kinston on the morning of March 14, 1865. For details of the march and the Battle of Kinston, see below, Operations in the Department of North Carolina, Advance of Schofield's Army to Goldsboro, North Carolina (Battle of Kinston or Wise's Forks). While at Kinston, March 18, 1865, Cox was relieved from command of the District of Beaufort, but retained command of the troops in the field. Palmer, who had been ill since March 10, 1865, was assigned command of the District of Beaufort, and was directed to report to Headquarters Department of North Carolina. Palmer assumed command of the district March 21, 1865.

All of the troops of the provisional division formerly commanded by Meagher, and who were returning to the armies of the Cumberland and the Tennessee, were ordered to report to George S. Greene, and they were then organized into a provisional division under Greene. Greene, who was on his way to join Sherman's army, had caught up with Cox at Gum Swamp, and was moving forward with him at the time of the reorganization.

Harland's First Brigade, First Division, District of Beaufort was detached from Cox's command, and Harland was assigned command of the post of Kinston. The other troops of First Division, District of Beaufort who were serving with Cox in the field were ordered to report to Samuel P. Carter to be consolidated with the troops of his Second Division, District of Beaufort. These troops were to replace those who had been transferred to Greene's Provisional Division. Carter's new division was designated as the Division of the District of Beaufort, and it was organized into two brigades as follows:

Division of the District of Beaufort, Samuel P. Carter
First Brigade, Peter J. Claassen
Second Brigade, James S. Stewart, Jr.

Note 1. First Brigade was formed from one regiment each of Upham's and Splaine's former brigades, which were then discontinued.
Note 2. Second Brigade was organized from one regiment each from Malloy's and Splaine's former brigades, and one regiment from Harland's brigade. Malloy's brigade was then discontinued.

When this reorganization was completed, Cox's Provisional Corps consisted of Ruger's First Division, Twenty-Third Corps; Carter's Division of the District of Beaufort; and Greene's Provisional Division. With this command, Cox left Kinston March 20, 1865, and occupied Goldsboro the next afternoon.

Sherman's army arrived at Goldsboro from its march through the Carolinas March 23–24, 1865, and the troops of Greene's Provisional Division then rejoined their proper commands in the Army of the Tennessee and the Army of the Cumberland. The latter was officially designated Army of Georgia March 28, 1865. Greene's division was discontinued March 24, 1865, and Greene was assigned command of Third Brigade, Third Division, Fourteenth Corps, Army of the Cumberland.

March 24, 1865, Carter's division was assigned as the garrison of Goldsboro. Ruger's First Division, Twenty-Third Corps was transferred from Cox's Provisional Corps to Couch's command, and Couch, with First Division and his Second Division, Twenty-Third Corps, moved back and took position on the railroad, about halfway to Kinston, to cover the roads from Moseley Hall and Kinston. Cox's own Third Division, Twenty-Third Corps, then commanded by James W. Reilly, was ordered to report to Cox to replace Ruger's division. Cox then had under his command only Reilly's division and Carter's Division of the District of Beaufort.

March 27, 1865, Cox was assigned by the president to the permanent command of Twenty-Third Corps, and when he assumed command March 31, 1865, Cox's Provisional Corps, Army of the Ohio was discontinued. The regiments of Carter's division were assigned to the three divisions of Twenty-Third Corps, and April 7, 1865, Carter was assigned command of Third Division, Twenty-Third Corps in place of Reilly, who had resigned.

Nineteenth Corps. Early in March 1865, while troops of Schofield's command were advancing from the coast toward Goldsboro, two brigades of Henry W. Birge's Second Division, Nineteenth Corps were ordered from the District of Savannah, Department of the South to North Carolina. Birge's command consisted of the following :

Second Division, Nineteenth Corps, Henry W. Birge
  Second Brigade, Nicholas W. Day, to March 17, 1865
    Harvey Graham
  Third Brigade, James P. Richardson, to March 17, 1865
    Nicholas W. Day

Note. Henry D. Washburn's First Brigade, Second Division was left in the District of Savannah.

Birge's command arrived at Morehead City March 10–14, 1865, and at first the regiments of the brigades were considerably scattered on special service, as train guards, assisting the quartermaster department, and in repairing roads. In general, however, during the period up to April 10, 1865, Day's Third Brigade and division headquarters were at New Berne; and Graham's Second Brigade was at Morehead City, where it was assigned to Langdon C. Easton, assistant chief quartermaster of the Military Division of the Mississippi, to assist in handling stores that were to be forwarded to Goldsboro.

When Tenth Corps was organized under Alfred H. Terry April 2, 1865, Graham's brigade (at Morehead City) was designated as First Brigade, First Division, Tenth Corps; and Day's brigade (at New Berne) became Third Brigade, First Division, Tenth Corps. Birge was assigned command of First Division, Tenth Corps.

April 10, 1865, the day Sherman's army began its march from Goldsboro toward Raleigh, Birge moved with his headquarters and Day's brigade to Goldsboro, where he assumed command of the post. Joseph E. Johnston surrendered his army to Sherman April 26, 1865, and the next day Birge was ordered to return with his two brigades to Savannah. He was relieved at Goldsboro May 1, 1865 by Charles J. Paine's Third Division, Tenth Corps, and two days later he sailed with his two brigades from Morehead City for Savannah.

For additional information, see the following: Tenth Corps, Department of North Carolina, below; and also Carolinas Campaign, Goldsboro to Raleigh, North Carolina (Surrender of Joseph E. Johnston's Army).

Tenth Corps, Department of North Carolina. By a presidential order of March 27, 1865, Tenth Corps was reconstituted to consist of all troops in North Carolina, except those belonging to Sherman's Army of the Military Division of the Mississippi, and Jacob D. Cox's Twenty-Third Corps (*note.* Cox did not assume command of the corps until March 31, 1865). Alfred H. Terry was assigned command March 27, 1865, and assumed command April 2, 1865. He then announced the organization of Tenth Corps as follows (the complete organization was announced April 9, 1865):

TENTH CORPS, DEPARTMENT OF NORTH
  CAROLINA, Alfred H. Terry

First Division, Henry W. Birge
  First Brigade, Harvey Graham
  Second Brigade, Joseph C. Abbott
  Third Brigade, Nicholas W. Day
  Artillery
    22nd Battery, Indiana Light Artillery, George W.
    Alexander

Note 1. Birge was formerly commander of Second Division, Nineteenth Corps at Savannah, Georgia. He arrived in North Carolina March 14, 1865.
Note 2. First Brigade was formerly Graham's Second Brigade, Second Division, Nineteenth Corps, and was stationed at Morehead City.
Note 3. Second Brigade was formerly Second Brigade, First Division, Twenty-Fourth Corps of Terry's Provisional Corps, and was at and about Wilmington, North Carolina.
Note 4. Third Brigade was formerly Day's Third Brigade, Second Division, Nineteenth Corps, and was at New Berne, North Carolina.

Second Division, Adelbert Ames
    First Brigade, Rufus Daggett
    Second Brigade, William B. Coan, to April 5, 1865
        John S. Littell
    Third Brigade, G. Frederick Granger
    Artillery
        16th Battery, New York Light Artillery, Richard H. Lee

Note. Second Division was formerly Ames' Second Division, Twenty-Fourth Corps of Terry's Provisional Corps.

Third Division, Charles J. Paine
    First Brigade, Delevan Bates
    Second Brigade, Samuel A. Duncan
    Third Brigade, John H. Holman

Note. Third Division was formerly Third Division, Twenty-Fifth Corps of Terry's Provisional Corps.

Unattached Artillery
    Battery E, 3rd United States Artillery, John R. Myrick

By an order of April 1, 1865, Terry's Tenth Corps, Department of North Carolina and Jacob D. Cox's Twenty-Third Corps, Army of the Ohio were designated as the "center" of Sherman's army, and John M. Schofield was assigned command. This organization was to be in effect while Schofield's two corps were engaged in operations with the Army of the Tennessee (Right Wing) and the Army of Georgia (Left Wing) of Sherman's army. For the complete organization of Sherman's army at that time, see Carolinas Campaign.

From April 1–10, 1865, Graham's First Brigade and Day's Third Brigade, First Division were encamped at New Berne, and Ames' Second Division and Paine's Third Division were at Faison's Station (or Depot) on the Wilmington and Weldon Railroad, south of Goldsboro. April 7, 1865, Sherman issued orders for the advance of the army toward Raleigh and Johnston's army. The movement began April 10, 1865, and that day Headquarters First Division, Tenth Corps, and Day's Third Brigade moved to Goldsboro, where Birge assumed command of the post. Ames' First Brigade, First Division remained at Morehead City, and Abbott's Second Brigade, First Division at Wilmington. That same day, Terry with Second Division and Third Division, Tenth Corps marched from Faison's Station by way of Bentonville toward Goldsboro, and he arrived there April 15, 1865.

Sherman halted all troop movements April 16, 1865, while he and Johnston conferred near Durham Station the next day. An agreement was signed April 18, 1865, and Tenth Corps remained near Raleigh during the truce that followed. This agreement was disapproved by the president in a communication dated April 21, 1865 and received by Sherman April 25, 1865, but Johnston finally surrendered his army April 26, 1865.

The day after Johnston's surrender, Paine's division was ordered back to Goldsboro to relieve Birge and Day's brigade. Upon being relieved, Birge was directed to assemble his troops of Nineteenth Corps at Morehead City in preparation for their return to the Department of the South. Paine left Raleigh with his division April 29, 1865, and arrived at Goldsboro and assumed command May 1, 1865. Birge moved his two brigades to Morehead City, and left there for Savannah May 3, 1865. First Division, Tenth Corps was thus discontinued, and Abbott's brigade remained at Wilmington as a detached brigade. Ames' Second Division remained on garrison duty at Raleigh, and July 6, 1865, Ames was assigned command of the District of Raleigh.

June 2, 1865, the troops of Third Division, Tenth Corps were assigned to new positions as follows: Nathan Goff was sent with his brigade to Wilmington to report to Joseph R. Hawley, commander of the District of Wilmington; Paine, with Duncan's Second Brigade and Bates' First Brigade, was ordered to relieve all white troops serving in the District of Beaufort, and to relieve Innis N. Palmer in command of the district. Duncan's brigade took post at New Berne and Kinston, and Bates' brigade at Morehead City.

June 6, 1865, Abbott was ordered to move with his brigade from Wilmington to Goldsboro, and three days later Goff relieved Abbott in command of the post of Wilmington. For additional information, see District of Wilmington, Department of North Carolina.

Tenth Corps, Department of North Carolina was discontinued August 1, 1865.

Sherman's Army of the Military Division of the Mississippi. The head of Sherman's army entered North Carolina from Cheraw, South Carolina about March 8, 1865, and occupied Fayetteville March 11, 1865. The army was then engaged at Averasboro and Bentonville, and did not join John M.

Schofield's Army of the Ohio at Goldsboro until March 23–24, 1865. April 1, 1865, Sherman announced a reorganization of his army as follows:

SHERMAN'S ARMY, William T. Sherman

Right Wing (Army of Tennessee), Oliver O. Howard
   Fifteenth Corps, John A. Logan
   Seventeenth Corps, Frank P. Blair, Jr.

Center (Army of the Ohio), John M. Schofield
   Tenth Corps, Alfred H. Terry
   Twenty-Third Corps, Jacob D. Cox

Left Wing (Army of Georgia), Henry W. Slocum
   Fourteenth Corps, Jefferson C. Davis
   Twentieth Corps, Alpheus S. Williams

Third Cavalry Division, Judson Kilpatrick

This army remained near Goldsboro until April 10, 1865 to refit, and it then advanced toward Raleigh. Hostilities ended when Johnston surrendered his army April 26, 1865. Schofield, with his Tenth Corps and Twenty-Third Corps, was ordered to remain in North Carolina after the surrender, and so was Kilpatrick's cavalry of Sherman's army, but on April 27, 1865, Sherman, with the rest of his command, began his final march toward Washington, D.C., and by May 4, 1865 had left the Department of North Carolina. For additional information, see Carolinas Campaign, Goldsboro to Raleigh, North Carolina (Surrender of Joseph E. Johnston's Army).

Kilpatrick's Third Cavalry Division, Sherman's Army. On April 27, 1865, after the surrender of Joseph E. Johnston's army at Durham Station, Kilpatrick's cavalry division, which had accompanied Sherman's army through the Carolinas, was transferred to the Department of North Carolina. It remained at Durham Station until May 7, 1865, and then moved to Greensboro, where it halted for a few days. It then took position at Lexington, North Carolina. The division was discontinued in June and July 1865 by the muster out and transfer of regiments.

OPERATIONS IN THE DEPARTMENT OF NORTH CAROLINA

When John M. Schofield assumed command of the newly constituted Department of North

Carolina, he was instructed by Grant to occupy Goldsboro, open the railroad between that point and New Berne, and accumulate supplies for Sherman's army when it should arrive in North Carolina. Further, Schofield was directed to assemble the troops under his command at or near Goldsboro and join Sherman when he reached that point. The operations carried out by Schofield's forces during February and March 1865 were the direct result of these instructions.

When Schofield assumed command of the Department of North Carolina, Federal troops under Alfred H. Terry held Federal Point and the posts at the mouth of the Cape Fear River, but the important port city of Wilmington, North Carolina, which was about twenty-eight miles upriver from Fort Fisher, was within the enemy lines. Not only was Wilmington an important seaport, but it was the terminus of the Wilmington and Weldon Railroad. This road ran north to Goldsboro, about eighty miles from Wilmington, and then on to Weldon, North Carolina. Innis N. Palmer, commanding the District of North Carolina, occupied New Berne and Morehead City, and that part of the Atlantic and North Carolina Railroad that ran between these two points; but beyond New Berne the railroad, which ran on through Kinston to Goldsboro, was in possession of the enemy. Thus, to comply with Grant's orders, it was necessary for Schofield to capture Wilmington, and to seize and repair the railroad from New Berne to Goldsboro. These operations are described in the following sections.

Capture of Wilmington, North Carolina, February 16–22, 1865. When Schofield arrived at Federal Point February 8, 1865 with the head of Jacob D. Cox's Third Division, Twenty-Third Corps, Alfred H. Terry with about 8,000 men held Fort Fisher and a line of entrenchments across the peninsula between the Cape Fear River and the Atlantic Ocean, about two miles north of the fort, and also occupied Smithville and Fort Caswell on the west side of the Cape Fear River. Terry's command consisted of Adelbert Ames' Second Division, Twenty-Fourth Corps; Charles J. Paine's Third Division, Twenty-Fifth Corps; and Joseph C. Abbott's Second Brigade, First Division, Twenty-Fourth Corps. In addition, a naval squadron under Rear Admiral David D. Porter held positions in the

Cape Fear River and off the Atlantic Coast covering the flanks of Terry's line.

Opposing Terry, and protecting Wilmington, was Robert Hoke's division of Braxton Bragg's Confederate Department of North Carolina. Johnson Hagood's brigade occupied Fort Anderson and adjacent works on the west side of the Cape Fear River, and Thomas L. Clingman's brigade, William W. Kirkland's brigade, and Alfred H. Colquitt's brigade (commanded by Charles T. Zachry) held a strong line directly across the river at Sugar Loaf. This line extended from the Cape Fear River on the right to Masonboro Sound on the left.

While awaiting the arrival of the rest of Twenty-Third Corps, Schofield ordered Terry to make a reconnaissance in force on the east side of the Cape Fear River. Terry's command, supported by Cox's Third Division, Twenty-Third Corps, advanced and drove back the enemy skirmishers and found Hoke's three brigades strongly entrenched at Sugar Loaf Hill. Paine's division and Abbott's brigade did most of the fighting that day, but they made no direct assault. Instead, they entrenched a line about 400 yards in front of the enemy works and remained there in a threatening position until February 19, 1865. When Terry's troops were safely entrenched, Cox withdrew his division to the old line previously held by Paine's division and Abbott's brigade, about a mile and a half in rear of Terry's new line.

On February 12, 1865, and again on February 14, 1865, Schofield attempted to move Ames' division and Cox's division to the rear of Hoke's line, but heavy seas delayed the movement of the pontoons which were necessary for the operation, and the attempt was abandoned. Schofield then decided to advance against the enemy right flank on the west side of the Cape Fear River, where he would have more room for maneuver.

February 16, 1865, Cox's division crossed to Smithville, where it was joined by Battery D, 1st Ohio Light Artillery and Orlando H. Moore's First Brigade of Darius N. Couch's Second Division, Twenty-Third Corps. Moore's brigade had arrived at Smithville from Alexandria, Virginia February 15, 1865, and it was temporarily attached to Cox's division the next day. The brigades of Cox's division were commanded as follows: First Brigade, Oscar W. Sterl; Second Brigade, John S. Casement; and Third Brigade, Thomas J. Henderson.

At 8:00 A.M. February 17, 1865, Cox advanced with his four brigades along the river road toward Wilmington and, after skirmishing most of the day, camped for the night about two miles from Fort Anderson. The Federal plan of attack called for a joint army-navy attempt to capture Fort Anderson, and Porter was asked to open fire on the fort when the land forces advanced. This he did with good effect.

Cox again moved forward on February 18, 1865, and drove the enemy skirmishers back into their works, which extended westward from Fort Anderson, near the Cape Fear River, for a distance of about 800 yards to the foot of Orton Pond. Cox soon came under artillery fire, and after a careful study of the enemy position decided that it was too strong to be taken by a frontal assault. He then ordered a line of entrenchments to be prepared in front of the Confederate line, and when these works were sufficiently strong, he left Moore's and Henderson's brigades to occupy them, and at 2:00 P.M. moved with Casement's and Sterl's brigades by a crossroad (the Brunswick Road) to the southwest toward the head of Orton's Pond (which was actually a small lake several miles long) in an attempt to gain the rear of Fort Anderson. After marching about six miles, Cox arrived at Moore's Creek, which flowed into Orton's Pond. At this point, the Wilmington and Lockwood's Folly Road crossed the swamp on a causeway at the head of the pond. The crossing was defended, but after a sharp skirmish lasting about a half hour, Cox forced a passage and crossed his command to the north, back of the stream, about 9:00 P.M.

Meantime, Ames' division of Terry's command had been sent across the river to support Cox, and it had landed at Smithville during the afternoon of February 18, 1865. It had then marched out on the Wilmington Road about five miles to Westcotts', where it took the left fork of the road and joined Cox that evening near the head of Orton's Pond. Ames was placed temporarily under the command of Cox.

On the morning of February 19, 1865, Cox marched with his two brigades and Ames' division along the north side of Orton's Pond toward the rear of Fort Anderson. En route, he learned that the fort had been evacuated during the night, and that it had been occupied at daylight by troops of Moore's and Henderson's brigades. After the enemy garrison had withdrawn from the fort, it had taken up a strong position behind Town Creek, about eight miles to the north. At the same time, Hoke's troops east of the river had fallen back to a new line opposite the mouth of Town Creek.

Cox, with his four brigades and Ames' division, followed Hagood's brigade up the west side of the river to Town Creek. His leading brigade, under Henderson, pushed back the enemy skirmishers close to the creek, and the other three brigades camped for the night in rear of Henderson. Meantime, during the afternoon of February 19, 1865, Ames was ordered back with his division to Fort Anderson, where he recrossed the river and rejoined Terry in front of Hoke's new position.

Early on February 20, 1865, Casement, with his own brigade and that of Sterl, moved down Town Creek to a point near where it flowed into the Cape Fear River, and by noon had crossed his two brigades to the north bank of the creek. The two brigades were then in position to march toward the rear of the enemy line. Meantime, while this movement was in progress, Henderson made a strong demonstration at the road crossing of the creek at the bridge upstream. Cox then joined Casement with Moore's brigade and assumed command of the three brigades. Cox moved his brigades obliquely to the right through some rice swamps to high ground, and then by a plantation road to the Wilmington Road, where they arrived about 4:00 P.M. two miles north of Town Creek.

Cox sent Moore's brigade west about a mile to another road that ran from Town Creek to Wilmington to cut off a possible enemy retreat in that direction. Then, with the brigades of Casement and Sterl, Cox moved down the road toward the rear of the enemy position along the creek. Cox's troops then charged, broke the enemy line, and captured 375 prisoners, including Charles H. Simonton, who was in charge of the brigade during the absence of Hagood. Moore, however, was unable to reach the road to which he had been directed, and the remainder of the enemy force escaped. Cox pursued the retreating enemy toward Wilmington until dark.

Henderson's brigade crossed Town Creek during the night and joined Cox on the morning of February 21, 1865. The entire command then pushed forward toward Wilmington. Cox reached Mill Creek, about six miles north of Town Creek, about noon, and was then delayed two hours while a bridge was being built. When this was completed, he moved forward to Brunswick Ferry, where he was able to secure a portion of the bridge across the Brunswick River (an arm of the Cape Fear River west of Eagle Island). Then, by using boats, he succeeded in putting some troops on Eagle Island, across the river from Wilmington. From this point, Cox was able to threaten a crossing above the city.

Meantime, on February 20, 1865, Terry pushed the enemy back to a point about four miles from Wilmington, but there Hoke occupied a good defensive position, and resisted so strongly that Terry was unable to advance February 21, 1865.

On February 21, 1865, because of Cox's menacing position, Hoke fired the military and naval stores, the cotton and tobacco in Wilmington, and the boats on the river, and during the night retired toward Goldsboro. Soon after daylight the next morning, Terry's command (known as Terry's Provisional Corps since February 21, 1865) entered the city. Terry did not remain there, however, but passed on through in pursuit of the retreating enemy, and halted that night at Northeast River, about ten miles north of Wilmington. Cox's brigades crossed into Wilmington during the afternoon of February 22, 1865, and they were assigned as a temporary garrison of the city.

The organization of Schofield's command during the operations against Wilmington was as follows:

TROOPS OF TWENTY-THIRD CORPS WEST OF THE CAPE FEAR RIVER, Jacob D. Cox

Second Division
    Second Brigade, Orlando H. Moore

Third Division, Jacob D. Cox
    First Brigade, Oscar W. Sterl
    Second Brigade, John S. Casement
    Third Brigade, Thomas J. Henderson

PROVISIONAL CORPS, Alfred H. Terry

First Division, Twenty-Fourth Corps
    Second Brigade, Joseph C. Abbott

Note. Abbott reported to Ames February 11, 1865, then to Charles J. Paine February 19, 1865, and finally he reported directly to Terry February 20, 1865.

Second Division, Twenty-Fourth Corps, Adelbert Ames
First Brigade, Rufus Daggett
Second Brigade, James A. Colvin
Third Brigade, G. Frederick Granger

Third Division, Charles J. Paine
First Brigade, Delevan Bates
Second Brigade, John W. Ames
Third Brigade, Elias Wright, to February 20, 1865, wounded
John A. Holman

Advance of Schofield's Army to Goldsboro (Battle of Kinston or Wise's Forks), March 1–21, 1865.

On February 10, 1865, the day after he assumed command of the Department of North Carolina, John M. Schofield ordered Innis N. Palmer to advance from New Berne with the troops of his District of North Carolina and gain possession of the Atlantic and North Carolina Railroad, which ran westward toward Goldsboro. Palmer delayed, however, and when he had not moved by February 25, 1865, Schofield ordered Jacob D. Cox, then commanding Third Division, Twenty-Third Corps at Wilmington, to go to New Berne and assume command of the newly constituted District of Beaufort. He was then to organize a force there, and with it advance and open the railroad and put it in running order. Cox assumed command of the district March 1, 1865, and that day organized a provisional corps and issued orders for its advance. For details of Cox's command, see above, Troops in the Department of North Carolina, Cox's Provisional Corps.

Peter J. Claassen, who commanded the outposts on Batchelder's Creek, about nine miles west of New Berne, was the first to move, and March 1, 1865 advanced with his command (later designated Second Brigade of Palmer's First Division, District of Beaufort) to Core Creek, about eighteen miles west of New Berne. The rest of the Provisional Corps advanced as follows: Palmer's First Division, District of Beaufort and Samuel P. Carter's Second Division, District of Beaufort arrived at Core Creek on the evening of March 4, 1865; and Thomas H. Ruger's First Division, Twenty-Third Corps, which did not leave New Berne until March 3, 1865, arrived at Core Creek on the evening of March 5, 1865.

March 6, 1865, Palmer's and Carter's divisions continued on about seven miles to Gum Swamp and camped there. Ruger's division remained at Core Creek. During the afternoon of March 6, 1865,

Claassen's Second Brigade of Palmer's division was sent on to Wise's Forks, at the junction of the Dover Road and the Trent Road, two miles from Southwest Creek. Claassen arrived at that point about 4:30 P.M.

The next day, March 7, 1865, Claassen moved forward on a reconnaissance, while the other two brigades of Palmer's division advanced along the railroad to establish a line from which to operate against an enemy position that had been reported to be behind Southwest Creek. Edward Harland's First Brigade, which was in the lead, was ordered to move toward the Neuse Road crossing of Southwest Creek, and Horace Boughton's Third Brigade was to advance toward the railroad crossing of the creek. Ruger's division was directed to march from Core Creek to Gum Swamp.

Also on March 7, 1865, Carter's division was ordered to Wise's Forks, and when it arrived there, Charles L. Upham's Second Brigade was sent down the British Road to relieve Claassen's brigade of Palmer's division. Upham was then to hold the east bank of Southwest Creek near Jackson's Mill on the Dover Road, about two miles west of Wise's Forks, Adam G. Malloy's First Brigade of Carter's division was placed in line just west of Wise's Forks on the Dover Road, with its right extending across the Trent Road. Henry Splaine's Third Brigade was formed on the left of the Dover Road, and generally continued the line of Malloy's brigade.

Harland's brigade of Palmer's division encountered enemy skirmishers near the British Road, and by 2:00 P.M. had driven them into their works beyond Southwest Creek. During the afternoon, Palmer put his troops in line as follows: Harland's brigade was on the right of the railroad, at the railroad crossing of the British Road, with its right extending down the British Road toward the Neuse Road; Boughton's brigade was on the left of the railroad, connecting on the right with Harland's brigade, and on the left with Carter's division; and Claassen's brigade, after being relieved by Upham's brigade about 4:00 P.M., moved from Wise's Forks and formed on the right of Harland's brigade. Thus, on the evening of March 7, 1865, Carter's and Palmer's divisions were in line facing the enemy across Southwest Creek; Upham's brigade was about a mile and a half in advance of the main line, on the extreme left; and Ruger's division was about four miles to the rear at Gum Swamp.

When Cox approached Southwest Creek on March 7, 1865, he was opposed only by troops of Robert F. Hoke's division of Braxton Bragg's Confederate Department of North Carolina, which had only recently arrived after its evacuation of Wilmington. A short time later, however, Hoke was strongly reinforced by troops of the Confederate Army of Tennessee, then serving in the east under Joseph E. Johnston. That evening, Daniel H. Hill, then commanding Stephen D. Lee's Corps, arrived with his own division, temporarily commanded by John G. Coltart, and Edmund W. Pettus' brigade of Carter L. Stevenson's division. Early the next morning, Hill relieved Hoke's division in the trenches at Southwest Creek, and the latter moved out on a flank movement toward the left of Cox's line. Henry D. Clayton also arrived that morning, March 8, 1865, with his division of Lee's corps, and he was sent to cooperate with Hoke in his movement to the right. Lawrence S. Baker, commanding the North Carolina Reserves of the Second District of Bragg's department, also joined Hill during the morning; and finally, on March 10, 1865, a part of Alexander P. Stewart's Corps, commanded by Edward C. Walthall, also came up.

About noon March 8, 1865, Upham's isolated division was struck by Hoke's division, supported by Clayton's division, and was thrown back in disorder and then driven from the field with considerable loss. While this attack was in progress, Hill demonstrated on the front of Palmer's division, but made no serious attack.

About 11:30 A.M., when Cox learned of the threat to his left, he ordered Ruger to march from Gum Swamp to Wise's Forks to support Carter, who was covering the Trent and Dover roads. When Ruger arrived with John M. Orr's First Brigade and John C. McQuiston's Second Brigade, he was sent to the right of Carter's division to occupy the space between Carter and Palmer. Minor T. Thomas' Third Brigade of Ruger's division also marched to Wise's Forks, but it arrived there after the other two brigades, and was held in reserve until evening.

After the destruction of Upham's brigade, the enemy advanced to the front of Carter's and Ruger's lines, but did not continue the attack. That night Hoke entrenched the position gained during the afternoon.

There was constant skirmishing during March 9,

1865, but neither side attempted to advance. The next day, however, the enemy again moved forward against the left and center of the Federal line. The attack struck the left of Carter's division on the Trent Road about noon, but after an hour's fighting it was repulsed. When Carter became engaged, Orr's brigade of Ruger's division was extended so as to relieve McQuiston's brigade, and the latter then moved to the left of Carter. It then aided in repelling the Confederate attack by advancing against the enemy's right flank. An attack was also made on Orr's attenuated line, but that too was unsuccessful. Thomas' brigade, which had been sent to the extreme right to support Palmer March 9, 1865, was quickly brought back to the left about 10:30 A.M. March 10, 1865, and it joined in stopping the enemy attack. Bragg made no further attempts on Cox's line, and that night withdrew his command across the Neuse River. The engagement of March 8–10, 1865 has been called the Battle of Kinston or Wise's Forks.

Two days after Cox began his advance from New Berne March 1, 1865, Darius N. Couch, commanding Second Division and Third Division of Twenty-Third Corps at Wilmington, was ordered to join Cox near Kinston, about eighty miles to the north. Couch left Wilmington March 6, 1865, and moved up the Coast Road to the vicinity of Onslow (Jacksonville), North Carolina, and then proceeded directly toward Kinston. March 10, 1865, the day of Bragg's last attack on Cox's position near Wise's Forks, Couch was about twelve miles from the battlefield, at the crossing of the Trent River. Two days later, he had arrived within a mile of Cox, and March 13, 1865, he was ordered to move his divisions to the Dover Road, within supporting distance of Cox's left.

Cox's Provisional Corps and Couch's two divisions remained in camp until March 14, 1865, and then they marched toward Kinston. The bridges over the Neuse River had been destroyed, and the troops were unable to cross until a pontoon bridge was laid the next day. They then advanced and occupied Kinston. Cox remained in camp there until March 20, 1865, while repairs on the railroad were completed from New Berne to the Neuse River.

On March 18, 1865, while still at Kinston, Cox announced the reorganization of his Provisional Corps. Palmer had been ill since March 10, 1865, and March 19, 1865 he was assigned command of the District of Beaufort, relieving Cox. Cox, however, retained command of all troops remaining in the field. All troops of Meagher's former Provisional Division, which had been broken up to provide troops for Cox's Provisional Corps, were assigned to a new provisional division under the command of George S. Greene. For additional information, see above, Troops in the Department of North Carolina, Cox's Provisional Corps and Meagher's Provisional Division. Greene, who was on his way to report to Henry W. Slocum in Sherman's army, had joined Cox at Gum Swamp, and had served as a volunteer aide to Cox during the fighting at Wise's Forks March 10, 1865.

Harland's First Brigade of Palmer's division was detached from Cox's Provisional Corps, and was assigned as the garrison of Kinston. All the remaining old troops belonging to the District of Beaufort were organized into a division, which was designated as the Division of the District of Beaufort, and was assigned to Samuel P. Carter. March 20, 1865, Cox advanced with his reorganized Provisional Corps and Couch's two divisions toward Goldsboro, and he arrived there the next day without serious opposition.

During Cox's advance from New Berne toward Kinston, Terry's Provisional Corps remained near Wilmington, where it had been since the occcupation of the city February 22, 1865. On March 14, 1865, Schofield, conforming to his orders to concentrate his army near Goldsboro, ordered Terry to march with his available force toward Kinston, but two days later he directed Terry to move instead to Faison's Station on the Wilmington and Weldon Railroad, about sixty miles north of Wilmington. Terry left Abbott's brigade behind to garrison Wilmington and Smithville and the forts at the mouth of the Cape Fear River, and assembled Ames' and Paine's divisions at the railroad crossing of Northeast River. Terry then marched with these divisions by roads east of the railroad, by way of South Washington and Island Creek, to Kenansville. He then crossed the railroad at Mount Olive, and continued on to Cox's Bridge on the Neuse River, where he arrived March 21, 1865.

At that time, Sherman's army was approaching Cox's Bridge from Fayetteville on its way to Goldsboro. Terry then laid a pontoon bridge across the river for Sherman's passage, and sent Samuel A. Duncan's Second Brigade of Paine's division across to the north bank of the river to fortify the approaches. Sherman crossed March 23–24, 1865, and marched on to Goldsboro. On the following day, Terry's command moved to Faison's Station, where it stayed until April 10, 1865. On March 28, 1865, G. Frederick Granger's Third Brigade of Ames' division was sent to Magnolia to guard the railroad between Faison's Station and Northeast River. While at Faison's Station, on April 2, 1865, the designation of Terry's Provisional Corps was changed to Tenth Corps, Department of North Carolina, Army of the Ohio.

By March 24, 1865, Schofield's forces of the Department of North Carolina and Sherman's Army of the Military Division of the Mississippi were united in the vicinity of Goldsboro, under Sherman's command, and preparations were begun for the next phase of the campaign. As a part of Sherman's army, Tenth Corps and Twenty-Third Corps, under the command of Schofield, took part in the final movements of the Carolinas Campaign, which ended with the surrender of Joseph E. Johnston's army near Durham Station, North Carolina April 26, 1865. For details, see Carolinas Campaign, Greensboro to Raleigh, North Carolina (Surrender of Joseph E. Johnston's Army).

Stoneman's Raid into Southwestern Virginia and Western North Carolina, March 21, 1865–April 25, 1865. During the period March 21, 1865–April 25, 1865, George Stoneman, with a cavalry division from the District of Eastern Tennessee, Department of the Cumberland, conducted a raid into western North Carolina and southwestern Virginia for the purpose of destroying railroads and the military resources of the region. He succeeded in wrecking the East Tennessee and Virginia Railroad between Wytheville and Salem (near Roanoke), Virginia; the Piedmont Railroad between Danville, Virginia and Greensboro, North Carolina; and the North Carolina Railroad between Greensboro and Salisbury, North Carolina. In addition, Stoneman destroyed large quantities of stores and supplies of military value to the Confederacy.

Stoneman's raid was not carried out by troops of John M. Schofield's Department of North Carolina, but it is included here because it was conducted in the western part of the state of North Carolina while

Sherman's army was near Goldsboro and Raleigh. For details of this raid, see Stoneman's Raid into Southwestern Virginia and Western North Carolina.

DEPARTMENT OF NORTHEASTERN VIRGINIA

After Virginia passed an ordinance of secession April 17, 1863, only the Potomac River separated Washington, D.C. from enemy territory. To provide for greater protection of the capital, Winfield Scott, commander in chief of the army, decided to occupy Alexandria, Virginia and the southern approaches to the city. Early on the morning of May 24, 1861, Union troops crossed the Potomac in three columns as follows:

The right column crossed at the Aqueduct, and consisted of Michael Corcoran's 69th New York State Militia, Christian Schwartzwalder's 5th New York State Militia, Edward Burns' 28th New York State Militia, the pioneers of A. M. Woods' 14th New York, one company of cavalry, and one section of artillery. The 69th New York remained near the canal, but the 5th and 28th New York moved out on the Leesburg Road about one and a half miles in advance of 69th New York.

The center column crossed at the Long Bridge, and consisted of Marshall Lefferts' 7th New York State Militia, Daniel Butterfield's 12th New York State Militia, Theodore Runyon's New Jersey Brigade (1st, 2nd, 3rd, and 4th New Jersey regiments), Orlando B. Willcox's 1st Michigan, pioneers, one company of cavalry, and one section of artillery. The 7th New York took position at the head of Long Bridge, and 25th New York moved out on the Columbia Turnpike to the Tollgate and Vose's Hill. The New Jersey Brigade and 12th New York occupied the Alexandria Road as far as Four-Mile Run, and the 1st Michigan moved on to Alexandria.

On the left, Elmer E. Ellsworth's 11th New York moved by water to Alexandria, and that regiment and 1st Michigan occupied the town. May 25, 1861, the 5th Massachusetts crossed the river and took position between Four-Mile Run and Alexandria, and the next day 8th New York State Militia occupied Arlington Heights.

The first troops that crossed into Virginia were from Joseph K. F. Mansfield's Department of Washington, and the movement was made under the direction of Samuel P. Heintzelman, inspector general of the department. Heintzelman, accompanied by Horatio G. Wright of the United States Engineers, was at Long Bridge; and Charles P. Stone, commanding the District of Columbia Volunteers, secured the Virginia end of the bridge for the crossing. The posting of the above regiments was the beginning of the Defenses of Washington South of the Potomac, and this line was strengthened by additional regiments that were sent into Virginia as they arrived in Washington.

May 22, 1861, Charles W. Sandford, major general of the New York State Militia, was assigned command of all New York regiments in the District of Columbia, and in that capacity, he accompanied the center column into Virginia. This created a problem because Virginia was outside the limits of the Department of Washington, and also Sandford was a militia general and was for this reason considered unsuitable for that command. To correct this situation, Irvin McDowell was made a major general of United States Volunteers, to date from May 14, 1861. May 27, 1861, the Department of Northeastern Virginia was constituted, and McDowell was assigned command. By definition this department included all of that part of Virginia east of the Allegheny Mountains and north of the James River, except Fort Monroe and the country around it for a distance of sixty miles. This territory was taken from the Department of the East. McDowell assumed command May 28, 1861, with headquarters in the field.

The Army of Northeastern Virginia. As new regiments arrived in the Department of Northeastern Virginia from Washington, they were organized into brigades as follows: Stone's Brigade, commanded by Charles P. Stone, organized May 28, 1861; Heintzelman's Brigade, Samuel P. Heintzelman, May 28, 1861; Hunter's Brigade, David Hunter, May 28, 1861; Tyler's Brigade, Daniel Tyler, June 3, 1861; Schenck's Brigade, Robert C. Schenck, June 12, 1861; Franklin's Brigade, William B. Franklin, July 1, 1861; Willcox's Brigade, Orlando B. Willcox, July 1, 1861; and Porter's Brigade, Andrew Porter, July 1, 1861. William T. Sherman was ordered to relieve Hunter June 30, 1861, and Erasmus D. Keyes was ordered to relieve Tyler July 1, 1861.

Three other brigades were formed in the Department of Washington by order of Mansfield. These were: Burnside's Brigade, commanded by Ambrose E. Burnside, organized July 2, 1861; Richardson's Brigade, Israel B. Richardson, July 2, 1861; and Blenker's Brigade, Louis Blenker, July 3, 1861.

July 6, 1861, Dixon S. Miles was assigned command of a newly created division, which was to consist of two brigades, commanded by Oliver O. Howard and Thomas A. Davies. These brigades were not completed at that time, however, and when the divisional organization of the army was finally announced July 8, 1861, Howard's brigade was assigned to Heintzelman's division and Davies' brigade to Miles' division.

The organization of the Army of Northeastern Virginia as announced July 8, 1861, was as follows:

ARMY OF NORTHEASTERN VIRGINIA, Irvin McDowell

First Division, Daniel Tyler
  First Brigade, Erasmus D. Keyes
  Second Brigade, Robert C. Schenck
  Third Brigade, William T. Sherman
  Fourth Brigade, Israel B. Richardson

Note. J. Howard Carlisle's Battery E, 2nd United States Artillery was attached to Schenck's brigade; Romeyn B. Ayres' Battery E, 3rd United States Artillery to Sherman's brigade; and John Edwards' Battery M, 2nd United States Artillery to Richardson's brigade.

Second Division, David Hunter
  First Brigade, Andrew Porter
  Second Brigade, Ambrose E. Burnside

Note. Charles Griffin's Battery D, 5th United States Artillery was attached to Porter's brigade; and J. Albert Monroe's Battery A, 1st Rhode Island Light Artillery was attached to Burnside's brigade.

Third Division, Samuel P. Heintzelman
  First Brigade, William B. Franklin
  Second Brigade, Orlando B. Willcox
  Third Brigade, Oliver O. Howard

Note. James B. Ricketts' Battery I, 1st United States Artillery was attached to Franklin's brigade; and Richard Arnold's Battery D, 2nd United States Artillery was attached to Willcox's brigade.

Fourth (or Reserve) Division, Theodore Runyon

Note. Fourth Division consisted of four three-month New Jersey regiments and four three-year New Jersey regiments.

Fifth Division, Dixon S. Miles
  First Brigade, Louis Blenker
  Second Brigade, Thomas A. Davies

Note 1. Fifth Division was broken up July 25, 1861, after the Battle of Bull Run.
Note 2. Charles Bookwood's battery of the 8th New York Militia and John C. Tidball's Battery A, 2nd United States Artillery were attached to Blenker's brigade; and Oliver D. Greene's Battery G, 2nd United States Artillery was attached to Davies' brigade.

The original order of July 8, 1861, organizing the army, assigned four three-month New Jersey regiments and three three-year New Jersey regiments to Runyon's Fourth Division, but gave no brigade organization. A short time later, however, 1st, 2nd, 3rd, and 4th New Jersey, all three-month regiments, were assigned to First Brigade, Fourth Division, and 1st, 2nd, and 3rd New Jersey, all three-year regiments, and 41st New York were assigned to Second Brigade, Fourth Division.

The above was the organization of McDowell's army that fought at Bull Run July 21, 1861. McDowell suffered a serious defeat that day, and the troops fled in complete disorder to their former camps near Washington. For details of the Battle of Bull Run, see Bull Run Campaign, Virginia (First Battle of Bull Run or Manassas).

The confusion resulting from the Federal defeat at Bull Run necessitated a complete reorganization of the army, and to secure the advantages of a unified command in the area around Washington, the Military Division of the Potomac (see) was created July 25, 1861, to consist of the Department of Washington and the Department of Northeastern Virginia, and George B. McClellan was assigned command. McClellan assumed command July 27, 1861, with headquarters in Washington.

August 17, 1861 (ordered August 15, 1861), the Military Division of the Potomac was discontinued, and the departments of Washington, Northeastern Virginia, and the Shenandoah were merged into the newly created Department of the Potomac. McClellan was assigned command, with headquarters at Washington. McDowell's former command thus became the Army of the Potomac.

DEPARTMENT OF PENNSYLVANIA APRIL 27, 1861–AUGUST 24, 1861 (PROBABLE)

April 19, 1861, the same day that a mob in Baltimore clashed with the 6th Massachusetts Regiment as it passed through the city en route to Washington, the limits of the Department of Washington (see Department of Washington, April 9, 1861–August 17, 1861) were extended to include the states of Pennsylvania and Delaware. Robert Patterson was assigned command, and he was charged with securing the rail line through Baltimore and on to Washington.

April 27, 1861, the Department of Pennsylvania and the Department of Annapolis were formed from a part of the territory of the Department of Washington. The Department of Pennsylvania consisted of the states of Pennsylvania and Delaware, and all of the state of Maryland not included in the departments of Washington and Annapolis. Patterson assumed command of the Department of Pennsylvania April 29, 1861, and transferred his headquarters from Washington to Philadelphia.

The department was reduced in size May 9, 1861, when the western part of the state of Pennsylvania was transferred to the Department of the Ohio. The western boundary of the department was then described as a line that began at the junction of the western boundary of Maryland and the Pennsylvania state line, and extended in a northerly direction to the northeast corner of McKean County in Pennsylvania.

June 2, 1861, Patterson moved his headquarters to Chambersburg, Pennsylvania, and there he began organizing a force for the invasion of Virginia. When this task was completed, he moved across the Potomac River at Williamsport, Maryland with his Army of the Department of Pennsylvania June 16, 1861, but he returned to the north bank the following night. He crossed again July 2, 1861, and advanced as far as Bunker Hill before turning east toward Harper's Ferry. He arrived there July 21, 1861,

without having accomplished anything of importance.

The failure of Patterson's campaign and the defeat of Irvin McDowell's Army of Northeastern Virginia at the Battle of Bull Run July 21, 1861 resulted in extensive changes in the command of the Union forces in the east, and also in the organization of the territory that they occupied. A number of these changes affected the Department of Pennsylvania.

By an order dated July 19, 1861, Patterson was honorably discharged from the service of the United States, and this order was to take effect July 27, 1861, when his tour of duty expired. July 22, 1861, Nathaniel P. Banks, then in command of the Department of Annapolis, was ordered to Harper's Ferry to relieve Patterson, who had just arrived there and was in command of the post.

John A. Dix relieved Banks in command of the Department of Annapolis July 23, 1861, and that same day the designation of Dix's command was changed to the Department of Maryland. Two days later, however, the Department of Maryland was discontinued, and a part of its territory was merged into the Department of Pennsylvania. Dix then relieved Patterson in command of the Department of Pennsylvania, but maintained his headquarters at Baltimore. It should be noted, however, that Dix continued to head his communications as "Headquarters Department of Maryland" until July 31, 1861.

Banks relieved Patterson in command at Harper's Ferry July 25, 1861, and Banks' new command was designated as the Department of the Shenandoah. That same day the Department of Pennsylvania was extensively reorganized as follows: Western Pennsylvania, as described above, was transferred from the Department of the Ohio to the Department of Pennsylvania; Washington and Allegany counties in Maryland were transferred to the new Department of the Shenandoah; Prince George's, Montgomery, and Frederick counties in Maryland were transferred to the Department of Washington; and a part of the Department of Maryland was absorbed in the Department of Pennsylvania. That department then consisted of the states of Pennsylvania and Delaware, and all of Maryland not included in the departments of Washington and of the Shenandoah.

August 17, 1861, the Department of the Potomac was constituted under George B. McClellan, and was to consist of the territory of the departments of the Shenandoah, of Washington, and of Northeastern Virginia, and also the states of Delaware and Maryland. In effect, with this order, the Department of Pennsylvania was discontinued, but the state of Pennsylvania was not formally added to the Department of the Potomac until February 1, 1862. It appears, however, that by an order of August 24, 1861, from headquarters of the army, Dix's command, formerly the Department of Pennsylvania, was assigned to the Department of the Potomac. On the other hand, the army register of September 10, 1861 shows the state of Pennsylvania assigned to the Department of the East. It should be further noted that it was not until November 8, 1861 that Dix changed the heading of his orders from "Headquarters Department of Pennsylvania" to "Headquarters Division." As noted above, the state of Pennsylvania (and also New Jersey) was not formally transferred to the Department of the Potomac until February 1, 1861.

The principal posts occupied by troops of Dix's command in August 1861 were Annapolis; Annapolis Junction; Baltimore; Federal Hill; Fort McHenry; Havre de Grace; McKims' Mansion; Mount Clare; the North Central Railroad; Patterson's Park; the Philadelphia, Baltimore, and Wilmington Railroad; Relay House; and West Baltimore Street.

TROOPS AND OPERATIONS IN THE DEPARTMENT OF PENNSYLVANIA

Organization of the Army of the Department of Pennsylvania. When Patterson assumed command of the Department of Pennsylvania, he was engaged principally in recruiting and organizing three-month regiments of Pennsylvania Volunteers. In addition to this duty, he was instructed by Winfield Scott, commander in chief of the army, to formulate plans for the occupation of Baltimore and the opening of the rail line between Philadelphia and Washington. While the latter project was under consideration, Benjamin F. Butler, with troops of his Department of Annapolis, and acting without orders, occupied Baltimore May 13, 1861, and thereby rendered unnecessary any further action by Patterson in this area.

May 24, 1861, Scott ordered Patterson to organize a force near Chambersburg, Pennsylvania for the purpose of advancing on Frederick, Hagerstown, and Cumberland in Maryland, and also threatening Harper's Ferry. This operation was intended to support Union sentiment in Western Virginia. May 28, 1861, Patterson sent five regiments to report to William H. Keim, then in command at Chambersburg, and he ordered an additional eight regiments to follow. He also ordered George H. Thomas to move from Carlisle to Chambersburg with four companies of regular infantry and his 2nd United States Cavalry.

June 2, 1861, Patterson moved his headquarters Department of Pennsylvania from Philadelphia to Chambersburg, and assumed personal direction of organizing the troops assembling there. By June 10, 1861, he had organized five brigades as follows:

First Brigade, George H. Thomas
Second Brigade, George C. Wynkoop
Third Brigade, Alpheus S. Williams
Fourth Brigade, Dixon S. Miles
Fifth Brigade, James S. Negley

The next day the above brigades were organized into two divisions as follows:

First Division, George Cadwalader
    First Brigade, George H. Thomas
    Third Brigade, Alpheus S. Williams
    Fourth Brigade, Dixon S. Miles

Note. June 18, 1861 Miles left for Washington with the 2nd, 3rd, and 8th United States Infantry of Thomas' brigade, and July 6, 1861, Miles was assigned command of a division in Irvin McDowell's Army of Northeastern Virginia.

Second Division, William H. Keim
    Second Brigade, George C. Wynkoop
    Fifth Brigade, James S. Negley

Artillery
    Battery A, 1st Rhode Island Light Artillery, William H. Reynolds
    Company F, 4th United States Artillery, Delevan D. Perkins
    Company E, 1st United States Artillery, Abner Doubleday

June 20, 1861, a Sixth Brigade was organized under John J. Abercrombie. This brigade was assigned to Keim's Second Division, and consisted of the 1st Wisconsin Regiment and 11th Pennsylvania Regiment, both from Negley's brigade, and also the 4th Connecticut Regiment. At the same time the 24th Pennsylvania was transferred from Wynkoop's brigade to Negley's brigade.

The brigade and division commanders held rank as follows: Thomas, colonel, 2nd United States Cavalry; Wynkoop, brigadier general, Pennsylvania Volunteers; Williams, brigadier general, United States Volunteers; Miles, colonel, 2nd United States Infantry; Negley, brigadier general, Pennsylvania Volunteers; Cadwalader, major general, Pennsylvania Volunteers; and Abercrombie, colonel, 7th United States Infantry.

A number of officers serving with Patterson's army, other than the division and brigade commanders, are also of interest because they later rose to higher command in the Union Army. These were: Ambrose E. Burnside, colonel, 1st Rhode Island; James Nagle, colonel, 6th Pennsylvania; and John F. Ballier, colonel, 21st Pennsylvania; all in Thomas' First Brigade. Joshua T. Owen, colonel, 24th Pennsylvania was in Wynkoop's Second Brigade, and later in Negley's Fifth Brigade. Thomas A. Rowley, colonel, 13th Pennsylvania was in Miles' Fourth Brigade. John C. Starkweather, colonel, 1st Wisconsin was in Negley's Fifth Brigade, and later in Abercrombie's Sixth Brigade. David B. Birney, lieutenant colonel, 23rd Pennsylvania was in Thomas' First Brigade. Lewis Wallace, with his 11th Indiana, occupied Cumberland, Maryland and came under Patterson's orders, but he was not assigned to a brigade. Abner Doubleday arrived at Hagerstown, Maryland June 18, 1861 with a battery of artillery, and still later other regiments joined the army with commanders who became well known. These were George H. Gordon, Charles S. Hamilton, Halbert E. Paine, and Daniel Butterfield.

The troops that Patterson organized and commanded in June and July 1861 have been called the Army of Pennsylvania, the Army of the Department of Pennsylvania, and also the Army of the Shenandoah. Generally, however, they have been known simply as Patterson's Army.

Advance of the Army into Virginia, June 16, 1861.
June 1, 1861, Patterson submitted a plan to army headquarters in which he proposed to cross the Potomac River at Williamsport, Maryland, and then advance and occupy Martinsburg, Virginia. In this way, he would turn the enemy position at Harper's Ferry and force its evacuation. When this was accomplished, Patterson would advance on Winchester, Virginia.

As a preliminary to this operation, Thomas advanced June 7, 1861 from Chambersburg toward Hagerstown with his cavalry, one battalion of 8th United States Infantry, and the three regiments of his First Brigade. He camped that night at Greencastle, Pennsylvania, and was joined there the next day by Williams' Third Brigade. Miles' Fourth Brigade was ordered to follow Williams.

June 15, 1861, Patterson moved his headquarters to Hagerstown, and that day issued orders for the advance of the army into Virginia. That same day Joseph E. Johnston evacuated Harper's Ferry and fell back to Bunker Hill, north of Winchester. June 16, 1861, Cadwalader's division crossed the Potomac and moved forward to Falling Waters. When Scott learned of the enemy's withdrawal from Harper's Ferry he did not order a pursuit, but instead directed Patterson to send to Washington the regulars under Miles; Thomas, with his 2nd Cavalry; and Burnside, with his 1st Rhode Island.

On the night of June 17, 1861, Patterson received a report from Cadwalader that Johnston was said to be at Martinsburg with about 15,000 men. Accordingly, Patterson promptly halted his advance and, at the same time, ordered Cadwalader to recross with his division to the north side of the river. The next morning, after Cadwalader had safely withdrawn his troops from Virginia, Miles, with the 2nd, 3rd, and 8th United States Infantry, and Burnside, with his 1st Rhode Island Regiment, departed for Washington.

Engagement at Falling Waters (Hoke's Run, or Hainesville), Virginia, July 2, 1861.
After Patterson's first attempt to invade Virginia, his army remained near Williamsport until July 2, 1861, and then again it crossed into Virginia. At daylight that morning, Abercrombie's brigade of Keim's Second Division began crossing the Potomac, and shortly after 7:00 A.M. the infantry was across. Abercrombie then took the main road toward Martinsburg, and he was followed by Thomas' brigade, and then Negley's brigade. About a mile from the ford, Negley's brigade was moved to the right to meet any

enemy force that might be advancing from the direction of Hedgesville, and also to protect Patterson's right flank. Patterson's left flank was on the Potomac River.

While Patterson was advancing from the river crossing, Johnston was with the main force of his army at Winchester, about thirty-five miles to the southwest. A brigade under the command of Thomas J. Jackson was encamped about two miles north of Martinsburg, and James E. B. (Jeb) Stuart was scouting the country in front of Jackson with the 1st Virginia Cavalry.

Soon after beginning their march, Abercrombie and Negley encountered enemy skirmishers, but despite some opposition Abercrombie continued his advance about four miles to Falling Waters and Hoke's Run. About a mile beyond the run, Federal skirmishers moved into an open field of the Porterfield farm, on the right of the road, and there they came under enemy fire. That morning Jackson had formed most of the 5th Virginia Infantry of his brigade along the edge of a woods on the south side of the Porterfield field, largely on the Confederate left of the road. These were the troops who fired on the advancing Federals.

Abercrombie then deployed his brigade, with the 1st Wisconsin across the road and the 11th Pennsylvania on its right. Abercrombie and Jackson then exchanged fire for about an hour until Thomas came up with his brigade about 10:00 A.M. Thomas then deployed his troops on the left side of the road, where he hoped to turn the enemy's right flank. Delevan D. Perkins then brought up his Battery F, 4th United States Artillery. A short time later, Jackson, who was under orders only to delay the Federal advance, began to withdraw. Thomas and Abercrombie followed slowly, with some exchange of fire, until about noon, but then Patterson halted his command, and bivouacked that night on Jackson's campground of the night before. Jackson's command halted that evening about two miles south of Martinsburg.

Patterson's engagement of July 2, 1861, which actually was little more than a skirmish, has been called the Battle of Falling Waters, and also the Battle of Hoke's Run, Hainesville, and Martinsburg.

* * * * * * * * * * * * * * * *

On the morning of July 3, 1861, Patterson marched into Martinsburg, but instead of continuing on he remained there until July 15, 1861. On July 4, 1861, Patterson learned of McDowell's intention of moving his Army of Northeastern Virginia toward Manassas, but apparently Scott was not for some time concerned about Patterson's attempting to hold Johnston's command at Winchester. Finally, on July 13, 1861, Scott ordered Patterson to detain Johnston in the Shenandoah Valley and to prevent him from marching eastward to join the Confederate forces near Centerville. On July 15, 1861, Patterson advanced to Bunker Hill, but the next day, instead of continuing on toward Johnston at Winchester, he turned to the left and marched to Charlestown, Virginia. This move left Johnston free to leave the valley to reinforce Pierre G. T. Beauregard's Confederate Army of the Potomac, which was the objective of McDowell's advance from Washington. Johnston arrived at Manassas with his Army of the Shenandoah in time to take part in the Battle of Bull Run, and aid in the defeat of McDowell July 21, 1861.

Meantime, reinforcements were on the way to join Patterson. On June 8, 1861, Scott organized a small secondary expedition from Washington under Charles P. Stone to cooperate with Patterson when the latter advanced into Virginia. This force, which was known as the Rockville Expedition, was of brigade strength, and it left Washington June 10, 1861. It moved up the Potomac River to Poolesville, Maryland, and remained there until July 2, 1861, watching the fords and ferries on the river. On June 30, 1861, Stone's expedition was ordered to join Patterson's army, and July 2, 1861, it moved to Point of Rocks. It then moved by way of Williamsport and arrived at Martinsburg July 8, 1861. That day the Rockville Expedition was organized as Seventh Brigade of Patterson's army under the command of Stone, and it was temporarily attached to Keim's division.

In addition to Stone's command, four New York regiments were ordered from Washington to Martinsburg. The 19th and 28th New York arrived July 8, 1861, and were temporarily attached to Wynkoop's brigade. Charles W. Sandford, major general of the New York Militia, arrived with the 5th and 12th New York July 10, 1861, and that day a new Third Division was organized under Sandford as follows:

Third Division, Charles W. Sandford
  Seventh Brigade, Charles P. Stone
  Eighth Brigade, Daniel Butterfield

Eighth Brigade was organized July 10, 1861 from the 5th, 12th, 19th, and 28th New York regiments. Butterfield, commander of the 12th New York, was the senior officer of the brigade.

In addition to the above reinforcements, four other regiments also joined Patterson's army. George H. Gordon with the 2nd Massachusetts arrived at Williamsport July 14, 1861, and was assigned to Abercrombie's Sixth Brigade; Lewis Wallace brought up his 11th Indiana from Cumberland, Maryland, and arrived at Charlestown July 19, 1861; and July 20, 1861, Charles S. Hamilton's 3rd Wisconsin and Halbert E. Paine's 4th Wisconsin were ordered to join Patterson.

When Patterson reached Charlestown July 17, 1861, the terms of enlistment of eighteen of his three-month Pennsylvania regiments were due to expire within the next eight days, and they refused to serve any longer. Patterson marched on to Harper's Ferry, where he arrived July 21, 1861, and by July 25, 1861 most of his Pennsylvania troops had departed, and his army as originally organized had ceased to exist. Williams and Wynkoop accompanied the Pennsylvania regiments to Harrisburg for muster out, and the following officers were mustered out of the Pennsylvania service: Cadwalader, July 19, 1861; Negley, July 20, 1861; and Keim, July 21, 1861. All three later received commissions in the United States Volunteers.

With the failure of Patterson's army in the Shenandoah Valley and its disintegration by muster out, some organizational and command changes were made in the troops remaining. By an order of July 19, 1861, Patterson, of the Pennsylvania Volunteers, was to be honorably discharged from the service of the United States, to take effect July 27, 1861, the date on which his term of duty expired. July 25, 1861 (ordered July 22, 1861), Nathaniel P. Banks arrived at Harper's Ferry from Baltimore, Maryland, and assumed command of Patterson's force. Banks' new command was designated as the Department of the Shenandoah. For additional information, see Department of the Shenandoah, July 19, 1861–August 17, 1861.

Banks then proceeded to organize the Department of the Shenandoah by assigning the troops remaining of Patterson's army as follows: 2nd United States Cavalry of the former First Brigade, First Division; 19th and 28th New York of the former Eighth Brigade, Third Division; and two new regiments were assigned to George H. Thomas' First Brigade, Department of the Shenandoah. The 4th Connecticut and 2nd Massachusetts of the former Sixth Brigade, Second Division; and three new regiments were assigned to John J. Abercrombie's Second Brigade, Department of the Shenandoah. The 1st New Hampshire and 83rd New York (9th New York State Militia) of the former Seventh Brigade, Third Division; and one new regiment were assigned to Charles P. Stone's Third Brigade, Department of the Shenandoah.

DEPARTMENT OF PENNSYLVANIA DECEMBER 1, 1864–JUNE 27, 1865

The Department of Pennsylania was re-created December 1, 1864 as a part of the Middle Military Division. It consisted of the state of Pennsylvania and the counties of Columbiana, Jefferson, and Belmont in Ohio, and was organized simply by changing the name of the Department of the Susquehanna to the Department of Pennsylvania. Darius N. Couch relinquished command of the Department of the Susquehanna December 1, 1864, and George Cadwalader assumed command of the Department of Pennsylvania. Cadwalader established his headquarters at Chambersburg, but on December 3, 1864 he moved to Philadelphia.

In the reorganization of the military divisions and geographical departments of the army June 27, 1865, the Department of Pennsylvania was discontinued and the state of Pennsylvania was assigned to the reorganized Middle Department, Military Division of the Atlantic; and the counties in Ohio were transferred to the Department of the Ohio, Military Division of the Mississippi.

POSTS AND DISTRICTS IN THE DEPARTMENT OF PENNSYLVANIA

When the Department of the Susquehanna was

discontinued, there were four districts within its limits, and they were retained in the Department of Pennsylvania. These were the districts of Juniata, Lehigh, Philadelphia, and the Monongahela. The important posts that were transferred to the Department of Pennsylvania were Carlisle (Camp Biddle and the Cavalry Depot), Bloody Run (present-day Everett), Chambersburg, Chelton Hill (Camp William Penn), Greencastle, Harrisburg, McConnellsburg, Philadelphia, Pittsburgh, Scranton, Stroudsburg, and York.

Juniata District. When transferred to the Department of Pennsylvania December 1, 1863, the eastern boundary of the district was, from north to south, the Williamsport and Elmira Railroad to Williamsport, the line of the Susquehanna River to its intersection with the Blue Ridge Mountains, near the mouth of the Juniata River, and then along the Blue Ridge Mountains to the Maryland state line. At its southern end, the boundary followed the western boundary of Franklin County. December 1, 1864, the counties of Adams, Cumberland, Franklin, and York were annexed to the district. These constituted the southern tier of counties in Pennsylvania lying between the Blue Ridge Mountains and the Susquehanna River. The western boundary of the district was the Laurel Hill range of mountains, which was also the eastern boundary of the District of the Monongahela. The Laurel Hill range began on the south near the junction of the western boundary of Maryland with the Pennsylvania state line, and ran in a northerly direction, passing a short distance west of Johnstown.

Orris S. Ferry was in command of the district when it was transferred to the Department of Pennsylvania December 1, 1864, and on that date he moved his headquarters from Bedford to Chambersburg. December 16, 1864, Ferry was assigned as military commander of Philadelphia, and John T. Morgan assumed command of the District of the Juniata. Morgan remained in command until the end of the war.

The principal posts in the district were Bloody Run (Everett), Chambersburg, Greencastle, and McConnellsburg. These posts were manned by three companies of Pennsylvania troops, the Patapsco Guards (at Chambersburg), a detachment of the United States Signal Corps, and a detachment of the 1st New York Light Artillery.

Lehigh District. When the Lehigh District was transferred to the Department of Pennsylvania December 1, 1864, there were only two companies of Pennsylvania troops in the district. One company was at Scranton and the other was at Stroudsburg, but these were soon withdrawn. On June 2, 1865, however, the district was reconstituted to consist of the counties of Berks, Carbon, Lehigh, Luzerne, Monroe, Northampton, Schuylkill, and Wyoming. Headquarters of the district was at Tamaqua, in Schuylkill County.

District of the Monongahela. When transferred to the Department of Pennsylvania December 1, 1864, the District of the Monongahela consisted of that part of the state of Pennsylvania west of the Laurel Hill range of mountains, and it also included the counties of Columbiana, Belmont, and Jefferson in Ohio. Thomas A. Rowley was in command of the district, with headquarters at Pittsburgh. Greenlief P. Davis commanded the post of Pittsburgh. Rowley resigned December 29, 1864, and Davis assumed command of the district. Davis remained in command until the end of the war.

In December 1864, the troops in the district consisted of a detachment of Battery A, 1st New York Light Artillery and two companies of the United States Veteran Reserve Corps, but later the only troops present consisted of one company of the Veteran Reserve Corps.

District of Philadelphia. When the District of Philadelphia was transferred to the Department of Pennsylvania December 1, 1863, it was commanded by George Cadwalader. Cadwalader, however, assumed command of the new department, and December 16, 1864, Orris S. Ferry was assigned as military commander of Philadelphia. December 31, 1864, the district was defined as consisting of the city and county of Philadelphia, except Fort Mifflin; and the counties of Bucks, Chester, Delaware, and Montgomery. Ferry was assigned command of the district, with headquarters at Philadelphia, and he remained in command until the end of the war.

In December 1864, the troops in the district consisted of the 186th Pennsylvania Regiment and nine companies of the 2nd Battalion of the United States Veteran Reserve Corps. In April 1865, only the

186th Pennsylvania and Battery A, 1st New York Light Artillery remained.

TROOPS IN THE DEPARTMENT OF PENNSYLVANIA

The troop organizations in the districts and at the posts of the department were generally no larger than companies or detachments. The troops in the districts have already been mentioned above. In addition, at the time of organization of the department, there were at Chelton Hill (Camp William Penn) two regiments of recruits of United States Colored Troops and three companies of United States Colored Troops. At Harrisburg and York there were three companies of the United States Veteran Reserve Corps, and at Scranton and Stroudsburg there was at each post one company of Pennsylvania troops. These numbers were considerably reduced by April 1864.

DEPARTMENT OF THE POTOMAC

The Department of the Potomac was constituted August 17, 1861 to consist of the departments of Washington, Northeastern Virginia, and the Shenandoah. Included within its limits were the states of Delaware and Maryland, the District of Columbia, and that part of Virginia east of the Allegheny Mountains and north of the James River, except Fort Monroe and the country around it for a distance of sixty miles. George B. McClellan assumed command August 20, 1861 (assigned August 17, 1861), with headquarters at Washington, D.C. By General Order No. 1, dated August 20, 1861, McClellan assumed command of the Army of the Potomac, which was composed of the troops within the limits of the newly created Department of the Potomac. Thereafter, McClellan and his successors issued orders and communications under the heading "Headquarters Army of the Potomac," rather than "Headquarters Department of the Potomac." The two designations were, however, generally regarded as synonymous, but the latter designation was seldom used. In fact, the last reference to the Department of the Potomac in the Official Records of the Rebellion was dated February 1, 1862, when the states of New Jersey and Pennsylvania were added to the department. Some references are simply "Department (or Army) of the Potomac." In describing territorial limits in this section, however, it is more significant to refer to the Department of the Potomac.

There were numerous changes in the boundaries of the department during the war, and these are described as follows:

The Department of Western Virginia was created September 19, 1861, to include that part of the state of Virginia west of the Blue Ridge Mountains. The western boundary of the Department of the Potomac was thus moved eastward from the Allegheny Mountains to the Blue Ridge Mountains. The Department of Western Virginia was redefined November 9, 1861 to include the territory north and west of the Greenbrier River, and west of a line extending northward from the Greenbrier to the southwest corner of Maryland, and thence northward along the western boundary of Maryland to the Pennsylvania border. A correction was issued January 23, 1862, to establish the eastern boundary of the Department of Western Virginia (the western boundary of the Department of the Potomac) along the western slope of the Allegheny Mountains.

February 1, 1862, the states of Maryland and Pennsylvania were added to the Department of the Potomac. The territory of New Jersey was taken from the Department of the East.

March 3, 1862, the eastern limits of the Department of Western Virginia were extended to include the valley of the Cow Pasture Branch of the James River, the valley of the James River to Balcony Falls, the valley of the Roanoke River west of the Blue Ridge, and the New River Valley. This established the western boundary of the Department of the Potomac as follows: beginning at the northern end, it followed the Flintstone Creek in Maryland; and in Virginia, it ran southward from the Potomac River, opposite the mouth of Flintstone Creek, along the South Branch Mountain, Town Hill Mountain, Branch Mountain (or Big Ridge), North or Shenandoah Mountain, Purgatory Mountain, and the Blue Ridge and Allegheny mountains to the border of North Carolina.

The Department of the Potomac was reduced in

size March 22, 1862, when the Middle Department was created to consist of the states of New Jersey, Delaware, and Pennsylvania; the Eastern Shore of Maryland; the Eastern Shore of Virginia; and the counties of Cecil, Harford, Baltimore, and Anne Arundel in Maryland. This left in the Department of the Potomac that part of Maryland east of Flintstone Creek, except the Eastern Shore and the counties of Cecil, Harford, Baltimore, and Anne Arundel, and that part of Virginia east of the boundary just described, except Fort Monroe and the country around within sixty miles of that place.

On April 4, 1862, after the Army of the Potomac had departed from Washington for the Peninsula, most of the territory of the Department of the Potomac was assigned to the newly created departments of the Rappahannock and the Shenandoah. That part of Maryland lying between the Potomac and Patuxent rivers, the District of Columbia, and that part of Virginia east of the Blue Ridge Mountains and west of the railroad running south from Fredericksburg through Richmond and Petersburg to Weldon, North Carolina was assigned to the Department of the Rappahannock. That part of Maryland and Virginia west of the Blue Ridge Mountains and east of the Mountain Department (created March 11, 1862) was assigned to the Department of the Shenandoah.

The advance corps of the Army of the Potomac arrived at Fort Monroe March 23, 1862, and from that date until August 1862, the army operated in the Department of Virginia. On June 1, 1862, the limits of the Department of Virginia were extended to include that part of the state of Virginia south of the Rappahannock River and east of the railroad from Fredericksburg to Weldon, and all the Federal forces within this territory were placed under the command of George B. McClellan, as commander of the Army of the Potomac. With the transfer of the country east of the railroad to the Department of Virginia, there was no territory specifically assigned to the Department of the Potomac.

June 26, 1862, the forces belonging to the departments of the Rappahannock and the Shenandoah and to the Mountain Department were consolidated to form the Army of Virginia under John Pope. Pope exercised control over the territory of the three former departments until September 2, 1862.

During the latter part of August 1862, the Army of the Potomac moved from the Peninsula to Fredericksburg and Alexandria, and a part of the army was with the Army of Virginia during the closing battles of Pope's Virginia Campaign. After Pope's defeat at Bull Run August 30, 1862, both armies retired within the defenses of Washington, and there, during the period September 2–5, 1862, they were consolidated by merging the Army of Virginia into the Army of the Potomac. Pope was relieved September 5, 1862, and McClellan was left in command of the combined armies.

When Pope's Army of Virginia was discontinued, a large part of the state of Virginia belonged to no department, and was under the jurisdiction of no army commander. In the East, the Eastern Shore (the counties of Accomac and Northampton) was in the Middle Department, and that part of the state south of the Rappahannock River and east of the railroad running from Fredericksburg to Weldon was in the Department of Virginia. September 19, 1862, all of Western Virginia was assigned to the Department of the Ohio. All the rest of Virginia that was north of the James River and was covered by the Army of the Potomac in its operations constituted the Department of the Potomac. Thereafter, the Department (or Army) of the Potomac was generally defined as the territory not included in other departments, but covered by the army in its operations.

There were several departmental changes during the rest of the war that involved territory of the state of Virginia, but only one affected the Department of the Potomac. On February 2, 1863, the Department of Washington was created to consist of the country north of the Potomac River bounded by a line from Piscataway Creek to Annapolis Junction, and from that point to the mouth of the Monocacy River; and also that part of Virginia bounded by a line that ran south from the Potomac along Goose Creek and the Bull Run Mountains, and then to the mouth of the Occoquan River.

From September 1862 to April 1865, with two exceptions, the operations of the Army of the Potomac were confined to the state of Virginia. During the latter part of 1862, the army was in Maryland during the Antietam Campaign; and in June and July 1863, it was in Maryland and Pennsylvania during the Gettysburg Campaign. The territory covered by the army during this period is briefly described as follows:

The Maryland Campaign. When the Army of Northern Virginia began crossing the Potomac River into Maryland September 4, 1862, McClellan moved out from Washington with the Army of the Potomac to drive it from the state. He marched northwest through Montgomery and Frederick counties to Frederick, and then turned west into Washington County, where he was engaged at the Battle of Antietam September 17, 1862.

Antietam to Fredericksburg. Following the Battle of Antietam, the Army of the Potomac remained in the vicinity of Sharpsburg until October 26, 1862. On that date, it began crossing the Potomac River into Virginia at Berlin (present-day Brunswick), and it then marched southward through Loudoun and Fauquier counties, and arrived at Warrenton November 6, 1862. The army remained there until November 15, 1862, and then, under the command of Ambrose E. Burnside, it moved to Falmouth, opposite Fredericksburg. It was engaged at Fredericksburg September 11–15, 1862, and then went into winter quarters north and east of Falmouth in Stafford County.

The Chancellorsville Campaign. On April 27, 1863, the Army of the Potomac, then commanded by Joseph Hooker, moved out of its winter quarters at the beginning of the Spring Campaign of 1863, but it was defeated at the Battle of Chancellorsville, a short distance west, May 1–4, 1863. It then returned to the Falmouth area, and remained there until the beginning of the Gettysburg Campaign in June 1863.

The Gettysburg Campaign. June 14, 1863, the Army of the Potomac left the line of the Rappahannock River to follow Robert E. Lee's army, which was then advancing toward the lower Shenandoah Valley and Maryland. Hooker moved northward through Virginia, east of the Bull Run Mountains, and crossed the Potomac into Maryland at and near Edwards Ferry. George G. Meade relieved Hooker of the command of the Army of the Potomac June 28, 1863 at Frederick, and then advanced with it into Pennsylvania, where it was engaged at the Battle of Gettysburg July 1–3, 1863. Meade then followed Lee's defeated army into Virginia, and arrived on the Rappahannock River in

the vicinity of Warrenton at the end of July 1863. During the period June 25, 1863–July 19, 1863, the Army of the Potomac operated in the counties of Montgomery, Frederick, Carroll, and Washington in Maryland; and in Adams County in Pennsylvania.

August 1863 to May 4, 1864. After arriving at Warrenton, the Army of the Potomac operated generally along the line of the Orange and Alexandria Railroad until May 4, 1864. In mid-September 1863, it advanced from the Rappahannock to Culpeper Court House and the Rapidan River, and it remained in position there until early October 1863. At that time, Lee took the offensive, and during the Bristoe, Virginia Campaign of October 9–22, 1863, Meade fell back to the Centerville area. Lee followed, but then withdrew, and Meade again moved back to the Rappahannock November 7–8, 1863. The army then crossed the river and took position on a line extending from Kelly's Ford, through Brandy Station, to Welford's Ford on Hazel River. Mead remained generally in this region during the winter of 1863–1864, except for a brief period when the army moved south of the Rapidan and into the Wilderness during the Mine Run Campaign of November 26, 1863–December 2, 1863.

The Virginia Campaigns of 1864–1865. On May 4, 1864, the Army of the Potomac moved south in Virginia at the beginning of the final effort against Richmond and Lee's army. Led by Grant, it moved by way of the Wilderness, Spotsylvania Court House, Hanover Court House, and Cold Harbor to the James River. It then moved on to Petersburg, where it remained in position in front of the town from June 16, 1864 to April 3, 1865. Then, when Lee evacuated Petersburg, the army pursued the Army of Northern Virginia to Appomattox Court House, where hostilities ended April 9, 1865.

The commanders of the Department (or Army) of the Potomac were as follows:

George B. McClellan	August 20, 1862 to November 9, 1862
Ambrose E. Burnside	November 9, 1862 to January 26, 1863
Joseph Hooker	January 26, 1863 to June 28, 1863
George G. Meade	June 28, 1863 to December 30, 1864

John G. Parke	December 30, 1864 to January 11, 1865
George G. Meade	January 11, 1865 to June 28, 1865

Note. The Army of the Potomac was discontinued June 28, 1865.

DEPARTMENT OF THE RAPPAHANNOCK

Concern for the safety of Washington following the battle of Kernstown, Virginia March 23, 1862 (see Shenandoah Valley Campaign [Jackson], 1862) was responsible for the creation of the departments of the Rappahannock and the Shenandoah April 4, 1862. The Department of the Rappahannock consisted of that part of Virginia east of the Blue Ridge Mountains and west of the Richmond, Fredericksburg, and Potomac Railroad, including the District of Columbia; and the country between the Potomac and Patuxent rivers, which included the counties of Montgomery, Prince George's, Charles, and Saint Mary's in Maryland. This territory was taken from the Department of the Potomac. Irvin McDowell, at that time in command of First Corps, Army of the Potomac, was assigned command of the Department of the Rappahannock, with headquarters in the field. McDowell's command was created to defend the northern and eastern parts of Virginia.

During the period of their existence, the boundaries of the departments of the Rappahannock and the Shenandoah, and also of the Mountain Department, which was constituted March 11, 1862, were not always strictly adhered to. Some army movements west of the Blue Ridge Mountains made it necessary to disregard departmental lines. Thus, during much of the period June 1–8, 1862, while Thomas J. (Stonewall) Jackson was operating in the Shenandoah Valley, troops from all three of the above departments were present in the Luray and Shenandoah valleys.

The Department of the Rappahannock was placed under the orders of the War Department March 11, 1862, when George B. McClellan was relieved as general in chief of the armies in anticipation of his taking the field during the Peninsular Campaign.

June 8, 1862, near the end of Jackson's Valley Campaign, the Department of the Rappahannock was reduced in size. That day McDowell was ordered to move his command toward Fredericksburg in preparation for a movement toward Richmond to cooperate with McClellan, who was then threatening the city. Also on June 8, 1862, Nathaniel P. Banks, commander of the Department of the Shenandoah, was directed to occupy the positions formerly held by John W. Geary's brigade (see below) along the Manassas Gap Railroad as far east as Manassas Junction. It was therefore necessary to move the eastern boundary of the Department of the Shenandoah (the Blue Ridge Mountains) eastward to include the Piedmont district and the Bull Run Mountains. This area was formerly in the Department of the Rappahannock. For details of the military situation at this time, see Shenandoah Valley Campaign (Jackson), 1862, and Peninsular Campaign.

The Department of the Rappahannock was discontinued June 26, 1862, when it was merged into John Pope's Army of Virginia as Third Corps.

DISTRICT IN THE DEPARTMENT OF THE RAPPAHANNOCK

Military District of Washington. The Department of the Rappahannock was not divided into districts, but at the time of its creation the Military District of Washington was included within its limits. The Military District of Washington was created March 17, 1862, when the Army of the Potomac was departing for the Peninsula, and James S. Wadsworth was assigned command. The District of Washington consisted of the District of Columbia, the city of Alexandria, the post of Fort Washington, and the ground in front of, and in the vicinity of, the defensive works south of the Potomac River, from the Occoquan River to Difficult Creek.

The powers assigned Wadsworth by Headquarters Army of the Potomac were not restricted or modified by the creation of the Department of the Rappahannock. The limits of his command were, however, subject to change if the department commander should be absent. In that event, Wadsworth was to have charge of that part of the department east of the Potomac River, and such parts of the counties of Fairfax, Loudoun, and Prince William in Virginia as were not occupied by the divisions commanded by William B. Franklin, George A. McCall, and Rufus King, of the former First Corps, Army of the Potomac. In May 1862, Wadsworth was assigned the duty of guarding the line of the Manassas Gap Railroad, and the Orange and Alexandria Railroad from White Plains to Alexandria, Virginia.

TROOPS IN THE DEPARTMENT OF THE RAPPAHANNOCK

When the Army of the Potomac left Washington for the Peninsula during the latter part of March 1862, Irvin McDowell's First Corps was detained near Alexandria because President Abraham Lincoln did not believe that McClellan had left sufficient troops to ensure the safety of the capital. Then, on April 4, 1862, First Corps was detached from the Army of the Potomac and was merged into the newly created Department of the Rappahannock, which was assigned to McDowell. The organization of First Corps at that time was as follows:

FIRST CORPS, Irvin McDowell

First Division, William B. Franklin
First Brigade, Philip Kearny
Second Brigade, Henry W. Slocum
Third Brigade, John Newton
Artillery
1st Battery (A), Massachusetts Light Artillery, Josiah Porter
Battery F, 1st New York Light Artillery, William R. Wilson
1st Battery, New Jersey Light Artillery, William Hexamer
Battery D, 2nd United States Artillery, Emory Upton

Second Division, George A. McCall
First Brigade, John F. Reynolds
Second Brigade, George G. Meade
Third Brigade, Edward O. C. Ord, to May 16, 1862
Truman Seymour
Artillery
Battery A, 1st Pennsylvania Light Artillery, Hezekiah Easton
Battery B, 1st Pennsylvania Light Artillery, James H. Cooper
Battery G, 1st Pennsylvania Light Artillery, Frank P. Amsden

Battery C, 5th United States Artillery, Henry V. De Hart

Third Division, Rufus King
First Brigade, Christopher C. Augur
Second Brigade, Marsena R. Patrick
Third Brigade, Lysander Cutler
Artillery
Battery B, 4th United States Artillery, John Gibbon
Battery D, 1st Rhode Island Light Artillery, J. Albert Monroe
Battery A, New Hampshire Light Artillery, George A. Gerrish
Battery D, Pennsylvania Light Artillery, George W. Durell

Note. Cutler was in temporary command of Third Brigade, and was relieved by John Gibbon May 7, 1862.

When McDowell assumed command of the Department of the Rappahannock, he first moved his command to Catlett's Station, in the direction of Culpeper Court House, and then moved toward Fredericksburg to occupy the town as his advanced position in front of Washington. At Fredericksburg he would also be in position to move south, if ordered to do so, and cooperate with McClellan in his advance on Richmond. Christopher C. Augur's First Brigade, McDowell's leading brigade, arrived near Falmouth, Virginia, April 15, 1862, and May 2, 1862, McDowell occupied Fredericksburg. A short time later he established his headquarters at Falmouth.

The organization of the troops under McDowell's command changed significantly a number of times during the short period of existence of the Department of the Rappahannock. The most important of these are described in the following paragraphs.

William B. Franklin's division was detached April 10, 1862, and was ordered to join McClellan on the Peninsula. It arrived at Yorktown April 22, 1862, and was engaged at Eltham's Landing May 7, 1862. The division was assigned to the new Sixth Provisional Corps, Army of the Potomac May 18, 1862, and that day Franklin assumed command of the corps. For further information, see Peninsular Campaign, and also Sixth Corps, Army of the Potomac.

April 30, 1862, George L. Hartsuff was assigned command of John J. Abercrombie's Second Brigade of Alpheus S. Williams' Division, Department of the Shenandoah, and Hartsuff was then sent with his brigade to the Department of the Rappahannock. He reported to McDowell May 1, 1862, and was ordered to Catlett's Station. There, on May 10, 1862, he was ordered to join McDowell at Fredericksburg, and May 16, 1862, his brigade was assigned as Third Brigade to Edward O. C. Ord's newly formed division (see below).

May 5, 1862, James B. Ricketts was assigned command of a brigade in the Department of the Rappahannock. It was composed of regiments from the Defenses of Washington, which were posted at Aquia Creek, Virginia. Ricketts moved his brigade to Fredericksburg May 8, 1862, and May 16, 1862, it was assigned as First Brigade of Ord's new division of the Department of the Rappahannock (see below).

On May 6, 1862, John W. Geary's Advance Brigade was transferred from the Department of the Shenandoah to the Department of the Rappahannock. Geary's brigade had been operating as an independent brigade in Loudoun and Fauquier counties in Virginia since February 25, 1862. After that date, Geary's brigade had been, first, a part of Banks' Division, Army of the Potomac; then a part of Fifth Corps, Army of the Potomac; and finally, a part of the Department of the Shenandoah. At the time of his transfer to the Department of the Rappahannock, Geary was engaged in guarding the Manassas Gap Railroad from Strasburg in the Shenandoah Valley to Manassas Junction. He continued in this service under McDowell. May 25, 1862, Geary was placed under the orders of James S. Wadsworth, commander of the District of Washington. June 22, 1862, he was again ordered to report to Banks.

Also on May 6, 1862, a brigade under Abner Doubleday was transferred to the Department of the Rappahannock from the Defenses North of the Potomac, Military District of Washington. This brigade was ordered to take position opposite Fredericksburg May 21, 1862.

Early in May 1862, a brigade commanded by Abram Duryee (also Duryea) was transferred from Cloud's Mill in the Military District of Washington to McDowell's field command. It moved to Catlett's Station, and then remained on the Orange and Alexandria Railroad until the end of the month. The brigade was placed under Wadsworth's control May 25, 1862, and a few days later it was assigned to Ord's division as Second Brigade.

In an order dated May 16, 1862, a new division of the Department of the Rappahannock was constituted, and Edward O. C. Ord was assigned command. Originally it was to have consisted of the brigades of Hartsuff and Ricketts (see above) and George D. Bayard's newly formed cavalry brigade, but as finally organized it was as follows:

Ord's Division, Edward O. C. Ord, to June 10, 1862
  James B. Ricketts, to June 26, 1862
  First Brigade, James B. Ricketts, to June 10, 1862
    Abram Duryee, to June 26, 1862
  Second Brigade, Abram Duryee, to June 10, 1862
    Zealous B. Tower, to June 26, 1862
  Third Brigade, George L. Hartsuff, to June 26, 1862
  Artillery
    2nd Battery (B), Maine Light Artillery, James A. Hall
    5th Battery (E), Maine Light Artillery, George F. Leppien
    Battery C, Pennsylvania Light Artillery, James Thompson
    Battery F, Pennsylvania Light Artillery, Captain Matthews

Note. When Ord was assigned command of the new division May 16, 1862, Truman Seymour relieved him in command of Third Brigade of George A. McCall's division.

On May 1, 1862, after the departure of Franklin's division for the Peninsula, James Shields was ordered, with his division of Nathaniel P. Banks' Department of the Shenandoah, to the Department of the Rappahannock. Shields was unable to move, however, until relieved by Banks' troops from Harrisonburg, but finally, on May 12, 1862, Shields left New Market in the Shenandoah Valley to join McDowell's command, and he arrived near Falmouth May 22, 1862. Shields' Division, as organized in the Department of the Shenandoah, consisted of three brigades, and at the time of the transfer, Nathan Kimball commanded the First Brigade; Orris S. Ferry, the Second Brigade; and Erastus B. Tyler, the Third Brigade. In the Department of the Rappahannock, however, the division was reorganized into four brigades. Three regiments of Tyler's brigade were transferred to Samuel S. Carroll's new Fourth Brigade, and two regiments of Ferry's brigade were transferred to Tyler's brigade. Carroll's brigade was completed by the transfer of one regiment from Kimball's brigade. When the reorganization was completed, Shields' Division was organized as follows:

Shields' Division, James Shields
First Brigade, Nathan Kimball
Second Brigade, Orris S. Ferry
Third Brigade, Erastus B. Tyler
Fourth Brigade, Samuel S. Carroll
Artillery
  Battery A, 1st West Virginia (Virginia) Light Artillery, John Jenks
  Battery B, 1st West Virginia (Virginia) Light Artillery, John V. Keeper
  Battery H, 1st Ohio Light Artillery, James F. Huntington
  Battery L, 1st Ohio Light Artillery, Lucius N. Robinson
  Battery E, 4th United States Artillery, Joseph C. Clark

May 17, 1862, McDowell was ordered to move down the Richmond, Fredericksburg, and Potomac Railroad to cooperate with McClellan, who was then approaching Richmond. On May 23, 1862, however, Thomas J. (Stonewall) Jackson suddenly appeared before Front Royal and captured the town, and McDowell's order was immediately suspended. McDowell was then ordered to move to the Shenandoah Valley with the divisions of Shields and King, and upon arrival there he was to cooperate with John C. Fremont's command of the Mountain Department, which was approaching the valley from the west in an attempt to cut off Jackson's retreat up the valley. Ord's division was substituted for King's division for this movement, and McCall's division was ordered to demonstrate south of the Rappahannock. May 29, 1862, Bayard's Cavalry Brigade was ordered to Front Royal from Catlett's Station. It then joined Fremont's command near Strasburg and moved south with it in the pursuit of Jackson.

Shields' Division arrived at Front Royal May 30, 1862, and that day Ord's division was at Piedmont. Ord, who was ill, turned over the division to Ricketts, who moved it to Front Royal, but Ord resumed command June 3, 1862. Three days later, however, he left for Washington, and Ricketts again assumed command of the division. During Jackson's retreat up the valley, Shields' Division moved southward in the Luray Valley in an attempt to intercept his column. On the morning of June 9, 1862, Jackson attacked the brigades of Carroll and Tyler at the Lewis plantation, northeast of Port Republic, and drove them back down the Luray Valley. For details of the operations in the Shenendoah Valley in May and June of 1862, see Shenandoah Valley Campaign (Jackson), 1862.

June 8, 1862, when Jackson's threat in the lower Shenandoah Valley had apparently ended, McDowell was again ordered to move with his available force toward Richmond. King's division, which was at Fredericksburg, was ordered to start at once. Then, when Fremont and Shields became engaged at Cross Keys and Port Republic June 8–9, 1862, King's movement was delayed, and he was instructed to be prepared to march to Front Royal if needed. The fighting was not renewed, however, and June 17, 1862, Jackson began to leave the valley on his way to join Lee near Richmond. The divisions of Shields and Ricketts, and Bayard's Cavalry Brigade, then moved back into the Department of the Rappahannock at Manassas and Bristoe Station, and King's division returned to Fredericksburg. Although McDowell's command was thus concentrated, it was not, for several reasons, sent to join McClellan's army in front of Richmond.

In the early part of June 1862, McCall's division was ordered to the Peninsula to reinforce the Army of the Potomac. It arrived there June 12–13, 1862, and June 18, 1862, it was attached to Fitz John Porter's Fifth Provisional Corps as Third Division.

A Reserve Corps was constituted June 18, 1862, to consist of troops in and around Washington. Samuel D. Sturgis was assigned command, and he was directed to report to James S. Wadsworth, commander of the Military District of Washington. The troops in the district at the end of May 1862 consisted of Amiel W. Whipple's Brigade; Samuel D. Sturgis' Brigade; William E. Doster's Provost Guard; and unbrigaded infantry, cavalry, and artillery. The Reserve Corps was not fully organized, and June 26, 1862, it was merged into John Pope's Army of Virginia.

When the Army of Virginia was organized, the troops of the Department of the Rappahannock were transferred as follows:

Shields' Division was broken up, and Kimball's brigade was sent to the Army of the Potomac on the Peninsula, and about July 6, 1862, it was attached to Sixth Corps. Then, on July 15, 1862, it was transferred to Second Corps as Kimball's Independent Brigade. Ferry's brigade was also sent to the Army of the Potomac, and July 5, 1862, it was designated as Third Brigade, Second Division, Fourth Corps. Tyler's brigade was assigned temporarily to Sturgis' command at Alexandria June 28, 1862. Five days later it was ordered to Banks' Second Corps, Army of Virginia, and August 2, 1862, it was consolidated with Geary's Second Brigade, First Division, and this command was designated as First Brigade, Second Division, with Geary assigned command. Carroll's brigade was also assigned temporarily to Sturgis' command at Alexandria June 28, 1862. Then, on July 23, 1862, it was assigned to McDowell's Third Corps, Army of Virginia as Fourth Brigade, Second Division.

Ricketts' Division was redesignated as Second Division, Third Corps, Army of Virginia. First brigade became Second Brigade, Second Division; Second Brigade became First Brigade, Second Division; and Third Brigade became Third Brigade, Second Division.

King's Division was redesignated as First Division, Third Corps. First Brigade became First Brigade, First Division; Second Brigade became Third Brigade, First Division; and Third Brigade became Fourth Brigade, First Division. Doubleday's unassigned brigade was designated as Second Brigade, First Division.

Bayard's Cavalry Brigade was transferred as Cavalry Brigade, Third Corps.

DEPARTMENT OF THE SHENANDOAH
JULY 19, 1861–AUGUST 17, 1861

July 19, 1861, Nathaniel P. Banks was ordered to Harper's Ferry to relieve Robert Patterson in command of the Army of the Department of Pennsylvania (also called Army of the Shenandoah). For information about this army, see Department of Pennsylvania, April 27, 1861–August 24, 1861. Banks' new command was designated as the Department of the Shenandoah, and it was defined as consisting of that part of the valley of Virginia occupied by Patterson's army. This territory was in the lower Shenandoah Valley, and was taken from the Department of the East. Banks assumed command July 25, 1861, with headquarters in the field.

The department was then redefined as consisting of the valley of Virginia, the counties of Washington and Allegany in Maryland, and such other parts of Virginia as might be covered by Banks' army in its operations.

Upon assuming command, Banks announced the organization of the troops in his department as follows: First Brigade, George H. Thomas; Second Brigade, John J. Abercrombie; and Third Brigade, Charles P. Stone. Stone was relieved from duty in the Department of the Shenandoah August 8, 1861, and Charles S. Hamilton was assigned command of Third Brigade. John W. Stiles was in temporary command of the brigade for a short time after Stone's departure. Thomas' First Brigade was organized from the 2nd United States Cavalry and the 2nd Rhode Island Battery of First Brigade, First Division of Patterson's army; the 2nd Pennsylvania Regiment of Second Brigade, First Division of Patterson's army; 19th New York and 28th New York of 8th Brigade, Third Division of Patterson's army; and two new regiments. Abercrombie's Second Brigade was organized from the 4th Connecticut and 2nd Massachusetts of Sixth Brigade, Second Division of Patterson's army, and three new regiments. Stone's Third Brigade was organized from 1st New Hampshire and 83rd New York (9th New York State Militia) of 7th Brigade, Third Division of Patterson's army, and one new regiment.

Most of the troops of Patterson's original command consisted of three-month regiments. These were mustered out in July 1861 and were replaced by new regiments.

Banks remained at Harper's Ferry until July 28, 1861, and then, concerned about his vulnerable position south of the Potomac, moved with most of his command across the river to Pleasant Valley near Sandy Hook. He continued to occupy Harper's Ferry and various posts along the Potomac. August 6, 1861, Banks moved his supply base to Frederick, Maryland, and August 15, 1861 marched with his main force toward a point east of the Monocacy River between Frederick and the Potomac. He left one regiment at each of the following posts: Harper's Ferry, Sharpsburg, Berlin (present-day Brunswick), and Point of Rocks. With the rest of his command, Banks arrived at Hyattstown, Maryland August 21, 1861.

The Department of the Shenandoah was discontinued August 17, 1861, when it was merged into the newly created Department of the Potomac. The troops in the department then with Banks became Banks' Division, Army of the Potomac. For further information about this command, see Army of the Potomac, Banks' Division.

DEPARTMENT OF THE SHENANDOAH
APRIL 4, 1862–JUNE 26, 1862

In March 1862, Thomas J. (Stonewall) Jackson marched down the Shenandoah Valley with his army of the Confederate Valley District and caused considerable concern among the authorities in Washington. Jackson was defeated at Kernstown, Virginia by James Shields' division of Nathaniel P. Banks' Fifth Corps, Army of the Potomac, but because of fear for the safety of the capital, the president created two new departments April 4, 1862. These were the Department of the Shenandoah and the Department of the Rappahannock (see).

The Department of the Shenandoah was defined as consisting of that part of the states of Maryland and Virginia lying west of the Blue Ridge Mountains and east of the eastern boundary of the Mountain Department, which was created March 11, 1862. The latter boundary began, at the north, on Flintstone Creek in Maryland, and then ran southward along South Branch Mountain, Town Hill Mountain, Branch Mountain (or Big Ridge), the North or Shenandoah Mountain, Purgatory Mountain, and the Blue Ridge and Allegheny mountains to the border of North Carolina. This territory was taken from the Department of the Potomac.

Nathaniel P. Banks assumed command of the department April 12, 1862 (assigned April 4, 1862), and at that time his headquarters was at Woodstock, Virginia. Banks reported directly to, and received orders from, the War Department, because George B. McClellan had been relieved from command of the armies of the United States March 11, 1862, in anticipation of his taking the field with the Army of the Potomac on the Peninsula.

The limits of the departments of the Shenandoah and the Rappahannock and the Mountain Department, as originally defined, were not always strictly adhered to. During Jackson's Shenandoah Valley Campaign of 1862, some army movements west of the Blue Ridge Mountains made it necessary to disregard departmental boundaries, and during most of the period June 1–8, 1862, troops of all three departments operated in the Luray and Shenandoah valleys.

June 8, 1862, as Jackson's Valley Campaign was drawing to a close, the boundaries of the Department of the Shenandoah were changed. Irvin McDowell was ordered to concentrate his forces of the Department of the Rappahannock (see) in the direction of Fredericksburg in preparation for a movement southward toward Richmond to cooperate with McClellan, who was then threatening the city. At the same time Banks was directed to move the main part of his force of the Department of the Shenandoah to Front Royal, and occupy the positions held by John W. Geary's Independent Brigade along the Manassas Gap Railroad, as far east as Manassas Junction. Because McDowell was to withdraw his troops from the country east of the Blue Ridge Mountains as far as Bristoe, Manassas, and Fredericksburg, and also because the railroad east of the Blue Ridge ran through territory of the Department of the Rappahannock, the eastern boundary of the Department of the Shenandoah was moved eastward to include the Piedmont district and the Bull Run range of mountains. This territory was thus transferred from the Department of the Rappahannock to the Department of the Shenandoah.

At the same time, June 8, 1862, John C. Fremont's army of the Mountain Department was in the Shenandoah Valley, and, because of this, the western boundary of the Department of the Shenandoah was moved eastward so as to leave Fremont in the Mountain Department, which he then commanded. The new western boundary of the Department of the Shenandoah, and the new eastern boundary of the Mountain Department, then ran south from Williamsport, Maryland, along the road through Martinsburg, Virginia, Winchester, Strasburg, and Harrisonburg to Staunton (Staunton was included in the Mountain Department), and from there it continued southward in the same direction to the Blue Ridge Mountains, along which it ran to the southern border of Virginia. The territory west of this line and east of the original eastern boundary of the Mountain Department was transferred from the Department of the Shenandoah to the Mountain Department.

The Department of the Shenandoah was discontinued June 26, 1862, when it was merged into John Pope's newly created Army of Virginia as Second Corps.

TROOPS AND OPERATIONS IN THE DEPARTMENT OF THE SHENANDOAH

The Department of the Shenandoah was organized April 12, 1862 from Nathaniel P. Banks' Fifth Corps, Army of the Potomac (see Fifth Corps, Army of the Potomac [Banks]), which at that time was organized as follows:

FIFTH CORPS, Nathaniel P. Banks

First Division, Alpheus S. Williams
    First Brigade, Dudley Donnelly
    Second Brigade, John J. Abercrombie
    Third Brigade, George H. Gordon
    Artillery
        Battery F, 4th United States Artillery, Clermont L. Best
        Battery F, Pennsylvania Light Artillery, Robert B. Hampton
        Battery M, 1st New York Light Artillery, George W. Cothran
        Battery E, Pennsylvania Light Artillery, Joseph M. Knap

Second Division, James Shields
    First Brigade, Nathan Kimball
    Second Brigade, Jeremiah C. Sullivan
    Third Brigade, Erastus B. Tyler
    Artillery
        Battery A, 1st West Virginia Light Artillery, John Jenks
        Battery B, 1st West Virginia Light Artillery, John V. Keeper
        Battery H, 1st Ohio Light Artillery, James F. Huntington
        Battery L, 1st Ohio Light Artillery, Lucius N. Robinson
        Battery E, 4th United States Artillery, Joseph C. Clark

Geary's Independent (or Detached) Brigade, John W. Geary

April 6, 1862, Shields' division and Gordon's brigade of Williams' division were near Edenburg; Donnelly's brigade of Williams' division was at the Narrow Passage; and Abercrombie's brigade was at Warrenton Junction. Geary's brigade was detached and was guarding the Manassas Gap Railroad between Strasburg and Manassas.

Banks' command was soon reduced in numbers by the transfer of troops to McDowell's Department of the Rappahannock. April 30, 1862, George L. Hartsuff was assigned command of Abercrombie's brigade, and he moved with it to Catlett's Station, where he came under McDowell's orders May 1, 1862. That day, May 1, 1862, Shields' division was also ordered to the Department of the Rappahannock, but he did not move until Banks reached Strasburg with the rest of his command. Finally, May 12, 1862, Shields left New Market in the Shenandoah Valley for Fredericksburg. May 6, 1862, Geary's brigade was also transferred to the Department of the Rappahannock. For further information about Shields' division and Abercrombie's and Geary's brigades, see Department of the Rappahannock. In mid-May 1862, Banks' command consisted only of Williams' division of two brigades and a cavalry brigade commanded by John P. Hatch. Donnelly commanded Williams' First Brigade and Gordon his Third Brigade.

After Jackson's defeat at Kernstown, Virginia March 23, 1862, his army retreated up the Shenandoah Valley to Harrisonburg, and then moved to the valley of Elk Run in Swift Run Gap. Jackson remained there quietly until April 28, 1862, and then, reinforced by the division of Richard S. Ewell, he again took the offensive by advancing against Robert H. Milroy's brigade of John C. Fremont's Mountain Department at McDowell, Virginia. Jackson was engaged at McDowell with Milroy's brigade and Robert C. Schenck's brigade of the Mountain Department, both under Schenck, and when the latter retreated, Jackson pursued as far as Franklin before returning to the valley.

Suddenly, on May 23, 1862, Jackson appeared before Front Royal, and after a vigorous attack captured the town. At that time Banks' command was at Strasburg, about ten miles west of Front Royal, and the next day he marched on the Valley Pike through Middletown and Newtown to Winchester. Banks was strongly attacked there May 25, 1862 and was driven from the town, and his troops did not stop until they had crossed the Potomac River at Williamsport, Maryland. Jackson followed to the Potomac, and to within a few miles of Harper's Ferry, and he remained there until May 30, 1862.

As Jackson advanced into the lower Shenandoah Valley, the administration took prompt measures to secure Harper's Ferry, which was then held only by a few troops of Dixon S. Miles' Railroad Brigade of the Middle Department (see). May 24, 1862, Rufus Saxton was ordered to Harper's Ferry with two regiments from Washington, and with instructions to assume command of the post. Saxton arrived the next day and assumed command May 26, 1862. Also on May 24, 1862, James Cooper was ordered to Harper's Ferry with three regiments and a battery from Baltimore, and when he arrived there he was assigned command of a brigade that was formed from his regiments and two regiments from Washington. John P. Slough, recently arrived in Washington from Colorado, was assigned command of a brigade formed from two regiments from Washington, one regiment from the Railroad Brigade, one regiment from the Middle Department, and one new regiment from New York.

May 25, 1862, when the War Department learned of Banks' defeat in the Shenandoah Valley, Edwin M. Stanton ordered McDowell at Falmouth, Virginia to send the divisions of James Shields and Edward O. C. Ord from the Department of the Rappahannock to Front Royal, and he also ordered Fremont to move with his army of the Mountain Department toward Strasburg. These two columns were to attempt to cut off Jackson's expected retreat up the valley. Jackson began to withdraw from the Potomac May 30, 1862, and that day moved with his main force through Winchester to Strasburg. Jackson passed through Strasburg before Shields and Fremont could join and stop him, and he then continued on up the valley to Cross Keys, where he arrived June 5, 1862. Jackson left Ewell's division at Cross Keys, and moved on with his division to Port Republic.

Fremont followed Jackson along the South Branch of the Shenandoah River to Cross Keys, and he was engaged there with Ewell June 8, 1862. Shields' division of the Department of the Rappahannock moved south along the Luray Valley in an effort to intercept Jackson's column. Samuel S. Carroll's and Erastus B. Tyler's brigades advanced to the Lewis plantation near Port Republic, and were defeated there by Jackson's division June 9, 1862. Shields' brigades retreated to Luray, and then the division moved back to Front Royal. Shields' and Ord's divisions were withdrawn from Front Royal to the Bristoe-Manassas area in the latter part of June 1862, but Fremont remained in the Shenandoah Valley.

June 1, 1862, Franz Sigel was assigned command of the forces at Harper's Ferry, which were then assigned to the Department of the Shenandoah. Sigel organized his troops into a division, to be known as Sigel's Division, which consisted of a First Brigade under Cooper and a Second Brigade under Slough. June 4, 1862, Banks returned to Winchester from Williamsport, and that day Sigel advanced with his command toward the same place. By June 8, 1862, the same day that Fremont was engaged with Ewell at Cross Keys, the remains of Banks' division and Slough's brigade were at Winchester, and Cooper's brigade was at Kernstown.

The engagement at Port Republic June 9, 1862 ended the fighting in the campaign, and June 17, 1862, Jackson began leaving the valley to join Lee at Richmond. For details of the organization and movements of the troops in the Department of the Shenandoah during this period, see Shenandoah Valley Campaign (Jackson), 1862. In mid-June 1862, Banks' troops in the Department of the Shenandoah were organized as follows:

Sigel's Division, Franz Sigel
  First Brigade, James Cooper
  Second Brigade, John P. Slough

Note. John A. Reynolds' Battery L, 1st New York Light Artillery was attached to Cooper's brigade; and Lorenzo Crounse's Battery K, 1st New York Light Artillery was attached to Slough's brigade.

Williams' Division, Alpheus S. Williams
  First Brigade, Samuel L. Crawford
  Third Brigade, George S. Greene
  Artillery
    Battery M, 1st New York Light Artillery, George W. Cothran
    Battery F, Pennsylvania Light Artillery, Robert B. Hampton
    Battery F, 4th United States Artillery, Clermont L. Best

Note. Crawford relieved Donnelly and Greene relieved Gordon May 27, 1862. Gordon was ordered to relieve Greene in command of Third Brigade June 18, 1862.

The Department of the Shenandoah was merged into John Pope's Army of Virginia June 26, 1862 as Second Corps. The troops were reassigned as follows: First Brigade of Williams' Division was designated as First Brigade, First Division, Second Corps; Third Brigade of Williams' Division was designated as Third Brigade, First Division; First Brigade of Sigel's Division was designated as First Brigade, Second Division, Second Corps; and Second Brigade of Sigel's Division was designated as Second Brigade, Second Division. Hatch's cavalry was also assigned to Second Corps. June 22, 1862, Geary's Independent Brigade was transferred from the Department of the Rappahannock to the Department of the Shenandoah, and June 26, 1862, it was assigned to Banks' Second Corps, Army of Virginia.

DEPARTMENT OF THE SOUTH

Because of the complexity of the organization of the Department of the South and the changes in its organization during the period of its existence from 1862 to 1865, it seems desirable to give a brief general summary of the organization of the department, and then follow with a more detailed history arranged in four distinct periods. These are:

Part I.   South Carolina Expedition (Thomas W. Sherman), November 3, 1861–March 31, 1862
Part II.   Department of the South, March 31, 1862–September 3, 1862
Part III. Department of the South, Tenth Corps, September 3, 1862–April 25, 1864
Part IV. Department of the South, April 25, 1864–June 27, 1865

The department was created by an order dated March 15, 1862, to consist of the states of South Carolina, Georgia, and Florida, and also the forces under the command of Thomas W. Sherman that were on the coast of South Carolina. By this order, the Department of Florida and the Department of Key West were merged into the Department of the South. David Hunter was assigned command, with headquarters at Hilton Head, and he assumed command March 31, 1862. Although the department was defined as consisting of the above-mentioned states, in fact, until 1865, it consisted only of a narrow strip of seacoast that was held by United States forces in these states.

The major events producing changes in the boundaries and organization of the department were as follows:

March 31, 1862, Hunter assumed command of the department and announced the organization of three districts— the Northern District, the Southern District, and the Western District. These districts were discontinued June 21, 1862. For details, see Part II, Department of the South.

August 8, 1862, the former District of West Florida was transferred to the Department of the Gulf.

September 3, 1862, Tenth Corps was created to consist of the troops in the Department of the South.

September 5, 1862, John M. Brannan assumed command of the Department of the South by right of seniority.

September 17, 1862, Ormsby M. Mitchell was assigned command of the department.

October 16, 1862, a part of northern Georgia was transferred to the Department of the Cumberland.

October 27, 1862, John M. Brannan again assumed command of the department, when Mitchell became ill with yellow fever. Mitchell died in Beaufort October 30, 1862.

Hunter resumed command of the department January 20, 1863.

March 16, 1863, the department was reduced in size when Key West and the Tortugas Islands were transferred to the Department of the Gulf.

June 12, 1863, Quincy A. Gillmore assumed command of the department (assigned June 3, 1863), with headquarters at Hilton Head.

In April 1864, Tenth Corps was largely transferred to the Department of Virginia and North Carolina, and Tenth Corps was discontinued in the Department of the South. This was followed by a reorganization of the department April 25, 1865.

May 1, 1864, John P. Hatch was assigned temporary command of the Department of the South, and he was relieved by John G. Foster May 26, 1864 (assigned May 5, 1864).

January 12, 1865, the limits of the department were extended to include the state of North Carolina, which was transferred from the Department of Virginia and North

Carolina. January 16, 1864, the state of North Carolina was designated as the District of North Carolina, Department of the South.

January 12, 1865, the Department of the South was placed under the orders and control of William T. Sherman, commander of the Military Division of the Mississippi.

January 21, 1865, Savannah, Georgia was attached to the Department of the South as the District of Savannah. For details, see Part IV, Department of the South, Districts in the Department of the South.

January 31, 1865, the state of North Carolina was transferred from the Department of the South to the Department of North Carolina.

February 9, 1865, Quincy A. Gillmore was assigned command of the Department of the South, relieving Foster. On April 16, 1865, Edward O. C. Ord was ordered to relieve Gillmore, but this order was revoked April 19, 1865.

May 17, 1865, the state of Florida was transferred to the Department of the Gulf.

In the reorganization of the military divisions and departments of the army June 27, 1865, the Department of the South was broken up and its former territory was reassigned as follows: the state of Florida was constituted as the Department of Florida, which was assigned to the Military Division of the Gulf; the state of Georgia was constituted as the Department of Georgia, which was assigned to the Military Division of the Tennessee; and the state of South Carolina was constituted as the Department of South Carolina, which was assigned to the Military Division of the Atlantic.

Headquarters Department of the South was at Hilton Head, South Carolina during most of the war. It was moved to Folly Island July 8, 1863, at the beginning of Federal operations on Charleston Harbor, and it was then transferred to Morris Island July 15, 1863. Headquarters was again established on Folly Island September 25, 1863, and it remained there until late December 1863, when it was moved back to Hilton Head.

COMMANDERS OF THE DEPARTMENT OF THE SOUTH

Thomas W. Sherman March 15, 1862 to March 31, 1862
David Hunter March 31, 1862 to September 5, 1862

John M. Brannan September 5, 1862 to September 17, 1862
Ormsby M. Mitchell September 17, 1862 to October 27, 1862
John M. Brannan October 27, 1862 to January 20, 1863
David Hunter January 20, 1863 to June 12, 1863
Quincy A. Gillmore June 12, 1863 to May 1, 1864
John P. Hatch May 1, 1864 to May 26, 1864
John G. Foster May 26, 1864 to February 9, 1865
Quincy A. Gillmore February 9, 1865 to June 27, 1865

Note 1. During the period September 3, 1862–April 1864, the commander of the department was also commander of Tenth Corps.
Note 2. Gillmore was still in command of the Department of the South July 5, 1865, indicating that some time elapsed before the reorganization of June 27, 1865 was complete.

PART I.
SOUTH CAROLINA EXPEDITION (THOMAS W. SHERMAN) NOVEMBER 3, 1861–MARCH 31, 1862

August 2, 1861, Thomas W. Sherman was ordered to New York to organize, in cooperation with Samuel F. Du Pont of the navy, an expedition to the southern Atlantic coast. The object of this expedition was to seize important harbors on the coast, and to hold them for the protection of the blockading squadron, and also to create a diversion for the armies in the field. The troops, numbering about 12,000 men, were to be supplied by the New England states, and were to assemble at Hempstead, Long Island (Camp Winfield Scott).

September 19, 1861, the Expeditionary Corps was organized into three brigades as follows: Egbert L. Viele's First Brigade; Isaac I. Stevens' Second Brigade; and Horatio G. Wright's Third Brigade. Early in October 1861, the three brigades were transferred to Annapolis, Maryland, and from there they moved to Hampton Roads, Virginia October 21, 1861. The expedition was delayed there by bad weather, but it sailed for Port Royal Sound, South Carolina October 29, 1861. After weathering a severe storm en route, the fleet arrived off Hilton Head November 3, 1861.

Fort Beauregard on Bay Point, and Fort Walker on Hilton Head Island, Port Royal Sound were captured by the navy November 7, 1861, and the army then went ashore on Hilton Head Island and began preparations to secure the region. Fort Beauregard was renamed Fort Seward, and Fort Walker was renamed Fort Welles.

The organization of Sherman's Expeditionary Corps October 28, 1861, was as follows:

EXPEDITIONARY CORPS, Thomas W. Sherman

First Brigade
    8th Maine, Lee Strickland
    3rd New Hampshire, Enoch Q. Fellows
    46th New York, Rudolph Rosa
    47th New York, Henry Moore
    48th New York, James H. Perry

Second Brigade, Isaac I. Stevens
    8th Michigan, William M. Fenton
    79th New York, William H. Noble
    50th Pennsylvania, Benjamin C. Christ
    100th Pennsylvania, Daniel Leasure

Third Brigade, Horatio G. Wright
    6th Connecticut, John L. Chatfield
    7th Connecticut, Alfred H. Terry
    9th Maine, Rishworth Rich
    4th New Hampshire, Thomas J. Whipple

Not brigaded
    1st New York Engineers, Edward W. Serrell
    3rd Rhode Island, Nathaniel W. Brown
    Battery E, 3rd United States Artillery, John Hamilton

The following regiments were a part of Sherman's command on Hilton Head Island in February 1862, but they were not organized into brigades: William Montieth's 28th Massachusetts; Thomas Welsh's 45th Pennsylvania; John M. Power's 76th Pennsylvania; and Robert Williams' 1st Massachusetts Cavalry.

Stevens, with his Second Brigade, Expeditionary Corps, occupied Beaufort, South Carolina and Port Royal Island, which was evacuated by Southern forces November 8, 1861. Stevens' command was known as the District of Beaufort (and also Port Royal District).

Union forces occupied Saint Helena Sound by mid-November 1861, and Rudolph Rosa's 46th New York Regiment moved onto Tybee Island near Savannah, Georgia early in December 1861. By mid-December 1861, Sherman's command held the southern Atlantic coast from South Edisto Island to Tybee Island, and in January 1862, there were 600 Union troops on Saint Helena Island, 3,000 on Port Royal Island, 200 at Fort Seward, 1,400 on Tybee Island, and 9,500 on Hilton Head Island.

In January 1862, operations were begun under the direction of Captain Quincy A. Gillmore, chief engineer of the Expeditionary Corps, for the capture of Fort Pulaski, which was on Cockspur Island in the Savannah River. Early in the month, Viele's First Brigade was sent to Daufuskie Island as a part of these operations. For details, see below, Capture of Fort Pulaski.

On February 1, 1862, Wright embarked at Hilton Head with his Third Brigade for an expedition to the Florida coast. He reached Wassaw Sound February 2, 1862, and then waited there until the end of the month for the navy to cooperate in this movement. Then, on February 28, 1862, the combined land and naval force sailed from Wassaw Sound for the coast of Florida. Wright occupied Saint Andrews Sound, Florida March 2, 1862, and Fernandina, Florida three days later. He established his headquarters at Fernandina. Wright then continued on and occupied Saint Augustine March 8, 1862, and Jacksonville March 12, 1862. Meantime, on February 11, 1862, Henry Moore occupied Edisto Island with his 47th New York Infantry. Thus, by mid-March 1862, Union forces were in possession of the entire southern Atlantic coast from Edisto Island, South Carolina to Saint Augustine, Florida.

Capture of Fort Pulaski, Georgia, December 1861–April 1862. Savannah, Georgia on the Savannah River was one of the more important posts on the east coast of the Confederacy and was protected from an approach by water by Fort Pulaski, which was a strong masonry fort on Cockspur Island in the Savannah River, below the city.

Shortly after landing his Expeditionary Corps on Hilton Head Island, Thomas W. Sherman initiated steps for the capture of the fort. November 29, 1861, he directed Quincy A. Gillmore, chief engineer on his staff, to make an examination of the fort and also Tybee Island, which was just across the river to the south. When he had completed his examination, Gillmore recommended the immediate occupation of Tybee Island, and early in December 1861, Rudolph Rosa landed on the island with his 46th New York Regiment.

By mid-January 1862, Gillmore began operations

for investing Fort Pulaski by erecting batteries above the fort on the Savannah River. Viele's First Brigade of the Expeditionary Corps, with the cooperation of naval forces under John Rogers, landed on Daufuskie Island in January 1862, and a land force under Wright, together with a naval force under Charles H. Davis, moved up from the south side of the Savannah River. The river was closed to traffic February 11, 1862, when a battery was established on Venus Point, James Island, and another battery was erected on Bird Island, opposite Venus Point.

February 19, 1862, Gillmore was ordered to Tybee Island to organize the defenses there, and to begin preparations for the bombardment of Fort Pulaski. The first vessel with ordnance and stores arrived at Tybee Island February 21, 1862, and from that time until April 9, 1862, all troops on the island were engaged in working on the batteries that were to open fire on the fort. The troops thus employed consisted of Alfred H. Terry's 7th Connecticut, Rosa's 46th New York, Viele's First Brigade, Expeditionary Corps, three companies of volunteer engineers, and two companies of the 3rd Rhode Island Regiment. Wright's Third Brigade was present, but it sailed for Florida February 28, 1862.

The bombardment of Fort Pulaski began April 10, 1862, and it surrendered the next day. From that time until the end of the war, the fort remained as a Federal post in the Department of the South.

Thomas W. Sherman was in command of the troops in South Carolina at the beginning of operations against Fort Pulaski, but when David Hunter assumed command of the newly created Department of the South March 31, 1862, he designated Sherman's former command as the Northern District, Department of the South. The same order that created the Northern District also relieved Sherman from command and assigned Henry W. Benham in his place. At the time of the surrender of the fort, the forces on Tybee Island were a part of Benham's Northern District of Hunter's Department of the South.

PART II.
DEPARTMENT OF THE SOUTH
MARCH 31, 1862–SEPTEMBER 3, 1862

The Department of the South was constituted March 15, 1862, to consist of the states of South Carolina, Georgia, and Florida, and the forces belonging to Thomas W. Sherman's Expeditionary Corps. David Hunter assumed command of the department March 31, 1862, with headquarters at Hilton Head. Because the troops in the department, as then defined, were widely separated in three areas, Hunter divided the department March 31, 1862, into three districts as follows:

Northern District. The Northern District consisted of the states of South Carolina and Georgia, and that part of Florida lying north and east of a line extending to the northwest from Cape Canaveral to the Gulf Coast, just north of Cedar Keys and its dependencies, and from that point north to the Georgia state line. The district constituted the territory held by the troops of Thomas W. Sherman's Expeditionary Corps (South Carolina Expedition). Henry W. Benham was assigned command, with headquarters at Hilton Head.

At the time of its organization, the posts of the Northern District were as follows:

Hilton Head, South Carolina
Beaufort, South Carolina, Isaac I. Stevens

Note. Stevens' command was formerly Second Brigade, Expeditionary Corps.

Savannah River, Egbert L. Viele
  Daufuskie Island
  Bird Island, South Carolina
  Jones' Island, South Carolina

Note. Viele's command was formerly First Brigade, Expeditionary Corps.

Fernandina, Florida, Horatio G. Wright

Note. Wright's command was formerly Third Brigade, Expeditionary Corps. At the end of April 1862, Wright occupied Otter Island, South Carolina and the area of the North Edisto River.

Tybee Island, Quincy A. Gillmore
Jacksonville, Florida, Henry R. Guss

Note. Jacksonville was evacuated by United States forces April 9, 1862.

Saint Augustine, Florida, Louis Bell
Mouth of Saint John's River
Bay Point, South Carolina

In April 1862, Benham organized the troops of his command as First Division, Northern District, Department of the South, as follows:

First Division, Northern District, Henry W. Benham
   First Brigade, Alfred H. Terry
   Second Brigade, Isaac I. Stevens
   Third Brigade, Horatio G. Wright

Note 1. First Brigade was organized from the United States Forces at Hilton Head, Cockspur Island, Tybee Island, Daufuskie Island, and Fort Pulaski.
Note 2. Second Brigade was organized from Second Brigade, Expeditionary Corps.
Note 3. Third Brigade was organized from Third Brigade, Expeditionary Corps.

In May 1862, a force consisting of two divisions was organized in the Northern District for an expedition against Charleston, South Carolina. Hunter commanded the expedition, and Benham was in immediate command of the two divisions, which in turn were commanded by Horatio G. Wright and Isaac I. Stevens. Hunter's force moved to James Island early in June 1862, but an attempt by Benham to carry the enemy works at Secessionville June 16, 1862 ended in failure, and no further offensive operations were undertaken at that time. Benham was relieved from command of the Northern District June 21, 1862, and the Federal troops were evacuated from James Island June 28, 1862–July 7, 1862. For details of Hunter's Expedition, see below, Engagement at Secessionville, South Carolina.

The Northern District was discontinued June 21, 1862.

Western District. The Western District was defined March 31, 1862 as consisting of that part of Florida lying west of a line running north from a point on the Gulf Coast just north of Cedar Keys, Florida to the Georgia state line. Lewis G. Arnold was assigned command, with headquarters at Fort Pickens, Florida. Until May 12, 1862, the troops in the Western District were stationed on Santa Rosa Island at Fort Pickens, Camp Seward, and Camp Lincoln. On that date, Confederate forces evacuated Pensacola, Florida, and Union troops occupied Pensacola and Fort Barrancas on the mainland.

The district was discontinued June 21, 1862, and Arnold's command was designated as Fort Pickens and Pensacola, or simply as Pensacola Harbor. The former district was transferred to the Department of the Gulf August 8, 1862 as the District of Fort Pickens and Pensacola.

Southern District. The Southern District was constituted March 31, 1862 to consist of all of the state of Florida south of a line extending to the northwest from Cape Canaveral to the Gulf Coast at a point just north of Cedar Keys and its dependencies. John M. Brannan was assigned command, with headquarters at Key West. The troops in the district were at Key West, Key West Barracks, Fort Taylor, and Fort Jefferson (Tortugas).

The Southern District was discontinued June 21, 1862, and Brannan's command was designated simply as Key West, Florida. As Key West and Tortugas, the former Southern District was transferred to the Department of the Gulf March 16, 1863.

When the district organization of the Department of the South was discontinued June 21, 1862, all returns from the various posts were made directly to Headquarters Department of the South.

Engagement at Secessionville, South Carolina, June 16, 1862. Shortly after Hunter assumed command of the Department of the South, he formulated a plan for the capture of Charleston, South Carolina. This called for the transfer of two infantry divisions from his command to James Island, south of Charleston, and then an advance on the city. In April and May 1862, Hunter assembled his troops from the various posts of the department, and he then organized them into two divisions as follows:

NORTHERN DISTRICT, Henry W. Benham

First Division, Horatio G. Wright
   First Brigade, John L. Chatfield
   Second Brigade, Thomas Welsh

Second Division, Isaac I. Stevens
   First Brigade, William M. Fenton
   Second Brigade, Daniel Leasure
   Third Brigade, Robert Williams

Artillery, John Hamilton
   1st Battery, Connecticut Light Artillery, Alfred P. Rockwell
   Company E, 3rd United States Artillery, Dunbar R. Ransom

Note. When Stevens left to join the expedition against

Charleston, John M. Brannan assumed command at Beaufort, South Carolina.

Hunter accompanied the expedition to James Island, but Benham was in immediate command of the invasion force. Benham's troops were transported by way of Stono Inlet to James Island. Stevens' Second Division landed on the southwest shore of the island June 2, 1862, and camped about three miles southwest of the village of Secessionville. Hunter and Benham landed several days later with Wright's First Division, and camped at Grimballs' Plantation, about one and a half miles to the north and west of Stevens' division, and west of Secessionville. There was skirmishing along Benham's front June 2–12, 1862, and then Hunter returned to Hilton Head to seek reinforcements.

Despite specific orders not to do so, Benham decided to attack the fort near Secessionville, which was at the southern end of the Confederate lines on James Island. The enemy troops in front of Benham were under the command of Nathan G. Evans, commander of the Second Military District of South Carolina, and T. G. Lamar, colonel of the 1st South Carolina Artillery, was in command of the fort.

Stevens' division was selected as the assaulting column for the attack, and at 4:00 A.M. June 16, 1862, it advanced toward the enemy works, with William M. Fenton's First Brigade in front and Daniel Leasure's Second Brigade in support. When Stevens advanced, Benham also moved forward from Grimballs' with Wright's division and Robert Williams' Third Brigade of Stevens' division to support Stevens' two brigades, and to protect their left and rear. A force of about 2,500 men from the two divisions was left to guard the camps.

The front of Stevens' attack was limited to about 200 yards, because both flanks of the enemy line rested on swampy ground. Fenton was thus compelled to make a frontal attack, which he did with great determination against the enemy left; and, despite heavy losses he pressed close to the enemy works. Leasure's brigade was then brought up, and it joined in the attack. Union troops gained the parapet in some places, but after a short time both brigades were forced to fall back and re-form. Williams' brigade was then ordered up on the left, and the 3rd New Hampshire and a detachment of Edwin Metcalf's 3rd Rhode Island Heavy Artillery were advanced to keep down enemy fire while

Stevens made a second attack. In the meantime, however, about 2,000 enemy infantry had arrived to reinforce the troops already engaged, and Stevens' second attack was also repulsed. About 10:00 A.M., Benham ordered a withdrawal, and the troops returned to their camps. Wright's division was not engaged, but it was under artillery fire during the morning.

Because, as Hunter claimed, the assault of June 16, 1862 was carried out against his orders, Benham was relieved from command of the Northern District, Department of the South June 21, 1862, and ordered to New York.

Reorganization of the Department of the South, July 1862. In July 1862, after Hunter's unsuccessful attempt to capture Charleston by way of James Island, the Department of the South was completely reorganized. The divisions that had been organized by Hunter and moved to James Island were broken up and their regiments were reassigned. July 12, 1862, Stevens, former commander of Second Division, left Hilton Head with six regiments for Newport News to reinforce the Army of the Potomac, which was then on the Peninsula. Because a number of the regimental commanders later attained higher command in Ninth Corps, their names are given here: MacLelland Moore, 28th Massachusetts and William M. Fenton from First Brigade, Second Division; Rudolph Rosa, 46th New York, Addison Farnsworth, 79th New York, and Daniel Leasure, 100th Pennsylvania of Second Brigade, Second Division; and Benjamin C. Christ, 50th Pennsylvania from Beaufort, South Carolina. Thomas Welsh's 45th Pennsylvania of Second Brigade, First Division was also sent July 18, 1862.

On July 22, 1862, at Newport News, Ambrose E. Burnside assumed command of the newly constituted Ninth Corps, which was organized from Stevens' two brigades and other troops transferred from North Carolina. The former First Brigade, Second Division, Northern District became First Brigade, First Division, Ninth Corps; and the former Second Brigade, Second Division, Northern District became Second Brigade, First Division, Ninth Corps. Stevens was assigned command of First Division, Ninth Corps. For further information, see Ninth Corps.

In the reorganization, Wright's First Division and

Robert Williams' Third Brigade of Stevens' division were largely transferred to Hilton Head, where Williams assumed command. His force consisted of five infantry regiments, cavalry, artillery, and engineers. Wright did not accompany the troops of his former division, but resumed command of the United States Forces Edisto Island. July 20, 1862, troops were withdrawn from Fort Edisto, and July 29, 1862, Wright was relieved from duty in the Department of the South. August 19, 1862, Wright was assigned command of the Department of the Ohio.

At the end of July 1862, the troops in the Department of the South were organized as follows:

Beaufort, South Carolina, John M. Brannan
Hilton Head, South Carolina, Robert Williams
Pensacola Harbor, Florida, Lewis G. Arnold
Fort Pulaski, Georgia, Alfred H. Terry
Fernandina, Florida, Rishworth Rich
Fort Clinch, Florida, James E. Place
Fort Jefferson, Florida, Lewis W. Tinelli
Fort Old Town, Florida, Hiram Ferrand
Fort Taylor, Key West, Florida, Charles G. Clark
Key West Barracks, Florida, Joseph F. Morgan
Saint Augustine, Florida, Louis Bell

The limits of the Department of the South were reduced August 8, 1862, when the troops at Pensacola Harbor (the former Western District, Department of the South) were transferred to the Department of the Gulf.

Hunter left the department on leave August 22, 1862, and John M. Brannan assumed temporary command in his place. Tilghman H. Good succeeded Brannan in command at Beaufort. September 1, 1862, Ormsby M. Mitchell was assigned command of the Department of the South, and two days later Tenth Corps was constituted under Mitchell to consist of the troops in the Department of the South. See following section.

PART III.
DEPARTMENT OF THE SOUTH, TENTH CORPS
SEPTEMBER 3, 1862–APRIL 25, 1864

Tenth Corps was constituted September 3, 1862, to consist of all Union troops in the Department of the South. Ormsby M. Mitchell was assigned command, and he assumed command September 17, 1862, with headquarters at Hilton Head. At the end of October 1862, Tenth Corps was organized as follows:

Hilton Head and Fort Seward, Alfred H. Terry
Grahams' Plantation, John G. Thayer
Fernandina, Florida, Rishworth Rich
Fort Clinch, Florida, James E. Place
Beaufort, South Carolina, Tilghman H. Good
Fort Pulaski, Georgia, William B. Barton
Key West, Florida, Joseph S. Morgan
Old Town, Florida, Hiram Ferrand
Saint Augustine, Florida, Haldimand S. Putnam

In the spring of 1862, John M. Brannan, commander at Key West, Florida, was ordered to Beaufort, South Carolina with all the available men of his department to take part in David Hunter's campaign against Charleston, South Carolina in June of 1862. See Part II, Department of the South, above. Brannan did not return to Key West, and in October 1862 led two expeditions from Hilton Head Island. The first was to Saint John's Bluff, Florida, and the second was against the Charleston and Savannah Railroad.

Brannan's Expedition from Hilton Head, South Carolina to Saint John's Bluff, Florida, September 29, 1862–October 13, 1862. At the request of Samuel F. Du Pont, commander of the South Atlantic Blockading Squadron, an expedition was organized under the command of Brannan to capture the Confederate batteries at Saint John's Bluff, Florida, about seven miles above the mouth of the Saint John's River. Brannan left Hilton Head September 29, 1862, with a force consisting of Tilghman H. Good's 47th Pennsylvania, Joseph R. Hawley's 7th Connecticut, a section of 1st Connecticut Light Artillery, and a detachment of 1st Massachusetts Cavalry under Captain Case. Later, on October 4, 1862, he was joined by 300 men of Rishworth Rich's 9th Maine from Fernandina, Florida. The total number of men in Brannan's expedition was about 1,900. Brannan was accompanied on his movement to Florida by a fleet of gunboats commanded by Captain Charles Steedman of the navy.

Brannan's expedition arrived in the Saint John's River October 1, 1862, and that night it landed and took position on Mount Pleasant Creek. On October 3, 1862, Brannan found that the enemy had evacuated the works at Saint John's Bluff and, after removing the guns, he completely destroyed the fortifications. Brannan occupied Jacksonville October 5, 1862, and from there sent out an expedition to Lake Beresford October 6–9, 1862. His mission completed, he then returned to Hilton Head October 13, 1862.

Brannan's Expedition against the Charleston and Savannah Railroad near Pocotaligo, South Carolina, October 21–23, 1862. On the evening of October 21, 1862, Brannan left Hilton Head on an expedition to the Charleston and Savannah Railroad. His command consisted of John L. Chatfield's First Brigade and Alfred H. Terry's Second Brigade, and detachments of 48th New York Infantry, 3rd Rhode Island Artillery, 1st Massachusetts Cavalry, and a section of 1st United States Artillery and 3rd United States Artillery. The expedition moved up the Broad River to Pocotaligo Creek, and from there Brannan sent William B. Barton's 48th New York, a detachment of the 3rd Rhode Island Artillery, and a party of engineers to the Coosawhatchie River to destroy the railroad and railroad bridges. Then, on October 22, 1862, the infantry and artillery landed at Mackay's Point, at the junction of the Pocotaligo and Tuliffiny rivers, and marched toward Pocotaligo Bridge. First Brigade took the lead, and it was followed by Second Brigade. After marching about five and a half miles, Brannan encountered the enemy at Caston Plantation, and after a sharp engagement continued the advance. Chatfield was wounded in the action, and Tilghman H. Good assumed command of First Brigade. Brannan was again engaged about a mile farther out at Frampton Plantation, and then, after destroying the Pocotaligo Bridge, he returned to Mackay's Point, and finally arrived at Hilton Head October 23, 1862.

* * * * * * * * * *

October 27, 1862, Brannan was assigned to the temporary command of the Department of the South, Tenth Corps when Mitchell became ill. Mitchell died October 30, 1862, and Brannan continued in his assignment until David Hunter resumed command January 20, 1863.

November 18, 1862, Truman Seymour was ordered to the Department of the South, and was then assigned command of Port Royal Island. He assumed command December 26, 1862, and the designation of his command was changed from United States Forces at Beaufort, South Carolina to United States Forces at Port Royal Island, Tenth Corps. It was more commonly referred to as Port Royal Island.

The withdrawal of many regiments from the Department of the South in July 1862 to reinforce the Army of the Potomac on the Peninsula (see above, Part II, Department of the South) compelled Tenth Corps to limit its activities for the remainder of the year, and the troops that were left behind were occupied mainly in garrisoning the posts of the department.

At the end of December 1862, Brannan's Department of the South, Tenth Corps was organized as follows:

Saint Helena Island and Hilton Head, South Carolina, Alfred H. Terry
Port Royal Island, South Carolina, Truman Seymour
Fort Pulaski, Georgia, William B. Barton
Fernandina, Florida, Rishworth Rich
Old Town, Florida, Hiram Ferrand
Key West, Florida, Tilghman H. Good
Fort Clinch, Florida, James E. Place
Saint Augustine, Florida, Haldimand S. Putnam

Note 1. Hunter resumed command of the Department of the South January 20, 1863, and the next day Brannan was relieved from duty in the department, and was ordered to Washington, D.C. He was later assigned command of a division in the Army of the Cumberland.

Note 2. Terry's command at Hilton Head Island was designated as Second Brigade, Tenth Corps.

Note 3. On January 20, 1863, when Hunter resumed command of the department, Seymour was announced as chief of staff and chief of artillery on Hunter's staff. He remained on this duty until about April 27, 1863. February 9, 1863 Tilghman H. Good was assigned command of the post of Port Royal Island.

Note 4. January 12, 1863, Joseph R. Hawley was ordered to Fernandina, Florida with his 7th Connecticut Regiment to relieve the 9th Maine, commanded by Rishworth Rich.

Note 5. January 29, 1863, Joseph S. Morgan was ordered from Port Royal Island to Key West to relieve Good and his 47th Pennsylvania. February 23, 1863, Good was assigned command of Key West and Tortugas, and left Port Royal Island with his regiment that day. Key West and Tortugas was transferred to the Department of the Gulf March 16, 1863.

Activities in the Department of the South increased markedly during 1863. For some time the authorities in Washington had been considering the possibility of capturing Charleston, South Carolina, and early in the year they planned for a combined land and sea attack. For this purpose, in January 1863, they ordered that two divisions of Eighteenth Corps, Department of North Carolina be sent to Charleston Harbor under the command of John G. Foster, commander of the department. These troops embarked as scheduled, but when the naval preparations were delayed, they were landed on Saint Helena Island. They remained in camp there under the command of Henry M. Naglee. Naglee was relieved from duty in the Department of the South March 5, 1863, and on that date, Orris S. Ferry was assigned command of the United States Forces on Saint Helena Island.

At the end of March 1863, the Department of the South, Tenth Corps was organized as follows:

Saint Helena Island, South Carolina, Orris S. Ferry
    First Division, Detachment Eighteenth Corps, Orris S. Ferry
    Second Division, Detachment Eighteenth Corps, Charles A. Heckman
Hilton Head, South Carolina, Alfred H. Terry
    Detachment Tenth Corps, Alfred H. Terry
Port Royal Island (Beaufort), South Carolina, Rufus Saxton
    Detachment Tenth Corps, Rufus Saxton
Fort Pulaski, Georgia, William B. Barton
    48th New York Regiment, artillery, and engineers
Saint Augustine, Florida, Joseph C. Abbott
    Detachment 7th New Hampshire Regiment
Ossabaw Island, Georgia, David A. Allen
    47th New York Regiment, and engineers
Fernandina, Florida, Joseph R. Hawley
    7th Connecticut Regiment

Note 1. The troops of Eighteenth Corps on Saint Helena Island were organized into two divisions in March 1863.

Note 2. In early April 1863, Terry's command was organized into a division as a part of the force selected to support the naval attack on Fort Sumter. It was not engaged and was ordered back to Port Royal Harbor April 11, 1863.

Note 3. Rufus Saxton was assigned command of the post of Port Royal Island, relieving Tilghman H. Good, February 19, 1863.

Note 4. Joseph C. Abbott, lieutenant colonel of the 7th New Hampshire, was in command of five companies of the regiment at Saint Augustine, and the remaining companies were en route to Hilton Head under the command

of Colonel Haldimand S. Putnam (ordered March 26, 1863).

Note 5. An artillery brigade, Tenth Corps was formed March 28, 1863, under the command of Edwin Metcalf. This brigade consisted of 3rd Rhode Island Artillery and 3rd New York Artillery. It was discontinued April 11, 1863, and the batteries were reassigned.

Early in April 1863, the naval forces were finally ready to begin their attack on Fort Sumter, and the land forces moved up in support. The operations against Charleston Harbor, and the organizational changes in Tenth Corps resulting from these operations, are described in detail in the following section.

Operations at Charleston Harbor (Fort Sumter), South Carolina, April 1863–September 1863

For a number of reasons, an attack on Fort Sumter and Charleston, South Carolina had been seriously considered by the Navy Department since early in the war. In the first place, Charleston, South Carolina and Wilmington, North Carolina were the chief ports of entry on the Atlantic Coast for blockade runners, and further, Charleston was the second city in size in the South. In addition to these practical reasons, both the administration and the people of the North strongly desired the capture of Charleston, because of the role played by the people of the city and of the state of South Carolina in the secession movement.

A plan was approved in late 1862, which called for Rear Admiral Samuel Du Pont, commander of the South Atlantic Blockading Squadron, to reduce Fort Sumter by a naval attack, and then with his ships to pass up the channel to Charleston. It was then decided that the operations of the ironclads (monitors) would be greatly facilitated by the presence of a land force prepared to assist in the attack, and also to occupy the enemy works when reduced by the navy. To implement this plan, preparations were begun to assemble a suitable force in the Department of the South.

On December 24, 1862, the troops in the Department of North Carolina were organized into the Eighteenth Corps, under the command of John G. Foster. Foster was then instructed to organize a detachment of Eighteenth Corps, and with it move to Charleston Harbor in the Department of the South for the purpose of assisting the navy in its attack on Fort Sumter. Foster's command consisted of the following:

DETACHMENT EIGHTEENTH CORPS, John G. Foster

Second Division, Henry M. Naglee
  First Brigade, Charles A. Heckman
  Second Brigade, William W. H. Davis

Third Division, Orris S. Ferry
  First Brigade, Joshua B. Howell
  Second Brigade, Francis A. Osborn

Note. It appears from brigade returns that First Brigade and Second Brigade were consolidated by Hunter's order of March 26, 1863.

Foster's detachment of Eighteenth Corps sailed from North Carolina near the end of January 1863, and arrived at Beaufort, South Carolina February 1, 1863. It was then ordered to land on Saint Helena Island February 7, 1863. Foster had expected operations against Charleston to begin at once, but upon learning that the navy would not be ready for several weeks (actually, not until April 7, 1863), he turned over the command of Detachment Eighteenth Corps to Henry M. Naglee and returned to North Carolina February 10, 1863.

Hunter had resumed command of the Department of the South January 20, 1863, and on February 11, 1863, he assumed command of the Detachment Eighteenth Corps, which was then in his department, and assigned it as a part of Tenth Corps. A controversy ensued, because Naglee had understood that his detachment was to remain a distinct organization of Eighteenth Corps while in the Department of the South, and was subject to Hunter's orders only as a unit. February 23, 1863, Hunter's order was revoked, but Foster did not return to the Department of the South, and Naglee was relieved from duty there March 5, 1863.

In March 1863 (ordered February 28, 1863), the infantry of Detachment Eighteenth Corps on Saint Helena Island was organized into two divisions as follows:

First Division, Orris S. Ferry
  First Brigade, Thomas G. Stevenson
  Second Brigade, William W. H. Davis

Second Division, Charles A. Heckman
  First Brigade, Jacob J. De Forest
  Second Brigade, Joshua B. Howell
  Third Brigade, Thomas O. Osborn

Note 1. Stevenson was assigned command of Heckman's First Brigade, First Division when Heckman was assigned command of Second Division.
Note 2. Stevenson brought his Second Brigade, Fourth Division, Eighteenth Corps to the Department of the South from the Department of North Carolina in late March 1863 (embarked March 26, 1863). His brigade was commanded by Davis in the reorganization of the troops on Saint Helena Island, and De Forest assumed command of Davis' brigade.
Note 3. Except for Heckman's First Brigade, First Division, some regiments of all other brigades were reassigned.

Early in April 1862, the navy had completed its preparations for the attack on Fort Sumter, and Hunter had reorganized his forces and had them ready to cooperate with the navy. A part of Hunter's command was on Cole's Island and North Edisto Island, and some of his troops held Folly Island up to Light House Inlet. Other troops were embarked and ready to sail when ordered. Finally, on April 7, 1863, Du Pont made a brief but unsuccessful attack on the fort, but after all of their preparations the land forces were not engaged.

When Hunter learned from Du Pont that he would not renew the attack on Fort Sumter, he issued orders April 11, 1863 for the following disposition of his troops: Terry's division was to return to Port Royal Harbor; Hawley's 7th Connecticut to Fernandina; and Putnam's 7th New Hampshire to Saint Augustine. Israel Vogdes, with the four regiments of his brigade, Detachment Eighteenth Corps (commanded by Howell to April 8, 1863), was ordered to hold Folly Island. Vogdes was also assigned command of all forces that were to remain on the Stono River and in the vicinity. George B. Dandy's 100th New York was sent to occupy Cole's Island. Stevenson's brigade, Detachment Eighteenth Corps, was sent to Seabrook Island, which commanded Edisto Harbor. Davis' brigade was sent to Beaufort, South Carolina. Metcalf's Artillery Brigade was broken up, and the 3rd Rhode Island Artillery was sent to Hilton Head, and the companies of 3rd New York Artillery were sent to Folly Island, Saint Helena Island, Edisto, and Beaufort, South Carolina. Four days later, however, both Vogdes and Stevenson were ordered back with their brigades to Hilton Head Island.

April 12, 1863, Heckman was sent back to North Carolina with his brigade, formerly First Brigade, Second Division, Eighteenth Corps, to aid in the relief of John G. Foster, who was besieged at Washington, North Carolina. In May 1863, Hunter asked for the return of this brigade, but it did not again serve in the Department of the South.

In a letter dated April 13, 1863 (received by Hunter April 16, 1863), President Lincoln directed Du Pont and Hunter to continue their operations at Charleston Harbor. In compliance with this order, the navy prepared for a second attack on Fort Sumter. Du Pont pointed out, however, that for the attack to be successful it would be necessary for the army to occupy Morris Island and establish batteries there to aid in the reduction of the fort.

April 16, 1863, Hunter countermanded his orders for Vogdes and Stevenson to withdraw from Folly and Seabrook islands, and he further directed that the other troops recently returned to Hilton Head move back to Folly Island and the Stono River, to Seabrook Island, and Edisto Island. These troops were to be in place by April 20, 1863. Also on April 16, 1863, Detachment Eighteenth Corps was broken up by Hunter's orders, and the troops were reassigned to the various organizations of Tenth Corps.

April 25, 3rd New Hampshire and 76th Pennsylvania were ordered to Botany Bay under the senior colonel, who was directed to report to Stevenson for orders. On May 2, 1863, Henry R. Guss was relieved from duty with his 97th Pennsylvania Regiment, and was ordered to assume command of the troops at Botany Bay, and then report to Stevenson, who commanded the United States Forces on the Edisto. May 11, 1863, Orris S. Ferry, who had been absent from the department, returned and was assigned command of all forces on the Edisto, including Seabrook Island and Botany Bay Island. Stevenson, on being relieved, resumed command of his brigade on Seabrook Island.

May 25, 1863, Guss was ordered with his 97th Pennsylvania, 3rd New Hampshire, and 76th Pennsylvania to Saint Helena Island, and June 10, 1863 was ordered to establish a post there at Land's End. He was also ordered to assume command of all troops on the island, but June 13, 1863, George C. Strong relieved Guss in command on Saint Helena Island. Guss' brigade was designated as First

Brigade, Tenth Corps, but this was discontinued June 19, 1863, when the brigade organization of Tenth Corps was abolished.

April 25, 1863, Vogdes was reinforced on Folly Island by John L. Chatfield's 6th Connecticut and Louis Bell's 4th New Hampshire.

Late in May 1863, Quincy A. Gillmore was called to Washington, and was informed that the army was to cooperate with the navy in another attack at Charleston Harbor. The task of the army was to be the destruction of the offensive power of Fort Sumter. This was to be done by establishing batteries on Morris Island and subjecting the fort to a heavy bombardment. This action, it was hoped, would enable the fleet to pass up the channel to the city of Charleston. The army was not expected to make a land attack on the city. The army's part in this undertaking was to be as follows: first, to gain possession of the south end of Morris Island; then to storm or lay siege to Battery Wagner; and finally, on the positions secured, to establish batteries and destroy Fort Sumter.

Because the above operations would require considerable engineering skill, and also because of his success at Fort Pulaski, Gillmore was assigned temporary command of the Department of the South June 4, 1863, and he was entrusted with the attack on Morris Island and the reduction of Fort Sumter. Gillmore assumed command of the department June 12, 1863. Immediately thereafter, Gillmore began preparations for the movement on Morris Island, and these were continued until July 6, 1863. Some detached posts were abandoned and forces at others were reduced, so that in the end Gillmore's command consisted of about 10,000 men, 600 engineers, and 350 artillerists. Folly Island was selected as the assembly point for the attack on Morris Island, and June 17, 1863, the following temporary brigade organization was announced:

FOLLY ISLAND, Israel Vogdes

First Brigade, Haldimand S. Putnam
   7th New Hampshire, Haldimand S. Putnam
   62nd Ohio, Francis B. Pond

Second Brigade, Joshua B. Howell
   85th Pennsylvania, Joshua B. Howell
   6th Connecticut, John L. Chatfield
   39th Illinois, Thomas O. Osborn
   100th New York, George B. Dandy

Note. March 26, 1863, Howell's 85th Pennsylvania was assigned to Osborn's Third Brigade of Heckman's Second Division, Detachment Eighteenth Corps, and as senior colonel, Howell assumed command of the brigade. Osborn's brigade consisted of 39th Illinois, 62nd Ohio, and 67th Ohio. On April 8, 1863, Vogdes was assigned command of Howell's brigade.

July 4, 1863, Strong was ordered to Folly Island with four regiments from Saint Helena Island. These were: 48th New York, 3rd New Hampshire, 76th Pennsylvania, and 9th Maine. Also with Strong were the Independent Battalion of New York Volunteers (Enfans Perdus) and Charles R. Brayton's Company C, Third Rhode Island Heavy Artillery. During the week ending July 8, 1863, the troops of Strong's brigade and also Terry's division were assembled on Folly Island under the cover of darkness.

July 4, 1863, Truman Seymour was assigned command of the troops on Folly Island and on the adjacent islands, and he assumed command the next day. On July 6, 1863, the troops on Folly Island were organized temporarily as follows:

FOLLY ISLAND, Truman Seymour

First Brigade, Israel Vogdes
39th Illinois, Thomas O. Osborn
4th New Hampshire, Louis Bell
7th New Hampshire, Haldimand S. Putnam
100th New York, George B. Dandy
62nd Ohio, Francis B. Pond
67th Ohio, Alvin C. Voris
85th Pennsylvania, Joshua B. Howell
Independent New York Battalion
1st Massachusetts Cavalry (detachment)
3rd New York Light Artillery (detachment)
1st United States Artillery (detachment)

Second Brigade, George C. Strong
6th Connecticut, John L. Chatfield
7th Connecticut (four companies), Daniel C. Rodman
9th Maine, Sabine Emery
3rd New Hampshire, Richard S. Jackson
48th New York, William B. Barton
76th Pennsylvania, De Witt C. Strawbridge
Company C, 3rd Rhode Island Heavy Artillery, Charles R. Brayton

Note. The remaining six companies of 7th Connecticut were at Saint Augustine, Florida under Joseph R. Hawley.

Also on July 6, 1863, a new temporary organization was announced for Seymour's troops on Folly Island and adjacent islands, and for troops that were to arrive later, as follows:

First Division, Alfred H. Terry
First Brigade, Thomas G. Stevenson
Second Brigade, William W. H. Davis
Third Brigade (colored), James Montgomery

Note 1. First Brigade was organized from United States Forces Seabrook Island, and it was transferred to Third Brigade, United States Forces Folly Island July 19, 1863.

Note 2. Second Brigade was organized from regiments on Seabrook Island, on Folly Island, and from Beaufort, South Carolina. It was transferred (largely) to Davis' Brigade, Folly Island July 19, 1863.

Note 3. Third Brigade was organized from regiments of United States Forces Saint Helena Island and of United States Forces Hilton Head. It was transferred to Fourth Brigade, United States Forces Morris Island July 19, 1863.

Second Division, Truman Seymour
First Brigade, Israel Vogdes
Second Brigade, George C. Strong

Note 1. First Brigade was organized from First Brigade, United States Forces Folly Island. It was transferred to Second Brigade, United States Forces Morris Island July 19, 1863.

Note 2. Second Brigade was organized from Second Brigade, United States Forces Folly Island. It was transferred to First Brigade, United States Forces Morris Island July 19, 1863.

July 8, 1863, Headquarters Department of the South was established on Folly Island.

Occupation of Morris Island, and Assaults on Battery Wagner, July 10–18, 1863. Shortly after sunrise on the morning of July 10, 1863, Federal artillery on Folly Island, and also from a fleet of monitors, led by Rear Admiral John A. Dahlgren, opened fire on the enemy positions on Morris Island. Two hours later, Strong's Second Brigade of Seymour's division crossed Lighthouse Inlet in boats, and effected a landing on the south end of Morris Island. Strong's attacking force consisted of the 7th Connecticut, 48th New York, 9th Maine, 3rd New Hampshire, 76th Pennsylvania, and 6th Connecticut.

At the end of July 1863, the organization of troops in Gillmore's Department of the South was as follows:

The following troops were held in reserve on Folly Island, ready to support Strong's attack, and a short time later they too crossed to Morris Island and joined Strong: a part of William B. Barton's 48th New York, Haldimand S. Putnam's 7th New Hampshire, George B. Dandy's 100th New York, and Guy V. Henry's Battery B, 1st United States Artillery. The 7th New Hampshire belonged to Vogdes' Brigade, Folly Island, and 100th New York was detached from Terry's division. In addition to the above regiments, Pond's 62nd Ohio, Voris' 67th Ohio, and Howell's 85th Pennsylvania were held under arms, to be used if necessary, but they remained on Folly Island under the command of Vogdes.

By 9:00 A.M., Federal troops had captured the enemy batteries on the south part of Morris Island and had advanced to within musket range of Battery Wagner. This was a strong earthwork constructed on a narrow part of the island, a little less than a mile south of Battery Gregg, which was located on the northern tip of the island. Battery Wagner was about 800 feet long, and extended from the Atlantic Ocean on the east to Vincent's Creek on the west.

At daybreak July 11, 1863, Strong launched an attack on Battery Wagner. The battalion of 7th Connecticut was deployed in front, and it was supported by 76th Pennsylvania and 9th Maine, in that order. The column advanced under heavy fire along a low strip of sandy beach, about eighty feet wide. Men of the 7th Connecticut succeeded in reaching the parapet of the works, and the other two regiments advanced as far as the ditch, with 9th Maine coming up on the left, but after a short time, all gave way and retreated out of range.

To divert attention from Strong's attack on Morris Island, Terry's division (less 100th New York, which remained on Folly Island) sailed up the Stono River July 8, 1863, and landed on James Island at Grimballs' Plantation, near Secessionville. Terry demonstrated against the enemy position there, and was in turn attacked at Grimballs' July 16, 1863. Terry's mission was accomplished, however, and his forces were withdrawn July 17, 1863.

July 14, 1863, Seymour's forces on Morris Island, which then consisted of Strong's brigade, regiments of Vogdes' brigade from Folly Island, and 100th New York from Terry's division, were organized into two brigades under Strong and Putnam. These were constituted as Seymour's Division, Morris Island. Also that day, Vogdes was assigned command of the forces on Folly Island. When Terry

withdrew from James Island, Thomas G. Stevenson's First Brigade of his division was sent to Morris Island and was assigned to Seymour's Division. On July 18, 1863, Seymour's Division on Morris Island was organized as follows:

First Brigade, George C. Strong
  48th New York, William B. Barton
  76th Pennsylvania, John S. Littell
  3rd New Hampshire, Richard S. Jackson
  6th Connecticut, John L. Chatfield
  9th Maine, Sabine Emery
  54th Massachusetts (colored), temporarily attached,
    Robert G. Shaw

Note 1. This brigade was Strong's former Second Brigade of Seymour's First Division.
Note 2. The 54th Massachusetts of James Montgomery's Third Brigade, Terry's division had just arrived on Morris Island from James Island.

Second Brigade, Haldimand S. Putnam
  7th New Hampshire, Joseph C. Abbott
  100th New York, George B. Dandy
  62nd Ohio, Francis B. Pond
  67th Ohio, Alvin C. Voris

Third Brigade, Thomas G. Stevenson
  10th Connecticut, John L. Otis
  97th Pennsylvania, Henry R. Guss
  24th Massachusetts, Francis A. Osborn
  4th New Hampshire, Louis Bell

About twilight July 18, 1863, a second attack was launched against Battery Wagner. Seymour organized and commanded the assaulting column, which was formed with Strong's brigade in front and Putnam's brigade in support. Stevenson's brigade was held in reserve. After forming on the beach, the two brigades advanced, with Shaw's 54th Massachusetts leading Strong's brigade. As the column advanced, it came under heavy artillery fire from Battery Wagner, Battery Gregg, Fort Sumter, and Confederate works on James Island and on Sullivan's Island. As the leading troops approached Battery Wagner, the defenders opened with a destructive musketry fire.

When Strong had covered about half the distance to Battery Wagner, Seymour ordered Putnam to advance, but the latter refused for the reason that Gillmore had ordered him to remain where he was. As Strong advanced unsupported, he suffered heavy losses, and the leading regiment fell back on the troops in the rear. Fragments of the regiments, however, continued on, crossed the ditch, and gained the parapet of the works, and engaged the enemy inside. Most of First Brigade fell back, but detached portions, principally from 48th New York and 6th Connecticut, held fast to their positions at the fort.

Finally, without waiting for further orders, Putnam advanced most of his brigade to the support of the troops holding the parapet. The southeastern angle of the works was finally captured, and about 100 men under Putnam remained in the works for about an hour. These were aided by Dandy's 100th New York, Lewis Butler's 67th Ohio, William B. Coan's 48th New York, and Daniel Keim's 6th Connecticut. Strong and Chatfield were mortally wounded during the attack, and Shaw was killed. Putnam was also killed while awaiting reinforcements. Seymour was wounded during the advance of Putnam's brigade, and John W. Turner, Gillmore's chief of staff, assumed temporary command of Seymour's Division. Alfred H. Terry then assumed command of the forces on Morris Island.

The attack on Battery Wagner was unsuccessful, and no further effort was made to take the work by storm. Gillmore then began siege operations, and these were continued until September 7, 1863, when both Battery Wagner and Battery Gregg were evacuated, and they were occupied by Federal troops.

* * * * * * * * * *

At the end of July 1863, the organization of troops in Gillmore's Department of the South was as follows:

MORRIS ISLAND, Alfred H. Terry

Terry's Division, Alfred H. Terry
First Brigade, Israel Vogdes
Second Brigade, Joshua B. Howell
Third Brigade, Thomas G. Stevenson
Artillery
Battery B, 3rd New York Light Artillery (one section), Edward A. Wild
Battery B, 1st United States Artillery, Guy V. Henry
Battery C, 1st United States Artillery (detachment), James E. Wilson
Battery E, 3rd United states Artillery, John R. Myrick

Note 1. Vogdes assumed command of First Brigade July 19, 1863, in place of Strong, who was mortally wounded in the attack on Battery Wagner the day before.
Note 2. Vogdes was relieved from command of First

Brigade August 1, 1863, and he assumed command of the troops on Folly Island. The next day, 97th Pennsylvania, commanded by Henry R. Guss, was transferred from Third Brigade to First Brigade, and Guss, as senior colonel, assumed command of First Brigade.

FOLLY ISLAND, William W. H. Davis

Davis' Brigade, William W. H. Davis
Unbrigaded regiments
Artillery
1st Battery, Connecticut Light Artillery, Alfred P. Rockwell
Battery B, 3rd New York Light Artillery, James E. Ashcroft
Battery F, 3rd New York Light Artillery, Paul Birchmeyer

Note. Davis' Second Brigade of Terry's Division arrived on Folly Island July 18, 1863. Davis assumed command the next day, relieving Vogdes, who left for Morris Island. Vogdes returned August 1, 1863, and assumed command on Folly Island.

ROYAL ISLAND, Rufus Saxton

Unbrigaded infantry and cavalry
Artillery
Company A, 3rd Rhode Island Heavy Artillery, William H. Hamner
Battery D, 1st United States Artillery, John S. Gibbs
Battery M, 1st United States Artillery, Loomis L. Langdon

Note. Saxton was relieved from command of the post of Beaufort, South Carolina by William W. H. Davis June 14, 1863, but Saxton was placed in command of the United States Forces on Port Royal Island July 6, 1863.

HILTON HEAD ISLAND, Edwin Metcalf

Note 1. Metcalf relieved Terry in command July 6, 1863.
Note 2. The troops on Hilton Head Island consisted of unbrigaded infantry and cavalry regiments and detachments.

FERNANDINA, FLORIDA, Harris M. Plaisted
FORT PULASKI, GEORGIA, William Ames
SAINT AUGUSTINE, FLORIDA, Joseph R. Hawley

During August 1863, additional reinforcements arrived in the Department of the South, and Gillmore's forces underwent a further reorganization, as follows:

Three brigades were transferred from the Department of Virginia and North Carolina to Folly Island during the period July 29, 1863–August 9, 1863. Samuel M. Alford's brigade (formerly First Brigade, Second Division, Seventh Corps, Department of Virginia) arrived August 1, 1863; Robert S. Foster's brigade (formerly Second Brigade, First Division, Seventh Corps, Department of Virginia) and Edward A. Wild's brigade from Eighteenth Corps, Department of Virginia and North Carolina arrived August 2–9, 1863. These were organized into a division commanded by Israel Vogdes, see below.

First Division, Eleventh Corps, Army of the Potomac, under the command of George H. Gordon, was transferred from Warrenton Junction, Virginia to Folly Island August 6–15, 1863 as Gordon's Division, see below.

August 14, 1863, Folly Island was divided into two commands (or posts) as follows: United States Forces, Northern End of Folly Island under Israel Vogdes; and United States Forces, Southern End of Folly Island under George H. Gordon.

The organization of the troops on Morris Island and Folly Island at the end of August 1863 was as follows:

MORRIS ISLAND, Alfred H. Terry

Terry's Division, Alfred H. Terry
　　First Brigade, Henry H. Guss
　　Second Brigade, Joshua B. Howell
　　Third Brigade, Thomas G. Stevenson
　　Fourth Brigade (colored), James Montgomery
　　Davis' Brigade, William W. H. Davis
　　Artillery
　　　　Battery B, 3rd New York Light Artillery, James E. Ashcroft
　　　　Battery F, 3rd New York Light Artillery, Paul Birchmeyer
　　　　Company B, 3rd Rhode Island Heavy Artillery, Albert E. Greene
　　　　Company C, 3rd Rhode Island Heavy Artillery, Charles R. Brayton
　　　　Company D, 3rd Rhode Island Heavy Artillery, Richard G. Shaw
　　　　Company H, 3rd Rhode Island Heavy Artillery, Augustus W. Colwell
　　　　Company I, 3rd Rhode Island Heavy Artillery, Charles G. Strahan
　　　　Company M, 3rd Rhode Island Heavy Artillery, Joseph J. Comstock, Jr.
　　　　Battery B, 1st United States Artillery, Guy V. Henry
　　　　Battery C, 1st United States Artillery (detachment), James E. Wilson
　　　　Battery E, 3rd United States Artillery, John R. Myrick

Note 1. Terry's Division was also known as United States Forces Morris Island.

Note 2. Montgomery's brigade was formed August 24, 1863.

Note 3. Davis' Brigade was transferred from Folly Island August 30, 1863.

NORTHERN END OF FOLLY ISLAND, Israel Vogdes

Vogdes' Division, Israel Vogdes
　　Alford's Brigade, Samuel M. Alford
　　Foster's Brigade, Robert S. Foster
　　Wild's Brigade (African Brigade, colored), Edward A. Wild
　　Artillery
　　　　1st Battery, Connecticut Light Artillery, Alfred P. Rockwell

Note. Vogdes' Division was also known as United States Forces Northern End of Folly Island.

SOUTHERN END OF FOLLY ISLAND, George H. Gordon

Gordon's Division, George H. Gordon
　　First Brigade, Alexander Schimmelfennig
　　Second Brigade, Adelbert Ames

Note 1. Gordon's Division was also known as United States Forces Southern End of Folly Island.

Note 2. August 17, 1863, Ames' brigade was sent to Morris Island to assist in the siege of Battery Wagner. It returned to Folly Island August 29, 1863.

Meantime, batteries were being erected on Morris Island, and on August 17, 1863, they opened fire on Fort Sumter. The bombardment was continued until August 23, 1863, but the enemy still continued to hold the fort. Firing was resumed August 30, 1863, and was continued for three more days without success.

Siege operations were continued against Battery Wagner and Battery Gregg during the bombardments, but the works were evacuated on the night of September 6, 1863, and then Federal troops occupied all of Morris Island.

During the night of September 8, 1863, a naval force attempted the capture of Fort Sumter by assault, but it did not succeed. A further bombardment of the fort began October 23, 1863, and with its unsuccessful conclusion, all aggressive operations at Charleston Harbor ended for the year.

* * * * * * * * *

There were some changes in the command and organization of the troops of the Department of the South, Tenth Corps during the remainder of the year. These were as follows:

September 28, 1863, Francis A. Osborn was ordered to Saint Augustine, Florida with his 24th Massachusetts to relieve Dudley W. Strickland's 48th New York.

October 11, 1863, Henry R. Guss, with his 97th Pennsylvania, relieved Harris M. Plaisted's 11th Maine at Fernandina, Florida. Plaisted then assumed command of Guss' former First Brigade of Terry's Division, then commanded by Gilman E. Sleeper.

October 18, 1863, Truman Seymour assumed temporary command of the troops on Morris Island during the absence of Terry. Terry returned and resumed command November 9, 1863.

October 24, 1863, Gordon departed on leave of absence, and Alexander Schimmelfennig assumed command of Gordon's Division. Leopold Von Gilsa took charge of Schimmelfennig's brigade.

October 28, 1863, Howell's Third Division, Morris Island was transferred to Gordon's Division on Folly Island.

November 9, 1863, Robert S. Foster assumed temporary command of forces on the Northern End of Folly Island during the absence of Vogdes. That same day, William B. Barton relieved De Witt C. Strawbridge in command on Hilton Head Island, and was also assigned command of the troops at Fort Pulaski and on Tybee Island.

November 23, 1863, the brigade organization of Terry's Division on Morris Island was discontinued, and the troops were reorganized as follows:

First Brigade, Thomas G. Stevenson
Second Brigade, William W. H. Davis
Third Brigade (colored), James Montgomery

Note 1. First Brigade consisted of 3rd New Hampshire, 4th New Hampshire, 9th Maine, and 11th Maine.

Note 2. Second Brigade consisted of 53rd Pennsylvania, 104th Pennsylvania, 100th New York, and Independent Battalion of New York Volunteers.

Note 3. Third Brigade consisted of 2nd South Carolina, 54th Massachusetts, and 3rd United States Colored Troops.

December 5, 1863, Seymour was assigned command of Hilton Head Island, Saint Helena Island, Fort Pulaski, and Tybee Island. Joshua B. Howell's

Third Brigade of Gordon's Division on Folly Island was ordered to Hilton Head to report to Seymour, and was transferred there December 5–7, 1863.

The organization of the Department of the South, Tenth Corps at the end of December 1863 was as follows:

SEYMOUR'S COMMAND, Truman Seymour

Post of Hilton Head Island, William B. Barton
Howell's Brigade, Hilton Head Island, Joshua B. Howell
Saint Helena Island, Joseph R. Hawley
Fort Pulaski and Tybee Island, Edwin Metcalf

MORRIS ISLAND

Terry's Division, Alfred H. Terry
First Brigade, Thomas G. Stevenson
Second Brigade, William W. H. Davis
Third Brigade (colored), James Montgomery
Artillery
Battery B, 3rd New York Light Artillery, Edward A. Wild
3rd Rhode Island Heavy Artillery (six companies), William Ames

FOLLY ISLAND

Vogdes' Division, Israel Vogdes
Alford's Brigade, Samuel M. Alford
Third Brigade, James C. Beecher
Foster's Brigade, Jeremiah C. Drake
Light Artillery Battalion, John Hamilton
Battery F, 3rd New York Light Artillery, Samuel C. Day
Battery E, 3rd United States Artillery, John Hamilton
Unattached artillery
1st Battery Connecticut Light Artillery, Alfred P. Rockwell
Company A, 3rd Rhode Island Heavy Artillery, William H. Hamner
Gordon's Division, George H. Gordon
First Brigade, William Gurney
Second Brigade, William H. Noble

Note 1. Gurney assumed command of First Brigade November 28, 1863, when Schimmelfennig became ill.

Note 2. Noble assumed command of Second Brigade November 27, 1863, when Ames departed on leave.

Note 3. Howell's Third Brigade was transferred to Hilton Head Island December 5–7, 1863.

PORT ROYAL ISLAND, Rufus Saxton
FERNANDINA, FLORIDA, Henry R. Guss

SAINT AUGUSTINE, FLORIDA, Francis A. Osborn

Districts in the Department of the South, Tenth Corps

Early in 1864, the Department of the South was divided into three military districts and the post of Port Royal Island, and this organization was not changed until Tenth Corps was transferred to Virginia in April 1864.

Northern District, Tenth Corps. January 15, 1864, the Northern District, Tenth Corps was constituted to consist of that part of the Department of the South that was bounded on the north by Charleston Harbor, and on the south by Saint Helena Sound. Alfred H. Terry was assigned command. The troops of the district consisted of those on Morris Island and Folly Island. By an order of January 15, 1864, the two posts on Folly Island were merged into a single command under George H. Gordon. The next day, Headquarters Department of the South was transferred from Folly Island to Hilton Head. At the end of January 1864, the Northern District was organized as follows:

FOLLY ISLAND, Adelbert Ames

Gordon's Division, George H. Gordon
First Brigade, Leopold Von Gilsa
Second Brigade, William H. Noble

Note 1. Alexander Schimmelfennig assumed command at Folly Island during the first week of February 1864, and Ames resumed command of Second Brigade. Robert S. Foster commanded the forces on Folly Island during the absence of Schimmelfennig in February 1864.

Note 2. Second Brigade left the district February 23, 1864, and was transferred to the District of Florida (see below). Second Brigade was reorganized by the transfer of Samuel M. Alford's Second Brigade of Vogdes' Division, Folly Island.

Vogdes' Division, Robert S. Foster
First Brigade, Jeremiah C. Drake
Second Brigade, Samuel M. Alford
Third Brigade (colored), James C. Beecher
Light Artillery Battalion, John Hamilton
Unattached artillery

Note. Vogdes' Division was discontinued when Drake's (Foster's) First Brigade and Beecher's Third Brigade were transferred to the District of Florida February 13–23, 1864, and Alford's Second Brigade was transferred to Gordon's Division as Second Brigade.

MORRIS ISLAND, William W. H. Davis
First Brigade, Harris M. Plaisted
Second Brigade, Henry M. Hoyt

Note. These two brigades were from First Division, Tenth Corps.

April 4, 1864, Gillmore was ordered to send all available forces of Tenth Corps to Fort Monroe, Virginia for reorganization as a part of Benjamin F. Butler's Army of the James, and during the month eleven regiments left the Northern District. Only five regiments of the former organization remained, and these, together with four colored regiments, garrisoned Folly Island, Little Folly Island, and Morris Island. At the end of April 1864, Alexander Schimmelfennig commanded the Northern District, which was organized as follows:

Folly Island, Leopold Von Gilsa
41st New York, Leopold Von Gilsa
54th New York, Eugene A. Kozlay
74th Pennsylvania, Adolph Von Hartung

Note 1. These three regiments formerly belonged to First Brigade, Gordon's Division.
Note 2. 74th Pennsylvania was on Cole's Island.

Little Folly Island, William Heine
103rd New York, Frederick Turnt
55th Massachusetts (colored), Alfred S. Hartwell

Note. 103rd New York formerly belonged to Samuel M. Alford's Second Brigade, Folly Island.

Morris Island, William Gurney
127th New York, Stewart L. Woodford
54th Massachusetts (colored), Edward N. Hallowell
21st United States Colored Troops, Augustus G. Bennett
34th United States Colored Troops, James Montgomery

Note 1. 127th New York formerly belonged to Von Gilsa's First Brigade, Folly Island.
Note 2. March 26, 1864, 2nd South Carolina (colored) was designated as 34th United States Colored Troops.

Artillery
Battery B, 3rd New York Light Artillery, James E. Ashcroft
2nd Battalion, 3rd Rhode Island Heavy Artillery, George Metcalf

District of Hilton Head. In January 1864, Truman

Seymour's command, consisting of Hilton Head Island, Saint Helena Island, Fort Pulaski, and Tybee Island, was organized as the District of Hilton Head, as follows:

Post of Hilton Head, Redfield Duryee
Saint Helena Island, Joseph R. Hawley
Fort Pulaski, James E. Bailey
Artillery Brigade, Loomis L. Langdon
Barton's Brigade, William B. Barton
Howell's Brigade, Joshua B. Howell
Montgomery's Brigade, James Montgomery
Cavalry, Guy V. Henry

Barton's Brigade was organized January 28, 1864 from 47th New York, 48th New York, and 115th New York. Third South Carolina (colored) and 4th South Carolina (colored) were attached. Henry, with his 40th Massachusetts Mounted Infantry, was transferred from Noble's Second Brigade, Gordon's Division, from Folly Island to Hilton Head January 14, 1864; and the Independent Battalion of Massachusetts Cavalry, the other unit of Henry's cavalry command, consisted of four companies of 1st Massachusetts Cavalry which had been detached from the regiment in August 1863.

On February 6, 1864, Seymour embarked with a force from the district at Hilton Head for Jacksonville, Florida. He took with him Barton's Brigade, Montgomery's Brigade, Henry's Cavalry Brigade, and Langdon's artillery. For details, see following section, District of Florida (Seymour's Florida Expedition). While Seymour was absent on his expedition, Joshua B. Howell commanded the District of Hilton Head.

April 4, 1864, Gillmore was ordered to send all available troops of Tenth Corps to Fort Monroe, Virginia for reorganization as a part of Benjamin F. Butler's Army of the James. On April 24, 1864, 6th Connecticut and 76th Pennsylvania and four regiments of Howell's Brigade were ordered to leave the District of Hilton Head for Fort Monroe. Two days later, William W. H. Davis relieved Howell in command of the district, and the latter went north with his brigade.

At the end of April 1864, the troops in the District of Hilton Head consisted largely of colored troops, and were organized as follows:

Hilton Head, Charles R. Brayton
52nd Pennsylvania; 104th Pennsylvania; Company B,

Rhode Island Heavy Artillery; and Company C, 1st New York Engineers
Bayley's Brigade, Thomas Bayley
1st Michigan (colored), 9th and 32nd United States Colored Troops. This brigade was organized April 28, 1864.
Fort Pulaski and Tybee Island, James E. Bailey
Companies D, G, H, and L, 3rd Rhode Island Heavy Artillery; and Company C, 9th United States Colored Troops
Saint Helena Island, David C. Benjamin
Company G, 1st Michigan (colored); Company B, 9th United States Colored Troops; and an Invalid Detachment
Cavalry, David B. Keith
2nd Battalion, 4th Massachusetts Cavalry

District of Florida (Seymour's Florida Expedition). December 15, 1863, Gillmore proposed to Henry W. Halleck that he send an expedition to Florida, and gave as his purpose the recovery for the Union of the most valuable land in the state, the cutting off of supplies for the Confederacy from that region, and the recruiting of Negro troops in the area. January 13, 1864, President Lincoln expressed an interest in the expedition, and asked Gillmore to aid in reestablishing Florida as a loyal state. The expedition was approved January 22, 1864, and Seymour was assigned command.

February 4, 1864, Gillmore ordered Seymour to embark the troops of his command, then on Hilton Head Island, on Saint Helena Island, and at Fort Pulaski, and to be prepared to sail for Florida on the night of February 6, 1864. Gillmore's original order included the following troops for embarkation: William B. Barton's Brigade (7th Connnecticut, 7th New Hampshire, and 8th United States Colored Troops, temporarily attached); James Montgomery's Brigade (2nd South Carolina, 3rd United States Volunteers, and 54th Massachusetts, all colored); Guy V. Henry's Mounted Brigade (54th Massachusetts Mounted Infantry and the Independent Battalion of Massachusetts Cavalry). The following artillery, under the command of John Hamilton, chief of artillery, accompanied the expedition: Loomis Langdon's Battery M, 1st United States Artillery; Samuel S. Elder's Battery B, 1st United States Artillery (Elder's Horse Battery); John Hamilton's Company E, 3rd United States Artillery; and one section of Company C, 3rd Rhode Island Heavy Artillery (James' Rhode Island Battery), commanded by George O. Eddy.

Montgomery's Brigade was organized January 31, 1864 from Third Brigade, Morris Island, and was ordered to Hilton Head. The brigade that Barton was ordered to take to Florida consisted of, as noted above, Joseph R. Hawley's 7th Connecticut and the 7th New Hampshire, which were the regiments formerly under Hawley's command on Saint Helena Island. The 47th New York, William B. Barton's 48th New York, and the 115th New York, which were the regiments assigned to Barton's Brigade January 28, 1864, were not included in the initial order. It appears, however, that a short time later the above three New York regiments were also sent to Florida, and that on February 9, 1864, Barton assumed command of these regiments, and Hawley took charge of the brigade brought to Florida by Barton.

Seymour's Expedition, accompanied by a naval escort provided by Admiral John A. Dahlgren, arrived at the mouth of the Saint John's River February 7, 1864, and disembarked at Jacksonville the next day. Gillmore accompanied the expedition. On the afternoon of February 8, 1864, the army moved westward from Jacksonville, with Henry's Brigade on the right, Barton's Brigade in the center, and Hawley's Brigade on the left. That night Henry advanced and captured the enemy Camp Finegan, eight miles west of Jacksonville. The infantry came up and bivouacked at Camp Finegan, but Henry pushed on during the night, and at sunrise the next morning occupied Baldwin, Florida. This was at the junction of the Florida Railroad that ran from Fernandina to Cedar Key and the Florida, Atlantic, and Gulf Railroad that ran from Jacksonville to Lake City.

The infantry arrived at Baldwin the next day, and Henry was then ordered to continue his march westward. On February 10, 1864, he reached the ford of the South Fork of the Saint Mary's River at Barbers' plantation (present-day Macclenny), near the crossing of the Florida, Atlantic, and Gulf Railroad. Henry's force continued on and reached Sanderson, ten miles beyond Barbers', at 6:00 P.M. that evening, and the next day, the 7th Connecticut of Hawley's Brigade reached Sanderson after dark.

Meantime, Joseph Finegan, commanding the Confederate District of East Florida, had collected a small force, principally from middle Florida, at Lake City, and then had established a defensive position

about two and a half miles east of the town. Henry arrived in front of these works about 10:00 A.M. February 11, 1864, and after skirmishing for several hours, retired toward Sanderson. On February 13, 1864, Seymour's force at Sanderson fell back to Barbers'.

On February 13, 1864, Seymour sent Henry on a raid toward Gainesville, and a detachment of the 40th Massachusetts reached the town the next day, but it returned February 17, 1864, without accomplishing anything of significance. A raid on Callahan, between Baldwin and Fernandina, on February 14, 1864 was more productive, and resulted in the destruction of a part of the Florida Railroad and some bridges near that point.

Gillmore remained in Florida with Seymour until February 13, 1864, and then returned to Hilton Head. Two days later he constituted the District of Florida, which was to include that part of Florida lying within the limits of the Department of the South. The district was organized February 16, 1864, and Seymour was assigned command.

A short time later, Seymour ordered the concentration of his forces at Barbers' in preparation for an expedition toward Lake City to destroy the railroad communications between east and west Florida at the Suwannee River. His army, which totaled about 5,500 officers and men and sixteen pieces of artillery, consisted of the brigades of Barton, Hawley, and Montgomery, Henry's Mounted Brigade, and the artillery under John Hamilton, chief of artillery.

Engagement at Olustee (or Ocean Pond). Seymour's army began its advance toward Lake City at 6:00 on the morning of February 20, 1864, and marched westward on a road roughly parallel to the railroad. Henry's Mounted Brigade led the advance, and it was followed at 7:00 A.M. by Hawley's Brigade. Barton's Brigade came next, and Montgomery's Brigade, which was in charge of the trains, did not leave Barbers' until 8:30 A.M.

Around midday, while the column was passing Sanderson, Seymour learned that a Confederate force was in position some distance east of Lake City. This was a small army that Finegan had assembled near Olustee, Florida, and had organized from troops of his District of East Florida and from reinforcements that Pierre G. T. Beauregard had sent from Georgia and South Carolina. It consisted of Alfred H. Colquitt's First Brigade and George P. Harrison's Second Brigade, and some cavalry commanded by Caraway Smith. When Finegan learned of Seymour's approach, he sent Colquitt's brigade forward about two miles to the place where the main road crossed the railroad. There Colquitt formed his troops in line facing the oncoming Federals.

Between 2:00 and 3:00 P.M., Henry's cavalry ran into the enemy pickets at a point where the road on which Seymour was moving crossed from the south to the north side of the railroad. After crossing the railroad, the road diverged to the right, and at a point about three-fourths of a mile north of the railroad it crossed a swampy area. A little more than one-fourth mile west of the swamp the road branched. The main Jacksonville and Lake City Road ran to the southwest, to the left, for about two and one-half miles, and then crossed to the south side of the railroad at a point about two miles east of Olustee, near where Colquitt had posted his brigade. The right-hand road diverged somewhat to the north, and then ran southwest, roughly parallel to the main road, for about three miles, and it too struck the railroad.

When Henry met the enemy pickets at the road crossing, he halted his cavalry, while two companies of the 7th Connecticut, which was moving ahead of the rest of Hawley's Brigade, were advanced as skirmishers on both sides of the track. The rest of the regiment followed in reserve. The leading companies soon came up to the enemy skirmishers and forced them back about three miles. The other companies of the 7th Connecticut were then brought up, and they extended the regimental line some distance to the north of the railroad. The 7th Connecticut then advanced and struck Colquitt's line near the road crossing, and was sharply engaged there for some time, but then, with its ammunition nearly exhausted and no support in sight, the regiment withdrew about four hundred yards. At about this time Finegan's other brigade under Harrison arrived and formed on the left of Colquitt.

When the 7th Connecticut fell back, Seymour advanced the other two regiments of Hawley's Brigade, but while the 7th New Hampshire was forming between the two roads north of the railroad to support John Hamilton's battery (commanded by John R. Myrick), it broke and fell back in confusion and was of no further service that day. The 8th United States Colored Troops, which had been ad-

vancing along the railroad, formed on the left of the Federal line between the railroad on the left and the main road on the right. It quickly became engaged, but it too was slowly forced back.

A new phase of the battle developed when Barton's Brigade arrived. About twenty minutes after the firing started, this brigade was ordered forward, but it was then halted on a line extending across both branches of the road. After the rout of 7th New Hampshire, Barton advanced until the left regiments of his brigade occupied the position just vacated by the 7th New Hampshire. The 47th New York was on the left of Barton's line, with its left near the main road to Lake City; the 48th New York was in the center, with its right on the northern road; and 115th New York was on the right, north of the northern branch of the road. Barton's Brigade was soon heavily engaged, and although it offered stubborn resistance to the enemy attack, it was slowly driven back.

When 7th Connecticut had replenished its ammunition, it moved forward again to close a gap that existed between 8th United States Colored Troops on the left, and Barton's Brigade on the right. Montgomery's Brigade, which had been guarding the trains, began to arrive on the field, with the 54th Massachusetts coming up along the railroad and the 1st South Carolina on the main road.

When Barton's Brigade and the 8th United States Colored Troops began to give way, the 54th Massachusetts hurried forward, and then formed in line between the railroad and the main road. It then advanced about 200 yards to the position formerly held by the 8th United States Colored Troops, on the left of Barton. The 8th United States Colored Troops, which had earlier withdrawn, then formed in rear of the 54th Massachusetts. Montgomery's other regiment, the 1st South Carolina (colored), formed to the right of the main road, and then pushed forward between the 47th New York and the 48th New York of Barton's Brigade.

The final Union line was held as follows: the 7th Connecticut was across the main road, with the 1st South Carolina on its right and the 54th Massachusetts on its left. These three regiments probably saved Seymour's small army from a complete rout. After about two and a half hours of hard fighting, Barton's and Montgomery's brigades were forced to leave the field.

During the fighting that day, Henry's cavalry

watched the flanks of the army, and on the left stopped a movement by enemy cavalry that threatened that flank.

Between 6:00 and 7:00 P.M., Seymour gave the order to retire, and the army marched back by the way it had come, covered on the rear by the 7th Connecticut and the cavalry. Barton was in immediate command during the retreat, which continued until after midnight, and then the army halted at Barbers' plantation. The retreat was continued to Baldwin the next day, and finally the army arrived on McGirt's Creek at Jacksonville February 22, 1864.

A short time after the engagement at Olustee, Seymour's command in the District of Florida was strongly reinforced with troops from Folly Island. The following brigades left the island February 14–23, 1864, and by February 25, 1864 had arrived at Jacksonville: Adelbert Ames' Second Brigade, Gordon's Division, consisting of 17th Connecticut, 144th New York, 157th New York, 75th Ohio, and 107th Ohio; Robert S. Foster's First Brigade, Vogdes' Division, consisting of 13th Indiana, 112th New York, and 169th New York; James C. Beecher's Third Brigade (colored), Vogdes' Division, consisting of 55th Massachusetts and 1st North Carolina.

February 25, 1864, the troops of the District of Florida were temporarily organized as follows:

DISTRICT OF FLORIDA, Truman Seymour

First Division, Adelbert Ames
    First Brigade, William H. Noble
    Second Brigade, Joseph R. Hawley
    Third Brigade (colored), Milton S. Littlefield

Note. Noble was in command of Ames' brigade.

Second Division, Israel Vogdes, to February 28, 1864
    Robert S. Foster
    First Brigade, Robert S. Foster, to February 28, 1864
        Jeremiah C. Drake
    Second Brigade (colored), Benjamin C. Tilghman
    Third Brigade (colored), James Montgomery

Note. Vogdes was relieved from duty in the District of Florida February 28, 1864.

Unassigned
    Barton's Brigade, William B. Barton
    Henry's Cavalry (later called Light Brigade), Guy V. Henry

Artillery, John Hamilton

March 9, 1864, Barton, with his brigade and five companies of the 55th Massachusetts and two sections of James' Battery, left Jacksonville, and the next day he occupied Palatka, Florida, seventy-five miles up the Saint John's River. Barton's Brigade remained there on garrison duty until it was ordered to Fort Monroe in April 1864, and at that time the post of Palatka was abandoned.

Seymour asked to be relieved from duty in the Department of the South, and March 24, 1864, John P. Hatch was ordered to the District of Florida to succeed him. Hatch assumed command of the district about March 28, 1864, and April 13, 1864, Seymour was ordered to New York to await action on his request.

On April 4, 1864, Gillmore was ordered to send all available troops of Tenth Corps to Fort Monroe for reorganization as a part of Benjamin F. Butler's Army of the James. The troops sent from the District of Florida consisted of the regiments of the brigades of Foster, Barton, and Hawley, and Henry's 40th Massachusetts, a total of ten regiments. Ames' brigade remained in the district, but April 14, 1864, Ames, in person, was ordered to Fort Monroe. James Shaw, Jr. assumed command of Ames' brigade. The 17th Connecticut under William H. Noble occupied Saint Augustine, six companies of 157th New York under Philip H. Brown were at Fernandina, and four companies of 157th New York were at Picolata.

William Birney was relieved from duty at Beaufort, South Carolina April 15, 1864, and was assigned command of the District of Florida. He arrived at Jacksonville and relieved Hatch sometime around April 20, 1864.

The organization of the District of Florida at the end of April 1864 was as follows:

District of Florida, William Birney
    First Brigade, James Shaw, Jr.
    Jacksonville, Andrew L. Harris
    Fernandina, Philip P. Brown, Jr.
    Artillery Brigade, Ulysses Doubleday
    Yellow Bluff, Romanzo C. Bailey
    Saint Augustine, William H. Noble
    Picolata, James C. Carmichael

Beaufort and Port Royal Island, South Carolina.
Although not officially designated as a military district during the period January 1864–April 1864,

Port Royal Island was an important post in the Department of the South, Tenth Corps, under the command of Rufus Saxton. The troops present on the island in January 1864 were 8th Maine, 56th New York, 55th Pennsylvania, 1st South Carolina (colored), and Battery D, 1st United States Artillery. On March 26, 1864, the designation of 1st South Carolina was changed to 33rd United States Colored Troops. Other troops that were later sent to Beaufort were 4th New Hampshire, 9th United States Colored Troops, 26th United States Colored Troops, and 29th Connecticut (colored)—the latter two arrived April 13, 1864. The 9th United States Colored Troops was sent to Hilton Head April 6, 1864.

April 4, 1864, Gillmore was ordered to send all available troops of Tenth Corps to Fort Monroe to form a part of Benjamin F. Butler's Army of the James. The 8th Maine, 4th New Hampshire, and 55th Pennsylvania were sent from Port Royal Island, and at the end of April 1864, the troops remaining on the island were 56th New York, 26th United States Colored Troops, 33rd United States Colored Troops, and 29th Connecticut (colored).

* * * * * * * *

During April 1864, thirty-one regiments, totaling about 8,000 officers and men, were transferred from the Department of the South to Gloucester Point, Virginia, and there they were organized into Tenth Corps, Army of the James. For further information about these troops, see Tenth Corps, Army of the James, and Army of the James.

Following the departure of Tenth Corps, the Department of the South was reorganized as described in the following section.

PART IV.
DEPARTMENT OF THE SOUTH
APRIL 25, 1864–JUNE 27, 1865

Tenth Corps left the Department of the South in detachments during April 1864, and at the end of the month, the troops remaining consisted of seventeen white regiments or detachments and seventeen colored infantry regiments. In addition, there was a detachment of 4th Massachusetts Cavalry, a detachment of 1st New York Engineers, and nine batteries, battalions, and companies of artillery. These troops were organized into districts as follows:

Northern District
    Folly Island
    Morris Island
    Little Folly Island
Port Royal Island (in May 1864, designated as the District of Beaufort)
District of Florida
Hilton Head District

Gillmore left the Department of the South for Virginia May 1, 1864, and John P. Hatch assumed temporary command. John G. Foster relieved Hatch May 26, 1864.

October 26, 1864, the troops in the various districts were designated as separate brigades, as follows:

Northern District as First Separate Brigade
District of Beaufort as Second Separate Brigade
District of Hilton Head as Third Separate Brigade
District of Florida as Fourth Separate Brigade

Thereafter, both district and separate brigade designations were used in referring to the troops in the department.

During the winter of 1864–1865, affairs in the Department of the South were greatly influenced by the presence of William T. Sherman's Army of the Military Division of the Mississippi in the states of Georgia and South Carolina. Sherman left Atlanta November 15, 1864 on his march through Georgia, and he arrived near Savannah December 10, 1865. Then, after the capture of Savannah, he decided to march northward through the Carolinas to Virginia. This he proceeded to do, and arrived near Goldsboro, North Carolina in March 1865.

As a result of Sherman's movements, there were several organizational changes in the Department of the South, and a number of expeditions and demonstrations were carried out to aid Sherman on his march. Two new districts, the District of North Carolina and the District of Savannah, were created; and a Coast Division, two provisional divisions, and several provisional brigades were formed (see below). In addition, Charleston was evacuated by the enemy February 17, 1865, and the city and its dependencies were attached to the Northern District the next day.

Not all of Sherman's army entered territory of the Department of the South, then under control of Foster's forces, but in January 1865, Oliver O.

Howard's Right Wing moved from Savannah to Beaufort, South Carolina. It then advanced toward the Charleston and Savannah Railroad, and Frank P. Blair's Seventeenth Corps took position at Pocotaligo, and John A. Logan's Fifteenth Corps at Garden's Corners and Port Royal Ferry. These two corps departed February 1, 1865, and marched toward Columbia, South Carolina to join Sherman.

For additional information about Sherman's operations, see the following: Savannah Campaign (Sherman's March through Georgia); Carolinas Campaign; and Department of North Carolina, January 31, 1865–May 19, 1866. For details of affairs in the Department of the South during this period, see below, Districts in the Department of the South and Operations in the Department of the South.

February 9, 1865, Foster departed on leave because of disability from wounds, and he was succeeded in command of the department by Quincy A. Gillmore.

After Sherman's passage through Georgia and South Carolina, the areas in these states that were under Federal control were greatly increased, and this resulted in extensive redistricting in the Department of the South, as follows:

May 13, 1865, the District of Beaufort and the District of Hilton Head were consolidated and designated as the District of Port Royal.

June 5, 1865, that part of Georgia that was within the limits of the Department of the South, and not occupied by troops belonging to the Military Division of the Mississippi, was divided into three military districts as follows: District of South Georgia, District of Savannah, and District of Northern Georgia.

June 23, 1865, the state of South Carolina was divided into four military districts, as follows: District of Eastern South Carolina, District of Charleston, District of Western South Carolina, and District of Port Royal. For details of the organization and boundaries of these districts, see below, Postwar Districts in the Department of the South.

June 27, 1865, the districts of the department were designated as separate brigades as follows:

District of Charleston as First Separate Brigade
District of Port Royal as Second Separate Brigade
District of Eastern South Carolina as Third Separate Brigade

District of Western South Carolina as Fourth Separate Brigade
District of Southern Georgia as Fifth Separate Brigade
District of Savannah as Sixth Separate Brigade
District of Northern Georgia as Seventh Separate Brigade
District of Florida as Eighth Separate Brigade

By an order of June 27, 1865, the military divisions and departments of the army were reorganized, and the Department of the South was discontinued. The state of South Carolina was constituted as the Department of South Carolina, and it was assigned to the Military Division of the Atlantic; the state of Georgia was constituted as the Department of Georgia, and it was assigned to the Military Division of the Tennessee; and the state of Florida was constituted as the Department of Florida, and it was assigned to the Military Division of the Gulf. This reorganization was not in effect, however, until July 1865.

Wartime Districts in the Department of the South

District of Beaufort. After the departure of Tenth Corps from the Department of the South in April 1864, the troops on Port Royal Island under the command of Rufus Saxton consisted of 56th New York, 29th Connecticut (colored), 26th United States Colored Troops, 33rd United States Colored Troops, and Battery F, 3rd New York Light Artillery. In May 1864, this command was designated as the District of Beaufort (sometimes called Port Royal District). Headquarters of the district was at Beaufort, South Carolina.

October 26, 1864, the troops in the District of Beaufort were designated as Second Separate Brigade, Department of the South.

The district was discontinued May 13, 1865, when the District of Beaufort and the District of Hilton Head were consolidated and designated as the District of Port Royal. Headquarters was established at Hilton Head. For additional information, see District of Port Royal, below.

Rufus Saxton retained command of the District of Beaufort until relieved by Edward E. Potter January 23, 1865. On several occasions during this period, however, Saxton was absent from the district. On July 1, 1864, Saxton joined John P. Hatch with a brigade consisting of three regiments from the District of Beaufort on an expedition to Saint John's Island, and left Potter in command during his absence. On July 31, 1864, Potter was assigned command of the District of Hilton Head, but he also continued to exercise temporary control over the District of Beaufort until Saxton returned. Saxton resumed command of the district in August 1864, but September 1, 1864, he was ordered to relieve Alexander Schimmelfennig in command of the Northern District. Saxton also retained command of the District of Beaufort, with the senior officers of the post in immediate charge of affairs in the district. October 4, 1864, Saxton resumed immediate command of the District of Beaufort, and remained in charge until relieved by Potter January 23, 1865. April 1, 1865, Potter was ordered to Georgetown, South Carolina, where he organized a provisional division (see below). William B. Guernsey assumed command of the District of Beaufort. For additional information, see below, Operations in the Department of the South, Expedition to Georgetown, South Carolina, and Potter's Expedition against the Wilmington and Manchester Railroad and the South Carolina Railroad.

District of Florida. Late in April 1864, the District of Florida, Department of the South was organized from the former District of Florida, Department of the South, Tenth Corps. William Birney was assigned command, with headquarters at Jacksonville. The district was organized as follows:

First Brigade, James Shaw, Jr.
    107th Ohio, Detachment 75th Ohio, 144th New York, 7th United States Colored Troops
Artillery Brigade, Ulysses Doubleday
    3rd United States Colored Troops and Battery A, 3rd Rhode Island Heavy Artillery
Jacksonville, Andrew L. Harris
    75th Ohio, 35th United States Colored Troops, Signal Detachment
Fernandina, Philip P. Brown
    157th New York (six companies) and 21st United States Colored Troops
Yellow Bluff, Romanzo C. Bailey
    8th United States Colored Troops
Saint Augustine, William H. Noble
    17th Connecticut
Picolata, James C. Carmichael
    157th New York (four companies)

October 26, 1864, the troops in the District of Florida were designated as Fourth Separate Brigade, Department of the South, but both designations were used to the end of the war. The troops of Fourth Separate Brigade consisted of 17th Connecticut, 75th Ohio, 107th Ohio, 3rd United States Colored Troops, 34th United States Colored Troops, 35th United States Colored Troops, a battalion of 4th Massachusetts Cavalry, and Battery F, 3rd New York Light Artillery. In November 1864, the 34th and 35th United States Colored Troops, and the cavalry and artillery were sent to Hilton Head to join the Coast Division. See below, Operations in the Department of the South, Hatch's Expedition against the Charleston and Savannah Railroad (Battle of Honey Hill), and also Hatch's Advance from Pocotaligo to Charleston, South Carolina.

June 27, 1865, the troops in the District of Florida were designated as Eighth Separate Brigade, Department of the South. For a discussion of military operations in the District of Florida, see below, section on Operations in the Department of the South.

By an order of June 27, 1865, the District of Florida (or Eighth Separate Brigade) was discontinued by transfer to the newly created Department of Florida. Israel Vogdes, then commanding the district, did not relinquish command, however, until July 10, 1865, when he received official notice of the order transferring the state of Florida to the Military Division of the Gulf as the Department of Florida.

The commanders of the District of Florida during this period were as follows:

William Birney	April 1864 to May 5, 1864
George H. Gordon	May 5, 1864 to June 2, 1864
William Birney	June 2, 1864 to August 4, 1864
John P. Hatch	August 4, 1864 to November 14, 1864
Eliakim P. Scammon	November 14, 1864 to April 7, 1865
Benjamin C. Tilghman	April 7, 1865 to April 19, 1865
Israel Vogdes	April 19, 1865 to July 10, 1865

Note. William H. Noble was in temporary command of the district in July 1864, during the absence of William Birney on an expedition in South Carolina.

District of Hilton Head. The District of Hilton Head, Department of the South was organized in late

April 1864 from the District of Hilton Head, Department of the South, Tenth Corps. William W. H. Davis was assigned command, with headquarters at Hilton Head. The district was organized as follows:

Hilton Head, Charles R. Brayton
    53rd Pennsylvania, 104th Pennsylvania, Company C, 1st New York Engineers, and Company B, 3rd Rhode Island Heavy Artillery
Bayley's Brigade, Thomas Bayley
    1st Michigan (colored), 9th United States Colored Troops, 32nd United States Colored Troops. This brigade was constituted at Hilton Head Island April 28, 1864.
Seabrook Island, Nathaniel Houghton
    25th Ohio
Fort Pulaski and Tybee Island, James E. Bailey
    Company C, 9th United States Colored Troops and Companies D, G, H, and L, 3rd Rhode Island Heavy Artillery
Saint Helena Island, David C. Benjamin
    Company B, 9th United States Colored Troops; Company G, 1st Michigan (colored); and a detachment of Invalid Corps
Cavalry, David B. Keith
    Second Battalion, 4th Massachusetts Cavalry

The troops in the District of Hilton Head were designated as Third Separate Brigade, Department of the South October 26, 1864. Both designations were used, however, until May 13, 1865, when the District of Beaufort and the District of Hilton Head were consolidated to form the District of Port Royal (see below).

In October 1864, the troops in the district consisted of 144th New York; 157th New York; 25th Ohio (nine companies); 32nd United States Colored Troops; First Battalion, 1st New York Engineers; and a detachment of United States Veteran Reserve Corps. The 157th New York was at Fort Pulaski.

In November 1864, the two New York regiments and the 25th Ohio, 32nd United States Colored Troops were transferred to John P. Hatch's Coast Division as a part of Edward E. Potter's First Brigade. For details, see below, Operations in the Department of the South, Hatch's Expedition against the Charleston and Savannah Railroad (Battle of Honey Hill, South Carolina), and Hatch's Advance from Pocotaligo to Charleston, South Carolina.

May 27, 1865, the order designating the troops in the District of Beaufort as Second Separate Brigade, and the troops in the District of Hilton Head as Third Separate Brigade was revoked, and the troops in the District of Port Royal (formed by the consolidation of the other two districts) were designated as Second Separate Brigade.

The commanders of the District of Hilton Head during this period were as follows:

Joshua B. Howell	April 1864 to April 26, 1864
William W. H. Davis	April 26, 1864 to May 13, 1864
William Birney	May 13, 1864 to June 2, 1864
John P. Hatch	June 2, 1864 to August 1, 1864
Edward E. Potter	August 1, 1864 to October 26, 1864
Philip P. Brown, Jr.	October 26, 1864 to November 1, 1864
Eliakim P. Scammon	November 1, 1864 to November 16, 1864
Edward E. Potter	November 16, 1864 to November 28, 1864
Philip P. Brown, Jr.	November 28, 1864 to December 24, 1864
Milton S. Littlefield	December 24, 1864 to January 1865
Philip P. Brown, Jr.	January 1865 to February 22, 1865
Milton S. Littlefield	February 22, 1865 to May 13, 1865

District of North Carolina. January 12, 1865 the Department of the South was extended to include the state of North Carolina, which was taken from the Department of Virginia and North Carolina, and January 16, 1865, the state was organized as the District of North Carolina, Department of the South. The district was placed under the orders of William T. Sherman, commander of the Military Division of the Mississippi, who was then about to move northward through the Carolinas. Because of poor communications between North Carolina and Headquarters Department of the South, however, the state was detached January 31, 1865 and constituted as the Department of North Carolina, under the command of John M. Schofield.

Northern District. The Northern District, Department of the South was organized in late April 1864 from the Northern District, Department of the South, Tenth Corps. Alexander Schimmelfennig was assigned command, with headquarters on Folly Island. The district was organized as follows:

Folly Island, Leopold Von Gilsa
  41st New York, 54th New York, 74th Pennsylvania,
    and infantry detachments
Little Folly Island, William Heine
  55th Massachusetts (colored) and 103rd New York
Morris Island, William Gurney
  127th New York, 54th Massachusetts (colored), 21st
    United States Colored Troops, and 34th United
    States Colored Troops
Artillery
  Battery B, 3rd New Light Artillery, and Second Bat-
    talion, 3rd Rhode Island Heavy Artillery

October 26, 1864 the troops in the Northern District were designated as First Separate Brigade, Department of the South, but both designations were used to the end of the war.

On February 17, 1865, the day Sherman's army reached Columbia, South Carolina, Confederate forces evacuated Charleston, and the next day Charleston and its dependencies were attached to the Northern District. Two days later, February 20, 1865, the post of Morris Island was transferred to the post of Charleston, and that day the order creating the posts of Morris Island and Folly Island was revoked.

Commanders of the post of Folly Island were Leopold Von Gilsa, William Heine, Alfred S. Hartwell, and Eugene A. Kozwell. The post was discontinued February 20, 1865. Commanders of the post of Morris Island were William Gurney, Philip P. Brown, Jr., Edward N. Hallowell, and Augustus G. Bennett. The post was discontinued February 20, 1865, and was transferred to the post of Charleston. Commanders of Charleston were Augustus G. Bennett to February 24, 1865, and then William Gurney to June 27, 1865.

The Northern District was discontinued in late June 1865 by the creation of the District of Charleston June 23, 1865, and the Department of North Carolina June 27, 1865.

The commanders of the Northern District were as follows:

Alexander Schimmelfennig	April 1864 to September 2, 1864
Rufus Saxton	September 2, 1864 to October 3, 1864
Eliakim P. Scammon	October 3, 1864 to October 26, 1864
Edward E. Potter	October 26, 1864 to November 14, 1864
John P. Hatch	November 14, 1864 to November 28, 1864
Edward N. Hallowell	November 28, 1864 to December 8, 1864
Alexander Schimmelfennig	December 8, 1864 to February 26, 1865
John P. Hatch	February 26, 1865 to June 1865

Note 1. Saxton also retained command of the District of Beaufort while in command of the Northern District.

Note 2. Hallowell assumed temporary command of the Northern District when Hatch departed to command the Coast Division.

Note 3. When Hatch assumed command of the Northern District February 26, 1865, Schimmelfennig took charge of the defenses of Charleston.

District of Savannah. The city of Savannah, Georgia was held by Confederate forces until late December 1864, and it was then captured by troops of William T. Sherman's Army of the Military Division of the Mississippi, who had marched across Georgia from Atlanta. The city was occupied by John W. Geary's Second Division, Twentieth Corps. For details, see Savannah Campaign (Sherman's March through Georgia). To relieve Geary's division from occupation duty so that it could accompany Sherman's army northward through the Carolinas (see Carolinas Campaign), Cuvier Grover's Second Division, Nineteenth Corps, at that time serving with Philip H. Sheridan's forces of the Middle Military Division in Virginia, was ordered January 6, 1865 from the Shenandoah Valley to Baltimore for transfer to Georgia. The division arrived at Savannah January 17–20, 1865, and relieved Geary's division January 19, 1865.

January 18, 1865, the city of Savannah and its dependencies were assigned by Sherman to the Department of the South, and John G. Foster, then commanding the department, assumed command January 21, 1865. That same day, Foster constituted the District of Savannah to include the city, with its forts, lines of defenses, and communications, and also the islands and country adjacent that were under the military control of the garrison. Grover was assigned command of the district, with headquarters at Savannah. Grover's Second Division, Nineteenth Corps was organized as follows:

Grover's Division, Cuvier Grover, to February 12, 1865
  Henry W. Birge, to March 1865

First Brigade, Henry W. Birge, to February 12, 1865
  Henry D. Washburn, to June 8, 1865
Second Brigade, Edward L. Molineux, to February 17, 1865
  Nicholas W. Day, to March 1865
Third Brigade, James P. Richardson, to March 1865

Note 1. Second Brigade and Third Brigade were sent to North Carolina in March 1865, and they did not return to the Department of the South until May 1865. For details of the activities of these two brigades in North Carolina, see Carolinas Campaign; and also Department of North Carolina, January 31, 1865–May 19, 1866, Troops in the Department of North Carolina.

Note 2. First Brigade remained in the District of Savannah during this time, but in March 1865, it was designated as Washburn's Brigade.

March 24, 1865, 33rd and 103rd United States Colored Troops were organized as a brigade under William T. Bennett, and were ordered to Savannah. In April 1865, the troops in the district consisted only of Washburn's Brigade (formerly First Brigade, Second Division, Nineteenth Corps) and the two regiments under Bennett.

April 19–21, 1865, William Dwight's Provisional Division (formerly First Division. Nineteenth Corps) was transferred from near Harper's Ferry to Washington, D.C., and then on May 29, 1865, it was ordered to Savannah. The division, which consisted of George L. Beal's First Brigade, Edwin P. Davis' Second Brigade, and James D. Fessenden's Third Brigade, left Washington during the period June 5–25, 1865, and headquarters of the division left June 27, 1865. By the end of June 1865, the division had arrived in Savannah.

June 5, 1865, in the reorganization of the state of Georgia, the District of Savannah was redefined as consisting of Fort Pulaski and the counties of Chatham, Bryan, Effingham, Bulloch, Emanuel, and Screven. Henry W. Birge was assigned command, with headquarters at Savannah. At that time Birge was on detached duty, and Stewart L. Woodford was assigned temporary commander of the post and District of Savannah for a few days until Birge returned.

June 27, 1865, the troops serving in the District of Savannah were designated as Sixth Separate Brigade, Department of the South.

By an order of June 27, 1865, the district became a part of the newly created Department of Georgia.

Postwar Districts in the Department of the South

District of Charleston, South Carolina. The District of Charleston was organized June 23, 1865, to consist of the districts (counties) of Charleston, Colleton, Orangeburg, Lexington, Barnwell, and Richland. John P. Hatch was assigned command, with headquarters at Charleston. That part of the district lying along the Savannah River, and then occupied by troops under Edward L. Molineux, commander of the District of Northern Georgia, remained under Molineux's control.

June 27, 1865, the troops in the District of Charleston were designated as First Separate Brigade, Department of the South.

William Gurney commanded the post of Charleston June 23–30, 1865, and was succeeded by William T. Bennett.

District of Eastern South Carolina. The District of Eastern South Carolina was organized June 23, 1865, to consist of the districts (counties) of Horry, Georgetown, Marion, Williamsburg, Marlboro, Darlington, Sumter, Kershaw, and Chesterfield. George L. Beal was assigned command, with headquarters at Florence, South Carolina. The troops in the district consisted of Beal's Brigade, which was formerly First Brigade, First Division, Nineteenth Corps; and a battalion of cavalry.

June 27, 1865, the troops in the district were designated as Third Separate Brigade, Department of the South.

District of Northern Georgia. The District of Northern Georgia was organized June 5, 1865, to consist of those counties in Georgia not included in the District of South Georgia and the District of Savannah. Edward L. Molineux was assigned command, with headquarters at Augusta. The region of South Carolina along the Savannah River, and occupied by troops under Molineux's command, remained under the command of Molineux when the District of Western South Carolina was organized June 23, 1865. The troops in the district were designated as Seventh Separate Brigade, Department of the South June 27, 1865.

District of Port Royal. The District of Port Royal

was formed May 13, 1865, by the consolidation of the District of Hilton Head and the District of Beaufort. Edward E. Potter was assigned command, with headquarters on Hilton Head Island. The posts of Hilton Head and Beaufort were established May 15, 1865.

May 27, 1865, the order assigning the designation of Second Separate Brigade to the troops of the former District of Beaufort, and of Third Separate Brigade to the troops of the former District of Hilton Head was revoked, and the troops in the District of Port Royal were designated as Second Separate Brigade, Department of the South.

In a further reorganization of the state of South Carolina June 23, 1865, the District of Port Royal was constituted to comprise only the District of Beaufort. Edward E. Potter was assigned command of the district, with headquarters at Hilton Head. June 27, 1865, the troops in the district were designated as Second Separate Brigade.

District of Savannah. See above, Wartime Districts in the Department of the South.

District of Southern Georgia. The District of Southern Georgia was organized June 5, 1865, to consist of that part of the state of Georgia lying south of the northern boundaries of the counties of Liberty, Tattnall, Montgomery, Laurens, Pulaski, Dooly, Sumter, Webster, and Stewart. Cuvier Grover was assigned command, with headquarters at Doctor Town, Georgia. June 27, 1865, the troops in the district were designated as Fifth Separate Brigade, Department of the South.

District of Western South Carolina. The District of Western South Carolina was organized June 23, 1865, to consist of the districts (counties) of Lancaster, Fairfield, Chester, York, Union, Newberry, Edgefield, Abbeville, Laurens, Spartanburg, Greenville, Anderson, and Pickens. Charles H. Van Wyck was assigned temporary command, with headquarters at Alston, South Carolina. That part of the district lying along the Savannah River, and then occupied by troops of Edward L. Molineux's District of Northern Georgia, was to remain under Molineux's command. The troops in the district consisted of two infantry regiments, including Van Wyck's own, and one battalion of cavalry.

The troops in the District of Western South Carolina were designated as Fourth Separate Brigade, Department of the South June 27, 1865.

Troops in the Department of the South

During this period there was no corps organization in the Department of the South. In addition to the troops in the various districts, which have been described above, there were three infantry divisions that were organized for special purposes, and also some special forces that were the equivalent of a division, but were not officially so designated. The three divisions were as follows:

Coast Division. This division was organized under the command of John P. Hatch for operations against the Charleston and Savannah Railroad in cooperation with William T. Sherman's advance into the Carolinas. For details of the organization and operations of this command, see below, Operations in the Department of the South, Hatch's Expedition against the Charleston and Savannah Railroad (Battle of Honey Hill), South Carolina, and Hatch's Advance from Pocotaligo to Charleston, South Carolina.

Potter's Provisional Division. This division was organized for an expedition against the Wilmington and Manchester Railroad and the South Carolina Railroad. For the organization and operations of this division, see below, Operations in the Department of the South, Potter's Expedition against the Wilmington and Manchester Railroad and the South Carolina Railroad.

Prince's Provisional Division. When William T. Sherman left Atlanta with the Army of the Cumberland and the Army of the Tennessee on his march across Georgia, there were many men absent from the armies who were unable to rejoin their commands before they departed. These men were transferred to the east to return to their units when they arrived in the Carolinas. In late January 1865, about 5,000–8,000 of these troops were expected in South Carolina, where Sherman was beginning his march northward toward Virginia. Sherman ordered that they be stopped at Hilton Head, and be formed into a command to be used by John G. Foster, commander of the Department of the South, to demonstrate toward Charleston and Georgetown, or to reinforce Hatch's Coast Division if needed.

February 4, 1865, Henry Prince was ordered to take charge of these troops, and put them in camp between Beaufort and Pocotaligo. During February and March Prince's Division was at Blair's Landing on the Pocotaligo River guarding Sherman's communications with Port Royal. One brigade of the division was sent to report to Hatch, then commanding the Northern District, and March 12, 1865, it was assigned to the Defenses of Charleston South of the Ashley River.

April 10, 1865, Prince's Provisional Division was ordered to join Sherman's army, and April 14–21, 1865, it was transferred by sea to North Carolina. The division was discontinued April 27, near Raleigh, by the distribution of the troops among their proper commands.

Operations in the Department of the South

The Department of the South was relatively quiet during the period May 1864–November 1864. There were no major operations, but there were numerous skirmishes and expeditions, especially in the District of Florida, which were conducted generally for the purpose of driving small enemy forces from the various parts of the department, and for the destruction of railroads, bridges, and other installations, and also for acquiring cotton, cattle, and supplies. In November and December 1864 and the early part of 1865, however, while Sherman's army was moving through Georgia and the Carolinas, a number of demonstrations and expeditions were carried out to aid Sherman in his operations.

The more important military operations in the Department of the South during this period are described briefly in the following sections.

Expedition from Jacksonville to Lake Monroe, Florida, April 26, 1864–May 6, 1864. On April 26, 1864, William Birney, commander of the District of Florida, left Jacksonville on an expedition through the counties in Florida on the east side of the Saint John's River to Lake Monroe. He captured cotton, cattle, and two schooners, and returned to Jacksonville May 6, 1864.

Operations on the Saint John's River, Florida, May 19–27, 1864. George H. Gordon, commanding the District of Florida, learned from William H. Noble that an enemy force was advancing from Welaka, on the east side of the Saint John's River, and he set out from Jacksonville with detachments of 144th New York and 157th New York to find this force. He was joined at Picolata by six companies of James C. Beecher's 35th United States Colored Troops, and he then moved by boat to Palatka and, after disembarking, marched to Volusia. Gordon then concentrated his infantry at a point nine miles south of Saint Augustine, at Saint Augustine, and at Picolata, and then, believing that he had accomplished all that he could in the area, returned to Jacksonville.

Skirmish near Camp Finegan, Florida, May 25, 1864. On May 25, 1864, Gordon sent James Shaw, Jr. with a force of about 400 men on a reconnaissance in the direction of Baldwin to determine whether there were enemy troops on his front. Shaw encountered a force near Camp Finegan and was briefly engaged, and he then withdrew.

Expedition from Jacksonville to Camp Milton, Florida, May 31, 1864–June 3, 1864. Early in June 1864, Gordon led an expedition to capture enemy forces at Camp Milton, Florida, and to destroy the entrenched camp, which was formed across the railroad about twelve miles west of Jacksonville. Gordon concentrated his force at Jacksonville, and then advanced in two columns. One column under William H. Noble, consisting of about 1,400 men from the 17th Connecticut, 157th New York, 107th Ohio, and 3rd and 35th United States Colored Troops, moved by boat and landed about ten miles from the mouth of McGirt's Creek at 3:00 A.M. June 1, 1864. It then moved northward along the creek toward the rear of the enemy entrenchments. The second column, under James Shaw, Jr., consisting of about 1,100 men from from 144th New York, 75th Ohio (Mounted), 7th United States Colored Troops, and six guns of the 3rd Rhode Island Heavy Artillery, moved at about the same time by the road south of the railroad to threaten the front of the line of enemy entrenchments. Both columns arrived at about the same time, but upon their approach the enemy departed, leaving the camp unprotected. The Federal troops completely demolished the works, and then, the object of the expedition having been accomplished, they marched back toward Jacksonville, and arrived there June 3, 1864.

Foster's Demonstration against Charleston, South Carolina and the Charleston and Savannah Railroad, July 1–11, 1864. John G. Foster, with a force of about 5,000 infantry, 100 cavalry, and two sections of artillery, left Hilton Head on the evening of July 1, 1864 for a demonstration against the city of Charleston and the Charleston and Savannah Railroad. The next morning, the expedition entered the mouth of the Edisto River and landed a force under John P. Hatch on Seabrook Island. Hatch's command was composed of a brigade under Rufus Saxton from Beaufort, South Carolina, which consisted of the 56th New York and 9th and 26th United States Colored Troops, and Samuel C. Day's Battery F, 3rd New York Light Artillery; and a brigade under William W. H. Davis from Hilton Head, which consisted of 144th New York, 157th New York, and 104th Pennsylvania. Davis was wounded July 6, 1864, and Philip P. Brown, Jr. assumed command of the brigade.

Foster continued on up the Edisto River to White Point, and there he landed William Birney with 1,200 men and two pieces of artillery. Birney's orders were to destroy the Charleston and Savannah Railroad, and the bridges over the South Edisto and Ashepoo rivers, if possible. Birney's command consisted of the 7th United States Colored Troops, four companies of the 35th United States Colored Troops, and a small detachment of the 75th Ohio from his District of Florida, and 35th United States Colored Troops from Beaufort, South Carolina.

July 3, 1864, Birney advanced, with skirmishing, about three miles to a creek, where he came under artillery fire from an earthwork on the far side. He was unable to advance on the road because of this fire, and the swamps and difficult country on both sides of the road prevented him from making a flanking movement. Birney was then ordered to reembark his command and join Alexander Schimmelfennig's forces on James Island.

While Foster was advancing to John's Island,

Alexander Schimmelfennig left Morris Island with the 54th Massachusetts (Colored), 21st United States Colored Troops, and Edward A. Wild's Battery B, 3rd New York Light Artillery to join the expedition on James Island. These troops advanced on the night of July 1, 1864 and captured a battery on the enemy line, but they were unable to advance further. They finally returned to Morris Island July 11, 1864.

Meantime, Hatch's command had crossed to John's Island, and then marched across the island to the Stono River, where it occupied the west bank, opposite James Island, from the vicinity of Legareville to Fort (or Battery) Pringle. The latter was a short distance north of Grimballs' plantation, west of Secessionville. Foster was absent from the expedition July 6–8, 1864, and Hatch was in command during this period. Saxton was in charge of the forces on John's Island. Hatch was unable to cross the Stono to James Island, and after some fighting on July 7 and July 9, 1864, he withdrew to Legareville. He then reembarked July 10, 1864 for Hilton Head.

On the night of July 2, 1864, William Gurney, with a force from Morris Island, made a night assault from boats on the enemy's works at Johnson's Point, James Island, but this was quickly repulsed and Gurney withdrew. Gurney's command consisted of the 52nd Pennsylvania, 127th New York, and a detachment of the 3rd Rhode Island Heavy Artillery.

Expedition from Jacksonville to Trout Creek, Florida, July 15–20, 1864. On July 15, 1864, William Birney, commander of the District of Florida, landed a force consisting of 3rd United States Colored Troops and a company of the 4th Massachusetts Cavalry at the mouth of Trout Creek, a short distance below Jacksonville. He then moved up the creek to its source in the direction of Lewisville, and sent out parties toward the Saint Mary's River, and to Callahan, in Nassau County, on the Florida Railroad. After capturing supplies and various installations, and destroying all that could not be removed, the expedition returned to Jacksonville.

Expedition from Jacksonville to Baldwin, Florida, July 23–28, 1864. William Birney left Jacksonville July 23, 1864 on a raid to the Cedar

Keys and Lake City Railroad (the Florida Railroad) beyond Baldwin. He took with him the 17th Connecticut, 75th Ohio, and the 7th, 8th, and 35th United States Colored Troops, and a detachment of the 4th Massachusetts Cavalry. On July 25, 1864, he destroyed portions of the track, including some trestlework, and then occupied Baldwin and Camp Milton the next day. Birney ordered William H. Noble, commanding the United States Forces at Baldwin, to continue the work of destruction on the railroad.

Raid on the Florida Railroad and Action at Gainesville, Florida, August 15–19, 1864. August 15, 1864, Andrew L. Harris left Baldwin with about 250 men of the 75th Ohio, 4th Massachusetts Cavalry, and 3rd Rhode Island Heavy Artillery, and advanced along the Florida Railroad to Gainesville. There he was attacked by troops of the 2nd Florida Cavalry and completely routed, and the remnants of his command fled to Magnolia on the Saint John's River, south of Jacksonville. William H. Noble, who had been ordered to move toward Magnolia from Baldwin August 15, 1864, arrived there August 19, 1864 with 34th, 35th, and 102nd United States Colored Troops, a detachment of 75th Ohio, and a detachment of 3rd Rhode Island Heavy Artillery. With Noble's departure, the post of Baldwin was abandoned, and Noble then assumed command of the United States Forces at Magnolia, Florida.

Hatch's Expedition against the Charleston and Savannah Railroad (Engagement at Honey Hill), South Carolina, November 28, 1864–February 5, 1865. In a communication dated November 13, 1864, Henry W. Halleck informed John G. Foster, commander of the Department of the South, that William T. Sherman, with his Army of the Military Division of the Mississippi, would leave Atlanta, Georgia November 16, 1864, and march for the interior of Georgia or Alabama, as circumstances might dictate. He further informed Foster that if Sherman marched through Georgia he probably would arrive on the Atlantic Coast in the early part of December 1864. In that event, he, Halleck, wanted Foster to cut the Charleston and Savannah Railroad near Pocotaligo, if possible, at about the same time so as to prevent enemy reinforcements from reaching Savannah from the north.

Accordingly, in November 1864, Foster organized an expedition on Hilton Head Island by bringing in regiments from Folly Island and Morris Island, and from the districts of Hilton Head, Beaufort, and Florida. This force, which consisted of about 5,000 largely inexperienced troops, was designated as the Coast Division, Department of the South, and was organized as follows:

First Brigade, Edward E. Potter
   56th New York from Morris Island; 127th New York from Beaufort; and 157th New York, 25th Ohio, and 32nd United States Colored Troops from Hilton Head

Second Brigade, Alfred S. Hartwell
   54th Massachusetts (colored) from Morris Island; 55th Massachusetts (colored) from Folly Island; 34th and 35th United States Colored Troops from the District of Florida; and 102nd United States Colored Troops from Beaufort.

Naval Brigade, George H. Preble
   Sailor Battalion of Infantry, James O'Kane
   Battalion of Marines, George G. Stoddard
   Artillery Battalion, Edmund O. Matthews

Artillery Brigade, William Ames
   Company A (one section), 3rd Rhode Island Artillery, William H. Hamner
   Battery B, 3rd New York Artillery, Thomas J. Mesereau
   Battery F, 3rd New York Artillery, Edgar H. Titus

Foster's expedition left Hilton Head on the night of November 28, 1864, and steamed up the Broad River in a dense fog. Most of the transports and gunboats became lost or ran aground, but the leading troops arrived at Boyd's Neck, a strip of land between two tributaries of the Broad River, and disembarked November 28, 1864. That day, John P. Hatch was placed in command of the Coast Division, with orders to push on and destroy the railroad near Grahamville Station.

The Naval Brigade landed first at 9:00 A.M., and was then sent out about two miles to hold the junction of the road from the landing with the River Road, which ran roughly parallel with the Broad River. The 32nd United States Colored Troops was ordered out to support the Naval Brigade.

When Hatch realized that all of his command would not be ashore until the next day, he decided to take the four regiments that had landed and some cavalry, and march to Grahamville that evening. Hatch left the landing at 4:00 P.M., and upon reaching the River Road turned to the right and marched about two miles before realizing that he was moving in the wrong direction. He then marched back on the River Road about three miles to Bolan Church, where the Honey Hill Road (toward Grahamville) branched off to the right. Instead of turning off on this road, however, Hatch continued on about four miles on the River Road before he realized that he again had taken the wrong road. He then turned back to Bolan Church, where he bivouacked at 2:00 A.M. November 30, 1864. He had marched about fifteen miles that evening and night, and was still seven miles from Grahamville.

On the morning of November 30, 1864, the Naval Brigade and the artillery came up, and Hatch then advanced toward Grahamville. The cavalry moved out in front, and it was followed by Potter's First Brigade, which was supported by the Naval Brigade. Only two regiments and four companies of another of Hartwell's brigade had arrived, but these followed the Naval Brigade.

About 9:15 A.M., after marching less than a mile, Hatch encountered enemy skirmishers that were supported with a battery of artillery. Potter then opened the action by advancing the 127th New York as skirmishers, and he supported them with 25th Ohio, 144th New York, and 157th New York. Potter slowly forced the enemy back for about three and a half miles, and then about 11:00 A.M. the head of his column arrived at a point where the road made a sharp turn to the left, and another road came in from the right. There he found the main body of the enemy entrenched across the road at Honey Hill on the crest of a low ridge. The works consisted of two redoubts for artillery, constructed by Robert E. Lee two years before, and a line of rifle pits that extended out beyond the redoubts on each side of the road. Occupying these works were troops of Charles J. Colcock's Third Military District of South Carolina, and Gustavus W. Smith's Georgia Militia, which had just arrived from Savannah. A small creek, bounded by a marsh that was covered by dense undergrowth, flowed across the front of the enemy line.

As Hatch's troops arrived, the 127th New York was formed about 200 yards in front of the redoubts, with its right on the road. Four companies of the 54th Massachusetts were across the road on the right, and three companies of the 55th Massachusetts were to the right of the 54th Massachusetts. The 35th United States Colored Troops was placed on the road in support of the 127th New York. Potter then arrived at the front and took charge.

The left of Potter's brigade, reinforced by two companies of the 54th Massachusetts and a part of the 55th Massachusetts, all led by Hartwell, made two desperate attacks on the enemy works, but these were repulsed with heavy losses, including Hartwell, who was wounded. The 32nd United States Colored Troops and 144th New York, which were advancing on the right of 55th Massachusetts, came under fire and wavered, but the 25th Ohio charged through their lines and drove the enemy back. About noon the Marine Battalion was sent to support the right wing. The Federal line was then formed as follows: On the left of the road, from left to right, were the 157th New York, 57th New York, and 127th New York; the artillery was on the road, and in rear of the artillery was the Naval Brigade; and on the right of the road, from left to right, were four companies of the 54th Massachusetts, three companies of the 55th Massachusetts, 25th Ohio, 144th New York, and the Marine Battalion. Henry L. Chapman arrived from the landing with his 102nd United States Colored Troops at 1:00 P.M., and he assumed command of Hartwell's brigade. Edward L. Hallowell relieved Chapman in command of Second Brigade December 8, 1864.

Hatch's right wing was the next to advance, with orders to swing around to the left and strike the enemy left flank or rear if possible, but this movement was soon halted by dense undergrowth and deep swamps. On the Federal left, deep swamps and an abatis in front of the enemy works made a forward movement in that area impossible. Fighting continued into the afternoon, but at 3:30 Hatch decided to hold his position until dark and then withdraw. The regiments began to fall back toward Bolan Church about dusk, and the troops camped that night about two miles from Boyd's Neck.

Hatch's Advance from Pocotaligo to Charleston, South Carolina, February 5–26, 1865. After the Engagement at Honey Hill, South Carolina, Hatch's Coast Division remained near the Charleston and ton and Savannah Railroad until February 1865. On January 2, 1865, Oliver O. Howard's Army of the Tennessee was ordered from Savannah, Georgia to Beaufort, South Carolina, and was then directed to move out to the head of the Broad River and concentrate near Pocotaligo before beginning its march through the Carolinas with Sherman. Howard occupied Pocotaligo January 15, 1865, and Hatch was ordered to prepare his Coast Division for offensive operations in cooperation with Howard's army when Sherman began his northward march.

There was a command change in the Coast Division January 23, 1865. On that date, Edward E. Potter was assigned command of the District of Beaufort, and he was succeeded in command of First Brigade, Coast Division by Charles H. Van Wyck.

February 1, 1865, Sherman ordered Hatch to march along the railroad toward Charleston as soon as the enemy withdrew, and to destroy the track as far as the Edisto River if possible. Four days later the Confederate forces departed from Hatch's front, and he then moved forward and on February 17, 1865 arrived at Jacksonboro and Willstown on the Edisto. This was on the same day that Sherman occupied Columbia, South Carolina, and that enemy forces evacuated Charleston. Hatch then moved on to Charleston, and February 26, 1865, he assumed command of the Northern District, Department of the South. The Coast Division was broken up and the regiments were transferred to the various districts of the department.

Potter's Expedition to Bull's Bay, South Carolina, February 11–20, 1865. Early in February 1865, as Sherman's army was advancing into South Carolina, Sherman ordered Foster to watch Charleston closely, and to make a diversion at Bull's Bay, about twenty-five miles northeast of Charleston Harbor. A Federal force in this area would also hold the roads by which the enemy might escape from Mount Pleasant, just east of Charleston.

February 11, 1865, an expedition commanded by Edward E. Potter left Stono Inlet and arrived at Bull's Bay the next morning. Potter's force consisted of a brigade commanded by Alfred S. Hartwell, which was composed of 144th New York, 32nd United States Colored Troops, and 55th Massachusetts (colored). Because of bad weather the expedition did not land until February 17, 1865, and

the next day the 32nd United States Colored Troops occupied Andersonville. Potter then learned that Confederate forces had evacuated Charleston, and February 19, 1865 marched with his command toward the city. March 12, 1865, Hartwell's brigade was posted in the defenses of Charleston at Charleston Neck.

Expedition to Georgetown, South Carolina, February 22, 1865. February 22, 1865, Alexander Schimmelfennig, commander of the post of Charleston, sent Philip P. Brown, Jr. with the 157th New York to make a diversion toward Georgetown, and then, if practicable, to move up the Santee River, with cooperation by the navy, and join Edward E. Potter's force that was operating in the area. For additional information, see above, Potter's Expedition to Bull's Bay, South Carolina. A second regiment was sent to Georgetown February 28, 1865, and Brown was assigned command of the post.

Hartwell's Expedition to the Santee River, South Carolina, April 5–15, 1865. April 5, 1865, Alfred S. Hartwell was ordered to march with his Provisional Brigade on an expedition to the Santee River to support Edward E. Potter, who was moving through the area north of the river from Georgetown toward Sumterville (Sumter) and Camden, South Carolina. Hartwell was directed to remain on the Santee River so as to be in position to aid Potter if the latter was forced back to the river. See Potter's Expedition against the Wilmington and Manchester Railroad and the South Carolina Railroad, following section. Hartwell started from Four-Mile House, near Charleston, on the morning of April 6, 1865. His command consisted of the 54th New York, 55th Massachusetts (colored), and a section of 3rd New York Artillery; and he halted for the night on Goose Creek, near the Northeastern Railroad, about eighteen miles from Charleston. He then marched by Monk's (Monch's) Corner to Pineville, and he arrived on Eutaw Creek, near Nelson's Ferry, April 9, 1865. The expedition returned to Charleston April 15, 1865.

Potter's Expedition against the Wilmington and Manchester Railroad and the South Carolina Railroad, April 5–25, 1865. March 27, 1865, Edward E. Potter, commanding the District of

Beaufort, was ordered to report to John P. Hatch to assume command of an expedition to destroy the Wilmington and Manchester Railroad and the South Carolina Railroad between Camden and Florence. On March 24, 1865, a brigade was formed under Edward N. Hallowell, consisting of 54th Massachusetts (colored) and 102nd United States Colored Troops, and it was ordered to Georgetown for the expedition. The 25th Ohio was sent April 1, 1865, and 32nd United States Colored Troops and five companies of 56th New York were sent the next day. Potter went to Georgetown April 1, 1865, and organized the troops assembled there, totaling about 2,700 men, into a provisional division of two brigades as follows:

PROVISIONAL DIVISION, Edward E. Potter

First Brigade, Philip P. Brown, Jr.
    25th Ohio, 107th Ohio, 157th New York, and a detachment of 56th New York

Second Brigade, Edward N. Hallowell
    54th Massachusetts (colored), 32nd and five companies of 102nd United States Colored Troops

Detachment 4th Massachusetts Cavalry
Detachment 1st New York Engineers
Section of Battery E, 3rd New York Artillery

Potter left Georgetown April 5, 1865, and marched up the Black River to Sumterville (Sumter), which he occupied April 9, 1865. He then destroyed locomotives, cars, railroad facilities, and bridges on the railroad, and he also burned cotton and captured government stores. Potter then moved on to Manchester on April 11, 1865, where he destroyed more locomotives, cars, track, and trestlework. On April 15, 1865, Potter moved on toward Statesburg, driving back the enemy as he advanced, to the main road connecting Sumterville and Camden. He then occupied Camden, and arrived at Middleton Depot April 19, 1865, having continued to destroy the railroad as he marched. April 21, 1865, Potter moved toward Georgetown, and at noon that day Gillmore informed Potter that a convention signed by Joseph E. Johnston and William T. Sherman had ended hostilities, and that the work of destruction of the railroads should end. That day Potter turned over the Provisional Division to Brown and returned to Hilton Head. Brown led the expedition back to Georgetown, where it arrived April 25, 1865. The Provisional Division was then broken up, and Hallowell returned to Charleston. Brown remained in command of the United States Forces at Georgetown, which was continued as an active post until June 1865. Brown was later relieved by James C. Carmichael.

Hartwell's Expedition to Orangeburg, South Carolina, May 4–20, 1865. May 4, 1865, John P. Hatch, commanding the Northern District, Department of the South, ordered Alfred S. Hartwell to assume command of a provisional brigade, and to lead it on an expedition to Orangeburg, South Carolina. The brigade was formed from the 25th Ohio, 54th New York, 55th Massachusetts (colored), 102nd United States Colored Troops, and a section of Battery B, 3rd New York Artillery. Hartwell left Charleston May 7, 1865, and reached Sumterville (Sumter) the next day. May 18, 1865, the 25th Ohio occupied Orangeburg, and the 102nd United States Colored Troops occupied Branchville. The 55th New York and 55th Massachusetts (colored) were also sent to Orangeburg, and Hartwell established his headquarters at that place May 20, 1865. May 23, 1865, the 25th Ohio was ordered to Columbia, South Carolina.

DEPARTMENT OF SOUTH CAROLINA

By an order of June 27, 1865 which reorganized the military divisions and geographical departments of the army, the Department of the South was discontinued, and its former territory was assigned to other departments. The Department of South Carolina was constituted by the above order to consist of the state of South Carolina, and Quincy A. Gillmore was assigned command, with headquarters at Hilton Head. Gillmore assumed command July 18, 1865. Also by the above order, the Department of South Carolina was assigned to the Military Division of the Atlantic. The department was merged into the Department of the Carolinas May 19, 1866.

DEPARTMENT OF THE SUSQUEHANNA

In the early part of June 1863, the administration became convinced from reports received that the state of Pennsylvania was threatened with invasion by Confederate forces from Virginia. To provide better administration of the troops that would be called upon to defend the state, the secretary of war decided to create two new departments. June 10, 1863, Edwin M. Stanton issued an order constituting the Department of the Susquehanna and the Department of the Monongahela.

The Department of the Susquehanna was formed from territory taken from the Middle Department and consisted of that part of the state of Pennsylvania lying east of Johnstown and the Laurel Hill range of mountains. This range begins in the south near the junction of the western boundary of Maryland and the Pennsylvania state line, and it extends in a northerly direction, passing a short distance west of Johnstown. Darius N. Couch was assigned command, with headquarters at Chambersburg. Couch assumed command June 11, 1863, and three days later moved his headquarters to Harrisburg.

The invasion of Pennsylvania took place as expected. Robert E. Lee's Army of Northern Virginia entered the state at Greencastle from Boonsboro, Maryland, and advanced along the Cumberland Valley to Chambersburg, with a part of Richard S. Ewell's corps going by the way of Waynesboro. Ewell continued his march to Carlisle, and some of his troops advanced to the Susquehanna River at Wrightsville and White Hall (Camp Hill), opposite Harrisburg. The rest of Lee's army marched to Cashtown. Meantime, the Army of the Potomac moved northward through Maryland; and July 1, 1863, the two armies met at Gettysburg. They were engaged there during the first three days of July, and on the night of the fourth Lee began his retreat toward Virginia. George G. Meade, then commanding the Army of the Potomac, followed to the Potomac River at Williamsport, Maryland and Falling Waters, West Virginia, where Lee recrossed into Virginia on the night of July 13, 1863.

Meade's army crossed the river at Harper's Ferry and Berlin (present-day Brunswick), and moved into the Loudoun Valley in pursuit of Lee. When the last of the Army of the Potomac had crossed, Meade left troops in Maryland to guard the line of the Potomac River, and these he placed under Couch's command. Thus that part of Washington County in Maryland between, and including, Clear Spring and Harper's Ferry was in effect included in the Department of the Susquehanna. On August 3, 1863, however, all of the state of Maryland west of the Monocacy River was transferred to Benjamin F. Kelley's Department of West Virginia, and all troops in this territory, then under Couch, were assigned to Kelley's command. For additional information, see below, Troops and Operations in the Department of the Susquehanna.

April 6, 1864, the Department of the Monongahela was discontinued and merged into the Department of the Susquehanna, which then included within its limits the entire state of Pennsylvania and the counties of Columbiana, Jefferson, and Belmont in Ohio.

August 7, 1864, the Middle Military Division was created under Philip H. Sheridan, and included in the division were the departments of the Susquehanna, Washington, and West Virginia, and the Middle Department.

The Department of the Susquehanna was discontinued December 1, 1864 by a change of designation to the Department of Pennsylvania. Couch remained in command of the Department of the Susquehanna until December 1, 1863, and he then was succeeded in command of the Department of Pennsylvania by George Cadwalader.

Headquarters of the Department of the Susquehanna changed several times, especially during the Gettysburg Campaign. It was at Chambersburg June 11–12, 1863; Harrisburg June 13, 1863 to July 8, 1863; Chambersburg July 10, 1863 to July 31, 1864; Harrisburg July 31, 1864 to about August 20, 1864; and Chambersburg from about August 10, 1864 to December 1, 1864.

DISTRICTS IN THE DEPARTMENT OF THE SUSQUEHANNA

Prior to August 20, 1863, there was no district organization in the Department of the Susquehanna. The troops were simply assigned to the various posts of the department. After that date, however, four districts were constituted as follows:

Lehigh District. The Lehigh District was constituted August 20, 1863, to consist of the counties of Berks, Lehigh, Schuylkill, Northampton, Carbon, Monroe, Luzerne, and Columbia in Pennsylvania. This was an irregular block of counties in the east-central part of the state. Franz Sigel was assigned command, with headquarters at Reading. The principal posts in the district were Bloomsburg, Easton, Hazelton, Pottsville, Reading, Scranton, and Stroudsburg. The district retained its organization until the department was discontinued December 1, 1864, and it was then continued as a district in the Department of Pennsylvania.

Commanders of the district were: Franz Sigel, August 20, 1863 to February 29, 1864, when he was assigned command of the Department of West Virginia; Orris S. Ferry, February 29, 1864 to May 1864, when he was ordered to the Department of Virginia and North Carolina; Josiah C. Hullinger, May 1864 to November 9, 1864, when he was ordered to Stroudsburg; and Thomas S. Mather, November 9, 1864 to December 1, 1864.

Brandywine District. The Brandywine District was constituted July 31, 1864, to consist of that part of the Department of the Susquehanna lying between the Blue Ridge Mountains and the Susquehanna River (including generally the counties of Franklin, Adams, York, and Cumberland), and also the counties of Dauphin, Lancaster, Chester, Delaware, Philadelphia, Montgomery, and Bucks. The latter was composed of a tier of counties east of the Susquehanna, in the extreme southeastern part of the state. George Cadwalader was assigned command, with headquarters at Harrisburg. The district was discontinued August 18, 1864, and Cadwalader resumed his command at Philadelphia. Troops of the Brandywine District were generally posted at Chambersburg, Fort Washington, York, Philadelphia, Mercersburg, and Hagerstown in Maryland. Troops also occupied the mountain passes between McConnellsburg and Loudon (Fort Loudon).

District of the Monongahela. The District of the Monongahela was constituted June 27, 1864, to consist of that part of the Department of the Susquehanna lying west of the Laurel Hill range of mountains. Thomas A. Rowley was assigned command, with headquarters at Pittsburgh. The principal posts in the district were Pittsburgh and Uniontown. The district retained its organization until the Department of the Susquehanna was discontinued December 1, 1864, and it was then continued in the newly constituted Department of Pennsylvania.

Juniata District. The Juniata District was constituted September 6, 1864. Its western boundary was the Laurel Hill range of mountains, which was also the eastern boundary of the District of the Monongahela. Its eastern boundary, beginning at the north, was the Williamsport and Elmira Railroad, south to Williamsport; and then along the Susquehanna River to its intersection with the Blue Ridge Mountains (near the mouth of the Juniata River); and from there along the Blue Ridge to the Maryland state line. At its southern end the district line followed the western boundary of Franklin County. Orris S. Ferry was assigned command of the district, with headquarters at Bedford, Pennsylvania. The principal posts in the district were Chambersburg, Bloody Run (present-day Everett), Greencastle, McConnellsburg, and Bedford. The district retained its organization until the Department of the Susquehanna was discontinued, and it was then transferred to the newly created Department of Pennsylvania.

TROOPS AND OPERATIONS IN THE DEPARTMENT OF THE SUSQUEHANNA

When the Department of the Susquehanna was organized in June 1863, there were within its limits only about 1,300 men, and these were stationed at Harrisburg, Philadelphia, and York. June 15, 1863, Ewell's Corps of Lee's army, which was then advancing toward the Potomac River at the beginning of the Gettysburg Campaign, defeated a Union force under Robert H. Milroy at Winchester, Virginia, and captured the town. That same day the administration sent out calls for troops to aid in the defense of Pennsylvania. Secretary of War Stanton asked Governor Horatio Seymour of New York for 20,000 troops, and President Abraham Lincoln issued a proclamation calling into the service of the United States 100,000 militia from the states of Maryland,

Pennsylvania, Ohio, and West Virginia to serve for a maximum of six months. Other states were also asked to send any available troops.

June 15, 1863, Governor Seymour responded to Stanton's request by offering immediately 8,000–10,000 men of the New York National Guard. These were to serve for a period of not more than three months. The first regiment left New York June 17, 1863, and during the next week twenty more regiments departed for Pennsylvania. In all, twenty-six regiments were sent by July 3, 1863. Most of these were from New York City and Brooklyn. The troops from New York City belonged to Charles W. Sandford's First Division, New York National Guard, and consisted of the following: Charles Yates' Second Brigade (six regiments), William Hall's Third Brigade (five regiments), and John Ewen's Fourth Brigade (two regiments). The troops from Brooklyn belonged to Second Division, New York National Guard, and consisted of Philip S. Crooke's Fifth Brigade (two regiments) and Jesse C. Smith's Eleventh Brigade (three regiments). The New York regiments were sent to Harrisburg.

The Pennsylvania Militia was organized more slowly, but by the end of June 1863 eight regiments had reported for service. By the end of July 1863 there were about thirty-two infantry regiments in service. There were also many detachments, and some cavalry and artillery.

Some of the New York regiments arriving at Harrisburg were sent across the Susquehanna to begin construction of a fortification directly opposite the city. When these works were completed, they were named Fort Washington. Others were posted at various points on the river. A few were held at Camp Curtin, which had been established at Harrisburg in 1861 as a reception center for new troops. On June 18, 1863, this was placed under the command of Joseph A. Beaver, who at that time was in Harrisburg recovering from a wound received at Chancellorsville. Later these regiments were sent across the river to points farther west.

As Lee advanced into Pennsylvania during the Gettysburg Campaign, Couch believed that he would attempt to cross the Susquehanna River at some point between Conowingo, about six miles above the mouth of the river, and Marysville, six miles north of Harrisburg. The most probable crossings were at Harrisburg and Columbia, which was across the river from Wrightsville. Couch promptly began preparations for the defense of the river line. June 15, 1863, Charles C. Haldeman, of Columbia County, Pennsylvania, was authorized to raise and command troops for the defense of Columbia and the bridges, fords, and dams in the vicinity. The next day Emlen Franklin, of Lancaster, Pennsylvania, was assigned to watch the fords and bridges below Columbia on the Susquehanna as far down as Conowingo. Both Haldeman and Franklin were relieved from their duties, however, when on June 24, 1863 Jacob Frick was assigned with his 27th Pennsylvania Militia to take charge of the defenses of all fords and bridges on the river in Lancaster County. To complete the preparations for the defense of the river, Charles Yates, with two regiments of the New York National Guard, was sent June 22, 1863 to Marysville and to Fenwick, at the junction of the Dauphin and Susquehanna rivers, about six miles north of Harrisburg, to guard the two railroad bridges crossing the Susquehanna there.

Steps were also taken to protect the line of the Juniata River, along which ran the Pennsylvania Railroad, and also the mountain passes to the south. Henry Coppee of Philadelphia offered his services to the state and was sent to Altoona to arrange with the officials of the railroad for the defense of the bridges there. Joseph W. Hawley was at Mount Union, about eighty-five miles west of Harrisburg on the railroad, with a regiment of Pennsylvania Militia that had rendezvoused there. June 25, 1863, he was reinforced by two regiments of the New York National Guard from Camp Curtin. These regiments constituted the Thirty-First Brigade of the New York National Guard under Watson A. Fox. Hawley assumed command of all troops at Mount Union. Twelve miles farther west, at Huntingdon, Nelson A. Miles, who had been recuperating at Harrisburg from a wound received at Chancellorsville, was assigned command of two regiments of Pennsylvania Militia and some detachments of others.

In addition to the troops guarding the rivers, others were sent out to the west to observe the approaching enemy. June 18, 1863 two regiments of New York National Guard were sent from Harrisburg to Shippensburg as a brigade under Joshua M. Varian, the senior colonel. Joseph F. Knipe, a resident of Harrisburg, who was not on active duty at the time because of a wound, offered his services to

Couch, and June 20, 1863 was sent to Shippensburg, where he assumed command of Varian's brigade. Knipe then advanced to Chambersburg, but as the Confederates approached he was forced to fall back to Carlisle, where he arrived June 23, 1863. He remained there until Ewell's corps came up June 27, 1863, and then withdrew to a point near Harrisburg.

Couch sent Granville O. Haller, of the 7th United States Infantry, to Gettysburg to organize the defenses of the town. Haller found there only a few companies of Pennsylvania troops, but June 24, 1863, he was joined by William Jennings' 26th Pennsylvania Militia from Camp Curtin. Two days later, however, when Elijah V. White's Confederate cavalry and John B. Gordon's infantry brigade of Jubal A. Early's division approached on the Chambersburg Pike, Jennings rapidly retired to Harrisburg and Haller to York.

During the period June 18–19, 1863, Couch received additional reinforcements indirectly from another direction. When Milroy's Second Division, Eighth Corps was wrecked by Ewell's corps at Stephenson's Depot (Winchester) June 15, 1863, about 1,000 cavalry and 2,000 infantry escaped to the northwest and, under James A. Galligher, crossed to the north side of the Potomac near Hancock, Maryland. Galligher's command continued on and arrived at Bloody Run (present-day Everett), Pennsylvania June 19, 1863. Milroy proceeded to Bloody Run and assumed command of the troops there, but was relieved by Lewis B. Pierce June 26, 1863. Pierce's command consisted of four infantry and two cavalry regiments, and numerous detachments of other units. One regiment of Pennsylvania Militia also joined Pierce at Bloody Run.

Back in Harrisburg, William F. Smith reported to Couch June 20, 1863, and was assigned to inspect the defenses of the Susquehanna. He was then sent west to Bloody Run, and June 24–25, 1863 inspected Milroy's command. Meantime, Couch had decided to organize the troops in the department into brigades and divisions. A new First Division was assigned to Smith, and was to consist of the troops then in the vicinity of Fort Washington, and also additional regiments that were to be sent there later. June 23, 1863 William Hall of the New York National Guard was assigned to the temporary command of all troops at Fort Washington until Smith returned from Bloody Run. Two days later Smith

was assigned command of all troops in the Department of the Susquehanna on the west side of the river in the vicinity of Harrisburg, and these were organized as First Division, Department of the Susquehanna, as follows:

First Division, William F. Smith
  First Brigade, Joseph F. Knipe
  Second Brigade, Philip St.G. Cooke
  Third Brigade, Jesse C. Smith
  Fourth Brigade, John Ewen
  Fifth Brigade, William Brisbane
  Sixth Brigade, Jacob G. Frick

Note. Frick's Sixth Brigade was organized July 4, 1863.

There were about 15,000 men present in Smith's division. The first four brigades were composed of regiments of New York National Guard, and the last two of regiments of Pennsylvania Militia.

A Second Division, Department of the Susquehanna was included in Couch's plans, but it was not organized until later because there were not sufficient troops. June 26, 1863 Napoleon J. T. Dana was assigned to organize and command the Pennsylvania Millitia and volunteer forces, and also the defenses of Philadelphia. He was in command at Philadelphia when he was ordered to Chambersburg July 8, 1863. Three days later, he was assigned command of the new Second Division at Chambersburg. It was organized July 12, 1863, as follows:

Second Division, Napoleon J. T. Dana
  First Brigade, Charles Yates
  Second Brigade, James Nagle
  Third Brigade, Emlen Franklin

First Brigade consisted of four regiments of Pennsylvania Militia and the two regiments of New York National Guard that Yates had brought forward from Fenwick, Pennsylvania. Second Brigade and Third Brigade were formed from regiments of Pennsylvania Militia.

There were no cavalry organizations in the department during this period. June 22, 1863 James S. Brisbin was assigned temporarily as chief of cavalry, but was relieved by John E. Wynkoop June 28, 1863. Then, July 2, 1863, Julius Stahel arrived from the Army of the Potomac and assumed command of the cavalry in the department. In addition to the two regiments and three companies of cavalry with Pierce at Bloody Run there were only a few companies of Pennsylvania Cavalry in the department at that time. July 6, 1863 Wynkoop was assigned to the temporary command of ten companies of cavalry attached to the department, and he established his headquarters at Carlisle. Two days later he was assigned to command the 20th Pennsylvania Cavalry, which was organized from his former temporary command, and he was then ordered toward Chambersburg. The designation of his regiment was changed to 19th Pennsylvania Cavalry.

The Gettysburg Campaign. During June 27–28, 1863, Ewell, with the divisions of Edward Johnson and Robert E. Rodes, arrived at Carlisle, and June 28, 1863 Jubal A. Early's division arrived at York. John B. Gordon's brigade of Early's division immediately advanced to the defenses of Wrightsville, which covered the western approaches to the Columbia Bridge over the Susquehanna River. The defending troops under Frick and Haller, who had fallen back from York, were slightly engaged during the evening of June 28, 1863, but they then crossed the river into Columbia and burned the bridge. June 29, 1863, under orders from Lee, Ewell withdrew from Carlisle and York, and marched back to join the other two corps of the Army of Northern Virginia at Gettysburg.

July 1, 1863, during the first day of the Battle of Gettysburg, William F. Smith advanced up the Cumberland Valley from near Harrisburg with John Ewen's Fourth Brigade and William Brisbane's Fifth Brigade of his First Division, and arrived at Carlisle during the afternoon and evening. Joseph F. Knipe was under orders to join later with his First Brigade.

Late in the afternoon of July 1, 1863, Fitzhugh Lee's brigade of James E. B. (Jeb) Stuart's cavalry division approached Carlisle on the York Road, and found the town occupied by Smith's troops. Smith refused a demand for its surrender, and Lee opened fire with his artillery. The firing continued until about 1:00 A.M. July 2, 1863, and then, after burning Carlisle Barracks, the Confederate cavalry withdrew toward Gettysburg. Smith moved his command to Carlisle Barracks that day, and remained there July 3, 1863, while he waited for provisions. Knipe's brigade arrived at Carlisle that day.

July 3, 1863, Couch ordered Pierce to move for-

ward with his command from Bloody Run toward Chambersburg and Greencastle to approach the rear of Lee's army. Pierce marched at once toward Mc-Connellsburg and arrived there the next day.

When George G. Meade assumed command of the Army of the Potomac June 28, 1863, he was authorized to exercise control over the troops of the Department of the Susquehanna. These troops, however, were not transferred to the Army of the Potomac, but were simply made subject to Meade's orders. Late in the evening of July 3, 1863, after the fighting at Gettysburg had ended, Meade informed Couch that he did not expect Lee to attack again, and that it was possible that he might retreat toward Virginia. In that event Couch was to march in pursuit along the Cumberland Valley.

July 4, 1863, Smith moved south from Carlisle with the brigades of Brisbane, Ewen, and Knipe to Mount Holly, and then on to Pine Grove (Pine Grove Furnace). Jacob G. Frick's Sixth Brigade was organized that day. During the night of July 4, 1863, Lee began his retreat toward the Potomac River. July 5, 1863, Smith's brigades covered the roads leading to Shippensburg, and the next day they marched by different roads to Newman's Pass on the Gettysburg-Chambersburg Turnpike, four miles east of Cashtown. July 7, 1863 Smith marched to Altodale (Alto Furnace), and then on to Waynesboro the next afternoon.

Meantime, on July 5, 1863, Pierce sent out his cavalry from Mercersburg toward Williamsport, and near Greencastle it attacked Lee's wagon train and captured about 100 wagons, three pieces of artillery, and about 600 prisoners, mostly wounded.

Smith remained at Waynesboro July 9 and 10, 1863, but he sent Frick's brigade to Ringgold in Maryland. July 11, 1863 Smith left Brisbane's brigade at Waynesboro and at dusk moved with the rest of his command to Leitersburg, Maryland. The next day Brisbane's brigade marched from Waynesboro; Frick's brigade moved from Ringgold to Chewsville; and the rest of Smith's command moved to Cavetown, Maryland. July 13, 1863, Smith's command, temporarily under Knipe, moved to a point near Smoketown, and the next day to Benevola, where Beaver Creek crosses the Boonsboro-Hagerstown Turnpike about three miles northwest of Boonsboro.

July 5, 1863, Joseph W. Hawley was ordered with

one regiment of the New York National Guard and three companies of Pennsylvania Militia from Mount Union to Chambersburg. He arrived at Loudon, Pennsylvania two days later, and was then ordered by Couch (through Pierce) to Clear Spring, Maryland, where he arrived July 10, 1863. Pierce replaced Hawley at Clear Spring, and Hawley returned to Loudon July 13, 1863. His command was discontinued the next day when his 74th New York Regiment was ordered to return home.

It has already been noted that July 8, 1863, Dana was ordered to report to Couch in the field. He arrived at Chambersburg July 11, 1863, and was assigned command of the new Second Division, Department of the Susquehanna, which he organized the next day.

For additional information on troop movements during this period, see Gettysburg Campaign, Part III, Pursuit of Lee, From Gettysburg to Falling Waters.

Beginning July 14, 1863, the composition and organization of the forces in the Department of the Susquehanna changed rapidly. Late on the evening of July 12, 1863, Andrew T. McReynolds was ordered by Couch at Chambersburg to take command of Pierce's troops, which were a part of Milroy's former Second Division, Eighth Corps. McReynolds was to assemble these troops, which were at and near Chambersburg, Loudon, and Greencastle, and with them join the Army of the Potomac. McReynolds arrived at Hagerstown July 14, 1863, but when the Army of the Potomac left the Williamsport-Falling Waters area the next day, McReynolds' command was left behind to watch the Potomac River between Harper's Ferry and Williamsport.

July 15, 1863, the emergency in Pennsylvania over and the Draft Riots raging in New York, all regiments of the New York National Guard marched toward Frederick, Maryland to return to New York. As a result, the First, Second, Third, and Fourth brigades of Smith's First Division, which were composed wholly of New York National Guard regiments, were discontinued. William Brisbane, commander of the Fifth Brigade, First Division, was appointed military governor of Hagerstown, and other Pennsylvania Militia regiments, in addition to those in his own brigade, that were ordered to join him there.

Dana's Second Division, Department of the Susquehanna was composed of Pennsylvania Militia regiments, except for two New York National Guard regiments of Yates' First Brigade. These returned to New York with Yates. Emlen Franklin's Third Brigade, Second Division was sent to Hagerstown and Williamsport, and later in July 1863 the designation was changed to Second Brigade of Smith's reorganized First Division (see below). James Nagle's Second Brigade, Second Division was later redesignated as First Brigade, Second Division.

July 19, 1863, the last troops of the Army of the Potomac left Maryland on their march toward Warrenton, Virginia in pursuit of Lee. Before departing, however, Meade left troops behind to watch the Potomac River, and these were placed under Couch's orders. McReynolds' brigade picketed the Potomac from Sharpsburg to Williamsport; Wynkoop's cavalry was at Falling Waters; Franklin's brigade of six Pennsylvania Militia regiments was at Williamsport; Brisbane's Fifth Brigade of Smith's division was in the vicinity of Hagerstown; and Henry H. Lockwood's division occupied Harper's Ferry and Maryland Heights. Although not a part of Couch's command, Benjamin F. Kelley's troops of the Department of West Virginia guarded the fords above Williamsport.

Lockwood, with the Maryland regiments of his Second Brigade, First Division, Twelfth Corps, Army of the Potomac, had been transferred to Harper's Ferry, where he had relieved Henry M. Naglee in command July 18, 1863. The next day the troops of Lockwood's command were, by Meade's orders, assigned to Couch's direction. Lockwood's troops consisted of a First Brigade under George D. Wells and a Second Brigade under William P. Maulsby.

July 21, 1863, Couch assigned William F. Smith at Hagerstown to command all troops in Maryland from, and including, Harper's Ferry to Clear Spring. Some confusion resulted from this order because the garrison at Harper's Ferry was formerly a part of Robert C. Schenck's Middle Department, Eighth Corps. This was clarified, however, when Henry W. Halleck, general in chief of the army, announced July 22, 1863 that so long as operations continued along the Potomac all troops in the field, regardless of departmental boundaries, were under Meade's orders, and that Meade had placed Lockwood's command under Couch's orders.

In late July 1863, First Division and Second Division of the Department of the Susquehanna were organized as follows:

First Division, William F. Smith
    First Brigade, Andrew T. McReynolds
    Second Brigade, Emlen Franklin
    Cavalry, John E. Wynkoop
    Artillery, Batteries B and E, 5th United States Artillery

Second Division, Fitz Henry Warren, to July 31, 1863
    William D. Whipple
    First Brigade, Melchior H. Horn
    Second Brigade, James Chamberlin

Note 1. Horn's brigade was formerly James Nagle's Second Brigade, Second Division, and it was posted at Reading and Pottsville.

Note 2. Chamberlin's brigade was formerly Brisbane's Fourth Brigade, First Division, and it was posted at Chambersburg and Loudon.

August 3, 1863, the Department of West Virginia was extended to include all of Maryland west of the Monocacy River, and that day all of the troops of the Department of the Susquehanna in Maryland, and all troops on the Potomac River above the Monocacy were transferred to the Department of West Virginia. Thereafter there was no brigade or division organization in the department. Instead the troops were distributed by companies, regiments, and detached forces at the various posts in the department. The principal posts were: Bloomsburg, Carlisle, Carlisle Barracks, Chambersburg, Chelton Hill (Camp William Penn), Easton, Fort Washington, Harrisburg, Hazelton, Huntingdon, McConnellsburg, Mercersburg, Philadelphia, Pittsburgh, Pottsville, Reading, Scranton, Stroudsburg, West Chester, and York. Generally these posts were not all occupied at the same time, but they were at one time or another during the existence of the department. The posts that were permanently occupied were Chambersburg, Harrisburg, Philadelphia, and York. There was a hospital at the latter place.

DEPARTMENT OF VIRGINIA
MAY 22, 1861–JULY 15, 1863

Benjamin F. Butler assumed command at Fort Monroe, Virginia May 22, 1861, and announced that his authority extended over all territory of southeastern Virginia and northeastern North Carolina that he could occupy and control. He called his command the Department of Virginia and North Carolina, and established his headquarters at Fort Monroe. He later changed the designation to the Department of Virginia, and defined it as consisting of Fort Monroe and the country around within a radius of sixty miles. The territory of this department was taken from the Department of the East. The boundary began at Drummondtown (present-day Accomac) on the north, passed near Petersburg on the west, and ended at Elizabeth City on the south.

January 7, 1862, that part of North Carolina originally included in the country lying within a sixty-mile radius of Fort Monroe was transferred to the Department of North Carolina.

June 1, 1862, during the Peninsular Campaign, the limits of the Department of Virginia were extended to include that part of Virginia south of the Rappahannock River, and east of the railroad that ran south from Fredericksburg, through Richmond and Petersburg, to Weldon, North Carolina. This territory was taken from the Department of the Potomac. All forces in the department, which then included the Army of the Potomac, were placed under the command of George B. McClellan. The important posts were Fort Monroe, Camp Hamilton, Newport News, Yorktown, Suffolk, Norfolk, and Portsmouth.

July 15, 1863, the Department of Virginia and the Department of North Carolina were consolidated to form the Department of Virginia and North Carolina, and the Department of Virginia was discontinued.

COMMANDERS OF THE
DEPARTMENT OF VIRGINIA

Benjamin F. Butler	May 22, 1861 to August 17, 1861
John Wool	August 17, 1861 to June 2, 1862
John A. Dix	June 2, 1862 to April 6, 1863
Erasmus D. Keyes	April 6, 1863 to April 14, 1863
John A. Dix	April 14, 1863 to July 16, 1863

Note 1. When ordered to command the Department of Virginia June 1, 1861, Wool was in command of the Middle Department. He left for Fort Monroe the next day.

Note 2. General Orders No. 7, Adjutant General's

Office, dated June 1, 1862, assigned McClellan to command the Department of Virginia. It also ordered Dix, then commanding the Middle Department, to assume command at Fort Monroe and to report to McClellan for orders. Apparently McClellan did not officially assume command of the department, but he did exercise some control over the territory. Dix reported to McClellan June 2, 1862, and was ordered to assume command of the troops at Fort Monroe, Norfolk, Portsmouth, and Suffolk, and in the vicinity of those places. He was to exercise within his command the functions of the commander of a division or a separate brigade. Dix assumed command June 2, 1862. He continued to issue orders and communications under the heading "Fort Monroe" until he was assigned command of the newly created Seventh Corps July 22, 1862, and he then used the heading "Headquarters Seventh Corps." It was not until September 27, 1862 that Dix used as the heading for his communications "Headquarters Department of Virginia, Seventh Corps."

Note 3. Keyes commanded the department temporarily in April 1863 while Dix was on leave in Washington.

Note 4. George Getty commanded the department July 16–18, 1863, until John G. Foster arrived and assumed command of the newly created Department of Virginia and North Carolina.

TROOPS AND OPERATIONS IN THE DEPARTMENT OF VIRGINIA

When Butler assumed command at Fort Monroe May 22, 1861, the following troops were present: John W. Phelps' 1st Vermont Regiment, Joseph B. Carr's 2nd New York, Justin Dimick's 2nd United States Artillery (seven companies), and parts of 3rd Massachusetts and 4th Massachusetts Militia (nine-month regiment) under Ebenezer W. Peirce. A short time later, Butler was reinforced by William H. Allen's 1st New York, Frederick Townsend's 3rd New York, Abram Duryee's 5th New York (Zouaves), and John E. Bendix's 7th New York. It is interesting to note that Gouverneur K. Warren was lieutenant colonel of 5th New York and Judson Kilpatrick was commander of Company H of the same regiment. The troops of Butler's command were stationed at Fort Monroe; Camp Hamilton, which was across Mill Creek, near fort Monroe; and Newport News.

Engagement of Big Bethel, June 10, 1861. In May 1861, John B. Magruder was assigned to command military operations on the lower Peninsula, with headquarters at Yorktown. On June 6, 1861, he

advanced Daniel H. Hill with his 1st North Carolina Regiment to Big Bethel, a church on the Hampton Road, about eleven miles from Fort Monroe. Hill established a fortified outpost at Big Bethel, and also posted troops at Little Bethel Church, about three miles farther out on the Hampton Road.

Hill's position at Big Bethel served as a base for raids on Newport News and Hampton, and Butler decided to organize an expedition to drive the enemy back and destroy their outposts. This movement was to be made in two columns and was to be under the command of Ebenezer W. Peirce (also spelled Pierce) of the Massachusetts Militia. At the time, Peirce was in command of Camp Hamilton at Hampton, and one column was to start from that point. Abram Duryee's 5th New York was to be ferried over Hampton Creek at 1:00 A.M. June 10, 1861, and was then to move by way of New Market Bridge to a position between Little Bethel and Big Bethel, and attack the Confederate camp at the latter place. Peirce, with Frederick Townsend's 3rd New York and two mountain howitzers of Joseph B. Carr's 2nd New York, was to march from Hampton an hour later in support of Duryee.

At the same time, Butler directed John W. Phelps, commanding at Newport News, to send out a battalion of 1st Vermont under Peter T. Washburn to demonstrate in front of Little Bethel. John E. Bendix was to support Washburn with his 7th New York, and Bendix and Townsend were to join at the fork of the road running from Hampton to Newport News.

Butler's troops moved out as directed, and Peirce, with Townsend's 3rd New York, reached New Market Bridge and then moved on toward Little Bethel. While this regiment was marching in column on the road, Bendix's 7th New York came up and, not recognizing the Federal troops, opened fire with infantry and artillery, and caused Townsend to recross the bridge. When Duryee and Washburn heard this firing, they marched back on their reserves. Peirce then sent to Butler for reinforcements, and William H. Allen's 1st New York was ordered forward.

Meantime, Peirce resumed his advance and found Little Bethel vacated. Duryee destroyed the enemy camp there, and then continued on toward Big Bethel, with Judson Kilpatrick's skirmishers in advance. At this point, Peirce learned that Big Bethel was held in strong force, and he halted within a mile of the County Bridge. He then decided to attack, and moved Duryee's 5th New York to the right of the road, where it formed in line of battle. The attack began about 9:30 A.M. The troops from Newport News formed in a second line to the left of the road, but soon moved across the road to support Duryee, who then marched by the flank to the right through, and covered by, a woods. Peirce again asked for reinforcements, and Carr's 2nd New York moved forward.

While the above-described movements were in progress, Townsend was ordered to take position in a lane that branched off at a right angle to the main road, which ran up to the enemy works. Townsend advanced to a point where the skirmishers were engaged, but by the time he was in position, Peirce decided that the enemy had been strongly reinforced and that further effort was useless. Townsend then withdrew, and a short time later Peirce directed that all of his troops retire. When Duryee's regiment pulled back, Allen's 1st New York, then coming up, was formed in line on the left of the road, and Carr's 2nd New York occupied the position vacated by Duryee.

During the retreat Duryee led the column, and he was followed by Townsend and the forces from Newport News. The regiments of Allen and Carr formed the rear guard. Despite some fighting, the Federal attack was not pressed vigorously, as is indicated by the fact that the total Union casualties were only seventy-nine men.

Expedition to Hatteras Inlet, August 26–29, 1861. John E. Wool succeeded Butler in command of the Department of Virginia August 17, 1861, and four days later Butler was assigned command of the volunteer forces in the department, exclusive of those at Fort Monroe. Present at that time at Camp Hamilton and Camp Butler were the following: 1st, 2nd, 7th, 9th, and 20th New York; a battalion of Massachusetts Volunteers; the Union Coast Guard (99th New York); and Mounted Rifles. August 25, 1861, Wool ordered Butler to prepare an expedition to proceed to Hatteras Inlet and capture the Confederate batteries located there. This was one of North Carolina's most important ports, a haven for blockade runners, and also a major channel for supplies for Confederate forces in Virginia. The attack was to be a joint land-sea operation, with Butler commanding the land forces, and Silas H. Stringfellow, flag officer of the Atlantic Blockading Squadron, commanding the naval force.

Butler sailed from Fort Monroe at 1:00 P.M. August 26, 1861 with a detachment of Max Weber's 20th New York, a detachment of Rush C. Hawkins' 9th New York, Richard Nixon's Union Coast Guard, and a detachment of 2nd United States Artillery under Frank J. Larned. August 28, 1862, the navy began the bombardment of Fort Clark and Fort Hatteras, which was west of Fort Clark and on ground that commanded the sea channel, and the troops began landing the same day. The landing was delayed by bad weather, but the forts were surrendered by Flag Officer Samuel Baron August 29, 1861. Butler and Stringham then departed for Fort Monroe, but they left a naval detachment and detachments of 9th and 20th New York regiments at Hatteras Inlet to garrison the captured forts. Weber's detachment was withdrawn September 9, 1861, and the rest of Hawkins' regiment was sent to take its place. Hawkins assumed command of the post.

John F. Reynolds was ordered to the Department of Virginia to take command at Hatteras Inlet, but when he arrived at Fort Monroe September 13, 1861, he received an order dated September 12, 1861 assigning him to the Army of the Potomac. Joseph K. F. Mansfield was then ordered to assume command at Hatteras Inlet October 5, 1861. October 13, 1861, Thomas Williams assumed command of the troops at Hatteras Inlet and vicinity, relieving Mansfield. At this time Williams' command consisted of two regiments.

An order of January 7, 1862 directing Ambrose E. Burnside to proceed with his expedition to the coast of North Carolina assigned the post of Hatteras Inlet to his command, and when he assumed command of the newly created Department of North Carolina at Hatteras Inlet January 13, 1862, Williams' brigade was transferred to the Department of North Carolina. For additional information, see Department of North Carolina, January 7, 1862–July 15, 1863, Burnside's Expedition to North Carolina.

September 10, 1861, Butler was authorized to raise and organize a special force in New England, and he left the department for New York. Butler's New England command eventually moved to New Orleans in the Department of the Gulf.

* * * * * * * * * *

Mansfield was assigned command of a brigade at Camp Hamilton October 14, 1861, but he turned over this brigade to Max Weber November 23, 1861 and relieved John W. Phelps in command at Newport News. Phelps was assigned command of an expedition to Ship Island in the Gulf of Mexico, and left the department November 27, 1861. Phelps' command was a detachment of Butler's New England force, and was the first to arrive in the Department of the Gulf.

March 3, 1862 Mansfield's command at Newport News was constituted as a separate brigade, and was designated as First Brigade, First Division, Department of Virginia.

George B. McClellan's Army of the Potomac arrived on the Peninsula in the latter part of March and early April 1862, and remained in the Department of Virginia until mid-August 1862. McClellan was given control over Fort Monroe and all of Wool's troops there, but this order was annulled April 3, 1862. March 19, 1862, McClellan requested that a division be formed from troops of the Department of Virginia, and that Mansfield be assigned command. This was ordered by Wool March 20, 1862, but this order was revoked April 2, 1862. For additional information, see Peninsular Campaign.

Occupation of Norfolk, Portsmouth, and Suffolk, Virginia, May 10, 1862. May 9, 1862, as the Army of the Potomac moved up the Peninsula toward Richmond, Confederate forces evacuated Norfolk. Immediately, Wool organized a force from regiments at Fort Monroe, Camp Hamilton, and Newport News, and with it occupied Norfolk the next day. Egbert L. Viele was appointed military governor of the town, and was assigned command of all troops in and near Norfolk and Portsmouth. Also, on May 10, 1862, Viele was assigned command of a newly organized Second Brigade, Department of Virginia, and Max Weber was assigned command of a new Third Brigade. The *Merrimac* was destroyed by the Confederates May 11, 1862.

Joseph B. Carr, commanding at Camp Hamilton, was ordered to take his troops to Norfolk, and there he was assigned command of the defenses of Portsmouth. Carr's troops remained near Norfolk until June 1, 1862, and then they were sent to the Army of the Potomac at Fair Oaks, Virginia.

May 16, 1862, the Union forces at Norfolk were organized into three brigades, commanded by Egbert L. Viele, Max Weber, and John C. Robinson. Robinson's brigade was broken up May 28, 1862, and Robinson with his 1st Michigan Regiment was assigned to Fitz John Porter's Fifth Corps, Army of the Potomac. Viele's brigade was broken up in June 1862, and the regiments were also sent to the Army of the Potomac. Weber's brigade remained intact until July 22, 1862, when Seventh Corps, Department of Virginia was created.

May 17, 1862, Wool sent a force consisting of the 16th Massachusetts Regiment, a section of Frederick M. Follett's Battery D, 4th United States Artillery under Stephen Whitney, and one squadron of 11th Pennsylvania Cavalry to take post at Suffolk, Virginia. Suffolk was situated at the head of the Nansemond River and was an important rail junction. It was on the Seaboard and Roanoke Railroad and on the Norfolk and Petersburg Railroad, which ran to the interior, and was the key to all approaches to the mouth of the James River on the north side of the Dismal Swamp.

June 1, 1862, the Department of Virginia was expanded (see above), and McClellan was assigned command of all forces in the department. These consisted of Wool's command of about 14,000 men and the Army of the Potomac. Also on June 1, 1862, John A. Dix was assigned command of the troops at Fort Monroe, Norfolk, Portsmouth, and Suffolk, and in the vicinity of these places. Dix assumed command June 2, 1862, relieving Wool. June 12, 1862, McClellan extended Dix's command to include Yorktown, Gloucester, and Williamsburg.

Organization of Ninth Corps, July 22, 1862. When the administration learned of McClellan's difficulties during the Seven Days' Battles before Richmond, Ambrose E. Burnside, then commanding the Department of North Carolina, was ordered July 3, 1862 to bring all of his available forces to the Peninsula to reinforce the Army of the Potomac. July 6, 1862, Burnside moved with the divisions of Jesse L. Reno and John G. Parke to Newport News, and he was joined there by Isaac I. Stevens with his division from the Department of the South. Meantime the Army of the Potomac had arrived safely at Harrison's Landing on the James River, and, because he was no longer needed, Burnside was directed to remain at Newport News. There, on July 22, 1862, the three divisions were organized into Ninth Corps, and Burnside was assigned command. On August 1, 1862, Ninth Corps was ordered to embark for Falmouth, Virginia, and it left the Department of Virginia. For further information, see Pope's Northern Virginia Campaign, and Ninth Corps.

Organization of Seventh Corps, Department of Virginia, July 22, 1862. July 22, 1862, the troops in the Department of Virginia, exclusive of the Army of the Potomac and Burnside's command at Newport News, were organized into Seventh Corps, Department of Virginia. John A. Dix was assigned command of the department and Seventh Corps. The organization of Seventh Corps at that time was as follows:

SEVENTH CORPS, John A. Dix

Fort Monroe, Joseph Roberts
Camp Hamilton
Norfolk, Egbert L. Viele
 Viele's Brigade
Division at Suffolk, Joseph K. F. Mansfield
 Weber's Brigade, Max Weber

Note. Weber's Brigade was organized July 22, 1862.

Organizational Changes in the Department of Virginia, August 1862–April 1863. There were numerous changes in the composition and organization of the troops in the Department of Virginia during the period August 1862–April 1863.

In mid-August 1862 the Army of the Potomac was transferred from the Peninsula to northern Virginia. Erasmus D. Keyes' Fourth Corps, however, was left behind at Yorktown in the Department of Virginia. At the end of August 1862, Darius N. Couch's First Division, Fourth Corps was detached and sent to northern Virginia, and there on September 3, 1862 it rejoined the Army of the Potomac. John J. Peck's Second Division, Fourth Corps remained at Yorktown. Henry M. Naglee commanded First Brigade of Peck's division; Henry W. Wessells, Second Brigade; and Orris S. Ferry, Third Brigade.

August 23, 1862, the brigades of Wessells and Ferry were ordered to Fort Monroe to report to Dix. Ferry's brigade was then sent to Suffolk, and Wessells' brigade to Camp Hamilton. In September 1862, the designation of Ferry's brigade was changed to Ferry's Brigade, Division at Suffolk.

At the end of August 1862, the organization of the troops in the Department was as follows:

Fort Monroe, Joseph Roberts
Camp Hamilton, Henry W. Wessells

Note. The troops at Camp Hamilton consisted of the 92nd and 96th New York regiments and the 85th, 101st, and 103rd Pennsylvania regiments of Fourth Corps, and the 5th Maryland Infantry; Company C, 11th Pennsylvania Cavalry; and the 7th Battery, New York Light Artillery of Seventh Corps.

Newport News, Reuben V. King
Norfolk, Egbert L. Viele
 Viele's Brigade

Note. Frederick M. Follett's Battery D, 4th United States Artillery was attached to Viele's command.

Suffolk, Joseph K. F. Mansfield
 Weber's Brigade, Seventh Corps, Max Weber
 Ferry's Third Brigade, Second Division, Fourth Corps, Orris S. Ferry

Note. There was also a mixed command of Seventh Corps at Suffolk consisting of 1st New York Mounted Rifles, 11th Pennsylvania Cavalry, and Battery L, 4th United States Artillery.

Fort Wool, Ira Winans
Sewell's Point, John C. Lee

FOURTH CORPS, Erasmus D. Keyes

Yorktown
 Second Division, John J. Peck
 Seventh Corps (detachment), James H. Van Alen
  Independent Battalion New York Volunteers
  4th Pennsylvania Cavalry (detachment)
  Battery F, 1st New York Light Artillery

Note 1. Only Henry M. Naglee's First Brigade was with Peck's division.
Note 2. October 11, 1862 Van Alen was relieved from duty with Seventh Corps and left the department.

Williamsburg, David Campbell
Gloucester Point, J. Watts De Peyster (of Fourth Corps artillery)

Mansfield was assigned command at Suffolk shortly after its occupation, and he remained in command there until September 8, 1862, and then was ordered to Washington and was assigned command of Twelfth Corps, Army of the Potomac. He was killed September 17, 1862 at the Battle of Antietam. Mansfield was succeeded in command at Suffolk by Ferry. Also on September 8, 1862, Weber's Brigade was transferred to the Army of the Potomac, and it took part in the Battle of Antietam as Third Brigade of William H. French's Third Division, Edwin V. Sumner's Second Corps. The brigade suffered heavy losses, and Weber was wounded during the fighting.

In September 1862, Suffolk was threatened by an enemy force under John J. Pettigrew from Samuel G. French's command on the Blackwater River. As a result, on September 22, 1862, Peck was ordered to Suffolk with Wessells' Second Brigade of his Second Division, Fourth Corps. Upon arrival there, the designation of Wessells' brigade was changed to Wessells' Brigade, Division at Suffolk. Peck assumed command of the Division at Suffolk, and for the next six months was engaged in constructing fortifications and in preparing for the defense of the town. September 23, 1862, a brigade known as Foster's Provisional Brigade, Seventh Corps was organized at Suffolk under Robert S. Foster. October 6, 1862, Francis B. Spinola was ordered to Suffolk, and was assigned command of a brigade, designated as Spinola's Brigade, which was organized from New York regiments at Suffolk.

December 5, 1862, Wessells was detached from the Department of Virginia, and left Suffolk with his brigade to reinforce John G. Foster in the Department of North Carolina. For further information about this brigade, see Department of North Carolina, January 7, 1862–July 15, 1863, Troops and Operations in the Department of North Carolina.

Also on December 5, 1862, Alfred Gibbs assumed command of a brigade at Suffolk, which was designated as Second Provisional Brigade. Foster's brigade was designated as First Provisional Brigade.

In October 1862, Nathaniel P. Banks was sent to New England to organize an expedition to the Department of the Gulf. Some of the regiments for this expedition were ordered to assemble at Fort Monroe. In late September 1862, William H. Emory was sent from Baltimore, Maryland to Fort Monroe with five regiments, and there he assumed command of the troops assigned to Banks' expedition. October 31, 1862 a brigade under Michael Corcoran (Corcoran's Brigade or Irish Legion) was ordered from New York to Fort Monroe to join the expedition. Upon arrival there, Corcoran's Brigade was moved to Newport News. Emory's command, which was then called Emory's Division, sailed for the Gulf early in December 1862, but Corcoran's Brigade was left behind in the Department of Virginia.

December 15, 1862, Richard Busteed was ordered to report to Dix, and was assigned command of a brigade organized at Yorktown. This brigade was known as Busteed's Brigade, and was part of Keyes' command at Yorktown.

December 16, 1862, Corcoran's Brigade was placed under Dix's command as a part of Seventh Corps, Department of Virginia, and December 29, 1862, it was sent to Suffolk. Ferry, who was then under orders to proceed with his brigade to the Department of North Carolina, turned over the command at Suffolk to Corcoran December 30, 1862.

During the period December 29, 1862–January 2, 1863, Naglee's brigade of Fourth Corps from Yorktown, and Spinola's Brigade and Ferry's Brigade from Suffolk were sent to the Department of North Carolina. The brigades sent to the Department of South Carolina were replaced in the Department of Virginia by about seventeen regiments.

At the end of December 1862, the Department of Virginia was organized as follows:

Fort Monroe, Samuel A. Alford
Camp Hamilton, Anthony Conk
Norfolk, Egbert L. Viele
Suffolk, John J. Peck
    Corcoran's Brigade, Michael Corcoran
    First Provisional Brigade, Robert S. Foster
    Second Provisional Brigade, Alfred Gibbs

Note. December 26, 1862, Henry D. Terry was ordered to report to Dix, and was assigned command of Gibbs' brigade.

Yorktown, Erasmus D. Keyes
    Busteed's Brigade, Richard Busteed

At the end of January 1863, the organization was as follows:

Fort Monroe, Samuel M. Alford
Camp Hamilton, Anthony Conk

Norfolk, Egbert L. Viele
Suffolk, John J. Peck
   Corcoran's Brigade, Michael Corcoran
   Terry's Brigade, Henry D. Terry
   Provisional Brigade, Robert S. Foster
Yorktown, Erasmus D. Keyes
   Busteed's Brigade, Richard Busteed
   Reserve Artillery, Fourth Corps, Edward H. Flood

February 4, 1863, Ninth Corps, then commanded by William F. Smith, was ordered to Fort Monroe to report to Dix, and the corps was transferred from the Army of the Potomac at Falmouth, Virginia to Newport News February 6–21, 1863. Burnside was ordered to assume command of Ninth Corps March 17, 1863, and was directed to take the corps to Kentucky. First Division left March 19, 1863, and Second Division followed March 25–26, 1863. George W. Getty's Third Division remained in Virginia, and March 13–16, 1863, moved to Suffolk. When Getty arrived, Peck's command at Suffolk was organized as follows:

Suffolk, Virginia, John J. Peck
   Division at Suffolk
      Corcoran's Brigade, Michael Corcoran
      Terry's Brigade, Henry D. Terry
      Foster's Brigade, Robert S. Foster

Getty's Division (Third Division, Ninth Corps), George W. Getty
   First Brigade, Harrison S. Fairchild
   Second Brigade, Edward Harland
   Third Brigade, Arthur H. Dutton
   Artillery
      Battery A, 1st Pennsylvania Light Artillery, John G. Simpson
      Battery A, 5th United States Artillery, James Gilliss

Note. Rush C. Hawkins commanded First Brigade April 23, 1863 to May 2, 1863.

Unassigned
   1st New York Mounted Rifles, Benjamin F. Onderdonk
   11th Pennsylvania Cavalry, Samuel P. Spear
   7th Battery, Massachusetts Light Artillery, Phineas A. Davis
   3rd Pennsylvania Heavy Artillery (battalion), John A. Blake
   Battery D, 4th United States Artillery, Frederick M. Follett
   Battery L, 4th United States Artillery, Henry C. Hasbrouck
   2nd Battery, Wisconsin Light Artillery, Charles Beger

   4th Battery, Wisconsin Light Artillery, John F. Vallee

April 9, 1863, the three brigades of the Division at Suffolk were organized into First Division, Seventh Corps as follows:

First Division, Seventh Corps, Michael Corcoran
   First Brigade, Henry D. Terry
   Second Brigade, Robert S. Foster
   Third Brigade, Mathew Murphy

Note 1. First Brigade was broken up in July 1863, and two regiments were assigned to First Brigade, First Division, First Corps, Army of the Potomac.
Note 2. Second Brigade was transferred to Folly Island, Tenth Corps, Department of the South July 7, 1863.
Note 3. Third Brigade was assigned to the Department of Washington July 11, 1863, and there it became Corcoran's Brigade of Rufus King's Division, Twenty-Second Corps.

There were also some changes in the forces at Yorktown in April 1863. April 1, 1863, the designation of Busteed's Brigade was changed to King's Brigade when Rufus King assumed command. April 12, 1863, another brigade was organized at Yorktown under Robert M. West, and it was designated as West's Advance Brigade.

Siege of Suffolk, Virginia, April 11, 1863–May 3, 1863. For a long time Confederate authorities in Richmond had been concerned about the safety of North Carolina, which was particularly susceptible to raids by Union forces from along its lengthy coast line. Then, when Ninth Corps was detached from the Army of the Potomac and sent to Hampton (Fort Monroe) early in February 1863, these fears were intensified. In mid-February 1863, Robert E. Lee detached George E. Pickett's division of James Longstreet's corps, and sent it toward Richmond to be in position to aid either North Carolina or southeastern Virginia if needed. A few days later, John B. Hood's division of the same corps followed Pickett. Then, on February 18, 1863, Longstreet left Lee's army, accompanied by his staff, to command in person his two divisions, and February 26, 1863, he assumed command of the Confederate Department of Southern Virginia and North Carolina. He established his headquarters at Petersburg.

While at Petersburg, Longstreet learned that there were abundant and much-needed supplies of food and forage inside the Union lines in eastern Virginia and North Carolina. To collect and remove these supplies, however, it would be necessary to advance his divisions so as to cover the country and hold the Federal forces near their fortified positions along the coast. Accordingly, early in April 1863, Longstreet moved the divisions of Pickett and Hood to the Blackwater River in preparation for an advance on Suffolk, Virginia. There they joined a force under Samuel G. French, who was in command of the Confederate Department of Southern Virginia.

At that time Suffolk was protected by a strong defensive line that had been constructed by John J. Peck after he had assumed command of the post in September 1862. The line of works began on the right, on the lower Nansemond River north of Suffolk, and then followed the river in a great curve to the west and south to the crossing of the Norfolk and Petersburg Railroad at Fort Nansemond. From that point the line ran eastward along the south side of the railroad for a short distance, and then it curved in a great loop to the southeast to Fort Union, and from there around to the northeast to Fort Halleck, which was situated southeast of Suffolk on the Jerico Canal, near the railroad.

A number of defensive works were constructed along Peck's line. Beginning on the Union left, south of Suffolk, and in order from left to right these were: Fort Halleck; Fort Dix, southwest of Fort Halleck; Fort Union, west of Fort Dix; Fort McClellan, northwest of Fort Union and just south of the Norfolk and Petersburg Railroad; and Fort Nansemond, west of Fort McClellan, and near the crossing of the Nansemond River. The remaining works were along the Nansemond River. North of Fort Nansemond was Battery South Quay, about midway between the Norfolk and Petersburg Railroad and the Seaboard and Roanoke Railroad. North of Battery South Quay was Battery Rosecrans, which was near the crossing of the Nansemond River by the Seaboard and Roanoke Railroad, and also near the point where the river begins to turn back to the east. Northeast of Battery Rosecrans was Battery Mansfield, and farther to the east, at the mouth of Jerico Creek, was Battery Onondaga. East of Battery Onondaga was Fort Dutton, and other forts and batteries were constructed to the north along the river.

Four roads radiated from Suffolk to the north, west, and south toward enemy-held territory. The Providence Church Road ran out to the northwest; the South Quay Road ran to the southwest, past the battery of the same name, to the south of, and nearly parallel to, the Seaboard and Roanoke Railroad; the Edenton Road ran south past Fort Dix and on to North Carolina; and the Somerton Road ran to the southwest between the South Quay Road and the Edenton Road.

The Federal troops at Suffolk under Peck held the following positions on the defensive line during the siege: Michael Corcoran's division was on the Union left, and occupied the ground from Fort Halleck to a point to the left of Battery Onondaga. Mathew Murphy's brigade was on the left from Fort Halleck to Fort Union; Robert S. Foster's brigade was on the center of the division line from Fort Union to Fort Nansemond, facing to the south and the southwest; and Henry D. Terry's brigade was on the right of the division line from Fort Nansemond to Battery Rosecrans, facing west. Brigadier General Charles C. Dodge, formerly colonel of the 1st New York Mounted Rifles, was assigned April 11, 1863 to command the southeast front between Forts Union and Halleck.

George W. Getty's division was on the right of Corcoran, and it held the line of the Nansemond River below Battery Onondaga for a distance of about eight miles. April 11, 1863, Edward Harland's Second Brigade was in position to support either Foster or Terry, but at noon the next day it was ordered to occupy the line between Forts Union and McClellan. This movement was completed by April 14, 1863. Arthur H. Dutton's Third Brigade was in position from the right of Corcoran's division to Battery Onondaga until April 18–19, 1863, and then it was relieved by Harland's brigade and assigned to the line of the Nansemond down to Doctor Council's house. Harrison S. Fairchild's First Brigade (commanded by Rush C. Hawkins part of the time) generally did not serve as a unit during the siege, but the regiments of the brigade were assigned to different parts of the line as needed. These positions included Fort Halleck, Fort Nansemond, a position to the right of Fort Union, and the line of the Nansemond River.

Union gunboats commanded by William B. Cushing, Roswell H. Lamson, and T. A. Harris of Rear Admiral S. Phillips Lee's North Atlantic Blockading Squadron held the Nansemond River below Getty's division, and cooperated with the land forces during the siege.

April 14, 1863, William Gurney was ordered from the Department of Washington with Second Brigade and Third Brigade of John J. Abercrombie's division to the Department of Virginia. Gurney's command arrived April 16, 1863, and was designated as Reserve Division at Suffolk. Burr Porter commanded Second Brigade and Robert S. Hughston Third Brigade. Gurney commanded Third Brigade until he assumed command of the two brigades and took them to Virginia.

April 24, 1863, a reserve brigade was organized at Suffolk under David W. Wardrop. He was relieved May 13, 1863, by Isaac J. Wistar, and the brigade was attached to Getty's division. In June 1863, this brigade was broken up and reorganized into Wistar's Independent Brigade and Wardrop's Independent Brigade of Seventh Corps.

The cavalry at Suffolk consisted of Benjamin F. Onderdonk's 1st New York Mounted Rifles and Samuel P. Spear's 11th Pennsylvania Cavalry. Also present at Suffolk were six batteries of light artillery under Frederick M. Follett, and John A. Blake's 2nd Battalion of 3rd Pennsylvania Heavy Artillery.

April 29, 1863, George H. Gordon was ordered to report to Peck at Suffolk He arrived May 1, 1863, three days before the siege ended, and assumed command of Gurney's Reserve Division. Gurney resumed command of his brigade. The Reserve Division was not engaged at the siege of Suffolk.

On April 11, 1863, Longstreet began his advance from the Blackwater toward Suffolk, which was about twenty miles distant. Hood's division approached the town on the South Quay Road, and the next day Pickett's division followed on the Somerton Road. Micah Jenkins' brigade of French's division moved up from the south on the Edenton Road, and another column advanced on the Providence Church Road from the northwest. There was skirmishing all along the roads as the enemy approached, but there was no heavy fighting. Longstreet made some preliminary attempts on the Federal lines, but these were all repulsed. He then began siege operations that lasted twenty-two days. Hood's division formed in front of the Federal right, and Pickett's division opposite the Federal left. During the weeks that followed, there were demonstrations, reconnaissances, and skirmishing

along the lines, but there were no major assaults. April 19, 1863, a detachment of Getty's division captured a Confederate battery at Hill's Point. Longstreet finally abandoned the siege at 9:00 P.M. May 3, 1863, and withdrew to the Blackwater. As the enemy moved back, Corcoran and Dodge pursued on the Edenton Road, Foster on the Somerton Road, and the cavalry under Spear and Onderdonk followed on several roads.

Reorganization of Fourth Corps, June 17, 1863. After the siege of Suffolk, George H. Gordon's division (formerly William Gurney's Reserve Division of Seventh Corps) was transferred from Suffolk to West Point, Virginia. It was then placed under Keyes' command and was reorganized as Second Division, Fourth Corps. First Brigade was organized from Gurney's Third Brigade of the division, and Second Brigade was organized from Porter's Second Brigade. Gurney thus commanded First Brigade and Porter the Second Brigade. The division was discontinued in July 1863, and the regiments of the two brigades under Gordon were transferred to Eleventh Corps, Army of the Potomac.

June 17, 1863, First Division, Fourth Corps was reorganized from regiments of Seventh Corps as follows:

First Division, Fourth Corps, Rufus King
   First Brigade, Hector Tyndale
   Second Brigade, George E. Church
   Third Brigade, Charles Kleckner

Note. Tyndale assumed command June 17, 1863.

The brigades of the division were posted as follows: First Brigade at Gloucester Point, Second Brigade at Williamsburg, and Third Brigade, probably at Yorktown.

Corcoran succeeded Peck in command at Suffolk June 17, 1863, and Terry's and Foster's brigades were moved to the White House. Murphy's brigade remained at Suffolk. Also at the White House in June 1863 were Getty's division, Wardrop's Provisional Brigade, and Spinola's Brigade (Keystone Brigade). Wistar's Brigade was at West Point.

In July 1863, the troops of Keyes' Fourth Corps, Spinola's Brigade, and Corcoran's Brigade (Irish Legion) were transferred to the Department of Washington. The regiments of Spinola's Brigade were mustered out in July and August of 1863. Foster's Second Brigade of Corcoran's First Division, Seventh Corps was transferred to Getty's Second Division, Seventh Corps.

Fourth Corps and Seventh Corps were discontinued August 1, 1863, and the troops were merged into Eighteenth Corps, Department of Virginia and North Carolina.

DEPARTMENT OF VIRGINIA
JANUARY 18, 1865–AUGUST 6, 1866

In January 1865, William T. Sherman's Army of the Military Division of the Mississippi left Savannah, Georgia and began its advance through the Carolinas toward Goldsboro, North Carolina. To secure better cooperation of the Union forces in North Carolina with Sherman's advancing columns, the Department of the South was extended January 12, 1865 to include the state of North Carolina. Prior to that time, North Carolina had been a part of Edward O. C. Ord's Department of Virginia and North Carolina. When North Carolina was transferred to the Department of the South, only that part of southeastern Virginia that was controlled by the Army of the James was under Ord's command, and January 18, 1865, the designation was changed to the Department of Virginia, Army of the James. Ord, however, continued to issue communications from "Headquarters Department of Virginia and North Carolina" and Army of the James until February 6, 1863, when he was officially assigned by the secretary of war to command the Department of Virginia. Ord's headquarters was north of the James River, about three miles from Aiken's Landing. For additional information relating to the reorganization of the Department of Virginia, see the following: Department of Virginia and North Carolina; Department of the South; Department of North Carolina, January 31, 1865–May 19,1866; Army of the James; and Carolinas Campaign.

After Robert E. Lee's surrender of the Army of Northern Virginia at Appomattox Court House April 9, 1865, Ord's command was greatly extended to include most of the state of Virginia. April 12, 1865, headquarters of the Department of Virginia was established at Richmond.

April 19, 1865, the Military Division of the James was constituted to include the Department of Virginia, the Army of the Potomac, and that part of North Carolina not occupied by Sherman's army. Henry W. Halleck assumed command of the Military Division April 22, 1865, and after that date the commanding officer of the Department of Virginia reported to Headquarters Military Division of the James.

On June 10, 1865, the Department of Virginia was re-created to consist of the entire state of Virginia, except Fairfax County, which was across the Potomac River from Washington and was included in the Department of Washington. Alfred H. Terry was assigned command of the Department of Virginia, with headquarters at Richmond. Terry relieved Ord June 14, 1865, and June 27, 1865, the latter was assigned command of the Department of the Ohio, which included the states of Ohio, Indiana, Michigan, and Illinois. The Army of the James was discontinued as a result of the order of June 10, 1865.

In the general reorganization of the Army of the United States June 27, 1865, the Department of Virginia was redefined to include the state of Virginia, except Fairfax County, and the line of the Baltimore and Ohio Railroad. Terry was assigned command, with headquarters at Richmond. The order of June 27, 1865 also attached the Department of Virginia to the Military Division of the Atlantic.

The Military Division of the James was discontinued June 30, 1865, and the commanding officer of the Department of Virginia, at that time Terry, was ordered to report directly to the adjutant general at Washington.

August 6, 1866, the Department of Virginia was merged into the Department of the Potomac.

COMMANDERS OF THE DEPARTMENT OF VIRGINIA

Edward O. C. Ord was in command from February 7, 1865 to June 14, 1865, and he was then succeeded by Alfred H. Terry. John Gibbon was in temporary command of the department on several occasions during the winter of 1864–1865, while Ord was absent on department business in the District of Eastern Virginia. On April 16, 1865, Halleck was assigned command of the Department of

Virginia and Ord was assigned command of the Department of the South. Three days later, however, this order was revoked, and Halleck was assigned command of the Military Division of the James.

DISTRICTS AND POSTS IN THE DEPARTMENT OF VIRGINIA

Prior to April 3, 1865, there were only two districts in the Department of Virginia, the Defenses of Bermuda Hundred and the District of Eastern Virginia. After that date, both Petersburg and Richmond were occupied by Federal troops, and they became special commands of the department.

Defenses of Bermuda Hundred. When the Department of Virginia was reconstituted early in February 1865, the Defenses of Bermuda Hundred was organized as follows:

Defenses of Bermuda Hundred, Edward Ferrero
    First Brigade, William Heine
    Second Brigade, James B. Campbell
    Provisional Brigade, William M. McClure

Charles K. Graham assumed temporary command of the Defenses February 19, 1865, while Ferrero was on leave. March 19, 1865, George L. Hartsuff relieved Graham, and the next day reorganized the Defenses as follows:

Defenses of Bermuda Hundred, George L. Hartsuff
    Infantry Division, Edward Ferrero
        First Brigade, Gilbert H. McKibbin
        Second Brigade, George C. Kibbe
    Artillery Brigade, George B. Cook, to March 21, 1865
        Henry L. Abbot
        1st Connecticut Heavy Artillery (four companies), George B. Cook
        3rd Pennsylvania Heavy Artillery (two companies)
        7th Battery, New York Light Artillery, Martin V. McIntyre

On April 4–5, 1865, after the evacuation of Richmond and Petersburg by the enemy, Hartsuff left Abbot's artillery brigade in the Defenses of Bermuda Hundred, and with Ferrero's Infantry Division moved to Petersburg, where he relieved the troops of Ninth Corps that were occupying the city. For

further information about Hartsuff's command, see United States Forces, Petersburg, below.

The Defenses of Bermuda Hundred was discontinued as an organization April 21, 1865, when Abbot was ordered with his artillery brigade to Fort Darling, Virginia. Abbot's siege artillery had been attached to the Army of the Potomac December 24, 1864, and May 5, 1865, it was detached from the Army of the Potomac and was assigned to duty in the Department of Virginia.

District of Eastern Virginia. The District of Eastern Virginia was constituted May 27, 1864 as a district of the Department of Virginia and North Carolina. It consisted of Fort Monroe, the Defenses of Yorktown, Williamsburg, Norfolk, Portsmouth, and the Eastern Shore of Virginia. It was continued as a district in the Department of Virginia after the state of North Carolina was transferred to the Department of the South, and it remained in existence until after the war. George H. Gordon relieved George F. Shepley in command of the district February 11, 1865, and remained in command until mustered out in August 1865.

April 27, 1865, the Sub-District of the Peninsula was constituted, and its commander, Benjamin C. Ludlow, was ordered to report to Gordon, the commander of the District of Eastern Virginia. The District of Fort Monroe was constituted May 21, 1865, and in the general reorganization of the districts of the department May 25, 1865, the Sub-District of the Peninsula was transferred from the District of Eastern Virginia to the District of Fort Monroe. For additional information, see below on Postwar Districts and Sub-Districts in the Department of Virginia.

The posts in the district at the end of April 1865 were as follows: Defenses of Norfolk and Portsmouth (commanded by Charles K. Graham until March 20, 1865, when he was relieved by Israel Vogdes), Getty's Station, Suffolk, Fort Hazlett, Fort Monroe, the Eastern Shore of Virginia, and the Sub-District of the Peninsula (see below, Postwar Districts and Sub-Districts in the Department of Virginia).

In a general reorganization of the districts of the Department of Virginia May 25, 1865, the District of Eastern Virginia was reconstituted to include the counties of Princess Anne, Norfolk, Nansemond,

Southampton, and Isle of Wight. Gordon was assigned command, with headquarters at Norfolk.

United States Forces, Petersburg, Virginia. When the Army of Northern Virginia evacuated Petersburg April 3, 1865, troops of John G. Parke's Ninth Corps occupied the city. These troops, however, were needed to guard the South Side Railroad during Grant's pursuit of Lee, and George L. Hartsuff was ordered to move from Bermuda Hundred with Edward Ferrero's Infantry Division to relieve them. Hartsuff arrived at Petersburg April 4–5, 1865 and assumed command there April 6, 1865. The designation of his command was United States Forces, Petersburg, and the designation of Ferrero's Infantry Division, Defenses of Bermuda Hundred was changed to Ferrero's Division, United States Forces, Petersburg, Virginia. Henry L. Abbot's artillery brigade was left behind in the Defenses of Bermuda Hundred, which was not discontinued until April 21, 1865 (see Defenses of Bermuda Hundred, above).

April 7, 1865, Hartsuff was assigned command of the forces at City Point, Petersburg, Bermuda Hundred, and the South Side Railroad as far west as Sutherland's Station. The next day he was also directed to assume command of Charles S. Russell's brigade (formerly Attached Brigade, First Division, Twenty-Fifth Corps), which was then at City Point. This entire command was included in United States Forces, Petersburg. The organization of Hartsuff's command at the end of April 1865 was as follows:

UNITED STATES FORCES, PETERSBURG, George L. Hartsuff

Ferrero's Division, Edward Ferrero
  First Brigade, Gilbert H. McKibbin
  Second Brigade, George C. Kibbe
  Artillery, Alger M. Wheeler

Artillery Brigade (at Bermuda Hundred), Henry L. Abbot

United States Forces, City Point, Charles S. Russell

On April 17–18, 1865, after Lee's surrender at Appomattox Court House, Philip H. Sheridan's cavalry moved to Petersburg to refit, and then on April 24, 1865, it was sent toward North Carolina to join William T. Sherman's Army of the Military Division of the Mississippi. Upon arriving at South Boston on the Dan River, however, Sheridan learned of the surrender of Joseph E. Johnston's army in North Carolina, and he then returned to Petersburg, where he arrived May 3, 1865. A week later the cavalry left for Alexandria, Virginia, but Charles H. Smith's Third Brigade of George Crook's Second Cavalry Division, Army of the Potomac remained behind with Hartsuff's command. May 12, 1865, Smith's brigade was detached from Sheridan's cavalry, and it was assigned to duty in the Department of Virginia.

May 22, 1865, Hartsuff's command was merged into the newly constituted District of the Nottoway (see below), and United States Forces, Petersburg and Ferrero's Division, United States Forces, Petersburg were discontinued.

Richmond, Virginia. The Confederates evacuated Richmond on the night of April 2, 1865, and the next morning Godfrey Weitzel advanced with his Detachment Army of the James to the outskirts of the city. Weitzel's command consisted of August Kautz's First Division, Twenty-Fifth Corps; Charles Devens' Third Division, Twenty-Fourth Corps; and Charles F. Adams' 5th Massachusetts Cavalry (colored). Edward H. Ripley's First Brigade of Devens' division was sent into Richmond as provost guard, and the rest of Weitzel's command camped near the city. April 15, 1865, George F. Shepley, Weitzel's chief of staff, was appointed military governor of Richmond.

April 12, 1865, Edward O. C. Ord arrived at Richmond from Appomattox Court House, and established there his headquarters of the Department of Virginia and of the Army of the James. That day he ordered Twenty-Fifth Corps to move to the south of Petersburg, and the next day Weitzel left the city with Kautz's division. Shepley relinquished his duties as military governor and left with Weitzel.

After Lee's surrender April 9, 1865, Ord's responsibilities were greatly expanded to include most of the state of Virginia. On April 12, 1865, Grant directed that Marsena R. Patrick, provost marshal general of the armies that had been operating against Richmond, be appointed provost marshal general of the Department of Virginia to have special and immediate control of affairs at Richmond. Patrick, whose headquarters was at City Point, arrived at Richmond April 15, 1865 and assumed the duties of military governor in his capacity as provost marshal general of the Department of Virginia.

April 17, 1865, Ord placed Devens in command of all United States forces in and about Richmond, and directed him to place them in camps outside the city. April 25, 1865, Frederick T. Dent, formerly aide de camp on Grant's staff, was assigned to duty as military commander of the city of Richmond and to the command of all troops within the city. Dent remained on this duty until May 18, 1865.

The Military Division of the James, which included the Department of Virginia, was constituted April 19, 1865, and Henry W. Halleck assumed command April 22, 1865. He established his headquarters in Richmond.

April 24–25, 1865, John Gibbon arrived at Richmond from Appomattox Court House with the divisions of Robert S. Foster and John W. Turner of Twenty-Fourth Corps, and Ranald S. Mackenzie's cavalry of the Army of the James. Gibbon placed his command in camps north of the city.

May 25, 1865, the District of Henrico was constituted, and included in its territory was the city of Richmond. Patrick was assigned command of the district.

Postwar Districts and Sub-Districts in the Department of Virginia

Following the surrender of the Army of Northern Virginia at Appomattox Court House April 9, 1865, a number of districts and sub-districts were formed to provide a better administration of affairs in the state of Virginia during postwar occupation by United States troops. These were as follows:

Sub-District of the Appomattox. For details, see District of the Nottoway, below, this section.

Sub-District of the Blackwater. For details, see District of the Nottoway, below, this section.

District of Eastern Virginia. For details, see District of Eastern Virginia, above, in Districts and Posts in the Department of Virginia.

District of Fort Monroe. The District of Fort Monroe was constituted May 21, 1865, to include the

peninsula between the York and James rivers, as far west as Henrico and Hanover counties, and also the counties of Mathews, Gloucester, Accomac, and Northampton. The former two counties were north of the York River, and the latter two constituted the Eastern Shore of Virginia. Nelson A. Miles was assigned command of the district, with headquarters at Fort Monroe.

In a general reorganization of the districts in the Department of Virginia May 25, 1865, the District of Fort Monroe was redefined to include the counties of Accomac and Northampton, Fort Monroe, and the Sub-District of the Peninsula. For more information about the latter, see below, this section. Miles remained in command of the district.

District of Henrico. In the general reorganization of the districts of the Department of Virginia May 25, 1865, the District of Henrico was constituted to consist of the county of that name. This county included the city of Richmond and the adjacent country north of the James River. Marsena R. Patrick was assigned command, with headquarters at Richmond. John W. Turner succeeded Patrick in command of the district June 9, 1865. July 13, 1865, the city of Manchester, which was located on the south bank of the James, opposite Richmond, was included in the District of Henrico. Troops of Twenty-Fourth Corps and Mackenzie's cavalry were in the district, in the vicinity of Richmond, until they were discontinued.

District (Sub-District) of Lynchburg. May 9, 1865, Samuel B. M. Young, commanding J. Irvin Gregg's Second Brigade, Second Cavalry Division, was sent to Lynchburg to restore order in the town and surrounding country. Gregg soon relieved Young and assumed command of the district. In the reorganization of the districts in the Department of Virginia May 25, 1865, the District of Lynchburg was constituted to consist of the counties of Nelson, Amherst, Bedford, Campbell, Appomattox, Pittsylvania, Henry, Patrick, and Franklin. Gregg was assigned command, with headquarters at Lynchburg. It should be noted that Gregg signed his communications under the heading "Headquarters Sub-District of Lynchburg."

The counties of the District of Lynchburg were included in the District of Southwestern Virginia, which was constituted July 13, 1865. The District of Lynchburg was discontinued as of that date.

District of Northeastern Virginia.

July 10, 1865, the District of Northeastern Virginia was constituted to consist of the Sub-District of the Rappahannock, as then constituted (see below, this section), and the counties of Loudoun, Prince William, Fauquier, Stafford, Rappahannock, Culpeper, Madison, King George, Westmoreland, Northumberland, Richmond, and Lancaster. Charles Devens was assigned command, with headquarters at Fredericksburg. Also on July 10, 1865, the First Independent Brigade, Twenty-Fourth Corps was organized from First Brigade, Third Division, Twenty-Fourth Corps, and under the command of Thomas M. Harris, it was ordered to report to Devens at Fredericksburg.

District of the Nottoway.

The District of the Nottoway was organized May 22, 1865 from George L. Hartsuff's United States Forces, Petersburg (see above), and Hartsuff was assigned command, with headquarters at Petersburg. By an order of the same day, Hartsuff subdivided the district as follows:

Sub-District of the Roanoke, to consist of the counties of Mecklenburg, Lunenburg, Prince Edward, Nottoway, Charlotte, and Halifax. These counties were to the south and west of Petersburg. Edward Ferrero was assigned command of the sub-district.

Sub-District of the Appomattox, to consist of the counties of Chesterfield, Amelia, Powhatan, Cumberland, and Buckingham. These counties were west of Petersburg, and were between the Sub-District of the Roanoke on the south and the James River on the north. Charles H. Smith was assigned command of the sub-district.

Sub-District of the Blackwater, to consist of the counties of Sussex, Surry, Greenville, Brunswick, Dinwiddie, and Prince George. These counties were to the southeast of Petersburg, and extended to the District of Eastern Virginia (see above). Gilbert H. McKibbin was assigned command of the sub-district.

The city of Petersburg was organized as a separate post of the District of the Nottoway, and was assigned to the command of Edward Martindale.

District (Sub-District) of the Peninsula.

The District of the Peninsula was constituted April 13, 1865, to include the territory between the James River and the York River and its northern branches. Benjamin C. Ludlow was asigned command, with headquarters at Williamsburg. Ludlow was also assigned supervision of Negro affairs in the district.

April 27, 1865, the order constituting the district was modified to change the designation of the District of the Peninsula to the Sub-District of the Peninsula, and also to change its boundaries as follows: it was to be bounded on the north by the York and Pamunkey rivers, including Gloucester and Mathews counties; on the east by the Chesapeake Bay; on the south by the James River; and on the west by the Richmond, Fredericksburg, and Potomac Railroad, excluding the city of Richmond and Forts Pocahontas and Monroe. Ludlow was assigned command of the sub-district, and he reported to George H. Gordon, commander of the District of Eastern Virginia.

In the general reorganization of the districts of the Department of Virginia May 25, 1865, the Sub-District of the Peninsula was redefined to include the counties of Mathews, Gloucester, New Kent, King William, Charles City, James City, York, Warwick, and Elizabeth City, excluding Fort Monroe. The sub-district was transferred to the District of Fort Monroe, and Ludlow was assigned command.

Sub-District of the Rappahannock.

April 27, 1865, Edwin V. Sumner, with his 1st New York Mounted Rifles (7th New York Cavalry), was sent to Fredericksburg, Virginia to maintain law and order in the area. In the general reorganization of the districts in the Department of Virginia May 25, 1865, the Sub-District of the Rappahannock was constituted to include the counties of Middlesex, King and Queen, Essex, Caroline, Spotsylvania, and Orange. Sumner was assigned command, with headquarters at Fredericksburg. Sumner reported directly to Edward O. C. Ord, commander of the Department of Virginia. July 10, 1865, the Sub-District of the Rappahannock was merged into the newly created District of Northeastern Virginia (see above).

Sub-District of the Roanoke. For details, see District of the Nottoway, above.

Sub-District of the South Anna. Shortly after the return of Twenty-Fourth Corps from Appomattox to Richmond, Alvin C. Voris, with his 67th Ohio Regiment of Thomas O. Osborn's First Brigade of Robert S. Foster's First Division, was sent out on the Virginia Central Railroad with orders to extend his command as far west as the mountains. Later, the 62nd Ohio of the same brigade was sent to join Voris. By May 4, 1865, Voris was at Louisa Court House, with his command established along the railroad.

In the general reorganization of the districts in the Department of Virginia May 25, 1865, the Sub-District of the South Anna was constituted to include the counties of Hanover, Louisa, and Albemarle, through which the railroad passed, and also the contiguous counties of Goochland, Fluvanna, and Greene. Voris was assigned command of the sub-district, and he reported directly to Edward O. C. Ord, commander of the Department of Virginia and Army of the James.

District of Southwestern Virginia. July 13, 1865, the District of Southwestern Virginia was constituted to consist of the counties of Nelson, Amherst, Bedford, Campbell, Appomattox, Pittsylvania, Henry, Patrick, Franklin, Augusta, Bath, Rockbridge, Botetourt, Montgomery, Grayson, Wythe, Tazwell, Russell, Lee, Washington, Highland, Alleghany, Roanoke, Craig, Giles, Pulaski, Carroll, Floyd, Smyth, Wise, and Buchanan. N. Martin Curtis was assigned command, with headquarters at Lynchburg. The territory of the former District (Sub-District) of Lynchburg was included in this new district, and the District of Lynchburg was discontinued.

TROOPS IN THE DEPARTMENT OF VIRGINIA, ARMY OF THE JAMES

When the Department of Virginia was re-created under Edward O. C. Ord early in February 1865, the troops in the department were known as the Army of the James, and the designation of Ord's command was Department of Virginia, Army of the James. At the end of January 1865, the department (and army) was organized as follows:

GENERAL HEADQUARTERS

Naval Brigade, Charles K. Graham
Signal Corps, Lemuel B. Norton
1st New York Engineers, Edward W. Serrell
4th Massachusetts Cavalry, Arnold A. Rand

Note. The Naval Brigade was turned over to the navy February 14, 1865. It was reorganized later under George H. Gordon at Norfolk, Virginia, and was then discontinued by an order dated May 26, 1865.

TWENTY-FOURTH CORPS, John Gibbon

First Division, Joseph R. Hawley
    First Brigade, Thomas O. Osborn
    Third Brigade, Harris M. Plaisted
    Fourth Brigade, James Jourdan

Note 1. Alfred H. Terry was the commander of First Division, but at the end of January 1865, he was absent on an expedition to Fort Fisher, North Carolina. Robert S. Foster assumed command February 1, 1865, relieving Hawley.
Note 2. Joseph C. Abbott's Second Brigade, First Division was absent on an expedition to Fort Fisher, but was still carried on the roster of Twenty-Fourth Corps.

Second Division, Adelbert Ames

Note. Ames' division was absent on an expedition to Fort Fisher, but was still carried on the roster of Twenty-Fourth Corps. For details, see Army of the James, Terry's Expedition to Fort Fisher, North Carolina.

Third Division, Charles Devens
    First Brigade, Edgar M. Cullen
    Second Brigade, Valentine G. Barney
    Third Brigade, Guy V. Henry, to January 29, 1865
        Samuel L. Roberts

Independent Division, Thomas M. Harris
    First Brigade, Thomas F. Wildes
    Second Brigade, William B. Curtis
    Third Brigade, Moses B. Hall

Artillery, Charles C. Abell

Note. For the batteries in Abell's command, see Twenty-Fourth Corps.

TWENTY-FIFTH CORPS, Godfrey Weitzel

First Division, Edward A. Wild
    First Brigade, Alonzo G. Draper
    Second Brigade, Charles S. Russell

Third Brigade, Henry G. Thomas

Note. Weitzel was absent in Washington after January 20, 1865, and Charles A. Heckman was in temporary command of Twenty-Fourth Corps.

Second Division, William Birney
First Brigade, James Shaw, Jr.
Second Brigade, Ulysses Doubleday
Third Brigade, Edward Martindale

Third Division, Charles J. Paine

Note. Paine's division was absent on an expedition to Fort Fisher, but was still carried on the roster of Twenty-Fifth Corps. For details, see Army of the James, Terry's Expedition to Fort Fisher, North Carolina.

Artillery Brigade, Richard H. Jackson

Note. For the batteries in Jackson's command, see Twenty-Fifth Corps, Army of the James.

Cavalry Division, August V. Kautz
First Brigade, Robert M. West
Second Brigade, Samuel P. Spear
Third Brigade, Andrew W. Evans

Defenses of Bermuda Hundred, Edward Ferrero
First Brigade, William Heine
Second Brigade, James B. Campbell
Provisional Brigade, William M. McClure
Siege Artillery, Henry L. Abbot

Note 1. Charles K. Graham commanded the Defenses of Bermuda Hundred after February 19, 1865, while Ferrero was on leave.
Note 2. The siege artillery was permanently attached to the Army of the Potomac December 24, 1864. George B. Cook was in temporary command at the end of January 1865 while Abbot was on leave.

Separate Brigade, Joseph B. Carr
Fort Pocahontas, William H. Tantum
Harrison's Landing, Wardwell G. Robinson
Fort Powhatan, William J. Sewell

District of Eastern Virginia, George F. Shepley
Defenses of Norfolk and Portsmouth, Israel Vogdes
Fort Monroe, Joseph Roberts
Eastern Shore, Frank J. White
Newport News, Loren Burritt
Fort Magruder (Williamsburg), Joseph J. Morrison

Note 1. Benjamin C. Ludlow relieved Morrison in command at Fort Magruder in February 1865.
Note 2. George H. Gordon assumed command of the

District of Eastern Virginia February 11, 1865, relieving Shepley.

The Army of the James was assigned a part in Grant's spring offensive in 1865, and in preparation for this, a number of organizational and command changes were made in the army. March 21, 1865, Ranald S. Mackenzie assumed command of the cavalry division, relieving August V. Kautz, and March 27, 1865, Kautz was assigned command of First Division, Twenty-Fifth Corps to relieve Edward A. Wild. March 28, 1865, the cavalry division was reduced to two brigades by merging Andrew W. Evans' Third Brigade into Samuel P. Spear's Second Brigade. During the month, two cavalry regiments were assigned to the Department of Virginia as unattached commands. March 19, 1865, Edwin V. Sumner's 1st New York Mounted Rifles returned to the army from Samuel H. Roberts' raids to Fredericksburg and Westmoreland County, Virginia (see Army of the James); and March 28–29, 1865, Charles F. Adams' 5th Massachusetts Cavalry (colored) arrived in the department from Point Lookout, Maryland.

March 27, 1865, Charles S. Russell was assigned command of a new brigade, which was designated as Attached Brigade, First Division, Twenty-Fifth Corps. This brigade was formed from regiments of Third Brigade, Second Division, Twenty-Fifth Corps, and joined First Division on the line of entrenchments in front of Richmond.

On the night of March 27, 1865, Ord marched from the north of the James River with Robert S. Foster's First Division and John W. Turner's Independent Division (formerly Thomas M. Harris' division) of John Gibbon's Twenty-Fourth Corps; William Birney's Second Division of Twenty-Fifth Corps; and Mackenzie's Cavalry Division, Army of the James to join the Army of the Potomac in the final effort to capture Petersburg. Ord arrived near Hatcher's Run, south of Petersburg, on the evening of March 28, 1865, and the next morning relieved Second Corps, Army of the Potomac on the left of the Union line of entrenchments. During the ensuing fighting at Petersburg and the Appomattox Campaign, Ord's command was known as the Army of the James.

The Army of the James participated in the fighting of April 2, 1865, which resulted in the breakthrough of the Confederate lines and the evacuation of Petersburg, and it then joined in the pursuit of the Army of Northern Virginia. It advanced on the left of Grant's army and contributed materially in forcing Lee's surrender at Appomattox Court House April 9, 1865. For additional information, see Appomattox Campaign, and also Army of the James.

When Ord left the Richmond front to join the Army of the Potomac, he left behind in the entrenchments Godfrey Weitzel with Devens' Third Division, Twenty-Fourth Corps; Kautz's First Division, Twenty-Fifth Corps; and Adams' 5th Massachusetts Cavalry. Weitzel's command was known as Detachment, Army of the James. Weitzel remained on the lines near Chaffin's farm until the enemy evacuated Richmond on the night of April 2, 1865, and then the next morning advanced and occupied the city. For further information, see Appomattox Campaign, Federal Occupation of Petersburg and Richmond.

There were some changes in the command and organization of the Army of the James during the Appomattox Campaign. On April 1, 1865, at Dinwiddie Court House, Mackenzie's cavalry division was temporarily assigned to Philip H. Sheridan's command, and it generally served with Sheridan's cavalry until Lee's surrender. During this period, about April 5, 1865, Mackenzie's division was reduced to a single brigade, and April 8, 1865, it was temporarily attached to George Crook's Second Cavalry Division, Army of the Potomac.

April 4–5, 1865, George L. Hartsuff, with Edward Ferrero's Infantry Division from the Defenses of Bermuda Hundred, occupied Petersburg and relieved troops of John G. Parke's Ninth Corps. Hartsuff assumed command April 6, 1865, and his command was designated as United States Forces, Petersburg. For additional information see the following: United States Forces, Petersburg; and Defenses of Bermuda Hundred, in section on Districts and Posts in the Department of Virginia, above.

April 8, 1865, Ord relieved William Birney from the command of Second Division, Twenty-Fifth Corps, and the division was temporarily broken up by the assignment of the brigades to Foster's and Turner's divisions of Twenty-Fourth Corps. Two days later, however, at Appomattox Court House, the division was re-formed under the command of Richard H. Jackson.

The Army of the James did not again reassemble as a unit after Lee's surrender at Appomattox Court House. April 12, 1865, Weitzel was ordered to move his Twenty-Fifth Corps to Petersburg, perhaps to remove the colored troops from the vicinity of Richmond, and to place the troops in camps south of the town. The next day, Weitzel marched with Kautz's First Division, and by April 16, 1865 he had his troops in camp along the old Military Railroad. He was joined there by Jackson's Second Division from Appomattox Court House. Gibbon's Twenty-Fourth Corps and Mackenzie's cavalry remained at Appomattox Court House and at Lynchburg until April 17, 1865. They then marched to Richmond, where they arrived April 24–25, 1865 and camped north of the city.

May 1, 1865, Ord directed that all colored troops in the Department of Virginia be assigned to Twenty-Fifth Corps, and that the corps be placed in a camp of instruction at City Point. Grant then decided to send Twenty-Fifth Corps to Texas, and May 18, 1865 ordered Weitzel to prepare his command for embarkation. This began May 23, 1865, and the last of Weitzel's troops left the Department of Virginia June 26, 1865.

May 24, 1865, the posts of Fort Pocahontas and Harrison's Landing were broken up, and their garrisons, which belonged to Joseph B. Carr's Separate Brigade, moved to City Point. Upon arrival there, Carr assumed command of the post of City Point.

When the Department of Virginia was re-created June 10, 1865, under the command of Alfred H. Terry, the Army of the James was discontinued. The troops remaining wih the army at that time, however, continued to serve in the department under Terry.

Gibbon's Twenty-Fourth Corps was broken up June 10, 1865 and Gibbon departed, but the corps was not officially discontinued until August 1, 1865. In the interim, the troops of Twenty-Fourth Corps were under the direction of John W. Turner, commander of the District of Henrico.

July 10, 1865, Devens' Third Division, Twenty-Fourth Corps, which had been in camp near Richmond since April 3, 1865, was discontinued, and Devens was assigned command of the newly constituted District of Northeastern Virginia. At that time, Third Division consisted of only two brigades, because Third Brigade had been discontinued in June 1865, largely by muster out of regiments. The regiments of First Brigade, Third Division were assigned to First Independent Brigade, Twenty-Fourth Corps, which was commanded by Thomas M. Harris. Harris was sent with his brigade to report to Devens at Fredericksburg. The regiments of Second Brigade, Third Division were assigned to Second Independent Brigade, which was commanded by James C. Briscoe, and this brigade served at Lynchburg and in central Virginia.

A new Second Brigade, Second Division, Twenty-Fourth Corps was organized July 10, 1865, and Joseph H. Potter was assigned command. Twenty-Fourth Corps was discontinued August 1, 1865.

For additional information about the troops in the Department of Virginia, see the following: Army of the James; Twenty-Fourth Corps, Army of the James; Twenty-Fifth Corps, Army of the James; and also Districts and Sub-Districts in the Department of Virginia, above.

DEPARTMENT OF VIRGINIA AND NORTH CAROLINA

July 15, 1863, John A. Dix, commander of the Department of Virginia, was ordered to New York during the Draft Riots to assume command of the Department of the East. No successor was assigned for Dix, and instead the departments of Virginia and North Carolina were consolidated to form a new Department of Virginia and North Carolina. John G. Foster, commander of the Department of North Carolina, was assigned command of the new department. Dix left Fort Monroe July 16, 1863, and George W. Getty served temporarily as department commander until Foster arrived and assumed command July 18, 1863.

Before the consolidation, the Department of Virginia included that part of the state of Virginia south of the Rappahannock River and east of the railroad running from Fredericksburg, through Richmond and Petersburg, to Weldon, North Carolina. The Department of North Carolina was originally created to consist of the entire state of North Carolina, but in July 1863 that part of the state under Federal control was limited to the eastern part in the vicinity of the posts of Hatteras Inlet, Roanoke Island, New Berne, Beaufort, Caroline City, Fort Macon, Morehead City, Newport, Plymouth, Washington, and Portsmouth.

Benjamin F. Butler relieved Foster in command of the Department of Virginia and North Carolina November 11, 1863.

December 21, 1863, the deprtment was extended to include Saint Mary's County, including the prison camp at Point Lookout (the District of Saint Mary's), in Maryland; and the counties of Northampton and Accomac (the Eastern Shore) in Virginia. This territory was taken from the Middle Department. June 27, 1864, Saint Mary's County was transferred to the Department of Washington.

January 12, 1865, the state of North Carolina was assigned to the Department of the South, where it was designated as the District of North Carolina. The Department of Virginia and North Carolina was discontinued January 18, 1865, when it was merged into the Department of Virginia and the Department of the South. Edward O. C. Ord, then commanding the Department of Virginia and North Carolina, continued to sign his communications under the heading "Headquarters Department of Virginia and North Carolina" (and also "Department of Virginia" and "Army of the James") until January 31, 1865. Ord was officially assigned command of the Department of Virginia February 6, 1865.

COMMANDERS OF THE DEPARTMENT OF VIRGINIA AND NORTH CAROLINA

George W. Getty	July 16, 1863 to July 18, 1863
John G. Foster	July 18, 1863 to November 11, 1863
Benjamin F. Butler	November 11, 1863 to August 27, 1864
Edward O. C. Ord	August 27, 1864 to September 5, 1864
David B. Birney	September 5, 1864 to September 7, 1864
Benjamin F. Butler	September 7, 1864 to December 14, 1864
Edward O. C. Ord	December 14, 1864 to December 24, 1864
Benjamin F. Butler	December 24, 1864 to January 8, 1865
Edward O. C. Ord	January 8, 1865 to January 18, 1865

Note. Ord was officially assigned command of the Department of Virginia February 6, 1865.

DISTRICTS IN THE DEPARTMENT OF VIRGINIA AND NORTH CAROLINA

Districts in North Carolina

District of the Albemarle. The District of the Albemarle was organized May 3, 1863 from Henry W. Wessells' Fourth Division, Eighteenth Corps, Department of North Carolina. The district was retained in the Department of Virginia and North Carolina, with the same limits that were established April 27, 1863. Wessells was assigned commmand, with headquarters at Plymouth, North Carolina. For the description of the district, see Department of North Carolina, Districts in the Department of North Carolina. A new District of North Carolina, Department of Virginia and North Carolina was constituted August 21, 1863 to have the same boundaries as the former Department of North Carolina. The designation of the District of the Albemarle was then changed to Sub-District of the Albemarle, District of North Carolina. For additional information, see District of North Carolina, below, in this section.

District of Beaufort. The District of Beaufort was organized May 2, 1863 from Henry M. Naglee's Second Division, Eighteenth Corps, Department of North Carolina, which at that time consisted only of Charles A. Heckman's First Brigade. Heckman was assigned command, with headquarters at Beaufort, North Carolina. The District of Beaufort was retained in the Department of Virginia and North Carolina, with the same limits that were established April 27, 1863. For a description of the district, see Department of North Carolina, Districts in the Department of North Carolina. Heckman commanded the district until July 21, 1863, and then was in charge of the Defenses of New Berne until August 14, 1863. He then resumed command of the District of Beaufort. Thomas J. C. Amory commanded the district during the absence of Heckman. A new District of North Carolina, Department of Virginia and North Carolina was constituted August 21, 1863, which was to have the same boundaries as the former Department of North Carolina. The designation of the district was then changed to the Sub-District of Beaufort, District of North Carolina. For additional information, see District of North Carolina, below.

Defenses of New Berne. New Berne, North Carolina was an important post in the Department of North Carolina, and headquarters of the department was located there. In July 1863, when the Department of Virginia and North Carolina was constituted, the troops reported for the post were as follows: Thomas J. C. Amory's First Division, James Jourdan's brigade, Edward A. Wild's colored troops, George W. Lewis' Cavalry Brigade, four nonbrigaded infantry regiments, and some artillery. This appears to have been a large force, but in fact it was comparatively small. Eight regiments of the post had left New Berne for muster out during June 1863, leaving only three infantry regiments in First Division. On April 13, 1863 Wild was authorized to raise four regiments of black soldiers in North Carolina, and April 24, 1863 he went to New Berne to begin the organization of his so-called "African Brigade." His regiments were only in the process of organization and training in July 1863, and numbered only about 1,000 men.

July 21, 1863, the designation of the post and garrison of New Berne was changed to Forces and Defenses of New Berne, and Charles A. Heckman was assigned command. Innis N. Palmer relieved Heckman, and remained in command of the Defenses until March 5, 1864, when the designation was changed to Sub-District of New Berne, District of North Carolina, Department of Virginia and North Carolina. For further information, see below, in this section, District of North Carolina. Thomas J. C. Amory commanded the Defenses temporarily from October 7, 1863 to November 7, 1863, while Palmer was absent.

August 2–9, 1863, Wild's Brigade, which then consisted of 1st North Carolina, 2nd North Carolina, and one company of 3rd North Carolina, was sent to Charleston Harbor in the Department of the South. Wild was relieved from duty there October 10, 1863, and he returned to New Berne to complete the organization of the 3rd North Carolina. Wild remained at New Berne until November 2, 1863, and then reported to James Barnes, commanding at Norfolk and Portsmouth (see Norfolk and Portsmouth, below, in this section), for assignment to command the colored troops in that district.

The garrison of the Defenses of New Berne was largely engaged in securing the area, and in carrying out a number of expeditions, especially in July and October 1863. For additional information see below, Operations in the Department of Virginia and North Carolina.

District of the Pamlico. The District of the Pamlico was constituted April 23, 1863 and organized from Henry Prince's Fifth Division, Eighteenth Corps, Department of North Carolina. The two brigades of Fifth Division were soon transferred from the district, and early in July 1863, only two regiments of infantry and some artillery under the command of Joseph M. McChesney remained. The District of the Pamlico was retained in the Department of Virginia and North Carolina, with the same limits established April 27, 1863. McChesney remained in command of the district, with headquarters at Washington, North Carolina. In the latter part of July 1863 Orson Moulton relieved McChesney. For a description of the district, see Department of North Carolina, Districts in the Department of North Carolina. A new District of North Carolina, Department of Virginia and North Carolina was organized August 21, 1863, to have the same boundaries as the former Department of North Carolina. The designation of the District of the Pamlico was then changed to the Sub-District of the Pamlico, District of North Carolina. For additional information, see District of North Carolina, below.

District of the Currituck. The District of the Currituck was constituted December 11, 1863 to consist primarily of the county of Currituck, in the extreme northeastern part of North Carolina. Although the territory of the district was in North Carolina, it was within the limits of George W. Getty's (and later Charles A. Heckman's) command of Portsmouth, Virginia (see below, Districts and Posts in Virginia, Norfolk and Portsmouth). James H. Ledlie was assigned command of the district, and his force consisted of three New York infantry regiments, a squadron of 5th Pennsylvania Cavalry, and one company of 3rd New York Cavalry. Ledlie was engaged primarily in freeing the district of guerrillas, and in securing control of the country. The posts occupied were Pongo, Currituck Court House, Coinjack Bridge, and Northwest Landing in Virginia.

In January 1864, the District of the Currituck was assigned to Heckman's Division at Portsmouth, Virginia, and in March 1864 it was designated as First Brigade, Heckman's Division at Portsmouth, Department of Virginia and North Carolina.

In February 1864 Samuel H. Roberts, with his 139th New York Regiment, was sent from Yorktown to the District of the Currituck, and Roberts relieved Ledlie in command. Early in March 1864, Roberts was reinforced by the 10th New Hampshire Regiment.

District of North Carolina. August 21, 1863, it was officially announced that the Department of Virginia and North Carolina was divided into two districts—the District of Virginia and the District of North Carolina. Despite the date of announcement, John J. Peck assumed command of the District of North Carolina August 14, 1863 (assigned August 12, 1863). The District of North Carolina had the same boundaries as the former Department of North Carolina, and headquarters was established at New Berne. The former districts of the Albemarle, the Pamlico, and Beaufort then became sub-districts in the District of North Carolina. The Defenses of New Berne was also included in the District of North Carolina as the Sub-District of New Berne. Innis N. Palmer relieved Peck in command of the district April 25, 1864 (assigned April 19, 1864).

The District of North Carolina was designated as a separate brigade October 21, 1864.

Sub-Districts of the District of North Carolina

Sub-District of the Albemarle. The designation of the District of the Albemarle was changed to the Sub-District of the Albemarle, District of North Carolina August 21, 1863, and Henry W. Wessells was assigned command, with headquarters at Plymouth, North Carolina. The troops at Plymouth at that time consisted of a First Brigade of infantry under Theodore F. Lehmann, one company of cavalry, and a battery of artillery. In January 1864, Edward Harland's Second Brigade of George W. Getty's Division at Portsmouth, then under the command of Francis Beach, was sent to Plymouth to reinforce Wessells' command. This brigade was broken up in April 1864.

April 20, 1864, an enemy force under Robert F. Hoke captured Plymouth, and with it Wessells and his command. Reinforcements had arrived at the mouth of the Roanoke River, but they were too late to aid in the defense of the town, and they were sent to Roanoke Island, where headquarters of the Sub-District of the Albemarle was reestablished. David W. Wardrop assumed command of the sub-district. For details of the capture of Plymouth, see Operations in the Department of Virginia and North Carolina, below. November 6, 1864, Jones Frankle, with three companies of the 2nd Massachusetts, was ordered to reoccupy Plymouth, and was assigned as military governor of the town. Later in the year, Theodore F. Lehmann relieved Wardrop in command. The sub-district was discontinued January 5, 1865, and the posts of Plymouth and Roanoke Island reported directly to Innis N. Palmer, commander of the District of North Carolina, at New Berne.

Sub-District of Beaufort. The Sub-District of Beaufort, District of North Carolina was organized when the District of North Carolina was constituted in August 1863. This was simply a change of designation of the District of Beaufort, Department of Virginia and North Carolina. Charles A. Heckman assumed command August 18, 1863. Posts in the sub-district were Beaufort, Caroline City, Fort Macon, Morehead City, Croatan Station, and Newport Barracks. Commanders of the sub-district were as follows:

Charles A. Heckman	August 18, 1863 to October 11, 1863
James Jourdan	October 11, 1863 to June 27, 1864
Thomas J. C. Amory	June 27, 1864 to October 7, 1864
Joseph M. McChesney	October 7, 1864 to January 14, 1865

Sub-District of New Berne. March 5, 1864, the designation of Innis N. Palmer's command was changed from Forces and Defenses of New Berne to the Sub-District of New Berne, District of North Carolina. Palmer assumed command of the District of North Carolina April 25, 1864 (assigned April 19, 1864), and was succeeded in command at New Berne by Thomas J. C. Amory. May 2, 1864, when the Sub-District of the Pamlico was discontinued,

the command at Hatteras Inlet was attached to the Sub-District of New Berne. Edward Harland relieved Amory May 3, 1864, and remained in command until January 1865.

Sub-District of the Pamlico. The Sub-District of the Pamlico was constituted August 21, 1863 by a change in designation of the District of the Pamlico (see above) to the Sub-District of the Pamlico, District of North Carolina. Orson Moulton was in command, with headquarters at Washington, North Carolina. The only posts in the sub-district were Washington and Hatteras Inlet, and the troops consisted of several regiments of infantry and some cavalry and artillery.

On the evening of April 26, 1864, Edward Harland, then in command at Washington, received orders from headquarters of the District of North Carolina to evacuate the town, because Robert F. Hoke had captured Plymouth, North Carolina April 20, 1864. Hoke appeared before Washington April 27, 1864, but he made no effort to storm the works because reports indicated that Federal troops were withdrawing from the town. Hoke retired the next day. Harland began the evacuation April 27, 1864, and the last troops departed at 4:00 P.M. April 30, 1864. The only Federal troops left in the Sub-District of the Pamlico were those of the garrison at Hatteras Inlet. The sub-district was discontinued May 2, 1864, and the command at Hatteras Inlet was attached to the Sub-District of New Berne.

Commanders of the Sub-District of the Pamlico were as follows:

Orson Moulton	August 21, 1863 to September 8, 1863
Josiah Pickett	September 8, 1863 to October 26, 1863
Joseph M. McChesney	October 26, 1863 to March 11, 1864
Edward Harland	March 11, 1864 to May 2, 1864

Districts and Posts in Virginia

District of Virginia. The Department of Virginia and North Carolina was divided into two districts August 21, 1863—the District of Virginia and the District of North Carolina (above). The District of Virginia had essentially the same limits as the former Department of Virginia. Henry M. Naglee was assigned command, with headquarters at Norfolk. The troops in the district were organized as follows:

Fort Monroe, Joseph Roberts
Norfolk, George M. Guion
Portsmouth, George W. Getty
  Getty's Division, George W. Getty
    Second Brigade, Edward Harland
    Third Brigade, William H. P. Steere
    Artillery
      Battery A, 1st Pennsylvania Light Artillery, John G. Simpson
      Battery A, 5th United States Artillery, James Gilliss

Note. Samuel M. Alford's First Brigade was detached and serving in the Department of the South.

Unattached
  Artillery, Frederick M. Follett
    Company F, 3rd Pennsylvania Heavy Artillery, John A. Blake
    Company G, 3rd Pennsylvania Heavy Artillery, Joseph W. Sanderson
    Company M, 3rd Pennsylvania Heavy Artillery, Francis H. Reichard
    Battery D, 4th United States Artillery, Frederick M. Follett
    Battery L, 4th United States Artillery, Robert V. W. Howard
  Cavalry
    11th Pennsylvania Cavalry, Samuel P. Spear
    1st Mounted Rifles, Benjamin F. Onderdonk

Yorktown and Vicinity, Isaac J. Wistar
  Wistar's Brigade, Isaac J. Wistar
  Cavalry, William Lewis
  Artillery
    8th Battery, New York Light Artillery, Butler Fitch
    16th Battery, New York Light Artillery, Frederick L. Hiller
    1st Pennsylvania (field and staff), Robert M. West
    Battery E, 1st Pennsylvania Light Artillery, Thomas G. Orwig
    2nd Battery, Wisconsin Light Artillery, Carl Schultz
    4th Battery, Wisconsin Light Artillery, George B. Easterly

Note. This command included Yorktown, Gloucester Point, Newport News, and Williamsburg.

Naglee disagreed with Federal policy of confiscation of property belonging to persons unwilling to take the oath of allegiance to the United States, and apparently to eliminate this problem, the District of Virginia was discontinued September 23, 1863. Naglee was ordered to Cincinnati, Ohio, and was mustered out of the service April 4, 1864.

Meantime, the troops of Naglee's former command were reorganized into three separate districts, each to report directly to headquarters of the Department of Virginia and North Carolina. These were: the District of Portsmouth, commanded by George W. Getty; the towns of Norfolk and Portsmouth, commanded by Edward E. Potter; and Yorktown and Vicinity, commanded by Isaac J. Wistar.

Post of Newport News. October 9, 1863, Charles A. Heckman, then commanding the Sub-District of Beaufort, District of North Carolina, was ordered to Newport News, Virginia with five regiments from the District of North Carolina. He was joined there by two additional infantry regiments, also from the District of North Carolina, and two regiments from the District of Virginia. The post of Newport News was organized October 18, 1863, and Heckman was assigned command.

A short time later, troops were detached from the post and sent to other commands. November 6, 1863, two infantry regiments, a squadron of cavalry, and a battery were sent to George W. Getty's command at Portsmouth, Virginia; December 11, 1863, three New York regiments and two companies of cavalry were detached and organized as the District of the Currituck, Department of Virginia and North Carolina (see above); and during January 1864, four additional regiments were transferred to other posts, leaving only a small force at Newport News. Arthur H. Dutton, colonel of the 21st Connecticut, relieved Heckman in January 1864. Dutton's regiment was sent to the Sub-District of Beaufort February 5, 1864, and then to New Berne February 16, 1864. Only a battery commanded by Richard H. Lee remained at Newport News in May 1864. Newport News was made a part of the District of Eastern Virginia May 27, 1864.

Norfolk and Portsmouth. After Confederate forces evacuated Norfolk, Virginia May 9, 1862, Egbert L. Viele was assigned as military governor of the town, and he was still in command there when the Department of Virginia and North Carolina was organized

July 18, 1863. Viele was ordered to command the Depot for Drafted Men at Cleveland, Ohio August 22, 1863, and he was succeeded in command at Norfolk by George M. Guion.

After the successful Union defense of Suffolk, Virginia in April and May 1863, Michael Corcoran's Third Brigade (Corcoran's Brigade) of First Division, Seventh Corps remained there until the town was evacuated July 3, 1863. Corcoran's Brigade then moved back to the line of defenses at Portsmouth, Virginia, which it occupied until ordered to Washington, D.C. July 11, 1863. George W. Getty's Second Division, Seventh Corps, which had been at White House, Virginia, then replaced Corcoran's Brigade at Portsmouth.

When the troops of the discontinued District of Virginia were reorganized September 23, 1863, Getty's Line of Defenses (called Portsmouth in Federal reports) was given the status of a district that reported directly to headquarters of the Department of Virginia and North Carolina. Getty was assigned command of all Federal troops in the country between the James River and Albemarle Sound, excluding the towns of Norfolk and Portsmouth, which were constituted as a separate district and placed under the command of Edward A. Potter. Getty's district consisted of the counties of Princess Anne, Norfolk, and Nansemond in Virginia, and Currituck, Camden, Pasquotank, Perquimans, Chowan, and Gates in North Carolina. This command was commonly referred to as "Getty's Line." Getty's Division was organized as follows:

Getty's Division, George W. Getty
    Second Brigade, Edward Harland
    Third Brigade, William H. P. Steere
    Cavalry Brigade, Samuel P. Spear
    Artillery Brigade, Frederick M. Follett

Note 1. Samuel M. Alford's First Brigade was detached and was serving in the Department of the South.

Note 2. Spear was placed in command of Getty's cavalry November 10, 1863. He was transferred to Yorktown in January 1864, and Newton B. Lord assumed command of the cavalry brigade.

Note 3. James Barnes commanded Getty's line temporarily in late September 1863, and Edward Harland commanded temporarily in October 1863.

January 12, 1864 Getty was relieved from command of his division and also from duty in the Department of Virginia and North Carolina. Later he was assigned to the Army of the Potomac, where he commanded Second Division, Sixth Corps. He was succeeded in command of the division at Portsmouth by Charles A. Heckman, and the designation of the division was changed to Heckman's Division.

January 25, 1864 Harland's Second Brigade of Heckman's Division, then under Francis Beach, was transferred to the Sub-District of the Albemarle, District of North Carolina, and James H. Ledlie's District of the Currituck (see above) was assigned to Heckman's Division, which was then organized as follows:

Heckman's Division, Charles A. Heckman
    Third Brigade, William H. P. Steere
    District of the Currituck, James H. Ledlie
    Cavalry Brigade, David M. Evans (commanding temporarily for Newton B. Lord)
    Artillery Brigade, Frederick M. Follett

Second Brigade of Heckman's Division was reorganized March 2, 1864 from regiments at Norfolk and Portsmouth, and Horace C. Lee was assigned command. On March 15, 1864, the District of the Currituck, then commanded by Samuel H. Roberts, was discontinued, and the designation of that command was changed to First Brigade, Heckman's Division. The division then consisted of Roberts' First Brigade, Lee's Second Brigade, and Steere's Third Brigade. Heckman's Division remained in the district until it was transferred to Yorktown in late April 1864, during the reorganization of Eighteenth Corps, Army of the James. For details, see Army of the James; and also Eighteenth Corps, Army of the James.

April 20, 1864, August V. Kautz was announced as chief of cavalry of the Department of Virginia and North Carolina, and was ordered to report to Heckman and assume command of all cavalry in the Portsmouth district.

September 23, 1863, the towns of Norfolk and Portsmouth were, in effect, constituted as a district that was to report directly to headquarters of the Department of Virginia and North Carolina. Edward E. Potter was assigned command, but he was relieved October 1, 1863 by James Barnes. November 2, 1863 Edward A. Wild was ordered to report to Barnes, and to assume command of all colored troops in the district. Wild's command was called the African Brigade, and it consisted of the 2nd North Carolina, 3rd North Carolina, 1st United States Colored Troops (USCT), 5th USCT, 10th USCT, and detachments of 1st North Carolina and 55th Massachusetts (colored). John H. Holman succeeded Wild in command of the African Brigade January 19, 1864, and he was followed by Abial G. Chamberlain February 5, 1864. Barnes was ordered to the Army of the Potomac January 6, 1864, and he was succeeded in command at Norfolk and Portsmouth by Wild January 12, 1864.

April 20, 1864, Wild was ordered to Camp Hamilton, Virginia, and Charles K. Graham assumed command of all troops in Norfolk and Portsmouth. Graham was thus placed in command of the troops that were to man Heckman's inner defense line near the towns. Heckman retained command of the district, and also as much of Norfolk and Portsmouth as was necessary to complete an inner line of defenses. Heckman remained until this work was finished, and then April 26, 1864 moved with his infantry to Yorktown, where the Army of the James was being organized. Graham, who had been left in command of the district and all of the defenses, was sent to North Carolina because of enemy activity there, and George F. Shepley was assigned command. April 27, 1864, Israel Vogdes was placed in command of the immediate defenses of Norfolk and Portsmouth, and Shepley remained in command of the district.

The cavalry of the district remained as an independent command under Kautz, who reported to headquarters of the Department of Virginia and North Carolina.

The brigades of Heckman's Division were assigned to the reorganized Eighteenth Corps as follows: First Brigade, as First Brigade, First Division, Eighteenth Corps; Second Brigade, as First Brigade, Second Division, Eighteenth Corps; and two regiments of Third Brigade and two additional regiments, as Second Brigade, First Division, Eighteenth Corps.

May 27, 1864, Norfolk and Portsmouth were assigned to the newly constituted District of Eastern Virginia (see below).

Yorktown, Virginia (and Sub-District of Yorktown).

When the Department of Virginia and North Carolina was organized July 18, 1863, Isaac J. Wistar was assigned command of the United States Forces at Yorktown and in the vicinity. The troops of this command consisted of an infantry brigade of four regiments, known as Wistar's Brigade, and six batteries of artillery. These were posted at Yorktown, Gloucester Point, Newport News, and Williamsburg. When the department was divided into the District of Virginia and the District of North Carolina August 21, 1863, Wistar's command was designated as the Sub-District of Yorktown, District of Virginia. On September 23, 1863, however, the District of Virginia was discontinued, and thereafter Wistar's command was known simply as Yorktown, or Yorktown and Vicinity. Wistar remained in command until April 1864, although Robert M. West commanded temporarily from December 22, 1863 to January 22, 1864, and also from February 16, 1864 to March 8, 1864 while Wistar was absent.

During the latter part of January 1864, the troops at Yorktown were organized into three brigades as follows: Robert M. West's First Brigade; Samuel A. Duncan's Second Brigade of United States Colored Troops; and Samuel P. Spear's Cavalry Brigade. Wistar led these three brigades from Williamsburg February 6, 1864 on an expedition toward Richmond, but after some skirmishing on the Chickahominy River at Bottom's Bridge, they returned to Williamsburg. For additional information, see Operations in the Department of Virginia and North Carolina, below. West's brigade was discontinued February 16, 1864, and on that date, the designation of Duncan's brigade was changed to Brigade of United States Colored Troops, United States Forces at Yorktown.

March 4, 1864, Judson Kilpatrick's cavalry command, which was returning from its unsuccessful raid on Richmond, arrived at Yorktown. It then began to embark to rejoin the Army of the Potomac, and the last of the troopers departed March 12, 1864. See Kilpatrick's Expedition against Richmond, Virginia. March 9, 1864, Wistar led an expedition into King and Queen County, Virginia, where a part of Kilpatrick's command under Ulric Dahlgren had been destroyed, and Dahlgren had been killed. About 400 of Kilpatrick's cavalrymen accompanied the expedition, but all returned to Yorktown March 12, 1864 without having accomplished anything of significance. For more information, see Operations in the Department of Virginia and North Carolina, below.

In preparation for the campaign in Virginia in the spring of 1864, Ulysses S. Grant, then commanding the Armies of the United States, ordered the transfer of Tenth Corps from the Department of the South to Butler's Department of Virginia and North Carolina, and he also ordered the reorganization of Eighteenth Corps into a field force. These two corps and Kautz's Cavalry Division were to constitute Butler's Army of the James, which was to operate against Richmond from the south side of the James River. April 21, 1864, William F. Smith assumed command of all troops and camps of instruction at Yorktown and Gloucester Point (assigned April 19, 1864), and relieved Wistar in command at Yorktown. Smith supervised the reorganization of Tenth Corps at Gloucester Point and Eighteenth Corps at Yorktown, and when the work was completed, he assumed command of Eighteenth Corps May 2, 1864. On the night of May 4, 1864, the Army of the James, under the command of Butler, left Yorktown for Bermuda Hundred to begin operations against Richmond. For further information, see Army of the James, and also Tenth Corps, Army of the James and Eighteenth Corps, Army of the James.

After the Army of the James had departed, only 1st and 2nd United States Colored Cavalry, 16th New York Heavy Artillery, and two batteries were left at Yorktown and Williamsburg. The designation of this command was changed to Defenses of Yorktown (and Williamsburg). Joseph B. Carr, who was relieved from duty with the Army of the Potomac May 2, 1864, assumed command at Yorktown one week later. May 27, 1864, Carr's command became a part of George F. Shepley's newly constituted District of Eastern Virginia (see below).

District of Eastern Virginia. The District of Eastern Virginia was constituted May 27, 1864 to consist of Fort Monroe, the Defenses of Yorktown, Williamsburg, Norfolk, Portsmouth, and the Eastern Shore of Virginia. George F. Shepley was assigned command, with headquarters at Norfolk. Israel Vogdes commanded at Portsmouth, Dexter E. Clapp at Norfolk, Joseph Roberts at Fort Monroe, Joseph B. Carr at Yorktown, Richard H. Lee at Newport News, and William H. P. Steere at Fort Magruder (Williamsburg). The Defenses of Yorktown was discontinued July 19, 1864.

The district was enlarged July 18, 1864 to include all territory east of the Chowan River and north of Albemarle Sound.

District in Maryland

District of Saint Mary's. Saint Mary's County in Maryland was constituted as a Separate District of Saint Mary's July 23, 1863 under the command of Gilman Marston, who reported directly to the War Department. August 1, 1863, a prisoner-of-war camp was established in the district. See District of Saint Mary's. December 21, 1863, the District of Saint Mary's, with the prison camp, was transferred to the Department of Virginia and North Carolina. At the end of June 1864, it was assigned to the Department of Washington.

Commanders of the district while it was in the Department of Virginia and North Carolina were as follows:

Gilman Marston   July 23, 1863 to April 3, 1864
Edward W. Hinks   April 3, 1864 to April 20, 1864
Alonzo G. Draper April 20, 1864 to July 2, 1864

Note. James Barnes relieved Draper July 2, 1864.

TROOPS IN THE DEPARTMENT OF VIRGINIA AND NORTH CAROLINA

When the Department of Virginia and North Carolina was constituted July 15, 1863, the troops present belonged to Seventh Corps of the former Department of Virginia, and Eighteenth Corps of the former Department of North Carolina. Fourth Corps, also of the Department of Virginia, was officially in existence until discontinued August 1, 1863, but it had been broken up about two weeks earlier by the transfer of most of its regiments to commands outside the department. The few remaining troops were assigned to Eighteenth Corps. For details of the organization of these corps, see Fourth Corps, Department of Virginia; Seventh Corps, Department of Virginia; and Eighteenth Corps, Department of Virginia and North Carolina.

In July 1863, Michael Corcoran's First Division, Seventh Corps was discontinued. Henry D. Terry's First Brigade was broken up, and the regiments were transferred from the department; Robert S. Foster's

Second Brigade was assigned to George W. Getty's Second Division, Seventh Corps; and Mathew Murphy's Third Brigade (Corcoran's Brigade) was sent to Washington, where it became Corcoran's Brigade of Rufus King's Division, Twenty-Second Corps.

Getty's Second Division, Seventh Corps, which early in July had been at Yorktown, was sent to Norfolk. Samuel M. Alford commanded First Brigade; Edward Harland, Second Brigade; and William H. P. Steere, Third Brigade. Robert S. Foster's Second Brigade, First Division and Samuel P. Spear's Independent Cavalry command of Seventh Corps were also attached to Getty's Division. During the period July 29, 1863–August 2, 1863, Alford's First Brigade was transferred to the Department of the South, and was assigned to Folly Island. Foster's Second Brigade, First Division was also sent to Folly Island.

In addition to Getty's Division, which was at Norfolk, Portsmouth, and vicinity, troops of Seventh Corps were stationed at Fort Monroe and Camp Hamilton, and Isaac J. Wistar's brigade was at Yorktown and Gloucester Point.

Seventh Corps was discontinued August 1, 1863. and the remaining troops were assigned to Eighteenth Corps. After that date all troops in the Department of Virginia and North Carolina belonged to Eighteenth Corps.

The commanders of Seventh Corps, Department of Virginia and North Carolina were as follows:

George W. Getty	July 16, 1863 to July 18, 1863
John G. Foster	July 18, 1863 to July 20, 1863
George W. Getty	July 20, 1863 to July 25, 1863
Henry M. Naglee	July 25, 1863 to August 1, 1863

The troops in the Department of North Carolina at the time of its consolidation with the Department of Virginia were designated as Eighteenth Corps. These troops were stationed as follows: at New Berne, the department and corps headquarters; in the District of Beaufort; at Plymouth, in the District of the Albemarle; and at Washington, in the District of the Pamlico. After August 1, 1863, when Seventh Corps was discontinued, all troops in the Department of Virginia and North Carolina belonged to Eighteenth Corps. For additional information, see the following: Department of Virginia, May 22, 1861–July 15, 1863; Department of North Carolina,

January 7, 1862–July 15, 1863; and Eighteenth Corps, Department of Virginia and North Carolina.

There were no major changes in the organization of the troops in the department until April 1864. At that time, in preparation for Grant's spring campaign in Virginia, Tenth Corps was transferred from the Department of the South to Gloucester Point, and the available troops of Eighteenth Corps were organized into a field force of three infantry divisions at Yorktown. A cavalry division was also organized under Kautz. Benjamin F. Butler assumed command of the two corps and Kautz's cavalry division, which were designated as the Army of the James, and on the night of May 4, 1864 moved with them to Bermuda Hundred to begin operations against Richmond from the south side of the James. For details, see Army of the James.

The Army of the James continued as the field force of the Department of Virginia and North Carolina until the latter was discontinued in January 1865. December 3, 1864, it was reorganized; Tenth Corps and Eighteenth Corps were discontinued, and two new corps were created in their place. The Twenty-Fourth Corps was formed from the white troops of Tenth Corps and Eighteenth Corps, Department of Virginia and North Carolina; and Twenty-Fifth Corps was formed from the black troops of the two corps.

One special organization deserves mention. Butler, commanding the department, decided to create a naval force under his command and organized a Naval Brigade as a part of the Army of the James. Charles K. Graham, who had been wounded and captured at Gettysburg, was exchanged in September 1863, and November 16, 1863 was ordered to the Department of Virginia and North Carolina. He was then assigned command of the army gunboats at Fort Monroe. February 9, 1864, he was placed in command of all army gunboats in the department, and his force was designated as the Naval Brigade, Department of Virginia and North Carolina.

The Naval Brigade was engaged in a number of expeditions on the James River and on the various creeks and inlets of the area, and was principally occupied in destroying supplies, installations, and boats of the enemy, and in operating against small bands of soldiers and guerrillas. It also supported various Federal troop movements in the department. Graham's boats moved ahead of the transports that carried Butler's Army of the James from Yorktown to Bermuda Hundred May 4–5, 1864, at the beginning of operations against Richmond. At that time, the designation of Graham's command was changed to Naval Brigade, Army of the James. Graham was also active on the James and Appomattox rivers during Grant's campaign at Petersburg. Graham remained in command of the Naval Brigade until the Department of Virginia and North Carolina was discontinued, and then held the same command in the newly reorganized Department of Virginia.

OPERATIONS IN THE DEPARTMENT OF VIRGINIA AND NORTH CAROLINA

The only major operations by troops of the Department of Virginia and North Carolina were carried out by the Army of the James. Butler's command cooperated with the Army of the Potomac during Grant's campaign against Richmond in the spring and summer of 1864, and also in the operations about Petersburg and Richmond from June 1864 to April 1865. Troops of the Army of the James also participated in the Appomattox Campaign in April 1865. For details of these operations, see Richmond, Virginia Campaign, 1864; Operations about Petersburg and Richmond, 1864–1865; and Appomattox Campaign.

In addition to the above, troops of the Army of the James took part in two expeditions against Fort Fisher, North Carolina, the latter of which resulted in the capture of the fort. For details, see Army of the James, Butler's Expedition to Fort Fisher, North Carolina, and also Army of the James, Terry's Expedition to Fort Fisher, North Carolina.

There were also some comparatively minor expeditions and some defensive operations against attempts by enemy forces to capture Federal posts in North Carolina. These were as follows:

Pickett's Expedition against New Berne, North Carolina, January 30, 1864–February 3, 1864. In January 1864, at Robert E. Lee's suggestion, enemy forces in North Carolina attempted to capture New Berne. Innis N. Palmer was then commanding the Defenses of New Berne in John J. Peck's District of North Carolina. Palmer's command consisted of the following: Thomas J. C. Amory's 17th Massachusetts, Hiram Anderson's 92nd New York, David D. Wardrop's 99th New York, Peter J. Claassen's 132nd New York, Rollin M. Strong's 19th Wisconsin (nine companies), James W. Savage's 12th New York (eight companies), 3rd New York Light Artillery, 3rd Rhode Island Heavy Artillery (seven companies), and 2nd Massachusetts Heavy Artillery. A detachment of 2nd North Carolina was also attached to 132nd New York. Claassen was in charge of the outposts west of New Berne, and with him were the 17th Massachusetts; 99th New York; 132nd New York; Company F, 2nd North Carolina; 12th New York Cavalry; and Battery K, 3rd New York Light Artillery.

George E. Pickett was selected to lead the enemy expedition, and during January 1864, he concentrated a force of approximately 13,000 men and seven navy cutters at Kinston, North Carolina. He then divided his troops into three columns, and on the morning of January 30, 1864 moved toward New Berne. Seth M. Barton was assigned command of the right column, which consisted of his own brigade and that of James L. Kemper, three regiments of Matthew W. Ransom's brigade, and some cavalry and artillery. Barton was ordered to cross the Trent River near Trenton, and then advance along the south side of the river to Brice's Creek. This stream flowed into the Trent River a short distance above its confluence with the Neuse River, below New Berne. Barton was to cross the creek, capture the forts along the Neuse River, and then enter New Berne by the railroad bridge. James A. Dearing commanded the left column, which consisted of two regiments of Montgomery D. Corse's brigade, the 67th North Carolina, and some cavalry and artillery. Dearing was directed to move down the north side of the Neuse River and capture Fort Anderson on the north bank, directly opposite New Berne. Pickett was with the center column, which consisted of Robert F. Hoke's brigade, and the remainder of his (Pickett's) force, and he was to advance directly on New Berne between the Trent and Neuse rivers. He was to drive off the Federal outpost on Batchelder's (Batchelor's) Creek and enter the town from that direction.

The three columns were to attack New Berne February 1, 1864. On the night of January 31, 1864, Hoke's command camped at Stewart's Creek, approximately ten miles from New Berne, and two miles from one of Claassen's outposts. At 1:00 A.M. February 1, 1864 Hoke advanced and soon encountered Claassen's pickets. These were driven back, but their warning enabled the troops guarding the crossing to destroy the bridge over Batchelder's Creek. Finding the Federal troops strongly entrenched on the far side of the creek, Hoke halted and waited for dawn. He then crossed his command on felled trees, and drove Claassen's line back toward New Berne. Hoke advanced to within about a mile of the town, and then halted to await the sounds of Barton's attack on the opposite side of the Trent River. Both Barton and Dearing, however, upon arriving before the Federal fortifications found them too strong to storm, and because of their failure, Pickett withdrew February 3, 1864 and returned to Kinston.

Two days before Pickett began his advance on New Berne, James G. Martin's brigade of William H. C. Whiting's Confederate Department of the Cape Fear marched out from Washington, North Carolina, and February 2, 1864 captured the Federal garrison at Newport Barracks near Shepherdsville.

Wistar's Expedition from Yorktown against Richmond, Virginia, February 6–8, 1864. Early in February 1864, Isaac J. Wistar, commanding at Yorktown, led an expedition toward Richmond in an attempt to surprise and capture the city. After dark on the evening of February 5, 1864, he assembled the troops selected for this expedition behind the Union lines at Williamsburg. These consisted of Robert M. West's First Brigade; Samuel A. Duncan's Second Brigade of United States Colored Troops; Samuel P. Spear's Cavalry Brigade; John S. Hunt's Battery L, 4th United States Artillery; and James Belger's Battery F, 1st Rhode Island Light Artillery.

The two infantry brigades advanced at 9:00 the next morning, and Spear's cavalry brigade marched two hours later. Spear was directed to arrive at Bottom's Bridge on the Chickahominy River, twelve miles from Richmond, at 3:00 A.M. February 7, 1864. Spear arrived at the bridge a little before 3:00 A.M., but while on the march, he had failed to capture the Confederate pickets at Baltimore Cross Roads, and they escaped to give the alarm. Consequently, when the Federal troopers ar-

rived on the Chickahominy they found the bridge held in strong force by troops of Eppa Hunton's brigade of the Confederate Department of Richmond.

James A. Wheelan, with a detachment of Benjamin F. Onderdonk's 1st New York Mounted Rifles, made an unsuccessful charge on the bridge. Then Spear reconnoitered the fords above and below the bridge and found them all strongly guarded. He skirmished along the river for a time, but was unable to cross. The infantry arrived at New Kent Court House at 2:00 A.M. February 7, 1864 and, after a halt of three hours, pushed on toward the Chickahominy. As the column advanced, Wistar heard the firing at Bottom's Bridge, and at 11:00 A.M. he realized that Spear had been unsuccessful and that surprise was no longer possible. He then ordered Spear to withdraw, but continued on to be in position to support him if needed. About seven miles from the bridge, Wistar met Spear returning, and he then ordered the entire expedition to withdraw toward Williamsburg. The enemy followed and overtook the Federal rear guard at Baltimore Store, but they were driven back. Wistar bivouacked at New Kent Court House that night and then continued on to Williamsburg, arriving there February 8, 1864.

Wistar's Expedition to King and Queen County, Virginia, March 9–12, 1864. During the early part of March 1864, Wistar led an expedition from Yorktown into King and Queen County in Virginia, where a part of Judson Kilpatrick's cavalry under the command of Ulric Dahlgren had been destroyed on its return from an unsuccessful raid on Richmond (see Kilpatrick's Expedition against Richmond, Virginia, and Custer's Raid into Albemarle County, Virginia). Wistar's mission was to capture the enemy forces responsible for this attack or drive them from the area.

Wistar organized a force consisting of infantry and cavalry, and some artillery. The infantry consisted of Samuel A. Duncan's brigade of United States Colored Troops and Joseph B. Kiddoo's 22nd United States Colored Troops. For the cavalry, Benjamin F. Onderdonk, with his 1st New York Mounted Rifles, was ordered from Williamsburg to Yorktown, and there he was directed by Samuel P. Spear, commanding the cavalry brigade, to assume command of his own regiment and 11th Pennsylvania Cavalry, and report to Kilpatrick at Gloucester Point. Kilpatrick was then assigned to lead the cavalry of the expedition, which consisted of Onderdonk's two regiments; Addison W. Preston's Second Brigade of Kilpatrick's Third Division, Army of the Potomac; and portions of James Belger's and John S. Hunt's batteries. Kilpatrick with Preston's brigade were only temporarily in the district while en route to join the army of the Potomac.

At 2:00 P.M. March 9, 1864, Wistar, with the infantry, left Yorktown on transports and arrived at Sheppard's Landing on the Mattapony River at 8:30 that evening. Kilpatrick's cavalry, under the command of Preston, moved from Gloucester Point at 3:00 A.M. that same day under orders to be at Sheppard's Landing at daylight March 10, 1864, and not before that time. By this arrangement Wistar hoped to arrive ahead of the cavalry and to intercept the enemy force retiring before Kilpatrick's advance. Preston, however, led the cavalry directly to Sheppard's Landing, and arrived there hours ahead of the infantry. Kilpatrick did not accompany the cavalry, but went upriver on a gunboat.

From Sheppard's Landing, Wistar pushed on up the Mattapony River. He decided that the enemy would probably make a stand at King and Queen Court House, and he ordered Kilpatrick to move on to that point at daylight. Kilpatrick advanced to Plymouth, about six or seven miles from the court house, and then sent Onderdonk with his command to engage the enemy. When Wistar arrived at Plymouth, he ordered Kilpatrick to move east to the New Dragon Bridge on the Piankatank River near Saluda, and he also ordered Onderdonk to meet him there. The combined force was then to move on into Middlesex County. March 11, 1864, Kilpatrick was ordered to rejoin Wistar at Old Dragon Bridge, farther down the river.

The 11th Pennsylvania Cavalry destroyed King and Queen Court House and other public buildings, and then joined Onderdonk and his 1st New York Mounted Rifles, who had advanced to Carleton's Store. Onderdonk attacked and drove an enemy force from near the store, and pursued until recalled by Kilpatrick. All movements during the expedition were difficult because of heavy rains and high water,

and some river crossings were impossible. Finally, Wistar ordered his command to return to Yorktown.

Capture of Plymouth, North Carolina, April 17–20, 1864. After the failure of Pickett's attempt to capture New Berne January 28, 1864–February 10, 1864 (see above), Pickett returned to Virginia, and Hoke assumed command of the Confederate forces in North Carolina. One of his first actions was to prepare plans for an attack on Plymouth, in the Sub-District of the Albemarle. The town was situated on the Roanoke River, not far from where it flowed into Albemarle Sound, and it was an important depot for Union land forces in eastern North Carolina.

The defenses at Plymouth consisted of a series of forts that ringed the town on the land side, and these were connected by strong redoubts, breastworks, and obstructions. The main works began at Battery Worth, on the river above Plymouth, and they then curved around the town to the south and east to Coneby Creek, below the town. The country was open to the east, but was protected by Fort Comfort and two redoubts, which covered the Columbia Road. Fort Williams was on the south center of the line of defenses, and commanded the front to the right and left of the fort. Two and one half miles upriver from Plymouth was a detached work on the river bank called Fort Gray. This was separated from the main defensive line by Welch's Creek and the marshy ground bordering it. About a mile to the southwest of the main line was another detached work called Fort Wessells, and also sometimes referred to as the "85th Redoubt."

At the time of Hoke's attack, Henry W. Wessells commanded the garrison at Plymouth, which consisted of four infantry regiments and a detachment of another, a part of the 12th New York Cavalry, and the 2nd Massachusetts Heavy Artillery and 24th New York Independent Battery. In addition to the land forces, Lieutenant Commander Charles W. Flusser was in command of two Union gunboats and some smaller vessels on the Roanoke River. The line of defenses was held by the following: Francis Beach's 16th Connecticut, Enrico Fardella's 85th New York, Alexander M. Taylor's 101st Pennsylvania, Theodore F. Lehmann's 103rd Pennsylvania, two companies of 2nd North Carolina, two companies of 12th New York Cavalry, and the 24th New York Independent Battery. The line was divided into three approximately equal parts, with Fardella commanding on the right, Lehmann on the center, and Beach on the left.

Because of its location, Hoke believed that Plymouth could be captured only with the aid of naval force to attack on the river side of town. At that time, the Confederate ironclad ram *Albemarle* was under construction at Edwards Ferry on the Roanoke River, and at the end of March 1864, it was moved two miles downriver for completion. In a conference with Hoke, Commander James W. Cooke agreed to cooperate in an attack when the vessel was in condition to fight. When informed that the *Albemarle* was ready, Hoke advanced toward Plymouth with his own brigade and the brigades of Matthew W. Ransom and James L. Kemper, the latter commanded by John T. Mercer. At 4:00 P.M. April 17, 1864, Hoke's advance arrived on the Washington road at a point about five miles southwest of the town, and he then moved to invest the land side of Wessells' position. The only Federal response to this movement was by the artillery, which continued to fire until dark.

On the morning of April 18, 1864, the enemy opened with a heavy bombardment on Fort Gray, but the Federal defenders retained possession of the work. Late that afternoon Hoke's brigade, commanded by Mercer, attacked Fort Wessells, and at the same time Ransom's brigade moved to the right and demonstrated in force with artillery fire on the Union line east of Fort Williams. Ransom continued his fire from 6:00 to 10:00 P.M. and then withdrew to his morning position of the day before. Meantime, troops of the 85th New York, commanded by Nelson Chapin, repulsed several attacks by Mercer's column on Fort Wessells, but finally the fort was captured. During the attack, Chapin was killed and Mercer was mortally wounded.

The *Albemarle* finally arrived at a point about three miles above Plymouth at 10:00 P.M. April 18, 1864, and at 2:30 the next morning steamed downriver toward the town. It then engaged Flusser's United States Navy Flotilla, sank one gunboat, and drove the other vessels out of the river and into Albemarle Sound. The *Albemarle* then shelled the Federal fortifications well into the night.

The land fighting April 19, 1864 was largely an exchange of artillery fire, but late in the afternoon, Hoke ordered Ransom with his brigade to cross Coneby Creek to the east, and then march around to the Columbia Road and attack Plymouth from the east. The attack was delayed because of darkness, but at daybreak the next morning Ransom's infantry moved forward as the artillery opened on the Federal works on both sides of the Columbia Road. At the same time, Hoke began a bombardment on the west side of the town. Ransom soon captured Fort Comfort and the two redoubts, and then pushed on into Plymouth, driving the defenders into Fort Williams. Hoke demanded the surrender of the fort, but Wessells refused. The Confederate artillery then opened with a heavy fire from all sides, and finally Wessells was forced to surrender at 10:00 A.M. April 20, 1864.

DEPARTMENT OF WASHINGTON
APRIL 9, 1861–AUGUST 17, 1861

For better administration of the troops then in, and expected to arrive at, Washington, D.C., the Department of Washington was constituted April 9, 1861 to consist of the District of Columbia to its original boundaries and the state of Maryland. This territory was taken from the existing Department of the East. Charles F. Smith, lieutenant colonel of the 10th United States Infantry, assumed command of the department April 10, 1861, with headquarters at Washington. The department was extended April 19, 1861 to include, in addition to the District of Columbia and Maryland, the states of Delaware and Pennsylvania. Robert Patterson assumed command of the enlarged department April 22, 1861.

The department was reduced in size April 27, 1861 by the reassignment of a part of its territory. The Department of Washington was redefined to include the District of Columbia to its original boundaries, Fort Washington, and the state of Maryland as far as Bladensburg, inclusive. Joseph K. F.

Mansfield, inspector general, assumed command April 28, 1862. That part of Maryland along the railroad between Washington and Annapolis, Maryland was assigned to Benjamin F. Butler as the Department of Annapolis. The Department of Pennsylvania was constituted to consist of the states of Delaware and Pennsylvania, and all of Maryland not included in the other two departments. Robert Patterson was assigned command.

July 25, 1861 the Department of Washington was increased in size by the addition of the counties of Prince George's, Montgomery, and Frederick in Maryland.

The Military Division of the Potomac was constituted July 25, 1861, after the battle of Bull Run, to consist of the Department of Washington and the Department of Northeastern Virginia. George B. McClellan assumed command of the Military Division of the Potomac July 27, 1861.

August 17, 1861 (ordered August 15, 1861), the Department of Washington was discontinued when the Department of the Potomac was constituted to consist of the departments of Washington, the Shenandoah, and Northeastern Virginia.

Troops in the Department of Washington. The first troops in the Department of Washington consisted of companies of United States Regulars. Those present at the end of April 1861 were:

At Washington, D.C.
> Light Company I, 1st United States Artillery, Absalom Baird
> West Point Battery, Charles Griffin
> Company E, 2nd United States Artillery, J. Howard Carlisle
> Companies D and H, 2nd United States Cavalry, Innis N. Palmer
> Company I, 1st United States Infantry, John H. King

Note. Baird arrived January 29, 1861; Griffin February 1, 1861; Carlisle February 7, 1861; Palmer April 14, 1861; and King April 14, 1861.

At Washington Arsenal
> Company F, 4th United States Artillery, Nathaniel H. McLean

The first of many volunteer regiments also began to arrive in Washington in April 1861; the regiments present at the end of the month, with their dates of arrival, were as follows:

At the Capitol
> 6th Massachusetts, Edward F. Jones (April 19, 1861)
> 7th New York, Marshall Lefferts (April 25, 1861)
> 8th Massachusetts, Timothy Munroe (April 26, 1861)
At the Navy Yard
> 71st New York, Abram S. Vosburgh (April 27, 1861)
At Inauguration Hall
> 5th Pennsylvania, Robert P. McDowell (April 27, 1861)
At the Treasury
> 5th Massachusetts, Samuel C. Lawrence (April 28, 1861)
At the Patent Office
> 1st Rhode Island, Ambrose E. Burnside (April 26 and 28, 1861)
At the Assembly Rooms
> 12th New York, Daniel Butterfield (April 28, 1861)
At Casparis' House, Capitol Hill
> 25th New York, Michael K. Bryan (April 29, 1861)

In addition to the above, five companies of Pennsylvania Volunteers arrived April 18, 1861, and about 3,000 District of Columbia Volunteers were also stationed at various points in the district.

During the following months many new regiments arrived from the north, and these, too, at first encamped near Washington. Then on May 24, 1861, the first Federal troops crossed the Potomac into Virginia, and three days later the Department of Northeastern Virginia was constituted under Irvin McDowell. Thus these troops, formerly a part of the Department of Washington, were placed under McDowell's command. Three brigades were organized in the Department of Washington by Mansfield's orders, and these were sent to Virginia to become a part of the Army of Northeastern Virginia that was being organized under McDowell. These brigades were:

Burnside's Brigade, Ambrose E. Burnside, organized July 2, 1861
Richardson's Brigade, Israel B. Richardson, organized July 2, 1861
Blenker's Brigade, Louis Blenker, organized July 3, 1861

For information about the organization of other troops south of the Potomac, see Department of Northeastern Virginia and Bull Run Campaign (First Battle of Bull Run or Manassas).

July 30, 1861, Andrew Porter was assigned as provost marshal in Washington, and he assumed command of the regular troops in the city.

DEPARTMENT OF WASHINGTON FEBRUARY 2, 1863–MARCH 16, 1869

By late January 1863, the functions of the Army of the Potomac and those of the troops of the Military District of the Defenses of Washington, which was a district of the Army of the Potomac, had become so different that the two organizations had little in common. As a matter of fact, at that time the commander of the Defenses of Washington was acting almost entirely under the orders of the general in chief of the army, or of the War Department, and not of the commander of the Army of the Potomac. Therefore, to provide for better administration of the territory around Washington, on February 2, 1863, the Department of Washington was constituted to have essentially the same boundaries as those of the Military District of the Defenses of Washington, which at that time was discontinued. The same order that created the Department of Washington, also designated the troops included within its limits as Twenty-Second Corps, Department of Washington.

The limits of the new department were defined as follows: In Maryland, the boundary ran northward from Piscataway to Annapolis Junction, and from that point westward to the mouth of the Monocacy River. In Virginia, beginning near Edwards Ferry on the Potomac River, it ran southward along Goose Creek and the Bull Run Mountains to Thoroughfare Gap, and then southeast to the mouth of the Occoquan River, about fifteen miles below Alexandria. This territory was taken from the Department of the Potomac.

Samuel P. Heintzelman assumed command of the department and Twenty-Second Corps February 7, 1863 (assigned February 2, 1863), with headquarters at Washington, D.C. Christoper C. Augur relieved Heintzelman October 14, 1863, and remained in command until the end of the war.

June 24, 1864, that part of the department in Maryland was enlarged to include the territory between the Patuxent River, Chesapeake Bay, and the Potomac River, including the prisoner-of-war camp at Point Lookout in Saint Mary's County. Saint Mary's County was taken from the Department of Virginia and North Carolina, and the rest of the new territory was taken from the Department of the Potomac.

The Department of Washington was attached to the Middle Military Division August 7, 1864.

In the reorganization of the military divisions and departments of the army June 27, 1865, the Department of Washington was defined as consisting of the District of Columbia, the counties of Anne Arundel, Prince George's, Calvert, Charles, and Saint Mary's in Maryland, and Fairfax County in Virginia. The new department was formed from parts of the old Middle Department, the Department of Washington, and the Department of the Potomac. Augur was assigned command, with headquarters at Washington.

The Department of Washington was discontinued March 16, 1869 and merged into the Department of the East.

COMMANDERS OF THE DEPARTMENT OF WASHINGTON

Samuel P. Heintzelman	February 7, 1863 to October 14, 1863
Christopher C. Augur	October 14, 1863 to June 7, 1865
John G. Parke	June 7, 1865 to June 26, 1865
Christopher C. Augur	June 26, 1865 to August 13, 1866
Edward R. S. Canby	August 13, 1866 to August 31, 1867
William H. Emory	August 31, 1867 to August 14, 1868
Edward R. S. Canby	August 14, 1868 to November 12, 1868
Horace Brooks	November 12, 1868 to March 13, 1869
William H. Emory	March 13, 1869 to March 16, 1869

DISTRICTS IN THE DEPARTMENT OF WASHINGTON

District of Alexandria. The District of Alexandria was originally a district in the Military District of the Defenses of Washington, and it was continued in the Department of Washington when the latter was constituted February 2, 1863. It consisted of the city of Alexandria and the surrounding country. John P. Slough, who formerly commanded the district, remained in command.

Until June 1863, the principal posts of the district were the city of Alexandria and the camps for convalescents, paroled prisoners, and distribution. After June 1863, these posts were listed as separate commands of the Department of Washington, Twenty-Second Corps. Henry S. Briggs was ordered to Alexandria to superintend the removal of drafted men from that place to the Army of the Potomac, and his command was called the Camp for Drafted Men.

There was no significant change in the district until April 26, 1865, when Augur announced the organization of the districts of the department. At that time the District of Alexandria was enlarged to consist of that part of the Department of Washington, and the troops serving therein, lying south of the Potomac River, except the "Northern Neck," south of the railroad from Fredericksburg to Aquia Creek Landing. For a description of the "Northern Neck," see below, District of the "Northern Neck." John G. Parke was assigned command of the District of Alexandria, with headquarters at Alexandria. The District of the "Northern Neck" was discontinued May 18, 1865, and its territory was transferred to the District of Alexandria, which was discontinued July 20, 1865.

The commanders of the District of Alexandria, Department of Washington were as follows:

John P. Slough	February 2, 1863 to November 21, 1864
Henry H. Wells	November 21, 1864 to January 1865
John P. Slough	January 1865 to April 26, 1865
John G. Parke	April 26, 1865 to June 7, 1865
John P. Slough	June 7, 1865 to July 20, 1865

Generally the troops of the District of Alexandria served as city guards at Alexandria, and at the camps for convalescents, paroled prisoners, distribution, and drafted men. These consisted only of un-brigaded regiments or detachments until April 15, 1863, when Horatio G. Sickel, with his Second Brigade, Pennsylvania Reserves, was assigned to the District of Alexandria. This brigade remained in the district until April 1864, and then it was broken up and the regiments were reassigned. For additional information, see Pennsylvania Reserve Corps (Division), below in section on Troops in the Department of Washington.

In April 1864, Frederick D. Sewall commanded a number of companies and battalions of regiments of the United States Veteran Reserve Corps in the District of Alexandria, and May 17, 1864, a Second Brigade, United States Veteran Reserve Corps was organized under William H. Browne. The regiments of the brigade were soon detached, however, and in July 1864 it was discontinued. For additional information, see United States Veteran Reserve Corps, Twenty-Second Corps, in section on Troops in the Department of Washington, below.

May 12, 1864, during Grant's Virginia Campaign, Robert O. Tyler's Division, which was on the Orange and Alexandria Railroad west of Alexandria, was broken up. The regiments of Arthur H. Grimshaw's First Brigade of this division, however, remained on the railroad, but it reported directly to Slough, the military governor of Alexandria.

Ninth Corps, Army of the Potomac was ordered to Washington after Lee's surrender at Appomattox Court House, and Second Division and Third Division of this corps were sent to Alexandria. The district was then reorganized under John G. Parke, commander of Ninth Corps, as the District of Alexandria, Ninth Corps, Department of Washington. Slough was assigned command of a Separate Brigade, which was composed of troops of his former command of the District of Alexandria. Parke's command consisted of all troops south of the Potomac River, which were organized as follows:

DISTRICT OF ALEXANDRIA, NINTH CORPS, John G. Parke

Second Division, Ninth Corps, Joseph J. Bartlett
  First Brigade, John I. Curtin
  Second Brigade, Simon G. Griffin
Third Division, Ninth Corps, John F. Hartranft
  First Brigade, Alfred B. McCalmont
  Second Brigade, Joseph A. Mathews
Artillery Brigade, John C. Tidball
De Russy's Division, Gustavus A. De Russy
  First Brigade, Joseph N. G. Whistler
  Second Brigade, Charles Barnes
  Third Brigade, Samuel C. Hart
  Fourth Brigade, Charles C. Meservey
First Separate Brigade, William Gamble
Separate Brigade, John P. Slough

District of Washington. The District of Washington was in existence in the Military District of the Defenses of Washington, and was continued in the Department of Washington when the latter was re-created February 2, 1863. John H. Martindale, former commander of the district, remained in command as military governor of the District of Columbia. December 15, 1864, Moses Wisewell, who had succeeded Martindale, was relieved of his command by Christopher C. Augur, who assumed his duties. The district was discontinued.

The district was reorganized by an order of April 26, 1865, to include that part of the Department of Washington north of the Potomac River, except the city of Washington and all troops serving therein, and the country between the Potomac and the Patuxent rivers lying south of the Piscataway River (the District of the Patuxent). Orlando B. Willcox was assigned command, with headquarters at Washington. The District of the Patuxent was discontinued May 18, 1865, and its territory was transferred to the District of Washington.

The District of Washington was discontinued August 2, 1865.

The commanders of the District of Washington were as follows:

John H. Martindale	February 2, 1863 to May 2, 1864
Moses N. Wisewell	May 2, 1864 to December 15, 1864
Orlando B. Willcox	April 26, 1865 to August 2, 1865

Note. Martindale was ordered to the Army of the James, and was assigned command of Second Division, Eighteenth Corps.

The District of Washington, Department of Washington was organized in February 1863 from the District of Washington, the Military District of the Defenses of Washington, and the regiments of Clarence Buell's Provisional Brigade of John J. Abercrombie's Division. Originally, the troops of the district consisted of five unbrigaded regiments and some additional companies.

There was a change in the composition of the troops in the district in April 1863. April 11, 1863, Joseph F. Fisher's Third Brigade of the Pennsylvania Reserves was attached to the District of Washington, and it remained in the district until it rejoined the Pennsylvania Reserve Division June 1, 1863. April 15, 1863, four regiments, including those of Buell's Provisional Brigade, were transferred to Seventh Corps, Department of Virginia, at Suffolk.

In May 1863, two regiments of Albert B. Jewett's Brigade, Twenty-Second Corps were added to the

district, and these were followed in October 1863 by three regiments of the Veteran Reserve Corps.

There was no brigade organization in the district until March 23, 1864. On that date, a brigade was organized from regiments of the Veteran Reserve Corps, and it was designated First Brigade, United States Veteran Reserve Corps, District of Washington, or more simply, First Brigade, District of Washington. Thereafter, until the district was discontinued December 15, 1864, the troops of the district consisted of First Brigade and unbrigaded regiments. When the district was re-created April 26, 1865, First Brigade served as the City Guards of Washington, and was not included in the district. In May 1865, the designation of the brigade was changed to Garrison of Washington.

The troops serving in the reorganized District of Washington April 26, 1865 were as follows:

DISTRICT OF WASHINGTON, Orlando B. Willcox

First Division, Ninth Corps, Orlando B. Willcox
    First Brigade, Samuel Harriman
    Second Brigade, Ralph Ely
    Third Brigade, Elisha G. Marshall

Dwight's Division, William Dwight
    First Brigade, George L. Beall
    Second Brigade, Edwin P. Davis
    Third Brigade, James D. Fessenden

Note. Dwight's Division formerly served in the Shenandoah Valley.

Hardin's Division, Martin D. Hardin
    First Brigade, Charles H. Long
    Second Brigade, William S. Abert
    Third Brigade, George S. Worcester
Horse Artillery, James M. Robertson
Fort Washington, Maryland, Horace Brooks
Cavalry Forces, Upper Potomac, John L. Thompson

District of Saint Mary's. The District of Saint Mary's was transferred to the Department of Washington from the Department of Virginia and North Carolina at the end of June 1864. Alonzo G. Draper commanded the district, with headquarters at Point Lookout, Maryland, but he was relieved by James Barnes, who was assigned command July 2, 1864. The principal post of the district was the prisoner-of-war camp at Point Lookout. The district was designated as a separate brigade September 7, 1864.

Point Lookout was discontinued as a garrisoned post June 13, 1865 (ordered June 2, 1865), and from that time until August 1865, it was designated as Post of Point Lookout, Maryland.

District of the Patuxent. In the reorganization of the districts of the Department of Washington April 26, 1865, the District of the Patuxent was announced as including the country lying between the Potomac River and the Patuxent River, south of Piscataway Creek, and all troops serving therein, except those at Point Lookout and vicinity. Henry H. Wells was assigned temporary command, with headquarters near Port Tobacco, Maryland. The troops of the district were announced as a separate brigade May 9, 1865, to date from April 26, 1865. The district was discontinued May 18, 1865, and its territory was transferred to the District of Washington.

District of the "Northern Neck." In the reorganization of the districts of the Department of Washington April 26, 1865, the District of the Northern Neck was announced as consisting of country between the Potomac River and the Rappahannock River, and south of the railroad from Fredericksburg to Aquia Landing. This territory included the counties in Virginia of King George, Westmoreland, Richmond, Northumberland, and Lancaster. Nelson B. Sweitzer was assigned temporary command. The district was discontinued May 18, 1865, and its territory was transferred to the District of Alexandria.

TROOPS IN THE DEPARTMENT OF WASHINGTON

In the order of February 2, 1863 which created the Department of Washington, the troops serving therein were designated as Twenty-Second Corps. Thus, at that time, Twenty-Second Corps consisted of the troops serving in the Military District of the Defenses of Washington.

Like Eighth Corps of the Middle Department, Twenty-Second Corps was not organized as a field combat unit, but rather was formed to provide for more efficient administration of the troops serving in the Department of Washington. The functions of these troops varied significantly. There were those that were normally employed in the defensive lines about the city of Washington; as city and provost guards; in the hospitals, camps, and other posts in the department; and as guards on the railroads near Washington and Alexandria. In addition to the above, there were the new regiments arriving in the department for organization, equipment, and training (the provisional brigades) in preparation for transfer to the Army of the Potomac, and for other services with the army. There were also troops from the Army of the Potomac, such as dismounted cavalry and depleted regiments, that were sent to Washington to rest and refit before returning to the army. Because of the diverse nature of the troops serving in the department, the composition and organization of Twenty-Second Corps changed frequently during the remainder of the war.

When the Department of Washington was organized from the Military District of the Defenses of Washington in February 1863, Twenty-Second Corps consisted of the following troops:

DEPARTMENT OF WASHINGTON, TWENTY-SECOND CORPS, Samuel P. Heintzelman

Abercrombie's Division, John J. Abercrombie
Second Brigade, Robert Cowdin
Third Brigade, William Gurney
Provisional Brigade, Clarence Buell

Note. Abercrombie's Division was posted at Chain Bridge, Minor's Hill, and Upton's Hill.

Casey's Division, Silas Casey
First Brigade, Francis Fessenden
Second Brigade, Edwin H. Stoughton
Third Brigade, Alexander Hays
Provisional Brigade, Joseph T. Copeland

Note. Casey's Division was posted at Centerville, Fairfax Court House, Fort Albany, Union Mills, Washington, D.C., and Wolf Run Shoals.

Cavalry Brigade, R. Butler Price
Artillery Defenses of Alexandria, Robert O. Tyler
Cogswell's Artillery Brigade, Milton Cogswell
Unbrigaded regiments

Note. The defenses consisted of Forts Barnard, Blenker, Ellsworth, Lyons, Richardson, Scott, Ward, and Worth.

Defenses North of the Potomac, Joseph A. Haskin
First Brigade, Augustus P. Gibson
Second Brigade, Lewis O. Morris

Third Brigade, William R. Pease

Artillery Camp of Instruction, William F. Barry
Jewett's Brigade, Albert B. Jewett

Note. This brigade was at Offutt's Cross Roads, Maryland.

Annapolis Junction, Benjamin F. Tracy
Fort Washington, Maryland, Charles S. Merchant

To provide a better understanding of the rather complex history of Twenty-Second Corps, a brief chronological outline of the more important changes in the composition of the corps is given below, and this is followed by a more detailed description of the many organizations that served in the Department of Washington. Beginning with the organization of Twenty-Second Corps given above, the more significant changes that occurred during the remainder of the war were as follows:

February 1863–June 1863

February 5–12, 1863, the division of Pennsylvania Reserves (Third Division, First Corps, Army of the Potomac) was transferred from the army, while near Fredericksburg, to Alexandria. Upon arrival there, the designation was changed to Pennsylvania Reserve Division, Twenty-Second Corps. In exchange for this division, Pennsylvania regiments then serving in the Department of Washington were sent to First Corps, Army of the Potomac and organized into a new Third Division.

March 21, 1863, Julius Stahel was assigned command of a newly organized cavalry division, with headquarters at Fairfax Station.

April 15, 1863, Abercrombie's Division was sent to Seventh Corps at Suffolk, in the Department of Virginia. That same day, Casey's Division was discontinued by assignment to the command of Abercrombie. It was organized April 17, 1863 as Abercrombie's Division.

April 17, 1863, the Defenses of Washington South of the Potomac was organized from the Artillery Defenses of Alexandria. Robert O. Tyler was assigned command, but he was succeeded by Thomas R. Tannatt April 26, 1863.

June 25–26, 1863, during the Gettysburg Campaign, Abercrombie's Division, Stahel's Cavalry

Division, Samuel W. Crawford's division of Pennsylvania Reserves, and Jewett's Brigade were transferred to the Army of the Potomac.

At the end of June 1863, the Department of Washington, Twenty-Second Corps was organized as follows:

DEPARTMENT OF WASHINGTON, Samuel P. Heintzelman

Defenses North of the Potomac, Joseph A. Haskin
  First Brigade, Augustus A. Gibson
  Second Brigade, Lewis O. Morris
  Third Brigade, Alexander Piper

Defenses South of the Potomac, Gustavus A. De Russy
  First Brigade, Thomas A. Tannatt
  Second Brigade, Leverette W. Wessells
  Third Brigade, Henry L. Abbot
  Fourth Brigade, Henry H. Hall

Artillery Camp of Instruction, William F. Barry
Railway Guard, Benjamin F. Tracy
City Guards of Alexandria, John P. Slough
City Guards of Washington, John H. Martindale
Fort Washington, Charles S. Merchant
Camp Convalescent and Paroled Prisoners, Samuel McKelvy
Provisional Brigades, Silas Casey
Cavalry, Percy Wyndham

July 1863–May 1864

July 18, 1863, Rufus King was assigned command of a newly organized division, which was to serve on the Orange and Alexandria Railroad. Michael Corcoran relieved King in command of the division October 17, 1863, and the designation was changed to Corcoran's Division. The name of the division was again changed to Tyler's Division December 30, 1863, when Robert O. Tyler relieved Corcoran in command. The division was discontinued May 12, 1864.

On January 6, 1864, a cavalry division was organized at Camp Stoneman under the command of John B. McIntosh. This was not a combat division, however, but was formed from dismounted detachments from the Army of the Potomac and some new regiments. William Gamble relieved McIntosh May 2, 1864.

May 10, 1864, the Cavalry Depot at Giesboro

Point, Maryland was placed under the command of Augur, commander of the Department of Washington.

May 18, 1864, the designation of the Defenses North of the Potomac was changed to Haskin's Division, and that of the Defenses South of the Potomac was changed to De Russy's Division.

In May and early June of 1864, during Grant's campaign in Virginia, there were heavy withdrawals of troops from the Department of Washington to reinforce the Army of the Potomac. The details of these reinforcements are given in a separate section, below.

At the end of May 1864, the Department of Washington was organized as follows:

DEPARTMENT OF WASHINGTON, TWENTY-SECOND CORPS, Christopher C. Augur

Haskin's Division, Joseph A. Haskin
    First Brigade, William H. Hayward
    Second Brigade, Hiram Miller
    Third Brigade, John H. Oberteuffer

Note. First Brigade and Second Brigade were composed largely of Ohio Militia regiments.

De Russy's Division, Gustavus A. De Russy
    First Brigade, John C. Lee
    Second Brigade, W. Smith Irwin

District of Washington, Moses N. Wisewell
    First Brigade, United States Veteran Reserve Corps, Moses N. Wisewell
    Unbrigaded regiments

Light Artillery Camp of Instruction, Albion P. Howe
District of Alexandria, John P. Slough
Cavalry Division, Army of the Potomac, William Gamble
Cavalry Depot, George A. H. Blake
Rendezvous for Drafted Men, Henry S. Briggs
Rendezvous for Distribution, Samuel McKelvy
Provisional Brigades, Silas Casey
Cavalry Brigade, Charles R. Lowell, Jr.

June 1864–April 1865

At the end of June 1864, the District of Saint Mary's was attached to the Department of Washington.

November 19, 1864, a separate brigade was formed to serve on the Orange and Alexandria Rail-road. It was a mixed brigade of infantry, cavalry, and artillery, and was assigned to William Gamble. It was later designated as First Separate Brigade.

April 14, 1865, William Dwight's First Provisional Division, formerly First Division, Nineteenth Corps in the Shenandoah Valley, was ordered from near Harper's Ferry to Washington. Upon arrival there it was designated as Dwight's Division, Twenty-Second Corps.

During the period April 20–26, 1865, Ninth Corps was transferred from the Army of the Potomac to the Washington area, and it was assigned to the District of Washington and the District of Alexandria.

Organizations Serving in the Department of Washington

A brief description of each of the organizations that served in the Department of Washington is given in the following sections. These organizations are listed generally in chronological order.

Abercrombie's Division. Abercrombie's Division was organized in October 1862 in the Defenses of Washington, and when the Department of Washington was created February 2, 1863, it became Abercrombie's Division, Twenty-Second Corps. At that time it was organized as follows:

Abercrombie's Division, John J. Abercrombie
    Second Brigade, Robert Cowdin, to March 31, 1863
        Burr Porter, to April 17, 1863
    Third Brigade, William Gurney
    Provisional Brigade, Clarence Buell

The division was posted at Chain Bridge, Minor's Hill, and Upton's Hill. February 10, 1863, the Provisional Brigade was broken up, and the regiments were reassigned to the District of Washington. On that date, Cowdin's brigade was near Arlington; and Gurney's brigade, then commanded by Robert S. Hughston, was near the Seminary.

April 15, 1863, Abercrombie's Division was sent to Suffolk, Virginia, and was then assigned to Seventh Corps, Department of Virginia. Abercrombie's Division, Twenty-Second Corps was reorganized April 17, 1863 (ordered April 15, 1863) from Casey's Division, Twenty-Second

Corps, as follows (for details of Casey's Division, see below):

Abercrombie's Division, John J. Abercrombie
  First Brigade, Francis Fessenden
  Second Brigade, George J. Stannard
  Third Brigade, Alexander Hays

Note. Stannard succeeded Asa Blunt in command of Second Brigade (Vermont Brigade) April 17, 1863.

Headquarters of the division was at Centerville, and the troops picketed the line of Bull Run and the Occoquan River, and guarded the Orange and Alexandria Railroad from Alexandria to Cedar Run.

Abercrombie's Division was ordered to join the Army of the Potomac June 25, 1863, as the latter advanced toward Gettysburg. Francis Fessenden's First Brigade was sent home for muster out in late June 1863, and it did not join the Army of the Potomac. George J. Stannard's Second Brigade marched June 25, 1863, with orders to join John F. Reynolds' First Corps. It caught up with the corps at Gettysburg late on July 1, 1863, and the next day was assigned as Third Brigade, Third Division. Alexander Hays' Third Brigade was ordered to join Winfield S. Hancock's Second Corps at Gum Springs, Virginia June 26, 1863, and upon arrival was assigned to Third Division as Third Brigade. Hays was then assigned command of Third Division, Second Corps, in place of William H. French, who was placed in command at Harper's Ferry. George L. Willard succeeded Hays in command of Third Brigade. The regiments of Fessenden's brigade were mustered out July 10–17, 1863, and the nine-month regiments of Stannard's brigade were mustered out during the latter part of July and early August 1863.

Casey's Division. Casey's Division was organized in the Defenses of Washington in October 1862, and when the Department of Washington was created February 2, 1863, the division was organized as Casey's Division, Twenty-Second Corps as follows:

Casey's Division, Silas Casey
  First Division, Francis Fessenden
  Second Brigade, Edwin H. Stoughton, to March 9, 1863
    Asa Blunt
  Third Brigade, Alexander Hays
  Provisional Cavalry Brigade, Joseph T. Copeland

Note. Copeland's cavalry brigade was attached to Casey's Division, but was relieved from duty with the division March 21, 1863, and was assigned to Stahel's new cavalry division (see below).

In March 1863, headquarters of the division was established at Centerville, and the brigades were posted as follows: First Brigade at Chantilly; Second Brigade at Wolf Run Shoals and Union Mills; and Third Brigade at Centerville.

April 17, 1863, Abercrombie's Division was transferred to the Department of Virginia. Abercrombie, however, did not accompany the division, and that day he relieved Casey in command of Casey's Division, which was then redesignated as Abercrombie's Division (see above).

Corps of Observation (Jewett's Independent Brigade). Albert B. Jewett commanded a brigade on the upper Potomac, in the Military District of the Defenses of Washington. When the Department of Washington was created February 2, 1863, this force was continued as Corps of Observation, or Jewett's Independent Brigade, Twenty-Second Corps. It generally occupied positions at Edwards Ferry, White's Ferry, Poolesville, and Seneca Locks.

June 24, 1863, during the Gettysburg Campaign, Jewett's Brigade was transferred to Erastus B. Tyler's command at Maryland Heights in the Middle Department. The brigade was then broken up, and the regiments were reassigned. June 26, 1863, William H. French assumed command of Tyler's force, which was then designated as French's Division, Army of the Potomac.

Stahel's Cavalry Division. On March 21, 1863, Julius Stahel was assigned command of a newly organized cavalry division of the Department of Washington. It was organized as follows:

Cavalry Division, Department of Washington, Julius
  Stahel
  First Brigade, Joseph T. Copeland
  Second Brigade, R. Butler Price
  Third Brigade, Robert Johnstone, to April 9, 1863
    Othneil De Forest

As the Army of the Potomac moved northward through Virginia during the Gettysburg Campaign, Stahel's cavalry division was placed under Joseph Hooker's orders, and June 21, 1863, it was sent out on a reconnaissance in force toward Warrenton and the upper Rappahannock. It returned to Fairfax Court House June 23, 1863, and the next day was ordered to join the Army of the Potomac The division was reorganized June 28, 1863, near Frederick, Maryland, as Third Cavalry Division, Cavalry Corps, Army of the Potomac. Judson Kilpatrick was assigned command of the division, and Stahel was ordered to the Department of the Susquehanna.

Defenses North of the Potomac. The troops and fortifications north of the Potomac River were first organized in August 1862 as the Defenses North of the Potomac, Military District of the Defenses of Washington, Army of the Potomac. The designation of this command was changed to Defenses North of the Potomac, Twenty-Second Corps February 2, 1863, when the Department of Washington was created; and Joseph A. Haskin was assigned command. At that time Haskin's command was organized as follows:

Defenses North of the Potomac, Joseph A. Haskin
First Brigade, Augustus A. Gibson
Second Brigade, Lewis O. Morris
Third Brigade, William R. Pease

First Brigade was posted at Battery Jameson, Fort Lincoln, and Fort Slocum; Second Brigade was at Advance Battery, Fort Alexander, Fort Reno, and Fort Simmons; and Third Brigade, under Alexander Piper, was at Fort Baker and Fort Stevens. For the location of the forts, see Miscellaneous Organizations, Defenses of Washington, D.C., Defensive Works and Troops Guarding Washington.

No significant changes occurred in the defenses until May 1864, when Grant advanced with the Army of the Potomac at the beginning of the Virginia Campaign. The army suffered heavy losses in the Wilderness and at Spotsylvania Court House, and it became necessary to send the heavy artillery regiments, then manning the defenses north of the Potomac, as infantry reinforcements. These troops were replaced largely by regiments of the Ohio National Guard and other artillery units. For additional information, see below, Organizational Changes in the Troops of the Department of Washington during the Campaigns in Virginia, Maryland, and Pennsylvania.

May 18, 1864, the designation of the Defenses North of the Potomac was changed to Haskin's Division, Twenty-Second Corps. See following section.

Haskin's Division, Twenty-Second Corps. May 18, 1864, the designation of Joseph A. Haskin's Defenses North of the Potomac was changed to Haskin's Division, which was organized as follows: The troops occupying the line formerly held by First Brigade, Defenses North of the Potomac (Forts Lincoln and Stevens) were designated as First Brigade, Haskin's Division, and this brigade was assigned to William B. Hayward; the troops occupying the line formerly held by Second Brigade, Defenses North of the Potomac (Fort De Russy and Battery Cameron) were designated as Second Brigade, Haskin's Division, and this brigade was assigned to Hiram Miller, but in June 1864, John M. C. Marble was in command; the troops occupying the line formerly held by Third Brigade, Defenses North of the Potomac (from Fort Mahan to Fort Greble, inclusive) were designated as "Forces South of the Eastern Branch," and later, this command was designated as Third Brigade, Haskin's Division, and it was assigned to John H. Oberteuffer.

There was no significant change in the division until Martin D. Hardin was assigned command July 9, 1864, and then the designation was changed to Hardin's Division, Twenty-Second Corps. See following section.

Hardin's Division, Twenty-Second Corps. July 9, 1864, Martin D. Hardin was assigned command of Haskin's Division, Twenty-Second Corps, and thereafter this command was known as Hardin's Division, Twenty-Second Corps. On that same date, the designations of First Brigade and Second Brigade were changed as follows: First Brigade, Haskin's Division became Second Brigade, Hardin's Division; and Second Brigade, Haskin's Division became First Brigade, Hardin's Division. Hardin's Division was then organized as follows:

Hardin's Division, Martin D. Hardin
First Brigade, James M. Warner
Second Brigade, Joseph A. Haskin
Third Brigade, John A. Oberteuffer

Note 1. First Brigade was formerly Second Brigade,

Haskin's Division, and was commanded by John M. C. Marble. Warner was assigned command July 9, 1864.

Note 2. Second Brigade was formerly First Brigade, Haskin's Division, and was commanded by William H. Hayward. Haskin was assigned command July 9, 1864.

Note 3. Third Brigade consisted of only eight independent companies of Massachusetts heavy artillery. This command later became the 3rd Massachusetts Heavy Artillery.

During the emergency created by the appearance of Jubal A. Early's Confederate army before Washington in July 1864, Hardin, with his First Brigade and Second Brigade, occupied the line of defenses from the Potomac River above Washington to Fort Reno near Tennallytown. Oberteuffer's Third Brigade was at Fort Baker, east of Washington, and was under the command of Abner Doubleday, who was in charge of the line south of the Eastern Branch. Headquarters of the division was at Fort Reno, and it was then moved to Tennallytown.

July 10, 1864, First Brigade, United States Colored Troops from the District of Washington, under Moses N. Wisewell (commander of the district), was temporarily attached to Warner's First Brigade, Hardin's Division at Tennallytown. The troops of the Veteran Reserve Corps were ordered to De Russy's Division July 13, 1864.

During July 1864, there were several changes in the brigade commanders of Hardin's Division. July 13, 1864, Haskin was announced as chief of artillery, Department of Washington, and he was succeeded in command of Second Brigade by William H. Hayward. July 25, 1864, Warner was assigned command of Second Brigade, relieving Hayward, and John M. C. Marble was assigned command of Warner's First Brigade. The next day, however, Warner was ordered to Sixth Corps, Army of the Potomac with his 1st Vermont Heavy Artillery (11th Vermont Volunteers), and Hayward again assumed command of Second Brigade.

Hardin's Division served in the defenses of Washington until August 2, 1865.

Artillery Defenses of Alexandria (and Artillery Brigade South of the Potomac), Twenty-Second Corps.

The Artillery Defenses of Alexandria was organized under Robert O. Tyler in November 1862, in the Military District of the Defenses of Washington, Army of the Potomac. The designation was changed February 2, 1863, when the Department of Washington was created, to Artillery Defenses of Alexandria, Department of Washington, Twenty-Second Corps. Tyler remained in command.

The troops of Tyler's command consisted of the following: Thomas R. Tannatt's 1st Massachusetts Heavy Artillery (formerly 14th Massachusetts Infantry); 2nd New York Heavy Artillery; 3rd New York Heavy Artillery (one battalion); 1st Wisconsin Heavy Artillery (one company); 19th Connecticut Infantry (designation changed to 2nd Connecticut Heavy Artillery November 23, 1863); and George D. Wells' 34th Massachusetts Infantry. These troops occupied Forts Barnard, Blenker, Ellsworth, Lyon, Richardson, Scott, Ward, and Worth. For information about the location of the forts, see Miscellaneous Organizations, Defenses of Washington, D.C., Defensive Works and Troops Guarding Washington.

April 17, 1863, the designation of the Artillery Defenses of Alexandria was changed to Defenses of Washington South of the Potomac.

An artillery brigade was formed in the Military District of the Defenses of Washington under Milton Cogswell, and this organization was retained when the Department of Washington was created February 2, 1863. The brigade consisted of 1st Massachusetts Heavy Artillery and 2nd New York Heavy Artillery, and was called Artillery Brigade South of the Potomac, Twenty-Second Corps. Tannatt assumed command April 9, 1863. The designation was changed to First Brigade, Defenses South of the Potomac when the latter was organized April 17, 1863.

Artillery Brigade South of the Potomac, Twenty-Second Corps.
See Artillery Defenses of Alexandria, Twenty-Second Corps, above.

Defenses of Washington South of the Potomac.
This command was organized April 17, 1863 from the Artillery Defenses of Alexandria. Robert O. Tyler assumed command, with headquarters at Arlington, Virginia. As originally organized, it consisted of Thomas R. Tannatt's First Brigade, which was organized from the Artillery Brigade of the Artillery Defenses of Alexandria; and George D. Wells' Second Brigade, which was organized from

other regiments of the Artillery Defenses of Alexandria. April 26, 1863, Tyler was ordered to the Army of the Potomac, and Tannatt assumed temporary command of the Defenses until relieved by Gustavus A. De Russy May 25, 1863. A Third Brigade was organized May 12, 1863 under Henry L. Abbot, and a Fourth Brigade was organized July 2, 1863.

At the end of July 1863, De Russy's command was organized as follows:

Defenses South of the Potomac, Gustavus A. De Russy
    First Brigade, Thomas R. Tannatt
    Second Brigade, Leverette W. Wessells
    Third Brigade, Henry L. Abbot
    Fourth Brigade, Henry H. Hall

Note. Fourth Brigade consisted of only 4th New York Heavy Artillery.

The troops of De Russy's command occupied the line of defenses as follows: First Brigade at Forts Albany, Bennett, Cass, Corcoran, Craig, De Kalb, Haggerty, C. F. Smith, Tillinghast, Whipple, and Woodruff; Second Brigade at Forts Ellsworth and Lyon, and redoubts A, B, C, and D; Third Brigade at Battery Garesche and Forts Barnard, Blenker, Richardson, Scott, Ward, and Worth; and Fourth Brigade at Battery Martin Scott and Forts Ethan Allen and Marcy.

It should be noted that the composition of the brigades changed frequently, and consequently so did the brigade commanders, who were generally the senior colonels of the regiments present in each of the brigades. For example, in August 1863, the brigades were commanded as follows: Joseph N. G. Whistler, First Brigade; Leverette W. Wessells, Second Brigade; Henry L. Abbot, Third Brigade; and Thomas Allcock, Fourth Brigade. In December 1863, brigade commanders were: Thomas R. Tannatt, First Brigade; Henry L. Abbot, Second Brigade; John C. Tidball, Third Brigade; and Louis Schirmer, Fourth Brigade.

In May 1864, the designation of the Defenses of Washington South of the Potomac was changed to De Russy's Division (see following section), but De Russy's command had been called De Russy's Division since November 1863.

De Russy's Division, Twenty-Second Corps. In May 1864, during Grant's Virginia Campaign, all of

the troops of De Russy's command south of the Potomac, except one company of cavalry and a battalion of heavy artillery, were sent to reinforce the Army of the Potomac and the Army of the James; and as a result, all of De Russy's four brigades were discontinued. The troops of these brigades were replaced largely by Ohio infantry regiments, and numerous batteries of artillery. For additional information, see section below on Organizational Changes in the Troops of the Department of Washington during the Campaigns in Virginia, Maryland, and Pennsylvania.

At the end of May 1864, De Russy's Division consisted of a First Brigade commanded by John C. Lee, and a Second Brigade commanded by W. Smith Irwin. It was reorganized in July 1864 as follows: a new Third Brigade and a new Fourth Brigade were formed from the regiments and batteries of the former Second Brigade; a new Second Brigade was reorganized from the former First Brigade; and a new First Brigade was reorganized from new regiments. The division then consisted of the following:

De Russy's Division, Gustavus A. De Russy
    First Brigade, Joseph N. G. Whistler
    Second Brigade, Thomas Wilhelm
    Third Brigade, W. Smith Irwin
    Fourth Brigade, Charles C. Meservey

The division consisted of four brigades during the remainder of the war.

Provisional Brigades, Twenty-Second Corps. The Provisional Brigades were first organized August 25, 1861, under Fitz John Porter in the Department of the Potomac. The purpose of this organization was to receive, equip, and train new regiments arriving in Washington before they were sent out to the various units of the field army. The Provisional Brigades, as an organization, remained in existence from that time; and when the Department of Washington was created February 2, 1863, the designation became Provisional Brigades, Twenty-Second Corps. They were under the command of Silas Casey until discontinued March 24, 1865. During 1864 and 1865, the regiments of the brigades were composed largely of United States Colored Troops.

Artillery Camp of Instruction (Light Artillery Camp of Instruction). The Artillery Camp of Instruction, later Light Artillery Camp of Instruction, was established under William F. Barry in the Military District of the Defenses of Washington, Army of the Potomac in October 1862. It was still in existence when the Department of Washington was created February 2, 1863, and was continued as a part of the department until the latter was discontinued July 20, 1865. Barry remained in command until relieved by Albion P. Howe March 3, 1864 (ordered February 29, 1864). Howe was in command of the Artillery Depot, and was in charge of the office of inspector of artillery in Washington. Barry was sent west to report to Ulysses S. Grant, commander of the Military Division of the Mississippi. Howe remained in command of the camp of instruction until July 20, 1865, although he was relieved temporarily by James A. Hall July 9, 1864–August 9, 1864; September 22, 1864–October 12, 1864; and October 26, 1864–November 1, 1864.

The principal post of this command was Camp Barry, which was commanded by James A. Hall. The post of Camp Barry was announced as a separate brigade November 11, 1864.

Fort Washington, Twenty-Second Corps. Fort Washington was an obsolete stone and brick fort on the Maryland side of the Potomac River below Alexandria, Virginia. It was an independent command of Twenty-Second Corps, and was manned by a small artillery force throughout the war. It was also headquarters of the 4th United States Artillery. Commanders of the fort were as follows: Charles S. Merchant, February 2, 1863–August 30, 1863; Charles R. Deming, temporarily in September 1863; and Horace Brooks, from September 1863 to the end of the war.

Railroad Guard, Twenty-Second Corps. This command was known as the Post of Annapolis Junction, Railway Guards, or Railway Brigade. The latter name is misleading, however, because the Railway Guard consisted only of a single regiment (the 109th New York), under the command of Benjamin F. Tracy. From February 1863 to October 1863 his headquarters was at Annapolis Junction, and then the regiment moved to Falls Church and Mason's Island. In April 1864, it was assigned to First Brigade, Third Division, Ninth Corps. Troops of the Veteran Reserve Corps later served as the Railroad Guard.

Pennsylvania Reserve Corps (Division), Twenty-Second Corps. On February 5, 1863, the Pennsylvania Reserve Division (Third Division, First Corps, Army of the Potomac), which had been seriously depleted by hard fighting in the major battles of the war up to that time, was ordered to Washington to rest and recruit. In exchange, Pennsylvania regiments from the Department of Washington were sent to First Corps, where they were organized into a new Third Division under the command of Abner Doubleday. During the period February 5–12, 1863, the Pennsylvania Reserves were transferred from near Fredericksburg to Alexandria, and there their designation was changed to Pennsylvania Reserve Division, Twenty-Second Corps. It was organized as follows:

Pennsylvania Reserve Division, Twenty-Second Corps, Horatio G. Sickel
First Brigade, William McCandless
Second Brigade, Henry C. Bolinger, to April 15, 1863
Horatio G. Sickel
Third Brigade, Joseph W. Fisher

Note 1. There was no commander of the division from April 15, 1863 to June 1, 1863.
Note 2. William Sinclair commanded First Brigade from March 29, 1863 to May 29, 1863.
Note 3. Bolinger commanded Second Brigade temporarily while Sickel was in command of the division.

Upon arrival at Alexandria, the Pennsylvania Reserves were assigned positions as follows: First Brigade at Fairfax Court House; Second Brigade to relieve William Gurney's Brigade of Abercrombie's Division at Upton's Hill; and Third Brigade to relieve Robert Cowdin's Brigade of Abercrombie's Division at Minor's Hill.

April 15, 1865, Sickel resumed command of his Second Brigade, and with it was assigned to Alexandria. Third Brigade was assigned to the District of Washington, and only Sinclair's First Brigade of the division reported directly to Headquarters Department of Washington. There was no division commander until June 1, 1863.

At the end of May 1863, First Brigade was at Carroll's Hill in the District of Columbia; Second Brigade was in the District of Alexandria; and Third Brigade was at Fairfax Station. June 1, 1863, Samuel W. Crawford was assigned command of First Brigade and Third Brigade, which then constituted the Pennsylvania Reserve Division. Crawford established headquarters at Fairfax Station, and moved First Brigade to that point and Third Brigade to Upton's Hill. Later, Crawford moved his headquarters to Upton's Hill.

June 26, 1863, as the Army of the Potomac advanced into Maryland during the Gettysburg Campaign, Crawford reported with his two brigades to Joseph Hooker, and two days later joined George G. Meade's (later George Sykes') Fifth Corps as Third Division. Sickel's Second Brigade was left in the District of Alexandria, Twenty-Second Corps. The organization of Crawford's division was as follows:

Third Division, Fifth Corps, Army of the Potomac, Samuel W. Crawford
First Brigade, William McCandless
Third Brigade, Joseph W. Fisher

In January 1864, two regiments of Sickel's Second Brigade were sent to West Virginia. April 9, 1864, they were assigned to First Provisional Brigade, First Infantry Division, and then on April 28, 1864, they were assigned to a new Third Brigade, Third Division, Department of West Virginia. Sickel was assigned command of the brigade. The other regiments of Second Brigade remained in the District of Alexandria until April 1864. The brigade was then discontinued, and the regiments were sent to rejoin the other Pennsylvania Reserves in Third Division, Fifth Corps. For additional information, see Miscellaneous Organizations, Pennsylvania Reserves.

King's Division, Twenty-Second Corps. July 15, 1863, following the Battle of Gettysburg, Rufus King was assigned command of all infantry then in Washington awaiting transportation to Frederick, Maryland; and was directed to organize them into a division. He was to march with this division by way of Alexandria along the Orange and Alexandria Railroad to repair and hold the road. Charles R. Lowell, Jr. was assigned command of the available cavalry of the Department of Washington, and was ordered to report to King and move in front of the infantry as it advanced. July 18, 1863, King assumed command and established headquarters at Fairfax Court House and also at Centerville. He organized his division as follows:

King's Division, Rufus King
First Brigade (Irish Legion), Michael Corcoran

Second Brigade, Arthur H. Grimshaw
Cavalry, Charles R. Lowell, Jr.

Note 1. First Brigade was organized from Mathew Murphy's Third Brigade, First Division, Seventh Corps, Department of Virginia.
Note 2. Second Brigade consisted largely of Pennsylvania drafted militia.
Note 3. The cavalry under Lowell was organized into a cavalry brigade August 1, 1863.

King was appointed minister to Rome, and resigned from the army October 20, 1863. He was succeeded in command of his division by Michael Corcoran October 17, 1863, and thereafter until December 30, 1863, the division was known as Corcoran's Division. See following section.

Corcoran's Division, Twenty-Second Corps. Michael Corcoran relieved Rufus King in command of King's Division October 17, 1863, and two days later announced the organization of Corcoran's (formerly King's) Division, as follows:

Corcoran's Division, Michael Corcoran
Murphy's Brigade (Irish Legion), Mathew Murphy
Unbrigaded infantry, cavalry, and artillery

Note. Murphy's Brigade was formerly commanded by Corcoran.

The mission of the division remained the same as under King. Headquarters was at Fairfax Court House.

The name of the division was changed again December 30, 1863, when Robert O. Tyler was assigned command. See following section.

Tyler's Division, Twenty-Second Corps. December 23, 1863, Robert O. Tyler was relieved from duty in the Army of the Potomac, and was ordered to report to Christopher C. Augur, commander of the Department of Washington. December 30, 1863, Tyler was assigned command of Corcoran's Division, which was then organized as Tyler's Division as follows:

Tyler's Division, Robert O. Tyler
Irish Legion, James P. McIvor
Cavalry Brigade, Charles R. Lowell, Jr.
Unbrigaded regiments

Note 1. Charles M. Alexander commanded the division temporarily until January 1, 1864, when Tyler assumed command.

Note 2. Mathew Murphy's Irish Legion was under the temporary command of McIvor.

The division was reorganized in January 1864, as follows:

Tyler's Division, Robert O. Tyler
    First Brigade, Arthur H. Grimshaw
    Second Brigade, Mathew Murphy
    Cavalry Brigade, Charles R. Lowell, Jr.

Note 1. First Brigade was organized from unbrigaded regiments, and Second Brigade was formed from the Irish Legion.
Note 2. Charles M. Alexander commanded First Brigade temporarily during March and April 1864.

The division was in position to protect the southern and western approaches to Washington, and headquarters was at Fairfax Court House.

May 12, 1864, during Grant's Virginia Campaign, the Orange and Alexandria Railroad beyond Bull Run was abandoned, and Tyler's Division was discontinued. Murphy's Second Brigade was sent to the Army of the Potomac, which it joined near Spotsylvania Court House May 17, 1864. Murphy's brigade, together with 8th New York Heavy Artillery, was then organized as Fourth Brigade, Second Division, Second Corps. James P. McIvor assumed command of the brigade May 18, 1864. The 2nd District of Columbia and 4th Delaware regiments of Grimshaw's First Brigade of Tyler's Division remained on the railroad, but they reported to John P. Slough, military governor of Alexandria, and became a part of his command. Charles R. Lowell with one regiment was posted at Fairfax Court House, and he reported to Augur, commander of the Department of Washington. Tyler was ordered to Belle Plain to assume command of the regiments of heavy artillery from the Defenses of Washington that were assembling there for transfer to the Army of the Potomac. For additional information, see below, Organizational Changes in the Troops in the Department of Washington during the Campaigns in Virginia, Maryland, and Pennsylvania.

United States Veteran Reserve Corps, Twenty-Second Corps. A number of regiments of the United States Veteran Reserve Corps were organized in the Department of Washington, primarily as garrison troops and for duty in the hospitals in the area. Generally, they served as regiments or as detach-ments, but two brigades were formed in the department.

In May 1864, a First Brigade, United States Veteran Reserve Corps was organized under Richard H. Rush, and it was assigned to duty in the District of Washington. For that reason, it was also called First Brigade, District of Washington. Moses N. Wisewell, military governor of Washington, succeeded Rush in command May 21, 1864, and he in turn was succeeded by George W. Gile July 6, 1864. Gile remained in command until May 1865. During the emergency created by the appearance of Jubal A. Early's army before Washington in July 1864, Gile's brigade was temporarily attached to James M. Warner's brigade of Martin D. Hardin's Division, near Tennallytown.

The District of Washington was discontinued in December 1864, and First Brigade came under the direct control of Augur, commander of the Department of Washington. When the District of Washington was re-created April 26, 1865, First Brigade was excluded, and its designation was changed to Garrison of Washington.

A Second Brigade, United States Veteran Reserve Corps was organized from regiments of the Veteran Reserve Corps May 17, 1864. Headquarters of the brigade was at Alexandria, but William H. Browne, the temporary commander of the brigade, was under orders to report directly to headquarters Department of Washington. May 20, 1864, Richard H. Rush was ordered to Alexandria to assume command of the brigade. In June 1864, four regiments were sent to Point Lookout, the Camp of Distribution, and to Washington, leaving only two regiments with the brigade at Alexandria. The brigade was discontinued in July 1864.

First Separate Brigade, Twenty-Second Corps. November 19, 1864, a separate brigade was formed to serve on the Orange and Alexandria Railroad. William Gamble was assigned command, with headquarters at Fairfax Court House. Gamble's command was a mixed force consisting of infantry, cavalry, and artillery regiments. November 29, 1864, it was announced as First Separate Brigade, Twenty-Second Corps. Gamble commanded the brigade until June 22, 1865, and he was then succeeded by William Wells. Wells remained in command until July 7, 1865.

Dwight's Division, Twenty-Second Corps. Nineteenth Corps, which had been with Philip H. Sheridan's army in the Shenandoah Valley, was discontinued March 20, 1865, and William Dwight's First Division was redesignated as First Provisional Division, Army of the Shenandoah. In the early part of April 1865, this division was posted on the railroad near Harper's Ferry. Following Robert E. Lee's surrender of the Army of Northern Virginia at Appomattox Court House, many soldiers and paroled prisoners began moving toward Washington; and to prevent possible disturbances there, Dwight's division was ordered to the city April 14, 1865. When it arrived, the designation was changed to Dwight's Division, Twenty-Second Corps. It consisted of three brigades: George L. Beal's First Brigade; Edwin P. Davis' Second Brigade; and James D. Fessenden's Third Brigade.

Dwight's Division served in the District of Washington, which at that time was commanded by Orlando B. Willcox of Ninth Corps. May 29, 1865, it was ordered to Savannah, Georgia, where it became Dwight's Division, Department of the South.

Ninth Corps. At the time of Lee's surrender at Appomattox Court House, John G. Parke's Ninth Corps, Army of the Potomac was on duty on the South Side Railroad west of Petersburg, Virginia. April 20, 1865, it was ordered to City Point for transfer to Alexandria. Embarkation began the next day, and by April 26, 1865, the corps had arrived at Washington and Alexandria. On that date, the District of Alexandria was reorganized under Parke, and Joseph J. Bartlett's Second Division and John F. Hartranft's Third Division of Ninth Corps were included in the district. Also on April 26, 1865, the District of Washington was organized under Orlando B. Willcox, commander of First Division, Ninth Corps, and Willcox's division was included in the district.

Cavalry Forces of Twenty-Second Corps. When the Department of Washington was organized February 7, 1863, there were two cavalry organizations carried over from the Military District of the Defenses of Washington: one was the Provisional Brigade of Casey's Division, under Joseph T. Copeland, and the other was a large Independent Brigade under R. Butler Price. A number of other cavalry organizations were later formed in the department. These were:

Stahel's Cavalry Division. March 17, 1863, Julius Stahel was relieved from duty in the Army of the Potomac, and was ordered to report to Samuel P. Heintzelman, commander of the Department of Washington. March 21, 1863, he was assigned command of a cavalry division to operate south of the Potomac River. This division was organized from troops of Copeland's and Price's brigades, as follows:

Stahel's Cavalry Division, Julius Stahel
  First Brigade, Joseph T. Copeland
  Second Brigade, R. Butler Price
  Third Brigade, Robert Johnstone, to April 9, 1863
    Othneil De Forest

Note 1. First Brigade was formerly Copeland's Provisional Brigade of Casey's Division.
Note 2. Second Brigade were formed from Price's Independent Cavalry Brigade.
Note 3. Timothy M. Bryan, Jr. was originally assigned command of Third Brigade.

April 21, 1863, Stahel was ordered to establish his headquarters at Fairfax Station, and with his cavalry cover the front from the Occoquan, along Bull Run, and to the mouth of Goose Creek.

June 21–23, 1863, during the march of the Army of the Potomac toward Gettysburg, Stahel's division made a reconnaissance from Fairfax Court House through Centerville, Gainesville, Buckland Mills, and New Baltimore to Warrenton, and then returned to Fairfax Court House. June 24, 1863, it moved to Dranesville, and the next day moved north to join the Army of the Potomac at Frederick, Maryland. It arrived there June 27, 1863, and that day Stahel was relieved from duty in the Army of the Potomac, and was ordered to the Department of the Susquehanna.

June 28, 1863, Judson Kilpatrick was assigned command of Stahel's Division, which was then organized as Third Division, Cavalry Corps, Army of the Potomac as follows:

Third Division, Judson Kilpatrick
  First Brigade, Elon J. Farnsworth
  Second Brigade, George A. Custer

Note 1. Custer's Second Brigade was formerly Copeland's First Brigade of Stahel's division.
Note 2. Farnsworth's First Brigade was formed largely

from regiments of De Forest's Third Brigade of Stahel's division.

Note 3. Price's Second Brigade of Stahel's division was broken up, and the regiments were reassigned.

Wyndham's Cavalry, District of Columbia. June 29, 1863, during the Gettysburg Campaign, Percy Wyndham was assigned command of all mounted and dismounted cavalry in the District of Columbia. When the emergency had ended, Wyndham returned to his command, the 1st New York Cavalry, with the Army of the Potomac.

Lowell's Cavalry Brigade. August 1, 1863, the cavalry under Charles R. Lowell, Jr. that was attached to King's Division, Twenty-Second Corps (see above), was organized into a cavalry brigade consisting of Lowell's 2nd Massachusetts Cavalry and two new cavalry regiments. This brigade remained attached to King's Division (and its successors, Corcoran's Division and Tyler's Division) until the division was discontinued in May 1864. Lowell's brigade was generally in position south and west of Washington, with headquarters at Centerville, Vienna, and Falls Church. It was largely employed against John S. Moseby's Partisan Rangers in the area between Washington and the Blue Ridge Mountains. Lowell commanded the brigade until February 1864, and then he was relieved by Henry M. Lazelle.

Lowell returned to command in April 1864, but was detached with his regiment July 10, 1864 during Jubal A. Early's raid on Washington and sent north of the Potomac. His cavalry covered the country in front of Martin D. Hardin's Division, which was in the Defenses of Washington between the Potomac River and Fort Reno. When Early withdrew from in front of Washington, Lowell accompanied Horatio G. Wright's force that was sent in pursuit. For details, see Early's Washington Raid (and Operations in the Shenandoah Valley, Maryland, and Pennsylvania).

After Lowell's departure, Lazelle commanded the cavalry brigade until his resignation October 19, 1864. John Burdsall commanded temporarily for a few days, and was then relieved by Henry S. Gansevoort. The brigade was discontinued November 19, 1864, and most of the regiments were transferred to William Gamble's Separate Brigade (later First Separate Brigade), Twenty-Second Corps.

Camp Stoneman, District of Columbia. A cavalry division was organized at Camp Stoneman January 9, 1864, under John B. McIntosh. It was organized for administrative purposes only, and consisted of detachments of dismounted cavalry from the Cavalry Corps, Army of the Potomac. William Gamble succeeded McIntosh in command May 2, 1864. The organization of the division followed that of the divisional organization of the Cavalry Corps. The composition of Gamble's command was constantly changing as troops were received, remounted, and returned to the army. The following organization for August 1864 is typical:

CAVALRY DIVISION, CAMP STONEMAN, William Gamble

First Division, Captain Benjamin F. Rockafellow
  First Brigade, Lieutenant Charles A. Packer
  Second Brigade, Lieutenant William J. Allen
  Reserve Brigade, Lieutenant Marcellus E. Jones

Second Division, Captain James T. Peale
  First Brigade, Lieutenant George W. Brooks
  Second Brigade, Lieutenant Robert A. Robertson

Third Division, Major Henry W. Sawyer
  First Brigade, Captain Robert London
  Second Brigade, Lieutenant George W. Byard

The Cavalry Division was designated as a separate brigade September 7, 1864, and was discontinued in January 1865.

Cavalry Depot, Giesboro Point, District of Columbia. A cavalry depot was established at Giesboro Point August 12, 1863, under the general supervision of the Cavalry Bureau, which was attached to the War Department. The general purpose of the depot was to organize and equip the cavalry forces of the army, and to provide mounts and remounts. In connection with the depot at Giesboro Point, there was a dismounted camp where new cavalry regiments were sent to be mounted, armed, and equipped, and where men of old regiments were remounted and prepared for the field. May 10, 1864, the depot at Giesboro Point was placed under the supervision of Christopher C. Augur, commander of the Department of Washington, and George A. H. Blake was assigned command.

Cavalry Forces, Upper Potomac. November 21, 1864, Joseph F. Andrews assumed command of the cavalry forces on the upper Potomac, which consisted of of six companies of his own 1st New Hampshire Cavalry and the 1st Delaware Cavalry. Andrews' headquarters was on the river at Muddy Branch, south of Darnestown, Maryland. His command was designated Cavalry Forces, Upper Potomac. It was later commanded by Erasmus C. Dunning and John L. Thompson and, with some changes in composition, was continued until the end of the war,

Chapman's Cavalry Division (Brigade). April 20, 1865, George H. Chapman's Cavalry Brigade of the Army of the Shenandoah was sent to Washington. It was carried on the roster of the department as a cavalry division, although it consisted of only two regiments and a battery.

Cavalry Corps, Twenty-Second Corps. May 17, 1865, the cavalry forces commanded by Philip H. Sheridan, which consisted of cavalry divisions belonging to the Army of the Shenandoah and the Army of the Potomac, arrived near Washington from Petersburg, Virginia, and camped near Alexandria. The dismounted men were sent on to Washington. May 17, 1865, Sheridan was assigned to the general command of the territory west of the Mississippi and south of the Arkansas River. The designation of Sheridan's former command was changed to Cavalry Corps, Twenty-Second Corps, and was organized as follows:

CAVALRY CORPS, TWENTY-SECOND CORPS, George Crook

First Division, Thomas C. Devin
First Brigade, Peter Stagg
Second Brigade, Charles L. Fitzhugh
Reserve Brigade (Third Brigade), Alfred Gibbs

Note. First Division was organized from First Cavalry Division, Army of the Shenandoah.

Second Division, Henry E. Davies
First Brigade, Henry E. Davies

Note 1. Second Division was organized from George Crook's Second Division, Army of the Potomac.
Note 2. Davies' First Brigade was placed under George A. Custer's command during the march from Petersburg to Alexandria, and it accompanied his Third Division.
Note 3. J. Irvin Gregg's Second Brigade, under the command of Samuel B. M. Young while Gregg was on

leave, was assigned to duty in the Department of Virginia May 12, 1865, and was sent to Lynchburg, Virginia.
Note 4. Third Brigade, under the command of Charles H. Smith, was assigned to duty in the Department of Virginia May 12, 1865, and remained at Petersburg.

Third Division, George A. Custer
First Brigade, William Wells
Second Brigade, Henry Capehart

Note. Third Division was organized from Custer's Third Cavalry Division, Army of the Shenandoah.

Miscellaneous Commands of Twenty-Second Corps. During the war there were a number of special "camps" in the department of Washington. These were: Camp Convalescent, Camp for Deserters, Camp Distribution, Camp for Drafted Men, Camp for Paroled Prisoners, and Camp for Recruits and Stragglers. The camps for convalescents, paroled and exchanged prisoners, and recruits and stragglers were established in the District of Alexandria, Military District of the Defenses of Washington, and in January 1863, these were commanded, respectively, by Samuel McKelvy, Gabriel de Korponay, and John J. Upham. These camps were continued in the Department of Washington as a part of the District of Alexandria. In June 1863, McKelvy was put in charge of Camp Convalescent, Camp Distribution, Camp Paroled Prisoners, and also a detachment of Pennsylvania Reserves. This was constituted as a special command of the Department of Washington. In addition to overall command, McKelvy was also in command of Camp Convalescent, John S. Davis was in command of Camp Distribution, and Guy H. Watkins was in command of Camp Paroled Prisoners. There was no change in McKelvy's command until December 1863, when Camp Paroled Prisoners was replaced by a Camp for Deserters. In April 1864, McKelvy's command was called the Rendezvous for Distribution, and apparently the designation of the camps as separate organizations was discontinued. McKelvy remained in command until the organization was discontinued at the end of the war.

August 22, 1863, Henry S. Briggs was ordered to Alexandria to superintend the removal of drafted men from that place to the Army of the Potomac. Brigg's' command was called Camp for Drafted Men, and was located in the District of Alexandria. In May 1864, it became an independent command of Twenty-Second Corps, and was designated as

Rendezvous for Drafted Men. It was commanded by Briggs.

An organization known as Hospital Guards in the Department of Washington was composed largely of troops of the United States Veteran Reserve Corps, and it was commanded by Surgeon Robert O. Abbott.

In August 1864, a provost detachment was organized under the command of Henry H. Wells, provost marshal general of the Defenses South of the Potomac.

ganized as Third Division, Cavalry Corps; Albert B. Jewett's Brigade (Corps of Observation), which was on the upper Potomac near Poolesville, Maryland early in June 1863, was assigned to Erastus B. Tyler's force at Harper's Ferry (after June 26, 1863, known as William H. French's Division, Army of the Potomac).

On June 29, 1863, Percy Wyndham was assigned command of all mounted and dismounted cavalry in the District of Columbia.

ORGANIZATIONAL CHANGES IN THE DEPARTMENT OF WASHINGTON DURING THE CAMPAIGNS IN VIRGINIA, MARYLAND, AND PENNSYLVANIA

On several occasions during the war, the composition and organization of the troops near Washington was markedly affected by Confederate troop movements that threatened the capital, and by the campaigns and battles of the Union armies operating nearby in Virginia, Maryland, and Pennsylvania. This was especially true in the Department of Washington, Twenty-Second Corps during the Gettysburg Campaign in 1863, during Grant's Virginia Campaign in 1864, and during Jubal A. Early's raid on Washington in July 1864. The more important organizational changes in Twenty-Second Corps, both temporary and permanent, during these periods are given in the following sections.

The Gettysburg Campaign, June 1863–July 1863. On June 26, 1863, as Joseph Hooker's Army of the Potomac was moving northward into Maryland during the Gettysburg Campaign, the following organizations of the Department of Washington were transferred to Hooker's command: Samuel W. Crawford's Division of Pennsylvania Reserves, then consisting of First Brigade and Third Brigade, was assigned to Fifth Corps as Third Division; the brigades of John J. Abercrombie's Division were assigned to First Corps and Second Corps; Julius Stahel's Cavalry Division was transferred to the Army of the Potomac and was reor-

Grant's Virginia Campaign, 1864. The Army of the Potomac crossed the Rapidan River May 4, 1864, at the beginning of the spring campaign against Robert E. Lee's Army of Northern Virginia. At the Battle of the Wilderness, May 5–7, 1864, it suffered approximately 18,000 casualties, and during the assaults at Spotsylvania Court House May 10 and 12, 1864, it lost an additional 11,000 men, for a total of 29,000 in eight days of fighting. In the assaults at Cold Harbor, 7,000 more were added to the casualty lists. Altogether, in the first month of fighting, the army lost about 50,000 men.

In order to continue the advance toward Richmond, Grant required heavy reinforcements. During the period May 1, 1864–June 3, 1864, forty-three regiments (ten of them heavy artillery regiments serving as infantry), two provisional brigades from the Rendezvous of Distribution, and seven battalions and many detachments from the Department of Washington were sent to the Army of the Potomac and the Army of the James. This resulted in significant changes in the composition and organization of Twenty-Second Corps.

May 11, 1864, John J. Abercrombie was sent to take command at Belle Plain, Virginia. His responsibilities were to receive and forward troops to the Army of the Potomac, to protect the stores collected there, to receive and take care of the wounded brought in from the battlefields, and also to take charge of the prisoners sent back from the front.

May 12, Robert O. Tyler's Division (see above) on the Orange and Alexandria was discontinued, and Mathew Murphy's Irish Legion was sent to the Army of the Potomac. It later became a part of Fourth Brigade, Second Division, Second Corps. May 13, 1864, Tyler was sent to Belle Plain to assume command of the regiments of heavy artillery from the Defenses of Washington that were assembling there for transfer to the Army of the Potomac. These regiments, which were then serving as infantry, were: Thomas R. Tannatt's 1st Massachusetts Heavy Artillery and Joseph N. G. Whistler's 2nd New York Heavy Artillery from De Russy's Division; Daniel Chapman's 1st Maine Heavy Artillery and Lewis O. Morris' 7th New York Heavy Artillery from Haskin's Division; and Peter A. Porter's 8th New York Heavy Artillery, which had arrived in Washington from Baltimore.

Tyler's command at Belle Plain was called Tyler's Division of Heavy Artillery, but after it joined the Army of the Potomac May 17–18, 1864, it was attached to Winfield S. Hancock's Second Corps as Fourth Division (Heavy Artillery). May 29, 1864, Fourth Division, Second Corps was broken up, and the regiments were assigned to the other divisions of the corps as follows: 2nd New York Heavy Artillery to First Brigade, First Division; 7th New York Heavy Artillery to Fourth Brigade, First Division; 8th New York Heavy Artillery to Fourth Brigade, Second Division; 1st Massachusetts Heavy Artillery to Second Brigade, Third Division; and 1st Maine Heavy Artillery to Third Brigade, Third Division.

A Fourth Brigade, Second Division, Second Corps was formed May 29, 1864 from Peter A. Porter's 8th New York Heavy Artillery and Mathew Murphy's Irish Legion (transferred from Robert O. Tyler's Division, Twenty-Second Corps), and Tyler was assigned command of the brigade. Also, when Tannatt's 1st Massachusetts Heavy Artillery was assigned to Second Brigade, Third Division, Second Corps, Tannatt assumed command of the brigade.

In addition to the above heavy artillery regiments, others were also transferred from the Department of Washington as follows: Alexander Piper's 10th New York Heavy Artillery from De Russy's Division to Second Brigade, Third Division, Eighteenth Corps, Army of the James; Joseph Welling's 9th New York Heavy Artillery from De Russy's Division to Second Brigade, Third Division, Sixth Corps; Augustus A. Gibson's 2nd Pennsylvania Heavy Artillery from De Russy's Division to Provisional Brigade, First Division, Ninth Corps; Henry L. Abbot's 1st Connecticut Heavy Artillery from Fourth Brigade, De Russy's Division to the Siege Artillery, Department of Virginia and North Carolina, Army of the James;

Elisha S. Kellogg's 2nd Connecticut Heavy Artillery from Fourth Brigade, De Russy's Division to Second Brigade, First Division, Sixth Corps; and James M. Warner's 1st Vermont Heavy Artillery from First Brigade, Haskin's Division to Second Brigade, Second Division, Sixth Corps.

When the above transfers were completed, there was left in De Russy's Division only one cavalry regiment and a battalion of Wisconsin Heavy Artillery; and in Haskin's Division only the Third Brigade remained. It was therefore necessary to reorganize these two divisions, and this was generally done by replacing the heavy artillery regiments with regiments of the Ohio National Guard and other units of artillery. For additional information, see Haskin's Division and De Russy's Division, above.

Early's Washington Raid, July 1864. The appearance of Jubal A. Early's Confederate army in Maryland during the early part of July 1864 resulted in a number of important, though temporary, changes in the composition and organization of the troops in the Department of Washington. Early crossed the Potomac River into Maryland July 5–6, 1864 and marched to Frederick, Maryland, where he arrived on the morning of July 9, 1864. That afternoon he met and defeated a Federal force under Lewis Wallace along the Monocacy River, and then moved on toward Washington. Early arrived in front of the northern defenses of Washington near Silver Spring, Maryland July 11, 1864. There was some fighting around Fort Stevens the next day, and that night, July 12, 1864, Early withdrew westward, and two days later recrossed the Potomac into Virginia near Leesburg. See Early's Washington Raid (and Operations in the Shenandoah Valley, Maryland, and Pennsylvania).

During the period July 10–14, 1864, there was intense activity in Washington as the authorities prepared for the defense of the city. Strong reinforcements were sent to Washington, and a number of temporary organizations were formed from troops of Twenty-Second Corps, civilians, navy personnel, and military organizations of the District of Columbia.

The reinforcements sent to Washington were: Second Division and Third Division of Sixth Corps from the Army of the Potomac, near Petersburg, Virginia; detachments from First Division and Second Division, Nineteenth Corps, which was then arriving at Fort Monroe from the Department of the Gulf; and about 2,500 dismounted cavalrymen from Philip H. Sheridan's Cavalry Corps, Army of the Potomac. The temporary organizations formed at Washington for service during the emergency were as follows: Alexander McD. McCook's command; Montgomery C. Meigs' Reserve Division; Quincy A. Gillmore's command; Admiral Louis M. Goldsborough's Navy Yard command; dismounted cavalry; employees at Giesboro Point; Charles M. Alexander's Brigade; Loyal Legions of Washington; and George C. Thomas' Militia of the District of Columbia.

July 12, 1864, the day of the fighting near Fort Stevens, the disposition of the Union forces in the defenses north of the Potomac River was as follows: Hardin's Division, Twenty-Second Corps held the front from the Potomac River to Fort Reno, near Tennallytown; Meigs' Reserve Division occupied the line from Forts De Russy and Kearny to Fort Totten, including the dependent batteries; Gillmore commanded the line from Fort Slemmer to the Eastern Branch; and Abner Doubleday commanded the fortifications south of the Eastern Branch. Augur was in command of the Defenses of Washington, and McCook exercised general supervision over the line of defenses from the Potomac River to the Eastern Branch. Horatio G. Wright's two divisions of Sixth Corps were generally held in reserve, but two brigades were in action at Fort Stevens July 11 and 12, 1864.

July 13, 1864, Wright was assigned supreme command of all troops that were to move out of the defenses to engage Early, regardless of rank, but he was not placed over Augur, who commanded the defenses. On the other hand, Augur and McCook, and the general officers under him, were not to leave the defenses.

A brief description of the organizations present in the Department of Washington during the emergency, and which at that time were not regular organizations of Twenty-Second Corps, is given in the following sections.

Sixth Corps, Army of the Potomac. When Early advanced into Maryland early in July 1864, James B. Ricketts' Third Division, Sixth Corps was ordered from the Army of the Potomac, then before Petersburg, to Baltimore, Maryland. Ricketts arrived there July 7, 1864, and immediately moved out toward Frederick to reinforce a small force from the Middle Department that was in position on the Monocacy River under the command of Lewis Wallace. Following the defeat of Wallace's command at the Battle of the Monocacy July 9, 1864, Ricketts retired to Baltimore, where he remained until Early withdrew from in front of the defenses of Washington.

July 9, 1864, as the threat from Early increased, Grant ordered Wright to take the other two divisions of his Sixth Corps, David A. Russell's First Division and George W. Getty's Second Division, to Washington. Wright, with the advance of his troops, arrived there at noon July 11, 1864, and that night he moved into position in reserve near Fort Stevens. Wright was placed under McCook's orders. Frank Wheaton's First Brigade, Second Division was slightly engaged. The next day, the remainder of the Sixth Corps troops arrived, and Wheaton's brigade and Daniel Bidwell's Third Brigade, Second Division were engaged near Fort Stevens.

Early retired from before Washington on the night of July 12, 1864, and marched back toward the Shenandoah Valley. The next day, Wright was assigned command of all troops that were to pursue his army, and with these he marched toward Edwards Ferry. Wright left the defenses of Washington with his First Division and Second Division of Sixth Corps, the detachments of Nineteenth Corps that had reached Washington, and some cavalry under Charles R. Lowell, Jr. He arrived at Poolesville, Maryland July 14, 1864, and halted there until Ricketts' Third Division, Sixth Corps came up from Baltimore, and also until some additional troops of Nineteenth Corps arrived from Tennallytown. Wright's command crossed the Potomac River to Leesburg, Virginia July 16, 1864, and left the Department of Washington.

Wright followed Early to the Shenandoah Valley, and then abandoned the pursuit. He marched back toward Washington, and arrived near Tennallytown July 23, 1864. Three days later, however, he departed for Monocacy Junction when Confederate troops again moved down the Shenandoah Valley.

For additional information, see Early's Washington Raid (and Operations in the Shenandoah Valley, Maryland, and Pennsylvania).

Nineteenth Corps. On July 2, 1864, a detachment of Nineteenth Corps, consisting of First Division and

Second Division, began embarkation at New Orleans, in the Department of the Gulf, for duty in Virginia. The first troops of First Division arrived at Fort Monroe July 10, 1864, the day after the Federal defeat at the Monocacy, and they were immediately sent on to Washington. These were followed by other troops of Nineteenth Corps as they came into Fort Monroe. As these troops arrived in Washington, they were placed under the command of Quincy A. Gillmore, who placed them in camp near Fort Saratoga. Early departed from in front of Washington during the night of July 12, 1864, and the next day Gillmore was directed to take the troops of Nineteenth Corps to Tennallytown, and to encamp them there prior to joining Wright's force in the pursuit of Early. On the night of July 13, 1864, Gillmore was disabled by a fall at Offutt's Cross Roads, and William H. Emory succeeded him in command. See also Gillmore's Command, below.

The organization of that part of Nineteenth Corps that was in the Department of Washington during Early's raid was as follows:

NINETEENTH CORPS (DETACHMENT), Quincy A. Gillmore, July 11–14, 1864
William H. Emory

First Division, William Dwight
First Brigade, George L. Beal

Note 1. Only a part of Second Brigade, under Stephen Thomas, was present with the forces opposing Early. The remainder of the brigade, under James W. McMillan, was with Benjamin F. Butler's Army of the James. The brigade was united at Monocacy Junction July 31, 1864.

Note 2. Third Brigade, under Leonard D. H. Currie, was also with the Army of the James, and it rejoined the division at Monocacy Junction July 31, 1864.

Second Division
Third Brigade, Jacob Sharp

Note. The other two brigades of Second Division were serving on the James River.

As a part of Wright's "Army of Operations," Emory's command joined in the pursuit of Early toward the Shenandoah Valley, and returned to Washington July 24, 1864, after the pursuit was abandoned. Emory was ordered to report with his force to Augur, but two days later, when Early again became active in the valley, Wright's command was re-formed, and it marched into Maryland to reinforce David Hunter's troops from the Department of West Virginia (then commanded by George Crook).

July 26–27, 1864, the rest of First Division, Nineteenth Corps was ordered to Washington from the Army of the James, and July 31, 1864, the two remaining brigades of Cuvier Grover's Second Division, also with the Army of the James, were ordered to follow. The brigades of First Division passed through Washington, and joined the other troops of the division at Monocacy Junction July 31, 1864.

Henry W. Birge's First Brigade and Edward L. Molineux's Second Brigade of Grover's division did not join Nineteenth Corps at this time, but encamped in the Department of Washington near Tennallytown August 2, 1864. August 8, 1864, Grover was ordered to report to Augur for temporary duty, but August 14, 1864, he departed with his command for Berryville, Virginia to join Philip H. Sheridan's army, which was then forming in the Shenandoah Valley.

For additional information, see Early's Washington Raid (and Operations in the Shenandoah Valley, Maryland, and Pennsylvania).

Dismounted Cavalry. July 6, 1864, about 2,500 dismounted cavalry from Philip H. Sheridan's Cavalry Corps, Army of the Potomac were ordered to Baltimore, Maryland under Myron H. Beaumont. Beaumont's command arrived there July 7–8, 1864, and was then sent to Camp Stoneman, which was commanded by William Gamble. July 11, 1864, 1,500 dismounted men were sent from there to McCook's Reserve Camp near Crystal Spring, Maryland. Other dismounted men were mounted and organized and also sent out during the emergency.

McCook's Command. July 10, 1864, Alexander McD. McCook arrived in Washington and was assigned command of a Reserve Camp near Crystal Spring, Maryland, on Fourteenth Street at the crossing of Piney Branch. There, during the next day, McCook received 1,500 dismounted cavalry, the 2nd District of Columbia Regiment, the 9th, 12th, and 14th regiments of United States Veteran Reserve Corps, the 147th Ohio National Guard, and some batteries.

Also on July 11, 1864, McCook was assigned

command of the line of defenses from the Potomac River on the left to the Eastern Branch, which was then held by the brigades of James M. Warner and Joseph A. Haskin of Martin D. Hardin's Division. That same day, Montgomery C. Meigs, quartermaster general of the army, ordered all employees of the quartermaster's department to report to McCook. The next day, July 12, 1864, Meigs was given command of all forces assigned to McCook, and he organized these into a force called Meigs' Reserve Division. Meigs was directed to report to McCook.

July 13, 1864, Gillmore left the line of defenses near Fort Lincoln with the troops of Nineteenth Corps, and McCook, then at Fort Stevens, assumed command of the entire line. Halbert E. Paine was assigned command of Gillmore's former front. The next day, McCook was ordered to relieve Goldsborough's Naval Command (see below) and Meigs' division, and to send them back to Washington. McCook was relieved from duty in the Department of Washington July 16, 1864.

Meigs' Reserve Division. July 11, 1864, when Early's troops appeared north of Washington on the Seventh Street Road, Montgomery C. Meigs, quartermaster general of the army, ordered all employees of the quartermaster's department to join McCook near Fort Stevens. The next day, Meigs was assigned command all forces under McCook at Fort Stevens. These troops consisted of all regiments, batteries, and detachments of all arms on the line of defenses from Fort Stevens to Fort Totten, including those forts and also Fort Slocum. Daniel H. Rucker, commanding the quartermaster's depot in Washington; Joseph A. Haskin, commanding Second Brigade of Martin D. Hardin's Division; and Halbert E. Paine were ordered to report to Meigs. Meigs assumed command July 12, 1864, and organized his force as follows:

Meigs' Reserve Division, Montgomery C. Meigs
    First Brigade, Daniel H. Rucker
    Second Brigade, Halbert E. Paine
    Third Brigade, Addison Farnsworth

Note. Third Brigade was formerly a reserve under Francis Price, Jr.

Paine's Second Brigade was placed on the left of the line, and Rucker's First Brigade on the right.

Price's command, later Third Brigade under Farnsworth, was formed in reserve.

July 12, 1864, Meigs' Division was extended to include the line from Fort Totten to Forts De Russy and Kearny, including the dependent batteries. July 13, 1864, Charles M. Alexander was assigned command of two regiments of Paine's Second Brigade, and was ordered to relieve Paine in the rifle pits between Forts Stevens and Slocum. Paine was assigned three regiments, and with this brigade remained near Fort Slocum.

July 14, 1864, Meigs returned to Washington with the quartermaster clerks and employees of his division. Rucker's brigade was relieved first, and his former position was occupied by the Reserve Brigade. Paine assumed command of the remainder of Meigs' division. Paine was relieved from duty in the Department of Washington July 16, 1864, and was assigned for court martial service.

Gillmore's Command. Quincy A. Gillmore reported to Headquarters Department of Washington July 11, 1864, and was assigned command of the troops of Nineteenth Corps then arriving in Washington. He was ordered to take these troops to Fort Saratoga and prepare them for field service. About 600 of these men were placed in the rifle pits on the line of defenses north of Washington July 12, 1864, but these were taken out of the line a short time later. That day, Gillmore, whose headquarters was near Fort Lincoln, was ordered to take command of the forts from the Eastern Branch westward to, and including, Fort Slemmer. Also, on July 12, 1864, about 1,000–1,500 men from the Navy Yard under Admiral Louis M. Goldsborough were ordered to the trenches near Fort Lincoln, and Gillmore was instructed to place them in position.

July 13, 1864, Gillmore was ordered with the troops of Nineteenth Corps (about 650 men) to march to Tennallytown to join a force being assembled for the pursuit of Early as he retired from in front of Washington. The remainder of Gillmore's troops were left on the line of defenses. McCook, then at Fort Stevens, was given command of the entire front, and Paine was assigned command of the front vacated by Gillmore. Goldsborough's command returned to the Navy Yard July 14, 1864

Goldsborough's Naval Command. See Gillmore's Command, above.

Employees at Giesboro Point. July 10, 1864, all employees of the Cavalry Bureau and at Giesboro Point were organized into companies and regiments for the defense of the depot and stables located there. They did not go to the front, however, and were not used.

Alexander's Brigade. July 13, 1864, Charles M. Alexander, commander of the 2nd Delaware Volunteers, was assigned command of a provisional brigade, consisting of two provisional regiments, formerly of Second Brigade of Montgomery C. Meigs' Reserve Division. Alexander was ordered to relieve Halbert E. Paine's troops in the rifle pits between Forts Stevens and Slocum.

Loyal Legions of Washington. July 12, 1864, Abner Doubleday was assigned command of the defenses of Washington south of the Eastern Branch, and he was also ordered to organize the Loyal Legions of Washington. The latter were ordered to report to Doubleday when organized. Doubleday was relieved from duty in the Department of Washington July 16, 1864.

Lowell's Cavalry. July 10, 1864, Charles R. Lowell, Jr., then commanding an independent cavalry brigade at Falls Church, Virginia, was ordered with his 2nd Massachusetts Cavalry to report to Augur in Washington. He was then sent to scout and cover the country in front of Martin D. Hardin's Division, north of the Potomac River. Lowell's cavalry accompanied Horatio G. Wright's command July 13, 1864, in the pursuit of Early toward the Shenandoah Valley, and left the Department of Washington.

Militia, District of Columbia. July 11, 1864, George C. Thomas, commander of the militia of the District of Columbia, was ordered to turn out eight infantry regiments of the militia of the district and assume command. These troops were mustered out two days later.

Kenly's Brigade. Edward O. C. Ord, with John R. Kenly's Brigade of the Middle Department, Eighth Corps, moved through the Department of Washington from Baltimore July 14–16, 1864, to join Wright's "Army of Operations" near Leesburg, Virginia as it was moving in pursuit of Early toward the Shenandoah Valley. The brigade was then attached to Nineteenth Corps July 17, 1864.

DEPARTMENT OF WEST VIRGINIA

In June 1863, Robert C. Schenck's Middle Department extended westward along the Baltimore and Ohio Railroad all the way to the Ohio River, and when Robert E. Lee began his invasion of Maryland and Pennsylvania during the latter part of the month, Schenck could no longer exercise effective control over the western part of his command. Accordingly, on June 24, 1863, the Middle Department was divided, and that part west of Hancock, Maryland was included in the newly created Department of West Virginia. As originally constituted, the Department of West Virginia included all of Maryland west of a north-south line through Hancock; all of West Virginia lying west of the north-south line through Hancock, except the counties of Hancock, Brooke, and Ohio, which were in the Department of the Monongahela; and the counties in Ohio of Monroe, Washington, Athens, Meigs, Gallia, and Lawrence, which bordered on the Ohio River from below Wheeling, West Virginia to a point opposite the mouth of the Big Sandy River. The territory of the Department of West Virginia was taken from the Middle Department and the Department of the Ohio. Benjamin F. Kelley assumed command June 28, 1863 (assigned June 24, 1863), with headquarters at Clarksburg, West Virginia. Later changes in the department were as follows:

August 3, 1863, the department was expanded to include all of the state of Maryland west of the Monocacy River, and that part of Virginia in the vicinity of Harper's Ferry. The territory in Maryland west of the Monocacy River was taken from the Department of the Potomac, and that part of Virginia about Harper's Ferry was taken from the Middle Department.

October 12, 1863, the counties of Hancock, Brooke, and Ohio were transferred from the Department of the Monongahela to the Department of West Virginia.

November 16, 1863, headquarters of the Department of West Virginia was moved to Cumberland, Maryland.

January 12, 1864, the counties in Ohio bordering on the Ohio River were transferred from the Department of West Virginia to the newly created Northern Department.

There was no further change in the limits of the department during the rest of the war. By an order of June 10, 1864, the Middle Department was extended to include Harper's Ferry, but this order was revoked three days later.

On August 7, 1864, the Department of West Virginia, together with the Middle Department, the Department of Washington, and the Department of the Susquehanna, was included in Philip H. Sheridan's newly created Middle Military Division, and it remained a part of the division until the end of the war.

In the reorganization of the military divisions and departments of the army June 27, 1865, the state of West Virginia and that part of Maryland previously in the Department of West Virginia were included in Winfield S. Hancock's reorganized Middle Department. This reorganization was not effected immediately, and William H. Emory, who had assumed command of the Department of West Virginia April 24, 1865, was still in command in July 1865.

COMMANDERS OF THE DEPARTMENT OF WEST VIRGINIA

Benjamin F. Kelley	June 28, 1863 to March 10, 1864
Franz Sigel	March 10, 1864 to May 21, 1864
David Hunter	May 21, 1864 to August 8, 1864
Julius Stahel	August 8, 1864 to August 9, 1864
George Crook	August 9, 1864 to February 21, 1865, captured
John D. Stevenson	February 21, 1865 to February 27, 1865
Winfield S. Hancock	February 27, 1865 to March 1, 1865
Samuel S. Carroll	March 1, 1865 to March 8, 1865
Winfield S. Hancock	March 8, 1865 to March 20, 1865
George Crook	March 20, 1865 to March 22, 1865
Winfield S. Hancock	March 22, 1865 to April 24, 1865
William H. Emory	April 24, 1865 to July 1865

Some explanation is required for the dates of command given above. Hunter left the army on leave August 8, 1864, and Crook assumed temporary command during his absence. Hunter did not return, however, and was relieved from his command August 30, 1864, and Crook assumed permanent command September 1, 1864. The situation became somewhat more complicated after February 27, 1865. On February 26, 1865, Hancock was assigned command of the Department of West Virginia by order of the president, and he also was in temporary command of the Middle Military Division during the absence of Philip H. Sheridan, who was on an expedition from Winchester to Petersburg, Virginia. The next day, February 27, 1865, at Winchester, Hancock assumed command of the Middle Military Division and also of the Department of West Virginia. Hancock, however, was unable to leave his Headquarters Middle Military Division at that time, and that day Hancock assigned Carroll to command the Department of West Virginia, with headquarters at Cumberland. Carroll assumed command March 1, 1865, but Hancock moved his Headquarters Middle Military Division to Cumberland March 6, 1865, and apparently assumed command of the Department of West Virginia, because a short time later Carroll was in command of Second Infantry Division, Department of West Virginia. March 8, 1865, Hancock moved his Headquarters Middle Military Division back to Winchester. George Crook, who was captured February 21, 1865, was exchanged March 20, 1865, and by an order from the adjutant general's office resumed command of the Department of West Virginia. Hancock reacted vigorously, pointing out that he had been assigned command of the department by an order of the president, and as a result, Crook was ordered by the secretary of war to report to Ulysses S. Grant at City Point. Crook relinquished command of the Department of West Virginia March 22, 1865. Hancock apparently exercised control over the department until April 22, 1865, and then, when he moved his Headquarters Middle Military Division to Washington, William H. Emory assumed command.

DISTRICT IN THE DEPARTMENT OF WEST VIRGINIA

District of Harper's Ferry. The District of Harper's Ferry was the only officially organized district in the Department of West Virginia during the period June 1863–July 1865. It was created July 7, 1864, during Jubal A. Early's invasion of Maryland, to consist of all troops on the line of the Baltimore and Ohio Railroad from the Monocacy River west to Hancock. At the time, these troops belonged to Max Weber's command of Franz Sigel's Reserve Division, Department of West Virginia. Albion P. Howe assumed command of the new district July 8, 1864, and at that time the Reserve Division was discontinued. Benjamin F. Kelley, however, continued in command of the troops on the railroad west of Sleepy Creek, and some sources show Kelley in command of Reserve Division West of Sleepy Creek for some time thereafter.

In January 1865, the troops of the District of Harper's Ferry were organized into a new Third Infantry Division, and Stevenson was assigned command. In effect, the District of Harper's Ferry was discontinued, and it does not again appear on the rosters of the Department of West Virginia, but Stevenson's command was referred to as the District of Harper's Ferry as late as March 1865.

For additional information, see below, Operations of the Troops of the Department of West Virginia, Early's Washington Raid, July 1864; and see also Shenandoah Valley Campaign (Sheridan).

TROOPS IN THE DEPARTMENT OF WEST VIRGINIA

There were numerous changes in the organization and distribution of the troops in the Department of West Virginia during the period June 1863–July 1865, and these are best described by considering them in significant time periods.

June 1863 to October 1863

When the Department of West Virginia was organized at the end of June 1863, the troops included within its limits consisted of a division commanded by Eliakim P. Scammon, and brigades commanded by William W. Averell, Nathan Wilkinson, James A. Mulligan, and Jacob M. Campbell. Benjamin F. Kelley was in command of the department.

Scammon's division of two brigades, formerly Third Division, Eighth Corps of the Middle Department, was serving in western West Virginia. The First Brigade, commanded by Rutherford B. Hayes, was at Camp White; and Second Brigade, commanded by Carr B. White, was at Fayetteville. Generally this organization was known as Scammon's Division, and later as Third Division, Department of West Virginia. July 8, 1863, a Third Brigade, consisting of cavalry regiments, was organized under John T. Toland. Toland was killed July 18, 1863, and Freeman E. Franklin assumed command of the brigade. Alfred N. Duffie was assigned to the Department of West Virginia August 14, 1863, and upon his arrival he relieved Franklin in command of Third Brigade. At the end of July 1863, the troops of Scammon's Division were stationed at Camp Piatt, Camp White, Coal's Mouth, Fayetteville, and Gauley Bridge. Headquarters of the division was at Charleston, West Virginia.

Averell's large brigade was formerly Fourth Separate Brigade, Eighth Corps, Middle Department, and in the Department of West Virginia it was called Fourth Separate Brigade. In June 1863, this brigade was posted along the Baltimore and Ohio Railroad, with headquarters at Grafton. Detachments of the brigade were at Beverly, Buckhannon, Bulltown, New Creek, Philippi, Webster, and Weston.

Campbell's former Fourth Brigade, First Division, Eighth Corps; Mulligan's former Fifth Brigade, First Division, Eighth Corps; and Wilkinson's Sixth Brigade, First Division, Eighth Corps became separate commands in June 1863, and they were known simply as Campbell's Brigade, Mulligan's Brigade, and Wilkinson's Brigade. The troops of these commands were generally stationed on the Baltimore and Ohio Railroad and the Northwestern Railroad, west of Sleepy Creek.

On August 3, 1863 (announced by Kelley August 10, 1863), the Department of West Virginia was extended to include all of the state of Maryland west of the Monocacy River, and also that part of Virginia in the vicinity of Harper's Ferry. By this order, all troops near Harper's Ferry, and on the Baltimore and Ohio Railroad between the Monocacy and Hancock, Maryland were transferred from the Department of the Susquehanna to the Department of West Virginia. These included Andrew T. McReynolds' command along the Potomac River, and Henry H. Lockwood's division at Harper's Ferry (Maryland Heights). This division was organized as follows:

Lockwood's Division (or Maryland Heights Division), Henry H. Lockwood
  First Brigade, George D. Wells
  Second Brigade, William P. Maulsby

Note 1. Peter A. Porter commanded Second Brigade until Lockwood assumed command of the division July 18, 1863. Maulsby was in command of one of the Maryland regiments transferred to Harper's Ferry with Lockwood.
Note 2. Milton L. Miner's 17th Battery, Indiana Light Artillery and Jeremiah McCarthy's Battery C, 1st Pennsylvania Light Artillery were attached to Wells' brigade; and Alonzo Snow's Battery B, Maryland Light Artillery and Charles Kusserow's 32nd Battery, New York Light Artillery were attached to Maulsby's brigade.

Post of Martinsburg, West Virginia, Andrew T. McReynolds
  Infantry Brigade, Thomas F. Wildes
  Unattached cavalry
  Artillery
    30th Battery, New York Light Artillery, Alfred Von Kleiser

At the end of August 1863, the troops in the Department of West Virginia were stationed as follows: Scammon's Division was in the Kanawha Valley; Lockwood's Division was at Harper's Ferry and Maryland Heights; McReynolds' command was at Martinsburg; Averell's Brigade (or Fourth Separate Brigade) was at Beverly; Campbell's Brigade was at Moorefield, Petersburg, and Romney; Mulligan's Brigade was at New Creek, Petersburg, and Romney; and Wilkinson's Brigade was at Clarksburg, Grafton, and Parkersburg. Other posts served by detachments were Green Spring Run and Sir John's Run in West Virginia, and Hagerstown in Maryland.

October 1863 to March 1864 (Reorganization of October 1863)

In October 1863, the troops of the Department of West Virginia were reorganized into three divisions and one separate brigade as follows:

First Division, Department of West Virginia. By an order of October 12, 1863, the troops at Harper's

Ferry and Martinsburg, and those guarding the line of the Baltimore and Ohio Railroad from the Monocacy River to Sleepy Creek were organized into a new First Division, Department of West Virginia. Jeremiah C. Sullivan was assigned command, with headquarters at Harper's Ferry. By this order Lockwood's Division (or Maryland Heights Division) and McReynolds' former command at Martinsburg, then under Lewis B. Pierce, were discontinued and included in Sullivan's new division, which was organized as follows:

First Division, Jeremiah C. Sullivan
  First Brigade, George D. Wells
  Second Brigade, William P. Maulsby
  Third Brigade, Robert S. Rodgers
  Cavalry Brigade, William H. Boyd
  Heavy Artillery, Gustavus F. Merriam
    3rd Battalion, 5th New York Heavy Artillery
    Tyler's (Pennsylvania) Battery, Horatio K. Tyler
    Battery H, 1st West Virginia Light Artillery, James H. Holmes

Note. Andrew Rosney's Battery D, 1st Pennsylvania Light Artillery and George When Furst's Battery A, 1st West Virginia Light Artillery were assigned to First Brigade; Alfred Von Kleiser's 30th Battery, New York Light Artillery and Charles Kusserow's 32nd Battery, New York Light Artillery were attached to Second Brigade; and Henry A. Du Pont's Battery B, 5th United States Artillery was attached to Third Brigade.

Sullivan assumed command of First Division. Lockwood was relieved from duty in the Department of West Virginia, and was ordered to report to the commander of the Middle Department at Baltimore, Maryland.

In December 1863, Wells' First Brigade advanced up the Shenandoah Valley to Harrisonburg to threaten Staunton during Averell's and Scammon's raid on the Virginia and Tennessee Railroad. For details see below, Operations of the Troops of the Department of West Virginia, Raid on the Virginia and Tennessee Railroad, and Demonstrations up the Shenandoah Valley, and from the Kanawha Valley. In January 1864, Wells' brigade was broken up by the transfer of regiments.

Frank Wheaton's Third Brigade, Third Division, Sixth Corps of the Army of the Potomac arrived at Harper's Ferry January 2, 1864, and it was attached to Sullivan's First Division. The division then consisted of Maulsby's Second Brigade, Rodgers'

Third Brigade, Wheaton's Brigade (commanded by John F. Ballier), and the Cavalry Brigade, commanded by Charles Fitz Simmons (also Fitz Simons). Wheaton's Brigade left the Department of West Virginia to rejoin the Army of the Potomac March 25, 1864.

Second Division, Department of West Virginia.

On October 21, 1863, a Second Division, Department of West Virginia was organized from the troops stationed on the Baltimore and Ohio Railroad and the Northwestern Railroad from Sleepy Creek west to the Ohio River. These troops belonged to the brigades of Campbell, Mulligan, and Wilkinson (see above). Mulligan was assigned command of the division, with headquarters at New Creek. The division was organized as follows:

Second Division, James A. Mulligan
  First Brigade, Jacob M. Campbell
  Second Brigade, Joseph Thoburn
  Third Brigade, Nathan Wilkinson

Note 1. First Brigade was formerly Fourth Brigade, First Division, Eighth Corps; Second Brigade was Fifth Brigade, First Division, Eighth Corps; and Third Brigade was Sixth Brigade, First Division, Eighth Corps.

Note 2. Francis M. Lowry's Battery E, 1st West Virginia Light Artillery was attached to First Brigade; John Rourke's Battery L, 1st Illinois Light Artillery and John Carlin's Battery D, 1st West Virginia Light Artillery were attached to Second Brigade; and George W. Graham's Battery F, 1st West Virginia Light Artillery was attached to Third Brigade.

The troops of Second Division remained generally on the line of the railroad, with advanced posts at Philippi, Buckhannon, Bulltown, Glenville, and Wirt Court House.

Third Division, Department of West Virginia.

Scammon's Third Division in the Kanawha Valley was unchanged in the reorganization of the troops in the department in October 1863. It took part, together with Averell's First Separate Brigade, in an expedition to Lewisburg in November 1863, and also on a raid on the Virginia and Tennessee Railroad in December 1863. For details of these expeditions, see below, Operations of the Troops of the Department of West Virginia.

Scammon was captured on the morning of February 3, 1864, while asleep on board a steamboat on the Kanawha River, and Alfred N. Duffie assumed temporary command of Third Division. On February 13, 1864, George Crook arrived and assumed command of the division. March 25, 1864, Crook was ordered to report to Ulysses S. Grant at Culpeper Court House for consultation, and Duffie again commanded the division for a few days during his absence.

At the end of March 1864, the troops of Third Division were stationed largely at Charleston, Fayetteville, Gauley Bridge, and Barboursville.

First Separate Brigade.

In the reorganization of October 1863, the designation of Averell's Fourth Separate Brigade was changed to First Separate Brigade, Department of West Virginia, with Averell remaining in command. In November 1863, Averell's brigade joined Scammon's Third Division in an expedition to Lewisburg, and was engaged at Droop Mountain November 6, 1863. Averell and Scammon also made a raid on the Virginia and Tennessee Railroad in December 1863. For details of these expeditions, see below, Operations of the Troops of the Department of West Virginia. First Separate Brigade was discontinued January 6, 1864 by a change of designation to Fourth Division, Department of West Virginia.

Fourth Division, Department of West Virginia.

A Fourth Division, Department of West Virginia was constituted by an order of December 31, 1863, and it was organized from Averell's First Separate Brigade. Benjamin F. Kelley, commander of the Department of West Virginia, announced the change of designation January 6, 1864. The division was organized as follows:

Fourth Division, William W. Averell
  First Brigade, Moses Hall
      Augustus Moor
  Second Brigade, John Schoonmaker
  Third Brigade, John H. Oley
  Artillery
      Battery B, 1st West Virginia Light Artillery, John V. Keeper
      Battery G, 1st West Virginia Light Artillery, Chatham T. Ewing

Note. Both Second Brigade and Third Brigade were composed of cavalry regiments.

March 15, 1864, Averell was ordered to take command of all cavalry attached to his own Fourth Division and to Sullivan's First Division, and organize them for service as cavalry outposts for both divisions. The infantry of Fourth Division remained under Averell's control. Fourth Division was discontinued March 23, 1864 (see following section).

Cavalry Division, Department of West Virginia. About March 18, 1864, Averell began calling his command "Cavalry Division, Department of West Virginia." Franz Sigel, then in command of the Department of West Virginia, questioned this change in designation from Fourth Division to Cavalry Division, but on March 23, 1864, he gave his approval, and Fourth Division was discontinued. Averell remained in command of the Cavalry Division at Martinsburg until it was discontinued by the organization of First Cavalry Division, Department of West Virginia from its regiments April 12, 1864 (see below).

At the end of March 1864, Averell's Cavalry Division was stationed near Martinsburg, with a line of outposts extending from the Shenandoah River to Back Creek. Two regiments of infantry that were attached to the division were placed at Beverly under Augustus Moor.

April 1864 to June 1864
(Reorganization of April 1864)

March 10, 1864, Franz Sigel was assigned command of the Department of West Virginia, relieving Kelley, and that same day the president assigned Ulysses S. Grant to the command of the Armies of the United States. In his preparation for the spring campaign of 1864 in Virginia, Grant included Sigel in his plans. During the latter part of March and in April 1864, the Department of West Virginia was completely reorganized to provide a force for field service, to be used as circumstances might dictate. When completed, the new organization consisted of two infantry divisions, two cavalry divisions, and a reserve division, and two separate brigades. These were organized as follows:

First Infantry Division, Department of West Virginia. April 6, 1864, Jeremiah C. Sullivan was

assigned command of a division, then assembling at Webster, Grafton, and Clarksburg, and including the infantry regiments under Augustus Moor at Beverly. April 9, 1864, this division was designated as First Infantry Division, Department of West Virginia, and was organized as follows:

First Infantry Division, Jeremiah C. Sullivan
  First Brigade, Augustus Moor, to June 8, 1864
    George D. Wells
  Second Brigade, Joseph Thoburn

Note 1. Moor's brigade was formed largely from regiments of the former First Division, Department of West Virginia.
Note 2. Thoburn's brigade was formed largely from regiments of the former Second Division, Department of West Virginia.
Note 3. Moor left with his 28th Ohio Regiment to escort prisoners from Staunton, Virginia to Indianapolis, Indiana June 9, 1864. He returned and resumed command of First Brigade at the end of the month.

The organization of First Infantry Division proceeded slowly, and during the latter part of April 1864, the troops were sent to Martinsburg to complete the concentration there. It was not until April 27, 1864 that Sullivan was relieved from duty at Webster and was ordered to Martinsburg to assume command.

During the period April 29, 1864–May 17, 1864, Sigel moved up the Shenandoah Valley with Sullivan's First Infantry Division and Julius Stahel's First Cavalry Division (see below) to New Market, Virginia, and there he was defeated May 15, 1864 by a Confederate force under John C. Breckinridge. Sigel then withdrew down the valley and camped at Cedar Creek. For details of this campaign, see below, Operations of the Troops of the Department of West Virginia, Sigel's Movement up the Shenandoah Valley (Engagement at New Market, Virginia).

The First Infantry Division took part in David Hunter's Lynchburg Campaign in May and June 1864. For details, see below, Operations of the Troops of the Department of West Virginia, Hunter's Lynchburg, Virginia Campaign.

Second Infantry Division, Department of West Virginia. As a part of the reorganization of April 1864, a new Second Infantry Division was organized from George Crook's Third Division,

Department of West Virginia and other troops. This was done as follows: April 26, 1864, Alfred N. Duffie's Third Brigade, Third Division was transferred to William W. Averell's new Second Cavalry Division, Department of West Virginia (see below), where it was designated as First Brigade. Two days later, a new Third Brigade was organized from two regiments of the Pennsylvania Reserves from Alexandria, Virginia, Department of Washington, and two regiments of the former Second Division, Department of West Virginia. Horatio G. Sickel, colonel of the 3rd Pennsylvania Reserves, was assigned command of the new Third Brigade. After this reorganization was completed, the designation of Third Division, Department of West Virginia was changed to Second Infantry Division, Department of West Virginia, which was organized as follows:

Second Infantry Division, George Crook
    First Brigade, Rutherford B. Hayes
    Second Brigade, Carr B. White
    Third Brigade, Horatio G. Sickel, to June 9, 1864
        Jacob M. Campbell
    Artillery, James R. McMullin
        1st Battery, Ohio Light Artillery, James R. McMullin

Crook's Second Infantry Division took part in David Hunter's Lynchburg Camapign in May and June 1864. For details, see below, Operations of the Troops of the Department of West Virginia, Hunter's Lynchburg, Virginia Campaign.

First Cavalry Division, Department of West Virginia. April 12, 1864, a new First Cavalry Division was formed from seven cavalry regiments belonging to William W. Averell's former Cavalry Division, Department of West Virginia (see above). These regiments were organized into two brigades, but April 18, 1864, Averell was ordered to take two of his regiments to Charleston, and report to George Crook, commanding Third Division, Department of West Virginia. He was then assigned command of a new Second Cavalry Division that was to be organized at Charleston. Averell departed April 19, 1864, and Robert F. Taylor assumed command of the cavalry remaining at Martinsburg. Then, on April 26, 1864, First Cavalry Division was organized from the cavalry serving in central and eastern West Virginia. Julius Stahel, chief of cavalry

of the Department of West Virginia, was relieved from that duty, and was ordered to Martinsburg to assume command of the division, which was organized as follows:

First Cavalry Division, Julius Stahel, to June 5, 1864, wounded
    Andrew T. McReynolds, to June 9, 1864
    Alfred N. Duffie
    First Brigade, William B. Tibbits, to June 1, 1864
        Robert F. Taylor
    Second Brigade, John Wynkoop
    Artillery
        Battery G, 1st West Virginia Light Artillery, Chatham T. Ewing

First Cavalry Division took part in Franz Sigel's advance up the Shenandoah Valley in April and May 1864, and was present at the Battle of New Market May 15, 1864. For details, see below, Operations of the Troops of the Department of West Virginia, Sigel's Movement up the Shenandoah Valley (Engagement at New Market, Virginia). It also accompanied David Hunter on his Lynchburg Campaign, and was engaged at the Battle of Piedmont June 5, 1864. Stahel was wounded that day, and Duffie assumed command of the division June 9, 1864 at Staunton, Virginia. For details, see below, Operations of the Troops of the Department of West Virginia, Hunter's Lynchburg, Virginia Campaign.

Second Cavalry Division, Department of West Virginia. April 19, 1864, William W. Averell, then commanding the Cavalry Division, Department of West Virginia at Martinsburg, left with two regiments of his command to report to George Crook, commanding Third Division, Department of West Virginia at Charleston. Averell was then assigned command of a new cavalry division that was to consist of eight regiments, including the two that he had brought from Martinsburg. Averell's command was also to include Alfred N. Duffie's former Third Brigade of Crook's Third Division, which consisted of cavalry regiments. On April 26, 1864, the organization of Second Cavalry Division was announced as follows:

Second Cavalry Division, William W. Averell
    First Brigade, Alfred N. Duffie
    Second Brigade, James M. Schoonmaker
    Third Brigade, John H. Oley

It should be noted that during the expedition against the Virginia and Tennessee Railroad May 2–19, 1864, in which Second Cavalry Division took part, Duffie's brigade retained its former designation of Third Brigade, Third Division. On May 30, 1864, however, while the cavalry division was encamped at Bunger's Mills near Lewisburg, West Virginia, the designation of Duffie's brigade was changed to First Brigade. For details of the expedition to the Virginia and Tennessee Railroad, see below, Operations of the Troops of the Department of West Virginia, Expedition against the Virginia and Tennessee Railroad (Engagement at Cloyd's Mountain).

On June 8, 1864, Averell's division joined Hunter's command at Staunton, Virginia, and then advanced with it to Lynchburg. It also accompanied Hunter when he retreated to the Kanawha Valley. For details, see below, Operations of the Troops of the Department of West Virginia, Hunter's Lynchburg, Virginia Campaign.

There were two reorganizations of the division in June 1864. On June 9, 1864, while Hunter's army was at Staunton, Duffie, commanding First Brigade, was assigned command of First Cavalry Division in place of Stahel, who was wounded at Piedmont June 5, 1864. The division was then reorganized as follows:

Second Cavalry Division, William W. Averell
    First Brigade, James M. Schoonmaker
    Second Brigade, John Oley
    Third Brigade, William H. Powell

Again, on June 25, 1864, near the end of the retreat from Lynchburg, the division was reorganized by the reassignment of regiments, but the brigade commanders remained the same.

Separate Brigades, Department of West Virginia. April 6, 1864, Second Division, Department of West Virginia was discontinued by the transfer of its regiments to other commands, principally to First Infantry Division. By an order of the same date, the infantry and artillery remaining in Second Division were organized into Second Separate Brigade, under the command of James A. Mulligan. Mulligan later left to command First Infantry Division, and Nathan Wilkinson assumed command of Second Separate Brigade. Wilkinson's troops were generally stationed on the Baltimore and Ohio Railroad west of Sleepy Creek.

April 9, 1864, Max Weber was assigned command of the Defenses of Harper's Ferry, and of all troops stationed on the Baltimore and Ohio Railroad from the Monocacy River to Sleepy Creek. Weber's command was designated as First Separate Brigade.

The two separate brigades were discontinued April 26, 1864, when their troops were organized as the Reserve Division, Department of West Virginia (see next section).

Reserve Division, Department of West Virginia. April 26, 1864, the troops of First Separate Brigade and Second Separate Brigade were consolidated to form a division, designated as Reserve Division, Department of West Virginia. Max Weber was assigned command, with headquarters at Harper's Ferry. On May 21, 1864, David Hunter relieved Sigel in command of the Department of West Virginia, and the next day Sigel was assigned command of the Reserve Division. Sigel assumed command May 24, 1864, and Weber was given the command of the troops on the railroad from the Monocacy River to Sleepy Creek, and Benjamin F. Kelley from Sleepy Creek west to the Ohio River.

Weber's headquarters was at Harper's Ferry, and his troops were at Monocacy, Point of Rocks, Harper's Ferry, Maryland Heights, Bolivar Heights, Duffield's Depot, Martinsburg, Back Creek, Cherry Run, and Sleepy Creek. Kelley's headquarters was at Cumberland, Maryland, and his troops were at Green Spring Run, Paw Paw, Cumberland, New Creek, Greenland Gap, Grafton, Buckhannon, and Clarksburg. Mulligan was in command at New Creek, Thomas M. Harris at Beverly, and Wilkinson at Clarksburg.

When Sigel withdrew his troops from the railroad to form his divisions for field service, he left the line vulnerable to enemy attack, and during the period May 5–8, 1864, fifteen one-hundred-day regiments of Ohio militia were sent to posts on the railroad as follows: three regiments to Parkersburg, three regiments to New Creek, two regiments to Cumberland, and three regiments to Harper's Ferry. Four regiments were also sent to Charleston. In June 1864, four of the Ohio regiments were sent to Grant at City Point and Bermuda Hundred, but the rest remained generally on the railroad until their terms expired at the end of August 1864.

July 8, 1864, during Jubal A. Early's invasion of Maryland, the District of Harper's Ferry was organized under Albion P. Howe, and the Reserve Division was discontinued. Kelley continued in command of the forces west of Sleepy Creek, and some sources refer to his command as Reserve Division, West of Sleepy Creek.

Artillery Brigade, Department of West Virginia. On May 24, 1864, Henry A. Du Pont was announced as chief of artillery of the Department of West Virginia, and he then assumed command of an artillery brigade, which he continued to command during the rest of the war. The brigade consisted of the following: Alonzo Snow's Battery B, Maryland Light Artillery; Conrad Carrolien's 30th Battery, New York Light Artillery; John Carlin's Battery D, 1st West Virginia Light Artillery; and Henry A. Du Pont's Battery B, 5th United States Artillery.

July 1864 (Army of the Kanawha)

When David Hunter arrived in the Kanawha Valley at the end of June 1864 on his return from the unsuccessful Lynchburg, Virginia campaign, it was necessary to refit his command for further service. As a first step, on July 2, 1864, he assigned George Crook to the command of all troops in the Kanawha Valley, and in West Virginia, west of the Allegheny Mountains and south of the Baltimore and Ohio Railroad. Alfred N. Duffie was ordered to report with his First Cavalry Division to Hunter, and to receive orders directly from Headquarters Department of West Virginia. William W. Averell was ordered to report with his Second Cavalry Division to Crook. Crook assumed command July 3, 1864, and by an order of that date designated his command as the Army of the Kanawha.

Almost immediately, however, Jubal A. Early arrived at Winchester, Virginia with a Confederate force, and Hunter was directed to send his available troops by rail from Parkersburg to Harper's Ferry and Martinsburg to protect the line of the Baltimore and Ohio Railroad. When Early arrived at Winchester, the only Federal troops on his front were those of the Reserve Division, commanded by Sigel, Weber, and Stahel. Sigel was at Martinsburg,

Weber at Harper's Ferry, and Stahel at Smithfield and Bunker Hill. As Early advanced, Sigel and Stahel withdrew into the defenses of Harper's Ferry July 4, 1864.

July 4, 1864, Albion P. Howe, then at the Artillery Camp of Instruction in Washington, was ordered to assume command of the 170th Ohio National Guard Regiment, a battalion of dismounted cavalry, and proceed with them to Harper's Ferry. On July 7, 1864, Howe was ordered to assume command of a new District of Harper's Ferry, which was to consist of all troops on the line of the Baltimore and Ohio Railroad from the Monocacy River west to Hancock, Maryland. Howe assumed command July 8, 1864, and because he was then serving in the Department of West Virginia, he was subject to Hunter's orders. The order of July 7, 1864 assigning Howe to the command of the District of Harper's Ferry also relieved Sigel and Stahel from further duty in the Department of West Virginia, and directed them to report to Hunter's headquarters at Cumberland, Maryland. Weber was assigned command at Maryland Heights. The Reserve Division was discontinued when the District of Harper's Ferry was organized July 8, 1864, but Kelley continued in command of the troops west of Sleepy Creek.

Early did not move to Harper's Ferry, but instead crossed the Potomac River into Maryland and advanced to Frederick. He then appeared on the north front of Washington July 11, 1864 and threatened the city, but on the night of July 12, 1864, he withdrew and marched by way of Leesburg, Virginia toward the Shenandoah Valley. He was followed from Washington by Horatio G. Wright, who had assumed command of a special force consisting of his own Sixth Corps, Army of the Potomac, a detachment of Nineteenth Corps, John R. Kenly's Brigade from the Middle Department, and some cavalry.

As Hunter's troops arrived at Harper's Ferry from the west, they were sent out of the department into Virginia, in the direction of Leesburg, to join Wright. Crook arrived at Harper's Ferry July 15, 1864, and was assigned command of all the forces leaving the Department of West Virginia to join Wright. Crook assumed command at Hillsboro, Virginia July 16, 1864, and at that time called his command the Army of the Kanawha. Under Crook at Hillsboro were Jeremiah C. Sullivan's First Infantry Division (commanded by Joseph Thoburn after July 16, 1864), Alfred N. Duffie's First Cavalry Division, Daniel Frost's Third Brigade of Crook's Second Infantry Division, and James A. Mulligan's Brigade (formerly commanded by Thomas M. Harris) of the Reserve Division, Department of West Virginia. William W. Averell's Second Cavalry Division and Isaac H. Duval's Second Brigade, Second Infantry Division (formerly commanded by Carr B. White), both under Averell, were ordered to remain at Martinsburg to protect the railroad. Rutherford B. Hayes' First Brigade was sent to Purcellville to join Crook.

On July 18, 1864, Crook's army, then attached to Wright's command, succeeded in crossing the Shenandoah River at Snicker's Ferry (or Parker's Ford), and Early's troops withdrew up the valley to Strasburg. Wright then returned to Washington with his special force, and July 22, 1864, Crook assembled his Army of the Kanawha at Winchester. He then reported to Hunter as commander of the Department of West Virginia.

After Wright had returned to Washington from the Shenandoah Valley, Early again advanced down the valley and defeated Crook at Kernstown July 24, 1864. Two days later Crook withdrew his army to the north side of the Potomac at Williamsport, and then moved toward Harper's Ferry. The cavalry remained north of the Potomac watching the fords. Early moved on into the lower valley of the Shenandoah, and then sent John McCausland with his cavalry into Pennsylvania, where he burned Chambersburg July 30, 1864. After the burning of Chambersburg, there was concern that Early might again invade Maryland from the west, and Hunter moved with the Army of the Kanawha and Wright's command to the east side of South Mountain to watch the passes. By August 2, 1864, it became clear that Early did not intend to invade Maryland, and was instead withdrawing up the valley. Shortly thereafter, Hunter began the concentration of his forces, which included the Army of the Kanawha, Sixth Corps, and Detachment Nineteenth Corps at Halltown, near Harper's Ferry. Crook's Army of the Kanawha was encamped at Halltown when Philip H. Sheridan assumed command of Hunter's former field force at Harper's Ferry August 6, 1864. Two days later, Sheridan changed the designation of Crook's command to the Army of West Virginia.

For details of the organization and operations of the troops of the Department of West Virginia during July 1864, see Early's Washington Raid (and Operations in the Shenandoah Valley, Maryland, and Pennsylvania).

August 1864 to September 1864 (Army of West Virginia)

During the greater part of this period, most of the troops of the Department of West Virginia were with Philip H. Sheridan's army in the Shenandoah Valley, and while there they were outside the limits of their department. When on August 6, 1864 Sheridan assumed command of the troops formerly commanded by David Hunter during Early's Washington Raid and his later operations in the lower Shenandoah Valley, Maryland, and Pennsylvania, George Crook's Army of the Kanawha was encamped at Halltown, four miles southwest of Harper's Ferry. On August 8, 1864, Sheridan designated Crook's command, which then consisted of First Infantry Division and Second Infantry Division, Department of West Virginia, as the Army of West Virginia. During August and September 1864, Crook's army was under Sheridan's orders and took part in his Shenandoah Valley Campaign against Early. For details of the organization and operations of the Army of West Virginia during this period, see Shenendoah Valley Campaign (Sheridan).

On August 9, 1864, Crook was assigned temporary command of the Department of West Virginia, in addition to the Army of West Virginia, during the absence of Hunter, who was on leave. Hunter did not return to the department, however, and was relieved from command August 30, 1864. Crook assumed command of the department September 1, 1864.

There were troops in the Department of West Virginia that were not with Sheridan during the Shenandoah Valley Campaign. These consisted of the forces in the Kanawha Valley, Kelley's forces on the railroad west of Sleepy Creek, the troops in the District of Harper's Ferry, and Duffie's First Cavalry Division. A brief description of these commands follows:

Kanawha Valley (First Separate Brigade). August 6, 1864, Jeremiah Sullivan was ordered to Charleston to assume command of the troops in the Kanawha Valley. He did not arrive there until late in the month, and meantime the one-hundred-day regiments of Ohio Militia had departed for muster out. At the end of the month Sullivan had under his command only John H. Oley's 7th West Virginia Cavalry. On September 5, 1864, however, Robert S. Taylor was sent with his 1st New York Veteran Cavalry of First Brigade, First Cavalry Division from Cumberland, Maryland to join Sullivan.

September 22, 1864, the troops serving in the Kanawha Valley were designated as First Separate Brigade, Department of West Virginia, and Sullivan was assigned command. On October 9, 1864, however, Sullivan was ordered to turn over his command to Oley and to report to Sheridan for orders. Sullivan was ordered to Hagerstown, Maryland October 27, 1864, and he apparently received no further command.

Oley remained in command of First Separate Brigade, consisting of 7th West Virginia Cavalry, 1st New York Veteran Cavalry, and a battery of 1st West Virginia Light Artillery, until after the war. The brigade was discontinued by muster out in July and August 1865.

District of Harper's Ferry. On the day that Sheridan assumed command at Harper's Ferry, August 6, 1864, Albion P. Howe, the commander of the District of Harper's Ferry, was ordered back to Washington. He departed two days later, and Max Weber assumed command of the district. He was relieved by John D. Stevenson August 15, 1864.

The troops of the district were not generally organized into brigades, but at the end of July 1864, William P. Maulsby commanded an infantry brigade that was composed of his own 1st Maryland Potomac Home Brigade (a regiment) under Roger E. Cook, and three one-hundred-day regiments of Ohio Militia. The other troops of the district consisted largely of artillery and some cavalry. The Ohio regiments departed for muster out in August 1864, and Maulsby resigned August 25, 1864.

On August 9, 1864, John R. Kenly's Brigade from the Middle Department, Eighth Corps, then attached to Detachment Nineteenth Corps, was assigned to the District of Harper's Ferry when Sheridan's army made its first advance of the Shenandoah Valley Campaign toward Berryville, Virginia. Kenly was relieved from duty in the District of Harper's Ferry September 13, 1864, and he then reported to Headquarters Middle Department, Eighth Corps. Kenly's Brigade in the district was discontinued.

August 28, 1864, Leonard D. H. Currie's Third Brigade, First Division, Nineteenth Corps was detached from the corps, and was then ordered to report to Stevenson at Harper's Ferry. Most of Currie's service was outside the district, however, because his brigade was employed in escorting wagon trains from Harper's Ferry and Martinsburg to the front. Currie's brigade was relieved from duty with the wagon train October 27, 1864, and it rejoined Detachment Nineteenth Corps.

September 30, 1864, Stevenson was reassigned to the command of the District of Harper's Ferry, including Martinsburg and the lower Shenandoah Valley.

Kelley's Forces West of Sleepy Creek. During the Shenandoah Valley Campaign, Kelley remained in command of the troops left to guard the Baltimore and Ohio Railroad west of Sleepy Creek. Although the composition of this force varied from time to time, it generally consisted of about seven infantry and cavalry regiments (or detached companies or battalions of regiments), and four batteries of artillery. At times, when the line was threatened, units of the West Virginia State Militia were called out. Nathan Wilkinson commanded the important post of Clarksburg.

First Cavalry Division. When Duffie's First Cavalry Division returned to the lower Shenandoah Valley from Hancock, Maryland, it was ordered to Charlestown, West Virginia in mid-August 1864, and it was then moved to Point of Rocks, Maryland. On August 24, 1864, Duffie was ordered to dismount the division (except two regiments, which were reassigned), and then to remount his troopers under the department commander. Four days later, Duffie was ordered to take his division to Cumberland, Maryland, and August 29, 1864 departed with about 2,500 men. John E. Wynkoop, who at that time was in command of the dismounted troops at Harper's Ferry, was ordered to join Duffie. The organization of First Cavalry Division was as follows:

First Cavalry Division, Alfred N. Duffie
    First Brigade, Robert F. Taylor
    Second Brigade, John E. Wynkoop

Note. First Brigade consisted of 1st New York Veteran Cavalry and 15th New York Cavalry, and Second Brigade of 20th Pennsylvania Cavalry and 21st New York Cavalry.

September 5, 1864, Taylor, with his 1st New York Veteran Cavalry, was ordered to report to Jeremiah C. Sullivan in the Kanawha Valley, and with his departure, First Brigade was discontinued.

October 20, 1864, Duffie left Cumberland with orders to assume command of all dismounted cavalry, and to assume a remount camp at Hagerstown. Duffie, however, was captured by John S. Mosby's men near Bunker Hill October 24, 1864.

Wynkoop assumed command of First Cavalry Division October 20, 1864, but the division then consisted only of his own Second Brigade of two regiments and a battery of light artillery. November 1, 1864, the 15th New York Cavalry was sent to Martinsburg to join Torbert, and First Cavalry Division was discontinued. Wynkoop remained on duty with his 20th Pennsylvania Cavalry.

December 1864 to July 1865

On December 19, 1864, Thomas M. Harris' First Infantry Division, Department of West Virginia left Winchester for City Point, Virginia, and December 24, 1864 it was attached to Benjamin F. Butler's Army of the James as Independent Division, Twenty-Fourth Corps. Also on December 10, 1864, Isaac H. Duval's Second Infantry Division moved up to occupy the positions vacated by Harris at Stephenson's Depot and at the crossing of the Opequon by the Front Royal Road. Late in the month, the designation of Second Infantry Division was changed to First Infantry Division.

December 19, 1864, Torbert set out on a raid from Winchester toward Gordonsville and the railroads in the vicinity, with William H. Powell's Second Cavalry Division, Department of West Virginia and Wesley Merritt's First Cavalry Division of the Army of the Shenandoah. The raid was unsuccessful, and the expedition returned to Winchester December 28,

1864. The cavalry then went into winter quarters. For details of this expedition, see Army of the Shenandoah, Torbert's Expedition from Winchester to Gordonsville, Virginia; and Custer's Demonstration in the Shenandoah Valley (Engagement at Lacey's Springs).

December 30, 1864, First Infantry Division moved to Martinsburg, and that same day Duval proceeded on to Cumberland with Rutherford B. Hayes' First Brigade. Daniel Johnson's Second Brigade of the division, which was then reduced to one regiment by detachments, was discontinued, and the remaining regiment was left at Martinsburg.

The organization of the troops in the Department of West Virginia at the end of December 1864 was as follows:

DEPARTMENT OF WEST VIRGINIA, George Crook

First Infantry Division, Isaac H. Duval
    First Brigade, Rutherford B. Hayes

Note 1. Headquarters of the division was at Cumberland, Maryland. Until late December 1864, its designation was Second Infantry Division.
Note 2. Daniel Johnson's Second Brigade was discontinued December 30, 1864.

Second Cavalry Division, William H. Powell
    First Brigade, William B. Tibbits
    Second Brigade, Henry Capehart

Note. Second Cavalry Division was in winter quarters at Winchester, Virginia.

District of Harper's Ferry, John D. Stevenson
    Unbrigaded infantry, cavalry, and artillery
    Artillery Brigade, Henry A. Du Pont

Forces West of Hancock, Maryland, Benjamin F. Kelley
First Separate Brigade (Kanawha Valley), John H. Oley
Wheeling, West Virginia, James Washburn

Reorganization of January 1865. The troops of the Department of West Virginia were extensively reorganized in January 1865. Early in the month a new Second Infantry Division was organized from Kelley's command west of Hancock. Kelley was assigned command, with headquarters at Cumberland, Maryland. The division was organized as follows:

Second Infantry Division, Benjamin F. Kelley
    First Brigade, Nathan Wilkinson

Second Brigade, Jacob Higgins

Note. Joseph A. J. Lightburn was ordered to relieve Higgins January 10, 1865.

Kelley's division was posted along the Baltimore and Ohio Railroad from Cumberland to Parkersburg, West Virginia, with regiments at New Creek, Grafton, Philippi, Buckhannon, and Beverly.

Also in January 1865, a Third Infantry Division was organized under John D. Stevenson from troops of the District of Harper's Ferry. The troops of this division guarded the Baltimore and Ohio Railroad from the Monocacy River to Hancock, with garrisons at Harper's Ferry, Maryland Heights, and Martinsburg. The division was organized as follows:

Third Infantry Division, John D. Stevenson
  First Brigade, William H. Seward, Jr.
  Second Brigade, Samuel Graham
  Third Brigade, Roger E. Cook

Note. A First Separate Brigade, Third Division was organized from four batteries of artillery of the District of Harper's Ferry in January 1865, and was discontinued in April of that year.

In effect, the District of Harper's Ferry was discontinued by the organization of Third Infantry Division, and it did not again appear on the rosters of the Department of West Virginia, but in the records there are references to Stevenson's command as the District of Harper's Ferry as late as March 1865.

The First Infantry Division at Cumberland, which consisted of Hayes' First Brigade and two unattached regiments, was not affected by the reorganization of January 1865. Hayes was assigned temporary command of the division February 15, 1865, when Duval departed on leave, and Hiram F. Devol assumed temporary command of First Brigade.

January 13, 1865, George H. Chapman, formerly commander of Second Brigade of George A. Custer's Third Cavalry Division, Army of the Shenandoah, relieved Powell in command of Second Cavalry Division, Department of West Virginia.

February 21, 1865, Crook, commander of the department, and Kelley, commander of Second Infantry Division, were captured at Cumberland, Maryland by a party of enemy cavalry under Jesse McNeil. Stevenson, as the senior officer present, assumed temporary command of the department, and Lightburn assumed command of Second Infantry Division. William H. Seward took charge at Harper's Ferry while Stevenson was at department headquarters at Cumberland.

On February 8, 1865, Grant had instructed Sheridan to move with his cavalry on the Virginia Central Railroad and the James River Canal as soon as the weather would permit, and finally, on February 27, 1865, the movement began. Sheridan took with him First Cavalry Division and Third Cavalry Division of the Army of the Shenandoah, and he did not again return to the valley. On the day of his departure, Sheridan transferred Capehart's Second Brigade, Second Cavalry Division, Department of West Virginia to George A. Custer's Third Cavalry Division as Third Brigade. This left Chapman in command of Second Cavalry Division, Department of West Virginia with only Tibbits' First Brigade. For details of Sheridan's expedition, see Sheridan's Expedition from Winchester to Petersburg, Virginia.

On February 26, 1865, as Sheridan prepared to leave on his expedition, Winfield S. Hancock was assigned command of the Department of West Virginia, and also to the temporary command of all troops of the Middle Military Division not under the immediate control of Sheridan. Hancock assumed command the next day.

Beginning early in March 1865, fourteen new regiments were ordered to Harper's Ferry to report to Stevenson, and these in turn were sent on to Halltown and Charlestown for organization. John R. Brooke was assigned command at Halltown and arrived there March 13, 1865. Thomas W. Egan assumed command at Charlestown March 19, 1865. By the end of the month the regiments at Halltown were organized into First Provisional Division under Brooke, and those at Charlestown into Second Provisional Division under Egan.

Reorganization of April 1865. By an order of April 2, 1865, the troops serving in the Department of West Virginia, and also those of the Army of the Shenandoah were completely reorganized. The Army of the Shenandoah was not a part of the Department of West Virginia, but it is included here because the reorganization affected both commands.

Duval's Brigade, which was the only brigade with First Infantry Division, Department of West Virginia, was transferred to a new Fourth Provisional Brigade, Army of the Shenandoah as First Brigade. First Infantry Division, Department of West Virginia was thus discontinued. Samuel S. Carroll, then in command of Second Infantry Division, Department of West Virginia, was assigned command of Fourth Provisional Division.

First Infantry Division, Department of West Virginia was then reorganized from Second Infantry Division, Department of West Virginia simply by a change in designation, and in turn, a new Second Infantry Division, Department of West Virginia was reorganized from Third Infantry Division, Department of West Virginia, again, simply by a change of designation. Third Infantry Division was thus discontinued.

For more complete information on the reorganization of April 1865, see Army of the Shenandoah.

March 20, 1865, Nineteenth Corps, of which only William Dwight's First Brigade remained in Virginia, was discontinued. By the order of April 2, 1865, reorganizing the Department of West Virginia, William H. Emory, the former corps commander, was ordered to Cumberland to relieve Carroll in command of Second Infantry Division, Department of West Virginia (redesignated April 2, 1865 as First Infantry Division). James W. McMillan, commander of the former Second Brigade, First Division, Nineteenth Corps, was ordered to report to Emory for assignment. Emory assumed command of the new First Infantry Division, Department of West Virginia April 3, 1865, and McMillan was sent to Clarksburg, apparently to command temporarily Wilkinson's First Brigade, First Infantry Division.

April 19 or 20, 1865, Chapman's cavalry brigade was sent to Washington and left the department.

April 22, 1865, Hancock moved his Headquarters Middle Military Division from Winchester to Washington. Torbert was assigned command of the Army of the Shenandoah at Winchester, and Emory was assigned command of the Department of West Virginia at Cumberland. McMillan was assigned command of First Infantry Division April 22, 1865. McMillan resigned May 18, 1865, and Francis Fessenden commanded the division May 18–22, 1865, and then he was relieved by William P. Carlin.

At the end of April 1865, the troops in the Department of West Virginia were organized as follows:

DEPARTMENT OF WEST VIRGINIA, William H. Emory

First Infantry Division, James W. McMillan
  First Brigade, Nathan Wilkinson
  Second Brigade, Rutherford B. Hayes
  Wheeling, West Virginia, James Washburn

Second Infantry Division, John D. Stevenson
  First Brigade, Roger E. Cook
  Second Brigade, Samuel Graham
  Unbrigaded regiments

Note. In April 1865, Cook's Third Brigade was discontinued, and Cook was assigned command of First Brigade in place of William H. Seward, Jr.

First Separate Brigade (Kanawha Valley), John H. Oley
Artillery Brigade, Henry A. Du Pont
  Battery L, 1st Ohio Light Artillery, Frank C. Gibbs
  Battery B, 5th United States Artillery, Henry A. Du Pont

May 25, 1865, Hancock ordered all West Virginia and Maryland troops guarding the railroad to be mustered out, and May 30, 1865, he further ordered that all troops in the Department of West Virginia whose terms of enlistment expired between May 30, 1865 and September 1, 1865 be discharged immediately. By July 1865, the troops in the department consisted of a regiment at Harper's Ferry, a regiment and some cavalry at Cumberland, a regiment and some cavalry at Clarksburg, a regiment at Wheeling, and an infantry regiment and a cavalry regiment in the Kanawha Valley.

OPERATIONS OF THE TROOPS OF THE DEPARTMENT OF WEST VIRGINIA

Gettysburg Campaign, July 1863. Benjamin F. Kelley assumed command of the Department of West Virginia at New Creek June 28, 1863, and two days later established his headquarters at Clarksburg. On July 4, 1863, the day after the Battle of Gettysburg, Kelley was ordered to move eastward with the infantry brigades of Jacob M. Campbell and James A. Mulligan and the mounted troops of William W. Averell's Fourth Separate Brigade, and concentrate at Hancock, Maryland. The purpose of this movement was to have a force in position to harass Robert E. Lee's retreating column if it should attempt to recross the Potomac River at Williamsport on its return to Virginia.

Kelley left Clarksburg with the infantry July 5, 1863, and Averell with the cavalry left Beverly two days later. Kelley reached Hancock July 9, 1863, and then moved on to Fairview, near Cherry Run on the Potomac, July 13, 1863. Averell also advanced, and pushed on to Williamsport July 14, 1863, but upon arriving there he learned that Lee had crossed the river the night before. Averell then marched back and joined the infantry at Cherry Run the next day. Kelley crossed the Potomac July 16–17, 1863 and advanced to Hedgesville, but he retired to Cherry Run July 20, 1863. He again crossed the river and marched to Hedgesville July 25, 1863. From there Averell sent Thomas Gibson's Independent Battalion of cavalry to Winchester, and it occcupied the town July 26, 1863. Averell marched with the rest of his command by way of Martinsburg and Bunker Hill and arrived at Winchester July 30, 1863.

Kelley remained at Hedgesville with the infantry until August 1, 1863, and then marched by way of Romney to New Creek, and was once again in the Department of West Virginia. Averell stayed at Winchester until August 5, 1863, and then he marched west by way of Wardensville and Moorefield, and arrived at Petersburg, in Grant County, West Virginia August 9, 1863. For a further account of the activities of Averell's command, see following sections.

Averell's Raid in West Virginia (Engagement at Rocky Gap, or White Sulfur Springs), August 18–31, 1863.

While at Petersburg, West Virginia on August 15, 1863, Averell received an order from Benjamin F. Kelley (dated August 12, 1863) directing him to move with his command by way of Franklin, West Virginia and Monterey, Virginia to Huntersville, in Pocahontas County, West Virginia. Upon his arrival there, he was to destroy or drive out of the country the Confederate force of William L. Jackson that was reported to be stationed there. Averell was also to destroy the saltpeter works and powder works in Pendleton County.

Averell was delayed in starting until August 18, 1863, while he waited for supplies. He then marched by way of Franklin, where he destroyed the salt works the next day, and he then reached Monterey August 20, 1863. The next day he continued on toward Huntersville, and encountered the enemy about three miles from town. He by-passed this force by a side road and entered the town on the morning of August 22, 1863.

Jackson's cavalry brigade had been encamped at Camp Northwest, near Huntersville, and this camp was captured and destroyed by a cavalry force under John Oley after Jackson had withdrawn. On August 24, 1863, Averell's column resumed the march toward Warm Springs, in Bath County, Virginia, and, with some skirmishing, drove Jackson out of Pocahontas County, through Warm Springs, and over the mountains to the east toward Millboro. Averell decided that he could not overtake Jackson, and he changed his line of march toward Lewisburg, West Virginia.

August 25, 1863, Averell reached Callaghans' in Alleghany County, Virginia, and destroyed salt and saltpeter works on the way. At 4:00 the next morning, he started for White Sulfur Springs, with his troops on the road in the following order, from front to rear: advance guard, 2nd West Virginia Mounted Infantry, 8th West Virginia Mounted Infantry, Thomas Gibson's battalion of cavalry, Chatham T. Ewing's Battery G, 1st West Virginia Light Artillery, 14th Pennsylvania Cavalry, and 3rd West Virginia Mounted Infantry. At 9:30 A.M., twelve miles from Callaghans', the advance guard encountered strong resistance and learned that the enemy was ahead in force. These troops belonged to George S. Patton's brigade of Samuel Jones' Confederate Department of Western Virginia.

Averell's column advanced through a narrow pass into a small valley about one mile long and enclosed on both sides by rugged, rocky heights. On entering the valley, the Federal troopers came under artillery fire. The 2nd West Virginia was ordered to dismount and move up to the summit of the ridge on the right, and a part of the 8th West Virginia was sent to the top of the ridge on the left. The detachment of 8th West Virginia, however, lost its way, and finally joined 2nd West Virginia on the right. Then the main body of 8th West Virginia, under its commander, John H. Oley, moved up the hill on the left.

Meantime, a section of Ewing's battery had been brought up, and it quickly opened fire. Averell's column was about four miles long, and Ewing held off the enemy until all of the Federal regiments had arrived at the front. The 3rd West Virginia and 14th Pennsylvania then dismounted and formed on the right and left of the road. Averell's line was then formed as follows: Oley's 8th West Virginia Mounted Infantry was on the extreme left, about one-half mile from White Sulfur Springs; Francis W. Thompson's 3rd West Virginia Mounted Infantry was on the right of Oley, with its right on the road; Ewing's battery was on the right of Thompson; George R. Latham's 2nd West Virginia Mounted Infantry was to the right of Ewing; and James N. Schoonmaker's 14th Pennsylvania was on the extreme right of the line.

As the Federal line formed, the enemy retired to a second line, about a half mile in rear of the first. Averell then advanced on this new line, but was soon stopped. Firing continued for about three hours, with neither side being able to advance. At 4:00 P.M. Averell decided to make another effort to take the enemy position, and a squadron of 14th Pennsylvania under Captain John Bird was sent forward with the understanding that he would be supported by the rest of the command. No such united effort was made, however, and Bird was driven back. At that time it was nearly dark. Scammon's division from the Kanawha Valley had been expected to come up during the day, but it did not appear. Averell could do nothing but wait for morning.

When daylight came, the enemy was found to be still in position, and there was no word from Scammon. To complicate matters, ammunition was running low, and Averell learned that enemy reinforcements were coming up from the direction of Lewisburg. The battle was renewed, and while the fighting was in progress, Averell made preparations in the rear for a withdrawal. The enemy reinforcements arrived at 10:00 A.M. and made an attempt to turn the Federal left, but this was repulsed. Averell began his retreat at 10:30 A.M. The engagement of August 26–27, 1863 has been called the Engagement at Rocky Gap, or the Engagement at White Sulfur Springs.

Averell's command reached Callaghans' and halted at 5:00 P.M. Fires were built, and the men ate an evening meal, and then, after dark, with the fires still burning, the column took the road toward Warm Springs. The march continued by way of Gatewoods' to Huntersville, and then past Greenbrier Bridge to Big Spring, and finally the column arrived at Beverly August 31, 1863.

Expedition from Beverly and Charleston to Lewisburg (Battle of Droop Mountain), West Virginia, November 1–17, 1863. Late in October 1863, Benjamin F. Kelley, commander of the Department of West Virginia, ordered William W. Averell, commander of First Separate Brigade at Beverly, West Virginia, to organize a force to move on Lewisburg in Greenbrier County to attack and capture, or drive away, a Confederate force reported to be in that vicinity. At Lewisburg, Averell was to be joined by a detachment of Eliakim P. Scammon's division, under Alfred N. Duffie, from the Kanawha Valley. Then Averell, with all the mounted troops, was to proceed by way of Union, West Virginia to the Virginia and Tennessee Railroad at or near Dublin, Virginia for the purpose of destroying the bridge over New River.

On November 1, 1863, Averell left Beverly with the following troops:

Infantry, Augustus Moor
    28th Ohio, Augustus Moor
    10th West Virginia, Thomas M. Harris

Mounted Regiments
    14th Pennsylvania Cavalry, James M. Schoonmaker
    2nd West Virginia Mounted Infantry, Alexander Scott
    3rd West Virginia Mounted Infantry, Francis C. Thompson
    8th West Virginia Mounted Infantry, John H. Oley
    Gibson's Independent Battalion of Cavalry, Thomas Gibson

Artillery
    Battery B, 1st West Virginia Light Artillery, John V. Keeper
    Battery G, 1st West Virginia Light Artillery, Chatham T. Ewing

Averell marched southward on the most direct road to Lewisburg and on November 5, 1863 encountered William L. Jackson's Confederate brigade at Mill Point. Jackson then withdrew to Droop Mountain, about thirty miles from Lewisburg, and he was joined there the next day by John Echols with his brigade and a part of Albert G. Jenkins' brigade, commanded by Milton J. Ferguson. All the enemy troops belonged to Samuel Jones' Department of Western Virginia. Echols assumed command of the combined force, and George S. Patton assumed command of Echols' brigade.

When Averell arrived in front of Droop Mountain, he found the enemy occupying a strong position on the summit. On the morning of November 6, 1863, he ordered Moor to move to the right with his two infantry regiments and a company of cavalry and attack Echols' right and rear. When Moor launched his attack, the three mounted infantry regiments were to dismount and advance against the front of the enemy position.

After a march of nine miles, Moor arrived at his assigned position, and at about 1:45 P.M. began his attack, with Harris' 10th West Virginia on the right and Moor's 28th Ohio on the left. While Moor was getting into position, Schoonmaker brought up his 14th Pennsylvania Cavalry and formed it on the road that ran across the mountain, on the extreme Federal left. John V. Keeper posted his battery on the left and rear of Schoonmaker. They were directed to make a demonstration on the enemy right to divert attention from Moor's movement. The three regiments of mounted infantry were put in position between Moor and Schoonmaker as follows, from right to left: Thompson's 3rd West Virginia on the left of Moor, Scott's 2nd West Virginia in the center, and Oley's 8th West Virginia on the left next to Schoonmaker. The attacks on both the enemy left and right flanks were successful, and about 3:00 P.M. Echols' command was driven from the summit, and Echols' brigade was virtually destroyed.

Meantime, Duffie had started out from Charleston November 3, 1863, with the 34th Ohio Mounted Infantry and 2nd West Virginia Cavalry of his Third Brigade of Scammon's division, and a section of artillery, and arrived at Gauley Bridge the next day. He then marched on the Lewisburg Pike by way of Hamilton to Tyree, where he was joined November 5, 1863 by Carr B. White, with 12th Ohio and 91st Ohio of his Second Brigade of Scammon's division. Duffie then moved on by way of Meadow Bluff, and arrived at Lewisburg on the morning of November 7, 1863. Averell came up from Droop Mountain that evening.

The enemy retreated toward Union, but when Averell attempted to follow he found the road blocked with fallen timber, and then when Duffie reported that his command was unfit for further active service, Averell decided to follow his discretionary orders, which permitted him to return to New Creek if he felt that this was necessary. Averell ordered Duffie to return to the Kanawha Valley, and he directed Moor to march to Beverly with Averell's infantry and a battery, and to take with him the prisoners, wounded, and captured materials. Averell, with the mounted troops, marched by way of White Sulfur Springs and Rocky Gap to Callaghans', and from there by way of the South Branch Valley to New Creek, where he arrived November 17, 1863.

Expeditions against the Virginia Central and the Virginia and Tennessee Railroads

During the spring of 1864, the military activities in the Department of West Virginia were largely related to the importance of the three railroads that ran through the area. These were, from north to south: (1) the Baltimore and Ohio Railroad, which ran across the northern part of the department and connected Baltimore and Washington with the Ohio River and the West; (2) the Virginia Central Railroad, which crossed the Shenandoah Valley through Staunton, and then continued on to the east by way of Rockfish Gap and Charlottesville to Richmond, Virginia; and (3) the Virginia and Tennessee Railroad, which ran just beyond the southern boundary of the department, and connected Richmond with the western part of the Confederacy.

The military planning relating to these railroads included provisions for the protection of the Baltimore and Ohio, and the interruption of traffic on the other two. The continued operation of the Baltimore and Ohio was always of primary interest to the authorities in Washington and to the department commander, and before any attempt could be made to block enemy communications with the West by means of the Virginia and Tennessee Railroad, sufficient troops must be made available to ensure its protection.

In the latter part of 1863, at Henry W. Halleck's request, two expeditions were sent out for the purpose of destroying the Virginia and Tennessee Railroad. The first expedition, which was made in

November 1863, did not reach the railroad; but the second expedition, made during December 1863, succeeded in breaking the track at Salem, Virginia. A description of these expeditions follows.

Raid on the Virginia and Tennessee Railroad, and Demonstrations in the Shenandoah Valley, and from the Kanawha Valley, December 8–24, 1863. On December 5, 1863 in accordance with instructions from Henry W. Halleck, Benjamin F. Kelley, commander of the Department of West Virginia, ordered William W. Averell to move with all available forces of his First Separate Brigade, Department of West Virginia against the Virginia and Tennessee Railroad. He was to march from New Creek by way of Petersburg, Franklin, and Monterey to the line of the railroad at Bonsack's Station or at Salem, Virginia, and upon arrival there he was to destroy the track as completely as possible. When Averell's mission was completed, he was to return to any station on the Baltimore and Ohio between New Creek and Harper's Ferry. To aid in this movement, Joseph Thoburn, commanding Second Brigade of James A. Mulligan's Second Division, Department of West Virginia, was ordered to report to Averell with two infantry regiments. These were to be left at some point on the route of march to guard the forage trains and support Averell's column on its return from the expedition.

Two other movements were planned to divert the enemy's attention while Averell advanced toward the railroad. On December 1, 1863, Eliakim P. Scammon, commander of Third Division, Department of West Virginia, was ordered to advance from the Kanawha Valley by way of Lewisburg and Union to threaten the Virginia and Tennessee Railroad at New River. December 8, 1863, Jeremiah C. Sullivan, commanding First Division, Department of West Virginia, was directed to send all of his cavalry force, with two infantry regiments and a battery, up the Shenandoah Valley and occupy Harrisonburg. From that point the cavalry was to be sent to threaten Staunton. Sullivan's force was to remain at Harrisonburg until December 23, 1863.

In addition to the above troops, Augustus Moor was ordered, on December 7, 1863, to report to Averell with two infantry regiments of First Separate Brigade, and to move forward from Beverly to Droop Mountain for the purpose of cooperating with Scammon in his expected attack on Lewisburg.

On the morning of December 8, 1863, Averell moved out from New Creek with the following troops:

2nd West Virginia Mounted Infantry, Alexander Scott
3rd West Virginia Mounted Infantry, Francis W. Thompson
8th West Virginia Mounted Infantry, John H. Oley
14th Pennsylvania Cavalry, William Blakely
Gibson's Independent Battalion of Cavalry, Thomas Gibson
Battery G, 1st West Virginia Light Artillery, Chatham T. Ewing

On December 10, 1863, Thoburn joined Averell at Petersburg in Hardy County, West Virginia, and together they marched to a point near Monterey. There, Thoburn was placed in charge of the trains and was ordered to take the road to McDowell. Averell continued on, and at Callaghans' learned that Scammon had occupied Lewisburg, and that the enemy had retreated toward Union. Averell then marched by way of Sweet Springs and New Castle and reached Salem on the morning of December 16, 1863. He then destroyed about sixteen miles of track and five important bridges on the line, burned the depot and other railroad buildings, and also the public buildings, and destroyed large quantities of stores accumulated there for the use of Longstreet's army in East Tennessee. At 4:00 P.M. that same day, Averell started on his return along the same route used in his advance. He arrived at Beverly December 24, 1863.

The other movements that had been ordered were carried out as follows: After separating from Averell near Monterey December 12, 1863, Thoburn moved east by way of McDowell and threatened Staunton, in the Shenandoah Valley. He then returned with the trains to Petersburg, West Virginia. Moor advanced from Beverly to Droop Mountain as ordered, but he was unable to communicate with Scammon at Lewisburg, and he marched back to Beverly, where he arrived December 17, 1863. Scammon also advanced as ordered from the Kanawha Valley, and reached Meadow Bluff December 11, 1863. He then moved on, and against some opposition from John Echols' Confederate brigade, he occupied Lewisburg the next day. There he learned that reinforcements were on the way to join Echols, and

December 14, 1863, he left Duffie with his cavalry and a section of artillery to occupy Lewisburg, and withdrew with his main body to Meadow Bluff. Duffie rejoined the infantry at Meadow Bluff about December 17, 1863, and Scammon then returned to the Kanawha Valley.

The demonstration in the Shenandoah Valley was led by George D. Wells, who left Harper's Ferry December 10, 1863 with two regiments of his First Brigade of Sullivan's division, two batteries, and 700 cavalry under William H. Boyd. Wells marched by way of Charlestown, Berryville, and Winchester, and occupied Strasburg December 12, 1863. The cavalry reached Harrisonburg December 19, 1863, and the infantry arrived the next day. While advancing to Harrisonburg, Wells received reports that Fitzhugh Lee's cavalry and infantry under Jubal A. Early were in the valley and that they were attempting to get in his rear and block his retreat route. Accordingly, Wells withdrew from Harrisonburg December 21, 1863, and after marching back through Strasburg and Winchester, arrived at his former camps December 24, 1863.

Expedition against the Virginia and Tennessee Railroad (Engagement at Cloyd's Mountain, May 9, 1864). In preparation for the 1864 campaign in Virginia, Ulysses S. Grant directed Franz Sigel, then commanding the Department of West Virginia, to form two columns and move south against the enemy. One column was to be commanded by George Crook in the Kanawha Valley, and the other, under the personal command of Sigel, in the Shenandoah Valley. Crook was ordered to break the Virginia and Tennessee Railroad by destroying the New River Bridge near Newbern Court House, Virginia, and also the salt works at Saltville if possible. Sigel was to move up the Shenandoah Valley and attempt to draw troops from in front of Crook by threatening the Virginia Central Railroad at Staunton. Both movements were to begin when the Army of the Potomac moved out from around Culpeper Court House toward the Rapidan River and the Wilderness.

On May 2, 1864, Crook left the Kanawha River and, with his Second Infantry Division, Department of West Virginia, started toward New River Bridge on the Virginia and Tennessee Railroad. On the same day, William W. Averell left Camp Piatt, ten miles above Charleston, and marched toward Saltville.

Crook's command was organized as follows:

Second Infantry Division, Department of West Virginia, George Crook
First Brigade, Rutherford B. Hayes
Second Brigade, Carr B. White
Third Brigade, Horatio G. Sickel
1st Battery, Ohio Light Artillery, James R. McMullin
1st Battery, Kentucky Light Artillery, Daniel W. Glassie

Note. Four hundred cavalry under John H. Oley, which started with Averell, joined Crook's column at Shannon's Bridge May 8, 1864.

Averell's column consisted of James M. Schoonmaker's Second Brigade and Alfred N. Duffie's First Brigade of the Second Cavalry Division, Department of West Virginia, and 400 men of the 5th and 7th West Virginia Cavalry. The latter, as noted above, joined Crook's column at Shannon's Bridge. During this expedition, Duffie's brigade retained its former designation of Third Brigade, Third Division (Crook's former command) until May 31, 1864. On that date, at Bunger's Mills, the designation was changed to First Brigade, Second Cavalry Division, Department of West Virginia.

Crook passed through Fayetteville May 3, 1864, and then for the next three days marched southeast without opposition. Then, on May 6, 1864, he encountered enemy skirmishers near Princeton, West Virginia. They were driven back, and Crook reached Shannon's Bridge, about seven miles from Dublin, Virginia. There he was joined by Oley's cavalry from Crook's column. At Shannon's Bridge, Crook learned that Confederate troops were in position at Cloyd's Mountain, about two miles ahead.

The next day, May 9, 1864, Crook moved up to the summit of the mountain with White's Second Brigade and two regiments of Sickel's Third Brigade. Upon arriving there, he found the enemy in position on a spur of the mountain, about three-fourths of a mile ahead. These troops, commanded by Albert G. Jenkins of the Confederate Department of Western Virginia, were posted behind a broad field, and their line commanded the road at a point where it emerged from the mountain. Crook sent White's brigade to the left to turn Jenkins' right flank, and with Sickel's two regiments joined the remainder of his command, which had by that time come up and was about to begin the descent of the mountain. Crook sent Hayes' First Brigade to the left to form on the right of White's brigade, and then sent Sickel to take position on the right of Hayes. When White began his attack, the other two brigades charged across the open field under musketry and artillery fire, and then, after pausing at the base of the ridge on which the enemy forces were posted, charged and drove them from the field. Jenkins was mortally wounded in the attack, and John Mc-Causland succeeded him in command.

After the Battle of Cloyd's Mountain, Crook marched on to Dublin and destroyed the military stores found there. The next day, May 10, 1864, he destroyed New Bridge. Then, his principal mission accomplished, Crook began his return march. He passed through Blacksburg and arrived at Union, where he was joined by Averell's cavalry May 15, 1864. He continued on and arrived at Meadow Bluff, about fifty miles southeast of Gauley Bridge, May 19, 1864, and placed his troops in camp.

While Crook was executing his part of the mission, Averell marched southward through Logan Court House, and arrived at Wyoming Court House May 6, 1864. From there he sent Oley to join Crook, and then with his main column continued on through Abb's Valley in Tazewell County, and arrived at Tazewell Court House May 8, 1864. While there, Averell learned that John H. Morgan and William E. Jones were at Saltville with about 4,500 men. He believed that it would be impossible to capture the town without infantry and artillery, and, accordingly, he turned eastward toward Wytheville, Virginia. Averell arrived near Wytheville May 10, 1864, and ran into Morgan's command and some troops of Jones' brigade. Schoonmaker attacked while Duffie formed his brigade in line of battle. The enemy then advanced, and after four hours of fighting, the Federal troopers still held their ground. It was then dark, and the enemy withdrew. Averell resumed his march and passed through Dublin and Christiansburg, where he destroyed the railroad to a point about four miles east of the town, and also the depot and shops. Averell joined Crook's column at Union May 15, 1864, and then placed his division in camp at Bunger's Mills, near Lewisburg, about May 18, 1864.

Sigel's Movement up the Shenandoah Valley (Engagement at New Market, Virginia, May 15, 1864)

During the latter part of April 1864, Franz Sigel began preparations for an advance up the Shenendoah Valley. This movement was not intended as an offensive operation, and Sigel was, according to Grant's instructions of May 2, 1864, to proceed no farther than Cedar Creek, where he was to watch the country to the south for enemy troop movements.

Sigel arrived at Martinsburg from Cumberland April 25, 1864. The next day he relieved Julius Stahel as chief of cavalry of the department, and ordered him to Martinsburg to assume command of his own First Cavalry Division and Jeremiah C. Sullivan's First Infantry Division, both of which were assembling there. Robert F. Taylor commanded the cavalry division while Stahel was in charge of both divisions.

Sigel's column left Martinsburg April 29, 1864 and marched to Bunker Hill, and then on to Winchester May 1, 1864. Taylor's cavalry was sent on to Cedar Creek and Strasburg to scout the front and flanks of the march. At Winchester, Sigel learned that only John D. Imboden's cavalry and mounted infantry were in the valley, and he decided to continue on toward Staunton and attempt to draw off a part of the enemy forces confronting Crook and Averell on their expeditions to the Virginia and Tennessee Railroad. Before Sigel left Winchester, he sent Jacob Higgins with a detachment of the 23rd Pennsylvania Cavalry from Benjamin F. Kelley's command (West of Sleepy Creek) to Wardensville to protect his right flank, and he also sent William H. Boyd with 300 cavalry into the Luray Valley to cover the left flank. Both detachments were defeated by Imboden, and were of little further service during the advance to New Market. May 9, 1864, Sullivan's infantry division joined the cavalry at Cedar Creek, and then Sigel moved forward through Strasburg to Woodstock, where the cavalry arrived May 10, 1864.

On the morning of May 14, 1864, Augustus Moor left Woodstock with two regiments of infantry from Joseph Thoburn's Second Brigade, 600 cavalry under Timothy Quinn of the 1st New York (Lincoln)

Cavalry, and two sections of artillery. In addition, 300 cavalry under John E. Wynkoop also came up, and one infantry regiment of Moor's First Brigade joined at Edenburg. Moor's troops encountered a part of Imboden's cavalry near Mount Jackson, but they pushed on, with skirmishing, across the Shenandoah River, and followed the enemy as far as New Market, seven miles beyond Mount Jackson and nineteen miles from Sigel at Woodstock. After the infantry arrived, Moor's skirmishers occupied a part of New Market. That evening, Moor formed a line across the road on an elevation north of New Market, between the Shenandoah River on the right and Smith's Creek on the left. Moor was attacked by Imboden's cavalry several times during the evening, but he held his position that night.

After dark, Imboden fell back to a strong position about four miles southwest of New Market, and there during the night he was joined by John C. Breckinridge, commanding the Confederate Department of Western Virginia, with the brigades of John Echols and Gabriel C. Wharton. Also joining that night was the Corps of Cadets of Virginia Military Institute, which consisted of a battalion of four companies of infantry and a section of artillery, under the command of Scott Shipp. Breckinridge had set out to join Imboden May 6, 1864, and had left Staunton for New Market May 13, 1864. On the morning of May 15, 1864, Breckinridge formed his brigades and the cadets in two lines near Shirley's Hill, about one and one-half to two miles southwest of New Market, between the Shenandoah River and the Valley Pike.

When Sigel learned of Moor's encounter with Imboden the day before, he moved out of Woodstock at 5:00 A.M. May 15, 1864 and marched for New Market. Stahel arrived near New Market on the morning of May 15, 1864 and assumed command. Sigel also arrived a short time later, about noon. Moor was ordered to fall back about one-half mile to a new position, and Sullivan's First Infantry Division arrived on the new line at about the same time as Moor.

Sigel formed his line of battle on the slopes of Bushong's Hill, about a mile and a half north of New Market. Alonzo Snow's Battery B, Maryland Light Artillery was on the extreme right, next to the Shenandoah River, and John Carlin's Battery D, 1st West Virginia Light Artillery was on the left of

Snow. One company of George D. Wells' 34th Massachusetts and two companies of William B. Curtis' 12th West Virginia were placed in support of the artillery. Thoburn's Second Brigade was formed between Carlin's battery and the Valley Pike, with Wells' 34th Massachusetts on the right, Jacob Weddle's 1st West Virginia in the center, and Jacob M. Campbell's 54th Pennsylvania on the left, next to the road. Curtis' 12th West Virginia and Henry A. Du Pont's Battery B, 5th United States Artillery were in reserve. Albert Von Kleiser's 30th Battery, New York Light Artillery was put in position across the road, several hundred yards in front of Thoburn's right; and Moor's two regiments, Henry Peale's 18th Connecticut and Horace Kellogg's 123rd Ohio, were placed on the right and left of this battery. Chatham T. Ewing's Battery G, 1st West Virginia Light Artillery was placed on the left of Sigel's line, and Stahel's cavalry was in rear of the left, watching Sigel's left flank.

During the morning of May 15, 1864, Breckinridge remained in position, expecting Sigel to attack. Finally, however, at about 11:00 A.M. he ordered his line to advance. This movement coincided more or less with Moor's withdrawal to the new Federal line. The advancing Confederate troops occupied New Market, and there was an exchange of artillery fire for the next hour. At 2:00 P.M. Breckinridge renewed the advance and struck the first Federal line and drove it back in confusion. Then the attack became general all along Sigel's line. The batteries on the right of Thoburn were driven off the hill, but for a time the infantry on the center of the line held their position. Sigel then ordered a counterattack, and Thoburn's infantry moved forward. The Virginia Military Institute cadets, who up to that time had advanced in reserve, were put in line and aided in driving the Federals back. Breckinridge's line immediately followed. By this time Sigel's right had been turned, and the advancing enemy soon overran Von Kleiser's battery and made a final charge against Thoburn's position. Finally, at about 3:00 P.M., the disorganized remnants of Sigel's command were driven from the field, and although there was intermittent fighting for the next two hours, the battle was over. Du Pont's battery, which was unsupported, covered the more or less orderly retreat.

Sigel's column arrived at Mount Jackson a little

before 7:00 that evening, May 15, 1864, and, after a short rest, continued on to Edenburg, where it arrived at 7:00 the next morning. Again Sigel halted for only a short time, and then marched on and reached Strasburg at 5:00 that evening, May 16, 1864. Early the next morning, Sigel's command crossed Cedar Creek and moved on to the heights beyond, where the troops returned to the same camps that they had occupied at the beginning of the campaign.

May 21, 1864, David Hunter relieved Sigel in command of the Department of West Virginia. The next day, Sigel departed to assume command of the Reserve Division (see above), and he established headquarters at Martinsburg.

The organization of the troops at the Engagement at New Market, Virginia was as follows:

UNION FORCES, Franz Sigel

First Infantry Division, Jeremiah C. Sullivan
    First Brigade, Augustus Moor
    Second Brigade, Joseph Thoburn

First Cavalry Division, Julius Stahel
    First Brigade, William B. Tibbits
    Second Brigade, John E. Wynkoop

Artillery Brigade, Henry A. Du Pont
    Battery B, Maryland Light Artillery, Alonzo Snow
    30th Battery, New York Light Artillery, Albert Von Kleiser
    Battery D, 1st West Virginia Light Artillery, John Carlin
    Battery G, 1st West Virginia Light Artillery, Chatham T. Ewing
    Battery B, 5th United States Artillery, Henry A. Du Pont

Hunter's Lynchburg, Virginia Campaign
May 26, 1864–June 29, 1864

On May 20, 1864, the day before David Hunter assumed command of the Department of West Virginia, Grant informed Halleck that, in his opinion, Hunter's available force could be used to the best advantage by moving up the Shenandoah Valley toward Staunton and the Virginia Central Railroad, and, if possible, advancing as far as Staunton and Gordonsville or Charlottesville. He further stated that Hunter would perform a very useful service if he could hold on his front an enemy force at least equal in size to his own. Accordingly, orders were issued for Hunter to carry out this movement.

Hunter assigned Franz Sigel to replace Max Weber in command of the Reserve Division, and gave him the duty of guarding the Baltimore and Ohio Railroad. Weber, who was given command of the troops on the railroad between the Monocacy River and Sleepy Creek, and Benjamin F. Kelley, who commanded the troops on the railroad west of Sleepy Creek, were directed to report to Sigel. When this arrangement was completed, Hunter prepared to march with the remainder of his command.

On May 26, 1864, Hunter, whose Headquarters Department of West Virginia had been established at Martinsburg, joined the troops of Sigel's former command at Cedar Creek, where they had been in camp since their defeat at New Market May 15, 1864. This command, which consisted of Jeremiah C. Sullivan's First Infantry Division, Julius Stahel's First Cavalry Division, and Henry A. Du Pont's Artillery Brigade, had been reinforced to about 8,500 men and twenty-one guns.

May 26, 1864, Hunter advanced to Woodstock, where he was informed by Halleck that Grant wished him to push on, if possible, to Charlottesville and Lynchburg, and destroy the railroads and the James River Canal. When this was accomplished, he was to either return to the lower Shenandoah Valley, or join Grant's army by way of Gordonsville.

From Woodstock, Hunter marched by way of Mount Jackson and Rude's Hill to New Market, where he remained May 29–30, 1864 while he collected forage. He continued on to Harrisonburg June 2, 1864, and found that John D. Imboden's cavalry was posted about seven miles ahead on the Valley Pike at Mount Crawford. Imboden's line of defense was behind the North River, with its right at Rockland Mills and its left at Bridgewater. Hunter decided not to attack this position, but instead he moved by a road to the southeast to Port Republic, and there he crossed the South Fork of the Shenandoah River and passed the right flank of Imboden's line.

Engagement at Piedmont, Virginia, June 5, 1864. Hunter camped about a mile south of Port Republic on the night of June 4, 1864, and early the next morning advanced on the road running from Port Republic to Staunton (the East Road). About 6:00 A.M., William B. Tibbits' First Brigade of Stahel's First Cavalry Division encountered enemy pickets near Mount Meridian. Tibbits was reinforced by troops of John E. Wynkoop's Second Brigade, First Cavalry Division, and he then pushed forward about a mile, before he was checked by Imboden's cavalry, which had moved up to delay Hunter's march while William E. Jones prepared a defensive position in its rear. Jones had marched from Staunton with three infantry regiments during the night and early morning of June 4, 1864, and was then preparing a line of works on the high ground near Piedmont. The village of Piedmont was about seven miles southwest of Port Republic, and was two miles north of New Hope. It was on the East Road, which ran from Port Republic to Staunton, near the junction of a crossroad that ran northwest to the Valley Pike, about four miles distant.

Imboden resisted the Federal advance for about an hour, but was finally driven back to Crawford's Run, about a mile in front of Jones' position. Jones formed his defensive line as follows: he placed his infantry about one-half mile north of the crossroad running to the Valley Pike, generally facing north, with its left on a loop of Middle River and its right on the East Road. John C. Vaughan's cavalry and mounted infantry took position in the edge of a woods, which extended eastward from a point on the East Road just south of Piedmont, and along the south side of an open field. The left of Vaughan's line rested on the road about three-fourths of a mile south of the right flank of the infantry. By this arrangement, there was a wide gap between the cavalry and the infantry, whose right flank was thus exposed to a Federal attack. When Imboden's cavalry came in, it was formed on the right of Vaughan, with its line curved back, first to the south, and then to the west, and it ended at Round Top Hill, south of New Hope.

Hunter's command arrived in front of Jones' infantry and formed to the right of the East Road. Augustus Moor's First Brigade of Sullivan's division was on the right of the line, and Joseph Thoburn's Second Brigade took position on high ground between the left of Moor's brigade and the East Road. Stahel's cavalry was massed to the right and rear of Moor.

The battle began with artillery fire about 9:00 A.M. June 5, 1864. An hour later, Moor's brigade advanced and drove the enemy back to their main line of works, which were constructed of fallen timber and fence rails. During this action, Du Pont's artillery succeeded in driving back the Confederate batteries from their positions along the East Road. At 1:00 P.M., Moor again attacked but was thrown back, and an enemy counterattack that followed almost reached Thoburn's line. At 1:30 P.M., Hunter sent Thoburn's brigade up a ravine to the southeast to a position on the right flank of Jones' infantry. A half hour later, the enemy made a determined attack on the front of Moor's brigade, but with help from Alfred Von Kleiser's battery and a crossfire from two Federal batteries on the left, the line held.

Finally, Thoburn launched an attack on Jones' exposed right flank, and simultaneously Moor and Wynkoop charged over the works from the front, and the enemy line completely disintegrated. About 1,000 of the enemy were captured, and the rest who were able fled from the field in confusion. Jones was killed during the attack, and Vaughan replaced him in command. It is not clear why, but Vaughan's and Imboden's cavalry did not take part in this engagement, despite an order from Jones to do so when Thoburn attacked. After assuming command, Vaughan led his shattered force to Waynesboro, abandoning Staunton, and he then moved west to Fisherville. Stahel was wounded during the fighting, and Andrew T. McReynolds assumed temporary command of First Cavalry Division. Sullivan was placed in charge of both his own First Infantry Division and First Cavalry Division.

* * * * * * * * * *

On June 6, 1864, the day after the Battle of Piedmont, Hunter occupied Staunton

Meantime, George Crook's Second Infantry Division and William W. Averell's Second Cavalry Division had been ordered from West Virginia to join Hunter at Staunton. Crook left Meadow Bluff May 31, 1864, and Averell started from his camps at Bunger's Mills, near Lewisburg, June 3, 1864. They marched by way of Warm Springs, Goshen, Pond Gap, and Middlebrook, and arrived at Staunton June 8, 1864. There was almost constant skirmishing with enemy scouts and guerrillas during the march, and at Middlebrook John McCausland's and Albert G. Jenkins' brigades attempted to delay the column, but it pressed on.

When reinforced by Crook and Averell, Hunter had with him approximately 18,000 men and thirty guns, and he was then ready to advance toward Lynchburg. Before leaving Staunton, Hunter destroyed factories and supplies, and also several miles of the Virginia Central Railroad, both east and west of the town. June 9, 1864, Moor was sent back by way of Buffalo Gap to Beverly, West Virginia with the 1,000 prisoners captured at Piedmont. These were escorted by 800 men, including Moor's 28th Ohio Regiment, whose terms of enlistment were about to expire. George D. Wells assumed command of Moor's First Brigade, First Infantry Division.

There was also a significant change in the cavalry while the army was at Staunton. On June 9, 1864, Alfred N. Duffie was relieved from command of First Brigade, of Averell's Second Cavalry Division, and was assigned command of Stahel's First Cavalry Division. Stahel had been wounded at Piedmont, and Andrew T. McReynolds was in temporary command of the division until Duffie assumed command. The next day, June 10, 1864, Second Cavalry Division was reorganized by the reassignment of regiments as follows:

Second Cavalry Division, William W. Averell
  First Brigade, James M. Schoonmaker
  Second Brigade, John H. Oley
  Third Brigade, William H. Powell

On June 7, 1864, after the Battle of Cold Harbor, and while Hunter was still at Staunton, Grant sent Philip H. Sheridan with two cavalry divisions on a raid against the Virginia Central Railroad. Sheridan was to join Hunter at Charlottesville, and together the two commands were to wreck the railroad from that point to Hanover Junction. Sheridan became engaged with enemy cavalry at Trevilian Station June 11, 1864, and also again the next day a short distance west of there, and then, being unable to join Hunter, he turned back to rejoin the Army of the Potomac. For additional information, see Sheridan's Trevilian Station Raid, Virginia.

While at Staunton, Hunter learned of Sheridan's inability to reach Charlottesville, and he also was informed that Rockfish Gap, through which he would have to pass to reach Charlottesville, was strongly defended by a force under John C. Breckinridge. He was further informed that a large enemy force was on its way to the valley. After considering this information, Hunter decided not to move on Lynchburg by way of Charlottesville, but through the comparatively open country by the Peaks of Otter.

Early on the morning of June 10, 1864, Hunter left Staunton and marched up the valley toward Lexington on four roughly parallel roads. Duffie's First Cavalry Division moved to the left and, after demonstrating in front of Waynesboro, marched by a road along the western base of the Blue Ridge Mountains to the Tye River Gap. Crook's Second Infantry Division took the Lexington Road on the right, by way of Middlebrook and Brownsburg, and Averell's Second Cavalry Division marched on a parallel road to the right of Crook. Sullivan's First Infantry Division and the artillery brigade advanced on a road through Greenville, midway between Duffie and Crook.

Hunter's command, less Duffie's division, arrived before Lexington June 11, 1864, and found the town defended by McCausland's cavalry. Hunter soon forced McCausland to retire, however, and then occupied the town. While there, Hunter's troops destroyed large quantities of military stores and supplies, and several iron works in the vicinity, and they also burned the Virginia Military Institute and the home of Governor John Letcher.

Meantime, Duffie had crossed the mountains by the Tye River Gap and destroyed a portion of the Charlottesville and Lynchburg Railroad (Orange and Alexandria Railroad) at Arrington's Station (Depot). He then moved on to Amherst Court House, where he received orders from Hunter to rejoin the main force at once. Duffie then marched by way of White's Gap, and arrived at Lexington at noon June 13, 1864. Hunter had lost valuable time while awaiting Duffie's return, and this ultimately may well have prevented his capture of Lynchburg. On June 13, 1864, while Hunter was waiting for news from Duffie, he sent Averell forward to Buchanan to drive McCausland out of the way and secure the bridge over the James River at that place.

June 14, 1864, Hunter moved to Buchanan, and the next day crossed the Blue Ridge by the Peaks of Otter Road. Powell's brigade, which was in the lead, occupied Liberty (present-day Bedford), which was twenty-four miles west of Lynchburg on the Virginia and Tennessee Railroad. June 16, 1864 Hunter marched through Liberty toward Lynchburg. Duffie marched to the left on the Forest (Forestville) Road; Crook advanced along the railroad, destroying the track as he went; and Averell, followed by Sullivan and the reserve artillery, moved forward on the Bedford Turnpike (also called the Salem Turnpike), which was the main road to Lynchburg.

On the morning of June 17, 1864, Crook marched to the Bedford Road at New London, and arrived on the road at 10:00 A.M., eight miles from Lynchburg. He then halted until 4:00 P.M. for Sullivan's division to come up, and then together they moved forward toward Lynchburg, with Crook's division in front. Averell's division advanced on a road to the right that joined the Bedford Pike four miles from Lynchburg. Averell passed the junction before Crook arrived, and, moving ahead on the Bedford Pike, he encountered the enemy in position at the Quaker Church (called in some reports Stone Church). After a brief reconnaissance Averell decided to attack. At first, the division advanced mounted, with James M. Schoonmaker's First Brigade in the center, and the other two brigades in column. John H. Oley's Second Brigade was on the right, and William H. Powell's Third Brigade was on the left. At the church the advancing troopers came under fire, and Schoonmaker and Oley dismounted their men and drove the enemy nearly a mile toward Lynchburg.

At Averell's request, Crook, whose division was following Averell, sent Carr B. White's Second Brigade to support Oley, and also sent Jacob M. Campbell's Third Brigade to the left of the cavalry to protect that flank. By that time it was dark, and Sullivan's division arrived and relieved Crook. All camped on the field that night.

Meantime, Duffie's division had advanced on the Forest (Forestville) Road on the extreme left, and it became engaged about 1:30 P.M. The cavalry fought dismounted, and the action continued for two hours. Duffie then halted for the night at Clay's Mills.

The troops opposing Hunter's advance at Lynchburg on June 17, 1864 were under the command of John C. Breckinridge. After Sigel's defeat at New Market May 15, 1864, Breckinridge, with the brigades of John Echols and Gabriel C. Wharton, was sent to the North Anna River to reinforce Robert E. Lee's Army of Northern Virginia, which was struggling with Grant's army as it advanced toward Richmond. Then, when William E. Jones was defeated by Hunter at Piedmont June 5, 1864, Breckinridge and his two brigades were moved back to Rockfish Gap to reinforce John C. Vaughan. When Hunter moved on up the valley beyond Staunton, Breckinridge moved to Lynchburg and occupied the entrenchments there with his two brigades, Vaughan's command, and some Home Guards and convalescents.

On June 13, 1864, Lee sent Richard S. Ewell's Second Corps of the Army of Northern Virginia, then commanded by Jubal A. Early, to the Shenandoah Valley. Early, with Stephen D. Ramseur's division and one brigade of John B. Gordon's division, arrived at Lynchburg from Charlottesville on the afternoon of June 17, 1864, and the rest of the corps came up the next day. These troops were immediately sent out to meet Hunter. The Confederate works were then manned as follows: Gordon's troops were south of the Bedford (Salem) Pike, just east of the toll gate, with their right on the road; Ramseur's division was on the right of Gordon, north of the road; Breckinridge's command was on the right of Ramseur, with its right south of the Forest (Forestville) Road; and McCausland was on that road.

On the morning of June 18, 1864, Federal skirmishers advanced along the Bedford Pike as far as the toll gate, about two miles from Lynchburg, and there they found the enemy occupying entrenchments. There was only skirmishing along the front there during the afternoon. Crook made a reconnaissance to the right that morning and then returned and took position to support Sullivan, who was on the Bedford Pike. Averell moved out on a demonstration against the Campbell Court House Road, which ran southward out of Lynchburg on the extreme Federal right. Duffie was more active on the Federal left. That morning, he resumed his advance on the Forest Road, and at 9:00 found the enemy at the railroad crossing, four miles from Lynchburg. At 10:30 A.M. he attacked, with Robert F. Taylor's First Brigade on the right of the road, the Horse Artillery on the road, and John E. Wynkoop's Second Brigade on the left. The enemy then retired within their line of entrenchments, two miles from the city. Duffie followed to within one-half mile of these works at Blackwater Creek. He was engaged there during the afternoon, but was unable to advance farther.

Farther south, Early attacked Hunter's position on the Bedford Pike, but he was driven back by Sullivan's division, with help from Campbell's brigade of Crook's division. Breckinridge made repeated attempts to turn the left flank of Hunter's infantry by advancing between Sullivan's division and Duffie's cavalry on the Forest Pike, but after about one and a half hours he was driven back into his works. The fighting ended there at 2:00 P.M. On the Federal right, the enemy also made an attack on Powell's brigade of Averell's division, but this was quickly repulsed.

From prisoners taken during the day, Hunter learned that all of Ewell's Corps (commanded by Early) had arrived at Lynchburg, or were nearby, and, based on this information, he decided to abandon his efforts to take the town. Hunter began his withdrawal during the night of June 18, 1864, and marched through Liberty (Bedford) and Bonsack's Station on the Virginia and Tennessee Railroad to Salem, where he arrived at sunrise June 21, 1864. He then continued on by way of Catawba Valley, New Castle, Sweet Springs, White Sulfur Springs, and Lewisburg, and arrived at Meadow Bluff June 25, 1864. He halted at Gauley Bridge June 27–29, 1864, and then reached Charleston June 29, 1864. Hunter did not long remain in the Kanawha Valley. After pursuing the retreating Federals from Lynchburg for some distance, Early turned north and advanced down the Shenandoah Valley to Winchester, and then crossed the Potomac River into Maryland to threaten Baltimore and Washington. Federal authorities reacted quickly to this threat, and Hunter was ordered to move east with his command to the lower Shenandoah Valley. This movement was made by boat to Parkersburg, and then by the Baltimore and Ohio Railroad to Harper's Ferry and Martinsburg. For further information, see Early's Washington Raid (and Operations in the Shenandoah Valley, Maryland, and Pennsylvania).

The organization of Hunter's forces that took part in the Lynchburg Campaign was as follows:

DEPARTMENT OF WEST VIRGINIA, David Hunter

First Infantry Division, Jeremiah C. Sullivan
    First Brigade, Augustus Moor, to June 9, 1864
        George D. Wells
    Second Brigade, Joseph Thoburn

Second Infantry Division, George Crook
    First Brigade, Rutherford B. Hayes
    Second Brigade, Carr B. White
    Third Brigade, Jacob M. Campbell
    Artillery, James R. McMullin
        1st Battery, Kentucky Light Artillery, Daniel W. Glassie
        1st Battery, Ohio Light Artillery, James R. McMullin

First Cavalry Division, Julius Stahel, to June 5, 1864, wounded
    Andrew T. McAndrews, to June 9, 1864
    Alfred N. Duffie
    First Brigade, William B. Tibbits, May 1864
        Robert F. Taylor
    Second Brigade, John E. Wynkoop

Second Cavalry Division, William W. Averell
    First Brigade, Alfred N. Duffie, to June 9, 1964
        James M. Schoonmaker
    Second Brigade, John H. Oley
    Third Brigade, William H. Powell

Artillery Brigade, Henry A. Du Pont
    Battery B, Maryland Light Artillery, Alonzo Snow
    30th Battery, New York Light Artillery, Conrad Carrolien
    Battery D, 1st West Virginia Light Artillery, John Carlin
    Battery B, 5th United States Artillery, Henry A. Du Pont

* * * * * * * * * *

Early's Washington Raid, July 1864

After Hunter's withdrawal from Lynchburg June 18, 1864, Jubal A. Early followed the retreating Federals as far as Liberty (present-day Bedford), and there, on June 23, 1864, he abandoned the pursuit, and moved down the Shenandoah Valley toward Winchester. He reached Winchester undetected July 2, 1864, but that day Franz Sigel at Martinsburg received reports that the enemy was moving in force down the valley, and this was largely confirmed the next day.

Meantime, Hunter had arrived in the Kanawha Valley, and by July 2, 1864 had been reorganized for further service. George Crook was assigned command of all troops in the Kanawha Valley, and in West Virginia, west of the Allegheny Mountains and south of the Baltimore and Ohio Railroad. Duffie, with his First Cavalry Division, was ordered to report to Hunter and receive orders directly from Headquarters Department of West Virginia; and Averell, with his Second Cavalry Division, was ordered to report to Crook. Crook assumed command July 3, 1864, and by an order of that date designated his new command as the Army of the Kanawha.

Also on July 2, 1864, Grant ordered Hunter to send all of his forces not required to hold the Kanawha Valley back to the Baltimore and Ohio Railroad to protect the line and to prevent enemy raids into Maryland. John H. Oley, with his 7th West Virginia Cavalry, was detached from Second Brigade, Second Cavalry Division (Oley also commanded the brigade), and Oley was assigned command of all Federal forces left in the Kanawha Valley. These consisted of 7th West Virginia Cavalry and four regiments of one-hundred-day regiments of Ohio Militia. That same day, July 2, 1864, Sullivan's First Infantry Division and the artillery brigade were ordered to Martinsburg.

On July 3, 1864, Early arrived in front of Martinsburg, and Sigel withdrew his forces there and at Leetown and crossed the Potomac at Shepherdstown. Max Weber evacuated the Virginia side of the river at Harper's Ferry July 4, 1864, and that evening Sigel arrived with his command at Maryland Heights.

Early did not approach Harper's Ferry, but bypassed the town and crossed the Potomac into Maryland at Shepherdstown July 5–6, 1864, and marched toward Frederick.

Hunter arrived at Parkersburg, West Virginia from Charleston July 4, 1864, and the next day was ordered to take immediate charge of all operations against the enemy forces that were threatening the Baltimore and Ohio Railroad. Hunter remained at Parkersburg until July 8, 1864, sending his forces east to New Creek and Cumberland, and that night he left for Cumberland, where he arrived the next morning. He remained at Cumberland until July 14, 1863, forwarding troops from the west, and he then moved on by way of Martinsburg, and arrived at Harper's Ferry that night.

Meantime, while Hunter's movement eastward across West Virginia was in progress, Early arrived in front of Washington July 11, 1864. He remained there only until the following night, and then marched by way of Leesburg toward the Shenandoah Valley. He was followed by Horatio G. Wright, who had assumed command of a special force consisting of his own Sixth Corps, Army of the Potomac, a detachment of Nineteenth Corps, John R. Kenly's brigade from the Middle Department, and some cavalry.

Jeremiah C. Sullivan's First Infantry Division arrived at Martinsburg July 10, 1864, and then moved on to Harper's Ferry July 13, 1864. The next day, Sullivan assumed command of all troops at Harper's Ferry and vicinity, including Howe's District of Harper's Ferry. Upon assuming command, Sullivan assigned James A. Mulligan to the command of Thomas M. Harris' brigade of the Reserve Division, Department of West Virginia. July 15, 1864, Sullivan left a garrison at Harper's Ferry, and with the remainder of his command, which consisted of his own First Infantry Division and Mulligan's Brigade (formerly Harris') of the Reserve Division, marched to join Wright's command in Virginia. Sullivan crossed the Potomac near Berlin (present-day Brunswick) and moved to Hillsboro, in the direction of Leesburg. When he crossed the Potomac, Sullivan left the Department of West Virginia and came under Wright's orders. Duffie arrived at Harper's Ferry July 15, 1864, with his First Cavalry Division, and was ordered on to report to Sullivan at Hillsboro.

Crook arrived at Harper's Ferry during the night of July 15, 1864, with Daniel Frost's Third Brigade of Second Infantry Division (formerly commanded by Jacob M. Campbell), and there assumed command of all troops of the Department of West Virginia that were under orders to join Wright's command in Virginia. Crook arrived at Hillsboro July 16, 1864, and relieved Sullivan in command of the forces of the Department of West Virginia that were assembled there. Sullivan was directed to report to Hunter at Harper's Ferry. Crook's command consisted of the following:

First Infantry Division, Joseph Thoburn

First Brigade, George D. Wells
Second Brigade, William G. Ely

Second Infantry Division
Third Brigade, Daniel Frost

Reserve Division
Mulligan's Brigade, James A. Mulligan

First Cavalry Division, Alfred N. Duffie
First Brigade, William B. Tibbits
Second Brigade, George Middleton

Note 1. Thoburn assumed command of First Infantry Division when Sullivan was relieved by Crook.
Note 2. Ely assumed command of Second Brigade, First Infantry Division when Crook was assigned command of the division.
Note 3. Frost assumed command of Third Brigade, Second Infantry Division, relieving Jacob M. Campbell, when the brigade arrived at Camp Piatt from Lynchburg.
Note 4. Middleton was in command of John E. Wynkoop's Second Brigade, First Cavalry Division, but he was relieved by Jacob Higgins July 22, 1864.

When the remainder of Crook's Second Infantry Division arrived from Parkersburg, Isaac H. Duval's Second Brigade (Carr B. White was honorably mustered out of the service July 11, 1864) was ordered to remain at Martinsburg, and July 18, 1864, Rutherford B. Hayes' First Brigade was sent to Purcellville to join Crook. Averell's Second Cavalry Division arrived at Martinsburg July 17–22, 1864, and remained there and in the vicinity to protect the Baltimore and Ohio Railroad. Averell was assigned command of all forces at Martinsburg, and Duval with his brigade reported to him for orders. Averell reported directly to Hunter, because Crook was operating outside of the department. At this time Crook called his command the Army of the Kanawha.

When Wright's command, which then included Crook's forces, advanced to the Shenandoah River, Joseph Thoburn was placed in command of his First Infantry Division and Frost's Third Brigade, Second Infantry Division, and was ordered to effect a crossing of the river. Thoburn was successfully engaged at Snicker's Ferry (or Parker's Ford) July 18, 1864, and he established his command on the west bank of the river, but was recalled that night. Frost was mortally wounded during the fighting.

July 19, 1864, Averell advanced from Martinsburg with Duval's brigade and three regiments of his cavalry division to Stephenson's Depot, and then moved on and occupied Winchester two days later. During the night of July 19, 1864, Early withdrew up the Shenandoah Valley toward Strasburg; and the next day, Wright, considering his mission accomplished, marched back toward Washington with Sixth Corps and Detachment Nineteenth Corps. After Wright's departure, Crook again reported to Hunter.

Crook then moved with his command to Winchester, where he joined Averell July 22, 1864, and assumed command of the entire force. That day he reorganized the infantry of his Army of the Kanawha into three divisions of two brigades each as follows:

ARMY OF THE KANAWHA, George Crook

First Division, Joseph Thoburn
First Brigade, George D. Wells
Second Brigade, William G. Ely

Second Division, Isaac H. Duval
First Brigade, Rutherford B. Hayes
Second Brigade, Daniel D. Johnson

Note. Johnson assumed command of Second Brigade July 22, 1864, when Duval assumed command of the division.

Third Division, James A. Mulligan
First Brigade, Thomas M. Harris
Second Brigade, John P. Linton

Note 1. Third Division was organized July 22, 1864.
Note 2. Harris' brigade was organized from regiments on the line of the Baltimore and Ohio Railroad near Harper's Ferry.
Note 3. Linton's brigade was organized from Third Brigade, Second Infantry Division, formerly commanded by Jacob M. Campbell.

Artillery
30th Battery, New York Light Artillery, Conrad Carrolien
1st Battery F, 1st West Virginia Light Artillery, George W. Graham
1st Battery, Ohio Light Artillery, George P. Kirtland

On July 23, 1864, Early, who had halted at Strasburg, learned that Wright had returned to Washington; and he immediately advanced against Crook's Army of the Kanawha at Winchester. The next day Early defeated Crook at Kernstown and drove him back to the Potomac River, which he crossed at Williamsport July 26, 1864. Crook left his cavalry to guard the Potomac and moved with the infantry to Pleasant valley.

When news of Early's advance and Crook's defeat reached Washington, Wright again assumed command of Sixth Corps and Detachment Nineteenth Corps, and marched by way of the Rockville, Maryland Road to join Hunter. Wright arrived on the Monocacy River July 28, 1864, and that day the order of July 13, 1864 temporarily assigning Hunter's troops to Wright's command during the pursuit of Early from Washington, was rescinded. Also that day, Crook again reorganized the infantry of his Army of the Kanawha. Third Division was discontinued, and its First Brigade and Second Brigade were consolidated and assigned to First Infantry Division as Third Brigade under the command of Jacob M. Campbell. On July 28, Hunter ordered Wright to Harper's Ferry, and he arrived there the next day and went into camp at Halltown near Crook.

After defeating Crook at Kernstown, Early moved on down the valley to the Potomac River, and then sent John McCausland with his Confederate cavalry northward into Pennsylvania, where he burned Chambersburg July 30, 1864. Averell's Second Cavalry Division pursued McCausland to Hancock, Maryland, crossed the Potomac, and advanced by way of Romney to a point near Moorefield. There, on August 7, 1864, Averell attacked and routed the enemy cavalry. Duffie's First Cavalry Division moved west to Hancock to support Averell, but it did not proceed further.

Meantime, after the burning of Chambersburg, the authorities were concerned that Early might again invade Maryand from the west, and Hunter ordered all of his forces, except the cavalry divisions and the garrison of Harper's Ferry, to move from Halltown to the east side of South Mountain to watch the passes. Crook's and Wright's commands moved to the vicinity of Frederick, Maryland, but by August 2, 1864, it was clear that Early did not intend to invade Maryland, and was instead withdrawing up the valley toward Winchester. On August 2, 1864, Hunter with Crook moved to Monocacy Junction, where he established headquarters, and then his command was broken up. August 2, 1864, Detachment Nineteenth Corps was assembled under Wil-

liam H. Emory at Monocacy Junction, and on August 4, 1864, it was sent by Hunter to Harper's Ferry to reinforce Howe. Wright's Sixth Corps was ordered to march back to Washington, but it was halted the next day in the vicinity of Buckeystown, Maryland. On August 5, 1864, Grant directed Hunter to move with his available force to Halltown, four miles southwest of Harper's Ferry, and that night Crook with his two infantry divisions moved to that point. At 9:00 A.M. August 6, 1864, Emory with his First Division and Third Brigade, Second Division of Detachment Nineteenth Corps arrived at Halltown from Harper's Ferry, and Wright with Sixth Corps joined the other troops there that same day. For details of Early's Washington raid, and the operations of Crook's forces in the Shenandoah Valley, including the engagements at Snicker's Ferry and Kernstown, see Early's Washington Raid (and Operations in the Shenandoah Valley, Maryland, and Pennsylvania).

Sheridan's Shenandoah Valley Campaign August 7, 1864–November 28, 1864

On August 6, 1864, Sheridan arrived at Harper's Ferry from the Army of the Potomac, and assumed command of all troops in the field, which consisted of the troops that Hunter had assembled at Halltown. The next day, Sheridan was assigned command of the newly created Middle Military Division, which consisted of the Middle Department and the departments of West Virginia, Washington, and the Susquehanna. This brought all of the troops of the Department of West Virginia under Sheridan's control.

August 8, 1864, Sheridan designated Crook's command, which consisted of First and Second Infantry Divisions, Department of West Virginia, as the Army of West Virginia. It should be noted here that during the Shenandoah Valley Campaign Crook's command was commonly called Eighth Corps, because many of the troops formerly belonged to that corps. It may be that the latter designation was used because it was shorter and more convenient than Army of West Virginia, but whatever the reason, it was not officially correct because Eighth Corps was properly the designation for the troops serving in the Middle Department.

On August 8, 1864, two days after Sheridan assumed command of the troops at Harper's Ferry in preparation for his Shenandoah Valley Campaign, Howe was ordered to Washington, and Max Weber was assigned temporary command of the District of Harper's Ferry. He was relieved by John D. Stevenson August 15, 1864.

While Sheridan was operating south of Winchester during the Valley Campaign, Stevenson was given the responsibility for guarding the line of communications from Harper's Ferry to the front; and September 30, 1864, he was reassigned command of the District of Harper's Ferry, including Martinsburg and the lower Shenandoah Valley.

Before embarking on his Shenandoah Valley Campaign, Sheridan's army was strongly reinforced. When Sheridan assumed command at Harper's Ferry, Averell's Second Cavalry Division, Department of West Virginia was near Moorefield, West Virginia, and Duffie's First Cavalry Division was at Hancock, Maryland. Sheridan ordered both divisions to report to him without delay in the lower valley. The rest of Detachment Nineteenth Corps, two cavalry divisions from the Army of the Potomac, and a provisional brigade under Charles R. Lowell, Jr. also joined the army.

In September 1864, Sheridan began his advance against Early. Accompanying him were Crook's Army of West Virginia and Averell's Second Cavalry Division as a part of what came to be known as the Army of the Shenandoah. Crook was under the direct orders of Sheridan, and Averell was under the direction of Alfred T. A. Torbert, Sheridan's chief of cavalry.

The army was engaged at the Battle of Opequon Creek September 19, 1864, and at Fisher's Hill September 21–22, 1864, and it then advanced to Harrisonburg, Virginia. Sheridan withdrew to Cedar Creek, and there his army, temporarily under the command of Horatio G. Wright, was attacked early on the morning of October 19, 1864 and driven back beyond Middletown. At that point, Sheridan rejoined the army and in an attack that afternoon routed Early's forces and drove them up the valley.

Crook's Army of West Virginia played a conspicuous part in the Federal successes at the Opequon and at Fisher's Hill, but it was surprised and completely disorganized during the early morning attack at Cedar Creek. Averell's Second Cavalry Division was present at Opequon Creek and at Fisher's Hill, but Sheridan was not pleased with Averell's performance and replaced him in command of the division by William H. Powell September 23, 1864. Only Alpheus S. Moore's First Brigade of Powell's division was engaged at Cedar Creek.

The organization of the troops of the Department of West Virginia that served with Sheridan during the period August 1864–November 1864 was as follows:

ARMY OF WEST VIRGINIA, George Crook

First Infantry Division, Joseph Thoburn, to October 19, 1864, killed
  Thomas M. Harris
  First Brigade, George D. Wells, to October 13, 1864, mortally wounded
    Thomas F. Wildes
  Second Brigade, William G. Ely, to September 18, 1864
    Robert S. Northcott, to October 1864
    William B. Curtis
  Third Brigade, Thomas M. Harris, to October 19, 1864
    Milton Wells

Note. Second Brigade was not engaged during this period, but was guarding the trains, and was on duty at Winchester.

Second Infantry Division, Isaac H. Duval, to September 19, 1864, wounded
  Rutherford B. Hayes
  First Brigade, Rutherford B. Hayes, to September 18, 1864
    Hiram F. Devol
  Second Brigade, Daniel D. Johnson, to September 19, 1864, wounded
    Benjamin F. Coats

Artillery Brigade, Henry A. Du Pont

The Second Cavalry Division, which reported to Alfred T. A. Torbert, chief of cavalry of the Middle Military Division, was organized as follows:

Second Cavalry Division, William W. Averell, to September 23, 1864
  William H. Powell, to September 26, 1864
  George A. Custer, to September 30, 1864
  William H. Powell
  First Brigade, James M. Schoonmaker, to October 1864

Alpheus S. Moore
Second Brigade, Henry Capehart

Note. Moore commanded First Brigade at the Battle of Cedar Creek October 19, 1864.

Sheridan's army, including Crook's infantry and Powell's cavalry, remained in camp on Cedar Creek until November 9, 1864, and it then moved back and went into camp near Kernstown. It remained there until late November 1864, when the campaigning for the year ended.

For details of the organization and operations of the Army of West Viginia and of Second Cavalry Division during the period August 7, 1864–November 28, 1864, see Shenandoah Valley Campaign (Sheridan).

DEPARTMENT OF WESTERN VIRGINIA

The Department of Western Virginia was created September 19, 1861, to consist of that part of the state of Virginia west of the Blue Ridge Mountains. The territory of the new department was taken from parts of the departments of the East, the Potomac, and the Ohio. William S. Rosecrans was assigned command, with headquarters in the field. The troops then operating within the limits of the Department of Western Virginia formerly belonged to Rosecrans' Army of Occupation of Western Virginia, Department of the Ohio. Rosecrans assumed command of the new department October 11, 1861, and that day announced the organization of the department. For details of the organization and operations of the Army of Occupation prior to October 11, 1861, see Western (West) Virginia Operations, May 26, 1861–October 11, 1861.

November 9, 1861, the department was redefined to consist of that part of the state of Virginia originally included in the Department of the Ohio. This region was bounded on the south by the Great Kanawha River; and on the east by the Greenbrier River, and a line from the river to the southwest corner of Maryland, and from there along the western boundary of Maryland to the Pennsylvania state line, and from that point northward to the

northeast corner of McKean County in Pennsylvania. Headquarters of the department was established at Wheeling December 11, 1861.

In a general order from headquarters of the army dated January 23, 1862, George B. McClellan noted that the boundaries of the department were incorrectly defined in the Army Register for 1862, and stated that they should be defined as follows: on the west, the western boundary of Virginia; on the north and east, the boundaries of Pennsylvania and Maryland; on the east, the western slope of the Allegheny Mountains; and on the south, the Tennessee state line.

The eastern limit of the department was extended March 3, 1862 to include the valleys of the South Branch of the Potomac River, the Cow Pasture Branch of the James River to the Balcony Falls, the Roanoke River west of the Blue Ridge, and the New River. The eastern boundary of the Department of Western Virginia was then defined as follows: beginning at the north, the Flintstone Creek in Maryland; and in Virginia, the South Branch Mountain, Town Hill Mountain, Branch Mountain or Big Ridge, the North or Shenandoah Mountain, Purgatory Mountain, and the Blue Ridge and Allegheny Mountains to the border of North Carolina. The added territory was taken from the Department of the Potomac.

The Department of Western Virginia was merged into the Mountain Department March 11, 1862 (ordered March 3, 1862).

DISTRICTS IN THE DEPARTMENT OF WESTERN VIRGINIA

Affairs in the Department of Western Virginia were administered largely by the creation of several military districts. These were:

Cheat Mountain District. When the Department of Western Virginia was created, Joseph J. Reynolds, commanding First Brigade, Army of Occupation of Western Virginia, Department of the Ohio, was in charge of the region around Cheat Mountain and Elkwater. Reynolds remained in command until December 20, 1861, when the Cheat Mountain District was formed. Robert H. Milroy was assigned command of the district, which was bounded on the north by the Baltimore and Ohio Railroad; on the east by, and including, Cheat Mountain; and on the south by the District of the Kanawha (see below). The principal posts in the district were Beverly, Elkwater, and Huttonsville. There was no change in the district until the department was merged into the Mountain Department March 11, 1862.

District of Grafton. The District of Grafton was organized in the Department of the Ohio, and consisted of the troops guarding the Baltimore and Ohio Railroad and the Northwestern Railroad. Benjamin F. Kelley was assigned command. October 22, 1861, Kelley was ordered with his command to Romney, Virginia to assume temporary command of the Department of Harper's Ferry and Cumberland until the arrival of Frederick W. Lander, who had been assigned command, but was wounded at Edwards Ferry that day. In the reorganization of the Department of Western Virginia December 20, 1861, Kelley was assigned command of the newly constituted Railroad District (see below). The principal posts in the District of Grafton were Parkersburg, Clarksburg, Grafton, Wheeling, and Rowlesburg.

District of the Kanawha. The District of the Kanawha was constituted December 20, 1861, to consist of both banks of the Gauley and Kanawha rivers, and all of that part of the department south of these rivers. Jacob D. Cox assumed command December 27, 1861 (assigned December 20, 1861). The principal posts in the district were Point Pleasant, Buffalo, Charleston, Gauley Bridge, Summersville, and Fayetteville (also called Fayette and Fayette Court House). There was no change in the district until the Department of Western Virginia was merged into the Mountain Department March 11, 1862.

Railroad District. The Railroad District was organized from the District of Grafton December 20, 1861, and it consisted of the railroads of the department and all posts along the lines. Benjanim F. Kelley was assigned command. The principal posts were Parkersburg, Clarksburg, Grafton, Wheeling, and Rowlesburg. There was no change in the district until the Department of Western Virginia was merged into the Mountain Department March 11, 1862.

TROOPS IN THE DEPARTMENT OF WESTERN VIRGINIA

In October 1861, when the Department of Western Virginia was organized, the following troops were present within its limits:

Joseph J. Reynolds commanded a brigade, whose troops were at Cheat Mountain, Elkwater, and Beverly. December 20, 1861, this command was organized as the Cheat Mountain District, and Robert H. Milroy was assigned command.

Troops of the District of Grafton were posted along the Baltimore and Ohio Railroad and the Northwestern Railroad, and were commanded by Benjamin F. Kelley. December 20, 1861, these troops were organized as the Railroad District under Kelley.

Henry W. Benham commanded a brigade at Camp McNeil, near Gauley Bridge, and Robert L. McCook commanded a brigade at Camp Anderson, also near Gauley Bridge. Both brigades were discontinued when the troops went into winter quarters.

Robert C. Schenck commanded a brigade at Camp Ewing, ten miles east of Gauley Bridge. In November 1861, Schenck, who was seriously ill, left for home, and Eliakim P. Scammon assumed command of his brigade. At the end of November 1861, Scammon's brigade was at Fayetteville.

Jacon D. Cox's Kanawha Brigade was in the Kanawha River Valley.

John L. Ziegler was at Ceredo with six West Virginia regiments. George Crook, with his 36th Ohio Regiment, was at Summersville, and regiments were stationed at the following places: Buckhannon, Camp Carlile, Camp Montgomery, Clarksburg, Cross Lanes, Parkersburg, Sutton, Red's House, and near Charleston.

The composition of the forces in the Western Department changed materially during the fall and winter of 1861–1862 by the transfer of regiments to Kentucky and to the Army of the Potomac, and also by the arrival of new regiments. In November 1861, the following regiments were sent to Don Carlos Buell's army of the Department of the Ohio, which was then forming in Kentucky: George D. Wagner's 15th Indiana, Milo S. Hascall's 17th Indiana, John Beatty's 3rd Ohio, William K. Bosley's 6th Ohio, Robert L. McCook's 9th Ohio, William H. Lytle's

10th Ohio, William S. Smith's 13th Ohio, and Jacob Ammen's 24th Ohio. McCook, Ammen, and Hascall were assigned to command brigades in Buell's army.

September 6, 1861, Frederick W. Lander was ordered to report for duty in the Army of the Potomac, and he was assigned command of a brigade. He generally served along the Potomac and the Baltimore and Ohio Railroad until wounded at Edwards Ferry October 22, 1861. On January 1, 1862, Thomas J. (Stonewall) Jackson left Winchester, on an expedition to Romney, Virginia, and Rosecrans was ordered to rush troops from the Department of Western Virginia to aid Lander, who had returned to duty, and was then in command along the Baltimore and Ohio Railroad in the vicinity of Hancock, Maryland. Jackson arrived opposite Hancock January 4, 1862 and shelled the town, but after a few days moved on and occupied Romney, which had been evacuated by Union troops.

In January 1862, seven regiments from the Railroad District and three regiments from the Cheat Mountain District of the Department of Western Virginia were assembled under Lander, and these were organized into a division of three brigades, known as Lander's Division, Army of the Potomac. Nathan Kimball, colonel of 14th Indiana, was assigned command of First Brigade; Jeremiah C. Sullivan, colonel of 13th Indiana, was assigned command of Second Brigade; and Erastus B. Tyler, colonel of 7th Ohio, was assigned command of Third Brigade. The 13th Indiana, 14th Indiana, and 7th Ohio were from the Cheat Mountain District, and these three regiments were assigned, one each, to the three brigades of the division. Their commanders, as senior colonels, were assigned command of the brigades.

To replace the regiments transferred to Kentucky and to the Army of the Potomac, ten newly organized West Virginia regiments, three new Ohio regiments, one Illinois regiment, and two regiments of the Maryland Home Brigades were assigned to the Department of Western Virginia.

OPERATIONS IN THE DEPARTMENT OF WESTERN VIRGINIA

There were many skirmishes and expeditions by small parties of Union troops in Western Virginia during the period October 11, 1861–March 11, 1862, but there were only a few more serious operations. This was due in part to the fact that during much of this time the troops of the department were in winter quarters.

Operations in the Kanawha and New River Region, November 1–19, 1861. After the Engagement at Carnifix Ferry September 10, 1861 (see Western [West] Virginia Operations, May 26, 1861–October 11, 1861), John B. Floyd withdrew with his Confederate Army of the Kanawha to Big Sewell Mountain, and then on to Meadow Bluff, Virginia. On October 6, 1861, Robert E. Lee, who then was directing military affairs in Western Virginia, devised a plan to drive Rosecrans' forces from their camps near Gauley Bridge, and thereby open the way into the Kanawha Valley. According to this plan, Floyd was to move from Meadow Bluff to the south bank of the Kanawha River and cut the line of communications of the Union forces on the Gauley and New rivers. Lee was then to advance on Rosecrans' front with William W. Loring's Army of the Northwest and, with the help of Floyd, drive the Federals out of the Kanawha Valley.

Floyd began his advance October 6, 1861. He crossed the New River and moved down the left bank through Fayetteville, and November 1, 1861 arrived on the heights of Cotton Hill, opposite Gauley Bridge. He opened fire with his artillery, but he did not attempt to cross.

Loring's command at Big Sewell Mountain was unable to move because of a lack of supplies, and also because of bad roads, and finally, on October 20, 1861, Lee called off his proposed movement. Ten days later Lee left Western Virginia for Richmond, and Floyd was thus left alone between New River and the Kanawha.

About October 27, 1861, Rosecrans learned that Floyd was moving from Raleigh Court House (Beckley) toward his line of communications, and he was aware of the possibility that Lee might make a frontal attack while Floyd moved against his rear. When Floyd opened fire from the hills across from Gauley Bridge on November 1, 1861, Rosecrans formulated a plan to cut off and destroy this force before Lee could interfere. At that time the Federal troops were in position as follows: Robert C.

Schenck's brigade was at Camp Ewing, about ten miles east of Gauley Bridge; Robert L. McCook's brigade was about eight miles east of Gauley Bridge, near Miller's Ferry on New River; Henry W. Benham's brigade was six miles east, in rear of McCook; and Jacob D. Cox's Kanawha Brigade was largely at Gauley Bridge.

The plan proposed by Rosecrans was as follows: McCook's brigade was to remain opposite Miller's Ferry, where it would threaten to cross, and would also be in position to hold in check any force under Lee that might advance on the Lewisburg Road. Schenck's brigade was to cross the river at Bowyer's Ferry, or at some point below it, and march to Cotton Hill. Benham's brigade, which was encamped below McCook, was to move by night down East River to Gauley Bridge, and then on down the Kanawha River to a point opposite Loop Creek. Benham was then to cross the river and advance toward the flank and rear of Floyd's command. Cox's brigade was to remain at Gauley Bridge.

Rosecrans' movement started slowly, principally because of bad weather and high water. Benham crossed at Loop Creek, as ordered, November 6, 1861, but he then made very slow progress. On the morning of November 10, 1861, a part of Cox's brigade was sent across the river, and the next day it occupied Cotton Hill and Huddleston, which was on the road to Fayetteville. Benham did not reach Cotton Hill, eight miles from Loop Creek, until 3:00 P.M. November 12, 1861.

When the Federal forces advanced on Cotton Hill, Floyd fell back to Fayetteville, and on November 13, 1861 continued his retreat. That night Benham's brigade occupied the town. Earlier that day, Schenck's brigade crossed New River and bivouacked at Huddleston. Benham pursued Floyd for about fourteen miles beyond Fayetteville, and then returned to his camp November 15, 1861. Schenck's brigade remained at Fayetteville, but Schenck became ill and Eliakim P. Scammon assumed command of his brigade. November 26, 1861, Benham was arrested for neglect of duty, and he then left for New York on a surgeon's certificate.

Engagement at Camp Allegheny, Virginia, December 13, 1861. During the winter of 1861–1862, Confederate forces under Edward Johnson, colonel of the 12th Georgia, occupied a camp on the summit of Allegheny Mountain. His position extended across the Staunton-Parkersburg Pike, and was located just off present-day Route 250 in Pocahontas County. Robert H. Milroy, commander of the Cheat Mountain District, decided to attack and destroy Johnson's camp; and he organized an expedition consisting of troops from the 9th Indiana, 13th Indiana, 25th Ohio, 32nd Ohio, and 2nd West Virginia, and also James R. Bracken's cavalry. Milroy advanced with these troops up Allegheny Mountain, and attacked the enemy camp. There were charges and countercharges during most of the day, with no decisive results. Finally, however, Federal troops began to straggle toward the rear, and when the attack could no longer be sustained, Milroy returned with his command to his camps.

FIELD ARMIES

★ ★ ★ ★

ARMY OF THE DEPARTMENT OF PENNSYLVANIA (PATTERSON)

The force that Robert Patterson organized at Chambersburg, Pennsylvania and led into Virginia at Williamsport, Maryland during the Bull Run Campaign of July 1861, has been called the Army of the Department of Pennsylvania, the Army of Pennsylvania, and the Army of the Shenandoah. For details of the organization and operations of this army, see Department of Pennsylvania, April 27, 1861–August 24, 1861.

ARMY OF THE DISTRICT OF NORTH CAROLINA

Shortly after John J. Peck assumed command of the District of North Carolina, Department of Virginia and North Carolina in August 1863, he issued orders under the heading Headquarters Army and District of North Carolina. Thus, in effect the troops in the District of North Carolina became the Army of the District. These troops were not at any time assembled as a field force, but were assigned as garrisons of the various posts in the sub-districts of North Carolina. When Innis N. Palmer relieved Peck April 25, 1864, he referred to his command simply as the District of North Carolina. For a description of the troops under Peck's command, see the following: Department of Virginia and North Carolina, Districts in the Department of Virginia and North Carolina, District of North Carolina; and

Department of Virginia and North Carolina, Operations in the Department of Virginia and North Carolina.

ARMY OF GEORGIA

In September 1864, after the Federal occupation of Atlanta, Georgia, John B. Hood marched northward from Lovejoy's Station with his Confederate Army of Tennessee toward Tennessee. He hoped by this move to force William T. Sherman to move northward out of Georgia to protect the state. Sherman left Henry W. Slocum's Twentieth Corps, Army of the Cumberland to garrison Atlanta, and with the remainder of his army marched in pursuit of Hood as far as Gaylesville, Alabama. There, he sent David S. Stanley's Fourth Corps, Army of the Cumberland and John M. Schofield's Twenty-Third Corps, Army of the Ohio to reinforce George H. Thomas in Tennessee; and with Jefferson C. Davis' Fourteenth Corps, Army of the Cumberland and John A. Logan's Fifteenth Corps and Frank P. Blair's Seventeenth Corps of the Army of the Tennessee returned to the vicinity of Atlanta. Sherman made his headquarters at Kingston, Georgia, and began preparations for his march through Georgia to Savannah. November 9, 1864, Sherman organized the four corps of his army into two wings as follows: a Right Wing under Oliver O. Howard, consisting of Fifteenth Corps and Seventeenth Corps of the Army of Tennessee; and a Left Wing under Henry W. Slocum, consisting of Fourteenth Corps and Twentieth Corps of the Army of the Cumberland. When Slocum assumed command of

Alpheus S. Williams took charge of Twentieth Corps.

The designations used to describe Sherman's army during the Savannah Campaign and the Campaign of the Carolinas are somewhat confusing. On November 10, 1864, Slocum's command was announced as the Left Wing, Army of Georgia, and this implies that the name given to Sherman's army was the Army of Georgia, and that Howard's two corps constituted the Right Wing, Army of Georgia. This is further supported by the fact that some communications from Headquarters Military Division of the Mississippi were directed to Howard as commander of the Right Wing, Army of Georgia. Thus it seems virtually certain that the army that Sherman organized for the march through Georgia was known as the Army of Georgia, and that Howard commanded the Right Wing and Slocum the Left Wing. On the other hand, during the Savannah Campaign and the march through the Carolinas, Howard signed his orders and official communications under the heading "Headquarters Army of the Tennessee," and his command was referred to as the Right Wing, or as the Army of the Tennessee. During the same period, Slocum signed his official papers under the heading "Headquarters Left Wing, Army of Georgia," but his command was commonly called, although unofficially, the Army of Georgia. Finally, on March 28, 1865, after Sherman's army had reached Goldsboro, North Carolina, Fourteenth Corps and Twentieth Corps were officially constituted by a presidential order as the Army of Georgia. A further note should be added here: until March 28, 1865, the troops of Slocum's two corps technically belonged to George H. Thomas' Department of the Cumberland, because they had not officially been transferred from it.

Sherman's army left Atlanta November 15, 1864, arrived near the coast about December 10, 1864, and after a short siege occupied Savannah December 21, 1864. For details of the organization and operations of the Army of Georgia during this period, see Savannah Campaign (Sherman's March through Georgia). Slocum's Left Wing, Army of Georgia left Savannah in January 1865, and marched on the left of Sherman's army through South Carolina, and arrived at Fayetteville, North Carolina March 11, 1865. It then left Fayetteville for Goldsboro March 15, 1865, and was engaged at Averasboro March 16,

1865, and at Bentonville March 19–21, 1865. Slocum's command arrived at Goldsboro March 23, 1865.

While at Goldsboro, on March 28, 1865, Sherman reorganized his army for further operations as follows:

Right Wing (Army of the Tennessee), Oliver O. Howard
Center (Army of the Ohio), John M. Schofield
Left Wing (Army of Georgia), Henry W. Slocum

Note. Schofield's Army of the Ohio had been transferred from Tennessee to the Department of North Carolina, and it joined Sherman's army at Goldsboro. See Department of North Carolina, January 31, 1865–May 19, 1866, Troops in the Department of North Carolina.

The Army of Georgia advanced with the rest of Sherman's army to Raleigh, North Carolina April 10–13, 1865, and then on April 26, 1865, Joseph E. Johnston surrendered his army to Sherman, and thus ended the war in the East. For details of the organization and operations of the Army of Georgia during the period January 1865 to April 1865, see Carolinas Campaign.

The army left Raleigh for Washington April 30, 1865–May 1, 1865, and marched on different roads by way of Oxford, North Carolina to Taylor's Ferry on the Roanoke River. From there, Fourteenth Corps proceeded by way of Boydton and Nottoway Court House to Richmond, Virginia. Twentieth Corps moved to the same point by way of the Boydton Plank Road and Blacks and Whites (present-day Blackstone). From Richmond, Fourteenth Corps marched by way of Hanover Court House, Chilesburg, Raccoon Ford on the Rapidan River, Stevensburg, Rappahannock Station, and Centerville, and arrived near Alexandria, Virginia May 18, 1865. Twentieth Corps also passed through Hanover Court House, and then moved by way of Ashland, Spotsylvania Court House, Chancellorsville, United States Ford on the Rappahannock River, Brentstville, and Fairfax Station, and arrived at Alexandria May 19, 1865.

The Army of Georgia marched in the Grand Parade in Washington May 24, 1865, and then camped near the city. June 4, 1865, the western regiments serving with Twentieth Corps were organized into a temporary division under Alpheus S. Williams, and this was assigned to Fourteenth

Corps. The next day, twelve eastern regiments with Twentieth Corps were transferred to Christopher C. Augur's Department of Washington, and the remaining regiments with Twentieth Corps were mustered out by June 13, 1865. On that date, Twentieth Corps was discontinued. Fourteenth Corps was ordered to Louisville, Kentucky to report to John A. Logan's Army of the Tennessee, and it left Washington June 9–12, 1865. The Army of Georgia was officially discontinued June 17, 1865, and Slocum was assigned to command the Department of Mississippi June 27, 1865.

ARMY OF THE JAMES

Organization of the Army. Ulysses S. Grant was assigned command of the Armies of the United States March 9, 1864, and the next day announced that he would make his headquarters with George G. Meade's Army of the Potomac. His plan for the spring campaign called for a simultaneous advance of the Federal field armies, both East and West, against the Confederate armies opposing them. In the East the objective of the Army of the Potomac was to be Robert E. Lee's Army of Northern Virginia, and Grant proposed to move forward in Virginia toward Richmond to meet and destroy it. April 2, 1864, Grant ordered Benjamin F. Butler, commander of the Department of Virginia and North Carolina, to organize in his department a field force to cooperate with Meade's movement. According to Grant's instructions Butler was to seize City Point, move his command to the south side of the James River, and then operate against Richmond from that direction.

Butler's army, later to be known as the Army of the James, was to consist of about 10,000 men of Tenth Corps from Quincy A. Gillmore's Department of the South, and about 23,000 men of Eighteenth Corps from Butler's own Department of Virginia and North Carolina. Tenth Corps was ordered to assemble at Gloucester Point, Virginia, and Eighteenth Corps at nearby Yorktown. April 21, 1864, William F. Smith assumed command at Yorktown (assigned April 19, 1864) and of all troops in the vicinity, and was given the task of supervising the reorganization of the two corps.

During the period April 14–29, 1864, the troops of Tenth Corps were transferred from the Department of the South to Gloucester Point, and there they were reorganized under the immediate direction of Alfred H. Terry. After supervising the embarkation of the troops, Gillmore arrived at Gloucester Point May 4, 1864, and assumed command that day.

During the latter part of April 1864, the garrisons of the posts and districts of the Department of Virginia and North Carolina were reduced in size, and the troops of Eighteenth Corps thus obtained were assembled near Yorktown. There they were reorganized into a field force of three divisions under William F. Smith.

While near Yorktown, during the period April 30, 1864 to May 4, 1864, the Army of the James was organized as follows:

ARMY OF THE JAMES
William F. Smith, to May 2, 1864
Benjamin F. Butler

TENTH CORPS, Alfred H. Terry, to May 4, 1864
Quincy A. Gillmore

First Division, Robert S. Foster, to May 4, 1864
Alfred H. Terry
First Brigade, Francis B. Pond, to May 2, 1864
Joshua B. Howell
Second Brigade, Harris M. Plaisted, to May 2, 1864
Joseph R. Hawley
Third Brigade, Joseph R. Hawley, to May 2, 1864
Harris M. Plaisted
Artillery Brigade, Alfred P. Rockwell
1st Battery, 1st Connecticut Light Artillery, Alfred P. Rockwell
5th Battery, New Jersey Light Artillery, Zenas C. Warren

Note 1. Robert S. Foster was assigned as chief of staff of Tenth Corps May 6, 1864.
Note 2. May 2, 1864, the designation of Plaisted's Second Brigade was changed to Third Brigade, and Hawley's Third Brigade to Second Brigade.

Second Division, Samuel M. Alford, to May 2, 1864
John W. Turner
First Brigade, Guy V. Henry, to May 2, 1864
Samuel M. Alford
Second Brigade, William B. Barton
Artillery Brigade, George T. Woodbury
4th Battery, New Jersey Light Artillery, George T. Woodbury
Battery B, 1st United States Artillery, Samuel S. Elder

Battery D, 1st United States Artillery, John S. Gibbs

Third Division, Adelbert Ames
First Brigade, Richard White
Second Brigade, John D. Rust, to May 2, 1864
Jeremiah C. Drake
Artillery Brigade, Alger M. Wheeler
33rd Battery, New York Light Artillery, Alger M. Wheeler
Battery C, 3rd Rhode Island Heavy Artillery, Martin S. James

EIGHTEENTH CORPS, Benjamin F. Butler, to May 2, 1864
William F. Smith

First Division, William T. H. Brooks
First Brigade, Gilman Marston
Second Brigade, Hiram Burnham
Third Brigade, Horace T. Sanders
Artillery Brigade, Theodore H. Schenck
Batteries K and M, 3rd New York Light Artillery, James R. Angel
Battery L, 4th United States Artillery, John S. Hunt
Battery A, 5th United States Artillery, Charles P. Muhlenberg
4th Battery, Wisconsin Light Artillery, George B. Easterly

Second Division, Isaac J. Wistar, to May 4, 1864
Godfrey Weitzel
First Brigade, Charles A. Heckman
Second Brigade, Griffin A. Stedman, Jr., to May 7, 1864
Isaac J. Wistar
Artillery Brigade, Frederick M. Follett
7th Battery, New York Light Artillery, Peter C. Regan
Battery F, 1st Rhode Island Light Artillery, James Belger
Battery D, 4th United States Artillery, James Thompson

Division of United States Colored Troops, Edward W. Hinks (also Hincks)
First Brigade, Edward A. Wild
Second Brigade, Samuel A. Duncan
Battery B, 2nd United States Colored Light Artillery

Cavalry Division, August V. Kautz
First Brigade, Simon H. Mix
Second Brigade, Samuel P. Spear

Note. Kautz's division was organized April 28, 1864.

Charles K. Graham commanded a naval force,

which was organized February 9, 1864 from the army gunboats in the Department of Virginia and North Carolina; and this was later designated as the Naval Brigade, Army of the James. This brigade was active on the James and Appomattox rivers during the advance of the army to Drewry's Bluff, and also during the operations about Petersburg. For further information about the organization of the Army of the James, see Tenth Corps, Army of the James, and also Eighteenth Corps, Army of the James.

Movement of the Army to Bermuda Hundred, May 4–6, 1864. On the night of May 4, 1864, Tenth Corps and Eighteenth Corps embarked on transports, and early the next morning moved up the James River. They were convoyed by ships of S. Phillips Lee's North Atlantic Blockading Squadron and Graham's Naval Brigade of army gunboats. The transports arrived at Bermuda Hundred, at the confluence of the James and Appomattox rivers, during the evening of May 5, 1864, and by the next morning the Army of the James had disembarked. Edward A. Wild's First Brigade of Edward W. Hinks' division of Eighteenth Corps landed at Fort Powhatan on the south bank of the James, and at Wilson's Wharf, about five miles below, on the north bank of the river. Hinks' other brigade, Samuel A. Duncan's Second Brigade, landed at City Point on the south bank of the James at the mouth of the Appomattox River.

Kautz's Cavalry Division remained near Portsmouth, Virginia until May 5, 1864, and then marched by way of Suffolk on an expedition to cut the Petersburg and Weldon Railroad at the crossings of Stony Creek, Rowanty Creek, and the Nottoway River.

On the morning of May 6, 1864, the Army of the James advanced about six miles, and took position at a narrow point of Bermuda Hundred Neck, with its right resting on the James River and its left on the Appomattox River near Port Walthall. This line, which was about three miles in length, was strongly entrenched and was held as a defensive position until the end of the war. The line was about two and one-half miles from the Richmond and Petersburg Railroad, and when first occupied was held by Smith's Eighteenth Corps on the right and Gillmore's Tenth Corps on the left.

While the above-described movements of the Army of the James were in progress, the Army of the Potomac was engaged with Lee's army at the Battle of the Wilderness.

Operations against the Railroads, May 6–11, 1864.

May 6, 1864, Charles A. Heckman's First Brigade, Second Division, Eighteenth Corps was sent out on a reconnaissance toward Petersburg. The next day William T. H. Brooks, with the brigades of William B. Barton, Jeremiah C. Drake, and Harris M. Plaisted of Tenth Corps and Hiram Burnham's brigade of Eighteenth Corps, advanced to Port Walthall Junction for the purpose of destroying the Richmond and Petersburg Railroad. Brooks was sharply engaged the next day, and about sunset withdrew to the entrenched lines without accomplishing his mission. That same day, May 7, 1864, Kautz destroyed the Petersburg and Weldon Railroad bridge over Stony Creek.

Butler was inactive May 8, 1864, but the next day he advanced toward the Richmond and Petersburg Railroad with the following troops: Godfrey Weitzel's Second Division, Eighteenth Corps; Brooks, with Gilman Marston's and Burnham's brigades of his First Division, Eighteenth Corps; Terry, with Joshua B. Howell's and Joseph R. Hawley's brigades of his First Division, Tenth Corps; Samuel M. Alford's brigade of John W. Turner's Second Division, Tenth Corps; and Richard White's brigade of Adelbert Ames' Third Division, Tenth Corps. When Butler's command reached the railroad, Weitzel's division and Brooks' two brigades moved south toward Petersburg, but they were stopped by strong enemy positions behind Swift Creek. Terry's two brigades destroyed some track May 9, 1864, and they were engaged at Chester Station the next day. The Federal troops remained on Swift Creek and at Chester Station that night and returned to their camps the next day.

Meantime, Kautz's cavalry had destroyed the railroad bridge over the Nottoway River, and then marched back to City Point May 10, 1864.

May 1, 1864, Robert M. West was assigned command of an unattached cavalry force consisting of two colored regiments, and this was assigned to William F. Smith's command at Yorktown. West remained at Williamsburg when the Army of the James departed, but he joined Butler at Bermuda Hundred May 9, 1864. His brigade consisted of Jeptha Garrard's 1st United States Colored Cavalry and George W. Coles' 2nd United States Colored Cavalry.

Engagement at Drewry's Bluff, May 16, 1864. On the morning of May 12, 1864, Butler left his entrenched line at Bermuda Hundred and advanced along the Richmond-Petersburg Pike toward Richmond. His command consisted of the divisions of Brooks and Weitzel of Smith's Eighteenth Corps, and Terry's and Turner's divisions of Gillmore's Tenth Corps. A force was left behind under the command of Howell to man the line of defenses, and Hinks' division remained along the James River. Most of Ames' division was posted at Port Walthall Junction to cover the rear of the army from the direction of Petersburg. Richard White, commanding the First Brigade of Ames' division, accompanied Terry's division with two regiments of his brigade; and later, May 16, 1864, Drake reinforced Weitzel with two regiments of his Second Brigade of Ames' division.

When Butler began his advance, Kautz started with his cavalry division on a raid from Chester Station against the Richmond and Danville Railroad and the South Side (Petersburg-Lynchburg) Railroad.

During Butler's advance toward Drewry's Bluff on May 12, 1864, Turner's division of Tenth Corps was temporarily placed under Smith's control. Smith's divisions were on the right of the pike, with Brooks near the road, Weitzel on his right, and Turner on the extreme right near the James River. Gillmore, with Terry's division, moved on the left of the pike. Butler halted that night on Procter's Creek, and the next morning resumed his advance along the pike toward the enemy works at Drewry's Bluff. Gillmore, with Terry's division and Marston's brigade of Brooks' division of Eighteenth Corps, marched to the left in an effort to turn the right of the enemy entrenchments at the head of Procter's Creek. About noon, Turner's division moved from the right of Smith's line to the left of the pike, where it rejoined Tenth Corps, and advanced on the right of Terry. Smith moved forward between the pike and the river, with Brooks' division on the left and Weitzel's division on the right. At that time, Brooks' division consisted only of Burnham's Second Brigade and half of Horace T. Sanders' Third Brigade. Two regiments of Third Brigade were serving as camp guard, and Marston's First Brigade was with Gillmore on the left of Butler's line.

The enemy entrenchments ran west from Drewry's Bluff for about two and a half miles so as to enclose the Richmond and Petersburg Pike and the railroad, and they then continued on to the north along the west side of the railroad. An exterior (or advanced) line branched off from the main (or interior) line near Drewry's Bluff, and ran to the southwest to Procter's Creek. There it crossed the creek near the railroad bridge, about one mile in front of the main line, and continued on to Wooldridge Hill, about one-half mile west of the railroad.

May 13, 1864, Terry's division arrived at Wooldridge Hill, on the extreme enemy right of the exterior line. The 3rd New Hampshire Regiment of Hawley's brigade charged the works on the hill, but it was driven back. At about the same time White, with two regiments of his brigade (temporarily attached to Terry's division), attacked the enemy position from the front. Terry was preparing for a second attack with Hawley's brigade when the enemy abandoned their entrenchments and retired toward Drewry's Bluff. Gillmore's troops followed until dark and gained possession of about one mile of the outer line.

The next morning Gillmore continued to move down the line of works and formed a junction with Turner's division, which was on the left of Smith's line. Brooks' division moved into a part of the outer works east of the pike, and then Brooks', Terry's, and Turner's divisions held about two and one-half miles of this line. The enemy, however, remained in full possession of the interior line. Weitzel's division did not occupy any part of the enemy entrenchments, but it constructed breastworks in front of the junction point of the two enemy lines near Drewry's Bluff. Heckman's First Brigade was on the right of Weitzel's position, and Isaac J. Wistar's Second Brigade was on the left.

There was skirmishing along Butler's front May 15, 1864, but there were no further attacks that day. Smith realized that the right of his line was exposed to a flank attack, and he moved Heckman's brigade back to cover the road running to the Federal entrenchments at Bermuda Hundred. As a further precaution, three regiments of Ames' division, which were at the Half-Way House, were placed at Smith's disposal.

The Confederate forces at Drewry's Bluff were commanded by Pierre G. T. Beauregard, and consisted of about 17,000 men organized into three divisions. A Right Division was commanded by Robert F. Hoke, a Left Division by Robert Ransom, Jr., and a Reserve Division by Alfred H. Colquitt. At 4:45 on the morning of May 16, 1864, Ransom's brigade advanced in a dense fog near Drewry's Bluff and struck Weitzel's division on Butler's right flank. Heckman's brigade was surprised and, after several hours of confused fighting, was forced to withdraw. Heckman and several hundred of his men were captured, and George J. Stannard assumed command of First Brigade. Wistar's brigade, on the left of Heckman, was also driven back; but Brooks' division, which then consisted only of Burnham's Second Brigade and a part of Sanders' Third Brigade, held its ground. Farther to the left, Hoke's division attacked Gillmore's line but was repulsed. Soon after the fighting started, Drake came up to reinforce Weitzel with two regiments of his Second Brigade of Ames' division.

The enemy continued its attempts to turn Weitzel's right, and Smith finally withdrew to a new position across the pike, about three-fourths of a mile from the Confederate outer line. Smith remained in this position during the remainder of the day. Meantime, Gillmore had ordered Terry and Turner to move to the right and attack the flank of the enemy forces that were engaged with Smith. About 10:00 A.M., however, Butler ordered Gillmore to fall back, and then to move to the right and form in the rear of Smith's line near the Half-Way House. This was done to hold open the road back to Bermuda Hundred. Gillmore reached his assigned position about noon, but toward evening Butler retired with his entire command to the entrenched line at Bermuda Hundred. Beauregard came up on the morning of May 17, 1864, and established a fortified line in front of Butler's position. This effectively prevented any further advance of the Army of the James toward Richmond, or toward Petersburg from the north.

During Butler's operations near Drewry's Bluff, Kautz destroyed stores, track, and installations on the Richmond and Danville Railroad at Coalfield,

Powhatan, and Chula; and then completed some destruction of the South Side Railroad at Blacks and Whites (present-day Blackstone), Wellville, and Wilson's Station. Kautz returned to City Point during the evening of May 17, 1864.

There were several command changes in the Army of the James during the latter part of May 1864. Richard White was captured May 16, 1864, and Louis Bell succeeded him in command of First Brigade, Third Division, Tenth Corps. Two days later Henry R. Guss succeeded Bell. Heckman was also captured May 16, 1864, and George J. Stannard succeeded him in command of First Brigade, Second Division, Eighteenth Corps. May 17, 1864, Arthur H. Dutton succeeded Horace T. Sanders in command of Third Brigade, First Division, Eighteenth Corps. Weitzel was assigned chief of engineers of the Army of the James May 20, 1864, and John H. Martindale succeeded him in command of Second Division, Eighteenth Corps. Apparently Butler was not pleased with Wistar's handling of his Second Brigade, Second Division, Eighteenth Corps at Drewry's Bluff, and he replaced him with Griffin A. Stedman May 18, 1864. It appears that Wistar held no further command, and he resigned September 15, 1864.

The Defenses of Bermuda Hundred. When the Army of the James reoccupied the entrenchments at Bermuda Hundred after the Engagement at Drewry's Bluff, Gillmore's Tenth Corps took position on the right and Smith's Eighteenth Corps on the left. On Gillmore's part of the line, Terry's First Division was on the right, next to the James River; Ames' Third Division was on the left; and Turner's Second Division was in reserve. On Smith's line, Brooks' First Division was on the left of Ames' division; and Martindale's Second Division (formerly commanded by Weitzel) was on the left of Brooks, next to the Appomattox River. Butler immediately began work strengthening the line of defenses, and this was continued during the rest of the month. During this time there was skirmishing along the front, with occasional limited attacks. May 20, 1864, the enemy launched a strong attack on the pickets covering the front of Terry's and Ames' divisions and occupied the advance rifle pits. The attack was soon halted, however, and the rifle pits in front of Terry's division were retaken by Howell's brigade.

Battle of Cold Harbor, June 1–3, 1864. May 22, 1864, while the Army of the Potomac was moving from Spotsylvania Court House toward the North Anna River, Grant learned of Butler's defeat at Drewry's Bluff. He then ordered Butler to keep sufficient men to hold City Point and the defenses at Bermuda Hundred, and to send all of his available troops to join the Army of the Potomac. William F. Smith was assigned command of the force that was to join Grant. The order was repeated May 25, 1864, and Smith was directed to move his command by water and disembark at White House on the Pamunkey River. Smith took with him Brooks' First Division and Martindale's Second Division of Eighteenth Corps, and Turner's Second Division and Ames' Third Division of Gillmore's Tenth Corps, and during the night of May 28, 1864 and the morning of May 29, 1864, this force embarked at Bermuda Hundred and City Point for White House. On May 30, 1864, before Smith joined the Army of the Potomac, the two divisions of Tenth Corps were consolidated to form a temporary Third Division, Eighteenth Corps under Charles Devens, Jr. Smith's corps participated in the attacks at Cold Harbor June 1–3, 1864, and then returned to Bermuda Hundred June 14, 1864. For details of the organization of Eighteenth Corps and its operations May 30, 1864 to June 12, 1864, see Richmond, Virginia Campaign, 1864, Operations about Cold Harbor.

The troops of the Army of the James that were left behind with Butler when Smith departed for Cold Harbor consisted of Terry's First Division, Tenth Corps; Hinks' division, Eighteenth Corps; Kautz's Cavalry Division; and two unassigned regiments of United States Colored Cavalry, which were formerly a part of Robert M. West's command at Williamsburg, Virginia. Terry's division remained in its former position at Bermuda Hundred on the right of the line of defenses, next to the James River. Wild's brigade of Hinks' division was at Wilson's Wharf and Fort Powhatan on the James River, and Duncan's brigade of Hinks' division was at City Point and Spring Hill, on the south bank of the Appomattox River below Port Walthall. Kautz's cavalry was near Bermuda Landing.

On May 26, 1864, in anticipation of Smith's departure for Cold Harbor, Butler began preparations for the occupation of that part of his line of defenses that would be vacated by the divisions of Ames, Brooks, and Martindale. Turner's division was in reserve at the time and not in the entrenchments. Terry's division of Tenth Corps was to remain in the defenses, and this division, together with all men of Tenth Corps not able to march, was to hold the right of the line. Kautz was ordered to dismount his cavalry, and his two dismounted brigades were to occupy the line then held by Brooks' division. Kautz was assigned command of the line then occupied by Smith's two divisions. Francis B. Pond was assigned command of a temporary brigade composed of his own 62nd Ohio Regiment, Horace T. Sanders' 19th Wisconsin, and George W. Cole's dismounted 2nd United States Colored Cavalry. Cole's and Sanders' regiments were to replace Martindale's division in the line, and 62nd Ohio was to form a reserve for Pond's brigade. Pond was placed under Kautz's orders. Three regiments of Duncan's brigade, Hinks' division were assigned as a reserve for Kautz's line. In addition, all men of Eighteenth Corps unable to march were ordered to report to Kautz. Gillmore was assigned command of the entire line of defenses.

Three days later, however, Butler modified his orders of May 26, 1864 for the occupation of the defenses at Bermuda Hundred. Kautz was assigned command of the dismounted brigades of Simon H. Mix and Samuel P. Spear on the left of Terry's division, and also of the artillery on that part of the line. Turner, who was left without a command when his Second Division, Tenth Corps was assigned to Eighteenth Corps May 30, 1864, was assigned command of the forces of all arms on the left of Kautz's command. Turner assumed command of his part of the line May 30, 1864, and his force consisted of Pond's brigade; Duncan's Second Brigade, Hinks' division; Benjamin F. Onderdonk's 1st New York Mounted Rifles; and Frederick M. Follett's artillery. Both Kautz and Turner, and also Terry, reported to Gillmore. May 31, 1864, Duncan's brigade was sent to Spring Hill when that post was attacked, but it returned to the defenses June 2, 1864.

May 29, 1864, Henry L. Abbot, colonel of 1st Connecticut Heavy Artillery, was announced as chief of artillery for the Line of Defenses. Earlier, on May 17, 1864, Abbot had been assigned command of the Siege Artillery, Army of the James.

Engagement at Petersburg, June 9, 1864. June 8, 1864, Butler assigned Gillmore to the command of an expedition to attempt the capture of Petersburg. Early the next morning Gillmore, with Hawley's Second Brigade of Terry's division, advanced toward Petersburg on the City Point Road; and Hinks, with two regiments of his division, marched on the Jordan's Point Road, to the left of Hawley. After proceeding for some distance, Gillmore halted without attacking, and at 1:00 P.M. withdrew his command. Kautz, with Spear's brigade and Everton J. Conger's 1st District of Columbia Cavalry of Mix's brigade, moved that morning to the left of Hawley and to the south of Petersburg, and then advanced on the Jerusalem Plank Road toward the city. Kautz carried some of the enemy works but was finally halted. When Gillmore failed to attack on his right, Kautz withdrew. That evening all of Gillmore's command returned to Bermuda Hundred.

Assault at Petersburg, June 15–18, 1864. As an aftermath of his fiasco at Petersburg June 9, 1864, Gillmore was relieved of command of Tenth Corps June 14, 1864, and Alfred H. Terry was assigned temporary command. Robert S. Foster, Gillmore's chief of staff, was assigned temporary command of Terry's former First Division, Tenth Corps. At Grant's suggestion, Butler's order of June 14, 1864 relieving Gillmore was withdrawn; and June 17, 1864, a new order was issued in which Gillmore was relieved at his own request. William T. H. Brooks, commanding First Division, Eighteenth Corps, assumed command of Tenth Corps June 18, 1864, relieving Terry.

June 12–14, 1864, ten regiments of the Ohio National Guard, which were composed of one-hundred-day men, arrived at Bermuda Hundred to reinforce Butler, and these were assigned positions in the line of defenses. June 13, 1864, 148th Ohio National Guard and 1st Maryland Cavalry were assigned to Kautz's line, and were constituted as a brigade under Andrew W. Evans.

June 14, 1864, Smith's Eighteenth Corps arrived at Bermuda Landing on its return from Cold Harbor. Grant then ordered Smith to cross with his command to the south side of the Appomattox River, and advance the next morning against the enemy lines in front of Petersburg. Kautz's cavalry division was withdrawn from the line of defenses that day, June 14, 1864, and it was ordered to cross the Appomattox and take position so as to guard the left of the army. The works vacated by Kautz, which were on the left of Hawley's brigade of Terry's division, were then occupied by three Ohio National Guard regiments. These were placed under the command of Joseph C. Abbott, commander of the 7th New Hampshire of Hawley's brigade.

Early on the morning of June 15, 1864, Smith crossed the Appomattox with his Eighteenth Corps and Kautz's cavalry division, and advanced toward Petersburg. The troops of the Army of the James left in the defenses of Bermuda Hundred were placed under the command of Terry. These consisted of Terry's own First Division, Tenth Corps under Robert S. Foster; the artillery of the three divisions of Tenth Corps (two of which were detached); William B. Barton's First Brigade of Adelbert Ames' temporary Third Division, Eighteenth Corps (formerly commanded by Charles Devens, Jr.); a brigade under John W. Turner; and a number of unattached regiments, largely of the Ohio National Guard.

When Smith arrived in front of the Confederate works at Petersburg, he formed his troops, in order from right to left, as follows: Martindale's division, Brooks' division, Hinks' command, and N. Martin Curtis' Second Brigade and Louis Bell's Third Brigade of Ames' division. Late in the afternoon of June 15, 1864, Brooks' division and Hinks' command, supported by the brigades of Bell and Curtis, attacked and captured a part of the enemy works, which they held during the night. At that time, the leading troops of the Army of the Potomac were approaching Petersburg from Cold Harbor after having crossed the James River near Windmill Point. Troops of Winfield S. Hancock's Second Corps relieved Hinks' command and the brigades of Bell and Martin, but they all remained on the field. Thomas H. Neill's Second Division, Sixth Corps relieved Brooks' division June 17, 1864.

David A. Russell's First Division and James B. Ricketts' Third Division of Sixth Corps, Army of the Potomac were sent to reinforce Butler at Bermuda Hundred while Eighteenth Corps was absent south of the Appomattox. They arrived June 16–17, 1864, and remained in the defenses until June 19, 1864. Beginning on June 17, 1864, troops of Eighteenth Corps began to move back to Bermuda Hundred, where they relieved the two divisions of Sixth Corps. The latter then moved to Petersburg, where they relieved Martindale's division and Samuel A. Duncan's brigade of Hinks' division, which was attached to it.

For details of the operations of Eighteenth Corps and Kautz's cavalry during this period, see Operations about Petersburg and Richmond, Virginia, 1864–1865, Operations of June 1864, Assaults at Petersburg, June 15–18, 1864.

Reorganization of the Army of the James, June 1864. By an order of June 19, 1864, the two corps of the Army of the James were reorganized. Tenth Corps, which prior to that date consisted only of First Division and some miscellaneous troops, was reorganized to consist of three divisions. First Division was unchanged. A new Second Division was organized from the temporary Third Division, Eighteenth Corps, which had been formed by the consolidation of the former Second Division and Third Division of Tenth Corps May 30, 1864, while Smith's command was on the way to Cold Harbor. A new Third Division was organized from one-hundred-day regiments of the Ohio National Guard, and Orris S. Ferry was assigned command. For additional information see Tenth Corps, Army of the James. The reorganization of Eighteenth Corps was not so extensive. First Division was unchanged. A new Third Brigade, Second Division was organized under Augustus Gibson, but Adelbert Ames assumed command June 20, 1864. Hinks' division of United States Colored Troops was reorganized as Third Division, Eighteenth Corps. For additional information, see Eighteenth Corps, Army of the James. When the reorganization was completed, the Army of the James consisted of the following:

TENTH CORPS, Alfred H. Terry, to June 18, 1864
  William T. H. Brooks

First Division, Robert S. Foster, to June 18, 1864
  Alfred H. Terry
  First Brigade, Joshua B. Howell
  Second Brigade, Joseph R. Hawley
  Third Brigade, Harris M. Plaisted

Artillery Brigade, Loomis L. Langdon
  1st Battery, Connecticut Light Artillery, James B. Clinton
  5th Battery, New Jersey Light Artillery, Zenas C. Warren
  Battery C, Third Rhode Island Heavy Artillery, Martin S. James
  Battery M, 1st United States Artillery, Loomis L. Langdon

Second Division, John W. Turner
  First Brigade, N. Martin Curtis
  Second Brigade, William B. Barton
  Third Brigade, Louis Bell
  Artillery, George T. Woodbury
    4th Battery, New Jersey Light Artillery, Charles R. Doane
    4th Battery, Wisconsin Light Artillery, Martin McDevitt
    Battery D, 1st United States Artillery, Robert M. Hall
    Battery E, 3rd United States Artillery, John R. Myrick
    Battery D, 4th United States Artillery, Frank Powell

Note. The artillery of Second Division was attached to Third Division.

Third Division, Orris B. Ferry
  First Brigade, Gilman Marston
  Second Brigade, James B. Armstrong
  33rd Battery, New York Light Artillery, Alger M. Wheeler

Cavalry, Atherton H. Stevens, Jr.

EIGHTEENTH CORPS, William F. Smith

First Division, William T. H. Brooks, to June 18, 1864
  Gilman Marston, to June 20, 1864
  George J. Stannard
  First Brigade, Gilman Marston, to June 18, 1864
    Edgar M. Cullen
  Second Brigade, Hiram Burnham
  Third Brigade, Guy V. Henry

Note 1. Brooks was assigned to command Tenth Corps June 18, 1864.
Note 2. Marston was assigned to Tenth Corps June 20, 1864.

Second Division, John H. Martindale
  First Brigade, George J. Stannard, to June 20, 1864
    Alexander Piper
  Second Brigade, Griffin A. Stedman, Jr.

Third Brigade, Augustus A. Gibson, to June 20, 1864
  Adelbert Ames

Third Division, Edward W. Hinks
  First Brigade, Edward A. Wild, to June 23, 1864
    John H. Holman
  Second Brigade, Samuel A. Duncan
  Artillery Brigade, Henry S. Burton
    Battery E, 3rd New York Light Artillery, Lewis H. Mowers
    Battery K, 3rd New York Light Artillery, James R. Angel
    Battery M, 3rd New York Light Artillery, John H. Howell
    7th Battery, New York Light Artillery, Martin V. McIntyre
    16th Battery, New York Light Artillery, Richard H. Lee
    Battery F, 1st Rhode Island Light Artillery, Thomas Simpson
    Battery C, 3rd Rhode Island Heavy Artillery, Martin S. James
    Battery B, 1st United States Artillery, Michael Leahy
    Battery L, 4th United States Artillery, Henry B. Beecher
    Battery A, 5th United States Artillery, Israel Ludlow

On the Lines at Petersburg and Bermuda Hundred. June 21, 1864, the reorganized Eighteenth Corps returned to the Petersburg entrenchments to relieve Sixth Corps, Army of the Potomac, which at that time held the right of the Union line. Two days later Turner's Second Division, Tenth Corps was temporarily attached to Eighteenth Corps, and early on June 24, 1864 relieved Orlando B. Willcox's Third Division, Ninth Corps, Army of the Potomac, on the left of Martindale's division of Eighteenth Corps.

June 23, 1864, Harris M. Plaisted's Third Brigade of Terry's First Division, Tenth Corps was moved from the lines at Bermuda Hundred to Deep Bottom to guard the pontoon bridges that crossed the James River there. When the brigade arrived, Robert S. Foster assumed command at Deep Bottom.

During the latter part of June and throughout July 1864, Terry's division remained on the right of the line of entrenchments at Bermuda Hundred. Hinks' Third Division, Tenth Corps was divided, with Second Brigade in the line of entrenchments and First Brigade along the James River at Fort Powhatan, Wilson's Wharf, and Bermuda Landing.

A number of important command changes occurred in the army during July 1864. Brooks resigned and was relieved from command of Tenth Corps July 18, 1864. Terry was in temporary charge of Tenth Corps until July 23, 1864, and then David B. Birney, formerly commanding Third Division, Second Corps, Army of the Potomac, assumed command. Smith was relieved from command of Eighteenth Corps July 19, 1864, and John H. Martindale assumed temporary command. Edward O. C. Ord relieved Martindale July 22, 1864.

During the month, Eighteenth Corps remained in the entrenchments before Petersburg. July 29, 1864, Gershom Mott's Third Division, Second Corps relieved Eighteenth Corps in the trenches, and the latter, with Turner's division of Tenth Corps, moved to the rear of Ambrose E. Burnside's Ninth Corps to support it in an assault that was to follow the explosion of the mine on the morning of July 30, 1864. Turner's division supported Burnside's attack at the "Crater," but it was not heavily engaged and withdrew during the afternoon. The next day Eighteenth Corps returned to its former positions in the entrenchments at Petersburg, relieving Mott, and Turner's division rejoined Tenth Corps at Bermuda Hundred. For details, see Operations about Petersburg and Richmond, Virginia, 1864–1865, Operations of July 1864, The Petersburg Mine Assault of July 30, 1864.

In July 1864, troops of Nineteenth Corps served briefly with the Army of the James. At the first of the month, Nineteenth Corps was at Morganza, Louisiana in the Department of the Gulf, but July 5, 1864, William H. Emory was assigned command of First Division and Second Division and was ordered to New Orleans, where he embarked with his command for Fort Monroe, Virginia. Emory's command was designated Detachment Nineteenth Corps. When Emory arrived at Fort Monroe with the advance of his troops, he was immediately ordered on to Washington, D.C., which was then threatened by a Confederate force under Jubal A. Early. See Early's Washington Raid (and Operations in the Shenandoah Valley, Maryland, and Pennsylvania). The brigades that followed Emory to Fort Monroe, however, were sent on to Bermuda Hundred. During the period July 20–25, 1864, James W. McMillan's Second Brigade and Leonard D. H. Currie's Third Brigade of First Division, and Henry W. Birge's First Brigade and Edward L. Molineux's Second Brigade of Second Division, Detachment Nineteenth Corps were attached to the Army of the James. From July 21 to July 31, 1864, the brigades of Birge and Molineux were temporarily attached to Tenth Corps.

July 21, 1864, Birge's brigade was placed in reserve in rear of the line of defenses at Bermuda Hundred between batteries No. 4 and 7; and July 27, 1864, it was sent to reinforce Hancock's Second Corps, which was then demonstrating north of the James River near Deep Bottom. Molineux's brigade occupied the position vacated by Birge. See Operations about Petersburg and Richmond, Virginia, 1864–1865, Operations of July 1864, Demonstration on the North Bank of the James River, Engagement at Deep Bottom (or Darbytown, Strawberry Plains, and New Market Road), Virginia.

In late July 1864, Early again became active and advanced into the lower Shenandoah Valley, and defeated a Federal force commanded by George Crook at Kernstown July 24, 1864. The four brigades of Detachment Nineteenth Corps then with the Army of the James were ordered to Washington. July 26, 1864, McMillan's brigade, then under Isaac Dyer, was sent to City Point to embark, and Currie's brigade followed the next day. Birge's brigade remained at Deep Bottom to hold the bridgehead for the next few days, and it arrived at City Point July 31, 1864. Molineux's brigade arrived there from Bermuda Hundred the same day. For additional information, See Early's Washington Raid (and Operations in the Shenandoah Valley, Maryland, and Pennsylvania).

The organization of the Army of the James at the end of July 1864 was as follows:

ARMY OF THE JAMES
Benjamin F. Butler

TENTH CORPS, David B. Birney

First Division, Alfred H. Terry
  First Brigade, Francis B. Pond
  Second Brigade, Joseph R. Hawley
  Third Brigade, Robert S. Foster
  Artillery Brigade, Zenas C. Warren

Second Division, John W. Turner
  First Brigade, N. Martin Curtis
  Second Brigade, William B. Coan

Third Brigade, Louis Bell
Artillery Brigade, Frederick M. Follett

Third Division, Orris S. Ferry
First Brigade, Gilman Marston
Second Brigade, James B. Armstrong
33rd Battery, New York Light Artillery, Alger M. Wheeler

EIGHTEENTH CORPS, Edward O. C. Ord

First Division, Hiram Burnham, to August 3, 1864
Joseph B. Carr
First Brigade, Aaron F. Stevens
Second Brigade, Edgar M. Cullen
Third Brigade, Guy V. Henry

Second Division, Adelbert Ames
First Brigade, James Stewart, Jr.
Second Brigade, Griffin A. Stedman, Jr.
Third Brigade, Harrison S. Fairchild

Third Division, Joseph B. Carr, to August 3, 1864
Charles J. Paine
First Brigade, Jeptha Garrard
Second Brigade, Samuel A. Duncan

Artillery Brigade, Eighteenth Corps, Henry S. Burton, to July 24, 1864
Alexander Piper

Cavalry Division, August V. Kautz
First Brigade, Robert M. West
Second Brigade, Samuel P. Spear

Naval Brigade, Charles K. Graham

Siege Artillery, Henry L. Abbot

During most of August 1864, the Army of the James was relatively quiet on the lines of entrenchments at Petersburg and at Bermuda Hundred. Two new brigades were organized during this period. July 31, 1864, William Birney was relieved from duty in the Department of the South, and was ordered to report to Butler at Bermuda Hundred. August 12, 1864, Birney was assigned command of a Separate Brigade, Army of the James. August 31, 1864, Gilman Marston was assigned command of all troops on the James River between City Point and Fort Monroe, and this command was designated as First Separate Brigade, Army of the James.

August 13, 1864, David B. Birney moved with most of his Tenth Corps from the lines at Bermuda

Hundred to the north side of the James River at Deep Bottom. There he joined Winfield S. Hancock's Second Corps and David McM. Gregg's Second Cavalry Division, Army of the Potomac in a demonstration against the Confederate works in front of Richmond. When this mission was completed, Birney returned to Bermuda Hundred August 21, 1864. For details, see Operations about Petersburg and Richmond, Virginia, 1864–1865, Operations of August 1864, Demonstration on the North Bank of the James River at Deep Bottom (Combats at Fussell's Mill, Gravel Hill, Bailey's Creek [or Run], White's Tavern, Charles City Road, and New Market Road), Virginia.

Early in August 1864, Ord's Eighteenth Corps held the line of entrenchments at Petersburg on the right of Ninth Corps and Fifth Corps. When Fifth Corps was withdrawn in mid-August 1864 for a movement against the Weldon Railroad, Ninth Corps and Eighteenth Corps were extended to the left to cover its former front. Eighteenth Corps then occupied the line from the Appomattox River to the site of the Petersburg Mine. Ames' Second Division was on the left; Charles J. Paine, with Elias Wright's Second Brigade of his Third Division, was on the center; and Joseph B. Carr's First Division was on the right. On the night of August 18, 1864, two brigades of Ord's reserves relieved Willcox's division of Ninth Corps to the left of the Crater.

During the two months that Eighteenth Corps had served in the trenches, it had become seriously depleted in numbers, and August 21, 1864 Ord asked that it be relieved. This request was approved, and three days later Tenth Corps was ordered to cross the Appomattox and take the place of Ord's command. At that time Tenth Corps was in position at Bermuda Hundred as follows: Terry's division was on the right next to the James River; Turner's division (commanded by Robert S. Foster after August 23, 1864) was on the center; and William Birney's Separate Brigade was on the left, next to the Appomattox River. Birney occupied the positions formerly held by the hundred-day regiments of the Ohio National Guard. Foster's brigade of Terry's division (commanded by Plaisted after August 23, 1864) was at Deep Bottom. Terry's division was the first to move to the relief of Eighteenth Corps. August 24, 1864, First Brigade and Second Brigade crossed the Appomattox and relieved Ames' Second

Division on the left of Eighteenth Corps' line. Ames' division then returned to Bermuda Hundred. Plaisted's Third Brigade at Deep Bottom did not join the division at Petersburg until August 27, 1864. When Terry's brigades departed, Foster's Second Division, Tenth Corps took their place in the defenses at Bermuda Hundred.

Coinciding almost exactly with the exchange of positions by Tenth Corps and Eighteenth Corps, and influenced by it, Third Division, Tenth Corps and Third Division, Eighteenth Corps were extensively reorganized. During the period August 25–27, 1864, the hundred-day regiments of the Ohio National Guard, which formed Ferry's Third Division, Tenth Corps, went home for muster out, and Ferry's division was discontinued. A short time later, Third Division, Tenth Corps was reorganized from colored regiments. At that time William Birney commanded a Separate Brigade of Tenth Corps, composed of colored troops, at Bermuda Hundred. August 25, 1864, he was ordered to assume command of all colored regiments camped in the vicinity of the Signal Tower, near Point of Rocks. He was then to proceed with these regiments and his own Separate Brigade to Petersburg, and there relieve Paine's Third Division, Eighteenth Corps in the trenches. When Birney arrived at Petersburg, his command was organized as Third Division, Tenth Corps. His own Separate Brigade, then under James Shaw, Jr., was designated as First Brigade, Third Division. Included in the troops brought from near the Signal Tower were the regiments of Paine's First Brigade, Third Division, Eighteenth Corps, and these were designated as Second Brigade, Third Division, Tenth Corps. John H. Holman was assigned command. It should be noted that, for the reason given above, Holman's brigade was carried on the rosters of both Tenth Corps and Eighteenth Corps at the end of August 1864.

When Paine was relieved at Petersburg, he marched with Wright's brigade of his division to Deep Bottom. There he relieved Plaisted's brigade and assumed command of the Defenses at Deep Bottom August 27, 1864. Plaisted then rejoined Terry's division at Petersburg.

At 7:30 P.M. August 26, 1864, David B. Birney assumed command of the line at Petersburg formerly held by Ord's troops. He then reported for orders to George G. Meade, commander of the Army of the Potomac. The disposition of Birney's command was as follows: Terry's First Division, Tenth Corps was on the left next to Gershom Mott's division of Second Corps; William Birney's new Third Division, Tenth Corps was in the center; and Joseph B. Carr's First Division, Eighteenth Corps, which had not yet been replaced, was on the right. Carr's division marched back to Bermuda Hundred the next day, but Foster's Second Division, Tenth Corps did not arrive on the right of David B. Birney's line until August 28, 1864.

When established north of the Appomattox, Ord's Eighteenth Corps was in position as follows: Carr's First Division and Ames' Second Division held the line of defenses at Bermuda Hundred, with Carr's division on the right between the James River and Battery No. 5, and Ames' division on the left, between Carr's division and the Appomattox River. Paine's Third Division was at Deep Bottom.

Kautz's cavalry division was generally on picket duty during the month. West's First Brigade covered the ground from the Weldon Railroad eastward toward Fort Powhatan on the James River. Spear's Second Brigade was principally in Prince George County, on a line from Mount Sinai Church to Cooke's Mill. August 18, 1864 Spear's brigade moved to the Weldon Railroad and served for a time with Gouverneur K. Warren's Fifth Corps near Globe Tavern. Spear then reported to Hancock, whose Second Corps was on the railroad near Reams' Station. August 23, 1864, Spear joined David McM. Gregg's Second Cavalry Division, which was then on the left of Hancock. Spear's brigade was engaged with Second Corps at the Battle of Reams' Station August 25, 1864, and the next day Spear was ordered, with his brigade, to report to Kautz. For more information about the activities of Spear's brigade, see Operations about Petersburg and Richmond, Virginia, 1864–1865, Operations of August 1864.

August 27, 1864, Butler left the army on leave to take care of business in Boston. Ord commanded the army temporarily until September 5, 1864, and then he too departed on leave. This left David B. Birney in command of the Army of the James until September 7, 1864, when Butler returned.

At the end of August 1864, the Army of the James was organized as follows:

ARMY OF THE JAMES
Benjamin F. Butler

TENTH CORPS, David B. Birney

First Division, Alfred H. Terry
    First Brigade, Joshua B. Howell
    Second Brigade, Joseph R. Hawley
    Third Brigade, Harris M. Plaisted

Second Division, Robert S. Foster
    First Brigade, N. Martin Curtis
    Second Brigade, William B. Barton
    Third Brigade, Francis A. Osborn

Third Division, William Birney
    First Brigade, James Shaw, Jr.
    Second Brigade, John H. Holman

Artillery Brigade, Tenth Corps, Freeman McGilvery

EIGHTEENTH CORPS, Edward O. C. Ord

First Division, Joseph B. Carr
    First Brigade, Aaron F. Stevens
    Second Brigade, Edgar M. Cullen
    Third Brigade, Samuel H. Roberts

Second Division, Adelbert Ames
    First Brigade, James Stewart, Jr.
    Second Brigade, George M. Guion
    Third Brigade, Harrison S. Fairchild

Third Division, Charles J. Paine
    First Brigade, John H. Holman
    Second Brigade, Alonzo G. Draper
    Third Brigade, Samuel A. Duncan

Note 1. Holman's brigade was also reported as Second Brigade, Third Division, Tenth Corps.
Note 2. Elias Wright commanded Second Brigade during August 1864.

Artillery Brigade, Eighteenth Corps, Alexander Piper

Cavalry Division, August V. Kautz
    First Brigade, Robert M. West
    Second Brigade, Samuel P. Spear

Naval Brigade, Charles K. Graham

Siege Artillery, Henry L. Abbot

Also included in Butler's Department of Virginia and North Carolina were the following:

District of Eastern Virginia, George F. Shepley

District of North Carolina, Innis N. Palmer
Sub-District of New Berne, Edward Harland

Battle of Chaffin's Farm, Virginia, September 29–30, 1864. The Army of the James, which had not functioned as a unit since the end of May 1864, remained scattered until near the end of September 1864. Two divisions of Eighteenth Corps manned the Defenses of Bermuda Hundred, and Paine's division was at Deep Bottom, with detachments at Dutch Gap, City Point, and other posts down the James River. Tenth Corps was in the trenches at Petersburg, and Kautz's Cavalry Division was on picket duty, covering the rear of the Union line from the Norfolk and Petersburg Railroad toward Fort Powhatan on the James.

Late in September 1864, as a part of Grant's autumn offensive, the Army of the James was given the task of attempting the capture of Richmond from the north side of the James River. Accordingly, orders were issued for the assembly of the army at Bermuda Hundred and Deep Bottom. Joseph H. Potter was assigned command of a Provisional Brigade, Eighteenth Corps, consisting of newly arrived and inexperienced one-year regiments. Potter was to relieve veteran troops on garrison duty so that they could join the forces preparing to advance on Richmond. David B. Birney's Tenth Corps was relieved at Petersburg on the night of September 24–25, 1864, and marched toward Deep Bottom. Kautz was relieved on the picket line September 27, 1864, and he also moved toward the James River.

In preparation for the advance on Richmond, Butler divided his army into two wings. Ord was assigned command of the Left Wing, which consisted of George J. Stannard's First Division and Charles A. Heckman's Second Division of Eighteenth Corps. This wing advanced from Aiken's Landing on the James River toward the enemy entrenchments at Chaffin's farm. David B. Birney was assigned command of the Right Wing, which consisted of his Tenth Corps and Charles J. Paine's Third Division, Eighteenth Corps. The Right Wing moved northward from Deep Bottom against the enemy entrenchments on New Market Heights, and toward the Charles City Road. Ord captured Fort Harrison and the adjacent entrenchments on both sides of the fort and held them firmly. Birney captured the works on New Market Heights, and then moved up on the left of Ord and occupied the Confederate Exterior Line up to the Darbytown Road. Kautz's cavalry division moved forward on the right of the Right Wing, and was engaged in front of Richmond. For details of Butler's advance north of the James, and also the organization of the Army of the James during this period, see Operations about Petersburg and Richmond, Virginia, 1864–1865, Operations of September 1864, Battle of Chaffin's Farm (Combats at Fort Harrison, Fort Gilmer, Fort Gregg, New Market Heights, and Laurel Hill).

There were several command changes in Eighteenth Corps that resulted from the fighting at Chaffin's farm and New Market Heights September 29, 1864. Ord was wounded, and Heckman commanded Eighteenth Corps temporarily during the rest of the day. That evening Godfrey Weitzel assumed command of the corps. Aaron Stevens, commanding First Brigade, First Division, was wounded and John B. Raulston assumed command of his brigade. Hiram Burnham, commanding Second Brigade, First Division, was killed, and Michael T. Donohoe assumed command of his brigade. Donohoe was also wounded later. Samuel Roberts, commanding Third Brigade, First Division, became ill and Edgar M. Cullen assumed command of his brigade. Samuel A. Duncan, commanding Third Brigade, Third Division, was wounded and was succeeded by John W. Ames. September 30, 1864, George M. Guion succeeded James Stewart, Jr. in command of First Brigade, Second Division.

Line of Defenses North of the James River. When the fighting at Chaffin's farm ended October 2, 1864, the Army of the James constructed a strong defensive line north of the James River facing the Confederate entrenchments southeast of Richmond. The line began at Signal Hill (later the site of Fort Brady) on the James River, and extended northward along the west side of the Varina Road to Fort Harrison (later renamed Fort Burnham). It then continued on to the north along the old Confederate Exterior Line, past the Clyne house on the New Market Road, to Johnson's farm on the Darbytown Road. Eighteenth Corps held the line from the river to, and including, Fort Harrison; Tenth Corps from Fort Harrison to Clynes' farm; and Kautz's Cavalry Division from Clynes' farm to Johnson's farm. For further information, see Operations about Petersburg and Richmond, Virginia, 1864–1865, Operations of October 1864, Siege of Petersburg, Entrenchments of the Army of the James.

The army generally remained on this line during October 1864, but on three occasions troops were withdrawn for active operations. October 7, 1864, the enemy attacked Kautz's cavalry on the Darbytown Road and drove it from its position at Johnson's farm. Terry's division of Tenth Corps was sent to Kautz's assistance, and it soon restored the Federal line. October 31, 1864, Terry, then commanding Tenth Corps, marched out with Ames' First Division and William Birney's Third Division in an attempt to break up the enemy defenses on the Darbytown Road. Finally, on October 27–28, 1864, most of the Army of the James left the entrenchments and demonstrated on the front of the Richmond defenses on the Darbytown and Williamsburg roads. After each of these movements, the troops returned to their former positions. For details of the above activities, see Operations about Petersburg and Richmond, Virginia, 1864–1865, Operations of October 1864.

There were some organizational and command changes during October 1864. October 14, 1864, a new Third Brigade of Kautz's Cavalry Division was organized from 1st New York Mounted Rifles and 1st Maryland Cavalry, and Andrew W. Evans was assigned command. The next day Charles K. Graham was, in addition to his command of the Naval Brigade, assigned command of all troops belonging to the Department of Virginia and North Carolina then occupying the lines between the James and the Appomattox rivers, including the garrison of Redoubt Converse and the 1st Connecticut Heavy Artillery. This command was designated as a Provisional Division. The Provisional Division consisted of Joseph H. Potter's Provisional Brigade and Henry L. Abbot's Siege Artillery. October 3, 1864, Gilman Marston became ill, and Joab N. Patterson assumed command of his Separate Brigade, which consisted of troops at Fort Powhatan, Fort Pocahontas, and Harrison's Landing. October 10, 1864, Alfred H. Terry relieved David B. Birney, who was ill, in command of Tenth Corps. Adelbert Ames assumed command of Terry's First Division, Tenth Corps. Birney died in Philadelphia, Pennsylvania October 18, 1864.

A number of regiments of United States Colored Troops arrived during October 1864 to reinforce the

Army of the James. Among these were six regiments from Kentucky, totaling about 5,000 men. Lorenzo Thomas, adjutant general of the army, began organizing these regiments about July 1, 1864, and during the latter part of October 1864 he brought them to Baltimore, Maryland to be forwarded to Deep Bottom. October 28, 1864, three of these regiments—107th, 117th, and 118th United States Colored Troops—were organized into a new Provisional Brigade under Edward Martindale.

In early November 1864, as the day of the presidential election drew near, the authorities in Washington became concerned that disturbances might occur in New York, and that Jacob Thompson with his Confederate followers might enter the United States from Canada. Accordingly, Secretary of War Edwin M. Stanton asked Grant to send troops to New York to prevent any disorders there and also to protect the public property. November 2, 1864, Grant directed Butler to go to New York and report to John A. Dix for duty in the Department of the East. He was also to be assigned command of the troops in the Harbor and City of New York that were to be sent there from the Army of the James. That same day Grant ordered Terry, who had assumed command of the Army of the James after Butler's departure, to send 3,000 troops from Tenth Corps and Eighteenth Corps to New York. Joseph R. Hawley, commander of Second Brigade, First Division, Tenth Corps, was to command this force. Hawley organized his regiments into a Provisional Division, Army of the James, which consisted of two brigades. The First Brigade was assigned to Joseph C. Abbott, and the Second Brigade to John B. Raulston. First Brigade was formed from regiments of Tenth Corps as follows: four from Hawley's Second Brigade, First Division; two (consolidated) from Third Brigade, First Division; and one each from First Brigade, Second Division and Third Brigade, Second Division. Second Brigade was formed from regiments of Eighteenth Corps as follows: two from Raulston's First Brigade, First Division; and one each from First Brigade, Second Division and Second Brigade, Second Division. Three regiments from Edgar M. Cullen's Second Brigade, First Division, Eighteenth Corps were designated to go, but they were delayed at Deep Bottom by a lack of transportation, and apparently they did not join the forces in New York. When

Hawley's command arrived in New York, Raulston, with two regiments of his brigade, was sent on to Watervliet Arsenal, and Alfred P. Rockwell assumed command of Raulston's brigade.

November 11, 1864, after the election, Hawley was ordered to return with his command to the Army of the James. Embarkation began at New York November 14, 1864, and by the next day all troops had departed. Raulston resumed command of Second Brigade for the return. The transports began arriving at Fort Monroe November 16, 1864, and as the regiments came in, they rejoined their respective commands. For additional information, see Department of the East, January 3, 1863–June 27, 1865, November Election of 1864 in New York.

Reorganization of the Army of the James, December 1864. As early as November 15, 1864, Grant had announced his intention to reorganize the Army of the James into two new army corps. One was to be composed of the white troops of Tenth Corps and Eighteenth Corps, and the other of the colored troops of the Department of Virginia and North Carolina. As a preliminary to this reorganization, Grant directed that the colored troops of Edward Ferrero's Third Division, Ninth Corps, Army of the Potomac be transferred to the Army of the James, and that in exchange the Pennsylvania regiments of Joseph H. Potter's Provisional Brigade of Charles K. Graham's Provisional Division, Army of the James be sent to Ninth Corps at Petersburg. November 18, 1864, two regiments of Ferrero's division were ordered to Bermuda Hundred to report to Butler, and a week later two regiments of Potter's brigade joined Ninth Corps. The remainder of Ferrero's division left the Petersburg front on the morning of November 26, 1864, and the next day it occupied the line of defenses formerly held by Potter's brigade. Ferrero's command was designated as Ferrero's Division, Defenses of Bermuda Hundred. Potter's brigade joined Ninth Corps about November 28, 1864. When this transfer was completed, all colored troops with Grant's army at Petersburg and Richmond were serving in the Army of the James.

At Bermuda Hundred a brigade consisting of 29th and 31st United States Colored Troops, commanded by Henry C. Ward, held the right of the line of entrenchments at the time Ferrero's division arrived.

Delevan Bates' First Brigade and Henry G. Thomas' Second Brigade of Ferrero's division were then placed on the left of Ward, and they occupied the left and center of the line.

Potter did not accompany his regiments to Ninth Corps but remained with the Army of the James. In the reorganization of December 3, 1864 (see below), Potter was ordered with his 12th New Hampshire Regiment to report to Charles Devens, commanding First Division, Eighteenth Corps, for assignment to Edgar M. Cullen's Second Brigade. He then relieved Cullen in command of the brigade. William M. McClure was assigned command of the reorganized Provisional Brigade and relieved Potter. McClure's Provisional Brigade consisted of his own 2nd Pennsylvania Heavy Artillery and one company of the 13th New Hampshire Regiment.

November 30, 1864, Butler proposed to Grant that the Army of the James be reorganized as follows: that Tenth Corps and Eighteenth Corps be discontinued; the white infantry of these two corps, then with the Army of the James, be consolidated and organized into a new corps, to be designated as Twenty-Fourth Corps; and the colored troops of the Department of Virginia and North Carolina be organized into a new corps to be called the Twenty-Fifth Corps. An order to this effect was issued by the secretary of war December 3, 1864; Edward O. C. Ord was assigned command of Twenty-Fourth Corps, and Godfrey Weitzel was assigned command of Twenty-Fifth Corps. The corps staff and artillery of Eighteenth Corps were transferred to Twenty-Fourth Corps, and the corps staff and artillery of Tenth Corps were transferred to Twenty-Fifth Corps.

The two corps were organized as follows:

TWENTY-FOURTH CORPS, Edward O. C. Ord

First Division, Robert S. Foster
First Brigade, Thomas A. Osborn
Second Brigade, Joseph R. Hawley
Third Brigade, Harris M. Plaisted
Fourth Brigade, James Jourdan

Note. First, Second, and Third brigades formerly belonged to Adelbert Ames' First Division, Tenth Corps. Fourth Brigade was formed from regiments of Heckman's Second Division, Eighteenth Corps, which was discontinued in the reorganization.

Second Division, Adelbert Ames

First Brigade, N. Martin Curtis
Second Brigade, Galusha Pennypacker
Third Brigade, Louis Bell

Note. Second Division was formerly Robert S. Foster's Second Division, Tenth Corps.

Third Division, Charles Devens
First Brigade, John B. Raulston
Second Brigade, John H. Potter
Third Brigade, Guy V. Henry

Note. Third Division was formerly Devens' First Division, Eighteenth Corps.

Artillery, Twenty-Fourth Corps, Charles C. Abell
    Battery E, 3rd New York Light Artillery, George E. Ashby
    Battery H, 3rd New York Light Artillery, William J. Riggs
    Battery K, 3rd New York Light Artillery, James R. Angel
    Battery M, 3rd New York Light Artillery, John H. Howell
    7th Battery, New York Light Artillery, Martin V. McIntyre
    16th Battery, New York Light Artillery, Richard H. Lee
    17th Battery, New York Light Artillery, Hiram D. Smith
    Battery A, 1st Pennsylvania Light Artillery, William Stitt
    Battery F, 1st Rhode Island Light Artillery, Robert B. Smith
    Battery L, 4th United States Artillery, Richard Wilson
    Battery A, 5th United States Artillery, Charles P. Muhlenberg
    Battery F, 5th United States Artillery, Leonard Martin

TWENTY-FIFTH CORPS, Godfrey Weitzel

First Division, Charles J. Paine
First Brigade, Delevan Bates
Second Brigade, John W. Ames
Third Brigade, Elias Wright

Note. December 31, 1864, the designation of First Division was changed to Third Division, and First Division was reorganized by the change of designation of Third Division to First Division.

Second Division, William Birney
First Brigade, Charles S. Russell
Second Brigade, Ulysses Doubleday

Third Brigade, Henry C. Ward

Third Division, Edward A. Wild
  First Brigade, Alonzo G. Draper
  Second Brigade, Edward Martindale
  Third Brigade, Henry G. Thomas

Note 1. In the organization of Twenty-Fifth Corps, the former brigades of Ninth Corps, Tenth Corps, and Eighteenth Corps were not transferred intact, but were broken up and their regiments reassigned.

Note 2. December 31, 1864, the designation of Third Division was changed to First Division, and Third Division was reorganized by the change of designation of First Division to Third Division.

Artillery Brigade, Richard S. Jackson
  1st Battery, 1st Connecticut Light Artillery, James B. Clinton
  4th Battery, New Jersey Light Artillery, Charles R. Doane
  5th Battery, New Jersey Light Artillery, Henry H. Metcalf
  16th New York Heavy Artillery (Detachment), Silas J. Truax
  Battery E, 1st Pennsylvania Light Artillery, Henry Y. Wildey
  Battery C, 3rd Rhode Island Light Artillery, Martin S. James
  Battery D, 1st United States Artillery, Redmond Tully
  Battery M, 1st United States Artillery, Loomis L. Langdon
  Battery E, 3rd United States Artillery, John R. Myrick
  Battery D, 4th United States Artillery, Frederick M. Follett

The reorganization of the corps of the army also affected the Defenses of Bermuda Hundred. December 4, 1864, Edward Ferrero was assigned command of the Defenses of Bermuda Hundred, relieving Graham. Graham later accompanied Butler's expedition to Fort Fisher, North Carolina (see below), and was in charge of disembarking and reembarking the troops there. Graham's Provisional Division was discontinued, and Ferrero's command was designated as the Defenses of Bermuda Hundred. When Ferrero's colored troops were transferred to Twenty-Fifth Corps by the order of December 3, 1864, they were replaced in the Defenses of Bermuda Hundred by two brigades of J. Howard Kitching's Provisional Division from the Middle Military Division. Kitching was wounded October 19, 1864 at the Battle of Cedar Creek in the Shenandoah Valley, and William Heine assumed temporary

command of the division. Kitching died of his wound January 10, 1865.

Delevan Bates' brigade, formerly of Ferrero's division of Ninth Corps, was ordered to report to Alonzo Draper's Third Division, Twenty-Fifth Corps December 28, 1864, and Heine's brigade of Kitching's division, which had just arrived at Bermuda Hundred, took its place in the line. Ward's brigade was ordered to join Second Division, Twenty-Fifth Corps December 30, 1864, and the next day G. DePeyster Arden's brigade of Kitching's division arrived and relieved Henry G. Thomas' brigade, formerly of Ferrero's division. Thomas' brigade reported to Weitzel as Third Brigade, Third Division, Twenty-Fifth Corps. December 31, 1864, the newly arrived regiments of Kitching's division were organized into a provisional division of two brigades. First Brigade, consisting of three New York regiments, was commanded by Heine; and Second Brigade, consisting of two New York Heavy Artillery regiments, was commanded by Arden. The Defenses of Bermuda Hundred was then organized as follows:

Defenses of Bermuda Hundred, Edward Ferrero
  First Brigade, William Heine
  Second Brigade, G. DePeyster Arden
  Provisional Brigade, William McClure

Note. Henry L. Abbot's Siege Artillery of the Defenses of Bermuda Hundred was permanently attached to the Army of the Potomac by an order of December 24, 1864.

The Army of the James received an additional reinforcement from the Shenandoah Valley December 23, 1864. That day Thomas M. Harris' First Infantry Division, Army of West Virginia (formerly commanded by Joseph Thoburn, who was killed at Cedar Creek) arrived at City Point and was attached to Twenty-Fourth Corps. For additional information, see Twenty-Fourth Corps, Army of the James; and also Shenandoah Valley Campaign (Sheridan).

Butler's Expedition to Fort Fisher, North Carolina, December 7–30, 1864. By late 1864, Wilmington, North Carolina was the last open seaport of the Confederacy, and to prevent its use by blockade runners Grant ordered an expedition to attempt the capture of Fort Fisher, which guarded the entrance to the Cape Fear River, on which Wilmington was situated. This was to be a joint land-sea operation, and Grant selected Godfrey Weitzel to command the land forces. The naval force, which was to consist of more than fifty warships, was to be under the command of Rear Admiral David D. Porter, commander of the North Atlantic Blockading Squadron. The start was delayed for some time, but finally on the evening of December 7, 1864, about 7,000 men belonging to Adelbert Ames' Second Division, Twenty-Fourth Corps and Charles J. Paine's First Division, Twenty-Fifth Corps were temporarily detached from the Army of the James and, under Weitzel, were moved that evening to the left of the lines at Bermuda Hundred. The next morning Weitzel embarked his command at Bermuda Hundred for Fort Monroe, where he was to be joined by Porter's naval force. At City Point, Butler requested of Grant that, as commander of the Army of the James, he be permitted to accompany the expedition as commander of the land forces. Grant assented to this request, but Weitzel remained in immediate command of the troops.

The expedition remained at Fort Monroe until December 13, 1864, waiting for the navy to complete its preparations and for the weather to improve. Finally, early on the morning of December 13, 1864, the transports carrying the expedition moved up the Potomac River to Mathias Point to confuse the enemy as to their true destination, and that night they steamed back to the south and arrived off the rendezvous at Masonboro Inlet on December 15, 1864. The fleet lay there until the evening of December 18, 1864, when Admiral Porter arrived. Then, because of high winds and rough seas, most of the vessels of the transport fleet were forced to take refuge in Beaufort Harbor, and they remained there until December 24, 1864. After taking on coal and water, the transports left Beaufort early that morning for New Inlet, where they arrived at 4:00 that afternoon. The navy had earlier exploded a powder ship off the beach near Fort Fisher at 1:40 P.M., and it was then engaged in shelling the enemy works. Neither the explosion nor the shelling had any significant effect on the fortifications.

About noon December 25, 1864, a reconnaissance force of about 500 men from N. Martin Curtis' First Brigade of Ames' division, under the immediate command of Curtis, landed on the beach a few miles north of Fort Fisher to determine the practicability of an assault. The landing was covered by

the navy, and was directed by Charles K. Graham of the Naval Brigade. Curtis promptly pushed forward a skirmish line to within a short distance of Fort Fisher, capturing the garrison at Flag Pole Battery as he advanced. Ames went ashore when Galusha Pennypacker's Second Brigade landed, and as soon as Louis Bell's Third Brigade reached the beach, Ames moved forward with Bell along the shore to support Curtis. Pennypacker's brigade and the rest of Curtis' brigade remained on the beach to protect the landing.

Butler and Weitzel made a careful examination of the enemy works and concluded that a successful assault was not possible, and Butler then ordered the reembarkation of his troops. This was completed on the morning of December 27, 1864, and Ames' division returned to its camps at Chaffin's farm the next day. Paine's division followed and arrived December 29–30, 1864. December 30, 1864, Weitzel relieved Ames' command from duty with the Expeditionary Corps, and ordered it to report to Alfred H. Terry, then commanding Twenty-Fourth Corps.

Weitzel's expedition was organized as follows:

EXPEDITIONARY CORPS, ARMY OF THE JAMES, Godfrey Weitzel

Second Division, Twenty-Fourth Corps, Adelbert Ames
    First Brigade, N. Martin Curtis
    Second Brigade, Galusha Pennypacker
    Third Brigade, Louis Bell

First Division, Twenty-Fifth Corps, Charles J. Paine
    First Brigade, Delevan Bates
    Second Brigade, John W. Ames
    Third Brigade, Elias Wright

Terry's Expedition to Fort Fisher, North Carolina, January 3–17, 1865 (Capture of Fort Fisher). Soon after the return of Butler's unsuccessful expedition to capture Fort Fisher and close the port of Wilmington, Grant decided to make a second attempt. He assigned Alfred H. Terry, then commanding Twenty-Fourth Corps, to command the new expedition. Terry was to take with him 3,300 picked men from Adelbert Ames' Second Division, Twenty-Fourth Corps; 3,300 men from Charles J. Paine's Third Division, Twenty-Fifth Corps; and 1,400 men from Joseph C. Abbott's Second Brigade, First Division, Twenty-Fourth Corps, which was to be attached to Ames' division. Terry was to proceed with this force as rapidly as possible and report to David D. Porter, whose fleet was then lying off the Cape Fear River.

At noon January 3, 1865, the troops that were to accompany Terry began to withdraw from the works north of the James River, and they then marched to Bermuda Hundred and bivouacked for the night. The detachments of Ames' division that were left behind were organized into a provisional brigade under G. Frederick Granger, and this was attached to Charles Devens' Third Division, Twenty-Fourth Corps. Devens assumed command of that part of the line of entrenchments previously held by Ames' division.

The transports to carry the troops did not arrive at Bermuda Hundred until late in the afternoon of January 4, 1865, and embarkation was not completed until noon the next day. As soon as the boats were loaded, they moved to Fort Monroe, where the entire transport fleet was assembled in Hampton Roads. At 4:00 A.M. on January 6, 1865, the transports sailed for the rendezvous with Porter's fleet at a point about twenty-five miles off Beaufort, North Carolina, but because of bad weather, they did not arrive at their destination until January 8, 1865. Four days later, Terry sailed toward Federal Point at the mouth of the Cape Fear River, where he arrived a short time before dark on the evening of January 12, 1865.

At 4:00 the next morning, the navy stood in close to the beach about five miles north of Fort Fisher to cover the landing of Terry's troops, and at 8:00 A.M. they started ashore. By 3:00 that afternoon, about 8,000 men had disembarked, and their necessary supplies were also ashore. Pickets immediately moved out to the front, and there was some exchange of fire, but there was no serious engagement that day.

The Confederate forces in the area belonged to Braxton Bragg's Confederate Department of North Carolina. William H. C. Whiting commanded the Third Military District of the department, with headquarters at Wilmington, and Louis Hebert commanded the defenses at the mouth of the Cape Fear River. William Lamb was in immediate command of the Garrison of Fort Fisher. Robert F. Hoke's division, which on December 20, 1864 had been sent to North Carolina from the defensive lines before Richmond, was in position north of Fort Fisher, on the peninsula between the Cape Fear River and the Atlantic Ocean, to oppose any land force that might disembark in that region.

Shortly after 5:00 P.M. January 13, 1865, Abbott's brigade, which was temporarily attached to Ames' division, was left to guard the stores accumulated at the landing, and the remainder of Terry's command set out toward the fort to form a defensive line across the peninsula from the Cape Fear River to the sea, facing Wilmington. This was to be done to protect the rear of the Federal forces that later were to attempt the capture of Fort Fisher farther south. The position finally selected was about two miles north of the fort, and Paine's division, which was to hold this line, arrived on the site about 2:00 A.M. January 14, 1865. By 8:00 A.M. a breastwork had been constructed and was in a defensible condition.

During the morning of January 14, 1865, N. Martin Curtis' First Brigade of Ames' division moved down toward Fort Fisher, and at noon reached a small unfinished outwork in front of the fort, and near the Cape Fear River. On January 14, 1865, Henry L. Abbot was assigned as chief of artillery of the expedition, and that day and the following night the artillery was landed and placed in position, most of it near the river, to protect the right of Terry's line.

On January 14, 1865, Terry, Curtis, and Cyrus B. Comstock, chief engineer of the expedition, made a careful reconnaissance of the enemy works, and Terry then ordered an assault for the next day. The navy was to open with a heavy bombardment on the morning of January 15, 1865, and this was to continue until the land assault began. Then the ships were to direct their fire to other parts of the fort. The assault was to begin at 3:00 P.M. by Ames' division, which was to move against the western half of the land face of the fort. At the same time, a column of sailors and marines was to attack at the northeast bastion. The naval assault force was placed under the command of Lieutenant Commander K. Randolph Breese, and it consisted of 2,000 volunteers assembled from the entire fleet. Prior to the attack, the sailors were organized into three divisions, each composed of men from the corresponding division squadrons of the fleet, as follows: First Division, commanded by Lieutenant Commander C. H. Cushman; Second Division, commanded by Lieutenant

Commander James Parker; and Third Division, commanded by Lieutenant Commander T. O. Selfridge, Jr. A Marine Division was commanded by Captain L. L. Dawson.

At 8:00 A.M. January 15, 1865, the navy opened fire from all vessels of the fleet, except from those of the division left to aid the troops on the northern defensive line, and during the bombardment the land forces prepared for the attack. Paine was placed in command of the defensive line, which was held by his own division and Abbott's brigade. Curtis' brigade was already in position near the fort at the outwork previously mentioned and in the adjacent trenches. At noon, Galusha Pennypacker's and Louis Bell's brigades were brought up within supporting distance of Curtis' brigade.

Preparations for the final assault began at about 2:00 P.M. Under cover of some sharpshooters who had been sent forward, Curtis advanced his brigade to within 475 yards of the fort and entrenched. Pennypacker's brigade then moved up and occupied the outwork just vacated by Curtis, and Bell's brigade advanced and formed in line about 200 yards in rear of Pennypacker. A short time later Curtis again advanced to a line just behind the sharpshooters, and Pennypacker moved up to Curtis' last line. Bell then moved forward and occupied the outwork.

At 3:30 P.M. Terry ordered Ames to move forward with his division, and at the same time the navy changed the direction of its fire. Curtis' brigade dashed forward and to the right to envelop the land front of the works, and a short time later gained the parapet of Fort Fisher. Simultaneously, Breese's sailors and marines rushed forward along the beach toward the northeast bastion. They were exposed to a murderous fire from the fort and were unable to get up on the parapet. There was a severe struggle for a time, but, after suffering heavy losses, the naval column was finally forced to withdraw.

When Curtis gained a foothold on the parapet, Pennypacker moved up to support him and, moving to the right, drove the enemy from a palisade that extended from the end of the land face of the fort to the river. Then both brigades pushed on to their left and captured about one-fourth of the land face of the fort. Bell's brigade then came up and attacked between the fort and the river. There was no regular parapet on the river side of the fort, but a series of traverses extending back from the land face served as strong defensive positions from which the enemy opposed Ames' attack. There was desperate hand-to-hand fighting across these traverses, but Ames' men pushed them back from one after another until nine of them had been captured.

When Bell's brigade joined in the fighting, Abbott's brigade was replaced on the northern defensive line by the naval force, and this brigade, together with Albert M. Blackman's 27th United States Colored Troops of Paine's division, marched down the peninsula and reported to Ames about dark. These fresh troops were sent to the rear of the fort, where they were immediately engaged. Fighting continued until about 9:00 P.M., and during this time two more traverses had been taken; then a part of Abbott's brigade drove the enemy from their last stronghold, and finally, Union forces were in complete possession of Fort Fisher. Abbott and Blackman immediately pushed on toward Battery Buchanan, where many of the enemy had fled after leaving Fort Fisher. Terry's men soon captured this work and took a number of prisoners, including Lamb and Whiting. Bell was mortally wounded during the fighting near the palisade, and Curtis and Pennypacker were wounded in attempting to take the traverses.

The enemy made no serious effort to break through Paine's northern line during the attack on Fort Fisher, but about 4:00 P.M., just after Ames' attack had started, Hoke advanced to the front of the entrenchments and was engaged in skirmishing with Paine's pickets. That was the extent of the fighting on the northern front. During the day, Henry L. Abbot was occupied in landing artillery and ammunition, and in preparing for siege operations if Ames' attack should fail. The artillery, however, was not needed, and January 22, 1865, Abbot was ordered to return to City Point. The siege train was ordered to return two days later.

During the night of January 15–16, 1865, the Confederates blew up and abandoned Fort Caswell, and they also abandoned their extensive works on Smith's Island at Smithville, and on Reeves' Point. By so doing, they cleared the way for Union forces to occupy all the works that they had constructed to defend the mouth of the Cape Fear River.

Terry's troops did not return to the Army of the James after the capture of Fort Fisher, but they remained for a time in camp on Federal Point, where they were known as United States Forces at Fort Fisher. On January 24, 1865, all detachments of regiments and batteries that were with Terry at Fort Fisher, and which had been left behind at the beginning of the expedition, were ordered to rejoin their commands. The area occupied by Terry became a part of the Department of North Carolina when the latter was organized February 9, 1865 (constituted January 31, 1865), and Terry's command was thus transferred to the Department of North Carolina. On February 21, 1865, it was organized as Terry's Provisional Corps, Department of North Carolina, and this in turn was reorganized April 2, 1865 as Tenth Corps, Department of North Carolina, with Terry in command. For further information about Terry's command, see Department of North Carolina, January 31, 1865–May 19, 1866, Troops in the Department of North Carolina.

The organization of the detachment of the Army of the James commanded by Alfred H. Terry at Fort Fisher January 13–15, 1865 was as follows:

EXPEDITION TO FORT FISHER,
NORTH CAROLINA
Alfred H. Terry

TWENTY-FOURTH CORPS

First Division
  Second Brigade, Joseph C. Abbott

Note. Abbott's brigade was temporarily attached to Ames' Second Division.

Second Division, Adelbert Ames
  First Brigade, N. Martin Curtis, to January 15, 1864, wounded
    Ezra Walrath
  Second Brigade, Galusha Pennypacker, to January 15, 1865, wounded
    Oliver P. Harding
  Third Brigade, Louis Bell, to January 15, 1865, mortally wounded
    Alonzo Alden

TWENTY-FIFTH CORPS

Third Division, Charles J. Paine
  Second Brigade, John W. Ames
  Third Brigade, Elias Wright

Note. Delevan Bates' First Brigade consisted of 1st, 30th, and 107th United States Colored Troops. During the Fort Fisher Expedition, 1st Regiment was attached to Wright's Third Brigade, and the 30th Regiment was attached to John W. Ames' Second Brigade. Bates remained on the line of entrenchments in front of Richmond with the 107th Regiment and the detachments that did not accompany their proper organizations to Fort Fisher.

ARTILLERY, Henry L. Abbot
  Companies B, G, and L, 1st Connecticut Heavy Artillery, William G. Pride
  16th Battery, New York Light Artillery, Richard H. Lee
  Battery E, 3rd United States Artillery, John R. Myrick

Roberts' Expedition from Fort Monroe to Fredericksburg, Virginia, March 5–8, 1865. During the winter of 1864–1865, Grant received information that a sizable contraband trade was carried on across the Potomac River by way of the Northern Neck of Virginia, and from there through Fredericksburg to Richmond. March 4, 1865, Samuel H. Roberts was ordered to take his Third Brigade, Third Division, Twenty-Fourth Corps and a detachment of cavalry; to proceed up the Rappahannock River on transports; and to break up that trade. Roberts was also authorized to go to the Potomac River or to any other point where goods in transit might be found. He was further directed to break up as much as possible of the railroad between Fredericksburg and Richmond.

Roberts embarked his brigade at Deep Bottom for Fort Monroe March 4, 1865 and, upon arriving there, he was joined by a detachment of 300 men of the 1st New York Mounted Rifles under Edwin V. Sumner. The transports, convoyed by four gunboats, left Fort Monroe the next day and arrived at Fredericksburg on the evening of March 6, 1865. Roberts occupied the town and destroyed the railroad bridge, buildings, and track. He also captured and removed large amounts of tobacco and other materials, and then returned to Fort Monroe late on March 8, 1865.

Roberts' Expedition from Fort Monroe into Westmoreland County, Virginia, March 11–13, 1865. Under the authority of the order of March 4, 1865 (see preceding section), Roberts' expedition again left Fort Monroe on the morning of March 11, 1865, for the Potomac River. The next morning it proceeded up the Yeocomico River and landed at Kinsale, and then marched to Hague. Roberts found little of value at the latter place and returned to

Kinsale. He then sailed to Point Lookout, where he turned over his prisoners to the prisoner-of-war camp located there. While at Point Lookout, on March 12, 1865, he was ordered up the York River, in company with gunboats, as a convoy for 100,000 rations that were being sent to the White House. These were intended for Philip H. Sheridan's two cavalry divisions, which at that time were marching toward City Point from the Shenandoah Valley. For additional information about Sheridan's march, see Sheridan's Expedition from Winchester to Petersburg, Virginia.

Reorganization of the Defenses of Bermuda Hundred, March 1865. March 19, 1865, George L. Hartsuff relieved Charles K. Graham in command of the Defenses of Bermuda Hundred. Graham was then assigned command of the post of Norfolk and Portsmouth and its defenses, in the District of Eastern Virginia, Department of Virginia. March 20, 1865, Hartsuff reorganized the Defenses as follows:

DEFENSES OF BERMUDA HUNDRED, George L. Hartsuff

Infantry Division, Edward Ferrero
First Brigade, Gilbert H. McKibbin
Second Brigade, George C. Kibbe
Artillery Brigade, George B. Cook

Reinforcements for the Army of the Potomac. The Army of the James was comparatively active until late March 1865, when, in preparation for Grant's final offensive at Petersburg, Ord marched from the north side of the James River with a force to join the Army of the Potomac south of Petersburg. His command consisted of Robert S. Foster's First Division and John W. Turner's Independent Division (formerly commanded by Thomas M. Harris) of John Gibbon's Twenty-Fourth Corps; William Birney's Second Division of Twenty-Fifth Corps; Ranald S. Mackenzie's Cavalry Division (formerly commanded by August V. Kautz); and three batteries of artillery.

Under cover of darkness, March 27, 1865, Ord's command was withdrawn from its camps north of the James and started on its way toward Petersburg. Gibbon's two divisions, with Turner's division in the lead, crossed the James River at Deep Bottom and marched to Broadway Landing on the Appomattox River. Gibbon was joined there by William

Birney's division, which had crossed the James at Varina.

By 7:40 A.M. March 28, 1865, the last of Ord's infantry had crossed the Appomattox River, and Turner's division had resumed the march toward the south of Petersburg. Weary from their night march, the troops of Foster's and Birney's divisions rested until noon, and then followed on the road behind Turner. Foster overtook Turner during the afternoon, and at dark both divisions went into camp at Fort Siebert. Birney's division halted that evening at Humphreys' Station on the Military Railroad. That night, Ord's infantry was in the rear of that part of the Union line of entrenchments held by Andrew A. Humphreys' Second Corps, Army of the Potomac, which it was to relieve the next day.

Mackenzie's cavalry left its camps on the evening of March 28, 1865, and marched to join Ord. It crossed the James River at Varina and the Appomattox River at Point of Rocks, and arrived at Hancock's Station at daylight the next morning.

When Ord departed, he left behind Charles Devens' Third Division, Twenty-Fourth Corps to hold the corps line. He also left August V. Kautz's First Division, Twenty-Fifth Corps and the Artillery Brigade at Chaffin's farm, on the Twenty-Fifth Corps' line. Hartsuff's command remained at Bermuda Hundred. Godfrey Weitzel was placed in command of the troops left north of the James, and these were designated as Detachment Army of the James. Ord's command at Petersburg was called the Army of the James.

Appomattox Campaign, March 29, 1865–April 9, 1865. On the morning of March 29, 1865, Ord's infantry relieved Humphreys' Second Corps on the Petersburg line of entrenchments near Hatcher's Run, and Mackenzie's cavalry moved to Reams' Station to guard the wagon trains of the Army of the Potomac. April 1, 1865, Mackenzie marched to Dinwiddie Court House and reported to Philip H. Sheridan, and during the day he served under Sheridan on the White Oak Road, and then on the right of Fifth Corps at the Battle of Five Forks. For details of Mackenzie's movements that day, see Appomattox Campaign, Battle of Five Forks.

Horatio G. Wright's Sixth Corps launched an attack on the enemy works at Petersburg early on April 2, 1865, and this attack was supported on the left by John Gibbon's Twenty-Fourth Corps. When Sixth Corps broke through the line and drove the defenders toward the Appomattox River, Ord's three divisions moved to the right and advanced toward Petersburg. That afternoon Foster's and Turner's divisions attacked the Confederate Inner Line and, after a severe struggle, captured Fort Gregg and Fort Baldwin (or Fort Whitworth).

When Petersburg was found to be evacuated the next morning, April 3, 1865, the Army of the James marched westward along the South Side Railroad toward Burkeville. Birney's division halted at Blacks and Whites (present-day Blackstone), but Gibbon's Corps reached Burkeville late that night. Mackenzie's cavalry, still under Sheridan, advanced toward Amelia Court House, where Lee's army was gathering, and arrived near the town April 4, 1865.

April 6, 1865, Ord advanced to Rice's Station, and there he was joined by Birney's division. The next day, the Army of the James followed James Longstreet's retreating column to Farmville. While at Farmville, Ord relieved Birney from command of Second Division, Twenty-Fifth Corps, and broke up the division by assigning its brigades to Foster's and Turner's divisions. Ord remained south of the Appomattox River at Farmville April 7, 1865 but, during the next day and most of the following night, Gibbon's Twenty-Fourth Corps marched toward Appomattox Station on the South Side Railroad in an attempt to head off the Army of Northern Virginia. On the way, at Prospect Station, Charles Griffin's Fifth Corps joined the Army of the James, and came under Ord's orders.

April 6, 1865, Mackenzie's cavalry division, then reduced to a single brigade, marched to Burkeville, and the next morning it moved on by way of Prince Edward Court House to the vicinity of Prospect Station. There, on April 8, 1865, Mackenzie was ordered to report to George Crook, commanding the Second Division of Sheridan's cavalry. Mackenzie remained under Crook's orders during the remainder of the campaign.

Ord arrived with Twenty-Fourth Corps and Fifth Corps near Appomattox Court House early on the morning of April 9, 1865, just in time to relieve Sheridan's hard-pressed cavalry, which was struggling to hold the Lynchburg Road. Ord then advanced and drove back the enemy forces that were attempting to open the way toward Lynchburg. That afternoon Lee surrendered the Army of Northern Virginia. Griffin's Fifth Corps, Gibbon's Twenty-Fourth Corps, and Mackenzie's cavalry were assigned to remain at Appomattox Court House until the surrendered soldiers were paroled and the public property was secured and moved to Farmville. Ord, in person, left Appomattox Court House for Richmond April 10, 1865. For details of the operations of the Army of the James during the period March 29, 1865–April 9, 1865, see Appomattox Campaign.

Meantime, there had been some activity in Weitzel's Detachment Army of the James. Early on the morning of April 3, 1865, Weitzel learned that the enemy lines in front of Richmond had been abandoned, and he promptly ordered his troops forward on several roads leading to the city. All halted, according to orders, on the outskirts while Weitzel proceeded on to receive the surrender at 8:15 A.M. Edward H. Ripley's First Brigade of Devens' Third Division, Twenty-Fourth Corps was assigned as provost guard of Richmond, and George F. Shepley, Weitzel's chief of staff, was appointed as military governor of the city. The other troops remained along the inner line of redoubts around Richmond. For additional information, see Appomattox Campaign, Federal Occupation of Petersburg and Richmond.

At Bermuda Hundred, Hartsuff also found the enemy works empty on the morning of April 3, 1865. Gilbert H. McKibbin's First Brigade of Ferrero's Infantry Division then advanced to Chesterfield Court House. On April 4–5, 1865, Ferrero's division moved to Petersburg, and relieved Ralph Ely's Second Brigade of Willcox's First Division, Ninth Corps as provost guard. Most of the division was posted on the outskirts of the city, picketing the approaches from the south and west. The line was established between the Appomattox River on the right and the Jerusalem Plank Road on the left. Hartsuff's artillery, under Henry L. Abbot, was left to garrison the works at Bermuda Hundred.

Hartsuff assumed command at Petersburg April 6, 1865, and that day the designation of Ferrero's Infantry Division, Defenses of Bermuda Hundred was changed to Ferrero's Division, United States Forces at Petersburg. By April 6, 1865, all Ninth Corps troops had been withdrawn from the South Side Railroad between Petersburg and Sutherland's Station, and these were replaced by troops of

Hartsuff's command. The next day Grant assigned Hartsuff to the command of all forces at City Point, Bermuda Hundred, Petersburg, and on the South Side Railroad as far west as Sutherland's Station.

April 6, 1865, Charles S. Russell's Attached Brigade of Kautz's division of Twenty-Fifth Corps was ordered to City Point to relieve the troops of the Army of the Potomac that were garrisoning the defenses there. It was not until April 10, 1865, however, that Russell relieved Charles H. T. Collis in command of the post of City Point, and that day Collis, and also Henry W. Benham with his engineers, marched toward Burkeville to join the Army of the Potomac.

The organization of the Army of the James during the Appomattox Campaign was as follows:

ARMY OF THE JAMES
Edward O. C. Ord

DEFENSES OF BERMUDA HUNDRED, George L. Hartsuff

Infantry Division, Edward Ferrero
First Brigade, Gilbert H. McKibbin
Second Brigade, George C. Kibbe
33rd Battery, New York Light Artillery, Alger M. Wheeler

Artillery, Henry L. Abbot
Companies A and H, 13th New York Heavy Artillery, William Pendrell
7th Battery, New York Light Artillery, Martin V. McIntyre
Company E, 3rd Pennsylvania Heavy Artillery, Erskine H. Miles
Company M, 3rd Pennsylvania Heavy Artillery, Sylvester W. Marshall

Note. April 6, 1865 the designation of Infantry Division was changed to Ferrero's Division.

SEPARATE BRIGADE, Joseph B. Carr
Fort Pocahontas, Ashbel W. Angel
Harrison's Landing, Wardwell G. Robinson
Fort Powhatan, William J. Sewell

CAVALRY DIVISION, Ranald S. Mackenzie
First Brigade, Robert M. West
Second Brigade, Samuel P. Spear, to April 1, 1865, wounded
Andrew W. Evans
4th Battery, Wisconsin Light Artillery, Dorman L. Noggle

UNATTACHED CAVALRY
4th Massachusetts Cavalry (three companies), Francis Washburn
5th Massachusetts Cavalry (colored), Charles F. Adams, Jr.
7th New York (1st Mounted Rifles), Edwin V. Sumner

Note. 7th New York Cavalry was detached on an expedition to North Carolina.

TWENTY-FOURTH CORPS, John Gibbon

First Division, Robert S. Foster
First Brigade, Thomas O. Osborn
Third Brigade, George B. Dandy
Fourth Brigade, Harrison S. Fairchild

Note. Second Brigade accompanied Terry's expedition to Fort Fisher and was no longer in the department.

Third Division, Charles Devens
First Brigade, Edward H. Ripley
Second Brigade, Michael T. Donohoe
Third Brigade, Samuel H. Roberts

Note. Second Division accompanied Terry's expedition to Fort Fisher and was no longer in the department.

Independent Division, John W. Turner
First Brigade, Andrew Potter
Second Brigade, William B. Curtis
Third Brigade, Thomas M. Harris

Artillery, Charles C. Abell
Battery E, 3rd New York Light Artillery, George E. Ashby
Battery H, 3rd New York Light Artillery, Enoch Jones
Battery K, 3rd New York Light Artillery, James R. Angel
Battery M, 3rd New York Light Artillery, John H. Howell
17th Battery, New York Light Artillery, George T. Anthony
Battery A, 1st Pennsylvania Light Artillery, William Stitt
Battery F, 1st Rhode Island Light Artillery, Charles E. Guild
Battery B, 1st United States Artillery, Samuel S. Elder
Battery L, 4th United States Artillery, Henry C. Hasbrouck
Battery A, 5th United States Artillery, Charles P. Muhlenberg
Battery F, 5th United States Artillery, Henry B. Beecher

TWENTY-FIFTH CORPS, Godfrey Weitzel

First Division, August V. Kautz

First Brigade, Alonzo G. Draper
Second Brigade, Edward A. Wild
Third Brigade, Henry G. Thomas
Attached Brigade, Charles S. Russell

Note. The Attached Brigade was detached from Third Brigade, Second Division.

Second Division, William Birney, to April 8, 1865, relieved
First Brigade, James Shaw, Jr.
Second Brigade, Ulysses Doubleday
Third Brigade, William W. Woodward

Third Division

Note. Third Division acompanied Terry's expedition to Fort Fisher and left the department.

Artillery Brigade, Loomis L. Langdon
  1st Battery, Connecticut Light Artillery, James B. Clinton
  4th Battery, New Jersey Light Artillery, Charles R. Doane
  5th Battery, New Jersey Light Artillery, Zenas C. Warren
  Battery E, 1st Pennsylvania Light Artillery, Henry Y. Wildey
  Battery C, 3rd Rhode Island Heavy Artillery, Martin S. James
  Battery D, 1st United States Artillery, Redmond Tully
  Battery M, 1st United States Artillery, Egbert W. Olcott
  Battery D, 4th United States Artillery, Frederick M. Follett

Early on April 8, 1865, Ord relieved Birney in command of Second Division and ordered him to City Point. Second Division was broken up temporarily: Doubleday's brigade was assigned to Foster's First Division, Twenty-Fourth Corps, and Woodward's brigade to Turner's Independent Division, Twenty-Fourth Corps. Shaw's brigade had been detached April 4, 1865 to hold Sutherland's Station until the arrival of Ninth Corps, and it did not rejoin Ord's command until April 9, 1865. It was then assigned to Turner's division. Second Division was reorganized April 10, 1865 under Richard H. Jackson, Ord's chief of staff, to consist of the original three brigades.

After Appomattox. After Lee's surrender at Appomattox the Army of the James did not operate again as a distinct organization, but was simply included in the designation of Ord's command as the Department of Virginia, Army of the James.

Weitzel's Twenty-Fifth Corps was placed in camps south of Petersburg until May 1, 1865, when it was ordered to City Point. It embarked there for Texas May 23, 1865–June 26, 1865, and it did not again return to the Department of Virginia. Twenty-Fourth Corps and Mackenzie's cavalry camped north af Richmond after returning from Appomattox, and remained near the city until Twenty-Fourth Corps was discontinued August 1, 1865.

COMMANDERS OF THE ARMY OF THE JAMES

William F. Smith	April 30, 1864 to May 2, 1864
Benjamin F. Butler	May 2, 1864 to August 27, 1864
Edward O. C. Ord	August 27, 1864 to September 5, 1864
David B. Birney	September 5, 1864 to September 7, 1864
Benjamin F. Butler	September 7, 1864 to October 16, 1864
Godfrey Weitzel	October 16, 1864 to October 18, 1864
Benjamin F. Butler	October 18, 1864 to November 2, 1864
Alfred H. Terry	November 2, 1864 to November 18, 1864
Benjamin F. Butler	November 18, 1864 to December 8, 1864
Alfred H. Terry	December 8, 1864 to December 28, 1864
Benjamin F. Butler	December 28, 1864 to January 8, 1865
Edward O. C. Ord	January 8, 1865 to June 14, 1865
Alfred H. Terry	June 14, 1865 to August 1, 1865

ARMY OF THE KANAWHA

About July 1, 1864, David Hunter's Army of the Department of West Virginia arrived in the Kanawha Valley on its retreat from Lynchburg, Virginia after its unsuccessful attempt to capture the town. For details, see Department of West Virginia, Operations of the Troops of the Department of West Virginia, Hunter's Lynchburg, Virginia Campaign. July 2, 1864, Hunter assigned George Crook, then commanding Second Infantry Division, Department of West Virginia, to assume command of all troops in the Kanawha Valley, and in West Virginia west of the Allegheny Mountains and south of the Baltimore and Ohio Railroad. Crook assumed command July 3, 1864, with headquarters at Charleston, West Virginia, and by an order of that date designated his command as the Army of the Kanawha.

Crook, however, had little time to exercise control over the territory defined in his orders. During the first week of July 1864, Jubal A. Early appeared at Winchester, Virginia with an army of about 14,000 men, and then crossed the Potomac above Harper's Ferry and advanced across Maryland toward Washington, D.C. Immediately, Hunter, with his two infantry divisions and two cavalry divisions, was sent east to Martinsburg and Harper's Ferry to guard the railroad and cooperate with other troops then moving against Early. Jeremiah C. Sullivan's First Infantry Division and Alfred N. Duffie's First Cavalry Division were the first troops to arrive at Harper's Ferry, and they were promptly sent into Virginia toward Leesburg to join Horatio G. Wright, who was in command of a force then pursuing Early from Washington toward the Shenandoah Valley.

Crook arrived at Harper's Ferry July 15, 1864, and was assigned command of all troops of the Department of West Virginia that were leaving the department to march against Early in Virginia. Crook, with Jacob M. Campbell's Third Brigade of Crook's division (commanded by Daniel Frost), arrived at Hillsboro, Virginia July 16, 1864, and there he assumed command. He then moved on to Purcellville, where he reported to Wright. Rutherford B. Hayes' First Brigade of Crook's division remained at Halltown until July 19, 1864, and then marched to join the division. William W. Averell's Second Cavalry Division and Crook's other brigade, under Isaac H. Duval, were left at Martinsburg to guard the railroad.

Wright returned to Washington July 20, 1864, after Early retreated up the valley toward Strasburg, and July 22, 1864, Crook assembled his army at Winchester. That day Crook reorganized the infantry of his command into three divisions of two brigades each, and called his army the Army of the Kanawha. It was organized as follows:

ARMY OF THE KANAWHA
George Crook

First Division, Joseph Thoburn

First Brigade, George D. Wells
Second Brigade, William G. Ely

Second Division, Isaac H. Duval
First Brigade, Rutherford B. Hayes
Second Brigade, Daniel D. Johnson

Third Division, James A. Mulligan
First Brigade, Thomas M. Harris
Second Brigade, John P. Linton

Note. Third Division was discontinued July 28, 1864, and the regiments were consolidated into a new Third Brigade, First Division under Jacob M. Campbell.

First Cavalry Division, Alfred H. Duffie
First Brigade, William B. Tibbits
Second Brigade, Jacob Higgins

Second Cavalry Division, William W. Averell
First Brigade, James M. Schoonmaker
Second Brigade, William H. Powell

Artillery Brigade, Henry A. Du Pont
Battery B, 5th United States Artillery, Henry A. Du Pont
Battery D, 1st West Virginia Light Artillery, John Carlin
Battery E, 1st West Virginia Light Artillery, Francis M. Lowry

July 24, 1864, Crook's army was defeated by Early at Kernstown, Virginia, and was forced to retire to the north bank of the Potomac at Williamsport, Maryland. Crook then marched to Halltown, where he joined Wright's command, which had again advanced from Washington. July 30, 1864, Confederate cavalry under John McCausland burned Chambersburg, Pennsylvania, and then Hunter, with the infantry under Crook and Wright, moved to the vicinity of Frederick, Maryland to guard against a possible invasion from the west. Crook's cavalry marched toward Hancock, Maryland in pursuit of McCausland.

Early withdrew from the Potomac toward Winchester August 2, 1864, and Crook with his two infantry divisions moved to the vicinity of Harper's Ferry. There, four days later, Philip H. Sheridan assumed command of all Federal forces in the area in preparation for his Shenandoah Valley Campaign. August 8, 1864, Crook's First Infantry Division and Second Infantry Division were designated as the Army of West Virginia. The Army of the Kanawha was thus discontinued.

For details of the organization and operations of the Army of the Kanawha during July and early August 1864, see the following: Early's Washington Raid (and Operations in the Shenandoah Valley, Maryland, and Pennsylvania); and Department of West Virginia, Troops in the Department of West Virginia, July 1864 (Army of the Kanawha).

ARMY OF NORTHEASTERN VIRGINIA

The Army of Northeastern Virginia was the army commanded by Irvin McDowell in the Department of Northeastern Virginia from May 27, 1861 to August 17, 1861, and was the Union army that fought at the First Battle of Bull Run July 21, 1861. For details of its organization and operations, see the following: Department of Northeastern Virginia; and Bull Run Campaign, Virginia (First Battle of Bull Run or Manassas).

ARMY OF OCCUPATION OF WESTERN VIRGINIA, DEPARTMENT OF THE OHIO

When Virginia seceded from the Union in April 1861, regiments from Indiana, Ohio, and Kentucky were sent into the western part of the state to protect the strongly pro-Union people of the area, and also to guard the line of the Baltimore and Ohio Railroad. The troops first sent were three-month regiments, but as their terms of enlistment expired they were replaced by three-year volunteer regiments. There were also some loyal Virginia (Western Virginia) regiments organized in the state. These troops, which belonged to the Department of the Ohio, were under the command of George B. McClellan and later William S. Rosecrans, and were known as the Army of Occupation of Western Virginia, Department of the Ohio.

There were no corps or divisional organizations in the army, and the largest units were brigades. Many of the operations of the army were carried out by regiments and by smaller units of one or two companies. In general, during the period June to September 1861, the troops of the Army of Occupation of Western Virginia were engaged in guarding the railroad, and in occupying and holding the Kanawha Valley and the Cheat Mountain-Elkwater region of Western Virginia. The army was discontinued September 19, 1861 when it was merged into the newly created Department of Western Virginia.

For details of the organization and operations of the Army of Occupation of Western Virginia, see Western (West) Virginia, Operations in, May 26, 1861–October 11, 1861.

ARMY OF PENNSYLVANIA (PATTERSON)

The force that Robert Patterson organized at Chambersburg, Pennsylvania and led into Virginia at Williamsport, Maryland during the Bull Run Campaign of July 1861, has been called the Army of Pennsylvania, the Army of the Department of Pennsylvania, and the Army of the Shenandoah. For details of the organization and operations of this army, see Department of Pennsylvania, April 27, 1861–August 24, 1861.

ARMY OF THE POTOMAC

PERIOD OF ORGANIZATION AUGUST 17, 1861–MARCH 17, 1862

The Army of the Potomac had its origin in Irvin McDowell's Army of the Department of Northeastern Virginia, and its organization began, although not by that name, when George B. McClellan assumed command of the Military Division of the Potomac July 27, 1861, following McDowell's defeat at Bull Run. There followed a period of change, during which the three-month volunteer forces were replaced by regiments that had enlisted for three-year service, and during this time all military operations were necessarily generally discontinued. Washington, and particularly the fortified area held by Union forces on the Virginia side of the Potomac River, became a great military camp; and there, under McClellan's personal supervision, the Army of the Potomac came into being. The Army and Department of the Potomac were created August 17, 1861, and McClellan was assigned. He assumed command August 20, 1861, and continued the reorganization of the army that he had begun as commander of the Military Division of the Potomac. For additional information, see Military Division of the Potomac.

Brigade Organization of the Army

When the Army of the Potomac was organized August 20, 1861, the brigades that were constituted by McClellan as commander of the Military Division of the Potomac were retained in the new organization. These brigades, which were known by the names of the brigade commanders, were as follows:

Hunter's Brigade. David Hunter commanded this brigade, but he was in ill health, and August 22, 1861 was ordered to the Western Department. His brigade was broken up, and the regiments were assigned to other brigades.

Sherman's Brigade. William T. Sherman commanded this brigade until August 24, 1861, when he was assigned to the Department of the Cumberland.

Heintzelman's Brigade. Samuel P. Heintzelman commanded this brigade.

Kearny's Brigade. This brigade was organized from Second Brigade of Theodore Runyon's Fourth Division, Army of Northeastern Virginia, and Philip Kearny was assigned command.

Hooker's Brigade. This brigade was commanded by Joseph Hooker.

Keyes' Brigade. This brigade was organized from new regiments, and was commanded by Erasmus D. Keyes.

Franklin's Brigade. This brigade was organized from Thomas A. Davies' Second Brigade, Fifth Division, Army of Northeastern Virginia, and was commanded by William B. Franklin.

Blenker's Brigade. This brigade was organized from First Brigade, Fifth Division, Army of Northeastern Virginia, and was commanded by Louis Blenker.

Richardson's Brigade. This brigade was organized from Fourth Brigade, First Division, Army of Northeastern Virginia, and was commanded by Israel B. Richardson.

Stone's Brigade. This brigade was commanded by Charles P. Stone.

Smith's Brigade. This brigade was commanded by William F. Smith.

Couch's Brigade. This brigade was commanded by Darius N. Couch.

McCall's Brigade. This brigade was organized August 2, 1861, and was commanded by George A. McCall.

Sickles' Brigade. This brigade was organized August 5, 1861, and was commanded by Daniel E. Sickles.

King's Brigade. This brigade was organized August 9, 1861, and was commanded by Rufus King.

Howard's Brigade. This brigade was organized in August 1861 from Howard's Third Brigade, Third Division, Army of Northeastern Virginia, and was commanded by Oliver O. Howard.

As new regiments arrived in Washington, they too were equipped and organized into new brigades. These are given below under Division Organization of the Army.

Division Organization of the Army
August 17, 1861–March 13, 1862

A week after assuming command of the Department of the Potomac, McClellan began organizing the brigades of the army into divisions. A brief description of the organization of these divisions follows, and they are given in the order of the dates the divisions were constituted. It should be noted that originally a cavalry regiment was generally assigned to each division. For more information, see Cavalry Corps, Army of the Potomac.

Banks' Division. This division was organized August 17, 1861 by transfer from the Department of the Shenandoah. At that time the division was in Maryland guarding the line of the Potomac River from Harper's Ferry to the mouth of the Monocacy River. In September 1861, this line was extended to cover the country above Williamsport, Maryland. The division was organized as follows:

Banks' Division, Nathaniel P. Banks
    First Brigade, George H. Thomas
    Second Brigade, John J. Abercrombie
    Third Brigade, John W. Stiles, temporarily
        Charles S. Hamilton

Thomas was ordered to the Department of the Cumberland August 24, 1861, and in September 1861 the division was reorganized, with John J. Abercrombie commanding First Brigade; John W. Stiles, Second Brigade; and George H. Gordon, Third Brigade.

November 28, 1861, Banks' Division was ordered to Frederick, Maryland, where, with the exception of Third Brigade, it remained until February 1862. Dudley Donnelly, in temporary command of Third Brigade, was ordered to Hancock, Maryland to report to Frederick Lander. Alpheus S. Williams assumed command of Third Brigade after it arrived at Hancock.

In February 1862, Banks' Division was ordered to cross the Potomac at Harper's Ferry and occupy Winchester, Virginia. At that time, John J. Abercrombie commanded First Brigade; Charles S. Hamilton, Second Brigade; and Alpheus S. Williams, Third Brigade.

Gordon relieved Hamilton in command of Second Brigade March 13, 1862, when the latter left to assume command of Third Division, Third Corps, Army of the Potomac. In the reorganization of the division, Gordon was assigned command of Third Brigade, Banks' Division. The next day, while at Winchester, Banks reorganized his division, and then Williams commanded First Brigade; Abercrombie, Second Brigade; and George H. Gordon, Third Brigade.

In September 1861, John W. Geary was assigned command of troops guarding the Potomac near Sandy Hook, Maryland. His command was called Geary's Independent Brigade. This brigade remained along the river intil February 25, 1862, and then it crossed into Virginia in conjunction with the movement of Banks' Division toward Winchester. See Shenandoah Valley Campaign (Jackson), 1862. Geary occupied Loudoun Heights, and then moved eastward to Leesburg, and from that point he moved south through Loudoun County to Upperville. While there, on March 13, 1862, the creation of Fifth Corps, Army of the Potomac was announced (Banks assumed command of the corps March 20, 1862), and Geary's Brigade and Banks' Division became a part of Fifth Corps. During its operations in Loudoun County, Geary's Brigade was called Advance Brigade, and also Detached Brigade.

In the reorganization of the army March 13, 1862, Banks' Division became Williams' Division (commanded by Alpheus S. Williams) of Fifth Corps, Army of the Potomac.

McDowell's Division. This division was constituted August 24, 1861, to consist of the brigades of Erasmus D. Keyes and James S. Wadsworth. The division was not organized until October 3, 1861, and at that time a Third Brigade under Rufus King was assigned.

McDowell's Division, Irvin McDowell
    First Brigade, Erasmus D. Keyes
    Second Brigade, James S. Wadsworth
    Third Brigade, Rufus King

Note 1. Keyes was assigned command of Buell's Division November 9, 1861, and he was succeeded in command of First Brigade by Christopher C. Augur.

Note 2. Wadsworth was assigned military governor of the District of Columbia March 12, 1862, and was succeeded in command of Second Brigade by Marsena R. Patrick.

Note 3. King's and Wadsworth's brigades were organized in October 1861.

In the reorganization of the army March 13, 1862, McDowell's Division was assigned to First Corps, Army of the Potomac as Third Division.

Franklin's Division. This division was constituted August 28, 1861, to consist of the brigades of William B. Franklin and Philip Kearny. September 9, 1861, Henry W. Slocum was assigned command of the brigade formerly commanded by Heintzelman, and this was added to the division. As finally announced in October 1861, Franklin's Division was organized as follows:

Franklin's Division, William B. Franklin
    First Brigade, Philip Kearny
    Second Brigade, Henry W. Slocum
    Third Brigade, John Newton

Note 1. Newton's brigade was formerly commanded by Franklin.
Note 2. Franklin was also in command of the Defenses in Front of Alexandria. In September and October 1861, Franklin's Division was also called the Alexandria Division.
Note 3. There is also a record of Newton commanding Fifth Brigade and Slocum commanding Seventh Brigade of Franklin's Division until February 1862.

In the reorganization of the army March 13, 1862, Franklin's Division was assigned to First Corps, Army of the Potomac as First Division.

Porter's Division. This division was constituted August 28, 1861, to consist of the brigades of George W. Morell and John H. Martindale. When the division was finally organized in October 1861, a Third Brigade under Daniel Butterfield was added. The division was then organized as follows:

Porter's Division, Fitz John Porter
    First Brigade, George W. Morell
    Second Brigade, John H. Martindale
    Third Brigade, Daniel Butterfield

Note 1. Morell's brigade was organized in October 1861, largely from Sherman's Brigade, Military Division of the Potomac. It was assigned to Porter's Division September 4, 1861.
Note 2. Martindale's brigade was organized in October 1861.
Note 3. Butterfield's brigade was constituted September 27, 1861, and was assigned to Porter's Division October 4, 1861.

In the reorganization of the army March 13, 1862, Porter's Division was assigned to Third Corps, Army of the Potomac as First Division.

McCall's Division. This division was organized in September 1861 from regiments of the Pennsylvania Reserves. At first, it consisted of the brigades of John F. Reynolds and George G. Meade, but a Third Brigade under Edward O. C. Ord was added November 14, 1861. The division was then organized as follows:

McCall's Division, George A. McCall
    First Brigade, John F. Reynolds
    Second Brigade, George G. Meade
    Third Brigade, Edward O. C. Ord
    1st Pennsylvania Reserve Cavalry, George D. Bayard

Note 1. Second Brigade was assigned September 5, 1861.
Note 2. First Brigade was assigned September 16, 1861.
Note 3. Third Brigade was assigned November 14, 1861.

During the winter of 1861–1862, McCall's Division was encamped at Camp Pierpoint, near Langley, Virginia. December 20, 1861, Ord's brigade was engaged at Dranesville, Virginia with a Confederate force under James E. B. (Jeb) Stuart. For details, see Engagement at Dranesville, Virginia.

In the reorganization of the army March 13, 1862 McCall's Division was assigned to First Corps, Army of the Potomac as Second Division.

Buell's Division. This division was constituted September 14, 1861, to consist of the brigades of Darius N. Couch and Lawrence P. Graham. As finally organized in October 1861, a Third Brigade under John J. Peck was assigned. The organization of the division was as follows:

Buell's Division, Don Carlos Buell
    First Brigade, Darius N. Couch
    Second Brigade, Lawrence P. Graham
    Third Brigade, John J. Peck

Note 1. Buell was assigned command of the Department of the Ohio November 9, 1861, and was succeeded in command of the division by Erasmus D. Keyes. Thereafter, the division was known as Keyes' Division.
Note 2. Couch's brigade was organized from Couch's Brigade, Military Division of the Potomac.
Note 3. Graham's brigade was organized September 9, 1861.
Note 4. Peck's brigade was organized from new regi-

ments September 13, 1861, and was assigned to Buell's Division October 5, 1861.

In the reorganization of the army March 13, 1862, this division, at that time Keyes' Division, was assigned to Fourth Corps, Army of the Potomac as First Division.

William F. Smith's Division. This division was constituted September 28, 1861, to consist of a brigade composed of Vermont regiments, to be commanded by the senior colonel; Isaac I. Stevens' Brigade; and Winfield S. Hancock's Brigade. The division was organized as follows:

Smith's Division, William F. Smith
  First Brigade, William T. H. Brooks
  Second Brigade, Isaac I. Stevens
  Third Brigade, Winfield S. Hancock

There were some changes in command during the fall and winter of 1861–1862. Stevens was assigned command of a brigade in Thomas W. Sherman's South Carolina Expedition October 27, 1861 (see Department of the South, Part I, South Carolina Expedition [Thomas W. Sherman]), and John M. Brannan was assigned command of Second Brigade. In January 1862, the brigade designations were changed, and in March 1862, Hancock commanded First Brigade; Brooks, Second Brigade; and John W. Davidson, who had succeeded Brannan, Third Brigade.

In the reorganization of the army March 13, 1862, Smith's Division was assigned to Fourth Corps, Army of the Potomac as Second Division.

Heintzelman's Division. This division was constituted October 3, 1861, to consist of Israel B. Richardson's Brigade, John Sedgwick's Brigade, and Charles D. Jameson's Brigade, which was temporarily attached to Franklin's Division. The division was organized as follows:

Heintzelman's Division, Samuel P. Heintzelman
  First Brigade, Israel B. Richardson
  Second Brigade, John Sedgwick, to February 19, 1862
    David B. Birney
  Third Brigade, Charles D. Jameson
  1st New Jersey Cavalry, Colonel Halsted

Note 1. Sedgwick was assigned command of Charles P. Stone's Division February 19, 1862, and was succeeded in command of Second Brigade by Birney.

Note 2. Third Brigade was formed from new regiments, and Jameson was assigned command October 4, 1861.

Note 3. Sedgwick's brigade was organized from Oliver O. Howard's Brigade, Military Division of the Potomac.

In the reorganization of the army March 13, 1862, Heintzelman's Division was assigned to Third Corps, Army of the Potomac as Third Division.

Hooker's Division. This division was constituted October 11, 1861 to consist of the brigades of Joseph Hooker and Daniel E. Sickles. It was organized as follows:

Hooker's Division, Joseph Hooker
  First Brigade, Henry M. Naglee
  Second Brigade, Daniel E. Sickles

Note 1. First Brigade was formerly commanded by Hooker.
Note 2. Second Brigade was formed from new New York regiments.
Note 3. A Third Brigade was constituted November 28, 1861, to consist of four New Jersey regiments under the command of the senior colonel, Samuel H. Starr. Earlier, this had been Silas Casey's brigade.
Note 4. Regimental records indicate that Louis Blenker's Brigade was attached to Hooker's Division until December 1861, although Blenker's Division was constituted October 12, 1861. The latter consisted of the brigades of Julius Stahel and Adolph Von Steinwehr, organized in part from Blenker's Brigade. In the organization of the army of the Potomac October 15, 1861, Blenker's Brigade was listed as unattached.

In the reorganization of the army March 13, 1862, Hooker's Division was assigned to Third Corps, Army of the Potomac as Second Division.

Blenker's Division. This division was constituted October 12, 1861, to consist of the brigades of Julius Stahel and Adolph Von Steinwehr. The division apparently was not organized until November 1861, and at that time a Third Brigade under Henry Bohlen was assigned. The division was then organized as follows:

Blenker's Division, Louis Blenker
  First Brigade, Julius Stahel
  Second Brigade, Adolph Von Steinwehr
  Third Brigade, Henry Bohlen

Note 1. Stahel's brigade was formerly commanded by Blenker.

Note 2. Second Brigade was organized largely from regiments of Casey's Provisional Brigades.

Note 3. Regimental records indicate that Blenker's Brigade was attached to Hooker's Division in October 1861.

In the reorganization of the army March 13, 1862, Blenker's Division was assigned to Second Corps, Army of the Potomac, but it was left behind when the army moved to the Peninsula in late March 1862. Blenker remained with his division at Hunter's Chapel, near Washington, until ordered to the Shenandoah Valley April 1, 1862. Upon arriving there, it moved on and joined John C. Fremont's command in the Mountain Department May 4–11, 1862.

Stone's Division. The Corps of Observation on the Upper Potomac was formed August 17, 1861 as an organization of the Military Division of the Potomac, and Charles P. Stone was assigned command. When the Department of the Potomac was created August 17, 1861, the designation of Stone's command was changed to Corps of Observation, Department of the Potomac. Stone was assigned command, with headquarters at Poolesville, Maryland. The troops of this command were organized as Stone's Division, Army of the Potomac in October 1861, but the designation of Corps of Observation was used until December of that year. Stone's Division was organized as follows:

Stone's Division, Charles P. Stone, to February 9, 1862
    Willis A. Gorman, to February 19, 1862
    John Sedgwick
    First Brigade, Frederick W. Lander, to October 1861
      (see Note 1, below)
    Second Brigade, Willis A. Gorman
    Third Brigade (or Baker's Brigade), Edward D. Baker, to October 21, 1861, killed
      Milton Cogswell, to October 25, 1861
      William W. Burns

Note 1. Lander's brigade was organized Septmber 9, 1861, and was ordered to report to Stone for duty. Later, Lander, in person, accompanied Gorman's brigade at Edwards Ferry as a volunteer, and was wounded there October 22, 1861 (see section on Battles and Campaigns, Part II, Engagement at Ball's Bluff). Edward W. Hinks commanded First Brigade temporarily at that time, and he was succeeded by Ira R. Grosvenor.

Note 2. Stone formerly commanded Gorman's brigade.

Note 3. Cogswell commanded Baker's Brigade tem-porarily after Baker was killed at the Engagement at Ball's Bluff, October 21, 1861.

February 9, 1862, Stone was placed under arrest on charges stemming from his part in the Engagement at Ball's Bluff. Willis A. Gorman exercised temporary command of the division until relieved by John Sedgwick February 19, 1862. Thereafter the division was known as Sedgwick's Division.

Sedgwick's Division. As noted above, John Sedgwick assumed command of Stone's Division February 19, 1862, and after that date the division was known as Sedgwick's Division. It was organized as follows:

Sedgwick's Division, John Sedgwick
    First Brigade, Napoleon J. T. Dana
    Second Brigade, Willis A. Gorman
    Third Brigade, William W. Burns

The brigades of Gorman and Burns were ordered to Harper's Ferry February 24, 1862 to support the crossing of Banks' Division into Virginia. For further information, see Shenandoah Valley Campaign (Jackson), 1862. A short time later, on March 27, 1862, Sedgwick's Division was transferred to McClellan's army on the Peninsula as Second Division, Second Corps, Army of the Potomac.

Keyes' Division. November 9, 1861, Erasmus D. Keyes was assigned command of Don Carlos Buell's Division (see above), which was then known as Keyes' Division.

Sumner's Division. This division was constituted November 25, 1861, to consist of Oliver O. Howard's Brigade, William H. French's Brigade, and a third brigade, which was to be added later. Thomas F. Meagher's Brigade was organized in November 1861, and was assigned to Sumner's Division as Second Brigade February 8, 1862. The division was then organized as follows:

Sumner's Division, Edwin V. Sumner
    First Brigade, Oliver O. Howard
    Second Brigade, Thomas F. Meagher
    Third Brigade, William H. French

Note 1. First Brigade was organized October 25, 1861, and was ordered to report to Silas Casey's Division. It was then assigned to Sumner's Division in November 1861.

Note 2. All three brigades of this division were formed from new regiments.

In the reorganization of the army March 13, 1862, this division, then under the command of Israel B. Richardson, was assigned to Second Corps, Army of the Potomac as First Division.

Casey's Division. In October 1861, a provisional division was formed under the command of Silas Casey. This division was organized as follows:

Casey's Division, Silas Casey
    First Brigade, Oliver O. Howard
    Second Brigade, George Sykes

Note 1. October 3, 1861, Sykes was assigned to duty in Washington under Andrew Porter, provost marshal.
Note 2. October 25, 1861, Howard's Brigade was ordered to report to Casey, but in November 1861, it was assigned to Sumner's Division.

In January 1862, Casey's Division was reorganized as follows:

Casey's Division, Silas Casey
    First Brigade, Henry M. Naglee
    Second Brigade, William H. Keim
    Third Brigade, Innis N. Palmer
    Provisional Brigades, Silas Casey
    Sykes' Brigade, George Sykes
    Cooke's Brigade of Regular Cavalry, Philip St. George Cooke
    Unbrigaded regiments

Casey's Brigade (not the Provisional Brigades) was organized in Washington from four New Jersey regiments October 9, 1861, and it was transferred to Hooker's Division November 28, 1861 as Third Brigade under Samuel H. Starr.

In the reorganization of the army March 13, 1862, Casey's Division was assigned to Fourth Corps, Army of the Potomac as Third Division.

Lander's Division. This division was organized January 5, 1862 from regiments from the Department of Western Virginia and some new regiments. Generally, this division was in position along the line of the upper Potomac River from Cumberland to Hancock, Maryland. The division was organized as follows:

Lander's Division, Frederick W. Lander, to March 2,

1862, died
Nathan Kimball, temporarily to March 6, 1862
James Shields
    First Brigade, Nathan Kimball
    Second Brigade, Jeremiah C. Sullivan
    Third Brigade, Erastus B. Tyler

Note. Kimball, Sullivan, and Tyler commanded regiments that were transferred to the Army of the Potomac from the Cheat Mountain District, Department of Western Virginia.

When McClellan decided to occupy the lower Shenandoah Valley in February 1862, he directed Lander February 28, 1862 to march with his division from Hancock, Maryland to Martinsburg, Virginia and join Alpheus S. Williams' Third Brigade of Banks' Division. Lander died March 2, 1862, but James Shields assumed command of his division, and joined Williams' brigade as ordered. Banks occupied Winchester March 12, 1862, and there Shields' Division (formerly Lander's) was assigned to the newly created Fifth Corps, Army of the Potomac as Second Division.

Richardson's Division. Israel B. Richardson was assigned command of Sumner's Division March 13, 1862, and the division was then called Richardson's Division. That day it was assigned to Second Corps, Army of the Potomac as First Division.

Hamilton's Division. Charles S. Hamilton was assigned command of Heintzelman's Division March 13, 1862, and it then became known as Hamilton's Division. That day it was assigned to Third Corps, Army of the Potomac as Third Division.

Couch's Division. Darius N. Couch was assigned command of Keyes' Division March 13, 1862, and it was then called Couch's Division. That day it was assigned to Fourth Corps, Army of the Potomac as First Division.

King's Division. Rufus King was assigned command of McDowell's Division March 13, 1862, and it then became known as King's Division. That day it was assigned to First Corps, Army of the Potomac as Third Division.

Dix's Division. The troops under the command of John A. Dix at Baltimore, Maryland were referred to as Dix's Division, but they were not organized as a combat division of the Army of the Potomac, and it does not appear that they were formally organized into brigades. On August 31, 1861, Abram Duryee, recently arrived from Camp Hamilton, Virginia, was assigned command of a large brigade consisting of thirteen regiments, but the purpose of this organization was for drill and instruction. March 16, 1862, Dix was directed to organize a brigade in the vicinity of Baltimore for active service, and this was to be commanded by Henry H. Lockwood.

March 22, 1862, Dix's command at Baltimore was included in the newly created Middle Department.

* * * * * * * * * * * * * * *

In addition to the divisions described above, there were also several other organizations formed in the army. These were:

Cavalry, Army of the Potomac. In the process of organizing the army, McClellan assigned the cavalry regiments of his command to the infantry divisions. There was no brigade or division organization of the cavalry at that time. One cavalry brigade was formed under the command of John P. Hatch December 16, 1861, and it consisted of the 5th New York Cavalry and 1st Vermont Cavalry. This was simply a training organization, however, and when the campaigning season opened in the spring of 1862, the two regiments were sent to the field separately. March 16, 1862, Hatch was ordered to report to Irvin McDowell to command the cavalry of his First Corps, Army of the Potomac. George Stoneman commanded the equivalent of a cavalry brigade in September and October of 1861, and from October 1861 to March 1862, he was chief of cavalry, Army of the Potomac.

November 28, 1861, Philip St. George Cooke was assigned command of the regular cavalry serving in the Army of the Potomac. Later, this command was designated as the Cavalry Reserve. The function and mission of the Cavalry Reserve are not clear, but it appears that it was simply an administrative arrangement for the cavalry not assigned to the infantry divisions.

Artillery Reserve. Henry J. Hunt was announced as chief of artillery, Department of Northeastern Virginia July 23, 1861. He then served as commander of the Artillery Reserve, Army of the Potomac until September 5, 1862, when he was appointed chief of artillery, Army of the Potomac.

Infantry Reserve. When McClellan assumed command of the army, he began to assemble the available regular infantry to constitute an infantry reserve for the army. Beginning with a small battalion that was with McDowell's Army of Northeastern Virginia (known as "Sykes' Regulars" at First Bull Run), this force grew to about 1,000 men at the end of August 1861, to almost 5,000 at the end of April 1862. Sykes was assigned to duty with Andrew Porter, provost marshal at Washington, October 3, 1861, and his command was assigned as Second Brigade of Silas Casey's Division. These troops went to the Peninsula as Sykes' Infantry Reserve (Regular Brigade), and May 17, 1862 were assigned to Fitz John Porter's Fifth Provisional Corps for organization into a division.

Provost Guard. Andrew Porter was assigned command of the Provost Guard of the army, which was organized in October 1861, and was composed largely of regular army units. It was assigned to the Infantry Reserve, Army of the Potomac in March 1862.

Corps of Observation on the Upper Potomac. For details of this organization, see Stone's Division, above.

Railroad Brigade (or Railroad Guard). This organization was formed in November 1861 under Robinson for the purpose of guarding the Baltimore and Ohio Railroad. Robinson was relieved by Dixon S. Miles, who remained in command until March 22, 1862, when the brigade was transferred to the newly created Middle Department.

Engineer Brigade. This brigade was formed in March 1862 from the 15th New York Engineers, the 50th New York Engineers, and a battalion of United States Engineers. Daniel P. Woodbury commanded the New York Volunteers, and James C. Duane commanded the regulars.

* * * * * * * * * * * * * * *

In October 1861, the troops of the Army of the Potomac were assigned as follows: Troops in and about Washington; the Garrison of Washington; the Garrison of Alexandria; the City Guard of Washington; Forces on the Maryland Shore of the Potomac below Washington; Forces on the Maryland Shore of the Potomac above Washington as Far as Cumberland, Maryland; and Troops under Dix at Baltimore and Its Dependencies.

The divisions of the army were generally located as follows: Hooker's Division was at Budd's Ferry on the lower Potomac; Heintzelman's Division, at Fort Lyon and vicinity; Franklin's Division, near Alexandria Theological Seminary; McDowell's Division, at Upton's Hill and Arlington; Fitz John Porter's Division, at Hall's Hill and Miner's Hill; Smith's Division, at Mackall's Hill; McCall's Division, at Langley, Virginia; Buell's Division, at Tennallytown, Meridian Hill, and Emory's Chapel, on the left bank of the Potomac; Casey's Division, at Washington; Stoneman's cavalry, at Washington; Hunt's artillery, at Washington; Banks' Division, at Darnestown, with detachments at Point of Rocks, Sandy Hook, and Williamsport in Maryland; Stone's Division, at Poolesville, Maryland; and Dix's Division, at Baltimore, Maryland.

Army Corps Organization
March 13, 1862

On March 8, 1862, shortly before the Army of the Potomac left for the Peninsula, President Lincoln directed that the active portion of the army be organized into four army corps as follows: First Corps, to be commanded by Irvin McDowell; Second Corps, to be commanded by Edwin V. Sumner; Third Corps, to be commanded by Samuel P. Heintzelman; and Fourth Corps, to be commanded by Erasmus D. Keyes. A Fifth Corps was also to be organized from the divisions of Nathaniel P. Banks and James Shields, which were then serving in the lower Shenandoah Valley. Banks was assigned command of Fifth Corps. The troops that were left for the defense of Washington after the army had departed were placed under the command of James S. Wadsworth, who was also assigned as military governor of the District of Columbia.

March 13, 1862, the organization of the five corps was announced as follows:

First Corps was to consist of the divisions of Franklin, McCall, and King (formerly McDowell's); Second Corps, of the divisions of Richardson (formerly Sumner's), Blenker, and Sedgwick (formerly Stone's); Third Corps, of the divisions of Fitz John Porter, Hooker, and Charles S. Hamilton (formerly Heintzelman's); Fourth Corps, of the divisions of Couch (formerly Keyes'), Smith, and Casey; and Fifth Corps, of the divisions of Alpheus S. Williams (formerly Banks') and Shields (formerly Lander's).

PENINSULAR CAMPAIGN
APRIL 1862–AUGUST 1862

At the end of January 1862, President Lincoln issued an order directing McClellan to advance with the Army of the Potomac from its camps around Washington toward Joseph E. Johnston's Confederate army at Manassas Junction. Instead of accepting Lincoln's plan, however, McClellan submitted another plan for the spring campaign in which he proposed to transport the Army of the Potomac by water to Urbanna, Virginia, on the Rappahannock River, and then move overland toward Richmond. The plan finally adopted was to move the army by water to Fort Monroe, and then to move up the Peninsula between the York and James rivers toward Richmond. In giving his approval to this plan, Lincoln directed McClellan to leave an adequate force in front of Washington to protect the capital. Thus, at the beginning of operations in the spring of 1862, the troops of the Department of the Potomac were divided into two forces: the one sent to the Peninsula, and the other that was retained in northern Virginia for the protection of Washington.

When the Army of the Potomac left Washington for the Peninsula, the following troops were left behind to protect the capital: McDowell's First Corps, near Alexandria; Banks' Fifth Corps, in the Shenandoah Valley; Wadsworth's command, in the District of Washington; Dix's Division, at Baltimore; and Blenker's Division of Second Corps, near Washington. This force was reduced when Dix's command at Baltimore was transferred to the newly created Middle Department March 22, 1862, and it was further reduced May 1, 1862, when Blenker's Division was ordered to the Shenandoah Valley, and eventually to join John C. Fremont in the Mountain Department.

The organization of First Corps, Fifth Corps, and the District of Washington was as follows:

FIRST CORPS, Irvin McDowell

King's Division, Rufus King
    Cutler's Brigade, Lysander Cutler
    Augur's Brigade, Christopher C. Augur
    Patrick's Brigade, Marsena R. Patrick

Note 1. King's Brigade was formerly McDowell's Brigade
Note 2. Cutler's Brigade was formerly King's Brigade.
Note 3. Patrick's Brigade was formerly Wadsworth's Brigade. Patrick was ordered to report to King March 23, 1862.

Franklin's Division, William B. Franklin
    First Brigade, Philip Kearny
    Second Brigade, Henry W. Slocum
    Third Brigade, John Newton

McCall's Division, George A. McCall
    First Brigade, John F. Reynolds
    Second Brigade, George G. Meade
    Third Brigade, Edward O. C. Ord

First Corps was merged into the newly created Department of the Rappahannock April 4, 1862. For further information, see Department of the Rappahannock.

FIFTH CORPS, Nathaniel P. Banks

Williams' Division, Alpheus S. Williams
    First Brigade, Dudley Donnelly
    Second Brigade, John J. Abercrombie
    Third Brigade, George H. Gordon

Note. Williams' Division was formerly Banks' Division.

Shields' Division, James Shields
    First Brigade, Nathan Kimball
    Second Brigade, Jeremiah C. Sullivan
    Third Brigade, Erastus B. Tyler

Note. Shields' Division was formerly Lander's Division.

Fifth Corps was made independent of the Army of the Potomac March 15, 1862, and it was merged into the Department of the Shenandoah April 4,

1862. For further information, see Department of the Shenandoah, April 4, 1862–June 26, 1862, and also Shenandoah Valley Campaign (Jackson), 1862.

DISTRICT OF WASHINGTON, James S. Wadsworth

Note. March 17, 1862, the same day that embarkation of the Army of the Potomac for Fort Monroe began, James S. Wadsworth was assigned as military governor of the District of Columbia. In addition, he was also assigned as military commander of the defenses, both north and south of the Potomac River, in the vicinity of Washington. The limits of his command were defined as follows: the District of Columbia; the city of Alexandria; the territory in front of and in the vicinity of the defensive works south of the Potomac from the Occoquan River to Difficult Run; and the post of Fort Washington. This command was called the District of Washington. Wadsworth was also placed in charge of the provisional brigades of new troops arriving in Washington, and also the troops present in the city.

The troops originally sent to the Peninsula consisted of the following:

Second Corps (less Blenker's Division), Edwin V. Sumner
Third Corps, Samuel P. Heintzelman
Fourth Corps, Erasmus D. Keyes
Cavalry Reserve, Philip St. G. Cooke
    Emory's Brigade, William H. Emory
    Blake's Brigade, George A. H. Blake
Artillery Reserve, Henry J. Hunt
Engineer Troops
    Volunteers, Daniel P. Woodbury
    Regulars, James C. Duane
Infantry Reserve (Regular Brigade), George Sykes
Artillery Troops with Siege Trains (1st Connecticut Artillery), Robert O. Tyler

Note. For the organization of the corps artillery, in this and later sections, see the various corps that served with the Army of the Potomac.

Embarkation of these troops began at Alexandria, Virginia March 17, 1862, and they were transferred to Fort Monroe by way of the Potomac River and Chesapeake Bay as rapidly as transportation became available. Headquarters of the Army of the Potomac was moved to the vicinity of Fort Monroe April 1–2, 1862. April 4, 1862, the Department of the Rappahannock and the Department of the Shenandoah were created (the Middle Department was created March 22, 1862), and after that date, the only troops remaining in the Army of the Potomac were those serving with McClellan on the Peninsula.

McClellan's army moved slowly up the Peninsula from Fort Monroe, with an engagement at Williamsburg May 5, 1862, and arrived at White's House on the Pamunkey River May 16, 1862. While at White's House, on May 18, 1862, McClellan reorganized his army by forming a Fifth Provisional Corps under Fitz John Porter, and a Sixth Provisional Corps under William B. Franklin. The Army of the Potomac then consisted of the following corps, with which it operated during the remainder of the Peninsular Campaign: Sumner's Second Corps, Heintzelman's Third Corps, Keyes' Fourth Corps, Porter's Fifth Provisional Corps, and Franklin's Sixth Provisional Corps.

McClellan then continued his advance toward Richmond, and when he arrived on the Chickahominy River, he divided his army into two parts. He kept the corps of Porter, Franklin, and Sumner on the northeast side of the river and sent the corps of Keyes and Heintzelman across to the other side. The latter two corps were strongly attacked at Fair Oaks and Seven Pines by troops of Joseph E. Johnston's army May 31, 1862, and Sumner's corps was sent to their assistance. Johnston was severely wounded, and Gustavus W. Smith was in command until relieved June 1, 1862 by Robert E. Lee.

For the next several weeks, both armies remained relatively quiet. But on June 25, 1862, the fighting before Richmond that became known as the Seven Days' Battles (or Campaign) began. The first engagement, which was a relatively minor one, was known as Oak Grove, King's School-House, the Orchard, or French's Field. The heavy fighting began at Mechanicsville June 26, 1862, and then continued at Gaines' Mill June 27, 1862; Savage's Station, June 29, 1862; Frayser's Farm or Glendale, June 30, 1862; and Malvern Hill, July 1, 1862. After the reverses suffered at Gaines' Mill at the beginning of the Seven Days, McClellan retreated to Harrison's Landing on the James River, where he arrived safely July 2, 1862, after the Battle of Malvern Hill. His army remained there in an entrenched position until the latter part of August 1862, when it was transferred to northern Virginia during John Pope's Virginia Campaign.

July 22, 1862, Fifth Provisional Corps and Sixth Provisional Corps were officially confirmed, and their designations were changed to Fifth Corps and Sixth Corps. (*note.* Banks' former Fifth Corps, Army of the Potomac had been merged into the

Department of the Shenandoah April 4, 1862.) Also on July 22, 1862, Ninth Corps was created under the command of Ambrose E. Burnside from troops at Newport News, which had been sent there from the Department of North Carolina and the Department of the South to reinforce McClellan. Ninth Corps was not at that time a part of McClellan's army, but it was later assigned to the Army of the Potomac.

For details of the organization and operations of the Army of the Potomac during the period March 17, 1862, to the time of its withdrawal from the Peninsula in the latter part of August 1862, see Peninsular Campaign.

POPE'S NORTHERN VIRGINIA CAMPAIGN
AUGUST 16, 1862–SEPTEMBER 2, 1862

During the latter part of August 1862, the Army of the Potomac was withdrawn from Harrison's Landing, on the Peninsula, and was sent to aid Pope's Army of Virginia in opposing Lee's advance in northern Virginia toward Washington. Burnside's Ninth Corps, which was not then a part of the Army of the Potomac but was on the Peninsula, was ordered to Fredericksburg August 1, 1862, and Second Corps, Third Corps, Fifth Corps, and Sixth Corps were ordered to Aquia Creek and Alexandria. Later Couch's Division of Fourth Corps was also ordered to Alexandria. John J. Peck's Division of Fourth Corps was left behind at Yorktown. The units of the Army of the Potomac arrived in northern Virginia August 22–29, 1862, and marched to join Pope's command.

Heintzelman's Third Corps, Porter's Fifth Corps, and two divisions of Ninth Corps, then under Jesse L. Reno, were with Pope during the battles of Groveton and Second Bull Run (Second Manassas) August 28–30, 1862, but Sumner's Second Corps and Franklin's Sixth Corps arrived at Centerville too late to be engaged. Isaac I. Stevens' First Division, Ninth Corps and Philip Kearny's First Division, Third Corps were also engaged at Chantilly or Ox Hill September 1, 1862. Both Stevens and Kearny were killed that day. From the time they joined Pope's Army of Virginia until the retreat from Centerville ended at Washington, the troops of the

Army of the Potomac were under the command of Pope.

For details of the organization of the troops of the Army of the Potomac during the latter part of August 1862, and also of their operations while with the Army of Virginia, see the following: Pope's Northern Virginia Campaign, and also the various corps involved.

IN THE DISTRICT OF THE DEFENSES OF WASHINGTON, ARMY OF THE POTOMAC SEPTEMBER 1–7, 1862

Following the Second Battle of Bull Run, the Army of Virginia and the corps of the Army of the Potomac retreated to within the Defenses of Washington, then commanded by John G. Barnard. Because of the transfer of the corps of the army of the Potomac to the Army of the James, and of the events that followed, there is a curious uncertainty about the command of the Army of the Potomac during the period immediately following Pope's defeat at the Second Battle of Bull Run. On September 1, 1862, when Pope was at or near Centerville, McClellan was in camp near Alexandria with only his staff and about 100 men under his personal direction. That day he went into Washington, and there Henry W. Halleck instructed him, verbally, to assume command of the Defenses of Washington, but limited his jurisdiction to the defensive works and their garrisons, and he specifically prohibited him from exercising any control over the troops then actively engaged at the front under Pope. McClellan was thus detached from the Army of the Potomac, although he was still technically in command because no order had been issued officially relieving him. According to McClellan, he met with Halleck and the president on the morning of September 2, 1862, and was instructed, again verbally, by the president to assume command of the entire city and of the troops falling back to it from the front.

September 3, 1862, Lincoln assigned Halleck the task of putting the army once again in condition for active field operations. That day McClellan sent some of the returning troops to the north side of the Potomac River, and apparently because of this movement, Halleck cautioned McClellan that his command was limited to the Defenses of Washington, and that it did not extend to any active column that might move outside of the works. In addition he was advised that there had been no decision as to the command of the active army. McClellan later asserted that he had never received any specific instructions to take command of the field army, but there are several reasons for believing that he did. At a later date, Halleck stated that at some time between September 2 and September 5, 1862, Lincoln did ask McClellan to take command of the army that was to march into Maryland. As further evidence, in a letter written September 5, 1862 to his wife, McClellan said that "Again I have been called upon to save the country. The case is desperate. . . ." It should also be noted that McClellan's orders until September 6, 1862 were under the simple heading "Headquarters, Washington"; but the next day, when he moved his headquarters to Rockville and started the army toward Frederick, Maryland, he again used the heading "Headquarters Army of the Potomac." There is also the presidential order of November 5, 1862 in which Lincoln relieved McClellan from the command of the "Army of the Potomac," which clearly implies that McClellan was indeed in command.

Whatever specific orders were issued, McClellan assumed command of the District of the Defenses of Washington, and immediately began to prepare for the defense of the capital, and to reorganize and reequip the army for field service.

September 3, 1862, Lee's Army of Northern Virginia withdrew from the Washington front and marched northward toward the Potomac River. September 4–7, 1862, it crossed into Maryland at the fords near Leesburg, Virginia, and marched toward Frederick, where it arrived Sept 7, 1862. At this time McClellan received information that led him to believe that Lee intended to cross the upper Potomac into Maryland, and on September 3, 1862 he sent his cavalry to the fords near Poolesville to watch the enemy and impede their crossing; and sent Second Corps, Army of the Potomac and Second Corps, Army of Virginia (later Twelfth Corps, Army of the Potomac) to Tennallytown, District of Columbia; and Ninth Corps to a position on Seventh Street Road, a short distance north of Washington. The remainder of the army was left on the Virginia side of the Potomac. The records are not clear, but it appears that the army remained in these positions during September 4, 1862 and a part of September 5, 1862. By September 6, 1862, Darius N. Couch's division of Fourth Corps and William B. Franklin's Sixth Corps were at Tennallytown and Offutt's Cross Roads; Second Corps, Army of the Potomac and Second Corps, Army of Virginia were at Rockville; and Third Corps, Army of Virginia (later to be designated First Corps, Army of the Potomac) were at Leesboro, north of Washington. Also on September 6, 1862, George Sykes' division of Porter's Fifth Corps was ordered to Tennallytown to constitute a reserve for the army. Sykes reported directly to McClellan.

During the first two weeks of September, there were several command and organizational changes in the army as follows:

On September 1, 1862, Alfred Pleasonton arrived at Alexandria from the Peninsula with his cavalry brigade, and William W. Averell followed with his cavalry brigade September 5, 1862. The regiments of these two brigades, plus other cavalry regiments from the Defenses of Washington, were organized into a cavalry division of five brigades. Pleasonton was assigned command of the division. The brigades were commanded as follows: First Brigade, Charles J. Whiting; Second Brigade, John F. Farnsworth; Third Brigade, Richard H. Rush; Fourth Brigade, Andrew T. McReynolds; and Fifth Brigade, Benjamin F. Davis. With five brigades, this appears to have been a strong organization, but actually it was not. There were only twelve regiments in the division, and of these, thirty-three companies were not under divisional control. For more information, see Cavalry Corps, Army of the Potomac.

September 3, 1862, Alpheus S. Williams was assigned command of Second Corps, Army of Virginia, relieving Nathaniel P. Banks, who was ill. On the same day, Jesse L. Reno was assigned command of Ninth Corps. Ambrose E. Burnside, former commander of Ninth Corps, was at Falmouth, Virginia, and he was ordered to bring John G. Parke's Third Division, Ninth Corps to Washington to rejoin the corps.

September 4, 1862, John F. Reynolds' Division, formerly Third Division, Fifth Corps while on the Peninsula, and which was then attached to Irvin McDowell's Third Corps, Army of Virginia during Pope's recent campaign, was ordered to rejoin Fifth Corps, Army of the Potomac. This order was not carried out, however, and Reynolds' Division remained with Third Corps, Army of Virginia until September 12, 1862, when the latter was reorganized as First Corps, Army of the Potomac. The designation of Reynolds' Division was then changed to Third Division, First Corps, Army of the Potomac. A new Third Division, Fifth Corps was organized September 12, 1862 (see below).

September 5, 1862, the Army of the Potomac and the Army of Virginia were consolidated, and Pope was relieved from command. This was no more than an official order, however, because Pope had exercised no effective command since September 1, 1862. Also on September 5, 1862, Fitz John Porter and William B. Franklin were relieved from duty with the army until charges against them for their conduct at Second Bull Run could be examined. Joseph Hooker was assigned command of Porter's Fifth Corps, and Franklin's Sixth Corps was attached to Heintzelman's Third Corps, Army of the Potomac. At McClellan's request, however, this order was suspended, because of the emergency created by Lee's invasion of Maryland.

For better control of his forces during the impending campaign in Maryland, McClellan ordered the organization of the Army of the Potomac into a Right Wing, Center, and Left Wing as follows:

The Right Wing consisted of Third Corps, Army of Virginia (later to be designated First Corps, Army of the Potomac) and Ninth Corps, Army of the Potomac, and was commanded by Ambrose E. Burnside. The two corps were ordered to assemble at Leesboro, Maryland. September 7, 1862, Joseph Hooker relieved Irvin McDowell in command of Third Corps, Army of Virginia (ordered September 6, 1862). That same day, Samuel D. Sturgis, formerly commander of the Reserve Corps, Army of Virginia, was ordered to report to Burnside at Leesboro, and was then assigned command of Second Division, Ninth Corps. September 8, 1862, Jacob D. Cox's Kanawha Division marched from Upton's Hill, south of the Potomac River, to Leesboro, and was then attached to Ninth Corps.

September 5, 1862, Second Corps, Army of the Potomac and Second Corps, Army of Virginia (later to be designated Twelfth Corps, Army of the Potomac) were moved to Rockville, Maryland to form the Center, Army of the Potomac. Edwin V. Sumner, commander of Second Corps, Army of the Potomac, was assigned command.

The Left Wing was assigned to William B. Franklin, commander of Sixth Corps, Army of the Potomac, and it consisted of Sixth Corps and Darius N. Couch's First Division of Fourth Corps. September 5, 1862, Couch moved his division to Offutt's Cross Roads, and the next day Sixth Corps marched from Alexandria to Tennallytown, District of Columbia.

On September 6, 1862, thirty-six new regiments were assigned to the different corps of the army to make good the losses sustained in the recent campaign in Virginia.

By September 7, 1862, the army was largely reorganized and was assembled northwest of Washington in readiness to move in pursuit of Lee in Maryland.

Franz Sigel's First Corps, Army of Virginia (later designated as Eleventh Corps, Army of the Potomac), Samuel P. Heintzelman's Third Corps, Army of the Potomac, and Fitz John Porter, with George W. Morell's division of Fifth Corps, Army of the Potomac, were left in the Defenses of Washington, on the south side of the Potomac. For the organization and disposition of the forces left by McClellan for the protection of the capital during the Maryland Campaign, see Miscellaneous Organizations, Military District of the Defenses of Washington.

MARYLAND CAMPAIGN (SOUTH MOUNTAIN AND ANTIETAM) SEPTEMBER 3, 1862–SEPTEMBER 20, 1862

September 7, 1862, McClellan's army left its encampments north and west of Washington and advanced into Maryland in pursuit of Lee. Second Corps and Ninth Corps, Army of the Potomac and Second Corps and Third Corps, Army of Virginia marched toward Frederick, Maryland; and Sixth Corps and Couch's division of Fourth Corps, Army of the Potomac advanced on the left along the Potomac River.

September 12, 1862, the Army of Virginia was officially discontinued, and the corps of that army were redesignated as follows:

First Corps became Eleventh Corps, Army of the Potomac
Second Corps became Twelfth Corps, Army of the Potomac
Third Corps became First Corps, Army of the Potomac

Note. Instead of the new designations, however, the corps numbers assigned in the Army of Virginia were generally used until after the Battle of Antietam.

McClellan's field force of the Army of the Potomac then consisted of First Corps; Second Corps; Couch's First Division, Fourth Corps; Fifth Corps; Sixth Corps; Ninth Corps; Twelfth Corps; and the cavalry. Left behind near Washington were Third Corps and Eleventh Corps.

McClellan advanced with the army to Frederick, Maryland, and then, when he learned that Lee had divided his army by sending Thomas J. (Stonewall) Jackson to capture Harper's Ferry, he moved rapidly westward toward Boonsboro to strike James Longstreet's command before it could be reinforced. September 14, 1862, Hooker's First Corps and Reno's Ninth Corps were engaged at South Mountain, and Franklin's Sixth Corps attacked and captured Crampton's Gap in South Mountain, farther south. After clearing the gaps in South Mountain, McClellan pressed on and took position in front of Lee's army, which was then in position beyond Antietam Creek, near Sharpsburg, Maryland. Most of the Army of the Potomac was engaged at the Battle of Antietam September 17, 1862. Fifth Corps was present but was not engaged, and only a part of Sixth Corps was in action. For details of the organization and the operations of the Army of the Potomac during the period September 7–18, 1862, see Maryland Campaign (South Mountain and Antietam).

ANTIETAM CREEK, MARYLAND TO WARRENTON, VIRGINIA SEPTEMBER 19, 1862–NOVEMBER 7, 1862

When Lee retreated into Virginia following the Battle of Antietam, McClellan did not follow. He gave as his reasons the exhaustion of his troops and the need to refit and reequip the army. Despite frequent urgings from Washington, McClellan did not move. Lincoln then paid McClellan a visit at Sharpsburg and, in an order dated October 6, 1862, directed him "to cross the Potomac and give battle to the enemy or drive him south." This order was repeated October 21, 1862, but it was not until October 26, 1862 that the army began its advance into Virginia.

Thus, for approximately five weeks after the Battle of Antietam, the Army of the Potomac remained inactive along the Potomac River in Maryland. During this time all was generally quiet, except for a brief interruption when James E. B. (Jeb) Stuart led an enemy cavalry force in his second ride around the Army of the Potomac. Stuart crossed the Potomac October 10, 1862, and rode through Maryland and Pennsylvania, by way of Chambersburg and Emmitsburg, to the mouth of the Monocacy River, near which he recrossed into Virginia October 12, 1862.

The Army of the Potomac remained near the battlefield of Antietam for a few days after Lee's departure, and then the corps were assigned to take positions as follows: Twelfth Corps at Harper's Ferry, September 19, 1862; Couch's Division of Fourth Corps (then attached to Sixth Corps) at Williamsport, September 20, 1862; Sixth Corps at Williamsport, September 21, 1862; and Second Corps at Harper's Ferry, September 22, 1862.

September 20, 1862, Richard H. Rush's Third Cavalry Brigade and Andrew T. McReynolds' Fourth Cavalry Brigade of Pleasonton's Cavalry Division were ordered to Williamsport, and on September 28, 1862, McReynolds' brigade moved on to Cumberland, Maryland. October 8, 1862, McClellan moved his headquarters to Knoxville, Maryland, near Harper's Ferry.

Ninth Corps remained near the mouth of Antietam Creek until October 7, 1862, and then (less the Kanawha Division) it moved to Harper's Ferry. First Corps remained near Sharpsburg until October 26, 1862, and Fifth Corps near the same place until October 30, 1862. On those two dates, respectively, First Corps and Fifth Corps were ordered to join the rest of the Army of the Potomac, which was then crossing the Potomac River on its advance toward Warrenton, Virginia.

In the meantime, there were some changes in the

composition and organization of the army. These were:

October 8, 1862 the Kanawha Division under the command of George Crook was detached from Ninth Corps, and was sent to Clarksburg in Western Virginia. Later in the month, two infantry divisions from the Defenses of Washington were transferred to the army in the field. October 10, 1862, George Stoneman's First Division, Third Corps, then at Poolesville, Maryland, was placed under McClellan's orders, and October 20, 1862, it was assigned to Ninth Corps. October 22, 1862, Amiel W. Whipple's Division of the Defenses of Washington reported to McClellan, and was assigned to Twelfth Corps as Third Division. For additional information regarding the changes of organization in the corps of the army, see Miscellaneous Organizations, Military District of the Defenses of Washington; and also the various corps of the army.

The organization of McClellan's cavalry was also changed in October 1862. October 3, 1862, First Cavalry Brigade, which Averell had commanded on the Peninsula, was reorganized under Averell, and was assigned to duty on the upper Potomac. October 21, 1862, Pleasonton, who was then in command of the Cavalry Division, Army of the Potomac, was assigned command of a reorganized Second Cavalry Brigade, which he had commanded on the Peninsula. The regiments for these two brigades were transferred from the Cavalry Division, which, as a result, was unofficially discontinued. For additional information, see Cavalry Corps, Army of the Potomac.

A temporary command of the army was established October 13, 1862, when Ambrose E. Burnside was assigned command of the Defenses of Harper's Ferry, and Second Corps, Ninth Corps, and Twelfth Corps were placed under his direction. This arrangement was continued until October 26, 1862.

There were also some important changes in the corps commanders during this period. September 29, 1862, John F. Reynolds returned from Pennsylvania, where he had been on duty during the Maryland Campaign, and assumed command of First Corps. October 7, 1862, Darius N. Couch assumed command of Second Corps, relieving Edwin V. Sumner, who departed on a leave of absence. Sumner died in Syracuse, New York March 21,

1863. October 8, 1862, Orlando B. Willcox relieved Jacob D. Cox in command of Ninth Corps. October 20, 1862, Henry W. Slocum was assigned command of Twelfth Corps to relieve Alpheus S. Williams, who had commanded the corps temporarily since the death of Joseph K. F. Mansfield at Antietam.

McClellan began his long-delayed advance into Virginia October 26, 1862. Pleasonton's Cavalry Brigade, Whipple's division of Twelfth Corps, Reynolds' First Corps, and Burnside's Ninth Corps (then commanded by Willcox) crossed the Potomac River at Berlin (present-day Brunswick), Maryland between October 26, 1862 and October 29, 1862. Stoneman's division of Ninth Corps crossed near Leesburg, Virginia October 27, 1862, and occupied the town. Franklin's Sixth Corps remained near Hagerstown, Maryland until October 30, 1862, and it then marched to Berlin, where it was the last corps to cross, November 2, 1862. Couch's Second Corps and Porter's Fifth Corps crossed the river at Harper's Ferry during the period October 29, 1862 to November 1, 1862. Once in Virginia, the army marched southward along the valley between the Blue Ridge Mountains and the Bull Run Mountains, and began arriving in the Warrenton area September 3, 1862. Pleasonton's cavalry moved along the eastern base of the Blue Ridge Mountains, covering the gaps leading into the Shenandoah Valley.

On October 29, 1862, Stoneman's division of Ninth Corps and Whipple's division of Twelfth Corps were detached from their respective corps and, together with Ninth Corps (then commanded by Willcox), were formed into a special force under Burnside. This force was designated as the Left or Left Wing of the Army of the Potomac. It was discontinued while the army was at Warrenton.

During McClellan's advance, Jackson's Corps of Lee's army remained in the Shenandoah Valley near Winchester, Virginia, but Longstreet's Corps moved southward, and arrived at Culpeper Court House November 3, 1862.

There were some changes in the cavalry early in November 1862. George D. Bayard's Cavalry Brigade, from the Defenses of Washington, joined McClellan near Warrenton October 31, 1862. October 29, 1862, Averell's Cavalry Brigade was ordered back from the upper Potomac, where it had been on duty, and it joined the army in Virginia November 3, 1862. Then on November 6, 1862,

Pleasonton's Cavalry Brigade was organized into a cavalry division of two brigades under Pleasonton. First Brigade was commanded by John F. Farnsworth; and Second Brigade, by David McM. Gregg. The cavalry with the Army of the Potomac then consisted of the cavalry brigades of Averell and Bayard, and Pleasonton's division. For additional information about the organization and movements of the cavalry during the advance of the army to Warrenton, see Cavalry Corps, Army of the Potomac.

By November 7, 1862, the army was near Warrenton. First Corps was at Warrenton; Second Corps was near Rectortown, and was under orders to advance to Waterloo; Fifth Corps was at White Plains; Sixth Corps was near Upperville, and was under orders to march to New Baltimore; and Ninth Corps was near Waterloo. Pleasonton's cavalry was at Little Washington and Sperryville; Averell's Cavalry Brigade was in the Little Washington-Sperryville area; and Bayard's Cavalry Brigade was on the line of the Rappahannock River from Waterloo to the Orange and Alexandria Railroad.

On November 7, 1862, Burnside, who was then near Waterloo, received an order dated November 5, 1862, assigning him to the command of the Army of the Potomac. That night, at Rectortown, McClellan turned over the command of the army to Burnside. It is important to note, however, that although Burnside did not issue a formal order assuming command until November 9, 1862, he was in command from the night of November 7, 1862.

When McClellan left the line of the Potomac River as he advanced toward Warrenton, steps were taken immediately to supply the army in Virginia from Washington and Alexandria by way of the Orange and Alexandria Railroad and the Manassas Gap Railroad. For this purpose it was necessary to repair and protect the line of the railroad, and Sigel's Eleventh Corps of the Defenses of Washington was sent forward for this purpose. In September 1862, Eleventh Corps had been advanced from the Defenses of Washington to the Centerville-Fairfax area as a corps of observation. George D. Bayard's Cavalry Brigade was attached to Sigel's command, and was operating on its front. October 31, 1862, Bayard arrived near Warrenton and reported to McClellan, and with his brigade joined the Army of the Potomac. Two days later, Eleventh Corps was ordered to Thoroughfare Gap, which it occupied November 5, 1862. Eleventh Corps remained in the Thoroughfare Gap-Gainesville area with the Army of the Potomac until November 17, 1862, when the latter advanced toward Falmouth at the beginning of Burnside's Fredericksburg Campaign. Eleventh Corps then moved eastward along the railroad to its former position near Fairfax and Centerville. For additional information, see Miscellaneous Organizations, Military District of the Defenses of Washington.

Defenses of the Upper Potomac. On October 30, 1862, as the army was leaving its positions along the Potomac, George W. Morell was relieved from command of First Division, Fifth Corps, Army of the Potomac, and the next day he was assigned command of the troops left by McClellan to guard the upper Potomac. Morell's command was designated Defenses of the Upper Potomac, and his headquarters was at Hagerstown, Maryland. This command was under McClellan's control, and was, in effect, a district of the Army of the Potomac.

When first defined, October 30, 1862, the Defenses of the Upper Potomac was to extend from the mouth of Opequon Creek to Cumberland, Maryland, but this order was amended the next day to define the Defenses as the territory between the mouth of Antietam Creek and Cumberland. Morell assumed command at Hagerstown November 1, 1862.

When organized, the troops of the Defenses of the Upper Potomac consisted of the following: George H. Gordon's Third Brigade, First Division, Twelfth Corps, which was detached from Slocum's command at Harper's Ferry, was on the left of Morell's line, near Sharpsburg; John R. Kenly's Maryland Brigade was in the center of the line at Williamsport; and Benjamin F. Kelley's Railroad Division of the District of Western Virginia, Department of the Ohio was on the right at Cumberland, and at New Creek, twenty-three miles farther west. Andrew T. McReynolds' Fourth Cavalry Brigade of the Army of the Potomac, which was at Cumberland, was transferred to the Defenses of the Upper Potomac.

Morell's command was enlarged November 14, 1862, when he was assigned command of all forces in the vicinity of Harper's Ferry and on the upper Potomac. The troops on the line of the Baltimore and

Ohio Railroad in early December 1862 were as follows: Kenly's Maryland Brigade was at Williamsport; Kelley's Railroad Division, at Cumberland and New Creek; John W. Geary's Second Division, Twelfth Corps, on Bolivar Heights; Joseph F. Knipe's First Brigade, First Division, Twelfth Corps, on Maryland Heights; Thomas L. Kane's Second Brigade, First Division, Twelfth Corps, in the Loudoun Valley near Loudoun Heights; and George H. Gordon's Third Brigade, First Division, Twelfth Corps, at Sharpsburg. Whipple's former Third Division, Twelfth Corps was with Third Corps, Army of the Potomac in Virginia.

In the reorganization of the Army of the Potomac before the Battle of Fredericksburg, Virginia, Henry W. Slocum's Twelfth Corps was assigned to Franz Sigel's Reserve of the army, and December 9, 1862, it was ordered to a position covering Washington, on the south side of the Potomac River. Morell was instructed to relieve Slocum's troops at Harper's Ferry. By December 11, 1862, Twelfth Corps, including Gordon's brigade, had departed for Harper's Ferry, leaving two regiments behind. That day, December 11, 1862, Morell sent Kenly with two regiments of his Maryland Brigade to Harper's Ferry, but he kept the other two regiments of the brigade to watch the line near Williamsport. December 20, 1862, Morell sent Kenly's other two regiments to Harper's Ferry.

The Defenses of the Upper Potomac continued as a part of the Army of the Potomac until December 1862. Then, on December 17, 1862, Robert C. Schenck was assigned command of of the Middle Department (assumed command December 22, 1862), and on the same day, December 17, 1862, Schenck was charged with the protection of the Baltimore and Ohio Railroad as far west as the Ohio River. By this order the Defenses of the Upper Potomac was, in effect, transferred to the Middle Department, Eighth Corps. For further information, see Middle Department.

FREDERICKSBURG CAMPAIGN NOVEMBER 7, 1862–DECEMBER 15, 1862

Immediately upon assuming command of the

Army of the Potomac, Burnside proposed a new plan of operations. Instead of continuing the advance of the army toward Culpeper Court House and Gordonsville, as McClellan had been doing slowly for the past two weeks, he suggested that the line of march be shifted eastward to Fredericksburg, and from that point southward toward Richmond. This plan was approved November 14, 1862, and on that date, Burnside announced the reorganization of the army into three grand divisions and a reserve as follows:

LEFT GRAND DIVISION, William B. Franklin
  First Corps, John F. Reynolds
  Sixth Corps, William F. Smith

Note. Smith relieved Franklin in command of Sixth Corps when the latter assumed command of the Left Grand Division.

CENTER GRAND DIVISION, Joseph Hooker
  Third Corps, George Stoneman
  Fifth Corps, Daniel Butterfield

Note 1. Third Corps was reorganized at this time under Stoneman.
Note 2. Hooker had relieved Porter in command of Fifth Corps November 12, 1862, when the latter was called to Washington to stand trial for his conduct at the Second Battle of Bull Run.
Note 3. Butterfield relieved Hooker in command of Fifth Corps when the latter assumed command of the Center Grand Division.

RIGHT GRAND DIVISION, Edwin V. Sumner
  Second Corps, Darius N. Couch
  Ninth Corps, Orlando B. Willcox

Note. Couch relieved Sumner in command of Second Division when the latter assumed command of the Right Grand Division.

RESERVE, Franz Sigel
  Eleventh Corps, Franz Sigel

On November 21, 1862, while the army was near Falmouth, Pleasonton's Cavalry Division was assigned to the Right Grand Division; Bayard's Cavalry Brigade, to the Left Grand Division; and Averell's Cavalry Brigade, to the Center Grand Division.

The forward movement of the army from Warrenton began promptly November 15, 1862, and four days later it was in position along the Rappa-

hannock River, opposite Fredericksburg. Burnside was unable to cross, however, because pontoon trains that had been ordered earlier from Washington had not arrived, and also because of heavy rains that made the fords of the river impassable for infantry. Then, although the pontoons finally arrived November 24, 1862, Burnside made no effort to cross until December 11, 1862.

Meantime, during this period, heavy reinforcements were ordered forward to the army. These were as follows:

Daniel E. Sickles' Second Division, Third Corps, of the Defenses of Washington, remained in position along the Orange and Alexandria when the other two divisions of the corps, under Stoneman, marched from Warrenton for Hartwood Church November 17, 1862. Then, on November 25, 1862, Sickles was ordered to move from his positions at Union Mills and Wolf Run Ford to join Stoneman, who had moved to Potomac Creek November 22, 1862.

Early in December 1862, about 15,000 troops were sent to the army at Falmouth by Samuel P. Heintzelman, commander of the Defenses of Washington. This force consisted of three brigades as follows: a provisional brigade under Henry M. Bossert (the senior colonel), which was formed from six regiments of Joseph A. Haskin's Division, Defenses of Washington North of the Potomac; William W. Jennings' Brigade of John J. Abercrombie's Division, Defenses of Washington South of the Potomac; and Dexter E. Wright's Brigade of Silas Casey's Division, Defenses of Washington South of the Potomac. December 1, 1862, these three brigades marched from Washington down the Maryland side of the Potomac, by way of Port Tobacco, to Liverpool Point, opposite Aquia Creek. They were then ferried across the Potomac, and continued on to Falmouth, where they arrived December 9, 1862. Bossert's brigade was assigned to Marsena R. Patrick's Provost Guard, Army of the Potomac, and the other two brigades were broken up and their regiments reassigned.

Three additional regiments and a battery were also sent to the army from the Middle Department, by way of Washington, December 5, 1862.

When Burnside left Warrenton for Falmouth, Sigel's Eleventh Corps was withdrawn from its forward position at Thoroughfare Gap to the Centerville-Fairfax area. On December 9, 1862, as Burnside was preparing to cross the Rappahannock at Fredericksburg, Eleventh Corps and Slocum's Twelfth Corps, the latter then at Harper's Ferry, were ordered forward to Dumfries, about twenty miles south of Washington, as a reserve. Sigel arrived there December 12, 1862, and the next day he was ordered to Falmouth, but he did not arrive in time to take part in the battle on December 13, 1862. December 14, 1862, Eleventh Corps marched to Stafford Court House. Twelfth Corps was at Fairfax Court House on the day of the Battle of Fredericksburg.

The Army of the Potomac crossed the Rappahannock December 11–13, 1862, and on the thirteenth was repulsed with heavy losses when it attempted to take the heights behind Fredericksburg. It remained in position across the river until the night of December 15, 1862, when it withdrew to the north bank. It then went into winter quarters. For details of the Battle of Fredericksburg, see Fredericksburg, Virginia Campaign.

WINTER OF 1862–1863
DECEMBER 15, 1862–APRIL 1863

During the first few weeks following the Battle of Fredericksburg, the army was engaged in constructing permanent housing for the winter. For Burnside, however, campaigning for the season was not yet over. December 26, 1862, he issued orders in preparation for another movement to cross the Rappahannock and engage Lee. The intended point of crossing is uncertain, but it may have been Muddy Creek, seven miles below Fredericksburg. This plan was canceled, however, when Lincoln forbade any movement of which he had not previously been informed.

The Mud March. Once again, Burnside decided to cross the Rappahannock and drive the Confederates from their positions at Fredericksburg. On January 20, 1863, he issued orders for Hooker's and Franklin's grand divisions to march westward along the north bank of the Rappahannock, then cross the river and turn back and attack the enemy on the heights west of Fredericksburg, at their northern end. Rain started to fall on the night of January 20,

1863, as the army moved toward the crossing sites, and continued to fall steadily until the roads and streams were virtually impassable. Finally, on January 23, 1863, Burnside called off the movement, and ordered the army to return to its camps around Falmouth. This brief campaign was the celebrated "Mud March" of the Army of the Potomac.

****

Following this abortive effort, the army generally stayed quietly in its camps during the remainder of the winter, except for the usual picket, outpost, and scouting duties. The corps camps were located as follows: First Corps was at Stoneman's Switch and near White Oak Church; Sixth Corps was also near White Oak Church; Second and Third corps were near Falmouth; Fifth Corps was on the Richmond, Fredericksburg and Potomac Railroad between Potomac Creek and near Falmouth; Eleventh Corps was near Brooke Station; Twelfth Corps was at Stafford Court House; and in February 1862, First Cavalry Division was near Stafford Court House, Second Cavalry Division was near Brooke Station, and Third Cavalry Division was near Belle Plain.

The infantry picket line of the army was established as follows: Beginning on the Potomac east of Belle Plain, it ran south to a point opposite Moss Neck; then along the north bank of the Rappahannock to the west of Falmouth; and finally, generally northward, covering Falmouth, Stafford Court House, and Dumfries. The cavalry picket line started to the west of Falmouth, and ran northward about five miles in front of the infantry pickets.

On January 10, 1863, a fourth grand division was organized. On that date, Franz Sigel assumed command of the Reserve Grand Division, which was defined by an order of January 20, 1863 as consisting of Eleventh Corps and Twelfth Corps. This order was stated to be in effect from the date that Sigel was authorized to assume command of both corps, which was December 9, 1862. Perhaps this is the reason that Sigel's Reserve has been called the Reserve Grand Division before the January date. Louis P. Di Cesnola's cavalry brigade was assigned to the Reserve Grand Division.

There was much dissatisfaction among some of the higher officers of the army following the Battle of Fredericksburg. Burnside had lost the confidence of a number of his subordinate officers, and he offered to resign. Some of these men behaved in a manner that Burnside considered to be disloyal and insubordinate. John Newton, a division commander, and John Cochrane, a brigade commander in Newton's division of William F. Smith Sixth Corps of William B. Franklin's Left Grand Division, went to Washington to explain to the president that the situation in the army had deteriorated to the point that it needed his attention. Both Smith and Franklin were aware of the purpose of this visit.

The fiasco of the "Mud March" added greatly to Burnside's woes, and on January 23, 1863, he composed General Order No. 8, in which he proposed to rid the army of those that he considered to be his detractors and disloyal subordinates. These were: Joseph Hooker, commander of the Center Grand Division; William B. Franklin, commander of the Left Grand Division; William F. Smith, commander of Sixth Corps; William T. H. Brooks, commander of First Division, Sixth Corps; John Newton, commander of Third Division, Sixth Corps; Samuel D. Sturgis, commander of Second Division, Ninth Corps; John Cochrane, commander of First Brigade, Third Division, Sixth Corps; and Edward Ferrero, commander of Second Brigade, Second Division, Ninth Corps. Burnside presented this order to the president, and asked that it be approved, stating that if it were not, his resignation was the only alternative.

In an order dated January 25, 1863, the president relieved Burnside, at his own request, and assigned Joseph Hooker to the command of the Army of the Potomac. The same order relieved Franklin from duty with the army, and also relieved Edwin V. Sumner, at his own request. The execution of this order resulted in a number of changes in the higher command of the army, and these were announced the next day as follows: Hooker relieved Burnside in command of the Army of the Potomac; George G. Meade succeeded Hooker in command of the Center Grand Division, and Charles Griffin was placed in temporary command of Fifth Corps, relieving Meade; Darius N. Couch succeeded Sumner in command of the Right Grand Division; Oliver O. Howard relieved John Sedgwick in command of Second Corps (note. Sedgwick had relieved Orlando B. Willcox in command of Ninth Corps January 16, 1863); and William F. Smith relieved Franklin in command of the Left Grand Division, and John Newton succeeded Smith in command of Sixth Corps.

Reorganization of the Army of the Potomac, February 1863. There were several organizational changes in the army in February 1863, following Hooker's assumption of command. The more significant of these are described in the following paragraphs.

Since its organization under McClellan September 2, 1862, the Defenses of Washington had been a military district of the Army of the Potomac. After that date, the commander of the Army of the Potomac was at some distance from the Washington area, and to provide for better administration of this district, the Defenses of Washington was merged into the newly created Department of Washington February 2, 1863. Samuel P. Heintzelman, commander of the Defenses of Washington, assumed command of the new department February 7, 1863. The Military District of the Defenses of Washington was then dropped from the roster of the Army of the Potomac. For further information, see Miscellaneous Organizations, Military District of the Defenses of Washington, and also Department of Washington, February 2, 1863–March 16, 1869.

On February 5, 1863 Hooker abolished the grand division organization of the army, and the corps commanders were directed to report to Headquarters Army of the Potomac. The corps commanders were assigned as follows: First Corps, John F. Reynolds; Second Corps, Darius N. Couch; Third Corps, Daniel E. Sickles; Fifth Corps, George G. Meade; Sixth Corps, John Sedgwick; Ninth Corps, William F. Smith; Eleventh Corps, Franz Sigel; Twelfth Corps, Henry W. Slocum. These appointments were temporary until confirmed by the president, which was not done until April 15, 1863.

February 5, 1863, Hooker consolidated the cavalry forces of the army into a cavalry corps, and assigned George Stoneman to command. Stoneman assumed command February 7, 1863, and February 12, 1863 announced the organization of the corps as follows:

Cavalry Corps, George Stoneman
  First Division, Alfred Pleasonton
  Second Division, William W. Averell
  Third Division, David McM. Gregg

Reserve Brigade, John Buford

For addditional information, see Cavalry Corps, Army of the Potomac.

During the period February 5–12, 1863, Third Division, First Corps (the Pennsylvania Reserve Division) was transferred to the Department of Washington to rest and recruit. A new Third Division, First Corps was then organized under Abner Doubleday from Pennsylvania regiments sent to the army from the Department of Washington. For additional information, see the following: First Corps, Army of the Potomac; Department of Washington, February 2, 1863–March 16, 1869; and Miscellaneous Organizations, Pennsylvania Reserves.

As early as December 31, 1862, the commander of the Ninth Corps was directed to prepare his command for transfer to the Department of Virginia. Final orders were received February 4, 1863, and William F. Smith was assigned command of the corps. The transfer was completed February 6–21, 1863, and Ninth Corps did not again join the Army of the Potomac until May 24, 1864. For further information, see Ninth Corps.

From February 1863 to September 1863, which period included the Chancellorsville and Gettysburg campaigns, the Army of the Potomac consisted of the following corps: First Corps, Second Corps, Third Corps, Fifth Corps, Sixth Corps, Eleventh Corps, Twelfth Corps, and the Cavalry Corps.

CHANCELLORSVILLE CAMPAIGN
APRIL 27, 1863–MAY 6, 1863

Hooker's Army of the Potomac generally remained in winter quarters about Falmouth until April 27, 1863, when the opening movements of the Chancellorsville campaign got under way. The Cavalry Corps, under George Stoneman, had left its camps April 13, 1863 to begin a raid toward Richmond, which was to be a part of the campaign, but it was delayed near Warrenton Junction by bad weather until April 29, 1863. It then crossed the Rappahannock with the infantry, which was marching toward Chancellorsville, and continued on its way south.

Fifth Corps, Eleventh Corps, and Twelfth Corps,

with Pleasonton's cavalry brigade, marched to Chancellorsville by way of Kelly's Ford. They were joined there by Second Corps and Third Corps, which arrived from near Falmouth by way of United States Ford. All of these corps were heavily engaged in the Battle of Chancellorsville May 1–3, 1863 and were driven back from their initial positions, but finally succeeded in halting the enemy advance. Hooker did not renew the fighting, however, but withdrew to a defensive position in front of United States Ford. First Corps had come up in the meantime and occupied the right of the defensive line. The army held this line until the night of May 5, 1863, and it then recrossed the Rappahannock during the night and returned to its old quarters.

Sedgwick's Sixth Corps, which had been left below Fredericksburg when the army marched to Chancellorsville, moved forward south of the Rappahannock to join Hooker. It captured Marye's Heights, in the rear of Fredericksburg, May 3, 1863, and was engaged at Salem Church May 3–4, 1863. Sedgwick was unable to advance farther, however, and, being threatened on three sides, finally recrossed to the north side of the Rappahannock at Banks' Ford at 2:00 A.M. May 5, 1863. Sixth Corps also returned to its former camps.

For details of the organization and activities of the army during the period April 27, 1863 to May 5, 1863, see Chancellorsville, Virginia Campaign.

GETTYSBURG CAMPAIGN
MAY 1863–JULY 1863

During the month following the Battle of Chancellorsville, the Army of the Potomac remained more or less quietly in its positions around Falmouth and Stafford Court House, confronting the Army of Northern Virginia across the Rappahannock River, near Fredericksburg. There were, however, some activities during this time. In mid-May 1863, Lee began moving his cavalry to the vicinity of Culpeper Court House, and Hooker countered by moving his cavalry to the upper Rappahannock. By the end of the month the greater part of the Cavalry Corps was in position along the Orange and Alexandria Railroad between the Rappahannock and Cedar Run, and near the upper fords of the Rappahannock. This part of the cavalry was under the command of John

Buford, the senior officer present. Because of the poor condition of the cavalry at that time, and because of the increasing strength of the enemy forces in Culpeper County, Meade's Fifth Corps was ordered to march from its camps on Potomac Creek and relieve the cavalry pickets on the Rappahannock. Fifth Corps was then occupied in guarding the river from Banks' Ford to Kelly's Ford. For additional information, see the following: Fifth Corps, Gettysburg Campaign; and Cavalry Corps, Army of the Potomac, Gettysburg Campaign.

When the above movements were completed, the Army of the Potomac was encamped as follows: First Corps and Sixth Corps were near White Oak Church; Second Corps and Third Corps were near Falmouth; Fifth Corps, as noted above, was guarding the fords of the Rappahannock; Eleventh Corps was near Brooke's Station on the Richmond, Fredericksburg, and Potomac Railroad; and Twelfth Corps was near Stafford Court House and Aquia Landing. All of the cavalry, except First Division, was in the vicinity of Warrenton Junction under John Buford. First Cavalry Division was near Brooke's Station. The Reserve Artillery and the Engineer Brigade were near Falmouth.

The March to Gettysburg. During May 1863, Hooker apparently formed no plan for future operations. Meantime, however, Lee had decided on the invasion of Maryland and Pennsylvania, and by the end of the month had completed arrangements for this movement. Lee's advance began June 3, 1863, when the corps of Richard S. Ewell and James Longstreet withdrew from Fredericksburg and from along the Rapidan, and marched toward Culpeper Court House. The initiative thus passed to Lee, and Hooker's future movements necessarily conformed to those of his adversary.

The Army of the Potomac became increasingly active during the first two weeks of June 1863. By June 5, 1863, Hooker became aware that the enemy was leaving his front, but he was without positive information as to the extent of this movement and its meaning. That day he sent Sedgwick's Sixth Corps across the Rappahannock at Franklin's old crossing to find out whether the main body of Lee's army had left Fredericksburg, and if so, in what direction it was moving. From the information so obtained, Sedgwick concluded that most of Lee's army was still near Fredericksburg. Sixth Corps

remained on the river near Franklin's Crossing until June 13, 1863, when the army began its withdrawal toward Centerville. For additional information, see the following: Sixth Corps, Army of the Potomac, Skirmishes at Franklin's Crossing (or Deep Run); and Gettysburg Campaign, Part I, From the Rappahannock to Gettysburg.

June 9, 1863, Pleasonton's Cavalry Corps, with some infantry support, was sent across the Rappahannock River toward Culpeper Court House, and it was engaged that day with Stuart's cavalry at Fleetwood Hill, near Brandy Station. Late that evening Pleasonton withdrew across the river and rejoined the army. For details of this engagement, see Gettysburg Campaign, Part I, From the Rappahannock to Gettysburg, Battle of Brandy Station (Fleetwood Hill).

Hooker remained without definite information about Lee's movements, but June 11, 1863, he began moving his infantry to the north and west to increase his force on the upper Rappahannock. Third Corps was ordered to Bealeton, and the next day First Corps was moved to Deep Run to act as a reserve to Third Corps and Fifth Corps. Also on June 12, 1863, Eleventh Corps was started toward Catlett's Station. Hooker then assigned John F. Reynolds to the command of a temporary right wing of the army, which consisted of the four infantry corps and the Cavalry Corps that were concentrated along the Rappahannock. This wing was discontinued June 16, 1863.

June 13, 1863, ten days after Lee had started his march northward, Hooker learned of Confederate forces near Winchester, Virginia, and he finally issued orders for the Army of the Potomac to withdraw from the Rappahannock to positions along the Orange and Alexandria Railroad in front of Washington. By June 17, 1863, the army was along the railroad from Warrenton Junction to Fairfax Station. The army then advanced to the north and west and formed a line facing west, extending from Thoroughfare Gap northward to Leesburg.

Lee's army began crossing the Potomac River into Maryland June 16, 1863; and June 25, 1863, Hooker had advanced into Maryland, crossing the Potomac at Edwards Ferry. By June 28, 1863, all but two corps were in position in Maryland on a line facing north, from Middletown eastward through Frederick. Sixth Corps and Twelfth Corps were in the rear, but north of the Potomac.

Early on the morning of June 28, 1863, George G.

Meade relieved Hooker in command of the Army of the Potomac, and George Sykes succeeded Meade in command of Fifth Corps.

The day after Meade assumed command, he started the army forward on an extended front in search of Lee. The cavalry marched on the flanks and covered the front of the infantry. On June 30, 1863, Judson Kilpatrick's Third Cavalry Division encountered Stuart's cavalry at Hanover, Pennsylvania, and a sharp fight ensued. For details, see Gettysburg Campaign, Part I, From the Rappahannock to Gettysburg, Meade's Advance from Frederick to Gettysburg, Cavalry Action at Hanover, Pennsylvania. That same day, June 30, 1863, Buford arrived at Gettysburg with two brigades of his First Cavalry Division.

For details of the march of the army from the Rappahannock to Gettysburg, see Gettysburg Campaign, Part I, From the Rappahannock to Gettysburg.

Organizational Changes in the Army, May and June 1863. There were several changes in the organization of the army during May and June 1863. There were two principal reasons for this. The first was the serious depletion of the army caused by the heavy losses at the Battle of Chancellorsville, and by the subsequent muster out of many nine-month and two-year regiments. The second was the arrival of reinforcements for the army in late June and early July 1863.

During May and June 1863, fifty-four regiments left the army because of the expiration of their terms of enlistment. This, together with the more than 17,000 casualties suffered at Chancellorsville, reduced the number of men serving with the army by approximately 47,000, which amounted to about one-third of its former strength. As a result, the number of infantry divisions was reduced from twenty-one at Chancellorsville to eighteen (before reinforcements arrived) in late June, and the number of brigades from fifty-six to forty-six during the same period. In addition, there was a fairly extensive transfer of regiments from one brigade to another in an attempt to achieve a relatively uniform brigade strength. As a result of this reorganization, Third Corps, Fifth Corps, and Sixth Corps each lost one division; and in addition to the brigades included in these divisions, First Corps lost two brigades, and Second Corps and Twelfth Corps each lost one.

Only Eleventh Corps was relatively unchanged. For details of these changes in organization, see the various corps of the army.

The strength of the cavalry had also been greatly reduced since April 1863, and June 11, 1863, two days after the Battle of Brandy Station, Pleasonton issued orders for the reorganization of the Cavalry Corps, which reduced the number of divisions in the corps from three to two. These were commanded by John Buford and David McM. Gregg. For details of the reorganization, see Cavalry Corps, Army of the Potomac, Chancellorsville to Gettysburg.

The artillery was also affected in the reorganization of the army. As a consequence of the reduction in the number and strength of the infantry divisions, the artillery attached to the corps was consolidated and reduced. Hooker ordered a reorganization of the artillery May 12, 1863. At Chancellorsville the artillery served with the infantry divisions, but in the reorganization it was assigned to the corps, with the artillery of each corps forming a brigade under the direction of the chief of artillery of the corps. The whole was under Henry J. Hunt, chief of artillery of the army. The brigade thus became the coordinating unit for the batteries. Each battery usually had six guns, and most brigades consisted of five batteries. There were fourteen artillery brigades with the army at this time, and eight of these were assigned to the infantry corps as follows: Charles S. Wainwright's brigade to First Corps; John G. Hazard's brigade to Second Corps; George E. Randolph's brigade to Third Corps; Augustus P. Martin's brigade to Fifth Corps; Charles H. Tompkins' brigade to Sixth Corps; Michael Wiedrich's brigade to Eleventh Corps; Edward D. Muhlenberg's brigade to Twelfth Corps; and James M. Robertson's Horse Artillery Brigade to the Cavalry Corps.

The remaining artillery brigades, under the command of Robert O. Tyler, constituted the Artillery Reserve of the army, which at the end of May 1863 consisted of the following:

ARTILLERY RESERVE, Robert O. Tyler

Regular Division
  First Brigade, Dunbar R. Ransom
  Second Brigade, John C. Tidball

Volunteer Division, John A. Tompkins
  First Brigade, Freeman McGilvery
  Second Brigade, Thomas W. Osborn
  Third Brigade, Richard Waterman

Fourth Brigade, Robert H. Fitzhugh

Note. The Volunteer Division was organized May 16, 1863.

Late in June 1863, about 25,000–26,000 reinforcements were sent from the Department of Washington and from the Middle Department to join the Army of the Potomac, and most of these were incorporated into its organization. The troops sent from Washington consisted of the following: John J. Abercrombie's Division, two brigades of Samuel W. Crawford's Pennsylvania Reserves, Julius Stahel's Cavalry Division, and Albert B. Jewett's Brigade from Poolesville, Maryland; and from the Middle Department, Daniel Tyler's (later William H. French's) command at Harper's Ferry, and Henry H. Lockwood's Provisional Brigade from Baltimore. A more detailed description of these commands, and their assignments after they joined the Army of the Potomac, is given in the following paragraphs:

June 24, 1863, Abercrombie's Division was ordered from its positions near Centerville to join the Army of the Potomac as it moved northward in Virginia toward the Potomac in pursuit of Lee. Frank Fessenden's First Brigade consisted of only two regiments, and these were soon to be mustered out. It was therefore discontinued, and the regiments remained for a time in the Defenses of Washington. George J. Stannard's Second Brigade left its positions on the Occoquan River June 25, 1863 and marched to join First Corps, Army of the Potomac. It arrived on the field of Gettysburg July 1, 1863, too late to take part in the battle that day. It joined First Corps the following morning, and was assigned as Third Brigade, Third Division, First Corps. For further information, see First Corps, Army of the Potomac, Gettysburg Campaign. Alexander Hays' Third Brigade marched from Centerville to join Second Corps, Army of the Potomac near Gum Springs June 26, 1863. Hays was then assigned command of Third Division, Second Corps. George L. Willard succeeded Hays in command of the brigade, which was then attached to Second Corps as Third Brigade, Third Division. For additional information, see Second Corps, Army of the Potomac, Gettysburg Campaign.

June 26, 1863, Samuel W. Crawford, with William McCandless' First Brigade and Joseph W.

Fisher's Third Brigade of Pennsylvnia Reserves, left Upton's Hill and Fairfax Station in the Department of Washington; and, marching by way of Vienna, Goose Creek, and Edwards Ferry, joined Fifth Corps at Ballinger's Ferry, near Frederick, Maryland, June 28, 1863. Crawford's command was then assigned to Fifth Corps as Third Division. Horatio G. Sickel's Second Brigade of Pennsylvania Reserves was left in the Department of Washington. For additional information, see Fifth Corps, Army of the Potomac, Gettysburg Campaign.

June 19, 1863, Julius Stahel was ordered to concentrate his cavalry division of the Department of Washington at Fairfax Court House, and two days later he was sent by Hooker to make a reconnaissance in force in the direction of Warrenton and the upper Rappahannock. He was instructed to go to Warrenton, and from there to send out parties to Waterloo, Sulfur Springs, Beverly Ford, and Rappahannock Station, and to drive back any enemy forces found in the area. Stahel encountered no serious opposition, and returned to Fairfax Court House June 23, 1863. His division consisted of three brigades as follows: Joseph T. Copeland's First Brigade (5th, 6th, and 7th Michigan Cavalry); R. Butler Price's Second Brigade (1st Michigan Cavalry, 2nd Pennsylvania Cavalry, and 18th Pennsylvania Cavalry); and Othneil De Forest's Third Brigade (5th New York Cavalry, 1st Vermont Cavalry, and 1st West Virginia Cavalry).

June 24, 1863, Stahel was ordered with his division to join William H. French's command at Harper's Ferry. This order was changed, however, and June 25, 1863, Stahel crossed the Potomac River at Young's Island Ford, and marched to join John F. Reynolds' Right Wing of the army, then near Poolesville, Maryland. He then moved northward toward Frederick, with his left near South Mountain, scouting in front of Reynolds' infantry. Stahel arrived at Frederick June 27, 1863, and the next day, his division was reorganized into a new division of two brigades under Judson Kilpatrick, and was assigned to the Cavalry Corps as Third Division. Elon J. Farnsworth commanded the First Brigade, and George A. Custer the Second Brigade. For additional information, see Cavalry Corps, Army of the Potomac, Gettysburg Campaign.

Albert B. Jewett's Brigade had for some time been posted along the Potomac from the Monocacy

River to Great Falls, with headquarters at Pooles-ville, Maryland. June 24, 1863, Samuel P. Heintzel-man, commanding the Department of Washington, ordered Jewett to move with his brigade to join Daniel Tyler's (later William H. French's) com-mand at Harper's Ferry. Upon arriving there, the brigade was broken up and the regiments were reas-signed.

On June 24, 1863, the Middle Department was divided, and the state of West Virginia and all of Maryland west of Hancock were assigned to the newly created Department of West Virginia. At that time the divisional organization of Eighth Corps (the troops in the Middle Department) was discontinued. Three brigades from Benjamin F. Kelley's First Division, Eighth Corps were transferred to Daniel Tyler's command at Harper's Ferry (Maryland Heights). The other three brigades of First Division, and Eliakim P. Scammon's Third Division, Eighth Corps were transferred to the Department of West Virginia. For additional information, see the follow-ing: Middle Department; Gettysburg Campaign; and Department of West Virginia.

June 23, 1863, Hooker ordered William H. French, commanding Third Division, Second Corps, Army of the Potomac, to relieve Tyler at Harper's Ferry. French assumed command June 26, 1863, while Hooker's army was crossing the Potomac into Maryland at Edwards Ferry. He then organized the approximately 10,000 men of his command into four brigades as follows:

French's Division, William H. French
    Elliott's Brigade, Washington L. Elliott
    Smith's Brigade, Benjamin F. Smith
    Kenly's Brigade, John R. Kenly
    Third Provisional Brigade, William H. Morris

This division was not present at Gettysburg, but did perform important duties in the rear of the army during that period. For additional information, see the following: Middle Department, and Gettysburg Campaign.

June 25, 1863, Henry H. Lockwood was assigned command of a provisional brigade, formed from troops at Baltimore, and he was ordered with this command to Monocacy Bridge to report to Hooker for duty with the Army of the Potomac. From Monocacy Bridge, Lockwood moved on to the field of Gettysburg, where he arrived at 8:00 A.M. July

2, 1863, and reported to First Division, Twelfth Corps. Lockwood was senior to Thomas H. Ruger, who was in temporary command of First Division, and for that reason Lockwood's brigade was not assigned during the battle, but received orders directly from headquarters of Twelfth Corps, Army of the Potomac. For additional information, see the following: Middle Department; and Twelfth Corps, Army of the Potomac, Gettysburg Campaign.

* * * * * * * * * * * * * * * *

As the new organizations from the Department of Washington and from the Middle Department came under Hooker's control, he apparently was not satis-fied with their leaders, and these were soon disposed of by replacement or by breaking up their commands as follows: French replaced Daniel Tyler in com-mand of the troops at Harper's Ferry; Stahel's cav-alry division was reorganized as Third Division, Cavalry Corps under Kilpatrick, and Stahel was sent to the Department of the Susquehanna; Abercrom-bie lost his division when it was broken up, and its brigades were assigned to First Corps and Second Corps; and Jewett's Brigade was also broken up and the regiments were assigned to French's command.

Command Changes in the Army during May and June 1863. A number of important changes oc-curred in the command of the Army of the Potomac while it was on the Rappahannock and on the march to Gettysburg. These were as follows:

June 18, 1863, Hooker's command was greatly enlarged. On that date, Hooker was informed by Halleck that he was to assume control of all forces of the Middle Department that were within the sphere of his operations, and that to secure the necessary cooperation he was to communicate directly with Robert C. Schenck, the department commander. Hooker was also instructed to call on Samuel P. Heintzelman, commander of the Depart-ment of Washington, for any necessary assistance. In response to a request by Hooker for a clarification of this order, Halleck, on June 22, 1863, placed that part of the Middle Department east of Cumberland, Maryland under Hooker's direct orders. The Depart-ment of Washington, however, was to remain as before under the direct command of Heintzelman. Hooker could call on Heintzelman for aid, but the latter was not obligated to comply. In case of any difficulty, and such did occur, Heintzelman was to report to Halleck for instructions.

Then, on June 28, 1863, there was a change in the commander of the Army of the Potomac. On the night of June 27, 1863, Hooker asked to be relieved of the command, and that same night, by the authority of the president, Halleck issued an order relieving Hooker and assigning George G. Meade in his place. For additional information, see the Gettysburg Campaign, Part I, From the Rappahannock to Gettysburg.

There were also some changes in the corps commanders. Throughout May and June 1863, only John Sedgwick (Sixth Corps), Oliver O. Howard (Eleventh Corps), and Henry W. Slocum (Twelfth Corps) remained in command of their corps. The other corps were commanded as follows:

John F. Reynolds, commanding First Corps, was relieved temporarily on three occasions to command a temporary wing of the army: a Right Wing, June 12, 1863–June 16, 1863; a Right Wing, June 25, 1863–June 28, 1863; and a Left Wing (or Advanced Wing), June 30, 1863–July 1, 1863. Abner Doubleday commanded First Corps on these occasions.

Darius N. Couch commanded Second Corps at Falmouth until June 9, 1863, when he was called to Pennsylvania to assume command of the Department of the Susquehanna. Winfield S. Hancock succeeded him in command of Second Corps.

Shortly after the Battle of Chancellorsville, Daniel E. Sickles left the army on leave, and David B. Birney assumed temporary command of his Third Corps. Birney remained in command until about noon June 28, 1863, when Sickles returned and resumed command of the corps.

George G. Meade commanded Fifth Corps until early on the morning of June 28, 1863, when he assumed command of the Army of the Potomac. He was succeeded in command of Fifth Corps by George Sykes.

On May 20, 1863, George Stoneman, commander of the Cavalry Corps, was granted a leave of absence, and two days later Alfred Pleasonton was assigned temporary command during his absence. Stoneman did not return to the army, however, and Pleasonton remained in command.

There were also numerous changes in the commanders of divisions and brigades in the army during this period. For these, see the corps of the army, from the time of the Battle of Chancellorsville to the Battle of Gettysburg.

Battle of Gettysburg, July 1–3, 1863. The Battle of Gettysburg began on the morning of July 1, 1863, when the advancing infantry of Ambrose P. Hill's Confederate Corps encountered John Buford's cavalry on the ridges west of the town. First Corps and Eleventh Corps then came up and and were heavily engaged, and that evening were driven back to Cemetery Hill. Third Corps and Twelfth Corps arrived on the field late on July 1, 1863, and were seriously engaged the next day, Third Corps on the Union left, and Twelfth Corps on the Union right, at Culp's Hill. Second Corps and Fifth Corps arrived early on the morning of July 2, 1863, and both corps joined Third Corps in the fighting on the Union left that evening. Sixth Corps arrived during the afternoon of July 2, 1863, but was only slightly engaged. Twelfth Corps was engaged at Culp's Hill again on the morning of July 3, 1863, and Second Corps bore the brunt of the Pickett-Pettigrew-Trimble assault on the afternoon of July 3, 1863. The cavalry also took an active part in the battle. Buford's division opposed Hill's advance on the first day, and on the third day there were two separate cavalry actions. Two brigades were engaged on the far Union left near the Big Round Top, and parts of Kilpatrick's and Gregg's divisions took part in the Cavalry Battle east of the town. For details of the Battle of Gettysburg, see Gettysburg Campaign, Part II, Battle of Gettysburg.

The Pursuit of Lee. The fighting at Gettysburg ended on the evening of July 3, 1863, and on the following day, except for the cavalry, the army remained quietly in its positions, facing the enemy. On July 4, 1863, Buford's and Kilpatrick's cavalry divisions were sent out toward the right and rear of Lee's army on Seminary Ridge. This was done to strike at Lee's lines of communications, and also to be in position to harass his retreating columns if he should decide to withdraw into Virginia.

When Meade discovered, on the morning of July 5, 1863, that Lee had begun his march toward the Potomac River, he issued orders for the movement of the army toward Williamsport and Hagerstown in an attempt to prevent the escape of the enemy into

Virginia. This movement was interrupted for a time when Sixth Corps found the enemy in force near Fairfield, Pennsylvania on July 5, 1863, but by July 9, 1863, the Army of the Potomac had advanced to a line extending from Rohrersville to Boonsboro, west of South Mountain. Meantime, the cavalry had been active in front of the infantry at Williamsport, Hagerstown, and Boonsboro.

Meade continued to advance, and by July 12, 1863, was in position on a line roughly parallel to the Hagerstown-Sharpsburg Pike, from Hagerstown on the right to Bakersville on the left. July 13, 1863, Meade examined the enemy lines that had been formed on the heights above Marsh Creek, and he made plans for a reconnaissance in force for the morning of July 14, 1863. Lee, however, who had been prevented from crossing the Potomac for several days because of high water, finally began crossing on the night of July 13, 1863; and, except for some rear-guard action at Falling Waters with Buford's and Kilpatrick's cavalry, completed the withdrawal without incident.

On the morning of July 15, 1863, the Army of the Potomac moved toward the Potomac River near Harper's Ferry and Berlin (present-day Brunswick) in preparation for following Lee into Virginia. The army crossed the river July 17–19, 1863, and marched southward in three columns toward Warrenton, Virginia. While on the march, Meade learned that Lee was withdrawing from the lower Shenandoah Valley, where he had remained for a time after recrossing the Potomac from Maryland. Meade then ordered a part of his army, with Third Corps in the lead, to advance and push through Manassas Gap and attempt to cut off at least a part of the retreating column. Third Corps arrived in Manassas Gap July 23, 1863; and finally, late in the day, succeeded in driving the enemy force guarding the gap back into the valley. By this time, however, it was too late for the Federals to interfere significantly with Lee's retreat. Lee continued his march to the vicinity of Culpeper Court House, and Meade moved on toward Warrenton.

The Army of the Potomac arrived in the Warrenton-Warrenton Junction area between July 23, 1863 and July 26, 1863, and then took up positions along the Rappahannock River, with the cavalry posted on the flanks. Then on July 31, 1863, the corps of the army were assigned positions as follows: Sixth Corps was to guard the river from Waterloo to Sulfur Springs, with one division on the river, one division at Warrenton, and one division at New Baltimore; Third Corps was to hold the Rappahannock from Sulfur Springs to the forks of the river near Beverly Ford; First Corps was to form on the river from Beverly Ford to Wheatley's Ford (about one mile north of Kelly's Ford), with one division near Rappahannock Station, one division near Beverly Ford, and one division at Bealeton Station to watch the railroad from Warrenton Junction to the river; Twelfth Corps was to watch the river from Wheatley's Ford to Ellis' Ford, with headquarters at Kelly's Ford; Fifth Corps was to mass at Fayetteville, about three miles northwest of Bealeton; Second Corps was to move to Morrisville, with one division to take position at Elk Run, and one of the brigades of the division at Bristerburg; and Eleventh Corps was to occupy Greenwich, Bristoe Station, and Brentsville, and to establish a force on Cedar Run to patrol and picket the rear of the army.

The Artillery Reserve was near Warrenton Junction. Gregg's Second Cavalry Division was at Amissville, on the right of the army; Kilpatrick's Third Cavalry Division (then under Custer) picketed the country from Ellis' Ford on the Rappahannock to Aquia Creek; and Buford's First Cavalry Division was on the Rappahannock near Rappahannock Station.

August 1, 1863 has generally been regarded as the end of the Gettysburg Campaign.

For details of the troop movements, organization of the army, and other information about the army for the period July 4, 1863–August 1, 1863, see the following: the several corps of the army; and Gettysburg Campaign, Part III, Pursuit of Lee.

Reinforcements for the Army of the Potomac. The ranks of the Army of the Potomac were seriously depleted in early July 1863, because of the approximately 23,000 casualties suffered at the Battle of Gettysburg, and also because of the muster out of nine-month regiments, especially those of George J. Stannard's Vermont Brigade of First Corps. Immediately after the battle, reinforcements were started forward to join the army.

The most readily available troops were those of William H. French's Division of Eighth Corps, then at Frederick, Maryland and Tennallytown, District of Columbia. In late June 1863, French's Division, then at Harper's Ferry, was placed under the orders of the commander of the Army of the Potomac, but it was not transferred from Eighth Corps to Hooker's army. During the Battle of Gettysburg, two brigades of the division, under French, were at Frederick; and the other two brigades, under Washington L. Elliott, were at Tennallytown. For additional information, see the following: Middle Department, Gettysburg Campaign; and Gettysburg Campaign, Part I, From the Rappahannock to Gettysburg.

July 6, 1863, John R. Kenly's Brigade of French's Division was sent from Frederick to Harper's Ferry, and the next day it reoccupied Maryland Heights. By July 7, 1863, Elliott's two brigades had rejoined French at Frederick; and that day French's Division, less Kenly's Brigade, was assigned to Third Corps. The three brigades, numbering about 8,000–9,000 men, joined Third Corps on Antietam Creek in the vicinity of Jones' Cross Roads (present-day Lappans) July 10, 1863. French assumed command of Third Corps July 9, 1863, and the next day his division, commanded by Washington L. Elliott, was assigned to Third Corps as Third Division. First Brigade was commanded by William H. Morris; Second Brigade, by J. Warren Keifer; and Third Brigade, by Benjamin F. Smith.

Most of the other early reinforcements for the army consisted of nine-month regiments from John G. Foster's Eighteenth Corps in North Carolina. The terms of enlistment of these regiments were about to expire, and they were then serving in Virginia, prior to being sent home. These troops were assigned as follows:

To take the place of French's Division of Eighth Corps, which was sent to the Army of the Potomac, Robert C. Schenck, commander of the Middle Department, transferred about 3,900 men from Baltimore to Harper's Ferry. These troops were included in a newly organized brigade under the command of Henry S. Briggs, which consisted of two new six-month Maryland regiments, the thirty-day 7th New York Militia, and artillery. In addition to the above were some troops from Virginia. Henry M. Naglee had arrived at Baltimore July 6, 1863, with a temporary brigade of three nine-month Massachusetts regiments from Virginia, which had formerly belonged to First Division, Eighteenth Corps at New Berne. Although the terms of enlist-

ment of these regiments were about to expire, the men agreed to continue in service during the emergency. These regiments were attached to Briggs' brigade, which arrived at Harper's Ferry July 7, 1863. The next day, Naglee was assigned command of the posts of Maryland Heights and Harper's Ferry, and upon arrival there reported 6,400 men present, but of these 4,200 were due to be mustered out soon.

On July 7, 1863, Francis B. Spinola's Brigade (Keystone Brigade), formerly of Henry Prince's District of Pamlico, Eighteenth Corps, embarked in Virginia for Washington; and from there they moved on to Harper's Ferry July 10, 1863.

July 10, 1863, Kenly's Brigade was assigned to First Corps, Army of the Potomac, and that same day it left Naglee's command at Harper's Ferry to join First Corps at Beaver Creek, Maryland. The next day, Kenly's Brigade was assigned to Third Division, First Corps as Third Brigade. Kenly then assumed command of Third Division, and was succeeded in command of his brigade by Nathan T. Dushane.

July 11, 1863, Spinola's Brigade was sent from Harper's Ferry to the South Mountain passes, but it did not join the Army of the Potomac. Two days later, the brigade, then under Everard Bierer, was ordered to Frederick, Maryland, where one regiment, the 168th Pennsylvania, left for muster out. The other two regiments, 158th Pennsylvania and 171st Pennsylvania, were assigned to guard the depots at Frederick and Monocacy Junction, although they too were due for muster out.

July 12, 1863, a brigade of about 1,600 men under Briggs was assigned to First Corps. This brigade consisted of the three Massachusetts regiments brought to Baltimore from Virginia by Naglee, and also the 39th Massachusetts from the Department of Washington. This brigade joined First Corps at Funkstown, Maryland July 12–13, 1863, but the three nine-month regiments were sent home for muster out July 15, 1863, July 17, 1863, and July 26, 1863, respectively. Briggs' brigade was thus discontinued, and 39th Massachusetts was assigned to First Brigade, Second Division, First Corps.

July 13, 1863, Naglee's command at Harper's Ferry was reorganized to consist of two brigades. George D. Wells was assigned command of First Brigade, and Peter A. Porter, of Second Brigade.

As the Army of the Potomac prepared to cross the Potomac in pursuit of Lee, Schenck requested that the three Maryland regiments with Henry H. Lockwood's Second Brigade, First Division, Twelfth Corps be left behind because they were needed in Maryland. On July 17, 1863, these regiments, under Lockwood, were ordered to reinforce the garrison on Maryland Heights, and the next day Lockwood relieved Naglee in command of the troops and defenses at Maryland Heights. Lockwood's brigade in Twelfth Corps was thus discontinued.

On July 14, 1863, strong reinforcements began to arrive from southeastern Virginia. Most of Erasmus D. Keyes' Fourth Corps of the Department of Virginia was transferred to the Army of the Potomac, and was assigned to Eleventh Corps. July 10, 1863 Hector Tyndale arrived at Washington from Fort Monroe with a temporary brigade that was composed of one regiment of his former First Brigade, First Division, Fourth Corps; and the two regiments of Charles Kleckner's Third Brigade, First Division, Fourth Corps. The next day Tyndale's brigade moved to Frederick, Maryland. Two regiments of George H. Gordon's Second Division, Fourth Corps arrived at Frederick July 12, 1863, and were attached to Tyndale's brigade. This brigade was broken up, however, when it joined Eleventh Corps, and the regiments were assigned to the different divisions of the corps. Tyndale was assigned command of First Brigade, Third Division, Eleventh Corps July 13, 1863.

Gordon's Second Division of Keyes' Fourth Corps began embarking at Norfolk and Yorktown, Virginia July 10, 1863, and the leading brigades arrived at Washington the next day. On July 14, 1863, the division was assigned to Eleventh Corps, which it joined a few days later at Berlin (present-day Brunswick), Maryland. The division was not assigned as a unit, but instead was broken up and the regiments were assigned to First Division and Third Division. Gordon was assigned command of First Division, Eleventh Corps July 17, 1863, but it should be noted that this was the reorganized former First Division, Eleventh Corps and not the division that Gordon brought from Virginia.

Two Pennsylvania regiments from Egbert L. Viele's command at Norfolk, Virginia were also sent to the Army of the Potomac, and July 13, 1863,

one regiment was assigned to Eleventh Corps and one to Twelfth Corps.

Michael Corcoran brought his Third Brigade and three other regiments of First Division, Seventh Corps, Department of Virginia to Washington July 11, 1863, but he did not join the Army of the Potomac. Corcoran's command did, however, perform a useful service to the army. When Meade marched down the Loudoun Valley after Lee had retreated into Virginia July 13–14, 1863, it became necessary to change the base for the army so as to receive supplies from Alexandria, Virginia by way of the Orange and Alexandria Railroad and the Manassas Gap Railroad. Rufus King, formerly commander of First Division, Fourth Corps, was assigned command of a division of the Department of Washington, and was ordered to advance along the railroad and repair it and protect it from enemy raids. Corcoran's Brigade was assigned as a part of this division.

For information about the organization of the troops in Virginia and North Carolina prior to the Battle of Gettysburg, and the reinforcement of the Army of the Potomac, see the following: Department of Virginia, May 22, 1861–July 15, 1863, Troops and Operations in the Department of Virginia; and Department of North Carolina, January 7, 1862–July 15, 1863, Troops and Operations in the Department of North Carolina.

FROM THE RAPPAHANNOCK TO THE RAPIDAN
AUGUST 1, 1863–OCTOBER 10, 1863

During August and the early part of September 1863, the Army of the Potomac remained in position along the Rappahannock River. During this period, the army was considerably reduced by the transfer of troops to other commands. On August 5, 1863, George H. Gordon's First Division, Eleventh Corps was sent to Morris Island, South Carolina to reinforce Quincy A. Gillmore's forces in the Department of the South. For additional information, see Eleventh Corps, Army of the Potomac; and also Department of the South, Part III, Department of the South, Tenth Corps.

During the last days of July and the early part of

August 1863, Romeyn B. Ayres' Second Division of regulars of Fifth Corps; Lewis A. Grant's Vermont Brigade of Sixth Corps; and an additional twenty regiments of Second Corps, Third Corps, Sixth Corps, and Twelfth Corps were sent to report to Edward R. S. Canby in New York to aid in controlling the disturbances that resulted from the draft. Many of these regiments, however, returned to their proper commands before the army began its advance to the Rapidan River in mid-September 1863. For additional information, see the above-mentioned corps; and also Department of the East, January 3, 1863–June 27, 1865, Draft Riots in New York, 1863.

The army was further diminished September 25, 1863, when Eleventh Corps and Twelfth Corps were detached and sent west to Tennessee to reinforce the Army of the Cumberland, which was under siege at Chattanooga. For further information, see below, and also Eleventh Corps and Twelfth Corps, Army of the Potomac.

Early in September 1863, there were some indications that Lee's army was moving back from its positions beyond the Rappahannock; and September 12, 1863, Meade ordered a reconnaissance in force to determine what, if anything, was happening. This was to be made by Pleasonton's Cavalry Corps, which was to be supported by Gouverneur K. Warren's Second Corps, Army of the Potomac.

Early on the morning of September 13, 1863, Kilpatrick's cavalry division crossed the river at Kelly's Ford and moved toward Stevensburg. Buford's cavalry division crossed at Beverly Ford and, followed by Second Corps, marched toward Brandy Station. Gregg's cavalry division marched toward Culpeper Court House from its camps between Sulfur Springs and Jefferson (Jeffersonton). Kilpatrick and Buford joined near Brandy Station, and then moved on toward Culpeper Court House against determined resistance by enemy cavalry. By 1:00 P.M. the enemy had been driven from the court house, and the two cavalry divisions then continued on toward Raccoon Ford on the Rapidan River. Gregg's division approached Culpeper Court House about 5:30 P.M., and it was then sent out on the Cedar Mountain Road, where it encountered some resistance. Warren's infantry arrived at Culpeper Court House about 5:00 P.M., and Alexander S. Webb's Second Division occupied the town. The

rest of the corps camped that night just east of the town.

By September 14, 1863, Pleasonton had driven the enemy across the Rapidan, and had tried unsuccessfully to cross the river at Raccoon Ford, Somerville Ford, and at Mitchell's Ford, at the railroad crossing. Kilpatrick's division and Buford's division remained on the river at Racoon and Somerville fords, and Gregg's division at Mitchell's Ford, near Cedar Mountain.

September 16, 1863, Meade's infantry, less Eleventh Corps, crossed the Rappahannock and took position as follows: Henry W. Slocum's Twelfth Corps crossed at Kelly's Ford and took position on the left of Meade's line at Stevensburg; John Newton's First Corps crossed at Rappahannock Station and took position between Stevensburg and Culpeper Court House; George Sykes' Fifth Corps crossed at Beverly Ford and formed in rear of Culpeper Court House; William H. French's Third Corps crossed at Freeman's Ford, and took position between Culpeper Court House and Stone House Mountain, which was on the Culpeper Court House-Sperryville Road between the court house and Griffinsburg; John Sedgwick's Sixth Corps crossed at Sulfur Springs and took position on the right of the army at Stone House Mountain; and Warren's Second Corps occupied a ridge in front of Culpeper Court House. Oliver O. Howard's Eleventh Corps remained north of the Rappahannock guarding the army's line of communications at the bridges at Rappahannock Crossing, Catlett's Station, and Bristoe Station.

September 16, 1863, Twelfth Corps advanced to Raccoon Ford and relieved the cavalry pickets guarding the river from Somerville down to Morton's Ford. Second Corps moved up on the right of Twelfth Corps and relieved the cavalry pickets from Somerville Ford to Cedar Mountain, including both places. Fifth Corps then advanced and occupied the position vacated by Twelfth Corps on the ridge in front of Culpeper Court House. Buford's cavalry division shifted to the left of Twelfth Corps; and Kilpatrick's cavalry division, to the right of Second Corps. Gregg's cavalry division moved to Watery Mountain, near Warrenton.

September 21–23, 1863, Buford's and Kilpatrick's divisions conducted a successful reconnaissance across the Rapidan, with skirmishes at

Madison Court House, White's Ford, Orange Court House, Raccoon Ford, Liberty Mills, and Robertson's Ford. These reconnaissances revealed that there were two corps of Confederate infantry north of Gordonsville. At that time, Lee, with Richard S. Ewell's and Ambrose P. Hill's corps, was at Gordonsville and Orange Court House, with strong advanced posts entrenched behind the fords along the Rapidan. James Longstreet's corps had been detached September 9, 1863, and sent to reinforce Braxton Bragg's army near Chattanooga.

At 2:30 A.M. September 14, 1863, Meade received orders to prepare Eleventh Corps and Twelfth Corps for a movement by rail to Tennessee to aid in the relief of the Army of the Cumberland, which was then under siege at Chattanooga. At 11:00 A.M., First Corps was ordered to relieve Twelfth Corps along the Rapidan, and this was completed by 5:30 P.M. Twelfth Corps then marched to the Orange and Alexandria Railroad at Bealeton Station, and from there moved by rail to Alexandria. It began the journey west September 27–28, 1863. For additional information, see Twelfth Corps, Army of the Potomac. Eleventh Corps was already on the railroad at Rappahannock Station, Catlett's Station, and Bristoe Station, with some troops on duty in Alexandria. These detachments assembled at Manassas Junction, and departed for Alexandria September 25, 1863. For additional information, see Eleventh Corps, Army of the Potomac.

During the period September 1863–March 1864, the Army of the Potomac consisted of the following corps: First Corps, Second Corps, Third Corps, Fifth Corps, Sixth Corps, and the Cavalry Corps.

When Eleventh Corps left the line of the railroad, Gregg's cavalry division assumed the duty of guarding the bridges at Bristoe Station, Catlett's Station, and Rappahannock Station. October 1, 1863, Albion Howe's Second Division of Sixth Corps was ordered to relieve Gregg's cavalry in guarding the bridges. When relieved, Horace B. Sargent's First Brigade of Gregg's division was ordered to Hartwood Church to establish a line of pickets from Falmouth to Kelly's Ford. Gregg, with J. Irvin Gregg's Second Brigade, moved to Bealeton Station.

October 5, 1863, Sedgwick's Sixth Corps relieved Second Corps on the Rapidan, and then picketed the river from Somerville Ford to near Robertson's Ford on Robertson's River. Second Corps moved back and took position on the heights in rear of Culpeper Court House.

When the above changes were completed, the army was disposed as follows: First and Sixth Corps were on the Rapidan; Second and Fifth Corps were near Culpeper Court House; Third Corps was between Culpeper Court House and Stone House Mountain. Howe's Second Division of Sixth Corps was on the railroad east of the Rappahannock; Buford's First Cavalry Division was on the left of the infantry, near the Rapidan; and Kilpatrick's Third Cavalry Division was on the right of the army, facing the Rapidan.

As early as October 2, 1863, there were signs of enemy movements south of the Rapidan, and these seemed to indicate a withdrawal from the right of the Confederate line. On October 8, 1863, earlier reports by Sedgwick that an enemy movement was in progress toward the Federal right were confirmed. Henry Prince's Second Division of Third Corps was sent to James City, about eight miles out of Culpeper Court House, on the road to Madison Court House.

On October 9, 1863, Meade was uncertain whether Lee was withdrawing from the Rapidan, or was conducting a flanking movement toward his right. Accordingly, he issued orders for a part of his army to cross to the south bank of the river, and to follow Lee if he was indeed retreating, and he also posted Kilpatrick's cavalry division to watch for and oppose any movement from the direction of Madison Court House, on the right. Also on October 9, 1863, Meade ordered Gregg to concentrate his cavalry division, and march as quickly as possible to Culpeper Court House.

The movement south of the Rapidan was to be carried out as follows: John Buford, with his cavalry division, was to force a crossing of the river at Germanna Ford; and then move upriver and uncover Morton's Ford, in front of John Newton's First Corps, by daylight October 10, 1863. George Sykes' Fifth Corps was to move forward and be near Newton's headquarters at that time. When Buford had uncovered the ford, First Corps, followed by Fifth Corps, was to cross and move upriver. John Sedgwick's Sixth Corps was also to follow when the fords in its front were in turn uncovered. Apparently Buford did not receive his order to advance until the morning of October 10, 1863, and he then crossed the river at Germanna Ford, but he did not arrive at Morton's Ford until about 8:00 that evening.

BRISTOE, VIRGINIA CAMPAIGN OCTOBER 10, 1863–OCTOBER 22, 1863

On the morning of October 10, 1863, Meade learned definitely that strong enemy forces were advancing from Madison Court House toward his right, and he promptly made some changes in the disposition of his troops. He placed Second Corps in position near Stone House Mountain to oppose any enemy advance from Sperryville, and to cooperate with William H. French's Third Corps, which was on the road to Madison Court House. He also called off his movement south of the Rapidan, and that evening withdrew First Corps, Fifth Corps, and Sixth Corps from along the river to the vicinity of Culpeper Court House and Stevensburg. Later that night, Meade issued orders for the withdrawal of the army to a new position behind the Rappahannock. This movement was completed by the evening of October 11, 1863.

During the afternoon of October 12, 1863, Meade learned from Gregg, who had been fighting that day around Jefferson (Jeffersonton) and Sulfur Springs (Warrenton Springs), that columns of Confederate infantry were crossing the Rappahannock upstream, beyond his right, and that night he ordered the further withdrawal of the army to the Centerville area, where it was assembled by early morning October 15, 1863. Warren's Second Corps, which was the rear corps of the army, was attacked at Bristoe Station on the evening of October 16, 1863 by Henry Heth's division of Ambrose P. Hill's Confederate corps. Heth was repulsed with heavy losses, and Second Corps continued on that night to Centerville.

Lee followed the Army of the Potomac only as far as Broad Run. He then destroyed the Orange and Alexandria Railroad from Bristoe Station to the river, and October 18, 1863 withdrew to the line of the Rappahannock River. Meade followed from Centerville October 19, 1863, and assembled his army in the Gainesville area the next day. Lee then withdrew to the south bank of the Rappahannock, and the Federal cavalry followed to the river.

For details of the organization and operations of the Army of the Potomac during the period October 10, 1863 to October 22, 1863, see Bristoe, Virginia Campaign.

ADVANCE OF THE ARMY ACROSS THE RAPPAHANNOCK NOVEMBER 1863

After Lee retired behind the Rappahannock at the end of the Bristoe Campaign, several weeks elapsed before Meade could resume active operations. Before any movement against Lee could be undertaken, it was necessary to complete repairs on the Orange and Alexandria Railroad so that supplies could be brought forward to the Army of the Potomac. By November 2, 1863, trains were running as far as the Rappahannock, and on that day Meade proposed to Halleck that the army make a rapid advance and cross the Rappahannock at Banks' Ford and Fredericksburg, and seize the heights beyond the town. In this way Meade hoped to force Lee to abandon his line between the Rappahannock and the Rapidan and accept battle under unfavorable conditions. Because this move would necessitate a change of base for the army, however, both Lincoln and Halleck disapproved. Meade then decided to force a passage of the Rappahannock and then advance on the enemy positions in front of Culpeper Court House.

Engagements at Rappahannock Station and Kelly's Ford, November 7, 1863. When Lee recrossed the Rappahannock in late October 1863, he left a strongly fortified bridgehead north of the river at Rappahannock Station. Meade's first step before crossing the river and advancing against Lee's army was to eliminate this bridgehead. In preparation for his advance, on November 6, 1863, Meade divided the army into two columns or wings. He placed Sedgwick in command of the right wing, which consisted of Sykes' Fifth Corps and Sedgwick's own Sixth Corps, temporarily under Horatio G. Wright. This wing was assigned the task of capturing the bridgehead at Rappahannock Station. Meade assigned French to command the left wing, which consisted of his own Third Corps, temporarily under David B. Birney; Warren's Second

Corps; and two divisions of Newton's First Corps. French was to advance to Kelly's Ford, cross the river, and then march upstream to the rear of the enemy forces holding the bridgehead across the river.

On the morning of November 7, 1863, the army advanced as ordered, and by early afternoon the troops of Third Corps were across the river at Kelly's Ford. Shortly after dark, the troops of Sixth Corps stormed and captured the enemy works at Rappahannock Station and about 1,600 prisoners.

The cavalry also advanced to aid the infantry in this operation. Buford's division crossed the Rappahannock at the upper fords, and moved on the right flank of the army to assist Sedgwick's column. On November 3, 1863, Kilpatrick's division had been sent to Fredericksburg, where enemy cavalry had crossed the river. This force was soon driven back, and November 6, 1863, Kilpatrick marched back by way of Ellis' Ford to cooperate with French's column. Gregg's division was held in reserve at Bealeton and Morrisville, where it guarded the trains. For details of the above operations, see Engagements at Rappahannock Station and Kelly's Ford.

After the Confederate defeat at Kelly's Ford and Rappahannock Station, Lee fell back to a new line about two miles in front of Culpeper Court House. Federal troops did not begin the pursuit until the morning of November 8, 1863. Then Third Corps, followed by Second Corps, advanced to Brandy Station. Sedgwick left Henry D. Terry's Third Division, Sixth Corps on the Rappahannock to guard the trains and the crossings, and with the other two divisions of Sixth Corps also moved to Brandy Station. Fifth Corps crossed the river at Kelly's Ford and bivouacked for the night near Paoli Mills on Mountain Run. Lee then considered his position near Culpeper Court House unsuitable for defense, and on the night of November 8, 1863, he withdrew behind the Rapidan River.

At noon November 9, 1863, the wing organization of the army was discontinued, and the commanders of the corps reported directly to army headquarters. That same day, Meade issued orders for the army to take position on a line from Kelly's Ford, through Brandy Station, to Welford's Ford on Hazel River. Positions were assigned as follows: French's Third Corps was to remain at Brandy Station; Sykes was to send Joseph J. Bartlett's First Division of Fifth Corps back to the Rappahannock to relieve Terry's Third Division, Sixth Corps, and Sykes was to place Romeyn B. Ayres' Second Division and Samuel W. Crawford's Third Division of his Fifth Corps on the north side of Mountain Run at Paoli Mills; Warren's Second Corps was to take position between Paoli Mills and Brandy Station; and Sedgwick's Sixth Corps was to move to Welford's Ford. Newton's First Corps was to remain on the Rappahannock and along the railroad as follows: Lysander Cutler's First Division at Beverly Ford; John C. Robinson's Second Division at Bealeton, Liberty, and near the crossing of Licking Run; and John R. Kenly's Third Division was guarding the railroad from Manassas to Warrenton Junction. Cutler's and Robinson's divisions were assigned to cover the trains passing along the railroad, and also the working parties on the road.

Gregg's Second Cavalry Division was assigned to watch the flanks of the infantry along the railroad and the Rappahannock. One brigade was sent to Morrisville on the left, and the other to Fayetteville to watch the right beyond Waterloo. Kilpatrick's Third Division was sent to Stevensburg to picket the crossings of the Rapidan below the railroad crossing; and Buford's First Division, to Culpeper Court House to picket the crossings of Robertson's River, and to the Federal right. The Artillery Reserve remained in the vicinity of Rappahannock Station.

There was no significant change in position of the Army of the Potomac until the beginning of the Mine Run Campaign November 26, 1863.

MINE RUN CAMPAIGN
NOVEMBER 26, 1863–DECEMBER 2, 1863

Before Meade could undertake another forward movement, it was necessary to repair the Orange and Alexandria Railroad south of the Rappahannock. This work was completed as far as Brandy Station by November 19, 1863, and Meade then prepared to resume the offensive. Meade was familiar with the position occupied by Lee south of the Rapidan, and it was, in his opinion, too strong for a successful frontal attack. For this reason he decided to move around its eastern flank by crossing the river at the lower fords, and then advancing westward toward

Orange Court House and the enemy rear. The movement was to begin November 24, 1863, but was delayed for two days by bad weather.

On November 26, 1863, the army finally advanced in three columns, and crossed the Rapidan at Jacob's Ford, Germanna Ford, and Culpeper Ford (or Culpeper Mine Ford). According to schedule, the corps were to unite in the vicinity of Locust Grove (Robertson's, or Robinson's, Tavern) by the morning of November 27, 1863, and they were then to move toward the rear of Lee's positions. The army moved much more slowly than Meade had anticipated, however, and it was not in position to attack that day. French's Third Corps, while on the march from Jacob's Ford to join Warren's Second Corps at Locust Grove, became sharply engaged with the enemy at Payne's farm and was held up until dark. This action also delayed Sedgwick's Sixth Corps, which was on the road behind French.

Finally, on the morning of November 28, 1863, the army was assembled, and it then advanced to attack, but it soon discovered that the enemy had withdrawn from its front the night before. As the advance continued, Lee's army was found in a strong position on the west side of Mine Run, a tributary of the Rapidan River. Meade then formed his command on a line on the east side of Mine Run, in front of the new enemy works. Instead of delivering a frontal assault on November 29, 1863, Meade sent Warren with his Second Corps and one division of Sixth Corps on a flank march to attack the extreme right of the enemy line. Two divisions of Third Corps were later sent to Warren, who then had under his command six divisions, or about half of the infantry of the army.

Meade's plan was to launch two attacks against the enemy works on the morning of November 30, 1863—one by Warren on the enemy right, and the other by Fifth Corps and Sixth Corps, both under Sedgwick, on the enemy left. On the morning of the scheduled attack, however, Warren reexamined the positions on his front, and then advised Meade that his attack on the enemy right should not be made. Meade promptly called off the attack, and also that of Sedgwick, which was subsidiary to Warren's attack.

The army remained in position until the night of December 1, 1863, and then, because there seemed to be no prospect of further success, Meade began to withdraw toward the Rapidan. The army recrossed the river during the night of December 1, 1863, and the next day returned to its camps. For details of this operation, see Mine Run Campaign, Virginia.

WINTER OF 1863–1864

After the Army of the Potomac returned from the Mine Run Campaign, it went into winter quarters at the camps it had previously occupied. Two corps, however, were assigned different positions. Before Mine Run, First Corps had been scattered along the Orange and Alexandria Railroad north of the Rappahannock, and Kenly's Third Division remained there, and did not accompany the rest of the corps when it advanced to Mine Run. On December 3, 1863, First Corps was ordered to Paoli Mills, and Sykes' Fifth Corps, which was formerly in position there, was sent to relieve Kenly's division and assume the duty of guarding the railroad. Kenly rejoined First Corps at Paoli Mills. The other corps went into camp as follows: Second Corps on Mountain Run; Third Corps at Brandy Station; and Sixth Corps in the vicinity of Welford's Ford. The Cavalry Corps resumed the duty of picketing the front and flanks of the army. The line extended from Hazel River on the right to Morton's Ford, then along the Rapidan, and to Kemper's Dam on the Rappahannock. Gregg's Second Cavalry Division was near Warrenton and Warrenton Junction.

There was only one significant change in the above positions during the winter. On December 22, 1863, First Corps moved to the vicinity of Culpeper Court House, with one division kept forward to support the cavalry picketing the Rapidan. For additional information, see the various corps of the army.

During the last months of 1863, the authorities in Washington and the commanders in the field were confronted by a serious problem. The oldest, and generally the best, regiments of the armies consisted of men who had enlisted in 1861 for a period of three years, which meant that their terms of service would expire in 1864. Of the 956 volunteer infantry regiments then in service, the times of enlistment would be up for 455 of them. The loss of these regiments would result not only in a dangerous shortage in manpower, but also in the services of the most experienced and skillful soldiers in the armies. In the Army of the Potomac alone, 78 regiments were due to leave by September 1, 1864, and this would result in a loss of about 40,000 men, present and absent.

To avoid this situation, if possible, the government asked the volunteers to reenlist, and offered them as an inducement a bounty of four hundred dollars, a thirty-days leave, the right to be called a "Veteran Volunteer," and an honorable-service chevron to be worn on the sleeve. In response to this offer, about 27,000 veterans of the Army of the Potomac reenlisted, or about one-half of those whose terms were about to expire. The troops who did reenlist, however, together with the new troops assigned to the army, were adequate to provide an efficient fighting force for the approaching spring and summer campaign. About sixty-six of the seventy-eight regiments due to be mustered out by September 1, 1864 were present at the Battle of the Wilderness early in May 1864, but many left the service during the summer as their terms expired. About twenty-five regiments qualified as "Veteran Regiments," and they remained in service to the end of the war, but some of these were reduced in size to a single battalion, or to only a few companies.

For the most part, the Army of the Potomac remained quietly in its winter quarters until early May 1864, at the beginning of Grant's Virginia Campaign. The army was engaged in the usual scouting and picket duties during the winter, but in addition there were several more significant operations. The more important of these are given in the following sections:

Demonstration on the Rapidan River, February 6–7, 1864. On January 28, 1864, troops under George E. Pickett, commander of the Confederate Department of North Carolina, advanced from Kinston toward New Berne in an attempt to capture that important Federal base. For details of this operation, see Department of Virginia and North Carolina, Operations in the Department of Virginia and North Carolina, Pickett's Expedition against New Berne, North Carolina. Benjamin F. Butler, commanding the Union Department of Virginia and North Carolina, learned February 3, 1864 that Pickett had attacked the Federal outposts at New Berne two days earlier, and suggested to Halleck and Stanton that a demonstration by the Army of the Potomac

might relieve some of the pressure on his, Butler's, command. Accordingly, at Halleck's request, John Sedgwick, then temporarily in command of the Army of the Potomac, ordered a vigorous demonstration along the Rapidan River to be carried out February 6, 1864 by two infantry corps and two divisions of the Cavalry Corps.

On the morning of February 6, 1864, John Newton's First Corps moved to the vicinity of Raccoon Ford and prepared to cross, but did not do so. Gouverneur K. Warren's Second Corps advanced to Morton's Ford, and during the afternoon Alexander Hays' Third Division crossed to the south bank of the river. It repulsed a determined attack that evening, and was then relieved by Alexander S. Webb's Second Division, after which it recrossed the river. Webb's division also withdrew later that night. Second Division remained in position on the north bank during the next day, and then returned to its camps. For additional information, see Second Corps, Army of the Potomac, Winter of 1863–1864.

While the infantry was demonstrating on the center of the line, the cavalry was performing a similar service on the flanks. Wesley Merritt's First Cavalry Division advanced to Barnett's Ford, and skirmished as if preparing to cross. Kilpatrick's Third Cavalry Division crossed the Rapidan at Culpeper (Culpeper Mine) Ford, and demonstrated against the enemy right. The cavalry withdrew the next day, February 7, 1864. During the operations on February 6–7, 1864, Third Corps and Sixth Corps were under orders to be prepared to move forward and support the other troops if needed.

Cavalry Expeditions and Raids. The cavalry performed the most vigorous service of the army during the winter. In addition to the usual outpost and picket duty, it conducted numerous scouts, and was sent out on a number of expeditions. The more significant of these were: an expedition from Bealeton to Luray, Virginia by a cavalry brigade under Charles H. Smith, December 21–24, 1863; an expedition from Warrenton toward Winchester, Virginia by Second Cavalry Division under John E. Taylor, January 1–4, 1864; Kilpatrick's Expedition against Richmond, Virginia, with his reinforced Third Cavalry Division, February 28, 1864–March 4, 1864; and Custer's raid into Albemarle County, Virginia, February 28, 1864–March 2, 1864. For details of Smith's and Taylor's expedition, see Cavalry Corps, Army of the Potomac, Winter of 1863–1864; and for Kilpatrick's and Custer's raids, see Kilpatrick's Expedition against Richmond, Virginia, and Custer's Raid into Albemarle County, Virginia.

When Custer moved out on his raid February 28, 1864, John Sedgwick's Sixth Corps advanced to Madison Court House to support the cavalry if needed. At the same time David B. Birney's First Division, Third Corps marched to James City to be in supporting distance of Sedgwick and Custer. These troops returned to their camps March 2, 1864.

REORGANIZATION OF THE ARMY, MARCH 1864

March 4, 1864, Meade recommended to the secretary of war that the five infantry corps of the army be consolidated into three corps. He gave as his reason the reduced strength of nearly all infantry regiments of the army. He probably was also influenced by the knowledge that the Army of Northern Virginia had been well managed with only three corps, and there was the additional fact that some of his corps commanders had on several occasions given less than satisfactory performances.

The proposed reorganization was effected by an order dated March 23, 1864, and was completed by March 26, 1864. Second Corps, Fifth Corps, and Sixth Corps were retained in the new organization, but First Corps and Third Corps were discontinued, and their regiments were transferred to the remaining three corps. The reorganization was carried out as follows:

Second Corps. The old Second Corps was consolidated into two divisions, which were numbered as First Division and Second Division. Then, First Division and Second Division of Third Corps were transferred to Second Corps, and renumbered as Third Division and Fourth Division of Second Corps.

Fifth Corps. The old Fifth Corps was consolidated into two divisions, which were numbered First Division and Third Division. The three divisions of First Corps were consolidated into two divisions,

and these were transferred to Fifth Corps as Second Division and Fourth Division of Fifth Corps.

Sixth Corps. The two divisions then with Sixth Corps retained their designations as First Division and Second Division, and Third Division, Third Corps was transferred to Sixth Corps as a new Third Division of that corps.

As a result of this reorganization, First Corps and Third Corps were discontinued, and the batteries belonging to these two corps were assigned to the remaining three corps so that each corps had eight batteries. The excess was assigned to the Artillery Reserve. For further details of the reorganization, see First Corps, Reorganization of the Army of the Potomac, 1864; Second Corps, Reorganization of the Army of the Potomac, 1864; Third Corps, Reorganization of the Army of the Potomac, 1864; Fifth Corps, Reorganization of the Army of the Potomac, 1864; and Sixth Corps, Reorganization of the Army of the Potomac, March 1864.

The new corps organization of the Army of the Potomac on April 30, 1864, was as follows:

Second Corps, Winfield S. Hancock
    First Division, Francis C. Barlow
    Second Division, John Gibbon
    Third Division, David B. Birney
    Fourth Division, Joseph B. Carr

Fifth Corps, Gouverneur K. Warren
    First Division, Charles Griffin
    Second Division, John C. Robinson
    Third Division, Samuel W. Crawford
    Fourth Division, James S. Wadsworth

Sixth Corps, John Sedgwick
    First Division, Horatio G. Wright
    Second Division, George W. Getty
    Third Division, James B. Ricketts

By an order dated March 29, 1864, the artillery of the Army of the Potomac under Henry J. Hunt was also reorganized into brigades as follows:

Artillery Brigade of Second Corps, John C. Tidball, eight batteries
Artillery Brigade of Fifth Corps, Charles S. Wainwright, eight batteries
Artillery Brigade of Sixth Corps, Charles H. Tompkins, eight batteries
Artillery Reserve, Henry S. Burton, seventeen batteries

Horse Artillery, James M. Robertson
　First Brigade, James M. Robertson
　Second Brigade, Alanson M. Randol

Note. One brigade of the Horse Artillery was with the cavalry, and the other with the Artillery Reserve. The Horse Artillery consisted of twelve batteries and sixty guns.

Robert O. Tyler, formerly commander of the Artillery Reserve, was relieved from duty with the Army of the Potomac December 23, 1863, and January 1, 1864, was assigned command of a newly constituted division, known as Tyler's Division, at Fairfax Court House. James Brady then assumed command of the Artillery Reserve until relieved by Henry S. Burton January 27, 1864.

The reorganization of the army resulted in a number of changes in the officers commanding corps, divisions, and brigades. On March 24, 1864, George Sykes, William H. French, John Newton, Solomon Meredith, John R. Kenly, and Francis B. Spinola were relieved from duty with the Army of the Potomac, and were ordered to report to the adjutant general of the army. Sykes was ordered to report to Samuel R. Curtis in the Department of Kansas; French was ordered to Philadelphia, was mustered out of the volunteer service May 6, 1864, and did not again serve as a field commander; Newton reported to William T. Sherman, commander of the Military Division of the Mississippi, and was assigned command of Second Division in Oliver O. Howard's Fourth Corps, Department of the Cumberland; Kenly reported to Lewis Wallace at Baltimore for assignment in the Middle Department; Meredith was assigned command of the post of Cairo, Illinois; and Spinola was assigned to recruiting duty in New York. March 25, 1864, John C. Caldwell was also relieved from duty with the Army of the Potomac, and three days later was detailed as a member of a military commission meeting in New York.

A number of officers returned to the army at this time after having been absent for some time. Winfield S. Hancock, who was wounded at Gettysburg, and was later assigned to special recruiting duty for Second Corps at Harrisburg, Pennsylvania, returned to the army March 24, 1864 and resumed command of Second Corps, relieving Warren. Warren was in turn assigned command of Fifth Corps in place of Sykes. Francis C. Barlow, who was also wounded at Gettysburg, and who later served in the Department of the South, was relieved from duty there January 26, 1864, and was ordered to report to Hancock in Harrisburg for recruiting duty. March 25, 1864, he was assigned command of First Division, Second Corps. John Gibbon, also wounded at Gettysburg, was later placed in command of the Draft Depot at Philadelphia. He remained there until recalled to the army in March 1864, and he then was assigned command of Second Division, Second Corps.

James S. Wadsworth, who commanded First Division, First Corps at Chancellorsville and Gettysburg, left the army on a leave of absence July 17, 1863. He later served as inspector for colored troops on the Mississippi River during the period October 9, 1863–November 18, 1863, and then on a board of inquiry from January 9, 1864 to February 23, 1864, examining the conduct of Alexander McD. McCook, Thomas L. Crittenden, and James S. Negley at the Battle of Chickamauga. He returned to the army March 25, 1864, and was assigned command of Fourth Division, Fifth Corps.

Horatio G. Wright, commander of First Division, Sixth Corps, was absent much of the winter on detached service, but he returned to the army in March 1864, and resumed command of his division. George W. Getty was relieved from duty in the Department of Virginia and North Carolina January 6, 1864, and three weeks later he was assigned to temporary duty as acting inspector general of the Army of the Potomac. He was assigned command of Second Division, Sixth Corps March 25, 1864. James B. Ricketts was wounded at Antietam, and upon recovery was appointed to Fitz John Porter's court martial. His reputation suffered as a result, and he did not return to the field until March 25, 1864, when he was relieved from a military commission meeting in New York. He then reported to Meade, and was assigned command of Third Division, Sixth Corps.

Alfred Pleasonton was relieved from duty with the Army of the Potomac in late March 1864, and April 4, 1864, Philip H. Sheridan was assigned command of the Cavalry Corps, Army of the Potomac.

Another important command change greatly affected the Army of the Potomac. By an act approved on February 29, 1864, Congress revived the grade of lieutenant general in the army, and authorized the president to assign the officer of that grade to the command of the Armies of the United States. Ulysses S. Grant received the commission March 9, 1864, and was assigned command of the Armies of the United States by an executive order dated March 10, 1864. Henry W. Halleck was relieved from duty as general in chief, and was assigned as chief of staff March 12, 1864.

On March 10, 1864, Grant visited Meade at the latter's headquarters near Brandy Station on the Orange and Alexandria Railroad, and announced his intention of making his headquarters with the Army of the Potomac during the coming campaign in Virginia. Grant then returned to the West to complete his business there, and he returned to join the Army of the Potomac in the field March 24, 1864. He established his headquarters at Culpeper Court House.

The organization of the Army of the Potomac April 30, 1864, on the eve of Grant's Virginia Campaign, was as follows:

ARMY OF THE POTOMAC, George G. Meade

General Headquarters
   Provost Guard, Marsena R. Patrick
   Volunteer Engineer Brigade, Henry W. Benham
   United States Engineer Battalion, George H. Mendell
   Signal Corps, Benjamin F. Fisher
   Ordnance Officer, Morris Schaff

Second Corps, Winfield S. Hancock
Fifth Corps, Gouverneur K. Warren
Sixth Corps, John Sedgwick
Cavalry Corps, Philip H. Sheridan
Artillery, Henry J. Hunt
   Artillery Reserve, Henry S. Burton
   First Brigade, J. Howard Kitching
   Second Brigade, John A. Tompkins
   Third Brigade, Robert H. Fitzhugh

   Horse Artillery
      First Brigade, James M. Robertson
      Second Brigade, Dunbar R. Ransom

Note. First Brigade was detached and was with the Cavalry Corps.

In April 1864, Ambrose E. Burnside's Ninth Corps was not a part of the Army of the Potomac, but it was cooperating with it under the direct orders of Grant. Ninth Corps had served with the army at Antietam and Fredericksburg, but was then transferred to the Department of Virginia February 4, 1863. Leaving George W. Getty's Third Division behind in Virginia, Ninth Corps then went west in late March 1863, to the Department of the Ohio. It spent the winter of 1863–1864 in East Tennessee, and on March 14, 1864 it was ordered to Annapolis, Maryland to fill up its ranks and reorganize. For information about Ninth Corps while in the West, see Ninth Corps.

On April 23, 1864, the reorganized Ninth Corps, then consisting of four divisions, was ordered to relieve Fifth Corps, and guard the Orange and Alexandria Railroad from Bull Run to the Rappahannock River. By April 30, 1864, Ninth Corps was in position on the railroad, with headquarters at Warrenton Junction. Ninth Corps followed the Army of the Potomac when it crossed the Rapidan River May 4, 1864, and it was engaged at the Battle of the Wilderness, but it did not officially become a part of the Army of the Potomac until assigned May 24, 1864. For the organization of Ninth Corps during May 1864, see Richmond, Virginia Campaign, 1864, Battle of the Wilderness.

GRANT'S RICHMOND, VIRGINIA CAMPAIGN
MAY 3, 1864–JUNE 17, 1864

During the afternoon and night of May 3, 1864 and the morning of May 4, 1864, the Army of the Potomac left its camps around Culpeper Court House, Stevensburg, and Brandy Station, and marched toward the fords of the Rapidan, at the beginning of Grant's campaign against Richmond. The army then consisted of Hancock's Second Corps, Warren's Fifth Corps, Sedgwick's Sixth Corps, and Sheridan's Cavalry Corps. It entered the Wilderness, south of the river, May 4, 1864, and was joined there by Burnside's Ninth Corps, which arrived from its positions on the Orange and Alexandria Railroad May 5–6, 1864. Ninth Corps accompanied the Army of the Potomac as a separate organization under Grant's direct orders until May 24, 1864. It then became a part of the Army of the Potomac, and was placed under Meade's orders.

The Army of the Potomac and Ninth Corps were engaged at the Battle of the Wilderness May 5–6, 1864, and suffered approximately 18,000 casualties.

For details, see Richmond, Virginia Campaign, 1864, Battle of the Wilderness.

During the night of May 7–8, 1864, the army left the Wilderness and advanced toward Spotsylvania Court House, and it was almost constantly engaged around the court house during the period May 8, 1864 to May 20, 1864. As the army approached Spotsylvania Court House, there was fighting at Todd's Tavern, Corbin's Bridge, Alsop's farm (Laurel Hill), and on the Po River. There were several assaults on the entrenched Confederate lines in front of the court house, including Emory Upton's attack on the evening of May 10, 1864, and Hancock's attack at the "Angle" on the salient near the McCool house, on the morning of May 12, 1864. In these two attacks, the army lost an additional 11,000 men. There was another engagement at the Harris farm May 19, 1864.

On May 9, 1864, John Sedgwick was killed by a sharpshooter, and Horatio G. Wright assumed command of Sixth Corps. David A. Russell succeeded Wright in command of First Division, and Henry L. Eustis assumed command of Russell's Third Brigade, First Division.

On May 13, 1864, J. Howard Kitching's First Brigade of the Artillery Reserve, which had been serving with the infantry, was transferred to Fifth Corps as the Heavy Artillery Brigade. May 16, 1864, the other two brigades of the Artillery Reserve were broken up, and the batteries of which they were composed were sent back to Washington.

For details of the operations of the army and Ninth Corps around Spotsylvania Court House, see Richmond, Virginia Campaign, 1864, Operations about Spotsylvania Court House.

Sheridan's Cavalry Corps did not participate in the fighting around Spotsylvania Court House, because it was absent on a raid toward Richmond, Virginia. It left the rear of the army on the morning of May 9, 1864, and it did not rejoin the infantry until May 24, 1864, when it arrived near Chesterfield, Virginia on the North Anna River. For details of the cavalry operations during this period, see Sheridan's Richmond, Virginia Raid.

During the night of May 20, 1864 and the morning of May 21, 1864, the Army of the Potomac left its entrenched positions near Spotsylvania Court House and marched toward the North Anna River, where it arrived May 23, 1864. There was consider-able fighting along the North Anna, but there were no major assaults. Most of the army crossed to the south bank of the river, but the enemy positions there were so unfavorable for a Federal attack that it was withdrawn on the night of May 26, 1864, and started for the crossings of the Pamunkey River in the vicinity of Hanovertown. For details see Richmond, Virginia Campaign, 1864, Spotsylvania Court House to the North Anna River.

May 24, 1864, Ninth Corps became officially a part of the Army of the Potomac, and from that time until July 1864, the army consisted of Second Corps, Fifth Corps, Sixth Corps, Ninth Corps, and the Cavalry Corps.

After leaving the North Anna, the army crossed the Pamunkey and by May 29, 1864 had advanced to the Totopotomoy Creek. There was some fighting along the creek, and at Bethesda Church, but on May 31, 1864, the army began moving to the left to take position at Cold Harbor and at Bethesda Church. Sixth Corps arrived at Cold Harbor June 1, 1864, and was joined there by William F. Smith's Eighteenth Corps from Benjamin F. Butler's Army of the James at Bermuda Hundred. Eighteenth Corps was placed under Meade's orders June 1, 1864.

Sixth Corps and Eighteenth Corps launched an unsuccessful attack on the enemy entrenchments at Cold Harbor on the evening of June 1, 1864, and two days later, Second Corps, Sixth Corps, and Eighteenth Corps made a second attack at Cold Harbor, while Fifth Corps and Ninth Corps were engaged near Bethesda Church. All Federal attacks were repulsed with very heavy losses. The army then entrenched close to the enemy lines, and remained in position there until June 12, 1864. It then began to move south toward the James River and Petersburg. For details, see Richmond, Virginia Campaign, 1864, Operations about Cold Harbor.

To facilitate the movement of the army toward the James River by drawing off the enemy cavalry, and also by destroying the Virginia Central Railroad, Sheridan's cavalry was sent on a raid toward Charlottesville, Virginia. On June 7, 1864, Sheridan left Newcastle Ferry with the divisions of David McM. Gregg and Alfred T. A. Torbert and marched westward. He reached Trevilian Station on the Virginia Central Railroad June 11, 1864, and during the day defeated Confederate forces under Wade Hampton and Fitzhugh Lee. Sheridan was also engaged the next day, and he then marched back to rejoin the army. He did not arrive until the army had crossed the James River. For details of the expedition, see Sheridan's Trevilian Station Raid, Virginia.

On June 12, 1864, Smith's Eighteenth Corps left the army at Cold Harbor to embark at White's House for the return to Bermuda Hundred and the Army of the James. Beginning that night, the Army of the Potomac crossed the Chickahominy River and marched to the James River in the vicinity of Charles City Court House. On June 14, 1864 it began to cross the river to Windmill Point from Wilson's Wharf, Wilcox's Landing, Douthat's Landing, and Fort Powhatan, and by June 17, 1864, it had arrived on the southern bank. The army was then ready to move toward Petersburg. On June 16, 1864, two divisions of Sixth Corps were detached and sent to reinforce Butler's command at Bermuda Hundred. For details, see Richmond, Virginia Campaign, 1864, Cold Harbor to the James River.

The trains of the army were escorted from the Wilderness to the James River by Ferrero's Fourth Division, Ninth Corps, and they arrived on the river June 16, 1864. The trains crossed that day, and Ferrero's division crossed the following day.

During the advance of the army from the Wilderness to the James, Grant established a number of depots to provide the necessary supplies. May 10, 1864, John J. Abercrombie was ordered to Belle Plain to establish a depot there, and he was assigned command of all troops at Belle Plain and Fredericksburg, and in the vicinity. He assumed command May 12, 1864, and was given the authority of a post and district commander. When the army left Spotsylvania Court House for the North Anna River, Abercrombie was directed to move the depot at Belle Plain to Port Royal, Virginia, on the Rappahannock below Fredericksburg. The transfer was completed May 22–25, 1864. The depot was next moved to White's House on the Pamunkey River. This took place at the end of May 1864, as the Army of the Potomac was approaching Cold Harbor. Abercrombie arrived at White's House and assumed command of the depot June 1, 1864. After the army had crossed the James River and advanced on Petersburg, the depot was again moved, this time to City Point. George W. Getty relieved Abercrombie in command at White's House June 20, 1864, and the next day Sheridan arrived there with his cavalry on his return from the Trevilian Station Raid. June 22, 1864, Sheridan broke up the depot at White's House, and escorted the train of about 900 wagons to the James River, which it crossed June 26–29, 1864.

During the first month of Grant's Richmond Campaign, the Army of the Potomac suffered a total loss of about 50,000 men in the fighting from the Wilderness through Cold Harbor. To compensate for this loss, strong reinforcements were sent forward to the army. Before Grant left Spotsylvania Court House, he had received about 16,000–17,000 men from Washington. On May 12, 1864, Robert O. Tyler's Division of the Department of Washington, which had been on duty on the Orange and Alexandria Railroad, was broken up; and Corcoran's Legion (or Irish Legion), then under Mathew Murphy, was sent to Hancock's Second Corps, which it joined May 17, 1864. At Belle Plain, Tyler assumed command of a temporary division of five large regiments of heavy artillery, then serving as infantry, from the Defenses of Washington. This division joined the army May 17–18, 1864, and it was attached to Second Corps as Fourth Division.

Altogether, by June 7, 1864, after the Battle of Cold Harbor, more than 48,000 men had been sent to the army from Washington as reinforcements. These included ten large regiments of heavy artillery, serving as infantry; more than forty regiments of infantry and cavalry; two provisional brigades and four provisional battalions, plus detachments, from the Rendezvous of Distribution; three additional battalions; and numerous detachments. One group of detachments, consisting of about 5,000 men, was sent forward under the command of Louis P. Di Cesnola.

OPERATIONS ABOUT PETERSBURG, 1864–1865

On June 15, 1864, while the Army of the Potomac was crossing the James River at Windmill Point, William F. Smith's Eighteenth Corps and August V. Kautz's Cavalry Division of Butler's Army of the James crossed the Appomattox River from Bermuda Hundred and captured a part of the enemy entrenchments in front of Petersburg. Starting that morning, the Army of the Potomac, led by Hancock's Second

Corps, marched toward Petersburg, and upon arrival took position in front of the enemy works south of the City Point Railroad. The army launched a number of assaults on the Petersburg lines June 16–18, 1864, and when these failed the troops entrenched on the positions gained. Thus began siege operations on the Petersburg front that lasted until April 2, 1865. For details of these assaults, see Operations about Petersburg and Richmond, Virginia, 1864–1865, Operations of June 1864, Assaults at Petersburg, Virginia, June 15–18, 1864.

During the remainder of June and through July 1864, Grant ordered a number of movements in an attempt to extend his lines, and to tighten the investment of Petersburg. These were: a cavalry raid on the South Side (Lynchburg) Railroad and the Richmond and Danville Railroad, June 22, 1864–July 2, 1864, by James H. Wilson's cavalry division, Army of the Potomac and Kautz's Cavalry Division, Army of the James; a movement by Hancock's Second Corps and Wright's Sixth Corps against the Weldon Railroad, June 21–23, 1864; and a demonstration on the north side of the James River at Deep Bottom June 27–29, 1864, by Hancock's Second Corps, and Sheridan with Gregg's and Torbert's cavalry divisions of the Army of the Potomac, and Kautz's Cavalry Division of the Army of the James.

In addition to the above operations, a mine was exploded under the enemy works at Petersburg July 30, 1864, and this was followed by an unsuccessful assault by Burnside's Ninth Corps, supported by a division of Tenth Corps (temporarily attached to Eighteenth Corps). For details of these operations, see Operations about Petersburg and Richmond, Virginia, 1864–1865, Operations of June 1864, and also Operations of July 1864.

Sixth Corps served with the Army of the Potomac for only a short time during this period. Only Thomas H. Neill's Second Division crossed the James and marched with the army to Petersburg. The other two divisions were sent to Butler's Army of the James at Bermuda Hundred June 16, 1864. They rejoined the army at Petersburg June 19, 1864, and relieved troops of Eighteenth Corps, who then returned to Bermuda Hundred. Three days later, the reassembled Sixth Corps moved to a position on the left of the army, near the Weldon Railroad. During late June and early July 1864, Jubal A. Early moved down the Shenandoah Valley with a Confederate army, and July 5, 1864 crossed the Potomac River above Harper's Ferry. He then advanced to Frederick, Maryland, where he was in position to threaten Baltimore and Washington. Grant reacted quickly to this threat, and July 6, 1864 sent James B. Ricketts' Third Division, Sixth Corps to City Point, where it embarked for Baltimore. Upon arrival there, it joined a force under Lewis Wallace on the Monocacy River near Frederick, and there the combined force was defeated by Early July 9, 1864. The next day, Wright, with the other two divisions of Sixth Corps, embarked at City Point for Washington. Sixth Corps remained to take part in the operations against Early, and did not rejoin the Army of the Potomac until December 1864. See Early's Washington Raid (and Operations in the Shenandoah Valley, Maryland, and Pennsylvania).

During July 1864, the Army of the Potomac consisted of Second Corps, Fifth Corps, Ninth Corps, and the Cavalry Corps.

Early retreated from before Washington to the Shenandoah Valley, and by July 20, 1864, the threat appeared to be over. A short time later, however, Early again advanced down the valley, and July 24, 1864 defeated George Crook's forces of the Department of West Virginia at Kernstown, Virginia. Then, a short time later John McCausland crossed the Potomac with an enemy cavalry force and July 30, 1864 burned Chambersburg, Pennsylvania. The next day, Sheridan was ordered to send a cavalry division to Washington, and August 1–6, 1864, Alfred T. A. Torbert's First Cavalry Division embarked for that destination. August 5, 1864, James H. Wilson's Third Cavalry Division was also ordered to City Point for transfer to Washington. Later these two divisions served as a part of Sheridan's army in his battles against Early in the Shenandoah Valley.

After the departure of the divisions of Torbert and Wilson, only David McM. Gregg's Second Cavalry Division, Army of the Potomac and August V. Kautz's Cavalry Division, Army of the James remained with Grant's forces before Petersburg and Richmond. Gregg reported directly to Meade.

August 2, 1864, Sheridan was relieved from duty with the Cavalry Corps, Army of the Potomac, and was ordered to Washington. On August 7, 1864, he was assigned to the temporary command of the newly created Middle Military Division, which consisted of the Middle Department and the departments of the Susquehanna, Washington, and West Virginia.

For details of the organization and operations of the Army of the Potomac during the period June 15, 1864–July 31, 1864, see the following: Operations about Petersburg and Richmond, Virginia, 1864–1865, Operations of June 1864, and also Operations of July 1864; Army of the James; and the various corps of the Army of the Potomac.

The Army of the Potomac continued to press the siege of Petersburg through the month of August 1864. During the first two weeks of the month, Fifth Corps and Ninth Corps, together with Eighteenth Corps, occupied the entrenchments between the Appomattox River and the Jerusalem Plank Road. Second Corps was in reserve in rear of the line. During the latter part of the month, the army renewed its activities. On August 13, 1864, Hancock, with his Second Corps, Gregg's cavalry division, and most of David B. Birney's Tenth Corps, was sent to the north side of the James River at Deep Bottom to demonstrate against the enemy entrenchments in front of Richmond. On the night of August 14, 1864, Warren's Fifth Corps was withdrawn from the lines at Petersburg, and August 18, 1864, it marched to the Petersburg and Weldon Railroad (the Weldon Railroad) at Globe Tavern to cut this line of communication between Richmond and Petersburg and the South. The enemy strongly attacked Fifth Corps on August 18, 19, and 21, 1864, but with help from Ninth Corps, Warren repulsed these attacks and remained firmly in possession of the railroad. He thus extended the line of entrenchments south of Petersburg, westward to Globe Tavern. Ninth Corps occupied the entrenched line between the Weldon Railroad and the Jerusalem Plank Road.

August 20, 1864, Hancock's forces were withdrawn from north of the James River, and the next day Hancock was ordered with two of his divisions of Second Corps to move to the left of Warren to destroy the Weldon Railroad as far south as Rowanty Creek. Gershom Mott's Third Division of Second Corps was left behind to hold a part of the entrenchments. Before Hancock's work of destruction was completed, he was heavily attacked at Reams' Station August 25, 1864 by Confederate troops under Ambrose P. Hill, and was forced to withdraw to the vicinity of the Jerusalem Plank Road.

August 26, 1864, Meade was authorized to command and direct the movements of all troops operating against Petersburg south of the Appomattox. During the period August 24–28, 1864, Birney's Tenth Corps relieved Eighteenth Corps on the line of entrenchments at Petersburg, and Tenth Corps then came under Meade's orders. Eighteenth Corps withdrew to the north side of the Appomattox and replaced Tenth Corps in the defenses at Bermuda Hundred and Deep Bottom.

There were some important command changes during August 1864. Following the poor performance of Ninth Corps at the Battle of the "Crater," John G. Parke relieved Burnside in command of Ninth Corps August 14, 1864; and earlier, on August 5, 1864, Julius White relieved James H. Ledlie in command of First Division, Ninth Corps. John F. Hartranft assumed temporary command of First Division, Ninth Corps August 28, 1864.

For details of the organization and operations of the Army of the Potomac during August 1864, see the following: Operations about Petersburg and Richmond, Virginia, 1864–1865, Operations of August 1864; and Second Corps, Fifth Corps, and Ninth Corps, Army of the Potomac.

The Army of the Potomac remained on the line of entrenchments at Petersburg without significant change until late September 1864. At that time Grant began preparations for an autumn offensive, which was to consist of an attack by the Army of the James on the defenses of Richmond, north of the James River, and an advance by the Army of the Potomac against Lee's communications south and west of Petersburg. On the night of September 24, 1864, Nelson A. Miles' and John Gibbon's divisions of Second Corps, which had been in reserve, relieved Birney's Tenth Corps, Army of the James in the Petersburg trenches to make it available for Butler's operation north of the James. When this exchange was completed, the Army of the Potomac occupied the entire siege line from the Appomattox River to the Weldon Railroad. A short time later, Meade assembled the following troops near Globe Tavern, on the Weldon Railroad: Parke, with Robert B. Potter's and Orlando B. Willcox's divisions of his Ninth Corps; Warren, with Charles Griffin's and Romeyn B. Ayres' divisions of his Fifth Corps; and

Gregg's Second Cavalry Division, Army of the Potomac. On September 30, 1864, this force marched westward toward Poplar Spring Church in the direction of Lee's communications. Meade was heavily engaged that day at Peebles' farm and Pegram's farm, and gained some initial successes, but he was then halted and finally driven back. For the details of these battles, see Operations about Petersburg and Richmond, Virginia, 1864–1865, Operations of September 1864, The Battle of Poplar Spring Church (Combats at Wyatt's Farm, Peebles' Farm, Chappell's House, Pegram's Farm, and Vaughan Road).

During the month of September 1864, there were some organizational and command changes in the army. The only significant organizational changes were the reorganizations of Fifth Corps and Ninth Corps to consist of three divisions each. For details, see Fifth Corps, Army of the Potomac and Ninth Corps. On the evening of September 1, 1864, Meade left the army for Philadelphia on leave, and Parke, as senior officer present, assumed command of the Army of the Potomac, and also of all troops operating south of the Appomattox River. Meade returned to the army and resumed command September 10, 1864.

Grant left City Point for the Shenandoah Valley September 14, 1864 to confer with Sheridan. Butler left the Army of the James September 14, 1864 for a few days, and Meade was authorized to command both the Army of the Potomac, and also the Army of the James if that became necessary. Grant returned to City Point September 19, 1864. During the first two days of October 1864, most of the Army of the Potomac was engaged in the operations around Poplar Spring Church (see above). The fighting ended October 2, 1864, and that night the troops of Fifth Corps, Ninth Corps, and Mott's division of Second Corps began work on a new entrenched line to cover the ground gained during the advance of September 30, 1864–October 2, 1864. This extended the Petersburg entrenchments from Fort Wadsworth, formerly the left of the line, to Pegram's farm and Peebles' farm. For details, see Operations about Petersburg and Richmond, Virginia, 1864–1865, Operations of October 1864, Siege of Petersburg.

Most of the month, the army was occupied in manning and strengthening the works, but October 27, 1864, Meade, at Grant's direction, made another attempt to cut Lee's communications west of Petersburg. Early that morning, most of the Army of the Potomac pulled out of the entrenchments and marched to the left in an attempt to pass the enemy right and reach the South Side Railroad east of Sutherland's Station.

Hancock and Gregg reached the vicinity of Burgess' Mill on Hatcher's Run, and were strongly attacked there that afternoon. The attack was repulsed, but because of the slow progress of the army that day, the movement was called off, and the troops returned to their former positions the next day. Fifth Corps and Ninth Corps also advanced on October 27, 1864, and moved close to the enemy entrenchments on their left, but they did not attempt a frontal assault. They also returned to their former positions on October 28, 1864. For details, see Operations about Petersburg and Richmond, Virginia, 1864–1865, Operations of October 1864, Engagement at the Boydton Plank Road (or Hatcher's Run), Virginia.

In December 1864, Horatio G. Wright's Sixth Corps returned to the Army of the Potomac from the Shenandoah Valley, and from that time until the end of the war the army consisted of Second Corps, Fifth Corps, Sixth Corps, Ninth Corps, and Second Cavalry Division. During the Appomattox Campaign, however, the Second Cavalry Division was under Sheridan's direct control and not Meade's.

From the end of October 1864 to the beginning of the spring campaign of 1865, the activities of the Army of the Potomac were confined largely to the defense and extension of the line of entrenchments, to reconnaissances, and to limited offensive movements to prevent the detachment of troops to be sent south to oppose Sherman's advance in the Carolinas. There were also some attempts against the enemy lines of communications. The most significant of these were as follows:

December 1, 1864, Gregg's cavalry division advanced to Stony Creek Station on the Weldon Railroad; after destroying the station and some other buildings, and large quantities of supplies, it returned to its camps near the Jerusalem Plank Road.

December 7–12, 1864, Warren led an expedition to Hicksford, Virginia to break up the Weldon Railroad. His command, which consisted of his own Fifth Corps, Mott's division of Second Corps, and

Gregg's cavalry division, destroyed about eighteen miles of track, and then returned to its former positions. For details, See Operations about Petersburg and Richmond, Virginia, 1864–1865, Winter of 1864–1865, Warren's Expedition to Hicksford, Virginia.

On December 9, 1864, while Warren was absent on his Hicksford expedition, Nelson A. Miles, with his First Division, Second Corps, was sent down the Vaughan Road to Hatcher's Run to learn what he could of the enemy activities in that area. About dark, Frank Wheaton arrived with parts of First Division and Third Division of Sixth Corps, and formed on the right of Miles. The next day, both Miles and Wheaton returned to their former positions. For additional information, see Operations about Petersburg and Richmond, Virginia, 1864–1865, Winter of 1864–1865, Reconnaissance to Hatcher's Run, Virginia.

There was little activity in January 1865, but early in February 1865, a large part of the army participated in a major movement to the left, which resulted in some hard fighting and ultimately the extension of the line of entrenchments from Fort Sampson, on the left of the old line, to the Vaughan Road Crossing of Hatcher's Run. On February 5, 1865, Gregg's cavalry division was sent out to Dinwiddie Court House to break up the enemy wagon trains believed to be using the Boydton Plank Road. Warren's Fifth Corps was moved up to the J. Hargrave house in support, and two divisions of Andrew A. Humphreys' Second Corps were advanced to Armstrong's Mill to be in supporting distance of Warren. Humphreys was attacked at Armstrong's Mill on the afternoon of February 5, 1865, but with help from Second Corps, Sixth Corps, and Ninth Corps, he held his position. Warren was recalled to Hatcher's Run that night. The next day, two divisions of Fifth Corps that had been advanced to Dabney's Mill were attacked and driven back to the Vaughan Road, south of Hatcher's Run, but there the enemy was stopped.

The fighting ended February 7, 1865, and Humphreys was then ordered to entrench his position. Warren was directed to watch the crossings of Hatcher's Run, and cover the left and rear of Second Corps' new line. After this action, Meade held a new line about five miles in advance of his former positions in this area. For details, see Operations about Petersburg and Richmond, Virginia, 1864–1865, Winter of 1864–1865, Battle of Hatcher's Run (or Dabney's Mill, Armstrong's Mill, Rowanty Creek, and Vaughan Road), Virginia.

The most serious fighting of the period occurred early on the morning of March 25, 1865, just before the opening of the spring campaign. A Confederate force under John B. Gordon attacked the Union line at Fort Stedman, on the front of Ninth Corps, and captured the fort and the adjacent works from Battery No. 9 to Fort Haskell. The line was restored during the morning, but the attack resulted in vigorous activity along the entire front of the Army of the Potomac. Some divisions were sent to aid Ninth Corps in repelling Gordon's attack, but they were not engaged. Other divisions were directed to make probing attacks along the right of the enemy line, and to attack if they discovered any weakness. The entrenched enemy picket line was captured, but no attack on the main line was attempted. For details, see Operations about Petersburg and Richmond, Virginia, 1864–1865, Winter of 1864–1865, Assault at Fort Stedman.

In November 1864, some troops of the Army of the Potomac, and also from the Army of the James, were sent to New York to help preserve order there during the election that month. Meade ordered the organizations of United States Infantry serving in Fifth Corps to proceed to New York by regiments and battalions, and November 2, 1864, these troops, numbering about 1,200 men, left the army for City Point, where they embarked for New York. Upon arrival, the regulars were sent north to Buffalo to watch the border, to Elmira to guard the prisoners held there, and to Watervliet Arsenal, near Albany. The regulars did not return to the army after election day, but they remained in upstate New York. For details, see Department of the East, January 3, 1863–June 27, 1865, Election of 1864 in New York.

During the period December 4–16, 1864, Sixth Corps, which had been serving with Sheridan's army in the Shenandoah Valley during the summer and fall, returned to the army at Petersburg. Upon its arrival, it relieved Fifth Corps in the entrenchments, and remained on duty there during the remainder of the winter. For details, see Operations about Petersburg and Richmond, Virginia, 1864–1865, The Winter of 1864–1865, Siege of Petersburg, The Petersburg Lines.

There was another addition to the army December 24, 1864, when Henry L. Abbot's Siege Artillery was permanently transferred from the Army of the James. December 27, 1864, it was placed under the orders of Henry J. Hunt, chief of artillery, Army of the Potomac.

On February 27, 1865, Philip H. Sheridan left Winchester, Virginia with First Cavalry Division and Third Cavalry Division, Army of the Shenandoah (also called Sheridan's Cavalry Command), and arrived at Petersburg March 27, 1865. For details of Sheridan's march, see Sheridan's Expedition from Winchester to Petersburg, Virginia. On the day of Sheridan's arrival, Second Cavalry Division, Army of the Potomac, then under George Crook, was assigned to his command, thus relieving the last division of the former Cavalry Corps from Meade's control. Sheridan's three cavalry divisions formed a separate command under the direct orders of Grant.

During the period November 1, 1864–March 29, 1865, the Army of the Potomac consisted of the following:

Provost Guard. This was commanded by Marsena R. Patrick until March 16, 1865, and then by George N. Macy.

Engineer Brigade. Henry Benham commanded the Engineer Brigade, and in addition he was also in charge of the Defenses of City Point. March 16, 1865, Meade made some changes in Benham's command. Charles H. T. Collis was assigned command of the post of City Point, and Benham remained in command of the defenses. The detachment of the Army of the Potomac under Collis was designated as a provisional brigade (independent brigade). On January 18, 1865, Benham was ordered to New York to procure engineer supplies, and also to inspect the Engineer Depot at Washington. He was instructed to return by February 15, 1865. Wesley Brainerd assumed command of the Engineer Brigade during Benham's absence.

Battalion of United States Engineers. Franklin Harwood commanded the battalion, but during the latter part of November 1864, Charles W. Howell commanded the engineers while Harwood was absent.

Artillery. Henry J. Hunt was chief of artillery of the army, and his command consisted of the Artillery Reserve and the Siege Artillery. Ezekiel R. Mayo commanded the Artillery Reserve until February 1865, and he then was succeeded by Calvin Shaffer. Henry L. Abbot commanded the Siege Artillery. Edward R. Warner was in temporary command of the artillery of the army from January 22, 1865 to February 1865 while Hunt was on leave. In addition to the Artillery Reserve of the army, an artillery brigade served with each of the corps. The Siege Artillery, which was transferred from the Army of the James to the Army of the Potomac December 27, 1864, remained at Broadway Landing, and was also carried on the roster of Edward Ferrero's Defenses of Bermuda Hundred.

Signal Corps. Benjamin F. Fisher commanded the Signal Corps until December 26, 1864, and then he was relieved from duty with the Army of the Potomac, and was placed in charge of the office of the Signal Corps in Washington. Charles L. Davis succeeded Fisher in command.

Second Corps. Winfield S. Hancock commanded the corps until November 26, 1864. In November 1864 the secretary of war proposed that Hancock come north and undertake the organization of a new corps, to be composed entirely of veteran soldiers. Hancock left the army November 26, 1864, and was succeeded in command of Second Corps by Andrew A. Humphreys, until that time chief of staff of the Army of the Potomac.

Fifth Corps. Gouverneur K. Warren commanded the corps.

Sixth Corps. Horatio G. Wright commanded the corps, which joined the Army of the Potomac from the Shenandoah Valley December 4–16, 1864.

Ninth Corps. John G. Parke commanded the corps.

Second Cavalry Division. David McM. Gregg commanded the division until February 10, 1865. Gregg's resignation, which had been tendered February 3, 1865, was accepted by the president, and he was relieved from duty with the Army of the Potomac by an order of February 9, 1865. The next day Gregg turned over the command of the division to J. Irvin Gregg, the senior officer present, and departed for Washington. At that time, Henry E. Davies, who ranked J. Irvin Gregg, was absent on leave, and when he returned he assumed command of the division. George Crook took over the command March 27, 1865. That day, Second Cavalry Division reported to Sheridan's cavalry command, which was under Grant's direct orders, and it thus left the Army of the Potomac.

For more complete details of the organization of the army during this period, see Second Corps, Fifth Corps, Sixth Corps, Ninth Corps, and Cavalry Corps, Army of the Potomac.

Meade left the army on leave December 30, 1864, and John G. Parke commanded temporarily until he returned January 11, 1865. Parke again commanded the army temporarily from January 24, 1865 until February 2, 1865, while Meade was absent, and then from February 22, 1865, when he left because of the death of his son, until February 28, 1865.

APPOMATTOX CAMPAIGN
MARCH 29, 1865–APRIL 9, 1865

March 29, 1865, the Army of the Potomac, the Army of the James, and Sheridan's cavalry, all under the command of Grant, began the spring offensive against Lee's army at Petersburg. This was to end twelve days later, with the surrender of the Army of Northern Virginia at Appomattox Court House, about eighty-five miles to the west. The corps of the army that had arrived before Petersburg in June 1864, under Meade, were all present on March 29, 1865, but during the Appomattox Campaign they did not function as a unit under Meade's control. First, Crook's cavalry division, Army of the Potomac had been taken from Meade before the campaign began, and assigned to Sheridan's cavalry command, which was under Grant's direct orders. Then, from April 1, 1865, four days after the campaign started, Meade was not in reality in command of the Army of the Potomac; and after that date the corps of the army was never together again. From the beginning of operations, Grant largely issued orders to Meade, Sheridan, and Edward O. C. Ord, and at one time or another during most of this period, Second Corps, Fifth Corps, and Sixth Corps were under Sheridan's or Ord's orders.

March 29, 1865, Warren's Fifth Corps and Humphreys' Second Corps moved out from the left of the army toward the enemy right, and by March 31, 1865 had gained possession of the White Oak Road west of Hatcher's Run. Sheridan's cavalry, which had moved forward to Dinwiddie Court House as the infantry advanced, was roughly handled by the enemy near there March 31, 1865; and early the next morning, Fifth Corps was sent to reinforce the cavalry. Upon reporting to Sheridan April 1, 1865, Warren came under Sheridan's orders. Meade's command was thus reduced to Second Corps, Sixth Corps, and Ninth Corps, and also the troops remaining at City Point.

Sheridan, with his three cavalry divisions and Fifth Corps, won a decisive victory over a combined cavalry and infantry force under George E. Pickett at Five Forks, Virginia April 1, 1865, and as a consequence, Sixth Corps and Ninth Corps, with help from Ord's Army of the James, launched a successful attack the next morning on the Confederate defenses at Petersburg. Parke's Ninth Corps captured a part of the outer works along the Jerusalem Plank Road, and Wright's Sixth Corps broke through completely on a front extending from Fort Welch to Fort Fisher, and captured the entire line of enemy works to the southwest of the Boydton Plank Road near Petersburg.

Second Corps, Sixth Corps, and Ord's command then advanced toward Petersburg, and by nightfall the city was completely encircled on the south from the Appomattox River on the east, around to the river on the west. Fifth Corps, then under the command of Charles Griffin, remained with Sheridan April 2, 1865, and that night camped to the west and north of Sutherland's Station, not far from the cavalry. Because Second Corps was in position west of Petersburg, with one division at Sutherland's Station, Humphreys was placed under Sheridan's orders late that evening, and received from him marching orders for the next day. Thus, during the night of April 2, 1865 and the next day, only Sixth Corps and Ninth Corps were under Meade's direction.

Lee's army evacuated Petersburg during the night of April 2, 1865, and early the next morning Grant started his command in pursuit. Sheridan, with his cavalry, Second Corps, and Fifth Corps, marched along the south side of the Appomattox River toward Jetersville, on the Richmond and Danville Railroad.

Sixth Corps followed Sheridan's column. At 4:30 that afternoon Meade resumed command of Second Corps.

Parke's Ninth Corps, which remained under Meade's command during the campaign, marched along the South Side Railroad as the infantry advanced, guarding the trains and picketing the road. By April 9, 1865, the day of Lee's surrender at Appomattox Court House, Ninth Corps was along the railroad from Sutherland's Station to Burkeville, and the next day one brigade advanced to Farmville.

Sheridan with the cavalry and Fifth Corps, and Meade with Second Corps and Sixth Corps arrived at Jetersville April 4–5, 1865 and entrenched on a line across the railroad facing Amelia Court House, where the Army of Northern Virginia was assembled. Meade resumed command of Fifth Corps about midnight April 5, 1865. That night Lee's army moved westward on the road through Deatonsville toward Rice's Station on the South Side Railroad, and the next morning Grant's army started in pursuit. Meade, with Second Corps and Fifth Corps, moved forward on the right of the army. Second Corps followed Lee through Deatonsville, and Fifth Corps moved north to Painesville (Paine's Cross Roads), and then west on the right of Second Corps to Ligonton (Ligontown). Sheridan hurried forward with the cavalry on the road from Jetersville to Pride's Church, which ran south of, and nearly parallel to, Lee's line of march in an attempt to intercept the Confederate column. Sixth Corps, which was placed temporarily under Sheridan's orders, followed the cavalry.

During the afternoon, Wesley Merritt, then in command of all the cavalry, got ahead of Richard H. Anderson's Confederate Corps on the road to Rice's Station; and Sheridan, who was directing Sixth Corps near Hott's Corners, closed up on the rear of Richard S. Ewell's command just east of Little Saylor's Creek, on the same road. During the ensuing battle at Little Saylor's Creek, Sixth Corps captured most of Ewell's command, and the cavalry virtually destroyed Anderson's corps. That same evening, Second Corps defeated John B. Gordon's corps at Locketts' farm, east of Saylor's Creek, and a few miles north of Sixth Corps' battle, and destroyed a large part of the enemy wagon train.

When the army pushed on toward Farmville April 7, 1865, Meade resumed direction of Sixth Corps (although Sheridan believed that Grant intended that he, Sheridan, was to remain in control of Sixth Corps), and during the day he exercised command of all four infantry corps of the army. But not for long. On April 7, 1865, Griffin's Fifth Corps was transferred from the extreme right of the army to the extreme left, at Prince Edward Court House. The next day Fifth Corps joined Ord and John Gibbon's Twenty-Fourth Corps at Prospect Station. Ord, as the senior officer, then assumed control of Fifth Corps, and Griffin continued to receive orders from Ord until after Lee's surrender at Appomattox Court House April 9, 1865.

Back on the right flank, Second Corps followed Gordon's troops across the Appomattox River at High Bridge April 7, 1865. Later that day, Francis C. Barlow's division was engaged with Gordon's rear guard north of Farmville, and Nelson A. Miles' division attempted unsuccessfully to drive the enemy from a position near Cumberland Church, north of Farmville. Sixth Corps marched to Farmville on the south side of the Appomattox, and that night crossed to the north bank, and encamped not far from Second Corps.

Once again the enemy pulled out during the night, and the next morning Grant resumed the pursuit. On the right, Meade with Second Corps and Sixth Corps followed the Army of Northern Virginia on the road to Appomattox Court House. On the left, Ord with Twenty-Fourth Corps, Army of the James and Fifth Corps, Army of the Potomac, preceded by Sheridan's cavalry, marched throughout the day of April 8, 1865 and most of the night on the road from Farmville to Appomattox Station in an effort to get ahead of Lee and block his escape route toward Lynchburg. That night Meade halted with his two corps in rear of Longstreet's corps, a short distance from Appomattox Court House. Sheridan's cavalry captured Appomattox Station, and formed a defensive line across the Lynchburg Road, a short distance west of Appomattox Court House.

On the morning of April 9, 1865, Second Corps, followed by Sixth Corps, advanced toward the court house, and Meade was preparing for an attack on Longstreet's position, when hostilities ceased under a flag of truce. On the west side of Appomattox Court House, Lee attempted to break through Sheridan's line, and was pushing forward when Ord arrived with his two infantry corps and relieved the cavalry. The infantry stopped the enemy advance, and were moving forward when the fighting ended.

That afternoon, Lee surrendered to Grant his Army of Northern Virginia.

While most of the Army of the Potomac had marched in pursuit of Lee April 3, 1865, some troops had remained for a time at Petersburg and City Point. Orlando B. Willcox's division of Ninth Corps served as the garrison of Petersburg until April 5, 1865, when it was relieved by Edward Ferrero's Infantry Division from George L. Hartsuff's Defenses of Bermuda Hundred, Army of the James. Willcox's division had then moved to Sutherland's Station, and guarded the South Side Railroad during the remainder of the Appomattox Campaign.

At City Point, a part of Henry W. Benham's Engineer Brigade and Charles H. T. Collis' Independent Brigade, both of the Army of the Potomac, had been left behind to guard the post. On April 2, 1865, Warren, who had been relieved from command of Fifth Corps the day before at Five Forks, was assigned command of the Defenses of City Point and Bermuda Hundred. Hartsuff, commanding at Bermuda Hundred, was senior to Warren, however, and the next day Warren was reassigned to command all troops at City Point, Petersburg, and on the railroad. Warren's command was soon reduced when Hartsuff arrived at Petersburg April 6, 1865 and assumed command of Ferrero's division, which occupied the town.

On April 4, 1865, Benham was assigned command of the Defenses of City Point, and was also directed to guard the railroad between City Point and Petersburg. This command was a part of the Army of the Potomac, and was under Meade's orders. On April 7, 1865, however, by Grant's orders, Godfrey Weitzel, commanding the Detachment Army of the James in front of Richmond, assigned Hartsuff to the command of all forces at City Point, Bermuda Hundred, Petersburg, and on the South Side Railroad as far west as Sutherland's Station. This relieved Meade of the responsibility for this area, but Benham's engineers and Collis' Independent Brigade remained for a time at City Point. Collis' brigade was relieved by Charles S. Russell's Attached Brigade of August V. Kautz's First Division, Twenty-Fifth Corps, Army of the James April 10, 1865, and that day Collis and Benham marched with their brigades to join the Army of the Potomac at Burkeville. Hartsuff's assignment of April 7, 1865 also relieved Warren of all of his command except

for a cavalry picket, and he remained awaiting orders until May 1, 1865, when he was assigned command of the Department of Mississippi, relieving Napoleon J. T. Dana.

For details of the operations of the Army of the Potomac during the period March 29, 1865–April 9, 1865, see Appomattox Campaign.

AFTER APPOMATTOX COURT HOUSE
APRIL 10, 1865–JUNE 28, 1865

After Lee's surrender at Appomattox Court House April 9, 1865, Joseph E. Johnston remained in the field with about 30,000 men confronting William T. Sherman's Army of the Military Division of the Mississippi in North Carolina. There was uncertainty at army headquarters as to whether Johnston would surrender or continue the fight. Accordingly, Grant prepared for the latter eventuality. Before leaving Appomattox Court House for Washington April 10, 1865, he assigned Fifth Corps and Twenty-Fourth Corps to remain at the court house until paroles were issued, and the surrendered property was removed to the railroad for transportation to Washington; and he ordered the rest of the army to move to Burkeville, where it would be in position to march to North Carolina if necessary.

The army assembled at Burkeville during the period April 13–17, 1865. Meade, with Second Corps and Sixth Corps, left Appomattox Court House April 11, 1865, and arrived at Burkeville two days later. Benham's Engineer Brigade, which left City Point April 10, 1865, reported to Meade April 14, 1865. Griffin's Fifth Corps completed its work at the surrender site April 15, 1865, and then marched to Burkeville and reported to Meade two days later.

As already noted, Ninth Corps was on duty at this time along the South Side Railroad from Sutherland's Station to Farmville, and with the arrival of Fifth Corps, Meade had, for the last time, the four corps of the Army of the Potomac under his immediate command. As had happened before during the Appomattox Campaign, this arrangement soon ended. April 19, 1865, Parke was ordered to move his Ninth Corps to Washington. It was relieved on the line of the railroad by Fifth Corps April 20–21, 1865, and then moved to City Point to embark for Alexandria, where it arrived April 24–26, 1865. Ninth Corps was permanently detached from the Army of the Potomac, and was assigned to the Department of Washington. Parke was then under the command of Christopher C. Augur, commander of the department. It should be noted that Ninth Corps did return briefly to Meade's command, when it marched with the Army of the Potomac in the Grand Review in Washington May 23, 1865.

Two other units of the Army of the Potomac were not with Meade when Ninth Corps departed for Washington. Henry L. Abbot's Artillery Brigade, which was then at Broadway Landing, was under the command of George L. Hartsuff, and was ordered by him April 21, 1865 to move his headquarters to Fort Darling, near Drewry's Bluff. Abbot's artillery did not rejoin the Army of the Potomac, but May 4, 1865, it was detached and assigned to duty in the Department of Virginia. Two days later, Abbot was announced as chief of artillery, Department of Virginia (he retained command of the artillery brigade), and he established his headquarters in Richmond. The other unit was Collis' Independent Brigade, which remained at City Point for a time in charge of prisoners being sent there from the front, before being sent to Burkeville April 20, 1865. Collis arrived there four days later, and his brigade was broken up, with the regiments assigned to Romeyn B. Ayres' division of Fifth Corps.

On April 22, 1865, Wright's Sixth Corps was placed under Sheridan's command, and both the cavalry and Sixth Corps were ordered to move at once toward Greensboro, North Carolina. Sixth Corps left Burkeville April 23, 1865, and marched along the Richmond and Danville Railroad to Danville, Virginia, where it arrived April 27, 1865. Sheridan marched from Petersburg and arrived at South Boston Station on the Richmond and Danville Railroad the next day. Sheridan and Wright learned on April 28, 1865 of the surrender of Johnston's army two days earlier at Durham's Station, North Carolina, and they did not continue their march southward. Sheridan returned to Petersburg with the cavalry, but Sixth Corps did not follow at once. Frank Wheaton's First Division was sent back to guard the railroad between Burkeville and Sutherland's Station, and Wright remained with George W. Getty's Second Division and James B. Ricketts' Third Division at Danville, and on the railroad back to Burkeville, until mid-May 1865.

Meantime, on April 30, 1865, Grant ordered Meade to move with the Army of the Potomac, except Sixth Corps, to Washington. Second Corps, Fifth Corps, the Engineer Brigade, and the Artillery Reserve departed May 2, 1865, and arrived in camp south of Washington May 12–13, 1865. May 16, 1865, Sixth Corps was ordered to follow Second Corps and Fifth Corps to Washington.

On May 17, 1865, the War Department issued an order that was soon to bring an end to the Army of the Potomac. This order directed that all white troops in the Army of the Potomac whose terms of service expired between that date and September 30, 1865 be mustered out immediately.

On May 23, 1865, the Army of the Potomac marched for the last time in the Grand Review in Washington. Ninth Corps and the cavalry, which at that time were not a part of Meade's Army of the Potomac, marched with it in the parade as they had done so many times in the past. The order of march was as follows:

First, Headquarters Army of the Potomac and escort;
Second, Cavalry Corps under Wesley Merritt;
Third, Provost Marshal's Brigade under George N. Macy;
Fourth, Engineer Brigade under Henry W. Benham;
Fifth, Ninth Corps, with William Dwight's division of
    Nineteenth Corps attached, under John G. Parke;
Sixth, Fifth Corps under Charles Griffin;
Seventh, Second Corps under Andrew A. Humphreys.

Sixth Corps did not arrive in the vicinity of Washington until June 2, 1865.

After the Grand Review the size of the army rapidly dwindled. June 3, 1865, all western troops with the army were sent under the command of Henry A. Morrow to report to John A. Logan at Louisville, Kentucky. These troops included one regiment each from Ohio, Indiana, and Minnesota; three from Wisconsin; and four from Michigan. In addition to these regiments, many eastern regiments were also mustered out.

Finally, on June 28, 1865, Grant directed Meade to consolidate each of the existing corps, Second Corps, Fifth Corps, and Sixth Corps, into a single division, and to organize these divisions into a provisional corps under the command of Horatio G. Wright. All officers relieved by this order were directed to return to their homes, and to report for orders to the adjutant general of the army. The troops not then to be mustered out were consolidated as follows:

PROVISIONAL CORPS, Horatio G. Wright

First Division (from troops of Sixth Corps), George W. Getty
First Brigade, Truman Seymour
Second Brigade, Frank Wheaton
Third Brigade, Joseph E. Hamblin

Second Division (from troops of Second Corps), Gershom Mott
First Brigade, P. Regis De Trobriand
Second Brigade, Byron R. Pierce
Third Brigade, George N. Macy

Third Division (from troops of Fifth Corps), Romeyn B. Ayres
First Brigade, Joshua L. Chamberlain
Second Brigade, Henry Baxter
Third Brigade, Joseph Hayes

General Order No. 35, Headquarters Army of the Potomac, issued June 28, 1865, declared that by virtue of the order that directed the consolidation of the troops of the army into the Provisional Corps, the Army of the Potomac ceased to exist. The consolidation was completed by July 1, 1865.

The Provisional Corps under Wright was ordered to go into camp at a suitable point on the Baltimore and Ohio Railroad, west of the Monocacy River, and when established there Wright was directed to report to Winfield S. Hancock, commander of the Middle Department. The regiments composing the Provisional Corps were mustered out about mid-July 1865.

June 26, 1865, George G. Meade was assigned command of the newly constituted Military Division of the Atlantic, which included the Department of the East, the Middle Department, and the departments of Virginia, North Carolina, and South Carolina.

For additional information about the closing days of the Army of the Potomac, see the following: Second Corps, Fifth Corps, Sixth Corps, Ninth Corps, Cavalry Corps, Army of the James, Depart-

ment of Virginia, and Department of Washington, February 2, 1863–March 16, 1869.

COMMANDERS OF THE ARMY OF THE POTOMAC

George B. McClellan	August 15, 1861 to November 7, 1862
Ambrose E. Burnside	November 7, 1862 to January 26, 1863
Joseph Hooker	January 26, 1863 to June 28, 1863
George G. Meade	June 28, 1863 to September 1, 1864
John G. Parke	September 1, 1864 to September 10, 1864
George G. Meade	September 10, 1864 to December 30, 1864
John G. Parke	December 30, 1864 to January 11, 1865
George G. Meade	January 11, 1865 to January 24, 1865
John G. Parke	January 24, 1865 to February 2, 1865
George G. Meade	February 2, 1865 to February 22, 1865
John G. Parke	February 22, 1865 to February 28, 1865
George G. Meade	February 28, 1865 to June 28, 1865

Note 1. Burnside announced his official assumption of command November 9, 1862, but he was actually in command from the night of November 7, 1862.

Note 2. During the latter part of August 1862, most of the Army of the Potomac was with John Pope's Army of Virginia, and was not under McClellan's orders. McClellan began to assume control again September 1, 1862, in the Defenses of Washington.

ARMY OF THE SHENANDOAH (PATTERSON)

The force that Robert Patterson organized at Chambersburg, Pennsylvania and led into Virginia at Williamsport, Maryland during the Bull Run Campaign of July 1861 has been called the Army of the Shenandoah, the Army of the Department of Pennsylvania, and the Army of Pennsylvania. For details of the organization and operations of this army, see Department of Pennsylvania, April 27, 1861–August 24, 1861.

ARMY OF THE SHENANDOAH (SHERIDAN)

There were at least three Union armies during the war that were called the Army of the Shenandoah. The first of these consisted of the troops that Robert Patterson led from Pennsylvania into the lower Shenandoah Valley in the summer of 1861. For a description of this army, see Department of Pennsylvania, April 27, 1861–August 24, 1861. The second army to bear this name was David Hunter's army of the Department of West Virginia, which he led up the Shenandoah Valley to Lynchburg, Virginia in May and June of 1864. For details of this army, see Department of West Virginia, Operations of the Troops of the Department of West Virginia. The third Army of the Shenandoah, and apparently the only one to be officially so designated, was the army that Philip H. Sheridan commanded during the Shenandoah Valley Campaign of August 7, 1864–November 28, 1864. A brief account of the organization and operations of this army is given below, but for more detailed information, see Shenandoah Valley Campaign (Sheridan).

In July 1864, Jubal A. Early, with an army of about 14,000 men, invaded Maryland from the Shenandoah Valley and threatened Washington, and then returned to the valley. A short time later Early again moved down the valley and defeated George Crook's Army of the Kanawha at Kernstown, Virginia July 24, 1864, and then advanced to the Potomac River. To oppose Early, an army was assembled, which consisted of the following: Horatio G. Wright's Sixth Corps from the Army of the Potomac; a part of William H. Emory's Detachment Nineteenth Corps, which was then arriving at Fort Monroe from the Department of the Gulf; David Hunter's field force from the Department of West Virginia; and a cavalry force under Charles R. Lowell, Jr. All were under the command of Hunter, and were encamped near Harper's Ferry when John McCausland's Confederate cavalry burned Chambersburg, Pennsylvania at the end of July 1864.

Hunter then moved his command back to the vicinity of Frederick, Maryland to counter a possible enemy advance through the passes of South Mountain. Early, however, withdrew with his army toward Winchester, Virginia, and at the suggestion of Ulysses S. Grant, Hunter concentrated his forces at Halltown, West Virginia, near Harper's Ferry, August 4–5, 1864. For details of the organization and operations of the Union forces opposing Early in July 1864, see Early's Washington Raid (and Operations in the Shenandoah Valley, Maryland, and Pennsylvania).

As a result of Early's activities during July 1864, Grant decided to put an end to the Confederate threat in the Shenandoah Valley. For this purpose he sent Philip H. Sheridan from the Army of the Potomac to assume command of Hunter's army at Halltown, and with it to clear the valley of enemy troops and render it untenable for further aggressive operations. Sheridan arrived at Harper's Ferry August 6, 1864 and assumed command, and he then began preparations for an advance up the valley. The next day he was assigned command of the newly created Middle Military Division that consisted of the Middle Department and the departments of Washington, West Virginia, and the Susquehanna. On August 8, 1864, he designated the troops under Crook, then serving in Sheridan's army, as the Army of West Virginia.

In preparation for the advance of the army up the Shenandoah Valley, the troops assembled near Harper's Ferry were strongly reinforced. The cavalry divisions of Alfred N. Duffie and William W. Averell of the Department of West Virginia, which had pursued McCausland's cavalry from Chambersburg through Hancock, Maryland, were near Hancock and Moorefield, West Virginia in early August 1864. These were ordered to rejoin the army in the lower Shenandoah Valley. Sheridan's cavalry force was greatly strengthened when Wesley Merritt's First Cavalry Division and James H. Wilson's Third Cavalry Division of the Cavalry Corps, Army of the Potomac arrived in the Shenandoah Valley. These two divisions, together with Averell's Second Cavalry Division, Department of West Virginia, were organized into a single cavalry force under the command of Alfred T. A. Torbert, Sheridan's chief of cavalry. In addition, an independent cavalry brigade was formed under Charles

R. Lowell, Jr. Cuvier Grover's Second Division, Detachment Nineteenth Corps, which had been detained in the Department of Washington, was also sent to reinforce Sheridan's infantry force.

The army organized by Sheridan was generally known as the Army of the Shenandoah, and it was officially so designated November 17, 1864. It consisted of the following:

ARMY OF THE SHENANDOAH, Philip H. Sheridan

Sixth Corps, Horatio G. Wright
    First Division, David A. Russell
    Second Division, George Getty
    Third Division, James B. Ricketts

Detachment Nineteenth Corps, William H. Emory
    First Division, William Dwight
    Second Division, Cuvier Grover

Army of West Virginia, George Crook
    First Division, Joseph Thoburn
    Second Division, Isaac H. Duval

Cavalry, Alfred T. A. Torbert
    First Division, Wesley Merritt
    Second Cavalry Division, Department of West Virginia, William W. Averell
    Third Division, James H. Wilson

To avoid misunderstanding in reading some reports of the operations of the Army of the Shenandoah, it should be noted here that Crook's Army of West Virginia was frequently called Eighth Corps, probably because many of the troops of Crook's command formerly belonged to that corps. This was not a proper designation, however, because Eighth Corps was formed to consist of the troops of the Middle Department, and this definition was never officially changed.

The organization given above was that of the army led by Sheridan during the Shenandoah Valley Campaign of August 7, 1864–November 28, 1864, and which was engaged at the Battle of Opequon Creek September 19, 1864, Fisher's Hill September 21–22, 1864, and Cedar Creek October 19, 1864. For details of the organization, command, and operations of the Army of the Shenandoah during this period, see Shenandoah Valley Campaign (Sheridan).

The army remained along Cedar Creek after the battle of October 19, 1864 until November 9, 1864, and then it moved back to Kernstown and went into camp at what became known as Camp Russell.

There were few changes in the army during that time. On October 28, 1864, the Provisional Division under William Heine (organized earlier in the month as J. Howard Kitching's Provisional Division) moved to Winchester to report to Oliver Edwards, commander of the post. Edwards' Third Brigade, First Division, Sixth Corps, which had been serving as garrison of the post, then rejoined Sixth Corps. On November 7, 1864, Nineteenth Corps, Department of the Gulf was discontinued, and the designation of Emory's Detachment Nineteenth Corps was then changed to Nineteenth Corps, and Emory was assigned command. As noted above, on November 17, 1864, Sheridan's army was officially designated as Army of the Shenandoah.

There was little further military activity by Sheridan's command that winter except for some cavalry expeditions outside the valley. The two most important of these are described in the following sections.

Merritt's Expedition from Winchester into Fauquier and Loudoun Counties in Virginia, November 28, 1864–December 3, 1864. During the entire Shenandoah Valley Campaign, guerrilla bands under John S. Mosby, Elijah V. White, Harry Gilmor, and others had been active and had seriously reduced Sheridan's combat strength by forcing him to use large infantry escorts for the supply trains. Mosby, whose force came from the country around Upperville, east of the Blue Ridge Mountains, caused the most trouble. Finally, on November 27, 1864, when the infantry campaigning was about over for the year, Merritt was ordered with his First Cavalry Division to the Loudoun Valley to destroy all forage and subsistence, to burn all barns and their contents, and to drive off all horses, cattle, sheep, and hogs in an area bounded on the north by the Potomac River, on the east by the Bull Run Mountains, and on the south by the Manassas Gap Railroad. Merritt's mission also included the capture or destruction of Mosby and his command.

On the morning of November 28, 1864, Merritt left Winchester with Peter Stagg's First Brigade and Thomas C. Devin's Second Brigade and moved to Ashby's Gap. After passing through the gap, two regiments of the Second Brigade were ordered to move north along the foot of the mountains, spreading out well over the country toward Bloomfield, while a regiment of the First Brigade was sent out by way of Grigsby's Store to the west of Piedmont. These regiments met the division that evening near Upperville, where it camped that night. The next morning, First Brigade moved to Rectortown, and from there three columns were sent out to Salem and White Plains. The entire force was assembled at Middleburg, and from there it marched by way of Philomont to Snickersville, with strong columns out on the right toward Millville and on the left through Bloomfield to the foot of the mountains. By that evening, the country had been devastated as far north as the Little River Turnpike.

Very early on the morning of November 29, 1864, Casper Crowninshield's Reserve Brigade of Merritt's division, which was at that time near Stephenson's Depot, marched into Loudoun Valley, and then proceeded by way of Bloomfield, Union, and Philomont to join Merritt near Snickersville.

On the morning of November 30, 1864, Devin moved by way of Philomont, Circleville, and Hamilton to Waterford, and then along Catoctin Creek to the Potomac River. He then moved to Lovettsville, where he was joined by a part of the Reserve Brigade. The regiments of the Reserve Brigade did not operate together that day. A part of the brigade marched north from Snickersville through Hillsboro to Cave Head on the Potomac, and from there along the river to Lovettsville, where it joined Devin. Another part marched down the Shenandoah River between the river and the Blue Ridge Mountains as far as Rockford and then returned to Snicker's Gap. On November 30, 1864, First Brigade marched from Philomont to Snickersville with the cattle that it had collected, and at the same time sent out parties to complete the work of destruction.

December 1, 1864, Devin, with a part of the Reserve Brigade, marched from Lovettsville through Hillsboro and Purcelleville and reached Snickersville that evening. After some further destruction and attempts to engage Mosby, Merritt's command returned to its camps near Kernstown, where he arrived December 3, 1864.

Torbert's Expedition from Winchester to Gordonsville, Virginia, December 19–28, 1864, and Custer's Demonstration in the Shenandoah Valley (Engagement at Lacey's Springs, December 19, 1864). On December 12, 1864, Grant repeated a request to Sheridan that the cavalry be sent to destroy the Virginia Central Railroad, and by this action prevent much-needed supplies from reaching Lee's army at Petersburg. Accordingly, on December 19, 1864, in very bad weather, Torbert left Winchester with 5,000 men of Merritt's First Cavalry Division and William H. Powell's Second Cavalry Division, Department of West Virginia, and marched by way of Front Royal to Chester Gap in the Blue Ridge Mountains. He camped there that night, and the next day continued on through Little Washington, Gaines' Cross Roads, and Sperryville toward Criglersville, and that night Second Division camped on Hughes River and First Division on the Hazel River. The weather was terrible, with hail and sleet falling all night. At daylight December 21, 1864, Torbert resumed the march by way of Criglersville toward Madison Court House. The march was made over nearly impassable roads and in a hail and snow storm that lasted all day. First Division arrived at Madison Court House and, after a brief engagement, drove William L. Jackson's Confederate cavalry brigade from the town. Second Division camped on Robertson's River, near Criglersville.

December 22, 1864, Torbert advanced on the pike toward Liberty Mills and Gordonsville. He drove back the brigades of Jackson and John McCausland, both under Lunsford L. Lomax, and forced them across the Rapidan River at Liberty Mills, but because of strong opposition he was unable to cross there. He finally managed to cross, however, both above and below Liberty Mills, and forced the enemy to withdraw toward Gordonsville after dark that night.

Fighting was resumed the next morning as Torbert advanced, but he finally arrived within two and one-half miles of Gordonsville before he was stopped at the gap in Southwest Mountain. While Torbert was attempting to flank this position, Confederate infantry began to arrive from Richmond and replace the cavalry in the defensive works. Torbert, believing that he would be unable to advance against infantry, decided to withdraw. He retired during the afternoon and evening to Madison Court House and Robertson's River, and he then continued on by way of Rixeyville and the Fauquier White Sulfur Springs to Warrenton. There he divided his column, and Second Division marched by way of Salem, Piedmont, and Paris; and First Division by way of New Baltimore, White Plains, and Middleburg; and then on to Winchester, where they arrived December 27–28, 1864, in bad condition from the cold and wet weather. The cavalry then went into winter quarters.

When Torbert left for Gordonsville December 19, 1864, George A. Custer moved up the Shenandoah Valley with his Third Division toward Staunton, Virginia on a demonstration to hold Jubal A. Early's troops in the valley. Custer halted at Woodstock that night and the next day moved on to Lacey's Springs, nine miles from Harrisonburg. He halted there on the night of December 20, 1864, with Alexander C. M. Pennington's First Brigade encamped in front, on the left of the pike, with regiments out on roads to the front and left; and George H. Chapman's Second Brigade was behind Pennington, with pickets out to the right.

When Early learned of Torbert's movement, however, he sent Lomax with his cavalry division to Gordonsville, and at the same time sent Thomas L. Rosser's division to meet Custer. Custer was surprised very early the following morning when Rosser attacked with William H. Payne's brigade, and then Wickham's brigade, commanded by William A. Morgan. Both sides claimed victory, but Custer then retired up the valley without being successful in preventing Early from sending troops to Gordonsville to oppose Torbert.

* * * * * * * * *

The Army of the Shenandoah remained relatively unchanged until December 1864, and then, during the period December 1864–February 1865, it was largely broken up by detachments, although the designation of Army of the Shenandoah was retained. The principal detachments were as follows:

December 1–9, 1864, Wright's Sixth Corps left the valley to rejoin the Army of the Potomac at Petersburg.

December 19, 1864, Thomas M. Harris' First Infantry Division, Army of West Virginia left to join the Army of the James on the Richmond front, where it was assigned as Harris' Independent Division, Twenty-Fourth Corps.

December 21, 1864, William Heine's Provisional Division was relieved from duty at Winchester, and it was sent to Twenty-Fourth Corps, Army of the James, and was assigned to the Defenses of Bermuda Hundred.

December 30, 1864, Isaac H. Duval's Second Infantry Division, Army of West Virginia (redesignated First Infantry Division after the departure of Harris' division) was sent to Cumberland, Maryland, and there it came under the orders of the commander of the Department of West Virginia.

January 6, 1865, Cuvier Grover's Second Division, Nineteenth Corps was sent to Savannah, Georgia.

February 27, 1865, Sheridan left Winchester with Merritt's First Cavalry Division, commanded by Thomas C. Devin, and Custer's Third Division, both commanded by Merritt, on an expedition against the Virginia Central Railroad and the James River Canal. Sheridan did not return to the valley, but continued on and joined Grant's army at Petersburg March 28, 1865. For details of Sheridan's expedition, see Sheridan's Expedition from Winchester to Petersburg, Virginia.

While Sheridan was leading his two cavalry divisions to Petersburg, he referred to his command as the Army of the Shenandoah. In fact, the only troops of Sheridan's former Army of the Shenandoah remaining in the lower valley at that time were William Dwight's First Division, Nineteenth Corps and a small cavalry force under Torbert, which included George H. Chapman's Second Cavalry Division, Department of West Virginia, consisting of only one brigade. When Sheridan left the valley on his expedition February 27, 1865, Winfield S. Hancock assumed temporary command of the Middle Military Division, and thus exercised direct control over what was left of the Army of the Shenandoah.

In March 1865, fourteen new regiments were ordered to report to John D. Stevenson, commanding at Harper's Ferry, in the Department of West Virginia, and these regiments were then sent to Halltown and Charlestown to be organized into divisions. March 13, 1865, John R. Brooke assumed command of the troops organizing at Halltown, and March 19, 1865, Thomas W. Egan took charge of the troops at Charlestown. At the end of the month, Brooke's command was organized as First Provisional Division, and Egan's command was organized as Second Provisional Division.

March 20, 1865, Nineteenth Corps was discontinued, and First Division of the corps, the only one then serving under Hancock, became simply Dwight's Division, and served under the direct orders of Hancock.

On April 2, 1865, the troops of the Army of the Shenandoah were reorganized as follows: Dwight's Division was redesignated as First Division, Army of the Shenandoah. The designation of Brooke's First Provisional Division was changed to Second Provisional Division, Army of the Shenandoah; and Egan's Second Provisional Division was changed to Third Provisional Division, Army of the Shenandoah. A new Fourth Provisional Division, Army of the Shenandoah was organized under Samuel S. Carroll from Isaac H. Duval's brigade of the former First Infantry Division, Department of West Virginia, and three regiments of United States Veteran Volunteers (First Corps) from the Department of Washington. When the reorganization of the army was completed, it consisted of the following:

ARMY OF THE SHENANDOAH, Winfield S. Hancock

First Division, William Dwight
    First Brigade, George L. Beal
    Second Brigade, Edwin P. Davis

Second Provisional Division, John R. Brooke
    First Brigade, George M. Love
    Second Brigade, Richard C. Duryea

Third Provisional Division, Thomas W. Egan
    First Brigade, Anson G. McCook
    Second Brigade, Green B. Raum

Fourth Provisional Division, Samuel S. Carroll
    First Brigade, Isaac H. Duval
    Second Brigade, Oliver Wood

Second Cavalry Division, George H. Chapman

Artillery Brigade, Albert W. Bradbury
    17th Battery, Indiana Light Artillery, Laban Sparks
    5th Battery (E), Maine Light Artillery, Greenleaf T. Stevens
    5th Battery, New York Light Artillery, John V. Grant
    Battery D, 1st Rhode Island Light Artillery, Elmer L. Corthell

This army remained in existence with some changes until discontinued by muster out in July and August 1865.

When Lee evacuated Petersburg and Richmond early in April 1865, Hancock moved all of his infantry, totaling about 18,000 men, to Kernstown to be put in condition for any movement that might be required in the valley.

April 19–20, 1865, Dwight's division and Chapman's cavalry were transferred to the Department of Washington, Twenty-Second Corps, and Marcus A. Reno was left in command of the cavalry remaining with the Army of the Shenandoah.

April 22, 1865, Hancock moved his headquarters of the Middle Military Division to Washington, and left Alfred T. A. Torbert in command of the Army of the Shenandoah, with headquarters at Winchester.

May 4, 1865, Carroll was ordered with the three regiments of United States Veteran Volunteers (Second Brigade, Fourth Provisional Division) of his command to march to Camp Stoneman near Washington. This left only Duval's First Brigade remaining in Fourth Provisional Division, and it was mustered out in July 1865. When Carroll arrived at Camp Stoneman, he assumed command of First Division, First Corps May 21, 1865.

In May 1865, the word "Provisional" was dropped from the designations of the divisions of the Army of the Shenandoah, and thereafter these were known as Brooke's Second Division, Egan's Third Division, and Duval's Fourth Division. Second Division was discontinued by muster out in August 1865, Third Division in July and August 1865, and Fourth Division in July 1865.

ARMY OF VIRGINIA (POPE)

In March and April 1862, Federal forces operating in northern Virginia were divided into separate commands by the creation of three departments, the Mountain Department, the Department of the Shenandoah, and the Department of the Rappahannock; and the lack of effective cooperation among the commanders of these departments was responsible, at least in part, for the success of Thomas J. (Stonewall) Jackson in his Shenandoah Valley Campaign of May and June of that year.

As a means of providing unity of command over

the field forces in northern Virginia, the Army of Virginia was created June 26, 1862, by the consolidation of the three departments. John C. Fremont's Mountain Department became First Corps, Army of Virginia; Nathaniel P. Banks' Department of the Shenandoah became Second Corps, Army of Virginia; and Irvin McDowell's Department of the Rappahannock became Third Corps, Army of Virginia. John Pope, who was brought to Washington from the western theater, was assigned command of the army. In addition to the above three corps, two divisions of Ambrose E. Burnside's Ninth Corps; John F. Reynolds' division of Pennsylvania Reserves; Samuel P. Heintzelman's Third Corps, Army of the Potomac; Fitz John Porter's Fifth Corps, Army of the Potomac; and two brigades joined the army before the Second Battle of Bull Run, August 30, 1862. After that date, five more divisions arrived, but they were too late to influence the outcome of Pope's campaign in northern Virginia.

The Army of Virginia had a short life, and it was engaged in only one campaign, which ended disastrously at the Second Battle of Bull Run. Troops of the army were engaged at Cedar Mountain August 9, 1862; Bull Run Bridge August 27, 1862; Thoroughfare Gap August 28, 1862; Gainesville August 28, 1862; Groveton August 29, 1862; Bull Run August 30, 1862; and Chantilly September 1, 1862. The army then retreated within the Defenses of Washington, and Pope was relieved from command September 5, 1862. The army was officially discontinued September 12, 1862, when it was merged into the Army of the Potomac, then at Frederick, Maryland. First Corps, Army of Virginia became Eleventh Corps, Army of the Potomac; Second Corps, Army of Virginia became Twelfth Corps, Army of the Potomac; and Third Corps, Army of Virginia became First Corps, Army of the Potomac.

For details of the organization and operations of the Army of Virginia, see Pope's Northern Virginia Campaign.

ARMY OF WEST VIRGINIA

August 6, 1864, Philip H. Sheridan arrived at

Harper's Ferry from the Army of the Potomac, and was assigned command of the field force assembled there. The troops of this force had been commanded by David Hunter during Jubal A. Early's advance into the lower Shenandoah Valley in late July 1864, and they consisted of Horatio G. Wright's Sixth Corps, one division of William H. Emory's Detachment Nineteenth Corps, and two infantry divisions under George Crook from the Department of West Virginia (Army of the Kanawha). For additional information, see Early's Washington Raid (and Operations in the Shenandoah Valley, Maryland, and Pennsylvania). Sheridan's army was later known as the Army of the Shenandoah, but was not officially so designated until November 17, 1864.

By an order dated August 8, 1864, the troops under Crook's command, then serving in Sheridan's army, were designated as the Army of West Virginia. (*note*. The original order designated Crook's command as the Army of Western Virginia.) At the beginning of the Shenandoah Valley Campaign, the Army of West Virginia was organized as follows:

ARMY OF WEST VIRGINIA
George Crook

First Infantry Division, Joseph Thoburn
  First Brigade, George D. Wells
  Second Brigade, Robert S. Northcott
  Third Brigade, Thomas M. Harris
Second Infantry Division, Isaac H. Duval
  First Brigade, Rutherford B. Hayes
  Second Brigade, Daniel H. Johnson
Artillery Brigade, Henry A. Du Pont
  Battery L, 1st Ohio Light Artillery, Frank C. Gibbs
  Battery D, 1st Pennsylvania Light Artillery, William Munk
  Battery B, 5th United States Artillery, Henry A. Du Pont

Crook's command served in the Army of the Shenandoah during Sheridan's Shenandoah Valley Campaign August 7, 1864 to November 28, 1864, and was engaged at the Battle of Opequon Creek September 19, 1864, at Fisher's Hill September 22, 1864, and at Cedar Creek October 19, 1864.

It should be noted that during the Valley Campaign the Army of West Virginia was commonly called Eighth Corps. Many of the troops of this army had belonged to Eighth Corps before the Department of West Virginia was organized, and possibly because the name Eighth Corps was shorter and easier to use than the Army of West Virginia, it was preferred by some. This usage was incorrect, however, because Eighth Corps was officially defined as the troops belonging to the Middle Department.

The Army of West Virginia remained under Sheridan's control, first in camp at Cedar Creek until November 9, 1864, and then near Kernstown until the end of December 1864. It was discontinued December 19, 1864, and the First Infantry Division, then under Thomas M. Harris, was sent to the Army of the James, where it was assigned to Twenty-Fourth Corps as Harris' Independent Division. For further information, see Army of the James. December 30, 1864, Duval's Second Infantry Division (redesignated as First Infantry Division after Harris' departure), then reduced to only one brigade, was moved to Cumberland, Maryland, where it remained as First Infantry Division, Department of West Virginia.

For details of the organization and operations of the Army of West Virginia, see Shenandoah Valley Campaign (Sheridan); and also Department of West Virginia, Troops in the Department of West Virginia, August 1864 to September 1864.

ARMY CORPS

⭐ ⭐ ⭐ ⭐

FIRST CORPS, ARMY OF THE POTOMAC
MARCH 13, 1862–APRIL 4, 1862

First Corps was created by a presidential order of March 8, 1862, which also created Second Corps, Third Corps, Fourth Corps, and Fifth Corps, Army of the Potomac. The corps was organized March 13, 1862, and Irvin McDowell assumed command that day (assigned March 8, 1862). It was organized as follows:

FIRST CORPS, Irvin McDowell

First Division, William B. Franklin
  First Brigade, Philip Kearny
  Second Brigade, Henry W. Slocum
  Third Brigade, John Newton
  Artillery
    Battery D, 2nd United States Artillery, Edward R. Platt
    Battery A, Massachusetts Light Artillery, Josiah Porter
    Battery A, New Jersey Light Artillery, William Hexamer
    Battery F, 1st New York Light Artillery, William R. Wilson

Second Division, George A. McCall
  First Brigade, John F. Reynolds
  Second Brigade, George G. Meade
  Third Brigade, Edward O. C. Ord
  Artillery
    Battery C, 5th United States Artillery, Truman Seymour
    Battery A, 1st Pennsylvania Light Artillery, Hezekiah Easton

    Battery B, 1st Pennsylvania Light Artillery, James H. Cooper
    Battery G, 1st Pennsylvania Light Artillery, Mark Kerns

Third Division, Rufus King
  First Brigade, Christopher C. Augur
  Second Brigade, James S. Wadsworth
  Third Brigade, Lysander Cutler
  Artillery
    Battery B, 4th United States Artillery, John Gibbon
    Battery D, 1st Rhode Island Light Artillery, J. Albert Monroe
    Battery A, Hew Hampshire Light Artillery, George A. Gerrish
    Battery B, Pennsylvania Light Artillery, George W. Durrells

Note 1. Third Division was formerly McDowell's Division, Army of the Potomac. When McDowell was assigned command of First Corps, King assumed command of the division, and Cutler took charge of King's Third Brigade.
Note 2. Wadsworth was assigned command of the District of Washington March 17, 1862, and Marsena R. Patrick succeeded him in command of Second Brigade.

For additional information, see Army of the Potomac, Period of Organization.

When George B. McClellan moved the Army of the Potomac to the Peninsula in late March and early April 1862, President Lincoln decided that the force left to protect the capital was not adequate, and accordingly First Corps was detached and ordered to remain in front of Washington near Alexandria, Virginia.

First Corps was discontinued April 4, 1862, and was merged into the newly created Department of the Rappahannock. McDowell, as commander of new department, moved the divisions of the former First Corps to Fredericksburg, Virginia. For further information, see Department of the Rappahannock.

FIRST CORPS, ARMY OF THE POTOMAC SEPTEMBER 12, 1862–MARCH 23, 1864

Reorganization—The Maryland Campaign, September 12, 1862–September 20, 1862. The Department of the Rappahannock was discontinued June 26, 1862, and the troops under McDowell, except those in the city of Washington and its fortifications, were reorganized as Third Corps of John Pope's Army of Virginia. McDowell's Third Corps took part in Pope's Virginia Campaign, which ended with the Second Battle of Bull Run (or Second Manassas) and Chantilly August 30, 1862–September 1, 1862. The Army of the Potomac, which had returned from the Peninsula and had joined the Army of Virginia, retreated with the latter into the Defenses of Washington, and there both were reformed under George B. McClellan. For details, see Pope's Northern Virginia Campaign.

At the beginning of the Maryland Campaign, when McClellan reorganized the Army of the Potomac, Third Corps, Army of Virginia and Ninth Corps, Army of the Potomac were assigned to the Right Wing of the army, which was commanded by Ambrose E. Burnside. September 12, 1862, when the Right Wing was near Frederick, Maryland as it was moving against Robert E. Lee's invading army, the designation of Third Corps, Army of Virginia was changed to First Corps, Army of the Potomac. Joseph Hooker, who had relieved McDowell in command of Third Corps, Army of Virginia September 7, 1862, was assigned command of the reorganized First Corps. First Corps then marched with Ninth Corps to South Mountain and was engaged there on the north side of the National Road September 14, 1862. The Right Wing organization was discontinued after the Battle of South Mountain, and First Corps marched to Antietam Creek, where it was placed on the extreme right of the Union line

along the Sharpsburg-Hagerstown Road. From this position, it advanced and opened the Battle of Antietam on the morning of September 17, 1862. Hooker was wounded during the fighting, and George G. Meade assumed command of First Corps. Ninth Corps, which earlier had been associated with First Corps, was sent to the extreme left of the Union line, where it was engaged that afternoon. For details, see Maryland Campaign (South Mountain and Antietam).

The organization of First Corps during the period September 12–17, 1862 was as follows:

FIRST CORPS, Joseph Hooker, to September 17, 1862, wounded
George G. Meade

First Division, Rufus King, to September 14, 1862, relieved
John P. Hatch, September 14, 1862, wounded
Abner Doubleday
First Brigade, John P. Hatch, to September 14, 1862
  Walter Phelps, Jr.
Second Brigade, Abner Doubleday, to September 14, 1862
  William W. Wainwright, to September 17, 1862, wounded
  J. William Hofmann
Third Brigade, Marsena R. Patrick
Fourth Brigade, John Gibbon
Artillery, J. Albert Monroe
  1st Battery, New Hampshire Light Artillery, Frederick M. Edgell
  Battery D, 1st Rhode Island Light Artillery, J. Albert Monroe
  Battery C, 1st New York Light Artillery, John A. Reynolds
  Battery B, 1st United States Artillery, Joseph M. Campbell
  Joseph Stewart

Second Division, James B. Ricketts
First Brigade, Abram Duryee (also spelled Duryea)
Second Brigade, William A. Christian
  Peter Lyle
Third Brigade, George L. Hartsuff, to September 17, 1862, wounded
  Richard Coulter
Artillery
  Battery F, 1st Pennsylvania Light Artillery, Ezra M. Matthews
  Battery C, Pennsylvania Light Artillery, James Thompson

Third Division, George G. Meade, to September 17, 1862
  Truman Seymour
  First Brigade, Truman Seymour, to September 17, 1862
    R. Biddle Roberts
  Second Brigade, Albert L. Magilton
  Third Brigade, Thomas F. Gallagher, to September 14,
    1862, wounded
    Robert Anderson
  Artillery
    Battery A, 1st Pennsylvania Light Artillery, John G.
      Simpson
    Battery B, 1st Pennsylvania Light Artillery, James
      H. Cooper
    Battery G, 1st Pennsylvania Light Artillery, Frank
      P. Amsden
    Battery C, 5th United States Artillery, Dunbar R.
      Ransom

Note. Amsden's battery was on detached service at Washington after September 6, 1862.

Antietam to Warrenton, Virginia, September 19, 1862–November 7, 1862. After the Battle of Antietam, First Corps remained near Sharpsburg, Maryland until October 26, 1862, when the Army of the Potomac began crossing the Potomac River at the beginning of its long-delayed advance into Virginia. That day First Corps, then commanded by John F. Reynolds, was ordered from its camps near Sharpsburg to Berlin (present-day Brunswick), Maryland, where it arrived October 28, 1862. Two days later it crossed the Potomac and advanced through Middleburg, Virginia and the Piedmont-Salem area, and arrived at Warrenton November 6, 1862. For additional information, see Army of the Potomac, Antietam to Warrenton, Virginia.

There were several command changes in the corps during its stay along the Potomac and during its advance to Warrenton. September 29, 1862, Reynolds returned to the army from detached duty in Pennsylvania and relieved Meade in command of First Corps. Meade then resumed command of Third Division, First Corps, relieving Truman Seymour. Seymour then returned to the command of First Brigade, Third Division, relieving R. Biddle Roberts. October 3, 1862, Abram Duryee departed on leave and Thomas F. McCoy assumed command of First Brigade, Second Division. George L. Hartsuff was wounded at Antietam, and Richard Coulter assumed command of his Third Brigade, Second Division. October 4, 1862 Nelson Taylor relieved Coulter in command of the brigade. Oc-

tober 6, 1862, Marsena R. Patrick, commanding Third Brigade, First Division, was assigned as provost marshal general of the Army of the Potomac, and William F. Rogers was assigned as temporary commander of Patrick's brigade. Gabriel R. Paul relieved Rogers October 14, 1862. November 5, 1862, James B. Ricketts was relieved from duty with the Army of the Potomac, and John Gibbon was assigned command of Second Division, First Corps. Lysander Cutler assumed command of Gibbon's Fourth Brigade, First Division. November 7, 1862, Christopher C. Augur was assigned command of First Division, but three days later he was ordered to report to Nathaniel P. Banks, commander of the Defenses of Washington. November 9, 1862, William P. Wainwright, who was wounded at South Mountain, returned to the army and resumed command of Second Brigade, First Division, relieving J. William Hofmann.

Fredericksburg Campaign, November 7, 1862–December 15, 1862. On the night of November 7, 1862, Ambrose E. Burnside relieved McClellan in command of the Army of the Potomac, and he then submitted to Henry W. Halleck a plan for moving the army toward Richmond by way of Fredericksburg. This plan was approved November 14, 1862, and that day Burnside announced the reorganization of the army into three grand divisions and a reserve. First Corps and Sixth Corps were assigned to the Left Grand Division, which was placed under the command of William B. Franklin. A short time later, the army advanced toward Fredericksburg. First Corps marched to Stafford Court House, about six miles northeast of Fredericksburg, and arrived there November 18, 1862.

December 12, 1862, First Corps crossed the Rappahannock with the Left Grand Division and took position below Fredericksburg on the extreme left of the Union line. Meade's Third Division and Gibbon's Second Division were heavily engaged at the Battle of Fredericksburg December 13, 1862 and suffered heavy losses. Doubleday's First Division was in position on Meade's left flank and was under fire but was not seriously engaged. First Corps recrossed the Rappahannock on the night of December 15, 1862, and returned to its former camps. For details of the battle, see Fredericksburg, Virginia Campaign.

The organization of First Corps at Fredericksburg was as follows:

FIRST CORPS, John F. Reynolds

First Division, Abner Doubleday
First Brigade, Walter Phelps, Jr.
Second Brigade, James Gavin
Third Brigade, William F. Rogers
Fourth Brigade, Solomon Meredith, to afternoon December 13, 1862, relieved
Lysander Cutler
Artillery, George A. Gerrish, wounded
John A. Reynolds
1st Battery, New Hampshire Light Artillery, Frederick M. Edgell
Battery L, 1st New York Light Artillery, John A. Reynolds
Battery B, 4th United States Artillery, James Stewart

Note 1. Charles S. Wainwright was the chief of the corps artillery.
Note 2. Meredith was assigned command of Fourth Brigade November 25, 1862.

Second Division, John Gibbon, to December 13, 1862, wounded
Nelson Taylor
First Brigade, Adrian R. Root
Second Brigade, Peter Lyle
Third Brigade, Nelson Taylor, to December 13, 1862
Samuel H. Leonard
Artillery, George F. Leppien
2nd Battery (B), Maine Light Artillery, James A. Hall
5th Battery (E), Maine Light Artillery, George F. Leppien
Battery C, Pennsylvania Light Artillery, James Thompson
Battery F, 1st Pennsylvania Light Artillery, R. Bruce Ricketts

Third Division, George G. Meade
First Brigade, William Sinclair, to December 13, 1862, wounded
William McCandless
Second Brigade, Albert L. Magilton
Third Brigade, C. Feger Jackson, to December 13, 1862, killed
Joseph W. Fisher
Robert Anderson
Artillery
Battery A, 1st Pennsylvania Light Artillery, John G. Simpson
Battery B, 1st Pennsylvania Light Artillery, James H. Cooper

Battery G, 1st Pennsylvania Light Artillery, Frank P. Amsden
Battery C, 5th United States Artillery, Dunbar R. Ransom

Winter of 1862–1863. Following the Battle of Fredericksburg, First Corps went into winter quarters near Belle Plain. On January 20, 1863, however, it left its camps and moved with the army up the Rappahannock toward Banks' Ford at the beginning of Burnside's ill-fated "Mud March." The campaign was abandoned a few days later when constant rains made the roads impassable. First Corps then returned to its quarters and was relatively quiet during the remainder of the winter. For additional information, see Army of the Potomac, Winter of 1862–1863.

There were some organizational changes in the corps during the winter. In December 1862, following the Battle of Fredericksburg, Henry M. Bossert brought a provisional brigade to Falmouth, Virginia from the Defenses of Washington. It was assigned to Marsena R. Patrick's Provost Guard, Army of the Potomac. In January 1863, the regiments of Gabriel R. Paul's Third Brigade, First Division were transferred to the Provost Guard as a provisional brigade under William F. Rogers, the senior colonel, and Paul's Third Brigade was reorganized from Bossert's Provisional Brigade.

The division of Pennsylvania Reserves (Third Division, First Corps) had been seriously depleted by hard fighting in the earlier battles of the war, and February 5, 1863, it was ordered to Washington to rest and recruit. Led by Horatio G. Sickel, the division was transferred to the Department of Washington during the period February 5–12, 1863. A new Third Division, First Corps, consisting of two brigades, was organized February 15, 1863 from Pennsylvania regiments from the Department of Washington, and Abner Doubleday was assigned command. The First Brigade was at first commanded by the senior colonel, but March 27, 1863, Thomas A. Rowley was assigned command. The Second Brigade was commanded by Roy Stone. The Pennsylvania Reserves did not rejoin the Army of the Potomac; and, consequently, Third Brigade, Third Division was discontinued. For additional information, see Pennsylvania Reserves, and also Department of Washington, February 2, 1863–March 16, 1869.

Joseph Hooker assumed command of the Army of the Potomac January 26, 1863, and February 5, 1863, he abolished the grand divisions of the army. Thereafter, the commanders of the various corps of the army reported directly to Headquarters Army of the Potomac.

There were some command changes in the corps during the winter. George G. Meade was assigned command of Fifth Corps December 23, 1862 (assumed command December 26, 1862), and Horatio G. Sickel, as the senior officer of the division present, assumed command of Meade's Third Division. December 27, 1862, James S. Wadsworth relieved Doubleday in command of First Division. Doubleday resumed command of Second Brigade, First Division, relieving George H. Biddle. Wadsworth commanded First Corps temporarily January 2–4, 1863, during the absence of Reynolds. John C. Robinson was assigned command of Second Division December 29, 1862, relieving Nelson Taylor, who had assumed temporary command after Gibbon was wounded December 13, 1862.

Chancellorsville Campaign, April 27, 1863–May 6, 1863. Reynolds' First Corps played a relatively minor role in the Battle of Chancellorsville. On April 28, 1863, it was sent with Third Corps and Sixth Corps to the Rappahannock River below Fredericksburg to threaten a Federal attack from that quarter. First Corps moved that day to the mouth of White Oak Creek, near Pollack's Mill, and the following morning Wadsworth's First Division crossed the river and established a bridgehead. The other two divisions of the corps remained on the north bank. There was no change of position until early on May 2, 1863, when the corps was ordered to report to Hooker at Chancellorsville. First Corps marched immediately to the Rappahannock and crossed at United States Ford late that evening and during the night. By early morning May 3, 1863, it occupied a defensive position behind Hunting Creek, between the Ely's Ford Road and the Rapidan River, on the extreme right of the Union line. It remained there without being seriously engaged until the army withdrew across the Rappahannock during the night of May 5–6, 1863. It then returned to its old camps. For additional information, see Chancellorsville, Virginia Campaign.

The organization of First Corps during the Chancellorsville Campaign was as follows:

FIRST CORPS, John F. Reynolds

First Division, James S. Wadsworth
First Brigade, Walter Phelps, Jr.
Second Brigade, Lysander Cutler
Third Brigade, Gabriel R. Paul
Fourth Brigade, Solomon Meredith
Artillery, John A. Reynolds
  1st Battery, New Hampshire Light Artillery, Frederick M. Edgell
  Battery L, 1st New York Light Artillery, John A. Reynolds
  Battery B, 4th United States Artillery, James Stewart

Second Division, John C. Robinson
First Brigade, Adrian R. Root
Second Brigade, Henry Baxter
Third Brigade, Samuel H. Leonard
Artillery, Dunbar R. Ransom
  2nd Battery (B), Maine Light Artillery, James A. Hall
  5th Battery (E), Maine Light Artillery, George F. Leppien
    Edmund Kirby
    Greenleaf T. Stevens
  Battery C, Pennsylvania Light Artillery, James Thompson
  Battery C, 5th United States Light Artillery, Dunbar R. Ransom

Third Division, Abner Doubleday
First Brigade, Thomas A. Rowley
Second Brigade, Roy Stone
Artillery, Ezra W. Matthews
  Battery B, 1st Pennsylvania Light Artillery, James H. Cooper
  Battery F, 1st Pennsylvania Light Artillery, R. Bruce Ricketts
  Battery G, 1st Pennsylvania Light Artillery, Frank P. Amsden

Reorganization of First Corps, May–June 1863. After the Battle of Chancellorsville, First Corps remained more or less quietly in its camps near White Oak Church until June 12, 1863, when the army began its march northward at the beginning of the Gettysburg Campaign. During this period there were several changes in the organization and command of the corps. During May and June of 1863, fourteen nine-month and two-year regiments were sent home for muster out, and because of this, a reorganization of the corps became necessary.

Second Division was reorganized May 20, 1863, when two regiments of Second Brigade departed for home. One regiment of Third Brigade was transferred to First Brigade, and the remaining four regiments of Third Brigade were transferred to Second Brigade. By this arrangement, Third Brigade was discontinued. Second Division was then organized as follows:

Second Division, John C. Robinson
    First Brigade, Thomas F. McCoy, to May 21, 1863
        Samuel H. Leonard
    Second Brigade, Henry Baxter

Note. Leonard commanded Third Brigade until it was discontinued May 20, 1863, and was then assigned command of First Brigade.

First Division was reorganized June 16, 1863. First Brigade was broken up when three New York regiments went home for muster out, and the remaining regiment was assigned to Second Brigade, First Division. A new First Brigade was then reorganized from the regiments of Fourth Brigade, which was discontinued. Third Brigade was also discontinued when four New Jersey regiments and one Pennsylvania regiment departed for muster out. First Division was then organized as follows:

First Division, James S. Wadsworth
    First Brigade, Edward B. Fowler, to June 16, 1863
        Solomon Meredith
    Second Brigade, Lysander Cutler

Note 1. First Brigade was discontinued June 16, 1863, and was then reorganized from Meredith's Fourth Brigade, which was thus discontinued.
Note 2. Third Brigade was discontinued June 16, 1863, and its commander, Gabriel R. Paul, was assigned to First Brigade, Second Division.

Third Division remained unchanged and was organized as follows:

Third Division, Abner Doubleday
    First Brigade, Thomas A. Rowley
    Second Brigade, Roy Stone

At this time, there were only two brigades in each of the three divisions of First Corps. June 25, 1863, George J. Stannard's Second Brigade (the Vermont Brigade) of John J. Abercrombie's Division of the Department of Washington was ordered to join the Army of the Potomac. This brigade arrived on the field of Gettysburg on the evening of July 1, 1863, and the next morning was assigned to First Corps as Third Brigade, Third Division.

Gettysburg Campaign, May 1863–July 1863. June 3, 1863, Robert E. Lee began moving the Army of Northern Virginia northward from Fredericksburg, Virginia at the beginning of his planned invasion of Maryland and Pennsylvania. June 9, 1863, Alfred Pleasonton's cavalry was engaged with enemy cavalry under James E. B. (Jeb) Stuart at Brandy Station (Fleetwood), and two days later Joseph Hooker, commanding the Army of the Potomac, received information that large forces of enemy infantry had been at Culpeper Court House and Brandy Station the day before. June 12, 1863, Hooker moved Reynolds' First Corps from near White Oak Church to Deep Run, south of Somerville, to act as a reserve for Third Corps and Fifth Corps, which were in position along the Rappahannock River. That same day, Reynolds was assigned command of the Right Wing of the army, which consisted of First Corps, Third Corps, Fifth Corps, Eleventh Corps, and the Cavalry Corps. Doubleday assumed temporary command of First Corps.

June 13, 1863, Hooker learned that enemy forces were in the Shenandoah Valley near Winchester, and finally he issued orders for the withdrawal of the army to positions along the Orange and Alexandria Railroad in front of Washington. That same day, First Corps moved to Morrisville and camped that night at Liberty. It then continued on toward the railroad with Reynolds' Right Wing and arrived at Manassas Junction June 14, 1863. Two days later, Hooker resumed direct control of the separate corps of the army, and Reynolds resumed command of First Corps.

A Confederate force under Richard S. Ewell defeated Robert H. Milroy's command at Winchester and Stephenson's Depot June 13–15, 1863, and beginning June 17, 1863, Hooker advanced the army from its positions along the railroad to the west and north to form a line extending from Thoroughfare Gap to Leesburg, Virginia. First Corps marched to Herndon Station and Guilford Station on the Alexandria, Loudoun, and Hampshire Railroad, west of Dranesville, Virginia.

June 25, 1863, this time in preparation for the

advance of the army into Maryland, Reynolds was again assigned command of the Right Wing of the army, which this time consisted of First Corps, Third Corps, and Eleventh Corps. Doubleday assumed temporary command of First Corps.

That same day, June 25, 1863, First Corps crossed the Potomac into Maryland at Edwards Ferry. It then marched northward on the left of the army through Barnesville, Jefferson, and Middletown, and arrived at Frederick three days later. That day, June 28, 1863, George G. Meade relieved Hooker in command of the Army of the Potomac, and he then abolished the Right Wing organization of the army. Reynolds resumed command of the First Corps, and the next day marched northward with Eleventh Corps on the left of the army to Emmitsburg, Maryland. First Corps continued on to Marsh Creek the next day, and there, on June 30, 1863, Reynolds was once more assigned command of a wing of the army. This time his command was designated the Left Wing, and it consisted of First Corps, Third Corps, and Eleventh Corps. The next day, July 1, 1863, First Corps, then under the command of Doubleday, marched to the field of Gettysburg. For additional information on the advance of the army to Gettysburg, see Gettysburg Campaign, Part I, From the Rappahannock to Gettysburg.

First Corps was the first infantry corps to arrive at Gettysburg. James S. Wadsworth's First Division came up on the morning of July 1, 1863, and it immediately went into action with John Buford's cavalry on McPherson's Ridge west of the town. The other two divisions soon followed, and the entire corps was engaged on McPherson's Ridge and Seminary Ridge that afternoon. First Corps fought valiantly and sustained severe losses, but it was finally forced back that evening to Cemetery Hill. George J. Stannard with his Second Brigade of John J. Abercrombie's Division, Department of Washington marched from the Occoquan River June 25, 1863 and arrived on the battlefield on the evening of July 1, 1863, too late to take part in the fighting that day. Stannard reported to Doubleday the next morning, and his brigade was assigned to Third Division as Third Brigade.

During the remainder of the battle, First Corps was, for all practical purposes, temporarily broken up, and it did not again fight as a unit at Gettysburg. Wadsworth's division was placed on the north side of Culp's Hill, where it aided in repulsing Ewell's attack on the evening of July 2, 1863, and again on the morning of July 3, 1863. John C. Robinson's Second Division and Abner Doubleday's Third Division were first placed in reserve on Cemetery Hill, but during the enemy attack on the line of Winfield S. Hancock's Second Corps late in the evening of July 2, 1863, both divisions were sent to support Hancock. Robinson's division soon returned to Cemetery Hill, but Doubleday's division remained in line on the left of Hancock. Stannard's Third Brigade, Third Division and a part of Rowley's First Brigade, Third Division aided Hancock in repulsing the Pickett-Pettigrew-Trimble assault July 3, 1863. For additional information, see Gettysburg Campaign, Part II, Battle of Gettysburg.

The organization of First Corps at the Battle of Gettysburg July 1–3, 1863 was as follows:

FIRST CORPS, Abner Doubleday, to July 2, 1863
    John Newton

First Division, James S. Wadsworth
    First Brigade, Solomon Meredith, to July 1, 1863, disabled
    William W. Robinson
    Second Brigade, Lysander Cutler

Note 1. John F. Reynolds, the permanent commander of First Corps, was killed July 1, 1863 while in command of the Left Wing of the army, and Newton was assigned command of the corps July 2, 1863.

Note 2. William W. Robinson assumed command of First Brigade during the evening of July 1, 1863 on Cemetery Hill.

Second Division, John C. Robinson
    First Brigade, Gabriel R. Paul, to July 1, 1863, wounded
        Samuel H. Leonard, July 1, 1863, wounded
        Adrian R. Root, July 1, 1863, wounded
        Richard Coulter
    Second Brigade, Henry Baxter

Note. Coulter assumed command of First Brigade on the evening of July 1, 1863. He was wounded July 3, 1863 but remained with the brigade and soon resumed command. Peter Lyle commanded the brigade temporarily during Coulter's absence.

Third Division, Thomas A. Rowley, July 1, 1863
    Abner Doubleday
    First Brigade, Chapman Biddle, July 1, 1863
        Thomas A. Rowley
    Second Brigade, Roy Stone, July 1, 1863, wounded

Langhorne Wister, July 1, 1863, wounded
Edmund L. Dana
Third Brigade, George J. Stannard, to July 1, 1863,
wounded
Francis V. Randall

Note 1. Doubleday was in command of First Corps July 1, 1863.
Note 2. Stannard's brigade was formerly Second Brigade of John J. Abercrombie's Division, Department of Washington.

Artillery Brigade, Charles S. Wainwright
2nd Battery (B), Maine Light Artillery, James A. Hall
5th Battery (E), Maine Light Artillery, Greenleaf T. Stevens
Edward N. Whittier
Battery L, First New York Light Artillery, Gilbert H. Reynolds
George Breck
Battery B, 1st Pennsylvania Light Artillery, James H. Cooper
Battery B, 4th United States Artillery, James Stewart

Note. Battery E, 1st New York Light Artillery was attached to Battery L, 1st New York Light Artillery.

The divisions of First Corps remained in their positions near Gettysburg July 4, 1863, and the men spent their time collecting and caring for the wounded. The next day, in preparation for the pursuit of Lee's army toward Virginia, Meade organized a temporary Right Wing of the army, under the command of John Sedgwick. This wing consisted of First Corps, Third Corps, and Sedgwick's own Sixth Corps. July 5, 1863, Sedgwick advanced Sixth Corps to Fairfield, Pennsylvania, and there encountered some enemy resistance. First Corps was held at Gettysburg in support, but the next day, July 6, 1863, it moved to Emmitsburg, Maryland, where it joined the other two corps of the Right Wing. Starting July 7, 1863, First Corps marched by way of Hamburg to Turner's Gap in South Mountain, where it arrived July 8, 1863. Two days later it moved on to Beaver Creek and then to Funkstown, Maryland July 12, 1863. The Army of Northern Virginia withdrew across the Potomac River during the night of July 13, 1863, and the next day First Corps moved up to Williamsport. For additional information relating to the advance of the army from Gettysburg to the Potomac River, see Gettysburg Campaign, Part III, The Pursuit of Lee, Gettysburg to Falling Waters.

Reinforcements joined First Corps during its advance to the Potomac River, and this resulted in some organizational and command changes. July 10, 1863, while the corps was at Beaver Creek, John R. Kenly arrived with a brigade formerly belonging to William H. French's Division at Harper's Ferry. Earlier, on July 8, 1863, while First Corps was at Middletown, Stannard's Third Brigade, Third Division, then commanded by Francis V. Randall, was transferred to Second Division, and Third Brigade, Third Division was thus discontinued. July 11, 1863, Kenly assumed command of Third Division. Third Brigade, Third Division was then reorganized from Kenly's brigade, which at that time was commanded by Nathan T. Dushane. Doubleday, formerly commander of Third Division, was relieved from duty with the Army of the Potomac by an order dated July 5, 1863. Third Division was then organized as follows:

Third Division, John R. Kenly
First Brigade, Chapman Biddle
Second Brigade, Edmund L. Dana
Third Brigade, Nathan T. Dushane

Note. Biddle relieved Rowley in command of First Brigade July 5, 1863.

While First Corps was at Funkstown, it was joined July 12–13, 1863, by Henry S. Briggs with a brigade from Harper's Ferry. Three of the four regiments of the brigade formerly belonged to First Division, Department of North Carolina. They were brought to Baltimore earlier in the month by Henry M. Naglee, and then were taken to Harper's Ferry by Briggs. Briggs' Brigade was assigned to Second Division, First Corps, which was then organized as follows:

Second Division, John C. Robinson
First Brigade, Richard Coulter, to July 5, 1863
Peter Lyle
Second Brigade, Henry Baxter
Stannard's Brigade, Francis V. Randall
Briggs' Brigade, Henry S. Briggs

Note 1. Stannard's Brigade consisted of nine-month regiments, and these were sent home for muster out July 15–18, 1863. The brigade was discontinued.
Note 2. Briggs' Brigade also consisted of nine-month regiments, and these returned home for muster out July 15–26, 1863. The brigade was discontinued, and Briggs

was assigned command of First Division, First Corps. He did not assume command until August 5, 1863.

July 15, 1863, the Army of the Potomac marched toward the Potomac River near Harper's Ferry in preparation for crossing into Virginia. First Corps marched by way of Rohrersville and arrived at Berlin (present-day Brunswick), Maryland the next day.

July 17, 1863, Wadsworth left the army on a leave of absence and Lysander Cutler assumed command of First Division. From October 9, 1863 to November 18, 1863, Wadsworth was on duty in the Mississippi Valley inspecting colored troops. Then from January 9, 1864 to February 23, 1864, he served on a court of inquiry on the conduct of Generals Alexander McD. McCook, Thomas L. Crittenden, and James S. Negley at the Battle of Chickamauga.

July 18, 1863, First Corps crossed the Potomac at Berlin and moved south, on the left of the army, along the west side of the Bull Run Mountains. It marched through Waterford, Hamilton, Middletown, and White Plains and arrived at Warrenton July 23, 1863. Two days later it moved to Warrenton Junction, and from there Robinson's Second Division proceeded on to Bealeton. July 30, 1863, Kenly's Third Division was sent to Rappahannock Station. The next day, First Corps was ordered to hold and picket the Rappahannock from the forks of the river near Beverly Ford to Wheatly's Ford, which was about one mile north of Kelly's Ford. One division was placed near Beverly Ford, one division near Rappahannock Station, and one division at Bealeton Station. The latter was to take charge of the Orange and Alexandria Railroad from Warrenton Junction to the river. Pickets of the corps were to connect with those of Third Corps on the right and those of Twelfth Corps on the left.

The Gettysburg Campaign is generally regarded as ending August 1, 1863.

Advance to the Rapidan River, and the Bristoe, Virginia Campaign, August 1, 1863–October 22, 1863. First Corps remained along the Rappahannock until September 1863. There were some command changes in the corps during this time. James C. Rice relieved Briggs in command of First Division August 23, 1863; and September 21, 1863, Cutler resumed command of the division, relieving Rice. Rice then assumed command of Second Brigade, First Division. Langhorne Wister, who was wounded at Gettysburg, returned to the army, and

August 22, 1863 relieved Dana, who was in command of Second Brigade, Third Division.

September 16, 1863, the the army crossed the Rappahannock River and advanced to Culpeper Court House, where it formed on a line facing the Rapidan River. First Corps took position on the left of the line between Stevensburg and Culpeper Court House. It remained there until September 24, 1863, and was then ordered to relieve Twelfth Corps, which was picketing the Rapidan between Somerville and Morton's Ford. For additional information, see Army of the Potomac, Gettysburg Campaign.

October 9, 1863, Meade became aware of a Confederate movement toward his right, but he was uncertain whether this was the beginning of a withdrawal or of a flanking movement. That evening he ordered Buford's cavalry division, Newton's First Corps, George Sykes' Fifth Corps, and John Sedgwick's Sixth Corps, in that order, to cross the Rapidan, and if they found the enemy to be withdrawing, they were to follow. Only Buford's cavalry had crossed the next day when Meade learned definitely that Lee was moving in heavy force against his right flank. He then called off the crossing of the three infantry corps and that evening issued orders for the withdrawal of the army to the line of the Rappahannock.

Newton's First Corps withdrew after dark to Stevensburg, and the next day marched to Kelly's Ford. It then crossed to the north bank of the river, remained there until October 12, 1863, and then marched to Warrenton Junction. Meantime, Lee had advanced on Meade's extreme right flank and threatened to interpose his army between the Army of the Potomac and Washington. Meade then ordered the army to retire to Centerville. October 13, 1863, First Corps marched with Fifth Corps and Sixth Corps along the Orange and Alexandria Railroad to Bristoe Station, and the next day it moved on to Centerville. First Corps remained at Centerville until October 19, 1863, and then, after Lee's withdrawal to the Rappahannock, advanced with the army to Hay Market. The next day it marched through Thoroughfare Gap to Georgetown and October 22, 1863 moved to Bristoe Station on the railroad. For additional information, see Bristoe, Virginia Campaign.

Rappahannock Station and Kelly's Ford, November 7, 1863. First Corps remained at Bristoe

Station until October 26, 1863 and then moved to Catlett's Station. From there, on October 29, 1863, one brigade was sent to Kettle Run Bridge to hold the railroad as far as Catlett's Station.

November 5, 1863, in preparation for an advance of the army against enemy positions at Kelly's Ford and Rappahannock Station, Kenly's Third Division, First Corps was left to guard the railroad from Manassas to Warrenton Junction, and Cutler's First Division and Robinson's Second Division were concentrated at Catlett's Station. Two days later, First Corps, Second Corps, and Third Corps were assigned to a temporary Left Wing of the army, commanded by William H. French. French was under orders to march to Kelly's Ford and force a passage of the Rappahannock River at that point. Third Corps marched first, and it was followed by Second Corps. Newton with his First Division and Second Division marched by way of Elk Run to Morrisville, where he remained in readiness to move forward if needed. Third Corps cleared the ford without difficulty, however, and Newton remained at Morrisville during the action. For additional information, see Engagements at Rappahannock Station and Kelly's Ford, Virginia.

November 9, 1863, the temporary wing organization of the army was discontinued, and that day First Corps was ordered back to the railroad. Cutler's division was placed at Rappahannock Station, with a brigade at Beverly Ford. The three brigades of Robinson's division were stationed at Bealeton, Liberty, and near the railroad crossing of Licking Run. Kenly's division continued to guard the railroad from Manassas to Warrenton Junction. One of Kenly's brigades was at Bristoe Station, one at Warrenton Junction, and one was guarding the bridges over Cedar Run and Kettle Run.

Mine Run Campaign, November 26, 1863–December 2, 1863. In November 1863, following the Bristoe, Virginia Campaign, Meade decided on a movement by which he hoped to maneuver Lee out of his position behind the Rapidan River. November 22, 1863, in preparation for this movement, Cutler's and Robinson's divisions and the artillery were concentrated at Rappahannock Station. Kenly's division was left to guard the railroad with one brigade and a battery at Rappahannock Station and infantry detachments at Bealeton, Warrenton Junction, Catlett's Station or Cedar Run

Bridge, Nokesville, Kettle Run Bridge, Bristoe Station, and Manassas Junction.

The army advanced toward the Rapidan River November 26, 1863. Newton marched with First Division of First Corps, then commanded by Solomon Meredith, and Robinson's Second Division to Paoli Mills on Mountain Run, and from there he followed Fifth Corps by way of Richardsville to Culpeper Ford (Culpeper Mine Ford) on the Rapidan River. Newton then crossed the river and advanced with the army to the vicinity of Locust Grove (Robertson's or Robinson's Tavern) in the Wilderness. First Corps arrived there during the evening of November 27, 1863, and then advanced to Mine Run, a tributary of the Rapidan. It remained there in front of the enemy works, on the center of Meade's line, until November 30, 1863. Meade then decided that an attack on the enemy entrenchments was impracticable and ordered the army to return to its camps. That evening Newton retired with his two divisions to Germanna Ford. In this movement he covered the withdrawal of Fifth Corps and Sixth Corps, which crossed the river on the night of December 1, 1863. The next day Newton left a brigade at Germanna Ford and one at Mitchell's Ford, and with the rest of his command withdrew to Stevensburg. The brigade left at Germanna Ford soon rejoined the corps. Newton then moved to Paoli Mills, where he arrived about noon December 3, 1863. From there he sent a brigade to Kelly's Ford. December 2, 1863, George Sykes, commanding Fifth Corps, was ordered to relieve Kenly's division on the railroad, and when this change was completed, Kenly rejoined the corps at Paoli Mills. For additional information, see Mine Run Campaign, Virginia.

The organization of First Corps during the Mine Run Campaign was as follows:

FIRST CORPS, John Newton

First Division, Lysander Cutler
    First Brigade, William W. Robinson
    Second Brigade, James C. Rice

Second Division, John C. Robinson
    First Brigade, Samuel H. Leonard
    Second Brigade, Henry Baxter

Third Division, John R. Kenly
    First Brigade, Chapman Biddle

Second Brigade, Langhorne Wister
Third Brigade, Nathan T. Dushane

Artillery, Charles S. Wainwright
    5th Battery (E), Maine Light Artillery, Greenleaf T. Stevens
    Battery A, Maryland Light Artillery, James H. Rigby
    Battery H, 1st New York Light Artillery, Charles E. Mink
    Batteries E and L, 1st New York Light Artillery, Gilbert H. Reynolds
    Battery B, 1st Pennsylvania Light Artillery, James H. Cooper
    Battery B, 4th United States Artillery, James Stewart

Winter of 1863–1864. December 22, 1863, Newton was ordered to move First Corps to Culpeper Court House, and to post one division south of the town to support the cavalry that was picketing the Rapidan from Raccoon Ford toward the right. The other two divisions were to maintain a special guard around the court house, and they were, in turn, to relieve the division supporting the cavalry. Henry Baxter's Second Division was assigned as the first to support the cavalry; and on December 24, 1863, it moved by way of Stevensburg to South Pony Mountain. One brigade moved forward to Mitchell's Station to connect with the cavalry pickets to the right and the left, and the other brigade remained about one and a half miles north of the station. First Division and Third Division marched by way of Brandy Station to Culpeper Court House.

First Corps remained generally in the vicinity of Culpeper Court House until it was discontinued March 24, 1864. During a demonstration of the army on the Rapidan River February 6–7, 1864, First Corps advanced on the morning of February 6, 1864 to the vicinity of Raccoon Ford and bivouacked for the night. It remained there until the next evening and then returned to its camps. See Army of the Potomac, Winter of 1863–1864.

December 28, 1863, Third Division was reorganized to consist of two brigades. Second Brigade was discontinued by the transfer of its regiments to First Brigade, and Second Brigade was then reorganized by a change of designation of Third Brigade to Second Brigade. In this way, Third Brigade was discontinued. Third Division was then organized as follows:

Third Division, John R. Kenly
    First Brigade, Langhorne Wister

Second Brigade, Nathan T. Dushane

Note. At the end of December 1863, Kenly was temporarily absent, and Dushane commanded the division. Charles E. Phelps temporarily commanded Second Brigade.

Reorganization of the Army of the Potomac, March 1864. By General Order No. 115, Adjutant General's Office, dated March 23, 1864, the Army of the Potomac was reorganized into three corps. First Corps and Third Corps were discontinued, and the regiments of First Corps were assigned to Fifth Corps. John Newton, who had commanded First Corps since Gettysburg, was relieved from duty with the Army of the Potomac, and was sent to the Department of the Cumberland. There, on April 14, 1864, he was assigned command of the Second Division of Oliver O. Howard's Fourth Corps. March 24, 1864, the three divisions of First Corps, which at that time consisted of two brigades each, were consolidated to form two new divisions. These were transferred to Fifth Corps and designated as Second Division and Fourth Division. The troops of these two divisions retained their First Corps badges and their division badges in their new organizations.

The consolidation of the three divisions of First Corps was effected by discontinuing Kenly's Third Division and reassigning its two brigades. Dushane's Second Brigade was assigned as Third Brigade of Robinson's Second Division, First Corps, and Dana's First Brigade was assigned as Third Brigade of Cutler's First Division. First Corps was then organized as follows:

First Division, Lysander Cutler
    First Brigade, William W. Robinson
    Second Brigade, James C. Rice
    Third Brigade, Edmund L. Dana

Second Division, John C. Robinson
    First Brigade, Samuel H. Leonard
    Second Brigade, Henry Baxter
    Third Brigade, Andrew W. Denison

Note. Denison's Third Brigade was formerly commanded by Dushane.

When this reorganization was completed, Cutler's First Division, First Corps was redesignated as Fourth Division, Fifth Corps. James S. Wadsworth, former commander of First Division, First Corps, who had been absent from the army since July 17, 1863, returned March 25, 1864 and assumed command of the new Fourth Division, Fifth Corps. Cutler resumed command of First Brigade, Fourth Division. Rice remained in command of Second Brigade, but Roy Stone was assigned command of Dana's Third Brigade. Robinson's Second Division, First Corps was redesignated as Second Division, Fifth Corps. For further information, see Fifth Corps, Army of the Potomac, Reorganization of the Army of the Potomac, March 1864.

COMMANDERS OF FIRST CORPS, ARMY OF THE POTOMAC

Irvin McDowell	March 13, 1862 to April 4, 1862
Joseph Hooker	September 12, 1862 to September 17, 1862
George G. Meade	September 17, 1862 to September 29, 1862
John F. Reynolds	September 29, 1862 to January 2, 1863
James S. Wadsworth	January 2, 1863 to January 4, 1863
John F. Reynolds	January 4, 1863 to March 1, 1863
James S. Wadsworth	March 1, 1863 to March 25, 1863
John F. Reynolds	March 25, 1863 to June 12, 1863
Abner Doubleday	June 12, 1863 to June 16, 1863
John F. Reynolds	June 16, 1863 to June 25, 1863
Abner Doubleday	June 25, 1863 to June 29, 1863
John F. Reynolds	June 29, 1863 to June 30, 1863
Abner Doubleday	June 30, 1863 to July 2, 1863
John Newton	July 2, 1863 to July 12, 1863, sick
James S. Wadsworth	July 12, 1863 to July 14, 1863
John Newton	July 14, 1863 to March 24, 1864

FIRST CORPS, ARMY OF VIRGINIA JUNE 22, 1862–SEPTEMBER 12, 1862

June 22, 1862, the Army of Virginia was created under John Pope, and was composed of troops taken from the Mountain Department and the departments of the Rappahannock and the Shenandoah. First Corps, Army of Virginia was organized from John C. Fremont's Mountain Department. Fremont refused to serve under Pope, who was his junior in rank, and Franz Sigel assumed command June 30, 1862. First Corps was originally organized as follows:

FIRST CORPS, ARMY OF VIRGINIA, Franz Sigel

First Division, Robert C. Schenck
  First Brigade, Julius Stahel
  Second Brigade, Nathaniel C. McLean

Note 1. First Brigade was organized from the First Brigade of Louis Blenker's Division, Mountain Department.
Note 2. Second Brigade was organized from Robert C. Schenck's Brigade, Mountain Department.
Note 3. Louis Schirmer's 2nd Battery, New York Light Artillery (also commanded by Theodore Blume) was attached to First Brigade, and George B. Haskin's Battery K, 1st Ohio Light Artillery was attached to Second Brigade.

Second Division, Adolph Von Steinwehr
  First Brigade, John A. Koltes
  Second Brigade, William R. Lloyd

Note 1. First Brigade was organized from Second Brigade, Blenker's Division, Mountain Department.
Note 2. Second Brigade was organized from unattached units of the Mountain Department.

Third Division, Carl Schurz
  First Brigade, Henry Bohlen
  Second Brigade, Wladimir Krzyzanowski

Note 1. First Brigade was organized from one new regiment and regiments of the Mountain Department.
Note 2. Second Brigade was organized from Third Brigade, Blenker's Division, Mountain Department.
Note 3. Robert B. Hampton's Battery F, Pennsylvania Light Artillery was attached to First Brigade; Jacob Roemer's Battery L, Hamilton's New York Artillery was attached to Second Brigade; and Hubert Dilger's Battery I, 1st Ohio Light Artillery served with the division unattached.

Milroy's Independent Brigade, Robert H. Milroy

Note. Milroy's Independent Brigade was organized from Milroy's Brigade, Mountain Department.

Cavalry Brigade, John Beardsley

Note. The Cavalry Brigade was organized from cavalry units from the Mountain Department and the departments of the Rappahannock and the Shenandoah.

At the end of July 1862, Pope joined the army in the field, and ordered the concentration of his command near Culpeper Court House. Shortly thereafter he became engaged in a series of battles and maneuvers, commonly known as Pope's Northern Virginia Campaign. Sigel's corps was near Culpeper Court House during the Battle of Cedar Mountain August 9, 1862, and was not engaged. When the Army of Virginia retired from the Rapidan River to a position behind the Rappahannock during Robert E. Lee's advance after Cedar Mountain, Henry Bohlen's First Brigade, Third Division and Milroy's Independent Brigade were engaged on the right of Pope's line. Bohlen was killed August 22, 1862, and Alexander Schimmelfennig succeeded him in command of the brigade.

Sigel spent most of the last week in August in marching and maneuvering as Lee's army advanced, but his entire corps was engaged at the Battle of Groveton August 29, 1862, and also the next day at the Second Battle of Bull Run (Manassas). Schenck, commanding First Division, was wounded August 30, 1862, and Julius Stahel assumed command of his division. Adolphus Buschbeck assumed command of Stahel's First Brigade. John A. Koltes, commanding First Brigade, Second Division, was killed August 30, 1862, and George A. Muhleck succeeded him in command of the brigade. During the fighting August 30, 1862, Koltes' brigade was temporarily attached to Carl Schurz's Third Division.

For details of the operations and changes in command of First Corps, Army of Virginia during the period of its existence, see Pope's Northern Virginia Campaign; and see also Maryland Campaign (South Mountain and Antietam).

First Corps was not again engaged during the campaign, and it retired with the rest of the Army of Virginia into the Defenses of Washington September 2, 1862. It was then sent to the vicinity of Fort Ethan Allen to guard the roads leading to the Chain Bridge.

When the reorganized Army of the Potomac left Washington at the beginning of the Maryland Campaign, Sigel's corps was left behind in the Defenses of Washington South of the Potomac. In the reorganization of the Army of the Potomac September 12, 1862, the designation of First Corps, Army of Virginia was changed to Eleventh Corps, Army of the Potomac. The brigade and division designations remained the same as in First Corps, Army of Virginia. Milroy's Independent Brigade was broken up and the regiments were assigned to the Defenses of Washington and Eleventh Corps.

The commanders of First Corps, Army of Virginia were as follows:

John C. Fremont	June 26, 1862 to June 28, 1862
Robert C. Schenck	June 28, 1862 to June 30, 1862
Franz Sigel	June 30, 1862 to July 7, 1862
Robert C. Schenck	July 7, 1862 to July 12, 1862
Franz Sigel	July 12, 1862 to September 12, 1862

FIRST VETERAN CORPS (HANCOCK)

By an order of November 28, 1864, a Veteran Army Corps was authorized. It was to consist of able-bodied men who had served honorably for not less than two years, and who would enlist for not less than one year. Organization of the corps was to begin December 1, 1864 in the District of Columbia, and Winfield S. Hancock was assigned command, with headquarters in Washington, D.C. The corps was commonly called Hancock's First Corps or Hancock's Veteran First Corps.

Enlistments were far below expectations and at the end of the year totaled only 174 officers and men. By April 1865 only 4,422 had enlisted. The men were organized into regiments of United States Veteran Volunteers, and apparently only six of these regiments were formed.

In March 1865, the 1st and 2nd United States Veteran Volunteers were sent to Harper's Ferry, and the following month these two regiments and the 3rd United States Veteran Volunteers were organized at Winchester, Virginia as Oliver Wood's Second Brigade of Samuel S. Carroll's Fourth Provisional Division, Army of the Shenandoah. May 2, 1865, Carroll, with Wood's brigade, was ordered back to Camp Stoneman in the District of Columbia, where the First Veteran Corps was stationed. Upon arriving there, Carroll assumed command of First Division, First Veteran Corps.

The corps remained in existence until December 1865, when the terms of enlistment of the troops began to expire, and then they were mustered out.

SECOND CORPS, ARMY OF THE POTOMAC

Second Corps, Army of the Potomac was created by a presidential order of March 8, 1862, which also created First Corps, Third Corps, Fourth Corps, and Fifth Corps. The corps was organized March 13, 1862, under the command of Edwin V. Sumner, and it originally consisted of the divisions of Israel B. Richardson (formerly commanded by Sumner), John Sedgwick, and Louis Blenker. The organization of the corps was announced as follows:

SECOND CORPS, Edwin V. Sumner

First Division, Israel B. Richardson
First Brigade, Oliver O. Howard
Second Brigade, Thomas F. Meagher
Third Brigade, William H. French
Artillery
Batteries A and C, 4th United States Artillery, F. N. Clarke, George W. Hazzard
Battery B, 1st New York Light Artillery, Rufus D. Pettit
Battery G, 1st New York Light Artillery, John D. Frank
Battery A, 2nd Battalion New York Artillery, William A. Hogan

Second Division, John Sedgwick
First Brigade, Willis A. Gorman
Second Brigade, William W. Burns
Third Brigade, Napoleon J. T. Dana
Artillery
Battery A, 1st Rhode Island Light Artillery, Charles H. Tompkins
Battery B, 1st Rhode Island Light Artillery, Walter O. Bartlett
Battery G, 1st Rhode Island Light Artillery, Charles D. Owens

Third Division, Louis Blenker
First Brigade, Julius Stahel
Second Brigade, Adolph Von Steinwehr
Third Brigade, Henry Bohlen

8th Pennsylvania Cavalry, John F. Farnsworth

When the army was ordered to the Peninsula in March 1862, the divisions of Second Corps were rather widely separated. Sedgwick's division was in the lower Shenandoah Valley, on a line from Charlestown to Berryville. Richardson's division was in advance of the army, with William H. French's brigade at Manassas, and the other two brigades within supporting distance along Bull Run. Blenker's division was at Fairfax Court House, where Sumner had his headquarters. Later, Sumner advanced with Richardson's and Blenker's divisions to Warrenton Junction. Sedgwick's division was ordered to Alexandria, where it embarked for the Peninsula in March 1862. On April 1, 1862, Blenker's division was detached from Second Corps, and also from the Army of the Potomac, and was sent to John C. Fremont's Mountain Department. The next day Richardson's division moved back to Alexandria, where it embarked for the Peninsula.

Peninsular Campaign, April 1862–August 1862. By April 2, 1862, Sedgwick's division had arrived at Fort Monroe; and two days later, Richardson's division having not yet arrived, it was temporarily assigned to Samuel P. Heintzelman's Third Corps. It then marched with Third Corps toward Yorktown. Upon arrival there, Sedgwick occupied the center of McClellan's line, with Heintzelman's Third Corps on the right and Erasmus D. Keyes' Fourth Corps on the left. On April 6, 1862, Sumner was assigned command of the left wing of the army, which consisted of Sedgwick's division and Fourth Corps. On April 16, 1862, Richardson's division joined Sumner and replaced Sedgwick's division on the front line.

The enemy evacuated Yorktown May 3, 1862, and Second Corps embarked there and moved up the York River to the vicinity of West Point on the Pamunkey River. During this movement, Napoleon J. T. Dana's Third Brigade of Sedgwick's division was present with William B. Franklin's division during the Engagement at Eltham's Landing (Barhamsville, or West Point) May 7, 1862, but it was not engaged.

While the army was assembling at White's House in mid-May 1862, Sumner's two divisions remained near Eltham's Landing. The army was reorganized May 18, 1862, with the formation of Fifth Provisional Corps under Fitz John Porter and Sixth Provisional Corps under William B. Franklin. When the reorganization was completed, the army continued its advance toward Richmond. Fourth Corps, supported by Third Corps, crossed to the south side of the Chickahominy River and moved to the Seven Pines-Fair Oaks area; Fifth Corps and Sixth Corps took position on the north side of the river near Gaines' Mill and Mechanicsville; and Second Corps remained near the York River Railroad, on the north bank of the Chickahominy.

Keyes' Fourth Corps was attacked at Seven Pines and Fair Oaks May 31, 1862 and driven back, and then Sumner crossed the Chickahominy and, with Heintzelman's Third Corps, aided Keyes in halting the enemy's advance. Oliver O. Howard, commanding First Brigade of Richardson's division, was wounded, and Thomas J. Parker assumed command of his brigade. May 29, 1862, John C. Caldwell, who had been serving in Silas Casey's Division in Washington, was assigned to duty with the Army of the Potomac, and June 4, 1862 was assigned to the temporary command of Howard's brigade, relieving Parker. Lieutenant Colonel William C. Massett of the 61st New York was killed at the Battle of Fair Oaks, and it is interesting to note that on May 31, 1862, to fill this vacancy, the governor of that state selected Lieutenant Nelson A. Miles of the 22nd Massachusetts because of his service on the Peninsula. Miles later commanded First Division, Second Corps.

The organization of Second Corps at Fair Oaks and Seven Pines was as follows:

SECOND CORPS, Edwin V. Sumner

First Division, Israel B. Richardson
    First Brigade, Oliver O. Howard, wounded
        Thomas J. Parker
    Second Brigade, Thomas F. Meagher
    Third Brigade, William H. French
    Artillery Brigade, George W. Hazzard
        Battery B, 1st New York Light Artillery, Rufus D. Pettit
        Battery G, 1st New York Light Artillery, John D. Frank
        Batteries A and C, 4th United States Artillery, George W. Hazzard

Second Division, John Sedgwick
    First Brigade, Willis A. Gorman
    Second Brigade, William W. Burns
    Third Brigade, Napoleon J. T. Dana
    Artillery Brigade, Charles H. Tompkins
        Battery A, 1st Rhode Island Light Artillery, Charles H. Tompkins
        Battery B, 1st Rhode Island Light Artillery, Walter O. Bartlett
        Battery G, 1st Rhode Island Light Artillery, Charles D. Owen
        Battery I, 1st United States Artillery, Edmund Kirby

During the battles of Mechanicsville and Gaines' Mill June 26 and 27, 1862, Second Corps was near Fair Oaks, south of the Chickahominy, and was not engaged. Late in the evening of May 27, 1862, near the end of the Battle of Gaines' Mill, Thomas F. Meagher's Second Brigade and William H. French's Third Brigade of Richardson's division were sent north of the river to reinforce Porter, but they were too late to take part in the battle. They did, however, support George Sykes' division of Fifth Corps in covering the retreat across the Chickahominy.

In the general withdrawal of the army toward the James River following the defeat at Gaines' Mill, Sumner's Second Corps remained in position near Fair Oaks until the night of June 28, 1862, and then it began to pull back toward the crossings of White Oak Swamp. It was engaged at Allen's farm during the morning of June 29, 1862, and then moved on to Savage Station, where it arrived about 2:00 that afternoon. The Battle of Savage Station, which began about 5:00 that evening, was fought largely by Sedgwick's division of Second Corps. William W. Burns' Second Brigade and the 1st Minnesota of Gorman's brigade (then commanded by Alfred Sully because of the illness of Gorman) sustained the first enemy attack, and they were later supported by other regiments of the corps. For details of this battle, See Peninsular Campaign, Seven Days' Battles, Battle of Savage Station.

After the Battle of Savage Station, Second Corps withdrew across White Oak Swamp as the retreat to the James River continued. Sedgwick's division was placed in reserve near Riddell's Shop, behind the Federal line in the Glendale area. Richardson's division was formed on the west side of the road at White Oak Bridge to assist William F. Smith's division of William B. Franklin's Sixth Corps in resisting Thomas J. (Stonewall) Jackson's attempt to force a crossing of the swamp. For a time Sully's brigade and Dana's brigade of Sedgwick's division were also with Franklin at the bridge.

Sedgwick's division became engaged at the Battle of Glendale June 30, 1862, when a Confederate attack broke through George A. McCall's line. Burns' brigade, which had been held on Nelson's farm, was ordered up; Dana and Sully were recalled from White Oak Swamp; and these three brigades then helped reestablish McCall's line. John C. Caldwell's First Brigade of Richardson's division was also sent down from White Oak Swamp to support Philip Kearny's Third Division, Third Corps, and with Caldwell's help, Kearny held his position.

On July 1, 1862, Second Corps was placed in reserve behind the Union line on Malvern Hill. During the battle that day, Meagher's and Caldwell's brigades of Richardson's division were sent to reinforce Darius N. Couch's First Division, Fourth Corps. When the battle was over, Second Corps retired with the Army of the Potomac to Harrison's Landing on the James River.

Division and brigade commanders during the Seven Days were the same as at Fair Oaks, except that Caldwell commanded First Brigade, First Division, and Sully commanded First Brigade, Second Division in place of Willis A. Gorman, who was sick. James Shields' Division of the Department of the Rappahannock was broken up June 26, 1862, and Nathan Kimball's brigade was sent to the Army of the Potomac on the Peninsula. It was assigned to Sixth Corps, but was then reassigned to Second Corps July 15, 1862, as Kimball's Independent Brigade. For additional information about the activities of Second Corps on the Peninsula, see Peninsular Campaign.

With Pope's Army of Virginia (Campaign in Northern Virginia), August 16, 1862–September 2, 1862. Second Corps remained at Harrison's Landing until the latter part of August 1862, and then the Army of the Potomac was withdrawn from the Peninsula. Second Corps was the last corps to leave, and it embarked at Newport News for Aquia Creek, where it arrived August 26, 1862. The next day it was sent on to Alexandria. From there it moved out to Centerville during the evening of August 30, 1862, but it was too late to take part in the Second Battle of Bull Run. It was placed in position near Chantilly, but was not engaged in the battle there September 1, 1862. In the withdrawal of the army

after the Battle of Chantilly, Sumner, with his Second Corps, covered the retreat on the Vienna and Langley Road. When the corps reached the vicinity of Washington, it took position on the Virginia side of the Potomac River, but the next day, September 3, 1862, it was ordered to Tennallytown. Two days later, Second Corps, Army of the Potomac and Second Corps, Army of Virginia (later to become Twelfth Corps, Army of the Potomac) were moved to Rockville, Maryland, where they were organized as the Center of McClellan's army under Sumner.

Maryland Campaign, September 3, 1862–September 20, 1862. On September 7, 1862, Second Corps marched with the Army of the Potomac toward Frederick, Maryland to engage Robert E. Lee's army, which had invaded the state. At this time Second Corps consisted of Richardson's First Division, Sedgwick's Second Division, and Kimball's Independent Brigade. Three days later, however, a new Third Division was organized under William H. French, who formerly commanded Third Brigade, First Division, Second Corps. It will be remembered that originally a Third Division under Louis Blenker was assigned to Second Corps, but that it never joined the corps. The new division was organized as follows:

Third Division, William H. French
  First Brigade, Nathan Kimball
  Second Brigade, Dwight Morris
  Third Brigade, Max Weber

Note 1. First Brigade was organized from Kimball's Independent Brigade, Second Corps.
Note 2. Second Brigade was formed from new regiments.
Note 3. Third Brigade was organized from Weber's Brigade, Division at Suffolk, Seventh Corps, Department of Virginia. This brigade had just arrived in Maryland from Virginia.

With the addition of Third Division, Second Corps was organized as follows:

SECOND CORPS, Edwin V. Sumner

First Division, Israel B. Richardson
  First Brigade, John C. Caldwell
  Second Brigade, Thomas J. Meagher
  Third Brigade, John R. Brooke

Second Division, John Sedgwick
 First Brigade, Willis A. Gorman
 Second Brigade, Oliver O. Howard
 Third Brigade, Napoleon J. T. Dana

Note. In July 1862, William W. Burns left the army on sick leave, and Joshua T. Owen and De Witt C. Baxter commanded Second Brigade until August 27, 1862. On that date, Howard returned to the army after recovering from a wound received at the Battle of Fair Oaks, and assumed command of Burns' former Second Brigade at Falmouth.

Third Division, William H. French
 First Brigade, Nathan Kimball
 Second Brigade, Dwight Morris
 Third Brigade, Max Weber

There were no significant changes in the organization of Second Corps until April 1863, but there were numerous changes in command during this period.

The corps was not present at the Battle of South Mountain September 14, 1862, but it was heavily engaged on the Union center, along "Bloody Lane," during the fighting at Antietam three days later. For details of the operations and organization of Second Corps during this period, see Maryland Campaign (South Mountain and Antietam). There were several command changes resulting from the Battle of Antietam. Richardson was mortally wounded, and Caldwell assumed temporary command of First Division until relieved by Winfield S. Hancock later in the day. Hancock was transferred from the command of First Brigade, Second Division, Sixth Corps to the command of Richardson's division. Thomas F. Meagher, commanding Second Brigade, First Division, was temporarily disabled, and was succeeded temporarily by John Burke, but Meagher returned to command the next day. Sedgwick was wounded and was succeeded temporarily in command of Second Division by Oliver O. Howard. Joshua T. Owen commanded Howard's Second Brigade for a short time until De Witt C. Baxter returned to the brigade from another part of the field that afternoon. Baxter then assumed command of Second Brigade, Second Division. Napoleon J. T. Dana was wounded and was succeeded in command of Third Brigade, Second Division by Norman J. Hall. Max Weber, commander of Third Brigade, Third Division, was also wounded and was succeeded by John W. Andrews. Three regimental commanders who were wounded are mentioned here because they were later promoted and exercised higher command. Francis C. Barlow, colonel of 61st New York, was absent because of his wound for more than a year, but he returned to the army to lead a division in Grant's Richmond Campaign in 1864. Isaac J. Wistar, colonel of the 71st Pennsylvania, and Edward W. Hinks, colonel of 19th Massachusetts, did not return to Second Corps after recovering from their wounds, but they were promoted and served in other corps.

The organization of Second Corps during the period September 14–17, 1862 was as follows:

SECOND CORPS, Edwin V. Sumner

First Division, Israel B. Richardson, to September 17, killed
 John C. Caldwell, temporarily
 Winfield S. Hancock
 First Brigade, John C. Caldwell
 Second Brigade, Thomas F. Meagher
  John Burke
 Third Brigade, John R. Brooke
 Artillery
  Battery B, 1st New York Light Artillery, Rufus D. Pettit
  Batteries A and C, United States Artillery, Evan Thomas

Second Division, John Sedgwick, to September 17, 1862, wounded
 Oliver O. Howard
 First Brigade, Willis A. Gorman
 Second Brigade, Oliver O. Howard
  Joshua T. Owen
  De Witt C. Baxter
 Third Brigade, Napoleon J. T. Dana, to September 17, 1862, wounded
  Norman J. Hall
 Artillery
  Battery A, 1st Rhode Island Light Artillery, John A. Tompkins
  Battery I, 1st United States Artillery, George A. Woodruff

Third Division, William H. French
 First Brigade, Nathan Kimball
 Second Brigade, Dwight Morris
 Third Brigade, Max Weber, to September 17, 1862, wounded
  John W. Andrews

Unattached Artillery
 Battery G, 1st New York Light Artillery, John D. Frank

Battery B, 1st Rhode Island Light Artillery, John G. Hazard

Battery G, 1st Rhode Island Light Artillery, Charles D. Owen

Antietam to Warrenton, September 19, 1862–November 7, 1862.

Second Corps remained near the battlefield of Antietam until September 22, 1862, and it was then ordered to Harper's Ferry to take position on Bolivar Heights. Upon arrival there Sumner was placed in command at Harper's Ferry.

On October 7, 1862, Sumner was granted a leave of absence, and Darius N. Couch was assigned command of Second Corps. Couch's First Division, Fourth Corps had been attached to Sixth Corps during the Maryland Campaign, and October 22, 1862, it was assigned to Sixth Corps as Third Division. Couch assumed command of Second Corps October 9, 1862, and under his command the corps remained on Bolivar Heights for several weeks, with headquarters at Harper's Ferry.

October 13, 1862, Ambrose E. Burnside was assigned command of the Defenses of Harper's Ferry, which included Second Corps, Ninth Corps, and Twelfth Corps. Second Corps remained in the Defenses until the Army of the Potomac began its advance into Virginia. On October 30, 1862, Second Corps crossed the Shenandoah River from Bolivar Heights, passed around the base of Loudoun Heights, and marched into the Loudoun Valley. It then moved toward Snickersville, covering Snicker's Gap. On November 2, 1862, Second Corps continued on and reached the vicinity of Upperville November 4, 1862, and two days later arrived at Rectortown. At this point, Sumner rejoined the army, but he did not resume command of Second Corps. Burnside, who was assigned command of the Army of the Potomac November 7, 1862, decided to reorganize the army into grand divisions, and Sumner was to receive command of the Right Grand Division.

There were several command changes during this period. On October 6, 1862, Samuel K. Zook relieved John R. Brooke in command of Third Brigade, First Division. William W. Burns resumed command of Second Brigade, Second Division, relieving De Witt C. Baxter, October 10, 1862. Burns was relieved from duty with Second Corps November 2, 1862, and was assigned command of First Division, Ninth Corps. Burns was succeeded in command of Second Brigade, Second Division by Joshua T. Owen.

October 29, 1862, Alfred Sully relieved Willis A. Gorman in command of First Brigade, Second Division.

Fredericksburg Campaign, November 7, 1862–December 15, 1862.

On November 7, 1862, Burnside received an order (dated November 5, 1862) directing him to relieve McClellan in command of the Army of the Potomac. He assumed command that night, and then submitted to Henry W. Halleck a plan for moving the army toward Richmond by way of Fredericksburg. This plan was approved November 14, 1862, and on that day Burnside reorganized the army to consist of three grand divisions and a reserve. Sumner was assigned command of the Right Grand Division, which was to consist of Second Corps and Ninth Corps. The next day the two corps left Warrenton, with Second Corps in the lead, and during the afternoon of November 17, 1862 they arrived at Falmouth, opposite Fredericksburg. The rest of the army also marched into the area near Falmouth at about the same time.

The operations against Fredericksburg were then delayed for several weeks, while Burnside waited for pontoon trains to arrive from Washington so that he could cross the Rappahannock. Finally, on December 11, 1862, the army began moving over the river. That day Couch's Second Corps began to cross on the bridges that had been constructed at Fredericksburg. These troops remained in the town until the morning of December 13, 1862, and they then marched out and formed for an attack on the enemy positions at Marye's Heights. The first attacks were launched at 11:00 A.M. by French's Third Division, and these were followed in quick succession by assaults from Hancock's First Division and Howard's Second Division. All of these attacks, as well as those by other divisions, were repulsed with very heavy losses. That evening the troops of Second Corps withdrew into Fredericksburg, and they remained there until the night of December 15, 1862, when they recrossed to the north bank of the river. For details of the battle, see Fredericksburg, Virginia Campaign.

There were some command changes in Second Corps resulting from the Battle of Fredericksburg: John C. Caldwell was wounded and was succeeded in command of First Brigade, First Division by George Von Schack; Nathan Kimball was wounded, and John S. Mason assumed command of his First Brigade, Third Division; John W. Andrews was disabled during the fighting, and turned over the command of Third Brigade, Third Division to John W. Marshall. William Jameson commanded Third Brigade briefly until Marshall arrived from detached service.

The organization of Second Corps at the Battle of Fredericksburg, December 11–15, 1862, was as follows:

SECOND CORPS, Darius N. Couch

First Division, Winfield S. Hancock
  First Brigade, John C. Caldwell
    George W. Von Schack
  Second Brigade, Thomas F. Meagher
  Third Brigade, Samuel K. Zook
  Artillery
    Battery B, 1st New York Light Artillery, Rufus D. Pettit
    Battery C, 4th United States Artillery, Evan Thomas

Second Division, Oliver O. Howard
  First Brigade, Alfred Sully
  Second Brigade, Joshua T. Owen
  Third Brigade, Norman J. Hall
    William R. Lee
  Artillery
    Battery A, 1st Rhode Island Light Artillery, William A. Arnold
    Battery B, 1st Rhode Island Light Artillery, John G. Hazard

Third Division, William H. French
  First Brigade, Nathan Kimball, to December 13, 1862, wounded
    John S. Mason
  Second Brigade, Oliver H. Palmer
  Third Brigade, John W. Andrews, disabled
    William Jameson
    John W. Marshall
  Artillery
    Battery G, 1st New York Light Artillery, John D. Frank
    Battery G, 1st Rhode Island Light Artillery, Charles D. Owen

Artillery Reserve, Charles H. Morgan
  Battery I, 1st United States Artillery, Edmund Kirby
  Battery A, 4th United States Artillery, Rufus King, Jr.

Winter of 1862–1863. When the army withdrew from the south side of the Rappahannock after the Battle of Fredericksburg, Second Corps went into winter quarters near Falmouth. It did not accompany Hooker's and Franklin's grand divisions on their famous "Mud March" up the Rappahannock January 20, 1862 (see Army of the Potomac, Winter of 1862–1863), but it was sent to the lower Rappahannock to divert attention from Burnside's flanking march. When this was called off because of bad weather, Second Corps returned to its camps.

During the winter there were some organizational changes and also many command changes, other than those that resulted from the customary winter leaves. On December 15, 1862, William R. Lee, who had been absent because of illness, returned to duty and relieved Norman J. Hall in command of Third Brigade, Second Division. Two days later, however, Lee resigned his commission, and Hall resumed command of the brigade. Couch, who had been in poor health for some time, was obliged to relinquish command of Second Corps; and on December 26, 1862, John Sedgwick, who had returned to the army after recovering from his Antietam wound, was assigned command. On January 26, 1863, Joseph Hooker relieved Burnside in command of the Army of the Potomac. Also that day, Sumner, who had been suffering from ill health, left the army, and Oliver O. Howard relieved Sedgwick in command of Second Corps when Sedgwick was assigned command of Eleventh Corps.

The grand divisions were abolished February 5, 1863, and Couch resumed command of Second Corps. Thereafter the corps commanders reported directly to Headquarters Army of the Potomac.

There were some changes in the divisional and brigade commanders during the winter. Samuel K. Zook was in temporary command of First Division from January 24, 1863 to February 20, 1863, while Hancock was on leave. Richard P. Roberts commanded Third Brigade, First Division during this period. When Howard assumed temporary command of Second Corps, Joshua T. Owen succeeded him in command of Second Division, and De Witt C. Baxter succeeded Owen in command of Second Brigade, Second Division. When Couch resumed command of Second Corps February 5, 1863, Howard returned to the command of Second Division. Howard assumed command of Eleventh Corps April 2, 1863, relieving Franz Sigel, and Owen commanded Second Division temporarily until April 11, 1863, when John Gibbon, who was transferred from First Corps, assumed command. Owen then resumed command of Second Brigade, relieving De Witt C. Baxter. February 12, 1863, William Hays, long connected with the Artillery Reserve of the Army of the Potomac, relieved Morris in command of Second Brigade, Third Division. John D. McGregor relieved Marshall in command of Third Brigade, Third Division after December 13, 1862.

Sully commanded Third Division in December 1862. Before that time, Sully commanded First Brigade, Second Division. Turner G. Morehead commanded First Brigade, Second Division in December 1862, and then in January Frederick D. Sewall commanded in place of Morehead (Sewall resigned February 19, 1863). John S. Mason, who commanded First Brigade, Third Division after Kimball was wounded December 13, 1862, was promoted to brigadier general and was sent west, where he was assigned command of the District of Ohio in the Department of the Ohio. Samuel S. Carroll, commanding 8th Ohio, and who had remained with Third Corps when his regiment was transferred to Second Corps, rejoined his regiment in April 1863, and by seniority assumed command of First Brigade. When Kimball recovered from his wound, he was sent west in the spring of 1863, and he led a division of Sixteenth Corps in the Vicksburg Campaign. On April 13, 1863, John R. Brooke, because of his good performance at the Battle of Fredericksburg, was assigned command of a new brigade that was formed from regiments of First Brigade and Third Brigade of First Division. This was designated as Fourth Brigade, First Division.

Chancellorsville Campaign, April 27, 1863–May 6, 1863. Only Hancock's and French's divisions of Second Corps took part in the Battle of Chancellorsville. Couch, with these two divisions, moved from near Falmouth to Banks' Ford on the Rappahannock April 28, 1863, and the next day marched on to United States Ford. On April 30, 1863, he joined Hooker and the rest of the army near Chancellorsville. Gibbon's division remained near Falmouth.

Late on the morning of May 1, 1863, Fifth Corps advanced from Chancellorsville toward Fredericksburg, with Sykes' division marching on the turnpike. Sykes soon encountered strong resistance, and Hancock's division moved up in support.

Sykes was then ordered to retire, and Hancock arrived in time to aid in his withdrawal. That night the two divisions of Second Corps were formed in line in front of Chancellorsville, facing east, and extending southward in front of Chancellorsville from the right of Fifth Corps near the Chandler house to the left of Twelfth Corps, near the Plank Road. The next day the corps remained in much the same position as the night before. Couch was under frequent attack on May 2, 1863, but easily held his ground. That evening, during Thomas J. (Stonewall) Jackson's attack on Hooker's right flank, west of Chancellorsville, William Hays' Second Brigade of French's Third Division was sent to support David B. Birney's division of Third Corps, which was attempting to halt Jackson's advance.

On the morning of May 3, 1863, Samuel S. Carroll's First Brigade and Charles Albright's Third Brigade of French's Third Division were moved to the right of Daniel E. Sickles' Third Corps, which was under heavy attack by Jackson's corps north of the Plank Road. French's two brigades then moved forward and drove the enemy back for some distance before they in turn were forced to retire. Hancock's division, together with a part of Twelfth Corps, continued to hold the advanced line east of Chancellorsville until about 10:00 A.M., at which time both divisions of Second Corps were ordered to fall back to a new defensive position north of Chancellorsville. There they were placed between Third Corps and Eleventh Corps.

Meantime, Gibbon's division had crossed the Rappahannock from Falmouth and joined John Sedgwick's Sixth Corps in Fredericksburg. Gibbon was placed on the right of Sedgwick's line in front of Marye's Heights, but it was only slightly engaged in the attack on the heights May 3, 1863. When Sedgwick marched west toward Salem Church, Gibbon remained in Fredericksburg, and then later withdrew to Falmouth. The other two divisions of Second Corps remained in Hooker's defensive line in front of United States Ford until the army recrossed the Rappahannock on the night of May 5–6, 1863, and they then returned to their former camps. For details of the Battle of Chancellorsville, see Chancellorsville, Virginia Campaign.

The organization of Second Corps at the Battle of Chancellorsville was as follows:

SECOND CORPS, Darius N. Couch

First Division, Winfield S. Hancock
First Brigade, John C. Caldwell
Second Brigade, Thomas F. Meagher
Third Brigade, Samuel K. Zook
Fourth Brigade, John R. Brooke
Artillery, Rufus D. Pettit
Battery B, 1st New York Light Artillery, Rufus D. Pettit
Battery C, 4th United States Artillery, Evan Thomas

Note. A provisional brigade under Edward F. Cross was formed at United States Ford April 30, 1863. It was composed of three regiments taken from First Brigade and Second Brigade, and was sometimes called Fifth Brigade.

Second Division, John Gibbon
First Brigade, Alfred Sully, to May 1, 1863
Henry W. Hudson, to May 3, 1863
Byron Laflin
Second Brigade, Joshua T. Owen
Third Brigade, Norman J. Hall
Artillery
Battery A, 1st Rhode Island Light Artillery, William A. Arnold
Battery B, 1st Rhode Island Light Artillery, T. Frederick Brown

Note. Sully was relieved May 1, 1863, for disobedience of orders. Hudson commanded the brigade for only a short time, and early on May 3, 1863, Laflin was in command.

Third Division, William H. French
First Brigade, Samuel S. Carroll
Second Brigade, William Hays, to May 3, 1863, wounded and captured
Charles J. Powers
Third Brigade, John D. MacGregor, to May 2, 1863, sick
Charles Albright
Artillery
Battery G, 1st New York Light Artillery, Nelson Ames
Battery G, 1st Rhode Island Light Artillery, George W. Adams

Reserve Artillery
Battery I, 1st United States Artillery, Edmund Kirby
Battery A, 4th United States Artillery, Alonzo H. Cushing

Gettysburg Campaign, May 1863–July 1863.

After the Battle of Chancellorsville, Second Corps remained near Falmouth and picketed the line of the Rappahannock River until the army began its withdrawal toward the Orange and Alexandria Railroad at the beginning of the Gettysburg Campaign. It covered the rear of the army until all government property had been removed, and then, late on June 14, 1863, it too marched northward.

There was some reorganization in Second Corps during May and June 1863. Four regiments of the corps were sent home for muster out, and three of these were from Third Division. Of these three, two were from Third Brigade, Third Division, and this left only one regiment in the brigade. It was transferred to Second Brigade May 23, 1863, and Third Brigade was thus discontinued. Charles Albright, commander of Third Brigade, departed with his 132nd Pennsylvania, which was one of the regiments sent home for muster out. Third Brigade was reorganized June 26, 1863 (see below).

In May the division artillery of the corps was broken up, and a Second Corps Artillery Brigade was constituted from Battery A and Battery B, 1st Rhode Island Artillery; Battery I, 1st United States Artillery; and Battery A, 4th United States Artillery. John G. Hazard, 1st Rhode Island Artillery, was assigned command.

An important command change also took place while the corps was near Falmouth. On June 9, 1863, Couch was relieved from command of Second Corps at his own request because he was unwilling to serve any longer under Hooker. Winfield S. Hancock assumed command of the corps, and John C. Caldwell succeeded Hancock in command of First Division. Edward E. Cross assumed command of Caldwell's First Brigade, First Division. Couch did not return to Second Corps.

When Second Corps left Falmouth to follow the rest of the army toward Gettysburg, it marched by way of Aquia and Dumfries and arrived at Sangster's Station on the Orange and Alexandria Railroad June 17, 1863. It then moved westward to help form a defensive line along the Bull Run Mountains, in front of Washington. It occupied Thoroughfare Gap June 21–25, 1863, and then joined the rest of the army on the march into Maryland. While at Thoroughfare Gap, Gibbon had placed Joshua T. Owen under arrest, and as the division was leaving, Alexander S. Webb, who had only that day arrived at the front, was assigned command of Owen's Second Brigade, Second Division. In June 1863, the 34th New York Regiment of First Brigade, Gibbon's division went home for muster out, and with it went its colonel, Byron Laflin.

Alexander Hays' Third Brigade of John J. Abercrombie's Division, Department of Washington joined Second Corps near Gum Springs (present-day Arcola) while the corps was on the march, and June 26, 1863, the brigade was designated as Third Brigade, Third Division, Second Corps. This brigade had formed a part of the force captured at Harper's Ferry the year before. Hays was assigned command of Third Division, relieving French, who was assigned command at Harper's Ferry, and George L. Willard assumed command of the newly organized Third Brigade of the division.

Second Corps crossed the Potomac into Maryland at Edwards Ferry, and arrived at Monocacy Junction June 28, 1863. It then marched northward through Uniontown and arrived at Taneytown about 11:00 A.M. July 1, 1863, the opening day of the Battle of Gettysburg. While there, Hancock turned over the command of the corps temporarily to Gibbon, and hurried forward that afternoon to Gettysburg, with orders to take command of all troops on the field. At that time, these were under the direction of Oliver O. Howard, commander of Eleventh Corps, who had assumed command as the senior officer present when John F. Reynolds was killed that morning. About dark that evening, Hancock turned over the command of the troops at Gettysburg to Henry W. Slocum. Meantime, during the afternoon of July 1, 1863, Second Corps, under Gibbon, marched toward Gettysburg, and it was halted by Hancock about three miles from the town. It arrived on the field about daylight July 2, 1863. It was first placed in position behind Cemetery Hill, and then, between 7:00 and 8:00 A.M., it was moved forward to Cemetery Ridge, where it formed with its right on the Emmitsburg Road, just west of Cemetery Hill, and its left on the ridge about one mile to the south.

When James Longstreet's corps attacked Daniel E. Sickles' Third Corps on the Union left during the afternoon of July 2, 1863, Caldwell's First Division, Second Corps was sent to its support, and was heavily engaged that evening in the vicinity of the Wheatfield and in the adjoining woods. Caldwell was finally driven back from that part of the field, along with Third Corps and Fifth Corps, and it did not rejoin Second Corps that day. The next morning it was again placed in position on Cemetery Ridge, but it was separated from the other two divisions of the corps by Abner Doubleday's Third Division, First Corps, which had come up into line the evening before during Longstreet's attack.

Gibbon's Second Division and Alexander Hays' Third Division of Second Corps bore the brunt of of the Pickett-Pettigrew-Trimble assault on the afternoon of July 3, 1863, and with help from the artillery and other infantry units succeeded in holding their positions on Cemetery Ridge. Gibbon was wounded near the close of the action, and Hancock was wounded a short time later. Hancock remained on the field, however, until the enemy had been repulsed, and he then turned over the command of the corps to Caldwell. Later that day, William Hays (not to be confused with Alexander Hays) was assigned command of Second Corps.

Carroll's First Brigade of Hays' Third Division, less the 8th Ohio Regiment, had been sent to aid Eleventh Corps in repelling Jubal A. Early's attack on Cemetery Hill on the evening of July 2, 1863, and was not present on Cemetery Ridge during the battle the next day. The 8th Ohio, however, rendered valuable service by striking the left flank of the enemy during the attack on Cemetery Ridge. For details of the Battle of Gettysburg, see Gettysburg Campaign, Part II, Battle of Gettysburg.

July 4, 1863, Second Corps remained in its positions on Cemetery Ridge, but the next day it joined the rest of the army as it moved toward the Potomac River in pursuit of Lee. In the marching orders for July 5, 1863, Second Corps was placed under the direction of Henry W. Slocum, commander of Twelfth Corps, and was to march with Twelfth Corps toward Middletown, Maryland. Second Corps left Gettysburg July 5, 1863, and marched by way of Two Taverns, Taneytown, and Frederick, and arrived at Rohrersville July 9, 1863. It continued on to near Tilghmanton, and then moved to the vicinity of Jones' Cross Roads (present-day Lappans) July 11, 1863. It remained there until the Army of Northern Virginia had recrossed the Potomac into Virginia during the night of July 13, 1863, and the next day it moved up to Falling Waters.

The Army of the Potomac then followed Lee into Virginia. Second Corps moved to Sandy Hook, Maryland July 15, 1863, and three days later crossed the Potomac at Harper's Ferry. It then advanced with Third Corps and Twelfth Corps along the eastern base of the Blue Ridge Mountains through Wood Grove, Bloomfield, and Paris to Linden Station in Manassas Gap, where it arrived July 23, 1863. It remained there during the day in support of Third Corps, which was trying to force its way through the gap, but it was not engaged. The next day, Second Corps moved eastward through White Plains, and July 26, 1863, it reached a point near Germantown, about four miles northeast of Fayetteville. It remained there until July 30, 1863, and then marched by way of Elk Run to Morrisville. The next day one division was ordered to Elk Run, with one of its brigades to march to Bristerburg. The pickets of Second Corps were to connect with those of Twelfth Corps. August 1, 1863 is generally regarded as the end of the Gettysburg Campaign. For details of the operations of Second Corps during June and July 1863, see Gettysburg Campaign.

The organization of Second Corps during the period May–July 1863 was as follows:

SECOND CORPS, Darius N. Couch, to May 9, 1863
    Winfield S. Hancock, to July 1, 1863
    John Gibbon, July 1, 1863
    Winfield S. Hancock, to July 3, 1863, wounded
    John C. Caldwell, briefly July 3, 1863
    William Hays

First Division, Winfield S. Hancock, to June 9, 1863
    John C. Caldwell
    First Brigade, John C. Caldwell, to June 9, 1863
        Edward E. Cross, to evening of July 2, 1863, mortally wounded
        H. Boyd McKeen, to July 18, 1863
        Robert McFarlane, temporarily July 18, 1863
        James A. Beaver, July 19–28, 1863
        Nelson A. Miles
    Second Brigade, Thomas F. Meagher, to May 8, 1863
        Patrick Kelly
    Third Brigade, Samuel K. Zook, to May 15, 1863
        Orlando H. Morris, to May 25, 1863
        Samuel K. Zook, to evening of July 2, 1863, mortally wounded
        John Fraser
        Paul Frank
    Fourth Brigade, John R. Brooke, to May 20, 1863
        William P. Baily, to June 12, 1863
        John R. Brooke

Second Division, John Gibbon, to July 1, 1863
    William Harrow, July 1, 1863
    John Gibbon, to July 3, 1863, wounded
    William Harrow

    First Brigade, Byron Laflin, to May 13, 1863
        Turner G. Morehead, to June 8, 1863
        William Harrow, to July 1, 1863
        Francis E. Heath
    Second Brigade, Joshua T. Owen, to June 28, 1863
        Alexander S. Webb
    Third Brigade, Norman J. Hall, to July 18, 1863
        R. Penn Smith

Note. Hall was sent to New York during the Draft Riots.

Third Division, William H. French, to June 26, 1863
    Alexander Hays
    First Brigade, Samuel S. Carroll, to July 1863
        Joseph Snider
    Second Brigade, Charles J. Powers, to May 16, 1863
        Thomas A. Smyth, to July 3, 1863, wounded
        Francis E. Pierce, temporarily July 3, 1863
        Thomas A. Smyth
    Third Brigade, Charles Albright, to May 23, 1863
        George L. Willard, May 26, 1863 to July 2, 1863, killed
        Eliakim Sherrill, to July 3, 1863, killed
        James M. Bull, to July 17, 1863
        John Coons

Note 1. Carroll with two of his regiments was sent to New York during the Draft Riots, and Snider commanded the remainder of the brigade. Carroll did not return to the army until September.

Note 2. Third Brigade was discontinued May 23, 1863, and was reorganized May 26, 1863 from Alexander Hays' Third Brigade, Abercrombie's Division, Department of Washington. Hays was assigned command of Third Division, and Willard assumed command of the brigade.

Artillery Brigade, John G. Hazard
    Battery B, 1st New York Light Artillery, Albert S. Sheldon
        James McKay Rorty
        Robert E. Rogers
    Battery A, 1st Rhode Island Light Artillery, William A. Arnold
    Battery B, 1st Rhode Island Light Artillery, T. Frederick Brown
        Walter S. Perrin
    Battery I, 1st United States Artillery, George A. Woodruff
        Tully McCrea
    Battery A, 4th United States Artillery, Alonzo H. Cushing
        Frederick Fuger

Note. Battery B, 1st New York Light Artillery was transferred from the Artillery Reserve July 1, 1863, with 14th New York Battery attached.

From the Rappahannock to the Rapidan, August 1, 1863–October 10, 1863. After arriving on the Rappahannock River at the end of July 1863, Second Corps remained in camp at Morrisville and Elk Run until mid-September 1863. On August 16, 1863, Gouverneur K. Warren assumed temporary command of Second Corps (assigned August 12, 1863) during the absence of Hancock, who was wounded at Gettysburg. Warren, who relieved William Hays, was formerly chief topographical engineer of the Army of the Potomac on Meade's staff, and August 8, 1863, he was appointed major general in recognition of his services at Gettysburg.

During the stay of the army along the Rappahannock, Second Corps was temporarily reduced in numbers when five regiments were sent to New York because of the disturbances caused by the Draft Riots. Three of the regiments were from Samuel S. Carroll's First Brigade, Third Division, leaving only 7th West Virginia in the brigade, which was commanded by Joseph Snider. The regiments of First Brigade returned to the army September 5, 1863. For additional information, see Army of the Potomac, From the Rappahannock to the Rapidan; and also Department of the East, January 3, 1863–June 27, 1865, Draft Riots in New York, 1863.

On September 13, 1863, Second Corps, then under the command of Warren, crossed the Rappahannock and marched to Culpeper Court House in support of Alfred Pleasonton's Cavalry Corps, which was conducting a reconnaissance in force toward the Rapidan River. Three days later, Second Corps advanced to the Rapidan and relieved the cavalry pickets along the river from Somerville Ford to Cedar Mountain, including both places. October 5, 1863, John Sedgwick's Sixth Corps relieved Second Corps, and the latter moved back to the heights in rear of Culpeper Court House. It remained there until October 10, 1863. On that day, Meade learned definitely that the enemy was moving in heavy force against his right flank, and that night he issued orders for the withdrawal of the army to the line of the Rappahannock. For additional information, see Army of the Potomac, From the Rappahannock to the Rapidan.

The organization of Second Corps during the period August 1, 1863–October 10, 1863 was as follows:

SECOND CORPS, William Hays, to August 16, 1863

Gouverneur K. Warren, to August 26, 1863?
John C. Caldwell, to September 2, 1863
Gouverneur K. Warren, to October 10, 1863
John C. Caldwell, to October 12, 1863
Gouverneur K. Warren

First Division, John C. Caldwell
  First Brigade, Nelson A. Miles
  Second Brigade, Patrick Kelly
  Third Brigade, Paul Frank, to October 10, 1863
    James A. Beaver
  Fourth Brigade, John R. Brooke, to August 29, 1863
    James A. Beaver, to September 20, 1863
    John R. Brooke

Note 1. William Hays commanded First Division briefly, shortly after being relieved from command of Second Corps.
Note 2. Paul Frank commanded First Division temporarily during the periods when Caldwell commanded Second Corps.

Second Division, William Harrow, to August 15, 1863
  Alexander S. Webb
  First Brigade, Francis E. Heath, to August 1863
    De Witt C. Baxter, to September 1863
    R. Penn Smith, to October 6, 1863
    Francis E. Heath
  Second Brigade, Alexander S. Webb, to August 15, 1863
    William L. Curry, to September 2, 1863
    De Witt C. Baxter
  Third Brigade, R. Penn Smith, to August 1863
    Ansel D. Wass
    James E. Mallon

Note. Harrow's resignation was accepted October 3, 1863, but was revoked November 24, 1863.

Third Division, Alexander Hays
  First Brigade, Joseph Snider, to September 7, 1863
    Samuel S. Carroll
  Second Brigade, Thomas A. Smyth, to August 14, 1863
    Thomas H. Davis, to September 3, 1863
    Thomas A. Smyth
  Third Brigade, John Coons, to August 15, 1863
    Joshua T. Owen

Note 1. Dwight Morris, former commander of Second Brigade, Third Division, resigned August 14, 1863.
Note 2. Joseph Snider was discharged September 7, 1863.

Artillery Brigade, John G. Hazard
  Battery G, 1st New York Light Artillery, Nelson Ames
  Batteries F and G, 1st Pennsylvania Light Artillery, R. Bruce Ricketts

Battery A, 1st Rhode Island Light Artillery, William A. Arnold

Battery B, 1st Rhode Island Light Artillery, Walter S. Perrin

Battery I, 1st United States Artillery, Frank S. French

Note. The organization of the Artillery Brigade is given as of August 31, 1863.

Bristoe, Virginia Campaign, October 10, 1863– October 22, 1863. When Lee began his movement around the Union right October 9, 1863, Second Corps, under the command of John C. Caldwell, was on the heights in the rear of Culpeper Court House. The next day it was sent out to the vicinity of Stone's House Mountain, to the west of Culpeper Court House, to meet any enemy advance from the direction of Sperryville. Then, when the army began its withdrawal October 11, 1863, Second Corps marched with Fifth Corps and Sixth Corps along the Orange and Alexandria Railroad to Rappahannock Station, where it crossed to the north bank of the river. The next day Warren resumed command of Second Corps, relieving Caldwell.

During the afternoon of October 12, 1863, Second Corps, Fifth Corps, and Sixth Corps, all under the command of Sedgwick, recrossed the Rappahannock and advanced to Brandy Station, but Sedgwick withdrew later that evening. Second Corps was then sent to Bealeton to support David McM. Gregg's Second Cavalry Division, and to cover Third Corps, which was at Freeman's Ford. The corps joined Gregg at Fayetteville at about 1:00 A.M. October 13, 1863, and that day marched on to Auburn (Auburn Mills). It was engaged there with Stuart's cavalry early on the morning of October 14, 1863, and then proceeded on by way of Catlett's Station to Bristoe Station on the Orange and Alexandria Railroad. That afternoon the corps was strongly attacked by Henry Heth's division of Ambrose P. Hill's Confederate corps, which was decisively repulsed with heavy loss. James E. Mallon was killed during the fighting, and Ansel D. Wass assumed command of his Third Brigade, Second Division.

That night Second Corps marched on and arrived near Centerville early on the morning of October 15, 1863. It remained there until after Lee's army withdrew, and on October 19, 1863, it advanced with the Army of the Potomac to Milford on Broad Run, near Bristoe Station. The next day it marched to Auburn, and on October 21, 1863 moved to the Warrenton Branch Railroad at the crossing of Turkey Run. For additional information, see Bristoe, Virginia Campaign.

The organization of Second Corps during the Bristoe Campaign was as follows:

SECOND CORPS, John C. Caldwell, to October 12, 1863
Gouverneur K. Warren

First Division, Paul Frank, to October 12, 1863
John C. Caldwell
First Brigade, Nelson A. Miles
Second Brigade, Patrick Kelly
Third Brigade, James A. Beaver, to October 12, 1863
Paul Frank
Fourth Brigade, John R. Brooke

Second Division, Alexander S. Webb
First Brigade, Francis E. Heath
Second Brigade, De Witt C. Baxter
Third Brigade, James E. Mallon, to October 14, 1863, killed
Ansel D. Wass

Third Division, Alexander Hays
First Brigade, Samuel S. Carroll
Second Brigade, Thomas A. Smyth
Third Brigade, Joshua T. Owen

Artillery, John G. Hazard
Battery G, 1st New York Light Artillery, Nelson Ames
Battery H, 1st Ohio Light Artillery, James F. Huntington
Batteries F and G, 1st Pennsylvania Light Artillery, R. Bruce Ricketts
Battery A, 1st Rhode Island Light Artillery, William A. Arnold
Battery B, 1st Rhode Island Light Artillery, T. Frederick Brown
Battery I, 1st United States Artillery, Frank S. French

Mine Run Campaign, November 26, 1863– December 2, 1863. After the Bristoe Campaign, the Army of the Potomac remained quietly north of the Rappahannock at Bristoe Station, Catlett's Station, New Baltimore, and Warrenton, and Second Corps was on the Warrenton Branch Railroad at the crossing of Turkey Run. Then Meade again decided to advance toward Culpeper Court House, and on November 7, 1863, the army moved up to the crossings of the Rappahannock. For this operation, Meade temporarily organized the army into two wings. The Left Wing was commanded by William H. French, and consisted of First Corps, Second Corps, and Third Corps. Third Corps advanced to Kelly's Ford and drove the enemy from the crossing, and then crossed to the west bank of the river. Second Corps followed Third Corps by way of Morrisville to Kelly's Ford but was not engaged. That evening Sixth Corps of the right wing captured the Confederate bridgehead at Rappahannock Station. Then the army passed over the river and moved forward in the direction of Culpeper Court House. On November 8, 1863, Second Corps advanced to the vicinity of Brandy Station. On November 9, 1863 the wing organization was discontinued, and Second Corps was ordered to take position between Paoli Mills and Brandy Station. For details of these operations, see Engagements at Rappahannock Station and Kelly's Ford, Virginia.

In November 1863, Meade decided on another offensive operation before putting the army in winter quarters. His plan was to move across the Rapidan River and into the Wilderness, and attempt to strike the right flank of Lee's army, which was in position along the Rapidan near Orange Court House. On the morning of November 26, 1863, Second Corps left its camps on Mountain Run and marched to Germanna Ford on the Rapidan. The next day it joined the other corps of the army at Locust Grove (Robertson's or Robinson's Tavern). On November 28, 1863, the army moved westward through the Wilderness, with Second Corps in the center along the old turnpike, and it soon found the enemy strongly posted on the high ground on the west bank of Mine Run, a tributary of the Rapidan. The enemy works appeared too strong for a frontal attack, and Warren's Second Corps, with a division of Sixth Corps, was sent south to the Plank Road to strike the enemy's right flank. On the evening of November 29, two divisions of Third Corps were sent to reinforce Warren, who was to attack the next morning. Upon reexamining the enemy works on November 30, 1863, however, Warren concluded that they could not be taken. He reported this to Meade, who then called off the attack. The army then recrossed the Rapidan and returned to its former camps. For details of the movement to Mine Run, see Mine Run Campaign, Virginia.

The organization of Second Corps at the time of the Mine Run Campaign was as follows:

SECOND CORPS, Gouverneur K. Warren

First Division, John C. Caldwell
  First Brigade, Nelson A. Miles
  Second Brigade, Patrick Kelly
  Third Brigade, James A. Beaver
  Fourth Brigade, John R. Brooke

Second Division, Alexander S. Webb
  First Brigade, De Witt C. Baxter
  Second Brigade, Arthur F. Devereux
  Third Brigade, Turner G. Morehead

Third Division, Alexander Hays
  First Brigade, Samuel S. Carroll
  Second Brigade, Thomas A. Smyth
  Third Brigade, Joshua T. Owen

Artillery Brigade, J. Albert Monroe
  Battery G, 1st New York Light Artillery, Nelson Ames
  Battery C, Pennsylvania Light Artillery, James Thompson
  Battery F, Pennsylvania Light Artillery, James Stephenson
  Batteries F and G, 1st Pennsylvania Light Artillery, Beldin Spence
  Battery A, 1st Rhode Island Light Artillery, William A. Arnold
  Battery B, 1st Rhode Island Light Artillery, T. Frederick Brown
  Battery C, 5th United States Artillery, Richard Metcalf

Winter of 1863–1864. Four days after the army had returned from the Mine Run Campaign, Second Corps moved to Stevensburg and picketed the front from the Stevensburg-Morton's Ford Road to the Rappahannock River, and then up that river to Kelly's Ford. On December 22, 1863, two brigades of the corps were sent foward to support the cavalry that was picketing the Rapidan to the left of Morton's Ford. One brigade was posted in the vicinity of Sheppard's Grove Post Office, and the other was south of Stevensburg. The corps generally remained in these positions during the remainder of the winter.

On December 16, 1863, Warren left on a fifteen-day leave, and John C. Caldwell assumed temporary command of Second Corps. Hancock returned to the army December 29, 1863 and resumed command, but he left again January 8, 1864, and Warren once more took charge of the corps. On January 26, 1864, corps headquarters was informed that Francis C.

Barlow, who had been wounded while serving with Eleventh Corps at Gettysburg, was assigned to duty with Second Corps. Barlow did not immediately join the corps, but instead he was ordered to report to Hancock at Harrisburg for recruiting duty.

Second Corps took a prominent part in the demonstration by the army on the Rapidan February 6–7, 1864. On February 6, 1864, Second Corps, then under the temporary command of Caldwell (Warren was sick but resumed command that afternoon), advanced to the Rapidan at Morton's Ford. Alexander Hays' Third Division, which was the leading division, arrived near the river a little before noon. Owen's Third Brigade then crossed and, after moving forward for a short distance, came under enemy fire. Carroll's First Brigade joined Owen about 1:15 P.M., and Second Brigade (commanded temporarily by Charles J. Powers during the absence of Thomas A. Smyth) came up about an hour later. Hays' division was strongly attacked about 5:00 P.M. and was engaged for about an hour before the fighting ceased. Meantime, Caldwell's First Division arrived and formed on the left of the Morton's Ford Road, and Webb's Second Division and the artillery, which were following, came up and took position on the right of the road. About 6:30 P.M. De Witt C. Baxter's First Brigade of Webb's division was sent over the river to reinforce Hays, and by 8:00 P.M. the rest of Webb's division had crossed. At that time, Hays was ordered to withdraw his division, and about midnight Webb also recrossed his division. Second Corps remained near Morton's Ford during February 7, 1864, and that evening returned to its camps.

Reorganization of the Army of the Potomac, March 1864. An order issued March 23, 1864 reduced the number of corps of the army from five to three. Second Corps was retained in the new organization, but it was extensively reorganized by an order of March 26, 1864. The number of divisions of Second Corps was first reduced from three to two, and these were designated as First Division and Second Division. Then a new Third Division and a new Fourth Division were organized from troops transferred from Third Corps, which was thus discontinued. Winfield S. Hancock, who was wounded at Gettysburg, returned to the army at this time and resumed command of Second Corps. He relieved Warren, who was assigned command of Fifth Corps.

The reorganization of Second Corps was effected as follows: Caldwell's First Division, Second Corps retained its designation in the new organization, but it was assigned to Francis C. Barlow. Nelson A. Miles' First Brigade, Richard Byrnes' Second Brigade, and John R. Brooke's Fourth Brigade also retained their designations, but Thomas A. Smyth was assigned command of Byrnes' brigade. Paul Frank's Third Brigade was broken up and the regiments were assigned to Brooke's Fourth Brigade, and to a new Third Brigade, First Division. The latter was organized from Joshua T. Owen's Third Brigade, Third Division and three regiments of Frank's brigade. Frank was assigned command of the new Third Brigade, First Division. Caldwell was relieved from duty with the Army of the Potomac, and was sent to New York, where he was assigned to a military commission meeting in that city.

Webb's Second Division also retained its designation in the new organization, but it was assigned to John Gibbon, who had been wounded at Gettysburg and had just returned to the army. De Witt C. Baxter's First Brigade and Turner G. Morehead's Third Brigade were consolidated and designated as First Brigade, Second Division. Webb was assigned command of this brigade. Second Brigade retained its designation, but Joshua T. Owen, formerly commander of Third Brigade, Third Division, was assigned command. A new Third Brigade, Second Division was formed by the consolidation of Samuel S. Carroll's First Brigade, and Thomas A. Smyth's Second Brigade of Third Division, and Carroll was assigned command of this brigade. By this transfer of troops, Third Division, Second Corps was discontinued.

A new Third Division, Second Corps was organized by the transfer to Second Corps of David B. Birney's First Division, Third Corps. A new Fourth Division, Second Corps was organized by the transfer to Second Corps of Henry Prince's Second Division, Third Corps. Joseph B. Carr was assigned command of the new Fourth Division.

At the end of April 1864, a short time before Grant's campaign in Virginia began, the organization of Second Corps was as follows:

SECOND CORPS, Winfield S. Hancock

First Division, Francis C. Barlow
First Brigade, Nelson A. Miles

Second Brigade, Thomas A. Smyth
Third Brigade, Paul Frank
Fourth Brigade, John R. Brooke

Note. Third Brigade was formerly Joshua T. Owen's Third Brigade, Third Division, Second Corps.

Second Division, John Gibbon
First Brigade, Alexander S. Webb
Second Brigade, Joshua T. Owen
Third Brigade, Samuel S. Carroll

Note. Third Brigade was formed by the consolidation of First Brigade and Second Brigade of Third Division, Second Corps.

Third Division, David B. Birney
First Brigade, J. H. Hobart Ward
Second Brigade, Alexander Hays

Note. Third Division was formerly David B. Birney's First Division, Third Corps.

Fourth Division, Joseph B. Carr
First Brigade, Gershom Mott
Second Brigade, William R. Brewster

Note 1. Fourth Division was formerly Henry Prince's Second Division, Third Corps (later commanded by Carr).
Note 2. Carr was assigned to the Department of Virginia and North Carolina May 2, 1864, and Mott assumed command of Fourth Division the next day. Robert McAllister assumed command of Mott's First Brigade.

Artillery Brigade, John C. Tidball
  6th Battery (F), Maine Light Artillery, Edwin B. Dow
  10th Battery, Massachusetts Light Artillery, J. Henry Sleeper
  1st Battery, New Hampshire Light Artillery, Frederick M. Edgell
  Battery G, 1st New York Light Artillery, Nelson Ames
  3rd Battalion, 4th New York Heavy Artillery, Thomas Allcock
  Battery F, 1st Pennsylvania Light Artillery, R. Bruce Ricketts
  Battery A, 1st Rhode Island Light Artillery, William A. Arnold
  Battery B, 1st Rhode Island Light Artillery, T. Frederick Brown
  Battery K, 4th United States Artillery, John W. Roder
  Batteries C and I, 5th United States Artillery, James Gilliss

Grant's Richmond, Virginia Campaign, 1864.

When Ulysses S. Grant was assigned command of the Armies of the United States March 9, 1864, he viewed the military problem as basically quite simple. In order to win the war, it was necessary to destroy the two major armies of the Confederacy—Robert E. Lee's Army of Northern Virginia and Joseph E. Johnston's Army of Tennessee, which was then in northern Georgia. Grant decided to make his headquarters with Meade's Army of the Potomac, and with it move south toward Richmond to force a decision with Lee. At the same time, William T. Sherman was to advance toward Atlanta, Georgia with the armies of the Tennessee, of the Cumberland, and of the Ohio to attempt the destruction of Johnston's army.

Early on the morning of May 4, 1864, the Army of the Potomac left its camps and marched toward the Rapidan River at the beginning of Grant's campaign in the East. Second Corps left its encampments near Stevensburg and followed David McM. Gregg's cavalry division by way of Ely's Ford to Chancellorsville, where it camped that night. It continued on the next morning, and had arrived at Todd's Tavern that afternoon when it was ordered back to the junction of the Brock Road and the Orange Court House Plank Road during the first day of the Battle of the Wilderness. It was engaged that evening and again the next morning, May 6, 1864, along the Plank Road, where it suffered heavy losses. For details of the participation of Second Corps in the Battle of the Wilderness, see Richmond, Virginia Campaign, 1864, Battle of the Wilderness.

The organization of Second Corps at the Battle of the Wilderness was as follows:

SECOND CORPS, Winfield S. Hancock

First Division, Francis C. Barlow
  First Brigade, Nelson A. Miles
  Second Brigade, Thomas A. Smyth
  Third Brigade, Paul Frank
  Fourth Brigade, John R. Brooke

Second Division, John Gibbon
  First Brigade, Alexander S. Webb
  Second Brigade, Joshua T. Owen
  Third Brigade, Samuel S. Carroll

Third Division, David B. Birney
  First Brigade, J. H. Hobart Ward
  Second Brigade, Alexander Hays, to May 5, 1864, killed
    John S. Crocker

Fourth Division, Gershom Mott
  First Brigade, Robert McAllister
  Second Brigade, William R. Brewster

Artillery Brigade, John C. Tidball

Note. The Artillery Brigade consisted of the same batteries of as April 1, 1864 (see above).

During the night of May 7, 1864, the Army of the Potomac resumed its march southward toward Spotsylvania Court House. Second Corps remained in position along the Brock Road to cover this movement, but the next morning it followed Fifth Corps to Todd's Tavern. For the next few days the corps did not operate as a unit. On May 8, 1864, Gibbon's division was sent to support Warren's Fifth Corps, which was engaged at Alsop's farm (Laurel Hill), and Nelson A. Miles' First Brigade of Barlow's division moved out to Corbin's Bridge. Miles became engaged while he was retiring that evening, and John R. Brooke's Fourth Brigade marched out to his support.

On May 9, 1864, Hancock left Mott's division at Todd's Tavern and advanced with the divisions of Barlow, Gibbon, and Birney to the Po River, on the right of Warren. Hancock crossed the Po River that evening and advanced on the Block House Road against the left of Lee's line near Spotsylvania Court House. That afternoon Mott moved to the left of Sixth Corps, which was on the left of Fifth Corps.

The next day, Gibbon's and Birney's divisions were withdrawn from south of the Po to take part in an assault on the enemy line on Laurel Hill. Barlow's division also recrossed the Po that evening, after repulsing strong enemy attacks. The attack on Laurel Hill that evening was unsuccessful. During the night of May 11, 1864, Hancock moved to the left, passing in rear of Fifth Corps and Sixth Corps, to the vicinity of the Brown house, where he joined Mott's division. He then deployed his corps and the next morning launched a successful attack on the apex of the salient in the enemy line just south of the Landrum (also Landron) house. Hancock's men captured the enemy breastworks on their front, and continued to advance until stopped by a second line that had been constructed across the base of the salient.

May 13, 1864, Mott's Fourth Division was discontinued, and the two brigades were assigned to Third Division as follows: Robert McAllister's First

Brigade, Fourth Division became Third Brigade, Third Division, with Mott in command; and William R. Brewster's Second Brigade, Fourth Division was redesignated as Fourth Brigade, Third Division. Brewster retained command of the brigade.

May 15, 1864, Second Corps moved farther to the left and took position near the Fredericksburg-Spotsylvania Court House Road. During the period May 17–19, 1864, Second Corps received strong reinforcements, as follows: Mathew Murphy's Corcoran Legion (or Irish Legion) from the Department of Washington; Robert O. Tyler's temporary division of heavy artillery regiments (serving as infantry) from the Defenses of Washington; 8th New York Heavy Artillery (serving as infantry); and the 36th Wisconsin Regiment. The Corcoran Legion was assigned to Gibbon's Second Division as Fourth Brigade, and Tyler's Division was assigned to Second Corps as Fourth Division.

May 18, 1864, Hancock, with the divisions of Barlow, Birney, and Gibbon, moved to the vicinity of Anderson's Mill on the Ny River. Tyler's division remained near the Harris farm on the Fredericksburg Road, and the next day it was engaged with Richard S. Ewell's Confederate corps on the Harris farm. Birney's division was sent back to its support.

For details of the operations of Second Corps around Spotsylvania Court House, see Richmond, Virginia Campaign, 1864, Operations about Spotsylvania Court House.

The organization of Second Corps during the operations about Spotsylvania Court House May 8–21, 1864 was as follows:

SECOND CORPS, Winfield S. Hancock

First Division, Francis C. Barlow
  First Brigade, Nelson A. Miles
  Second Brigade, Thomas A. Smyth, to May 17, 1864
    Richard Byrnes
  Third Brigade, Paul Frank, to May 10, 1864
    Hiram L. Brown, to May 12, 1864, captured
    Clinton D. MacDougall
  Fourth Brigade, John R. Brooke

Note 1. Smyth was assigned command of Third Brigade, Second Division when Samuel S. Carroll was wounded May 13, 1864. Byrnes, who had just arrived from Fredericksburg, assumed command of Second Brigade, First Division.

Note 2. Paul Frank was relieved from command of Third Brigade and placed under arrest May 10, 1864.

Second Division, John Gibbon
First Brigade, Alexander S. Webb, to May 12, 1864, wounded
H. Boyd McKeen
Second Brigade, Joshua T. Owen
Third Brigade, Samuel S. Carroll, to May 13, 1864, wounded
Theodore G. Ellis, to May 17, 1864
Thomas A. Smyth
Fourth Brigade, Mathew Murphy, to May 18, 1864, wounded
James P. McIvor

Note 1. Smyth commanded Second Brigade, First Division until transferred to Second Division May 17, 1864.

Note 2. Fourth Brigade was organized May 17, 1864 from four New York regiments belonging to the so-called Corcoran's Legion or Irish Legion, which Murphy had just brought to the army from Washington.

Third Division, David B. Birney
First Brigade, J. H. Hobart Ward, to May 12, 1864
Thomas W. Egan
Second Brigade, John S. Crocker, to May 18, 1864
Elijah Walker

Note 1. Ward was relieved from command of First Brigade May 12, 1864, for misbehavior (running away and intoxication) during the Battle of the Wilderness. He was arrested May 12, 1864, and was dismissed from the service without trial July 18, 1864.

Note 2. Fourth Division was discontinued May 13, 1864, and its two brigades were assigned to Third Division as Third Brigade and Fourth Brigade. Third Division then consisted of Thomas W. Egan's First Brigade, John S. Crocker's Second Brigade, Gershom Mott's Third Brigade, and William R. Brewster's Fourth Brigade.

Fourth Division, Gershom Mott, to May 13, 1864
First Brigade, Robert McAllister, to May 13, 1864
Second Brigade, William R. Brewster, to May 13, 1864

Note 1. May 9, 1864, John Ramsey was assigned command of a Provisional Brigade, Fourth Division. This brigade was composed largely of regiments from McAllister's First Brigade.

Note 2. Hancock was dissatisfied with the performance of Fourth Division under Mott, and May 13, 1864, he ordered the division discontinued. He assigned the two brigades to Third Division (see above).

Note 3. Fourth Division was reorganized temporarily May 18, 1864 from Robert O. Tyler's Heavy Artillery Division. This division consisted of five heavy artillery regiments, serving as infantry, that had joined the army that day from the Defenses of Washington. The division was not organized into brigades.

Artillery Brigade, John C. Tidball

Note. The same batteries were present in the Artillery Brigade as at the Battle of the Wilderness, but in addition the following batteries were transferred to the brigade from the Artillery Reserve May 16, 1864: A. Judson Clark's Battery B, New Jersey Light Artillery; James E. Burton's 11th Battery, New York Light Artillery; and George F. McKnight's 12th Battery, New York Light Artillery.

On the night of May 20, 1864, the Army of the Potomac left its positions near Spotsylvania Court House and marched toward the North Anna River. Second Corps followed Alfred T. A. Torbert's cavalry, which reported to Hancock during the march, and advanced by way of Guiney's Station and Milford Station to Chesterfield (Telegraph) Bridge on the North Anna. It arrived there during the afternoon of May 23, 1864. That evening Thomas W. Egan's First Brigade and Elijah Walker's Second Brigade of Birney's Third Division captured the enemy bridgehead on the north bank of the North Anna at Chesterfield Bridge. The next day Second Corps crossed to the south bank of the river and took position to the Union left of Ox Ford, in front of the enemy entrenchments. It remained there until the night of May 26, 1864, when Grant resumed his flanking movement to the left. Second Corps marched down the Pamunkey River toward Hanover Town, then crossed to the south bank of the river, and on May 29, 1864 advanced to the Totopotomoy River. The next evening Barlow's division of Second Corps attacked the enemy positions on its front for the purpose of relieving the pressure on Warren's Fifth Corps, which was engaged near Bethesda Church.

On the night of June 1, 1864, Second Corps started for Cold Harbor. It arrived there the next day and formed on the left of Sixth Corps, near the Chickahominy River. The corps took part in the assault at Cold Harbor June 3, 1864, and suffered heavy losses. There was no change in position until the night of June 12, 1864, and then the army began to move toward the James River. That night Second Corps and Sixth Corps withdrew to a newly prepared line of defenses in rear of Cold Harbor to cover the withdrawal of the rest of the army. When this was completed, Second Corps marched by way of Long Bridge, Saint Mary's Church, and Charles City Court House, and arrived at Willcox's Landing on the James June 13, 1864. Second Corps was the first corps to cross the river, and by the morning of June 15, 1864, it was assembled at Windmill Point on the south bank.

For details of the operations of Second Corps from the time it left Spotsylvania Court House until it crossed the James River, see Richmond, Virginia Campaign, 1864, Spotsylvania Court House to the North Anna River, Operations on the Pamunkey River, Operations on the Totopotomoy River, Totopotomoy River to Cold Harbor, Operations about Cold Harbor, and Cold Harbor to the James River.

The organization of Second Corps during the period May 22, 1864–June 15, 1864, including operations on the North Anna River, Pamunkey River, and Totopotomoy River, and the Battle of Cold Harbor, was as follows:

SECOND CORPS, Winfield S. Hancock

First Division, Francis C. Barlow
First Brigade, Nelson A. Miles
Second Brigade, Richard Byrnes, to June 3, 1864, wounded
Patrick Kelly
Third Brigade, Clinton D. MacDougall
Fourth Brigade, John R. Brooke, to June 3, 1864, wounded
Orlando H. Morris, June 3, 1864, killed
Lewis O. Morris, to June 4, 1864, killed
James A. Beaver

Second Division, John Gibbon
First Brigade, H. Boyd McKeen, to June 3, 1864, killed
Frank A. Haskell, June 3, 1864, killed
Byron R. Pierce, assigned June 4, 1864
Second Brigade, Joshua T. Owen, to June 12, 1864
John Fraser
Third Brigade, Thomas A. Smyth
Fourth Brigade, James P. McIvor, to May 29, 1864
Robert O. Tyler, to June 3, 1864, wounded
James P. McIvor, to June 7, 1864
John Ramsey

Note. Owen was charged with disobedience of orders, both at Spotsylvania Court House and at Cold Harbor, and Grant ordered him to Fort Monroe in arrest. He was mustered out of the service July 18, 1864.

Third Division, David B. Birney
First Brigade, Thomas W. Egan
Second Brigade, Elijah Walker, to May 23, 1864

Byron R. Pierce, to May 29, 1864
Thomas R. Tannatt
Third Brigade, Gershom Mott
Fourth Brigade, William R. Brewster

Fourth Division, Robert O. Tyler

Note. Fourth Division was not organized in brigades. It consisted of 1st Maine Heavy Artillery, 1st Massachusetts Heavy Artillery, 2nd New York Heavy Artillery, 7th New York Heavy Artillery, and 8th New York Heavy Artillery, all serving as infantry. The division was broken up May 29, 1864, and the regiments were assigned to the other divisions of the corps.

Artillery Brigade, John C. Tidball
10th Battery, Massachusetts Light Artillery, J. Henry Sleeper
Battery G, 1st New York Light Artillery, Nelson Ames
4th New York Heavy Artillery, John B. Vande Wiele
11th Battery, New York Light Artillery, John E. Burton
12th Battery, New York Light Artillery, George F. McKnight
Battery F, 1st Pennsylvania Light Artillery, R. Bruce Ricketts
Battery A, 1st Rhode Island Light Artillery, William A. Arnold
Battery B, 1st Rhode Island Light Artillery, T. Frederick Brown
Battery K, 4th United States Artillery, John W. Roder
Batteries C and I, 5th United States Artillery, James Gilliss

Operations about Petersburg, June 1864. Hancock's Second Corps marched from Windmill Point to the vicinity of Petersburg on June 15, 1864, and that night Birney's and Gibbon's divisions relieved troops of Eighteenth Corps on the line that they had gained in an attack that evening. Barlow's division, which had marched with the trains, arrived about daylight May 16, 1864, and formed on the left of Birney's division.

Second Corps was engaged in attacks on the enemy entrenchments May 16, 1864. That morning, Egan's First Brigade of Birney's division advanced and drove the enemy from his positions near the Dunn house and captured Battery No. 12. Egan was wounded and was succeeded in command of the brigade by Henry J. Madill. That evening, Second Corps launched a heavy attack on the Hare House Hill, where Fort Stedman was later built. For this attack, Birney was reinforced by John Fraser's Second Brigade and John Ramsey's Fourth Brigade of Gibbon's division and by the brigades of Louis Bell and Guy V. Henry of Eighteenth Corps. Simon G. Griffin's brigade and John F. Hartranft's brigade of Ninth Corps supported Barlow. The attack resulted in the capture of Batteries Nos. 13 and 14, but losses among the brigade commanders were heavy. In First Division, Kelly was killed and Beaver was wounded; in Second Division, John Fraser was wounded; and in Third Division, Tannatt, Levi P. Duff, and John Willian were all wounded while leading Second Brigade.

On June 17, 1864, all three divisions of Second Corps made unsuccessful attacks on the enemy works, and the corps also participated in the final assaults the next day. Hancock then entrenched his command on a line across the Prince George Court House Road near the Hare house, between John H. Martindale's command of Eighteenth Corps on the right and Ninth Corps on the left. For details of the operations of Second Corps during the attacks at Petersburg, see Operations about Petersburg and Richmond, Virginia, 1864–1865, Operations of June 1864, Assaults at Petersburg, June 15–18, 1864.

At 2:15 A.M. June 18, 1864, Hancock, who was suffering from the effects of the wound received at Gettysburg, turned over the command of Second Corps to Birney. Mott assumed command of Birney's Third Division, and Daniel Chaplin took command of Mott's Third Brigade. Hancock resumed command of the corps June 27, 1864.

After the final unsuccessful assaults at Petersburg, Grant ordered that the army begin siege operations. He decided to strengthen the investment of the town by extending the line of entrenchments westward toward the Petersburg and Weldon (Weldon) Railroad. Second Corps and Sixth Corps were selected for this operation. On June 20, 1864, Second Corps, then commanded by Birney, was relieved on the line of entrenchments and the next day marched beyond the left flank of the army toward the Weldon Railroad. Sixth Corps followed Second Corps.

On June 22, 1864, while Second Corps was attempting to come into line on the left of Fifth Corps, west of the Jerusalem Plank Road, Ambrose P. Hill's Confederate corps struck its left flank and rear and drove it back in some confusion to its positions of the night before. The next day Second Corps

advanced with little opposition to the left of Fifth Corps and entrenched its position. For details of this movement, and the engagement near the Jerusalem Plank Road, see Operations about Petersburg and Richmond, Virginia, 1864–1865, Operations of June 1864, Movement against the Petersburg and Weldon (Weldon) Railroad (Engagement near the Jerusalem Plank Road, June 22, 1864).

Sixth Corps advanced on the left of Second Corps June 22, 1864, but it was not engaged. The next day it took position on the left of Second Corps. June 23, 1864, Fifth Corps relieved Gibbon's division of Second Corps, and the latter moved to the left of Sixth Corps. On June 29, 1864, Sixth Corps advanced to Reams' Station on the Weldon Railroad, and then Gibbon's division moved back to the left of the other divisions of Second Corps, where it occupied the works vacated by Sixth Corps.

The organization of Second Corps during the last two weeks of June 1864 was as follows:

SECOND CORPS, Winfield S. Hancock, to June 18, 1864, disabled
    David B. Birney, to June 27, 1864
    Winfield S. Hancock

First Division, Francis C. Barlow
    First Brigade, Nelson A. Miles
    Second Brigade, Patrick Kelly, to June 16, 1864, killed
    Third Brigade, Clinton D. MacDougall
    Fourth Brigade, James A. Beaver, to June 16, 1864, wounded
        John Hastings, to June 21, 1864
        John Fraser, to June 22, 1864, captured
        John Hastings

Note. On June 27, 1864, Second Brigade and Third Brigade were consolidated under the command of MacDougall. First Division then consisted of Miles' First Brigade, MacDougall's Consolidated Brigade, and Hastings' Fourth Brigade.

Second Division, John Gibbon
    First Brigade, Byron R. Pierce, to June 22, 1864
        Major William F. Smith, to June 27, 1864
        Francis E. Pierce
    Second Brigade, John Fraser, to June 21, 1864
        Timothy O'Brien, to June 26, 1864
        James McIvor
    Third Brigade, Thomas A. Smyth
    Fourth Brigade, John Ramsey, to June 12, 1864, wounded
        James P. McIvor, to June 20, 1864

William Blaisdell, to June 23, 1864, killed

James P. McIvor, to June 26, 1864, brigade discontinued

Note 1. Byron R. Pierce was relieved from command of First Brigade, and was assigned command of Second Brigade, Third Division June 24, 1864.

Note 2. Second Division was reorganized June 26, 1864. Second Brigade was broken up, and the regiments were assigned to First Brigade and Third Brigade. The designation of Fourth Brigade was then changed to Second Brigade, Second Division.

Third Division, David B. Birney, to June 18, 1864

  Gershom Mott, to June 27, 1864

  David B. Birney

  First Brigade, Thomas W. Egan, to June 16, 1864, wounded

    Henry J. Madill

  Second Brigade, Thomas R. Tannatt, to June 16, 1864, wounded

    Levi B. Duff, June 16, 1864

    John Willian, June 16, 1864

    Robert McAllister, to June 24, 1864

    Byron R. Pierce

  Third Brigade, Gershom Mott, to June 18, 1864

    Daniel Chaplin, to June 27, 1864

    Gershom Mott

  Fourth Brigade, William R. Brewster

  Artillery Brigade, John C. Tidball

    6th Battery (F), Maine Light Artillery, Edwin B. Dow

    10th Battery, Massachusetts Light Artillery, J. Henry Sleeper

    1st Battery, New Hampshire Light Artillery, Frederick M. Edgell

    Battery B, 1st New Jersey Light Artillery, A. Judson Clark

    3rd Battery, New Jersey Light Artillery, Christian Woerner

    4th New York Heavy Artillery, John Vande Wiele

    Battery G, 1st New York Light Artillery, Nelson Ames

    11th Battery, New York Light Artillery, John E. Burton

    12th Battery, New York Light Artillery, George F. McKnight

    Battery F, 1st Pennsylvania Light Artillery, R. Bruce Ricketts

    Battery A, 1st Rhode Island Light Artillery, G. Lyman Dwight

    Battery B, 1st Rhode Island Light Artillery, T. Frederick Brown

    Battery K, 4th United States Light Artillery, John W. Roder

    Batteries C and I, 5th United States Artillery, James Gilliss

Note. The 1st and 2nd battalions of the 4th New York Heavy Artillery were assigned, respectively, to First Brigade and Second Brigade, Third Division, June 25, 1864.

Operations about Petersburg and Richmond, July 1864. During July 1864, Second Corps was relatively inactive until late in the month. On July 12, 1864, the troops destroyed their works on the left of Fifth Corps, and the next day moved to the vicinity of Deserted House, in rear of Fifth Corps, as a reserve. On July 17, 1864, Second Division, Second Corps moved out and occupied the left of the Federal line of entrenchments. On July 26, 1864, Hancock marched with his corps for a demonstration on the north side of the James River. Accompanied by Torbert's and Gregg's cavalry divisions, Second Corps crossed the James at Deep Bottom and advanced to the New Market Road. Hancock skirmished with the enemy along Bailey's Creek July 27–29, 1864, but he did not order an assault on the entrenchments.

On the night of July 28, 1864, Hancock sent Mott's division back to the Petersburg front to relieve Eighteenth Corps in the entrenchments. The latter was needed to support Ninth Corps in an assault scheduled for July 30, 1864, after the explosion of a mine under the enemy works. During the night of July 29, 1864, Hancock recrossed the James River with the other two divisions of Second Corps, and marched to the lines at Petersburg, where he massed troops in rear of Ninth Corps. Second Corps was not engaged in the Battle at the "Crater" July 30, 1864, and that evening it moved back to the vicinity of Deserted House, where it was again placed in reserve.

For details of Hancock's movement north of the James River, see Operations about Petersburg and Richmond, Virginia, 1864–1865, Operations of July 1864, Demonstration on the North Bank of the James River, Engagement at Deep Bottom (or Darbytown, Strawberry Plains, New Market Road), Virginia, July 27–29, 1864.

The organization of Second Corps during the month of July 1864 was as follows:

SECOND CORPS, Winfield S. Hancock

First Division, Francis C. Barlow, to July 29, 1864, sick

  Nelson A. Miles

First Brigade, Nelson A. Miles, to July 29, 1864
  James C. Lynch
Consolidated Brigade, Clinton D. MacDougall, to July 3, 1864
  Levin C. Crandell
Fourth Brigade, John Hastings, to July 25, 1864
  K. Oscar Broady

Second Division, John Gibbon, to July 18, 1864
  Thomas A. Smyth, to July 23, 1864
  John Gibbon, to July 31, 1864
  Thomas A. Smyth
  First Brigade, Francis E. Pierce
  Second Brigade, James P. McIvor, to July 14, 1864
    Mathew Murphy
  Third Brigade, Thomas A. Smyth, to July 18, 1864
    Henry A. Cook, to July 23, 1864
    Thomas A. Smyth, to July 31, 1864
    Samuel A. Moore

Third Division, David B. Birney, to July 23, 1864
  Gershom Mott
  First Brigade, Henry J. Madill, to July 12, 1864
    P. Regis De Trobriand
  Second Brigade, Byron R. Pierce, to July 26, 1864, sick
    Daniel Chaplin, to July 28, 1864
    Henry J. Madill
  Third Brigade, Gershom Mott, to July 23, 1864
    Robert McAllister
  Fourth Brigade, William R. Brewster, to July 5, 1864

Note 1. Birney was assigned command of Tenth Corps July 23, 1864.

Note 2. Brewster's Fourth Brigade was discontinued July 5, 1864, and the regiments were assigned to the three remaining brigades of the division.

Artillery Brigade, John C. Tidball, to July 6, 1864
  John G. Hazard

Note 1. Tidball was relieved from duty in the Army of the Potomac July 6, 1864, and was assigned as commandant of cadets at West Point.

Note 2. The batteries with Second Corps in July 1864 were the same as for June 1864.

Operations about Petersburg and Richmond, August 1864.

Second Corps remained in reserve near Deserted House, in rear of the entrenchments, until August 12, 1864, and it then marched toward City Point, en route to Deep Bottom for another demonstration on the north bank of the James River. It arrived at Deep Bottom on the morning of August 14, 1864, and was joined there by Birney's Tenth Corps, Army of the James and Gregg's cavalry division. This force, under the command of Hancock, was under orders to advance on the Confederate works covering Richmond and stage a demonstration. Hancock's troops were engaged in considerable skirmishing and in some severe fighting during the next few days, but they were unable to penetrate the enemy defenses.

Mott's division returned to the Petersburg front August 18, 1864, and the next morning relieved the divisions of Julius White and Robert B. Potter of Ninth Corps on the left of the line of entrenchments, near the Jerusalem Plank Road. Mott remained on this part of the line during the remainder of the month. White's and Potter's divisions, when relieved, moved toward the Weldon Railroad to support Warren's Fifth Corps, which was engaged near Globe Tavern at that time. On the afternoon of August 20, 1864, Hancock, with the divisions of Barlow (commanded by Miles) and Gibbon, recrossed the James River, and early the next morning arrived at his old camps near Deserted House.

For details of Hancock's second demonstration, see Operations about Petersburg and Richmond, Virginia, 1864–1865, Operations of August 1864, Demonstration on the North Bank of the James River at Deep Bottom (Combats at Fussell's Mill, Gravel Hill, Bailey's Creek, Deep Run [or Creek], White's Tavern, Charles City Road, and New Market Road), Virginia, August 13–20, 1864.

Hancock paused only briefly at Deserted House, and on the afternoon of August 21, 1864, he marched on toward the Weldon Railroad with orders to destroy the road as far south as Rowanty Creek. Samuel P. Spear's brigade of August V. Kautz's Cavalry Division, Army of the James was ordered to report to Hancock and cover the front of the infantry. Miles' division began the work of destruction August 22, 1864, and two days later it had reached a point a few miles south of Reams' Station. Gibbon's division relieved Miles' troops, and August 25, 1864, was ordered out on a reconnaissance and also to continue the destruction of the road. That morning, however, a strong force of enemy cavalry and infantry appeared, and both Miles and Gibbon took up a defensive position at Reams' Station. Hancock's command was strongly attacked that afternoon and was driven from its works, and finally, at dark, it withdrew to a position near the Williams house. For details of the activities of Second Corps during this period, and also of the Battle of Reams' Station, see Operations about Petersburg and Richmond, Virginia, 1864–1865, Operations of August 1864, Battle of Reams' Station, Virginia.

Miles' and Gibbon's divisions remained near the Williams house until August 27, 1864, and they then moved to the vicinity of the Jones house, near the Jerusalem Plank Road. While there, they supported various parts of the line of entrenchments and furnished details to work on the fortifications.

The organization of Second Corps during August 1864 was as follows:

SECOND CORPS, Winfield S. Hancock

First Division, Francis C. Barlow, to August 17, 1864, sick
  Nelson A. Miles, to August 23, 1864
  Francis C. Barlow, to August 24, 1864, sick
  Nelson A. Miles
  First Brigade, Nelson A. Miles, to August 17, 1864
    James C. Lynch, to August 23, 1864
    Nelson A. Miles, to August 24, 1864
    James C. Lynch
  Consolidated Brigade, Levin C. Crandell, to August 29, 1864
    Nelson Penfield
    William Wilson
  Fourth Brigade, K. Oscar Broady, to August 25, 1864, wounded
    William Glenny

Note 1. On the evening of August 24, 1864, Crandell was ordered to take charge of the picket line at Reams' Station, and was thus separated from his brigade during the engagement the next day. Captain Penfield was left in command of the brigade. About noon August 25, 1864, Broady assumed control of both his own First Brigade and the Consolidated Brigade.

Note 2. During August 1864, reports frequently referred to the Irish Brigade (Second Brigade) and Third Brigade of First Division, although at that time they had no such official designation. These were the two brigades that were combined to form the Consolidated Brigade. The above designations apparently referred to the former association of the regiments involved.

Second Division, Thomas A. Smyth, to August 22, 1864
  John Gibbon
  First Brigade, Francis E. Pierce, to August 13, 1864
    George N. Macy, to August 14, 1864, disabled
    Horace P. Rugg
  Second Brigade, Mathew Murphy
  Third Brigade, Samuel A. Moore, to August 14, 1864

  Francis E. Pierce, to August 23, 1864
  Thomas A. Smyth

Third Division, Gershom Mott
  First Brigade, P. Regis De Trobriand
  Second Brigade, Henry J. Madill, to August 11, 1864
    Calvin Craig, to August 16, 1864, killed
    John Pulford, to August 26, 1864
    Byron R. Pierce
  Third Brigade, Robert McAllister

Artillery Brigade, John G. Hazard

Note 1. A. Judson Clark assumed temporary command of the Artillery Brigade August 12, 1864, during the absence of Hazard.

Note 2. The batteries with Second Corps during August 1864 were essentially the same as those with the corps during June 1864.

Operations about Petersburg, September and October 1864. During most of September and October 1864, Second Corps occupied the line of entrenchments at Petersburg, or was in reserve. Mott's Third Division held the line from the Strong house, about one mile west of the Jerusalem Plank Road (Fort Alexander Hays), to the Norfolk and Petersburg Railroad. Miles' First Division and Gibbon's Second Division were held in reserve, and were engaged principally in constructing defensive works, especially on the rear line from the Jerusalem Plank Road eastward to the Norfolk and Petersburg Railroad. After September 10, 1864, Miles' division was in camp near Deserted House, and Gibbon's division (then commanded by Smyth) was near the Jones house and the Chieves house.

On the night of September 24, 1864, Miles' and Gibbon's divisions relieved Tenth Corps on the right of the line of works, so that the latter could take part in Benjamin F. Butler's movement with the Army of the James against Richmond. Miles' division held the right of the line from Battery No. 13 to the Appomattox River, and Gibbon's division extended to the left from Battery No. 13 to the Norfolk and Petersburg Railroad, where it connected with the right of Mott's division. Second Corps then occupied the entrenchments from the Appomattox River to Fort Alexander Hays, west of the Jerusalem Plank Road. Headquarters of the corps was established at Deserted House September 25, 1864.

On September 30, 1864, Grant began an autumn offensive against Lee's communications south and southwest of Petersburg. On that date, Fifth Corps and Ninth Corps moved out from the Weldon Railroad toward Poplar Spring Church, while Second Corps remained to hold the entrenchments. Early on the morning of October 1, 1864, however, Mott's division was withdrawn from the line and was sent west to reinforce Fifth Corps and Ninth Corps, which were then engaged around Poplar Spring Church, west of the Weldon Railroad. When Mott departed, the other two divisions of Second Corps extended to the left to cover the front as far as Fort Davis. Miles' division then held the front from the Appomattox to Fort Meikel, and Gibbon's division from Fort Meikel to Fort Davis. Edward Ferrero's Third Division, Ninth Corps occupied that part of Mott's former line from Fort Alexander Hays to Fort Davis and also extended to the left to the vicinity of the Weldon Railroad.

Mott arrived at Peebles' farm on the evening of October 1, 1864, and was assigned temporarily to John G. Parke's Ninth Corps. The next morning Mott advanced with his division on the left of Ninth Corps, and was engaged later in the day in the combat along the Harman Road, near Mrs. Hart's house. He withdrew that night and formed on the extreme left of the new Union line at Peebles' farm, near the Clements house. Mott was relieved by Ferrero's division October 5, 1864, and he then rejoined Second Corps on the line of entrenchments. For details of the operations around Poplar Spring Church and the operations of Mott's division October 1–2, 1864, see Operations about Petersburg and Richmond, Virginia, 1864–1865, Operations of September 1864, Battle of Poplar Spring Church (Combats at Wyatt's Farm, Peebles' Farm, Chappell's House, Pegram's Farm, and Vaughan's Road), Virginia.

During most of October 1864, Second Corps occupied the Petersburg entrenchments as follows: Mott's division from Fort Hays to Fort Sedgwick, Gibbon's division from Fort Sedgwick to Fort Morton, and Miles' division from Fort Morton to the Appomattox River. Late in the month, Grant made another effort to cut Lee's communications south and west of Petersburg, and Second Division and Third Division of Second Corps were selected to accompany this movement. During the night of October 24, 1864, these two divisions were relieved in the trenches by First Division, and they then moved back and camped near Southalls' house. This was between the United States Military Railroad and the Norfolk and Petersburg Railroad, a short distance south of their intersection. First Division was left to hold the entrenchments from the Appomattox River to Battery No. 24.

At 2:00 P.M. October 26, 1864, Hancock marched with his Second Division (temporarily commanded by Thomas W. Egan) and his Third Division by way of the Widow Smith's house, the Williams house, and the Gurley house, and bivouacked that night near the Lewis house and the Perkins house, in the vicinity of Fort Dushane on the Weldon Railroad. The next day he marched around the left of the army to the Boydton Plank Road, and was engaged that afternoon near Burgess' Mill on Hatcher's Run. Hancock's divisions repulsed a strong Confederate attack by William Mahone's and Henry Heth's infantry divisions and Wade Hampton's cavalry, and at 10:00 that night began to withdraw by the route that they had followed that morning. On October 28, 1864, Second Division arrived at Fort Bross and Third Division at Southalls' house. For details of this operation, see Operations about Petersburg and Richmond, Virginia, 1864–1865, Operations of October 1864, Engagement at the Boydton Plank Road (or Hatcher's Run), Virginia.

On the night of October 30, 1864, Mott's division relieved Miles' First Division garrisons in Battery No. 24, Forts Hays, Davis, Sedgwick, Rice, Meikel, and Morton, and Battery No. 14. The replaced troops of First Division were then sent to garrison the forts on the rear line of entrenchments, relieving Gibbon's Second Division. On the night of October 31, 1864, Gibbon's division relieved the rest of the troops of Miles' division in Forts Haskell and Stedman, Battery No. 10 and Battery No. 9, Fort McGilvery, Battery No. 5 and Battery No. 4, and the Dunn House Battery.

The organization of Second Corps during September and October 1864 was as follows:

SECOND CORPS, Winfield S. Hancock

First Division, Nelson A. Miles
   First Brigade, James Lynch, to October 6, 1864
      William Wilson, October 27, 1864
      K. Oscar Broady

Consolidated Brigade, William Wilson, to September 12, 1864

    James E. McGee, to October 13, 1864

    George N. Macy, to October 27, 1864

    Clinton D. MacDougall

Fourth Brigade, William Glenny, to October 7, 1864

    Hiram L. Brown, to October 15, 1864

    St. Clair Mulholland

Second Division, John Gibbon, to September 4, 1864

    Thomas A. Smyth, September 6, 1864 to September 25, 1864

    John Gibbon, to October 8, 1864, on leave

    Thomas W. Egan, to October 29, 1864

    John Gibbon

    First Brigade, Horace P. Rugg, to September 26, 1864

        Thomas W. Egan, to October 8, 1864

        Horace P. Rugg, to October 29, 1864

        Thomas W. Egan

    Second Brigade, Mathew Murphy, to October 1864

        James M. Willett, temporarily in late October 1864

        James P. McIvor, commanding at the end of October

    Third Brigade, Thomas A. Smyth, to September 6, 1864

        Francis E. Pierce, to September 25, 1864

        Thomas A. Smyth

Third Division, Gershom Mott, to October 8, 1864, on leave

    P. Regis De Trobriand, to October 21, 1864

    Gershom Mott

    First Brigade, P. Regis De Trobriand, to October 8, 1864

        William R. Brewster, to October 21, 1864

        P. Regis De Trobriand

    Second Brigade, Byron R. Pierce

    Third Brigade, Robert McAllister

Artillery Brigade, John G. Hazard

Note 1. Frederick M. Edgell assumed temporary command of the brigade September 4, 1864, during the absence of Hazard.

Note 2. The batteries serving with Second Corps during September and October 1864 were essentially the same as at the end of June 1864.

Winter of 1864–1865. On November 25, 1864, Hancock, who was still suffering from the wound received at Gettysburg, was granted a leave of absence. Three days later he was assigned command of a new Veteran Volunteer Corps, to be designated as First Corps, and was ordered to Washington to recruit and organize this new corps. Organization was to begin December 1, 1864, but progress was slow, and February 27, 1865, Hancock assumed command of the Middle Military Division and also the Department of West Virginia. He did not return to Second Corps. He was succeeded in temporary command of Second Corps November 26, 1864 by Andrew A. Humphreys, at that time chief of staff to George G. Meade. It was not until March 27, 1865 that Humphreys was assigned by the president to the permanent command of Second Corps.

Until November 30, 1864, Second Corps occupied the line of entrenchments on the right of the army, from the Appomattox River to Battery No. 24, near the Strong house. Gibbon's Second Division was on the right, from the river to Fort Meikel, on the Norfolk and Petersburg Railroad; Mott's Third Division was on the left, from Fort Meikel to Battery No. 24; and Miles' First Division was in reserve near the Southall house.

By an order of November 28, 1864, Second Corps and Ninth Corps exchanged places on the line of entrenchments. Miles' division marched from its camps near Southalls' and relieved Orlando B. Willcox's First Division and Robert B. Potter's Second Division of Ninth Corps, and then took their place on the line from Fort Fisher, on the Church Road, to Fort Sampson, including both forts, and also Forts Gregg and Welch. Potter and Willcox then moved to the right and relieved the other two divisions of Second Corps in the entrenchments. Willcox relieved Gibbon's division, and Potter relieved Mott's division. Mott and Gibbon then marched to the left and, with Miles' division, occupied the works previously held by Ninth Corps. When the transfer was completed, Gibbon's division was on the left, from Fort Seibert to a point about midway between Fort Clarke and Fort Dushane; Mott's division was between Fort Seibert and Fort Cummings; and Miles, as noted above, was on the right from Fort Cummings to Fort Fisher. Headquarters of Second Corps was established at Peebles' house. Second Corps generally remained on this line until February 9, 1865, although troops were withdrawn on three occasions to take part in operations to the south of the entrenchments.

On December 7, 1864, Mott's division accompanied an expedition under Gouverneur K. Warren to Hicksford (present-day Emporia), Virginia to destroy the Weldon Railroad. It did not return to its position in front of Forts Clarke and Seibert until December 12, 1864. For details of this expedition, see Operations about Petersburg and Richmond, Virginia, 1864–1865, Winter of 1864–1865, Warren's Expedition to Hicksford, Virginia.

On December 9, 1864, while Mott's division was absent with Warren, Miles was sent with his First Division down the Vaughan Road on a reconnaissance to Hatcher's Run to learn what he could of enemy troop movements in that area. Miles returned to his position on the line of entrenchments the next day. For details of this movement, see Operations about Petersburg and Richmond, Virginia, 1864–1865, Winter of 1864–1865, Reconnaissance to Hatcher's Run, Virginia.

The organization of Second Corps at the end of December 1864 was as follows:

SECOND CORPS, Andrew A. Humphreys

First Division, Nelson A. Miles
First Brigade, George N. Macy
Second Brigade, Robert Nugent
Third Brigade, Clinton D. MacDougall
Fourth Brigade, William Glenny

Second Division, John Gibbon
First Brigade, James M. Willett
Second Brigade, Mathew Murphy
Third Brigade, Francis E. Pierce

Third Division, Gershom Mott
First Brigade, P. Regis De Trobriand
Second Brigade, Byron R. Pierce
Third Brigade, John Ramsey

Artillery Brigade, John G. Hazard
6th Battery (F), Maine Light Artillery, William H. Rogers
10th Battery, Massachusetts Light Artillery, J. Henry Sleeper
Battery M, 1st Hew Hampshire Light Artillery, Frederick M. Edgell
Battery B, 1st New Jersey Light Artillery, A. Judson Clark
3rd Battery, New Jersey Light Artillery, Christian Woerner
Battery G, 1st New York Light Artillery, Samuel A. McClellan
Battery C, 4th New York Heavy Artillery, James H. Wood
Battery L, 4th New York Heavy Artillery, Richard Kennedy
11th Battery, New York Light Artillery, George W. Davey
12th Battery, New York Light Artillery, William S. Bull
Battery F, 1st Pennsylvania Light Artillery, John F. Campbell
Battery B, 1st Rhode Island Light Artillery, T. Frederick Brown
Battery K, 4th United States Artillery, John W. Roder
Batteries C and I, 5th United States Artillery, W. Butler Beck

There was no significant activity on the lines of Second Corps during January 1865, but early in the following month the corps took part in an operation that resulted in some sharp fighting, and an extension to the left of the Union siege line. On the morning of February 7, 1865, David McM. Gregg's Second Cavalry Division, Army of the Potomac advanced to Dinwiddie Court House to break up wagon trains reported to be using the Boydton Plank Road, and Warren's Fifth Corps moved up in support. That same morning, Humphreys, with Thomas A. Smyth's Second Division (Gibbon had been assigned command of Twenty-Fourth Corps January 15, 1865) and Gershom Mott's Third Division, marched down the Vaughan Road to Hatcher's Run, at the road crossing, and to Armstrong's Mill. Humphreys then took up a defensive position a few miles in rear of Warren. John Ramsey's Fourth Brigade of Miles' First Division came up and joined Humphreys later in the day. That afternoon the enemy launched several attacks against the Second Corps' new line, but all were repulsed. George Von Schack's Third Brigade of Miles' division was also sent up from the line of entrenchments in support, but, not being needed, it returned to its former position that night. A division of Sixth Corps and a division of Ninth Corps were sent to reinforce Humphreys that evening, and they formed on the right of Second Corps. Second Corps remained in position during February 6 and 7, 1865, while Fifth Corps and Gregg's cavalry were engaged south of Hatcher's Run. For details of the above operations, see Operations about Petersburg and Richmond, 1864–1865, Winter of 1864–1865, Battle of Hatcher's Run (or Dabney's Mill, Armstrong's Mill, Rowanty Creek, Vaughan Road), Virginia.

The organization of Second Corps at the Battle of Hatcher's Run was as follows:

SECOND CORPS, Andrew A. Humphreys

First Division, Nelson A. Miles
First Brigade, George N. Macy
Second Brigade, Robert Nugent, to January 29, 1865, on leave
Richard C. Duryea
Third Brigade, Henry J. Madill, to January 28, 1865, on leave
George Von Schack
Fourth Brigade, John Ramsey

Note. First Division was not engaged at the Battle of Hatcher's Run.

Second Division, Thomas A. Smyth
First Brigade, William A. Olmsted
Second Brigade, Mathew Murphy, to February 5, 1865, mortally wounded
James P. McIvor
Third Brigade, Francis E. Pierce

Note. John Gibbon was relieved from command of Second Division, and January 15, 1865 was assigned command of Twenty-Fourth Corps, Army of the James.

Third Division, Gershom Mott
First Brigade, P. Regis De Trobriand
Second Brigade, Byron Pierce, to January 24, 1865, on leave
George W. West
Third Brigade, Robert McAllister

Artillery Brigade, John G. Hazard
10th Battery, Massachusetts Light Artillery, J. Webb Adams
Battery K, 4th United States Artillery, John W. Roder

Note 1. Only the above two batteries were taken with the corps on this expedition.
Note 2. One section of Battery B, 1st Rhode Island Light Artillery was attached to 10th Battery, Massachusetts Light Artillery on this expedition.

On February 9, 1865, Meade ordered the construction of a new line of entrenchments along the front recently gained by Humphreys' command, and that day Miles' division and Mott's division occupied this position, which began at Fort Sampson on the old line and extended toward Hatcher's Run. Two days later, Smyth's division, which was watching the fords, moved back from Armstrong's Mill and occupied the left of the new line that extended along Hatcher's Run to the Vaughan Road Crossing.

For additional information, see Operations about Petersburg and Richmond, Virginia, 1864–1865, Winter of 1864–1865, Siege of Petersburg, Virginia.

There was little change in position of Second Corps until March 29, 1865, when Grant began his final offensive at Petersburg. There was, however, considerable activity along the siege line March 25, 1865. That morning, a Confederate force under John B. Gordon attacked on the front held by Ninth Corps, and captured Fort Stedman and all of the front-line works from Battery No. 9 to Fort Haskell. That afternoon, Humphreys was ordered to make a demonstration on his front to determine whether the enemy lines had been weakened by supporting Gordon; and, if this was found to be so, to attack. All three divisions advanced skirmishers, which were strongly supported. They captured the enemy's entrenched picket line, and took many prisoners. The enemy's main line, however, was found to be too strongly held for a successful attack, and that night Second Corps returned to their former positions. For details of the action of March 25, 1865, see Operations about Petersburg and Richmond, Virginia, 1864–1865, Winter of 1864–1865, Assault at Fort Stedman, Virginia.

There was only one significant organizational change in Second Corps during the winter. It has been noted that on June 27, 1864, Second Brigade and Third Brigade were consolidated into a single brigade because of the heavy losses that they had suffered during the early weeks of the Campaign of 1864. By an order of November 2, 1864, these two brigades were again separately organized, primarily because of the return of Robert Nugent, who, on October 30, 1864, had been recommissioned as colonel of his old regiment, the 69th New York. The brigades were brought up to strength by the transfer of 28th Massachusetts from First Brigade, First Division and the 7th New York Heavy Artillery from Fourth Brigade, First Division to the new Second Brigade. Nugent was assigned command of Second Brigade, and George N. Macy was assigned command of Third Brigade. The order assigning Macy was rescinded November 4, 1864, and Clinton D. MacDougall was assigned command of Third Brigade. On November 7, 1864, Macy was assigned command of First Brigade, relieving William Wilson. First Division was then organized as follows:

First Division, Nelson A. Miles

First Brigade, George N. Macy
Second Brigade, Robert Nugent
Third Brigade, Clinton D. MacDougall
Fourth Brigade, St. Clair A. Mulholland

Note. The above reorganization was proposed October 31, 1864, and Nugent assumed command of Second Brigade November 1, 1864, and the brigade was organized on that date.

Appomattox Campaign, March 29, 1865–April 9, 1865. Grant began his spring offensive at Petersburg on March 29, 1865. That morning, Humphreys' Second Corps was relieved on the line of entrenchments by three divisions of the Army of the James under the command of Edward O. C. Ord. Humphreys then moved his corps to the south side of Hatcher's Run and moved up to a new position on the right of Warren's Fifth Corps. His line then extended from the Crow house to the vicinity of Burgess' Mill on the Boydton Plank Road. The Fifth Corps line extended westward from the left of Second Corps along the White Oak Road. Second Corps supported Fifth Corps in the engagement on the White Oak Road March 31, 1865, and then remained in position along Hatcher's Run until the morning of April 2, 1865. For additional information, see Appomattox Campaign, The Opening Moves, Engagement at the Lewis House, Advance to Hatcher's Run, and Engagement at the White Oak Road (or White Oak Ridge), Virginia.

During the night of April 1, 1865, following the Battle of Five Forks, Miles' division of Second Corps was sent out on the White Oak Road to reinforce Sheridan. The next morning, after Sixth Corps had broken through the enemy line on his right, Humphreys ordered his two remaining divisions to advance against the enemy works on their front. These were soon abandoned, and Second Corps joined in the general advance of the army toward the city of Petersburg.

Miles' division, which had joined Sheridan at Five Forks early that morning, April 2, 1865, then returned on the White Oak Road and moved up the Claiborne Road in pursuit of the enemy troops that were retiring after having been driven from their works. That afternoon, Miles found these troops entrenched near Sutherland's Station and, after several attacks, drove them back toward the Appomattox River. Henry J. Madill was wounded in this action, and he was succeeded in command of Third Brigade by Clinton D. MacDougall. Humphreys, with the divisions of Hays and Mott, arrived before the inner defenses of Petersburg, and took position on the left of the Union line, west of the city. About 10:30 that night, in preparation for the movements of the next day, Second Corps was placed under Sheridan's orders. For details of the activities of April 2, 1865, see Appomattox Campaign, Breakthrough at Petersburg.

Petersburg was evacuated by the enemy during the night of April 2, 1865; and early the next morning, Sheridan, with his cavalry, Second Corps, and Fifth Corps, moved west along the south side of the Appomattox River toward Jetersville on the Richmond and Danville Railroad. Second Corps marched under Sheridan's orders during the day, but at 4:30 that afternoon Meade resumed control of the corps. George Crook's cavalry division and Fifth Corps were the first troops to arrive at Jetersville, and they formed a defensive line across the railroad. This was done to prevent Lee's army, which was then assembling at Amelia Court House, from escaping to Danville by marching along the railroad. Second Corps arrived during the afternoon of April 5, 1865, and formed on the left of Fifth Corps.

During the night of April 5, 1865, Lee moved west by the road through Deatonsville, toward Rice's Station on the South Side Railroad, and early on the morning of April 6, 1865, Sheridan's cavalry and Meade's infantry started in pursuit. Second Corps marched through Deatonsville and skirmished with Lee's rear guard during most of the day. Mott was wounded that morning near Amelia Springs, and De Trobriand succeeded him in command of Third Division.

As Humphreys approached Little Sayler's Creek that afternoon, he turned off to the right on the Jamestown Road, and followed John B. Gordon's Confederate corps, which was guarding the army trains. That evening, while Sixth Corps was engaged with Richard S. Ewell's command a few miles to the south, Second Corps attacked and defeated Gordon's corps at Locketts' farm. It also destroyed much of the enemy wagon train and captured many prisoners. For details, see Appomattox Campaign, Pursuit of the Army of Northern Virginia, and also Appomattox Campaign, Battle of Sayler's Creek.

On the morning of April 6, 1865, William Hays, commanding Second Division, was assigned command of the Artillery Reserve of the Army of the Potomac, and Thomas A. Smyth assumed temporary command of the division. Francis C. Barlow arrived about an hour later and relieved Smyth.

On the morning of April 7, 1865, Second Corps marched along the south bank of the Appomattox and followed the remnants of Gordon's command across the river at High Bridge. Barlow's division then moved on after Gordon along the South Side Railroad toward Farmville. Humphreys, with the divisions of Miles and De Trobriand, marched to the northwest to the vicinity of Cumberland Church, about three miles north of Farmville. Miles' division attacked the enemy position at Cumberland Church that afternoon but was repulsed. Barlow's division had a sharp engagement with Gordon's rear guard near Farmville, during which Smyth was mortally wounded. He was succeeded in command of Third Brigade by Daniel Woodall. Barlow's division rejoined the corps at Cumberland Church that evening.

During the night of April 7, 1865, Lee resumed his retreat toward Appomattox Court House, and early the next morning Meade followed with Second Corps and Sixth Corps. Second Corps marched by way of New Store and camped on the night of April 8, 1865 about nine miles from Appomattox Court House and three miles in rear of Longstreet's corps. The next morning, Second Corps advanced toward Appomattox Court House, and was preparing for an attack on Longstreet's line when the fighting ended under a flag of truce. That afternoon, April 9, 1865, Lee surrendered to Grant the Army of Northern Virginia. For additional information, see Appomattox Campaign, Movements of the Armies to Appomattox Court House, April 7–9, 1865.

The organization of Second Corps during the Appomattox Campaign was as follows:

SECOND CORPS, Andrew A. Humphreys

First Division, Nelson A. Miles
   First Brigade, George W. Scott
   Second Brigade, Robert Nugent
   Third Brigade, Henry J. Madill, to April 2, 1865, wounded
     Clinton D. MacDougall
   Fourth Brigade, John Ramsey

Second Division, William Hays, to April 6, 1865
   Thomas A. Smyth, April 6, 1865

   Francis C. Barlow
   First Brigade, William A. Olmsted
   Second Brigade, James P. McIvor
   Third Brigade, Thomas A. Smyth, to April 6, 1865
     Daniel Woodall
     Thomas A. Smyth, to April 7, 1865, mortally wounded
     Daniel Woodall

Note 1. Hays was assigned command of the Artillery Reserve of the Army of the Potomac about 9:00 A.M. April 6, 1865, and Smyth assumed temporary command of Second Division. About one hour later, Barlow arrived and relieved Smyth.

Note 2. Smyth was mortally wounded April 7, 1865 in an engagement near Farmville.

Third Division, Gershom Mott, to April 6, 1865, wounded
   P. Regis De Trobriand
   First Brigade, P. Regis De Trobriand, to April 6, 1865
     Russell B. Shepherd
   Second Brigade, Byron R. Pierce
   Third Brigade, Robert McAllister

Note. Mott was wounded during skirmishing near Amelia Springs April 6, 1865.

Artillery Brigade, John G. Hazard
   10th Battery, Massachusetts Light Artillery, J. Webb Adams
   Battery M, 1st New Hampshire Light Artillery, George K. Dakin
   Battery B, 1st New Jersey Light Artillery, A. Judson Clark
   11th Battery, New York Light Artillery, James A. Manning
   Company C, 4th New York Heavy Artillery, Richard Kennedy
   Company L, 4th New York Heavy Artillery, Frank Seymour
   Battery B, 1st Rhode Island Light Artillery, William B. Westcott
   Battery K, 4th United States Artillery, John W. Roder

After Appomattox. After the surrender of the Army of Northern Virginia at Appomattox Court House April 9, 1865, Joseph E. Johnston remained in the field with an army of about 30,000 men confronting William T. Sherman in North Carolina. It was not known at that time whether Johnston would also surrender or continue fighting; consequently, Grant prepared for the latter eventuality. He directed Charles Griffin's Fifth Corps, Army of the Potomac and John Gibbon's Twenty-Fourth Corps, Army of the James to remain at Appomattox Court House until paroles were issued and the surrendered property was removed to the railroad; and he then ordered the rest of the army to move to Burkeville, Virginia, where it would be in position to march into North Carolina if necessary.

April 11, 1865, Second Corps left Appomattox Court House and marched by way of New Store, Curdsville, and Farmville on its way to Burkeville. It arrived there and went into camp April 13, 1865. When Johnston surrendered his army to Sherman near Durham Station, North Carolina April 26, 1865, there was no longer any need for the Army of the Potomac to remain in the field, and it was ordered to proceed to Washington, D.C.

Second Corps departed May 2, 1865, marched by way of Jetersville and Goode's Bridge, and arrived at Manchester, near Richmond, three days later. It continued on through Richmond May 6, 1865, and then marched by way of Hanover Court House, Chesterfield Station, Massaponax Church, Fredericksburg, and Wolf Run Shoals on the Occoquan River, and arrived at Bailey's Cross Roads May 13, 1865. Two days later, it moved to Four-Mile Run, and it remained in camp there until late June 1865. While there, it participated in the Grand Review of the Army of the Potomac in Washington May 23, 1865.

An order dated May 17, 1865 directed that all volunteer organizations of white troops in the Army of the Potomac whose terms of service expired between that date and September 30, 1865 be mustered out immediately. As a result, the number of troops present in each of the corps of the army was greatly reduced. Because of this, on June 28, 1865, a further order directed that all troops not then under orders for muster out be consolidated in each of the corps of the army into a division of three brigades. With this order, the Army of the Potomac ceased to exist. The three divisions to be formed in this manner (one each from Second Corps, Fifth Corps, and Sixth Corps) were to be organized temporarily into a provisional corps under the command of Horatio G. Wright. The division formed from troops of Second Corps was organized July 1, 1865, as follows:

Second Division, Provisional Corps, Gershom Mott
  First Brigade, P. Regis De Trobriand
  Second Brigade, Byron R. Pierce
  Third Brigade, George N. Macy

The Provisional Corps was placed in camp on the Baltimore and Ohio Railroad west of the Monocacy River, and Wright reported to Winfield S. Hancock, commander of the Middle Department. In time the troops of Mott's division were also mustered out.

Second Corps was discontinued June 28, 1865.

COMMANDERS OF SECOND CORPS, ARMY OF THE POTOMAC

Edwin V. Sumner	March 13, 1862 to October 7, 1862
Darius N. Couch	October 7, 1862 to December 26, 1862
John Sedgwick	December 26, 1862 to January 26, 1863
Oliver O. Howard	January 26, 1863 to February 5, 1863
Darius N. Couch	February 5, 1863 to May 22, 1863
Winfield S. Hancock	May 22, 1863 to July 1, 1863
John Gibbon	July 1, 1863, temporarily
Winfield S. Hancock	July 1, 1863 to July 3, 1863
John C. Caldwell	July 3, 1863, briefly
William Hays	July 3, 1863 to August 16, 1863
Gouverneur K. Warren	August 16, 1863 to October 10, 1863
John C. Caldwell	October 10, 1863 to October 12, 1863
Gouverneur K. Warren	October 12, 1863 to December 16, 1863
John C. Caldwell	December 16, 1863 to December 29, 1863
Winfield S. Hancock	December 29, 1863 to January 8, 1864
Gouverneur K. Warren	January 8, 1864 to February 6, 1864
John C. Caldwell	February 6, 1864, temporarily
Gouverneur K. Warren	February 6, 1864 to March 24, 1864
Winfield S. Hancock	March 24, 1864 to June 18, 1864
David B. Birney	June 18, 1864 to June 27, 1864
Winfield S. Hancock	June 27, 1864 to November 26, 1864
Andrew A. Humphreys	November 26, 1864 to February 15, 1865
Gershom Mott	February 15, 1865 to February 17, 1865
Nelson A. Miles	February 17, 1865 to February 25, 1865
Andrew A. Humphreys	February 25, 1865 to April 22, 1865

Francis C. Barlow	April 22, 1865 to May 5, 1865
Andrew A. Humphreys	May 5, 1865 to June 9, 1865
Gershom Mott	June 9, 1865 to June 20, 1865
Andrew A. Humphreys	June 20, 1865 to June 28, 1865

SECOND CORPS, ARMY OF VIRGINIA
JUNE 26–SEPTEMBER 12, 1862

June 26, 1862, the Army of Virginia was created under John Pope, and was composed of troops from the Mountain Department and the departments of the Rappahannock and the Shenandoah. Second Corps was organized from Nathaniel P. Banks' Department of the Shenandoah, and Banks was assigned command. The corps was originally organized as follows:

SECOND CORPS, ARMY OF VIRGINIA, Nathaniel P. Banks

First Division, Alpheus S. Williams
  First Brigade, Samuel W. Crawford
  Third Brigade, George H. Gordon

Note 1. First Brigade was organized from First Brigade, First Division, Department of the Shenandoah.
Note 2. Third Brigade was organized from Third Brigade, First Division, Department of the Shenandoah.
Note 3. There was no Second Brigade. May 1, 1862, John J. Abercrombie's Second Brigade, First Division, Department of the Shenandoah, then under the command of George L. Hartsuff, was transferred to the Department of the Rappahannock.

Second Division, James Cooper, to July 11, 1862
  Christopher C. Augur
  First Brigade, James Cooper
  Second Brigade, John P. Slough, to July 7, 1862
    Gustavus A. Scroggs
    Henry Prince
  Geary's Brigade, John W. Geary

Note 1. First Brigade was organized from First Brigade, Sigel's Division, Department of the Shenandoah.
Note 2. Second Brigade was organized from Second Brigade, Sigel's Division, Department of the Shenandoah.

Cavalry Brigade, John P. Hatch

Note. The Cavalry Brigade was organized from Hatch's Cavalry Brigade, Department of the Shenandoah.

Artillery, Clermont L. Best
  4th Battery (D), Maine Light Artillery, O'Neil W. Robinson
  6th Maine Battery (F), Maine Light Artillery, Freeman McGilvery
  Battery K, 1st New York Light Artillery, Lorenzo Crounse
  Battery M, 1st New York Light Artillery, George W. Cothran
  Battery L, Hamilton's New York Artillery, Jacob Roemer
  10th Battery, New York Light Artillery, Charles T. Bruen
  Battery E, Pennsylvania Light Artillery, Joseph M. Knap
  Battery F, 4th United States Artillery, Edward D. Muhlenberg

August 2, 1862, Second Division was reorganized. Erastus B. Tyler's Brigade, formerly Third Brigade of James Shields' Division, Department of the Rappahannock, and which had been serving during July 1862 in Samuel D. Sturgis' Reserve Corps at Alexandria, Virginia, arrived at Sperryville, Virginia August 1, 1862, and was assigned to Second Corps. It was then consolidated with John W. Geary's Brigade, and the resulting new brigade was designated as First Brigade, Second Division, and was assigned to Geary. Cooper's former First Brigade was redesignated as Second Brigade, and was assigned to Henry Prince. A new Third Brigade was organized from Prince's former Second Brigade, and it was assigned to George S. Greene. Second Division was then organized as follows:

Second Division, Christopher C. Augur
  First Brigade, John W. Geary
  Second Brigade, Henry Prince
  Third Brigade, George S. Greene

August 9, 1862, Banks' Second Corps was engaged at Cedar Mountain with Thomas J. (Stonewall) Jackson's Confederate Corps, and suffered heavy losses. In the Second Division Augur was wounded and was succeeded by Henry Prince. David P. De Witt assumed command of Prince's Second Brigade. Then Prince was captured, and Greene assumed command of Second Division. James A. Tait took command of Greene's Third Brigade. Geary was also wounded, and Charles Candy assumed command of First Brigade. At the end of the battle Second Division was commanded as follows:

Second Division, George S. Greene
    First Brigade, Charles Candy
    Second Brigade, David P. De Witt
    Third Brigade, James A. Tait

When Robert E. Lee's Army of Northern Virginia advanced against Pope's army after Cedar Mountain, Banks' Second Corps withdrew from the line of the Rapidan with the other two corps, and while at Warrenton, Virginia on August 27, 1862, it was assigned the duty of guarding the army trains. It did no further fighting during the Northern Virginia Campaign, but marched with the trains into the Defenses of Washington early in September 1862. For details of the operations of Second Corps, see Pope's Northern Virginia Campaign.

Upon arriving at Washington, Second Corps was sent north of the Potomac to Tennallytown, D.C., and then on September 5, 1862, it moved to Rockville, Maryland. While there Second Corps, Army of Virginia and Edwin V. Sumner's Second Corps, Army of the Potomac were organized as the Center of George B. McClellan's Army of the Potomac.

Meantime, Banks became too sick to accompany the army into Maryland, and September 3, 1862, he was relieved from command of Second Corps, Army of Virginia by Alpheus S. Williams. The corps advanced with the Army of the Potomac into Maryland at the beginning of the Maryland Campaign, and near Frederick, September 12, 1862, its designation was changed to Twelfth Corps, Army of the Potomac. Brigade and division designations remained the same as in Second Corps, Army of Virginia.

The Cavalry Brigade of Second Corps, which had been under the command of John Buford since July 27, 1862, was redesignated as Cavalry Brigade, Defenses of Washington in the reorganization of September 12, 1862.

The commanders of Second Corps, Army of Virginia were as follows:

Nathaniel P. Banks   June 26, 1862 to September 3, 1862
Alpheus S. Williams   September 3, 1862 to September 12, 1862

THIRD CORPS, ARMY OF THE POTOMAC

Third Corps, Army of the Potomac was created by a presidential order of March 8, 1862, which also created First Corps, Second Corps, Fourth Corps, and Fifth Corps. The corps was organized March 13, 1862 under Samuel P. Heintzelman, as follows:

THIRD CORPS, Samuel P. Heintzelman

First Division, Fitz John Porter
    First Brigade, John H. Martindale
    Second Brigade, George W. Morell
    Third Brigade, Daniel Butterfield
    Artillery
        Battery D, 1st United States Artillery, Charles Griffin
        Battery C, 1st Rhode Island Light Artillery, William B. Weeden
        3rd Battery (C), Massachusetts Light Artillery, Augustus P. Martin
        5th Battery (E), Massachusetts Light Artillery, George D. Allen

Second Division, Joseph Hooker
    First Brigade, Cuvier Grover
    Second Brigade, Nelson Taylor
    Third Brigade, Samuel H. Starr, to May 3, 1862
        Francis E. Patterson
    Artillery
        Battery H, 1st United States Light Artillery, Charles H. Webber
        4th Battery, New York Light Artillery, James E. Smith
        6th Battery, New York Light Artillery, Walter M. Bramhall
        Battery D, 1st New York Light Artillery, Thomas W. Osborn

Third Division, Charles S. Hamilton, to April 30, 1862
    Philip Kearny
    First Brigade, Charles D. Jameson
    Second Brigade, David B. Birney
    Third Brigade, Hiram G. Berry
    Artillery
        Battery G, 2nd United States Artillery, James Thompson
        Battery B, New Jersey Light Artillery, John E. Beam
        Battery E, 1st Rhode Island Light Artillery, George E. Randolph

Note. Hamilton was assigned to the Department of the

Mississippi, where he assumed command of Third Division, Army of the Mississippi at Corinth.

3rd Pennsylvania Cavalry, William W. Averell

Peninsular Campaign, April 1862–August 1862. Heintzelman's Third Corps accompanied George B. McClellan's Army of the Potomac when it moved to the Peninsula in the spring of 1862. Charles D. Hamilton's Third Division was the first division of the army to go, and it left Alexandria, Virginia March 17, 1862. Fitz John Porter's First Division followed a short time later, but Joseph Hooker's Second Division did not arrive on the Peninsula until April 10, 1862.

When the army began its advance from the vicinity of Fort Monroe April 4, 1862, Heintzelman moved forward on the right with the divisions of Hamilton and Porter (Hooker's division had not yet arrived) to the front of Yorktown. Hooker arrived later, and with the other two divisions of the corps took part in the siege of Yorktown. After the enemy evacuated Yorktown, Heintzelman left Porter's division there, and with the divisions of Hooker and Philip Kearny (commanding Hamilton's former division) joined in the pursuit of John B. Magruder's forces as they retired up the Peninsula. Both of Heintzelman's divisions took part in the Battle of Williamsburg May 5, 1862, and then advanced with the army to White House on the Pamunkey River, where they arrived in mid-May 1862. Porter's division moved up the York River from Yorktown, and rejoined the corps at White House. During the advance to White House, on May 11, 1862, John J. Abercrombie relieved Nelson Taylor in command of Second Brigade, Second Division. Daniel Sickles relieved Abercrombie May 24, 1862.

While at White House, the Army of the Potomac was reorganized by the creation of two new corps— Fifth Provisional Corps and Sixth Provisional Corps. Fifth Provisional Corps was formed from Porter's First Division, Third Corps and a new division under George Sykes, which consisted of Sykes' brigade of regulars and two additional regiments. Porter was assigned command of the corps. Third Corps then consisted only of Hooker's Second Division and Kearny's Third Division.

From White House the army advanced to the Chickahominy River, and May 20–23, 1862, Erasmus D. Keyes' Fourth Corps crossed to the south bank and took position at Seven Pines. On May 25, 1862, Third Corps followed Fourth Corps across the river. Hooker's division moved on south to guard the crossings of White Oak Swamp, and Kearny's division took position to cover Bottom's Bridge on the Chickahominy. On May 31, 1862, Keyes was strongly attacked at Seven Pines and driven back, and at about 3:00 P.M., Kearny was moved up in support. All three of Kearny's brigades were engaged in repelling the enemy attack. Hooker's division was moved forward, but it was not in action that day. Sickles' Second Brigade and Samuel H. Starr's Third Brigade (Francis H. Patterson was sick) were slightly engaged the next morning.

Third Corps was again engaged at Oak Grove June 25, 1862. Hooker was ordered to drive in the Confederate outposts in front of the corps, and when his division was stopped, Birney's Second Brigade of Kearny's division moved up in support. The advance was not resumed, however, because the Seven Days' Battles began the next day. During the battles of Mechanicsville and Gaines' Mill, Third Corps remained inactive near Fair Oaks, south of the Chickahominy.

When orders for the withdrawal of the army to the James River were issued on the night of June 27, 1862, Heintzelman was directed to remain near Fair Oaks with Third Corps until the following night, and then, together with William B. Franklin's Sixth Provisional Corps and Edwin V. Sumner's Second Corps, he was to retire by way of Savage Station toward the crossings of White Oak Swamp. The Battle of Savage Station was fought June 29, 1862, but Third Corps was not present. Heintzelman arrived at the station before the fighting began, but he did not remain there with Sumner's corps and William F. Smith's division of Franklin's corps. Instead, he marched on and crossed White Oak Swamp, and took position in the Glendale area.

On June 30, 1862, Kearny's division and Cuvier Grover's First Brigade of Hooker's division were engaged in severe fighting at the Battle of Glendale. At Malvern Hill the next day, the divisions of Kearny and Hooker were in line between Darius N. Couch's First Division, Fourth Corps and Franklin's Sixth Provisional Corps, which was on the extreme right of the Federal position. Sickles' Second Brigade of Hooker's division was sent to reinforce Couch, and it relieved some regiments of that division. The fighting began to the left of Third Corps, and finally extended to Kearny's front, but this largely involved only skirmishers and artillery.

The organization of Third Corps during the Seven Days was as follows:

THIRD CORPS, Samuel P. Heintzelman

Second Division, Joseph Hooker
First Brigade, Cuvier Grover
Second Brigade, Daniel E. Sickles
Third Brigade, Joseph E. Carr
Artillery
Battery D, 1st New York Light Artillery, Thomas W. Osborn
4th Battery, New York Light Artillery, Joseph E. Nairn
Battery H, 1st United States Artillery, Charles H. Webber

Note. Carr relieved Samuel H. Starr in command of Third Brigade June 1, 1862.

Third Division, Philip Kearny
First Brigade, John C. Robinson
Second Brigade, David B. Birney
Third Brigade, Hiram G. Berry
Artillery
Battery E, 1st Rhode Island Light Artillery, George E. Randolph
Battery G, 2nd United States Artillery, James Thompson

Note. Robinson relieved Charles D. Jameson in command of First Brigade June 12, 1862.

Artillery Reserve, Gustavus A. De Russy
6th Battery, New York Light Artillery, Walter M. Bramhall
2nd Battery (B), New Jersey Light Artillery, John E. Beam
Battery K, 4th United States Artillery, Francis W. Seeley

First Division, Third Corps was reorganized August 5, 1862 by the change of designation of Third Division to First Division, and as a result, Third Division was discontinued.

For additional information about the organization and operations of Third Corps, Army of the Potomac during the period April 1862–August 1862, see Peninsular Campaign.

With Pope's Army of Virginia (Campaign in Northern Virginia), August 16, 1862–September 2, 1862. After the Battle of Malvern Hill, the Army of the Potomac withdrew to Harrison's Landing on the James River, and it remained there until August 1862. Then, in the general withdrawal of the army from the Peninsula, Third Corps was ordered to Alexandria, Virginia. It arrived there August 22, 1862, and then marched to Warrenton Junction, where it joined Pope's Army of Virginia August 26, 1862. The corps was engaged at the Battle of Groveton August 29, 1862, and at the Second Battle of Bull Run (Manassas) the next day. Kearny's First Division supported Reno's Ninth Corps at Chantilly (Ox Hill) September 1, 1862. Kearny was killed in that battle, and was succeeded in command of the division by David B. Birney.

The organization of Third Corps while attached to the Army of Virginia was as follows:

THIRD CORPS, Samuel P. Heintzelman

First Division, Philip Kearny, to September 1, 1862, killed
David B. Birney
First Brigade, John C. Robinson
Second Brigade, David B. Birney, to September 1, 1862
J. H. Hobart Ward
Third Brigade, Orlando M. Poe
Artillery
Battery E, 1st Rhode Island Light Artillery, George E. Randolph
Battery K, First United States Artillery, William M. Graham

Second Division, Joseph Hooker
First Brigade, Cuvier Grover
Second Brigade, Nelson Taylor
Third Brigade, Joseph B. Carr
Artillery
Battery E, 4th United States Artillery, Joseph C. Clark

For details of the operations of Third Corps while with Pope's Army of Virginia, see Pope's Northern Virginia Campaign .

In the District of the Defenses of Washington, September 2, 1862–October 10, 1862. Following the Battle of Chantilly, Third Corps retreated with Pope's army into the District of the Defenses of

Washington, and took position near Alexandria. The corps was so depleted at that time that it did not accompany the reorganized Army of the Potomac when it moved into Maryland in pursuit of Lee's Army of Northern Virginia, and it was not present at the Battle of Antietam. It remained in the Defenses of Washington to rest and recruit, and while there it occupied the left of the Federal defensive line south of the Potomac.

When Heintzelman's Third Corps arrived at Alexandria, it consisted of only the divisions of Hooker and Birney (formerly Kearny's). On September 7, 1862, Hooker relieved Irvin McDowell in command of Third Corps, Army of Virginia (on September 12, 1862, designated First Corps, Army of the Potomac), and Daniel E. Sickles assumed command of Second Division, Third Corps, Army of the Potomac. September 9, 1862, Heintzelman was placed in command of all troops in the Defenses of Washington South of the Potomac, and these included the two divisions of Third Corps.

September 15, 1862, George Stoneman assumed command of First Division, Third Corps (ordered September 13, 1862), and Birney resumed command of his Second Brigade of the division, relieving Ward. On the day that he assumed command, Stoneman was ordered to move, with Birney's Second Brigade, to Poolesville, Maryland to guard the crossings of the Potomac River from Great Falls to Point of Rocks. Stoneman also assumed command of some regiments already along the river, and his combined command was designated as Stoneman's Corps of Observation, Upper Potomac. It was also called Stoneman's Provisional Division. On October 10, 1862, during James E. B. (Jeb) Stuart's cavalry raid into Maryland and Pennsylvania, the other two brigades of First Division, Robinson's First Brigade and Berry's Third Brigade (commanded by Orlando M. Poe), were ordered up from Alexandria to Poolesville. Despite this reinforcement, Stuart eluded Stoneman and returned safely to Virginia.

Also on October 10, 1862, Stoneman was directed to report to, and receive orders from, George B. McClellan, and by this order, First Division, Third Corps was transferred from the District of the Defenses of Washington to McClellan's Field Army of the Potomac. It was then assigned to Ambrose E. Burnside's Ninth Corps. This left only Sickles'

Second Division, Third Corps under Heintzelman's control, and when the latter relieved Nathaniel P. Banks in command of the District of the Defenses of Washington October 27, 1862, Third Corps, for all practical purposes, ceased to exist, although it was not officially discontinued.

Sickles' Second Division remained in the District of the Defenses of Washington. Another troop transfer is of significance here because of its relationship to Third Corps. On October 17, 1862 (ordered October 10, 1862), Amiel W. Whipple's Division of the District of the Defenses of Washington was detached and sent to join McClellan's army in the field. It arrived at Knoxville, Maryland, near Harper's Ferry, October 22, 1862, and was then assigned to Twelfth Corps. Later, when Third Corps was reorganized under Stoneman, Whipple's Division was assigned to Third Corps.

McClellan's Advance into Virginia, September 19, 1862–November 7, 1862. When McClellan began his long-delayed advance into Virginia after the Battle of Antietam, Ninth Corps (including Stoneman's division) and Whipple's Division of Twelfth Corps were among the first troops to cross the Potomac River. On October 29, 1862, while the army was on the march, Stoneman's division and Whipple's Division were detached, respectively, from Ninth Corps and Twelfth Corps, and, together with Ninth Corps, were constituted as a special force under Ambrose E. Burnside. This arrangement was continued until the army reached the Warrenton area early in November 1862.

Sickles' division of Third Corps was also affected by McClellan's advance toward Warrenton. Franz Sigel's Eleventh Corps of the District of the Defenses of Washington had for some time been guarding the line of the Orange and Alexandria Railroad, with headquarters at Fairfax Court House. When the Army of the Potomac approached the Manassas Gap Railroad, Sigel was ordered on November 2, 1862 to move toward Thoroughfare Gap and occupy the line of the railroad. That same day, Sickles marched from his positions in the Defenses of Washington to relieve Eleventh Corps on the Orange and Alexandria Railroad. Joseph B. Carr's First Brigade (formerly commanded by Cuvier Grover) occupied the line from Burke's Station to Bull Run Bridge, including the post of Centerville; Francis E.

Patterson's Third Brigade from Bull Run Bridge to Manassas; George B. Hall's Second Brigade (commanded by Nelson Taylor to September 5, 1862) from Manassas to Kettle Run; and a provisional brigade commanded by William Blaisdell held the line from Kettle Run to Warrenton Junction. Sickles' division continued in this service until after the Army of the Potomac, under Ambrose E. Burnside, had left Warrenton in mid-November 1862, on its march to Falmouth, Virginia. For additional information about Third Corps during this period, see the following: Army of the Potomac, Antietam Creek, Maryland to Warrenton, Virginia; and Miscellaneous Orgnizations, Military District of the Defenses of Washington, Army of the Potomac.

Fredericksburg Campaign, November 7, 1862–December 15, 1862. When the Army of the Potomac arrived near Warrenton on November 7, 1862, Ambrose E. Burnside relieved McClellan in command of the army, and he immediately proposed a plan, which was accepted by the president, to change the direction of march so as to move toward Richmond by way of Fredericksburg. In preparation for this movement, on November 14, 1862, Burnside reorganized the army into three grand divisions and a reserve. At the same time he reorganized Third Corps and assigned Stoneman to command. The new Third Corps and Fifth Corps were assigned to Joseph Hooker's Center Grand Division.

When the army advanced from Warrenton toward Fredericksburg in November 1862, the Center Grand Division, which consisted of Stoneman's Third Corps and Daniel Butterfield's Fifth Corps, marched toward Hartwood Church, which was opposite United States Ford on the Rappahannock River, and arrived there November 19, 1862. Stoneman had with him only Birney's First Division and Whipple's Third Division. Sickles' Second Division remained on the Orange and Alexandria Railroad until November 25, 1862, and it then joined the army at Potomac Creek December 5, 1862.

Burnside halted his operations for several weeks while he waited for pontoons to arrive from Washington, but finally the bridges were laid, and the army began crossing the Rappahannock December 11–12, 1862 for an attack on the Army of Northern Virginia, which was in position beyond Fredericksburg. Third Corps and Fifth Corps remained on the north bank during those two days, but both crossed December 13, 1862, while the battle was in progress. Birney's and Sickles' divisions crossed at the lower bridges below Fredericksburg (Franklin's Crossing) to reinforce William B. Franklin's Left Grand Division. Birney arrived just in time to assist in stopping an enemy counterattack that followed the repulse of an assault by John F. Reynolds' First Corps near Hamilton's Crossing. Sickles' division came up a short time later and formed on the right of Birney. Both divisions maintained their positions during the rest of the day, but they were not again engaged.

Whipple's division crossed the river at Fredericksburg about noon December 13, 1862. A. Sanders Piatt's First Brigade formed a picket line in the northwestern part of the town, and Samuel S. Carroll's Second Brigade moved to the left after crossing into Fredericksburg , and formed behind Samuel D. Sturgis' Second Division of Ninth Corps. Later, Carroll's brigade attacked with Ninth Corps, and gained some high ground beyond the town. Piatt was disabled December 13, 1862, and Emlen Franklin assumed temporary command of his brigade.

Third Corps recrossed the Rappahannock with the rest of the army during the night of December 15, 1862. For additional information about the operations of Third Corps during the Battle of Fredericksburg, see Fredericksburg, Virginia Campaign.

The organization of Third Corps during the Fredericksburg Campaign was as follows:

THIRD CORPS, George Stoneman

First Division, David B. Birney
  First Brigade, John C. Robinson
  Second Brigade, J. H. Hobart Ward
  Third Brigade, P. Regis De Trobriand, to November 1862
    Hiram G. Berry
  Artillery, George E. Randolph
    Battery E, 1st Rhode Island Light Artillery, Pardon S. Jastram
    Batteries F and K, 3rd United States Artillery, John G. Turnbull

Note 1. First Division was originally First Division, Third Corps, but more recently had been Stoneman's Division of Burnside's Special Command.

Note 2. December 29, 1862, Robinson was assigned command of Second Division, First Corps (formerly John Gibbon's division), and Samuel B. Hayman assumed command of First Brigade.

Second Division, Daniel E. Sickles
First Brigade, Joseph B. Carr
Second Brigade, George B. Hall
Third Brigade, Francis E. Patterson, to November 22, 1862, sick
Joseph W. Revere
Provisional Brigade, William Blaisdell
Artillery, James E. Smith
  2nd Battery (B), New Jersey Light Artillery, A. Judson Clark
  4th Battery, New York Light Artillery, Joseph E. Nairn
  Battery H, 1st United States Artillery, Justin E. Dimick
  Battery K, 4th United States Artillery, Francis W. Seeley

Note 1. Second Division remained on the Orange and Alexandria Railroad until November 25, 1862, and then joined the corps at Falmouth, before the Battle of Fredericksburg.

Note 2. When Second Division was withdrawn from the railroad on its march to Falmouth, the Provisional Brigade was discontinued, and Blaisdell resumed command of his 11th Massachusetts Regiment at Fredericksburg.

Note 3. Gershom Mott was assigned to Third Corps December 24, 1862, and relieved Revere in command of Third Brigade. Revere, in turn, relieved Hall in command of Second Brigade.

Third Division, Amiel W. Whipple
First Brigade, A. Sanders Piatt, to December 13, 1862, disabled
Emlen Franklin
Second Brigade, Samuel S. Carroll
Artillery
  10th Battery, New York Light Artillery, John T. Bruen
  11th Battery, New York Light Artillery, Albert A. von Puttkammer
  Battery H, 1st Ohio Light Artillery, George W. Norton

Note. Third Division was organized in the District of the Defenses of Washington, and was then assigned to Twelfth Corps. It was then assigned as Whipple's Division of Burnside's Special Command (see above).

Winter of 1862–1863. After the Battle of Fredericksburg, the Army of the Potomac went into winter quarters in the vicinity of Falmouth, and

Third Corps established its camps near the town. The corps was called out again January 20, 1863, when Burnside again attempted to lead the army across the Rappahannock and engage the enemy. Hooker's and Franklin's grand divisions marched to the vicinity of Banks' Ford, but they were unable to proceed farther because constant rain had made the roads impassable. The movement, commonly known as the "Mud March," was called off January 24, 1863, and the troops returned to their quarters.

During the winter, there were several command and organizational changes that affected Third Corps. January 26, 1863, Joseph Hooker relieved Burnside in command of the Army of the Potomac, and a short time later made two significant changes in the organization of the army. February 5, 1863, he abolished the grand division organization, and thereafter the corps commanders received orders directly from, and reported to, Headquarters Army of the Potomac. That same day he issued orders for the consolidation of the cavalry of the army into a cavalry corps, and he assigned Stoneman, then commanding Third Corps, to its command. Stoneman assumed command February 7, 1863, and this necessitated some command changes in Third Corps. Daniel E. Sickles, commanding Second Division, assumed temporary command of Third Corps February 12, 1863 (assigned February 5, 1863); and Joseph B. Carr, who was in temporary command of Second Division during the absence of Sickles, remained in command of Second Division until Hiram G. Berry, who was assigned February 5, 1863, assumed command.

The organization of Third Corps at the end of January 1863, including the more important command changes in February 1863, was as follows:

THIRD CORPS, George Stoneman, to February 7, 1863
Daniel E. Sickles

First Division, David B. Birney
First Brigade, Samuel B. Hayman
Second Brigade, P. Regis De Trobriand
Third Brigade, Thomas B. Roberts
Artillery

Note 1. In February 1863, Hayman relieved Roberts in command of Third Brigade, and Charles H. T. Collis assumed temporary command of First Brigade. Charles K. Graham was assigned command of First Brigade March 23, 1863.

Note 2. January 26, 1863, De Trobriand assumed tem-

porary command of Second Brigade during the absence of J. H. Hobart Ward.

Note 3. Roberts was in temporary command of Third Brigade during the absence of Hiram G. Berry. Berry was assigned command of Second Division February 5, 1863, and Roberts remained in command of Third Brigade until relieved by Hayman.

Note 4. The batteries with the division were the same as at the Battle of Fredericksburg.

Second Division, Joseph B. Carr, to February 8, 1863
    Hiram G. Berry
    First Brigade, William Blaisdell, to February 8, 1863
    Second Brigade, Joseph W. Revere
    Third Brigade, Gershom Mott
    Artillery, James E. Smith

Note 1. Carr assumed temporary command of Second Division in January 1863, during the temporary absence of Sickles. Sickles was assigned command of Third Corps February 5, 1863, and Berry was assigned command of Second Division.

Note 2. The batteries with Second Division were the same as at the Battle of Fredericksburg.

Third Division, Amiel W. Whipple
    First Brigade, A. Sanders Piatt
    Second Brigade, Joseph H. Potter
    Artillery

Note 1. Benajah P. Bailey commanded First Brigade from February to April 1863, and was then succeeded by Emlen Franklin.

Note 2. Hiram Berdan was assigned command of Second Brigade February 19, 1863, and March 13, 1863, he was relieved by Samuel M. Bowman.

Note 3. The batteries with Third Division were the same as at the Battle of Fredericksburg.

Third Division was reorganized by Whipple in March 1863. Samuel S. Carroll, commanding Second Brigade, had left the army on sick leave January 14, 1863, and in March 1863, as the campaigning season drew near, he had not returned. At that time, there were only two regiments left in Second Brigade. Whipple attached one of these regiments to Bailey's First Brigade, and the other, with two additional regiments, he organized into a new Second Brigade under Joseph H. Potter. Then, on March 13, 1863, he organized a new Third Brigade from 1st United States Sharpshooters and 2nd United States Sharpshooters, and assigned Hiram Berdan to its command. There was little further change in the organization of the corps during the remainder of the winter.

Chancellorsville Campaign, April 27, 1863–May 6, 1863. On April 27, 1863, Hooker's Army of the Potomac advanced from its camps at the beginning of the Chancellorsville Campaign. Third Corps did not move that day, but the next day it marched from near Falmouth to the vicinity of the crossings of the Rappahannock below Fredericksburg to support First Corps and Sixth Corps, which were establishing bridgeheads there on the south bank of the river.

April 30, 1863, Sickles was ordered to march upriver with his command and report to Hooker at Chancellorsville. He arrived there the next day, and was directed to picket the rear of the army while Fifth Corps and Twelfth Corps advanced eastward from Chancellorsville toward the rear of Fredericksburg. Late that evening, after Fifth Corps and Twelfth Corps had been recalled, Third Corps moved up and took position near the Plank Road, in rear of the junction of Eleventh Corps and Twelfth Corps. On the morning of May 2, 1863, Third Corps moved south of the Plank Road and occupied the space between the right of Twelfth Corps and the left of Eleventh Corps.

During the morning of May 2, 1863, Thomas J. (Stonewall) Jackson's flanking column was observed moving westward past Catharine Furnace (Wellford's Furnace), and about noon Sickles was sent southward with the divisions of Birney and Whipple to investigate. Sickles was engaged that evening with enemy forces near the furnace when he learned of Jackson's defeat of Eleventh Corps on the right of the army. He immediately hurried back to help in stopping the enemy advance along the turnpike.

Early on the morning of May 3, 1862, the Federal line was again heavily attacked and forced back, and finally it was withdrawn to a new defensive line that Hooker had prepared covering United States Ford. Third Corps was ordered to fall back at 9:00 A.M., and it then moved into the new line between Second Corps and Fifth Corps. Third Corps recrossed the Rappahannock with the rest of the army during the night of May 5, 1863, and returned to its former quarters.

Third Corps was engaged in some of the heaviest fighting of any of the corps at Chancellorsville and suffered more than 4,000 casualties. Berry was killed on the morning of May 3, 1863, and he was succeeded in command of Second Division by

Joseph B. Carr. Whipple was killed by a sharpshooter May 4, 1863, and Charles K. Graham assumed command of his Third Division. Gershom Mott, commanding Third Brigade, Second Division, was wounded, and was succeeded in command of the brigade by William J. Sewell. For details of the Third Corps at Chancellorsville, see Chancellorsville, Virginia Campaign.

The organization of Third Corps during the Battle of Chancellorsville was as follows:

THIRD CORPS, Daniel E. Sickles

First Division, David B. Birney
First Brigade, Charles K. Graham, to May 4, 1863
Thomas W. Egan
Second Brigade, J. H. Hobart Ward
Third Brigade, Samuel B. Hayman
Artillery, A. Judson Clark
Battery B, New Jersey Light Artillery, Robert Sims
Battery E, 1st Rhode Island Light Artillery, Pardon S. Jastram
Batteries F and K, 3rd United States Artillery, John G. Turnbull

Note. Graham was assigned command of Third Division after its commander, Amiel W. Whipple, was killed May 4, 1863.

Second Division, Hiram G. Berry, to May 3, 1863, mortally wounded
Joseph B. Carr
First Brigade, Joseph B. Carr, to May 3, 1863
William Blaisdell
Second Brigade, Joseph W. Revere
J. Egbert Farnum
Third Brigade, Gershom Mott, to May 3, 1863, wounded
William J. Sewell
Artillery, Thomas W. Osborn
Battery D, 1st New York Light Artillery, George B. Winslow
4th Battery, New York Light Artillery, George F. Barstow
William T. McLean
Battery H, 1st United States Artillery, Justin E. Dimick
James A. Sanderson
Battery K, 4th United States Artillery, Francis W. Seeley

Note. Revere was relieved from duty with the Army of the Potomac for leaving the field with his brigade during the battle. He was convicted by a court martial and dismissed from the service, but he was permitted to resign.

Third Division, Amiel W. Whipple, to May 4, 1863, killed
Charles K. Graham
First Brigade, Emlen Franklin
Second Brigade, Samuel M. Bowman
Third Brigade, Hiram Berdan
Artillery, Albert A. von Puttkammer
James F. Huntington
10th Battery, New York Light Artillery, Samuel Lewis
11th Battery, New York Light Artillery, John E. Burton
Battery H, 1st Ohio Light Artillery, James F. Huntington

Note. Whipple was killed by a sharpshooter while on the lines near the Chandler house, north of Chancellorsville.

Gettysburg Campaign, May 1863–July 1863. After the Battle of Chancellorsville, Third Corps remained in its camps near Falmouth until June 11, 1863, at the beginning of the Gettysburg Campaign. During this period, there were extensive changes in both the organization and command of the corps. Much of this was due to the muster out of regiments, whose terms of enlistment had expired.

In May 1863, Sickles left the army temporarily, and David B. Birney assumed command of Third Corps. Birney was in command during the march of the army northward into Maryland in pursuit of Lee, but Sickles returned and resumed command at Frederick June 28, 1863. While Birney was in command of the corps, J. H. Hobart Ward commanded Birney's First Division, and P. Regis De Trobriand was in charge of Ward's Second Brigade, First Division. There were also other command changes in First Division. In May 1863, Thomas W. Egan's 40th New York was transferred from First Brigade to Third Brigade, and Andrew H. Tippin assumed command of First Brigade, relieving Egan. Charles K. Graham's Third Division was discontinued in June 1863 (see below), and then Graham was assigned command of First Brigade, First Division, relieving Tippin. In June 1863, Samuel B. Hayman's 37th New York and De Trobriand's 38th New York left the army and were mustered out of the service June 22, 1863. De Trobriand remained with Third Corps, however, and was assigned command of Third Brigade, First Division, relieving Hayman. Apparently, Hiram Berdan succeeded De Trobriand in command of Second Brigade, First Division.

Andrew A. Humphreys, whose Third Division, Fifth Corps was discontinued in late May 1863 (see Fifth Corps, Army of the Potomac), was assigned command of Second Division, Third Corps, relieving Joseph B. Carr. Carr then resumed command of his First Brigade, Second Division, relieving William Blaisdell. In May 1863, William R. Brewster relieved J. Egbert Farnum in command of Second Brigade, Second Division. On June 11, 1863, Samuel A. Bowman's 84th Pennsylvania was transferred from Second Brigade, Third Division to Third Brigade, Second Division, and by seniority Bowman relieved William J. Sewell in command of Third Brigade. Then on June 14, 1863, 84th New York was assigned to First Brigade, Second Division, and George C. Burling assumed command of Third Brigade, Second Division. On May 8, 1863, A. Van Horne Ellis relieved Emlen Franklin in command of First Brigade, Third Division when Franklin's 122nd Pennsylvania left the army for Washington and muster out.

In June 1863, Graham's Third Division was discontinued, and the regiments were assigned to First Division and Second Division. The two regiments that remained of Ellis' First Brigade, Third Division, including Ellis' 124th New York and the two regiments of United States Sharpshooters of Berdan's Third Brigade, Third Division, were transferred to Second Brigade, First Division. Two regiments of Bowman's Second Brigade, including Bowman's 84th New York, were transferred to Second Division, and one regiment to Third Brigade, First Division.

When the reorganization described above was completed, Third Corps consisted of the following:

THIRD CORPS, David B. Birney

First Division, J. H. Hobart Ward
   First Brigade, Charles K. Graham
   Second Brigade, Hiram Berdan (probably)
   Third Brigade, P. Regis De Trobriand

Second Division, Andrew A. Humphreys
   First Brigade, Joseph B. Carr
   Second Brigade, William R. Brewster
   Third Brigade, George C. Burling

Artillery Brigade, George E. Randolph

* * * * * * * * * *

On June 11, 1863, Third Corps was sent from Falmouth to strengthen the Federal forces on the upper Rappahannock, and the next day it arrived at Bealeton, Virginia. It then took position on the right of Fifth Corps, and Humphreys' Second Division was immediately moved up to the river.

That same day, June 12, 1863, Third Corps was assigned, together with Fifth Corps, Eleventh Corps, and the Cavalry Corps, to the Right Wing of the Army of the Potomac, to which John F. Reynolds, commander of First Corps, was assigned command.

On June 13, 1863, as the van of Lee's army approached Winchester on its march toward Maryland, Hooker began to withdraw the Army of the Potomac northward from its positions near the Rappahannock toward the Orange and Alexandria Railroad. Third Corps marched with the Right Wing to Manassas Junction, where it remained for a short time to guard the crossings of the Occoquan River until the corps coming up from Falmouth had safely crossed to the north bank. Third Corps then advanced to Gum Springs (present-day Arcola), where it remained until June 25, 1863.

In the marching orders issued for the army June 17, 1863, Reynolds' Right Wing had been broken up, but on June 25, 1863, in preparation for a renewal of the advance of the army into Maryland, Reynolds was again assigned a wing of the army, which was called the Advance Wing and also Left Wing. This wing consisted of First Corps, Third Corps, Eleventh Corps, and Julius Stahel's Cavalry Division from the Department of Washington.

Third Corps crossed the Potomac River at Edwards Ferry June 25, 1863, and then marched on the left of the army through Jefferson to Middletown, Maryland, where it arrived June 27, 1863. Sickles, who had been absent from the army since May 1863, rejoined the corps at Frederick about noon June 28, 1863, and resumed command. Birney returned to the command of First Division and relieved Ward, who resumed command of his Second Brigade, First Division. Also that day, June 28, 1863, George G. Meade relieved Joseph Hooker in command of the Army of the Potomac.

Acting under Reynolds' orders, as a part of the Left Wing, Sickles advanced his Third Corps from the vicinity of Frederick through Woodsboro and Taneytown, and arrived at Bridgeport June 30, 1863. It then marched through Emmitsburg to Gettysburg, Pennsylvania. Birney's division arrived on the south end of the battlefield, north of Little Round Top, about 5:30 P.M. July 1, 1863, and Humphreys' Second Division arrived at the southern end of Cemetery Ridge about 1:00 A.M. the next morning. De Trobriand's brigade of First Division and Burling's brigade of Second Division had been left behind to guard the trains at Emmitsburg, but they came up and rejoined their divisions between 9:00 and 10:00 A.M. July 2, 1863.

During the early afternoon of July 2, 1863, Sickles, in a controversial move, advanced his line to an exposed position that extended from the Devil's Den, past the Wheatfield to Sherfeys' Peach Orchard on the Emmitsburg Road, and then along the road to a point near the Codori house. A short time after 4:00 P.M. July 2, 1863, Sickles' line was assailed by James Longstreet's corps, and, although strongly reinforced by Fifth Corps and a division from Second Corps, Third Corps was driven from the field. Sickles was severely wounded, and Birney assumed command of the corps, and Ward assumed command of Birney's First Division. Graham, commanding First Brigade, First Division, was wounded and captured, and Andrew H. Tippin succeeded him in command of the brigade. On the evening of July 3, 1863, Henry J. Madill relieved Tippin.

The remnants of Third Corps re-formed on the night of July 2, 1863 behind the main line of battle, and Winfield S. Hancock was assigned the direction of Birney's Third Corps, as well as his own Second Corps. Third Corps served the next day as a reserve during the Pickett-Pettigrew-Trimble assault on Cemetery Ridge, but it was not further engaged.

The organization of Third Corps at the Battle of Gettysburg was as follows:

THIRD CORPS, Daniel E. Sickles, to July 2, 1863, wounded
David B. Birney

First Division, David B. Birney, to July 2, 1863
J. H. Hobart Ward
First Brigade, Charles K. Graham, to July 2, 1863, wounded and captured
Andrew H. Tippin, to July 3, 1863
Henry J. Madill
Second Brigade, J. H. Hobart Ward, to July 2, 1863
Hiram Berdan
Third Brigade, P. Regis De Trobriand

Second Division, Andrew A. Humphreys

First Brigade, Joseph B. Carr
Second Brigade, William R. Brewster
Third Brigade, George C. Burling

Artillery Brigade, George E. Randolph, to July 2, 1863, wounded
A. Judson Clark
2nd Battery, New Jersey Light Artillery, A. Judson Clark
Robert Sims
Battery D, 1st New York Light Artillery, George B. Winslow
4th Battery, New York Light Artillery, James E. Smith
Battery E, 1st Rhode Island Light Artillery, John K. Bucklyn
Benjamin Freeborn
Battery K, 4th United States Artillery, Francis W. Seeley
Robert James

Third Corps remained on the battlefield of Gettysburg for a few days after the fighting had ended, and the men spent the time in caring for the wounded, burying the dead, and collecting arms. In the marching orders issued July 5, 1863 for the Army of the Potomac, Third Corps was assigned with First Corps and Sixth Corps to the Right Wing of the army. These corps were placed under the direction of John Sedgwick, commander of Sixth Corps, for the march to Middletown, Maryland. That day, however, Sixth Corps was advanced to Fairfield, Pennsylvania, where it encountered the enemy rear guard, and First Corps and Third Corps were ordered to remain in position at Gettysburg to support Sixth Corps, if necessary. Finally, on July 7, 1863, conforming to orders of July 5, 1863, Third Corps marched by way of Emmitsburg, Mechanicstown (present-day Thurmont), and Frederick, Maryland toward Fox's Gap in South Mountain. It arrived there July 9, 1863, and the next day continued on through Boonsboro to Antietam Creek, in the vicinity of Jones' Cross Roads (present-day Lappans). It remained there until July 15, 1863, two days after Lee's army had recrossed the Potomac into Virginia.

There were several important changes in command and organization in Third Corps during the march from Gettysburg. On July 8, 1863, Humphreys was assigned as Meade's chief of staff, Army of the Potomac, and he assumed that duty the next day. Carr assumed temporary command of Humphreys' Second Division, Third Corps. Henry

Prince, formerly commander of the District of the Pamlico, Eighteenth Corps, Department of North Carolina, joined Third Corps at Fox's Gap July 9, 1863, and the next day assumed command of Third Corps, relieving Carr.

July 7, 1863, the troops of William H. French's Division (except John R. Kenly's Brigade), formerly of the Middle Department, Eighth Corps, were assigned to Third Corps. The same order assigned French to the command of Third Corps. French, with the brigades of Benjamin F. Smith and Washington L. Elliott, from Middletown, and the brigade of William H. Morris, from Turner's Gap, joined Third Corps at Fox's Gap July 9, 1863. French then assumed command of the corps, and Birney resumed command of First Division, relieving Ward. Ward then resumed command of his Second Brigade, First Division, relieving Berdan.

July 10, 1863, while Third Corps was on Antietam Creek, a new Third Division was organized from the brigades of French's Division. Elliott was assigned command of Third Division, and J. Warren Keifer assumed command of Elliott's brigade. The new Third Division was organized as follows:

Third Division, Washington L. Elliott
  First Brigade, William H. Morris
  Second Brigade, J. Warren Keifer
  Third Brigade, Benjamin F. Smith

Note 1. First Brigade was organized from Morris' Third Provisional Brigade (Morris' Brigade), French's Division.

Note 2. Second Brigade was organized from Elliott's First Brigade, French's Division.

Note 3. Third Brigade was organized from two regiments of Smith's Third Brigade, French's Division, and two regiments formerly belonging to Robert H. Milroy's Second Division, Eighth Corps from the Department of the Susquehanna.

Francis C. Spinola, former commander of the District of Beaufort, Eighteenth Corps, Department of North Carolina, joined Third Corps on Antietam Creek July 11, 1863, and was assigned command of William R. Brewster's Second Brigade, Second Division. Brewster departed on sick leave and did not return until August 10, 1863.

When Meade's army marched toward the Potomac River July 15, 1863 in preparation for crossing into Virginia, Third Corps marched through the battlefield of Antietam to Pleasant Valley, near Sandy Hook, Maryland, where it arrived the next day. It crossed the Potomac at Harper's Ferry July 17, 1863, and camped a short distance beyond the river. It then marched toward Warrenton, together with Second Corps and Twelfth Corps, on the right of the army, along the eastern base of the Blue Ridge Mountains. Third Corps moved through Hillsboro, Wood Grove, Upperville, and Piedmont to Linden Station in Manassas Gap. There, on July 23, 1863, French attempted to force his way through the gap to intercept a part of Lee's army, which was then moving from the Shenandoah Valley toward Culpeper Court House. Ward's Division made the attack about 2:00 P.M., with the divisions of Prince and Elliott following in reserve. Ward drove Ambrose R. Wright's brigade of Ambrose P. Hill's corps from Wapping Heights, the hills at the western end of the gap, but it was stopped when the enemy formed a second line in the valley beyond. Prince's division then came up, and about 4:00–5:00 P.M. Spinola's brigade attacked and forced Wright's brigade back to a third line formed by Robert E. Rodes' division of Richard S. Ewell's corps, which had just arrived. The fighting soon ended for the day. Spinola was wounded in the attack, and J. Egbert Farnum assumed command of Second Brigade, Second Division.

Third Corps resumed its march July 25, 1863 and, passing through Salem, arrived near Warrenton the next day. While at Warrenton, on July 27, 1863, Farnum was ordered on detached duty in New York during the Draft Riots, and Thomas Rafferty assumed command of Farnum's brigade. The corps remained at Warrenton until July 31, 1863, and was then ordered to hold and picket the Rappahannock River from Sulfur Springs to the forks of the river near Beverly Ford. The pickets connected with Sixth Corps on the right and with First Corps on the left.

For details of the operations of Third Corps during the period May 1863–July 1863, see Gettysburg Campaign.

From the Rappahannock to the Rapidan, August 1, 1863–October 10, 1863. Third Corps remained in position along the Rappahannock River from August 1, 1863 to mid-September 1863. During this period the corps was temporarily reduced in strength when six regiments were sent to New York because of the disturbances resulting from the draft. For more detailed information about the forces sent to New York, see Army of the Potomac, From the Rappahannock to the Rapidan; and also Department of the East, January 3, 1863–June 27, 1865, Draft Riots in New York, 1863.

There were also several command changes during August and September 1863. William R. Brewster returned from sick leave August 10, 1863, and resumed command of Second Brigade, Second Division, relieving Rafferty. J. Warren Keifer was on detached service in New York from August 14, 1863 to September 14, 1863, and John W. Horn commanded Second Brigade, Third Division. Gershom Mott, who was wounded at Chancellorsville, returned to the army in August 1863 and resumed command of his Third Brigade, Second Division, relieving George C. Burling. George E. Randolph, who was wounded at Gettysburg, also returned to the army in August 1863, and resumed command of the Artillery Brigade, relieving A. Judson Clark. Also in August 1863, Charles H. T. Collis relieved Henry J. Madill in command of First Brigade, First Division. Lorenzo D. Carver was in temporary command of Second Brigade, First Division during the absence of Ward in August and September 1863.

The Army of the Potomac advanced from the line of the Rappahannock September 16, 1863, and formed on a line through Culpeper Court House, facing the Rapidan River. During this movement, Third Corps crossed the Rappahannock at Freeman's Ford, marched through Culpeper Court House, and took position about midway between the latter place and Stone House Mountain. While in position there, on October 3, 1863, Washington L. Elliott was relieved from duty with the Army of the Potomac, and was ordered west to report to William S. Rosecrans, commander of the Department and Army of the Cumberland. Joseph B. Carr, commanding First Brigade, Second Division, Third Corps, was assigned command of Elliott's Third Division, and Robert McAllister assumed command of Carr's brigade.

By October 8, 1863, Meade had become aware of an enemy movement toward the right of the army, and that day Prince's Second Division, Third Corps was sent to James City to support Judson Kilpatrick's cavalry. James City was about eight miles west of Culpeper Court House on the road to Madison Court House.

Bristoe, Virginia Campaign, October 10, 1863–October 22, 1863. Robert E. Lee, whose headquarters was at Orange Court House, realized that the Federal position on the ridge north of the Rapidan River was too strong for a successful frontal attack, and he decided to move around its right flank and force Meade to withdraw or be attacked under unfavorable conditions. Accordingly, Ewell's and Hill's Confederate corps crossed the upper Rapidan October 9, 1863, and marched to Madison Court House. When Meade learned of the presence of enemy infantry on his right, Birney's First Division and Carr's Third Division of Third Corps were formed in line of battle on the right of Second Corps, facing west. On the night of October 10, 1863, however, Meade issued orders for the withdrawal of the army to the line of the Rappahannock, and early the next morning the movement began. Third Corps marched back by way of Welford's Ford on Hazel River, to the vicinity of Freeman's Ford on the Rappahannock, and there it took position on the north bank of the river.

When Lee continued his flanking movement, the Army of the Potomac withdrew toward Centerville. During the night of October 12, 1863, Third Corps marched back by way of Fayetteville and Auburn (Auburn Mills) and arrived at Greenwich the following night. It then marched to Milford October 14, 1863, and from there it continued on along the Orange and Alexandria Railroad to Centerville. On October 15, 1863, two divisions of the corps were placed at Union Mills, and the other division at Fairfax Station to watch McLean's Ford.

Lee followed the Army of the Potomac toward Centerville, but soon withdrew to the Rappahannock. On October 19, Meade moved forward in pursuit. Third Corps advanced to Bristoe Station that day, and then continued on through Gainesville to Auburn. On October 21, 1863, the corps marched to the vicinity of Catlett's Station, with one brigade posted at Bristoe Station. After the Bristoe Campaign, Third Corps remained at Catlett's Station until October 30, 1863, and it then moved to Warrenton Junction, with one brigade left on the Orange and Alexandria Railroad from Catlett's Station to Warrenton Junction. For more detailed information, see Bristoe, Virginia Campaign.

The organization of Third Corps October 10, 1863 was as follows:

THIRD CORPS, William H. French

First Division, David B. Birney
  First Brigade, Charles H. T. Collis
  Second Brigade, J. H. Hobart Ward
  Third Brigade, P. Regis De Trobriand

Second Division, Henry Prince
  First Brigade, Robert McAllister
  Second Brigade, William R. Brewster
  Third Brigade, Gershom Mott

Third Division, Joseph B. Carr
  First Brigade, William H. Morris
  Second Brigade, J. Warren Keifer
  Third Brigade, Benjamin F. Smith

Artillery, George E. Randolph
  4th Battery (D), Maine Light Artillery, O'Neil W. Robinson, Jr.
  10th Battery, Massachusetts Light Artillery, J. Henry Sleeper
  Battery B, New Jersey Light Artillery, A. Judson Clark
  Battery D, 1st New York Light Artillery, George B. Winslow
  12th Battery, New York Light Artillery, George K. Dauchy
  Battery E, 1st Rhode Island Light Artillery, James K. Bucklyn
  Battery K, 4th United States Artillery, Robert James

Engagements at Rappahannock Station and Kelly's Ford, Virginia, November 7, 1863. On November 6, 1863, in preparation for an advance to Rappahannock Station and Kelly's Ford, Meade organized the army into two temporary wings or columns. First Corps, Second Corps, and Third Corps were assigned to the left wing, and French was assigned command of the wing. Birney assumed temporary command of Third Corps.

Early on the morning of November 7, 1863, Third Corps, which was the leading corps of French's wing, marched by way of Elk Run and Morrisville to Kelly's Ford. De Trobriand's Third Brigade, First Division arrived near the ford about noon and then, supported by the artillery, crossed the river and

gained possession of the crossing. During this time, Collis' First Brigade and Ward's Second Brigade supported the artillery with infantry fire. Prince's Second Division and Carr's Third Division arrived near the river, but they were not engaged. At 3:00 P.M., Third Corps began crossing the Rappahannock at Kelly's Ford. That same evening, November 7, 1863, Fifth Corps and Sixth Corps, which formed John Sedgwick's left wing, captured the Confederate bridgehead at Rappahannock Station, about five miles upstream from Kelly's Ford. For details, see Engagements at Rappahannock Station and Kelly's Ford, Virginia.

On the morning of November 8, 1863, Third Corps advanced to Brandy Station, where it remained until November 26, 1863. The wing or column organization was discontinued November 9, 1863.

Mine Run Campaign, Virginia, November 26, 1863–December 2, 1863. In late November 1863, Meade led the Army of the Potomac across the Rapidan River and into the Wilderness in an attempt to strike the right flank of Lee's army, which was in position along the south bank of the Rapidan River near Orange Court House. When this movement began on the morning of November 26, 1863, Third Corps marched from Brandy Station by way of Ross' Mill to the Rapidan River, where it crossed that evening at Jacob's Ford. The next morning, French marched south with orders to join Second Corps at Locust Grove (or Robertson's Tavern). On the way, however, Third Corps encountered Edward Johnson's Confederate division near Payne's farm, and was sharply engaged during the afternoon. As a result, it was delayed and did not reach Locust Grove until early on the morning of November 28, 1863.

That morning, the army advanced and found the enemy in a strong position on the west side of Mine Run, a tributary of the Rapidan. Third Corps followed Sixth Corps in this movement, and was then sent to the left of Meade's line, where it took position between the Turnpike and the Plank Road. The Confederate works appeared too strong for a successful frontal attack, and November 29, 1863, Meade sent Gouverneur K. Warren with his Second Corps and a division of Sixth Corps to make a flank attack on the enemy right. That evening he sent

Prince's division and Carr's division of Third Corps to join Warren. Meade also sent Birney's division to join John Newton's First Corps in a demonstration against the enemy center.

Early on the morning of November 30, 1863, however, Warren concluded that he could not successfully attack the enemy works on his front, and he so advised Meade. The attack for that day was then called off, and that evening the divisions of Third Corps returned to French's control. On the evening of December 1, 1863, the army began to withdraw toward the Rapidan. Third Corps crossed the river at Culpeper Ford that night and the next morning, and then returned to its camps at Brandy Station December 2–3, 1863. For additional information, see Mine Run Campaign, Virginia.

The division and brigade commanders in Third Corps during the Mine Run Campaign were, with two exceptions, the same as during the Bristoe, Virginia Campaign. Shortly before the beginning of the Mine Run Campaign, probably on November 22, 1863, Thomas W. Egan replaced De Trobriand in command of Third Brigade, First Division; and sometime after the Bristoe Campaign, William Blaisdell replaced Robert McAllister in command of First Brigade, Second Division.

Winter of 1863–1864. During the period January 9–13, 1864, Third Corps moved to Rixeys' farm, which was located between Brandy Station and Culpeper Court House, and about two and a half miles from the latter place. It then picketed the front from the vicinity of Culpeper Court House to the Stevensburg-Morton's Ferry Road. The corps remained generally in this position until it was discontinued March 24, 1864.

French departed on leave in January 1864, and Birney was in temporary command of the corps until he returned in February 1864.

There was some activity February 6–7, 1864, when the Army of the Potomac made a demonstration on the Rapidan River. Third Corps, commanded at that time by Birney, took part in this movement. Ward's First Division marched toward Raccoon Ford and camped near Pony Mountain, Prince's Second Division marched by way of Stevensburg to the vicinity of Morton's Ford, and Carr's Third Division marched by way of Culpeper Court House to Mitchell's Station. All three divisions returned to

their camps the next day. For additional information, see Army of the Potomac, Winter of 1863–1864.

On February 28, 1864, Judson Kilpatrick led a cavalry expedition against Richmond, Virginia, and at the same time George A. Custer conducted a raid into Albemarle County, Virginia to create a diversion. For details, see Kilpatrick's Expedition against Richmond, Virginia, and Custer's Raid into Albemarle County, Virginia. To support Custer, John Newton advanced his Sixth Corps to Madison Court House, and Birney moved with his First Division, Third Corps to James City to be in position to cooperate with Sedgwick. Birney remained at James City until March 2, 1864, and he then returned to camp. This was the last operation of the Army of the Potomac in which Third Corps took part.

Reorganization of the Army of the Potomac, March 1864. By an order of March 23, 1864, issued by the secretary of war, the number of infantry corps composing the Army of the Potomac was reduced from five to three. By this order First Corps and Third Corps were to be discontinued, and the troops of these two corps were to be distributed among the remaining three corps.

A following order from the War Department, dated March 24, 1864, directed that the troops of Second Corps, Fifth Corps, and Sixth Corps be consolidated into two divisions each, and it also assigned the divisions of First Corps and Third Corps as follows: the divisions of First Corps to Fifth Corps; Birney's First Division and Prince's Second Division of Third Corps to Second Corps as Third Division and Fourth Division, respectively; and Carr's Third Division, Third Corps to Sixth Corps as Third Division.

The divisions of Third Corps were not transferred with their former organizations of three brigades each, but they were reorganized as follows: In First Division, Collis' First Brigade, Ward's Second Brigade, and Egan's Third Brigade were all broken up, and their regiments were reassigned to a new First Brigade, Third Division, Second Corps under Ward; and a new Second Brigade, Third Division, Second Corps under Alexander Hays. Hays formerly commanded Third Division, Second Corps. Birney was assigned command of the new Third Division, Second Corps.

In Second Division, Third Corps, Blaisdell's First

Brigade and Mott's Third Brigade were consolidated to form a new First Brigade, Fourth Division, Second Corps, and Mott was assigned command of this brigade. Brewster's Second Brigade was simply redesignated as Second Brigade, Fourth Division, Second Corps, and remained under the command of Brewster. Carr, formerly commander of Third Division, Third Corps, was assigned command of the new Fourth Division, Second Corps. For additional information, see Second Corps, Army of the Potomac.

In Third Division, Third Corps, Benjamin F. Smith's Third Brigade was broken up, and its regiments were assigned to the other two brigades of the division. William H. Morris' First Brigade, thus reinforced, was redesignated as First Brigade, Third Division, Sixth Corps, and Morris remained in command of the brigade. Keifer's Second Brigade, Third Division, also reinforced, was redesignated as Second Brigade, Third Division, Sixth Corps. David A. Russell was assigned command of this brigade, but he was later replaced by Benjamin F. Smith. Prince, former commander of Second Division, Third Corps, was assigned command of the new Third Division, Sixth Corps. but he was later relieved by James B. Ricketts. For additional information, see Sixth Corps, Army of the Potomac.

The former troops of Third Corps were permitted to retain their corps and division badges and distinctive marks in the new organizations.

French was relieved from duty with the Army of the Potomac March 23, 1864, and was ordered to Philadelphia to report to the adjutant general of the army.

COMMANDERS OF THIRD CORPS, ARMY OF THE POTOMAC

Samuel P. Heintzelman	March 13, 1862 to November 7, 1862
George Stoneman	November 7, 1862 to February 7, 1863
Daniel E. Sickles	February 7, 1863 to May 1863
David B. Birney	May 1863 to June 28, 1863
Daniel E. Sickles	June 28, 1863 to July 2, 1863
David B. Birney	July 2, 1863 to July 9, 1863
William H. French	July 9, 1863 to November 6, 1863
David B. Birney	November 6, 1863 to November 9, 1863
William H. French	November 9, 1863 to January 28, 1864
David B. Birney	January 28, 1864 to February 17, 1864
William H. French	February 17, 1864 to March 24, 1864

THIRD CORPS, ARMY OF VIRGINIA
JUNE 26, 1862–SEPTEMBER 12, 1862

June 26, 1862, the Army of Virginia was created under John Pope, and was composed of troops of the Mountain Department and the departments of the Shenandoah and the Rappahannock. Third Corps, Army of Virginia was organized from Irvin McDowell's Department of the Rappahannock, and McDowell was assigned command. The corps was originally organized as follows:

THIRD CORPS, ARMY OF VIRGINIA, Irvin McDowell

First Division, Rufus King
  First Brigade, Christopher C. Augur, to July 11, 1862
    Timothy Sullivan, to July 27, 1862
    John P. Hatch
  Second Brigade, Abner Doubleday
  Third Brigade, Marsena R. Patrick
  Fourth Brigade, John Gibbon
  Artillery, Joseph B. Campbell
    1st Battery, New Hampshire Light Artillery, George A. Gerrish, captured
    Frederick M. Edgell
    Battery D, 1st Rhode Island Light Artillery, J. Albert Monroe
    Battery L, 1st New York Light Artillery, John A. Reynolds
    Battery B, 4th United States Artillery, Joseph B. Campbell

Note 1. First Brigade was organized from First Brigade, Third Division, Department of the Rappahannock.

Note 2. Second Brigade was organized from Doubleday's Brigade, Department of the Rappahannock.

Note 3. Third Brigade was organized from Second Brigade, Third Division, Department of the Rappahannock.

Note 4. Fourth Brigade was organized from Third Brigade, Third Division, Department of the Rappahannock.

Second Division, James B. Ricketts
  First Brigade, Abram Duryee
  Second Brigade, Zealous B. Tower
  Third Brigade, George L. Hartsuff
  Fourth Brigade, Samuel S. Carroll

Note 1. First Brigade was organized from Third Brigade, Third Division, Department of the Rappahannock.
Note 2. Second Brigade was organized from First Brigade, Edward O. C. Ord's Division, Department of the Rappahannock.
Note 3. Third Brigade was organized from Third Brigade, Edward O. C. Ord's Division, Department of the Rappahannock.
Note 4. Fourth Brigade was formerly Fourth Brigade of James Shields' Division, Department of the Rappahannock, and during July 1862 it had served in Samuel D. Sturgis' Reserve Corps at Alexandria, Virginia. It joined Third Corps at Warrenton July 25, 1862, and was assigned to Ricketts' division August 4, 1862.

During most of the time that Third Corps was in existence the divisions of the corps did not operate together. When Pope assumed command of the Army of Virginia, Ricketts' division was near Manassas and King's division was at Falmouth. July 3, 1862, Ricketts' division was ordered to Warrenton, but King's division was left near Fredericksburg. When Pope began to concentrate his army near Culpeper Court House, preparatory to moving on Gordonsville, Ricketts marched to Culpeper Court House August 6, 1862, three days before the Battle of Cedar Mountain. Ricketts' division moved to the battlefield near the end of the fighting and was under fire for a time, but was not otherwise engaged. King's division also joined the army at Culpeper Court House August 11, 1862.

Samuel S. Carroll's former Fourth Brigade of James Shields' Division, Department of the Rappahannock joined Pope's army at Warrenton July 25, 1862, and joined Ricketts' division on the Aestham River August 5, 1862. It was assigned to the division as Fourth Brigade. Carroll was wounded near the Rapidan River, after the Battle of Cedar Mountain, and Joseph Thoburn assumed command of the brigade.

Third Corps withdrew with the rest of the army from the Rapidan River when Robert E. Lee advanced at the beginning of the Northern Virginia Campaign, and it took position behind the Rappahannock.

John F. Reynolds' division (formerly George McCall's) of Fitz John Porter's Fifth Corps, Army of the Potomac arrived from the Peninsula and joined the army at Warrenton August 22, 1862. It was attached temporarily to Third Corps, Army of Virginia.

During Lee's flanking march around the right of Pope's army, Third Corps marched to the vicinity of Gainesville, and then the divisions of the corps were again separated. Ricketts' division was sent to oppose Longstreet's march through Thoroughfare Gap, and the other two divisions marched toward Manassas Junction. The march order was then changed, and on the evening of August 28, 1862, Gibbon's and Doubleday's divisions were engaged with Thomas J. (Stonewall) Jackson's Confederate corps near Gainesville (at Brawner's farm). During the night, Ricketts' division marched to Bristoe Station, King's division to Manassas Junction, and Reynolds' division camped near Groveton. King then became too ill to command, and John P. Hatch assumed command of Second Division. Timothy Sullivan took charge of Hatch's First Brigade.

At the Battle of Groveton August 29, 1862, Reynolds' division was with Franz Sigel's First Corps during the fighting that day. Hatch, with King's division, arrived on the battlefield late in the afternoon and was in action on the Warrenton Turnpike. Ricketts' division did not arrive on the field until late in the evening, and was not engaged.

The entire corps took part in the Second Battle of Bull Run August 30, 1862, but it was not under McDowell's control. During the Federal attack that afternoon, Ricketts' division was attached to Samuel P. Heintzelman's Third Corps, Army of the Potomac, and Reynolds' and Hatch's divisions were attached to Fitz John Porter's Fifth Corps, Army of the Potomac.

For details of the operations and changes in command of Third Corps, Army of Virginia during the period of its existence, see Pope's Northern Virginia Campaign, and see also Maryland Campaign (South Mountain and Antietam).

Third Corps retreated with the rest of the army into the Defenses of Washington September 2, 1862, and upon arrival there took position at Ball's

Crossroads, on the road south from the Aqueduct Bridge. September 6, 1862, the corps moved from the south side of the Potomac River to Leesboro, Maryland, where it joined Jesse L. Reno's Ninth Corps, Army of the Potomac. The next day, Joseph Hooker relieved McDowell in command of Third Corps, Army of Virginia, and that same day, September 7, 1862, Ambrose E. Burnside assumed command of the Right Wing of the Army of the Potomac, which consisted of Hooker's Third Corps and Reno's Ninth Corps.

The army then advanced into Maryland in pursuit of the Army of Northern Virginia, which had moved into the state after the Battle of Bull Run. On September 12, 1862, while the army was near Frederick, Maryland at the beginning of McClellan's Maryland Campaign, the designation of Hooker's Third Corps, Army of Virginia was changed to First Corps, Army of the Potomac. The brigade and division designations were unchanged. Carroll's Fourth Brigade, Second Division, Third Corps, Army of Virginia had been detached from the division August 31, 1862, and had been sent to Fairfax Station to guard commissary stores. It did not rejoin the division, but in the reorganization of September 12, 1862, it was assigned to Amiel W. Whipple's Division, Defenses of Washington.

The commanders of Third Corps, Army of Virginia were as follows:

Irvin McDowell   June 26, 1862 to September 7, 1862
Joseph Hooker   September 7, 1862 to September 12, 1862

FOURTH CORPS, ARMY OF THE POTOMAC

Fourth Corps, Army of the Potomac was created by a presidential order of March 8, 1862, which also created First Corps, Second Corps, Third Corps, and Fifth Corps. Fourth Corps was organized March 13, 1862 under the command of Erasmus D. Keyes, as follows:

FOURTH CORPS, Erasmus D. Keyes

First Division, Darius N. Couch

Graham's Brigade (First Brigade), Lawrence P. Graham
Peck's Brigade (Second Brigade), John J. Peck
Briggs' Brigade (Third Brigade), Henry S. Briggs
Artillery
  Battery C, 1st Pennsylvania Light Artillery, Jeremiah McCarthy
  Battery D, 1st Pennsylvania Light Artillery, Edward H. Flood
  Battery E, 1st Pennsylvania Light Artillery, Theodore Miller
  Battery H, 1st Pennsylvania Light Artillery, James Brady

Smith's Division (Second Division), William F. Smith
First Brigade, Winfield S. Hancock
Second Brigade, William T. H. Brooks
Third Brigade, John W. Davidson
Artillery
  Battery F, 5th United States Artillery, Romeyn B. Ayres
  3rd Battery, New York Light Artillery, Thaddeus P. Mott
  Battery E, 1st New York Light Artillery, Charles C. Wheeler
  1st Battery, New York Light Artillery, Terence J. Kennedy

Casey's Division (Third Division), Silas Casey
First Brigade, Henry M. Naglee
Second Brigade, William H. Keim
Third Brigade, Innis N. Palmer
Artillery
  7th Battery, New York Light Artillery, Peter C. Regan
  8th Battery, New York Light Artillery, Butler Fitch
  Battery A, 1st New York Light Artillery, Thomas H. Bates
  Battery H, 1st New York Light Artillery, Joseph Spratt

The corps moved to the Peninsula in late March 1862 with George B. McClellan's Army of the Potomac, and it took part in the siege of Yorktown April 5, 1862–May 4, 1862, and the Battle of Williamsburg May 5, 1862, where it suffered only slight loss. At Williamsburg, First Division was organized as follows:

First Division, Darius N. Couch
Graham's Brigade (First Brigade), Julius W. Adams
Peck's Brigade (Second Brigade), John J. Peck
Third Brigade, Charles Devens, Jr.

Note 1. Graham became ill in late April 1862, and Adams assumed temporary command of his brigade.

Note 2. Devens assumed command of Third Brigade about May 1, 1862, and Briggs resumed command of his 10th Massachusetts Infantry.

After the Battle of Williamsburg, Fourth Corps moved up the Peninsula to the vicinity of White House, and by mid-May 1862, Smith's Division was at White House, and Couch's and Casey's divisions were at New Kent Court House.

The Army of the Potomac was reorganized by an order of May 18, 1862, and Smith's Division was detached from Fourth Corps and assigned to William B. Franklin's newly created Sixth Provisional Corps as Second Division. Franklin assumed command of Sixth Provisional Corps May 23, 1862.

The army continued its advance from White House toward Richmond, and May 20, 1862, Fourth Corps arrived at Bottom's Bridge on the Chickahominy River. It then crosssed and marched to Seven Pines and Fair Oaks, in front of Richmond. Fourth Corps was supported by Samuel P. Heintzelman's Third Corps.

On May 31, 1862, a large enemy force commanded by Joseph E. Johnston strongly attacked Fourth Corps at Seven Pines. Casey's and Couch's divisions were engaged in severe fighting and were driven from their initial positions. Heintzelman's Third Corps and Edwin V. Sumner's Second Corps came up in support of Fourth Corps, and they finally halted the enemy advance.

At the Battle of Seven Pines, Fourth Corps was organized as follows:

FOURTH CORPS, Erasmus D. Keyes

First Division, Darius N. Couch
First Brigade, John J. Peck
Second Brigade, Henry W. Wessells, to May 24, 1862
John J. Abercrombie
Third Brigade, Charles Devens, Jr., May 31, 1862, wounded
Charles H. Innes
Artillery Brigade, Robert M. West
Battery C, 1st Pennsylvania Light Artillery, Jeremiah McCarthy
Battery D, 1st Pennsylvania Light Artillery, Edward H. Flood
Battery E, 1st Pennsylvania Light Artillery, Theodore Miller
Battery H, 1st Pennsylvania Light Artillery, James Brady

Note. Wessells relieved Julius W. Adams in command of Graham's Brigade May 19, 1862, and May 24, 1862 was assigned command of Second Brigade in Casey's Division. Abercrombie succeeded Wessells in command of Second Brigade, First Division May 24, 1862.

Third Division, Silas Casey
First Brigade, Henry M. Naglee
Second Brigade, William H. Keim, to May 18, 1862, died
Joshua B. Howell, to May 24, 1862
Henry W. Wessells
Third Brigade, Innis N. Palmer
Artillery, Guilford D. Bailey, to May 31, 1862, killed
D. H. Van Valkenburg, May 31, 1862, killed
Peter C. Regan
Battery A, 1st New York Light Artillery, George P. Hart
Battery H, 1st New York Light Artillery, Joseph Spratt, wounded
Charles E. Mink
7th Battery, New York Light Artillery, Peter C. Regan
8th Battery, New York Light Artillery, Butler Fitch

8th Pennsylvania Cavalry, David McM. Gregg

Fourth Corps was reorganized June 7, 1862. The three brigades of Casey's division were consolidated into two brigades under Wessells and Naglee, and the designation of Third Division was changed to Second Division, Fourth Corps. In this way, Third Division was discontinued. Fourth Corps was then organized as follows:

FOURTH CORPS, Erasmus D. Keyes

First Division, Darius N. Couch
First Brigade, John J. Peck
Second Brigade, John J. Abercrombie
Third Brigade, Innis N. Palmer

Note 1. Palmer was assigned June 7, 1862 to command Devens' Third Brigade. He relieved Charles H. Innes, who commanded the brigade temporarily after Devens was wounded at Seven Pines,

Note 2. Peck was assigned command of Casey's Second Division June 23, 1862, and Albion P. Howe was assigned command of Peck's brigade.

Second Division, Silas Casey
First Brigade, Henry M. Naglee
Second Brigade, Henry M. Wessells

Note. John J. Peck relieved Casey in command of Second Division June 24, 1862.

June 25, 1862, Heintzelman's Third Corps advanced at Oak Grove, south of the Chickahominy River, as a preliminary movement in McClellan's plan to continue his march toward Richmond. Late in the day, Palmer's brigade of Couch's division, Fourth Corps was sent forward in support of Heintzelman, but it was not seriously engaged.

During the opening battles of the Seven Days at Mechanicsville and Gaines' Mill June 26–27, 1862, Fourth Corps remained near Seven Pines on the extreme left of the Union line. It then moved to the south side of White Oak Swamp, where it remained for the next two days to protect the army wagon train, which was then moving from White House to Harrison's Landing during McClellan's retreat to the James River.

Fourth Corps moved to Malvern Hill June 30, 1862, and from there Peck's division marched on to Harrison's Landing. Couch's division remained with the rest of the army, and was engaged at the Battle of Malvern Hill July 1, 1862. It then retired with the army to Harrison's Landing.

For details of the operations of Fourth Corps on the Peninsula, see Peninsular Campaign.

The organization of Fourth Corps during the Seven Days' Battles was as follows:

FOURTH CORPS, Erasmus D. Keyes

First Division, Darius N. Couch
  First Brigade, Albion P. Howe
  Second Brigade, John J. Abercrombie
  Third Brigade, Innis N. Palmer
  Artillery
    Battery C, 1st Pennsylvania Light Artillery, Jeremiah McCarthy
    Battery D, 1st Pennsylvania Light Artillery, Edward H. Flood

Second Division, John J. Peck
  First Brigade, Henry M. Naglee
  Second Brigade, Henry W. Wessells
  Artillery
    Battery H, 1st New York Light Artillery, Charles E. Mink
    7th Battery, New York Light Artillery, Peter C. Regan

Reserve Artillery, Robert M. West
  8th Battery, New York Light Artillery, Butler Fitch
  Battery E, 1st Pennsylvania Light Artillery, Theodore Miller

Battery H, 1st Pennsylvania Light Artillery, James Brady
Battery M, 5th United States Artillery, James McKnight

In July 1862, while on the James River, Fourth Corps was again reorganized. The designation of Abercrombie's Second Brigade, First Division was changed to Third Brigade, First Division, and John Cochrane was assigned command; the designation of First Brigade, First Division was changed to Second Brigade, First Division; and the designation of Third Brigade, First Division was changed to First Brigade, First Division. In addition to the reorganization of First Division, Orris S. Ferry's Second Brigade of James Shields' First Division, Department of the Rappahannock arrived at Harrison's Landing July 2, 1862, and was assigned to Second Division, Fourth Corps as Third Brigade. Fourth Corps was then organized as follows:

FOURTH CORPS, Erasmus D. Keyes

First Division, Darius N. Couch
  First Brigade, Innis N. Palmer, to July 26, 1862
    Charles Devens, Jr.
  Second Brigade, Albion P. Howe
  Third Brigade, John Cochrane

  Note 1. First Brigade was formerly Third Brigade, First Division.
  Note 2. Second Brigade was formerly First Brigade, First Division.
  Note 3. Third Brigade was formerly Second Brigade, First Division.

Second Division, John J. Peck
  First Brigade, Henry M. Naglee, to July 6, 1862
    William H. Emory
  Second Brigade, Henry W. Wessells
  Third Brigade, Orris S. Ferry

When the Army of the Potomac left the Peninsula during the latter part of August 1862 to join John Pope's Army of Virginia, Fourth Corps was ordered to Yorktown, Virginia. There the two divisions of the corps were separated. Couch's First Division was sent on to Alexandria with the Army of the Potomac; and Keyes, with Peck's Second Division, remained on the Peninsula in the Department of Virginia.

Couch's division arrived at Alexandria August 30, 1862–September 1, 1862, and September 13,

1862 it was attached to Sixth Corps as First Division, Fourth Corps. It accompanied the army during the Maryland Campaign, and some of its regiments were engaged at the Battle of Antietam. After the battle, on September 26, 1862, the division was permanently attached to Sixth Corps as Third Division, Sixth Corps. Couch was assigned command of Second Corps October 7, 1862, and John Newton was assigned command of Couch's division.

For further information about Keyes' command at Yorktown, see Fourth Corps, Department of Virginia.

FOURTH CORPS, DEPARTMENT OF VIRGINIA

When the Army of the Potomac left the Peninsula in late August 1862 to join John Pope's Army of Virginia, Erasmus D. Keyes, commanding Fourth Corps, Army of the Potomac, was left behind at Yorktown with John J. Peck's Second Division, Fourth Corps. Darius N. Couch, with his First Division, Fourth Corps, accompanied the army north and did not rejoin the corps.

When Fourth Corps joined the Department of Virginia, Peck's division, which was posted at Yorktown, Williamsburg, and Gloucester Point, was organized as follows:

Second Division, Fourth Corps, John J. Peck
  First Brigade, Henry M. Naglee
  Second Brigade, Henry W. Wessells
  Third Brigade, Orris S. Ferry
  Artillery
    Battery H, 1st New York Light Artillery, Charles E. Mink
    7th Battery, New York Light Artillery, Peter C. Regan

Robert M. West's Artillery Reserve, Fourth Corps was also transferred to the Department of Virginia. This consisted of 8th Battery, New York Light Artillery; Battery E, 1st Pennsylvania Light Artillery; Battery H, 1st Pennsylvania Light Artillery; and Battery M, 5th United States Artillery.

August 23, 1862, the brigades of Ferry and Wessells were ordered to Fort Monroe to report to John

A. Dix, commander of the Department of Virginia and Seventh Corps. Ferry's brigade was then sent to Suffolk, where it became Ferry's Brigade, Division at Suffolk, Seventh Corps. In September 1862, Wessells' brigade also moved to Suffolk, and became Wessells' Brigade, Division at Suffolk, Seventh Corps. In the latter part of September 1862, Peck was assigned command at Suffolk. Naglee's brigade remained at Yorktown until the end of December 1862, and it was then sent to report to John G. Foster in the Department of North Carolina.

On December 15, 1862, Richard Busteed was ordered to report to Dix, and was assigned command of a brigade organized from regiments at Yorktown. This brigade was known as Busteed's Brigade until April 1, 1863, and then the designation was changed to King's Independent Brigade, under the command of Rufus King. On April 12, 1863, another brigade, known as West's Advance Brigade, was organized at Yorktown under the command of Robert M. West. The brigades of King and West were commanded by Keyes.

In May 1863, Fourth Corps was reorganized as follows:

FOURTH CORPS, Erasmus D. Keyes

First Division, Erasmus D. Keyes
  Advance Brigade, Robert M. West
  King's Brigade, Rufus King

    Note. First Division was at Yorktown.

Second Division, George H. Gordon
  First Brigade, William Gurney
  Second Brigade, Burr Porter

    Note. Gordon assumed command of the division (formerly John J. Abercrombie's) at Suffolk, Virginia May 4, 1863, and left with his command for West Point, Virginia the next day. The division remained at West Point until May 31, 1863, and then moved to Yorktown.

Reserve Artillery, James McKnight

    Note. The Reserve Artillery was at Yorktown.

First Division, Fourth Corps was reorganized June 17, 1863, as follows:

First Division, Fourth Corps, Rufus King
  First Brigade, Hector Tyndale
  Second Brigade, George H. Church
  Third Brigade, Charles Kleckner

Note. First Brigade was at Gloucester Point, Second Brigade was at Williamsburg, and Third Brigade was probably at Yorktown.

Fourth Corps was broken up in July 1863, and was officially discontinued August 1, 1863. The regiments of Third Brigade, First Division; Gordon's Second Division; and some regiments of Tyndale's First Brigade, First Division were transferred to Eleventh Corps, Army of the Potomac. Some of Tyndale's regiments were transferred to the Department of Washington, Twenty-Second Corps; and Church's Second Brigade. First Division was assigned to Yorktown, Department of Virginia and North Carolina.

For additional information about the organization and operations of Fourth Corps, see the following: Peninsular Campaign; and Department of Virginia, May 22, 1861–July 15, 1863.

FIFTH CORPS, ARMY OF THE POTOMAC (BANKS)

In the reorganization of the Army of the Potomac March 13, 1862 (see Army of the Potomac, Period of Organization), Nathaniel P. Banks' command in the Department of the Shenandoah was designated as Fifth Corps, Army of the Potomac. Banks assumed command March 20, 1862 (assigned March 13, 1862). At that time, Banks' Division and James Shields' Division (formerly Frederick W. Lander's) of the Army of the Potomac had just crossed the Potomac River from Maryland into Virginia, and Banks' Division occupied Winchester in the Shenandoah Valley.

The organization of Fifth Corps was as follows:

FIFTH CORPS, Nathaniel P. Banks

First Division, Alpheus S. Williams
First Brigade, Dudley Donnelly
Second Brigade, John J. Abercrombie
Third Brigade, George H. Gordon
Artillery
    Battery F, 4th United States Artillery, Clermont L. Best
    Battery F, Pennsylvania Light Artillery, Robert B. Hampton

Battery M, 1st New York Light Artillery, George W. Cothran
Battery E, Pennsylvania Light Artillery, Joseph M. Knap

Note 1. First Division was formerly Banks' Division of the Army of the Potomac.
Note 2. Gordon replaced Charles S. Hamilton in command of Third Brigade when the latter was assigned command of Third Division, Third Corps, Army of the Potomac.

Second Division, James Shields
First Brigade, Nathan Kimball
Second Brigade, Jeremiah C. Sullivan
Third Brigade, Erastus B. Tyler
Artillery
    Battery A, 1st West Virginia Light Artillery, John Jenks
    Battery B, 1st West Virginia Light Artillery, Samuel Davey
    Battery H, 1st Ohio Light Artillery, James F. Huntington
    Battery L, 1st Ohio Light Artillery, Lucius N. Robinson
    Battery E, 4th United States Artillery, Joseph C. Clark

Cavalry Command, John P. Hatch

Note. Hatch was assigned command March 28, 1862.

Geary's Independent Brigade, John W. Geary

Geary's command, which formerly belonged to Banks' Division, Army of the Potomac, was also called Geary's Brigade, Advance Brigade, and Detached Brigade. At the time Fifth Corps was formed, it was operating in Loudoun County, Virginia; and, March 13, 1862, it was at Upperville. For more information, see Shenandoah Valley Campaign (Jackson), 1862.

Banks advanced with his command down the Shenandoah Valley, but was halted at Strasburg March 20, 1862, after its occupation by Shields' division. George B. McClellan, who was then moving the Army of the Potomac to the Peninsula, ordered Banks to move to the vicinity of Manassas and fortify the area. Accordingly, Williams' division moved out of the valley toward Manassas, and Shields' division returned to Winchester. When Thomas J. (Stonewall) Jackson learned of Williams' movement, he marched down the valley to Kernstown, and there on March 23, 1862 he was defeated by Shields' division, commanded that day by Nathan Kimball. For details, see Shenandoah Valley Campaign (Jackson), 1862.

Banks' Fifth Corps was discontinued April 4, 1862 when, after an existence of a little more than two weeks, it was merged into the newly created Department of the Shenandoah (see).

FIFTH PROVISIONAL CORPS, ARMY OF THE POTOMAC

Fifth Corps was reorganized provisionally May 18, 1862, during the Peninsular Campaign, from Fitz John Porter's First Division, Third Corps; George Sykes' Independent Brigade of regulars, and Gouverneur K. Warren's Provisional Brigade, Army of the Potomac. Porter was assigned command. The corps was first known as Fifth Provisional Corps, and under this designation served during the remainder of the Peninsular Campaign until July 17, 1862. On that date George B. McClellan, commanding the Army of the Potomac, announced the change of designation to Fifth Corps, and this was officially confirmed by the secretary of war July 22, 1862.

For details of the organization and operations of Fifth Provisional Corps, see Fifth Corps, Army of the Potomac, and also Peninsular Campaign.

FIFTH CORPS, ARMY OF THE POTOMAC

Organization—Peninsular Campaign, May 18, 1862–August 1862. Fifth Corps was re-created provisionally May 18, 1862, during George B. McClellan's Peninsular Campaign. At that time, the Army of the Potomac was near White House, on the Pamunkey River. The corps was formed from Fitz John Porter's First Division, Third Corps and a division of regular army units under the command of George Sykes. The corps was designated as Fifth Provisional Corps, and Porter was assigned command. It was not until July 17, 1862 that McClellan announced a change of designation to Fifth Corps,

and this was officially confirmed July 22, 1862. In June 1862, the corps was organized as follows:

FIFTH PROVISIONAL CORPS, Fitz John Porter

First Division, George W. Morell
First Brigade, John H. Martindale
Second Brigade, James McQuade, to June 26, 1862
Charles Griffin
Third Brigade, Daniel Butterfield
1st United States Sharpshooters (unattached), Hiram Berdan
Artillery, William B. Weeden
3rd Battery (C), Massachusetts Light Artillery, Augustus P. Martin
5th Battery (E), Massachusetts Light Artillery, John H. Hyde
Battery C, 1st Rhode Island Light Artillery, William B. Weeden
Battery D, 5th United States Artillery, Henry W. Kingsbury
3rd Pennsylvania Cavalry, William W. Averell

Note 1. First Division was formerly Porter's First Division, Third Corps.
Note 2. McQuade assumed temporary command of Second Brigade when Morell assumed command of the division, and he was relieved by Griffin June 26, 1862.

Second Division, George Sykes
First Brigade, Robert C. Buchanan
Second Brigade, William Chapman, to June 27, 1862
Charles S. Lovell
Third Brigade, Gouverneur K. Warren
Artillery, Stephen H. Weed
Batteries L and M, 3rd United States Artillery, John Edwards
Battery I, 5th United States Artillery, Stephen H. Weed

Note. Second Division was organized from a brigade commanded by George Sykes, which was variously known as Reserve Brigade, the Infantry Reserve, and the Brigade of Regular Infantry. It was composed of regiments of regular infantry and Gouverneur K. Warren's 5th New York Infantry. Third Brigade was organized from 5th New York and the 1st Connecticut Heavy Artillery, then serving as infantry. Later the 1st Connecticut Heavy Artillery was replaced by the 10th New York Infantry.

Artillery Reserve, Army of the Potomac, Henry J. Hunt

Note. The Artillery Reserve, Army of the Potomac was assigned to duty with Fifth Corps May 20, 1862, and Hunt was ordered to report to Porter May 21, 1862. For the organization of the Artillery Reserve, see Peninsular Campaign, Reorganization of the Army, May 18, 1862.

During McClellan's advance on Richmond from White House, Fifth Corps moved along the north side of the Chickahominy River to Mechanicsville so as to be in position to link up with Irvin McDowell's command of the Department of the Rappahannock (formerly First Corps, Army of the Potomac), which was expected to march south from Fredericksburg.

May 26, 1862, Porter was ordered to lead an expedition to Hanover Court House and clear the country of enemy troops up to, or beyond, that point. Porter took with him Morell's division, William H. Emory's First Brigade of the Cavalry Reserve, and a provisional brigade commanded by Gouverneur K. Warren that had been organized May 24, 1862. After some sharp engagements with Confederate forces commanded by James H. Lane and Lawrence O'B. Branch on May 27, 1862, Porter drove them from the area, and on May 29, 1862 returned to his position on the right of the army. Warren's Provisional Brigade was discontinued May 31, 1862. For details of this operation, see Peninsular Campaign, Engagement at Hanover Court House.

June 12–13, 1862, George McCall's division of Pennsylvania Reserves, from McDowell's Department of the Rappahannock, arrived on the Peninsula, and June 18, 1862, it was attached to Fifth Provisional Corps as Third Division. McCall's division was not, however, detached from the Department of the Rappahannock, but it continued to serve under Porter's command during the Peninsular Campaign. First Brigade of McCall's division was commanded by John F. Reynolds, Second Brigade by George G. Meade, and Third Brigade by Truman Seymour. Also attached to McCall's division was James H. Childs' 4th Pennsylvania Cavalry and John F. Farnsworth's 8th Illinois Cavalry.

Porter's corps remained near Mechanicsville during most of June 1862, but June 26, 1862, it was then strongly attacked in its positions along Beaver Dam Creek by Confederate troops under Ambrose P. Hill, at the beginning of the Seven Days' Battles. Porter repulsed all attacks, but fell back during the night to a new position near Gaines' Mill. It was heavily assailed there the next day by the greater part of Robert E. Lee's army, and late in the evening was driven from the field. It crossed to the south side of the Chickahominy that night, and then moved on south toward the James River. Reynolds was captured during the battle, and was succeeded in command of First Brigade, Third Division by Seneca G. Simmons.

Morell's and Sykes' divisions reached Malvern Hill June 30, 1862, but McCall's division was left in position near Glendale, on the Long Bridge Road, to aid in covering the retreat of the army toward the James River. During the Battle of Glendale that day, McCall's division was powerfully attacked, and driven back with heavy losses. Losses among the officers of the division were particularly serious. McCall was captured, and Truman Seymour assumed command of the division. C. Feger Jackson relieved Seymour in command of Third Brigade. Simmons was killed, and R. Biddle Roberts succeeded him in command of First Brigade. George G. Meade was wounded, and Albert L. Magilton took charge of Second Brigade.

During the Battle of Malvern Hill July 1, 1862, Fifth Provisional Corps occupied the western end of the Union line. The enemy attacks fell largely on Morell's First Division and also on Darius N. Couch's First Division of Fourth Corps. During the fighting, Sykes' division was sent to support Morell. For details of the operations of Fifth Provisional Corps during the Seven Days, see Peninsular Campaign, Seven Days' Battles.

The organization of Fifth Provisional Corps during the Seven Days was as follows:

FIFTH PROVISIONAL CORPS, Fitz John Porter

First Division, George W. Morell
  First Brigade, John H. Martindale
  Second Brigade, Charles Griffin
  Third Brigade, Daniel Butterfield
  1st United States Sharpshooters, Hiram Berdan
  Artillery, William B. Weeden
      3rd Battery (C), Massachusetts Light Artillery, Augustus P. Martin
      5th Battery (E), Massachusetts Light Artillery, John H. Hyde
      Battery C, 1st Rhode Island Light Artillery, William B. Weeden
      Battery D, 5th United States Artillery, Henry W. Kingsbury

Second Division, George Sykes
  First Brigade, Robert C. Buchanan
  Second Brigade, George H. Chapman, to June 27, sick
      Charles S. Lovell

Third Brigade, Gouverneur K. Warren

Artillery, Stephen H. Weed

Batteries L and M, 3rd United States Artillery, John Edwards

Battery I, 5th United States Artillery, Stephen H. Weed

Third Division, George McCall, to June 30, captured
Truman Seymour

First Brigade, John F. Reynolds, to June 27, 1862, captured

Seneca G. Simmons, to June 30, 1862, killed

R. Biddle Roberts

Second Brigade, George G. Meade, to June 30, 1862, wounded

Albert L. Magilton

Third Brigade, Truman Seymour, to June 30, 1862

C. Feger Jackson

Artillery, Henry V. De Hart

Battery A, 1st Pennsylvania Light Artillery, John G. Simpson

Battery B, 1st Pennsylvania Light Artillery, James H. Cooper

Battery G, 1st Pennsylvania Light Artillery, Frank P. Amsden

Battery C, 5th United States Artillery, Henry V. De Hart

4th Pennsylvania Cavalry, James H. Childs

8th Illinois Cavalry, John F. Farnsworth

After the Battle of Malvern Hill, Fifth Provisional Corps retired with the rest of the army to Harrison's Landing on the James River, where it remained until mid-August 1862. While there, on July 22, 1862, its designation as Fifth Corps was officially confirmed.

With Pope's Army of Virginia (Campaign in Northern Virginia), August 16, 1862–September 2, 1862. By the second week of August 1862, Robert E. Lee concluded that McClellan did not intend to renew active operations on the James River, and he decided to send reinforcements to Thomas J. (Stonewall) Jackson, who was then to advance against John Pope's Army of Virginia, which was in position in front of Washington. Accordingly, on August 13, 1862, Lee sent James Longstreet's corps and James E. B. (Jeb) Stuart's cavalry to Gordonsville to join Jackson, and then, on August 16, 1862, he advanced toward the Army of Virginia, which was in position along the north bank of the Rapidan River and on the railroad toward Culpeper Court House.

That same day, the Army of the Potomac began to withdraw from the Peninsula to join Pope. Fifth Corps was the first to leave, embarking August 19–20, 1862, and it arrived at Aquia Creek August 21–22, 1862. Meantime, Pope had been forced to withdraw to the east bank of the Rappahannock. Seymour's Third Division (formerly McCall's) moved to Fredericksburg August 21, 1862, and there it was reorganized as follows: John F. Reynolds, who was captured at Gaines' Mill June 27, 1862 and exchanged August 8, 1862, was assigned command of the division; George G. Meade's Second Brigade was designated as First Brigade; Seymour was assigned command of John F. Reynolds' First Brigade, which was then designated as Second Brigade; and C. Feger Jackson, who had succeeded Seymour in command of Third Brigade when the latter assumed command of the division at the Battle of Glendale, was left in command of Third Brigade. Reynolds' division then marched to Warrenton, where it was attached temporarily to Irvin McDowell's Third Corps, Army of Virginia as Reynolds' Division. It should be noted here that this division had formerly belonged to McDowell's command, and had never been officially detached from it.

Porter, with the divisions of Morell and Sykes, then constituting Fifth Corps, arrived at Aquia Creek August 22, 1862, and marched to Warrenton Junction, where he joined the Army of Virginia August 27, 1862. Fifth Corps guarded the trains that day, and then marched to join Pope, who had by that time retreated to Groveton. A. Sanders Piatt's Brigade of Samuel D. Sturgis' Reserve Corps, Army of Virginia was attached to Fifth Corps at that time.

On August 29, 1862, during the Battle of Groveton, Porter's corps was in position on Dawkins' Branch, south of the Manassas Gap Railroad, and about two and one-half miles south of Groveton. It was not engaged that day. Reynolds' division, however, which was then with McDowell's corps of the Army of Virginia, did take part in the battle. That night, Fifth Corps marched to join Pope, and arrived on the battlefield at daybreak the next morning. By mistake, Morell went to Centerville that day with Piatt's Brigade and Charles Griffin's Second Brigade of First Division. Piatt's Brigade rejoined the corps on the battlefield, but Morell and Griffin's brigade remained at Centerville and was not present during the Second Battle of Bull

Run, September 30, 1862. For additional information, see Pope's Northern Virginia Campaign.

The organization of Fifth Corps while with the Army of Virginia was as follows:

FIFTH CORPS, Fitz John Porter

First Division, George W. Morell
 Daniel Butterfield, September 30, 1862
 First Brigade, Charles W. Roberts
 Second Brigade, Charles Griffin
 Third Brigade, Daniel Butterfield, to September 30, 1862
  Henry S. Lansing, September 30, 1862, sick
  Henry A. Weeks, September 30, 1862, wounded
  James C. Rice, September 30, 1862
  Daniel Butterfield
 Artillery
  3rd Battery (C), Massachusetts Light Artillery, Augustus P. Martin
  Battery C, 1st Rhode Island Light Artillery, Richard Waterman
  Battery D, 5th United States Artillery, Charles E. Hazlett

Note. Morell was with Griffin's division at Centerville September 30, 1862, and Daniel Butterfield commanded First Brigade and Third Brigade at the Second Battle of Bull Run that day.

Second Division, George Sykes
 First Brigade, Robert C. Buchanan
 Second Brigade, William Chapman
 Third Brigade, Gouverneur K. Warren
 Artillery, Stephen H. Weed
  Batteries E and G, 1st United States Artillery, Alanson M. Randol
  Battery I, 5th United States Artillery, Stephen H. Weed
  Battery K, 5th United States Artillery, John R. Smead, to August 30, 1862, killed
   William E. Van Reed

Maryland Campaign, September 3, 1862–September 20, 1862. Porter's Fifth Corps retreated with the Army of Virginia into the Defenses of Washington, following Pope's defeat at the Second Battle of Bull Run, and it then took position at Hall's Hill, south of the Potomac River. George B. McClellan was then called upon to reorganize the troops of the Army of the Potomac and of the Army of Virginia. For additional information, see Military District of the Defenses of Washington, Army of the Potomac.

September 4, 1862, Reynolds' Division (formerly Third Division, Fifth Corps), which had been attached to McDowell's Third Corps, Army of Virginia since August 26, 1862, was ordered to rejoin Fifth Corps. This order was not carried out, however, and Reynolds' Division remained with Third Corps, Army of Virginia until September 12, 1862, when the latter was reorganized as First Corps, Army of the Potomac. Its designation then became Third Division, First Corps, and it was commanded by George G. Meade.

On September 4, 1862, the Army of Northern Virginia crossed the Potomac River into Maryland at White's Ford, and advanced toward Frederick. McClellan then began to shift troops to the north side of the Potomac. September 6, 1862, George Sykes' Second Division, Fifth Corps was ordered to Tennallytown to constitute a reserve for the army that McClellan was then assembling to follow Lee into Maryland. Sykes' division was detached from Fifth Corps, and was ordered to report directly to McClellan. This left Porter with only Morell's First Division, south of the Potomac. At that time Morell's brigades were commanded as follows: Martindale's First Brigade, by James Barnes; Second Brigade, by Charles Griffin; and Butterfield's Third Brigade, by Thomas B. W. Stockton.

On the day that Sykes' division was detached from Fifth Corps, September 6, 1862, a new division was organized and assigned to Porter. This division consisted of Erastus B. Tyler's Brigade from the Defenses of Washington, and A. Sanders Piatt's Brigade. Samuel D. Sturgis was assigned command, but the next day Sturgis was ordered to report to Ninth Corps. The new division was then enlarged by the addition of Peter H. Allabach's Brigade from the Defenses of Washington, and it was assigned to the command of Amiel W. Whipple. September 11, 1862, Porter received orders to report with Fifth Corps, then consisting only of Morell's First Division, to McClellan at Brookville, Maryland. The next day, a new division was organized in the Defenses of Washington from Whipple's Division, and it was assigned to Fifth Corps as Third Division, under the command of Andrew A. Humphreys. It consisted of Tyler's First Brigade and Allabach's Second Brigade. Whipple and Piatt's Brigade remained in the Defenses of Washington.

When McClellan advanced with his army to Frederick at the beginning of the Maryland Campaign, Sykes' division of Fifth Corps followed, and then, after the Battle of South Mountain, September 14, 1862, it marched toward Sharpsburg. It arrived on Antietam Creek on the evening of September 15, 1862. Morell's division followed Sykes and joined him during the afternoon of the following day. Both divisions were on the field during the Battle of Antietam, September 17, 1862, but they were held in reserve and were not engaged. Humphreys' new Third Division started late from Washington, and did not join the other two divisions until the day after the battle. For details of the operations in Maryland, see Maryland Campaign (South Mountain and Antietam).

The organization of Fifth Corps at the time of the Battle of Antietam was as follows:

FIFTH CORPS, Fitz John Porter

First Division, George W. Morell
    First Brigade, James Barnes
    Second Brigade, Charles Griffin
    Third Brigade, Henry S. Lansing, to September 18, 1862
        Thomas B. W. Stockton
    Artillery
        Battery C, Massachusetts Light Artillery, Augustus P. Martin
        Battery C, 1st Rhode Island Light Artillery, Richard Waterman
        Battery D, 5th United States Artillery, Charles E. Hazlett

Second Division, George Sykes
    First Brigade, Robert C. Buchanan
    Second Brigade, William Chapman
    Third Brigade, Gouverneur K. Warren
    Artillery
        Batteries E and G, 1st United States Artillery, Alanson M. Randol
        Battery I, 5th United States Artillery, Stephen H. Weed
        Battery K, 5th United States Artillery, William E. Van Reed

Third Division, Andrew A. Humphreys
    First Brigade, Erastus B. Tyler
    Second Brigade, Peter H. Allabach
    Artillery, Lucius N. Robinson
        Battery C, 1st New York Light Artillery, Almont Barnes

Battery L, 1st Ohio Light Artillery, Lucius N. Robinson

Artillery Reserve, William Hays
    Battery A, 1st Battalion New York Light Artillery, Bernhard Wever
    Battery B, 1st Battalion New York Light Artillery, Alfred Von Kleiser
    Battery C, 1st Battalion New York Light Artillery, Robert Langner
    Battery D, 1st Battalion New York Light Artillery, Charles Kusserow
    5th Battery, New York Light Artillery, Elijah D. Taft
    Battery K, 1st United States Artillery, William M. Graham
    Battery G, 4th United States Artillery, Marcus P. Miller

Antietam to Warrenton, Virginia, September 19, 1862–November 7, 1862. After the Battle of Antietam, Porter's Fifth Corps remained near Sharpsburg until the end of October 1862. The Army of the Potomac began crossing the Potomac River October 26, 1862 on its advance into Virginia, and October 30, 1862, Porter was ordered to Harper's Ferry. Fifth Corps crossed the river there October 31, 1862–November 1, 1862, and followed Darius N. Couch's Second Corps to Snickersville, Virginia. It then moved south through Middleburg and arrived at White Plains November 7, 1862. Two days later it marched to Waterloo.

There were some changes in command during this period. Morell was assigned command of the Defenses of the Upper Potomac (see Army of the Potomac, Antietam Creek, Maryland to Warrenton, Virginia) October 30, 1862. Charles Griffin commanded First Division temporarily November 1, 1862, and then Daniel Butterfield assumed command. Thomas B. W. Stockton commanded Butterfield's Third Brigade. First Brigade, First Division was generally referred to during this period as Martindale's Brigade. Porter had preferred charges against Martindale August 3, 1862, and the latter was absent from his command, although not relieved, from that time until the end of a court of inquiry that was held October 8–31, 1862. The charges against Martindale were disapproved, but he was relieved from command of First Brigade November 1, 1862. He was then assigned as commander of the District of Columbia and as military governor November 20, 1862. Charles S. Lovell relieved William Chapman in command of Second Brigade, Second Division in

October 1862, and the following month George L. Andrews relieved Lovell.

Fredericksburg, Virginia Campaign, November 7, 1862–December 15, 1862.

Two important command changes occurred in the army during the early part of November 1862, while it was near Warrenton. On the night of November 7, 1862, Ambrose E. Burnside relieved McClellan in command of the Army of the Potomac, and by an order dated November 10, 1862 (presidential order of November 5, 1862), Fitz John Porter was relieved from command of Fifth Corps and ordered to Washington. There he was tried by court martial on charges preferred by John Pope because of his conduct at the Second Battle of Bull Run. He was found guilty by the court, which convened November 27, 1862, and was cashiered from the army. Joseph Hooker succeeded Porter in command of Fifth Corps November 12, 1862.

Upon assuming command of the Army of the Potomac, Burnside submitted to Henry W. Halleck a plan for moving the army eastward to Fredericksburg, and from that point south toward Richmond. This plan was approved November 14, 1862, and that same day Burnside reorganized the army into three grand divisions and a reserve. Fifth Corps and the newly reorganized Third Corps, commanded by George Stoneman, were assigned to the Center Grand Division. November 16, 1862, Hooker was given the command of the Center Grand Division, and Daniel Butterfield assumed command of Fifth Corps. Charles Griffin succeeded Butterfield in command of First Division, Fifth Corps, and Jacob B. Sweitzer took charge of Griffin's Second Brigade, First Division.

Hooker, with his two corps, followed Edwin V. Sumner's Right Grand Division toward Falmouth, and arrived near Hartwood Church, opposite United States Ford on the Rappahannock River, November 19, 1862. Then, after a rapid start, Burnside remained relatively inactive until the second week of December 1862, while he waited for pontoons to arrive from Washington so that he could cross the Rappahannock. The pontoons finally arrived, and the army began crossing December 11, 1862. Fifth Corps and Third Corps did not cross with the rest of the army December 11–12, 1862, but remained on the north bank, near the bridges.

Sumner launched a series of unsuccessful attacks on the Confederate positions in front of Marye's Hill during the morning of December 13, 1864, and about 2:00 P.M. Fifth Corps was sent across the river into Fredericksburg to make another effort. Griffin's First Division attacked about 3:30 P.M., and Humphreys' Third Division about a half-hour later, but both were repulsed with great loss. Sykes' Second Division also moved into Fredericksburg but did not attack. During the night, it moved out and covered the line in front of Fredericksburg, and it remained there the following day.

Fifth Corps withdrew across the Rappahannock with the rest of the army during the night of December 15, 1862. For details of the operations of the army and of Fifth Corps during the period November 15, 1862–December 15, 1862, see Fredericksburg, Virginia Campaign.

The organization of Fifth Corps at the Battle of Fredericksburg was as follows:

FIFTH CORPS, Daniel Butterfield

First Division, Charles Griffin
First Brigade, James Barnes
Second Brigade, Jacob B. Sweitzer
Third Brigade, Thomas B. W. Stockton
Artillery
 3rd Battery (C), Massachusetts Light Artillery, Augustus P. Martin
 5th Battery (E), Massachusetts Light Artillery, Charles A. Phillips
 Battery C, 1st Rhode Island Light Artillery, Richard Waterman
 Battery D, 5th United States Artillery, Charles E. Hazlett

Second Division, George Sykes
First Brigade, Robert C. Buchanan
Second Brigade, George L. Andrews, to December 15, 1862
Charles S. Lovell
Third Brigade, Gouverneur K. Warren
Artillery
 Battery L, 1st Ohio Light Artillery, Frederick Dorries
 Battery I, 5th United States Artillery, Malbone F. Watson

Note. Lovell returned from leave, and resumed command of Second Brigade on the morning of December 15, 1862.

Third Division, Andrew A. Humphreys
   First Brigade, Erastus B. Tyler
   Second Brigade, Peter H. Allabach
   Artillery
      Battery C, 1st New York Light Artillery, William H.
       Phillips
      Batteries E and G, 1st United States Artillery, Alanson M. Randol

Winter of 1862–1863. After Fifth Corps returned to the north bank of the Rappahannock December 15, 1862, it went into winter quarters along the Richmond, Fredericksburg, and Potomac Railroad, between Falmouth and Potomac Creek. Its rest was of short duration, however, because Burnside attempted once more to lead his army across the Rappahannock and engage the enemy. January 20, 1863, he marched up the Rappahannock with Hooker's and William B. Franklin's grand divisions with the intention of crossing the river at Banks' Ford and then advancing against the left and rear of Lee's army at Fredericksburg. Shortly after starting, it began to rain, and by the time the army reached the vicinity of Banks' Ford it was unable to continue because the roads had become impassable. This movement, which has been called the "Mud March" of the Army of the Potomac, was called off January 24, 1863, and Fifth Corps and the other corps returned to their camps.

There was no significant change in the organization of Fifth Corps during the winter, but there were some important command changes. December 26, 1862, George G. Meade, formerly commander of Third Division, First Corps, relieved Butterfield in command of Fifth Corps. January 26, 1863, Joseph Hooker relieved Burnside in command of the Army of the Potomac, and January 29, 1863, Butterfield was announced as Hooker's chief of staff. George Sykes temporarily commanded Fifth Corps February 1–5, 1863, during the absence of Meade. February 5, 1863, the grand divisions were abolished, and the corps commanders then reported directly to Headquarters Army of the Potomac. February 16, 1863, Meade left the army on a leave of absence, and Sykes again assumed temporary command of Fifth Corps. Andrew A. Humphreys relieved Sykes February 23, 1863, when the latter was called for court martial duty in New York, and remained in command of Fifth Corps until Meade returned February 27, 1863. There were also some changes in command in Second Division. February 5, 1863, Gouverneur K. Warren was assigned as chief topographical engineer at Hooker's headquarters, and Patrick H. O'Rorke assumed command of Third Brigade, Second Division. In March 1863, Sidney Burbank succeeded George L. Andrews in command of Second Brigade, Second Division; April 19, 1863, Romeyn B. Ayres was relieved from command of the Artillery Reserve of the army, and two days later, relieved Richard S. Smith in command of First Brigade, Second Division.

Chancellorsville, Virginia Campaign, April 27, 1863–May 6, 1863. After assuming command of the Army of the Potomac, Hooker began preparations for the spring campaign of 1863. His objective was Lee's army at Fredericksburg, and he developed a plan to attack and drive it from the town. According to this plan, John Sedgwick's Sixth Corps was to demonstrate below Fredericksburg, while three corps moved around Lee's left flank and struck his left and rear. The flanking column, commanded by Henry W. Slocum, was to consist of George G. Meade's Fifth Corps, Oliver O. Howard's Eleventh Corps, and Slocum's Twelfth Corps, and it was to move around to the right, pass through the Wilderness, and strike the left of the Army of Northern Virginia at Fredericksburg. Slocum's column marched to Kelly's Ford on the Rappahannock April 27–28, 1863, and after Fifth Corps had crossed the river, Meade marched with Charles Griffin's First Division and George Sykes' Second Division by way of Ely's Ford on the Rapidan River to Chancellorsville, where they arrived April 30, 1863. Andrew A. Humphreys' Third Division remained at Kelly's Ford April 29, 1863 to cover the passage of the trains and aid in taking up the bridges, and it then followed the other two divisions to Chancellorsville, and joined them there on the morning of April 31, 1863.

About 11:00 A.M. May 1, 1863, Meade moved his Fifth Corps eastward toward Fredericksburg. The divisions of Griffin and Humphreys advanced on the River Road, and Sykes' division moved forward on the Turnpike to the south. Sykes soon encountered strong enemy resistance and was forced to retire. The other two divisions advanced without opposition to a point near Banks' Ford, but when Sykes fell back, Griffin and Humphreys also withdrew, and returned to the vicinity of Chancellorsville late that evening. That night, Humphreys' division was formed on the extreme left of the Union line, along Mineral Spring Road; Griffin's division was on the left of Winfield S. Hancock's First Division of Darius N. Couch's Second Corps, and it extended northward to the Mineral Spring Road; and Sykes' division was southeast of Chancellorsville, on a line parallel to the Turnpike and facing south, between Hancock's division and Henry W. Slocum's Twelfth Corps.

On May 2, 1863, Fifth Corps was united behind the Mineral Spring Road, on a line that extended from Scott's Dam on the Rappahannock to Chancellorsville. It was not engaged during the day, but that night it moved to a new position along the Ely's Ford Road that extended from the Chandler house on the left, to the left of First Corps, near Hunting Run. This line faced southwest, in the direction of Thomas J. (Stonewall) Jackson's advance.

Erastus B. Tyler's First Brigade and Peter H. Allabach's Second Brigade of Humphreys' Third Division, Fifth Corps were engaged during the morning of May 3, 1863 in support of William H. French's Third Division, Second Corps, but the rest of the corps did not advance. Later in the day, Third Corps formed on the left of Fifth Corps on the new line.

Fifth Corps withdrew across the Rappahannock with the rest of the Army of the Potomac on the night of May 5, 1863, and it then returned to its former quarters near Falmouth. For details of the operations of Fifth Corps and the Army of the Potomac during the period May 27, 1862–May 7, 1863, see Chancellorsville, Virginia Campaign.

The organization of Fifth Corps during the Chancellorsville Campaign was as follows:

FIFTH CORPS, George G. Meade

First Division, Charles Griffin
  First Brigade, James Barnes
  Second Brigade, James McQuade, to May 4, 1863, disabled
    Jacob B. Sweitzer
  Third Brigade, Thomas B. W. Stockton
  Artillery, Augustus P. Martin
    3rd Battery (C), Massachusetts Light Artillery, Augustus P. Martin
    5th Battery (E), Massachusetts Light Artillery, Charles A. Phillips

    Battery C, 1st Rhode Island Light Artillery, Richard Waterman
    Battery D, 5th United States Artillery, Charles E. Hazlett

Second Division, George Sykes
  First Brigade, Romeyn B. Ayres
  Second Brigade, Sidney Burbank
  Third Brigade, Patrick H. O'Rorke
  Artillery, Stephen H. Weed
    Battery L, 1st Ohio Light Artillery, Frank C. Gibbs
    Battery I, 5th United States Artillery, Malbone F. Watson

Third Division, Andrew A. Humphreys
  First Brigade, Erastus B. Tyler
  Second Brigade, Peter H. Allabach
  Artillery, Alanson M. Randol
    Battery C, 1st New York Light Artillery, Almont Barnes
    Batteries E and G, 1st United States Artillery, Alanson M. Randol

Gettysburg Campaign, May 1863–July 1863. After the Battle of Chancellorsville, Meade's Fifth Corps took up a position north of Falmouth on a line that extended from Potomac Creek, near High Bridge, to the head of Clairburn Run, and remained there until the end of May 1863. During the month, Fifth Corps lost by muster out a total of eleven regiments. Six of these were from Humphreys' Third Division, leaving him with only two regiments. These were transferred to Third Brigade, Second Division, which had also been left with only two regiments, and May 25, 1863, Third Division, Fifth Corps was discontinued. Humphreys was assigned to the command of the late Hiram G. Berry's Second Division, Third Corps. Berry had been killed at Chancellorsville May 3, 1863.

The organization of Fifth Corps at the end of May 1863 was as follows:

FIFTH CORPS, George Meade

First Division, James Barnes
  First Brigade, William S. Tilton
  Second Brigade, Jacob B. Sweitzer
  Third Brigade, Thomas B. W. Stockton, to May 18, 1863, resigned
    Strong Vincent

Note. Barnes was in command of First Division during the absence of Charles Griffin, who was sick.

Second Division, George Sykes
First Brigade, Romeyn B. Ayres
Second Brigade, Sidney Burbank
Third Brigade, Patrick H. O'Rorke

Artillery Brigade, Augustus P. Martin
3rd Battery (C), Massachusetts Light Artillery, Augustus P. Martin
Battery C, 1st New York Light Artillery, Almont Barnes
Battery L, 1st Ohio Light Artillery, Frank C. Gibbs
Battery D, 5th United States Artillery, Charles E. Hazlett
Battery I, 5th United States Artillery, Malbone F. Watson

May 28, 1863, Barnes' First Division left its camps near the Telegraph Road to relieve Alfred Pleasonton's cavalry pickets along the Rappahannock. Strong Vincent's Third Brigade covered the river from Banks' Ford to the mouth of Deep Run, Jacob B. Sweitzer's Second Brigade from that point to Kelly's Ford, and William S. Tilton's First Brigade was placed in reserve at Morrisville. June 4, 1863, Sykes' Second Division was also ordered up to the Rappahannock. Two brigades of the division covered the river from Banks' Ford to Richard's Ford, and the other brigade was placed in reserve at Benson's Mills. Barnes' division then concentrated on the right of Sykes, and guarded the river toward Kelly's Ford. Fifth Corps remained on the river until June 13, 1863.

On June 12, 1863, Hooker assigned John F. Reynolds to command a temporary right wing of the army, which consisted of First Corps, Third Corps, Fifth Corps, Eleventh Corps, and the Cavalry Corps.

Meantime, Lee had decided to take the offensive by moving his army northward into Maryland and Pennsylvania. On June 3, 1863, he began to withdraw his troops from Fredericksburg and from along the Rapidan River in preparation for their march toward the Potomac River and Maryland. Hooker was aware that some movement was in progress, but it was not until June 13, 1863 that he became convinced that Lee was indeed marching northward, and at that time was in the Shenandoah Valley. He then issued orders for the Army of the Potomac to pull back from the line of the Rappahannock to the Orange and Alexandria Railroad. That day Fifth Corps left its positions along the Rappahannock and moved back with Reynolds'

Right Wing to Manassas Junction, where it arrived June 15, 1863. Two days later, it marched westward to Gum Springs and Aldie. On June 26, 1863, Fifth Corps crossed the Potomac into Maryland at Edwards Ferry with the rest of the army, and the next day encamped at Ballinger's Creek, near Frederick. While there, on June 28, 1863, Third Division, Fifth Corps was reorganized from Samuel W. Crawford's division of Pennsylvania Reserves, which had arrived from the Department of Washington. Crawford, with William McCandless' First Brigade and Joseph W. Fisher's Third Brigade, had left the vicinity of Washington, D.C. June 25, 1863, and arrived on Ballinger's Creek three days later. Horatio G. Sickel's Second Brigade was left in the Department of Washington.

Early on the morning of June 28, 1863, George G. Meade, commander of Fifth Corps, was assigned command of the Army of the Potomac, and he relieved Joseph Hooker that day. George Sykes assumed command of Fifth Corps, and Romeyn B. Ayres moved up to command Sykes' Second Division, Fifth Corps. Hannibal Day assumed command of Ayres' First Brigade, Second Division.

On June 29, 1863, when Meade began his advance on a wide front in search of Lee, Fifth Corps marched on the right flank, and was at Hanover, Pennsylvania July 1, 1863, when the Battle of Gettysburg began. It then headed for Gettysburg, and arrived on the field of battle on the morning of July 2, 1863. For details of the march to Gettysburg, see Gettysburg Campaign, Part I, From the Rappahannock to Gettysburg. Sometime before 8:00 A.M. July 2, 1863, Barnes' First Division and Ayres' Second Division arrived on the field near Wolf's Hill, to the right of Twelfth Corps. A short time later, they moved across Rock Creek, and massed near Power's Hill. Crawford's Third Division came up and joined the corps about noon. Probably about 3:00 P.M., Sykes was ordered to move his Fifth Corps to left of Meade's line, and was charged with the responsibility of protecting that flank.

Barnes' division arrived near the Wheatfield about an hour later, and was soon fighting desperately while contesting the advance of James Longstreet's corps, which had attacked on the Federal left that afternoon. William S. Tilton's First Brigade and Jacob Sweitzer's Second Brigade advanced across the Wheatfield to a point near the

Rose house, but they were soon outflanked and driven back. Later, Sweitzer advanced with John C. Caldwell's First Division, Second Corps, but was finally driven from the field with the other troops on that part of the line.

Strong Vincent's Third Brigade of Barnes' division was sent to Little Round Top, where it aided in a successful defense of the hill. Vincent was mortally wounded, and James C. Rice assumed command of his brigade. Ayres' division came up near Little Round Top while the fighting was going on, and Stephen H. Weed's Third Brigade was sent to aid Vincent's brigade in its defense. Weed was mortally wounded, and Kenner Garrard assumed command of his brigade. Hannibal Day's First Brigade and Sidney Burbank's Second Brigade of Ayres' division advanced toward the Devil's Den, on the left of Sweitzer, and helped for a time to check the enemy advance on that part of the field. A short time later, however, they were forced to retire to the line of the Round Tops. Late in the day, Joseph W. Fisher's Third Brigade of Crawford's division was sent to the Round Tops, and William McCandless' First Brigade of Crawford's division took position to the right of Little Round Top. McCandless' brigade made a successful charge and drove the enemy back into the Wheatfield, and then remained in position that night, a short distance west of Plum Run.

There was no change in position of the troops of Fifth Corps on July 3, 1863, except that Tilton's brigade was sent to relieve Rice's brigade on Little Round Top. The day was spent principally in burying the dead. For details of the Battle of Gettysburg, see Gettysburg Campaign, Part II, Battle of Gettysburg.

The organization of Fifth Corps during the Battle of Gettysburg was as follows:

FIFTH CORPS, George Sykes

First Division, James Barnes
  First Brigade, William S. Tilton
  Second Brigade, Jacob B. Sweitzer
  Third Brigade, Strong Vincent, to July 2, 1863, mortally wounded
    James C. Rice

Note. Barnes had been in command of First Division during the march to Gettysburg, and during the battle, due to the illness of its permanent commander, Charles Grif-
fin. Griffin returned to the army at Gettysburg July 3, 1863, and the next day relieved Barnes, who was suffering from a wound received during the battle.

Second Division, Romeyn B. Ayres
  First Brigade, Hannibal Day
  Second Brigade, Sidney Burbank
  Third Brigade, Stephen H. Weed, to July 2, 1863, mortally wounded
    Kenner Garrard

Third Division, Samuel Crawford
  First Brigade, William McCandless
  Third Brigade, Joseph W. Fisher

Note. Horatio G. Sickel's Second Brigade of Crawford's division was at Alexandria, Virginia in the Department of Washington.

Artillery Brigade, Augustus P. Martin
  3rd Battery (C), Massachusetts Light Artillery, Aaron F. Walcott
  Battery C, 1st New York Light Artillery, Almont Barnes
  Battery L, 1st Ohio Light Artillery, Frank C. Gibbs
  Battery D, 5th United States Artillery, Charles E. Hazlett
    Benjamin F. Rittenhouse
  Battery I, 5th United States Artillery, Malbone F. Watson
    Charles C. MacConnell

Fifth Corps remained in its positions near the Round Tops July 4, 1863, and that night Lee began his withdrawal from Gettysburg toward the Potomac River, and Virginia. The next day, Meade started the Army of the Potomac in pursuit. For this purpose he divided the army into three columns for the march to Middletown, Maryland. First Corps, Sixth Corps, and Third Corps were to move on the right by Mechanicsville (present-day Thurmont) and Lewistown to Middletown; Twelfth Corps and Second Corps were to march on the left by way of Taneytown, Middleburg, and Frederick; and Fifth Corps and Eleventh Corps, both under the command of Oliver O. Howard, were to march between the other two columns through Emmitsburg.

Fifth Corps left Gettysburg July 5, 1863, and moved to Marsh Creek. The next day it continued on to Moritz's Cross Roads, and July 7, 1863, it advanced through Emmitsburg, Creagerstown, and Utica to Middletown. From there it passed through Fox's Gap in South Mountain and arrived near

Boonsboro July 9, 1863. The next day it moved on to Delaware Mills on Antietam Creek and went into camp. On the night of July 13, 1863, the Army of Northern Virginia re-crossed the Potomac River into Virginia at Falling Waters and Williamsport, and the next day Fifth Corps moved up to Williamsport. For further information, see Gettysburg Campaign, Part III, Pursuit of Lee, From Gettysburg to Falling Waters.

July 15, 1863, Meade's army marched toward the Potomac River near Harper's Ferry, in preparation for crossing into Virginia in pursuit of Lee. Fifth Corps marched by way of Burkittsville and arrived at Berlin (present-day Brunswick), Maryland the next day. It crossed the river at Berlin July 17, 1863, and marched with Sixth Corps along the Loudoun Valley, in the center of the army, toward Warrenton, Virginia. Fifth Corps passed through Lovettsville, Purcellville, Philomont, Union, and Rectortown to Manassas Gap. There, on July 23, 1863, it formed in support of William H. French's Third Corps, which was attempting to push through the gap, but it was not engaged. The corps then moved on by way of Farrowsville and Barbee's Cross Roads, and arrived near Warrenton, Virginia July 26, 1863. Crawford's Third Division was sent on to Fayetteville. Fifth Corps remained in these positions during the remainder of the month, but on July 31, 1863, it was ordered to assemble at Fayetteville. For additional information about the march to Warrenton, see Gettysburg Campaign, Part III, Pursuit of Lee, From Williamsport and Falling Waters to the Rappahannock River.

From the Rappahannock to the Rapidan, August 1, 1863–October 10, 1863. Fifth Corps remained along the Rappahannock River with little activity until mid-September 1863. During the disturbances caused by the draft, the strength of the corps was temporarily reduced by about 4,000 men when Ayres was sent to New York for several weeks with the two brigades of regulars of his division. For additional information, see Department of the East, January 3, 1863–June 27, 1865, Draft Riots in New York, 1863.

On September 16, 1863, the Army of the Potomac crossed the Rappahannock and advanced to Culpeper Court House, where it formed on a line through the town, facing the Rapidan River. Fifth Corps crossed the Rappahannock at Beverly Ford and took position in rear of Culpeper Court House. Second Corps occupied a ridge in front of the court house, and when it advanced to relieve the cavalry pickets on the Rapidan, Fifth Corps moved up and took its place on the ridge.

On October 9, 1863, Meade became aware of an enemy movement toward his right, but he was uncertain whether this was the beginning of a withdrawal or of a flanking movement. That evening, he ordered John Buford's cavalry division, John Newton's First Corps, George Sykes' Fifth Corps, and John Sedgwick's Sixth Corps, in that order, to cross to the south side of the Rapidan, and if they found that Lee was withdrawing, they were to follow him. In preparation for this movement, Fifth Corps was ordered to move to the vicinity of Newton's headquarters, near Morton's Ford, and be ready to cross by daylight October 10, 1863. Only Buford's cavalry had crossed on October 10, 1863, when Meade learned definitely that Lee was not withdrawing, but was moving in heavy force against his right flank. The crossing of the three infantry corps was then called off, and about mid-afternoon Fifth Corps was called back to its position near Culpeper Court House. That night, Meade issued orders for the army to retire to a new line behind the Rappahannock River. For additional information, see Army of the Potomac, From the Rappahannock to the Rapidan.

There were some changes in organization and command during August and September 1863. August 17, 1863, James C. Rice, commanding Third Brigade, First Division, was promoted to brigadier general, and August 23, 1863 assumed command of First Division, First Corps. He was succeeded in command of the brigade by Joshua L. Chamberlain. In September 1863, Second Brigade of Ayres' Second Division, then commanded by Sidney Burbank, was discontinued, and the two regiments remaining in the brigade were assigned to First Brigade. Burbank, as the senior officer, assumed command of First Brigade. There were also some temporary changes of command in Third Division. In August 1863, William McCandless commanded Third Division during the absence of Crawford, and William C. Talley assumed command of

McCandless' First Brigade. In September 1863, Martin D. Hardin relieved Joseph W. Fisher in command of Third Brigade.

Bristoe, Virginia Campaign, October 10, 1863–October 22, 1863. As noted above, Fifth Corps withdrew from the Rapidan to a position near Culpeper Court House October 10, 1863, when Meade learned that the Army of Northern Virginia was moving against his right flank. The next day, as Meade's army moved back toward the Rappahannock River, Fifth Corps marched with Second Corps and Sixth Corps along the Orange and Alexandria Railroad to Rappahannock Station, where it crossed to the east bank of the river. Then, on the afternoon of October 12, 1863, these three corps recrossed the river and advanced to Brandy Station on a reconnaissance in force, but they withdrew that evening. Lee continued his advance and began to threaten the right of Meade's line along the Rappahannock, and October 13, Fifth Corps marched to the northeast with First Corps and Sixth Corps along the Orange and Alexandria Railroad toward Centerville. Fifth Corps halted that night at Walnut Run, a short distance east of Catlett's Station, and resumed the march the next morning. It had just passed Bristoe Station when Gouverneur K. Warren's Second Corps, the rear corps of the army, was attacked there by troops of Ambrose P. Hill's Confederate corps. Sykes turned back to aid Warren, but he was not needed, and then continued the march during the night, and arrived at Centerville on the morning of October 15, 1863. From there he moved to Fairfax Court House.

Lee did not pursue beyond Bristoe Station, and soon began to withdraw toward the Rappahannock. On October 19, 1863, Fifth Corps advanced with the army from Centerville to Groveton, and the next day it moved to Gainesville. It then followed Sixth Corps toward Warrenton, and on October 21, 1863, it was at New Baltimore. For details of the operations of Fifth Corps during the period October 10–21, 1863, see Bristoe, Virginia Campaign.

The organization of Fifth Corps October 10, 1863 was as follows:

FIFTH CORPS, George Sykes

First Division, Charles Griffin

First Brigade, James Barnes
Second Brigade, Jacob B. Sweitzer
Third Brigade, Joshua L. Chamberlain

Second Division, Romeyn B. Ayres
First Brigade, Sidney Burbank
Third Brigade, Kenner Garrard

Third Division, William McCandless
First Brigade, William C. Talley
Third Brigade, Martin D. Hardin

Artillery, Augustus P. Martin
3rd Battery (C), Massachusetts Light Artillery, Aaron F. Walcott
5th Battery (E), Massachusetts Light Artillery, Charles A. Phillips
Battery C, 1st New York Light Artillery, Almont Barnes
Battery L, 1st Ohio Light Artillery, Frank C. Gibbs
Battery D, 5th United States Artillery, Benjamin F. Rittenhouse

Engagement at Rappahannock Station, Virginia, November 7, 1863. Early in November 1863, Meade ordered an advance of the army against Kelly's Ford and the Confederate bridgehead on the east side of the Rappahannock River at Rappahannock Station. On November 6, 1863, in preparation for this movement, Sykes' Fifth Corps, then at New Baltimore, was assigned with Sixth Corps to a temporary left column, or wing, of the army, which was to be commanded by John Sedgwick. Early the next morning, Joseph J. Bartlett relieved Charles Griffin in command of First Division, Fifth Corps, and the corps marched by way of Germantown and Bealeton Station to the front of the enemy works at Rappahannock Station. There it deployed on the left of Sixth Corps, with its right on the Orange and Alexandria Railroad. About 3:30 that afternoon, 900 skirmishers belonging to the pickets of the three divisions advanced under the command of Kenner Garrard along the east side of the railroad. They soon reached the Rappahannock River, and then proceeded to clear the river bank of enemy troops for a distance of about a half mile. Otherwise, Fifth Corps was not engaged that day. It did not participate with Sixth Corps in the latter's successful attack on the enemy redoubts west of the railroad that evening. For details of this operation, see

Engagements at Rappahannock Station and Kelly's Ford, Virginia.

November 8, 1863, Fifth Corps crossed the Rappahannock at Kelly's Ford and bivouacked that night near Paoli Mills, on Mountain Run. The next day, the temporary organization of the army into columns was discontinued. That evening Bartlett's First Division was sent back to the left bank of the river to protect Kelly's Ford, Norman's Ford, and the road leading to Bealeton. Bartlett's division relieved Henry D. Terry's Third Division, Sixth Corps at the fords. Fifth Corps remained in these positions until November 26, 1863.

Mine Run Campaign, November 26, 1863–December 2, 1863. In late November 1863, before the campaigning season ended for the year, Meade led the Army of the Potomac across the Rapidan River and into the Wilderness in an attempt to strike the right flank of Lee's army, which was in position along the south bank of the river. Sykes' Fifth Corps left Paoli Mills early on the morning of November 26, 1863, and marched by way of Richardsville to Culpeper Ford (Culpeper Mine Ford) on the Rapidan, and it was across the river by noon. It waited there for Second Corps and Third Corps to cross upstream at Germanna Ford and Jacob's Ford, and then resumed the march at 3:00 P.M. It camped that night near Wilderness Tavern, at the intersection of the Germanna Plank Road and the Orange Court House Turnpike.

The next morning, Fifth Corps continued on by way of Parker's Store to New Hope Church, where it arrived about 4:00 P.M. It then relieved David McM. Gregg's Second Cavalry Division, which was engaged with enemy cavalry, and marched on during the night to Locust Grove. It arrived there early on the morning of November 28, 1863. At 4:00 A.M. November 29, 1863, Fifth Corps relieved Second Corps, and took position across the Turnpike, in front of the enemy works on the far side of Mine Run, a tributary of the Rapidan.

Meade decided against a frontal assault on the enemy lines at Mine Run, but prepared for attacks on both flanks for the morning of November 30, 1863. Warren, with his strongly reinforced Second Corps, was to advance on Lee's right, and Fifth Corps and Sixth Corps were to march about two miles to the right and strike the enemy left flank. On the morning of November 30, 1863, however, Warren reported to Meade that the enemy works on his front were too strong for a successful attack, and both attacks were called off. After dark that night, Fifth Corps returned to its former position across the Turnpike. Meade then ordered the withdrawal of the army, and at 6:00 P.M. December 1, 1863, it began to move back toward the Rapidan. Fifth Corps recrossed the river at Germanna Ford and marched to Stevensburg. For details of this campaign, see Mine Run Campaign, Virginia.

The organization of Fifth Corps during the Mine Run Campaign was as follows:

FIFTH CORPS, George Sykes

First Division, Joseph J. Bartlett
  First Brigade, William S. Tilton
  Second Brigade, Jacob B. Sweitzer
  Third Brigade, Joseph Hayes

Second Division, Romeyn B. Ayres
  First Brigade, Sidney Burbank
  Third Brigade, Kenner Garrard

Third Division, Samuel W. Crawford
  First Brigade, William McCandless
  Third Brigade, Martin D. Hardin

Artillery Brigade, Augustus P. Martin
  3rd Battery (C), Massachusetts Light Artillery, Aaron F. Walcott
  5th Battery (D), Massachusetts Light Artillery, Charles A. Phillips
  Battery C, 1st New York Light Artillery, Almont Barnes
  Battery L, 1st Ohio Light Artillery, Frank C. Gibbs
  Batteries F and K, 3rd United States Artillery, George F. Barstow
  Battery D, 5th United States Artillery, Benjamin F. Rittenhouse

Winter of 1863–1864. At the close of the Mine Run Campaign, Fifth Corps did not return to its old camps at Paoli Mills, but instead relieved John R. Kenly's Third Division, First Corps, whiich was guarding the Orange and Alexandria Railroad. The corps remained along the railroad until relieved by Ambrose E. Burnside's Ninth Corps during the latter part of April 1864. There were some changes in position during the winter, but generally First Division was near Rappahannock Station, Second Division was near Warrenton Junction, and Third Division was near Warrenton Junction, and Third

Division was farther east, along the road from Bristoe Station to Bull Run Bridge and Manassas Junction. The posts held were Rappahannock Station, Beverly Ford, Bealeton, Liberty, Elk Run Bridge, Germantown, Warrenton Junction, Bristoe Station, Catlett's Station (or Cedar Run), Nokesville, Kettle Run Bridge, and Manassas Junction. The corps also picketed the fords of the Rappahannock from Norman's Ford to Freeman's Ford.

On December 4, 1863, Kenner Garrard, commanding Third Brigade, Second Division, was relieved from duty with the Army of the Potomac, and his brigade was discontinued by a change of designation to Second Brigade, Second Division. Edgar M. Gregory, colonel of the 91st Pennsylvania of Garrard's former brigade, assumed command of the new Second Brigade.

In the reorganization of Fifth Corps March 25, 1864 (see below), Third Division was discontinued, leaving only Griffin's First Division and Crawford's Third Division guarding the railroad. The new Second Division and Fourth Division, organized from troops of Third Corps, were camped near Rixeys' farm (not far from Culpeper Court House), and Brandy Station. Headquarters of Fifth Corps was moved to Culpeper Court House March 25, 1864. There was no further significant change in position until the army began its advance across the Rapidan River May 4, 1864, at the beginning of Grant's spring campaign in Virginia.

Reorganization of the Army of the Potomac, March 1864. By an order of March 23, 1864, the president of the United States directed that the number of corps of the Army of the Potomac be reduced from five to three, and that Second Corps, Fifth Corps, and Sixth Corps be retained in the new organization. These corps, however, were extensively reorganized. By an order of March 24, 1864, Meade directed that the regiments of Fifth Corps be consolidated into two divisions; and he further directed that the three divisions then forming First Corps be transferred to Fifth Corps, and that upon joining Fifth Corps, they be consolidated into two divisions. Also on March 24, 1864, George Sykes was relieved from command of Fifth Corps, and from duty with the Army of the Potomac, and Gouverneur K. Warren assumed command of Fifth Corps (assigned March 23, 1864).

The reorganization of Fifth Corps was effected as follows: Charles Griffin's First Division, then commanded by Joseph J. Bartlett, retained its designation in the new organization, and Griffin remained in command. William S. Tilton's First Brigade, First Division was broken up, and the regiments were asssigned to Jacob B. Sweitzer's Second Brigade, First Division and Joseph Hayes' Third Brigade, First Division. These two brigades retained their designations in the new organization. Sweitzer remained in command of Second Brigade, but Bartlett was assigned command of Third Brigade, relieving Hayes. A new First Brigade, First Division was formed by consolidating the regiments of Luther B. Bruen's First Brigade and George Ryan's Second Brigade of Romeyn B. Ayres' Second Division, and Second Division, Fifth Corps was thus discontinued. Ayres was assigned command of the new First Brigade, First Division. Samuel W. Crawford's Third Division of Pennsylvania Reserves, Fifth Corps was unchanged and retained its designation in the new organization. It consisted of William McCandless' First Brigade and Joseph W. Fisher's Third Brigade.

The three divisions of First Corps, each with two brigades, were reduced to two divisions with three brigades each. This was done by transferring one of the brigades of Third Division to First Division, and the other brigade of Third Division to Second Division. Third Division was thus discontinued. John C. Robinson's Second Division was then redesignated as Second Division, Fifth Corps. Lysander Cutler's First Division, First Corps was redesignated as Fourth Division, Fifth Corps, and James S. Wadsworth was assigned command. For details of the reorganization of the divisions of First Corps, see First Corps, Army of the Potomac, and also roster, below.

When the reorganization was complete, Fifth Corps was organized as follows:

FIFTH CORPS, Gouverneur K. Warren

First Division, Charles Griffin
  First Brigade, Romeyn B. Ayres
  Second Brigade, Jacob B. Sweitzer
  Third Brigade, Joseph J. Bartlett

Note 1. First Brigade was formerly Second Division, Fifth Corps.

Note 2. James Barnes was assigned command of Second Brigade, but apparently he did not assume command.

Second Division, John C. Robinson
    First Brigade, Samuel H. Leonard
    Second Brigade, Henry Baxter
    Third Brigade, Andrew W. Denison

Note 1. First Brigade was formerly First Brigade, Second Division, First Corps.
Note 2. Second Brigade was formerly Second Brigade, Second Division, First Corps.
Note 3. Third Brigade was formerly Nathan T. Dushane's Second Brigade, Third Division, First Corps.

Third Division, Samuel W. Crawford
    First Brigade, William McCandless
    Third Brigade, Joseph W. Fisher

Note. Second Brigade was not with the Army of the Potomac.

Fourth Division, James S. Wadsworth
    First Brigade, Lysander Cutler
    Second Brigade, James C. Rice
    Third Brigade, Roy Stone

Note 1. First Brigade was formerly William W. Robinson's First Brigade, First Division, First Corps.
Note 2. Second Brigade was formerly Rice's Second Brigade, First Division, First Corps.
Note 3. Third Brigade was formerly Edmund L. Dana's First Brigade, Third Division, First Corps.

Artillery Brigade, Charles S. Wainwright
    3rd Battery (C), Massachusetts Light Artillery, Aaron F. Walcott
    5th Battery (D), Massachusetts Light Artillery, Charles A. Phillips
    Battery D, 1st New York Light Artillery, George B. Winslow
    Batteries E and L, 1st New York Light Artillery, Gilbert H. Reynolds
    Battery H, 1st New York Light Artillery, Charles E. Mink
    2nd Battalion, 4th New York Heavy Artillery, William Arthur
    Battery B, 1st Pennsylvania Light Artillery, James H. Cooper
    Battery B, 4th United States Artillery, James Stewart
    Battery D, 5th United States Artillery, Benjamin F. Rittenhouse

In April 1864, another minor problem was resolved in the division of Pennsylvania Reserves (Third Division, Fifth Corps). When this division joined the Army of the Potomac in June 1863, during the Gettysburg Campaign, Horatio G. Sickel's Second Brigade remained in the Department of Washington. In January 1864, two regiments of the brigade (3rd and 4th Pennsylvania Reserves) were sent to the Department of West Virginia, and two regiments (7th and 8th Pennsylvania Reserves) remained in the District of Alexandria, Department of Washington. On April 18, 1864, Second Brigade, Pennsylvania Reserves, then consisting of only the 7th and 8th regiments, and commanded by Henry C. Bolinger, joined Third Division, Fifth Corps. Then, on April 25, 1864, Bolinger's 7th Pennsylvania Reserves was assigned to First Brigade, Third Division, and the 8th Pennsylvania Reserves to Third Brigade, Third Division. The brigades of Third Division were not renumbered, but the Second Brigade was discontinued. Bolinger was in temporary command of First Brigade while McCandless commanded Third Division, and Joseph W. Fisher was in command of Third Brigade.

Grant's Richmond, Virginia Campaign, 1864.
Early in May 1864, the Army of the Potomac marched toward the Rapidan River at the beginning of Ulysses S. Grant's spring campaign in Virginia. About midnight May 3, 1864, Warren's Fifth Corps left Culpeper Court House and marched toward Stevensburg, and then followed James H. Wilson's cavalry division to Germanna Ford on the Rapidan River. It crossed to the south bank May 4, 1864, and then moved past Old Wilderness Tavern to the Lacy house, where it bivouacked for the night. The next morning it advanced on the Orange Court House Turnpike, and soon encountered troops of Richard S. Ewell's Confederate corps about two miles from Wilderness Tavern. About noon Charles Griffin's First Division attacked, and gained some initial successes, but it was soon forced back. During the afternoon, James S. Wadsworth's Fourth Division of Fifth Corps was sent to aid Winfield S. Hancock's Second Corps, which was fighting on the Plank Road to the south, but it became lost and was driven back when the enemy struck its exposed right flank. The other two divisions of Fifth Corps were also engaged that afternoon.

On the morning of May 6, 1864, Warren again attacked on the Turnpike, but without success. Wadsworth's division was engaged with Hancock

May 6, 1864, and during the fighting Wadsworth was mortally wounded. Lysander Cutler assumed command of Fourth Division, and William W. Robinson assumed command of Cutler's First Brigade, Fourth Division. At daybreak May 6, 1864, J. Howard Kitching reported to Warren at the Lacy house with his First Brigade of Henry S. Burton's Artillery Reserve of the Army, and it was sent to join Wadsworth in his attack. For details of Fifth Corps' participation in the Battle of the Wilderness, see Richmond, Virginia Campaign, 1864, Battle of the Wilderness.

The organization of Fifth Corps during the Battle of the Wilderness was as follows:

FIFTH CORPS, Gouverneur K. Warren

First Division, Charles Griffin
  First Brigade, Romeyn B. Ayres
  Second Brigade, Jacob B. Sweitzer
  Third Brigade, Joseph J. Bartlett

Second Division, John C. Robinson
  First Brigade, Samuel H. Leonard, to May 6, 1864, sick
    Peter Lyle
  Second Brigade, Henry Baxter, to May 6, 1864, wounded
    Richard Coulter
  Third Brigade, Andrew W. Denison

Third Division, Samuel W. Crawford
  First Brigade, William McCandless
  Second Brigade, Joseph W. Fisher

Fourth Division, James S. Wadsworth, to July 6, 1864, mortally wounded
  Lysander Cutler
  First Brigade, Lysander Cutler, to May 6, 1864
    William W. Robinson
  Second Brigade, James C. Rice
  Third Brigade, Roy Stone, to May 6, 1864, disabled
    Edward S. Bragg

Artillery Brigade, Charles S. Wainwright

Note. The batteries with the brigade were the same as listed above under the reorganization of the army in March 1864.

The Battle of the Wilderness was not renewed on May 7, 1864, and that night the army marched south toward Spotsylvania Court House. Fifth Corps led the way on the Brock Road, and arrived near Todd's Tavern the next morning. It then pressed on, and became engaged with troops of Richard H.

Anderson's (Longstreet's) corps near Alsop's farm (Laurel Hill) that day. John C. Robinson was seriously wounded, and was succeeded in command of Second Division by Richard Coulter. Fifth Corps was unable to advance farther, and May 9, 1864, Sixth Corps came up and formed on its left and Second Corps moved up on its right.

During the evening of May 9, 1864, Second Division was temporarily discontinued. Peter Lyle's First Brigade was assigned to Cutler's Fourth Division, Coulter's Second Brigade to Crawford's Third Division, and Andrew W. Denison's Third Brigade (then commanded by Richard N. Bowerman) was made an independent command that was ordered to report directly to Warren.

Fifth Corps remained in position on the right of Sixth Corps until the morning of May 12, 1864, and then it advanced on the right of Sixth Corps to support Hancock's Second Corps, which had overrun the Confederate breastworks at the salient of their line, north of Spotsylvania Court House. Warren, however, accomplished little, and Griffin's and Cutler's divisions were taken from him, and sent to the left to report to Horatio G. Wright for orders. This left only Crawford's division and Kitching's heavy artillery brigade to hold Warren's line. The divisions of Griffin and Cutler returned to Fifth Corps the next morning.

On the night of May 13, 1864, Fifth Corps moved to the left along the rear of the army, and arrived the next morning on the left of Ninth Corps, which was in position on the Spotsylvania Court House-Fredericksburg Road. Fifth Corps was then relatively inactive until May 18, 1864, and at that time it moved to the right to join in an attack by the army on the enemy lines, but little was accomplished by this movement. Coulter was wounded while leading Second Brigade, and was succeeded by James L. Bates. The corps then returned to its positions of the day before.

J. Howard Kitching's First Brigade of the Artillery Reserve, consisting of 6th New York Heavy Artillery and 15th New York Heavy Artillery, had been attached to Fifth Corps at the Wilderness July 6, 1864, and had been serving with the corps since that time. Then, on May 13, 1864, it was transferred from the Artillery Reserve to Fifth Corps as an unattached brigade. On May 19, 1864, Kitching's brigade was posted with Robert O. Tyler's Heavy

Artillery Division of Second Corps near the Harris farm on the Spotsylvania Court House-Fredericksburg Road. Ewell's Confederate corps, while advancing to turn Warren's right flank, struck Kitching's brigade and Tyler's division, and a sharp struggle ensued. Bowerman's Third Brigade, Second Division, Fifth Corps came up, and together they repulsed the enemy attack.

The army remained on the lines at Spotsylvania Court House until May 21, 1864, but there was no further serious fighting. For details of the operations of the army around Spotsylvania Court House, see Richmond, Virginia Campaign, 1864, Operations about Spotsylvania Court House.

The organization of Fifth Corps during the operations around Spotsylvania Court House was as follows:

FIFTH CORPS, Gouverneur K. Warren

First Division, Charles Griffin
    First Brigade, Romeyn B. Ayres
    Second Brigade, Jacob B. Sweitzer
    Third Brigade, Joseph J. Bartlett

Second Division, John C. Robinson, to May 8, 1864, wounded
    Richard Coulter, to May 9, 1864
    First Brigade, Peter Lyle, to May 9, 1864
    Second Brigade, Richard Coulter, to May 8, 1864
        James L. Bates, to May 9, 1864
    Third Brigade, Andrew W. Denison, to May 8, 1864, wounded
        Charles E. Phelps, May 8, 1864, wounded and captured
        Richard N. Bowerman, to May 9, 1864.

Note. Second Division was temporarily discontinued May 9, 1864, and the brigades were reassigned.

Third Division, Samuel W. Crawford
    First Brigade, William McCandless, to May 8, 1864, wounded
        William C. Talley, May 8, 1864, captured
        Wellington H. Ent
        Samuel M. Jackson, to May 18, 1864
        Martin D. Hardin
    Second Brigade, Joseph W. Fisher
    Second Brigade, Second Division, Richard Coulter, to May 18, 1864, wounded
        James L. Bates

Note 1. Talley was recaptured by Philip H. Sheridan's cavalry at Beaver Dam Station May 9, 1864, and then,

with 600 recaptured officers and men, he marched to Belle Plain. This command left Belle Plain May 22, 1864 as guard for a train going to the Army of the Potomac.

Note 2. Coulter's Second Brigade, Second Division was temporarily attached to Third Division May 9, 1864.

Fourth Division, Lysander Cutler
    First Brigade, William W. Robinson
    Second Brigade, James C. Rice, to May 10, 1864, killed
        Edward B. Fowler, to May 21, 1864
        J. William Hofmann
    Third Brigade, Edward S. Bragg
    First Brigade, Second Division, Peter Lyle

Note 1. The term of service of Fowler's 84th New York of Second Brigade was about to expire, and the regiment was sent on special duty to Fredericksburg.

Note 2. Lyle's First Brigade, First Division was temporarily attached to Fourth Division May 9, 1864.

Third Brigade, Second Division, Richard C. Bowerman

Note. Bowerman's brigade was made a temporary independent brigade May 9, 1864. Bowerman reported directly to Headquarters Fifth Corps.

Heavy Artillery Brigade, J. Howard Kitching

Note. Kitching's First Brigade of the Artillery Reserve of the army was attached to Fifth Corps May 6, 1864, but was unassigned. On May 13, 1864, this brigade was transferred from the Artillery Reserve to Fifth Corps as an unattached brigade.

Artillery Brigade, Charles S. Wainwright
    3rd Battery (C), Massachusetts Light Artillery, Aaron F. Walcott
    5th Battery (D), Massachusetts Light Artillery, Charles A. Phillips
    9th Battery, Massachusetts Light Artillery, John Bigelow
    Battery B, 1st New York Light Artillery, Albert S. Sheldon
    Battery C, 1st New York Light Artillery, Almont Barnes
    Battery D, 1st New York Light Artillery, Lester I. Richardson
    Batteries E and L, 1st New York Light Artillery, George Breck
    Battery H, 1st New York Light Artillery, Charles E. Mink
    5th Battery, New York Light Artillery, Elijah D. Taft
    15th Battery, New York Light Artillery, Patrick Hart
    2nd Battalion, 4th New York Heavy Artillery, William Arthur
    Battery B, 1st Pennsylvania Light Artillery, James H. Cooper
    Battery B, 4th United States Artillery, James Stewart

Battery D, 5th United States Artillery, Benjamin F. Rittenhouse

May 21, 1864, the Army of the Potomac began to leave its positions at Spotsylvania Court House and march toward the North Anna River. Fifth Corps moved by way of Guiney's Station, and arrived on the river at Jerico Mills shortly after noon May 23, 1864. It crossed during the afternoon, and then advanced a short distance and prepared a defensive line. About 6:00 that evening, troops of Ambrose P. Hill's corps attacked Warren's position and, after a sharp struggle, forced the right of the line back, but otherwise Fifth Corps held its ground.

May 25, 1864, Warren moved down the river three or four miles to the main enemy line, but he did not attack. Grant then decided to continue the movement of the army to the left from the line of the North Anna, and started his corps down the Pamunkey River toward Hanovertown. On the night of May 25, 1864, Fifth Corps recrossed the North Anna at Quarles' Mills and marched down the north side of the Pamunkey to Hanovertown. It then crossed the river and May 28, 1864 advanced to the Totopotomoy River. On May 30, 1864, Griffin's division advanced toward Shady Grove Church, driving back the skirmishers of Robert E. Rodes' Confederate Division, and Martin D. Hardin's brigade of Crawford's division then moved out to drive away enemy troops that were threatening the left of the Fifth Corps line. Hardin encountered a strong enemy force near Bethesda Church and was driven back. Hardin was soon supported by Crawford's other brigade under Joseph W. Fisher, and Lysander Cutler's Fourth Division, and together they checked Rodes' advance. For details of the operations of the army, and of Fifth Corps, during the advance from Spotsylvania Court House to Cold Harbor, see Richmond, Virginia Campaign, 1864, the following sections: From Spotsylvania Court House to the North Anna River; Operations on the Pamunkey River; Operations on the Totopotomoy River; From the Totopotomoy River to Cold Harbor.

On May 29, 1864, Warren assigned Henry H. Lockwood, who had just reported to the corps, to the command of Second Division, Fifth Corps, which had been temporarily discontinued since May 9, 1864. The division was to consist of the three brigades that formerly belonged to the division. These were Peter Lyle's First Brigade, James L. Bates' Second Brigade, and Nathan T. Dushane's Third Brigade. Lockwood assumed command May 30, 1864, and the division was reorganized that day.

At the end of May 1864, Crawford's Third Division was composed of nine regiments of Pennsylvania Reserves whose terms of enlistment were about to expire, and during the period May 31, 1864–June 1, 1864, they left for Pennsylvania, and muster out, under the command of Hardin. Third Division was temporarily discontinued, but a new brigade was formed under William R. Hartshorne May 31, 1864, which consisted of the 190th Pennsylvania (1st Pennsylvania Veteran Reserves) and the 191st Pennsylvania (2nd Pennsylvania Veteran Reserves). These regiments were formed from veterans and recruits of the Pennsylvania Reserves. In the reorganization of Fifth Corps June 6, 1864 (see below), this brigade, under James Carle, was designated as Third Brigade, Third Division. Kitching's brigade of heavy artillery joined Third Division May 30, 1864, but was transferred to Second Division June 2, 1864.

May 31, 1864, Fifth Corps advanced to the vicinity of Bethesda Church, and remained in position there on the left of Ninth Corps during the Battle of Cold Harbor. Ninth Corps and Fifth Corps were separated by a few miles from Meade's main line of battle to the south at Cold Harbor. Fifth Corps did not take part in the assaults of June 1, 1864 and June 3, 1864 at Cold Harbor, but it was engaged near Bethesda Church during these two days. For details of the Battle of Cold Harbor, see Richmond, Virginia Campaign, 1864, Operations about Cold Harbor.

The organization of Fifth Corps at the time of the Battle of Cold Harbor was as follows:

FIFTH CORPS, Gouverneur K. Warren

First Division, Charles Griffin
First Brigade, Romeyn B. Ayres
Second Brigade, Jacob B. Sweitzer
Third Brigade, Joseph J. Bartlett

Second Division, Henry H. Lockwood, to June 2, 1864
Samuel W. Crawford
First Brigade, Peter Lyle
Second Brigade, James L. Bates
Third Brigade, Nathan T. Dushane

Fourth Division, Lysander Cutler

First Brigade, William W. Robinson
Second Brigade, J. William Hofmann
Third Brigade, Edward S. Bragg

Heavy Artillery Brigade, J. Howard Kitching

Artillery Brigade, Charles S. Wainwright
    3rd Battery (C), Massachusetts Light Artillery, Aaron
        F. Walcott
    5th Battery (E), Massachusetts Light Artillery, Charles
        A. Phillips
    Battery B, 1st New York Light Artillery, Albert S.
        Sheldon, to June 1, killed
        Robert E. Rogers
    Battery C, 1st New York Light Artillery, Almont
        Barnes
    Battery D, 1st New York Light Artillery, Lester I.
        Richardson
    Batteries E and L, 1st New York Light Artillery,
        George Breck
    Battery H, 1st New York Light Artillery, Charles E.
        Mink
    15th Battery, New York Light Artillery, Patrick Hart
    Battery B, 1st Pennsylvania Light Artillery, James H.
        Cooper
    Battery B, 4th United States Artillery, James Stewart
    Battery D, 5th United States Artillery, Benjamin F.
        Rittenhouse

On the night of June 5, 1864, Fifth Corps was withdrawn from Bethesda Church to the vicinity of the Leary house as a reserve. The next day, Fifth Corps was extensively reorganized into four divisions, commanded by Charles Griffin, Romeyn B. Ayres, Samuel W. Crawford, and Lysander Cutler. The new organization was as follows:

FIFTH CORPS, Gouverneur K. Warren

First Division, Charles Griffin
    First Brigade, Edward S. Bragg
        Joshua Chamberlain
    Second Brigade, Jacob B. Sweitzer
    Third Brigade, Joseph J. Bartlett

Note. First Brigade was formerly Bragg's Third Brigade, Fourth Division.

Chamberlain was assigned command June 6, 1864. Ayres' former First Brigade, First Division was assigned to Second Division as First Brigade under the command of Edgar M. Gregory.

Second Division, Romeyn B. Ayres
    First Brigade, Edgar M. Gregory
    Second Brigade, Nathan T. Dushane
    Third Brigade, J. Howard Kitching

Note 1. Gregory's First Brigade was formerly Ayres' First Brigade, First Division. Lyle's former First Brigade, Second Division was assigned to Third Division as First Brigade.
Note 2. Dushane's Second Brigade, Second Division was formerly Dushane's Third Brigade, Second Division. Bates' former Second Brigade, Second Division was assigned to Third Division as Second Brigade.
Note 3. Third Brigade was formerly Kitching's Brigade of Heavy Artillery, which was attached to Third Division May 30, 1864, and was then transferred to Second Division June 2, 1864

Third Division, Samuel W. Crawford
    First Brigade, Peter Lyle
    Second Brigade, James L. Bates
    Third Brigade, James Carle

Note 1. First Brigade was formerly First Brigade, Second Division.
Note 2. Second Brigade was formerly Second Brigade, Second Division.
Note 3. Third Brigade was organized from Veteran Pennsylvania Reserves and recruits.

Fourth Division, Lysander Cutler
    First Brigade, William W. Robinson, to June 7, 1864
        Edward S. Bragg
    Second Brigade, J. William Hofmann

Note. Bragg's former Third Brigade, Fourth Division was transferred to First Division as First Brigade, and was assigned to Joshua L. Chamberlain.

Artillery Brigade, Charles S. Wainwright

June 7, 1864, the divisions of Griffin and Cutler were sent to the extreme left of the army to picket the line of the Chickahominy River. Ayres and Crawford, with their divisions, remained near Cold Harbor to support Burnside's Ninth Corps, but on June 11, 1864, they were ordered to Moodys' house, about two and a half miles northeast of Dispatch Station, and south of the Richmond and York River Railroad. This was done in preparation for the movement of the Army of the Potomac to the James River, which was to begin the next day.

On the evening of June 12, 1864, Fifth Corps moved to Long Bridge on the Chickahominy River and, after crossing, followed James H. Wilson's cavalry division toward White Oak Swamp Bridge. It then took position near Riddell's Shop, with its right at White Oak Bridge, to cover the passage of the rest of the army to the James. When this movement was completed, Fifth Corps withdrew on the evening of June 13, 1864, and marched by way of Saint Mary's Church to Charles City Court House, where it arrived the next day. It then crossed to the south side of the James River June 16, 1864. For details of this movement, see Richmond, Virginia Campaign,1864, Cold Harbor to the James River.

Operations about Petersburg, June and July 1864. Warren's Fifth Corps was ferried across the James River at Windmill Point during the night of June 15, 1864, and it then marched by way of Prince George Court House toward Petersburg. It arrived near the rear of the Union lines, just established in front of the town, the following night. June 17, 1864, Cutler's division was sent to the far left, and the other three divisions were massed in rear of the center of the line. That evening, Crawford's division was sent forward, and at 9:00 P.M. it supported an attack by James H. Ledlie's First Division, Ninth Corps on the enemy works. James Carle's Third Brigade of Third Division led Crawford's attack, and it was supported by Peter Lyle's First Brigade and James L. Bates' Second Brigade.

The attacks on the enemy lines were renewed on June 18, 1864. Fifth Corps was first engaged in clearing the enemy troops from the deep cut of the Norfolk and Petersburg Railroad, and it then joined in the final, unsuccessful assault that afternoon. Joshua L. Chamberlain was wounded in the first attack, and was succeeded in command of First Brigade, First Division by William S. Tilton. For details of these attacks, see Operations about Petersburg and Richmond, Virginia, 1864–1865, Operations of June 1864, Assaults at Petersburg, June 15–18, 1864.

After the attack of June 18, 1864, Grant ordered the army to entrench on the line it then held, and prepare for further operations. Fifth Corps entrenched on the line that it had gained on June 18, 1864, with its left near the Norfolk and Petersburg Railroad, and its right connecting with Ninth Corps. Warren then shifted his troops to the left, and by the evening of June 21, 1864, the left of the corps was on the Jerusalem Plank Road, and the right joined

Ninth Corps near the Norfolk and Petersburg Railroad. The next day, Second Corps, which was then attempting to advance to the Weldon Railroad, came up on the left of Fifth Corps, with John Gibbon's division of Second Corps next to the Jerusalem Plank Road. June 23, 1864, Willcox's division of Ninth Corps relieved Crawford's division, which was on the right of Fifth Corps, and Crawford then moved to the left and relieved Gibbon's division, thus extending the Fifth Corps line still further to the left. Fifth Corps remained generally in this position until Sixth Corps, and then Second Corps, were withdrawn from its left in July 1864. On July 6–10, 1864, Sixth Corps departed for Washington during Jubal A. Early's raid in Maryland, and after it was gone, Hancock destroyed the Second Corps line of entrenchments, and moved into reserve in the vicinity of Deserted House. Warren then refused the left of his line by drawing it back to the east of the Jerusalem Plank Road, and facing it south.

The organization of Fifth Corps during the period June 15, 1864–July 31, 1864 was as follows:

FIFTH CORPS, Gouverneur K. Warren

First Division, Charles Griffin, to July 21, 1864
  Joseph J. Bartlett
  First Brigade, Joshua L. Chamberlain, to June 18, 1864, wounded
    William S. Tilton
  Second Brigade, Jacob B. Sweitzer, to July 3, 1864
    Edgar M. Gregory
  Third Brigade, Joseph J. Bartlett, to July 21, 1864
    Norval E. Welch

Second Division, Romeyn B. Ayres
  First Brigade, Edgar M. Gregory, to June 20, 1864
    Joseph Hayes
  Second Brigade, Nathan T. Dushane
  Third Brigade, J. Howard Kitching

Third Division, Samuel W. Crawford
  First Brigade, Peter Lyle
  Second Brigade, James L. Bates, to June 25, 1864
    Henry Baxter
    Charles Wheelock
  Third Brigade, James Carle, to July 26, 1864
    William R. Hartshorne

Note. Bates' term of enlistment expired June 25, 1864.

Fourth Division, Lysander Cutler
  First Brigade, Edward S. Bragg

Second Brigade, J. William Hofmann
Artillery Brigade, Charles S. Wainwright

Note. The batteries with the brigade were essentially the same as at Cold Harbor.

Operations about Petersburg, August 1864. Warren's Fifth Corps remained in position on the left of the line of entrenchments until the night of August 14–15, 1864, and it then moved back and camped generally on a line from the Chieves house to Deserted House. This was done in preparation for a planned movement against the right of the enemy line south of Petersburg. For additional information about the positions of the army during the period August 1–19, 1864, see Operations about Petersburg and Richmond, Virginia, 1864–1865, Operations of August 1864, Siege of Petersburg, August 1864.

On the morning of August 18, 1864, Fifth Corps marched westward to the Weldon Railroad, with Griffin's First Division in the lead. It was followed by Ayres' Second Division, Crawford's Third Division, and Cutler's Fourth Division, in that order. Griffin took position on the railroad at Globe Tavern, to cover the position to the south and west. Ayres advanced north along the railroad for about a mile and found the enemy in line of battle, and Crawford's division was then ordered up to take position on the right of Ayres. During the afternoon, however, before Crawford arrived, Henry Heth's Confederate division strongly attacked Ayres and forced him to fall back. Peter Lyle's First Brigade of Crawford's division was also hit during this attack. Ayres fought stubbornly, and finally drove the enemy back. J. William Hofmann's Second Brigade of Cutler's division was sent to support Ayres.

About 4:15 P.M. August 19, 1864, the enemy, reinforced by William Mahone's division, again attacked. This blow fell on the fronts of Ayres' and Crawford's divisions, and Edward S. Bragg's First Brigade of Cutler's division, which had been brought up on the right. The enemy succeeded in driving back Crawford and Bragg in considerable confusion, but with help from Ninth Corps, Warren was able to hold his ground. A third enemy attack, on August 21, 1864, was also repulsed, and with that effort the battle ended. For details, see Operations about Petersburg and Richmond, Virginia, 1864–1865, Operations of August 1864, Battle of Globe

Tavern (or Yellow House, Yellow Tavern, Blick's House [or Station], Weldon Railroad), Virginia.

After the Battle of Globe Tavern, Fifth Corps remained along the Weldon Railroad until the end of the month. Griffin's division was at Globe Tavern and Ayres' division was on his right, with both divisions facing west. Crawford's division was on the left of Griffin, and generally faced south.

There were several significant organizational changes in Fifth Corps during the month. J. Howard Kitching's Third Brigade of Ayres' Second Division consisted of two regiments of heavy artillery until August 13, 1864. On that date, Kitching was ordered, with his 6th New York Heavy Artillery, to Washington, D.C., and this left only Michael Wiedrich's 15th New York Heavy Artillery in the brigade. This regiment was engaged at Globe Tavern as Third Brigade, and was under Ayres' orders. Wiedrich was wounded during the battle, and Louis Eiche assumed command of the regiment. The brigade was discontinued August 20, 1864, when Eiche's regiment was assigned to First Brigade of Ayres' division.

William R. Hartshorne's Third Brigade of Crawford's Third Division was also discontinued as a result of the Battle of Globe Tavern. The brigade consisted of only two regiments of Veteran Pennsylvania Reserves, and most of these troops were captured, along with Hartshorne, during the fighting of August 19, 1864. The remnants of the two regiments were transferred to Lyle's First Brigade of Crawford's division. Both Third Brigade, Second Division and Third Brigade, Third Division were reorganized a short time later.

During the fighting at Globe Tavern, both brigades of Cutler's Fourth Division were assigned to other commands. On August 18, 1864, Hofmann's Second Brigade was sent to aid Second Division, which was then under attack, and it remained under Ayres' command until August 20, 1864. On August 19, 1864, Bragg's First Brigade was sent to establish connection between Crawford's division and Ninth Corps on its right, and it was placed under Crawford's orders. On August 20, 1864, both brigades were returned to Cutler's command, and were engaged west of the railroad August 21, 1864, between the divisions of Griffin and Ayres. Cutler was wounded that day, and Bragg assumed command of the division, which was then placed under Ayres' direction. Mark Finnicum was then the senior officer in Bragg's brigade.

On August 24, 1864, Hofmann's brigade was temporarily assigned to Ayres' Second Division as Third Brigade, and Bragg's brigade was temporarily assigned to Crawford's Third Division as Third Brigade. The headquarters staff and provost guard of Fourth Division reported to Headquarters Fifth Corps.

The organization of Fifth Corps during August 1864 was as follows:

FIFTH CORPS, Gouverneur K. Warren

First Division, Joseph J. Bartlett, to August 9, 1864
  Charles Griffin
  First Brigade, William S. Tilton, to August 22, 1864
    William A. Throop
  Second Brigade, Edgar M. Gregory
  Third Brigade, Norval E. Welch, to August 9, 1864
    Joseph J. Bartlett, to August 17, 1864
    James Gwyn

Second Division, Romeyn B. Ayres
  First Brigade, Joseph Hayes, to August 19, 1864, captured
    Frederick Winthrop, to August 22, 1864
    Charles P. Stone
  Second Brigade, Nathan T. Dushane, to August 21, 1864, killed
    Samuel A. Graham
  Third Brigade, J. Howard Kitching, to August 13, 1864
    Louis Eiche, to August 20, 1864
    J. William Hofmann, August 24, 1864 to August 31, 1864

Note. Third Brigade was discontinued August 20, 1864, when the one remaining regiment of the brigade was transferred to First Brigade, Second Division. Third Brigade, Second Division was reorganized August 24, 1864 by the transfer of Hofmann's Second Brigade of Cutler's Fourth Division to Second Division.

Third Division, Samuel W. Crawford
  First Brigade, Peter Lyle, to August 25, 1864, sick
    Thomas F. McCoy
  Second Brigade, Henry Baxter, to August 15, 1864
    Richard Coulter, to August 18, 1864, sick
    Charles Wheelock, to August 29, 1864
    Henry Baxter
  Third Brigade, William R. Hartshorne, to August 19, 1864, captured
    Edward S. Bragg, August 24, 1864 to August 31, 1864

Note. Third Brigade was discontinued August 21, 1864. Hartshorne and most of his men had been captured during the Battle of Globe Tavern August 19, 1864, and two days later the remnants of the two regiments of the brigade were transferred to First Brigade, Third Division. Third Brigade, Third Division was reorganized August 24, 1864 by the transfer of Bragg's First Brigade of Cutler's Fourth Division to Third Division.

Fourth Division, Lysander Cutler, to August 21, 1864, wounded
  Edward S. Bragg, August 22, 1864 to August 24, 1864
  First Brigade, Edward S. Bragg
  Second Brigade, J. William Hofmann

Note. Cutler was wounded August 21, 1864, and Ayres assumed the direction of Fourth Division as well as his own Second Division. On August 24, 1864, First Brigade was assigned to Third Division, and Second Brigade was assigned to Second Division, but the division was not discontinued.

Artillery Brigade, Charles S. Wainright

Note. There was little change in the Artillery Brigade during August 1864.

Operations about Petersburg (Reorganization of Fifth Corps), September 1864. On September 1, 1864, Meade ordered Warren to reorganize Fifth Corps into three divisions, as soon as practicable, and he specified that one division should be composed exclusively of troops that originally belonged to the old First Corps. The reorganization was delayed for some time because of the temporary absence of Meade from the army, but September 12, 1864, Warren issued the necessary orders. The reorganization was relatively complex, and was effected as follows:

First Division

First Brigade. First Brigade was reduced to one regiment when five regiments, formerly belonging to First Corps, were assigned to First Brigade and Third Brigade of Third Division. First Brigade was then reorganized September 24, 1864, under Horatio G. Sickel, from a new Pennsylvania regiment and one regiment from Second Brigade, First Division.

Second Brigade. Except for the transfer of one regiment to First Brigade, First Division, Second Brigade was unchanged.

Third Brigade. Third Brigade was unchanged.

Second Division

First Brigade. First Brigade was unchanged.

Second Brigade. Second Brigade was unchanged.

Third Brigade. This brigade, formerly J. William Hofmann's Second Brigade, Fourth Division until August 24, 1864, was considerably changed. Four of its regiments, formerly belonging to First Corps, were transferred to Third Brigade, Third Division September 13, 1864. Third Brigade, Second Division was then reorganized the next day from two Delaware regiments that remained in the brigade; two Pennsylvania regiments from First Brigade, Third Division; and 210th Pennsylvania, which was organized September 12–24, 1864.

Third Division

First Brigade. First Brigade was discontinued when five regiments were transferred to Second Brigade, Third Division, and two regiments to Third Brigade, Second Division. It was reorganized September 13, 1864 from three regiments of the former First Brigade, First Division, and three regiments of Third Brigade, Third Division (formerly Bragg's First Brigade, Fourth Division, Fifth Corps).

Second Brigade. One regiment of Second Brigade was transferred to the new Third Brigade, Third Division, and in turn it received five regiments from the former First Brigade, Third Division. The regiments of the original Second Brigade were from First Corps.

Third Brigade. Third Brigade (formerly Bragg's First Brigade, Fourth Division) was discontinued September 13, 1864, when its three regiments were transferred to First Brigade, Third Division. Third Brigade was reorganized that same day from four regiments of Third Brigade, Second Division

(formerly Hofmann's Second Brigade, Fourth Division, Fifth Corps), two regiments from the former First Brigade, First Division, and one regiment from Second Brigade, Third Division. The regiments of the original Third Brigade were from First Corps.

Fourth Division

On August 24, 1864, the two brigades of Cutler's Fourth Division were transferred to Second Division and Third Division of Fifth Corps. Thus, only Cutler's headquarters remained of Fourth Division, and it continued to report to Warren. On September 12, 1864, however, Fourth Division was discontinued, and Cutler, who was suffering from a wound and ill health, was relieved from duty with the Army of the Potomac September 13, 1864.

The organization of Fifth Corps during September 1864 was as follows:

FIFTH CORPS, Gouverneur K. Warren

First Division, Charles Griffin
  First Brigade, William A. Throop, to September 15, 1864
    Horatio G. Sickel
  Second Brigade, Edgar M. Gregory
  Third Brigade, James Gwyn

Second Division, Romeyn B. Ayres
  First Brigade, Charles P. Stone, to September 1864
    Frederick Winthrop, to September 30, 1864
    Elwell S. Otis, to October 1, 1864, wounded
    James Grindlay
  Second Brigade, Samuel A. Graham
  Third Brigade, J. William Hofmann, to September 14, 1864
    Arthur H. Grimshaw

Note. Grimshaw commanded the reorganized Third Brigade, Second Division after September 14, 1864, and Hofmann assumed command of the reorganized Third Brigade, Third Division.

Third Division, Samuel W. Crawford
  First Brigade, Thomas F. McCoy, to September 13, 1864
    Edward S. Bragg
  Second Brigade, Henry Baxter
  Third Brigade, Edward S. Bragg, to September 13,

1864
J. William Hofmann

Note 1. Bragg assumed command of First Brigade when the regiments of his former Third Brigade were transferred to First Brigade.

Note 2. Hofmann assumed command of Third Brigade when the regiments of his former Third Brigade, Second Division were transferred to Third Division as Third Brigade.

Fourth Division.

Note. This division, which consisted only of the headquarters staff in early September 1864, was discontinued September 12, 1864.

Artillery Brigade, Charles S. Wainwright

Fifth Corps remained along the Weldon Railroad until September 30, 1864, and was engaged principally in constructing defensive works and guarding a long picket line on the left flank of the army. On September 15, 1864, Baxter, with his Second Brigade, Third Division, moved out on a reconnaissance along the Vaughan Road to develop the position of the enemy. The next day, Baxter's brigade was detached and ordered to garrison Fort Wadsworth, Fort Dushane, and Fort Davison. From September 25, 1864, Fifth Corps held the line from Fort Howard around to the Gurley house. On September 29, 1864, Baxter's brigade conducted another reconnaissance, this time westward from Fort Dushane on the Poplar Spring Road. Baxter found the enemy in strength near Peebles' farm, and then returned to Fort Dushane.

September 29, 1864, as a part of Grant's autumn offensive, Benjamin F. Butler's Army of the James launched an attack on the Confederate defenses of Richmond, north of the James River. While this movement was in progress, Grant prepared to send Fifth Corps and Ninth Corps westward from the Weldon Railroad, south of Petersburg, toward the Boydton Plank Road. Griffin's First Division, Ayres' Second Division, and J. William Hofmann's Third Brigade, Third Division, which was temporarily attached to Ayres' division, were to form a part of the mobile force that was to make this movement. First Division and Second Division of Ninth Corps were also assigned to this force, and they were replaced on the entrenchments, to the right of Fifth Corps, by Edward Ferrero's Third Division, Ninth

Corps. Ferrero's division was unable to cover the original Ninth Corps' front, and Edward Bragg's First Brigade, Third Division, Fifth Corps was placed between the Weldon Railroad and Fort Howard. Crawford's Third Division (less Hofmann's brigade) was left to hold the Fifth Corps' line of entrenchments along the Weldon Railroad.

On the morning of September 30, 1864, Ayres' and Griffin's divisions were ready to move. Ayres' brigades were in position as follows: Elwell S. Otis' First brigade was on the west side of the Weldon Railroad, near Fort Wadsworth; and across the railroad, and in rear of the siege line held by Bragg and the left of Ferrero's division, were Arthur H. Grimshaw's Third Brigade, Samuel A. Graham's Second Brigade, and J. William Hofmann's Third Brigade, Third Division, in that order from west to east. Griffin's three brigades were in line between the left of Otis' brigade and Fort Dushane, facing west.

At 9:00 A.M. September 30, 1864, Warren's divisions, with Griffin in the lead, marched south on the Halifax Road to the Poplar Spring Road, and there they turned west toward Poplar Spring Church. The divisions of Ninth Corps followed Warren. Griffin found the enemy in position near Poplar Spring Church, and then his division charged and captured the line of entrenchments on Peebles' farm. Ninth Corps moved up on the left and drove the enemy from their works on Pegram's farm. There was a severe engagement that afternoon on the lines gained by Fifth Corps and Ninth Corps, but they generally held their ground. Ayres' division moved to the left and assumed a new position on the Squirrel Level Road. That day, Ferrero was ordered to extend his Ninth Corps line from Fort Howard to Fort Wadsworth to relieve Bragg's brigade of Crawford's division, and early the next morning, Bragg was sent to Flowers' house, on the Vaughan Road, to help hold the new line between the right of Ayres' division and Fort Wadsworth. During the first two days of October 1864, all the troops of Fifth Corps, except Bragg's and Baxter's brigades of Crawford's Third Division, continued active operations about Poplar Spring Church. Bragg's brigade was on the Vaughan Road at Flowers' house, and the regiments of Baxter's brigade garrisoned Fort Wadsworth, Fort Dushane, and Fort Davison. On October 3, 1864, Hofmann's brigade, which had been attached to Ninth Corps, rejoined Third Division. For details of the operations around Poplar Spring Church September 30, 1864–October 2, 1864, see Operations about Petersburg and Richmond, Virginia, 1864–1865, Operations of September 1864, Battle of Poplar Spring Church (Combats at Wyatt's Farm, Peebles' Farm, Chappell's House, Pegram's Farm, and Vaughan Road), Virginia.

When the fighting around Poplar Spring Church ended October 2, 1864, the two divisions of Fifth Corps did not return to their former positions on the Weldon Railroad, but instead they entrenched on the line gained during their advance of the past three days. This extended the line of the Petersburg entrenchments westward from Fort Wadsworth, past the Flowers house and the Chappell house to Pegram's farm. There were some changes in the positions of the troops of Fifth Corps during the next few days, but by the evening of October 5, 1864, they were in line as follows: Griffin's division was on the left, from the Church Road, just east of the Pegram house, to the Squirrel Level Road at the Chappell house; Ayres' division was on the center, and extended eastward from the right of Griffin to the Vaughan Road at the Flowers house; and Crawford's division was on the right, and it held the line from the Flowers house to Fort Wadsworth. Troops of Crawford's division also held the works on the Weldon Railroad. On October 16, 1864, Griffin extended his line to the right to a point about midway between the Squirrel Level Road and the Vaughan Road. At the same time, Ayres also moved to the right to cover the front from the right of Griffin to Fort Wadsworth. Baxter's division then occupied the line from Fort Wadsworth to Battery No. 24.

Operations about Petersburg, October 1864. During the period October 7–21, 1864, Warren was absent from the army on leave, and Crawford was in temporary command of Fifth Corps. Henry Baxter took temporary charge of Third Division during this time.

Fifth Corps remained on the line from the Church Road to Battery No. 24 until early on the morning of October 27, 1864, when the army again moved out in an attempt to seize the South Side Railroad. Warren left Baxter's brigade to hold the line of entrenchments, and with the rest of Fifth Corps moved about two miles down the Squirrel Level Road to the Clements house, and from there to the Duncan Road and Hatcher's Run, above Armstrong's Mill. Warren then advanced on the left of Ninth Corps, and moved up close to the enemy works, while Second Corps moved forward on the left of Fifth Corps, across Hatcher's Run. Parke informed Meade that he would probably not be able to force the enemy lines, and the latter then directed Warren to send a part of his command across Hatcher's Run and, with Second Corps, attempt to turn the enemy right flank. While Ninth Corps and Griffin, with his division and two brigades of Ayres' division, remained near the enemy works, Crawford's division, reinforced by Andrew W. Denison's Second Brigade (Maryland Brigade) of Ayres' division, crossed at Armstrong's Mill and advanced along the south side of Hatcher's Run. Crawford was engaged most of the afternoon, and progress was slow, and when Meade learned that Hancock had been attacked with great violence that afternoon, he called off the whole operation. The next day, Fifth Corps returned to its former positions. For details of the operations of Fifth Corps during the period October 27–28, 1864, see Operations about Petersburg and Richmond, Virginia, 1864–1865, Operations of October 1864, Engagement at the Boydton Plank Road (or Hatcher's Run), Virginia.

The organization of Fifth Corps during the engagement at the Boydton Plank Road was as follows:

FIFTH CORPS, Gouverneur K. Warren

First Division, Charles Griffin
    First Brigade, Horatio G. Sickel
    Second Brigade, Edgar M. Gregory
    Third Brigade, Joseph J. Bartlett

Second Division, Romeyn B. Ayres
    First Brigade, Frederick Winthrop
    Second Brigade, Andrew W. Denison
    Third Brigade, Arthur H. Grimshaw

Third Division, Samuel W. Crawford
    First Brigade, Edward S. Bragg
    Second Brigade, Henry Baxter
    Third Brigade, J. William Hofmann

Note. Baxter's Second Brigade remained in the trenches, and was not present at Hatcher's Run.

Artillery Brigade, Charles S. Wainwright

5th Battery (E), Massachusetts Light Artillery, Charles A. Phillips

9th Battery, Massachusetts Light Artillery, Richard S. Milton

Battery B, 1st New York Light Artillery, Robert E. Rogers

Battery C, 1st New York Light Artillery, David F. Ritchie

Battery D, 1st New York Light Artillery, James B. Hazelton

Battery E, 1st New York Light Artillery, Angell Matthewson

Battery H, 1st New York Light Artillery, Charles E. Mink

Battery L, 1st New York Light Artillery, George Breck

15th Battery, New York Light Artillery, Andrew R. McMahon

Battery B, 1st Pennsylvania Light Artillery, William C. Miller

Battery B, 4th United States Artillery, James Stewart

Battery D, 5th United States Artillery, William E. Van Reed

Winter of 1864–1865. During November 1864, the divisions of Fifth Corps continued to occupy the positions that they had assumed October 16, 1864, between Battery No. 24, on the right, and the Church Road, on the left. In addition, troops of Fifth Corps also held the rear line west of Fort Davison, and November 12, 1864, this position was extended to include the line from Fort McMahon to Fort Dushane, inclusive. December 5, 1864, Frank Wheaton's First Division of Sixth Corps, which had just rejoined the Army of the Potomac from the Shenandoah Valley, relieved Crawford's division on the line of works, and the next day, Truman Seymour's Third Division, Sixth Corps arrived and relieved Ayres' division. Also on December 6, 1864, John Gibbon's Second Division, Second Corps relieved Griffin's division temporarily. George W. Getty's Second Division, Sixth Corps arrived at Petersburg December 13–16, 1864 and relieved Gibbon's division, which then rejoined Second Corps.

When Warren's divisions were thus relieved, they were concentrated between the Halifax Road and the Jerusalem Plank Road, and early on the morning of December 7, 1864, Warren set out with his own Fifth Corps, Gershom Mott's Third Division, Second Corps, and David McM. Gregg's Second Cavalry Division on an expedition toward Hicksford

(present-day Emporia), Virginia to destroy the Weldon Railroad south of Stony Creek. Warren reached the Meherrin River December 9, 1864, and, after destroying seventeen to eighteen miles of track, started back the next day to rejoin the army. Fifth Corps returned from the expedition December 12, 1864, and the next day went into camp about midway between the Halifax Road and the Jerusalem Plank Road. For details of this expedition, see Operations about Petersburg and Richmond, Virginia, 1864–1865, Winter of 1864–1865, Warren's Expedition to Hicksford, Virginia.

On December 12, 1864, First Brigade, Third Division, Fifth Corps was discontinued when Edward S. Bragg left the army with the brigade for Baltimore, Maryland. There the regiments were to be assigned to duty at camps for drafted men. At City Point, while the brigade was en route to Baltimore, the 6th Wisconsin and 7th Wisconsin regiments were detached and returned to Fifth Corps. On February 14, 1865, these two regiments were organized as First Provisional Brigade, Third Division, which was placed under the command of John A. Kellogg, colonel of the 6th Wisconsin. March 3, 1865, the 91st New York arrived and was assigned to Kellogg's brigade. March 15, 1865, the term "Provisional" was dropped from the brigade designation, which then became First Brigade, Third Division. Of the four regiments of the original First Brigade that went north, 143rd Pennsylvania was sent to Hart's Island in New York Harbor; 149th and 150th Pennsylvania to Elmira, New York; and the 24th Michigan to Springfield, Illinois. Bragg remained in Baltimore and did not again return to the army.

Fifth Corps relieved the cavalry pickets on the line between the Weldon Railroad and the Jerusalem Plank Road, but otherwise the troops remained quietly in their camps until February 5, 1865. That day Gregg's cavalry division marched toward Dinwiddie Court House to break up the enemy wagon trains that were reported to be using the Boydton Plank Road, and Fifth Corps marched out to the intersection of the Vaughan Road and the Quaker Road to support the cavalry. Also that day, Andrew A. Humphreys' Second Corps advanced to Hatcher's Run, to be within a few miles of Fifth Corps. That afternoon, Humphreys was attacked at Armstrong's Mill, and during the night Gregg's cavalry and Warren's Fifth Corps were ordered to join Second Corps on Hatcher's Run. Warren arrived by way of the Vaughan Road early on the morning of February 6, 1865, and that afternoon Ayres' Second Division and Crawford's Third Division advanced to Dabney's Mill. These two divisions were soon vigorously attacked, and were driven back toward the Vaughan Road. The next morning Crawford advanced his division and recovered most of the ground lost the day before. The battle, however, was not resumed. For details of the Battle of Hatcher's Run, see Operations about Petersburg and Richmond, Virginia, 1864–1865, Battle of Hatcher's Run (or Dabney's Mill, Armstrong's Mill, Rowanty Creek, Vaughan Road), Virginia.

The organization of Fifth Corps at the Battle of Hatcher's Run was as follows:

FIFTH CORPS, Gouverneur K. Warren

First Division, Charles Griffin
First Brigade, Horatio G. Sickel, wounded February 6, 1865
Second Brigade, Allen L. Burr
Third Brigade, Alfred L. Pearson

Note 1. Joshua L. Chamberlain left on sick leave January 13, 1865, and Sickel commanded First Brigade temporarily until Chamberlain returned February 27, 1865.
Note 2. Edgar M. Gregory departed January 22, 1865 on leave, and Burr commanded Second Brigade until Gregory returned February 25, 1865.
Note 3. Joseph J. Bartlett left the army on sick leave January 6, 1865, and Pearson was in temporary command until Bartlett returned in March 1865.

Second Division, Romeyn B. Ayres
First Brigade, Frederick Winthrop
Second Brigade, Richard N. Bowerman
Third Brigade, James Gwyn

Note. Andrew W. Denison left on sick leave, and Bowerman commanded Second Brigade until he returned February 14, 1865.

Third Division, Samuel W. Crawford
First Brigade, Edward S. Bragg
Second Brigade. Henry Baxter
Third Brigade, Henry A. Morrow, to February 6, 1865, wounded
Thomas F. McCoy

Note. J. William Hofmann departed on leave January

24, 1865, and Morrow commanded Third Brigade temporarily until he was wounded February 6, 1865. McCoy then commanded the brigade until Hofmann returned February 9, 1865.

Artillery, Robert H. Fitzhugh
9th Battery, Massachusetts Light Artillery, George W. Foster
Battery D, 1st New York Light Artillery, James B. Hazelton
Battery L, 1st New York Light Artillery, George Breck

Note. Fitzhugh commanded the artillery brigade while Charles S. Wainwright was on leave. Fitzhugh took only the above batteries of his brigade to Hatcher's Run.

February 9–11, 1865, Second Corps was ordered to occupy a new line of entrenchments that was to begin at Fort Sampson on the old line, extend along the positions gained by Humphreys in his recent advance, and end at the Vaughan Road crossing of Hatcher's Run. Fifth Corps held the crossing until the new Second Corps line was completed, and it then camped near Hatcher's Run to watch the left and rear of the new line.

Fifth Corps remained in camp near Hatcher's Run until March 25, 1865. That morning a Confederate column under John B. Gordon attacked the Federal entrenchments on the front of Ninth Corps and captured Fort Stedman and the main line of works from Battery No. 9 to Fort Haskell. Ayres' and Crawford's divisions were then sent north to support Ninth Corps, but they were stopped en route when it was learned that Fort Stedman had been recaptured and that the Ninth Corps line had been restored. They then returned to their camps. For details of the assault at Fort Stedman, see Operations about Petersburg and Richmond, Virginia, 1864–1865, Assault at Fort Stedman, Virginia.

Following the attack on Fort Stedman, Humphreys' Second Corps was ordered to advance that afternoon to make a demonstration on the right of the enemy line to determine whether it had been weakened by the withdrawal of troops for Gordon's attack. If so, Humphreys was directed to attack. Griffin's division of Fifth Corps was sent to support Humphreys in this movement. Humphreys captured the entrenched enemy picket line, but he did not attack the main line. Bartlett's brigade of Griffin's division was engaged, along with Second Corps, near the Watkins house that evening. That night all the divisions of Fifth Corps returned to their camps, and they remained there until the beginning of Grant's final offensive at Petersburg March 29, 1865.

Appomattox Campaign, March 29, 1865–April 9, 1865. On the morning of March 29, 1865, Warren's Fifth Corps, with Second Corps on its right, advanced on the south side of Hatcher's Run toward the right flank on the enemy line of entrenchments beyond Burgess' Mill. That afternoon, while on the march, Griffin's division became engaged on the Quaker Road (or Military Road), north of Gravelly Run, but the corps pushed on, and that night reached the Boydton Plank Road. The next day Ayres' division moved out to a point near the White Oak Road, and Crawford's division formed a short distance to the rear. Griffin's division was farther to the rear, near the Plank Road.

During the morning of March 31, 1865, the enemy attacked Ayres' division, and then struck Crawford's division, and both were driven back to a position near the Boydton Plank Road. That afternoon, however, Fifth Corps, with help from Second Corps, advanced and finally gained possession of the White Oak Road. Andrew W. Denison, commanding Second Brigade of Ayres' division, was wounded, and Richard N. Bowerman succeeded him in command of the brigade.

On the morning of March 31, 1865, a Confederate force under George E. Pickett attacked Philip H. Sheridan's cavalry command north of Dinwiddie Court House and drove it back to a defensive position just in front of the court house. That night Warren received orders to march with his command and report to Sheridan, and take position on the right and rear of Pickett's line. Pickett, however, withdrew during the night to Five Forks, where he entrenched a position along the White Oak Road.

Warren arrived early the next morning, April 1, 1865, on the Dinwiddie Court House-Five Forks Road, and then became subject to Sheridan's orders. During the afternoon, he, marched north to the vicinity of Gravelly Run Church, about one mile from Five Forks, and at 4:00 P.M., while the cavalry attacked on the enemy front and right, Warren advanced against the left and rear of the enemy works east of Five Forks. Sheridan's attack was completely successful, and Fifth Corps, with the aid of the cavalry, drove the enemy completely from the field. Frederick Winthrop, commanding First Brigade of Ayres' division, was mortally wounded, and was succeeded in command of the brigade by James Grindlay. Richard Bowerman, commanding Second Brigade of Ayres' division, was wounded and succeeded by David L. Stanton.

Sheridan was dissatisfied with Warren's performance during the day, both before and during the battle, and that evening, near the close of the action, summarily relieved him from command of Fifth Corps and replaced him with Charles Griffin. Joseph J. Bartlett succeeded Griffin in command of First Division, and Alfred L. Pearson relieved Bartlett in command of Third Brigade, First Division. For details of the operations of Fifth Corps before and during the Battle of Five Forks, see Appomattox Campaign, Virginia, The Opening Moves, and also Battle of Five Forks.

Early on the morning of April 2, 1865, Sheridan started toward Hatcher's Run with Ayres' and Crawford's divisions of Fifth Corps, but he soon led them back to Five Forks, where they were united with Bartlett's division. Then Griffin, still under Sheridan's orders, marched north with Fifth Corps, crossed the South Side Railroad, and halted for the night at the intersection of the Namozine and the River roads. Later, Crawford's division was sent to support the cavalry at the crossing of the Namozine River.

Lee evacuated Petersburg and Richmond on the night of April 3, 1865, and the next day Grant's army took up the pursuit. Fifth Corps followed Sheridan's cavalry along the south side of the Appomattox River in the direction of Jetersville on the Richmond and Danville Railroad. Griffin arrived there during the afternoon of April 4, 1865, and entrenched a line across the railroad to prevent the Army of Northern Virginia, which was then arriving at Amelia Court House, from escaping by that route to Danville. Meade, with Second Corps and Sixth Corps, arrived at Jetersville April 5, 1865, and late that night Meade resumed control of Fifth Corps.

Lee did not attack the Federal line at Jetersville, but instead turned west, and throughout the night of April 5, 1865 marched by way of Deatonsville, on the road to Rice's Station on the South Side Railroad. The next morning, Sheridan's cavalry and Meade's infantry again started in pursuit. Fifth

Corps marched north to Paineville, where it turned west and moved forward on the extreme right of the army to Ligonton (Ligontown), near the Appomattox River. As Griffin's command was arriving at this point, Humphreys' Second Corps, Wright's Sixth Corps, and Sheridan's cavalry were engaged in a successful battle several miles to the south along Little Sayler's Creek, but Fifth Corps was not involved. For details of the movements of the army that day, see Appomattox Campaign, Virginia, Battle of Sayler's Creek.

On April 7, 1865, Fifth Corps marched from the extreme right of the army at Ligonton to the extreme left at Prince Edward Court House. It arrived there at 7:30 that evening, and the next morning moved on to Prospect Station on the South Side Railroad. It arrived there about noon and joined the Army of the James, and then came under the orders of Edward O. C. Ord, commander of the Army of the James. That afternoon, Fifth Corps continued on, and followed John Gibbon's Twenty-Fourth Corps along the route taken by Sheridan's cavalry toward Appomattox Station. The cavalry reached the station late in the afternoon, ahead of Lee's retreating army, and moved into position across the Lynchburg Road, west of Appomattox Court House. Fifth Corps and Twenty-Fourth Corps hurried forward during most of the night and arrived near Appomattox Station between 4:00 and 6:00 A.M. April 9, 1865. The infantry then relieved the cavalry, which was under attack as the enemy attempted to break through and escape. Fifth Corps relieved Thomas C. Devin's cavalry division, and then advanced, with Twenty-Fourth Corps on the left, and drove the enemy back toward Appomattox Court House. A short time later, the fighting ended under a flag of truce, and that afternoon Lee surrendered the Army of Northern Virginia.

For details of the operations of Fifth Corps from March 29, 1864 to April 9, 1865, see Appomattox Campaign, Virginia.

The organization of Fifth Corps during the Appomattox Campaign was as follows:

FIFTH CORPS, Gouverneur K. Warren, to April 1, 1865
Charles Griffin

First Division, Charles Griffin, to April 1, 1865
Joseph J. Bartlett
First Brigade, Joshua L. Chamberlain

Second Brigade, Edgar M. Gregory
Third Brigade, Joseph J. Bartlett, to April 1, 1865
Alfred L. Pearson

Second Division, Romeyn B. Ayres
First Brigade, Frederick Winthrop, to April 1, 1865, mortally wounded
James Grindlay, to April 3, 1865
Joseph Hayes
Second Brigade, Andrew W. Denison, to March 31, 1865, wounded
Richard Bowerman, to April 1, 1865, wounded
David L. Stanton
Third Brigade, James Gwyn

Third Division, Samuel W. Crawford
First Brigade, John A. Kellogg
Second Brigade, Henry Baxter
Third Brigade, Richard Coulter

Artillery Brigade, Charles S. Wainwright
Battery B, 1st New York Light Artillery, Robert E. Rogers
Battery D, 1st New York Light Artillery, Deloss M. Johnson
Battery H, 1st New York Light Artillery, Charles E. Mink
Company M, 15th New York Heavy Artillery, William D. Dickey
Battery B, 4th United States Artillery, John Mitchell, to March 29, 1865, wounded
William P. Vose
Batteries B and D, 5th United States Artillery, Jacob B. Rawles

Note. Other batteries formerly with Fifth Corps had been transferred to the Artillery Reserve of the army.

After Appomattox. After the surrender of the Army of Northern Virginia on April 9, 1865, Fifth Corps and Twenty-Fourth Corps were assigned to remain at Appomattox Court House to issue paroles and to look after the public property. While there, on April 12, 1865, First Division, Fifth Corps received the surrendered arms, guns, and colors of Lee's army. Joseph J. Bartlett was then in command of First Division, but Joshua L. Chamberlain was designated to command the parade at the formal surrender. Chamberlain had commanded First Brigade, First Division during the Appomattox Campaign, but for the formal surrender he asked that he be given command of Third Brigade, First Division, which he had commanded at Gettysburg, and with which he had been associated during the first two years of the war. He was assigned command of Third Brigade April 10, 1865, and Alfred L. Pearson took charge of First Brigade.

A short time after Lee's surrender, Second Corps, Sixth Corps, and Sheridan's cavalry were sent to Burkeville, where they would be in position to move against Joseph E. Johnston's army in North Carolina if it continued active operations. Fifth Corps remained at Appomattox Court House for two days after the formal surrender April 12, 1865, and spent the time in removing the surrendered property to the railroad for transfer to Washington. When this work was completed, Fifth Corps marched on April 15, 1865 along the South Side Railroad through Prospect Station and Farmville to Burkeville. On April 14, 1865, Charles H. T. Collis, with his Independent Brigade, arrived at Nottoway Court House from City Point, and his regiments were later assigned to Ayres' division. On April 17, 1865, the corps camped on Sandy Run, about three miles east of the town. It remained there until April 20, 1865, and then moved to Nottoway Court House. Upon arriving there, it relieved Ninth Corps of the duty of guarding the South Side Railroad from Burkeville to Sutherland's Station. Ayres' Second Division remained at Sutherland's Station; Crawford's Third Division took position at Blacks and Whites (present-day Blackstone); and First Division, commanded by Chamberlain after April 20, 1865, moved to Wilson's Station. When relieved by Fifth Corps, Ninth Corps marched to City Point to embark for Alexandria, and it left the Army of the Potomac.

Johnston surrendered his army to William T. Sherman near Durham Station, North Carolina April 26, 1865, and there then being no further need for the Army of the Potomac to remain near Burkeville, it was ordered to proceed to Washington, D.C. On May 1, 1865, Fifth Corps assembled near Wilson's Station, and the next day it began its march north. It moved by way of Sutherland's Station, Petersburg, and Drewry's Bluff, and May 4, 1865 arrived at Manchester, near Richmond. It marched with the rest of the army through Richmond May 6, 1865, and then continued on by way of Concord Church, Milford's Station, Fredericksburg, and Dumfries, and it camped at Fairfax Station on the night of May 11, 1865. The next day it moved to the Columbia Pike and camped on Four-Mile Run, and it remained

there until June 28, 1865. While there, it participated in the Grand Review of the Army of the Potomac in Washington May 23, 1865.

An order dated May 17, 1865 directed that all volunteer organizations of white troops in the Army of the Potomac whose terms of service expired between that date and September 30, 1865 be mustered out immediately. Compliance with this order greatly reduced the number of troops present in each of the corps of the army; and as a result, on June 28, 1865, a further order directed that all troops not then eligible for muster out be consolidated, in each corps of the army, into a division of three brigades. The three divisions thus formed (one each from Second Corps, Fifth Corps, and Sixth Corps) were to be organized temporarily into a provisional corps, that was to be commanded by Horatio G. Wright. The troops of Fifth Corps were organized in Third Provisional Division as follows:

Third Provisional Division, Romeyn B. Ayres
   First Brigade, Joshua L. Chamberlain
   Second Brigade, Henry Baxter
   Third Brigade, Joseph Hayes

Wright's Provisional Corps was placed in camp on the Baltimore and Ohio Railroad, west of the Monocacy River, and Wright reported to Winfield S. Hancock, commander of the Middle Department. In time, the troops of Ayres' Provisional Division were also mustered out.

With the order of June 28, 1865, the Army of the Potomac ceased to exist, and Fifth Corps was discontinued.

The organization of Fifth Corps during the period April 10, 1865 to June 28, 1865 was as follows:

FIFTH CORPS, Charles Griffin

First Division, Joseph J. Bartlett, to April 20, 1865
   Joshua L. Chamberlain
   First Brigade, Joshua L. Chamberlain, to April 11, 1865
      Alfred L. Pearson
   Second Brigade, Edgar M. Gregory
   Third Brigade, Alfred L. Pearson, to April 11, 1865
      Joshua L. Chamberlain, to April 20, 1865
      J. Cushing Edmands

Note. Bartlett was assigned command of Second Division, Ninth Corps April 22, 1865.

Second Division, Romeyn B. Ayres

First Brigade, Joseph Hayes
Second Brigade, David L. Stanton, to May 16, 1865
   Andrew W. Denison
Third Brigade, James Gwyn

Note. Second Brigade was discontinued by muster out of regiments May 31, 1865.

Third Division, Samuel W. Crawford
   First Brigade, John A. Kellogg, to April 28, 1865
      Henry A. Morrow
   Second Brigade, Henry Baxter
   Third Brigade, Richard Coulter, to May 13, 1865
      Adrian Root

Note 1. Henry A. Morrow, colonel of the 24th Michigan Regiment, who had been wounded at the Battle of Dabney's Mill in early February 1865, rejoined his regiment at Camp Butler, near Springfield, Illinois, and April 14, 1865, was ordered east to command First Brigade.
Note 2. On June 5, 1865, Morrow was sent to Louisville, Kentucky with ten western regiments that had been serving in the Army of the Potomac, with orders to report to John A. Logan, commanding the Army of the Tennessee.

Artillery Brigade, Charles S. Wainwright

COMMANDERS OF FIFTH CORPS, ARMY OF THE POTOMAC

Fitz John Porter	May 18, 1862 to November 10, 1862
Joseph Hooker	November 10, 1862 to November 16, 1862
Daniel Butterfield	November 16, 1862 to December 25, 1862
George G. Meade	December 25, 1862 to January 26, 1863
Charles Griffin	January 26, 1863 to February 1, 1863
George Sykes	February 1, 1863 to February 5, 1863
George G. Meade	February 5, 1863 to February 16, 1863
George Sykes	February 16, 1863 to February 23, 1863
Andrew A. Humphreys	February 23, 1863 to February 27, 1863
George G. Meade	February 27, 1863 to June 28, 1863
George Sykes	June 28, 1863 to August 5, 1863
Samuel W. Crawford	August 5, 1863 to August 8, 1863
George Sykes	August 8, 1863 to March 23, 1864
Gouverneur K. Warren	March 23, 1864 to January 2, 1865
Samuel W. Crawford	January 2, 1865 to January 27, 1865
Gouverneur K. Warren	January 27, 1865 to April 1, 1865
Charles Griffin	April 1, 1865 to June 28, 1865

SIXTH PROVISIONAL CORPS, ARMY OF THE POTOMAC

Sixth Corps was organized provisionally May 18, 1862, during the Peninsular Campaign, from William B. Franklin's Division of the Department of the Rappahannock and William F. Smith's Second Division, Fourth Corps, Army of the Potomac. Franklin was assigned command. The corps was first known as Sixth Provisional Corps, and under this designation served during the remainder of the Peninsular Campaign until July 17, 1862. On that date, George B. McClellan, commander of the Army of the Potomac, announced the change of designation to Sixth Corps, and this was officially confirmed by the secretary of war July 22, 1862.

For details of the organization and operations of Sixth Provisional Corps, see Sixth Corps, Army of the Potomac, Peninsular Campaign, and Department of the Rappahannock.

SIXTH CORPS, ARMY OF THE POTOMAC
MAY 18, 1862–JULY 10, 1864

Peninsular Campaign, May 18, 1862–August 1862. Sixth Corps was provisionally organized May 18, 1862, while the Army of the Potomac was near White House during the Peninsular Campaign. It was formed from William B. Franklin's Division of the Department of the Rappahannock, which had arrived on the Peninsula from Manassas April 22, 1862, and William F. Smith's Second Division of

Erasmus D. Keyes' Fourth Corps, Army of the Potomac. Franklin was assigned command of the corps May 18, 1862, and assumed command May 23, 1862. The corps was organized as follows:

SIXTH PROVISIONAL CORPS, William B. Franklin

First Division, Henry W. Slocum
  First Brigade, George W. Taylor
  Second Brigade, Joseph J. Bartlett
  Third Brigade, John Newton
  Artillery, Edward R. Platt
    1st Battery, Massachusetts Light Artillery, Josiah Porter
    1st Battery (A), New Jersey Light Artillery, William Hexamer
    Battery D, 2nd United States Artillery, Emory Upton

Note. When Franklin assumed command of Sixth Corps, Slocum assumed command of Franklin's division, and Bartlett assumed command of Slocum's brigade.

Second Division, William F. Smith
  First Brigade, Winfield S. Hancock
  Second Brigade, William T. H. Brooks
  Third Brigade, John W. Davidson
  Artillery, Romeyn B. Ayres
    Battery E, 1st New York Light Artillery, Charles C. Wheeler
    1st Battery, New York Light Artillery, Andrew Cowan
    3rd Battery, New York Light Artillery, Thaddeus P. Mott
    Battery F, 5th United States Artillery, Romeyn B. Ayres

When the army advanced from White House toward Richmond, Sixth Provisional Corps and Fifth Provisional Corps moved along the north side of the Chickahominy River to the Mechanicsville-Gaines' Mill area. Sixth Provisional Corps was moved to the south side of the river June 19, 1862. It remained there during the Battle of Mechanicsville June 26, 1862, but late the next afternoon Slocum's division recrossed the river to support Fitz John Porter's Fifth Provisional Corps during the Battle of Gaines' Mill.

During the evening of June 27, 1862, troops of John B. Magruder's Confederate command made a strong attack on Winfield S. Hancock's First Brigade of William F. Smith's Second Division at Garnett's and Golding's farms. A part of William T. H. Brooks' Second Brigade of Smith's division was

also involved. The attack was renewed the next day without success.

On June 28, 1862, after the Battle of Gaines' Mill, George B. McClellan began the withdrawal of his army to Harrison's Landing on the James River. Sixth Provisional Corps, Second Corps, and Third Corps remained in position south of the Chickahominy River, facing Richmond, while Fourth Corps, Fifth Corps, and the wagon train crossed White Oak Swamp. Franklin, who occupied the right of the line south of the Chickahominy, withdrew a short distance, and concentrated his corps at Golding's farm.

During the night of June 28, 1862, Sixth Provisional Corps left Golding's farm and began its march, by way of Savage Station, toward White Oak Swamp. Henry W. Slocum's First Division reached Savage Station about 5:00 the next morning, and then moved on and crossed to the south side of the swamp. William F. Smith's Second Division arrived at Savage Station about noon June 29, 1862, and then took position on the Williamsburg Road, south of the station. William T. H. Brooks' Second Brigade moved forward and formed on the left of Second Corps, south of the road. Troops of Second Corps did most of the fighting at the Battle of Savage Station that afternoon, but Brooks' brigade was also engaged.

After crossing White Oak Swamp, Slocum's division was placed north of the Charles City Road, about one mile west of the crossroads at Glendale. Smith's division withdrew from Savage Station on the night of June 29, 1862 and, after crossing the swamp, formed on the east side of the road at White Oak Bridge to guard the crossing at that point. Israel B. Richardson's division of Second Corps was on the west side of the road, and on the left of Smith's division.

The Confederate attack at Glendale on the evening of June 30, 1862 was launched to the south of Slocum's division, which was not fully engaged during the battle. Late in the evening, however, Slocum advanced Joseph J. Bartlett's Second Brigade to relieve the pressure on Philip Kearny's division of Third Corps, which was hard pressed on his left. Later, he also sent George W. Taylor's First Brigade to support Kearny. Both brigades were engaged.

On the night of June 30, 1862, Sixth Provisional

Corps moved to Malvern Hill, and was placed on the right of McClellan's line, facing Western Run. It was not engaged in the Battle of Malvern Hill July 1, 1862. For details of the operations of Sixth Provisional Corps during McClellan's campaign on the Peninsula, see Peninsular Campaign.

After the Battle of Malvern Hill, Franklin's corps withdrew to Harrison's Landing on the James River, and it remained there until the army was withdrawn in August 1862. In the meantime, on June 26, 1862, when the Army of Virginia was created under John Pope, James Shields' Division of the Department of the Rappahannock was broken up, and Nathan Kimball's brigade was sent to the Army of the Potomac. It was assigned to Sixth Provisional Corps July 6, 1862, but it was transferred to Second Corps as Kimball's Independent Brigade July 15, 1862.

In an order dated July 17, 1862, McClellan changed the designation of Sixth Provisional Corps to Sixth Corps, Army of the Potomac, and this action was officially confirmed by a presidential order of July 22, 1862.

When the Army of the Potomac withdrew from the Peninsula during the latter part of August 1862, Sixth Corps was sent to Alexandria, Virginia. Slocum's division arrived there August 24, 1862, the day before Thomas J. (Stonewall) Jackson began his flanking march around John Pope's Army of Virginia. When it was learned that James E. B. (Jeb) Stuart's Confederate cavalry had captured Manassas Station, Slocum sent George W. Taylor's First Brigade to reconnoiter. August 27, 1862, Taylor found Confederate forces at Bull Run Bridge, near Union Mills, and in the ensuing engagement Taylor was mortally wounded. Alfred T. A. Torbert assumed command of First Brigade.

The rest of Sixth Corps, which had arrived at Alexandria by August 29, 1862, then marched toward Centerville to join Pope's army. It arrived there during the evening of the next day, but it was too late to take part in the Second Battle of Bull Run, which was fought that day. Sixth Corps then retired with the defeated Union army into the Defenses of Washington, where it took position near Alexndria. For details of the movements of Sixth Corps during August 1862, see Pope's Northern Virginia Campaign, and also Military District of the Defenses of Washington, Army of the Potomac.

Maryland Campaign, September 3, 1862–September 20, 1862. Sixth Corps remained only briefly near Alexandria. Lee's army had crossed the Potomac River into Maryland at White's Ford September 4, 1862, and two days later Sixth Corps was ordered to Tennallytown, D.C. to join the forces that McClellan was assembling there to march in pursuit. Franklin was assigned command of the Left Wing of the army, which was to consist of his own Sixth Corps and Darius N. Couch's First Division, Fourth Corps. Couch's division joined Sixth Corps temporarily September 13, 1862, but it retained its designation as Fourth Corps for the time being. It served with Sixth Corps during the Maryland Campaign, and then, on September 26, 1862, it was permanently attached to Sixth Corps as Third Division.

During the advance of McClellan's army from Washington into Maryland in September 1862, Sixth Corps, with Couch's division, moved forward on the left along the Potomac River through Licksville and Burkittsville to Crampton's Gap in South Mountain. On September 14, 1862, Slocum's division attacked an enemy force holding the gap and after a sharp engagement forced a passage, and then Sixth Corps advanced into Pleasant Valley. It remained near Rohrersville until the morning of September 17, 1862, and then Franklin, with the divisions of Slocum and Smith, marched toward Keedysville to join the Army of the Potomac on Antietam Creek. Franklin sent Couch's division southward to occupy Maryland Heights, but after marching for some distance, it too was ordered to march toward Sharpsburg. Because of the long distance Couch was forced to travel, he did not reach the battlefield until early on the morning of September 18, 1862, the day after the Battle of Antietam.

Sixth Corps was not strongly engaged at the Battle of Antietam. Slocum's First Division was in line and was exposed to artillery fire, and Smith's Second Division supported William H. French's and Israel B. Richardson's divisions of Second Corps in the fighting at "Bloody Lane." For details of the involvement of Sixth Corps at the Battle of Antietam, see Maryland Campaign (South Mountain and Antietam).

The organization of Sixth Corps and Couch's division of Fourth Corps at the Battle of Antietam was as follows:

SIXTH CORPS, William B. Franklin

First Division, Henry W. Slocum
First Brigade, Alfred T. A. Torbert
Second Brigade, Joseph J. Bartlett
Third Brigade, John Newton
Artillery, Emory Upton
Battery A, Maryland Light Artillery, John W. Wolcott
Battery A, Massachusetts Light Artillery, Josiah Porter
1st Battery (A), New Jersey Light Artillery, William Hexamer
Battery D, 2nd United States Artillery, Edward B. Williston

Second Division, William F. Smith
First Brigade, Winfield S. Hancock, September 17, 1862
Amasa Cobb
Second Brigade, William T. H. Brooks
Third Brigade, William H. Irwin
Artillery, Romeyn B. Ayres
Battery B, Maryland Light Artillery, Theodore J. Vanneman
1st Battery, New York Light Artillery, Andrew Cowan
3rd Battery, New York Light Artillery, William Stuart
Battery F, 5th United States Artillery (to September 17, 1862), Leonard Martin

Note. Hancock was assigned command of First Division, Second Corps September 17, 1862.

First Division, Fourth Corps, Darius N. Couch
First Brigade, Charles Devens, Jr.
Second Brigade, Albion P. Howe
Third Brigade, John Cochrane
Artillery
Battery C, 1st Pennsylvania Light Artillery, Jeremiah McCarthy
Battery D, 1st Pennsylvania Light Artillery, Michael Hall
Battery G, 2nd United States Artillery, John H. Butler
3rd Battery, New York Light Artillery (from September 17, 1862), William Stuart

Antietam to Warrenton, Virginia, September 19, 1862–November 7, 1862. Sixth Corps remained only briefly near Sharpsburg after the Battle of Antietam. Couch's First Division, Fourth Corps, then temporarily attached to Sixth Corps, moved to Williamsport, Maryland September 20, 1862, and

Sixth Corps followed the next day. September 26, 1862, Couch's division was permanently attached to Sixth Corps as Third Division.

Sixth Corps remained on the upper Potomac, occupying such points as Hagerstown, Hancock, and Cherry Run, until the end of October 1862. On October 30, 1862, Franklin was ordered with his Sixth Corps to Berlin, Maryland (present-day Brunswick) to join the rest of the Army of the Potomac, which was then moving southward into Virginia. Sixth Corps crossed the Potomac November 1–2, 1862, and then marched south along the Loudoun Valley to the New Baltimore-Greenwich area, where it arrived November 7, 1862.

The organization of Sixth Corps during this period was as follows:

SIXTH CORPS, William B. Franklin

First Division, Henry W. Slocum, to October 15, 1862
John Newton, to October 18, 1862
William T. H. Brooks
First Brigade, Alfred T. A. Torbert
Second Brigade, Joseph J. Bartlett
Third Brigade, John Newton, to September 21, 1862
Roderick Matheson, to October 1862
Edwin H. Stoughton

Note 1. Slocum was assigned command of Twelfth Corps October 15, 1862.
Note 2. On September 21, 1862, Newton was relieved, at his own request, from duty with the Army of the Potomac. On October 15, 1862, he was assigned command of Slocum's former First Division, and three days later he was assigned command of Third Division, Sixth Corps.

Second Division, William F. Smith
First Brigade, Amasa Cobb, to September 1862
Calvin E. Pratt
Second Brigade, William T. H. Brooks, to October 18, 1862
Henry Whiting
Third Brigade, Ernest Von Vegesack, to September 1862
Francis L. Vinton

Third Division, Darius N. Couch, to October 18, 1862
John Newton
First Brigade, Charles Devens, Jr., to October 1862
John Cochrane
Second Brigade, Albion P. Howe, to October 1862
Charles Devens, Jr.

Third Brigade, John Cochrane, to October 1862
    Albion P. Howe

Note 1. Newton succeeded Couch in command of Third Division when the latter was assigned command of Second Corps.

Note 2. In October 1862, Third Division was reorganized as follows: First Brigade was redesignated as Second Brigade, and First Brigade was reorganized from regiments of Third Brigade; Second Brigade was redesignated as Third Brigade, and Second Brigade was reorganized from regiments of First Brigade. This accounts for the changes in the brigade commanders in October 1862.

There was little change in the organization of the artillery serving with Sixth Corps during this period

Fredericksburg Campaign, November 7, 1862– December 15, 1862. On the night of November 7, 1862, while the Army of the Potomac was near Warrenton, Virginia, Ambrose E. Burnside relieved McClellan in command, and he then submitted to Henry W. Halleck a plan for moving the army eastward to Fredericksburg, and from there to advance on Richmond from the north. This plan was approved November 14, 1862, and on that date Burnside reorganized the army into three grand divisions and a reserve. Franklin was assigned command of the Left Grand Division, which consisted of his own Sixth Corps and John F. Reynolds' First Corps. Franklin assumed command November 16, 1862, and he was succeeded in command of Sixth Corps by William F. Smith. Albion P. Howe assumed command of Smith's Second Division.

Burnside immediately put the army in motion toward Falmouth, Virginia, and a few days later it arrived on the north bank of the Rappahannock River, opposite Fredericksburg. Franklin's Left Grand Division arrived at Stafford Court House November 18, 1862. There was then a long delay while Burnside waited for the arrival of the pontoon trains from Washington, but finally bridges were laid across the river, and all was in readiness for the army to cross.

On December 11, 1862, Sixth Corps moved to the bridges near the mouth of Deep Run, and it crossed there with First Corps the next day. Sixth Corps then moved into position along the Richmond Stage Road, with First Corps on its left and Ninth Corps on its right. It remained there, under fire, during the Battle of Fredericksburg December 13, 1862, but it

was not engaged in any offensive operations. Daniel E. Sickles' Second Division and David B. Birney's First Division of Third Corps were sent to aid Reynolds during the afternoon, and John Newton's Third Division, Sixth Corps was sent to support them, but it was not engaged. Sixth Corps recrossed the Rappahannock with the rest of the army on the night of December 15, 1862. For details of the Battle of Fredericksburg, see Fredericksburg, Virginia Campaign.

The organization of Sixth Corps during the Battle of Fredericksburg was as follows:

SIXTH CORPS, William F. Smith

First Division, William T. H. Brooks
    First Brigade, Alfred T. A. Torbert
    Second Brigade, Henry L. Cake
    Third Brigade, David A. Russell
    Artillery
        Battery A, Maryland Light Artillery, James H. Rigby
        1st Battery (A), Massachusetts Light Artillery, William H. McCartney
        1st Battery, New Jersey Light Artillery, William Hexamer
        Battery D, 2nd United States Artillery, Edward B. Williston

Second Division, Albion P. Howe
    First Brigade, Calvin E. Pratt
    Second Brigade, Henry Whiting
    Third Brigade, Francis L. Vinton, wounded
        Robert F. Taylor
        Thomas H. Neill
    Artillery
        Battery B, Maryland Light Artillery, Alonzo Snow
        1st Battery, New York Light Artillery, Andrew Cowan
        3rd Battery, New York Light Artillery, William A. Harn
        Battery F, 5th United States Artillery, Leonard Martin

Third Division, John Newton
    First Brigade, John Cochrane
    Second Brigade, Charles Devens, Jr.
    Third Brigade, Thomas A. Rowley
        Frank Wheaton
    Artillery
        Battery C, 1st Pennsylvania Light Artillery, Jeremiah McCarthy
        Battery D, 1st Pennsylvania Light Artillery, Michael Hall
        Battery G, 2nd United States Light Artillery, John H. Butler

Winter of 1862–1863. After the Battle of Fredericksburg, Sixth Corps went into winter quarters at White Oak Church, east of Falmouth. On January 20, 1863, however, Burnside began another offensive movement against Lee's army. Franklin's and Joseph Hooker's grand divisions marched up the Rappahannock River to a point near Banks' Ford, with the intention of crossing the river and then attacking the enemy's left and rear at Fredericksburg. This movement, which became known as the infamous "Mud March" of the Army of the Potomac, was called off January 24, 1863, when incessant rains rendered the roads virtually impassable. For additional information, see Army of the Potomac, Winter of 1862–1863. After this fiasco, the army returned to its camps and was relatively quiet during the rest of the winter.

There were several organizational and command changes in Sixth Corps during the winter. William B. Franklin was in command of the Left Grand Division on January 25, 1863, when he was relieved from duty with the Army of the Potomac. William F. Smith, then commanding Sixth Corps, was assigned command of the Left Grand Division, and John Newton assumed command of Sixth Corps. The grand divisions were abolished February 5, 1863, and John Sedgwick was assigned command of Sixth Corps. Smith did not return to Sixth Corps, but was assigned command of Ninth Corps.

On January 26, 1863, a new brigade was organized in Albion P. Howe's Second Division, and Calvin Pratt was assigned command. Robert F. Taylor assumed command of Pratt's First Brigade, Second Division. Pratt's new brigade was designated as the Light Brigade, and it consisted of three infantry regiments from First Brigade and an independent battery. On February 3, 1863, the brigade was increased to five infantry regiments and organized as a division for special service. It was designed to act in emergencies. It was sometimes referred to as the Light Division, and also as Fourth Division, Sixth Corps, although it consisted of only one brigade of five regiments. In later reports it was called both Light Brigade and Light Division. It was discontinued May 11, 1863. One regiment was sent home for muster out, and the other regiments were transferred to First Division and Second Division of the corps. First Brigade, Second Division was discontinued March 24, 1863, and the two regiments then remaining in the brigade were assigned to Third Brigade, First Division, Sixth Corps.

Lewis A. Grant succeeded Henry Whiting in command of Second Brigade (Vermont Brigade), Second Division in February 1863.

Chancellorsville Campaign, April 27, 1863–May 6, 1863. At the beginning of the Chancellorsville Campaign in the latter part of April 1863, Joseph Hooker, then commanding the Army of the Potomac, divided the army into two wings. The Right Wing, consisting of Fifth Corps, Eleventh Corps, and Twelfth Corps, marched by way of Kelly's Ford on the Rappahannock to the Rapidan River, and it then advanced into the Wilderness toward Chancellorsville. On April 28, 1863, the Left Wing, consisting of First Corps, Third Corps, and Sixth Corps, marched to the Rappahannock below Fredericksburg to attempt to hold Lee in his entrenchments above Fredericksburg while the Right Wing moved on his rear. First Corps marched about noon, and Sixth Corps followed about three hours later. First Corps halted at Fitzhugh's Crossing about 5:30 P.M. and Sixth Corps at Franklin's Crossing about 9:00 P.M. Third Corps came up between the two, and somewhat to their rear. Darius N. Couch's Second Corps remained near Falmouth.

The next day, William T. H. Brooks' First Division, Sixth Corps crossed the Rappahannock and established a bridgehead on the south bank. There was no further change in the position of Sixth Corps until the evening of May 1, 1863, and then Hiram Burnham's Light Division (or Light Brigade) crossed the river and joined Brooks. Third Corps marched toward Chancellorsville April 30, 1863, and First Corps followed May 2, 1863, leaving Sixth Corps alone below Fredericksburg.

On the evening of May 2, 1863, Howe's and Newton's divisions crossed the Rappahannock and joined Brooks and Burnham south of the river. That night Sedgwick marched toward Fredericksburg with his Sixth Corps, and arrived there the next morning. At about that time, John Gibbon's division of Second Corps entered Fredericksburg from Falmouth and reported to Sedgwick.

At 10:30 A.M. May 3, 1863, Sixth Corps attacked and carried Marye's Heights, and that afternoon it marched westward on the Plank Road toward Chancellorsville. About 4:00 P.M. Brooks' division, which was leading the corps, encountered the enemy in position near Salem Church, and after a severe engagement, it was forced to retire a short distance to the Toll House (Toll Gate). There Brooks was joined by Newton's Third Division and a part of Howe's Second Division. Gibbon's division remained at Fredericksburg.

During May 4, 1863, Sixth Corps remained on the defensive on a line extending along the Plank Road, with the right flank refused and facing Salem Church, and the left flank refused and facing the heights above Fredericksburg. Brooks and Howe were strongly attacked about 6:00 P.M. that day, but they were able to maintain their positions. The corps withdrew that night, and recrossed the Rappahannock at Banks' Ford at 2:00 A.M. the next morning. It then returned to its former quarters. For details of the operations of Sixth Corps near Fredericksburg, see Chancellorsville, Virginia Campaign.

The organization of Sixth Corps during the Chancellorsville Campaign was as follows:

SIXTH CORPS, John Sedgwick

First Division, William T. H. Brooks
    First Brigade, Henry W. Brown, to May 3, 1863, wounded
        William H. Penrose, May 3, 1863
        Samuel L. Buck, May 3–4, 1863, disabled
        William H. Penrose
    Second Brigade, Joseph J. Bartlett
    Third Brigade, David A. Russell
    Artillery, John A. Tompkins
        1st Battery (A), Massachusetts Light Artillery, William H. McCartney
        Battery A, New Jersey Light Artillery, Augustin N. Parsons
        Battery A, Maryland Light Artillery, James H. Rigby
        Battery D, 2nd United States Artillery, Edward B. Williston

Second Division, Albion P. Howe
    Second Brigade, Lewis A. Grant
    Third Brigade, Thomas H. Neill
    Artillery, J. Watts De Peyster
        1st Battery, New York Light Artillery, Andrew Cowan
        Battery F, 5th United States Artillery, Leonard Martin

Note. First Brigade was discontinued March 24, 1863.

Third Division, John Newton
    First Brigade, Alexander Shaler
    Second Brigade, William H. Browne, to May 3, 1863, wounded
        Henry L. Eustis
    Third Brigade, Frank Wheaton
    Artillery, Jeremiah McCarthy
        Batteries C and D, 1st Pennsylvania Light Artillery, Jeremiah McCarthy
        Battery G, 2nd United States Artillery, John H. Butler

Light Division (or Light Brigade), Calvin A. Pratt, to April 30, 1863, resigned
    Hiram Burnham

Note 1. The Light Division was attached to Newton's division during the march to Fredericksburg.
Note 2. William A. Harn's 3rd Battery, New York Light Artillery was attached to Burnham's brigade.

During May 1863, Sixth Corps lost nine regiments by muster out, but there was no extensive reorganization in the corps. On May 11, 1863, Hiram Burnham's Light Division was discontinued when one regiment left for muster out, and the remaining infantry regiments were assigned to First Division and Second Division, and the artillery to Third Division. Third Brigade, First Division was reorganized at that time. Two regiments were mustered out, and one was transferred to Second Brigade, First Division, but this loss was made good by the transfer of two regiments of the Light Division to this brigade. Third Brigade, Second Division was also reorganized. It lost two regiments by muster out, but these were replaced by two regiments from the Light Division.

Skirmishes at Franklin's Crossing (or Deep Run), Virginia, June 5–13, 1863. After the Battle of Chancellorsville, Sixth Corps remained relatively inactive near White Oak Church until early in June 1863. At that time Lee's Army of Northern Virginia began to leave its positions near Fredericksburg on its march toward Pennsylvania. Hooker then ordered Sedgwick to make a reconnaissance in force across the Rappahannock below Fredericksburg to determine the strength and positions of the enemy forces remaining in the area. Lewis A. Grant's Second Brigade of Howe's Second Division left its camp near White Oak Church about noon June 5, 1863, and marched to the Rappahannock at

Franklin's old crossing near the mouth of Deep Run. Enemy fire from across the river prevented for a time the laying of pontoon bridges, but finally the 5th Vermont and 26th New Jersey regiments went over in boats and drove the enemy from their rifle pits and away from the river. The 2nd, 3rd, and 4th Vermont regiments followed in boats while the first bridge was being completed, and then 6th Vermont also crossed. A number of prisoners from Ambrose P. Hill's corps were taken in this operation, and this led Sedgwick to believe that most of Lee's army was still in position at Fredericksburg.

Skirmishers of Grant's brigade occupied an advanced line that night and the next day. This line extended from the river on the left, at the Bernard house (Mansfield), across the Bowling Green Road (Fredericksburg-Bowling Green-Richmond Road), and on to Deep Run. During the afternoon of June 6, 1863, Thomas H. Neill's Third Brigade of Howe's division, temporarily commanded by Daniel D. Bidwell, crossed the river and joined the Vermont Brigade on the south bank. Also on June 6, 1863, First Division, commanded by Horatio G. Wright since May 23, 1863, and Newton's Third Division of Sixth Corps advanced to Franklin's Crossing, where they took position on the north side of the river. The next day Wright crossed over and relieved Howe, and June 9, 1863, Newton relieved Wright. Only one division at a time was sent across the river, because that was a large enough force for the purpose intended, and it was considered unsafe to commit the entire corps in the presence of what was believed to be a strong enemy force.

On June 10, 1863, Howe's division, then on the north bank of the Rappahannock, was sent back to Aquia Creek, and two days later Hooker ordered Sedgwick to withdraw Newton's division from across the river. The crossing began about 10:00 that evening, and the bridges had been taken up shortly after midnight.

Gettysburg Campaign, May 1863–July 1863. On June 13, 1863, Hooker finally realized that Lee's army was moving northward toward the Potomac River, and that day he issued orders for the Army of the Potomac to march toward Centerville and the Orange and Alexandria Railroad. At that time Howe's Second Division was at Aquia Creek, and Wright's First Division and Newton's Third

Division were at Franklin's Crossing. June 13, 1863, First Division and Third Division moved back to Potomac Creek, and the next day they continued on to Stafford Court House. On June 15, 1863, all three divisions of Sixth Corps marched to Dumfries. From there they moved on by way of Fairfax Court House to Germantown, where they arrived June 18, 1863. Two days later, Second Division was sent to Bristoe Station. June 24, 1863, Third Division moved to Centerville, and it was joined there the next day by Second Division from Germantown.

The rest of the Army of the Potomac was already crossing the Potomac River into Maryland when Sixth Corps began its march toward Edwards Ferry June 26, 1863. It marched through Dranesville, crossed the river the next day, and arrived at Hyattstown June 28, 1863. That day George G. Meade relieved Hooker in command of the Army of the Potomac. When the advance continued the next day, Sixth Corps moved to the right flank of the army, and arrived at Manchester June 30, 1863. For details of the movements of the army to Gettysburg, see Gettysburg Campaign, Part I, From the Rappahannock to Gettysburg.

Sixth Corps was only lightly engaged at the Battle of Gettysburg, and it suffered a total loss of only 242 men. When the battle began on the morning of July 1, 1863, the corps was at Manchester, Maryland, on the extreme right of Meade's advance; and it was only by hard marching that the divisions arrived on the field of Gettysburg between 3:00 and 6:00 P.M. July 2, 1863. Shortly thereafter the brigades of the corps were detached and sent to various parts of the field as needed. About 6:00 P.M. Thomas H. Neill's Third Brigade of Albion P. Howe's Second Division was sent to Power's Hill to support the artillery that was posted there. Just before dark, Henry L. Eustis' Second Brigade and David J. Nevin's Third Brigade of Frank Wheaton's Third Division, and Joseph J. Bartlett's Second Brigade of Horatio G. Wright's First Division were advanced into line with George Sykes' Fifth Corps, and they assisted in turning back James Longstreet's final advance that evening. These brigades of Sixth Corps were joined about 7:00 P.M. by Alexander Shaler's First Brigade, Third Division. Lewis A. Grant's Second Brigade, the remaining brigade of Second Division, was sent to the east of Big Round Top, on the extreme left of the Union line. Alfred T. A. Torbert's First Brigade and David A. Russell's Third Brigade of First Division were held in reserve.

The break-up of Sixth Corps was completed on the morning of July 3, 1863. About 8:00 A.M. Shaler's brigade of Third Division arrived near Culp's Hill to reinforce Twelfth Corps, which was engaged with Edward Johnson's reinforced Confederate division. Russell's brigade of First Division was sent to the left of Meade's line to join Grant's brigade, and Wright was placed in command of both of these brigades. Torbert's brigade and Eustis' brigade were placed in the main line of battle on Cemetery Ridge, where they were under the direction of John Newton, commander of First Corps. Bartlett was in command of his own brigade and Nevin's brigade, which were in position along the Taneytown Road, to the north of Little Round Top. When these dispositions were completed, Sedgwick, Howe, and Wheaton were left with no troops under their command. For details of the Battle of Gettysburg, see Gettysburg Campaign, Part II, Battle of Gettysburg.

The organization of Sixth Corps at the Battle of Gettysburg was as follows:

SIXTH CORPS, John Sedgwick

First Division, Horatio G. Wright
   First Brigade, Alfred T. A. Torbert
   Second Brigade, Joseph J. Bartlett
   Third Brigade, David A. Russell

Note. On July 3, 1863, Bartlett commanded Third Brigade, Third Division in addition to his own brigade.

Second Division, Albion P. Howe
   Second Brigade, Lewis A. Grant
   Third Brigade, Thomas H. Neill

Note. There was no First Brigade in Second Division.

Third Division, John Newton, to July 2, 1863
   Frank Wheaton
   First Brigade, Alexander Shaler
   Second Brigade, Henry L. Eustis
   Third Brigade, Frank Wheaton, to July 2, 1863
     David J. Nevin

Note. Newton was assigned command of First Corps July 2, 1863.

Artillery Brigade, Charles H. Tompkins
   1st Battery (A), Massachusetts Light Artillery, William H. McCartney
   1st Battery, New York Light Artillery, Andrew Cowan
   3rd Battery, New York Light Artillery, William A. Harn
   Battery C, 1st Rhode Island Light Artillery, Richard Waterman
   Battery G, 1st Rhode Island Light Artillery, George W. Adams
   Battery D, 2nd United States Artillery, Edward B. Williston
   Battery G, 2nd United States Artillery, John H. Butler
   Battery F, 5th United States Artillery, Leonard Martin

The brigades of Sixth Corps, which were scattered over the field at the end of the fighting at Gettysburg, remained in their various positions during July 4, 1863. That day Joseph J. Bartlett was assigned command of Third Division, relieving Wheaton, and Emory Upton was assigned command of Bartlett's Second Brigade, First Division. That night, Lee withdrew from his positions at Gettysburg and began his retreat toward Virginia. Sixth Corps was reassembled July 5, 1863 and, under the command of Sedgwick, advanced to Fairfield, Pennsylvania in pursuit of Lee's retreating columns. That day, Meade placed Sedgwick in charge of First Corps, Third Corps, and Sixth Corps, and directed him to march with these three corps on the right of the army toward Middletown, Maryland. On July 6, 1863, at Fairfield, Neill was assigned command of a Light Division, consisting of his own Third Brigade, Second Division, Sixth Corps, John B. McIntosh's First Brigade of David McM. Gregg's Second Cavalry Division, and a rifled battery, and he was directed to follow closely the retreating Confederates and report their movements.

That night the rest of Sixth Corps moved to Emmitsburg, where it joined First Corps and Third Corps for the march to Middletown. Sixth Corps marched by way of Mountain Pass, near Hamburg, and Middletown, and arrived at Boonsboro July 9, 1863. It then moved to Beaver Creek July 10, 1863, and to Funkstown two days later. Neill's brigade of Sixth Corps, which had marched with the Light Division by way of Waynesboro and Leitersburg, rejoined the corps at Funkstown July 12, 1863. The next day, Sixth Corps advanced to the vicinity of Hagerstown. That night the Army of Northern Virginia recrossed the Potomac River at Williamsport and Falling Waters, and the next day Sixth Corps advanced to the vicinity of Williamsport.

Early on July 15, 1863, the Army of the Potomac

began its march toward the Potomac River near Harper's Ferry, where it was to cross into Virginia in pursuit of Lee. Sixth Corps advanced through Boonsboro and arrived at Berlin (present-day Brunswick), Maryland the next day. It crossed the river at Berlin July 19, 1863, and marched with Fifth Corps, in the center of the army, down the Loudoun Valley toward Warrenton, Virginia. Sixth Corps marched by way of Wheatland and Beaver Dam to Rectortown, and from there, on July 23, 1863, the divisions proceeded by different routes. Wright's First Division marched by way of White Plains to New Baltimore; Howe's Second Division marched by way of Barbee's Cross Roads and Markham's Station to Orleans; and Bartlett's Third Division accompanied Second Division to Barbee's Cross Roads, and from there it moved to Thumb Run. The corps was concentrated at Warrenton July 25, 1863.

July 31, 1863, Sixth Corps was ordered to hold the Waterloo Crossing of the Rappahannock, and to picket the river from Waterloo to Sulfur Springs. One division was assigned to the crossing, one division was to remain at Warrenton, and the other division was to go to New Baltimore.

For details of the movements of the army from Gettysburg to the Rappahannock, see Gettysburg Campaign, Part III, Pursuit of Lee.

From the Rappahannock to the Rapidan, August 1, 1863–October 10, 1863. Sixth Corps remained in its positions along the Rappahannock until mid-September 1863. During this period, the corps was temporarily reduced in numbers when Lewis A. Grant's Second Brigade, Second Division and two other regiments were sent to New York because of the disturbances caused by the draft. For additional information, see Army of the Potomac, From the Rappahannock to the Rapidan, and also Department of the East, January 3, 1863–June 27, 1865, Draft Riots in New York,1863.

On September 16, 1863, the Army of the Potomac advanced from the Rappahannock, and formed on a line passing through Culpeper Court House, facing the Rapidan River. Sixth Corps crossed the Rappahannock at Sulfur Springs, and took position on the right of the army near Stone House Mountain.

On October 1, 1863, Howe's Second Division was sent to relieve David McM. Gregg's Second Cavalry Division, which was guarding the line of the Orange and Alexandria Railroad, including the bridges at Bristoe Station, Catlett's Station, and Rappahannock Station. Then, on October 5, 1863, Sixth Corps relieved Gouverneur K. Warren's Second Corps, which was on duty along the Rapidan, and it picketed the river from Somerville to near Robertson's Ford on Robertson's (or Robertson) River.

October 9, 1863, Meade learned of a Confederate movement toward his right, but he was uncertain whether this was the beginning of an enemy withdrawal or of a flanking movement against the right of his line. That evening he ordered John Buford's First Cavalry Division, Newton's First Corps, Sykes' Fifth Corps, and Sedgwick's Sixth Corps, in that order, to cross the Rapidan to find out what was going on, and, if they found Lee to be withdrawing, they were to follow him and report back. Only Buford's cavalry division crossed the river October 10, 1863, and then Meade learned definitely that Lee was not withdrawing, but was advancing in heavy force against his right flank. He promptly called off the movement south of the Rapidan, and that night he issued orders for the withdrawal of the army to the line of the Rappahannock. For additional information, see Army of the Potomac, From the Rappahannock to the Rapidan.

Bristoe, Virginia Campaign, October 10, 1863–October 22, 1863. When Lee began his movement around the Federal right flank October 9, 1863, Sixth Corps was in position along the north bank of the Rapidan from Somerville Ford to a point near Robertson's Ford on Robertson's River. During the evening of October 10, 1863, it was withdrawn to the line of the Orange and Alexandria Railroad behind Culpeper Court House, and the next day it marched with Second Corps and Fifth Corps along the railroad to Rappahannock Station, where it crossed to the north bank of the Rappahannock River. On the afternoon of October 12, 1863, Second Corps, Fifth Corps, and Sixth Corps recrossed the river and advanced to Brandy Station, but they withdrew later that evening.

Meantime, Lee continued his advance and again threatened the right of Meade's new line along the Rappahannock. When Meade became aware of this, he ordered the army to fall back toward Centerville.

On October 13, 1863, Sixth Corps marched with First Corps and Fifth Corps along the railroad toward Centerville, and it arrived that night at Kettle Run. It continued on to Centerville the next day, and October 15, 1863, it was on the Little River Turnpike near Chantilly. Lee did not follow to Centerville, but soon fell back to the Rappahanock River. October, 19, 1863, the Army of the Potomac again advanced, and during this movement Sixth Corps moved to Gainesville. For details of the operations of the army during this period, see Bristoe, Virginia Campaign.

The organization of Sixth Corps during the Bristoe Campaign was as follows:

SIXTH CORPS, John Sedgwick

First Division, Horatio G. Wright
First Brigade, Alfred T. A. Torbert
Second Brigade, Joseph J. Bartlett
Third Brigade, David A. Russell

Second Division, Albion P. Howe
Second Brigade, Lewis A. Grant
Third Brigade, Thomas H. Neill

Note. There was no First Brigade in Second Division at this time.

Third Division, Henry D. Terry
First Brigade, Alexander Shaler
Second Brigade, Henry L. Eustis
Third Brigade, Frank Wheaton

Note. Terry relieved Wheaton in command of Third Division August 4, 1863.

Artillery, Charles H. Tompkins
1st Battery (A), Massachusetts Light Artillery, William H. McCartney
1st Battery, New York Light Artillery, Andrew Cowan
3rd Battery, New York Light Artillery, William A. Harn
Battery C, 1st Rhode Island Light Artillery, Richard Waterman
Battery G, 1st Rhode Island Light Artillery, George W. Adams
Battery F, 5th United States Artillery, Leonard Martin
Battery M, 5th United States Artillery, James Mc-Knight

Engagement at Rappahannock Station and Kelly's Ford, Virginia, November 7, 1863. On October 20, 1863, at the close of the Bristoe Cam-

paign, Sixth Corps occupied Warrenton, and it remained there until early in November 1863. At that time, Meade planned an advance to capture Kelly's Ford and the Confederate bridgehead at Rappahannock Station. On November 6, 1863, in preparation for this movement, Meade divided the army into two temporary columns or wings, and he assigned Sixth Corps and Fifth Corps to the Right Column. He also assigned Sedgwick to command this column, and Wright assumed temporary command of Sixth Corps. David A. Russell temporarily commanded Wright's First Division, and Peter C. Ellmaker commanded Russell's Third Brigade. Joseph J. Bartlett was transferred to Fifth Corps, where he was assigned command of First Division. Emory Upton assumed command of Bartlett's Second Brigade, First Division, Sixth Corps.

On the morning of November 7, 1863, Sixth Corps marched by way of Fayetteville to Rappahannock Station, and formed in front of the enemy bridgehead. It took position on the west side of the railroad and connected with Fifth Corps on its left. During the afternoon, Howe's Second Division, to which Shaler's brigade of Terry's Third Division was attached, advanced and captured a ridge to the right of the railroad. Howe then brought up artillery and opened fire on the redoubts. This had little effect on the enemy's defensive works; and shortly after dark, Ellmaker's Third Brigade and Upton's Second Brigade of Russell's First Division, which was next to the railroad, advanced and captured the redoubts and about 1,600 prisoners. For details, see Engagements at Rappahannock Station and Kelly's Ford, Virginia.

The next day, Russell's and Howe's divisions marched to Brandy Station, and Terry's division was left to guard the trains and the crossings of the Rappahannock. Shaler's brigade was sent to Norman's Ford, and Terry, with the brigades of Eustis and Wheaton, remained at Kelly's Ford.

On November 9, 1863, the column organization of the army was discontinued, and that day Sixth Corps was ordered to the right of the army, where it took position at Welford's Ford on Hazel River. Sedgwick moved there directly with the divisions of Russell and Howe, but Terry's division remained on the Rappahannock until relieved by Bartlett's First Division of Fifth Corps November 11, 1863. It then marched to Welford's Ford. Shaler's brigade rejoined the corps from Norman's Ford November 11, 1863, and Terry with the brigades of Eustis and Wheaton arrived the next day.

Mine Run Campaign, Virginia, November 26, 1863–December 2, 1863. In late November 1863, Meade led the Army of the Potomac across the Rapidan River in an attempt to strike the right flank of Lee's army, which was in position along the south bank of the river. On the morning of November 26, 1863, at the beginning of the Mine Run Campaign, Sedgwick's Sixth Corps marched from Welford's Ford by way of Brandy Station to Jacob's Ford on the Rapidan. It arrived there after dark, and crossed the river that night. The next morning, it followed William H. French's Third Corps toward Locust Grove (Robertson's or Robinson's Tavern), where they were to join Gouverneur K. Warren's Second Corps. About 11:00 that morning, however, Third Corps became engaged with Edward Johnson's Confederate division near Payne's farm, and both divisions were held up there for the rest of the day. During the fighting, Sixth Corps moved forward in support of French, but it was not engaged. That night Sixth Corps moved to Locust Grove, and on the morning of November 28, 1863, it took position on the right of Warren's Second Corps, which was astride the Old Turnpike.

That day, Sixth Corps advanced with the army to Mine Run, a tributary of the Rapidan, where Lee's army was entrenched in a strong position on the west bank. Meade decided against a frontal attack, and ordered two flank attacks to be made on the morning of November 30. A large part of the army was assigned to Warren, who was to attack the enemy right; and Fifth Corps and Sixth Corps, both commanded by Sedgwick, were to attack the enemy left. About 2:00 A.M. November 30, 1863, Fifth Corps and Sixth Corps moved about two miles to their right and formed for their attack. Sixth Corps left two brigades and a battery to hold the lines vacated by the two corps. Warren prepared for his attack, but after a further examination of the enemy's works he advised Meade against an advance on his front. Meade then called off Warren's attack, and also that of Sedgwick, which was subsidiary to Warren's. After dark that night Sixth Corps returned to its former position. Then, on the night of December 1, 1863, it withdrew from the Wilderness with the rest

of the army. It recrossed the Rapidan at Germanna Ford and halted at Stevensburg early the next morning. It returned to its camps at Welford's Ford December 3, 1863. For details of this operation, see Mine Run Campaign, Virginia.

Winter of 1863–1864. Sixth Corps remained in the vicinity of Welford's Ford, Brandy Station, and Culpeper Court House until early in May 1864, and it then moved south with the army at the beginning of Ulysses S. Grant's Virginia Campaign of 1864. Its principal duty during the winter was to picket the front from Freeman's Ford on the Rappahannock to the Rixeyville Road, about three miles from Culpeper Court House.

During George A. Custer's raid into Albemarle County, Virginia February 28, 1864 to March 1, 1864, Sixth Corps advanced to Robertson's River and Madison Court House to be in position to support the cavalry. It left its camps February 27, 1864, and arrived at its assigned positions on the river the next day. It remained there until March 2, 1864, and then returned to Welford's Ford. This was the only significant movement of the corps during the winter. For details, see Kilpatrick's Expedition against Richmond, Virginia, and Custer's Raid into Albemarle County, Virginia.

In January 1864, Third Division, Sixth Corps was broken up, but it was not discontinued, when the brigades were assigned to other duties. During William W. Averell's raid on the Virginia Central Railroad in December 1863, Jubal A. Early demonstrated against Winchester, Virginia, and he also sent cavalry into Hardy and Hampshire counties. In response to this threat, Frank Wheaton's Third Brigade was sent by way of Washington to reinforce Jeremiah C. Sullivan's command at Harper's Ferry. There, under the command of John F. Ballier, it was designated as Wheaton's Brigade of Sullivan's First Division, Department of West Virginia. The brigade remained in the Department of West Virginia until near the end of March 1864, and it then returned to the Army of the Potomac. It was assigned to the reorganized Sixth Corps (see below, Reorganization of the Army of the Potomac, March 1864) as First Brigade, Second Division. January 6, 1864, Henry D. Terry, commanding Third Division, was ordered to take Shaler's First Brigade of the division to Sandusky, Ohio. Shaler's brigade served as a guard for the prisoners of war at Johnson's Island, and January 13, 1864, Terry was assigned command of Johnson's Island. Shaler's brigade returned to the Army of the Potomac late in April 1864, and it was assigned to First Division, Sixth Corps as a new Fourth Brigade. Eustis' Second Brigade was the only brigade of Third Division left with the corps, and it was temporarily attached to Second Division, Sixth Corps as Fourth Brigade. This arrangement was made permanent in the reorganization of the army March 24, 1864 (see below).

A number of important command changes occurred in Sixth Corps during the winter. As noted above, Henry D. Terry, commander of Third Division, was transferred to Johnson's Island, Ohio, where he assumed command January 13, 1864. There was no commander of Third Division until the reorganization of the army March 24, 1864. On March 25, 1864, James B. Ricketts was relieved from duty on a military commission then meeting in New York, and was ordered to the Army of the Potomac. A short time later he assumed command of Third Division, Sixth Corps.

February 29, 1864, Albion P. Howe, commanding Second Division, was assigned to command the Artillery Depot in Washington, D.C, and was also placed in charge of the office of inspector of artillery in that city. Henry L. Eustis assumed temporary command of Howe's division. January 6, 1864, George W. Getty was relieved from duty in Benjamin F. Butler's Department of Virginia and North Carolina, and was ordered to the Army of the Potomac. He was assigned temporarily as acting inspector general of the Army of the Potomac January 27, 1864, and then on March 19, 1864, he was assigned command of Second Division, Sixth Corps.

Although not relieved from command of First Division, Sixth Corps, Horatio G. Wright was absent from his command during most of the period from December 19, 1863 to the end of March 1864. During this time David A. Russell served as temporary commander of the division. During the winter, Wright served as a member of a Board of Engineers in Washington. On February 26, 1864, he was ordered to return temporarily to his command when Sixth Corps advanced to Madison Court House during Custer's raid into Albemarle County,

Virginia, but after Custer rejoined the army March 2, 1864, Wright returned to Washington.

In addition to the above command changes, there were others that were made during the reorganization of the army March 24, 1864. See following section.

Reorganization of the Army of the Potomac, March 1864. An order issued March 23, 1864 reduced the number of infantry corps of the Army of the Potomac from five to three. Second Corps, Fifth Corps, and Sixth Corps were retained in the new organization, but all three were extensively reorganized by an order of March 24, 1864. At that time there were only two divisions of Sixth Corps present for duty. As noted above, the three brigades of Third Division had been assigned to other service, and Third Division existed in name only. In the reorganization of the corps March 24, 1864, Third Division, Sixth Corps was discontinued, and a new Third Division was organized by the transfer of Third Division, Third Corps.

The complete reorganization of Sixth Corps was effected as follows:

First Division. Horatio G. Wright's First Division, then commanded by David A. Russell, retained its designation, but was increased to four brigades. The new Fourth Brigade was to be Alexander Shaler's First Brigade, Third Division, Sixth Corps, which was then on duty at Johnson's Island, Ohio. Only three of its regiments had returned to the army by the end of April 1864, and it was then designated as Fourth Brigade, First Division.

Second Division. Second Division, formerly Howe's, but under the command of George W. Getty since March 19, 1864, also retained its former designation in Sixth Corps. Until January 1864, Second Division consisted only of Lewis A. Grant's Second Brigade and Thomas H. Neill's Third Brigade. In January, however, Henry L. Eustis' Second Brigade of Third Division was assigned to Second Division, and it was temporarily organized as Fourth Brigade. This assignment was made permanent March 24, 1864. A new First Brigade, Second Division was organized by the transfer of Frank Wheaton's Third Brigade, Third Division, which had been serving at

Harper's Ferry in the Department of West Virginia. Wheaton's brigade returned to the army March 29, 1864.

Third Division. A new Third Division, Sixth Corps was organized from Joseph B. Carr's Third Division, Third Corps. Henry Prince was assigned to the temporary command of the new Third Division March 25, 1864, but he was relieved a few days later by James B. Ricketts, who had been absent from the army since the Battle of Antietam.

For additional information about the reorganization of the army, see Army of the Potomac, Reorganization of the Army, March 1864.

The organization of Sixth Corps at the end of April 1864 was as follows:

SIXTH CORPS, John Sedgwick

First Division, Horatio G. Wright
  First Brigade, Henry W. Brown
  Second Brigade, Emory Upton
  Third Brigade, David A. Russell
  Fourth Brigade, Alexander Shaler

Note. Alfred T. A. Torbert, formerly the commander of First Brigade, was assigned April 10, 1864 to command First Cavalry Division, Cavalry Corps, Army of the Potomac.

Second Division, George W. Getty
  First Brigade, Frank Wheaton
  Second Brigade, Lewis A. Grant
  Third Brigade, Thomas H. Neill
  Fourth Brigade, Henry L. Eustis

Third Division, James B. Ricketts
  First Brigade, William H. Morris
  Second Brigade, Benjamin F. Smith

Note. The two brigades of this division were organized from the regiments of Joseph B. Carr's Third Division, Third Corps.

Artillery Brigade, Charles H. Tompkins
  4th Battery (D), Maine Light Artillery, Melville C. Kimball
  1st Battery (A), Massachusetts Light Artillery, William H. McCartney
  1st Battery, New York Light Artillery, Andrew Cowan
  3rd Battery, New York Light Artillery, William A. Harn
  1st Battalion, 4th New York Heavy Artillery, Thomas D. Sears
  Battery C, 1st Rhode Island Light Artillery, Richard Waterman
  Battery E, 1st Rhode Island Light Artillery, William B. Rhodes
  Battery G, 1st Rhode Island Light Artillery, George W. Adams
  Battery M, 5th United States Artillery, James McKnight

Grant's Richmond, Virginia Campaign, 1864.
Early in May 1864, George G. Meade's Army of the Potomac, under the personal direction of Ulysses S. Grant, moved toward the Rapidan River at the beginning of the Richmond, Virginia Campaign. Sedgwick's Sixth Corps left its camps near Welford's Ford, Brandy Station, and Culpeper Court House and marched to Stevensburg, and from there followed Fifth Corps to Germanna Ford. It crossed the Rapidan that evening and bivouacked for the night along the Germanna Plank Road, south of the river. The next morning, Getty's Second Division was sent on to hold the intersection of the Brock Road and the Orange Court House Plank Road. That afternoon, May 5, 1864, Getty joined Winfield S. Hancock's Second Corps in an attack along the Plank Road, and again the next morning it attacked with Second Corps, also along the Plank Road. Getty was wounded May 6, 1864, and Neill assumed command of the division.

Meantime, on May 5, 1864, Sedgwick, with Wright's First Division and Ricketts' Third Division, advanced on the right of Fifth Corps, and took position north of the Orange Court House Turnpike, on the extreme right of the army. These two divisions were engaged in skirmishing during the afternoon and also the next day. Then on the evening of May 6, 1864, the right of Sedgwick's line was vigorously attacked and driven back, and that night it was forced to retire to a new line. Neill's division rejoined the corps the next day.

For details of the operations of Sixth Corps during the Battle of the Wilderness, see Richmond, Virginia Campaign, 1864, Battle of the Wilderness.

The organization of Sixth Corps at the Battle of the Wilderness was as follows:

SIXTH CORPS, John Sedgwick

First Division, Horatio G. Wright
   First Brigade, Henry W. Brown
   Second Brigade, Emory Upton
   Third Brigade, David A. Russell
   Fourth Brigade, Alexander Shaler, to May 6, 1864,
     captured
     Nelson Cross

Second Division, George W. Getty, to May 6, 1864,
   wounded
   Thomas H. Neill
   First Brigade, Frank Wheaton
   Second Brigade, Lewis A. Grant
   Third Brigade, Thomas H. Neill, to May 6, 1864
     Daniel D. Bidwell
   Fourth Brigade, Henry L. Eustis

Third Division, James B. Ricketts
   First Brigade, William H. Morris
   Second Brigade, Truman Seymour, to May 6, 1864,
     captured
     Benjamin F. Smith

Note. Seymour was relieved from duty in the Department of the South, and April 20, 1864 was ordered to report to John A. Dix, commander of the Department of the East, for temporary duty inspecting and forwarding troops to the field. May 5, 1864, Seymour joined the Army of the Potomac, and that morning relieved Smith in command of Second Brigade.

Artillery Brigade, Charles H. Tompkins
   4th Battery (D), Maine Light Artillery, Charles W. White
   5th Battery (E), Maine Light Artillery, Greenleaf T. Stevens
   1st Battery (A), Massachusetts Light Artillery, William H. McCartney
   Battery A, 1st New Jersey Light Artillery, William Hexamer
   1st Battery, New York Light Artillery, Andrew Cowan
   3rd Battery, New York Light Artillery, William A. Harn
   2nd Battalion, 9th New York Heavy Artillery, James W. Snyder
   Battery H, 1st Ohio Light Artillery, Stephen W. Dorsey
   Battery C, 1st Rhode Island Light Artillery, Richard Waterman
   Battery E, 1st Rhode Island Light Artillery, William B. Rhodes
   Battery G, 1st Rhode Island Light Artillery, George W. Adams
   Battery E, 5th United States Artillery, John R. Brinckle
   Battery M, 5th United States Artillery, James McKnight

During the night of May 7, 1864, Sixth Corps left Old Wilderness Tavern and marched by way of Chancellorsville to the intersection of the Piney Branch Road and the Brock Road. The next day it moved to the left of Fifth Corps near Alsop's farm (Laurel Hill), and that evening William H. Penrose's First Brigade, First Division was engaged with Fifth Corps in an attack at Alsop's farm.

On May 9, 1864, while directing operations of Sixth Corps in front of Spotsylvania Court House, Sedgwick was killed by an enemy sharpshooter, and Wright assumed command of the corps. Russell succeeded Wright in command of First Division, and Eustis succeeded Russell in command of Third Brigade, First Division. William H. Morris was wounded May 9, 1864, and was succeeded in command of First Brigade, Third Division by John W. Schall.

On May 10, 1864, Emory Upton organized a special force of twelve regiments, and that afternoon he made an attack on the western side of the "Angle" in the Confederate works at Spotsylvania Court House. Upton's men carried the first and second lines of the enemy entrenchments, but when they received no support, they were forced to withdraw after dark that night.

Early on the morning of May 12, 1864, Hancock's Second Corps launched a heavy attack on the Angle at Spotsylvania Court House and broke through the works at that point. Sixth Corps joined in this battle by attacking the line on the right of Second Corps. The struggle, which continued all through the day and until 3:00 the next morning, was desperate, and both sides suffered heavy losses.

May 14, 1864, Sixth Corps moved to the left of the line, and formed on the left of Ambrose E. Burnside's Ninth Corps, a short distance west of Anderson's Mill. Then, on the night of May 17, 1864, Sixth Corps, together with Fifth Corps, moved back to the works captured in the attack of May 12, 1864, and the next day assaulted the new Confederate line at the base of the old salient. This attack was unsuccessful, and Sixth Corps marched back to the southeast of Spotsylvania Court House and formed on the left of Warren's Fifth Corps. It remained in this position until May 21, 1864, and then marched with the army toward the North Anna River.

For details of the operations of Sixth Corps since leaving the Wilderness, see Richmond, Virginia

Campaign of 1864, Operations about Spotsylvania Court House.

The organization of Sixth Corps during the period May 8–21, 1864 was as follows:

SIXTH CORPS, John Sedgwick, to May 9, 1864, killed
Horatio G. Wright

First Division, Horatio G. Wright, to May 9, 1864
David A. Russell
First Brigade, Henry W. Brown, to May 9, 1864
William H. Penrose
Second Brigade, Emory Upton
Third Brigade, David A. Russell, to May 9, 1864
Henry L. Eustis
Fourth Brigade, Nelson Cross

Second Division, Thomas H. Neill
First Brigade, Frank Wheaton
Second Brigade, Lewis A. Grant
Third Brigade, Daniel D. Bidwell
Fourth Brigade, Henry L. Eustis, to May 9, 1864
Oliver Edwards

Third Division, James B. Ricketts
First Brigade, William H. Morris, to May 9, 1864, wounded
John W. Schall, to May 14, 1864
William S. Truex
Second Brigade, Benjamin F. Smith

Artillery Brigade, Charles H. Tompkins

Note. The batteries serving with Sixth Corps during the operations around Spotsylvania Court House were essentially the same as those with the corps at the Battle of the Wilderness.

On May 21, 1864, Sixth Corps followed Ninth Corps to Stanard's Mill on the Po River, and there, about sundown, repulsed an enemy attack. It then moved on by way of Guiney's Station and arrived at Jerico Mills (or Jerico Ford) on the North Anna River May 23, 1864. The next morning it crossed the river to support Fifth Corps, which was already in position on the south side.

Grant withdrew the army from the line of the North Anna River on the night of May 26, 1864, and Sixth Corps recrossed at Quarles Mill and marched toward Hanovertown on the Pamunkey River. Russell's First Division was detached from the corps early on May 26, 1864, and it accompanied the trains to Chesterfield Station. From there it marched to Hanovertown, crossed the Pamunkey, and on the

morning of May 27, 1864 joined Philip H. Sheridan's cavalry. Wright, with Neill's Second Division and Ricketts' Third Division, marched down the Pamunkey, and on the morning of May 28, 1864 crossed to the south bank of the river about one mile below the mouth of Crump's Creek. Here, Russell's division rejoined the corps.

Sixth Corps remained near Crump's Creek and Hanover Court House until May 30, 1864, covering the right and rear of the army. It then advanced to the Totopotomoy River, and took position on the right of Second Corps, on the extreme right of the Union line. On the night of May 31, 1864, Sixth Corps withdrew from the line of the Totopotomoy and marched across the rear of the army to Cold Harbor.

On June 1, 1864, Sixth Corps arrived at Cold Harbor, and that evening, together with William F. Smith's Eighteenth Corps of Benjamin F. Butler's Army of the James, unsuccessfully attacked the Confederate positions there. Sixth Corps also joined Second Corps and Eighteenth Corps in the assault of June 3, 1864, which was repulsed with very heavy losses.

The organization of Sixth Corps at the Battle of Cold Harbor was as follows:

SIXTH CORPS, Horatio G. Wright

First Division, David A. Russell
First Brigade, William H. Penrose
Second Brigade, Emory Upton
Third Brigade, Henry L. Eustis, to June 12, 1864
Gideon Clark
Fourth Brigade, Nelson Cross

Second Division, Thomas H. Neill
First Brigade, Frank Wheaton
Second Brigade, Lewis A. Grant
Third Brigade, Daniel D. Bidwell
Fourth Brigade, Oliver Edwards

Third Division, James B. Ricketts
First Brigade, William S. Truex, to June 1, 1864, wounded
Caldwell K. Hall, to June 2, 1864
John W. Schall, to June 3, 1864, wounded
Caldwell K. Hall
Second Brigade, Benjamin F. Smith

Artillery Brigade, Charles H. Tompkins
4th Battery (D), Maine Light Artillery, Charles W. White

5th Battery (E), Maine Light Artillery, Greenleaf T. Stevens

1st Battery (A), Massachusetts Light Artillery, William H. McCartney

Battery A, 1st New Jersey Light Artillery, William Hexamer

1st Battery, New York Light Artillery, Andrew Cowan

3rd Battery, New York Light Artillery, William A. Harn

Battery H, 1st Ohio Light Artillery, Stephen W. Dorsey

Battery C, 1st Rhode Island Light Artillery, Richard Waterman

Battery E, 1st Rhode Island Light Artillery, William B. Rhodes

Battery M, 5th United States Artillery, James McKnight

After the failure of the assaults at Cold Harbor, Grant decided against further frontal attacks, and ordered the army to move to the left and cross to the south side of the James River. Sixth Corps remained in position near the enemy lines at Cold Harbor until the night of June 12, 1864, and then it moved back with Second Corps to newly prepared defensive lines in rear of Cold Harbor. It remained there until the withdrawal of the other corps was successfully completed, and then it marched by way of Jones' Bridge, on the Chickahominy, and Vaiden's to Charles City Court House, where it arrived June 14, 1864. It then remained on the north bank of the James River to cover the crossing of the rest of the army.

On the evening of June 16, 1864, Second Division was detached from the corps, and it crossed the James on the pontoon bridge to the vicinity of Windmill Point, where it came under Meade's direct orders. Wright, with First Division and Third Division, embarked on transports at Wilson's Wharf, Wilcox's Wharf (or Landing), and Harvey's Landing for Bermuda Hundred, where he was to report to Benjamin F. Butler, commanding the Department of Virginia and North Carolina, Army of the James.

For details of the operations of Sixth Corps from the time that it left Spotsylvania Court House until it arrived on the James River, see Richmond, Virginia Campaign, 1864.

There were some changes in command during this period. Henry L. Eustis was relieved from command of Third Brigade, First Division June 12, 1864, and was ordered to Washington. He appears to have been told that charges of neglect of duty and general inefficiency would be brought against him if he did not resign. His resignation was accepted June 27, 1864. Impaired health has also been given as the reason for his resignation. After Eustis' departure, Gideon Clark assumed command of his brigade. William S. Truex, commanding First Brigade, Third Division, was wounded June 1, 1864, and Caldwell K. Hall commanded until June 2, 1864. John W. Schall then assumed command, but he was wounded June 3, 1864, and Hall again assumed command of the brigade.

Operations about Petersburg, June 15, 1864– July 9, 1864. Neill's Second Division crossed the James River at dark June 16, 1864, and the next day marched toward the Union lines in front of Petersburg. When it arrived there, it immediately relieved William T. H. Brooks' First Division, Eighteenth Corps, Army of the James, which held the works near the City Point Railroad. Russell's and Ricketts' divisions moved by transport to Bermuda Hundred June 16–17, 1864, to help hold Butler's defensive lines there during the absence of Eighteenth Corps at Petersburg.

Sixth Corps was not seriously engaged during the assaults on the Petersburg lines June 15–18, 1864. On the final day, Neill's division, then under the temporary direction of John H. Martindale, commander of Second Division, Eighteenth Corps, advanced with some skirmishing, but it did not attack the main enemy works. June 19, 1864, Ricketts' and Russell's divisions arrived on the Petersburg lines from Bermuda Hundred, and that day and the next they relieved Martindale's division, which returned to Bermuda Hundred. Sixth Corps then occupied the right of the Union works, with its right on the Appomattox River and its left connecting with Second Corps near the Hare house on the Prince George Court House Road.

After the final assaults at Petersburg June 18, 1864, Grant decided to strengthen the investment of the town by extending his line of entrenchments south of Petersburg to the west toward the Petersburg and Weldon Railroad and the South Side (Lynchburg) Railroad. Sixth Corps and Second Corps were assigned to carry out this operation. On June 21, 1864, Eighteenth Corps, which had been reorganized two days before, returned to Petersburg and relieved Sixth Corps on the line of entrench-ments. That day Second Corps, followed by Sixth Corps, marched toward the Weldon Railroad. The advance was continued June 22, 1864, with Sixth Corps moving up on the left of Second Corps, which was wheeling to the right, with its right pivoting on the left of Fifth Corps. During the advance, Sixth Corps and Second Corps became separated, and Ambrose P. Hill's corps advanced into the interval, struck the left and rear of Second Corps, and drove it back to the positions that it had occupied that morning. The next morning, Second Corps again advanced and entrenched on the left of Fifth Corps, but the movement of the two corps toward the rail-roads was halted. Sixth Corps entrenched on the left of Second Corps on a line generally facing the Weldon Railroad, and about one and one-half miles from it. The pickets of the corps were pushed out near the railroad. Sixth Corps remained in this posi-tion until June 29, 1864, and it then advanced to Reams' Station on the Weldon Railroad. The next day it destroyed about three miles of track, and then moved back to the Jerusalem Plank Road. July 2, 1864, the corps moved back to its former position on the left of Second Corps.

For details of the operations of Sixth Corps from the time it crossed the James River until the end of June 1864, see Operations about Petersburg and Richmond, Virginia, 1864–1865, Operations of June 1864.

The organization of Sixth Corps while at Petersburg in June and early July 1864 was as follows:

SIXTH CORPS, Horatio G. Wright

First Division, David A. Russell
First Brigade, William H. Penrose
Second Brigade, Emory Upton
Third Brigade, Gideon Clark, to July 7, 1864
Oliver Edwards
Fourth Brigade, Nelson Cross, to June 20, 1864, or-dered home for muster out
Joseph E. Hamblin

Second Division, Thomas H. Neill, to June 21, 1864
Frank Wheaton, to June 28, 1864
George W. Getty
First Brigade, Frank Wheaton, to June 21, 1864
John F. Ballier, to June 28, 1864
Frank Wheaton
Second Brigade, Lewis A. Grant

Third Brigade, Daniel D. Bidwell
Fourth Brigade, Oliver Edwards, to July 6, 1864

Note 1. Neill was transferred to Eighteenth Corps June 21, 1864, and was assigned to the staff of that corps.
Note 2. Fourth Brigade was discontinued July 6, 1864. Two regiments departed for muster out, and the other two regiments were assigned to Third Brigade, First Division.

Third Division, James B. Ricketts
First Brigade, William S. Truex
Second Brigade, Benjamin F. Smith

Cavalry Detachment, Timothy M. Bryan, Jr.
Artillery Brigade, Charles H. Tompkins

Sixth Corps during Early's Washington Raid, July 6, 1864–August 2, 1864. During the first week in July 1864, Jubal A. Early moved down the Shenandoah Valley with an army, crossed the Potomac River into Maryland, and marched eastward to Frederick, where he threatened Bal-timore and Washington. Grant, at Petersburg, reacted promptly to this threat, and ordered Sixth Corps to be sent north to reinforce the troops in the Middle Department and the Department of Washington. July 6, 1864, Ricketts' division marched from the left of the line of entrenchments at Petersburg to City Point, where it embarked for Baltimore. It arrived there July 8, 1864, and marched out to the Monocacy River near Frederick to join Lewis Wallace, who was in command of a force from the Middle Department, Eighth Corps. Early advanced from Frederick and defeated Wallace at the Battle of the Monocacy July 9, 1864, and Rick-etts returned to Baltimore with the rest of Wallace's command. Two regiments and part of a third of Benjamin F. Smith's Second Brigade did not arrive at the battlefield, and Matthew R. McClennan com-manded the troops of that brigade that were present during the battle.

When Grant learned of Early's victory on the Monocacy, he ordered the other two divisions of Sixth Corps to Washington. July 9, 1864, Wright, with the divisions of Russell and Getty, marched to City Point, and embarked the next day. He arrived at Washington July 11–12, 1864, just as Early's army appeared in front of the fortifications north of the city. Early withdrew toward Leesburg late on July 12, 1864, and the next day Wright was assigned command of all Federal troops that were ordered to go in pursuit. Wright's command consisted of the three divisions of Sixth Corps, which were commanded by Ricketts; some troops of William H. Emory's Detachment Nineteenth Corps; John R. Kenly's Maryland Brigade; and the cavalry of Charles R. Lowell, Jr. George Crook's army from the Department of West Virginia (Army of the Kanawha) joined Wright at Purcellville, Virginia. Wright followed Early to the Shenandoah Valley, but when the latter retreated toward Strasburg, Wright left Crook's army of the Department of West Virgina to watch Early and, with the rest of his command, began his return march to Washington.

After Wright had departed, Early again marched down the valley and defeated Crook's forces at Kernstown July 24, 1864, and then continued on to Martinsburg and the Potomac River. On the day of the Battle of Kernstown, Wright's command was broken up, and Sixth Corps was ordered to return to the Army of the Potomac. Two days later, however, Wright was ordered to resume command of the same troops that he had earlier led to the Shenandoah Valley, including Sixth Corps, and move with them through Maryland toward the Monocacy River and join Crook's army. Wright arrived on the Monocacy July 28, 1864, crossed the river, and the next day moved to Halltown, West Virginia. When Wright crossed the Monocacy, he moved into the Department of West Virginia, and came under the orders of David Hunter, the department commander.

July 30, 1864, Confederate cavalry under John McCausland burned Chambersburg, Pennsylvania, and Hunter promptly ordered his army to the east side of South Mountain to oppose a possible enemy advance from the west. Sixth Corps arrived at Frederick, Maryland August 1, 1864; but the next day, when it was learned that Early was not advancing, Wright's command was again broken up, and Sixth Corps was ordered to Washington for transfer to Petersburg. Grant decided to eliminate the threat of Early's command in the Shenandoah Valley, however, and Sixth Corps was halted on the Monocacy River. It was to form a part of an army to be assembled for this purpose, under the command of Philip H. Sheridan.

For details of the operations of Sixth Corps and the other troops opposing Early during July 1864, see Early's Washington Raid (and Operations in the Shenandoah Valley, Maryland, and Pennsylvania).

The organization of Sixth Corps at the end of July 1864 was as follows:

SIXTH CORPS, Horatio G. Wright

First Division, David A. Russell
First Brigade, William H. Penrose
Second Brigade, Emory Upton
Third Brigade, Oliver Edwards
Artillery
1st Battery, Massachusetts Light Artillery, William H. McCartney

Second Division, George W. Getty
First Brigade, Frank Wheaton
Second Brigade, Lewis A. Grant
Third Brigade, Daniel D. Bidwell
Artillery
1st Battery, New York Light Artillery, Andrew Cowan

Third Division, James B. Ricketts
First Brigade, William Emerson
Second Brigade, John F. Staunton
Artillery
Battery M, 5th United States Artillery, James McKnight

Note. Ricketts commanded Sixth Corps during most of the month while Wright commanded the combined forces opposing Early. Frank Wheaton commanded Third Division.

Independent Brigade, John R. Kenly

Artillery Brigade, Charles H. Tompkins
5th Battery, Maine Light Artillery, Greenleaf T. Stevens
Battery C, 1st Rhode Island Light Artillery, Richard Waterman
Battery G, 1st Rhode Island Light Artillery, George W. Adams

Note. The other batteries of the former Artillery Brigade remained with the Army of the Potomac at Petersburg.

For further information about the organization and operations of Wright's Sixth Corps, see Sixth Corps, Army of the Shenandoah, and see also Shenandoah Valley Campaign (Sheridan).

COMMANDERS OF SIXTH CORPS, ARMY OF THE POTOMAC, MAY 18, 1862 to AUGUST 7, 1864

William B. Franklin	May 23, 1862 to November 16, 1862
William F. Smith	November 16, 1862 to January 25, 1863
John Newton	January 25, 1863 to February 5, 1863
John Sedgwick	February 5, 1863 to April 6, 1864
James B. Ricketts	April 6, 1864 to April 13, 1864
John Sedgwick	April 13, 1864 to May 9, 1864, killed
Horatio G. Wright	May 9, 1864 to July 13, 1864
James B. Ricketts	July 13, 1864 to July 24, 1864
Horatio G. Wright	July 24, 1864 to July 26, 1864
James B. Ricketts	July 26, 1864 to August 2, 1864
Horatio G. Wright	August 2, 1864 to August 7, 1864

Note 1. On November 16, 1862, Franklin was assigned command of the Left Grand Division of the Army of the Potomac, and Smith assumed command of Sixth Corps.

Note 2. Franklin was relieved from duty with the Army of the Potomac January 25, 1863, and Smith succeeded him in command of the Left Grand Division. John Newton assumed command of Sixth Corps in place of Smith.

Note 3. The grand divisions were abolished February 5, 1863. Smith did not return to Sixth Corps, but was assigned command of Ninth Corps. Sedgwick was assigned command of Sixth Corps.

Note 4. During the period July 13, 1864–July 24, 1864, Wright was in command of a combined force that was sent in pursuit of Jubal A. Early after his Washington raid. Then, during the period July 26, 1864–August 2, 1864, Wright was again in command of the same force, and was sent to reinforce David Hunter, commander of the Department of West Virginia, when Early threatened once more in the Shenandoah Valley.

SIXTH CORPS, ARMY OF THE POTOMAC DECEMBER 16, 1864–JUNE 30, 1865

At Petersburg, Winter of 1864–1865. Wheaton's division arrived at City Point from the Shenandoah Valley December 4, 1864, and the next day marched to the south of Petersburg. It then relieved Samuel W. Crawford's Third Division, Fifth Corps, which held the line of entrenchments from Battery No. 24, near the Strong house, to Fort Wadsworth. Seymour arrived at City Point December 6, 1864, and that evening relieved Romeyn B. Ayres' Second Division, Fifth Corps on the line from Fort Wadsworth to a point about midway between the Squirrel Level Road and the Vaughan Road.

Meantime, on December 6, 1864, John Gibbon's Second Division, Second Corps had temporarily relieved Charles Griffin's First Division, Fifth Corps in the entrenchments so that it could accompany Fifth Corps on an expedition to Hicksford (present-day Emporia), Virginia to destroy the Weldon Railroad. When Getty's division arrived at Petersburg December 13–16, 1864, it relieved Gibbon's division, which then held the line from the left of Seymour's division to the vicinity of Fort Fisher, near the Church Road. All three divisions of Sixth Corps were then on the line of entrenchments, connecting on the right with Ninth Corps and on the left with Second Corps. Wright did not arrive in person at Petersburg until December 12, 1864, and during his absence Wheaton and Seymour reported to Andrew A. Humphreys, commanding Second Corps. For additional information, see Operations about Petersburg and Richmond, Virginia, 1864–1865, Winter of 1864–1865, Siege of Petersburg, Virginia.

Sixth Corps remained relatively inactive during the remainder of the winter, but on several occasions troops of the corps participated in operations with other units of the army. On December 9, 1864, while Warren was absent with his Fifth Corps on an expedition to Hicksford, Nelson A. Miles' First Division, Second Corps advanced on the Vaughan Road to Hatcher's Run on a reconnaissance to determine whether enemy troops were moving in Warren's direction. During the afternoon, Wheaton was sent to support Miles with a part of his division and a part of Seymour's division. Wheaton formed his troops along the Squirrel Level Road on the right of Miles to keep open the Vaughan Road. For additional information, see Operations about Petersburg and Richmond, Virginia, 1864–1865, Winter of 1864–1865, Reconnaissance to Hatcher's Run, Virginia.

On February 5, 1865, David McM. Gregg's Second Cavalry Division was sent out to Dinwiddie

Court House to break up enemy wagon trains that were reported to be using the Boydton Plank Road. At the same time, Warren's Fifth Corps advanced toward Dinwiddie Court House in support, and Humphreys' Second Corps moved up to Hatcher's Run in rear of Warren. These movements led to the Battle of Hatcher's Run, in which Sixth Corps played a minor role. That afternoon, Humphreys was strongly attacked near Armstrong's Mill, but he was able to hold his ground. At 8:00 P.M. Wright ordered Wheaton to move with his First Division, Sixth Corps and report to Humphreys. John F. Hartranft's Third Division, Ninth Corps had preceded Wheaton, and had formed on the right of Second Corps. When Wheaton's division came up it took position along the Squirrel Level Road, on the right of Hartranft.

During the night of February 5, 1865, Warren's Fifth Corps was ordered back to Hatcher's Run at the Vaughan Road crossing, and the next afternoon Warren was attacked at Dabney's Mill and driven back. About noon February 7, 1865, Samuel W. Crawford's Third Division of Fifth Corps advanced and occupied most of the battlefield of the previous day. Joseph E. Hamblin's Third Brigade of Wheaton's division was sent to the south side of Hatcher's Run to support Crawford, and a short time later James Hubbard's Second Brigade followed Hamblin, but neither brigade was engaged. Wheaton withdrew his division about midnight and returned to his camps on the right of the corps line, where he arrived the next morning. For additional information, see Operations about Petersburg and Richmond, Virginia, Winter of 1864–1865, Battle of Hatcher's Run (or Dabney's Mill, Armstrong's Mill, Rowanty Creek, Vaughan Road), Virginia.

Following the Battle of Hatcher's Run, the Union line of entrenchments was extended to the left, from Fort Sampson on the old line to the Vaughan Road crossing of Hatcher's Run. Second Corps was assigned to hold this line and the old line from Fort Sampson to Fort Gregg. On February 8, 1865, as a result of this change, Sixth Corps was assigned to new positions on the line of entrenchments. First Division held the line from Fort Howard to Fort Keene, on the Vaughan Road, not including the latter fort, and the division also furnished garrisons for Forts Davison and McMahon on the rear line. Second Division was on the line from Fort Keene to

Fort Fisher, not including the latter fort, and the division also provided the garrison for Fort Dushane on the rear line. Third Division occupied Fort Fisher and Fort Gregg, and the line of entrenchments between the two forts.

On the morning of March 25, 1865, a Confederate force led by John B. Gordon attacked the Union line on the front of Ninth Corps, and captured Fort Stedman and the batteries and trenches from Battery No. 9 to Fort Haskell. Wheaton, with his First Division, Sixth Corps, was immediately ordered to that part of the line, but it had only reached a point about midway between Hancock's Station and Meade's Station on the Army Railroad when he learned that Fort Stedman had been recaptured and the line of works restored. Wheaton was no longer needed by Ninth Corps, and he was sent to the left to cover the front between Fort Howard and Fort Fisher. During the afternoon of March 25, 1865, Sixth Corps and Second Corps made a strong demonstration on the right of the enemy lines. Sixth Corps advanced in front of Fort Fisher and captured the entrenched enemy picket line near the Jones house on the Church Road, and held this position until it withdrew that night. The main enemy line was strongly held and was not attacked. Participating in this operation were Getty's Second Division; Hamblin's Second Brigade and Oliver Edwards' Third Brigade of First Division, which were sent at 3:00 P.M. to support Getty; and Keifer's Second Brigade, Third Division. For details of the operations on March 25, 1865, see Operations about Petersburg and Richmond, Virginia, 1864–1865, Winter of 1864–1865, Assault at Fort Stedman, Virginia.

Appomattox Campaign, March 29, 1865–April 9, 1865. Sixth Corps was engaged in no further activities until the beginning of Grant's final offensive at Petersburg March 29, 1865. Early that morning Warren's Fifth Corps, Humphreys' Second Corps, and Sheridan's cavalry moved forward on the left of the army, south of Hatcher's Run, in an effort to reach the right and rear of the Confederate works. While this movement was in progress, Sixth Corps, Ninth Corps, and Twenty-Fourth Corps, Army of the James remained in position on the line of works, with orders to be ready to follow up any successes of the flanking column. When Grant learned of

Sheridan's victory at Five Forks April 1, 1865, he issued orders for an assault on the enemy entrenchments the next morning.

Wright's Sixth Corps attacked at 4:40 A.M. April 2, 1865, on a front extending from Fort Welsh to Fort Fisher, and it quickly broke through the enemy line and advanced to the Boydton Plank Road. It then turned to the left and moved along the rear of the captured works toward Hatcher's Run. When the area was cleared of enemy troops, Sixth Corps faced about and marched toward Petersburg. Hamblin's Second Brigade, First Division was left behind to hold the trenches where Sixth Corps had broken through, but it was relieved by Robert S. Foster's First Division, Twenty-Fourth Corps and was then sent to aid Ninth Corps in its attack that day. When Sixth Corps arrived near Petersburg on its return from Hatcher's Run, Getty's division took position near the Whitworth house, on the left of Twenty-Fourth Corps; Wheaton's division, less Hamblin's brigade, halted on the South Side Railroad, about two miles west of Petersburg; and Seymour's division was detached and sent to the right to cover the left flank of Ninth Corps. Hamblin's brigade remained with Ninth Corps until the next day, and then rejoined the corps about 8:00 P.M. For details of the operations of Sixth Corps April 2, 1865, see Appomattox Campaign, Virginia, Breakthrough at Petersburg.

Lee evacuated Petersburg during the night of April 2, 1865, and early the next morning Grant's army moved forward in pursuit. Meade, with Sixth Corps and Second Corps, followed Sheridan's cavalry and Fifth Corps along the south side of the Appomattox River toward Jetersville, on the Richmond and Danville Railroad. Sixth Corps was delayed on the road by the cavalry, which had priority, and did not reach Jetersville until late in the afternoon of April 5, 1865. It then joined Second Corps and Fifth Corps on a defensive line to prevent Lee's army, which was then at Amelia Court House, from moving south to Danville by way of Burkeville. That night, however, Lee turned aside and marched by way of Deatonsville toward Rice's Station on the South Side Railroad.

On the morning of April 6, 1865, Sheridan's cavalry and Meade's infantry started in pursuit. Sheridan marched westward, south of Lee's retreat route, on the road from Jetersville to Pride's Church;

and Sixth Corps, which that day was marching under Sheridan's orders, followed the cavalry. During the afternoon, Sheridan's cavalry, temporarily under the command of Wesley Merritt, blocked the road to Rice's Station ahead of Richard H. Anderson's Confederate corps, west of Little Sayler's Creek, while Sheridan brought up Sixth Corps to the Hillsman farm and prepared to attack the forces under Richard S. Ewell. In the ensuing Battle of Sayler's Creek, Wheaton's and Seymour's divisions of Sixth Corps attacked and defeated Ewell, and captured most of his command. At about the same time, Merritt virtually destroyed Anderson's corps. Getty's division came up near the close of the battle, but it was not engaged. For details of the operations of Sixth Corps during the period April 3–6, 1865, see Appomattox Campaign, Pursuit of the Army of Northern Virginia, April 3–5, 1865, and also Battle of Sayler's Creek, April 6, 1865.

The remnants of Lee's army resumed the retreat toward Farmville during the night of April 6, 1865, and early the next morning Grant's army followed. Wright's Sixth Corps moved from Sayler's Creek to Rice's Station, and from that point followed Edward O. C. Ord's Army of the James on the road toward Farmville. Sixth Corps had been under Sheridan's orders April 6, 1865, and it was Sheridan's understanding that this arrangement was to continue, but on the morning of April 7, 1865, Meade resumed control of its movements. Shortly after noon April 7, 1865, Ord and Wright arrived near Farmville, and they were ordered to cross the Appomattox River at that point and attack enemy forces that had halted north of the town. The bridges at Farmville had been destroyed, however, and it was not until after dark that a pontoon bridge had been completed and Sixth Corps began to cross.

Lee moved on toward Appomattox Court House during the night of April 7, 1865, and the next day Meade followed close behind with Second Corps and Sixth Corps.

The rest of the army advanced south of the Appomattox River toward Appomattox Station, and that night Sheridan's cavalry succeeded in blocking Lee's escape route on the Lynchburg Road near Appomattox Court House. On the morning of April 9, 1865, Sixth Corps and Second Corps advanced against the rear of Lee's army near Appomattox Court House, and were preparing to attack when the fighting ended under a flag of truce. That afternoon Lee surrendered to Grant the Army of Northern Virginia. For additional information, see Appomattox Campaign, Virginia, Movement of the Armies to Appomattox Court House, Virginia, April 7–9, 1865, and also Surrender of the Army of Northern Virginia.

The organization of Sixth Corps during the Appomattox Campaign was as follows:

SIXTH CORPS, Horatio G. Wright

First Division, Frank Wheaton
First Brigade, William H. Penrose
Second Brigade, Joseph E. Hamblin
Third Brigade, Oliver Edwards

Second Division, George W. Getty
First Brigade, James M. Warner
Second Brigade, Lewis A. Grant, to April 2, 1865, wounded
  Amasa S. Tracy, April 2, 1865
  Charles Mundee, April 2, 1865
  Amasa S. Tracy, to April 4, 1865
  Lewis A. Grant
Third Brigade, Thomas W. Hyde

Note. Lewis A. Grant was wounded about 2:00 A.M. April 2, 1865, while under fire waiting to attack. Tracy then assumed command of Second Brigade and led it during the assault that broke the enemy line. When the brigade was re-formed, Mundee, the assistant adjutant general of Getty's division, assumed command and directed the operations of the brigade during the remainder of the day. At nightfall he turned over the command of the brigade to Tracy.

Third Division, Truman Seymour
First Brigade, William S. Truex
Second Brigade, J. Warren Keifer

Artillery Brigade, Andrew Cowan
  Battery A, 1st New Jersey Light Artillery, Augustin N. Parsons
  1st Battery, New York Light Artillery, Orsamus R. Van Etten
  3rd Battery, New York Light Artillery, William A. Harn
  Company L, 9th New York Heavy Artillery, S. Augustus Howe
  Battery G, 1st Rhode Island Light Artillery, George W. Adams
  Battery H, 1st Rhode Island Light Artillery, Crawford Allen, Jr.
  Battery E, 5th United States Artillery, John R. Brinckle

Company D, 1st Vermont Heavy Artillery, Charles J. Lewis

After Appomattox. The surrender of Lee at Appomattox Court House did not immediately end the war in the East. Joseph E. Johnston remained in North Carolina with an army of about 30,000 men confronting William T. Sherman, and it was not known at that time whether Johnson would also surrender or continue fighting. Accordingly, Grant prepared for the latter eventuality. He ordered Charles Griffin's Fifth Corps and John Gibbon's Twenty-Fourth Corps to remain at Appomattox Court House until paroles were issued and the surrendered property was removed to the railroad, and he directed the rest of the army to move to Burkeville, Virginia, where it would be in position to march into North Carolina if necessary.

After the surrender, Wright's Sixth Corps remained in camp at Clover Hill, a short distance north of Appomattox Court House, until April 11, 1865, and it then marched to Burkeville, where it arrived two days later. Johnston's army remained in the field, and Grant decided to send a force to join Sherman to force its early surrender. On April 22, 1865, Grant placed Sixth Corps under Sheridan's orders, and directed the latter to proceed toward North Carolina with his cavalry and Wright's infantry. Sixth Corps left Burkeville April 23, 1865, and marched to the southwest along the Richmond and Danville Railroad by way of Keysville, Charles' Ferry on the Staunton River, Halifax Court House, and Brooklyn, and arrived at Danville, Virginia, near the state line, April 27, 1865. The cavalry advanced from Petersburg on the Boydton Plank Road to South Boston on the Dan River. Johnston surrendered his army to Sherman near Durham Station, North Carolina April 26, 1865, and upon receiving this information, Grant halted Sheridan's command. The cavalry then left South Boston for Petersburg, but Sixth Corps remained until mid-May 1865 at Danville, and along the railroad between that point and Burkeville. Meantime, the other corps of the Army of the Potomac left the line of the South Side Railroad for Washington. When they departed, Wheaton's First Division, Sixth Corps moved to the railroad and took position between Burkeville and Sutherland's Station.

Finally, on May 16, 1865, Sixth Corps was ordered to follow the rest of the army toward Washington. It moved by rail to Manchester, Virginia, near Richmond, and arrived there May 17–20, 1865. It marched in review through Richmond May 24, 1865, and then continued on toward Washington. Its progress was slowed by heavy rains, but it passed through Hanover Court House, Milford Station, and Fredericksburg to Wolf Run Shoals on the Occoquan River, and on June 2, 1865 it went into camp between Hall's Hill and Ball's Cross Roads, south of Washington. Sixth Corps was on the march May 23, 1865, when the Grand Review of the Army of the Potomac was held in Washington, but on June 8, 1865, it had its own parade in the city.

An order dated May 17, 1865 directed that all volunteer organizations of white troops in the Army of the Potomac whose terms of service expired between that date and September 30, 1865 be mustered out immediately. Compliance with this order greatly reduced the number of troops present in each of the corps. As a result, on June 28, 1865, it was further ordered that all troops not then eligible for muster out were, in each of the three corps of the Army of the Potomac, to be consolidated into a division of three brigades. With this order the Army of the Potomac ceased to exist. The three divisions formed in this manner from Second Corps, Fifth Corps, and Sixth Corps were organized temporarily into a provisional corps, which was commanded by Horatio G. Wright. The troops of Sixth Corps were organized June 30, 1865, as follows:

First Division, Provisional Corps, George W. Getty
    First Brigade, Truman Seymour
    Second Brigade, Frank Wheaton
    Third Brigade, Joseph E. Hamblin

The Provisional Corps was placed in camp on the Baltimore and Ohio Railroad, west of the Monocacy River, and Wright reported to Winfield S. Hancock, commander of the Middle Department. In time, the troops of Getty's division were also mustered out.

Sixth Corps was discontinued by the order of June 28, 1865, but the consolidation of the remaining troops into a single division was not completed until June 30, 1865.

The organization of Sixth Corps during the period April 10, 1865 to June 28, 1865 was as follows:

SIXTH CORPS, Horatio G. Wright

First Division, Frank Wheaton
    First Brigade, William H. Penrose
    Second Brigade, Joseph E. Hamblin
    Third Brigade, Oliver Edwards, to June 21, 1865

Second Division, George W. Getty
    First Brigade, James M. Warner, to April 21, 1865, on leave
        Charles W. Eckman, to May 2, 1865
        James M. Warner
    Second Brigade, Lewis A. Grant
    Third Brigade, Thomas W. Hyde

Third Division, Truman Seymour, to April 16, 1865
        James B. Ricketts
    First Brigade, William S. Truex, to April 17, 1865
        Truman Seymour
    Second Brigade, J. Warren Keifer

Note. Ricketts, who was wounded at the Battle of Cedar Creek October 19, 1864, returned to the army and was assigned command of Third Division April 14, 1865.

Artillery Brigade, Andrew Cowan

COMMANDERS OF SIXTH CORPS, ARMY OF THE POTOMAC, DECEMBER 16, 1864 to JUNE 28, 1865

Horatio G. Wright	December 16, 1864 to January 16, 1865, on leave
George W. Getty	January 16, 1865 to February 11, 1865
Horatio G. Wright	February 11, 1865 to June 28, 1865

SIXTH CORPS, ARMY OF THE SHENANDOAH AUGUST 7–DECEMBER 16, 1864

After Early's second threat from the Shenandoah Valley in July 1864, Grant decided to form a new army under the command of Philip H. Sheridan for the purpose of destroying Early's army or driving it from the valley. August 5, 1864, Grant ordered the concentration of Hunter's army near Harper's Ferry, and Wright's Sixth Corps joined Crook's army of the Department of West Virginia and Emory's Detachment Nineteenth Corps in a strong defensive position at Halltown.

Sheridan, the former commander of the Cavalry Corps, Army of the Potomac, arrived at Harper's Ferry from Petersburg August 6, 1864, and the next day assumed temporary command of the newly constituted Middle Military Division. He immediately began preparations for operations against Early in the Shenandoah Valley. He began his first advance August 10, 1864. Sixth Corps moved south to Berryville, and two days later it advanced to Cedar Creek, where it remained until August 17, 1864. It then moved to Opequon Creek, on the Berryville Pike. During this movement William H. Penrose's First Brigade, First Division was left at Winchester, with a part of Alfred T. A. Torbert's cavalry as a rear guard. This force was strongly attacked by a part of Early's command that evening, but it held its position until late at night. The next day Sixth Corps moved to Charlestown, repulsed an enemy attack there August 21, 1864, and then returned to Halltown. For details, see Shenandoah Valley Campaign (Sheridan), Sheridan's First Advance up the Valley.

Sheridan again advanced in September 1864. Sixth Corps moved to Charlestown September 1, 1864, and two days later to Clifton, where it remained until September 19, 1864. It then marched to the Opequon and took part in the battle that was fought there that day. For details, see Shenandoah Valley Campaign (Sheridan), Battle of Opequon Creek (or Winchester), Virginia.

The organization of Sixth Corps at the Battle of Opequon Creek, September 19, 1864, was as follows:

SIXTH CORPS, Horatio G. Wright

First Division, David A. Russell, killed
  Emory Upton, wounded
  Oliver Edwards
  First Brigade, Edward L. Campbell
  Second Brigade, Emory Upton
    Joseph E. Hamblin
  Third Brigade, Oliver Edwards
    Isaac C. Bassett

Second Division, George W. Getty
  First Brigade, Frank Wheaton

Second Brigade, James M. Warner
  Amasa S. Tracy
Third Brigade, Daniel D. Bidwell

Note. Tracy commanded a part of the line during the battle.

Third Division, James B. Ricketts
  First Brigade, William Emerson
  Second Brigade, J. Warren Keifer

Artillery Brigade, Charles H. Tompkins
  5th Battery (E), Maine Light Artillery, Greenleaf T. Stevens
  1st Battery (A), Massachusetts Light Artillery, William H. McCartney
  1st Battery, New York Light Artillery, William H. Johnson
    Orsamus R. Van Etten
  Battery C, 1st Rhode Island Light Artillery, Jacob H. Lamb
  Battery G, 1st Rhode Island Light Artillery, George W. Adams
  Battery M, 5th United States Artillery, James McKnight

Following his defeat at the Opequon, Early retired up the valley, and Sheridan followed. Sixth Corps marched to Strasburg September 20, 1864, and then took part in the Battle of Fisher's Hill September 22, 1864. For details, see Shenandoah Valley Campaign (Sheridan), Battle of Fisher's Hill, Virginia.

The organization of Sixth Corps at the Battle of Fisher's Hill, September 21–22, 1864, was as follows:

SIXTH CORPS, Horatio G. Wright

First Division, Frank Wheaton
  First Brigade, Edward L. Campbell
  Second Brigade, Joseph B. Hamblin
  Third Brigade, Oliver Edwards

Note. Third Brigade was not engaged at Fisher's Hill, but was serving as a guard at Winchester, Virginia.

Second Division, George W. Getty
  First Brigade, James M. Warner
  Second Brigade, George P. Foster
  Third Brigade, Daniel D. Bidwell

Third Division, James B. Ricketts
  First Brigade, William Emerson
  Second Brigade, J. Warren Keifer

Artillery Brigade, Charles H. Tompkins

Note. The batteries of Tompkins' brigade were the same as at the Battle of the Opequon.

Early's army was routed by Sheridan's attack at Fisher's Hill, and the victorious Federals pursued. Sixth Corps marched up the valley through Woodstock, Edenburg, and New Market, and arrived at Harrisonburg September 25, 1864. September 29, 1864, it moved forward to Mount Crawford, and returned to Harrisonburg the next day. The corps remained at Harrisonburg until October 6, 1864, and it then marched back down the valley to Strasburg. While there, on October 10, 1864, Sixth Corps was ordered to Front Royal for transfer to Alexandria to rejoin the Army of the Potomac at Petersburg. Once more, however, Early threatened, and October 14, 1864, Sixth Corps was sent back to Cedar Creek, where it encamped on the north bank until October 19, 1864. The next day it was engaged in the Battle of Cedar Creek, during which Early achieved some initial successes, but was finally decisively defeated. For details, see Shenandoah Valley Campaign (Sheridan), Battle of Cedar Creek, Virginia.

The organization of Sixth Corps at the Battle of Cedar Creek, October 19, 1864, was as follows:

SIXTH CORPS, James B. Ricketts, wounded
    George W. Getty
    Horatio G. Wright

Note. Wright commanded the Army of the Shenandoah during the temporary absence of Sheridan in the early part of the battle.

First Division, Frank Wheaton
    First Brigade, William H. Penrose, wounded
        Edward L. Campbell, wounded
        Baldwin Hufty
    Second Brigade, Joseph E. Hamblin, wounded
        Ranald S. Mackenzie, wounded
        Egbert Olcott
    Third Brigade, Oliver Edwards

Note. Third Brigade was at Winchester, Virginia, and was not engaged in the battle.

Second Division, George W. Getty
    Lewis A. Grant
    George W. Getty
    First Brigade, James M. Warner
    Second Brigade, Lewis A. Grant

        Amasa S. Tracy
        Lewis A. Grant
    Third Brigade, Daniel D. Bidwell, killed
        Winsor B. French

Third Division, J. Warren Kiefer
    First Brigade, William Emerson
    Second Brigade, William H. Ball

Artillery Brigade, Charles H. Tompkins

Note. The batteries with Topmpkins' brigade were the same as at the Battle of the Opequon.

Sixth Corps remained in camp at Cedar Creek until November 4, 1864, and then it withdrew with the rest of the army to Camp Russell near Kernstown. Finally, in December 1864, when the weather prevented further campaigning by the infantry, Sixth Corps left the Shenandoah Valley to return to the Army of the Potomac. On December 1, 1864, Wheaton's First Division marched to Stephenson's Depot on the Winchester and Potomac Railroad, and from there it traveled by rail to Washington, where it embarked the next day for City Point. Seymour's Third Division left Kernstown December 3, 1864, and followed Wheaton's division by the same route to City Point. Getty's Second Division was retained at Kernstown until December 9, 1864. That day John B. Gordon's and John Pegram's Confederate divisions left the valley for Petersburg (Joseph B. Kershaw's division had left November 15, 1864), and with their departure, Getty's division followed the other two divisions of Sixth Corps to City Point, where it arrived December 13–16, 1864.

COMMANDERS OF SIXTH CORPS, ARMY OF THE SHENANDOAH AUGUST 7–DECEMBER 16, 1864

Horatio G. Wright	August 7, 1864 to October 16, 1864
James B. Ricketts	October 16, 1864 to October 19, 1864, wounded
George W. Getty	October 19, 1864
Horatio G. Wright	October 19, 1864 to December 16, 1864

Note. Philip H. Sheridan left the Shenandoah Valley for Washington October 16, 1864, and Wright was in tem-

porary command of the Army of the Shenandoah during his absence. Sheridan returned to the army on October 19, 1864, during the Battle of Cedar Creek, and resumed command of the army, and Wright returned to the command of Sixth Corps.

SEVENTH CORPS, DEPARTMENT OF VIRGINIA

July 22, 1862, the troops in the Department of Virginia, except those belonging to the Army of the Potomac, which was then on the Peninsula, and those belonging to Ambrose E. Burnside's Ninth Corps (organized July 22, 1862) at Newport News, were organized into Seventh Corps, Department of Virginia. This was not a mobile command, but was employed largely in garrison duty in southeastern Virginia. John A. Dix was assigned command. Seventh Corps was discontinued August 1, 1863, and was merged into the Department of Virginia and North Carolina. For details of the organization of Seventh Corps, see Department of Virginia, May 22, 1861–July 15, 1863.

EIGHTH CORPS, MIDDLE DEPARTMENT

July 22, 1862, the troops in the Middle Department were designated as Eighth Corps. This corps was not organized into brigades and divisions for field service, but was disposed as brigades and smaller units among the districts and posts of the department. For details of the organization of the troops of Eighth Corps, see Middle Department, Eighth Corps.

Some confusion may result from the fact that George Crook's Army of West Virginia (see), which was a part of Philip H. Sheridan's command during the Shenandoah Valley Campaign of 1864, was also sometimes called Eighth Corps. Crook's army consisted in part of troops formerly belonging to Eighth Corps, and apparently to avoid the use of the more cumbersome name "the Army of West Virginia," this command was commonly called Eighth Corps. It should be emphasized, however, that the official

designation of that organization was, by order of August 8, 1864, the Army of West Virginia.

NINTH CORPS

On June 28, 1862, during the Seven Days' Battles on the Peninsula, Ambrose E. Burnside, commander of the Department of North Carolina, was ordered to take such troops as could be spared from his department, and move with them to Virginia to reinforce George B. McClellan's Army of the Potomac. On July 6, 1862, Burnside proceeded to Newport News with Jesse L. Reno's Second Division and John G. Parke's Third Division of the Department of North Carolina. He was joined there later in July 1862 by Isaac I. Stevens, who arrived from Hilton Head Island with First Brigade and Second Brigade of his Second Division, Department of the South.

Meantime, McClellan had completed his successful retreat to Harrison's Landing on the James River, and, the immediate danger being over, Burnside's command remained for a time at Newport News. There, on July 22, 1862, it was organized into a new Ninth Corps as follows:

NINTH CORPS, Ambrose E. Burnside

First Division, Isaac I. Stevens
    First Brigade, William M. Fenton, to August 3, 1862?
        Benjamin C. Christ
    Second Brigade, Daniel Leasure, to August 3, 1862?
        Thomas Welsh

Second Division, Jesse L. Reno
    First Brigade, James Nagle
    Second Brigade, Edward Ferrero

Third Division, John G. Parke
    First Brigade, Rush C. Hawkins, to August 3, 1862
        Harrison S. Fairchild
    Second Brigade, Edward Harland

For details of the earlier organizations of the troops from which Ninth Corps was formed, see Department of North Carolina, January 7, 1862–July 15, 1863, Troops and Operations in the Department of North Carolina; and also see Department of the South, Part II, Department of the South, March 31, 1862–September 3, 1862.

NINTH CORPS
(With the Army of Virginia)

On August 1, 1862, Ninth Corps was ordered to embark at Newport News for Aquia Creek, and then to take position at Falmouth, Virginia, opposite Fredericksburg. The corps began arriving at Falmouth August 3, 1862, and Stevens' division arrived three days later. A detachment of Ninth Corps consisting of Stevens' First Division and Reno's Second Division, both under Reno, marched from Falmouth August 13, 1862, and joined John Pope's Army of Virginia at Culpeper Court House the next day. Reno's command remained with the Army of Virginia during the remainder of the month. Burnside stayed near Fredericksburg with Parke's Third Division to forward troops to Pope's army as they arrived from the Peninsula. After the Second Battle of Bull Run (Manassas), he was ordered to Alexandria.

Reno's detachment was engaged at the Battle of Groveton August 29, 1862, and at the Second Battle of Bull Run August 30, 1862. Reno marched from Centerville on the morning of August 29, 1862, and formed his command behind Franz Sigel's First Corps, Army of Virginia south of Sudley Springs, on the right of Pope's line. He then supported an attack by Philip Kearny's division of Third Corps during the late afternoon. When James Longstreet's Confederate corps attacked on the Union left on the afternoon of August 30, 1862, Thomas J. (Stonewall) Jackson's corps also advanced against the Union right, and it was opposed by Reno's detachment and Samuel P. Heintzelman's Third Corps. Later, Reno was moved to the Union left and helped in opposing Longstreet's advance. When Pope's line collapsed that evening, Ninth Corps covered the retreat of the army to Centerville. Ninth Corps was again engaged in severe fighting at the Battle of Chantilly, or Ox Hill, September 1, 1862, and during the battle Stevens, commanding First Division, was killed. Benjamin C. Christ assumed command of the division. For additional information, see Pope's Northern Virginia Campaign.

The organization of Ninth Corps during this period was as follows:

DETACHMENT NINTH CORPS, Jesse L. Reno

First Division. Isaac I. Stevens, to September 1, 1864, killed
Benjamin C. Christ
First Brigade, Benjamin C. Christ, to September 1, 1862
Frank Graves, temporarily
William M. Fenton
Second Brigade, Daniel Leasure, to August 30, 1862, wounded
David A. Leckey
Third Brigade, Addison Farnsworth, to August 30, 1862
David Morrison
Artillery
8th Battery, Massachusetts Light Artillery, Asa M. Cook
Battery E, 2nd United States Artillery, Samuel N. Benjamin

Note. Third Brigade was organized for the Virginia Campaign under Farnsworth. It was discontinued after the Battle of Chantilly, and its two regiments were assigned to First Brigade, First Division.

Second Division, Jesse L. Reno
First Brigade, James Nagle
Second Brigade, Edward Ferrero

NINTH CORPS
(With the Army of the Potomac)

After the Battle of Chantilly, Reno's detachment of Ninth Corps retreated with Pope's army into the Defenses of Washington, and it was then ordered to Leesboro, Maryland. Reno was assigned command of Ninth Corps September 3, 1862, and Edward Ferrero assumed temporary command of Second Division. At that time, Burnside, former commander of Ninth Corps, was at Aquia Creek, with orders to bring the remaining regiments of the corps to Washington.

Jacob D. Cox's Kanawha Division, which had been ordered from Western Virginia to join Pope's army during the Northern Virginia Campaign, arrived in late August 1862, and was placed in the Defenses of Washington at Munson's Hill and Perkins' Hill. It was then ordered to Leesboro, and was attached to Ninth Corps September 7–8, 1862. It remained with Ninth Corps during McClellan's Maryland Campaign.

Maryland Campaign, September 3, 1862–September 20, 1862. Robert E. Lee's Army of Northern Virginia crossed the Potomac River into Maryland at White's Ford on September 4, 1862, and then advanced to Frederick. McClellan immediately began preparations for his army to go in pursuit. For this purpose he organized his army into three wings. Third Corps, Army of Virginia (later designated First Corps, Army of the Potomac), under the command of Joseph Hooker, was also sent to Leesboro. This corps and Ninth Corps were assigned to the Right Wing of the Army of the Potomac, which was placed under the command of Burnside. John G. Parke, commander of Third Division, Ninth Corps, which had arrived from Aquia Creek, was appointed as Burnside's chief of staff, and Isaac P. Rodman assumed command of Third Division.

Ninth Corps advanced with the army to Frederick, Maryland, and then marched to South Mountain, where it was engaged at Fox's Gap during the Battle of South Mountain September 14, 1862. Reno was killed that day, and was succeeded in command of Ninth Corps by Jacob D. Cox. Eliakim P. Scammon assumed command of Cox's Kanawha Division. Ninth Corps was also engaged on the Union left at the Battle of Antietam September 17, 1862. After several unsuccessful attempts, the corps finally crossed Antietam Creek at "Burnside's Bridge," east of Sharpsburg, and also at Snavely's Ford, a short distance downstream; and it then advanced to the outskirts of Sharpsburg before being driven back late in the day. Rodman was killed during the attack and Edward Harland assumed command of Third Division. For details of the operations, see Maryland Campaign (South Mountain and Antietam).

The organization of Ninth Corps during the Maryland Campaign was as follows:

NINTH CORPS, Jesse L. Reno, to September 14, 1862, killed
Jacob D. Cox

First Division, Benjamin C. Christ, to September 8, 1862
Orlando B. Willcox
First Brigade, William M. Fenton, to September 8, 1862
Benjamin C. Christ
Second Brigade, Thomas Welsh
Artillery
8th Battery, Massachusetts Light Artillery, Asa M. Cook

Battery E, 2nd United States Artillery, Samuel N. Benjamin

Second Division, Edward Ferrero, September 3–7, 1862
Samuel D. Sturgis
First Brigade, James Nagle
Second Brigade, John F. Hartranft, September 3–7, 1862
Edward Ferrero
Artillery
Battery D, Pennsylvania Light Artillery, George W. Durell
Battery E, 4th United States Artillery, Joseph C. Clark

Third Division, Isaac P. Rodman, to September 17, 1862, killed
Edward Harland
First Brigade, Harrison S. Fairchild
Second Brigade, Edward Harland
Artillery
Battery A, 5th United States Artillery, Charles P. Muhlenberg

Note. George W. Getty assumed command of Third Division October 4, 1862. Getty was Burnside's chief of artillery, and was made brigadier general September 25, 1862.

Kanawha Division, Jacob D. Cox, to September 14, 1862
Eliakim P. Scammon
First Brigade, Eliakim P. Scammon, to September 14, 1862
Hugh Ewing
Second Brigade, Augustus Moor, to September 13, 1862, captured
George Crook

Note. James R. McMullin's 1st Battery, Ohio Light Artillery was attached to First Brigade, and Seth J. Simmonds' Battery, Kentucky Light Artillery was with Second Brigade.

John G. Parke, former commander of Third Corps, served as chief of staff with Burnside during the Maryland Campaign.

The Right Wing of the army was discontinued after the Battle of South Mountain, but Burnside did not return to the command of Ninth Corps. He did, however, exercise general control on the left of the Union line at the Battle of Antietam.

After the Battle of Antietam, Ninth Corps camped near the mouth of Antietam Creek. While there, in the latter part of September 1862, a new Third

Brigade, First Division was organized from Thomas Welsh's 45th Pennsylvania, 100th Pennsylvania from Second Brigade, First Division, and one new regiment. At that time Welsh was in command of Second Brigade, but when transferred, he assumed command of Third Division. Benjamin C. Christ succeeded him in command of Second Brigade.

On October 4, 1862, Jacob D. Cox, commanding Ninth Corps, was ordered to Western Virginia; and three days later the corps marched to Harper's Ferry, where it camped nearby in Pleasant Valley. When Ninth Corps left Antietam Creek, the Kanawha Division (commanded by George Crook since October 1, 1862) was left behind, and October 8, 1862, it was ordered by way of Cumberland, Maryland to Clarksburg in Western Virginia. It was not again associated with Ninth Corps. Also on October 8, 1862, Orlando B. Willcox superseded Cox in command of Ninth Corps, and William M. Fenton succeeded Willcox in command of First Division. October 13, 1862, Burnside was assigned command of the Defenses of Harper's Ferry, and the troops assigned to the Defenses were Second Corps, Ninth Corps, and Twelfth Corps.

October 20, 1862, George Stoneman's First Division, Third Corps, then near Poolesville, Maryland, in the Defenses of Washington, was assigned to Ninth Corps.

Antietam to Warrenton, Virginia, September 19, 1862–November 7, 1862. On October 26, 1862, McClellan's Army of the Potomac began its advance into Virginia. Ninth Corps followed Amiel W. Whipple's division of Twelfth Corps across the Potomac at Berlin (present-day Brunswick), Maryland to lead the Army of the Potomac into the Loudoun Valley. The next day, Stoneman's division, then attached to Ninth Corps, crossed the river at Edwards Ferry, and marched to Leesburg, Virginia. By October 29, 1862, Willcox's Ninth Corps had arrived near Hillsboro, Virginia. That day, Stoneman's division was detached from Ninth Corps and Whipple's division from Twelfth Corps, and a special command was formed under Burnside that consisted of Ninth Corps, Stoneman's Division, and Whipple's Division.

On November 2, 1862, while the corps was near Wheatland, William W. Burns was assigned command of First Division, and he relieved Daniel Leasure, who was in temporary command of the division. Burns had been wounded at Savage Station during the Peninsular Campaign, while commanding a brigade in Second Corps, and had recently returned to the army.

Burnside advanced with his command by way of Upperville to Piedmont, with Stoneman's Division marching from Upperville to Rectortown, and by November 5, 1862, he was in position between Piedmont and Salem. Two days later, it was in the vicinity of Waterloo, Virginia.

Fredericksburg Campaign, November 7, 1862–December 15, 1862. On November 7, 1862, Burnside received an order dated September 5, 1862 assigning him to the command of the Army of the Potomac. He relieved McClellan that night, and then submitted to Henry W. Halleck a new plan of operations. He proposed to move the army eastward to Fredericksburg, and from that point south toward Richmond. This plan was approved November 14, 1862, and that day Burnside reorganized the Army of the Potomac into three grand divisions and a reserve. He assigned Darius N. Couch's Second Corps and Willcox's Ninth Corps to Edwin V. Sumner's Right Grand Division. The next day Sumner left Warrenton with his two corps, and two days later arrived at Falmouth, opposite Fredericksburg. He was unable to cross the Rappahannock because expected pontoons had not arrived from Washington, and he remained with the rest of the army near Falmouth until December 11, 1862, when the bridges were completed. Then the army began crossing the river in preparation for the Battle of Fredericksburg. Only Rush C. Hawkins' First Brigade of Getty's Third Division, Ninth Corps crossed into Fredericksburg that day. The rest of the corps crossed December 12, 1862.

On the morning of December 13, 1862, Ninth Corps formed along the south bank of the Rappahannock, between Fredericksburg and the mouth of Deep Run. William F. Smith's Sixth Corps was on the left of Ninth Corps, and Couch's Second Corps was on the right. William W. Burns' First Division was on the left of the corps line, George W. Getty's Third Division was on the center, and Samuel D. Sturgis' Second Division was on the right. Late in the morning, Sturgis' division joined in the attacks by Second Corps against the Confederate positions in front of Marye's Hill, but it was driven back. About noon, Getty's division attacked Marye's Hill from the east, but it too was driven back. During the day, Burns' division was placed at the disposal of William B. Franklin, commanding the Left Grand Division, but it was not engaged. Ninth Corps withdrew to the north bank of the Rappahannock during the night of December 15, 1862, and went into camp. For details of the Battle of Fredericksburg, see Fredericksburg Campaign, Virginia.

The organization of Ninth Corps during the Battle of Fredericksburg was as follows:

NINTH CORPS, Orlando B. Willcox

First Division, William W. Burns
  First Brigade, Orlando M. Poe
  Second Brigade, Benjamin C. Christ
  Third Brigade, Daniel Leasure
  Artillery
    Battery D, 1st New York Light Artillery, Thomas W. Osborn
    Batteries L and M, 3rd United States Artillery, Horace J. Hayden

Second Division, Samuel D. Sturgis
  First Brigade, James Nagle
  Second Brigade, Edward Ferrero
  Artillery
    Battery L, 2nd New York Light Artillery, Jacob Roemer
    Battery D, Pennsylvania Light Artillery, George W. Durell
    Battery D, 1st Rhode Island Light Artillery, William W. Buckley
    Battery E, 4th United States Artillery, George Dickenson John Egan

Third Division, George W. Getty
  First Brigade, Rush C. Hawkins
  Second Brigade, Edward Harland
  Artillery
    Battery E, Second United States Artillery, Samuel N. Benjamin
    Battery A, 5th United States Artillery, James Gilliss

NINTH CORPS
(In the Department of Virginia)

January 16, 1863, John Sedgwick relieved Willcox in command of Ninth Corps, and Willcox

resumed command of First Division. The organization of the corps at the end of January 1863 was as follows:

NINTH CORPS, John Sedgwick

First Division, William W. Burns
  First Brigade, William M. Fenton
  Second Brigade, George W. Mindil
  Third Brigade, Thomas Welsh
  Artillery
    Battery D, 1st New York Light Artillery, Thomas W. Osborn
    Batteries L and M, 3rd United States Artillery, William C. Bartlett

Note 1. February 8, 1863, Burns was ordered to report to William S. Rosecrans, commander of the Department of the Cumberland, at Murfreesboro, Tennessee.
Note 2. Mindil commanded Second Brigade temporarily during the absence of Benjamin C. Christ.
Note 3. Welsh commanded Third Brigade temporarily during the absence of Daniel Leasure.

Second Division, Samuel D. Sturgis
  First Brigade, James Nagle
  Second Brigade, Edward Harland
  Artillery
    Battery D, Pennsylvania Light Artillery, George W. Durell
    Battery D, 1st Rhode Island Light Artillery, George C. Harkness
    Battery E, 4th United States Artillery, Samuel S. Elder

Third Division, George W. Getty
  First Brigade, Rush C. Hawkins
  Second Brigade, Edward Ferrero
  Third Brigade, Aaron F. Stevens
  Artillery
    Battery L, 2nd New York Light Artillery, Jacob Roemer
    Battery E, 2nd United States Artillery, William P. Graves
    Battery A, 5th United States Artillery, George W. Crabb

Note. Third Brigade was organized in January 1863 from two regiments of First Brigade, Third Division, including Stevens' 13th New Hampshire, and two regiments of Second Brigade, Third Division.

On February 4, 1863, William F. Smith relieved Sedgwick, and was ordered to report with the corps to John A. Dix, commander of the Department of Virginia. Embarkation for Fort Monroe began at

Aquia Creek February 6, 1863, and by February 16, 1863, the transfer had been completed and the corps assembled at Newport News.

March 8, 1863, Orlando B. Willcox relieved William F. Smith in command of Ninth Corps. Smith's removal was the result of a letter written by him and William B. Franklin to the president, criticizing Burnside's plan for the future campaign. A contributing factor in his removal was undoubtedly the fact that he was a close friend of George B. McClellan.

About two weeks after Ninth Corps had assembled at Newport News, Getty's Third Division was ordered to Suffolk, Virginia, and it was moved there by water March 13–16, 1863.

NINTH CORPS
(In the Department of the Ohio)

On March 16, 1863, Burnside, then in Washington, was ordered to resume command of Ninth Corps, and to proceed immediately to Cincinnati and relieve Horatio G. Wright in command of the Department of the Ohio. He was further instructed to leave one division of Ninth Corps in the Department of Virginia, and move the other two divisions to Ohio. Burnside, while still in Washington, assumed command March 17, 1863, and ordered John G. Parke, his former chief of staff of the Army of the Potomac, to proceed to Virginia and take command of the two divisions that were to go west. Parke assumed command March 19, 1863, and that same day began to embark his command for the trip north.

Willcox's First Division broke camp at Newport News March 19, 1863, and during the period March 19–24, 1863 embarked for Baltimore, Maryland. From there it moved on by rail, and arrived at Cincinnati March 24–30, 1863. Orlando M. Poe's First Brigade was sent to Bardstown; Benjamin C. Christ's Second Brigade to Camp Dick Robinson; and Daniel Leasure's Third Brigade to Mount Sterling, all in Kentucky.

Samuel D. Sturgis' Second Division embarked at Newport News for Baltimore March 25–26, 1863, and from there moved by rail by way of Harrisburg, Pennsylvania, Columbus, Ohio, and Cincinnati to

Lexington, Kentucky. James Nagle's First Brigade was then sent on to Mount Sterling, and Edward Ferrero's Second Brigade remained at Lexington.

Getty's division was detached and assigned to Dix's Department of Virginia, and its designation was changed to Getty's Division, Department of Virginia. It did not again join Ninth Corps. For further information about Getty's division, see Department of Virginia, May 22, 1861–July 15, 1863.

Ninth Corps remained in Kentucky for about two months, and was then ordered to join Ulysses S. Grant's army at Vicksburg, Mississippi. There were some changes in command in the corps during its stay in Kentucky. April 4, 1863, Orlando B. Willcox assumed temporary command of Ninth Corps, relieving John G. Parke. On April 10, 1863, Willcox relieved Quincy A. Gillmore in command of the District of Central Kentucky, and Thomas Welsh assumed command of Willcox's First Division, Ninth Corps. Late in May 1863, John F. Hartranft relieved Samuel D. Sturgis in command of Second Division, Ninth Corps, and June 4, 1863, Sturgis assumed command of the District of Central Kentucky, Twenty-Third Corps.

NINTH CORPS
(In the Department of the Tennessee)

In the latter part of May 1863, Willcox, then in command of of the District of Central Kentucky, was considering a movement toward Cumberland Gap, and on June 3, 1863, Thomas Welsh's First Division was at Columbia and John F. Hartranft's Second Division was at Stanford. On that date, the two divisions were ordered to Vicksburg, and they immediately marched northward to Cincinnati and Louisville for transfer to the Mississippi. On June 5, 1863, John G. Parke was assigned command of Ninth Corps, and while at Cincinnati, on the way south, Robert B. Potter relieved Hartranft in command of Second Division. Willcox was then ordered to Indiana, where he assumed command at Indianapolis June 8, 1863. Willcox was not present with the corps at Vicksburg, and Welsh remained in command of his division. There was also an organizational change in the corps as it moved toward

Vicksburg. Benjamin C. Christ's Second Brigade, First Division was transferred to Second Division and redesignated as Third Brigade. This left First Division with only First Brigade and Third Brigade.

Parke, with his Ninth Corps, arrived at Vicksburg, in the Department of the Tennessee, June 14–17, 1863, and then moved up the Yazoo River to Snyder's Bluff, where the corps disembarked June 17, 1863. It then took position in the valley of the Skilliaklia Bayou, with the left of the corps near Snyder's Bluff, and the right near the Templeton plantation. Park established his headquarters at Milldale, near the center of his line. Ninth Corps served as a reserve for the rest of the line, and was not engaged during the siege.

John C. Pemberton surrendered at Vicksburg July 4, 1863, and that afternoon Parke marched with William T. Sherman's Expeditionary Army toward Jackson, Mississippi, against Confederate forces commanded by Joseph E. Johnston. The corps arrived at Jackson July 16, 1863, and advanced with the rest of the army, against some opposition, toward the enemy works. They again advanced the next day and found the enemy had retired. Edward Ferrero's Second Brigade, Second Division occupied the town until relieved by Frank P. Blair's Second Division, Fifteenth Corps. During this movement, William Sooy Smith's First Division, Sixteenth Corps was temporarily attached to Ninth Corps. On the morning of July 20, 1863, Parke started with his two divisions to return to his former position at Milldale and Snyder's Bluff. He arrived there on the evening of July 23, 1863, and was then ordered to return to Kentucky.

The organization of Ninth Corps at Vicksburg was as follows:

NINTH CORPS, John G. Parke

First Division, Thomas Welsh
First Brigade, Henry Bowman
Third Brigade, Daniel Leasure
Artillery
Battery D, Pennsylvania Light Artillery, George W. Durell

Note. Durell's battery was transferred from Second Division June 25, 1863.

Second Division, Robert B. Potter
First Brigade, Simon G. Griffin

Second Brigade, Edward Ferrero
Third Brigade, Benjamin C. Christ
Artillery
Battery L, 2nd New York Light Artillery, Jacob Roemer

Artillery Reserve
Battery E, 2nd United States Artillery, Samuel N. Benjamin

Ninth Corps embarked at Snyder's Bluff for the return to Kentucky August 3–8, 1863, and First Division arrived at Covington, Kentucky August 12, 1863. Second Division arrived there August 20, 1863.

NINTH CORPS
(In East Tennessee, Department of the Ohio)

In August 1863, Burnside began a long-contemplated advance into East Tennessee. He left Cincinnati August 10, 1863, and then joined George L. Hartsuff's Twenty-Third Corps, which began its march August 16, 1863. The main body advanced on the main road to Kingston, and arrived at Knoxville September 3, 1863. Burnside also captured Cumberland Gap September 9, 1863.

Meantime, Ninth Corps had arrived at Covington, Kentucky on its return from Vicksburg. First Division had encamped there until August 18, 1863, and had then moved by way of Nicholasville to Crab Orchard, where it arrived August 26, 1863. Second Division had also encamped at Covington, and had left there August 26, 1863 for Nicholasville.

There were some changes in command and organization in Ninth Corps after it left Vicksburg. When First Division reached Cairo on its return, Welsh left the division August 12, 1863, because of illness, and Edward Ferrero assumed command. Welsh died two days later, probably from malaria contracted while at Vicksburg.

August 22, 1863, Benjamin C. Christ's Third Brigade, Second Division, which had been transferred earlier from First Division, was returned to First Division under its former designation of Second Brigade. It was commanded temporarily by

Ebenezer W. Peirce. On August 25, 1863, Robert B. Potter relieved Parke, who was ill, in command of Ninth Corps.

The organization of Ninth Corps at the end of August 1863 was as follows:

NINTH CORPS, Robert B. Potter

First Division, Edward Ferrero
    First Brigade, David Morrison
    Second Brigade, Ebenezer W. Peirce
    Third Brigade, Cornelius Byington
    Artillery
        Batteries L and M, 3rd United States Artillery, John Edwards, Jr.

Note. Byington was in temporary command of Third Brigade during the absence of Daniel Leasure.

Second Division, Simon G. Griffin
    First Brigade, Zenas R. Bliss
    Second Brigade, Edwin Schall
    Artillery
        Battery L, 2nd New York Light Artillery, Jacob Roemer
        Battery D, Pennsylvania Light Artillery, George W. Durell

Note. Third Brigade was discontinued August 22, 1863, by transfer to First Division as Second Brigade.

September 15, 1863, Parke returned to the army from sick leave, and was assigned command of Ninth Corps. A short time later, however, he was reassigned as Burnside's chief of staff.

On September 17, 1863, Burnside ordered Ninth Corps to join him in East Tennessee, and by September 30, 1863 it had arrived at Knoxville. Orlando B. Willcox returned from duty in Indiana, and on October 6, 1863 reported to Burnside with four regiments from that state. Willcox did not rejoin Ninth Corps at that time, but was instead assigned command of a division of troops in East Tennessee. Ninth Corps under Potter moved up the valley of the Holston River to Bull's Gap, and it was joined there by Willcox's command October 8, 1863. Together, they drove the enemy beyond the Wautuga River, and Ninth Corps then returned to Knoxville October 14–15, 1863.

On October 20, Ninth Corps advanced to Loudoun, Tennessee, and then fell back to Lenoir's Station. On November 14, 1863, it again advanced to Loudoun to meet James Longstreet's corps, which was advancing toward Knoxville from Chattanooga.

Ninth Corps was engaged in skirmishing with the enemy November 15, 1863, after which it returned to Lenoir's Station. Second Division was then sent back to Knoxville, and the next day First Division retired to Campbell's Station. On November 16, 1863, First Division repulsed a strong attack, and then it too returned to Knoxville. The next day Ninth Corps and Twenty-Third Corps began the construction of a line of works for the defense of the city. This line began, on the left, about 450 yards below the mouth of Second Creek, which flowed southward along the western side of Knoxville. From there it ran northward to Fort Sanders, and then eastward along the north side of Knoxville, roughly parallel to the East Tennessee and Georgia Railroad, and on to Maybry's Hill. There it turned back to the southeast and ended on the Holston River, about 1,000 yards above the mouth of First Creek, which flowed southward along the eastern side of Knoxville. Ferrero's division was placed on the left of this line, and held the ground from the river to the point where the East Tennessee and Georgia Railroad crossed Second Creek. Hartranft's division was on the right of Ferrero, and held the line between Second Creek and First Creek. Troops of Twenty-Third Corps were in the entrenchments from the right of Hartranft to the river above Knoxville.

Longstreet's troops arrived in front of Knoxville on the morning of November 18, 1863, but there was little action along the line until November 29, 1863. On that day the enemy launched an assault on Fort Sanders, which was held by troops of Ferrero's division, but this attack was repulsed with heavy enemy losses. That was the last serious effort to penetrate Burnside's line. Longstreet gave up the siege December 4, 1863, and marched with his corps to the northeast toward Rogersville. Parke was then assigned as commander of United States Forces in the Field, and December 7, 1863 started in pursuit with Ninth Corps and Twenty-Third Corps. Parke reached Rutledge December 14, 1863, and that day, Longstreet, who had marched back from Rogersville, attacked the Federal cavalry at Bean's Station and drove it back. Parke then retired to Blain's Cross Roads, about eighteen miles from Knoxville. He then moved to Strawberry Plains January 18, 1864, and at the end of the month returned to Knoxville.

On November 16, 1863, John G. Foster was ordered to relieve Burnside in command of the Department and Army of the Ohio. A short time later Burnside was besieged at Knoxville, and Foster was directed to go to Cumberland Gap and, with the forces there, march, as one of three columns, to his relief. Foster arrived at Cumberland Gap at the end of November 1863, and then moved with his command to Tazewell shortly before the siege was lifted. On November 11, 1863, while Parke was marching in pursuit of Longstreet, Foster arrived at Knoxville, and the next day relieved Burnside of his command. January 7 (and also 12), 1864, Burnside was assigned to recruiting duty to to fill up the old regiments of Ninth Corps. On February 9, 1864, Robert B. Potter was detailed as chief of recruiting service in the state of New York, and the same day Edward Harland was assigned a similar service in the state of Connecticut.

January 18, 1864, Potter left the corps on a thirty-day leave, and Willcox was assigned command of Ninth Corps. At that time Second Division was temporarily attached to First Division. On January 26, 1864, Parke was assigned command of Ninth Corps, and Willcox was directed to assume command of Second Division, which was then relieved from duty with First Corps. At the end of January 1864, Ninth Corps was organized as follows:

NINTH CORPS, John G. Parke

First Division, Edward Ferrero
    First Brigade, David Morrison
    Second Brigade, Ebenezer W. Peirce
    Artillery
        Batteries L and M, 3rd United States Artillery, Erskine Gittings
        Battery D, 1st Rhode Island Light Artillery, William W. Buckley

Note. William Humphrey's Third Brigade was discontinued in January 1864, by the assignment of its regiments to First Brigade and Second Brigade.

Second Division, Orlando B. Willcox
    First Brigade, Joshua K. Sigfried
    Second Brigade, Moses N. Collins

NINTH CORPS
(With the Army of the Potomac)

March 14, 1864, Ulysses S. Grant ordered Ninth

Corps from East Tennessee to Annapolis, Maryland, and also directed that all veterans of the corps rendezvous at that place. He further ordered Burnside, who was on recruiting duty in New York, to send all regiments to Annapolis. On March 16, 1864, Parke was ordered to join Butler in New York, and Willcox was assigned temporary command of Ninth Corps during his absence. Also on March 16, 1864, Ninth Corps was relieved from duty in the Department of the Ohio and ordered east. It was at Morristown, Tennessee when the order was received, and it promptly moved to Knoxville in preparation for its departure. The corps left Knoxville March 21, 1864, and marched by way of Cumberland Gap for Kentucky. It proceeded by way of Barboursville and Camp Nelson to Covington, and then on to Pittsburgh, Pennsylvania. From there it traveled by the Pennsylvania Central Railroad to Harrisburg, and then moved on to Annapolis.

Burnside resumed command of Ninth Corps April 13, 1864, and April 19, 1864, he ordered the reorganization of the corps into four divisions, which were to be commanded as follows: First Division, Thomas G. Stevenson; Second Division, John G. Parke; Third Division, Orlando B. Willcox; and Fourth Division, Edward Ferrero. This reorganization was not completed for some time.

On April 19, 1864, Grant ordered Burnside to move his corps to the Orange and Alexandria Railroad and relieve Gouverneur K. Warren's Fifth Corps, Army of the Potomac from the duty of guarding the road from Bull Run to the Rappahannock River. He also ordered Burnside to divert all troops then on the way to Annapolis, and those yet to start, to Alexandria to join the corps. Burnside ordered Ninth Corps to start from Annapolis on the morning of April 23, 1864, with the divisions moving in the order of their division numbers. John G. Parke was assigned command of the column, but the day before he was too sick to command, and he was replaced by Orlando B. Willcox.

On April 30, 1864, Stevenson's First Division established headquarters at Bealeton Station, and relieved Charles Griffin's division of Fifth Corps, which was guarding the railroad from Licking Run to Warrenton Junction. Willcox's Third Division relieved Romeyn B. Ayres' division of Fifth Corps on the railroad between Warrenton Junction and Licking Run. Second Division took position at Bristoe Station, and Fourth Division at Manassas Junction.

At the end of April 1864, Ninth Corps was organized as follows:

NINTH CORPS, Ambrose E. Burnside

First Division, Thomas G. Stevenson
First Brigade, Sumner Carruth
Second Brigade, Daniel Leasure
Artillery
  2nd Battery (B), Maine Light Artillery, Albert F. Thomas
  14th Battery, Massachusetts Light Artillery, Joseph W. B. Wright

Second Division, Simon G. Griffin
First Brigade, Joshua K. Sigfried
Second Brigade, Herbert B. Titus
Artillery
  11th Battery, Massachusetts Light Artillery, Edward J. Jones
  19th Battery, New York Light Artillery, Edward W. Rogers

Note 1. Robert B. Potter assumed command of Second Division May 1, 1864, and Griffin assumed command of Second Brigade.
Note 2. John G. Parke, who had been assigned command of Second Division, returned to the army May 5, 1864, after having recovered from his illness, but was assigned as Burnside's chief of staff.
Note 3. Sigfried was assigned command of First Brigade, Fourth Division May 4, 1864, and Zenas R. Bliss assumed command of First Brigade, Second Division.

Third Division, Orlando B. Willcox
First Brigade, John F. Hartranft
Second Brigade, Benjamin C. Christ
Artillery
  7th Battery (G), Maine Light Artillery, Adelbert B. Twitchell
  34th Battery, New York Light Artillery, Jacob Roemer

Fourth Division, Edward Ferrero

Note. Fourth Division consisted of five regiments of United States Colored Troops and 30th Connecticut (colored), but was not organized into brigades until May 4, 1864. Then, a First Brigade was organized under Joshua K. Sigfried, and a Second Brigade under Henry G. Thomas. Sigfried was formerly in command of First Brigade, Second Division.

Artillery
  3rd Battery, Vermont Light Artillery, Romeo H. Start

Reserve Artillery, John Edwards, Jr.
  27th Battery, New York Light Artillery, John B. Eaton
  Battery H, 1st Rhode Island Light Artillery, Crawford Allen, Jr.
  Battery D, Pennsylvania Light Artillery, George W. Durell
  Battery E, 2nd United States Artillery, James S. Dudley
  Battery G, 3rd United States Artillery, Herbert F. Guthrie
  Batteries L and M, 3rd United States Artillery, John Edwards, Jr.

About May 1, 1864, Elisha G. Marshall was assigned command of a provisional brigade that consisted of his own 14th New York Heavy Artillery and two new regiments. This brigade was unattached and was under Burnside's direct orders.

Grant's Richmond, Virginia Campaign, 1864.
On the morning of May 4, 1864, Grant began his spring campaign in Virginia against Robert E. Lee's Army of Northern Virginia and Richmond. Burnside was ordered to send troops to guard the crossings of the Rapidan River at Ely's Ford, Culpeper Mine Ford, and Germanna Ford, and these were to be on the river by the morning of May 5, 1864. Stevenson's First Division left Bealeton Station and Rappahannock Station May 4, 1864, and the next morning crossed the Rapidan at Germanna Ford. It remained near the Army of the Potomac May 5, 1864 during the Battle of the Wilderness, but it was not engaged. Potter's Second Division left Bealeton Station, and Willcox's Third Division left Rappahannock Station May 5, 1864, and both divisions crossed the river at Germanna Ford that afternoon. Willcox then relieved James B. Ricketts' division of Sixth Corps, which had been guarding the ford. Marshall's Provisional Brigade also arrived at Germanna Ford that day, from near Rappahannock Station. Ferrero's Fourth Division, which was at Manassas Junction, and had the greatest distance to travel, began its march May 4, 1864, and did not arrive at Germanna Ford until May 6, 1864. The division was then detached from the corps and assigned to guard the trains of the army. It did not again come under Burnside's orders until July 1864.

When Ninth Corps joined the Army of the Potomac at the Wilderness, both Burnside and Parke, his chief of staff, held superior rank to that of George G. Meade, commander of the Army of the Potomac, and to avoid the problem that this created, Grant did not assign the corps to Meade's army but retained it under his personal direction.

On the morning of May 6, 1864, during the second day of the Battle of the Wilderness, Stevenson's division was detached and sent to support Winfield S. Hancock's Second Corps, which was then attacking on the Plank Road. Stevenson's division took part in Hancock's battle that day, but rejoined Ninth Corps May 7, 1864. Burnside, with the divisions of Potter and Willcox, was ordered into action May 6, 1864, and he moved forward along the Parker's Store Road, between Hancock's command on the Plank Road and Warren's Fifth Corps on the Turnpike. When Hancock attacked on the Plank Road, Burnside was to join in the attack on his right. Burnside was unable to get his command in position until some time after noon, however, and by that time Hancock had been driven back. For details of the operations of Ninth Corps during the Battle of the Wilderness, see Richmond, Virginia Campaign, 1864, Battle of the Wilderness.

The organization of Ninth Corps at the Battle of the Wilderness was as follows:

NINTH CORPS, Ambrose E. Burnside

First Division, Thomas G. Stevenson
First Brigade, Sumner Carruth, to May 6, 1864, sunstroke
Jacob P. Gould

Note 1. Gould assumed command on the morning of May 7, 1864.
Note 2. The artillery with First Division was the same as at the end of April 1864.

Second Division, Robert B. Potter
First Brigade, Zenas R. Bliss, to May 6, 1864, sunstroke
John I. Curtin
Second Brigade, Simon G. Griffin

Note. The artillery with Second Division was the same as at the end of April 1864.

Third Division, Orlando B. Willcox
First Brigade, John F. Hartranft
Second Brigade, Benjamin C. Christ

Note. The artillery with Third Division was the same as at the end of April 1864.

Fourth Division, Edward Ferrero
First Brigade, Joshua K. Sigfried
Second Brigade, Henry G. Thomas
Artillery
Battery D, Pennsylvania Light Artillery, George W. Durell
3rd Battery, Vermont Light Artillery, Romeo H. Start

Note. Fourth Division was detached from the corps, guarding the trains of the army, and was not engaged at the Battle of the Wilderness.

Provisional Brigade, Elisha G. Marshall

Reserve Artillery, John Edwards, Jr.
27th Battery, New York light Artillery, John B. Eaton
Battery D, 1st Rhode Island Light Artillery, William W. Buckley
Battery H, 1st Rhode Island Light Artillery, Crawford Allen, Jr.
Battery E, 2nd United States Artillery, Samuel B. McIntire

Cavalry (four regiments)

During the night of May 7, 1864, the army began to leave its positions in the Wilderness, as it continued the march southward toward Spotsylvania Court House. Early the next morning, Ninth Corps moved back to the vicinity of Chancellorsville, and remained there until the morning of May 9, 1864. At that time, Willcox's division advanced to the far left of the army at the Gayle House, where the Spotsylvania Court House-Fredericksburg Road crossed the Ny River, about one and one-half miles northeast of the court house. Stevenson's division followed Willcox, and joined him about noon. Potter's division and Marshall's Provisional Brigade came up the next day.

On May 10, 1864, Stevenson's division moved out on a reconnaissance toward Spotsylvania Court House, and during the morning, Stevenson was killed by an enemy sharpshooter. He was succeeded temporarily in command of the division by Daniel Leasure, who remained in command until Thomas L. Crittenden, who had been ordered to report to Burnside April 28, 1864, arrived and relieved him May 12, 1864. That day, Marshall's Provisional Brigade was discontinued as an unattached command and was assigned to First Division.

Early on the morning of May 12, 1864, Hancock's Second Corps launched a successful assault on the salient of the Confederate works north of Spotsylvania Court House. Ninth Corps joined in this attack by advancing on the left of Second Corps. Burnisde's three divisions made repeated attacks on the east side of the salient, but they made no significant progress.

There was skirmishing along the front of Ninth Corps until May 18, 1864, and then the corps joined in an attack with Fifth Corps and Sixth Corps against the new enemy line at the base of the old salient. This attack was a failure, and the three corps returned to their former positions. The next day, Ninth Corps moved to the left and took position on the left of Sixth Corps, with its line extending southward to within about a mile of the Po River. It remained in this position until the army began its movement toward the North Anna River May 21, 1864. For details of the operations of Ninth Corps at Spotsylvania Court House, see Richmond, Virginia Campaign of 1864, Operations about Spotsylvania Court House.

The organization of Ninth Corps during the fighting around Spotsylvania Court House was as follows:

NINTH CORPS, Ambrose E. Burnside

First Division, Thomas G. Stevenson, to May 10, 1864, killed
   Daniel Leasure, to May 12, 1864
   Thomas L. Crittenden
   First Brigade, Jacob P. Gould, to May 8, 1864, sick
     Stephen M. Weld, to May 13, 1864
     James H. Ledlie
   Second Brigade, Daniel Leasure, to May 10, 1864
     Gilbert P. Robinson, to May 12, 1864
     Daniel Leasure, to May 14, 1864, sick
     Gilbert P. Robinson
   Provisional Brigade, Elisha G. Marshall

Note. Marshall's Provisional Brigade was discontinued as an unattached command and was assigned to First Division May 12, 1864.

Second Division, Robert B. Potter
   First Brigade, John I. Curtin
   Second Brigade, Simon G. Griffin

Third Division, Orlando B. Willcox
   First Brigade, John F. Hartranft
   Second Brigade, Benjamin C. Christ, to May 12, 1864
     William Humphrey

Fourth Division, Edward Ferrero
   First Brigade, Joshua K. Sigfried
   Second Brigade, Henry G. Thomas

Note. During the battles around Spotsylvania Court House, Fourth Division was generally along the Fredericksburg Plank Road, guarding the trains, and was not engaged.

The artillery with Ninth Corps was the same as at the Battle of the Wilderness.

May 21, 1864, Grant resumed his movement to the left, and that day Ninth Corps, followed by Sixth Corps, marched to Stanard's Mill on the Po River. Sixth Corps was attacked that evening, and Willcox's division was sent to its assistance. That night and the next morning Ninth Corps continued its march through Guiney's Station to Bethel Church, and on May 23, 1864 it arrived at Ox Ford on the North Anna River.

As noted earlier, since May 5, 1864, Ninth Corps had been serving with the army as an independent command under the direct orders of Grant. This had not been a satisfactory arrangement, and both Burnside and Parke, his chief of staff, waived superiority of rank over Meade. At Burnside's suggestion, Grant issued an order May 24, 1864, incorporating Ninth Corps into the Army of the Potomac.

Burnside found the enemy position at Ox Ford a strong one, and he did not attempt to force a crossing. Instead, he kept Willcox's division in position north of the river, and sent the other two divisions that were with him to the south bank. Potter's division crossed at Chesterfield Bridge and moved to the right of Second Corps, which had crossed earlier, and was then placed temporarily under Hancock's orders. Crittenden's division crossed upstream at Quarles' Mill, and then moved downstream in an attempt to clear Ox Ford so that Willcox's division could cross. Crittenden attacked the enemy positions above the ford, but was soon stopped, and in a counterattack he was driven back to Quarles' Mill. He then took up a position near the mill with Samuel W. Crawford's division of Fifth Corps, and remained there under Warren's orders until the army withdrew from the south side of the North Anna. Both Potter and Crittenden recrossed the river during the night of May 26, 1864, and the next day Ninth Corps was reassembled near Mount Carmel Church.

Once more, Grant moved the army to the left, and on the afternoon of May 27, 1864, Ninth Corps started along the north side of the Pamunkey River toward Hanovertown. During the night of May 28, 1864 the corps crossed to the south side of the river at Hanovertown, and the next morning it moved out to a position between Second Corps and Fifth Corps, with its right near Haw's Shop. On the morning of May 30, 1864, Ninth Corps moved south and crossed the Totopotomoy River, and then occupied a gap that existed between Second Corps and Fifth Corps, which had also advanced to the Totopotomoy. Ninth Corps remained generally in this area until June 2, 1864, and then it moved to the northeast of Bethesda Church and formed on the right of Fifth Corps, which was in position near Cold Harbor. While this movement was in progress, the corps was strongly attacked, but Crittenden's division, which was bringing up the rear, held the enemy in check until the new line was established.

During Grant's assault at Cold Harbor on the morning of June 3, 1864, Ninth Corps also advanced, but it was some distance to the north of Eighteenth Corps, Sixth Corps, and Second Corps, which made the main assault. After the attacks had failed, Ninth Corps remained in position on the right of the army until June 12, 1864, and then Grant began the movement of the army toward the James River. On June 9, 1864, Crittenden was relieved from command of First Division, Ninth Corps at his own request, and he was succeeded by James H. Ledlie.

During the night of June 12, 1864, Ninth Corps left its entrenched lines near Bethesda Church, and marched by way of Tunstall's Station and Baltimore Cross Roads to Jones' Bridge on the Chickahominy River. It was delayed there until the morning of June 14, 1864 by the passage of Sixth Corps, and then it continued on its way past Vaiden's and Charles City Court House to Wilcox's Landing on the James River. It crossed there on the pontoon bridge during the night of June 15, 1864, and marched toward Petersburg. Ferrero's Fourth Division, which had been guarding the trains during the campaign, arrived on the James River, and crossed June 17, 1864. It too moved toward Petersburg. For details of the operations of Ninth Corps from the time it left Spotsylvania Court House until it crossed the James River, see Richmond, Virginia Campaign, 1864.

The organization of Ninth Corps during this period was as follows:

NINTH CORPS, Ambrose E. Burnside

First Division, Thomas L. Crittenden, to June 9, 1864, relieved
James H. Ledlie
First Brigade, James H. Ledlie, to June 9, 1864
  Jacob P. Gould
Second Brigade, Gilbert P. Robinson, to May 31, 1864
  Joseph M. Sudsburg, to June 4, 1864
  Ebenezer W. Peirce
Third Brigade, Elisha G. Marshall

Note 1. Crittenden was relieved from command of First Division June 8, 1864, at his own request. His reason for this action was that his division was not equal to his rank, and that many of his juniors held higher commands.
Note 2. Marshall's Provisional Brigade, First Division was redesignated June 11, 1864 as Third Brigade, First Division.

Second Division, Robert B. Potter
  First Brigade, John I. Curtin
  Second Brigade, Simon G. Griffin

Third Division, Orlando B. Willcox
  First Brigade, John F. Hartranft
  Second Brigade, William Humphrey, to about May 30, 1864
    Benjamin C. Christ

Fourth Division, Edward Ferrero
  First Brigade, Joshua K. Sigfried
  Second Brigade, Henry G. Thomas

Reserve Artillery, John Edwards, Jr.

Note. The artillery with Ninth Corps was essentially the same as at the Battle of the Wilderness.

Operations about Petersburg, June 1864. After crossing the James River on the night of June 15, 1864, Ninth Corps marched by way of Old Court House toward Petersburg, where it arrived near the enemy lines early the next morning. On the afternoon of June 16, 1864, the corps took position in front of the enemy works on the left of Second Corps, and on the extreme left of the Union line. Ferrero's division did not arrive from guarding the trains until June 19, 1864, and it was then sent to Prince George Court House to watch that area. That evening, Second Corps launched an attack on the Hare House Hill, and Simon G. Griffin's brigade of Potter's division and Hartranft's brigade of Willcox's division reported to Francis C. Barlow, and supported his division of Second Corps in the attack.

Ninth Corps was heavily engaged in the attacks at Petersburg June 17, 1864. Potter's division advanced and captured the ridge on which the Shand house stood; and Willcox's division, supported on its right by Barlow's division of Second Corps, advanced on Battery No. 14, but was stopped after suffering severe losses. That evening, Ledlie's division advanced over the same ground as that covered by Willcox's attack earlier in the day, and for a time occupied a part of the enemy line, but it was soon driven out. Benjamin C. Christ, commanding Second Brigade of Willcox's division, was wounded during the fighting of June 17, 1864, and William C. Raulston assumed command of his brigade. Elisha G. Marshall, commanding Third Brigade of Ledlie's division, was also wounded June 17, 1864, and Benjamin G. Barney assumed command of his brigade.

Ninth Corps also participated in the fighting of June 18, 1864. It advanced to a deep cut of the Norfolk and Petersburg Railroad, and was engaged there for some time before being driven out. It then moved forward again and joined in the final assault on the main enemy line that afternoon. Willcox had the lead in this attack, and was supported by Potter, but despite serious losses, these divisions were unable to enter the enemy works. During this assault, Willcox and Potter were under the personal direction of John G. Parke, Burnside's chief of staff. Raulston, who had replaced Christ in command of Second Brigade of Willcox's division the day before, was wounded, and George W. Travers assumed command of the brigade. Travers was also wounded, and was succeeded by Walter C. Newberry. John I. Curtin, commanding First Brigade of Potter's division, was wounded, and he was succeeded by Henry Pleasants.

For details of the attacks at Petersburg in June 1864, see Operations about Petersburg and Richmond, Virginia, 1864–1865, Operations of June 1864, Assaults at Petersburg, June 15–18, 1864.

The organization of Ninth Corps during the period June 15–30, 1864 was as follows:

NINTH CORPS, Ambrose E. Burnside

First Division, James H. Ledlie
  First Brigade, Jacob P. Gould
  Second Brigade, Ebenezer W. Peirce, to June 17, 1864
    Joseph H. Barnes
  Third Brigade, Elisha G. Marshall, to June 17, 1864, wounded
    Benjamin G. Barney
  Artillery, John B. Eaton
    2nd Battery (B), Maine Light Artillery, Albert F. Thomas
    14th Battery, Massachusetts Light Artillery, Joseph W. B. Wright
    27th Battery, New York Light Artillery, John B. Eaton

Second Division, Robert B. Potter
  First Brigade, John I. Curtin, to June 18, 1864, wounded
    Henry Pleasants
  Second Brigade, Simon G. Griffin
  Artillery
    11th Battery, Massachusetts Light Artillery, Edward J. Jones
    19th Battery, New York Light Artillery, Edward W. Rogers

Third Division, Orlando B. Willcox
  First Brigade, John F. Hartranft
  Second Brigade, Benjamin F. Christ, to June 17, 1864, wounded
    William C. Raulston, to June 18, 1864, wounded
    George W. Travers, June 18, 1864, wounded
    Walter C. Newberry, to June 19, 1864
    William Humphrey, assigned from First Brigade
  Artillery
    7th Battery (G), Maine Light Artillery, Albert B. Twitchell
    34th Battery, New York Light Artillery, Jacob Roemer

Fourth Division, Edward Ferrero
  First Brigade, Joshua K. Sigfried
  Second Brigade, Henry G. Thomas
  Artillery
    Battery D, Pennsylvania Light Artillery, George W. Silvis
    3rd Battery, Vermont Light Artillery, Romeo H. Start

On June 18, 1864, First Division, Ninth Corps was reorganized. The regiments of Second Brigade (except 29th Massachusetts) were transferred to First Brigade, and Third Brigade (with 29th Massachusetts added) was redesignated as Second Brigade. Third Brigade was thus discontinued in the division. On July 23, 1864, First Division was again reorganized by the transfer of regiments. The 3rd Maryland Regiment (commanded by Gilbert P. Robinson) and the 179th New York were transferred from First Brigade to Second Brigade, and the 29th Massachusetts (commanded by Joseph H. Barnes) was transferred from Second Brigade to First Brigade. That same day, William F. Bartlett relieved Jacob P. Gould in command of First Brigade, First Division. In the assault at the crater of the Petersburg Mine July 30, 1864, Bartlett was taken prisoner, and Barnes assumed command of First Brigade. Elisha G. Marshall, commanding Second Brigade, First Division, was also captured at the crater, and Robinson, as senior officer, assumed command of the brigade.

After the attack of June 18, 1864, Grant decided against any further frontal attacks on the enemy works, and he ordered the army to prepare a line of defenses in front of Petersburg, and prepare for further operations. With this order, the siege of Petersburg began. Ninth Corps entrenched on the ground that it had gained beyond the cut on the Norfolk and Petersburg Railroad. David B. Birney's Second Corps was on the right, and Warren's Fifth Corps was on the left. Second Corps was withdrawn from the line June 20, 1864, and Ninth Corps was extended to the right to the vicinity of the Hare house, where Willcox's division relieved a division of Second Corps, and connected on the right with Sixth Corps. A short time later, Eighteenth Corps relieved Sixth Corps, and June 23, 1864, John W. Turner's division of Tenth Corps relieved Willcox. This left Ledlie's division in contact with Turner. When relieved, Willcox moved to the left and relieved Crawford's division of Fifth Corps. Potter's division was on the center of the corps line. The corps remained on the line of entrenchments during July 1864. Ferrero's division occupied various positions on the left and rear of the army during the month, and one time or another it was attached to Second Corps and Fifth Corps.

Operations about Petersburg, July 1864—Battle of the Crater.

Work on a mine under the enemy works was started June 25, 1864, behind that part of the line held by Potter's division, and it was completed and ready for charging July 23, 1864. An attack was scheduled for Ninth Corps immediately after the explosion of the mine. On June 29, 1864, Ferrero's division was moved to the vicinity of Burnside's headquarters in preparation for the attack the next day. The mine was exploded under Elliott's Salient early on the morning of July 30, 1864, and this was followed by an assault at the "Crater" by Ledlie's division, with Potter's division advancing on its right. Willcox's division then moved up and attacked, and Ferrero's division followed a short time later. The Ninth Corps troops were unable to advance beyond the crater, and they were finally forced to withdraw to their former positions after suffering very heavy losses. The whole affair was badly managed, and Burnside and Ledlie were soon replaced. On August 4, 1864, Ledlie was relieved, and the next day he was succeeded in command of First Division by Julius White, who at the time was serving temporarily as Burnside's chief of staff. On the evening of August 13, 1864, Burnside was relieved from command of Ninth Corps, and John G. Parke assumed command the next day.

For details of the attacks following the explosion of the mine, see Operations About Petersburg and Richmond, Virginia, 1864–1865, Operations of July 1864, Petersburg Mine Assault.

The organization of Ninth Corps during July 1864, including the Battle of the "Crater," was as follows:

NINTH CORPS, Ambrose E. Burnside

First Division, James H. Ledlie
  First Brigade, Jacob P. Gould, to July 21, 1864
    William F. Bartlett, to July 30, 1864, captured
    Joseph H. Barnes
  Second Brigade, Ebenezer W. Peirce, to July 21, 1864
    Elisha G. Marshall, to July 30, 1864, captured
    Gilbert P. Robinson

Second Division, Robert B. Potter
  First Brigade, Henry Pleasants, to July 4, 1864
    Zenas R. Bliss, to July 11, 1864
    William H. P. Steere, to July 25, 1864
    Zenas R. Bliss
  Second Brigade, Simon G. Griffin

Third Division, Orlando B. Willcox
  First Brigade, John F. Hartranft
  Second Brigade, William Humphrey

Fourth Division, Edward Ferrero, to July 21, 1864
  Julius White, to July 29, 1864

Edward Ferrero
First Brigade, Joshua K. Sigfried
Second Brigade, Henry G. Thomas

Note. Ferrero's appointment as brigadier general was not confirmed by the Senate, and July 21, 1864, he was ordered to Washington. Then, on July 29, 1864, he was again ordered to report to Burnside.

Artillery Brigade, J. Albert Monroe

Operations about Petersburg, August 1864. During the greater part of the month of August 1864, Ninth Corps was on duty on the line of entrenchments at Petersburg. Early in the month, it was in position on the center of the line, between Eighteenth Corps on the right and Fifth Corps on the left, with its front extending to the north and south of the crater. Fifth Corps was withdrawn from the entrenchments on the night of August 14, 1864, and Ninth Corps and Eighteenth Corps extended to the left so as to occupy the entire line from the Appomattox River to the Jerusalem Plank Road. Ninth Corps was in position between the crater and the Plank Road.

Warren's Fifth Corps advanced to the Weldon Railroad August 18, 1864, and that afternoon it was engaged to the north of Globe Tavern. That night Willcox's Third Division was relieved in the trenches by Eighteenth Corps, and it then marched to Globe Tavern and reported for duty to Warren. On the morning of August 19, 1864, Gershom Mott's division of Second Corps relieved Julius White's First Division and Potter's Second Division in the entrenchments, and these two divisions also joined Warren. Parke remained in the entrenchments with Ferrero's Fourth Division.

On the afternoon of August 19, 1864, the enemy attacked the right of Fifth Corps and drove it back in confusion. White and Willcox then advanced their divisions, and after severe fighting aided Fifth Corps in recovering its former positions. Potter's division was nearby, but was not engaged. After the fighting had ended, White's division and Potter's division began to entrench on a line that extended from near the Weldon Railroad toward the position of Mott's division in the vicinity of the Strong house, near the Jerusalem Plank Road. Willcox's division was sent to the vicinity of the Blick house, near the Weldon Railroad, and it helped Warren in repulsing the Confederate attacks of August 21, 1864. That

afternoon, Willcox's division was withdrawn to the east of the railroad, where it was held in reserve.

On August 22, 1864, Parke moved his headquarters forward and resumed command of Ninth Corps. Three days later, he sent Willcox's division by way of the Jerusalem Plank Road and Shay's Tavern to support Hancock's Second Corps, which was engaged in destroying the Weldon Railroad to the south. During the afternoon of August 25, 1864, a strong enemy force attacked Hancock at Reams' Station and drove him from his position, and back toward the Plank Road. Willcox did not arrive until the fighting had ended, but he remained on the field until midnight to cover the withdrawal of Second Corps. Later that night, he returned to his former position in reserve.

August 25, 1864, Ferrero's division moved from the entrenchments toward the left, in the direction of the Weldon Railroad, and it then took position on the right of the divisions of Potter and White, connecting on its right with Mott's division near the Strong house. Two days later, Willcox relieved Ferrero's division, which then went into camp near the Gurley house. At the end of the month, Ninth Corps occupied the newly extended line of entrenchments from the Weldon Railroad, on the left, to vicinity of the Jerusalem Plank Road, on the right. Potter's division was on the left of the corps line near the railroad, White's division was on the center, and Willcox's division was on the right, next to Gershom Mott's division of Second Corps.

For details of the operations of Ninth Corps during August 1864, see Operations about Petersburg and Richmond, Virginia, 1864–1865, Operations of August 1864.

Operations about Petersburg, September 1864–October 1864. During most of September 1864, Ninth Corps remained in the positions that it had occupied at the end of August 1864. On September 1, 1864, Parke was ordered to reduce the number of divisions in the corps from four to three, and that day he issued the order for the reorganization. Julius White's First Division, which had become seriously depleted in numbers, was discontinued, and the regiments were transferred to Second Division and Third Division as follows: from First Brigade, First Division, two regiments were assigned to John I. Curtin's First Brigade, Second Division, one regiment was assigned to Simon G. Griffin's Second Brigade, Second Division, and the remaining regiments were assigned to Third Division; from Second Brigade, First Division, two regiments were assigned to Second Brigade, Second Division, and two regiments to Third Division. The regiments assigned to Third Division were organized as a new Third Brigade, Third Division, which was commanded by Napoleon B. McLaughlen. On August 28, 1864, White left the army on a leave of absence because of ill health. The reorganization was completed September 13, 1864, when First Division was reorganized by a change of designation of Willcox's Third Division to First Division, and the designation of Ferrero's Fourth Division was changed to Third Division. Fourth Division was thus discontinued.

On September 1, 1864, Parke assumed temporary command of the Army of the Potomac during the absence of Meade, and Orlando B. Willcox assumed command of Ninth Corps. John F. Hartranft was assigned command of Third Division September 2, 1864. Parke resumed command of Ninth Corps September 10, 1864, and Willcox resumed command of Third Division. Hartranft resumed command of Second Brigade.

In late September 1864, Grant ordered a new offensive against Lee's communications south and west of Petersburg, and two divisions of Ninth Corps were selected to accompany Fifth Corps on this movement. At daylight September 28, 1864, Potter's Second Division moved from its position in reserve to the Gurley house, where it remained until the advance of the army began September 3, 1864. At 4:00 P.M. September 29, 1864, Hartranft's First Division marched from its encampment just west of the Jerusalem Plank Road, and joined Potter's division at the Gurley house. Willcox assumed command of First Division the next day.

At 10:00 A.M. September 30, 1864, Parke, with his two divisions, crossed the Weldon Railroad and followed Fifth Corps along the Poplar Spring Road toward Poplar Spring Church. Later that day, Ninth Corps was engaged at the Jones farm, and was driven back to the vicinity of Oscar Pegram's farm. During the first two days of October 1864, Parke, with Willcox's First Division and Potter's Second Division, continued active operations west of the Weldon Railroad, and on the left of Fifth Corps, at Peebles' farm and Pegram's farm. On October 1,

1864, Gershom Mott's Third Division, Second Corps arrived at Peebles' farm, and was temporarily attached to Ninth Corps.

The next day, Parke advanced on the Harman Road, with his two divisions of Ninth Corps and Mott's division, and that afternoon a part of Willcox's division and a part of Mott's division were engaged near Mrs. Hart's house. That night, Parke withdrew his three divisions, and took up a defensive position on the left of Fifth Corps, extending along Arthur's Swamp from the Pegram house to the Clements house. As a result of the fighting of the past few days, Grant had succeeded in extending his line of investment at Petersburg to the left to the Clements house on the Squirrel Level Road. For details of the fighting around Poplar Spring Church, see Operations about Petersburg and Richmond, Virginia, 1864–1865, Operations of September 1864, Battle of Poplar Spring Church (Combats at Wyatt's Farm, Peebles' Farm, Chappell's House, Pegram's Farm, and Vaughan Road, Virginia).

The organization of Ninth Corps from September 13, the date when the reorganization of Ninth Corps was completed, to October 3, 1864 was as follows:

NINTH CORPS, John G. Parke

First Division, Orlando B. Willcox, to September 13, 1864, on leave
  John F. Hartranft, to September 30, 1864
  Orlando B. Willcox
  First Brigade, Benjamin C. Christ, to September 30, 1864, mustered out
    Samuel Harriman
  Second Brigade, William Humphrey, to September 30, 1864, mustered out
    John F. Hartranft
  Third Brigade, Joseph H. Barnes, to September 15, 1864
    Napoleon B. McLaughlen

Second Division, Robert B. Potter
  First Brigade, John I. Curtin
  Second Brigade, Simon G. Griffin

Third Division, Edward Ferrero
  First Brigade, Joshua K. Sigfried, to September 30, 1864, mustered out
    Ozora P. Stearns
  Second Brigade, Charles S. Russell
    Henry G. Thomas

Artillery Brigade, J. Albert Monroe

7th Battery (G), Maine Light Artillery, Albert B. Twitchell

11th Battery, Massachusetts Light Artillery, Edward J. Jones

19th Battery, New York Light Artillery, Edward W. Rogers

27th Battery, New York Light Artillery, Peter L. Moore

34th Battery, New York Light Artillery, Jacob Roemer

Battery D, Pennsylvania Light Artillery, Samuel H. Rhoads

While Parke was engaged around Poplar Spring Church, Ferrero's Third Division remained in the Petersburg entrenchments, where it held the line from near the Weldon Railroad to Fort Davis on the Jerusalem Plank Road. On October 5, 1864, Ferrero marched to Poplar Spring Church and relieved Mott's division, which returned to its former position on left of Second Corps. When this exchange was completed, Willcox's First Division and Potter's Second Division held the line from Fort Fisher at the Church Road, on the right, to Fort Cummings, near the Clements house, on the left. Potter's division was on the right, and Willcox's division was on the left, along Arthur's Swamp. Ferrero's Third Division was on the rear line from Fort Cummings to near Fort Dushane. For more detail, see Operations about Petersburg and Richmond, Virginia, 1864–1865, Operations of October 1864, Siege of Petersburg.

Late in October 1864, Grant ordered a movement from the left of the army for the purpose of cutting the Boydton Plank Road and the South Side Railroad. Hancock, with two divisions of his Second Corps, was to cross Hatcher's Run on the Vaughan Road, and then to march by way of Dabney's Mill to the Boydton Plank Road. Parke, with his Ninth Corps, was to attack the enemy entrenchments north of Hatcher's Run, and Warren's Fifth Corps was to advance between Hancock and Parke, and support Ninth Corps. The movement began early on the morning of October 27, 1864, and at that time Ninth Corps moved out from Fort Cummings on Route 673, with Willcox's First Division in the lead. Willcox passed J. Hawk's house and moved on to the Watkins farm, at the west end of Route 673, at the Duncan Road. First Division then extended to the left to connect with Fifth Corps, which was across the Duncan Road, near Hatcher's Run. Ferrero's Third Division came up on the right of Willcox, and formed in front of the Williamson

house. Potter's Second Division extended the line from the right of Ferrero to the Union line of entrenchments. Parke found the enemy works too strong for a successful attack, and, according to his instructions, he moved up close to the line and waited for Second Corps and Fifth Corps to turn the enemy right flank. Hancock and Warren were unable to advance far enough to help Parke, however, and the movement was called off. The troops then returned to their former positions. For details of this movement, see Operations about Petersburg and Richmond, Virginia, 1864–1865, Operations of October 1865, Engagement at the Boydton Plank Road (or Hatcher's Run), Virginia.

Winter of 1864–1865. In November 1864, Ninth Corps held the line of entrenchments on the left of the army. Potter's division was in the works near the Pegram house, Willcox's division extended from the left of Potter to Fort Cummings, and Ferrero's division was on the line between Fort Cummings and Fort Dushane.

On November 17, 1864, Grant decided to send the colored troops of Ferrero's Third Division, Ninth Corps to the Army of the James, and the next day the 29th and 31st regiments of United States Colored Troops were ordered to Point of Rocks, Virginia to report to Benjamin F. Butler, commander of the Army of the James. These regiments were replaced November 22, 1864 by 207th Pennsylvania and 209th Pennsylvania of Joseph H. Potter's Provisional Brigade, Army of the James. The remaining regiments of Ferrero's division left the Ninth Corps' front on the morning of November 26, 1864, and marched to Bermuda Hundred. Upon arrival there, the designation of Ferrero's Third Division, Ninth Corps was changed to Ferrero's Division, Defenses of Bermuda Hundred. On November 28, 1864, four additional Pennsylvania regiments of Potter's Provisional Brigade arrived from Bermuda Hundred, and camped in rear of the entrenchments between Fort Cummings and Fort Seibert. The regiments of Potter's former Provisional Brigade, Army of the James were organized into the Provisional Brigade, Ninth Corps, and John F. Hartranft was assigned command.

On November 29, 1864, Nelson A. Miles' First Division, Second Corps relieved the divisions of Potter and Willcox on the line of entrenchments, and they then moved to the extreme right of the line and relieved the other two divisions of Second Corps. When the transfer was completed, First Division, Ninth Corps held the line from the Appomattox River to the Norfolk and Petersburg Railroad, and Second Division from the railroad to Battery No. 24, near the Strong house, where it connected with the right of Fifth Corps. November 30, 1864, Mott's division of Second Corps relieved Hartranft's Provisional Brigade, which then moved to the rear of Ninth Corps in reserve. For additional information, see Operations about Petersburg and Richmond, Virginia, 1864–1865, Winter of 1864–1865, Siege of Petersburg.

Ninth Corps remained in position on the right of the line of entrenchments without significant change until April 1, 1865, except for brief periods during which some units of Ninth Corps participated in operations conducted by other parts of the army. On the morning of December 7, 1864, Gouverneur K. Warren, commander of Fifth Corps, led an expedition toward Hicksford (present-day Emporia), Virginia to destroy the Weldon Railroad below Stony Creek Station. Parke was ordered to organize a force from Ninth Corps to march out and be in position to assist Warren on his return. On December 8, 1865, he placed Robert B. Potter, commanding Second Division, Ninth Corps, in command of a force selected from Ninth Corps, and ordered him to have it ready to move at a moment's notice. Potter's command consisted of the reserve of his own division, that of First Division, and Hartranft's Provisional Brigade. The regiments of First Division's reserve (3rd Maryland, 57th Massachusetts, 37th Wisconsin, 109th New York, and 60th Ohio) were organized into a provisional brigade under the command of Gilbert P. Robinson of the 3rd Maryland. On the afternoon of December 10, 1864, Potter marched with his command about twenty miles to the left to Hawkinsville, near the Nottoway River, to await the arrival of Warren. During the absence of the reserve of Ninth Corps, Henry W. Benham took their place temporarily with the reserve from City Point. Warren joined Potter December 11, 1864, and the next day he continued on to the camps of Fifth Corps. Potter returned to Ninth Corps December 13, 1864, and the next day Robinson's Provisional Brigade was discontinued. For details of Warren's expedition, see Operations

about Petersburg and Richmond, Virginia, 1864–1865, Winter of 1864–1865, Warren's Expedition to Hicksford, Virginia.

On December 15, 1864, Hartranft's Provisional Brigade was organized into a division of two brigades, and was designated as Third Division, Ninth Corps. First Brigade was commanded by Charles W. Diven, and consisted of 200th, 208th, and 209th Pennsylvania regiments. Second Brigade was commanded by Joseph A. Mathews, and consisted of 205th, 207th, and 211th Pennsylvania regiments.

February 5, 1865, Hartranft's Third Division was sent to the left to support Andrew A. Humphreys' Second Corps, which was attacked that day near Armstrong's Mill on Hatcher's Run. Hartranft remained under Humphreys' orders until the evening of February 10, 1865, and then returned with his division to his former camps. For details of Humphreys' engagement, see Operations about Petersburg and Richmond, Virginia, 1864–1865, Winter of 1864–1865, Battle of Hatcher's Run (Dabney's Mill, Armstrong's Mill, Rowanty Creek, or Vaughan Road), Virginia.

The organization of Ninth Corps at the end of February 1865 was as follows:

NINTH CORPS, John G. Parke

First Division, Orlando B. Willcox
    First Brigade, Samuel Harriman
    Second Brigade, Byron M. Cutcheon
    Third Brigade, Gilbert P. Robinson

Note. Willcox was on leave from February 20, 1864 to March 7, 1864, and Napoleon B. McLaughlen, commander of Third Brigade, commanded the division temporarily during his absence.

Second Division, Robert B. Potter
    First Brigade, John I. Curtin
    Second Brigade, Simon G. Griffin

Third Division, John F. Hartranft
    First Brigade, Alfred B. McCalmont
    Second Brigade, Joseph A. Mathews

Note. Third Division was reorganized December 15, 1864 from the regiments of Hartranft's Provisional Brigade.

Artillery Brigade, John C. Tidball

Note. The batteries with the Artillery Brigade were the same as during the Appomattox Campaign, which are given below.

On the morning of March 25, 1865, a Confederate force under John B. Gordon launched a sudden attack on the line of entrenchments held by Willcox's division. It succeeded in capturing Fort Stedman and the adjacent works, and for a time held the main Union line from Battery No. 9 to Fort Haskell. Willcox continued to resist, however, and with help from Hartranft's division, which moved up from its reserve position, soon drove the enemy from the captured works and reestablished the broken line. Four days later, on March 29, 1865, Grant began his final offensive at Petersburg. For details of the attack at Fort Stedman, see Operations about Petersburg and Richmond, Virginia, 1864–1865, Winter of 1864–1865, Assault at Fort Stedman, Virginia.

The organization of Ninth Corps at Fort Stedman March 25, 1865 was as follows:

NINTH CORPS, John G. Parke

First Division, Orlando B. Willcox
    First Brigade, Samuel Harriman
    Second Brigade, Ralph Ely
    Third Brigade, Napoleon B. McLaughlen, captured
        Gilbert P. Robinson

Note 1. First Brigade was not actively engaged in the attack at Fort Stedman.
Note 2. Ely assumed command of Second Brigade March 10, 1865.

Second Division, Robert B. Potter
    First Brigade, John I. Curtin
    Second Brigade, Simon G. Griffin

Note. Second Division was not engaged.

Third Division, John F. Hartranft
    First Brigade, Charles W. Diven, wounded
        William H. H. McCall
    Second Brigade, Joseph A. Mathews

Artillery, John C. Tidball

Appomattox Campaign, Virginia, March 29, 1865–April 9, 1865. Grant opened his spring offensive at Petersburg by sending Humphreys' Second Corps, Warren's Fifth Corps, and Philip H. Sheridan's cavalry to the south and west of the city to attack the right of Lee's defensive line.

Horatio G. Wright's Sixth Corps, Parke's Ninth Corps, and Edward O. C. Ord's Army of the James were left on the line of entrenchments, with orders to be prepared to take advantage of any successes of the flanking column. When Grant learned of Sheridan's victory at Five Forks April 1, 1865, he ordered an assault on the enemy works, all along the line, for the following morning.

At 4:40 A.M. April 2, 1865, Parke launched an attack by Ninth Corps from in front of Fort Stedman. Potter's division advanced on the left of the Jerusalem Plank Road, and Hartranft's division on the right of the road. Samuel Harriman's First Brigade of Willcox's division was attached to Hartranft's command for this attack. The other two brigades of Willcox's division demonstrated on their fronts during the day. Parke's divisions captured a part of the enemy's outer line, but they were unable to reach the inner line. Potter was wounded in the attack, and was succeeded in command of Second Division by Simon G. Griffin. Walter Harriman assumed command of Griffin's Second Brigade.

Reinforcements were ordered to Ninth Corps, and two brigades under Henry W. Benham arrived from City Point shortly after noon. Charles H. T. Collis, with his Independent Brigade, Army of the Potomac, reported to Griffin, and moved into the captured works on the right of Fort Mahone. Wesley Brainerd, with a provisional brigade composed of engineers and mounted and dismounted cavalry from City Point, also came up, and was placed in reserve by Benham, in position to support Willcox's division. Later in the afternoon, Joseph E. Hamblin's brigade of Sixth Corps joined Ninth Corps, and reported to Hartranft, who placed it in the captured trenches near Fort Mahone.

During the day, Sixth Corps and John Gibbon's Twenty-Fourth Corps, Army of the James (less Charles Devens' division) attacked on the left of Ninth Corps and broke through the enemy line. After clearing the lines on their front, they moved north and advanced close to Petersburg on the south and west. That night Lee evacuated Petersburg and Richmond, and withdrew toward Amelia Court House. When troops of Ninth Corps advanced early on the morning of April 3, 1865, they found that the enemy had departed, and they entered Petersburg at 4:00 A.M. Troops of Ralph Ely's Second Brigade of Willcox's division were the first, or among the first, to arrive, and Ely received the formal surrender.

Later that afternoon, Hamblin's brigade of Sixth Corps, and Samuel Harriman's brigade of Willcox's division, then temporarily attached to Hartranft's division, were ordered to join their proper commands. Collis' Independent Brigade, then serving with Griffin's division, was ordered to return to City Point. Benham remained with the engineers during most of April 3, 1865, rebuilding bridges across the Appomattox River, and he returned to City Point the next day.

Parke left Willcox's division to garrison Petersburg, and he marched through the city with the divisions of Potter and Hartranft and followed Sixth Corps along the River Road in pursuit of Lee's retreating army. Parke continued to follow Sixth Corps until the afternoon of April 4, 1865, and he was then ordered to cross over to the Cox Road, and march westward on that road, guarding the trains and picketing the South Side Railroad in rear of the army. Willcox remained at Petersburg only two days, and was then relieved on the morning of April 5, 1865 by Edward Ferrero's Infantry Division, Defenses of Bermuda Hundred. George L. Hartsuff, commander of the Defenses of Bermuda Hundred, assumed command of the United States Forces at Petersburg April 5, 1865, and relieved Willcox in command of the city. When relieved, Willcox marched with his division to Sutherland's Station April 5, 1865, and joined the other two divisions of Ninth Corps on the South Side Railroad.

As Grant's army moved westward in pursuit of Lee, Ninth Corps followed along the railroad. Willcox's division continued to hold the line from Petersburg to Sutherland's Station until April 6, 1865, and he was then relieved by troops of Hartsuff's command. By April 9, 1865, the day of Lee's surrender at Appomattox Court House, Willcox's division held the road from Sutherland's Station to Wellville Depot, Hartranft's division was at Nottoway Court House, and Simon G. Griffin's Second Division was at Burkeville. John I. Curtin's First Brigade of Griffin's division advanced to Farmville the next day.

The organization of Ninth Corps during the Appomattox Campaign was as follows:

NINTH CORPS, John G. Parke

First Division, Orlando B. Willcox
  First Brigade, Samuel Harriman
  Second Brigade, Ralph Ely
  Third Brigade, Gilbert P. Robinson, to April 2, 1865
    James Bintliff

Second Division, Robert B. Potter, to April 2, 1865, wounded
  Simon G. Griffin
  First Brigade, John I. Curtin
  Second Brigade, Simon G. Griffin, to April 2, 1865
    Walter Harriman

Third Division, John F. Hartranft
  First Brigade, William H. H. McCall
    Alfred B. McCalmont
  Second Brigade, Joseph A. Mathews

Artillery Brigade, John C. Tidball
  7th Battery (G), Maine Light Artillery, Adelbert B. Twitchell
  11th Battery, Massachusetts Light Artillery, Edward J. Jones
  19th Battery, New York Light Artillery, Edward W. Rogers
  27th Battery, New York Light Artillery, John B. Eaton
  34th Battery, New York Light Artillery, Jacob Roemer
  Battery D, Pennsylvania Light Artillery, Samuel H. Rhoads

NINTH CORPS
(In the Department of Washington)

After Lee's surrender at Appomattox Court House April 9, 1865, Ninth Corps continued to guard the South Side Railroad until it was ordered to Washington, D.C. April 20, 1865. That day and the next it was relieved by Fifth Corps, and it then marched to City Point to embark for Alexandria. At Petersburg, April 22, 1865, while the corps was on the march to City Point, Joseph J. Bartlett, formerly commander of First Division, Fifth Corps, relieved Simon G. Griffin in command of Second Division, Ninth Corps. April 24, 1865, while the transfer of the corps was in progress, Ninth Corps was detached from the Army of the Potomac, and was placed under the orders of Christopher C. Augur, commander of the Department of Washington, Twenty-Second Corps.

First Division disembarked at Alexandria April 22–24, 1865, and encamped at Fowles' farm, near Alexandria, on the Old Fairfax Road. Third Division arrived April 25, 1865, and Second Division arrived April 26, 1865, and both encamped near Alexandria. On April 26, 1865, Willcox's First Division marched through Washington to Tennallytown, and established camp there. While at Tennallytown, detached regiments of the division guarded the city of Washington. Also on April 26, 1865, Willcox was assigned command of the District of Washington, and his First Division, Ninth Corps was included in that district. That same day, Parke was announced as commander of the District of Alexandria, and Bartlett's Second Division and Hartranft's Third Division were included in that district.

Ninth Corps returned briefly to the Army of the Potomac May 23, 1865 to march with that organization in the Grand Review in Washington, but it then resumed its duties in the Department of Washington. The corps was discontinued July 27, 1865. For additional information about Ninth Corps while in the Department of Washington in April 1865, see Department of Washington, February 2, 1863–March 16, 1869.

The organization of Ninth Corps from April 10, 1865 to July 27, 1865 was as follows:

NINTH CORPS, John G. Parke, to June 7, 1865
    Orlando B. Willcox, to June 26, 1865
    John G. Parke

Note. Parke was in temporary command of the Department of Washington June 7–26, 1865.

First Division, Orlando B. Willcox, to June 7, 1865
    Napoleon B. McLaughlen, to June 17, 1865
    William F. Bartlett, to June 26, 1865
    First Brigade, Samuel Harriman, to July 17, 1865
        John Green
    Second Brigade, Ralph Ely, to June 11, 1865
        William H. Telford, to July 1, 1865
        Samuel K. Schwenck
    Third Brigade, James Bintliff, to April 24, 1865
        Elisha G. Marshall, to June 17, 1865
        Napoleon B. McLaughlen

Note. First Brigade and Second Brigade were discontinued by muster out in July 1865.

Second Division, Simon G. Griffin, to April 22, 1865
    Joseph J. Bartlett, May 3, 1865
    Simon G. Griffin
    First Brigade, John I. Curtin, to May 3, 1865
        Sumner Carruth, to June 9, 1865
        Isaac F. Brannon, to July 8, 1865
        John I. Curtin
    Second Brigade, Walter Harriman, to April 22, 1865
        Simon G. Griffin, to May 3, 1865
        Herbert B. Titus, to June 11, 1865
        Stephen M. Weld, Jr.

Note 1. Joseph J. Bartlett was assigned command of the District of the Patuxent May 3, 1865.

Note 2. Second Brigade was discontinued by muster out in July 1865.

Third Division, John F. Hartranft, to May 3, 1865, on detached service
    John I. Curtin, to July 8, 1865
    First Brigade, Alfred B. McCalmont, to June 1, 1865
    Second Brigade, Joseph A. Mathews, to June 2, 1865

Note. Third Division was discontinued by muster out of regiments in June 1865.

COMMANDERS OF NINTH CORPS

Ambrose E. Burnside	July 22, 1862 to September 3, 1862
Jesse L. Reno	September 3, 1862 to September 14, 1862, killed
Jacob D. Cox	September 14, 1862 to October 8, 1862
Orlando B. Willcox	October 8, 1862 to January 16, 1863
John Sedgwick	January 16, 1863 to February 4, 1863
William F. Smith	February 4, 1863 to March 8, 1863
Orlando B. Willcox	March 8, 1863 to March 17, 1863
Ambrose E. Burnside	March 17, 1863 to March 19, 1863
John G. Parke	March 19, 1863 to April 4, 1863
Orlando B. Willcox	April 4, 1863 to June 5, 1863
John G. Parke	June 5, 1863 to August 25, 1863
Robert B. Potter	August 25, 1863 to January 18, 1864
Orlando B. Willcox	January 18, 1864 to January 26, 1864

John G. Parke	January 26, 1864 to March 16, 1864
Orlando B. Willcox	March 16, 1864 to April 13, 1864
Ambrose E. Burnside	April 13, 1864 to August 13, 1864
Orlando B. Willcox	August 13, 1864 to August 14, 1864
John G. Parke	August 14, 1864 to September 1, 1864
Orlando B. Willcox	September 1, 1864 to September 10, 1864
John G. Parke	September 10, 1864 to December 30, 1864
Orlando B. Willcox	December 30, 1864 to January 12, 1865
John G. Parke	January 12, 1865 to January 24, 1865
Orlando B. Willcox	January 24, 1865 to February 2, 1865
John G. Parke	February 2, 1865 to February 22, 1865
Robert B. Potter	February 22, 1865 to March 1, 1865
John G. Parke	March 1, 1865 to June 7, 1865
Orlando B. Willcox	June 7, 1865 to June 26, 1865
John G. Parke	June 26, 1865 to July 27, 1865

Note. Parke left the corps August 25, 1863 on sick leave. When he returned September 15, 1863, he was assigned command of Ninth Corps, but was then reassigned as chief of staff to Burnside.

TENTH CORPS, DEPARTMENT OF THE SOUTH

Tenth Corps was constituted September 3, 1862, to consist of the troops in the Department of the South. Ormsby M. Mitchell was assigned command, with headquarters at Hilton Head. At that time the United States forces in the department did not have the usual corps organization of divisions and brigades, but were serving as garrisons of the various posts in South Carolina, Georgia, and Florida. These commands were as follows: United States Forces Beaufort, South Carolina, Tenth Corps; United States Forces Hilton Head, South Carolina; United States Forces Savannah River (Headquarters at Fort Pulaski), Georgia; and garrisons at Saint Augustine, Fernandina, and Key

West in Florida. For additional information about affairs in the Department of the South before the organization of Tenth Corps, see Department of the South, Part I, South Carolina Expedition (Thomas W. Sherman), and also Department of the South, Part II, Department of the South.

Mitchell became ill October 27, 1862 (died October 30, 1862 at Beaufort), and John M. Brannan assumed command of the Department of the South, with headquarters at Hilton Head. The organization of the troops in the Department of the South at the end of October 1862 was as follows:

DEPARTMENT OF THE SOUTH, TENTH CORPS, John M. Brannan

Hilton Head and Fort Seward, South Carolina, Alfred H. Terry
Beaufort, South Carolina, Tilghman H. Good
Fort Pulaski, Georgia, William B. Barton
Grahams' Plantation, John G. Thayer
Fort Clinch, Florida, James E. Place
Old Town, Florida, Hiram Ferrand
Key West, Florida, Joseph S. Morgan
Fernandina, Florida, Rishworth Rich
Saint Augustine, Florida, Haldimand S. Putnam

Truman Seymour assumed command of the United States Forces at Beaufort, South Carolina December 26, 1862, and the designation of his command was changed to United States Forces, Port Royal Island.

There were several expeditions, minor engagements, and skirmishes during the winter, but no major operations. Early in 1863, however, preparations were begun for operations to secure possession of Charleston Harbor. The plan adopted called for the use of the troops of Tenth Corps, Department of the South, in cooperation with the navy, to reduce the Confederate batteries on Morris Island, and thus force the evacuation of Fort Sumter. If this could be accomplished, the Federals would control Charleston Harbor.

On January 20, 1863, David Hunter assumed command of the Department of the South, and late in the month, Tenth Corps was strongly reinforced when Henry M. Naglee's Second Division and Orris S. Ferry's Third Division, both under the command of John G. Foster, were detached from Eighteenth Corps, Department of North Carolina, and were sent to the Department of the South. These troops disembarked at Saint Helena Island, and remained there awaiting transfer to Morris Island. The operations at Charleston Harbor were delayed for several weeks, however, and March 10, 1863, Foster turned over the command of Detachment Eighteenth Corps to Henry M. Naglee and returned to North Carolina. Charles A. Heckman assumed command of Naglee's division. In March 1863, while on Saint Helena Island, Naglee's command was organized into two divisions as follows:

First Division, Detachment Eighteenth Corps, Orris S. Ferry
First Brigade, Thomas G. Stevenson
Second Brigade, William W. H. Davis

Note. In late March 1863, Stevenson's Second Brigade, Fourth Division, Eighteenth Corps was also transferred from the Department of North Carolina to Saint Helena Island, and was assigned to First Division, Detachment Eighteenth Corps as First Brigade.

Second Division, Detachment Eighteenth Corps, Charles A. Heckman
First Brigade, Jacob J. DeForest
Second Brigade, Joshua B. Howell
Third Brigade, Thomas O. Osborn

In addition to the above two divisions, Alfred H. Terry also commanded a force of division strength at Hilton Head.

Naglee's and Ferry's divisions did not return to the Department of North Carolina, but were broken up by Hunter, and the units were incorporated into Tenth Corps, Department of the South.

Operations at Charleston Harbor, April 1863– September 1863. During the spring of 1863, the administration waited impatiently for operations to begin at Charleston Harbor, and finally, on June 4, 1863, Quincy A. Gillmore was ordered to relieve Hunter in command of the Department of the South, and instructed him to move on the defenses of Charleston Harbor as soon as possible. Gillmore began preparations at once, and these were continued until July 6, 1863, when approximately 11,000 troops were assembled and ready to move.

Because the organization, as well as the changes in organization, of Gillmore's forces during the summer of 1863 was complex, only a general summary is given here. For a more detailed description of the organization and operations of Gillmore's

command, see Department of the South, Part III, Department of the South, Tenth Corps.

Folly Island was selected as the assembly point for the attack on Morris Island, and the troops there were first organized as follows:

Folly Island, Israel Vogdes
First Brigade, Haldimand S. Putnam
Second Brigade, Joshua B. Howell

In addition to these two brigades, four regiments under George C. Strong soon arrived on the island. July 5, 1863, Truman Seymour was assigned command of all troops on Folly Island and adjacent islands, and his command was designated as United States Forces Folly Island. That same day, Alfred H. Terry's division was relieved from duty at Hilton Head and was transferred to Folly Island. On July 6, 1863, the troops on Folly Island and on the adjacent islands were organized into divisions as follows:

First Division, Alfred H. Terry
First Brigade, Thomas G. Stevenson
Second Brigade, William W. H. Davis
Third Brigade (colored), James Montgomery

Second Division, Truman Seymour
First Brigade, Israel Vogdes
Second Brigade, George C. Strong

July 10, 1863, Seymour's division crossed onto Morris Island, and Terry moved his division to James Island on a demonstration to divert attention from Seymour's advance. The next day, Seymour launched an unsuccessful attack on Battery Wagner, and July 14, 1863, he reorganized his division as follows:

Seymour's Division, Morris Island, Truman Seymour
First Brigade, George C. Strong
Second Brigade, Haldimand S. Putnam
Third Brigade, Thomas G. Stevenson

A second attack on Battery Wagner July 18, 1863 was repulsed, and Gillmore then began siege operations. Seymour was wounded in the attack of July 18, 1863, and his division was incorporated into Terry's division. Terry assumed command of the troops on Morris Island the next day. Further operations at Charleston Harbor after the assault of July 18, 1863 consisted largely of advancing siege lines and bombardments of Fort Sumter. This was continued until September 7, 1863, when the enemy evacuated Battery Gregg and Battery Wagner.

The organization of the troops of Tenth Corps at the end of July 1863 was as follows:

MORRIS ISLAND, Alfred H. Terry

Terry's Division
    First Brigade, Israel Vogdes
    Second Brigade, Joshua B. Howell
    Third Brigade, Thomas G. Stevenson
    Artillery
        Battery B, 3rd New York Light Artillery (one section), Edward A. Wild
        Battery F, 3rd New York Light Artillery, Paul Birchmeyer
        Battery B, 1st United States Artillery, Guy V. Henry
        Battery C, 1st United States Artillery (detachment), James E. Wilson
        Battery E, 3rd United States Artillery, John R. Myrick

FOLLY ISLAND, William W. H. Davis

Davis' Brigade, William W. H. Davis
Unbrigaded regiments
Artillery
    1st Battery, Connecticut Light Artillery, Alfred P. Rockwell
    Battery B, 3rd New York Light Artillery, James E. Ashcroft
    Battery F, 3rd New York Light Artillery, Paul Birchmeyer

HILTON HEAD ISLAND, Edwin Metcalf

Note. The troops on Hilton Head Island consisted of unbrigaded regiments and detachments of infantry regiments, two companies of cavalry, and four companies of 3rd Rhode Island Heavy Artillery.

PORT ROYAL ISLAND, Rufus Saxton

Note. The troops on Port Royal Island consisted of unbrigaded regiments of infantry, some cavalry, John S. Gibbs' Battery D, 1st United States Artillery, and Loomis L. Langdon's Battery M, 1st United States Artillery.

Fernandina, Harris M. Plaisted

Fort Pulaski, William Ames

Saint Augustine, Joseph R. Hawley

Early in August 1863, three brigades, commanded by Samuel L. Alford, Robert S. Foster, and Edward

A. Wild, were transferred from the Department of Virginia and North Carolina to Folly Island, and these were organized into a division commanded by Israel Vogdes. Also during the period August 6–15, 1863, George H. Gordon's First Division, Eleventh Corps, Army of the Potomac was transferred from Warrenton Junction, Virginia to Folly Island. At the end of August 1863, the troops on Folly Island and Morris Island were organized as follows:

MORRIS ISLAND, Alfred H. Terry

Terry's Division, Alfred H. Terry
    First Brigade, Henry R. Guss
    Second Brigade, Joshua B. Howell
    Third Brigade, Thomas G. Stevenson
    Fourth Brigade (colored), James Montgomery
    Davis' Brigade, William W. H. Davis
    Artillery
        Battery B, 3rd New York Light Artillery, James E. Ashcroft
        Battery F, 3rd New York Light Artillery, Paul Birchmeyer
        Company B, 3rd Rhode Island Heavy Artillery, Albert E. Greene
        Company C, 3rd Rhode Island Heavy Artillery, Charles R. Brayton
        Company D, 3rd Rhode Island Heavy Artillery, Richard G. Shaw
        Company H, 3rd Rhode Island Heavy Artillery, Augustus W. Colwell
        Company I, 3rd Rhode Island Heavy Artillery, Charles G. Strahan
        Company M, 3rd Rhode Island Heavy Artillery, Joseph J. Comstock, Jr.
        Battery B, 1st United States Artillery, Guy V. Henry
        Battery C, 1st United States Artillery (detachment), James E. Wilson
        Battery E, 3rd United States Artillery, John R. Myrick

NORTH END OF FOLLY ISLAND

Vogdes' Division, Israel Vogdes
    Alford's Brigade, Samuel M. Alford
    Foster's Brigade, Robert S. Foster
    Wild's Brigade (African Brigade), Edward A. Wild
    1st Battery, Connecticut Light Artillery, Alfred P. Rockwell

SOUTH END OF FOLLY ISLAND

Gordon's Division, George H. Gordon
    First Brigade, Alexander Schimmelfennig
    Second Brigade, Adelbert Ames

In addition to the above, there were comparatively large forces at Port Royal Island, under the command of Rufus Saxton, and at Hilton Head Island, under the command of De Witt C. Strawbridge. There were also garrisons at Fort Pulaski, Fernandina, and Saint Augustine.

Seymour's Florida Expedition, February 5–22, 1864. December 5, 1863, Seymour was assigned command of Hilton Head Island, Saint Helena Island, Fort Pulaski, and Tybee Island. Joshua B. Howell's brigade of Terry's Division at Morris Island was ordered to report to Seymour at Hilton Head. At the end of December 1863, the troops of Tenth Corps, Department of the South were posted as follows:

Seymour's Command, Truman Seymour
  Post of Hilton Head, William B. Barton
  Howell's Brigade, Hilton Head Island, Joshua B. Howell
  Saint Helena Island, Joseph R. Hawley
  Fort Pulaski and Tybee Island, Edwin Metcalf

Morris Island, Alfred H. Terry
  Terry's Division, Alfred H. Terry

Folly Island
  Vogdes' Division, Israel Vogdes
  Gordon's Division, George H. Gordon

Port Royal Island, Rufus Saxton
Fernandina, Henry R. Guss
Saint Augustine, Francis A. Osborn

Beginning on February 5, 1864, Seymour led an expedition to Florida to establish Federal control over the northeastern part of the state. Seymour's command consisted of the following:

Barton's Brigade, William B. Barton
Montgomery's Brigade (colored), James Montgomery
Hawley's Brigade, Joseph B. Hawley
Henry's Mounted Brigade, Guy V. Henry
Artillery, John Hamilton
  Battery E, 3rd United States Artillery, John R. Myrick
  Battery M, 1st United States Artillery, Loomis L. Langdon
  Company C, 3rd Rhode Island Heavy Artillery, Henry H. Metcalf

Seymour occupied Jacksonville, Florida February 7, 1864, and then moved west about twenty miles to the rail junction of Baldwin. He then sent out an expedition to the vicinity of Lake City and Gainesville, and by February 14, 1864 had concentrated his force at Baldwin. Seymour returned to the vicinity of Jacksonville, and February 15, 1864, he was assigned command of the newly constituted District of Florida, Department of the South. On February 20, 1864, Seymour advanced with his army toward Sanderson, and that day he was defeated at the Battle of Olustee (or Ocean Pond). He then withdrew and established his headquarters at Jacksonville. The principal posts of the District of Florida were Jacksonville, Fernandina, Yellow Bluff, Saint Augustine, Picolata, and Palatka. For details of Seymour's activities in Florida, see Department of the South, Part III, Department of the South, Tenth Corps, District of Florida (Seymour's Florida Expedition).

After Seymour's defeat at Olustee, he was strongly reinforced with troops transferred from Folly Island. On February 25, 1864, the troops of the District of Florida were organized into two divisions as follows:

DISTRICT OF FLORIDA, Truman Seymour

First Division, Adelbert Ames
  First Brigade, William H. Noble
  Second Brigade, Joseph R. Hawley
  Third Brigade, Milton S. Littlefield
  Barton's Brigade, William B. Barton

Second Division, Israel Vogdes
  First Brigade, Robert S. Foster, to February 28, 1864
    Jeremiah C. Drake
  Second Brigade (colored), Benjamin C. Tilghman
  Third Brigade (colored), James Montgomery

There was little further activity by the troops of Tenth Corps in the Department of the South. In April 1864, when Ulysses S. Grant ordered Gillmore to send all available troops of Tenth Corps to Virginia to be reorganized for participation in the spring campaign against Richmond, most of the troops left the department.

COMMANDERS OF TENTH CORPS, DEPARTMENT OF THE SOUTH

Ormsby S. Mitchell September 3, 1862 to October 27, 1862

John M. Brannan   October 27, 1862 to January 20, 1863
David Hunter   January 20, 1863 to June 12, 1863
Quincy A. Gillmore June 12, 1863 to May 1, 1864

Note. Mitchell relinquished command October 27, 1862 because of illness, and he died October 30, 1862.

TENTH CORPS, ARMY OF THE JAMES

In the spring of 1864, Ulysses S. Grant planned to move southward with the Army of the Potomac from near Culpeper Court House toward Richmond, Virginia. As a part of this operation, he ordered Benjamin F. Butler, commander of the Department of Virginia and North Carolina, to organize a field force for the purpose of operating against Richmond at the same time from the south side of the James River. On April 4, 1864, Grant also directed Quincy A. Gillmore, commander of the Department of the South, to send all available troops of Tenth Corps to the Department of Virginia and North Carolina to reinforce Butler's Eighteenth Corps. These two corps, together with August V. Kautz's Cavalry Division of the Department of Virginia and North Carolina, were to constitute Butler's Army of the James. April 21, 1864, William F. Smith was assigned command at Yorktown, Virginia, and was ordered to take charge of the troops of Tenth Corps and Eighteenth Corps that were assembling in the vicinity and to supervise their reorganization.

During the period April 14–29, 1864, about 8,000 men of Tenth Corps were transferred from the various posts and districts of the Department of the South to Gloucester Point, Virginia, where they were reorganized for the coming campaign. Gillmore, who commanded Tenth Corps and the Department of the South, remained behind to look after the forwarding of troops, and April 17, 1864, he sent Alfred H. Terry to Virginia to report to Butler and take charge of the reorganization of Tenth Corps. During the period April 20–26, 1864, Gillmore also sent to Virginia Samuel M. Alford, Adelbert Ames, John W. Turner, Robert S. Foster, and Joshua B. Howell to aid in the reorganization of Tenth Corps and to assume command of brigades and divisions in the new organization. Gillmore

finally relinquished command of the Department of the South May 1, 1864 and left for Fort Monroe to join Tenth Corps.

On April 30, 1864, the organization of Tenth Corps, Army of the James at Gloucester Point was as follows:

TENTH CORPS, Alfred H. Terry, to May 4, 1864
   Quincy A. Gillmore

First Division, Robert S. Foster, to May 4, 1864
   Alfred H. Terry
   First Brigade, Francis B. Pond, to May 2, 1864
      Joshua B. Howell
   Second Brigade, Harris M. Plaisted
   Third Brigade, Joseph R. Hawley
   Artillery, Alfred P. Rockwell
      1st Battery, Connecticut Light Artillery, Alfred P. Rockwell
      5th Battery, New Jersey Light Artillery, Zenas C. Warren

Note 1. First Brigade was organized from Howell's Brigade, United States Forces at Hilton Head, South Carolina. Howell rejoined his brigade and relieved Pond May 2, 1864.

Note 2. Plaisted's brigade was organized from regiments of the District of Florida; from the post of Saint Augustine, Florida; and from Morris Island, South Carolina. The designation of Second Brigade was changed to Third Brigade, First Division May 2, 1864.

Note 3. Hawley's Third Brigade was organized from Hawley's Brigade, District of Florida. The designation of Third Brigade was changed to Second Brigade, First Division May 2, 1864.

Note 4. Robert S. Foster was announced as Gillmore's chief of staff May 6, 1864.

Second Division, Samuel M. Alford, to May 2, 1864
   John W. Turner
   First Brigade, Guy V. Henry, to May 2, 1864
      Samuel M. Alford
   Second Brigade, William B. Barton
   Artillery Brigade, George T. Woodbury
      4th Battery, New Jersey Light Artillery, George T. Woodbury
      Battery B, 1st United States Artillery, Samuel S. Elder
      Battery D, 1st United States Artillery, John S. Gibbs

Note 1. Henry's First Brigade was organized from regiments of Henry's Light Brigade, District of Florida, and three regiments from the Northern District, Department of the South.

Note 2. Barton's Second Brigade was organized from Barton's Brigade, District of Florida.

Third Division, Adelbert Ames
  First Brigade, Richard White
  Second Brigade, John D. Rust, to May 2, 1864
    Jeremiah C. Drake
  Artillery Brigade, Alger M. Wheeler
    33rd Battery, New York Light Artillery, Alger M. Wheeler
    Battery E, 3rd United States Artillery, Joseph E. Sanger

Note 1. First Brigade was organized from regiments from Morris Island, South Carolina; Beaufort, South Carolina; Fernandina, Florida; and Robert S. Foster's Brigade, District of Florida.

Note 2. Second Brigade was organized from Foster's First Brigade, Vogdes' Second Division, District of Florida.

At Bermuda Hundred (Operations against the Railroads, and Engagement at Drewry's Bluff), May 6, 1864–May 27, 1864. On the night of May 4, 1864, the Army of the James, consisting of Tenth Corps and Eighteenth Corps and commanded by Benjamin F. Butler, embarked and moved up the James River to Bermuda Hundred. The army was ashore by May 6, 1864, and that day it advanced and took position at a narrow part of Bermuda Hundred Neck, between the James and the Appomattox rivers. Gillmore's Tenth Corps was placed on the right of this line, next to the James River, and Eighteenth Corps on the left.

On May 7 and 9, 1864, Tenth Corps advanced with the army against the Richmond and Petersburg Railroad, and then on May 12–16, 1864, it took part in Butler's advance along the railroad toward Richmond. It was engaged at the Battle of Drewry's Bluff, and then retired with the army to the lines at Bermuda Hundred. For details of these operations, see Army of the James, Operations against the Railroads, and also Engagement at Drewry's Bluff.

The organization of Tenth Corps at Drewry's Bluff May 12–16, 1864 was as follows:

TENTH CORPS, Quincy A. Gillmore

First Division, Alfred H. Terry
  First Brigade, Joshua B. Howell
  Second Brigade, Joseph R. Hawley
  Third Brigade, Harris M. Plaisted
  Artillery, Alfred P. Rockwell
    1st Battery, Connecticut Light Artillery, Alfred P. Rockwell
    5th Battery, New Jersey Light Artillery, Zenas C. Warren

Second Division, John W. Turner
  First Brigade, Samuel M. Alford
  Second Brigade, William B. Barton
  Artillery Brigade, George T. Woodbury
    4th Battery, New Jersey Light Artillery, George T. Woodbury
    Battery B, 1st United States Artillery, Samuel S. Elder
    Battery D, 1st United States Artillery, John S. Gibbs

Third Division, Adelbert Ames
  First Brigade, Richard White, to May 16, 1864, captured
    Louis Bell, to May 18, 1864
    Henry R. Guss
  Second Brigade, Jeremiah C. Drake
  Artillery, Alger M. Wheeler
    33rd Battery, New York Light Artillery, Alger M. Wheeler
    Battery C, Rhode Island Heavy Artillery, Charles R. Brayton

Note. Only White, with two regiments of his brigade of Third Division, accompanied Tenth Corps to Drewry's Bluff. The rest of the division covered the rear of Butler's army. Two regiments under Drake were sent to reinforce Godfrey Weitzel's division of Eighteenth Corps May 16, 1864.

After the engagement at Drewry's Bluff, Tenth Corps and Eighteenth Corps returned to the entrenched lines at Bermuda Hundred. Tenth Corps again occupied the right of the line, with Terry's division on the right and Ames' division on the left. Turner's division was in reserve. The enemy closely followed Butler's retiring army, and established a strong line of works in front of the defenses of Bermuda Hundred. On May 20, 1864, they launched a strong attack on the pickets of Ames' Third Division and a part of Terry's First Division. They captured the advanced line of rifle pits, but these were retaken on Terry's front by Howell's reinforced First Brigade.

With the Army of the Potomac at Cold Harbor, May 27, 1864–June 15, 1864. On May 27, 1864, Turner's Second Division and Ames' Third Division were detached from Tenth Corps, and were assigned to duty with William F. Smith's Eighteenth Corps. Smith was under orders to join the Army of the Potomac, which was then approaching Cold Harbor. During the night of May 28, 1864, the two divisions of Tenth Corps embarked with Eighteenth

Corps for White House on the Pamunkey River. Terry's First Division, Tenth Corps was left behind to hold the line of defenses at Bermuda Hundred. Gillmore, then left with only one division, was assigned command of the line of defenses. For additional information about Gillmore's command, see Army of the James, Defenses of Bermuda Hundred.

On May 30, 1864, Ames' and Turner's divisions, while en route to join the Army of the Potomac, were consolidated to form a temporary Third Division, Eighteenth Corps under Charles Devens, Jr. This reorganization was effected as follows:

Third Division, Charles Devens, Jr., to June 4, 1864, sick
  Adelbert Ames
  First Brigade, William B. Barton
  Second Brigade, Jeremiah C. Drake
  Third Brigade, Adelbert Ames, to June 4, 1864
    Henry R. Guss

Note. 1. Devens formerly commanded Third Brigade, First Division, Eighteenth Corps.

Note 2. First Brigade was organized from Barton's Second Brigade, Second Division, Tenth Corps.

Note 3. Second Brigade was organized from Drake's Second Brigade, Third Division, Tenth Corps.

Note 4. Third Brigade was organized from Samuel M. Alford's First Brigade, Second Division, Tenth Corps, and was assigned to the command of Adelbert Ames, formerly commander of Third Division, Tenth Corps.

Note 5. Henry R. Guss' First Brigade, Third Division, Tenth Corps was broken up, and the regiments were assigned to the three brigades of the new Third Division, Eighteenth Corps.

As a part of Eighteenth Corps, the troops formerly of Tenth Corps, constituting the new Third Division, took part in the assaults at Cold Harbor on June 1 and June 3, 1864, and then remained on the entrenched lines close to the enemy until June 12, 1864. That day, the army began its withdrawal from Cold Harbor as it marched toward the James River. When the army departed, Eighteenth Corps reembarked at White House, and returned to Bermuda Hundred June 14–15, 1864. For details of the operations of Eighteenth Corps while with the Army of the Potomac, see Richmond, Virginia Campaign, 1864, Operations about Cold Harbor.

The organization of Third Division, Eighteenth Corps at Cold Harbor was as follows:

Third Division, Charles Devens, Jr., to June 4, 1864, sick
  Adelbert Ames
  First Brigade, William B. Barton

Second Brigade, Jeremiah C. Drake, to June 1, 1864, mortally wounded
  Zina H. Robinson, to June 5, 1864
  Alexander Piper, to June 9, 1864
  N. Martin Curtis
Third Brigade, Adelbert Ames, to June 4, 1864
  Henry R. Guss
  Louis Bell

Meantime, on June 9, 1864, Gillmore had led an unsuccessful expedition against Petersburg, and June 14, 1864, Butler removed him from command. Terry, as the senior officer, assumed temporary command of Tenth Corps, and also of the line of defenses at Bermuda Hundred. Robert S. Foster, Gillmore's chief of staff, was assigned command of Terry's First Division. On June 18, 1864, William T. H. Brooks was relieved from command of First Division, Eighteenth Corps, and ordered to relieve Terry in command of Tenth Corps.

Operations about Petersburg and Richmond, June 1864–July 1864. When Smith arrived at Bermuda Hundred from White House June 14, 1864, he received orders to cross the Appomattox River with his Eighteenth Corps and attack the enemy defenses in front of Petersburg. Ames, commanding the temporary Third Division, Eighteenth Corps (composed of troops of Tenth Corps), was assigned command of the Central Section of the line of defenses at Bermuda Hundred, and he took with him the regiments of William B. Barton's First Brigade of the division. N. Martin Curtis' Second Brigade and Louis Bell's Third Brigade, however, accompanied Eighteenth Corps to Petersburg, and participated in the assaults there June 15, 1864. These two brigades remained at Petersburg until June 18, 1864, and then returned to Bermuda Hundred. The next day, Bell was ordered to report with the two brigades to William T. H. Brooks, who had assumed command of Tenth Corps June 18, 1864. For details of the participation of Curtis' and Bell's brigades in the assaults at Petersburg, see Operations about Petersburg and Richmond, Virginia, 1864–1865, Operations of June 1864, Assaults at Petersburg, June 15–18, 1864.

During the fighting at Petersburg June 15, 1864, Tenth Corps remained at Bermuda Hundred. When Smith's command attacked and captured a part of the outer line of the enemy defenses that day, Pierre G. T. Beauregard, commanding the Confederate forces at Petersburg, withdrew the troops from in front of the Federal defenses at Bermuda Hundred to reinforce the troops at Petersburg. The next day, Foster's First Division of Tenth Corps and the brigades of Ames and Turner occupied the trenches vacated by the enemy. Terry was in command of the entire force. Foster's division then advanced to the Richmond and Petersburg Turnpike to check the enemy reinforcements that were moving south toward Petersburg. Foster remained on the turnpike until dark, and then returned to Bermuda Hundred. In addition, Ames' and Turner's brigades, covered by First Division, destroyed more than two miles of the Richmond and Petersburg Railroad near Port Walthall Junction. June 17, 1864, the enemy returned and moved into the works that they had abandoned the day before.

The organization of Tenth Corps during the early part of June 1864 was as follows:

TENTH CORPS, Quincy A. Gillmore, to June 14, 1864
Alfred H. Terry, to June 18, 1864
William T. H. Brooks

First Division, Alfred H. Terry, to June 14, 1864
Robert S. Foster
First Brigade, Joshua A. Howell, to June 17, 1864, sick
Joseph C. Abbott
Second Brigade, Joseph R. Hawley
Third Brigade, Harris M. Plaisted
Artillery Brigade, Loomis L. Langdon

Artillery of Second Division and Third Division

By an order of June 19, 1864, Tenth Corps was reorganized to consist of three divisions as follows:

TENTH CORPS, William T. H. Brooks

First Division, Robert S. Foster, to June 21, 1864
Alfred H. Terry
First Brigade, Joshua B. Howell
Second Brigade, Joseph R. Hawley
Third Brigade, Harris M. Plaisted, to June 23, 1864
Robert S. Foster
Artillery Brigade, Loomis L. Langdon
1st Battery, Connecticut Light Artillery, James B. Clinton
5th Battery, New Jersey Light Artillery, Zenas C. Warren
Battery C, 3rd Rhode Island Heavy Artillery, Martin S. James
Battery M, 1st United States Artillery, Loomis L. Langdon

Second Division, John W. Turner
First Brigade, N. Martin Curtis
Second Brigade, William B. Barton, to June 30, 1864
Edward Eddy, Jr.
Third Brigade, Louis Bell
Artillery Brigade, George T. Woodbury
4th Battery, New Jersey Light Artillery, Charles R. Doane
4th Battery, Wisconsin Light Artillery, Martin McDevitt
Battery D, 1st United States Artillery, Robert M. Hall
Battery E, 3rd United States Artillery, John R. Myrick
Battery D, 4th United States Artillery, Frank Powell

Note 1. Second Division was the division formed by the consolidation of Second Division and Third Division of Tenth Corps May 30, 1864, and the one that served with Eighteenth Corps at Cold Harbor as Third Division. Adelbert Ames commanded the division when it returned from Cold Harbor, and Turner assumed command June 22, 1864, when the division was redesignated as Second Division, Tenth Corps.

Note 2. Curtis' First Brigade was organized June 21, 1864 from three regiments of Third Brigade and one regiment of Second Brigade of Ames' temporary Third Division, Eighteenth Corps. It was essentially the same as the original First Brigade, Second Division, Tenth Corps.

Note 3. Barton's Second Brigade was organized from First Brigade of Ames' temporary Third Division, Eighteenth Corps, and this was essentially the same as Barton's original Second Brigade, Second Division, Tenth Corps.

Note 4. Bell's Third Brigade was organized June 20, 1864 from three regiments of Second Brigade and two regiments of Third Brigade of Ames' temporary Third Division, Eighteenth Corps. It was composed of regiments of the original Third Division, Tenth Corps that was discontinued when the temporary Third Division, Eighteenth Corps was organized May 30, 1864.

Note 5. Barton was relieved from command of Second Brigade because of poor performance in preparing for an assault on the afternoon of June 30, 1864 at Bermuda Hundred.

Note 6. The Artillery Brigade was attached to Third Division.

Third Division, Orris S. Ferry
First Brigade, Gilman Marston
Second Brigade, James B. Armstrong
Artillery
33rd Battery, New York Light Artillery, Alger M. Wheeler

Note 1. Third Division was organized June 19, 1864 from nine one-hundred-day regiments of the Ohio National Guard, which had arrived at Bermuda Hundred June

12–14, 1864, and which had been serving under Butler. These regiments were mustered out between August 20, 1864 and September 22, 1864, and the division was discontinued September 24, 1864.

Note 2. The Artillery Brigade of Second Division was attached to Third Division.

When the reorganization of Tenth Corps was completed, Terry's First Division was on the right of the line of defenses at Bermuda Hundred, between the James River and Battery No. 4, with Hawley's brigade on the right, next to the river, and Howell's brigade on the left. Plaisted's brigade was in reserve. Turner's Second Division and James B. Armstrong's Second Brigade of Orris S. Ferry's Third Division held the left of the line from the left of Terry's division to the Appomattox River. Curtis' brigade of Turner's division was on the right, next to First Division; Armstrong's brigade of Ferry's division was on the left of Curtis; and Barton's brigade of Turner's division was on the left of Armstrong, and on the left of the line. Gilman Marston's First Brigade of Ferry's division was stationed on the James River at Fort Powhatan, Wilson's Wharf, and Bermuda Landing.

June 21, 1864, Terry relieved Foster in command of First Division, and Foster was sent to Deep Bottom to assume command of the one-hundred-day Ohio regiments, which were stationed there. He was ordered to construct an entrenched line on the north bank of the James River at Deep Bottom to cover the two pontoon bridges at that point. Two days later, Plaisted's Third Brigade, First Division was also sent to Deep Bottom, where it came under the command of Foster.

An important troop movement took place June 23, 1864. Turner's Second Division was withdrawn from the line of defenses at Bermuda Hundred, and was assigned to temporary duty with Smith's Eighteenth Corps in the entrenchments at Petersburg. Turner's division moved into the line on the left of Eighteenth Corps, relieving Orlando B. Willcox's division of Ninth Corps in the trenches. The next day, Ferry was ordered to assume command of that part of the line of defenses at Bermuda Hundred that extended from the left of Terry to the Appomattox River. Second Division remained in the trenches at Petersburg during the rest of June and all of July 1864, temporarily attached to Eighteenth Corps.

During the latter part of July 1864, William H. Emory, commanding a detachment of Nineteenth Corps, consisting of First Division and Second Division, arrived at Fort Monroe from the Department of the Gulf. A part of this command was immediately sent on to Washington, D.C., which was then threatened by a Confederate army under Jubal A. Early, but four brigades joined the Army of the James at Bermuda Hundred. From July 21–31, 1864, Henry W. Birge's First Brigade and Edward L. Molineux's Second Brigade of Second Division, Detachment Ninteenth Corps were temporarily attached to Tenth Corps, and were placed in reserve behind the line of defenses. July 27, 1864, Birge's brigade was sent to reinforce Hancock's Second Corps, Army of the Potomac, which was then operating north of the James River, near Deep Bottom. That day, the other two brigades of Nineteenth Corps, commanded by Leonard D. H. Currie and James W. McMillan, were ordered to Washington. July 30, 1864, the brigades of Birge and Molineux were also ordered to Washington, and they departed the next day.

On July 30, 1864, Turner's Second Division, Tenth Corps supported the assaulting column of Ambrose E. Burnside's Ninth Corps that attacked the enemy's works at Petersburg after the explosion of the mine. The next day Turner's division was relieved from duty with Eighteenth Corps at Petersburg and returned to Bermuda Hundred.

The organization of Tenth Corps during July 1864 was as follows:

TENTH CORPS, William T. H. Brooks, to July 18, 1864
    Alfred H. Terry, to July 23, 1864
    David B. Birney

First Division, Alfred H. Terry, to July 18, 1864
    Robert S. Foster, to July 23, 1864
    Alfred H. Terry
    First Brigade, Joshua B. Howell, to July 29, 1864, sick
      Francis B. Pond
    Second Brigade, Joseph R. Hawley
    Third Brigade, Robert S. Foster, to July 18, 1864
      Harris M. Plaisted, to July 23, 1864
      Robert S. Foster
    Artillery Brigade, Loomis L. Langdon, to July 28, 1864
      Zenas C. Warren

Note 1. Brooks' resignation was accepted July 15, 1864, to take effect July 14, 1864. He relinquished command of Tenth Corps July 18, 1864.

Note 2. The batteries with First Division were the same as in June 1864.

Second Division, John W. Turner
    First Brigade, N. Martin Curtis
    Second Brigade, Edward Eddy, Jr., to July 2, 1864
        William B. Coan
    Third Brigade, Louis Bell
    Artillery Brigade, Frederick M. Follett

Note. The batteries with Second Division were the same as in June 1864, except the 4th Battery, Wisconsin Light Artillery, which had been detached.

Third Division, Orris S. Ferry
    First Brigade, Gilman Marston
    Second Brigade, James B. Armstrong
    33rd Battery, New York Light Artillery, Alger M. Wheeler

Cavalry
    4th Massachusetts Cavalry (detachment), Francis Washburn

Operations about Petersburg and Richmond, August 1864. Tenth Corps spent most of the month of August 1864 on the line of defenses at Bermuda Hundred and at Deep Bottom. Troops of the corps, however, took part in some operations during this period. On August 13, 1864, David B. Birney marched to Deep Bottom with First Brigade and Second Brigade of Terry's First Division; Second Brigade and Third Brigade of Turner's Second Division; and William Birney's Separate Brigade of Tenth Corps, which had been organized the day before from regiments of United States Colored Troops. David B. Birney's command joined Hancock's Second Corps and David McM. Gregg's Second Cavalry Division, Army of the Potomac at Deep Bottom for a demonstration north of the James River, on the enemy works in front of Richmond. Robert S. Foster's Third Brigade of Terry's division, which had been on duty guarding the bridges at Deep Bottom, joined its division for this demonstration. When David B. Birney joined Hancock, the troops of Tenth Corps became subject to Hancock's orders. While with Hancock, the troops of Tenth Corps were engaged in daily skirmishing and some more serious fighting, after which they then returned to Bermuda Hundred August 21, 1864.

For details of Hancock's demonstration north of the James River, see Operations about Petersburg and Richmond, Virginia, 1864–1865, Operations of August 1864, Demonstration on the North Bank of the James River at Deep Bottom (Combats at Fussell's Mill, Gravel Hill, Bailey's Creek, Deep Run [or Creek], White's Tavern, Charles City Road, and New Market Road), Virginia.

Turner did not accompany the brigades of his division to Deep Bottom, but remained at Bermuda Hundred in charge of the line of defenses. These were manned by Curtis' First Brigade of Turner's division, the one-hundred-day regiments of the Ohio National Guard, dismounted cavalry, troops of Charles K. Graham's Naval Brigade, and such other troops as were available.

On August 24, 1864, Tenth Corps was ordered to Petersburg to relieve Eighteenth Corps in the entrenchments. The transfer was completed during the period August 24–28, 1864, and Tenth Corps then occupied the line from the Appomattox River to a point near the crater of the Petersburg Mine, where it connected with Gershom Mott's Third Division, Second Corps. Robert S. Foster's Second Division (commanded by John W. Turner until August 23, 1864) was on the right of the line, William Birney's newly organized Third Division (see below) was on the center, and Alfred H. Terry's First Division was on the left. When relieved, Eighteenth Corps returned to Bermuda Hundred, and Charles J. Paine's Third Division relieved Harris M. Plaisted's Third Brigade, First Division, Tenth Corps (commanded by Robert S. Foster until August 24, 1864) at Deep Bottom. Plaisted then joined the division at Petersburg with his brigade. For additional information, see Army of the James, On the Lines at Petersburg and Bermuda Hundred.

There were some changes in the organization of Tenth Corps during August 1864, particularly in Third Division. During the period August 25–27, 1864, the one-hundred-day regiments of of Orris S. Ferry's Third Division were sent home for muster out, and the division was discontinued. This occurred during the exchange of positions by Tenth Corps and Eighteenth Corps. At that time, William Birney commanded a Separate Brigade of Tenth Corps that consisted of United States Colored Troops. Birney was then ordered to assume command of the colored regiments of John H. Holman's First Brigade, Third Division, Eighteenth Corps, which were camped at the Signal Tower near Point of Rocks, and take them and his own brigade to Petersburg. There, he was to relieve Elias Wright's Second Brigade of Charles J. Paine's Third Division, Eighteenth Corps in the entrenchments.

On August 27, 1864, William Birney organized his new command as Third Division, Tenth Corps. His own Separate Brigade of Tenth Corps was designated as First Brigade, Third Division, and was commanded by James Shaw, Jr. The regiments of Holman's First Brigade, Third Division, Eighteenth Corps were designated as Second Brigade, Third Division, Tenth Corps, with Holman in command. Although serving with Tenth Corps, and carried on the Tenth Corps roster for August 1864, Holman's brigade was also carried on the Eighteenth Corps roster as First Brigade, Third Division.

The organization of Tenth Corps during August 1864 was as follows:

TENTH CORPS, David B. Birney

First Division, Alfred H. Terry
    First Brigade, Francis B. Pond, to August 16, 1864, sick
      Alvin C. Voris, to August 18, 1864
      Joshua B. Howell
    Second Brigade, Joseph R. Hawley
    Third Brigade, Robert S. Foster, to August 23, 1864
      Harris M. Plaisted

Second Division, John W. Turner, to August 23, 1864
    Robert S. Foster
    First Brigade, N. Martin Curtis
    Second Brigade, William B. Coan, to August 27, 1864
      William B. Barton
    Third Brigade, Louis Bell, to August 13, 1864
      Francis A. Osborn, to August 16, 1864, wounded
      Ezra L. Walrath, to August 16, 1864, wounded
      Frank W. Parker, to August 16, 1864, wounded
      Robert J. Gray, to August 20, 1864
      Francis A. Osborn

Third Division, Orris S. Ferry, to August 27, 1864
    First Brigade, Gilman Marston
    Second Brigade, Samuel C. Armstrong

Note 1. Marston was in command of the post of Wilson's Wharf on the James River.
Note 2. Ferry's division was discontinued August 27, 1864, when the regiments of which it was composed went home for muster out.

Third Division (reorganized), William Birney
    First Brigade, James Shaw, Jr.
    Second Brigade, John H. Holman

Note 1. Third Division was reorganized under William Birney August 27, 1864.
Note 2. First Brigade was formerly William Birney's Separate Brigade, Tenth Corps (see below).
Note 3. Second Brigade was formerly Holman's First Brigade, Third Division, Eighteenth Corps.

Separate Brigade, William Birney

Note. Birney's Separate Brigade was organized August 12, 1864, and consisted of regiments of the United States Colored Troops and 29th Connecticut (colored). It was discontinued August 27, 1864 and redesignated as First Brigade, Third Division, Tenth Corps, under the command of James Shaw, Jr.

Artillery Brigade, Freeman McGilvery
    1st Battery, Connecticut Light Artillery, James B. Clinton
    4th Battery, New Jersey Light Artillery, Charles R. Doane
    5th Battery, New Jersey Light Artillery, Zenas C. Warren
    Battery E, 3rd New York Light Artillery, George E. Ashby
    Battery H, 3rd New York Light Artillery, William J. Riggs
    16th Battery, New York Light Artillery, Richard H. Lee
    33rd Battery, New York Light Artillery, Alger M. Wheeler
    Battery A, 1st Pennsylvania Light Artillery, William Stitt
    Battery E, 1st Pennsylvania Light Artillery, Thomas G. Orwig
    Battery C, 3rd Rhode Island Heavy Artillery, Martin S. James
    Battery D, 1st United States Artillery, Joseph P. Sanger
    Battery M, 1st United States Artillery, Loomis L. Langdon
    Battery E, 3rd United States Artillery, John R. Myrick
    Battery D, 4th United States Artillery, Frederick M. Follett

Operations about Petersburg and Richmond, September 1864–October 1864. David B. Birney's Tenth Corps remained on the line of entrenchments at Petersburg until late September 1864, covering the front from the Appomattox River to the Norfolk and Petersburg Railroad. As a part of Grant's autumn offensive, Butler was ordered to assemble his Army of the James and attempt to capture Richmond by advancing against the eastern fortifications of the city, north of the James River. Accordingly, on the night of September 24, 1864, Second Corps, Army of the Potomac relieved Tenth Corps in the trenches at Petersburg, and the latter moved back about one mile and massed near corps headquarters at the Friend house in preparation for joining Butler north of the Appomattox. Tenth Corps remained there until the afternoon of September 28, 1864, and then marched toward Deep Bottom, where it crossed the James River the next morning. Birney then marched northward toward New Market Heights with his Tenth Corps and Charles J. Paine's Third Division, Eighteenth Corps, which was temporarily attached to Birney's command. Paine's division attacked New Market Heights on the morning of September 29, 1864, while Tenth Corps pressed the Confederate left. The fighting was severe, and the Federal troops were driven back. They again advanced, however, and reached the crest, but found that the enemy had withdrawn. They had been ordered back when Edward O. C. Ord's Eighteenth Corps marched up the Varina Road and threatened Fort Harrison at Chaffin's farm. Later that day, after capturing Fort Harrison, Tenth Corps marched up the Charles City Road and unsuccessfully attacked Fort Gilmer and Fort Gregg. For details of the operations of Tenth Corps and the Army of the James September 29–30, 1864, see Operations about Petersburg and Richmond, Virginia, 1864–1865, Operations of September 1864, Battle of Chaffin's Farm (Combats at Fort Harrison, Fort Gilmer, Fort Gregg, New Market Heights, and Laurel Hill), Virginia.

There was one significant change in the organization of Tenth Corps during the month. On September 1, 1864, John H. Holman, commanding Second Brigade, Third Division, was ordered with his regiment (1st United States Colored Troops) to Broadway Landing on the Appomattox River. The other regiment of Second Brigade, the 22nd United States Colored Troops, was ordered to Fort Powhatan September 5, 1864. This left only one brigade in Third Division, and September 24, 1864 (ordered September 17, 1864), the troops composing Third Division were designated as First Brigade, Third Division. William Birney commanded the new First Brigade, and James Shaw, the former commander of First Brigade, resumed command of his regiment (7th United States Colored Troops). The new First Brigade, Third Division was the only brigade of the division, and after September 24, 1864, it was called Birney's Brigade, or the Colored Brigade. It was treated as a separate brigade, and it reported directly to Headquarters Tenth Corps.

The organization of Tenth Corps during the fighting at New Market Heights and Chaffin's farm September 29–30, 1864 was as follows:

TENTH CORPS, David B. Birney

First Division, Alfred H. Terry
    First Brigade, Francis B. Pond
    Second Brigade, Joseph C. Abbott
    Third Brigade, Harris M. Plaisted

Second Division, Robert S. Foster
    First Brigade, Rufus Daggett
    Second Brigade, Galusha Pennypacker
    Third Brigade, Louis Bell

Note 1. Daggett assumed temporary command of First Brigade September 17, 1864, during the absence of N. Martin Curtis.
Note 2. William B. Barton was detached from Second Division September 14, 1864, and was assigned to other duties. He was succeeded in command of Second Brigade by Pennypacker.
Note 3. Bell was relieved from arrest September 23, 1864, and relieved Francis A. Osborn in command of Third Brigade.

Birney's Brigade (or Colored Brigade), William Birney

Artillery Brigade, Richard H. Jackson
    1st Battery, Connecticut Light Artillery, James B. Clinton
    4th Battery, New Jersey Light Artillery, Charles R. Doane
    5th Battery, New Jersey Light Artillery, Henry H. Metcalf
    16th New York Heavy Artillery (detachment), Silas J. Truax
    Battery E, 1st Pennsylvania Light Artillery, Henry Y. Wildey
    Battery C, 3rd Rhode Island Heavy Artillery, Martin S. James
    Battery D, 1st United States Artillery, Redmond Tully
    Battery M, 1st United States Artillery, Loomis L. Langdon
    Battery E, 3rd United States Artillery, John R. Myrick
    Battery D, 4th United States Artillery, Frederick M. Follett

At the end of the fighting around Chaffin's farm October 2, 1864, the Army of the James remained on the ground gained during its advance September 29, 1864. The troops then prepared a defensive line extending from Signal Hill (later the site of Fort Brady) on the James River, northward past Fort Harrison (later renamed Fort Burnham), to the Darbytown Road. Eighteenth Corps occupied the left of this line from the river to, and including, Fort Harrison. Tenth Corps was in position to the right of Fort Harrison, and along the old Confederate Exterior Line to a point a short distance north of the New Market Road at the Clyne house. August V. Kautz's Cavalry Division was on the right of the army, on the Darbytown Road. For additional information, see Operations about Petersburg and Richmond, Virginia, 1864–1865, Operations of October 1864, Siege of Petersburg.

Tenth Corps remained generally in this position during the rest of October 1864, except for three brief periods when it was withdrawn from the defensive line for active operations. The first of these occurred October 7, 1864, when the enemy attacked Kautz's cavalry at Johnson's farm and drove it back to the New Market Road. Terry's First Division was moved back along that road to meet the enemy advance, and repulsed two attacks. The enemy then withdrew, and Terry followed a short distance, but then returned to his former position. For details of Terry's engagement, see Operations about Petersburg and Richmond, Virginia, 1864–1865, Operations of October 1864, Engagement at the Darbytown Road and the New Market Road (Johnson's Farm and Four-Mile Creek [or Run]), Virginia. On October 13, 1864, Terry, then commanding Tenth Corps, moved out on the Darbytown Road with First Division, then commanded by Adelbert Ames, and William Birney's Third Division in a limited attempt to break up the enemy works that were being constructed there. Finding the works too strong to be taken with his command, Terry returned to his camps. For details, see Operations about Petersburg and Richmond, Virginia, 1864–1865, Operations of October 1864, Engagement at the Darbytown Road, Virginia. On October 27, 1864, Tenth Corps, in conjunction with Eighteenth Corps, moved out for a demonstration against the enemy entrenchments. Tenth Corps advanced on the Darbytown Road and, after considerable skirmishing, returned to its camps the next morning. For details, see Operations about Petersburg and Richmond, Virginia, 1864–1865, Operations of October 1864,

Engagement at the Darbytown Road (Fair Oaks), Virginia.

There were some command and organizational changes in Tenth Corps during October 1864. David B. Birney became ill October 10, 1864, and returned to his home in Philadelphia, where he died October 18, 1864. Alfred H. Terry assumed temporary command of Tenth Corps October 10, 1864, and Adelbert Ames took command of Terry's First Division. It will be remembered that on September 17, 1864, William Birney's Third Division, Tenth Corps was reduced to a single brigade, which was designated as First Brigade, Third Division. This was usually called simply Birney's Brigade or Colored Brigade. On October 3, 1864, the 127th United States Colored Troops arrived and was assigned to Birney's Brigade. Two days later an order was issued for the reorganization of Third Division, which was to consist of two brigades of three colored regiments each. William Birney was assigned command of the new Third Division, Alvin C. Voris of First Brigade, and Francis A. Osborn of Second Brigade. Osborn's assignment was revoked, however, and when Second Brigade was organized October 6, 1864, Samuel C. Armstrong was assigned command. The next day Armstrong was relieved by Ulysses Doubleday. Elias Wright relieved Doubleday October 29, 1864.

Winter of 1864–1865. During November 1864, Tenth Corps continued to hold the same positions as it did the preceding month, but there was little significant activity on its front. On November 2, 1864, Grant ordered 3,000 men of the Army of the James to New York to preserve order and protect the public property during the presidential election of November 8, 1864. Joseph R. Hawley, commander of Second Brigade, First Division, Tenth Corps, was assigned command of this force, which consisted of eight regiments of Tenth Corps and four regiments of Eighteenth Corps. The regiments of Tenth Corps were commanded by Joseph C. Abbott. After the election, on November 14, 1864, Hawley's force began embarking at New York for the return to the army, and as the regiments arrived at City Point, they rejoined their proper commands. For additional information, see Army of the James, Line of Defenses North of the James River; and also Department of the East, January 3, 1863–June 27, 1865, November Election of 1864 in New York.

The organization of Tenth Corps during November 1864 was as follows:

TENTH CORPS, Alfred H. Terry, to November 4, 1864
    Adelbert Ames, to November 18, 1864
    Alfred H. Terry

Note. Terry commanded the Army of the James while Butler was in New York during the election of November 1864.

First Division, Adelbert Ames, to November 4, 1864
    Alvin C. Voris, to November 18, 1864
    Adelbert Ames
    First Brigade, Alvin C. Voris, to November 4, 1864
        Francis B. Pond, to November 6, 1864
        James C. Briscoe, to November 18, 1864
        Alvin C. Voris
    Second Brigade, Joseph R. Hawley, to November 4, 1864
        Joseph C. Abbott, to November 18, 1864
        Joseph R. Hawley
    Third Brigade, Harris M. Plaisted, to November 2, 1864
        George B. Dandy

Note. Pond was honorably discharged from the service, at his own request, November 6, 1864, while temporarily commanding First Brigade.

Second Division, Robert S. Foster
    First Brigade, Albert M. Barney, to November 14, 1864
        N. Martin Curtis
    Second Brigade, Galusha Pennypacker
    Third Brigade, Louis Bell

Third Division, William Birney
    First Brigade, James Shaw, Jr.
    Second Brigade, Elias Wright, to November 6, 1864
        Ulysses Doubleday

Note. Wright was assigned to Charles J. Paine's Third Division, Eighteenth Corps.

By an order of December 3, 1864, Tenth Corps and Eighteenth Corps were discontinued, and the white troops of the two corps were assigned to the newly constituted Twenty-Fourth Corps. The colored troops of the Department of Virginia and North Carolina were assigned to a new Twenty-Fifth Corps. The troops of Tenth Corps were assigned to Twenty-Fourth Corps and Twenty-Fifth Corps as

follows: First Division, Tenth Corps was redesignated as First Division, Twenty-Fourth Corps, and the brigade numbers remained the same. Second Division, Tenth Corps was redesignated as Second Division, Twenty-Fourth Corps, and the brigade numbers remained the same. The brigades of Third Division, Tenth Corps were largely broken up, and the regiments were assigned to Second Division and Third Division of Twenty-Fifth Corps. Three regiments of Ulysses Doubleday's Second Brigade, Third Division, Tenth Corps were assigned as Second Brigade, Second Division, Twenty-Fifth Corps. For additional information, see Twenty-Fourth Corps and Twenty-Fifth Corps, Army of the James.

COMMANDERS OF TENTH CORPS, ARMY OF THE JAMES

Alfred H. Terry	April 22, 1864 to May 4, 1864
Quincy A. Gillmore	May 4, 1864 to June 15, 1864
Alfred H. Terry	June 15, 1864 to June 18, 1864
William T. H. Brooks	June 18, 1864 to July 18, 1864
Alfred H. Terry	July 18, 1864 to July 23, 1864
David B. Birney	July 23, 1864 to October 10, 1864
Alfred H. Terry	October 10, 1864 to November 4, 1864
Adelbert Ames	November 4, 1864 to November 18, 1864
Alfred H. Terry	November 18, 1864 to December 3, 1864

Note. Birney became ill October 10, 1864, and died in Philadelphia October 18, 1864.

TENTH CORPS, DEPARTMENT OF NORTH CAROLINA

In February 1865, John M. Schofield arrived in North Carolina from Tennessee with his Twenty-Third Corps, Army of the Ohio, and February 9, 1865 assumed command of the Department of North Carolina. Then, in response to an order from William T. Sherman, who was moving north with his army through the Carolinas, Schofield advanced with the available troops of the Department of North Carolina from Wilmington and New Berne toward Goldsboro, where he arrived March 20–21, 1865. His command consisted of Jacob D. Cox's Provisional Corps, Army of the Ohio; Darius N. Couch, with two divisions of Twenty-Third Corps, Army of the Ohio; and Alfred H. Terry's Provisional Corps, Department of North Carolina. During March 23–24, 1865, William T. Sherman's Army of the Military Division of the Mississippi also arrived at Goldsboro from its march through the Carolinas.

In preparation for further operations, Sherman ordered Schofield to organize the troops of his department into two army corps, and to prepare them for field service. By a presidential order dated March 27, 1865, Tenth Corps was reconstituted to consist of all troops in North Carolina not belonging to Sherman's army or Twenty-Third Corps. Terry was assigned command of the corps. Further, on April 1, 1865, Terry's Tenth Corps and Cox's Twenty-Third Corps were designated as the Center of Sherman's army, and Schofield was assigned command of the two corps. This organization was to be in effect while the two corps were operating with Oliver O. Howard's Army of the Tennessee (Right Wing) and Henry W. Slocum's Army of Georgia (Left Wing).

Terry assumed command of Tenth Corps April 2, 1865, and announced its organization as follows:

TENTH CORPS, Alfred H. Terry

First Division, Henry W. Birge
 First Brigade, Harvey Graham
 Second Brigade, Joseph C. Abbott
 Third Brigade, Nicholas W. Day
 Artillery
  22nd Battery, Indiana Light Artillery, George W. Alexander

Note 1. Birge, formerly commander of Second Division, Nineteenth Corps at Savannah, Georgia, arrived in North Carolina March 14, 1865.
Note 2. First Brigade was formerly Second Brigade, Second Division, Nineteenth Corps, which was stationed at Morehead City, North Carolina.
Note 3. Second Brigade was formerly Second Brigade, First Division, Twenty-Fourth Corps of Terry's Provisional Corps, Department of North Carolina. It was stationed in and about Wilmington, North Carolina.
Note 4. Third Brigade was formerly Third Brigade, Second Division, Nineteenth Corps. Birge remained at New Berne with Third Brigade until April 10, 1865, and he then moved to Goldsboro and assumed command of First Division.

Second Division, Adelbert Ames
 First Brigade, Rufus Daggett
 Second Brigade, William B. Coan, to April 5, 1865
  John S. Littell
 Third Brigade, G. Frederick Granger
  16th Battery, New York Light Artillery, Richard H. Lee

Note. Second Division was formerly Ames' Second Division, Twenty-Fourth Corps of Terry's Provisional Corps, Department of North Carolina.

Third Division, Charles J. Paine
 First Brigade, Delevan Bates
 Second Brigade, Samuel A. Duncan
 Third Brigade, John H. Holman

Note. Third Division was formerly Paine's Third Division, Twenty-Fifth Corps of Terry's Provisional Corps, Department of North Carolina.

Unattached
 Battery E, 3rd United States Artillery, John R. Myrick

Terry, with his Second Division and Third Division of Tenth Corps, was in camp at Faison's Station on the Wilmington and Weldon Railroad until April 10, 1865, and he then joined Sherman's army in its advance against Joseph E. Johnston's Confederate forces at Smithfield, North Carolina. When Sherman approached, however, Johnston retired toward Raleigh, with the Federal troops following. Tenth Corps left Faison's Station April 10, 1865, marched south along the Neuse River, by way of Bentonville, and arrived at Raleigh April 15, 1865. All further troop movements were then suspended while Sherman and Johnston met near Durham's Station to discuss terms for ending hostilities. Johnston surrendered his army April 26, 1865, and thus ended the war in the East. For additional information, see Carolinas Campaign, Goldsboro to Raleigh, North Carolina (Surrender of Joseph E. Johnston's Army).

On April 27, 1865, Sherman's Army of the Tennessee and Army of Georgia began their march northward toward Washington, D.C., and they soon left the state. Tenth Corps and Twenty-Third Corps, however, remained in North Carolina until they were discontinued. April 27, 1865, Paine's Third Division was ordered back to Goldsboro to relieve Birge in command of the post, and Birge was, in turn, ordered to assemble his two brigades of First Division, Tenth Corps and return with them to the

Department of the South. Paine left Raleigh April 29, 1865, and arrived at Goldsboro and assumed command May 1, 1865. Birge then moved with his brigades to Morehead City, where he embarked for Savannah May 3, 1865. On that date, First Division, Tenth Corps was discontinued. Abbott's Second Brigade, First Division remained at Wilmington, North Carolina as a detached brigade.

Ames' Second Division remained on garrison duty at Raleigh. Terry was granted a leave of absence, and May 23, 1865, Ames assumed command of Tenth Corps. On July 6, 1865, Ames was assigned command of the newly constituted District of Raleigh.

June 2, 1865, Paine's Third Division, Tenth Corps was reassigned. Nathan Goff, then commanding Third Brigade, was ordered to the District of Wilmington. Paine, with Delevan Bates' First Brigade and Samuel A. Duncan's Second Brigade, was assigned to the District of Beaufort, where Paine assumed command. Duncan's brigade was sent to New Berne and Kinston, and Bates' brigade to Morehead City. On June 6, 1865, Goff relieved Abbott's brigade at Wilmington, and Abbott then moved to Goldsboro.

Tenth Corps was discontinued August 1, 1865, and all troops not mustered out were transferred to the Department of North Carolina.

The organization of Tenth Corps, Department of North Carolina during the period April 27, 1865–August 1, 1865 was as follows:

TENTH CORPS, Alfred H. Terry, to May 13, 1865, on leave
  Adelbert Ames

Note. Terry was later assigned command of the Department of Virginia and did not return to Tenth Corps.

First Division, Henry W. Birge, to July 4, 1865
  First Brigade, Harvey Graham, to July 4, 1865
  Second Brigade, Joseph C. Abbott, to July 4, 1865
  Third Brigade, Nicholas W. Day, to July 4, 1865

Note. First Division was discontinued July 4, 1865.

Second Division, Adelbert Ames, to May 13, 1865
  Rufus Daggett, to June 8, 1865, mustered out
  John S. Littell, to July 18, 1865, mustered out
  William B. Coan
  First Brigade, Rufus Daggett, to May 13, 1865
    Albert M. Barney, to June 7, 1865
    Frank W. Parker, July 20, 1865 to August 1, 1865

Second Brigade, John S. Littell, to June 9, 1865
  William B. Coan, to July 18, 1865
  Christopher R. McDonald
Third Brigade, G. Frederick Granger, to June 12, 1865
  Alonzo Alden, to July 18, 1865

Note 1. First Brigade was discontinued June 7, 1865 by muster out of regiments. It was reorganized July 20, 1865 by transfer of the 4th New Hampshire and 13th Indiana regiments from Third Brigade, Second Division.

Note 2. Third Brigade was discontinued July 18, 1865 by the muster out of three regiments and the transfer of 4th New Hampshire and 13th Indiana to First Brigade, Second Division.

Third Division, Charles J. Paine, to July 6, 1865
  Delevan Bates, to August 1, 1865
  First Brigade, Delevan Bates, to July 6, 1865
    William H. Revere, to August 1, 1865
  Second Brigade, Samuel A. Duncan, to June 14, 1865
    Ozora P. Stearns, to August 1, 1865
  Third Brigade, Albert M. Blackman, to May 12, 1865
    Nathan Goff, Jr., June 9, 1865
    Abial G. Chamberlain, to July 1, 1865
    Nathan Goff, Jr.

Note 1. Charles J. Paine was assigned command of the District of New Berne July 6, 1865.

Note 2. Third Division consisted of nine regiments of United States Colored Troops, and these were transferred to the Department of North Carolina August 1, 1865.

ELEVENTH CORPS, ARMY OF THE POTOMAC

After John Pope's disastrous defeat at the Second Battle of Bull Run August 30, 1862, Franz Sigel's First Corps, Army of Virginia retreated with the rest of the army into the Defenses of Washington. It was then placed on the right of the line of defenses, south of the Potomac River, at Fort Ethan Allen. On September 6, 1862, Sigel's front was extended from Forts Ethan Allen and Marcy to the vicinity of Fort De Kalb, and he was charged with the defense of the roads running out from Chain Bridge. Sigel's corps was left in this position when George B. McClellan's Army of the Potomac left Washington at the beginning of the Maryland Campaign. On September 12, 1862, the designation of Sigel's command was officially changed from First Corps, Army of Virginia to Eleventh Corps, Army of the Potomac. At that time it was organized as follows:

ELEVENTH CORPS, Franz Sigel

First Division, Julius Stahel
  First Brigade, Leopold Von Gilsa
  Second Brigade, Nathaniel C. McLean

Second Division, Adolph Von Steinwehr
  First Brigade, George A. Muhleck

  Note. A Second Brigade was organized under Orland Smith October 25, 1862.

Third Division, Carl Schurz
  First Brigade, Alexander Schimmelfennig
  Second Brigade, Wladimir Krzyzanowski

Cavalry Brigade, John Beardsley

Milroy's Independent Brigade, Robert H. Milroy

  Note. Milroy's brigade was detached from the corps September 24, 1862, and sent to Western Virginia.

September 22–24, 1862, Sigel advanced his Eleventh Corps to Fairfax and Centerville, Virginia as a corps of observation, and in October 1862, troops occupied the following posts, which were generally along the Orange and Alexandria Railroad: Fairfax Station, Fairfax Court House, Burke's Station, Union Mills, Bull Run Bridge, Chantilly, Brentsville, Catlett's Station, Bristoe, and Greenwich. For additional information, see Miscellaneous Organizations, Military District of the Defenses of Washington, Army of the Potomac.

October 27, 1862, Eleventh Corps was reorganized, largely by reassignment of regiments. A new Second Brigade, Second Division was organized under the command of Orland Smith. First Brigade and Second Brigade of Third Division were reorganized by first transferring the old regiments to the other divisions, and then reorganizing the two brigades largely from new regiments.

After the Battle of Antietam, the Army of the Potomac remained along the Potomac River, generally in the vicinity of Harper's Ferry, until October 26, 1862. On that date, McClellan began crossing the river into Virginia at Berlin, Maryland (present-day Brunswick) at the beginning of McClellan's march along the Loudoun Valley toward Warrenton. At that time preparations were started for the repair and protection of the Orange and Alexandria and Manassas Gap railroads, which would be needed for the supply of the Army of the

Potomac as it approached Warrenton. As a part of this undertaking, on November 2, 1862, Eleventh Corps moved forward toward Thoroughfare Gap, which it occupied three days later. Schurz's Third Division took position at the gap, Von Steinwehr's Second Division was at Carter's Switch, and Stahel's First Division was at Gainesville. For additional information, see Army of the Potomac, Antietam Creek, Maryland to Warrenton, Virginia.

Fredericksburg Campaign, November 7, 1862–December 15, 1862. Ambrose E. Burnside assumed command of the Army of the Potomac November 7, 1862, and one week later reorganized the army to consist of three grand divisions and a reserve. The reserve was to consist of Sigel's Eleventh Corps and any other troops that might be assigned later. When the reorganization was complete, Burnside started the army forward toward Fredericksburg. On November 17, 1862, as the army was leaving the Warrenton area, Eleventh Corps was ordered to fall back toward Washington from its advanced positions. Stahel's division moved to Chantilly, Von Steinwehr's division to near Germantown, and Schurz's division to Centerville. Sigel's headquarters was at Fairfax Court House. The corps remained in that general area, covering Washington, until December 9, 1862, and then it was ordered to join Burnside's army at Fredericksburg. Its place in front of Washington was taken by Henry W. Slocum's Twelfth Corps, which was then approaching from Harper's Ferry. Because of the poor condition of the roads, the leading troops of Eleventh Corps had only reached Dumfries December 13, 1862, the day of the Battle of Fredericksburg. Eleventh Corps then went into winter quarters at Stafford Court House. Later in the month Von Steinwehr's Second Division moved to the vicinity of Falmouth and established headquarters there.

Winter of 1862–1863. Eleventh Corps remained generally inactive in its camps during the winter except for the usual picket and reconnaissance duties. Alexander Schimmelfennig's First Brigade, Third Division was involved during James E. B. (Jeb) Stuart's raid on Dumfries and Fairfax Station December 27–29, 1862, and the corps also took part in Burnside's unsuccessful "Mud March" on the Rappahannock January 20–24, 1863, but other activities were comparatively minor.

There were no significant changes in the organization of the corps during the winter, but there were some command changes. December 18, 1862, Sigel departed for Washington and left Headquarters Eleventh Corps in the charge of his assistant adjutant general, Theodore A. Meysenburg. Stahel was assigned command of the troops stationed between Chopawamsic Creek and Potomac Creek; and both Stahel and Von Steinwehr, whose Second Division was near Falmouth, were instructed to report to Headquarters Army of the Potomac. Schurz's Third Division was at Stafford Court House, and was under Stahel's control.

The organization of Eleventh Corps at the end of December 1862 was as follows:

ELEVENTH CORPS, Julius Stahel

First Division, Nathaniel C. McLean
    First Brigade, Leopold Von Gilsa
    Second Brigade, Nathaniel C. McLean
    Cavalry Brigade, Louis P. Di Cesnola
    Artillery, William L. De Beck
        2nd Battery, New York Light Artillery, Louis Schirmer
        13th Battery, New York Light Artillery, Julius Dieckmann
        Company K, 1st Ohio Light Artillery, William L. De Beck

Second Division, Adolph Von Steinwehr
    First Brigade, Adolphus Buschbeck
    Second Brigade, Orland Smith
    Artillery
        Battery I, 1st New York Light Artillery, Michael Wiedrich
        12th Battery, Ohio Light Artillery, Aaron C. Johnson

Note 1. One return for the corps listed Buschbeck as commanding Second Division.
Note 2. Headquarters Second Division was at Falmouth, Virginia.

Third Division, Carl Schurz
    First Brigade, Alexander Schimmelfennig
    Second Brigade, Wladimir Krzyzanowski

Note. Hubert Dilger's Battery I, 1st Ohio Light Artillery was attached to First Brigade, and Wallace Hill's Battery C, 1st West Virginia Light Artillery was attached to Second Brigade.

January 10, 1863, Sigel assumed command of the Grand Reserve Division of the Army of the Potomac, and Stahel replaced him in command of Eleventh Corps. On January 19, 1863, Stahel was assigned command of the cavalry of the Grand Reserve Division, and Schurz assumed command of Eleventh Corps. Schimmelfennig relieved Schurz in command of Third Division, and Gotthilf Bourry succeeded Schimmelfennig in command of First Brigade, Third Division. This was not the end of the shifts in command in Eleventh Corps that winter. February 6, 1863, Sigel resumed command of the corps when the grand divisions of the army were abolished, and Schurz again commanded Third Division. Then, on February 12, 1863, Sigel asked to be relieved from command of Eleventh Corps, which he deemed unsuitable because of its small size, and his request was granted. February 22, 1863, Von Steinwehr assumed temporary command of the corps, and Buschbeck assumed command of Second Division. Clemens Soest took charge of First Brigade, Second Division. March 5, 1863, Schurz relieved Von Steinwehr in command of Eleventh Corps, and Schimmelfennig assumed command of Third Division. George Von Amsberg assumed command of Schimmelfennig's First Brigade, Third Division. Oliver O. Howard was assigned to the temporary command of Eleventh Corps March 31, 1863 (assumed command April 2, 1863), and then received permanent assignment April 15, 1863.

There were also three other significant command changes in Eleventh Corps before the opening of the spring campaign. Stahel was assigned to the Department of Washington March 20, 1863, and left the Army of the Potomac. Francis C. Barlow succeeded Orland Smith in command of Second Brigade, Second Division April 17, 1863, and Charles Devens, Jr. was assigned command of First Division April 20, 1863.

Chancellorsville Campaign, April 27, 1863–May 6, 1863. As a part of his plan for the spring campaign of 1863, Hooker organized a flanking column consisting of George G. Meade's Fifth Corps, Oliver O. Howard's Eleventh Corps, and Henry W. Slocum's Twelfth Corps, which was to move around through the Wilderness and strike the left of Lee's army at Fredericksburg. The column marched to Kelly's Ford April 27–28, 1863, and from there Eleventh Corps followed Twelfth Corps across Germanna Ford on the Rapidan River, and then turned to the southeast toward Chancellorsville. On this march both corps were under Slocum's command. Howard's corps arrived in the vicinity of Dowdall's Tavern at 4:00 P.M. April 30, 1863, and camped that night along the Old Turnpike, on the extreme right of the army.

On May 1, 1863, Hooker ordered a general advance of the army toward Fredericksburg, but the order for Eleventh Corps to take part in this movement was countermanded soon after it began, and the corps returned to its former positions.

On May 2, 1863, Thomas J. (Stonewall) Jackson's Confederate corps was observed to the south of Chancellorsville as it marched westward on its flanking movement toward Wilderness Tavern, and Daniel E. Sickles' Third Corps was sent down to attack what was believed to be a part of Lee's retreating army. During the afternoon, Barlow's Second Brigade of Von Steinwehr's division was sent to support Sickles, who was then near Catharine Furnace. Later that evening, Jackson assailed Howard's exposed flank and drove it from its positions west of Chancellorsville. The corps was reorganized that night near Chancellorsville, and the next day it was sent to occupy the positions recently vacated by Fifth Corps on the left of the Union line.

Later, on May 3, 1863, when Hooker had withdrawn the army to a new defensive position covering United States Ford, Eleventh Corps was placed between Second Corps and Twelfth Corps, the latter then being on the extreme left of the army. Eleventh Corps recrossed the Rappahannock with the rest of the army on the night of May 5–6, 1863, and returned to its former camps. For details of the Battle of Chancellorsville, see Chancellorsville, Virginia Campaign.

The organization of Eleventh Corps during the Chancellorsville Campaign was as follows:

ELEVENTH CORPS, Oliver O. Howard

First Division, Charles Devens, Jr., to May 2, 1863, wounded
Nathaniel C. McLean
First Brigade, Leopold Von Gilsa
Second Brigade, Nathaniel C. McLean, to May 2, 1863
John C. Lee
Artillery
13th Battery, New York Light Artillery, Julius Dieckmann

Second Division, Adolph Von Steinwehr
First Brigade, Adolphus Buschbeck

Second Brigade, Francis C. Barlow
Artillery
Battery I, 1st New York Light Artillery, Michael Wiedrich

Third Division, Carl Schurz
First Brigade, Alexander Schimmelfennig
Second Brigade, Wladimir Krzyzanowski
Artillery
Battery I, 1st Ohio Light Artillery, Hubert Dilger

Reserve Artillery, Louis Schirmer
2nd Battery, New York Light Artillery, Hermann Jahn
Battery K, 1st Ohio Light Artillery, William L. De Beck
Battery C, 1st West Virginia Light Artillery, Wallace Hill

Gettysburg Campaign, May 1863–July 1863.
After the Battle of Chancellorsville, Eleventh Corps returned to its former positions near Brooke's Station on the Richmond, Fredericksburg, and Potomac Railroad, and it remained there until June 12, 1863. On that date, the Army of the Potomac started northward at the beginning of the Gettysburg Campaign. That day, Eleventh Corps marched to join First Corps, Third Corps, Fifth Corps, and Alfred Pleasonton's cavalry on the upper Rappahannock. Proceeding by way of Hartwood Church, the corps arrived at Catlett's Station on the Orange and Alexandria Railroad June 13, 1863, and there it came under the orders of John F. Reynolds, commanding the newly organized Right Wing of the army. The next day, Eleventh Corps moved to Manassas Junction, and then on to Centerville June 15, 1863.

Hooker then moved his army westward to the Bull Run Mountains, and, conforming with this movement, Eleventh Corps marched on June 17, 1863 to Goose Creek, about four miles south of Leesburg. It remained there until June 24, 1863, and then moved to the Potomac River at Edwards Ferry preparatory to crossing into Maryland. The next day, Reynolds was again assigned command of the Right Wing of the army, which this time consisted of First Corps, Third Corps, and Eleventh Corps. Under Reynolds' direction, Eleventh Corps moved northward on the left of the army from the Potomac to Middletown. It remained there June 26–27, 1863, and then marched to Frederick June 28, 1863. That day George G. Meade relieved Hooker in command of the Army of the Potomac.

During the advance of the army toward Pennsylvania, which began the next day, Eleventh Corps marched with First Corps to Emmitsburg June 29, 1863. The next day First Corps marched on to Marsh Creek, but Eleventh Corps remained at Emmitsburg. Early on the morning of July 1, 1863, both First Corps and Eleventh Corps marched toward Gettysburg. For details of the march of the army to Gettysburg, see Gettysburg Campaign, Part I, From the Rappahannock to Gettysburg.

There were no significant changes in the organization of Eleventh Corps during May and June 1863, but there were some changes in command. The organization of Eleventh Corps during this period was as follows:

ELEVENTH CORPS, Oliver O. Howard

First Division, Nathaniel C. McLean, to May 1863
  Francis C. Barlow
  First Brigade, Leopold Von Gilsa, to May 25, 1863
    Gotthilf Bourry, to June 6, 1863
    Leopold Von Gilsa
  Second Brigade, John C. Lee, to May 1863
    Adelbert Ames

Second Division, Adolph Von Steinwehr
  First Brigade, Adolphus Buschbeck, to June 10, 1863
    Charles R. Coster
  Second Brigade, Francis C. Barlow, to May 1863
    Orland Smith

Third Division, Carl Schurz
  First Brigade, Alexander Schimmelfennig
  Second Brigade, Wladimir Krzyzanowski

Artillery Brigade, Michael Wiedrich

The Battle of Gettysburg began on the morning of July 1, 1863, when John Buford's Federal cavalry encountered the advancing troops of Ambrose P. Hill's corps on the ridges west of the town. John F. Reynolds, then commanding the Left Wing of Meade's army, soon arrived from Marsh Creek with First Corps and relieved the cavalry, and then continued to rest stubbornly until reinforcements arrived. Eleventh Corps, which had a longer march than First Corps, was some distance away but was advancing on the Emmitsburg Road and the Taneytown Road.

Howard arrived in person at Gettysburg about 10:30–11:00 on the morning of July 1, 1863, and there he learned of the death of Reynolds a short time before. As ranking officer, Howard assumed command of all Union troops then on the field, and also those of his own Eleventh Corps, which were approaching the town. Schurz arrived with his staff about noon, and Howard turned over the command of Eleventh Corps to him.

Schimmelfennig took charge of Schurz's Third Division, and George Von Amsberg replaced Schimmelfennig in command of First Brigade, Third Division.

Schurz's Third Division, then commanded by Schimmelfennig, arrived in Gettysburg about 1:00 P.M., and Barlow's First Division followed a short time later. Meantime, Howard had learned that enemy troops were approaching from the north and northeast, and he sent these two divisions to the north of town, where they formed a line to meet this threat. Schimmelfennig's division was on the left and Barlow's division was on the right. Von Steinwehr's Second Division arrived near the town about 2:00 P.M., and it was placed in reserve on Cemetery Hill.

About mid-afternoon, Eleventh Corps was heavily attacked by Jubal A. Early's division and George Dole's brigade of Robert E. Rodes' division, both of Richard S. Ewell's corps, and it was finally driven back through Gettysburg to Cemetery Hill. Charles R. Coster's First Brigade of Von Steinwehr's division was sent forward to attempt to check the enemy advance, but it was also driven back with the rest of the corps.

Eleventh Corps was posted on Cemetery Hill that evening, and it remained there until its departure from Gettysburg on the evening of July 5, 1863. During the late evening of July 2, 1863, Adelbert Ames' First Division, which was in position on the northeastern slopes of Cemetery Hill, was attacked by two brigades of Early's division, but with aid from Samuel S. Carroll's brigade of Second Corps and other troops of Eleventh Corps, this attack was repulsed.

For details of the fighting at Gettysburg, see Gettysburg Campaign, Part II, Battle of Gettysburg.

The organization of Eleventh Corps at the Battle of Gettysburg was as follows:

ELEVENTH CORPS, Oliver O. Howard, to about noon July 1, 1863
  Carl Schurz, to about 4:30 P.M. July 1, 1863
  Oliver O. Howard

First Division, Francis C. Barlow, to July 1, 1863, wounded

Adelbert Ames

First Brigade, Leopold Von Gilsa

Second Brigade, Adelbert Ames, to July 1, 1863

Andrew L. Harris

Second Division, Adolph Von Steinwehr

First Brigade, Charles R. Coster

Second Brigade, Orland Smith

Third Division, Carl Schurz, to about noon July 1, 1863

Alexander Schimmelfennig, to about 4:30 P.M. July 1, 1863

Carl Schurz

First Brigade, Alexander Schimmelfennig, to about noon July 1, 1863

George Von Amsberg

Second Brigade, Wladimir Krzyzanowski

Artillery Brigade, Thomas W. Osborn

Battery I, 1st New York Light Artillery, Michael Wiedrich

13th Battery, New York Light Artillery, William Wheeler

Battery I, 1st Ohio Light Artillery, Hubert Dilger

Battery K, 1st Ohio Light Artillery, Lewis Heckman

Battery G, 4th United States Artillery, Bayard Wilkeson, to July 1, 1863, mortally wounded

Eugene A. Bancroft

On the night of July 4, 1863, the Army of Northern Virginia withdrew from its positions at Gettysburg and began its retreat toward the Potomac River. In the marching orders for the pursuit, issued by Meade the next day, Eleventh Corps and Fifth Corps were placed under the direction of Howard, who was instructed to march in the center of the army toward Middletown, Maryland. Eleventh Corps camped on Rock Creek on the night of July 5, 1863, and then marched by way of Emmitsburg and Middletown, and arrived at Turner's Gap in South Mountain July 8, 1863. From there, Schurz's division was sent on to Boonsboro to reinforce Buford, whose cavalry was engaged there and was hard pressed. The corps advanced to Beaver Creek July 10, 1863, and on to Funkstown two days later. On July 12, 1863, Ames' First Division and Judson Kilpatrick's Third Cavalry Division occupied Hagerstown. Lee's army recrossed the Potomac into Virginia on the night of July 13, 1863, and the next day Eleventh Corps advanced to Williamsport.

Meade then ordered the army to advance to the Potomac near Harper's Ferry in preparation for crossing into Virginia in pursuit of Lee. July 15, 1863, Eleventh Corps returned to Hagerstown from Williamsport, and then marched through Middletown to Berlin (present-day Brunswick), Maryland, where it arrived the next day. The corps crossed the river at Berlin July 19, 1863, and then, together with First Corps, marched southward on the left of the army along the western side of the Bull Run Mountains. Eleventh Corps advanced by way of Hamilton and Mount Gilead to Mountville, where it halted July 20–22, 1863. It then moved on through New Baltimore and arrived at Warrenton Junction July 25, 1863, and went into camp.

July 31, 1863, Eleventh Corps was ordered to occupy Greenwich, Bristoe Station, and Brentsville, and also to place a sufficient force on Cedar Run, about four or five miles from the Orange and Alexandria Railroad, to patrol and picket the rear of the army. Eleventh Corps was to connect with the pickets of the detachment of Sixth Corps at New Baltimore, and the pickets of Second Corps at Bristerburg. For details of the operations of the Army of the Potomac and of Eleventh Corps from July 5, 1863 to August 1, 1863, see Gettysburg Campaign, Part III, Pursuit of Lee.

During July 1863, Eleventh Corps received strong reinforcements from Virginia. These consisted largely of regiments from Erasmus D. Keyes' Fourth Corps, Department of Virginia. On July 13, 1863, a temporary brigade under Hector Tyndale, composed of regiments taken from First Brigade and Third Brigade of Rufus King's First Division, Fourth Corps, joined Eleventh Corps at Funkstown. Tyndale's brigade was broken up, and the regiments were assigned to the three divisions of the corps. Tyndale was assigned command of First Brigade, Third Division, Eleventh Corps.

July 14, 1863, George H. Gordon's Second Division, Fourth Corps was assigned to Eleventh Corps, and it joined the corps at Berlin, Maryland July 17, 1863. That day, Gordon assumed command of First Division, Eleventh Corps, but this was not his former Second Division, Fourth Corps. The division that Gordon had brought from Virginia was broken up, and the regiments were assigned to First Division and Third Division, Eleventh Corps.

The organization of Eleventh Corps during the latter part of July 1863 was as follows:

ELEVENTH CORPS, Oliver O. Howard

First Division, Adelbert Ames, to July 14, 1863
  Alexander Schimmelfennig, to July 17, 1863
  George H. Gordon
  First Brigade, Leopold Von Gilsa, to July 17, 1863
    Alexander Schimmelfennig
  Second Brigade, Andrew L. Harris, to July 4, 1863
    William H. Noble
    Philip P. Brown, Jr., to July 14, 1863
    Adelbert Ames

Second Division, Adolph Von Steinwehr
  First Brigade, Charles R. Coster
    Adolphus Buschbeck
  Second Brigade, Orland Smith

Note. Smith was in temporary command of Second Division for a time after the Battle of Gettysburg.

Third Division, Carl Schurz
  First Brigade, Alexander Schimmelfennig, to July 13, 1863
    Hector Tyndale
  Second Brigade, Wladimir Krzyzanowski

Note. Schurz was ordered to Washington July 29, 1863, and Tyndale was in temporary command of Third Division for a few days.

Artillery Brigade, Thomas W. Osborn

Along the Orange and Alexandria Railroad, August 1, 1863–September 25, 1863. Eleventh Corps remained generally in position along the Orange and Alexandria Railroad during August and September 1863. When the Army of the Potomac advanced from its positions along the Rappahannock to Culpeper Court House and the Rapidan River September 13–16, 1863, Eleventh Corps was left along the railroad to protect the army's line of communications, especially with forces posted to guard the bridges at Rappahannock Crossing, Catlett's Station, and Bristoe Station.

During August 1863, the corps was reduced to two divisions. On August 5, 1863, George H. Gordon's First Division was ordered from Warrenton Junction to Alexandria, Virginia. It was to embark there for Morris Island, South Carolina, in the Department of the South, to reinforce Quincy A. Gillmore's forces at Charleston Harbor. It was permanently detached from Eleventh Corps August 7, 1863, and transferred to Tenth Corps, where it was

designated as United States Forces South End of Folly Island. For further information, see Department of the South, Part III, Department of the South, Tenth Corps. The other two divisions of Eleventh Corps remained on the railroad until September 25, 1863.

Transfer of Eleventh Corps and Twelfth Corps to the Army of the Cumberland, September 1863. Upon learning of the defeat of William S. Rosecrans' Army of the Cumberland at Chickamauga, Tennessee September 19–20, 1863, Secretary of War Edwin McM. Stanton became concerned about the possible loss of Chattanooga, and on the night of September 23, 1863, he called a meeting at the War Department, to which President Lincoln was invited. There it was decided to send two corps from the Army of the Potomac to reinforce the Army of the Cumberland. The next morning the president directed that Eleventh Corps and Twelfth Corps be sent to Tennessee under the command of Joseph Hooker.

Eleventh Corps, which was then already on the Orange and Alexandria Railroad, moved first. During September 25, 1863, the troops entrained at Bristoe Station and Manassas Junction and traveled to Washington, D.C. From there they proceeded on west by the Baltimore and Ohio Railroad to Benwood, West Virginia. By 9:15 A.M. September 27, 1863, 12,600 men, 33 cars of artillery, and 21 cars of baggage had left Washington, and the first train had arrived at Benwood. At that time, Twelfth Corps began entraining at Bealeton Station on the Orange and Alexandria Railroad to follow Eleventh Corps west.

After crossing the Ohio River to Bellaire, Ohio, Eleventh Corps continued on by way of the Central Ohio and Indiana Central railroads, through Columbus, Ohio to Indianapolis, Indiana. The first train reached Indianapolis on the evening of September 28, 1863, as the last troops of Twelfth Corps were leaving Bealeton Station. From Indianapolis, Eleventh Corps moved on to Jeffersonville, crossed the Ohio River to Louisville, Kentucky, and from there it proceeded on by the Louisville and Nashville Railroad to Nashville, Tennessee. It then moved on to Stevenson and Bridgeport in Alabama. The first four trains arrived at Bridgeport September 30, 1863, but they were unable to continue farther because the bridge over the Tennessee had been destroyed. On that day, the last troop trains reached Benwood from Washington. The last troops of Eleventh Corps arrived at Bridgeport October 2, 1863, and the next day, Hooker arrived at Stevenson and established headquarters of his command. Howard joined Eleventh Corps at Bridgeport October 4, 1863.

By October 8, 1863, the movement of Eleventh Corps and Twelfth Corps was completed. The baggage of the two corps, including horses, wagons, ambulances, and commissary, followed over the same route during the first two weeks of October 1863.

COMMANDERS OF ELEVENTH CORPS, ARMY OF THE POTOMAC

Franz Sigel	September 12, 1862 to January 10, 1863
Julius Stahel	January 10, 1863 to January 19, 1863
Carl Schurz	January 19, 1863 to February 6, 1863
Franz Sigel	February 6, 1863 to February 22, 1863
Adolph Von Steinwehr	February 22, 1863 to March 5, 1863
Carl Schurz	March 5, 1863 to April 2, 1863
Oliver O. Howard	April 2, 1863 to July 1, 1863
Carl Schurz	Temporarily July 1, 1863
Oliver O. Howard	July 1, 1863 to September 25, 1863

Note. Sigel left the army for Washington December 18, 1862, and left Theodore A. Meysenburg, his assistant adjutant general, in charge of corps headquarters, and Julius Stahel in command of the troops of Eleventh Corps.

TWELFTH CORPS, ARMY OF THE POTOMAC

Following John Pope's defeat at the Second Battle of Bull Run August 30, 1862, Nathaniel Banks' Second Corps, Army of Virginia retreated with the rest of the army into the Defenses of Washington, where it took position south of the Potomac River. On September 3, 1862, Alpheus S. Williams relieved Banks, who was ill, and on the same day he moved the corps across the Potomac River to Tennallytown in the District of Columbia. On September 4, 1862, the Army of Northern Virginia crossed the Potomac River at White's Ford and moved northward into Maryland. The next day Williams' corps, and also Edwin V. Sumner's Second Corps, Army of the Potomac, moved to Rockville, Maryland, where both were in a strong position on September 6, 1862. Second Corps, Army of Virginia and Second Corps, Army of the Potomac were then assigned as the Center of the army that George B. McClellan was organizing for the pursuit of Lee in Maryland. Sumner was assigned command of the two corps.

McClellan advanced his army to Frederick, Maryland, and while there, on September 12, 1862, the designation of Williams' corps was changed from Second Corps, Army of Virginia to Twelfth Corps, Army of the Potomac. Joseph K. F. Mansfield was assigned command, but Williams continued to exercise control until September 15, 1862, when Mansfield arrived from the Department of Virginia and assumed command at South Mountain. When organized, Twelfth Corps consisted of the following:

TWELFTH CORPS, Alpheus S. Williams, to September 15, 1862
Joseph K. F. Mansfield

First Division, Samuel W. Crawford, to September 15, 1862
Alpheus S. Williams
First Brigade, Joseph F. Knipe, to September 15, 1862
Samuel W. Crawford
Third Brigade, George H. Gordon

Note. There was no Second Brigade in First Division at this time. The former Second Brigade, First Division, Department of the Shenandoah had been transferred to the Department of the Rappahannock May 1, 1862.

Second Division, George S. Greene
First Brigade, Charles Candy, to September 17, 1862
Hector Tyndale
Second Brigade, Thomas B. Van Buren, to September 15, 1862
Henry J. Stainrook
Third Brigade, William B. Goodrich

Twelfth Corps was near South Mountain during the battle of September 14, 1862, but it was not engaged. On the following morning, Mansfield arrived and assumed command of the corps, which then marched on through Boonsboro and Keedysville, and took up a position along Antietam Creek, near Sharpsburg, Maryland. On the afternoon of September 16, 1862, Joseph Hooker's First Corps moved westward from Keedysville to the Hagerstown Pike, on the extreme right of McClellan's line, and during the night, Twelfth Corps followed Hooker, and camped about a mile to his left and rear.

Hooker launched the initial attack of the Battle of Antietam at daylight September 17, 1862 by advancing down the Hagerstown Pike toward Sharpsburg. A short time later Twelfth Corps advanced on his left. Mansfield was mortally wounded early in the action, and Williams again assumed command. Twelfth Corps advanced to the vicinity of the Dunker (Dunkard) Church before it was stopped by heavy enemy fire. Samuel W. Crawford's First Division was taken out of the line about 9:00 A.M., but George S. Greene's Second Division held its position near the church until 1:30 that afternoon before he was forced to retire. About 5:30 P.M., Twelfth Corps took position in rear of William B. Franklin's Sixth Corps, which was then in line of battle in the East Woods, facing west. For details of the Battle of Antietam, see Maryland Campaign (South Mountain and Antietam).

The organization of Twelfth Corps at the Battle of Antietam, September 17, 1862, was as follows:

TWELFTH CORPS, Joseph K. F. Mansfield, mortally wounded
Alpheus S. Williams

First Division, Alpheus S. Williams
Samuel W. Crawford, wounded
George H. Gordon
First Brigade, Samuel W. Crawford
Joseph F. Knipe
Third Brigade, George H. Gordon
Thomas H. Ruger

Second Division, George S. Greene
First Brigade, Hector Tyndale, wounded
Orrion J. Crane
Second Brigade, Henry J. Stainrook
Third Brigade, William B. Goodrich, killed
Jonathan Austin

Artillery, Clermont L. Best

4th Battery (D), Maine Light Artillery, O'Neil W. Robinson
6th Battery (F), Maine Light Artillery, Freeman McGilvery
Battery M, 1st New York Light Artillery, George W. Cothran
10th Battery, New York Light Artillery, John T. Bruen
Battery E, Pennsylvania Light Artillery, Joseph M. Knap
Battery F, Pennsylvania Light Artillery, Robert B. Hampton
Battery F, 4th United States Artillery, Edward D. Muhlenberg

Note. Williams did not officially assume command of Twelfth Corps until September 18, 1862. Prior to that date, he had used as the designation of his command Second Corps, Army of Virginia, although Twelfth Corps had been created by an order of September 12, 1862.

At Harper's Ferry, September 21, 1862–December 9, 1862. Twelfth Corps remained near the battlefield of Antietam only until September 19, 1862, and then it was ordered to Harper's Ferry. Two days later it occupied Maryland Heights, and then First Division was sent to Sandy Hook and Second Division to Loudoun Heights. The corps remained in the general area of Harper's Ferry until December 9, 1862, and then it was ordered to Dumfries, Virginia to guard the Washington front during the Fredericksburg Campaign.

October 4, 1862, eight new regiments were assigned to Twelfth Corps, and these were temporarily organized into a brigade designated as Second Brigade, First Division, which was assigned to George L. Andrews. This organization was discontinued two days later, however, and the regiments were assigned to two new brigades. Four of the regiments were organized into a new brigade designated as Fourth Brigade, First Division to be commanded by Andrews; and the other four regiments were organized into a Second Brigade, First Division under Thomas L. Kane. Thus on October 6, First Division was organized as follows:

First Division, George H. Gordon
First Brigade, Joseph F. Knipe
Second Brigade, Thomas L. Kane
Third Brigade, Thomas H. Ruger
Fourth Brigade, George L. Andrews

Note. Fourth Brigade was discontinued October 26, 1862 by the transfer of its regiments to Third Brigade, Second Division, and to the Defenses of Washington.

October 13, 1862, Ambrose E. Burnside was assigned command of the Defenses of Harper's Ferry, and Second Corps, Ninth Corps, and Twelfth Corps were placed under his control. This arrangement was continued until October 26, 1862, when the Army of the Potomac crossed the river and began its advance toward Warrenton, Virginia.

On October 20, 1862, Henry W. Slocum assumed command of Twelfth Corps (assigned command October 15, 1862) and Williams resumed command of First Division.

October 22, 1862, Amiel W. Whipple's Division from the Defenses of Washington arrived at McClellan's headquarters at Knoxville, Maryland, near Harper's Ferry, and it was assigned to Twelfth Corps as Third Division. This division was one of the first to cross the Potomac when the army began its advance into Virginia October 26, 1862. It was then detached from Twelfth Corps October 29, 1862, and assigned to a special force under Burnside. This consisted of Ninth Corps, George Stoneman's Division (detached from Ninth Corps), and Whipple's Division (its new designation). Whipple's Division did not rejoin Twelfth Corps, but was asssigned to Third Corps as Third Division in November 1862.

Twelfth Corps did not accompany the army on its advance into Virginia, but it was detached and left behind in the vicinity of Harper's Ferry to watch the Potomac.

October 26, 1862, Twelfth Corps was extensively reorganized, largely by the transfer of regiments among the brigades of the corps. In this process Fourth Brigade, First Division was broken up and discontinued. The corps was then organized as follows:

TWELFTH CORPS, Henry W. Slocum

First Division, Alpheus S. Williams
    First Brigade, Joseph F. Knipe
    Second Brigade, Thomas L. Kane
    Third Brigade, George H. Gordon

Second Division, John W. Geary
    First Brigade, Thomas H. Ruger
    Second Brigade, Nathaniel J. Jackson
    Third Brigade, George L. Andrews, to October 31, 1862
        George S. Greene

Note. Geary, who had been wounded at Cedar Mountain, rejoined the corps and assumed command of Second Division October 15, 1862. Greene left on sick leave at that time.

October 29, 1862, Gordon's Third Brigade, First Division was sent from Maryland Heights to relieve Fitz John Porter's Fifth Corps near Sharpsburg. The next day, Gordon's Brigade was detached from Twelfth Corps and placed under the command of George W. Morell, who that same day was assigned command of the Defenses of the Upper Potomac. Third Brigade remained with Morell until December 9, 1862, when it left with Twelfth Corps to join Franz Sigel as a part of the Reserve of the Army of the Potomac.

October 30, 1862, Slocum's territorial command was extended to include the troops at Frederick, Maryland. In early December 1862, the troops of Twelfth Corps were posted as follows: Joseph F. Knipe's First Brigade, First Division was on Maryland Heights; Thomas L. Kane's Second Brigade, First Division was in the Loudoun Valley, near Loudoun Heights; George H. Gordon's Third Brigade, First Division (detached) was near Sharpsburg; and John W. Geary's Second Division was on Bolivar Heights.

Fredericksburg Campaign, November 7, 1862– December 15, 1862. In early December 1862, Sigel's Eleventh Corps was generally in the Centerville-Fairfax Court House area and along the Orange and Alexandria Railroad, covering Washington. On December 9, 1862, Sigel was ordered to join the Army of the Potomac, then commanded by Ambrose E. Burnside, near Falmouth, Virginia, where it was preparing to advance against Lee's army at Fredericksburg. That same day, Slocum was ordered to march with his Twelfth Corps from Harper's Ferry toward Dumfries, Virginia to join Sigel's Reserve, which at that time consisted only of Eleventh Corps. Eleventh Corps left its positions in front of the Defenses of Washington December 10–11, 1862 and marched toward Dumfries and Fredericksburg.

On December 13, 1862, the day of the Battle of Fredericksburg, Slocum's leading division arrived at Fairfax Court House. Slocum then came under Sigel's orders as a part of the Reserve of the army.

That day, Twelfth Corps was ordered to Fredericksburg, but December 16, 1862, it was assigned to positions at Fairfax Court House, Wolf Run Shoals, and Dumfries.

Winter of 1862–1863. Twelfth Corps remained along the Fairfax Court House-Wolf Run Shoals-Dumfries line, with headquarters at the latter place, until January 19, 1863. The principal posts were at Fairfax Court House and Dumfries. The corps was employed principally in aiding in the defense of Washington against Confederate cavalry raids on posts in the vicinity. The most threatening of these was James E. B. (Jeb) Stuart's raid on Dumfries and Fairfax Court House December 27–29, 1862. Charles Candy's First Brigade, Second Division, which was at Dumfries at that time, was engaged December 27, 1862.

The organization of Twelfth Corps at the end of December 1862 was as follows:

TWELFTH CORPS, Henry W. Slocum

First Division, Alpheus S. Williams
  First Brigade, Joseph F. Knipe
  Second Brigade, Thomas L. Kane
  Third Brigade, John K. Murphy
  Artillery, Robert H. Fitzhugh
    Battery K, 1st New York Light Artillery, Edward L. Bailey
    Battery M, 1st New York Light Artillery, Charles E. Winegar
    Battery F, 4th United States Artillery, Edward D. Muhlenberg

Second Division, John W. Geary
  First Brigade, Charles Candy
  Second Brigade, Joseph M. Sudsburg
  Third Brigade, George S. Greene
  Artillery, Luther Kieffer
    6th Battery (F), Maine Light Artillery, Edwin Dow
    Battery E, Pennsylvania Light Artillery, Joseph M. Knap
    Battery F, Pennsylvania Light Artillery, R. B. Hampton

Note. Sudsburg commanded Second Brigade temporarily during the absence of Nathaniel J. Jackson, who resumed command January 3, 1863.

January 10, 1863, Sigel's Reserve of the Army of the Potomac, then consisting of Eleventh Corps and Twelfth Corps, was redesignated as the Grand Reserve Division of the army, and Sigel remained in command. When the grand divisions were abolished by Joseph Hooker February 5, 1863, Slocum was directed to report directly to Headquarters Army of the Potomac

January 19, 1863, Slocum was ordered to move with his Twelfth Corps to Stafford Court House, and that day Williams' First Division and Geary's Second Division (less Candy's brigade) marched for Dumfries. First Division arrived at Stafford Court House January 23, 1863, and Second Division followed the next day. This march, which was made at the same time as Burnside's famous "Mud March," was extremely difficult because of high water and muddy roads. Both divisions established winter quarters, and were engaged in guard duty for the next month.

In early February 1863, Twelfth Corps extended its line of pickets from Potomac Creek to Aquia Creek. First Division and one brigade of Second Division were near Stafford Court House, facing west; one brigade of Second Division was at Aquia Creek Landing; and Candy's brigade of Second Division (commanded part of the time by William R. Creighton) was at Dumfries. On April 14, 1863, in preparation for Hooker's spring campaign, the brigade at Dumfries was ordered to Stafford Court House.

Chancellorsville Campaign, April 27, 1863–May 6, 1863. As a part of his plan for the spring campaign of 1863, Hooker organized a flanking column consisting of George G. Meade's Fifth Corps, Oliver O. Howard's Eleventh Corps, and Henry W. Slocum's Twelfth Corps, which was to move across the Rappahannock River and around through the Wilderness to strike the left flank of Lee's army at Fredericksburg. Twelfth Corps and the other two corps marched to Kelly's Ford April 27–28, 1863, and from there Twelfth Corps, followed by Eleventh Corps, marched to Germanna Ford on the Rapidan River. During this movement, Slocum was in command of both corps. After crossing the river, Slocum marched to the southeast toward Chancellorsville, and his Twelfth Corps arrived there about 2:00 P.M. April 30, 1863. Slocum then placed his corps in position on the left of Eleventh Corps, with its left extending to the Orange Plank Road south of Chancellorsville. Williams' division was on the right and Geary's division on the left of this line.

On May 1, 1863, Hooker ordered Meade's Fifth Corps to advance eastward toward Fredericksburg, and he directed Slocum to move forward with his Twelfth Corps along the Plank Road, on the right of George Sykes' Second Division, Fifth Corps. About two hours after starting, however, Hooker ordered Twelfth Corps to return to its original position.

On May 2, 1863, Geary advanced his division, but he soon encountered strong resistance and withdrew. Also that afternoon, Williams' division was sent forward to support Daniel E. Sickles' Third Corps, which had moved down to Catharine Furnace when Thomas J. (Stonewall) Jackson's flanking column was observed passing across some open space to the south. Later that evening, when Howard's Eleventh Corps was routed by Jackson's attack, Williams' division returned to the Plank Road and, with Sickles' divisions, aided in halting the Confederate advance. Jackson was wounded late that evening, and during the night James E. B. (Jeb) Stuart assumed command of his corps.

Williams' division was heavily engaged south of the Plank Road during the early morning of May 3, 1863, when Stuart resumed the attacks on Hooker's right flank, but it finally retired from the field with Geary's division about 9:00 A.M. Twelfth Corps was then ordered to the extreme left of Hooker's new defensive line, and it was formed with its left on the Rappahannock and its right connecting with Eleventh Corps. It remained in this position until the army withdrew across the Rappahannock River on the night of May 5–6, 1863, and it then returned to its former camps. For details of the Battle of Chancellorsville, see Chancellorsville, Virginia Campaign.

The organization of Twelfth Corps at the Battle of Chancellorsville was as follows:

TWELFTH CORPS, Henry W. Slocum

First Division, Alpheus S. Williams
  First Brigade, Joseph F. Knipe
  Second Brigade, Samuel Ross
  Third Brigade, Thomas H. Ruger
  Artillery, Robert H. Fitzhugh
    Battery K, 1st New York Light Artillery, Edward L. Bailey
    Battery M, 1st New York Light Artillery, Charles E.

Winegar, to May 3, 1863, captured
      John D. Woodbury
    Battery F, 4th United States Artillery, Franklin B. Crosby, to May 3, 1863, killed
      Edward D. Muhlenberg

Second Division, John W. Geary
  First Brigade, Charles Candy
  Second Brigade, Thomas L. Kane
  Third Brigade, George S. Greene
  Artillery, Joseph M. Knap
    Battery E, Pennsylvania Light Artillery, Charles A. Atwell, to May 2, 1863, wounded
      James D. McGill
    Battery F, Pennsylvania Light Artillery, Robert F. Hampton, to May 3, 1863, mortally wounded
      James P. Fleming

Gettysburg Campaign, May 1863–July 1863. After the Battle of Chancellorsville, Twelfth Corps returned to the vicinity of Stafford Court House and Aquia Landing, and it remained there until June 13, 1863. During this period there was some reorganization in Twelfth Corps. In May 1863, First Brigade, First Division was reduced to two regiments when two regiments of the brigade were sent home for muster out. Second Brigade, First Division, which consisted of four regiments, was temporarily attached to First Brigade May 13, 1863. In June 1863, Second Brigade was discontinued by the transfer of its regiments to First Brigade.

On June 3, 1863, Lee's Army of Northern Virginia began to withdraw from its positions at Fredericksburg and along the Rapidan River as it began its march toward Culpeper Court House and the Shenandoah Valley, on its way toward Maryland and Pennsylvania. Finally, on June 13, 1863, Hooker became convinced that Lee was moving northward, and he began to move the Army of the Potomac back from the line of the Rappahannock to the Orange and Alexandria Railroad. During this movement, Twelfth Corps marched by way of Dumfries, and reached Fairfax Court House June 15, 1863. Two days later, the army moved to the west and northwest toward the Bull Run Mountains and the Potomac River. As a part of this movement, Twelfth Corps marched through Dranesville to Leesburg, and it occupied the town from June 18, 1863 to June 25, 1863.

On June 25, 1863, the army began its advance into Maryland. The next day, Twelfth Corps crossed the

Potomac at Edwards Ferry and marched to Frederick, where it arrived June 28, 1863. On that date, George G. Meade relieved Hooker in command of the Army of the Potomac. The next day Meade started the army northward toward Pennsylvania on an extended front, and Twelfth Corps marched on the center of this line. It passed through Taneytown, Littlestown, and Two Taverns, and arrived on the field of Gettysburg about 5:00–5:30 on the afternoon of July 1, 1863. For details of the march to Gettysburg, see Gettysburg Campaign, Part I, From the Rappahannock to Gettysburg.

The organization of Twelfth Corps during May and June 1863 was as follows:

TWELFTH CORPS, Henry W. Slocum

First Division, Alpheus S. Williams
   First Brigade, Joseph F. Knipe, to May 1863
      Archibald L. McDougall
   Second Brigade, Samuel Ross, to May 13, 1863
      Archibald L. McDougall
   Third Brigade, Thomas H. Ruger

Note. May 13, 1863, Second Brigade was attached to First Brigade, and in June 1863, it was discontinued when it was merged into First Brigade.

Second Division, John W. Geary
   First Brigade, Charles Candy
   Second Brigade, Thomas L. Kane, to May 1863, sick
      George A. Cobham, Jr.
   Third Brigade, George S. Greene

Artillery Brigade, Edward D. Muhlenberg

Twelfth Corps marched from Two Taverns on the afternoon of July 1, 1863, and approached the rear of the Union positions on Cemetery Hill about 5:00 that evening. Geary's Second Division marched on across Rock Creek and formed on the high ground north of Little Round Top, where it spent the night. Williams' First Division, temporarily under Ruger, halted east of Rock Creek, to the right and rear of the position of James S. Wadsworth's First Division, First Corps on Culp's Hill. Early on the morning of July 2, 1863, the two divisions of Twelfth Corps were sent to Culp's Hill on the Union right. Geary's division was formed along the crest of the hill on the right of Wadsworth's division, and Ruger's division continued the line on down the hill to Rock Creek, near the crossing of the Baltimore Pike.

At about this time, Henry H. Lockwood with a Provisional Brigade arrived from Baltimore and reported to Williams, who was in temporary command of Twelfth Corps. His arrival created a command problem. Lockwood was senior in rank to Ruger, who was in temporary command of First Division, Twelfth Corps, and Williams was unwilling to turn over the command of First Division to a man of unknown capability, and he could not ask Lockwood to serve under his junior in rank. To solve this problem, Williams kept Lockwood's brigade as an unassigned command, and personally directed Lockwood's brigade and Ruger's division during the battle. On July 5, 1863, however, after Williams had resumed command of First Division and Ruger had returned to Third Brigade, First Division, Lockwood's Provisional Brigade was assigned to First Division as Second Brigade.

During James Longstreet's attack on the Union left late in the afternoon of July 2, 1863, Williams personally led Ruger's division and Lockwood's brigade to support the line on the lower part of Cemetery Ridge, near Freeman McGilvery's artillery position. Lockwood immediately charged the enemy approaching on his front, and drove them back almost to the Peach Orchard. Ruger formed his division in line of battle on the ridge, but he was not engaged. Geary was directed to follow Williams, with the brigades of Candy and Kane (then commanded by Cobham), but on the way he took the wrong road and did not arrive on the Union left that evening. After the departure of Twelfth Corps for the left of Meade's line, troops of Edward Johnson's division of Richard S. Ewell's corps moved up Culp's Hill and occupied the works that Williams' troops had just vacated.

Soon after dark, while the fighting was still in progress, Williams and Geary were ordered back to Culp's Hill, but when they returned shortly after midnight they found their former positions held by the enemy. Williams' two divisions then took up new positions on and near the hill. On the morning of July 3, 1863, Geary's division was engaged in repelling renewed attacks by Johnson's division on Culp's Hill, and finally, when Ruger's division came up, they succeeded in driving the enemy back and restoring their former positions. For details of the fighting at Gettysburg, see Gettysburg Campaign, Part II, Battle of Gettysburg.

The organization of Twelfth Corps at the Battle of Gettysburg was as follows:

TWELFTH CORPS, Alpheus S. Williams

First Division, Thomas H. Ruger
 First Brigade, Archibald L. McDougall
 Third Brigade, Silas Colgrove

Note 1. Slocum, the permanent commander of Twelfth Corps, was in command of the Right Wing of the Army July 1–4, 1863, and Williams was in temporary command of Twelfth Corps during the same period. While Williams commanded Twelfth Corps, Ruger commanded his First Division, and Colgrove commanded Ruger's Third Brigade.

Note 2. There was no Second Brigade, First Division during the Battle of Gettysburg, although Lockwood's Provisional Brigade was sometimes referred to as such. This brigade reported to First Division about 8:00 A.M. July 2, 1863 from Baltimore in the Middle Department, but it was unassigned until July 5, 1863, and then it was attached to First Division as Second Brigade. At Gettysburg, Lockwood was under Williams' direct orders.

Second Division, John W. Geary
 First Brigade, Charles Candy
 Second Brigade, George A. Cobham, Jr.
  Thomas L. Kane
  George A. Cobham, Jr.
 Third Brigade, George S. Greene

Note. Kane, who was ill, joined Twelfth Corps at 6:00 A.M. July 2, 1863, and assumed command of Second Brigade. Because of his illness, however, he relinquished command a short time later, and Cobham resumed command. Kane remained on the field, and perhaps for this reason many reports refer to Kane's brigade, although Cobham was actually in command except for a brief time.

Lockwood's Provisional Brigade, Henry H. Lockwood

Artillery Brigade, Edward D. Muhlenberg
 Battery M, 1st New York Light Artillery, Charles E. Winegar
 Battery E, Pennsylvania Light Artillery, Charles A. Atwell
 Battery F, 4th United States Artillery, Sylvanus T. Rugg
 Battery K, 5th United States Artillery, David H. Kinzie

On July 4, 1863, Twelfth Corps remained in its positions on Culp's Hill, and spent the time in burying the dead and collecting arms. That night, the Army of Northern Virginia left its positions at Gettysburg and began its retreat toward the Potomac River.

The orders for the movement of the Army of the Potomac in pursuit of Lee, issued by Meade on July 5, 1863, directed Slocum to assume control of his own Twelfth Corps and Winfield S. Hancock's Second Corps (then commanded by William Hays), and march on the left of the army toward Middletown, Maryland. Twelfth Corps left Gettysburg July 5, 1863, and marched through Littlestown, Walkersville, and Jefferson, and arrived at Rohrersville, Maryland July 9, 1863. It then advanced on the extreme left of the army, first to Bakersville, and then to Fair Play and Jones' Cross Roads (present-day Lappans). It remained in the latter two places from July 11, 1863 to July 14, 1863. Lee's army recrossed the Potomac River into Virginia on the night of July 13, 1863, and Twelfth Corps moved up to Falling Waters and Williamsport. For additional information, see Gettysburg Campaign, Part III, Pursuit of Lee, From Gettysburg to Falling Waters.

Early on the morning of July 15, 1863, Meade began the movement of the army to the Potomac River near Harper's Ferry in preparation for crossing into Virginia. Twelfth Corps reached Sandy Hook that day, and the next day moved into Pleasant Valley. The corps crossed the Potomac at Harper's Ferry July 19, 1863, and then marched south, together with Second Corps and Third Corps, along the eastern base of the Blue Ridge Mountains. Twelfth Corps advanced by way of Hillsboro and Woodgrove to Snickersville, where it halted July 20, 1863. Then, on July 23, 1863, it resumed its march and passed Ashby's Gap and Markham's Station, and arrived at Linden in Manassas Gap July 24, 1863. Third Corps was engaged there the day before, but Twelfth Corps came up too late to join in the action. Twelfth Corps then countermarched by way of Markham's Station and reached Piedmont that day. July 25, 1863, the corps marched eastward by way of Rectortown and White Plains to Thoroughfare Gap, and the next day continued on through Greenwich and Catlett's Station to Warrenton Junction. July 31, 1863, Twelfth Corps advanced to Kelly's Ford, and Ruger's Third Brigade, First Division was sent on to Ellis' Ford. Twelfth Corps was then assigned to hold and picket the line of the Rappahannock River from Wheatley's Ford, about a mile north of Kelly's Ford, to Ellis' Ford. For additional information about the movements of the army in Virginia during this period, see Gettysburg Campaign, Part III, Pursuit of Lee, From Williamsport and Falling Waters to the Rappahannock River.

The organization of Twelfth Corps during the movement from Gettysburg to the Rappahannock was as follows:

TWELFTH CORPS, Henry W. Slocum

First Division, Alpheus S. Williams
  First Brigade, Archibald L. McDougall, to July 1863
    Joseph F. Knipe
  Second Brigade, Henry H. Lockwood
  Third Brigade, Thomas H. Ruger

Note. Lockwood's Provisional Brigade was designated as Second Brigade, First Division July 5, 1863. The brigade was discontinued July 15, 1863, when Lockwood and the Maryland regiments of the brigade were transferred to Harper's Ferry.

Second Division, John W. Geary
  First Brigade, Charles Candy
  Second Brigade, George A. Cobham, Jr.
  Third Brigade, George S. Greene

Artillery Brigade, Edward D. Muhlenburg
  John D. Woodbury

From the Rappahannock to the Rapidan, August 1, 1863–October 10, 1863.

During August and early September 1863, Twelfth Corps remained in position along the Rappahannock River from Wheatley's Ford to Ellis' Ford. During this time, Twelfth Corps was temporarily reduced in numbers when some troops were sent to New York to aid in controlling the disturbances caused by the draft. August 16, 1863, Thomas H. Ruger was ordered to New York with seven regiments of Twelfth Corps, including four Ohio regiments of Charles Candy's First Brigade, Second Division, and two regiments each from Second Corps and Third Corps. All the Twelfth Corps regiments were assigned to Edward R. S. Canby's command as a part of Second Brigade, New York City. Ruger commanded this brigade. September 9, 1863, Ruger was ordered to return with his troops to the Army of the Potomac, and Ruger and the Twelfth Corps regiments rejoined the corps at Kelly's Ford September 12, 1863. For additional information, see Department of the East,

January 3, 1863–June 27, 1865, Draft Riots in New York, 1863.

September 13, 1863, Alfred Pleasonton's Cavalry Corps, Army of the Potomac, supported by Gouverneur K. Warren's Second Corps, crossed the Rappahannock River and occupied Culpeper Court House. It then moved south and drove the enemy cavalry across the Rapidan River. Three days later, the rest of Meade's army (except Eleventh Corps) moved forward and formed a line through Culpeper Court House, facing the Rapidan. Twelfth Corps advanced to Stevensburg, and that same day, September 16, 1863, it was ordered to Raccoon Ford on the Rapidan to relieve the cavalry pickets along the river from Somerville down to Morton's Ford.

The organization of Twelfth Corps during the period August 1, 1863–September 25, 1863 was as follows:

TWELFTH CORPS, Henry W. Slocum, to August 13, 1863
  Alpheus S. Williams, to August 15, 1863
  Henry W. Slocum, to August 31, 1863
  Alpheus S. Williams, to September 13, 1863
  Henry W. Slocum, to September 25, 1863

First Division, Alpheus S. Williams, to August 13, 1863
  Joseph F. Knipe, to August 15, 1863
  Alpheus S. Williams, to August 31, 1863
  Joseph F. Knipe, to September 13, 1863
  Alpheus S. Williams, to September 25, 1863
  First Brigade, Joseph F. Knipe, to August 13, 1863
    Samuel Ross, to August 15, 1863
    Joseph F. Knipe, to August 31, 1863
    Samuel Ross, to September 13, 1863
    Joseph F. Knipe, to September 25, 1863
  Third Brigade, Thomas H. Ruger, to August 16, 1863
    Ezra Carman, to September 16, 1863
    Thomas H. Ruger, to September 25, 1863

Note 1. Williams commanded Twelfth Corps temporarily August 13–15, 1863, while Slocum was in charge of Headquarters Army of the Potomac; and he also was in command of the corps August 31, 1863–September 13, 1863, while Slocum was in Washington, and then on leave.

Note 2. Ruger, with three regiments of his brigade, was on duty in New York August 16, 1863–September 16, 1863, during the disturbances caused by the draft.

Second Division, John W. Geary
  First Brigade, Charles Candy, to August 16, 1863
    Ario Pardee, Jr., to September 6, 1863
    Charles Candy, to September 25, 1863

Second Brigade, George A. Cobham, Jr.
Third Brigade, George S. Greene

Note. Candy, with four regiments of his brigade, was on duty in New York August 16, 1863–September 6, 1863, during the disturbances caused by the draft.

Artillery, John D. Woodbury
    John A. Reynolds

Note. The batteries with Twelfth Corps were the same as at the Battle of Gettysburg.

Transfer of Eleventh Corps and Twelfth Corps to the Army of the Cumberland, September 1863. Twelfth Corps remained in position along the Rapidan until September 24, 1863, and that day Eleventh Corps and Twelfth Corps were detached from the Army of the Potomac and ordered to Tennessee to reinforce William S. Rosecrans' Army of the Cumberland, then besieged at Chattanooga. Also that day Joseph Hooker was assigned command of the two corps.

On the afternoon of September 24, 1863, Twelfth Corps was relieved along the Rapidan by John Newton's First Corps, and about 5:30 it marched for Brandy Station on the Orange and Alexandria Railroad for transfer to Washington, D.C. The corps arrived at Brandy Station the next day but, finding no cars there, moved on that evening to Bealeton Station, where it entrained September 27–28, 1863. Eleventh Corps, which was in position on the line of the Orange and Alexandria Railroad when ordered west, left first on September 25, 1863, and Twelfth Corps followed as both corps moved west across West Virginia, Ohio, and Indiana, and then south through Kentucky to Tennessee. For more details of the route followed, see Eleventh Corps, Army of the Potomac. Some regiments of Twelfth Corps arrived at Bridgeport, Alabama with Eleventh Corps about October 1, 1863, but the corps proper did not arrive at Nashville, Tennessee until several days later. On October 3, 1863, Hooker arrived at Stevenson, Alabama and established headquarters for his two corps.

COMMANDERS OF TWELFTH CORPS, ARMY OF THE POTOMAC

Alpheus S. Williams	September 12, 1862 to September 15, 1862
Joseph K. F. Mansfield	September 15, 1862 to September 17, 1862, killed
Alpheus S. Williams	September 17, 1862 to October 20, 1862
Henry W. Slocum	October 20, 1862 to July 1, 1863
Alpheus S. Williams	July 1, 1863 to July 4, 1863
Henry W. Slocum	July 4, 1863 to August 13, 1863
Alpheus S. Williams	August 13, 1863 to August 15, 1863
Henry W. Slocum	August 15, 1863 to August 31, 1863
Alpheus S. Williams	August 31, 1863 to September 13, 1863
Henry W. Slocum	September 13, 1863 to September 25, 1863

EIGHTEENTH CORPS, DEPARTMENT OF NORTH CAROLINA

Eighteenth Corps was created by a presidential order of December 24, 1862, to consist of the troops in the Department of North Carolina. John G. Foster was assigned command. The corps was organized December 28, 1862, as follows:

EIGHTEENTH CORPS, John G. Foster

First Division, Henry W. Wessells
    First Brigade, Lewis C. Hunt
    Second Brigade, Thomas G. Stevenson

Note. First Brigade was organized from Wessells' Brigade, Division at Suffolk, Seventh Corps.

Unattached Brigades
    Amory's Brigade, Thomas J. C. Amory
    Lee's Brigade, Horace C. Lee
    Heckman's Brigade, Charles A. Heckman
    Artillery Brigade, James H. Ledlie
        3rd New York Light Artillery, Henry M. Stone
        23rd Battery, New York Light Artillery, Alfred Ransom
        24th Battery, New York Light Artillery, Jay E. Lee
        Battery F, 1st Rhode Island Light Artillery, James Belger
        Battery C, 1st United States Artillery, Cornelius Hook, Jr.

Cavalry
    3rd New York Cavalry, Simon H. Mix

Note. Henry M. Naglee's First Brigade of Peck's Division, Fourth Corps was also in the Department of North Carolina.

Early in January 1863, three brigades were sent from Seventh Corps, Department of Virginia to Eighteenth Corps, Department of North Carolina. These were transferred as follows: Henry M. Naglee's First Brigade of John J. Peck's Division, Fourth Corps from Yorktown, Virginia to New Berne, North Carolina; and Orris S. Ferry's Brigade and Francis B. Spinola's Brigade from Suffolk, Virginia were also sent to New Berne.

By an order of January 2, 1863, the troops of Eighteenth Corps were organized into five divisions as follows:

First Division, Innis N. Palmer
    First Brigade, Thomas J. C. Amory
    Second Brigade, Horace C. Lee

Note 1. First Brigade was organized from Amory's Unattached Brigade, Department of North Carolina.
Note 2. Second Brigade was organized from Lee's Unattached Brigade, Department of North Carolina.

Second Division, Henry M. Naglee
    First Brigade, Charles A. Heckman
    Second Brigade, William W. H. Davis

Note 1. First Brigade was formed from regiments of Naglee's First Brigade, Peck's Division, Fourth Corps, and Heckman's Unattached Brigade.
Note 2. Second Brigade was organized from Naglee's Brigade, Department of North Carolina (formerly of Fourth Corps, Department of Virginia).

Third Division, Orris S. Ferry
    First Brigade, Thomas O. Osborne
    Second Brigade, Joshua B. Howell

Note 1. First Brigade was organized from Ferry's Brigade, Division at Suffolk, Seventh Corps.
Note 2. Second Brigade was organized from regiments of the Department of North Carolina.

Fourth Division, Henry W. Wessells
    First Brigade, Lewis C. Hunt
    Second Brigade, Thomas G. Stevenson

Note 1. Fourth Division was formerly First Division, Eighteenth Corps (see above).

Fifth Division, Henry Prince
    First Brigade, Francis B. Spinola
    Second Brigade, James Jourdan

Note 1. First Brigade was organized from Spinola's Brigade, Division at Suffolk, Seventh Corps.
Note 2. Second Brigade was organized from regiments of Heckman's Unattached Brigade, Department of North Carolina and Spinola's Brigade, Division at Suffolk, Seventh Corps.

In addition to the five infantry divisions, James H. Ledlie commanded the Artillery Brigade, which consisted of the same five batteries as given in the organization for December, 1862.

In late January 1863, Naglee's Second Division and Ferry's Third Division were detached from Eighteenth Corps and sent to South Carolina under the command of John G. Foster. The two divisions sailed from Beaufort, North Carolina to reinforce the troops in the Department of the South for operations against Fort Sumter and Charleston, South Carolina. When these operations were delayed for several weeks, Foster turned over the command of his detachment to Henry M. Naglee, and February 10, 1863 returned to North Carolina. Naglee's and Ferry's divisions did not return to Eighteenth Corps, but they were broken up and the units incorporated into Tenth Corps, Department of the South. In addition to these two divisions, Thomas G. Stevenson was also sent with a part of his Second Brigade, Fourth Division to the Department of the South. For additional information, see Department of the South; and also Department of North Carolina, January 7, 1862–July 15, 1863.

Confederate forces laid siege to Washington, North Carolina March 30, 1863, and April 12, 1863, Heckman was sent back to New Berne with his First Brigade of Naglee's former Second Division, Eighteenth Corps. Four days later, Naglee also returned to North Carolina and resumed command of his reorganized Second Division, which at that time consisted only of Heckman's brigade. The siege of Washington was ended April 20, 1863. For details, see Department of North Carolina, January 7, 1862–July 15, 1863, Department of North Carolina, Eighteenth Corps, Siege of Washington, North Carolina.

Eighteenth Corps was again reorganized by an order of April 23, 1863, and also an amended form of April 27, 1863. Second Division was discontinued May 2, 1863, by a change of designation to the District of Beaufort, and Naglee was assigned command of the district the next day. Fourth Division was discontinued by a change of designation to District of the Albemarle, and Wessells was assigned command of the district. Fifth Division was discontinued by a change of designation to the District of the Pamlico, and Henry Prince was assigned command. For additional information about this reorganization, see Department of North Carolina, January 7, 1862–July 15, 1863, Districts in the Department of North Carolina. At the end of May 1863, Eighteenth Corps was organized as follows:

EIGHTEENTH CORPS, John G. Foster

First Division, Innis N. Palmer
First Brigade, Thomas J. C. Amory
Second Brigade, Horace C. Lee

Note 1. First Division was at New Berne.
Note 2. The First Division return for May 1863 reports Amory in command of the division, Charles L. Holbrook in command of First Brigade, and George H. Pierson in command of Second Brigade.

Independent Brigades at New Berne
Jourdan's Brigade, James Jourdan
Lee's Brigade, Francis L. Lee
Cavalry Brigade, Simon H. Mix
Artillery Brigade
3rd New York Light Artillery, Terance J. Kennedy
Battery F, 1st Rhode Island Light Artillery, James Belger

Note 1. Jourdan's Brigade was organized April 22, 1863 from Second Brigade, Fifth Division, Eighteenth Corps.
Note 2. Lee's Brigade was organized in May 1863, largely from Second Brigade, Fourth Division, Eighteenth Corps, and it was then broken up in June 1863.
Note 3. The Cavalry Brigade was organized in May 1863.

District of the Albemarle, Henry Wessells
District of Beaufort, Henry M. Naglee
District of the Pamlico, Henry Prince, to May 29, 1863
Francis B. Spinola

Note. Jay E. Lee's 24th Battery, New York Light Artillery was in the District of the Albemarle; Battery C, 1st United States Artillery was in the District of Beaufort; and Alfred Ransom's 23rd Battery, New York Light Artillery was in the District of the Pamlico.

Edward A. Wild arrived in the Department of North Carolina May 19, 1863, with orders to raise and organize a brigade of colored troops. By July 1, 1863, Wild's force numbered about 1,000 men.

The number of troops in the Eighteenth Corps was greatly reduced in June 1863, when twelve nine-month regiments (eight from Massachusetts and four from Pennsylvania) left the Department of North Carolina on their way home for muster out. The Pennsylvania regiments were from Spinola's District of the Pamlico. Prince went north with a brigade of Massachusetts regiments, three from Amory's First Brigade of Palmer's First Division, two each from Horace C. Lee's Second Brigade of Palmer's division and Jourdan's Independent Brigade, and one from Francis L. Lee's Independent Brigade.

At the end of June 1863, Eighteenth Corps was organized as follows:

EIGHTEENTH CORPS, John G. Foster

New Berne, North Carolina

First Division, Thomas J. C. Amory
First Brigade, Luther Day
Second Brigade, Horace C. Lee

Note. The above organization given for First Division is misleading. Eight Massachusetts regiments left the division June 6–24, 1863 for muster out, and this left only one regiment in First Brigade and two regiments in Second Brigade.

Jourdan's Brigade, James Jourdan
Unbrigaded infantry
United States Colored Troops, Edward A. Wild
Cavalry Brigade, George W. Lewis
Artillery
3rd New York Light Artillery, Terance J. Kennedy
Battery F, 1st Rhode Island Light Artillery, Thomas Simpson

District of Beaufort, Charles A. Heckman
District of the Albemarle, Henry W. Wessells
Infantry Brigade, Theodore F. Lehmann
District of the Pamlico, Joseph M. McChesney

July 15, 1863, the Department of North Carolina was discontinued when it was merged with the Department of Virginia to form the Department of Virginia and North Carolina. The designation of Eighteenth Corps was then changed to Eighteenth Corps, Department of Virginia and North Carolina. The only commander of Eighteenth Corps during the period December 24, 1862–July 15, 1863 was John G. Foster.

EIGHTEENTH CORPS, DEPARTMENT OF VIRGINIA AND NORTH CAROLINA

July 15, 1863, the Department of Virginia and North Carolina was constituted to consist of the territory of the former Department of Virginia and of the Department of North Carolina. The organization of Eighteenth Corps remained essentially the same as it was in the Department of North Carolina until August 1, 1863. At that time, Seventh Corps, formerly of the Department of Virginia, was discontinued; and its troops were assigned to Eighteenth Corps. Fourth Corps was also discontinued August 1, 1863, but at that time the troops formerly of this command had been transferred to other corps. Thus, as of August 1, 1863, Eighteenth Corps consisted of the troops present in the Department of Virginia and North Carolina.

The troops from Seventh Corps were posted at Fort Monroe, Norfolk, Portsmouth and vicinity, and Yorktown and vicinity. The only divisional organization present at that time was George W. Getty's Division at Portsmouth, and it was organized as follows:

Getty's Division, George W. Getty
First Brigade, Samuel M. Alford
Second Brigade, Edward Harland
Third Brigade, William H. P. Steere
Artillery
Battery A, 1st Pennsylvania Light Artillery, John G. Simpson
Battery A, 5th United States Artillery, James Gilliss

Alford's brigade of Getty's Division was sent to the Department of the South (reported August 1, 1863); and August 2–9, 1863, Wild's Colored Brigade, consisting of 1st North Carolina, 2nd North Carolina, and one company of 3rd North Carolina, was sent to Charleston Harbor, Department of the South. The troops of the former Department of North Carolina were serving in the Defenses of New Berne, and in the districts of Beaufort, of the Albemarle, and of the Pamlico. The only divisional

organization was Amory's First Division at the post of New Berne.

August 21, 1863, the Department of Virginia and North Carolina was reorganized to consist of two districts, the District of Virginia and the District of North Carolina. The former had essentially the same boundaries as the former Department of Virginia, and the latter the same boundaries as the former Department of North Carolina. At the end of August 1863, the organization of the Department of Virginia and North Carolina, Eighteenth Corps was as follows:

DISTRICT OF VIRGINIA, Henry M. Naglee

Norfolk, Virginia, George M. Guion
Portsmouth, Virginia, George W. Getty
Getty's Division, George W. Getty
Second Brigade, Edward Harland
Third Brigade, William H. P. Steere
Artillery
Battery A, 1st Pennsylvania Light Artillery, John G. Simpson
Battery A, 5th United States Artillery, James Gilliss

Note. First Brigade of Getty's Division was serving in the Department of the South.

Unattached Artillery, Frederick M. Follett
Unattached Cavalry, Samuel P. Spear

Yorktown and Vicinity, Isaac J. Wistar
Wistar's Brigade, Isaac J. Wistar
Artillery
8th Battery, New York Light Artillery, Butler Fitch
16th Battery, New York Light Artillery, Frederick L. Hiller
1st Pennsylvania Light Artillery (field and staff), Robert M. West
Battery E, 1st Pennsylvania Light Artillery, Thomas G. Orwig
2nd Battery, Wisconsin Light Artillery, Carl Schulz
4th Battery, Wisconsin Light Artillery, George B. Easterly

Cavalry, William Lewis

Note. Also included in Wistar's command were Gloucester Point, Newport News, and Williamsburg.

DISTRICT OF NORTH CAROLINA, John J. Peck

Defenses of New Berne, Innis N. Palmer
Sub-District of the Albemarle, Henry W. Wessells
First Brigade, Theodore F. Lehmann

Sub-District of Beaufort, Charles A. Heckman
Sub-District of the Pamlico, Oscar Moulton

Note 1. Peck assumed command of the district August 14, 1863.

Note 2. Palmer relieved Heckman in command of the Defenses of New Berne August 14, 1863.

Note 3. The troops of Wessells' command were at Plymouth, North Carolina.

Note 4. Heckman assumed command of the Sub-District of Beaufort August 18, 1863. The troops of his command were at Beaufort, Caroline City, Fort Macon, Morehead City, and Newport Barracks.

Note 5. The troops of the Sub-District of the Pamlico were at Washington, North Carolina.

Note 6. Charles H. Stewart's 3rd New York Light Artillery (seven companies); Thomas Simpson's Battery F, 1st Rhode Island Light Artillery; and Henry T. Sisson's 5th Rhode Island Heavy Artillery were in the Defenses of New Berne. A. Lester Cady's 24th Battery, New York Light Artillery was in the Sub-District of the Albemarle; Redmond Tully's Battery C, 1st United States Artillery was in the Sub-District of Beaufort; and Alfred Ransom's 23rd Battery, New York Light Artillery was in the Sub-District of the Pamlico.

There was another reorganization September 23, 1863, when the District of Virginia was discontinued. The troops formerly belonging to this district were organized into three new districts that were to report directly to Headquarters Department of Virginia and North Carolina. These were the District of Portsmouth (or Getty's Line of Defenses), the towns of Norfolk and Portsmouth, and Yorktown and vicinity. There were no major changes in the organization of Eighteenth Corps until April 1864, at which time preparations were begun for Grant's spring campaign against Richmond.

Benjamin F. Butler relieved John G. Foster in command of the Department of Virginia and North Carolina, Eighteenth Corps November 11, 1863.

The organization of Butler's Department of Virginia and North Carolina at the end of January 1864 was as follows:

Fort Monroe, Joseph Roberts
Norfolk and Portsmouth, Edward A. Wild
  African Brigade, John A. Holman
Portsmouth, Charles A. Heckman
  Heckman's Division, Eighteenth Corps
    Third Brigade, William H. P. Steere
    District of the Currituck, James H. Ledlie
    Cavalry Brigade, David M. Evans
    Artillery, Frederick M. Follett
      Battery M, 3rd New York Light Artillery, John H. Howell

      Battery A, 1st Pennsylvania Light Artillery, William Stitt
      Battery D, 4th United States Artillery, Frederick M. Follett
      Battery A, 5th United States Artillery, Charles P. Muhlenberg
      4th Battery, Wisconsin Light Artillery, George B. Easterly
      Company A, 13th New York Heavy Artillery, George A. Bulmer
      Company B, 13th New York Heavy Artillery, William Hoffman
      Company C, 13th New York Heavy Artillery, George F. Potter
      Company D, 13th New York Heavy Artillery, Moses Stevens

Note 1. Heckman assumed command of Getty's Division when the latter was ordered to join the Army of the Potomac January 6, 1864.

Note 2. First Brigade of Heckman's Division was at Charleston, South Carolina, and Second Brigade was at Albemarle, North Carolina.

Yorktown and Vicinity, Isaac J. Wistar
  First Brigade, Robert M. West
  Second Brigade, Samuel A. Duncan
  Cavalry Brigade, Samuel P. Spear
  Artillery, Robert M. West
    8th Battery, New York Light Artillery, James D. Ladd
    Battery E, 1st Pennsylvania Light Artillery, Henry Y. Wildey
    Battery F, 1st Rhode Island Light Artillery, James Belger
    Battery L, 4th United States Artillery, John S. Hunt
    Battery H, 3rd New York Light Artillery, William J. Riggs
    16th Battery, New York Light Artillery, Frank H. Gould

Newport News, Arthur H. Dutton
Drummondtown, Edward H. Powell
District of Saint Mary's, Gilman Marston

District of North Carolina, John J. Peck
  Defenses of New Berne, Innis N. Palmer
  Sub-District of the Albemarle, Henry W. Wessells
    Harland's Brigade, Francis Beach
  Sub-District of Beaufort, James Jourdan
  Sub-District of the Pamlico, Joseph M. McChesney

On April 9, 1864, Ulysses S. Grant, then commanding the Armies of the United States, ordered Butler to reduce the garrisons of the various posts and districts of the Department of Virginia and

North Carolina and to organize the troops so obtained into an effective field force. These troops of Eighteenth Corps were to assemble at Yorktown for the reorganization. Grant also ordered that troops of Tenth Corps be transferred from the Department of the South to Gloucester Point. These two corps were to be reorganized and form the newly created Army of the James, which was to cooperate with the Army of the Potomac during the spring campaign in Virginia. When the reorganization was completed May 2, 1864, the designation of Eighteenth Corps was again changed to Eighteenth Corps, Army of the James.

The commanders of Eighteenth Corps, Department of Virginia and North Carolina were as follows:

John G. Foster	July 15, 1863 to July 29, 1863
Innis N. Palmer	July 29, 1863 to August 14, 1863
John J. Peck	August 14, 1863 to August 21, 1863
John G. Foster	August 21, 1863 to November 11, 1863
Benjamin F. Butler	November 11, 1863 to May 2, 1864

Note. William F. Smith was assigned command of all forces at Yorktown and Gloucester Point April 19, 1864, and he assumed command two days later. He officially assumed command of the reorganized Eighteenth Corps May 2, 1864.

EIGHTEENTH CORPS, ARMY OF THE JAMES

When Ulysses S. Grant assumed command of the Armies of the United States March 17, 1864, he decided on an overall plan for the operations of the armies in the spring of 1864. As a part of this plan, George G. Meade was to advance with the Army of the Potomac from the Rapidan River toward Lee's army and Richmond; and to aid in this movement, he ordered Benjamin F. Butler to organize an army in his Department of Virginia and North Carolina, and to move with it against Richmond from the south side of the James River. This army, which was called the Army of the James, was to consist of Tenth Corps from the Department of the South, and a reorganized Eighteenth Corps from the Department of Virginia and North Carolina.

Accordingly, on April 9, 1864, Grant ordered

Butler to reduce the garrisons of the various posts and districts of the department and to organize the troops so obtained into an effective field force, which was to be commanded by William F. Smith. Smith, who had been serving in the West with Grant as chief engineer of the Army of the Cumberland, and later of the Military Division of the Mississippi, was ordered east and, April 19, 1864, was assigned command of all forces that were at Yorktown and Gloucester Point. Troops of Eighteenth Corps were assembling at Yorktown, and troops of Tenth Corps from the Department of the South were assembling at Gloucester Point. Smith assumed command April 21, 1864, and then supervised the reorganization of Tenth Corps and Eighteenth Corps. When this work was completed, he assumed command of Eighteenth Corps May 2, 1864.

In addition to Smith, a number of officers were sent to Yorktown from other areas to command brigades and divisions in the new Eighteenth Corps. William T. H. Brooks, who commanded the Department of the Monongahela until it was discontinued April 6, 1864, was ordered to the Department of Virginia and North Carolina, and he was assigned command of the new First Division, Eighteenth Corps. Gilman Marston was relieved from the command of the District of Saint Mary's (Point Lookout, Maryland) April 3, 1864, and April 20, 1864 was ordered to Yorktown, where he was assigned command of First Brigade, First Division, Eighteenth Corps. Hiram Burnham was relieved from duty with the Army of the Potomac April 14, 1864, and was ordered to Yorktown April 21, 1864. He was then assigned command of Second Brigade, First Division, Eighteenth Corps. Godfrey Weitzel was relieved from duty in the Department of the Gulf about April 1, 1864, and was assigned to Eighteenth Corps May 4, 1864. He then relieved Isaac J. Wistar in command of Second Division, Eighteenth Corps. On April 29, 1864, George J. Stannard, commanding the United States Troops at New York Harbor, and John H. Martindale, military governor of Washington, were ordered to report to Butler for assignment to command in Eighteenth Corps.

By an order of April 21, 1864, the regiments of Eighteenth Corps were organized into two divisions as follows:

First Division, William T. H. Brooks
  First Brigade, Gilman Marston

Second Brigade, Hiram Burnham
Third Brigade, Horace T. Sanders
Artillery Brigade, Theodore H. Schenck
    Batteries K and M, 3rd New York Light Artillery,
      James R. Angel
    Battery L, 4th United States Artillery, John S. Hunt
    Battery A, 5th United States Artillery, Charles P.
      Muhlenberg
    4th Battery, Wisconsin Light Artillery, George B.
      Easterly

Note 1. First Brigade was formed from the reorganized First Brigade (formerly the District of Currituck) of Heckman's Division (formerly Getty's Division) at Portsmouth.

Note 2. Seond Brigade was organized from regiments of William H. P. Steere's Second Brigade of Heckman's Division at Portsmouth, plus one regiment each from the United States Forces at Yorktown and the Sub-District of the Albemarle.

Note 3. Third Brigade was organized about April 25, 1864 from regiments from the District of North Carolina.

Second Division, Isaac J. Wistar
    First Brigade, Charles A. Heckman
    Second Brigade, Griffin A. Stedman, Jr.
    Artillery Brigade, Frederick M. Follett
      7th Battery, New York Light Artillery, Peter C.
        Regan
      Battery F, 1st Rhode Island Light Artillery, James
        Belger
      Battery D, 4th United States Artillery, James
        Thompson

Note 1. Godfrey Weitzel relieved Wistar in command of Second Division May 4, 1864. When relieved, Wistar was assigned command of Second Brigade, but he did not officially relieve Stedman until May 7, 1864.

Note 2. Heckman's First Brigade was formed from the reorganized Second Brigade of Heckman's Division at Portsmouth, which was then under the command of Horace C. Lee (see Department of Virginia and North Carolina, Districts in the Department of Virginia and North Carolina, Norfolk and Porstmouth).

Note 3. Second Brigade consisted of four regiments, two from the District of Saint Mary's and two from Yorktown.

April 20, 1864, Edward W. Hinks was relieved from the District of Saint Mary's (Point Lookout, Maryland) and two days later was assigned to Camp Hamilton, near Fort Monroe. The next day he was placed in command of a newly organized division of United States Colored Troops, which was organized as follows:

Hinks' Division, Edward W. Hinks
    First Brigade, Edward A. Wild

Second Brigade, Samuel A. Duncan
Artillery
    Battery B, 2nd United States Colored Light Artillery, Francis C. Choate

Hinks' Division was also called Division of United States Colored Troops. The designation of this division was changed to Third Division, Eighteenth Corps by a reorganization order of June 19, 1864 (see below), but it was sometimes called Third Division before that date.

The organization of the Army of the James was completed by May 4, 1864, and that night Tenth Corps and Eighteenth Corps, under the command of Butler, boarded transports and were carried up the James River to Bermuda Hundred, where they arrived May 6, 1864. Butler then advanced his command and established an entrenched line between the Appomattox River and the James River. For additional information, see Army of the James, Organization of the Army; and also Movement of the Army to Bermuda Hundred.

Operations South of the James River (Engagement at Drewry's Bluff), May 6–16, 1864. As a part of the Army of the James, Eighteenth Corps took part in Butler's operations against the Richmond and Petersburg Railroad May 7 and 9, 1864, and also in his expedition against Richmond May 12–16, 1864, which ended in defeat near Drewry's Bluff. For details of the operations of Eighteenth Corps during these operations, see Army of the James, Operations against the Railroads; and also Engagement at Drewry's Bluff.

The organization of Eighteenth Corps during the period May 4–30, 1864 was as follows:

EIGHTEENTH CORPS, William F. Smith

First Division, William T. H. Brooks
    First Brigade, Gilman Marston
    Second Brigade, Hiram Burnham
    Third Brigade, Horace T. Sanders, to May 17, 1864
      Arthur H. Dutton, to May 26, 1864, mortally
        wounded
      Thomas F. Burpee, temporarily
      Charles Devens, Jr., May 26–30, 1864
    Artillery Brigade, Theodore H. Schenck
      3rd New York Light Artillery, Theodore H. Schenck
      4th Battery, Wisconsin Light Artillery, George B.
        Easterly
      Battery L, 4th United States Artillery, John S. Hunt

Battery A, 5th United States Artillery, Henry B. Beecher

Note. When Devens was assigned command of the newly organized Third Division, Eighteenth Corps May 30, 1864, Guy V. Henry was assigned command of Third Brigade.

Second Division, Isaac J. Wistar, to May 4, 1864
  Godfrey Weitzel, to May 20, 1864
  John H. Martindale
  First Brigade, Charles A. Heckman, to May 16, 1864, captured
  George J. Stannard
  Second Brigade, Griffin A. Stedman, Jr., to May 7, 1864
  Isaac J. Wistar, to May 18, 1864
  Griffin A. Stedman, Jr.
  Artillery Brigade, Frederick M. Follett
    7th Battery, New York Light Artillery, Peter C. Regan
    Battery E, 3rd New York Light Artillery, George E. Ashby
    Battery F, 1st Rhode Island Light Artillery, James Belger
    Battery D, 4th United States Artillery, James Thompson

Hinks' Division, Edward W. Hinks
  First Brigade, Edward A. Wild
  Second Brigade, Samuel A. Duncan
  Artillery
    Battery K, 3rd New York Light Artillery, James R. Angel
    Battery M, 3rd New York Light Artillery, John H. Howell
    Battery B, 2nd United States Colored Light Artillery, Francis C. Choate

Note. This division was also called Division of United States Colored Troops.

With the Army of the Potomac at Cold Harbor, May 28, 1864–June 12, 1864.

After the engagement at Drewry's Bluff, Eighteenth Corps retired to its former position on the right of the line of defenses at Bermuda Hundred. It remained there until May 28, 1864, and then Smith was ordered to take four divisions of the Army of the James to White House on the Pamunkey River and join the Army of the Potomac. Smith took with him Brooks' First Division and Martindale's Second Division of Eighteenth Corps, and left Hinks' Division behind. In its place, Smith took John W. Turner's Second Division and Adelbert Ames' Third Division of

Tenth Corps, but on May 30, 1864, he consolidated these two divisions to form a new temporary division that was designated as Third Division, Eighteenth Corps. Charles Devens, Jr. was assigned command of this new division, which was organized as follows:

Third Division, Eighteenth Corps, Charles Devens, Jr.
  First Brigade, William B. Barton
  Second Brigade, Jeremiah C. Drake
  Third Brigade, Adelbert Ames

Note 1. First Brigade was formerly Barton's Second Brigade, Second Division, Tenth Corps.
Note 2. Second Brigade was formerly Drake's Second Brigade, Third Division, Tenth Corps.
Note 3. Third Brigade was formerly Samuel M. Alford's First Brigade, Second Division, Tenth Corps.
Note 4. Henry R. Guss' First Brigade, Third Division, Tenth Corps was broken up in the reorganization, and the regiments were assigned to the three brigades of the new Third Division, Eighteenth Corps.
Note 5. When Devens was assigned command of Third Division, Eighteenth Corps, Guy V. Henry was assigned command of Devens' former Third Brigade, First Division, Eighteenth Corps.

On June 1, 1864, Smith's Eighteenth Corps was placed temporarily under George G. Meade's orders, and it joined the Army of the Potomac at Cold Harbor. It then participated in the assault on the enemy entrenchments that evening and again on June 3, 1864. Adelbert Ames' Third Brigade, Third Division was left at White House to guard the landing, and it did not rejoin the corps until the night of June 3, 1864. The next day, Ames relieved Devens, who was ill, in command of Third Division, Eighteenth Corps. Henry R. Guss assumed command of Ames' brigade. Eighteenth Corps remained in the trenches at Cold Harbor until June 12, 1864, when the Army of the Potomac began its march toward the James River.

For details of the operations of Eighteenth Corps during the time it was detached at Cold Harbor, see Army of the James, Battle of Cold Harbor; and also Richmond, Virginia Campaign, 1864, Operations about Cold Harbor, and also Cold Harbor to the James River.

The organization of Eighteenth Corps at Cold Harbor was as follows:

EIGHTEENTH CORPS, William F. Smith

First Division, William T. H. Brooks

First Brigade, Gilman Marston
Second Brigade, Hiram Burnham
Third Brigade, Guy V. Henry

Second Division, John H. Martindale
First Brigade, George J. Stannard
Second Brigade, Griffin A. Stedman, Jr.

Third Division, Charles Devens, Jr., to June 4, 1864, sick
Adelbert Ames
First Brigade, William B. Barton
Second Brigade, Jeremiah C. Drake, to June 1, 1864,
mortally wounded
James A. Colvin, June 1, 1864
Zina H. Robinson, to June 5, 1864
Alexander Piper, to June 9, 1864, relieved
N. Martin Curtis
Third Brigade, Adelbert Ames, to June 4, 1864
Henry R. Guss
Louis Bell

Artillery Brigade, Samuel S. Elder
Battery B, 1st United States Artillery, Samuel S. Elder
Battery L, 4th United States Artillery, John S. Hunt
Battery A, 5th United States Artillery, Henry B.
Beecher

Operations at Petersburg, June 15, 1864–July 31, 1864. On June 12, 1864, when the Army of the Potomac marched for the James River, Eighteenth Corps returned from Cold Harbor to White House and reembarked for Bermuda Hundred, where it arrived June 14–15, 1864. When Smith arrived at Bermuda Hundred June 14, 1864, he received orders from Butler to cross the Appomattox River the next day and assault the enemy works in front of Petersburg. Smith advanced on the morning of June 15, as ordered, from the vicinity of Point of Rocks with the divisions of Brooks and Martindale; a part of Hinks' Division; the brigades of N. Martin Curtis and Louis Bell of Ames' temporary Third Division; and August V. Kautz's Cavalry Division, Army of the James. Ames was placed in command of the Central Section of the Defenses of Bermuda Hundred, and he was assigned the regiments of Barton's brigade of his division. Smith attacked that evening and captured a part of the enemy works south of the City Point Railroad.

When Eighteenth Corps was sent to the south side of the Appomattox, Grant thought that the enemy might possibly attack the weakened defenses at Bermuda Hundred, and he sent David A. Russell's and

James B. Ricketts' divisions of Sixth Corps, Army of the Potomac up the James River by transport to report to Butler and reinforce Tenth Corps on the line of defenses.

On the night of June 15, 1864, Winfield S. Hancock's Second Corps, which had arrived near Petersburg that evening, moved up and relieved a part of Eighteenth Corps in the positions that had been gained that afternoon. June 17, 1864, Thomas H. Neill's division of Sixth Corps arrived at Petersburg and relieved Brooks' division in the works south of the City Point Railroad. Brooks' division; Curtis' and Bell's brigades, both under Bell; and a part of Hinks' Division were sent back to Bermuda Hundred to reorganize. Russell's and Ricketts' divisions then moved from Bermuda Hundred to Petersburg June 19, 1864, and that day and the next relieved Martindale's division on the lines at Petersburg. Martindale then returned to Bermuda Hundred.

For details of the operations of Eighteenth Corps at Petersburg during this period, see Operations about Petersburg and Richmond, Virginia, 1864–1865, Operations of June 1864.

On June 18, 1864, Brooks was assigned command of Tenth Corps at Bermuda Hundred, and he was succeeded temporarily in command of First Division, Eighteenth Corps by Gilman Marston. Edgar M. Cullen assumed command of Marston's First Brigade, First Division. The next day orders were issued for the reorganization of Eighteenth Corps. First Division was not changed, but a new Third Brigade, Second Division was organized by this order. In addition, the temporary Third Division, Eighteenth Corps that was organized for Second Division and Third Division, Tenth Corps just before the Battle of Cold Harbor, was transferred to Tenth Corps as Second Division of that corps. A new Third Division, Eighteenth Corps was then organized from Hinks' Division of United States Colored Troops. The organization of Eighteenth Corps for the remainder of June 1864 was as follows:

EIGHTEENTH CORPS, William F. Smith

First Division, William T. H. Brooks, to June 18, 1864
Gilman Marston, to June 20, 1864
George J. Stannard
First Brigade, Gilman Marston, to June 18, 1864
Edgar M. Cullen

Second Brigade, Hiram Burnham
Third Brigade, Guy V. Henry

Note 1. Brooks was assigned command of Tenth Corps June 17, 1864, and he assumed command the next day.
Note 2. Marston was transferred to Tenth Corps June 20, 1864.

Second Division, John H. Martindale
    First Brigade, George J. Stannard, to June 20, 1864
      Alexander Piper
    Second Brigade, Griffin Stedman, Jr.
    Third Brigade, Augustus A. Gibson, to June 20, 1864
      Adelbert Ames

Note 1. Stannard was assigned command of First Division June 20, 1864.
Note 2. Third Brigade was organized by the order of June 19, 1864 to consist of three regiments, one each from the Middle Department; Defenses South of the Potomac, Twenty-Second Corps; and First Brigade, Second Division, Eighteenth Corps.

Third Division, Edward W. Hinks
    First Brigade, Edward A. Wild, to June 23, 1864
      John H. Holman
    Second Brigade, Samuel A. Duncan

Note. Wild was in arrest at the time of the reorganization for insubordination.

Artillery Brigade, Henry S. Burton
    Battery E, 3rd New York Light Artillery, Lewis H. Mowers
    Battery K, 3rd New York Light Artillery, James R. Angel
    Battery M, 3rd New York Light Artillery, John H. Howell
    7th Battery, New York Light Artillery, Martin V. McIntyre
    16th Battery, New York Light Artillery, Richard H. Lee
    Battery F, 1st Rhode Island Light Artillery, Thomas Simpson
    4th Battery, Wisconsin Light Artillery, Martin McDevitt
    Battery B, 1st United States Artillery, Michael Leahy
    Battery L, 4th United States Artillery, Henry B. Beecher
    Battery A, 5th United States Artillery, Israel Ludlow
    Battery B, 2nd United States Colored Light Artillery, Francis C. Choate

June 21, 1864, the reorganized Eighteenth Corps returned to Petersburg and relieved Wright's Sixth Corps on the right of the line of entrenchments. Two days later, John W. Turner's Second Division, Tenth Corps was temporarily assigned to Eighteenth Corps, and on the morning of June 24, it relieved Orlando B. Willcox's division of Ninth Corps on the left of Martindale's division of Eighteenth Corps.

The situation in which William F. Smith served under Butler had, for some time, proved troublesome, and July 7, 1864, an order from the adjutant general's office (ordered by the president) announced that the troops of the Department of Virginia and North Carolina then serving with the Army of the Potomac in the field, constituted the Eighteenth Corps under the command of Smith. This included Turner's division of Tenth Corps. Butler was assigned command of the rest of the troops in the department, with headquarters at Fort Monroe. This order had been requested by Grant July 6, 1864. It was suspended by Grant July 18, 1864, however, and the next day Smith was relieved from command of Eighteenth Corps and ordered to New York. John H. Martindale was assigned temporary command of Eighteenth Corps July 19, 1864, and he assumed command the next day. July 21, 1864, Edward O. C. Ord was assigned command of Eighteenth Corps, subject to the approval of the president, and he assumed command the next day. The appointment was approved July 28, 1864.

Eighteenth Corps remained in the entrenchments at Petersburg until July 29, 1864, and it was then relieved temporarily by Gershom Mott's division of Hancock's Second Corps. That night, Eighteenth Corps moved to the rear of Ninth Corps to support the latter in its assault the next day, following the explosion of the "Petersburg Mine." Turner's division of Tenth Corps, temporarily attached to Eighteenth Corps, attacked at the "Crater" in support of Ninth Corps July 30, 1864, and so did Griffin Stedman's Second Brigade, Second Division, Eighteenth Corps. Burnside's assault was unsuccessful, and that evening and the following night Ord's command returned to its former positions on the line of entrenchments. On July 31, 1864, Turner's division returned to Tenth Corps at Bermuda Hundred. For details of the Petersburg Mine explosion, see Operations about Petersburg and Richmond, Virginia, 1864–1865, Operations of July 1864, Petersburg Mine Assault.

The organization of Eighteenth Corps during July 1864 was as follows:

EIGHTEENTH CORPS, William F. Smith, to July 9, 1864

John H. Martindale, to July 21, 1864
Edward O. C. Ord

First Division, George J. Stannard, to July 31, 1864, on
  leave
  Hiram Burnham
  First Brigade, Edgar M. Cullen, to July 31, 1864
    Aaron Stevens
  Second Brigade, Hiram Burnham, to July 31, 1864
    Edgar M. Cullen
  Third Brigade, Guy V. Henry

*Note. Smith was in nominal command of Eighteenth
Corps until July 19, 1864. He was granted a ten-day leave
of absence July 9, 1864, however, and was relieved temporarily by Martindale on that date. The order relieving
Smith from command of the corps was issued July 19,
1864, and the next day Martindale reassumed command
temporarily until Ord arrived.*

Second Division, John H. Martindale, to July 9, 1864
  Adelbert Ames
  First Brigade, Alexander Piper, to July 24, 1864
    James Stewart, Jr.
  Second Brigade, Griffin Stedman, Jr.
  Third Brigade, Adelbert Ames, to July 11, 1864
    Harrison S. Fairchild

*Note. Piper was assigned command of the Artillery
Brigade July 24, 1864.*

Third Division, Edward W. Hinks, to July 1, 1864
  John H. Holman, to July 27, 1864
  Samuel A. Duncan, to July 29, 1864
  Joseph B. Carr
  First Brigade, John H. Holman, to July 2, 1864
    Jeptha Garrard
  Second Brigade, Samuel A. Duncan

*Note 1. Hinks was granted a leave of absence because
of disability July 1, 1864.*
*Note 2. Holman left on a thirty-day leave of absence
July 27, 1864.*
*Note 3. Wild, formerly commanding First Brigade, was
in arrest until July 24, 1864, and then he was relieved and
ordered to Fort Monroe.*

Artillery Brigade, Henry S. Burton, to July 24, 1864
  Alexander Piper

Operations at Petersburg, August 1864. There
were some changes in Third Division during August
1864. On August 3, 1864, the division was reorganized, and Charles J. Paine succeeded Joseph B.
Carr in command. Since June 1864, Third Division
had consisted of only two brigades that were com-

posed of regiments of United States Colored Troops.
In the reorganization there was a general reassignment of these regiments, and Samuel A. Duncan,
formerly commander of Second Brigade, Third
Division, was assigned command of the newly organized Third Brigade. Elias Wright assumed command of Second Brigade. Duncan's brigade
consisted of the 4th and 6th United States Colored
Troops of his former Second Brigade and the unattached 10th United States Colored Troops. On
August 3, 1864, Duncan's brigade was ordered to
the trenches at Petersburg. On August 16, 4th and
6th United States Colored Troops were sent to Dutch
Gap, where a canal was being cut across a narrow
neck of land at a great loop in the James River.

Eighteenth Corps continued to occupy the line of
entrenchments at Petersburg until late August 1864.
On the night of August 14–15, 1864, Fifth Corps
withdrew from the line in preparation for a movement against the Weldon Railroad, and Ninth Corps
and Eighteenth Corps moved to the left to cover the
lines just vacated. When this movement was completed, Eighteenth Corps was on the line from the
Appomattox River to a point near the crater of the
Petersburg Mine. Ames' Second Division was on
the left next to Ninth Corps; Elias Wright's Second
Brigade of Third Division, then commanded by
Charles J. Paine, was in the center; and First
Division, then commanded by Joseph B. Carr, was
on the right. On the night of August 18, 1864, Ord
relieved Ninth Corps on the left of the crater with
two of his reserve brigades, and Eighteenth Corps
then held a front of about three miles.

After about two months of continuous service in
the trenches, Eighteenth Corps was greatly reduced
in strength, largely because of sickness, and August
21, 1864, Ord asked that the corps be relieved and
allowed to rest and recuperate. This request was
approved, and August 24, 1864, David B. Birney's
Tenth Corps was ordered to Petersburg to take the
place of Eighteenth Corps in the trenches. The transfer took some time (August 24–28, 1864), because
it was done one division at a time, but when completed Eighteenth Corps had moved to the north side
of the Appomattox and into the works vacated by
Tenth Corps. Carr's First Division and Ames'
Second Division manned the line of defenses at
Bermuda Hundred, with Carr on the right and Ames
on the left. Paine's Third Division was ordered to

Deep Bottom. August 25, 1864, Paine's Third Division headquarters moved to Deep Bottom, but only Elias Wright's Second Brigade (later commanded by Alonzo G. Draper) joined him there. Headquarters of Eighteenth Corps was at the Hatcher farm, near Bermuda Hundred. On August 25, 1864, while Eighteenth Corps and Tenth Corps were exchanging positions, William Birney, then commanding a separate brigade of Tenth Corps, was assigned command of the regiments of John H. Holman's First Brigade, Third Division, which were encamped at the Signal Tower near Point of Rocks. He was then ordered to move with these regiments and his own brigade to the entrenchments at Petersburg. Birney's new command was then organized as Third Division, Tenth Corps, and Holman's brigade was redesignated as Second Brigade of this division. Holman's brigade, however, was also carried on the roster of Eighteenth Corps for August 1864, as First Brigade, Third Division. On August 26, 1864, Duncan's Third Brigade headquarters was moved to Deep Bottom. The 4th and 6th United States Colored Troops of the brigade were at Dutch Gap, and the 10th United States Colored Troops was ordered to City Point.

The organization of Eighteenth Corps during August 1864 was as follows:

EIGHTEENTH CORPS, Edward O. C. Ord

First Division, Hiram Burnham, to August 3, 1864
  Joseph B. Carr
  First Brigade, Aaron Stevens
  Second Brigade, Edgar M. Cullen
  Third Brigade, Guy V. Henry, to August 12, 1864
    Samuel H. Roberts

Second Division, Adelbert Ames
  First Brigade, James Stewart, Jr.
  Second Brigade, Griffin Stedman, Jr., to August 5, 1864, mortally wounded
    George M. Guion
  Third Brigade, Harrison S. Fairchild

Third Division, Joseph B. Carr, to August 3, 1864
  Charles J. Paine
  First Brigade, Jeptha Garrard, to August 3, 1864
    John H. Holman
  Second Brigade, Samuel A. Duncan, to August 3, 1864
    Elias Wright, to about August 26, 1864
    Alonzo G. Draper
  Third Brigade, Samuel A. Duncan

Note. Third Brigade was organized August 3, 1864 under Duncan.

Artillery Brigade, Alexander Piper

Operations North of the James River, September 1864–December 1864. During the greater part of September 1864, Eighteenth Corps was in the Defenses of Bermuda Hundred and at Deep Bottom, with detachments at Dutch Gap, City Point, and other points on the James River. As noted above, 4th and 6th United States Colored Troops of Duncan's Third Brigade, Third Division were at Dutch Gap, and September 10, 1864, headquarters of the brigade was moved there. The 22nd United States Colored Troops were also ordered to Dutch Gap September 16, 1864.

There were several command changes in Eighteenth Corps during September 1864. Ord left the corps September 4, 1864, because of illness, and John Gibbon, commander of Second Division, Second Corps, was in command during his absence. Also in September 1864, George J. Stannard resumed command of First Division, and Hiram Burnham succeeded Edgar M. Cullen in command of Second Brigade, First Division. September 19, 1864, Charles A. Heckman assumed command of Second Division when Adelbert Ames departed on leave, and that same day Edward H. Ripley relieved George M. Guion in command of Second Brigade, Second Division. Ord resumed command of Eighteenth Corps September 22, 1864, relieving Gibbon, but he was wounded at the Battle of Chaffin's Farm September 29, 1864, and was succeeded temporarily by Charles A. Heckman. Heckman remained in command until early the next morning, when Godfrey Weitzel was assigned command. Heckman then resumed command of Second Division. Also, about September 25, 1864, a new provisional brigade consisting of new one-year regiments was organized under the command of Joseph H. Potter, and September 28, 1864, it was ordered to report to Eighteenth Corps.

As a part of Grant's autumn offensive against Lee's army and Richmond, Butler was directed to assemble his Army of the James in preparation for an attack on the enemy works east of the city from north of the James River. On the night of September 28, 1864, Ord marched with his First Division and Second Division from Bermuda Hundred to the

James River, and crossed to the north bank at Aiken's Landing. The next day, he moved up the Varina Road toward the enemy works, and after a severe engagement Stannard's First Division captured Fort Harrison. Further attempts to advance from the fort, however, were unsuccessful. The enemy attempted to retake Fort Harrison on the afternoon of September 30, 1864, but because of Stannard's stubborn resistance the attack failed. Stannard was wounded while directing the defense, and Edgar M. Cullen assumed temporary command of First Division.

Paine's division, which had been guarding the bridgehead at Deep Bottom during the month, joined David B. Birney's Tenth Corps there on the morning of September 29, 1864, and with it advanced against the enemy positions on New Market Heights. Paine's division captured the works there and drove the enemy back, and then marched with Tenth Corps up the New Market Road, and formed on the right of Eighteenth Corps. The next day, the wing arrangement, under which the battle of September 29, 1864 was fought, was discontinued, and Paine's division returned to Eighteenth Corps. For details of the above operations, see Operations about Petersburg and Richmond, Virginia, 1864–1865, Operations of September 1864, Battle of Chaffin's Farm (Combats at Fort Harrison, Fort Gilmer, Fort Gregg, New Market Heights, and Laurel Hill), Virginia.

The organization of Eighteenth Corps at the Battle of Chaffin's Farm, September 29–30, 1864, was as follows:

EIGHTEENTH CORPS, Edward O. C. Ord, to September 29, 1864, wounded
Charles A. Heckman, to the morning of September 30, 1864
Godfrey Weitzel

First Division, George J. Stannard, to September 30, 1864, wounded
Edgar M. Cullen, temporarily
James Jourdan
First Brigade, Aaron F. Stevens, to September 29, 1864, wounded
John B. Raulston
Second Brigade, Hiram Burnham, to September 29, 1864, killed
Michael T. Donohoe, September 29, 1864, wounded
Edgar M. Cullen, temporarily

Stephen Moffitt (probably)
Edgar M. Cullen, temporarily
Third Brigade, Samuel H. Roberts, to September 29, 1864, disabled by illness
Edgar M. Cullen, temporarily
Stephen Moffitt

Second Division, Charles A. Heckman, to September 29, 1864
Harrison S. Fairchild (probably), September 29, 1864
Charles A. Heckman
First Brigade, James Stewart, Jr., to September 30, 1864
George M. Guion
Second Brigade, Edward H. Ripley
Third Brigade, Harrison S. Fairchild

Third Division, Charles J. Paine
First Brigade, John H. Holman
Second Brigade, Alonzo G. Draper, to September 30, 1864, sick
John W. Ames
Third Brigade, Samuel A. Duncan, to September 29, 1864, wounded
John W. Ames, to September 30, 1864
Augustus Boernstein

Artillery Brigade, George B. Cook
Battery E, 3rd New York Light Artillery, George E. Ashby
Battery H, 3rd New York Light Artillery, William J. Riggs
Battery K, 3rd New York Light Artillery, James R. Angel
7th Battery, New York Light Artillery, Martin V. McIntyre
16th Battery, New York Light Artillery, Richard H. Lee
17th Battery, New York Light Artillery, George T. Anthony
Battery A, 1st Pennsylvania Light Artillery, William Stitt
Battery F, 1st Rhode Island Light Artillery, Philip S. Chase
Battery B, 1st United States Artillery, Robert M. Hall
Battery L, 4th United States Artillery, Henry B. Beecher
Battery A, 5th United States Artillery, Charles P. Muhlenberg
Battery F, 5th United States Artillery, Leonard Martin

At the end of the fighting around Chaffin's farm, October 2, 1864, the Army of the James remained on the ground gained during its advance September 29, 1864, and it proceeded to prepare a defensive line that extended from Signal Hill on the James

River (later the site of Fort Brady) to the northwest, past Fort Harrison (later renamed Fort Burnham), to the Darbytown Road. This line generally faced west. Eighteenth Corps occupied this line from the river up to, and including, Fort Harrison, and Tenth Corps continued the line northward from the right of Fort Harrison, along the old Confederate Exterior Line, to the New Market Road. August V. Kautz's Cavalry Division covered the right of Tenth Corps. For additional information, see Operations about Petersburg and Richmond, Virginia, 1864–1865, Operations of October 1864, Siege of Petersburg.

Eighteenth Corps remained generally in the same position during most of October 1864. On October 1, 1864, David B. White's Independent Brigade, which came up to reinforce Butler's army during the fighting at Chaffin's farm, probably picketed the space from Signal Hill to the Kingsland Road, near its intersection with the Varina Road. It was soon withdrawn, however, and Paine extended his pickets southward to the river. On the morning of October 7, 1864, the enemy made an attack on Kautz's cavalry, and a part of Alfred H. Terry's division of Tenth Corps was sent to its support. White's brigade then relieved a part of William Birney's brigade of Tenth Corps, so that it could move from it position on the right of Fort Harrison and occupy that part of the line vacated by Terry. Edward H. Ripley, with a regiment of his Second Brigade, Second Division, Eighteenth Corps, also moved to the right of Fort Harrison, and he then assumed command of White's Brigade, as well as that of his own regiment. White's Brigade was discontinued later that day, and his regiments returned to their respective commands. For details of Kautz's engagement, see Operations about Petersburg and Richmond, Virginia, 1864–1865, Operations of October 1864, Engagement at the Darbytown Road and the New Market Road (Johnson's Farm and Four-Mile Creek [or Run]), Virginia.

There were some command changes in Eighteenth Corps during October 1864. As noted above, George J. Stannard was wounded September 30, 1864, and James Jourdan assumed temporary command of First Division. The next day, Gilman Marston (then commanding a Separate Brigade that consisted of the troops garrisoning Fort Powhatan, Fort Pocahontas, and Harrison's Landing) was assigned command of First Division. That day, how-ever, Marston became ill and was forced to remain at Fort Pocahontas for a week until he recovered. Meantime, Jourdan continued in command of First Division until Marston assumed command about October 8, 1864. Charles Devens, Jr. assumed command at the end of the month. Samuel H. Roberts was intermittently sick during the month, and Joab N. Patterson and Edgar M. Cullen relieved him in command of Third Brigade, First Division. Guy V. Henry assumed command of Third Brigade, First Division at the end of October 1864. Charles J. Paine commanded Third Division until mid-October, and was then relieved by John H. Holman. After Holman was wounded during Weitzel's demonstration October 28, 1864 (see below), Alonzo G. Draper assumed command of Third Division, and Dexter E. Clapp assumed command of his Second Brigade, Third Division.

On the morning of October 26, 1864, Gilman Marston's First Division; two brigades of Charles A. Heckman's Second Division; and two brigades of Third Division, Eighteenth Corps were withdrawn from the line and concentrated on the Cox farm in preparation for joining Butler's demonstration against Richmond October 27–28, 1864. These troops were under the personal direction of Weitzel. John H. Holman was in command of Third Division, but October 26, 1864, he was assigned to command only First Brigade, Third Division. Alonzo G. Draper's Second Brigade was ordered to report to Heckman's division at the Cox farm for this operation. John W. Ames' Third Brigade, Third Division was left to cover the left of the Eighteenth Corps line. George W. Cole, with his unattached 2nd United States Colored Cavalry, occupied the redoubt on the extreme left. All other troops remaining, including the regiments of First Brigade, Second Division, held Fort Burnham (formerly Fort Harrison) and the line to the first redoubt on the left. James Jourdan was assigned command of all troops remaining on the entrenched line of Eighteenth Corps during the absence of Weitzel.

On October 28, 1864, Weitzel's command of Eighteenth Corps, preceded by Kautz's cavalry, marched north past the New Market, Darbytown, and Charles City roads to the Williamsburg Road, where it demonstrated against the enemy works that afternoon. Holman's brigade was sent to the Nine-Mile Road, and was engaged there that evening.

Holman was wounded during the action, and Abial G. Chamberlain assumed command of First Brigade. Weitzel marched back with his command that night, and the next day his troops returned to their former positions on the left of the entrenched line. For details of this movement, see Operations about Petersburg and Richmond, Virginia, 1864–1865, Operations of October 1864, Engagement at the Darbytown Road (Fair Oaks), Virginia.

October 28, 1864, a provisional brigade was organized under the command of Edward Martindale from three new regiments of United States Colored Troops. These regiments were withdrawn from the line of entrenchments and encamped on the field of the Cox farm, where they were drilled and disciplined for further service. This brigade reported to Headquarters Eighteenth Corps.

The organization of Eighteenth Corps at the end of October was as follows:

EIGHTEENTH CORPS, Godfrey Weitzel

First Division, Charles Devens, Jr.
First Brigade, John B. Raulston
Second Brigade, Edgar M. Cullen
Third Brigade, Guy V. Henry

Second Division, Charles A. Heckman
First Brigade, William H. McNary
Second Brigade, Edward H. Ripley
Third Brigade, Harrison S. Fairchild

Third Division, Alonzo G. Draper
First Brigade, Abial G. Chamberlain
Second Brigade, Dexter E. Clapp
Third Brigade, John W. Ames
Unattached Cavalry (colored), George W. Cole

Provisional Brigade, Edward Martindale

Artillery Brigade, Alexander Piper

During November 1864, Eighteenth Corps occupied the left of the line of entrenchments in front of Richmond, from the vicinity of Fort Burnham southward to the James River, but there was little significant activity on its front during the month.

On November 2, 1864, Grant ordered 3,000 troops from the Army of the James to New York to preserve order and protect the public property during the presidential election of November 8, 1864. Joseph R. Hawley of Tenth Corps was assigned command of this force, which included four regiments from Eighteenth Corps and eight regi-

ments from Tenth Corps. John B. Raulston, commander of First Brigade, First Division, was assigned command of the regiments of Eighteenth Corps. November 14, 1864, after the election, Hawley's command began embarking at New York for its return to the Army of the James. As the regiments arrived at City Point, they left to rejoin their respective brigades. For additional information, see Army of the James, Line of Defenses North of the James River; and also Department of the East, January 3, 1863–June 27, 1865, November Election of 1864 in New York.

Early in November 1864, James Jourdan resumed command of First Brigade, Second Division, relieving William H McNary; and Charles J. Paine resumed command of Third Division, relieving Alonzo G. Draper. When relieved, Draper resumed command of Second Brigade, Third Division. On November 6, 1864, Elias Wright returned from duty with Tenth Corps, and relieved Abial G. Chamberlain in command of First Brigade, Third Division. Edward Martindale's Provisional Brigade of colored troops was in the vicinity of Deep Bottom during the month, and Martindale was assigned command of the post of Deep Bottom November 28, 1864.

By an order of December 3, 1864, Tenth Corps and Eighteenth Corps were discontinued, and the troops of the two corps were assigned to the newly constituted Twenty-Fourth Corps and Twenty-Fifth Corps. The white troops of Tenth Corps and Eighteenth Corps were assigned to Twenty-Fourth Corps, and the black troops of the Department of Virginia and North Carolina were assigned to Twenty-Fifth Corps.

In the process of reorganization, the troops of Eighteenth Corps were reassigned as follows: First Brigade, First Division, Eighteenth Corps became First Brigade, Third Division, Twenty-Fourth Corps; Second Brigade, First Division, Eighteenth Corps became Second Brigade, Third Division, Twenty-Fourth Corps; and Third Brigade, First Division, Eighteenth Corps became Third Brigade, Third Division, Twenty-Fourth Corps. First Brigade, Second Division, Eighteenth Corps, with one regiment each from Second Brigade and Third Brigade, Second Division, Eighteenth Corps, became Fourth Brigade, First Division, Twenty-Fourth Corps. Second Brigade, Second Division,

Eighteenth Corps was broken up, and one regiment was assigned to Fourth Brigade, First Division, Twenty-Fourth Corps, and one regiment to Second Brigade, Third Division, Twenty-Fourth Corps. Third Brigade, Second Division, Eighteenth Corps was also broken up. One regiment was assigned to Fourth Brigade, First Division, Twenty-Fourth Corps; one regiment to McClure's Provisional Brigade, Defenses of Bermuda Hundred; and one regiment was assigned to First Brigade, Third Division, Twenty-Fourth Corps. All three brigades of Third Division, Eighteenth Corps were broken up, and the regiments were assigned to First Division, Twenty-Fifth Corps and to First Brigade, Third Division, Twenty-Fifth Corps.

For additional information about the reorganization, see Twenty-Fourth Corps and Twenty-Fifth Corps, Army of the James.

COMMANDERS OF EIGHTEENTH CORPS, ARMY OF THE JAMES

Benjamin F. Butler	April 21, 1864 to May 2, 1864
William F. Smith	May 2, 1864 to July 9, 1864
John H. Martindale	July 9, 1864 to July 21, 1864
Edward O. C. Ord	July 21, 1864 to September 4, 1864
John Gibbon	September 4, 1864 to September 24, 1864
Edward O. C. Ord	September 24, 1864 to September 29, 1864
Charles A. Heckman	September 29, 1864 to October 1, 1864
Godfrey Weitzel	October 1, 1864 to December 3, 1864

Note 1. April 19, 1864, William F. Smith was assigned command of all troops of Eighteenth Corps and Tenth Corps assembling at Yorktown and Gloucester Point, and supervised their reorganization for field service. He officially assumed command of Eighteenth Corps, Army of the James May 2, 1864.

Note 2. September 4, 1864, Ord was granted a fifteen-day leave of absence because of disability; and John Gibbon, then commanding Second Division, Second Corps, Army of the Potomac, was assigned temporary command of Eighteenth Corps.

Note 3. Ord was wounded at the Battle of Chaffin's Farm September 29, 1864.

Note 4. Weitzel was chief engineer of Butler's Army of the James at the time of his assignment to command Eighteenth Corps.

DETACHMENT NINETEENTH CORPS

In July 1864, William H. Emory sailed from New Orleans with First Division and Second Division of Nineteenth Corps, Department of the Gulf for Fort Monroe, Virginia. Upon its departure, Emory's command was designated as Detachment Nineteenth Corps, and under this designation its troops served briefly with Benjamin F. Butler's Army of the James, with Horatio G. Wright's force that marched in pursuit of Jubal A. Early at the end of his Washington raid, and with Philip H. Sheridan's Army of the Shenandoah during his campaign in the valley. On November 7, 1864, the organization known as Nineteenth Corps, Military Division of West Mississippi, then operating in Arkansas, was discontinued, and the designation of Emory's Detachment Nineteenth Corps was changed to Nineteenth Corps. For details of the organization and operations of Detachment Nineteenth Corps while in the East, see Nineteenth Corps (With the Eastern Armies).

NINETEENTH CORPS (WITH THE EASTERN ARMIES)

Nineteenth Corps was organized under an order dated January 5, 1863, but retroactive to December 14, 1862. It was defined to consist of all troops in the Department of the Gulf, which at that time comprised the state of Texas, all of the coast of the Gulf of Mexico west of Apalachicola, including West Florida, and so much of the Gulf States as might be occupied by the forces under Nathaniel P. Banks. Banks assumed command of the corps January 16, 1863, with headquarters at New Orleans, Louisiana.

In December the troops of the Department of the Gulf consisted of Cuvier Grover's division at Baton Rouge; Thomas W. Sherman's division at Carrollton, Louisiana; Godfrey Weitzel's Reserve Brigade in the District of La Fourche; Thomas W. Cahill's Defenses of New Orleans; Neal Dow's District of Pensacola, Florida; and some unassigned regiments. These forces were strongly reinforced, especially with the addition of Nathaniel P. Banks' expedition from New York and Fort Monroe, which arrived in Louisiana in December 1862. The reinforcements consisted of thirty-nine New England regiments, twenty-two New York regiments, and the 47th Pennsylvania Regiment.

Nineteenth Corps was organized to consist of two separate parts: a mobile column for field operations, and another part to provide for the administration of the garrisons of the defenses and the permanent detachments for guard and provost duties. The main body of troops consisted of four divisions of three brigades each. Christopher C. Augur's division was designated as First Division, Thomas W. Sherman's division as Second Division, William H. Emory's division as Third Division, and Cuvier Grover's division as Fourth Division.

After a demonstration against Port Hudson in March 1863, Banks led an expedition into western Louisiana. Grover's division, Emory's division, and Godfrey Weitzel's Second Brigade, First Division assembled at Brashear City early in April 1863, and then, under the command of Banks, crossed Berwick Bay and moved up the Bayou Teche and the Atchafalaya River. After engagements at Fort Bisland and Irish Bend, Banks reached Opelousas, Louisiana April 20, 1863, and then moved on to Alexandria. May 17, 1863, he pushed on to the Mississippi River, which he crossed at Bayou Sara May 23, 1863, and arrived before Port Hudson the next day. Banks launched two assaults on the fortifications at Port Hudson, and then conducted siege operations until the enemy surrendered July 8, 1863.

Soon after the surrender of Port Hudson, the terms of enlistment of twenty-two nine-month regiments expired, and they left for home. As a result of this reduction in strength, Nineteenth Corps was reorganized to consist of three divisions instead of four. In the ensuing nine months, from July 1863 to March 1864, the troops of Nineteenth Corps served on post or garrison duty in the Department of the Gulf, with some reconnaissances and expeditions into enemy-held territory. William B. Franklin assumed command of the corps August 20, 1863, and during October and November 1863, he led an expedition from New Iberia and Berwick Bay up the Bayou Teche. His force consisted of a detachment of Thirteenth Corps, and Weitzel's First Division and Grover's Third Division of Nineteenth Corps.

March 15, 1864, Banks began his expedition up the Red River toward Shreveport, Louisiana. Accompanying Banks were Emory's First Division, Nineteenth Corps, and Thomas E. G. Ransom, with Third Division and Fourth Division of Thirteenth Corps. Franklin commanded Nineteenth Corps on this expedition, but only Emory's division and Grover's Second Division of the corps were with Banks. Third Division remained in the Defenses of New Orleans, and Second Division was left at Alexandria. Only First Division of Nineteenth Corps was present with the detachment of Thirteenth Corps at the Battle of Sabine Cross Roads (Mansfield), and at Pleasant Hill.

At the end of April 1864, Banks' defeated army was back at Alexandria, and in May 1864, both Nineteenth Corps and the detachment of Thirteenth Corps continued the retreat toward Morganza. Emory succeeded Franklin in command of Nineteenth Corps May 2, 1864, and May 20, 1864, he was assigned command of the combined forces of Thirteenth Corps and Nineteenth Corps. Emory arrived with his command at Morganza May 22, 1864, and that day Joseph J. Reynolds assumed command of the forces assembled there.

June 27, 1864, Nineteenth Corps at Morganza was again reorganized as follows:

NINETEENTH CORPS, William H. Emory

First Division, Benjamin S. Roberts
    First Brigade, George L. Beal
    Second Brigade, James W. McMillan
    Third Brigade, Leonard D. H. Currie

Second Division, Cuvier Grover
    First Brigade, Henry W. Birge
    Second Brigade, Edward L. Molineux
    Third Brigade, Jacob Sharpe

Third Division, Michael K. Lawler
    First Brigade, Albert L. Lee
    Second Brigade, Robert A. Cameron
    Third Brigade, Frederick W. Moore

Note. Third Division was reorganized from troops of Third Division and Fourth Division of Thirteenth Corps.

June 30, 1864, First Division and Second Division, Nineteenth Corps began moving down the Mississippi River to New Orleans for transfer to Virginia. Benjamin S. Roberts, commanding First Division, did not accompany the division, but remained behind at Morganza to supervise the forwarding of the troops. July 3, 1864, Emory assumed command of the two divisions, which thereafter were designated as Detachment Nineteenth Corps. First Division began embarking at Algiers July 3, 1864, and the last regiment of Third Brigade departed July 11, 1864. Grover's Second Division began its embarkation about July 10, 1864, and the last troops left about July 20, 1864.

On July 10, 1864, the transports began arriving at Fort Monroe at a critical time. The day before, a Confederate force under Jubal A. Early had defeated a small Union army under Lewis Wallace at the Battle of the Monocacy in Maryland, and Early was then moving toward Washington. The leading troops of Emory's Detachment Nineteenth Corps were immediately sent on to Washington, where they began arriving the next day, just as Early was approaching the city. The first arrivals, totaling about 600 men, were placed under the temporary command of Quincy A. Gillmore; and they were moved to the northern line of defenses of Washington, near Fort Saratoga, July 12, 1864. That night Early withdrew from in front of the Defenses of Washington and began his march back toward the Shenandoah Valley. The next day, Gillmore's force, which had been increased to about 4,600 men by new arrivals, was ordered to Tennallytown, and there on July 14, 1864, Emory arrived and relieved Gillmore in command. William Dwight then assumed command of First Division.

During July 11–12, 1864, Horatio G. Wright also arrived in Washington from the Petersburg front with First Division and Second Division of his Sixth Corps, and after Early's departure, he was assigned command of all Union forces that were ordered to go in pursuit. Wright started out with the two divisions of Sixth Corps, a part of Emory's Detachment Nineteenth Corps, and some cavalry under Charles R. Lowell, Jr. Near Leesburg, Virginia, he was joined by Third Division, Sixth Corps from Baltimore, and also by a new brigade from the Middle Department, Eighth Corps under the command of John R. Kenly. Kenly's Brigade was attached to Detachment Nineteenth Corps July 17, 1864. Wright's command followed Early as far as Snicker's Ferry in the Shenandoah Valley, and then it returned to Washington July 24, 1864.

The organization of Emory's force while under Wright's command was as follows:

DETACHMENT NINETEENTH CORPS, William H. Emory

First Division, William Dwight
　First Brigade, George L. Beal
　Second Brigade (part), Stephen Thomas

Note. The remainder of Second Brigade and all of Third Brigade were with the Army of the James at Bermuda Hundred.

Second Division
　Third Brigade, Jacob Sharpe

Note 1. Cuvier Grover commanded Second Division, but he had not yet arrived.
Note 2. First Brigade and Second Brigade of Second Division were with the Army of the James at Bermuda Hundred.

Kenly's Brigade, John R. Kenly

Meantime, during the latter part of July 1864, while Wright was in pursuit of Early, the remainder of Emory's Detachment Nineteenth Corps disembarked at Fort Monroe. It then moved to Bermuda Hundred, where it reported to Benjamin F. Butler, commander of the Army of the James. Henry W. Birge's First Brigade, Second Division arrived at Bermuda Hundred July 21, 1864, and was placed in reserve in rear of the line of defenses. Also on July 21, 1864, James W. McMillan arrived at Bermuda Hundred with a part of Second Brigade, First Division. Leonard D. H. Currie's Third Brigade, First Division arrived at Deep Bottom on the James River July 24, 1864, and reported to Robert S. Foster, who commanded the bridgehead at that point. Edward L. Molineux's Second Brigade, Second Division arrived at Bermuda Hundred July 25, 1864.

July 26, 1864, Birge's brigade and Isaac Dyer, then commanding that part of McMillan's brigade that was at Bermuda Hundred, were ordered to report to Orris S. Ferry, commanding Third Division, Tenth Corps, and Molineux's brigade was ordered to report to Alfred H. Terry, commanding First Division, Tenth Corps. July 27, 1864, Birge's brigade was sent to reinforce Winfield S. Hancock's Second Corps, Army of the Potomac, which was then operating north of the James River near Deep Bottom, and Molineux's brigade moved up to occupy the position vacated by Birge. For details of Hancock's operations, see Operations about

Petersburg and Richmond, Virginia, 1864–1865, Operations of July 1864, Demonstration on the North Bank of the James River, Engagement at Deep Bottom (or Darbytown, Strawberry Plains, New Market Road), Virginia.

July 26, 1864, Early again became active in the lower Shenandoah Valley, and Wright was once more ordered to move forward with his command to meet this new threat. This time he was ordered to march toward the Monocacy River to counter a possible enemy advance into Maryland. That same day orders were issued for the troops of Detachment Nineteenth Corps arriving from the Gulf to proceed directly to Washington, and also for Emory's troops then with the Army of the James to be sent to Washington. That day, the part of McMillan's brigade then under Isaac Dyer was ordered to City Point to embark for Washington, and Currie's brigade followed Dyer the next day. Birge's brigade remained at Deep Bottom to hold the bridgehead there, and then moved to City Point to embark July 31, 1864. Molineux, who was at Bermuda Hundred, also moved to City Point for embarkation July 31, 1864.

Meantime, on July 26, 1864, Wright's command moved forward from Washington toward Rockville, Maryland, and two days later it reached the Monocacy River near Frederick. Wright had with him the same force that he had commanded in the pursuit of Early to the Shenandoah Valley earlier in the month, but William Dwight then commanded the troops of Detachment Nineteenth Corps with Wright, while Emory remained in Washington to receive the other brigades of Nineteenth Corps as they arrived from the Army of the James.

Wright moved on from the Monocacy, through Jefferson, Maryland, and assembled his entire command at Halltown, near Harper's Ferry, July 30, 1864. When Wright advanced beyond the Monocacy River, he came under the orders of David Hunter, commander of the Department of West Virginia.

July 30, 1864, John McCausland's Confederate cavalry burned Chambersburg, Pennsylvania, and that day Hunter ordered all of his available force, except the garrison of Harper's Ferry, to move along the east side of South Mountain toward Frederick, and to occupy the passes in the mountain so as to prevent an enemy advance from the west. That same day, Emory was ordered from Washington to Monocacy Junction with about 4,600 infantry belonging to McMillan's and Currie's brigades of First Division, Detachment Nineteenth Corps that had arrived from Bermuda Hundred. Emory arrived at Monocacy Junction the next day.

Hunter's command, including Sixth Corps, troops of Detachment Nineteenth Corps, and Kenly's Brigade, reached Jefferson on the night of July 30, 1864, and the next day it arrived at Frederick. This force was broken up when it was learned that Early was not advancing into Maryland, and August 2, 1864, that part of Detachment Nineteenth Corps that had been serving with Wright, together with Kenly's Brigade, was ordered to report to Emory at Monocacy Junction. First Division was thus reassembled under Dwight, and Emory resumed command of the troops of Detachment Nineteenth Corps that were at Monocacy Junction. These were organized as follows:

DETACHMENT NINETEENTH CORPS, William H. Emory

First Division. William Dwight
  First Brigade, George L. Beal
  Second Brigade, James W. McMillan
  Third Brigade, Leonard D. H. Currie
  Artillery
    Battery D, 1st Rhode Island Light Artillery, William W. Buckley

Note. Edwin P. Davis commanded First Brigade July 27–31, 1864, inclusive.

Second Division
  Third Brigade, Jacob Sharpe

Note. First Brigade and Second Brigade were en route from Bermuda Hundred to Washington, and they arrived August 2, 1864 and went into camp at Tennallytown.

On August 4, 1864, Hunter ordered Emory to proceed with Dwight's First Division and Sharpe's brigade of Second Division and Kenly's Brigade to reinforce the troops at Harper's Ferry. Emory arrived there the next day and moved on to Halltown August 6, 1864. There he took position, with Crook's Army of West Virginia on the left and Wright's Sixth Corps on the right. For additional information about the operations of Detachment

Nineteenth Corps during July and early August 1864, see Early's Washington Raid (and Operations in the Shenandoah Valley, Maryland, and Pennsylvania), and also Army of the James.

Meantime, back at Headquarters of the Army at City Point, Ulysses S. Grant had decided to put an end to the constant threat posed by Confederate forces in the Shenandoah Valley; and August 2, 1864, he had relieved Philip H. Sheridan, commander of the Cavalry Corps, from duty with the Army of the Potomac and ordered him to Washington to assume command of all troops that were opposing Early. He also ordered two cavalry divisions from the Army of the Potomac to join Sheridan's command. On August 6, 1864, Sheridan arrived at Harper's Ferry and assumed command of the field forces assembled in the vicinity by David Hunter, and the next day he assumed temporary command of the newly created Middle Military Division. This consisted of the departments of Washington, West Virginia, and the Susquehanna and the Middle Department, and its formation assured cooperation among the various forces of Sheridan's command. Sheridan was under orders to clear the Shenandoah Valley of enemy forces, and during the period August 7, 1864–November 28, 1864, he led his army in a successful campaign.

Emory remained with his command at Halltown until August 10, 1864, and then Sheridan advanced with his army to a line extending from Berryville, on the left, to Clifton, on the right. At that time, Emory's command consisted only of Dwight's First Division and Sharpe's Third Brigade, Second Division, and it took position near Berryville. Kenly was detached from Emory's command by an order of August 9, 1864, and he remained with his brigade at Halltown after Emory had departed.

On August 8, 1864, Grover, whose two brigades of Second Division, Detachment Nineteenth Corps were still at Tennallytown, was ordered to report to Christopher C. Augur, commander of the Department of Washington, Twenty-Second Corps, for temporary duty. August 10, 1864, however, Grover was ordered to join Sheridan, and August 14, 1864, he left Washington for Berryville to rejoin Emory's command. In August 1864, a new Fourth Brigade, Second Division was formed from the 8th and 18th Indiana and 24th and 28th Iowa regiments, taken from Third Brigade, Second Division, and David

Shunk, colonel of the 8th Indiana, was assigned command.

August 11, 1864, Sheridan advanced to Opequon Creek, and Emory took position at the ford on the Berryville Pike. Early then retreated through Strasburg to Fisher's Hill, and part of Sheridan's command followed as far as Strasburg. Detachment Nineteenth Corps halted at Cedar Creek, and there, on August 14, 1864, Currie's Third Brigade, First Division was sent back to Winchester as escort for a wagon train going to Harper's Ferry.

Sheridan learned that reinforcements were on their way to join Early, and on the morning of August 15, 1864, he decided to withdraw to Halltown, where there was a good defensible position. Emory began to fall back that night to Winchester, and he then moved on to Berryville. Grover arrived at Berryville from Washington on the night of August 17, 1864 with his two brigades and joined Emory. Emory then had under his command Dwight's First Division and Grover's Second Division, Detachment Nineteenth Corps. Sheridan continued the retreat down the valley and arrived at Halltown on the morning of August 22, 1864. He then moved his infantry back to the Berryville-Clifton line September 3, 1864.

Sheridan remained in this position until he learned on the evening of September 16, 1864 that Joseph B. Kershaw's division was on the march toward Front Royal on its return to Lee's army, and he then decided to attack Early's weakened army. He advanced on the morning of September 19, 1864, and was soon engaged in the severe Battle of Opequon Creek, which ended with the retreat of Early. The organization of Emory's command during the battle that day was as follows:

DETACHMENT NINETEENTH CORPS, William H. Emory

First Division, William Dwight
  First Brigade, George L. Beal
  Second Brigade, James W. McMillan
  Artillery
    5th Battery, New York Light Artillery, John V. Grant

Note. Leonard D. H. Currie's Third Brigade was detached from the division August 14, 1864, during Sheridan's first advance up the Shenandoah Valley, and it was assigned the duty of guarding the wagon trains

supplying the army at the front. August 28, 1864, the brigade was ordered to report to John D. Stevenson, commanding the District of Harper's Ferry, Department of West Virginia. Currie's brigade was relieved from the duty of guarding the trains October 26, 1864.

Second Division, Cuvier Grover
    First Brigade, Henry W. Birge
    Second Brigade, Edward L. Molineux
    Third Brigade, Jacob Sharpe, wounded
        Alfred Neafie, September 21, 1864
        Daniel Macauley
    Artillery
        1st Battery (A), Maine Light Artillery, Albert W. Bradbury

Reserve Artillery, Elijah D. Taft
    17th Battery, Indiana Light Artillery, Milton L. Miner
    Battery D, 1st Rhode Island Light Artillery, Frederick Chase

Following his defeat at Opequon Creek, Early withdrew to Fisher's Hill, and there, on September 22, 1864, his army was routed by Sheridan and driven up the valley. The organization and command of Detachment Nineteenth Corps at Fisher's Hill were the same as at the Battle of the Opequon.

Sheridan pursued Early up the valley as far as Harrisonburg and Mount Crawford, and then returned to Cedar Creek and went into camp. Sheridan's army was surprised there in an attack launched early on the morning of October 19, 1864, and suffered an initial defeat, but it rallied later in the day, and upon the return of Sheridan from Washington, attacked and once more drove Early's army in disorder up the valley. The organization of Detachment Nineteenth Corps at the Battle of Cedar Creek October 19, 1864 was as follows:

DETACHMENT NINETEENTH CORPS, William H. Emory

First Division, James W. McMillan, until 2:00 P.M.
    William Dwight
    First Brigade, Edwin P. Davis
    Second Brigade, Stephen Thomas, until 2:00 P.M.
        James W. McMillan
    Artillery
        5th Battery, New York Light Artillery, Elijah D. Taft

Second Division, Cuvier Grover, wounded
    Henry W. Birge
    First Brigade, Henry W. Birge
        Thomas W. Porter

Second Brigade, Edward L. Molineux
Third Brigade, Daniel Macauley, wounded
    Alfred Neafie
Fourth Brigade, David Shunk
Artillery
    1st Battery (A), Maine Light Artillery, Eben D. Haley, wounded
    John S. Snow

Reserve Artillery
    17th Battery, Indiana Light Artillery, Hezekiah Hinkson
    Battery D, 1st Rhode Island Light Artillery, Frederick Chase

For details of the operations of Detachment Nineteenth Corps during the period August 1864–November 1864, see Shenandoah Valley Campaign (Sheridan).

Emory's command remained in camp near Cedar Creek after the battle of October 19, 1864 until November 9, 1864. At the end of October 1864, it was organized as follows:

DETACHMENT NINETEENTH CORPS, William H. Emory

First Division, William Dwight
    First Brigade, George M. Love
    Second Brigade, James D. Fessenden
    Third Brigade, Nathan A. M. Dudley

Note 1. October 10, 1864, James D. Fessenden arrived at Harper's Ferry from Portland, Maine, and October 12, 1864, he was assigned command of Second Brigade, First Division during the absence of McMillan. November 1, 1864, Fessenden was assigned to the permanent command of Third Brigade, First Division.

Note 2. October 12, 1864, Dudley was assigned command of Leonard D. H. Currie's Third Brigade, which on October 26, 1864 rejoined the division from detached service at Harper's Ferry. November 1, 1864, Dudley was assigned command of First Brigade, First Division during the absence of Beal, and that day Fessenden was assigned command of Third Brigade.

Second Division, Henry W. Birge
    First Brigade, Thomas W. Porter
    Second Brigade, Nicholas W. Day
    Third Brigade, Alfred Neafie
    Fourth Brigade, David Shunk

Artillery Brigade, Albert M. Bradbury
    17th Battery, Indiana Light Artillery, Hezekiah Hinkson

1st Battery, New York Light Artillery, Elijah D. Taft

Battery D, 1st Rhode Island Light Artillery, Frederick Chase

1st Battery (A), Maine Light Artillery, John S. Snow

On November 7, 1864, while the army was on Cedar Creek, the organization known as Nineteenth Corps, Military Division of West Mississippi, then operating in Arkansas, was abolished, and the designation of Emory's Detachment Nineteenth Corps was changed to Nineteenth Corps.

On November 9, 1864, Sheridan's army moved back to Camp Russell, near Kernstown. During the second week in December 1864, Sixth Corps rejoined the Army of the Potomac at Petersburg, and December 19, 1864, George Crook's Army of West Virginia was broken up. Thomas M. Harris' division was detached and and sent to City Point, and at the end of December 1864, Isaac H. Duval's division was sent to West Virginia. This left only Nineteenth Corps and Alfred T. A. Torbert's cavalry with Sheridan in the valley. Because of the reduced size of his force, and also because of the severity of the winter, Sheridan decided to occupy a line nearer to the base of supplies at Harper's Ferry. Accordingly, on December 29, 1864, Nineteenth Corps moved back from near Kernstown to Stephenson's Depot, north of Winchester, where it established another camp, called Camp Sheridan.

At the end of December 1864, Nineteenth Corps was organized as follows:

NINETEENTH CORPS, William H. Emory

First Division, William Dwight
  First Brigade, George L. Beal
  Second Brigade, James W. McMillan
  Third Brigade, James D. Fessenden

Second Division, Cuvier Grover
  First Brigade, Henry W. Birge
  Second Brigade, Edward L. Molineux
  Third Brigade, James P. Richardson
  Fourth Brigade, Henry D. Washburn

Note. Washburn relieved David Shunk in command of Fourth Brigade in November 1864, and Shunk died of disease February 21, 1865. Early in January 1865, Fourth Brigade was broken up, and 8th Indiana and 18th Indiana were assigned to First Brigade, Second Division. Washburn, colonel of 8th Indiana, then assumed command of First Brigade. Harvey Graham's 22nd Iowa was assigned to Second Brigade, and 24th Iowa to Third Brigade.

Artillery Brigade, Albert W. Bradbury
  17th Battery, Indiana Light Artillery, Hezekiah Hinkson
  1st Battery (E), Maine Light Artillery, Greenleaf T. Stevens
  5th Battery, New York Light Artillery, Elijah D. Taft
  Battery D, 1st Rhode Island Light Artillery, Elmer L. Cothrell

January 5, 1865, Fessenden's Third Brigade, First Division (formerly Currie's) was again detached and sent to Winchester. The next day Fessenden was assigned command at Winchester, and his brigade served as garrison of the post. McMillan's brigade was at Summit Point, and Beal's brigade, with Emory's and Dwight's headquarters, was at Stephenson's Depot.

January 6, 1864, Grover's Second Division, Nineteenth Corps left the Shenandoah Valley for Baltimore, Maryland to embark for Savannah, Georgia. February 27, 1865, Sheridan also left the Shenandoah Valley with three divisions of cavalry on an expedition toward Petersburg, where it later joined Grant's army. When Sheridan departed, Winfield S. Hancock assumed temporary command of the Middle Military Division, including Emory's Nineteenth Corps, which then consisted only of Dwight's division.

By a presidential order of March 20, 1865, Nineteenth Corps was discontinued, and Emory was sent to Cumberland, Maryland to command the troops of the Department of West Virginia west of Sleepy Creek.

The Army of the Shenandoah was reorganized April 2, 1865, and Dwight's division was redesignated as First Division (First Provisional Division), Army of the Shenandoah. Two days later, Hancock sent Dwight's division back to Camp Russell, where he would be in position to prevent the escape of any enemy troops moving northward on the Valley Pike. April 7, 1865, however, Dwight was pulled back to Winchester, where he encamped on the banks of Abraham's Creek. On April 10, 1865, after the authorities learned of Lee's surrender, Dwight's division marched eighteen miles to Summit Point, and there boarded trains for Washington. The division arrived there the next morning, and went into camp at Tennallytown. Its designation was then changed to Dwight's Division, Twenty-Second Corps. A week later Dwight moved to the vicinity of Bladensburg and camped. Upon arrival in Washington, Dwight's Division was assigned to Orlando B. Willcox's District of Washington. During May 1865, he furnished heavy details to guard the prison and the grounds of the Arsenal, where President Lincoln's assassins were being held.

When the Army of the Potomac arrived in Washington from its successful campaign in Virginia, Dwight's Division was ordered to report to Orlando B. Willcox, then commanding Ninth Corps, and to follow that corps in the Grand Review of the Army in Washington. May 22, 1865, Dwight broke camp near Bladensburg and marched to a point east of the capital, near the Congressional Cemetery, where it bivouacked with Ninth Corps. The division then marched in the Grand Review May 23, 1865.

The break-up of Dwight's Division began June 1, 1865, when 114th and 116th New York regiments of Beal's brigade and the 133rd New York from Fessenden's brigade left for muster out. The 8th Vermont had already been transferred to Sixth Corps to join the Vermont Brigade. May 29, 1865, the rest of Dwight's Division began embarking for Savannah, Georgia to join Grover's division.

Meantime, Grover's division had begun embarking at Baltimore January 10, 1865, and the advance troops began landing at Savannah January 19, 1865. The rest of the division soon followed. January 21, 1865, Grover was assigned command of the District of Savannah, Department of the South, and Birge assumed command of Second Division, Nineteenth Corps. The organization of Grover's command was as follows:

DISTRICT OF SAVANNAH, Cuvier Grover

Second Division, Nineteenth Corps, Henry W. Birge
First Brigade, Henry D. Washburn
Second Brigade, Nicholas W. Day
Third Brigade, James P. Richardson

Birge's division remained at Savannah on garrison and police duty until about March 4, 1865, and then it was ordered to report to John M. Schofield, commanding the Department of North Carolina. On March 1, 1865, Schofield advanced from near the coast with the available troops of his command toward Goldsboro. There it was to join William T. Sherman's Army of the Military Division of the Mississippi, which was then moving northward through the Carolinas. Birge was ordered with two of his brigades to North Carolina to reinforce Schofield. His command was organized as follows:

Second Division, Nineteenth Corps, Henry W. Birge
Second Brigade, Nicholas W. Day, to March 17, 1865
Harvey Graham
Third Brigade, James P. Richardson, to March 17, 1865
Nicholas W. Day

Note. Henry D. Washburn's First Brigade was left behind in the District of Savannah.

Birge's command arrived at Morehead City, North Carolina March 10–14, 1865, and at first the regiments were scattered on special service as train guards, repairing roads, and assisting the Quartermaster's Department. In general, however, during the period March 10, 1865–April 10, 1865, Day's Third Brigade and Birge's headquarters were at New Berne, and Graham's Second Brigade was at Morehead City, where it was assigned to Landon C. Easton, assistant quartermaster general of the Military Division of the Mississippi. Their duty was to assist Easton in handling stores to be forwarded to Goldsboro.

On March 20, 1865, Nineteenth Corps was discontinued, and Birge's Second Division became Birge's Division, District of Savannah.

On April 2, 1865, Tenth Corps was reorganized under Alfred H. Terry at Faison's Station, near Goldsboro, and Birge's two brigades were assigned temporarily to that corps. Harvey Graham's former Second Brigade, Second Division, Nineteenth Corps was redesignated as First Brigade, First Division, Tenth Corps, and Day's former Third Brigade, Second Division, Nineteenth Corps (at New Berne) became Third Brigade, First Division, Tenth Corps. Birge was assigned command of First Division, Tenth Corps.

April 10, 1865, Sherman's army advanced from Goldsboro toward Raleigh, North Carolina, and that day Birge moved with his First Division headquarters and Day's Third Brigade to Goldsboro, where he assumed command of the post. Joseph E. Johnston surrendered his army to Sherman at Durham's Station, North Carolina April 26, 1865, and the war in the East came to an end. The next day, Birge was ordered to return with his two brigades to Savannah, and First Division, Tenth Corps was thus discontinued. Birge was relieved at Goldsboro May 1, 1865, and he sailed with his two brigades from Morehead City two days later. For additional information, see Department of North Carolina, January 31, 1865–May 19, 1866, Nineteenth Corps; and also Tenth Corps, Department of North Carolina.

May 11, 1865, Birge's Division marched for Augusta, Georgia, leaving behind at Savannah Day with all of his regiments except 24th Iowa and 128th New York. On June 5, 1865, that part of the state of Georgia lying within the limits of the Department of the South was divided into three districts. Grover was assigned command of the District of Southern Georgia, with headquarters at Doctor Town; Birge was assigned command of the District of Savannah, with headquarters in the city of Savannah; and Molineux was assigned command of the District of Northern Georgia, with headquarters at Augusta.

June 7, 1865, Birge's brigade returned to Savannah from Augusta, and two days later Day's brigade marched back to replace it.

Meantime, the government had ordered that all regiments whose terms of enlistment expired before November 1, 1865 be mustered out, but by June 5, 1865, the reenlisted veterans of Dwight's Division began arriving at Savannah. Upon their arrival, Dwight's command was designated as Dwight's Division, Department of the South.

From this time the break-up of the Federal forces in Georgia proceeded rapidly. What was left of the divisions of Dwight and Grover continued to occupy Savannah and Augusta, Georgia, and Charleston, South Carolina for some time, but they too finally finally left for home.

TWENTY-SECOND CORPS, DEPARTMENT OF WASHINGTON

In the order of February 2, 1863 constituting the Department of Washington, the troops in the department were designated as Twenty-Second Corps. This corps was not a mobile force for field duty, but served instead as a permanent garrison for the Federal capital, and also as a force ready for service in the Union Department and District of Washington. Samuel P. Heintzelman was assigned

command. For details of the organization of Twenty-Second Corps during the war, see Department of Washington, February 2, 1863–March 16, 1869.

TWENTY-THIRD CORPS, ARMY OF THE OHIO
(In the Department of North Carolina)

In the spring of 1863, Ambrose E. Burnside was assigned command of the Department of the Ohio, which included Kentucky and East Tennessee, and Ninth Corps left Virginia at that time for the Department of the Ohio. Burnside planned for an active campaign in East Tennessee, and to provide more troops for this purpose he organized Twenty-Third Corps from regiments then stationed in Kentucky. The corps was formed April 27, 1863, and George L. Hartsuff was assigned command.

In the latter part of August 1863, Burnside moved into East Tennessee with the Second, Third, and Fourth divisions of Twenty-Third Corps and occupied Knoxville September 3, 1863. The corps remained in East Tennessee during the winter, and in April 1864, John M. Schofield was assigned command. Also that month, a newly designated First Division joined the corps.

Schofield's Army of the Ohio, then consisting of only Twenty-Third Corps, took part in William T. Sherman's Atlanta Campaign, and after the capture of Atlanta, it was sent back to Tennessee when John B. Hood threatened an invasion of that state. Later, when Hood advanced into Tennessee, Twenty-Third Corps was engaged at the Battle of Franklin and later at the Battle of Nashville. After Nashville, Schofield joined in the pursuit of Hood's defeated army until it left the state, and then on January 9, 1865 moved to Clifton, Tennessee. While there he was ordered with his corps to Washington, D.C. for transfer to North Carolina, where he would be in position to cooperate with Sherman's Army of the Military Division of the Mississippi as it marched northward through the Carolinas. Twenty-Third Corps began embarkation at Clifton January 15, 1865, and it then moved eastward by way of the Tennessee and Ohio rivers past Louisville to Cincinnati. From there it traveled by rail to Washington, where it arrived at the end of the month. It then embarked for North Carolina.

Schofield was assigned command of the Department of North Carolina January 31, 1865. He left Alexandria with Jacob D. Cox's Third Division as soon as the Potomac River was navigable, arrived at the mouth of the Cape Fear River February 9, 1865, and landed near Fort Fisher. That day, Schofield assumed command of the Department of North Carolina. He then issued orders under the heading "Headquarters Department of North Carolina, Army of the Ohio." Included in his command was Alfred H. Terry's force of about 8,000 men, formerly belonging to the Army of the James, that had captured Fort Fisher, and which at that time occupied a line about two miles north of the fort.

After an unsuccessful attempt to advance toward Wilmington on the east side of the Cape Fear River, Schofield sent Cox's division and Adelbert Ames' division of Terry's command across the river to Smithville, where they were joined by Orlando H. Moore's First Brigade of Darius N. Couch's Second Division, Twenty-Third Corps, which had just disembarked. This force then advanced against Fort Anderson, which was evacuated on the night of February 18, 1865. Ames' division recrossed the river on the night of February 19, 1865, but Cox continued the advance toward Wilmington. He forced the evacuation of the enemy position on Town Creek, and then occupied Wilmington without opposition on the morning of February 22, 1865. Terry made some progress east of the river, but he was unable to penetrate the enemy defenses south of Wilmington. For details of the capture of Wilmington, see Department of North Carolina, January 31, 1865–May 19, 1866, Operations in the Department of North Carolina, Capture of Wilmington, North Carolina.

Couch with his Second Brigade and Third Brigade arrived at the mouth of the Cape Fear River February 22–23, 1865, and he was sent on to Wilmington. His divisions were assembled by February 26, 1865. Thomas H. Ruger's First Division, Twenty-Third Corps also arrived at Fort Fisher February 22–23, 1865, but it was ordered to New Berne, where it arrived during the period February 28, 1865–March 1, 1865.

The organization of Twenty-Third Corps when it arrived in North Carolina was as follows:

TWENTY-THIRD CORPS, John M. Schofield

First Division, Thomas H. Ruger
First Brigade, John M. Orr
Second Brigade, John C. McQuiston
Third Brigade, Minor T. Thomas
Artillery
22nd Battery, Indiana Light Artillery, George W. Alexander
Battery F, 1st Michigan Light Artillery, Byron D. Paddock

Second Division, Darius N. Couch
First Brigade, Orlando H. Moore
Second Brigade, John Mehringer
Third Brigade, Nathaniel C. McLean
Artillery
15th Battery, Indiana Light Artillery, Alonzo D. Harvey
19th Battery, Ohio Light Artillery, Frank Wilson

Third Division, Jacob D. Cox
First Brigade, Oscar W. Sterl
Second Brigade, John S. Casement
Third Brigade, Thomas J. Henderson
Artillery
23rd Battery, Indiana Light Artillery, James H. Myers
Battery D, 1st Ohio Light Artillery, Giles J. Cockerill

Note 1. Sterl was in temporary command of First Brigade during the absence of James W. Reilly.
Note 2. George W. Schofield was in command of the artillery.

February 25, 1865, Cox was assigned command of the newly constituted District of Beaufort, with headquarters at New Berne. When Cox left Wilmington for his new assignment, James W. Reilly assumed temporary command of his Third Division. February 28, 1865, Couch assumed command of Second Division and Third Division, Twenty-Third Corps, and Nathaniel C. McLean took charge temporarily of Second Division.

At New Berne on March 1, 1865, Cox organized a provisional corps for the purpose of advancing along the Atlantic and North Carolina Railroad toward Goldsboro and putting the road in running order to that point. Ruger's First Division, Twenty-Third Corps was included in Cox's corps, and it was engaged at the Battle of Kinston (or Wise's Forks) March 8–10, 1865. Couch left Wilmington with Second Division and Third Division March 6, 1865, and joined Cox's command near Kinston March

13–14, 1865. Cox remained near Kinston until the railroad was repaired to that place, and March 20, 1865 marched with his Provisional Corps and Couch's two divisions toward Goldsboro, where it arrived the next day. For details of Cox's movement, see Department of North Carolina, January 31, 1865–May 19, 1866, Operations in the Department of North Carolina, Advance of Schofield's Army to Goldsboro (Battle of Kinston or Wise's Forks).

Sherman's Army of the Military Division of the Mississippi arrived at Goldsboro from its march through the Carolinas March 23–24, 1865, and it was joined there by Schofield's army. March 24, 1865, Reilly's Third Division replaced Ruger's First Division in Cox's Provisional Corps, and was assigned as the garrison of Goldsboro. Couch, with First Division and Second Division, then moved back along the railroad to a point about midway between Goldsboro and Kinston, and established headquarters at Moseley Hall.

March 31, 1865, Cox was assigned by the president to the permanent command of Twenty-Third Corps, and Cox's Provisional Corps was discontinued. Thus, for the first time since their arrival in North Carolina the three divisions of Twenty-Third Corps were united as a single command. At this time Ruger was in command of First Division, Couch of Second Division, and Reilly of Third Division.

April 1, 1865, in preparation for further operations by his army, Sherman designated Cox's Twenty-Third Corps and Alfred H. Terry's newly reorganized Tenth Corps as the Center of the army. Schofield, as commander of the Army of the Ohio, was assigned command. This organization was to be in effect while Schofield's two corps were operating with the Army of the Tennessee (the Right Wing) and the Army of Georgia (the Left Wing).

April 7, 1865, James W. Reilly resigned, and Samuel P. Carter was assigned command of Third Division of Twenty-Third Corps.

April 9, 1865, Ruger's First Division and Couch's Second Division marched from Moseley Hall to Goldsboro, and the next day the corps advanced as a part of Sherman's army to engage Joseph E. Johnston's Confederate command in North Carolina, which at that time was near Smithfield. When Sherman began his advance, Johnston retired toward Raleigh, and he was closely pursued by Sherman's troops. Twenty-Third Corps arrived at Raleigh and went into camp April 13–14, 1865.

All movements were suspended April 15, 1865 while Sherman and Johnston met near Durham Station, North Carolina to discuss terms for the ending of hostilities. Johnston surrendered his army April 26, 1865, and the war in the East was ended.

The Army of the Tennessee and the Army of Georgia began their final march toward Washington, D.C. and muster out April 27, 1865, but Tenth Corps and Twenty-Third Corps remained in the Department of North Carolina until they were discontinued. Twenty-Third Corps stayed in its camps at Raleigh until May 4, 1865, and it then marched to Greensboro. Ruger's division continued on to Charlotte, North Carolina, where it arrived May 11–16, 1865. It remained there until it was discontinued August 1, 1865. Joseph A. Cooper relieved Couch in command of Second Division about May 8, 1865, and he was sent on with this division to Salisbury, North Carolina. Second Division remained there until it was discontinued July 4, 1865. Carter's Third Division moved from Raleigh to Greensboro May 6, 1865, and it was there when it was discontinued July 4, 1865. Two days later Carter was assigned command of the District of Greensboro. For details of the final movements of the armies in North Carolina, see Carolinas Campaign, Goldsboro to Raleigh, North Carolina (Surrender of Joseph E. Johnston's Army).

Twenty-Third Corps was officially discontinued to date from August 1, 1865.

The organization of Twenty-Third Corps during the time it was in North Carolina was as follows:

TWENTY-THIRD CORPS, John M. Schofield, to March 31, 1865
    Jacob D. Cox, to June 19, 1865
    Thomas H. Ruger, to June 27, 1865
    Samuel P. Carter, to July 12, 1865

First Division, Thomas H. Ruger, to June 19, 1865
    Minor T. Thomas, to July 11, 1865, mustered out
    George W. Schofield
    First Brigade, John M. Orr, to March 14, 1865
        Israel N. Stiles, to May 1865
        John M. Orr, to June 1865
        Allen W. Prather
    Second Brigade, John C. McQuiston
    Third Brigade, Minor T. Thomas, to June 19, 1865
        James Tucker, to July 1865, mustered out

Second Division, Darius N. Couch, to February 28, 1865
    Nathaniel C. McLean, to April 4, 1865

Orlando H. Moore, to April 8, 1865
Darius N. Couch, to April 20, 1865
Joseph A. Cooper, to April 26, 1865
Darius N. Couch, to about May 8, 1865, resigned
Joseph A. Cooper, to June 12, 1865
George W. Schofield, to July 4, 1865
First Brigade, Joseph A. Cooper, to March 6, 1865
    Orlando H. Moore, to April 4, 1865
    Joseph A. Cooper, to April 20, 1865
    Orlando H. Moore, to April 26, 1865
    Joseph A. Cooper, to about May 8, 1865
    Orlando H. Moore, to June 24, 1865, mustered out
    John B. Conyngham, to July 4, 1865
Second Brigade, Orlando H. Moore, to February 27, 1865
    John Mehringer, to June 12, 1865
    Oliver L. Spaulding, to June 28, 1865, mustered out
Third Brigade, Nathaniel C. McLean, to February 28, 1865
    Silas A. Strickland, to June 12, 1865
    John Mehringer, to June 26, 1865, mustered out
    George W. Hoge, to July 4, 1865

Note 1. Second Division was discontinued July 4, 1865.
Note 2. Second Brigade was discontinued June 28, 1865 by muster out of its regiments.

Third Division, Jacob D. Cox, to February 25, 1865
James W. Reilly, to April 7, 1865
Samuel P. Carter, to June 27, 1865
James Stewart, Jr., to July 4, 1865
First Brigade, Oscar W. Sterl, to June 18, 1865, relieved
    Laurence H. Rousseau, to June 28, 1865
    William S. Stewart, to July 4, 1865
Second Brigade, John S. Casement, to February 25, 1865
    Arthur T. Wilcox, to March 1865
    John S. Casement, to May 1, 1865
    George W. Schofield, to June 12, 1865
    Arthur T. Wilcox, to June 24, 1865, mustered out
    James Stewart, Jr., to June 28, 1865
    Laurence H. Rousseau, to July 4, 1865
Third Brigade, Thomas J. Henderson

Note 1. Third Division was discontinued July 4, 1865.
Note 2. It is important to note regarding the commanders of First Brigade and Second Brigade that the designations of these two brigades were exchanged by an order of June 28, 1865. On that date, the designation of First Brigade was changed to Second Brigade, and the designation of Second Brigade was changed to First Brigade.
Note 3. The organization of the artillery was essentially unchanged during this period.

TWENTY-FOURTH CORPS, ARMY OF THE JAMES

Twenty-Fourth Corps, Army of the James was constituted December 3, 1864, and was to consist of the white troops of Tenth Corps and Eighteenth Corps of Benjamin F. Butler's Army of the James. The latter two corps were discontinued by the same order. The troops of Tenth Corps were assigned to First Division and Second Division, Twenty-Fourth Corps, and the troops of Eighteenth Corps were assigned to Third Division, Twenty-Fourth Corps. Edward O. C. Ord was assigned command, and he assumed command December 4, 1864. The corps was organized as follows:

TWENTY-FOURTH CORPS, Edward O. C. Ord, to December 6, 1864
    Alfred H. Terry, to December 10, 1864
    Edward O. C. Ord

First Division, Alfred H. Terry, to December 6, 1864
    Robert S. Foster, to December 10, 1864
    Alfred H. Terry
    First Brigade, Alvin C. Voris, to December 8, 1864
        Thomas O. Osborn
    Second Brigade, Joseph R. Hawley
    Third Brigade, Harris M. Plaisted
    Fourth Brigade, James Jourdan

Note 1. First Brigade was organized from First Brigade, First Division, Tenth Corps.
Note 2. Second Brigade was organized from Second Brigade, First Division, Tenth Corps.
Note 3. Third Brigade was organized from Third Brigade, First Division, Tenth Corps.
Note 4. Fourth Brigade was organized from Second Brigade, Second Division, Eighteenth Corps.

Second Division, Adelbert Ames
    First Brigade, N. Martin Curtis
    Second Brigade, Galusha Pennypacker
    Third Brigade, Louis Bell

Note 1. Ames assumed command of Second Division December 5, 1864.
Note 2. First Brigade was organized from First Brigade, Second Division, Tenth Corps.
Note 3. Second Brigade was organized from Second Brigade, Second Division, Tenth Corps, and Pennypacker assumed command December 5, 1864.
Note 4. Third Brigade was organized from Third Brigade, Second Division, Tenth Corps.

Third Division, Charles Devens
　First Brigade, John B. Raulston
　Second Brigade, Joseph H. Potter
　Third Brigade, Guy V. Henry

Note 1. First Brigade was organized from First Brigade, First Division, Eighteenth Corps plus the 11th Connecticut and 19th Wisconsin of Second Brigade, Second Division, Eighteenth Corps. Raulston assumed command December 5, 1864.

Note 2. Second Brigade was organized from Second Brigade, First Division, Eighteenth Corps plus 9th Vermont from Second Brigade, Second Division, Eighteenth Corps and 5th Maryland from Third Brigade, Second Division, Eighteenth Corps.

Note 3. Third Brigade was organized from Third Brigade, First Division, Eighteenth Corps, and Henry was assigned command December 11, 1864.

Artillery Brigade, Charles C. Abell
　Battery E, 3rd New York Light Artillery, George E. Ashby
　Battery H, 3rd New York Light Artillery, William J. Riggs
　Battery K, 3rd New York Light Artillery, James R. Angel
　Battery M, 3rd New York Light Artillery, John B. Howell
　7th Battery, New York Light Artillery, Martin V. McIntyre
　16th Battery, New York Light Artillery, Richard H. Lee
　17th Battery, New York Light Artillery, Hiram D. Smith
　Battery A, 1st Pennsylvania Light Artillery, William Stitt
　Battery F, 1st Rhode Island Light Artillery, Robert B. Smith
　Battery L, 4th United States Artillery, Richard Wilson
　Battery A, 5th United States Artillery, Charles P. Muhlenberg
　Battery F, 5th United States Artillery, Leonard Martin

On the Lines North of the James River. Twenty-Fourth Corps occupied the line of entrenchments north of the James River that were previously held by Tenth Corps, and which extended from the vicinity of Fort Burnham to the New Market Road.

In October 1864, Ulysses S. Grant planned for a joint army-navy expedition against Wilmington, North Carolina, the last open Confederate seaport on the Atlantic Coast. He postponed this venture until December 1864, however, when the chances of success seemed more favorable. Grant chose Godfrey Weitzel, commanding Twenty-Fifth Corps

of the Army of the James, to lead this expedition, but at the last minute Butler assumed command. A part of Adelbert Ames' Second Division was detached temporarily from Twenty-Fourth Corps and assigned to Weitzel's expedition. Butler's attempt to capture Fort Fisher, at the mouth of the Cape Fear River below Wilmington, was unsuccessful, and his command returned to the lines in front of Richmond. Ames' division returned to its camps December 28, 1864 and rejoined the corps. For details, see Army of the James, Butler's Expedition to Fort Fisher, North Carolina.

During the absence of Butler at Fort Fisher, reinforcements arrived for the Army of the James. On December 19, 1864, Thomas M. Harris' First Infantry Division, Army of West Virginia left Camp Russell near Winchester in the Shenandoah Valley, with orders to report to Butler at Bermuda Hundred. This division was formerly commanded by Joseph Thoburn, who was killed October 19, 1864 at the Battle of Cedar Creek, Virginia. Harris' division arrived at City Point and Bermuda Hundred December 22–23, 1864, and, during the absence of Ames' division, it was temporarily attached to Twenty-Fourth Corps December 24, 1864. When Milton Wells' Third Brigade arrived December 23, 1864, it reported to Edward Ferrero, commanding the Defenses of Bermuda Hundred, but January 2, 1865, it rejoined the division north of the James River. Harris' division was organized as follows:

First Infantry Division, Department of West Virginia, Thomas M. Harris
　First Brigade, Thomas F. Wildes
　Second Brigade, William B. Curtis
　Third Brigade, Milton Wells, to December 31, 1864
　　Moses S. Hall

Note. This division was also called Harris' Division, but in January 1865 it was designated as Independent Division, Twenty-Fourth Corps.

January 1, 1865, Robert S. Foster departed on leave, and Joseph R. Hawley assumed command of First Division, Twenty-Fourth Corps. Joseph C. Abbott was then assigned command of Hawley's Second Brigade, First Division. The next day Alfred H. Terry, then in command of Twenty-Fourth Corps, was assigned command of a second expedition to Fort Fisher. He took with him a part of Ames'

Second Division and Abbott's Second Brigade, First Division of Twenty-Fourth Corps, and Charles J. Paine's Third Division, Twenty-Fifth Corps. The expedition embarked at Bermuda Hundred for North Carolina January 4–5, 1865, and January 15, 1865 assaulted and captured the fort. Most of the fighting was done by troops of Twenty-Fourth Corps. For details of the capture of Fort Fisher, see Army of the James, Terry's Expedition to Fort Fisher, North Carolina.

Terry's command did not rejoin the Army of the James, but remained for a time on Federal Point as United States Forces at Fort Fisher. On February 9, 1865, Terry's forces were transferred to the Department of North Carolina, and later were included in the newly reorganized Tenth Corps.

When Terry left Twenty-Fourth Corps, Ord was absent on leave, and Charles Devens assumed temporary command of the corps. Then when Ord returned, he relieved Butler in command of the Department of Virginia and North Carolina and the Army of the James January 8, 1865. Devens continued in temporary command of Twenty-Fourth Corps until relieved by John Gibbon January 15, 1865.

On December 7, 1864, the troops of Second Division that did not accompany Ames on Butler's first Fort Fisher expedition were organized as a provisional brigade under G. Frederick Granger, and this brigade was temporarily attached to Devens' Third Division. On January 1, 1865, Granger's Provisional Brigade was relieved from duty with Devens' division and was ordered to report to Ames, who had returned from Fort Fisher a few days earlier. On January 3, 1865, however, Ames' division again departed on Terry's expedition to Fort Fisher, and as before, the detachments that were left behind were organized as a provisional brigade and attached to Devens' division. This brigade remained with Devens until January 30, 1865, and it then rejoined the division at Fort Fisher.

Twenty-Fourth Corps remained on the line of entrenchments north of the James River until March 27, 1865. Then, in preparation for Grant's spring offensive south of Petersburg, Ord marched with a large part of the Army of the James to reinforce Meade's Army of the Potomac. He took with him Robert S. Foster's First Division and John W. Turner's Independent Division (formerly Harris'

division) of Twenty-Fourth Corps, William Birney's Second Division of Twenty-Fifth Corps, and Ranald S. Mackenzie's Cavalry Division, Army of the James (formerly commanded by Kautz). Ord's command was designated as the Army of the James. Devens' Third Division, Twenty-Fourth Corps and Kautz's First Division, Twenty-Fifth Corps were left to hold the trenches in front of Richmond. Both divisions were under the command of Godfrey Weitzel, commander of Twenty-Fifth Corps, and his command was known as Detachment Army of the James.

The organization of Twenty-Fourth Corps for the period December 3, 1864–March 29, 1865 was as follows:

TWENTY-FOURTH CORPS, Edward O. C. Ord, December 3–6, 1864
Alfred H. Terry, to December 10, 1864
Edward O. C. Ord, to December 28, 1864
Alfred H. Terry, to January 3, 1865
Charles Devens, to January 15, 1865
John Gibbon

First Division, Alfred H. Terry, to December 6, 1864
Robert S. Foster, to January 1, 1865, on leave
Joseph R. Hawley, to February 1, 1865
Robert S. Foster
First Brigade, Alvin C. Voris, to December 8, 1864
Thomas O. Osborn
Second Brigade, Joseph R. Hawley
Joseph C. Abbott
Third Brigade, Harris M. Plaisted, to February 2, 1865
George B. Dandy
Fourth Brigade, James Jourdan, to March 17, 1865, resigned
Harrison S. Fairchild

Note. Second Brigade was detached from First Division January 5, 1865, and it accompanied Terry's expedition to Fort Fisher, North Carolina. This brigade did not rejoin the division, but was carried on the rolls as detached until it became a part of Terry's Provisional Corps, Department of North Carolina.

Second Division, Adelbert Ames
First Brigade, N. Martin Curtis
Second Brigade, Galusha Pennypacker
Third Brigade, Louis Bell

Note. Second Division was detached from Twenty-Fourth Corps January 5, 1865, and it accompanied Terry's expedition to Fort Fisher, North Carolina. This division did not rejoin the corps, but was carried on the rolls as detached until it became a part of Terry's Provisional Corps, Department of North Carolina. For additional information, see Army of the James, Terry's Expedition to Fort Fisher.

Third Division, Charles Devens, Jr.
  First Brigade, John B. Raulston, to January 15, 1865, mustered out of service
    William Kreutzer, to January 16, 1865
    Edgar M. Cullen, to March 22, 1865, honorably discharged
    Edward H. Ripley
  Second Brigade, Joseph H. Potter, to January 17, 1865
    Valentine G. Barney, to February 6, 1865
    John E. Ward
  Third Brigade, Guy V. Henry, December 11, 1864–January 29, 1865
    Samuel H. Roberts

Note 1. Devens was in temporary command of Twenty-Fourth Corps January 3–15, 1865.
Note 2. Potter was assigned as chief of staff, Twenty-Fourth Corps January 18, 1865.
Note 3. Henry left the army on leave January 29, 1865, and March 23, 1865, he was assigned to the Department of Missouri.

Independent Division, Thomas M. Harris, to March 20, 1865
  John M. Turner
  First Brigade, Thomas F. Wildes, to March 1865
    Andrew Potter
  Second Brigade, William B. Curtis
  Third Brigade, Milton Wells, to December 31, 1864
    Moses S. Hall, to March 25, 1865
    Thomas M. Harris

Note 1. Harris' division arrived from the Shenandoah Valley, and was attached to Twenty-Fourth Corps December 24, 1864.
Note 2. Turner was chief of staff of Ord's Army of the James when assigned command of the Independent Division.

Artillery Brigade, Charles C. Abell

Appomattox Campaign, Virginia. From late March 1865 to the end of the war, Gibbon's Twenty-Fourth Corps did not serve as a unit. As noted above, Gibbon, with the divisions of Foster and Turner, was sent to Grant at Petersburg, and they joined in the pursuit of the Army of Northern Virginia from Petersburg to Appomattox Court House. Gibbon's other division, under Devens, was left behind as a part of Weitzel's Detachment Army of the James, which occupied the line of entrenchments in front of Richmond.

Ord's Army of the James arrived near Hatcher's Run from north of the James River on March 28, 1865, and the next morning Foster's division relieved Humphreys' Second Corps on the left of the Union line of entrenchments, from Fort Sampson to Hatcher's Run. Turner's division was placed in reserve near Hatcher's Run. On March 30, 1865, William Birney's division of Twenty-Fifth Corps was attached to Gibbon's command.

Turner's division briefly supported the advance of Second Corps south of Hatcher's Run March 30, 1865, but otherwise Twenty-Fourth Corps remained in the entrenchments until April 2, 1865. That morning, Sixth Corps, supported by Twenty-Fourth Corps, broke through the enemy lines on a front extending from Fort Welch to Fort Fisher. Then, while Sixth Corps cleared the works to the left, Twenty-Fourth Corps moved to the right and advanced toward Petersburg. That afternoon, Foster's and Turner's divisions attacked and captured Fort Gregg and Fort Baldwin (or Whitworth), and opened the way to the Confederate inner line of defenses south and west of Petersburg.

Lee's army evacuated Petersburg and Richmond during the night of April 2, 1865, and the next day, Ord's Army of the James joined the Army of the Potomac and Sheridan's cavalry in pursuit. Ord advanced along the South Side Railroad toward Burkeville to head off Lee if he attempted to escape to Danville along the Richmond and Danville Railroad. Ord reached Burkeville late on the night of April 5, 1865, and learned that Lee was moving westward and not toward Danville. Ord then marched on through Rice's Station and arrived at Farmville April 7, 1865. While at Farmville, William Birney's division of Twenty-Fifth Corps was broken up and the brigades were assigned to Foster's and Turner's divisions.

All through the day of April 8, 1865 and during most of the night, Gibbon's Twenty-Fourth Corps followed Sheridan's cavalry toward Appomattox Station on the South Side Railroad. Sheridan arrived at the station that evening, ahead of Lee's army, and promptly formed a line across the Lynchburg Road, which was Lee's only escape route to the west and south. Twenty-Fourth Corps arrived at Appomattox Station on the morning of April 9, 1865, just in time to relieve Sheridan's cavalry, which was then hard pressed by John B. Gordon's infantry and Fitzhugh Lee's cavalry. These troops continued for a time in their final attempt to open the way for the rest of the army, but Gibbon then advanced and pushed them back toward Appomattox Court House. The fighting then ended, and that afternoon Lee surrendered to Grant his Army of Northern Virginia. For details of the operations of Twenty-Fourth Corps during this period, see Appomattox Campaign, Virginia.

Meantime, back near Chaffin's farm, Devens' division had continued to hold the entrenchments until the morning of April 3, 1865. Then, when skirmishers found that the enemy works had been evacuated during the night, Weitzel advanced toward Richmond with the divisions of Devens and Kautz and Charles F. Adams' regiment of cavalry. Authorities surrendered the city that morning, and Edward H. Ripley's brigade of Devens' division was assigned as provost guard. The remainder of Devens' division remained on the outskirts of the city, on the old inner line of defenses. For additional information, see Appomattox Campaign, Virginia, Federal Occupation of Petersburg and Richmond.

The organization of Twenty-Fourth Corps during the period of the Appomattox Campaign was as follows:

TWENTY-FOURTH CORPS, John Gibbon

First Division, Robert S. Foster
   First Brigade, Thomas O. Osborn
   Third Brigade, George B. Dandy
   Fourth Brigade, Harrison S. Fairchild

Note. Ulysses Doubleday's Second Brigade of William Birney's Second Division, Twenty-Fifth Corps was temporarily attached to Foster's division April 8–10, 1865.

Third Division, Charles Devens
   First Brigade, Edward H. Ripley
   Second Brigade, Michael T. Donohoe
   Third Brigade, Samuel H. Roberts

Independent Division, John W. Turner
   First Brigade, Andrew Potter
   Second Brigade, William B. Curtis
   Third Brigade, Thomas M. Harris

Note. William W. Woodward's Third Brigade of William Birney's Second Division, Twenty-Fifth Corps was temporarily attached to Turner's division April 8–10, 1865. James Shaw's First Brigade of Birney's division arrived at Appomattox Station April 9, 1865 from

detached duty, and April 9–10, 1865, it was also attached to Turner's division.

Artillery, Charles C. Abell

Note. The batteries of Abell's command were essentially the same as those given above.

After Appomattox. After Lee's surrender, Devens' Third Division, which had occupied Richmond on the morning of April 3, 1865, remained in its camps on the outskirts of the city until July 10, 1865, and then it was discontinued (see below). Gibbon, with the divisions of Foster and Turner, was assigned to remain at Appomattox Court House (with Fifth Corps, Army of the Potomac and Mackenzie's cavalry) until the terms of surrender had been carried into effect and the surrendered property had been collected and moved to the railroad for transfer to Washington. Gibbon, Wesley Merritt, and Charles Griffin were appointed April 9, 1865 as commissioners to arrange the details of the surrender.

On April 10, 1865, before leaving the army for Washington, Grant ordered Gibbon to march with Twenty-Fourth Corps and Mackenzie's cavalry to Lynchburg to parole the garrison and secure the public property there. Mackenzie entered the town April 12, 1865, and Turner's division followed the next day. Gibbon, in person, joined them April 14, 1865. Foster's division did not accompany Gibbon, but remained encamped near Appomattox Court House. Charles Griffin, commander of Fifth Corps, assumed temporary charge of Foster's division while Gibbon was absent at Lynchburg. Gibbon resumed command April 15, 1865.

Turner's division completed its work at Lynchburg and returned to Appomattox Court House April 16, 1865, and the next day Gibbon, with his two divisions and Mackenzie's cavalry, left for Richmond. Gibbon marched by way of Prospect Station and Farmville, and reached Burkeville April 19, 1865. He remained there until April 22, 1865, and then marched on through Jetersville and Amelia Court House and arrived at Manchester two days later. April 25, 1865, Gibbon's command moved through Richmond and camped on the old intermediate line of works north of the city. It remained near Richmond during May and June 1865, and some units were on duty there until the corps was officially discontinued August 1, 1865.

The organization of Twenty-Fourth Corps at the end of April 1865 was as follows:

TWENTY-FOURTH CORPS, John Gibbon

First Division, Robert S. Foster
    First Brigade, Thomas O. Osborn
    Third Brigade, George B. Dandy
    Fourth Brigade, Harrison S. Fairchild

Note 1. Gibbon was absent for a few days in Washington beginning April 27, 1865, and John W. Turner was in temporary command of the corps.
Note 2. Osborn was in temporary command of First Division during the absence of Foster, who left about May 5, 1865. James C. Briscoe assumed temporary command of Osborn's First Brigade.

Third Division, Charles Devens
    First Brigade, Edward H. Ripley
    Second Brigade, Michael Donohoe
    Third Brigade, Samuel H. Roberts

Note. George F. Nichols was in temporary command of First Brigade from April 16, 1865 to May 5, 1865, during the absence of Ripley.

Independent Division, Thomas M. Harris
    First Brigade, William S. Lincoln
    Second Brigade, William B. Curtis
    Third Brigade, John W. Holliday

Note 1. John W. Turner was in command of the Independent Division until he relieved Gibbon temporarily in command of Twenty-Fourth Corps. Harris, then commanding Third Brigade, assumed command of the division. Holliday temporarily commanded Third Brigade while Harris was in charge of the division.
Note 2. Lincoln succeeded Andrew Potter in command of First Brigade April 27, 1865.

Artillery, Charles C. Abell

Twenty-Fourth Corps retained its organization until mid-June 1865. It was then broken up, but it was not officially discontinued until August 1, 1865. Gibbon relinquished command and departed June 13, 1865, and there appears to have been no official assignment of a new commander for the corps. On June 9, 1865, however, John W. Turner was assigned command of the District of Henrico, which included the city of Richmond and the area north of the James River where the troops of Twenty-Fourth Corps were encamped.

There were several significant changes in the corps during the period May–August 1865. First Division remained relatively intact and was not seriously affected by the muster out of troops, but May 20, 1865, the designation of Fairchild's brigade was changed from Fourth Brigade to Second Brigade. First Division then consisted of Briscoe's First Brigade, Fairchild's Second Brigade, and Dandy's Third Brigade (commanded from May 12, 1865 to June 12, 1865 by Edwin S. Greely).

It has been noted that the former Second Division, Twenty-Fourth Corps under Adelbert Ames left the corps with Alfred H. Terry's expedition to Fort Fisher in January 1865 and did not return. Its place in the corps was taken by a division under Thomas M. Harris from the Shenandoah Valley, and this division (later commanded by John W. Turner) was designated as Independent Division, Twenty-Fourth Corps, and it was so called during the Appomattox Campaign. In mid-April, however, Turner referred to his command as Second Division, Twenty-Fourth Corps, although for some time thereafter it was known as both Independent Division and Second Division. Thus in its latter days Twenty-Fourth Corps consisted of Foster's First Division, Harris' Second Division, and Devens' Third Division.

Second Division (or Independent Division) was reorganized in June and July 1865, largely as the result of muster out of regiments. All three regiments of First Brigade were mustered out June 12–16, 1865, but the brigade was reorganized by the transfer of two regiments from Second Brigade and one regiment from Third Brigade. The other regiments of Second Brigade and Third Brigade were mustered out June 14–17, 1865, and both brigades were discontinued. Thus for a time, Second Division consisted of only one brigade. On July 10, 1865, however, Joseph H. Potter was relieved from duty as chief of staff of Twenty-Fourth Corps and was assigned command of a new brigade consisting of three regiments of regular United States Infantry. This brigade was attached to Second Division as Second Brigade. Second Division was discontinued later in the month.

Third Brigade, Third Division was discontinued in June 1865 by the muster out and reassignment of regiments, and July 10, 1865, Third Division was discontinued. The regiments of First Brigade were assigned to a new First Independent Brigade under Thomas M. Harris, and the regiments of Second

Brigade were assigned to a new Second Independent Brigade under James C. Briscoe. Charles Devens, the former commander of Third Division, was assigned July 10, 1865 to the command of the newly constituted District of Northeastern Virginia, with headquarters at Fredericksburg. Harris' Independent Brigade was ordered to report to Devens at Fredericksburg, and Briscoe's Independent Brigade served at Lynchburg and in central Virginia. Twenty-Fourth Corps was officially discontinued August 1, 1865.

For further information about military affairs in Virginia during this period, see Department of Virginia, January 18, 1865–August 6, 1866; and also Army of the James.

COMMANDERS OF TWENTY-FOURTH CORPS, ARMY OF THE JAMES

Edward O. C. Ord	December 3, 1864 to December 6, 1864
Alfred H. Terry	December 6, 1864 to December 10, 1864
Edward O. C. Ord	December 10, 1864 to December 28, 1864
Alfred H. Terry	December 28, 1864 to January 3, 1865
Charles Devens	January 3, 1865 to January 15, 1865
John Gibbon	January 15, 1865 to June 13, 1865
John W. Turner	

TWENTY-FIFTH CORPS, ARMY OF THE JAMES

Twenty-Fifth Corps was created by an order of December 3, 1864, to consist of the colored troops of the Department of Virginia and North Carolina. Godfrey Weitzel was assigned command December 4, 1864. Twenty-Fourth Corps was created at the same time, and these two corps replaced Tenth Corps and Eighteenth Corps, which were discontinued in the Army of the James by the order of December 3, 1864. Twenty-Fifth Corps was organized as follows:

TWENTY-FIFTH CORPS, Godfrey Weitzel

First Division, Charles J. Paine
First Brigade, Delevan Bates
Second Brigade, Samuel A. Duncan
Third Brigade, Elias Wright

Note 1. First Division was organized by a confidential order from Headquarters Department of Virginia and North Carolina December 1, 1864.
Note 2. First Brigade was organized December 2, 1864 from the 1st United States Colored Troops of First Brigade, Third Division, Eighteenth Corps, and 27th United States Colored Troops and 30th United States Colored Troops of First Brigade, Third Division, Ninth Corps.
Note 3. Second Brigade was organized from 4th United States Colored Troops and 6th United States Colored Troops of Third Brigade, Third Division, Eighteenth Corps, and 39th United States Colored Troops of First Brigade, Third Division, Ninth Corps.
Note 4. Third Brigade was organized from the following regiments of Third Division, Eighteenth Corps: 5th United States Colored Troops of Second Brigade, 10th United States Colored Troops of Third Brigade, 37th United States Colored Troops of First Brigade, and 107th United States Colored Troops of the Provisional Brigade.

Second Division, William Birney
First Brigade, James Shaw, Jr., to December 8, 1864
  Charles S. Russell
Second Brigade, Ulysses Doubleday
Third Brigade, Charles S. Russell, to December 8, 1864
  Henry C. Ward

Note 1. Second Division was organized December 4, 1864, and Birney was assigned command that same day.
Note 2. First Brigade was organized from the following regiments: 7th United States Colored Troops from First Brigade, Third Division, Tenth Corps; 109th United States Colored Troops from the Department of Kentucky; 116th United States Colored Troops, an unattached regiment from Tenth Corps; and 117th United States Colored Troops from the Provisional Brigade of Eighteenth Corps.
Note 3. Second Brigade was organized from Second Brigade, Third Division, Tenth Corps.
Note 4. Third Brigade was organized from Second Brigade, Third Division, Ninth Corps.

Third Division, Charles A. Heckman
First Brigade, Alonzo G. Draper
Second Brigade, Edward Martindale
Third Brigade, Henry G. Thomas

Note 1. First Brigade was organized from regiments of Third Division, Eighteenth Corps as follows: 32nd United States Colored Troops from First Brigade, 36th United States Colored Troops and 38th United States Colored

Troops from Second Brigade, and 118th United States Colored Troops from the Provisional Brigade.

Note 2. Second Brigade was organized December 5, 1864 from regiments of Third Division, Tenth Corps as follows: 29th Connecticut (colored) and 9th United States Colored Troops from First Brigade, and 41st United States Colored Troops from Second Brigade.

Note 3. Thomas was ordered to report to Heckman for assignment December 11, 1864. His Third Brigade was organized from regiments of Third Division, Ninth Corps as follows: 19th United States Colored Troops and 23rd United States Colored Troops from Second Brigade, and 43rd United States Colored Troops from First Brigade.

Cavalry Brigade, Benjamin C. Ludlow

Artillery Brigade, Richard H. Jackson, to December 7, 1864
Loomis L. Langdon
1st Battery, Connecticut Light Artillery, James B. Clinton
4th Battery, New Jersey Light Artillery, Charles R. Doane
5th Battery, New Jersey Light Artillery, Henry H. Metcalf
16th New York Heavy Artillery (detachment), Silas J. Truax
Battery E, 1st Pennsylvania Light Artillery, Henry Y. Wildey
Battery C, 3rd Rhode Island Heavy Artillery, Martin S. James
Battery D, 1st United States Artillery, Redmond Tully
Battery M, 1st United States Artillery, Loomis L. Langdon
Battery E, 3rd United States Artillery, John R. Myrick
Battery D, 4th United States Artillery, Frederick M. Follett

On the Lines North of the James River. At the time of its organization, Twenty-Fifth Corps occupied the line of entrenchments previously held by Eighteenth Corps at Chaffin's farm, from Fort Burnham to the James River.

On December 7, 1864, Paine's First Division was temporarily detached from Twenty-Fifth Corps and was assigned as a part of Godfrey Weitzel's expedition for the capture of Fort Fisher, North Carolina, at the mouth of the Cape Fear River. Benjamin F. Butler, commander of the Department of Virginia and North Carolina, assumed command of the expedition, but failed to capture the fort, and with his troops rejoined the Army of the James. Paine's division returned to its camps December 29–30, 1864 and rejoined the corps. For details, see Army of the James, Butler's Expedition to Fort Fisher, North Carolina.

Twenty-Fifth Corps was reorganized December 31, 1864 by changing the designation of First Division to Third Division, and that of Third Division to First Division. The corps was then organized as follows:

TWENTY-FIFTH CORPS, Godfrey Weitzel

First Division, Edward A. Wild
    First Brigade, Alonzo G. Draper
    Second Brigade, Edward Martindale
    Third Brigade, Henry G. Thomas

Second Division, William Birney
    First Brigade, Charles S. Russell
    Second Brigade, Ulysses Doubleday
    Third Brigade, Henry C. Ward

Note. Russell was assigned command of Third Brigade December 31, 1864, and he assumed command the next day, relieving Ward. James Shaw, Jr. succeeded Russell in command of First Brigade.

Third Division, Charles J. Paine
    First Brigade, Delevan Bates
    Second Brigade, John W. Ames
    Third Brigade, Elias Wright

Artillery Brigade, Richard H. Jackson

A second expedition to capture Fort Fisher was organized January 2, 1865 under the command of Alfred H. Terry, and this consisted of Paine's Third Division, Twenty-Fifth Corps, Adelbert Ames' Second Division, Twenty-Fourth Corps, and Joseph C. Abbott's Second Brigade, First Division, Twenty-Fourth Corps. The expedition embarked for North Carolina at Bermuda Landing January 4–5, 1865 and went ashore near Fort Fisher January 13, 1865. Paine's division was assigned to hold a defensive position north of Fort Fisher to protect the rear of the forces advancing on the fort; and it did not take part in the final assault that resulted in the capture of the fort January 15, 1865. For details, see Army of the James, Terry's Expedition to Fort Fisher.

Terry's command did not again serve with the Army of the James, but it remained for a time on Federal Point, North Carolina as United States Troops at Fort Fisher. This district was included in the Department of North Carolina, which was organized February 9, 1865, and consequently, Terry's forces were transferred to that department. February 21, 1865, Terry's command became Terry's Provisional Corps, Department of North Carolina, and this was reorganized April 2, 1865 as Tenth Corps, Department of North Carolina.

Paine's Third Division remained on the roster of Twenty-Fifth Corps during the remainder of the winter, but it did not again join the corps. There was no change in the organization of the division during this period, but in February 1865, Samuel A. Duncan assumed command of Second Brigade, and John H. Holman assumed command of Third Brigade.

After the departure of Third Division, Edward A. Wild's First Division and William Birney's Second Division of Twenty-Fifth Corps remained quietly on the line of entrenchments north of the James River until March 27, 1865. At that time, in preparation for Grant's spring offensive south of Petersburg, Ord marched south with Birney's Second Division, Twenty-Fifth Corps; Robert S. Foster's First Division and John W. Turner's Independent Division of Twenty-Fourth Corps; and Ranald S. Mackenzie's Cavalry Division to reinforce Meade's Army of the Potomac. On the night of March 28, 1865, Ord camped near Hatcher's Run, in rear of the front line positions of Andrew A. Humphreys' Second Corps, which he had been ordered to relieve the next day. Ord called his command the Army of the James. On March 27, 1865, August V. Kautz relieved Wild in command of First Division, Twenty-Fifth Corps, and this division and Charles Devens' Third Division, Twenty-Fourth Corps were left behind by Ord to occupy the line of entrenchments in front of Richmond. Weitzel was in command of these two divisions, which were called Detachment Army of the James.

The organization of Twenty-Fifth Corps during the period January 1865–March 1865 was as follows:

TWENTY-FIFTH CORPS, Godfrey Weitzel, to about
    January 2, 1865
    Charles A. Heckman, to February 7, 1865
    Godfrey Weitzel

First Division, Edward A. Wild, to March 27, 1865
    August V. Kautz
    First Brigade, Alonzo G. Draper

Second Brigade, Charles S. Russell, to February 27,
    1865, on leave
    Thomas Bayley
    Thomas D. Sedgwick, to March 28, 1865
    Edward A. Wild
Third Brigade, Henry G. Thomas
Attached Brigade, Charles S. Russell

Note 1. Weitzel was on leave from about January 2, 1865, and January 20, 1865, he was ordered to Washington to appear before the Joint Committee on the Conduct of the War.

Note 2. Apparently Heckman held no further command after February 7, 1865, and March 23, 1865, he was relieved from duty in the Department of Virginia and was ordered home.

Note 3. The Attached Brigade was formed March 27, 1865 from 10th United States Colored Troops and 28th United States Colored Troops. It was placed on the line of entrenchments after the departure of Ord, with his three divisions of the Army of the James, for Petersburg .

Second Division, William Birney, to February 20, 1865,
    on leave
    James Shaw, Jr., to March 1865
    William Birney
    First Brigade, James Shaw, Jr., to February 20, 1865
        Orion A. Bartholomew, to March 1865
        James Shaw, Jr.
    Second Brigade, Ulysses Doubleday
    Third Brigade, Charles S. Russell, to January 1865
        Edward Martindale, to March 1865
        William W. Woodward

Artillery Brigade, Richard H. Jackson
    Loomis L. Langdon

Appomattox Campaign, Virginia. As noted above, Ord arrived with his Army of the James on Hatcher's Run, in rear of Humphreys' Second Corps, Army of the Potomac, on the evening of March 28, 1865. The next morning, Ord relieved Second Corps on the line of entrenchments at Petersburg, and March 30, 1865, Birney's division was assigned to Gibbon's command of Twenty-Fourth Corps. On April 2, 1865, Ord supported Horatio G. Wright's Sixth Corps in an assault that broke through the enemy lines, and after the breakthrough, Birney's division advanced toward Petersburg on the right of Gibbon's two divisions.

When the enemy evacuated Petersburg on the night of April 2, 1865, Birney's division advanced with Ord's command along the South Side Railroad toward Burkeville. It was detached to hold the railroad at Blacks and Whites (present-day Blackstone) until relieved by Ninth Corps. It rejoined Ord's Army of the James at Rice's Station April 6, 1865, and marched with it to Farmville. There on the morning of April 8, 1865, Birney was relieved from command, and his division was temporarily broken up by the assignment of the brigades to Foster's and Turner's divisions. For additional information, see Appomattox Campaign, Virginia.

Kautz's First Division, Twenty-Fifth Corps remained in the trenches at Chaffin's farm until the morning of April 3, 1865, and then, after skirmishers reported that the enemy works had been abandoned, it marched with Charles Devens' division of Twenty-Fourth Corps and the cavalry toward Richmond. These troops were halted outside the city until the surrender had been completed, and they were then placed in camps along the old inner line of works. They remained there during Grant's pursuit of Lee's army to Appomattox Court House. For more detailed information, see Appomattox Campaign, Virginia, Federal Occupation of Petersburg and Richmond.

After Appomattox. When hostilities ended at Appomattox Court House April 9, 1865, only Kautz's First Division of Twenty-Fifth Corps remained organized and under Weitzel's command, and it was at that time encamped on the outskirts of Richmond. As already noted, Charles J. Paine's Third Division was detached in January 1865, and was later transferred to the Department of North Carolina. On April 8, 1865, as the army was marching toward Appomattox Court House, William Birney was relieved from command of Second Division, and the brigades were transferred temporarily to the divisions of Foster and Turner of Twenty-Fourth Corps. Second Division was not discontinued by this action, however, and April 10, 1865, at Appomattox Court House, the division was re-formed when the two colored brigades with Foster and Turner were ordered to report to Richard H. Jackson of Weitzel's staff. Jackson assumed command of the revived Second Division, with orders to march with it to Richmond. On April 12, 1865, however, Weitzel was ordered to move his Twenty-Fifth Corps to the vicinity of Petersburg, and Jackson changed his direction of march toward that point. He marched through Burkeville and arrived at Petersburg April 17, 1865. Meantime, in obedience to his orders of the day before, Weitzel marched on April 13, 1865, with Kautz's division, from Richmond toward Petersburg, and by April 17, 1865, the corps was encamped on the line of the Military Railroad, with headquarters at Poplar Grove Church. On April 21, 1865, Twenty-Fifth Corps changed camps, with Kautz's division moving to the Cox Road, west of J. Read's house, and Jackson's division to a line extending from the Boydton Plank Road at the Wells house to the Cox Road at the Read house.

May 1, 1865, Henry W. Halleck, then commanding the Military Division of the James, assigned all colored troops in the Department of Virginia to Twenty-Fifth Corps, which was to be placed in a camp of instruction at City Point. All detached companies and regiments were ordered to report to Weitzel at that place.

A number of reports had pointed out that Twenty-Fifth Corps was not a suitable force to maintain order in the Department of Virginia, and these had suggested that it be replaced by other troops. These complaints may have been only an excuse to remove the colored troops from Virginia, but whatever the reason, on May 18, 1865, Weitzel received orders from Grant to prepare for the transfer of Twenty-Fifth Corps to Texas to join the Army of Occupation in that state. Embarkation began at City Point May 23, 1865, and the last troops departed on transports June 26, 1865. Second Division arrived in Texas June 13, 1865, and First Division followed June 26, 1865. The troops were stationed at Indianola, Brazos Santiago, Corpus Christi, and other points in the state.

The organization of Twenty-Fifth Corps from April 10, 1865 until its departure for Texas was as follows:

TWENTY-FIFTH CORPS, Godfrey Weitzel

First Division, August V. Kautz
 First Brigade, Alonzo Draper
 Second Brigade, Edward A. Wild, to April 18, 1865
  Thomas D. Sedgwick
 Third Brigade, Henry G. Thomas, to April 27, 1865, on leave
  Stephen B. Yeoman

Second Division, Richard H. Jackson

First Brigade, James Shaw, Jr.
Second Brigade, Ulysses Doubleday
Third Brigade, William W. Woodward

Cavalry Brigade, George W. Cole

Detached Brigade at City Point, Charles S. Russell

Artillery Brigade, Loomis L. Langdon
  1st Battery, Connecticut Light Artillery, James B. Clinton
  4th Battery, New Jersey Light Artillery, Charles R. Doane
  5th Battery, New Jersey Light Artillery, Zenas C. Warren
  Battery E, 1st Pennsylvania Light Artillery, Henry Y. Wildey
  Battery C, 3rd Rhode Island Heavy Artillery, Martin S. James
  Battery D, 1st United States Artillery, Redmond Tully
  Battery M, 1st United States Artillery, Loomis L. Langdon
  Battery D, 4th United States Artillery, Frederick M. Follett

Note 1. The cavalry brigade was organized May 14, 1865, to consist of 1st United States Colored Cavalry and 2nd United States Colored Cavalry.

Note 2. The Detached Brigade at City Point was formerly Russell's Attached Brigade, First Division, Twenty-Fifth Corps.

Note 3. June 8, 1865, Langdon was appointed assistant inspector general of Twenty-Fifth Corps, on Weitzel's staff.

A number of changes occurred in the organization of Twenty-Fifth Corps while it was in Texas. July 6, 1865, Third Division was reorganized as follows:

Third Division, Alonzo G. Draper
  First Brigade, Charles S. Russell
  Second Brigade, James Given
  Third Brigade, George W. Cole

Note 1. Second Brigade was organized July 20, 1865.
Note 2. Third Brigade was organized from Cole's Cavalry Brigade.

There was a general reorganization of the corps in October 1865, due to muster out and reassignment of regiments. At the end of October 1865, the corps was organized as follows:

TWENTY-FIFTH CORPS, Godfrey Weitzel

First Division, Giles A. Smith

First Brigade, Thomas Bayley
Second Brigade, Robert M. Hall

Note 1. Giles A. Smith was relieved from duty in the Army of the Tennessee May 29, 1865, and was assigned to duty with Twenty-Fifth Corps.
Note 2. Third Brigade was discontinued by muster out and transfer of regiments.

Second Division, Richard H. Jackson
  First Brigade, James Shaw, Jr.
  Second Brigade, Theodore H. Barrett

Note. Second Brigade was discontinued by muster out, and the designation of Third Brigade was changed to Second Brigade. By this change of designation, Third Brigade was discontinued.

Third Division, William T. Clark
  First Brigade, Charles S. Russell
  Second Brigade, J. Ham Davidson

Note 1. Clark was relieved from duty with the Army of the Tennessee June 17, 1865, and was assigned to Twenty-Fifth Corps.
Note 2. Third Brigade was discontinued in October 1865.

Twenty-Fifth Corps, which was the last of the Union corps to be mustered out, was discontinued January 8, 1866.

CAVALRY CORPS, ARMY OF THE POTOMAC

At the outbreak of war, there were only five mounted regiments in the United States service, and these were generally scattered in small units at the many army posts throughout the West. These regiments were:

First Regiment of Dragoons, Thomas T. Fauntleroy
Second Regiment of Dragoons, Philip St. George Cooke
Regiment of Mounted Riflemen, William W. Loring
First Cavalry, Robert E. Lee
Second Cavalry, Albert Sidney Johnston

A sixth regiment, designated as Third Cavalry, was organized May 4, 1861 and was officially confirmed July 29, 1861. The colonel of the regiment was David Hunter and the lieutenant colonel was William H. Emory.

Winfield Scott, general in chief of the army, believed that the war would be of short duration, and for that reason no additional cavalry would be needed. In his opinion, there would not be sufficient time to organize, equip, and train cavalry regiments, and consequently no volunteer cavalry was called for in President Lincoln's first call for troops. In fact, it was not until after mid-June 1861 that the War Department would accept volunteer cavalry regiments, and these did not begin to join the army in appreciable numbers until after the Battle of Bull Run in July 1861.

At the Battle of Bull Run there were only seven companies of regular cavalry attached to Irvin McDowell's Army of Northeastern Virginia. These were two companies of First United States Cavalry, four companies of Second United States Cavalry, and one company of Second Dragoons. All were under the command of Innis N. Palmer. These troops served as escorts and couriers, and they also supported the batteries of artillery. They covered the retreat of the army after the battle.

By an act of Congress August 3, 1861, the six regiments of mounted troops were organized into a single, uniform mounted force that was to be known as "Cavalry," and the designations of the regiments were changed as follows:

First Regiment of Dragoons became First United States Cavalry

Second Regiment of Dragoons became Second United States Cavalry

Regiment of Mounted Riflemen became Third United States Cavalry

First Cavalry was renumbered as Fourth United States Cavalry

Second Cavalry was renumbered as Fifth United States Cavalry

Third Cavalry was renumbered as Sixth United States Cavalry

These regiments were commanded as follows: First Cavalry, Benjamin L. Beall; Second Cavalry, Philip St. George Cooke; Third Cavalry, John S. Simonson; Fourth Cavalry, John Sedgwick; Fifth Cavalry, George H. Thomas; and Sixth Cavalry, David Hunter.

August 14, 1861, George B. McClellan appointed George Stoneman as chief of cavalry of the Army of the Potomac, and this was announced August 20, 1861. One of Stoneman's duties was to receive the new cavalry regiments arriving in Washington, but in general his duties appear to have been purely administrative, and he had little or no command authority, except by superior orders.

The new cavalry regiments that joined the army were not organized into cavalry brigades and divisions for field service, as were the infantry regiments. Instead, they were assigned without brigade organization to the newly organized infantry divisions of the army, and in turn, the cavalry regiments were divided among the brigades of the divisions to provide escorts and to perform other duties at headquarters.

October 15, 1861, the volunteer cavalry regiments present with the army were attached to the divisions as follows: Nathaniel P. Banks' Division, 3rd New York Cavalry (four companies), and 1st Michigan Cavalry was assigned later; Louis Blenker's Division, Christian F. Dickel's 4th New York Cavalry (Mounted Rifles); William B. Franklin's Division, Andrew T. McReynolds' 1st New York Cavalry (Lincoln); Samuel P. Heintzelman's Division, William Halstead's (and later Percy Wyndham's) 1st New Jersey Cavalry; Joseph Hooker's Division, Scott Carter's (and later George H. Chapman's) 3rd Indiana Cavalry (eight companies); Erasmus D. Keyes' Division, no cavalry assigned; George A. McCall's Division, George D. Bayard's 1st Pennsylvania Reserve Cavalry; Irvin McDowell's Division, J. Mansfield Davies' 2nd New York Cavalry (Harris Light); Fitz John Porter's Division, William W. Averell's 3rd Pennsylvania Cavalry and David McM. Gregg's 8th Pennsylvania Cavalry; William F. Smith's Division, Max Friedman's (and later David Campbell's) 5th Pennsylvania Cavalry (Cameron Dragoons); Charles P. Stone's Division, James H. Van Alen's 3rd New York Cavalry (six companies); John A. Dix's Division (at Baltimore, Maryland), one company of Pennsylvania Cavalry; Don Carlos Buell's Division, no cavalry assigned.

The above arrangement remained essentially unchanged during the winter of 1861–1862. In addition to the above, however, there were at that time some other cavalry units with the army. Two companies of the 4th United States Cavalry were with the Washington City Guard under Andrew Porter. Stoneman's command consisted of 5th United States Cavalry, 4th Pennsylvania Cavalry, Oneida Cavalry (1st Company), 11th Pennsylvania Cavalry, and one company of Barker's Illinois Cavalry. In November 1861, Stoneman's Cavalry was at Washington and Fairfax Court House. Later, the 8th Illinois Cavalry under John F. Farnsworth was attached to Edwin V. Sumner's Division.

November 28, 1861, Philip St. George Cooke was assigned command of the regular cavalry serving with the Army of the Potomac. This consisted of 1st United States Cavalry, 2nd United States Cavalry (seven companies), 4th United States Cavalry (two companies), 5th United States Cavalry, and 6th United States Cavalry. Cooke's command was known as the Cavalry Reserve, Army of the Potomac, and for a time it was attached to Silas Casey's Division as Cooke's Cavalry Brigade.

December 16, 1861, a cavalry brigade consisting of 5th New York and 1st Vermont was formed under John P. Hatch, but this was simply a training organization, and when the campaigning season opened in the spring of 1862, the two regiments were sent to the field separately.

On March 24, 1862, after the corps organization of the army had been announced, McClellan expanded his cavalry organization. A cavalry force of from two to five regiments, without brigade organization, was assigned to each corps, and a chief of cavalry was also assigned to each corps as follows: The 1st New York and 2nd New York Cavalry were assigned to First Corps, and John P. Hatch was made chief of cavalry; the 3rd New York, 8th Illinois, and one squadron of 6th New York Cavalry were assigned to Second Corps, but no chief of cavalry was named; the 3rd Pennsylvania and 1st New Jersey Cavalry were assigned to Third Corps, and William W. Averell was assigned as chief of cavalry; the 1st Pennsylvania, 5th Pennsylvania, and 4th New York Cavalry were assigned to Fourth Corps, and George D. Bayard was assigned as chief of cavalry; and 5th New York, 1st Vermont, 1st Michigan, 1st New England, and 1st Maine were assigned to Fifth Corps, and Othneil De Forest was assigned as chief of cavalry of the corps.

By the above arrangement, each corps had a cavalry force of brigade size, but it was not under a central control. The regiments generally were broken up to provide orderlies and couriers for the divisions and corps of the army. It should be noted that the above assignments were not all completely carried out, and the assignments were somewhat different when the army was on the Peninsula in April 1862 (see below).

There were still other cavalry assignments. Five squadrons of cavalry were sent to James Shields' Division, and Cooke's Cavalry Reserve was expanded to consist of two brigades as follows: a First Brigade under William H. Emory, and a Second Brigade under George A. H. Blake. Emory's brigade consisted of 5th United States Cavalry, 6th United States Cavalry, and Richard H. Rush's 6th Pennsylvania Cavalry; and Blake's brigade consisted of 1st United States Cavalry, David McM. Gregg's 8th Pennsylvania Cavalry, Barker's Squadron of Illinois Cavalry, and Mann's 5th Company of Oneida Cavalry. The Cavalry Reserve appears to have been formed only as an administrative convenience for the cavalry not assigned to infantry divisions or corps, and McClellan retained this organization under his personal control.

By an order of March 26, 1862, the duties of the chief of cavalry were defined as "exclusively administrative," and were confined to inspecting units, handling reports and other paperwork, and communicating orders of the commanding general. He was not to exercise command unless specifically directed to do so. By this order, the chief of cavalry became merely a staff officer.

On April 1, 1862, at the beginning of McClellan's Peninsular Campaign, the cavalry with the army on the Peninsula was assigned as follows: to Sumner's Second Corps, John F. Farnsworth's 8th Illinois Cavalry and one squadron of the 6th New York Cavalry; to Heintzelman's Third Corps, William W. Averell's 3rd Pennsylvania Cavalry; and to Keyes' Fourth Corps, the 2nd United Sates Cavalry, with the Provost Guard at General Headquarters, two companies of the 4th United States Cavalry, and one company of Oneida Cavalry, New York Volunteers.

The cavalry remaining in northern Virginia was assigned as follows:

McDowell's First Corps: Andrew T. McReynolds' 1st New York Cavalry; J. Mansfield Davies' Second New York Cavalry (Harris Light); David Campbell's' 4th New York Cavalry; and George D. Bayard's 1st Pennsylvania Cavalry.

(note. McDowell's corps was merged into the Department of the Rappahannock April 4, 1862.)

Banks' Fifth Corps: Samuel H. Allen's 1st Maine Cavalry, Jonas P. Holliday's 1st Vermont Cavalry, Thornton F. Brodhead's 1st Michigan Cavalry, Robert B. Lawton's 1st Rhode Island Cavalry, Othneil De Forest's 5th New York Cavalry, Samuel J. Crook's 8th New York Cavalry, Key's Battalion of Pennsylvania Cavalry, and some companies of Maryland and Virginia cavalry. (note. Banks' corps was merged into the Department of the Shenandoah April 4, 1862.)

James S. Wadsworth's Military District of Washington: Percy Wyndham's 1st New Jersey Cavalry at Alexandria, and the 4th Pennsylvania Cavalry at the capital.

John A. Dix's Command at Baltimore, Maryland: 1st Maryland Cavalry and a detachment of the Purnell Legion.

Peninsular Campaign, April 1862–August 1862. Cavalry operations during the Peninsular Campaign were generally of limited importance. This was due primarily to the fact that the cavalry was not organized as a single fighting force, but in addition the country on the Peninsula was not suitable for cavalry operations. Altogether on the Peninsula there were eight complete cavalry regiments and sixteen odd companies, representing five different cavalry regiments. Not only did the eight regiments not serve in a single cavalry command, but actually a regiment seldom served as a unit. Instead, the cavalry was usually assigned as companies, or as groups of two or three companies on detached service. Generally one regiment was assigned to each corps.

The cavalry saw its first service as a larger unit immediately after the evacuation of Yorktown by Confederate forces. On May 4, 1862, McClellan ordered George Stoneman, his chief of cavalry, to assemble his available cavalry and artillery and pursue the retreating enemy up the Williamsburg Road. Stoneman's command, called the Advance Guard, consisted of the following: William H. Emory's First Brigade, Cavalry Reserve, and William W. Averell's 3rd Pennsylvania Cavalry; Philip St. George Cooke, with 6th United States Cavalry of First Brigade, Cavalry Reserve, and 1st United States Cavalry of Second Brigade, Cavalry Reserve; William Hays' Brigade of four batteries of Horse Artillery; Barker's Squadron; and John F. Farnsworth's 8th Illinois Cavalry.

Stoneman was engaged in front of Williamsburg on the evening of May 4, 1862. Emory's command, with Barker's Squadron, attempted to cut off the retreating enemy column before it reached the town, but was unable to do so. Although Stoneman's cavalry was at Williamsburg, it did not function under his control. In his words, he was a "mere spectator" during the fighting, and contributed nothing to the result. For details of the Battle of Williamsburg and subsequent operations during the campaign, see Peninsular Campaign.

Emory's First Brigade of the Cavalry Reserve accompanied Fitz John Porter on an expedition to Hanover Court House May 27–29, 1862, and was present during the engagement of May 27, 1862. Emory was under Porter's orders at that time.

Stoneman remained in command of the Advance Guard during McClellan's advance up the Peninsula until June 1862. June 12, 1862, James E. B. (Jeb) Stuart, with about 1,200 men, left Richmond on his first ride around the Army of the Potomac. The next day he passed beyond Porter's Fifth Provisional Corps, which formed the right of McClellan's line, and near Hanover Old Church he ran into a part of the 5th United States Cavalry under William B. Royall. Stuart promptly attacked and scattered Royall's troopers and then moved on. The Federal cavalry commanded by Cooke did not begin the pursuit until late that evening, and by that time Stuart was out of reach. After riding completely around the army, Stuart returned to Richmond June 15, 1862. The day after Stuart's return, the Cavalry Reserve and the troops under Stoneman were placed under Porter's orders.

On June 20, 1862, cavalry regiments were assigned to the corps as follows: Averell's 3rd Pennsylvania Cavalry to Third Corps, Gregg's 8th Pennsylvania Cavalry to Fourth Corps, Farnsworth's 8th Illinois Cavalry to Fifth Provisional Corps, and McReynolds' 1st New York Cavalry to Sixth Provisional Corps. During the Seven Days' Battles, these regiments served with the corps as assigned; and in addition Duncan McVicar, with four companies of his 6th New York Cavalry, was with Second Corps. At the beginning of the Seven Days, the 1st New York Cavalry and James H. Childs' 4th Pennsylvania Cavalry, which was attached to Third Division, Fifth Provisional Corps, were used as couriers and to prevent straggling. The following were at McClellan's headquarters: 2nd United States Cavalry, two companies of 4th United States Cavalry, two unattached companies of volunteer cavalry, the McClellan Dragoons (Illinois), and the Oneida (New York) Cavalry. Five companies of the 11th Pennsylvania were at White House.

On June 25, 1862, Stoneman was assigned command of a special force near New Bridge, with which he was to operate on the right flank of the army. This force consisted of two cavalry regiments under Emory, the 8th Illinois Cavalry, one light battery, and the 17th New York Infantry, and 18th Massachusetts Infantry from George W. Morell's First Division, Fifth Provisional Corps. That day Stoneman picketed the front from Mechanicsville to the Pamunkey River, but he was cut off from Porter's corps when the enemy advanced and attacked at Mechanicsville and Gaines' Mill. Stoneman was then ordered to White House to secure the government property there, but he later rejoined Porter's command.

A part of Cooke's Cavalry Reserve was engaged at Gaines' Mill on the evening of June 27, 1862. When Porter had formed his Fifth Corps behind Boatswain's Swamp, he had placed Cooke's command in rear of his left flank, on a nearly level plain that ran down to the Chickahominy River. The cavalry force was quite small: it consisted of five companies of Charles J. Whiting's 5th United States Cavalry and six companies of the 6th Pennsylvania Cavalry of Richard H. Rush's First Brigade, and four under-strength companies of William N. Grier's 1st United States Cavalry of George A. H. Blake's Second Brigade. Cooke was on a ridge near three Federal batteries when he saw Porter's line begin to give way. He then led the 5th United States and 1st United States to the front and deployed them in rear of the interval between the two right batteries. There is some question as to the orders given to Whiting, and also his interpretation of them, but one report states that Cooke directed him to charge the enemy when the support and safety of the batteries required it, and Cooke also ordered Blake and Rush to support him. Whatever the orders, Whiting charged the advancing enemy infantry, and his command was virtually destroyed. He lost 150 of the 250 men of his regiment, and because of this disaster, Cooke was later relieved from duty with the army.

The cavalry was not significantly involved in any of the remaining battles of the Seven Days, but it retreated with the army to Harrison's Landing on the James River. There, on July 5, 1862, Cooke was relieved of his command, and that same day Stoneman left on sick leave. Also that day, William W. Averell was appointed acting brigadier general and was placed in command of the cavalry of the army. He then issued orders for the reorganization of the cavalry forces into a cavalry division of two brigades. The next day, Emory was relieved from duty with the Cavalry Reserve and was assigned to the temporary command of Henry M. Naglee's First Brigade of John J. Peck's Second Division, Fourth Corps.

Stoneman returned to duty July 6, 1862 and assumed command of the Cavalry Division. It was then organized as follows:

Cavalry Division, Army of the Potomac, George Stoneman
First Brigade, William W. Averell
Second Brigade, David McM. Gregg, to July 16, 1862
Alfred Pleasonton

Even after its organization, the cavalry division did not operate as a unit. Averell's brigade was assigned to the right wing of the army, and Gregg's brigade to the left wing.

August 22, 1862, Stoneman was relieved as commander of the cavalry division, and the two brigades then reported separately to McClellan's headquarters. During the latter part of August 1862, the Army of the Potomac was withdrawn from the Peninsula, and early in September 1862, the cavalry brigades of Averell and Pleasonton were transferred to Alexandria, Virginia.

In the Defenses of Washington. The Defenses of Washington were constituted September 2, 1862 under McClellan as a military district of the Army of the Potomac. John Pope's Army of Virginia retired within the Defenses following its defeat at the Second Battle of Bull Run, and with it were the cavalry brigades of John Beardsley, John Buford, and George D. Bayard. These had been attached, respectively, to Franz Sigel's First Corps, Nathaniel P. Banks' Second Corps, and Irvin McDowell's

Third Corps. Buford was announced as chief of cavalry, Army of the Potomac September 10, 1862, and he was succeeded in command of his brigade by R. Butler Price. Bayard's and Price's brigades were assigned to cover the front of the central part of the Defenses South of the Potomac. Beardsley's brigade remained with First Corps, Army of Virginia, which on September 12, 1862 became Eleventh Corps, Army of the Potomac.

A Cavalry Division, Army of the Potomac was organized in the Defenses of Washington early in September and accompanied the army when it departed on the Maryland Campaign that month. For details, see following section.

On October 1, 1862, a cavalry division was organized in the Defenses of Washington, and Bayard was assigned command. It was organized as follows:

Bayard's Cavalry Division, George D. Bayard
First Brigade, J. Mansfield Davies
Second Brigade, R. Butler Price
Third Brigade, John Beardsley

Bayard's cavalry was employed in scouting the country to the south and southwest of Washington. When Sigel's Eleventh Corps moved out from the Defenses of Washington to Centerville and Fairfax Court House September 22–24, 1862, the cavalry division was attached to Eleventh Corps. Percy Wyndham commanded a cavalry brigade at Chantilly from October to December 1862, and this too operated with Eleventh Corps.

On October 31, 1862, Bayard's cavalry was ordered to report to the Army of the Potomac, which was then approaching Warrenton, Virginia on its march from Harper's Ferry. Price's cavalry brigade, however, did not accompany Bayard but remained in the Defenses of Washington. A Provisional Cavalry Brigade was organized in the Defenses of Washington in December 1862, and January 13, 1863, it was assigned to Joseph T. Copeland. The brigade was attached to Silas Casey's Division.

Maryland Campaign, September 3, 1862–September 20, 1862. Following the defeat of Pope's Army of Virginia at the Second Battle of Bull Run, the Army of the Potomac was reorganized by McClellan early in September 1862 in the Defenses of Washington. A new Cavalry Division, Army of the Potomac was a part of this reorganization. Alfred Pleasonton's Second Cavalry Brigade, Army of the Potomac arrived at Alexandria from the Peninsula September 1, 1862, and William W. Averell's First Brigade followed two days later. These two brigades, plus four additional regiments, were organized into a cavalry division of five brigades as follows:

Cavalry Division, Army of the Potomac, Alfred Pleasonton
First Brigade, Charles J. Whiting
Second Brigade, John F. Farnsworth
Third Brigade, Richard H. Rush
Fourth Brigade, Andrew T. McReynolds
Fifth Brigade, Benjamin F. Davis
Artillery
Battery A, 2nd United States Artillery, John C. Tidball
Batteries B and L, 2nd United States Artillery, James M. Robertson
Battery M, 2nd United States Artillery, Peter C. Hains
Batteries C and G, 3rd United States Artillery, Horatio G. Robertson

This division served with McClellan's army during the Maryland Campaign.

Because it is listed as consisting of five brigades it appears to have been a strong force, but this was not the case, and it played only a minor role in the Maryland Campaign. Farnsworth's brigade consisted of four regiments, but the other brigade had only two regiments each, thus making a total of only twelve regiments in the division. This number, too, is misleading, because a part of every regiment was serving on escort or provost duty with the various corps and divisions of the army. Twenty-five companies, about one-sixth of the total number, were absent from their regiments. In addition, eight companies of the 8th New York Cavalry were serving with Ninth Corps. McReynolds' Fourth Brigade did not accompany the army to Antietam, but it was sent north from Frederick, Maryland to Gettysburg. Benjamin F. Davis, with the 8th New York Cavalry, was at Harper's Ferry until the night before the surrender of Dixon S. Miles' forces there, and he then led the cavalry of that post northward to join the Army of the Potomac.

At the Battle of Antietam, the cavalry, with the horse artillery, was ordered to support the left of

Edwin V. Sumner's Second Corps. The batteries of Horatio G. Gibson, James M. Robertson, John C. Tidball, and Peter C. Hains were put in position near the Sharpsburg Road, above the Middle Bridge, and these were supported on the right and left by the 5th United States Cavalry, Farnsworth's Second Brigade, Rush's Third Brigade, and Davis' Fifth Brigade.

Antietam to Warrenton, Virginia, September 19, 1862–November 7, 1862. After the Battle of Antietam, Pleasonton's Cavalry Division was soon scattered, and it was finally discontinued with little notice. On September 20, 1862, from his headquarters at Keedysville, Maryland, Pleasonton sent Rush's Third Brigade and McReynolds' Fourth Brigade to Williamsport, Maryland and Whiting's First Brigade to the vicinity of Harper's Ferry. On September 28, 1862, McReynolds' brigade moved on to Cumberland, Maryland, where it served until transferred to the newly created Defenses of the Upper Potomac October 30, 1862.

On October 3, 1862, Averell was assigned command of a new brigade. This had the same designation, and consisted of the same regiments, as the former First Cavalry Brigade, Army of the Potomac that he had commanded on the Peninsula. The regiments for Averell's brigade were taken from the Cavalry Division, and when they were transferred, Whiting's First Brigade and Davis' Fifth Brigade were left with one regiment each. Rush's Third Brigade had only two regiments and Farnsworth's Second Brigade had three. Averell's brigade was at Williamsport, but October 6, 1862, it was moved to Cumberland. It remained on the upper Potomac until the end of the month, and it was then ordered to rejoin the army, which had then advanced into Virginia.

October 21, 1862, another new cavalry brigade was organized from regiments of the Cavalry Division, and it was assigned to Pleasonton. It consisted largely of regiments that were originally with Second Cavalry Brigade, Army of the Potomac, which Pleasonton had commanded on the Peninsula. The new brigade was given this same designation. With this transfer, there were no regiments left in First Brigade, Second Brigade, and Fifth Brigade of the Cavalry Division. As already noted, McReynolds's Fourth Brigade was transferred a

short time later to the Defenses of the Upper Potomac. Thus, although apparently not officially discontinued, Pleasonton's Cavalry Division, Army of the Potomac simply ceased to exist at that time.

When the Army of the Potomac began its long-delayed advance into Virginia after the Battle of Antietam, Pleasonton's Cavalry Brigade crossed the Potomac River at Berlin (present-day Brunswick), Maryland October 26, 1862, and scouted the country in front of the infantry. On October 29, 1862, McClellan also ordered Averell's Cavalry Brigade to leave the upper Potomac and join the army on the march in Virginia. The brigade left Hagerstown two days later.

Pleasonton moved forward through Lovettsville and Purcelleville and arrived at Upperville November 3, 1862. Meantime, Averell, who was then marching to join Pleasonton, had passed through Philomont the day before and reached Piedmont Station on the Manassas Gap Railroad November 3, 1862. Pleasonton arrived at Piedmont Station the next day and assumed command of both brigades. He then moved on with the two brigades to the Sperryville-Little Washington area. During the advance in Virginia, the cavalry was engaged at Snicker's Gap, Upperville, Aldie, Mountville, Philomont, Manassas Gap, and Barbee's Cross Roads.

On November 6, 1862, Pleasonton's brigade, plus 6th New York Cavalry, was reorganized into a cavalry division of two brigades. The First Brigade, commanded by John F. Farnsworth, consisted of 3rd Indiana, 8th Illinois, and 8th New York Cavalry; the Second Brigade, commanded by David McM. Gregg, consisted of 6th New York and 8th Pennsylvania Cavalry. Pleasonton established his headquarters at Corbin's Cross Roads, near Amissville, November 8–11, 1862. Averell was sick during this period and was absent from his command for a time.

Meantime, the cavalry of the Army of the Potomac had been increased by the addition of George D. Bayard's Brigade from the Defenses of Washington. During October 1862, Bayard had been operating in front of Franz Sigel's Eleventh Corps, which at that time was posted on the Orange and Alexandria Railroad in the Centerville-Fairfax Court House area. On October 31, 1862, Bayard was ordered to report with his brigade to McClellan, whose Army of the Potomac was then nearby and approaching Warrenton from Harper's Ferry. On November 7, 1862, the day that Ambrose E. Burnside relieved McClellan in command of the army, Bayard's cavalry was on the line of the Rappahannock River from Waterloo to the Orange and Alexandria Railroad; Pleasonton's Cavalry Division was in the Sperryville-Little Washington area; and Averell's brigade was with Pleasonton.

Fredericksburg Campaign, November 7, 1862– December 15, 1862. Immediately after assuming command of the Army of the Potomac, Burnside offered a new plan of operations to Henry W. Halleck. According to this plan, the army was to march eastward to Fredericksburg and, after securing communications with Washington, turn south toward Richmond. This plan was approved November 14, 1862, and that day Burnside announced the reorganization of the army into three grand divisions and a reserve. A few days later the army began its march to the Rappahannock River, opposite Fredericksburg.

On November 21, 1862, Burnside assigned the cavalry to the grand divisions as follows: Bayard's Brigade to William B. Franklin's Left Grand Division; Averell's Brigade to Joseph Hooker's Center Grand Division; and Pleasonton's Cavalry Division to Edwin V. Sumner's Right Grand Division.

Burnside was delayed opposite Fredericksburg while he waited for the arrival of pontoon bridges from Washington, but finally, on December 12, 1862, he began moving his troops into position for the expected battle the next day.

The cavalry played only a small part in the Battle of Fredericksburg. On December 12, 1862, Bayard's Brigade crossed the Rappahannock at the lower bridges with Franklin's Left Grand Division and covered the advance of John F. Reynolds' First Corps as it moved into position below Fredericksburg. Bayard was killed during the battle the next day, when struck by a piece of shell while at Franklin's headquarters. David McM. Gregg, then commanding Second Brigade of Pleasonton's division, was assigned command of Bayard's Brigade; and Thomas C. Devin assumed command of Gregg's former brigade. Pleasonton's Cavalry Division remained on the north side of the Rappahannock during the battle of December 13, 1862,

massed behind a ridge, where it covered the upper crossings of the river. Averell's brigade also remained north of the river, and it was not engaged.

Winter of 1862–1863. During January and February 1863, the cavalry was constantly employed on picket duty, in reconnoitering, and in watching the fords of the Rappahannock. While engaged in this service there was frequent skirmishing with the enemy, particularly at Grove Church, Fairfax Court House, Rappahannock Bridge, and Somerville.

The cavalry remained attached to the grand divisions until February 5, 1863, when they were discontinued by Joseph Hooker, then commanding the Army of the Potomac. In the same order that restored the corps organization of the army, the cavalry forces were consolidated into a cavalry corps that was to be commanded by George Stoneman. This was a long-overdue improvement because it provided the organization necessary for a more effective use of the cavalry. Stoneman assumed command February 7, 1863, and February 12, 1863, he issued the order that assembled the Cavalry Corps, Army of the Potomac in the form that it would retain during most of the remainder of the war. The organization was announced as follows:

CAVALRY CORPS, Army of the Potomac, George
  Stoneman

First Division, Alfred Pleasonton
  First Brigade, Benjamin F. Davis
  Second Brigade, Thomas C. Devin

Second Division, William W. Averell
  First Brigade, Alfred N. Duffie
  Second Brigade, John B. McIntosh

  Note 1. First Brigade was organized February 25, 1863.
  Note 2. McIntosh assumed command of Second Brigade February 17, 1863.

Third Division, David McM. Gregg
  First Brigade, Judson Kilpatrick
  Second Brigade, Eugene Von Kielmansegge, to March
    1863
    Percy Wyndham

  Note. Third Brigade was organized into brigades February 16, 1863.

Reserve Brigade (Regulars), John Buford

Horse Artillery Brigade, James M. Robertson
    Batteries B and L, 2nd United States Artillery, Albert
    O. Vincent
    Battery M, 2nd United States Artillery, Robert Clarke
    Battery E, 4th United States Artillery, Samuel S. Elder

6th Pennsylvania Cavalry (Rush's Lancers), Richard H.
Rush

*Note. The 6th Pennsylvania Cavalry was under direct
orders from headquarters of the Cavalry Corps.*

The divisions of the corps were organized from
the regiments formerly belonging to Pleasonton's
division, Averell's brigade, and Gregg's brigade
(formerly Bayard's), and Louis P. Di Cesnola's
Brigade. The latter was formerly commanded by
John Beardsley of Pope's Army of Virginia, and
since September it had been attached to Sigel's
Eleventh Corps of the Reserve Grand Division of the
army. First Division was formed from the regiments
of Pleasonton's division and two regiments from Di
Cesnola's Brigade; Second Division was formed
from the regiments of Averell's brigade and two
regiments from Di Cesnola's Brigade; and Third
Division was formed from the regiments of Gregg's
Brigade and one regiment from Di Cesnola's
Brigade.

February 12, 1863, First Division was designated
as the Right of the Cavalry Corps, and headquarters
was established near Aquia Creek Church; Second
Division was designated as the Center of the corps,
with headquarters at Brooke's Station on the Richmond, Fredericksburg, and Potomac Railroad; and
Third Division was designated as the Left of the
corps, with headquarters near Belle Plain. The
Reserve Brigade was encamped in the vicinity of
corps headquarters, near White Oak Church.

On February 15, 1863, the territory surrounding
the army was assigned to the cavalry as follows:
Pleasonton's First Division was to watch the country
lying south of the Occoquan River and Cedar Run,
and extending as far south as the Southern Branch
of Aquia Creek; Averell's Second Division was
assigned to the country on the left of Pleasonton,
south of the Southern Branch of Aquia Creek, and
between this line and the Richmond,
Fredericksburg, and Potomac Railroad; Buford's
Reserve Brigade was to picket the Rappahannock

River between the railroad and Corbin, opposite
Moss Neck; and Gregg's Third Division was assigned to the left of the Reserve Brigade, to cover
the country between the Potomac and the Rappahannock rivers.

March 2, 1863, the assignments of First Division
and Second Division were modified. Second
Division was directed to establish a picket line,
beginning on the left with the infantry pickets on the
Rappahannock near Falmouth, and extending up the
river to a point near Rockypen Creek, and from there
northward in front of Berea Church to Gray's Old
Tavern, about four miles west of Stafford Court
House, and then on a few miles to the headwaters of
Accakeek Creek. There it was to connect with the
left of First Division, which was to extend the line
northward to a point two or three miles in front of
the outposts of a Federal force at Dumfries.

The first major engagement of the newly organized Cavalry Corps occurred March 17, 1863,
when Averell's Second Division crossed the Rappahannock River at Kelly's Ford and engaged
Fitzhugh Lee's Confederate cavalry. After some
sharp fighting during the afternoon, and achieving
some success, Averell withdrew. Although not a
major battle, Kelly's Ford was notable because it
was the first purely cavalry battle in the East in
which more than small forces were employed on
both sides. For details of this engagement, see
Engagement at Kelly's Ford (Kellysville), Virginia.

After the engagement at Kelly's Ford, the cavalry
was employed only in routine service until the Army
of the Potomac opened its spring campaign in late
April 1863. At that time the army began its march
toward Chancellorsville and Fredericksburg.

**Chancellorsville Campaign, April 27, 1863–May
6, 1863.** On April 27, 1863, the day that Hooker's
Army of the Potomac began its movement toward
Chancellorsville, George Stoneman was at
Warrenton Junction, with his Cavalry Corps encamped along the Orange and Alexandria Railroad.
A short time later, the corps was assigned different
missions, and it did not again serve as a unit during
the campaign.

On April 29, 1863, Pleasonton reported with
Thomas C. Devin's Second Brigade of his division
to Henry W. Slocum, who was in command of a
flanking column consisting of Fifth Corps, Eleventh

Corps, and Twelfth Corps that was marching toward Chancellorsville. One regiment of Devin's brigade was then assigned to each of the three corps. Pennock Huey's 8th Pennsylvania Cavalry and one troop of the 1st Michigan Cavalry moved out in front of George G. Meade's Fifth Corps; Duncan McVicar's 6th New York Cavalry performed a similar service with Slocum's Twelfth Corps; and Josiah H. Kellogg's 17th Pennsylvania Cavalry advanced in front of Oliver O. Howard's Eleventh Corps. On April 30, 1863, when the three corps reached the vicinity of Chancellorsville, Devin's brigade was re-formed, and it then picketed the right and front of Slocum's command.

Stoneman was sent with the remainder of the corps on a raid toward Richmond to destroy the enemy communications, and also to be in position to intercept Lee's army if it was forced to retreat from its position at Fredericksburg. Stoneman crossed the Rappahannock River April 29, 1863, and then divided his force. He detached Averell with his Second Cavalry Division, Benjamin F. Davis' First Brigade of Pleasonton's First Cavalry Division, and John C. Tidball's Battery A, 2nd United States Artillery, and sent him by way of Culpeper Court House to Rapidan Station. Stoneman then marched on toward Richmond with Gregg's Third Division, Buford's Reserve Brigade, and one section each of the three batteries of James M. Robertson's Horse Artillery Brigade. He crossed the Rapidan at Raccoon Ford and advanced to Louisa Court House, and from there he sent out detachments to destroy portions of the Virginia Central Railroad, the Richmond, Fredericksburg, and Potomac Railroad, and the James River Canal. Averell did not rejoin the main column, but May 1, 1863, he was ordered back to United States Ford by Hooker. He arrived at Ely's Ford on the Rapidan the next day and remained there until May 3, 1863. Stoneman began his return march May 5, 1863 and arrived at Falmouth May 10, 1863. Judson Kilpatrick, with the 2nd New York Cavalry of his brigade, and Hasbrouck Davis, with the 12th Illinois Cavalry of Percy Wyndham's brigade, did not return with Gregg but marched eastward to Gloucester Point before returning to the army from Yorktown.

Pleasonton rendered valuable aid to Hooker's infantry during the Battle of Chancellorsville. On May 2, 1863, he was ordered with Devin's brigade to assist Daniel E. Sickles' Third Corps in pursuing the enemy wagon trains during Thomas J. (Stonewall) Jackson's flanking march to the right of Hooker's line. Pleasonton soon returned, however, and took position north of Scott's Run, on the left of Howard's Eleventh Corps. When Eleventh Corps was routed by Jackson's attack that evening, Pleasonton sent Pennock Huey with his 8th Pennsylvania Cavalry in a desperate charge that for a time checked Jackson's infantry on the Plank Road. Meantime, Pleasonton had collected twenty-three pieces of artillery and placed them in position at Hazel Grove. These guns, supported by two squadrons of cavalry, succeeded in forcing the enemy to withdraw from their immediate front.

On May 3, 1863, two regiments of cavalry were placed near Chancellorsville to stop stragglers. Huey's 8th Pennsylvania Cavalry crossed the Rappahannock at United States Ford to picket the road from Hartwood Church to Kelly's Ford. It later returned and bivouacked that night, with Kellogg's 17th Pennsylvania Cavalry, near United States Ford. McVicar's 6th New York Cavalry, then commanded by William E. Beardsley, remained in rear of Hooker's line of battle.

About 1:00 P.M. May 3, 1863, Averell crossed the Rapidan at Ely's Ford with his division and marched to United States Ford, where he reported to Hooker. He was then sent to support Howard's Eleventh Corps, which had been reassembled on the left of the Union line near the river. Averell was ordered to Washington that day, and Pleasonton was directed to assume command of Averell's division, in addition to his own, but the order was probably not received until the next day. Later, Averell was relieved from duty with the Army of the Potomac and was sent to West Virginia.

On May 5, 1863, Pleasonton was directed to secure the fords and crossings of the Rappahannock on the north side of the river, and that day the Army of the Potomac recrossed the river and marched back to its old camps in the vicinity of Falmouth. The next day Pleasonton's two divisions also returned to their former camps.

For details of the operations of the infantry and the cavalry during the Battle of Chancellorsville, see Chancellorsville, Virginia Campaign.

Along the Rappahannock River, May 1863.

During the month of May 1863, the Cavalry Corps was gradually concentrated on the right of the army on the Rappahannock River. After the Battle of Chancellorsville, Pleasonton formed his command along the river on a line extending from a point ten to twelve miles below Fredericksburg to Rappahannock Station. He also sent some cavalry to protect the rear of the army as far north as Dumfries.

On May 11, 1863, Gregg's Third Cavalry Division returned from its raid toward Richmond and went into camp on Potomac Creek, near Potomac Creek Bridge. It then took up the duty of patrolling and scouting against guerrillas and bushwhackers. Three days later, however, Gregg was ordered to Bealeton. His new responsibility was to cover the country from the right of the infantry pickets of Darius N. Couch's Second Corps near Falmouth to Samuel P. Heintzelman's pickets of the Department of Washington. Gregg's line extended along the Rappahannock from near Falmouth to the bridge of the Orange and Alexandria Railroad, and then along the railroad to the bridge over Cedar Run.

On May 24, 1863, Second Cavalry Division, then commanded by Alfred N. Duffie, was ordered to Bealeton to report to Gregg, who was assigned command of all cavalry forces on the Orange and Alexandria Railroad and along the Rappahannock River. Duffie arrived May 27, 1863 and was assigned the duty of guarding the river on Gregg's front. Third Division was ordered to guard the line of the Rappahannock and the fords of the river above the railroad bridge.

After Chancellorsville, Buford's Reserve Brigade was occupied for a short time in picketing the Rappahannock between Falmouth and Rappahannock Station, but on May 17, 1863, it was sent from the vicinity of Hartwood Church to Potomac Creek Bridge. It then moved to Dumfries May 25, 1863 to clear the area of bushwhackers, guerrillas, and enemy scouts.

On May 28, 1863, Stuart was reported near Culpeper Court House with three brigades of his cavalry, and also the brigades of Beverly Robertson from North Carolina and William E. ("Grumble") Jones from the Shenandoah Valley. Stuart was becoming increasingly aggressive, and on that day Confederate scouts were reported north of the Rappahannock at Warrenton and Warrenton Springs. This activity was regarded by Federal commanders as an almost certain indication that some enemy movement was imminent. Therefore, on May 28, 1863, Buford was ordered to move his Reserve Brigade from Dumfries to Bealeton and as senior officer present, to assume command of all Federal cavalry in the area. He was further directed to drive the enemy back across the Rappahannock and to keep him there. Buford arrived at Bealeton and assumed command May 30, 1863.

While the movements described above were in progress, there were some important command changes in the Cavalry Corps. On May 20, 1863, Stoneman was granted a leave of absence because of illness, and two days later Pleasonton was assigned temporary command of the Cavalry Corps during his absence. Alfred N. Duffie, as senior officer, was assigned command of Second Cavalry Division, and Benjamin F. Davis assumed temporary command of First Cavalry Division. Stoneman was relieved from duty with the Army of the Potomac by an order dated June 5, 1863, and Pleasonton then became the commander of the Cavalry Corps.

The Horse Artillery Brigade of the Cavalry Corps was broken up by an order of May 24, 1863, but this order was modified as follows: The brigade organization was retained for all matters relating to reports, returns, and requisitions, but the brigade commander became essentially a staff officer on duty at headquarters of the Cavalry Corps. The batteries of the brigade were assigned to cavalry divisions and the Reserve Brigade, with one battery attached to each. These batteries were under the direction of the division and Reserve Brigade commanders.

The cavalry had become very seriously depleted by the campaigning during the month of May, and on May 27, 1863, Meade was ordered to relieve the cavalry pickets along the Rappahannock from Banks' Ford to Kelly's Ford with infantry pickets of his Fifth Corps. When this exchange was completed, the cavalry was concentrated around Bealeton and on the Rappahannock above Kelly's Ford.

At the end of May 1863, the organization of the Cavalry Corps was as follows:

CAVALRY CORPS, Alfred Pleasonton

First Cavalry Division, Benjamin F. Davis
  First Brigade, Benjamin F. Davis

Second Brigade, Josiah H. Kellogg
   6th Battery, New York Light Artillery, Joseph W. Martin

Second Cavalry Division, Alfred N. Duffie
   First Brigade, Horace B. Sargent
   Second Brigade, J. Irvin Gregg
   Battery M, 2nd United States Artillery, Alexander C. M. Pennington

Third Cavalry Division, David McM. Gregg
   First Brigade, Calvin S. Douty
   Second Brigade, Percy Wyndham

Note. Judson Kilpatrick was at Yorktown with the 2nd New York Regiment of his First Brigade, and Hasbrouck Davis with the 12th Illinois Regiment.

Reserve Brigade, Charles J. Whiting

Note 1. Samuel S. Elder's Battery E, 4th United States Artillery was attached to the Reserve Brigade.
Note 2. John Buford was in command of Second Division, Third Division, and the Reserve Brigade, and May 30, 1863, Whiting relieved Buford temporarily in command of the Reserve Brigade.

Artillery, James M. Robertson
   Battery B, 2nd United States Artillery, Albert O. Vincent
   Battery L, 2nd United States Artillery, Leroy L. Janes

Gettysburg Campaign, May 1863–July 1863.

Confederate troops of Lee's Army of Northern Virginia began to leave Fredericksburg June 3, 1863 in the opening moves of the Gettysburg Campaign. At that time, most of Pleasonton's cavalry, under the command of John Buford, was on the upper Rappahannock in the vicinity of Warrenton. On June 5, 1863, Buford reported to Hooker that there were five enemy cavalry brigades under Stuart in Culpeper County. Two days later, Hooker ordered Pleasonton to take all of his cavalry and 3,000 infantry and cross the Rappahannock near Brandy Station, on the Orange and Alexandria Railroad, and disperse and destroy this force. Pleasonton crossed the river early on the morning of June 9, 1863, and soon ran into Stuart's cavalry. After fighting most of the day around Beverly Ford, St. James Church, and Fleetwood Hill, near Brandy Station, both sides had had enough, and that evening the Federal cavalry withdrew across the river and marched to Warrenton Junction. For details of the Battle of Brandy Station,

and of the organization of Pleasonton's command, see Gettysburg Campaign, Part I, From the Rappahannock to Gettysburg.

After Brandy Station, the cavalry resumed its picket duty; and skirmishes, some severe, were an almost daily occurrence. Some of the most significant of these were at Bealeton Station, Herndon, Occoquan, Little River Turnpike, Broad Run, Middleburg, Burlington, Purgitsville, Rappahannock Bridge, Kelly's Ford, Wilford's Ford, and Beverly Ford.

As a result of almost constant fighting, the Cavalry Corps was reduced to fewer than 7,000 men, and this was less than the number needed for three divisions and a Reserve Brigade. Therefore, on June 11, 1863, with Hooker's approval, Pleasonton ordered the reorganization of the corps into two divisions. A new First Cavalry Division was organized under John Buford from regiments belonging to Davis' First Cavalry Division and the Reserve Brigade, and a new Second Cavalry Division was organized under David McM. Gregg from regiments of Duffie's Second Cavalry Division and Gregg's Third Cavalry Division The division commanders were authorized to work out the brigade organization, and this was completed by June 15, 1863.

Also on June 11, 1863, John C. Tidball's Second Brigade, Regular Division of the Artillery Reserve of the army (organized as Second Brigade, Horse Artillery) was ordered to report to Pleasonton and relieve Robertson's First Brigade, Horse Artillery, then with the cavalry. Tidball arrived at Warrenton Junction June 14, 1863, and three days later Robertson's artillery was sent to Fort Runyon in the Defenses of Washington to refit.

As finally reorganized, the Cavalry Corps consisted of the following:

CAVALRY CORPS, Alfred Pleasonton

First Cavalry Division, John Buford
   First Brigade, William Gamble
   Second Brigade, Thomas C. Devin
   Reserve Brigade, Samuel H. Starr

Note. Starr relieved Charles J. Whiting in command of the Reserve Brigade June 9, 1863.

Second Cavalry Division, David McM. Gregg
   First Brigade, John B. McIntosh
   Second Brigade, Judson Kilpatrick, to June 28, 1863
     Pennock Huey

Third Brigade, J. Irvin Gregg

Second Brigade, Horse Artillery, John C. Tidball
Battery E, 1st United States Artillery, Alanson M. Randol
Battery G, 1st United States Artillery, Egbert W. Olcott
Battery K, 1st United States Artillery, William M. Graham
Battery A, 2nd United States Artillery, John C. Tidball
Battery C, 3rd United States Artillery, James R. Kelly

McIntosh's First Brigade, Second Cavalry Division was formerly Wyndham's Second Brigade, Third Cavalry Division. Wyndham was sent to Washington, where he was engaged in mounting and equipping all the cavalry in the area and forwarding them to Pleasonton. Kilpatrick's Second Brigade was organized from regiments taken from the three former cavalry divisions. J. Irvin Gregg's Third Brigade was organized from Calvin S. Douty's First Brigade, Third Cavalry Division.

Troops of Richard S. Ewell's corps and James Longstreet's corps had been on the move from Fredericksburg and the line of the Rapidan since June 3, 1863, but it was not until June 13, 1863 that Hooker was finally convinced that Lee's army was marching northward toward the Shenandoah Valley. Accordingly, on that date, Hooker issued orders for the Army of the Potomac to leave its camps near Falmouth and along the Rappahannock and move to the vicinity of Centerville, where it would be in position to protect Washington and Baltimore.

The Cavalry Corps remained in the neighborhood of Warrenton Junction from June 10 to 15, 1863, except Wyndham's brigade of Gregg's division, which was sent to Warrenton June 13, 1863. June 15, 1863, the Cavalry Corps (except Wyndham) moved to Union Mills and Bristoe Station. That day, Wyndham marched from Warrenton to Manassas Junction, and June 16, 1863, the Cavalry Corps moved to Manassas Junction and Bull Run.

On June 17, 1863, Hooker ordered Pleasonton to take his corps to Aldie, Virginia, and after arriving there he was to determine the positions and movements of the Army of Northern Virginia, which was then on its way toward the fords of the upper Potomac. This movement resulted in five days of almost constant fighting, including the series of engagements at Aldie (June 17, 1863), Middleburg (June 17–18, 1863), and Upperville (June 21, 1863). For details, see Gettysburg Campaign, Part I, From the Rappahannock to Gettysburg, Advance of the Army to the Bull Run Mountains. The day after the engagement at Upperville, the cavalry withdrew to Aldie and spent the next few days on outpost duty and refitting for the advance into Maryland in pursuit of Lee.

Meantime, the infantry of the Army of the Potomac had been moving northward. It moved first to the line of the Orange and Alexandria Railroad, and then to a position in front of Washington, facing west. This line extended from Thoroughfare Gap through Aldie, Gum Springs, and Goose Creek to Leesburg, Virginia. After remaining there a short time, the infantry again moved north, and during the period June 25–27, 1863 crossed the Potomac into Maryland at Edwards Ferry.

The Cavalry Corps remained south of the river to cover the crossing until the infantry was over, and it then marched to Leesburg and followed the rest of the army into Maryland. After crossing the Potomac, the two cavalry divisions separated. Buford's First Cavalry Division marched northward through Jefferson to Middletown to cover the left of the army, which was concentrating near Frederick. Gregg's Second Cavalry Division marched through Frederick to New Market and Ridgeville, on the Baltimore Pike, to be in position to protect the right of the army.

Julius Stahel commanded a cavalry division in the Department of Washington, and for some time in June 1863 this had been under Hooker's control. On June 21, 1863, Hooker ordered Stahel out on a reconnaissance toward Warrenton and the upper Rappahannock. Stahel returned two days later, and June 24, 1863, he was ordered to join the Army of the Potomac, which was then moving into Maryland. Stahel's division was organized into three brigades as follows: First Brigade, commanded by Joseph T. Copeland, consisted of the 5th, 6th, 7th, and 9th Michigan Cavalry; Second Brigade, commanded by R. Butler Price, consisted of the 1st Michigan Cavalry, 2nd Pennsylvania Cavalry, and 18th Pennsylvania Cavalry; and Third Brigade, commanded by Othneil De Forest, consisted of the 5th New York Cavalry, 1st Vermont Cavalry, and 1st West Virginia Cavalry.

Stahel's division arrived in Frederick June 27, 1863, and the next day it was assigned to the Cavalry Corps as Third Division. Judson Kilpatrick assumed command June 29, 1863, and the division was then reorganized to consist of two brigades. Elon J. Farnsworth was assigned command of First Brigade, and George A. Custer of Second Brigade. Both Farnsworth and Custer were made brigadier generals June 29, 1863. De Forest's brigade of Stahel's division was placed under the command of Farnsworth and designated as First Brigade, Third Division. De Forest's 5th New York Cavalry was assigned to First Brigade. Copeland's brigade of Stahel's division was given to Custer and designated as Second Brigade, Third Division. Copeland was relieved from duty with the Army of the Potomac July 4, 1863, and one week later was assigned command of the Depot for Drafted Men at Annapolis Junction, Maryland. Price's Brigade of Stahel's division was broken up and the regiments were reassigned. Price, with his 2nd Pennsylvania Cavalry, was assigned to Marsena R. Patrick's Provost Marshal General's command, and the other two regiments were assigned to First Brigade and Second Brigade of Third Division. On June 28, 1863, Stahel was relieved from duty with the Army of the Potomac and ordered to report to Darius N. Couch, commander of the Department of the Susquehanna. Stahel was directed to organize and command the cavalry of that department.

On June 21, 1863, Robertson's brigade of horse artillery was ordered to march from Fort Runyon, where it had been refitting, and rejoin the Cavalry Corps. It arrived at Frederick June 28, 1863, and while there the artillery of the corps, plus Jabez J. Daniels' 9th Michigan Battery, was reorganized into two brigades under James M. Robertson and John C. Tidball. Robertson's First Brigade, Horse Artillery consisted of five batteries, and Tidball's Second Brigade, Horse Artillery of four batteries. Also on June 28, 1863, Wesley Merritt (commissioned brigadier general June 29, 1863) was assigned command of the Reserve Brigade, relieving Samuel H. Starr.

On June 29, 1863, George G. Meade, then in command of the Army of the Potomac, started the army northward on an extended front to find Lee. The cavalry covered the flanks, and also moved in front of the center of the army as it advanced. Buford

with the brigades of Gamble and Devin crossed South Mountain to Boonsboro, and then marched north through Cavetown to Fairfield, Pennsylvania. Merritt's Reserve Brigade, also of Buford's division, accompanied the division trains to Mechanicstown (present-day Thurmont), where it remained until July 2, 1863. On June 30, 1863, Buford's two brigades moved on from Fairfield to Gettysburg, where they were engaged the next day at the opening of the battle.

On June 29–30, 1863 Gregg's cavalry division moved to the east of the army through New Windsor, Westminster, and Manchester, and on July 1, 1863 it continued on to Hanover Junction. From that point, McIntosh's and J. Irvin Gregg's brigades proceeded on to Hanover, but Huey's brigade returned to Manchester. McIntosh and J. Irvin Gregg arrived on the field of Gettysburg July 2, 1863. Huey remained at Manchester, but the next day moved to Westminster.

Kilpatrick assumed command of his new Third Division June 29, 1863, at its bivouac about three miles north of Frederick. At that time the regiments were widely scattered on scouting duty on a front extending from the vicinity of Turner's Gap along the eastern side of the Catoctin Mountains to Gettysburg. Kilpatrick waited until the evening of that day, when most of his regiments had assembled, and he then marched to Littlestown, where he arrived about 10:00 P.M. He made his evening march in an attempt to head off Stuart's cavalry, which was known to have been near Rockville that morning and was believed to be marching toward Westminster.

Meantime, early on the morning of June 25, 1863, as the Army of the Potomac was marching toward Edwards Ferry, Stuart left Salem, Virginia with three cavalry brigades on a march to join Ewell's Confederate corps in Pennsylvania. He passed around the rear of Hooker's army, crossed the Potomac River not far from Washington, and reached Westminster during the evening of June 29, 1863. While Kilpatrick was in bivouac at Littlestown that night, Stuart marched on toward Union Mills.

The next morning, June 30, 1863, both Kilpatrick and Stuart marched toward Hanover, Pennsylvania. Kilpatrick arrived first, and about 10:00 A.M., as the rear of his division was passing through the town, it was struck by the head of Stuart's column and scattered. The Federal troopers, however, rallied and, reinforced by the other regiments of Farnsworth's brigade, strongly attacked and recaptured the town. Both Kilpatrick and Stuart remained in position during the remainder of the day, but that night Stuart detoured to the east toward Jefferson and York, Pennsylvania. On the morning of July 1, 1863, Kilpatrick moved to Berlin, Pennsylvania, and the next day marched to Gettysburg. For details of the engagement at Hanover, see Gettysburg Campaign, Part I, From the Rappahannock to Gettysburg, Meade's Advance from Frederick to Gettysburg.

Buford arrived at Gettysburg with his two brigades on the morning of June 30, 1863, and camped there that night. The next morning, Buford encountered the advance of Henry Heth's division of Ambrose P. Hill's Confederate corps on the ridges west of town and held the enemy in check until relieved by the infantry of John F. Reynolds' First Corps. Gamble's brigade, which had been fighting on the left of Devin, continued to fight on the left of First Corps during the rest of the day. When Devin's brigade was relieved by First Corps on Seminary Ridge, it moved to the right of the Union line. Then, after Oliver O. Howard's Eleventh Corps arrived at Gettysburg early in the afternoon and had taken position north of the town, Devin took position on the right of Howard's corps. During the evening of July 1, 1863, Buford's two brigades moved to the vicinity of the Round Tops and spent the night there. The next day, when Daniel E. Sickles' Third Corps arrived on the Union left, Buford was ordered to take his two brigades to Westminster to guard the army trains assembled there.

David McM. Gregg, with the brigades of McIntosh and J. Irvin Gregg of his division, arrived near Gettysburg about noon July 2, 1863. He was then sent to the extreme right of the Union line, where he formed his command on the Hanover Road, to the east of Benner's Hill. That evening, Gregg was engaged east of Culp's Hill with James A. Walker's Confederate brigade (the Stonewall Brigade) of Edward Johnson's division. Huey's brigade was at Manchester and Westminster during the battle and was not engaged.

Kilpatrick's division arrived east of Gettysburg about 2:00 P.M. July 2, 1863, and was then ordered out to the York Road to help protect the right flank of the army. He arrived near Hunterstown about 4:00 P.M. and was soon engaged with Wade Hampton's brigade of Stuart's cavalry. The action continued until after dark, and then Hampton withdrew. That night Kilpatrick marched to Two Taverns and arrived there about daylight July 3, 1863.

There were two cavalry actions during the afternoon of July 3, 1863. Gregg, with McIntosh's brigade of his division and Custer's brigade of Kilpatrick's division, was engaged with Stuart's cavalry in the fields near the junction of Hanover Road and the Low Dutch (or Salem Church) Road, about three miles east of Gettysburg. Neither side could claim a victory in this engagement, but Gregg was able to prevent Stuart from advancing into the rear areas of Meade's army.

About 8:00 A.M. July 3, 1863, Kilpatrick was ordered to move with his division to a new position on the extreme enemy right, south of Gettysburg. By some mistake, Custer was ordered to report with his brigade to David McM. Gregg, and he did not join Kilpatrick that day. At 1:00 P.M., Farnsworth reached the right and rear of the enemy position west of the Round Tops, and his skirmishers were soon in action. He then formed a line east of the Emmitsburg Road, facing north, and about three-fourths of a mile west and a little south of Big Round Top. About 3:00 P.M., Merritt, who had been approaching from Emmitsburg with his Reserve Brigade of Buford's division, came up on the left of Farnsworth and formed a line astride the Emmitsburg Road. At about 5:30 P.M., Kilpatrick ordered an attack by both brigades. Farnsworth charged with his brigade into the rear of Evander Law's division of Longstreet's corps, which was facing the western slopes of the Round Tops. Under almost constant infantry fire, Farnsworth drove deep into the rear area of Law's position, but this did not significantly affect the outcome of the battle. At the same time Merritt's brigade attempted to advance, fighting dismounted, but it made little progress. Farnsworth was killed in the charge, and Nathaniel P. Richmond assumed command of his brigade.

For details of the operations of the cavalry at Gettysburg, see Gettysburg Campaign, Part II, Battle of Gettysburg, The Third Day, July 3, 1863.

The organization of the Cavalry Corps at the Battle of Gettysburg was as follows:

CAVALRY CORPS, Alfred Pleasonton

First Cavalry Division, John Buford
  First Brigade, William Gamble
  Second Brigade, Thomas C. Devin
  Reserve Brigade, Wesley Merritt

Second Cavalry Division, David McM. Gregg
  First Brigade, John B. McIntosh
  Second Brigade, Pennock Huey
  Third Brigade, J. Irvin Gregg

Third Cavalry Division, Judson Kilpatrick
  First Brigade, Elon J. Farnsworth, to July 3, killed
  Second Brigade, George A. Custer

Horse Artillery
  First Brigade, James M. Robertson
    9th Battery, Michigan Light Artillery, Jabez J. Daniels
    6th Battery, New York Light Artillery, Joseph W. Martin
    Batteries B and L, 2nd United States Artillery, Edward Heaton
    Battery M, 2nd United States Artillery, Alexander C. M. Pennington, Jr.
    Battery E, 4th United States Artillery, Samuel S. Elder
  Second Brigade, John C. Tidball
    Batteries E and G, 1st United States Artillery, Alanson M. Randol
    Battery K, 1st United States Artillery, William M. Graham
    Battery A, 2nd United States Artillery, John H. Calef
    Battery C, 3rd United States Artillery, William D. Fuller

The fighting at Gettysburg ended on the evening of July 3, 1863, but the infantry corps of both armies continued to hold their positions during the next day. The Federal cavalry, however, was sent toward Lee's right and rear to strike at his lines of communications, and to be in position to harass his marching columns if he should withdraw toward Virginia. On the morning of July 4, 1863, Buford was at Westminster with the brigades of Gamble and Devin, and Merritt's Reserve Brigade was at Gettysburg. That day, all of Buford's brigades marched toward Frederick, where they arrived the next afternoon. On July 4, 1863, Kilpatrick's division marched from Gettysburg to Monterey, Pennsylvania, where it was joined from Westminster by Huey's brigade of Gregg's division. J. Irvin Gregg's

brigade of Gregg's division moved to Hunterstown, and McIntosh's brigade of the same division remained at Gettysburg.

During the night of July 4, 1863, Kilpatrick's division, with Huey's brigade, was engaged with Beverly H. Robertson's cavalry brigade at Monterey Gap, and at 3:00 A.M. the next morning it made a successful attack on Ewell's wagon train. Later that day, Kilpatrick and Huey moved on through Smithsburg to Boonsboro.

On July 6, 1863, both Buford and Kilpatrick were seriously engaged with the enemy along Lee's retreat route. Buford marched to Williamsport and late that evening attempted to capture Lee's trains, which were then under the protection of John D. Imboden's cavalry brigade. Buford pushed forward to within one-half mile of the town, but he could go no farther. While Buford was advancing toward Williamsport, Kilpatrick's division and Huey's brigade moved to Hagerstown and drove the enemy from the town. Leaving Farnsworth's brigade, then under Richmond, to protect his rear, Kilpatrick marched toward Williamsport to aid Buford in his attack on Imboden.

Richmond was soon confronted by both cavalry and infantry, and he was forced to retire to Boonsboro. Kilpatrick, with Custer's brigade, joined Buford; but a short time later both were compelled to withdraw from before Williamsport when enemy cavalry and infantry came up in rear of Kilpatrick. Under cover of darkness, Buford and Kilpatrick retired to Jones' Cross Roads (present-day Lappans), and the next day they moved on to Boonsboro. Both divisions managed to hold their advanced positions around Boonsboro July 8–9, 1863, despite almost constant fighting with Stuart. Meade's infantry then came up and relieved the cavalry.

On July 10, 1863, Buford and Kilpatrick moved to Funkstown, Maryland, and Huey's brigade of Gregg's division was sent to Jones' Cross Roads to cover the front of Twelfth Corps. The next day Kilpatrick moved up to near Hagerstown, and Buford marched to Bakersville on the extreme left of the Union line. July 12, 1863, Kilpatrick's cavalry division and Adelbert Ames' First Division, Eleventh Corps occupied Hagerstown. When Lee withdrew across the Potomac into Virginia on the night of July 13, 1863, Kilpatrick advanced from

Hagerstown and Buford from Bakersville, and the next morning both divisions were engaged with the Confederate rear guard at Falling Waters, Maryland.

During the pursuit of Lee from Gettysburg, Gregg's Second Cavalry Division did not serve as a unit, but the brigades were usually separated on different assignments. As noted above, Huey's brigade was detached and served with Kilpatrick's division until it rejoined Second Division July 9, 1863. It was again detached July 11, 1863 and sent to the front of Twelfth Corps. McIntosh's brigade was also detached at Gettysburg July 4, 1863, and two days later, at Fairfield, Pennsylvania, it was assigned to Thomas H. Neill's temporary Light Division, which was organized to follow and report on the movements of Lee's retreating army. McIntosh moved with the Light Division through Waynesboro and Leitersburg, and rejoined Second Cavalry Division at Boonsboro July 12, 1863. J. Irvin Gregg's brigade was detached July 5, 1863 and followed in rear of the army to Boonsboro, where it rejoined the division July 11, 1863. For a more detailed account of the movements of the Army of the Potomac during the period July 4–14, 1863, see Gettysburg Campaign, Part III, Pursuit of Lee, From Gettysburg to Falling Waters.

On July 14, 1863, when it was learned that Lee had returned to Virginia, David McM. Gregg marched with McIntosh's brigade and J. Irvin Gregg's brigade to Harper's Ferry, and the next day he advanced with constant skirmishing to Shepherdstown, West Virginia. During the afternoon of July 16, 1863, the two brigades became engaged with Stuart's cavalry, and the fighting continued until dark. Huey's brigade arrived at Shepherdstown about 7:00 that evening, but it was not engaged. The next morning, all three brigades of Gregg's division returned to Harper's Ferry.

On July 15, 1863, Buford's and Kilpatrick's divisions started for the Potomac River. That day, at Falling Waters, Custer assumed temporary command of Third Division during the absence of Kilpatrick. Custer then marched with the division by way of Williamsport, Hagerstown, and Boonsboro and arrived at Berlin, Maryland (present-day Brunswick) on the river July 16, 1863. Othneil De Forest, who had succeeded Nathaniel P. Richmond in command of First Brigade (formerly Farnsworth's) July 15, 1863, then proceeded on to

Harper's Ferry. Buford's division marched directly from Falling Waters to Berlin, and arrived there July 15, 1863. The next day it proceeded on to Petersville.

The Army of the Potomac began crossing the river into Virginia July 17, 1863. Buford's division was assigned to cover the front of the army as it moved south along the Loudoun Valley, and Custer's division was ordered to advance on the right front of the army, along the base of the Blue Ridge Mountains. Gregg's division remained at Harper's Ferry until July 19, 1863. Custer's division crossed the Potomac at Berlin and Harper's Ferry July 17, 1863; it marched by way of Purcellville, Upperville, and Piedmont and arrived at Amissville July 23, 1863. It remained there picketing the right of the army until July 30, 1863.

Buford's division crossed the Potomac at Berlin July 18, 1863 and marched through Purcelleville and Philomont to Rectortown, where it arrived July 20, 1863. From there Buford sent Gamble's brigade to Chester Gap, Merritt's Reserve Brigade to Manassas Gap, and Devin's brigade with the trains to Salem. The three brigades rejoined at Barbee's Cross Roads July 22, 1863. Four days later Buford's division took position at Warrenton and Fayetteville, and was assigned the duty of picketing the Rappahannock River from Sulfur Springs to Kelly's Ford.

Meantime, on July 19, 1863, McIntosh's brigade was detached from Gregg's division and was assigned to positions in the rear of the advancing army. It followed the infantry through Hillsboro, Snickersville, Upperville, Middleburg, White Plains, and New Baltimore, and reported to Pleasonton at Warrenton on the evening of July 27, 1863. Also on July 19, 1863, Gregg, with the other two brigades of his division, Huey's and J. Irvin Gregg's, started south with orders to protect the Orange and Alexandria Railroad, which would soon be needed to supply the army as it neared Warrenton. Gregg marched through Leesburg and Manassas Junction and arrived at Bristoe Station July 22, 1863. He then moved on to Warrenton Junction, where he was joined by McIntosh's brigade July 18, 1863. Two days later, Gregg's division relieved Custer's division at Amissville, and the latter moved to Warrenton Junction for supplies and to refit. Custer was then ordered to establish a picket line from the Rappahannock River at Ellis' Ford to Aquia Creek.

This was completed by August 2, 1863. For more detailed information about the movements of the army, including the Cavalry Corps, during its advance from the Potomac to Warrenton, see Gettysburg Campaign, Part III, Pursuit of Lee, From Williamsport and Falling Waters to the Rappahannock River.

The organization of the Cavalry Corps at the end of July 1863 was as follows:

CAVALRY CORPS, Alfred Pleasonton

First Cavalry Division, John Buford
　First Brigade, William Gamble
　Second Brigade, Thomas C. Devin
　Reserve Brigade, Wesley Merritt

Second Cavalry Division, David McM. Gregg
　First Brigade, John B. McIntosh
　Second Brigade, Pennock Huey
　Third Brigade, J. Irvin Gregg

Third Cavalry Division, George A. Custer
　First Brigade, Edward B. Sawyer
　Second Brigade, Charles H. Town

　　Note. Kilpatrick returned to the army from leave August 4, 1863 and resumed command of Third Cavalry Division. Custer resumed command of Second Brigade.

Horse Artillery
　First Brigade, James M. Robertson
　Second Brigade, John C. Tidball

Cavalry Bureau of the War Department. By an order of the secretary of war dated July 28, 1863, a bureau was attached to the War Department and designated as the Cavalry Bureau. George Stoneman was assigned as chief of the new bureau, which was to have charge of the organization and equipment of the cavalry force of the army and the provision of mounts and remounts for the troopers. Shortly after assuming his duties August 1, 1863, Stoneman established a cavalry depot at Giesboro Point on the Potomac River, a short distance below Washington. Stoneman served as the chief of the bureau until January 2, 1864, and was then relieved by Kenner Garrard. Garrard was in turn relieved by James H. Wilson January 26, 1864. Wilson was reassigned April 7, 1864 and was ordered to join the Army of the Potomac to command a cavalry division. On April 14, 1864, the Cavalry Bureau was placed under the charge of the chief of the army staff, Henry W. Halleck. The duties of organization, equipping, and inspection of the cavalry were performed by a cavalry officer, and the duties of purchase, inspection, and transportation of horses and providing subsistence were performed by an officer of the Quartermaster Department. There were no further significant changes in the Cavalry Bureau during the rest of the war.

From the Rappahannock to the Rapidan, August 1, 1863–October 10, 1863. Pleasonton's cavalry remained generally along the Rappahannock River during August and the early part of September 1863, and was engaged principally in picketing and scouting duty. Gregg's division picketed the right of the army, Kilpatrick's division the left, and Buford's division (commanded part of the time by Merritt) the center.

August 1, 1863, Buford crossed the river at Rappahannock Station and pushed forward to within a mile and a half of Culpeper Court House to determine the position of the enemy. He was opposed during his advance by William E. Jones' and Wade Hampton's cavalry brigades, commanded by Stuart, and near Culpeper he encountered enemy infantry of Ambrose P. Hill's corps. Buford was finally forced back to Brandy Station, and then moved to a point near Rappahannock Station.

There were several command and organization changes in the Cavalry Corps during August 1863. About August 9, 1863, Wesley Merritt assumed command of First Cavalry Division during the temporary absence of Buford. Buford returned to command August 22, 1863, and during this time Alfred Gibbs commanded the Reserve Brigade.

August 12, 1863, Pennock Huey's Second Brigade, Second Cavalry Division was broken up, and its regiments were assigned to the other two brigades of the division. This brigade was reorganized that same day from J. Irvin Gregg's Third Brigade, Second Cavalry Division. Third Brigade was thus discontinued by the change of designation. J. Irvin Gregg commanded the new Second Brigade. August 15, 1863, the Reserve Brigade was ordered to Washington to report to George Stoneman, chief of the Cavalry Bureau, to fill up the brigade and to obtain remounts. It left the army about August 22, 1863 and rejoined the corps at Bristoe Station October 13, 1863. August 24, 1863, J. Irvin Gregg assumed temporary command of Second Cavalry Division during the absence of David McM. Gregg. Huey commanded Second Brigade until September 4, 1863, when J. Irvin Gregg resumed command. There were also two other changes in brigade commanders during August 1863. Henry E. Davies, Jr. relieved Edward B. Sawyer in command of First Brigade, Third Division August 22, 1863, and at the end of August 1863, George H. Chapman relieved William Gamble in command of First Brigade, First Cavalry Division.

At the end of August 1863, the Cavalry Corps was organized as follows:

CAVALRY CORPS, Alfred Pleasonton

First Cavalry Division, John Buford
    First Brigade, George H. Chapman
    Second Brigade, Thomas C. Devin
    Reserve Brigade, Wesley Merritt

Note. The Reserve Brigade was in Washington, D.C. and was not with the army.

Second Cavalry Division, J. Irvin Gregg
    First Brigade, John B. McIntosh
    Second Brigade, Pennock Huey

Note. David McM. Gregg was absent from the army until September 4, 1863, and J. Irvin Gregg was in temporary command of the division. J. Irvin Gregg resumed command of Second Brigade September 4, 1863.

Third Cavalry Division, Judson Kilpatrick
    First Brigade, Henry E. Davies, Jr.
    Second Brigade, George A. Custer
    Second Brigade, Horse Artillery, William M. Graham

Note. August 29, 1863, Graham was ordered to relieve James M. Robertson's First Brigade, Horse Artillery.

On September 1, 1863, Kilpatrick marched with his division to Port Conway, on the lower Rappahannock, where he drove back an enemy force that he found there, and he also destroyed two enemy gunboats.

September 13, 1863, the Cavalry Corps crossed the Rappahannock and, supported by Gouverneur K. Warren's Second Corps, made a reconnaissance in force to Brandy Station. By 4:00 P.M. Buford and Kilpatrick had driven the enemy from Culpeper Court House and were in pursuit on the road to Raccoon Ford on the Rapidan River. Gregg's division arrived at Culpeper Court House about 5:30

that afternoon from its camps between Sulfur Springs and Jefferson (Jeffersonton), and it then moved out on the Cedar Mountain Road.

By September 14, 1863, Pleasonton had cleared the north bank of the Rapidan and had tried unsuccessfully to cross at the fords. He then assigned Kilpatrick's and Buford's divisions to picket the river in the vicinity of Raccoon Ford and Somerville Ford, and Gregg's division to a similar duty at Mitchell's Ford, near the Orange and Alexandria Railroad crossing.

On September 16, 1863, the infantry of the Army of the Potomac, less Eleventh Corps, moved up behind the cavalry and formed on a line through Culpeper Court House, facing the Rapidan River. That day, Twelfth Corps advanced to Raccoon Ford and relieved the cavalry pickets watching the river from Somerville Ford down to Morton's Ford. Second Corps moved up on the right of Twelfth Corps and relieved the cavalry pickets from Somerville Ford to Cedar Mountain. When relieved, Buford's cavalry division took position on the left of Twelfth Corps, and Kilpatrick's cavalry division on the right of Second Corps. Gregg's cavalry division moved back to Watery Mountain, near Warrenton.

September 21, 1863, Buford's and Kilpatrick's divisions crossed the Rapidan on a reconnaissance to determine the enemy strength and to locate the enemy's left flank. While out, they were engaged in a number of skirmishes and returned in good condition two days later.

Eleventh Corps, which had been guarding the line of the Orange and Alexandria Railroad, departed September 24, 1863 for transfer to Tennessee. Gregg's cavalry division was assigned the duty of protecting the bridges at Bristoe Station, Catlett's Station, and Rappahannock Station. Gregg was relieved from this duty by Albion P. Howe's Second Division, Sixth Corps October 1, 1863. When relieved, Horace B. Sargent's First Brigade of Gregg's division was sent to Hartwood Church to establish a line of pickets from Falmouth to Kelly's Ford; and Gregg, with J. Irvin Gregg's Second Brigade, moved to Bealeton Station.

Bristoe, Virginia Campaign, October 10, 1863–October 22, 1863. Meade's Army of the Potomac remained rather quietly near Culpeper Court House and along the Rapidan until October 9, 1863, the day that Lee's army crossed the Rapidan and marched toward Madison Court House at the beginning of the Bristoe, Virginia Campaign. That day, Gregg's Second Cavalry Division was some distance to the rear, along the Rappahannock, and Merritt's Reserve Brigade of First Cavalry Division was at the Cavalry Depot near Washington. When Meade learned of Lee's movements, he immediately ordered Gregg and Merritt to rejoin the army near Culpeper. Buford's other two brigades were on the Rapidan on the left of the army, and Kilpatrick's division was directly in the path of the approaching Confederates, on the right of the army.

During the day of October 9, 1863, Meade was aware that there was a shifting of enemy troops toward his right, but he was uncertain whether this was the beginning of a withdrawal from his front or of a flanking movement against his right. That evening he ordered Buford to force a crossing of the Rapidan at Germanna Ford, and then to move upriver and clear Morton's Ford so that First Corps and Fifth Corps could cross and follow Lee. Sixth Corps was also to cross and join the other two corps upstream. At that time Kilpatrick was in position on Crooked Run, with Custer's Brigade at James City. On October 10, 1863, Buford's division crossed the Rapidan as ordered, but it was unable to reach Morton's Ford until after dark. By that time Meade had learned definitely that Lee was not withdrawing, and he then called off the movement south of the Rapidan before the infantry had crossed. At the same time, he recalled Buford's division.

J. Irvin Gregg's Second Brigade of Gregg's division left Bealeton at daylight October 10, 1863, and arrived at Culpeper Court House about 11:00 A.M. He was immediately sent to Wayland's Mill to support Kilpatrick's command, which was then disposed as follows: Custer's brigade was on the Culpeper Court House-Madison Court House Road; Davies' brigade was between the right of Custer and the Sperryville Pike; and after J. Irvin Gregg's brigade arrived, it was sent to picket the country between Thoroughfare Mountain and Cedar Mountain. Late on October 10, 1863, Davies reported heavy columns of enemy infantry moving toward Woodville, and Kilpatrick then fell back to the front of the Federal infantry pickets. That night Meade issued orders for the Army of the Potomac to retire behind the Rappahannock River. For additional information, see Army of the Potomac, Advance of the Army Across the Rappahannock, November 1863.

On October 11, 1863, the army moved back toward the Rappahannock, and Pleasonton's cavalry covered the retreat. Kilpatrick's division followed Fifth Corps along the railroad to Brandy Station, where it was joined by Buford's division coming up from the Rapidan. The two divisions were strongly attacked by Stuart's cavalry at Brandy Station and at Fleetwood Hill, but they held their ground until evening and then followed the infantry across the river. That day, J. Irvin Gregg's Second Brigade of Gregg's division marched from near Culpeper Court House to the vicinity of Sulfur Springs (Warrenton Springs), where it was joined by John P. Taylor's First Brigade of the same division (commanded by Sargent until early October 1863). Gregg's two brigades were engaged October 12, 1863 at Welford's Ford and at Jefferson (Jeffersonton) and were finally forced to retire across the Rappahannock

Because of increasing pressure on his right, Meade began the withdrawal of the army toward Centerville on the night of October 12, 1863. Kilpatrick's cavalry division marched in front of William H. French's Third Corps by way of Auburn (Auburn Mills) to Greenwich, and Gregg's division followed Gouverneur K. Warren's Second Corps to Auburn. Buford's division, which was at Warrenton, was assigned to guard the army trains and to march with them to Brentsville. On October 14, 1863, Gregg's division followed Second Corps to Bristoe Station to protect its left flank and rear. Kilpatrick was ordered to march by way of Hay Market to Sudley Springs and to hold that point. Wesley Merritt's Reserve Brigade of Buford's division arrived from the Cavalry Depot at Washington and rejoined the army near Bristoe Station October 13, 1863. It then marched to Sudley Springs, and then on to Centerville October 15, 1863. It did not rejoin First Cavalry Division, but remained on the Orange and Alexandria Railroad at Bristoe Station and at Catlett's Station during the remainder of the campaign. October 15, 1863, after the army had reached Centerville, Buford's division was assigned to picket the Occoquan River, and the rest of the cavalry covered the right and front of Meade's position.

During the retreat of the army from the Rappahannock, the Confederate cavalry pursued closely to the vicinity of Centerville, but the infantry halted at Broad Run. At that point, Lee decided that little more could be accomplished by a further advance, and on October 18, 1863 he withdrew to the Rappahannock. The next day Meade advanced on the Warrenton Turnpike, with Kilpatrick's cavalry out in front and Buford and Gregg covering the flanks. That day, October 19, 1863, Stuart's cavalry struck the head of Kilpatrick's column at Buckland Mills, and a short time later Fitzhugh Lee's brigade moved up on its flank and rear. Kilpatrick's division was routed, and it was not until that evening that it was re-formed on the infantry supports at Gainesville and Hay Market.

When Meade approached Lee's position at Broad Run, the latter withdrew across the Rappahannock. Buford's division followed and occupied the north bank of the river from Kelly's Ford to Beverly Ford. Gregg's division came up on the right of Buford and extended the line from Beverly Ford to Waterloo. Kilpatrick's division remained on the right of the army, north of Warrenton. For additional information, See Bristoe, Virginia Campaign.

The organization of the Cavalry Corps October 10, 1863 was as follows:

CAVALRY CORPS, Alfred Pleasonton

First Cavalry Division, John Buford
    First Brigade, George H. Chapman
    Second Brigade, Thomas C. Devin

Note. Wesley Merritt's Reserve Brigade was at the Cavalry Depot at Washington at this time, but it joined the army at Bristoe Station October 13, 1863.

Second Cavalry Division, David McM. Gregg
    First Brigade, John P. Taylor
    Second Brigade, J. Irvin Gregg

Third Cavalry Division, Judson Kilpatrick
    First Brigade, Henry E. Davies, Jr.
    Second Brigade, George A. Custer

First Brigade, Horse Artillery, James M. Robertson

Rappahannock Station and Kelly's Ford, November 7, 1863. November 3, 1863, Kilpatrick was sent to the lower Rappahannock to drive back some enemy cavalry who had crossed the river near

Fredericksburg. Four days later, the Army of the Potomac advanced to Rappahannock Station and Kelly's Ford to force a crossing of the river. Kilpatrick, who had been successful in his mission, left Falmouth November 7, 1863; and after crossing the Rappahannock at Ellis' Ford, moved up on the left of William H. French's Left Column of the army, which consisted of First Corps and Third Corps and was then advancing toward Kelly's Ford. Buford's division advanced on the right of the army, crossed at the upper fords of the Rappahannock, and then marched by way of Rixeyville to cooperate with John Sedgwick's Right Column, which consisted of Fifth Corps and Sixth Corps and was advancing toward Rappahannock Station. Gregg's division covered the front of Sedgwick's column until it reached Rappahannock Station; and then, after the infantry came up, it moved to Bealeton and Morrisville to guard the trains.

After the Union successes at Kelly's Ford and Rappahannock Station, the army crossed the river, and during the next two days advanced to a line that extended from Kelly's Ford, through Brandy Station, to Welford's Ford on Hazel River. Kilpatrick's division moved to Stevensburg and picketed the fords of the Rapidan below the railroad crossing. Davies' brigade was sent to Deep Run, between Hartwood Church and Grove Church on the Morrisville Road. Buford's division moved to the vicinity of Culpeper Court House and picketed the crossings of Robertson's River and the country toward the right. Devin's brigade was near Culpeper Court House, on the Madison Court House Road; Merritt's Reserve Brigade was in front of Culpeper Court House, in the direction of Cedar Mountain (Slaughter Mountain); and Chapman's brigade was on the left of Merritt, picketing toward the Rapidan. Gregg's division remained in rear of the army to guard the flanks of the troops along the railroad, and also the fords of the Rappahannock. One brigade was placed on the left at Morrisville, and one brigade was on the right at Fayetteville, where it watched the country beyond Waterloo. The cavalry remained generally in these positions until November 26, 1863.

Mine Run Campaign, November 26, 1863–December 2, 1863. On the morning of November 26, 1863, the Army of the Potomac left its camps and advanced toward the Rapidan River at the beginning of the Mine Run Campaign. The movement had been scheduled for November 24, 1863, but it had been postponed for two days because of bad weather. On November 24, 1863, Gregg's division marched from Morrisville and crossed the Rappahannock at Ellis' Ford, and then continued on to Ely's Ford on the Rapidan. Gregg withdrew to Richardsville and Ellis' Ford when the march of the army was delayed, but on November 26, 1863, Gregg again advanced. He crossed the Rapidan and marched to the headwaters of the Po River, near the road from Spotsylvania Court House to Parker's Store. The division arrived there about 8:00 that evening and bivouacked for the night.

Kilpatrick's cavalry division, then under the temporary command of Custer, was ordered to take position on the right of the army to watch the fords and to demonstrate against the enemy. On November 26, 1863, Custer advanced from Stevensburg to the Rapidan, and upon arriving there, Davies' brigade took position near Raccoon Ford, and Custer's brigade, then commanded by Charles H. Town, moved to Morton's Ford. The division patrolled the river from Germanna Ford to Somerville Ford.

A short time before Meade's advance began, Merritt relieved Buford in command of First Cavalry Division, and Alfred Gibbs assumed command of the Reserve Brigade. Buford left the army on sick leave to rest in General Stoneman's home in Washington, and he died there December 16, 1863, reportedly of typhoid fever. On November 26, 1863, Merritt marched with his division from the vicinity of Culpeper Court House to Richardsville, and the next day he sent Gibbs' brigade to guard the fords from Germanna Ford down to the mouth of the Rapidan River, and also Richards' Ford. Chapman's brigade was assigned as a part of the force left to guard the army trains near Richardsville, and Devin's brigade remained north of the Rapidan until November 29, 1863.

On the morning of November 27, 1863, Gregg moved on to Parker's Store, and then marched west on the Orange Plank Road, ahead of George Sykes' Fifth Corps, which had just arrived. Taylor's brigade encountered skirmishers of the enemy cavalry at New Hope Church and drove them back on their infantry supports, who halted Gregg's advance.

Fifth Corps came up that afternoon and relieved Gregg's division, which was then pulled back to watch the roads to the rear. Taylor's brigade was placed at Wilderness Tavern, with two regiments at Parker's Store; and J. Irvin Gregg's brigade, then commanded by Pennock Huey, remained at New Hope Church.

November 29, 1863, Devin's brigade of Merritt's division crossed the Rapidan at Ely's Ford and took position to cover the approaches to the ford. The next day it marched to Wilderness Tavern and joined Gregg's division. It relieved Taylor's brigade, which was in position there, and Taylor's regiment assembled at Parker's Store.

Meantime, the infantry corps of the army had come up and were in position at Robertsons' in the Wilderness. Meade then advanced and found the enemy in a strong position on the high ground beyond Mine Run, a tributary of the Rapidan River. He then made dispositions for an assault on the enemy works; but Warren, who commanded the troops that were to make the effort, reported that the the position was too strong to carry, and the attack was then called off. On the night of December 1, 1863, the army began to withdraw toward the crossings of the Rapidan. Gregg's division and Devin's brigade of Merritt's division, together with three infantry brigades of Third Corps, covered the retreat. The next day Gregg's division returned to Culpeper Court House, and December 3, 1863, Custer's division moved back to Stevensburg. Gregg's division remained to picket the lower fords of the Rapidan until December 10, 1863, and then it was ordered to Warrenton and Bealeton.

Winter of 1863–1864. When the Army of the Potomac went into winter quarters at the end of the Mine Run Campaign, the Cavalry Corps resumed the duty of picketing the front and flanks of the infantry positions. Merritt's division camped near Culpeper Court House and picketed the right of the army from the vicinity of Raccoon Ford on the Rapidan, along Cedar Run to the west of Culpeper, and on to Hazel River. Kilpatrick's division, commanded by Custer until December 20, 1863, was on the Rapidan, near Raccoon Ford, on the left of Merritt, and on the right of Gregg's division. Gregg was on the left and front of the army, with a brigade at Sheppard's Post Office picketing Jacob's Ford and Germanna Ford, and a brigade at Richardsville picketing the lower fords of the Rapidan.

December 10, 1863, Kilpatrick's division relieved Gregg on the lower Rapidan, and Gregg moved back to Warrenton and Bealeton. Kilpatrick then picketed a line from Morton's Ford to Germanna Ford on the Rapidan, and then across the neck of land between the Rapidan and the Rappahannock to Kemper's Dam on the Rappahannock. Kilpatrick's troopers also patrolled the roads to Ellis' Ford and Ely's Ford.

The cavalry remained essentially in these same positions until the beginning of Grant's spring campaign, early in May 1863. There were, however, frequent scouts, demonstrations, and expeditions by the cavalry during the remainder of the winter. The principal ones were as follows:

Expedition from Bealeton to Luray, Virginia. On the morning of December 21, 1863, Charles H. Smith left Bealeton with four regiments of his Second Brigade of Gregg's division on an expedition to Luray, Virginia. He marched by way of Sulfur Springs, Amissville, and Sperryville, and entered Luray during the morning of December 23, 1863. He destroyed all works and supplies of military value to the enemy, and returned to camp December 24, 1863.

Expedition toward Winchester, Virginia. During William W. Averell's raid from West Virginia toward the Virginia and Tennessee Railroad December 8–25, 1863, Jubal A. Early advanced down the Shenandoah Valley with infantry and cavalry on a demonstration against Winchester, Virginia. On January 1, 1864, John P. Taylor, then in temporary command of Gregg's Second Cavalry Division, was ordered to Winchester in an attempt to intercept Early. He left Bealeton with a part of Charles H. Smith's Second Brigade and marched to Warrenton, where he was joined by his First Brigade, then under the temporary command of John W. Kester. Taylor left Warrenton that afternoon and marched on the Waterloo Pike to Hedgman's River, and then on to Orleans, where he arrived after dark and bivouacked for the night. At daylight the next morning he resumed the march and, after passing through Chester Gap, arrived at Front Royal after dark. Taylor learned the next morning, January 3, 1864,

that he would be unable to continue on to Winchester because of high water in the Shenandoah River, and that afternoon he began the return march to camp. He passed through Manassas Gap and Salem and arrived at Warrenton during the afternoon of January 4, 1864.

Demonstration on the Rapidan. On February 6, 1864, three infantry corps of the Army of the Potomac carried out a demonstration on the Rapidan River. Warren's Second Corps moved to Morton's Ford and Newton's First Corps and French's Third Corps, the latter commanded temporarily by David B. Birney, advanced to the vicinity of Raccoon Ford. Two of the divisions of the Cavalry Corps also participated in this demonstration. Merritt's First Cavalry Division marched on the right of the infantry to Barnett's Ford, where it skirmished for a time with the enemy before returning to its camps. Kilpatrick's Third Cavalry Division advanced on the left of the infantry and crossed the Rapidan at Ely's Ford, Culpeper (Culpeper Mine) Ford, and Germanna Ford. Kilpatrick demonstrated south of the river the next day, February 7, 1864, and then marched back to its camps. For additional information, see Army of the Potomac, Winter of 1863–1864.

Kilpatrick's Expedition against Richmond, Virginia. February 28, 1864, Judson Kilpatrick left Stevensburg with his Third Cavalry Division, reinforced to 4,000 men, on an expedition to Richmond, Virginia. The purpose of this expedition was to distribute copies of President Lincoln's Amnesty Proclamation and to release prisoners held at Richmond. Kilpatrick failed in his attempt to free the prisoners, and his command returned to Stevensburg, where all had arrived by March 19, 1864. For details of this expedition, see Kilpatrick's Expedition against Richmond, Virginia, and Custer's Raid into Albemarle County, Virginia.

Custer's Raid into Albemarle County, Virginia. On the same day that Kilpatrick left Stevensburg for Richmond, February 28, 1864, Custer set out with 1,500 cavalrymen on a raid by way of Madison Court House toward Charlottesville, Virginia. The purpose of this raid was to create a diversion during Kilpatrick's advance toward Richmond. Custer arrived within a few miles of Charlottesville, and then withdrew. For details, see Kilpatrick's Raid against Richmond, Virginia, and Custer's Raid into Albemarle County, Virginia.

Reorganization of the Cavalry Corps, April 1864. In preparation for active campaigning in the spring of 1864, the Cavalry Corps of the Army of the Potomac was extensively reorganized. March 24, 1864, Alfred Pleasonton was relieved from duty with the Army of the Potomac and was ordered to Saint Louis, Missouri to report to William S. Rosecrans, then in command of the Department of the Missouri. The next day, David McM. Gregg assumed temporary command of the Cavalry Corps. On March 23, 1864, Philip H. Sheridan, then in command of Second Division, Fourth Corps in East Tennessee, was ordered to Washington, and there on April 4, 1864 he was assigned command of the Cavalry Corps. He assumed command the next day, and Gregg resumed command of Second Cavalry Division.

During the past winter, James H. Wilson, then serving on Grant's staff in the West, was assigned command of the Cavalry Bureau of the War Department in Washington. He was relieved from that duty April 7, 1864, and April 13, 1864 he was ordered to join the Army of the Potomac. On April 17, 1864, he assumed command of Third Cavalry Division at Stevensburg. Because of problems of seniority, however, it was necessary to make some command and organizational changes in the cavalry before Wilson could assume command. Judson Kilpatrick, then commanding Third Cavalry Division, was relieved from duty with the Army of the Potomac and was sent west, where he later commanded a cavalry division during William T. Sherman's Atlanta Campaign. Wesley Merritt, George A. Custer, and Henry E. Davies, the latter two commanding brigades in Third Division, all held higher rank than Wilson, and it was necessary that they be reassigned. Alfred T. A. Torbert, formerly commander of First Brigade, First Division, Sixth Corps, was assigned command of First Cavalry Division April 10, 1864, and Merritt resumed command of the Reserve Brigade, relieving Alfred Gibbs. Henry E. Davies, commanding First Brigade, Third Cavalry Division, was assigned command of First Brigade, Second Cavalry Division, and John P. Taylor, who had been

commanding this brigade, resumed command of the 1st Pennsylvania Cavalry. Timothy M. Bryan, Jr., commanding the 18th Pennsylvania Cavalry in First Brigade, Third Cavalry Division, replaced Davies in command of First Brigade. A further change was made in order to remove Custer from Third Cavalry Division. He, with his Second Brigade of the division, was transferred to First Cavalry Division, and his brigade was redesignated as First Brigade, First Cavalry Division. The former First Brigade, First Cavalry Division under George H. Chapman was transferred to Third Cavalry Division and redesignated as Second Brigade, Third Cavalry Division, with Chapman in command.

The organization of the Cavalry Corps at the end of April 1864 was then as follows:

CAVALRY CORPS, Philip H. Sheridan

First Cavalry Division, Alfred T. A. Torbert
    First Brigade, George A. Custer
    Second Brigade, Thomas C. Devin
    Reserve Brigade, Wesley Merritt

Second Cavalry Division, David McM. Gregg
    First Brigade, Henry E. Davies, Jr.
    Second Brigade, J. Irvin Gregg

Third Cavalry Division, James H. Wilson
    First Brigade, Timothy M. Bryan, Jr., to May 5, 1864
      John B. McIntosh
    Second Brigade, George H. Chapman
    First Brigade, Horse Artillery, James M. Robertson
      6th Battery, New York Light Artillery, Joseph W. Martin
      Batteries B and L, 2nd United States Artillery, Edward Heaton
      Battery D, 2nd United States Artillery, Edward B. Williston
      Battery M, 2nd United States Artillery, Alexander C. M. Pennington, Jr.
      Battery A, 4th United States Artillery, Frederick Fuger
      Batteries C and E, 4th United States Artillery, Charles L. Fitzhugh

Grant's Richmond, Virginia Campaign, 1864. During the first days of May 1864, the Cavalry Corps was assembled in preparation for its part in Grant's spring campaign in Virginia. Torbert's First Cavalry Division and Wilson's Third Cavalry Division were at Stevensburg, and Gregg's Second Cavalry Division was at Paoli Mills. Beginning on the afternoon of May 3, 1864, the cavalry led the way southward toward the crossings of the Rapidan River. Gregg left Paoli Mills and, followed by Winfield S. Hancock's Second Corps, marched toward Ely's Ford. He crossed the river there the next day and moved to the vicinity of Chancellorsville. Wilson started toward Germanna Ford on the night of May 3, 1864, and Gouverneur K. Warren's Fifth Corps followed. The next morning, Wilson crossed the Rapidan and advanced to Parker's Store on the Orange Plank Road. On the morning of May 5, 1864, he moved south to the Catharpin Road, and there he was attacked at Craig's Meeting House by Wade Hampton's cavalry division and Thomas L. Rosser's brigade and was forced to retire to Todd's Tavern. He was joined there by Gregg's division, which had advanced from the Aldrich farm, near Chancellorsville.

Meantime, Meade's three infantry corps had crossed the Rapidan and moved into the Wilderness. That afternoon and evening Fifth Corps and Sixth Corps were heavily engaged with Richard S. Ewell's corps of the Army of Northern Virginia on the Orange Turnpike; and Second Corps, reinforced by troops of the other corps, battled Ambrose P. Hill's corps on the Orange Plank Road.

Torbert's cavalry division, which had been left in the rear of the army when it marched to the Rapidan, moved up and arrived at Chancellorsville May 5, 1864. The next day, while the infantry was engaged in the second day's battle in the Wilderness, Custer moved down the Furnace Road with his own brigade and Devin's brigade of Torbert's division to the Brock Road; and then took position on the left of Second Corps. Custer was then attacked by Hampton's cavalry, but he maintained his position. He later moved back to Catharine Furnace to protect the trains.

During May 6, 1864, Gregg's division skirmished with Fitzhugh Lee's cavalry at Todd's Tavern, but it was not seriously engaged. That day Torbert was disabled by an abscess on his back, and May 7, 1864, he turned over the command of First Cavalry Division to Wesley Merritt and left for Washington. Alfred Gibbs assumed temporary command of the Reserve Brigade.

For detailed information about the Battle of the Wilderness, see Richmond, Virginia Campaign, 1864, Battle of the Wilderness.

The infantry did not renew the fighting in the Wilderness May 7, 1864, but the cavalry was engaged at Todd's Tavern that day. Merritt, commanding Tobert's division, joined Gregg's division at Todd's Tavern, and both divisions attacked the enemy cavalry of Hampton and Fitzhugh Lee. For this attack, the Federal cavalry was formed as follows: J. Irvin Gregg's Second Brigade, Second Cavalry Division was on the right, on the Catharpin Road; Gibbs' Reserve Brigade, First Cavalry Division was on the Spotsylvania Court House Road; and Davies' First Brigade, Second Cavalry Division was on the left, on the Piney Branch Road. Devin's Second Brigade, First Cavalry Division was in reserve. After some sharp fighting, the enemy was driven back, and the Federal cavalry pursued almost to Spotsylvania Court House before they were halted by darkness.

During the night of May 7, 1864, the Army of the Potomac left its positions in the Wilderness and moved southward toward Spotsylvania Court House. Wilson's cavalry division was at Alsop's house that day, and it was ordered to move out the next morning to Spotsylvania Court House, and then continue on to Snell's Bridge on the Po River. Gregg and Merritt were ordered to the same point by way of Corbin's Bridge and the Block House.

May 8, 1864, Wilson advanced to Spotsylvania Court House as ordered and occupied the town. He remained there for some time, but was finally driven out by enemy infantry of James Longstreet's corps, then commanded by Richard H. Anderson. The orders to the other two divisions were changed, and Gregg was directed to hold Corbin's Bridge, and Merritt's division was to cover the front of the infantry as it advanced toward Spotsylvania Court House. Merritt moved ahead of Warren's Fifth Corps toward Alsop's farm, but he was unable to clear the way and was relieved by infantry.

In response to a complaint by Sheridan that his cavalry was not being used properly during the advance of the army, Grant, through Meade, ordered Sheridan on May 8, 1864 to make a raid with his Cavalry Corps around the left of the army toward Richmond and engage Stuart's cavalry. During the night of May 8, 1864, Sheridan assembled his divisions near Aldriches', on the Fredericksburg Plank Road, and the next morning set out toward Richmond. At Yellow Tavern on May 11, 1864,

Sheridan defeated the enemy cavalry, and during the engagement Stuart was killed. Sheridan moved on almost to Richmond, and then turned off and proceeded to Haxall's Landing on the James River, where he obtained supplies from Benjamin F. Butler's Army of the James. When resupplied, he marched back by way of Jones' Bridge on the Chickahominy, White House, and Ayletts' and rejoined the army near Chesterfield on May 24, 1864. At that time the battles around Spotsylvania had been fought, and the army was maneuvering to cross the North Anna River. For details, see Sheridan's Richmond, Virginia Raid.

Meantime, on May 16, 1864, Torbert had rejoined the army and had assumed command of all cavalry that had not accompanied Sheridan on his raid. Torbert's command had led the way when the army left Spotsylvania Court House for the North Anna River on the night of May 20, 1864. Torbert was near the North Anna when Sheridan arrived from his raid, and May 26, 1864, he resumed command of his First Cavalry Division, relieving Merritt.

May 25, 1864, Wilson's division was sent to the right of the army and there made a reconnaissance south of the North Anna as far as Little River. Gregg's and Merritt's divisions remained near Pole Cat Station on the Richmond, Fredericksburg, and Potomac Railroad until May 26, 1864. At that time the army departed from the line of the North Anna, and started for the crossings of the Pamunkey River at and near Hanovertown. Torbert's and Gregg's divisions, with David A. Russell's First Division of Horatio G. Wright's Sixth Corps, took the lead, to secure the crossings of the river. The next morning, Custer's brigade of Torbert's division crossed to the south bank of the Pamunkey at Dabney's Ferry and drove back an enemy force posted there. The rest of the division followed Custer, and a short distance from Hanovertown Torbert met and defeated James B. Gordon's brigade of William H. F. Lee's cavalry division. Gordon withdrew toward Hanover Court House and was followed by Torbert to Crump's Landing. A short time later Gregg joined Torbert at Crump's Landing.

On May 28, 1864, Gregg moved out on a reconnaissance in the direction of Mechanicsville. About three-fourths of a mile beyond Haw's Shop he met Confederate cavalry under Williams C. Wickham and Thomas L. Rosser and promptly attacked. There was stubborn fighting most of the day, without decided advantage to either side, but late in the evening Custer's brigade of Torbert's division arrived and, together with Gregg's division, charged and forced the enemy to withdraw. The other two brigades of Torbert's division remained on the line of Crump's Creek until relieved by Sixth Corps, and they then marched to Haw's Shop that afternoon. They demonstrated on the right of Gregg, but they were not seriously engaged. After dark, the cavalry moved back to the rear of the infantry, which was only a short distance behind, and went into camp in the vicinity of Old Church. For details of the engagement at Haw's Shop, see Richmond, Virginia Campaign, 1864, Operations on the Pamunkey River

Wilson's division, which had followed the infantry from the North Anna, remained on the north bank of the Pamunkey River until May 30, 1864. Then George H. Chapman's Second Brigade crossed at New Castle Ferry and marched to Crump's Creek, where it took position between the river and the right of the infantry. John B. McIntosh's First Brigade halted until the trains of the army had passed, and then it too crossed the river and joined Chapman. On the morning of May 31, 1864, Wilson's division advanced toward Hanover Court House. It met an enemy force at Dr. Price's house and drove it back beyond Mechump's Creek.

That evening, Wilson received orders to destroy the bridges over the South Anna River and also to destroy the track of the Virginia Central Railroad and the Richmond, Fredericksburg, and Potomac Railroad. He immediately advanced on the enemy positions on the ridge west of Mechump's Creek, near Hanover Court House. McIntosh's brigade, supported by Chapman's brigade, moved forward in the dark and, fighting dismounted, drove the enemy from the field. The next morning, Wilson continued his advance. McIntosh reached Ashland and was engaged there; and Chapman proceeded up the south bank of the South Anna River, destroying bridges as he went. Wilson then withdrew to his former camps near Dr. Price's. His command had been fighting continuously for two days.

Meantime, on May 30, 1864, after Sheridan had reached Old Church, he had ordered Gregg and Torbert to advance with their divisions toward Cold Harbor. It was essential that Grant occupy this important road junction to secure a line of communications with White House on the Pamunkey River, which was to be the new supply base for the army. Not far from Old Church, on the road to Cold Harbor, a Confederate force was in position at the crossing of Matadequin Creek. Torbert attacked this force and drove it back to Cold Harbor. Torbert then halted for the night about a mile and a half from that place. The next afternoon he advanced to Cold Harbor, which was occupied by Fitzhugh Lee's cavalry, and after a sharp fight gained possession of that important crossroads. During the action, Gregg moved up in support of Torbert.

About dusk, enemy infantry came up to support the cavalry, and during the night Sheridan withdrew from Cold Harbor. He soon received imperative orders, however, to hold that point at all costs, and he promptly moved back and fortified a position there. Just after daylight June 1, 1864, the enemy attacked Sheridan's line, but his troopers continued to resist until 10:00 A.M., when Wright's Sixth Corps arrived and secured the position. When relieved by the infantry, Torbert's and Gregg's divisions moved down the Chickahominy River to cover the left of the army, and they camped on the night of June 1, 1864 at and near Prospect Church. These two divisions were relieved by Hancock's Second Corps on the afternoon of June 2, 1864, and they then moved farther downstream to Bottom's Bridge.

While Sheridan was engaged at Cold Harbor, Wilson's division was posted on the right of the army near the headwaters of the Totopotomoy River. On the night of June 2, 1864, it moved to Linneys' house, near the right of Meade's line at Cold Harbor. The next day it recrossed the Totopotomoy and drove some Confederate cavalry from Haw's Shop and pursued to Mount Carmel Church. McIntosh's brigade was left at Haw's Shop, and Chapman's brigade marched past P. Norman's house to the Totopotomoy. There Chapman attacked an enemy force that was in front of Ambrose E. Burnside's Ninth Corps, near Mrs. Via's house, and drove it off. On June 4, 1864, Wilson camped near New Castle Ferry and picketed a line from the right of the infantry to the Pamunkey River. Also that day, Torbert's division was ordered back from the Chickahominy to Old Church. Two days later, Chapman's brigade moved to Bottom's Bridge to relieve Gregg's division, and McIntosh's brigade

crossed the Totopotomoy and camped at Old Church to cover the right and rear of the army. When Gregg's division was relieved at Bottom's Bridge by Chapman, it too moved back to the vicinity of Old Church.

By June 6, 1864, after the Union failure at Cold Harbor, Grant had decided to continue his movement by the left flank to the south bank of the James River. To aid in this movement by drawing off the enemy cavalry while it was in progress, Sheridan was ordered to take two divisions of his cavalry on a raid toward Charlottesville, Virginia to cut the line of the Virginia Central Railroad. This order was later modified to include a junction at Charlottesville, if possible, of Sheridan's command with an army under David Hunter, which was then advancing up the Shenandoah Valley.

On June 7, 1864, Sheridan, with the divisions of Torbert and Gregg, marched westward along the north bank of the Pamunkey River and of the North Anna River toward Charlottesville. Wilson's division was left behind and was directed to report to and receive orders from Headquarters Army of the Potomac. As Sheridan approached Trevilian Station on the Virginia Central Railroad, he was confronted by Confederate cavalry under Wade Hampton and Fitzhugh Lee, and after an all-day engagement on June 11, 1864, the enemy withdrew, and that night Sheridan camped along the railroad at Trevilian Station. There Sheridan learned that Hunter apparently was not marching toward Charlottesville, and he decided to proceed no farther. He was engaged again the next day while attempting to return to the army by way of Mallory's Ford, and was forced to return to the North Anna River by the way that he had come. After destroying some of the track on the Virginia Central Railroad, Sheridan began his return march on the night of June 12, 1864. He arrived at White House on the Pamunkey River June 21, 1864. He then broke up the army base there and escorted the wagons carrying the supplies from the abandoned base to the James River. Sheridan crossed the James during the night of June 27, 1864 and rejoined the Army of the Potomac near Petersburg, Virginia June 28–29, 1864. For details of Sheridan's expedition, see Sheridan's Trevilian Station Raid, Virginia.

After Sheridan's departure for Trevilian Station, Wilson's division remained near Cold Harbor until

June 12, 1864, the day that the army began its march to the James River. Chapman's brigade continued to picket the Chickahominy near Bottom's Bridge until the night of June 12, 1864, and it then crossed the river against some opposition and moved ahead of Fifth Corps to White Oak Swamp. It remained in that area watching the roads toward Richmond while the army passed in its rear on the way to the James River. Chapman then withdrew and crossed the James on the morning of June 17, 1864. McIntosh's brigade remained at Old Church until June 12, 1864, and that night and the next day it covered the rear of the army as it marched from Cold Harbor to the James River. It crossed the Chickahominy at Long Bridge and arrived at Charles City Court House June 14, 1864. McIntosh then moved back to Saint Mary's Church and was engaged the next day at Smith's Store. He then withdrew to Saint Mary's Church and remained there until his brigade crossed the James River on the morning of June 17, 1864. For additional information relating to the crossing of the James River, see Richmond, Virginia Campaign, 1864, Cold Harbor to the James River.

The organization of the Cavalry Corps during the Richmond, Virginia Campaign of 1864, including Sheridan's Richmond, Virginia Raid and Sheridan's Trevilian Station Raid, was as follows:

CAVALRY CORPS, Philip H. Sheridan

First Cavalry Division, Alfred T. A. Torbert, to May 7,
  1864, on sick leave
  Wesley Merritt, to May 26, 1864
  Alfred T. A. Torbert
  First Brigade, George A. Custer
  Second Brigade, Thomas C. Devin
  Reserve Brigade, Wesley Merritt, to May 7, 1864
    Alfred Gibbs, to May 26, 1864
    Wesley Merritt

Second Cavalry Division, David McM. Gregg
  First Brigade, Henry E. Davies, Jr.
  Second Brigade, J. Irvin Gregg

Third Cavalry Division, James H. Wilson
  First Brigade, Timothy Bryan, Jr., to May 5, 1864
    John B. McIntosh
  Second Brigade, George H. Chapman

First Brigade, Horse Artillery, James M. Robertson

Operations about Petersburg and Richmond, Virginia, June–July 1864. Wilson's Third Cavalry Division, which was with the army when it moved from Cold Harbor to the James River, crossed near Fort Powhatan June 17, 1864 and marched toward Petersburg. Wilson camped on the Blackwater River, southeast of Petersburg, June 20, 1864, and two days later he marched with his own division and August V. Kautz's Cavalry Division, Army of the James on a raid to Burkeville, Virginia to destroy the South Side Railroad and the Richmond and Danville Railroad. He successfully completed this part of his mission, and June 25, 1864, while at Roanoke Station on the Danville Railroad, he decided to return to the army. He started out toward the Weldon Railroad on the morning of June 26, 1864, and two days later reached the crossing of Stony Creek near Sappony Church. He was attacked there by Hampton's cavalry, which had been sent out to intercept him. He marched on to Reams' Station and was again strongly attacked, this time by both infantry and cavalry. As a result, he was forced to withdraw to the south to Jarrett's Station on the Weldon Railroad. Wilson managed to move on east, and then north, and finally arrived at Light House Point (or Jordan's Point) July 2, 1864. There he joined Sheridan, who had just returned from the Trevilian Station Raid with the other two divisions of the Cavalry Corps. For additional information about Wilson's raid, see Operations about Petersburg and Richmond, Virginia, 1864–1865, Operations of June 1864, Wilson's Cavalry Raid on the South Side (Lynchburg) Railroad and the Richmond and Danville Railroad.

Wilson's cavalry remained on picket duty in the vicinity of Light House Point and in the country to the south until July 29, 1864, and it then marched to the Jerusalem Plank Road. It was there when the Petersburg Mine was exploded on the front of Burnside's Ninth Corps near Petersburg July 30, 1864.

Meantime, on June 28, 1864, Sheridan's two divisions had crossed the James River on their return from Trevilian Station. Torbert had crossed at Windmill Point and marched to Prince George Court House. On July 3, 1864, he moved to Light House Point and remained in the area until the evening of July 26, 1864. Gregg's division crossed and camped that night near Fort Powhatan. The next day it marched to the Jerusalem Plank Road, and July 2, 1864, it moved to Prince George Court House. He then picketed the country about the court house and Light House Point until July 11, 1864. On July 12, 1864, Gregg again moved to the left of the army and remained near the Jerusalem Plank Road until relieved by Torbert's division July 16, 1864. It then marched to Light House Point and camped.

July 25, 1864, Grant ordered a demonstration on the north side of the James River, which was to be made in conjunction with a proposed expedition down the Weldon Railroad. The troops selected for the demonstration were Hancock's Second Corps and a cavalry force under Sheridan, consisting of two divisions of the Cavalry Corps and Kautz's Cavalry Division of the Army of the James. The principal object of this expedition was the destruction of the Virginia Central Railroad. On the evening of July 26, 1864, Sheridan, with the divisions of Torbert and Gregg, marched to Jones' Neck, and the next morning followed Second Corps across the James River at Deep Bottom. Hancock's infantry was soon engaged north of the river, and Sheridan then moved to the right and advanced to the New Market Road and the Central Road, which led to Richmond. Gregg was attacked by enemy infantry on the New Market Road July 28, 1864 and driven back, but he then dismounted his men and soon recovered the lost ground. Hancock was unable to reach the Virginia Central Railroad, and on July 29, 1864 withdrew his command to the south side of the James. The cavalry followed the infantry across the next day.

The explosion of the mine on Burnside's front was scheduled for July 30, 1864, and Gregg's division marched across the rear of Ninth Corps toward Lee's Mill to be in position to operate on the extreme left of the army in the event that Burnside's attack should be successful. The attack failed, however, and Gregg's movement was halted. Gregg's division was relieved by Torbert's division at 11:00 on the night of July 30, 1864, and the next day it formed a picket line in rear of the army from the Norfolk and Petersburg Railroad to the James River. Division headquarters was at Prince George Court House. On July 30, 1864, William Stedman relieved Davies, who was sick, in command of First Brigade, Second Cavalry Division.

Transfer of First Division and Third Division to the Shenandoah Valley, August 1864. When Jubal

A. Early became active in the Shenandoah Valley in late July 1864, Grant sent two divisions of the Cavalry Corps and the corps commander, Philip H. Sheridan, to Washington, D.C. Torbert's First Cavalry Division was ordered to City Point for embarkation July 31, 1864, and James H. Wilson's Third Cavalry Division followed August 4, 1864. Sheridan was relieved from command of the Cavalry Corps, and also from duty with the Army of the Potomac August 2, 1864, and he departed for Washington. On August 6, 1864, he was assigned command of all troops in the Department of West Virginia, and the next day he was assigned command of the newly constituted Middle Military Division. When Sheridan left the army at Petersburg, David McM. Gregg assumed command of the Cavalry Corps, and J. Irvin Gregg replaced him in command of Second Cavalry Division. David McM. Gregg remained in command of the Cavalry Corps until First Cavalry Division and Third Cavalry Division were transferred to Sheridan's command, and August 12, 1864, he resumed command of Second Cavalry Division. J. Irvin Gregg then relieved Michael Kerwin, who had commanded Second Brigade during his absence. For details of the operations of Sheridan's two cavalry divisions, see Shenandoah Valley Campaign (Sheridan).

Gregg's Second Division at Petersburg, August 1864. After Sheridan's departure, the cavalry left with Grant's army at Richmond and Petersburg consisted of Gregg's Second Cavalry Division, Army of the Potomac and Kautz's Cavalry Division, Army of the James. Gregg's division was on picket duty on the left of the infantry at Petersburg, but was relieved by Kautz's division August 12, 1864. That day, Hancock was ordered to make another demonstration against Richmond, north of the James River. The troops assigned for this expedition were Hancock's Second Corps, David B. Birney's Tenth Corps, Army of the James, and Gregg's cavalry division. August 13, 1864, Gregg's division marched by way of Point of Rocks toward Deep Bottom, where it was to join Hancock. Gregg arrived at Deep Bottom the next day, and then marched on the right of the infantry to the Charles City Road. He remained there, and was engaged in skirmishing and some more serious fighting, until August 20, 1864. J. Irvin Gregg was wounded August 16, 1864, and

Michael Kerwin assumed temporary command of his Second Brigade. Charles H. Smith arrived August 20, 1864 and relieved Kerwin.

On August 19, 1864, William Stedman's First Brigade (Davies was sick) was ordered back to the south side of the James to report to Meade. Stedman recrossed the river the next day and arrived at his camp at Prince George Court House at daylight August 21, 1864. He then marched across the Jerusalem Plank Road to the Weldon Railroad and took position on the left of Warren's Fifth Corps, which had been engaged at Globe Tavern since August 18, 1864.

On the morning of August 22, 1864, Gregg, with the Second Brigade of his division, then commanded by Charles H. Smith, joined Stedman's brigade on the Weldon Railroad. That day, Gregg's reunited division made a reconnaissance to Reams' Station. It then covered the left and front of the infantry of Hancock's Second Corps, who were then engaged in destroying the track in that area. At that time, Samuel P. Spear's Second Brigade of Kautz's cavalry division was serving with Second Corps, and August 24, 1864, Spear was placed under Gregg's orders.

Spear's brigade was on outpost duty at Malone's Crossing, south of Reams' Station, during the night of August 24, 1864, and the next morning it became engaged with Wade Hampton's cavalry. Spear was pushed back slowly to Reams' Station, where he reported to Gregg. That morning, August 25, 1864, Stedman's brigade was at the junction of the Dinwiddie Court House and Reams' Station roads, and Smith's brigade was picketing and in reserve on the left of Hancock's infantry, which was then in line of battle near Reams' Station. That afternoon a strong enemy force consisting of Hampton's cavalry and two divisions of infantry of Ambrose P. Hill's Confederate corps advanced on Hancock's line. Smith's and Spear's brigades were dismounted and placed behind the works on the left of the infantry. When the latter were driven back, the cavalry was withdrawn and remounted, and it then covered the rear of the infantry and formed a picket line extending to the Jerusalem Plank Road. Stedman's brigade remained on the Dinwiddie Court House Road until the next morning. After the Battle of Reams' Station, Spear's brigade departed to rejoin Kautz's division. Gregg's division took position between the

Gurley house and the Plank Road, and remained there during the rest of the month. For additional information about the activities of the cavalry during August 1864, see Operations about Petersburg and Richmond, Virginia, 1864–1865, Operations of August 1864, Battle of Reams' Station, Virginia.

During September 1864, Gregg's cavalry division was encamped in the vicinity of the Williams house, near the Jerusalem Plank Road, and most of the time it was engaged in picketing the left of the army, between the Weldon Railroad and the Norfolk and Petersburg Railroad. It was also engaged in a number of reconnaissances, and September 16–17, 1864, it made an unsuccessful attempt to intercept Hampton's cavalry as it was returning from a raid on a herd of grazing cattle near Coggin's Point. For details of the latter, see Operations about Petersburg and Richmond, Virginia, 1864–1865, Operations of September 1864, Siege of Petersburg.

The organization of Gregg's Second Cavalry Division during September 1864 was as follows:

Second Cavalry Division, David McM. Gregg, to September 15, 1864, on leave
    Henry E. Davies, Jr., to September 25, 1864
    David McM. Gregg
    First Brigade, William Stedman, to September 13, 1864
        Henry E. Davies, Jr., to September 15, 1864
        William Stedman, to September 25, 1864
        Henry E. Davies, Jr.
    Second Brigade, Charles H. Smith
    Artillery
        Battery A, 2nd United States Artillery, Robert Clarke

Note. Davies returned from sick leave September 13, 1864 and resumed command of First Brigade.

On September 30, 1864, Grant launched an autumn offensive against Lee's communications south and west of Petersburg. He sent Warren's Fifth Corps and Parke's Ninth Corps westward from the Weldon Railroad toward Poplar Spring Church, and ordered Gregg's cavalry division to advance on the left of the infantry along the Wyatt Road toward the Vaughan Road. Gregg remained on the Vaughan Road during the first three days of October 1864, during the infantry battles around Poplar Spring Church, Peebles' farm, and Pegram's farm. On October 4, 1864, Gregg returned to his old camps on the Jerusalem Plank Road and established a picket line that extended from the left of Ninth Corps, near the Weldon Railroad, eastward across the Plank Road. He was also under instructions to watch the main roads leading to the rear of the army between the Plank Road and the James River. The cavalry division remained on this line until late October 1864. For details of the operations of the army during the period September 29, 1864–October 3, 1864, see Operations about Petersburg and Richmond, Virginia, 1864–1865, Operations of September 1864, Battle of Poplar Spring Church (Combats at Wyatt's Farm, Peebles' Farm, Chappell's House, Pegram's Farm, and Vaughan Road), Virginia.

October 18, 1864, Gregg's Second Cavalry Division was reorganized to consist of three brigades. Charles H. Smith's 1st Maine Cavalry and 21st Pennsylvania Cavalry (the latter had been serving dismounted with the infantry before being remounted) were detached from Second Brigade and assigned to a new Third Brigade, which was to be commanded by Smith. Michael Kerwin succeeded Smith in command of Second Brigade. The 6th Ohio Cavalry was detached from First Brigade October 24, 1864, and assigned to Third Brigade. The division was then organized as follows:

Second Cavalry Division, David McM. Gregg
  First Brigade, Henry E. Davies, Jr.
  Second Brigade, Michael Kerwin
  Third Brigade, Charles H. Smith
  Artillery
    Battery I, 1st United States Artillery, Edwin L. Garvin
    Battery A, 2nd United States Artillery, William N. Dennison

Late in October 1864, Grant directed Meade to make another attempt to reach the South Side Railroad. Winfield S. Hancock was assigned command of the expedition, and he was to take with him two divisions of his Second Corps and Gregg's cavalry division. Hancock, with the infantry, was to advance on the Vaughan Road, and then by way of Dabney's Mill to the Boydton Plank Road. From there he was to move out on the White Oak Road, and then turn north toward the railroad. Gregg, who was under Hancock's orders, was to advance on the left of Second Corps by way of Rowanty Post Office and the Quaker Road. At 3:00 P.M. October 26, 1864,

Gregg's cavalry left the Jerusalem Plank Road and bivouacked that night in the vicinity of the Perkins house, near the Weldon Railroad. The next morning, both Gregg and Hancock advanced toward the Boydton Plank Road. Hancock arrived near Burgess' Mill, on Hatcher's Run, about noon; Gregg came up on the Quaker Road a short time later, and took position on the left of Second Corps. While halted near Hatcher's Run, Hancock's divisions were heavily attacked by Confederate infantry about 4:00 P.M., and they were driven back in some confusion, but with help from Kerwin's dismounted brigade on the left and Smith's brigade, also dismounted, on the right, Hancock was able to hold his position.

While Hancock was thus engaged, Wade Hampton's cavalry attacked the 21st Pennsylvania Cavalry of Smith's brigade, which was holding the Boydton Plank Road to the rear of Hancock's line. The other two regiments of Smith's brigade and three regiments of Kerwin's brigade were rushed to its assistance, and with their help Gregg held the road until night. Davies' brigade was still farther to the rear near Gravelly Run. That night, October 27, 1864, Gregg's division retired with Second Corps, and the next morning it returned to its camps on the Jerusalem Plank Road. It then reestablished its picket line in the rear of the army. For details of Hancock's advance to the Boydton Plank Road October 27–28, 1864, see Operations about Petersburg and Richmond, Virginia, 1864–1865, Operations of October 1864, Engagement at the Boydton Plank Road (or Hatcher's Run), Virginia.

Winter of 1864–1865. Gregg's cavalry division spent most of the winter on picket duty, covering the left and rear of the army, but it was also engaged in a number of reconnaissances and expeditions. During November and the early part of December 1864, it was encamped near the Jerusalem Plank Road with its picket line extending from the Weldon Railroad to the James River

December 1, 1864, Gregg marched out by way of Lee's Mill to the Jerusalem Plank Road on an expedition to Stony Creek Station (Depot), on the Weldon Railroad. He left Smith's Third Brigade to hold the bridge at Rowanty Creek and Davies' First Brigade at Duval's Station to hold the Halifax Road, and with J. Irvin Gregg's Second Brigade he pressed on and captured Stony Creek Station. Gregg destroyed the depot, shops, cars, public buildings, and large quantities of supplies. He then began his return and arrived at his camps about 11:00 that night. For additional information, see Army of the Potomac, Operations about Petersburg and Richmond, Virginia, 1864–1865, Winter of 1864–1865.

On December 7, 1864, Gregg's cavalry division joined Warren's Fifth Corps and Mott's division of Second Corps, all under Warren, on an expedition to destroy the Weldon Railroad below Stony Creek Station, toward Hicksford (present-day Emporia), Virginia. The cavalry moved ahead of the infantry on the march, and then cleared the way along the railroad during the work of destruction. The expedition reached the Meherrin River opposite Hicksford December 9, 1864, and then began its return to the army the next day. J. Irvin Gregg's brigade covered the front of the column, and the other two brigades brought up the rear. Gregg's troopers returned to their camps December 11, 1864. For details, see Operations about Petersburg and Richmond, Virginia, 1864–1865, Winter of 1864–1865, Warren's Expedition to Hicksford, Virginia.

When Warren's Fifth Corps returned to its camps between the Halifax Road and the Jerusalem Plank Road after its expedition to Hicksford, it relieved the cavalry from picket duty on the line between the two roads. December 13, 1864, Gregg was assigned to picket the country from the Jerusalem Plank Road where it connected with Fifth Corps, to the James River. Davies' First Brigade was on a line from the plank road at Gray's Church to the Norfolk and Petersburg Railroad; J. Irvin Gregg's Second Brigade extended the line from the railroad to a point east of Prince George Court House, on a road running north from Sinai Church; and Smith's Third Brigade continued the line on to the James River.

On February 5, 1865, Gregg's division was given another assignment. It marched westward by way of Reams' Station to Dinwiddie Court House to break up enemy wagon trains that were reported to be using the Boydton Plank Road to transport supplies from the Weldon Railroad to Petersburg. Gregg, however, found little activity on the Boydton Plank Road, and returned that evening to Malone's Bridge on Rowanty Creek. Meantime, Humphreys' Second Corps and Warren's Fifth Corps had moved up to be within supporting distance of Gregg if needed.

Humphreys' corps was attacked that afternoon at Armstrong's Mill on Hatcher's Run, and both Gregg and Warren were ordered to Hatcher's Run. In this movement, the cavalry covered the rear of Fifth Corps as it marched up the Vaughan Road to join Humphreys. Gregg was engaged most of February 6, 1865 in holding the Vaughan Road and driving the enemy back to Gravelly Run. During the fighting that day, Davies and J. Irvin Gregg, both commanding brigades, were wounded, and Hugh H. Janeway, colonel of the 1st New Jersey Cavalry and senior officer after Davies in First Brigade, was also wounded. Walter C. Newberry assumed command of First Brigade, and Michael Kerwin of Second Brigade. Kerwin's brigade remained in position across the Vaughan Road, but the other two brigades crossed Hatcher's Run and moved to the Halifax Road to cover the approaches from Reams' Station and Monk's Neck Bridge. Second Cavalry Division returned to its camps February 8, 1865 and resumed its picket duty on the left and rear of the army. For details of the activities of February 5–7, 1865, see Operations about Petersburg and Richmond, Virginia, 1864–1865, Winter of 1864–1865, Battle of Hatcher's Run (or Dabney's Mill, Armstrong's Mill, Rowanty Creek, Vaughan Road), Virginia.

When Gregg returned to camp February 8, 1865, he learned that his resignation, which had been submitted earlier, had been accepted, and the next day he was relieved from duty with the Army of the Potomac. Henry E. Davies, the senior officer remaining with the division, was absent on leave, and February 10, 1865, J. Irvin Gregg assumed temporary command of Second Cavalry Division. Davies returned to the army and assumed command of the division February 24, 1865. He remained in command until relieved by George Crook March 27, 1865. Crook, with Benjamin F. Kelley, had been captured at Cumberland, Maryland February 21, 1865, and had been exchanged March 20, 1865.

Return of Sheridan from the Shenandoah Valley, March 1865. March 27, 1865, Philip H. Sheridan arrived at Petersburg from the Shenandoah Valley with Thomas C. Devin's First Cavalry Division and George A. Custer's Third Cavalry Division of the Army of the Shenandoah. These two divisions constituted a special corps under the command of Wesley Merritt. They went into camp at Hancock's

Station on the Military Railroad, in front of Petersburg. By an order of March 26, 1865, Davies' Second Cavalry Division, Army of the Potomac was placed under Sheridan's orders, and was thereby removed from Meade's control.

At this time, the official status of Sheridan's command was somewhat hazy. It was treated as a separate army and received orders directly from Grant—not Meade, although the three cavalry divisions had previously belonged to the Cavalry Corps, Army of the Potomac. As organized at the end of March 1865, however, First Cavalry Division and Third Cavalry Division belonged to the Army of the Shenandoah, although they still retained the designations that they had borne in the Cavalry Corps, Army of the Potomac, and it appears that they were never officially transferred from the latter. Crook's Second Cavalry Division definitely belonged to the Army of the Potomac, but it was not under Meade's command.

Appomattox Campaign, March 29, 1865–April 9, 1865. Early on the morning of March 29, 1865, Grant's army at Petersburg began the opening movements of the campaign that would end at Appomattox Court House April 9, 1865. On the opening day, Humphreys' Second Corps and Warren's Fifth Corps moved out toward the right of the Confederate line of entrenchments at Petersburg, and Sheridan's cavalry advanced on their left toward Dinwiddie Court House. Sheridan left Custer's Third Cavalry Division at Malone's Crossing at Rowanty Creek to guard the wagon train, and with Devin's and Crook's divisions, marched on and camped that night within a mile of Dinwiddie Court House.

During March 31, 1865, Merritt moved northward from Dinwiddie Court House toward the White Oak Road with Devin's division and Davies' First Brigade of Crook's division. That afternoon he was assailed on his left flank by a strong enemy force commanded by George E. Pickett, and was driven eastward to the Boydton Plank Road. Pickett continued to advance toward Dinwidde Court House, but he was strongly opposed by Gibbs' Reserve Brigade of Devin's division and Gregg's Second Brigade and Smith's Third Brigade of Crook's division until late that evening. At that time, Custer's division came up and, together with the rest of Sheridan's cavalry, finally stopped the enemy thrust. Pickett withdrew his command to Five Forks during the night, and there he entrenched a line along the White Oak Road.

The next day, April 1, 1865, Sheridan's cavalry advanced toward Five Forks, while Warren's Fifth Corps, which earlier had arrived near Dinwiddie Court House from Hatcher's Run, moved forward on its right. Late that afternoon, Warren and Sheridan launched a heavy attack on Pickett's line at Five Forks. While the cavalry advanced on the enemy right and front of this line, Fifth Corps struck on the enemy left and rear, and together they drove Pickett's forces from the field and captured many prisoners. Meantime, Ranald S. Mackenzie's Cavalry Division, Army of the James had reported to Sheridan that morning at Dinwiddie Court House, and had been sent northward to the White Oak Road at a point east of Pickett's position. During the attack that evening, Mackenzie advanced on the right of Fifth Corps. For details of the operations of Sheridan's cavalry during the period March 29, 1865–April 1, 1865, see Appomattox Campaign, Virginia, The Opening Moves, Battle of Dinwiddie Court House, and Battle of Five Forks.

April 2, 1865, Sheridan moved northward from the battlefield of Five Forks, crossed the South Side Railroad near Ford's Church, and camped that night near Scott's Forks at the crossing of the Namozine River. Mackenzie's division joined Sheridan's column that day while on the march.

The Army of Northern Virginia evacuated Petersburg during the night of April 3, 1865, and early the next morning Grant's army started in pursuit. Sheridan, with the cavalry and Fifth Corps (then commanded by Charles Griffin), marched west along the south side of the Appomattox River toward the Richmond and Danville Railroad to block a possible attempt by Lee to escape to Danville by that route. Crook's cavalry division and Fifth Corps arrived near Jetersville April 4, 1865 and entrenched a position across the railroad, facing toward Amelia Court House, where Lee's forces were gathering. Custer and Devin joined Crook and Griffin the next morning. Mackenzie moved up to a point near Amelia Court House April 4, 1865, and remained in position there the next day to watch Lee. Meade, with Second Corps and Sixth Corps, arrived at Jetersville during the afternoon of April 5, 1865.

On April 5, 1865, Davies' brigade of Crook's division made a reconnaissance to a point beyond Paineville (Paine's Cross Roads), where it destroyed an enemy wagon train. Davies then marched back to rejoin his division, but he was soon in trouble. His rear guard was almost constantly engaged during the return until he reached Amelia Springs, where he was relieved by the other two brigades of the division.

When Lee found his way to Danville blocked at Jetersville, he turned west and during the night of April 5, 1865 marched through Deatonsville toward Rice's Station on the South Side Railroad. The next morning, Sheridan's cavalry, followed by Sixth Corps, moved out from Jetersville on a road that ran south of Lee's retreat route toward Pride's Church and the Rice's Station Road beyond. That afternoon, April 6, 1865, while Sheridan was directing Wright's Sixth Corps in the action along Little Sayler's Creek, Merritt led the three cavalry divisions on toward Rice's Station and a short distance west of the creek forced Richard H. Anderson's Confederate corps to halt. Then in a series of attacks, Merritt drove off Anderson with heavy losses in prisoners. For additional information, see Appomattox Campaign, Virginia, Pursuit of the Army of Northern Virginia, April 3–5, 1865, and also Battle of Sayler's Creek, Virginia.

The next day, the cavalry marched to the road from Rice's Station to Farmville, and followed the enemy cavalry toward the latter place. After proceeding a short distance beyond Rice's Station, Sheridan moved back with Merritt's two divisions to Prince Edward Court House. He did this to prevent a possible movement by Lee toward Danville on a road running through the latter place. Crook's division continued on toward Farmville.

Meantime, during the morning of April 7, 1865, Lee's army had crossed to the north bank of the Appomattox River, and that afternoon was assembled north of Farmville. When Crook arrived at Farmville, he crossed the river and moved out on the Maysville (or Buckingham Court House) Plank Road. A few miles north of the river Gregg's brigade attacked a guarded wagon train but was driven back. Then the enemy attacked and drove Gregg back on the rest of the division. Gregg was captured during the action, and Samuel B. M. Young assumed command of his brigade.

When Sheridan arrived at Prince Edward Court House, he found Mackenzie's cavalry occupying the town, and then, after learning from Crook that Lee was not moving in that direction, he ordered Merritt and Mackenzie to move on toward Prospect Station on the South Side Railroad. Sheridan arrived at Prospect Station on the morning of April 8, 1865, and there he assigned Mackenzie's division, then reduced to a single brigade, to Crook's division. Then, with his three cavalry divisions, he marched rapidly toward Appomattox Station in an attempt to head off Lee, who was marching toward that point on the road to Lynchburg. Edward O. C. Ord, of the Army of the James, followed the cavalry with John Gibbon's Twenty-Fourth Corps, Army of the James and Charles Griffin's Fifth Corps, Army of the Potomac.

Custer's division, which was at the head of Sheridan's column, arrived at Appomattox Station late in the evening of April 8, 1865, and captured three trains loaded with provisions for Lee's army. Custer also captured twenty five guns and William H. F. Lee's wagon train. Sheridan then formed his cavalry across the enemy's line of retreat. The next morning he was attacked in front of Appomattox Court House by John B. Gordon's infantry corps and Fitzhugh Lee's cavalry, who were attempting to break through his lines and continue the march toward Lynchburg. The Federal cavalry resisted stubbornly until relieved by Ord's infantry, who stopped the enemy advance. When the cavalry was relieved, it moved to the right of the infantry and prepared to attack the extreme left of the enemy position near Appomattox Court House. While these preparations were in progress the fighting ended, and that afternoon Lee surrendered the Army of Northern Virginia. For details of the operations of the cavalry during the final days of the campaign, see Appomattox Campaign, Virginia, Movement of the Armies to Appomattox Court House, Virginia, April 6–9, 1865.

The organization of Sheridan's cavalry during the Appomattox Campaign was as follows:

CAVALRY, Philip H. Sheridan

Army of the Shenandoah, Wesley Merritt

First Cavalry Division, Thomas C. Devin
First Brigade, Peter Stagg

Second Brigade, Charles L. Fitzhugh
Reserve Brigade, Alfred Gibbs
Artillery
    Batteries C and E, 4th United States Artillery, Marcus P. Miller

Third Cavalry Division, George A. Custer
    First Brigade, Alexander C. M. Pennington
    Second Brigade, William Wells
    Third Brigade, Henry Capehart

Army of the Potomac

Second Cavalry Division, George Crook
    First Brigade, Henry E. Davies, Jr.
    Second Brigade, J. Irvin Gregg, to April 7, 1865, captured
        Samuel B. M. Young
    Third Brigade, Charles H. Smith

Note. James H. Lord's Battery A, 2nd United States Artillery was attached to First Brigade. Chandler P. Eakin's Batteries H and L, 1st United States Artillery were assigned to Second Brigade, but were detached with Ninth Corps during the campaign.

Army of the James

Cavalry Division, Ranald S. Mackenzie
    First Brigade, Robert M. West
    Second Brigade, Samuel P. Spear. to April 1, 1865, wounded
        Andrew W. Evans
    Artillery
        4th Battery, Wisconsin Light Artillery, Dorman L. Noggle

Note 1. Mackenzie was under Edward O. C. Ord's orders until April 1, 1865, when his division was assigned to Sheridan's command.

Note 2. This division was reduced to a single brigade April 6, 1865, and West resumed command of his 5th Pennsylvania Cavalry, and Evans of his 1st Maryland Cavalry.

After Appomattox. After the surrender of the Army of Northern Virginia April 9, 1865, Joseph E. Johnston remained in the field with an army of about 30,000 men, confronting William T. Sherman in North Carolina. It was not known at that time whether Johnston would also surrender or continue to resist, and it was necessary that Grant prepare for the latter eventuality. He directed that Griffin's Fifth Corps and Gibbon's Twenty-Fourth Corps remain at Appomattox Court House until paroles were issued

and the surrendered property was removed to the railroad, and he ordered the rest of the army to move to Burkeville, where it would be in position to move onto North Carolina, if necessary.

April 11, Sheridan's command left Appomattox Court House and marched toward Burkeville. It arrived there the next day, and April 13, 1865 moved on to Nottoway Court House to refit. Merritt had been appointed as one of the commissioners (with John Gibbon and Charles Griffin) to arrange the details of the surrender of Lee's army, and during the march of the cavalry to Nottoway Court House, Custer temporarily commanded First Cavalry Division and Third Cavalry Division, Army of the Shenandoah, and Henry Capehart commanded Custer's Third Cavalry Division. Because of the poor condition of the railroad running from City Point to Nottoway Court House, Sheridan was unable to obtain supplies in sufficient quantity to refit his command and feed his horses, and so he moved his cavalry to Petersburg April 17–18, 1865.

It was Grant's intention to send the cavalry to join Sherman in South Carolina, but the start was necessarily delayed because of the poor condition of the horses and men. Finally, on April 22, 1865, Wright's Sixth Corps was placed under Sheridan's orders, and both the cavalry and infantry were ordered to proceed immediately toward Greensboro, North Carolina. Sheridan with the cavalry was to march from Petersburg by way of Boydtown and join Sixth Corps (which was to march from Burkeville along the Richmond and Danville Railroad) near the junction of the Dan River and the Staunton River.

Sheridan marched April 24, 1865 on the Boydton Plank Road by way of Dinwiddie Court House and Burchett's Bridge on the Nottoway River to the Meherrin River, where he arrived the next day. He then continued on by way of Boydton and Abbyville, and arrived at South Boston Station on the Richmond and Danville Railroad at the Dan River. Sixth Corps, which had started earlier and had a shorter distance to travel, had arrived the day before at Danville, Virginia, about thirty miles to the west and south of Boston Station.

On April 28, 1865, both Sheridan and Wright received dispatches, sent by Henry W. Halleck, and transmitted through Meade, which informed them that Johnston had surrendered to Sherman at Durham's Station two days earlier and that there was no further reason to continue their march toward North Carolina. Wright was directed to remain at Danville for the time being, but Sheridan was to return immediately to Petersburg.

Sheridan left South Boston Station April 29, 1865 and arrived at Petersburg May 3, 1865. From this time, the cavalry began to lose its identity as an organized force. May 6, 1865 at Petersburg, Sheridan turned over the command of the cavalry to Crook and departed for Washington. The next day, Crook was ordered to move the cavalry to Alexandria, Virginia. Before leaving, however, Crook detached two brigades and left them behind. As early as May 4, 1865, Sheridan had been informed of acts of lawlessness at Lynchburg, Virginia and in the vicinity, and May 9, 1865, Samuel B. M. Young's Second Brigade of Crook's Second Cavalry Division was sent there by way of Burkeville as a peace-keeping force. Young arrived at Lynchburg May 15, 1865. Charles H. Smith's Third Brigade of Crook's division was also left at Petersburg. These two brigades were officially detached from the Army of the Potomac and assigned to duty in the Department of Virginia.

The order that was finally to bring an end to the old Cavalry Corps was issued May 8, 1865. It directed that all volunteer soldiers of the cavalry command whose terms of service expired before October 1, 1865 be mustered out immediately, and that the remaining troops be consolidated into regiments.

On the morning of May 10, 1865, Crook left Petersburg for Alexandria. With him were Thomas C. Devin's First Cavalry Division and George A. Custer's Third Cavalry Division of Wesley Merritt's Army of the Shenandoah, and Henry E. Davies' First Brigade of Crook's Second Cavalry Division, Army of the Potomac. During the march, Davies' brigade was temporarily attached to Custer's division. Crook's column marched north through Richmond to the Orange and Alexandria Railroad, and then on through Catlett's Station and Fairfax Station to the vicinity of Alexandria, where all were in camp by May 17, 1865. Two days later, however, the cavalry crossed the Potomac and set up camp at Bladensburg, Maryland.

Sheridan, who had formerly led the Cavalry Corps, was relieved from command of the Middle Military Division May 17, 1865, and was assigned to the general command of the territory west of the Mississippi River and south of the Arkansas River. He left Washington before the Grand Review of the Army of the Potomac, which was held May 23, 1865, and did not ride with the cavalry on that occasion.

There is considerable confusion as to whether Crook or Merritt commanded the cavalry while it was in camp near Washington. Crook, the senior of the two officers, was clearly in command of the column during the march from Petersburg, but he was reporting progress to Sheridan as late as May 14, 1865. On May 19, 1865, however, Theodore S. Bowers of Grant's staff ordered Merritt, "commanding cavalry," to move his command to Bladensburg. In the same order, he directed Merritt to report to Meade, commanding the Army of the Potomac, for instructions regarding the Grand Review. The matter is further complicated by the fact that on the same day, May 19, 1865, Orville E. Babcock, also of Grant's staff, ordered Crook to report to Meade with his command for the Grand Review. It was Merritt who arranged the order of march for the review, and this was issued May 21, 1865 from "Headquarters Cavalry Corps." That same day, however, Bowers ordered Crook to send Peter Stagg's First Brigade, First Cavalry Division, which was Devin's division—not Crook's—to Saint Louis to report to John Pope, commander of the Military Division of the Missouri. It may be that Crook was in command of the cavalry, and that Merritt was assigned to arrange the order of march, because at that time all of the cavalry except that of Davies belonged to Merritt's Army of the Shenandoah. On the other hand, on May 22, 1865, George H. Chapman's cavalry division, then serving in the Department of Washington, was ordered to report for duty with the cavalry force at Bladensburg, which, according to the order, was under Merritt's command. It is also interesting to note that when Merritt assigned positions to the divisions and brigades in the parade, Crook's name was not mentioned, and that Davies was listed as commanding Second Cavalry Division.

A short time after the Grand Review, the Cavalry Corps as an organization ceased to exist. Sheridan was already gone, and May 22, 1865, Custer and Merritt were ordered to report to him in New Orleans. As noted above, Second Brigade and Third

Brigade of Second Cavalry Division had been detached and were serving the Department of Virginia. Stagg's First Brigade, First Cavalry Division had been sent to Missouri, and later it was sent on to Fort Leavenworth, Kansas. During the last week of May 1865, the remaining brigades of the corps were discontinued or transferred. Charles L. Fitzhugh's Second Brigade, First Cavalry Division and Alfred Gibbs' Reserve Brigade, First Cavalry Division were discontinued by muster out, consolidation, and transfer of regiments. May 26, 1865, Henry E. Davies' First Brigade, the one remaining brigade of Crook's Second Cavalry Division, was assigned to duty in the Department of Washington, and reported to Christopher C. Augur, commander of the department. The three brigades of Third Cavalry Division were discontinued, largely by muster out of the regiments.

The cavalry remaining in the Department of Washington was commanded by Crook until June 27, 1865, and then he was relieved and ordered home to report to the adjutant general of the army. Crook's command was designated as Cavalry Corps, Department of Washington.

COMMANDERS OF THE CAVALRY CORPS, ARMY OF THE POTOMAC

George Stoneman	February 7, 1863 to May 22, 1863
Alfred Pleasonton	May 22, 1863 to January 22, 1864
David McM. Gregg	January 22, 1864 to February 12, 1864
Alfred Pleasonton	February 12, 1864 to March 25, 1864
David McM. Gregg	March 25, 1864 to April 4, 1864
Philip H. Sheridan	April 4, 1864 to August 2, 1864

The Cavalry Corps, Army of the Potomac was, for all practical purposes, discontinued during the first week of August 1864. August 2, 1864, Sheridan was relieved from duty with the Cavalry Corps, and departed to assume command of the Middle Military Division and the Army of the Shenandoah. Also that week, First Cavalry Division and Third Cavalry Division left Petersburg to join Sheridan in the Shenandoah Valley. Only David McM. Gregg's Second Cavalry Division remained with the Army of the Potomac. Sheridan returned to Petersburg March 25, 1865, and brought with him, under the command of Wesley Merritt, First Cavalry Division and Third Cavalry Division. The designation of Sheridan's command, however, was Army of the Shenandoah, and it remained so until the end of the war. It was not a part of the Army of the Potomac. Sheridan commanded Grant's cavalry until May 6, 1865, and then turned it over to George Crook. Crook remained in command of what was left of cavalry until June 27, 1865, but at that time almost all of Sheridan's former command had long since departed.

MISCELLANEOUS ORGANIZATIONS

✮✮✮✮

BURNSIDE'S EXPEDITIONARY CORPS

In October 1861, Ambrose E. Burnside obtained approval for the organization of a special division for operations along the Atlantic Coast. The troops for this expedition assembled at Annapolis, Maryland, and there they were organized into a division consisting of three brigades. These were commanded by John G. Foster, Jesse L. Reno, and John G. Parke.

Early in January 1862, Burnside embarked his command on light draft vessels suitable for amphibious operations, and, supported by a naval force under Admiral Louis M. Goldsborough, sailed for the coast of North Carolina. Burnside assumed command of the newly created Department of North Carolina January 13, 1862 (assigned January 7, 1862), and then proceeded to establish Federal authority in the state. He captured Roanoke Island February 8, 1862, New Berne March 14, 1862, and Beaufort April 26, 1862, and thus secured the eastern part of the state. For more detailed information, see Department of North Carolina, January 7, 1862–July 15, 1863, Burnside's Expedition to North Carolina.

COX'S PROVISIONAL CORPS, DEPARTMENT OF NORTH CAROLINA

See Department of North Carolina, January 31, 1865–May 19, 1866.

DEFENSES OF THE UPPER POTOMAC (MORELL)

When Robert E. Lee's army recrossed the Potomac River into Virginia after the Battle of Antietam, George B. McClellan, commander of the Army of the Potomac, did not follow. Instead he ordered his corps into camp at Harper's Ferry, the mouth of Antietam Creek, Sharpsburg, Williamsport, and Hagerstown in Maryland.

The army was generally inactive until late October 1862, and then it crossed the Potomac at the beginning of its advance toward Warrenton, Virginia. When McClellan left Maryland, he relieved George W. Morell from command of First Division of Fitz John Porter's Fifth Corps, and assigned him to the command of the troops remaining on the river between the mouth of Antietam Creek and Cumberland, Maryland. Morell's new command was designated as the Defenses of the Upper Potomac. Henry W. Slocum's Twelfth Corps was left by McClellan at Harper's Ferry, but this was not included in Morell's command.

Morell assumed command November 1, 1862. At that time his force consisted of the following: George H. Gordon's Third Brigade, First Division, Twelfth Corps, which was detached from the corps, was on the left near Sharpsburg; John R. Kenly's Maryland Brigade was at Williamsport, on the center of Morell's line; and Benjamin F. Kelley's Railroad Division of the District of Western Virginia, Department of the Ohio was on the right at Cumberland and New Creek. In addition, Andrew T. McReynolds' Fourth Cavalry Brigade, Army of the Potomac, which was at Cumberland, was transferred to the Defenses of the Upper Potomac. Morell's command was enlarged November 14, 1862 when he was assigned command of all forces in the vicinity of Harper's Ferry and on the upper Potomac.

The Defenses of the Upper Potomac was under McClellan's control and was, in effect, a district of the Army of the Potomac until it was discontinued in December 1862. December 16, 1862, Morell was directed to turn over his command to Kelley, who was then assigned command of all forces on the upper Potomac, and was also charged with the defense of the Baltimore and Ohio Railroad to the west. December 22, 1862, Robert C. Schenck, commander of the Middle Department and Eighth Corps, was assigned command of the railroad from Baltimore to the Ohio River, and Kelley was placed under his control.

For additional information, see the following: Army of the Potomac, Antietam to Warrenton, Virginia; and Middle Department, Troops in the Middle Department, Eighth Corps.

DEFENSES OF WASHINGTON, D.C.

From the firing on Fort Sumter to the end of the war, the protection of Washington, D.C. was of primary concern to the Federal authorities. Not only was it the national capital, but, especially during the early part of the war, it was also the assembly point for troops and supplies that were to form and maintain the Union armies in the East. No important campaign or troop movements were undertaken without first providing for the safety of Washington. In addition, it provided a fortified rear area upon which a defeated army could retire, as after the First and Second Battles of Bull Run (Manassas), and it also afforded such security for the Army of the Potomac at Antietam, Fredericksburg, Chancellorsville, Gettysburg, and the beginning of Grant's Virginia Campaign of 1864.

DEFENSIVE WORKS

At the outbreak of war Washington was virtually defenseless. The only fortification was Fort Washington, an obsolete work located about eleven miles below the city on the Maryland side of the Potomac River. Then, on May 23–24, 1861, Union regiments crossed the Potomac from Washington and occupied the nearby hills in Virginia, covering the southern approaches to the city.

After the defeat of Irvin McDowell's army at Bull Run in July 1861, the importance of a better system of defenses was clearly recognized, and earthworks were then built in the most strategic positions on the hills surrounding Washington.

In December 1862, recommendations were submitted for the completion of the system of fortifications, and by the end of the war in 1865, the defenses of Washington consisted of sixty-eight enclosed forts and batteries located on a total perimeter of thirteen miles. In addition, there were ninety-three unarmed batteries for field guns and twenty miles of rifle trenches connecting the principal works. The entire circuit, from Fort Willard below Alexandria around to Fort Greble on the opposite side of the Potomac, was thirty-four miles.

These defenses were generally divided into two subordinate commands. These were the Defenses North of the Potomac and the Defenses South of the Potomac.

Below are listed the principal forts in the Defenses of Washington. These are given in order, from left to right, beginning at Fort Willard on the Virginia side of the Potomac, below Alexandria, and ending at Fort Greble on the Maryland side of the river below Washington.

Defenses South of the Potomac

From the Potomac River to Cameron Run (the Orange and Alexandria Railroad)
Fort Willard; Fort Lyon.

From Cameron Run to Four-Mile Creek (the Loudoun and Hampshire Railroad)
Fort Ellsworth (near Alexandria on the Little River Turnpike); Fort Worth (in front of Fort Ellsworth near the Little River Turnpike); Fort Ward (just south of the Leesburg Turnpike); Fort Blenker (just north of the Leesburg Turnpike).

From Four-Mile Run to the Columbia Turnpike
Fort Barnard (near the Loudoun and Hampshire

Railroad); Fort Richardson (south of the Columbia Turnpike); Fort Albany and Fort Runyon (behind Fort Richardson, on the Columbia Turnpike, near the south end of Long Bridge).

From the Columbia Turnpike to the road running from Aqueduct Bridge to Ball's Cross Roads and Falls Church

Fort Craig; Fort McPherson; Fort Tillinghast; Fort Whipple; Fort Cass; Fort Woodbury.

The above forts are located generally on a north-south line in front of Arlington, Virginia.

From the Aqueduct Bridge Road to the Potomac River, one mile west of Georgetown

Fort DeKalb (on the west side of the Aqueduct Bridge Road); Fort Haggerty; Fort Corcoran; and Fort Bennett (in rear of Fort Woodbury and Fort DeKalb, and in front of the Aqueduct Bridge to Georgetown); Fort Strong; Fort C. F. Smith.

Near Chain Bridge

Fort Ethan Allen; Fort Marcy (on the Leesburg and Georgetown Turnpike).

Defenses North of the Potomac

From the Potomac River to the Rockville Road

Fort Sumner (located on the Potomac above Chain Bridge, and was formed when three small works—Fort Alexander, Fort Franklin, and Fort Ripley—were combined in 1863); Fort Mansfield; Fort Simmons; Fort Bayard (near the Rockville Road).

Rockville Road to the Seventh Street Road, which ran to Silver Spring, Maryland

Fort Reno (formerly Fort Pennsylvania, near Tennallytown); Fort Kearny; Fort DeRussy (commanded the valley of Rock Creek); Fort Stevens (originally constructed as Fort Massachusetts in August 1861, but was enlarged and renamed Fort Stevens in 1863. It was located on the Seventh Street Road, just south of Silver Spring).

Seventh Street Road to the Washington Branch of the Baltimore and Ohio Railroad

Fort Slocum; Fort Totten (on the Bladensburg Road); Fort Slemmer; Fort Bunker Hill; Fort Saratoga; Fort Thayer.

Washington Branch of the Baltimore and Ohio Railroad to the Eastern Branch (Anacostia River)

Fort Lincoln (overlooked the Baltimore Turnpike).

Eastern Branch to the Potomac River

Fort Mahan (on the Benning Road in front of Benning Bridge over the Eastern Branch); Fort Meigs; Fort Dupont; Fort Davis; Fort Baker; Fort Wagner; Fort Ricketts; Fort Stanton; Fort Snyder; Fort Carroll; Fort Greble.

TROOPS GUARDING WASHINGTON

The troops responsible for the protection of Washington might generally be regarded as belonging to two types of organizations. First, there were the garrison troops of the fortifications, who were capable of defending the city from small raids. In addition, during most of the war, there were mobile forces deployed in Virginia and Maryland for the purpose of defending the city from more determined attacks by larger enemy forces. The latter consisted of the field armies and the troops of the several departments that, at various times, included Washington or the territory near the city. A brief outline of these commands follows.

Department of Washington, April 9, 1861–August 17, 1861. During this period the troops in and near Washington belonged to the Department of Washington. May 23–24, 1861, a volunteer force from the Department of Washington crossed the Potomac River into Virginia, and occupied Alexandria and Arlington Heights. For details, see Department of Washington, April 9, 1861–August 17, 1861.

Department of Northeastern Virginia. Three days after the occupation of Alexandria and Arlington Heights, the Department of Northeastern Virginia was created and assigned to the command of Irvin McDowell. The southern approaches to Washington were included in McDowell's department, and in this area he assembled the forces arriving in

Washington and organized them into brigades and divisions as the Army of Northeastern Virginia. This was the army that fought at Bull Run in July 1861. For details, see Department of Northeastern Virginia.

Military Division of the Potomac. On July 25, 1861, after McDowell's defeat at Bull Run, George B. McClellan was called to Washington from Western Virginia to assume command of the new Military Division of the Potomac. This consisted of the departments of Washington and Northeastern Virginia. McClellan assumed command July 27, 1861, and continued the work which had been begun by McDowell in organizing the regiments arriving in Washington into what became known as the Army of the Potomac. For details, see Army of the Potomac.

Department of the Potomac. August 17, 1861, the Department of Washington and the Department of Northeastern Virginia were merged into the Department of the Potomac under McClellan. During the fall and winter of 1861–1862, the Army of the Potomac remained near Washington and along the Potomac River as it prepared for offensive operations in the spring. For details, see Army of the Potomac.

When the Army of the Potomac was transferred to the Peninsula in late March and early April 1862, McClellan was directed to leave behind sufficient troops to protect Washington. The troops assigned for this purpose consisted of Irvin McDowell's First Corps, Nathaniel P. Banks' Fifth Corps, and Louis Blenker's division of Edwin V. Sumner's Second Corps. McDowell's corps was near Alexandria and later moved to Fredericksburg. Banks' corps was in the Shenadoah Valley. Blenker's division was in front of Washington for a time, and was then sent to the Shenandoah Valley and later joined John C. Fremont in the Mountain Department.

District of Washington. March 17, 1862, James S. Wadsworth was assigned as military governor of the District of Columbia and was directed to assume military command of the city of Washington and of the defenses north and south of the Potomac River in the vicinity of Washington. The limits of his command were described as consisting of the District of Columbia, the city of Alexandria, the ground in front of and in the vicinity of the defensive works south of the Potomac from the Occoquan to Difficult Creek, and the post of Fort Washington. He was also placed in charge of the Provisional Brigades, which were composed of new troops arriving in Washington, and also of the other troops in the city.

Department of the Rappahannock. The Department of the Rappahannock was created April 4, 1862, and the District of Washington was included within its limits. McDowell was assigned command of the new department, and he then moved his former First Corps, Army of the Potomac to Fredericksburg to cover the southern approaches to Washington.

Department of the Shenandoah. The Department of the Shenandoah was created April 4, 1862, under the command of Nathaniel P. Banks. The troops in this department belonged to Banks' former Fifth Corps, Army of the Potomac, and they were retained in the Shenandoah Valley to guard against a possible enemy advance on Washington from that direction.

Army of Virginia (Pope). The Army of Virginia was constituted June 26, 1862, to consist of the troops of the Mountain Department and the departments of the Rappahannock and the Shenandoah. John Pope was assigned command. The army was assembled in the Culpeper Court House area, and a part of it was engaged with Thomas J. (Stonewall) Jackson's corps at Cedar Mountain August 9, 1862. Pope was then outmaneuvered by Robert E. Lee's army, and forced to fall back to Bull Run, where he was defeated August 29–30, 1862. At that time a part of the Army of the Potomac had joined Pope and shared in his defeat. Pope's forces then retreated into the safety of the Defenses of Washington. For details, see Pope's Northern Virginia Campaign.

When the Department of the Rappahannock was merged into the Army of Virginia as Third Corps, Wadsworth's District of Washington was not included. During the Northern Virginia Campaign of July and August 1862, Wadsworth continued in command at Washington, under Pope's jurisdiction.

Army of the Potomac. During Lee's advance against Pope's army in Virginia in August 1862, troops of the the Army of the Potomac were arriving from the Peninsula at Aquia Creek and Alexandria, and they joined the Army of Virginia in covering the southern approaches to Washington. Following the defeat of Pope at the Second Battle of Bull Run, both armies retired within the Defenses of Washington, where they were reorganized by George B. McClellan into the Army of the Potomac.

Military District of the Defenses of Washington. August 20, 1862, John G. Barnard assumed command of the fortifications of Washington and the troops assigned to their defense. September 2, 1862, Barnard's command became the Military District of the Defenses of Washington, Army of the Potomac. McClellan relieved Barnard September 2, 1862, and remained in command until the departure of the army September 8, 1862, at the beginning of the Maryland Campaign. Nathaniel P. Banks commanded the district from September 8, 1862 until October 27, 1862, when he was relieved by Samuel P. Heintzelman. This command was continued as a district of the Army of the Potomac until it was reorganized as the Department of Washington February 7, 1863 (ordered February 2, 1863). During the period September 2–8, 1862, the troops of the Army of Virginia and the Army of the Potomac were reorganized under McClellan into the Army of the Potomac that he led at the battles of South Mountain and Antietam. For details, see the following: Military District of the Defenses of Washington, and Maryland Campaign (South Mountain and Antietam).

Department of Washington, Twenty-Second Corps. February 7, 1863, the Department of Washington was organized from the Military District of the Defenses of Washington, and the troops in the new department were designated as Twenty-Second Corps. Samuel P. Heintzelman assumed command of the department and Twenty-Second Corps February 7, 1863 (assigned February 2, 1863), and he was relieved by Christopher C. Augur October 14, 1863. This department remained in existence until after the end of the war. For details, see Department of Washington, February 2, 1863–March 16, 1869. Also, for additional information, see the following: Middle Department, Gettysburg Campaign, and Early's Washington Raid (and Operations in the Shenandoah Valley, Maryland, and Pennsylvania).

MILITARY DISTRICT OF THE DEFENSES OF WASHINGTON, ARMY OF THE POTOMAC SEPTEMBER 2, 1862–FEBRUARY 2, 1863

The term "Defenses of Washington" was generally used throughout the war to refer to the fortifications constructed to protect the national capital and the troops assigned to occupy them. For a comparatively brief but very important period, however, the Defenses of Washington were specifically organized as a military district, which was designated as the Military District of the Defenses of Washington, Army of the Potomac. The district was discontinued February 2, 1863, when it was merged into the Department of Washington, and the troops of the Department of Washington, formerly of the District of the Defenses of Washington, were designated as Twenty-Second Corps.

The commanders of the district were as follows:

John G. Barnard	August 19, 1862 to September 2, 1862
George B. McClellan	September 2, 1862 to September 8, 1862
Nathaniel P. Banks	September 8, 1862 to October 27, 1862
Samuel P. Heintzelman	October 27, 1862 to February 2, 1863

TROOPS IN THE DISTRICT OF THE DEFENSES OF WASHINGTON

The organization and activities of the troops serving in the District of the Defenses of Washington during the period of its existence were very complex and almost constantly changing. When first organized, the only troops present were those manning the defensive lines north and south of the Potomac River, those in the District of Washington, and Silas Casey's Provisional Brigades. Thereafter, however, many organizations, ranging from armies to regiments, entered the district, departed from it, or passed through it, and this caused an almost constant change in the composition of the forces serving there. The description of these troops is presented in the following sections.

The Defenses under Barnard
August 18, 1862–September 2, 1862

In July and August 1862, Washington was the principal base for John Pope's Army of Virginia, which was then operating in Virginia, southwest of the city. When Robert E. Lee's Army of Northern Virginia advanced against Pope and forced him to withdraw eastward, first from the line of the Rapidan River and then from the Rappahannock River, the authorities in Washington made preparations for a better organization of the defenses of the city. On August 19, 1862, John G. Barnard of the engineers was assigned command (assumed command August 20, 1862) of the fortifications and the troops provided for their defense. These works consisted of a ring of forts completely surrounding the city, and a line of outer works south of the Potomac on such high points as Munson's Hill, Upton's Hill, Hall's Hill, and Perkins' Hill. For a description of these works, see above, Defenses of Washington, D.C.

The troops defending the fortifications, as organized under Barnard in August 1862, were as follows:

DEFENSES OF WASHINGTON, John G. Barnard

Defenses South of the Potomac, Amiel W. Whipple
    Whipple's Division, Amiel W. Whipple
        First Brigade, William B. Greene
        Second Brigade, Thomas D. Doubleday
        Fellows' Brigade, Enoch Q. Fellows
        Van Valkenburg's Brigade, Robert B. Van Valkenburg

Note 1. Doubleday's brigade was designated as Third Brigade in September 1862, and during the same month became Second Brigade of John J. Abercrombie's Division (see below).

Note 2. From September 1862 to February 1863, Greene's brigade was known as First Artillery Brigade, Defenses of Washington and was commanded by Greene and Milton Cogswell.

Note 3. Whipple's command extended from Four-Mile

Run (the line of the Alexandria, Loudoun, and Hampshire Railroad) northward along the line of the forts to the Potomac River beyond Chain Bridge.

Defenses North of the Potomac, Joseph A. Haskin
    Unbrigaded troops consisting of infantry regiments and artillery

District of Washington, James S. Wadsworth
    Provisional Brigades, Silas Casey

Beginning on August 31, 1862, the troops of Pope's Army of Virginia, and McClellan's Army of the Potomac, which had joined Pope's army from the Peninsula, began to arrive in the Defenses of Washington, and these were quickly disposed to meet a possible attack from Lee's victorious Army of Northern Virginia. The positions taken by these troops are given below under the headings of the different organizations present.

Kanawha Division. August 30, 1862, Jacob D. Cox's Kanawha Division, which had just arrived from Western Virginia, was ordered into the outer defenses south of the Alexandria, Loudoun, and Hampshire Railroad. Eliakim P. Scammon's First Brigade occupied Munson's Hill, and Augustus Moor's Second Brigade took position on Perkins' Hill.

Abercrombie's Division. A brigade under John J. Abercrombie arrived at Alexandria September 1, 1862, and the next day it marched, together with some troops of Darius N. Couch's First Division, Fourth Corps, to the vicinity of Chain Bridge. There, Abercrombie was assigned command of nearby Fort Ethan Allen and Fort Marcy. His command, which then consisted of his own brigade and Thomas D. Doubleday's Second Brigade, formerly of Amiel W. Whipple's Division, was designated as Abercrombie's Division, Defenses of Washington.

Woodbury's Independent Command. On September 1, 1862, an independent command was constituted under Daniel P. Woodbury, commander of the Engineer Brigade. Woodbury's command consisted of the fortifications and troops guarding the western approaches to Alexandria from Four-Mile Run (the Alexandria, Loudoun, and Hampshire Railroad) at Fort Blenker, southward across Cameron Run (the Orange and Alexandria Railroad) to Fort Lyon, including Fort Ward and Fort Worth. This command consisted of the following: Woodbury's Engineer Brigade at Fort Lyon, Erastus B. Tyler's Brigade of new regiments, Peter H. Allabach's Provisional Brigade at Fort Ward, Robert O. Tyler's 1st Connecticut Heavy Artillery, and 16th Connecticut Infantry. Also present at Alexandria were 33rd Massachusetts, 34th Massachusetts, and 68th Illinois. These regiments were under the command of John M. Slough, military governor of the city.

Army of Virginia. When the three corps of the Army of Virginia arrived at Washington after their defeat at Bull Run, they were assigned positions in the Defenses as follows: Franz Sigel's First Corps was sent to Fort Ethan Allen to guard the roads leading to the Chain Bridge; Nathaniel P. Banks' Second Corps was ordered north of the Potomac to Rockville, Maryland; and Irvin McDowell's Third Corps was assigned position at Ball's Cross Roads, on the road south from Aqueduct Bridge.

The three cavalry brigades of the Army of Virginia accompanied the army into the Defenses of Washington. These were John Beardsley's brigade of Sigel's First Corps, John Buford's brigade of Banks' Second Corps, and George D. Bayard's brigade of McDowell's Third Corps. Buford was announced as chief of cavalry, Army of the Potomac September 10, 1862, and was succeeded in command of his brigade by R. Butler Price. Bayard's and Buford's (later Price's) brigades covered the ground in front of Porter's command on the line of defenses (see below), and Beardsley's brigade remained with First Corps, Army of Virginia.

Army of the Potomac. The corps of the Army of the Potomac, which came into Washington with the Army of Virginia, were assigned positions as follows: Edwin V. Sumner's Second Corps was sent north of the Potomac to Rockville, Maryland; Samuel P. Heintzelman's Third Corps took position at Fort Lyon; Fitz John Porter's Fifth Corps was stationed at Hall's Hill; and William B. Franklin's Sixth Corps was at the Theological Seminary near Alexandria. On September 4, 1862, Erastus B. Tyler's brigade of the Defenses of Washington was ordered to report to Franklin.

Darius N. Couch's First Division, Fourth Corps,

Army of the Potomac arrived at Alexandria from the Peninsula August 30, 1862–September 1, 1862, and the leading troops were sent out toward Centerville to guard the Orange and Alexandria Railroad. The rest of the division marched with John J. Abercrombie's brigade to the vicinity of Chain Bridge.

On September 1, 1862, Alfred Pleasonton's Cavalry Brigade, Army of the Potomac arrived at Alexandria from the Peninsula; and William W. Averell's cavalry brigade, also of the Army of the Potomac, followed September 5, 1862. Shortly thereafter, the regiments of these brigades, together with some regiments from the Defenses of Washington, were organized into a cavalry division of the Army of the Potomac under the command of Alfred Pleasonton. This division did not serve in the Defenses of Washington, but accompanied the Army of the Potomac on its campaign in Maryland. For details of the organization of the cavalry division, see Maryland Campaign (South Mountain and Antietam).

Ninth Corps. Jesse L. Reno's Detachment Ninth Corps, which consisted of his own Second Division and First Division, temporarily commanded by Benjamin C. Christ, arrived in Washington with the Army of Virginia and was sent north of the city to Leesboro, Maryland. On August 31, the day after Pope's defeat at Bull Run, Ambrose E. Burnside, then at Falmouth, Virginia, was ordered to bring John G. Parke's Third Division, Ninth Corps to Washington. This division, consisting of Harrison S. Fairchild's First Brigade and Edward Harland's Second Brigade, embarked at Aquia Creek September 4–6, 1862 and rejoined the corps. Parke was assigned as Burnside's chief of staff, and Isaac P. Rodman assumed command of Third Division.

Defenses of Washington under McClellan September 2, 1862–September 8, 1862

Following the defeat of John Pope's army at Bull Run (Manassas) August 30, 1862, George B. McClellan, who was then at Alexandria without command, was called to Washington, and September 2, 1862 relieved Barnard in command of the Defenses of Washington. At that time, the defenses were constituted as the Military District of the Defenses of Washington, Army of the Potomac. That same day, the limits of the district were extended to include that part of Maryland lying within a line from Fort Washington on the Potomac, northward to Annapolis Junction, and then west to the mouth of Seneca Creek. This territory remained in the Defenses of Washington until the Department of Washington was created February 2, 1863.

When McClellan assumed command, he was faced with an extremely difficult situation. During the first few days of September 1862, the somewhat disorganized corps of the Army of Virginia and of the Army of the Potomac retreated to within the comparative safety of the defensive works south of the Potomac. Lee's intentions were not known, but it was clearly necessary to organize and prepare Pope's army and the garrison of the Defenses of Washington for a possible attack by the Army of Northern Virginia. The attack did not materialize, however, because on September 3, 1862, Lee's army disappeared from the Washington front and marched toward the fords of the Potomac near Leesburg, and there it crossed into Maryland September 4–7, 1862. With this new threat in Maryland, McClellan began the necessary reorganization of the Army of the Potomac for field service to go in pursuit of Lee and, at the same time, to arrange for the security of the capital after his army had departed.

As a first step in the reorganization, the Army of Virginia and the Army of the Potomac were consolidated September 5, 1862 by an order from the adjutant general's office, and Pope was directed to report to the secretary of war.

McClellan also began to shift additional troops from the south to the north side of the Potomac for his field army. On September 4, 1862, Couch's division of Fourth Corps was ordered to Tennallytown, D.C. to guard the northwestern approaches to Washington, and the next day Cox was sent to Leesboro, Maryland with his Kanawha Division for assignment to Reno's command of Ninth Corps. On September 6, 1862, McDowell's Third Corps, Army of Virginia also moved to Leesboro, and William B. Franklin's Sixth Corps and George Sykes' Second Division of Fitz John Porter's Fifth Corps, Army of the Potomac were sent to Tennallytown. Sykes'

division was to constitute a reserve for the Army of the Potomac, and Sykes then reported directly to McClellan. Earlier, Banks' Second Corps, Army of Virginia and Edwin V. Sumner's Second Corps, Army of the Potomac had been sent to Rockville, Maryland.

On September 7, 1862, McClellan, with his field forces of the Army of the Potomac, left the vicinity of Washington and marched toward Frederick, Maryland. For details of the reorganization of the army, which was completed on the march, and also of its operations in Maryland during September 1862, see Maryland Campaign (South Mountain and Antietam). When McClellan departed, he left behind in Virginia for the protection of the capital Heintzelman's Third Corps, Army of the Potomac; Sigel's First Corps, Army of Virginia (after September 12, 1862, designated as Eleventh Corps, Army of the Potomac); George W. Morell's First Division, Fifth Corps, Army of the Potomac; the cavalry brigades of Bayard and Buford; and the garrison troops of the Defenses South of the Potomac. In addition, John F. Reynolds' division of McDowell's Third Corps, Army of Virginia was temporarily detached and left briefly at Fort Albany near Long Bridge, but it then rejoined the corps.

Defenses of Washington under Banks and Heintzelman September 8, 1862–February 2, 1863

While in the Defenses of Washington, Banks, commanding Second Corps, Army of Virginia, became ill, and September 3, 1862, Alpheus S. Williams assumed temporary command of the corps. When the Army of the Potomac departed for Frederick September 7, 1862, Banks was unable to march with his corps and was assigned command of the District of the Defenses of Washington in place of McClellan, who left with the army. Banks assumed command September 8, 1862, and the next day Heintzelman was placed in command of the Defenses South of the Potomac, subject to Banks' orders. Banks remained in command of the district until October 27, 1862, and he then left the army to assume command of the Department of the Gulf. He was succeeded in command of the district by Heintzelman, who remained in command until

February 2, 1862, when the District of the Defenses of Washington was discontinued.

When Banks assumed command, the defensive line of works south of the Potomac was organized as follows: Porter's command, which consisted of Morell's First Division, Fifth Corps and Whipple's Division of the Defenses of Washington, occupied all the forts from Fort De Kalb, southwest of Georgetown, D.C. to Hunting Creek (Cameron Run) near Alexandria. Porter also issued orders to Bayard's and Buford's cavalry brigades, which were operating on his front. Sigel's First Corps, Army of Virginia was on the right of the line, with its left connecting with Porter near Fort De Kalb; and Heintzelman's Third Corps, Army of the Potomac occupied the left of the Union line from Hunting Creek to the Potomac River below Alexandria. North of the Potomac River, Joseph A. Haskin was in charge of the works from the river above Washington to the Eastern Branch, and Woodbury was in command of the forts from the Eastern Branch to the river below Washington.

During the period September 8, 1862–February 2, 1863, when the district was discontinued, there were many changes in the organization and disposition of the troops in the Defenses of Washington. These can best be understood by reference to the following general summary.

When McClellan departed on his Maryland Campaign, he left behind about 47,000 men belonging to the Army of Virginia and the Army of the Potomac. There were also about 15,000 men of the garrison of the Defenses of Washington, and about 11,000 men of Casey's Provisional Brigades, and this made a grand total of about 73,000 men—approximately one-half of McClellan's entire army. This number was rapidly increased by new levies to more than 80,000 before Porter's Fifth Corps was sent to McClellan September 12, 1862. About 36,000 men, however, were sent to the army in the field during the last three weeks of September, and another 29,000 in October 1862. These troops belonged to the following organizations: Porter's Fifth Corps (Morell's and Andrew A. Humphreys' divisions) (15,500); twenty new regiments under Henry S. Briggs (18,500); George Stoneman's First Division, Third Corps and Whipple's Division, Defenses of Washington (15,000); and convalescents and stragglers (16,000).

In addition to the above, Bayard's Cavalry Brigade; Daniel E. Sickles' Second Division, Third Corps; Sigel's Eleventh Corps (formerly First Corps, Army of Virginia); and 12,000 more men from the Defenses of Washington were sent to the army during November and December 1862.

The organizations serving in the District of the Defenses of Washington during the period September 8, 1862–February 2, 1863, and a brief description of their composition, command, and service are given in the following sections.

Fifth Corps, Army of the Potomac. Only First Division of Fifth Corps was with Porter early in September 1862; John F. Reynolds' Third Division (formerly George McCall's) was transferred to McDowell's Third Corps, Army of Virginia August 26, 1862, during Pope's Virginia Campaign; and George Sykes' Second Division was detached September 6, 1862, and was sent to Tennallytown as reserve for the Army of the Potomac. September 8, 1862, Sykes was ordered into Maryland to join the army, and after that date Sykes reported directly to McClellan. Porter's First Division was organized as follows:

FIFTH CORPS, Fitz John Porter

First Division, George W. Morell
  First Brigade, James Barnes
  Second Brigade, Charles Griffin
  Third Brigade, Thomas B. W. Stockton

Note 1. Barnes commanded First Brigade in place of John H. Martindale, who was absent.
Note 2. Stockton commanded Third Brigade in place of Daniel Butterfield, who was absent.

September 11, 1862, Porter was ordered, with Morell's division, to join the army in the field, and the next day he left for Brookville, Maryland. A new Third Division, Fifth Corps was organized September 12, 1862 from Erastus B. Tyler's Brigade and Peter H. Allabach's Brigade, both of Whipple's Division, District of the Defenses of Washington. Andrew A. Humphreys was assigned command of the division. The two brigades left for Brookville September 14, 1862 to join Porter. Whipple, with A. Sanders Piatt's brigade of his division, was left in the Defenses of Washington. For information about Whipple's Division, see below.

Third Corps, Army of the Potomac. The organization of Third Corps, Army of the Potomac in the Defenses of Washington in early September 1862 was as follows:

THIRD CORPS, Samuel P. Heintzelman

First Division, Philip Kearny, to September 1, 1862, killed
   David B. Birney, to September 15, 1862
   George Stoneman
   First Brigade, John C. Robinson
   Second Brigade, David B. Birney, to September 1, 1862
      J. H. Hobart Ward, to September 15, 1862
      David B. Birney
   Third Brigade, Orlando M. Poe
      Hiram Berry

Second Division, Joseph Hooker, to September 5, 1862
   Cuvier Grover, to October 1862
   Daniel E. Sickles
   First Brigade, Cuvier Grover, to September 5, 1862
      Joseph B. Carr
   Second Brigade, Nelson Taylor, to September 5, 1862
      George B. Hall
   Third Brigade, Francis E. Patterson

Note. Sickles had been sent to New York on recruiting service July 10, 1862, and was not present with the army during Pope's Virginia Campaign.

When Porter's Fifth Corps left the Defenses of Washington to join the Army of the Potomac in Maryland, Third Corps was extended to occupy the lines as follows: David B. Birney's First Division was moved to the right to occupy Porter's former positions north of Cameron Run (the Orange and Alexandria Railroad), and Cuvier Grover's Second Division held the line from Cameron Run to the Potomac River below Alexandria.

After George Stoneman assumed command of First Division, Third Corps September 15, 1862, he was sent with Birney's Second Brigade to Poolesville, Maryland as a corps of observation. His command consisted of Birney's brigade and two regiments (10th Vermont and 39th Massachusetts) under Albert Jewett, which had been on the upper Potomac for some time. On October 10, 1862, James E. B. (Jeb) Stuart led a cavalry force across the Potomac River on a raid through Maryland and Pennsylvania, and around the Army of the Potomac. Stoneman was given the important assignment of guarding the fords of the Potomac to prevent Stuart

from recrossing into Virginia. In this he was unsuccessful, however, and Stuart crossed to safety at White's Ford, near the mouth of the Monocacy River, October 12, 1862. On the day that Stuart crossed into Maryland, the other two brigades of Stoneman's division were ordered to Poolesville from their positions near Alexandria. John C. Robinson's First Brigade arrived October 12, 1862, and Hiram G. Berry's Third Brigade, then commanded by Orlando M. Poe, followed soon after, but neither brigade arrived in time to interfere with Stuart's movements. Henry G. Staples was in temporary command of Birney's Second Brigade October 10–12, 1862, and he in turn was relieved by J. H. Hobart Ward. Stoneman's division, thus reunited, took positions along the Potomac from the mouth of Seneca Creek to the mouth of Monocacy.

The same order of October 10, 1862 that directed the concentration of Stoneman's division at Poolesville also detached the division from the District of the Defenses of Washington and assigned it to McClellan's Army of the Potomac in the field. Before the division reported to McClellan, the two regiments originally at Poolesville (10th Vermont and 39th Massachusetts) were detached and formed into a brigade under Jewett to guard the upper Potomac. Cuvier Grover relieved Jewett October 14, 1862, and the brigade was then called Grover's Brigade. Stoneman's First Division, Third Corps was attached to Ninth Corps, Army of the Potomac, but it was then detached and assigned to a special force under Ambrose E. Burnside as Stoneman's Division. For more information about this command, see Army of the Potomac, Antietam to Warrenton, Virginia.

After Stoneman's departure, only Daniel E. Sickles' Second Division of Third Corps was left in the District of the Defenses of Washington. Grover, who had been relieved in command of the division by Sickles, was assigned to Jewett's detached brigade at Poolesville, which was then designated as Grover's Independent Brigade. Grover was relieved from duty with the Army of the Potomac by an order of November 10, 1862, and he left a short time later to report to Nathaniel P. Banks for assignment in the Department of the Gulf.

During October 1862, Franz Sigel's Eleventh Corps was on duty along the Orange and Alexandria

Railroad (see below), and on November 2, 1862, it was ordered forward on the Manassas Gap Railroad to Thoroughfare Gap. Sickles' Second Division, Third Corps was then moved forward from its positions near Alexandria to relieve the troops of Eleventh Corps. Sickles established his headquarters at Manassas Junction, and posted his brigades as follows: Joseph B. Carr's First Brigade was on the railroad from Burke's Station to Bull Run Bridge; Francis E. Patterson's Third Brigade extended the line from Bull Run Bridge to Manassas; George B. Hall's Second Brigade from Manassas to Kettle Run; and a Provisional Brigade under William Blaisdell was in position from Kettle Run to Warrenton Junction.

November 25, 1862, Sickles was ordered to move with his division to Potomac Creek, north of Falmouth, Virginia to rejoin Third Corps, which had been reorganized with the Army of the Potomac under Stoneman. For additional information, see Fredericksburg, Virginia Campaign. When Sickles' division left the District of the Defenses of Washington, it was replaced along the railroad by troops of Casey's Division, Defenses of Washington.

Eleventh Corps, Army of the Potomac. On September 12, 1862, the designation of Franz Sigel's First Corps, Army of Virginia, which had been left in the Defenses of Washington when McClellan marched into Maryland, was changed to Eleventh Corps, Army of the Potomac. The corps was organized as follows:

ELEVENTH CORPS, Franz Sigel

First Division, Julius Stahel
First Brigade, Adolphus Buschbeck, to September 12, 1862
Leopold Von Gilsa
Second Brigade, Nathaniel C. McLean

Second Division, Adolph Von Steinwehr
First Brigade, George A. Muhleck
Unbrigaded cavalry regiments and artillery

Note. A Second Brigade was organized October 25, 1862, under Orland Smith.

Third Division, Carl Schurz
First Brigade, Alexander Schimmelfennig
Second Brigade, Wladimir Krzyzanowski

Cavalry Brigade, John Beardsley

On September 22–24, 1862 Eleventh Corps was advanced from its positions in front of Chain Bridge to Centerville and Fairfax Court House as a corps of observation.

On October 26, 1862, the Army of the Potomac, which was then near Harper's Ferry, began its long-delayed crossing of the Potomac into Virginia at the beginning of a campaign that ended at the Battle of Fredericksburg December 13, 1862. The troops of the District of the Defenses of Washington immediately became involved. A new line of communication would be necessary to supply the army as it advanced from the line of the Baltimore and Ohio Railroad, and the most suitable route as it neared Warrenton would be westward from Alexandria by way of the Orange and Alexandria Railroad and the Manassas Gap Railroad. Before this route could be used, however, it would be necessary to repair and protect the lines of the two railroads.

For some time past, troops of Sigel's Eleventh Corps had occupied the following posts: Fairfax Court House, Fairfax Station, Burke's Station, Union Mills, Bull Run Bridge, Chantilly, Brentsville, Bristoe Station, Catlett's Station, and Greenwood. Bayard's cavalry covered the front of this line. On November 1, 1862, Sigel was ordered to advance along the Manassas Gap Railroad toward Thoroughfare Gap, which he occupied November 5, 1862. That day, Eleventh Corps was detached from the District of the Defenses of Washington and was attached to McClellan's Army of the Potomac.

November 9, 1862, Ambrose E. Burnside succeeded McClellan in command of the army of the Potomac, and shortly thereafter began his march toward Falmouth, Virginia, opposite Fredericksburg. Sigel's Eleventh Corps did not accompany Burnside's army, but it was left behind and remained generally along the railroad, with headquarters at Gainesville. For further information, see Fredericksburg, Virginia Campaign.

Troops of the Defenses South of the Potomac

Whipple's Division, Defenses of Washington. A new division was formed September 6, 1862 from troops of the garrison of the Defenses of Washington. When William B. Franklin's Sixth Corps left Alexandria that day, Erastus B. Tyler's brigade, which had been serving under Franklin's orders, was directed to report to Fitz John Porter at Hall's Hill. Tyler's brigade and A. Sanders Piatt's brigade, then attached to Porter's command, were constituted as a division under Samuel D. Sturgis. The next day, however, Sturgis was ordered to report to Jesse L. Reno at Leesboro, Maryland, and he was then assigned command of Second Division, Ninth Corps. When Sturgis departed to join Ninth Corps, Amiel W. Whipple was assigned command of Sturgis' division. September 8, 1862, Peter H. Allabach's brigade was added to Sturgis' former division, which then was designated as Whipple's Division, Defenses of Washington.

September 12, 1862, a new Third Division, Fifth Corps was organized from Tyler's Brigade and Allabach's brigade of Whipple's Division, and Andrew A. Humphreys was assigned command. Humphreys' division then left the District of the Defenses of Washington to join Fifth Corps in Maryland with the Army of the Potomac. Whipple, with Piatt's brigade, remained in the Defenses of Washington.

In September 1862, Samuel S. Carroll's brigade, formerly Fourth Brigade, Second Division, Third Corps, Army of Virginia, was transferred to Whipple's command, which was then reorganized as Whipple's Division. It consisted of Piatt's Brigade and Carroll's Brigade.

October 10, 1862, Whipple was ordered to report with his division to McClellan, who was then at Knoxville, Maryland, near Harper's Ferry. The movement was delayed, however, until October 17, 1862, while a new division was organized under John J. Abercrombie to replace Whipple's Division in the Defenses. After joining McClellan, Whipple's Division was assigned to Twelfth Corps, Army of the Potomac, but it was then detached and assigned to Ambrose E. Burnside's Special Force as Whipple's Division. For further information, see Army of the Potomac, Gettysburg Campaign, The Pursuit of Lee.

Abercrombie's Division, Defenses of Washington. October 10, 1862, John J. Abercrombie was assigned command of a new division that was to be formed from regiments of Casey's Provisional Brigades. It was to consist of two brigades that were to be commanded by their senior colonels. First Brigade, as originally formed, was broken up and its regiments were reassigned. October 14, 1862, Robert Cowdin was assigned command of Second Brigade. A Third Brigade was organized October 17, 1862, and William Gurney was assigned command. The division was organized as follows:

Abercrombie's Division, John J. Abercrombie
  Second Brigade, Robert Cowdin
  Third Brigade, William Gurney

October 28, 1862, two regiments were assigned to the division as a nucleus for a new brigade. The entire division was formed from new regiments. A provisional brigade was organized December 22, 1862 under Clarence Buell, and it was attached to Abercrombie's Division.

Casey's Division, Defenses of Washington. September 16, 1862, Casey's Provisional Brigades were concentrated on the Virginia side of the Potomac and were given the designation of Casey's Division. Usually, however, Casey's command was called Provisional Brigades. On October 28, 1862, Casey was assigned command of a newly organized provisional division, designated as Casey's Provisional Division, Reserve Corps, Defenses of Washington. It was organized as follows:

Casey's Provisional Division, Silas Casey
  First Brigade, Dexter R. Wright, to December 1, 1862
    Frederick G. D'Utassy, December 1862
    Francis Fessenden
  Second Brigade, Asa P. Blunt, to November 6, 1862
    Edwin H. Stoughton
  Third Brigade, Francis Fessenden, to December 31, 1862
    Frederick G. D'Utassy, temporarily to January 6, 1863
    Alexander Hays

Note 1. First Brigade and Third Brigade were south of the Potomac in Virginia, and Second Brigade was on Capitol Hill.

Note 2. First Brigade was transferred to the Army of the Potomac December 1, 1862. It was then broken up and the regiments were assigned to Ninth Corps. It was reorganized from regiments of Third Brigade.

Note 3. Second Brigade was organized from new Vermont regiments and was sometimes called the Vermont Brigade.

Note 4. Third Brigade was organized from new Maine regiments. It was broken up in December 1862, largely by transfer of regiments to First Brigade.

Note 5. Casey was in command of a provisional brigade consisting of regiments captured at Harper's Ferry and recently exchanged at Camp Douglas, Illinois. This brigade was assigned to Casey's Division as Third Brigade December 31, 1862. It was commanded temporarily by D'Utassy until relieved by Alexander Hays January 6, 1863.

Casey also commanded a provisional brigade consisting of New Jersey regiments until December 1862, and then it was transferred to the Provost Guard, Army of the Potomac. A provisional cavalry brigade was organized in December 1862, and Joseph T. Copeland was assigned command January 13, 1863. This brigade was attached to Casey's Division.

On December 6, 1862, the Defenses South of the Potomac was discontinued as a sub-district of the District of the Defenses of Washington, and the various units of that command were ordered to report directly to Headquarters District of the Defenses of Washington.

Troops of the Defenses North of the Potomac River

The defensive works north of the Potomac River were manned by unbrigaded infantry regiments and artillery that had joined the District of the Defenses of Washington in August and early September 1862. These troops were under the command of Joseph A. Haskin. September 12, 1862, John G. Barnard was assigned command of the troops for the immediate defense of Washington north of the Potomac, but this order was revoked the next day and Barnard was assigned as chief engineer of all the defenses, to date from September 3, 1862. Haskin and Woodbury remained in command north of the Potomac.

In October 1862, Haskin's command was organized into a division of three brigades as follows:

Haskin's Division, Joseph A. Haskin
First Brigade, Augustus A. Gibson
Second Brigade, Louis O. Morris
Third Brigade, William R. Pease

This command was commonly referred to simply as the Defenses North of the Potomac. The brigade organization remained unchanged during the rest of the period of existence of the District of the Defenses of Washington. In December 1862 and January 1863, however, the designations of a number of infantry regiments were changed to regiments of heavy artillery.

November 12, 1862, Daniel P. Woodbury, commander of the Engineer Brigade, who was in command of the Defenses North of the Potomac east of the Eastern Branch, was ordered with his brigade and the pontoon train to report to Burnside at Falmouth, Virginia. When Woodbury departed, Haskin assumed command of all defenses north of the Potomac.

Other Organizations in the Defenses of Washington

Bayard's Cavalry Division. October 1, 1862, a cavalry division was organized at Upton's Hill under the command of George D. Bayard, as follows:

Cavalry Division, George D. Bayard
First Brigade, J. Mansfield Davies
Second Brigade, R. Butler Price
Third Brigade, John Beardsley

Note. September 10, 1862, John Buford was announced as chief of cavalry, Army of the Potomac, and was succeeded in command of his brigade by Price.

Bayard's cavalry was employed primarily in scouting the country to the west and southwest of Washington, and when Franz Sigel's Eleventh Corps moved out from near Washington to Centerville and Fairfax Court House, the cavalry division was attached to Sigel's command. Percy Wyndham commanded a cavalry brigade at Chantilly, Virginia during the period October 1862–December 1862, and this too operated with Eleventh Corps.

As the Army of the Potomac advanced into Virginia in late October 1862, Bayard was ordered, on the last day of the month, to report to McClellan, and Bayard's Brigade then left the District of the Defenses of Washington. Price's Second Brigade, however, did not accompany Bayard, but remained in the Defenses of Washington.

Provisional Brigades. Silas Casey, who was in command of the Provisional Brigades at Washington, had been assigned the duty of receiving, organizing, and instructing the new regiments that arrived in Washington. When ready for duty, these regiments were assigned to the various units of the army. During the time that it was a part of the District of the Defenses of Washington, more than 100,000 men passed through Casey's command. For example, September 29, 1862, Henry S. Briggs took twenty regiments from the Provisional Brigades to the Army of the Potomac as reinforcements; and in October 1862, John J. Abercrombie's Division of the Defenses of Washington was formed from regiments of the Provisional Brigades.

District of Washington. The District of Washington, originally constituted March 17, 1862, was included in the District of the Defenses of Washington when the latter was organized August 20, 1862. James S. Wadsworth, the military governor of Washington, remained in command of the district until he was relieved by John H. Martindale November 20, 1862. The troops in the district consisted generally of unbrigaded regiments.

District of Alexandria. August 25, 1862, John P. Slough was appointed military governor of Alexandria, Virginia, and he continued in this command until the end of the war. In October 1862, Slough's command was designated as the District of Alexandria. On September 15, 1862, Slough was directed to organize a camp for convalescents, stragglers, and recruits near Alexandria. To emphasize the importance of this operation, approximately 52,000 men were cared for at the camp during the period September 17, 1862 (when the organization of the camp was completed) to January 1, 1863. During this same period, 41,000 men were returned to duty.

Artillery Defenses of Alexandria. On January 8, 1863, Robert O. Tyler, commander of the Artillery Defenses of Alexandria, was assigned command of a brigade of heavy artillery, consisting of 1st Connecticut Heavy Artillery, 19th Connecticut Heavy Artillery, and 1st Wisconsin Heavy Artillery. In addition to the brigade, Tyler was assigned command at Fort Lyon January 14, 1863.

Artillery Camp of Instruction. An artillery camp of instruction was established near Washington in October 1862, and William F. Barry, chief of artillery of the Defenses of Washington, was assigned command.

Division of Reinforcements for the Army of the Potomac. On November 31, 1862, about 12,000 men from the District of the Defenses of Washington were sent to Ambrose E. Burnside's Army of the Potomac at Falmouth, Virginia. These troops were organized into brigades under the command of their senior colonels as follows: William W. Jennings' Brigade from Abercrombie's Division, Dexter R. Wright's First Brigade of Casey's Division, and Henry M. Bossert's command of six regiments from Joseph A. Haskin's Defenses North of the Potomac. Bossert's Brigade was later assigned as Provisional Brigade, Provost Guard, Army of the Potomac

ORGANIZATION OF THE DISTRICT IN JANUARY 1863

At the end of January 1863, the District of the Defenses of Washington was organized as follows:

Defenses North of the Potomac, Joseph A. Haskin
    First Brigade, Augustus A. Gibson
    Second Brigade, Louis O. Morris
    Third Brigade, William R. Pease

Abercrombie's Division, John J. Abercrombie
    Second Brigade, Robert Cowdin
    Third Brigade, William Gurney
    Provisional Brigade, Clarence Buell

Note. The troops of this division were at Chain Bridge, Minor's Hill, and Upton's Hill.

Casey's Division, Silas Casey
    First Brigade, Francis Fessenden
    Second Brigade, Edwin H. Stoughton
    Third Brigade, Alexander Hays
    Provisional Cavalry Brigade, Joseph T. Copeland

Note. The troops of Casey's Division were posted at Centerville, Fairfax Court House, Fort Albany, Union Mills, Wolf Run Shoals, and Washington.

Cavalry Brigade, R. Butler Price

Note. Price's brigade was posted at Centerville, Chantilly, Dranesville, and Occoquan.

District of Alexandria, John P. Slough
Camps for convalescents, stragglers, and recruits

Artillery Defenses of Alexandria, Robert O. Tyler
Cogswell's Brigade, Milton Cogswell
2nd New York Heavy Artillery and 14th Massachusetts Heavy Artillery
Tyler's Brigade, Robert O. Tyler
1st Connecticut Heavy Artillery, 19th Connecticut Heavy Artillery, and 1st Wisconsin Heavy Artillery

Note. The troops of Tyler's command were stationed at Forts Barnard, Blenker, Ellsworth, Lyon, Richardson, Scott, Ward, and Worth.

District of Washington, John H. Martindale, Military Governor
Artillery Camp of Instruction, William F. Barry
Jewett's Brigade, Alfred B. Jewett

Note. Jewett's Brigade, formerly commanded by Cuvier Grover, was at Offutt's Cross Roads, Maryland.

Annapolis Junction, Maryland, Benjamin F. Tracy
Fort Washington, Charles S. Merchant

The Military District of the Defenses of Washington was merged into the Department of Washington February 2, 1863.

DISTRICT OF SAINT MARY'S

July 23, 1863, the county of Saint Mary's, Maryland was detached from the Middle Department and was constituted as a separate district, reporting to the War Department. Gilman Marston was assigned command, and August 1, 1863, he established a prisoner-of-war camp at Point Lookout on a low peninsula formed by the junction of the Potomac River with the Chesapeake Bay. This became the largest prison in the North, and at times as many as 20,000 prisoners were confined there. Marston's headquarters was at Point Lookout.

December 21, 1863, the District of Saint Mary's (Saint Mary's County), with the prisoner-of-war camp at Point Lookout, was transferred to Benjamin F. Butler's Department of Virginia and North Carolina. Marston remained in command until April 3, 1864, and then was relieved by Edward W. Hinks. Alonzo G. Draper replaced Hinks April 10, 1864.

At the end of June 1864, the District of Saint Mary's was transferred to the Department of Washington, and James Barnes was assigned command July 2, 1864. Barnes remained in command until April 26, 1865. The District of Saint Mary's was designated as a separate brigade September 7, 1864.

The district was discontinued June 13, 1865 (ordered June 2, 1865), and from that time the command was designated as the post of Point Lookout, Maryland.

For additional information, see Department of Virginia and North Carolina, Middle Department, and also Department of Washington, February 2, 1863–March 16, 1869.

INVALID CORPS

See Veteran Reserve Corps.

KITCHING'S PROVISIONAL DIVISION, SHERIDAN'S ARMY OF THE SHENANDOAH

See Shenandoah Valley Campaign (Sheridan), Fisher's Hill to Cedar Creek, Virginia.

PENNSYLVANIA RESERVE CORPS

See Pennsylvania Reserves, below.

PENNSYLVANIA RESERVES

When the first calls for troops were sent out from Washington at the beginning of the war, the response was so great that more regiments were formed than had been requested, or that could be equipped and supplied by the federal government.

This was true in Pennsylvania, as in most other Northern states, and when the excess Pennsylvania Militia regiments were not accepted into Federal service, they were organized by Governor Andrew G. Curtin into thirteen regiments of Pennsylvania Reserves. These regiments were designated as the 1st through 13th Pennsylvania Reserves, and they were equipped and trained at the state's expense. When later they were accepted into Federal service, they were assigned volunteer designations of 30th through 42nd Pennsylvania Volunteers. These regiments, however, were generally known as Pennsylvania Reserves during their terms of service.

October 3, 1861, the Pennsylvania Reserve regiments were organized into three brigades to form a division of the Army of the Potomac under George A. McCall. John F. Reynolds was assigned command of First Brigade; George G. Meade, of Second Brigade; and Edward O. C. Ord, of Third Brigade. Truman Seymour relieved Ord in command of Third Brigade May 16, 1862. Throughout its term of service, McCall's division (later commanded by other officers) was generally called the Pennsylvania Reserves, the Pennsylvania Reserve Division, and also the Pennsylvania Reserve Corps, although it also carried the usual numerical division designation in the larger organizations of which it was a part. The 1st Pennsylvania Cavalry (14th Pennsylvania Reserves) and the 1st Pennsylvania Light Artillery (15th Pennsylvania Reserves) were originally a part of the Pennsylvania Reserve Division, but in March 1862 they were detached for duty in the newly organized corps of the Army of the Potomac.

Ord's Third Brigade was engaged at Dranesville, Virginia December 20, 1861, and the other two brigades of the division were nearby. For details, see Engagement at Dranesville, Virginia.

When the corps organization of the Army of the Potomac was announced March 13, 1862, McCall's division was assigned as the Second Division of Irvin McDowell's First Corps. First Corps was detached from the army at the beginning of the Peninsular Campaign, and April 4, 1862, McDowell's command became the Department of the Rappahannock. McCall's division then became Second Division, Department of the Rappahannock. The division remained near Fredericksburg, Virginia until ordered to join the army on the Peninsula, and there, on June 12, 1862, it was assigned to Fitz John Porter's Fifth Provisional Corps (later Fifth Corps) as Third Division.

McCall's division was engaged during the Seven Days' Battles at Mechanicsville, Gaines' Mill, and Glendale, but was in reserve at Malvern Hill. Reynolds was captured at Gaines' Mill, and McCall was captured and Meade wounded at Glendale. At the end of the fighting July 1, 1862, the Pennsylvania Reserves were commanded as follows: Truman Seymour commanded the division; R. Biddle Roberts, First Brigade; Albert L. Magilton, Second Brigade; and C. Feger Jackson, Third Brigade.

After leaving the Peninsula in August 1862, the Pennsylvania Reserves were reorganized under John F. Reynolds, and August 23, 1862, they were transferred to McDowell's Third Corps of John Pope's Army of Virginia. Meade commanded First Brigade; Seymour, Second Brigade; and Jackson, Third Brigade. The division was engaged at the battles of Groveton and Second Bull Run. For details, see Pope's Northern Virginia Campaign.

September 12, 1862 Third Corps, Army of Virginia was discontinued by a change of designation to First Corps, Army of the Potomac, which was assigned to Joseph Hooker. The Pennsylvania Reserve Division, then commanded by Meade, became Third Division, First Corps. Meade commanded the division at the battle of South Mountain, and at the Battle of Antietam until Hooker was wounded September 17, 1862. Meade then assumed command of First Corps, and Seymour succeeded him in command of the Pennsylvania Reserves. R. Biddle Roberts took charge of Seymour's First Brigade. Thomas F. Gallagher was wounded at South Mountain September 14, 1862, and was succeeded in command of Third Brigade by Robert Anderson.

Meade commanded Third Division, First Corps at the Battle of Fredericksburg December 13, 1862. William Sinclair, then commanding First Brigade, was wounded and was succeeded by William McCandless. C. Feger Jackson was killed while commanding Third Brigade, and was succeeded by Joseph W. Fisher. Fisher was then relieved by Robert Anderson.

The Pennsylvania Reserves were engaged in almost all major battles of 1862, and early in February 1863, the division was ordered to Washington to rest and recruit. There, under the command of Horatio

G. Sickel, they became the Pennsylvania Reserve Division, Twenty-Second Corps. April 15, 1863, Sickel's Second Brigade was transferred to the District of Alexandria as Second Brigade, Pennsylvania Reserves, District of Alexandria; and Third Brigade of the division was attached to the District of Washington. For additional information, see Department of Washington, February 2, 1863–March 16, 1869.

June 1, 1863, Samuel W. Crawford was assigned command of the Pennsylvania Reserve Division, which then consisted of McCandless' First Brigade and Fisher's Third Brigade. Headquarters was established at Fairfax Station. Crawford's two brigades volunteered to rejoin the Army of the Potomac for the defense of Pennsylvania during Lee's invasion of the state, and June 26, 1863 they joined the army as it was moving into Maryland. Two days later Crawford's command was assigned to Meade's Fifth Corps (George Sykes assumed command of Fifth Corps June 28, 1863) as Third Division.

As a part of Fifth Corps, the Pennsylvania Reserves were engaged at Gettysburg, and were with the army during the Bristoe, Virginia Campaign in October 1863 and the Mine Run Campaign in November 1863. They were also engaged in the Battle of the Wilderness and the Battle of Spotsylvania in the spring of 1864. The last action of this organization as a unit was at Bethesda Church June 1, 1864. Meantime, the Second Brigade, Pennsylvania Reserves, which had been left in the District of Alexandria when the other two brigades marched to Gettysburg, was essentially discontinued in April 1864. In January 1864, two regiments of the brigade were sent to the Department of West Virginia, where in April of that year they were assigned to Third Brigade, Second Infantry Division, Department of West Virginia. With that brigade they were engaged at Cloyd's Mountain May 9–19, 1864. The other two regiments of the brigade rejoined the Pennsylvania Reserves of Third Division, Fifth Corps in April 1864.

The first of the Pennsylvania Reserve regiments left the army for muster out May 4, 1864, just before the Battle of the Wilderness, and the last of the regiments was mustered out June 17, 1864. There were veteran volunteers and recruits of the Reserves who were not due for muster out, and during March and April of 1864, a part of these were organized in the field into the 190th Pennsylvania Regiment. In May 1864, the rest were organized into the 191st Pennsylvania Regiment. These two regiments were also known as the 190th and 191st Veteran Reserves. In June 1864, they were organized into a Third Brigade of Crawford's Third Division, Fifth Corps. This brigade, also known as the Veteran Reserve Brigade, was commanded by William R. Hartshorne to June 6, 1864, and he was succeeded by James Carle. This brigade was slightly engaged at Cold Harbor. For further information, see the following: Army of the Potomac; Department of Washington, February 2, 1863–March 16, 1869; and also Department of West Virginia.

PROVISIONAL BRIGADES, WASHINGTON, D.C.

August 25, 1861, George B. McClellan, commander of the Army and Department of the Potomac, assigned Fitz John Porter the duty of receiving new regiments arriving in Washington; organizing them into provisional brigades; and placing them in camps in the suburbs for equipment, instruction, and discipline. As soon as the new recruits were in suitable condition for transfer to the forces encamped across the Potomac, they were assigned to the brigade organization of the army. Porter's command was designated as Provisional Brigades, and it was continued in existence to the end of the war, although under different commanders. It performed the same service of preparing regiments for transfer to the army. It was, successively, in the Department of the Potomac, the Department of the Rappahannock, Pope's Army of Virginia, the Military District of the Defenses of Washington, the Army of the Potomac, and the Department of Washington, Twenty-Second Corps. The organization of the Provisional Brigades was discontinued March 24, 1865. The commanders were as follows:

Fitz John Porter   August 25, 1861 to September 3, 1861

Ambrose E. Burnside   September 3, 1861 to October 23, 1861

Silas Casey	October 23, 1861 to March 17, 1862
James S. Wadsworth	March 17, 1862 to August 12, 1862
Silas Casey	August 12, 1862 to March 24, 1865

Note. Wadsworth commanded as military governor of the District of Columbia and of the District of Washington.

PROVISIONAL CORPS (WRIGHT)

After the surrender of the armies commanded by Robert E. Lee and Joseph E. Johnston, the field armies of the United States were no longer needed. An order from the War Department dated May 17, 1865 directed that all volunteer organizations of white troops in the Army of the Potomac whose terms of enlistment expired between that date and September 30, 1865 be mustered out immediately. Compliance with this order greatly reduced the number of troops present with the army, and June 28, 1865, another order directed that all troops not then scheduled for muster out were to be consolidated in each corps of the army into a division of three brigades. With this order the Army of the Potomac ceased to exist. The three divisions, formed respectively from Second Corps, Fifth Corps, and Sixth Corps, were then to be organized temporarily into a provisional corps to be commanded by Horatio G. Wright. The consolidation was completed by June 30, 1865, and the Provisional Corps was organized as follows:

PROVISIONAL CORPS, Horatio G. Wright

First Division (from Sixth Corps), George W. Getty
    First Brigade, Truman Seymour
    Second Brigade, Frank Wheaton
    Third Brigade, Joseph E. Hamblin

Second Division (from Second Corps), Gershom Mott
    First Brigade, P. Regis De Trobriand
    Second Brigade, Byron R. Pierce
    Third Brigade, George N. Macy

Third Division (from Fifth Corps), Romeyn B. Ayres

    First Brigade, Joshua L. Chamberlain
    Second Brigade, Henry Baxter
    Third Brigade, Joseph Hayes

The Provisional Corps was placed in camp on the Baltimore and Ohio Railroad west of the Monocacy River, and Wright reported to Winfield S. Hancock, commander of the Middle Department. The corps was discontinued about mid-July 1865 when the troops were mustered out of the service.

SHERMAN'S EXPEDITIONARY CORPS (THOMAS W. SHERMAN)

August 2, 1861 Thomas W. Sherman was ordered to New York to organize, in cooperation with Samuel F. Du Pont of the navy, an expedition to the coast of South Carolina. The purpose of this expedition was to seize Port Royal and establish there a large naval base and also a base for subsequent operations along the coast of South Carolina, Georgia, and Florida. Sherman was to assemble on Long Island Sound a force of about 12,000 men, obtained from the northeastern states, to accompany the warships of the navy. This force was called the Expeditionary Corps, Sherman's Expeditionary Corps, or South Carolina Expeditionary Corps, and it was organized into three brigades commanded by Egbert L. Viele, Isaac I. Stevens, and Horatio G. Wright.

Sherman transferred this command to Hampton Roads, Virginia, and from there it sailed October 29, 1861 for the coast of South Carolina. It was accompanied by a naval force under Flag Officer Du Pont, who had been assigned command of the Atlantic Blockading Squadron. The expedition arrived off Port Royal November 4, 1861, and, after a naval bombardment November 7, 1861, landed and took possession of Fort Walker on Hilton Head and Fort Beauregard at Bay Point on Phillips Island. A short time later, Federal troops also occupied Beaufort, South Carolina and pushed out along the coast. For more detailed information, see Department of South Carolina, Part I, South Carolina Expedition (Thomas W. Sherman).

SOUTH CAROLINA EXPEDITIONARY CORPS (THOMAS W. SHERMAN)

This organization was also called Sherman's Expeditionary Corps. For details of its organization and operations, see Department of the South, Part I, South Carolina Expedition (Thomas W. Sherman).

TERRY'S PROVISIONAL CORPS, DEPARTMENT OF NORTH CAROLINA

Alfred H. Terry, with troops from the Army of the James, captured Fort Fisher, North Carolina January 15, 1865. Terry did not return with his command to the Richmond front, but remained on Federal Point (formerly Confederate Point) garrisoning Smithville and the forts at the mouth of the Cape Fear River. While on this duty Terry's command was first called United States Forces at Fort Fisher, and then Terry's Provisional Corps. This corps, together with troops of Twenty-Third Corps, Army of the Ohio, advanced on Wilmington, North Carolina February 16–22, 1865, and captured the town. Terry's Provisional Corps remained there and in the vicinity until March 14, 1865, and then marched toward Goldsboro. It arrived at Faison's Station on the Wilmington and Weldon Railroad March 25, 1865, and there, on April 2, 1865, its designation was changed to Tenth Corps, Department of North Carolina. Terry was assigned command.

For details of the organization and operations of Terry's Provisional Corps, see the following: Army of the James, Terry's Expedition to Fort Fisher, North Carolina; Department of North Carolina, January 31, 1865–May 19, 1866, Troops in the Department of North Carolina and Operations in the Department of North Carolina; Tenth Corps, Department of North Carolina; and Carolinas Campaign.

VETERAN RESERVE CORPS

An organization to be known as the Invalid Corps was authorized by the War Department April 28, 1862. This was to consist of officers and enlisted men of commands then in the field, either present or temporarily absent, who, because of wounds received in action or disease contracted in the line of duty, were unfit for field service but were capable of garrison duty or other light service that might be required. These troops were to be organized into companies, and were to be under the control of the bureau of the provost marshal general.

An order of May 26, 1863 announced the formation of three battalions of the Invalid Corps, the members of each of which were to be determined by their degree of physical fitness. Those most able-bodied and capable of using a musket, performing guard duty, and making light marches were to be assigned to the First Battalion. Those of the next degree of physical fitness were to be used as hospital personnel, such as cooks and nurses, and were to be assigned to the Second Battalion. The least effective were to be assigned to the Third Battalion. Although proposed in the order forming the three battalions, the Third Battalion appears not to have been organized. The companies of the Invalid Corps, when organized, were assigned to the First and Second battalions.

The points of assembly for the troops of the Invalid Corps were announced June 11, 1863, as follows: officers and men on the rolls of the corps of the Army of the Potomac and the Department of Washington were to report to Samuel McKelvey at the Convalescent Camp near Alexandria, Virginia; those on the rolls of the Department of the Gulf, the Department of the South, and the Department of North Carolina were to report to New York City; those on the rolls of John A. Dix's Seventh Corps and Erasmus D. Keyes' Fourth Corps were to report to Charles M. Prevost, commander of the depot at Harrisburg, Pennsylvania; those on the rolls of the corps in Kentucky and in the Department of the Cumberland were to report to William Sidell at Louisville, Kentucky; and those on the rolls of the Department of the Tennessee and of the Department of the Missouri were to report to Edmund B. Alexander at Saint Louis, Missouri.

September 3, 1863, the provost marshal general was authorized to organize companies of the Invalid Corps into regiments. Each regiment was to consist of six companies of the First Battalion and four companies of the Second Battalion, and was thus capable of performing both provost and hospital duty wherever formed. By the end of 1863 the corps numbered 20,000 men, and December 31, 1863, enlistment in the Second Battalion was stopped because no more troops of that category were needed. A total of 24 regiments and 188 separate companies were formed, and these relieved many able-bodied soldiers for combat duty.

The name "Invalid Corps" had an unpleasing connotation, and on March 18, 1864, the designation was changed to Veteran Reserve Corps. The various organizations of the Veteran Reserve Corps were generally reported on departmental rosters. For additional information refer to the departments of the army.

BATTLES AND CAMPAIGNS

☆ ☆ ☆ ☆

INTRODUCTION

An explanation is required for the arrangement of the material of this section, which relates to the campaigns, battles, engagements, expeditions, raids, and reconnaissances in which the eastern armies participated. Originally, it was intended that the descriptions of all operations in the East would be presented here in alphabetical sequence, but as the writing progressed, practical considerations suggested another method. Many of the operations described here were carried out by troops belonging to a military department, and not to one of the major armies, and so it seemed advantageous to include in the description of that department a subdivision in which are described the organization of the troops of that department and their operations. By so doing, a comprehensive background is available for a better understanding of the troop organizations and their operations than would have been the case if the operations had been presented separately in this section. Thus, Operations at Charleston Harbor in 1863, Seymour's Expedition to Florida and the Battle of Olustee, and the numerous expeditions in Georgia and Florida are best described in the history of the Department of the South. Similarly, much is gained by including, for example, the Battle of Drewry's Bluff and Terry's Expedition to Fort Fisher in the description of the Army of the James.

Further, for each major campaign included here, the separate battles and engagements are included in the history of the campaign instead of being listed one by one in a separate section and arranged in alphabetical order. This arrangement has been adopted because it provides a better continuity to the history of the campaign than would have been possible if the battles were described separately elsewhere. Thus, for example, the battles of the Wilderness, Spotsylvania Court House, and Cold Harbor, and such engagements as at Alsop's Farm, Harris' Farm, the North Anna, and Haw's Shop, are described in the Richmond, Virginia Campaign, 1864, in their chronological order.

Based on the above considerations, the descriptions of some of the operations of the eastern armies are to be found in other parts of the book, and to make them readily accessible, this section has been divided in two parts as follows: Part I consists of a list of all operations described in this volume, arranged in alphabetical order, with a cross-reference for each indicating where the full account of the operation is to be found; and Part II consists of all major campaigns conducted by the eastern armies during the war, and also some lesser operations that could not logically be included elsewhere.

PART I: LIST OF CAMPAIGNS, BATTLES, ENGAGEMENTS, AND EXPEDITIONS

Aenon Church (or Haw's Shop), Virginia, Engagement at, May 28, 1864. See Richmond, Virginia Campaign, 1864, Operations on the Pamunkey River, Engagement at Haw's Shop (Aenon, or Enon Church).

Albemarle County, Virginia, Custer's Raid into, February 28, 1864–March 2, 1864. See Part II, below, Kilpatrick's Expedition against Richmond, Virginia, and Custer's Raid into Albemarle County, Virginia.

Aldie, Virginia, Action at, June 17, 1863. See Gettysburg Campaign, Part I, From the Rappahannock to Gettysburg, Advance of the Army to the Bull Run Mountains.

Allegheny Mountain (or Camp Allegheny), Virginia, Engagement at, December 13, 1861. See Department of Western Virginia, Operations in the Department of Western Virginia, Engagement at Camp Allegheny, Virginia.

Allen's Farm (or Peach Orchard), Virginia, Engagement at, June 29, 1862. See Peninsular Campaign, Seven Days' Battles, Engagement at Allen's Farm (or Peach Orchard).

Alsop's Farm (or Laurel Hill), Virginia, Engagement at, May 8, 1864. See Richmond, Virginia Campaign, 1864, Operations about Spotsylvania Court House.

Antietam (or Sharpsburg), Maryland, Battle of, September 17, 1862. See Maryland Campaign (South Mountain and Antietam), Battle of Antietam (Sharpsburg).

Appomattox Campaign, Virginia, March 29, 1865–April 9, 1865. See Part II, below.

Appomattox Court House, Virginia, Engagement at, April 9, 1865. See Appomattox Campaign, Virginia, Surrender of the Army of Northern Virginia.

Appomattox Station, Virginia, Engagement at, April 8, 1865. See Appomattox Campaign, Virginia, Movement of the Armies to Appomattox Court House, Virginia, April 7–9, 1865.

Armstrong's Mill (or Hatcher's Run), Virginia, Battle of, February 5–7, 1865. See Operations about Petersburg and Richmond, Virginia, 1864–1865, Winter of 1864–1865, Battle of Hatcher's Run (or Dabney's Mill, Armstrong's Mill, Rowanty Creek, Vaughan Road).

Auburn, Virginia, Action at, October 13, 1863. See Bristoe, Virginia Campaign.

Averasboro (or Taylor's Hole Creek), North Carolina, Battle of, March 16, 1865. See Carolinas Campaign, Fayetteville to Goldsboro, North Carolina.

Averell's Raid in West Virginia (Engagement at Rocky Gap, or White Sulfur Springs), August 18–31, 1863. See Department of West Virginia, Operations of the Troops of the Department of West Virginia.

Bailey's Creek, Virginia, Combat at, August 16, 1864. See Operations about Petersburg and Richmond, Virginia, 1864–1865, Operations of August 1864, Demonstration on the North Bank of the James River at Deep Bottom (Combats at Fussell's Mill, Gravel Hill, Bailey's Creek, Deep Run [or Creek], White's Tavern, Charles City Road, and New Market Road), Virginia.

Ball's Bluff, Virginia, Engagement at, October 21, 1861. See Part II, below.

Barhamsville, Virginia, Engagement at, May 7, 1862. See Peninsular Campaign, Advance of the Army to White House, Virginia, Engagement at Eltham's Landing (West Point, or Barhamsville).

Battery Wagner (or Fort Wagner), Charleston Harbor, South Carolina, Assaults on, and Siege of, July 1863. See Department of the South, Part III, Department of the South, Tenth Corps, Operations at Charleston Harbor (Fort Sumter), Occupation of Morris Island and Assaults on Battery Wagner.

Beaver Dam Creek (or Mechanicsville, Ellerson's Mill [or Ellison's Mill]), Virginia, Battle of, June 26, 1862. See Peninsular Campaign, Seven Days' Battles, Battle of Mechanicsville.

Bentonville, North Carolina, Battle of, March 19–21, 1865. See Carolinas Campaign, Fayetteville to Goldsboro, North Carolina.

Bethesda Church, Virginia, Engagement at, May 30, 1864. See Richmond, Virginia Campaign of 1864, Operations on the Totopotomoy River.

Big Bethel, Virginia, Engagement at, June 10, 1861. See Department of Virginia, May 22, 1861–July 15, 1863, Troops and Operations in the Department of Virginia.

Blackburn's Ford, Virginia, Action at, July 18, 1861. See Bull Run Campaign, Virginia (First Battle of Bull Run or Manassas).

Blick's House (or Station), Virginia, Battle of, August 18–21, 1864. See Operations about Petersburg and Richmond, Virginia, 1864–1865, Operations of August 1864, Battle of Globe Tavern (or Yellow House, Yellow Tavern, Blick's House [or Station], Weldon Railroad), Virginia.

Boydton Plank Road (or Hatcher's Run), Virginia, Engagement at, October 27–28, 1864. See Operations about Petersburg and Richmond, Virginia, 1864–1865, Operations of October 1864, Engagement at the Boydton Plank Road (or Hatcher's Run), Virginia.

Brandy Station (or Fleetwood Hill), Virginia, Battle of, June 9, 1863. See Gettysburg Campaign, Part I, From the Rappahannock to Gettysburg.

Brawner's Farm (or Gainesville), Virginia, Battle of, August 28, 1862. See Pope's Northern Virginia Campaign, Battle of Gainesville (or Brawner's Farm).

Bristoe, Virginia Campaign, October 10, 1863–October 22, 1863. See Part II, below.

Bristoe Station, Virginia, Engagement at, October 14, 1863. See Bristoe, Virginia Campaign.

Bull Run Campaign, Virginia (First Battle of Bull Run or Manassas), July 16–22, 1861. See Part II, below.

Bull Run (or Manassas), Virginia, First Battle of, July 21, 1861. See Bull Run Campaign, Virginia (First Battle of Bull Run or Manassas).

Bull Run (or Manassas), Virginia, Second Battle of (or Groveton Heights), August 30, 1862. See Pope's Northern Virginia Campaign, Second Battle of Bull Run (or Groveton Heights, Second Manassas).

Bull Run Bridge, Virginia, Action at, August 27, 1862. See Pope's Northern Virginia Campaign.

Burnside's Expedition to North Carolina, January 1862. See Department of North Carolina, January 7, 1862–July 15, 1863, Troops and Operations in the Department of North Carolina, Burnside's Expedition to North Carolina.

Butler's Expedition to Fort Fisher, North Carolina, December 7–30, 1864. See Army of the James, Butler's Expedition to Fort Fisher.

Camden (or South Mills), North Carolina, Engagement at, April 19, 1862. See Department of North Carolina, January 7, 1862–July 15, 1863, Troops and Operations in the Department of North Carolina, Department of North Carolina, April 2, 1862–December 24, 1862, Engagement at South Mills, Camden County.

Camp Allegheny, Virginia, Engagement at, December 13, 1861. See Department of Western Virginia, Operations in the Department of Western Virginia.

Campaign in Northern Virginia, August 16, 1862–September 2, 1862. See Part II, below, Pope's Northern Virginia Campaign.

Carnifix Ferry, Western Virginia, Engagement at, September 10, 1861. See Western (West) Virginia Operations, May 26, 1861–October 11, 1861, Engagement at Carnifix Ferry, Gauley River, Virginia.

Carolinas Campaign, January 1, 1865–April 26, 1865. See Part II, below.

Carrick's Ford (or Corrick's Ford), Western Virginia, Action at, July 13, 1861. See Western (West) Virginia Operations, May 26, 1861–October 11, 1861, McClellan's Western Virginia Campaign (Engagement at Rich Mountain).

Cedar Creek, Virginia, Battle of, October 19,

1864. See Shenandoah Valley Campaign (Sheridan), Battle of Cedar Creek, Virginia.

Cedar Mountain (Slaughter's Mountain, or Cedar Run), Virginia, Battle of, August 9, 1862. See Pope's Northern Virginia Campaign, Battle of Cedar Mountain (Slaughter's Mountain, or Cedar Run).

Cedar Run (Cedar Mountain, or Slaughter's Mountain), Virginia, Battle of, August 9, 1862. See Pope's Northern Virginia Campaign, Battle of Cedar Mountain (Slaughter's Mountain, or Cedar Run).

Cedarville (Front Royal, or Guard Hill), Virginia, Engagement at, August 16, 1864. See Shenandoah Valley Campaign (Sheridan), Sheridan's First Advance up the Valley.

Chaffin's Farm, Virginia, Battle of, September, 29–30, 1864. See Operations about Petersburg and Richmond, Virginia, 1864–1865, Operations of September 1864, Battle of Chaffin's Farm (Combats at Fort Harrison, Fort Gilmer, Fort Gregg, New Market Heights, and Laurel Hill), Virginia.

Chambersburg, Pennsylvania, Burning of, July 30, 1864. See Early's Washington Raid (and Operations in the Shenandoah Valley, Maryland, and Pennsylvania), Burning of Chambersburg, Pennsylvania.

Chancellorsville, Virginia, Battle of, May 1–4, 1863. See Part II, below, Chancellorsville, Virginia Campaign.

Chancellorsville, Virginia Campaign, April 27, 1863–May 6, 1863. See Part II, below.

Chantilly (or Ox Hill), Virginia, Battle of, September 1, 1862. See Pope's Northern Virginia Campaign, Battle of Chantilly or Ox Hill.

Chappell's House, Virginia, Combat at, October 1, 1864. See Operations about Petersburg and Richmond, Virginia, 1864–1865, Operations of September 1864, Battle of Poplar Spring Church (Combats at Wyatt's Farm, Peebles' Farm, Chappell's House, Pegram's Farm, and Vaughan Road), Virginia.

Charles City Road, Virginia, Battle of, June 30, 1862. See Peninsular Campaign, Seven Days' Battles, Engagement at White Oak Swamp Bridge and Battle of Glendale (or White Oak Swamp, Charles City Road, New Market Road, Nelson's Farm, Frayser's Farm [or Frazier's Farm], Willis' Church).

Charles City Road, Virginia, Combat at, August 13, 1864. See Operations about Petersburg and Richmond, Virginia, 1864–1865, Operations of August 1864, Demonstration on the North Bank of the James River at Deep Bottom (Combats at Fussell's Mill, Gravel Hill, Bailey's Creek, Deep Run [or Creek], White's Tavern, Charles City Road, and New Market Road).

Charleston Harbor (Fort Sumter), South Carolina, Operations at, 1863. See Department of the South, Part III, Department of the South, Tenth Corps, Operations at Charleston Harbor (Fort Sumter), South Carolina.

Charleston and Savannah Railroad, South Carolina, Operations against, November–December 1864 (Engagement at Honey Hill). See Department of the South, Part IV, Operations in the Department of the South, Hatch's Expedition against the Charleston and Savannah Railroad (Engagement at Honey Hill), South Carolina.

Charlottesville, Virginia, Custer's Raid toward, February 28, 1864–March 2, 1864. See Kilpatrick's Expedition against Richmond, Virginia, and Custer's Raid into Albemarle County, Virginia.

Cheat Mountain, Western Virginia, Operations at, September 11–17, 1861. See Western (West) Virginia Operations, May 26, 1861–October 11, 1861, Operations at Cheat Mountain, Virginia.

Chickahominy (Gaines' Mill, or First Cold Harbor), Virginia, Battle of, June 27, 1862. See Peninsular Campaign, Seven Days' Battles, Battle of Gaines' Mill (or First Cold Harbor, Chickahominy).

Cloyd's Mountain (or Cloyd's Farm), Virginia, Engagement at, May 9, 1864. See Department of West Virginia, Operations of the Troops of the Department of West Virginia, Expeditions against the Virginia Central Railroad and the Virginia and Tennessee Railroad, Expedition against the Virginia and Tennessee Railroad (Engagement at Cloyd's Mountain).

Cold Harbor, First Battle of (Gaines' Mill, or Chickahominy), Virginia, June 27, 1862. See Peninsular Campaign, Seven Days' Battles, Battle of Gaines' Mill (or First Cold Harbor, Chickahominy).

Cold Harbor, Virginia, Battle of, June 1–3, 1864. See Richmond, Virginia Campaign, 1864, Operations about Cold Harbor.

Columbia, South Carolina, Occupation of, February 17, 1865. See Carolinas Campaign, Savannah, Georgia to Fayetteville, North Carolina.

Corbin's Bridge, Virginia, Engagement at, May 8, 1864. See Richmond, Virginia Campaign, 1864, Operations about Spotsylvania Court House, Virginia.

Corrick's Ford (or Carrick's Ford), Western Virginia, Action at, July 13, 1861. See Western (West) Virginia Operations, May 26, 1861–October 11, 1861, McClellan's Western Virginia Campaign (Engagement at Rich Mountain).

Cox's Kanawha Valley Campaign, Western Virginia, July 11–29, 1861. See Western (West) Virginia Operations, May 26, 1861–October 11, 1861, Kanawha Valley Campaign, July 1861.

Cox's Advance from the Kanawha Valley to East River and Lewisburg, West Virginia, May 1862. See Mountain Department, Troops and Operations in the Mountain Department.

Crampton's Gap (or Crampton's Pass), Maryland, Battle of, September 14, 1862. See Maryland Campaign (South Mountain and Antietam).

Crater at Petersburg, Virginia, Assault at, July 30, 1864. See Operations about Petersburg and Richmond Virginia, 1864–1865, Operations of July 1864, Petersburg Mine Assault.

Crew's Farm (Malvern Hill, or Poindexter's Farm), Virginia, Battle of, July 1, 1862. See Peninsular Campaign, Seven Days' Battles, Battle of Malvern Hill (or Crew's Farm, Poindexter's Farm).

Cross Keys, Virginia, Battle of, June 8, 1862. See Shenandoah Valley Campaign (Jackson), 1862, Engagements at Cross Keys and Port Republic, Virginia.

Cumberland Church, Virginia, Action at, April 7, 1865. See Appomattox Campaign, Virginia, Movement of the Armies to Appomattox Court House, Virginia.

Custer's Demonstration in the Shenandoah Valley (and Engagement at Lacey's Springs), Virginia, December 19–22, 1864. See Army of the Shenandoah (Sheridan), Torbert's Expedition from Winchester to Gordonsville, Virginia, December 19–28, 1864, and Custer's Demonstration in the Shenandoah Valley (Engagement at Lacey's Springs), December 19–22, 1864.

Custer's Raid into Albemarle County, Virginia, February 28, 1864–March 2, 1864. See Kilpatrick's Expedition against Richmond, Virginia, and Custer's Raid into Albemarle County, Virginia.

Dabney's Mill (or Hatcher's Run), Virginia, Battle of, February 5–7, 1865. See Operations about Petersburg and Richmond, Virginia, 1864–1865, Winter of 1864–1865, Battle of Hatcher's Run (or Dabney's Mill, Armstrong's Mill, Rowanty Creek, Vaughan Road).

Daniel H. Hill's Expedition against New Berne, North Carolina, March 8–16, 1863. See Department of North Carolina, January 7, 1862–July 15, 1863, Troops and Operations in the Department of North Carolina, Department of North Carolina, Eighteenth Corps.

Darbytown (Deep Bottom, Strawberry Plains, or New Market Road), Virginia, Engagement at, July 27, 1864. See Operations about Petersburg and Richmond, Virginia, 1864–1865, Operations of July 1864, Demonstration on the North Bank of the James River, Engagement at Deep Bottom (or Darbytown, Strawberry Plains, New Market Road), Virginia.

Darbytown Road and New Market Road, Virginia, Engagement at, October 7, 1864. See Operations about Petersburg and Richmond, Virginia, 1864–1865, Operations of October 1864, Engagement at Darbytown Road and the New Market Road (Johnson's Farm and Four-Mile Creek [or Run]), Virginia.

Darbytown Road, Virginia, Engagement at, October 13, 1864. See Operations about Petersburg and Richmond, Virginia, 1864–1865, Operations of October 1864, Engagement at the Darbytown Road, Virginia.

Darbytown Road (Fair Oaks), Virginia, Engagement at the, October 27–28, 1864. See Operations about Petersburg and Richmond, Virginia, 1864–1865, Operations of October 1864, Engagement at the Darbytown Road (Fair Oaks), Virginia.

Deep Bottom, Virginia, Engagement at, July 27, 1864. See Operations about Petersburg and Richmond, Virginia, 1864–1865, Operations of July 1864, Demonstration on the North Bank of the James River, Engagement at Deep Bottom (or Darbytown, Strawberry Plains, New Market Road), Virginia.

Deep Bottom, Virginia, Demonstration on the North Bank of the James River at, August 13–20, 1864. See Operations about Petersburg and Richmond, Virginia, 1864–1865, Operations of August 1864, Demonstration on the North Bank of the James River at Deep Bottom (Combats at Fussell's Mill, Gravel Hill, Bailey's Creek, Deep Run [or Creek], White's Tavern, Charles City Road, and New Market Road), Virginia.

Deep Run (or Franklin's Crossing), Virginia, Skirmish at, June 5, 1863. See Gettysburg Cam-paign, Part I, From the Rappahannock to Gettysburg; also see Sixth Corps, Army of the Potomac, Skirmishes at Franklin's Crossing (or Deep Run).

Deep Run (or Deep Creek), Virginia, Combats at, August 13–20, 1864. See Operations about Petersburg and Richmond, Virginia, 1864–1865, Operations of August 1864, Demonstration on the North Bank of the James River at Deep Bottom (Combats at Fussell's Mill, Gravel Hill, Bailey's Creek, Deep Creek [or Run], White's Tavern, Charles City Road, and New Market Road), Virginia.

Demonstration on the Rapidan River, February 6–7, 1864. See Army of the Potomac, Winter of 1863–1864, Demonstration on the Rapidan River.

Dinwiddie Court House, Virginia, Battle of, March 31, 1865. See Appomattox Campaign, Virginia, Battle of Dinwiddie Court House.

Draft Riots in New York, July 1863. See Department of the East, January 3, 1863–June 27, 1865, Draft Riots in New York, July 1863.

Dranesville, Virginia, Engagement at, December 20, 1861. See Part II, below.

Drewry's Bluff (or Fort Darling), Virginia, Engagement at, May 12–16, 1864. See Army of the James, Engagement at Drewry's Bluff.

Droop Mountain, West Virginia, Engagement at, November 6, 1863. See Department of West Virginia, Operations of the Troops of the Department of West Virginia, Expedition from Beverly and Charleston to Lewisburg (Battle of Droop Mountain), West Virginia.

Early's Washington Raid (and Operations in the Shenandoah Valley, Maryland, and Pennsylvania). See Part II, below.

Eastern North Carolina, Expedition to the Counties of Washington and Hyde, October 31, 1862–November 12, 1862. See Department of North Carolina, January 7, 1862–July 15, 1863, Troops and Operations in the Department of North Carolina,

Department of North Carolina, April 2, 1862–December 24, 1862.

Ellerson's Mill, Virginia, Battle of, June 26, 1862. See Peninsular Campaign, Seven Days' Battles, Battle of Mechanicsville (or Beaver Dam Creek, Ellerson's Mill [or Ellison's Mill]).

Ellison's Mill, Virginia, Battle of, June 26, 1862. See Peninsular Campaign, Seven Days' Battles, Battle of Mechanicsville (Beaver Dam Creek, Ellerson's Mill [or Ellison's Mill]).

Eltham's Landing (West Point, or Barhamsville), Virginia, Engagement at, May 7, 1862. See Peninsular Campaign, Advance of the Army to White House, Virginia.

Enon Church (or Haw's Shop), Virginia, Engagement at, May 28, 1864. See Richmond, Virginia Campaign, 1864, Operations on the Pamunkey River, Engagement at Haw's Shop (Aenon or Enon Church).

Fair Oaks-Seven Pines, Virginia, Battle of, May 31, 1862. See Peninsular Campaign, Battle of Fair Oaks-Seven Pines, Virginia.

Fair Oaks (Darbytown Road), Virginia, Engagements at, October 27–28, 1862. See Operations about Petersburg and Richmond, Virginia, 1864–1865, Operations of October 1864, Engagement at the Darbytown Road (Fair Oaks), Virginia.

Falling Waters (Hoke's Run, or Hainesville), Virginia, Engagement at, July 2, 1861. See Department of Pennsylvania, April 27, 1861–August 24, 1861, Engagement at Falling Waters (Hoke's Run, or Hainesville), Virginia.

Fisher's Hill, Virginia, Battle of, September 22, 1864. See Shenandoah Valley Campaign (Sheridan), Battle of Fisher's Hill, Virginia.

Five Forks, Virginia, Battle of, April 1, 1865. See Appomattox Campaign, Virginia, Battle of Five Forks.

Fleetwood Hill (or Brandy Station), Virginia, Battle of, June 9, 1863. See Gettysburg Campaign, Part I, From the Rappahannock to Gettysburg, Battle of Brandy Station (or Fleetwood Hill).

Florida Expedition (Truman Seymour) (Engagement at Olustee or Ocean Pond), February 5–22, 1864. See Department of the South, Part III, Department of the South, Tenth Corps, Districts in the Department of the South, Tenth Corps, District of Florida (Seymour's Florida Expedition).

Fort Anderson, North Carolina, Capture of, February 19, 1865. See Department of North Carolina, January 31, 1865–May 19, 1866, Operations in the Department of North Carolina, Capture of Wilmington, North Carolina.

Fort Darling (or Drewry's Bluff), Virginia, Engagement at, May 12–16, 1864. See Army of the James, Engagement at Drewry's Bluff.

Fort Fisher, North Carolina, Butler's Expedition to, December 7–30, 1864. See Army of the James, Butler's Expedition to Fort Fisher, North Carolina.

Fort Fisher, North Carolina, Terry's Expedition to, January 3–17, 1865. See Army of the James, Terry's Expedition to Fort Fisher, North Carolina.

Fort Gilmer, Virginia, Combat at, September 29, 1864. See Operations about Petersburg and Richmond, Virginia, 1864–1865, Operations of September 1864, Battle of Chaffin's Farm (Combats at Fort Harrison, Fort Gilmer, Fort Gregg, New Market Heights, and Laurel Hill), Virginia.

Fort Gregg, Virginia, Combat at, September 29, 1864. See Operations about Petersburg and Richmond, Virginia, 1864–1865, Operations of September 1864, Battle of Chaffin's Farm (Combats at Fort Harrison, Fort Gilmer, Fort Gregg, New Market Heights, and Laurel Hill), Virginia.

Fort Harrison, Virginia, Combats at, September 29–30. 1864. See Operations about Petersburg and Richmond, Virginia, 1864–1865, Operations of September 1864, Battle of Chaffin's Farm (Combats at Fort Harrison, Fort Gilmer, Fort Gregg, New Market Heights, and Laurel Hill), Virginia.

Fort McAllister, Georgia, Capture of, December 13, 1864. See Savannah Campaign (Sherman's March through Georgia).

Fort Macon, North Carolina, Siege of, March 23, 1862–April 26, 1862. See Department of North Carolina, January 7, 1862–July 15, 1863, Troops and Operations in the Department of North Carolina, Burnside's Expedition to North Carolina.

Fort Pulaski, Georgia, Capture of, April 10, 1862. See Department of the South, Part I, South Carolina Expedition (Thomas W. Sherman).

Fort Stedman, Virginia, Assault on, March 25, 1865. See Operations about Petersburg and Richmond, Virginia, 1864–1865, Winter of 1864–1865, Assault at Fort Stedman.

Fort Stevens, District of Columbia, Action near, July 12, 1864. See Early's Washington Raid (and Operations in the Shenandoah Valley, Maryland, and Pennsylvania), Early's Army before Washington, D.C.

Fort Sumter, South Carolina, Bombardment and Evacuation of, April 12–13, 1861. See Part II, below, Bombardment and Evacuation of Fort Sumter, South Carolina.

Fort Sumter, South Carolina, Operations against, 1863. See Department of the South, Part III, Department of the South, Tenth Corps, Operations at Charleston Harbor (Fort Sumter), South Carolina.

Fort Wagner (or Battery Wagner), Charleston Harbor, South Carolina, Assault on, and Siege of, July 1863. See Department of the South, Part III, Department of the South, Tenth Corps, Occupation of Morris Island and Assaults on Battery Wagner.

Four-Mile Creek (or Run), Virginia, Engagement at, October 7, 1864. See Operations about Petersburg and Richmond, Virginia, 1864–1865, Operations of October 1864, Engagement at the Darbytown Road and the New Market Road (Johnson's Farm and Four-Mile Creek [or Run]), Virginia.

Fox's Gap, South Mountain, Maryland, Battle of, September 14, 1862. See Maryland Campaign (South Mountain and Antietam), Battle of South Mountain (Fox's Gap and Turner's Gap).

Franklin's Crossing (or Deep Run), Virginia, Skirmish at, June 5, 1863. See Gettysburg Campaign, Part I, From the Rappahannock to Gettysburg; and also Sixth Corps, Army of the Potomac, Skirmishes at Franklin's Crossing (or Deep Run).

Frayser's Farm (or Frazier's Farm), Virginia, Battle of, June 30, 1862. See Peninsular Campaign, Seven Days' Battles, Engagement at White Oak Swamp Bridge and the Battle of Glendale (or White Oak Swamp, Charles City Road, New Market Road, Nelson's Farm, Frayser's Farm [or Frazier's Farm], Willis' Church).

Fredericksburg, Virginia, Battle of, December 13, 1862. See Fredericksburg, Virginia Campaign.

Fredericksburg, Virginia Campaign, November 15, 1862–December 15, 1862. See Part II, below.

Fredericksburg (or Marye's Heights), Virginia, Battle of, May 3–5, 1863. See Chancellorsville, Virginia Campaign, Battle of Fredericksburg (or Marye's Heights) and Battle of Salem Church (or Salem Heights).

Fredericksburg, Virginia, Roberts' Expedition from Fort Monroe to, March 5–8, 1865. See Army of the James, Roberts' Expedition from Fort Monroe to Fredericksburg, Virginia.

French's Field (or Oak Grove, Henrico, King's School House, The Orchard), Virginia, Engagement at, June 25, 1862. See Peninsular Campaign, The Seven Days' Battles, Engagement at Oak Grove (or French's Field, Henrico, King's School House, The Orchard), Virginia.

Front Royal, Virginia, Action at, May 23, 1862. See Shenandoah Valley Campaign (Jackson), 1862, Engagements at Front Royal and Winchester, Virginia.

Front Royal (Cedarville, or Guard Hill), Virginia, Engagement at, August 16, 1864. See

Shenandoah Valley Campaign (Sheridan), Sheridan's First Advance up the Valley.

Fussell's Mill, Virginia, Combat at, August 13, 1864. See Operations about Petersburg and Richmond, Virginia, 1864–1865, Operations of August 1864, Demonstration on the North Bank of the James River at Deep Bottom (Combats at Fussell's Mill, Gravel Hill, Bailey's Creek, Deep Run [or Creek], White's Tavern, Charles City Road, and New Market Road).

Gaines' Mill, Virginia, Battle of, June 27, 1862. See Peninsular Campaign, Seven Days' Battles, Battle of Gaines' Mill (or First Cold Harbor, Chickahominy).

Gainesville (or Brawner's Farm), Virginia, Battle of, August 28, 1862. See Pope's Northern Virginia Campaign, Battle of Gainesville (or Brawner's Farm).

Garnett's Farm and Golding's Farm, Virginia, Action at, June 27–28, 1862. See Peninsular Campaign, Seven Days' Battles, Action at Garnett's Farm and Golding's Farm.

Gettysburg, Pennsylvania, Battle of, July 1–3, 1863. See Gettysburg Campaign, Part II, Battle of Gettysburg.

Gettysburg, Pennsylvania, Cavalry Battle at, July 3, 1863. See Gettysburg Campaign, Part II, Battle of Gettysburg.

Glendale, Virginia, Battle of, June 30, 1862. See Peninsular Campaign, The Seven Days' Battles, Engagement at White Oak Swamp Bridge, and the Battle of Glendale (or White Oak Swamp, Charles City Road, New Market Road, Nelson's Farm, Frayser's Farm [or Frazier's Farm], Willis' Church).

Globe Tavern, Virginia, Battle of, August 18–21, 1864. See Operations about Petersburg and Richmond, Virginia, 1864–1865, Operations of August 1864, Battle of Globe Tavern (or Yellow House, Yellow Tavern, Blick's House [or Station], Weldon Railroad), Virginia.

Golding's Farm and Garnett's Farm, Virginia, Action at, June 27–28, 1862. See Peninsular Campaign, Seven Days' Battles, Action at Garnett's Farm and Golding's Farm.

Goldsboro, North Carolina, Expedition from New Berne to, December 11–20, 1862. See Department of North Carolina, January 7, 1862–July 15, 1863, Troops and Operations in the Department of North Carolina, Department of North Carolina, April 2, 1862–December 24, 1862, Expedition from New Berne to Goldsboro.

Gordonsville, Virginia, Torbert's Expedition from Winchester to, December 19–28, 1864. See Army of the Shenandoah (Sheridan), Torbert's Expedition from Winchester to Gordonsville, Virginia, December 19–28, 1864, and Custer's Demonstration in the Shenandoah Valley (Engagement at Lacey's Springs, December 19–22, 1864).

Gravel Hill, Virginia, Combat at, August 13, 1864. See Operations about Petersburg and Richmond, Virginia, 1864–1865, Operations of August 1864, Demonstration on the North Bank of the James River at Deep Bottom (Combats at Fussell's Mill, Gravel Hill, Bailey's Creek, Deep Run [or Creek], White's Tavern, Charles City Road, and New Market Road), Virginia.

Greenbrier River, Western Virginia, Engagement at, October 3, 1861. See Western (West) Virginia Operations, May 26, 1861–October 11, 1861, Engagement at Greenbrier River, Virginia.

Griswoldville, Georgia, Engagement at, November 22, 1864. See Savannah Campaign (Sherman's March through Georgia).

Groveton (or Manassas Plains), Virginia, August 29, 1862. See Pope's Northern Virginia Campaign, Battle of Groveton (or Manassas Plains).

Groveton Heights (Second Bull Run, or Second Manassas), Virginia, Battle of, August 30, 1862. See Pope's Northern Virginia Campaign, Second Battle of Bull Run (or Groveton Heights, Second Manassas).

Guard Hill (Cedarville, or Front Royal), Virginia, Engagement at, August 16, 1864. See Shenandoah Valley Campaign (Sheridan), Sheridan's First Advance up the Valley.

Hainesville (Falling Waters, or Hoke's Run), Virginia, Engagement at, July 2, 1861. See Department of Pennsylvania, April 27, 1861–August 24, 1861, Engagement at Falling Waters (Hoke's Run, or Hainesville), Virginia.

Hanover, Pennsylvania, Cavalry Action at, June 30, 1863. See Gettysburg Campaign, Part I, From the Rappahannock to Gettysburg, Meade's Advance from Frederick to Gettysburg.

Hanover Court House, Virginia, Engagement at, May 27, 1862. See Peninsular Campaign, Engagement at Hanover Court House, Virginia.

Harper's Ferry, Virginia (West Virginia), Capture of, September 15, 1862. See Maryland Campaign (South Mountain and Antietam), Capture of Harper's Ferry, Virginia.

Harris Farm, Virginia, Engagement at, May 19, 1864. See Richmond, Virginia Campaign, 1864, Operations about Spotsylvania Court House, Operations of May 19, 1864 (Engagement at the Harris Farm, Virginia).

Hatch's Expedition against the Charleston and Savannah Railroad (Engagement at Honey Hill), South Carolina, November–December 1864. See Department of the South, Part IV, Department of the South, Operations in the Department of the South.

Hatcher's Run (or Boydton Plank Road), Virginia, Engagement at, October 27–28, 1864. See Operations about Petersburg and Richmond, Virginia, 1864–1865, Operations of October 1864, Engagement at the Boydton Plank Road (or Hatcher's Run), Virginia.

Hatcher's Run, Virginia, Reconnaissance to, December 9–10, 1864. See Operations about Petersburg and Richmond, Virginia, 1864–1865, Winter of 1864–1865, Reconnaissance to Hatcher's Run, Virginia.

Hatcher's Run, Virginia, Battle of, February 5–7, 1865. See Operations about Petersburg and Richmond, Virginia, 1864–1865, Winter of 1864–1865, Battle of Hatcher's Run (or Dabney's Mill, Armstrong's Mill, Rowanty Creek, Vaughan Road), Virginia.

Hatteras Inlet, North Carolina, Expedition to, August 22–29, 1861. See Department of Virginia, May 22, 1861–July 15, 1863, Troops and Operations in the Department of Virginia, Expedition to Hatteras Inlet.

Haw's Shop (Aenon, or Enon Church), Virginia, Engagement at, May 28, 1864. See Richmond, Virginia Campaign, 1864, Operations on the Pamunkey River.

Henrico (or Oak Grove, French's Field, King's School House, The Orchard), Virginia, Engagement at, June 25, 1862. See Peninsular Campaign, The Seven Days' Battles, Engagement at Oak Grove (or French's Field, Henrico, King's School House, The Orchard).

Hicksford, Virginia, Warren's Expedition to, December 7–12, 1864. See Operations about Petersburg and Richmond, Virginia, 1864–1865, Winter of 1864–1865, Warren's Expedition to Hicksford, Virginia.

High Bridge, Virginia, Action at, April 6, 1865. See Appomattox Campaign, Virginia, Action at High Bridge.

Hill's Expedition against New Berne, North Carolina, March 8–16, 1863. See Department of North Carolina, January 7, 1862–July 15, 1863, Troops and Operations in the Department of North Carolina, Department of North Carolina, Eighteenth Corps, December 24, 1862–July 15, 1863.

Hoke's Run (Falling Waters, or Hainesville), Virginia, Engagement at, July 2, 1861. See Department of Pennsylvania, April 27, 1861–August 24, 1861, Engagement at Falling Waters (Hoke's Run, or Hainesville), Virginia.

Honey Hill, South Carolina, Engagement at, November 30, 1864. See Department of the South, Part IV, Department of the South, Operations in the Department of the South, Hatch's Expedition against the Charleston and Savannah Railroad (Engagement at Honey Hill), South Carolina.

Hunter's Lynchburg, Virginia Campaign, May 26, 1864–June 29, 1864. See Department of West Virginia, Operations of the Troops of the Department of West Virginia, Expeditions against the Virginia Central Railroad and the Virginia and Tennessee Railroad, Hunter's Lynchburg, Virginia Campaign.

Hupp's Hill (Strasburg), Virginia, Skirmish at, October 14, 1864. See Shenandoah Valley Campaign (Sheridan), Fisher's Hill to Cedar Creek, Virginia.

Jerico Mills (or Ford), Virginia, Engagement at, May 25, 1864. See Richmond, Virginia Campaign, 1864, From Spotsylvania Court House to the North Anna River, Battle of the North Anna River (Including the Combat at Jerico Mills [Jerico Bridge, or Jerico Ford]).

Jerusalem Plank Road, Virginia, Engagement at, June 22, 1864. See Operations about Petersburg and Richmond, Virginia, 1864–1865, Operations of June 1864, Movements against the Petersburg and Weldon (Weldon) Railroad (Engagement near the Jerusalem Plank Road).

Johnson's Farm, Virginia, Engagement at, October 7, 1864. See Operations about Petersburg and Richmond, Virginia, 1864–1865, Operations of October 1864, Engagement at the Darbytown Road and the New Market Road (Johnson's Farm, and Four-Mile Creek [or Run]), Virginia.

Kanawha Valley Campaign, Western Virginia, July 11–29, 1861. See Western (West) Virginia Operations, May 26, 1861–October 11, 1861, Kanawha Valley Campaign, July 1861.

Kanawha Valley and New River Region, Western Virginia, Operations in, November 1–19, 1861. See Department of Western Virginia, Operations in the Department of Western Virginia, Operations in the Kanawha and New River Region.

Kanawha Valley, Cox's Advance from, to East River and Lewisburg, West Virginia, May 1862. See Mountain Department, Troops and Operations in the Mountain Department.

Kearneysville, West Virginia, Action near, August 25, 1864. See Shenandoah Valley Campaign, Sheridan), Sheridan's First Advance up the Valley.

Kelly's Ford (or Kellysville), Virginia, Engagement at, March 17, 1863. See Part II, below.

Kelly's Ford, Virginia, Action at, November 7, 1863. See Part II, below, Engagements at Rappahannock Station and Kelly's Ford, Virginia.

Kellysville (or Kelly's Ford), Virginia, Engagement at, March 17, 1863. See Part II, below, Action at Kelly's Ford (Kellysville).

Kernstown (or Winchester), Virginia, Battle of, March 23, 1862. See Shenandoah Valley Campaign (Jackson), 1862, Battle of Kernstown (or Winchester), Virginia.

Kernstown (or Winchester), Virginia, Battle of, July 24, 1864. See Early's Washington Raid (and Operations in the Shenandoah Valley, Maryland, and Pennsylvania), Early Threatens Again in the Valley, Battle of Kernstown (or Winchester), Virginia.

Kilpatrick's Expedition against Richmond, Virginia, and Custer's Raid into Albemarle County, Virginia, February 28, 1864–March 4, 1864. See Part II, below.

King and Queen County, Virginia, Wistar's Expedition to, March 9–12, 1864. See Department of Virginia and North Carolina, Operations in the Department of Virginia and North Carolina, Wistar's Expedition to King and Queen County, Virginia.

King's School House (or Oak Grove, Henrico, French's Field, The Orchard), Virginia, Engagement at, June 25, 1862. See Peninsular Campaign, The Seven Days' Battles, Engagement at Oak Grove (or French's Field, Henrico, King's School House, The Orchard).

Kinston (or Wise's Forks), North Carolina, Battle of, March 8–10, 1865. See Department of North Carolina, January 31, 1865–May 19, 1866, Operations in the Department of North Carolina, Advance of Schofield's Army to Goldsboro (Battle of Kinston or Wise's Forks).

Lacey's Springs, Virginia, Engagement at, December 19, 1864. See Army of the Shenandoah (Sheridan), Torbert's Expedition from Winchester to Gordonsville, Virginia, December 19–28, 1864, and Custer's Demonstration in the Shenandoah Valley (Engagement at Lacey's Springs, December 19, 1864).

Laurel Hill (or Alsop's Farm), Virginia, Engagement at, May 8, 1864. See Richmond, Virginia Campaign, 1864, Operations about Spotsylvania Court House, Engagement at Alsop's Farm (Laurel Hill).

Laurel Hill, Virginia, Combat at, September 29, 1864. See Operations about Petersburg and Richmond, Virginia, 1864–1865, Operations of September 1864, Battle of Chaffin's Farm (Combats at Fort Harrison, Fort Gilmer, Fort Gregg, New Market Heights, and Laurel Hill), Virginia..

Lynchburg, Virginia Campaign (Hunter), May 26, 1864–June 29, 1864. See Department of West Virginia, Operations of the Troops of the Department of West Virginia, Hunter's Lynchburg, Virginia Campaign.

Lynchburg, Virginia, Engagement at, June 17–18, 1864. See Department of West Virginia, Operations of the Troops of the Department of West Virginia, Hunter's Lynchburg, Virginia Campaign.

McClellan's Western Virginia Campaign, July 6–17, 1861. See Western (West) Virginia Operations, May 26, 1861–October 11, 1861, McClellan's Western Virginia Campaign (Engagement at Rich Mountain).

McDowell, Virginia, Engagement at, May 8, 1862. See Shenandoah Valley Campaign (Jackson), 1862, Engagement at McDowell, Virginia.

Malvern Cliff (or Turkey Bridge), Virginia, Engagement at, June 30, 1862. See Peninsular Campaign, Seven Days' Battles, Occupation of Malvern Hill (Engagement at Malvern Cliff or Turkey Bridge).

Malvern Hill (Crew's Farm, or Poindexter's Farm), Virginia, Battle of, July 1, 1862. See Peninsular Campaign, Seven Days' Battles, Battle of Malvern Hill (or Crew's Farm, Poindexter's Farm).

Manassas (or Bull Run), Virginia, First Battle of, July 21, 1861. See Bull Run Campaign, Virginia (First Battle of Bull Run or Manassas).

Mannassas (Bull Run, or Groveton Heights), Virginia, Second Battle of, August 30, 1862. See Pope's Northern Virginia Campaign, Second Battle of Bull Run (or Groveton Heights, Second Manassas).

Manassas Gap (or Wapping Heights), Virginia, Action at, July 23, 1863. See Gettysburg Campaign, Part III, Pursuit of Lee, From Williamsport and Falling Waters to the Rappahannock River.

Manassas Plains (or Groveton), Virginia, Battle of, August 29, 1862. See Pope's Northern Virginia Campaign, Battle of Groveton (or Manassas Plains).

Marye's Heights (or Fredericksburg), Virginia, Battle of (Chancellorsville Campaign), May 3–5, 1863. See Chancellorsville, Virginia Campaign, Battle of Fredericksburg (or Marye's Heights) and Battle of Salem Church (or Salem Heights).

Maryland Campaign (South Mountain and Antietam), September 3, 1862–September 20, 1862. See Part II, below.

Mechanicsville (or Beaver Dam Creek, Ellerson's Mill [or Ellison's Mill]), Virginia, Battle of, June 26, 1862. See Peninsular Campaign, Seven Days' Battles, Battle of Mechanicsville (or

Beaver Dam Creek, Ellerson's Mill [or Ellison's Mill]).

Merritt's Expedition from Winchester into Fauquier and Loudoun Counties, Virginia, November 28, 1864–December 3, 1864. See Army of the Shenandoah (Sheridan).

Middleburg, Virginia, Skirmishes at, June 17–18, 1863. See Gettysburg Campaign, Part I, From the Rappahannock to Gettysburg, Advance of the Army to the Bull Run Mountains.

Middleburg, Virginia, Action at, June 19, 1863. See Gettysburg Campaign, Part I, From the Rappahannock to Gettysburg, Advance of the Army to the Bull Run Mountains.

Military Road (or Quaker Road), Virginia, Skirmish on, March 29, 1865. See Appomattox Campaign, Virginia, The Opening Moves, and Engagement at the Lewis House.

Mine Run Campaign, Virginia, November 26, 1863–December 2, 1863. See Part II, below.

Monocacy, Maryland, Battle of the, July 9, 1864. See Early's Washington Raid (and Operations in the Shenandoah Valley, Maryland, and Pennsylvania), Battle of the Monocacy, Maryland.

Monroe's Cross Roads, South Carolina, Engagement at, March 10, 1865. See Carolinas Campaign, Savannah, Georgia to Fayetteville, North Carolina, Engagement at Monroe's Cross Roads, South Carolina.

Monterey Gap, Pennsylvania, Action at, July 4, 1863. See Gettysburg Campaign, Part III, Pursuit of Lee, From Gettysburg to Falling Waters; and also Cavalry Corps, Army of the Potomac, Gettysburg Campaign.

Moorefield, West Virginia, Engagement near, August 7, 1864. See Early's Washington Raid (and Operations in the Shenandoah Valley, Maryland, and Pennsylvania), Early Threatens Again in the Valley, Burning of Chambersburg, Pennsylvania.

Morton's Ford, Virginia, Engagement at, February 6, 1864. See Army of the Potomac, Winter of 1863–1864, Demonstration on the Rapidan River. See also Second Corps, Army of the Potomac, Winter of 1863–1864.

Mud March, Virginia, January 20–23, 1863. See Army of the Potomac, Winter of 1862–1863, The Mud March.

Nelson's Farm, Virginia, Battle of, June 30, 1862. See Peninsular Campaign, Seven Days' Battles, Engagement at White Oak Swamp Bridge and the Battle of Glendale (or White Oak Swamp, Charles City Road, New Market Road, Nelson's Farm, Frayser's Farm [or Frazier's Farm], Willis' Church).

New Berne, North Carolina, Battle of, March 14, 1862. See Department of North Carolina, January 7, 1862–July 15, 1863, Troops and Operations in the Department of North Carolina, Burnside's Expedition to North Carolina.

New Berne, North Carolina, Expedition to Goldsboro from, December 1–20, 1862. See Department of North Carolina, January 7, 1862–July 15, 1863, Troops and Operations in the Department of North Carolina, Department of North Carolina, April 2, 1862–December 24, 1862.

New Berne, North Carolina, Daniel H. Hill's Expedition against, March 8–16, 1863. See Department of North Carolina, January 7, 1862–July 15, 1863, Troops and Operations in the Department of North Carolina, Department of North Carolina, Eighteenth Corps, December 24, 1862–July 15, 1863.

New Berne, North Carolina, Pickett's Expedition against, January 30, 1865–February 3, 1864. See Department of Virginia and North Carolina, Operations in the Department of Virginia and North Carolina, Pickett's Expedition against New Berne, North Carolina.

New Market, Virginia, Engagement at, May 15, 1864. See Department of West Virginia, Operations of the Troops of the Department of West Virginia,

Expeditions against the Virginia Central and Virginia and Tennessee Railroads, Sigel's Movement up the Shenandoah Valley (Engagement at New Market), Virginia.

New Market Heights, Virginia, Combat at, September 29, 1864. See Operations about Petersburg and Richmond, Virginia, 1864–1865, Operations of September 1864, Battle of Chaffin's Farm (Combats at Fort Harrison, Fort Gilmer, Fort Gregg, New Market Heights, and Laurel Hill), Virginia.

New Market Road, Virginia, Battle of, June 30, 1862. See Peninsular Campaign, Seven Days' Battles, Engagement at White Oak Swamp Bridge, and the Battle of Glendale (or White Oak Swamp, Charles City Road, New Market Road, Nelson's Farm, Frayser's Farm [or Frazier's Farm], Willis' Church).

New Market Road, Virginia, Engagement at, July 27, 1864. See Operations about Petersburg and Richmond, Virginia, 1864–1865, Operations of July 1864, Demonstration on the North Bank of the James River, Engagement at Deep Bottom (or Darbytown, Strawberry Plains, New Market Road), Virginia.

New Market Road, Virginia, Combat at, August 14, 1864. See Operations about Petersburg and Richmond, Virginia, 1864–1865, Operations of August 1864, Demonstration on the North Bank of the James River at Deep Bottom (Combats at Fussell's Mill, Gravel Hill, Bailey's Creek, Deep Run [or Creek], White's Tavern, Charles City Road, and New Market Road), Virginia.

New Market Road, Virginia, Engagement at, October 7, 1864. See Operations about Petersburg and Richmond, Virginia, 1864–1865, Operations of October 1864, Engagement at the Darbytown Road and the New Market Road (Johnson's Farm and Four-Mile Creek [or Run], Virginia).

New York, Draft Riots in, July 1863. See Department of the East, January 3, 1863–June 27, 1865, Draft Riots in New York, July 1863.

New York, The November Election of 1864 in. See Department of the East, January 3, 1863–June 27, 1865, Election of 1864 in New York. See also Army of the James, Line of Defenses North of the James River.

North Anna River, Virginia, Operations about, May 23–27, 1864. See Richmond, Virginia Campaign, 1864, From Spotsylvania Court House to the North Anna River.

Northern Virginia Campaign, Pope's, July 26, 1862–September 2, 1862. See Part II, below, Pope's Northern Virginia Campaign.

Oak Grove (or French's Field, Henrico, King's School House, The Orchard), Virginia, Engagement at, June 25, 1862. See Peninsular Campaign, Seven Days' Battles.

Ocean Pond (or Olustee), Florida, Engagement at, February 20, 1864. See Department of the South, Part III, Department of the South, Tenth Corps, Districts in the Department of the South, Tenth Corps, District of Florida (Seymour's Florida Expedition).

Olustee (or Ocean Pond), Florida, Engagement at, February 20, 1864. See Department of the South, Part III, Department of the South, Tenth Corps, Districts in the Department of the South, Tenth Corps, District of Florida (Seymour's Florida Expedition).

Opequon Creek (or Winchester), Virginia, Battle of, September 19, 1864. See Shenandoah Valley Campaign (Sheridan), Battle of Opequon Creek (or Winchester).

Orchard, The (or Oak Grove, French's Field, Henrico, King's School House), Virginia, Engagement at, June 25, 1862. See Peninsular Campaign, Seven Days' Battles, Engagement at Oak Grove (or French's Field, Henrico, King's School House, The Orchard).

Ox Hill (or Chantilly), Virginia, Battle of, September 1, 1862. See Pope's Northern Virginia Campaign, Battle of Chantilly (or Ox Hill).

Pamunkey River, Virginia, Operations on, May 28–31, 1864. See Richmond, Virginia Campaign,1864, Operations on the Pamunkey River.

Parker's Ford (or Snicker's Ferry), Virginia, Engagement at, July 18, 1864. See Early's Washington Raid (and Operations in the Shenandoah Valley, Maryland, and Pennsylvania), Engagement at Snicker's Ferry (or Parker's Ford), Virginia.

Patterson's Shenandoah Valley Campaign of July 1861. See Department of Pennsylvania, April 27, 1861–August 24, 1861.

Payne's Farm, Virginia, Engagement at, November 27, 1863. See Mine Run Campaign, Virginia.

Peach Orchard (or Allen's Farm), Virginia, Engagement at, June 29, 1862. See Peninsular Campaign, Seven Days' Battles, Engagement at Allen's Farm (or Peach Orchard).

Peebles' Farm, Virginia, Combats at, September 29, 1864–October 2, 1864. See Operations about Petersburg and Richmond, Virginia, 1864–1865, Operations of September 1864, Battle of Poplar Spring Church (Combats at Wyatt's Farm, Peebles' Farm, Chappell's House, Pegram's Farm, and Vaughan Road), Virginia.

Pegram's Farm, Virginia, Combats at, September 29, 1864–October 2, 1864. See Operations about Petersburg and Richmond, Virginia, 1864–1865, Operations of September 1864, Battle of Poplar Spring Church (Combats at Wyatt's Farm, Peebles' Farm, Chappell's House, Pegram's Farm, and Vaughan Road), Virginia.

Peninsular Campaign, Virginia, March 17, 1862–September 2, 1862. See Part II, below.

Petersburg, Virginia, Engagement at, June 9, 1864. See Army of the James, Engagement at Petersburg, June 9, 1864.

Petersburg, Virginia, Operations about, June 9, 1864–June 18, 1864. See Army of the James, Engagement at Petersburg, June 9, 1864, and also Assaults at Petersburg, June 15–18, 1864.

Petersburg, Virginia, Assaults at, June 15–18, 1864. See Operations about Petersburg and Richmond, Virginia, 1864–1865, Operations of June 1864, Assaults at Petersburg, June 15–18, 1864.

Petersburg, Virginia, Operations about, June 18, 1864–March 29,1865. See Part II, below, Operations about Petersburg and Richmond, Virginia, 1864–1865; and also Army of the James.

Petersburg, Virginia, Siege of, June 18, 1864–March 29, 1865. See Operations about Petersburg and Richmond, Virginia, 1864–1865.

Petersburg, Virginia, Operations about, March 29, 1865–April 3, 1865. See Appomattox Campaign, Virginia.

Petersburg Mine Asssault, Virginia, July 30, 1864. See Operations about Petersburg and Richmond, Virginia, 1864–1865, Operations of July 1864, Petersburg Mine Assault.

Philippi, Western Virginia, Action at, June 3, 1861. See Western (West) Virginia Operations, May 26, 1861–October 11, 1861, Action at Philippi, Western Virginia.

Pickett's Expedition against New Berne, North Carolina, January 30, 1864–February 3, 1864. See Department of Virginia and North Carolina, Operations in the Department of Virginia and North Carolina, Pickett's Expedition against New Berne, North Carolina.

Piedmont, Virginia, Engagement at, June 5, 1864. See Department of West Virginia, Operations of Troops of the Department of West Virginia, Hunter's Lynchburg, Virginia Campaign.

Plymouth, North Carolina, Capture of, April 17–20, 1864. See Department of Virginia and North Carolina, Operations in the Department of Virginia and North Carolina, Capture of Plymouth, North Carolina.

Poindexter's Farm (or Malvern Hill, Crew's Farm), Virginia, Battle of, July 1, 1862. See Peninsular Campaign, Seven Days' Battles, Battle of Malvern Hill (or Crew's Farm, Poindexter's Farm).

Pope's Northern Virginia Campaign, July 30, 1862–September 2, 1862. See Part II, below.

Poplar Spring Church, Virginia, Battle of, September 29, 1864–October 2, 1864. See Operations about Petersburg and Richmond, Virginia, 1864–1865, Operations of September 1864, Battle of Poplar Spring Church (Combats at Wyatt's Farm, Peebles' Farm, Chappell's House, Pegram's Farm, and Vaughan Road), Virginia.

Port Republic, Virginia, Engagement at, June 9, 1862. See Shenandoah Valley Campaign (Jackson), 1862, Engagements at Cross Keys and Port Republic, Virginia.

Port Royal Expedition, South Carolina, November 1861. See Department of the South, Part I, South Carolina Expedition (Thomas W. Sherman).

Quaker Road (Military Road, or Lewis' Farm), Virginia, Skirmish on, March 29, 1865. See Appomattox Campaign, Virginia, The Opening Moves, and also Engagement at the Lewis Farm.

Rapidan River, Virginia, Demonstration on, February 6–7, 1864. See Army of the Potomac, Winter of 1863–1864, Demonstration on the Rapidan River. See also Second Corps, Army of the Potomac, Winter of 1863–1864.

Rappahannock Station, Virginia, Engagement at, November 7, 1863. See Part II, below, Engagement at Rappahannock Station and Kelly's Ford, Virginia.

Reams' Station, Virginia, Engagement at, June 29, 1864. See Operations about Petersburg and Richmond, Virginia, 1864–1865, Operations of June 1864, Wilson's Cavalry Raid on the South Side (Lynchburg) Railroad and the Richmond and Danville Railroad.

Reams' Station, Virginia, Battle of, August 25, 1864. See Operations about Petersburg and Richmond, Virginia, 1864–1865, Operations of August 1864, Battle of Reams' Station, Virginia.

Rich Mountain, Western Virginia, Engagement at, July 11, 1861. See Western (West) Virginia Operations, May 26, 1861–October 11, 1861, McClellan's Western Virginia Campaign (Engagement at Rich Mountain).

Richmond, Virginia Campaign, 1864. See Part II, below.

Richmond, Virginia, Wistar's Expedition from Yorktown against, February 6–8, 1864. See Department of Virginia and North Carolina, Operations in the Department of Virginia and North Carolina, Wistar's Expedition from Yorktown against Richmond, Virginia.

Richmond, Virginia, Operations about, May 6, 1864–June 15, 1864. See Army of the James, Engagement at Drewry's Bluff.

Richmond, Virginia, Sheridan's Raid to, May 9–24, 1864. See Part II, below, Sheridan's Richmond, Virginia Raid.

Richmond, Virginia, Operations About, June 15, 1864–March 29, 1865. See Part II, below, Operations about Petersburg and Richmond, Virginia, 1864–1865; and also Army of the James.

Roanoke Island, North Carolina, Battle, of February 8, 1862. See Department of North Carolina, January 7, 1862–July 15, 1863, Troops and Operations in the Department of North Carolina, Burnside's Expedition to North Carolina.

Rocky Gap (or White Sulfur Springs), West Virginia, Engagement at, August 26–27, 1863. See Department of West Virginia, Operations of the Troops of the Department of West Virginia, Averell's Raid in West Virginia (Engagement at Rocky Gap, at White Sulfur Springs).

Rowanty Creek (or Hatcher's Run), Virginia, Battle of, February 5–7, 1865. See Operations about Petersburg and Richmond, Virginia, 1864–1865, Winter of 1864–1865, Battle of Hatcher's Run (or Dabney's Mill, Armstrong's Mill, Rowanty Creek, Vaughan Road), Virginia.

Salem Church (or Salem Heights), Virginia, Battle of, May 3, 1863. See Chancellorsville, Virginia Campaign, Battle of Fredericksburg (or Marye's Heights) and Battle of Salem Church (or Salem Heights).

Salem Heights (or Salem Church), Virginia, Battle of, May 3, 1863. See Chancellorsville, Virginia Campaign, Battle of Fredericksburg (or Marye's Heights) and Battle of Salem Church (or Salem Heights).

Santa Rosa Island, Florida, Action at, October 9, 1861. See Department of Florida, April 11, 1861–March 15, 1862.

Savage Station (or Savage's Station), Virginia, Battle of, June 29, 1862. See Peninsular Campaign, Seven Days' Battles, Battle of Savage Station.

Savannah Campaign (Sherman's March through Georgia). See Part II, below.

Savannah, Georgia, Siege of, December 10–21, 1864. See Savannah Campaign (Sherman's March through Georgia).

Savannah, Georgia, Occupation of, December 21, 1864. See Savannah Campaign (Sherman's March through Georgia).

Sayler's Creek, Virginia, Battle of, April 6, 1865. See Appomattox Campaign, Virginia, Battle of Sayler's Creek.

Scarey Creek, Western Virginia, Action at, July 17, 1861. See Western (West) Virginia Operations, May 26, 1861–October 11, 1861, Kanawha Valley Campaign, July 1861.

Secessionville, South Carolina, Engagement at, June 16, 1862. See Department of the South, Part II, Department of the South, Engagement at Secessionville, South Carolina.

Seven Days' Battles, Virginia, June 25, 1862–July 1, 1862. See Peninsular Campaign, Seven Days' Battles.

Seven Pines–Fair Oaks, Virginia, Battle of, May 31, 1862. See Peninsular Campaign, Battle of Fair Oaks–Seven Pines, Virginia.

Seymour's Florida Expedition (Engagement at Olustee or Ocean Pond), Florida, February 5–22, 1864. See Department of the South, Part III, Department of the South, Tenth Corps, Districts in the Department of the South, Tenth Corps, District of Florida (Seymour's Florida Expedition).

Sharpsburg (or Antietam), Maryland, Battle of, September 17, 1862. See Maryland Campaign (South Mountain and Antietam), Battle of Antietam (Sharpsburg), Maryland.

Shenandoah Valley Campaign of July 1861 (Patterson). See Department of Pennsylvania, April 27, 1861–August 24, 1861.

Shenandoah Valley Campaign (Jackson), 1862. See Part II, below.

Shenandoah Valley Campaign (Sheridan), August 7, 1864–November 28, 1864. See Part II, below.

Sheridan's Expedition from Winchester to Petersburg, Virginia, February 27, 1865–March 28, 1865. See Part II, below.

Sheridan's Richmond, Virginia Raid, May 9–24, 1864. See Part II, below.

Sheridan's Shenandoah Valley Campaign, Virginia, August 7, 1864–November 28, 1864. See Shenandoah Valley Campaign (Sheridan).

Sheridan's Trevilian Station Raid, Virginia, June 7–28, 1864. See Part II, below.

Sherman's Carolinas Campaign, January 1, 1865–April 26, 1865. See Carolinas Campaign.

Sherman's March through Georgia, November 15, 1864–December 21, 1864. See Savannah Campaign (Sherman's March through Georgia).

Slaughter's Mountain (Cedar Mountain, or Cedar Creek), Virginia, Battle of, August 9, 1862. See Pope's Northern Virginia Campaign, Battle of Cedar Mountain (Slaughter's Mountain, or Cedar Run).

Snicker's Ferry (or Parker's Ford), Virginia, Engagement at, July 18, 1864. See Early's Washington Raid (and Operations in the Shenandoah Valley, Maryland, and Pennsylvania), Engagement at Snicker's Ferry (or Parker's Ford), Virginia.

South Carolina Expedition (Thomas W. Sherman). See Department of the South, Part I, South Carolina Expedition (Thomas W. Sherman).

South Mills, Camden County, North Carolina, Engagement at, April 19, 1862. See Department of North Carolina, January 7, 1862–July 15, 1863, Troops and Operations in the Department of North Carolina, Department of North Carolina, April 2, 1862–December 24, 1862.

South Mountain, Maryland, Battle of, September 14, 1862. See Maryland Campaign (South Mountain and Antietam), Battle of South Mountain (Fox's Gap and Turner's Gap).

Southwest Mountain (Cedar Mountain, or Slaughter's Mountain), Virginia, Battle of, August 9, 1862. See Pope's Northern Virginia Campaign, Battle of Cedar Mountain (Slaughter's Mountain, or Cedar Run).

Spotsylvania Court House, Battle of, May 8–19, 1864. See Richmond, Virginia Campaign, 1864, Operations about Spotsylvania Court House.

Spotsylvania Court House, Operations about, May 8–20, 1864. See Richmond, Virginia Campaign, 1864, Operations about Spotsylvania Court House.

Stephenson's Depot (or Winchester), Virginia, Battle of, June 15, 1863. See Gettysburg Campaign, Part I, From the Rappahannock to Gettysburg, Withdrawal of the Army to the Orange and Alexandria Railroad, Engagement at Winchester, Virginia, and Engagement at Stephenson's Depot (or Station), Virginia.

Stoneman's Raid (Chancellorsville Campaign), Virginia, April 29, 1863–May 7, 1863. See Chancellorsville, Virginia Campaign, Stoneman's Raid.

Stoneman's Raid into Southwestern Virginia and Western North Carolina, March 21, 1865–April 25, 1865. See Part II, below.

Stony Creek Station, Virginia, Expedition to, December 1, 1864. See Operations about Petersburg, Virginia, 1864–1865, Winter of 1864–1865.

Strasburg (Hupp's Hill), Virginia, Skirmish at, October 14, 1864. See Shenandoah Valley Campaign (Sheridan), Fisher's Hill to Cedar Creek, Virginia.

Strawberry Plains, Virginia, Engagement at, July 27, 1864. See Operations about Petersburg and Richmond, Virginia, 1864–1865, Operations of July 1864, Demonstration on the North Bank of the James River, Engagement at Deep Bottom (or Darbytown, Strawberry Plains, New Market Road), Virginia.

Suffolk, Virginia, Siege of, April 11, 1863–May 4, 1863. See Department of Virginia, May 22, 1861–July 15, 1863, Troops and Operations in the Department of Virginia.

Taylor's Hole Creek (or Averasboro), North Carolina, Battle of, March 16, 1865. See Carolinas Campaign, Fayette to Goldsboro, North Carolina, Battle of Averasboro (or Taylor's Hole Creek).

Terry's Expedition to Fort Fisher, North Carolina, January 3–17, 1865. See Army of the James, Terry's Expedition to Fort Fisher, North Carolina.

Tom's Brook, Virginia, Engagement at, October 9, 1864. See Shenandoah Valley Campaign (Sheridan), Fisher's Hill to Cedar Creek, Virginia.

Torbert's Expedition from Winchester to Gordonsville, Virginia, December 19–28, 1864. See Army of the Shenandoah (Sheridan), Torbert's Expedition from Winchester to Gordonsville, Virginia, December 19–28, 1864, and Custer's Demonstration in the Shenandoah Valley (Engagement at Lacey's Springs), December 19, 1864.

Totopotomoy River, Virginia, Operations about, May 28–31, 1864. See Richmond, Virginia Campaign,1864, Operations on the Totopotomoy River.

Trevilian Station, Virginia, Combat at, June 11, 1864. See Part II, below, Sheridan's Trevilian Station Raid, Virginia.

Turkey Bridge (or Malvern Cliff), Virginia, Engagement at, June 30, 1862. See Peninsular Campaign, Seven Days' Battles, Occupation of Malvern Hill (Engagement at Malvern Cliff or Turkey Bridge).

Turner's Gap, South Mountain, Maryland, Battle of, September 14, 1862. See Maryland Campaign (South Mountain and Antietam), Battle of South Mountain (Fox's Gap and Turner's Gap).

Upperville, Virginia, Engagement at, June 21, 1863. See Gettysburg Campaign, Part I, From the Rappahannock to Gettysburg, Advance of the Army to the Bull Run Mountains.

Vaughan Road, Virginia, Combat at, October 1, 1864. See Operations about Petersburg and Richmond, Virginia, 1864–1865, Operations of September 1864, Battle of Poplar Spring Church (Combats at Wyatt's Farm, Peebles' Farm, Chappell's House, Pegram's Farm, and Vaughan Road), Virginia.

Vaughan Road (or Hatcher's Run), Virginia, Battle of, February 5–7, 1865. See Operations about Petersburg and Richmond, Virginia, 1864–1865, Winter of 1864–1865, Battle of Hatcher's Run (or Dabney's Mill, Armstrong's Mill, Rowanty Creek, Vaughan Road), Virginia.

Virginia Central Railroad, Expeditions against. See Department of West Virginia, Operations of the Troops of the Department of West Virginia, Expeditions against the Virginia Central and the Virginia and Tennessee Railroads.

Virginia and Tennessee Railroad, Expeditions against. See Department of West Virginia, Operations of the Troops of the Department of West Virginia, Expeditions against the Virginia Central and the Virginia and Tennessee Railroads.

Wapping Heights (or Manassas Gap), Virginia, Action at, July 23, 1863. See Gettysburg Campaign, Part III, Pursuit of Lee, From Williamsport and Falling Waters to the Rappahannock River.

Warren's Expedition to Hicksford, Virginia, December 7–12, 1864. See Operations about Petersburg and Richmond, Virginia, 1864–1865, Winter of 1864–1865, Warren's Expedition to Hicksford, Virginia.

Washington, D.C., Early's Raid on, June 23, 1864–August 3, 1864. See Early's Raid on Washington (and Operations in the Shenandoah Valley, Maryland, and Pennsylvania), Early's Army before Washington, D.C.

Washington, North Carolina, Siege of, March 30, 1863–April 20, 1863. See Department of North Carolina, January 7, 1862–July 15, 1863, Troops and Operations in the Department of North Carolina, Department of North Carolina, Eighteenth Corps, December 24, 1862–July 15, 1863.

Watkins House, Virginia, Action at, March 25, 1865. See Operations about Petersburg and Richmond, Virginia, 1864–1865, Winter of 1864–1865, Assault at Fort Stedman, Virginia.

Waynesboro, Virginia, Engagement at, March 2, 1865. See Sheridan's Expedition from Winchester to Petersburg, Virginia.

Weldon Railroad, Virginia, Movement against, June 21–23, 1864. See Operations about Petersburg and Richmond, Virginia, 1864–1865, Operations of June 1864, Movement against the Petersburg and Weldon (Weldon) Railroad (Engagement near the Jerusalem Plank Road).

Weldon Railroad (or Globe Tavern), Virginia, Battle of, August 18–21, 1864. See Operations about Petersburg and Richmond, Virginia, 1864–1865, Operations of August 1864, Battle of Globe Tavern (or Yellow House, Yellow Tavern, Blick's House [or Station], Weldon Railroad), Virginia.

West Point (Barhamsville, or Eltham's Landing), Virginia, Engagement at, May 7, 1862. See Peninsular Campaign, Advance of the Army to White House, Engagement at Eltham's Landing (West Point, or Barhamsville).

Western Virginia Campaign (McClellan), July 6–17, 1861. See Western (West) Virginia Operations, May 26, 1861–October 11, 1861, McClellan's Western Virginia Campaign (Engagement at Rich Mountain).

Western (West) Virginia, Operations in, May 26, 1861–October 11, 1861. See Part II, below.

Western Virginia, Union Occupation of, 1861. See Western (West) Virginia Operations, May 26, 1861–October 11, 1861.

Westmoreland County, Virginia, Roberts' Expedition into, from Fort Monroe, Virginia, March 11–13, 1865. See Army of the James, Roberts' Expedition from Fort Monroe into Westmoreland County, Virginia.

White Oak Ridge (or White Oak Road), Virginia, Engagement at, March 31, 1865. See Appomattox Campaign, Virginia, The Opening Moves, and also Engagement at the White Oak Road (or White Oak Ridge).

White Oak Road (or White Oak Ridge), Virginia, Engagement at, March 31, 1865. See Appomattox Campaign, Virginia, The Opening Moves, and also Engagement at the White Oak Road (or White Oak Ridge).

White Oak Swamp Bridge, Virginia, Engagement at, June 30, 1862. See Peninsular Campaign, Seven Days' Battles, Engagement at White Oak Bridge and the Battle of Glendale (White Oak Swamp, Charles City Road, New Market Road, Nelson's Farm, Frayser's Farm [or Frazier's Farm], Willis' Church).

White Sulfur Springs (or Rocky Gap), West Virginia, Engagement at, August 26–27, 1863. See Department of West Virginia, Operations of the Troops of the Department of West Virginia, Averell's Raid in West Virginia (Engagement at Rocky Gap or White Sulfur Springs).

White's Tavern, Virginia, Combat at, August 16, 1864. See Operations about Petersburg and Richmond, Virginia, 1864–1865, Operations of August 1864, Demonstration on the North Bank of the James River at Deep Bottom (Combats at Fussell's Mill, Gravel Hill, Bailey's Creek, Deep Run [or Creek], White's Tavern, Charles City Road, and New Market Road), Virginia.

Wilderness, Virginia, Battle of, May 5–6, 1864. See Richmond, Virginia Campaign, 1864, Battle of the Wilderness.

Williamsburg, Virginia, Battle of, May 5, 1862. See Peninsular Campaign, Battle of Williamsburg, Virginia.

Williams' Farm, Virginia, Engagement at, June 22, 1864. See Operations about Petersburg and Richmond, Virginia, 1864–1865, Operations of June 1864, Movement against the Petersburg and Weldon (Weldon) Railroad (Engagement near the Jerusalem Plank Road).

Wilmington, North Carolina, Capture of, February 16–22, 1865. See Department of North Carolina, January 31, 1865–May 19, 1866, Operations in the Department of North Carolina, Capture of Wilmington, North Carolina.

Wilson's Cavalry Raid on the South Side (Lynchburg) Railroad and the Richmond and Danville Railroad, June 22, 1864–July 2, 1864. See Operations about Petersburg and Richmond, Virginia, 1864–1865, Operations of June 1864.

Winchester (or Kernstown), Virginia, Engagement at, March 23, 1862. See Shenandoah Valley Campaign (Jackson), 1862, Battle of Kernstown (or Winchester), Virginia.

Winchester, Virginia, Engagement at, May 25, 1862. See Shenandoah Valley Campaign (Jackson), 1862, Engagements at Front Royal and Winchester, Virginia.

Winchester (and Stephenson's Depot), Virginia, Battle of, June 13–15, 1863. See Gettysburg Campaign, Part I, From the Rappahannock to Gettysburg, Withdrawal of the Army to the Orange and Alexandria Railroad, Engagement at Winchester, Virginia, and Engagement at Stephenson's Depot (or Station), Virginia.

Winchester (or Kernstown), Virginia, Battle of, July 24, 1864. See Early's Washington Raid (and Operations in the Shenandoah Valley, Maryland, and Pennsylvania), Early Threatens Again in the Valley, Battle of Kernstown (or Winchester), Virginia.

Winchester (or Opequon Creek), Virginia, Battle of, September 19, 1864. See Shenandoah Valley Campaign (Sheridan), Battle of Opequon Creek (or Winchester), Virginia.

Wise's Forks (or Kinston), North Carolina, Battle of, March 8–10, 1865. See Department of North Carolina, January 31, 1865–May 19, 1866, Operations in the Department of North Carolina, Advance of Schofield's Army to Goldsboro (Battle of Kinston or Wise's Forks).

Wyatt's Farm, Virginia, Combat at, September 29, 1864. See Operations about Petersburg and Richmond, Virginia, 1864–1865, Operations of September 1864, Battle of Poplar Spring Church (Combats at Wyatt's Farm, Peebles' Farm, Chappell's House, Pegram's Farm, and Vaughan Road), Virginia.

Yellow House (or Globe Tavern), Virginia, Battle of, August 18–21, 1864. See Operations about Petersburg and Richmond, Virginia, 1864–1865, Operations of August 1864, Battle of Globe Tavern (or Yellow House, Yellow Tavern, Blick's House [or Station], Weldon Railroad), Virginia.

Yellow Tavern (or Globe Tavern), Virginia, Battle of, August 18–21, 1864. See Operations about

Petersburg and Richmond, Virginia, 1864–1865, Operations of August 1864, Battle of Globe Tavern (or Yellow House, Yellow Tavern, Blick's House [or Station], Weldon Railroad), Virginia.

Yellow Tavern, Henrico County, Virginia, Engagement at, May 11, 1864. See Sheridan's Richmond, Virginia Raid.

Yorktown, Virginia, Siege of, April 5, 1862–May 4, 1862. See Peninsular Campaign, Siege of Yorktown, Virginia.

PART II:
BATTLES AND CAMPAIGNS

APPOMATTOX CAMPAIGN, VIRGINIA, MARCH 29, 1865–APRIL 9, 1865

As the winter of 1864–1865 drew to a close, Ulysses S. Grant's principal concern was that the Army of Northern Virginia might pull out of its entrenchments in front of Petersburg and Richmond and withdraw into the interior and join Joseph E. Johnston's army in North Carolina. If this should happen, the Army of the Potomac would be forced to follow and operate at a serious disadvantage because of the greater distance from its base. To avoid this possibility, Grant was determined to begin his planned spring offensive before the ground was dry enough to enable an army to move readily across country, and by so doing he would prevent Lee from taking advantage of good roads and starting before the Union army was ready to move.

Accordingly, on March 24, 1865, Grant issued orders for the army to move out to the left on the morning of March 29, 1865, for the dual purpose of turning the enemy out of his positions in front of Petersburg and of ensuring the success of a cavalry expedition under Philip H. Sheridan, which was to start at the same time. Sheridan was to attempt to destroy the South Side Railroad and the Danville Railroad, which were essential for the continued subsistence of Robert E. Lee's army, and which also provided an important route to Johnston's army in North Carolina if Lee should decide to move in that direction.

According to the march orders of March 24, 1865, Andrew A. Humphreys' Second Corps and Gouverneur K. Warren's Fifth Corps, Army of the Potomac were to move to the left in two columns, cross Hatcher's Run, and advance toward Dinwiddie Court House. Sheridan, with his cavalry, was to move on the far left to Dinwiddie Court House, and then act according to further instructions. John G. Parke, commander of Ninth Corps, was placed in command of all troops left to hold the lines about Petersburg and City Point, and was subject to George G. Meade's orders. Ninth Corps was to remain in the works that it then occupied for as long as the entire line of entrenchments was held, but if the troops to the left of Ninth Corps were withdrawn, Parke was authorized to pull back the left of the corps so as to occupy the position held by the army prior to the capture of the Weldon Railroad.

The orders issued by Grant March 24, 1865 also directed Edward O. C. Ord to detach three divisions from his Army of the James, and with them march to the left of the Army of the Potomac below Petersburg. Godfrey Weitzel, commanding Twenty-Fifth Corps, Army of the James, was placed in charge of all troops of the Army of the James left behind in the entrenchments in front of Richmond.

At the beginning of Grant's offensive, the Confederate main line of defenses in front of Petersburg was located as follows: Beginning at the Appomattox River on the left, the line ran southward to the Jerusalem Plank Road and then westward to the Boydton Plank Road at Fort Lee; there it turned to the southwest and ran in front of, and roughly parallel to, the Boydton Plank Road to Hatcher's Run, at a point about a mile east of Burgess' Mill on the Plank Road; from there it extended along Hatcher's Run to Burgess' Mill and westward on the White Oak Road to the Claiborne Road; and from there it curved back to the north, west of the Claiborne Road, and ended on Hatcher's Run.

The Confederate line was occupied as follows: John B. Gordon's Second Corps, Army of Northern Virginia was on the enemy left and held a front of about four miles, which extended from the Appomattox River to the point where Lieutenant's Creek passed through the line between Confederate Batteries Nos. 35 and 36, about one mile east of the Weldon Railroad; Cadmus M. Wilcox's division of Ambrose P. Hill's Third Corps held the line from the right of Gordon's corps to a point roughly opposite Fort Welch, a distance of about four and a half miles; and Henry Heth's division, also of Hill's corps, was on the line from from the right of Wilcox's division to Burgess' Mill, a distance of about three and a half miles. Richard H. Anderson's corps, which then consisted of little more than Bushrod R. Johnson's division, held the line beyond Burgess' Mill, for a distance of about three miles.

The Opening Moves. Promptly on the morning of March 29, 1865, Grant started his army forward. Romeyn B. Ayres' Second Division of Warren's Fifth Corps was on the road by 3:00 A.M., and the rest of the corps soon followed. Ayres crossed Hatcher's Run at the W. Perkins house, and arrived at Monk's Neck Bridge on Rowanty Creek at 4:45 A.M. The bridge had been destroyed, but Ayres soon crossed and marched westward on the Stage Road (Monk's Neck Road) to its junction with the Vaughan Road. The head of Ayres' column arrived at the road junction at 8:15 A.M.

Warren then deployed his command, and Ayres' division proceeded on to the junction of the Vaughan Road and the Quaker Road (or Military Road). Ayres formed one of his brigades in line of battle a short distance up the Quaker Road and held the other two brigades near the junction of the two roads. The brigades of Charles Griffin's First Division were posted on the Hargrave, Scott, and Chappell farms. Samuel W. Crawford, commanding Third Division, Fifth Corps, left Richard Coulter's Third Brigade at the junction of the Stage Road and the Vaughan Road to guard the trains, and placed John A. Kellogg's First Brigade and Henry Baxter's Second Brigade in a position to watch a country road that ran out to the R. Boisseau farm on the Boydton Plank Road.

Meantime, there was activity in the other corps of the army. Early on the morning of March 29, 1865, Ord's Army of the James relieved Humphrey's Second Corps on the left of the Union line of entrenchments. Robert S. Foster's First Division of John Gibbon's Twenty-Fourth Corps occupied the works from Fort Sanders to Hatcher's Run. Thomas

O. Osborn's First Brigade of Foster's division relieved Nelson A. Miles' First Division, Second Corps; and Harrison S. Fairchild's Fourth Brigade of Foster's division relieved Gershom Mott's Third Division, Second Corps; George B. Dandy's Third Brigade of Foster's division occupied the encampment of a part of William Hays' Second Division, Second Corps; and John W. Turner's Independent Division of Twenty-Fourth Corps was placed in reserve at Hatcher's Run. William Birney's Second Division, Twenty-Fifth Corps, which had accompanied Gibbon's Twenty-Fourth Corps from the Richmond front to Petersburg, remained at Humphreys' Station throughout the day.

When relieved by Ord, Second Corps broke camp, and at 6:30 A.M. March 29, 1865, a half hour late, Hays' Second Division moved out and marched down the Vaughan Road toward Hatcher's Run. Hays then crossed the stream and moved out about a half mile to the west, where he deployed his division about a half mile north of the road. Thomas A. Smyth's Third Brigade and James P. McIvor's Second Brigade were formed in line of battle, with McIvor's brigade on the right, next to Hatcher's Run. William A. Olmsted's First Brigade was in reserve.

Mott's Third Division, which had been following Hays, moved on and halted about a mile west of Hatcher's Run, where it deployed north of the Vaughan Road. Byron R. Pierce's Second Brigade was on the right, connecting with Hays' division, and Robert McAllister's Third Brigade was on the left. P. Regis De Trobriand's First Brigade was in reserve.

Miles' First Division, which had been camped near the Squirrel Level Road, followed closely behind Mott and was across Hatcher's Run by 8:30 A.M. Miles then marched on about a mile and formed in line of battle north of the Vaughan Road. George W. Scott's First Brigade was on the right, next to Mott's division; Henry J. Madill's Third Brigade was in the center; and John Ramsey's Fourth Brigade was on the left, near Gravelly Run, about one-half mile from the Quaker Road. Robert Nugent's Second Brigade was in reserve. When deployed, Second Corps was in position to cover the Vaughan Road, and was about three-fourths of a mile from Dabney's Mill, where the enemy was reported to be entrenched.

Simultaneously with the advance of Second Corps and Fifth Corps on the morning of March 29, 1865, Sheridan's cavalry moved out on the far left of the army toward Dinwiddie Court House. Sheridan had just rejoined the Army of the Potomac from the Shenandoah Valley March 27, 1865, and had brought with him Thomas C. Devin's First Cavalry Division and George A. Custer's Third Cavalry Division of the Army of the Shenandoah, both under the direct command of Wesley Merritt; and that same day, George Crook, commanding the Second Cavalry Division, Army of the Potomac (formerly David McM. Gregg's division), was assigned to Sheridan's command.

On March 29, 1865, Sheridan left Hancock's Station with his three divisions and marched southward on the Jerusalem Plank Road on his way toward Dinwiddie Court House. He passed by Gray's Church and Reams' Station on the Weldon Railroad, and at Webbs' farm he turned onto the road to Malone's Crossing on Rowanty Creek. Sheridan's orders were to reach the right and rear of Lee's army as soon as possible. He was not, however, to attack the enemy in its entrenched positions, but was to attempt to force them out into the open by his flanking movement. If the Union cavalry was attacked, or if the enemy moved out where they could be attacked, Sheridan was to strike with his entire force and rely on the cooperation of the army. If, on the other hand, the enemy remained in their entrenchments, Sheridan was authorized to cut loose and destroy the Danville Railroad and the South Side Railroad, which at that time were Lee's only significant lines of supply. When, and if, the railroads were destroyed, Sheridan was either to return to the Army of the Potomac, or to move on and join Sherman's army in North Carolina, whichever he decided would produce the best results.

While on the march that day, Sheridan learned that a strong force of enemy cavalry was south of Stony Creek, and because of this, he left Custer's division at Malone's Crossing to assist and protect the wagon trains, which were moving slowly because of the muddy roads. Sheridan continued on with the divisions of Devin and Crook to Dinwiddie Court House, where he arrived at 5:00 P.M. and camped for the night. He then placed detachments of the two divisions where they would cover the

Vaughan Road, the Flat Foot Road, the Boydton Plank Road, and the Adams Road.

Engagement at the Lewis Farm, March 29, 1865.

At 10:20 A.M., Warren received an order from Meade directing him to move with his corps up the Quaker Road to the crossing of Gravelly Run. Upon arriving there, Warren was to form his corps, facing north, and connecting with Andrew A. Humphreys' Second Corps on his right. His mission was to hold the Boydton Plank Road if possible. Because of a misunderstanding of the order, Warren did not begin his advance until about noon, and he then directed Griffin to move with his division up the Quaker Road. At the same time, he also ordered Crawford to hold his division in readiness to support Griffin's advance.

About noon March 29, 1865, Johnson learned that a strong Federal force was advancing up the Quaker Road, and he was authorized by Richard H. Anderson, his corps commander, to advance with his division and drive this force back to the Vaughan Road. When Johnson led his troops out of the entrenchments and started toward Gravelly Run, he deployed Henry A. Wise's brigade in line of battle and directed William H. Wallace, Young M. Moody, and Matthew Ransom to march with their brigades in column, in that order, in rear of Wise's line. Wise encountered Warren's skirmishers just beyond the point where the Quaker Road joined the Boydton Plank Road. He then pressed on and soon met the leading troops of Griffin's division.

At that time, Griffin was advancing up the Quaker Road, with Joshua L. Chamberlain's First Brigade in the lead. When Chamberlain reached Gravelly Run, he was ordered by Griffin to form his brigade in line of battle and advance on some rifle pits that could be seen on the opposite bank. After crossing the run, Chamberlain sent forward Edwin A. Glenn with his battalion of the 198th Pennsylvania as skirmishers, and formed the rest of his command in line, with the 198th Pennsylvania on the right of the road and 185th New York on the left of the road. Glenn drove the enemy skirmishers out of their works, and then followed them through the woods as far as the Lewis house, about a mile and a half beyond Gravelly Run. There Chamberlain found the enemy on the far side of the clearing in considerable force, and he halted Glenn's command until he could bring up the rest of his brigade to within supporting distance.

When Griffin arrived at the Lewis farm, he ordered Edgar M. Gregory to move his Second Brigade up on the left of Chamberlain, and directed Chamberlain to resume his advance. Chamberlain then brought up his line of battle to the Lewis house, where he re-formed his regiments, reinforced his skirmishers, and then began a rapid advance with his entire command. Before his line reached the woods on the far side of the clearing, it came under a heavy fire from Wise's brigade, but it pressed on and drove a part of Wise's command about a mile back into the woods.

Gregory's brigade, which was to have advanced on the left of Chamberlain, did not keep pace and fell behind. While Chamberlain was waiting for Gregory to come up, he was strongly assailed between 3:00 and 4:00 P.M. by the brigades of Wise and Wallace, and after resisting for a half hour, he was finally forced to fall back out of the woods when the enemy turned his left flank. Chamberlain took a new position parallel to the Quaker Road, and there he was again violently attacked. Although delayed by obstructions on the road, John Mitchell's Battery B, 4th United States Artillery arrived at the Lewis house and opened fire with canister on Wise's brigade. Moody's brigade then attacked on Chamberlain's right and center, and Chamberlain's situation became desperate. He then called for help, and Griffin sent the 1st Michigan, 16th Michigan, and 155th Pennsylvania of Joseph J. Bartlett's Third Brigade, and Gregory sent the 188th New York of his brigade to aid Chamberlain. They arrived just as Chamberlain's brigade was falling back on the Lewis house to support the artillery. The new regiments passed through Chamberlain's line and advanced on the enemy. The three regiments of Bartlett's brigade, commanded by Alfred L. Pearson, moved directly toward the enemy line, and the 188th New York followed Pearson's regiments. About 5:00 P.M., when the fresh Federal troops appeared, Johnson withdrew his brigades to a new position across the Boydton Plank Road, in the edge of the woods to the north and east of the Bevill house. He remained there until dusk, and then retired into the breastworks adjacent to Burgess' Mill and west of Hatcher's Run.

Advance to Hatcher's Run. A country lane crossed the Quaker Road a short distance south of the Lewis house, and while Griffin was engaged, Warren sent his escort, Company C, 4th Pennsylvania Cavalry, out along this lane toward the Boydton Plank Road. The cavalrymen had not gone very far when they were fired on by the enemy, and Warren then ordered Crawford to move out with his division and support them. Crawford deployed Baxter's brigade in line of battle, with its right on the left of Griffin's division, and brought up Kellogg's brigade to the rear of Baxter. Crawford then advanced and, against slight opposition, reached the Boydton Plank Road.

Two of Ayres' brigades followed Crawford across Gravelly Run, but they were not needed during Griffin's engagement that afternoon, and were halted in reserve near the R. Spain house. Ayres' other brigade remained on the south side of Gravelly Run.

About 4:00 P.M., while Warren was attempting to advance on the Quaker Road, Humphreys was directed to move up with his Second Corps and advance on the right of Warren. Earlier, reconnaissances had been sent out on the front of Second Corps, and these had revealed that there were only a few troops ahead. Thus, when Humphreys was ordered to advance, he expected no serious resistance.

When Humphreys heard the sounds of Griffin's battle, he was directed to support the right of Griffin's line with Miles' division. As Miles advanced on the left of the Second Corps line, his left brigade, commanded by John Ramsey, succeeded in establishing contact with the right of Warren, and generally remained in contact during the rest of the day.

When the fighting ended on the Quaker Road March 29, 1865, Griffin, with the brigades of Bartlett and Gregory, followed Johnson's rear guard up the road for about a mile to its junction with the Boydton Plank Road. Griffin then entrenched, with one brigade at the J. Stroud house and the other nearby. Chamberlain's brigade remained on the battlefield that night and the next day.

The advance of Crawford's Third Division of Fifth Corps was delayed by the thick woods through which it had to pass, but it came up on the left of Griffin about dark and took position with its right near the Stroud house and its left on Gravelly Run.

Ayres' division was held in reserve near the R. Spain house, well to the rear of the front line, to watch that area.

McIvor's brigade, which advanced on the left of Hays' division during the day, had maintained contact with troops of Twenty-Fourth Corps on the east side of Hatcher's Run, and it had reached Armstrong's Mill by nightfall. Smyth's brigade, Hays' left brigade, arrived at Dabney's Mill and relieved some troops of Olmsted's brigade, which were in position at the mill, and Olmsted then moved his brigade to the left. That night, Mott's division was on a line that was at nearly a right angle to Hays' line. Pierce's brigade was on the right of the division, on the left of Olmsted, and McAllister's brigade was on the left of Pierce. In advancing that day, a gap had developed between Pierce and McAllister, and two regiments of De Trobriand's brigade were moved up to fill this interval. At dark, Miles' division was still in contact with Fifth Corps on its left.

Encouraged by the successful advances of Fifth Corps and Second Corps during March 29, 1865, Grant decided to change his plans and move against the right flank of Lee's line. That night he instructed Sheridan to ignore that part of his orders that called for a raid on the railroads, and instead ordered him to attempt a movement around the right of Lee's line of entrenchments for an attack on the enemy right rear the next day. Grant also decided to force the enemy back into his line of works along Hatcher's Run and the White Oak Road, and at 9:20 that night, he ordered Warren to advance at 6:00 the next morning. He was to keep his right across the Quaker Road, and to extend his left out as far as possible and yet be able to protect the left of the corps line. He also ordered Humphreys to advance and, while doing so, keep his contact with Warren on his left. Both corps were to halt when they encountered enemy resistance.

That night it began to rain, and it continued to rain during most of the next day. As a result, troop movements could be carried out only with great difficulty because of the muddy roads and fields and the swollen streams.

During the morning of March 29, 1865, Lee received word that Federal infantry and cavalry had crossed Hatcher's Run and were then marching westward toward his right flank. He was not certain of their objective, but he began preparations to strengthen that flank. Earlier, George E. Pickett's division had been ordered from north of the James River to support John B. Gordon's assault on Fort Stedman March 25, 1865, but only George H. Steuart's brigade had reached Petersburg on the morning of the attack. It was not called into action, but was held temporarily near the city. Montgomery D. Corse's and William R. Terry's brigades of Pickett's division were halted on Swift Creek, north of Petersburg. Eppa Hunton's brigade was still north of the James River. On March 29, 1865, Lee ordered Pickett to move to Petersburg with his two brigades from Swift Creek, pick up Steuart's brigade there, and then move by rail to Sutherland's Station, ten miles west of Petersburg on the South Side Railroad. The last of Pickett's troops arrived there late on the night of March 29, 1865. Pickett then marched to the south, across Hatcher's Run, and he took position in the trenches along the Claiborne Road, facing west. That same day, Fitzhugh Lee arrived at Petersburg with his cavalry division from Nine-Mile Creek, east of Richmond, and reported to Lee. Lee also ordered William H. F. Lee and Thomas L. Rosser to march with their cavalry divisions from the extreme right of the Confederate line and join Fitzhugh Lee. Fitzhugh Lee was to take charge of the Confederate cavalry corps when they arrived. William H. F. Lee and Rosser, however, had to move from Stony Creek by a wide detour to the west of Dinwiddie Court House, and they were unable to join Fitzhugh Lee until the evening of March 30, 1865.

In addition to the above changes in positions, Lee ordered Samuel McGowan's Brigade of Cadmus M. Wilcox's division from the line of defenses east of Hatcher's Run to that part of the line west of Burgess' Mill that was held by Anderson's corps.

On the morning of March 30, 1865, Lee rode out to Sutherland's Station, and, upon arriving there decided to send Pickett with his three brigades, Ransom's and Wallace's brigades of Johnson's division, and six guns of William J. Pegram's Artillery Battalion to Five Forks. He was to meet Fitzhugh Lee's cavalry, and then march on Dinwiddie Court House.

Early that same morning, Merritt, with Devin's division, moved up from Dinwiddie Court House on the Five Forks Road to J. Boisseau's house, which was about two miles from the court house, near the junction of the Five Forks Road with the Crump Road. From there, he sent out reconnaissances toward Five Forks and the White Oak Road. As a result, Sheridan soon learned that enemy forces were in some strength on his front and that they apparently intended to hold the White Oak Road. Henry E. Davies' First Brigade of Crook's cavalry division, which had spent the night on the Boydton Plank Road, also sent out a reconnaissance. It communicated with Warren's Fifth Corps, and that afternoon the brigade marched toward Five Forks to support Merritt. It was not engaged, however, and that night it encamped with Merritt and Devin near J. Boisseau's. During the day, Crook, with Charles H. Smith's Third Brigade and J. Irvin Gregg's Second Brigade, covered the crossings of Stony Creek south of Dinwiddie Court House. Custer's division was still at Rowanty Creek trying to move the trains forward.

Meantime, Pickett had been marching westward on the White Oak Road, and at about 4:30 P.M. March 30, 1865, he arrived with his command at Five Forks. He was joined there about dark by the cavalry divisions of William H. F. Lee and Rosser. Pickett's orders were to move south toward Dinwiddie Court House with his infantry, which was to be supported by the cavalry, and to attack the Federal troops that had been reported in the area. By the time Pickett's command was assembled, however, it was too late to start that evening, and the entire force camped for the night at Five Forks.

About 8:30 on the morning of March 30, 1865, Meade directed Warren to extend his line to the left from the Boydton Plank Road. Complying with that order, Warren moved Frederick Winthrop's First Brigade of Romeyn B. Ayres' Second Division out toward the White Oak Road, but the other two brigades of Ayres' division were held near Mrs. Butler's house That evening, Winthrop encountered enemy resistance and, conforming to his instructions, halted for the night near the S. Dabney house, which was about 600 yards south of the junction of the Claiborne Road with the White Oak Road. Griffin's division then advanced to cover the junction of the Dabney's Mill Road with the Boydton Plank Road.

Early that morning Turner's division crossed Hatcher's Run and moved into position on the right of Second Corps, between Dabney's Mill and

Hatcher's Run. Then Second Corps, with Turner's division on its right, advanced and drove the enemy back into their main line of entrenchments on Hatcher's Run. Between 8:30 and 9:00 A.M., Humphreys and Turner had reached a line that extended from the vicinity of the Crow house, on the right, to Mrs. Ramsey's house at the junction of the Quaker Road and the Boydton Plank Road, on the left. Humphreys halted his advance early in the afternoon.

Later, Miles and Mott, with their divisions of Second Corps, and Griffin's division of Fifth Corps moved into position to cover all of the Dabney's Mill Road. During the afternoon, Turner's division recrossed Hatcher's Run and reported to Gibbon, commanding Twenty-Fourth Corps, but Hays' division continued to maintain its connection with Turner across the run. There was skirmishing close to the enemy works throughout that rainy day, but there were no major attacks.

During the evening of March 30, 1865, Griffin's division of Fifth Corps was in position as follows: It extended from the left of Second Corps at the Boyd-.on Plank Road to a point about one-fourth mile west of the road; it then bent back to the rear to the Boydton Plank Road near its junction with the Quaker Road; and from there it ran down the Plank Road a few hundred yards to a large branch of Gravelly Run.

Engagement at the White Oak Road (or White Oak Ridge), March 31, 1865. At 4:00 P.M. March 30, 1865, Warren had sent Meade a message stating that he could move with his corps and cut the White Oak Road. When Grant learned of this, he issued an order at 8:30 P.M. directing Humphreys to relieve Griffin's division of Fifth Corps with Miles' division of his Second Corps, and he then ordered Warren to move the divisions of Griffin and Crawford to within supporting distance of Ayres' troops, which had earlier been sent out near the White Oak Road. At 9:45 P.M., Sheridan informed Grant that Pickett's command was then deployed along the White Oak Road, with its right near Five Forks and its left extending toward Petersburg.

At daybreak March 31, 1865, Ayres began massing his division on the open ground near the S. Dabney house by calling up the brigades of Denison and Gwyn, which had spent the night near Mrs.

Butler's, on the left bank of the branch of Gravelly Run. At 7:00 A.M., Warren ordered Crawford to concentrate his division at the Holliday house, which was about 500 yards in rear of Ayres' division, on a wood road that ran from Mrs. Butler's house on the Boydton Plank Road to W. Dabney's house on the White Oak Road, near the junction of the latter with the Claiborne Road.

There was also activity in Second Corps on the morning of March 31, 1865. Early that morning, Hays called up Smyth's brigade of his division from reserve, and Smyth halted in the rear of Pierce's brigade of Mott's division, which was holding the trenches on the right of Mott's line. At dawn, Smyth moved up and relieved Pierce's brigade, and Mott then shifted his division to the left and occupied the works that had been held by Miles' division. McAllister's brigade was on the left of the division, next to the Boydton Plank Road, and Pierce's brigade was on the right, next to Hays' division, at the Taylor house. De Trobriand's brigade was massed near the Rainey house, where it could support Miles' division. When relieved by Mott, Miles moved across the Boydton Plank Road and relieved Griffin's division of Fifth Corps. The brigades of Ramsey and Madill relieved Griffin's troops in the breastworks, and the brigades of Nugent and Scott were held in reserve. Griffin then massed his division near Mrs. Butler's, about 1,000 yards in rear of Crawford's position, on the south and east side of the branch of Gravelly Run, which, because of heavy rains, was difficult to cross.

At 8:15 A.M. Warren informed Ayres that Pickett was at Five Forks, only about four miles distant to his left, and he was cautioned to prepare for an attack on his left flank as well as on his front. Ayres then formed his division east of S. Dabney's, in the field of the H. Butler farm. The H. Butler farm was bounded on the north by the White Oak Road, and the farm buildings were just south of the White Oak Road and just west of its junction with the Claiborne Road. Winthrop's brigade was north of the Holliday house, facing north, and Gwyn's brigade was en echelon to the right, also facing north. Both brigades were about one-fourth mile south of the White Oak Road. Denison's brigade was placed along a ravine, facing west, to the left of Winthrop. Richard Coulter's Third Brigade of Crawford's division was sent forward to report to Ayres and support him, and it was placed in rear of Winthrop, near the center of Ayres' line.

Crawford arrived at Holliday's at 10:00 A.M., and after Coulter had departed to join Ayres, he massed Baxter's brigade of his division in column in the thick woods south of the H. Butler field, and Kellogg's brigade, also in column, on the right of Baxter.

The rain, which had stopped falling during the afternoon of March 30, 1865, began again at about 3:00 the next morning, and at 7:40 that morning, Grant ordered that all troop movements were to be suspended because of the almost impassable conditions of the roads, fields, and streams, and that troops were to remain in substantially the same positions that they then occupied. This order, however, was not passed on by Meade to the corps commanders until 8:25 A.M.

At 9:40 A.M., Warren informed Meade that the enemy's pickets covered the White Oak Road, and that he had ordered Ayres to move out and drive them back and determine what enemy troops held the road. In reply, Meade informed Warren that if after advancing he believed that he could get possession of the road and hold it, he was authorized to do so, despite the order halting all movements.

Robert E. Lee, who was present on the White Oak Road that morning, had observed Ayres' exposed position and had made preparations to advance and strike his left flank. The troops selected for this purpose consisted of Moody's brigade (commanded by Martin L. Stansel while Moody was ill) of Johnson's division, Hunton's brigade of Pickett's division, and McGowan's brigade of Wilcox's division. Wise's brigade of Johnson's division was assigned to support this movement on the left. Johnson was placed in command of the entire attacking force. All of Johnson's brigades were in position as Ayres prepared to advance, but they were concealed in the woods north of the White Oak Road.

At about 11:00 A.M., Winthrop moved forward, with Gwyn's brigade in support on his left, and was within about fifty yards of the White Oak Road when Johnson's line of battle moved out of the woods from the northwest. Hunton and Stansel struck Winthrop's line and quickly drove it back. Gwyn then moved up and for a time checked the Confederate onslaught, and during this time Winthrop rallied his brigade. Hunton then advanced on

Gwyn's line, while Stansel advanced on Winthrop's flank. Winthrop then fell back in disorder to the branch of Gravelly Run. Gwyn's brigade held for a time, but when Winthrop withdrew, its position became untenable, and it fell back on Crawford's division.

While Winthrop and Gwyn were having their troubles, McGowan's brigade advanced and attacked Denison's brigade on the left of Ayres' line. Denison checked the first attack, and Coulter moved up to his support. McGowan reached a point from which he could enfilade Denison's line, and soon drove the brigade from the ravine and back on Coulter. Denison, however, was unable to halt his troops, and they were not re-formed until they had crossed the branch of Gravelly Run. Denison was wounded in the attack and was succeeded in command of Second Brigade, Second Division by Richard N. Bowerman. Coulter's brigade attempted to make a stand, but was soon outflanked and driven back in confusion. Attempts were made to re-form the shattered brigade as they retired, but the whole of Ayres' division retreated in disorder across the run.

When Crawford learned that Ayres' division was being attacked, he deployed his two brigades in the woods north of the Holliday house, with Baxter's brigade on the right and Kellogg's brigade on the left. The enemy continued their advance across the H. Butler field, however, and soon struck Crawford's line. Crawford's troops fought stubbornly for a time, and then Baxter's brigade gave way. Kellogg's brigade soon followed, and Crawford's division did not stop until it too had crossed the branch of Gravelly Run. Warren arrived on the field about 10:30 A.M. and made every effort to rally his panic-stricken men, but was unable to do so. He then recrossed the run and began the task of re-forming his demoralized troops.

When Griffin heard the sounds of battle from the direction of the White Oak Road, he moved with his division toward the point of danger. He soon reached some high ground overlooking the branch of Gravelly Run, toward which Ayres' disorganized troops were fleeing, and put his troops in position behind the run. With great difficulty, DeLoss M. Johnson's Battery D, 1st New York Light Artillery and Charles E. Mink's Battery H, 1st New York Light Artillery of Charles S. Wainwright's Artillery Brigade of

Fifth Corps were brought up to help Griffin. Mink posted his guns on a slight elevation in a small field where he had a good field of fire, but Johnson could find no suitable position and was forced to place his guns in the woods, where they were of little help that day. When the enemy approached along the wood road toward Griffin's line, Mink's guns opened fire, and this, together with a heavy infantry fire, forced them to fall back about 400 yards.

When Humphreys heard the firing on Warren's front, and when stragglers began coming back through the lines, he ordered Miles to move forward with his division and strike the left flank of the attacking force. Miles received the order from Humphreys to support Fifth Corps about 12:30 P.M., and Henry J. Madill's Third Brigade and John Ramsey's Fourth Brigade were selected to make the attack. They were to be supported by Robert Nugent's Second Brigade, and George W. Scott's First Brigade was brought up from reserve to relieve the brigades of Madill and Ramsey in the line of works. Madill and Ramsey swung around to the left and advanced into the woods west of the Boydton Plank Road and soon reached the bank of the branch of Gravelly Run beyond Warren's right flank. Ramsey's brigade, which was on the left of Miles' line, crossed the run and advanced about a hundred yards and then met Wise's brigade near the crest of a ridge. After a sharp fight, one of Wise's regiments gave way, and then the entire brigade was forced back to a new line along the crest of the ridge. For some reason, Madill's brigade did not advance with Ramsey, but after Ramsey's fight, Miles sent Madill across the run. Madill then moved to the right until he had passed Wise's left flank, and he then wheeled his brigade to the left, struck Wise's exposed flank, and drove his brigade back in confusion. While Madill was making his flank march, Ramsey had been moving up on the front of Wise's brigade, and when Wise's brigade broke under Madill's attack, Ramsey charged and occupied the ridge.

When Miles attacked Wise's brigade, Hunton's brigade shifted to the left to support him, and Stansell's brigade then extended its front to cover the line of Fifth Corps. After the collapse of Wise's brigade, Johnson's command was withdrawn to the line of breastworks south of the White Oak Road, near W. Dabney's, that had been constructed by the men of Ayres' division the evening before.

After Miles had driven Wise's brigade from the ridge north of the branch of Gravelly Run, he informed Humphreys that if he was reinforced by another brigade he would be able to carry the line of Confederate fortifications. Humphreys then ordered De Trobriand to move up and relieve Scott in the works west of the Boydton Plank Road, and when relieved, Scott moved forward and joined Miles' division, which at that time was advancing slowly through the woods toward the Confederate earthworks that covered the approaches to the White Oak Road. Ramsey's division was on the left of Miles' line, with its left on the eastern edge of the H. Butler field; Madill's brigade was on the right of Ramsey; Scott's brigade was placed to the right and rear of Madill; and Nugent's brigade was in reserve. As the line advanced, however, a gap developed between Madill and Scott, and Nugent was moved up between the two brigades.

By 3:30 P.M., Miles had arrived in front of the Confederate works, but he then concluded that they were too strong to attack. Meantime, Miles had lost contact with Mott's division on his right, and he then moved his entire division by the right flank until he connected with De Trobriand's brigade of Mott's division. Miles then re-formed his command, with the brigades in order from left to right as follows: Scott's, Ramsey's, Madill's, and Nugent's.

Meantime, Humphreys had ordered some limited attacks on the enemy lines on his front by troops of the divisions of Mott and Hays. This was done in an effort to prevent the enemy from detaching troops to oppose Miles. He directed Mott to make a reconnaissance in force of the enemy works east of the Boydton Plank Road, and McAllister and Pierce prepared to assault the enemy works on their respective fronts. At 2:30 P.M., Pierce attacked with two regiments of his brigade, but was stopped by the abatis in front of the works. McAllister attacked with two regiments and a battalion of a third, and was supported by another regiment. He advanced on the enemy works covering Burgess' Mill, and he overran several outposts and got close up to the works, but was finally stopped. Then both brigades withdrew.

By 1:00 P.M., Warren was certain that his corps could be able to hold its position, and he then began preparations for a counterattack. Griffin's division was to make the attack, and it was to be supported on the left by the troops collected and re-formed by Ayres. These were placed on the left and rear of Griffin. The portions of Crawford's division that had re-formed since their defeat that morning were placed on the right and rear of Griffin to watch his right flank. Chamberlain was assigned the task of regaining the ground lost by Ayres and Crawford earlier in the day, and the direction of his attack was along the woods road running out from Mrs. Butler's to the W. Dabney house.

Warren gave the order for the attack at 2:30 P.M., and then Chamberlain's brigade crossed the run and formed for the advance. Gregory's brigade followed Chamberlain across the run and formed on his right. Bartlett then crossed and massed his brigade on the left rear of Chamberlain's line. Chamberlain reached the Holliday house without difficulty, and then advanced onto the southern edge of the H. Butler field. There, Chamberlain's men received a heavy fire from Hunton's brigade, which then occupied the works constructed earlier by troops of Ayres' division. He was also under fire from enemy troops in the woods on the east side of the field. Warren then directed Chamberlain to entrench his position, but when the latter proposed that he push ahead, Warren granted him permission to do so. At that point, Gregory came up and moved into the woods on the right. Chamberlain then charged against the front of the enemy works while Gregory turned their left, and together they drove Hunton back into the enemy's main line of defense on the Claiborne Road. Then McGowan, with his own and Stansel's brigade, also fell back to the main line. Griffin's troops advanced about 300 yards beyond the White Oak Road and halted about 4:00 P.M. The most significant results of Warren's victory over Johnson's command was that the enemy had lost control of the important White Oak Road, and that the direct line of communication between Pickett's command near Five Forks and Johnson's division had been severed.

Miles' division of Second Corps also attacked with Chamberlain that afternoon, and it too crossed the White Oak Road about 3:30 P.M.

Ayres' division, which was not engaged during the advance, was halted just south of the White Oak Road, near W. Dabney's, and took position facing west toward Five Forks. Crawford's division was posted to the north and east of the Holliday house to watch the gap between the right of Griffin and the left of Miles.

While Fifth Corps and Second Corps were engaged along the White Oak Road that day, Sheridan's cavalry was fighting a desperate battle with Pickett's command near Dinwiddie Court House. Warren's Fifth Corps remained on the White Oak Road only until that night, and then it was sent to support Sheridan at Dinwiddie Court House.

Battle of Dinwiddie Court House, March 31, 1865. At 9:00 A.M. March 31, 1865, Merritt ordered Devin to make reconnaissances to the north to gain information about the Confederate positions covering the White Oak Road. Devin sent Charles L. Fitzhugh's Second Brigade of his division, which had been dismounted, up the Adams Road (or Dinwiddie Court House Road), which ran from Dinwiddie Court House to Five Forks; and he sent Peter Stagg's First Brigade up the Crump Road, to the right of Fitzhugh. Alfred Gibbs' Reserve Brigade was massed at the junction of the Brooks Road with the Adams Road, about a half mile south of J. Boisseau's house, where it was in position to support Stagg and Fitzhugh if needed.

Henry E. Davies' First Brigade of Crook's division, which had been ordered to the front the day before, was to advance on the left of Devin to cover his flank and watch the country west of Chamberlain's Creek (or Chamberlain's Bed). The other two brigades of Crook's division remained near Dinwiddie Court House.

When Stagg neared the White Oak Road, he found the enemy in force, and he then withdrew to a position on the Crump Road, a short distance north of Gravelly Run.

Fitzhugh encountered the enemy about a mile southeast of Five Forks, and deployed his dismounted brigade across the road. When Devin learned that Pickett's division and at least one cavalry division were at Five Forks, he ordered Fitzhugh to hold his position and open communications with Davies, who was then operating on his left.

That same morning, Fitzhugh Lee's Confederate cavalry moved out on the direct road from Five Forks toward Dinwiddie Court House and soon met the troopers of Devin's division. At that time, Pickett had not yet started his infantry toward Dinwiddie

Court House, but only a short time later he had his column on the road. Fitzhugh Lee, with William H. F. Lee's and Rosser's cavalry divisions, led the way, and they were followed by Pickett's and Johnson's infantry divisions. Pickett left Thomas T. Munford, with Fitzhugh Lee's cavalry division, near Five Forks to confront Devin.

Pickett's command marched along the west side of Chamberlain's Creek, down the Scott Road to Little Five Forks, which was at the junction of the Ford's Station Road, and there it turned eastward on the latter road toward Fitzgerald's and Danse's crossings of Chamberlain's Creek. Fitzgerald's Ford was about one and three-fourths miles northwest of Dinwiddie Court House, measured on a straight line, but about two and a half miles by road. Danse's Ford was about a mile north of Fitzgerald's. It was Pickett's intention to cross Chamberlain's Creek at these two crossings and attack Sheridan's left flank.

Meantime, Crook had moved Charles H. Smith's brigade to Fitzgerald's Ford to cover Merritt's left, and he had placed J. Irvin Gregg's brigade on the right of Smith, on the low ground along the east side of Chamberlain's Creek. Davies' pickets covered Danse's Ford.

William H. F. Lee's cavalry arrived at Fitzgerald's Ford, in front of Smith's brigade, at 11:00 A.M., and then attempted to force a crossing of the creek, but was strongly repulsed. Finally, at about 2:00 P.M., Pickett's infantry, led by Corse's brigade, appeared in front of Danse's Ford. Davies, whose brigade had been in that area, had dismounted his men and moved down the creek when Smith's brigade was threatened at Fitzgerald's Ford, but he had left Walter R. Robbins with a battalion of the 1st New Jersey Cavalry to watch Danse's Ford. Corse attempted to force a crossing of the creek, but was checked by Robbins' battalion. Then, a part of Corse's brigade crossed the creek above the ford and moved down against Robbins' flank, while at the same time the rest of the brigade attacked his front. In a short time the Federal troopers were driven in total disorder from the ford.

When Davies reached Fitzgerald's Ford, he found that he was not needed there, and was just returning to Danse's Ford when Corse was beginning to cross the creek. Davies attempted to check the enemy advance with his 10th New York Cavalry and what

was left of Robbins' battalion, but was finally forced to fall back to the Adams Road. Davies left Hugh H. Janeway, with two battalions of the 1st New Jersey Cavalry, to cover the retreat, and a regiment of Stagg's brigade was soon sent to support him.

There was little activity on Devin's front until 2:00 P.M., and then Devin ordered Fitzhugh to move back with his brigade from its advanced position near Five Forks. Fitzhugh then withdrew about a half mile and took position in front of the junction of the Adams Road and the Gravelly Church Road. Devin did not become aware of Pickett's flanking march until shortly after 2:00 P.M., when he heard the sounds of the firing to the southwest as the enemy tried to cross Chamberlain's Creek. A little after 2:30 P.M., Janeway asked Devin for help, and a regiment from Stagg's brigade was sent to aid him. Meantime, most of Stagg's brigade had retired to the J. Boisseau farm.

Devin went to the front with Stagg's regiment, and when he was unable to rally Davies' men, he ordered Fitzhugh to move with his brigade by the left flank to the road leading to Danse's Ford. There Fitzhugh joined Janeway, dismounted his men, and deployed them across the road near the Williams house. Janeway then left to rejoin Davies' brigade, which was then re-forming near the J. Boisseau house; and Stagg's regiment that had gone to the support of Janeway returned to its brigade.

As soon as Corse's brigade had secured a position on the east side of Chamberlain's Creek, Pickett's other brigades began to cross. Corse then moved out from the ford to the northwest, but was stopped by Fitzhugh's new line. At about that time Munford moved down the Adams Road with his division. He was opposed only by the 6th New York Cavalry of Fitzhugh's brigade, and a little later by a part of one of Stagg's regiments, but they were able to hold their line only briefly, and were soon driven back. Then the Confederate attack intensified. Pickett sent Terry's brigade forward to join Corse, and this, combined with Munford's advance, placed Fitzhugh's brigade in an untenable position. On Devin's order, Fitzhugh withdrew a short distance, and Stagg's brigade then came up and took position on his left. Munford continued his movement down the Dinwiddie Court House Road, and soon struck the right of Fitzhugh's brigade and forced it to fall back. Fitzhugh then formed a new line extending across the Dinwiddie Court House Road, and Stagg was left to confront Pickett's infantry. Finally, however, both brigades fell back to the J. Boisseau farm, where Davies was attempting to re-form his brigade. Devin's two brigades were formed on the right of a new line at that point, and Davies' brigade was placed on the left.

As Pickett's infantry advanced, it passed between the troops of Merritt and Crook, and finally gained possession of the Adams Road between J. Boisseau's and Dinwiddie Court House, thus isolating Sheridan's brigades at these two locations. Devin was then ordered to move across country with his two brigades to the Boydton Plank Road. Upon arriving at the A. Dabney farm, just north of the junction of the Brooks Road and the Boydton Plank Road, Devin deployed his brigades in line of battle to cover the plank road. A short time later, Davies' brigade joined Devin on the Boydton Plank Road, and as the senior officer present, Davies assumed command of all three brigades. He then ordered Devin to march down the Boydton Plank Road to Dinwiddie Court House, and Davies, whose troopers were still dismounted, marched to the same place.

When Pickett's infantry reached the junction of the Adams Road and the Crump Road after its advance from Chamberlain's Creek, Pickett deployed his brigades in line of battle. He then made a partial wheel to the left and advanced in pursuit of Merritt's cavalry. During the early part of that afternoon, Gibbs' Reserve Brigade of Devin's division had been held in reserve on the Adams Road, near the junction with the Brooks Road, about two miles north of Dinwiddie Court House. When Pickett's line wheeled to the left, it exposed its right and rear to Gibbs' waiting brigade, and Gibbs promptly charged and struck the rear of enemy's unprotected flank. At the same time, Gregg's brigade, which had been ordered up from Chamberlain's Creek, attacked on the left of Gibbs. These attacks forced Pickett to abandon the pursuit of Merritt and face about to meet this new threat.

By that time, it was about 4:00 P.M., and Sheridan had been making every effort to avert a serious defeat by concentrating his forces near Dinwiddie Court House. He had ordered Merritt to bring his brigades to Dinwiddie Court House by the Boydton Plank Road, and he had also ordered Custer to hurry forward to the same place with two of his brigades. When Custer received this order, he detached William Wells' Second Brigade to guard the trains, and then rode toward Dinwiddie Court House with Henry Capehart's Third Brigade and Alexander C. M. Pennington's First Brigade. Sheridan also directed Smith, who was still confronting William H. F. Lee's cavalry at Fitzgerald's Crossing, to move back slowly, while still resisting, to Dinwiddie Court House.

When Pickett was finally forced to break off the pursuit of Merritt and face his infantry to the rear, he attacked the brigades of Gibbs and Gregg in overwhelming numbers. These two brigades continued to resist for almost two hours, but they were slowly forced back toward Dinwiddie Court House.

Sheridan had selected a defensive position on which to make a stand about three-fourths of a mile to the north of the court house. When Custer arrived with Henry Capehart's brigade, it was placed on the left of the Adams Road, on the crest of a low ridge. Smith's brigade withstood the enemy attacks at Fitzgerald's Ford until about 5:30 P.M., and by that time the retirement of Gregg and Gibbs had uncovered his rear. Smith then fell back, closely followed by William H. F. Lee's cavalry, and was then directed to form on the left of Capehart. James H. Lord's Battery A, 2nd United States Artillery was brought up and placed in a field to the left of the Adams Road.

A little before sundown, Pennington's brigade arrived, and the 2nd Ohio and 3rd New Jersey of the brigade were formed in line of battle on the right of the road, to the front and right of Capehart's brigade. Pennington's 2nd Connecticut had not arrived, and the 2nd New York had been sent to guard the Boydton Plank Road crossing of Stony Creek.

Under the steady pressure of Pickett's infantry, Gregg's and Gibbs' brigades finally came in and passed through Custer's lines. Gregg's brigade was placed on the right of Pennington's brigade, and Gibbs' brigade was sent to the rear. A short time later, Pickett launched a strong attack on Pennington's regiments, which were out in front of the Federal line, and forced them to give way. They re-formed, however, on the crest of the ridge, on the right of Capehart's brigade. Pickett then made two more attacks on Custer's line, and both were repulsed. Custer then launched a counterattack and drove the Confederate skirmishers back on their main line of battle.

Near sunset, Fitzhugh Lee's cavalry launched a strong attack on Smith's brigade before it was in position, but this was repulsed, largely by a heavy flank fire from Capehart's brigade. Smith held his position, despite heavy losses, until nearly dark; and then, when his ammunition was exhausted, he fell back and re-formed on the Adams Road.

Devin's two brigades and Davies' brigade arrived near Dinwiddie Court House about dark, and Gibbs' brigade rejoined Devin at the Crump farm. When the fighting ended that evening, the troopers of Gregg's and Smith's brigades were remounted, and they then marched out about three miles to the east to Great Cattail Creek at the Vaughan Road, where they were joined by Davies' brigade. Crook's division camped there that night.

Pickett's troops remained in position in front of Sheridan's line during the night, but they retired the next morning. Only Custer's two brigades remained in position on Sheridan's front during the night.

Battle of Five Forks, April 1, 1865. Until the late afternoon of March 31, 1865, Warren had carried out his operations on the Boydton Plank Road and the White Oak Road independently of Sheridan's cavalry, which, as already noted, had arrived at Dinwiddie Court House two days earlier. Then, at 5:15 March 31, 1865, Warren, who was then at W. Dabney's near the White Oak Road, heard the sounds of Sheridan's battle off to the southwest, and it seemed to him that the sounds were receding. This led Warren to believe that the cavalry was being driven back, and he then directed Griffin to send Bartlett, with his brigade, directly across country and attack the advancing Confederates on their flank. At army headquarters, however, the sounds of battle seemed to be approaching, instead of receding; and at 5:15 P.M., shortly after Bartlett had moved out, Warren received an order from Meade directing him to send a brigade out on the White Oak Road to open it for Sheridan and support him if necessary. Before this order could be executed, however, Warren learned definitely that Sheridan had been attacked near Dinwiddie Court House by infantry and cavalry and was being driven back. At 6:30 P.M., Warren received another order, instructing him to send the brigade that had been ordered

out on the White Oak Road to move down the Boydton Plank Road instead. It was too late to recall Bartlett, but all the corps artillery and three regiments of Bartlett's brigade, commanded by Alfred L. Pearson, had been left on the Boydton Plank Road. Warren then directed Pearson to march on the Plank Road to Dinwiddie Court House. Pearson, however, was compelled to stop at Gravelly Run because the bridge was out and the water in the run was very high.

Bartlett advanced as ordered, but halted at dark on the high ground at Dr. Boisseau's, on the Crump Road, about a half mile north of Gravelly Run. Later that night, Bartlett withdrew his brigade and rejoined the division.

At 9:30 P.M. March 31, 1865, Warren was ordered to withdraw his command from the White Oak Road and mass his divisions on the Boydton Plank Road. He was also ordered to send Griffin's division by the Plank Road to report to Sheridan at Dinwiddie Court House. At the same time, Humphreys was ordered to withdraw his Second Corps to the line that it had occupied that morning. Some time was required for Warren to get his troops back from their advanced positions, and at 11:00 that night he decided to send Ayres' division to Sheridan instead of Griffin's division, because Ayres was the first to arrive on the Boydton Plank Road. Ayres was delayed until 2:00 A.M. April 1, 1865, however, while he waited for the completion of a bridge over Gravelly Run, and it was nearly daylight when he turned off the Boydton Plank Road onto the Brooks Road at R. Boisseau's house. He then followed the Brooks Road to its junction with the Dinwiddie Court House-Five Forks Road (Adams Road), at the point where Gibbs' brigade had been posted the day before. Ayres reported to Sheridan at about 4:30 A.M. April 1, 1865.

Between 5:00 and 6:00 A.M. April 1, 1865, Warren started from the Boydton Plank Road with the divisions of Griffin and Crawford, and marched across country to J. Boisseau's at the junction of the Crump Road with the Adams Road. Warren arrived at the crossroads with the head of Griffin's division about 7:00 A.M. and communicated with Sheridan. He did not, however, meet with Sheridan until 11:00 A.M. Griffin's division was about a half mile north of Ayres' position. When Warren arrived, his Fifth Corps was subject to Sheridan's orders.

Meantime, at about 10:00 on the night of March 31, 1865, Pickett had learned of the presence of Bartlett's brigade on the left and rear of his line in front of Dinwiddie Court House; and then, fearing that a large Federal infantry force was approaching his rear, he began to withdraw his command toward Five Forks. The ambulances, ammunition trains, and artillery started first, and then the infantry followed on the Adams Road. Montgomery D. Corse's infantry brigade and Munford's cavalry brigade were the last troops to leave Pickett's lines north of Dinwiddie Court House, and they got away at just about daylight. They had scarcely passed the J. Boisseau house when Warren's Fifth Corps began to arrive.

When Sheridan advanced on the morning of April 1, 1865, Pickett's withdrawal was well under way, and his only opposition was some rear guard action. Merritt followed the enemy closely, with Devin's division on the right and Custer's dismounted cavalry on the left. Devin advanced on the Adams Road, and Custer moved up along Chamberlain Creek, and later Bear Swamp, toward the Gilliam house, southwest of Five Forks. Crook's division remained in the rear and was not engaged at Five Forks that afternoon. Smith's brigade was at Fitzgerald's Ford on Chamberlain's Creek; Gregg's brigade was out about a mile to the northwest on the Ford's Station Road, near Little Five Forks; and Davies' brigade was near Dinwiddie Court House, watching the crossings of Stony Creek.

Early that morning, Ranald S. Mackenzie, with his Cavalry Division of the Army of the James, arrived at Dinwiddie Court House and reported to Sheridan. About 11:00 A.M., under orders from Sheridan, Mackenzie rode up the Adams Road to J. Boisseau's, and then northward on the Crump Road to its junction with the White Oak Road. Mackenzie's instructions were to gain and hold the White Oak Road. He encountered enemy pickets about 1:00 P.M., and a short time later was sharply engaged with William P. Roberts' brigade of William H. F. Lee's cavalry division. Mackenzie pushed on and soon had possession of the White Oak Road. Samuel P. Spear, commanding Mackenzie's Second Brigade, was killed during the action, and he was succeeded by Andrew W. Evans. Mackenzie then moved west on the White Oak Road to join Sheridan at Five Forks.

By 2:00 P.M., Pickett's command was back in position behind the line of works on the White Oak Road. These works ran from a point about a mile west of Five Forks, through Five Forks, and then on beyond for about three-fourths of a mile to the east. At the eastern end of the line, there was a return that extended northward from the road for a distance of less than 150 yards. William H. F. Lee's cavalry held the enemy right, along the west side of Gilliams' field, and then, in succession from the Confederate right to left, were the brigades of Montgomery D. Corse, William R. Terry (then commanded by Robert M. Mayo), and George H. Steuart of Pickett's division; and the brigades of William H. Wallace and Matt W. Ransom of Johnson's division. Pegram's guns were placed on the right, center, and left of the line where there were good fields of fire. Munford's cavalry brigade was dismounted and placed on the enemy left, between Ransom's brigade and Hatcher's Run. Rosser's cavalry was with the trains on the north side of Hatcher's Run, near Ford Road.

As Sheridan's cavalrymen approached Five Forks, they were formed in line, facing the enemy works on the White Oak Road. Custer's division was on the left, with Henry Capehart's Third Brigade on the left of the division and Pennington's First Brigade on the right, near the Scott Road. Devin's division was formed on the right of Custer, with Fitzhugh's Second Brigade on the left of the division, between the Scott Road and the Adams Road; Gibbs' Reserve Brigade (Third Brigade) in the center; and Stagg's brigade on the right. William Wells' Second Brigade of Custer's division came up with Sheridan's trains about 11:00 A.M., and after resting two hours, Wells' brigade was placed on the left of Custer's line.

When Sheridan had determined the position of Pickett's line along the White Oak Road, he decided on a plan for his attack later that day. According to this plan, the cavalry was to feint as if to turn the Confederate right flank, and then, after Warren's Fifth Corps had moved up from J. Boisseau's, Warren was to attack the enemy left flank with his infantry and drive Pickett's entire command away from Petersburg. When Fifth Corps advanced, Sheridan's cavalry was to deliver a frontal attack on Pickett's line.

At 2:00 P.M., Warren received orders from Sheridan (issued at 1:00 P.M.) to move up to the front with his Fifth Corps, and he soon had his troops in motion. He marched up the Adams Road from J. Boisseau's to the Gravelly Run Church Road, and then up that road to the vicinity of the Gravelly Run Church, which was a little more than a fourth of a mile from the White Oak Road and about a mile from the crossroads of Five Forks. Warren then deployed his divisions as they came up on a line facing to the northwest. It was in that direction that the left flank of the enemy position was supposed to be.

Crawford's division arrived first, and it was deployed on the right of the Gravelly Run Church Road. John A. Kellogg's First Brigade was on the left, with its left on the road, and Henry Baxter's Second Brigade was on the right. Richard Coulter's Third Brigade was formed in rear of the interval between the two brigades on the front line. All three brigades were formed in double line of battle. Griffin's division came up next, and it was massed to the right and rear of Crawford. Joseph J. Bartlett's Third Brigade was on the left and Joshua L. Chamberlain's First Brigade was on the right, and both brigades were formed in triple line of battle. Edgar M. Gregory was ordered to report to Chamberlain with his Second Brigade. Chamberlain then assigned Gregory's regiments to positions with his own Second Brigade. He formed one regiment in line of battle on the right of his brigade, sent out another regiment as skirmishers in front of his brigade, and placed Gregory's other regiment in position to cover the right flank of his brigade. Ayres' division was the last to arrive, and it was deployed on the left of Crawford, west of the Gravelly Run Church Road, with Richard N. Bowerman's Second Brigade on the left and James Gwyn's Third Brigade on the right, next to the road. Frederick Winthrop's First Brigade was placed in rear of the interval between the other two brigades of the division. All three brigades were formed in double line of battle.

When Warren's line advanced to the attack about 4:15 P.M., a serious problem soon developed. The Confederate breastworks did not extend to the east as far as expected, and as a result, Warren's divisions crossed the White Oak Road about 800 yards to the right of, instead of directly against the angle of, the line and the return on the north side of the road. As Ayres' division continued its march beyond the road

in the original direction to the northwest, it suddenly received a heavy flank fire on its left from Ransom's brigade, which held the refused part of the enemy line. Ayres immediately changed front, moved Bowerman's brigade to the left until it was in front of the return, and brought up Winthrop's brigade into the front line on the left of Bowerman. Gwyn's brigade later came up on the right of the division. When these new dispositions were completed, Ayres advanced and attacked the left of the Confederate works.

Soon after crossing the White Oak Road, Crawford's division lost its connection with Ayres on its left, and marched on to the open ground of the Sydnor farm, which was about midway between the White Oak Road and Hatcher's Run, and 800 yards north of the refused extension of the enemy works. Crawford brought up Coulter's brigade and placed it on the left of his division in an attempt to link up with Ayres. He then changed the direction of his march to the left and moved across the Sydnor farm toward the rear of the enemy line.

Griffin's division marched about a mile without encountering any serious opposition, and reached the southeast corner of the Sydnor farm after Crawford had passed. Then Chamberlain, hearing the heavy firing of Ayres' battle off to his left, marched his brigade in that direction. Gregory and Bartlett followed, and soon all three brigades joined in the fighting on the right of Ayres. Ayres' division soon carried the works at the angle and, with Winthrop's brigade in the lead, moved on toward Five Forks along the rear of the enemy main line on the north side of the White Oak Road. Griffin's division, on the right, also pushed on toward the Ford Road. Winthrop was mortally wounded while charging the works, and James Grindlay assumed command of First Brigade. Bowerman was wounded, and David L. Stanton took charge of his Second Brigade.

Mackenzie's brigade, after defeating Roberts' brigade earlier in the day, marched west on the White Oak Road, and arrived near the battlefield just as Warren was attacking. Mackenzie was then directed to move to the extreme right of the infantry and occupy the Ford Road at the crossing of Hatcher's Run.

When Crawford's division continued its advance from the Sydnor farm, it marched far to the right of Griffin, driving Munford's cavalry ahead of it. It finally arrived at the the B. (or D.) Boisseau (or C. Young) farm, which was on the Ford Road about midway between Five Forks and Hatcher's Run. Upon arriving there, Crawford received a heavy fire on his left and center, and was ordered by Warren to advance down the Ford Road toward Five Forks. Coulter's brigade was selected to make the attack, and it was to be supported by the other two brigades of the division.

The enemy quickly adjusted to meet Warren's attack. William R. Terry's brigade (commanded by Joseph Mayo) was pulled back from the enemy main line to aid Wallace and Ransom in attempting to check the divisions of Ayres and Griffin that were approaching the Ford Road from the east, and also Crawford's division, which was coming down the road from the north. The Federal advance continued, however, and the enemy was soon driven in disorder toward Gilliams' field, west of Five Forks.

From the beginning of the battle, Merritt's cavalry had been pressing the front of the enemy line, but they had had little success until troops were withdrawn to protect their rear against the Federal advance. Then Fitzhugh's and Pennington's brigades broke through at Five Forks and aided Warren's infantry in driving the enemy.

By that time it was late in the evening, and the division commanders of Fifth Corps collected their troops as best they could and pursued the fleeing enemy forces westward from Five Forks. Ayres' division was south of the White Oak Road, Griffin's division was on the road, and Crawford's division was on the right of Griffin. A final charge at the Gilliam field, a mile west of Five Forks, ended all resistance for the day, but the cavalry pursued the remnants of Pickett's troops for about six miles to the west, and finally halted long after dark. Pickett's command was driven from the field in complete disorder, and lost most of its artillery and perhaps as many as 5,000–6,000 prisoners. With the loss of the vital crossroads of Five Forks and the virtual destruction of the force assigned to protect it, Lee's position at Petersburg became untenable.

During the day, Sheridan had become dissatisfied with Warren's performance, both before and during the battle, and toward the close of the fighting that evening, he summarily relieved him from command of Fifth Corps and assigned Charles Griffin in his place. Joseph J. Bartlett then assumed command of

Griffin's First Division, and Alfred L. Pearson succeeded Bartlett in command of Third Brigade, First Division.

Immediately after the fighting ceased at Five Forks, Sheridan ordered Griffin to assemble his Fifth Corps and march with Ayres' and Crawford's divisions to the Gravelly Run Church Road. Upon arriving there, Griffin was to put these two divisions in position at a right angle to the White Oak Road, facing Petersburg. Bartlett's First Division, Fifth Corps remained on the field at Five Forks and covered the Ford Road to Hatcher's Run. Mackenzie's cavalry division took position on the Ford Road at the crossing of Hatcher's Run, and Merritt's cavalry camped on the Gilliam farm.

Toward dusk April 1, 1865, while Sheridan was engaged at Five Forks, Humphreys moved Miles' division of Second Corps forward, and to the left of the Boydton Plank Road, to the vicinity of the junction of the Claiborne Road and the White Oak Road. This was done to hold the White Oak Road and to prevent Lee from sending reinforcements to Pickett at Five Forks. Humphreys extended Mott's division of Second Corps to maintain connection with Miles' division. Miles remained in this position until 11:00 P.M., and then marched by way of the White Oak Road to the vicinity of Five Forks, where he camped for the night.

During the evening of April 1, 1865, Grant learned of Sheridan's victory at Five Forks, and between midnight and 1:00 A.M. April 2, 1865, he ordered Miles to join Sheridan and help hold the newly won position. Miles immediately marched west on the White Oak Road toward Five Forks.

Breakthrough at Petersburg, April 2, 1865. At 4:00 P.M. April 1, 1865, Grant issued orders, through Meade, for an assault by Wright's Sixth Corps and Parke's Ninth Corps on the enemy entrenchments south of Petersburg at 4:00 the next morning. Ord was also ordered to advance with his Army of the James and attack the enemy works, or support Sixth Corps, as circumstances might dictate. About 7:00 P.M. April 1, 1865, Grant learned of Sheridan's victory, and two hours later he modified his original order. He directed Parke and Wright to open at once with their artillery and send a strong skirmish line forward. At the same time, he repeated his order for the assault the next morning.

At 9:30 P.M., Meade instructed Humphreys to be prepared to move with Hays' and Mott's divisions of Second Corps, and if the enemy began to leave the entrenchments on his front, he was to join in the attack with Ord and Wright.

The assault on the morning of April 2, 1865 was delayed until 4:30–4:45, when it was light enough to see, and then Sixth Corps and Ninth Corps moved forward. On Parke's front, Orlando B. Willcox's First Division opened with a feint attack on the right at 4:00 A.M., and a half hour later the main attack began on the front of Fort Sedgwick, along the Jerusalem Plank Road. The assaulting column consisted of Robert B. Potter's Second Division and John F. Hartranft's Third Division. Potter's division was on the left of the Jerusalem Plank Road, with Simon G. Griffin's Second Brigade in front and John I. Curtin's First Brigade in its rear. Hartranft's division was on the right of the road, with Joseph A. Mathews' Second Brigade in the lead and William H. H. McCall's First Brigade close behind. Samuel Harriman's First Brigade of Willcox's division was temporarily attached to Hartranft's division, and it advanced on Hartranft's right. Parke's column passed over the enemy picket line and captured the main works for a distance of about 400 yards on each side of the Plank Road, including Fort Mahone and some other forts and redans. It was unable to carry the inner line and, after the initial effort, made no further attempt to advance. Potter was severely wounded during the attack and was succeeded in command of the division by Simon G. Griffin. Walter Harriman assumed command of Griffin's Second Brigade, Second Division.

During the night of April 1, 1865, Horatio G. Wright formed his Sixth Corps on a line that extended from Fort Welch to Fort Fisher in preparation for an attack on the enemy works the next morning. Truman Seymour's Third Division was on the immediate left of Fort Welch, with William S. Truex's First Brigade on the left of the division line and J. Warren Keifer's Second Brigade on the right. George W. Getty's Second Division was on the right of Seymour, and to the right of Fort Welch, with Lewis A. Grant's Second Brigade on the left, Thomas W. Hyde's Third Brigade in the center, and James M. Warner's First Brigade on the right. Frank Wheaton's First Division was on the right of Getty, and on the right of the corps line, and it extended toward Fort Fisher. Oliver Edward's Third Brigade was on the left, William H. Penrose's First Brigade was on the right and rear of Edwards' line, and Joseph E. Hamblin's Second Brigade was on the right and rear of Penrose.

The Confederate trenches in front of Wright's and Ord's commands were held by the divisions of Cadmus M. Wilcox and Henry Heth of Hill's corps. The brigades of Edward L. Thomas and James H. Lane of Wilcox's division occupied the line directly in front of Sixth Corps, and they were simply overwhelmed by the attack. Farther to the southwest, near Hatcher's Run, were the brigades of Joseph R. Davis and William McComb of Heth's division. Later in the day, Davis' brigade and a part of McComb's were captured. The brigades of Samuel McGowan and Alfred M. Scales (commanded by Joseph H. Hyman) of Wilcox's division and John R. Cooke's brigade and a part of William McRae's brigade of Heth's division were near Burgess' Mill.

Wright's corps moved forward at 4:40 A.M. and quickly broke through the enemy main line near the Jones house on the Church Road, and soon captured the enemy works along the entire front of the attack. Immediately after Sixth Corps broke through, Seymour turned to the left and advanced along the line of the enemy works toward Hatcher's Run. Getty's division re-formed on the Boydton Plank Road, about a mile beyond the captured works, and then it too moved toward Hatcher's Run, on the right of Seymour. Wheaton left Hamblin's brigade of his division to hold the captured works and, with his other two brigades, moved to the left with the rest of the corps. When Wright reached Hatcher's Run, opposite the front of the Army of the James, he found the enemy trenches empty, and he also learned that both Second Corps and Fifth Corps were moving in his direction. It was therefore unnecessary for Sixth Corps to proceed farther to the south and west, and at about 9:00 A.M., Wright faced his corps about and marched back toward Petersburg.

April 1, 1865, Ord's Army of the James was in position on the line of entrenchments between Hatcher's Run on the left and the right of Sixth Corps on the right. John W. Turner's Independent Division was on the left, with Thomas M. Harris' Third Brigade on the left of the division, next to Hatcher's Run, and Andrew Potter's First Brigade on the right. William B. Curtis' Second Brigade was in reserve. Robert S. Foster's First Division, Twenty-Fourth Corps was on the right of Turner, with George B. Dandy's Third Brigade on the left, Harrison S. Fairchild's Fourth Brigade in the center, and Thomas O. Osborn's First Brigade on the right. William Birney's Second Division of United States Colored Troops held the line between Foster's division on the left and Sixth Corps on the right. That night, complying with Ord's orders, Turner massed the brigades of Curtis and Andrew Potter on the right of Dandy's brigade of Foster's division in preparation for the attack ordered for the next morning.

Early on the morning of April 2, 1865, the order for the attack by Twenty-Fourth Corps was countermanded, and at 6:50 A.M. Ord directed Gibbon to send his available troops to Fort Welch to support Sixth Corps in its attack. At 8:00 A.M., Foster moved to the right with his division and relieved Hamblin's brigade, which was holding the works captured earlier by Wright. Turner, with the brigades of Curtis and Andrew Potter, also moved to the right and took position at the signal tower near Fort Gregg (Union) to support Sixth Corps.

Shortly after Turner had departed on his march to support Wright, Thomas M. Harris' Third Brigade of Turner's division advanced and captured the enemy line on its front. William Birney's Second Division, Twenty-Fifth Corps, which had been under Gibbon's orders since March 30, 1865, also moved forward and occupied the captured works. Harris and Birney were then in contact with Sixth Corps, which was moving toward Hatcher's Run. When Sixth Corps turned back that morning, Harris and Birney accompanied it toward Petersburg.

At 6:00 that morning, Humphreys learned of the successes of Parke and Wright, and he then ordered Hays and Mott to advance with their divisions. At 7:30, Robert McAllister's Third Brigade of Mott's division captured the entrenched picket line on its front; and about a half hour later, Hays' division captured the Crow House Redoubt, on the right of Humphreys' line, and it then extended its front to the left in the enemy trenches. At that point, Heth withdrew his troops from the front of Second Corps, and Hays and Mott pushed on to join in the advance of the army toward Petersburg.

About 9:00 that morning, Humphreys learned that Miles' division, which had joined Sheridan at Five Forks earlier in the day, was returning and was approaching on the White Oak Road. Humphreys also learned that Miles was under orders to move up the Claiborne Road and attack the enemy troops that were retreating on that road. Sheridan was following Miles with Ayres' and Crawford's divisions of Fifth Corps. A curious situation then developed. When Humphreys and Sheridan met, Humphreys understood that Miles' division was to be returned to Second Corps, but he was informed by Sheridan that he, Sheridan, had not intended to give up the division. As a result of this meeting, Sheridan left Miles' division on the White Oak Road and returned to Five Forks with the divisions of Hays and Mott. Humphreys, too, departed, and with the divisions of Hays and Mott started up the Boydton Plank Road toward Petersburg. Miles was thus left alone to carry out his previous orders, and he then proceeded up the Claiborne Road toward Sutherland's Station on the South Side Railroad.

Meantime, the enemy was becoming aggressive on the front of Ninth Corps, and Parke asked for reinforcements. A little after 10:00 A.M., Henry W. Benham's Engineer Brigade and Charles H. T. Collis' Independent Brigade were ordered up from City Point; and Hamblin's Second Brigade of Wheaton's division of Sixth Corps was ordered to join Ninth Corps when relieved by Foster's division of Twenty-Fourth Corps.

The enemy counterattacked on Parke's front about 11:00 A.M., and then continued the attacks until about 3:00 P.M., when they recaptured a part of their former line on the left of Simon G. Griffin's Second Division (commanded by Potter until he was wounded earlier in the day). Collis' brigade (commanded temporarily by Andrew H. Tippin until about 1:00 P.M.) arrived at Fort Sedgwick at 2:00 P.M. and reported to Griffin. Griffin then sent Collis to the threatened part of the line, and with his help, the Federals finally drove the enemy from their lodgment on the left.

Wesley Brainerd, in command of a provisional brigade consisting of the 15th New York Engineers (of Benham's Engineer Brigade) and some dismounted cavalry, also arrived from City Point, and was sent to support Willcox on the right. Hamblin arrived with his brigade on the left of Ninth Corps between 4:00 and 5:00 P.M. and reported to Hartranft, who placed them in the trenches near captured Fort Mahone.

With Parke's line on the right thus stabilized and the enemy works on the left in Union hands, the rest of Grant's army moved up toward the inner line of the Confederate defenses at Petersburg, which were only one and a half to two miles from the city. After Foster had reached the point of Wright's breakthrough and had relieved Hamblin's brigade about noon, he deployed his division in line of battle, facing Petersburg. Osborn's brigade was on the left, Dandy's brigade was on the center, and Fairchild's brigade was on the left. When the line was completed, Foster advanced toward the city. He soon arrived in front of Confederate Fort Gregg and Fort Baldwin (also called Fort or Battery Whitworth). These two works were located at the southern end of an outer defensive line that was about 1,000 yards in front of the inner line of works. The latter ran northward along the east side of Indian Town (or Old Town) Creek from the old main line of works to the Appomattox River. Shortly after Foster was in position in front of Fort Gregg and Fort Baldwin, Turner came up with the brigades of Andrew Potter and Curtis and formed in Foster's rear.

At 2:00 P.M., Gibbon ordered an assault on the two forts. Just before the attack began, Harris' brigade of Turner's division came up from Hatcher's Run with Sixth Corps, and formed on the left of Foster's line. Harris then reported to Foster. Foster's division, supported by Turner's two brigades, immediately charged toward Fort Gregg and soon gained the parapet of the works. Then, after a desperate hand-to-hand struggle, which lasted about a half hour, Foster's men finally captured the fort. Harris' brigade moved up in front of Fort Baldwin, and was advancing to attack when Fort Gregg fell. The enemy then began to evacuate Fort Baldwin, and Harris moved in and occupied the works. A short time later, however, Harris withdrew and rejoined Turner's division.

When Sixth Corps began its march back toward Petersburg after its advance to Hatcher's Run, Getty's Second Division, which was in the lead, moved to the northeast, with its right on the Boydton Plank Road. When it arrived in front of the enemy works, it formed on the left of Twenty-Fourth Corps. It then advanced to a point near the Whitworth house and halted. Wheaton, with the brigades of Penrose and Edwards, came up on the left of Getty and halted about 1:00 P.M. on the South Side Railroad, about

two miles west of Petersburg. Seymour's Third Division of Sixth Corps was detached and sent to the right to cover the left flank of Ninth Corps. When the above changes in position were finally completed, there was a gap of about a half mile between the right of Getty's division and the left of Foster's division. Mott's division of Second Corps arrived later, and it then moved up to fill this gap. William Birney's division of Twenty-Fifth Corps also advanced inside the line of the abandoned enemy works and took position on the right of Twenty-Fourth Corps. It then connected on its right with Seymour's Third Division, Sixth Corps. Ulysses Doubleday's Second Brigade, which was on the left of Birney's line, was in front of Confederate Battery No. 45, which was located about midway between Confederate Fort Gregg and the Weldon Railroad. Later that evening, Seymour's division moved back and spent the night on the old enemy picket line in front of Fort Fisher and to the right of it.

While Humphreys, with the divisions of Hays and Mott, advanced on the Boydton Plank Road toward Petersburg, Miles continued his march on the Claiborne Road and followed the enemy to a point near Sutherland's Station. The enemy force consisted of four brigades of Hill's corps that had been cut off from Petersburg by Wright's attack that morning. These were John R. Cooke's brigade and a part of William McRae's brigade of Heth's division and Samuel McGowan's brigade and Alfred M. Scales' brigade (commanded by Joseph H. Hyman) of Wilcox's division, all under Heth's command. Near Sutherland's Station, Heth's column joined the remnants of Pickett's and Johnson's divisions, both under Richard H. Anderson, and Fitzhugh Lee's Cavalry Corps.

When Miles arrived near Sutherland's Station, he found the enemy strongly posted behind breastworks. Robert Nugent's Second Brigade and Henry J. Madill's Third Brigade promptly attacked but were driven back. Madill was wounded and was succeeded in command of Third Brigade by Clinton D. MacDougall. At 12:30 P.M., MacDougall launched a second attack, but it too was unsuccessful. Finally, at 2:45 John Ramsey's Fourth Brigade charged the left flank of the line and captured the works and a large number of prisoners.

When Humphreys' other divisions arrived in front of the enemy entrenchments behind Indian

Town Creek, Mott's division, as noted above, was placed in a gap that existed between the divisions of Foster and Getty. At 2:30 P.M., before Hays' division was in position, Humphreys received word that Miles needed support, and he immediately moved with Hays' division out the Cox Road toward Sutherland's Station. Mott's division was placed under Wright's control during Humphreys' absence. Humphreys had reached a point on the Cox Road about two miles east of Sutherland's Station when he learned that Miles had defeated the commands of Heth and Anderson, and that he no longer needed assistance. Humphreys did not return immediately to Petersburg, but halted in the position he then occupied.

About 5:00 P.M. April 2, 1865, Wheaton, with the brigades of Penrose and Edwards of his First Division, Sixth Corps, marched out and formed on the left of Hays. Edwards' brigade was on the right, next to Hays, and Penrose's brigade was on the left, with its left on the Appomattox River. At about 9:30 that night, Second Corps was placed under Sheridan's orders.

After Sheridan left Miles on the White Oak Road that morning, he returned to Five Forks, and from there he marched north with Griffin's Fifth Corps on the Ford Road to Ford's Station on the South Side Railroad. Griffin continued on to the north to the Cox Road, and then marched on that road toward Sutherland's Station. He turned off on the Namozine Road and halted for the night near Williamsons' at the intersection of the Namozine Road and the River Road.

Merritt's cavalry, at Sheridan's direction, also moved out from Five Forks on the morning of April 2, 1865. The two divisions marched west on the White Oak Road for about three miles, and then turned off to the right and continued on to a point near Ford's Church on the South Side Railroad, about midway between Ford's Station and Sutherland's Station. Merritt destroyed some track, and then moved on about five miles to the north to Scott's Cross Roads, at the intersection of the Namozine Road and the Sutherland Station Road. Mackenzie's cavalry division joined Merritt's column on this march and continued on with his column.

Crook's brigades did not accompany Merritt's command that day, but they marched by different routes to the north. Gregg's Second Brigade generally followed Merritt from the White Oak Road, and joined him near the Namozine Road later that day. Davies' First Brigade marched from Dinwiddie Court House to the Claiborne Road crossing of Hatcher's Run, where it halted for the night. Smith's Third Brigade also marched from Dinwiddie Court House in the direction of Sutherland's Station, and camped on Hatcher's Run that night.

On the night of April 2, 1865, Grant's army was in position close to Petersburg as follows: Wheaton's First Division, Sixth Corps was on the left, with Penrose's First Brigade on the left of the division next to the Appomattox River, and Edwards' Third Brigade on the right, connecting with Hays' Second Division, Second Corps, which was on the Cox Road. Hamblin's Second Brigade of Wheaton's division was serving that evening with Parke's Ninth Corps near the Jerusalem Plank Road. Getty's Second Division, Sixth Corps was on the right of Hays, with its right on the Boydton Plank Road. Seymour's Third Division, Sixth Corps was camped on the old enemy picket line in front of Fort Fisher and to its right.

Mott's Third Division, Second Corps was on the right of Getty, and on the right of the Boydton Plank Road. It connected on its right with Foster's First Division, Twenty-Fourth Corps, which was on the line of Fort Baldwin and Fort Gregg (Confederate). Turner's Independent Division, Twenty-Fourth Corps extended from the right of Fort Gregg to the vicinity of Confederate Battery No. 45, which was about midway between Fort Gregg and the Weldon Railroad. William Birney's Second Division, Twenty-Fifth Corps was on the right of Turner, with Doubleday's left brigade near Battery No. 45, and James Shaw's right brigade connecting with Ninth Corps. Ninth Corps continued the line to the Appomattox River east of Petersburg, with Simon G. Griffin's First Division (Potter's division) on the left, between Shaw's brigade and the Jerusalem Plank Road; John Hartranft's Third Division in the center, on the right of the Jerusalem Plank Road; and Willcox's First Division on the right, between the right of Hartranft and the river.

Miles' First Division, Second Corps was at Sutherland's Station, and as noted above, Griffin's Fifth Corps was at the Williamson house. Crawford's Third Division, Fifth Corps was supporting Merritt's cavalry, which was at the crossing of the Namozine River, northwest of Sutherland's Station.

North of the Appomattox River, George L. Hartsuff, with Edward Ferrero's infantry division and Henry L. Abbot's artillery brigade, occupied the Defenses of Bermuda Hundred. North of the James River, Godfrey Weitzel held the line of entrenchments from the river, past Chaffin's farm, to the New Market Road with Charles Devens' Third Division, Twenty-Fourth Corps and August V. Kautz's First Division, Twenty-Fifth Corps.

Federal Occupation of Petersburg and Richmond, April 3, 1865. The condition of the Army of Northern Virginia had steadily deteriorated during the winter of 1864–1865, and after the failure of Gordon's attack at Fort Stedman March 25, 1865, it was apparent to Lee that the time for the evacuation of Petersburg was not far off. Then, after the destruction of his Right Wing at Five Forks on the evening of April 1, 1865 and the breakthrough of his line of entrenchments by Sixth Corps the next morning, Lee knew that he could delay no longer.

During the morning of April 2, 1865, Lee notified the authorities at Richmond of his intention to abandon the lines in front of Petersburg and Richmond, and at 3:00 P.M. he issued orders for the withdrawal, to begin at 8:00 that night. He hoped to effect a junction with Joseph E. Johnston's army in North Carolina, and to that end he directed the various units of his army to concentrate at Amelia Court House on the Richmond and Danville Railroad in preparation for a retreat to the south through Burkeville.

As soon as it was dark, the Confederate army began to pull out of its entrenchments all along the line, and it then marched toward Amelia Court House, where it arrived during the period from the afternoon of April 4, 1865 to noon April 5, 1865. James Longstreet, with Charles W. Field's division of his corps and Henry Heth's and Cadmus M. Wilcox's division of Ambrose P. Hill's corps (Hill was killed early on the morning of April 2, 1865), crossed the Appomattox River on the pontoon bridge at the Battersea factory in Petersburg, and took the River Road, north of the river, toward Bevill's (also Bevil's) Bridge over the Appomattox. John B. Gordon's corps crossed the river at the

Pocahontas Bridge and at the railroad bridge, and followed Longstreet to the forks of the road, about a mile from the bridge, and there it took the Hickory Road to the right. This road rejoined the River Road farther on, and when later Gordon again came into the latter road, he followed Longstreet toward Bevill's Bridge. The approaches to this bridge were flooded, however, and Longstreet and Gordon were rerouted to Goode's Bridge farther north. There they recrossed the Appomattox River and arrived at Amelia Court House during the afternoon of April 4, 1865.

William Mahone's division of Hill's corps, which was holding the Howlett Line in front of Bermuda Hundred, marched west to Chesterfield Court House, and then by way of Old Colville to Goode's Bridge. Mahone remained there during the night of April 4, 1865 to hold the bridge, and he then crossed and followed Gordon's route to Amelia Court House.

Fitzhugh Lee's cavalry and Richard H. Anderson's command, which consisted of the remnants of Pickett's and Johnson's divisions, marched from the Namozine Road, west of Petersburg, along the south side of the Appomattox River, and arrived at Amelia Court House during the morning of April 5, 1865.

Richard S. Ewell's command at Richmond consisted of Joseph B. Kershaw's division of Longstreet's corps; G. W. Custis Lee's division (largely heavy artillery); and Ewell's Reserve Corps of Local Defense Troops and Reservists. With these troops, Ewell crossed the James River at and below Richmond and, followed by Martin W. Gary's cavalry, took the Broad Rock Road that passed by Branch Church and Gregory's, and then the Genito Road toward Genito's Bridge on the Appomattox River. When Ewell arrived at the crossing, however, he found that a pontoon bridge that was supposed to be in place had not been laid, and he crossed his command on the Richmond and Danville Railroad bridge at Mattoax. He then marched into Amelia Court House April 5, 1865.

While Lee was retreating toward Amelia Court House, the Union forces had also been very active. During the night of April 2, 1865, Grant ordered an assault all along the Petersburg and Richmond lines to begin the next morning. About 3:00 A.M., however, skirmishers found that the enemy works had been abandoned by all except a few pickets, and when this was reported, Federal troops began advancing toward the two cities. About 4:00 A.M., troops of Ninth Corps had finally succeeded in penetrating the enemy picket line in front of Petersburg and had occupied the empty works. Ralph Ely's Second Brigade of Willcox's division was apparently the first to enter the city, which it did near the Appomattox River, and Ely received the formal surrender at 4:25 A.M. April 3, 1865. William Birney also claimed that troops of his Second Division, Twenty-Fifth Corps were the first to enter Petersburg. Orlando B. Willcox was assigned commander of the city, and was ordered to garrison the post with his First Division, Ninth Corps. Willcox's division and the troops at City Point were placed under the command of Gouverneur K. Warren, who had been relieved from command of Fifth Corps at Five Forks April 1, 1865.

North of the James River, Weitzel also learned during the night that the enemy was abandoning the line on his front, and he ordered his command to be prepared to move at daylight. Then, at about 5:00 A.M. April 3, 1865, Devens reported that his picket line was in possession of the enemy works. All of this indicated that Richmond was being evacuated, and Weitzel sent Major Atherton H. Stevens and Major Eugene E. Graves, both of his staff, to receive the surrender of the city. At the same time he started his troops toward Richmond. Kautz's First Division, Twenty-Fifth Corps marched up the Osborne Pike; Devens' Third Division, Twenty-Fourth Corps on the New Market Road; and the cavalry under Charles F. Adams, Jr. on the Darbytown and the Charles City roads. All were directed to halt at the outskirts of the city and await further orders.

Weitzel rode ahead of the troops on the Osborne Pike and entered Richmond, where he received the surrender of the city at City Hall at 8:15 A.M. Stevens and Graves had arrived a little after 7:00 A.M. and had occupied the city with their cavalry. Edward H. Ripley's First Brigade of Devens' division was then assigned as provost guard of Richmond, and all other troops were ordered to take position along the inner line of redoubts around the city.

Pursuit of the Army of Northern Virginia, April 3–5, 1865. Grant was virtually certain that Lee would attempt to move by the South Side (or Lynchburg) Railroad or the Richmond and Danville Railroad to reach the interior, and Grant's marching orders, issued April 3, 1865, were such as to place his army in positions to interrupt any movement by either of these two routes. His orders were as follows: Sheridan was to march west with his cavalry and Griffin's Fifth Corps along the south side of the Appomattox River, keeping close to the river, to strike the Richmond and Danville Railroad somewhere between Mattoax and Burkeville. At the latter point, the Richmond and Danville Railroad crossed the South Side Railroad. Meade, with Humphreys' Second Corps and Wright's Sixth Corps, was to follow Sheridan, and then to move toward the Richmond and Danville Railroad at Amelia Court House. During most of the day, Humphreys marched under Sheridan's orders, but at 4:30 P.M. Meade resumed the direction of Second Corps. Ord was to move along the South Side Railroad to Burkeville with Gibbon's Twenty-Fourth Corps and Birney's Second Division, Twenty-Fifth Corps. Parke was to follow Ord with Simon G. Griffin's and Hartranft's divisions of Ninth Corps.

Early on the morning of April 3, 1865, the cavalry left its bivouac near Scott's Cross Roads, and followed Anderson's Confederate command along the south side of the Appomattox River throughout the day. William Wells' Second Brigade of Custer's division was engaged with Fitzhugh Lee's rear guard at Namozine Church, and about dark, Merritt attacked the enemy rear guard of cavalry and infantry at Deep Creek. The cavalry camped that night at Deep Creek, near Bridgeforth Mill, and Fifth Corps, which had followed the cavalry closely during the day, camped nearby. Second Corps halted for the night, with Hays' division near Namozine Church and Miles' and Mott's divisions about three miles farther on. Sixth Corps halted at Mount Pleasant Church, near Sutherland's Station, on the Namozine Road.

Parke advanced along the South Side Railroad toward Burkeville with the divisions of Simon G. Griffin and Hartranft of his Ninth Corps. Griffin, after sending Collis' brigade back to City Point, left Petersburg early in the afternoon and marched west on the River Road and the Namozine Road. He followed Sixth Corps during the afternoon, and bivouacked that night about ten miles west of

Petersburg. At 7:30 that morning, Hartranft relieved Hamblin and his brigade from further service with Ninth Corps and directed him to rejoin Wheaton's division of Sixth Corps, which was then moving westward on the River Road. Then, at about 3:00 P.M., Hartranft's division, which had been held near the Avery house, marched through Petersburg and on west, following Griffin's division. It moved along the South Side Railroad, guarding the wagon trains of the army, and halted for the night five miles from the city.

Early on April 4, 1865, Sheridan learned that Lee appeared to be concentrating his army at Amelia Court House, and he then directed Crook to move his cavalry division to the Richmond and Danville Railroad between Burkeville and Jetersville, and then to advance on the railroad toward the latter place. Mackenzie's cavalry division marched directly toward Amelia Court House that day and reached Five Forks (not the Five Forks of Sheridan's battle), which was about a mile south of Amelia Court House. Mackenzie camped there that night and then remained in the vicinity watching and demonstrating against the enemy. Sheridan also ordered Charles Griffin to move with his Fifth Corps directly toward Jetersville. Both Crook and Griffin arrived there late in the afternoon, and then entrenched on a line that extended across the railroad to enable them to hold the position until the rest of the army came up.

Meade followed closely behind Fifth Corps April 4, 1865 until 11:00 A.M.; he was then delayed when Merritt's cavalry came into the road, and he was not able to reach Deep Creek until that night. Parke also resumed his advance at daylight that morning with his two divisions. Simon G. Griffin's division moved from the Namozine Road to the Cox Road, and continued its march on the latter road during the day. It halted that night, with one brigade at Picketts' and the other at Ford's Station on the South Side Railroad. Hartranft's division also continued its march by slow stages, and had only reached Nottoway Court House April 9, 1865, the day that Lee surrendered the Army of Northern Virginia.

April 4, 1865, Devin's cavalry division marched to Drummond's Mills, where it was engaged during the day. That night Devin marched toward Jetersville, where he arrived about 10:00 the next morning. Custer's division, which had been following Fitzhugh Lee's cavalry, camped on Sweathouse Creek during the night of April 4, 1865, and from that point it marched on toward Jetersville and arrived there at 7:00 the next morning.

At Jetersville, Sheridan learned that Lee's army was at Amelia Court House, eight miles to the northeast, and when Meade was informed of this, he ordered Humphreys to march with his Second Corps for Jetersville at 1:00 A.M. April 5, 1865. He also ordered Wright to follow Humphreys with his Sixth Corps. Shortly after starting, however, Humphreys was delayed when Merritt, who had marched from the vicinity of Bevill's Bridge, entered the road ahead of him; and Second Corps, closely followed by Sixth Corps, did not begin to arrive at Jetersville until 2:30 that afternoon. As Second Corps arrived, it was put in position on the left of Griffin's Fifth Corps, and when Sixth Corps came up it was placed on the left of Griffin. Mackenzie's cavalry took position on the right of this line and Merritt's cavalry on the left. In this way a solid barrier was formed across Lee's escape route to Danville.

On the morning of April 5, 1865, Sheridan sent Davies' brigade of Crook's cavalry division to Paineville (or Paine's Cross Roads), about five miles north of Amelia Springs (Amelia Sulfur Springs), to determine whether the enemy was moving in that direction. A few miles beyond Paineville, Davies found the enemy wagon train from Richmond, escorted by Gary's cavalry, and after driving off the escort, destroyed the train. Shortly after Davies left Paineville on his return to the army, Gary attacked his rear guard, and a running fight continued as far as Amelia Springs. At that point, Smith's and Gregg's brigades of Crook's division arrived in support, and Davies returned safely to his camp.

When Lee arrived at Amelia Court House, he found that supplies that had been ordered to that place had not arrived, and he was then forced to remain there for twenty-four hours while he attempted to collect subsistence for both men and horses. Finally, during the afternoon of April 5, 1865, after he had assembled his army, Lee marched toward Jetersville in an attempt to break through what he hoped to be a line held only by Sheridan's cavalry, and in this way reach Burkeville on the road to Danville. Lee had not gone very far, however, when he learned that Sheridan's cavalry had been reinforced by infantry, and he then turned back toward a bridge over Flat Creek near Amelia Springs, about three miles from Jetersville. Longstreet, who was leading Lee's column, began to arrive at the springs about sunset.

Ord, with Gibbon's Twenty-Fourth Corps, arrived at Burkeville late at night April 5, 1865, and further secured the Richmond and Danville Railroad. Ord had left Birney's division of Twenty-Fifth Corps at Blacks and Whites (present-day Blackstone) on the South Side Railroad. The troops of Ninth Corps also continued their advance along the railroad. Curtin's brigade of Griffin's division advanced to Morgansville, and Harriman's brigade of the same division reached Wellville. That day, Willcox's division of Ninth Corps, which had been serving as garrison of Petersburg, marched out to Sutherland's Station. There it connected with Hartranft's division, and moved westward along the railroad as the army advanced until on April 9, 1865, it extended from Sutherland's Station to Wellville. Parke continued to advance, guarding the trains and picketing the railroad up to the rear of the army, until Lee's surrender.

The Army of Northern Virginia continued its retreat toward the west during the night of April 5, 1865, and Longstreet's command, which was still leading, passed through Deatonsville, crossed Sayler's Creek, and began arriving at Rice's Station on the South Side Railroad about sunrise the next morning. The rest of the army was on the road, in order behind Longstreet, as follows: Anderson's command, Ewell's command, the army trains, and Gordon's corps, which was serving as rear guard. At daylight April 6, 1865, Fitzhugh Lee's cavalry, which had halted for the night at Amelia Springs, marched toward Rice's Station, where it joined Longstreet later that day.

Grant's movements began early on April 6, 1865. Meade, believing Lee was still at Amelia Court House, moved forward in that direction, with Fifth Corps on the railroad, Second Corps on the left, and Sixth Corps on the right. By 10:00 A.M., however, Meade had received information that convinced him that Lee had been moving westward past his left flank during the night, and he changed the direction of his march. He directed Humphreys to move forward toward Deatonsville; Griffin with Fifth Corps through Paineville, on the right of Second Corps; and Wright with Sixth Corps through Jetersville to take position on the left of Second Corps.

As Humphreys advanced, he followed Gordon's corps and skirmished almost constantly with its rear guard. Mott was wounded near Amelia Springs, and P. Regis De Trobriand assumed command of Third Division, Second Corps. Russell B. Shepherd took charge of De Trobriand's First Brigade, Third Division. Another command change occurred in Second Corps that day. William Hays assumed command of the Artillery Reserve of the army, and at 9:00 A.M. Thomas A. Smyth took temporary charge of Hays' Second Division. About an hour later, however, Francis C. Barlow rejoined the army after a long absence on sick leave, and assumed command of Second Division. Smyth then resumed command of his Third Brigade, Second Division.

On the morning of April 6, 1865, Crook marched out of Jetersville on the Pride's Church Road toward Deatonsville, and Merritt followed with the divisions of Custer and Devin. Wright's Sixth Corps marched on the same road behind the cavalry. When Crook approached Deatonsville, he found the enemy trains, strongly escorted by infantry and cavalry, passing through the village on the Jamestown Road. Then Crook, followed by Merritt and Wright, pushed on along the Pride's Church Road, while attempting to find a suitable place to attack the trains. This road ran generally westward from one to three miles south of, and roughly parallel to, the road on which Lee's army was marching to Pride's Church. At that point the road branched. The road to the right ran north for about three-fourths of a mile, and then to the northwest to intersect the Deatonsville-Rice's Station Road at Hott's (or Holt's) Corner, about three miles west of Deatonsville and one-fourth mile northeast of Little Sayler's Creek. (*note.* At the time of the battle of April 6, 1865, this stream was incorrectly called Sailor's Creek, and on more recent maps it is designated as Big Sayler's Creek.) At Hott's Corner, the Jamestown Road turned to the right and continued on to Jamestown on the Appomattox River. The road that turned to the left at Pride's Church ran to the southwest, then to the west, and after crossing Little Sayler's Creek at Gill's Mill, it ran on to the northwest toward Lockett's Mill. About one mile beyond Gill's Mill, it intersected the Deatonsville-

Rice's Station Road, less than one-fourth of a mile west of the Marshall house.

When Crook arrived at Pride's Church, he turned north, and about noon arrived near Hott's Corner. There he found Anderson's troops in position along the Deatonsville-Rice's Station Road, protecting the trains. Crook attacked but was repulsed. The head of Ewell's column, which was about a mile behind Anderson, then came up and aided Anderson in repelling a second attack, in which Merritt's cavalry also took part. Anderson then moved on and crossed Little Sayler's Creek. The attacks on the trains that day had considerably slowed the progress of Anderson's and Ewell's commands, and as a result a serious gap developed that afternoon between Longstreet and Anderson.

Sheridan retained Peter Stagg's First Brigade of Devin's cavalry division for special service with him near Hott's Corner, and sent the rest of the cavalry on to the west in an attempt to get across the enemy line of retreat. Merritt was placed in command of all the cavalry (except Stagg's brigade) while Sheridan was directing affairs at Hott's Corner, and he then moved back with his command to Pride's Church, where he marched west on the left-hand fork of the road. He crossed Little Sayler's Creek at Gill's Mill, and then continued on to the northwest on the road to Lockett's Mill until he arrived on the front and flank of Anderson's command.

Anderson then deployed his command in a defensive position along the Deatonsville-Rice's Station Road. The left of this position was at the crossroads of the roads to Rice's Station and Lockett's Mill, about one-fourth mile west of the Marshall house. A little less than a mile west of the crossroads, another road ran off to the north from the Rice's Station Road, and Anderson's left was on this road. Pickett's division was on the left of Anderson's line, and his brigades were, in order from left to right, as follows: Corse's, Hunton's, Terry's, and Steuart's. The first three of these brigades were along the road, facing south, and Steuart's faced to the southwest. Johnson's line was on the right of the line and was posted north of the Rice's Station Road, with its left near the road and its right on the road that ran north from the Rice's Station Road. Johnson's line was in position across the angle formed by the two roads, and faced to the southwest. Johnson's brigades

were, in order from left to right, as follows: Wise's, Wallace's, Moody's, and Ransom's.

Merritt formed his command about three-fourths of a mile south of the Price's Station Road, with Devin's division on the left and Custer's division on the right. Devin's line faced north toward the brigades of Steuart and Terry, and its right was about midway between the G. Harper house and the J. Harper house. Fitzhugh's brigade was on the left, and Gibbs' brigade was on the right. Custer's division was on the right of Devin, with Pennington's brigade on the left, next to Gibbs, and Capehart's brigade on the right. Wells' brigade was in rear of Capehart, in reserve.

Crook's division marched across country from Hott's Corner and formed on the left of Merritt, and ahead of Anderson. Crook's line was across the road that ran to Longstreet's position at Rice's Station. Gregg's brigade was north of the road, and west of the road that ran north from the Rice's Station Road. It faced to the northeast toward the right of Johnson's position. Davies' brigade was on the right of Gregg, south of the Rice's Station Road, and faced north toward the left of Johnson's line. Smith's brigade was on the right of Davies, well to the south of the Rice's Station Road, and it faced to the northeast toward Steuart's brigade.

Back at Hott's Corner, Ewell ordered the wagon train to turn off to the right from the road to Rice's Station, and to continue its movement on the Jamestown Road toward a lower crossing of Sayler's Creek, near the Appomattox River. Then, after giving this order, Ewell, with his own command, followed Anderson down the road toward Rice's Station. When Gordon's corps arrived at Hott's Corner, it too turned to the right and followed the trains. By that movement, Gordon left the rear of Ewell's corps completely unprotected. Humphreys' Second Corps, which had been following Gordon all day, also turned to the right on the Jamestown Road and continued to follow Gordon.

Battle of Sayler's Creek, April 6, 1865. At about the same time that Merritt's cavalry was approaching Anderson's front, off to the left, Wright's Sixth Corps was nearing Pride's Church. When Sixth Corps was directed to follow Sheridan's cavalry that morning, it was placed under Sheridan's orders, and Sheridan, who had remained at Hott's Corner that afternoon, sent an order to Wright at Pride's Church to bring up his Sixth Corps as rapidly as possible. Wright then hurried forward in person, and was followed, in order, by the divisions of Seymour, Wheaton, and Getty.

Engagement at the Hillsman Farm. Troops of Keifer's brigade of Seymour's division were the first of Sixth Corps to arrive at Hott's Corner, and they were promptly sent after Ewell, down the road toward Little Sayler's Creek. After advancing a short distance, however, Keifer found Kershaw's rear guard in line near the Hillsman house and, after deploying, drove the enemy back across the creek to Ewell's entrenched line, which was on the hillside beyond, a few hundred yards to the southwest. Seymour's other brigade, under Truex, then came up, and the division was formed on the right of the road, about halfway between the Hillsman house and Little Sayler's Creek. Keifer's brigade was on the right of the division line, and Truex's brigade was on the left, next to the road. Wheaton's division then arrived and was placed on the left of Seymour, with Edwards' brigade on the right, next to the road, and Hamblin's brigade was on the left. Wheaton's other brigade, under Penrose, had been detached the day before to guard the trains, and it was not present during the battle that evening.

The guns of Andrew Cowan's Artillery Brigade of Sixth Corps were posted on a ridge in front of the Hillsman house. These belonged to the following batteries: John R. Brinckle's Battery E, 5th United States Artillery; George W. Adams' Battery G, 1st Rhode Island Light Artillery; Crawford Allen's Battery H, 1st Rhode Island Artillery; Orsamus R. Van Etten's 1st Battery, New York Light Artillery; and Augustin N. Parsons' Battery A, 1st New Jersey Light Artillery.

At Sheridan's direction, Stagg's cavalry brigade of Devin's division was placed in the interval between the left of Wheaton and the right of Merritt's cavalry.

Cowan's artillery opened on Ewell's line about 5:15 P.M., and at 6:00 P.M., without waiting for Getty's division, Wright began his attack. His line advanced and crossed Little Sayler's Creek, but then the center was momentarily checked and driven back. It recovered, however, and together with the troops on both flanks, charged and captured almost all of Ewell's command. Toward the end of the fighting, Getty's division arrived and was posted near the Hillsman house, but it was not engaged.

Engagement on the Rice's Station Road. Late in the evening, simultaneously with Wright's attack on Ewell, Merritt advanced on Anderson's position, which was about a mile south of Ewell's line. Gregg's brigade of Crook's division, fighting dismounted, struck the right flank of Johnson's line and quickly drove it back. Then Custer, after several attempts, finally broke through Pickett's position by a charge with Capehart's brigade, which was supported by a part of Pennington's brigade. Anderson's command was completely broken, and the troops fled across country in complete disorder. This happened just as Wright completed his successful assault on Ewell's line. Most of Anderson's command was destroyed, with only Henry A Wise's brigade and a few other troops escaping. Most of the rest were captured.

Engagement at the Lockett Farm. There was still a third engagement along Little Sayler's Creek that evening. While Sixth Corps and the cavalry were engaged along the road to Rice's Station, Gordon's corps was following the trains along the Jamestown Road about two miles to the north toward a crossing at the confluence of Little Sayler's Creek and Sayler's Creek. Humphreys' Second Corps was close behind Gordon and was skirmishing with his rear guard. While the trains were crossing the creek, the bridge collapsed, and Gordon's column east of the creek was forced to halt. Gordon then prepared for a stand on the high ground of the Lockett farm, a half mile to the east of Sayler's Creek.

Humphreys brought up his Second Corps and prepared for an attack. He formed Miles' division in two lines north of the road just west of the Christian house, facing west. MacDougall's brigade was on the right, and Scott's brigade was on the left of the first line. Ramsey's brigade was in rear of MacDougall, and Nugent's brigade was in rear of Scott on the second line. De Trobriand's division (formerly Mott's) was deployed on the left of Miles, south of the road. Pierce's brigade was on the right, next to Scott, and McAllister's brigade was on the left. Shepherd's brigade (formerly De Trobriand's) was in reserve behind Pierce. Barlow's division (commanded by Hays until that morning) covered the right of Miles' division and was not engaged that evening. When Humphreys had his troops in position, he advanced and drove Gordon back across Sayler's Creek and to the high ground beyond. The fighting continued until dark, and Gordon lost about 1,700 men as prisoners and 200 wagons.

After the fighting had ended along the road to Rice's Station, Devin's division advanced to Sayler's Creek (not Little Sayler's Creek where the battle was fought) and halted for the night. Mahone's Confederate division, which had been sent back from Rice's Station by Longstreet, took position on the opposite side of the creek. Crook's and Custer's divisions camped near the battlefield. Getty's division of Sixth Corps, which had not been engaged that evening, also advanced to Sayler's Creek, about two miles beyond the battlefield. Wheaton and Seymour closed up on Getty during the night.

During the day, April 6, 1865, Griffin had marched north with his Fifth Corps from Jetersville to Paineville, then turned west and advanced on the right of the army toward the Appomattox River. He halted that evening about a half mile south of Ligonton (Ligontown) near the river. At that time, Griffin was about two miles north of the Christian house, where Humphreys was forming for his attack on Gordon. Fifth Corps then moved south and was arriving on the right of Second Corps while it was engaged with Gordon, but it did not take part in the action.

Action at High Bridge, April 6, 1865. The Army of the James was also active on the left flank of the army April 6, 1865. At 4:00 P.M., Ord sent out from Burkeville a force of 580 infantry and cavalry under Francis Washburn to destroy the South Side Railroad bridge over the Appomattox River (the "High Bridge"), which was about four miles east and north of Farmville. The destruction of this bridge could seriously interfere with the retreat of Lee's army. Washburn's command consisted of two infantry regiments from Turner's division of Twenty-Fourth Corps and three companies of cavalry from Washburn's own 4th Massachusetts Cavalry of Ord's headquarters escort. Horace Kellogg, lieutenant colonel of the 123rd Ohio Infantry, was in immediate command of the infantry.

Soon after the expedition departed, Ord learned that Lee's army was approaching the area, and he sent Theodore Read, his chief of staff, to warn Washburn. When Read joined the column, he assumed command and continued on through Farmville toward the bridge. Meantime, Longstreet had learned of Read's advance and had sent Rosser, with his own cavalry division and Munford's (formerly Fitzhugh Lee's) division, in pursuit. Rosser found Read's infantry near the Watson house, about a mile from the High Bridge, and prepared to attack.

Washburn's cavalry, which had moved on toward the bridge, then returned and charged the advancing enemy line. A bitter engagement then ensued, during which the Federal cavalry was destroyed. Read and Washburn were mortally wounded, and most of the cavalry officers were killed or wounded. Confederate losses were also severe. James Dearing, commanding a brigade in Rosser's division, and Reuben B. Boston, commanding a brigade in Munford's division, were killed. The infantry continued to resist for some time, but finally surrendered without accomplishing its purpose.

Movement of the Armies to Appomattox Court House, April 6–9, 1865. After dark April 6, 1865, the Army of Northern Virginia, or what was left of it, started for Farmville, where food for the hungry soldiers had been sent. Longstreet, with Field's division and the broken divisions of Heth and Wilcox, marched on the road from Rice's Station and arrived at Farmville around 9:00 the next morning. He then crossed to the north bank of the Appomattox River and halted to cook the expected rations. Fitzhugh Lee with the cavalry followed Longstreet to Farmville.

Gordon's corps, with the survivors of Anderson's defeated command, marched from near Sayler's Creek during the night of April 6, 1865 to High Bridge; and early the next morning, crossed to the north bank of the Appomattox by the wagon bridge at the base of the railroad bridge. Gordon then marched on the River Road toward Farmville. Mahone's division, which had covered the retreat of Gordon's command during the night, also crossed at High Bridge after Gordon.

At noon April 6, 1865, after Washburn had departed for High Bridge, Ord advanced with

Gibbon's two divisions along the South Side Railroad, on the Farmville Road, toward Rice's Station. About 3:00 P.M., Foster's division, which was in the lead, came up to Longstreet's corps, which was entrenched across the road, blocking the way. Foster then deployed in front of Longstreet, with Fairchild's brigade on the right of the road and Osborn's brigade on the left, with its left extending across the railroad. It was dark before Foster was in position, and it was then too late to attack. Turner's division arrived during the night and formed on the left of Foster. Dandy's brigade of Foster's division, which had been attempting to establish contact with Sheridan's cavalry on the right, reported to Foster about 9:00 that night and was placed in reserve. Birney's division of Twenty-Fifth Corps also arrived near Gibbon's position during the night.

Mackenzie's Cavalry Division, Army of the James, which had been on the right of Meade's infantry beyond Jetersville April 5, 1865, marched the next day to Burkeville and camped there that night. Very early on the morning of April 7, 1865, Mackenzie was ordered to march to Prince Edward Court House. The control of Mackenzie's cavalry division during the Appomattox Campaign was varied. It was under Ord's orders until April 1, 1865, when it reported to Sheridan at Dinwiddie Court House, and then came under Sheridan's orders. When it was sent to Burkeville, it was to rejoin the Army of the James, but upon arrival there it was sent on to Prince Edward Court House by Grant's orders. At the latter place, April 7, 1865, Sheridan again took charge and ordered Mackenzie to Prospect Station. That same day, Mackenzie reported to Ord, but April 8, 1865, his division, then consisting of only a single brigade, was ordered by Sheridan to report to Crook. Mackenzie served under Crook's direction during the rest of the campaign.

Federal troops resumed their pursuit of Lee early on April 7, 1865. Sheridan's cavalry moved to the road from Rice's Station to Farmville, and then followed Fitzhugh Lee's cavalry to the latter place. After proceeding a short distance, Sheridan discovered that the Army of the James was not in position to prevent Lee's escape on the road to Danville that ran through Prince Edward Court House, and he ordered Merritt with his two divisions to that point. Crook, however, pushed on toward Farmville and closely followed Fitzhugh Lee's cav-

alry. Crook was so close, in fact, that he forced Lee to make a stand on the outskirts of the town, and then again in the streets of the town to gain time for Longstreet's rear guard and the stragglers to cross the Appomattox.

Federal infantry also pressed forward after Longstreet and Fitzhugh Lee on the Farmville Road. Ord, who had spent the night near Rice's Station, started at daylight with the divisions of Foster, Turner, and Birney, and followed Crook's cavalry. Wright's Sixth Corps marched that morning from the vicinity of the battlefield of the evening before, and when it reached Rice's Station it fell in behind Ord's column. Sixth Corps had been under Sheridan's orders during the Battle of Sayler's Creek, and Sheridan believed that it was Grant's intention that he, Sheridan, would retain control of the corps in the succeeding operations. Whether this was correct or not, on the morning of April 9, 1865, Meade assumed control of the movements of Wright's corps.

Before reaching Farmville, Sixth Corps passed Ord's column and moved onto the hills that overlooked the town from the south. The enemy then fired the bridges over the Appomattox before Rosser's and Munford's cavalry could cross, and Lee ordered the immediate resumption of the retreat. Longstreet's command then moved up the road about two and a half miles to the Piedmont Coal Pits (Dalby's). Upon arrival there, Lee found his cavalry, which had crossed the Appomattox at a ford (probably Sandy Ford) about four miles above the Buckingham Court House Plank Road (or Maysville Plank Road) bridge.

Sixth Corps remained on the hills south of the river until that night, and then crossed the river on a newly constructed foot bridge and went into camp.

Meantime, Humphreys' Second Corps had resumed its advance at 5:30 A.M. April 7, 1865, and had moved by roads nearest to the Appomattox to High Bridge. It arrived there just after the enemy rear guard had set fire to the railroad bridge and also to the wagon bridge below. Barlow's Second Division, which had the advance, secured the wagon bridge, put out the fire, and then began to cross. Mahone, who had not yet departed with his division, attempted to retake the bridge but failed, and then he set out for Farmville behind Gordon.

Humphreys believed that Lee was moving toward

Lynchburg by the Old Stage Road, north of the Appomattox, and in an attempt to intercept him, marched out with the divisions of Miles and De Trobriand on the Jamestown Road. This road ran northwest from High Bridge and intersected the Old Stage Road about four miles north of Farmville. Humphreys was not certain about Lee's route, however, and he sent Barlow's division along the railroad to follow Gordon and Mahone toward Farmville. Barlow overtook Mahone's rear guard about 11:00 A.M., and in the sharp engagement that ensued, Thomas A. Smyth was mortally wounded. He was succeeded in command of Third Brigade, Second Division by Daniel Woodall. Upon advancing close to the town, Barlow found Farmville still occupied by the enemy, and he halted to await orders.

Most of the survivors of the Army of Northern Virginia were at that time near Farmville, where they hoped to obtain rations and prepare food. William T. Poague was sent with his artillery up the Cumberland Court House Road to Cumberland Church, which was about three miles north of Farmville, near the junction with the Jamestown Road on which Humphreys was approaching. Later, Mahone was sent to join Poague, and he placed his division around the church, facing north and east, so as to protect the trains coming up from Farmville.

About 1:00 P.M., Humphreys arrived with his two divisions on the left and front of Mahone's division, near the junction of the Jamestown Road and the Cumberland Court House Road, and there he came under fire from Poague's artillery. Miles' First Division was deployed on the right of the corps line, across the Cumberland Court House Road just north of the road junction, facing south. De Trobriand's Third Division was on the left, south of the Jamestown Road, facing west toward Cumberland Church. Barlow's Second Division, which was then on the South Side Railroad near Farmville, was ordered to rejoin the corps. It did not arrive near Cumberland Church until 6:30 P.M., and then took position on the right of Humphreys' line, west of the Cumberland Court House Road.

By about 2:00 P.M., Wright's Sixth Corps and Ord, with Gibbon's divisions of Twenty-Fourth Corps and Birney's division of Twenty-Fifth Corps, were in the vicinity of Farmville, south of the Appomattox River. Ord's command was then operating in close proximity to the Army of the Potomac, and it was placed under Meade's orders. When Meade learned of the situation that afternoon, he issued orders for Sixth Corps to cross the Appomattox at Farmville and advance and strike the enemy while Humphreys attacked at Cumberland Church. Wright was unable to comply, however, because the bridges had been destroyed, and the river was too deep for the infantry ford. Bridges were constructed, but it was almost dark before Sixth Corps began to cross.

About 3:00 P.M., Humphreys, believing that Sixth Corps was across the river and advancing, decided to attack. Scott's First Brigade of Miles' division then moved down the road from the north and attacked the left flank of Mahone's division, which was then supported by George T. Anderson's brigade of Field's division. This attack was repulsed, and, although there was skirmishing until sundown, there was no further major attack. When Humphreys attacked at Cumberland Church, Lee halted all of his infantry and sent both Longstreet and Gordon to help Mahone.

At about the time of Humphreys' attack, Crook's cavalry had an encounter about a mile and a half to the southwest. When Crook arrived at Farmville and found the bridges burned, he crossed the river by a ford and, during the afternoon, moved northward on the Buckingham Court House (or Maysville) Plank Road. Gregg's brigade was in the lead, and it was followed by the brigades of Davies and Smith. About two miles up the road, Gregg found enemy cavalry protecting an enemy wagon train. It was then about 4:00 P.M. The 4th Pennsylvania Cavalry charged but was repulsed, and then Munford's and Rosser's cavalry charged and drove Gregg back in disorder on Davies' brigade. Gregg was captured, and Samuel B. M. Young assumed command of the Second Brigade of Crook's division. Young rallied Gregg's men and, with Davies' brigade on his right, again advanced. By that time the enemy cavalry was supported by infantry, and Crook was forced to fall back. He later recrossed the river at Farmville, and that night marched along the South Side Railroad to Prospect Station, where he halted shortly after midnight.

When Sheridan arrived with the divisions of Custer and Devin at Prince Edward Court House about 3:00 P.M. April 7, 1865, he found Mackenzie's cavalry had already arrived there from

Burkeville about noon. Sheridan then ordered Mackenzie to move on, cross the Buffalo River, and make a reconnaissance toward Prospect Station to find out whether Lee was moving in that direction. Sheridan then learned from Crook that Lee had crossed to the north side of the Appomattox River and was not moving south, and Sheridan then directed Merritt to move on toward Appomattox Station. Merritt camped that night on the Buffalo River, about four miles from Prospect Station.

At 7:30 that evening, after the cavalry had departed, Griffin's Fifth Corps arrived at Prince Edward Court House. Griffin had marched that day from Ligonton, which was on the extreme right of the army, to a position on the extreme left.

About 9:30 P.M. April 7, 1865, at or near Cumberland Church, Lee received Grant's communication, written at Farmville at 5:00 that afternoon, proposing the surrender of the Army of Northern Virginia. That night, Lee's army pulled out of its positions north of Farmville and marched in the direction of New Store. Mahone left the vicinity of Cumberland Church about 11:00 P.M., and Longstreet marched at midnight on the Old Lynchburg Wagon Road. The rest of the army moved on the Buckingham Court House Plank Road. Fitzhugh Lee's cavalry brought up the rear. Lee's marching columns did not stop until they reached the vicinity of New Store, some twenty miles from Farmville. His army moved on during April 8, 1865, and that evening halted northeast of Appomattox Court House. Gordon's division was within a mile of the village, and Longstreet's rear guard was about six miles out.

Grant's forces resumed the pursuit early on the morning of April 8, 1865. At 5:30 A.M., Second Corps marched from Cumberland Church to the Piedmont Coal Pits, and then took the Lynchburg Road (the Appomattox Court House Stage Road) toward New Store. Humphreys continued on beyond that point and, after a rest of two or three hours, marched on and camped at midnight about three miles behind Longstreet.

Wright's Sixth Corps did not move until after 8:00 A.M., but it soon overtook Second Corps. Sixth Corps did not follow Second Corps all day, however, but turned off on the Buckingham Court House Plank Road and marched by way of Curdsville before coming in again behind Second Corps at New Store. Wright camped there that night. Meade accompanied Second Corps and Sixth Corps on the march that day, and remained with them until after Lee's surrender.

On the other flank, south of the Appomattox River, the rest of the army was hurrying forward toward Appomattox Station. Early on April 8, 1865, Merritt's two cavalry divisions and Mackenzie's cavalry division (then reduced to a single brigade) moved from the Buffalo River to Prospect Station. There they joined Crook's division, which had arrived there during the previous night. Sheridan then placed Mackenzie's cavalry under Crook's orders. From Prospect Station, Sheridan advanced on the road along the South Side Railroad toward Appomattox Station. The divisions were on the road, in order from front to rear, as follows: Custer, Devin, Crook, and Mackenzie.

Ord's Army of the James remained near Farmville during the night of April 7, 1865, and at daylight the next morning marched up the road toward Appomattox Station. Before leaving, however, Ord relieved Birney from command of Second Division, Twenty-Fifth Corps, and directed him to report for duty at City Point. Birney's division was temporarily broken up as follows: Ulysses Doubleday's Second Brigade was assigned to Foster's division of Twenty-Fourth Corps; and William W. Woodward's Third Brigade to Turner's division of Twenty-Fourth Corps. James Shaw's First Brigade of Birney's division had been detached April 4, 1865 to hold Sutherland's Station until Ninth Corps arrived, and it did not rejoin Ord's command April 9, 1865 at Appomattox Station. It was then assigned temporarily to Turner's division.

Ord arrived at Prospect Station about noon April 8, 1865, and there he found Griffin's Fifth Corps waiting to join him. Fifth Corps, which was then under Sheridan's immediate direction, had just come up from Prince Edward Court House that morning. Ord, as senior officer, then assumed the direction of Fifth Corps as well as his own Twenty-Fourth Corps. In fact, Ord was the senior officer on the left flank, and was therefore in command of all troops there, including Sheridan's cavalry. Ord promptly moved on with his column and followed Sheridan toward Appomattox Station. Gibbon's Twenty-Fourth Corps had the lead, with Turner's division in front, and Fifth Corps followed Gibbon.

Custer's cavalry division reached Appomattox Station during the late evening of April 8, 1865, and captured three trains loaded with food for Lee's army. These had been sent back from Farmville the day before when Federal troops arrived before rations could be distributed. Without stopping, Custer pushed on and drove back some enemy troops that had reached the vicinity of the station, and then captured twenty-five guns of Lindsay R. Walker's surplus artillery, and William H. F. Lee's wagon train. Devin's cavalry division came up at about that time, and Stagg's and Fitzhugh's brigades were dismounted and put in on the right of Custer. The cavalry engagement lasted until 9:00 P.M., and during the evening the enemy was driven back to the vicinity of Appomattox Court House. Crook's division arrived that night, and Smith's brigade was sent to hold the road running from Appomattox Court House to Lynchburg. Smith formed his brigade across the road, and the rest of the division camped that night not far from Appomattox Station. Sheridan's cavalry was then squarely across the line of Lee's retreat, and at 9:20 that evening, Sheridan sent a dispatch to Grant apprising him of the situation, and urging that Ord's infantry be hurried forward as rapidly as possible to support him.

Ord's troops had been advancing steadily throughout the day, and Gibbon's Twenty-Fourth Corps did not halt until midnight. At that time, it was about four miles from Appomattox Station. Griffin's Fifth Corps, following Gibbon, marched twenty-nine miles, and finally camped at 2:00 A.M. April 9, 1865 along the railroad at the Abbitt house. It was then only two miles from Appomattox Station. Thus, before daylight April 9, 1865, Lee's route of retreat to the west and south was blocked, and Humphreys' Second Corps and Wright's Sixth Corps were closing in on the rear of the Army of Northern Virginia.

Meantime, while the rest of the army had been marching and fighting, Parke's Ninth Corps remained in the rear guarding the line of the South Side Railroad west of Petersburg. April 9, 1865, Willcox's First Division was on the line from Sutherland's Station to Blacks and Whites (present-day Blackstone); Simon G. Griffin's Second Division was at Burkeville (Curtin's First Brigade advanced to Farmville the next day); and Hartranft's Third Division was at Nottoway Court House, about midway between Blacks and Whites and Burkeville.

Surrender of the Army of Northern Virginia, April 9, 1865. After discussing the situation with Gordon and Fitzhugh Lee during the night of April 8, 1865, Lee decided to make a final attempt early the next morning to break through Sheridan's lines and continue the retreat to the west and south. It was generally recognized that this effort would be successful if only Federal cavalry barred the way, and that if Ord's infantry was in position across the road, it would be too strong to be driven away. In the latter event, the only alternative left would be the surrender of the army.

During the early hours of April 9, 1865, the remains of Gordon's infantry corps and Fitzhugh Lee's cavalry were formed in line of battle about a half mile west of Appomattox Court House, on the road to Lynchburg. Gordon's infantry was on the left of the line, and Fitzhugh Lee's cavalry on the right. The cavalry was disposed as follows: William H. F. Lee's division was on the left, next to the infantry; Rosser's division was in the center; and Munford's division was on the right. Fitzhugh Lee was to open the attack at 5:00 A.M., and Gordon was to support him.

Meantime there had been some changes in the positions of Sheridan's cavalry in front of Appomattox Court House. Devin's division, which had spent the night on the Lynchburg Road west of the court house, was relieved at daybreak by Crook's division. Smith's brigade of Crook's division relieved Fitzhugh's brigade of Devin's division on the road; and Devin, with the brigades of Stagg and Fitzhugh, then took position on the right of Crook.

A little after 5:00 A.M., Gordon's infantry advanced on the front and both flanks of Smith's brigade, while Fitzhugh Lee's cavalry attempted to reach its rear. Mackenzie's brigade then arrived on the left of Smith; and Davies' brigade, which had been sent out on a reconnaissance to the left, attacked the enemy cavalry as it advanced. Young's brigade (formerly Gregg's) also came up, and when Young could not find Crook, he reported to Davies and was engaged with his brigade on the left that morning. Devin, with the brigades of Stagg and Fitzhugh, were also soon engaged, and Gibbs' Reserve Brigade was brought up in support.

While the cavalry was thus engaged, Ord arrived at Sheridan's headquarters with Gibbon's Twenty-Fourth Corps and Griffin's Fifth Corps. Twenty-Fourth Corps appeared at 4:00 A.M. and immediately marched toward the left, with Foster's division leading, to relieve Crook's cavalry. Gibbon arrived on the Lynchburg Road about 6:00 A.M. and deployed Foster's division across the road. He placed Osborn's brigade on the right of the road, Dandy's brigade on the left of Osborn, and Woodward's brigade (formerly of William Birney's division) on the extreme left. He placed Fairchild's brigade in support of Osborn, but when he discovered enemy forces advancing on the left, he moved Fairchild to that flank. Then Foster moved his whole line in that direction until it reached the Bent Creek (or Oakdale) Road, and then took position along the road.

Ulysses Doubleday's brigade (formerly of Birney's division) was on the Lynchburg Road in rear of Foster's line when a part of the Federal cavalry that had not been relieved gave way. Doubleday then formed his brigade in line of battle on the right and pushed the enemy back. A short time later Doubleday rejoined Foster's division near the Bent Creek Road.

Because of heavy enemy pressure on the Federal right of the Lynchburg Road, Turner's division was sent in that direction, and it was deployed on the right of Foster, with William B. Curtis' Second Brigade on the left, next to Osborn; Andrew Potter's First Brigade in the center; and Thomas M. Harris' Third Brigade on the right.

Ord supervised the placement of Gibbon's divisions, and he then rode back to Griffin's Fifth Corps, which arrived at Appomattox Station at 6:00 A.M. Ord then directed Griffin to take position on the right of Twenty-Fourth Corps. Ayres' Second Division, which was leading, deployed on the right of Turner, with David L. Stanton's Second Brigade on the left, Joseph Hayes' First Brigade (commanded by James Grindlay to April 3, 1865) on the right. James Gwyn's Third Brigade was formed on a second line, supporting Stanton. Ayres arrived just in time to rescue Devin's cavalry division and check Gordon's advance. Bartlett's First Division of Fifth Corps took position on the right of Ayres, with Edgar M. Gregory's Second Brigade on the left, Alfred L. Pearson's Third Brigade (formerly Bartlett's) in the center, and Joshua L. Chamberlain's First Brigade on the right. Crawford's Third Division did not arrive until 8:00 A.M., and was not engaged.

When Fifth Corps was finally deployed, it advanced and relieved Devin's division, which then moved off to the right and, with Custer's division, took position opposite the extreme left of the enemy line. These two divisions then began preparations for an attack on the enemy left.

About 8:00 A.M., Gordon reported to Lee that he could do no more without help from Longstreet, but the latter could do little because at that time he was seriously threatened by the approach of Humphreys and Wright from New Hope Church. Lee then decided that the surrender of his army could no longer be delayed, and he set out toward the rear to meet with Grant. Gordon was not aware of Lee's decision, however, and he continued fighting for a time as Ord's lines steadily advanced. Ord finally reached a ridge that overlooked Appomattox Court House, and then, under a flag of truce, hostilities were suspended.

Lee was unable to meet with Grant as expected, because the latter had left the road on which Second Corps was approaching, and at that time he was riding toward Appomattox Station on the road from Farmville. Lee then sent a message through the lines to Grant, which the latter received on the road about four miles west of Walker's Church at 11:50 that morning. Grant replied, agreeing to meet Lee at a place of the latter's selection, and he then hurried forward for the meeting. Lee left his headquarters about 12:30 P.M. April 9, 1865 and rode into Appomattox Court House, where the home of Wilmer McLean had been chosen as the meeting place. Grant did not arrive until 1:30 P.M., and the surrender was completed at about 3:45 P.M.

After Appomattox. With the surrender of the Army of Northern Virginia, the war in Virginia came to an end. Joseph E. Johnston's army in North Carolina, however, remained in the field until it too surrendered April 26, 1865, and then the war in the East was over. It was not until the end of June 1865, however, that the armies were finally disbanded and the soldiers had returned to their homes.

Because of Johnston's presence in North Carolina, Grant's army did not remain long at Appomattox Court House after the surrender of Lee.

Grant and Ord, in person, left the army at noon April 10, 1865, and Grant went to Washington and Ord to Richmond, Virginia. John Gibbon, Charles Griffin, and Wesley Merritt were appointed commissioners to arrange the details of the surrender. Gibbon's Twenty-Fourth Corps, Griffin's Fifth Corps, and Mackenzie's cavalry were designated to remain at Appomattox Court House to take charge of the public property and remove it to Farmville, and to wait until paroles were issued to the surrendered soldiers.

Humphreys' Second Corps, Wright's Sixth Corps, and Sheridan's cavalry were not present at the formal surrender, because they marched on the morning of April 11, 1865 toward Burkeville, in preparation for moving to North Carolina. April 12, 1865, Turner's division of Twenty-Fourth Corps and Mackenzie's cavalry marched to Lynchburg, where they paroled prisoners and took possession of large quantities of public property.

April 12, 1865 was the day of the formal surrender of the arms and colors of the Army of Northern Virginia. Joshua L. Chamberlain was appointed to command the parade of the surrender, and Joseph J. Bartlett's First Division, Fifth Corps was selected for that service. When the surrender was completed and all public property had been removed, Fifth Corps left April 15, 1865, for Burkeville. Turner's division and Mackenzie's cavalry left Lynchburg April 17, 1865, and with Foster's division, which joined at Appomattox Court House, also marched toward Burkeville. For a further description of the service and organization of the troops composing Grant's army at Appomattox Court House, see Army of the Potomac and Army of the James.

Organization of the Union Forces Commanded by Ulysses S. Grant during the Appomattox Campaign March 29, 1865–April 9, 1865.

ARMY OF THE POTOMAC
George G. Meade

Provost Guard, George N. Macy
Engineer Brigade, Henry W. Benham
Battalion United States Engineers, Franklin Harwood
Artillery, Henry J. Hunt
 Siege Train, Henry L. Abbot
  1st Connecticut Heavy Artillery, George Ager, to

April 6, 1865
George B. Cook
3rd Battery, Connecticut Light Artillery, Thomas L. Gilbert

Artillery Reserve, Calvin Shaffer, to April 6, 1865
 William Hays
 2nd Battery (B), Maine Light Artillery, Charles E. Stubbs
 3rd Battery (C), Maine Light Artillery, Ezekiel R. Mayo
 4th Battery (D), Maine Light Artillery, Charles W. White
 6th Battery (F), Maine Light Artillery, William H. Rogers
 5th Battery (E), Massachusetts Light Artillery, Charles A. Phillips
 9th Battery, Massachusetts Light Artillery, Richard S. Milton
 14th Battery, Massachusetts Light Artillery, Joseph W. B. Wright
 3rd Battery, New Jersey Light Artillery, Christian Woerner
 Battery C, 1st New York Light Artillery, David F. Ritchie
 Battery E, 1st New York Light Artillery, George H. Barse
 Battery G, 1st New York Light Artillery, Samuel A. McClellan
 Battery L, 1st New York Light Artillery, DeWitt M. Perine
 George Breck
 12th Battery, New York Light Artillery, Charles A. Clark
 Battery H, 1st Ohio Light Artillery, Stephen W. Dorsey
 Battery B, 1st Pennsylvania Light Artillery, William McClelland
 Battery F, 1st Pennsylvania Light Artillery, John F. Campbell
 Battery E, 1st Rhode Island Light Artillery, Ezra K. Parker
 3rd Battery, Vermont Light Artillery, Romeo H. Start
 Batteries C and I, 5th United States Artillery, Valentine H. Stone

SECOND CORPS, Andrew A. Humphreys

First Division, Nelson A. Miles
 First Brigade, George W. Scott
 Second Brigade, Robert Nugent
 Third Brigade, Henry J. Madill, to April 2, 1865, wounded
  Clinton D. MacDougall
 Fourth Brigade, John Ramsey

Second Division, William Hays, to April 6, 1865
    Thomas A. Smyth, April 6, 1865
    Francis C. Barlow
    First Brigade, William A. Olmsted
    Second Brigade, James P. McIvor
    Third Brigade, Thomas A. Smyth, to April 6, 1865
        Daniel Woodall, April 6, 1865
        Thomas A. Smyth, to April 7, 1865, mortally
            wounded
        Daniel Woodall

Note. Hays was assigned command of the Artillery Reserve of the army about 9:00 A.M. April 6, 1865. Smyth then assumed temporary command of Second Division, but he was relieved about an hour later by Barlow, who had just returned to the army from sick leave.

Third Division, Gershom Mott, to April 6, 1865, wounded
    P. Regis De Trobriand
    First Brigade, P. Regis De Trobriand, to April 8, 1865
        Russell B. Shepherd
    Second Brigade, Byron R. Pierce
    Third Brigade, Robert McAllister

Artillery Brigade, John G. Hazard
    10th Battery, Massachusetts Light Artillery, J. Webb
        Adams
    Battery M, 1st New Hampshire Artillery, George K.
        Dakin
    Battery B, 1st New Jersey Light Artillery, A. Judson
        Clark
    11th Battery, New York Light Artillery, James A.
        Manning
    Company C, 4th New York Heavy Artillery, Richard
        Kennedy
    Company L, 4th New York Heavy Artillery, Frank
        Seymour
    Battery B, 1st Rhode Island Light Artillery, William B.
        Westcott
    Battery K, 4th United States Artillery, John W. Roder

FIFTH CORPS, Gouverneur K. Warren, to April 1, 1865,
    relieved at Five Forks
    Charles Griffin

First Division, Charles Griffin, to April 1, 1865
    Joseph J. Bartlett
    First Brigade, Joshua L. Chamberlain
    Second Brigade, Edgar M. Gregory
    Third Brigade, Joseph J. Bartlett, to April 1, 1865
        Alfred L. Pearson

Second Division, Romeyn B. Ayres
    First Brigade, Frederick Winthrop, to April 1, 1865,
        mortally wounded

Joseph Grindlay, to April 3, 1865
Joseph Hayes
Second Brigade, Andrew W. Denison, to March 31,
    1865, wounded
    Richard Bowerman, to April 1, 1865, wounded
    David L. Stanton
Third Brigade, James Gwyn

Third Division, Samuel W. Crawford
    First Brigade, John A. Kellogg
    Second Brigade, Henry Baxter
    Third Brigade, Richard Coulter

Artillery Brigade, Charles S. Wainwright
    Battery B, 1st New York Light Artillery, Robert E.
        Rogers
    Battery D, 1st New York Light Artillery, DeLoss M.
        Johnson
    Battery H, 1st New York Light Artillery, Charles E.
        Mink
    Battery M, 15th New York Heavy Artillery, William
        D. Dickey
    Battery B, 4th United States Artillery, John Mitchell,
        to March 29, 1865, wounded
        William P. Vose
    Batteries D and G, 5th United States Artillery, Jacob B.
        Rawles

SIXTH CORPS, Horatio G. Wright

First Division, Frank Wheaton
    First Brigade, William H. Penrose
    Second Brigade, Joseph E. Hamblin
    Third Brigade, Oliver Edwards

Second Division, George W. Getty
    First Brigade, James M. Warner
    Second Brigade, Lewis A. Grant, to April 2, 1865,
        wounded
        Amasa S. Tracy, April 2, 1865
        Charles Mundee, April 2, 1865
        Amasa S. Tracy, to April 4, 1865
        Lewis A. Grant
    Third Brigade, Thomas W. Hyde

Note. Grant was wounded about 2:00 A.M. April 2, 1865, while under fire, waiting to attack. Tracy then assumed command of the brigade and led it during the assault that broke through the enemy line. When the brigade was re-formed after the attack, Mundee, who was assistant adjutant general of Getty's division, relieved Tracy and directed the brigade during the remainder of the day. He turned over the command to Tracy that night.

Third Division, Truman Seymour
    First Brigade, William S. Truex

Second Brigade, J. Warren Keifer

Artillery Brigade, Andrew Cowan
  Battery A, 1st New Jersey Light Artillery, Augustin N. Parsons
  1st Battery, New York Light Artillery, Orsamus R. Van Etten
  3rd Battery, New York Light Artillery, William A. Harn
  Company L, 9th New York Heavy Artillery, S. Augustus Howe
  Battery G, 1st Rhode Island Light Artillery, George W. Adams
  Battery H, 1st Rhode Island Light Artillery, Crawford Allen, Jr.
  Battery E, 5th United States Light Artillery, John R. Brinckle
  Company D, 1st Vermont Heavy Artillery, Charles J. Lewis

NINTH CORPS, John G. Parke

First Division, Orlando B. Willcox
  First Brigade, Samuel Harriman
  Second Brigade, Ralph Ely
  Third Brigade, Gilbert P. Robinson, to April 2, 1865
    James Bintliff

Second Division, Robert B. Potter, to April 2, 1865, wounded
  Simon G. Griffin
  First Brigade, John I. Curtin
  Second Brigade, Simon G. Griffin, to April 2, 1865
    Walter Harriman

Third Division, John F. Hartranft
  First Brigade, William H. H. McCall, to April 3, 1865
    Alfred B. McCalmont
  Second Brigade, Joseph A. Mathews, to April 2, 1865, sick
    Robert C. Cox, April 2, 1865
    Joseph Mathews

Note. McCalmont arrived at division headquarters late in the evening of April 2, 1865 from leave of absence, and he assumed command of First Brigade at 3:00 A.M. April 3, 1865.

Artillery Brigade, John C. Tidball
  7th Battery (G), Maine Light Artillery, Adelbert B. Twitchell
  11th Battery, Massachusetts Light Artillery, Edward J. Jones
  19th Battery, New York Light Artillery, Edward W. Rogers
  27th Battery, New York Light Artillery, John B. Eaton

  34th Battery, New York Light Artillery, Jacob Roemer
  Battery D, Pennsylvania Light Artillery, Samuel H. Rhoads

INDEPENDENT BRIGADE AT CITY POINT, Charles H. T. Collis

CAVALRY
Philip H. Sheridan

ARMY OF THE SHENANDOAH, Wesley Merritt

First Cavalry Division, Thomas C. Devin
  First Brigade, Peter Stagg
  Second Brigade, Charles L. Fitzhugh
  Reserve Brigade, Alfred Gibbs

Third Cavalry Division, George A. Custer
  First Brigade, Alexander C. M. Pennington
  Second Brigade, William Wells
  Third Brigade, Henry Capehart

ARMY OF THE POTOMAC

Second Cavalry Division, George Crook
  First Brigade, Henry E. Davies, Jr.
  Second Brigade, J. Irvin Gregg, to April 7, 1865, captured
    Samuel B. M. Young
  Third Brigade, Charles H. Smith

ARMY OF THE JAMES

Cavalry Division, Ranald S. Mackenzie
  First Brigade, Robert M. West
  Second Brigade, Samuel P. Spear, to April 1, 1865, wounded
    Andrew W. Evans

Note. Mackenzie's Cavalry Division was attached to Sheridan's cavalry command April 1, 1865.

ARMY OF THE JAMES
Edward O. C. Ord

Engineers, James F. Hall
Pontoniers, John Pickering, Jr.
Unattached Cavalry
  4th Massachusetts Cavalry (Companies I, L, and M), Francis Washburn
  5th Massachusetts Cavalry (colored), Charles F. Adams, Jr.
  7th New York Cavalry (1st Mounted Rifles), Edwin V. Sumner

Note. During the Appomattox Campaign, the 7th New York Cavalry was on an expedition into North Carolina.

DEFENSES OF BERMUDA HUNDRED, George L. Hartsuff

Infantry Division, Edward Ferrero
  First Brigade, Gilbert H. McKibbin
  Second Brigade, George C. Kibbe
  3rd Battery, New York Light Artillery, Alger M. Wheeler

Artillery, Henry L. Abbot
  Companies A and H, New York Heavy Artillery, William Pendrell
  7th Battery, New York Light Artillery, Martin V. McIntyre
  Company E, 3rd Pennsylvania Heavy Artillery, Erskine H. Miles
  Company M, 3rd Pennsylvania Light Artillery, Sylvester W. Marshall

SEPARATE BRIGADE, Joseph B. Carr
  Fort Pocahontas, Ashbel W. Angel
  Harrison's Landing, Wardwell G. Robinson
  Fort Powhatan, William J. Sewell

TWENTY-FOURTH CORPS, John Gibbon

First Division, Robert S. Foster
  First Brigade, Thomas O. Osborn
  Third Brigade, George B. Dandy
  Fourth Brigade, Harrison S. Fairchild

Note. Second Brigade was detached in North Carolina.

Third Division, Charles Devens
  First Brigade, Edward H. Ripley
  Second Brigade, Michael T. Donohoe
  Third Brigade, Samuel H. Roberts

Independent Division, John W. Turner
  First Brigade, Andrew Potter
  Second Brigade, William B. Curtis
  Third Brigade, Thomas M. Harris

Artillery, Charles C. Abell
  Battery E, 3rd New York Light Artillery, George E. Ashby
  Battery H, 3rd New York Light Artillery, Enoch Jones
  Battery K, 3rd New York Light Artillery, James R. Angel
  Battery M, 3rd New York Light Artillery, John H. Howell
  17th Battery, New York Light Artillery, George T. Anthony
  Battery A, 1st Pennsylvania Light Artillery, William Stitt

Battery F, 1st Rhode Island Light Artillery, Charles E. Guild
Battery B, 1st United States Artillery, Samuel S. Elder
Battery L, 4th United States Artillery, Henry C. Hasbrouck
Battery A, 5th United States Artillery, Charles P. Muhlenberg
Battery F, 5th United States Artillery, Henry B. Beecher

TWENTY-FIFTH CORPS, Godfrey Weitzel

First Division, August V. Kautz
  First Brigade, Alonzo G. Draper
  Second Brigade, Edward A. Wild
  Third Brigade, Henry G. Thomas
  Attached Brigade, Charles S. Russell

Note. Russell's Attached Brigade was formed from two regiments of United States Colored Troops that were detached from Third Brigade, Second Division.

Second Division, William Birney
  First Brigade, James Shaw, Jr.
  Second Brigade, Ulysses Doubleday
  Third Brigade, William W. Woodward

Note. April 8, 1865, Birney was relieved from command of Second Division, while at Farmville, and ordered to City Point. The division was then temporarily broken up. Doubleday's brigade was assigned to Foster's First Division, Twenty-Fourth Corps; and Woodward's brigade was assigned to Turner's Independent Division of Twenty-Fourth Corps. At that time Shaw's brigade was absent, having been left behind to guard the South Side Railroad, but it arrived at Appomattox Court House April 9, 1865 and was assigned to Turner's division. Second Division was re-formed April 10, 1865, under the command of Richard H. Jackson of Ord's staff.

Artillery Brigade, Loomis L. Langdon
  1st Battery, Connecticut Light Artillery, James B. Clinton
  4th Battery, New Jersey Light Artillery, Charles R. Doane
  5th Battery, New Jersey Light Artillery, Zenas C. Warren
  Battery E, 1st Pennsylvania Light Artillery, Henry Y. Wildey
  Battery C, 3rd Rhode Island Heavy Artillery, Martin S. James
  Battery D, 1st United States Artillery, Redmond Tully
  Battery M, 1st United States Artillery, Egbert W. Olcott
  Battery D, 4th United States Artillery, Frederick M. Follett

CAVALRY DIVISION, Ranald S. Mackenzie
  First Brigade, Robert M. West

Second Brigade, Samuel P. Spear, to April 1, 1865, wounded
Andrew W. Evans
4th Battery, Wisconsin Light Artillery, Dorman L. Noggle

Note. Mackenzie's division was temporarily attached to Sheridan's cavalry command at Dinwiddie Court House April 1, 1865.

ENGAGEMENT AT BALL'S BLUFF, VIRGINIA
OCTOBER 21, 1861

In the autumn of 1861, Charles P. Stone's Division (Corps of Observation), Department of the Potomac was in the vicinity of Poolesville, Maryland watching the fords and ferries on the Potomac River. Stone's division consisted of three brigades commanded by Willis A. Gorman, Frederick A. Lander, and Edward D. Baker.

October 19, 1861, George B. McClellan, commanding the Department and Army of the Potomac, ordered George A. McCall to move with his division, then near Washington, on an expedition to Dranesville, Virginia, and he directed Stone to observe Leesburg, Virginia to see if this movement resulted in a Confederate withdrawal from the town. McClellan also suggested to Stone that a "slight demonstration" might be helpful to McCall.

At 1:00 P.M. October 20, 1861, Stone proceeded to Edwards Ferry with Gorman's brigade, the 7th Michigan Regiment of Lander's brigade, two troops of James H. Van Alen's 3rd New York Cavalry, and the Putnam Rangers. At the same time, he sent to Harrison's Island and vicinity William R. Lee with a battalion of the 20th Massachusetts of Lander's brigade and four companies of Charles P. Devens' 15th Massachusetts. One company of 15th Massachusetts was already on the island. Harrison's Island was about a mile and a half in length, and was situated in the Potomac River about midway between the Maryland and Virginia shores. It was three and a half to four miles upstream from Edwards Ferry, and about three miles northwest of Leesburg. Stone also sent to Conrad's Ferry, a short distance above Harrison's Island, Milton Cogswell's 42nd New York (Tammany) Regiment and a section of

Thomas F. Vaughan's Battery B, 1st Rhode Island Artillery. A section of Bunting's 6th New York Independent Battery under Walter M. Bramhall was already on duty at Conrad's Ferry. Edmund Kirby's Battery I, 1st United States Artillery (formerly commanded by James B. Ricketts) was posted at Edwards Ferry under George A. Woodruff.

Stone then ordered Devens at Harrison's Island to send Chase Philbrick with twenty men of the 15th Massachusetts across the Potomac into Virginia to advance by a path through the woods in the direction of Leesburg to learn what he could of the enemy positions in that direction. At dark October 20, 1861, Stone ordered Gorman's brigade and the 7th Michigan back to their camps, but he held the 42nd New York, the companies of 15th Massachusetts, and the artillery near Conrad's Ferry to await the results of Philbrick's scout. Stone remained at Edwards Ferry. Philbrick returned sometime before 10:00 P.M. and reported that he had proceeded unmolested to within about a mile of Leesburg and had discovered an enemy camp.

At 10:30 P.M. Stone issued orders for the disposition of his troops. Devens was to cross the river with five companies of his 15th Massachusetts and move that night toward Leesburg so as to be in position to attack at daylight the next morning the camp reported by Philbrick. Immediately after Devens' departure, William R. Lee, colonel of the 20th Massachusetts, was to occupy Harrison's Island with four companies of his regiment, and he was then to send one company across the Potomac to occupy the heights on the far side to cover Devens' return. Frank S. French of Kirby's Battery was to take two mountain howitzers across to the far side of Harrison's Island and report to Lee. Baker was to send Isaac J. Wistar's 71st Pennsylvania (commonly called the 1st California Regiment or simply the California Regiment) of his brigade to Conrad's Ferry, and he was to have the rest of his brigade ready to move early the next morning. Finally, George H. Ward of the 15th Massachusetts was to move with a battalion of the regiment to the river bank opposite Harrison's Island in preparation for crossing to the island.

Devens crossed the Potomac from Harrison's Island to the Virginia side of the river about midnight October 20, 1861 with five companies of his regiment, as ordered, and all were over by four o'clock the next morning. The landing place selected was at the base of a steep bluff that rose to a height of fifty to seventy-five feet above the river and extended for some distance along the Virginia shore opposite Harrison's Island. This was known as Ball's Bluff. At the top of the bluff was an open field variously estimated as six to ten acres in extent. This clearing was surrounded on the north, west, and south by woods. Crossing the field, parallel to the river and about midway between the top of the bluff and the woods beyond, was a road that ran along the river from Edwards Ferry to Conrad's Ferry. Branching off from this road near the northern end of the field, and close to the J. P. Smart house, was another road that ran off to the southwest toward Leesburg, a little more than two miles distant.

Devens' command climbed the bluff after coming ashore, and then halted until daybreak in the field at the top. There it was joined by Lee with two companies of the 20th Massachusetts. Lee was instructed to remain at Ball's Bluff to hold the ground until Devens' return. At daybreak Devens pushed forward about a mile from the river to the reported site of the enemy camp, but he found that Philbrick was in error and that there was no camp. Devens remained in the area until about 10:00 A.M. and, after some skirmishing, fell back and rejoined Lee near the bluff. Around 11:00 A.M., Ward joined Devens with the other companies of the 15th Massachusetts. Then about noon, or a little after, Devens advanced a second time and took position about one mile from the bluff.

Meantime, to distract attention from Devens' advance toward Leesburg, and at the same time to make a reconnaissance toward that place, Stone had directed Gorman to send out a small force on the Leesburg Road early on the morning of October 21, 1861. John Mix, of the 3rd New York Cavalry, with some troopers of his regiment and two companies of the 1st Minnesota Regiment, crossed the Potomac at Edwards Ferry at 7:00 A.M. and advanced to the Monroe house, about two miles from the ferry. After some skirmishing, Mix withdrew and rejoined his command. During the rest of that day and that night, Gorman moved his entire brigade to the south side of the river.

Early on the morning of October 21, 1861, Baker arrived at Conrad's Ferry with Wistar's 71st Pennsylvania (California Regiment) as directed, and he had the rest of his brigade ready to march. Between 9:00 and 9:30 A.M., Stone sent Baker to Harrison's Island to assume command of all troops on the right of Stone's line. Baker assumed command at 10:00 A.M. In assigning Baker to this command, Stone authorized him to make such use as he saw fit of the following troops: Baker's own brigade; Cogswell's 42nd New York Regiment; Edward W. Hinks' (also spelled Hincks) 19th Massachusetts Regiment of Lander's brigade; a part of Lee's 20th Massachusetts Regiment of Lander's brigade; and the artillery. Baker was also given the discretion, after viewing the ground, of withdrawing the troops from the Virginia side of the river or of sending over troops to support them, whichever he thought best. After Baker arrived at Harrison's Island, apparently without examining the ground across the river, he proceeded to cross his entire force as rapidly as possible. This, however, was necessarily a slow process because of a shortage of boats.

Between 12:30 and 1:00 P.M., the enemy appeared in force in front of Devens' advanced line, and a sharp skirmish ensued. The Confederate force at Leesburg, and the one that advanced against Devens, belonged to Nathan G. Evans' Seventh Brigade, First Corps, Army of the Potomac (Confederate). It consisted of William Barksdale's 13th Mississippi, Winfield S. Featherston's 17th Mississippi, E. R. Burt's 18th Mississippi, and Eppa Hunton's 8th Virginia. Walter H. Jenifer was also present in command of three companies of Virginia cavalry.

Devens' 15th Massachusetts skirmished for a time and then, unsupported and about to be outflanked, retired and took position about one-half to three-fourths mile in front of Lee's line near the bluff. Devens remained in this new position until about 2:00 P.M. and then fell back and took his place in line with Lee's 20th Massachusetts and Wistar's 71st Pennsylvania of Baker's brigade, which had just arrived. At this time, Cogswell's 42nd New York was coming over from Harrison's Island with two pieces of artillery. The entire 42nd New York had been transported to Harrison's Island, but the crossing to Virginia was so slow and tedious that only five companies succeeded in reaching Ball's Bluff. The rest remained on the island.

Sometime after 2:15 P.M., Baker arrived in person on the bluff. He then proceeded to form a line of battle, and after this was completed, he awaited an enemy attack. Devens' 15th Massachusetts was on the right of the line in the edge of the woods on the northern side of the field. The regiment was formed nearly at a right angle to the road crossing the field, with its left near that road. Lee's troops of the 20th Massachusetts were along the road in the field on the left of Devens' line. One company of the 20th Massachusetts was deployed as skirmishers in the woods on the right, one company was out on the left, and three companies were in reserve near the center of the line. Wistar's 71st Pennsylvania was in the field in front of the road to the left and front of Lee's line. Bramhall and French had, with much labor, brought their guns up the bluff. Bramhall, with his single piece of the 1st Rhode Island Artillery, was placed on the left of Wistar's line, and French, with his two mountain howitzers, was placed in front of the junction of Devens' and Lee's lines. In the fighting that began a short time later, both Bramhall and French were wounded and their guns were hauled to the rear to avoid capture.

Evans began his attack about 3:00 P.M. The whole Federal line was subjected to a heavy fire, but it was particularly heavy on the center and left. Cogswell arrived with a small part of his command during the fighting and quickly became engaged on the Federal left near the southern edge of the field. About 4:00 P.M. Devens sent two companies of his regiment to support the left of Baker's line and, at the same time, drew in his right to close the gap thus created.

About 4:00 P.M., Baker was killed and Lee assumed command. It was soon discovered, however, that Cogswell was the senior officer present, and he then took charge. Cogswell decided to make an attempt to cut through the enemy line and reach Edwards Ferry. The 15th Massachusetts was moved from the right to the left of the original line, and two or three companies of the 42nd New York, just then arriving, formed on Devens' left. By some mistake, 42nd New York and 15th Massachusetts charged the enemy line, but they received a murderous fire and were quickly recalled. By that time the movement to the left toward Edwards Ferry was no longer practicable, and Cogswell reluctantly gave the order to retire. The enemy pursued the retreating Federals to the edge of the bluff above the landing place, and opened with a heavy fire on the struggling men

attempting to cross back to the island. There were not enough boats to carry all the troops, and some boats were swamped when overloaded by frantic soldiers. Some men were able to swim back, but many were drowned and others were captured on the shore, including Cogswell and Lee. The result was a complete disaster, with 49 men reported killed, 158 wounded, and 700 missing.

Hinks' 19th Massachusetts of Lander's brigade was on Harrison's Island when the Federals retired, and Hinks took charge there during the retreat.

Stone was blamed for the mismanagement of the battle of Ball's Bluff. He was arrested February 9, 1862, and was subsequently confined for 189 days at Fort LaFayette and Fort Hamilton in New York Harbor. No charges were ever preferred. He was finally released August 6, 1862, without reparation or acknowledgment of error, but his military reputation was ruined. He was later given some employment, but he finally resigned September 13, 1864.

BRISTOE, VIRGINIA CAMPAIGN
OCTOBER 10–22, 1863

After the Gettysburg Campaign ended August 1,1863, the Army of the Potomac remained along the line of the Rappahannock River until mid-September 1863. At that time, it advanced and took position in the vicinity of Culpeper Court House, with two infantry corps and two cavalry divisions in advance on the north bank of the Rapidan River, where they confronted Robert E. Lee's Army of Northern Virginia on the far side. Except for the usual picket and reconnaissance duty, there was little further activity until the end of the first week of October 1863. For additional information about the advance of the army to the Rapidan, see Army of the Potomac, From the Rappahannock to the Rapidan.

Early in October 1863, there were increasing signs of enemy movements south of the Rapidan, and by October 8, 1863, it was clear that troops were withdrawing from the right of the Confederate line. It was not certain, however, whether Lee was beginning to withdraw from the line of the Rapidan, or was starting a flanking movement against the Army of the Potomac. During the morning and early afternoon of October 10, 1863, however, George G. Meade, commanding the army, learned definitely that a strong enemy movement was in progress against his right flank from the direction of Madison Court House.

At that time, John Newton's First Corps, George Sykes' Fifth Corps, and John Sedgwick's Sixth Corps were in line along the north bank of the Rapidan, and William H. French's Third Corps was west of Culpeper Court House, facing the enemy advance from the direction of Madison Court House. John C. Caldwell's Second Corps (Caldwell was relieved by Gouverneur K. Warren October 12, 1863) was moved from the heights in rear of Culpeper Court House to a position near Stone House Mountain, west of the town, to oppose any advance from the direction of Sperryville. John Buford's First Cavalry Division had crossed the Rapidan at Germanna Ford that morning and was approaching Morton's Ford on the south side of the river. Judson Kilpatrick's Third Cavalry Division, reinforced by J. Irvin Gregg's Second Brigade of David McM. Gregg's Second Cavalry Division that had just arrived from Bealeton, was out in front of Second Corps and Third Corps, facing James E. B. (Jeb) Stuart's cavalry.

At 3:15 on the afternoon of October 10, 1863, Fifth Corps was withdrawn from the river to its former position in front of Culpeper Court House, and at about 4:00 P.M. the trains of the army were ordered to the north side of the Rappahannock for safety. A short time later, First Corps and Sixth Corps were ordered to withdraw from the line of the Rapidan after dark, and First Corps was directed to move to Stevensburg, and Sixth Corps to the railroad beyond Culpeper Court House. Later, at 10:00 P.M., Sixth Corps was ordered to continue on to Rappahannock Station. Also during the night of October 10, 1863, Buford withdrew his cavalry division to the north side of the Rapidan and marched toward Culpeper Court House.

Late on October 10, 1863, Meade issued orders for the withdrawal of the Army of the Potomac to the east bank of the Rappahannock River. Third Corps was directed to march by way of Welford's Ford on the Hazel River to the vicinity of Freeman's Ford on the Rappahannock; Second Corps, Fifth Corps, and Sixth Corps were to march along the Orange and Alexandria Railroad to Rappahannock

Station; and First Corps was to move to Kelly's Ford. Third Corps, Fifth Corps, and the cavalry were to cover the withdrawal, with Third Corps on the road to Sperryville and Fifth Corps watching the front toward Rapidan Station.

On October 11, 1863, when Fifth Corps withdrew, Kilpatrick's cavalry division followed and at Brandy Station joined Buford's division, which had just arrived from the Rapidan. Kilpatrick formed on the right of Buford, and soon both divisions were engaged with Stuart's cavalry. There were several charges and countercharges during the afternoon as the Federal cavalry withdrew, until finally it recrossed the Rappahannock River that evening and went into camp at 8:00 P.M. By nightfall, all of the Army of the Potomac, except J. Irvin Gregg's cavalry brigade, was east of the Rappahannock. That day Gregg's brigade had marched from the Sperryville Pike to the vicinity of Sulfur Springs (Warrenton Springs), where it had halted and taken position to guard the approaches to the river. John P. Taylor's First Cavalry Brigade of Second Cavalry Division marched from Kelly's Ford and camped that night near Sulfur Springs, on the eastern bank of the Rappahannock.

Both armies were active October 12, 1863. Lee's two corps had arrived at Culpeper Court House the day before, and on the morning of the twelfth they advanced toward Warrenton in two columns. Richard S. Ewell's Second Corps moved on the direct road through Jefferson (Jeffersonton) and Sulfur Springs, and Ambrose P. Hill's Third Corps marched on the left by way of Sperryville, Amissville, and Waterloo. James Longstreet's corps had been sent west to reinforce Braxton Bragg's Army of Tennessee in Georgia. There was little activity in Meade's army during the morning, but Kilpatrick's division moved to Fayetteville to reinforce David McM. Gregg. About 1:00 P.M., for reasons that are not entirely clear, Meade ordered Second Corps, Fifth Corps, Sixth Corps, and Buford's cavalry division, all under the command of Sedgwick, to recross the Rappahannock and march toward Brandy Station to determine whether Lee had followed the army during its withdrawal along the railroad. First Corps was ordered to remain in position and be prepared to support Sedgwick if needed.

While Sedgwick's movement was in progress,

Stuart's cavalry, supported by infantry, attacked J. Irvin Gregg's cavalry brigade at Welford's Ford and Jefferson, and finally forced it to retire behind the Rappahannock. Gregg's brigade, supported by Taylor's brigade, continued to resist for some time, but finally the enemy forced a passage of the river at Sulfur Springs, and Robert E. Rodes' and Edward Johnson's Confederate divisions crossed and bivouacked for the night. This fact was reported to Meade by David McM. Gregg at about 5:00 P.M., and that evening Gregg moved with the brigades of J. Irvin Gregg and Taylor to Fayetteville.

Meantime, Sedgwick, with his column, had advanced to Brandy Station, and Buford's cavalry had penetrated to within a short distance of Culpeper Court House, but had encountered only a small body of cavalry. Then, when Meade learned that his right was menaced by heavy columns of Confederate infantry, he ordered Sedgwick to return to the east bank of the Rappahannock. He also directed Warren's Second Corps, which was nearest to the river, to march to Bealeton to support Gregg's Second Cavalry Division, and to cover French's Third Corps, which was at Freeman's Ford. Newton's First Corps, which was then no longer needed to support Sedgwick, was ordered at 10:45 P.M. October 12, 1863 to march to Warrenton Junction. Warren joined Gregg at Fayetteville about 1:00 A.M. October 13, 1863.

At 1:00 A.M. October 13, 1863, Meade issued orders for the army to retire toward Centerville. The movements of the army that day were as follows: Third Corps withdrew from Freeman's Ford and marched through Fayetteville and Auburn (Auburn Mills) to Greenwich, where it camped that night. Warren's Second Corps followed Third Corps to Auburn, and camped there that night on the west side of Cedar Run. Kilpatrick's cavalry, which had been covering the road from Fayetteville to Warrenton, was relieved by Gregg's Second Cavalry Division, and Kilpatrick marched by way of Hay Market to Sudley Springs to hold that point. After the infantry had withdrawn, Gregg brought up the rear and long after dark took position between Second Corps and Warrenton. Newton's First Corps, Sykes' Fifth Corps, and Sedgwick's Sixth Corps marched back along the Orange and Alexandria Railroad and camped on the night of October 13, 1863 as follows: First Corps at Bristoe Station; Fifth Corps at Walnut Run, a short distance east of Catlett's Station; and Sixth Corps at Kettle Run. Buford's cavalry division was at Warrenton Junction, and was assigned to guard the trains of the army, which were ordered to Brentsville.

Engagement at Bristoe Station, October 14, 1863. Meade's army continued on to the heights of Centerville October 14, 1863. First Corps marched along the railroad to Manassas Junction, and then by way of Mitchell's Ford to Centerville. Sixth Corps followed First Corps to Manassas Junction, and then crossed Bull Run at Blackburn's Ford and formed on the right of First Corps. Third Corps marched from Greenwich, through Milford to the railroad, and then by way of Manassas Junction and Mitchell's Ford to Centerville. It then took position on the left of First Corps. Fifth Corps followed Third Corps, and Second Corps brought up the rear.

About dawn October 14, 1863, Second Corps resumed its march from near Auburn, but with its direction changed from Greenwich to Catlett's Station. From there it was to proceed along the railroad to Centerville. John C. Caldwell's First Division had crossed Cedar Run, and Alexander Hays' Third Division was beginning to cross when Stuart's artillery opened fire on the rear of Caldwell's column. Caldwell, with help from Hays and R. Bruce Ricketts' battery, soon drove off the enemy, and Second Corps continued on to Catlett's Station. Shortly after noon, Warren was ordered to close up on Fifth Corps, which was on the road ahead, and the divisions of Webb, Hays, and Caldwell were started, in that order, along the railroad toward Bristoe Station. Gregg's cavalry division covered the rear and left flank.

Hill's Confederate corps had started northward from near Warrenton at about 5:00 A.M. October 14, 1863. It marched on the Warrenton-Alexandria Turnpike until it reached Broad Run Church, and there it took the road through Greenwich toward Bristoe Station. Fifth Corps was in the process of crossing Broad Run, east of the station, when Hill arrived on the high ground to the northwest. When he observed the Union troops on his front, he ordered Henry Heth's division forward, and formed it in line of battle, facing southeast toward the railroad crossing of Broad Run. Some time elapsed before Heth was ready to advance, and while he was moving into position the Confederate artillery opened fire on the Union troops ahead. Fifth Corps quickly moved on toward Centerville, and Heth started his men forward to press Sykes' retreating column.

The advance of Webb's division of Second Corps reached Bristoe Station about 2:00 P.M., as the rear of Fifth Corps was moving off beyond Broad Run, and as Heth's brigades were advancing toward the railroad. Webb formed his division in line behind the railroad embankment between Bristoe Station and Broad Run, with Francis E. Heath's First Brigade on the right and James E. Mallon's Third Brigade on the left. DeWitt C. Baxter's Second Brigade was detached as wagon guard and was not with the division. T. Fred Brown's Battery B, 1st Rhode Island Light Artillery, which was temporarily attached to Webb's division, was placed on a hill west of Broad Run and south of the railroad, but it was later moved across Broad Run to a position that enfiladed the approaching enemy line.

Hays' Third Division soon came up and formed on the left of Webb, behind the embankment and in the cuts of the railroad. Joshua T. Owen's Third Brigade was on the right, next to Webb, and Thomas A. Smyth's Second Brigade was on the left. Samuel S. Carroll's First Brigade was in the rear with the ammunition train. R. Bruce Ricketts, with his Batteries F and G of the 1st Pennsylvania Light Artillery, was temporarily attached to Hays' division, and was placed on the hill originally occupied by Brown's battery near the railroad bridge crossing Broad Run.

When Caldwell's division arrived, it formed on the left of Hays, with the brigades in order, from right to left, as follows: Paul Frank's Third Brigade, Patrick Kelly's Second Brigade, and John R. Brooke's Fourth Brigade. Nelson A. Miles' First Brigade was sent to support Brown's and Ricketts' batteries. William A. Arnold's Battery A, 1st Rhode Island Light Artillery was placed in rear of Caldwell's line. Sometime after 4:00 P.M. Samuel S. Carroll's First Brigade of Hays' division was brought up and placed on the left and rear of Brooke's brigade.

Hill was unaware of the presence of Second Corps behind the railroad embankment when he sent Heth's line forward, but as the brigades of John R. Cooke and William W. Kirkland advanced, they encountered Webb's skirmishers on their right, and they finally observed the Federal line of infantry along the railroad below. The enemy then changed the direction of their line of attack toward Bristoe Station, with Cooke's brigade on the right of the road leading to that point, and Kirkland's brigade on the left of the road. Their attack fell principally on the brigades of Heath, Mallon, and Owen, and it was decisively repulsed with a loss of about 1,900 men. The attack was not renewed. All of the brigades of Second Corps, except Baxter's brigade, were under fire during the engagement, and they suffered some losses, but the heaviest casualties were sustained by the brigades of Smyth, Brooke, Owen, Mallon, and Heath. Mallon was mortally wounded, and Ansel D. Wass assumed command of Third Brigade, Second Division.

During the fighting at Bristoe Station, Sykes started his Fifth Corps back to aid Warren, but the danger had passed before it arrived, and it then turned about and resumed its march toward Centerville. The corps arrived at Bull Run near Blackburn's Ford about midnight October 14, 1863, and went into camp. Second Corps remained near Bristoe Station for several hours after the fighting had ended, and it then marched toward Centerville. The last troops of the corps crossed Bull Run about 4:00 A.M. October 15, 1863.

* * * * * * * * * *

On October 15, 1863, the Army of the Potomac was in position as follows: Third Corps was at Union Mills, with First Division at Fairfax Station to watch McLean's Ford; Fifth Corps was at Fairfax Court House; Sixth Corps was on the Little River Turnpike near Chantilly; one division of First Corps was on the heights of Centerville, and the other two divisions were massed between this division and Sixth Corps; Second Corps was to the left of First Corps, on the heights of Centerville and at Blackburn's and Mitchell's fords on Bull Run. Buford's cavalry division was sent out to picket the Occoquan River, and the remaining cavalry covered the front and right of the army.

Except for his cavalry, Lee did not advance beyond Broad Run, and then, on October 18, 1863, he retired to the line of the Rappahannock. The next day, Meade moved forward to a line behind Broad Run that extended from Hay Market on the right to below Bristoe Station on the left. First Corps was at Hay Market; Sixth Corps was at Gainesville; Third Corps was at Bristoe Station, and extended south of the railroad; Second Corps was on Broad Run at Milford, on the right of Third Corps; and Fifth Corps was at Groveton. During the advance to this line, Buford and Gregg covered the flanks of the army. Kilpatrick's cavalry was out in front of the infantry on the Warrenton Turnpike. It advanced to Buckland Mills October 19, 1863, and while on the march it was attacked in front by Stuart's cavalry and on the flank and rear by Fitzhugh Lee's cavalry, and was quickly routed and driven from the field. Kilpatrick finally re-formed his command that evening on the infantry supports at Gainesville and Hay Market.

There were some indications that Meade might find the enemy near Warrenton, and at 9:00 P.M. October 19, 1863, he ordered the army to concentrate in the Gainesville area the next day. Second Corps was ordered to Gainesville to take position on the left of Sixth Corps, which was already in position there. Third Corps was to follow and form on the left of Second Corps. Fifth Corps was also ordered to Gainesville and was directed to mass in rear of First Corps and Sixth Corps.

On October 20, 1863, Sixth Corps moved forward toward Warrenton, and it was followed by Fifth Corps. Second Corps advanced to Auburn (Auburn Mills), and it was followed by Third Corps. That afternoon, First Corps moved through Thoroughfare Gap to Georgetown. As Meade advanced, Lee retreated across the Rappahannock, and at 8:00 P.M. the advance units of the Army of the Potomac occupied Warrenton without opposition.

While Lee was north of the Rappahannock, he destroyed the railroad from Bristoe Station to the river, and in order to supply the army in its forward position, Meade started repairs on the line immediately. Troops were sent to aid in the work and to guard the road. October 21, 1863, Third Corps was ordered to the vicinity of Catlett's Station, with one brigade to be sent to Bristoe Station. By October 23, 1863, the corps of the army were in position as follows: First Corps was at Georgetown, but it moved the next day to Bristoe Station and relieved the brigade of Third Corps; Second Corps was on the Warrenton Branch Railroad at the crossing of Turkey Run; Third Corps was at Catlett's Station;

Fifth Corps was at New Baltimore; and Sixth Corps was at Warrenton. The Reserve Artillery was near New Baltimore.

During the night of October 26, 1863, First Corps moved to Catlett's Station, and October 29, 1863, one brigade was sent to Kettle Run to guard the bridge there. The corps held the line of the railroad as far as Catlett's Station. October 30, 1863, Third Corps advanced to Warrenton Junction, with one brigade left to guard the depot at Catlett's Station, Cedar Run Bridge, and the railroad from Catlett's Station to Warrenton Junction. During this period, the cavalry was generally in position along the Rappahannock as follows: Buford's division was on the left from Kelly's Ford to Beverly Ford; Gregg's division was on the center of the line, from Beverly Ford to Waterloo; and Kilpatrick's division was on the right, north of Warrenton.

Repairs on the railroad were completed to Warrenton Junction November 1, 1863, and then supplies were brought forward for the army. On November 7, 1863, Meade advanced the army to the Rappahannock, where Third Corps forced a crossing of the river at Kelly's Ford; and Sixth Corps, supported by Fifth Corps, captured the Confederate bridgehead east of the river at Rappahannock Station. For details of this movement, see Engagements at Rappahannock Station and Kelly's Ford, Virginia. After Lee's setback November 7, 1863, he withdrew his army, first to a line in front of Culpeper Court House, and then to its old positions south of the Rapidan River, near Orange Court House. The Army of the Potomac then advanced to positions as follows: Fifth Corps at Paoli Mills, Second Corps between Paoli Mills and Brandy Station, Third Corps at Brandy Station, and Sixth Corps at Welford's Ford on the Hazel River. First Corps was left east of the river to guard the line of the Orange and Alexandria Railroad from Warrenton to Manassas. The army remained essentially in these positions until the beginning of the Mine Run Campaign in late November 1863.

The organization of the Army of the Potomac during the Bristoe Campaign October 9–22, 1863 was as follows:

ARMY OF THE POTOMAC, George G. Meade
    Provost Guard, Marsena R. Patrick
    Engineer Brigade, Henry W. Benham

FIRST CORPS, John Newton

First Division, Lysander Cutler
    First Brigade, William W. Robinson
    Second Brigade, James C. Rice

Second Division, John C. Robinson
    First Brigade, Thomas F. McCoy
    Second Brigade, Henry Baxter

Third Division, John R. Kenly
    First Brigade, Chapman Biddle
    Second Brigade, Langhorne Wister
    Third Brigade, Nathan T. Dushane

Artillery, Charles S. Wainwright
    2nd Battery (B), Maine Light Artillery, Albert F. Thomas
    5th Battery (E), Maine Light Artillery, Greenleaf T. Stevens
    Batteries E and L, 1st New York Light Artillery, Gilbert H. Reynolds
    Battery B, 1st Pennsylvania Light Artillery, James H. Cooper
    Battery B, 4th United States Artillery, James Stewart

SECOND CORPS, John C. Caldwell, to October 12, 1863
    Gouverneur K. Warren

First Division, Paul Frank, to October 12, 1863
    John C. Caldwell
    First Brigade, Nelson A. Miles
    Second Brigade, Patrick Kelly
    Third Brigade, James A. Beaver, to October 12, 1863
        Paul Frank
    Fourth Brigade, John R. Brooke

Second Division, Alexander S. Webb
    First Brigade, Francis E. Heath
    Second Brigade, DeWitt C. Baxter
    Third Brigade, James E. Mallon, to October 14, 1863, mortally wounded
        Ansel D. Wass

Third Division, Alexander Hays
    First Brigade, Samuel S. Carroll
    Second Brigade, Thomas A. Smyth
    Third Brigade, Joshua T. Owen

Artillery, John G. Hazard
    Battery G, 1st New York Light Artillery, Nelson Ames
    Battery H, 1st Ohio Light Artillery, James F. Huntington
    Batteries F and G, 1st Pennsylvania Light Artillery, R. Bruce Ricketts

Battery A, 1st Rhode Island Light Artillery, William A. Arnold
Battery B, 1st Rhode Island Light Artillery, T. Frederick Brown
Battery I, 1st United States Artillery, Frank S. French

THIRD CORPS, William H. French

First Division, David B. Birney
    First Brigade, Charles H. T. Collis
    Second Brigade, J. H. Hobart Ward
    Third Brigade, P. Regis De Trobriand

Second Division, Henry Prince
    First Brigade, Robert McAllister
    Second Brigade, William R. Brewster
    Third Brigade, Gershom Mott

Third Division, Joseph B. Carr
    First Brigade, William H. Morris
    Second Brigade, J. Warren Keifer
    Third Brigade, Benjamin F. Smith

Artillery, George E. Randolph
    4th Battery (D), Maine Light Artillery, O'Neil W. Robinson, Jr.
    10th Battery, Massachusetts Light Artillery, J. Henry Sleeper
    Battery B, New Jersey Light Artillery, A. Judson Clark
    Battery D, 1st New York Light Artillery, George B. Winslow
    12th Battery, New York Light Artillery, George K. Dauchy
    Battery E, 1st Rhode Island Light Artillery, John K. Bucklyn
    Battery K, 4th United States Artillery, Robert James

FIFTH CORPS, George Sykes

First Division, Charles Griffin
    First Brigade, James Barnes
    Second Brigade, Jacob B. Sweitzer
    Third Brigade, Joshua L. Chamberlain

Second Division, Romeyn B. Ayres
    First Brigade, Sidney Burbank
    Third Brigade, Kenner Garrard

Third Division, William McCandless
    First Brigade, William C. Talley
    Third Brigade, Martin D. Hardin

Artillery, Augustus P. Martin
    3rd Battery (C), Massachusetts Light Artillery, Aaron F. Walcott

5th Battery (E), Massachusetts Light Artillery, Charles A. Phillips

Battery C, 1st New York Light Artillery, Almont Barnes

Battery L, 1st Ohio Light Artillery, Frank C. Gibbs

Battery D, 5th United States Artillery, Benjamin F. Rittenhouse

SIXTH CORPS, John Sedgwick

First Division, Horatio G. Wright
First Brigade, Alfred T. A. Torbert
Second Brigade, Joseph J. Bartlett
Third Brigade, David A. Russell

Second Division, Albion P. Howe
First Brigade, Lewis A. Grant
Second Brigade, Thomas H. Neill

Third Division, Henry D. Terry
First Brigade, Alexander Shaler
Second Brigade, Henry L. Eustis
Third Brigade, Frank Wheaton

Artillery, Charles H. Tompkins
1st Battery (A), Massachusetts Light Artillery, William H. McCartney
1st Battery, New York Light Artillery, Andrew Cowan
3rd Battery, New York Light Artillery, William A. Harn
Battery C, 1st Rhode Island Light Artillery, Richard Waterman
Battery G, 1st Rhode Island Light Artillery, George W. Adams
Battery F, 5th United States Artillery, Leonard Martin
Battery M, 5th United States Artillery, James Mc-Knight

CAVALRY CORPS, Alfred Pleasonton

First Division, John Buford
First Brigade, George H. Chapman
Second Brigade, Thomas C. Devin

Note. Reserve Brigade of First Cavalry Division was at the Cavalry Depot near Washington August 12, 1863–October 11, 1863. It rejoined the army October 13, 1863 near Bristoe Station, but it did not rejoin the division during the campaign.

Second Division, David McM. Gregg
First Brigade, John P. Taylor
Second Brigade, J. Irvin Gregg

Third Division, Judson Kilpatrick
First Brigade, Henry E. Davies, Jr.

Second Brigade, George A. Custer

ARTILLERY, Henry J. Hunt

Artillery Reserve, Robert O. Tyler
First Regular Brigade, Alanson M. Randol
First Volunteer Brigade, Freeman McGilvery
Second Volunteer Brigade, Elijah D. Taft
Third Volunteer Brigade, Robert H. Fitzhugh
Second Brigade, Horse Artillery, William M. Graham

Note 1. For the batteries assigned to the Artillery Reserve, see Gettysburg Campaign.

Note 2. First Volunteer Brigade was temporarily attached to Second Corps.

Note 3. The batteries of First Brigade, Horse Artillery were attached to First, Second, and Third cavalry divisions.

BULL RUN CAMPAIGN, VIRGINIA (FIRST BATTLE OF BULL RUN OR MANASSAS) JULY 16–22, 1861

The strategic importance of Manassas Junction as a road and rail communications center was recognized by both Union and Confederate leaders from the beginning of hostilities. The Confederates moved first to secure this position. Philip St. George Cocke, commander of the southern forces at Culpeper Court House, Virginia, was ordered to send to Manassas Junction a force sufficient to defend it against a Federal advance from Washington. The enemy occupied Manassas Junction shortly after May 15, 1861, and thereafter additional troops were sent to that point to establish a defensive position along Bull Run. This came to be known as the "Alexandria Line." Pierre G. T. Beauregard assumed command of the force assembled around Manassas Junction, and June 1, 1861 it was designated by the Confederates as the Army of the Potomac.

Irvin McDowell, commander of the Union Department of Northeastern Virginia, made no immediate attempt to move on Manassas Junction. He was busy during June and early July 1861 organizing and training the troops under his command, which were in no condition to undertake field operations. During this period, however, there was an increasing insistence in the North, supported by journalists and politicians, that some offensive action be taken in a move toward Richmond. Both Robert Patterson's army at Hagerstown, Maryland and McDowell's army near Washington were composed largely of three-month regiments, and unless something was done soon, their terms of enlistment would expire before they could be used. Winfield Scott, commander of the United States Army, reluctantly yielded to this pressure and began to reinforce McDowell and prepare his army for the field.

June 24–25, 1861, McDowell proposed a plan of operations, which was to leave a small garrison in the defensive works near Washington, and to advance with the greater part of his army toward Manassas Junction. Initially, Scott set the date for the advance at July 8, 1861, but that was impossible because it was not until that day that McDowell was able to issue orders for the organization of his army. Finally, however, at 2:00 P.M. July 16, 1861, the march toward Centerville began.

Awaiting McDowell on the line at Bull Run was Beauregard's Army of the Potomac, which was organized into brigades as follows: Milledge L. Bonham's First Brigade, Richard S. Ewell's Second Brigade, David R. Jones' Third Brigade, James Longstreet's Fourth Brigade, Philip St. George Cocke's Fifth Brigade, Jubal A. Early's Sixth Brigade, and Nathan G. (Shanks) Evans' Seventh Brigade. Other Confederate forces were within supporting distance. Theophilus H. Holmes was in command of a force at Fredericksburg, about forty miles south of Manassas Junction, and Joseph E. Johnston commanded a division (sometimes called the Army of the Shenandoah) at Winchester, Virginia. Johnston's division consisted of four brigades as follows: Thomas J. Jackson's First Brigade, Francis S. Bartow's Second Brigade, Bernard E. Bee's Third Brigade, Kirby E. Smith's Fourth Brigade, and also James E. B. (Jeb) Stuart's 1st Virginia Cavalry.

Beauregard had established his defensive line behind Bull Run, and it extended from Union Mills on the right to Stone Bridge on the Warrenton Turnpike on the left. Three of his brigades were posted in front of the Bull Run line, toward Washington. Bonham's brigade was at Fairfax Court House, with some troops as far forward as Falls Church; Ewell's brigade was at Fairfax Station, on the Orange and Alexandria Railroad, about five miles south of the court house; and Cocke's brigade was at Centerville. Jones' brigade was along the Orange and Alexandria Railroad between Union Mills and Manassas Junction; Longstreet's brigade was near Blackburn's Ford; and Early's brigade was dispersed to cover the several crossings of Bull Run that might be used by an army approaching from Washington. Nathan G. Evans commanded a temporary brigade on the far left at the Stone Bridge.

In anticipation of McDowell's advance, Beauregard had issued orders July 8, 1861 for the forward brigades to fall back behind Bull Run when the Federal columns approached, and this they did July 17, 1861. When this retirement was completed, Beauregard's army was in position as follows: Ewell's brigade was at Union Mills; Jones' brigade was about one and one-half miles upstream at McLean's Ford, near Wilmer McLean's house; Longstreet's brigade was less than a mile beyond Jones at Blackburn's Ford; Bonham's brigade was at Mitchell's Ford, three-fourths of a mile upstream from Blackburn's Ford; Cocke's brigade covered Island Ford, Ball's Ford, and Lewis' Ford, between Mitchell's Ford and Stone Bridge; and Evans' brigade was near the Van Pelt house, covering the Stone Bridge. On July 18, 1861, Early's brigade was ordered to the McLean farm, where it remained until noon, and then moved to the road from the McLean farm to Blackburn's Ford, where it would be in position to support Jones, Longstreet, or Bonham as circumstances might require. Holmes' brigade, which had been ordered up from Fredericksburg July 17, 1861, arrived on the morning of July 19, 1861, and was placed in support of Ewell, on the road from Manassas to Union Mills. Also, on the night of July 17, 1861, Joseph E. Johnston was ordered from the Shenandoah Valley with his four infantry brigades and Stuart's cavalry, and this force arrived at Manassas during the period July 19–21, 1861, in time to take part in the Battle of Bull Run.

McDowell's Advance to Centerville, July 16–18, 1861.

As noted above, McDowell's advance began at 2:00 P.M. July 16, 1861. The march orders for the day were so prepared as to place a part of the troops in rear of Fairfax Court House, while the rest advanced to the front, and in this way it was hoped that Bonham's command might be captured. Bonham, however, withdrew to Bull Run July 17, 1861, and so escaped.

Daniel Tyler's First Division left its camps opposite Georgetown and advanced toward Vienna, where it camped that night. Israel B. Richardson's Fourth Brigade, First Division marched on the road from Chain Bridge by way of Langley, Louisville, and Old Court House, while the rest of the division moved on the Georgetown Turnpike and the Leesburg Pike. David Hunter's Second Division advanced from the Long Bridge on the Columbia Turnpike, and halted for the night near Annandale, just north of the Little River Turnpike. Samuel P. Heintzelman's Third Division left its positions in front of Alexandria, and advanced on the Old Fairfax Road, south of the Orange and Alexandria Railroad, and camped that night on the road, about three miles from Sangster's Cross Roads. Dixon S. Miles' Fifth Division marched from near Alexandria, on the Little River Turnpike, and halted that night at Annandale, where a road turned off to the left onto the Old Braddock Road. Theodore Runyon's Fourth Division, was left behind to guard the railroads. Runyon was assigned command of all troops that were not on the move toward the front, including those in the fortifications.

Early on the morning of July 17, 1861, McDowell's divisions resumed their march. Tyler's division moved south from Vienna and halted at Germantown, on the Warrenton Turnpike, less than two miles beyond Fairfax Court House. Tyler's leading brigade, under Richardson, camped that night along the Turnpike about three miles from Centerville. Miles' division turned to the left at Annandale, onto the Old Braddock Road, and then marched on that road, which ran west toward Centerville on a course roughly parallel to the Orange and Alexandria Railroad, and about two or three miles south of the Little River Turnpike. Miles halted about 3:00 P.M., south of Fairfax Court House, at the crossing of a road that ran from the court house to Fairfax Station. Hunter waited for Miles' division to pass through Annandale, and he then turned right onto the Little River Turnpike and, with Ambrose E. Burnside's brigade in the lead, advanced to Fairfax Court House. As noted earlier, Bonham had withdrawn from the village, and Burnside's troops moved in about 1:00 P.M. Heintzelman's movements on July 17, 1861 are not exactly clear, but it appears that that night Orlando B. Willcox's brigade camped at Fairfax Station, one

brigade at Sangster's Cross Roads, and one brigade at Sangster's Station.

Although all of his divisions had arrived at their assigned positions early in the afternoon, McDowell was unable to move his inexperienced troops any farther that afternoon. On July 18, 1861, however, all divisions marched toward Centerville, where they arrived during the day.

Action at Blackburn's Ford, July 18, 1861. At 8:15 A.M. July 18, 1861, as Richardson's leading brigade of Tyler's division was approaching Centerville, McDowell ordered Tyler to watch carefully the roads leading to Bull Run and to Gainesville, but he instructed him not to bring on an engagement. Richardson reached Centerville about 9:00 A.M., and then, instead of continuing on west on the Warrenton Turnpike, he turned off to the left on the road leading to Manassas. He then halted about a mile from Centerville, at a spring where there was water for the troops.

Tyler, in person, came up about noon, and decided to reconnoiter the ground to the south of Centerville. He took with him Richardson, George D. Wells, with companies G and H of the 1st Massachusetts, and a squadron of cavalry, and advanced about two miles, to within a short distance of Blackburn's Ford. There he discovered the enemy in a strong position on rising ground beyond the ford. Then, apparently ignoring McDowell's order not to bring on an engagement, Tyler decided to develop more fully the enemy position. He ordered up the rest of Richardson's brigade, and placed Samuel N. Benjamin's section of Battery B, 1st United States Artillery of Richardson's brigade on the right of the road and on the crest of a slope overlooking Blackburn's Ford. The artillery position was about one-half mile from Bull Run. Benjamin promptly opened fire on the enemy beyond the run.

While Benjamin's guns were in action, the rest of Richardson's brigade, and Romeyn B. Ayres' Battery E, 3rd United States Artillery of William T. Sherman's brigade, Tyler's division arrived. Ayres placed his guns next to Benjamin's and also opened fire. A short time later Ayres moved forward closer to Blackburn's Ford. At this time, Wells' two companies were about 500 yards in front of the artillery. They then advanced close to the ford, but were met with a heavy fire and were withdrawn to the artillery line. Richardson then placed Ezra L. Walrath's 12th New York on the left of Benjamin's guns, with orders to charge in the direction of the ford. He also placed 1st Massachusetts, 2nd Massachusetts, and 3rd Michigan on the right of the artillery.

The 12th New York then advanced and soon came under a very heavy fire from the enemy troops concealed in the woods and bushes along Bull Run. Walrath's men returned the fire for about a half hour, and then the line began to break. The men retired slowly at first, and then they turned about and fled in complete disorder. The enemy troops who had crossed the stream pursued, and they soon came up on the exposed flank of the 1st Massachusetts. They were engaged there for about a half-hour, and finally Tyler ordered Richardson to withdraw his brigade to a line behind Ayres' and Benjamin's guns, which continued to fire until about 4:00 P.M.

Meantime, shortly after noon, Sherman's brigade of Tyler's division, then at Centerville, had been ordered forward to support Richardson. Sherman reached the rear of Richardson's position just after Tyler had ordered the brigade to withdraw behind the guns. Sherman was placed on the left of Richardson but, except for being under artillery fire for a time, he was not engaged.

McDowell arrived on the field shortly before 4:00 P.M. and ordered Tyler to break off the action. Tyler then moved back with his two brigades, and camped that night south of Centerville.

While Tyler's troops were engaged in front of Blackburn's Ford, the rest of the Army of Northeastern Virginia arrived at Centerville. Robert C. Schenck's brigade of Tyler's First Division camped on the road west of Centerville, and Erasmus D. Keyes' brigade of the same division camped to the east of the village. Hunter's Second Division camped along the Warrenton Turnpike, with the head of the column near Centerville. Miles' Fifth Division was on the road from Sangster's Station, to the southeast of Centerville, and Heintzelman's Third Division was on the same road, in rear of Miles.

The army remained quietly in camp during July 19–20, 1861, while McDowell ordered reconnaissances to find a suitable route by which the Confederate position behind Bull Run could be turned. On July 20, 1861, two developments caused McDowell to issue orders for an attack the next day.

First, he learned that Johnston had arrived at Manassas from the Shenandoah Valley with reinforcements for Beauregard, and then, about noon that same day, McDowell's engineers, John G. Barnard and Daniel P. Woodbury, reported that they had found a way to the crossings of Bull Run above Stone Bridge, and that a movement against the enemy left flank was possible.

The orders issued on the evening of July 20, 1861 for the march of the army the next day were as follows: Tyler's division, except Richardson's brigade, was to advance at 2:30 A.M. July 21, 1861 on the Warrenton Turnpike and threaten a crossing of Bull Run at Stone Bridge. Hunter's division was to move out at 2:00 A.M. and follow Tyler toward Stone Bridge. After crossing Cub Run, however, he was to turn to the right on a road that led by a roundabout route to Sudley Ford. There, Hunter was to cross Bull Run, turn to the left, and move downstream. After clearing Poplar Ford (or Red House Ford) and the crossing at Stone Bridge, he was to bear to the right to make room for the following division. Heintzelman's division was to move out at 2:30 A.M. and march on the road taken by Hunter, but it was to cross at a lower ford, probably Poplar Ford, after it had been cleared by Hunter. After crossing Bull Run, it was to turn to the left and take position between Hunter's division and Bull Run. Miles' division, with Richardson's brigade temporarily attached, was to remain on the Centerville heights as a reserve, and also to threaten a crossing at Blackburn's Ford and Mitchell's Ford.

The above plan was generally followed on July 21, 1861, but with one important exception. After Hunter crossed Bull Run at Sudley Ford, instead of moving to the left along the run as directed, he took the Sudley Springs-Manassas Road to the right, and as the fighting developed, McDowell's entire turning column marched toward the right and away from Bull Run.

It should be noted here, to avoid confusion in the following discussion, that Sudley Ford on Bull Run was a short distance above Sudley Springs, where there was a mill and a hotel. Catharpin Run flows into Bull Run from the west just below Sudley Springs, and the Sudley Springs-Manassas Road crossed Catharpin Run just south of Sudley Springs Ford. It is sometimes difficult to determine which of these three points is indicated in reports of the battle, but this is of minor importance, because they were all close together.

Battle of Bull Run, July 21, 1861. The three divisions that were to advance on the morning of July 21, 1861 were ready between 2:00 and 2:30 A.M., but progress was very slow. Tyler's leading brigade, commanded by Schenck, did not move until 3:00 A.M., and it was not until three hours later that Tyler arrived in front of the Stone Bridge, three and one-half miles from Centerville, with the brigades of Schenck and Sherman and the batteries of Ayres and J. Howard Carlisle. Tyler placed Sherman's brigade on the right of the road, and Schenck's brigade on the left of the road, both facing Bull Run. This deployment was completed by about 6:30 A.M. Keyes' brigade was halted on the left of the Turnpike at a point just beyond the junction of the road that turned off to Sudley Ford, and about one-half mile from Bull Run. It has already been noted that Richardson's brigade was left near Centerville, and was attached to Miles' division.

Hunter's division, which was to lead the turning column, was ready to move at 2:00 A.M., but it was delayed by the passage of Tyler's division, and it was unable to march through Centerville until 4:30 A.M. Ambrose E. Burnside's leading brigade of Hunter's division was further delayed on the road by Tyler, and the rear of Tyler's division did not cross Cub Run until about 5:30 A.M. At about that time Keyes' brigade was ordered off the road to allow Burnside to move on. Andrew Porter's brigade followed Burnside. After crossing Cub Run, Burnside turned to the right on the road that led to Sudley Springs, and arrived at that place at 9:00–9:30 A.M.

Heintzelman began his march from beyond Centerville at 2:30 A.M., but upon reaching the village he was delayed three hours while he waited for Tyler and Hunter to pass. Heintzelman then followed Hunter, with William B. Franklin's brigade in the lead, and then the brigades of Orlando B. Willcox and Oliver O. Howard, in that order. Heintzelman was unable to find the lower ford assigned to him, and continued on to Sudley Ford, following Hunter, and arrived there about 11:00 A.M. Shortly after turning off from the Warrenton Turnpike, Howard's brigade was halted by McDowell's order, and it remained until noon about one mile from Cub Run. At that time Howard

received orders to move to the front by way of Sudley Springs.

Miles' division, with Richardson's brigade, remained near Centerville during the day, and did not take part in the battle. Louis Blenker's brigade occupied the village, and Richardson's brigade and Thomas A. Davies' brigade were advanced to the southwest toward Mitchell's Ford. Davies' brigade then took position on the left toward Blackburn's Ford and Richardson's brigade on the right toward Mitchell's Ford.

During the morning of July 21, 1861, Evans, whose brigade was watching the Stone Bridge, observed McDowell's movement toward his left and, recognizing Tyler's activities as a feint, marched northward at 9:00 A.M. to meet Hunter and Heintzelman. He moved first to the Carter house, and then to the left to the hill on which the Matthews house stood. Evans then deployed to the left, along a ridge that extended to the southwest from the Matthews house to the Stone House, which was located near the crossing of the Warrenton Turnpike and the Sudley Springs-Manassas Road (also called the Manassas Road, the Sudley Springs Road, and the Sudley Springs-New Market Road). Evans' line faced to the northwest, toward Hunter's line of march.

Shortly after reaching Sudley Springs, Burnside advanced on the road to Manassas with the 2nd Rhode Island Regiment of his brigade and its battery of artillery. About 9:15 A.M., after proceeding about one mile, Burnside came under fire from Evans' brigade. While Hunter was putting the 2nd Rhode Island in position, he was wounded, and Andrew Porter assumed command of Second Division. The rest of Burnside's brigade was then brought up and formed in line of battle, with the 2nd Rhode Island across the road, and the other three regiments extending to the northeast, facing Evans' line. The Federal artillery was placed on the right, near the road. Firing then began, and soon became general along the front.

McDowell, in person, arrived at Sudley Springs shortly after Burnside had crossed Bull Run, and he decided to strengthen the Federal attack before enemy reinforcements, which he believed were approaching, could arrive. He sent orders for Porter and Heintzelman to hurry forward, and for Tyler to attack at Stone Bridge. He also ordered Howard's brigade, which, as noted earlier, had been halted near Cub Run, to march toward Sudley Springs.

Porter's brigade, with Charles Griffin's Battery D, 5th United States Artillery, advanced from Sudley Ford between 10:30 and 11:00 A.M. with orders to take position on the right of Burnside, who was then engaged with Evans. Porter had only a part of his brigade in position when Evans launched an attack on the center of the Federal line. This attack was repulsed, but for a time it delayed Burnside's advance. Porter finally completed his deployment on the right of the Sudley Springs-Manassas Road, with his line extending along a crest that ran to the southwest toward the Dogan house, which stood on the Warrenton Turnpike about a half mile west of the intersection of the Warrenton Turnpike and the Sudley Springs-Manassas Road. Griffin's battery was placed farther to the right, and it opened fire about 11:15 A.M. Burnside's brigade began to waver from the effects of the enemy fire, and Porter sent George Sykes with his battalion of regulars to aid in holding its position.

Franklin's brigade of Heintzelman's division, which was following Hunter's column, arrived at Sudley Ford at 11:00 A.M., and then waited for Porter's brigade to cross. Franklin then sent 1st Minnesota to help hold Burnside's line, and with his two remaining regiments (5th Massachusetts and 11th Massachusetts) followed Porter and deployed on his right, with his own right not far from the Warrenton Turnpike. James B. Ricketts' Battery I, 1st United States Artillery of Franklin's brigade was posted on the extreme right of the line.

While Heintzelman was getting in position, heavy fighting continued along Evans' front, and his troops were becoming hard pressed. At 10:00 A.M. Evans asked for help, and the parts of Bee's and Bartow's brigades that had arrived from the Shenandoah Valley marched to his assistance. They arrived about 11:00 A.M. and were placed on the crest of Matthews' Hill. Bee's brigade was formed on the right of Evans, and Bartow's brigade on the right of Bee. When these new troops were in position, Evans' whole line attacked, but it was driven back, and then a short time later it began to crumble. About noon, the brigades of Evans, Bee, and Bartow gave way completely, and the troops streamed back toward the Warrenton Turnpike. They then fled eastward on the Turnpike and took shelter in a ravine on the eastern side of the northern spur of the Henry House Plateau, behind the Robinson house.

Willcox's brigade of Heintzelman's division, which followed Franklin, arrived at Sudley Ford about 12:30 P.M., after the enemy had been driven from its position north of the Warrenton Turnpike. Willcox then placed Richard Arnold's Battery D, 2nd United States Artillery on a hill covering the ford, with 1st Michigan in support, and his remaining two regiments (11th New York and 38th New York) marched at 1:00 P.M. down the Sudley Springs-Manassas Road and reached the vicinity of the Stone House about a half hour later. Ricketts' battery was then brought up and placed near the Dogan house.

About the time of Evans' collapse, Sherman's brigade of Tyler's division was crossing Bull Run and moving onto the battlefield. During the morning, Tyler, at the Stone Bridge, had followed the progress of the battle to his right and front, and between 9:00 and 10:00 A.M. had ordered Keyes' brigade from its position in reserve to a point about 800 yards above the bridge in preparation to cross with Sherman and go to the aid of Hunter. About noon, Sherman crossed the run by a ford that he had discovered about 200 yards below Poplar Ford (or Red Farm Ford), and then moved out of the woods bordering Bull Run and into an open field about one-half mile north of the Warrenton Turnpike. Sherman halted near the Carter house, and Keyes' brigade, which had followed Sherman, took position on his left. Tyler, in person, accompanied Keyes' brigade. Schenck's brigade and the batteries of Ayres and Carlisle were left on the east bank of Bull Run at the Stone Bridge.

While Evans, Bee, and Bartow were retreating before the advance of Hunter and Heintzelman, Thomas J. (later, Stonewall) Jackson's brigade of Johnston's army arrived on the Henry House Plateau from near the Lewis house. Jackson then formed his troops in line of battle at the center of the southern end of the plateau, facing to the northwest. Beauregard, who was in command on the field, and Johnston, who was the senior officer but had waived his rank, arrived in person on the plateau and promptly ordered up reinforcements. They then formed a new line that began on the right near where the Warrenton Turnpike crossed Young's Branch, a little more than a half mile west of the Stone Bridge, and a short distance east of the Robinson house. The line then ran to the southwest over the Henry House Hill, back of the Robinson house and the Henry house, and ended on the left at the Sudley Springs-Manassas Road, about three-fourths of a mile south of the Stone House. This line was completed shortly after 1:00 P.M., and was manned as follows: Jackson's brigade and two batteries were on the center; the remnants of the brigades of Evans, Bee, and Bartow, two regiments of Cocke's brigade, and Wade Hampton's Legion were on the right; and the regiments of Bonham's brigade, the remaining regiments of Cocke's brigade, and Stuart's cavalry were on the left, between Jackson's brigade and the Sudley Springs-Manassas Road. Later in the afternoon, as the battle was ending, E. Kirby Smith's brigade of Johnston's army and Early's brigade arrived and formed across the road, on the extreme Confederate left.

Between 1:00 and 2:00 P.M. there was a lull in the fighting as McDowell's troops advanced from the Carter house and the Sudley Springs Road across the valley of Young's Branch, and then re-formed along the Warrenton Turnpike in preparation for an attack on the Henry House Hill. On the Federal left, next to Bull Run, Keyes' brigade, accompanied by Tyler, moved to the left, away from Sherman, in the direction of the Stone Bridge. Keyes soon arrived before the Van Pelt House Hill, just north of the Warrenton Turnpike, and about 600 yards west of Bull Run. This was the position held by Evans that morning before moving to oppose Hunter, and it was still occupied by enemy troops. These opened fire on the approaching Federals, as did some guns posted farther south in the vicinity of the Lewis house. Keyes moved to his left to get his troops under the cover of the wooded bank of Bull Run, then moved slowly downstream, and had reached a point about one-half mile below the bridge when the battle ended. The brigade was not seriously engaged during the day.

As Keyes moved away toward the Stone Bridge, Sherman marched with his brigade from the Carter house to the southwest to Young's Branch. He crossed the stream and moved up the southern bank to the Warrenton Turnpike, where he sheltered his brigade for a time, just west of the Robinson house, in a depression along the road. At this point, Sherman was separated from Keyes by a distance of about a mile.

After Porter had become disengaged, he advanced to the southeast from the Sudley Springs-Manassas Road to the ridge occupied earlier by Evans' brigade. Then, from a point north and a little east of the Stone House, he turned south and halted on the Warrenton Turnpike to the right of Sherman. Porter's 8th New York, which had been badly broken in the earlier fighting, turned back and took no further part in the battle that day.

Burnside's brigade, except the 2nd New Hampshire, moved back into the woods and was not again engaged that day. Gilman Marston's 2nd New Hampshire was attached to Heintzelman's division, and although it was under fire, it was not again in action.

On McDowell's right, Franklin's and Willcox's divisions moved up the Warrenton Turnpike, as did the batteries of Ricketts and Griffin.

Upon his arrival on the Warrenton Turnpike, McDowell began preparations for an assault on the Henry House Hill. He decided, as a first step, to advance his artillery onto the hill to fire at close range, and then to bring up supports and move his infantry around toward the enemy left flank. At 2:00 P.M. Griffin moved his battery forward from a point to the right of the Dogan house, and then up the slopes of the hill. Ricketts followed with his battery, but because Griffin's battery was misdirected, Ricketts arrived first and took position immediately south of the Henry house, about 300 yards from the enemy line. Griffin then came up and took position on the left of Ricketts. Both batteries immediately opened fire.

The 11th New York (Fire Zouaves) of Willcox's brigade and a battalion of Marines under John G. Reynolds were sent to support the batteries, and the 14th New York of Porter's brigade was sent to protect the right flank of the Federal position. The Marines moved up in rear of the 14th New York. As noted above, about noon Porter moved up to the right of Sherman along the Warrenton Turnpike, but when the batteries moved up to the Henry house, the 14th New York, 27th New York, and the Marines, about all that remained of the brigade, were sent to the right to support them. This left Porter with virtually no command.

Heintzelman's two brigades on the right were then ordered to advance. Willcox crossed Young's Branch and moved up the Sudley Springs-Manassas Road to a point just west of the Henry house, about 700 yards south of the Warrenton Turnpike. Franklin followed Willcox for a time, and then obliqued to the left and up the hill to a position on the left of Willcox, and to the left and rear of the batteries.

Meantime, the batteries had been firing about fifteen minutes when Stuart's cavalry charged down the Sudley Springs-Manassas Road and scattered the 11th New York. At that time, Franklin was on his way up the hill. Just after Stuart's attack, Willis A. Gorman brought up his 1st Minnesota of Franklin's brigade and formed on the right of what remained of the 11th New York. Moments later, Arthur C. Cummings' 33rd Virginia of Jackson's brigade advanced, and when it was mistaken for a Federal regiment, it was allowed to approach to within about seventy yards of the batteries. It then delivered a devastating fire that killed or wounded most of the men and horses of both batteries. Ricketts was wounded and captured. The 11th New York and 1st Minnesota were routed by this attack, and when the 14th New York was brought up it too broke and fled. A heavy fire from Franklin's regiments drove the 33rd Virginia back to cover, and the batteries were temporarily recovered. Then Jackson advanced and penetrated the Federal center, while the Confederate right cleared the area about the Robinson house. Jackson reached the abandoned batteries, but he was driven back. Then, for the next two hours there was heavy and confused fighting on the plateau, largely for possession of Griffin's and Ricketts' guns.

Meantime, Sherman had begun putting his regiments into the fight. He left his position on the Warrenton Turnpike and started up the hill. His line of march was inclined to the right, up the slope, and he moved out onto the plateau about midway between the Henry house and the Robinson house, well to the left of Ricketts' battery. Sherman attacked with one regiment at a time, and each in turn was driven back and forced to take shelter under the crest of the hill.

About 3:00 P.M., Howard's brigade of Heintzelman's division, which had been halted near Cub Run early in the day, was approaching Young's Branch after crossing Bull Run at Sudley Ford. Howard was ordered to the right, where he formed his brigade in a ravine several hundred yards west of the Henry House Hill. He was then ordered forward, and he came onto the field at some distance to the right of the abandoned batteries. Sykes' regulars were also on the right of the line with Howard. Howard soon came under a heavy fire, and his line began to break up.

Sometime after 3:00 P.M., the enemy gained possession of the Robinson house and the Henry house. Then they launched a final attack at 3:45 P.M., and by 4:30 P.M. the last of McDowell's troops had been driven from the field. At about 4:00 P.M., E. Kirby Smith's brigade of Johnston's army, which had just arrived from the Shenandoah Valley, and Early's brigade, which was moving over from the Confederate right, were marching past the southern slope of the Henry House Hill toward McDowell's right, where Howard had just arrived. Smith was wounded as his brigade moved up, and Arnold Elzey assumed command. The brigade moved into position as Howard was on the point of retiring, and when Elzey charged, the Federals fled in confusion.

The Federal withdrawal began in fairly good order, but it soon degenerated into a panic-stricken flight. McDowell did not leave the battlefield until a little after 4:30 P.M., and when he arrived at Centerville, he found that very little had been done to prepare for holding the village until the defeated army had passed through. He promptly dismissed Miles and assumed direct personal control of the troops at Centerville. These consisted of the brigades of Israel B. Richardson, Louis Blenker, and Thomas A. Davies, and three regiments from Theodore Runyon's division, which had arrived from Washington. Later Miles was charged with drunkenness, but the charges were not upheld.

By 7:30 P.M. the last of the fugitives had finally passed through Centerville, and were streaming in complete disorder through Fairfax Court House toward the Potomac. Richardson's brigade, which brought up the rear of the army, left Centerville at 2:30 A.M. July 22, 1861, and that night all Federal troops were back where they had started from on July 16, 1861.

The organization of the Army of Northeastern

Virginia at Bull Run is given with more than the usual detail because it was the first major battle of the Civil War, and also because many of the field, company, and staff officers went on to higher command later in the war. In addition, some brigades did not always fight as units during the battle, but a number of regiments were assigned temporarily to other commands or to special service. For this reason the operations of these regiments have been noted above. The organization of the army July 21, 1861 was as follows:

ARMY OF NORTHEASTERN VIRGINIA, Irvin McDowell

First Division, Daniel Tyler
  First Brigade, Erasmus D. Keyes
    2nd Maine, Charles D. Jameson
    1st Connecticut, John Speidel
    2nd Connecticut, Alfred H. Terry
    3rd Connecticut, John L. Chatfield

Note. Captain Edward Harland commanded a company in the 3rd Connecticut.

  Second Brigade, Robert C. Schenck
    2nd New York, George W. B. Tompkins
    1st Ohio, Alexander McD. McCook
    2nd Ohio, Rodney Mason
    Battery E, 2nd United States Artillery, J. Howard Carlisle
  Third Brigade, William T. Sherman
    13th New York, Isaac F. Quinby
    69th New York, Michael Corcoran, wounded and captured
    79th New York (Highlanders), James Cameron, killed
    2nd Wisconsin, Harry W. Peck
    Battery E, 3rd United States Artillery, Romeyn B. Ayres

Note 1. Thomas F. Meagher was acting major in the 69th New York.
Note 2. Lieutenant Alexander Piper was acting assistant adjutant general on Sherman's staff.

  Fourth Brigade, Israel B. Richardson
    1st Massachusetts, Robert Cowdin
    12th New York, Ezra L. Walrath
    2nd Michigan, Adolphus W. Williams
    3rd Michigan, Daniel McConnell
    Battery G, 1st United States Artillery, John Edwards
    Battery M, 2nd United States Artillery, Henry J. Hunt

Note. Captain Edward A. Wild and Lieutenant Colonel George D. Wells served in the 1st Massachusetts, and Captain Byron R. Pierce commanded a company in the 3rd Michigan.

Second Division, David Hunter, wounded
  Andrew Porter
  First Brigade, Andrew Porter
    8th New York State Militia, George Lyons
    14th New York State Militia (84th New York), A. M. Wood, wounded and captured
    Edward B. Fowler
    27th New York, Henry W. Slocum, wounded
    Joseph J. Bartlett
    Battalion United States Infantry, George Sykes
    Battalion United States Marines, John G. Reynolds
    Battalion United States Cavalry, Innis N. Palmer
    Battery D, 5th United States Artillery, Charles Griffin

Note 1. Daniel P. Woodbury was chief engineer on Hunter's staff, and William W. Averell was acting assistant adjutant general.
Note 2. Lieutenant Adelbert Ames served with Griffin's artillery and was wounded.
Note 3. Sykes' regulars consisted of companies C and G, 2nd United States Infantry; companies B, D, G, H, and K, 3rd United States Infantry; and Company G, 8th United States Infantry.

  Second Brigade, Ambrose E. Burnside
    2nd New Hampshire, Gilman Marston, wounded
    Frank S. Fiske
    1st Rhode Island, Joseph P. Balch
    2nd Rhode Island, John S. Slocum, killed
    Frank Wheaton
    71st New York (Militia), Henry P. Martin

Note 1. 2nd Rhode Island had with it a battery of light artillery, and 71st New York had two howitzers.
Note 2. Captain Isaac P. Rodman served with 2nd Rhode Island, and Captain Simon G. Griffin commanded a company in 2nd New Hampshire..

Third Division, Samuel P. Heintzelman
  First Brigade, William B. Franklin
    5th Massachusetts, Samuel C. Lawrence
    11th Massachusetts, George Clark, Jr.
    1st Minnesota, Willis A. Gorman
    Battery I, 1st United States Artillery, James B. Ricketts, wounded and captured
    Edmund Kirby

Note 1. Captain Horatio G. Wright served as chief engineer on Heintzelman's staff.
Note 2. The term of enlistment of 4th Pennsylvania of Franklin's brigade expired, and the regiment was

mustered out and departed July 20, 1861. John F. Hartranft, colonel of the regiment, remained with the army and served with Franklin as aide de camp during the battle.

Second Brigade, Orlando B. Willcox, wounded and captured
J. H. Hobart Ward
11th New York (Fire Zouaves), Noah L. Farnham
38th New York, J. H. Hobart Ward
    Addison Farnsworth
1st Michigan, Alonzo F. Bidwell
4th Michigan, Dwight A. Woodbury
Battery D, 2nd United States Artillery, Richard Arnold
Third Brigade, Oliver O. Howard
3rd Maine, Henry G. Staples
4th Maine, Hiram G. Berry 5th Maine, Mark H. Dunnell
2nd Vermont, Henry Whiting

Note. George J. Stannard was lieutenant colonel of the 2nd Vermont.

Fourth Division, Theodore Runyon

Note. This division did not accompany the army to Bull Run, but the 41st New York, 1st New Jersey (three-year), and 2nd New Jersey (three-year) were advanced to Centerville on the evening of July 21, 1861, where they reported to McDowell. For additional information on the organization of Runyon's division, see Department of Northeastern Virginia.

Fifth Division, Dixon S. Miles
First Brigade, Louis Blenker
8th New York, Julius Stahel
29th New York, Adolph Von Steinwehr
39th New York, Frederick G. D'Utassy
27th New York, Max Einstein
Battery A, 2nd United States Artillery, John C. Tidball
Brookwood's New York Battery, Charles Brookwood
Second Brigade, Thomas A. Davies
16th New York, Samuel Marsh
18th New York, William A. Jackson
31st New York, Calvin E. Pratt
32nd New York, Roderick Matheson
Battery G, 2nd United States Artillery, Oliver D. Greene

In addition to the above-mentioned officers, a number of others who later became well-known served on the staff of McDowell. Major John G. Barnard was chief engineer, and assistants were Captain Amiel W. Whipple, Lieutenant Henry L. Abbot, and Lieutenant Haldimand S. Putnam. Major William F. Barry was chief of artillery, and assistant was Lieutenant Alexander S. Webb. Lieutenant George C. Strong was ordnance officer, and Major James S. Wadsworth and Guy V. Henry were aides de camp. While not on the staff, Lieutenant George A. Custer was detailed by Winfield Scott to carry dispatches to McDowell at Centerville.

CAROLINAS CAMPAIGN
JANUARY 1, 1865–APRIL 26, 1865

In mid-November 1864, William T. Sherman, with his Army of the Military Division of the Mississippi, set out from Atlanta on his march across Georgia toward Savannah. He arrived near the coast December 10, 1864, and occupied Savannah eleven days later. For details of this campaign, see Savannah Campaign (Sherman's March through Georgia).

After the capture of Savannah, Sherman began preparations for further operations. It was Ulysses S. Grant's original intention that Sherman move his army north by sea to join the Army of the Potomac and the Army of the James in Virginia in a final campaign to end the war, and Sherman received orders to that effect December 6, 1864. Sherman, however, believed that a march northward through the interior of the Carolinas, destroying the railroads and public property as he went, would serve a more useful purpose. On January 2, 1865, Sherman received authorization from Grant to proceed with his proposed plan, and the former immediately began preparations for the march north.

Sherman's first step was to organize his army for the coming campaign. He decided to retain the wing organization that had been used so effectively during the march across Georgia, and there was but one change in the commanders of the four corps of the army. On January 8, 1865, John A. Logan returned to the army, from which he had been absent since September 22, 1864, and relieved Peter J. Osterhaus, who had been in temporary command of Fifteenth Corps since that time.

Early in January 1865, as the army was prepared to march, it was organized as follows:

Right Wing (Army of the Tennessee), Oliver O. Howard
   Fifteenth Corps, John A. Logan
   Seventeenth Corps, Frank P. Blair, Jr.

Left Wing (Army of Georgia), Henry W. Slocum
   Fourteenth Corps, Jefferson C. Davis
   Twentieth Corps, Alpheus S. Williams

Third Cavalry Division, Military Division of the Mississippi, Judson Kilpatrick

Note 1. During the Savannah Campaign and the Carolinas Campaign, Slocum's command was unofficially called the Army of Georgia. Then, by a presidential order of March 28, 1865, Fourteenth Corps and Twentieth Corps were officially designated as the Army of Georgia, and this was announced April 2, 1865.

   Note 2. For details of the above organization and the division and brigade commanders, see roster at the end of this section.

Another necessary step was to provide for the security of Savannah after the departure of the army. January 6, 1865, Cuvier Grover's Second Division, Nineteenth Corps was ordered from the Shenandoah Valley, where it was then serving, to Savannah. It arrived there January 17–18, 1865 and relieved John W. Geary's Second Division, Twentieth Corps, which had been occupying the city since its capture. Geary was thus freed to accompany Twentieth Corps on the march north into South Carolina. January 21, 1865, Sherman transferred the command of Savannah and its dependencies to John G. Foster's Department of the South. For additional information, see Department of the South, Part IV, Department of the South, Wartime Districts in the Department of the South, District of Savannah.

There were also some necessary preparations carried out in North Carolina to receive Sherman's army when it arrived in the state. Sherman's march was to be directed toward Goldsboro, North Carolina, and it was essential that communications between that point and the coast be opened and secured so that Sherman's army could be supplied when it reached the town. To aid in accomplishing this important mission, John M. Schofield's Twenty-Third Corps, Army of the Ohio was ordered from Tennessee to North Carolina to reinforce the troops already serving there. In addition, the Department of North Carolina was constituted January 31, 1865, to provide for a more effective control of affairs in the state. Schofield was assigned command of the new department, subject to Sherman's orders, and he was directed to seize and repair the railroad running from New Berne to Goldsboro. He was also ordered to accumulate supplies for Sherman's army at Goldsboro, and to assemble his army near there to join Sherman upon his arrival. Schofield occupied Goldsboro March 21, 1865. For details of the organization of the troops in North Carolina and their operations during the period February 9, 1865– March 23, 1865, see Department of North Carolina, January 31, 1865–May 19, 1866, Operations in the Department of North Carolina.

Sherman's orders for the opening moves into South Carolina were designed to confuse the enemy as to his true objectives. All, or part, of Oliver O. Howard's Right Wing was to be transferred by sea to Beaufort, South Carolina, and was then to occupy Pocotaligo, where it would be in position to move on Charleston, South Carolina. At the same time, Henry W. Slocum's Left Wing and Judson Kilpatrick's Third Cavalry Division, Military Division of the Mississippi were to cross the Savannah River above Savannah at Sister's Ferry, and then move toward Augusta to threaten that city. When these opening moves were completed, the two wings of the army were to advance on Columbia, South Carolina.

The only significant bodies of Confederate troops confronting Sherman as he prepared to move into South Carolina belonged to William J. Hardee's corps of the Confederate Department of South Carolina, Georgia, and Florida; and Joseph Wheeler's cavalry corps, which had moved across Georgia as Sherman's army marched through the state. Hardee's corps, which consisted of the divisions of Lafayette McLaws, William B. Taliaferro, and Ambrose R. Wright, had moved into South Carolina after the evacuation of Savannah, and Hardee had established his headquarters at Charleston.

At the beginning of Sherman's advance, Wheeler was near Savannah, and he became active in contesting Kilpatrick's advance toward Augusta. January 19, 1865, Matthew C. Butler's cavalry division of Wade Hampton's cavalry was sent by Robert E. Lee from Virginia to South Carolina. Later, Hampton was permitted to go in person to aid in the defense of South Carolina, his native state. Hampton arrived in Hardee's Department of South

Carolina, Georgia, and Florida February 7, 1865, and was assigned command of Butler's and Pierce M. B. Young's cavalry divisions. Ten days later, Hampton was assigned as chief of cavalry, and was to command Wheeler's cavalry corps and Butler's cavalry division.

Early in February 1865, the remnants of John B. Hood's Army of Tennessee, which had been virtually destroyed at the Battle of Nashville, Tennessee December 15–16, 1865, were sent east from Tupelo, Mississippi to reinforce the troops in South Carolina.

Stephen D. Lee's leading corps, then commanded by Carter L. Stevenson (until March 2, 1865, after which Daniel H. Hill was in command), arrived at Branchville, South Carolina about February 5, 1865, and was placed in position to guard the North Branch of the Edisto River. The other two corps of the Army of Tennessee arrived later in South Carolina, but they were too late to offer any resistance to Sherman as he marched through the state.

SAVANNAH, GEORGIA TO FAYETTEVILLE, NORTH CAROLINA JANUARY 3, 1865–MARCH 11, 1865

Sherman began his opening movements early in January 1865. During the period January 3–11, 1865, Frank P. Blair moved his Seventeenth Corps by sea to Beaufort, South Carolina, and January 14, 1865, he advanced to Pocotaligo on the Charleston and Savannah Railroad. John A. Logan's Fifteenth Corps followed, and with the exception of John M. Corse's Fourth Division, it was established at Garden's Corners and Port Royal Ferry January 28, 1865. Corse had been ordered to move his division by land to join the rest of Fifteenth Corps in South Carolina, but because of floods and bad roads he was unable to march until January 27, 1865. At that time, he was directed to join Henry W. Slocum's Left Wing, and march by way of Sister's Ferry on the Savannah River.

On January 1, 1865, William T. Ward's Third Division of Alpheus S. Williams' Twentieth Corps crossed the Savannah River and camped near Hardeeville. Nathaniel J. Jackson's First Division, Twentieth Corps remained in camp at Savannah until January 17, 1865, and then it too crossed the

river and advanced to Purysburg, where it arrived two days later. John W. Geary's Second Division, Twentieth Corps, which was encamped in Savannah performing garrison duty, was relieved by Cuvier Grover's Second Division, Nineteenth Corps, just arrived from the Shenandoah Valley, and was ordered to join First Division and Third Division north of the Savannah River. Heavy rains, however, forced Geary to remain near Savannah until January 27, 1865, and he was then ordered to follow Jefferson C. Davis' Fourteenth Corps along the south side of the Savannah River to Sister's Ferry.

Davis' Fourteenth Corps, accompanied by Judson Kilpatrick's cavalry, began its march from Savannah January 20, 1865, but it did not arrive at Sister's Ferry, on the south side of the river, until January 29, 1865. Geary, who began his march January 27, 1865, joined Fourteenth Corps at Sister's Ferry two days later. Corse came up with his division and reported to Slocum January 30, 1865.

Meantime, on January 26, 1865, First Division and Third Division of Twentieth Corps began to move up the north side of the Savannah River, and they arrived at Robertsville, South Carolina January 29, 1865. They remained there until February 2, 1865, and then marched by way of Lawtonville, Buford's Bridge on the Salkehatchie River, and Graham's Station, and arrived at Blackville, February 9, 1865.

Kilpatrick's cavalry and Fourteenth Corps were finally able to cross the river by February 3, 1865, and they were followed the next day by Geary's division of Twentieth Corps and Corse's Fourth Division of Fifteenth Corps. After the crossing was completed, these troops marched to the vicinity of Robertsville. When Nathaniel J. Jackson's First Division, Twentieth Corps advanced from Robertsville February 2, 1865, James L. Selfridge's First Brigade was left behind to guard the depot at Sister's Ferry. When Geary's division crossed the river, Selfridge reported to Geary, and marched with him by way of Robertsville and Buford's Bridge to Blackville, where they rejoined Twentieth Corps February 9, 1865.

Howard's Right Wing left the vicinity of Pocotaligo February 1, 1865 and advanced toward the railroad from Augusta, Georgia to Charleston, South Carolina (the South Carolina Railroad). Fifteenth Corps marched by way of Buford's Bridge on the Salkehatchie River, while Seventeenth Corps moved on parallel roads to the right. The two corps joined on the railroad near Bamberg, South Carolina February 7, 1865. After destroying about twenty-four miles of track, Fifteenth Corps and Seventeenth Corps marched on, and arrived near Orangeburg, South Carolina February 12, 1865. Meantime, Corse's division, which had crossed the Savannah River at Sister's Ferry with the Left Wing, had marched northward and rejoined Fifteenth Corps February 11, 1865, while the latter was en route to Orangeburg.

While Howard's Right Wing was advancing toward Orangeburg, Kilpatrick's cavalry and Slocum's Left Wing left Robertsville and started on their advance toward Augusta. Kilpatrick moved out ahead of the infantry, generally along the line of the South Carolina Railroad, and pushed up close to Augusta, despite considerable opposition from Wheeler's cavalry. Kilpatrick arrived at Johnson's Station February 10, 1865, and demonstrated against Augusta the next day. He then turned toward Columbia and marched on the left of Fourteenth Corps, which was advancing toward Lexington, South Carolina. Fourteenth Corps had advanced from Robertsville by way of Barnwell, and it arrived near Williston Station on the South Carolina Railroad February 12, 1865. After destroying the track in the vicinity, it marched on toward Lexington, as noted above.

Twentieth Corps marched by way of Lawtonville, Buford's Bridge on the Salkehatchie River, Graham's Station, Blackville, Williston Station, and Coonville, and joined Fourteenth Corps at Lexington on the evening of February 15, 1865.

On February 16, 1865, both wings of the army were approaching Columbia, South Carolina, where the Saluda River and the Broad River join to form the Congaree. Logan's Fifteenth Corps and Blair's Seventeenth Corps arrived from Orangeburg and halted that evening on the south side of the Congaree, opposite Columbia. To the west, the Left Wing was marching that day from Lexington toward Columbia. Davis' Fourteenth Corps was moving on the direct road from Lexington, and Williams' Twentieth Corps on a road to the right. These two corps, however, did not enter Columbia. Instead, about three miles out, Slocum received orders to by-pass the city to the west, and to march to Winns-

boro, South Carolina. Fourteenth Corps, followed by Twentieth Corps, then crossed the Saluda River at Mount Zion Church, and the Broad River about five miles below Alston, and arrived at Winnsboro February 21, 1865. When the troops of Slocum's Left Wing arrived at Winnsboro, they began the destruction of the railroads around the town.

Kilpatrick's cavalry did not accompany the Left Wing on its march toward Columbia, but encamped near Lexington February 16, 1865. The next day it continued its advance on the left of the army. It crossed the Saluda River at Mount Zion Church, passed through Alston, and reached Monticello February 20, 1865.

Fifteenth Corps entered Columbia February 17, 1865. Seventeenth Corps also moved into the city, but only passed through, just after dark, and camped that night about a mile and a half to the north. The next day it moved on about six miles, and began destroying the track of the Charlotte and South Carolina Railroad. Seventeenth Corps continued its movement up the railroad, destroying the track as it advanced, and reached Winnsboro February 22, 1865.

A fire broke out in Columbia during the night of February 17, 1865, and most of the city was destroyed. During the next two days, Fifteenth Corps remained in the city and completed the work of destruction of public buildings and stores not consumed by the fire. Fifteenth Corps left Columbia February 20, 1865 and marched by roads to the right of the railroad, and also to the right of Seventeenth Corps, toward Peay's Ferry on the Catawba River, about fifteen miles northeast of Winnsboro. It moved by way of Longtown, Dutchman's Creek, and Poplar Spring Church, and arrived at the crossing of the Catawba February 22, 1865. When Seventeenth Corps had completed the work of destruction on the railroad from Columbia to Winnsboro, it moved on February 22, 1865 to Poplar Spring Church and camped near Fifteenth Corps. Thus, that day, Sherman's entire army was concentrated near Winnsboro, South Carolina. Its next destination was Cheraw, South Carolina.

When the Left Wing had completed the wrecking of the railroad, it moved out with the cavalry February 22, 1865 toward Rocky Mount Ferry on the Catawba or Wateree River, above Peay's Ferry. Kilpatrick's cavalry division was in the lead during this march, and it was followed by Twentieth Corps, and then Fourteenth Corps. The cavalry and Twentieth Corps crossed the river February 23–24, 1865, but Fourteenth Corps was delayed when the bridge was swept away by the swollen waters. It finally crossed February 27, 1865, and then both corps marched toward Cheraw. Twentieth Corps advanced by way of Hanging Rock Post Office, Chesterfield, and Sneedsboro, on the South Carolina-North Carolina line, and arrived at Cheraw March 6, 1865. It crossed the Peedee River the next day. Fourteenth Corps marched by Hanging Rock Post Office, Horton's Tavern, Taxipaw, McManus Bridge at Lynch's Creek, Blakeny's Cross Roads, Mount Croghan, and Sneedsboro, and on March 1–4, 1865 arrived on the Peedee River at Pegue's Ferry, ten miles above Cheraw and three miles below Sneedsboro. A bridge was completed March 6, 1865, and Kilpatrick's cavalry crossed that evening. Fourteenth Corps followed the next day.

February 22–23, 1865, Howard's Right Wing marched to the Wateree River at Peay's Ferry. Logan's Fifteenth Corps advanced February 22, 1865, with the left column passing by Poplar Springs to Peay's Ferry, and Charles R. Woods' division moving on the direct road to the ferry. Blair's Seventeenth Corps followed Logan the next day, and arrived at the ferry while Fifteenth Corps was crossing. Logan was over the river by 3:00 P.M., and then Seventeenth Corps began crossing. February 23, 1865, both corps began the march toward Cheraw. Seventeenth marched on the direct road by way of Liberty Hill and Flat Rock Post Office, and arrived at Cheraw March 2–4, 1865. Fifteenth Corps advanced on the right of Seventeenth Corps to Liberty Hill and was then divided into two columns so as to strike the system of roads running from Camden to Cheraw. The column on the left, consisting of Charles R. Woods' First Division and John E. Smith's Third Division, moved by way of Flat Rock Church to West's Cross Roads, and the column on the right, consisting of William B. Hazen's Second Division and John M. Corse's Fourth Division, marched by way of Red Hill Post Office to Big Pine Church on the Camden and Cheraw Road. Detachments from the right-hand column passed through Camden and destroyed all stores and public buildings in the town.

February 26, 1865, Fifteenth Corps marched to Lynch's Creek, with the Fourth Division and First Division moving to Tiller's Bridge, and Second Division and Third Division to Kelly's Bridge, and there they prepared to cross the stream. Corse's Fourth Division managed to cross that day, but the creek was too wide to bridge and too deep to ford, and the rest of the corps was forced to wait for some time. The other three divisions finally crossed Lynch's Creek March 2, 1865, and arrived at Cheraw two days later. Seventeenth Corps crossed the Peedee River at Cheraw March 4, 1865, and Fifteenth Corps followed the next day.

Sherman's next objective, after his army had crossed the Peedee, was Fayetteville, North Carolina, on the Cape Fear River. The advance began March 6–8, 1865 on several roads, which were all in very bad condition because of incessant rains. On March 6, 1865, Seventeenth Corps left Cheraw, and then turned to the right and marched to Bennettsville. On the following day the corps moved out by way of Gilopolis, toward Fayetteville. The march was greatly delayed by constant rain, and the corps did not arrive near Fayetteville until March 11, 1865. Fifteenth Corps started March 7, 1865, and used two roads that were about ten miles to the left of Seventeenth Corps. One road ran by Brightsville Post Office and Springfield to Laurel Hill, North Carolina, and the other road ran directly to Laurel Hill. The corps was near Laurel Hill on the night of March 8, 1865, and near Fayetteville March 12, 1865.

Fourteenth Corps advanced by way of Rockingham, North Carolina and Blue's (or Love's) Bridge at Lumber River, and reached Fayetteville March 11, 1865. While en route, on March 10, 1865, John G. Mitchell's Second Brigade of James D. Morgan's Second Division was sent to help Kilpatrick's cavalry, which was engaged at Monroe's Cross Roads, but it arrived after the fighting had ended (see below). It rejoined the division that night.

Twentieth Corps marched through Rockingham March 7, 1865, and then continued on by way of Mark's Station on the Wilmington, Charlotte, and Rutherford Railroad and McFarland's Bridge on the Lumber River, and arrived at Fayetteville March 11, 1865.

Engagement at Monroe's Cross Roads, South Carolina, March 10, 1865. Kilpatrick's cavalry had a somewhat more eventful march than the infantry after it left the Peedee River. It continued to move forward on the left of the army through Rockingham and on toward Fayetteville. On March 9, 1865, George E. Spencer's Third Brigade marched in advance of the division, from the headwaters of the Lumber River in Moore County, North Carolina to Solemn Grove, which was about midway between Rockingham and Fayetteville. When Spencer arrived there, he was about five miles in front of Thomas J. Jordan's First Brigade and Smith D. Atkins' Second Brigade, and he waited until 5:00 P.M. for them to come up. At that time, however, Kilpatrick ordered him to move on about twelve miles in the direction of Fayetteville, to Monroe's Cross Roads, which was located in the northwest corner of Cumberland County, North Carolina.

Before leaving Solemn Grove, Spencer was joined by William B. Way's Fourth Brigade, which consisted of dismounted men of Kilpatrick's division. Way's brigade followed Spencer to Monroe's Cross Roads, where both brigades camped about 9:00 that evening in a heavy rain. Way's brigade camped in line of battle, parallel to the main road, and in front of division headquarters, which was in the Charles Monroe house. Spencer's brigade camped to the right and rear of the dismounted men.

Early on the morning of March 10, 1865, the Federal troopers were completely surprised by sudden and simultaneous attacks on both camps by the cavalry divisions of Matthew C. Butler, William W. Allen, and William Y. C. Humes, which were under the command of Wade Hampton and Joseph Wheeler. The camp of Fourth Brigade and division and brigade headquarters, together with the wagons and artillery, were captured almost immediately. At the same time, the enemy cavalry advanced into Spencer's camp, and for a time held the greater part of it. The Federal forces reformed, however, and fought back stubbornly, and finally, after recovering two pieces of Ebenezer W. Stetson's section of the 10th Battery, Wisconsin Light Artillery, they opened fire on the enemy. Kilpatrick's men then advanced, and after close and desperate fighting that lasted for about an hour, the Southern forces withdrew about 7:30 A.M.

Largely because of the condition of the roads, the cavalry brigades of Jordan and Atkins did not join

the rest of the division until the fighting had ended. Kilpatrick's engagement, however, took place about five miles to the left of the line of march of Fourteenth Corps, and at 8:00 A.M. John G. Mitchell's Second Brigade, Second Division was sent to help the cavalry. Mitchell did not reach the field until after the enemy had retired, but he remained with the cavalry until about 1:30 P.M. and then rejoined the division on the Fayetteville Road at dark.

Spencer's and Way's brigades remained on the battlefield until the afternoon of March 10, 1865, and they then marched about five miles toward Fayetteville and joined the rest of the division. The next day, Kilpatrick marched toward Fayetteville, but finding the road occupied by the infantry, he camped a few miles from the town.

FAYETTEVILLE TO GOLDSBORO, NORTH CAROLINA
MARCH 15, 1865–MARCH 23, 1865

Sherman's march from Savannah to Fayetteville was made without any serious opposition, but there was daily skirmishing along the front of the advancing columns. Upon arrival of the army at Fayetteville, however, this was about to change. On February 25, 1865, Joseph E. Johnston assumed command of the Confederate Army of Tennessee and of all troops in the Department of South Carolina, Georgia, and Florida. At that time his forces were widely scattered, and the march of Sherman's army prevented their concentration at any point south of Fayetteville. William J. Hardee's corps was arriving at Cheraw from Charleston, which had been evacuated February 17, 1865; Braxton Bragg's troops of the Confederate Department of North Carolina were near Kinston, North Carolina; Carter L. Stevenson's corps of the Army of Tennessee was near Charlotte, North Carolina; and Alexander P. Stewart's and Benjamin F. Cheatham's corps of the Army of Tennessee were on the road between Newberry, South Carolina and Charlotte, North Carolina. After the Federal occupation of Fayetteville, however, Johnston ordered the concentration of his troops at Smithfield, North Carolina, about thirty miles northwest of Goldsboro, and on the road from Goldsboro to Raleigh. When Johnston had assembled his army at Smithfield, he was in position to oppose a Federal movement toward either Goldsboro or Raleigh.

Hardee, who had been keeping just ahead of Sherman's army on the march to the northeast from Cheraw, was directed to move to the vicinity of Averasboro, which was on the road from Fayetteville to Raleigh, and to remain there until the objective of Sherman's next movement was known. Wheeler's cavalry was north of Fayetteville, acting as a rear guard for Hardee's corps.

When Sherman reached Fayetteville, he was aware that most of the enemy troops with which he had to contend had arrived in North Carolina, and accordingly, he planned to continue his march in as compact a formation as possible so as to have his corps within easy supporting distance in case of attack. By March 1865, he had his entire force across the Cape Fear River near Fayetteville, and was ready to resume the advance toward Goldsboro. Sherman's immediate plans for the march were as follows: Kilpatrick was to move up the Plank Road along the east bank of the Cape Fear River to the vicinity of Averasboro, and Slocum was to follow with four divisions of his Left Wing. This movement was intended as a feint toward Raleigh, and after Kilpatrick and Slocum reached Averasboro, they were to turn eastward toward Bentonville. The four divisions were to march with only the minimum number of wagons necessary to fight a battle. The trains of the Left Wing were to proceed toward Bentonville, in charge of the remaining two divisions, by a more direct road to the south of the road leading from Kingsburg to Bentonville. Howard's Right Wing was to move toward Goldsboro by roads still farther to the right. John A. Logan's Fifteenth Corps was to march on the road by way of Beaman's Cross Roads to Faison's Station on the Wilmington and Weldon Railroad, and Frank P. Blair's Seventeenth Corps was to move still farther to the south on a road that ran by Owenville and Clinton to the same point.

Battle of Averasboro (or Taylor's Hole Creek), March 16, 1865. Early on the morning of March 15, 1865, Kilpatrick's cavalry moved out from Fayetteville toward Averasboro. Following Kilpatrick were William T. Ward's Third Division and Nathaniel J. Jackson's First Division of Alpheus S. Williams' Twentieth Corps, and after them came William P.

Carlin's First Division and James D. Morgan's Second Division of Jefferson C. Davis' Fourteenth Corps. All four divisions traveled in light marching order. John W. Geary's Second Division, Twentieth Corps accompanied the trains of Twentieth Corps on the march toward Bentonville, and Absalom Baird's Third Division of Fourteenth Corps followed with the trains of Fourteenth Corps.

At about 3:00 P.M., Smith D. Atkins, commanding Kilpatrick's leading brigade, encountered the enemy in strong force about seventeen miles north of Fayetteville, and six miles from Averasboro. Atkins put his brigade in position to the right of the Raleigh Road and threw up a barricade. As the other two brigades of the division came up, Atkins placed Jordan's brigade on his right and Spencer's brigade on his left, and they, too, erected barricades.

The troops that Kilpatrick had found belonged to Hardee's command, which had camped the night before at Smith's Mill, and which, upon learning of Kilpatrick's approach, had formed in line of battle across the road. William B. Taliaferro's division occupied the works directly ahead of Kilpatrick; Lafayette McLaws' division was on his left; and Wheeler's dismounted cavalry was on the right of Taliaferro. After examining the enemy position, Kilpatrick concluded that it was too strong for the cavalry to attack alone, and he sent back for infantry support. Slocum sent forward William Hawley's Second Brigade of Jackson's division, and during the night it arrived and relieved Atkins' cavalry brigade. The latter then withdrew to the rear of the Federal line. During the night of March 15, 1865, the four infantry divisions of Slocum's Left Wing camped near Taylor's Hole Creek, a few miles in rear of Kilpatrick's position.

At daylight the next morning, Kilpatrick moved out in line of battle, with Hawley's infantry brigade in the center and Atkins' brigade and Jordan's brigade on the right, both under the command of Atkins, and drove the enemy skirmishers back into their main line of works. After a careful reconnaissance, Kilpatrick again decided that he could not attack successfully, and he asked for additional infantry support. At about this time, however, the enemy advanced and strongly attacked Fielder A. Jones' 8th Indiana Cavalry of Jordan's brigade, which was covering the right flank of Hawley's line. Jones was able to hold his position until Jordan's and

Atkins' brigades came up, and together they repulsed the enemy attack. Then, with Hawley on the left, Jordan in the center, and Atkins on the right, Kilpatrick advanced and drove the enemy back into their works.

At about 10:00 A.M., the head of Slocum's infantry reached the field and began to deploy in line of battle. First to arrive was William T. Ward's Third Division, of Williams' Twentieth Corps. Ward placed Daniel Dustin's Second Brigade on the right of the Raleigh Road, in rear of Hawley, and William Cogswell's Third Brigade on the right of Dustin. At first, Henry Case's First Brigade was left behind to cover the trains, but it was soon brought forward to form on the right of Cogswell. When the deployment was completed, Ward moved forward to develop the enemy line. Dustin's brigade was then sent across the road to relieve Spencer's cavalry brigade, and Cogswell's brigade moved forward and relieved Hawley's brigade. When relieved, Hawley moved to the right of Cogswell.

Jackson's other two brigades of his First Division, Twentieth Corps then began to arrive, and were ordered to form on the right of Ward's division. James S. Robinson's Third Brigade came up first, and it was placed on the right of Hawley. As the line advanced, the right of Robinson's brigade became exposed, and it was forced to halt until James L. Selfridge's First Brigade arrived and relieved Jordan's cavalry on the right of Robinson. When relieved, Kilpatrick's cavalry moved to a position on the extreme right of the Federal line, where it faced McLaws' division.

While advancing, Case's brigade was ordered to move from the right of the Third Division line to the extreme left, and then, passing by the rear of the brigades of Cogswell and Dustin, it marched out to the left and front. It struck the right of the enemy line while at the same time Dustin and Cogswell attacked on its front. The maneuver was completely successful, and Taliaferro's line was driven back about a mile. Then, after making a brief stand on a second line, it again fell back to a strong third line of works. This line crossed the Raleigh Road in the vicinity of a fork in the road where the Smithfield Road turned off to the northeast. Ward then pushed forward to the abandoned second line, with Cogswell on the right, Dustin in the center, and Case on the left. By this time, Jackson's division was up on the right of

Ward, and with the understanding that James D. Morgan's Second Division, Fourteenth Corps was approaching on the left, Ward's line again advanced. Morgan did not appear, however, and when Ward's division was hit by a flank fire, it was forced to halt. At about 10:00 A.M., John G. Mitchell's Second Brigade of Morgan's division was sent forward, and it formed in line of battle on the left of the Raleigh Road. At noon, the two remaining brigades of Morgan's division—William Vandever's First Brigade and Benjamin D. Fearing's Third Brigade—were also ordered forward. Fearing took position on the left of Mitchell, and these two brigades engaged in a brisk skirmish. Vandever came up on the left of Fearing, but was struck by a destructive flank fire and was forced to withdraw to the rear of Fearing's brigade.

Meantime, William P. Carlin's First Division, Fourteenth Corps had followed in rear of Morgan and had massed in front of the first line that had been evacuated by the enemy. At 3:00 P.M., Harrison C. Hobart's First Brigade was sent forward to relieve Hawley, who then moved back in reserve. About 5:00 P.M., George P. Buell's Second Brigade and David Miles' Third Brigade of Carlin's division moved to the extreme left, and formed in rear of Morgan, supporting his left.

Much time had been required to advance and deploy Slocum's troops, largely because of the bad condition of the roads and the swampy nature of the country, and by the time that Fourteenth Corps was up and ready, it was too late in the day to launch another attack. The Federal troops bivouacked on the battlefield that night, but around 8:00 P.M. Hardee began to withdraw his troops and artillery up the Smithfield Road, and he left Wheeler's dismounted cavalry to cover the retreat.

The organization of the troops engaged at Averasboro March 16, 1865 was as follows:

LEFT WING (ARMY OF GEORGIA)
Henry W. Slocum

FOURTEENTH CORPS, Jefferson C. Davis

First Division, William P. Carlin
   First Brigade, Harrison C. Hobart
   Second Brigade, George P. Buell
   Third Brigade, David Miles

Note. Second Brigade and Third Brigade were in reserve.

Second Division, James D. Morgan
    First Brigade, William Vandever
    Second Brigade, John G. Mitchell
    Third Brigade, Benjamin D. Fearing

Note. Absalom Baird's Third Division was absent with the trains.

TWENTIETH CORPS, Alpheus S. Williams

First Division, Nathaniel J. Jackson
    First Brigade, James L. Selfridge
    Second Brigade, William Hawley
    Third Brigade, James S. Robinson

Third Division, William T. Ward
    First Brigade, Henry Case
    Second Brigade, Daniel Dustin
    Third Brigade, William Cogswell

Note. John W. Geary's Second Division was absent with the trains.

Third Cavalry Division, Military Division of the Mississippi, Judson Kilpatrick
    First Brigade, Thomas J. Jordan
    Second Brigade, Smith D. Atkins
    Third Brigade, George E. Spencer

Note. William B. Way's Fourth Brigade of dismounted men was guarding the trains March 16, 1865.

Battle of Bentonville, March 19–21, 1865. While Slocum was advancing toward Averasboro from Fayetteville March 15, 1865, and during the battle the next day, Howard marched with his Right Wing, according to his orders, toward Goldsboro by roads to Slocum's right. The four divisions of Logan's Fifteenth Corps marched unencumbered on the first road south of the direct Goldsboro Road and reached South River on the evening of March 15, 1865. Blair's Seventeenth Corps moved out on the road toward Owensville. After crossing South River the next morning, Logan took the first practicable left-hand road to the north, and that night camped on the Goldsboro Road. Blair reached Owensville that evening.

On March 17, 1865, Sherman's army resumed its march toward Goldsboro. After caring for the wounded and burying the dead, the troops of Slocum's Left Wing moved out from the vicinity of Averasboro and marched toward Bentonville on the direct road to Goldsboro. Davis' Fourteenth Corps took the lead, and it was followed by Williams' Twentieth Corps. Kilpatrick's cavalry division crossed Black River and took the Smithfield Road to the right and front of the infantry.

Fourteenth Corps advanced slowly because of muddy roads and frequent halts to build bridges, and it did not reach Mill Creek until the night of March 18, 1865. It camped that night about five or six miles from the Cole plantation, which was about two miles south of the hamlet of Bentonville, and on the road along which Slocum's troops were marching. Twentieth Corps camped that night on the road behind Fourteenth Corps.

While Slocum was moving toward Bentonville, Howard's Right Wing left Black River, about fifteen miles east of Fayetteville, and marched along roads to the south of Slocum toward Goldsboro. Blair's Seventeenth Corps marched to the right on the Clinton Road, by way of Owensville, and arrived at Troublefield's Store, south of Bentonville, on March 18, 1865. Joseph A. Mower's First Division then took the road to Everettsville, on the Wilmington and Weldon Railroad, and Manning F. Force's Third Division and Giles A. Smith's Fourth Division marched on the main road from Clinton to Goldsboro. John A. Logan's Fifteenth Corps moved by roads to the left of Seventeenth Corps, by way of Jenks' Cross Roads, and camped on the night of March 18, 1865 eleven miles south of Bentonville and not far from Troublefield's Store.

About daybreak March 18, 1865, Joseph E. Johnston learned from Wade Hampton that the Union army was marching toward Goldsboro by different roads, and concluded, from reports received, that the heads of Slocum's and Howard's columns were separated from one another by about a day's march. Based on this understanding, Johnston decided to attack Slocum's isolated wing the next morning. He then ordered his troops at Smithfield and Elevation to concentrate about twenty-five miles west of Goldsboro, between Bentonville and Slocum's line of march on the Goldsboro Road. That day, Johnston sent Hampton's cavalry forward to gain time for his forces to get in position. Fighting dismounted, Hampton's troopers engaged the skirmishers of William P. Carlin's division of Fourteenth Corps until sunset, and then both sides withdrew. At daybreak Hampton returned to his position of the evening before, and posted his pickets within a mile of the Federal advance. Almost immediately they became engaged with foragers of Fourteenth Corps that had moved out to the front early that morning.

Meantime, while Hampton delayed Slocum's advance, Johnston was able to get his troops in position. Robert F. Hoke's division, then under the immediate direction of Braxton Bragg, was the first to arrive, and it was deployed across the Goldsboro Road and perpendicular to it, less than a half mile east of the Cole house. The Army of Tennessee, then under the command of Alexander P. Stewart, came up next and formed on the right of Hoke. Stewart's line was north of the Goldsboro Road and at approximately a right angle to Hoke's line, and it extended to the west from the right of Hoke for about a mile. The Army of Tennessee consisted of the corps of Stewart, Stephen D. Lee, and Benjamin F. Cheatham, commanded respectively by William W. Loring, Daniel H. Hill, and William B. Bate. Hardee's corps had not yet arrived. In front of the Confederate line was a large, open field of the Cole plantation. When Johnston's deployment was completed, Hampton withdrew his cavalry through Bragg's line and moved to the extreme Confederate right, where he was joined by Wheeler's cavalry later in the day.

At 7:00 A.M. March 19, 1865, Slocum's Left Wing resumed its march, with William P. Carlin's First Division of Davis' Fourteenth Corps in the lead. Harrison C. Hobart's First Brigade was at the head of the division, and it was followed in order by George P. Buell's Second Brigade and David Miles' Third Brigade. Neither Sherman nor Slocum expected any serious opposition on the march to Goldsboro, and Sherman, who had been traveling with Slocum's wing, departed that morning to join Howard's column, and he left Slocum in charge on the Goldsboro Road that passed by Bentonville.

After advancing about three miles, Carlin overtook the foragers, who were still skirmishing with Hampton's cavalry. Progress was slow, and at about 10:00 A.M. Hobart deployed his brigade in two lines. The right wing of the brigade, consisting of the 88th Indiana, 33rd Ohio, and 94th Ohio regiments under Cyrus E. Briant, formed the first line; and the left wing, consisting of the 104th Illinois,

21st Wisconsin, and 42nd Indiana regiments under Michael H. Fitch, were on the second line. Hobart, with Briant's three regiments, immediately advanced and forced the enemy back across the fields of the Cole plantation and into their main line. Fitch was directed to follow and support the first line.

When Hobart's regiments reached the Cole house, in the center of the field, they came under artillery and musketry fire from Hoke's division, which was posted along the eastern edge of the field, about 200 yards distant. They immediately began constructing works in front of the house, but then Hobart moved his regiments to the left and temporarily sheltered them in a wooded ravine. Fitch's regiments, which had advanced about a mile, came up and took position on the right of Hobart, with their left on the Goldsboro Road, supporting Battery C, 1st Illinois Light Artillery, which had been placed about thirty yards in rear of the Cole house.

When Hobart deployed and moved forward, Buell, who was following Hobart, was ordered to move his brigade about a mile around the enemy's right flank, and then attack on the flank and rear. This order was soon suspended, however, and Buell was directed to move forward and take position on the left of Hobart's brigade. At about this time, Carlin deployed his other brigade, commanded by Miles, on the right of Fitch's regiments, south of the Goldsboro Road.

When these dispositions were completed, Davis ordered Buell to attack on the Confederate right, and he was to be supported by the rest of Carlin's division. After advancing about 400 yards, Buell found the enemy entrenched in a strong position, and after some furious fighting he was driven back. Hobart, with Briant's three regiments, advanced on the right of Buell, but he too was halted at the enemy works. Miles' brigade on the right fared no better. Carlin's brigades then fell back to the positions from which they had launched their attacks.

During this engagement, fighting was heavy on Hoke's front, and when Bragg became concerned about the safety of his line, Hardee, who was then approaching the field, sent his leading division, under Lafayette McLaws, to support Hoke. Hardee's other division, commanded by William B. Taliaferro, moved on to a position on the extreme Confederate right.

At about 11:00 A.M., James D. Morgan, whose

Second Division, Fourteenth Corps was following Carlin that morning, was ordered forward with two brigades to support him. When Morgan arrived, he placed John G. Mitchell's Second Brigade on the right of Miles' brigade, which was on the right of Carlin's line, and Benjamin D. Fearing's Third Brigade, in close column of regiments, to the right and rear of Mitchell. William Vandever's First Brigade, which had been left with the trains, was then brought up to a position on the right of Mitchell, with its right on a swamp. Fortunately, as events were soon to prove, Morgan threw up a line of strong log works.

When Carlin became engaged that morning, Slocum sent orders to Alpheus S. Williams to hasten forward with two divisions of his Twentieth Corps. Williams immediately directed Nathaniel J. Jackson, who commanded his leading First Division, to send up William Hawley's Second Brigade and James S. Robinson's Third Brigade, and shortly after noon he ordered James L. Selfridge's First Brigade to follow these two brigades. Hawley arrived on the field about 2:00 P.M., and placed his brigade in position about a mile east of the Harper house, and a mile and a half in rear of Carlin's division, with its right on the Goldsboro Road. A short time later, however, Hawley moved about a half mile to the left and entrenched on a line where he could protect the Federal left. Robinson's brigade arrived about 3:00 P.M., and was sent forward to occupy a gap between Hobart and Miles. The position occupied by Robinson was on the left of the Goldsboro Road, just west of the Cole house, and to the right and rear of Hobart's line. Robinson formed his brigade in two lines, with 61st Ohio, 82nd Ohio, and 31st Wisconsin on the first line and the 82nd Illinois and 143rd New York on the second line. He was just beginning to construct a breastwork to cover his front when the two reserve regiments were ordered to the rear to support Hawley's brigade. Three regiments were not sufficient to fill the gap in Carlin's line, and Robinson's three regiments were unable to make connection with the troops on either flank.

Kilpatrick, who was moving at the head of Twentieth Corps with his cavalry that morning, also moved forward when he heard the sound of Carlin's battle, and he took position on the far left of the Union line.

While Jackson's troops were getting in position, Johnston completed his preparations for an attack on the Federal line. His divisions were in line, from the Confederate right to left, as follows: Taliaferro's division of Hardee's corps; William B. Bate with two divisions of Cheatham's corps; Daniel H. Hill with three divisions of Stephen D. Lee's corps; William W. Loring's division of Stewart's corps; Edward C. Walthall's division, also of Stewart's corps, was to the left of the Cole field, supporting the artillery opposite the Cole house; and Bragg held the left of the line, with Hoke's division across the Goldsboro Road. McLaws' division of Hardee's corps was to the rear, in support of Hoke. Early that afternoon, Johnston had placed Hardee in temporary command of the Army of Tennessee, and then, shortly before the attack, he directed him to take charge of the Right Wing, which was composed of Taliaferro's division and the Army of Tennessee.

At 3:15 P.M. March 19, 1865, Hardee's Army of Tennessee moved forward toward Carlin's line. The Confederate infantry advanced about 600 yards, pushing back the Federal skirmishers, and then struck Carlin's works. Hill's troops struck the front of Hobart's brigade, passed through the gap on its right, and forced it to retire. Buell's brigade held for a time, but after Hobart's withdrawal, it was outflanked on the left by Taliaferro and on the right by Hill, and was also driven back. Robinson's line, which was about 300 yards beyond, was also swept away. The brigades of Hobart, Buell, and Robinson fell back in confusion on Twentieth Corps, which, as noted above, was deploying about a mile to the rear. Miles' brigade, which held the right of Carlin's line, changed front to the left and resisted for a while, and then moved by the left flank and connected with Mitchell's Second Brigade, Second Division, Fourteenth Corps, south of the Goldsboro Road. At this point Miles was wounded, and Arnold McMahan assumed command of the brigade.

Morgan's Second Division, Fourteenth Corps was not engaged during this first phase of the battle because Bragg's troops, which were on their front, did not advance with the Army of Tennessee. As the enemy pursued Carlin's troops westward toward Williams' Twentieth Corps, however, Davis ordered Morgan to move Fearing's reserve brigade to the left and occupy the ground left vacant by Carlin's withdrawal. When Fearing reached the Goldsboro

Road, he saw the Confederate troops following Carlin's men across the field on his front. He promptly advanced against the enemy's exposed left flank and pushed it back until he in turn was struck in front and on his right by superior forces and driven back. Fearing then moved to the rear about 300 yards and formed a new line, with its left resting on the Goldsboro Road. Thereafter, there was only skirmishing on Fearing's front. Fearing, who had been wounded during the fighting, turned over the command of the brigade to James W. Langley.

When Fearing was forced back to his new position, he left a large gap between his brigade and the other two brigades of Morgan's division. Three brigades of Hill's corps passed through this opening and moved against the rear of Morgan's breastworks. At that time, Bragg, whose troops had not taken part in the initial charge, ordered Hoke to assault the front of Morgan's line. Heavy fighting then took place around Morgan's position south of the Goldsboro Road, with Federal troops defending both the front and rear of their works.

Fortunately, at about 3:00 P.M., William Cogswell had been sent with his Third Brigade of William T. Ward's Third Division, Twentieth Corps to report to Davis, commanding Fourteenth Corps, and upon his arrival he was sent to fill the space between Fearing's and Mitchell's brigades. While moving forward beyond Fearing's right, Cogswell came up on the flank of Hill's men as they moved toward Morgan's rear. Cogswell immediately attacked, and the enemy fell back and formed a defensive line. Heavy fighting continued in the area until 8:30 P.M., and then Hill withdrew. Meantime, Morgan repulsed Hoke's attacks on the front of his works and inflicted heavy losses on the enemy.

While Morgan was engaged with Hoke and Hill, Hardee, north of the Goldsboro Road, prepared for an attack on Williams' Twentieth Corps. During the defeat and pursuit of Carlin and in fending off Fearing's flank attack, his troops had become considerably disorganized, and he had halted for a time to reorganize.

As noted above, in response to orders from Slocum, the troops of Twentieth Corps began to arrive on the battlefield about 2:00 P.M. Upon arrival there, Robinson's brigade and Cogswell's brigade were sent forward to support Fourteenth Corps, and they took part in the fighting later in the

afternoon. The other four brigades of the corps were used to form a second line in rear of Fourteenth Corps. Hawley's brigade of Jackson's division, as already described, was placed in position to protect the left flank, about a mile east of the Harper house, with its right about a fourth of a mile north of the Goldsboro Road. A little later Selfridge's brigade, also of Jackson's division, was placed on the left of Hawley. When Carlin's line was broken, however, Selfridge fell back and took position with his brigade across the Goldsboro Road, along which the enemy was advancing. Dustin's brigade of Ward's division then came up and occupied the ground vacated by Selfridge. Case's brigade, also of Ward's division, arrived and formed to the left and rear of Dustin, on the extreme left of the Federal line. Kilpatrick's cavalry was on beyond, watching the country to the left.

When Robinson, with his three regiments, was driven back from the vicinity of the Cole house, he halted on a new line south of Hawley's brigade, with his right on the Goldsboro Road, about 300 yards in front of Selfridge's line. The 143rd New York, one of the regiments of Robinson's brigade that had been sent earlier to support Hawley, returned to the brigade and was placed on the left of Robinson's line.

When the above dispositions were completed, there was still an interval of about 400 yards across open fields between the brigades of Robinson and Hawley. Major John A. Reynolds, commander of the artillery brigade of Twentieth Corps, placed all of his batteries to cover this space and also the open ground between the first and second lines. These were: Charles E. Winegar's Battery I, 1st New York Light Artillery; Edward P. Newkirk's Battery M, 1st New York Light Artillery; Jerome B. Stephens' Battery C, 1st Ohio Light Artillery; and Thomas S. Sloan's Battery E, Pennsylvania Light Artillery.

Later, the Twentieth Corps line was made more secure when Robinson's brigade connected on its right with Fearing's brigade, then commanded by Langley. To complete the defensive line in front and to the left of the Harper house, the defeated troops of Carlin's division, which had passed through Williams' lines, were reorganized and placed in reserve.

About 5:00 P.M., when Hardee's preparations for the second attack were completed, Bate's division, supported by McLaws' division, launched an attack on the front of Twentieth Corps. As enemy troops entered the field between the brigades of Robinson and Hawley, they were struck by a deadly fire from Reynolds' artillery and a crossfire from the infantry on the left of Robinson and the right of Hawley, and they were driven back in confusion and with heavy losses. Five times Hardee attempted to push through between the two Federal brigades, but each time he was driven back. The last attack was made about sundown, and the fighting finally ended at dark, with the Union line still intact.

Meantime, on March 19, 1865, Sherman had accompanied Howard's Right Wing as it marched toward Goldsboro. Sherman was aware during the day that Slocum was engaged near Bentonville, but as late as 5:00 that afternoon he did not believe that Johnson would commit his army to a major battle south of the Neuse River. He therefore allowed Howard's column's to move on, and that night Blair's Seventeenth Corps camped at Smith's Chapel, about seven miles west of Mount Olive, and Logan's Fifteenth Corps halted in the vicinity of Falling Creek Church, about three miles south of Cox's Bridge over the Neuse River. Howard and Sherman established headquarters at Falling Creek Church.

Late that evening, Sherman learned of Slocum's battle that day, and he immediately issued orders for the Right Wing to march toward Bentonville. He also authorized Slocum to call up the divisions of John W. Geary and Absalom Baird, which were guarding the trains of Twentieth Corps and Fourteenth Corps, respectively. During the night, Geary, commanding Second Division, Twentieth Corps, left George W. Mindil's Second Brigade with the corps trains, which were then at Canaan Church, about five miles south of Bentonville, and he marched with Ario Pardee's First Brigade and Henry A. Barnum's Third Brigade to rejoin the corps. Geary arrived about daybreak March 20, 1865 and was placed in reserve behind the left of the line. About 5:00 that morning, Baird left George P. Este's Third Brigade to guard the corps trains, then about six miles from Bentonville, and marched at daylight with Morton C. Hunter's First Brigade and Thomas Doan's Second Brigade to report to Davis. Baird's command was also placed in reserve.

There were some changes in the dispositions of

the troops on Slocum's line during the night and the following morning. Selfridge's brigade, which had been in reserve, had relieved Robinson's brigade on the line at about 7:00 the evening before. Carlin's reorganized division was sent to the right to relieve Langley's (formerly Fearing's) and Cogswell's brigades. When this transfer was completed, Langley moved his brigade to a position in reserve, behind Morgan's line. Hobart relieved Cogswell's brigade, which then moved back to a position in rear of the batteries of Twentieth Corps. Buell's brigade formed in rear of Hobart.

Howard's Right Wing, which had started for Bentonville during the night, began arriving early on the morning of March 20, 1865. William B. Hazen's Second Division, Fifteenth Corps, which had marched all night, reported to Slocum at daybreak, and was moved to the rear of Fourteenth Corps. About 11:00 A.M. Charles R. Woods' First Division, Fifteenth Corps approached the rear of Hoke's line on the Goldsboro Road, and Hoke was forced to move to a new position about a mile north of the road. John M. Corse then came up with his Fourth Division, and formed on the right of Woods. About noon, Theodore Jones' First Brigade of Hazen's division was placed in the front line, connecting on the left with Fourteenth Corps, and on the right with Charles R. Woods' division. John E. Smith's Third Division, which followed Corse, formed a second line in rear of Woods' division. Clark R. Wever's Second Brigade of Smith's division was left at Cox's Bridge with the trains, but it rejoined the division about 5:00 P.M.

Blair's Seventeenth Corps began its march from Smith's Chapel at 3:00 A.M. March 20, 1865, and followed Fifteenth Corps from Falling Creek Church along the Goldsboro Road toward Bentonville. Giles A. Smith's Fourth Division arrived around 4:00 P.M. and was placed on the right of Corse's division of Fifteenth Corps. Joseph A. Mower's First Division and Manning F. Force's Third Division followed and encamped that night in rear of Giles A. Smith's Fourth Division as a reserve.

On March 20, 1865, after Johnston's troops had withdrawn from their advanced positions of the evening before, they occupied a line that was roughly in the shape of a wide letter "V." The two sides were at approximately a right angle to one another, and each extended back at an angle of about forty-five degrees from the road that ran south from the bridge over Mill Creek near Bentonville to the Goldsboro Road. The junction of the two wings was about a mile north of the latter road. The Confederate right, which ran nearly parallel to the Goldsboro Road in an east-west direction, was held by Taliaferro's division of the Army of Tennessee. The left, which generally ran north and south, was held by the divisions of Hoke and McLaws, both under the command of Hardee. Hampton's cavalry guarded the right flank, and Wheeler's cavalry the left.

There was no major engagement on March 20, 1865, but there was sharp skirmishing along the entire front during most of the day. About noon, skirmishers of William Vandever's First Brigade of Morgan's Second Division, Fourteenth Corps entered Hoke's abandoned works, and Morgan's division then changed front and occupied Hoke's former position, facing to the northeast. About 3:00 P.M. Morgan's line was again changed to face toward the northwest. Carlin's division was on the left of Morgan, and Logan's Fifteenth Corps was brought up on the left.

On the morning of March 21, 1865, Blair moved Force's division from reserve to a position on the right of Giles A. Smith's division, and Mower's division to the right of Force, on the extreme right of of the Federal line. Fighting then flared up on the front of Seventeenth Corps as the entire line advanced to within range of the east face of the enemy works. Hazen's Second Division reported to Logan that morning and was placed on Fifteenth Corps' line, on the left of Woods. Logan also moved his corps up, with sharp fighting, to a position close to the enemy works.

There was intense skirmishing along the entire front March 21, 1865, especially on the Federal right and center. The most serious action of the day, however, occurred during the afternoon when Mower advanced with John W. Fuller's First Brigade and John Tillson's Third Brigade against the extreme Confederate left. By 4:00 P.M., Mower was approaching the bridge over Mill Creek near Bentonville, and had reached a point about three-fourths of a mile in advance of the nearest supporting troops. Because the Bentonville Bridge was on the only line of retreat for Johnston's army, the Confederates reacted quickly to Mower's threat. Alfred

Cumming's Georgia Brigade (commanded by Robert J. Henderson), Wheeler's cavalry, Hampton with Young's brigade (commanded by Gilbert J. Wright), and Hardee with 8th Texas Cavalry advanced and, in a series of counterattacks on Mower's front and flanks, forced him to fall back. He then established a new temporary defensive position some distance to the rear. Fuller's brigade, which had advanced on the right of Tillson's brigade, then moved to the left, across the rear of the latter, and established connection with Force's Third Division on the left and Tillson's brigade on the right. Mower was ordered to remain where he was and entrench. That night, Johnston's army withdrew across Mill Creek and retreated toward Smithfield.

Sherman directed Howard and the cavalry to remain at Bentonville through March 22, 1865 to bury the dead and remove the wounded, and with the rest of the army he resumed the march toward Goldsboro. When the work of the Right Wing was completed on the battlefield, it too marched toward Goldsboro. The army arrived there March 23–24, 1865.

The organization of Sherman's forces at the Battle of Bentonville March 19–21, 1865 was as follows:

RIGHT WING (ARMY OF THE TENNESSEE)
Oliver O. Howard

FIFTEENTH CORPS, John A. Logan

First Division, Charles R. Woods
  First Brigade, William B. Woods
  Second Brigade, Robert F. Catterson
  Third Brigade, George A. Stone

Second Division, William B. Hazen
  First Brigade, Theodore Jones
  Second Brigade, Wells S. Jones
  Third Brigade, John M. Oliver

Third Division, John E. Smith
  First Brigade, William T. Clark
  Second Brigade, Clark R. Wever

Note. Third Division was in reserve and was not engaged.

Fourth Division, John M. Corse
  First Brigade, Elliott W. Rice
  Second Brigade, Robert N. Adams
  Third Brigade, Frederick J. Hurlbut

Note. Fourth Division was partly in reserve, and suffered only 32 casualties.

Artillery, William H. Ross
    Battery H, 1st Illinois Light Artillery, Francis De Gress
    Battery B, 1st Michigan Light Artillery, Edward B. Wright
    Battery H, 1st Missouri Light Artillery, Charles M. Callahan
    12th Battery, Wisconsin Light Artillery, William Zickerick

SEVENTEENTH CORPS, Frank P. Blair, Jr.

First Division, Joseph A. Mower
    First Brigade, John W. Fuller
    Second Brigade, Milton Montgomery
    Third Brigade, John Tillson

Third Division, Manning F. Force
    First Brigade, Cassius Fairchild
    Second Brigade, Greenberry F. Wiles

Fourth Division, Giles A. Smith
    First Brigade, Benjamin F. Potts
    Third Brigade, William W. Belknap

Artillery, Allen C. Waterhouse
    Battery C, 1st Michigan Light Artillery, William H. Hyzer
    1st Battery, Michigan Light Artillery, William Z. Clayton
    15th Battery, Ohio Light Artillery, James Burdick

LEFT WING (ARMY OF GEORGIA)
Henry W. Slocum

FOURTEENTH CORPS, Jefferson C. Davis

First Division, William P. Carlin
    First Brigade, Harrison C. Hobart
    Second Brigade, George P. Buell
    Third Brigade, David Miles, to March 19, 1865, wounded
    Arnold McMahan

Second Division, James D. Morgan
    First Brigade, William Vandever
    Second Brigade, John G. Mitchell
    Third Brigade, Benjamin D. Fearing, to March 19, 1865, wounded
    James W. Langley

Third Division, Absalom Baird
    First Brigade, Morton C. Hunter
    Second Brigade, Thomas Doan

Third Brigade, George P. Este

Note. Third Division guarded the trains during the fighting of March 19, 1865. Baird then left Third Brigade to guard the trains, and marched with First Brigade and Second Brigade to the battlefield on the morning of March 20, 1865. These two brigades were held in reserve.

Artillery, Charles Houghtaling
    Battery C, 1st Illinois Light Artillery, Palmer F. Scovel
    Battery I, 2nd Illinois Light Artillery, Judson Rich
    19th Battery, Indiana Light Artillery, Clinton Keeler
    5th Battery, Wisconsin Light Artillery, Joseph McKnight

TWENTIETH CORPS, Alpheus S. Williams

First Division, Nathaniel J. Jackson
    First Brigade, James L. Selfridge
    Second Brigade, William Hawley
    Third Brigade, James S. Robinson

Second Division, John W. Geary
    First Brigade, Ario Pardee, Jr.
    Second Brigade, George W. Mindil
    Third Brigade, Henry A. Barnum

Note. Second Division guarded the corps trains during the fighting of March 19, 1865. Geary then left Second Brigade to guard the trains, and with First Brigade and Third Brigade marched to the battlefield the next morning. Geary's two brigades were held in reserve.

Third Division, William T. Ward
    First Brigade, Henry Case
    Second Brigade, Daniel Dustin
    Third Brigade, William Cogswell

Artillery, John A. Reynolds
    Battery I, 1st New York Light Artillery, Charles E. Winegar
    Battery M, 1st New York Light Artillery, Edward P. Newkirk
    Battery C, 1st Ohio Light Artillery, Jerome B. Stephens
    Battery E, Pennsylvania Light Artillery, Thomas B. Sloan

Note. Sloan's battery was not present on the field at Bentonville.

Third Cavalry Division, Judson Kilpatrick
    First Brigade, Thomas J. Jordan
    Second Brigade, Smith D. Atkins
    Third Brigade, George E. Spencer

Note. The cavalry division was posted on the far left of the army during the Battle of Bentonville, and was not engaged.

GOLDSBORO TO RALEIGH, NORTH CAROLINA (SURRENDER OF JOSEPH E. JOHNSTON'S ARMY) MARCH 14, 1865–APRIL 27, 1865

When Sherman arrived at Goldsboro March 23, 1865, he found the forces of John M. Schofield's Department of North Carolina encamped at and near the town. Alfred H. Terry's Provisional Corps was in position at Cox's Bridge on the Neuse River, and was the first to greet the approaching westerners. Jacob D. Cox's Provisional Corps, Army of the Ohio, consisting of George S. Greene's Provisional Division; Samuel P. Carter's Division of the District of Beaufort, Department of North Carolina; and Thomas H. Ruger's First Division, Twenty-Third Corps, Army of the Ohio, was in position beyond Goldsboro, with Greene on the left, Carter in the center, and Ruger on the right. Second Division and Third Division of Twenty-Third Corps, both under the command of Darius N. Couch, were also near Goldsboro. In addition to the troops at Goldsboro, Edward Harland's brigade of the District of Beaufort was at Kinston, North Carolina; Second Brigade and Third Brigade of Henry W. Birge's Second Division, Nineteenth Corps were at New Berne and Morehead City; and Joseph C. Abbott's Second Brigade, First Division, Twenty-Fourth Corps was at Wilmington. For details of the organization of these troops and their movements on the march to Goldsboro, see Department of North Carolina, January 31, 1865–May 19, 1866, Troops in the Department of North Carolina, and also Operations in the Department of North Carolina.

March 24, 1865, Greene's Provisional Division, which consisted of troops belonging to the Army of the Tennessee and the Army of the Cumberland that were on their way to join their respective armies in North Carolina, was discontinued when its troops rejoined their proper commands. Carter's division was brought in to garrison Goldsboro, and James W. Reilly's Third Division, Twenty-Third Corps was assigned to Cox's Provisional Corps in place of Ruger's division. Then Couch, with his Second Division and Ruger's Third Division of Twenty-Third Corps, was sent back about halfway to Kinston to cover the roads running from Mosely Hall and Kinston.

Sherman's army, after arriving from Cox's Bridge, marched through Goldsboro and camped north of the town, with Howard's Army of the Tennessee on the right, and Slocum's Army of Georgia on the left. After Sherman's troops had passed Cox's Bridge, Terry's Provisional Corps moved to Faison's Station (or Depot) on the Wilmington and Weldon Railroad, where it arrived March 25, 1865. Kilpatrick's cavalry division was sent to Mount Olive, about seven miles north of Faison's Station, on the railroad.

On March 24, 1865, Sherman ordered an important organizational change in the army. He directed Schofield to organize the troops of his command into the equivalent of two corps and to equip them for field service. When organized, this force, under the command of Schofield, was to be known as the "Center" of Sherman's army while operating with the Army of Tennessee and the Army of Georgia.

March 25, 1865, Sherman went north to consult with Grant at City Point, and he left Schofield, the senior officer present, in command of all forces around Goldsboro during his absence. Sherman returned to his headquarters on the night of March 30, 1865.

The organizational changes in Schofield's command ordered by Sherman were completed during the period March 27, 1865–April 2, 1865. March 27, 1865, Tenth Corps was reorganized from Terry's Provisional Corps, plus two brigades from Nineteenth Corps, and Terry was assigned command. Terry's Provisional Corps was thus discontinued. Terry assumed command of the new Tenth Corps April 2, 1865, and announced its organization as follows:

TENTH CORPS, Alfred H. Terry

First Division, Henry W. Birge
 First Brigade, Harvey Graham
 Second Brigade, Joseph C. Abbott
 Third Brigade, Nicholas W. Day

Note. First Brigade was at Morehead City and Second Brigade was at Wilmington. Day's brigade was at New Berne until April 10, 1865, and it then moved to Goldsboro.

Second Division, Adelbert Ames
 First Brigade, Rufus Daggett
 Second Brigade, William B. Coan, to April 5, 1865
  John S. Littell
 Third Brigade, G. Frederick Granger

Third Division, Charles J. Paine
  First Brigade, Delevan Bates
  Second Brigade, Samuel A. Duncan
  Third Brigade, John H. Holman

March 31, 1865, Jacob D. Cox received his presidential assignment (dated March 27, 1865) to the permanent command of Twenty-Third Corps, and he assumed command that day, although his official order for assuming command was dated April 2, 1865.

On March 31, 1865, Cox's Provisional Corps consisted of only Reilly's Third Division, Twenty-Third Corps and Carter's Division of the District of Beaufort. That day Reilly's division rejoined Twenty-Third Corps, the regiments of Carter's Division were assigned to the divisions of Twenty-Third Corps, and Cox's Provisional Corps was discontinued. April 7, 1865, Carter was assigned command of Third Division, Twenty-Third Corps.

On April 1, 1865, Sherman announced the organization of his army as follows:

Right Wing (Army of the Tennessee), Oliver O. Howard
  Fifteenth Corps, John A. Logan
  Seventeenth Corps, Frank P. Blair, Jr.

Center (Army of the Ohio), John M. Schofield
  Tenth Corps, Alfred H. Terry
  Twenty-Third Corps, Jacob D. Cox

Left Wing (Army of Georgia), Henry W. Slocum
  Fourteenth Corps, Jefferson C. Davis
  Twentieth Corps, Alpheus S. Williams, to April 2, 1865
    Joseph A. Mower

A significant change in this reorganization amounted to constituting the Left Wing as a distinct army to be known as the Army of Georgia. Prior to March 28, 1865, the two corps of Slocum's command remained technically a part of George H. Thomas' Army of the Cumberland. At the beginning of the Savannah Campaign in November 1864, the two corps commanded by Slocum were designated as the Left Wing, Army of Georgia, but generally during the march through Georgia and the Carolinas it was unofficially called the Army of Georgia. On March 28, 1865, however, as a part of Sherman's reorganization, Fourteenth Corps and Twentieth Corps were officially constituted by the president as

the Army of Georgia, and Slocum was assigned command.

Sherman's army remained around Goldsboro fifteen or sixteen days while food, forage, clothing, and other necessary supplies for further operations were brought up and distributed to the army. As the next step, Sherman planned to move rapidly northward, feint toward Raleigh, and then march directly toward Burkeville, Virginia to get between the armies of Robert E. Lee and Joseph S. Johnston, and thereby prevent their junction. On April 6, 1865, however, Sherman learned of the battles around Petersburg and of the fall of Richmond, and as a result, he realized that the entire military situation had changed. From that time, the armies of Lee and Johnston became the principal objectives of the United States forces in Virginia and in North Carolina. Grant, with the Army of the Potomac and the Army of the James, was capable of dealing with Lee, and Sherman's task was clearly that of capturing or destroying Johnston's army, which was then encamped about Smithfield, North Carolina. Sherman promptly issued orders for the various units of his army to be ready to march toward Smithfield and Raleigh on the morning of April 10, 1865, and at daybreak that morning the heads of all columns were started toward Johnston's army. Shortly after this movement began, Johnston began to withdraw from Smithfield toward Raleigh.

Kilpatrick's cavalry left its camps at Mount Olive and marched westward south of the Neuse River in an attempt to reach the North Carolina and Atlantic Railroad between Smithfield and Raleigh, where it would be on the rear of Johnston's army. Kilpatrick passed by Troublefield's Store, about sixteen miles west of Mount Olive, and then turned to the northwest and reached the railroad not far from Gulley's Store (present-day Clayton). Johnston, however, had already passed that point, and he arrived near Raleigh April 12, 1865.

Slocum's Army of Georgia took the two direct roads from Goldsboro to Smithfield. Davis' Fourteenth Corps, which was in the lead, entered the town at 10:00 A.M. the next morning, April 11, 1865, and Mower's Twentieth Corps was close behind. Slocum pushed on and reached Raleigh on the evening of April 13, 1865.

Howard's Right Wing moved forward from Goldsboro by roads to the north of Slocum's route.

Logan's Fifteenth Corps took the road along the Wilmington and Weldon Railroad to Pikeville, about seven miles north of Goldsboro, and there it turned to the left on a road roughly parallel to, and to the right of, the North Carolina and Atlantic Railroad. It passed by Lowell on Little River and reached Pineville April 12, 1865. Blair's Seventeenth Corps marched on a road along the left bank of Little River, which empties into the Neuse River just west of Goldsboro, then by way of Pine Level on the railroad, and joined Fifteenth Corps at Pineville April 12, 1865.

Terry, with the Second Division and Third Division of his Tenth Corps, left Faison's Station on the Wilmington and Weldon Railroad and marched along the south side of the Neuse River, following Kilpatrick's cavalry toward the North Carolina and Atlantic Railroad. Terry marched through Bentonville and arrived at Raleigh April 14–15, 1865. On April 10, 1865, Cox concentrated his Twenty-Third Corps near Goldsboro, and the next day marched on the Lower Raleigh Road (Old Neuse Road) in support of the left of Slocum's columns. Cox crossed the Neuse River at Turner's Bridge and arrived at a point about two miles east of Raleigh April 14, 1865.

When Sherman's army marched toward Raleigh April 10, 1865, Henry W. Birge moved up from New Berne to Goldsboro with his division headquarters and Nicholas W. Day's Third Brigade, First Division, Tenth Corps, and assumed command of the post.

During the night of April 12, 1865, Johnston marched out of Raleigh with all of his army except Wheeler's cavalry, and Wheeler left the next morning. The city was surrendered to Kilpatrick early on April 13, 1865, and soon thereafter he rode in at the head of his cavalry. He did not remain long, however, but pressed on in pursuit of Wheeler. About 7:30 that morning, Sherman, then traveling with Davis' Fourteenth Corps, arrived in Raleigh and set up his headquarters in the governor's mansion.

Kilpatrick's cavalry reached Morrisville, about twelve miles west of Raleigh, on the afternoon of April 13, 1865, and the next day pushed on to Durham's Station, and from there Kilpatrick sent Smith D. Atkins' Second Brigade on to Chapel Hill. Logan's Fifteenth Corps and Blair's Seventeenth Corps arrived at Raleigh April 14, 1865, and both corps passed through the city and camped a few

miles to the west. Fifteenth Corps followed the cavalry as far as Morrisville, and Seventeenth Corps halted at Jones' Station, a short distance behind.

Sherman believed that Johnston would continue his retreat along the North Carolina Railroad, which swung around in a great arc from Raleigh to the west and south through Hillsboro, Greensboro, Salisbury, and Charlotte, and he immediately moved to head him off. He ordered Kilpatrick to make a show of following Johnston, and directed Howard and Slocum to march across the arc so as to come onto the railroad at some point ahead of him. Howard was to turn left from the railroad at Jones' Station and march to Hackney's Cross Roads, and then due west through Pittsboro, Saint Lawrence, and Ashboro, in the direction of Salisbury. Slocum was to march southwest from Raleigh, through Martha's Vineyard, and cross the Cape Fear River at Aven's Ferry, a short distance beyond. From there, he was to push forward rapidly to the southwest, through Carthage, in the direction of Charlotte. Schofield was directed to hold Raleigh and the roads to the rear with a part of his corps and to follow the other columns, by an intermediate route, with the rest of his command.

By April 15, 1865, despite heavy rains and bad roads, Fourteenth Corps had arrived near Martha's Vineyard and had laid a pontoon bridge across the Cape Fear River at Aven's Ferry. Twentieth Corps was on the road a short distance behind. Fifteenth and Seventeenth corps were marching along the road toward Pittsboro, and Kilpatrick held Durham Station and Chapel Hill. They were, however, to go no farther.

On April 14, 1865, Sherman received, through Kilpatrick, a letter from Johnston, dated the day before, asking for a temporary suspension of active operations for the purpose of negotiating for the ending of hostilities. As a result of this communication, all troop movements were halted April 15, 1865, and Sherman agreed to confer with Johnston. On April 17, 1865, they met at the farmhouse of James Bennett, near Durham's Station. They reached no conclusive agreement that day but met again April 18, 1865. At this meeting, they signed an agreement that included the provision for an armistice for all armies in the field while superior authorities considered the terms. On April 24, 1865, Grant arrived at Sherman's headquarters and informed the latter that the basis for his agreement with Johnston was completely unacceptable to the Federal government, and that President Andrew Johnson and his cabinet had unanimously rejected the terms. The terms allowed by Sherman had gone far beyond strictly military considerations, and he had, in effect, dealt with the policy of reconstruction and had attempted to make a peace agreement. Sherman was directed to give Johnston forty-eight hours notice (the truce was to expire at 11:00 A.M. April 26, 1865), and then, if Johnston had not surrendered, he was to resume hostilities. In addition, Grant was instructed to direct future military operations, but publicly he allowed Sherman to do so.

At Johnston's request, another meeting was arranged for April 26, 1865, at the Bennett house, and on that day Johnston yielded to the inevitable and surrendered his army on essentially the same terms as those given by Grant to Lee at Appomattox Court House. With the surrender of Johnston's army, the Carolinas Campaign came to an end. Schofield was given the responsibility for carrying out the surrender terms in North Carolina, and James H. Wilson was entrusted with a similar task at Macon in western Georgia. There was some uncertainty in the instructions given to Wilson, and Sherman prepared to go to Savannah to see to it that there was no misunderstanding.

Before leaving, on April 27, 1865, Sherman ordered the following dispositions of the troops under his command in North Carolina: Tenth Corps and Twenty-Third Corps were to remain in the state; the two brigades of Birge's Second Division, Nineteenth Corps were to return to the Department of the South; Kilpatrick's cavalry division was transferred to the Department of North Carolina, and was ordered to report to Schofield; Howard was to conduct the Army of the Tennessee to Richmond, Virginia; and Slocum was to march with the Army of Georgia to the same place.

Sherman left Raleigh on the night of April 28, 1865 and arrived on the Savannah River May 1, 1865. He concluded his business in Savannah, and began his return to the army the next day. He arrived at Morehead City May 4, 1865, and rejoined the army May 9, 1865, at Manchester, Virginia, opposite Richmond.

For further information relating to the activities of the troops of Sherman's army and of the troops of the Department of North Carolina, see Department of North Carolina, January 31, 1865–May 19, 1866.

The Union Forces commanded by Sherman during the Carolinas Campaign of January 1865–April 1865 were organized as follows:

SHERMAN'S ARMY, MILITARY DIVISION OF THE MISSISSIPPI
William T. Sherman

Right Wing (Army of the Tennessee), Oliver O. Howard

FIFTEENTH CORPS, John A. Logan

First Division, Charles R. Woods
First Brigade, Milo Smith, to January 23, 1865
William B. Woods
Second Brigade, Robert F. Catterson, to March 28, 1865
Charles C. Walcutt, to April 4, 1865
Robert F. Catterson
Third Brigade, George A. Stone

Note. William B. Woods commanded First Division temporarily April 2–5, 1865.

Second Division, William B. Hazen
First Brigade, Theodore Jones
Second Brigade, Wells S. Jones
Third Brigade, John M. Oliver

Third Division, John E. Smith
First Brigade, William T. Clark
Second Brigade, Clark R. Wever, to April 7, 1865
John Tourtellotte

Note. Third Division was discontinued April 26, 1865, and the troops were transferred to the other three divisions of Fifteenth Corps.

Fourth Division, John M. Corse
First Brigade, Elliott W. Rice
Second Brigade, Robert N. Adams
Third Brigade, Frederick J. Hurlbut

Artillery, William H. Ross
Battery H, 1st Illinois Light Artillery, Francis De Gress
Robert S. Gray
Battery H, 1st Michigan Light Artillery, Edward B. Wright
Battery H, 1st Missouri Light Artillery, Charles M. Callahan
12th Battery, Wisconsin Light Artillery, William Zickerick

SEVENTEENTH CORPS, Frank P. Blair, Jr.

First Division, Joseph A. Mower, to April 3, 1865
　Manning F. Force
　First Brigade, Charles S. Sheldon, to January 25, 1865
　　John W. Fuller
　Second Brigade, John W. Sprague, to January 29, 1865
　　Milton Montgomery, to March 28, 1865
　　John W. Sprague
　Third Brigade, John Tillson, to March 26, 1865
　　Charles H. De Groat, to April 10, 1865
　　James S. Wright
　　John Tillson

Third Division, Mortimer D. Leggett, to January 15, 1865
　Manning F. Force, to March 31, 1865
　Mortimer D. Leggett
　First Brigade, Manning F. Force, to January 15, 1865
　　Cassius Fairchild, to March 31, 1865
　　Manning F. Force, to April 3, 1865
　　Charles Ewing
　Second Brigade, Greenberry F. Wiles, to March 28, 1865
　　Robert K. Scott

Fourth Division, Giles A. Smith
　First Brigade, Benjamin F. Potts
　Third Brigade, William W. Belknap

Artillery, Allen C. Waterhouse
　Frederick Welker
　Battery C, 1st Michigan Light Artillery, William W. Hyzer
　1st Battery, Minnesota Light Artillery, William Z. Clayton
　15th Battery, Ohio Light Artillery, Lyman Bailey
　James Burdick

Left Wing (Army of Georgia), Henry W. Slocum

FOURTEENTH CORPS, Jefferson C. Davis

First Division, William P. Carlin, to March 28, 1865
　George P. Buell, April 4, 1865
　Charles C. Walcutt
　First Brigade, Harrison C. Hobart
　Second Brigade, George P. Buell, to March 28, 1865
　　Michael H. Fitch, to April 4, 1865
　　George P. Buell
　Third Brigade, David Miles, to March 19, 1865, wounded
　　Arnold McMahan, to March 28, 1865
　　Henry A. Hambright

Second Division, James D. Morgan
　First Brigade, William Vandever

Second Brigade, John S. Pearce, to February 7, 1865
　John G. Mitchell
　Third Brigade, Benjamin D. Fearing, to March 19, 1865, wounded
　James W. Langley

Third Division, Absalom Baird
　First Brigade, Morton C. Hunter
　Second Brigade, Thomas Doan, to April 3, 1865
　　Newell Gleason
　Third Brigade, George P. Este, to March 29, 1865
　　Hubbard K. Milward, to April 9, 1865
　　George S. Greene

Artillery, Charles Houghtaling
　Battery C, 1st Illinois Light Artillery, Joseph R. Channel, Palmer F. Scovel
　Battery I, 2nd Illinois Light Artillery, Judson Rich
　19th Battery, Indiana Light Artillery, Samuel D. Webb, Clinton Keeler
　5th Battery, Wisconsin Light Artillery, Joseph McKnight, Elijah Booth, Jr.

TWENTIETH CORPS, Alpheus S. Williams, to April 2, 1865
Joseph A. Mower

First Division, Nathaniel J. Jackson, to April 2, 1865
　Alpheus S. Williams
　First Brigade, James L. Selfridge
　Second Brigade, William Hawley
　Third Brigade, James S. Robinson

Second Division, John W. Geary
　First Brigade, Ario Pardee, Jr., to March 30, 1865
　　George W. Mindil
　Second Brigade, George W. Mindil, to March 30, 1865
　　Patrick H. Jones
　Third Brigade, Henry A. Barnum

Third Division, William T. Ward
　First Brigade, Henry Case, to April 19, 1865
　　Benjamin Harrison
　Second Brigade, Daniel Dustin
　Third Brigade, Samuel Ross, to January 16, 1865
　　William Cogswell

Artillery, John A. Reynolds, to April 1, 1865
　Charles E. Winegar
　Battery L, 1st New York Light Artillery, Charles E. Winegar
　Warren L. Scott
　Battery M, 1st New York Light Artillery, Edward P. Newkirk
　Battery C, 1st Ohio Light Artillery, Jerome B. Stephens

Battery E, Pennsylvania Light Artillery, Thomas S. Sloan

CAVALRY

Third Division, Cavalry Corps, Military Division of the Mississippi, Judson Kilpatrick
First Brigade, Thomas J. Jordan
Second Brigade, Smith D. Atkins
Third Brigade, George Spencer, to about April 8, 1865, on leave
    Michael Kerwin, to April 21, 1865
    Thomas Heath
Fourth Brigade, William B. Way
Artillery
    23rd Battery, New York Light Artillery, Samuel Kittinger
    10th Battery, Wisconsin Light Artillery, Yates V. Beebe

Note. Fourth Brigade was organized provisionally January 25, 1865 from dismounted men of Third Cavalry Division. The 1st Regiment consisted of men belonging to First Brigade; 2nd Regiment of men from Second Brigade; and 3rd Regiment of men from Third Brigade.

Center (Army of the Ohio), John M. Schofield

TENTH CORPS, Alfred H. Terry

First Division, Henry W. Birge
    Third Brigade, Nicholas W. Day
    Artillery
        22nd Battery, Indiana Light Artillery, George W. Alexander

Note 1. Third Brigade was formerly Third Brigade, Second Division, Nineteenth Corps from Savannah, Georgia.
Note 2. First Brigade of First Division was at Morehead City, and Second Brigade, First Division was at Wilmington, North Carolina, and they were not with Sherman's army.

Second Division, Adelbert Ames
    First Brigade, Rufus Daggett
    Second Brigade, William B. Coan, to April 5, 1865
        John S. Littell
    Third Brigade, Frederick Granger
    Artillery
        16th Battery, New York Light Artillery, Richard H. Lee

Note. Second Division was formerly Second Division, Twenty-Fourth Corps.

Third Division, Charles J. Paine

First Brigade, Delevan Bates
Second Brigade, Samuel A. Duncan
Third Brigade, John H. Holman, to April 22, 1865
    Albert M. Blackman

Note. Third Division was formerly Third Division, Twenty-Fifth Corps.

Unattached Artillery
    Battery E, 3rd United States Artillery, John R. Myrick

TWENTY-THIRD CORPS, John M. Schofield, to March 31, 1865
Jacob D. Cox

First Division, Thomas H. Ruger
    First Brigade, Israel N. Stiles
    Second Brigade, John C. McQuiston
    Third Brigade, Minor T. Thomas
    Artillery
        22nd Battery, Indiana Light Artillery (to April 5, 1865), George W. Alexander
        Battery F, 1st Michigan Light Artillery, Byron D. Paddock
        Elgin Battery, Illinois Light Artillery, Andrew M. Wood

Note 1. Twenty-Third Corps was transferred from Tennessee to North Carolina during the latter part of January and in February 1865.
Note 2. Stiles commanded First Brigade after March 14, 1865.

Second Division, Nathaniel C. McLean, to April 4, 1865
    Orlando H. Moore, to April 8, 1865
    Darius N. Couch, to April 20, 1865
    Joseph A. Cooper, to April 26, 1865
    Darius N. Couch
    First Brigade, Orlando H, Moore, to April 26, 1865
        Joseph A. Cooper
    Second Brigade, John Mehringer
    Third Brigade, Silas A. Strickland
    Artillery
        15th Battery, Indiana Light Artillery, Alonzo D. Harvey
        19th Battery, Ohio Light Artillery, Frank Wilson

Third Division, James W. Reilly, to April 7, 1865, resigned
    Samuel P. Carter
    First Brigade, Oscar W. Sterl
    Second Brigade, John S. Casement
    Third Brigade, Thomas J. Henderson
    Artillery
        23rd Battery, Indiana Light Artillery, James H. Myers

Battery D, 1st Ohio Light Artillery, Giles J. Cockerill

Cecil C. Reed

District of Beaufort (Division), Samuel P. Carter
First Brigade, Peter J. Claassen
Second Brigade, James Stewart, Jr.
Artillery, William E. Mercer
Battery C, 3rd New York Light Artillery, E. Barton Wood
Battery I, 3rd New York Light Artillery, William Richardson

RESERVE ARTILLERY, William E. Mercer
Battery C, 3rd New York Light Artillery, E. Barton Wood
Battery D, 3rd New York Light Artillery, Stephen Van Heusen
Battery G, 3rd New York Light Artillery, William A. Kelsey
Battery I, 3rd New York Light Artillery, William Richardson

Note. The Reserve Artillery was organized April 5, 1865.

CHANCELLORSVILLE, VIRGINIA CAMPAIGN
APRIL 27, 1863–MAY 6, 1863

Following the Battle of Fredericksburg, the Army of the Potomac remained more or less quietly in its winter quarters in the vicinity of Falmouth, Virginia until spring. There were the usual skirmishes, scouts, and reconnaissances, and in the latter part of January 1863, Ambrose E. Burnside conducted his ill-fated "Mud March" in an attempt to move on the rear of Robert E. Lee's army at Fredericksburg. William W. Averell's Second Cavalry Division was also engaged at Kelly's Ford (Kellysville) March 17, 1863, with Fitzhugh Lee's cavalry brigade of James E. B. (Jeb) Stuart's cavalry division.

There were some important changes during the winter. Joseph Hooker relieved Burnside in command of the army January 26, 1863; the grand divisions were abolished February 5, 1863; the Cavalry Corps was organized under George Stoneman February 7, 1863; Ninth Corps was transferred to the Department of Virginia February 6–21, 1863; and

Eleventh Corps and Twelfth Corps moved up from the rear and rejoined the army.

As the rainy season in Virginia ended in April 1863, Hooker prepared his plans for the opening of the spring campaign. There was some urgency in beginning operations as soon as possible because it was essential that a major battle be fought before the terms of service of the nine-month and two-year regiments with the army expired. The plan finally adopted by Hooker was as follows: John Sedgwick, with three corps of the army, was to make a diversionary movement below Fredericksburg to hold the Army of Northern Virginia in its entrenchments near the town. Henry W. Slocum was to lead three corps and the cavalry on a wide turning movement, cross the Rappahannock River at Kelly's Ford, twenty-seven miles above Fredericksburg, then cross the Rapidan, march down the river toward the left flank of Lee's army, and open Banks' Ford. This would reunite the two wings of the army and secure a line of retreat in case of the defeat of Sedgwick's command. Darius N. Couch's Second Corps was to remain on the Rappahannock near Fredericksburg. To ensure surprise, John Gibbon's Second Division, Second Corps was left behind at Falmouth, because its encampment was in full view of the enemy on the opposite side of the river.

It was Hooker's plan to give battle in the open country near Banks' Ford, and take the Confederate line on the heights of Fredericksburg in reverse. His plan thus far was simply to defeat Lee's army, but he then took an additional step that he hoped would result in its capture. He directed Stoneman to start with his Cavalry Corps two weeks in advance of the main body of the army, cross the Rappahannock at the upper fords, and then move on Lee's communications with Richmond. Stoneman's primary mission was to destroy the railroads, canals, and telegraph lines, and to intercept supplies of all kinds destined for Lee's army. This, Hooker believed, might force Lee to withdraw, but if he did not and was defeated in the battle near Fredericksburg, Stoneman would be on his line of retreat where he could delay him until Hooker came up and forced his surrender.

Stoneman started April 13, 1863, but was detained on the upper Rappahannock by flood waters and bad roads until April 29, 1863. Finally when the floods had subsided, the infantry, cavalry, and artillery all crossed together. As a result of Stoneman's delay at the river, the Battle of Chancellorsville had ended in a Union defeat before the cavalry had accomplished its mission, and its operations had little or no effect in obstructing Lee's movements. For details of Stoneman's Raid, see below.

In late April 1863, Hooker ordered a number of demonstrations that were intended to confuse Lee as to his real intentions in the upcoming campaign. He threatened Kelly's Ford April 21, 1863, and sent expeditions to Port Conway and Port Royal, twenty miles below Fredericksburg, April 21–24, 1863, to make a pretense of crossing the Rappahannock.

The Turning Movement, April 27–30, 1863. The troops assigned to Hooker's turning movement consisted of George G. Meade's Fifth Corps, Oliver O. Howard's Eleventh Corps, and Henry W. Slocum's Twelfth Corps. In addition, Alfred Pleasonton, with Thomas C. Devin's Second Brigade, First Cavalry Division, was assigned to march with these corps.

Early on the morning of April 27, 1863, the three infantry corps marched from their camps to Hartwood Church, where they bivouacked for the night. Eleventh Corps advanced from Brooke Station on the Richmond, Fredericksburg, and Potomac Railroad, Twelfth Corps from Stafford Court House, and Fifth Corps from its positions along the railroad south of Potomac Creek. The next day, the Right Wing, with Eleventh Corps in the lead, marched to the vicinity of Mount Holly Church, about two miles from Kelly's Ford. Eleventh Corps went into camp there about 4:00 P.M., and Twelfth Corps and then Fifth Corps came in later. The latter did not arrive until after 10:00 that night.

At this point, Slocum was ordered to assume command of Eleventh Corps and Twelfth Corps, cross the Rappahannock at Kelly's Ford, and then move with them to Germanna Ford on the Rapidan River. Alpheus S. Williams assumed temporary command of Twelfth Corps for the march. Meade was also ordered to cross at Kelly's Ford the next day, and then march to Ely's Ford on the Rapidan. Both Sedgwick and Meade were to cross the Rapidan that day if possible. Pleasonton, with Devin's brigade of his First Cavalry Division, reported to Slocum at Kelly's Ford, and Devin's regiments were assigned to the three corps as

follows: Duncan McVicar's 6th New York Cavalry, to Twelfth Corps; Josiah H. Kellogg's 17th Pennsylvania Cavalry, to Eleventh Corps; and Pennock Huey's 8th Pennsylvania Cavalry and one troop of 1st Michigan Cavalry, to Fifth Corps. This arrangement was in effect until the Right Wing reached Chancellorsville.

At 10:00 that night, April 28, 1863, as soon as the pontoon bridge at Kelly's Ford was completed, Eleventh Corps began to cross, and a little before daylight the next morning it was over the river. It then established a defensive position to cover the crossing of the other two corps. As soon as Eleventh Corps had cleared the bridge, Twelfth Corps followed, and by 11:00 A.M. it was across. Twelfth Corps then immediately marched for Germanna Ford on the Rapidan, and it was preceded by the 6th New York Cavalry, under the personal direction of Pleasonton. Eleventh Corps followed Twelfth Corps and was protected on its right during the march by the 17th Pennsylvania Cavalry.

At 11:00 A.M., when the bridge was clear, George Sykes' Second Division and Charles Griffin's First Division of Meade's Fifth Corps began their crossing of the Rappahannock. Then Meade, with these two divisions, promptly marched for Ely's Ford on the Rapidan. They were preceded by the troopers of the 8th Pennsylvania Cavalry under the immediate direction of Devin.

Twelfth Corps reached Germanna Ford during the afternoon of April 29, 1863 and, after overcoming some slight enemy resistance, began crossing the river. The crossing continued until after dark, and the corps went into camp a short distance beyond the ford. Eleventh Corps followed Twelfth Corps over the river and was in camp by 4:00 on the morning of April 30, 1863.

Meade, with the head of Griffin's First Division, Fifth Corps, arrived at Ely's Ford at 5:00 P.M. April 29, 1863. Devin's cavalry then crossed the river, and First Division followed, but it did not complete the crossing until after dark. Second Division then crossed, and both divisions bivouacked on the right bank of the Rapidan by midnight.

Stoneman's Cavalry Corps, which, as has been noted, had been delayed on the upper Rappahannock by high water, arrived at Kelly's Ford at 8:00 A.M. April 29, 1863 and crossed the river that day by the ford at the same time that the infantry was crossing on the bridge. When across the river, Stoneman moved to the right toward Culpeper Court House and Stevensburg (see below, Stoneman's Raid).

Andrew A. Humphreys' Third Division, Fifth Corps was left at Kelly's Ford to cover the passage of the corps' trains, and to accompany the pontoon train to Ely's Ford. Humphreys crossed the river at 8:00 P.M., but the pontoons were not ready until 11:30 P.M., and at that time he marched for Ely's Ford. At 3:00 A.M. April 30, 1863, Humphreys was forced to halt until daylight, and he did not reach the Rapidan until between noon and 1:00 P.M that day. Meantime, at 3:00 A.M. April 30, 1863, at the time that Humphreys halted his column, Meade had ordered Devin to move forward with his cavalry toward Chancellorsville and United States Ford. Devin started out on the Chancellorsville Road, and just before reaching the intersection with the road leading to United States Ford, he encountered some resistance. He then charged and pushed on toward Chancellorsville. When Meade was informed of this, he ordered Sykes' division to United States Ford and sent Griffin's division on to Chancellorsville, where it arrived about 11:00 A.M. After Sykes reached United States Ford, he marched back about 1:00 P.M and joined Griffin at Chancellorsville. Both divisions bivouacked in line of battle, with the right resting on Chancellorsville and the left extending in a northeast direction toward the river. Humphreys' division left Ely's Ford shortly after noon, and halted for the night near Big Hunting Creek (or Run), about two miles from Chancellorsville.

Slocum's Twelfth Corps left its bivouac near Germanna Ford at daylight April 30, 1863, advanced on the Germanna Ford Road past Wilderness Tavern to the Orange Plank Road, and then followed that road toward Chancellorsville. When Slocum arrived there about 2:00 P.M., he formed his corps on a curving line that ran southeast from Old School House on the Orange Plank Road to a point east of Hazel Grove, and then on a line eastward to the Plank Road, about 600 yards south of Chancellorsville. Alpheus S. Williams' First Division was on the right of the corps line, with Joseph F. Knipe's First Brigade on the right, next to the Plank Road; Thomas H. Ruger's Third Brigade on the center; and Samuel Ross' Second Brigade on the left. John W. Geary's Second Division was on the left of the

corps, with George S. Greene's Third Brigade on the right of the division, next to Ross; Thomas L. Kane's Second Brigade on the center; and Charles Candy's First Brigade on the left, next to the Plank Road.

Howard's Eleventh Corps followed Twelfth Corps during the day, and about 4:00 P.M. reached Dowdall's Tavern (Melzi Chancellor's), about one-fourth of a mile east of the junction of the Plank Road and the Turnpike. Howard was ordered to cover the right of the army, and accordingly, he posted his command near Hunting Run, on the right of Twelfth Corps. Charles Devens' First Division occupied the right of Howard's line. Nathaniel C. McLean's Second Brigade was formed along the Turnpike at the Talley (Tally) farm, facing south, and Leopold Von Gilsa's First Brigade was about a half mile farther to the right, perpendicular to the road and facing northwest. Skirmishers covered the interval between Second Brigade and Third Brigade.

In the rear of Devens' division, on open ground of the Hawkins farm and about 500 yards north of the Turnpike, Carl Schurz formed his Third Division, facing westward. Wladimir Krzyzanowski's Second Brigade was just west of the Hawkins house, and Alexander Schimmelfennig's First Brigade was on the right of Second Brigade. Adolph Von Steinwehr's Second Division was formed along the Plank Road, and extended from the left of Devens' division to the right of Twelfth Corps at Old School House. Adolphus Buschbeck's First Brigade was on the right of the division near Dowdall's Tavern, and Francis C. Barlow's Second Brigade was on the left, next to Twelfth Corps.

When Slocum arrived at Chancellorsville on the afternoon of April 30, 1863, he assumed command of Meade's Fifth Corps, in addition to Eleventh Corps and Twelfth Corps. Hooker, with his staff, left Falmouth for Chancellorsville about 4:00 P.M., and arrived there sometime between 5:00 and 6:00 that evening. He then assumed direct command of the troops on that part of the field; Slocum resumed command of Twelfth Corps; and Williams returned to his First Division, Twelfth Corps.

After dark on the night of April 30, 1863, the 6th New York Cavalry, while on a reconnaissance on the Spotsylvania Court House Road, encountered Confederate cavalry of Fitzhugh Lee's brigade, and in the resulting fighting the commander of the regiment, Duncan McVicar, was killed.

Movements near Fredericksburg, April 28, 1863–May 1, 1863.

There was considerable activity among the troops near Fredericksburg April 28, 1863. John F. Reynolds' First Corps left its camps at Belle Plain and Fletcher's Chapel and marched to the rear of the crossing of the Rappahannock at the mouth of White Oak Creek (Pollock's Mill Creek), near Pollock's Mill. James S. Wadsworth's First Division crossed the river the next day, but the other two divisions remained on the north bank. There was no change in position of First Corps April 30, 1863. John Sedgwick's Sixth Corps also marched from its camps near White Oak Church to the vicinity of Franklin's Old Crossing, near the mouth of Deep Run. William T. H. Brooks' First Division crossed the Rappahannock the next day, but the other two divisions did not follow until the evening of May 2, 1863. Daniel E. Sickles' Third Corps broke camp near Falmouth April 28, 1863, and marched four miles down the river and took position between First Corps and Sixth Corps, and in supporting distance of both. The next day Sickles moved nearer the upper crossing.

Also on the morning of April 28, 1863, Darius N. Couch moved from near Falmouth to Banks' Ford with Winfield S. Hancock's First Division and William H. French's Third Division of his Second Corps. Samuel S. Carroll's First Brigade of French's division was sent to United States Ford that morning. John Gibbon's Second Division, Second Corps remained in position near Falmouth, and was subject to Hooker's direct orders. At 2:00 P.M. April 29, 1863, the divisions of Hancock and French marched to United States Ford, and spent the night and a part of the next day preparing for the crossing of the river. It was not until 3:15 the next afternoon that the pontoons were laid and the approaches were completed, and then Couch began to cross. The head of his column arrived at the Chandler house, about three-fourths of a mile north of Chancellorsville, at 10:00 that night. The divisions closed up and went into bivouac about midnight.

On April 28, 1863, Edward E. Cross, with his own 5th New Hampshire and 81st Pennsylvania of John C. Caldwell's First Brigade, First Division, Second Corps, was detached and assigned to picket the houses and roads to United States Ford to prevent the enemy from receiving information about Hooker's movements. Two days later, Cross with his two regiments marched from the vicinity of Banks' Ford to United States Ford, where he was joined by 88th New York of Thomas F. Meagher's Second Brigade, First Division, Second Corps. These three regiments were then organized into a provisional brigade of Second Corps under Cross. This brigade has also been referred to as Fifth Brigade of Hancock's First Division, Second Corps. Cross commanded the brigade throughout the campaign. It was left as a guard for the ammunition train until it crossed the river at United States Ford, and it then rejoined Hancock May 1, 1863. Meagher's brigade, less two regiments, was sent to the vicinity of Scott's Dam.

When it became evident that the enemy did not intend to attack the bridgeheads of First Corps and Sixth Corps below Fredericksburg, Hooker sent Sickles an order, which he received at 1:00 P.M. April 30, 1863, directing him to march with his Third Corps to United States Ford and then report to the commander of the army at Chancellorsville. Sickles marched to the vicinity of United States Ford that evening and went into camp, but the last of his troops did not come up until about midnight. The positions of First Corps and Sixth Corps were not changed April 30, 1863.

Battle of Chancellorsville, May 1, 1863.

During the morning of May 1, 1863, the troops that were under orders to join Hooker near Chancellorsville began to arrive. Humphreys' Third Division, Fifth Corps came up from Big Hunting Creek about 7:00 A.M. and joined the other two divisions of the corps. A half hour later, Third Corps began crossing the Rappahannock at United States Ford. David B. Birney's First Division crossed first, and it was followed by Amiel W. Whipple's Third Division, and then Hiram G. Berry's Second Division. Sickles reported in person to Hooker at Chancellorsville at 9:00 A.M., and two hours later Birney's division began arriving at the junction of the Ely's Ford Road and the United States Ford Road, near the Chandler house. Gershom Mott's Third Brigade of Berry's division was left behind at United States Ford, on the west bank, to guard the crossing.

About 8:00 A.M., French's Third Division of

Couch's Second Corps, with Rufus D. Pettit's Battery B, 1st New York Artillery of Hancock's division, was ordered to march to Todd's Tavern, about eight miles southwest of Chancellorsville. After advancing about one mile, French was delayed by troops of Twelfth Corps on the Plank Road, and he was then ordered back to his original position at Chandlers'. Between 9:00 and 10:00 A.M.,Cross' Provisional Brigade crossed the Rappahannock and joined Hancock's division about 4:00 that afternoon.

While the above-described movements of the Army of the Potomac were in progress, Confederate forces were assembling on Hooker's front. On the night of April 29, 1863, Richard H. Anderson's division of James Longstreet's corps was sent from Fredericksburg toward Chancellorsville. Anderson then learned that some of Hooker's troops had crossed the Rapidan and were approaching in considerable force. Accordingly, he retired on the morning of April 30, 1863 to the intersection of the Mine Road and the Plank Road, near Tabernacle Church, and entrenched.

The inactivity of First Corps and Sixth Corps below Fredericksburg indicated to Lee that the principal Federal attack would be made elsewhere. Retaining Jubal A. Early's division of Thomas J. (Stonewall) Jackson's corps and William Barksdale's brigade of Lafayette McLaws' division of Longstreet's corps at Fredericksburg, Lee sent McLaws with the remainder of his division to support Anderson. McLaws set out at midnight, and at 6:00 the next morning arrived and took position on the right of Anderson. Jackson followed McLaws at dawn May 1, 1863 with the remaining divisions of his corps, and he reached Anderson's position at 8:00 A.M. Upon arriving there, Jackson assumed command of all Confederate troops. At 11:00 A.M., near Tabernacle Church, McLaws and Anderson moved forward on the Turnpike and on the Plank Road, and Jackson followed Anderson on the Plank Road. Longstreet, with the divisions of John B. Hood and George E. Pickett, was in southeastern Virginia.

About 11:00 A.M. the troops that Hooker had assembled about Chancellorsville began their advance toward the open country in the direction of Fredericksburg. To guard the rear against enemy cavalry during the advance, Third Corps was formed on a line of outposts that extended from United States Ford to the Plank Road, facing west. Berry's division was on the right and Whipple's division was on the left. At about 11:00 A.M., Charles K. Graham's First Brigade of Birney's division, with John G. Turnbull's Batteries F and K, 3rd United States Artillery, was ordered from near Chancellorsville to picket the country to the left of Whipple. Graham moved to Dowdall's Tavern at 1:00 P.M., but upon arriving there he found his assigned position occupied by Eleventh Corps. Hooker then ordered Graham to halt at Dowdall's Tavern.

Between 10:00 and 11:00 P.M., Fifth Corps advanced toward Fredericksburg to uncover Banks' Ford. Griffin's First Division, followed by Humphreys' Third Division, moved forward on the River Road, while Sykes' Second Division marched on the Turnpike to the right. About noon, when Sykes had reached a point near Mrs. Lewis' house, a little more than two and one-half miles from Chancellorsville, he ran into William Mahone's brigade of Anderson's division and the brigades of William T. Wofford and Paul J. Semmes of McLaws' division. At that time, Edward A. Perry's brigade of Anderson's division was advancing toward Sykes' left, and Joseph B. Kershaw's brigade of McLaws' division was moving toward his right. On the Plank Road to the south and rear of Sykes were the brigades of Ambrose R. Wright and Carnot Posey of Anderson's division.

Sykes then deployed his division, with Sidney Burbank's Second Brigade in front and extending across the road; Patrick H. O'Rorke's Third Brigade in rear of Burbank, and also on the road; and Romeyn B. Ayres' First Brigade on the left of Burbank, north of the road. Sykes was completely isolated, being out of contact with Meade on his left and Slocum on his right. By 1:30 P.M., Meade had advanced on the River Road to the north of Sykes, and had reached the vicinity of Mott Run (Duerson Mill), a little more than two miles to the northeast of Sykes. Slocum's Twelfth Corps was about a mile to the right and rear near the Aldrich house on the Orange Plank Road. Thus, soon after 1:00 P.M., Sykes was in the presence of a large enemy force, and he was outflanked on both the right and left. When Hooker learned of this, he ordered Sykes to retire toward Chancellorsville, and at about the same time, he ordered Couch to support him. A short time later, Couch advanced with John C. Caldwell's First Brigade, Samuel K. Zook's Third Brigade, and John R. Brooke's Fourth Brigade of Winfield S. Hancock's First Division, Second Corps. Meagher's Second Brigade was near Scott's Dam. Sykes began his withdrawal, probably at about 1:30 P.M.

At about 11:00 P.M. Slocum's Twelfth Corps had advanced from south of Chancellorsville on the Plank Road toward Fredericksburg. About a mile out, Slocum encountered enemy skirmishers and formed his corps in line of battle. Geary's Second Division was on the right of the road, with Greene's Third Brigade on the left, next to the road, and Kane's Second Brigade on the right. Candy's First Brigade was in rear of Kane. Williams' First Division was on the left of the road, with Knipe's First Brigade on the right, next to the road, and Ruger's Third Brigade on the left. Ross' Second Brigade was placed in reserve. Slocum completed his deployment about 1:00 P.M., and then advanced about a mile to the Aldrich house, where he found the brigades of Wright and Posey of Anderson's division of Longstreet's corps, and Stephen D. Ramseur's brigade of Robert E. Rodes' division of Jackson's corps. Slocum's advance troops were pushed back on the main line, and the opposing batteries opened fire. Then, at about 1:30 P.M., Hooker ordered Twelfth Corps to return to its positions of the night before.

At noon May 1, 1863, Howard's Eleventh Corps was ordered to take part in the general advance of the army, and Howard was directed to move forward on the Plank Road and take position about one mile in rear of Twelfth Corps. Almost immediately, however, the order was countermanded, and the corps returned to its former positions.

A little after 2:00 P.M., Couch, who was advancing with Hancock's division on the Turnpike, met Sykes about one mile east of Chancellorsville. Sykes, who was withdrawing from Mott's Run at the time, passed to the rear of Hancock, and then returned to his position of the night before, on the left of Twelfth Corps. Hancock covered Sykes' withdrawal, and then he too was ordered to fall back to the position that he had occupied that morning. About 4:30 P.M. he arrived on that line, which was about three-fourths of a mile east of Chancellorsville.

About 1:00 P.M., Hooker sent an order for the two divisions of Fifth Corps, which were then advancing on the River Road, to return to Chancellorsville. The order apparently was not received, however, until about two hours later, at which time they had arrived at the Decker house, about two miles from Banks' Ford. Humphreys immediately turned back, but Griffin appears not to have received the order until between 5:00 and 6:00 P.M., and then he too hurried back.

After the collapse of his advance toward Fredericksburg, Hooker decided to abandon the offensive and form a defensive line and wait for an attack by Lee. At 4:20 P.M. he sent orders to that effect to the commanders of Eleventh Corps, Twelfth Corps, Second Corps, and Fifth Corps. The positions taken by these four corps on the evening of May 1, 1863 are described in the following paragraphs.

When Eleventh Corps returned from its brief advance on the Plank Road, in rear of Twelfth Corps, it resumed its former positions, with some changes. Devens' First Division remained on the right of the line, on the Turnpike, with Von Gilsa's brigade on the right and McLean's brigade on the left. That night, however, Von Gilsa was drawn in so as to connect on the left with McLean. One section of Julius Dieckmann's 13th Battery, New York Light Artillery was with Von Gilsa, and the rest of the battery was on the left of Devens' division. Schurz's Third Division, which earlier had been on the Hawkins farm, north of the Turnpike, was placed in line on the Turnpike, between Devens' division on the right and Von Steinwehr's Second Division on the left. Schimmelfennig's brigade was on the right of the division line, next to McLean's brigade, and Krzyzanowski's brigade was on the left, next to Buschbeck's brigade of Von Steinwehr's division. Hubert Dilger's Battery I, 1st Ohio Light Artillery, of Schurz's division, was placed at the junction of the Plank Road and the Turnpike, covering the Plank Road and the valley and woods beyond. Von Steinwehr's division was on the Plank Road, to the left of Schurz's division. Buschbeck's First Brigade was in the fields a short distance south of Dowdall's Tavern, with its right near the junction of the Plank Road and the Turnpike. Barlow's Second Brigade was north of the Plank Road, in rear of Howard's headquarters at Dowdall's Tavern. One section of Michael Wiedrich's Battery I, 1st New York Light Artillery of Von Steinwehr's division was placed in rear of Dowdall's Tavern. and the remaining guns of the battery were posted on high ground near the right of Buschbeck's line.

Twelfth Corps occupied essentially the same positions as the night before. Williams' division held the right of the line from a point on the Plank Road about one-fourth mile east of Old School House, to a point about 700 yards south and a little to the west of Fairview. Knipe's First Brigade was on the right, next to the Plank Road, facing west; Ruger's Third Brigade was on the center of the line, facing southwest, with two regiments entrenched in advance of the main line, just north of Hazel Grove; and Ross' Second Brigade was on the left, facing southwest and south. Geary's division was on the left of the corps line, and it held the ground from the left of Ross' brigade to a point about 400 yards south of Chancellorsville. Greene's Third Brigade was on the right, and Kane's Second Brigade was on the center of the line, and both brigades faced south. Candy's First Brigade was along the Plank Road, on the left, facing southeast, with two regiments on the left of the road, facing south. The artillery of Twelfth Corps, twenty-eight guns, was divided into two equal parts, and it was posted so as to cover the front of the corps. Joseph M. Knap's Battery E, Pennsylvania Light Artillery, Robert B. Hampton's Battery F, Pennsylvania Light Artillery, and Edward D. Muhlenberg's section of Franklin B. Crosby's Battery F, 4th United States Artillery were posted on the left of Geary's line, at the junction of the Plank Road and the Turnpike, near Chancellorsville. Charles E. Winegar's Battery M, 1st New York Light Artillery, Robert H. Fitzhugh's Battery K, 1st New York Light Artillery, and the other four pieces of Crosby's battery were posted in rear of the center of Slocum's line, on the high ground at Fairview. There was a gap of about one-half mile between the left of Eleventh Corps and the right of Twelfth Corps, but this part of the line was strengthened later in the day by troops of Daniel E. Sickles' Third Corps (see below).

When Sykes' division of Fifth Corps returned on the afternoon of May 1, 1863 from its advance toward Fredericksburg, it was formed along the Turnpike, with its right connecting with Twelfth Corps near Chancellorsville, and its left extending to the southeast to the crossing of Great Meadow Swamp. Sykes' line faced southwest, with Ayres' First Brigade on the right, Burbank's Second Brigade in the center, and O'Rorke's Third Brigade on the left. Only Malbone F. Watson's Battery I, Fifth United States Artillery accompanied Sykes when he advanced, and later that battery was put in position near the Chancellor house. The other battery of the division, Frank C. Gibbs' Battery L, 1st Ohio Light Artillery, did not arrive from United States Ford until 9:00 that night, and it then went into park near Chancellorsville.

When Hancock's division returned from covering Sykes' withdrawal at 4:30 P.M., it was formed on a line that extended almost due north from the left of Sykes' division at Great Meadow Swamp, and ended a short distance north of the River Road. The line faced east, with Brooke's Fourth Brigade on the right and Caldwell's First Brigade on the left. Zook's Third Brigade was held in rear on the River Road, and Meagher's Second Brigade was on detached duty at Scott's Dam. Cross, with his Provisional Brigade, arrived a short time later and was placed in reserve along the Turnpike, in rear of Sykes.

When French's Third Division, Second Corps returned to Chandlers' after being recalled from its reconnaissance toward Todd's Tavern, it remained massed there until evening. It was then advanced a short distance toward Chancellorsville, and deployed on a line parallel to the Plank Road. William Hays' Second Brigade was on the right of this line, and Carroll's First Brigade was on the left. John D. MacGregor's Third Brigade was held in rear near Chandlers'.

About dusk, Hooker directed Meade to form his Fifth Corps on a line extending from Chancellorsville to the Rappahannock River. Meade at once sent Humphreys' division to the left, to the vicinity of the Childs house, on the Old Mine (or Mountain) Road, to guard the approach to United States Ford by the River Road. Meagher's Second Brigade of Hancock's Second Division was already nearby, on the river at Scott's Dam, and Humphreys placed Erastus B. Tyler's First Brigade to the right and rear of Meagher, with its right on the Old Mine Road, a short distance northwest of the Childs house. Peter H. Allabach's Second Brigade was sent to the right of Tyler, with its right extending to the southwest along the Mineral Spring Road in the direction of Chancellorsville.

When Griffin's division returned from Deckers' that evening, it formed on a line that ran northward from the left of Hancock to Mineral Spring (or Mine) Creek. James Barnes' First Brigade was on the right of this line, next to Hancock; James McQuade's Second Brigade was on the left of Barnes; and Thomas B. W. Stockton's Third Brigade was on the left of McQuade, with its left on Mineral Spring Creek.

At 4:00 P.M. May 1, 1863, Sickles was ordered to bring up his entire Third Corps (except Gershom Mott's Third Brigade and Francis W. Seeley's Battery K, 4th United States Artillery, which were guarding United States Ford) and put them in position as quickly as possible on a line parallel to the Plank Road at Chancellorsville. Sickles withdrew Whipple's and Berry's outposts, and marched to join Birney's division near Chancellorsville.

Meantime, after Slocum's Twelfth Corps had withdrawn from its short advance on the Orange Plank Road earlier in the afternoon, Wright's brigade of Anderson's division was ordered to move across the Plank Road and then on to the left and attempt to get on Hooker's right flank and rear. Wright advanced on the line of an unfinished railroad to the Wellford (Catharine) Furnace Road, near the Wellford house (commonly spelled on maps as Welford or Catherine), and then he marched northward on the latter road to the Furnace, where he arrived about 4:30 P.M. A short distance north, he encountered the outposts of Williams' division and, with the help of Stuart's artillery, drove them back to their entrenchments on the northern edge of Hazel Grove. Wright then came under the fire of Winegar's battery and the section of Crosby's battery and was forced to retire.

At 5:00 P.M., while Wright was advancing on Slocum, Birney moved up with J. H. Hobart Ward's Second Brigade and Samuel B. Hayman's Third Brigade and took position in rear of Chancellorsville. Birney also sent to Dowdall's Tavern for the return of Graham's brigade, which had moved to that point earlier in the day. When Graham rejoined Birney, he was sent to the rear of Fairview to support Slocum's artillery, and also to be ready to aid Williams if that became necessary. About sunset, Birney marched westward along the Plank Road with the brigades of Ward and Hayman to the right of Twelfth Corps, and he bivouacked for the night near the interval between Twelfth Corps and Eleventh Corps. Two regiments of the division and three pieces of artillery were advanced to a forward position to the right of Williams' line. During the night, Sickles ordered Birney to move forward at daybreak the next morning and occupy the front line between Twelfth Corps and Eleventh Corps.

Whipple's division and Berry's division (less Mott's brigade) remained in reserve near Chancellorsville during the night. Berry's artillery (except Seeley's battery) was held in reserve near the junction of the Ely's Ford Road and the United States Ford Road, about a mile in rear of Chancellorsville.

Late in the evening, Devin's cavalry brigade, which had preceded the infantry movements during the day, assembled in camp on Little Hunting Creek to feed and rest. The 8th Pennsylvania Cavalry was near Chancellorsville.

Battle of Chancellorsville, May 2, 1863. Early on the morning of May 2, 1863, Hooker rearranged the left of his line east of Chancellorsville. At 1:30 A.M., Sykes' division of Fifth Corps withdrew from its position along the Turnpike and moved north, then entrenched along the Mineral Spring Road, with its right near the Chandler house. Immediately after Sykes had departed, Hancock's division of Second Corps moved back about a half mile and formed a new line. It connected on its right with Geary's division of Twelfth Corps near the Plank Road, and from that point it ran northeast about 400 yards to the Turnpike. There it turned back and ran in front of, and nearly parallel to, the road running up from Chancellorsville, past Chandlers', and on to United States Ford. Cross' Provisional Brigade was on the right, in the angle between the Plank Road and the Turnpike, facing southeast. Then, in order from right to left, were Caldwell's First Brigade, Brooke's Fourth Brigade, and Zook's Third Brigade. Zook's left was near the right of Sykes' new line near the Mineral Spring Road. Also during the morning, Meagher's Second Brigade appears to have been withdrawn from Scott's Dam to a position in rear of Humphreys' division of Fifth Corps.

During the early morning, Grffin's division of Fifth Corps moved northward and entrenched on the Mineral Spring Road between Sykes' division and Humphreys' division. Barnes' First Brigade was on the right, next to Sykes; Stockton's Third Brigade was on the center of the line; and McQuade's Second Brigade was on the left, next to Humphreys. With this rearrangement, Meade's Fifth Corps was united on a line along the Mineral Spring Road from Chandlers' to Scott's Dam on the Rappahannock.

Between 7:00 and 8:00 A.M., Carroll's First Brigade of French's Third Division, Second Corps moved up between the right of Sykes and the left of Hancock, and during the day it entrenched its new position. MacGregor's Third Brigade was massed in rear of Carroll, and Hays' Second Brigade was in line north of Chancellorsville, facing south.

There were also some changes on the right of Hooker's line on May 2, 1863. At daylight Birney, with the brigades of Ward and Hayman, moved forward and occupied a line south of the Plank Road, and along the crest north of Lewis' Creek (or Scott's Run) that extended from Hazel Grove westward toward Dowdall's Tavern. Ward's Second Brigade was on the right, next to Eleventh Corps, and Hayman's Third Brigade was on the left, next to Twelfth Corps. Graham's First Brigade, which had spent the night in rear of Fairview, rejoined the division shortly after daylight, and took position on the crest of Hazel Grove, on the left of Hayman. Birney's batteries also came up and bivouacked near the division. These were: A. Judson Clark's Battery B, New Jersey Light Artillery; Pardon S. Jastram, with George E. Randolph's Battery E, 1st Rhode Island Light Artillery; and John G. Turnbull's Batteries F and K, 3rd United States Artillery. Also that morning, Pleasonton's cavalry, with Joseph W. Martin's 6th Independent New York Horse Artillery, moved up from Hunting Creek to Chancellorsville.

At 2:00 on the morning of May 2, 1863, Hooker sent an order to John F. Reynolds, commanding First Corps below Fredericksburg, directing him to withdraw his troops from the south bank of the Rappahannock, take up the bridges, and report to Hooker at Chancellorsville. Reynolds received the order at 7:00 A.M., and two hours later John C. Robinson's Second Division and Abner Doubleday's Third Division started for United States Ford. As soon as James S. Wadsworth's First Division recrossed the river, it followed the other two divisions toward Chancellorsville. Robinson's division arrived at United States Ford about sunset, and Doubleday's division was close behind. With Reynolds' departure for Chancellorsville, the only Federal troops left south of the Rappahannock below Fredericksburg were William T. H. Brooks' First Division, Hiram Burnham's Light Brigade, and Edward B. Williston's Battery D, 2nd United States Artillery of Sixth Corps.

During the night of May 1, 1863, Lee made plans for the next day. He decided to send Jackson, with the three divisions of his corps, on a flanking march to the west in an effort to strike the right and rear of Hooker's line on the Turnpike. He directed Anderson and McLaws to remain with their divisions in position to the east and south of Chancellorsville to threaten the Federal troops then in position on their front, and also to divert attention from Jackson's movement.

About 7:00 A.M. May 2, 1863, Jackson began his march down the the the Furnace Road toward Wellford's (or Catharine) Furnace, with Daniel H. Hill's division, then commanded by Robert E. Rodes, in the lead. Isaac R. Trimble's division (formerly Jackson's), then commanded by Raleigh E. Colston, followed Rodes, and Ambrose P. Hill's division brought up the rear. Fitzhugh Lee's cavalry brigade, under the personal direction of Stuart, covered the march. On the east side of Lewis' Creek, close to the Furnace, the road ran over an elevation or hill that was visible from the Union lines. About 8:00 A.M., Birney observed the van of Jackson's column as it passed over the hill, and a section of Robert Sims' Battery B, New Jersey Light Artillery opened fire. Other guns of the battery were brought up and soon joined Sims.

Birney reported the enemy movement to Sickles, who in turn notified Hooker. Sickles also communicated this information to Howard and Slocum. Sickles also proposed to Hooker that he, Sickles, advance with his entire Third Corps and attack the enemy column. Hooker received Sickles' message about 9:00 A.M., but it was not until noon that he replied. At that time, he instructed Sickles to advance cautiously to the road on which the enemy was marching and harass the movement as much as possible, but to take with him only the divisions of

Birney and Whipple. Berry's division was to remain near Chancellorsville.

To lead his advance, Sickles brought up the 1st and 2nd United States Sharpshooters of Hiram Berdan's Third Brigade of Whipple's division, deployed them as skirmishers and flankers, and sent them forward. He then directed Birney to follow Berdan and gain possession of the Furnace Road, on which Jackson was moving.

When Jackson passed Wellford's Furnace, he left the 23rd Georgia of Rodes' division, commanded by Emory F. Best, to guard a trail that ran in from the direction of the Union lines to the north. Then, about noon, Posey's brigade of Anderson's division moved forward on the Furnace Road, from its position on the Plank Road, and formed on the Furnace Road about 500 yards from the Furnace, facing west.

About 12:30 P.M., Hayman's brigade, covered in front by his own and Berdan's skirmishers, crossed Lewis' Creek and headed for the point on the road where Jackson's column had been observed. The fire of the enemy skirmishers was so effective that at 1:00 P.M. Birney ordered Graham's brigade forward to support Hayman. At the same time, Sickles ordered Whipple to move his division to within supporting distance of Birney. Berdan and Hayman reached the Furnace about 2:00 P.M., and there Berdan's Sharpshooters captured a party of the 23rd Georgia. Best, however, with the remainder of the regiment, withdrew to the south to the shelter of a cut on the unfinished railroad, near the Wellford house.

At 2:00 P.M., Ward's brigade moved up to support Hayman and Graham, and at that time Whipple's division began arriving at Hazel Grove. Also at 2:00 P.M., Wright's brigade of Anderson's division moved forward to support Posey, and formed on his right, to the right of the Furnace Road. A half hour later, the brigades of Hayman and Graham started to move southward past the Furnace in pursuit of the 23rd Georgia, but they received a heavy flank fire from Posey's line to the left and a direct fire from an enemy battery near the Wellford house, and they were forced to halt.

By 2:00 P.M., Jackson's infantry had passed the Furnace, and Rodes' leading division was crossing the Plank Road to the northwest. Edward L. Thomas, commanding the rear brigade of Ambrose P. Hill's division and the last infantry brigade of Jackson's column, was then about one mile southwest of the Wellford house. The trains, however, had not yet passed, and when these were threatened, Thomas' brigade and James J. Archer's brigade returned to the Wellford house about 3:30 P.M. to protect them. By 4:45 P.M., the trains were safely on their way, and Archer with the two Confederate brigades hurried on after the rest of Jackson's column. The 23rd Georgia remained in position too long, however, and it was captured by Berdan's brigade.

About 4:00 P.M., Pleasonton's cavalry, which had been held near Chancellorsville during the earlier part of the day, was sent forward to cooperate with Third Corps in pursuit of the enemy wagon train. It proceeded by way of Hazel Grove, and at 5:00 P.M. arrived near Wellford's Furnace, where it reported to Sickles. Also at 4:00 P.M., Hooker ordered Howard to send a brigade of Eleventh Corps to support Sickles, and Howard, in person, accompanied by Von Steinwehr, went forward with Francis C. Barlow's Second Brigade of Von Steinwehr's Second Division.

Meantime, there had been considerable activity along the front of the Union line near the Plank Road and the Turnpike. This was largely the action by the skirmishers of both armies, but about 3:15 P.M., Wofford's brigade of McLaws' division made a vigorous attack along the Turnpike against that part of Hancock's line held by Nelson A. Miles' 61st New York of Caldwell's brigade. This attack, however, was soon repulsed.

About 3:00 P.M., Geary moved forward with two regiments of Candy's First Brigade on the left of the Plank Road, and Kane's Second Brigade on the right of the road. A section of Joseph M. Knap's Battery E, Pennsylvania Light Artillery, under the command of Charles A. Atwell, advanced on the road. The artillery suffered severely, and after proceeding only 200 yards, was ordered back. The infantry advanced about 500 yards and found the enemy entrenched and in heavy force, and it was ordered back to its entrenchments.

About 4:30 P.M., as Geary's command was returning to its lines, Slocum, with Hooker's permission, moved Williams' division out of its entrenchments and sent it forward to support Birney. There was an interval between Williams and Birney, and Sickles ordered Whipple to move forward with his division from Hazel Grove and fill this gap.

About 5:00 P.M. Barlow's brigade arrived on the right of Berdan, west of the Wellford house, and a short time later Howard and Von Steinwehr left Barlow to return to Eleventh Corps. At that time, the troops that had advanced toward the Furnace that afternoon were in position as follows: Berdan's brigade was just west of the Wellford house, facing south; Barlow's brigade was on the right of Berdan; Hayman's brigade was in rear of Berdan, also facing south; Ward's brigade was in line between the Furnace and Wellfords' house, facing Posey's brigade to the east: and Graham's brigade was just west of the Furnace, also facing east. Whipple's division was in line from the Furnace to the northeast, with Samuel W. Bowman's Second Brigade on the right and Emlen Franklin's First Brigade on the left, next to Williams' division. Williams' division extended to the northeast from the left of Whipple's division to a point about a half mile below Fairview. Knipe's First Brigade was on the right, next to Whipple; Ross' Second Brigade was on the left of Knipe; and Ruger's Third Brigade was on the left of Williams' line.

At 5:00 P.M., Pleasonton's cavalry was near the Furnace, but a short time later Sickles decided that the country was not suitable for cavalry, and after detaching Devin with the 6th New York Cavalry to report to Birney, he ordered Pleasonton, with the remainder of the cavalry, back to Hazel Grove. Soon after 5:00 P.M., Turnbull's battery, which was in action near the Furnace, exhausted its ammunition, and it was replaced by Jastram's battery of Birney's division. Turnbull's battery returned to Hazel Grove.

In the meantime, all through the day, Jackson's corps had been marching toward the exposed Union right near the Talley farm. With Rodes' division in the lead, the column marched to the southwest from the Furnace on the Furnace Road to the Brock Road, and upon arriving there, it moved south for about 600 yards to a country road that branched off to the right about one and a fourth miles north of Todd's Tavern. Rodes then turned onto this road and followed it around to the north on a course roughly parallel to, and about one-half mile west of, the Brock Road. Beyond the Trigg and Stevens (spelled Stephens on some maps) houses, and a little more than a mile south of the Plank Road, this road rejoined the Brock Road. After emerging from the

country road, Jackson's column marched up the Brock Road, crossed the Plank Road, and then moved on north and across the Germanna Plank Road (or Germanna Ford Road) until it struck the Turnpike, about three-fourths of a mile east of Wilderness Tavern.

Rodes' division reached that point about 4:00 P.M., and then turned to the right on the Turnpike toward Chancellorsville. Beyond the Luckett house, about three miles from Chancellorsville, Rodes formed his division in line of battle, perpendicular to the Turnpike and extending for about one mile on each side of the road. George Dole's brigade was on the Confederate right of the road, with Alfred H. Colquitt's on its right, next to the Germanna Plank Road. Edward A. O'Neal's brigade was on the left of the Turnpike, and Alfred Iverson's brigade was on the left of O'Neal.

Colston's division came up about 5:00 P.M., and it was formed on a second line, about 200 yards in rear of Rodes. Colston's brigade, commanded by Edward T. H. Warren, was on the right of the road, in rear of Dole, and Stephen D. Ramseur's brigade of Rodes' division was on the right of Warren, in rear of Colquitt. John R. Jones' brigade was on the left of the road, and Francis T. Nicholls' brigade was formed on the left of Jones, but by mistake it was to the rear of Jones on a third line. As Jackson's column crossed the Orange Plank Road, Elisha F. Paxton's brigade (Stonewall Brigade) of Colston's division was detached, with two batteries, and was posted at the Hickman house, near the junction of the Orange Plank Road and the Germanna Ford Road on the right and front of Colquitt's brigade. Paxton's assignment was to support Fitzhugh Lee's cavalry, which was about a half mile ahead at the Burton house, covering Jackson's march. Paxton was temporarily placed under Fitzhugh Lee's orders.

When Rodes' division was deployed and ready to move forward, only William D. Pender's brigade and Henry Heth's brigade of Ambrose P. Hill's division had arrived on the Turnpike in rear of Colston. Pender's brigade was deployed on the left of the Turnpike, with its right on the road near Lucketts', and Heth's brigade was formed on the left of Pender, and on the right of Nicholls' brigade. James H. Lane's brigade and Samuel McGowan's brigade were approaching in the rear, and had reached the intersection of the Brock Road and the

Turnpike. Archer's and Thomas's brigades, which had turned back to protect the trains at Wellfords', were far to the rear.

Jackson's line began to move forward at about 5:15 P.M. May 2, 1863. A short time later it struck the right of Von Gilsa's brigade, which was facing south, and it was quickly driven back in disorder through a line hastily formed by McLean's brigade near the Talley house. McLean's line was soon enveloped by three enemy brigades, and after a hopeless struggle of ten or fifteen minutes, it retreated rapidly toward Wilderness Church, which was about 200 yards north of the junction of the Plank Road and the Turnpike. About an hour after Jackson began his attack, Devens' First Division, Eleventh Corps had been wrecked, and enemy troops had gained possession of the high ground at the Talley farm.

At 6:00 P.M., when Schurz heard the firing on his right, he changed front with all of the regiments of his Third Division that were within reach, and formed a new line a short distance west of Wilderness Church, facing west. This line extended northward from a point near the junction of the Plank Road and the Turnpike, and it connected on the right with the 58th New York and 26th Wisconsin regiments of Krzyzanowski's brigade, both under the personal supervision of Krzyzanowski, which had been sent earlier in the day to the Hawkins farm. Schurz held his position for about twenty minutes, but as Jackson pushed forward with overwhelming force toward Dowdall's Tavern, he was forced to fall back toward the woods in rear of the Hawkins farm.

Buschbeck's brigade, the only brigade of Second Division remaining with Von Steinwehr, quickly took position along a shallow trench that ran north and south a short distance east of Dowdall's Tavern. This line was perpendicular to the Plank Road and extended northward from a short distance south of the road to a point about 700 yards east of the Hawkins house. Buschbeck's four regiments were joined on this line by some fragments of Devens' division and two regiments and two companies of Schimmelfennig's First Brigade and three regiments of Krzyzanowski's Second Brigade of Schurz's division.

Jackson's brigades continued their advance along the Turnpike and then the Plank Road, and from Wilderness Church and the Hawkins farm; they struck the troops of Schurz and Buschbeck in front and on both flanks, and at about 7:10 P.M. they had gained this third and last line of Howard's Eleventh Corps. Thousands of fugitives of Eleventh Corps that had been driven from the Turnpike had fled to the rear in the greatest confusion, but the troops manning the third defensive line retired in good order in two separate bodies. Schurz, with five regiments of his Third Division, fell back to the north of the Plank Road, and Buschbeck with his brigade moved to the south of the road. Hubert Dilger, with a single gun of his Battery I, 1st Ohio Light Artillery, fell back on the road. Buschbeck fell back to the works constructed earlier by Williams' division of Twelfth Corps, and then, not being pressed, continued on to Fairview, where he arrived at 7:45 P.M. There he posted his brigade, together with some men of McLean's brigade, in front of a line of guns that was then being formed by Clermont L. Best, chief of artillery of Twelfth Corps. Later, Buschbeck moved farther back and formed his command across the roads leading to the rear to stop the stragglers of Eleventh Corps, and he remained on this duty during the night. When Schurz, during his retreat, arrived at Williams' empty works, just abandoned by Buschbeck, he retired to the northeast by the Bullock Farm Road to the crossing of Little Hunting Creek, and then, at about 8:30 P.M., he moved on to the vicinity of Chancellorsville.

During the night of May 2, 1863, the disorganized troops of Eleventh Corps were collected and sent to the rear to re-form. When this was completed, they replaced Fifth Corps, which was withdrawn from the left of Hooker's line that night and early the next morning and sent to the Ely's Ford Road.

When Hooker, at his headquarters at Chancellorsville, learned of the route of Eleventh Corps on the evening of May 2, 1863, he promptly took measures to form a new defensive line that would ensure the safety of the army. The corps commanders cooperated vigorously in this effort. At about the same time that Jackson was beginning his attack, the leading brigade of Reynolds' First Corps arrived at United States Ford from below Fredericksburg. It crossed the river at 5:30 P.M., and by sunset, Robinson's Second Division and Doubleday's Third Division had followed and halted for a time south of the ford. Wadsworth's First Division was on the road about six miles back, and it did not come up until after daylight May 3, 1863. Reynolds, in person, reported to Hooker at Chancellorsville at 6:30. P.M., and he was directed to put his corps in position on the Ely's Ford Road to protect the right of the army and guard the approaches to United States Ford.

Reynolds' divisions then resumed their march. By 9:00 P.M., Robinson's division was proceeding on the Mineral Spring Road, between the Mine (or Mountain) Road and the Chandler house; and Doubleday's division, which was marching in rear of Robinson, was between United States Ford and the Mine Road. Reynolds continued the march during the night, but his corps was not established on its assigned positions until sunrise the next morning (see below).

Pleasonton, who had been sent back from Sickles' position near Wellford's Furnace with the 8th Pennsylvania Cavalry, 17th Pennsylvania Cavalry, and Martin's battery of horse artillery, arrived at Hazel Grove during Jackson's attack on Eleventh Corps. Pleasonton then aided Sickles in holding that position by supervising the placement of twenty-two guns belonging to Martin's battery; Samuel Lewis' 10th Battery, New York Light Artillery; John E. Burton's 11th Battery, New York Light Artillery; and James F. Huntington's Battery H, 1st Ohio Light Artillery. The last three batteries belonged to Whipple's division, and had been left behind under the command of Huntington when Whipple had advanced to join Birney near Wellford's Furnace. The batteries were soon placed in position and, firing canister, aided in halting Jackson's advance.

Sometime after 6:00 P.M., Pennock Huey, commanding the 8th Pennsylvania Cavalry, was ordered to report to Howard, who at the time was believed to be near Wilderness Church. At 6:45 P.M., Huey left Hazel Grove and marched northward toward the Plank Road, but upon arriving near the road, he found his way blocked by Jackson's victorious troops. It was then too late for Huey to turn back, and at about 7:30 P.M. he charged and cut his way through, but upon arriving at the Plank Road he found his return route to the east also in possession of enemy troops. Accordingly, he turned to the left, seeking a way out, and after advancing about a hundred yards, his command was struck by a murderous fire, which inflicted serious losses. The regiment then turned off the road to the right, and made

its way back to Fairview. For a time, it supported the artillery assembled there under Best, but when Huey was relieved in this duty by infantry, he fell back to Chancellorsville. Pleasonton later stated that he ordered Huey to charge the enemy to gain time for the placement of his artillery, but this claim does not appear to be supported by Huey or by other participants in the charge of the 8th Pennsylvania Cavalry.

When Hooker realized the danger created by the rout of Eleventh Corps, he ordered Berry's Second Division of Third Corps, then in reserve near Chancellorsville, to move westward on the Plank Road to check the enemy advance. Berry had with him only two brigades, but by 8:00 P.M. he had them in position along a ridge, facing west and northwest, with their left on the Plank Road and their right at the Bullock Farm Road crossing of Little Hunting Run. Joseph W. Revere's Second Brigade, with two regiments of Joseph B. Carr's First Brigade, formed the first line, and two regiments of Carr's brigade were to the rear, in reserve.

Gershom Mott's Third Brigade of Berry's division, which had been posted at United States Ford, marched at 10:00 that night for Chancellorsville, and arrived there about 2:00 A.M. the next morning, May 3, 1863. It was then sent to the south of the Plank Road, in rear of Williams' division of Twelfth Corps.

At 7:00 P.M., Williams' division, which was then preparing to attack south of Fairview, was ordered by Slocum to return to its original line to the south of the Plank Road. When Williams arrived near the road about 8:00 P.M., however, he found that the right of his former position was occupied by the enemy. He then formed a new line along the interior edge of the woods on the western rim of the ravine that separates the high ground of Fairview and of Hazel Grove. Ross' brigade took its former position on the left of the line, facing south, and Ruger's brigade formed on the right of Ross, and at a right angle to the latter's line, facing west. Two regiments of Knipe's brigade were on the right of Ruger, also facing west, and these connected with the left of Berry's division at the Plank Road. Three broken regiments of Knipe's brigade were placed in reserve 200 yards in rear of the two regiments on the front line.

When Best, commanding the Twelfth Corps artillery at Fairview, became aware of Howard's defeat, he placed his guns on a ridge a short distance to the west and in rear of Williams' division. These guns belonged to the batteries of Fitzhugh, Winegar, and Crosby. George B. Winslow's Battery D, 1st New York Light Artillery and two sections of Justin E. Dimick's Battery H, 1st United States Artillery, commanded by Philip D. Mason, and which had come up with Berry's division, were placed to the right of the Twelfth Corps' batteries. In addition, Hubert Dilger's battery of Schurz's division and one section of Wallace Hill's Battery C, 1st West Virginia Artillery of the Reserve Artillery of Eleventh Corps halted in their retreat and joined Best's line. This made a total of thirty-seven guns. (The number has also been reported as thirty-four, thirty-eight, and forty-three.)

At about 7:00 P.M., Sickles was notified of the attack on Eleventh Corps, and he was ordered to return at once with his two divisions of Third Corps toward the Plank Road. At that time Birney's division and Barlow's brigade of Eleventh Corps were to the west and south of Wellford's Furnace, and Whipple's division was in line to the northeast of the Furnace. Sickles began his return immediately, and by 9:00 P.M. Whipple's division, including Berdan's brigade, had arrived in rear of Pleasonton's cavalry and artillery at Hazel Grove. Birney's division had also arrived, and was forming in rear of Whipple. Barlow's brigade, which had to march back from about a mile south of the unfinished railroad, also began to arrive near Hazel Grove at 9:00 P.M. Devin, with his 6th New York Cavalry, which had been assigned to Birney, also returned and reported to Pleasonton. Sickles' position at Hazel Grove was outside of Slocum's established line in front of Chancellorsville, but when Sickles reported this fact to Hooker at 9:00 P.M., he was ordered to remain where he was and hold his ground.

When Meade, whose Fifth Corps occupied the left of the Union line along the Mineral Spring Road, learned of the disaster on the right, he sent Sykes with his Second Division to cover the roads leading to Ely's Ford and United States Ford. Sykes marched on the Ely's Ford Road to its junction with the road to United States Ford, about one-half mile northwest of Chandlers', and at about 6:15 P.M. (times given range from 5:00 to 7:00 P.M.) took

position, with Ayres' First Brigade across the road to United States Ford, about one-fourth mile north of the junction, facing north; and O'Rorke's Third Brigade across the Ely's Ford Road, 300 to 400 yards beyond the junction, facing west. Burbank's Second Brigade was along the road between Chandlers' and the road junction. When Sykes pulled out of Fifth Corps' line, Barnes' First Brigade of Griffin's division took his place on the Mineral Spring Road.

Sometime after 8:30 P.M., John D. McGregor's Third Brigade of French's division, Second Corps (commanded by Charles Albright in the absence of McGregor, who was sick) was sent forward from its bivouac between Chandlers' and Chancellorsville to support Carroll's brigade of the same division, east of Chandlers'. This movement left Berry's right flank unprotected, and at about 9:00 P.M. William Hays' Second Brigade of French's division was sent to support Berry. Hays' brigade was posted obliquely in rear of Berry's division, with its left near the Plank Road at a point almost due north of Fairview.

About 10:30 that night, William W. Averell arrived at Ely's Ford from Rapidan Station with his own Second Cavalry Division, Benjamin F. Davis' First Brigade of Pleasonton's First Cavalry Division, and John C. Tidball's Battery A, 2nd United States Artillery. He then went into bivouac on the north side of the river, and on the opposite bank was Stuart, with his available cavalry and an infantry regiment.

While Hooker was laboring to form a new defensive line, Jackson was making every effort to push his troops forward on the Plank Road that evening. As Rodes' and Colston's divisions moved eastward after overrunning Howard's last defensive line at Dowdall's Tavern, they became inextricably mixed and, as a result, almost impossible to control. Nevertheless, the two divisions arrived near the junction of the Bullock Farm Road and the Plank Road sometime before 8:00 P.M., and then Rodes, as the senior officer, ordered them to halt. At that time, his line was only a short distance from the works of Twelfth Corps that had been left vacant when Williams advanced toward Wellford's Furnace that afternoon, and some of Rodes' men pushed ahead and seized a portion of these works.

Rodes did not believe that it was possible to renew the attack with his disorganized command in the darkness of the woods, and he sent word to Jackson that he needed time to re-form his divisions. He also urged Jackson to send Ambrose P. Hill's fresh troops to the front to continue the pursuit. Hill then came up and began to deploy in front of Rodes and Colston, and at about 8:45 that evening, Lane's brigade was in position south of the Plank Road, in front of Williams' former line.

Jackson was determined to press on that night and seize the road to United States Ford, and he rode forward in the darkness with his couriers and guides to examine the ground. He met Lane at 9:00 P.M. and directed him to push on, and he then started back through his lines to hasten forward the other brigades of Hill's division. A short time later, his party was fired upon by troops of the 18th North Carolina of Lane's brigade, and Jackson was seriously wounded. He was taken to the rear, and Ambrose P. Hill assumed command of the corps. A short time later, Hill was disabled, and a messenger was sent to Stuart, then near Ely's Ford, directing him to come and take command of the corps. Stuart arrived, probably about midnight, and assumed command. While awaiting Stuart's arrival, Rodes exercised temporary command of the corps, but it made no further attacks that night.

At Hazel Grove, Sickles requested permission of Hooker to make a night attack in order to regain the Plank Road to the north, and also to recover some of Whipple's guns and caissons, and a part of his ammunition train that had been left outside the Federal lines earlier that evening. Permission was granted at 11:00 P.M., and then Sickles ordered Birney to advance. Ward's First Brigade formed the first line of the attacking column, and Hayman's Second Brigade the second line. Thomas W. Egan, colonel of the 40th New York, was given command of a special column that consisted of the 40th New York of Ward's brigade, 17th Maine of Hayman's brigade, and 63rd Pennsylvania of Graham's brigade, and he was directed to move forward on the left of Birney, along a road running perpendicular to the Plank Road.

Sickles' attack was generally in a northerly direction toward the Plank Road, and along the front of Williams' division on the right and Lane's Confederate brigade on the left. Birney's men were fired on in the darkness from both sides, but the center of his line succeeded in reaching the Plank Road. In a short time, however, these troops were driven back on the rest of the division. Sickles' attack, however, was not a complete failure, because he did succeed in bringing back Whipple's guns, caissons, and ammunition, and he did take and hold a more advanced position. From this new position, he was able to open a road and establish connection with Twelfth Corps.

Battle of Chancellorsville, May 3, 1863. During the night of May 2–3, 1863, both armies prepared for a renewal of the battle the next morning. As noted above, Stuart arrived at the front from Ely's Ford about midnight and assumed command of Jackson's corps, and at 3:00 A.M. Stuart received orders from Lee to attack as soon as possible and effect a junction of the two wings of the army by driving the Federal troops from Chancellorsville.

By dawn May 3, 1863, Henry Heth, then commanding Hill's division, had his brigades in line across, and perpendicular to, the Plank Road, one mile west of Chancellorsville, and facing east. The length of Heth's line was about one and one-fourth miles. South of the road, from the Confederate left to right, were the brigades of Lane, McGowan, and Archer, and these faced Williams' division of Twelfth Corps and the troops of Sickles' Third Corps at Hazel Grove. North of the road, from right to left, were the brigades of William D. Pender and Edward L. Thomas, which faced Berry's division of Third Corps. Astride the road, a short distance in rear of Lane and Pender, was a short second line composed of troops of Heth's brigade, then commanded by John M. Brockenbrough.

Extending across the Plank Road, about 200 yards west of Old School House, Colston's division formed Stuart's second line. South of the road, from the Confederate left to right, were Warren's brigade, then commanded by Titus V. Williams, and Jones' brigade, then commanded by Thomas S. Garnett. Warren was wounded May 2, 1863, and Jones had been disabled on the night of May 2, 1863. North of the road, from right to left, were Paxton's Stonewall Brigade and Nicholls' brigade, then commanded by Jesse M. Williams. Nicholls had been wounded May 2, 1863.

In rear of Colston's line, at Dowdall's Tavern, Rodes formed Stuart's third line, which also extended north and south across the Plank Road. South of the road, from the Confederate left to right, were the brigades of Ramseur, Doles, and Colquitt; and north of the road, from right to left, were the brigades of O'Neal and Iverson.

While Stuart was preparing for his attack on the morning of May 3, 1863, Hooker was also getting his troops in position for a renewal of the battle. At 1:00 A.M. May 3, 1863, Reynolds, with the divisions of Robinson and Doubleday, arrived on the ground to which he had been assigned, and between 3:00 and 4:00 that morning he formed his command on the extreme right of the army. Reynolds' line ran along the east side of Hunting Creek (or Run), which flowed into the Rapidan between Todd's Ford and Blind Ford. Robinson's division was on the right of the line, and Doubleday's division was on the left. On Robinson's line, Adrian R. Root's First Brigade was on the right, with its right about 600 yards from the river; Henry Baxter's Second Brigade was in the center; and Samuel H. Leonard's Third Brigade was on the left, with its left near the Bailey house. In Doubleday's division, Thomas A. Rowley's First Brigade was on the right, next to Leonard's brigade; and Roy Stone's Second Division was on the left, connecting with the right of Sykes' Second Division, Fifth Corps, near the junction of Big Hunting Creek and Little Hunting Creek.

While Reynolds was forming his line on Hunting Creek, Wadsworth came up from United States Ford with his First Division, First Corps, and Reynolds placed it in support of the other two divisions. Walter Phelps' First Brigade was sent to the right of Robinson's division to cover the gap between Root's brigade and the Rapidan; Gabriel R. Paul's Third Brigade was formed in rear of Robinson's division; Lysander Cutler's Second Brigade was sent to the rear of Sykes' division, west of Compback's Mill; and Solomon Meredith's Fourth Brigade was placed on the United States Ford Road, in rear of the left of Robinson's division.

Only James A. Hall's Battery C, Pennsylvania Light Artillery arrived with Reynolds that morning, and it was not placed in position until 6:00 A.M. To provide sufficient artillery for the First Corps line until the rest of the corps artillery came up, Charles A. Atwell's Battery E, Pennsylvania Light Artillery of Twelfth Corps, and the available artillery of Eleventh Corps, consisting of some twenty guns, were sent to Reynolds. Not all of the Eleventh Corps

batteries performed well, however, and some left the field.

As noted above, on the evening of May 2, 1863, Meade sent Sykes' division out to protect the roads to Ely's Ford and United States Ford, and it took position near the junction of the two roads. Toward morning, on May 3, 1863, the division moved farther out and formed along the Ely's Ford Road, on the left of Reynolds' First Corps. Ayres' First Brigade was on the right of Sykes' division, north of, and perpendicular to, the road, facing northwest. It connected on the right with Doubleday's division of First Corps, and its left rested on the road. Burbank's Second Brigade was along the Ely's Ford Road, facing southwest, and it extended from the left of Ayres' brigade to a point near Little Hunting Creek. O'Rorke's Third Brigade was in rear of Burbank's brigade.

Between 3:00 and 4:30 on the morning of May 3, 1863, Griffin's First Division of Fifth Corps was relieved from its position along the Mineral Spring Road, and it then moved to the west and formed along the Ely's Ford Road, on the left of Sykes' division. Stockton's Third Brigade was on the right, with its right connecting with Burbank's brigade, and McQuade's Second Brigade was on the left of Stockton. Barnes' First Brigade was first placed in rear of Sykes' division, but about two hours later it was moved to the left of Griffin's line at the Chandler house.

A little after 6:00 A.M. (ordered at 3:00 A.M.), Humphreys' Third Division, Fifth Corps, which was on the Mine Run Road (or Mountain Road) near Scott's Dam, was relieved by Schurz's Third Division, Eleventh Corps, and it then marched to Chandlers'. At 7:00 A.M., Humphreys massed his division in rear of Griffin's division, where it would be in position to support Sykes, Griffin, or French, whose Third Division, Second Corps was on the left of Griffin.

The infantry of Eleventh Corps that had been assembled during the night formed along the Mineral Spring Road on the ground vacated by Meade's Fifth Corps. Schurz's Third Division was on the left, next to the Rappahannock; Von Steinwehr's Second Division was on the center of the line; and Devens' First Division, then commanded by McLean, was on the right, with its right near Chandlers'. At first, Von Steinwehr had with him only Buschbeck's First Brigade, but Barlow's Second Brigade, which had been serving with Third Corps, was relieved from that duty on the morning of May 3, 1863 and rejoined its division that morning.

The rest of Hooker's army to the south remained in essentially the same positions that it had occupied at the end of the fighting the night before. Couch's Second Corps held the line that ran south and a little east from Chandlers' to the Turnpike east of Chancellorsville, and then to the southwest to connect with the left of Geary's division of Twelfth Corps at the Plank Road. French's Third Division was on the left of this line, with Carroll's First Brigade near Chandlers', and Charles Albright's Second Brigade (McGregor was sick) in rear of Carroll. It has been noted that Hays' Second Brigade of French's division had been sent on the evening of May 2, 1863 to support Berry's division of Third Corps near the Plank Road. Hancock's First Division was on the right of Couch's line, and its brigades were in line, from left to right, as follows: Zook's Third Brigade, Brooke's Fourth Brigade, Caldwell's First Brigade, and Cross' Provisional Brigade. Meagher's Second Brigade was still near Scott's Dam, and, it will be remembered, John Gibbon's Second Division was at Falmouth.

Geary's Second Division, Twelfth Corps was in its original position south of Chancellorsville and Fairview, facing south. Candy's First Brigade was on the left, next to the Plank Road; Kane's Second Brigade was in the center; and Greene's Third Brigade was on the right, connecting with Williams' First Division, Twelfth Corps.

On the main line west of Chancellorsville, the Federal troops that were facing Stuart's corps on the morning of May 3, 1863 were as follows: Berry's Second Division, Third Corps was north of the Plank Road, with William Hays' Second Brigade of French's Third Division, Second Corps in its rear. Hays was under Berry's orders. Williams' First Division, Twelfth Corps was on a line that ran south from the left of Berry's division at the Plank Road to a point near Hazel Grove, and there it turned eastward to connect with the right of Geary's division. Two regiments of Ross' Second Brigade were on the right next to Berry, and Ruger's Third

Brigade continued the line southward from Ross' regiments to the bend in the line opposite Hazel Grove. The 110th Pennsylvania of Whipple's division, Third Corps and two regiments of Ross' brigade completed Williams' line to its connection with Geary's division. Knipe's First Brigade had held the right of Williams' line during the night, but early on the morning of May 3, 1863, it was relieved by the two regiments of Ross' brigade, and it then moved back to a position about 200 yards in rear of the main line, near the Plank Road. Ross was wounded about 8:00 that morning, and Knipe assumed command of his brigade, as well as of his own. Clermont L. Best's artillery was at Fairview, south of the Plank Road.

About 3:00 A.M. May 3, 1863, Gershom Mott's Third Brigade of Berry's division and Seeley, with four guns of his Battery K, 4th United States Artillery, arrived at the front from United States Ford. Seeley's battery was held in reserve at Chancellorsville, but Mott's brigade was moved near the front, and formed with its right on the Plank Road, in rear of Williams' main line and in front of Knipe's brigade.

Sickles, with Birney's First Division and Whipple's Third Division of Third Corps and Barlow's Second Brigade of Von Steinwehr's Second Division, Eleventh Corps, had spent the night at Hazel Grove, in front of the main line, but at daylight May 3, 1863, Hooker ordered Sickles to withdraw his command to Fairview and occupy a new line of entrenchments. Sickles' artillery moved out first, and it was followed by Whipple's division, and then Birney's division. Barlow's brigade also accompanied the column. Graham's First Brigade of Birney's division, with Huntington's battery, covered the withdrawal.

When day dawned on the morning of May 3, 1863, both armies had completed their preparations for a renewal of the struggle. Between 5:30 and 6:00 A.M., Stuart ordered his first line to advance and his second and third lines to follow. Heth's division quickly crossed Slocum's original log works, and pushed on toward the positions of Berry and Williams. Archer's brigade, on the enemy right, advanced and occupied Hazel Grove just after Sickles had withdrawn. Archer then pressed forward and came up with Graham's rear guard near the ravine in front of Fairview, but Graham held his ground until Sickles reached Fairview, and then continued his withdrawal.

Birney's and Whipple's divisions were generally placed in support of Best's artillery line. Whipple's brigades were placed as follows: Berdan's Third Brigade, which had been relieved from duty with Birney's division, was sent north across the Plank Road to the right of Berry's line, across Little Hunting Run. Franklin's First Brigade was formed on the Plank Road in rear of the right of Best's artillery line, and Bowman's Second Brigade was placed on the left and front of the artillery, and in rear of the right of Greene's brigade of Twelfth Corps. Birney's brigades were on the left and rear of Best's line at Fairview. Graham's First Brigade was on the left of the artillery, and in rear of Bowman's brigade; Ward's Second Brigade was in the rear, just east of Fairview, and Hayman's Third Brigade was between Ward and Graham.

After Archer's brigade had reached Hazel Grove, it turned to the left and attacked that part of Williams' line held by Ross. It was sharply repulsed, and at 6:45 A.M. Archer returned to Hazel Grove to await reinforcements. Realizing the importance of the position at Hazel Grove, the enemy brought up thirty-one pieces of artillery with which they were able to enfilade the southern part of Twelfth Corps' lines. From this position, too, they were able to deliver an effective fire on Ruger's line on the west front, and on Best's artillery and its supports at Fairview. As McGowan advanced on the left of Archer he came up on the 37th New York, the rear regiment of Hayman's brigade, and drove it back in disorder. Farther on, McGowan struck Ruger's brigade and the 7th New Jersey of Mott's brigade, both of which had been advanced, and after a sharp engagement of about thirty minutes' duration, McGowan was driven back in disorder to Slocum's log works, closely followed by Ruger's brigade and the 7th New Jersey.

Lane's brigade, supported by the right wing of Brockenbrough's brigade, advanced along the south side of the Plank Road, accompanied on the north side by Pender's brigade, and about 7:00 A.M. attacked the left of Berry's line and the right of Williams' line. The 3rd Maryland of Ross' brigade, which was on the immediate left of Berry's division, gave way in some disorder, and Lane's men followed it into Williams' works. Lane was soon checked by the 5th and 8th New Jersey regiments of Mott's brigade, but Pender pressed on against Berry's exposed flank. Berry was mortally wounded in the fighting that morning and died about 7:30 A.M. Joseph B. Carr succeeded Berry in command of Second Division, Third Corps, and William Blaisdell assumed command of Carr's First Brigade of the division.

Carr then sent the 11th New Jersey of Blaisdell's First Brigade to support Justin E. Dimick's section of Battery H, 1st United States Artillery on the Plank Road, and at about the same time the 1st and 11th Massachusetts regiments of Blaisdell's brigade, which were on the left of Berry's (Carr's) line, gave way. As Pender, and then Thomas, who was advancing on Pender's left, struck Carr's line in quick succession, the rest of Carr's division, which consisted of Revere's Second Brigade and 16th Massachusetts and 28th Pennsylvania regiments of Blaisdell's brigade, broke off, regiment by regiment from the left, and fell back to the north. Ward's brigade of Birney's division was sent to form on the right of Carr and support him, but Ward was unable to find Carr in the confusion, and instead reported to French, who directed him to take position near the Chandler house.

Meantime, south of the Plank Road, Mott's brigade advanced against Lane, and the latter, who had suffered from the Federal artillery at Fairview, and who was then threatened on the right and rear by Ruger's brigade, fell back in confusion to Slocum's old works. Ruger's men followed the remnants of McGowan's, Lane's, and Brockenbrough's brigades to these works, and delivered a devastating fire. McGowan was wounded and was succeeded by Oliver O. Edwards. Edwards was also wounded, and Daniel H. Hamilton assumed command of his brigade.

Back on the north side of the road, Pender's brigade, followed by the left wing of Brockenbrough's brigade, broke through Carr's line and advanced to the front of Hays' Second Brigade of French's division, Second Corps. At this point, Pender was halted by heavy infantry and artillery fire, except for his left regiment, the 13th North Carolina. This regiment moved on with Thomas' brigade, which struck the right of Hays' brigade and pushed it back, capturing Hays and most of his staff.

Charles J. Powers assumed command of Hays' brigade.

At 7:00 A.M. French, with Couch's approval, withdrew the 7th West Virginia, 4th Ohio, 8th Ohio, and 14th Indiana of Carroll's brigade from the works on the left of Hancock's division, leaving the 24th and 28th New Jersey to hold the brigade line, and placed these four regiments in line on the open ground west of the road running from Chancellorsville to Chandlers'. This line faced southwest toward the Plank Road. French also formed Albright's brigade near Chandlers' to support the left of a line of Fifth Corps artillery.

At 7:30 A.M. Hooker ordered French to attack, and Carroll's four regiments advanced to the southwest, between the Bullock Farm Road and the Plank Road. French then brought up two regiments of Albright's brigade to the right of Carroll, and also ordered up the two remaining regiments of Carroll's brigade, which he placed en echelon on the right of Albright. French then moved forward and drove back the brigades of Pender and Thomas and the left wing of Brockenbrough's brigade, across Berry's former position to Slocum's log works. By 8:15 A.M. Carroll's brigade was on the Plank Road, at the junction of the Bullock Farm Road, and Albright's regiments were on his right. When Pender, Thomas, and Brockenbrough were driven back, Hays' brigade, then commanded by Powers, withdrew to Chandlers'. This left Franklin and Berdan, supported by Carr and Ward, covering the right of Best's artillery.

At about 7:45 A.M., as French was beginning his attack, Joseph W. Revere, believing that he was in command of Berry's division, withdrew with his own Second Brigade and a part of Blaisdell's brigade, and marched back to the vicinity of United States Ford, where he remained the rest of the day. What was left of Blaisdell's brigade was re-formed in rear of Emlen Franklin's First Brigade of Whipple's division, which was on the Plank Road, north of Fairview. Ward's Second Brigade of Birney's division then came up from near Chandlers' and, at about 8:45, took position on the right of the remains of Carr's division. At about the same time, Meagher's Second Brigade of Hancock's division arrived from near Scott's Dam and formed on the right of Ward. Berdan's Third Brigade of Whipple's division was pulled in from the right, near Little Hunting Creek, and was placed in front of Ward, and on the right of Franklin. Peter H. Allabach's Second Brigade of Humphreys' division, Fifth Corps was formed in line of battle along the Ely's Ford Road, in front of Chandlers'.

At 8:00 A.M., while Heth's shattered division was seeking protection behind Slocum's old works, Colston's division arrived near the front, and Rodes' third line was following close behind. Colston's right wing crowded in behind Heth's men at the log works and refused to go forward from there. To complicate matters for Stuart, it began to appear that Ruger's brigade might drive Heth's and Colston's men from their shallow trenches. To meet this threat, Paxton's Stonewall Brigade was ordered to the south side of the Plank Road, and Garnett's brigade, which was on the right of Colston's division, was ordered to advance. At the same time, Rodes' division was ordered to attack. Paxton moved up to Slocum's former line and then, with Garnett's brigade on his right, crossed the works and advanced toward Ruger's line. A very heavy fire quickly drove them back in disorder to Slocum's works. At the beginning of the attack, Paxton and Garnett were mortally wounded; John H. S. Funk succeeded Paxton in command of the Stonewall Brigade, and Alexander S. Vandeventer assumed direction of Garnett's brigade. At about the same time that Paxton advanced to support Lane's and McGowan's brigades, Jesse M. Williams, commanding Nicholls' brigade of Colston's division, advanced to support Pender and Thomas north of the Plank Road.

By this time, Ruger's brigade had been fighting for about three hours, and had repulsed three separate attacks by Archer, McGowan, and Paxton. Then, with its ammunition nearly exhausted, it was relieved by Graham's brigade, and moved back to Chancellorsville, and then on to United States Ford.

At about 8:15 A.M., Rodes began his attack. Ramseur's brigade advanced south of the Plank Road toward the brigades of Graham and Mott, and struck the right flank of Graham's brigade. O'Neal's brigade advanced on the left of Ramseur, north of the Plank Road, and about 8:30 A.M. launched an attack on Mott's brigade, which was to the right and rear of Graham, just south of the Plank Road. Mott was wounded at the beginning of the attack, and William J. Sewell assumed command of his brigade. O'Neal was also wounded, and Josephus M. Hall succeeded him in command. A part of Doles' brigade advanced on the right of Ramseur, toward that part of Williams' line held by the two regiments of Ross' brigade, then commanded by Knipe. Bowman sent two regiments forward to occupy the line on the right of Knipe. Doles advanced on the flank and rear of this line, and Ross' regiments, then out of ammunition, fell back in some disorder and left the field. Doles continued on and moved into the rear of Greene's Third Brigade of Geary's division of Twelfth Corps, and also of Sickles' Third Corps. At about 9:00 A.M. Carr's brigade withdrew to Chandlers'.

Graham was finally forced to retire to Williams' log works, and there, with Sewell's (Mott's) brigade on his right, he held out for about an hour, but finally Funk's Stonewall Brigade advanced on its front, while Ramseur continued his pressure on the right, and at 9:15 A.M. Graham's brigade began a disorderly retreat toward Chancellorsville. Hayman's brigade covered Graham's withdrawal, and then it too retired to Chancellorsville. Sewell's brigade moved back behind Best's artillery, and then on to Chancellorsville. Knipe, with what remained of his own brigade and Ross' brigade, fell back to Chancellorsville, and then on to United States Ford. Best's artillery continued to hold its position at Fairview until about 9:00 A.M., when it was finally compelled to withdraw. Bowman's brigade, which had been supporting the artillery, also retired at that time. Some of Best's guns went into action between Fairview and Chancellorsville, forming with artillery from other units a line of twenty-four pieces about the Chancellor house. About 9:30 A.M., Franklin's brigade, accompanied by remnants of Sewell's brigade, advanced and occupied for a time Best's vacated position, but it, too, soon withdrew.

Meantime, north of the Plank Road, French had been engaged for about an hour when he observed enemy forces forming on his right. He called for help, and Meade sent forward Erastus B. Tyler's First Brigade of Humphreys' division to form on the right of French. Tyler joined in the attack about 9:00 A.M. and forced Jesse M. Williams to change front to the left. Colquitt's brigade of Rodes' division was then sent to the left of Jesse M. Williams.

A short time after 9:00 A.M., Caldwell's First Brigade of Hancock's division was detached and ordered to report to Hooker, and it was then sent to the northwest of Chandlers' to take position on the right of Allabach's brigade. At about the same time, Hooker was momentarily stunned when a solid shot struck the pillar of the porch of the Chancellor house where he was standing. He did not, however, relinquish command of the army, although a half hour later he turned over to Couch the management of the withdrawal of the troops to the new defensive line. Hooker continued to receive reports and issue orders during the late morning and afternoon.

By 9:30 A.M., French and Tyler had pushed the enemy back north of the Plank Road to the works on Berry's former line. Caldwell's brigade then advanced, accompanied on its left by Meagher's brigade, and it soon met French falling back with Carroll's brigade. Caldwell's brigade also withdrew. Meagher's brigade moved forward only a short distance, and then, when it came under a heavy fire, returned to its original position.

While Stuart was attacking the Federal lines from the west, Anderson's division was moving up from the south, from the direction of Wellford's Furnace, and by 8:00 A.M. had passed east of Hazel Grove and was approaching Geary's line. Geary's division, which had suffered severely from the enemy artillery at Hazel Grove, and was then beginning to be pressed by Anderson's infantry, began to withdraw about 9:00 A.M. At that time, Greene's Third Brigade retired toward Chancellorsville, and it was followed forty-five minutes later by Kane's Second Brigade. Candy's First Brigade, with the 60th and 102nd New York regiments of Greene's brigade, continued to hold Geary's line until sometime after 10:00 A.M., and then it too withdrew. Supporting Candy at that time was Edward D. Muhlenberg with two sections of Samuel Lewis' 10th Battery, New Light Artillery, and one of Best's.

By 10:00 A.M., all of Hooker's troops, except Candy's brigade and his artillery, had withdrawn from the south side of the Plank Road. At that time, the Union line facing Stuart's troops ran from the southeast to the northwest along the front of Little Hunting Creek, beginning on the left within a few hundred yards of the Plank Road, north of Fairview, and extending to a point about 700 yards northwest of the Bullock Farm Road. Holding this line, from left to right, were the brigades of Caldwell, Albright, and Tyler. Meagher's brigade was in rear of Caldwell, along the west side of the road running from Chancellorsville to Chandlers', and Brooke's brigade of Hancock's division was on the left of Meagher, near Chancellorsville. These brigades were withdrawn a short time later to the rear of the line at Chandlers', where they rejoined their divisions. Cross' Provisional Brigade of Hancock's division was still on the left of Candy's brigade, facing McLaws' division. A little after 10:00 A.M., Couch ordered Hancock to withdraw, and Allabach advanced two regiments of his brigade into the woods south of Chandlers' to cover the withdrawal.

During the late morning and early afternoon of May 3, 1863, the regiments that had been separated from their brigades, the brigades from their divisions, and the divisions from their corps, rejoined their proper commands. The re-formed Second Corps, Third Corps, and Twelfth Corps were then assigned positions on the new defensive line. Couch's Second Corps, which had completed its withdrawal by noon, moved to the Mineral Spring Road and formed along the road, with its right near Chandlers' and its left connecting with Howard's Eleventh Corps. Howard had shortened his line to make room for the corps arriving from the front. French's Third Division was on the left of Couch's line, next to Eleventh Corps, and Hancock's First Division was on the right, next to Third Corps.

When Sickles' Third Corps had withdrawn from the line, it was first sent to the junction of the Ely's Ford Road and the United States Ford Road to support Meade's Fifth Corps, but it was soon ordered to occupy the front of the new line near Chandlers'. Third Corps was placed at the apex of the angle formed by the Ely's Ford Road and the Mineral Spring Road, connecting on the left with Second Corps and on the right with Fifth Corps. Whipple's division occupied the left of the salient, and Birney's division the right. Carr's division was formed in rear of the left of the corps line, in support of Whipple. Revere, who had led his troops from the front to United States Ford earlier in the day, was ordered back with his Second Brigade and part of Blaisdell's brigade of Carr's division, and he rejoined Carr about 2:30 P.M. Sickles promptly relieved Revere for leaving the field, and J. Egbert Farnum assumed command of Second Brigade.

Whipple was mortally wounded while supervising the construction of new works, and he was succeeded in command of Third Division, Third Corps by Charles K. Graham, formerly commander of First Brigade of Birney's division. Thomas W. Egan succeeded Graham in command of the brigade.

Slocum's Twelfth Corps first withdrew to the rear of Chandlers', and about 9:00 A.M. it was ordered to the extreme left of the army to cover the road leading to United States Ford. Williams' division was placed on the left, next to the Rappahannock River, and Geary's division on the right, connecting with Eleventh Corps about 500 yards southwest of the Old Mine (or Mountain) Road. Knipe's First Brigade of Williams' division was at United States Ford guarding prisoners.

On the shortened front of Eleventh Corps, Von Steinwehr's Second Division was on the left, McLean's First Division was on the right, and Schurz's Third Division was massed in rear of the line. Reynolds' First Corps and Meade's Fifth Corps remained in the same positions they had occupied that morning, on the right and right-center of Hooker's line.

During the fighting on the morning of May 3, 1863, Pleasonton's cavalry formed in line in rear of the battlefront to intercept stragglers, and the 8th Pennsylvania was sent to the Rappahannock to picket the road from Hartwood Church to Kelly's Ford. The 8th and 17th Pennsylvania regiments bivouacked near United States Ford that night, but the 6th New York remained in rear of the line of Federal works south of the river. That day, Averell moved with his Second Cavalry Division and Benjamin F. Davis' brigade of Pleasonton's First Cavalry Division from Ely's Ford to United States Ford.

Battle of Fredericksburg (or Marye's Heights) and Battle of Salem Church (or Salem Heights), May 3–5, 1863. Since April 28, 1863, John Sedgwick's Sixth Corps, Army of the Potomac had remained near the mouth of Deep Run in a threatening position below Fredericksburg. Then at 11:00 on the night of May 2, 1863, Sedgwick received a somewhat confusing order, dated 10:10 P.M. May 2, 1863, directing him to cross the Rappahannock and move toward Chancellorsville, so as to be in rear of Lee's army at daylight May 3, 1863. In fact, Sixth

Corps was already across the Rappahannock, about three miles below Fredericksburg, and was not at Falmouth as the order appears to have implied. Thus it was impossible for Sedgwick to be near Chancellorsville at daylight the next morning.

Nevertheless, Sedgwick had his corps on the Bowling Green Road, marching toward Fredericksburg shortly after midnight. John Newton's Third Division, with Alexander Shaler's First Brigade in front, led the column, and he was followed by Hiram Burnham's Light Brigade (sometimes called Light Division), which was attached to Newton's division. Next on the road was Albion P. Howe's Second Division, and it was followed by William T. H. Brooks' First Division. The head of Newton's column reached Fredericksburg about 3:00 A.M. May 3, 1863, but he did not occupy the town until daylight that morning. Howe's division was on the left of Hazel Run, and Brooks' division was in position along Deep Run to the rear.

Meantime, at 10:30 the night before, John Gibbon, then at Falmouth, had been ordered to take possession of Fredericksburg with his Second Division, Second Corps. Byron Laflin's First Brigade (formerly commanded by Alfred Sully) and Norman J. Hall's Second Brigade of Gibbon's division marched to the Rappahannock at 1:00 A.M. May 3, 1863, and then waited until daylight. After pontoon bridges were laid, Gibbon crossed into Fredericksburg with the brigades of Laflin and Hill and reported to Sedgwick. Joshua T. Owen's Second Brigade of the division was at Banks' Ford.

At dawn May 3, 1863, Newton deployed Frank Wheaton's Third Brigade and moved it forward on a demonstration to develop the enemy line. He then decided to attack the heights above Fredericksburg on a wide front. These were the same hills that Ambrose E. Burnside had attacked unsuccessfully the preceding December. That morning, however, the Fredericksburg Heights were held by Jubal A. Early's division of Jackson's corps and William Barksdale's brigade of Lafayette McLaws' division of Longstreet's corps. In addition, Cadmus M. Wilcox's brigade of Anderson's division, which had been watching Banks' Ford, moved up and occupied Taylor's Hill. This was on the left of Early's line, near the Rappahannock River. The Confederate brigades, from the right of Wilcox to the vicinity of Hamilton's Crossing, were in position as follows:

Barksdale at Marye's Heights and on the Telegraph Road to the right; Harry T. Hays on Barksdale's right; and then in order to the right, the brigades of Robert F. Hoke, William Smith, and John B. Gordon. When Sedgwick threatened to attack, Hays' brigade was moved to the left of Barksdale, at Stansbury Hill.

According to Sedgwick's plan of attack, Gibbon was to advance on the right and, if possible, turn the enemy left flank, Newton was to demonstrate against the enemy center, and Howe was to attack on the Federal left. Neither Gibbon nor Howe made any progress in their attacks, however, and about 10:00 A.M. Sedgwick prepared to make a direct assault on the heights.

Howe's division was formed in three columns on the left, south of Hazel Run, as follows: a First Column was commanded by Thomas H. Neill, and consisted of 7th Maine, 77th New York, 83rd New York, and a part of 21st New Jersey of his Third Brigade; a Second Column was commanded by Lewis A. Grant, and consisted of 2nd Vermont, 6th Vermont, and 26th New Jersey of his Second Brigade; and a Third Column was commanded by Thomas O. Seaver, and consisted of his own 3rd Vermont and 4th Vermont of Grant's brigade, and a part of 21st New Jersey of Neill's brigade.

The assaulting troops of Newton's division were organized as follows: a Right Column commanded by George C. Spear, which consisted of his own 61st Pennsylvania and 43rd New York of Hiram Burnham's Light Brigade (or Division), supported by 67th New York and 82nd Pennsylvania of Alexander Shaler's First Brigade; a Left Column commanded by Thomas D. Johns, which consisted of his own 7th Massachusetts and 36th New York of William H. Browne's Second Brigade; and a Line of Battle commanded by Hiram Burnham, which consisted of 5th Wisconsin, 6th Maine, and 31st New York of his Light Brigade, and 23rd Pennsylvania of Shaler's brigade.

Brooks' division was to the rear, along Deep Run, with Joseph J. Bartlett's Second Brigade at the Richmond, Fredericksburg, and Potomac Railroad crossing of Deep Run. This brigade was sharply engaged during the morning.

The attack began about 11:00 A.M., and Newton's two columns moved up the Plank Road and to the right of it, directly against the heights, and

Burnham's line advanced to the left of the Plank Road against the lower line of enemy rifle pits. Despite heavy losses, Newton's men charged over the entrenchments at the base of the heights, including the famous "Stone Wall," and after only ten or fifteen minutes of fighting drove the enemy from Marye's Hill. Howe's columns also advanced on the left of Hazel Run and on the left of Newton, and carried Willis' Hill.

After driving the enemy from the heights, Sedgwick did not move immediately toward Chancellorsville. Instead, he ordered Gibbon to hold Fredericksburg and cover the bridges there, and then proceeded to reorganize his command and wait for Brooks' division to come up from Deep Run. It was not until 3:00 P.M. that he resumed the advance.

When Lee at Chancellorsville learned that Sedgwick had carried the heights west of Fredericksburg, and that he was advancing on the Plank Road, he sent McLaws' division back to meet him. McLaws arrived near Salem Church, about three miles west of Fredericksburg, at 2:00 P.M., and there he formed in line of battle along a ridge, facing east. Cadmus M. Wilcox's brigade of Anderson's division, which had fallen back from Fredericksburg, was formed across the Plank Road near the church. To his left, in order, were Paul J. Semmes' brigade of McLaws' division and William Mahone's brigade of Anderson's division; and on the right of Wilcox, south of the road, were the brigades of Joseph B. Kershaw and William T. Wofford of McLaws' division.

Brooks' division took the lead in Sedgwick's advance on the Plank Road toward Chancellorsville, and against some opposition arrived in front of McLaws' line at Salem Church. Joseph J. Bartlett's Second Brigade and the 2nd New Jersey and 23rd New Jersey regiments of Henry W. Brown's First Brigade (the New Jersey Brigade) were south of the Plank Road, and the 1st, 3rd, and 15th New Jersey regiments of Brown's brigade and the 95th and 119th Pennsylvania regiments of David A. Russell's Third Brigade were north of the Plank Road. Russell's two regiments had been detached from the brigade earlier in the day, and they had accompanied Brooks' division during the march. Russell, with his other regiments, had remained at Fredericksburg to cover Sedgwick's withdrawal.

At 4:00 P.M. Brooks advanced his division and made several assaults on McLaws' line. Bartlett finally succeeded in occupying Salem Church and the adjacent school house, and by 5:30 P.M., as Brown moved up, the fighting became general. Brown was wounded about 6:30 that evening, and Samuel L. Buck assumed command of his First Brigade, Brooks' division. Brooks maintained his position for about an hour, and was then driven back about a half mile to the Toll House (or Toll Gate). Russell arrived from Fredericksburg with three regiments of his brigade, and he was assigned command of Brooks' first line, which was held by Russell's brigade, and some regiments of Newton's division. A part of Howe's division also came up and formed on the left of Brooks. The fighting finally ended at dark, and Sedgwick's troops held their positions during the night. William H. Browne, commanding the Second Brigade of Newton's division, was wounded that afternoon near Salem Church, and Henry L. Eustis assumed command of the brigade.

About 4:30 P.M., while Brooks was engaged at Salem Church, Joshua T. Owen, with his Second Brigade of Gibbon's division, crossed the Rappahannock at Scott's Ford and reported to Sedgwick. He was ordered to take position on the right of Sedgwick's line, near the Rappahannock, to guard the crossings of Scott's Ford and Blind Ford (not the Blind Ford on the Rapidan River).

On the morning of May 4, 1863, Sixth Corps was in a precarious position. During the night, Early had reoccupied the heights west of Fredericksburg, and by this movement he had cut off Sedgwick from Fredericksburg, and also threatened to interpose between him and Banks' Ford. To complicate matters, Hooker had instructed Sedgwick to look after the safety of Sixth Corps without additional help, and also to recross the river at Banks' Ford if that became necessary. That day, Sedgwick formed his corps on three sides of a rectangle in front of Banks' Ford. Howe's line generally faced east, and ran southward from Taylor's Hill, near the Rappahannock, to a point a short distance south of the Plank Road, where it connected with the left of Brooks' division. Brooks' line faced south and extended westward for about a mile, a short distance south of the Plank Road, to the Toll House. On the west, Sedgwick's line ran northward in front of Salem Church from the right of Brooks' line to the vicinity of Banks' Ford. Russell's brigade of Brooks' division was on the left of this line, south of the Plank Road, and Newton's division extended from the right of Russell to the vicinity of Banks' Ford. Burnham's Light Brigade, which was attached to Newton, was on the right of the line.

At daylight May 4, 1863, Anderson's Confederate division was ordered from Chancellorsville to Salem Church, and it arrived there about 11:00 A.M. It was then sent to the south of the Plank Road, where it took position in front of Brooks' division, between Early and McLaws. There was skirmishing throughout the day, and then at 6:00 P.M. the enemy attacked Brooks and Howe, on the center and right of Sedgwick's line. These attacks were repulsed, but at 6:45 Sedgwick issued orders for the withdrawal of the corps to the river. As soon as it was dark, Brooks' division, Newton's division, and Burnham's Light Brigade fell back to Banks' Ford and formed a defensive line to protect the crossing. Howe's division then retired and formed on the right of Newton.

At 2:00 A.M. May 5, 1863, Sedgwick received orders to recross the Rappahannock. He began crossing immediately, and then camped in the vicinity of the ford on the north side of the river. Samuel L. Buck, commanding Henry W. Brown's brigade of Brooks' division, was disabled during the crossing, and William H. Penrose assumed command of the brigade. At Fredericksburg, Gibbon's division also recrossed the Rappahannock and returned to Falmouth.

Withdrawal of the Army of the Potomac, May 4–6, 1863. There was little activity at Chancellorsville on May 4, 1863. Hooker was content to remain with the Army of the Potomac on its entrenched line in front of United States Ford awaiting developments, and Lee's army, which was disorganized and exhausted by three days of fighting, and which had been weakened when troops were sent back to Salem Church to deal with Sedgwick, was in no condition to continue on the offensive.

At daylight that morning, Hooker relieved Averell, who was then at United States Ford, from duty with the cavalry, and his Second Cavalry Division and Benjamin F. Davis' First Brigade of First Cavalry Division were placed under the command of Pleasonton. The next day, Pleasonton was

ordered to Falmouth to secure the crossings of the Rappahannock.

On May 5, 1863, Hooker issued orders for the withdrawal of the army, and in preparation for recrossing the Rappahannock, he ordered the construction of a new and shorter line of defenses that were to extend from Scott's Dam on the Rappahannock to the mouth of Hunting Run on the Rapidan. That night, Meade's Fifth Corps was assigned to man the new defensive line, and First Corps, Second Corps, Third Corps, Eleventh Corps, and Twelfth Corps marched to the vicinity of United States Ford. After issuing the orders for the army to cross the river, Hooker was one of the first to leave, and he thus left the handling of the army during the movement to the individual corps commanders. It was not until midnight that Couch, the senior corps commander, learned that he was in charge of the army. At the same time he learned that the bridges were unserviceable, and accordingly he suspended the order for crossing. Then at 2:00 A.M. May 6, 1863, the bridges were reopened, and Couch received an imperative order from Hooker to proceed with the crossing. This was completed during the morning of May 6, 1863. Fifth Corps was the last to cross. Humphreys' division went first, and it was followed by Sykes' division, and then Griffin's division. Barnes' First Brigade of Griffin's division waited for the pickets to cross, and was thus the last brigade of the army to leave the south bank of the Rappahannock. Romeyn B. Ayres of Sykes' division was field officer of the day, and it was he who brought in the pickets. When the Army of the Potomac was once again on the north side of the river, it returned to its old camps opposite Fredericksburg.

Stoneman's Raid, April 27, 1863–May 7, 1863. As a part of Hooker's plans for the spring campaign of 1863, George Stoneman, commanding the Cavalry Corps, Army of the Potomac, was ordered April 12, 1863 to make a major raid to the rear of Lee's army at Fredericksburg. He was to proceed by way of Culpeper Court House and Gordonsville to the vicinity of Hanover Court House, and destroy as much as possible the enemy communications in the area. In addition, Hooker expected to defeat Lee's army at, or near, Fredericksburg, and he wanted

Stoneman to be in position to interfere with its retreat until the Army of the Potomac could come up and complete its destruction.

Stoneman was directed to leave Thomas C. Devin's Second Brigade of Pleasonton's First Cavalry Division, under the personal direction of Pleasonton, with the Army of the Potomac, and to march with the rest of the Cavalry Corps, including four battalions of James M. Robertson's Horse Artillery Brigade. He was to move up the east bank of the Rappahannock River to the upper fords, and then, after crossing the river, he was to march to the southeast in the direction of Richmond.

Stoneman began his march April 13, 1863, and arrived at the fords in the vicinity of the Orange and Alexandria Railroad the next day. That evening, however, before the crossing began, it started to rain, and after a few hours the water had risen to such height that the depth at the fords made them impassable. Stoneman then moved his command back to Warrenton Junction, where it could be supplied more readily than on the river, and waited for the waters to subside. Finally, on the morning of April 29, 1863, Stoneman again arrived on the Rappahannock, and during the day crossed the river at Kelly's Ford. At the same time, Fifth Corps, Eleventh Corps, and Twelfth Corps were crossing there on the bridges, at the beginning of their flanking march to Chancellorsville.

Once across the river, Stoneman detached William W. Averell's Second Cavalry Division and Benjamin F. Davis' First Brigade of Pleasonton's First Cavalry Division, and a battery of artillery, and sent Averell by way of Brandy Station and Culpeper Court House toward Rapidan Station, on the Orange and Alexandria Railroad. The purpose of Averell's detachment from the corps was to divert attention from the march of Stoneman's main force, and to engage and destroy the Confederate cavalry force believed to be in the area. The order for Averell's movement was at best confusing, and was, by implication at least, in violation of Hooker's directive. This was to become a serious issue later in the campaign.

Early on the morning of April 30, 1863, Stoneman began his march toward Richmond. He took with him David McM. Gregg's Third Cavalry Division and John Buford's Regular Reserve Cavalry Brigade, to which Richard H. Rush's 6th Pennsylvania Cavalry Regiment (then commanded by Robert Morris, Jr.) was attached. Buford's brigade took the lead and, moving by way of Stevensburg, crossed the Rapidan River at Morton's Ford. Gregg's division followed, and crossed during the evening at Raccoon Ford. The next day, Stoneman resumed the march and arrived at Louisa Court House on the morning of May 2, 1863. There he destroyed bridges, culverts, water tanks, and several miles of the Virginia Central Railroad, and then moved on by way of Yanceyville and arrived that night at Thompson's Cross Roads, on the South Anna River. Stoneman then detached two companies of the 2nd United States Cavalry to watch the bridge at Thompson's Cross Roads, and early the next morning, he sent out several parties to continue the work of destruction. These were as follows:

Percy Wyndham, with the 1st New Jersey Cavalry and the 1st Maryland Cavalry of his Second Brigade of Gregg's division, marched to Columbia on the James River, near the mouth of the Rivanna River, and there he destroyed the aqueduct and the bridges over the James River Canal. Wyndham then moved eastward along the canal and destroyed locks, gates, and canal boats, and returned the same day.

Hasbrouck Davis, with his 12th Illinois Cavalry of Wyndham's brigade, advanced to Ashland Station on the Richmond, Fredericksburg, and Potomac Railroad, and Hanover Station on the Virginia Central Railroad, and destroyed buildings, trestles, and culverts on the railroads. He then moved on to the east and entered the Federal lines at Gloucester Point, opposite Yorktown.

Judson Kilpatrick, with the 2nd New York Cavalry of his First Brigade of Gregg's division, crossed the Richmond, Fredericksburg, and Potomac Railroad, caused some destruction, and then passed within two miles of Richmond. He burned Meadow Bridge on the Chickahominy River, destroyed railroad cars and wagons loaded with stores, and finally reached Gloucester Point.

Gregg, with the 1st Maine of Kilpatrick's brigade and 1st Maryland of Wyndham's brigade, moved down the South Anna River, destroying bridges as he advanced. Thomas Drummond, with 200 men of the 5th United States Cavalry, also moved down the

South Anna as far as Goochland Court House. Both parties returned to Thompson's Cross Roads the next day.

Stoneman retained at Thompson's Cross Roads 500 men of Buford's brigade to form a command upon which the other parties could rally if necessary.

On May 5, 1863, most of Stoneman's men, except those with Kilpatrick and Davis, were concentrated at Yanceyville, and he then began his return march. He followed the same route that he had used in his advance, and recrossed the Rapidan at Raccoon Ford on the night of May 7, 1863. The next day he moved to Bealeton Station on the Orange and Alexandria Railroad, and May 10, 1863 he marched to the vicinity of Falmouth.

To return to Averell, it appears that when he was detached from Stoneman's column on the night of April 29, 1863 and sent toward Culpeper Court House, he did not understand that he was to rejoin Stoneman's command. In any event, when Hooker learned that Averell was at Rapidan Station, and that he had accomplished nothing, he ordered him to march at once with his command to United States Ford and report in person to the commander of the army. Averell received this order May 2, 1863, and arrived at Ely's Ford about 10:30 that night. The next day he moved on to United States Ford, and there on May 4, 1863 he received an order dated May 3, 1863, relieving him from duty with the Army of the Potomac. The same order placed Pleasonton in charge of his division. Averell was sent to Western Virginia, where on May 18, 1863 he was assigned command of Fourth Separate Brigade (mounted infantry) of Robert C. Schenck's Middle Department, Eighth Corps.

Organization of the Army of the Potomac during the Battle of Chancellorsville, May 1–6, 1863.

ARMY OF THE POTOMAC, Joseph Hooker
Command of the Provost Marshal General, Marsena R. Patrick
Patrick's Brigade, William F. Rogers
Unbrigaded regiments
Engineer Brigade, Henry W. Benham
Signal Corps, Samuel T. Cushing
Ordnance Detachment, John R. Edie
Artillery, Henry J. Hunt, Chief of Artillery
Artillery Reserve, William M. Graham, to May 2, 1863
Robert O. Tyler

FIRST CORPS, John F. Reynolds

First Division, James S. Wadsworth
First Brigade, Walter Phelps, Jr.
Second Brigade, Lysander Cutler
Third Brigade, Gabriel R. Paul
Fourth Brigade, Solomon Meredith
Artillery, John A. Reynolds
1st Battery, New Hampshire Light Artillery, Frederick N. Edgell
Battery L, 1st New York Light Artillery, John A. Reynolds
Battery B, 4th United States Artillery, James Stewart

Second Division, John C. Robinson
First Brigade, Adrian R. Root
Second Brigade, Henry Baxter
Third Brigade, Samuel H. Leonard
Artillery, Dunbar R. Ransom
2nd Battery (B), Maine Light Artillery, James A. Hall
5th Battery (E), Maine Light Artillery, George F. Leppien, to May 3, 1863, killed
Edmund Kirby, wounded
Greenleaf T. Stevens
Battery C, Pennsylvania Light Artillery, James Thompson
Battery C, 5th United States Artillery, Dunbar R. Ransom

Third Division, Abner Doubleday
First Brigade, Thomas A. Rowley
Second Brigade, Roy Stone
Artillery, Ezra W. Matthews
Battery B, 1st Pennsylvania Light Artillery, James H. Cooper
Battery F, 1st Pennsylvania Light Artillery, R. Bruce Ricketts
Battery G, 1st Pennsylvania Light Artillery, Frank P. Amsden

SECOND CORPS, Darius N. Couch

First Division, Winfield S. Hancock
First Brigade, John C. Caldwell
Second Brigade, Thomas F. Meagher
Third Brigade, Samuel K. Zook
Fourth Brigade, John R. Brooke
Provisional Brigade, Edward E. Cross

Note. Cross commanded a temporary brigade consisting of 5th New Hampshire and 81st Pennsylvania of First Brigade and 88th New York of Second Brigade.

Artillery, Rufus D. Pettit
Battery B, 1st New York Light Artillery, Rufus D. Pettit

Battery C, 4th United States Artillery, Evan Thomas

Second Division, John Gibbon
First Brigade, Alfred Sully, to May 1, 1863
Henry W. Hudson, to May 3, 1863
Byron Laflin
Second Brigade, Joshua T. Owen
Third Brigade, Norman J. Hall

Note. Sully was relieved from command of First Brigade May 1, 1863, because he was unable to enforce discipline in the brigade.

Artillery
Battery A, 1st Rhode Island Light Artillery, William A. Arnold
Battery A, 1st Rhode Island Light Artillery, T. Fred Brown

Third Division, William H. French
First Brigade, Samuel S. Carroll
Second Brigade, William Hays, to May 3, 1863, captured
Charles J. Powers
Third Brigade, John D. McGregor, to May 2, 1863, sick
Charles Albright
Artillery
Battery G, 1st New York Light Artillery, Nelson Ames
Battery G, 1st Rhode Island Light Artillery, George W. Adams
Reserve Artillery
Battery I, 1st United States Artillery, Edmund Kirby
Battery A, 4th United States Artillery, Alonzo H. Cushing

THIRD CORPS, Daniel E. Sickles

First Division, David D. Birney
First Brigade, Charles K. Graham, to May 4, 1863
Thomas W. Egan
Second Brigade, J. H. Hobart Ward
Third Brigade, Samuel B. Hayman

Note. Graham was assigned command of Amiel W. Whipple's Third Division, Third Corps May 4, 1863.

Artillery, A. Judson Clark
Battery B, New Jersey Light Artillery, Robert Sims
Battery B, 1st Rhode Island Light Artillery, Pardon S. Jastram
Batteries F and K, 3rd United States Artillery, John G. Turnbull

Second Division, Hiram Berry, to May 3, 1863, killed
Joseph B. Carr
First Brigade, Joseph B. Carr, to May 3, 1863
William Blaisdell

Second Brigade, Joseph W. Revere, to May 3, 1863
J. Egbert Farnum
Third Brigade, Gershom Mott, to May 3, 1863, wounded
William J. Sewell

Note. Revere was relieved from command of Third Brigade May 3, 1863, for having led his brigade and a part of First Brigade from the field during the fighting earlier in the day.

Artillery, Thomas W. Osborn
Battery D, 1st New York Light Artillery, George B. Winslow
4th Battery, New York Light Artillery, George F. Barstow
William T. McLean
Battery H, 1st United States Artillery, Justin E. Dimick, to May 3, 1863, killed
James A. Sanderson
Battery K, 4th United States Artillery, Francis W. Seeley

Third Division, Amiel W. Whipple, to May 4, 1863, killed
Charles K. Graham
First Brigade, Emlen Franklin
Second Brigade, Samuel M. Bowman
Third Brigade, Hiram Berdan

Note. Whipple was killed by a sharpshooter while supervising the construction of new works near Chandlers'.

Artillery, Albert Von Puttkammer, to May 2, 1863
James F. Huntington
10th Battery, New York Light Artillery, Samuel Lewis
11th Battery, New York Light Artillery, John E. Burton
Battery H, 1st Ohio Light Artillery, James F. Huntington.

Note. Von Puttkammer left the field during Jackson's attack on the evening of May 2, 1863, and was later relieved from his command.

FIFTH CORPS, George G. Meade

First Division, Charles Griffin
First Brigade, James Barnes
Second Brigade, James McQuade, to May 4, 1863, disabled
Jacob B. Sweitzer
Third Brigade, Thomas B. W. Stockton

Artillery, Augustus P. Martin
3rd Battery (C), Massachusetts Light Artillery, Augustus P. Martin

5th Battery (E), Massachusetts Light Artillery, Charles A. Phillips

Battery C, 1st Rhode Island Light Artillery, Richard Waterman

Battery D, 5th United States Artillery, Charles E. Hazlett

Second Division, George Sykes
First Brigade, Romeyn B. Ayres
Second Brigade, Sidney Burbank
Third Brigade, Patrick H. O'Rorke
Artillery, Stephen H. Weed
Battery L, 1st Ohio Light Artillery, Frank C. Gibbs
Battery I, 5th United States Artillery, Malbone F. Watson

Third Division, Andrew A. Humphreys
First Brigade, Erastus B. Tyler
Second Brigade, Peter H. Allabach
Artillery, Alanson M. Randol
Battery C, 1st New York Light Artillery, Almont Barnes
Batteries E and G, 1st United States Artillery, Alanson M. Randol

SIXTH CORPS, John Sedgwick

First Division, William T. H. Brooks
First Brigade, Henry W. Brown, to May 3, 1863, wounded
William H. Penrose, May 3, 1863
Samuel L. Buck, to May 5, 1863, disabled
William H. Penrose
Second Brigade, Joseph J. Bartlett
Third Brigade, David A. Russell
Artillery, John A. Tompkins
1st Battery (A), Massachusetts Light Artillery, William H. McCartney
Battery A, New Jersey Light Artillery, Augustin N. Parsons
Battery A, Maryland Light Artillery, James H. Rigby
Battery D, 2nd United States Artillery. Edward B. Williston

Second Division, Albion P. Howe
Second Brigade, Lewis A. Grant
Third Brigade, Thomas H. Neill

Note. First Brigade was discontinued March 24, 1863, and its regiments were assigned to Third Brigade.

Artillery, J. Watts De Peyster
1st Battery, New York Light Artillery, Andrew Cowan

Battery F, 5th United States Artillery, Leonard Martin

Third Division, John Newton
First Brigade, Alexander Shaler
Second Brigade, William H. Browne, to May 3, 1863, wounded
Henry L. Eustis
Third Brigade, Frank Wheaton
Artillery, Jeremiah McCarthy
Batteries C and D, 1st Pennsylvania Light Artillery, Jeremiah McCarthy
Battery G, 2nd United States Artillery, John H. Butler

Light Brigade (or Light Division), Hiram Burnham

Note. Burnham's Light Brigade (or Light Division) was attached to Newton's Third Division during the operations at Fredericksburg and Salem Church May 3, 1863.

ELEVENTH CORPS, Oliver O. Howard

First Division, Charles Devens, to May 2, 1863, wounded
Nathaniel C. McLean
First Brigade, Leopold Von Gilsa
Second Brigade, Nathaniel C. McLean, to May 2, 1863
John C. Lee
13th Battery, New York Light Artillery, Julius Dieckmann

Second Division, Adolph Von Steinwehr
First Brigade, Adolphus Buschbeck
Second Brigade, Francis C. Barlow
Battery I, 1st New York Light Artillery, Michael Wiedrich

Third Division, Carl Schurz
First Brigade, Alexander Schimmelfennig
Second Brigade, Wladimir Krzyzanowski
Battery I, 1st Ohio Light Artillery, Hubert Dilger

Reserve Artillery, Louis Schirmer
2nd Battery, New York Light Artillery, Hermann Jahn
Battery K, 1st Ohio Light Artillery, William L. De Beck
Battery C, 1st West Virginia Light Artillery, Wallace Hill

TWELFTH CORPS, Henry W. Slocum

First Division, Alpheus S. Williams
First Brigade, Joseph F. Knipe
Second Brigade, Samuel Ross
Third Brigade, Thomas H. Ruger

Note. Ross was wounded on the morning of May 3, 1863, and Knipe commanded both First Brigade and Second Brigade.

Artillery, Robert H. Fitzhugh
  Battery K, 1st New York Light Artillery, Edward L. Bailey
  Battery M, 1st New York Light Artillery, Charles E. Winegar, to May 3, 1863, captured
    John D. Woodbury
  Battery F, 4th United States Artillery, Franklin B. Crosby, to May 3, 1863, killed
    Edward B. Muhlenberg

Second Division, John W. Geary
  First Brigade, Charles Candy
  Second Brigade, Thomas L. Kane
  Third Brigade, George S. Greene
  Artillery, Joseph M. Knap
  Battery E, Pennsylvania Light Artillery, Charles S. Atwell, to May 2, 1863, wounded
    James D. McGill
  Battery F, Pennsylvania Light Artillery, Robert B. Hampton, to May 3, 1863, mortally wounded
    James P. Fleming

CAVALRY CORPS, George Stoneman

First Cavalry Division, Alfred Pleasonton
  First Brigade, Benjamin F. Davis
  Second Brigade, Thomas C. Devin
  6th Battery, New York Light Artillery, Joseph W. Martin

Second Cavalry Division, William W. Averell, to May 4, 1863
  First Brigade, Horace B. Sargent
  Second Brigade, John B. McIntosh
  Battery A, 2nd United States Artillery, John C. Tidball

Note. Joseph Hooker was dissatisfied with Averell's performance during Stoneman's raid, and relieved him from duty with the Army of the Potomac May 4, 1863. Pleasonton assumed command of Second Cavalry Division as well as of his own First Cavalry Division.

Third Cavalry Division, David McM. Gregg
  First Brigade, Judson Kilpatrick
  Second Brigade, Percy Wyndham

Regular Reserve Cavalry Brigade, John Buford

  Artillery, James M. Robertson
  Batteries B and L, 2nd United States Artillery, Albert O. Vincent

Battery M, 2nd United States Artillery, Robert Clarke
Battery E, 4th United States Artillery, Samuel S. Elder

ENGAGEMENT AT DRANESVILLE, VIRGINIA DECEMBER 20, 1861

In December 1861, George A. McCall's Division, Army of the Potomac was encamped at Camp Pierpoint (also Camp Peirpoint) near Langley, Virginia. On the evening of December 19, 1861, McCall learned that enemy pickets had advanced to within four or five miles of his lines, and that they had carried off and threatened some Union men and had plundered their farms. He then ordered Edward O. C. Ord to move out with his Third Brigade, a battery, and two squadrons of cavalry toward Dranesville, a hamlet about twelve miles to the west on the Leesburg Pike (present-day State Route 7), to drive off the raiding parties, and also to bring back forage from that area. He also ordered John F. Reynolds to move forward with his First Brigade to support Ord if that became necessary.

At 6:00 A.M. December 20, 1861, Ord marched out on the Georgetown Road, which joined the Leesburg Pike a short distance east of Dranesville. At about the same time an enemy wagon train, protected by James E. B. (Jeb) Stuart with four infantry regiments and Richard C. F. Radford's cavalry, left Joseph E. Johnston's army at Centerville to collect forage west of Dranesville, about twelve miles to the north.

The leading elements of Ord's column arrived at Dranesville about noon. These consisted of Thomas L. Kane's 1st Pennsylvania Rifles (Bucktails), Conrad Feger Jackson's 9th Pennsylvania Reserves, Hezekiah Easton's Battery A, Pennsylvania Light Artillery, and two squadrons of Jacob Higgins' 1st Pennsylvania Reserve Cavalry. On the road behind were John S. McCalmont's 10th Pennsylvania Reserves, William M. Penrose's 6th Pennsylvania Reserves, and John H. Taggart's 12th Pennsylvania Reserves.

At 1:00 P.M., McCalmont, whose regiment was posted on the high ground north of the Leesburg Pike, observed Stuart's cavalry advancing to the south and southeast of Dranesville. At that time, the rear of Ord's column was approaching the junction of the Georgetown Road and the Leesburg Pike, and as the regiments came up, Ord formed them in line of battle along the Leesburg Pike. The 9th Pennsylvania Reserves was placed on the right, south of the pike, near the eastern edge of Dranesville. Next, to the left of Kane, were the 6th Pennsylvania Reserves and the 1st Pennsylvania Rifles. Both regiments were just south of the pike, and the left of the 1st Pennsylvania Rifles was near the junction of the Georgetown Road and the Leesburg Pike. The 12th Pennsylvania Reserves was placed on the pike, but later moved up between the 9th Pennsylvania Reserves and the 6th Pennsylvania Reserves. Easton's battery was to the left of the 1st Pennsylvania Rifles, in the angle formed by the junction of the Georgetown Road and the Leesburg Pike. It was supported by the 10th Pennsylvania Reserves. The 1st Pennsylvania Reserve Cavalry was placed on the extreme left of Ord's line, north of the pike.

When Stuart learned of the proximity of Ord's troops, his first concern was for the safety of the wagon train. He quickly sent orders for it to withdraw, and then brought up his infantry and Allen S. Cutts' battery. The latter was soon engaged with Easton's battery to the north. Stuart formed his infantry across the Centerville Road, with his regiments from the Confederate left to right, as follows: 1st Kentucky, 6th South Carolina, 10th Alabama, and 11th Virginia. When the deployment was completed, Stuart's line advanced but was soon halted by heavy infantry fire, probably from Kane's regiment. Stuart's infantry returned the fire, and held its position for about one-half hour. At that time, about 2:00 P.M., McCall arrived on the field in person from Camp Pierpont. Before leaving he had taken the precaution of ordering up Reynolds' brigade and also George G. Meade's Second Brigade to support Ord. They did not arrive on the field, however, until the fighting had ended.

About 3:00 P.M. Stuart decided that his train had withdrawn to safety, and he then directed his command to retire toward Centerville. McCall's Division remained at Dranesville that night, and then returned to camp the next day.

EARLY'S WASHINGTON RAID (AND OPERATIONS IN THE SHENANDOAH VALLEY, MARYLAND, AND PENNSYLVANIA) JUNE 23, 1864–AUGUST 3, 1864

EARLY'S WASHINGTON RAID

When Lynchburg, Virginia was threatened by David Hunter's advance up the Shenandoah Valley in June 1864, Jubal A. Early's Second Corps was detached from the Army of Northern Virginia and June 13, 1864 marched from near Gaines' Mill to reinforce the Confederate troops holding the town. Early arrived June 18, 1864, just in time to aid John C. Breckinridge in repulsing Hunter's attack. Aware of Early's approach, Hunter retreated to the west by way of Salem, White Sulfur Springs, Lewisburg, and Gauley Bridge, and arrived at Charleston, West Virginia June 30, 1864. For additional information, see Department of West Virginia, Operations in the Department of West Virginia, Hunter's Lynchburg Campaign.

Early followed Hunter as far as Liberty (present-day Bedford), and there, on June 23, 1864, he abandoned the pursuit. He then moved northward, down the Shenandoah Valley, in an offensive movement designed to divert Federal troops from the Richmond and Petersburg front. He reached Winchester, Virginia July 2, 1864, and then, by-passing Harper's Ferry, he crossed the Potomac River at Shepherdstown July 5–6, 1864, and marched toward Frederick, Maryland.

Battle of the Monocacy, Maryland, July 9, 1864. On July 5, 1864, Lewis (Lew) Wallace, commanding the Middle Department and Eighth Corps at Baltimore, learned that Early was north of the Potomac in Maryland, and by the evening of July 6, 1864, he had concentrated all available troops of his command, about 2,500 men, on the Monocacy River, not far from Frederick. Wallace's command consisted of the following:

First Separate Brigade, Eighth Corps, Erastus B. Tyler
3rd Maryland Home Brigade, Charles Gilpin

11th Maryland Regiment, William T. Landstreet

Regiment of Ohio National Guard, Allison L. Brown

1st Maryland Home Brigade (three companies), Charles J. Brown

Alexander's Maryland (Baltimore) Battery, Frederic W. Alexander

Note 1. The Regiment of Ohio National Guard consisted of seven companies of 149th Ohio National Guard and three companies of 144th Ohio National Guard, which were combined under Brown.

Note 2. All Ohio troops and those of the 11th Maryland were one-hundred-day men.

Some Federal cavalry also joined Wallace at Frederick. David R. Clendenin left Washington, D.C. on the evening of July 4, 1864 with 230 men of the 8th Illinois Cavalry, and moved up the Potomac River to Point of Rocks. There, at 11:30 A.M. July 6, 1864, he was ordered to march to Frederick to investigate reports that a Confederate force was at Boonsboro, Maryland. Clendenin arrived at Frederick at 8:00 P.M. and reported to Wallace, who was then at Monocacy Junction.

The next day Clendenin's cavalry, aided by a section of Alexander's battery that had been sent up from the Monocacy, skirmished with Early's advance as it moved forward from Middletown. Tyler then sent Charles Gilpin's 3rd Maryland Home Brigade to join the cavalry at Frederick, and Gilpin, as the senior officer, assumed command of the combined force. At midnight July 7, 1864, Tyler, with Allison L. Brown's regiment of Ohio National Guard, moved up to Frederick and prepared for an engagement that was expected on the following day.

At daybreak July 8, 1864, a portion of William S. Truex's First Brigade, Third Division, Sixth Corps, under the command of William A. Henry, was also sent to Frederick from Monocacy Junction, where it had just arrived from Baltimore.

Tyler's command skirmished with the enemy throughout the day of July 8, 1864, and during that time Clendenin was reinforced by Edward H. Lieb of the 5th United States Cavalry with about 100 mounted infantry, Charles A. Wells of the 1st New York Veteran Cavalry with about 250 men of various regiments, and the Independent Loudoun (Virginia) Rangers. Clendenin's command then consisted of the following:

Cavalry, David R. Clendenin

Detachment 8th Illinois Cavalry, David R. Clendenin

149th Ohio Regiment (100 men), Edward H. Lieb and Henry S. Allen

Detachment of Mixed Cavalry (25 men), Charles A. Wells

Loudoun (Virginia) Rangers

Note. The men of 149th Ohio Regiment served as mounted infantry.

Because of the conflicting reports of Early's strength and of his movements, Wallace also went to Frederick July 8, 1864, and from the information received while there, he decided to fall back to the Monocacy River and cover the roads to Baltimore and Washington. During the night of July 8, 1864, Wallace withdrew his command to the east side of the Monocacy River, across from Monocacy Junction, and there he was joined by James B. Ricketts' Third Division, Sixth Corps, which had just moved up from Baltimore.

When Ulysses S. Grant, then at City Point, Virginia, learned of Early's threat in Maryland, he immediately sent north reinforcements from the Army of the Potomac, which at that time was on the lines in front of Petersburg. Ricketts' Third Division, Sixth Corps embarked at City Point for Baltimore, where it arrived on the morning of July 8, 1864. It immediately moved forward by the Baltimore and Ohio Railroad to join Wallace on the Monocacy. Ricketts' division was organized as follows:

Third Division, Sixth Corps, James B. Ricketts

First Brigade, William S. Truex

14th New Jersey, Caldwell K. Hall

106th New York, Edward M. Paine

151st New York, William Emerson

87th Pennsylvania, James A. Stahle

10th Vermont, William W. Henry

Second Brigade, Matthew R. McClennan

9th New York Heavy Artillery, William H. Seward, Jr.

110th Ohio, Otho H. Binkley

122nd Ohio (detachment), Charles J. Gibson

126th Ohio, Aaron W. Ebright

138th Pennsylvania, Lewis A. May

Note. Benjamin F. Smith was in command of Second Brigade at Petersburg, but McClennan was in command of that part of the brigade that was present at the Battle of the Monocacy. The 6th Maryland, 67th Pennsylvania, and a part of the 122th Ohio, all under the command of John F. Staunton, were delayed and did not reach the battlefield.

Early on the morning of July 9, 1864, Wallace assumed command of the combined forces of Sixth Corps and Eighth Corps at Monocacy Junction, and placed them in position on the east bank of the Monocacy River to cover the crossings of the roads leading to Baltimore and Washington. Tyler's troops were placed on the right of the line, and their front extended from the Baltimore and Ohio Railroad on the left to the Stone Bridge on the Baltimore Pike on the right; Brown's regiment of Ohio National Guard and Leib's mounted infantry were posted at the Stone Bridge; three companies of Gilpin's 3rd Maryland Home Brigade were at Crum's Ford, about midway between the Baltimore Pike and the railroad; and Landstreet's 11th Maryland and the rest of Gilpin's regiment were held in reserve near the railroad.

Ricketts formed his two brigades across the Washington Road (Georgetown Road) south of the railroad so as to hold the rising ground there, and also the wooden bridge on the Washington Pike at the Monocacy River. The division generally faced toward the Monocacy River. Clendenin's cavalry was posted farther south to watch the left of Ricketts, and to guard the lower fords.

Early on the morning of July 9, 1864, Early's command moved forward toward the Monocacy River. Stephen D. Ramseur's division passed through Frederick and, driving the Federal skirmishers before it, deployed on the west bank of the river at the crossings of the railroad and the Washington Road. Ramseur then engaged in an artillery exchange with Alexander's guns. John C. Breckinridge's command, consisting of his own division and John B. Gordon's division, was in the rear, between Frederick and Monocacy Junction.

There was skirmishing along the line from 9:00 to 10:30 A.M., and the fighting at the Stone Bridge on the Baltimore Pike became serious, but Brown was able to hold his position with some difficulty. Then John McCausland moved his cavalry down the Monocacy, crossed the river at a ford about a mile below the bridge at the crossing of the Washington Pike, and advanced toward Ricketts' left flank. Ricketts' division then changed front to the left, and

formed on a single line that ran generally parallel to the Washington Pike and extended from the river, near the bridge, to the Thomas house, which was west of the road and about a mile south of the railroad bridge.

Ricketts forced McCausland back, and Early then ordered Breckinridge to hurry forward with Gordon's division and support the cavalry and follow up its attack. At 2:30 P.M. Gordon marched across the fields, out of range of the Federal artillery, and crossed the Monocacy at the ford used by McCausland. He promptly formed his division for an attack on Ricketts' line as follows: Clement A. Evans' brigade was on the right; the brigades of Harry T. Hays and Leroy A. Stafford, united under the command of Zebulon York, were on the left of Evans; and William Terry's brigade was placed to support the left of Gordon's line. While Ramseur skirmished on the front of Wallace's line, Gordon advanced and launched an attack on its left. Ricketts repulsed three Confederate attacks, but about 3:30 P.M. he was driven back, and finally at 4:00 P.M. he withdrew to the north to the Baltimore Pike.

It was of the greatest importance that Rodes be prevented from crossing the river at the Stone Bridge on the Baltimore Pike, because this was Wallace's line of retreat, and Tyler, with his reserve regiments, was ordered to that point to support Brown. The Federals retained possession of the bridge until 5:00 P.M., at which time Wallace's column was well on the way to New Market, on the road to Baltimore. Ramseur and Rodes then crossed the river and followed Wallace for a time, but soon abandoned the pursuit. Wallace in person reached Baltimore on the evening of July 10, 1864. His army arrived at Ellicott's Mills that same evening, and then moved on to Baltimore the next day.

July 11, 1864, Edward O. C. Ord was assigned command of Eighth Corps and of all troops in the Middle Department. Wallace remained in charge of administrative affairs of the department, but he reported to Ord, who was superior in all military operations and movements.

Early's Army before Washington, D.C., July 11–12, 1864. On the morning of July 10, 1864, after the Battle of the Monocacy, Early marched by way of Rockville, Maryland toward Washington, and arrived the next day north of the defenses of the city, near Silver Spring, Maryland. Also that day, David A. Russell's First Division and George W. Getty's Second Division of Sixth Corps, both under the command of Horatio G. Wright, began embarking at City Point for Washington. The leading elements of Wright's command began to arrive at the capital about noon July 11, 1864, and they immediately moved up into the fortifications in front of Early. The remainder of Sixth Corps arrived later that day and during the next.

Additional reinforcements also arrived in Washington on July 11, 1864. Earlier in the month, First Division and Second Division of Nineteenth Corps, Department of the Gulf, both under the command of William H. Emory, embarked at New Orleans, Louisiana for Virginia, and on July 10, 1864, the first of these troops began arriving at Fort Monroe. These were immediately ordered on to Washington, and they began disembarking there the next day. Quincy A. Gillmore was assigned command of the troops of Nineteenth Corps in Washington, which at that time consisted of only about 600 men.

Early learned that heavy reinforcements were moving into Washington, and he decided against any attempt to storm the defensive works. There was some fighting around Fort Stevens July 12, 1864, and the Federal troops involved belonged largely to Daniel D. Bidwell's Third Brigade of Getty's Second Division, Sixth Corps. That night Early withdrew to the west, and two days later he recrossed the Potomac into Virginia near Leesburg.

For details of the organization of the Union troops in the defenses of Washington during this period, see Department of Washington, February 2, 1863–March 16, 1869, Organizational Changes in the Department of Washington during Campaigns in Virginia, Maryland, and Pennsylvania, Early's Washington Raid.

Pursuit of Early, July 13–18, 1864. On July 13, 1864, Wright was assigned command of all forces that were to be ordered out in pursuit of Early, and on the same day, Emory was assigned command of Detachment Nineteenth Corps, which then consisted of 4,600 men. Wright assumed command, and with Russell's and Getty's divisions of Sixth Corps, Emory's Detachment Nineteenth Corps, and Charles R. Lowell's 2nd Massachusetts Cavalry

from the Defenses of Washington, followed Early toward Edwards Ferry. Wright crossed the Potomac there and arrived at Leesburg July 16, 1864.

Meantime, on July 14, 1864, Ord, at Baltimore, had assigned John R. Kenly to the command of Erastus B. Tyler's brigade of Eighth Corps, and that same day had moved by rail with Kenly's Brigade and Ricketts' Third Division of Sixth Corps to Washington. Kenly and Ricketts then moved on, following Wright's column, and joined it near Leesburg July 17, 1864. Ricketts' division then rejoined Sixth Corps, and the next day Ricketts assumed temporary command of the corps while Wright was in command of the expedition. Frank Wheaton assumed command of Third Division. Kenly's Brigade was assigned temporarily to Detachment Nineteenth Corps. For additional information relating to Kenly's Brigade and Ricketts' division, see Middle Department,. Military Operations in the Middle Department, Early's Washington Raid.

The organization of the troops that Wright led from Washington and Leesburg in pursuit of Early was as follows:

SIXTH CORPS, Horatio G. Wright, to July 17, 1864
  James B. Ricketts

First Division, David A. Russell
  First Brigade, William H. Penrose
  Second Brigade, Emory Upton
  Third Brigade, Oliver Edwards

Second Division, George W. Getty
  First Brigade, Frank Wheaton, to July 17, 1864
  Second Brigade, Lewis A. Grant
  Third Brigade, Daniel D. Bidwell

Third Division, James B. Ricketts, to July 17, 1984
  Frank Wheaton
  First Brigade, William S. Truex
  Second Brigade, Benjamin F. Smith

DETACHMENT NINETEENTH CORPS, William H. Emory

First Division, William Dwight
  First Brigade, George L. Beal
  Second Brigade (part)

Note. Only a part of James W. McMillan's Second Brigade, commanded by Stephen Thomas, was present with Wright.

Second Division
   Third Brigade, Jacob Sharpe

Kenly's Brigade (Maryland Brigade), John R. Kenly

Note. At Leesburg, Kenly's Brigade was temporarily attached to Detachment Nineteenth Corps.

2nd Massachusetts Cavalry, Charles R. Lowell, Jr.

In addition to the above troops, Wright was soon to be joined by David Hunter's Army of the Department of West Virginia. It has been noted above that Hunter had been forced to retire from before Lynchburg, Virginia when Early arrived there with reinforcements from Richmond June 17–18, 1864, and that he had marched back through West Virginia and had arrived at Charleston June 30, 1864. During this same period, Early had been marching down the Shenandoah Valley, and on July 4, 1864, he arrived in front of Bolivar Heights, near Harper's Ferry. That same day Hunter arrived with his command at Parkersburg from Charleston, and immediately began the transfer of his army eastward by way of the Baltimore and Ohio Railroad toward Martinsburg and Harper's Ferry.

At that time, Franz Sigel was in command of the Reserve Division, Department of West Virginia, which included troops on the Baltimore and Ohio Railroad westward from Monocacy Junction. Max Weber commanded that part of the line from Monocacy Junction to Sleepy Creek, and Benjamin F. Kelley was in charge from that point westward. The Reserve Division included brigades commanded by Thomas M. Harris, James A. Mulligan, and William P. Maulsby, and also some unbrigaded regiments. On July 8, 1864, Albion P. Howe assumed command of the newly created District of Harper's Ferry, which included the railroad from Monocacy Junction to Hancock, Maryland. Weber was placed in command of the Defenses of Maryland Heights. Jeremiah C. Sullivan's First Infantry Division, the leading division of Hunter's army, arrived at Martinsburg July 10, 1864, and then moved on to Harper's Ferry July 13, 1864. The next day, Sullivan assumed command of the available forces at Harper's Ferry and in the vicinity, including Howe's District of Harper's Ferry. On July 15, 1864, Sullivan left a garrison at Harper's Ferry, and with the remainder of his command, which consisted of his First Infantry Division, Department of West

Virginia and Mulligan's Brigade (formerly commanded by Harris) of the Reserve Division, Department of West Virginia, marched out to join Wright, who was approaching in pursuit of Early. Sullivan crossed the Potomac near Berlin (present-day Brunswick) and marched to Hillsboro, Virginia, in the direction of Leesburg.

Alfred N. Duffie, with his First Cavalry Division, Department of West Virginia, arrived at Harper's Ferry July 15, 1864, and was sent on to report to Sullivan at Hillsboro. George Crook arrived at Harper's Ferry at midnight July 15, 1864, and he was then assigned command of all troops of the Department of West Virginia that were under orders to join Wright. Crook assumed command of Sullivan's forces at Hillsboro the next day. His force there was organized as follows:

FIELD TROOPS OF THE DEPARTMENT OF WEST
   VIRGINIA, George Crook

First Infantry Division, Jeremiah C. Sullivan
   First Brigade, George D. Wells
   Second Brigade, Joseph Thoburn

Note. July 18, 1864, Thoburn assumed command of First Infantry Division, and William G. Ely assumed command of Second Brigade.

First Cavalry Division, Alfred N. Duffie
   First Brigade, William B. Tibbits
   Second Brigade, George Middleton

Mulligan's Brigade, Reserve Division, James A. Mulligan

Third Brigade, Second Infantry Division, Daniel Frost

Note. Frost was temporarily in command of Jacob M. Campbell's Third Brigade.

On July 16, 1864, Duffie assigned William Blakely, commander of the 14th Pennsylvania Cavalry, Second Cavalry Division, to command all detachments of Second Cavalry Division then in the Snickersville area, and designated Blakely's command as a separate brigade.

Although Hunter was unhappy at Crook's assignment to command, this had been done because Grant wished the forces under Wright and Hunter to be combined to defeat Early. Wright had the greater part of the force, and Hunter had the higher rank, and accordingly, Hunter was left in command of the Department of West Virginia, and Crook, who was junior to Wright, was given command of the field force of the Department of West Virginia. July 16, 1864, Crook, then under the orders of Wright, marched to Purcellville to join Sixth Corps and Detachment Nineteenth Corps. When the remainder of Crook's Second Infantry Division arrived from Parkersburg, Isaac H. Duval's Second Brigade (formerly commanded by Carr B. White) was ordered to remain at Martinsburg, and July 18, 1864, Rutherford B. Hayes' First Brigade was sent on to Purcellville to join Crook.

The advance of William W. Averell's Second Cavalry Division, Department of West Virginia arrived at Martinsburg July 17, 1864 (the remainder was up by July 22, 1864), and was directed to remain there to protect the railroad in the vicinity. Duval, with his brigade, reported to Averell, who was assigned command of all forces at Martinsburg. Averell then reported to Hunter, because Crook was no longer in the department.

Engagement at Snicker's Ferry (or Parker's Ford), Virginia, July 18, 1864. On July 17, 1864, Wright's headquarters was at Clark's Gap in Catoctin Mountain, three miles west of Leesburg. That day he issued orders for the advance of the army to the Shenandoah Valley, and he directed Crook to send a cavalry force, supported by infantry, to press the rear of Early's column and determine what route he had taken. Accordingly, Crook sent Duffie's cavalry and Mulligan's infantry brigade on this mission, and they found that the enemy had crossed the Shenandoah River at Snicker's Ferry and had possession of the crossing. At 4:00 the next morning, Crook followed with the remainder of his command on the Snickersville Pike, and through Snicker's Gap into the Shenandoah Valley. Ricketts, with Sixth Corps, was also ordered to move by the same route into the valley. Emory was directed to march at the same time, with Detachment Nineteenth Corps, to Clark's Gap, and then to follow Crook and Ricketts.

About 2:00 P.M. July 18, 1864, while passing through Snicker's Gap, Joseph Thoburn received orders to take a part of Crook's command and cross the Shenandoah River at Island Ford, about two miles below Snicker's Ferry, and dislodge the enemy troops in position there. Thoburn's command consisted of the following:

First Infantry Division, Department of West Virginia, Joseph Thoburn
First Brigade, George D. Wells
Second Brigade, Joseph Thoburn

Third Brigade, Second Infantry Division, Department of West Virginia, Daniel Frost

Note. Frost was in temporary command of Jacob M. Campbell's brigade, and was mortally wounded that afternoon

Wells' brigade arrived on the river first, and then crossed and drove the enemy from their position at the ford. Thoburn then joined Wells on the far side of the river with his other two brigades, and formed a defensive line with Thoburn's brigade on the right, Frost's brigade in the center, and Wells' brigade on the left. Robert E. Rodes' division of Early's command launched three unsuccessful attacks on Thoburn's line, and then withdrew. Thoburn had been promised that a division of Sixth Corps would be sent to support him, but when it did not arrive, Crook ordered Thoburn to recross the river.

Federal Occupation of Winchester, Virginia, July 21, 1864. On the morning of July 19, 1864, Averell, acting under discretionary orders, advanced from Martinsburg with Duval's brigade and three regiments of his Second Cavalry Division, and arrived that afternoon at Stephenson's Depot, about four miles from Winchester. The next day, Averell advanced and drove back a Confederate force under Stephen D. Ramseur, and July 21, 1864 he occupied Winchester, which had been evacuated during the night. July 20, 1864, the day of Averell's fight in front of Winchester, William H. Powell was ordered to Snicker's Gap with his Second Brigade of Averell's cavalry division to follow Early, who was then retreating up the valley.

Wright crossed the Shenandoah River with his Sixth Corps on the morning of July 20, 1864, and advanced to the vicinity of Berryville with the intention of engaging Early, but he soon learned that the enemy had retreated during the night on the road to Front Royal and Strasburg. Wright then decided that, according to his instructions, the object of his expedition was accomplished, and accordingly he led Sixth Corps, Detachment Nineteenth Corps, and Charles R. Lowell's cavalry back out of the valley and on to Washington. Crook, however, was left in the valley, and July 20, 1864, he was ordered to march with his entire command from Snicker's Ferry, by way of Berryville to Winchester. He joined Averell there about noon July 22, 1864, and assumed command of all forces in the town.

When Crook arrived at Charleston, West Virginia on July 2, 1864, at the end of the retreat of Hunter's army from Lynchburg, he was assigned command of all troops in that part of the Department of West Virginia west of the Allegheny Mountains and south of the Baltimore and Ohio Railroad. The next day, Crook designated his command as the Army of the Kanawha. When Crook arrived at Winchester July 22, 1864, he found himself in command of essentially the same troops that had been assigned to him while at Charleston, and he called his army the Army of the Kanawha. Crook's command, however, has been referred to as the Army of West Virginia and also the Army of the Department of West Virginia.

July 22, 1864, Crook announced the temporary reorganization of the infantry of his command as follows:

ARMY OF THE KANAWHA (infantry only)

First Division, Joseph Thoburn
    First Brigade, George D. Wells
    Second Brigade, William G. Ely

Second Division, Isaac H. Duval
    First Brigade, Rutherford B. Hayes
    Second Brigade, Daniel D. Johnson

Third Division, James A. Mulligan
    First Brigade, Thomas M. Harris
    Second Brigade, John P. Linton

Note 1. Harris' brigade was organized from regiments on the Baltimore and Ohio Railroad near Harper's Ferry.
Note 2. Linton's brigade was organized from Third Brigade, Second Infantry Division, formerly commanded by Jacob M. Campbell.

When Wright left the Shenandoah Valley to return to Washington, Crook came under Hunter's orders.

Also on July 22, 1864, Jacob Higgins relieved George Middleton in command of Second Brigade, First Cavalry Division, and Duval's infantry brigade, which had been serving with Averell since July 17, 1864, again reported to Crook.

EARLY THREATENS AGAIN IN THE VALLEY

Battle of Kernstown (Winchester), Virginia, July 24, 1864. After Early left Snicker's Ferry, he retired up the valley with his army to New Market, Virginia, and he was there when he learned of Ramseur's defeat at Winchester July 20, 1864. He immediately moved back down the valley with Rodes' division, concentrated his forces at Newtown July 21, 1864, and then advanced toward Winchester. William H. Powell's Second Brigade of Averell's Second Cavalry Division, which had been picketing the roads as far south as Middletown, was forced back to Kernstown on the evening of July 22, 1864, and it was relieved there that night by Duffie's cavalry division.

The infantry of the Army of the Kanawha was in position near Winchester July 22, 1864, and the next day Crook sent forward James A. Mulligan's newly organized Third Division on a reconnaissance. That night, July 23, 1864, it bivouacked at Kernstown, with Thomas M. Harris' First Brigade on the right and John P. Linton's Second Brigade on the left. Early the next morning, Crook moved the rest of his command forward, and deployed in line of battle on the north bank of a small stream called Hogg Run. Thoburn's First Infantry Division advanced, and formed in a woods on the right and rear of Mulligan, with George D. Wells' First Brigade on the right and William G. Ely's Second Brigade on the left of the division line. Hayes' First Brigade of Duval's Second Infantry Division also moved to the front and was formed on the left of Mulligan. Daniel D. Johnson's Second Brigade of Duval's division was sent out on the Romney Road to protect the right of the army, and it was not engaged until during the Federal retreat that afternoon.

On the morning of July 24, 1864, Duffie proceeded to Kernstown, where Tibbits' First Brigade of his cavalry division had been skirmishing with Early's advance, and upon arriving there he formed his two brigades, with Tibbits' on the right and Higgins' Second Brigade on the left, to hold the ground until the infantry arrived. Duffie was then ordered to guard the flanks of the infantry line with his cavalry. Also that morning, Averell was sent out on the Front Royal Road to pass around the enemy right and attempt to strike the rear of Early's advancing column. About two miles out, however, Averell encountered stiff opposition and was forced to retire to Winchester when the infantry gave way that afternoon.

Shortly after noon July 24, 1864, Early advanced, and soon Crook's entire line was under heavy attack. John B. Gordon's leading division made a strong demonstration on Crook's front, and while this was in progress, John C. Breckinridge, with Gabriel C. Wharton's division, swung around to the right and struck Crook's exposed left flank. At the same time, Stephen D. Ramseur's division advanced against the Federal right. Crook's men fought stubbornly, but with their left partially turned and their right threatened, they were forced to retreat, and this soon became a rout as the Union brigades fled down the Valley Pike toward Winchester.

Mulligan was mortally wounded that afternoon, and Linton, commanding Mulligan's Second Brigade, was disabled by a fall. No field officers were left in Linton's brigade, which was brought off by Captain John Suter. Jacob M. Campbell arrived at Winchester as the Federal troops were retreating through the town, and July 25, 1864, he was ordered to assume command of Mulligan's division.

Crook fell back to Bunker Hill that night, and Averell's cavalry covered the rear during the retreat. There was skirmishing during July 25, 1864, but that evening the army withdrew toward Williamsport, closely followed by Early. Crook crossed the Potomac at Williamsport July 26, 1864, and the infantry marched by way of Sharpsburg to Harper's Ferry. The cavalry was left to picket the crossings of the Potomac. Duffie's division was on the river from Harper's Ferry to Downsville, Maryland, with headquarters at Shepherdstown; and Averell's division extended the line upriver from Downsville, with headquarters at Hagerstown.

The organization of the Federal forces engaged at Kernstown and during the retreat was as follows:

ARMY OF THE KANAWHA, George Crook

First Infantry Division, Joseph Thoburn
First Brigade, George D. Wells
Second Brigade, William G. Ely

Second Infantry Division, Isaac H. Duval
First Brigade, Rutherford B. Hayes
Second Brigade, Daniel D. Johnson

Third Division, James A. Mulligan, to July 24, 1864, mortally wounded
Jacob M. Campbell
First Brigade, Thomas M. Harris
Second Brigade, John P. Linton, to July 24, 1864, disabled
John Suter

Note 1. Campbell assumed command of the division at Winchester July 25, 1864.
Note 2. Third Division was discontinued July 28, 1864. See below for details of the reorganization of Crook's infantry.

Artillery
30th Battery, New York Light Artillery, Conrad Carrolien
1st Battery, Ohio Light Artillery, George P. Kirtland
Battery F, West Virginia Light Artillery, George W. Graham

First Cavalry Division, Alfred N. Duffie
First Brigade, William B. Tibbits
Second Brigade, Jacob Higgins

Second Cavalry Division, William W. Averell
First Brigade, James M. Schoonmaker
Second Brigade, William H. Powell

Wright's Command Reactivated, July 25, 1864.
July 24, 1864, the same day that Crook was defeated at Kernstown, Horatio G. Wright's command that had pursued Early from Washington to the Shenandoah Valley was broken up by orders. Sixth Corps, then at Washington, was ordered to return to the Army of the Potomac, and Wright resumed command of Sixth Corps, and Ricketts returned to the command of Third Division. Detachment Nineteenth Corps, previously assigned to Wright, was directed to report to Christopher C. Augur, commander of the Department of Washington. The next day, however, the order to dissolve Wright's command was suspended because of Early's activities in the Shenandoah Valley, and Wright again resumed command of Sixth Corps, Emory's Detachment Nineteenth Corps, Kenly's Maryland Brigade, and Lowell's cavalry. Ricketts resumed command of Sixth Corps.

July 26, 1864, Wright was ordered to move forward with his command by way of Rockville and Hyattstown toward the Monocacy River, and join Crook's army of Hunter's Department of West Virginia. That same day, Grant ordered Benjamin F.

Butler to release such troops as he could spare of Detachment Nineteenth Corps that were then serving with him at Deep Bottom, Virginia, and to send them to Washington. Butler ordered James W. McMillan's Second Brigade, First Division to go that day and Leonard D. H. Currie's Third Brigade to follow the next day. July 26, 1864, Emory was ordered to remain in Washington to receive these brigades, and William Dwight was assigned command of Detachment Nineteenth Corps.

An administrative change in the army was ordered in late July 1864. For several days, Grant had been concerned about the time required for orders and communications to be transmitted between his headquarters at City Point and the commanders of the departments affected by Early's presence in the lower Shenandoah Valley. Therefore, on July 27, 1864, Grant placed all military operations necessary for the defense of the Middle Department, the Department of Washington, the Department of West Virginia, and the Department of the Susquehanna under the general command of Henry W. Halleck, Chief of Staff, United States Army, whose office was in Washington, D.C.

Wright, with his force, reached Monocacy Junction July 28, 1864, and then marched on to the vicinity of Jefferson, Maryland. When Wright crossed the Monocacy River, he moved into the Department of West Virginia and became subject to Hunter's orders. Because of this, the troops from Hunter's command that had been placed temporarily under Wright's direction July 15, 1864, during the pursuit of Early from Washington, were relieved from that assignment July 28, 1864.

While Wright was marching to Jefferson, Crook moved with his Army of the Kanawha to Pleasant Valley July 28, 1864, and that day he reorganized his infantry as follows:

ARMY OF THE KANAWHA (infantry only), George Crook

First Infantry Division, Joseph Thoburn
    First Brigade, George D. Wells
    Second Brigade, William G. Ely
    Third Brigade, Jacob M. Campbell

Note. In the reorganization of the infantry, First Brigade and Second Brigade of the former Third Division were combined and assigned to First Infantry Division as Third Brigade, and Third Division was discontinued.

Campbell was assigned command of the new Third Brigade.

Second Infantry Division, Isaac H. Duval
    First Brigade, Rutherford B. Hayes
    Second Brigade, Daniel D. Johnson

July 28, 1864, Halleck instructed Hunter that if Early had not crossed the Potomac into Maryland, he should concentrate his forces near Harper's Ferry, and that day Hunter ordered Wright to bring his command to that point. Wright arrived the next day and went into camp at Halltown, near Crook, who had arrived from Pleasant Valley a short time before.

Burning of Chambersburg, Pennsylvania, July 30, 1864. On July 29, 1864, the cavalry brigades of John McCausland and Bradley T. Johnson of Early's army crossed the Potomac at McCoy's Ford near Cherry Run, West Virginia, and marched through Mercersburg toward Loudon (Fort Loudon), Pennsylvania. At the same time Confederate cavalry also crossed the Potomac at Williamsport, Falling Waters, and Shepherdstown, and advanced toward Hagerstown. Averell, whose headquarters was in the latter town, was forced to fall back on the Greencastle Road.

At about 3:30 A.M. July 30, 1864, McCausland entered Chambersburg, Pennsylvania, with only slight opposition from troops of Darius N. Couch's Department of the Susquehanna. McCausland arrested a number of citizens and informed them that unless paid $500,000 in currency or $100,000 in gold, he would burn the town. When this demand was not complied with, and when McCausland learned that Averell was not many miles away and was approaching rapidly, he burned the town and marched westward toward McConnellsburg, where he camped that night. Later that morning, Averell reached Chambersburg, too late to save the town, and pushed on in pursuit of McCausland.

The reaction of the Federals to the burning of Chambersburg was immediate. July 30, 1864, Hunter ordered all of his available forces, except the garrison at Harper's Ferry, to move northward on the east side of South Mountain, and occupy the passes so as to prevent an enemy advance from the west. At 1:00 that afternoon, Wright started his command from Halltown toward Frederick, Maryland.

Lowell's cavalry marched first, and it was followed, in order, by Dwight's Detachment Nineteenth Corps, Kenly's Maryland Brigade, and Ricketts' Sixth Corps. The column crossed the Potomac at Harper's Ferry, and then marched by way of Jefferson to Frederick. Detachment Nineteenth Corps, with Kenly's Brigade, arrived at Frederick July 31, 1864, and George L. Beal's First Brigade, First Division moved out thirteen miles on the Emmitsburg Road. Sixth Corps arrived August 1, 1864 and camped at Frederick that night, and also August 2, 1864.

Hunter left Halltown with Crook's Army of the Kanawha and moved up the Middletown Road. Hunter established headquarters at Frederick July 31, 1864. Crook arrived at Wolfsville, Maryland, between Hagerstown and Frederick, and remained there August 1–2, 1864, before moving on to Frederick.

While these infantry movements were in progress, Averell followed McCausland to Hancock, Maryland and skirmished with him near the town July 31, 1864. McCausland was unable to cross the Potomac at that point, and the next day he marched on to Cumberland. Near there he was met by Benjamin F. Kelley, commander of the United States Troops on the Baltimore and Ohio Railroad West of Sleepy Creek. Kelley drove McCausland back eastward to Old Town (present-day Oldtown), where he recrossed the river into West Virginia August 2, 1864.

Averell crossed the Potomac at Hancock August 4, 1864, and reached Romney two days later. Then, at 5:00 A.M. August 7, 1864, he came up on the troops of McCausland and Johnson encamped near Moorefield, West Virginia, and in a series of attacks routed and dispersed the entire force. At the time of the engagement, Averell's Second Cavalry Division consisted of Thomas Gibson's First Brigade and William H. Powell's Second Brigade.

Meantime, on August 1, 1864, Hunter had ordered Crook to send Duffie west with his First Cavalry Division to join Averell in the pursuit of McCausland. Duffie arrived near Hancock August 3, 1864, but instead of continuing on, he remained there when Averell crossed the Potomac the next day on his way to Romney.

End of the Campaign. It has been noted earlier that

only a part of Emory's Detachment Nineteenth Corps served with Wright during July and early August 1864, while he was conducting operations against Early. These troops consisted of George L. Beal's First Brigade and a part of James W. McMillan's Second Brigade (commanded by Stephen Thomas), both of William Dwight's First Division; and Jacob Sharpe's Third Brigade of Cuvier Grover's Second Division. The rest of Detachment Nineteenth Corps, which had arrived at Fort Monroe from New Orleans, had been sent to Deep Bottom to join Benjamin F. Butler's Army of the James in its operations against Richmond.

After Crook's defeat by Early at Kernstown, the rest of McMillan's brigade and Leonard D. H. Currie's Third Brigade of First Division were ordered to Washington, where they arrived July 29, 1864 and reported to Emory. The next day, Emory was ordered to take these two brigades to Monocacy Junction, and he arrived there July 31, 1864. That same day, Wright's command began to arrive at Frederick from Halltown. The day after the burning of Chambersburg, July 31, 1864, the remainder of Grover's Second Division, Detachment Nineteenth Corps, consisting of Henry W. Birge's First Brigade and Edward L. Molineux's Second Brigade, was ordered to Washington from the Army of the James. These two brigades arrived at Washington August 2, 1864. By that time, however, Early's threat north of the Potomac had ended, and Grover's troops encamped at Tennallytown. August 7, 1864, Grover was ordered to report to Christopher C. Augur, commander of the Department of Washington, Twenty-Second Corps.

Grant recognized the inadequacies of Hunter's cavalry in dealing with affairs in the Shenandoah Valley and in the Department of West Virginia, and on July 31, 1864, he ordered Philip H. Sheridan to send a cavalry division from near Petersburg to City Point for immediate transfer to Washington. Alfred T. A. Torbert's First Cavalry Division, Cavalry Corps, Army of the Potomac was selected, and it embarked for Giesboro Point, D.C. August 1–6, 1864. Torbert arrived there by August 7, 1864, and then moved out to Tennallytown. His division was finally concentrated at Harper's Ferry August 9, 1864.

By August 2, 1864, it was clear that Early did not intend to invade Maryland, and was, in fact, at

Bunker Hill and Darkesville that day, at the beginning of his withdrawal up the valley. The threat of an advance through the passes of South Mountain thus being ended, Wright's command was again broken up. That day, August 2, 1864, that part of Detachment Nineteenth Corps that was serving with Wright, and Kenly's Brigade were ordered to report to Emory, commanding Detachment Nineteenth Corps, at Monocacy Junction. Upon arriving there, First Division was reunited. Also that day, Hunter moved his headquarters to Monocacy Junction.

Also on August 2, 1864, Wright was ordered to march with his Sixth Corps by the Rockville Road to Washington. This order was changed the next day, however, and Sixth Corps was halted in the vicinity of Buckeystown, Maryland, a few miles south of Monocacy Junction. The corps remained in camp there until August 5, 1864, and then moved to Monocacy Junction. Lowell's cavalry was sent to guard the Potomac River from Point of Rocks to Edwards Ferry.

·For further information about the organization and operations of the troops that were commanded by Hunter at the end of July 1864, and about the reinforcements that were ordered to join them, see Shenandoah Valley Campaign (Sheridan).

The Union forces commanded by David Hunter July 31, 1864 were as follows:

FORCES IN THE FIELD, DEPARTMENT OF WEST VIRGINIA, George Crook

First Infantry Division, Joseph Thoburn
First Brigade, George D. Wells
Second Brigade, William G. Ely
Third Brigade, Jacob M. Campbell

Second Infantry Division, Isaac H. Duval
First Brigade, Rutherford B. Hayes
Second Brigade, Daniel D. Johnson

Harper's Ferry and Defenses, Max Weber
Infantry Brigade, William P. Maulsby
Unbrigaded regiments

Note. This command was included in Albion P. Howe's District of Harper's Ferry.

West of Sleepy Creek, Benjamin F. Kelley
Unbrigaded regiments

Kanawha Valley, John H. Oley

Unbrigaded regiments

First Cavalry Division, Alfred N. Duffie
First Brigade, William B. Tibbits
Second Brigade, Andrew J. Greenfield

Note. The roster for July 1864 states that the regiments of Second Brigade were not brigaded, but an order of July 30, 1864 assigned Greenfield to succeed Jacob Higgins in command of Second Brigade.

Second Cavalry Division, William W. Averell
First Brigade
Second Brigade, William H. Powell

Note. Most of 8th Ohio Cavalry of First Brigade was at Beverly, West Virginia, and 14th Pennsylvania Cavalry of First Brigade was serving in detachments.

Artillery Brigade, Henry A. Du Pont
Battery B, 5th United States Artillery, Henry A. Du Pont
Battery D, 1st West Virginia Light Artillery, John Carlin
Battery E, 1st West Virginia Light Artillery, Francis M. Lowry

SIXTH CORPS, Horatio G. Wright

First Division, David A. Russell
First Brigade, William H. Penrose
Second Brigade, Emory Upton
Third Brigade, Oliver Edwards
Artillery
1st Battery, Massachusetts Light Artillery, William H. McCartney

Second Division, George W. Getty
First Brigade, Frank Wheaton
Second Brigade, Lewis A. Grant
Third Brigade, Daniel D. Bidwell
Artillery
1st Battery, New York Light Artillery, Andrew Cowan

Third Division, James B. Ricketts
First Brigade, William Emerson
Second Brigade, John F. Staunton
Artillery
Battery M, 5th United States Artillery, James McKnight

Maryland Brigade, John R. Kenly

Artillery Brigade, Charles H. Tompkins
5th Battery (E), Maine Light Artillery, Greenleaf T. Stevens

Battery C, 1st Rhode Island Light Artillery, Richard Waterman

Battery G, 1st Rhode Island Light Artillery, George W. Adams

DETACHMENT NINETEENTH CORPS, William H. Emory

First Division, William Dwight
    First Brigade, George L. Beal
    Second Brigade, James W. McMillan
    Third Brigade, Leonard D. H. Currie
    Artillery
        Battery D, 1st Rhode Island Light Artillery, William W. Buckley

Note 1. First Division was reunited at Monocacy Junction August 2, 1864.

Note 2. Edwin P. Davis commanded Beal's First Brigade July 27–31, 1864, inclusive.

BOMBARDMENT AND EVACUATION OF FORT SUMTER, SOUTH CAROLINA

In the autumn of 1860, the United States forces at Charleston Harbor, South Carolina were, for the most part, stationed at Fort Moultrie on Sullivan's Island. They were under the command of Colonel John L. Gardner. At that time Fort Moultrie was in a state of disrepair, and Fort Sumter, on an island in Charleston Harbor, had not yet been completed. November 15, 1860, Major Robert Anderson, 1st United States Artillery, then in New York City, was ordered to proceed to Fort Moultrie and relieve Gardner.

When Anderson arrived at Charleston Harbor, he became concerned for the safety of his troops on Sullivan's Island, and on the night of December 26, 1860 he secretly transferred his command from Fort Moultrie to Fort Sumter. He then erected batteries and attempted to put the fort in a defensible condition. With him in Fort Sumter were Captain Abner Doubleday's Company E, 1st United States Artillery and Captain Truman Seymour's Company H, 1st United States Artillery, both undersized. His command consisted of sixty-eight noncommissioned officers and privates, eight musicians, and forty-three noncombatant workmen. In addition, the following officers were present: Surgeon Samuel W. Crawford, First Lieutenant Theodore Talbot of Company H, First Lieutenant Jefferson C. Davis of the 1st United States Artillery, and Second Lieutenant Norman J. Hall of Company H.

Also present were Captain John G. Foster and First Lieutenant George W. Snyder of the Corps of Engineers. Foster was in charge of construction at the forts, and Snyder was assisting Foster in supervising the work at Fort Sumter. Foster was responsible to Engineer Headquarters in Washington, and not to Anderson.

When the South Carolinians learned of the movement of the United States troops to Fort Sumter, they were enraged at what they considered to be a threat to Charleston, and also at what they believed to be a breach of an agreement. Accordingly, they proceeded to occupy with state troops Fort Moultrie, Fort Johnson on James Island, and Castle Pinckney in Charleston Harbor. On December 30, 1860, South Carolina troops also occupied the United States arsenal in Charleston. Then all communication by the Sumter garrison with Charleston was severed, and no fresh provisions were permitted to enter the fort.

On January 5, 1861, an expedition under Charles R. Woods of the 9th United States Infantry sailed from New York on the *Star of the West* for the relief of Fort Sumter. On January 9, 1861, the unarmed vessel was fired on by batteries on Morris Island while it was attempting to reach the fort. Then the guns at Fort Moultrie opened fire, and finally the *Star of the West* turned about and returned to New York, arriving there January 12, 1861.

April 4, 1861, Gustavus V. Fox, formerly an officer in the United States Navy, was assigned command of a second expedition to provision Fort Sumter. Confederate authorities learned of this April 8, 1861, and two days later ordered Pierre G. T. Beauregard, then in command of the Southern troops at Charleston Harbor, to demand the evacuation of Fort Sumter. They further directed Beauregard that if Anderson refused their demand, he was to reduce the fort. Anderson did refuse, and early on the morning of April 12, 1861, the enemy batteries began the bombardment of Fort Sumter. Fox's expedition sailed from New York on the steamer *Baltic* April 10, 1861, and it arrived off Charleston Harbor two days later while the bombardment was in progress. It was then too late. Fort Sumter was forced to surrender at 2:30 P.M. April 13, 1861, but the formal surrender and evacuation of the fort took place the next day. Then Anderson and his men embarked for New York, where they arrived April 18, 1861.

FREDERICKSBURG, VIRGINIA CAMPAIGN NOVEMBER 15–DECEMBER 15, 1862

Following the Battle of Antietam in September 1862, Robert E. Lee's Army of Northern Virginia retreated into Virginia, and the Army of the Potomac under George B. McClellan followed to the Potomac River. McClellan remained relatively inactive in Maryland until October 26, 1862, and then, at President Lincoln's insistence, crossed the Potomac into Virginia to find Lee. The army marched southward along the Loudoun Valley between the Blue Ridge and Bull Run mountains, and arrived in the Warrenton area November 6–9, 1862. At that time James Longstreet's Confederate corps was at Culpeper Court House, and Thomas J. (Stonewall) Jackson's corps was in the Shenandoah Valley.

November 7, 1862, Ambrose E. Burnside was near Waterloo, Virginia in command of the Left Wing of the Army of the Potomac, which consisted of George Stoneman's division of Ninth Corps and Amiel W. Whipple's division of Twelfth Corps. This command had been organized for special service at the beginning of the advance of the army into Virginia. While at Waterloo Burnside received an order, dated November 5, 1862, assigning him to the command of the Army of the Potomac. It should be noted that, although Burnside did not issue a formal order assuming command until November 9, 1862, he was officially in command of the army from the night of November 7, 1862.

Burnside studied the situation for a few days and then presented to Henry W. Halleck a new plan of operations. He proposed to discontinue the advance of the army toward Culpeper Court House and Gordonsville, and thus to abandon the prospect of an early engagement with Lee. The advance toward Culpeper Court House was the plan that had been approved by the president, and was the one that McClellan had been slowly following since late October 1862. Instead Burnside proposed to shift the line of march eastward to Fredericksburg, Virginia, and then, after securing water and rail connections with Washington by way of Aquia Creek, to move south toward Richmond before Lee could effect the junction of his two corps. Halleck did not approve the change of plan, and November 12, 1862 visited Burnside at Warrenton and urged him to continue the original line of advance. Burnside insisted that his plan be approved, but Halleck informed him that the president would have to make the final decision, and returned to Washington. Then, November 14, 1862, Burnside was informed that Lincoln had assented to his plan, although it appears that he did so with some reluctance.

On November 14, 1862, in preparation for the advance toward Fredericksburg, Burnside announced the reorganization of the army into three grand divisions and a reserve as follows:

Right Grand Division, Edwin V. Sumner
  Second Corps, Darius N. Couch
  Ninth Corps, Orlando B. Willcox

Note 1. Sumner assumed command of the Right Grand Division November 14, 1862, and was succeeded in command of Second Corps by Couch.

Note 2. Alfred Pleasonton's cavalry division was attached to the Right Grand Division November 21, 1862.

Center Grand Division, Joseph Hooker
  Third Corps, George Stoneman
  Fifth Corps, Daniel Butterfield

Note 1. Hooker assumed command of the Center Grand Division November 16, 1862, and was succeeded in command of Fifth Corps by Butterfield.

Note 2. Third Corps was reorganized November 16, 1862 (see Third Corps, Army of the Potomac).

Note 3. William W. Averell's cavalry brigade was attached to the Center Grand Division November 21, 1862.

Left Grand Division, William B. Franklin
  First Corps, John F. Reynolds
  Sixth Corps, William F. Smith

Note 1. Franklin assumed command of the Left Grand Division November 16, 1862 and was succeeded in command of Sixth Corps by Smith.

Note 2. George D. Bayard's cavalry brigade was assigned to the Left Grand Division November 21, 1862.

Reserve, Franz Sigel
  Eleventh Corps, Franz Sigel

Note. December 9, 1862, Henry W. Slocum's Twelfth Corps, then at Harper's Ferry, was ordered toward Dumfries, Virginia to join the Reserve.

Burnside's plan called for a rapid march to Falmouth, Virginia and a crossing of the Rappahannock River there before a large Confederate force could be shifted to Fredericksburg to oppose him. To ensure a prompt crossing, Burnside informed Halleck at a meeting November 12, 1862 that the necessary pontoons for bridging the river should be sent from Washington to Falmouth. At this time the pontoons were at Berlin (present-day Brunswick), Maryland, and these were started for Washington November 12, 1862 by a delayed order of November 6, 1862.

Advance of the Army toward Fredericksburg. The march of the army toward Fredericksburg began shortly after the grand divisions were organized. Sumner, with the Second and Ninth corps of the Right Grand Division, left Warrenton November 15, 1862 and entered Falmouth two days later. Falmouth was about a mile upstream and across the river from Fredericksburg. Franklin's Left Grand Division began its advance November 17, 1862. First Corps marched from Fayetteville and Bealeton and Sixth Corps from New Baltimore, and they arrived at Stafford Court House November 18, 1862. Later, First Corps moved to Brooke's Station and Sixth Corps to near White Oak Church. Hooker's Center Grand Division advanced from Warrenton November 17, 1862, and the next day arrived at Hartwood Church, about eight miles northwest of Falmouth. It remained there until November 22, 1862, and it then moved to the Richmond, Fredericksburg, and Potomac Railroad crossing of Potomac Creek. Burnside, with his headquarters, arrived at Falmouth November 19, 1862.

When Sumner arrived on the Rappahannock November 17, 1862, the expected pontoons had not arrived. He asked permission to cross his command at the fords, but this was denied, although at the time Fredericksburg was only lightly held by the enemy. Heavy rains began two days later, and soon the water at the fords was too deep for infantry to cross. The pontoons began arriving in Washington from Berlin November 14, 1862, and these were ordered forward under the supervision of Daniel P. Woodbury, commander of the Engineer Brigade. The start of the first train for Fredericksburg, under the command of Ira Spaulding of the 50th New York Engineers, was delayed until November 19, 1862 because of difficulties in obtaining the necessary transportation from the quartermaster's department. It was then further delayed by bad roads; the first pontoons did not arrive near Fredericksburg until November 24, 1862, and the rest were not up until several days later.

Meantime, Longstreet's corps arrived at Fredericksburg from Culpeper Court House November 21–25, 1862, and Jackson's corps arrived from the Shenandoah Valley December 1, 1862. Thus, shortly after the pontoons arrived, Lee's army was concentrated along the west side of the Rappahannock in position to resist any attempt of the Army of the Potomac to cross. Burnside's chances for a rapid movement toward Richmond had vanished.

Frustrated by the failure of his initial plan for a quick crossing of the river, and unable to improvise a new alternative, Burnside remained idle for almost two and a half weeks before attempting to bridge the Rappahannock with his pontoons. Finally, however, Burnside decided to begin offensive operations, and December 9, 1862 issued orders for crossing the river and attacking Lee's army.

For a better understanding of the Battle of Fredericksburg, it is necessary to describe briefly the more important features of the ground over which it was fought. West of Fredericksburg was a range of hills that began on the Rappahannock at a point opposite Falmouth and extended southward for approximately five miles to Hamilton's Crossing on the Richmond and Fredericksburg Railroad, and a little more than a mile from Massaponax Creek. This line ran roughly parallel to the river.

Between the hills and the river was a broken plain that was only about 600 yards wide at the northern end, then widened to about two miles at Deep Run, and then narrowed to about one mile near Massaponax Creek. There were several streams that flowed across this plain toward the river, and two of these were large enough to be significant in affecting troop movements before and during the battle. Hazel

Run emerged from a ravine just south of Willis Hill and flowed into the Rappahannock just below the southern edge of Fredericksburg. Deep Run crossed the Mine Road about two and a half miles west of Hamilton's Crossing and flowed northeast and north into the Rappahannock about one-half mile below the mouth of Hazel Run.

The Richmond, Fredericksburg, and Potomac Railroad crossed from the eastern bank of the Rappahannock into the lower end of Fredericksburg, passed through the town, and near its western edge curved to the southwest through a cut and crossed Hazel Run. It then continued on to the south and southeast between the hills and the river to Hamilton's Crossing, where it curved to the south toward Richmond. The Old Richmond Stage Road ran south out of Fredericksburg, and continued on along the plain about midway between the railroad and the Rappahannock and on to Richmond.

The Battle of Fredericksburg was actually two separate battles, fought at about the same time, but without significant effect of one on the other. One battle was fought on the northern end of the plain between Fredericksburg and the hills beyond, and the other on the southern end of the plain beyond Deep Run. Additional details of the features of the two battlefields will be given later when the separate battles are described.

When Longstreet's corps arrived at Fredericksburg, it was placed along the range of hills from the river opposite Falmouth, on the left, to a point not far from Massaponax Creek, on the right. In order, from the Confederate left to right, were the divisions of Richard H. Anderson, Robert Ransom, Lafayette McLaws, George E. Pickett, and John B. Hood. Later, when Jackson's corps came up it was sent to the right of Longstreet to watch the southern flank. The divisions were posted as follows: Daniel H. Hill's at Port Royal, seventeen miles on a direct line downstream from Fredericksburg; Jubal A. Early's (Ewell's) division at Skinker's Neck, twelve miles southeast of Fredericksburg; Ambrose P. Hill's division at Yerbys' house, three miles to the right and rear of Longstreet's right; and William B. Taliaferro's division at Guiney's Station, four miles farther south on the Richmond, Fredericksburg, and Potomac Railroad. William H. F. Lee's cavalry was near Port Royal; Fitzhugh Lee's cavalry was near Hamilton's Crossing; Wade Hampton's cavalry was near Banks' Ford, above Fredericksburg; and Thomas L. Rosser's cavalry was in the rear near Wilderness Tavern.

In preparation for the crossing of the river, Henry J. Hunt, chief of artillery of the Army of the Potomac, was directed to post his artillery so as to protect the engineers while constructing the bridges, and also to cover the passage of the army. Two pontoon bridges were to be laid at the upper end of Fredericksburg, in front of the Lacy house (Chatham); and one bridge at the lower end of the town, below the railroad bridge. Two more bridges were to be constructed one and a half miles below the lower bridge at Fredericksburg for the passage of the Left Grand Division.

All of the artillery, except for one battery of each division, was taken from the divisions and attached to the Artillery Reserve. It should be noted here that the batteries of the divisional artillery were returned to their respective divisions when the divisions crossed the river. Hunt placed his batteries on the high ground east of the river (Stafford Heights), and divided his line into four divisions as follows: The right was under William Hays, aide de camp, and extended from Falmouth Dam to a ravine about one-fourth of a mile below Falmouth (forty guns). The right center was under Charles H. Tompkins, 1st Rhode Island Artillery, and it extended from the ravine to near the point selected for the middle bridge, about one-fourth of a mile below the railroad (thirty-eight guns). The left center was under Robert O. Tyler, 1st Connecticut Artillery, and it was formed on the crest of a ridge, beginning at the middle bridge and extending to a ravine near the center of the ridge (twenty-seven guns). The left was under Gustavus A. De Russy, 4th United States Artillery, and it occupied the crest of the high ridge and a low ridge that ended at Pollock's Mill, northeast of and across the river from Smithfield (forty guns). Hunt's guns were all in position by 11:00 P.M. on the night of December 10, 1862.

Crossing of the Rappahannock, December 11, 1862. Before daylight on the morning of December 11, 1862, the engineers began the construction of the pontoon bridges, and the troops assigned to make the crossing marched from their camps and took cover in rear of the crossing points. Sumner's Right Grand Division, consisting of Couch's Second Corps and

Willcox's Ninth Corps, took position opposite Fredericksburg. Franklin's Left Grand Division, consisting of Reynolds' First Corps and Smith's Sixth Corps, marched to a point in rear of the lower bridges, afterwards known as Franklin's Crossing. Hooker's Center Grand Division, consisting of Stoneman's Third Corps and Butterfield's Fifth Corps, remained in the rear and did not cross the river until December 13, 1862.

On the morning of December 11, 1862, Norman J. Hall's Third Brigade of Oliver O. Howard's Second Division, Second Corps, the leading brigade of the Right Grand Division, arrived near the river in preparation for crossing. It was then sent forward to report to Woodbury, commanding the Engineer Brigade, to support the engineers laying the bridges at Fredericksburg. The upper and middle bridges were completed to about mid-river soon after daylight, and then the work was interrupted by a heavy fire from men of William Barksdale's brigade of McLaws' division, who were concealed in buildings along the riverfront. Hunt's artillery on the heights opened fire and practically silenced the enemy infantry, but when work was resumed on the bridges, the pontoniers were again driven back. The artillery again shelled the town, but several later attempts to complete the bridges failed. Finally, at about 2:30 P.M. Henry Baxter with the 7th Michigan, and followed by 19th Massachusetts and 20th Massachusetts, all of Hall's brigade, crossed the river in pontoon boats and drove the sharpshooters from the town. Harrison S. Fairchild with his 89th New York of Rush C. Hawkins' First Brigade of George W. Getty's Third Division, Ninth Corps also aided in clearing the town.

The bridges were finally completed at 4:30 P.M. December 11, 1862, but only Howard's division of Second Corps was able to cross before dark. Hawkins' brigade of Ninth Corps also crossed that evening, and Howard and Hawkins occupied the lower part of Fredericksburg that night.

About sunrise December 12, 1862, William H. French's Third Division and Winfield S. Hancock's First Division of Couch's Second Corps crossed the bridges at Fredericksburg and took position in the streets of the town that ran parallel to the river. The rest of Willcox's Ninth Corps crossed the river immediately after Second Corps and occupied the lower (left) part of the town. These two corps remained in position along the streets during the rest of the day and that night.

Less difficulty was encountered at the lower bridges (Franklin's Crossing), where one bridge was completed by 9:00 A.M. December 11, 1862, and both were ready for crossing by 11:00 A.M. Five batteries, totaling twenty-two guns, were brought up near the bridges to drive off the enemy sharpshooters, and at 4:00 P.M. Franklin was ordered to cross with his entire command. This order was modified, however, and only Charles Devens' Second Brigade of John Newton's Third Division, Sixth Corps crossed that evening to protect the bridges. Devens held his position on the south bank of the river during the night.

At daylight December 12, 1862, Smith's Sixth Corps began crossing on the pontoons. William T. H. Brooks' First Division crossed first and moved to the front of Devens' brigade. The division was then formed in three lines, with David A. Russell's Third Brigade in front, Henry L. Cake's Second Brigade next, and Alfred T. A. Torbert's First Brigade in the rear. Brooks then slowly advanced until Russell's brigade was beyond Deep Run, Cake's brigade was on the Old Richmond Stage Road, and Torbert's brigade was in the valley of Deep Run. These brigades remained in these same positions while they were south of the Rappahannock. During the battle the next day, Edward B. Williston's battery was placed on the right of Deep Run so as to command the valley of the run; William Hexamer's battery was in rear of Williston near Deep Run; and William H. McCartney's battery was south and east of Deep Run.

Albion P. Howe's Second Division followed Brooks across the river and formed on the plateau immediately in front of the bridges, and on the left of Brooks. Howe's line was about 400 yards from the river. Calvin E. Pratt's First Brigade was deployed in front, Francis L. Vinton's Third Brigade was in rear of Pratt, and Henry Whiting's Second Brigade was in rear of Vinton, in column. The division advanced about 10:00 A.M. and occupied a ridge on the plateau about midway between the river and the hills in front, with its right resting on Deep Run. The left of Howe's line was about 1,500 yards from the hills, but the right was somewhat farther away because the hills receded there toward the head of Deep Run. During the battle Leonard

Martin's battery was placed on the right of the division, and Alonzo Snow's battery on the left. John H. Butler's battery of Newton's division and A. Judson Clark's battery of Daniel E. Sickles' Second Division, Third Corps were placed in front of Howe's line.

Newton's division, consisting of John Cochrane's First Brigade, Charles Devens' Second Brigade, and Thomas A. Rowley's (later Frank Wheaton's) Third Brigade, was held near the bridges in reserve on the south bank of the river.

John F. Reynolds' First Corps, followed by Bayard's cavalry brigade, crossed the river after Sixth Corps, and by 1:00 P.M. December 12, 1862, all of Franklin's Left Grand Division was on the south side of the Rappahannock. Bayard's cavalry moved ahead to reconnoiter, and Reynolds' corps moved southward along the Rappahannock for about a mile to a point beyond the Bernard house (Mansfield), where Franklin established his head-quarters. By 4:00 P.M. First Corps was in position as follows: John Gibbon's Second Division was on the left of Sixth Corps, in rear of the Old Richmond Stage Road, facing south; and George G. Meade's Third Division was on the left of Gibbon, with its left on the Rappahannock, facing south. Abner Doubleday's First Division was in reserve, in column, in rear of the left of Meade's line.

Stoneman's Third Corps was to have followed Sumner's Right Grand Division over the river at Fredericksburg on December 11, 1862, but because of the delay in completing the bridges, it was unable to do so. It bivouacked that night in rear of Sumner's headquarters at the Lacy house. On the morning of December 12, 1862, Third Corps moved down the river to follow Sumner's Right Grand Division into Fredericksburg. Sumner's troops were over by 2:00 P.M., and Amiel W. Whipple's Third Division, Third Corps was ordered to follow, but the town was so filled with Federal troops that Whipple was forced to remain on the north bank. Shortly before sundown, Stoneman was ordered to move downriver with David B. Birney's First Division and Daniel E. Sickles' Third Division to the lower bridges and report to Franklin. This movement was completed by 10:00 P.M., and the two divisions bivouacked for the night on the north bank. Whipple's division also remained north of the river guarding the ford at Falmouth.

Butterfield's Fifth Corps bivouacked north of the river on the night of December 11, 1862, with George Sykes' Second Division in rear of Falmouth, and Charles Griffin's First Division and Andrew A. Humphreys' Third Division near the Phillips house. Fifth Corps remained in these positions until December 13, 1862, when it crossed into Fredericksburg during the battle.

Bayard's brigade was the only cavalry to cross the river with the infantry. Bayard was killed during the fighting and was succeeded in command of the brigade by David McM. Gregg. Alfred Pleasonton's cavalry division of the Right Grand Division was massed in rear of a ridge, covering the approaches to the upper bridges, during the period December 11–14, 1862. William W. Averell's cavalry brigade of the Center Grand Division moved to the rear of Fifth Corps, whose positions have been noted above.

BATTLE OF FREDERICKSBURG, DECEMBER 13, 1862

As noted above, the Battle of Fredericksburg was actually two separate battles fought on opposite flanks of the army. Both were fought on the plain between the Rappahannock River and the range of hills to the west. One consisted of a series of Federal attacks on the heights at the northern end of the Confederate line, and the other was an attack by First Corps on the hills at the southern end of the enemy line, northwest of Hamilton's Crossing. For a better understanding of the action on December 13, 1862, the attacks on the two flanks are considered separately.

Federal Attack on the Southern Flank. Before proceeding with a discussion of Franklin's battle on the Union left, it is necessary to give a more detailed description of the field over which it was fought. Just a short distance south of the Rappahannock River at Franklin's Crossing, the ground rose sharply about thirty feet to an elevated plain that stretched away to the west and south to the range of hills that ran south from the rear of Fredericksburg. This plain was generally cultivated and open, but it was broken by ditches and hedges. The Old Richmond Stage Road (also called the Bowling Green Road) ran out of the south end of Fredericksburg and traversed the plain from north to south at a distance ranging from one-half to three-fourths of a mile from the river, and nearly parallel to it. The Richmond, Fredericksburg, and Potomac Railroad also ran out of Fredericksburg and across the plain about one half-mile beyond (southwest of) the Richmond Stage Road, and roughly parallel to it. South of Deep Run the railroad ran close to the hills through a hollow or depression several hundred yards in width, and for almost the entire distance along the Union front it was in a shallow cut. Between the Richmond Stage Road and the railroad the open plain extended southward to the Massaponax Creek.

Along the south side of the railroad, the slopes of the hills were wooded for about one and a half miles northwest of Hamilton's Crossing. Across the railroad to the north, the plain was open except for at one point in front of Meade's division, where the division began its attack. There, along a marshy stream, a narrow belt of woods extended across the railroad for about one-fourth mile toward the First Corps line. The plain on the Federal side was cultivated up to the hollow in front of the hills, and from there it fell away to the railroad.

Until December 12, 1862, the hills in front of Franklin's Left Grand Division had been held by Hood's division of Longstreet's corps. When Jackson, who was at Guiney's Station, was informed that pontoons had been thrown across the Rappahannock at Fredericksburg the day before, he ordered Ambrose P. Hill to move with his division at dawn December 13, 1862, and to occupy the position then held by Hood. Hood's division shifted to its left to make room for Hill, and took position with its left at Dr. Rennolds' house (misspelled as Reynolds on maps of the Civil War period). Dr. Rennolds' house was on the hills near Deep Run, about two miles west and a little north of Hamilton's Crossing, and about one-fourth mile north of Mine Road.

When Hill moved up on the right of Hood, Jackson also ordered the other divisions of his corps to march to the vicinity of Hamilton's Crossing to support him. Taliaferro's division formed in rear of Hill as a reserve. Early and Daniel H. Hill came up from farther down the Rappahannock, and arrived on the Confederate right about noon December 13, 1862. Early took position on the right of Taliaferro, with his right at Hamilton's Crossing, and Daniel H. Hill formed in rear of Early.

At 7:45 A.M. December 13, 1862, Franklin received a verbal order from Burnside (a written order arrived at 8:00 A.M.) to advance and attack the enemy position on his front. Reynolds' First Corps was assigned to carry out this order. Meade was directed to make the attack with his Third Division, and Gibbon was ordered to support Meade on the right with his Second Division. Doubleday's First Division was to advance and protect the left of the attacking columns.

About 8:30 A.M., Meade moved downriver 700 or 800 yards to his position of the night before. He then turned sharply to the right and advanced toward the strip of woods that extended northward across the railroad toward the Old Richmond Stage Road. A heavy fog covered the battlefield that morning, and the early part of Meade's advance was made under its protection. The fog began to lift between 9:00 and 10:00 A.M., and when the enemy observed Meade's column, John Pelham opened with an enfilade fire with a gun of James E. B. Stuart's Horse Artillery from a point near the intersection of the Richmond Stage Road and the Hamilton's Crossing Road. This unexpected fire caused Meade to halt until Pelham's gun was silenced by Federal artillery, but by 11:00 A.M. the line had advanced about one-half mile.

After crossing the Richmond Stage Road, Meade formed his division for an attack on the enemy position in the woods. William Sinclair's First Brigade was placed on the crest in front of the hollow, facing the railroad; Albert L. Magilton's Second Brigade was positioned 300 yards in rear of First Brigade; and C. Feger Jackson's Third Brigade was formed at a right angle to First Brigade, with its right near Sinclair's left. It faced down the Richmond Stage Road to guard against a possible enemy attack from that direction.

Meade ordered his artillery forward to a position on a slight elevation between the Richmond Stage Road and the railroad. John G. Simpson's battery was advanced to the front and left of Jackson's brigade, and John H. Cooper's and Dunbar R. Ransom's batteries were moved to the left of Sinclair's brigade. Cooper and Ransom then opened fire on the enemy batteries on the crest of the hills in front and on Pelham's gun on the left. The artillery, aided by John W. Wolcott's battery of Brooks' division, Sixth Corps, which at that time was attached to Doubleday's division, finally forced Pelham to withdraw. At about the same time Frank P. Amsden's battery arrived from the rear and was placed on the left of Cooper's battery.

Meantime, while Meade was making his dispositions, Gibbon's and Doubleday's divisions were advancing to support him. At 9:00 A.M. Gibbon moved forward from near the river and halted in rear of the Richmond Stage Road on the right of Meade's division and on the left of Smith's corps. Nelson Taylor's Third Brigade, preceded by skirmishers, then crossed the road and advanced toward the woods that were held by the enemy. The brigade halted under cover of a slight elevation about halfway across the field. Peter Lyle's Second Brigade moved forward to within supporting distance of Taylor's brigade. John A. Hall's battery was posted on the left of Lyle's brigade, and Adrian R. Root's First Brigade was formed in close column to the left and rear to support the battery. James Thompson's battery was placed on the right of the division, and George F. Leppien's battery was posted behind the Richmond Stage Road. Gibbon's division remained in this position until after noon.

Doubleday's First Division followed Meade down the river, and about a half mile below Smithfield halted and formed in line of battle, generally facing south. James Gavin's Second Brigade was on the right of the division and on the left of Meade's division, with his line in rear of, and parallel to, the Richmond Stage Road. Walter Phelps' First Brigade was on the left of Gavin, and was also in rear of the road. William F. Rogers' Third Brigade was on the left of Phelps, and it extended toward the river. Solomon Meredith's Fourth Brigade was on the left of Rogers, with its left resting on the river. (*note.* During the movements that day, Doubleday became dissatisfied with Meredith's performance and replaced him with Lysander Cutler.) John A. Reynolds' battery was posted to the left of Phelps' brigade, and George A. Gerrish's battery (commanded by Frederick M. Edgell) was placed to the right and rear of Rogers' brigade, near the Richmond Stage Road. James Stewart's battery was sent to the right of Gerrish's battery to support it. John W. Wolcott's battery of Brooks' division, Sixth Corps was detached from the corps and was sent to Doubleday, and served with his division that day.

By noon the artillery fire on Franklin's front, which during the morning had been fairly heavy, virtually ceased, and Meade then decided to attack. The batteries of Ransom, Amsden, Cooper, and Hall shelled the woods on their front for about forty minutes, and during this time Jackson's brigade changed front to the right and came into line on the left of Sinclair's brigade, facing the enemy positions on the hills. Finally, at 1:00 P.M. Meade's infantry moved forward.

Sinclair's brigade on the right advanced several hundred yards over cleared land to the strip of woods that extended beyond the railroad in front of Ambrose P. Hill's position. Sinclair continued on across the railroad and up the heights beyond. Although under heavy fire, it reached the crest of the hill, crossed the road running along the crest, and entered the open ground on the other side. There, despite a heavy fire on its front and right flank, it held on for some time, but finally, when no support arrived, it was forced to fall back. Magilton's brigade followed in rear of Sinclair's brigade to the railroad, but on passing through the woods it was strongly assaulted on its left. Magilton then changed his line of attack in that direction, and moved up the hill as Sinclair was retiring. Upon reaching the crest Magilton came under a very heavy fire at short range, and the whole line broke and fell back to its position of that morning. Jackson's brigade, after advancing about 100 yards, was struck by artillery fire from the hills, and it moved by the right flank to the cover of the woods. It then moved up the hill, while inclining to the left, in an attempt to take the enemy batteries. Like the other two brigades, however, it was soon driven back across the railroad and out of the woods. Sinclair was wounded during the fighting and was succeeded in command of First Brigade by William McCandless. Jackson was killed and was succeeded temporarily in command of Third Brigade by Joseph W. Fisher. Fisher was then relieved by Robert Anderson.

When Meade began his attack at 1:00 P.M., Gibbon's division also moved forward on his right. Taylor's Third Brigade advanced first and in a short time was under heavy fire. Its left was soon thrown back in confusion, and Lyle's Second Brigade was ordered up in support. It took position on the left of Taylor's right wing (97th New York and 88th Pennsylvania), which still held its ground, but Lyle too was soon driven back in disorder. Root's First Brigade then came up and advanced beyond the railroad, where it remained until about 2:30 P.M. When Meade's division began to fall back, Gibbon's division also retired. Gibbon was wounded about 3:30 P.M., and Taylor assumed command of the division. Samuel H. Leonard took charge of Taylor's brigade.

Meade's initial successes were gained against the brigades of Maxcy Gregg, James H. Lane, and James J. Archer of Ambrose P. Hill's division, but the Federal brigades were driven back when Hill's line was reinforced by the brigades of Alexander R. Lawton (commanded by E. N. Atkinson), Jubal A. Early (commanded by James A. Walker), and Isaac R. Trimble (commanded by Robert F. Hoke) of Early's division. Charles W. Field's brigade (commanded by John M. Brockenbrough) of Ambrose P. Hill's division was sent to aid Archer, and Edward L. Thomas' brigade of Ambrose P. Hill's division was sent to help Lane.

It has been mentioned earlier that late in the evening of December 12, 1862, George Stoneman, by Burnside's orders, arrived with David B. Birney's First Division and Daniel E. Sickles' Second Division of Third Corps on the north bank at the Rappahannock at Franklin's Crossing. At 10:30 the next morning Franklin directed Stoneman to send a division to support Reynolds. Stoneman immediately crossed the river with Birney's division and arrived on the field an hour later. He left Sickles' division on the north bank with orders to be prepared to move at any time. When Stoneman arrived near the scene of the fighting, Meade and Gibbon had driven the enemy back beyond the railroad, and at Reynolds' request Birney's division was formed to support Meade. J. H. Hobart Ward's Second Brigade was deployed on the right, and Hiram G. Berry's Third Brigade on the left. John C. Robinson's First Brigade, which did not cross the river until 1:00 P.M., had not yet arrived. Birney's division was under artillery fire for some time and suffered considerable loss, and was then ordered to withdraw to the embankment along the road. This movement was only partially completed when Meade called for help, and the division was turned back toward the front. A part of Ward's brigade

supported Meade's batteries, and the 38th and 40th New York were sent to Gibbon's left, but these were forced back when Gibbon retired. Berry's brigade returned to its former position on the left.

George E. Randolph's battery (commanded by Pardon S. Jastram) and and La Rhett L. Livingston's battery (commanded by John G. Turnbull) of Birney's division moved up and relieved Ransom's battery of Meade's division when its ammunition was exhausted. These two batteries immediately went into action under the direction of George E. Randolph, chief of artillery, First Division.

By this time Meade and Gibbon were in full retreat and had retired behind the Richmond Stage Road. Robinson's brigade was then arriving, and Birney formed a new line about midway between the Richmond Stage Road and the railroad. Berry's brigade was on the left, Robinson's brigade was in the center, and Ward's brigade was on the right. Birney's infantry and the artillery, firing canister, checked the Confederate forces following Meade and Gibbon, and drove them back to the cover of the woods.

Meantime, at 2:10 P.M., Sickles was ordered to cross his division at the lower bridges and await orders under cover of the river bank. A short time later he was directed to advance and form on the right of Birney's division. Sickles then moved up in column to the Richmond Road and reported to Stoneman, who sent him across the Stage Road to deploy on the ground previously occupied by Gibbon's division. Joseph B. Carr's First Brigade was on the right, and George B. Hall's Second Brigade was on the left of Sickles' first line. Joseph W. Revere's Third Brigade formed a second line, and was placed on the road. Francis W. Seeley's battery was posted in rear of the center of the first line, and Justin E. Dimick's battery was held in reserve near the road.

During the afternoon Newton's division of Sixth Corps moved from its position in reserve in front of the bridges to a point between the Bernard house (Mansfield) and Smithfield, and it then advanced and formed in three lines in rear of Berry's brigade. Newton's leading brigade formed just in front of the Richmond Stage Road. The skirmishers of Sixth Corps were almost constantly engaged, and the corps artillery was also in action, but otherwise

Smith's divisions were not involved in the fighting that day. Doubleday's division was also engaged in skirmishing and was under heavy artillery fire; it suffered moderate casualties but made no major attacks.

On the morning of December 13, 1862, William W. Burns' First Division of Willcox's Ninth Corps took position with its left on Deep Run, and on the right of Smith's Sixth Corps. Burns was placed under Smith's orders. At 3:00 P.M., after Reynolds' repulse, Burns crossed Deep Run and moved to cover the pontoon bridges, which had been left unguarded when Newton's division moved to the left to support Stoneman's line. Burns remained near the bridges that night, but the next morning he moved back and crossed Deep Run and rejoined Ninth Corps.

After the failure of Reynolds' attack, there was skirmishing and artillery fire along the front until dark, but there were no further major attacks on the southern part of the battlefield. The fighting on Franklin's front ended at dark.

Federal Attacks on the Northern Flank. Before proceeding with an account of the battle on the northern flank, a brief description of of the battlefield is presented here for a better understanding of the troop movements during the Federal attacks. At the time of the battle the town of Fredericksburg ran back from the river bank for about 600 yards, and from its western edge a broken plain extended another 600 yards to the base of the range of hills on which Longstreet had posted his infantry and artillery. The high ground occupied by Longstreet was broken by a number of ravines, with the result that a number of more or less prominent hills rose along the ridge to heights of forty or fifty feet above the plain. The heights immediately west of Fredericksburg and north of Hazel Run have loosely been called Marye's Heights, but instead of being a single elevation the heights actually consist of several hills, as noted above. From north to south these are: Taylor's Hill, near the Rappahannock River; Stansbury Hill, about three-fourths of a mile to the southeast; Marye's Hill (or Marye's Heights), a little more than a mile to the south and east of Stansbury Hill; and Willis Hill, which on its southern end slopes down to Hazel Run. Beyond Hazel Run, and a little more than a half mile south-

west of Willis Hill, was Telegraph Hill (or Lee's Hill).

The plain between Fredericksburg and the heights was generally open, but it was traversed, roughly from north to south, by the spillway of a canal. The canal proper originated at a dam on the Rappahannock about one mile above Falmouth at the head of Beck's Island (later called Hunter's Island). It then ran to the southeast to the northwestern corner of Fredericksburg, and there it turned back into the river below the rapids at the northern edge of town. At a point on the canal a few hundred yards from the outskirts of the town there was a mill that was fed by water from the canal. Past this mill the surplus water ran into the spillway mentioned above. This was the "ditch" or "canal" mentioned in the Federal reports of the battle. The spillway, or ditch, flowed close to the western side of Fredericksburg and emptied into Hazel Run about 500 yards from its mouth. The spillway was of such depth that it could be crossed only on the bridges, and its western bank was high enough to afford protection for the Federal troops forming for their attack on the heights.

Two major roads ran out from the western side of Fredericksburg toward the hills beyond. The Telegraph Road left the town on Hanover Street, crossed the spillway, and, after veering slightly to the left, reached the base of the hills just below the Marye house (Brompton). The road then turned sharply to the left and ran along the foot of Marye's Hill and Willis Hill through what would become the "Sunken Road." It then turned back toward the west around the base of Willis Hill, crossed Hazel Run, and then ran past Lee's Hill and on to Richmond. That part of the Telegraph Road that ran below Marye's Heights was cut from the lower part of the ridge, and there was a stone wall on both sides. The road itself ran through a shallow cut, and the outer wall, which faced Fredericksburg, was four feet high. This made a perfect parapet for infantry. The second road, known as the Plank Road, also ran out of the western side of Fredericksburg, north of, and parallel to, the Telegraph Road. It crossed the spillway and the plain beyond, and then over the heights and on by way of Salem Church and Chancellorsville to Orange Court House.

All Federal attacks on the northern flank during the afternoon of December 13, 1862 were made across the plain against the Confederate position behind the Stone Wall, and they were confined to the space between the Plank Road on the right and Hazel Run on the left. It has already been noted that the plain was relatively open, but it was obstructed at various places by fences and houses. One such point was about 150 yards from the Stone Wall, where the Telegraph Road branched off slightly to the left from the extension of Hanover Street, which continued on, parallel to the Plank Road, past the northern end of Marye's Hill. In the narrow triangle formed by the extension of Hanover Street, the Telegraph Road, and the base of Marye's Hill were several houses and gardens. Also, just south of, and parallel to, the Telegraph Road another road ran out to the Sunken Road, and on this road was a large, square brick house. A little in advance of the brick house was a slight rise in the ground that afforded some protection for infantry lying down.

On the morning of December 13, 1862, Longstreet's corps was in position along the range of hills from the Rappahannock above Fredericksburg to a point below Deep Run. Richard H. Anderson's division held the left of the line from the high ridge opposite Beck's Island to the Plank Road. Robert Ransom's division was in rear of the artillery on Marye's Hill and Willis Hill, between the Plank Road and Hazel Run, with the 24th North Carolina of Ransom's brigade advanced to the foot of the hills between the Plank Road and the extension of Hanover Street. Thomas R. R. Cobb's brigade of Lafayette McLaws' division occupied the Sunken Road below Marye's Heights, and was on the right of 24th North Carolina. The other brigades of McLaws' division extended from the southern end of the Sunken Road, past Howison's Mill, across Hazel Run, and over Lee's Hill to a point beyond the Howison house. George E. Pickett's division followed the curve of the hills from the right of McLaws to the vicinity of Dr. Rennolds' house near Deep Run. John B. Hood's division was beyond Deep Run, and on the right of Ambrose P. Hill's division of Jackson's Corps.

There were some changes in the enemy positions during the afternoon. When Couch's troops emerged from Fredericksburg in preparation for their attack, John R. Cooke's brigade of Ransom's division moved forward to the crest of the hill to aid Cobb.

Later, between noon and 1:00 P.M., two regi-ments of Cooke's brigade joined Cobb's troops in the Sunken Road, and Ransom brought up the rest of his brigade to the crest of the hill just south of the Plank Road. Just after the first Federal attack, Cobb was mortally wounded, and at almost the same time, Cooke was wounded. Robert McMillan assumed command of Cobb's brigade, and Edward D. Hall succeeded Cooke. McLaws then sent Joseph B. Kershaw with his brigade to the Sunken Road, and directed Kershaw to replace Cobb in command of the troops there. At 2:00 P.M., when Reynolds' attack on the southern flank was collapsing, Longstreet ordered Pickett to send two brigades to support Ransom and McLaws. James L. Kemper's brigade was used as a reserve for Ransom's division, and Micah Jenkins' brigade took the place in McLaws' line left vacant when Kershaw moved to the Sunken Road.

It will be remembered that on the night of December 12, 1862, Couch's Second Corps and Willcox's Ninth Corps of Sumner's Right Grand Division bivouacked in the streets of Fredericksburg after crossing the Rappahannock. Also, that Butterfield's Fifth Corps and Whipple's division of Stoneman's Third Corps of Hooker's Center Grand Division were massed on the east bank of the river in readiness to move to the support of Sumner if needed.

On the morning of December 13, 1862, Burnside directed Sumner to attack with one division, closely supported by a second division, along the Plank Road and the Telegraph Road and to attempt to gain possession of the heights in rear of Fredericksburg. Sumner remained at his headquarters on the east side of the river during the day, and left to Couch, the senior officer on the field, the direction of the Federal attacks on the other side of the river.

Before the fighting began, Burnside made some changes in the disposition of the troops of Ninth Corps. He ordered Willcox to extend to the left over Hazel Run and form his corps so as to connect with Franklin on the left and Couch on the right. He was to hold this ground and support the attacks by Franklin and Couch if that became necessary. Conforming to this order, Willcox placed Samuel D. Sturgis' Second Division on the right of the railroad in Fredericksburg, near Couch, and William W. Burns' First Division on the left between Hazel Run and Deep Run, with his left next to Franklin. Burns was instructed to hold himself subject to Franklin's orders if called upon for support. George W. Getty's Third Division was placed in the center of Willcox's line, to the right of Hazel Run, near the point where it flows into the Rappahannock. At 3:00 P.M. Burns' division was ordered by Franklin to cross Deep Run and cover the bridges at Franklin's Crossing, and it did not rejoin the corps until the next day.

At 8:15 A.M. December 13, 1862, Sumner ordered Couch to make the attack on the northern flank, and Couch selected William H. French's Third Division of his Second Corps to lead the way. He also directed Winfield S. Hancock to follow with his First Division, Second Corps and support French. Fog covered the ground until about 10:00 A.M., and an hour later French's division began moving out of Fredericksburg by two parallel streets that ran into the Plank Road and the Telegraph Road. Nathan Kimball's First Brigade was in front, and it was followed at 200-yard intervals by John W. Andrews' Third Brigade, and then Oliver H. Palmer's Second Brigade. The division crossed the spillway at the bridges, and deployed under cover of the rise of ground about midway between the edge of town and the foot of the heights.

French began his attack at 12:10 P.M., with his three brigades moving forward in succession toward the heights. Each brigade suffered severely, first from artillery fire as it emerged from the town, and then from infantry fire as it neared the Stone Wall. The leading troops advanced to within about 100 yards of the wall, and a part of Kimball's brigade got into the cluster of houses at the forks of the Telegraph Road and the extension of Hanover Street, but then the brigade lines simply melted away. Many men were killed or wounded, and some fell back to reassemble in the ravine along the spillway, but many simply lay down to secure whatever protection the ground offered. The latter remained in position near the front until about 4:30 P.M. and then withdrew into Fredericksburg. Kimball was wounded during the fighting and was succeeded in command of First Brigade by John S. Mason.

Hancock's division followed French, with Samuel K. Zook's Third Brigade in front, Thomas F. Meagher's Second Brigade next, and John C. Caldwell's First Brigade in the rear. About 1:00 P.M. Hancock came up with French's division, which was attempting to advance, but his brigades were also stopped with heavy losses. Zook's and Meagher's brigades got close to the Stone Wall and Caldwell's brigade reached the brick house, but they could go no farther, and the survivors joined French's men on the ground. They maintained their position there until late evening and then withdrew into the town. Caldwell was wounded in the attack, and was succeeded in command of First Brigade by George W. Von Schack.

The ground over which Couch attacked was not favorable for artillery, and the divisions moved out of town without their batteries. In a short time, however, artillery was requested, and George Dickenson's battery of Sturgis' division and William A. Arnold's battery of Howard's division were in action on the outer edge of the high ground on which Fredericksburg was located. Soon Dickenson was killed and a number of his men were killed or wounded, and Hunt sent Charles Kusserow's battery of the Artillery Reserve and Richard Waterman's battery of Charles Griffin's division, Fifth Corps, both under the command of Alexander Doull (inspector on Hunt's staff), across the Rappahannock to replace Dickenson's battery. Doull placed his batteries on the Plank Road and opened fire on the enemy guns on the heights. Meantime, Arnold continued to fire until his battery was masked by the advance of the infantry. Most of the Right Grand Division batteries remained in the streets of Fredericksburg.

About noon Willcox ordered Sturgis to advance with his Second Division, Ninth Corps to support Couch's attack, which was about to begin. Sturgis moved forward along the railroad to the western edge of town, and took position to the left and front of the brick kiln. At 12:30 P.M. Edward Ferrero's Second Brigade advanced under cover of Dickenson's battery, and followed Hancock's division toward the Stone Wall. It soon came under heavy fire and was forced to halt short of its objective. James Nagle's First Brigade was ordered to take position on the left of Ferrero but, being unable to do so, moved by the flank to support Ferrero. Sturgis' division was unable to advance farther, but continued to hold its ground until relieved by Griffin's division about 7:00 P.M. It then moved back to its position of the previous night.

Howard's Second Division, Second Corps, which had occupied the northern part of Fredericksburg the night of December 12, 1862, remained in the town until about 1:00 P.M. the next day. It was then ordered to the right of the Plank Road to attack on the right of French and Hancock. This order was immediately countermanded, however, and Howard was ordered to the left to support Hancock's attack.

It has been noted earlier that Amiel W. Whipple's First Division of Stoneman's Third Corps was left near Falmouth when Stoneman, with his other two divisions, moved downriver on the evening of December 12, 1862 to support Franklin. On the morning of December 13, 1862, Whipple received orders to cross the Rappahannock, and between 12:00 and 1:00 P.M. he moved with his division into Fredericksburg. Samuel S. Carroll's Second Brigade moved downriver to a point near the railroad in rear of Sturgis' division, and Carroll reported to Willcox, commanding Ninth Corps, at 1:30 P.M. A. Sanders Piatt's First Brigade took position upriver to the right of the upper bridge to guard the approaches to the town from the west, and also to protect the right of Howard's division, which was then under orders to attack. Piatt's brigade picketed the right of the army between the right of Howard's division and the river. Piatt was injured in a fall from his horse, and early on the morning of December 14, 1862, Emlen Franklin assumed command of the brigade.

Shortly after 1:00 P.M. Howard moved his division toward Hanover Street to advance in support of Hancock. Joshua T. Owen's Second Brigade moved out on Hanover Street, crossed the spillway, deployed, and began its attack. Like the other brigades that had preceded it, Owen's brigade was forced to halt and lie down in front of the Stone Wall. Norman J. Hall's Third Brigade followed Owen. It deployed to the right of Hanover Street and then advanced, but it too was soon stopped. Alfred Sully's First Brigade was held in the outskirts in readiness to support Owen and Hall. Two regiments were later sent to Hall, and one regiment attempted to reinforce Owen. Owen and Hall held their ground, with Owen in position from the right of Sturgis to the extension of Hanover Street, and Hall on the right of Owen. Howard's division was relieved between 11:00 P.M. December 13, 1862 and 1:00 A.M. December 14, 1862 by George Sykes' Second Division, Fifth Corps, and it moved back into Fredericksburg.

About 4:00 P.M., John G. Hazard's battery of Hancock's division advanced to the crest beyond the spillway, just in rear of Owen's brigade, and opened fire. John D. Frank's battery of French's division was also sent up to the left and rear of Hazard. These batteries continued to fire until Humphreys' attack failed, and then they were withdrawn. Charles Phillips' battery of Andrew A. Humphreys' division replaced Hazard's and Frank's batteries when they moved forward.

Daniel Butterfield's Fifth Corps of Hooker's Center Grand Division did not cross the river into Fredericksburg until the afternoon of December 13, 1862. At 1:00 P.M. Griffin's First Division was ordered to cross at the bridge just below the railroad and support Willcox's Ninth Corps. The head of Griffin's column arrived on the west bank of the river at 2:00 P.M., and the division halted in town, near the river, and on the left of the railroad. Humphreys' division crossed a little after 3:00 P.M., and Sykes' division at 4:00 P.M.

At 3:00 P.M. Butterfield ordered Griffin to move to the rear of Fredericksburg to support Sturgis' division. Carroll's brigade of Whipple's division was also ordered forward by Willcox at about the same time to support Sturgis. In moving through town Carroll encountered Griffin's column, and joined and moved forward with it. At 3:30 P.M. Griffin was ordered to relieve Ferrero's brigade, which had been in action for several hours. James Barnes' First Brigade, which was Griffin's leading brigade, then advanced and formed in line of battle in rear of Ferrero. At 4:00 P.M. Barnes moved up under heavy fire to the front of Sturgis' division, and remained in position there that night and the next day.

At 4:30 P.M. Griffin was ordered to attack the enemy works, and Jacob B. Sweitzer's Second Brigade, supported on the left by Carroll's brigade of Whipple's division, advanced and arrived near the Stone Wall before being driven back to a position behind the crest of a slight rise in the ground. Just before sundown Thomas B. W. Stockton's Third Brigade of Griffin's division, which had been held in reserve, to the left of the railroad in the lower part of town, arrived in support of Sweitzer and Carroll. It was nearly dark when Stockton arrived, and he was assigned a position about 500 yards from the Stone Wall, but at that time the fighting had ended. Sweitzer then advanced to the front of Barnes and Stockton, to the right of the Telegraph Road, and he held this position until 10:00 P.M. December 14, 1862. At that time Sturgis advanced and relieved Griffin's division, which then moved back into the streets of Fredericksburg. Stockton held his position that night and the next day.

When Griffin's division was detached and sent to support Ninth Corps, Butterfield was left with only the divisions of Humphreys and Sykes of his Fifth Corps. Hooker had under his direct control only Butterfield's two divisions and Piatt's brigade of Whipple's division of Third Corps. Humphreys' Third Division crossed the Rappahannock shortly after 2:30 P.M. and moved forward to the western edge of town on Hanover Street. There he formed his division in line, with Peter H. Allabach's Second Brigade on the left of the Telegraph Road and Erastus B. Tyler's First Brigade on the left of the Plank Road.

About 2:00 P.M. Joseph Hooker arrived on the field, and as the senior officer present, he was then in command of Second Corps and Ninth Corps, as well as the troops of his own Center Grand Division. About forty minutes later Hooker was ordered to attack with his entire force, but upon examining the ground, he expressed his opposition to any further advance. He then rode back to Burnside's headquarters to discuss the situation, and he did not return until around 4:00 P.M. When he departed, Couch resumed command of the troops on the field, which then included Humphreys' division.

At 4:00 P.M. Couch ordered Humphreys to attack, and Allabach's brigade then moved forward toward the Stone Wall over the same ground used earlier by French and Hancock. The brigade passed through many of the survivors of the earlier attacks, who were lying on the ground, but like its predecessors it was soon driven back by the murderous fire of the Confederate artillery on the hills and the infantry in the Sunken Road. Tyler's brigade then came up, and it too was repulsed. Humphreys then retired to a new position in the ravine along the spillway, on the right of the Telegraph Road, and at midnight moved back into town.

Shortly after 4:00 P.M., while Humphreys was still attacking, George W. Getty was ordered to attack on the left of Couch's divisions with his Third Division, Ninth Corps. He was to advance by the unfinished railroad that ran westward out of Fredericksburg along the north bank of Hazel Run. Getty marched northwest from his position on the river near the mouth of Hazel Run, with Rush C. Hawkins' First Brigade in the lead and Edward Harland's Second Brigade following. Hawkins crossed the spillway and then the railroad, just beyond the outskirts of the town, and charged against the Confederate right of the position at the Stone Wall, below the Willis house. Hawkins advanced close up to the enemy line, but when struck in front and flank by a destructive fire he fell back to the protection of the spillway. He later returned to his former position in the town. Harland's brigade advanced only to a position protected by a ridge bordering the railroad, and it remained there during the night. The next morning it too withdrew into Fredericksburg.

At 2:00 P.M. Sykes was ordered with his Second Division, Fifth Corps to cross the Rappahannock into Fredericksburg. He moved the division down to the upper bridges, and at 4:00 P.M. crossed over and marched through the town on Hanover Street to Prince George Street, where it was placed under cover. Directly after Humphreys' repulse, Robert C. Buchanan's First Brigade moved out and formed in line of battle under the cover of the ravine along the spillway, between the Telegraph Road and the Plank Road. George L. Andrews' Second Brigade formed on the left of Buchanan, on the left side of the Telegraph Road. This movement was completed at 5:15 P.M. Gouverneur K. Warren's Third Brigade remained in Fredericksburg.

At 11:00 P.M. Sykes moved his First Brigade and Second Brigade to the front to within about 100 yards of the Stone Wall, and around midnight relieved Howard's division. Howard then withdrew into Fredericksburg. Sykes remained in his advanced position until 11:00 P.M. December 14, 1862, and then he was relieved by five regiments of Howard's division under George N. Morgan.

The Battle of Fredericksburg was not resumed on December 14, 1862, although it was Burnside's intention to do so until dissuaded by some of his officers. The army remained in position on the west bank of the Rappahannock at Fredericksburg and in front of Franklin's Crossing December 14–15, 1862, and then on the night of December 15–16, 1862 it recrossed the river and returned to its former camps.

With a few exceptions, such as Burnside's famous "Mud March" of January 20–24, 1863, the Army of the Potomac remained quietly in the vicinity of Falmouth until the beginning of Joseph Hooker's Chancellorsville campaign in late April 1863.

Organization of the Union Forces during the Fredericksburg Campaign, December 11–15, 1862.

ARMY OF THE POTOMAC, Ambrose E. Burnside

Provost Guard, Marsena R. Patrick
Volunteer Engineer Brigade, Daniel P. Woodbury
Battalion of United States Engineers, Charles E. Cross
Artillery, Henry J. Hunt
    Artillery Reserve, William Hays
    Unattached Artillery, Thomas S. Trumbull

Note. In addition to the above, artillery was also assigned to the divisions of the army. Each corps had a chief of artillery as follows:

First Corps, Charles S. Wainwright
Second Corps, Charles H. Morgan
Third Corps, La Rhett L. Livingston
Fifth Corps, Stephen H. Weed
Sixth Corps, Romeyn B. Ayres
Ninth Corps, John Edwards, Jr.

RIGHT GRAND DIVISION
Edwin V. Sumner

SECOND CORPS, Darius N. Couch

First Division, Winfield S. Hancock
    First Brigade, John C. Caldwell, to December 13, 1862, wounded
        George W. Von Schack
    Second Brigade, Thomas F. Meagher
    Third Brigade, Samuel K. Zook
    Artillery
        Battery B, 1st New York Light Artillery, Rufus D. Pettit
        Battery C, 4th United States Artillery, Evan Thomas

Second Division, Oliver O. Howard
    First Brigade, Alfred Sully
    Second Brigade, Joshua T. Owen
    Third Brigade, Norman J. Hall, to December 15, 1862
        William R. Lee
    Artillery
        Battery A, 1st Rhode Island Light Artillery, William A. Arnold
        Battery B, 1st Rhode Island Light Artillery, John G. Hazard

Third Division, William H. French
    First Brigade, Nathan Kimball, to December 13, 1862, wounded
        John S. Mason
    Second Brigade, Oliver H. Palmer
    Third Brigade, John W. Andrews, to December 13, 1862, wounded
        William Jameson, temporarily until evening December 13, 1862
    Artillery
        Battery G, 1st New York Light Artillery, John D. Frank
        Battery G, 1st Rhode Island Light Artillery, Charles D. Owen

Corps Artillery Reserve, Charles H. Morgan
    Battery I, 1st United States Artillery, Edmund Kirby
    Battery A, 4th United States Artillery, Rufus King, Jr.

NINTH CORPS, Orlando B. Willcox

First Division, William W. Burns
    First Brigade, Orlando M. Poe
    Second Brigade, Benjamin C. Christ
    Third Brigade, Daniel L. Leasure
    Artillery
        Battery D, 1st New York Light Artillery, Thomas W. Osborn
        Batteries L and M, 3rd United States Artillery, Horace J. Hayden

Second Division, Samuel D. Sturgis
    First Brigade, James Nagle
    Second Brigade, Edward Ferrero
    Artillery
        Battery L, 2nd New York Light Artillery, Jacob Roemer
        Battery D, Pennsylvania Light Artillery, George W. Durell
        Battery D, 1st Rhode Island Light Artillery, William W. Buckley
        Battery E, 4th United States Artillery, George Dickenson, to December 13, 1862, killed
        John Egan

Third Division, George W. Getty
    First Brigade, Rush C. Hawkins
    Second Brigade, Edward Harland
    Artillery
        Battery E, 2nd United States Artillery, Samuel N. Benjamin
        Battery A, 5th United States Artillery, James Gilliss

Cavalry Division (attached to Right Grand Division)

Alfred Pleasonton
First Brigade, John F. Farnsworth
Second Brigade, David McM. Gregg, to December 13, 1862
Thomas C. Devin
Battery M, 2nd United States Artillery, Alexander C. M. Pennington, Jr.

Note. Gregg succeeded George D. Bayard in command of the Cavalry Brigade attached to the Right Grand Division. Bayard was killed December 13, 1862.

CENTER GRAND DIVISION
Joseph Hooker

THIRD CORPS, George Stoneman

First Division, David B. Birney
First Brigade, John C. Robinson
Second Brigade, J. H. Hobart Ward
Third Brigade, Hiram G. Berry
Artillery
    Battery E, 1st Rhode Island Light Artillery, Pardon S. Jastram
    Batteries F and K, 2nd United States Artillery, John G. Turnbull

Note 1. Stoneman was assigned command of Third Corps November 16, 1862.
Note 2. Birney was assigned command of First Division November 16, 1862.
Note 3. Ward was assigned command of Second Brigade November 26, 1862.

Second Division, Daniel E. Sickles
First Brigade, Joseph B. Carr
Second Division, George B. Hall
Third Brigade, Joseph W. Revere
Artillery, James E. Smith
    2nd Battery, New Jersey Light Artillery, A. Judson Clark
    4th Battery, New Jersey Light Artillery, Joseph E. Nairn
    Battery H, 1st United States Artillery, Justin E. Dimick
    Battery K, 4th United States Artillery, Francis W. Seeley

Third Division, Amiel W. Whipple
First Brigade, A. Sanders Piatt, to December 13, 1862, disabled
    Emlen Franklin, from morning of December 14, 1862
Second Brigade, Samuel S. Carroll
Artillery

10th Battery, New York Light Artillery, John T. Bruen
11th Battery, New York Light Artillery, Albert A. Von Puttkammer
Battery H, 1st Ohio Light Artillery, George W. Norton

FIFTH CORPS, Daniel Butterfield

First Division, Charles Griffin
First Brigade, James Barnes
Second Brigade, Jacob B. Sweitzer
Third Brigade, Thomas B. W. Stockton, to late December 15, 1862, sick
Strong Vincent
Artillery
    3rd Battery (C), Massachusetts Light Artillery, Augustus P. Martin
    5th Battery (E), Massachusetts Light Artillery, Charles A. Phillips
    Battery C, 1st Rhode Island Light Artillery, Richard Waterman
    Battery D, 5th United States Artillery, Charles E. Hazlett

Note. Joseph Hooker relieved Fitz John Porter in command of Fifth Corps November 12, 1862, and November 16, 1862 was assigned command of the Center Grand Division. Butterfield assumed command of Fifth Corps November 16, 1862, and Charles Griffin assumed command of First Division. Sweitzer assumed command of Second Brigade November 16, 1862.

Second Division, George Sykes
First Brigade, Robert C. Buchanan
Second Brigade, George L. Andrews, to December 15, 1862
Charles S. Lovell
Third Brigade, Gouverneur K. Warren
Artillery, Malbone F. Watson
    Battery L, 1st Ohio Light Artillery, Frederick Dorries
    Battery I, 5th United States Artillery, Malbone F. Watson

Third Division, Andrew A. Humphreys
First Brigade, Erastus B. Tyler
Second Brigade, Peter H. Allabach
Artillery, Alanson M. Randol
    Battery C, 1st New York Light Artillery, William H. Phillips
    Batteries E and G, 1st United States Artillery, Alanson M. Randol

Cavalry Brigade (attached to the Center Grand Division), William W. Averell

Artillery
  Batteries B and L, 2nd United States Artillery, James M. Robertson

LEFT GRAND DIVISION
William B. Franklin

FIRST CORPS, John F. Reynolds

First Division, Abner Doubleday
  First Brigade, Walter Phelps, Jr.
  Second Brigade, James Gavin
  Third Brigade, William F. Rogers
  Fourth Brigade, Solomon Meredith, to December 13, 1862
    Lysander Cutler
  Artillery, George A. Gerrish, to December 13, 1862, wounded
    John A. Reynolds
    1st Battery, New Hampshire Light Artillery, Frederick M. Edgell
    Battery L, 1st New York Light Artillery, John A. Reynolds
    Battery B, 4th United States Artillery, James Stewart

Second Division, John Gibbon, to December 13, 1862, wounded
  Nelson Taylor
  First Brigade, Adrian R. Root
  Second Brigade, Peter Lyle
  Third Brigade, Nelson Taylor, to December 13, 1862
    Samuel H. Leonard
  Artillery, George F. Leppien
    2nd Battery, Maine Light Artillery, James A. Hall
    5th Battery, Maine Light Artillery, George F. Leppien
    Battery C, Pennsylvania Light Artillery, James Thompson
    Battery F, 1st Pennsylvania Light Artillery, R. Bruce Ricketts

Third Division, George G. Meade
  First Brigade, William Sinclair, to December 13, 1862
    William McCandless
  Second Brigade, Albert L. Magilton
  Third Brigade, C. Feger Jackson, to December 13, 1862, killed
    Joseph W. Fisher, temporarily December 13, 1862
    Robert Anderson
  Artillery
    Battery A, 1st Pennsylvania Light Artillery, John G. Simpson
    Battery B, 1st Pennsylvania Light Artillery, James H. Cooper
    Battery G, 1st Pennsylvania Light Artillery, Frank P. Amsden

Battery C, 5th United States Artillery, Dunbar R. Ransom

SIXTH CORPS, William F. Smith

First Division, William H. T. Brooks
  First Brigade, Alfred T. A. Torbert
  Second Brigade, Henry L. Cake
  Third Brigade, Davis A. Russell
  Artillery
    Battery A, Maryland Light Artillery, John W. Wolcott
    1st Battery (A), Massachusetts Light Artillery, William H. McCartney
    1st Battery, New Jersey Light Artillery, William Hexamer
    Battery D, 2nd United States Artillery, Edward D. Williston

Second Division, Albion P. Howe
  First Brigade, Calvin E. Pratt
  Second Brigade, Henry Whiting
  Third Brigade, Francis L. Vinton, to December 13, 1862, wounded
    Robert F. Taylor, to noon December 13, 1862
    Thomas H. Neill
  Artillery
    Battery B, Maryland Light Artillery, Alonzo Snow
    1st Battery, New York Light Artillery, Andrew Cowan
    3rd Battery, New York Light Artillery, William A. Harn
    Battery F, 5th United States Artillery, Leonard Martin

Third Division, John Newton
  First Brigade, John Cochrane
  Second Brigade, Charles Devens, Jr.
  Third Brigade, Thomas A. Rowley
    Frank Wheaton
  Artillery
    Battery C, 1st Pennsylvania Light Artillery, Jeremiah McCarthy
    Battery D, 1st Pennsylvania Light Artillery, Michael Hall
    Battery C, 2nd United States Artillery, John H. Butler

Cavalry Brigade (attached to Left Grand Division), George D. Bayard, to December 13, killed
  David McM. Gregg
  Artillery
    Battery C, 3rd United States Artillery, Horatio G. Gibson

GETTYSBURG CAMPAIGN, PART I FROM THE RAPPAHANNOCK TO GETTYSBURG
JUNE 3, 1863–JULY 2, 1863

In May 1863, following the Battle of Chancellorsville, Robert E. Lee submitted to the authorities in Richmond a plan for the invasion of Maryland and Pennsylvania by the Army of Northern Virginia. This plan was finally approved, and June 3, 1863, Lee's leading divisions started north from their positions near Fredericksburg and on the Rapidan River. By June 8, 1863, James Longstreet's First Corps and Richard S. Ewell's Second Corps of Lee's army were concentrated around Culpeper Court House, where James E. B. (Jeb) Stuart's cavalry had been assembled since mid-May 1863. Ambrose P. Hill remained with his Third Corps near Fredericksburg to confuse Joseph Hooker, commanding the Army of the Potomac, as to Lee's intentions, and also to guard the line of the Rappahannock.

On June 5, 1863, two days after Lee's movement began, Hooker became aware that enemy troops were leaving his front near Fredericksburg, but he had no definite information as to their numbers or destination. That same day, Hooker ordered John Sedgwick, commanding Sixth Corps, to make a reconnaissance in force at Franklin's old crossing on the Rappahannock River, near the mouth of Deep Run, to determine the strength and positions of the Confederate forces in the area. Sedgwick moved Albion P. Howe's Second Division up to the river, and that afternoon Lewis A. Grant's Second Brigade crossed, drove back the enemy from the crossing, and took a number of prisoners. These were found to belong to Hill's corps, and this led Sedgwick to believe that Fredericksburg was still held in force. For additional information, see Sixth Corps, Army of the Potomac, Skirmishes at Franklin's Crossing (or Deep Run), Virginia.

BATTLE OF BRANDY STATION (OR FLEETWOOD HILL)
JUNE 9, 1863

In a report detailing the enemy troops' disposi-

tions prepared May 27, 1863, Hooker learned that there were three brigades of cavalry belonging to Stuart's cavalry division between Kelly's Ford and Culpeper Court House. Hooker was uncertain as to why they were there, but he believed that they had been assembled in preparation for a raid, or to cover and conceal the movements of other troops. In either case, Hooker was interested, and June 2, 1863, he ordered John Buford, who was in command of the Federal cavalry along the Rappahannock River, to cross the river and learn more about this force. Three days later, Buford reported that Stuart was indeed in Culpeper County, and that he had with him the entire available Confederate cavalry force. Buford's report was correct: Stuart's force consisted of Fitzhugh Lee's and Wade Hampton's brigades of Stuart's cavalry division, Beverly Robertson's cavalry brigade from North Carolina, and William E. ("Grumble") Jones' cavalry brigade from the Shenandoah Valley.

Hooker finally concluded that Stuart planned a raid to the north, possibly into Maryland, and June 7, 1863, he ordered Alfred Pleasonton, commanding the Cavalry Corps, Army of the Potomac, to move with all his cavalry and his artillery, cross the Rappahannock River at Beverly Ford and Kelly's Ford June 9, 1863, and march directly on Culpeper Court House. He was to disperse and destroy Stuart's cavalry, and also to destroy his trains and supplies. Hooker had also directed Pleasonton to divide his command for this expedition as he thought best. Because there was some uncertainty as to the strength of the enemy force confronting Pleasonton, Hooker decided to send with him two special infantry brigades.

Earlier, on June 6, 1863, Pleasonton divided his cavalry corps into two groups or wings as follows: he assigned John Buford to command the Right Wing, which consisted of Buford's First Division and Wesley Merritt's Reserve Brigade (temporarily commanded by Charles J. Whiting), which was composed of the Regular Cavalry and 6th Pennsylvania Cavalry. He assigned David McM. Gregg to command the Left Wing, which consisted of Alfred N. Duffie's Second Cavalry Division and Gregg's Third Cavalry Division.

Also on June 6, 1863, a special infantry brigade was formed at Spotted Tavern, beyond Hartwood Church, from two regiments of Third Corps, two regiments of Twelfth Corps, and one regiment of Eleventh Corps. Adelbert Ames, commanding First Brigade, First Division, Eleventh Corps, was assigned command of this brigade. That day it marched to join Buford's Right Wing. A second special infantry brigade was formed on the night of June 7, 1863 from 600 men of First Corps, 600 men of Sixth Corps, and 300 men of Second Corps. David A. Russell, commanding Third Brigade, First Division, Sixth Corps, was assigned command of this brigade. It marched to join Gregg's Left Wing. As a further precaution, Hooker instructed George G. Meade, commanding Fifth Corps, to have James Barnes' First Division, which was then guarding Kelly's Ford, ready to aid Pleasonton's cavalry if needed.

On the night of July 8, 1863, Pleasonton moved up with his command to the east bank of the Rappahannock. Buford's wing was at Beverly Ford, about one and one-half miles northwest of the Orange and Alexandria Railroad bridge, and Gregg's two cavalry divisions were assembled around the approaches to Kelly's Ford, about four miles southeast of the bridge. Both wings were under orders to cross the river at dawn. That night Stuart was camped on Fleetwood Hill, about one-half mile east of Brandy Station.

At 4:30 on the morning of June 9, 1863, Buford's command, with Benjamin F. Davis' First Brigade, First Cavalry Division in the lead, crossed the Rappahannock against some opposition, and advanced to Saint James Church, about two miles northeast of Brandy Station. A short time after crossing the river, Davis was killed and was succeeded in command of the brigade by William S. McClure. Later, William Gamble assumed command of the brigade. Pleasonton was with Buford until the two wings joined near Brandy Station, and during this time Buford commanded his own division. At Brandy Station, however, Pleasonton directed the movements of his entire force.

Buford encountered heavy resistance northeast of Saint James Church and was forced to fall back for a short distance. By 10:00 A.M. he was facing the greater part of Stuart's cavalry and could advance no farther. Meantime, Gregg had started several hours late that morning because Duffie had lost his way in marching to the ford. As a result, Gregg did not complete his crossing until after 8:00 A.M., at which time Buford's wing had been fighting for about four hours.

Once across the river, Gregg marched with his two divisions on the road toward Stevensburg. About halfway there, four and a half miles out, Gregg, with his Third Cavalry Division and Russell's infantry brigade, turned off on the road to Brandy Station, which was about seven miles to the northwest. Duffie proceeded on toward Stevensburg with his Second Cavalry Division. His mission was to protect the left flank of Pleasonton's main body as it advanced from Brandy Station toward Culpeper Court House.

Between 11:00 and noon Gregg's division, with Percy Wyndham's Second Brigade on the left and leading, and Judson Kilpatrick's First Brigade on the right, crossed the railroad a short distance west of Brandy Station and headed for Fleetwood Hill. By this movement, Gregg was approaching the rear of Stuart's force, which was then at Saint James Church to the northeast, facing Buford. Stuart immediately returned to meet Gregg, and charged the oncoming Federals. The fighting that ensued was bitter and completely disordered. There were numerous charges and countercharges by regiments, battalions, squadrons, and even smaller groups; and all organization on both sides was partially or totally lost. There were no established battle lines, but rather the fighting became what has generally been described as a melee. Gregg was finally forced back across the railroad, where he was joined by Duffie, who had returned from Stevensburg. Gregg, however, did not renew the attack.

Back at Saint James Church, Buford was preparing to advance again; but before he was ready, Gregg had been repulsed. With the threat from Gregg removed, Stuart established a line of battle along the length of Fleetwood Hill, facing Buford. There was some further fighting when Buford attacked the left flank of Stuart's position, but the enemy cavalry was able to hold its ground.

By late afternoon, both sides had had enough fighting for the day. Stuart had concentrated his force and was holding Fleetwood Hill, and Pleasonton did not have the strength to drive him off. Then Pleasonton learned of the approach of Confederate infantry and decided that it was time to withdraw. He issued the order between 4:00 and 5:00 P.M., and his weary troopers retired toward the Rappahannock. His command crossed the river about 7:00 P.M. without molestation by the enemy, and it then moved to the vicinity of Warrenton Junction.

It should be noted that this was the greatest cavalry battle of the war, but much of the fighting was done by dismounted cavalrymen acting as infantry. In addition, there were eight infantry regiments present during the battle, and Ames' brigade was engaged throughout the day with Buford's Right Wing. Russell's brigade was a few miles from the field during Gregg's battle, but it later moved up to the left of Buford and suffered some casualties.

Although Pleasonton was unsuccessful in the principal part of his mission, he did discover that enemy infantry were in the vicinity of Culpeper Court House.

The organization of Pleasonton's forces that were engaged at the Battle of Brandy Station (Fleetwood Hill), Beverly Ford, and Stevensburg June 9, 1863 was as follows:

CAVALRY CORPS, Alfred Pleasonton

First Cavalry Division, John Buford
    First Brigade, Benjamin F. Davis, killed June 9, 1863
       William S. McClure
    Second Brigade, Thomas C. Devin
    Reserve Brigade, Charles J. Whiting

Note. The Reserve Brigade was assigned to First Cavalry Division June 6, 1863.

Second Cavalry Division, Alfred N. Duffie
    First Brigade, Louis P. Di Cesnola
    Second Brigade, J. Irvin Gregg

Note. This division was engaged in a skirmish at Stevensburg.

Third Cavalry Division, David McM. Gregg
    First Brigade, Judson Kilpatrick
    Second Brigade, Percy Wyndham

Ames' Infantry Brigade, Adelbert Ames

Russell's Infantry Brigade, David A. Russell

Accompanying the cavalry to Brandy Station were the following batteries: Edward Heaton's Batteries B and L, 2nd United States Artillery was with First Brigade, First Cavalry Division; Samuel S. Elder's Battery E, 4th United States Artillery was with the Reserve Brigade, First Cavalry Division; Alexander C. M. Pennington's Battery M, 2nd United States Artillery was with Second Cavalry Division; and Joseph W. Martin's 6th Battery, New York Light Artillery was with Third Cavalry Division. All these batteries belonged to James M. Robertson's First Brigade, Horse Artillery. In addition, William M. Graham's Battery K, 1st United States Artillery of John C. Tidball's Second Brigade, Horse Artillery was with Ames' infantry brigade.

When Stoneman made his raid toward Richmond during the Chancellorsville Campaign, Judson Kilpatrick with the Harris Light Cavalry (2nd New York Cavalry) and Hasbrouck Davis with his 12th Illinois Cavalry did not return to the army with Stoneman, but instead they marched past Richmond to Gloucester Point and reported to John A. Dix, commander of the Department of Virginia. These regiments remained with Dix as a temporary brigade, commanded by Kilpatrick, until May 28, 1863, when he was ordered to march north and rejoin the Cavalry Corps. Kilpatrick reported with his regiment to David McM. Gregg, commanding Third Cavalry Division, and June 7, 1863, he was ordered to resume command of First Brigade, Third Division, to which he had been assigned February 16, 1863. The 12th Illinois Cavalry, then under the command of Arno Voss, was ordered to repor. 'o Bealeton June 8, 1863. Because this regiment had become so depleted during the recent campaign, it did not take part in the engagement at Brandy Station.

* * * * * * * * * *

On June 10, 1863, there were some changes in position in both armies. On the Union side, the Cavalry Corps moved to the neighborhood of Warrenton Junction, and the infantry supports that had accompanied the cavalry to Brandy Station left to rejoin their respective commands. Howe's Second Division, which had recrossed the Rappahannock at Franklin's Crossing, marched north from the river to Aquia Creek. There was also activity by the enemy at this time. After assembling Ewell's and Longstreet's corps at Culpeper Court House, Lee's next objective was the fords of the Upper Potomac, and these he proposed to reach by way of the Shenandoah Valley. He sent Ewell forward June 10, 1863 to secure these fords, and two days later Ewell's corps entered the valley by way of Chester Gap and marched toward Winchester.

Activity in the Army of the Potomac increased during the next few days. On June 11, 1863, Hooker ordered all corps commanders to be prepared to move on very short notice, and he then began to extend his right toward the Orange and Alexandria Railroad. That day, Third Corps, temporarily under the command of David B. Birney, marched from near Falmouth to take position on the right of George G. Meade's Fifth Corps to give Pleasonton's cavalry more support on the stretch of the Rappahannock between Kelly's Ford and Beverly Ford. At the same time, Pleasonton was directed to take position on the right of Third Corps and guard the river above Beverly Ford.

Also on June 1, 1863, Pleasonton ordered the reorganization of the Cavalry Corps into two divisions, which were to be commanded by John Buford and David McM. Gregg. For details, see Cavalry Corps, Army of the Potomac, Gettysburg Campaign.

Preparations for a major movement of the army continued June 12, 1863. First Corps, commanded by John F. Reynolds, marched from Fitzhughs' plantation and White Oak Church to Deep Run south of Somerville, near Embury Mill, to act as a reserve for Third Corps and Fifth Corps. Oliver O. Howard's Eleventh Corps left the vicinity of Brooke's Station on the Richmond, Fredericksburg, and Potomac Railroad and marched by way of Hartwood Church toward Catlett's Station. Also, the troops of Sixth Corps that were across the Rappahannock near Franklin's Crossing were ordered to return to the north bank.

On June 12, 1863, Hooker made a temporary organizational change in the army to provide for better control of the forces concentrating on the upper Rappahannock. Reynolds was assigned command of the Right Wing of the army, which was to consist of First Corps, Third Corps, Fifth Corps, and the Cavalry Corps. In addition, Howard's Eleventh Corps was to come under Reynolds' orders when it

arrived at Catlett's Station the next day. Reynolds' headquarters was at Bealeton.

WITHDRAWAL OF THE ARMY TO THE ORANGE AND ALEXANDRIA RAILROAD
JUNE 13–16, 1863

After Ewell had entered the Shenandoah Valley by way of Chester Gap June 12, 1863, he marched northward toward Winchester with the divisions of Jubal A. Early and Edward Johnson. Robert E. Rodes' division, with Albert G. Jenkins' cavalry brigade, moved toward Berryville. At that time Washington L. Elliott's First Brigade and William G. Ely's Second Brigade of Robert H. Milroy's Second Division, Eighth Corps of Robert C. Schenck's Middle Department occupied Winchester, and Andrew T. McReynolds' Third Brigade was at Berryville.

The principal defenses of Winchester were on a ridge to the north and northwest of the town. The Star Fort was on the Pughtown Road where it crossed the ridge, and the Main Fort, or Flag Fort, was on the same ridge farther south. There were also two smaller outposts, one north and one south of these forts. About three-fourths of a mile west of the fortified ridge was another ridge (Flint Ridge) on which were three unfinished earthworks. The largest and most southerly of these was the West Fort.

Engagement at Winchester, Virginia, June 13–14, 1863. A little before 8:00 A.M. June 13, 1863 Milroy learned of Early's approach toward Winchester, and he promptly sent Ely forward on the Front Royal Road with a part of his Second Brigade, and Elliott on the Valley Pike (Strasburg Road) with a part of his First Brigade. A little more than a mile south of town, Ely came under enemy artillery fire, and about 9:30 A.M. he retired to a position at the southern edge of Winchester, between the Front Royal Road and the Valley Pike.

About 2:00 P.M., J. Warren Keifer of Elliott's brigade advanced with his 110th Ohio Infantry Regiment, Joseph L. Moss' 12th Pennsylvania Cavalry, and a section of John Carlin's Battery D, 1st West Virginia Artillery to a point near Kernstown. There he encountered Early's advance, and was soon engaged. A short time later Keifer's left was threatened by the enemy on the Front Royal Road, and he withdrew and took position with Elliott south of Winchester, behind Abram's (also Abraham's) Creek, and on the west side of the Valley Pike.

About 3:00 P.M. John B. Klunk's 12th West Virginia of Ely's brigade came up on the right of Keifer's former position and became engaged with John B. Gordon's brigade of Early's division. Klunk continued to oppose Gordon for about two hours and then withdrew. There was no further serious fighting that evening, but there was skirmishing along the line until dark. That night the Federal troops south of Winchester were withdrawn into the southern suburbs. At 2:00 on the morning of June 14, 1863, most of the troops in Winchester were ordered to retire to the forts to the north and northwest of town. Ely with a part of his brigade was sent to a position in front of the forts on the east side of town.

During the morning of June 13, 1863, Milroy had ordered McReynolds to bring his brigade from Berryville to Winchester, and he arrived safely between 9:00 and 10:00 that night. About midnight McReynolds moved his command to the Star Fort and other works in the vicinity. The next morning, June 14, 1863, Elliott, with a part of his brigade and Klunk's 12th West Virginia of Ely's brigade, moved onto the ridge just to the northwest of Winchester. Elliott sent Keifer with his 110th Ohio, one company of 116th Ohio, and Edmund D. Spooner's Battery L, 5th United States Artillery to occupy the unfinished works on Flint Ridge.

About 7:00 A.M. June 14, 1863, fighting began on the east side of town as troops of Johnson's Confederate division feinted and threatened an attack on Ely's line. Johnson continued with this activity until 4:00 P.M. Meantime, Early, with the brigades of Harry T. Hays, William Smith, and Robert F. Hoke (the latter commanded by Isaac E. Avery), made a flanking march of eight to ten miles to a point beyond the positions of Elliott and McReynolds, west of Winchester. Then, at about 5:00 P.M., Hays' Louisiana brigade launched a strong attack on the West Fort. This was soon overrun and captured, and Keifer's troops were driven back to the main fortifications nearer the town. It was then growing dark, and the fighting ended for the day.

Engagement at Stephenson's Depot (or Station), Virginia, June 15, 1863. During the night of June 14, 1863, Milroy decided that his position at Winchester was untenable, and he issued orders for a withdrawal. About 1:00 A.M. June 15, 1863, he started his troops north on the Martinsburg Road. Elliott's brigade marched first, and it was followed by Ely's brigade, and then McReynolds' brigade. Meantime, about nightfall June 14, 1863, Ewell ordered Johnson to move with his division to the Martinsburg Road, four miles from Winchester, to prevent Milroy from retiring to either Martinsburg or Harper's Ferry. Johnson marched during the night by way of Jordan Springs, and the head of his column arrived near Stephenson's Depot at about 3:30 A.M. June 15, 1863, just as the van of Milroy's division was approaching from Winchester. Johnson then formed his division along a cut of the Winchester and Potomac Railroad, next to the Martinsburg Road. The line was on elevated ground in a woods east of the road, and in a field east of and adjoining the woods. George H. Steuart's brigade, which was in the lead, took position in the cut, with one regiment on the right of a small bridge over the cut, and two regiments on the left. When Francis T. Nicholls' brigade (then commanded by Jesse M. Williams) came up, it was formed in line perpendicular to the Charlestown Road, 300 yards to the rear of Steuart's position. When James A. Walker arrived with his Stonewall Brigade, he was sent to the extreme Confederate right.

Milroy's advance guard, the 12th Pennsylvania Cavalry, arrived near Stephenson's Depot about 4:00 A.M. and ran into the leading troops of Johnson's division. Elliott's brigade then came up and formed parallel to the road, and made three unsuccessful charges on Steuart's brigade along the railroad. When Ely's brigade arrived it moved against the enemy left. Ely launched two attacks, and was preparing for a third when Elliott was ordered to withdraw by way of the Martinsburg Road. Ely was directed to follow, and similar orders were sent to McReynolds, but the latter did not receive them. Ely was just starting his third attack when Walker's brigade arrived and advanced on the right of

Steuart's brigade. Walker moved forward through the woods and beyond the Martinsburg Road for about a half mile to the right of the Carter house, where he found Ely's brigade. By this time Milroy's division was completely demoralized, and Ely surrendered his brigade. Two regiments of Elliott's brigade were also captured there. Milroy, with Elliott, escaped to Harper's Ferry with about 1,200 men. Meantime, McReynold's brigade—consisting of only two infantry regiments, one cavalry regiment, and one battery—had arrived on the right of Milroy's line and had become engaged, but in the confusion on the field, the brigade simply disintegrated. McReynolds personally escaped to Harper's Ferry.

In addition to the men who escaped to Harper's Ferry, about 2,700 more retreated northward, and eventually crossed the Potomac at Hancock, Maryland. They then moved on and assembled at Bloody Run (present-day Everett) in Pennsylvania. Milroy suffered a loss of 4,443 men, of which 3,358 were captured, and his division was destroyed. For additional information, see Middle Department, Military Operations in the Middle Department, The Gettysburg Campaign.

While Ewell was engaged at Winchester, Robert E. Rodes' division of his corps, accompanied by Albert G. Jenkins' cavalry brigade, passed through Berryville and moved on toward Martinsburg and Williamsport.

* * * * * * * * *

June 13, 1863, Daniel Tyler was ordered from Baltimore to Harper's Ferry to assume command of all Federal troops there, including Benjamin F. Smith's Third Brigade of Benjamin F. Kelley's First Division, Eighth Corps, which was then at Martinsburg. Because of Ewell's threat at Winchester, Smith's brigade was withdrawn to Harper's Ferry the next day. Tyler then crossed the Potomac with all of his troops and occupied Maryland Heights. There he organized his command into three brigades that were commanded by John R. Kenly, Washington L. Elliott, and William H. Morris. Kelley was assigned command of all Federal troops west of Hancock, Maryland.

When Hooker learned that Milroy had been attacked at Winchester, he was finally convinced that Lee was marching toward the Potomac River and Maryland, and that day, June 13, 1863, he issued orders for the Army of the Potomac to move to the line of the Orange and Alexandria Railroad. He directed the four corps of Reynolds' Right Wing to march to the northeast to Manassas Junction, but he personally remained for a time with the Left Wing in the Falmouth-Stafford Court House-Aquia area to cover the removal of the government property, especially from the main base at Aquia Creek. The Left Wing consisted of Winfield S. Hancock's Second Corps (Darius N. Couch, the former commander of Second Corps, had been assigned command of the Department of the Susquehanna June 10, 1863), John Sedgwick's Sixth Corps, Henry W. Slocum's Twelfth Corps, and Robert O. Tyler's Reserve Artillery. When the government property had been secured, the Left Wing was to march by way of Dumfries to the Orange and Alexandria Railroad. Also at that time, the supply base for the army was moved to the Orange and Alexandria Railroad, with the main base at Alexandria, Virginia.

During the next few days the corps of the army moved back to the railroad. First Corps, Third Corps, and Eleventh Corps arrived at Manassas Junction June 14, 1863, and Fifth Corps came up the next day. When the movement of these corps to the railroad was completed, Reynolds' Right Wing was discontinued June 16, 1863, and Hooker resumed direct control of the four corps. The Cavalry Corps occupied positions along the railroad at Warrenton, Warrenton Junction, Manassas Junction, Union Mills, and Bristoe Station from June 10, 1863 to June 17, 1863, but Pleasonton's pickets did not leave the line of the Rappahannock until 1:00 A.M. June 15, 1863.

Twelfth Corps left Stafford Court House and Aquia Landing June 13, 1863, and marched by way of Dumfries to Fairfax Court House, where it arrived June 15, 1863. Horatio G. Wright's First Division and John Newton's Third Division of Sixth Corps moved back from Franklin's Crossing to Aquia Creek and joined Albion P. Howe's Second Division there June 13, 1863. Sixth Corps then marched by way of Dumfries to Fairfax Station, where it arrived June 16, 1863. The Artillery Reserve left Falmouth June 13, 1863 and moved to Fairfax Court House, where it remained from June

15, 1863 to June 25, 1863. Second Corps remained at Falmouth until late on June 14, 1863, and it then marched by way of Dumfries to Sangster's Station and arrived there June 17, 1863.

Headquarters Army of the Potomac left Falmouth June 14, 1863; it moved to Fairfax Station the next day, and remained there from June 18, 1863 to June 25, 1863.

ADVANCE OF THE ARMY TO THE BULL RUN MOUNTAINS JUNE 17–21, 1863

While the army of the Potomac was moving to the Orange and Alexandria Railroad, Lee's army continued its march northward toward the Potomac. On June 14, as soon as the Federal infantry began to leave the lines opposite Fredericksburg, Ambrose P. Hill's Confederate corps began to move out and follow Ewell's route northward toward the Shenandoah Valley. Longstreet remained at Culpeper Court House until June 15, 1863, and then he began to march northward along the eastern side of the Blue Ridge Mountains toward Ashby's Gap and Snicker's Gap. During his advance he was screened on the right by Stuart's cavalry, which was operating along the Bull Run Mountains and in the Loudoun Valley between the Bull Run and Blue Ridge mountains.

On June 16, 1863, the Army of Northern Virginia was disposed as follows: Ewell's divisions were at Williamsport, Sharpsburg, and Shepherdstown; Jenkins' cavalry brigade, which had crossed the Potomac at Williamsport the day before, had advanced to Chambersburg, Pennsylvania; Longstreet's corps was near Sperryville, and was marching toward Piedmont; and Hill's corps was near Culpeper Court House, on the march toward the Shenandoah Valley.

Up to this point, Hooker was unable to arrive at any definite conclusion as to Lee's intentions. Lee was in position to turn eastward and strike toward Washington and Baltimore, or to continue on northward into Maryland and Pennsylvania. On June 16, however, Darius N. Couch, commanding the Department of the Susquehanna, informed Edwin M. Stanton that Confederate troops were north of the Potomac River. That same day, Henry W. Halleck advised Hooker to move a part of his force toward Leesburg, and to place the remainder of the army in position to support it. Further, he directed Hooker to send out his cavalry to learn something definite about the size of the enemy force, where it then was, and where it seemed to be going.

On June 17, 1863, in response to Halleck's directive, Hooker sent Pleasonton's cavalry forward toward Aldie, Virginia to determine the whereabouts of the Army of Northern Virginia, and also to find out what he could about its movements. Pleasonton's attempts to penetrate Stuart's cavalry screen in the Loudoun Valley resulted in almost continuous skirmishing and fighting from that day until June 22, 1863, including a series of cavalry engagements at Aldie (June 17, 1863), Middleburg (June 17–18, 1863), and Upperville (June 21, 1863).

Action at Aldie, Virginia, June 17, 1863. Shortly after noon June 17, 1863, in obedience to orders from Hooker that morning, Pleasonton started his Cavalry Corps from its camps at Manassas Junction toward Aldie. About nine miles from the town, he ordered Gregg, whose Second Cavalry Division was in the lead, to send a brigade through Aldie Gap to scout the country to the west and southwest toward Front Royal. Kilpatrick's Second Brigade, which was at the front of the column, was selected for this purpose. The head of Kilpatrick's brigade arrived near Aldie about 4:00–4:30 P.M. and encountered Confederate pickets posted east of the gap. The leading squadron drove them back through the gap and through the town, but it was finally stopped by troopers of Fitzhugh Lee's brigade, then under the temporary command of Thomas T. Munford. This brigade had just arrived near Aldie and was preparing to camp for the night.

The rest of Kilpatrick's brigade came up, and then for four hours there was stubborn fighting between the two brigades. This consisted primarily of charges, usually by squadrons and regiments, that resulted in little advantage to either side. Finally, late in the day, Calvin S. Douty's 1st Maine Cavalry came up and joined in the action. This was Kilpatrick's only reinforcement. John B. McIntosh's First Brigade and J. Irvin Gregg's Third Brigade, both of Second Cavalry Division, were nearby during the fighting, but except for the 1st Maine Cavalry they were not engaged. About dark that evening, Munford withdrew toward Middleburg.

Skirmishes at and near Middleburg, Virginia, June 17–18, 1863. On the morning of June 17, 1863, before starting with the Cavalry Corps toward Aldie, Pleasonton detached Alfred N. Duffie's 1st Rhode Island Cavalry of Kilpatrick's brigade and ordered it to move by way of Thoroughfare Gap to Middleburg. Duffie was further directed that, after arriving at Middleburg, he was to communicate with Pleasonton, who was expected to be at Aldie, and then camp for the night. From there he was to make a reconnaissance through the Loudoun Valley, and finally, to rejoin Gregg's division at Noland's Ferry, near the mouth of the Monocacy River.

Duffie started out as ordered, and he encountered enemy pickets at Thoroughfare Gap at 9:30 A.M. He was not able to clear the gap until about 11:00 A.M. He then turned north to avoid John R. Chambliss' brigade of Confederate cavalry, which was approaching the gap from the west, and he arrived near Middleburg about 4:00 P.M. After an engagement of about a half hour, the enemy retreated and Duffie entered the town. He then attempted to communicate with Kilpatrick as ordered, but without success. Duffie's skirmishers were constantly engaged in resisting enemy pressure until about 7:00 P.M., when he decided to return by the way that he had come. He soon found Chambliss' cavalry blocking the road about one-half mile southwest of Middleburg, and he then dismounted his men and formed a defensive position. Duffie repulsed a number of attacks, but he soon discovered that he was surrounded by troopers of the brigades of Chambliss and Beverly Robertson, and he decided to fight his way out. He made the attempt about 3:00 A.M. June 18, 1863, and in the process the 1st Rhode Island Cavalry was virtually destroyed. Duffie, with only four officers and twenty-seven men, finally arrived at Centerville, Virginia about 1:30 that afternoon. A number of other men of his command, however, came in later.

Action at Middleburg, Virginia, June 19, 1863. June 18, 1863, the cavalry was sent out to the west on a number of reconnaissances in attempts to find Lee's army. Othneil De Forest's brigade of Julius Stahel's Cavalry Division, Department of Washington advanced toward Warrenton; Thomas C. Devin's Second Brigade of Buford's First Cavalry Division, toward Thoroughfare Gap; J. Irvin Gregg's Third Brigade of David McM. Gregg's Second Cavalry Division, to Middleburg; and William Gamble's First Brigade of Buford's division, toward Philomont.

After a brisk skirmish, J. Irvin Gregg's brigade entered Middleburg, but that evening it was ordered back to a point about midway between Middleburg and Aldie. The next day, June 19, 1863, Pleasonton received a third order to break through Stuart's cavalry screen. Accordingly, he ordered David McM. Gregg, with J. Irvin Gregg's brigade and Kilpatrick's brigade of his own division and Gamble's brigade of Buford's division, to advance from Aldie and capture Middleburg, and then to send on a force to Ashby's Gap. Gregg's other brigade, under McIntosh, was ordered to Hay Market. J. Irvin Gregg, supported by Kilpatrick, was ordered to advance on Middleburg, and Gamble was directed to move to the right toward Union.

J. Irvin Gregg moved out at 6:00 A.M., and about an hour later the 4th Pennsylvania Cavalry, Gregg's leading regiment, drove the enemy pickets through Middleburg and advanced to Stuart's position on a ridge about one mile west of the town. At 9:30 A.M., a part of Gregg's dismounted troopers charged with some success against Beverly Robertson's line. Gregg's men were pushed back by Chambliss' brigade, and then Kilpatrick with Gregg's reserves charged and forced Stuart to withdraw to the next ridge. There was no further attack that day, and the Federal cavalrymen bivouacked for the night.

June 20, 1863, Gamble's brigade, which was farther to the right, about three miles northwest of Middleburg, was attacked, but it was able to hold its position.

Engagement at Upperville, Virginia, June 21, 1863. On June 20, 1863, when Wade Hampton's cavalry brigade joined Stuart, all five of the brigades of his cavalry division were in the Loudoun Valley. Munford's brigade was near Snickersville; Chambliss' brigade and William E. Jones' brigade were at Union; and Hampton was with Robertson near Middleburg, on the ridge west of the town that Robertson had occupied the day before. James Longstreet's infantry corps occupied Ashby's and

Snicker's gaps in the Blue Ridge Mountains, across the valley to the west.

On June 20, 1863, Hooker approved a plan submitted by Pleasonton, according to which Pleasonton was to move with his Cavalry Corps and a division of infantry into the Loudoun Valley against Stuart. George G. Meade's Fifth Corps, Army of the Potomac had arrived at Aldie the day before, and James Barnes' First Division of three brigades was detached from Fifth Corps and assigned to accompany Pleasonton on this expedition.

At daylight June 21, 1863, Pleasonton moved west out of Aldie on the road to Ashby's Gap, with Gregg's Second Cavalry Division in the lead. At Middleburg, William S. Tilton's First Brigade and Jacob B. Sweitzer's Second Brigade of Barnes' division were left to guard Pleasonton's communications; and Gregg, with his cavalry division and Strong Vincent's Third Brigade of Barnes' division, proceeded on through the town. About 8:00 A.M., Gregg arrived in front of the position held by Hampton and Robertson, about three miles farther on to the west. Gregg then attacked, with Vincent's infantry brigade on his left, and forced the enemy to withdraw toward Upperville.

When Buford reached Middleburg about 7:00 A.M., he was joined there by Wesley Merritt's Reserve Brigade of his division, then commanded by Samuel H. Starr, which had been sent to Gregg the day before. Buford then turned to the right and marched along Goose Creek so as to come in on the enemy's left (northern) flank. Because of the nature of the country and of the opposition by Chambliss' and Jones' brigades, Buford was unable to reach the enemy flank. He had sent the Reserve Brigade, under Starr, across Goose Creek at Millville for this purpose, and he had intended to follow with the rest of the division, but he then decided to march with the brigades of Devin and Gamble toward Upperville. To avoid a loss of time while waiting for the Reserve Brigade to recross, Buford directed Starr to take the road to Rectortown and report to Gregg.

When Robertson and Hampton retired from Middleburg, they made a stand at Goose Creek, a short distance west of Rectortown, but when Vincent's brigade forced a crossing of Goose Creek, they retreated to Upperville, followed by Gregg's cavalry. The leading squadrons of Gregg's division arrived near Upperville about 3:00 P.M., and at about the same time, Buford's column came into view about a mile to the north.

When Buford came up with Gregg's division, he turned and marched to the northwest against an enemy force that appeared about a mile north of Upperville. Buford then became sharply engaged with Jones' brigade, which was supported by artillery. The fighting continued for some time, but finally, Jones broke off the action and withdrew into Ashby's Gap. Buford pursued until about sunset and then returned and bivouacked on the battlefield.

Meantime, on the turnpike to the south, Kilpatrick's brigade, followed by J. Irvin Gregg's brigade, advanced on Upperville. Stuart did not intend to make a stand there, and he placed Hampton's brigade south of the town to cover Robertson's withdrawal. Kilpatrick attacked just as Robertson was passing through the town toward the rear. After some fighting between parts of Hampton's and Kilpatrick's brigades, Hampton moved forward with his entire command against Kilpatrick, who had withdrawn to the edge of town. Kilpatrick promptly charged into the oncoming Confederates, and after furious fighting, both sides withdrew.

At about this time, Starr's Reserve Brigade arrived. It then dismounted and advanced on the south side of the road toward Hampton. Seeing this, and believing it to be advancing Federal infantry, Hampton withdrew. Kilpatrick made a final charge at 5:30 P.M. and occupied Upperville. Stuart's cavalry then retired to Ashby's Gap. Gregg remained at Upperville that night, and the next day Pleasonton's command returned to Aldie.

The following Federal forces were engaged at Upperville June 21, 1863:

CAVALRY CORPS, Alfred Pleasonton

First Cavalry Division, John Buford
   First Brigade, William Gamble
   Second Brigade, Thomas C. Devin
   Reserve Brigade, Samuel H. Starr

Second Cavalry Division, David McM. Gregg
   Second Brigade, Judson Kilpatrick
   Third Brigade, J. Irvin Gregg

Note. John B. McIntosh's First Brigade had been sent to Hay Market June 19, 1863. It marched to Upperville by way of Aldie June 21, 1863, but it was not engaged.

Attached Infantry, Strong Vincent

Note. Vincent commanded Third Brigade, First Division, Fifth Corps, which consisted of 20th Maine, 16th Michigan, 44th New York, and 83rd Pennsylvania Cavalry.

* * * * * * * * * *

On June 17, 1863, the infantry of the Army of the Potomac also began to move forward from its camps along the Orange and Alexandria Railroad. Second Corps, Third Corps, and Fifth Corps were sent west toward the Bull Run Mountains; and First Corps, Eleventh Corps, and Twelfth Corps were moved to the north and west, generally toward Leesburg. Sixth Corps remained in the Germantown-Centerville-Bristoe Station area until June 26, 1863, and that day it marched toward Edwards Ferry.

Second Corps occupied Gainesville and Thoroughfare Gap June 21–24, 1863; Fifth Corps was at Gum Springs June 17–18, 1863, and then at Aldie June 19–25, 1863; and Third Corps was at Gum Springs June 19–24, 1863. First Corps took position at Herndon Station and Guilford Station, on the line of the Alexandria, Loudoun, and Hampshire Railroad, between Dranesville and Leesburg, June 17–24, 1863; Eleventh Corps was at Goose Creek, south of Leesburg, June 17–23, 1863; and Twelfth Corps marched by way of Dranesville to Leesburg and remained there June 18–25, 1863.

ADVANCE OF THE ARMY TO FREDERICK, MARYLAND
JUNE 25–27, 1863

By mid-afternoon of June 24, 1863, Hooker was finally convinced that most of Lee's army was north of the Potomac River and that an invasion of Maryland and Pennsylvania was definitely in progress. It was not until the next day, however, that he issued the orders that set in motion the Army of the Potomac toward Edwards Ferry and Maryland.

Reynolds' Right Wing of the army had been broken up June 17, 1863, when the corps of which it was composed were dispersed by the marching orders of that day. On June 25, 1863, however, Reynolds was again assigned command of a wing of the army, which was composed of First Corps, Third Corps, and Eleventh Corps, and was designated as the Advance Wing or Left Wing. Abner Doubleday assumed temporary command of First Corps, while Reynolds was in command of the wing. Julius Stahel, commanding the Cavalry Division, Department of Washington, was ordered to Harper's Ferry from Fairfax Court House June 24, 1863, and the next day Stahel was ordered to report to Reynolds for orders. Reynolds was given the assignment of moving his three infantry corps and Stahel's cavalry to Middletown, Maryland, and was directed to occupy the gaps in South Mountain and to protect the left of the army as it advanced into Maryland.

First Corps and Eleventh Corps crossed the Potomac at Edwards Ferry June 25, 1863, and then marched through Jefferson to Middletown, Maryland, where they arrived the next day. Adolph Von Steinwehr's Second Division, Eleventh Corps was then sent to Turner's Gap in South Mountain. Third Corps followed the other two corps across the Potomac during the late afternoon of June 25, 1863, and it joined them at Middletown on the night of June 27, 1863. Stahel's cavalry crossed the Potomac at Young's Island Ford June 25, 1863, and then joined Reynolds' column. Stahel moved northward ahead of the infantry toward Middletown, covering the front eastward from South Mountain, and then moved on to Frederick June 27, 1863.

The remainder of the Army of the Potomac was ordered to march to Edwards Ferry June 26, 1863, and Second Corps, Fifth Corps, and Twelfth Corps crossed into Maryland that day. Fifth Corps and Twelfth Corps marched on to the mouth of the Monocacy River that night, but Second Corps bivouacked near the ford. The next day, Fifth Corps marched to Ballinger's Creek near Frederick, and Twelfth Corps moved upriver to Knoxville, Maryland, as a preliminary to a contemplated movement on Lee's line of communications. Second Corps proceeded directly from Edwards Ferry to Frederick, and arrived there June 28, 1863.

On June 25, 1863, while the above movements were in progress, William H. French, commanding Third Division, Second Corps, was assigned command at Harper's Ferry. He relieved Daniel Tyler in command there, and Tyler was assigned to duty at Baltimore. Also that day, a new brigade joined Second Corps, and was assigned to Third Division as Third Brigade. This was a brigade commanded by Alexander Hays, which consisted of four New

York regiments that had formed a part of the troops captured at Harper's Ferry during the Maryland Campaign of the year before. Upon joining the corps, Hays was assigned command of Third Division, replacing French, and George L. Willard assumed command of Third Brigade. Also on June 25, John Gibbon, commanding Second Division, Second Corps, placed Joshua T. Owen in arrest, and Alexander S. Webb, who had just that day arrived at the front, was assigned command of Owen's Second Brigade.

Sixth Corps was the last of the infantry to march. It left Germantown and Centerville June 26, 1863, and marched by way of Dranesville to Edwards Ferry, where it crossed the Potomac the next day. It then moved on by way of Poolesville, and arrived at Hyattstown, June 28, 1863.

The Cavalry Corps remained south of the Potomac to cover the crossing of the army, and it then followed the infantry into Maryland June 27, 1863. The two cavalry divisions then separated, with Buford's First Division going by way of Jefferson to Middletown to cover the left of the army, and Gregg's Second Division marching the same day through Frederick to New Market and Ridgeville on the Baltimore Pike to protect the right of the army.

The Artillery Reserve left Fairfax Court House June 25, 1863, and joined the army at Frederick two days later. Headquarters Army of the Potomac remained at Fairfax Court House through June 25, 1863. The next day it moved by way of Dranesville and Edwards Ferry to Poolesville, and then on to Frederick June 27, 1863.

Thus, on June 28, 1863, the Army of the Potomac, except Sixth Corps and Twelfth Corps, was concentrated in Maryland on a line generally facing north, and extending from Middletown eastward through Frederick. Sixth Corps was at Hyattstown, and Twelfth Corps was at Knoxville. That night, however, Twelfth Corps was also ordered to Frederick.

June 28, 1863, Stahel's Cavalry Division from the Department of Washington was assigned to the Cavalry Corps, Army of the Potomac, and it was then reorganized by Pleasonton as Third Division, Cavalry Corps. Judson Kilpatrick was assigned command of the division, and he relieved Stahel the next day. Stahel was assigned to duty in the Department of the Susquehanna. The new Third Division consisted of two brigades; Elon J. Farnsworth was assigned command of First Brigade and George A. Custer of Second Brigade. For additional information, see Cavalry Corps, Army of the Potomac, The Gettysburg Campaign.

There were no major movements by either army on June 28, 1863, but it was a significant day in the history of the Army of the Potomac. On that day George G. Meade relieved Joseph Hooker in command of the army. At the time of the crossing of the army into Maryland, Hooker appears to have formed a plan to move against Lee's communications and in this way force him to turn back toward Virginia. At 8:00 P.M. June 27, 1863, he sent an order to Slocum, commanding Twelfth Corps at Knoxville, to pick up two brigades of William H. French's command at Harper's Ferry early the next morning and to proceed with them and his Twelfth Corps to Williamsport, Maryland.

Because of this plan and his intended use of French's troops, Hooker became involved in a controversy with Halleck and, as a result, submitted his resignation. The trouble began when Hooker wished to abandon Harper's Ferry and use the garrison as a reinforcement for the Army of the Potomac. This was a move that Halleck was unwilling to approve. Hooker and Halleck had disliked one another intensely ever since their association in California before the war, and this feeling had already significantly affected their relationship during Hooker's command of the army. Although Hooker was Halleck's subordinate, he would not report information to or otherwise consult with him, but instead by-passed Halleck and dealt directly with President Lincoln. This unsatisfactory arrangement was continued until June 16, 1863, when Lincoln finally ordered Hooker to report directly to Halleck.

When Halleck would not agree to the abandonment of Harper's Ferry, Hooker countermanded his planned expedition to Williamsport at 8:30 P.M. on June 27, 1863, and ordered Twelfth Corps to Frederick. He then sent in his resignation, and stated as his reason that he did not have the means to defend both Harper's Ferry and Washington as he had been instructed to do. It may be that Hooker did not expect that his resignation would be accepted and that, by this action, he hoped to force Halleck to grant him greater freedom in the handling of the army. Whatever his reasoning, however, Lincoln did accept his resignation, and at 3:00 A.M. June 28, 1863, Meade was informed that he had been assigned command of the army by a presidential order dated June 27, 1863. Meade assumed command of the Army of the Potomac just before dawn on the morning of June 28, 1863. He immediately began to prepare plans for the advance of the army, which was to begin the next day. As a first step, he ordered Reynolds to move his Left Wing from Middletown to Frederick, which he did June 28, 1863.

MOVEMENTS OF THE ARMY OF NORTHERN VIRGINIA

While the Army of the Potomac was moving into Maryland toward Frederick, the Army of Northern Virginia was advancing along the Cumberland Valley to the north, with Ewell's corps in the lead. By June 28, 1863, Early's division was at York, Pennsylvania, and Rodes' and Johnson's divisions were at Carlisle, also in Pennsylvania. Hill's corps was at Fayetteville, west of the Cashtown Gap in South Mountain, and Longstreet's corps was behind Hill near Chambersburg, Pennsylvania.

In a discretionary order of June 22, 1863, Lee gave Stuart permission, under specified conditions, to take three of his five cavalry brigades into Maryland and join Ewell. Although the route he was to follow was not clearly defined, a later communication referred to Stuart as leaving the Loudoun Valley by way of Hopewell Gap, and then passing by the rear of Hooker's army. Stuart assembled the brigades of Wade Hampton, Fitzhugh Lee, and John R. Chambliss at Salem, Virginia, on the Manassas Gap Railroad, and at 1:00 A.M. June 25, 1863, he rode with them toward the Bull Run Mountains. His column soon encountered Hancock's Second Corps marching toward the north, and he decided to detour to the east and cross the Potomac on the far (eastern) side of Hooker's army. June 26, 1863, he marched eastward through Glasscock's Gap and then on by way of New Market to Wolf Run Shoals on the Occoquan River. From there he moved northward past Fairfax Station and Dranesville, and crossed the Potomac at Rowser's Ford at 3:00 A.M. June 28, 1863. From there he set out to join Ewell. Early that afternoon, Stuart captured a wagon train near Rockville, Maryland, and moved on to Brookeville that night. On the night of June 29, 1863, Stuart was at Union Mills, fourteen miles south of Hanover, Pennsylvania.

Late on the night of June 28, 1863, Lee learned that Meade was north of the Potomac with his entire army, and was approaching South Mountain, where he could threaten the Confederate communications in the Cumberland Valley. Accordingly, Lee recalled Ewell, who was preparing to cross the Susquehanna River and move on Harrisburg, and began to concentrate his army near Cashtown, Pennsylvania.

MEADE'S ADVANCE FROM FREDERICK TO GETTYSBURG JUNE 28, 1863–JULY 2, 1863

On June 28, 1863, while at Frederick, Meade learned that the last of the Confederate columns had passed through Hagerstown, apparently on the way to Chambersburg, but he had no certain knowledge of the exact location of Lee's army. In the absence of such information, Meade started forward on June 29, 1863, on a broad front that extended from the western side of South Mountain on the left to Westminster, Maryland on the right.

That day, Buford's First Cavalry division moved northward, covering the left flank of the army. Buford, with William Gamble's First Brigade and Thomas C. Devin's Second Brigade, crossed South Mountain to Boonsboro, and then marched northward along the western side of South Mountain, through Cavetown, Maryland to Fairfield, Pennsylvania. Wesley Merritt's Reserve Brigade was detached and, under Merritt, advanced through Mechanicstown (present-day Thurmont) to Emmitsburg, Maryland with the division trains. Gregg's Second Cavalry Division moved through Westminster, on the right flank of the army, and patrolled the country to the north. Kilpatrick's Third Cavalry Division (formerly Stahel's division) marched northeast from Frederick, in advance of the center of the army, and halted that night at Littlestown, Pennsylvania, about eight miles southwest of Hanover. That same night, Stuart's cavalry was at Union Mills, fourteen miles south of Hanover, Pennsylvania.

June 29, 1863, Meade's infantry moved forward as follows: Reynolds' three corps advanced on the left, with First Corps and Eleventh Corps marching from Frederick to Emmitsburg, and Third Corps from Woodsboro to Taneytown; Second Corps moved from Monocacy Junction by way of Liberty and Johnsville to Uniontown; Fifth Corps from Ballinger's Creek by way of Mount Pleasant to Liberty; Sixth Corps from Hyattstown by way of New Market and Ridgeville to New Windsor; and Twelfth Corps from Frederick to Taneytown and Bruceville. The Artillery Reserve advanced from Frederick to Bruceville, and headquarters of the army was established at Middleburg.

June 28, 1863, Halleck had informed Meade that French's command at Harper's Ferry was under his direct orders, and that he could make such changes there as he deemed necessary. Accordingly, the next day Meade ordered the evacuation of Harper's Ferry. French remained there until the evening of June 29, 1863, while the government property was being removed, and he then divided his command and marched with the brigades of Kenly and Morris to Frederick, where he arrived the next day. He left behind the brigades of Elliott and Smith, both under the command of Elliott, to complete the removal of the stores and to escort them to Washington. Elliott left Harper's Ferry June 30, 1863, and arrived in Washington July 4, 1863. Later that day he went into camp at Tennallytown, D.C. Elliott was under orders to rejoin French at Frederick.

French, with his two brigades, did not join the army at Gettysburg, but instead occupied the lines of communication running from Frederick to Washington, Baltimore, and Headquarters of the Army. French also manned posts of observation toward Williamsport, Emmitsburg, and Harper's Ferry. For additional information, see Middle Department, Military Operations in the Middle Department, The Gettysburg Campaign.

June 30, 1863, Buford, with Devin's and Gamble's brigades, continued his march northward and, passing through Emmitsburg, arrived at Gettysburg, Pennsylvania about 11:00 A.M. By chance, at the same time, James J. Pettigrew's brigade of Henry Heth's division, Hill's Third Confederate Corps was approaching the western outskirts of the town. Pettigrew withdrew toward Cashtown, and Buford took position near Gettysburg. That day, Gregg's cavalry division moved by way of Westminster to Manchester, Maryland.

Cavalry Action at Hanover, Pennsylvania, June 30, 1863. On the morning of June 30, 1863, both Kilpatrick and Stuart marched toward Hanover. Kilpatrick arrived there first, at 8:00 A.M., with George A. Custer's Second Brigade in the lead, and after pausing briefly to eat, moved on northward toward Abbottstown. Elon J. Farnsworth's First Brigade followed Custer and arrived at Hanover about an hour later, and it too halted in the town to eat. The two leading regiments of the brigade had finished their meal and, with Farnsworth in person, had moved on after Custer, when at about 10:00 A.M., Stuart's leading brigade, under John R. Chambliss, approached the town from the south. At that time, John Hammond's 5th New York Cavalry was still in the town, and the rear guard of the brigade—William P. Brinton's 18th Pennsylvania Cavalry—was entering the town from the west. The 2nd North Carolina of Chambliss' command immediately charged and drove the Federal troopers northward out of Hanover in some confusion, but they soon rallied and delivered a sharp counterattack. Farnsworth, who was then about a mile to the north, learned of Stuart's attack, and he promptly led his two regiments back along the Abbottstown Road; these regiments, together with the 5th New York, charged and reoccupied Hanover.

There was a lull in the fighting for several hours, during which time Kilpatrick returned with Custer's brigade. Custer then took position generally along the Littlestown Road, southwest of the center of Hanover. Fitzhugh Lee and Wade Hampton also came up with their brigades and took position with Chambliss to the south and west of Hanover. There was no further fighting during the afternoon, except for some skirmishing on the flanks. Stuart remained in position until dark, and then detoured to the east and marched that night to Jefferson, Pennsylvania.

Kilpatrick's Third Division, Cavalry Corps, Army of the Potomac was organized as follows:

Third Division, Judson Kilpatrick
  First Brigade, Elon J. Farnsworth
    5th New York Cavalry, John Hammond
    18th Pennsylvania Cavalry, William P. Brinton
    1st Vermont Cavalry, Addison W. Preston
    1st West Virginia Cavalry, Nathaniel P. Richmond

Second Brigade, George A. Custer
  1st Michigan Cavalry, Charles H. Town
  5th Michigan Cavalry, Russell A. Alger
  6th Michigan Cavalry, George Gray
  7th Michigan (ten companies), William D. Mann

* * * * * * * * * *

June 30, 1863, the Federal infantry advanced as follows: First Corps to Marsh Creek, about six miles south of Gettysburg; Third Corps to Bridgeport; Fifth Corps by way of Johnsville to Union Mills; Sixth Corps to Manchester; and Twelfth Corps to Littlestown, Pennsylvania. Second Corps remained at Uniontown, and Eleventh Corps at Emmitsburg. The Artillery Reserve and Meade's headquarters moved to Taneytown.

July 1, 1863, the Federal cavalry movements were as follows: Gamble's and Devin's brigades of Buford's division became engaged during the morning with the advance of Heth's Confederate division on the ridges west of Gettysburg (see Gettysburg Campaign, Part II, Battle of Gettysburg). Merritt's Reserve Brigade of Buford's division remained that day at Mechanicstown. Gregg's division marched to Hanover Junction, and from there John B. McIntosh's and J. Irvin Gregg's brigades moved on to Hanover, and Pennock Huey's brigade returned to Manchester. Kilpatrick's division moved by way of Abbottstown to Berlin (present-day East Berlin), on the York-Heidlersburg Road.

On July 1, 1863, Meade's infantry advanced as follows: First Corps arrived at Gettysburg about 10:00–10:30 A.M. and almost immediately became engaged with Heth's division west of the town; Second Corps marched through Taneytown to a point near Gettysburg; Third Corps advanced by way of Emmitsburg to the battlefield; Fifth Corps marched by way of Hanover to Bonaughtown (Bonneauville); Sixth Corps was en route from Manchester to Gettysburg; Eleventh Corps arrived on the field of Gettysburg about 1:00–1:30 P.M. and soon became heavily engaged north of the town; and Twelfth Corps marched by way of Two Taverns and reached the battlefield about 5:00–5:30 P.M. Dunbar R. Ransom's and Robert H. Fitzhugh's brigades of the Artillery Reserve also arrived near Gettysburg that day.

On July 2, 1863, Gamble's and Devin's brigades of Buford's cavalry division, which had been engaged the day before but had been relieved by the infantry of First Corps, were sent to Taneytown; and Merritt's Reserve Brigade was moved from Mechanicstown to Emmitsburg. McIntosh's and J. Irvin Gregg's brigades of David McM. Gregg's cavalry division and Kilpatrick's cavalry division arrived near Gettysburg.

The infantry moved up to the battlefield as follows: Second Corps arrived at daylight July 2, 1863; Fifth Corps at about 6:00–7:00 A.M.; and Sixth Corps about 4:00 P.M. Henry H. Lockwood, with his Provisional Brigade, arrived from Baltimore about 8:00 A.M. July 2, 1863, and he then reported to First Division, Twelfth Corps. The remaining brigades of the Artillery Reserve also arrived at Gettysburg July 2, 1863.

There is some uncertainty as to the time when Meade arrived on the field. It appears probable, however, that he left his headquarters at Taneytown shortly after midnight July 2, 1863, and that he arrived near the Gettysburg Cemetery, on the Baltimore Pike, sometime before dawn that morning, perhaps about 3:00 A.M. July 2, 1863.

GETTYSBURG CAMPAIGN, PART II
BATTLE OF GETTYSBURG

THE FIRST DAY, JULY 1, 1863

Morning of July 1, 1863. John Buford arrived at Gettysburg with two brigades of his First Cavalry Division on the morning of June 30, 1863. At about the same time, a Confederate brigade commanded by Johnson J. Pettigrew approached the western outskirts of the town, but upon discovering the Federal cavalrymen it quickly withdrew without bringing on an engagement. That night, William Gamble's First Brigade of Buford's division camped on Seminary Ridge, about three-fourths of a mile west of Gettysburg, with pickets out about three miles on the Chambersburg Pike (Cashtown Road) to watch the enemy's movements. Thomas C. Devin's Second Brigade bivouacked near Gettysburg, with pickets out to the north and east on the roads to Carlisle, Harrisburg, and York.

Henry Heth's division of Ambrose P. Hill's Confederate Third Corps was at Cashtown, Pennsylvania June 30, 1863, and at 5:00 the next morning Heth started toward Gettysburg on the Chambersburg Pike. His leading troops encountered Gamble's pickets about 8:00 A.M. July 1, 1863, and Buford immediately ordered Gamble to form his brigade in line of battle on Herr Ridge, about a mile west of the Seminary. Gamble promptly complied. His line began on the right at the cut of an unfinished railroad, about 150 yards north of the Chambersburg Pike, and it extended southward for about a mile and ended on the left near the Fairfield (Hagerstown) Road. Devin's brigade took position to the right of Gamble, and its line extended northward to the Mummasburg Road, where it connected with the Federal pickets to the north and east.

Gamble was soon engaged, and as the enemy pressure increased, he was forced back to McPherson's Ridge, less than half a mile west of Seminary Ridge. He continued to resist there, however, until the infantry of James S. Wadsworth's First Division of John F. Reynolds' First Corps arrived.

First Corps, then commanded by Abner Doubleday while Reynolds was in charge of the Left Wing of the army, had spent the night of June 30, 1863 on Marsh Creek, about five miles to the south and west of Gettysburg. The next morning, Reynolds ordered First Corps, and also Eleventh Corps, which was then at Emmitsburg, to march toward Gettysburg. All units of First Corps were on the road between 8:00 and 9:30 A.M., with Wadsworth's division in the lead. The corps moved along Marsh Creek to the Fairfield Road, and then approached Gettysburg from the west. Upon learning that Buford was engaged near Gettysburg, Reynolds rode on ahead and arrived on McPherson's Ridge about 10:00 A.M. He directed Buford to hold his position, and he then returned to the Fairfield Road to hurry forward the divisions of First Corps. Lysander Cutler's Second Brigade of Wadsworth's division was the first of the Federal infantry to arrive on McPherson's Ridge, and it was just in time. The cavalry was beginning to give way under the mounting pressure exerted by Joseph R. Davis' brigade, attacking north of the Chambersburg Pike, and by James J. Archer's brigade south of the pike.

Cutler quickly took position on McPherson's Ridge, with his line extending across the Chambersburg Pike. Two of his regiments were placed south of the pike, around the McPherson farm; James A. Hall's 2nd Battery (B), Maine Light Artillery, of the corps artillery, was put in between the pike and the railroad cut; and the other three regiments of the brigade, under the personal direction of Cutler, were formed on the right of Hall, and north of the railroad cut. The latter three regiments were almost immediately engaged with Davis' brigade.

Solomon Meredith, commanding First Brigade (Iron Brigade) of Wadsworth's division, was ordered to aid Cutler, and Lucius Fairchild, with his 2nd Wisconsin Regiment, hurried forward and arrived just in time to check the advance of Archer's brigade in McPherson's Woods. Just after 2nd Wisconsin went in, Reynolds was killed just inside the eastern edge of the woods. At that time, the rest of Meredith's brigade, except Rufus R. Dawes' 6th Wisconsin, came up and attacked, and drove the enemy from the woods and back to Herr Ridge. The Iron Brigade then returned to the west of McPherson's Ridge and formed on the left of Cutler.

Meanwhile, Cutler's three regiments north of the cut stubbornly resisted the attacks by Davis' brigade for some time, and then two regiments, under orders from Wadsworth, retired toward Seminary Ridge. They left behind the 147th New York, which did not receive the order to fall back. With Cutler's brigade thus in difficulty, Dawes, with his 6th Wisconsin of Meredith's brigade, was sent to support Cutler. Starting from the extreme left of the Union line, near the Fairfield Road, Dawes rapidly moved the regiment northward along the eastern side of McPherson's Ridge to the Chambersburg Pike. He arrived just as the enemy was passing his front in pursuit of Cutler's two retreating regiments. The 6th Wisconsin then opened fire and halted Davis' advance. Other regiments of Cutler's brigade then came up, and together they drove the attackers back beyond the ridge. It was then about noon, and there was little fighting for the next two hours.

Afternoon of July 1, 1863. During the lull that followed the morning battle on McPherson's Ridge, both armies hastened more men to the front and regrouped their forces for continuing the fight. The enemy brought up the remaining brigades of Heth's division, and William D. Pender's division, also of Hill's corps, was ordered forward to join Heth.

Early on the morning of July 1, 1863, two divisions of Richard S. Ewell's Second Corps of Lee's army, Robert E. Rodes' division from Carlisle, Pennsylvania and Jubal A. Early's division from York, Pennsylvania, arrived at Heidlersburg, where they had been ordered by Lee in preparation for joining the main part of the army. Edward Johnson's division had already marched toward Chambersburg when the order to join the corps was received. During the morning, after he had resumed the march, Ewell learned of Hill's intention to march toward Gettysburg that day, and, accordingly, he turned to march in that direction, with Early moving on the Heidlersburg Road and Rodes on the Middletown Road. Just north of Gettysburg, Rodes turned off to the west and marched across to Oak Hill, and by 2:00 P.M. he had formed his division in line of battle, facing to the south and southeast, with its center on the Mummasburg Road. Early continued his march on the Heidlersburg Road, and deployed to the north and east of Rock Creek, northeast of Gettysburg.

While the enemy was thus being reinforced, Third Division, First Corps, temporarily under the command of Thomas A. Rowley, was approaching Gettysburg on the Fairfield Road, and about 11:00 or 12:00 it reached a point south and west of Wadsworth's line on McPherson's Ridge. John C. Robinson's Second Division was following Rowley. Rowley's division then left the road and marched across the fields to join Wadsworth on McPherson's Ridge. Robinson's division marched on to Seminary Ridge, and took position there as a reserve for the other two divisions of the corps.

At about 2:00 P.M. First Corps was in position as follows: Chapman Biddle's First Brigade, Third Division held the line from the Fairfield Road to McPherson's Woods; Meredith's First Brigade, First Division occupied the woods; and Roy Stone's Second Brigade, Third Division was between the woods and the Chambersburg Pike. One regiment of Stone's brigade held the McPherson house and barn, and the other two regiments were refused on the right, and were in line parallel to the pike, facing north and northeast. Cutler's brigade of First Division extended the line to the north of the Chambersburg Pike, with its left on the pike a short dis-

tance east of Stone's right flank. On the extreme right of the infantry, beyond Cutler, was Dawes' 6th Wisconsin of Meredith's brigade. The Union line at this time extended only about one-fourth of a mile north of the railroad cut.

Devin's cavalry brigade remained on the right of the infantry until relieved by troops of Eleventh Corps that afternoon. When Gamble's brigade was relieved by First Corps, it was sent to the south of the Fairview Road to guard the left flank of First Corps' line.

Shortly after taking position near the Seminary with his Second Division, First Corps, Robinson learned that a heavy enemy force was advancing on the right of the corps' line of battle, and he sent Henry Baxter's Second Brigade to extend the line northward on Oak Ridge for about a half mile toward the Mummasburg Road. Gabriel R. Paul's First Brigade of Robinson's division remained for a time on Seminary Ridge, entrenching a position, but when Baxter became seriously threatened by Rodes' advance, Paul was sent to the right of Baxter to continue the Union line to the Mummasburg Road. One regiment on the right of Paul's brigade was, at times, refused and posted down the east slope of the ridge along the road.

As the infantry of First Corps arrived to occupy the ground between the Chambersburg Pike and the Mummasburg Road, Devin's cavalry brigade moved to the east of Oak Ridge and formed a line in the valley between the ridge and the Middletown Road. It remained there until relieved by Eleventh Corps about 2:00 P.M., and it then moved to the far right near the York Road.

Oliver O. Howard's Eleventh Corps began to arrive on the field about 1:00 P.M. July 1, 1863, after the First Corps' battle of that morning had ended. It had started from near Emmitsburg about 8:00 A.M. and had marched by different routes toward Gettysburg. Francis C. Barlow's First Division marched on the Emmitsburg Road, and Adolph Von Steinwehr's Second Division and Carl Schurz's Third Division took another route and entered Gettysburg on the Taneytown Road.

Howard, in person, arrived in Gettysburg as the fighting west of the town was ending. There, at about 11:30 A.M., he learned of the death of Reynolds, and as senior officer present, he assumed command of all Federal troops then on the field. Schurz arrived about a half hour later, having turned over the command of his Third Division to Alexander Schimmelfennig, and he was assigned by Howard to the temporary command of Eleventh Corps. George Von Amsberg moved up to the command of Schimmelfennig's First Brigade, Third Division.

About 12:30 P.M., Howard learned from Buford that enemy troops were massing to the north and northeast between the Heidlersburg and York roads, and when Schimmelfennig's (Schurz's) division arrived in Gettysburg about 1:00 P.M., it was sent on through the town to take up a position about a mile to the north to meet this threat. Barlow's division was following close behind, and it too was sent north to join Schimmelfennig. These divisions relieved Devin's cavalry brigade, which then moved to the extreme right of the Union line and took position east of Rock Creek and south of the York Road.

By 2:00 P.M., Schurz had completed the task of placing these two divisions in a defensive position. The left flank of Schurz's line was in the valley near the Mummasburg Road, about one-fourth of a mile east of the right flank of First Corps on Oak Ridge, and from there it extended about three-fourths of a mile to the north of east and ended on a slight elevation, now called Barlow's Knoll. This knoll was just to the northwest of the point where the Heidlersburg Road crossed Rock Creek. Schimmelfennig's division held this line from the Mummasburg Road to the Middletown Road, with Von Amsberg's First Brigade on the left and Wladimir Krzyzanowski's Second Brigade on the right. Leopold Von Gilsa's First Brigade of Barlow's division occupied the knoll, and Adelbert Ames' Second Brigade of Barlow's division held the ground between the knoll and the right of Schimmelfennig's division at the Middletown Road.

Von Steinwehr's division arrived near Gettysburg about 2:00 P.M., and was placed by Howard in reserve on Cemetery Hill, where Howard had established his headquarters.

About 2:30 P.M., Rodes moved forward from Oak Hill and with two brigades attacked the right of the First Corps line near the Mummasburg Road, but he was strongly repulsed by the men of Robinson's division. While this attack was in progress, John B. Gordon's brigade of Early's division struck Von Gilsa's brigade on the knoll and drove it back, thus exposing the right and rear of Ames' brigade. The brigades of Harry T. Hays and Isaac E. Avery of Early's division then advanced against the right and rear of Von Gilsa's brigade and routed it, and with that the entire Eleventh Corps line crumpled, and the brigades fled in disorder through Gettysburg to Cemetery Hill. Charles R. Coster's First Brigade of Von Steinwehr's Second Division was advanced to the northern edge of Gettysburg to help check the enemy advance, but it too was soon driven back to Cemetery Hill. Barlow was wounded during the attack that afternoon, and Ames assumed command of his First Division, Eleventh Corps. Andrew L. Harris succeeded Ames in command of Second Brigade, First Division.

Simultaneously with Early's attack on Eleventh Corps, the enemy advanced all along the line from the Fairfield Road to the Heidlersburg Road. Wadsworth's and Rowley's divisions of First Corps held fast for a time on McPherson's Ridge, but they were finally forced to withdraw to Seminary Ridge. Stone's brigade, then commanded by Edmund L. Dana, was the last Federal brigade to leave McPherson's Ridge. Robinson's division of First Corps continued to fight on Oak Ridge. The remnants of First Corps, with Gamble's cavalry brigade on their left, made a last stand on Seminary Ridge and Oak Ridge, but finally, between 4:00 and 4:30 P.M., the line gave way and the troops retreated through and to the south of Gettysburg to Cemetery Hill. Only about 12,000 survivors of the day's fighting assembled that evening on Cemetery Hill, and only about one-third of First Corps remained in the ranks. Casualties among the officers of First Corps were also heavy that day. Early in the battle, Meredith was disabled when his horse was killed and fell on him, and William W. Robinson assumed command of Meredith's First Brigade, First Division. That afternoon, Stone was wounded and Langhorne Wister assumed command of his Second Brigade, Third Division. A short time later Wister was wounded and Edmund L. Dana took charge of the brigade. Also during the afternoon, Gabriel R. Paul, commanding First Brigade, Second Division, was wounded, and he was succeeded by Samuel H. Leonard. Leonard was soon wounded, as was his successor Adrian R. Root, and Richard Coulter assumed command of the brigade about 5:00 P.M. after it had returned to Cemetery Hill.

Evening of July 1, 1863. During July 1, 1863, headquarters of the Army of the Potomac was at Taneytown, and it remained there until shortly after midnight while Meade directed the concentration of the army at Gettysburg. About 11:00 that morning, Winfield S. Hancock's Second Corps arrived there from Uniontown and prepared to bivouac. Sometime after noon, however, Meade learned of the fighting at Gettysburg, and of the death of Reynolds, and he then directed Hancock to turn over the command of Second Corps to John Gibbon and proceed immediately to Gettysburg. Upon arrival there, he was to assume command of First Corps and Eleventh Corps, and also of Third Corps, which was then at Emmitsburg. This order created a command problem because Hancock was junior in rank to Howard, commander of Eleventh Corps, and also to Daniel E. Sickles, commander of Third Corps. Another complication resulted from the fact that Gibbon was not the senior brigadier general in Second Corps. At about 1:30 P.M., however, Hancock left for Gettysburg when assured by Meade that he, Meade, had been authorized by the secretary of war, Edwin M. Stanton, to make any necessary changes in the commanders of the army. Hancock arrived near Gettysburg about 3:30 P.M. and assumed command as directed. Howard questioned his right to do so, but with reservations resumed command of Eleventh Corps, relieving Schurz, who again took charge of his Third Division, Eleventh Corps.

Hancock was on Cemetery Hill when the Union lines north and west of Gettysburg collapsed, and he, together with Howard, Buford, and Gouverneur K. Warren, chief of engineers of the army, labored to put the survivors of First Corps and Eleventh Corps in position to resist any further attacks by the enemy. Eleventh Corps was formed on Cemetery Hill as follows: Ames' division was on the right, generally facing north, with its left on the Baltimore Pike; Schurz's division was between the Baltimore Pike and the Taneytown Road, facing to the northwest; and Von Steinwehr's division was on the left, with its line extending southward along the Taneytown Road.

Wadsworth's division of First Corps was placed on Culp's Hill, with Cutler's brigade on the right and Meredith's brigade (then commanded by William W. Robinson) on the left. John C. Robinson's division was on the left of Eleventh Corps, on Cemetery Ridge; and Doubleday's division (commanded temporarily during the battle that day by Thomas A. Rowley) was held in reserve behind Cemetery Hill, with Biddle's brigade in front and Dana's brigade (formerly Stone's) to its rear. After the collapse of Eleventh Corps that afternoon, Devin's cavalry brigade, which had been operating on its right, was ordered to the extreme left of the Union line, where it bivouacked that night.

When Hancock was sent to take command at Gettysburg, he was asked to determine the suitability of that area as a place to engage Robert E. Lee. After examining the ground, Hancock decided to make a stand on Cemetery Hill, and he so notified the army commander. Meade then ordered the remaining troops of the army to march toward Gettysburg. Reinforcements had already been ordered up, and at about 5:00 P.M. they began to arrive. About 800 men of First Corps and Eleventh Corps, who had been left on guard duty at Emmitsburg, came up and rejoined their commands. A short time later, three regiments of George J. Stannard's Brigade arrived from the Department of Washington and reported to Doubleday, who was then commanding Third Division, First Corps. The next morning, Stannard's Brigade was assigned to Doubleday's division as Third Brigade.

At noon July 1, 1863, Henry W. Slocum's Twelfth Corps was about five miles southeast of Gettysburg, near Two Taverns, on the Baltimore Pike. When Slocum learned of the fighting at Gettysburg that day, he started forward at about 3:00–3:30 P.M., and two hours later he was approaching the rear of the Union position on Cemetery Hill. Alpheus S. Williams' First Division stopped for the night east of Rock Creek, and to the right and rear of Wadsworth's line on Culp's Hill. John W. Geary's Second Division marched on to a point near Cemetery Hill, and it was then placed by Hancock on the high ground to the north of Little Round Top, facing the Emmitsburg Road. Charles Candy's First Brigade was on the left of this line, near Little Round Top, and George S. Greene's Third Brigade was on the right. George A. Cobham's Second Brigade was held in reserve on the Baltimore Pike, probably near Power's Hill.

When Slocum arrived with his Twelfth Corps, he was the ranking major general on the field, and it was intended that he relieve Hancock and assume command of all troops then present at Gettysburg. Slocum did not assume command, however, until sometime between 5:30 and 6:30 P.M., and it was not until about 7:00 P.M. that Howard finally acknowledged his authority.

Sickles was at Emmitsburg with his Third Corps on the afternoon of July 1, 1863, when he received orders at about 2:00 P.M. to march with his corps to Gettysburg. Before leaving, he placed Charles K. Graham in command of P. Regis De Trobriand's Third Brigade, First Division; George C. Burling's Third Brigade, Second Division; and two batteries. Sickles directed Graham to remain at Emmitsburg to guard the flank and rear of the army and to protect the trains. Then, at about 3:00 P.M., Sickles started northward with the remaining brigades of David B. Birney's First Division and Andrew A. Humphreys' Second Division. Birney, with his two brigades, arrived about dusk on the Taneytown Road, and was assigned a position just to the north of Geary's division of Twelfth Corps. Humphreys took a different route with his two brigades, and was delayed when he found the enemy in possession of the road on which he was marching. As a result, he did not arrive on the battlefield until about midnight, and he then bivouacked to the east of the Emmitsburg Road, near the crest of Cemetery Ridge. The two brigades of Third Corps left at Emmitsburg that afternoon were ordered up at about 1:30–2:00 A.M. July 2, 1863, and they rejoined their commands near Gettysburg between 9:00 and 10:00 that morning.

By nightfall July 1, 1863, Slocum had under his command 27,000 men, and many others were not far away. Hancock's Second Corps, commanded temporarily by Gibbon, left Taneytown during the afternoon of July 1, 1863, and halted for the night on the Taneytown Road about three miles south of Gettysburg, where it was in position to protect the left flank of the army. Dunbar R. Ransom's First Regular Brigade and Robert H. Fitzhugh's Fourth Volunteer Brigade of Robert O. Tyler's Artillery Reserve also came up and camped that night near Second Corps.

Meade's other two corps, which were advancing on the far right of the army on July 1, 1863, also received orders late that afternoon to march toward Gettysburg. George Sykes' Fifth Corps left Hanover at 7:00 P.M. and camped at midnight at Bonaughtown (Bonneauville), about six miles from

Gettysburg. John Sedgwick's Sixth Corps started from near Manchester at about 9:00 P.M. and marched throughout the night and the next day, and arrived on the battlefield between 4:00 and 5:00 on the afternoon of July 2, 1863.

On July 1, 1863, after the death of Reynolds, John Newton, commander of Third Division, Sixth Corps, was assigned command of First Corps. Early the next morning, Newton turned over the command of his division to Frank Wheaton and hurried on to Cemetery Ridge, where he assumed command of First Corps a short time later.

THE SECOND DAY, JULY 2, 1863

Organization of the Union Position. Early on July 2, 1863, probably about 3:00 A.M., Meade arrived at the cemetery near Gettysburg and assumed personal direction of the troops already there, and also of those who were then approaching the battlefield. After an examination of the lines established the night before, he decided on the positions to be occupied by the various corps and then proceeded to establish his line of battle. He left Howard's Eleventh Corps unchanged on Cemetery Hill. He placed Hancock's Second Corps, which arrived about 5:30–6:30 that morning, behind Cemetery Hill, where it was in position to move rapidly to the right, which at that time appeared to be threatened. A short time later, however, between 7:00 and 8:00 A.M., he ordered Second Corps to take position on Cemetery Ridge. Hancock deployed his corps along the ridge, with its right on the Emmitsburg Road, just west of Cemetery Hill, where it connected with the left of Eleventh Corps, and its left on the ridge about a mile to the south. Alexander Hays' Third Division was on the right of the line, John Gibbon's Second Division was on the center, and John C. Caldwell's First Division was on the left.

There was little change in the disposition of Newton's First Corps that morning. Wadsworth's First Division remained on the right of Eleventh Corps on Culp's Hill. Doubleday's Third Division was posted in reserve behind Hays' division of Second Corps. Robinson's Second Division, which had spent the night on Cemetery Ridge to the left of Eleventh Corps, was relieved by Second Corps, and was placed in reserve on Cemetery Hill in rear of Schurz's division of Eleventh Corps.

About 5:00 A.M., Geary's Second Division, Twelfth Corps was ordered up from its position of the night before, just north of Little Round Top, to Culp's Hill. When it arrived, it formed on the right of Wadsworth's division and fortified a line that extended along the eastern crest of the hill, facing the valley of Rock Creek below. At 8:00 A.M., Williams was ordered to cross to the west side of Rock Creek with his First Division, Twelfth Corps and form on the right of Geary. He was thus to extend the line of Twelfth Corps down a spur on the southern side of Culp's Hill to the point where the Baltimore Pike crossed Rock Creek. At about this time, Henry H. Lockwood arrived from Baltimore with his Provisional Brigade of the Middle Department and reported to Williams. This brigade served with Twelfth Corps during the remainder of the battle as an unassigned brigade, but was later attached to First Division as Second Brigade. For additional information, see Twelfth Corps, Army of the Potomac, The Battle of Gettysburg.

Sometime before 8:00 A.M., James Barnes' First Division and Romeyn B. Ayres' Second Division of Sykes' Fifth Corps arrived on the right of Twelfth Corps, near Wolf's Hill. A short time later, these two divisions crossed to the west side of Rock Creek and closed up near Power's Hill so as to be in position to reinforce any part of Meade's line. Samuel W. Crawford's Third Division of Fifth Corps joined the other two divisions about noon.

During the morning, Sedgwick's Sixth Corps was approaching the rear of the army on the Baltimore Pike, but the leading elements did not arrive on the field until about 3:00 P.M.

By early morning July 2, 1863, Robert O. Tyler had brought up four of his five Artillery Reserve brigades from Taneytown and had them parked within a half mile of Meade's headquarters. Freeman McGilvery, commanding the First Volunteer Brigade of the Artillery Reserve, arrived with the remainder of the reserve batteries and reported to Tyler about 10:30 A.M.

It is necessary here, in discussing the arrival of Fifth, Sixth, and Twelfth corps on the battlefield, to attempt to clarify a somewhat confused command problem. Frequent references are made in accounts of the Gettysburg Campaign to Slocum's command of the Right Wing of the army, both during the march to Gettysburg and during the battle. The extent and duration of this command, however, were not clearly understood by Slocum. It appears that on the evening of June 30, 1863, Slocum was assigned control of Fifth Corps as well as his Twelfth Corps to ensure better control of the two corps, which were then marching on the extreme right of the army. In a later communication to Meade, moreover, Slocum stated that he had been in command of no fewer than two corps since June 28, 1863. On the morning of July 2, 1863, Meade issued an order placing Fifth Corps under Slocum's direction, and also Sixth Corps when it arrived on the field. This order placed Twelfth Corps, Fifth Corps, and Sixth Corps, or the Right Wing of the army, under Slocum's control. This was done because at that time Meade proposed to make an attack with these three corps against the left of Lee's line. This attack, however, was not made. It was Slocum's understanding that these three corps were to remain under his control during the battle, and because of this he turned over the command of Twelfth Corps to Williams. This arrangement was not what Meade had in mind. During Longstreet's attack on the afternoon of July 2, 1863, Meade sent both Fifth Corps and Sixth Corps to the left of the army to support Third Corps, and they did not later return to Slocum's part of the field. Meade presumed that Slocum would understand that his control of Fifth Corps and Sixth Corps was only temporary, and that it would end with their departure. In any event, Williams remained in charge of Twelfth Corps during the battle, and Thomas H. Ruger commanded Williams' First Division of the corps. Slocum exercised general command of the troops on the right of the Federal line.

There was some shifting of positions on the left of Meade's line during the morning and early afternoon of July 2, 1863. As noted above, Geary's division of Twelfth Corps, which during the night had occupied the Round Tops and the high ground to the north, was ordered at 5:00 A.M. to move to the right of the army. Geary departed at 5:30 A.M. with his division and marched to Culp's Hill.

Birney, with two brigades of his First Division, Third Corps, had spent the night on the right of Geary's division; and Humphreys, with two brigades of his Second Division, Third Corps, had bivouacked nearby on Cemetery Ridge. It was an hour or more after 5:30 A.M. before Birney began to move his troops to the left to occupy that part of the line vacated by Geary. Burling's brigade of Humphreys' division and De Trobriand's brigade of Birney's division, which had been left at Emmitsburg by Sickles the evening before, came up and rejoined Third Corps between 9:00 and 10:00 A.M.

When Meade established his line on the morning of July 2, 1863, he had intended that Third Corps would occupy the position southward from the left of Hancock's Second Corps to the Big Round Top. That morning, Sickles' two divisions were generally about where Meade wanted them to be. Birney's division was on Little Round Top, with its line extending northward toward Humphreys' division, which had bivouacked the night before on the crest of Cemetery Ridge in the area later occupied by Caldwell's division of Second Corps. Sickles, however, was reluctant to comply with Meade's instructions, and he delayed further movement for a time while he sought approval for a different and more advanced line. To complicate matters, Buford's two cavalry brigades, which were covering Sickles' left flank during the morning of July 2, 1863, were unaccountably withdrawn about noon by Alfred Pleasonton, commanding the Cavalry Corps, and they were sent to Westminster, but they were not replaced. Thus at a very critical time, Sickles was left without adequate information about affairs on his left and front.

Early on the afternoon of July 2, 1863, Sickles, on his own initiative, gradually advanced Birney's division to the line that he had wished to have approved earlier in the day. The deployment of this division was completed by 3:30 P.M., with J. H. Hobart Ward's Second Brigade on the left, covering the Devil's Den; Charles K. Graham's First Brigade holding an angle in the line at J. Sherfy's peach orchard (the Peach Orchard), on the Emmitsburg Road; and P. Regis De Trobriand's Third Brigade occupying the space between the other two brigades. De Trobriand's brigade was held in column of regiments in readiness to support Ward and Graham. Birney's line generally faced to the southwest, and was at an angle of about forty-five degrees with the Emmitsburg Road.

Shortly after noon, Sickles ordered Humphreys to advance his division and form it in line of battle near the foot of the western slope of Cemetery Ridge, between Caldwell's division of Second Corps on the right and Birney's division on the left. Humphreys formed his division in three lines, with Joseph B. Carr's First Brigade in front, William R. Brewster's Second Brigade in rear of Carr, and George C. Burling's Third Brigade in rear of Brewster. A little before 4:00 P.M., Burling's brigade was detached from Humphreys' division and moved to the right and rear of Birney's line, which at that time was being threatened. At about the same time, Humphreys advanced his remaining brigades to the Emmitsburg Road, and he then formed a line that extended along the road from the right of Graham's brigade, near the Peach Orchard, to a point near the Codori farm. Brewster's brigade was on the left, connecting with Birney's division, and Carr's brigade was on the right. Carr's right was unprotected, and was about a half mile in front of Hancock's Second Corps.

Between 4:00 and 5:00 P.M., Hancock sent Caldwell's division, which was on the left of the Second Corps line, to report to Sykes and to replace the brigades of Ward and De Trobriand on the left of Sickles' line. When Caldwell departed on this mission, Gibbon extended his Second Division to the left by bringing up William Harrow's First Brigade from its position in reserve. To protect the right flank of Humphreys' division, which, as noted above, was unprotected, Gibbon sent the 15th Massachusetts and 82nd New York regiments of Harrow's brigade out to the Emmitsburg Road, northeast of the Codori house. He also moved up T. Frederick Brown's Battery B, 1st Rhode Island Light Artillery of John G. Hazard's Artillery Brigade of Second Corps to a position to the right and rear of these two regiments.

The artillery that supported Third Corps during the battle that afternoon was posted along the Emmitsburg Road, at the Peach Orchard, and along the Fairfield Cross Road. The latter was a country road running southeast from the Peach Orchard on the Emmitsburg Road, past the northern edge of the Wheatfield, and on to the Taneytown Road, just north of Little Round Top. Three batteries of George E. Randolph's Third Corps Artillery Brigade were placed along the crossroad. James A. Smith's 4th

Battery, New York Light Artillery was on the left of the line near the Devil's Den; George B. Winslow's Battery D, 1st New York Light Artillery was on the right of Smith, and to the left of the Wheatfield; and A. Judson Clark's 2nd Battery, New Jersey Light Artillery was to the left of the Peach Orchard. Nelson Ames' Battery G, 1st New York Light Artillery of Robert H. Fitzhugh's Fourth Volunteer Brigade of Robert O. Tyler's Artillery Reserve reported to Sickles at 11:00 A.M., and was later posted in the Peach Orchard. John K. Bucklyn's Battery E, 1st Rhode Island Light Artillery and Francis W. Seely's Battery K, 4th United States Artillery of the Third Corps Artillery Brigade supported Humphreys' division along the Emmitsburg Road, with Bucklyn's battery on the left and Seely's battery on the right, about midway between the Peach Orchard and the Codori house.

About 3:30 P.M., Freeman McGilvery, commanding the First Volunteer Brigade of the Artillery Reserve, arrived with Charles A. Phillips' 5th Battery, Massachusetts Light Artillery; John Bigelow's 9th Battery, Massachusetts Light Artillery; and Patrick Hart's 15th Battery, New York Light Artillery. McGilvery placed Bigelow's battery on the Fairfield Cross Road, to the right of the Wheatfield, and Phillip's battery to the right of Bigelow, and to the left of A. Judson Clark's Battery B, 1st New Jersey Light Artillery of Third Corps. Hart's battery was placed in the Peach Orchard to the right and front of Ames' battery.

Close behind these batteries were James Thompson's Batteries C and F, 1st Pennsylvania Light Artillery of McGilvery's brigade and John W. Sterling's 2nd Battery, Connecticut Light Artillery of Elijah D. Taft's Second Volunteer Brigade of the Artillery Reserve. Thompson's brigade was placed on the right of Hart. Robert O. Tyler then brought up Evan Thomas' Battery C, 4th United States Artillery; John G. Turnbull's Batteries F and K, 3rd United States Artillery; and Gulian V. Weir's Battery C, 5th United States Artillery of Dunbar R. Ransom's First Regular Brigade of the Artillery Reserve to support Humphreys' line. Turnbull was placed on the right of Seely's battery, and Weir was near the right of the line, near Codoris'. Later, Malbone F. Watson's Battery I, 5th United States Artillery and Aaron F. Walcott's 3rd Battery (C),

Massachusetts Light Artillery of the Fifth Corps artillery were brought up to support Third Corps, although these batteries were needed elsewhere at that time.

Longstreet's Attack on the Union Left. During the evening of July 1, 1863, Lee decided to remain at Gettysburg and renew the offensive the next day if Meade's army still held its position on Cemetery Ridge. After carefully considering the situation, he decided to launch an attack the next morning against Meade's left flank, which he believed to be in the vicinity of the Peach Orchard. He selected John B. Hood's and Lafayette McLaws' divisions of James Longstreet's First Corps, Army of Northern Virginia to deliver the attack, and this was to be supported by an attack on their left by Richard H. Anderson's division of Ambrose P. Hill's Third Corps.

Despite Lee's hope for a morning attack, Longstreet's corps did not begin the march to its jumping-off place at the southern end of the battlefield until about 11:00 A.M., and it was not in position and ready to attack until 4:00 P.M. McLaws deployed his division on Seminary Ridge, about a quarter of a mile west of the Peach Orchard, facing east. Hood came up with his division on the right of McLaws and formed his line along the Warfield Ridge, which extended southward from the end of Seminary Ridge. Hood's line crossed the Emmitsburg Road at an acute angle about a half mile south of the Peach Orchard. When completed, Longstreet's line faced to the east and northeast, and ended on the south about three-fourths of a mile due west of Big Round Top.

When Meade discovered on the afternoon of July 2, 1863 that Sickles had compromised the safety of the army by advancing his Third Corps to a position that appeared to Meade to be too weak to defend, he promptly ordered reinforcements to that part of the line. It was probably about 3:00 P.M. when he sent Sykes with his Fifth Corps to the left of the army, and assigned to him the task of defending that flank. It is significant to note that Sykes was not directed to report to Sickles, but instead he was personally given the responsibility of handling his own corps.

Sykes, with Barnes' First Division, Fifth Corps, left his position near Power's Hill and, marching westward across the Taneytown Road and Cemetery

Ridge, arrived at a point northeast of the Wheatfield about 4:00 P.M. Ayres' Second Division followed by a different route and arrived at about the same time at the northern edge of Little Round Top. Crawford's Third Division followed Ayres.

About 4:00 P.M., Hood's division began its advance against the left of Birney's line, with Evander McIver Law's Alabama brigade on the right and Jerome B. Robertson's Texas brigade on the left. These two brigades moved eastward toward Big Round Top with the intention of enveloping the left of Sickles' line, which ended at the Devil's Den. As Law's brigade neared Big Round Top, it wheeled to the left, with some of its troops passing over the crest and western slopes of the hill and the rest advancing through the valley of Plum Run into the rear of Third Corps. Robertson's brigade, on the left of Law, struck Ward's brigade near the Devil's Den, but some of its regiments advanced with Law toward Little Round Top.

At about the same time that Hood began his advance, Gouverneur K. Warren, chief engineer of the Army of the Potomac, discovered that Little Round Top had been left unguarded when Sickles advanced his Third Corps earlier in the afternoon. Through Warren's vigorous efforts, Strong Vincent's Third Brigade of Barnes' division of Fifth Corps, and Charles E. Hazlett's Battery D, 5th United States Artillery of Augustus P. Martin's Artillery Brigade of Fifth Corps, were rushed to the hill just in time to repulse a strong attack by Law's brigade and two regiments of Robertson's brigade. A little later, when Vincent's brigade was threatened, Stephen H. Weed's Third Brigade of Ayres' division of Fifth Corps was also sent to Little Round Top. Patrick H. O'Rorke led the brigade to the summit during the brief absence of Weed, who was looking for Sickles. There was a desperate struggle for possession of the hill, including a heroic defense of the left of the line by Joshua L. Chamberlain's 20th Maine Regiment, but all of the enemy attacks failed. Weed, Hazlett, and O'Rorke were killed, and Vincent was mortally wounded in the defense of the position, which was still held by the troops of Fifth Corps at the end of the day. James C. Rice succeeded Vincent in command of Third Brigade, First Division; and Kenner Garrard took Weed's place in command of Third Brigade, Second Division. Benjamin F. Rittenhouse assumed command of Hazlett's Battery D, 5th United States Artillery.

The successful defense of Little Round Top prevented the envelopment of Sickles' left flank, but the Confederate attacks continued unabated for three hours as they gradually extended to the Federal right until finally the entire Third Corps line was in action. At first, Robertson confronted Ward at the Devil's Den with only two regiments, and he urged Henry L. Benning and George T. Anderson to bring up their brigades and support him. Hood was wounded at the beginning of the attack, and command of the division devolved on Law. Law, however, was at that time engaged at the front, and for a while the Confederate brigade commanders acted largely on their own initiative.

Benning had been following Robertson's brigade instead of Law's brigade, as Hood had directed, and as a result, he was then near Robertson's position and was able to join in the fighting with little delay. Anderson's brigade had been held in reserve on the left of the division, but when it received Robertson's request for help, Anderson moved forward immediately to support him. The attacks of these three brigades were then concentrated on the brigades of Ward and De Trobriand.

Burling's brigade of Humphreys' division, which shortly before 4:00 P.M. had been detached from the division and sent to the left as a reserve for Birney, had been placed in a woods northwest of the Wheatfield, and when Ward became hard-pressed, three regiments of Burling's brigade were sent to help him. A little later two regiments of the brigade were sent to Graham at the Peach Orchard, and the remaining regiment of the brigade was sent back to rejoin Humphreys' division. Burling was thus left without any troops to command, and he then reported with his staff to Humphreys for orders. De Trobriand, who had with him only two regiments, also moved to the left to support Ward at the Devil's Den.

Sykes then sent Barnes with William S. Tilton's First Brigade and Jacob B. Sweitzer's Second Brigade of First Division, Fifth Corps (Vincent's Third Brigade was on Little Round Top) from his position on the left of Third Corps to occupy the ground left vacant by the shift of De Trobriand's regiments to the left toward the Devil's Den. Barnes advanced with his two brigades across the Wheatfield and deployed in line of battle to the south of and near the Rose house, with Tilton's brigade on the right and Sweitzer's brigade on the left. Although these two brigades were on the Third Corps' line, they remained under Sykes' control, and they were not subject to the orders of either Birney or Sickles.

At this point, Longstreet directed McLaws to attack. McLaws had deployed his division in two lines, with Joseph B. Kershaw's brigade on the right and William Barksdale's brigade on the left of the front line, and the brigades of Paul J. Semmes and William T. Wofford on the second line. Kershaw advanced on the left of George T. Anderson's brigade of Hood's division to aid Hood in his attack. It crossed the Emmitsburg Road, passed the Rose house, and advanced toward Birney's line from the southwest. Semmes' brigade followed Kershaw. Tilton had scarcely arrived with his brigade at its position beyond the Wheatfield when he observed Kershaw's brigade approaching from the direction of the Rose house. Because Tilton's right was unprotected and would soon be outflanked by Kershaw, he moved back at about 6:00 P.M. This left the right of Sweitzer's line exposed. At that time Sweitzer was engaged with George T. Anderson's brigade, but he soon broke off the action and followed Tilton toward the rear. Both brigades withdrew across the Wheatfield and formed a new line north of the Fairfield Cross Road. Tilton's brigade was perpendicular to the road, facing west, and Sweitzer's brigade was on his left, parallel to the road and facing south.

Between 4:00 and 5:00 P.M., on Meade's orders, Hancock sent Caldwell's Second Division of Second Corps to report to Sykes and aid him in protecting the left of the army. Caldwell arrived near the Fairfield Cross Road, probably about 5:00 P.M. He had received instructions from an officer of Sykes' staff to attack near the center of Birney's line, which was then having difficulty in maintaining its position. Caldwell, however, was unable to find Sykes, or any other superior officer, and he then assumed command on that part of Third Corps' line. Caldwell deployed his brigades and moved forward. Edward E. Cross' First Brigade advanced across the Wheatfield, with its left on the woods bordering the field; Patrick Kelly's Second Brigade attacked on the right of First Brigade and entered the woods

south of the Wheatfield; and Samuel K. Zook's Third Brigade, which was still farther to the right, pushed on to a ridge to the west and southwest of the Wheatfield. Cross was killed in this attack and was succeeded by H. Boyd McKeen. Zook was also killed, and John Fraser assumed command of his brigade. John R. Brooke's Fourth Brigade was at first held in reserve, but later it was moved up to relieve First Brigade. Brooke was injured in this action, but he remained on the field. Sweitzer's brigade of Barnes' division, in response to a call for help, again advanced into the Wheatfield in support of Caldwell's line.

Finally, late in the afternoon, Ward and De Trobriand could no longer stand the pressure, and they were driven from the Devil's Den, closely followed by the enemy. When Ayres' Second Division of Sykes' corps arrived near Little Round Top that afternoon, it was placed on the right of Garrard's (Weed's) Third Brigade of the division, which had arrived earlier and was then on the crest of the hill. Hannibal Day's First Brigade and Sidney Burbank's Second Brigade extended the line down the northern slope to the Fairfield Cross Road. A short time later, Ayres advanced with the brigades of Day and Burbank and, wheeling to the left, came up on the left of Sweitzer's brigade, where he formed a line at a right angle to Garrard's position, facing the Devil's Den. Burbank's brigade was in front, and Day's brigade was in the rear. For a time, Ayres helped check Hood's advance in that area.

When Caldwell, Sweitzer, and Ayres came into action on the left of Birney's line, Ward and De Trobriand withdrew their brigades to the rear, where they bivouacked for the night

By 6:00 P.M., Caldwell had advanced to a point near the Rose house, Sweitzer's line was along the southern edge of the Wheatfield, and Ayres' line was still holding on the left near the Devil's Den.

At about 5:30 P.M., shortly after Tilton and Sweitzer had withdrawn from near the Rose house, and while Caldwell was beginning his advance at the Wheatfield, McLaws' division of Longstreet's corps moved forward against Graham's position at the angle in Sickles' line at the Peach Orchard. Graham's infantry and its supporting artillery resisted resolutely for some time, but under the heavy attacks by Kershaw on the left and Wofford on the right, and suffering from the heavy fire from

E. Porter Alexander's artillery, they were finally overwhelmed at about 6:00 P.M. and driven to the rear. Graham was wounded and captured, and Andrew H. Tippin assumed command of the remnants of the brigade and attempted to bring them off the field. McGilvery withdrew all his batteries in good order except Bigelow's. Bigelow withdrew with difficulty across the lane from the Trostle barn, and to the south of it; and then, on McGilvery's orders, he remained there in action from 6:00 to 6:30 P.M. to cover the retreat while McGilvery formed a new artillery line about 400 yards to the rear. This new line consisted of the remnants of McGilvery's First Volunteer Brigade, Edwin B. Dow's 6th Battery (F), Maine Light Artillery, and Malbone F. Watson's Battery I, 5th United States Artillery. When this line was completed, Bigelow's remaining men, with two guns, fell back and joined it.

Sickles was severely wounded at about 5:30 P.M., and Birney assumed command of Third Corps. Ward took charge of Birney's division. When Sickles was wounded, Meade ordered Hancock to assume command of Third Corps, in addition to his own Second Corps, but by that time Third Corps was finished for the day as an organized force.

The collapse at the angle of Sickles' line left a gap through which enemy troops poured to take in flank the left and rear of Humphreys' division along the Emmitsburg Road, and the right and rear of Caldwell's, Birney's, and Sykes' troops who were fighting near the Wheatfield, the Devil's Den, and in the adjoining woods. As a result, the entire left of the Union line south of the Fairfield Cross Road disintegrated, and all the troops fighting there were forced to fall back across Plum Run Valley to the comparative safety of the high ground beyond.

Meantime, Crawford's Third Division of Fifth Corps had arrived from its position near Power's Hill, and by 5:00 P.M. had formed on the eastern slope of the north ridge of Little Round Top. Joseph W. Fisher, with four regiments of his Third Brigade (one regiment was with William McCandless' First Brigade), was then sent to assist Rice's brigade (formerly Vincent's brigade) on Little Round Top. McCandless' brigade then moved up to occupy the north ridge. It was at about that time that the Union line at the Peach Orchard and to its left collapsed, and the fugitives were then streaming to the rear on

McCandless' front. When the pursuing enemy infantry approached from the Wheatfield, McCandless' brigade charged and drove them back across the valley and beyond a stone fence just west of Plum Run. The brigade remained in position there during the night and all the next day.

The fighting on Birney's front had been in progress for about two hours before it extended to the lines north of the Fairview Cross Road. Shortly after Kershaw advanced against Birney, Barksdale's brigade of McLaws' division and Richard H. Anderson's division of Hill's corps moved forward against Humphreys' line. Barksdale advanced on the left of McLaws, and he was followed in quick succession, from right to left, by the brigades of Cadmus M. Wilcox, David Lang (commanding Perrin's brigade), and Ambrose R. Wright. William Mahone's and Carnot Posey's brigades were not engaged.

Barksdale's advance, north of the Peach Orchard, threatened Humphreys' left, and on orders from Birney, then commanding Third Corps, Humphreys drew back his left to a new line that extended in the direction of Little Round Top. He had just completed this movement when he was ordered to retire to Cemetery Ridge. Thus, when Wilcox and Lang struck Humphreys' line they did not encounter strong resistance, because Humphreys was under orders to retire at that time, and he then proceeded to do so, fighting all of the way to Cemetery Ridge. The main attack by Wright's brigade was against the 82nd New York and 15th Massachusetts regiments of Harrow's brigade, which were on the Emmitsburg Road north of the Codori house. To the rear of these regiments were Evan Thomas' Battery C, 4th United States Artillery, supported by the 1st Minnesota Regiment of Harrow's brigade, and T. Frederick Brown's Battery B, 1st Rhode Island Light Artillery of the Second Corps Artillery Brigade, which was supported by the 19th Maine of Harrow's brigade. The 82nd New York and 15th Massachusetts were driven back, but Wright's attack was finally repulsed by the artillery and its supports.

Sometime between 5:00 and 6:00 P.M., Hancock was sent with George L. Willard's Third Brigade of Alexander Hays' Third Division, Second Corps from the north end of Cemetery Ridge to reinforce Birney. At the same time, James E. Mallon's 42nd

New York and 19th Massachusetts of Norman J. Hall's Third Brigade of Gibbon's division, both under Mallon, were sent to support Humphreys. While on his way with Willard's brigade to join Birney, Hancock learned that all troops of Third Corps had gone to the rear and that Birney had gone with them. This altered Hancock's mission, but he continued on and, at about 7:15 P.M., arrived at a point on the ridge just north of the Trostle Lane. At that time, the Trostle farm was held only by McGilvery's artillery, toward which Barksdale was rapidly moving. Willard deployed his brigade north of the lane, and immediately charged against the left flank of Barksdale's advancing line. A severe struggle ensued, during which Willard was killed and Barksdale was mortally wounded, and the enemy was driven back and up the west slope of the valley of Plum Run. Eliakim Sherrill assumed command of Willard's brigade and brought it back to Plum Run. It remained there until after dark, and then returned to the position that it had occupied that morning.

Shortly after Willard's successful attack, Williams, temporarily commanding Twelfth Corps, approached the rear of McGilvery's artillery line on Cemetery Ridge with Thomas H. Ruger's First Division and Lockwood's Provisional Brigade, which was attached to Twelfth Corps but was unassigned. Lockwood promptly formed his brigade and charged the enemy on his front. He drove forward almost to the Peach Orchard before he was stopped. Ruger also deployed his division, probably on Cemetery Ridge, but a short time later, Williams was ordered to return to Culp's Hill with his command.

Sometime after 4:00 P.M., Hancock asked for troops to help hold that part of the Second Corps' line that was left vacant when Caldwell's division left to join Birney. In response, Doubleday's Third Division and a part of Robinson's Second Division of First Corps were sent up from their positions in reserve, in rear of Cemetery Hill. They arrived on Cemetery Ridge as the fighting was ending, however, and they were only slightly engaged. Francis V. Randall, with his 13th Vermont Regiment of Stannard's leading brigade of Doubleday's division, advanced and recaptured Weir's battery and then pushed on to the Emmitsburg Road, capturing some prisoners and two guns. The regiment rejoined the brigade at dark. Doubleday remained on Cemetery Ridge during the night, but shortly after Robinson arrived he returned to his original position in reserve.

At no place that evening did enemy troops gain the crest of Cemetery Ridge, although Wright claimed that men of his brigade did. Most of the Confederate attackers advanced no farther than the bottom of the Plum Run Valley, on the south, or the lower ground between the eastern slope of the ridge along which the Emmitsburg Road ran and the western slope of Cemetery Ridge, on the north.

Sedgwick's Sixth Corps began to arrive on the left of the Union line about 3:00 P.M. July 2, 1863. Frank Wheaton's Third Division came up at about that time, and Horatio G. Wright's First Division followed about an hour later. Albion P. Howe's Second Division arrived about 5:00 P.M. David J. Nevin's Third Brigade (Wheaton's) and Henry L. Eustis' Second Brigade, both of Third Division, and Joseph J. Bartlett's Second Brigade of First Division moved up and took position between the divisions of Fifth Corps, and about dark aided in repelling the final advance of Longstreet's men in the Plum Run Valley. Bartlett was unable to take part in this action because his position was masked by Nevin's advance.

About 7:00 P.M., Alexander Shaler's First Brigade of Third Division, Sixth Corps was formed in line of battle behind Eustis' brigade. The remaining brigades of the corps were disposed that night as follows: David A. Russell's Third Brigade and Alfred T. A. Torbert's First Brigade of Wright's division were placed in reserve; Lewis A. Grant's Second Brigade of Howe's division was posted on the extreme left of the Union line between the Taneytown Road and Big Round Top; and Thomas H. Neill's Third Brigade of Howe's division, which had arrived about 6:00 P.M., was sent to the right to support some artillery, probably on Power's Hill. Neill's brigade was then sent to Culp's Hill to support the divisions of Geary and Wadsworth during Edward Johnson's attack on Culp's Hill and Cemetery Hill that evening (see below), but it returned to its original position about midnight. Charles P. Tompkins' Artillery Brigade of Sixth Corps was placed under the orders of Henry J. Hunt, chief of artillery of the army.

When Caldwell's division returned to Second Corps from its engagement at the Wheatfield, it moved to the rear of the main line, where it regrouped during the night. The next morning, Caldwell again moved into position on Cemetery Ridge, on the left of Doubleday's division of First Corps.

Sykes' Fifth Corps remained near the Round Tops that night, with Fisher's Third Brigade, Third Division on Big Round Top; Rice's Third Brigade, First Division (formerly Vincent's) on the low ground between the two Round Tops; and Garrard's Third Brigade, Second Division (formerly Weed's) on Little Round Top.

Birney's Third Corps was massed in rear of Cemetery Ridge, where it was re-formed during the night.

Ewell's Attack on Culp's Hill and Cemetery Hill. As a part of Lee's plan of attack for July 2, 1863, he gave Richard E. Ewell, commanding the Confederate Second Corps, a discretionary order to make a demonstration on the Union right when Longstreet began his attack on the opposite flank. In addition, he authorized Ewell to change his demonstration into a real attack if he found a favorable opportunity.

In conforming with this order, Ewell moved Edward Johnson's division to a position on the extreme left of the enemy line, to the north and east of Culp's Hill. Nicholls' brigade (commanded by Jesse M. Williams) was north of Culp's Hill, facing southwest toward the angle of the Union line where Wadsworth's division joined Greene's brigade of Geary's division; John M. Jones' brigade was on the left of Williams' line, facing Greene's brigade to the west; George H. Steuart's brigade was on the left of Jones, also facing west, directly in front of that part of the Twelfth Corps line that was vacated that evening when troops were sent to aid in stopping Longstreet's attack on the Union left; and James A. Walker's brigade was held in the rear to oppose the skirmishers of David McM. Gregg's cavalry division, which had just arrived on the battlefield.

Jubal A. Early placed the brigades of Hoke (commanded by Isaac E. Avery) and Harry T. Hays of his division north of Cemetery Hill between the Baltimore Pike and Rock Creek, with Hays' brigade on the right and Avery's brigade on the left, next to Rock Creek. Early brought up John B. Gordon's brigade to within supporting distance of Hays and Avery, and he left William Smith's brigade in the rear to guard the approach to the Confederate position from the York Road.

During the afternoon of July 2, 1863, the troops defending the right of Meade's line opposite Early and Johnston were in position from left to right as follows: Adelbert Ames' First Division (formerly Barlow's) of Howard's Eleventh Corps was on the northeast slope of Cemetery Hill; Greenleaf T. Stevens' 5th Battery (E), Maine Light Artillery occupied a knoll (now called Stevens' Knoll) between Cemetery Hill and Culp's Hill; Wadsworth's First Division of Newton's First Corps extended along a part of Culp's Hill near the crest; Geary's Second Division, Twelfth Corps was on a line that ran from the right of Wadsworth's division at the top of the hill down the slope along the eastern edge, facing the valley of Rock Creek; and Williams' First Division, Twelfth Corps (commanded temporarily by Thomas H. Ruger) continued the line on down the shoulder of Culp's Hill, past Spangler's Spring, to Rock Creek at the crossing of the Baltimore Pike. The positions occupied by Twelfth Corps were strongly protected by breastworks and trenches.

David McM. Gregg arrived on the battlefield about noon July 2, 1863, with John B. McIntosh's First Brigade and J. Irvin Gregg's Third Brigade of his Second Cavalry Division, and he then took position on the Gettysburg-Hanover Road on the extreme right of the Union line. Pennock Huey's Second Brigade of the division was left at Westminster.

The Federal artillery supporting the right of Meade's line was in position as follows: Henry J. Hunt, chief of artillery, placed the batteries of Edward D. Muhlenberg's Artillery Brigade of Twelfth Corps south of the cemetery gate, in the gap between First Corps and Second Corps. These were: Sylvanus T. Rugg's Battery F, 4th United States Artillery; Charles E. Winegar's Battery M, 1st New York Light Artillery; Charles A. Atwell's Battery E, Pennsylvania Light Artillery; and David H. Kinzie's Battery K, 5th United States Artillery. Later in the day these batteries were pulled out of line to accompany the infantry of Twelfth Corps when it went to aid in repelling Longstreet's attack on the left of the Union Line.

The batteries of Charles P. Wainwright's Artillery Brigade of First Corps and Thomas W. Osborn's Artillery Brigade of Eleventh Corps, badly depleted by the fighting of the day before, were placed to cover the fronts of Cemetery Hill and Culp's Hill, and additional batteries of the Reserve Artillery were brought up to reinforce them. James Stewart's Battery B, 4th United States Artillery of First Corps was placed in front of the cemetery gate, and James H. Cooper's Battery B, 1st Pennsylvania Light Artillery and Michael Wiedrich's Battery I, 1st New York Light Artillery of Eleventh Corps were placed on lower ground in advance of Stewart's battery. During the afternoon, Cooper was relieved by R. Bruce Ricketts' Batteries F and G of James F. Huntington's Third Volunteer Brigade of the Artillery Reserve. Some 200 yards to the right of Stewart's battery was Stevens' battery on the knoll, and Gilbert H. Reynolds' Battery L, 1st New York Light Artillery of First Corps (then commanded by George Breck) was also to the right of Stewart.

An artillery line was also formed to the left of the Baltimore Pike. Beginning on the right, next to the road, was Hubert Dilger's Battery I, 1st Ohio Light Artillery of Eleventh Corps; and then, in order from right to left, were the following: Eugene A. Bancroft's Battery G, 4th United States Artillery of Eleventh Corps; Chandler P. Eakin's Battery H, 1st United States Artillery of Dunbar R. Ransom's First Regular Brigade of the Artillery Reserve; William Wheeler's 13th Battery, New York Light Artillery of Eleventh Corps; Wallace Hill's Battery C, 1st West Virginia Light Artillery of Huntington's Third Volunteer Brigade of the Artillery Reserve; and James A. Hall's 2nd Battery (B), Maine Light Artillery of First Corps.

In addition to the above, the following batteries were also sent from the Artillery Reserve to Cemetery Hill as reinforcements: Frederick M. Edgell's 1st Battery, New Hampshire Light Artillery and George H. Norton's Battery H, 1st Ohio Light Artillery, both of Huntington's Third Volunteer Brigade ; and Elijah D. Taft's 5th Battery of New York Light Artillery from Taft's Second Volunteer Brigade. Edgell's battery was later moved to a position on the Baltimore Pike, where it was not engaged.

Late in the afternoon of July 2, 1863, during Longstreet's attack on the southern part of the battlefield, Meade directed Slocum to send both divisions of Twelfth Corps to the left to reinforce the troops fighting there. Ruger's First Division and Lockwood's unassigned Provisional Brigade left their positions at Culp's Hill sometime between 5:00 and 6:00 P.M. and, accompanied by Williams, the temporary corps commander, they marched to Cemetery Ridge and formed near McGilvery's artillery line, east of the Trostle farm. Geary left Greene's Third Brigade of his Second Division to cover, as best it could, the Twelfth Corps line, and set out with Candy's First Brigade and Cobham's Second Brigade to follow Williams. For some unexplained reason, Geary became lost. The first part of his march was along the Baltimore Pike, but instead of turning off to the right near Power's Hill toward the Taneytown Road, as Williams had done, he continued on, crossed Rock Creek, and marched away from the battlefield. When Geary finally realized that he was on the wrong road, he retraced his steps and bivouacked near the Rock Creek Bridge. He was there when messengers found him late that evening with orders to return to Culp's Hill.

When Ruger and Geary departed, they left the breastworks to the right of Greene without defenders, and they were empty when Ewell began his attack that evening. Greene was just beginning to extend his line to the right to occupy these positions when the enemy advanced.

During the late afternoon, when Johnson was finally given the order to attack, he experienced considerable difficulty in getting his troops in position, and it was nearly dark, about 7:30 P.M., when he reached the main Union defenses on Culp's Hill and started forward. The assault was so vigorous that Greene soon needed help. Although Wadsworth was himself engaged, he sent two regiments to Greene, and Carl Schurz, commanding Third Division, Eleventh Corps, sent four regiments (totaling only about 750 men) of George Von Amsberg's (Schimmelfennig's) First Brigade, Third Division. Neill's Third Brigade of Howe's division of Sixth Corps, which was at that time near Power's Hill, was also sent to support Greene and Wadsworth. Neill's brigade remained at Culp's Hill until midnight, after the fighting had ended for the day, and it then returned to its original position.

Repeated attempts by Johnson's two right

brigades, commanded by Jesse M. Williams and John M. Jones, failed to drive Greene and Wadsworth from their entrenchments; but on the right of Greene, Steuart's brigade encountered no resistance and moved into the empty Twelfth Corps works, where it remained during the rest of the night. The fighting ended on Culp's Hill at 10:30, although there was some firing along the line for another hour.

Ewell's plans for his attack on the Union right on the evening of July 2, 1863 called for simultaneous assaults by both Johnson's and Early's divisions. As soon as Johnson began his attack at Culp's Hill, Early was to advance two of his brigades and engage the Federal troops holding the northeast slope of Cemetery Hill. Therefore, about 8:00 P.M., the brigades of Hays and Hoke, the latter commanded by Avery, started forward toward that part of the Union line held by Ames' First Division, Eleventh Corps and artillery. Ames' division was protected by a stone wall at an angle in the line on the north and northeast slope of the hill. Leopold Von Gilsa's First Brigade was on the left, facing northwest, with its left on the Baltimore Pike. Andrew L. Harris' Second Brigade (formerly Ames') was on the right, and its line ran parallel to the Baltimore Pike, facing to the northeast. To the right and rear of Harris' line was Stevens' 5th Battery (E), Maine Light Artillery on the knoll between Culp's Hill and Cemetery Hill. To the left and rear of Stevens' battery was Adin B. Underwood's 33rd Massachusetts Regiment of Orland Smith's Second Brigade of Von Steinwehr's Second Division, Eleventh Corps in support of Harris' line. On Cemetery Hill, to the rear of the infantry line, were the batteries of Stewart, Wiedrich, Ricketts, and Reynolds (see artillery positions, above).

When Early attacked, Ames' brigades offered only a feeble resistance, and were quickly driven from the stone wall and up the hill. Some of the pursuing Confederates entered Wiedrich's battery, and for a time were engaged in furious hand-to-hand fighting with the artillerymen among their guns. To aid the gunners in the defense of their guns, Ames brought back some of the fleeing infantry to support them. The enemy also overran Ricketts' battery, and for a time there was desperate fighting among the guns. Help for the embattled gunners soon arrived.

Wladimir Krzyzanowski brought up the nearest two regiments of his Second Brigade, Third Division, Eleventh Corps, and with Schurz, the division commander, and his staff, they charged at a point near Wiedrich's battery and, with help from Charles S. Coster's First Brigade of Von Steinwehr's Second Division, Eleventh Corps, drove the enemy back down the hill.

Hancock sent Samuel S. Carroll's First Brigade of Alexander Hays' Third Division, Second Corps to support Eleventh Corps during Early's attack, and it arrived near Ricketts' battery at a very critical time. Carroll immediately charged Avery's men on his front and drove them off the hill. At that point, Harry T. Hays, who was then in temporary command of both of Early's brigades, called off the attack and withdrew. Carroll pursued for a time and then returned to the stone wall near the bottom of the hill. The firing on Cemetery Hill finally ceased at about 10:30 P.M. Despite Carroll's wish to return to Second Corps, his brigade was retained by Howard, and it continued to hold that position until the end of the battle.

When Longstreet's attack on the Union left ended about dark July 2, 1863, Williams and Geary were ordered to return with their divisions to their former positions on Culp's Hill. Ruger arrived in rear of the hill at 10:00 P.M. and discovered that a part of his breastworks on the right of Greene's brigade, held earlier by Archibald L. McDougall's First Brigade, was occupied by enemy troops. He also found that the breastworks south of Spangler's Spring were unoccupied. Ruger immediately advanced Silas Colgrove's Third Brigade, First Division (Ruger's brigade) to a rocky hill just south of the swampy ground around the spring, and with the rest of his division he formed a line westward from the hill to the vicinity of the Baltimore Pike, facing north. Lockwood's brigade was sent to Power's Hill to support the batteries of Muhlenberg's Artillery Brigade of Twelfth Corps, which were posted there.

When Williams returned to Culp's Hill about midnight from a meeting of the corps commanders at Meade's headquarters, he learned of the situation there and decided to wait until daylight before attempting to recapture the breastworks that Steuart had occupied the evening before.

Cobham's Second Brigade of Geary's Second Division (Thomas L. Kane's brigade) returned to Culp's Hill from the vicinity of Rock Creek Bridge, probably about 10:30 P.M., but it was unable to move into its former works because they too were occupied by the enemy. Instead, Cobham formed his brigade on a line that extended from the right of Greene's position toward the Baltimore Pike, facing south. Charles Candy's First Brigade of Geary's division also came up sometime after midnight, perhaps as late as 1:30 A.M. July 3, 1863, to support Greene.

When Twelfth Corps was reassembled, Williams, with help from Slocum and Geary, began preparations for a counterattack at Culp's Hill the next morning to restore their original line. Geary's division was to make the principal attack, and most of Ruger's division was to be ready to support Geary, or advance against the left of Johnson's line if circumstances were favorable. Geary's division was on the left of the corps, and was formed on a line that began at the top of the hill, ran down the southern slope, and then curved around to the west toward the Baltimore Pike. Greene's brigade was on the left of this line, Cobham's brigade on the center, and Candy's brigade on the right. Williams created an interval between Geary's division and Ruger's division by drawing back the left of Ruger's division to enable Muhlenberg's guns to fire without injury to infantry on their front. Williams then placed Charles A. Atwell's Battery E, Pennsylvania Light Artillery and James H. Rigby's Battery A, Maryland Light Artillery of Fitzhugh's Fourth Volunteer Brigade of the Artillery Reserve on Power's Hill, and Charles E. Winegar's Battery M, 1st New York Light Artillery on McAllister's Hill.

Ruger's division was on the right of Geary, with its right near Rock Creek and its left out on the open ground on a line at a right angle to the Baltimore Pike. The brigades of Colgrove and McDougall remained in about the same positions that they had occupied the previous night. Colgrove's brigade was on the right, and its line extended from the rocky hill out to the left across the low ground near Spangler's Spring. McDougall's brigade (except the 20th Connecticut) was held in reserve. Lockwood's brigade was along the Baltimore Pike, near Syl-

vanus T. Rugg's Battery F, 4th United States Artillery and David H. Kinzie's Battery K, 5th United States Artillery, and was also to serve as a reserve that might be needed either on the right or the left.

THE THIRD DAY, JULY 3, 1863

Battle on Culp's Hill. Early on the morning of July 3, 1863, the fighting on Culp's Hill was resumed. Williams' plan of attack called for a heavy artillery fire on the enemy position, and this was to be followed by a feint from the Union right, and then the main assault was to be made by Geary's division from Greene's position on the left.

Johnson had been reinforced during the night by William Smith's brigade of Early's division, Edward A. O'Neal's and Junius Daniel's brigades of Robert E. Rodes' division, and Walker's Stonewall Brigade of his own division, and his plan for the morning was simply to drive forward and capture the crest of the hill.

The Union artillery opened at 4:30 A.M. and continued firing for about fifteen minutes, and then the infantry battle began. There is some doubt as to whether Geary attacked as planned, because soon after the artillery fire had ended, Johnson launched a series of attacks on the line held by Greene and Cobham. The first attack failed, but it was followed during the morning by several other attempts, and all of these were in turn repulsed. O'Neal's brigade attacked at 8:00 A.M., Walker's brigade an hour or so later, and, finally, Steuart's and Daniel's brigades at 10:00 A.M.

During the enemy attacks, Williams sent forward more troops to reinforce Geary. These included Lockwood's brigade, three regiments of Candy's brigade, and Shaler's First Brigade of Wheaton's division of Sixth Corps, which had arrived from near Little Round Top that morning. Neill's Third Brigade of Howe's division of Sixth Corps, which had been sent to Twelfth Corps the evening before, was sent to the extreme right of the line near Wolf's Hill, but it was only slightly engaged. When the attacks by Steuart and Daniel collapsed, Geary's division, with several regiments of Ruger's division, launched a counterattack and finally forced the enemy to withdraw down the hill toward Rock Creek. The battle ended around 11:00 A.M., but heavy firing continued for some time thereafter.

Reorganization of the Union Line. While Twelfth Corps was fighting on Culp's Hill, the Union commanders on the line between between Cemetery Hill and Little Round Top were busily engaged in preparing a defense for an enemy attack that was expected there during the day. One of the first steps to be taken on the morning of July 3, 1863 was to make certain that the line was adequately manned. As a result of the fighting of the evening before, some units were more or less disorganized and not properly placed for defense. Also, as a consequence of the frequent shifting of troops to reinforce threatened parts of the line, some positions were left unoccupied and some units were separated from their proper commands. Every effort was made to rectify this situation, and finally, that morning, the troops on the Union center were in place and ready for an attack. On the right, Hays' Third Division and Gibbon's Second Division (the latter commanded temporarily that morning by Harrow) of Hancock's Second Corps occupied the same positions as the day before. These two divisions, with Hays on the right, held a line about 2,000 feet long, beginning at the edge of Ziegler's Grove on the Taneytown Road and extending southward on Cemetery Ridge to a point about 600 feet beyond the so-called "Clump of Trees." Hancock's headquarters was with these divisions. Caldwell's First Division, which had been sent to the left the previous evening, had not rejoined the corps. On the morning of July 3, 1863, Hancock was in charge of his own Second Corps, Newton's First Corps, and Birney's Third Corps. Gibbon was temporarily in command of Second Corps; and Harrow temporarily commanded Gibbon's Second Division, Second Corps. This arrangement was terminated about noon, and Hancock resumed command of Second Corps and Gibbon of his division.

Next in line on Cemetery Ridge, on the left of Gibbon, was Doubleday's Third Division of Newton's First Corps, with Newton's headquarters in rear of the division. During the morning, Newton discovered that there were no Federal troops in position on the ridge between the left of Doubleday's division and the troops of Fifth Corps and Sixth Corps, which were near the Round Tops

to the south. When Newton reported this fact to Meade, he was authorized to go to Sedgwick, commander of Sixth Corps, for men to fill this gap. While performing this duty, Newton found Caldwell's division, which had regrouped the night before in rear of the main line, and with Hancock's consent, he placed it on the left of Doubleday's division. Newton then brought Torbert's First Brigade of Wright's division of Sixth Corps and put it in line on the left of Caldwell. A little later, Eustis' Second Brigade of Wheaton's Third Division of Sixth Corps arrived and formed on the line with Torbert's brigade. Newton was authorized to direct the operations of both brigades, in addition to those of Doubleday's division of his own First Corps.

The remnants of Birney's Third Corps had been re-formed after the battle of the day before, and on the morning of July 3, 1863, the corps was massed in the rear of the junction of Doubleday's and Caldwell's divisions. It remained there during the day to provide support if needed on that part of the line.

Sykes' Fifth Corps was in position on and near the Round Tops. Fisher's Third Brigade of Crawford's Third Division was on Big Round Top; Barnes' First Division was on the lower ground to the north, and it connected on the right with Garrard's (formerly Weed's) Third Brigade of Ayres' Second Division, which was on Little Round Top. The other two brigades of Ayres' division were just to the east of Little Round Top. McCandless' First Brigade, Third Division was in position just west of Plum Run, and across the road that ran out to the Peach Orchard. Sykes' corps was supported on the right and rear by Bartlett's Second Brigade of Wright's First Division, Sixth Corps and Nevin's Third Brigade of Wheaton's Third Division, Sixth Corps. Both were under the command of Bartlett.

Grant's Second Brigade of Howe's Second Division, Sixth Corps and Russell's Third Brigade of Wright's First Division, Sixth Corps—both under Wright—extended the left of the Union line from the Big Round Top to a point a short distance east of the Taneytown Road.

Meade's line on the left and center was strongly supported by artillery. The batteries of Augustus P. Martin's Artillery Brigade of Fifth Corps were on and near the Round Tops. Frank C. Gibbs' Battery L, 1st Ohio Light Artillery was in position to cover the valley in front of the Round Tops, and Benjamin F. Rittenhouse's Battery D, 5th United States Artillery (formerly commanded by Hazlett) was on Little Round Top.

Next, to the north, were thirty-nine guns belonging to Freeman McGilvery's First Volunteer Brigade of the Artillery Reserve, which were on the lower part of Cemetery Ridge, where they had been engaged the evening before. On the right of McGilvery's line was Evan Thomas' Battery C, 4th United States Artillery of Dunbar R. Ransom's First Regular Brigade of the Artillery Reserve, and to the right of Thomas were the five batteries of John G. Hazard's Artillery Brigade of Second Corps. These were posted along that part of the crest of Cemetery Ridge occupied by the infantry of Gibbon's and Hays' divisions of Second Corps, and they were in order from left to right as follows: James McKay Rorty's Battery B, 1st New York Light Artillery; T. Frederick Brown's Battery B, 1st Rhode Island Light Artillery (commanded by Walter S. Perrin); Alonzo H. Cushing's Battery A, 4th United States Artillery; William A. Arnold's Battery A, 1st Rhode Island Light Artillery; and George A. Woodruff's Battery I, 1st United States Artillery.

Beyond the guns of Second Corps, on and near Cemetery Hill, the batteries were in positions as of the previous day. The batteries of Thomas W. Osborn's Artillery Brigade of Eleventh Corps were on Cemetery Hill, and those of Charles S. Wainwright's Artillery Brigade of First Corps were in front of the cemetery gate and north of the Baltimore Pike.

Twelve batteries of the Artillery Reserve had been ordered to the different corps July 2, 1863, and these were still in the positions to which they had been assigned. The rest were taken back out of range of the enemy fire until the assault on Cemetery Ridge that afternoon, and then they were all ordered back to the front.

James M. Robertson, commanding the First Brigade, Horse Artillery of the Cavalry Corps, was ordered to report to Robert O. Tyler that morning to assist him with the Artillery Reserve. One of Robertson's batteries, Jabez J. Daniels' 9th Michigan Battery, was sent to aid Newton. For a time Robertson was in command of the Artillery Reserve when Tyler suffered a sunstroke.

Meade completed the reorganization of his line on Cemetery Ridge about noon July 3, 1863, and then all was in readiness for the attack expected later in the day.

Pickett-Pettigrew-Trimble Assault (Pickett's Charge).

While Meade's defensive preparations were in progress on Cemetery Ridge, the enemy, across the fields on Seminary Ridge, were completing the dispositions of their forces for an assault on the Union center. This attack began at 1:00 P.M., when approximately 150 guns opened fire on Meade's line on Cemetery Ridge. The Federal batteries returned the fire for a time, but then, to conserve ammunition, they gradually ceased firing.

The troops selected for the infantry attack consisted of the brigades of George E. Pickett's division of Longstreet's First Corps and eight brigades of Hill's Third Corps. Four of Hill's brigades were from Henry Heth's division (then commanded by James J. Pettigrew), and two each from Richard H. Anderson's division and William D. Pender's division (then commanded by Isaac R. Trimble). After Pender was wounded July 2, 1863, James H. Lane assumed command of his division, but on July 3, 1863, just before the attack on Cemetery Ridge, Trimble relieved Lane in command of the division, and Lane resumed command of his brigade. Trimble led the brigades of Land and Alfred M. Scales (the latter commanded by William L. J. Lowrance) in the attack that afternoon. About 3:00 P.M. the Confederate artillery ceased firing, and the infantry began to move forward on a front of more than a thousand yards toward Cemetery Ridge .

When the enemy began its advance, the following Union batteries were moved up to the infantry line on Cemetery Ridge and put in position near the "Clump of Trees" and at the stone wall in front of Alexander S. Webb's brigade: Robert H. Fitzhugh's Battery K, 1st New York Light Artillery (with the 11th New York Battery attached) and Augustin N. Parsons' 1st Battery, New Jersey Light Artillery of Fitzhugh's Fourth Volunteer Brigade of the Artillery Reserve; Gulian V. Weir's Battery C, 5th United States Artillery of Dunbar R. Ransom's First Regular Brigade of the Artillery Reserve; and Andrew Cowan's 1st Battery, New York Light Artillery of Charles H. Tompkins' Artillery Brigade of Sixth Corps. Brown's and Arnold's batteries had been so badly crippled by the enemy fire that they were withdrawn and replaced by Cowan's battery.

That part of the Union line that was to receive the full impact of the enemy attack was held as follows: On the right were Thomas A. Smyth's Second Brigade and Eliakim Sherrill's Third Brigade (formerly Willard's) of Alexander Hays' Third Division, Second Corps. They were formed on a straight line from a point near the angle at the stone wall northward to, and perhaps a little beyond, the Bryan house and barn on the edge of Ziegler's Grove. Smyth's brigade was on the right and Sherrill's brigade was on the left. Carroll's First Brigade of Hays' division (except the 8th Ohio Regiment) had been detached the evening before and sent to aid Howard's Eleventh Corps, and it was still with Howard. Smyth was wounded during the cannonade, and Francis E. Pierce assumed command of his brigade. Sherrill was killed about 4:00 P.M. and was succeeded in command of Third Brigade by James M. Bull. It should be noted that Sherrill's and Smyth's brigades did not fight that afternoon as units, but instead their regiments were detached and used to aid in defending the line as they were needed.

Gibbon's Second Division, Second Corps was on the left of Hays, with the brigades in line from right to left as follows: Alexander S. Webb's Second Brigade occupied the angle of the line just to the right of the Clump of Trees, connecting on the right with Hays' division; Norman J. Hall's Third Brigade was next, on the center of the division front, to the left of the Clump of Trees; and William Harrow's First Brigade was on the left of the division.

The regiments of Doubleday's Third Division of First Corps extended the line into the lower ground to the left of Gibbon. Theodore B. Gates' 80th New York (20th New York Militia) was the right regiment of Doubleday's line, and next to it was the 151st Pennsylvania. Both regiments belonged to Thomas A. Rowley's First Brigade, but Gates, as the senior officer, was in command of both regiments. George J. Stannard, commanding the Third Brigade, Third Division (the Vermont Brigade), placed the 13th Vermont, 14th Vermont, and 16th Vermont regiments irregularly in front and to the left of Gates' regiments.

When the enemy advance began, Pettigrew, fol-lowed by Trimble, marched slightly to the right of straight ahead toward the Clump of Trees and the stone wall at the angle of the Union line. Pickett's division started forward about 350 yards to the right of Pettigrew, and generally headed for Doubleday's division. Near the Emmitsburg Road, however, Pickett turned his division about 45 degrees to the left, advanced along the road past the Codori house, and then turned back to the right and moved alongside Pettigrew's men toward the Clump of Trees. As these troops advanced across the fields, the Federal artillery opened with every gun that could be brought to bear, but although it did fearful damage, it did not halt their progress.

Edward A. Perry's brigade (commanded by David Lang) and Cadmus M. Wilcox's brigade, both of Richard H. Anderson's division of Hill's corps, started forward about twenty minutes after Pickett and to the right of the latter, but when they reached the Emmitsburg Road, they did not veer to the left as Pickett had done, but continued to move straight ahead. They advanced into the valley of Plum Run, to the west of the Weikert farm, under a heavy fire from McGilvery's guns and the musketry of the 14th and 16th Vermont regiments, which had turned about from their fight with Pickett's men and charged into the left flank of Lang. Both Lang and Wilcox then returned to Seminary Ridge.

The brigades of John M. Brockenbrough (commanded by Robert M. Mayo) and Joseph R. Davis of Pettigrew's division did not advance until sometime after Pettigrew's other two brigades, but they then moved forward on the left of the assaulting column, with Mayo on the left of Davis. Shortly after Mayo's brigade emerged from behind Seminary Ridge, it was struck by the full force of Osborn's thirty-one guns of Eleventh Corps on Cemetery Hill, and in addition, it came under a destructive flank fire from Franklin Sawyer's 8th Ohio Regiment of Carroll's brigade, which had advanced to a position west of the Emmitsburg Road. As a result of the combined effects of the artillery and infantry fire, Mayo soon withdrew. Davis' brigade advanced on the right of Mayo until it arrived in front of Hays' division, and then under fire of Hays from the front and 8th Ohio from the left, it too soon retired.

Pickett's and Trimble's troops approached to within a few hundred feet of Hancock's line and then, after halting briefly, they began their final assault. The brigades of Richard B. Garnett, James L. Kemper, and Lewis A. Armistead of Pickett's division; and the brigades of Pettigrew (commanded by James K. Marshall) and James J. Archer (led by Birkett D. Fry) of Pettigrew's division converged on the Clump of Trees. The brigades of Lane and Scales (the latter commanded by Lowrance) moved forward farther to the left and came up against the line held by Hays.

At this time, the troops of Doubleday's division rendered timely aid. The path followed by Pickett's division brought it in on the right of Stannard's brigade, and Stannard then advanced the 13th and 16th Vermont to the front, where they faced to the right and fired volley after volley into Pickett's right flank as it passed. Gates' two regiments of Rowley's brigade also added their fire to that of the Vermont regiments.

Armistead with a hundred or so men broke through the Union line at the Angle and forced Webb's men back, but with help from Hall, who came up with two regiments, and Harrow, with four regiments, they drove the enemy back and down the slope of the ridge, leaving Armistead dead among the guns. Garnett was also killed and Kemper was wounded in the attack. The brigades of Lane and Lowrance fared no better in their attack on Hays, and a short time later the survivors the of Confederate assault were streaming back across the fields toward Seminary Ridge, and the fighting on that part of the line was over.

Hancock and Gibbon were wounded during the attack on Cemetery Ridge, but Hancock remained on the field until the enemy had been repulsed. He then turned over the command of Second Corps to Caldwell and went to the rear. That evening William Hays (not to be confused with Alexander Hays) was assigned command of Second Corps, and Caldwell returned to the command of his division. Harrow assumed command of Gibbon's Second Division, and Francis E. Heath took charge of Harrow's brigade. Stannard was also wounded, and Francis V. Randall assumed command of the Vermont Brigade. The same order that assigned William Hays to the command of Second Corps also placed Newton in command of the entire line between Howard's Eleventh Corps on Cemetery Hill and Sykes' Fifth Corps near Little Round Top. Newton, however, retained his command of First Corps.

Cavalry Battle of July 3, 1863. David McM. Gregg, with John B. McIntosh's First Brigade and J. Irvin Gregg's Second Brigade of his Second Cavalry Division, arrived near Gettysburg about noon July 2, 1863 and moved to a position on the Hanover Road to the east of Benner's Hill, on the extreme right of the Union line. During the evening, Gregg's brigades were in contact with troops of James A. Walker's infantry brigade of Edward Johnson's division of Ewell's corps.

After his engagement with Judson Kilpatrick's cavalry at Hanover, Pennsylvania June 30, 1863, Stuart moved on northward with his cavalry by way of Jefferson and Dover, and on July 1, 1863 arrived near Carlisle. While there, he received orders from Lee to join the army at Gettysburg, and he promptly marched in that direction. Shortly after noon July 2, 1863, he passed through Hunterstown with the brigades of William H. F. Lee (commanded by John R. Chambliss), Fitzhugh Lee, and Wade Hampton, and he then halted on Brinkerhoff's Ridge, about two miles northeast of Gettysburg. Stuart then proceeded on to Gettysburg to report to Lee.

Lee's instructions to Stuart on this occasion are not definitely known, but from the events of the next twenty-four hours it is probable that he directed him to move into the rear area of the Army of the Potomac and create whatever disorder that he could while Lee attacked the center of Meade's line on Cemetery Ridge. Whatever his instructions, Stuart marched eastward on the York Road July 3, 1863 with his cavalry division and Albert G. Jenkins' Independent Cavalry Brigade, which had accompanied Ewell's corps into Pennsylvania. About two and a half miles east of Gettysburg he turned south and took position about midway between the York Road and the Hanover Road on a long ridge, known as the Cress Ridge, that ran up from the south. The northern end of the ridge was wooded, and behind these woods he placed the brigades of Fitzhugh Lee, Hampton, and Chambliss, and he sent forward as skirmishers Jenkins' dismounted troopers. Jenkins had been wounded the day before, and Milton J. Ferguson was in command of his brigade.

On the morning of July 3, 1863, as Stuart was

moving into position, the two brigades of Gregg's Second Cavalry Division were formed on a long skirmish line that extended from Wolf's Hill to the Hanover Road. George A. Custer's Second Brigade of Kilpatrick's Third Cavalry Division was behind Gregg's line at the crossing of the Low Dutch Road (or Salem Church Road) and the Hanover Road, about three miles east of Gettysburg. That morning, Pleasonton ordered Gregg to send Custer's brigade back to Kilpatrick, and in obedience to this order Gregg sent McIntosh's brigade of his own division back to relieve Custer. This left only J. Irvin Gregg's brigade to hold the Wolf's Hill-Hanover Road line.

Gregg accompanied McIntosh to his new position, and upon arriving there, he learned that a strong force of enemy cavalry was in position near the Rummel house on Cress Ridge. Realizing that an engagement was imminent, Gregg, on his own responsibility, directed Custer to remain with him. Thus, in front of Stuart were the two cavalry brigades of Custer and McIntosh, and with them were Alexander C. M. Pennington's Battery M, 2nd United States Artillery of James M. Robertson's First Brigade of Horse Artillery and Alanson M. Randol's Battery E, 1st United States Artillery of John C. Tidball's Second Brigade of the Horse Artillery.

When McIntosh arrived at Custer's position, he turned to the north from the Hanover Road on which he had been riding and formed his brigade along and to the west of the Low Dutch Road in the vicinity of the Lott house. Custer's brigade was to his left, near the Hanover Road. The cavalry action that was to be fought that afternoon took place in the open fields north of the Hanover Road and between the Rummel and Lott farms, which were about three-fourths of a mile apart.

Around 2:00 P.M., McIntosh advanced three regiments into the fields to a position along a branch of Little's Run. McIntosh's regiments, fighting dismounted, opened a firefight in the center of the field, during which reinforcements were sent in and the lines were extended. A short time later, the 1st Virginia Cavalry of Fitzhugh Lee's brigade advanced, but it was soon stopped by the 7th Michigan of Custer's brigade, which was fighting dismounted behind a stone wall. The 1st North Carolina and the Jeff Davis Legion of Hampton's brigade then came up to reinforce the 1st Virginia, and together they attacked and scattered the 7th Michigan. Soon, however, they in turn were driven back by flanking attacks and by artillery fire.

The main attack began at about 3:00 P.M., just as the enemy cannonade against Cemetery Ridge was ending. At that time Stuart advanced southward with most of his force between the Low Dutch Road and Little's Run, a stream about a mile to the west. His column first came under artillery fire, and was then attacked in front by the 1st Michigan Cavalry, led by Custer in person, and on both flanks by troopers of both Custer's and McIntosh's brigades. A wild melee followed in which neither side gained any decided advantage. Finally, as if by mutual consent, both sides retired to their original positions. The skirmishers and artillery continued to fire for some time, but the battle was over. While Gregg could not claim a victory, he did accomplish his primary purpose of preventing Stuart from advancing into the rear area of the army.

Soon after the engagement ended, Custer departed with his brigade to rejoin Kilpatrick, who was covering the Union left flank near Big Round Top with Elon J. Farnsworth's brigade.

Kilpatrick's Attack (Farnsworth's Charge), July 3, 1863. Judson Kilpatrick's Third Cavalry Division arrived near Gettysburg about 2:00 P.M. July 2, 1863, and was then sent to the York Road to protect the right flank of the army. His command was attacked that evening near Hunterstown by Stuart's cavalry, but the latter finally withdrew, and Kilpatrick bivouacked for the night. At 11:00 P.M., however, he was ordered to Two Taverns, and he arrived there about daylight July 3, 1863. Custer's brigade was placed two to three miles to the north, near the place where it was engaged in the cavalry battle with Stuart that afternoon (see above).

At 8:00 A.M. Kilpatrick received orders from Pleasonton to move on with his division from Two Taverns to the left of the Union line and take position beyond and to the south of Big Round Top. There he was to be joined by Wesley Merritt's Reserve Brigade of Buford's First Cavalry Division, and together they were to attack the right and rear of the enemy line, which was occupied by troops of Evander McIver Law's Confederate division (Hood's division) of Longstreet's corps. Kilpatrick marched with only Farnsworth's First Brigade of his division, because Custer's brigade was detained by Gregg that day, and he arrived near Big Round Top about 1:00 P.M. Farnsworth was soon engaged with the enemy skirmishers.

Merritt left his bivouac at Emmitsburg about noon July 3, 1863, and marched on the Emmitsburg Road toward Gettysburg. He arrived on the left of Farnsworth about 3:00 P.M., and together they advanced and drove the enemy back about a mile, with Merritt advancing on the road.

At 5:30 P.M. Kilpatrick ordered Farnsworth to take half of his brigade and charge against the center of Law's line. Farnsworth, with the 1st Vermont Cavalry and the 1st West Virginia Cavalry, quickly drove through the enemy skirmish line and penetrated well into the rear of Law's position. During their wild ride, however, the regiments were exposed almost constantly to the fire of the Confederate infantry, and finally, after making a complete circuit of the field, most of the troopers returned, but without Farnsworth. He was killed during the ride, and the next day Nathaniel P. Richmond was assigned command of his brigade.

Organization of the Army of the Potomac at Gettysburg, July 1–3, 1863.

ARMY OF THE POTOMAC
George G. Meade

Command of the Provost Marshal General, Marsena R. Patrick
Artillery, Henry J. Hunt
Engineer Brigade, Henry W. Benham

FIRST CORPS, Abner Doubleday, to July 2, 1863
John Newton

First Division, James S. Wadsworth
First Brigade, Solomon Meredith, to July 1, 1863, injured
William W. Robinson
Second Brigade, Lysander Cutler

Note. John F. Reynolds, commander of First Corps, was killed July 1, 1863 while in command of the Left Wing of the army. Doubleday commanded the corps during the fighting July 1, 1863, and he was relieved by Newton July 2, 1863 (assigned July 1, 1863).

Second Division, John C. Robinson
First Brigade, Gabriel R. Paul, July 1, 1863, wounded
Samuel H. Leonard, July 1, 1863, wounded

Adrian R. Root, July 1, 1863, wounded
Richard Coulter, evening of July 1, 1863, wounded
Peter Lyle
Richard Coulter
Second Brigade, Henry Baxter

Note. Coulter was wounded July 3, 1863, but remained with his brigade and soon resumed command. Meantime, Lyle was temporarily in charge of the brigade.

Third Division, Thomas A. Rowley, July 1, 1863
Abner Doubleday
First Brigade, Chapman Biddle, from June 30, 1863 to July 2, 1863
Thomas A. Rowley
Chapman Biddle
Second Brigade, Roy Stone, to July 1, 1863, wounded
Langhorne Wister, July 1, 1863, wounded
Edmund L. Dana
Third Brigade, George J. Stannard, to July 3, 1863, wounded
Francis V. Randall

Note. Stannard's brigade marched from the Defenses of Washington June 25, 1863, and joined First Corps on the battlefield during the evening of July 1, 1863. Stannard reported to Doubleday the next morning, and his brigade was assigned to Third Division as Third Brigade.

Artillery Brigade, Charles S. Wainwright
2nd Battery (B), Maine Light Artillery, James A. Hall
5th Battery (E), Maine Light Artillery, Greenleaf T. Stevens, to July 2, 1863, wounded
Edward N. Whittier
Battery L, 1st New York Light Artillery, Gilbert H. Reynolds, to July 1, 1863, wounded
George Breck
Battery B, 1st Pennsylvania Light Artillery, James H. Cooper
Battery B, 4th United States Artillery, James Stewart

SECOND CORPS, Winfield S. Hancock
John Gibbon, temporarily July 1, 1863
Winfield S. Hancock, to evening of July 3, 1863, wounded
John C. Caldwell, temporarily evening of July 3, 1863
William Hays

First Division, John C. Caldwell
First Brigade, Edward E. Cross, to evening of July 2, 1863, mortally wounded.
H. Boyd McKeen
Second Brigade, Patrick Kelly
Third Brigade, Samuel K. Zook, to evening of July 2, 1863, mortally wounded
Fourth Brigade, John R. Brooke

Second Division, John Gibbon, to evening of July 3, 1863, wounded
William Harrow
First Brigade, William Harrow, to evening of July 3, 1863
Francis E. Heath
Second Brigade, Alexander S. Webb
Third Brigade, Norman J. Hall

Third Division, Alexander Hays
First Brigade, Samuel S. Carroll
Second Brigade, Thomas A. Smyth, to July 3, 1863, wounded
Theodore G. Ellis, temporarily July 3, 1863
Francis E. Pierce
Third Brigade, George L. Willard, to July 2, 1863, killed
Eliakim Sherrill, to July 3, 1863, killed
James M. Bull

Note. Smyth, commanding Second Brigade, was wounded during the cannonade July 3, 1863, and the command of the brigade devolved on the senior officer, Francis E. Pierce of the 108th New York Regiment. This regiment was far to the right, however, and Ellis commanded the brigade during the assault on Cemetery Ridge that afternoon and until Pierce arrived at headquarters to assume command.

Artillery Brigade, John G. Hazard
Battery B, 1st New York Light Artillery, Albert S. Sheldon, to July 3, 1863, wounded
James McKay Rorty, July 3, 1863, killed
Robert E. Rogers
Battery A, 1st Rhode Island Light Artillery, William A. Arnold
Battery B, 1st Rhode Island Light Artillery, T. Frederick Brown, to evening July 2, 1863, wounded
Walter S. Perrin
Battery I, 1st United States Artillery, George A. Woodruff, to afternoon of July 3, 1863, mortally wounded
Tully McCrea
Battery A, 4th United States Artillery, Alonzo H. Cushing, to afternoon of July 3, 1863, killed
Frederick Fuger

THIRD CORPS, Daniel E. Sickles, to evening of July 2, 1863, wounded
David B. Birney

First Division, David B. Birney, to July 2, 1863
J. H. Hobart Ward
First Brigade, Charles K. Graham, to July 2, 1863, wounded and captured
Andrew H. Tippin

Second Brigade, J. H. Hobart Ward, to July 2, 1863
Hiram Berdan
Third Brigade, P. Regis De Trobriand

Second Division, Andrew A. Humphreys
First Brigade, Joseph B. Carr
Second Brigade, Jacob B. Sweitzer
Third Brigade, George C. Burling

Artillery Brigade, George E. Randolph, to July 2, 1863, wounded
A. Judson Clark
2nd Battery, New Jersey Light Artillery, A. Judson Clark, to July 2, 1863
Robert Sims
Battery D, 1st New York Light Artillery, George B. Winslow
4th Battery, New York Light Artillery, James E. Smith
Battery E, 1st Rhode Island Light Artillery, John K. Bucklyn, to evening of July 2, 1863, wounded
Benjamin Freeborn
Battery K, 4th United States Artillery, Francis W. Seely, to evening of July 2, 1863, wounded
Robert James

FIFTH CORPS, George Sykes

First Division, James Barnes
First Brigade, William S. Tilton
Second Brigade, Jacob B. Sweitzer
Third Brigade, Strong Vincent, to July 2, 1863, mortally wounded
James C. Rice

Second Division, Romeyn B. Ayres
First Brigade, Hannibal Day
Second Brigade, Sidney Burbank
Third Brigade, Stephen H. Weed, to July 2, 1863, mortally wounded
Kenner Garrard

Third Division, Samuel W. Crawford
First Brigade, William McCandless
Third Brigade, Joseph W. Fisher

Note 1. Crawford's division joined Fifth Corps from Washington June 28, 1863, and was assigned to the corps as Third Division.
Note 2. Second Brigade of the division was left in the Department of Washington.

Artillery Brigade, Augustus P. Martin
3rd Battery (C), Massachusetts Light Artillery, Aaron F. Walcott
Battery C, 1st New York Light Artillery, Almont Barnes

Battery L, 1st Ohio Light Artillery, Frank C. Gibbs
Battery D, 5th United States Artillery, Charles E. Hazlett, to July 3, 1863, killed
Benjamin F. Rittenhouse
Battery I, 5th United States Artillery, Malbone F. Watson, to July 2, 1863, wounded
Charles C. MacConnell

SIXTH CORPS, John Sedgwick

First Division, Horatio G. Wright
First Brigade, Alfred T. A. Torbert
Second Brigade, Joseph J. Bartlett
Third Brigade, David A. Russell

Note 1. On the evening of July 1, 1863, Emory Upton temporarily relieved Bartlett in command of Second Brigade, but Bartlett resumed command of the brigade as it marched toward Little Round Top the next afternoon.
Note 2. Bartlett also commanded Third Brigade, Third Division, as well as his own Second Brigade, First Division, July 3, 1863.

Second Division, Albion P. Howe
Second Brigade, Lewis A. Grant
Third Brigade, Thomas H. Neill

Note. There was no First Brigade in Second Division.

Third Division, John Newton, to July 2, 1863
Frank Wheaton
First Brigade, Alexander Shaler
Second Brigade, Henry L. Eustis
Third Brigade, Frank Wheaton, to July 2, 1863
David J. Nevin

Note. Newton was assigned command of First Corps July 2, 1863.

Artillery Brigade, Charles H. Tompkins
1st Battery (A), Massachusetts Light Artillery, William H. McCartney
1st Battery, New York Light Artillery, Andrew Cowan
3rd Battery, New York Light Artillery, William A. Harn
Battery C, 1st Rhode Island Light Artillery, Richard Waterman
Battery G, 1st Rhode Island Light Artillery, George W. Adams
Battery D, 2nd United States Artillery, Edward B. Williston
Battery G, 2nd United States Artillery, John H. Butler
Battery F, 5th United States Artillery, Leonard Martin

ELEVENTH CORPS, Oliver O. Howard
Carl Schurz
Oliver O. Howard

First Division, Francis C. Barlow, to afternoon of July 1, 1863, wounded
Adelbert Ames
First Brigade, Leopold Von Gilsa
Second Brigade, Adelbert Ames, to July 1, 1863
Andrew L. Harris

Second Division, Adolph Von Steinwehr
First Brigade, Charles R. Coster
Second Brigade, Orland Smith

Third Division, Carl Schurz
First Brigade, Alexander Schimmelfennig
Second Brigade, Wladimir Krzyzanowski

Note. During the period between the death of John F. Reynolds and the arrival of Winfield S. Hancock on the afternoon of July 1, 1863, all Federal troops near Gettysburg were under the command of Howard, and Schurz was in temporary command of Eleventh Corps. Also during this time, Schimmelfennig commanded Third Division and Von Amsberg commanded First Brigade, Third Division. Schimmelfennig was forced to hide in Gettysburg after the collapse of Eleventh Corps July 1, 1863, and he was unable to rejoin his command until July 4, 1863.

Artillery Brigade, Thomas W. Osborn
Battery I, 1st New York Light Artillery, Michael Wiedrich
13th Battery, New York Light Artillery, William Wheeler
Battery I, 1st Ohio Light Artillery, Hubert Dilger
Battery K, 1st Ohio Light Artillery, Lewis Heckman
Battery G, 4th United States Artillery, Bayard Wilkeson, to July 1, 1863, mortally wounded
Eugene A. Bancroft

TWELFTH CORPS, Henry W. Slocum
Alpheus S. Williams

First Division, Alpheus S. Williams
Thomas H. Ruger
First Brigade, Archibald L. McDougall
Third Brigade, Thomas H. Ruger
Silas Colgrove

Note 1. Henry W. Slocum, the permanent commander of Twelfth Corps, was in command of the right wing of the army July 1–4, 1863, and Williams was in temporary command of Twelfth Corps during the same period. While Williams was in command of Twelfth Corps, Ruger was in temporary command of First Division and Colgrove of Third Brigade, First Division.
Note 2. There was no Second Brigade, First Division during the Battle of Gettysburg, although Henry H. Lockwood's Provisional Brigade is sometimes listed as such. This brigade reported to First Division, Twelfth

Corps from Baltimore, Middle Department about 8:00 A.M. July 2, 1863, but it was unassigned until July 5, 1863, and it was then attached to First Division as Second Brigade.

Second Division, John W. Geary
First Brigade, Charles Candy
Second Brigade, George A. Cobham, Jr.
Thomas L. Kane
George A. Cobham, Jr.

Note. Kane joined the army and Twelfth Corps in an ambulance at 6:00 A.M. July 2, 1863, and assumed command of Second Brigade. He was ill at the time, however, and soon was forced to turn over the command again to Cobham. Kane remained on the field, and perhaps for this reason, in some reports, Second Brigade is referred to as Kane's brigade.

Artillery Brigade, Edward D. Muhlenberg
Battery M, 1st New York Light Artillery, Charles E. Winegar
Battery E, Pennsylvania Light Artillery, Charles A. Atwell
Battery F, 4th United States Artillery, Sylvanus T. Rugg
Battery K, 5th United States Artillery, David H. Kinzie

CAVALRY CORPS, Alfred Pleasonton

First Cavalry Division, John Buford
First Brigade, William Gamble
Second Brigade, Thomas C. Devin
Reserve Brigade, Wesley Merritt

Second Cavalry Division, David McM. Gregg
First Brigade, John B. McIntosh
Second Brigade, Pennock Huey
Third Brigade, J. Irvin Gregg

Note. Second Brigade was at Westminster during the battle and was not engaged.

Third Cavalry Division, Judson Kilpatrick
First Brigade, Elon J. Farnsworth, to July 3, 1863, killed
Nathaniel P. Richmond
Second Brigade, George A. Custer

Horse Artillery
First Brigade, James M. Robertson
9th Michigan Battery, Jabez J. Daniels
6th New York Battery, Joseph W. Martin
Batteries B and L, 2nd United States Artillery, Edward Heaton
Battery M, 2nd United States Artillery, Alexander C. M. Pennington, Jr.

Battery E, 4th United States Artillery, Samuel S. Elder
Second Brigade, John C. Tidball
Batteries E and G, 1st United States Artillery, Alanson M. Randol
Battery K, 1st United States Artillery, William M. Graham
Battery A, 2nd United States Artillery, John F. Calef
Battery C, 3rd United States Artillery, William D. Fuller

Note. Fuller's battery was with Huey's cavalry brigade at Westminster and was not engaged.

ARTILLERY RESERVE, Robert O. Tyler
James M. Robertson

First Regular Brigade, Dunbar R. Ransom
Battery H, 1st United States Artillery, Chandler P. Eakin, to July 2, 1863, wounded
Philip D. Mason
Batteries F and K, 3rd United States Artillery, John G. Turnbull
Battery C, 4th United States Artillery, Evan Thomas
Battery C, 5th United States Artillery, Gulian V. Weir

First Volunteer Brigade, Freeman McGilvery
5th Battery (E), Massachusetts Light Artillery, Charles A. Phillips
9th Battery, Massachusetts Light Artillery, John Bigelow, to July 2, 1863, wounded
Richard S. Milton
15th Battery, New York Light Artillery, Patrick Hart
Batteries C and F, Pennsylvania Light Artillery, James Thompson

Note. The 10th New York Battery was attached to Phillips' 5th Battery (E).

Second Volunteer Brigade, Elijah D. Taft
Battery B, 1st Connecticut Heavy Artillery, Albert F. Brooker
Battery M, 1st Connecticut Heavy Artillery, Franklin A. Pratt
2nd Battery, Connecticut Light Artillery, John W. Sterling
5th Battery, New York Light Artillery, Elijah D. Taft

Third Volunteer Brigade, James F. Huntington
1st Battery, New Hampshire Light Artillery, Frederick M. Edgell
Battery H, 1st Ohio Light Artillery, George W. Norton
Batteries F and G, Pennsylvania Light Artillery, R. Bruce Ricketts
Battery C, West Virginia Light Artillery, Wallace Hill

Fourth Volunteer Brigade, Robert H. Fitzhugh
  6th Battery (F), Maine Light Artillery, Edwin B. Dow
  Battery A, Maryland Light Artillery, James H. Rigby
  1st Battery, New Jersey Light Artillery, Augustin N. Parsons
  Battery G, 1st New York Light Artillery, Nelson Ames
  Battery K, 1st New York Light Artillery, Robert H. Fitzhugh

Note. The 11th New York Battery was attached to Fitzhugh's Battery K.

GETTYSBURG CAMPAIGN, PART III
PURSUIT OF LEE

FROM GETTYSBURG TO FALLING WATERS
JULY 5–14, 1863

The fighting at Gettysburg was not renewed July 4, 1863, and the two armies remained quietly in essentially the same positions that they had occupied the day before. The Federal cavalry, however, was ordered to march toward the rear of Lee's army to strike at its communications and generally to create difficulties if Lee should decide to retreat. The movements of the cavalry divisions were as follows: That day, John Buford's First Cavalry Division marched toward Frederick. The brigades of David McM. Gregg's Second Cavalry Division were separated at this time, and they were not reassembled until July 16, 1863 at Shepherdstown, West Virginia. John B. McIntosh's First Brigade was directed to remain at Gettysburg; J. Irvin Gregg's Third Brigade was sent to Hunterstown; and Pennock Huey's Second Brigade was temporarily assigned to Judson Kilpatrick's Third Cavalry Division. Kilpatrick's division, accompanied by Huey's brigade of Gregg's division, moved to Monterey, Pennsylvania, on the road to Waynesboro. Kilpatrick's division and Huey's brigade were engaged at Monterey Gap that evening and night, and at about 3:00 A.M. July 5, 1863, they made a successful attack on the trains of Richard S. Ewell's Second Corps.

Other than the movements described above, Meade made no other changes in the disposition of his troops July 4, 1863. Observations along his front during the day gave no indication of what Lee planned to do, and until Meade could learn more of Lee's intentions, he was reluctant to order any major movements for the army. He did, however, direct Gouverneur K. Warren, his chief of engineers, to take one division of Sixth Corps and move out early the next morning on a reconnaissance to learn what he could of the positions and movements of the enemy.

Before Warren started out, however, the Army of Northern Virginia began its retreat toward Virginia. After dark July 4, 1863, in a pouring rain, Ambrose P. Hill's Third Corps marched out on the Fairfield Road toward Hagerstown and Williamsport. James Longstreet's First Corps followed Hill, and Richard S. Ewell's Second Corps brought up the rear.

Early on the morning of July 5, 1863, a signal officer reported that positions held by the enemy the day before had been vacated, and from this information Meade concluded that Lee had decided to retreat. He promptly issued orders for the pursuit. His general plan was for the infantry, preceded by the cavalry, to advance on a broad front toward Middletown, Maryland, and then to make a wide wheel to the right and move forward toward the line of the Hagerstown-Williamsport Road. In this way he hoped to intercept Lee's retreating columns.

Meade also made use of William H. French's command, which was on the left of the army at Frederick, Maryland. He directed French to send a brigade to reoccupy Harper's Ferry and another brigade to occupy and hold Turner's Gap in South Mountain. Henry W. Halleck also ordered the other two brigades of French's Division, then at Tennallytown under the command of Washington L. Elliott, to move to Frederick.

To facilitate the advance of the Army of the Potomac, Meade divided the corps into three groups or wings and ordered them to move by different routes to Middletown, where they were to assemble about July 7, 1863. John Newton's First Corps, David B. Birney's Third Corps, and John Sedgwick's Sixth Corps, all under the direction of Sedgwick, were to march on the right of the army on the direct road through Emmitsburg, Mechanicstown (present-day Thurmont), Lewistown, and Hamburg to Middletown. George Sykes' Fifth Corps and Oliver O. Howard's Eleventh Corps, both under Howard, were to move on the left of the army on the Taneytown Road by way of Emmitsburg, Creagerstown, Utica, and High Knob Pass to Middletown. William Hays' Second Corps and Henry W. Slocum's Twelfth Corps, both commanded by Slocum, were to move by way of Taneytown, Middleburg, and Frederick to Middletown. Robert O. Tyler was to march with the Artillery Reserve by way of Taneytown and Middleburg.

Commissary and quartermaster's depots and supplies, which at the time of the battle were located at Westminster, at the railhead of the Hampshire Railroad from Baltimore, were to be moved to Frederick, where a new base for the army was to be established on the Baltimore and Ohio Railroad.

With Lee's departure from Gettysburg, Warren's planned reconnaissance for the morning of July 5, 1863 was changed to a pursuit, and about noon Warren advanced on the Fairfield Road with Sedgwick's entire Sixth Corps. During the late afternoon, Alfred T. A. Torbert's First Brigade of Horatio G. Wright's First Division—Sedgwick's leading division—came up to Ewell's rear guard near Fairfield, Pennsylvania. Warren then discovered that the enemy was in force beyond the town, and when he reported this to Meade, the latter halted the movement of the army toward Middletown.

The corps that had already started the march that morning spent the night as follows: Second Corps at Two Taverns, Fifth Corps on the Emmitsburg Road at Marsh Creek, Eleventh Corps on the Taneytown Road at Rock Creek, and Twelfth Corps at Littlestown. First Corps and Third Corps, which were under Sedgwick's orders, were held near Gettysburg to support Sixth Corps at Fairfield if they were needed.

The movements of the cavalry July 5, 1863 were as follows: Buford's division reached Frederick; Kilpatrick's division, with Huey's brigade of Gregg's division, marched through Smithsburg to Boonsboro; McIntosh's brigade of Gregg's division moved to Emmitsburg; and J. Irvin Gregg's brigade of David McM. Gregg's division arrived at Greenwood. The Artillery Reserve was at Littlestown.

While the above movements were in progress,

troops of Darius N. Couch's Department of the Susquehanna were advancing from the Susquehanna to cooperate with Meade. Before the Army of the Potomac crossed the Potomac River into Maryland, Joseph Hooker, commander of the army, was authorized to assume control of any troops within his sphere of operations. At that time, this order applied to the troops of Robert C. Schenck's Middle Department, Eighth Corps. When Meade assumed command of the army June 28, 1863, he was informed by Halleck that he had an authority similar to that of Hooker and that this was to include also the command and the direction of the movements of all troops in the Department of the Susquehanna.

About 10:00 P.M. July 3, 1863, Meade informed Couch that he did not expect Lee to attack again at Gettysburg, and that if Lee retreated, Couch was to pursue along the Cumberland Valley. The troops of Couch's department that were available to cooperate with Meade consisted of William F. Smith's First Division, Department of the Susquehanna, which was composed largely of regiments of the New York National Guard and of the Pennsylvania Militia, totaling about 9,000 men. In addition, there were about 2,000 cavalry and infantry at Bloody Run (present-day Everett) in Bedford County, Pennsylvania, which consisted largely of troops of Robert H. Milroy's old Second Division, Eighth Corps that had been destroyed at Winchester, Virginia by Ewell's corps at the beginning of the Gettysburg Campaign. In addition there was one regiment of Pennsylvania Militia at Bloody Run. The troops at Bloody Run were under the command of Lewis B. Pierce, who had succeeded Milroy June 28, 1863. There were other militia regiments forming in Pennsylvania, and there were also some New York regiments along the Susquehanna River. Some of these were later organized into a Second Division, Department of the Susquehanna under Napoleon J. T. Dana. For details of the organization of these forces, see Department of the Susquehanna, Troops and Operations in the Department of the Susquehanna.

On June 20, 1863, when Ewell began to withdraw toward Gettysburg from his advanced positions at York and Carlisle, Pennsylvania, Smith's First Division, Department of the Susquehanna followed from near Harrisburg and July 1, 1863 occupied Carlisle. On July 4, 1863, after receiving Meade's message of the night before, Couch ordered Smith to advance along the Cumberland Valley in pursuit of Lee. Smith's division passed through Mount Holly and Pine Grove and arrived at Newman's Pass in South Mountain July 6, 1863.

July 3, 1863, Couch ordered Pierce to move from Bloody Run with his command to the passes near McConnellsburg, and then to push up as close as possible to Mercersburg and Chambersburg. Chambersburg was across the mountains, about fifty miles east of Bloody Run, and there Pierce would be in position to harass the rear of Lee's army as it marched toward the Potomac. July 5, 1863, Pierce's cavalry captured about 100 wagons and 500 prisoners near Greencastle, and late on the evening of July 6, 1863, it arrived at Loudon. Pierce then remained in the area until July 12, 1863.

Only the cavalry of the Army of the Potomac advanced July 6, 1863, but it was a busy day for the divisions of Buford and Kilpatrick. Buford left Frederick at 4:00 A.M. and marched toward Williamsport, where he hoped to destroy a wagon train that was protected by John Imboden with his mounted force and some artillery. Buford arrived near Williamsport at 5:00 that afternoon, but was prevented by Imboden from reaching the town. Kilpatrick's division, and also Huey's brigade, arrived at Hagerstown from Boonsboro and, after some fighting, drove the cavalry brigades of John R. Chambliss and Beverly Robertson from the town. Later, however, Kilpatrick was forced to retire when Stuart's cavalry with infantry supports arrived. Kilpatrick then joined Buford at Williamsport, but both divisions were forced to withdraw when enemy cavalry and infantry approached on Kilpatrick's rear. That night the two divisions bivouacked at Jones' Cross Roads (present-day Lappans), at the intersection of the Hagerstown-Sharpsburg Turnpike and the road that ran from Williamsport through Boonsboro to Frederick. During July 6, 1863, Gregg's two cavalry brigades that had been left at the rear of the army also advanced. McIntosh's brigade joined Sedgwick at Fairfield, and J. Irvin Gregg's brigade moved from Greenwood to Marion, Pennsylvania. July 7, 1863, Buford and Kilpatrick moved back to Boonsboro, and for the next two days, despite almost constant fighting with Stuart's cavalry, they

continued to hold their ground until the infantry of the Army of the Potomac arrived.

July 6, 1863, Meade ordered the formation of a "Light Division" under the command of Thomas H. Neill. It consisted of Neill's Third Brigade of Albion P. Howe's Second Division, Sixth Corps; McIntosh's cavalry brigade; and Leonard Martin's Battery F, 5th United States Artillery. Neill's mission was to follow closely with his division and keep in direct contact with Lee's retreating army, and to send back constant information about its movements.

The rest of Sixth Corps remained in position at Fairfield until dark July 6, 1863, and it then marched to Emmitsburg, where it joined First Corps. Third Corps arrived from Gettysburg the next day, and thereafter these three corps, conforming to the marching orders of July 5, 1863, moved toward Middletown.

During the afternoon of July 6, 1863 and the following morning, the Army of Northern Virginia arrived at Hagerstown.

During the evening of July 6, 1863, Meade issued orders for the army to resume its march toward Middletown the next morning, and by 11:00 P.M. July 7, 1863, five of the seven corps were on or along the Catoctin Mountains as follows: Third Corps was at Mechanicstown (present-day Thurmont); Fifth Corps was east of the mountains at Utica, north of Frederick and on the Monocacy River; First Corps and Sixth Corps were in the mountain passes near Hamburg; and Eleventh Corps was west of the mountains at Middletown. Second Corps, which was bringing up the rear, was at Taneytown; Twelfth Corps was at Walkerville; the Artillery Reserve was at Woodsboro; and Neill's Light Division was at Waynesboro. Headquarters of the army was at Frederick.

July 8, 1863, First Corps and Eleventh Corps reached Turner's Gap in South Mountain, and from there Howard sent Carl Schurz's Third Division, Eleventh Corps on to Boonsboro; Third Corps arrived near Frederick; Fifth Corps and Sixth Corps reached Middletown; Twelfth Corps arrived at Jefferson; and Second Corps and the Artillery Reserve arrived at Middletown. Headquarters of the army moved to Middletown.

By July 9, 1863, the Army of the Potomac was

concentrated on a line about four miles in length that extended from Rohrersville, on the left, along South Mountain, to Boonsboro on the right. Second Corps and Twelfth Corps were at Rohrersville; Third Corps was at Fox's Gap in South Mountain; First Corps and Eleventh Corps were at Turner's Gap; Schurz's division of Eleventh Corps was at Boonsboro; and Fifth Corps and Sixth Corps were near Boonsboro. Neill's Light Division was at Waynesboro; J. Irvin Gregg's cavalry brigade had arrived at Middletown, in the rear of the army; and Meade's headquarters was at Turner's Gap.

During the period July 10–12, 1863, the army advanced to a line roughly parallel to the Hagerstown-Sharpsburg Pike. This line began on Antietam Creek on the right, just north of Funkstown, and extended southward to Fair Play on the left. First Corps, Sixth Corps, and Eleventh Corps advanced to Benevola (Beaver Creek) July 10, 1863, and then on to Funkstown two days later; John R. Kenly's Maryland Brigade of French's Division arrived from Maryland Heights and joined First Corps at Beaver Creek July 10, 1863; and Neill's brigade rejoined Sixth Corps at Funkstown July 12, 1863. The other corps of the army moved up as follows: Second Corps marched through Tilmanton to Jones' Cross Roads July 10–11, 1863; Third Corps to Jones' Cross Roads July 10, 1863; Fifth Corps to Delaware Mills on Antietam Creek July 10, 1863; and Twelfth Corps moved to the extreme left of the line at Bakersville, about two miles south of Fair Play, July 10, 1863. The next day Twelfth Corps moved north to Fair Play.

July 10, 1863, the cavalry movements were as follows: Buford's and Kilpatrick's divisions advanced to Funkstown; J. Irvin Gregg's brigade remained at Middletown; McIntosh's brigade was at Waynesboro; and Huey's brigade was sent to Jones' Cross Roads. The next day, William Gamble's First Brigade and Thomas C. Devin's Second Brigade of Buford's division moved from Funkstown to the left of the army, to take the place of Twelfth Corps at Bakersville. Kilpatrick's division advanced to a point near Hagerstown, and the Artillery Reserve moved to Beaver Creek.

Lee evacuated Hagerstown July 12, 1863, and Kilpatrick's Third Cavalry Division and Adelbert Ames' First Division, Eleventh Corps occupied the town. The next day, Sixth Corps also moved up near Hagerstown.

While the Army of the Potomac was advancing, first to the Rohrersville-Boonsboro line July 9, 1863, and then to the line of the Hagerstown-Sharpsburg Pike July 12, 1863, the cooperating forces of the Middle Department, the Department of the Susquehanna, and the Department of West Virginia were also in motion to assist Meade in preventing Lee's army from escaping across the Potomac River. July 6, 1863, Kenly's brigade of French's Division, Eighth Corps left Frederick for Maryland Heights, which it occupied the next day. It was joined there by a brigade under Henry S. Briggs from Baltimore. Also, on July 6, 1863, the two brigades of French's Division under Elliott left Tennallytown for Frederick, where they arrived July 7, 1863. That day, French was ordered to take the brigades of Washington L. Elliott, William H. Morris, and Benjamin F. Smith and join Birney's Third Corps; and French was directed to assume command of Third Corps when he arrived. French, with the brigades of Elliott and Benjamin F. Smith, marched to Middletown July 9, 1863, and the next day these two brigades and Morris' brigade from Turner's Gap joined Third Corps on Antietam Creek. French assumed command of Third Corps that day.

William F. Smith's First Division, Department of the Susquehanna arrived at Waynesboro July 8, 1863. The day before, Charles Yates, with two regiments of the New York State Militia, occupied Carlisle, and then July 8–9, 1863, he proceeded on with his command to Shippensburg. He was joined there by three regiments of Pennsylvania Militia, and his command was then designated as Second Division, Department of the Susquehanna. Yates was at Chambersburg July 11, 1863, when Napoleon J. T. Dana arrived and assumed command of Second Division, relieving Yates.

Smith's First Division arrived at Leitersburg, Maryland July 11, 1863, and it then marched on through Cavetown and reached Hagerstown July 14, 1863. Dana also continued to advance with Second Division, and was approaching Greencastle by the time that Lee had crossed the Potomac July 14, 1863.

Pierce's command remained at Chambersburg until July 12, 1863, and then it was transferred temporarily to the Army of the Potomac. Late that day, at Chambersburg, Couch ordered Andrew T. McReynolds, who had just arrived, to assume command of that part of Pierce's force that had formerly belonged to Milroy's division of Eighth Corps, and with it to join the Army of the Potomac. McReynolds arrived at Hagerstown with his command July 14, 1863.

On July 4, 1863, Halleck ordered Benjamin F. Kelley, commander of the Department of West Virginia, to concentrate the available forces of his department at Hancock, in western Maryland, so as to be in position to attack the flank of Lee's army if it should be forced to withdraw across the Potomac River. Lee began his withdrawal that night, and Kelley was directed to move eastward. By July 8, 1863 the brigades of Jacob M. Campbell and James A. Mulligan had arrived at Hancock, and Kelley then moved them on to Fairview on North Mountain. He was joined there July 13, 1863 by William W. Averell with the cavalry of his Fourth Separate Brigade, Department of West Virginia. Kelley's command was not under Meade's orders, but it was advancing to cooperate with him under Halleck's direction. July 14, 1863, Kelley advanced from Fairview to Williamsport, but he arrived there after Lee had recrossed the Potomac.

Meantime, while these other movements were in progress, there was almost constant skirmishing, with some severe engagements, on the front of the Army of the Potomac during the period July 6–14, 1863, as James E. B. (Jeb) Stuart's cavalry struggled to keep the area east of the Hagerstown-Williamsport Pike clear of Pleasonton's cavalry. This was very important to the Army of Northern Virginia, which at that time was assembled along the pike and was unable to cross the Potomac because of high water. The pontoon bridge at Falling Waters had been destroyed July 4, 1863 by a detachment of French's cavalry, and the water at the fords was too deep for the army to cross.

To cover the road and the crossings, Lee began, on July 11, 1863, to prepare a defensive line that began on the right near Downsville, Maryland and extended generally northward along the high ground above Marsh Creek, and ended on the left at a point about a mile and a half southwest of Hagerstown. These works were occupied July 12–13, 1863, with Longstreet on the right, Hill on the center, and Ewell on the left. Most of Stuart's cavalry was massed on the left flank.

During July 13, 1863, Meade made a careful examination of Lee's position and then began preparations for an attack. At 9:00 that evening he ordered Second Corps, Fifth Corps, Sixth Corps, and Twelfth Corps to make a reconnaissance in force at 7:00 the next morning, and he instructed the rest of the army to be ready for immediate action. By this time, however, the waters of the Potomac had subsided and a pontoon bridge at Falling Waters had been completed, and at dark July 13, 1863, Lee's army began crossing the river on its return to Virginia. Longstreet and Ewell crossed at Falling Waters, and Hill crossed at the ford at Williamsport. By the next morning, all were across except the divisions of Henry Heth and James H. Lane (Pender's division). Heth's division was in position on a ridge about a mile and a half from Falling Waters, covering the crossing, and Lane's division was in rear of this line awaiting its turn to cross. Upon arrival on the south side of the Potomac, Longstreet's and Hill's corps moved to Bunker Hill, West Virginia, and Ewell's corps arrived at Darkesville the next day.

Before the time announced by Meade for the reconnaissance on the morning of July 14, 1863, both Horatio G. Wright, commanding First Division, Sixth Corps, and Howard, commanding Eleventh Corps, received information that led them to believe that the enemy troops were withdrawing from their lines. Wright immediately advanced his skirmishers, and when they found the trenches empty, he moved his division forward toward Williamsport. The other two divisions of Sixth Corps followed. At 8:30 A.M., Meade ordered a general pursuit, but by that time most of Lee's army had arrived safely in Virginia.

About noon July 14, 1863, Kilpatrick's cavalry attacked Heth's line from the north, and Buford's division struck from the east, but Heth and Lane succeeded in withdrawing with the loss of only about 500 prisoners. James J. Pettigrew, commander of the North Carolina Brigade of Heth's division, was mortally wounded during the engagement.

During July 14, 1863, First Corps, Fifth Corps, Sixth Corps, Eleventh Corps, and Alpheus S. Williams' First Division of Twelfth Corps advanced to Williamsport. Second Corps advanced to the river near Falling Waters, and Third Corps moved up to Downsville. McIntosh's and J. Irvin Gregg's brigades of Gregg's cavalry division marched from Boonsboro to Harper's Ferry.

FROM WILLIAMSPORT AND FALLING WATERS TO THE RAPPAHANNOCK RIVER
JULY 14, 1863–AUGUST 1, 1863

The Army of the Potomac remained in the vicinity of Williamsport and Falling Waters during July 14, 1863, but the next morning they started for the crossings of the Potomac River near Harper's Ferry to be ready for an advance into Virginia. Before leaving, however, Meade made some necessary arrangements to secure the line of the Potomac River. July 14, 1863, he asked Couch to occupy Hagerstown and watch the river on his front. The next day, he assigned McReynolds, commanding the troops of Milroy's former Second Division, Eighth Corps, to picket the river from Williamsport to Harper's Ferry. Also on July 15, 1863, Meade detached from the Army of the Potomac McReynolds and his command, which had just joined the army the day before, and placed him under Couch's orders. Also on July 15, 1863, Meade relieved William F. Smith's troops from the Department of the Susquehanna from further service with the Army of the Potomac and returned them to Couch's command. For the time being, however, Meade retained Couch under his direction.

Couch's forces were greatly reduced July 15, 1863, when the regiments of the New York State National Guard were ordered home during the Draft Riots in New York. The first four brigades of William F. Smith's First Division, Department of the Susquehanna were composed of these regiments, and when they departed, Smith's division was discontinued. William Brisbane, commanding the Fifth Brigade of Smith's division, was assigned as military governor of Hagerstown. Brisbane had with him his own brigade of Pennsylvania Militia, and other Pennsylvania Militia regiments were ordered to report to him. Dana's Second Division, Depart-

ment of the Susquehanna was also discontinued, and Emlen Franklin's Third Brigade of that division was placed at Williamsport and near Hagerstown. For additional information, see Department of the Susquehanna, Troops and Operations in the Department of the Susquehanna.

July 14, 1863, while the rest of the Army of the Potomac was near Williamsport, David McM. Gregg, with the brigades of McIntosh and J. Irvin Gregg of his Second Cavalry Division, marched to Harper's Ferry, and the next day he advanced, with constant skirmishing, to Shepherdstown. There, at about 1:00 P.M. July 16, 1863, Gregg was attacked by Stuart's cavalry, and severe fighting continued through the rest of the afternoon and that evening. Gregg's other brigade, commanded by Huey, arrived about 7:00 P.M. That night, however, the enemy withdrew, and the next day Gregg's division returned to Harper's Ferry.

July 16, 1863, the infantry corps of the army arrived on the Potomac as follows: First Corps, Fifth Corps, Sixth Corps, and Eleventh Corps at Berlin (present-day Brunswick); Second Corps and Third Corps near Sandy Hook; and Twelfth Corps in Pleasant Valley. Buford's cavalry division arrived at Petersburg, Maryland; and Kilpatrick's division, temporarily commanded by George A. Custer, reached Berlin. Othneil De Forest's First Brigade of Kilpatrick's division (formerly Elon J. Farnsworth's) proceeded on to Harper's Ferry.

There were several command and organizational changes in the army during its advance from Gettysburg to the Potomac at Harper's Ferry. July 8, 1863, Andrew A. Humphreys, commanding Second Division, Third Corps, was assigned as Meade's chief of staff, and Joseph B. Carr was temporarily in charge of the division until July 10, 1863, when Henry Prince assumed command. July 11, 1863, Francis B. Spinola relieved William R. Brewster in command of Second Brigade, Second Division, Third Corps when the latter departed on sick leave. William H. French, with three brigades from the Middle Department, Eighth Corps, joined the army on Antietam Creek, and July 9, 1863, he assumed command of Third Corps, relieving Birney. Birney resumed command of First Division, Third Corps, and J. H. Hobart Ward returned to the command of Second Brigade, First Division. July 10, 1863, a new

Third Division, Third Corps was organized from French's Division from Harper's Ferry (less John R. Kenly's brigade), and Washington L. Elliott was assigned command. William H. Morris' brigade was designated as First Brigade; Elliott's brigade (then commanded by J. Warren Keifer) was designated as Second Brigade; and Benjamin F. Smith's brigade was designated as Third Brigade.

Kenly's brigade joined First Corps at Beaver Creek July 10, 1863, and the next day Kenly was assigned command of Third Division, First Corps. Abner Doubleday, the former commander of Third Division, had been relieved from duty with the Army of the Potomac July 5, 1863. George J. Stannard's Third Brigade, Third Division, First Corps was transferred to Second Division, First Corps, and July 4–18, the regiments were sent home for muster out and the brigade was discontinued. Kenly's brigade, under the command of Nathan T. Dushane, was then assigned to Third Division, First Corps as Third Brigade.

While in Maryland, Eleventh Corps was reinforced with ten regiments of George H. Gordon's Second Division, Fourth Corps from White House in the Department of Virginia, and these were incorporated into First Division and Third Division. Gordon arrived, in person, at Berlin, Maryland July 17, 1863, and was assigned command of First Division, Eleventh Corps, relieving Adelbert Ames.

There were also two changes of command in the Cavalry Corps. July 9, 1863, Nathaniel P. Richmond, commanding the First Brigade of Kilpatrick's cavalry division, was sent with his regiment to Frederick, Maryland on provost duty, and Othneil De Forest assumed command of his brigade, July 15, 1863, Kilpatrick left the army on leave, and George A. Custer assumed temporary command of Third Cavalry Division.

While the Army of the Potomac was assembling along the Potomac in preparation for crossing into Virginia, Kelley's force of the Department of West Virginia became active. July 15, 1863, it moved to Indian Springs, Maryland, and two days later it crossed the Potomac at Cherry Run. It then advanced along the Baltimore and Ohio Railroad to Hedgesville, West Virginia, about seven miles north of Martinsburg. July 19, 1863, however, Kelley withdrew when Ewell's corps approached his posi-

tion, and he recrossed the river at Cherry Run. He then remained on the north bank of the Potomac for some time, about eleven miles upstream from Williamsport.

Meade began crossing the Potomac into Virginia during the evening of July 17, 1863. Custer, commanding Kilpatrick's cavalry division, crossed at Berlin and at Harper's Ferry and advanced to Purcellville. Third Corps crossed at Harper's Ferry and camped a short distance beyond the river. Fifth Corps crossed at Berlin and marched to Lovettsville. The crossing continued the next day as follows: Buford's cavalry division crossed at Berlin and halted that night at Purcellville; First Corps also crossed at Berlin and moved on that day to Waterford; and Second Corps crossed at Harper's Ferry and marched to Hillsboro. The crossing was completed July 19, 1863, as follows: Sixth Corps and Eleventh Corps crossed at Berlin, and from there Sixth Corps marched to Wheatland and Eleventh Corps to Hamilton; and Twelfth Corps crossed at Harper's Ferry and advanced to Hillsboro.

As Meade was leaving the line of the Potomac River on his march into Virginia, he made some significant changes in the command of the troops that were left to watch the river. July 19, 1863, he placed Henry H. Lockwood, who two days earlier had replaced Henry M. Naglee in command of the troops at Maryland Heights and vicinity, under the orders of Darius N. Couch, commanding the Department of the Susquehanna. The next day, he assigned William F. Smith to the command of all troops in Maryland from, and including, Harper's Ferry to Hancock. These included the Pennsylvania Militia; Lockwood's force at Harper's Ferry; McReynolds' brigade, which was along the Potomac from Sharpsburg to Williamsport; and John E. Wynkoop's cavalry force of the Department of the Susquehanna.

To clarify a matter of jurisdiction concerning Lockwood's command, on July 21, 1863, Halleck informed Couch and also Schenck, commander of the Middle Department, that both department commanders had been placed under Meade's orders, without regard for departmental lines, and that as long as military operations continued along the Potomac, all troops in the field were under Meade's orders. It was not until August 1, 1863 that Meade, then at Warrenton, Virginia, finally relinquished control of the troops left on the Potomac, and at that time Lockwood was directed to report to Schenck.

Meantime, the Army of the Potomac began its march along the Loudoun Valley toward Warrenton in three columns. First Corps and Eleventh Corps moved on the left, along the western side of the Bull Run Mountains; Fifth Corps and Sixth Corps marched generally through the center of the valley; and Second Corps, Third Corps, and Twelfth Corps advanced on the right, along the eastern base of the Blue Ridge Mountains.

Buford's cavalry division covered the front of the advancing infantry, with Gamble's First Brigade moving to Chester Gap and Merritt's Reserve Brigade to Manassas Gap, before reassembling at Barbee's Cross Roads July 23–25, 1863. Custer's division marched on the right flank through Upperville and Piedmont before moving to Amissville July 23–30, 1863. Huey's and J. Irvin Gregg's brigades of Gregg's cavalry division marched by way of Lovettsville, Leesburg, Manassas Junction, and Bristoe Station, and arrived at Warrenton Junction July 24, 1863. They were sent there to protect the Orange and Alexandria Railroad. Gregg's other brigade, under McIntosh, followed in rear of the army. It marched through Hillsboro and Purcellville to Snickersville. It remained there July 23–25, 1863, and then moved on by way of Upperville, Middleburg, Warrenton, and Warrenton Junction, and arrived at Catlett's Station July 28, 1863. The three brigades of Gregg's division were united at Warrenton the next day.

While Meade was advancing east of the Blue Ridge Mountains, Lee's army began its march toward Culpeper Court House. Longstreet left Bunker Hill July 20, 1863, and Hill followed the next day. They took the same route and arrived near Culpeper Court House July 24–25, 1863. Ewell's corps moved back to Martinsburg during the night of July 21, 1863, when Kelley's command of the Department of West Virginia was reported at Hedgesville, but when Kelley withdrew, Ewell set out for Culpeper Court House July 22, 1863. He crossed the Blue Ridge at Thornton's Gap and Fisher's Gap and joined the other corps about August 1, 1863.

Action at Manassas Gap (Wapping Heights), July 23, 1863. As Custer moved south along the east side of the Blue Ridge Mountains with his cavalry, he sent detachments into Snicker's Gap and Ashby's Gap, and they discovered that the Confederate infantry was withdrawing from the lower Shenandoah Valley. When Meade learned of this July 22, 1863, he ordered a large part of the army, with Third Corps in the lead, to march toward Manassas Gap and attempt to intercept at least a part of Lee's army as it moved south. Merritt's Reserve Brigade had occupied the gap July 21, 1863, and had skirmished there with the enemy the next day. Ward's First Division, which was the leading division of Third Corps, arrived at Linden's Station in Manassas Gap at 11:00 P.M. July 22, 1863. Between 4:00 and 5:00 the next morning Ward moved up into the gap and relieved Merritt's cavalry, which then departed for Barbee's Cross Roads. At 10:00 that morning French arrived with the divisions of Prince and Elliott.

French then ordered Ward to push on through the gap and strike Lee's passing column. All of Longstreet's corps and most of Hill's corps had already passed Front Royal by that time, but Ewell's corps was still near Winchester on the night of July 22, 1863. Ward deployed his division in line of battle and, supported by the divisions of Prince and Elliott, advanced on the enemy positions on the hills (Wapping Heights) at the western entrance to the gap. These hills were occupied by Ambrose R. Wright's brigade (then commanded by Edward J. Walker) of Richard H. Anderson's division of Hill's corps, which had been detached to hold the gap until relieved by Ewell. About 2:00 P.M., Ward attacked and drove the enemy from Wapping Heights and into the valley beyond, but there they formed a second line and halted Ward's advance. About 4:00 or 5:00 P.M. Prince came up with his division, and then Spinola attacked with his Second Brigade of the division and broke through the center of the second line. Walker was again forced to retire, this time about 600 yards to a third line. This last line was held by Robert E. Rodes' division of Ewell's corps, which had just arrived from Winchester. Spinola was wounded in the attack, and he was succeeded in command of the brigade by J. Egbert Farnum. After

Walker's division had withdrawn, Rodes' artillery checked any further advance by Third Corps. Rodes withdrew during the night and continued his march south.

Second Corps and Fifth Corps also reached Manassas Gap July 23, 1863, and Twelfth Corps came up the next day, but by that time, the Army of Northern Virginia was beyond reach. The Confederate rear guard under Early was able to withdraw from Winchester through Strasburg and New Market. When Ewell moved south, Kelley's command of the Department of West Virginia again crossed the Potomac at Cherry Run, and then advanced through Hedgesville and Martinsburg and occupied Winchester July 26, 1863.

* * * * * * * * * *

After the engagement at Manassas Gap, the Army of the Potomac resumed its march toward Warrenton, and by July 27, 1863 had reached the following positions: Fifth Corps was between Warrenton and Fayetteville; Third Corps and Sixth Corps were near Warrenton; Second Corps was near Germantown; First Division and Third Division of First Corps were near Warrenton Junction; Second Division was at Bealeton; and Eleventh Corps and Twelfth Corps were near Warrenton Junction. For additional information about the routes followed by the army during its advance, see the various corps of the Army of the Potomac.

There were no further changes in the positions occupied by the army until July 30, 1863, and then Kenly's Third Division, First Corps moved to Rappahannock Station, and Second Corps moved to Elk Run. The next day, Second Corps marched to Morrisville; Howe's Second Division, Sixth Corps moved to near Waterloo; and Twelfth Corps to Kelly's Ford.

July 30, 1863, Gregg's Second Cavalry Division relieved Custer's Third Cavalry Division at Amissville, and the next day Custer moved to Warrenton Junction to obtain supplies and to refit. Buford's First Cavalry Division was near Rappahannock Station, with pickets on the river from near Kelly's Ford to Sulfur Springs.

August 1, 1863 has been the date generally accepted as the end of the Gettysburg Campaign. At that time the Army of the Potomac was in position along the upper Rappahannock from Waterloo Crossing on the right to Ellis' Ford on the left, with forces at Warrenton, New Baltimore, Brentsville, and Morrisville. Gregg's cavalry division was on the right at Amissville; Buford's division was on the river at Rappahannock Station; and Custer's division was on the left, picketing a line from Ellis' Ford to Aquia Creek. The Army of Northern Virginia was in the vicinity of Culpeper Court House. During August 1863, the two armies watched one another while they rested and refitted.

During the march to the Rappahannock, headquarters of the Army of the Potomac were established as follows: at Beaver Creek until July 14, 1863; at Berlin (present-day Brunswick) July 15–17, 1863; at Lovettsville July 18, 1863; at Wheatland July 19, 1863; at Union July 20–21, 1863; at Upperville July 22, 1863; at Linden Station in Manassas Gap July 23, 1863; at Salem July 24, 1863; and at Warrenton July 25, 1863.

For the organization of the Army of the Potomac during this period, see Army of the Potomac, Gettysburg Campaign, The Pursuit of Lee; and see also the various corps of the Army of the Potomac.

ENGAGEMENT AT KELLY'S FORD (KELLYSVILLE), VIRGINIA MARCH 17, 1863

On February 24, 1863, Fitzhugh Lee's cavalry brigade of James E. B. (Jeb) Stuart's Cavalry Division, Army of Northern Virginia crossed the Rappahannock River at Kelly's Ford on a reconnaissance. The next day Lee drove in the Federal cavalry pickets near Hartwood Church, and then attacked the main force and drove it back some distance. Lee's advance was reported to Headquarters Army of the Potomac, and Daniel Butterfield, Joseph Hooker's chief of staff, at once ordered William W. Averell, commanding Second Cavalry Division of George Stoneman's Cavalry Corps, to advance and drive back the enemy cavalry. At the same time, Butterfield directed Alfred Pleasonton to march rapidly up the Rappahannock with his First Cavalry Division and cut off Lee from the fords. Averell's specific instructions were to destroy Lee's cavalry. Orders to that same effect were later sent by Stoneman, who was called to headquarters to help direct the operation. For reasons that are not clearly understood, Lee was able to recross the river by the way that he had come, and escape with his prisoners and captured materials.

Three weeks later, Hooker ordered Averell to cross the Rappahannock with 3,000 men and a six-gun battery of horse artillery, and destroy Fitzhugh Lee's command, which, according to prisoners, was camped at Culpeper Court House. The troops to accompany Averell on this expedition were as follows: Averell's own Second Cavalry Division, consisting of Alfred N. Duffie's First Brigade and John B. McIntosh's Second Brigade; 1st United States Cavalry and three squadrons of 5th United States Cavalry, commanded by Marcus Reno, of John Buford's Reserve Brigade of the Cavalry Corps; and Joseph W. Martin's 6th Independent Horse Battery, commanded by George Browne, Jr.

Averell left the main body of the army March 16, 1863 and marched toward Morrisville, Virginia, which was about six miles from Kelly's Ford. He sent forward Captain William F. Hart of the 4th New York Cavalry with 100 men of the 4th New York and 5th United States Cavalry to Kelly's Ford as an advance guard. Hart's orders were to cross the Rappahannock at dawn March 17, 1863 and capture the enemy pickets on the south bank. The remainder of 4th New York was to support Hart's command. During the evening of March 16, 1863, the advance guard moved forward and took position near the river. Averell with his main force reached Morrisville at 11:00 that night, after a march of thirty-six miles.

Averell left Morrisville at 4:00 A.M. March 17, 1863 with about 2,100 men, and marched toward Kelly's Ford. Enemy cavalry had been reported north of the Rappahannock in the vicinity of Brentsville, and Averell left behind the 1st Massachusetts Cavalry of Duffie's brigade and four squadrons of 4th Pennsylvania Cavalry, a total of 900 men, to guard the fords and watch for the enemy cavalry. These troops were ordered to take position on the railroad between Bealeton and Catlett's Sta-

tion, and they were not present during the engagement at Kelly's Ford later that day.

When Averell approached the river on the morning of March 17, 1863, he found that the advance guard under Hart had not been able to cross. Hart, supported by 4th New York Cavalry, had made several unsuccessful attempts, but all had been driven back. The approaches to the ford on both banks were obstructed by abatis, and the southern bank was held by a detachment of Confederate sharpshooters. The head of Averell's column arrived at the ford at 6:00 A.M., and Averell assumed the direction of operations. In a final charge by a platoon of 1st Rhode Island Cavalry under Simeon A. Brown, followed by a party of axmen who had been clearing the approaches, the Federal troopers managed to cross. Pickets were then thrown out on all roads running out from the ford. Brown was quickly followed by the remainder of 1st Rhode Island Cavalry, the 6th Ohio Cavalry, and the 4th New York Cavalry of Duffie's First Brigade; then the 3rd Pennsylvania Cavalry and 16th Pennsylvania Cavalry of McIntosh's Second Brigade; and finally, Reno with the 1st and 5th United States Cavalry of the Reserve Brigade. Averell's advance had been delayed two hours at the crossing.

At about 7:30 A.M. Fitzhugh Lee, at Culpeper Court House, learned of Averell's attempts to cross the Rappahannock, and he immediately moved with his brigade by way of Brandy Station toward Kelly's Ford.

About 10:10 A.M. Averell had completed his preparations on the south bank of the river, and he then moved forward. He marched through Kellysville, a hamlet consisting of six houses and a mill, and took the road running northwest past the Brooks house, the Brannan house, and R. Dean's shop. Duffie's brigade was in the lead, with the 6th Ohio deployed as skirmishers and 4th New York and 1st Rhode Island following as supports.

About noon, the Federal skirmishers emerged from a strip of woods about a mile from the ford, and found a squadron of Lee's cavalry posted behind a stone fence, a short distance in front of the woods. Averell then deployed 4th New York of Duffie's brigade on the right of the road and 4th Pennsylvania of McIntosh's brigade on the left, and placed a section of artillery between them. The two dismounted regiments then advanced to the edge of the woods. The 1st Rhode Island was on the road in their rear. Averell then posted the rest of his cavalry as follows: He ordered McIntosh to deploy his 3rd Pennsylvania and 16th Pennsylvania on the right of 4th New York, and supported these two regiments with three squadrons of Reno's command and a section of artillery. Reno sent one squadron up the road to support Duffie's left wing, and retained the rest of his Reserve Brigade as a general reserve.

The 4th New York and 4th Pennsylvania then advanced against the Confederate cavalrymen posted behind the stone fence, and at the same time about 100 dismounted men of 16th Pennsylvania on the right moved in on their rear. The enemy quickly fell back, and 4th New York and 4th Pennsylvania then took position behind the stone fence. Fitzhugh Lee then came up with the 3rd Virginia and 5th Virginia of his brigade, and charged the Federal line at the fence. This attack was repulsed, and Lee then moved to his left and attacked McIntosh's regiments on the right of 4th New York, near the Wheatley house (Wheatleyville). He was again unsuccessful, and his two regiments fell back.

At about this time, Duffie on the Federal left, on his own responsibility, began to lead his brigade out in front of Averell's line. The 1st Rhode Island was forming to lead the column, when Lee again advanced, this time with his 1st and 4th Virginia Cavalry. The Federals waited until the enemy was within 50 to 100 yards, and then the 1st Rhode Island charged. It was followed on the right by 6th Ohio and two squadrons of 4th Pennsylvania, and on the left by two squadrons of 5th United States Cavalry. At the same time 3rd Pennsylvania threatened the flank and rear of Lee's advancing troopers. These were then in a difficult situation, and after firing a few shots, they turned about and withdrew. The 1st Rhode Island pursued for a time, but was soon recalled. Lee withdrew about a mile and formed his brigade in a line across the road on the north side of Carter's Creek (or Carter's Run).

Averell halted for about one-half hour to straighten out his line, and he then resumed his advance. His command passed through a belt of woods about three-fourths of a mile in width, and as it emerged from the shelter of the trees, Lee again attacked. The Federal troopers held their own, and

then they in turn advanced and forced back both flanks of Lee's line. By that time it was 5:30 P.M., and Averell decided to withdraw. This he did in good order, but without accomplishing his mission.

KILPATRICK'S EXPEDITION AGAINST RICHMOND, VIRGINIA, AND CUSTER'S RAID INTO ALBEMARLE COUNTY, VIRGINIA FEBRUARY 28, 1864–MARCH 4, 1864

December 8, 1863, President Abraham Lincoln issued his Proclamation of Amnesty and Reconstruction, pardoning those who took part in the rebellion if they took an oath to the Union. Lincoln wished to have this proclamation distributed within the enemy lines, and February 12, 1864 discussed with Judson Kilpatrick the practicability of accomplishing this by means of a cavalry expedition. George G. Meade, having learned that Richmond, Virginia was practically defenseless, approved the plan, and added as an objective the release of Union prisoners held near that city.

A picked cavalry force of 4,000 men was assigned to Kilpatrick, and this was assembled at Stevensburg, Virginia. It consisted of Kilpatrick's Third Cavalry Division; Major William P. Hall with a detachment of 700 men from 3rd Indiana Cavalry of First Brigade and the 4th New York Cavalry and 17th Pennsylvania Cavalry of Second Brigade of Wesley Merritt's First Cavalry Division; Major Constantine Taylor with a detachment of 500 men from the 1st Maine Cavalry, 4th Pennsylvania Cavalry, and 16th Pennsylvania Cavalry of Charles H. Smith's Second Brigade of David McM. Gregg's Second Cavalry Division; and Dunbar R. Ransom's Battery C, 3rd United States Artillery.

Kilpatrick's division was organized as follows:

Third Cavalry Division, Judson Kilpatrick
  First Brigade, Henry E. Davies, Jr.
  Second Brigade, Edward B. Sawyer
    Addison W. Preston

Before the expedition started, about 500 men were detached from the 1st Vermont Cavalry, 5th Michigan Cavalry, 2nd New York Cavalry, and 5th New York Cavalry of Kilpatrick's Third Cavalry Division, and from 1st Maine Cavalry of Second Brigade, Second Cavalry Division, and these were assigned to Ulrich Dahlgren, who was to lead the advance. Dahlgren, son of Admiral John A. Dahlgren, had served on Meade's staff at Gettysburg, and had been wounded while with Kilpatrick's cavalry division at Hagerstown during Robert E. Lee's retreat to Virginia. Dahlgren had recovered from his wound, and in February 1864 had returned to the army.

To create a diversion, and to prevent enemy reinforcements from being sent toward Richmond, George A. Custer was ordered to move on the same day as Kilpatrick with 1,500 men toward Charlottesville. At the same time, John Sedgwick, with two divisions of his Sixth Corps, was to advance to Madison Court House to support Custer. David B. Birney's First Division, Third Corps was ordered to move to James City, on the road to Madison Court House, and communicate with Sedgwick (see below).

Kilpatrick left Stevensburg at 7:00 on the evening of February 28, 1864, and the advance under Dahlgren reached the Rapidan River at Ely's Ford at 11:00 P.M. The column crossed the river that night and moved forward rapidly toward Spotsylvania Court House. Near that point, Dahlgren, with his 500 men, was detached and ordered to move on through Frederick's Hall, on the Virginia Central Railroad, to a point about eight miles east of Goochland on the James River. Dahlgren was then to cross the river, march downstream on the south bank, and, if possible, release the prisoners at Belle Isle. When this was accomplished, he was to rejoin Kilpatrick and the main force at Richmond at 10:00 A.M. March 1, 1864.

After Dahlgren had departed on this mission, Kilpatrick moved south from Spotsylvania Court House, through Chilesburg, to the Virginia Central Railroad, where he arrived at Beaver Dam Station during the day. After completing some destruction on that railroad and also on the Richmond, Fredericksburg, and Potomac Railroad, Kilpatrick marched on and crossed the South Anna River at Ground Squirrel Bridge. At 10:00 A.M. March 1,

1864, he arrived before the defenses of Richmond on the Brooke Pike, about five miles from the city. He drove back the pickets and approached the inner defenses, and then skirmished for several hours while he waited for Dahlgren to join. The latter, however, was far behind schedule, and was still to the west of Richmond at nightfall that day.

After leaving Kilpatrick, Dahlgren had marched southwest from Spotsylvania Court House, and by noon February 29, 1864 was on the Virginia Central Railroad east of Frederick's Hall Station. He destroyed some track and railroad facilities and then marched on, and crossed the South Anna River about 10:00 that night. Early the next morning, March 1, 1864, the column arrived on the James River Canal east of Goochland. While a detachment destroyed portions of the canal, locks, boats, and mills, Dahlgren moved on. He was, however, unable to find the ford by which he was to cross the James River, probably because of the treachery of his guide, and he was forced to continue along the north side of the river. That evening, when about five miles from Richmond, Dahlgren encountered enemy resistance, which increased and continued until dark. Dahlgren then gave the order to withdraw and rejoin the main force.

When Dahlgren failed to rejoin Kilpatrick during the day, the latter was uncertain as to what had happened and, believing that the enemy was being reinforced, withdrew at dark and camped near Mechanicsville (Wade Hampton says at Atlee's Station). About 10:00 P.M. Kilpatrick was attacked by Hampton's cavalry, and at 1:00 A.M. March 2, 1864, after some sharp fighting, withdrew to the crossroads north of Walnut Grove Church. That day he marched east by Old Church to Benjamin F. Butler's lines at New Kent Court House, and camped that night near Tunstall's Station. Butler was the commander of the Department of Virginia and North Carolina.

When Dahlgren began his withdrawal from before Richmond on the night of March 1, 1864, he moved out in front with a force of about 100 men under the command of Major Edwin F. Cooke, and Captain John F. B. Mitchell brought up the rear with about 300 men. During the night, Dahlgren, with the advance force, became separated from the main force and moved on alone. He crossed the Pamunkey River at Hanovertown and the Mattapony River at

Aylett's, and about 11:00 on the night of March 2, 1864, he was ambushed by a Confederate force between King and Queen Court House and King William Court House. Dahlgren was killed and most of his men were captured. Mitchell's command succeeded in breaking through the enemy lines, and the next day, March 2, 1864, joined Kilpatrick's troopers at Tunstall's Station, near White House. On the morning of March 3, 1864, Kilpatrick moved to New Kent Court House, and the next day he marched by way of Williamsburg to Yorktown, Virginia.

March 9, 1864, about 400 men of Kilpatrick's command, temporarily under Addison W. Preston, joined an expedition to King and Queen Court House to drive the enemy from the area and to destroy the town. The expedition was commanded by Isaac J. Wistar, commanding the United States Forces at Yorktown, Virginia in Butler's Department of Virginia and North Carolina. In addition to Kilpatrick's cavalry, Wistar took with him about 700 cavalry and 2,700 infantry of his command. Kilpatrick assumed command of all the cavalry the next day, but the expedition accomplished little and returned to Yorktown March 12, 1864. For additional information, see Department of Virginia and North Carolina, Operations in the Department of Virginia and North Carolina, Wistar's Expedition to King and Queen County, Virginia.

March 9, 1864, Henry E. Davies' First Brigade of Kilpatrick's Third Division embarked at Yorktown for Alexandria, Virginia, and the remainder of the expedition followed March 12, 1864. By March 15, 1864, all of Kilpatrick's command had returned to its former camps.

A serious controversy developed after Dahlgren's death. It was alleged that papers found on his body contained instructions for his command to kill Jefferson Davis and his cabinet, and to burn and destroy Richmond. Meade ordered an immediate investigation, and after examining all available evidence, he informed Robert E. Lee that neither the United States government, Meade himself, nor Kilpatrick had authorized or approved such acts as were described in the papers said to be found on Dahlgren's body.

It has been noted above that simultaneously with Kilpatrick's raid, George A. Custer was to conduct an expedition toward Charlottesville, Virginia. At 2:00 P.M. February 28, 1864, a few hours before Kilpatrick started toward Richmond, Custer, with 1,500 cavalrymen, left Pony Mountain on his march toward Charlottesville. Custer's command consisted of a detachment of 500 men from First Brigade of David McM. Gregg's Second Cavalry Division under William Stedman, and 1st United States Cavalry, 5th United States Cavalry, and 6th Pennsylvania Cavalry, all from Alfred Gibbs' Reserve Brigade of Wesley Merritt's First Cavalry Division.

Custer arrived in the vicinity of Madison Court House at 6:00 P.M., and then halted until 2:00 the next morning. He then resumed the march February 29, 1864, passed through Stanardsville at 8:15 A.M., and arrived on the Rivanna River at 3:00 P.M. There he encountered enemy pickets, but he crossed the South Fork of the river, at Naked Run, and drove them back to a point about two miles beyond the river, and to within two miles of the town. He then learned that one brigade of cavalry and one infantry division were at Charlottesville, and he decided to withdraw. He recrossed the Rivanna and halted about 9:00 that night, February 29, 1864, eight miles southwest of Stanardsville. He resumed the march about an hour later, with Stedman's detachment leading the way. The night was dark and rainy, and as a result Stedman's command became separated from the rest of the column, which became lost, and took the wrong road. Custer halted to wait for daylight, but Stedman, who was on the right road, continued on through Stanardsville toward Madison Court House.

At daylight March 1, 1864, Custer, with the main force, moved on to Stanardsville, and then took the road toward Madison Court House. He soon became engaged with Williams C. Wickham's cavalry brigade, under the personal direction of James E. B. (Jeb) Stuart, but after some fighting, continued on and crossed the Rapidan at Banks' Mill Ford. About five miles from Madison Court House, Stedman rejoined the main force, and then on March 2, 1864, the expedition returned to its camps.

When Custer was ordered out on his expedition, John Sedgwick was sent to Madison Court House with his Sixth Corps to be in position to support him if necessary. On February 27, 1864, David A. Russell's First Division and Henry L. Eustis' Second Division of Sixth Corps marched from

Welford's Ford on Hazel River to James City, and the next day they moved on to Robertson's River. There the two divisions were placed in position along the river, with one brigade in advance at Madison Court House. They returned to their camps at Welford's Ford March 2, 1864. David B. Birney's First Division, Third Corps was also sent forward to support Sixth Corps and Custer. March 28, 1864, Birney marched from Rixeys' farm, about two and one-half miles from Culpeper Court House, to James City, on the road to Madison Court House. He remained there, in communication with Sixth Corps, until March 2, 1864, and then returned with his division to his former quarters.

MARYLAND CAMPAIGN (SOUTH MOUNTAIN AND ANTIETAM) SEPTEMBER 3–20, 1862

On August 30, 1862, John Pope's Army of Virginia, which had been reinforced by most of the Army of the Potomac, suffered a crushing defeat by Robert E. Lee's Army of Northern Virginia at the Second Battle of Bull Run, and then, after another engagement at Chantilly September 1, 1862, it retreated to within the safety of the Defenses of Washington during the first days of September 1862. At that time, the army was considerably disorganized and reduced in numbers by the arduous campaigning of the past few weeks and by its recent defeat, and it was badly in need of reorganization.

George B. McClellan did not accompany the corps of the Army of the Potomac when they moved from the Peninsula to join Pope, but he arrived in person at Alexandria August 26, 1862. He had with him at that time only his staff and about 100 men. Then, on September 1, 1862, McClellan went into Washington, where Henry W. Halleck, general in chief of the army, verbally assigned him to the command of the Defenses of Washington. His command, however, was specifically limited to the works and garrisons of the Defenses, and he was to have no control over the troops then in the field with Pope. According to McClellan, however, on September 2, 1862, when President Abraham Lincoln learned that Pope's army was in full retreat toward

Washington, he asked McClellan to make preparations for the defense of the city, to take command of the army when it arrived near the defensive works, and to place the troops in position for the protection of the capital. For further information about the command of the army at that time, see Army of the Potomac, In the Military District of the Defenses of Washington.

On September 3, 1862, the president assigned to Halleck the task of putting the army in condition for field operations. On the same day, the army was assigned positions near Washington as follows: the cavalry was sent to the fords of the Potomac River near Poolesville, Maryland; Second Corps, Army of the Potomac and Second Corps, Army of Virginia (later Twelfth Corps, Army of the Potomac) were sent to Tennallytown, D.C.; Ninth Corps was assigned to a position on the Seventh Street Road, near Washington; and the remaining corps of the Army of the Potomac and the Army of Virginia were left on the Virginia side of the Potomac.

Reorganization of the Army in the Defenses of Washington. On September 3, 1862, Halleck informed Pope that the reorganization of the army would begin at once, and that McClellan, commanding the Defenses of Washington, would exercise general authority in this process as senior officer. By this announcement, Pope was left without a command. Also that day, Alpheus S. Williams was assigned command of Second Corps, Army of Virginia, relieving Nathaniel P. Banks, who was ill; and Jesse L. Reno was assigned command of Ninth Corps. Ambrose E. Burnside, former commander of Ninth Corps, who was at Falmouth, Virginia, was ordered to bring John G. Parke's Third Division to Washington and rejoin the corps.

Also on September 3, 1862, Lee's Army of Northern Virginia quietly left the Washington front and marched northward toward the Potomac River. Upon arrival there, it crossed at the fords near Leesburg September 4–7, 1862, and marched on to Frederick, Maryland.

September 4, 1862, John F. Reynolds' Division (formerly Third Division, Fifth Corps while on the Peninsula), which had been attached to Irvin McDowell's Third Corps, Army of Virginia in August 1862, was ordered to rejoin Fifth Corps, Army of the Potomac. This order was not carried out, however, and Reynolds' Division remained with Third Corps, Army of Virginia until September 12, 1862, when the latter was reorganized as First Corps, Army of the Potomac. The designation of Reynolds' Division was then changed to Third Division, First Corps, Army of the Potomac. A new Third Division, Fifth Corps was reorganized September 12, 1862 (see below).

September 5, 1862, the Army of the Potomac and the Army of Virginia were consolidated, and Pope was relieved from command. This was no more than an official order, however, because Pope had exercised no effective command since September 1, 1862. Also on September 5, 1862, Fitz John Porter, William B. Franklin, and Charles Griffin were relieved from duty with the army until charges against them for their conduct at Second Bull Run could be examined. Joseph Hooker was assigned command of Porter's Fifth Corps; Franklin's Sixth Corps was attached to Samuel P. Heintzelman's Third Corps, Army of the Potomac; and both corps were placed under the command of Heintzelman. At McClellan's request, however, this order was suspended because of the emergency created by Lee's invasion of Maryland, and also because Sixth Corps was then under orders to march.

For better control of his forces during the coming campaign in Maryland, McClellan decided on the organization of his army into a right wing, center, and left wing. On September 5, 1862, Second Corps, Army of the Potomac and Second Corps, Army of Virginia (later to become Twelfth Corps, Army of the Potomac) were moved to Rockville, Maryland, where they were to be organized as the Center of McClellan's army. Edwin V. Sumner, commander of Second Corps, Army of the Potomac, was assigned command of both corps.

The assembly point for the Right Wing was Leesboro, Maryland, and McDowell's Third Corps, Army of Virginia (later to become First Corps, Army of the Potomac) and Reno's Ninth Corps, Army of the Potomac, which were to constitute this command, were ordered to that point. On September 6, 1862, Third Corps, Army of Virginia was moved from the south side of the Potomac to Leesboro, where Ninth Corps had already assembled. The next day, Hooker relieved McDowell in command of Third Corps, Army of Virginia. On September 7 (or 8), 1862, Jacob D. Cox's Kanawha Division, recent-

ly arrived from Western Virginia, marched from Upton's Hill, south of the Potomac, to Leesboro, where it was attached to Ninth Corps.

The Left Wing of the army was assigned to Franklin, commander of Sixth Corps, Army of the Potomac, and it consisted of his own Sixth Corps and Darius N. Couch's First Division, Fourth Corps. On September 5, 1862, Couch moved to Offutt's Cross Roads, and the next day Sixth Corps marched from Alexandria, Virginia to Tennallytown, D.C.

September 6, 1862, George Sykes' Second Division of Porter's Fifth Corps was sent to Tennallytown to constitute a reserve for the army, and Sykes was ordered to report directly to McClellan. Also on September 6, 1862, thirty-six new regiments were assigned to the various corps of the army to replace the losses sustained in Pope's recent campaign in Virginia.

In late August 1862, Samuel D. Sturgis, commander of the Reserve Corps, Army of Virginia, with A. Sanders Piatt's Brigade of that corps, was attached to Porter's Fifth Corps, Army of the Potomac. Then on September 6, 1862, Sturgis was assigned command of a newly formed division, which was attached to Fifth Corps. The next day, however, Sturgis was ordered to report to Burnside at Leesboro, where he was assigned command of Second Division, Ninth Corps.

On September 1, 1862, Alfred Pleasonton's Cavalry Brigade arrived at Alexandria from the Peninsula, and it was followed September 5, 1862 by William W. Averell's Cavalry Brigade. The regiments of these two brigades, plus additional regiments from the Defenses of Washington, were then formed into a cavalry division of five brigades, and Pleasonton was assigned command. The division was organized as follows:

Cavalry Division, Alfred Pleasonton
   First Brigade, Charles J. Whiting
   Second Brigade, John F. Farnsworth
   Third Brigade, Richard H. Rush
   Fourth Brigade, Andrew T. McReynolds
   Fifth Brigade, Benjamin F. Davis

With five brigades, this appears to have been a strong division, but actually it was not. There were only twelve regiments in the division, and of these thirty-three companies were not under divisional control. For additional information, see Cavalry

Corps, Army of the Potomac, McClellan's Maryland Campaign of 1862. The cavalry played only a comparatively minor role in the Maryland Campaign.

By September 7, 1862, McClellan's army was largely reorganized, and was assembled northwest of Washington in Maryland ready for field service. It consisted of the following:

ARMY OF THE POTOMAC, George B. McClellan

Right Wing, Ambrose E. Burnside
    Third Corps, Army of Virginia, Joseph Hooker
    Ninth Corps, Army of the Potomac, Jesse L. Reno

Center, Edwin V. Sumner
    Second Corps, Army of Virginia, Alpheus S. Williams
    Second Corps, Army of the Potomac, Edwin V. Sumner

Left Wing, William B. Franklin
    Sixth Corps, Army of the Potomac, William B. Franklin
    First Division, Fourth Corps, Army of the Potomac, Darius N. Couch

Second Division, Fifth Corps, Army of the Potomac, George Sykes

Note. For the complete organization of the corps of the army, see below.

Before leaving Washington with his army to march into Maryland in pursuit of Lee, McClellan detached a part of his command and left it in the defensive works south of the Potomac for the protection of the capital. The troops selected for this purpose, in addition to the garrison troops of the defenses, were Franz Sigel's First Corps, Army of Virginia (later to become Eleventh Corps, Army of the Potomac); Samuel P. Heintzelman's Third Corps, Army of the Potomac; and Fitz John Porter, with George W. Morell's First Division, Fifth Corps, Army of the Potomac. Also, on September 7, 1862, McClellan assigned Nathaniel P. Banks to the immediate command of the defenses of the capital. For the organization and the positions occupied by the forces left by McClellan for the defense of the capital during the Maryland Campaign, see Military District of the Defenses of Washington, Army of the Potomac.

Advance of the Army—Completion of the Reorganization. On September 7, 1862, McClellan moved his headquarters to Rockville, Maryland and issued orders for the advance of his field army into Maryland in pursuit of Lee. The Right Wing and the Center were to move generally toward Lee's army, which was reported to be at Frederick, Maryland; and the Left Wing was to march to the south of the other two columns along the Potomac toward the lower Monocacy River. The cavalry was to cover the advance.

On September 9, 1862, Couch's division, on the extreme left, reached the Potomac at the mouth of Seneca Creek, and Franklin's Sixth Corps arrived at Darnestown; Sumner's Second Corps, Army of the Potomac and Williams' Second Corps, Army of Virginia arrived at Middleburg (or Middlebrook); Reno's Ninth Corps, Army of the Potomac and Hooker's Third Corps, Army of Virginia were at Brookville; and Sykes' division left Tennallytown for Clarksburg.

The army then continued its advance in search of Lee. The Right Wing and Center of the army moved forward toward Frederick as follows: Second Corps, Army of the Potomac marched by way of Middleburg, Clarksburg, and Urbana; Second Corps, Army of Virginia passed through Damascus, and then between Urbana and New Market; Ninth Corps marched by way of Damascus and New Market; and Third Corps, Army of Virginia, on the extreme right, marched through Cookesville and Ridgeville.

At 4:30 P.M. September 12, 1862, McClellan's leading troops, Cox's Kanawha Division, arrived at Frederick on the New Market Road and, after a short engagement, occupied the town, which was only lightly held. Augustus Moor, commanding Second Brigade of the Kanawha Division, was captured during this encounter, and George Crook assumed command of his brigade. At 5:00 P.M., Pleasonton's cavalry also entered Frederick on the Urbana Road, and with troops of Ninth Corps occupied all approaches to the town.

At daylight September 13, 1862, Pleasonton's cavalry moved out of Frederick on the National Road on a reconnaissance toward South Mountain, and that afternoon Cox moved to Middletown with the Kanawha Division in support of Pleasonton. Also that afternoon, Orlando B. Willcox's First Division and Samuel D. Sturgis' Second Division of Ninth Corps followed Cox to Middletown and camped that night just west of the town. Also that day, the rest of the Right Wing and the Center of McClellan's army arrived near Frederick.

On McClellan's left, Couch's division moved forward on the River Road, watching the fords of the Potomac, and it then followed and supported Sixth Corps. Couch and Franklin moved forward as follows: September 10–11, 1862, Sixth Corps was at Barnesville, and Couch's division at Poolesville; September 12, 1862, Sixth Corps was at Licksville, a place in the northern angle formed by the junction of the Monocacy River and the Potomac, and Couch's division at Barnesville; September 13, 1862, Sixth Corps was at Buckeystown, and Couch's division at Licksville; and September 14, both Sixth Corps and Couch's division were at Burkittsville.

Sykes' division, which had left Tennallytown September 9, 1862, advanced by way of Rockville, Middleburg, and Urbana, and arrived at Frederick September 13, 1862.

A number of significant changes in organization and command occurred in the army while McClellan was on the march toward Frederick. On September 11, 1862, Porter, then at Arlington, Virginia, received orders to report with his remaining division (Morell's First Division) to McClellan at Brookville, Maryland. The next day a new division was organized in the Defenses of Washington under the command of Andrew A. Humphreys, and it was assigned to Fifth Corps as Third Division. This division consisted of a First Brigade commanded by Erastus B. Tyler and a Second Brigade commanded by Peter H. Allabach. These two brigades were taken from Amiel W. Whipple's Division, Defenses of Washington. Whipple, with A. Sanders Piatt's Brigade of his division, remained in the Defenses of Washington. For additional information about Whipple's Division, see Military District of the Defenses of Washington, Army of the Potomac. At 6:00 A.M. September 12, 1862, Porter left Washington with Morell's division, and marched by way of Leesboro to join the army. Porter reported to McClellan September 14, 1862, and resumed command of Sykes' division. Humphreys' new Third Division left Washington September 14, 1862 to join Porter near Middletown, Maryland.

On September 11, 1862, John F. Reynolds was assigned to duty with the governor of Pennsylvania, because of the emergency created by Lee's invasion of neighboring Maryland, and George G. Meade was assigned command of Reynolds' Third Division, Third Corps, Army of Virginia.

September 12, 1862, while the army was near Frederick, the Army of Virginia was officially discontinued and merged into the Army of the Potomac. The designations of the corps of the Army of Virginia were then changed as follows: First Corps became Eleventh Corps, Army of the Potomac; Second Corps became Twelfth Corps, Army of the Potomac; and Third Corps became First Corps, Army of the Potomac. At the time of this order, the Army of the Potomac was in active pursuit of Lee, and consequently the above changes in designations were not immediately carried out. This should be understood in order to avoid the confusion that might result from reading the orders related to the various corps in the days to follow. Thus, for example, we find that on September 13, 1862, John Sedgwick was assigned temporary command of Second Corps, Army of Virginia, and two days later, Joseph K. F. Mansfield assumed command of Second Corps, Army of Virginia. When Mansfield was killed at Antietam September 17, 1862, Williams resumed command of Second Corps, Army of Virginia; and that same day, Meade assumed command of Third Corps, Army of Virginia after Hooker was wounded. It should be further noted that Williams did not officially assume command of Twelfth Corps, Army of the Potomac until September 18, 1862, the day after the Battle of Antietam.

Capture of Harper's Ferry, Virginia, September 15, 1862. When Lee crossed the Potomac River into Maryland September 4–7, 1862, Harper's Ferry was held by Dixon S. Miles with troops belonging to the Middle Department. These consisted of Miles' Railroad Brigade; and Julius White's Brigade, formerly commanded by A. Sanders Piatt, which had just arrived from Winchester, Virginia September 3, 1862. Additional troops were at Martinsburg under the command of Daniel Cameron.

Miles was ordered to defend Harper's Ferry, and September 5, 1862, he sent White to Martinsburg to relieve Cameron. That same day, Miles reorganized his command into a division of four brigades as follows:

Miles' Command (or Division) at Harper's Ferry, Dixon S. Miles

First Brigade, Frederick G. D'Utassy
Second Brigade, William H. Trimble
Third Brigade, Thomas H. Ford
Fourth Brigade, William G. Ward

Note 1. Fourth Brigade was composed largely of troops of the former Railroad Brigade.
Note 2. Ford, Trimble, and D'Utassy commanded regiments in White's Brigade at Winchester.

Lee was naturally concerned about leaving Miles' force in his rear while operating in Maryland, and he promptly took steps to secure his line of communications and also to shift his supply line from the more exposed route east of the Blue Ridge Mountains into the more protected Shenandoah Valley. On September 9, 1862, Lee issued Special Order No. 191 (the so-called "Lost Order") for the movements of the army the next day, including those for the troops assigned for the capture of Harper's Ferry. Thomas J. (Stonewall) Jackson was to march with three divisions of his corps and attempt the capture of Harper's Ferry. The divisions of Lafayette McLaws and Richard H. Anderson, of James Longstreet's corps, and John G. Walker's division were to cooperate with Jackson in the capture of Harper's Ferry by occupying Maryland Heights and Loudoun Heights in Virginia. Longstreet was ordered with the remainder of his corps to Boonsboro, where he was to halt and await developments. Daniel H. Hill's division, which had been attached to Jackson's corps, was to accompany Longstreet.

September 10, 1862, Jackson left Frederick with his three divisions and marched by way of Middletown and Boonsboro to Williamsport. He crossed the Potomac there the next day and advanced toward Martinsburg. White, who was in command of the post of Martinsburg, learned of Jackson's approach, and on the night of September 11, 1862, evacuated the town and retired toward Harper's Ferry. He arrived there the next morning and turned over his three regiments to Miles, who then assigned White as second in command of the garrison of Harper's Ferry. On September 12, 1862 Jackson arrived at Halltown, about three miles to the west and south of Harper's Ferry, and he halted there to await information about his cooperating columns.

On September 10, 1862, Longstreet marched westward on the National Road with his corps and D. H. Hill's division until he came to Middletown.

There, McLaws, with his own division and Anderson's division, turned off from the road and moved through Burkittsville and across South Mountain into Pleasant Valley. McLaws then overcame some slight opposition and occupied Maryland Heights at 4:30 P.M. September 13, 1862. Walker's division, which had been on duty along the Monocacy River, marched south, crossed the Potomac at Point of Rocks on the night of September 9, 1862, and then advanced through Hillsboro and occupied Loudoun Heights September 13, 1862. The investment of Harper's Ferry was then complete.

The Confederates then opened fire with their artillery on the defenses of Harper's Ferry on September 14, 1862, and that evening A. P. Hill's division of Jackson's corps made an unsuccessful attack on the left of Miles' line. That night, 1,300 Federal cavalry, led by Benjamin F. ("Grimes") Davis and Hasbrouck Davis, escaped almost certain capture by crossing the Potomac from Harper's Ferry and marching around the base of Maryland Heights and then on to the north toward Sharpsburg.

On the morning of September 15, 1862, Jackson again opened fire with batteries placed all around the town, and at 9:00 A.M. Miles surrendered the garrison, but asked White to arrange the terms of capitulation. While the white flag of surrender was still displayed, Miles was struck by a shell fragment and was mortally wounded. Jackson then left Hill to arrange the surrender and, with the rest of his corps, marched immediately toward Sharpsburg. McLaws and Walker also moved immediately toward Sharpsburg.

Battle of South Mountain (Fox's Gap and Turner's Gap), September 14, 1862.

Shortly after Lee's army left Frederick, the Army of the Potomac entered the town, and on September 13, 1862, a copy of Lee's Special Order No. 191 was found on an old campground used by the enemy. This was passed on to McClellan, who thus learned that Lee had divided his army and had thus presented him with the unusual opportunity of striking a part of the Army of Northern Virginia before the other could come to its assistance. To take advantage of this situation, McClellan prepared march orders for the next day.

That night, the Army of the Potomac was in camp on a broad front as follows: First Corps (formerly

Third Corps, Army of Virginia); Second Corps; Twelfth Corps (formerly Second Corps, Army of Virginia); Sykes' division of Fifth Corps; and Isaac P. Rodman's Third Division, Ninth Corps were at or near Frederick. The other three divisions of Ninth Corps were near Middletown; Sixth Corps was at Buckeystown; Couch's division of Fourth Corps was at Licksville; and Pleasonton's cavalry was out toward Turner's Gap in South Mountain. McClellan's march orders for the next day, September 14, 1862, were as follows: Franklin, with his Sixth Corps, was to push forward through Burkittsville and Crampton's Gap in South Mountain, and from there to march to the relief of Miles at Harper's Ferry; Burnside, with Ninth Corps and First Corps of his Right Wing, was to move west on the National Road to Turner's Gap in South Mountain; and the rest of the army was to follow Burnside to South Mountain. The execution of these orders resulted in the battles that took place at Turner's Gap, Fox's Gap, and Crampton's Gap in South Mountain September 14, 1862, and the Battle of Antietam, September 17, 1862.

Before describing the battles at South Mountain that took place September 14, 1862, it is necessary to note some of the more important features of the region at and near the battlefields. The National Road, on which McClellan's army marched westward from Frederick, passed through Middletown and Bolivar, and then, about two miles beyond Bolivar, it crossed South Mountain at Turner's Gap. It then ran on through Boonsboro, near the western base of the mountain, to Hagerstown. To the north of the road at Turner's Gap, South Mountain was divided into two crests by a narrow valley or ravine, which was deep near the National Road but was only a shallow depression about a mile to the north. It was in this area that Joseph Hooker's battle of September 14, 1862 was fought.

At Bolivar, two roads that ran up to the top of the mountain branched off from the National Road, one to the right and the other to the left. The right-hand road, the Old Hagerstown Road, ran northward up a ravine for about a mile to Mount Tabor Church, and it then curved around to the left through Frostburg (or Frosttown), which was about a half mile beyond the church. From there the road continued on in a westerly direction up and along the first, or eastern,

crest of the mountain mentioned above, and it then joined the National Road at the Mountain House near Turner's Gap. The left-hand road, the Old Sharpsburg Road, followed a somewhat circuitous route up the mountain to Fox's Gap (or Braddock's Gap), which was about a mile south of Turner's Gap. A crossroad ran from Fox's Gap along the mountaintop to Turner's Gap. The Battle of South Mountain was fought along or near the three roads described above—the Old Hagerstown Road on the right, the National Road in the center, and the Old Sharpsburg Road on the left.

As noted above, on September 13, 1862, Pleasonton advanced with his cavalry along the National Road from Frederick, and during the afternoon he arrived at the eastern base of South Mountain. During the day, he was opposed by James E. B. (Jeb) Stuart's cavalry, but late in the day the latter withdrew to Turner's Gap. Pleasonton concluded that he could not force a passage of the gap with his cavalry alone, and he sent back to Jesse L. Reno, commanding Ninth Corps at Middletown, for infantry support.

After the departure of McLaws and Anderson for Harper's Ferry September 10, 1862, Longstreet continued on from Middletown toward Boonsboro with the rest of his corps and D. H. Hill's division. Lee accompanied Longstreet's column. During the day Lee learned of a rumor, which proved to be false, that Federal troops were advancing from Pennsylvania toward Hagerstown. He then left D. H. Hill's division at Boonsboro to watch Turner's Gap and to block a possible Federal retreat from Harper's Ferry, and he marched with Longstreet's command to Hagerstown, which was about ten miles to the northwest.

When D. H. Hill learned on September 13, 1862 of Stuart's withdrawal toward South Mountain the day before, and of McClellan's advance on the National Road, he immediately informed Lee, and then sent Alfred H. Colquitt's brigade of his division to Turner's Gap to support Stuart. He also ordered Samuel Garland's brigade to follow Colquitt. When Lee received Hill's message, he immediately prepared to return from Hagerstown to Boonsboro. When Colquitt arrived on the mountain, he joined Stuart at Turner's Gap on the evening of September 13, 1862, and that night Stuart left for Crampton's Gap. Before leaving, however, he sent Thomas L.

Rosser with a detachment of cavalry and horse artillery to Fox's Gap to hold the Old Sharpsburg Road at that point.

Early on the morning of September 14, 1862, Jacob D. Cox, with Eliakim P. Scammon's First Brigade of his Kanawha Division, advanced on the National Road from Middletown to support Pleasonton. At Catoctin Creek, when Cox learned that the enemy was ahead in some force, he sent Scammon's brigade on toward the front and returned to Middletown to bring up Moor's Second Brigade, then commanded by George Crook. When Scammon arrived at Bolivar, Pleasonton sent him to the left on the Old Sharpsburg Road to move up to the top of the mountain at Fox's Gap. Upon arrival there, Scammon was to move to the right along the crest of the mountain to the National Road, where he would come in on the rear of Colquitt's brigade. Scammon left Bolivar for the mountaintop about 7:00 A.M., and Cox, who arrived with Crook's brigade about a half hour later, followed Scammon up the mountain.

Meantime, Pleasonton had placed a part of his artillery and some guns of Ninth Corps on high ground about a half mile in advance of Bolivar, and at 7:30 A.M. they opened fire on the enemy position at Turner's Gap.

When Scammon arrived within about a half mile of the summit about 9:00 A.M., he was fired on by Rosser's cavalry and artillery, and Scammon turned off on a country road still farther to the left and nearly parallel to the ridge. Cox joined Scammon at that point, and Crook's brigade came up a short time later. At about that time, Garland's brigade of D. H. Hill's division came up from Turner's Gap to support Rosser.

Scammon deployed his brigade a few hundred yards to the left of the Old Sharpsburg Road, and at about 10:00 A.M. advanced toward Fox's Gap, which was held by Rosser and Garland. There was heavy fighting for more than an hour, during which Garland was killed and his brigade was routed. Scammon's line then advanced across Wises' field, near the gap, and up the slope of the mountain beyond toward Turner's Gap. At about that time, Crook arrived on the mountain. He sent one regiment to the extreme left to watch that flank, and he moved with his other two regiments to support Scammon's line.

About a half hour after Garland's brigade was broken, George B. Anderson's brigade of D. H. Hill's division came up and attempted to recover the lost position but failed. Roswell S. Ripley's brigade, also of D. H. Hill's division, arrived and formed on the left of Anderson. D. H. Hill's last brigade, commanded by Robert E. Rodes, arrived at the Mountain House from Boonsboro about 2:00 P.M., and it was sent to the extreme left to occupy some high ground overlooking the National Road at Turner's Gap.

At about 11:00 A.M., Cox, then without close support and encountering stubborn resistance, decided to withdraw to the line that he had occupied at the beginning of the attack and to wait for the arrival of the other divisions of Ninth Corps. Following Cox's withdrawal, there was a lull in the fighting that lasted from noon until about 2:00 P.M. Orlando B. Willcox's First Division, Ninth Corps arrived on the mountain sometime before 2:00 P.M. and formed on the right of the Kanawha Division, with its right bent back at almost a right angle to the rest of the line. Thomas Welsh's Second Brigade was on the left of the road, connecting with the right of Cox's division, and Benjamin C. Christ's First Brigade was extended to the right across the road.

About 3:30 P.M., the leading troops of Longstreet's corps reached the mountaintop, and the brigades of George T. Anderson and Thomas F. Drayton of David R. Jones' division were sent to the Confederate right and placed on the left of Ripley. The enemy then made a strong attack on the angle of Willcox's line, and initially there was some confusion in the Federal ranks. Willcox, however, was able to re-form his division, and after a very severe contest, he advanced across the Old Sharpsburg Road, through Wises' field, and into the woods beyond.

It was nearly 4:00 P.M. when Samuel D. Sturgis arrived with his Second Division, Ninth Corps and deployed his brigades in line of battle. He placed Edward Ferrero's Second Brigade on both sides of the road and held James Nagle's First Brigade in reserve. Ferrero was almost immediately engaged with the Confederate brigades of Drayton and the two Andersons, and Nagle's brigade was brought up in support. When the troops of Willcox's division had exhausted their ammunition, Sturgis relieved Willcox.

Isaac P. Rodman's Third Division, Ninth Corps

was the last to arrive that day, and it did not fight as a unit. When Rodman came up, Cox's left was threatened, and he sent Harrison F. Fairchild's First Brigade to the extreme left to support Cox. Rodman personally supervised the placement of Edward Harland's Second Brigade on the right to support Sturgis and Willcox. As the divisions of Ninth Corps arrived on the mountain, they reported to Cox, who was the senior officer on the field. Reno, the corps commander, had remained behind to move the rear divisions to the front.

As Sturgis' and Rodman's divisions were arriving, the brigades of William T. Wofford and Evander McIver Law of John B. Hood's division came up and took position beside Drayton, about midway between Fox's Gap and Turner's Gap. Then, during the late afternoon, there was sharp fighting along the front as the enemy attempted to drive back the left and center of the Federal line, which was on the highest ground.

Soon after Rodman arrived, the entire Federal line was ordered forward to drive the enemy from the remaining summit and gain Turner's Gap. The troops on the center and left made good progress on the high ground, but on the right the attack was uphill and over rocky, broken ground, and progress was slow.

McClellan, Burnside, and Reno had come up to Pleasonton's position near Bolivar soon after Willcox's division had passed by, and they remained there during the afternoon and directed the battle from that central position. Shortly after sunset, Reno went up to Fox's Gap to attempt to speed up the advance of Cox's right, but he was killed in Wises' field about 7:00 P.M. during an enemy attack on Sturgis' division and the right of the Kanawha Division. Cox then assumed command of Ninth Corps, Scammon succeeded Cox in command of the Kanawha Division, and Hugh Ewing assumed command of Scammon's First Brigade, Kanawha Division. About dark, the enemy made a final attack on Fairchild's brigade on the left, but this was driven back. The fighting ended about 10:00 P.M. with the enemy still in possession of Turner's Gap.

During the morning and early afternoon of September 14, 1862, while Ninth Corps was fighting at Fox's Gap, McClellan, with Joseph Hooker's First Corps, Edwin V. Sumner's Second Corps, and Alpheus S. Williams' Twelfth Corps, was marching westward on the National Road from Frederick toward South Mountain. Hooker's corps of Burnside's Right Wing, which was leading the infantry column, reached Middletown, and halted there for a time while Hooker went forward to reconnoiter. At 2:00 P.M. Hooker, at McClellan's direction, ordered George G. Meade to make a diversion to the right of the road with his Third Division to aid Reno in his attack at Fox's Gap. McClellan then ordered Hooker to advance with the other two divisions of the corps and support Meade.

Meade marched up the road to Bolivar, and from there he moved northward about a mile to Mount Tabor Church. Upon arriving there, Meade turned to the left and deployed his division onto a line facing west toward South Mountain. Truman Seymour's First Brigade was on the right; Thomas F. Gallagher's Third Brigade was on the center; and Albert L. Magilton's Second Brigade was on the left. The right of Meade's line was about a mile and a half north of the National Road.

The other divisions of the corps deployed as they came up. John P. Hatch's First Division formed on the left of Meade's division in three lines, with one brigade on each line. Marsena R. Patrick's Third Brigade was deployed on the front line; Walter Phelps' First Brigade was behind Patrick; and Abner Doubleday's Second Brigade formed the third line. John Gibbon's Fourth Brigade had been detached by Burnside at Bolivar, and it had been ordered to make a demonstration up the National Road toward Turner's Gap. James B. Ricketts' Second Division arrived about 5:00 P.M. and was deployed to the rear as a reserve. Abram Duryee's (also Duryea) First Brigade was on the right; George L. Hartsuff's Third Brigade was on the center; and William A. Christian's Second Brigade was on the left.

As soon the deployment was completed, Hooker ordered the attack to begin at once. He directed Meade to advance with his division to the right of the Old Hagerstown Road and to move forward along the mountain toward Turner's Gap. Seymour's brigade, on the extreme right, was to move to the top of the slope on the right of the ravine, which was mentioned earlier and through which the road ran, and then move forward along the summit parallel to the road. The brigades of Gallagher and Magilton were to move along the slope and in the ravine on the left of Seymour. Hatch's division was to take the crest on the left of the ravine and on the left of Meade's line, and Ricketts' division was to follow in reserve.

The attack began about 6:00 P.M., and Hooker's line advanced slowly but steadily up the slopes against very determined resistance by Rodes' brigade. In Meade's division, Seymour's brigade reached the crest about dark, and the other brigades kept pace. Gallagher was wounded during the advance, and Robert Anderson succeeded him in command of Third Brigade. During the attack, Hooker received word that the enemy was attempting to turn Meade's right, and he sent Duryee's brigade of Ricketts' division to support Seymour.

On Meade's left, Hatch's division advanced up the slopes of the eastern ridge, and Phelps' brigade, which was leading the attack, succeeded in occupying a stone wall very close to the summit. It maintained this position for some time, and at dusk it was relieved by Doubleday's brigade. Hatch was wounded that evening and was succeeded in command of First Division by Doubleday. William P. Wainwright assumed command of Doubleday's brigade, but he was wounded and J. William Hofmann succeeded him in command of the brigade. At Hatch's request, Christian's brigade was sent to the extreme left to support First Division, then commanded by Doubleday. About dusk, Christian relieved Doubleday's brigade, then commanded by Hofmann. When relieved, Hofmann fell back to a position behind Phelps. Later, Ricketts personally brought up Hartsuff's brigade and about dark put it in position between Doubleday's brigade on the left and Meade's division on the right.

When the fighting ended at dark, Hooker's troops held the mountaintop, but they had failed to reach Turner's Gap. Earlier in the day, three brigades of David R. Jones' division, and Nathan G. Evans' Independent Brigade had been ordered to South Mountain to support Rodes, but they did not arrive until about dark and were too late to contribute significantly to the defense of Rodes' position.

As noted above, Gibbon's brigade of Hatch's division was detached by Burnside for a demonstration at Turner's Gap. Late in the afternoon, Gibbon advanced up the National Road directly toward the enemy position in front of Turner's Gap. The 19th Indiana Regiment was on the left of the road, and the 7th Wisconsin was on the right. The 6th Wisconsin

and 2nd Wisconsin followed in reserve, but as the attack developed, 6th Wisconsin moved up to support 7th Wisconsin, and 2nd Wisconsin moved to the left and joined 19th Indiana. Gibbon made some progress against strong opposition by Colquitt's men, but he was soon stopped on the mountainside, well below the summit.

Sumner's Second Corps came up in rear of Burnside's command during the evening and night of September 14, 1862. Israel B. Richardson's First Division, Second Corps was sent to Mount Tabor Church, and the rest of Second Corps and all of Williams' Twelfth Corps camped near Bolivar. After dark, Willis A. Gorman's First Brigade, Second Division of Sumner's corps moved up the mountain and relieved Gibbon's brigade. Sykes' Second Division, Fifth Corps and the Reserve Artillery of the army halted for the night at Middletown.

Lee began to withdraw his forces from South Mountain about 11:00 P.M. September 14, 1862, and they started back through Boonsboro and Keedysville toward Sharpsburg, Maryland. By the morning of September 17, 1862, the Army of Northern Virginia was near Sharpsburg, and occupied a defensive line on a ridge west of Antietam Creek.

The troops engaged at the Battle of South Mountain September 14, 1862 were organized as follows:

RIGHT WING, ARMY OF THE POTOMAC
Ambrose E. Burnside

FIRST CORPS, Joseph Hooker

First Division, John P. Hatch, wounded
  Abner Doubleday
  First Brigade, Walter Phelps, Jr.
  Second Brigade, Abner Doubleday
    William P. Wainwright, wounded
    J. William Hofmann
  Third Brigade, Marsena R. Patrick
  Fourth Brigade, John Gibbon

Note. Hatch relieved Rufus King in command of First Division at Catoctin, Maryland at 10:00 A.M. September 14, 1862.

Second Division, James B. Ricketts
  First Brigade, Abram Duryee (Duryea)
  Second Brigade, William A. Christian
  Third Brigade, George L. Hartsuff

Third Division, George G. Meade
  First Brigade, Truman Seymour

Second Brigade, Albert L. Magilton
Third Brigade, Thomas F. Gallagher, wounded
  Robert Anderson

NINTH CORPS, Jesse L. Reno, killed
  Jacob D. Cox

First Division, Orlando B. Willcox
  First Brigade, Benjamin C. Christ
  Second Brigade, Thomas Welsh

Second Division, Samuel D. Sturgis
  First Brigade, James Nagle
  Second Brigade, Edward Ferrero

Third Division, Isaac P. Rodman
  First Brigade, Harrison S. Fairchild
  Second Brigade, Edward Harland

Note. Harland's brigade was present on the battlefield but suffered no casualties.

Kanawha Division, Jacob D. Cox
  Eliakim P. Scammon
  First Brigade, Eliakim P. Scammon
    Hugh Ewing
  Second Brigade, George Crook

Note. Augustus Moor, commanding Second Brigade, was captured September 12, 1862 at Frederick, Maryland, and Crook assumed command of his brigade that day.

Battle of Crampton's Gap, September 14, 1862.

While Reno's Ninth Corps and Hooker's First Corps were attempting to seize Turner's Gap in South Mountain September 14, 1862, Franklin's Sixth Corps was also engaged about five miles to the south at Crampton's Gap.

When Lee divided his army at Frederick, Maryland September 10, 1862 to send a column to capture Harper's Ferry, Lafayette McLaws marched with his own division and that of Richard H. Anderson to occupy Maryland Heights. When he crossed South Mountain, McLaws left Paul J. Semmes' brigade and William Mahone's brigade, then commanded by William A. Parham, at Brownsville Gap to protect the rear of his intended position on Maryland Heights. McLaws then sent Parham with a battery and three infantry regiments of Mahone's brigade north to Crampton's Gap, where Stuart had already posted Beverly H. Robertson's cavalry brigade (then commanded by Thomas T. Munford). Munford, as the senior officer, assumed command

at Crampton's Gap. He then posted the infantry behind a stone wall at the eastern base of South Mountain and to the Confederate left of the road to Burkittsville. He placed his dismounted cavalry on both flanks, and supported the line with his artillery, which was in position on the mountain side. Later, McLaws sent back Howell Cobb with his brigade and with orders to take command and to hold Crampton's Gap.

In the march orders issued by McClellan September 13, 1862 after he learned that Lee had divided his army, he had directed Franklin to advance with his Sixth Corps and Couch's division of Fourth Corps through Crampton's Gap into Pleasant Valley. Upon arriving there, Franklin was to cut off and destroy or capture McLaws' command, and he was also to attempt the relief of Miles' force at Harper's Ferry.

On the morning of September 14, 1862, Franklin marched through Jefferson from his camps three miles east of the town, and about noon his leading division, Henry W. Slocum's First Division, arrived near Burkittsville, one and a half miles southeast of Crampton's Gap. Franklin then directed Slocum to move forward and attack the enemy forces holding the gap. Joseph J. Bartlett's Second Brigade moved out first and, after driving the enemy skirmishers out of Burkittsville, advanced on the road to the gap. John Newton's Third Brigade followed Bartlett, and Alfred T. A. Torbert's First Brigade followed Newton. Franklin held William F. Smith's Second Division in reserve, on the east side of Burkittsville, with instructions to be ready to support Slocum if needed.

Bartlett soon found the enemy in line behind the stone wall, and he then moved to the right and formed his brigade in line of battle. He began his attack about 3:00 P.M. and had been sharply engaged for about a half hour when Newton came up to support his line by placing two regiments of his brigade on the right of Bartlett's brigade and two regiments on the left. Torbert then took position on the left of Newton's two regiments, with the left of his brigade resting on the road to Crampton's Gap. Slocum's entire line, which then extended for about a mile to the north of the road, moved forward and drove the enemy from the wall, over the summit of the pass, and down the other side of the mountain.

When Slocum first became engaged, William T.

H. Brooks' Second Brigade of Smith's division was ordered up the mountain on the left of the road to protect Torbert's left. William H. Irwin's Third Brigade was sent up to support Brooks, who advanced to the crest simultaneously with Slocum. Irwin followed and reached the top of the mountain about dark. Winfield S. Hancock's First Brigade of Smith's division was held in reserve and was not engaged. The casualties in Smith's division were light. Couch's division of Fourth Corps did not arrive at Crampton's Gap until dark and did not take part in the battle.

Advance from South Mountain to Antietam Creek. When Federal pickets advanced at dawn September 15, 1862, they found that the enemy had withdrawn from Turner's Gap and Fox's Gap, and McClellan immediately started the army in pursuit. Richardson, whose First Division, Second Corps had spent the night in rear of First Corps at Mount Tabor Church, was directed to report to Hooker, and was assigned to lead the advance. Richardson's division and Pleasonton's cavalry moved forward on the National Road toward Boonsboro, and they were followed by Hooker's First Corps, Sumner's Second Corps, and Joseph K. F. Mansfield's Twelfth Corps. Mansfield had joined the army that morning at South Mountain and had assumed command of Twelfth Corps, relieving Williams, who resumed command of his First Division of the corps. Also that morning, First Corps was detached from Burnside's Right Wing, and McClellan issued orders directly to Hooker.

Richardson's division and the cavalry moved rapidly through Boonsboro and Keedysville, and as they approached Sharpsburg, they found Lee's army in position on a ridge west of Antietam Creek. D. H. Hill's division was on the high ground between Antietam Creek and the Sharpsburg Ridge to the west; David R. Jones' division of Longstreet's corps was on the right of Hill, occupying a position that covered the Sharpsburg-Boonsboro Pike and the Middle Bridge over the Antietam and was later extended to the right to some high ground above the Lower Bridge; and Hood's division, with some of Jones' brigades, was on the left of Hill on a line that extended from the Dunker Church into the West Wood. This line overlooked the road running from Sharpsburg to Hagerstown.

When Richardson observed Lee's line, he deployed his division along the east bank of the creek, and on the right of the road from Keedysville to Sharpsburg (the Boonsboro Pike), near the Middle Bridge. First Corps, Second Corps, and Twelfth Corps arrived near Keedysville during September 15, 1862 and massed near, and on both sides of, the Keedysville-Sharpsburg Road.

On the left, at Fox's Gap, Sykes' Second Division of Porter's Fifth Corps came up the mountain, passed through the troops of Cox's Ninth Corps, and marched on the Old Sharpsburg Road toward Sharpsburg. Ninth Corps then followed Sykes. When First Corps was taken from Burnside's control that morning, Burnside remained with Ninth Corps, but he did not resume command. Instead, for the next few days, he left Cox in charge, but under his direct supervision. Sykes' division arrived on Antietam Creek a short time after Richardson, and Sykes formed his line along the creek on the left of Richardson's division, and on the left of the Keedysville-Sharpsburg Road.

On the evening of September 15, 1862, Ninth Corps encamped in rear of the extreme left of the Army of the Potomac, close to the hills on the south side of the valley of Antietam Creek, and on the left of the road from Rohrersville to Sharpsburg.

Morell's First Division, Fifth Corps, which was then advancing from Frederick to rejoin the army, was on the road behind Ninth Corps, and it did not join Porter on the Antietam until about noon the next day. Humphreys' new Third Division, Fifth Corps was also on the march from Washington, but it did not join the army until September 18, 1862, the day after the Battle of Antietam.

Early on the morning of September 15, 1862, William F. Smith received orders to move with his division of Franklin's Sixth Corps from Crampton's Gap into Pleasant Valley and proceed toward Harper's Ferry. Slocum was directed to follow with his division of Sixth Corps and support Smith. Couch's division of Fourth Corps was ordered to Rohrersville. Franklin started out on his mission to relieve Harper's Ferry, which was surrendered to Jackson at 9:00 that morning, but he found that McLaws held a position that was too strong to attack. He then remained inactive in Pleasant Valley, without orders from McClellan, until the evening of September 16, 1862.

McClellan made no attempt to attack Lee's waiting army on September 16, 1862, but he spent the morning and the early part of the afternoon riding along the lines and attempting to formulate plans for the coming battle. This was a costly delay, however, because during this time the troops that Lee had sent to Harper's Ferry began to rejoin the army at Sharpsburg. Jackson arrived from Harper's Ferry on the morning of September 16, 1862 with his own division, commanded by John R. Jones, and Ewell's division, commanded by Alexander R. Lawton; and Walker's division came up from Loudoun Heights. Jackson's corps was placed on the Confederate left, behind Hood, and Walker's division was sent to the right. McLaws' division, followed by Richard H. Anderson's division, arrived from Maryland Heights and Pleasant Valley at sunrise September 17, 1862.

By 2:00 P.M. September 16, 1862, McClellan had completed his examination of the enemy position, and he then decided on his plan for an attack the next day. Hooker and Mansfield, supported by Sumner, and also by Franklin if necessary, were to advance against the left of the Confederate line. Then, at a time to be determined by the progress of the battle on the enemy left, Burnside's Ninth Corps, technically under the command of Cox, was to advance against the enemy right. If either of these two attacks succeeded, McClellan planned to strike the enemy center with whatever troops were available.

That afternoon, the Federal troops began moving to their assigned positions in preparation for the impending battle. At 4:00 P.M., Hooker's First Corps left the vicinity of Keedysville and marched westward toward the Sharpsburg-Hagerstown Road (usually called the Hagerstown Pike or Road) and the left of Lee's army. Meade's Third Division and Ricketts' Second Division crossed the Antietam at the bridge near Keedysville (the Upper Bridge), and Doubleday's First Division crossed at a ford a short distance below.

As Hooker advanced, he shifted his direction of march to the left, until finally he was facing south toward Sharpsburg. About 6:00 P.M. he encountered enemy pickets, and he then deployed his corps, with Meade's division in the center, Doubleday's division on the right, and Ricketts' division on the left. Hooker then pushed on slowly until dark and halted for the night a mile and a half to two miles north of Sharpsburg. During this advance he faced strong opposition by two brigades of Hood's division.

That night Hooker's troops were in position as follows: Doubleday's division was along the Hagerstown Pike, facing west, with Patrick's Third Brigade on the right, Hofmann's Second Brigade on the left, and Phelps' First Brigade and Gibbon's Fourth Brigade east of the road in reserve. Meade's line began at the left of Hofmann's brigade and ran eastward between Joseph Poffenberger's house and the North Woods. Anderson's Third Brigade was on the right, next to the Hagerstown Pike, and Magilton's Second Brigade was on the left of Anderson. Seymour's First Brigade was on the left of the division, but it was not on the line with the other two brigades. It bivouacked that night farther to the front on the Smoketown Road, just north of the East Woods. Ricketts' division halted on the Smoketown Road in rear of Seymour's brigade, with Hartsuff's Third Brigade deployed across the road. The other two brigades were in rear of Hartsuff, with Duryee's First Brigade on the right of the road, and Christian's Second Brigade on the left.

About 6:00 P.M., Mansfield was ordered to cross the Antietam with his Twelfth Corps and follow Hooker. Mansfield bivouacked that night about a mile north of Hooker's position, near the intersection of the Smoketown Road and the road that ran from Keedysville, through Smoketown, to the Hagerstown Pike.

On the far left of McClellan's line, Burnside also moved his Ninth Corps forward on the afternoon of September 16, 1862. The entire corps, except Willcox's First Division, which was held in reserve, advanced to the left front and took position on the rear slopes of the ridges just east of Antietam Creek. The center of the corps' line was nearly opposite the stone bridge over the creek on which the road from Rohrersville to Sharpsburg crossed. This bridge was generally referred to as the Lower Bridge, and is known today as "Burnside's Bridge." Crook's Second Brigade of Scammon's Kanawha Division was on the right front, and it was supported in the rear by Sturgis' Second Division; the artillery was posted on the center of the line; and Rodman's Third Division was on the left front, and it was supported in the rear by Ewing's First Brigade of Scammon's division. Samuel W. Benjamin's Battery E, 2nd

United States Artillery of Willcox's division was placed on the crest of a hill immediately in front of the Lower Bridge, and the remaining batteries of the corps were halted in rear of the crest, where they were under partial cover.

Sumner's Second Corps and Porter, with the divisions of Sykes and Morell (the latter had arrived on the field that afternoon) of his Fifth Corps, remained in bivouac on the night of September 16, 1862, in the positions that they had occupied during that day.

Battle of Antietam (or Sharpsburg), September 17, 1862. The Battle of Antietam began early on the morning of September 17, 1862, when Hooker's First Corps advanced against the left of the Confederate line. This was held by Jackson with his own division, commanded by John R. Jones, and Ewell's division, commanded by Alexander R. Lawton.

Doubleday's division, which led the attack, formed on the Hagerstown Pike, and then Gibbon's brigade, supported by Patrick's brigade, advanced along the west side of the road toward Sharpsburg. Gibbon was soon engaged in desperate fighting with Lawton's division in a cornfield on the David R. Miller farm (known today simply as "The Cornfield"), and also against Jones in the woods on the west side of the road. Patrick's brigade came up and supported Gibbon for a time and then moved to the right of the road to attack the enemy in the West Woods. Phelps' brigade was held back at first, but it was then sent forward to the rear of Gibbon's brigade in the cornfield. The infantry was well supported by Doubleday's artillery during the attack. Joseph B. Campbell's Battery B, 4th United States Artillery accompanied Gibbon through the woods and then went into action on the open space beyond. Frederick M. Edgell's 1st Battery, New Hampshire Light Artillery; J. Albert Monroe's Battery D, 1st Rhode Island Light Artillery; and John A. Reynolds' Battery L, 1st New York Light Artillery fired from the ridge where they had spent the night. Hofmann's brigade of Doubleday's division remained in its position of the night before and supported these batteries. In addition, James H. Cooper's Battery B, 1st Pennsylvania Light Artillery and John G. Simpson's Battery A, 1st Pennsylvania Light Artil-

lery of Meade's division joined Doubleday's batteries on the ridge.

Seymour's brigade of Meade's division became engaged at daylight in the East Woods, which bordered the cornfield on the east, and it maintained its position there until relieved by Ricketts' division. Ricketts advanced into the East Woods, with Hartsuff's brigade in the center of the division, Duryee's brigade on the right and rear of Hartsuff, and Christian's brigade on the left and rear of Hartsuff. The fighting in the woods was violent, and Ricketts lost about one-third of his division. Hartsuff's and Christian's brigades succeeded in reaching the outer edge of the woods, and they maintained their positions there until they had exhausted their ammunition. Duryee's brigade, on the right of the division, advanced into the cornfield, where it was engaged.

By 7:00 A.M., Hooker's divisions had driven Jackson's brigades from the northern part of the West Woods, the cornfield, and the East Woods and had inflicted and suffered appalling losses, but they were at that time threatening the entire left of Lee's line. The situation changed dramatically, however, when Hood's division emerged from the West Woods near the Dunker Church and charged into the cornfield and the East Woods. This impetuous attack by fresh troops stopped Hooker's advancing brigades and drove them back. The brigades of Anderson and Magilton of Meade's division had been held in reserve during the early part of the action, but when Hood attacked, they advanced to a position in rear of Doubleday. When they reached the cornfield they moved into a ravine that extended up from the pike. At that time, Hood was driving Doubleday's troops from the cornfield, and Anderson and Magilton formed their brigades in line of battle along a fence bordering the field to cover the withdrawal. Magilton was then sent to the left, to the East Woods, to reinforce Ricketts and Seymour, who were hard pressed, and Anderson was left to hold the fence. Gibbon placed Joseph B. Campbell's Battery B, 4th United States Artillery on the Hagerstown Pike, where it fired canister at almost point-blank range into the enemy infantry in the cornfield, and soon forced Hood to fall back.

Hooker's attack had virtually ended by 7:30

A.M., and by 9:00 A.M. most of First Corps had been withdrawn to the north of the field near the Hagerstown Pike to reorganize. Hooker was wounded during the fighting, and Meade assumed command of First Corps. Seymour succeeded Meade in command of Third Division, First Corps, and R. Biddle Roberts assumed command of Seymour's First Brigade.

At 7:00 A.M., while Hooker was engaged with Hood's division, Mansfield's Twelfth Corps began to arrive from its bivouac in rear of First Corps. Mansfield was mortally wounded while deploying his troops, and Williams again assumed command of Twelfth Corps. Samuel W. Crawford assumed command of Williams' First Division, and Joseph F. Knipe succeeded Crawford in command of First Brigade. It should be noted, however, that Knipe did not officially assume command of First Brigade until that afternoon.

Crawford's First Division advanced on the right and front of Twelfth Corps, with Knipe's First Brigade on the right, next to the Hagerstown Pike, and George H. Gordon's Third Brigade on the left. George S. Greene's Second Division came up on the Smoketown Road, to the left of Gordon, and advanced to the East Woods. While Greene's division was approaching the field, William B. Goodrich's Third Brigade, Second Division was detached and sent to the right to support Doubleday's division, west of the Hagerstown Road.

When Twelfth Corps was in position it moved forward. Gordon's brigade advanced past the Miller buildings and aided in driving the enemy from the cornfield, but Knipe's brigade on the right made little progress and later withdrew. Greene's division on the left pushed forward into the East Woods.

At that time, three brigades of D. H. Hill's division advanced from the vicinity of the Mumma house, and they then charged onto the Miller farm and into the East Woods against Williams' Twelfth Corps. After more than an hour of very hard fighting, Hill withdrew to a sunken road on the southern edge of the Mumma farm. Greene's division then moved forward to a position on open ground on a slight elevation opposite the Dunker Church, and across the Hagerstown Pike from the West Woods. By 9:00 A.M., Crawford's First Division was in position

approximately one-half mile north of the Dunker Church, with its line generally facing south; and Greene's Second Division was just east of the Dunker Church. Between these two divisions, on ground over which Sedgwick's division of Second Corps would soon pass, there were practically no Federal troops.

At 7:20 that morning, Edwin V. Sumner was ordered to move to the right with his Second Corps and support Hooker in his attack on the Confederate left. John Sedgwick's Second Division started immediately, and it was followed by William H. French's Third Division. Israel B. Richardson's First Division, then in position along Antietam Creek, did not move until later, when it was relieved by George W. Morell's First Division of Porter's Fifth Corps. The three divisions of Second Corps did not fight as a unit during the day, and the participation of each division in the battle will be considered separately.

Sedgwick's division, accompanied by Sumner in person, crossed the Antietam at the ford used the day before by First Corps and Twelfth Corps, and it then marched to the west in three columns toward the East Woods. They entered the woods from the south and then faced to the left, and formed in a column of three deployed brigades, facing west. Willis A. Gorman's First Brigade was in front; Napoleon J. T. Dana's Third Brigade was next; and William W. Burns' Second Brigade, then commanded by Oliver O. Howard, was in the rear. When the deployment was complete, Sumner ordered the division to advance. As Sedgwick moved forward, Crawford's division of Twelfth Corps, which was to the right of Sedgwick, withdrew to replenish its ammunition; and with its departure, all fighting on that part of the field ceased.

With no opposition at all, Sedgwick marched straight ahead, across the cornfield and the Hagerstown Pike. The division crossed the latter just north of the Dunker Church and then entered the West Woods beyond. At the western edge of the woods, Gorman encountered Jubal A. Early's brigade, which opened fire, and a short time later the two following brigades received a destructive fire on their left and rear from McLaws' division, which had just arrived from Pleasant Valley and formed on the left of Sedgwick's advancing column. Sedgwick's division was virtually destroyed, losing 2,200 men in a very short time. Most of the survivors escaped to the north and reassembled in the vicinity of the Miller farm. Gordon's brigade advanced to aid Sedgwick, but it was too late to affect the outcome of his battle. Sedgwick was wounded, and Howard succeeded him in command of Second Division. Joshua T. Owen assumed command of Howard's Second Brigade.

Not long after Sedgwick's defeat in the West Woods, Greene pushed forward from his position east of the Hagerstown Pike and moved into the West Woods at the Dunker Church. Henry J. Stainrook's Second Brigade was on the right and Hector Tyndale's First Brigade was on the left. Greene remained in this new position from 10:00 A.M. until noon, when he was forced to withdraw. Tyndale was wounded during the fighting, and he was succeeded in command of First Brigade by Orrin J. Crane. Goodrich, whose Third Brigade, Second Division, Twelfth Corps had been engaged on the right of McClellan's line, west of the Hagerstown Pike, was killed, and Jonathan Austin succeeded him in command of the brigade.

By 10:00 A.M., all hard fighting on the Federal right had ended, and all gains of the morning had been lost. Greene still held fast at the Dunker Church, but most of the remaining troops that had been engaged had been withdrawn to the east side of the Hagerstown Road. Meade's First Corps, Williams' Twelfth Corps, and Sedgwick's division of Second Corps had been heavily damaged and were to be of no further service that day.

At 10:00 A.M., William F. Smith's leading Second Division of Franklin's Sixth Corps arrived on the Antietam from Pleasant Valley, and a short time later it was sent to the right to support Sumner. As noted above, Smith was too late to help Sedgwick, but when his leading brigade, Hancock's First Brigade, arrived near the East Woods it was placed in support of three batteries which were in position a short distance east of the northeast corner of the cornfield, facing the Miller farm buildings and the Hagerstown Road. These batteries were Andrew Cowan's 1st Battery, New York Light Artillery of Smith's division; John D. Frank's Battery G, 1st New York Light Artillery of French's Third Division, Second Corps; and George W. Cothran's

Battery M, 1st New York Light Artillery of Twelfth Corps. Hancock's brigade remained in this position during the rest of the day, but early in the afternoon Hancock left to assume command of Richardson's First Division, Second Corps, and Amasa Cobb assumed command of Hancock's First Brigade.

When Irwin's Third Brigade of Smith's division came up, it was placed on the left of Hancock's brigade, and later Brooks' Second Brigade of the same division arrived on the left of Irwin. At that time, Brooks' brigade faced no opposition, but immediately after Irwin's brigade was deployed, Smith ordered Irwin to move out and attack an enemy force advancing on its front. The brigade passed through Evan Thomas' Batteries A and C, 4th United States Artillery, then charged the enemy, and succeeded in reaching the Hagerstown Pike abreast of the Dunker Church. Irwin's brigade maintained its ground near the church for some time, but was then roughly handled when it withdrew. A short time after this attack, Brooks' brigade was sent to the right of French's Third Division, Second Corps, and it remained there the rest of the day.

Slocum, with his First Division, Sixth Corps, arrived on the field from Pleasant Valley about noon and promptly moved to the right to join Smith's division. Upon arriving there, Newton's Third Brigade and Torbert's First Brigade were formed for an attack on the West Woods, to the right of the Dunker Church. When Slocum's brigades were deployed, Torbert's brigade was in position across the Smoketown Road; Newton's brigade was on the right of Torbert, with its right near the Miller cornfield; and Bartlett's Second Brigade was in reserve. Before Slocum's line moved forward, Sumner expressed his opposition to the attack, and when McClellan agreed, it was called off. Slocum's division remained in this same position during the rest of the day.

As the fighting on the Confederate left ended, the action shifted to the center of the line. At 7:30 A.M., French's Third Division of Sumner's Second Corps crossed the Antietam at the ford used by Sedgwick's Second Division, and then followed the latter closely for about a mile toward the East Woods. Then, instead of continuing on to support Sedgwick, French faced his command to the left and advanced over the William Roulette farm toward the enemy position along the Sunken Road. Max Weber's

Third Brigade was in the lead, and it was followed, in order, by Dwight Morris' Second Brigade and Nathan Kimball's First Brigade.

After advancing about three-fourths of a mile, Weber encountered enemy pickets, but he pushed on and and drove the Confederate infantry from the buildings of the Roulette farm, which were about 650 yards east of the Dunker Church. At about that time, Sumner ordered French to attack and create a diversion so as to aid Sedgwick, who, as described above, was in trouble in the West Woods. Kimball's brigade was then moved up to the left of Weber, where it formed on the lane running from the Roulette house to the Sunken Road, and it then moved up to the crest of a hill overlooking the road, which was held in force by troops of D. H. Hill's division.

The Sunken Road, which after the battle was called "Bloody Lane," was a narrow lane or road that branched off at nearly a right angle from the Hagerstown Pike, about a fourth of a mile south of the Dunker Church. It then ran a little north of east for about a fourth of a mile, then a little south of east for another fourth of a mile, and then it turned at almost a right angle to the south and ran through a series of curves and joined the Boonsboro Pike between Sharpsburg and the Middle Bridge. For the first approximately one-half mile east of the Hagerstown Pike, the bed of the road was generally below the level of the adjoining fields, and for this reason it was called the Sunken Road. It was, in effect, a shallow trench, and it formed a very strong natural defensive position.

Kimball's brigade attempted to advance from the ridge but was unable to do so because of the heavy fire from the Sunken Road; it did maintain its position for more than three hours, during which time there were several charges and countercharges along the line. Weber's brigade also advanced toward the Sunken Road, but after severe fighting, during which Weber was wounded, it was forced to fall back. John W. Andrews assumed command of Weber's brigade. Morris' brigade was held in reserve near the Roulette house during the early part of this action.

During the fighting at the Sunken Road, the enemy advanced and threatened the right of French's division. Brooks' brigade of Smith's division of Sixth Corps was then detached from the

left of Irwin's brigade and sent to the right of French's division. Morris' brigade, which had been placed under Kimball's orders, was then brought up from the Roulette house to support Brooks and Kimball.

Richardson's First Division of Second Corps, which had remained on the Antietam until relieved by Morell's division, crossed the creek at 9:30 A.M. at the ford used earlier by the other divisions of the corps, and then moved rapidly to the support of French's division. Richardson marched southward on a course parallel to the creek, and then deployed in a small valley on the left of French. Thomas F. Meagher's Second Brigade was on the right; John C. Caldwell's First Brigade was on the left; and John R. Brooke's Third Brigade was in reserve behind Meagher's brigade. Richardson then advanced to a position a short distance to the left of French and farther to the south. Meagher's brigade took position on the left of a lane running from the Clipp house to the Sunken Road, and then, with hard fighting, pushed forward to a ridge overlooking the Sunken Road, and also the Piper house about 700 yards beyond in the direction of Sharpsburg. Meagher's brigade was unable to advance farther, and Caldwell's brigade, which faced no enemy troops on its front, moved to the right and relieved Meagher. The latter then marched to the rear to obtain more ammunition. At about that time, Meagher was injured by a fall from his horse, and John Burke assumed command of his brigade.

Brooke's brigade remained in support of Caldwell, and at one point, when an enemy attack seriously threatened the left of Kimball's position, Brooke sent three regiments to help. These regiments, together with some other troops from the left of French, drove the enemy back and restored the line.

After Caldwell had relieved Meagher's brigade, he advanced and broke the enemy line except on the extreme right, where it was protected by the Sunken Road. Then Francis C. Barlow, commanding 61st and 64th New York, changed front, and from a position at the bend of the road where it turned south toward the Boonsboro Pike, he forced the surrender of most of the troops holding the Sunken Road by a destructive enfilade fire. Meantime, Caldwell, followed by Brooke, drove the enemy back through the Piper cornfield, which was south of the Sunken

Road, toward the Piper house and orchard. During the advance, Caldwell's left was threatened, and the left regiment, commanded by Edward C. Cross, moved to the left and drove the enemy back. Brooke's brigade was then moved up on the left of Caldwell to fill the gap between Cross and the rest of the brigade. Caldwell and Brooke pressed on and drove the enemy from the cornfield and finally gained possession of the Piper farm buildings and orchard.

The fighting ended on this part of the field about 1:00 P.M., but the troops remained under artillery fire for some time. Richardson withdrew his line a short distance from the Piper house and orchard to the crest of a hill, where it remained the rest of the day. While attending to these movements, Richardson was mortally wounded, and Caldwell assumed temporary command of the division. A short time later, Winfield S. Hancock, formerly commander of First Brigade of Smith's Second Division, Sixth Corps, arrived from the right of McClellan's line and relieved Caldwell. Barlow was also wounded near the Piper orchard, and he was succeeded in command of the two New York regiments by Nelson A. Miles. About 1:00 P.M., Meagher's brigade, then commanded by John Burke, came up from the rear and took position in the center of Richardson's line. Morris' brigade also came up in reserve.

On the morning of September 17, 1862, Alfred Pleasonton left Keedysville with his cavalry division and the horse batteries of artillery. His orders were to advance on the road toward Sharpsburg and form his command beyond Antietam Creek at some point where he could support the left of Sumner's line of battle. He crossed the creek at the Middle Bridge about noon and placed his guns on a ridge a short distance beyond. These belonged to John C. Tidball's Battery A, 2nd United States Artillery; James M. Robertson's Batteries B and L, Second United States Artillery; Peter C. Hains' Battery M, Second United States Artillery; and Horatio G. Gibson's Batteries C and G, 3rd United States Artillery. During the afternoon the artillery was engaged against the center of the enemy line that was on the site of the present National Cemetery, and it also provided some support to the left of Sumner's line, about a mile distant, and also to Ninth Corps on its left. During the afternoon,

Charles Kusserow's Battery D, 1st Battalion New York Light Artillery and Alanson M. Randol's Batteries E and G, 1st United States Artillery of Fifth Corps replaced Pleasonton's batteries while they replenished their ammunition. The cavalry and five battalions of infantry from Sykes' division of Fifth Corps supported the artillery. During the day, Pleasonton's command was the only Federal force between Sumner's corps on the right and Ninth Corps on the left.

The final Federal attacks of the day were made against the enemy right near Sharpsburg. At 7:00 A.M. September 17, 1862, Burnside received orders from McClellan to be ready to attack and force a passage at the Lower Bridge over the Antietam. It was not until 9:00 A.M., however, after the Federal left had been in action for several hours, that McClellan directed Burnside to advance. Jacob D. Cox, who was officially in command of Ninth Corps but was acting under the direct supervision of Burnside, issued the necessary orders between 9:00 and 10:00 A.M. According to these orders, Crook's Second Brigade of the Kanawha Division was to advance on the right and, with the support of Sturgis' Second Division, attempt to cross the bridge. Rodman, on the left, was to move downstream with his Third Division and Ewing's First Brigade (Scammon's) of the Kanawha Division and cross the Antietam at Snavely's Ford, about a third of a mile below the Lower Bridge. After crossing the creek, the two columns were to unite and advance on Sharpsburg.

The only enemy troops in position to oppose this attack were five brigades of David R. Jones' division of Longstreet's corps. On the high ground overlooking the Lower Bridge were two Georgia regiments of Robert Toombs' brigade, and to their right was the 50th Georgia of Thomas F. Drayton's brigade (temporarily assigned to Toombs), which was guarding a farm road running up from Snavely's Ford. Earlier, at the beginning of the Maryland Campaign, Toombs had been assigned to the command of a temporary division, but at Antietam the only brigade with him was his own brigade, then under the immediate supervision of Henry L. Benning. Behind Toombs was the rest of Jones' division. Its left was on the Boonsboro Road at the eastern edge of Sharpsburg, and it then curved around to the south and west to the Harper's Ferry Road, a little less than a third of a mile south of Sharpsburg.

On September 17, 1862, in preparation for Burnside's attack, Benjamin's battery was left in its original position on the crest of the hill, but the other batteries were moved up on the hills bordering the Antietam, where they overlooked the Middle Bridge and the high ground beyond the creek. Joseph C. Clark's Battery E, 4th United States Artillery and George W. Durell's Battery D, Pennsylvania Light Artillery of Sturgis' division were on the right and front of Benjamin. Stephen H. Weed's Battery I, 5th United States Artillery of Fifth Corps was on the right of Durell's battery, and Clark's battery was on the left. Charles P. Muhlenberg's Battery A, 5th United States Artillery of Rodman's division; Asa M. Cook's 8th Battery, Massachusetts Light Artillery of Willcox's division; and James R. McMullin's 1st Battery, Ohio Light Artillery of Ewing's Brigade, Kanawha Division were on the left and rear of Benjamin. One section of Seth J. Simmonds' Battery of Kentucky Light Artillery was with Crook's brigade, and one section was with Benjamin.

Burnside's first attack on the bridge was made at 10:00 A.M. by the 11th Connecticut, which was detached from Harland's Second Brigade of Rodman's division. Its mission was to secure a crossing for Crook's brigade, but it was unsuccessful in this attempt. When Crook finally came over the ridge on his advance to cross the creek, he was moving in the wrong direction, and he reached the Antietam a few hundred yards above the bridge. There he was forced to halt and return a heavy enemy fire.

After Crook's failure, Sturgis formed an assaulting column consisting of the 2nd Maryland and 6th New Hampshire from Nagle's First Brigade, and these regiments were to be supported by Ferrero's Second Brigade. The attack was made about noon, but it too failed. A new storming party was then organized from Ferrero's brigade, and it consisted of Robert B. Potter's 51st New York and John F. Hartranft's 51st Pennsylvania. At 1:00 P.M. these regiments, aided by Crook's artillery, carried the bridge and drove off the defenders. Sturgis' division then crossed the bridge, and when it arrived on the other side, Ferrero's brigade filed to the right and Nagle's brigade to the left. The division then moved up the hill and occupied the high ground above the bridge. Crook's brigade finally crossed at a ford

above the bridge, and took position to the right and rear of Sturgis.

Meantime, Rodman's advance had been delayed while scouts attempted to find the ford. When it finally was located, Fairchild's First Brigade crossed the creek and moved up to the high ground on the left of Sturgis. Harland's Second Brigade followed, and formed on the left of Fairchild. Scammon, with Ewing's brigade, crossed last and formed on the left of Harland. Thus, by shortly after 1:00 P.M., Burnside's command was across the Antietam and in position to move forward toward Sharpsburg. At that time, however, Sturgis reported that his division was without ammunition and that it was unable to advance. Then two hours of valuable time were lost while Willcox's division was brought up from reserve to relieve Sturgis. Finally, at 3:00 P.M., when most of the fighting had ended on the other parts of the field, Burnside's line advanced.

Willcox's division moved forward along the road to Sharpsburg, with Christ's First Brigade on the right of the road, and Thomas Welch's Second Brigade on the left of the road. Crook's brigade supported Willcox on the right. Rodman advanced on the left of Willcox, with Fairchild's brigade on the right of the division and Harland's brigade on the left. Scammon, with Ewing's brigade, supported Rodman on the left. Sturgis was left behind to hold the crest of the hill above the Lower Bridge.

Willcox's division advanced rapidly to the eastern outskirts of Sharpsburg, and gained the high ground where the National Cemetery now stands. On the left, however, Rodman encountered stiffer resistance from the enemy posted on the ridges to his left. He was thus forced to swing his front in that direction, and as he moved forward, a gap developed between the right of his line and the left of Willcox.

At some time after 3:00 P.M.—probably about 3:40 P.M.—A. P. Hill's division of Jackson's corps began to arrive from Harper's Ferry and move into the rear of the Confederate right, where it formed to the left of Rodman's division. When Scammon observed this, he changed front to the left and for a time protected Rodman's left from behind a line of stone fences. Then James J. Archer's brigade of A. P. Hill's division and Toombs' brigade of Jones' division charged and struck the left of Harland's brigade, while farther to the Confederate right the brigades of William D. Pender and Lawrence O'B.

Branch supported the attack with a heavy fire. Rodman was mortally wounded, and Harland's brigade was broken and pushed back in confusion. Fairchild, with his left thus exposed, was forced to fall back and change front to the left.

Cox, with his entire line endangered, ordered Willcox to fall back, and at the same time brought forward Sturgis' division. Scammon continued to hold the stone wall until Sturgis was in position on some high ground to his rear, but soon the entire Ninth Corps' line was withdrawn to a defensive position covering the Lower Bridge over the Antietam, with both flanks resting on the stream. At that time it was about 5:00 P.M., and the Battle of Antietem had finally come to an end. Both armies remained on the field that night and the next day, but on the night of September 18, 1862, the Army of Northern Virginia withdrew across the Potomac into Virginia. McClellan did not follow, and the Maryland Campaign came to an end.

The Army of the Potomac remained near the battlefield for a short time, and then moved into positions along the upper Potomac, generally on the Maryland side of the river. On September 19, 1862, Williams' Twelfth Corps was ordered to Harper's Ferry and Couch's division of Fourth Corps was sent to Williamsport, Maryland. Franklin's Sixth Corps followed Couch to Williamsport the next day. September 22, 1862, Sumner's Second Corps was ordered to Harper's Ferry to take position on Bolivar Heights. Ninth Corps, still under Cox, moved to the mouth of Antietam Creek and remained there until October 7, 1862. Later, it moved to Harper's Ferry and went into camp in Pleasant Valley . Meade's First Corps and Porter's Fifth Corps remained near the battlefield until late October 1862, when the Army of the Potomac began its belated advance into Virginia.

The organization of the troops engaged at the Battle of Antietam September 17, 1862 was as follows:

FIRST CORPS, Joseph Hooker, wounded
George G. Meade

First Division, Abner Doubleday
First Brigade, Walter Phelps, Jr.
Second Brigade, J. William Hofmann
Third Brigade, Marsena R. Patrick
Fourth Brigade, John Gibbon
Artillery, J. Albert Monroe

1st Battery, New Hampshire Light Artillery, Frederick M. Edgell
Battery G, 1st Rhode Island Light Artillery, J. Albert Monroe
Battery L, 1st New York Light Artillery, John A. Reynolds
Battery B, 4th United States Artillery, Joseph B. Campbell, wounded
James Stewart

Second Division, James B. Ricketts
First Brigade, Abram Duryee (Duryea)
Second Brigade, William A. Christian
Peter Lyle
Third Brigade, George L. Hartsuff, wounded
Richard Coulter
Artillery
Battery F, 1st Pennsylvania Light Artillery, Ezra W. Matthews
Battery C, Pennsylvania Light Artillery, James Thompson

Third Division, George G. Meade
Truman Seymour
First Brigade, Truman Seymour
R. Biddle Roberts
Second Brigade, Albert L. Magilton
Third Brigade, Robert Anderson
Artillery
Battery A, 1st Pennsylvania Light Artillery, John G. Simpson
Battery B, 1st Pennsylvania Light Artillery, James H. Cooper
Battery C, 5th United States Artillery, Dunbar R. Ransom

SECOND CORPS, Edwin V. Sumner

First Division, Israel B. Richardson, mortally wounded
John C. Caldwell, temporarily
Winfield S. Hancock
First Brigade, John C. Caldwell
Second Brigade, Thomas F. Meagher, injured
John Burke
Third Brigade, John R. Brooke
Artillery
Battery B, 1st New York Light Artillery, Rufus D. Pettit
Batteries A and C, 4th United States Artillery, Evan Thomas

Second Division, John Sedgwick, wounded
Oliver O. Howard
First Brigade, Willis A. Gorman
Second Brigade, Oliver O. Howard

Joshua T. Owen

De Witt C. Baxter

Third Brigade, Napoleon J. T. Dana, wounded

Norman J. Hall

Artillery

Battery A, 1st Rhode Island Light Artillery, John A. Tompkins

Battery I, 1st United States Artillery, George A. Woodruff

Note. Baxter's regiment was separated from Second Brigade during the fighting in the West Woods, but Baxter, as senior officer, assumed command of the brigade when he rejoined during the afternoon.

Third Division, William H. French

First Brigade, Nathan Kimball

Second Brigade, Dwight Morris

Third Brigade, Max Weber, wounded

John W. Andrews

Unattached Artillery

Battery G, 1st New York Light Artillery, John D. Frank

Battery B, 1st Rhode Island Light Artillery, John G. Hazard

Battery G, 1st Rhode Island Light Artillery, Charles D. Owen

FOURTH CORPS

First Division, Darius N. Couch

First Brigade, Charles Devens, Jr.

Second Brigade, Albion P. Howe

Third Brigade, John Cochrane

Note. Couch's division did not reach the battlefield until September 18, 1862, and it was not engaged in the battle. Cochrane's Third Brigade suffered a few casualties September 18, 1862.

FIFTH CORPS, Fitz John Porter

First Division, George W. Morell

First Brigade, James Barnes

Second Brigade, Charles Griffin

Third Brigade, Thomas B. W. Stockton

Artillery

Battery C, Massachusetts Light Artillery, Augustus P. Martin

Battery C, 1st Rhode Island Light Artillery, Richard Waterman

Battery D, 5th United States Artillery, Charles E. Hazlett

Second Division, George Sykes

First Brigade, Robert C. Buchanan

Second Brigade, Charles S. Lovell

Third Brigade, Gouverneur K. Warren

Artillery

Batteries E and G, 1st United States Artillery, Alanson M. Randol

Battery I, 5th United States Artillery, Stephen H. Weed

Battery K, 5th United States Artillery, William E. Van Reed

Third Division, Andrew A. Humphreys

First Brigade, Erastus B. Tyler

Second Brigade, Peter H. Allabach

Artillery, Lucius N. Robinson

Battery C, 1st New York Light Artillery, Almont Barnes

Battery L, 1st Ohio Light Artillery, Lucius N. Robinson

Artillery Reserve, William Hays

Battery A, 1st Battalion New York Light Artillery, Bernhard Wever

Battery B, 1st Battalion New York Light Artillery, Alfred Von Kleiser

Battery C, 1st Battalion New York Light Artillery, Robert Langner

Battery D, 1st Battalion New York Light Artillery, Charles Kusserow

5th Battery, New York Light Artillery, Elijah D. Taft

Battery K, 1st United States Artillery, William M. Graham

Battery G, 4th United States Artillery, Marcus P. Miller

Note. Only Sykes' Second Division and a part of the artillery was engaged. Morell's First Division was on the east side of Antietam Creek in reserve, and Humphreys' Third Division did not arrive and join the corps until September 18, 1862.

SIXTH CORPS, William B. Franklin

First Division, Henry W. Slocum

First Brigade, Alfred T. A. Torbert

Second Brigade, Joseph J. Bartlett

Third Brigade, John Newton

Artillery, Emory Upton

Battery A, Maryland Light Artillery, John P. Wolcott

Battery A, Massachusetts Light Artillery, Josiah Porter

Battery A, New Jersey Light Artillery, William Hexamer

Battery D, 2nd United States Artillery, Edward B. Williston

Second Division, William F. Smith
First Brigade, Winfield S. Hancock
Amasa Cobb
Second Brigade, William T. H. Brooks
Third Brigade, William H. Irwin
Artillery, Romeyn B. Ayres
Battery B, Maryland Light Artillery, Theodore J. Vanneman
1st Battery, New York Light Artillery, Andrew Cowan
Battery F, 5th United States Artillery, Leonard Martin

Note. Hancock was assigned command of First Division, Second Corps on the afternoon of September 17, 1862.

NINTH CORPS, Ambrose E. Burnside
Jacob D. Cox

First Division, Orlando B. Willcox
First Brigade, Benjamin C. Christ
Second Brigade, Thomas Welch
Artillery
8th Battery, Massachusetts Light Artillery, Asa M. Cook
Battery E, 2nd United States Artillery, Samuel N. Benjamin

Second Division, Samuel D. Sturgis
First Brigade, James Nagle
Second Brigade, Edward Ferrero
Artillery
Battery D, Pennsylvania Light Artillery, George W. Durell
Battery E, 4th United States Artillery, Joseph C. Clark, Jr.

Third Division, Isaac P. Rodman, mortally wounded
Edward Harland
First Brigade, Harrison S. Fairchild
Second Brigade, Edward Harland
Artillery
Battery A, 5th United States Artillery, Charles P. Muhlenberg

Kanawha Division, Eliakim P. Scammon
First Brigade, Hugh Ewing
Second Brigade, George Crook
Artillery
Batteries L and M, 3rd United States Artillery, John Edwards, Jr.

TWELFTH CORPS, Joseph K. F. Mansfield, mortally wounded
Alpheus S. Williams

First Division, Alpheus S. Williams

Samuel W. Crawford, wounded
George H. Gordon
First Brigade, Samuel W. Crawford
Joseph F. Knipe
Third Brigade, George H. Gordon
Thomas H. Ruger

Second Division, George S. Greene
First Brigade, Hector Tyndale, wounded
Orrin J. Crane
Second Brigade, Henry J. Stainrook
Third Brigade, William B. Goodrich, killed
Jonathan Austin

Artillery, Clermont L. Best
4th Battery, Maine Light Artillery, O'Neil W. Robinson
6th Battery, Maine Light Artillery, Freeman McGilvery
Battery M, 1st New York Light Artillery, George W. Cothran
10th Battery, New York light Artillery, John T. Bruen
Battery E, Pennsylvania Light Artillery, Joseph M. Knap
Battery F, Pennsylvania Light Artillery, Robert F. Hampton
Battery F, 4th United States Artillery, Edward D. Muhlenberg

CAVALRY DIVISION, ARMY OF THE POTOMAC, Alfred Pleasonton

First Brigade, Charles J. Whiting
Second Brigade, John F. Farnsworth
Third Brigade, Richard H. Rush
Fourth Brigade, Andrew T. McReynolds
Fifth Brigade, Benjamin F. Davis
Artillery
Battery A, 2nd United States Artillery, John C. Tidball
Batteries B and L, 2nd United States Artillery, James M. Robertson
Battery M, 2nd United States Artillery, Peter C. Hains
Batteries C and G, 3rd United States Artillery, Horatio G. Gibson

Note. Only the First, Second, and Third brigades of cavalry were engaged at Antietam.

MINE RUN CAMPAIGN, VIRGINIA NOVEMBER 26–DECEMBER 2, 1863

After the successful Union attacks at Kelly's Ford and Rappahannock Station November 7, 1863,

Robert E. Lee's Army of Northern Virginia withdrew to a line in front of Culpeper Court House, and then it moved on across the Rapidan River to the old positions that it had occupied before the Bristoe, Virginia Campaign. George G. Meade's Army of the Potomac followed and, November 9, 1863, established a line that extended from Kelly's Ford on the left, through Brandy Station, to Welford's Ford on Hazel River on the right. Meade waited until November 19, 1863 for the Orange and Alexandria Railroad to be repaired as far as Brandy Station, and he then prepared to resume the offensive before active operations ended for the winter.

Meade believed that Lee's position behind the Rapidan was too strong for a successful frontal attack, and he decided on an attempt to turn its right flank by crossing to the south side of the Rapidan at the lower fords and then advancing westward toward Orange Court House. The movement was scheduled to begin November 24, 1863, and orders were issued the night before for the corps to march as follows: Gouverneur K. Warren's Second Corps was to move from Mountain Run to Germanna Ford, then cross the river and march by way of the Germanna Plank Road and the Orange Turnpike to Locust Grove (also called Robertson's or Robinson's Tavern). George Sykes' Fifth Corps was to advance from Paoli Mills by the Ridge Road and Richardsville to Culpeper Ford (Culpeper Mine Ford), which was about midway between Germanna Ford and Ely's Ford. Sykes was to cross the river there, and then march by way of Wilderness Tavern and the Orange Plank Road to Parker's Store, and from there move to the northwest so as to come in on the left of Warren.

On November 20, 1863, in preparation for the advance of the army, Meade ordered John Newton, whose First Corps was north of the Rappahannock guarding the railroad, to be ready to concentrate the corps at Rappahannock Station. He was to leave John R. Kenly's Third Division, First Corps on the railroad and be prepared to march with his other two divisions. Meade's order of November 23, 1863 directed Newton to march with Solomon Meredith's First Division and John C. Robinson's Second Division to Paoli Mills. From that point, Newton was to follow Fifth Corps by way of Culpeper Ford and the Orange Plank Road and form in the rear of Fifth Corps near Locust Grove. The Reserve Artillery of the army was to follow First Corps. William H. French's Third Corps was to move from Brandy Station, cross Mountain Run at Ross' Mills, and then march on the Germanna Ford Road to within a short distance of the ford. French was then to turn to the right, cross the Rapidan at Jacob's Ford, and follow the road to Locust Grove, where he was to form on the right of Second Corps, on the road from Locust Grove to Raccoon Ford.

John Sedgwick's Sixth Corps was to march from its camps near Welford's Ford to Brandy Station, and from there it was to follow Third Corps by way of Jacob's Ford and take position in rear of Third Corps on the Jacob's Ford Road.

Meade's plan called for all three columns to cross the Rapidan at about the same time, and then for all corps to march to the vicinity of Locust Grove. From there they were to move forward together toward the rear of Lee's army.

Cavalry units were to precede each of the above columns. In addition, David McM. Gregg's Second Cavalry Division was to move forward on the left of the army; John Buford's First Cavalry Division, then commanded by Wesley Merritt, was assigned to guard the trains in the vicinity of Richardsville; and Judson Kilpatrick's Third Cavalry Division, then under George A. Custer, was to hold the fords of the Rapidan on the right of the army.

Heavy rains prevented the start of the campaign until November 26, 1863, and then the corps advanced along the routes previously described. Progress, however, was much slower than expected. Sykes' Fifth Corps reached Culpeper Ford at 10:30 A.M. November 26, 1863, and was across the river by noon that day. Warren, with his Second Corps, arrived at Germanna Ford at 9:30 A.M. and was joined there by Meade at 11:00 A.M. They then waited for French's Third Corps to arrive at Jacob's Ford before Second Corps continued its advance. Finally, at 1:30 P.M. two brigades of John C. Caldwell's First Division, Second Corps crossed the Rapidan to secure the south bank, and the rest of the corps followed after the completion of a pontoon bridge. Second Corps then advanced on the Germanna Plank Road and camped that night on Flat Run, about midway between Germanna Ford and Wilderness Tavern.

The head of French's Third Corps did not arrive at Jacob's Ford until about noon, and then it was forced to wait until a pontoon bridge was completed before crossing the river. Henry Prince's Second Division began crossing at 4:00 P.M., and it then moved out a short distance on the road to Locust Grove. David B. Birney's First Division and Joseph B. Carr's Third Division followed and camped south of the river at 7:00 P.M. Sedgwick's Sixth Corps, which had the greatest distance to travel, started at 6:00 A.M. November 26, 1863, but it was forced to wait at Brandy Station until 11:00 A.M. for Third Corps to clear the road. As a result, it did not arrive at Jacob's Ford until after dark.

Newton's First Corps reached Culpeper Ford during the afternoon of November 26, 1863, but only one of the two divisions was able to cross by 7:00 P.M. At that time the corps halted for the night.

Thus, on the night of November 26, 1863, Second Corps and Third Corps had not arrived at Locust Grove as planned, and consequently were not able to attack the next morning. In fact, no Union troops had advanced more than a few miles south of the Rapidan, and some had not yet crossed.

At 12:15 on the morning of November 27, 1863, Meade issued orders for the advance of the army that day. Second Corps was to march along the turnpike to Old Verdiersville; Third Corps was to march to Locust Grove and close up on Second Corps; Fifth Corps was to move on to New Verdiersville; and First Corps was to follow Fifth Corps and close up. Henry D. Terry's Third Division, Sixth Corps was to remain near the Rapidan to cover the bridges and trains at Germanna Ford; and Sedgwick, with Horatio G. Wright's First Division and Albion P. Howe's Second Division of Sixth Corps, was to follow Third Corps and close up. Robert O. Tyler's Reserve Artillery was to follow Second Corps and halt before reaching Locust Grove. Circumstances, however, were to prevent the completion of these movements as ordered.

On the morning of November 26, 1863, Lee learned of Meade's movement toward the upper fords, and that evening he decided to move his army eastward toward Spotsylvania Court House. Richard S. Ewell's Second Corps of Lee's army, commanded by Jubal A. Early, left its camps along the Rapidan that night and took position along a ridge west of Mine Run. Then at 4:00 the next morning, Early was ordered to move forward to Locust Grove. Early's division, then commanded by

Harry T. Hays, moved eastward on the turnpike; Robert E. Rodes' division marched on the road from Zoar Church to Locust Grove, which ran north of, and roughly parallel to, the turnpike; and Edward Johnson's division, which had been to the left and rear of Rodes, took the road running from Raccoon Ford by way of Bartlett's Mill on Walnut Run, to Locust Grove.

Also that morning, Ambrose P. Hill's Third Corps of Lee's army advanced on the Plank Road, with Henry Heth's division leading the way. Richard H. Anderson's division followed Heth, and Cadmus M. Wilcox's division brought up the rear. Stuart, with Wade Hampton's cavalry division, covered the advance.

Warren's Second Corps, with Alexander Hays' Third Division in front, began its march on the morning of November 27, 1863, but between 11:00 and 11:30 A.M. it encountered John B. Gordon's brigade of Harry T. Hays' Confederate division just west of Locust Grove Cross Roads. Samuel S. Carroll's First Brigade of Alexander Hays' division drove the enemy skirmishers back about 500 yards, and the rest of the division deployed south of the tunpike on the high ground near Locust Grove. Carroll's brigade was on the road, with Thomas A. Smyth's Second Brigade on its left and Joshua T. Owen's Third Brigade on the left of Smyth.

Alexander Webb's Second Division of Warren's corps then came up and formed north of the road on the right of Hays' division. Arthur F. Devereaux's Second Brigade was on the right of Carroll, Turner G. Morehead's Third Brigade was on the right of Devereaux, and DeWitt C. Baxter's First Brigade was on the right of Morehead. Caldwell's First Division of Warren's corps was massed in rear of Webb's line, about one mile east of Locust Grove. John R. Brooke's Fourth Brigade of Caldwell's division was detached and sent forward to report to Alexander Hays and support his Third Division. A little after 7:00 P.M., Newton arrived from Parker's Store with his First Corps and halted a short distance east of Locust Grove, on the left of Caldwell's division, to support Warren.

While Meade's troops were coming up to Locust Grove, the rest of Harry T. Hays' Confederate division arrived in front of Locust Grove and deployed a short distance to the west. Rodes' division also moved up and extended Hays' line to the north, but Early waited for Johnson's division before ordering an attack. Meade also hesitated, and he directed Warren to wait until Sykes' Fifth Corps arrived on his left and French's Third Corps on his right before he attacked. There was constant skirmishing along the front during the day, but there was no major attack on Warren's front. On the Federal left, Sykes was under orders to advance on the Plank Road to New Hope Church, and he reached Parker's Store about 9:00 A.M. At that point, Gregg's cavalry division came into the road, and Sykes halted to permit the cavalry to go forward. As a result, Sykes did not reach New Hope Church until 4:00 P.M., and it was then too late to join Warren in the proposed attack.

Gregg's cavalry division marched ahead of Sykes, and at New Hope Church troopers of John P. Taylor's First Brigade encountered skirmishers of James B. Gordon's brigade of Wade Hampton's cavalry, which was directed by James E. B. (Jeb) Stuart in person. Taylor drove back the enemy skirmishers, but he then came up to the infantry of Henry H. Walker's brigade of Heth's division and was forced to halt. Sykes then joined Gregg and advanced one of his divisions to relieve the cavalry, which had been engaged since 11:00 that morning. When relieved, Gregg's division retired to within Sykes' lines late that evening.

The most serious fighting of November 27, 1863 was done by Third Corps. Early that morning, French was only about four miles from Warren's Second Corps, which he was under orders to join at Locust Grove, but despite constant urging from Meade's headquarters, he did not do so. Third Corps started for Locust Grove that morning, with Prince's Second Division in the lead, Carr's Third Division following, and Birney's First Division bringing up the rear. After marching about a mile, Prince became uncertain as to which of two roads he was to take, and he then halted two hours while he attempted to determine the proper route.

Meantime, Johnson's Confederate division had started that morning on the Raccoon Ford-Locust Grove Road on its march toward Locust Grove, and it was strung out along the road when a Federal reconnaissance party sent out by Prince discovered Johnston's trains. When this party reached the road, three brigades of Johnston's division had already passed by, ahead of the trains, but George H. Steuart,

whose brigade was bringing up the rear, sent out skirmishers to meet the Federals who were threatening the trains. Steuart's skirmishers moved eastward, and when they arrived at the Payne farm they found William Blaisdell's First Brigade of Prince's division supporting two sections of John K. Bucklyn's Battery E, 1st Rhode Island Light Artillery. This artillery was later increased to two batteries. Johnson deployed Steuart's brigade and then sent for the other three brigades of his division to return. When they arrived, he placed them on the right of Steuart, in order from left to right, as follows: James A. Walker's brigade (Stonewall Brigade), Leroy A. Stafford's brigade, and John M. Jones' brigade. Jones' brigade was near the left of Rodes' division.

French, then in a state of uncertainty, delayed any further movement for two or three hours, and finally deployed two of his divisions near Payne's farm (the northernmost of two farms of that name). He placed Prince's division on the right and Carr's divison on the left of the open ground of the farm. Prince, who had only two of his brigades with him, deployed Blaisdell's First Brigade on the right and William R. Brewster's Second Brigade on the left. Gershom Mott's Third Brigade was in the rear at Jacob's Ford guarding the trains. Carr placed William H. Morris' First Brigade on the right of his line and J. Warren Keifer's Second Brigade on the left. At 4:00 P.M. he ordered up Benjamin F. Smith's Third Brigade and formed it on the left of Keifer's brigade.

Carr's division was scarcely in line when it was attacked by the three left brigades of Johnson's line. A part of Steuart's brigade also struck Prince's line. Prince and Carr were able to hold their positions, but the latter was hard pressed, and Smith's brigade was driven back. Meantime, Birney's First Division had moved around to the left and had formed a second line in rear of Carr. J. H. Hobart Ward's Second Brigade was on the right, Charles H. T. Collis' First Brigade was in the center, and Thomas W. Egan's Third Brigade was on the left. About sunset, Birney advanced Egan's brigade, and then Collis' brigade, to relieve Carr's troops, who were running short of ammunition. Birney's line then repulsed all attacks until the fighting ended at dark. French's battle that day has been known as the Battle (or Engagement) of Payne's Farm.

When Johnson's attacks on Third Corps began,

Sixth Corps was on the road to the rear, and Sedgwick sent forward Wright's First Division and Howe's Second Division in support. Terry's Third Division was near the Rapidan River at that time. Later, Peter C. Ellmaker's Third Brigade of Wright's division was advanced to the right of Ward's brigade, and Thomas H. Neill's Third Brigade of Howe's division and Emory Upton's Second Brigade of Wright's division moved up on the left and rear of Third Corps, but they were not engaged.

During the night of November 27, 1863, Meade decided to attack at dawn the next morning, and he issued the necessary orders for the disposition of his troops. By daylight November 28, 1863, Sixth Corps had arrived near Locust Grove and had formed on the right of Warren's Second Corps, and at about the same time First Corps had moved up on the left of Warren. During the night of November 27, 1863, Fifth Corps marched from New Hope Church and arrived at Locust Grove early the next morning. Also that morning, Third Corps arrived near Locust Grove from Payne's farm, and then massed on the right of Sixth Corps in reserve.

When Meade's line, consisting of First Corps, Second Corps, and Sixth Corps, advanced on the morning of November 28, 1863, the skirmishers found that the enemy had retired during the night. Meade pursued immediately, with Second Corps in front, and after marching about two miles found Lee's divisions occupying a strong position on high ground on the west side of Mine Run, a tributary of the Rapidan River. Meade then formed his corps in line along Mine Run, in order from right to left as follows: Sedgwick's Sixth Corps, Warren's Second Corps, Newton's First Corps, and French's Third Corps. Sykes' Fifth Corps was held in rear of this line.

A careful examination of the enemy positions revealed that there was little chance of a successful frontal assault, and on the evening of November 28, 1863, Meade decided to send Warren with his Second Corps and Terry's Third Division of Sixth Corps, plus about 300 cavalry, on a flank march to attack the right of Lee's line. He also ordered the other corps commanders to reconnoiter on their fronts to determine whether there were any other suitable points for attacks.

During the night of November 28, 1863, Warren withdrew from his position on the Union line, and at 4:00 the next morning, he was replaced there by Sykes' Fifth Corps. Warren then marched back with his Second Corps and Terry's division of Sixth Corps, totaling about 18,000 men, to Locust Grove. There he turned south to the Plank Road, then moved west on the road, and by 10:30 that morning he had reached Gregg's outposts. Warren then brought up Caldwell's First Division, and spent the next two hours deploying two brigades and a battery. He placed Patrick Kelly's Second Brigade, First Division (the Irish Brigade) on the right of the Plank Road and Nelson A. Miles' First Brigade, First Division on the left; and at 1:00 P.M. he pushed on toward the head of Mine Run. When Warren finally arrived before the enemy works and deployed, it was too late to advance that evening, and so he prepared for an attack the next morning.

About 6:00 P.M. November 29, 1863, Wright, commanding First Division, Sixth Corps, reported that there was a point on the extreme left of the enemy line where an attack would probably succeed. This, together with a report that Warren should encounter no difficulty on the enemy right, prompted Meade to order three assaults on the morning of November 30, 1863. Fifth Corps and Sixth Corps, both under Sedgwick, were to attack on the Federal right; First Corps and Third Corps were to advance on the center; and Warren with Second Corps and Terry's division of Sixth Corps were to attack the enemy right. French, however, did not report favorably on an attack to his front, and accordingly Meade modified his original plan. He decided to abandon his proposed attack by the Union center, and instead to attack only on the two flanks. At 10:30 P.M. November 29, 1863, Meade ordered French to send Prince's and Howe's divisions of his Third Corps to reinforce Warren. This gave Warren six divisions, or about one-half the infantry forces of the army.

Sedgwick, who was to have charge of the attack on Lee's left, detached two brigades and a battery of Sixth Corps to occupy the lines previously held by Fifth Corps and Sixth Corps, and during the night he moved with the rest of the two corps about two miles to the right so as to be in position to attack the next morning.

The battle was to begin with artillery fire at 8:00 A.M. November 30, 1863, and the infantry was to attack an hour later. In front of Warren, however, the enemy worked through the night to construct strong breastworks that were protected by abatis, and in placing artillery to cover the ground over which Warren would have to advance. Hill's corps, which occupied that part of the Confederate line, originally had Richard H. Anderson's division on the left, with its left on the Old Turnpike, and Wilcox's division on the right, with its right on the Catharpin Road. Heth's division was in reserve. On the morning of November 30, 1863, however, Hill shifted Wilcox's division to the right, with its right at Antioch Church, and he brought up Heth's division to occupy the space thus created on the center of the line.

After a careful examination of Hill's new works on the morning of November 30, 1863, Warren concluded that they could not be taken by assault, and he so reported to Meade at about 7:45 A.M. Meade then called off both Warren's and Sedgwick's attacks. That night Carr's and Prince's divisions rejoined Third Corps, and Fifth Corps and Sixth Corps returned to their original positions on the right of Meade's line.

The Army of the Potomac remained in position during December 1, 1863, but that night it began to withdraw toward the Rapidan. Meantime, while the infantry was maneuvering along Mine Run, the cavalry had made some changes in position. On November 30, 1863, Thomas C. Devin's Second Brigade of Wesley Merritt's First Cavalry Division, which had been guarding the trains of the army near Ely's Ford, rejoined Gregg's division and then moved to Wilderness Tavern, where it relieved Taylor's brigade. Taylor then moved to Parker's Store.

Gregg with his Second Cavalry Division, Devin's brigade of the First Cavalry Division, and two infantry brigades of Third Corps covered the retreat of the army. Taylor's First Brigade, Second Cavalry Division and Benjamin F. Smith's Third Brigade, Third Division, Third Corps covered the movement on the Culpeper Ford Road; J. Irvin Gregg's Second Brigade, Second Cavalry Division and William Blaisdell's First Brigade, Second Division, Third Corps were on the Ely's Ford Road; and Devin's Second Brigade, First Cavalry Division covered the Germanna Ford Road.

The army safely crossed the Rapidan during the night of December 1, 1863 and the next day and then returned to the positions occupied before the beginning of the campaign.

The organization of the Army of the Potomac during the Mine Run Campaign was as follows:

ARMY OF THE POTOMAC
George G. Meade

Provost Guard, Marsena R. Patrick
Engineer Brigade, Henry W. Benham

FIRST CORPS, John Newton

First Division, Lysander Cutler
First Brigade, William W. Robinson
Second Brigade, James C. Rice

Note. Solomon Meredith, who was relieved from duty with the Army of the Potomac October 17, 1863, was ordered to return November 3, 1863, and he arrived and was assigned command of First Division November 12, 1863. Cutler, however, was in command of First Division during the Mine Run Campaign.

Second Division, John C. Robinson
First Brigade, Samuel H. Leonard
Second Brigade, Henry Baxter

Third Division, John R. Kenly
First Brigade, Chapman Biddle
Second Brigade, Langhorne Wister
Third Brigade, Nathan T. Dushane

Note. Third Division did not accompany the army to Mine Run, but remained to guard the Orange and Alexandria Railroad north of the Rappahannock.

Artillery Brigade, Charles S. Wainwright
5th Battery (B), Maine Light Artillery, Greenleaf T. Stevens
Battery A, Maryland Light Artillery, James H. Rigby
Battery H, 1st New York Light Artillery, Charles E. Mink
Batteries E and L, 1st New York Light Artillery, Gilbert H. Reynolds
Battery B, 1st Pennsylvania Light Artillery, James H. Cooper
Battery B, 4th United States Artillery, James Stewart

SECOND CORPS, Gouverneur K. Warren

First Division, John C. Caldwell
First Brigade, Nelson A. Miles

Second Brigade, Patrick Kelly
Third Brigade, James A. Beaver
Fourth Brigade, John R. Brooke

Second Division, Alexander S. Webb
First Brigade, De Witt C. Baxter
Second Brigade, Arthur F. Devereux
Third Brigade, Turner G. Morehead

Third Division, Alexander Hays
First Brigade, Samuel S. Carroll
Second Brigade, Thomas A. Smyth
Third Brigade, Joshua T. Owen

Artillery Brigade, J. Albert Monroe
Battery G, 1st New York Light Artillery, Samuel A. McClellan
Battery C, Pennsylvania Light Artillery, James Thompson
Battery F, Pennsylvania Light Artillery, Nathaniel Irish
Batteries F and G, 1st Pennsylvania Light Artillery, Charles B. Brockway
Battery A, 1st Rhode Island Light Artillery, William A. Arnold
Battery B, 1st Rhode Island Light Artillery, John G. Hazard
Battery C, 5th United States Artillery, Richard Metcalf

THIRD CORPS, William H. French

First Division, David B. Birney
First Brigade, Charles H. T. Collis
Second Brigade, J. H. Hobart Ward
Third Brigade, Thomas W. Egan

Second Division, Henry Prince
First Brigade, William Blaisdell
Second Brigade, William R. Brewster
Third Brigade, Gershom Mott

Third Division, Joseph B. Carr
First Brigade, William H. Morris
Second Brigade, J. Warren Keifer
Third Brigade, Benjamin F. Smith

Artillery Brigade, George E. Randolph
4th Battery (D), Maine Light Artillery, O'Neil W. Robinson, Jr.
10th Battery, Massachusetts Light Artillery, J. Henry Sleeper
1st Battery, New Hampshire Light Artillery, Frederick M. Edgell
Battery B, 1st New Jersey Light Artillery, A. Judson Clark
Battery D, 1st New York Light Artillery, George B. Winslow

12th Battery, New York Light Artillery, George F. McKnight
Battery E, 1st Rhode Island Light Artillery, John K. Bucklyn
Battery K, 4th United States Artillery, John W. Roder

FIFTH CORPS, George Sykes

First Divison, Joseph J. Bartlett
First Brigade, William S. Tilton
Second Brigade, Jacob B. Sweitzer
Third Brigade, Joseph Hayes

Second Division, Romeyn B. Ayres
First Brigade, Sidney Burbank
Third Brigade, Kenner Garrard

Third Division, Samuel W. Crawford
First Brigade, William McCandless
Third Brigade, Martin D. Hardin

Artillery Brigade, Augustus P. Martin
3rd Battery (C), Massachusetts Light Artillery, Aaron F. Walcott
5th Battery (E), Massachusetts Light Artillery, Charles A. Phillips
Battery C, 1st New York Light Artillery, Ela H. Clark
Battery L, 1st Ohio Light Artillery, Frank C. Gibbs
Batteries F and K, 3rd United States Artillery, George F. Barstow
Battery D, 5th United States Artillery, Benjamin F. Rittenhouse

SIXTH CORPS, John Sedgwick

First Division, Horatio G. Wright
First Brigade, Alfred T. A. Torbert
Second Brigade, Emory Upton
Third Brigade, Peter C. Ellmaker

Second Division, Albion P. Howe
Second Brigade, Lewis A. Grant
Third Brigade, Thomas H. Neill

Third Division, Henry D. Terry
First Brigade, Alexander Shaler
Second Brigade, Henry L. Eustis
Third Brigade, Frank Wheaton

Artillery Brigade, Charles H. Tompkins
1st Battery (A), Massachusetts Light Artillery, William H. McCartney
1st Battery, New York Light Artillery, Andrew Cowan
3rd Battery, New York Light Artillery, William A. Harn

Battery C, 1st Rhode Island Light Artillery, Richard Waterman

Battery G, 1st Rhode Island Light Artillery, George W. Adams

Battery C, 4th United States Artillery, Charles L. Fitzhugh

Battery F, 5th United States Artillery, Alexander J. McDonald

Battery M, 5th United States Artillery, James McKnight

CAVALRY CORPS, Alfred Pleasonton

First Cavalry Division, Wesley Merritt
First Brigade, George H. Chapman
Second Brigade, Thomas C. Devin
Reserve Brigade, Alfred Gibbs
Artillery
Batteries B and L, 2nd United States Artillery, Edward Heaton
Battery D, 2nd United States Artillery, Edward B. Williston

Note 1. John Buford, who was sick, was relieved in command of First Cavalry Division by Wesley Merritt November 21, 1863. Buford died in Washington December 16, 1863, apparently of typhoid fever.

Note 2. During the Mine Run Campaign, the Reserve Brigade guarded the trains and the fords of the Rapidan from Germanna Ford down to the mouth of the river.

Second Division, David McM. Gregg
First Brigade, John P. Taylor
Second Brigade, Pennock Huey
Artillery
6th Battery, New York Light Artillery, Joseph W. Martin
Battery A, 4th United States Artillery, Rufus King, Jr.

Third Division, George A. Custer
First Brigade, Henry E. Davies, Jr.
Second Brigade, Charles H. Town
Artillery
Battery E, 4th United States Artillery, Edward Field
Battery M, 2nd United States Artillery, Alexander C. M. Pennington, Jr.

Note 1. Custer, commander of Second Brigade, relieved Kilpatrick in command of Third Division November 25, 1863.

Note 2. All batteries serving with the Cavalry Corps were from James M. Robertson's First Brigade, Horse Artillery of Robert O. Tyler's Artillery Reserve.

ARTILLERY, Henry J. Hunt

Reserve Artillery, Robert O. Tyler
First Volunteer Brigade, Freeman McGilvery
Second Volunteer Brigade, Elijah D. Taft
Third Volunteer Brigade, Robert H. Fitzhugh
First Brigade, Horse Artillery, James M. Robertson
Second Brigade, Horse Artillery, William M. Graham

Note 1. James M. Robertson's First Brigade, Horse Artillery served with the Cavalry Corps during the Mine Run Campaign.

Note 2. Hunt's command also included the artillery assigned to the corps of the army.

PENINSULAR CAMPAIGN
MARCH 1862–AUGUST 1862

Following the defeat of Irvin McDowell's Army of Northeastern Virginia at Bull Run July 21, 1861, George B. McClellan was called to Washington, and was there assigned command of the newly created Military Division of the Potomac. He assumed command July 27, 1861, and then entered upon a period of extensive reorganization of the army from new three-year regiments and of training and equipping the new troops for field service. He continued this work through the fall and winter of 1861–1862. For details, see Army of the Potomac, Period of Organization. During this time, however, McClellan issued no orders for the movement of his army, nor did he reveal any plans for its employment, although Joseph E. Johnston's Confederate Army of the Potomac remained in its entrenchments near Centerville, only a short distance southwest of Washington. President Lincoln strongly urged that the army be used in an offensive operation, and he favored a Manassas plan similar to that used by McDowell the preceding July. McClellan appeared to accept this idea, but nevertheless he remained inactive, and continued with his preparations for a campaign in the spring.

McClellan became ill in December 1861, and at that time no one, including the president, had any knowledge of his plans. McClellan was confined to his house in Washington for about a month, and during that time Lincoln was not permitted to see him. Finally, in desperation, on January 10, 1862, the president called an emergency meeting of General McDowell, General William B. Franklin, the secretary of war, and the secretary of the treasury to discuss the situation, and to determine their views. McDowell proposed an advance into Virginia against Johnston's army at Manassas, and Franklin suggested a movement against Richmond by way of the York River, but no plan was officially adopted.

On January 27, 1862, the president ordered a general advance of all armies of the United States, to begin on, or before, February 22, 1862. Four days later, January 31, 1862, he issued Special War Order No. 1, which directed McClellan to occupy a point on the Orange and Alexandria Railroad southwest of Manassas Junction, and to begin his movement on February 22, 1862.

When McClellan, who had recovered from his illness, was informed of Lincoln's proposed advance toward Manassas, he objected strongly, and instead, on February 3, 1862, he suggested another plan. He proposed to move the army down the Potomac River to the Chesapeake Bay, then up the Rappahannock River to Urbanna, and establish a base there that could be supplied by water. From Urbanna he would march rapidly to West Point at the head of the York River, and from there advance toward Richmond. Such movement, he contended, would place the Army of the Potomac between Johnston's army and Richmond, and would force the evacuation of Manassas without a battle. Lincoln did not approve McClellan's plan, however, primarily because it would cause further delays and would leave Washington unprotected against an enemy attack.

Finally, however, about mid-February 1862, Lincoln gave his reluctant approval of McClellan's plan for an amphibious operation against Richmond, but he agreed to this movement only with the stipulation that a sufficient force be left in northern Virginia to protect the capital. On February 27, 1862, Secretary of War Edwin M. Stanton issued an order for the assembly of the necessary transports to move the army down the Chesapeake Bay to Urbanna, and he placed John Tucker, assistant secretary of war, in charge of this work. On March 8, 1862, in War Order No. 3, the president directed that McClellan begin his movement March 18, 1862.

Then, on March 9, 1862, Johnston withdrew his army from Manassas and retired behind the Rappahannock River. When McClellan learned of this, he advanced his army to Centerville and established his headquarters at Fairfax Court House. On March 11, 1862, the president, thus considering that McClellan had taken the field with his army, relieved him from command of all departments except the Department of the Potomac. From that time on, McClellan was in charge only of the active operations of the Army of the Potomac.

Johnston's withdrawal from Manassas rendered the Urbanna plan impractical, and March 13, 1862, McClellan called a council of war, composed of his four corps commanders, at Fairfax Court house. As a result of this meeting, McClellan proposed that the army move farther down the Chesapeake and make Fort Monroe the base for its operations. From there he would move up the Peninsula between the York and James rivers toward Richmond. This plan was approved by the president that same day, and he issued an order that directed McClellan to do the following: (1) leave a sufficient force at Manassas to prevent its reoccupation by the enemy; (2) leave enough troops to make Washington completely secure; and (3) move with the rest of his force down the Potomac and establish a base at Fort Monroe, or, if he so desired, at any point between Washington and Fort Monroe.

For the organization of the Army of the Potomac on the eve of its departure for the Peninsula, see Army of the Potomac, Period of Organization.

Transfer of the Army to the Peninsula, March 17, 1862–April 4, 1862. On March 17, 1862, Charles S. Hamilton's Third Division of Samuel P. Heintzelman's Third Corps embarked at Alexandria for Fort Monroe, and Fitz John Porter's First Division of the same corps left five days later. The remaining divisions of the army followed as rapidly as transportation could be provided.

When the president learned, as he believed, that McClellan had not provided for a sufficient force to ensure the safety of the capital, he directed that McDowell's First Corps or Edwin V. Sumner's Second Corps be retained near Washington. McDowell's corps was selected, and it was held near Alexandria until April 4, 1862, and then it was detached and merged into the newly created Department of the Rappahannock. For further information about McDowell's command, see Department of the Rappahannock.

Louis Blenker's Division of Sumner's Second

Corps was also left behind near Washington when the army departed. On March 23, 1862, Thomas J. (Stonewall) Jackson threatened in the Shenandoah Valley when he attacked James Shields' First Division, Department of the Rappahannock, at Kernstown, and a week later Blenker's Division was detached and sent to join John C. Fremont's command in Western Virginia. For additional information, see Shenandoah Valley Campaign (Jackson), 1862.

Meantime, the movement of the army to the Peninsula continued. John E. Wool, commander of the Department of Virginia at Fort Monroe, received the troops as they arrived, and placed them in camps there, pending the arrival of McClellan. Wool's own command consisted of seventeen infantry regiments and one cavalry regiment. March 19, 1862, McClellan requested that some of Wool's troops be organized into a division, to be commanded by Joseph K. F. Mansfield. This was done the following day, by order of the secretary of war, but the order was revoked April 2, 1862. McClellan was then given complete control over Fort Monroe and all of Wool's forces there, but this order was annulled the next day, and Wool was again given command of Fort Monroe and the troops previously assigned to the Department of Virginia. McClellan was thus left in command of the troops belonging to the Army of the Potomac.

Because of the presence of the Confederate ironclad *Merrimac* at Norfolk, Virginia, Union naval vessels would not be able to protect transports if they attempted to move up the James River toward Richmond, and for this reason McClellan prepared to march his army overland, up the Peninsula. By April 3, 1862, the following troops of the Army of the Potomac had arrived at Fort Monroe: Porter's First Division and Hamilton's Third Division of Heintzelman's Third Corps; Darius N. Couch's First Division and William F. Smith's Second Division of Erasmus D. Keyes' Fourth Corps; John Sedgwick's Second Division of Sumner's Second Corps; George Sykes' brigade of regulars; and Henry J. Hunt's Artillery Reserve. Silas Casey's Third Division of Fourth Corps had also arrived, but it was unable to move because it was without wagons.

The Federal cavalry on the Peninsula at the beginning of the campaign consisted of the Cavalry Reserve under Philip St. George Cooke, which was organized into two brigades as follows: William H. Emory's First Brigade, consisting of 5th United States Cavalry, 6th United States Cavalry, and 6th Pennsylvania Cavalry; and George A. H. Blake's Second Brigade, consisting of 1st United States Cavalry, 8th Pennsylvania Cavalry, and the McClellan (Illinois) Dragoons. In addition, John F. Farnsworth's 8th Illinois Cavalry was assigned to Second Corps, and William W. Averell's 3rd Pennsylvania Cavalry was assigned to Third Corps. George Stoneman was McClellan's chief of cavalry.

The Confederate troops on the Lower Peninsula at the beginning of McClellan's campaign numbered only about 12,000 men, and they were commanded by John B. Magruder. To the best of his ability and with the means at his disposal, he had attempted to form a defensible line across the Peninsula from Yorktown, on the York River, to the James River. The line generally was along the Warwick River, which rose about a mile and a half from Yorktown and flowed diagonally across the Peninsula, through low swampy ground, to the James. At its head, the Warwick was a small stream, but a succession of dams had flooded the country to within a mile of Yorktown. As a result, it was impossible for troops to cross without bridges except at the dams, and these were defended by earthworks. The principal crossings were at Wynn's Mill, three miles below Yorktown; and at Lee's Mill, two and one half miles below Wynn's Mill, where the James River Road crossed the Warwick. Yorktown was strongly protected by earthworks, and the artillery in these works commanded the open space between the town and the head of the Warwick River.

When the Army of the Potomac began disembarking at Fort Monroe, in preparation for its march on Richmond, Confederate reinforcements were quickly sent to Magruder. March 3, 1862, Robert E. Lee was recalled from Charleston, South Carolina to serve as a military adviser in Virginia; and on March 13, 1862, he was charged by President Jefferson Davis with the conduct of military affairs in the armies of the Confederacy. His position appears to have been merely advisory, and was never clearly defined, but in his new capacity Lee began the reconcentration of the army on the Peninsula.

As noted above, on March 9, 1862, Johnston

withdrew from Manassas, and he then took position behind the Rappahannock River. Later he moved back to the line of the Rapidan River. At Magruder's request, Johnston detached some of his troops and sent them to the Peninsula, and by April 5, 1862, as McClellan began his advance from Fort Monroe, the divisions of Jubal A. Early, Daniel H. Hill, and David R. Jones had been ordered to join Magruder. On March 23, 1862, Gustavus W. Smith had been sent to Fredericksburg to relieve Theophilus H. Holmes in command of the Confederate troops there, and Jones had assumed command of Smith's division. This left only four divisions with Johnston's army: Thomas J. (Stonewall) Jackson's division at Mount Jackson in the Shenandoah Valley; Richard S. Ewell's division on the Rappahannock; James Longstreet's division at Orange Court House; and Gustavus W. Smith's division at Fredericksburg.

On April 10, 1862, President Davis ordered Johnston to make any defensive arrangements necessary in the region he then occupied and to march with the rest of his army to Richmond. Johnston left Jackson in the Shenandoah Valley and Ewell on the upper Rappahannock, and ordered Longstreet to move with his division to Richmond. He also directed Smith to leave the equivalent of a brigade in front of Fredericksburg and to bring his remaining regiments to Richmond.

April 12, 1862, Johnston, in person, arrived in Richmond, and April 17, 1862, he assumed command of all Confederate troops on the Peninsula, which at that time numbered about 53,000 men. These were organized into four divisions that were commanded by Magruder, Longstreet, Daniel H. Hill, and Smith. Magruder was assigned command of the Right Wing of the army, Longstreet the Center, and Hill the Left Wing. Smith's division was held in reserve.

Siege of Yorktown, Virginia, April 5, 1862–May 4, 1862. On April 4, 1862, McClellan began his advance from near Fort Monroe toward Richmond in two columns: one marched to the right on the direct road to Yorktown; and the other on the left, along the James River, toward Williamsburg. The column on the right consisted of Porter's and Hamilton's divisions of Heintzelman's Third Corps, Sedgwick's division of Sumner's Second Corps, and Averell's 3rd Pennsylvania Cavalry, all under the command of Heintzelman. The column on the left, which was commanded by Keyes, consisted of the divisions of William F. Smith and Couch of Keyes' Fourth Corps, with 5th United States Cavalry attached. The army marched ten to twelve miles that day, and that night the left column bivouacked at Young's Mills and the right column at Howard's Bridge and Cockletown. The Cavalry Reserve, Hunt's artillery, Stoneman's cavalry, and Sykes' brigade camped at Big Bethel.

March orders for April 5, 1862 directed Heintzelman to advance to within three or four miles of Yorktown and then halt and await orders; and Keyes to move by way of Warwick Court House to Halfway House, on the road between Yorktown and Williamsburg. The march of the army was resumed at 6:00 A.M. April 5, 1862, as ordered. On the right, Third Corps moved forward, with Porter's division in the lead, and about three miles beyond Cockletown it arrived near the defenses of Yorktown, where it was stopped by enemy fire. At that time, Heintzelman was near his assigned position, and he made no further attempt to advance. On the left, Keyes' divisions pushed forward through Warwick Court House on the road to Halfway House. William F. Smith's division was in the lead, and it soon arrived before Magruder's strong defensive position at Lee's Mill, about three miles beyond the court house, but it was unable to cross the Warwick River. Couch's division remained at Warwick Court House with a part of Casey's division.

McClellan then came forward and examined Magruder's defensive works and, noting their strength, decided to conduct siege operations against Yorktown instead of attempting a frontal assault. This operation was not to be a siege in the strict sense of the term, but his plan was to move troops forward by a system of approaches and, after seriously damaging the enemy works by the fire of heavy artillery, to carry them by assault.

By April 10, 1862, the three divisions of Third Corps and the three divisions of Fourth Corps were with the army. Joseph Hooker's Second Division, Third Corps began disembarking that day at Ship Point, near Yorktown. That day McClellan's army was in position as follows: Heintzelman's Third Corps was on the right of the line, in front of Yorktown, and it covered the front from the mouth of Wormley's Creek, a little more than two miles below Yorktown, to the Warwick Road, opposite Wynn's Mill. Porter's division was on the right, next to the river; Hooker's division was on the center of the line; and Hamilton's division was on the left. On April 6, Sumner had been assigned command of the Left Wing of the army, which was composed of his own Second Corps, of which only Sedgwick's division was then present, and Keyes' Fourth Corps. On April 10, 1862, Sedgwick's division was on the left of Hamilton; and Fourth Corps, which consisted of the divisions of Smith, Couch, and Casey, was on the left of Sedgwick, and its left extended down the Warwick to Lee's Mill and beyond. Israel B. Richardson's First Division, Second Corps reached the front April 16, 1862, and it was ordered up to relieve Sedgwick's division on the front line.

Meantime, preparations for the siege operations at Yorktown had been started. John G. Barnard, chief engineer of the Army of the Potomac, was given the responsibility for arming, and supplying with ammunition, all siege and field batteries; the construction of the approaches to the batteries and of the necessary roads, bridges, and depots was to be done by troops under the direction of Sumner and Heintzelman; and Porter, the director of the siege, was assigned the task of guarding the trenches, and assembling and distributing the necessary working parties.

During the night of May 3, 1862, just a few days before the siege works were completed, Johnston's army evacuated Yorktown and the line of the Warwick River, and began to fall back toward Richmond to a better defensive position behind the Chickahominy River.

The organization of the Army of the Potomac during the siege of Yorktown April 5, 1862–May 4, 1862, was as follows

ARMY OF THE POTOMAC
George B. McClellan

SECOND CORPS, Edwin V. Sumner

First Division, Israel B. Richardson
First Brigade, Oliver O. Howard
Second Brigade, Thomas F. Meagher
Third Brigade, William H. French
Artillery, George W. Hazzard
Battery B, 1st New York Light Artillery, Rufus D. Pettit

Battery G, 1st New York Light Artillery, John D. Frank
Battery A, 2nd Battalion New York Light Artillery, William H. Hogan
Battery A, 4th United States Artillery
Battery C, 4th United States Artillery, George W. Hazzard

Note. Hazzard commanded both Battery A and Battery C, 4th United State Artillery.

Second Division, John Sedgwick
First Brigade, Willis A. Gorman
Second Brigade, William W. Burns
Third Brigade, Napoleon J. T. Dana
Artillery, Charles H. Tompkins
Battery A, 1st Rhode Island Light Artillery, John A. Tompkins
Battery B, 1st Rhode Island Light Artillery, Walter O. Bartlett
Battery G, 1st Rhode Island Light Artillery, Charles D. Owen
Battery I, 1st United States Artillery, Edmund Kirby

8th Illinois Cavalry, John F. Farnsworth

THIRD CORPS, Samuel P. Heintzelman

First Division, Fitz John Porter
First Brigade, John H. Martindale
Second Brigade, George W. Morell
Third Brigade, Daniel Butterfield
Artillery, Charles Griffin
Battery C, Massachusetts Light Artillery, Augustus P. Martin
Battery E, Massachusetts Light Artillery, George D. Allen
Battery C, 1st Rhode Island Light Artillery, Richard Waterman
Battery D, 5th United States Artillery, Henry W. Kingsbury

Second Division, Joseph Hooker
First Brigade, Cuvier Grover
Second Brigade, Nelson Taylor, to May 11, 1862
John J. Abercrombie
Third Brigade, Samuel H. Starr, to May 3, 1862
Francis E. Patterson
Artillery, Charles S. Wainwright
Battery D, 1st New York Light Artillery, Thomas W. Osborn
4th Battery, New York Light Artillery, James E. Smith
6th Battery, New York Light Artillery, Walter M. Bramhall

Battery H, 1st United States Artillery, Charles H. Webber

Third Division, Charles S. Hamilton, to May 3, 1862
Philip Kearny
First Brigade, Charles D. Jameson
Second Brigade, David B. Birney
Third Brigade, Hiram G. Berry
Artillery, James Thompson
2nd Battery, New Jersey Light Artillery, John E. Beam
Battery E, 1st Rhode Island Light Artillery, George E. Randolph
Battery G, 2nd United States Artillery, James Thompson

3rd Pennsylvania Cavalry, William W. Averell

FOURTH CORPS, Erasmus D. Keyes

First Division, Darius N. Couch
First Brigade, Henry S. Briggs
Second Brigade, John J. Peck
Third Brigade, Lawrence P. Graham
Julius W. Adams
Artillery, Robert M. West
Battery C, 1st Pennsylvania Light Artillery, Jeremiah McCarthy
Battery D, 1st Pennsylvania Light Artillery, Edward H. Flood
Battery E, 1st Pennsylvania Light Artillery, Theodore Miller
Battery H, 1st Pennsylvania Light Artillery, James Brady

Note 1. Adams temporarily relieved Graham, who was ill, but Graham did not return to the army.
Note 2. At the end of the siege of Yorktown, First Division was reorganized. The designation of First Brigade was changed to Third Brigade, and Charles Devens was assigned command. The designation of Third Brigade was changed to First Brigade, and Adams was assigned command.

Second Division, William F. Smith
First Brigade, Winfield S. Hancock
Second Brigade, William T. H. Brooks
Third Brigade, John W. Davidson
Artillery, Romeyn B. Ayres
1st Battery, New York Light Artillery, Andrew Cowan
3rd Battery, New York Light Artillery, Thaddeus P. Mott
Battery E, 1st New York Light Artillery, Charles C. Wheeler
Battery F, 5th United States Artillery, Romeyn B. Ayres

Third Division, Silas Casey
First Brigade, Henry M. Naglee
Second Brigade, William H. Keim
Third Brigade, Innis N. Palmer
Artillery, Guilford D. Bailey
Battery A, 1st New York Light Artillery, Thomas H. Bates
Battery H, 1st New York Light Artillery, Joseph Spratt
7th Battery, New York Light Artillery, Peter C. Regan
8th Battery, New York Light Artillery, Butler Fitch

Brigade of Regular Infantry, George Sykes

Cavalry Reserve, Philip St. George Cooke
First Brigade, William H. Emory
Second Brigade, George A. H. Blake

Artillery Reserve, Henry J. Hunt
Brigade of Horse Artillery, William Hays
Second Brigade, George W. Getty

Siege Train (1st Connecticut Heavy Artillery), Robert O. Tyler

Volunteer Engineer Brigade, Daniel P. Woodbury

Battalion United States Engineers, James C. Duane

At McClellan's urgent request, the president ordered William B. Franklin's Division of Irvin McDowell's Department of the Rappahannock (formerly First Division, First Corps, Army of the Potomac) to report to McClellan on the Peninsula, but it did not reach the landing at Cheeseman's Creek, at the Poquosin River below Yorktown, until April 20, 1862. Then McClellan directed that preparations be started to disembark the division on the north side of the river, about three and a half miles below Gloucester Point, and attempt to take the enemy works there from the rear. Two weeks passed, however, and Franklin's division had not yet landed on the Gloucester side of the York River when the enemy evacuated Yorktown. Franklin then moved his division to Yorktown. His division was organized as follows:

Franklin's Division, William B. Franklin
First Brigade, George W. Taylor
Second Brigade, Henry W. Slocum
Third Brigade, John Newton

Battle of Williamsburg, Virginia, May 5, 1862.
When Johnston withdrew from Yorktown and the line of the Warwick River during the night of May 3, 1862, the divisions of Magruder and Longstreet fell back on the southern road, which ran from Hampton, Virginia by way of Lee's Mill to Williamsburg; and the divisions of Gustavus W. Smith and Daniel H. Hill marched on the direct road from Yorktown to Williamsburg. About noon May 4, 1862, the two columns were converging on Williamsburg. A line of redoubts, which had been constructed earlier by Magruder, extended across the Peninsula from the York to the James rivers, and crossed the Williamsburg Road about two miles east of town. The principal work on this line was situated in front of Williamsburg at the junction of the roads from Yorktown and Hampton, and about midway between the two rivers. Johnston did not intend to defend this position, but on his retreat from Yorktown had halted his command at Williamsburg to give the men a rest.

McClellan learned early on the morning of May 4, 1862 that the enemy had departed from his front, and he quickly began to organize a pursuit. He placed George Stoneman, his chief of cavalry, in command of an advance guard, and ordered him to move out on the Yorktown-Williamsburg Road to harass the enemy rear guard, and also attempt to cut off the enemy column that was retreating on the Hampton-Williamsburg Road. Stoneman's command consisted of 1st United States Cavalry, 6th United States Cavalry, 3rd Pennsylvania Cavalry, C. W. Barker's Illinois Squadron of cavalry, and William Hays' Artillery Brigade of four batteries of horse artillery. Emory, with his First Brigade of the Cavalry Reserve, Averell's 3rd Pennsylvania Cavalry, Barker's squadron, and Henry Benson's Battery M, 2nd United States Artillery, was sent to the left to the Hampton Road in an attempt to block the line of retreat of Magruder and Longstreet, but in this he was unsuccessful. Cooke, with the rest of the cavalry of his division, consisting of 6th United States Cavalry of First Brigade and 2nd United States Cavalry of Second Brigade, and Horatio G. Gibson's Battery C, 3rd United States Artillery, moved out on the Yorktown-Williamsburg Road, and at Halfway House, about 1:00 P.M., encountered James E. B. (Jeb) Stuart's cavalry and drove it back. When Johnston learned of

Stoneman's approach, he ordered his troops to occupy Fort Magruder on the Williamsburg Road and the nearby redoubts.

Hooker's division of Third Corps and Smith's division of Fourth Corps were ordered forward to support Stoneman. Hooker was to advance on the direct road from Yorktown to Williamsburg, and Smith was to move from his position opposite Dam No. 1, about midway between Wynn's Mill and Lee's Mill, and then take the Hampton Road toward Williamsburg. Philip Kearny's Third Division of Third Corps was ordered to follow Hooker, and Couch's and Casey's divisions of Fourth Corps were to follow Smith.

Hooker and Smith, however, encountered difficulties early on their march. Smith reached the Hampton Road, but was forced to halt at Skiff Creek when he found the bridge destroyed. Then, between 2:00 and 3:00 P.M. he was directed to move to the right to the road on which Hooker was advancing. Smith came into the road at Halfway House just before Hooker arrived, and the latter was forced to wait for three hours for Smith's column to pass. Finally, Hooker started again and followed Smith about three miles, and then turned off to the left and marched over to the Hampton Road. Because of this change of route, Smith approached Williamsburg on the right, on the Yorktown Road, and Hooker on the left, on the Hampton Road. Both divisions camped that night in front of the enemy works at Williamsburg.

Late in the afternoon of May 4, 1862, Longstreet relieved Magruder's troops in Fort Magruder and the nearby field works, and that evening Magruder's division, then commanded by Jones because of the illness of Magruder, resumed its march toward Richmond. Gustavus W. Smith's division, and then D. H. Hill's division were to have followed Jones, but because of darkness they did not move out until the following morning.

At 7:30 A.M. May 5, 1862, Hooker's Second Division of Third Corps opened the Battle of Williamsburg, which, from beginning to end, was badly managed. Hooker began his attack on the basis of orders received from McClellan before he left Yorktown the previous morning, and he did so before his entire division was up. Hooker also made his attack despite the fact that Sumner, who was in overall charge of the advance, and Heintzelman,

Hooker's corps commander, were on the field. In addition, William F. Smith and Keyes were also present at the beginning of the fighting. McClellan did not arrive on the field until 5:00 P.M. that day.

Immediately in front of Hooker's division, as he prepared to attack, were Fort Magruder and Longstreet's entire division. Cuvier Grover's First Brigade formed on the road, and when he moved forward he was quickly engaged. Nelson Taylor's Second Brigade came up at 9:00 A.M.; a part of the brigade supported Grover, and two regiments were sent to the left to protect that flank. Francis E. Patterson's Third Brigade arrived about 11:00 A.M. and formed on the left of Taylor and Grover.

At about the same time that Patterson came on the field, Longstreet advanced against Hooker's center and left. Kearny, who was approaching with his division of Third Corps, was ordered to support Hooker. No other troops on the rest of Sumner's line were severely engaged that morning. On the right, sometime after 10:00 A.M., Winfield S. Hancock, at Sumner's direction, took possession of an unoccupied redoubt with his own First Brigade of Smith's Second Division, Fourth Corps, and a part of John W. Davidson's Third Brigade of the same division. Davidson was sick, and his brigade was placed under Hancock's orders. Hancock then advanced about two-thirds of a mile and occupied a second redoubt, but when he was not reinforced, he fell back to the first redoubt.

D. H. Hill's division had left Williamsburg for Richmond that morning, and when Hooker began his attack on the Confederate works, Hill sent Jubal A. Early's brigade and Gabriel J. Rains' brigade back to report to Longstreet. Then Early, accompanied by Hill, attempted to drive Hancock from his redoubt, but he was repulsed with serious losses, including Early, who was wounded.

On the Federal left, Hooker's attack had stalled, and he was then slowly being driven back, although his troops continued to resist strongly. When Kearny came up, he deployed Hiram G. Berry's Third Brigade on the left of the road about 2:30 P.M., and David B. Birney's Second Brigade then arrived and was placed on the right. Charles D. Jameson's First Brigade, which brought up the rear, came up about 4:00 and deployed on a second line in rear of Berry and Birney. Darius N. Couch's First Division of

Fourth Corps also began to arrive about 2:00 P.M., and John J. Peck's Second Brigade deployed on the right of Hooker, and soon joined in the action. When Kearny's line was completed, Hooker withdrew his division and moved to the rear. Kearny attacked vigorously, and by nightfall had recovered the ground lost by Hooker during the day.

During the afternoon, the divisions of Sedgwick and Richardson of Sumner's Second Corps also moved up to Williamsburg, but Franklin's Division of the Department of the Rappahannock and Porter's First Division of Third Corps were left at Yorktown, from which point they were to move up the York River on transports.

Hooker's division did most of the fighting at Williamsburg, and of the total Union losses of 2,283 reported for the army, 1,575 were in Hooker's division. Kearny's division, also of Third Corps, lost 419 officers and men.

McClellan arrived on the field about 5:00 P.M., when most of the fighting had ended. The army was generally in good shape after the battle, and that evening McClellan ordered Sedgwick and Richardson back to Yorktown, from which point they were to follow Franklin and Porter by water to West Point. The rest of the army remained near Williamsburg. That night, the enemy withdrew from Williamsburg, and the divisions of D. H. Hill and Longstreet followed Magruder and Gustavus W. Smith toward Richmond.

The Union forces engaged at Williamsburg were as follows:

THIRD CORPS, Samuel P. Heintzelman

Second Division, Joseph Hooker
  First Brigade, Cuvier Grover
  Second Brigade, Nelson Taylor
  Third Brigade, Francis E. Patterson
  Artillery, Charles S. Wainwright

Third Division, Philip Kearny
  First Brigade, Charles D. Jameson
  Second Brigade, David B. Birney
  Third Brigade, Hiram G. Berry
  Artillery, James Thompson

FOURTH CORPS, Erasmus D. Keyes

First Division, Darius N. Couch

First Brigade, Julius W. Adams
Second Brigade, John J. Peck
Third Brigade, Charles Devens, Jr.
Artillery, Robert M. West

Note 1. Adams' First Brigade was formerly Lawrence P. Graham's Third Brigade, First Division.
Note 2. Devens' Third Brigade was formerly Henry S. Briggs' First Brigade, First Division.

Second Division, William F. Smith
First Brigade, Winfield S. Hancock
Second Brigade, William T. H. Brooks
Third Brigade, John W. Davidson
Artillery, Romeyn B. Ayres

Note. During the battle, Davidson was sick, and Hancock commanded both First Brigade and Second Brigade.

Third Division, Silas Casey
First Brigade, Henry M. Naglee
Second Brigade, William H. Keim
Third Brigade, Innis N. Palmer
Artillery, Guilford D. Bailey

Advance Guard, George Stoneman
Emory's Cavalry Command, William H. Emory
Cooke's Cavalry Command, Philip St. George Cooke
C. W. Barker's Squadron of Illinois Cavalry
Brigade of Horse Artillery, William Hays
3rd Pennsylvania Cavalry, William W. Averell

Advance of the Army to White House, Virginia, May 6–15, 1862. On May 6, 1862, the day after the Battle of Williamsburg, McClellan's Right Wing began its movement by water up the York River to the vicinity of West Point. The leading troops belonged to Franklin's Division, and they were followed by Sedgwick's and Richardson's divisions of Sumner's Second Corps and Porter's division of Heintzelman's Third Corps. The divisions of Hooker and Kearny of Third Corps, and the divisions of Smith, Couch, and Casey of Keyes' Fourth Corps remained at Williamsburg until May 8, 1862.

Engagement at Eltham's Landing (West Point, or Barhamsville), May 7, 1862. Franklin's Division left Yorktown on the morning of May 6, 1862, and at 3:00 that afternoon the transports arrived off West Point, at the confluence of the Pamunkey and the Mattapony rivers. During the afternoon and that night, the infantry and artillery disembarked at Eltham's Landing on the south bank of the Pamunkey. McClellan hoped that by this movement Johnston would be forced to abandon any works that he might have constructed below that point.

By early morning May 7, 1862, the infantry and artillery were ashore, and Franklin, accompanied by John Newton, commander of his Third Brigade, had made a careful reconnaissance of the position that he was to occupy. About five miles to the south of Eltham's Landing was the village of Barhamsville, which was on the road from Williamsburg to Richmond. Because this was the road on which Johnston's army was withdrawing from Williamsburg, Franklin was concerned about the safety of his relatively small command, which at the time was without close support. With this in mind, Franklin promptly began to form a defensive line that he could hold against a stronger force.

The landing place was a cleared area of about one square mile, with dense woods on three sides and the river at the rear. On the right, a road ran from the landing across the open space, and then through the woods to Barhamsville. Franklin was aware of the critical position in which his command would be placed if the enemy advanced into the clearing from Barhamsville, and then opened fire with his artillery on the landing and the transports on the river. To prevent this, Franklin proceeded to post his command so as to hold the road in the woods in front of the open ground. He placed Newton's brigade on the right of his line to hold the woods and the road to Barhamsville, and he supported Newton on the left with the 3rd New Jersey and 4th New Jersey of George W. Taylor's First Brigade, and the 5th Maine of Henry W. Slocum's Second Brigade. In rear of Newton's line, he placed the remainder of Taylor's brigade, the 1st New Jersey and 2nd New Jersey, to support William Hexamer's Battery A, 1st New Jersey Light Artillery and Emory Upton's Battery D, 2nd United States Artillery. Both batteries were under the command of Edward R. Platt. He also placed Napoleon J. T. Dana's Third Brigade of Sedgwick's division of Second Corps, which had arrived from Yorktown that morning, on the left of the line, with Josiah Porter's Battery A, Massachusetts Artillery on its left, near the river. Slocum commanded the center and left wing of Franklin's line. Slocum sent the 5th Maine, 16th New York, and 27th New York of his brigade to Newton, and his command then consisted of only the 96th Pennsylvania of his own Second Brigade, and Dana's brigade.

When Franklin's Division went ashore at Eltham's Landing, Gustavus W. Smith's Reserve of Johnston's army was at Barhamsville, and later the rest of Johnston's army came up and assembled in the vicinity. On the morning of May 7, 1862, Smith sent William H. C. Whiting's division of the Reserve north on the road to the landing to prevent Franklin from reaching Barhamsville until all of the trains of the army had passed that point. He directed Whiting to drive the Federal skirmishers from the thick woods and to attempt to reach the open ground near the river.

Whiting advanced as ordered, and about 9:00 A.M. became engaged with Newton's skirmishers. John B. Hood's Texas Brigade (First Brigade) attacked along the road leading to the landing, and he was supported on the right by the Hampton Legion and the 19th Georgia of Wade Hampton's Second Brigade. Later, Samuel R. Anderson's Tennessee Brigade came up and supported Hood on the left. Fighting became severe between 10:00 and 11:00 that morning, and it continued without significant result until 3:00 P.M., and then, with the trains safely on their way, Whiting returned to Barhamsville. Franklin remained near Eltham's Landing.

* * * * * * * * * * *

After the engagement at Eltham's Landing, Johnston's army resumed its retreat toward Richmond. Smith and Magruder marched by way of New Kent Court House, and Longstreet and Hill took the road by Long Bridge on the Chickahominy River. On the evening of May 9, 1862, Johnston halted on a line that extended from Long Bridge to Baltimore Cross Roads, which was on the New Kent Court House Road. The right of Longstreet's division covered the Long Bridge, and the left of Magruder's division was on the Richmond and York River Railroad. Johnston remained on this line five days and then moved back, and on May 17, 1862, the army encamped about three miles from Richmond, in front of the line of works constructed the year before. D. H. Hill's division was in the center of this line, across the Williamsburg Road; Longstreet's

division was on the right, covering the River Road; and Magruder's division was on the left and extending across the Nine-Mile Road toward the Chickahominy River. Smith's division was in reserve, behind the left of Hill and the right of Magruder.

On May 8, 1862, McClellan's left wing marched out of Williamsburg on the road to Richmond in pursuit of Johnston. Stoneman's cavalry moved first, and it was followed, in turn, by Keyes' Fourth Corps and Heintzelman's two divisions of Third Corps. Grover's brigade of Hooker's division remained at Williamsburg until May 12, 1862, and then it rejoined its division at Cumberland, near White House, on the Pamunkey River. McClellan's column passed through Barhamsville, and then on May 10, 1862 the two wings of the army were united. On May 15, 1862, the divisions of the Army of the Potomac were at the following places: Franklin's, Smith's, and Porter's divisions, and Sykes' brigade of regulars, which reported to Porter, were at Cumberland; Couch's and Casey's divisions were nearby, at Kent Court House; Hooker's and Kearny's divisions were near Roper's Church; and Richardson's and Sedgwick's divisions were near Eltham's Landing. On May 15–16, 1862, Franklin, Porter, Smith, and Sykes advanced to White House where the Richmond and York River Railroad crossed the Pamunkey River on its way to West Point. McClellan established his headquarters there, and also a large depot to supply the army.

Reorganization of the Army, May 18, 1862. On May 18, 1862, before continuing the advance on Richmond, McClellan reorganized the the Army of the Potomac by forming two new army corps. A Fifth Corps was organized provisionally, under the command of Fitz John Porter, from Porter's First Division, Third Corps and George Sykes' Regular Infantry Brigade. A Sixth Corps was organized provisionally, under the command of William B. Franklin, from William F. Smith's Second Division, Fourth Corps and Franklin's Division, Department of the Rappahannock (formerly First Division, First Corps, Army of the Potomac). The organization of McClellan's army from May 18, 1862 to May 31, 1862, the day of the Battle of Fair Oaks or Seven Pines, was as follows:

ARMY OF THE POTOMAC
George B. McClellan

SECOND CORPS, Edwin V. Sumner

First Division, Israel B. Richardson
First Brigade, Oliver O. Howard
Second Brigade, Thomas J. Meagher
Third Brigade, William H. French
Artillery, George W. Hazzard

Second Division, John Sedgwick
First Brigade, Willis A. Gorman
Second Brigade, William W. Burns
Third Brigade, Napoleon J. T. Dana
Artillery, Charles H. Tompkins

Note. Louis Blenker's Division, which had been detached from Second Corps, was transferred to John C. Fremont's command in Western Virginia March 31, 1862.

THIRD CORPS, Samuel P. Heintzelman

Second Division, Joseph Hooker
First Brigade, Cuvier Grover
Second Brigade, John J. Abercrombie, to May 24, 1862
Daniel E. Sickles
Third Brigade, Francis E. Patterson, to May 31, 1862
Samuel H. Starr
Artillery, Charles S. Wainwright

Note 1. First Division, Third Corps was transferred to Fifth Provisional Division as First Division May 18, 1862.
Note 2. Henry M. Naglee commanded First Brigade until April 27, 1862.
Note 3. Nelson Taylor commanded Second Brigade until May 11, 1862.

Third Division, Philip Kearny
First Brigade, Charles D. Jameson
Second Brigade, David Birney, to June 1, 1862
J. H. Hobart Ward
Third Brigade, Hiram G. Berry
Artillery, James Thompson

Note. Birney was placed in arrest at 7:00 A.M. June 1, 1862, and Ward was placed in temporary command of the brigade.

FOURTH CORPS, Erasmus D. Keyes

First Division, Darius N. Couch
First Brigade, John J. Peck
Second Brigade, Henry W. Wessells, to May 24, 1862
John J. Abercrombie
Third Brigade, Charles Devens, Jr., to May 31, 1862,

wounded
Charles H. Innes
Artillery, Robert M. West

Third Division, Silas Casey
First Brigade, Henry M. Naglee
Second Brigade, William H. Keim, to May 18, 1862, died
Joshua B. Howell, to May 24, 1862
Henry W. Wessells
Third Brigade, Innis N. Palmer
Artillery, Guilford D. Bailey, to May 31, 1862, killed
D. H. Van Valkenburgh, May 31, 1862, killed
Peter C. Regan

Note. William F. Smith's Second Division was transferred to Sixth Provisional Corps as Second Division May 18, 1862. After that, Casey's division was sometimes called Second Division of Fourth Corps.

FIFTH PROVISIONAL CORPS, Fitz John Porter

First Division, Fitz John Porter, to May 18, 1862
George W. Morell
First Brigade, John H. Martindale
Second Brigade, George W. Morell, to May 18, 1862
James McQuade
Third Brigade, Daniel Butterfield
Artillery, Charles Griffin

Note. First Division was First Division, Third Corps until transferred to Sixth Provisional Corps May 18, 1862.

Second Division, George Sykes
First Brigade, Robert C. Buchanan
Second Brigade, William Chapman
Artillery, Stephen H. Weed

Note 1. Until May 18, 1862, Second Division was designated as Sykes' Independent Brigade of Regulars, Army of the Potomac.

Provisional Brigade, Gouverneur K. Warren

Note. Warren's Brigade was formed May 24, 1862, just before Porter's expedition to Hanover Court House, and it was discontinued May 31, 1862.

May 20, 1862, Henry J. Hunt's Reserve Artillery was assigned to duty with Fifth Provisional Corps, and Hunt reported to Porter the next day. The organization of of the Reserve Artillery was as follows:

Reserve Artillery, Henry J. Hunt

First Brigade (Horse Artillery), William Hays
  Battery A, 2nd United States Artillery, John C. Tidball
  Batteries B and L, 2nd United States Artillery, James M. Robertson
  Battery M, 2nd United States Artillery, Henry Benson

Note. Batteries C and G, 3rd United States Artillery, Horatio G. Gibson, were detached with Silas Casey's command.

Second Brigade, George W. Getty
  Batteries E and G, 1st United States Artillery, Alanson M. Randol
  Battery K, 1st United States Artillery, Samuel S. Elder
  Battery G, 4th United States Artillery, Charles H. Morgan
  Battery A, 5th United States Artillery, Adelbert Ames
  Battery K, 5th United States Artillery, John R. Smead
Third Brigade, Albert Arndt
  Battery A, 1st New York Battalion, Otto Diedrichs
  Battery B, 1st New York Battalion, Adolph Voegelee
  Battery C, 1st New York Battalion, John Knieriem
  Battery D, 1st New York Battalion, Edward Grimm
Fourth Brigade, Edward R. Petherbridge
  Battery A, Maryland Light Artillery, John W. Wolcott
  Battery B, Maryland Light Artillery, Alonzo Snow
Fifth Brigade, J. Howard Carlisle
  5th Battery, New York Light Artillery, Elijah D. Taft
  Battery E, 2nd United States Artillery, J. Howard Carlisle
  Batteries F and K, 3rd United States Artillery, La Rhett L. Livingston

SIXTH PROVISIONAL CORPS, William B. Franklin

First Division, William B. Franklin, to May 18, 1862
  Henry W. Slocum
First Brigade, George W. Taylor
Second Brigade, Henry W. Slocum, to May 18, 1862
  Joseph J. Bartlett
Third Brigade, John Newton
Artillery, Edward R. Platt

Note. First Division was formerly Franklin's Division, Department of the Rappahannock.

Second Division, William F. Smith
  First Brigade, Winfield S. Hancock

Second Brigade, William T. H. Brooks
Third Brigade, John W. Davidson
Artillery, Romeyn B. Ayres

Note. Second Division was formerly Smith's Second Division, Fourth Corps.

Cavalry Reserve, Philip St. George Cooke
  First Brigade, William H. Emory
  Second Brigade, George A. H. Blake

Advance to the Chickahominy River and Seven Pines, May 20–25, 1862. When McClellan established the base for his army at White House on the Pamunkey River, he was committed to operating with his command on both the north and south sides of the Chickahominy River. It was necessary that he retain on the north bank a sufficient force to protect the base, and at the same time move troops to the south bank for an attack on Richmond. As an additional reason for maintaining troops north of the Chickahominy, McClellan expected McDowell to join him from Fredericksburg with his troops of the Department of the Rappahannock. In an order dated May 17, 1862, the secretary of war directed McDowell to march southward with his corps along the Richmond, Fredericksburg, and Potomac Railroad and cooperate with McClellan in his advance on Richmond, and on the same day he ordered McClellan to extend his line to the right so as to link up with McDowell when he arrived in the area. McDowell's movement was called off, however, because of Jackson's activities in the Shenandoah Valley, but on June 8, 1862, he was again ordered toward Richmond. This movement, too, was soon halted. For additional information about McDowell's part in the Peninsular Campaign, see Shenandoah Valley Campaign (Jackson), and also Department of the Rappahannock.

After concentrating the Army of the Potomac near White House, and with the above considerations in mind, McClellan issued orders for the advance of the army to the Chickahominy. The leading troops reached the north bank at Bottom's Bridge May 20, 1862, and by the next day the whole army was in position along the river facing Richmond, which was from seven to twelve miles distant. Franklin's new Sixth Provisional Corps held the right of the line, three miles from New Bridge, and it was supported by Porter's new Fifth Provisional Corps.

Stoneman's cavalry was on the right of Franklin, and within about a mile of New Bridge. Sumner's Second Corps occupied the center of the line, near the Tyler house, and connected on its left with Keyes' Fourth Corps, which held the left of the line near Bottom's Bridge. Heintzelman's Third Corps was in reserve.

On May 20, 1862, Henry M. Naglee's First Brigade of Casey's Second Division, Fourth Corps crossed the Chickahominy at Bottom's Bridge on a reconnaissance, and three days later Keyes crossed his Fourth Corps at the same bridge and then encamped two miles beyond. May 24, 1862, Naglee's brigade dislodged Robert Hatton's Tennessee Brigade of Gustavus W. Smith's division from a position on the Bottom's Bridge Road, about three miles from Seven Pines. The next day Keyes advanced and fortified a position near Seven Pines, where the Nine-Mile Road came into the Williamsburg Road.

On the same day, May 25, 1862, McClellan ordered Heintzelman to cross the river and take position two miles in advance of Bottom's Bridge, where he was to watch the crossings of White Oak Swamp and cover the left and rear of the left wing of the army. As senior officer, Heintzelman assumed command of both his own Third Corps and Keyes' Fourth Corps, which were then south of the Chickahominy and separated from the rest of the army by the river.

McClellan's Right Wing, which consisted of Porter's Fifth Provisional Corps, Franklin's Sixth Provisional Corps, Sumner's Second Corps, and Stoneman's cavalry, remained in position along the north bank of the river during this period, and May 24, 1862, Stoneman extended the line to Mechanicsville, which he occupied that day.

It will be remembered that at that time the Confederate forces facing McClellan in front of Richmond consisted of the divisions of Magruder, D. H. Hill, Longstreet, and Gustavus W. Smith. In addition, there were other enemy forces under Johnston's control that were not far distant, and which were soon brought to Richmond to aid in its defense. Joseph R. Anderson commanded a force of three brigades and four additional regiments, which was in position south of Fredericksburg on the Richmond, Fredericksburg, and Potomac Railroad watching McDowell. Lawrence O'B. Branch com-

manded a brigade at Hanover Court House, about fourteen miles north of Richmond. This brigade had been brought up from Gordonsville, where it had been placed in support of Richard S. Ewell's division. Benjamin Huger commanded a division at Petersburg, Virginia, where it had arrived about mid-May after the evacuation of Norfolk May 9, 1862.

May 26, 1862, Branch moved his brigade to a point about four miles south of Lebanon Church, near Peake's Turnout on the Virginia Central Railroad, which was about ten miles east of Ashland. Johnston also ordered Anderson to move south to Hanover Court House, and then on through Ashland to a position closer to Richmond.

Engagement at Hanover Court House, Virginia, May 27, 1862. On May 26, 1862, McClellan learned of the presence of Branch's brigade at Hanover Court House. He also was informed that Anderson had withdrawn from in front of Fredericksburg, and that McDowell was moving south and was at that time about eight miles from Fredericksburg. On the basis of this information, McClellan decided to move against Branch, who constituted a threat to the right of his line, and who also was in position to interfere with McDowell's advance. Accordingly, McClellan ordered Porter to move forward and drive the enemy from the area as far as Hanover Court House, or beyond. He was also to destroy the bridges over the South Anna and Pamunkey rivers, and to cut the Virginia Central Railroad so as to prevent the sending of reinforcements to Branch and Anderson, and also to Thomas J. (Stonewall) Jackson in the Shenandoah Valley.

When Porter left White House and advanced to the Chickahominy River, he left a regiment at Mount Airey, on the White House Road, to operate in conjunction with the 6th Pennsylvania Cavalry and destroy boats and bridges on the Pamunkey River. These forces were consolidated May 24, 1862 into a brigade consisting of 5th New York, 1st Connecticut, 6th Pennsylvania Cavalry, and William B. Weeden's Battery C, 1st Rhode Island Light Artillery. Gouverneur K. Warren was assigned command of this brigade, which was posted at Old Church. Warren proceeded to destroy all means of communication over the Pamunkey River from that point toward Hanover Court House.

At 4:00 A.M. May 27, 1862, Porter left New Bridge on the Chickahominy with George W. Morell's First Division, Fifth Provisional Corps, and marched by way of Mechanicsville toward Hanover Court House. Porter was preceded by an advance guard under William H. Emory, which consisted of 5th United States Cavalry, 6th United States Cavalry, and Henry Benson's Battery M, 2nd United States Artillery of the Horse Artillery. At the same time, Warren's brigade marched from Old Church toward Hanover Court House. According to Porter's plan, Morell was to attack on the front of the enemy position, while Warren, advancing along the Pamunkey, was to strike the flank and rear.

About noon, Emory's cavalry encountered a part of Branch's brigade at the junction of the Ashland Road and the Hanover Court House Road, near Dr. Kinney's house, and about a mile east of Peake's Station on the Virginia Central Railroad. John H. Martindale's First Brigade, First Division was sent on the road toward Ashland to guard Porter's left flank, and then Daniel Butterfield's Third Brigade advanced and cleared the way. At that point, Warren joined Porter from Old Church. Porter then ordered Martindale to move up the railroad and directed Warren to send out his cavalry to destroy the bridges over the Pamunkey, east of the railroad. Porter then moved with the rest of his command toward Hanover Court House. Shortly after Porter had started, Martindale became engaged with Branch's entire command at Peake's Station, and it was only with considerable difficulty that he was able to maintain his position.

The head of Porter's column had just reached Hanover Court House when Porter learned of Martindale's difficulties, and he immediately marched back to give assistance. Morell, leading his old brigade, then commanded by James McQuade, struck Branch on the front and flank, while a part of Butterfield's brigade moved on his rear. These two brigades, together with Martindale's brigade, drove Branch from the field and back to Ashland.

On May 27, 1862, a new Confederate division was formed under the command of Ambrose P. Hill. At the time of Porter's advance, Joseph R. Anderson's command was passing through Ashland on its way toward Richmond, and Hill was then assigned command of Branch's brigade and Anderson's three brigades.

Porter camped on the road to Ashland during the night of May 27, 1862, and the next day he continued the work of clearing the area of enemy troops and destroying the bridges over the South Anna and Pamunkey rivers. He returned with his command to its camps near the Chickahominy River on the evening of May 29, 1862.

Battle of Fair Oaks-Seven Pines, Virginia, May 31, 1862–June 1, 1862. During the afternoon of May 27, 1862, Johnston learned from Joseph R. Anderson that McDowell was moving south from Fredericksburg with about 40,000 men, and he decided to attack McClellan's Right Wing, north of the Chickahominy, before these reinforcements arrived. Johnston made preparations for the attack, but when these had been completed he learned that McDowell had turned back and was returning to Fredericksburg. Johnston then called off the attack and made other plans.

About noon May 30, 1862, Johnston decided to attack early the next morning and overwhelm the two Federal corps on the south side of the Chickahominy before help could arrive from across the river. The country east of Richmond, where the battle was soon to be fought, was flat and marshy, and was generally covered with timber and dense undergrowth; and at the time of the battle, it was flooded because of a heavy rainstorm on the afternoon and the night before. Through this area ran the Williamsburg Road, the Richmond and York River Railroad, the Nine-Mile Road, and the Charles City Road.

The Williamsburg Road left Richmond along the south side of Mount Chimbarazo and near the James River, and it then ran almost due east through Seven Pines to Bottom's Bridge on the Chickahominy River, and on beyond. This road was also known as the Seven-Mile Road and the "Old Stage Road," and it followed the route of present-day U.S. 60. The Charles City Road branched off the Williamsburg Road a short distance east of Richmond, and ran to the southeast, and south of White Oak Swamp. The Nine-Mile Road left Richmond about a mile northeast of the Williamsburg Road and ran a little north of east for about three miles to "Old Tavern," where a road branched off to the north to New Bridge on the Chickahominy, about a mile and a half distant. At Old Tavern, the Nine-Mile Road turned to the southeast and ran on an almost straight line for two and three-fourths miles and then joined the Williamsburg Road at Seven Pines. The Nine-Mile Road crossed the Richmond and York River Railroad at Fair Oaks Station, one mile northwest of Seven Pines.

The Richmond and York River Railroad ran eastward out of Richmond, between the Williamsburg Road and the Nine-Mile Road, and passed through Fair Oaks Station and Savage (Savage's) Station before crossing the Chickahominy about three-fourths of a mile above Bottom's Bridge. The Battle of Fair Oaks-Seven Pines was fought along these roads.

According to Johnston's plan of attack, Daniel H. Hill's division was to advance along the Williamsburg Road, and Longstreet's division along the Nine-Mile Road, and they were to attack the Union positions at Fair Oaks and Seven Pines. Huger's division, which had been brought up from Petersburg, was to march on the right of D. H. Hill, along the Charles City Road; and Gustavus W. Smith's division, then commanded by William H. C. Whiting (Smith remained on the field but left the direction of the division to Whiting), was to advance on the Nine-Mile Road to Old Tavern and await Longstreet's attack. Ambrose P. Hill's new division was on the left of Johnston's line at Meadow Bridge (or Bridges), and Magruder's division was on the right of Ambrose P. Hill along the Chickahominy east of Richmond. Neither division was to take part in the battle of May 31, 1862. For better control of the Confederate troops in the impending battle, Longstreet was assigned command of the Right Wing and Gustavus W. Smith of the Left Wing of Johnston's army.

On the morning of May 31, 1862, the Federal troops north of the Chickahominy were in position as follows: Porter's Fifth Provisional Corps was behind Beaver Dam Creek, with its right near Ellerson's (or Ellison's) Mill; Franklin's Sixth Provisional Corps faced New Bridge, on the left of Porter, with its left on Powhite Swamp; and

Sumner's Second Corps was to the right of Bottom's Bridge, with its right connecting with Franklin. Sedgwick's Second Division of Second Corps was to the right of the Tyler house, facing Sumner's Upper Bridge (Grapevine Bridge), and Richardson's First Division was to the left of the Tyler house, in front of Sumner's Lower Bridge. The Grapevine Bridge was almost due south of Cold Harbor.

The Federal positions south of the Chickahominy on the morning of May 31, 1862 were as follows: Silas Casey's Second Division of Keyes' Fourth Corps occupied a partially completed defensive line across the Williamsburg Road, about three-fourths of a mile west of Seven Pines, with a strong picket line about a half mile farther out near present-day Sandston. Innis N. Palmer's Third Brigade was on the left of Casey's line, south of the Williamsburg Road; Henry W. Wessells' Second Brigade was on the right of Palmer, on the road; and Henry M. Naglee's First Brigade was on the right, with a part of the brigade near Wessells' brigade, and the rest picketing a line through Fair Oaks to the Chickahominy. When the fighting started, Naglee's brigade was largely reassembled.

Darius N. Couch's First Division of Fourth Corps formed a second line in rear of Casey, at Seven Pines. John J. Peck's First Brigade was on the left, south of the Williamsburg Road; Charles Devens' Third Brigade was on the center of the division line; and John J. Abercrombie's Second Brigade was on the right of Devens, along the Nine-Mile Road. One regiment of Abercrombie's brigade was near Seven Pines; two regiments were along the Nine-Mile Road; and two regiments were at Fair Oaks, guarding the railroad crossing.

About one and one-half miles in rear of Seven Pines was an unoccupied third line, which had been constructed earlier during the Federal advance from the Chickahominy.

Farther to the rear, Philip Kearny's Third Division of Heintzelman's Third Corps occupied a position at the west end of Bottom's Bridge, and Joseph Hooker's Second Division was about three miles south, watching White Oak Bridge.

On the enemy side, there was considerable confusion during the preparations for the attack, probably because of a misunderstanding of orders, and it was not until 1:00 P.M. that D. H. Hill's division advanced to the attack. At that time Whiting's division (Gustavus W. Smith's) had moved up to its assigned position on the Nine-Mile Road, near the turnout of that road to New Bridge; and Longstreet's division, which was to have attacked on the Nine-Mile Road, had, by mistake, taken position on the Williamsburg Road in rear of Hill.

Samuel Garland's brigade, leading Hill's attack and supported by Winfield S. Featherston's brigade (commanded that day by George T. Anderson), struck Casey's line shortly after 1:00 P.M. Casey's division repulsed all attacks for a time, but it was finally driven back in disorder when the brigades of Robert E. Rodes and Gabriel J. Rains advanced against its left flank, south of the road. Nearly all of Naglee's brigade remained on the field and continued to fight, but the greater part of Palmer's and Wessells' brigades passed through Couch's line at Seven Pines, and continued on to the third position in the rear.

Hill's troops then pressed forward and continued the attack against Couch's second line. Longstreet detached George E. Pickett's brigade, and sent it to the north of D. H. Hill to cover the Richmond and York River Railroad, and he ordered forward the brigades of Richard H. Anderson (commanded by Micah Jenkins while Anderson directed three brigades of Longstreet's division) and James L. Kemper to support Hill's attack. Longstreet's three remaining brigades, commanded by Cadmus M. Wilcox, which had been on the Charles City Road, were also ordered to join Hill, but they did not arrive until about 5:00 P.M., and then were only slightly engaged.

On the day of the battle, as noted above, Kearny's division of Heintzelman's Third Corps held the bridgehead at Bottom's Bridge, on the west side of the Chickahominy River, and Hooker's division of Third Corps was three miles farther south at White Oak Bridge. At 3:00 P.M., in response to a call for help from Keyes, Heintzelman sent David B. Birney's Second Brigade and Hiram G. Berry's Third Brigade of Kearny's division westward along the Williamsburg Road toward the rear of Keyes' position. Birney marched to the third defensive line and then moved north a short distance to the railroad. Berry halted at the third line, about three-fourths of

a mile west of Savage Station. When Casey's division was driven back about 3:30 P.M., Heintzelman ordered Birney and Berry to move up and support Couch, who was then in position at the second line. At the same time, Heintzelman ordered forward Charles D. Jameson's First Brigade of Kearny's division, which had been in camp near Bottom's Bridge, three miles to the rear. Kearny, with Berry's brigade, marched to the left of the Williamsburg Road at Seven Pines, and advanced to a point south of Casey's camps, which were then occupied by the enemy. Berry was able to hold his position there, on D. H. Hill's right flank, until 5:30 P.M., and then he fell back toward the third line.

As Jameson approached Seven Pines, one of his regiments was sent to Peck and one to Birney, but he arrived at the scene of the fighting with two regiments about 4:00 P.M. He was sharply engaged for an hour and a half, and then he too was forced to fall back. Because of conflicting orders, Birney's brigade was kept marching and countermarching during the afternoon and evening, and consequently was unable to serve effectively.

At 3:00 P.M., at the same time that Kearny started forward from Bottom's Bridge, Hooker started forward from White Oak Swamp with Daniel Sickles' Second Brigade and Francis E. Patterson's Third Brigade of his division. Patterson was absent sick, and Samuel H. Starr was in command of his brigade. Cuvier Grover's First Brigade was left behind to hold the bridge across the swamp. Hooker arrived with his troops near the third line that evening, but he was too late to be engaged.

Meantime, under a steady pressure from D. H. Hill's division in front and from Jenkins' brigade on the right, Couch's line finally gave way about 6:00 P.M., and then the rest of Fourth Corps and the brigades of Third Corps also fell back about a mile and a half to the third line, which they held during the night.

When Hill began his attack about 1:00 P.M., the two regiments of Abercrombie's brigade at Fair Oaks were sent back to join the 65th New York and James Brady's Battery H, 1st Pennsylvania Light Artillery on the Nine-Mile Road to protect the right of Keyes' line. An hour later, as Hill's attack developed, Keyes ordered Couch to advance against the enemy left with two regiments of Abercrombie's brigade and to relieve the pressure on Casey's right.

Couch was soon engaged, and the 7th Massachusetts of Devens' brigade and the 62nd New York of Peck's brigade were sent forward to reinforce him. Then, when Casey's line fell back, Couch and Abercrombie were cut off with 31st Pennsylvania, 65th New York, and a part of 61st New York of Abercrombie's brigade, 7th Massachusetts of Devens' brigade, 62nd New York of Peck's brigade, and Brady's battery. When Couch realized that he would not be able to rejoin the main force, he fell back with his command to the right of the railroad, and then continued on for a half mile to the Courtney house on the road to Trents'. There Couch formed his regiments in line of battle, facing south toward Fair Oaks Station.

Meantime, at his headquarters north of the Chickahominy, McClellan learned of the fighting at Seven Pines, and at 2:30 P.M. he ordered Sumner to cross the river with the two divisions of his Second Corps and march to the support of Keyes and Heintzelman. John Sedgwick's Second Division began crossing at once at Grapevine Bridge (Sumner's Upper Bridge), and Israel B. Richardson's First Division started crossing at the Lower Bridge, about one mile below. After William H. French's Third Brigade, First Division had crossed, the bridge became unsafe because of the flood waters, and Oliver O. Howard's First Brigade and Thomas F. Meagher's Second Brigade moved up to Grapevine Bridge and followed Sedgwick's division over the river.

Sedgwick immediately took the road toward Fair Oaks, with Willis A. Gorman's First Brigade in the lead, and then, in order, William W. Burns' Second Brigade and Napoleon J. T. Dana's Third Brigade. Sedgwick's leading troops, Alfred Sully's 1st Minnesota of Gorman's brigade, arrived on the field at the Adams house about 4:30 P.M., and there they found Couch's regiments, under the immediate control of Abercrombie, engaged to the southwest of the Courtney house, which was about one-fourth mile west of the Adams house. Sully's regiment formed on the right of Abercrombie, and the rest of Gorman's brigade on the left, and soon all were engaged. Burns' brigade arrived a short time later and formed on the right of Sully, and to the right of the Courtney house. When Dana came up, he had with him only two regiments (the other regiment was in the rear with the batteries), and these were placed on the left of Gorman, with their left extending southward toward the railroad. Richardson's division, which was following Sedgwick, did not arrive on the battlefield until dark, and at that time the fighting had ended for the day.

Meantime, Whiting's division had moved up to a point near Old Tavern, and had remained inactive there until between 4:00 and 5:00 P.M. At that time Johnston, whose headquarters was nearby, ordered Whiting to move down the Nine-Mile Road and attack the right of the Federal line that was resisting Hill's advance. It was Whiting's division—which consisted of the brigades of John B. Hood, James J. Pettigrew, Wade Hampton, Robert Hatton, and Whiting's own brigade—that attacked Couch's and Sumner's troops north and east of Fair Oaks that evening. This engagement lasted from about 5:30 to 7:00 P.M., and it ended with the Federal troops holding their position. Hatton was killed during the fighting, Hampton was wounded, and Pettigrew was wounded and captured. Johnston was also wounded that evening, and Gustavus W. Smith assumed temporary command of the army. He remained in command until 2:00 P.M. the next day, June 1, 1862, and then Robert E. Lee was assigned command. From that time on Lee's army was known as the Army of Northern Virginia.

At nightfall, at the end of the first day's fighting at Seven Pines and Fair Oaks, the troops of Fourth Corps, Third Corps, and Second Corps were in position as follows: on the Williamsburg Road, on or near the third Federal line, were Keyes' Fourth Corps; Sickles' brigade of Hooker's division, Third Corps; two regiments of Starr's (Patterson's) brigade of Hooker's division (the other two regiments had been sent to guard the depot at Bottom's Bridge); and Berry's and Jameson's brigades of Kearny's division, Third Corps. Birney's brigade of Kearny's division was also on the line of the third position, but it was on the railroad to the north, about two miles east of Fair Oaks.

North of the railroad, Couch's troops of Fourth Corps and Sumner's Second Corps occupied the following positions: Couch, with Abercrombie, was in line, facing south, with his left near the Adams house; Burns' brigade of Sedgwick's division, Second Corps was to the right and rear of Couch; Gorman's and Dana's brigades of Sedgwick's division were in line along the road between the

Adams house and Fair Oaks, about a half mile to the southwest, and they faced a little to the north of west. Gorman's right connected with Couch at the Adams house, and Dana's brigade was on the left of Gorman, with its left near the railroad, and about 200 to 250 yards east of Fair Oaks.

As noted above, Richardson's division of Sumner's corps did not arrive on the battlefield until dark and was not engaged. French's brigade halted for the night just north of the railroad, near the Hyer house, which was about three-fourths of a mile east of Fair Oaks; Howard's brigade and Meagher's brigade bivouacked to the northeast of the Adams house, on the road leading in from Dr. Trent's, near the Chickahominy. That evening, Birney's brigade moved up the railroad from the right of the third line, and at 10:00 P.M. established connection with the left of French's brigade.

On the morning of June 1, 1862, Richardson formed his division in three lines on the left of Sedgwick's division. French's brigade, with one regiment of Howard's brigade, formed the first line, which ran from the left of Dana's brigade, diagonally across the railroad, and faced a little to the west of south. The center of the brigade line crossed the railroad about a half mile east of Fair Oaks, and its left was a short distance south of the Hyer house. Howard's brigade was in line behind French, and Meagher's brigade was in rear of Howard.

Birney's brigade, then commanded by J. H. Hobart Ward (Birney had been placed in arrest), was on the left of French, facing southwest. Birney's right was on the railroad just east of the Hyer house, and its left was about one-fourth mile south of the Allen house, which was on the railroad. Starr's two New Jersey regiments were on the left of Birney's brigade, and about one-fourth mile north of Sickles' brigade, which had advanced on the Williamsburg Road and was at that time confronting Cadmus M. Wilcox's and Roger A. Pryor's brigades of Longstreet's division.

Dana's and Gorman's brigades remained in about the same positions that they had occupied the night before, but Burns' brigade was sent back to protect the crossing of the Chickahominy.

Gustavus W. Smith renewed the enemy attack at 6:30 A.M. June 1, 1862 by advancing against the left of French's brigade with the brigades of Lewis A. Armistead and William Mahone of Benjamin Huger's division and George E. Pickett's brigade of Longstreet's division. About 8:00 A.M., Howard, with two regiments of his brigade, relieved the left of French's brigade, and then the Federals attacked. Ward, commanding Birney's brigade, advanced and struck the flank of Armistead's brigade, just as Howard attacked on its front. Pickett's line on the right held its ground, but Armistead's troops were driven back in disorder. Howard was wounded in the attack, and he was succeeded in command of the brigade by Thomas J. Parker.

There was some fighting that morning on the Williamsburg Road, and also to the north of the road, between the Confederate brigades of Wilcox and Pryor of Longstreet's division and the Federal brigades of Sickles and Starr of Hooker's division, but this ended about 11:00 A.M., and two hours later the enemy troops retired to the vicinity of the former camps of Casey's division. When the Federal pickets advanced at sunrise June 2, 1862, they found that the enemy had left their front and had retired toward Richmond.

The organization of the Union forces at the Battle of Seven Pines or Fair Oaks May 31, 1862–June 1, 1862, was as follows:

ARMY OF THE POTOMAC
George B. McClellan

SECOND CORPS, Edwin V. Sumner

First Division, Israel B. Richardson
  First Brigade, Oliver O. Howard, to June 1, 1862, wounded
    Thomas J. Packer, to June 4, 1862
    John C. Caldwell
  Second Brigade, Thomas F. Meagher
  Third Brigade, William H. French
  Artillery Brigade, George W. Hazzard
    Batteries A and C, 4th United States Artillery, George W. Hazzard
    Battery B, 1st New York Light Artillery, Rufus D. Pettit
    Battery G, 1st New York Light Artillery, John D. Frank

Second Division, John Sedgwick
  First Brigade, Willis A. Gorman
  Second Brigade, William W. Burns
  Third Brigade, Napoleon J. T. Dana
  Artillery Brigade, Charles H. Tompkins
    Battery I, 1st United States Artillery, Edmund Kirby

Battery A, 1st Rhode Island Light Artillery, John A. Tompkins

Battery B, 1st Rhode Island Light Artillery, Walter O. Bartlett

Battery G, 1st Rhode Island Light Artillery, Charles D. Owen

THIRD CORPS, Samuel P. Heintzelman

Second Division, Joseph Hooker
First Brigade, Cuvier Grover
Second Brigade, Daniel E. Sickles
Third Brigade, Francis Patterson, sick
Samuel H. Starr
Artillery Brigade, Charles S. Wainwright
Battery H, 1st United States Artillery, Charles H. Webber
Battery D, 1st New York Light Artillery, Thomas W. Osborn
4th New York Battery, James E. Smith
6th New York Battery, Walter M. Bramhall

Note. The battery commanders given here are those who were in command at the time of the Battle of Williamsburg.

3rd Pennsylvania Cavalry, William W. Averell

Note 1. Grover's brigade was at White Oak Bridge and was not engaged.

Note 2. Averell's cavalry was not engaged.

Third Division, Philip Kearny
First Brigade, Charles D. Jameson
Second Brigade, David B. Birney, to 7:00 A.M. June 1, 1862, placed in arrest
J. H. Hobart Ward
Third Brigade, Hiram G. Berry
Artillery
Battery G, 2nd United States Artillery, James Thompson
Battery E, 1st Rhode Island Artillery, George E. Randolph
2nd Battery, New Jersey Light Artillery, John E. Beam

FOURTH CORPS, Erasmus D. Keyes

First Division, Darius N. Couch
First Brigade, John J. Peck
Second Brigade, John J. Abercrombie
Third Brigade, Charles Devens, Jr., to May 31, 1862, wounded
Charles H. Innes
8th Pennsylvania Cavalry, David McM. Gregg
Artillery, Robert M. West

Battery C, 1st Pennsylvania Light Artillery, Jeremiah McCarthy

Battery D, 1st Pennsylvania Light Artillery, Edward H. Flood

Battery E, 1st Pennsylvania Light Artillery, Theodore Miller

Battery H, 1st Pennsylvania Light Artillery, James Brady

Third Division, Silas Casey
First Brigade, Henry M. Naglee
Second Brigade, Henry W. Wessells
Third Brigade, Innis N. Palmer
Artillery, Guilford D. Bailey, killed
D. H. Van Valkenburgh, killed
Peter C. Regan
Battery A, 1st New York Light Artillery, Thomas H. Bates (commanded by George P. Hart)
Battery H, 1st New York Light Artillery, Joseph Spratt, wounded
John H. Howell, wounded
Charles E. Mink
7th New York Battery, Peter C. Regan
8th New York Battery, Butler Fitch

Note. After the reorganization of the army May 18, 1862, Casey's Third Division was commonly called Second Division, or simply Casey's Division.

The Army before Richmond, Virginia, June 1862. There was little activity in the Army of the Potomac during June 1862, largely because of bad weather, but there were some organizational and command changes, and also some changes in position, during this period. June 1, 1862, the limits of the Department of Virginia were extended, and the department, including the post of Fort Monroe, was placed under the control of McClellan. At the same time, John A. Dix, who was then at Baltimore, was assigned command of the troops at Fort Monroe, Norfolk, Portsmouth, and Suffolk and vicinity, and he relieved John E. Wool June 2, 1862.

June 7, 1862, Silas Casey was ordered to consolidate the three brigades of his Third Division, Fourth Corps into two brigades. Henry M. Naglee was assigned command of the new First Brigade, and Henry W. Wessells of the new Second Brigade. The regiments of Wessells' former Second Brigade and of Innis N. Palmer's Third Brigade were consolidated to form the new Second Brigade. Palmer was assigned to the temporary command of Third Brigade, First Division, Fourth Corps during the absence of Charles Devens, Jr., who had been wounded at Seven Pines. The designation of Casey's division was then changed to Second Division, and Third Division, Fourth Corps was discontinued.

June 12–13, 1862, George McCall's division of Pennsylvania Reserves, which had been sent from Irvin McDowell's Department of the Rappahannock, arrived on the Peninsula, and June 18, 1862, it was attached to Porter's Fifth Provisional Corps as Third Division. By this arrangement, however, McCall's division was not officially detached from the Department of the Rappahannock, and it would again come under McDowell's orders if the latter should join McClellan's army at Richmond. On June 18, 1862, McDowell was again ordered to march overland from Fredericksburg and join McClellan near Richmond, but because of the terrible condition of the roads, the movement was suspended.

The organization of McCall's division was as follows:

Third Division, Fifth Provisional Corps, George McCall
   First Brigade, John F. Reynolds
   Second Brigade, George G. Meade
   Third Brigade, Truman Seymour

Note. Third Brigade was formerly commanded by Edward O. C. Ord.

On June 16, 1862, Philip St. George Cooke's Cavalry Reserve and Stoneman's Advance Guard were placed under Fitz John Porter's orders, and they were assigned the task of watching the country toward the Pamunkey River, on Porter's right flank.

June 23, 1862, Casey was ordered to White House to assume command of the army depot there, and John J. Peck, formerly the commander of First Brigade, First Division, Fourth Corps, assumed command of Casey's Second Division. Albion P. Howe was assigned command of Peck's former brigade.

In addition to the command changes given above, there were, during the month, some further changes in the commanders of brigades in the army. In Second Corps, John C. Caldwell was assigned June 4, 1862 to command First Brigade, First Division in place of Howard, who had been wounded at Seven Pines; and later Alfred Sully assumed command of Gorman's First Brigade, Second Division because of the illness of the latter. In Third Corps, Joseph B. Carr was assigned June 12, 1862 to the temporary command of Patterson's Third Brigade, Second Division; and a short time later John C. Robinson was assigned command of Charles D. Jameson's First Brigade, Third Division.

On June 19, 1862, Franklin's Sixth Provisional Corps was moved from the north to the south side of the Chickahominy River, thus leaving only Porter's Fifth Provisional Corps and the cavalry on the north side. When this transfer was completed, McClellan's troops south of the river occupied an entrenched line that began on the left at White Oak Swamp, passed to the west of Seven Pines and Fair Oaks, and ended on the right near the Chickahominy at Golding's farm.

On the eve of the Seven Days' Battles, which began June 25, 1862, McClellan's troops were in position as follows: Porter's Fifth Provisional Corps was north of the Chickahominy in the vicinity of Gaines' Mill, with McCall's division posted farther west at Mechanicsville and along Beaver Dam Creek. The cavalry, with Henry S. Lansing's 17th New York Infantry and James Barnes' 18th Massachusetts Infantry, both of Morell's division of Porter's corps, was on the right of Porter, guarding the region from the Pamunkey River to Meadow Bridge on the Chickahominy. Meadow Bridge was frequently called Meadow Bridges, because when McClellan arrived in the area there were two bridges over the river—the highway bridge and the bridge of the Virginia Central Railroad. These bridges were destroyed, but were later rebuilt.

South of the river, Franklin's Sixth Provisional Corps was on the right of the line, with William F. Smith's division on the right of the corps' line, and Slocum's division on the left. Smith's right rested on a hill overlooking the Chickahominy River, about two miles north of Fair Oaks, and near the Golding house. Slocum's division was in reserve at Courtneys', with pickets out in front.

Sumner's Second Corps, consisting of the divisions of Richardson and Sedgwick, was on the left of Franklin, in front of Fair Oaks Station; Heintzelman's Third Corps, consisting of the divisions of Hooker and Kearny, was on the left of Sumner, with Hooker's division on the Williamsburg Road, in front of Seven Pines, and Kearny's division on the left of Hooker; and Keyes'

Fourth Corps, consisting of the divisions of Couch and Peck, was in reserve.

During most of the month of June 1862, Robert E. Lee, as the new commander of the Army of Northern Virginia, was concerned primarily with the problem of halting the Federal advance on Richmond. In his opinion, it would be necessary to force the Army of the Potomac from behind its entrenchments to prevent McClellan from moving forward from one position to another, under the cover of his heavy guns, until he was within artillery range of the city. To draw McClellan out, he decided to advance against his line of communications, which ran along the north side of the Chickahominy from the front lines to White House on the Pamunkey River. As a preliminary to this movement, Lee sent James E. B. (Jeb) Stuart with his cavalry on a reconnaissance to the rear of McClellan's army to determine its position, and also the strength of Porter's Right Wing, which was guarding the army's supply line.

Stuart started north on the Brook Turnpike early on June 12, 1862, and late that afternoon he turned to the east and halted for the night west of Hanover Court House. Stuart continued on the next day, and at 11:00 A.M., as he approached the court house, he encountered Edward H. Lieb's company of the 5th United States Cavalry. Lieb was forced to withdraw, but he sent back word to William B. Royall, who commanded a squadron of the 5th United States Cavalry at Old Church. Royall in turn notified Cooke, the commander of the Cavalry Reserve, whose headquarters was at Gaines' Mill, of the presence of enemy cavalry at Hanover Court House.

Stuart continued on toward Old Church by way of Taliaferro's Mill and Aenon (Enon) Church to Haw's Shop. About a mile from Old Church he met Royall, who had moved out to investigate. Stuart scattered the Federal cavalry in brief combat, and then continued on to Old Church.

Cooke sent six squadrons of the 5th and 6th United States Cavalry to join Royall, and ordered the 6th Pennsylvania Cavalry (Rush's Lancers) and the 1st United States Cavalry to follow. These troopers arrived at Old Church about an hour after Stuart had departed, and were then directed to hold that position for the time being. Under the mistaken belief that Confederate infantry were with Stuart's cavalry, Gouverneur K. Warren was sent to Old Church with his Third Brigade of Sykes' division,

Fifth Provisional Corps and Stephen H. Weed's Battery I, 5th United States Artillery. Cooke also proceeded to Old Church, but he did not start in pursuit of Stuart until 4:00 the next morning.

Cooke's delay gave Stuart a twelve-hour start, and he moved on unmolested by way of Garlick's Landing on the Pamunkey, Tunstall's Station on the Richmond and York River Railroad, and he then crossed the Chickahominy River at Forge Bridge. From there he returned to Richmond by way of Charles City Court House and Malvern Hill June 15, 1862. Stuart reported to Lee the exact disposition of the Federal Right Wing and its approximate strength, and he further informed him that the ridge along Totopotomoy Creek was not fortified, and that he found no indication that McClellan intended to change his base of operations to the James River. Based on this information, Lee believed that his plan to attack McClellan's right wing would be successful, and the day after he received Stuart's report, he ordered Jackson to move with his army from the Shenandoah Valley and, at the earliest possible date, join the army of Northern Virginia near Richmond. Jackson left the valley with his command June 17, 1862.

June 23, 1862, Lee issued the following orders for the attack on Porter's corps, which was to begin June 26, 1862. Jackson was to march from Ashland, about sixteen miles north of Richmond, and camp at some convenient point west of the Virginia Central Railroad. Then at 3:00 A.M. June 26, 1862, he was to advance toward Cold Harbor on the road leading to Pole Green Church. By this movement, Jackson would turn the Beaver Dam Creek line, about one mile east of Mechanicsville, and thus render McCall's strong position along the creek untenable. Having accomplished this, Jackson was to continue on toward Cold Harbor.

Branch's brigade of Ambrose P. Hill's division was to cross the Chickahominy west of Mechanicsville at Half Sink, and then wait until Jackson had passed that point. Branch was then to march toward Mechanicsville and uncover the Meadow Bridge so that the rest of A. P. Hill's division could cross. Once across the river, Hill was to move directly toward Mechanicsville. When this movement uncovered the Mechanicsville Bridge, Daniel H. Hill and James Longstreet were to cross there with their divisions. D. H. Hill was then to march to the support of Jackson, and Longstreet was to move to the support of A. P. Hill on the right.

When these movements were completed, the Confederate divisions were to sweep down the north bank of the Chickahominy, en echelon, with Jackson's divisions in advance, on the left, and Longstreet's division nearest the river, in the rear. Stuart's cavalry was to protect Jackson's left flank, and the divisions of Huger and Magruder were to hold the lines in front of Richmond.

SEVEN DAYS' BATTLES
JUNE 25, 1862–JULY 1, 1862

McClellan's and Lee's armies had been forced to remain relatively inactive in front of Richmond for about a month, but then the weather improved and military operations were resumed. On June 25, 1862, Heintzelman's Third Corps was engaged on the Williamsburg Road west of Seven Pines, and this, as it happened, was the beginning of a week of almost constant fighting and marching. The operations during this period are now commonly known as the Seven Days' Battles, and the engagements fought were as follows:

Engagement at Oak Grove (or French's Field, Henrico, King's School House, The Orchard), June 25, 1862.
Battle of Mechanicsville (or Beaver Dam Creek, Ellerson's Mill [or Ellison's Mill]), June 26, 1862.
Battle of Gaines' Mill (or First Cold Harbor, Chickahominy), June 27, 1862.
Action at Garnett's Farm and Golding's Farm, June 27–28, 1862.
Engagement at Allen's Farm (or Peach Orchard), June 29, 1862.
Battle of Savage Station, June 29, 1862.
Engagement at White Oak Swamp Bridge and the Battle of Glendale (or White Oak Swamp, Charles City Road, New Market Road, Nelson's Farm, Frayser's Farm [or Frazier's Farm], Willis' Church), June 30, 1862.
Occupation of Malvern Hill (Engagement at Malvern Cliff or Turkey Bridge), June 30, 1862–July 1, 1862.
Battle of Malvern Hill (or Crew's Farm, Poindexter's Farm), July 1, 1862.

Engagement at Oak Grove (or French's Field, Henrico, King's School House, The Orchard),

June 25, 1862. Shortly after the Battle of Seven Pines or Fair Oaks, the Federal pickets were withdrawn from swampy and overgrown ground, which they had occupied at the end of the fighting, to a new position close to the main line of defenses along Casey's old entrenchments. On June 24, 1862, Heintzelman was ordered to advance his Third Corps and extend his pickets, so as to be in position to support a planned movement by Franklin's Sixth Provisional Corps toward Old Tavern, which was on the New River Road, about one mile in advance of the Sixth Corps line. Richardson's First Division of Sumner's Second Corps was also to advance on the right of Heintzelman.

At 8:00 A.M. June 25, 1862, Heintzelman moved forward and was soon engaged in what was to be the first of the Seven Days' Battles. Hooker's Second Division was on the right of the Third Corp line, and Kearny's Third Division was on the left. Sickles' Second Brigade of Hooker's division moved forward on both sides of the Williamsburg Road, west of Seven Pines, and Grover's First Brigade of the same division was on the left of Sickles. Joseph B. Carr's Third Brigade (Patterson's) remained behind to hold the line of defenses and to support Sickles or Grover, if needed. Robinson's First Brigade (formerly Jameson's) of Kearny's division advanced on the left of Hooker, and Berry's Third Brigade was on the left of Robinson. Berry's brigade covered the flank down to the western extension of White Oak Swamp. Birney's Second Brigade of Kearny's division remained on the line of entrenchments during the morning. Howe's First Brigade and Palmer's Third Brigade of Couch's First Division, Fourth Corps were ordered forward to support Hooker, but they were held in reserve until 2:30 P.M.

A half mile in front of Hooker, the ground was heavily wooded and was swampy in places. Beyond the woods was a cleared field that extended 500 yards to the west toward Richmond. Huger's Confederate division held the front ahead of Hooker, and occupied a line running southward from the Richmond and York River Railroad, across the cleared field and the Williamsburg Road, down to and beyond the Charles City Road. William Mahone's brigade was on the right of Huger's line; Ambrose R. Wright's brigade was on the center; and Lewis Armistead's brigade was on the left. Robert

Ransom's Second Brigade, Confederate Department of North Carolina joined Huger at 9:00 A.M. June 25, 1862, and was engaged later in the day.

Heintzelman's line advanced slowly, and it soon ran into strong opposition. Grover's skirmishers became engaged almost at once, and William A. Henry's 5th New Jersey of Carr's brigade was sent to support Grover. On the right, Sickles' brigade pressed forward, and between 9:00 and 10:00 A.M. it had arrived near the outer edge of the woods. It then came under a heavy fire and was reinforced on the right by Joseph W. Revere's 7th New Jersey of Carr's brigade. Grover soon came up on Sickles' line, and Robinson's First Brigade of Kearny's division moved up on the left of Grover.

Heintzelman's advance was stopped about 11:00 A.M., but the attack was renewed at 1:00 P.M. by McClellan's direct order. Shortly after 11:00 A.M. the 7th New Jersey returned to Carr's line, but when the attack was renewed, William A. Olmsted's 2nd New York of Carr's brigade was sent forward to replace 7th New Jersey.

At 2:30 P.M., Palmer's brigade of Couch's division, Fourth Corps arrived at the front, and then advanced with Hooker's division to the outer edge of the woods. About 5:00 P.M. Heintzelman's troops reached their assigned positions, and the line halted. About an hour later, the enemy made a strong attack on the left of Robinson's brigade, and it was only with difficulty that Robinson was able to hold his position. Birney's brigade was then brought up to support Robinson, and the threat at that point was ended. At dusk, Birney's brigade relieved Grover. At 7:00 P.M., Hooker withdrew his division and left Palmer's brigade to cover the front on the Williamsburg Road during the night. Robinson's and Birney's brigades also remained on the newly established line.

Heintzelman did not renew his attack on the east side of Richmond because the next day Lee began his offensive north of the Chickahominy against McClellan's line of communications .

Battle of Mechanicsville (or Beaver Dam Creek, Ellerson's Mill [or Ellison's Mill]), June 26, 1862.
On the morning of June 26, 1862, the Confederate divisions of Thomas J. Jackson, Ambrose P. Hill, Daniel H. Hill, and James Longstreet began to move to their assigned positions in preparation for their attack on McClellan's line north of the Chickahominy River. The only Federal troops in position to oppose this movement belonged to Porter's Fifth Provisional Corps, and also to the cavalry, which was at that time under Porter's direction.

Before giving the details of the enemy advance and the positions of Porter's command on June 26, 1862, it is important to note some of the more significant features of the area around Mechanicsville. About a mile east of the village, Beaver Dam Creek flowed generally southward through a small but distinct ravine on its way to the Chickahominy River. The creek was bordered on both sides by low, swampy ground. Two roads ran eastward from Mechanicsville and crossed the creek. The Mechanicsville Turnpike, running up from Richmond, crossed the Chickahominy at the Mechanicsville Bridge, and then continued on to the northeast to Mechanicsville, about a mile distant from the river. This road then ran onward from Mechanicsville to the north of east as the Old Church (or Bethesda Church) Road, and it crossed Beaver Dam Creek about a mile and a half north of the Chickahominy. The Cold Harbor Road left Mechanicsville in a southeasterly direction and crossed Beaver Dam Creek about three-fourths of a mile south of the crossing of the Old Church Road at Ellerson's Mill. From that point this road followed a winding course eastward toward Cold Harbor. In addition to these two roads, another ran northwest from Mechanicsville, past Atlee's Station on the Virginia Central Railroad, to Half Sink on the Chickahominy. A road from Meadow Bridge joined this road about a mile and a half northwest of Mechanicsville.

On the morning of June 26, 1862, John F. Reynolds' First Brigade and Truman Seymour's Third Brigade of George McCall's Third Division of Porter's corps, both under the command of Reynolds, were posted on the high ground on the east side of Beaver Dam Creek. Seymour's brigade held the heights on the left of the line, from near the Chickahominy to a point just north of Ellerson's Mill, and Reynolds' brigade continued the line to the north to a point beyond the Old Church Road. James H. Cooper's Battery B, 1st Pennsylvania Light Artillery was posted on the right of the Old Church Road; Henry V. De Hart's Battery C, 5th United States Artillery was on the center of the line, covering the road from Mechanicsville and the open fields west of the creek; and John R. Smead's Battery K, 5th United States Artillery was on the left of the line. Hezekiah Easton's Battery A, 1st Pennsylvania Light Artillery and John Edwards' Batteries L and M, 3rd United States Artillery were held in reserve, but were later brought up to support Reynolds. Mark Kerns' Battery G, 1st Pennsylvania Light Artillery was also engaged during the evening.

Lee delayed his crossing of the Chickahominy on the morning of June 26, 1862 while he waited for Jackson to arrive on Porter's right flank. Finally, however, A. P. Hill felt that he could wait no longer, and at 3:00 P.M. he began moving his division over the river at Meadow Bridge on the road toward Mechanicsville. Branch's brigade was not with Hill, but was posted farther up the river at Half Sink.

When McCall learned of Hill's advance, he came forward and assumed command of his two brigades that were in position on Beaver Dam Creek, and he also brought up George G. Meade's Second Brigade of the division and placed it in rear of Seymour. Porter also sent George W. Morell's First Division forward to support McCall's line. John H. Martindale's First Brigade deployed on the right of Reynolds, and Charles Griffin's Second Brigade formed in rear of Reynolds, where the Old Church Road crossed Beaver Dam Creek. Daniel Butterfield's Third Brigade was ordered to support the right of Cooke's cavalry, but was later sent to the right of Martindale's brigade. George Sykes' Third Division remained on the Gaines farm, where it watched the crossings of the Chickahominy, but it was prepared to move to any threatened point as needed.

After Hill's division had crossed at Meadow Bridge, it moved across to the Half Sink Road, and then marched to the southeast on the road to Mechanicsville. On arriving there, he came under the fire of the Federal artillery on the high ground beyond Beaver Dam Creek. Hill then moved to the left on the Old Church Road with three of his brigades, and into the valley of Beaver Dam Creek in front of Reynolds' brigade. Joseph R. Anderson's brigade advanced on the left, north of the road; James J. Archer's brigade on the center; and Charles W. Field's brigade on the right, with his line extending southward to the Cold Harbor Road. Maxcy Gregg's brigade was left in Mechanicsville as a

reserve. William D. Pender's brigade was not yet up from Meadow Bridge, and nothing had been heard from Branch's brigade.

Hill's brigades attacked Porter's line along Beaver Dam Creek, but they were completely stopped after suffering heavy losses from Federal infantry and artillery fire. Pender's brigade finally arrived, and it was sent south to support Field in an attempt of turn Seymour's left. Pender advanced with two of his regiments to the vicinity of Ellerson's Mill, and there his column was shattered by the destructive fire of Seymour's infantry and the artillery

When Lee observed A. P. Hill's advance, he sent orders to D. H. Hill and Longstreet to prepare to cross the Chickahominy with their divisions at the Mechanicsville Bridge. Roswell S. Ripley's brigade of D. H. Hill's division was the first to cross, and it immediately marched toward the scene of the action. Just before sundown, Lee made a final effort to turn McCall's left, and Ripley's brigade was sent to support Pender in the attack. By mistake, Ripley moved directly on Ellerson's Mill instead of around the Federal left, and his brigade was literally cut to pieces on the same field where Pender had been repulsed.

The Battle of Mechanicsville ended after dark, with all parts of Porter's line intact. Branch's brigade finally arrived on the field after dark, but was not engaged that evening. Jackson's division camped that evening at Hundley's Corner, and his presence had no effect on the outcome of the fighting along Beaver Dam Creek that day.

Battle of Gaines' Mill (or First Cold Harbor, Chickahominy), June 27, 1862. After the fighting ended about 9:00 P.M. June 26, 1862, the divisions of McCall and Morell remained in position along Beaver Dam Creek until early the next morning. During the night, McClellan learned with certainty that Jackson was moving toward the right and rear of Porter's position. He then issued orders for the change of his base from White House to Harrison's Landing on the James River, and he also ordered Porter to withdraw to a new position east of Powhite Creek and to hold fast during the day until the evacuation of the depot at White House could be completed.

Forter began his withdrawal from the line of

Beaver Dam Creek at 3:00 A.M. June 27, 1862, and McCall and Morell moved back, while Seymour's brigade and two horse batteries covered their rear. During the morning, Porter established a new line about five miles east of Beaver Dam Creek and one mile southeast of Gaines' Mill, which was located on Powhite Creek. Porter's new position was on the edge of a plateau that sloped upward to the north from the Chickahominy River, between Grapevine Bridge and New Bridge, and it was bounded on the north and west by a small creek called Boatswain's Swamp. This creek headed about 1,000 yards south of Old Cold Harbor, and then curved in a wide arc to the southwest and south for a distance of about two miles to a point a little more than a half mile north of the Chickahominy. There it turned abruptly to the east for one-fourth of a mile, and then turned south and emptied into the Chickahominy a short distance below New Bridge. Along the edge of the plateau, the ground dropped sharply into the valley of Boatswain's Creek.

The Cold Harbor Road ran to the southeast from Gaines' Mill for a little more than a half mile to the crossroads of New Cold Harbor, and from there a private road ran southeast toward Boatswain's Swamp. Before reaching the slope that ran down to the ravine through which the stream flowed, the road divided, with one branch running southeast to the McGhee house, and the other almost due south. The latter crossed Boatswain's Swamp, then ascended the slope of the plateau, and ended at the Watt house. This house stood near the crest of the plateau where it dropped down sharply into the swamp, and was Porter's headquarters during the Battle of Gaines' Mill. The main road ran on from New Cold Harbor to Old Cold Harbor, about a mile to the northeast. A road also ran south from Old Cold Harbor for about three miles, past the McGhee house and Barker's Mill to Grapevine Bridge on the Chickahominy.

Porter formed his new line long the rim of the plateau above Boatswain's Swamp. Morell's division was on the left, and it extended from the southern edge of the plateau, where the creek turns to the east, to a point about a fourth of a mile north of the Watt house, where a small ravine cuts into the plateau. Sykes' division was on the right of Morell, and its line extended along the crest to the McGhee house. McCall's division was held in reserve about a half mile in rear of Morell. On Morell's line,

Butterfield's brigade was on the left, Martindale's brigade was on the center, and Griffin's brigade was on the right. On Sykes' line, Gouverneur K. Warren's Third Brigade was on the left, next to Griffin; Robert C. Buchanan's First Brigade was on the right, and extended across the road that ran from Old Cold Harbor to Barker's Mill; and Charles S. Lovell's Second Brigade was in rear of the junction of Warren's and Buchanan's brigades.

Cooke's Cavalry Reserve was on the extreme left of Porter's line, on the low ground bordering the Chickahominy. The day before, June 26, 1862, as Jackson's divisions were approaching the right of Porter's line, Stoneman's force, which consisted of cavalry and two brigades of infantry, had retired down the Pamunkey River and had joined Casey's force at White House.

Early on the morning of June 27, 1862, Lee's army began the pursuit of Porter's retiring Fifth Provisional Corps. A. P. Hill's division advanced from Ellerson's Mill along the Cold Harbor Road toward Gaines' Mill. Longstreet's division marched along a road that was roughly parallel to Hill's route, but which was nearer the Chickahominy River, and which came out at the Gaines farm. D. H. Hill proceeded to the northeast from Mechanicsville on the Old Church Road to Bethesda Church, and there he turned to the south and southeast toward Old Cold Harbor. Jackson marched south from Hundley's Corner to Walnut Grove Church, which was south of the Old Church Road and about two miles east of Ellerson's Mill, and there he turned eastward to the road on which D. H. Hill was marching. He then followed Hill toward Old Cold Harbor.

D. H. Hill arrived near Old Cold Harbor at 11:00 A.M., and he was soon engaged with Sykes' regulars on the road to Barker's Mill. At 1:00 P.M., A. P. Hill's leading brigade, commanded by Maxcy Gregg, reached Gaines' Mill, where the Cold Harbor Road crossed Powhite Creek, and after a short engagement, crossed the creek and drove back a small Federal force that was posted there. The rest of A. P. Hill's division then came up and was deployed in line of battle along the road to Cold Harbor, facing south. Branch's brigade was placed on the right of Gregg, with its right on the Watt House Road. Then, in order to the right, the brigades of Joseph R. Anderson, Field, and Archer were formed across a wheatfield west of the road.

Pender's brigade, which had cleared the wheatfield of Hiram Berdan's sharpshooters, was relieved by Archer, and was then placed in reserve along the Cold Harbor Road in rear of Gregg and Branch. Longstreet's division then came up on the right of A. P. Hill and connected with Archer.

About 2:30 P.M., A. P. Hill's line advanced against the right and center of Morell's division and the left of Sykes' division. The attack was not well coordinated, and after almost two hours of severe fighting, Hill's division was repulsed with heavy losses.

About 3:30 P.M., during A. P. Hill's attack, McCall's division was brought up and put in on Morell's right and center to support Martindale and Griffin, who had borne the brunt of the enemy attack. Reynolds' brigade relieved Warren's brigade on the left of Sykes' line. Earlier Porter had asked for reinforcements, and at 2:00 P.M. Henry W. Slocum's First Division of Franklin's Sixth Provisional Corps was ordered to go to his assistance. John Newton's Third Brigade crossed the Chickahominy at Alexander's Bridge, and it was followed by George W. Taylor's First Brigade, and then Joseph J. Bartlett's Second Brigade. The division arrived in rear of Porter's line about 4:00 P.M., and the brigades of Newton and Taylor were put in between Morell and Sykes, and Bartlett's brigade was sent to support the right of Sykes' line, near the McGhee house.

Shortly after 4:00 P.M., Lee ordered Longstreet to make a diversion on the Confederate right so as to help A. P. Hill, but before this could be started, Richard S. Ewell's division of Jackson's command arrived near Old Cold Harbor and moved into the interval between A. P. Hill on the right and D. H. Hill on the left. Ewell then advanced on the left of A. P. Hill and struck the front of Sykes' line, but despite determined fighting during the remainder of the afternoon, he made little progress.

While Ewell was thus engaged, Longstreet began his diversion on Porter's left, but he quickly found that a diversion would accomplish nothing, and he then decided to make a full-scale assault. Meantime, A. P. Hill's division had become somewhat demoralized by the heavy fighting of the afternoon, and it was replaced by William H. C. Whiting's division on the left of Longstreet, who was then forming his division for the attack.

Jackson's division, after it arrived on the field, did not function as a unit during the fighting that evening. Charles S. Winder's brigade and Alexander R. Lawton's brigade were formed in the interval between A. P. Hill and Ewell, and John R. Jones' brigade (commanded by R. H. Cunningham) and Samuel V. Fulkerson's brigade were sent to the right. Jones' brigade later supported Longstreet, and Fulkerson's brigade supported Whiting.

The deployment of Longstreet, Whiting, and Lawton was not completed until after 6:00 P.M., and an hour later Lee's entire line moved forward in a final attack. Under this very heavy pressure, Morell's line broke near the Watt house, and when this happened, the left and center of Porter's line gave way, and his troops streamed away to the rear in disorder. Sykes' regulars, however, withdrew in good order, still fighting, toward Grapevine Bridge. Most of the corps crossed the Chickahominy by the bridges south of the Watt house. Reynolds was captured that night, and Seneca G. Simmons assumed command of Reynolds' brigade.

Meantime, at 5:00 P.M., William H. French, with his own Third Brigade and Thomas F. Meagher's Second Brigade of Israel B. Richardson's First Division, Second Corps, had been ordered to the north side of the Chickahominy to support Porter. The two brigades crossed the river at Grapevine Bridge and arrived on the field during the Federal withdrawal in time to help Sykes cover the retreat. French and Meagher remained north of the river during the night.

During Porter's withdrawal, Philip St. George Cooke's cavalry charged the advancing enemy in an attempt to prevent the capture of some of the reserve batteries that were posted in the lowlands south of the Watt house. Cooke's losses were heavy, and his charge later became a matter of considerable controversy, but apparently it did gain a little time for the artillerists.

Action at Garnett's Farm and Golding's Farm, June 27–28, 1862. On the morning of June 27, 1862, the pickets of Winfield S. Hancock's First Brigade of William F. Smith's Second Division, Franklin's Sixth Provisional Corps advanced from Golding's farm and occupied some unfinished rifle pits in a field overlooking the James Garnett house and adjacent fields. The enemy line at this point was held by the brigades of Robert Toombs and George T. Anderson of David R. Jones' division.

About 10:00 A.M., as Porter's corps was moving into position along Boatswain's Swamp on the other side of the Chickahominy, Jones' artillery opened fire on Hancock's line, but after a time it stopped. Then, during the afternoon, Magruder decided to make a demonstration on Smith's line, and about 6:30 P.M. again opened fire with his artillery. Following this, Toombs launched a furious assault on Hancock's line, but this was repulsed with help from the 4th Vermont and 6th Vermont of William T. H. Brooks' Second Brigade of Smith's division.

On the morning of June 28, 1862, Magruder's artillery again opened fire on the Federal lines on Golding's farm, and then the 7th Georgia and 8th Georgia of Anderson's brigade attacked from near the Garnett house, but this was repulsed by a section of artillery and the 33rd New York of John W. Davidson's Third Brigade and the 49th Pennsylvania of Hancock's First Brigade, which were on picket duty.

Beginning of the Retreat to the James River, June 28, 1862. During the night of June 27, 1862, all the troops that had been engaged at Gaines' Mill withdrew to the south side of the Chickahominy River. Slocum's division of Franklin's corps recrossed the river at 11:00 P.M. and rejoined the corps at Courtneys' farm. Porter's three divisions of Fifth Provisional Corps crossed during the night and bivouacked in the vicinity of the Trent house, where McClellan had established his headquarters, about one-half mile south of Alexander's Bridge. The brigades of French and Meagher remained north of the river during the night, but they were back on the south side by 4:00 A.M. June 28, 1862, and they then rejoined Sumner's Second Corps near Fair Oaks Station.

Meantime, McClellan had been formulating plans for his future movements. Since mid-June 1862, following Stuart's ride around the army, he had considered the possibility of moving his supply base from White House to the James River, and on June 18, 1862, he had ordered 800,000 rations to be sent up the James River so that they would be waiting when he arrived on the river. Then, following the Battle of Mechanicsville, and when the position of Jackson's approaching divisions had

definitely been determined, McClellan had issued the order to abandon the base at White House. Everything that could not be carried away was destroyed, and a train of 5,000 wagons was started southward across the Chickahominy River and White Oak Swamp toward the James River. Henry J. Hunt's Reserve Artillery and the beef herd were ordered to take the same road.

McClellan's immediate problem was to provide for the safe crossing of White Oak Swamp by the army and the trains, and also to arrange for the protection of the artillery and the trains during the retreat. During the evening of June 27, 1862, McClellan assembled his corps commanders at Dr. Trent's, and after explaining the situation to them, he issued orders for their movements the next day. His plan, generally, called for the placing of his troops on a succession of defensive lines, facing Lee's army, and behind which the trains and artillery could move southward in safety to the James River. In addition, it included the provision for forming a defensive position to protect the new base when it was established.

Keyes' Fourth Corps, which was then in position along the north side of White Oak Swamp, on the Williamsburg Road, and on the Richmond and York River Railroad near Bottom's Bridge, was assigned the task of protecting the wagon train during its passage of White Oak Swamp. McCall's division of Porter's corps was detached and ordered to accompany the Reserve Artillery. Porter, with the divisions of Morell and Sykes, was to follow Keyes, and while Fourth Corps guarded the bridges across White Oak Swamp, Porter was to cross and form his command at Glendale so as to cover the roads running out from Richmond to White Oak Swamp and Long Bridge. Franklin's Sixth Provisional Corps, Sumner's Second Corps, and Heintzelman's Third Corps were to remain in position near Golding's farm, Fair Oaks, and Seven Pines during June 28, 1862, to prevent an advance by Magruder and Huger. These three corps, however, were instructed to withdraw about a mile to give better protection to the important area around Savage Station on the Richmond and York River Railroad.

At 1:00 A.M. McClellan ordered Keyes to move three brigades of his corps across White Oak Swamp before daylight that morning and to cover the passage of the rest of the army. John J. Peck, commander of Second Division, Fourth Corps, started in advance with Henry W. Wessells' Second Brigade; and he was immediately followed by Darius N. Couch, commander of First Division, Fourth Corps, with Innis N. Palmer's Third Brigade. These brigades began crossing White Oak Swamp Bridge at daylight; and by noon they were in position about three miles beyond the bridge, and a mile beyond Glendale Cross Roads, where they could guard the Charles City Road, the Long Bridge Road, and the Willis' Church Road. Before noon, John J. Abercrombie's Second Brigade and Albion P. Howe's First Brigade of Couch's division had arrived and joined the rest of the corps. Keyes' line then extended from Brightwells' farm on the edge of White Oak Swamp southward to the Long Bridge Road.

Henry M. Naglee's First Brigade of Couch's division, with two batteries, was left behind to guard the Richmond and York River Bridge and Bottom's Bridge over the Chickahominy until the rest of the army had crossed, after which it was to destroy the bridges and rejoin its command. When this work was finally completed, Naglee marched to White Oak Swamp Bridge, where he was temporarily attached to Franklin's command.

During the afternoon of June 28, 1862, Porter, with the divisions of Morell and Sykes, marched by way of Savage Station to White Oak Swamp. Morell crossed the swamp before sunset and reported to Keyes, and the next morning was sent to occupy the road junction at Glendale. Sykes' division marched at 6:00 P.M. June 28, 1862, crossed the swamp at Brackett's Ford at dawn the next morning, and then joined Morell. McCall's division remained at Trents' house until 8:00 P.M. June 28, 1862, and then marched with the Reserve Artillery toward White Oak Swamp.

During the night of June 28, 1862 and the next morning, the three corps facing Richmond began to withdraw from the Golding's farm-Fair Oaks Station-Seven Pines line, and to march toward Savage Station on their way to White Oak Swamp. Franklin moved first, and he was followed by Sumner, and then Heintzelman. Slocum's First Division of Franklin's corps reached Savage Station about 5:00 A.M. June 29, 1862, and upon arriving there, he was directed by McClellan to move on and cross the swamp. Slocum crossed at 2:00 P.M., and three

hours later he was ordered to relieve the divisions of Couch and Peck of Keyes' corps. Keyes was already under orders to proceed on the the James River when relieved by Slocum. William F. Smith's Second Division of Franklin's corps moved to the Trent house at 7:00 A.M to cover the retreat of the rear of McClellan's wagon train, and after it had passed, Smith moved to a position in front of Savage Station. About noon, he moved back to the station.

Engagement at Allen's Farm (or Peach Orchard), June 29, 1862. Sumner's Second Corps abandoned its works at Fair Oaks at daylight on the morning of June 29, 1862, and moved back to Orchard Station on the Richmond and York River Railroad. Sumner had been ordered to destroy all government property that had been accumulated there, and when this duty had been completed, he moved on to the Allen field, about a mile east of Fair Oaks Station. He then formed in line of battle, with Israel B. Richardson's First Division on the right and John Sedgwick's Second Division on the left. Richardson had with him only John C. Caldwell's First Brigade and William H. French's Third Brigade. The day before, Thomas F. Meagher's Second Brigade had been ordered to report to McClellan at Savage Station. Meagher was then directed to hold a position at Meadow Station, but he rejoined the division on the evening of June 29, 1862 at Savage Station.

As Sumner's corps withdrew eastward, Magruder followed with his division from his position in front of Richmond, and at about 9:00 A.M. he advanced and delivered an attack on Sumner's line at Allen's farm. He struck the left of Richardson's division and the right of Sedgwick's division, but the fighting ended about noon when Magruder finally fell back. Heintzelman's Third Corps was posted on the left of Sumner, but it was not engaged.

Battle of Savage Station, June 29, 1862. At noon June 29, 1862, after the Engagement at Allen's Farm had ended, Sumner continued his withdrawal to Savage Station. Upon arriving there, as senior officer on the field, he ordered the concentration of his own Second Corps, Heintzelman's Third Corps, and Franklin's Sixth Provisional Corps. At that time only William F. Smith's Second Division of Franklin's corps was near the station.

Sumner formed his own corps in line of battle. Richardson's division was formed as a reserve in an open field north of the railroad, and just east of the station. At that time, Thomas F. Meagher, commander of Richardson's Second Brigade, was in temporary arrest, and Robert Nugent was in command of his brigade until 8:30 the next morning. Sedgwick's division held the center of the line and was in another field south of the station and between the Richmond and York River Railroad and the Williamsburg Road. William W. Burns' Second Brigade was on the front line about 700 yards west of the station, with its right near the railroad, and its left extending toward the Williamsburg Road. In rear of Burns, and to his left near the road, were Alfred Sully's First Brigade and Napoleon J. T. Dana's Third Brigade. Supporting this line were Rufus D. Pettit's Battery B, 1st New York Light Artillery, Thomas W. Osborn's Battery D, 1st New York Light Artillery, and George W. Hazzard's Batteries A and C, 4th United States Artillery. When it was discovered later, just before Magruder's attack, that Burns' brigade was unable to cover the front assigned to it, the 1st Minnesota Regiment of Willis A. Gorman's First Brigade (commanded by Alfred Sully during the illness of Gorman) was sent forward to occupy the ground between the left of Burns and the Williamsburg Road.

Smith's division of Franklin's corps was formed in rear of Sedgwick in a woods south of Savage Station. William T. H. Brooks' Second Brigade was placed on the left of the 1st Minnesota, south of the Williamsburg Road; Winfield S. Hancock's First Brigade was held in reserve about a half mile in rear of Burns' line, north of the Williamsburg Road; and John W. Davidson's Third Brigade was placed on the left of Hancock, south of the road. Davidson was disabled by sunstroke about 4:00 P.M. that day, and Robert F. Taylor assumed temporary command of the brigade. As noted above, Henry W. Slocum's First Division of Franklin's corps had not stopped at Savage Station, but had moved on to the south of White Oak Swamp.

Sumner had directed Heintzelman to form a defensive line on the left of Second Corps to prevent the enemy from advancing along the Williamsburg Road, but when Heintzelman arrived at Savage Station he decided to move on. He believed that the divisions of Richardson, Sedgwick, and Smith, which he found there, were sufficient to deal with Magruder, and he further believed that to add his two divisions to this force could, in the event of a Confederate success there, imperil McClellan's entire command. In his opinion, if Sumner were forced to withdraw under enemy pressure, the three corps could not possibly escape by the few existing roads, bridges, and fords. Accordingly, and contrary to Sumner's orders, Heintzelman moved on that afternoon and crossed White Oak Swamp. Hiram G. Berry's Third Brigade of Philip Kearny's Third Division crossed at Fisher's Ford, and the rest of the corps at Brackett's Ford. Third Corps arrived on the Charles City Road between 6:30 and 10:00 P.M. June 29, 1862. When Sumner learned that Heintzelman's corps had departed from his left, he ordered up Sully's and Dana's brigades to support Burns.

While Sumner was getting his troops in position at Savage Station, Magruder advanced slowly from Allen's farm, and when he approached Sumner's position, he formed his command in line of battle in front of Burns and Brooks, a little more than a half mile west of Savage Station. Paul J. Semmes' brigade of Lafayette McLaws' division was across the Williamsburg Road; Joseph B. Kershaw's brigade, also of McLaws' division, was on the left of Semmes, with its line extending northward through a woods to the railroad; Howell Cobb's brigade of Magruder's division was on the left of Kershaw, north of the railroad; and Richard Griffith's brigade of Magruder's division was in reserve on the railroad. Later two regiments of this brigade were brought up on the right of Semmes' brigade, south of the Williamsburg Road. Griffith had been mortally wounded that morning at Allen's farm, and William Barksdale was in command of his brigade. David R. Jones' division was on the left of Magruder's line, between Cobb's brigade and the Chickahominy River, but it was not engaged that day.

The Battle of Savage Station began at 5:00 P.M. June 29, 1862, when the brigades of Kershaw and Semmes advanced against the left of Sumner's line. Sumner immediately sent Burns forward along the north side of the road with the 72nd Pennsylvania and 106th Pennsylvania regiments of his brigade to meet this attack. As Magruder's attack developed, Burns' line was outflanked on both the right and left.

When the 1st Minnesota of Sully's brigade came up, it was formed across the road on the left of Burns. The 72nd Pennsylvania then moved to the right to cover the railroad, and this so weakened the center of Burns' line that Magruder threatened to break through. Meantime, other regiments of Second Corps had been started forward. The 82nd New York of Sully's brigade arrived just in time to reestablish the center of Burns' line. The fighting then moved southward to the Williamsburg Road, and there the 88th New York of Meagher's brigade of Richardson's division came up and succeeded in driving the enemy back. At about that time, 15th Massachusetts of Sully's brigade relieved the 106th Pennsylvania, and the 20th Massachusetts of Dana's brigade of Sedgwick's division relieved the 72nd Pennsylvania. To strengthen the left of the line, the 69th Pennsylvania of Meagher's brigade was sent to the left of the 1st Minnesota, and Brooks' brigade of Smith's division moved up to the left of 69th Pennsylvania, south of the Williamsburg Road. The 71st Pennsylvania (the so-called California Regiment) of Burns' brigade and the 7th Michigan of Dana's brigade also moved forward, but they were held in reserve. The fighting ended at dark, with the Union line unbroken, and the last of Sumner's regiments engaged were the 82nd and 88th New York and the 15th Massachusetts.

Engagement at White Oak Swamp Bridge and the Battle of Glendale (or White Oak Swamp, Charles City Road, New Market Road, Nelson's Farm, Frayser's Farm [or Frazier's Farm], Willis' Church), June 30, 1862. While Sumner and Franklin were holding back Magruder's force at Savage Station, McClellan was busily engaged in forming a defensive line south of White Oak Swamp to protect the trains and the artillery as they moved southward toward the James River. Keyes' Fourth Corps, which had completed its crossing of the swamp by noon June 28, 1862, was placed on a line facing Richmond, and about a mile and a half west of Glendale Cross Roads. Keyes' line extended from Brightwells' farm, near the swamp, on the right, southward to the Long Bridge Road.

Porter crossed the swamp with the divisions of Morell and Sykes of his Fifth Provisional Corps during the evening of June 28, 1862, and early the next morning he moved to Glendale, where he was in rear of Keyes' line. Porter remained there until sundown June 29, 1862, and then marched during the night toward Turkey Bend on the James River. Upon arrival there he was to select and hold a position, behind which the army and its trains could withdraw. Porter arrived at Malvern Hill at 9:00 A.M. June 30, 1862, and placed his command along the western crest to cover the River Road, which ran into Turkey Bend, and on which Benjamin Huger's Confederate division was approaching.

Slocum's division of Franklin's Sixth Provisional Corps crossed White Oak Swamp at 2:00 P.M. June 29, 1862, and at 5:00 P.M. it relieved the divisions of Couch and Peck of Keyes' Fourth Corps. That night, Keyes marched southward on the Willis' Church Road and camped on the James River below Turkey Bend Creek Bridge. He then established guards at the bridge. At the point where the Willis' Church Road joined the River Road, it crossed over Turkey Bend Creek, which flowed from the north into the James River at the top of a great loop of the river, just south of Malvern Hill.

McCall's division of Porter's corps crossed the swamp at White Oak Bridge with the Reserve Artillery about noon June 29, 1862, and when the artillery was then sent on toward Malvern Hill, McCall was directed to form his division to repel a possible attack from the direction of Richmond. McCall occupied several positions during the afternoon and evening, and that night he moved to a line on the Long Bridge Road, west of Frayser's farm.

Sumner's and Franklin's troops remained on and near the battlefield of Savage Station until 10:00 P.M. June 29, 1862, and then they began to withdraw toward White Oak Swamp Bridge. Smith's division of Franklin's corps started at 10:00 P.M. and crossed the swamp about 3:00 the next morning. Then, just after crossing, it took position on the high ground to the east of the road, facing north, to hold the crossing. Davidson's brigade was placed on the road, just south of the bridge, with Brooks' brigade to his right and rear, and Hancock's brigade was on the right of Brooks. Sedgwick's division of Sumner's corps followed Smith from Savage Station, and after crossing the swamp, it moved on south to Nelson's farm, where it halted on the morning of June 30, 1862. Richardson's division of Sumner's corps, which acted as the rear guard during the withdrawal from Savage Station, left there at 1:00 A.M. June 30, 1862 and, just after crossing White Oak Swamp Bridge, formed on the west side of the road, and on the left of Smith's division, to help hold the bridge. Naglee's brigade of Peck's division, Fourth Corps then came up from Bottom's Bridge, and was placed on the left of Davidson's brigade of Smith's division. Richardson's brigades were formed as follows: Meagher's Second Brigade was on the left of Naglee, just south of the swamp; Caldwell's First Brigade was on the west of the road behind Naglee, and in support of George W. Hazzard's Batteries A and C, 4th United States Artillery, and Rufus D. Pettit's Battery B, 1st New York Light Artillery; and French's Third Brigade was in rear of Meagher and on the left of Caldwell.

Late on the morning of June 30, 1862, probably about 10:30, McClellan called a meeting of his corps commanders at Glendale, and informed them of the positions their corps were to assume. Before continuing with a description of the troop movements and the positions held on June 30, 1862, however, it is necessary to digress briefly in order to avoid some of the confusion that might result from the names used for the roads and places in the area, as they appear in the reports of the battle that was fought that day. Glendale was the place name applied to the junction of the Charles City Road and the Long Bridge Road. It was also from this point that the Willis' Church Road ran south past Frayser's farm, Nelson's farm, and Willis' Church, and then on to Turkey Bend. There was no settlement at the Glendale Cross Roads, but the place was sometimes called Riddell's Shop, because of a blacksmith's shop located there. The Willis' Church Road was commonly called the Quaker Road in some battle reports, although there was another Quaker Road two miles to the west, which was an unused road running southward from the Long Bridge Road. The Long Bridge Road was also called the New Market Road, because some officers believed it to be an extension of the New Market Road that ran beyond New Market Heights. Another confusing point that should be noted here is that beyond New Market Heights, the New Market Road became the River Road.

Following McClellan's meeting at Glendale, the corps commanders proceeded to put their troops in position, according to his instructions, as follows: Smith's division of Franklin's corps, Richardson's division of Sumner's corps, and Naglee's brigade of Keyes' corps were left on the south side of White Oak Swamp to cover the crossing, and Franklin, in person, was sent back from Glendale to assume command of that part of McClellan's line. Slocum's division of Sumner's corps was placed about a mile northwest of Glendale, north of the Charles City Road, and near the junction of that road and a road running in from Brackett's Ford. Slocum's line faced a little to the north of west. John Newton's Third Brigade was on the left of this line, near the Charles City Road; Joseph J. Bartlett's Second Brigade was on the center of the line; and George W. Taylor's First Brigade was on the right, near the swamp. This line was supported by Emory Upton's Battery D, 2nd United States Artillery; William Hexamer's Battery A, New Jersey Light Artillery; and Josiah Porter's 1st Battery (A), Massachusetts Light Artillery. Sedgwick's division of Second Corps was at Glendale in reserve.

Kearny's division of Heintzelman's corps was on the left of Slocum, and its line extended southward almost to the Long Bridge Road. John C. Robinson's First Brigade was on the left; David B. Birney's Second Brigade was on the right; and Hiram G. Berry's Third Brigade was in reserve behind Birney. James Thompson's Battery G, 2nd United States Artillery was on the left of the division, and George E. Randolph's Battery E, 1st Rhode Island Light Artillery was with Birney.

It has already been noted that McCall's division moved during the night of June 29, 1862 to the Long Bridge Road, but the next morning it was formed across the road about a half mile beyond Glendale, facing southwest. George G. Meade's Second Brigade was on the right, north of the road, and next to Kearny; Truman Seymour's Third Brigade was on the left, south of the road; and John F. Reynolds' First Brigade, then commanded by Seneca G. Simmons, was in reserve. Later in the day, when McCall's division was attacked, Simmons was brought up to support Seymour, and he took position between Seymour and Meade. Alanson M. Randol's Battery E, 1st United States Artillery; Mark Kerns' Battery G, 1st Pennsylvania Light Artillery (commanded by Frank P. Amsden); and James H. Cooper's Battery B, 1st Pennsylvania Light Artillery were placed on the right of McCall's line. Two German batteries of Henry J. Hunt's Artillery

Reserve, Otto Diederichs' Company A, 1st New York Battalion and John Knieriem's Company C, 1st New York Battalion, were on the left.

Heintzelman had intended to put Hooker's division on the left of Kearny, but when he found McCall's division already there, he placed Hooker on the left of McCall. Hooker's line was west of, and roughly parallel to, the Willis' Church Road, and it extended southward from a point about one-fourth mile west of the Nelson house to and beyond Willis Church. Cuvier Grover's First Brigade was on the right; Joseph B. Carr's Third Brigade was on the center; and Daniel E. Sickles' Second Brigade was on the left. Hooker's batteries were sent on toward the James River to take position there.

All of McClellan's troops were on line between White Oak Swamp and Willis' Church by noon June 30, 1862, but the command situation was confused. After the late morning meeting at Glendale, McClellan departed for the James River to look after affairs there, and he did not exercise immediate control over the divisions that were engaged that evening. Franklin had been sent back to White Oak Swamp, and his immediate command consisted of Smith's division of his own Sixth Provisional Corps, Richardson's division of Second Corps, and Naglee's brigade of Fourth Corps. McCall's division of Porter's Fifth Provisional Corps was detached from the corps and served as a more or less independent division. Heintzelman's two divisions were separated by McCall's division, and Sumner was at Glendale with only Sedgwick's division.

Meantime, on the morning of June 29, 1862, Lee had discovered that McClellan had abandoned his lines in front of Richmond, both north and south of the Chickahominy River, and that he was in full retreat toward the James River. Lee then ordered his army forward in an attempt to destroy the Union army while on the march. His orders were as follows: Longstreet was to march with his own division, and that of A. P. Hill, by way of New Bridge and the Darbytown Road and strike McClellan's columns south of White Oak Swamp; Jackson was to advance with his command and D. H. Hill's division by way of Grapevine Bridge and Savage Station to White Oak Swamp Bridge; Magruder was to move eastward with his division on the Williamsburg Road toward Savage Station; Huger's division was to move forward toward Glen-

dale on the Charles City Road; and Holmes was to advance on the New Market Road and the River Road toward Malvern Hill.

Jackson's command crossed the Chickahominy River at Grapevine Bridge during the night of June 29, 1862, and it then marched through Savage Station and arrived on the north bank of White Oak Swamp, opposite Franklin's command, about noon June 30, 1862. About 2:00 P.M., Jackson opened fire with thirty guns on the Federal defenses across the swamp. The artillery continued its fire for about a half hour, then it slackened, and later it resumed firing intermittently during the rest of the day. Jackson, however, made no serious attempt to force a crossing with his infantry, and his artillery did no appreciable damage

When Jackson's artillery opened at White Oak Swamp, Sumner sent Dana's and Sully's brigades of Sedgwick's division, both under the command of Dana, back from Glendale to support Franklin. Sully was ill that day, and James A. Suiter commanded his brigade. William R. Lee commanded Dana's brigade while the latter was in charge of the two brigades. When Dana arrived at the swamp, he placed one of his brigades on the left of French's brigade and held the other in reserve. Jackson made no serious threat on Franklin's position, however, and when McCall's division was attacked that evening, Dana was ordered to rejoin Sedgwick, and the two brigades returned to Glendale about 5:00 P.M.

On the night of June 29, 1862, Longstreet and A. P. Hill camped at the junction of the Darbytown Road and the Long Bridge Road. The next morning, Longstreet's division—then commanded by Richard H. Anderson while Longstreet was in charge of the two divisions—advanced on the Long Bridge Road toward Glendale. About noon, the head of the column ran into McCall's pickets and quickly drove them back, and then, when Anderson's skirmishers advanced, they soon discovered the strong Union lines covering the roads south toward the James River. Longstreet then deployed his division and prepared to attack. He sent the brigades of Roger A. Pryor, Winfield S. Featherston, and Cadmus M. Wilcox to the left of the road, toward the right of McCall's division and the left of Kearny's division; and he sent to the right the brigades of George E. Pickett (commanded that day by Eppa Hunton and J. B. Strange), Richard H. Anderson (commanded by Micah Jenkins), and James L. Kemper, and they advanced toward the left of McCall's division and the right of Hooker's division. Lawrence O'B. Branch's brigade of A. P. Hill's division was ordered up to support Kemper, but the rest of Hill's division was held in reserve until late in the day.

When Longstreet had completed the formation of his line, he waited for Huger to begin his attack against the Federal right on the Charles City Road. When Longstreet heard Jackson's guns at White Oak Swamp, however, he assumed that it was Huger coming into action, and he immediately ordered his line to advance. Because of the nature of the ground, there was some confusion during Longstreet's advance, and his troops on the left began their attack at 4:00 P.M., and those on the right not until an hour later.

The heaviest blow fell on McCall's division, but Wilcox's brigade struck Meade's brigade on the right of McCall, and also Simmons' brigade, which was brought up from reserve in support. Soon a furious fight developed for possession of Randol's battery. McCall's right was driven back for some distance, and some guns were captured, but the line generally remained unbroken. Meade was wounded during the fighting, and Albert L. Magilton assumed command of his brigade. Simmons was killed and R. Biddle Roberts took charge of his brigade.

On the Confederate right, Kemper's brigade advanced against Seymour's brigade on McCall's left and Grover's brigade on the right of Hooker's division. The 12th Pennsylvania Reserves Regiment was driven back in great disorder, and the two German batteries posted on McCall's left quickly withdrew. The 10th Pennsylvania Reserves of Seymour's brigade and the 5th and a part of the 13th Pennsylvania Reserves (Bucktails) of Simmons' brigade were brought up to halt the enemy advance. Sedgwick, who was at Nelson's farm, sent forward Burns' brigade of his division, and while it advanced, John A. Tompkin's Battery A, 1st Rhode Island and Edmund Kirby's Battery I, 1st United States Artillery fired into the enemy line. Sedgwick also moved up his other two brigades (Dana's and Sully's), which had just returned from White Oak Swamp. Sedgwick's division, with help from Grover's brigade of Hooker's division, soon stabilized the situation. Burns was engaged with Pickett's brigade, which had moved up to relieve

Kemper. About dark, McCall was captured, and Seymour assumed command of his division. C. Feger Jackson assumed command of Seymour's brigade.

To the left of Wilcox, the brigades of Pryor and Featherston extended the front of the attack along Kearny's line. Kearny asked Heintzelman for help, and between 5:00 and 6:00 P.M. Caldwell's brigade of Richardson's division was sent to support Kearny, and about 7:00 P.M. Slocum also sent George W. Taylor's brigade to Kearny. The attack on Kearny was repulsed largely by Robinson's brigade and Thompson's artillery, but with some help from regiments of Birney's, Berry's, and Caldwell's brigades.

As reinforcements arrived near the front held by McCall and Kearny, the Federal commanders began to mount counterattacks against the spent enemy forces. Longstreet, who had received no help from Huger or Holmes, finally, just at sundown, ordered A. P. Hill to advance and support his line. Huger's division did not advance during the day, and except for an exchange of artillery fire and some action with Federal sharpshooters, it was not engaged.

The fighting finally ended about dark, with McClellan's divisions still holding their positions covering the roads to the James River.

Occupation of Malvern Hill (Engagement at Malvern Cliff or Turkey Bridge), June 30, 1862–July 1, 1862. Soon after the fighting ended at Glendale, Franklin and Heintzelman decided to retire to Malvern Hill, and Sumner was obliged to follow, although reluctantly. This movement was made without orders from McClellan, who was not on the field and had sent no orders to his corps commanders. Franklin moved first with Smith's division about 10:00 P.M., and he marched by a newly found road about two miles east of the Willis' Church Road. Richardson followed to cover the movement, but he had with him only French's brigade because the other two brigades had been detached that evening and sent to support Sumner at Glendale. The rest of the army marched south on the Willis' Church Road. Sedgwick moved sometime after 10:00 P.M., and Slocum followed about an hour later. Kearny and Seymour (then commanding McCall's division) moved out about midnight. Hooker's division remained in position until the rest of the army had passed by its rear on the Willis' Church Road, and then it joined the march south soon after daylight. Sumner's, Franklin's, and Heintzelman's troops arrived on Malvern Hill shortly after daylight July 1, 1862.

The position selected by Fitz John Porter to cover the final stage of McClellan's withdrawal to the James River was about three miles south of Glendale, on Malvern Hill. This was an open plateau, about fifty to sixty feet above the surrounding fields and woodlands, and it extended about a mile from north to south and was about three-fourths of a mile wide. On both the east and west sides of the plateau, it sloped down gently into adjacent valleys, except at the Crew house (also called the Mellert house, because Dr. J. H. Mellert was the owner), where the ground fell away quite abruptly. Through a marshy valley on the eastern side of Malvern Hill, a stream called Western Run flowed southward toward the James River. The banks of this stream were covered with trees and thick underbrush, which made the passage of troops through this area very difficult. On the western side, a small stream also flowed southward through low meadows toward the James. The Malvern house was located on the southwest corner of Malvern Hill, and about a mile to the north, on the western side of the plateau, was the Crew house. The high ground around the Crew house and its outbuildings was commonly called the Crew House Hill.

The Willis' Church Road ran to the southwest from Willis' Church to the northern base of Malvern Hill, and there it turned to the south and ran up and over the hill. An unnamed country road ran to the southeast from the Long Bridge Road, through the Carter farm, and then joined the Willis' Church Road at the point where it turned south and began the ascent of Malvern Hill. Southward from this road junction, the ground was open and sloped up gradually for about a fourth of a mile to a road or lane that ran eastward from the Crew house to the Willis' Church Road. On the east side of the Willis' Church Road was the West farm, and the West house was near the junction of that road and the lane from the Crew house.

For several hundred yards in all directions from the crest of the hill, the ground over which the enemy would have to move to approach the Federal position on the hill was cleared and generally cultivated; because of this, the Union artillery had a clear field of fire.

At 10:00 A.M. June 30, 1862, Morell's First Division of Porter's Fifth Provisional Corps arrived on the James River below Turkey Bridge, and bivouacked on the bank of the river. Sykes' Second Division came up about an hour later and was posted along the western edge of Malvern Hill, with its left near the Malvern house. In this position it covered the River Road, on which Theophilus H. Holmes' Confederate division was approaching. Warren's Third Brigade was placed on the low ground to the left and front of Sykes' main line to hold the River Road and cover the extensive open fields to the north along the base of the Crew House Hill. Warren was supported by the 11th United States Infantry, commanded by DeLancey Floyd-Jones, and later in the afternoon by Augustus P. Martin's Battery C, Massachusetts Light Artillery and a detachment of the 3rd Pennsylvania Cavalry.

Along the hill, and overlooking Warren's position and the fields to its right, Henry J. Hunt placed thirty-six guns belonging to Stephen H. Weed's Battery I, 5th United States Artillery; John Edwards' Batteries L and M, 3rd United States Artillery; J. Howard Carlisle's Battery E, 2nd United States Artillery; John R. Smead's Battery K, 5th United States Artillery; and Adolph Voegelee's Battery B, 1st Battalion New York Light Artillery. Later in the day, Robert O. Tyler arrived with the siege guns of his 1st Connecticut Heavy Artillery, and these were put in position near the Malvern house. Charles S. Lovell's Second Brigade of Sykes' division (commanded by William Chapman during the illness of Lovell) supported some of these batteries and, with Robert C. Buchanan's First Brigade on the right, extended Sykes' line northward to a point near the Crew house.

Morell's division was ordered up from its bivouac on the James River, and it was placed on the right of Sykes' line, along the lane running from the Crew house to the Willis' Church Road, facing north. Charles Griffin's Second Brigade formed the first line of Morell's position, and John H. Martindale's First Brigade and Daniel Butterfield's Third Brigade were placed in the rear in support.

The artillery, which was to play a very important part in the battle the next day, was massed along

Morell's front. This artillery consisted of four divisional batteries commanded by William B. Weeden, some batteries of the Artillery Reserve, and one battery of Third Corps. These batteries were: John Edwards' Batteries L and M, 3rd United States Artillery; La Rhett Livingston's Batteries F and K, 3rd United States Artillery; Henry W. Kingsbury's Battery D, 5th United States Artillery; Walter M. Bramhall's 6th New York Battery of Light Artillery of Third Corps; Adelbert Ames' Battery A, 5th United States Artillery; parts of William B. Weeden's Battery C, 1st Rhode Island Light Artillery, commanded by Richard Waterman; and George B. Allen's Battery E, Massachusetts Light Artillery, commanded by John B. Hyde. As other batteries arrived, they were placed in reserve south of the Crew House Hill and were later used to replace batteries that had exhausted their ammunition or were brought up and put in action at various points to strengthen the Federal line. On the morning of July 1, 1862, Charles Griffin, an old artilleryman, was assigned the general direction of the artillery on his front. Henry J. Hunt, in addition to his duties as commander of the Artillery Reserve, also supervised the placing of the guns on the line on Malvern Hill.

About 3:00 P.M. June 30, 1862, Holmes' division approached along the River Road toward the left of Porter's position. At 4:00 P.M. his artillery opened fire, and Henry A. Wise's brigade moved forward to attack Warren's position. This attack was quickly repulsed by the artillery on the crest of the hill, and by the fire of Union gunboats on the James River. Holmes made no further effort to advance that day. This affair has been called the Action at Turkey Bridge or Malvern Cliff.

On the night of June 30, 1862, Porter's troops remained in the positions that they had occupied during the day.

Meantime, during the night of June 29, 1862, Darius N. Couch's First Division of Keyes' Fourth Corps had marched to Haxall (or Haxall's), and between 3:00 and 4:00 P.M. the next day, when Holmes was advancing on the River Road, Couch was ordered forward to Malvern Hill to support Porter. When Holmes' threat subsided, Couch put his division in position for the night on the West farm, to the right of Morell's line. At dark, however, Couch was ordered to Glendale with Albion P. Howe's First Brigade and Innis N. Palmer's Third Brigade to report to Sumner. Couch reported to Sumner as ordered, but returned that night when Sumner left the battlefield and marched to Malvern Hill. Couch, with his two brigades, led the way, and when he arrived on Malvern Hill at daylight he resumed his former position, which began on the right of Morell's division, near the West house, and extended eastward for about a third of a mile. Palmer's brigade was on the left, next to Griffin's brigade of Morell's division; John J. Abercrombie's Second Brigade was on the center; and Howe's brigade was on the right, toward the slope of the hill above Western Run.

Battle of Malvern Hill (or Crew's Farm, Poindexter's Farm), July 1, 1862. During the night of June 30, 1862, after the fighting at Glendale had ended, the rest of the Army of the Potomac withdrew to Malvern Hill. McCall's division, then commanded by Seymour, which had suffered heavy losses during the past few days, was posted just in front of the Malvern house, and it remained there in reserve during the Battle of Malvern Hill.

Heintzelman's Third Corps was placed on the right of Couch, with Kearny's division on the left of the corps' line and Hooker's division on the right. Birney's brigade held the front line of Kearny's division, and it was supported by the brigades of Robinson and Berry. Grover's brigade was on the right of Hooker's line, Carr's brigade was on the left, and Sickles' brigade was in reserve, in rear of Grover.

Franklin's Sixth Provisional Corps was placed on the extreme right, facing Western Run, which flowed to the southeast along the base of the hill.

Sumner's Second Corps was held in reserve near the center of the Union line, between Hooker's division and the Binford house, which was about 600–700 yards in rear of the right of Couch's line. Sumner established contact with Franklin's corps to his right.

On the morning of July 1, 1862, the Army of Northern Virginia again moved forward in pursuit of McClellan's army. Jackson's command crossed White Oak Swamp and marched southward down the Willis' Church Road toward Malvern Hill. Jackson was followed by the brigades of William Mahone and Robert Ransom of Huger's division. The other two brigades of Huger's division, commanded by Lewis A. Armistead and Ambrose R. Wright, moved south from the Charles City Road to the Long Bridge Road, and then continued on to the southeast to the road junction in front of Malvern Hill, where they arrived about noon. They moved into position to the right of the unnamed country road, in front of Malvern Hill.

Whiting's division of Jackson's command arrived at the northern base of Malvern Hill about 9:00 A.M. July 1, 1862, and formed on the left of the Willis' Church Road, with its left at the Poindexter farm. D. H. Hill's division then came up and took position to the right of Whiting, and his line extended across the Willis' Church Road. Richard Taylor's brigade of Ewell's division was placed in the interval between D. H. Hill and Whiting, and the rest of Ewell's division was held in reserve.

Magruder was ordered to march by way of the Quaker Road and take position on the right of Jackson, but Magruder took the wrong Quaker Road (the Willis' Church Road, also called the Quaker Road, was the intended route), and he did not arrive at the front until late in the afternoon. Originally, Lee intended to put Magruder's division on the right of D. H. Hill, but when Magruder took the wrong road and did not arrive as early as expected, Lee placed the brigades of Ransom and Mahone there instead. When Magruder finally came up between 3:00 and 4:00 P.M., Lee placed this division in rear of the brigades of Armistead and Wright, on the extreme right of the enemy line. Magruder assumed command of these two brigades. Lee finally completed his line of battle about 5:00 P.M.

The first action at Malvern Hill began about 9:00 A.M., when the Federal artillery opened fire on the enemy troops as they moved into position along the northern base of the hill. This firing continued until about 1:00 P.M.. and then it diminished until the infantry attacks began late in the afternoon. There was also skirmishing along the front during the day, but there was no general attack until about 5:00 P.M.

When Lee first arrived on the field, he decided to attack about 1:30 P.M., drive McClellan's forces from Malvern Hill, and destroy them before they could reach the safety of the James River. His plan was to bring up his artillery and attempt to silence the Federal batteries on the crest of the hill, and when this had been accomplished, to advance with his infantry. The order for the attack directed Armistead, who could best observe the effects of Lee's artillery fire, to advance when the Federal batteries had been subdued, and the rest of the line was to await Armistead's signal, and then move forward with him. The Confederate artillery, however, was unequal to its task, and the infantry attack was delayed.

Later in the day, when Magruder arrived on the field, he received Lee's order written at 1:30 P.M. for Armistead's attack (which did not include the time that it was issued) and, believing that it applied to the time that he received it, ordered an attack on the Crew House Hill about 5:00 or 6:00 P.M. Wright and Armistead promptly advanced against Morell's line, but they were soon stopped by the heavy artillery fire from the hill. These two brigades once again attempted to storm the Crew House Hill and were supported by Howell Cobb's brigade of Magruder's division, William Mahone's brigade of Huger's division, the brigades of Paul J. Semmes and Joseph B. Kershaw of McLaws' division, and George T. Anderson's brigade of David R. Jones' division. This attempt also failed, and Magruder's troops were driven back with heavy losses.

After Magruder's attack on the Crew House Hill, Martindale's brigade was advanced from Morell's second line to support Griffin, and when Griffin's brigade was compelled to fall back, it was relieved by Butterfield's brigade. Sykes, who had been posted to the left and rear of Morell, marched to the front with the brigades of Buchanan and Lovell, and posted his brigades to cover the left of Morell's line. They were soon engaged. Earlier, Sumner had ordered Richardson to send Meagher's brigade to Porter, and at about dark, Meagher moved to the front of the Crew house and relieved Butterfield's men, who had expended all their ammunition. Warren's brigade of Sykes' division remained on the River Road during the day and was not engaged.

On the Confederate left, D. H. Hill, believing the sounds of Magruder's battle to be the signal for a general attack, advanced his division up the hill, along both sides of the Willis' Church Road, against the front of Couch's division and the left of Kearny's division. Samuel Garland's brigade formed the front line of Hill's attack, and Toombs' brigade of Jones' division was brought up in support. These were followed by the brigades of Robert E. Rodes (commanded by John B. Gordon), Alfred H. Colquitt, Roswell Ripley, and George B. Anderson (commanded by Charles C. Tew), but all were driven back with severe losses. The fighting on Couch's front was severe as D. H. Hill's troops attempted to break through his line and get among his guns. Between 5:00 and 6:00 P.M. Caldwell's brigade of Richardson's division was sent to support Couch, and it went into action on the extreme right of Couch's line. Heintzelman also sent Francis W. Seeley's Battery K, 4th United States Artillery and Sickles' brigade to support Couch. The battery was placed in front of Howe's line, and Sickles' regiments relieved troops on the line when their ammunition was exhausted. Finally, late in the day, a part of Robert Ransom's brigade (temporarily attached to Huger's division) and Charles S. Winder's brigade of Jackson's division, and also Ewell's division, came up, but they were too late to have any significant effect on the outcome of the battle. The fighting at Malvern Hill continued until 9:00 P.M., and then the enemy stopped their attacks. On all parts of the field, the enemy suffered a decisive defeat.

During the night, the Army of the Potomac withdrew and started for Harrison's Landing on the James River, seven miles distant. McClellan's retreat ended there July 2, 1862.

During the Battle of Malvern Hill, Keyes, with John J. Peck's Second Division, Fourth Corps, guarded the bridge at Carter's Mill and the approach to Haxall, where several roads converged. Peck's division served as rear guard of the army as it retreated to Harrison's Landing.

The organization of the Army of the Potomac during the Seven Days' Battles, June 25, 1862–July 2, 1862 was as follows:

ARMY OF THE POTOMAC
George B. McClellan

SECOND CORPS, Edwin V. Sumner

First Division, Israel B. Richardson
First Brigade, John C. Caldwell
Second Brigade, Thomas F. Meagher
  Robert Nugent
  Thomas F. Meagher

Third Brigade, William H. French
Artillery, George W. Hazzard, to June 30, 1862, mortally wounded
  Battery B, 1st New York Light Artillery, Rufus D. Pettit
  Batteries A and C, 4th United States Artillery, George W. Hazzard
  Rufus King, Jr.

Note. Meagher was in temporary arrest at Savage Station June 29, 1862, and until 8:30 the next morning, and Nugent commanded Second Brigade during his absence.

Second Division, John Sedgwick
First Brigade, Alfred Sully
Second Brigade, William W. Burns
Third Brigade, Napoleon J. T. Dana
Artillery, Charles H. Tompkins
  Battery A, 1st Rhode Island Light Artillery, Charles H. Tompkins
  Battery I, 1st United States Artillery, Edmund Kirby

Note. Willis A. Gorman was ill during the Seven Days, and Sully was in command of First Brigade.

Corps Artillery Reserve
  Battery G, 1st New York Light Artillery, John D. Frank
  Battery B, 1st Rhode Island Light Artillery, Walter O. Bartlett
  Battery G, 1st Rhode Island Light Artillery, Charles D. Owen

Cavalry
  Companies D, F, H, K, 6th New York Cavalry, Duncan McVicar

THIRD CORPS, Samuel P. Heintzelman

Second Division, Joseph Hooker
First Brigade, Cuvier Grover
Second Brigade, Daniel E. Sickles
Third Brigade, Joseph B. Carr
Artillery
  Battery D, 1st New York Light Artillery, Thomas W. Osborn
  4th Battery, New York Light Artillery, Joseph Nairn
  Battery H, 1st United States Artillery, Charles H. Webber

Third Division, Philip Kearny
First Brigade, John C. Robinson
Second Brigade, David B. Birney
Third Brigade, Hiram G. Berry
Artillery

Battery E, 1st Rhode Island Light Artillery, George E. Randolph

Battery G, 2nd United States Artillery, James Thompson

Corps Artillery Reserve, Gustavus A. De Russy
6th Battery, New York Light Artillery, Walter M. Bramhall
2nd Battery, New Jersey Light Artillery, John E. Beam, to July 1, 1862, killed
John B. Monroe
Battery K, 4th United States Artillery, Francis W. Seeley

3rd Pennsylvania Cavalry, William W. Averell

FOURTH CORPS, Erasmus D. Keyes

First Division, Darius N. Couch
First Brigade, Albion P. Howe
Second Brigade, John J. Abercrombie
Third Brigade, Innis N. Palmer
Artillery
Battery C, 1st Pennsylvania Light Artillery, Jeremiah McCarthy
Battery D, 1st Pennsylvania Light Artillery, Edward H. Flood

Second Division, John J. Peck
First Brigade, Henry M. Naglee
Second Brigade, Henry W. Wessells
Artillery
Battery H, 1st New York Light Artillery, Charles E. Mink
7th Battery, New York Light Artillery, Peter C. Regan

Corps Artillery Reserve, Robert M. West
8th Battery, New York Light Artillery, Butler Fitch
Battery E, 1st Pennsylvania Light Artillery, Theodore Miller
Battery H, 1st Pennsylvania Light Artillery, James Brady
Battery M, 5th United States Artillery, James Mc-Knight

8th Pennsylvania Cavalry, David McM. Gregg

FIFTH PROVISIONAL CORPS, Fitz John Porter

First Division, George W. Morell
First Brigade, John H. Martindale
Second Brigade, Charles Griffin
Third Brigade, Daniel Butterfield
1st United States Sharpshooters, Hiram Berdan
Artillery, William B. Weeden

3rd Battery, Massachusetts Light Artillery, Augustus P. Martin
5th Battery, Massachusetts Light Artillery, John B. Hyde
Battery C, 1st Rhode Island Light Artillery, Richard Waterman
Battery D, 5th United States Artillery, Henry W. Kingsbury

Second Division, George Sykes
First Brigade, Robert C. Buchanan
Second Brigade, Charles Lovell
Third Brigade, Gouverneur K. Warren
Artillery, Stephen H. Weed
Batteries L and M, 3rd United States Artillery, John Edwards
Battery I, 5th United States Artillery, Stephen H. Weed

Note. Lovell assumed command of Second Brigade June 27, 1862, during the absence of William Chapman, who was ill.

Third Division, George A. McCall, to June 30, 1862, captured
Truman Seymour
First Brigade, John F. Reynolds, to June 27, 1862, captured
Seneca G. Simmons, to June 30, 1862, killed
R. Biddle Roberts
Second Brigade, George G. Meade, to June 30, 1862, wounded
Albert L. Magilton
Third Brigade, Truman Seymour, to June 30, 1862
C. Feger Jackson
Artillery
Battery A, 1st Pennsylvania Light Artillery, Hezekiah Easton, to June 27, 1862, killed
Jacob L. Detrich
John G. Simpson
Battery B, 1st Pennsylvania Light Artillery, James H. Cooper
Battery G, 1st Pennsylvania Light Artillery, Mark Kerns, to June 27, 1862, wounded
Frank P. Amsden
Battery C, 5th United States Artillery, Henry V. De Hart, to June 27, 1862, mortally wounded
Eben G. Scott

4th Pennsylvania Cavalry, James H. Childs

8th Illinois Cavalry, John F. Farnsworth

Artillery Reserve, Army of the Potomac, Henry J. Hunt
First Brigade (Horse Artillery), William Hays
Second Brigade, George W. Getty

Third Brigade, Albert Arndt
Fourth Brigade, Edward R. Petherbridge
Fifth Brigade, J. Howard Carlisle
Siege Train (1st Connecticut), Robert O. Tyler

Note. On May 20, 1862, the Artillery Reserve was assigned to duty with Fifth Provisional Corps, and Hunt reported to Fitz John Porter.

SIXTH PROVISIONAL CORPS, William B. Franklin

First Division, Henry W. Slocum
First Brigade, George W. Taylor
Second Brigade, Joseph J. Bartlett
Third Brigade, John Newton
Artillery, Edward R. Platt
1st Battery, Massachusetts Light Artillery, Josiah Porter
1st Battery, New Jersey Light Artillery, William Hexamer
Battery D, 2nd United States Light Artillery, Emory Upton

Second Division, William F. Smith
First Brigade, Winfield S. Hancock
Second Brigade, William T. H. Brooks
Third Brigade, John W. Davidson
Artillery, Romeyn B. Ayres
Battery E, 1st New York Light Artillery, Charles C. Wheeler
1st Battery, New York Light Artillery, Andrew Cowan
3rd Battery, New York Light Artillery, Thaddeus P. Mott
Battery F, 5th New York Light Artillery, Romeyn B. Ayres

5th Pennsylvania Cavalry (Companies I and K), John O'Farrell

Cavalry Reserve, Philip St. George Cooke
First Brigade
6th Pennsylvania Cavalry, Richard Rush
5th United States Cavalry (five companies), Charles J. Whiting, captured
Joseph H. McArthur
Second Brigade, George A. H. Blake

Note. George Stoneman and William H. Emory were on the right flank of the army with a mixed command of infantry, artillery, and cavalry.

Volunteer Engineer Brigade, Daniel P. Woodbury
Troops at Depot at White House, Silas Casey

The Cavalry during the Peninsular Campaign.

Union cavalry operations during the Peninsular Campaign were of comparatively minor importance. There were several reasons for this, but the most significant was that the cavalry with the Army of the Potomac was not organized as a separate body, but instead was assigned as companies, regiments, or two or more regiments to special duties. Its principal service was on picket and outpost duties, and on scouting expeditions on the front and flanks of the army, but it was also used as escorts and orderlies for the corps and division commanders.

Generally during the campaign, a regiment or a part of a regiment was assigned to each corps. Initially, four companies of the 6th New York were assigned to Second Corps, the 3rd Pennsylvania to Third Corps, and the 8th Pennsylvania to Fourth Corps. Later two companies of the 5th Pennsylvania were assigned to Fifth Provisional Corps. The 1st New York Cavalry, commanded by Andrew T. McReynolds, and which appears to have been unattached, was broken up into detachments after landing at Fort Monroe and was not reassembled until at the beginning of the withdrawal of the army from the Peninsula in August 1862.

Originally, there was one separate cavalry organization of more than one regiment, and this was known as the Cavalry Reserve. This was commanded by Philip St. George Cooke and appears to have been formed only for administrative control of the cavalry that was not assigned to the different army corps. It was organized as follows:

Cavalry Reserve, Philip St. George Cooke
First Brigade, William H. Emory
5th and 6th United States Cavalry, and 5th Pennsylvania Cavalry
Second Brigade, George A. H. Blake
1st United States Cavalry, 8th Pennsylvania Cavalry, and McClellan (Illinois) Dragoons

After the enemy evacuated Yorktown, George Stoneman, chief of cavalry of the army, was assigned command of a cavalry force called the Advance of the Army, and with this command he followed the retiring Confederate column up the Peninsula toward Williamsburg, and beyond. Later, Stoneman was placed in command of a mixed force of cavalry, infantry, and artillery, and was assigned to watch the right of the army from Mechanicsville to the Pamunkey River. William H. Emory was assigned command of the cavalry with Stoneman. When Jackson advanced on McClellan's right toward Gaines' Mill at the beginning of the Seven Days' Battles, Stoneman's command retired down the Pamunkey River and joined Silas Casey's force at White House. The units of Stoneman's command did not rejoin their proper organizations until the army arrived at Harrison's Landing.

Cooke's Cavalry Reserve remained with the infantry north of the Chickahominy River, and was under Porter's control at the beginning of the Seven Days' Battles. Near the end of the Battle of Gaines' Mill, a part of Cooke's cavalry made an almost suicidal charge on the advancing enemy infantry in an attempt to save some of Porter's guns; but otherwise it did little more than watch the flanks of Porter's line during the battle and then join Fifth Provisional Corps in the retreat.

When the army arrived at Harrison's Landing, Cooke was relieved from command of the Cavalry Reserve, and Stoneman departed on sick leave. On July 5, 1862, William W. Averell was appointed acting brigadier general and was assigned to the temporary command of the cavalry with the Army of the Potomac. He then issued orders for the organization of the cavalry forces into a cavalry division and thus instituted the brigade organization of the cavalry with the army. Stoneman returned to the army that same day and resumed command July 6, 1862. That day Emory was relieved from duty with the Cavalry Reserve, and was assigned to the temporary command of Henry M. Naglee's First Brigade of John J. Peck's Second Division, Fourth Corps.

The new cavalry organization, as announced July 8, 1862, was as follows:

CAVALRY DIVISION, ARMY OF THE POTOMAC, George Stoneman

First Brigade, William W. Averell
  3rd Pennsylvania Cavalry, Samuel W. Owen
  1st New York Cavalry, Andrew T. McReynolds
  4th Pennsylvania Cavalry, James H. Childs

Second Brigade, David McM. Gregg
  8th Illinois Cavalry, William Gamble
  8th Pennsylvania Cavalry, David McM. Gregg
  6th New York Cavalry (two squadrons), Duncan McVicar

First Brigade was assigned to operate with the right wing of the army, and Second Brigade with the left wing.

July 16, 1862, Alfred Pleasonton, commanding the 2nd United States Cavalry, was promoted to brigadier general, and was assigned command of Second Brigade of the cavalry division, and Gregg resumed command of his 8th Pennsylvania Cavalry.

During July and August 1862, the cavalry was principally occupied in covering the front of the army encampment at Harrison's Landing, and in making reconnaissances into the surrounding countryside. It also covered the withdrawal of the army to Yorktown and Fort Monroe for embarkation when it left the Peninsula in the latter part of August 1862.

In a report of August 11, 1862, the organization of Stoneman's Cavalry Division was given as follows:

CAVALRY DIVISION, George Stoneman

First Brigade, William W. Averell
  3rd Pennsylvania Cavalry, Samuel W. Owen
  4th Pennsylvania Cavalry, James H. Childs
  1st New York Cavalry, Frederick Von Schickfuss
  5th United States Cavalry, Joseph H. McArthur

Second Brigade, Alfred Pleasonton
  1st United States Cavalry, Marcus A. Reno
  6th United States Cavalry, August V. Kautz
  8th Illinois Cavalry, David R. Clendenin
  8th Pennsylvania Cavalry, David McM. Gregg

One squadron of cavalry was also assigned to each of the army corps.

August 22, 1862, Stoneman was relieved from duty as commander of the Cavalry Division of the Army of the Potomac. The brigades were then to be commanded by the senior colonel of each then present for duty.

Harrison's Landing, Virginia, July–August 1862. After the Battle of Malvern Hill July 1, 1862, the Army of the Potomac retired to Harrison's Landing on the James River, and it remained there in a fortified position until ordered to withdraw from the Peninsula in August 1862. There were no further offensive operations by the army during this period, but there were several scouts and reconnaissances sent out into the surrounding area.

While at Harrison's Landing, there were some changes in the organization of the army, and there were also some important events elsewhere that were to have an effect on the affairs of the army. Most of the organizational changes, except in the cavalry (see preceding section), were comparatively minor. Darius N. Couch's First Division, Fourth Corps was reorganized by the change of designations of the brigades. Albion P. Howe's First Brigade became Second Brigade, and Howe remained in command; John J. Abercrombie's Second Brigade became Third Brigade, and John Cochrane, the senior colonel present, was assigned command; and Innis N. Palmer's Third Brigade, formerly commanded by Charles Devens, became First Brigade. When Devens returned to the army after recovering from a wound received at Seven Pines, he resumed command of the new First Brigade. Abercrombie commanded Couch's division temporarily in August 1862.

On June 26, 1862, at the beginning of the Seven Days' Battles, the Mountain Department and the departments of the Rappahannock and the Shenandoah were merged into the Army of Virginia, under the command of John Pope. At that time, James Shields' Division of the Department of the Rappahannock was broken up, and the brigades of Nathan Kimball and Orris S. Ferry were sent to the Peninsula to join the Army of the Potomac. Ferry's brigade arrived July 5, 1862 and was assigned to Second Division, Fourth Corps as Third Brigade. Kimball's brigade joined the next day, and was assigned to Sixth Provisional Corps, but July 15, 1862, it was transferred to Second Corps as Kimball's Independent Brigade.

When the news of the the Seven Days' Battles, and McClellan's retreat to the James River, reached Washington, Edwin M. Stanton, the secretary of war, urged Ambrose E. Burnside, commander of the Department of North Carolina, to send all available troops of the Department to Virginia to reinforce the Army of the Potomac. Two days after the Battle of Malvern Hill, Burnside was en route to Norfolk, Virginia with Jesse L. Reno's Second Division and John G. Parke's Third Division of the Department of North Carolina. From Norfolk, Burnside's two divisions were transferred to Newport News, and there, on July 22, 1862, these divisions, and Isaac I. Stevens' Division from the Department of the South

were organized into a new army corps, which was designated as Ninth Corps. Burnside was assigned command of the corps. By that time, however, it was clear that McClellan did not need Burnside's reinforcements, and on August 1, 1862, Ninth Corps was ordered from Newport News to support Pope's Army of Virginia. The corps arrived at Aquia Creek August 4, 1862, and then moved to the Rappahannock River, where it took position opposite Fredericksburg.

The order of July 22, 1862 that created the Ninth Corps also officially confirmed the existence of Fifth Corps and Sixth Corps, and thereafter the term "Provisional" was dropped from their designations. In addition, it also created two other new corps, which were designated as Seventh Corps and Eighth Corps. Seventh Corps was organized from troops of John A. Dix's Department of Virginia, which were stationed at Fort Monroe, Camp Hamilton, Norfolk, Portsmouth, and Yorktown. Eighth Corps was organized from troops of John A. Wool's Middle Department. For details of these two corps, see Department of Virginia, May 22, 1861–July 15, 1863; and also Middle Department.

On July 13, Jackson left Richmond with his own and Ewell's divisions and marched to Gordonsville, Virginia, where he arrived July 19, 1862. Later, on August 9, 1862, Jackson was engaged with Nathaniel P. Banks' corps of Pope's Army of Virginia at Cedar Mountain (see Pope's Northern Virginia Campaign). By August 13, 1862, Lee was convinced that the Army of the Potomac would soon withdraw from the Peninsula, and that day he issued orders for Daniel H. Hill's division to remain at Richmond to watch McClellan and for the rest of the Army of Northern Virginia to join Jackson's command at Gordonsville.

Withdrawal of the Army of the Potomac from the Peninsula, August 1862. On July 30, 1862, Henry W. Halleck ordered McClellan to send north the sick of his command, and on August 3, 1862 further directed him to prepare for the removal of the Army of the Potomac to Aquia Creek, Virginia. The army began to withdraw from Harrison's Landing August 14–15, 1862, and to march toward Fort Monroe, Yorktown, and Newport News for embarkation. The evacuation of Harrison's Landing was completed by August 16, 1862. Porter's Fifth Corps was the first to leave the Peninsula, and it departed August 19–20, 1862; Sumner's Second Corps was the last to go, and it left August 26, 1862. Couch's division of Fourth Corps accompanied the army when it went north, but Keyes with Peck's division remained at Yorktown. For further information about Keyes' command, see Department of Virginia, May 22, 1861–July 15, 1863; and also Fourth Corps, Army of the Potomac.

Porter's Fifth Corps arrived at Aquia Creek August 22, 1862 and disembarked there, but the other corps were ordered to continue on to Alexandria, Virginia. Heintzelman's Third Corps arrived at Alexandria August 22, 1862; Sumner's Second Corps, August 27, 1862; Franklin's Sixth Corps, August 29, 1862; and Couch's First Division, Fourth Corps arrived August 30, 1862–September 1, 1862. All corps were ordered forward to join the Army of Virginia, which was then engaged in operations that ended in Pope's defeat at the battles of Groveton, Second Manassas, and Chantilly. Third Corps, Fifth Corps, and also two divisions of Ninth Corps under Reno arrived on the field in time to take part in the final battles, and all were heavily engaged. For details, see Pope's Northern Virginia Campaign.

The Army of Virginia and the Army of the Potomac retreated from Centerville into the Defenses of Washington, and were reorganized there in early September 1862. When this was completed, the Army of the Potomac, again under McClellan, marched into Maryland on a campaign that ended with the Battle of Antietam. For further information, see Maryland Campaign (South Mountain and Antietam).

OPERATIONS ABOUT PETERSBURG AND RICHMOND, VIRGINIA, 1864–1865

OPERATIONS OF JUNE 1864

Assaults at Petersburg, Virginia, June 15–18, 1864. During the night of June 12, 1864, William F. Smith's Eighteenth Corps, Army of the James withdrew from its positions near Cold Harbor, and the next morning embarked for Bermuda Hundred. About sunset June 14, 1864, Smith arrived there and reported in person to Benjamin F. Butler, commanding the Army of the James and the Department of Virginia and North Carolina. At Butler's headquarters, Smith received orders to transfer his corps to the south side of the Appomattox River at daylight the next morning, and then to advance against the enemy works in front of Petersburg. Smith was directed to cross the river on a pontoon bridge that had been constructed near the left of the Federal lines at Bermuda Hundred, at Point of Rocks (or Broadway Landing), about two miles below Port Walthall.

Smith's transports arrived at Broadway Landing during the night, and about 10,000 men of his Eighteenth Corps disembarked. In addition, Butler's cavalry division, commanded by August V. Kautz, and about 3,700 men of Edward W. Hinks' (also spelled Hincks) division of the Army of the James that were available, were assigned to Smith's command. The rest of Hinks' division was stationed at Wilson's Landing, Fort Powhatan, City Point, and Bermuda Hundred.

The orders for the advance of Smith's force May 15, 1864 were as follows: Kautz's cavalry was to cross the river at 1:00 A.M. and march to the enemy entrenchments near the Norfolk and Petersburg Railroad to protect the left flank of the infantry; Hinks' command was to follow Kautz and take position across the Jordan's Point Road, near the enemy works; William T. H. Brooks' First Division, and Adelbert Ames' Third Division of Eighteenth Corps were to follow Hinks and deploy on his right; and John H. Martindale's Second Division, Eighteenth Corps was to march on the River Road to a point near the City Point Railroad and await orders.

The enemy entrenchments at Petersburg encircled the town at a distance of about two miles; they consisted of a series of redans or batteries that were connected by infantry parapets. This line began on the Confederate left at the Appomattox River, near the mouth of Harrison's Creek, which was a little more than a mile downstream from Petersburg. From there it ran east about a mile to the City Point Railroad; then south for about three miles to the Norfolk and Petersburg Railroad; then west for about four miles to a point one mile west of the Weldon Railroad; and from there it ran north and ended on the Appomattox River above Petersburg.

The batteries or redans on this line were numbered consecutively from left to right, beginning with Battery No. 1, on the Appomattox River. Their locations with respect to features on the field of operations mentioned in the reports of the campaign were as follows: Batteries Nos. 1–4 were between the Appomattox River and the City Point Railroad; Nos. 5–8 were between the City Point Railroad and the Jordan's Point Road, with No. 5 near the Jordan house, and No. 6 near the Friend (or Gibbon) house; Nos. 9 and 10 were on opposite sides of the Jordan's Point Road, at the place where the Prince George Court House Road joined from the southeast; Nos. 11–14 were between the Jordan's Point Road and the Shand house, with No. 11 near the Dunn house; Nos. 15–19 were between the Shand house and the Norfolk and Petersburg Railroad, with the Avery house in front of Nos. 16 and 17; and Nos. 20–23 were on the line running west, on the south side of the Norfolk and Petersburg Railroad.

At the time of Smith's advance, these works were occupied only from the Appomattox River below Petersburg to a point about midway between the Norfolk and Petersburg Railroad and the Jerusalem Plank Road, which crossed the line of entrenchments about a mile and one-fourth west of the railroad.

Smith began his advance after midnight June 15, 1864, when Kautz crossed the Appomattox River at Point of Rocks and marched south. Kautz moved on and crossed the City Point Road, the Jordan's Point Road, and the Prince George Court House Road, and arrived at the Norfolk and Petersburg Railroad about noon. He rested there until 3:00 P.M. and then advanced to within about 500 yards of the enemy works, where he became engaged. He remained in position there until about 5:30 P.M. and then withdrew to the Jordan's Point Road. Simon H. Mix, commanding Kautz's First Brigade, was mortally wounded and was succeeded by Robert M. West. Kautz continued to guard the left flank of Smith's line until after dark June 16, 1864, and then he was relieved by the infantry of Gouverneur K. Warren's Fifth Corps, Army of the Potomac. Kautz then returned to Bermuda Hundred.

Hinks' command followed the cavalry on the road south toward the City Point Railroad. It consisted of Samuel A. Duncan's Second Brigade of United States Colored Troops and a small provisional brigade commanded by John H. Holman. When Kautz's cavalry reached the railroad, it came under fire from an enemy position in the Baylor field, which commanded the road at a point where it emerged from a woods and swamp near Perkinson's saw mill, near the railroad. Kautz was forced to halt while Hinks was sent forward to force a passage of the swamp. Hinks then advanced, with Duncan's brigade in front and Holman's brigade following in support, and as they approached the Baylor field, the enemy retired toward Petersburg. At 9:00 A.M., Hinks resumed the march from the City Point Road toward the Jordan's Point Road, and upon arriving there, turned to the right toward Petersburg. Holman's brigade, which was in the lead, encountered enemy pickets on Bailey's Creek, near the Bryant house, and drove them back. Hinks then advanced his division to a position in front of the enemy works, and at 11:00 A.M. established a line of skirmishers that extended from a point across the junction of the Jordan's Point Road and the Suffolk Stage Road on the left, to, and beyond, the Peebles house on the right.

Brooks' division of Eighteenth Corps followed Hinks to the City Point Road, where it deployed and advanced along the road and the railroad toward Petersburg, with its right on the City Point Railroad and its left extending toward Hinks' command on the left. About 2:00 P.M., Hinks extended his line to the right to connect with Brooks.

When Ames' division arrived at Bermuda Hundred from White House, Ames was assigned command of the center section of Butler's line of defenses, and William B. Barton's Second Brigade of Ames' division and three additional regiments were assigned to him to man this part of the line. The other two brigades of Ames' division accompanied Eighteenth Corps toward Petersburg. Louis Bell's Third Brigade was at the rear of Brooks' division, and N. Martin Curtis' First Brigade was behind Bell. Apparently, as senior officer, Bell was in charge of both brigades. They took position on the left of the railroad about 11:00 A.M., with Bell in front, and advanced somewhat toward Petersburg.

Martindale's division followed Brooks, with George J. Stannard's First Brigade in front and

Griffin A. Stedman's Second Brigade close behind. When Martindale reached the City Point Railroad, it deployed to the right of the railroad and prepared to advance. Stannard's brigade was on the left, connecting with Brooks, and Stedman's brigade was on the right, with its pickets out to the Appomattox River.

When Smith approached the enemy works during the afternoon of June 15, 1864, Pierre G. T. Beauregard, commanding the Confederate Department of North Carolina and Southern Virginia, had for their defense only Henry A. Wise's brigade of 2,400 men, Fletcher H. Archer's militia, Battle's and Wood's battalions, James Dearing's cavalry, and some artillery.

Smith carefully examined the enemy positions during the afternoon, and it was not until about 7:00 P.M. that he launched an attack from the front of Brooks' line. After an artillery bombardment, skirmishers advanced and penetrated the line by passing through a ravine between batteries No. 6 and No. 7. Both Bell's brigade of Ames' division and Hiram Burnham's Second Brigade of Brooks' division are reported to have captured Battery No. 5. Curtis' brigade of Ames' division and Gilman Marston's First Brigade of Brooks' division, supported by Guy V. Henry's Third Brigade of Brooks' division, reported the capture of Battery No. 6. Both batteries were near the Jordan house.

At that critical time, help arrived for Beauregard. Robert F. Hoke came up from near Drewry's Bluff with the brigades of Johnson Hagood, Alfred H. Colquitt, and Thomas L. Clingman of his division, and these were placed in position in rear of the captured works. James G. Martin's brigade, also of Hoke's division, arrived June 17, 1864.

Hinks' command advanced on the left of Brooks, and captured batteries Nos. 7, 8, 9, 10, and 11. The last, Battery No. 11, was taken about 9:00 P.M. Bell's and Curtis' brigades then moved to the left and occupied Battery No. 7 and the connecting lines. Bell's brigade was on the right of the battery, and Curtis' brigade was on the left.

On the right of the City Point Railroad, Martindale's division also advanced at 7:00 P.M. Stannard's brigade was on the left, next to the railroad, and Stedman's brigade was on the right. Stannard captured Battery No. 3, and Stedman advanced to the enemy works at Harrison's Creek, but that

night both brigades withdrew. At the end of the day, Smith occupied about a mile and a half of the enemy entrenchments between the City Point Railroad and the Prince George Court House Road.

Meantime, Winfield S. Hancock's Second Corps, Army of the Potomac, which had crossed the James River at Wilcox's Landing June 14–15, 1864, had been advancing on the road from Windmill Point, and at 5:30 P.M. had arrived at a point on the Prince George Court House Road about four miles from the left of Smith's line. David B. Birney's Third Division then left the road and turned to the right toward Petersburg. John Gibbon's Second Division followed Birney. Francis C. Barlow's First Division marched with the trains to Old Court House, which was about six miles northeast of Petersburg on the City Point Road, and then it too marched toward Petersburg.

Birney's division, with Gibbon's division following, arrived at the Bryant house, on Bailey's Creek, about one mile in rear of Hinks' division, at 6:30 P.M. Birney and Gibbon then moved up and occupied a part of the line captured by Hinks' division that evening. Birney's division took position on the left at Battery No. 11, between the Prince George Court House Road and the Dunn house. Birney was in line by 11:00 P.M., but Gibbon did not arrive until between 2:00 and 3:00 A.M. June 16, 1864. Gibbon occupied the line between the ravine near the Friend house and the right of Birney's line on the Prince George Court House Road. Gibbon relieved the brigades of Bell and Curtis, which then moved back to the vicinity of the Friend house. There Bell formed a new line, with Curtis in reserve. Barlow's division arrived about daylight June 16, 1864 and took position on the left of Birney, with its left extending southward to the Norfolk and Petersburg Railroad.

Hinks' division remained on the line with Birney during the night of June 15, 1864, but the next morning it withdrew to the right to the junction of the Spring Hill Road and the City Point Road. Holman's brigade was sent to picket the Appomattox River from the right of Martindale's division to the gunboats on the river, and Duncan's brigade was held in reserve near the above-mentioned junction.

When Hancock's Second Corps marched toward Petersburg June 15, 1864, the rest of the Army of the Potomac followed. Ambrose E. Burnside's Ninth

Corps crossed the James River on the pontoon bridge during the night of June 15, 1864, and then marched toward Petersburg by way of Old Court House. It arrived near the enemy lines about 5:00 P.M. the next day, and it moved into position on the left of Second Corps. Orlando B. Willcox's Third Division was on the right of the corps' line, connecting with Second Corps; Robert B. Potter's Second Division was on the center, to the right of the Shand house, and in front of Battery No. 14; and James H. Ledlie's First Division was on the left, in front of batteries Nos. 15 and 16.

Warren's Fifth Corps was ferried across the James River to Windmill Point between 2:00 A.M. and 1:00 P.M. June 16, 1864, and it then set out toward Petersburg by way of Prince George Court House. Charles Griffin's First Division was in the lead, and it was followed in turn by Lysander Cutler's Fourth Division, Romeyn B. Ayres' Second Division, and Samuel W. Crawford's Third Division. The corps arrived near Petersburg during the afternoon and night, and the next day, June 17, 1864, Cutler's division was sent to the extreme left, where it connected on its right with Ninth Corps. The other three divisions of Fifth Corps were massed in the rear, near the center of the Union line.

At dark June 16, 1864, Thomas H. Neill's Second Division of Horatio G. Wright's Sixth Corps followed Fifth Corps across the James River and started toward Petersburg. David A. Russell's First Division and James B. Ricketts' Third Division of Sixth Corps were sent by transport up the James to Bermuda Hundred to help hold Butler's defensive lines there while Eighteenth Corps was absent at Petersburg. Neill's division arrived near Petersburg June 17, 1864, and it immediately relieved Brooks' division of Eighteenth Corps, which was holding the works near the City Point Railroad.

During the morning of June 16, 1864, Grant assigned Hancock to the command of all Federal troops in front of Petersburg, during the absence of George G. Meade, who had not yet arrived from the crossing of the James River.

At 6:00 A.M. June 16, 1864, Birney's and Gibbon's divisions of Second Corps advanced on a reconnaissance. Two hours later, Thomas W. Egan's First Brigade of Birney's division attacked the enemy in front of, and to the left of, the Dunn house, drove them back, and captured Battery No.

12. Egan was wounded during the attack and was succeeded in command of the brigade by Henry J. Madill. Martindale demonstrated that morning on the right of the Union line, but he did not attack.

Also on June 16, 1864, Beauregard received additional reinforcements. At dawn that morning, Bushrod R. Johnson's Confederate division was withdrawn from the lines in front of Bermuda Hundred and sent to Petersburg. It arrived there at 10:00 that morning and was placed on the line of works behind batteries Nos. 12, 13, and 14, on a ridge near the Shand house. Johnson's division consisted of the brigades of Stephen Elliott, Matt W. Ransom, Archibald Gracie, and Bushrod R. Johnson, the latter commanded by John S. Fulton. Hoke's division was then on the left of Johnson, with its left extending across the City Point Railroad. Wise's brigade, then commanded by Powhatan R. Page while Wise commanded the First Military District, was on the right of Johnson. Wise's brigade was across the Norfolk and Petersburg Railroad, and faced to the southeast.

Meade finally arrived at Petersburg during the afternoon of June 16, 1864 and ordered an attack for later in the day on the hill where the Hare house stood, and where later Fort Stedman would be built. Second Corps was strongly reinforced for this attack. During the evening, John Ramsey's Fourth Brigade and John Fraser's Second Brigade of Gibbon's division were ordered to report to Birney, whose division was to make the assault. In addition, Bell's brigade of Ames' division and Henry's brigade of Brooks's division, both of Eighteenth Corps, were also sent to Birney. Simon G. Griffin's Second Brigade of Potter's division and John F. Hartranft's First Brigade of Willcox's division, both of Ninth Corps, were sent to support Barlow's division of Second Corps.

At 6:00 P.M. Second Corps advanced to the front of the Hare house and captured batteries Nos. 13 and 14, together with their connecting lines. The principal attack was made by the divisions of Barlow and Birney, but Gibbon's division was also engaged. Fighting continued for about three hours, until dark, and then there were still further efforts that night as the enemy attempted to retake the captured positions. Federal losses were heavy and included a number of officers. Patrick Kelly, commander of Second Brigade of Barlow's division, was killed, and the following were wounded: James A. Beaver, commander of Fourth Brigade of Barlow's division; Thomas R. Tannatt, commander of Second Brigade of Birney's division; and John Ramsey, commander of Fourth Brigade of Gibbon's division. Beaver was succeeded by John Hastings; Ramsey by James P. McIvor; and Tannatt temporarily by Levi B. Duff and John Willian. Later that day, Robert McAllister was assigned command of Tannatt's brigade. No successor to Kelly is noted, but later his small brigade was consolidated with Clinton D. MacDougall's Third Brigade, First Division.

During the night of June 16, 1864, Beauregard abandoned most of his front line and moved his troops back to Harrison's Creek, where they again entrenched. This line extended from Battery No. 3, at the northern end, to the old Confederate works in the vicinity of the Norfolk and Petersburg Railroad on the south.

Fighting began early June 17, 1864, when Potter's division of Ninth Corps advanced against the batteries and lines on the Shand House Ridge. During the previous night, Griffin's and Curtin's brigades of Potter's division moved up into a ravine close to the enemy works on the ridge where the Shand house stood, and each formed his brigade in two lines for the attack. Griffin's brigade was on the left of Second Corps, and directly in front of the Shand house, which was about 100 yards distant. Curtin's brigade was on the left of Griffin and a short distance to the rear of Griffin's line, and it was in front of Battery No. 15. At daylight, Potter's line moved forward and surprised the enemy on the ridge, and captured their works there with almost no opposition. Potter then pushed on until he found the enemy in their new position on the west slope beyond Harrison's Creek. This new line extended from Battery No. 3, at the northern end, to the old Confederate works in the vicinity of the Norfolk and Petersburg Railroad on the south.

Willcox's division, supported on the right by Barlow's division of Second Corps, also advanced in front of Battery No. 14. Hartranft's brigade, which had returned from Second Corps that morning, charged and suffered very heavy losses. Benjamin C. Christ's Second Brigade, which advanced on the left of Hartranft, then halted and entrenched, and remained in position there during the rest of the

day. Elisha G. Marshall's Third Brigade of Ledlie's First Division was to have supported Willcox, but Marshall was wounded and the brigade gave no effective support. Benjamin G. Barney succeeded Marshall in command. Ledlie's division, which was to have supported Potter's division, was unable to move up because of difficult terrain, and it did not join in the attack. Birney's and Gibbon's divisions of Second Corps also moved forward on the right of Ninth Corps to Harrison's Creek, and drove the enemy from the Hare House Hill.

During the evening of June 17, 1864, Ledlie's division of Ninth Corps attacked over the same ground traversed by Willcox during his unsuccessful attack that morning. Jacob P. Gould's First Brigade and Ebenezer W. Peirce's Second Brigade (commanded that day by Joseph H. Barnes) were on the first line, and they were supported by Barney's Third Brigade (formerly Marshall's brigade). Ledlie was supported in his attack by Barlow's division of Second Corps, and by Christ's brigade of Willcox's division. Christ was wounded in the attack and was succeeded by William C. Raulston. At 9:00 P.M., Crawford's division of Fifth Corps came up on the left of Ledlie and joined in the attack.

Ledlie carried a part of the enemy line and held it until 10:00 P.M., and was then driven back. James C. Carle's Third Brigade led Crawford's attack, and he was supported by Peter Lyle's First Brigade and James L. Bates' Second Brigade. Carle moved up in front of Ledlie's line when the latter moved back, and he remained there for some time, but later he withdrew and formed on the left of Ledlie.

During the day June 17, 1864, Beauregard decided to withdraw that night to a new and shorter line some 500 to 1,000 yards to the rear of the Harrison Creek line. Then, at about 12:30 A.M. June 18, 1864, Beauregard pulled back to this new position near Taylor's Creek. This new line intersected the old line in the vicinity of the Jerusalem Plank Road, and ran northward to a point on the Norfolk and Petersburg Railroad about one-half mile southwest of the Hare house. It then crossed the railroad and continued on to the north along the east side of the railroad, crossed the City Point Railroad, and ended on the Appomattox River.

About 2:15 P.M. June 18, 1864, Hancock, who was suffering from an old wound received at Gettysburg, turned over the command of Second Corps to David B. Birney. Gershom Mott assumed command of Birney's Third Division, Second Corps, and Daniel Chaplin assumed command of Mott's Third Brigade, Third Division.

Late at night June 17, 1864, Meade issued orders for an attack at 4:00 the next morning. This was to be made by Second Corps, Fifth Corps, and Ninth Corps. Martindale's division of Eighteenth Corps and Neill's division of Sixth Corps were also to be prepared to support the attack. When the corps of the army advanced the next morning, however, they found that the enemy lines of the day before had been abandoned. Meade, believing that Beauregard was soon to be reinforced by troops of Robert E. Lee's Army of Northern Virginia, ordered the corps to press forward and attack before these fresh troops reached Petersburg. In fact, however, before the attacks could be started, the reinforcements had already arrived.

At 3:00 A.M. June 18, 1864, Joseph B. Kershaw's division of Richard H. Anderson's First Corps, Army of Northern Virginia marched from the lines in front of Bermuda Hundred for Petersburg, and it was closely followed by Charles W. Field's division of Anderson's corps. George E. Pickett's division, also of Anderson's corps, was left to hold the lines at Bermuda Hundred. Kershaw arrived at 7:30 A.M., and Field came up two hours later. Kershaw relieved Johnson's division and took position with his right near the Jerusalem Plank Road, and between noon and 1:00 P.M., Field's division was placed in line on the right of Kershaw. Also that day, Ambrose P. Hill arrived with the divisions of William Mahone and Cadmus M. Wilcox of his corps. These two divisions began to arrive before Meade's assault that afternoon, and they were put in line on the right of Anderson, with their right extending across the Weldon Railroad.

Meantime, Meade had been preparing for his attack. Birney's Second Corps was at the Hare house, only about 300 yards from the new enemy main line, and it was the first corps to be in position for the attack. Ninth Corps, which was on the left of Second Corps, had some distance to travel before it was in position to attack; and Fifth Corps, which was on the left of Ninth Corps, had a still greater distance to travel, over extremely difficult terrain, and it

experienced considerable difficulty in coming up on the left of Ninth Corps. When Meade learned of the delays by Burnside and Warren in reaching their assigned positions, he ordered that the attack be made all along the front at noon June 18, 1864.

As noted above, Birney was the only commander who had his corps in position at the appointed hour, and promptly at noon he launched two attacks with Gibbon's division on the right of the Prince George Court House Road. Daniel Chaplin's Third Brigade and William R. Brewster's Fourth Brigade of Mott's division (formerly Birney's) reported to Gibbon that morning and also participated in these attacks. In addition, Robert McAllister's Second Brigade of Mott's division, temporarily under Byron R. Pierce, also charged at noon in front of the Hare house, but all these attacks were repulsed with severe losses.

Between 4:00 and 4:30 P.M., Birney again attacked, with his divisions in line, in order from left to right, as follows: Barlow, Mott, Gibbon. Mott's division attacked on the left of the Prince George Court House Road with the brigades of Madill and Chaplin, and with McAllister's brigade in front of the Hare house. Mott was supported by McIvor's brigade of Gibbon's division on the right and by an attack by Barlow's division on the left, but all attacks were repulsed with heavy losses.

Meantime, at 4:00 A.M. June 18, 1864, Ninth Corps had begun its advance, with Willcox's division in the lead and Potter's division following in support. After finding that the enemy had withdrawn from their former line, Willcox continued his advance with his division and Curtin's brigade of Potter's division. About one mile from his starting point, Willcox encountered an enemy force posted beyond the Taylor house in a cut on the Norfolk and Petersburg Railroad, and in a ravine. This was not the new enemy main line, but was about 400–500 yards in front of, and nearly parallel to, it. After severe fighting, Willcox drove the enemy from a portion of the cut, and about 3:00 P.M., Willcox and Potter charged to within 100 yards of the new enemy line beyond the railroad, but they could go no farther. Losses were great, and included Raulston, commander of Second Brigade of Willcox's division, and also his successor, George W. Travers, both of whom were wounded. Walter C. Newberry assumed temporary command of the brigade, but William Humphrey was assigned command the next day. During the attack that evening, Willcox's and Potter's divisions were under the immediate direction of John G. Parke, Burnside's chief of staff.

At 5:00 A.M., Griffin's division moved forward and prepared to attack. Finally, about noon, Jacob B. Sweitzer's Second Brigade advanced down the Norfolk Turnpike, crossed the Norfolk and Petersburg Railroad, and then moved on to a ravine close under the enemy works. All regiments of Sweitzer's brigade, except one, were on the right of the road. Chamberlain then advanced with his brigade to the ravine and formed on the left of Sweitzer. Chamberlain was seriously wounded in this encounter, and William S. Tilton was assigned command of First Brigade. Joseph J. Bartlett's Third Brigade was then sent forward in support, and was formed on a second line in rear of Tilton's brigade. Some of Griffin's men were killed within twenty feet of the enemy works.

Cutler's division also advanced at daylight. It passed through the enemy line that had been abandoned the night before, then crossed the Norfolk and Petersburg Railroad and arrived in front of the enemy's new line. Cutler formed his Fourth Division on the left of the Norfolk and Petersburg Railroad. At 3:20 P.M., Cutler advanced in two lines, with his right on the railroad. Hofmann's Second Brigade was in front, on the left of Chamberlain's (later Tilton's) brigade, and Edward S. Bragg's First Brigade was in rear of Hofmann, on the second line. Cutler reached a point within about seventy-five yards of the enemy main line. He was unable to go farther, however, but remained in his position until dark, and then withdrew. Ayres' division then came up on the left of Cutler.

Crawford's division, which had advanced the evening before to support Ledlie's division of Ninth Corps, was on the right of Griffin's division during the attacks of June 18, 1864.

On June 18, 1864, Duncan's brigade of Hinks' division was temporarily attached to Martindale's division of Eighteenth Corps, which was still in position on the extreme right of the Union line. Hinks was partially disabled by old wounds and by an injury suffered in the fighting of June 15, 1864, and remained personally in the rear with the artillery. Martindale's division, Neill's division of Sixth

Corps, and Duncan's brigade were ordered to advance and demonstrate during the attacks by Second Corps, Fifth Corps, and Ninth Corps. Martindale, as senior officer, assumed command of all troops on his part of the field, including Charles H. Tompkins' Artillery Brigade of Sixth Corps. Martindale advanced about 3:00 P.M. Stedman's brigade moved forward along the City Point-Petersburg Road, and Stannard's brigade followed. Duncan's brigade advanced in rear of Stannard on the City Point Railroad. At Pages' house, not far from Harrison's Creek, Martindale deployed his command, with Neill's division on the left, Stedman's brigade on the right, and Stannard's brigade in support. Duncan's brigade moved up to support Stannard, and reported to him for orders. There was heavy skirmishing along the front, and Martindale's troops captured some rifle pits, but there was no general assault on the main enemy line. Martindale remained in the positions gained that afternoon, and entrenched his line.

For a description of Butler's command at Bermuda Hundred during this period, see Army of the James. The complete organization of the Union forces participating in the assaults at Petersburg June 15–18, 1864 is given below in the section on Organization of the Union Forces Operating about Petersburg, and at Bermuda Hundred, Virginia, June 15–30, 1864.

Siege of Petersburg, June 18–22, 1864. During the evening of June 18, 1864, after all attempts to penetrate the enemy lines that day had failed, Grant concluded that little could be accomplished by further assaults, and he ordered that all troops of the Army of the Potomac, who had been marching and fighting since May 4, 1864, be put under cover and allowed to get some much-needed rest. In this way, the "siege" of Petersburg began. The positions gained by the army June 18, 1864 were strongly entrenched, and the two opposing lines on that part of the field remained in substantially the same positions that they then occupied until the end of the war.

Beginning on June 17, 1864, the troops of Eighteenth Corps were sent back from the Petersburg front to Bermuda Hundred, where they were to relieve Russell's and Ricketts' divisions of Sixth Corps. That day Bell, with his own brigade and Curtis' brigade of the temporary Third Division of

Eighteenth Corps, started back to Bermuda Hundred; and that night, Neill's division of Sixth Corps relieved Brooks' division of Eighteenth Corps, which returned to Bermuda Hundred the next day. Upon his arrival there, Brooks assumed command of Tenth Corps, relieving Alfred H. Terry. June 19, 1864, Bell was assigned to Tenth Corps with his two brigades, and was ordered to report to Brooks.

When Russell's and Ricketts' divisions were relieved by troops of Eighteenth Corps at Bermuda Hundred, they were ordered to rejoin the Army of the Potomac at Petersburg. Early on the morning of June 19, 1864, they crossed the Appomattox and relieved Martindale's division and Hinks' troops on the right of the Union entrenchments. Russell's division relieved Hinks' troops (Duncan's brigade) and occupied the front line of the entrenchments. Hinks' command was near Point of Rocks during the afternoon of June 19, 1864. Neill's and Ricketts' divisions, which had relieved Martindale, were formed in the rear of Russell. The transfer was not completed until June 20, 1864, and then Martindale returned to Bermuda Hundred.

When these changes were completed, the disposition of the Union forces on the lines in front of Petersburg was as follows: Wright's Sixth Corps was on the right, with its right on the Appomattox River; Birney's Second Corps was across the Prince George Court House Road near the Hare house, connecting on the right with Sixth Corps; Burnside's Ninth Corps was on the left of Second Corps, in front of the Shand house; and Warren's Fifth Corps was on the left of the line, between the Norfolk and Petersburg Railroad and the left of Ninth Corps.

This arrangement, however, was soon changed. Realizing that Petersburg could not be taken by assault, Grant decided to extend his siege lines to the west, toward the Weldon Railroad, with the object of eventually encircling the city on the south with a line that extended from the Appomattox River on the east back to the river on the west.

Second Corps and Sixth Corps were selected for the movement toward the Weldon Railroad. In addition, Grant decided to send two cavalry divisions farther to the west to cut the enemy supply lines to the west and south. He hoped to accomplish this by destroying the South Side (Lynchburg) Railroad and the Richmond and Danville Railroad in the vicinity of Burkeville, Virginia. For details of these movements, see the following sections.

June 20, 1864, Birney's Second Corps was ordered out of the entrenchments and was assigned to a position in rear of the left center of the line. The withdrawal began after dark that night. Wright extended his Sixth Corps line to the left to the Prince George Court House Road at the Hare house to relieve one division of Second Corps, and Burnside relieved the remainder of Second Corps by extending his Ninth Corps to the right to connect with Sixth Corps at the Hare house.

Warren's Fifth Corps was on the left of Ninth Corps, and June 20, 1864, its line extended to a point beyond the Norfolk and Petersburg Railroad. That night Griffin's division was withdrawn from the center of the line, and the next day it was used to extend Warren's line to the Jerusalem Plank Road at a point where a short time later Fort Sedgwick would be built.

Smith's Eighteenth Corps was reorganized at Bermuda Hundred June 19, 1864, and two days later it returned to Petersburg and relieved Wright's Sixth Corps in the entrenchments. That night, June 21, 1864, Sixth Corps moved to the extreme left of the line of the army so as to be in position to advance toward the Weldon Railroad with Second Corps.

When the above movements were completed, the line of entrenchments was occupied as follows: Eighteenth Corps was on the right, from the Appomattox River to the Hare house; Ninth Corps was in position from the Hare house to the Norfolk and Petersburg Railroad, in front of the Shand house; and Fifth Corps held the line from the left of Ninth Corps, toward the southwest, to the Jerusalem Plank Road.

Meantime, James H. Wilson's Third Cavalry Division, which had been left with the Army of the Potomac when Philip H. Sheridan departed with the other two divisions of his Cavalry Corps on his raid to Trevilian Station, had crossed the James River near Fort Powhatan June 17, 1864, and had marched to a point beyond Prince George Court House. The next day it moved on and camped at Mount Sinai Church on the Blackwater River. It was then in position to move out on its raid against the railroads.

Movement against the Petersburg and Weldon (Weldon) Railroad, June 21–23, 1864 (Engage-

ment near the Jerusalem Railroad, June 22, 1864). June 21, 1864, Birney's Second Corps and Wright's Sixth Corps began their march toward the Weldon Railroad. Second Corps crossed the Jerusalem Plank Road and advanced to the Williams house, which was about midway between the Plank Road and the Gurley house, which was near the Weldon Railroad, and it then took position on the left of Fifth Corps, generally facing west. Sixth Corps followed Second Corps and bivouacked in rear of the latter that night. The distance between the Jerusalem Plank Road and the Weldon Railroad was about three miles.

According to orders for the next day, Birney was to execute an enveloping movement by advancing his left and center while pivoting on Gibbon's division on the right, which connected with Fifth Corps near the Jerusalem Plank Road. Birney was then to entrench close to the enemy works, which at that point ran roughly east and west south of Petersburg. Wright was to advance with his Sixth Corps past the Williams house and gain possession of the Weldon Railroad, and at the same time maintain a connection with Second Corps on his right.

Sixth Corps was slow in coming up on the left of Second Corps, and at 10:00 A.M., to prevent further delay, Birney was directed to proceed with his movement independently of Sixth Corps. Consequently, when Sixth Corps advanced toward Globe Tavern, on the Weldon Railroad, June 22, 1864, it lost its connection with Second Corps, and a gap soon developed between them. Birney's movements that day were necessarily slow because he had to pass through dense woods, but despite this difficulty, Barlow and Mott struggled forward in their wheel to the right. Gibbon's division, on the right of the corps line, had only a short distance to travel, and by late afternoon had entrenched on its part of the new line. About 4:00 P.M., Mott reached his assigned position and began to throw up defensive works. At that time, Barlow was still advancing on his left.

Meantime, on June 21, 1864, the movements of Birney and Wright had been reported to Robert E. Lee, who then directed Hill to move southward from the Petersburg lines and prevent the Federals from seizing the Weldon Railroad. Hill took with him the divisions of William Mahone and Cadmus M. Wilcox, and Bushrod R. Johnson's division followed in support. The next day, Hill sent Wilcox's division

down the railroad to Globe Tavern, where he was to turn eastward and stop Sixth Corps. Mahone's division, with Johnson in support, moved out from the railroad and, under cover of a ravine, reached a point near the Johnson house, three-fourths of a mile due south of what later became Confederate Fort Walker. By this movement, Mahone had entered the gap between Second Corps and Sixth Corps, and was then on the left and rear of Birney's advancing division.

Mahone deployed in line of battle, with John C. C. Sanders' and Ambrose R. Wright's brigades on the front line, and these were supported on the right by David A. Weisiger's brigade. About 3:00 P.M., Mahone advanced and struck Barlow's unprotected flank and rapidly rolled it up. Kelly's former Second Brigade, MacDougall's Third Brigade, and John Fraser's Fourth Brigade were driven back in disorder by this unexpected attack, and eventually they retired to their rifle pits of the night before. Nelson A. Miles' First Brigade was on the second line, on the left of the division, and it too was forced to fall back. Fraser, who had assumed command of Fourth Brigade only the day before, was captured, and John Hastings assumed command of the brigade. About 5:00 P.M., Nathan T. Dushane's Second Brigade of Ayres' division, Fifth Corps was sent to support Barlow, but Dushane's brigade returned to Fifth Corps that night. When Barlow's First Division broke and fled, Mott's division became unsteady, and it too soon returned to its line of the night before without making any attempt to change front and meet Mahone's attack.

The enemy continued to press forward down Birney's line, and it soon struck the left of Gibbon's division. Gibbon was entrenched in two lines, with Timothy O'Brien's Second Brigade (formerly commanded by John Fraser until the latter was assigned command of Fourth Brigade, First Division June 21, 1864) on the left and Byron R. Pierce's First Brigade on the right of the front line. Thomas A. Smyth's Third Brigade and William Blaisdell's Fourth Brigade were on the second line. O'Brien's brigade was broken by the enemy attack on its flank, and several of its regiments and George F. McKnight's 12th Battery, New York Light Artillery were captured. The left of Pierce's First Brigade was also disorganized by the attack, but the enemy was finally stopped by the 20th Massachusetts Regiment of

First Brigade. The troops of First Brigade were rallied, and a part of Fourth Brigade was sent to Pierce to retake the line and the battery. Pierce was so slow in mounting a counterattack that the enemy was able to establish a strong position, and Blaisdell, who was ordered to supersede him, found them too strong to be driven out. The next day, Blaisdell was mortally wounded while out on the picket line. The fighting ended late in the afternoon, but skirmishing continued along the line until dark. Hill left a force to hold the railroad and returned with the rest of his command to the entrenchments at Petersburg.

The next day, June 23, 1864, Second Corps moved forward and established itself on the line from which it had been driven by Hill's attack. Sixth Corps then formed a line on the left of Second Corps, facing west toward the Weldon Railroad, and about a mile and a half from it. Pickets were sent out close to the railroad.

For the organization of Second Corps and Sixth Corps during this period, see below, Organization of the Union Forces Operating against Petersburg, and at Bermuda Hundred, Virginia, June 15–30, 1864.

Wilson's Cavalry Raid on the South Side (Lynchburg) Railroad and the Richmond and Danville Railroad, June 22, 1864–July 2, 1864. June 21, 1864, James H. Wilson was ordered to move at 2:00 the next morning with his own Third Cavalry Division, Army of the Potomac and August V. Kautz's Cavalry Division, Army of the James on an expedition against the railroads to the west and south of Petersburg. He was to proceed to the intersection of the South Side Railroad and the Richmond and Danville Railroad at Burkeville, Virginia, and upon arriving there, to destroy as much as possible of both railroads.

Kautz reported to Wilson June 21, 1864, and the next day Wilson started out on his expedition with about 5,500 men. He marched by way of Reams' Station on the Weldon Railroad and Dinwiddie Court House, and that day reached the South Side Railroad in the vicinity of Ford's Station, about fourteen miles west of Petersburg. John B. McIntosh's First Brigade was busy until late that night destroying track in the vicinity. Wilson also captured and destroyed two trains, including locomotives and cars, and burned all railroad buildings, water tanks, and woodpiles.

The next morning, June 23, 1864, Wilson sent Kautz's division ahead to Burkeville, and then with his division he followed along the railroad, destroying track as he advanced. About 2:00 P.M., he was met by William H. F. Lee's cavalry at the crossing of the railroad near Nottoway Court House, between Blacks and Whites (present-day Blackstone) and Nottoway Creek, and during the remainder of the afternoon and that evening George H. Chapman's Second Brigade was almost constantly engaged.

While Kautz destroyed the railroads around Burkeville, Wilson crossed over to the Richmond and Danville Railroad near Meherrin Station, and was joined there by Kautz. Up to that time, Wilson's cavalry had destroyed thirty miles of the South Side Railroad. From Meherrin Station, Wilson advanced along the Richmond and Danville Railroad about thirty miles to Roanoke Station near the Staunton River, and destroyed the track as he moved forward. He arrived on the Staunton River about 6:00 P.M. June 25, 1864, and there he was again attacked by William H. F. Lee's cavalry. Chapman's brigade repulsed that attack.

Kautz was unable to capture the bridge at the Staunton River, and Wilson, who was then about 100 miles from Petersburg, decided that it was time to return to the army. Beginning at 12:30 on the morning of June 26, 1864, he marched eastward through Christianville and Greensboro to the Meherrin River at Saffold's Bridge. He crossed the river there, and arrived at the "Double Bridges" on the Nottoway River at 2:00 P.M. June 28, 1864. He was then about ten miles west of Jarrett's Station on the Weldon Railroad; at that time, the left of the Army of the Potomac was about two miles east of the railroad.

Wilson then crossed the Nottoway and marched to Stony Creek. When he arrived at the crossing of the Stony Creek Station-Dinwiddie Court House Road, near Sappony Church, he was vigorously attacked by Wade Hampton's cavalry, which had been sent south from Lee's lines to intercept him. Hampton joined William H. F. Lee June 28, 1864 and, as senior officer, assumed command of both divisions. Fighting continued until 10:00 that night, during which Chapman's brigade suffered severely. About daylight June 29, 1864, Wilson withdrew and marched on the Old Petersburg Stage Road (Halifax Road) toward Reams' Station. This road was roughly parallel to the Weldon Railroad, and was about a mile west of it at Reams' Station.

Kautz, whose division was in the lead, arrived opposite Reams' Station early on the morning of June 29, 1864, and found William Mahone of A. P. Hill's corps already there with the brigades of Joseph Finegan and John C. C. Sanders of his division. Fitzhugh Lee's cavalry division had also been ordered to Reams' Station. Kautz put his troopers in position facing the railroad about one-fourth mile west of Reams' Station, which was held by the enemy. When Wilson arrived, he placed McIntosh's brigade on some high ground just west of the Old Stage Road, and to the left and rear of Kautz's line. Chapman's brigade took position on the road, to the south of McIntosh.

Wilson soon learned that Federal troops did not hold the railroad as he had expected, and instead of being near the protection of the army, he was in an isolated position and was nearly surrounded by a large enemy force. He then prepared to withdraw. The movement began shortly after noon, and almost simultaneously, the enemy attacked. Mahone's infantry advanced on the front of Wilson's line, and broke in between Kautz and McIntosh. This placed the enemy on the flank and rear of McIntosh's line and threw the whole rear area of Wilson's line into confusion. At the same time, Fitzhugh Lee attacked on the left of the Federal line.

Wilson ordered that the wagons and caissons be destroyed, and he then retreated by the Stage Road to the south side of the Nottoway River. Kautz was unable to join the main column, but he succeeded in crossing the Weldon Railroad between Reams' Station and Rowanty Creek and reached the lines of the Army of the Potomac after dark.

Wilson continued his march back toward Jarrett's Station and, after marching all night, struck the Weldon Railroad at dawn June 30, 1864. He then marched east by way of Peter's Bridge on the Nottoway, and then Waverly, and reached Blunt's Bridge on the Blackwater River at midnight. Wilson crossed the Blackwater July 1, 1864, and the next afternoon rejoined the Cavalry Corps, Army of the Potomac at Light House Point.

Siege of Petersburg, June 23–30, 1864. Second Corps and Sixth Corps remained on the left of the army, between the Jerusalem Plank Road and the Weldon Railroad, during the rest of the month, but there were some changes in position. June 23, 1864, John W. Turner's Second Division, Tenth Corps (formerly commanded by Adelbert Ames) arrived at Petersburg from Bermuda Hundred and relieved Willcox's Third Division, Ninth Corps, which was on the right of the Ninth Corps' line. Willcox then moved to the left and relieved Crawford's division of Fifth Corps. Crawford, in turn, moved about three miles to the left and relieved Gibbon's division of Second Corps near the Plank Road. June 24, 1864, Gibbon took position on the left of Sixth Corps.

June 29, 1864, Sixth Corps advanced to Reams' Station on the Weldon Railroad, and its former place in the line was occupied by Gibbon's division. The next day, Sixth Corps destroyed about three miles of the railroad and then moved back to the Jerusalem Plank Road. All along the rest of the line, the troops were generally engaged in skirmishing and working on the entrenchments.

June 27, 1864, Hancock returned to the army and resumed command of Second Corps.

Organization of the Forces Operating against Petersburg, and at Bermuda Hundred, Virginia, June 15–30, 1864.

ARMY OF THE POTOMAC
George G. Meade

SECOND CORPS, Winfield S. Hancock, to June 18, 1864
  David B. Birney, to June 27, 1864
  Winfield S. Hancock

First Division, Francis C. Barlow
  First Brigade, Nelson A. Miles
  Second Brigade, Patrick Kelly, to June 16, 1864, killed
  Third Brigade, Clinton D. MacDougall, to June 27, 1864
  Fourth Brigade, James A. Beaver, to June 16, 1864, wounded
    John Hastings, to June 21, 1864
    John Fraser, to June 22, 1864, captured
    John Hastings

Note. Second Brigade and Third Brigade were consolidated June 27, 1864 to form the Consolidated Brigade, and MacDougall was assigned command.

Second Division, John Gibbon
  First Brigade, Byron R. Pierce, to June 22, 1864
  Major William F. Smith, to June 27, 1864

Francis E. Pierce
Second Brigade, John Fraser, to June 21, 1864
  Timothy O'Brien, to June 26, 1864
  James P. McIvor
Third Brigade, Thomas A. Smyth
Fourth Brigade, John Ramsey, to June 16, 1864, wounded
  James P. McIvor, to June 19, 1864
  William Blaisdell, to June 23, 1864, killed
  James P. McIvor, to June 26, 1864

Note. Second Division was reorganized June 26, 1864, as follows: Second Brigade was broken up and the regiments were assigned to First Brigade and Third Brigade; and the designation of Fourth Brigade was changed to Second Brigade.

Third Division, David B. Birney, to June 18, 1864
  Gershom Mott, June 27, 1864
  David B. Birney
First Brigade, Thomas W. Egan, to June 16, 1864
  Henry J. Madill
Second Brigade, Thomas R. Tannatt, to June 16, 1864, wounded
  Levi B. Duff, June 16, 1864
  John Willian, June 16, 1864
  Robert McAllister, to June 24, 1864
  Byron R. Pierce
Third Brigade, Gershom Mott, to June 18, 1864
  Daniel Chaplin, to June 27, 1864
  Gershom Mott
Fourth Brigade, William R. Brewster

Artillery Brigade, John C. Tidball
  John G. Hazard
  6th Battery (F), Maine Light Artillery, Edwin Dow
  10th Battery, Massachusetts Light Artillery, Henry J. Sleeper
  1st Battery, New Hampshire Light Artillery, Frederick M. Edgell
  Battery B, 1st New Jersey Light Artillery, A. Judson Clark
  3rd Battery, New Jersey Light Artillery, Christian Woerner
  4th New York Heavy Artillery, James H. Wood
  Battery G, 1st New York Light Artillery, Nelson Ames
  11th Battery, New York Light Artillery, John E. Burton
  12th Battery, New York Light Artillery, George F. McKnight
  Battery F, 1st Pennsylvania Light Artillery, R. Bruce Ricketts
  Battery A, 1st Rhode Island Light Artillery, G. Lyman Dwight
  Battery B, 1st Rhode Island Light Artillery, T. Frederick Brown

Battery K, 4th United States Artillery, John W. Roder
Batteries C and I, 5th United States Artillery, James Gilliss

FIFTH CORPS, Gouverneur K. Warren

First Division, Charles Griffin
  First Brigade, Joshua L. Chamberlain, to June 18, 1864, wounded
    William S. Tilton
  Second Brigade, Jacob B. Sweitzer
  Third Brigade, Joseph J. Bartlett

Second Division, Romeyn B. Ayres
  First Brigade, Edgar M. Gregory, to June 20, 1864
    Joseph Hayes
  Second Brigade, Nathan T. Dushane
  Third Brigade, J. Howard Kitching

Third Division, Samuel W. Crawford
  First Brigade, Peter Lyle
  Second Brigade, James L. Bates, to June 25, 1864
    Henry Baxter
  Third Brigade, James Carle

Note. Bates' term of service expired and he was relieved June 25, 1864.

Fourth Division, Lysander Cutler
  First Brigade, Edward S. Bragg
  Second Brigade, J. William Hofmann

Artillery Brigade, Charles S. Wainwright
  3rd Battery (C), Massachusetts Light Artillery, Aaron F. Walcott
  5th Battery (E), Massachusetts Light Artillery, Charles A. Phillips
  9th Battery, Massachusetts Light Artillery, John Bigelow
  Battery B, 1st New York Light Artillery, Robert E. Rogers
  Battery C, 1st New York Light Artillery, Almont Barnes
  Battery D, 1st New York Light Artillery, Lester I. Richardson
  Battery E, 1st New York Light Artillery, James B. Hazelton
  Battery H, 1st New York Light Artillery, Charles E. Mink
  Battery L, 1st New York Light Artillery, George Breck
  15th Battery, New York Light Artillery, Patrick Hart
  Battery B, 1st Pennsylvania Light Artillery, James H. Cooper
  Battery B, 4th United States Artillery, James Stewart

Battery D, 5th United States Artillery, Benjamin F. Rittenhouse

SIXTH CORPS, Horatio G. Wright

First Division, David A. Russell
First Brigade, William H. Penrose
Second Brigade, Emory Upton
Third Brigade, Gideon Clark
Fourth Brigade, Nelson Cross, to June 20, 1864
  Joseph E. Hamblin

Note. Cross was ordered home for muster out June 20, 1864.

Second Division, Thomas H. Neill, to June 21, 1864
  Frank Wheaton, to June 28, 1864
  George W. Getty
First Brigade, Frank Wheaton, to June 21, 1864
  Joseph F. Ballier, to June 28, 1864
  Frank Wheaton
Second Brigade, Lewis A. Grant
Third Brigade, Daniel D. Bidwell
Fourth Brigade, Oliver Edwards

Note. Neill was transferred to Eighteenth Corps June 21, 1864.

Third Division, James B. Ricketts
First Brigade, William S. Truex
Second Brigade, Benjamin F. Smith

Cavalry Detachment, Timothy M. Bryan, Jr.

Artillery Brigade, Charles H. Tompkins
  4th Battery (D), Maine Light Artillery, Charles W. White
  5th Battery (E), Maine Light Artillery, Greenleaf T. Stevens
  1st Battery (A), Massachusetts Light Artillery, William H. McCartney
  Battery A, 1st New Jersey Light Artillery, William Hexamer
  1st Battery, New York Light Artillery, Andrew Cowan
  3rd Battery, New York Light Artillery, William A. Harn
  2nd Battalion, 9th New York Heavy Artillery, James W. Snyder
  Battery H, 1st Ohio Light Artillery, Stephen W. Dorsey
  Battery C, 1st Rhode Island Light Artillery, Richard Waterman
  Battery E, 1st Rhode Island Light Artillery, William B. Rhodes
  Battery G, 1st Rhode Island Light Artillery, George W. Adams
  Battery E, 5th United States Artillery, John R. Brinckle

Battery M, 5th United States Artillery, James Mc-Knight

NINTH CORPS, Ambrose E. Burnside

First Division, James H. Ledlie
First Brigade, Jacob P. Gould
Second Brigade, Ebenezer W. Peirce, June 17, 1864
  Joseph H. Barnes, in command June 17, 1864
Third Brigade, Elisha G. Marshall, to June 17, 1864, wounded
  Benjamin G. Barney
Artillery
  2nd Battery (B), Maine Light Artillery, Albert F. Thomas
  14th Battery, Massachusetts Light Artillery, Joseph W. B. Wright
  27th Battery, New York Light Artillery, John B. Eaton

Note. First Division was reorganized June 18, 1864 as follows: The regiments of Second Brigade, except Ebenezer W. Peirce's 29th Massachusetts, were transferred to First Brigade; Third Brigade, to which 29th Massachusetts was added, was redesignated as Second Brigade; and Third Brigade, First Division was discontinued.

Second Division, Robert B. Potter
First Brigade, John I. Curtin, to June 18, 1864, wounded
  Henry Pleasants
Second Brigade, Simon G. Griffin
Artillery
  11th Battery, Massachusetts Light Artillery, Edward J. Jones
  19th Battery, New York Light Artillery, Edward W. Rogers

Third Division, Orlando B. Willcox
First Brigade, John F. Hartranft
Second Brigade, Benjamin C. Christ, to June 17, 1864, wounded
  William C. Raulston, to June 18, 1864, wounded
  George W. Travers, June 18, 1864, wounded
  Walter C. Newberry, to June 19, 1864
  William Humphrey
Artillery
  7th Battery (G), Maine Light Artillery, Adelbert B. Twitchell
  34th Battery, New York Light Artillery, Jacob Roemer

Fourth Division, Edward Ferrero
First Brigade, Joshua K. Sigfried
Second Brigade, Henry G. Thomas
Artillery

Battery D, Pennsylvania Light Artillery, George W. Durell

3rd Battery, Vermont Light Artillery, Romeo H. Start

Note. Fourth Division guarded the trains of the army during the Richmond Campaign, and rejoined Ninth Corps June 19, 1864.

CAVALRY CORPS, Philip H. Sheridan

First Cavalry Division, Alfred T. A. Torbert
First Brigade, George A. Custer
Second Brigade, Thomas C. Devin
Reserve Brigade, Wesley Merritt

Second Cavalry Division, David McM. Gregg
First Brigade, Henry E. Davies, Jr.
Second Brigade, J. Irvin Gregg

Third Cavalry Division, James H. Wilson
First Brigade, John B. McIntosh
Second Brigade, George H. Chapman

Horse Artillery Brigade, James M. Robertson
Batteries H and I, 1st United States Artillery, Alanson M. Randol
Battery K, 1st United States Artillery, Thomas Ward
Battery A, 2nd United States Artillery, Neil Dennison
Batteries B and L, 2nd United States Artillery, Edward Heaton
Battery D, 2nd United States Artillery, Edward B. Williston
Battery M, 2nd United States Artillery, Alexander C. M. Pennington, Jr.
Battery C, 3rd United States Artillery, Dunbar R. Ransom
Batteries C and E, 4th United States Artillery, Charles L. Fitzhugh

Note. Sheridan, with First Cavalry Division and Third Cavalry Division, crossed to the south side of the James River June 27–28, 1864, at the close of his Trevilian Station Raid. He moved to Reams' Station on the Weldon Railroad June 29, 1865.

ARMY OF THE JAMES
Benjamin F. Butler

Note. During the period June 15–30, 1864, the Army of the James consisted of Tenth Corps and Eighteenth Corps, but both corps were reorganized by an order of June 19, 1864. Therefore, it is necessary to give the organization of each corps for the periods, both before and after that date.

TENTH CORPS (June 15–19, 1864), William H. Terry, to June 18, 1864
William T. H. Brooks

First Division, Robert S. Foster
First Brigade, Joshua B. Howell
Second Brigade, Joseph R. Hawley
Third Brigade, Harris M. Plaisted

Artillery, Alfred P. Rockwell
Artillery of Second Division and Third Division

Note. For the batteries of Tenth Corps during this period, see below.

TENTH CORPS (June 19–30), William T. H. Brooks

First Division, Robert S. Foster, to June 23, 1864
Alfred H. Terry
First Brigade, Joshua B. Howell
Second Brigade, Joseph R. Hawley
Third Brigade, Harris M. Plaisted
Artillery, Loomis L. Langdon
1st Battery, Connecticut Light Artillery, James B. Clinton
5th Battery, New Jersey Light Artillery, Zenas C. Warren
Battery C, 3rd Rhode Island Heavy Artillery, Martin S. James
Battery M, 1st United States Artillery, Loomis L. Langdon

Note. June 23, 1864, Foster was assigned to command Third Brigade, and was sent to Deep Bottom to guard the pontoon bridges over the James River at that point.

Second Division, Adelbert Ames, to June 19, 1864
John W. Turner
First Brigade, N. Martin Curtis
Second Brigade, William B. Barton
Third Brigade, Louis Bell
Artillery, George T. Woodbury
4th Battery, New Jersey Light Artillery, Charles R. Doane
4th Battery, Wisconsin Light Artillery, Martin McDevitt
Battery D, 1st United States Artillery, Robert M. Hall
Battery E, 3rd United States Artillery, John B. Myrick
Battery D, 4th United States Artillery, Frank Powell

Note 1. Ames was assigned to Eighteenth Corps June 19, 1864.
Note 2. Second Division, Tenth Corps was formerly the temporary Third Division, Eighteenth Corps, which was

formed by the consolidation of Second Division and Third Division of Tenth Corps during the movement of Eighteenth Corps to Cold Harbor.

Note 3. Woodbury's artillery of Second Division was attached to Third Division, Tenth Corps.

Third Division, Orris S. Ferry
    First Brigade, Gilman Marston
    Second Brigade, James B. Armstrong
    Artillery
        33rd Battery, New York Light Artillery, Alger M. Wheeler

Note 1. Third Division was organized June 19, 1864 from one-hundred-day Ohio regiments that had arrived at Bermuda Hundred June 12–14, 1864 to reinforce Butler. These regiments were mustered out between August 20, 1864 and September 22, 1864.

Note 2. The artillery of Second Division was attached to Third Division.

EIGHTEENTH CORPS (June 15–19, 1864), William F. Smith

First Division, William T. H. Brooks, to June 18, 1864
    Gilman Marston
    First Brigade, Gilman Marston, to June 18, 1864
        Edgar M. Cullen
    Second Brigade, Hiram Burnham
    Third Brigade, Guy V. Henry

Note. Brooks was assigned command of Tenth Corps June 18, 1864.

Second Division, John H. Martindale
    First Brigade, George J. Stannard
    Second Brigade, Griffin A. Stedman

Third Division, Adelbert Ames
    First Brigade, William B. Barton
    Second Brigade, N. Martin Curtis
    Third Brigade, Louis Bell

Note 1. Second Brigade and Third Brigade took part in the assaults at Petersburg, but Ames, with Barton's brigade, remained on the lines at Bermuda Hundred.

Note 2. June 19, 1864, the designation of Third Division, Eighteenth Corps was changed to Second Division, Tenth Corps.

Note 3. Edward W. Hinks' division was nominally a part of Eighteenth Corps, but during the operations at Cold Harbor it was detached and under the direct orders of Butler.

EIGHTEENTH CORPS (June 19–30, 1864), William F. Smith

First Division, Gilman Marston, to June 20, 1864
    George J. Stannard
    First Brigade, Edgar M. Cullen
    Second Brigade, Hiram Burnham
    Third Brigade, Guy V. Henry

Note. Marston was assigned to Tenth Corps June 20, 1864.

Second Division, John H. Martindale
    First Brigade, George J. Stannard, to June 20, 1864
        Alexander Piper
    Second Brigade, Griffin A. Stedman
    Third Brigade, Augustus A. Gibson, to June 20, 1864
        Adelbert Ames

Note. Third Brigade was organized June 19, 1864 from William L. Schley's 5th Maryland from the Middle Department; Harrison S. Fairchild's 89th New York from First Brigade, Second Division, Eighteenth Corps; and Augustus A. Gibson's 2nd Pennsylvania Heavy Artillery from the Department of Washington.

Third Division, Edward W. Hinks
    First Brigade, Edward A. Wild, to June 23, 1864
        John H. Holman
    Second Brigade, Samuel A. Duncan

Note. By the reorganizational order of June 19, 1864, the former temporary Third Division, Eighteenth Corps was assigned to Tenth Corps as Second Division. The new Third Division was then reorganized from Hinks' regiments of United States Colored Troops.

Artillery Brigade, Henry S. Burton
    Battery E, 3rd New York Light Artillery, Lewis H. Mowers
    Battery K, 3rd New York Light Artillery, James R. Angel
    Battery M, 3rd New York Light Artillery, John H. Howell
    7th Battery, New York Light Artillery, Martin V. McIntyre
    16th Battery, New York Light Artillery, Richard H. Lee
    Battery F, 1st Rhode Island Light Artillery, Thomas Simpson
    Battery B, 1st United States Artillery, Michael Leahy
    Battery L, 4th United States Artillery, Henry B. Beecher
    Battery A, 5th United States Artillery, Israel Ludlow

In addition to Tenth Corps and Eighteenth Corps, the following were a part of Butler's Department of Virginia and North Carolina:

Signal Corps, Lemuel B. Norton

Naval Brigade, Charles K. Graham

First New York Engineers, Joseph Walker

Siege Artillery, Henry L. Abbot

  1st Connecticut Heavy Artillery, Henry L. Abbot

  12th New York Heavy Artillery (Companies A and H),
    William Pendrell

  3rd Pennsylvania Heavy Artillery (Company M),
    Frederick Korte

Cavalry Division, August V. Kautz

  First Brigade, Simon H. Mix, to June 15, 1864, killed
    Robert M. West

  Second Brigade, Samuel P. Spear

Unattached Troops

  36th United States Colored Troops, Alonzo G. Draper

  38th United States Colored Troops, Dexter E. Clapp

  1st New York Mounted Rifles, Benjamin F. Onderdonk

  13th Massachusetts Heavy Artillery, John Pickering,
    Jr.

  Battery E, 1st Pennsylvania Light Artillery, Thomas G.
    Orwig

  Battery B, 2nd United States Colored Light Artillery,
    Francis C. Choate

OPERATIONS OF JULY 1864

Siege of Petersburg, July 1, 1864–July 26, 1864.
During the greater part of July 1864, the army was
principally engaged in strengthening the entrenchments and skirmishing with the enemy, but there
were also some local attacks along the front. Near
the end of the month, two offensive operations were
undertaken. On July 26, 1864, Hancock's Second
Corps and Sheridan with two divisions of cavalry
were sent north of the James River to make a
demonstration against Richmond; and July 30,
1864, a mine was exploded under the Confederate
works on the front of Ninth Corps, and this was
followed by an unsuccessful attempt to break
through the enemy line and reach Petersburg. For
details of these operations, see below.

During the first week in July 1864, Jubal A. Early
invaded Maryland with a strong force, and then
marched eastward to threaten Baltimore and
Washington. Grant reacted promptly to this threat
by sending reinforcements to the troops defending
the capital. July 6, 1864, James B. Ricketts' Third
Division, Sixth Corps was withdrawn from the left
of the line of entrenchments at Petersburg, and sent

to Baltimore. Three days later, Early defeated a
Union force under Lewis Wallace, including
Ricketts' division, on the Monocacy River near
Frederick, Maryland. When Grant learned of this, he
sent Horatio G. Wright with the other two divisions
of his Sixth Corps to Washington. Sixth Corps did
not rejoin the army at Petersburg until December
1864. For further information about the organization
and activities of Sixth Corps after it left the Army of
the Potomac, see Early's Washington Raid (and
Operations in the Shenandoah Valley, Maryland,
and Pennsylvania); and also Shenandoah Valley
Campaign (Sheridan).

July 9, 1864, Meade directed that operations on
the front of Gouverneur K. Warren's Fifth Corps and
Ambrose E. Burnside's Ninth Corps be conducted
by regular siege approaches, and these two corps
remained in their entrenchments during the month.
On the right of Ninth Corps, John W. Turner's
Second Division, Tenth Corps and William F.
Smith's Eighteenth Corps continued to hold their
positions on the line until July 29, 1864.

After the departure of Sixth Corps from
Petersburg, the left flank of the army was drawn in
to the Jerusalem Plank Road to shorten the line.
Second Corps remained on the left of Fifth Corps
until July 12, 1864, and it then destroyed its works
and massed its divisions near the Williams house. It
then moved the next day to the vicinity of Deserted
House in the rear of Fifth Corps. Two days later,
John Gibbon's Second Division, Second Corps was
sent to the left of Meade's line. Second Corps
remained in those positions until the evening of July
26, 1864, and then it began its march to the north
side of the James River (see below).

During the month, Philip H. Sheridan's cavalry
divisions, which had rejoined the army from their
Trevilian Station Raid, remained near Lighthouse
Point, with one division on duty on the left of the
army. July 26, 1864, Sheridan, with Alfred T. A.
Torbert's First Cavalry Division and David McM.
Gregg's Second Cavalry Division, marched toward
Deep Bottom to join Hancock's infantry in the
demonstration north of the James River (see below).

Smith was relieved from command of Eighteenth
Corps July 19, 1864, and John H. Martindale com-
manded the corps temporarily until July 22, 1864.
On that date, Edward O. C. Ord assumed command.
There was also a change in command of Tenth Corps

during the month. July 18, 1864, Alfred H. Terry relieved William T. H. Brooks, and exercised temporary command of the corps until July 23, 1864, at which time he was relieved by David B. Birney. Francis C. Barlow assumed command of Birney's First Division, Second Corps.

For details of the organization of Grant's forces during this period, see below, at the end of this section on Operations of July 1864.

Demonstration on the North Bank of the James River, Engagement at Deep Bottom (or Darbytown, Strawberry Plains, New Market Road), Virginia, July 26–29, 1864. July 25, 1864, Grant decided to send Hancock's Second Corps and Sheridan with two cavalry divisions to the north bank of the James River at Deep Bottom. Once across the river, the cavalry was to make a dash toward Richmond if there appeared to be any chance of success, but if not, it was to move northward and destroy the Virginia Central Railroad and the Richmond, Fredericksburg, and Potomac Railroad from the vicinity of Richmond to to the North and South Anna rivers. August V. Kautz's Cavalry Division, Army of the James was also ordered to join Sheridan at Deep Bottom for this expedition. Second Corps was to move up to Chaffin's Bluff to support the cavalry if the latter reached Richmond, and it was also to prevent enemy troops from crossing the James River to engage Sheridan. As another objective of this expedition, it was hoped that Hancock would draw off enemy forces from the Petersburg front, and thus indirectly aid Ninth Corps in an assault that was scheduled to follow the explosion of a mine under the enemy works on July 30, 1864 (see below).

Hancock with his Second Corps and Sheridan with Torbert's and Gregg's cavalry divisions marched for Deep Bottom on the afternoon of July 26, 1864. Second Corps crossed the Appomattox River at Point of Rocks and the cavalry at Broadway Landing, and at 2:00 the next morning Second Corps, followed by the cavalry, began crossing the James River at Deep Bottom on the pontoon bridge below Bailey's Creek. Robert S. Foster, with his Third Brigade of Alfred H. Terry's First Division, Tenth Corps, held the bridgehead north of the James at the two bridges.

After crossing the river, Hancock advanced

toward the New Market Road. Francis C. Barlow's First Division was in the lead, and Gershom Mott's Third Division advanced on the right and John Gibbon's Second Division on the left. There was some skirmishing along the front, and the line paused, but it soon moved forward again with Gibbon's division in the lead. Hancock then swung to the left and advanced on the New Market Road to Bailey's Creek, where he found the enemy intrenched on the west bank of the creek, from its mouth to the vicinity of Fussell's Mill. This line was held by Cadmus M. Wilcox's and Joseph B. Kershaw's divisions of Richard H. Anderson's corps, which had arrived in the area before Hancock's movement began. These two divisions were joined by Henry Heth's division of Ambrose P. Hill's corps July 27, 1864. Gibbon's division held the advanced position on the New Market Road, and Barlow's and Mott's division were pushed forward to the Long Bridge Road, where they connected with Torbert's cavalry on the right. Gregg's cavalry was in the rear toward Malvern Hill, at Strawberry Plains.

At 5:00 on the morning of July 28, 1864, Henry W. Birge's First Brigade of Cuvier Grover's Second Division of Nineteenth Corps, which had just arrived from New Orleans in the Department of the Gulf, reported to Hancock and relieved Gibbon's division in its advanced position on the New Market Road. Sheridan was also placed under Hancock's orders July 28, 1864.

Grant had instructed Hancock to make no assault on the enemy works, but instead to attempt to turn their position with the cavalry while Second Corps and Foster's brigade demonstrated on the front of the entrenchments. On the morning of July 28, 1864, however, as Gregg advanced along the New Market Road, he was attacked by Kershaw's division and driven back. Gibbon's infantry division was sent to support Gregg, but Gregg's troopers, fighting dismounted, drove the enemy back before Gibbon arrived. Kautz's cavalry was engaged that day near Malvern Hill.

The mine on Burnside's front at Petersburg was to be exploded July 30, 1864, and on the night of July 28, 1864, Mott's division was sent back to the Petersburg lines to relieve Ord's Eighteenth Corps and John W. Turner's Second Division, Tenth Corps so that the latter would be available to support

Burnside's attack. Mott occupied the entrenchments from the right of Ninth Corps to the Appomattox River. The following night, Hancock and Sheridan recrossed the James River, and the two divisions of Second Corps marched to Petersburg, where they massed in rear of Ninth Corps.

The troops participating in the operations near Deep Bottom July 27–29, 1864 were as follows:

SECOND CORPS, Winfield S. Hancock

First Division, Francis C. Barlow
    First Brigade, Nelson A. Miles
    Consolidated Brigade, Levin Crandell
    Fourth Brigade, K. Oscar Broady

Note. The Consolidated Brigade was formed by the consolidation of Second Brigade and Third Brigade June 27, 1864. Clinton D. MacDougall commanded the brigade June 27 to July 2, 1864.

Second Division, John Gibbon
    First Brigade, Francis E. Pierce
    Second Brigade, Mathew Murphy
    Third Brigade, Thomas A. Smyth

Third Division, Gershom Mott
    First Brigade, T. Regis De Trobriand
    Second Brigade, Daniel Chaplin, to July 28, 1864
        Henry J. Madill
    Third Brigade, Robert McAllister

Artillery Brigade, John G. Hazard
    10th Battery, Massachusetts Light Artillery, J. Henry Sleeper
    Battery B, 1st Rhode Island Light Artillery. T. Frederick Brown
    Battery F, 1st Pennsylvania Light Artillery, R. Bruce Ricketts
    Batteries C and I, 5th United States Artillery, James Gilliss
    1st Battery, New Hampshire Light Artillery, Frederick M. Edgell
    6th Battery (F), Maine Light Artillery, Edwin B. Dow
    3rd Battery, New Jersey Light Artillery, Christian Woerner

Note. Sleeper's and Brown's batteries were assigned to First Division; Ricketts' and Gilliss' batteries were assigned to Second Division; and Edgell's, Dow's, and Woerner's batteries were assigned to Third Division.

TENTH CORPS

First Division
    Third Brigade, Robert S. Foster

NINETEENTH CORPS

Second Division
    First Brigade, Henry W. Birge

CAVALRY, Philip H. Sheridan

First Cavalry Division, Alfred T. A. Torbert
    First Brigade, George A. Custer
    Second Brigade, Thomas C. Devin
    Reserve Brigade, Wesley Merritt

Second Cavalry Division, David McM. Gregg
    First Brigade, Henry E. Davies, Jr.
    Second Brigade, J. Irvin Gregg

Kautz's Division, August V. Kautz
    First Brigade, Robert M. West
    Second Brigade, Samuel P. Spear

Note. Torbert's and Gregg's divisions belonged to the Cavalry Corps, Army of the Potomac, and Kautz's Division to the Army of the James.

Petersburg Mine Assault, July 30, 1864. As a result of the attacks of June 17–18, 1864, Burnside's Ninth Corps had gained a position beyond the deep cut of the Norfolk and Petersburg Railroad, which was within about 130 yards of the enemy line. This position was in front of a strong enemy work called Elliott's Salient (sometimes called Pegram's Salient because William J. Pegram's artillery was posted there), and it was almost due west of the place where Fort Morton was later built.

In the latter part of June 1864, Robert B. Potter, commander of Second Division, Ninth Corps, proposed to Burnside that a mine be excavated under Elliott's Salient. The idea was approved and work was started June 25, 1864, under the direction of Henry Pleasants, who originally suggested the plan to Potter, to whose division his regiment belonged. Pleasants was in command of the 48th Pennsylvania Infantry, a regiment composed largely of miners from the coal region of Schuylkill County, Pennsylvania. The mine was completed and ready for charging July 23, 1864, and plans were made for an infantry assault that was to follow the explosion, which was scheduled for 3:30 A.M. July 30, 1864. Burnside's Ninth Corps was to make the initial attack, and most of the army was to be prepared to follow up any penetration of the enemy line.

Preparations were made for the assault during the

night of July 29, 1864. The troops of Ninth Corps moved up to their assigned positions in front of Elliott's Salient. Warren, on the left of Ninth Corps, left Samuel W. Crawford's Third Division to hold the trenches on the Fifth Corps' line, and he concentrated the rest of the corps on the right of his position, next to Ninth Corps, to support the latter in its attack. Gershom Mott's Third Division, Second Corps, which had returned the night before from Hancock's expedition north of the James River, moved up and relieved Edward O. C. Ord's Eighteenth Corps and John W. Turner's Second Division, Tenth Corps in the trenches on the right of Ninth Corps. When this exchange was completed, Mott held the line of entrenchments from the right of Ninth Corps to the Appomattox River. Ord withdrew at dark and moved with Eighteenth Corps and Turner's division to the rear of Ninth Corps. Hiram Burnham's First Division and Joseph B. Carr's Third Division of Eighteenth Corps were then placed in the trenches on Burnside's front, where they relieved a part of Ninth Corps, for the attack the next morning. Carr was placed in command of both divisions. Adelbert Ames' Second Division, Eighteenth Corps and Turner's division of Tenth Corps were held in rear of Ninth Corps as reserve supports.

When Hancock returned from Deep Bottom with the rest of Second Corps, he moved into position in rear of Mott's division, where he would be in position to follow up the assault of Ninth Corps if it was successful. Hancock resumed command of Mott's division.

On the morning of July 30, 1864, the troops holding the Confederate line of entrenchments were in position as follows: Robert F. Hoke's division was on the left, and it extended southward from the Appomattox River for nearly a mile. Bushrod R. Johnson's was on the right of Hoke, and his brigades were, in order from left to right, as follows: Matt W. Ransom's, Stephen Elliott's, Henry A. Wise's (commanded by John T. Goode), and Alfred Colquitt's. Colquitt's brigade belonged to Hoke's division, but it was temporarily assigned to Johnson in place of Archibald Gracie's brigade, which was serving with Hoke. Johnson's line ended on the right at Rives' Salient, about one-fourth mile northeast of the point where the enemy line crossed the Jerusalem Plank Road. On the right of Johnson, west of Rives' Salient, was William Mahone's division and half of Cadmus M. Wilcox's division of A. P. Hill's corps.

The mine was on the front of Johnson's division at the center of Elliott's brigade, about 200 yards north of the Baxter Road. It was set to explode at 3:30 A.M., but there was a delay because the fuse failed to ignite at a place where it had been spliced, and it was not until 4:45 A.M., after the fuse had been repaired, that the explosion occurred. There was tremendous destruction in the vicinity of the mine and a large crater was formed, and for some time the enemy trenches were abandoned for a distance of 200–300 yards on both sides of the crater. Then, a few minutes later, Ledlie's division moved forward, with Elisha G. Marshall's Second Brigade in the lead and William F. Bartlett's First Brigade close behind. Contrary to Meade's orders, however, Ledlie's troops entered the crater instead of quickly passing on beyond as ordered. Thereafter, all attempts to advance from the crater failed.

Potter's division of Ninth Corps followed Ledlie, with Simon G. Griffin's Second Brigade in front. Griffin moved to the right of the crater and took possession of the partially abandoned entrenchments. After some severe fighting over the works, Zenas R. Bliss' First Brigade came up on the right of Griffin and drove the enemy back.

Orlando B. Willcox's Third Division followed Ledlie's division about 5:00 A.M. and advanced on his left. John F. Hartranft, with three regiments of his First Brigade, occupied the works on the left of the crater, and his other regiments remained in the rear. William Humphreys, after some effort, moved up with his Second Brigade and captured a part of the enemy line on the left of Hartranft. Willcox's men, however, were unable to proceed farther, and they withdrew about 2:30 P.M.

At 6:00 A.M., Turner's division of Tenth Corps and Edward Ferrero's Fourth Division of Ninth Corps, which consisted of regiments of United States Colored Troops, were also ordered to advance. Ferrero's division, however, did not get out of the trenches until 8:00 A.M. It had been ordered to pass the crater and move on beyond, but despite all efforts of the officers to prevent it, many of the men entered the crater, and many others halted in rear of it. All was confusion at that time, and to make matters worse, Ledlie and Ferrero did not accompany their men forward, but remained in the rear under cover.

Ord had trouble in getting his troops forward through the Ninth Corps' line, because the entrenchments had not been properly prepared for the attack, and also because they were crowded with men. Turner was forced to wait until Potter's division of Ninth Corps passed before he was able to advance, and then Louis Bell's Third Brigade moved forward to the right of Potter's division and gained possession of about a hundred yards of the enemy works. William B. Coan's Second Brigade moved still farther to the right and then attacked, but it was unable to drive the enemy from their works. N. Martin Curtis' First Brigade remained in rear of the other brigades. Adelbert Ames' Second Division of Eighteenth Corps was also ordered to attack, but because of the difficulty of moving forward through the trenches and the crowded conditions in front, it was unable to do so.

At 9:45 A.M., Meade suspended further offensive movements, and he sent orders to Burnside to withdraw his troops. A second order, sent at 10:00 A.M., directed Burnside to use discretion, and to withdraw his troops when he could safely do so.

Meantime, Lee had taken steps to recover the lost works. When he learned of the explosion of the mine, he ordered Mahone to bring up two of his brigades from the Wilcox farm, about two miles southwest of the crater, and to prepare them for a counterattack. The place selected for Mahone to form his brigades for the attack was in a swale or ravine that ran roughly parallel to the Confederate entrenchments, about midway between the entrenchments and the Jerusalem Plank Road to the west. Mahone started at once with the brigades of David A. Weisiger and Ambrose R. Wright, and a short time later, John C. C. Sanders' brigade, also of Mahone's division, was ordered to follow. Hill, the corps commander, accompanied Mahone's division to the front. While these troops were on the march, Wise's brigade (commanded by Goode) and the survivors of Elliott's brigade had, with the help of the artillery, succeeded in confining the Union troops to the area originally captured in their first advance three hours earlier.

Mahone, with Weisiger's brigade, arrived at his assigned position and at 9:00 A.M. began his counterattack. Weisiger struck Henry G. Thomas' Second Brigade of Ferrero's division as it was trying to advance, and drove it, and also Joshua K. Sigfried's First Brigade of the division, back in disorder. As these two brigades fell back, they carried with them many of Potter's troops, both brigades of Turner's division, and many of the troops that had been lying in rear of the crater. Weisiger regained nearly all of the captured entrenchments north of the crater, but he advanced no farther.

Wright's brigade came up next, and at 11:00 A.M. attacked on the right of Weisiger. As it advanced, it came under a heavy fire, and it moved to the left and failed to clear the crater. Finally, at 1:00 P.M., Sanders' brigade came up and joined in the attack. Aided by Elliott's and Wise's brigades, it succeeded in entering the crater. There ensued a short but deadly struggle, and finally the remaining Union troops surrendered. By 3:30 P.M., it was all over.

Federal losses were probably about 4,000, and most of these were from Ninth Corps. Many of those lost were prisoners. Among those captured were William F. Bartlett and Elisha G. Marshall, the two brigade commanders of Ledlie's division. Joseph H. Barnes assumed command of Bartlett's First Brigade, and Gilbert P. Robinson of Marshall's Second Brigade.

Because of the lack of proper preparations and the poor handling of the Federal troops at the Battle of the Crater, there were some important command changes in Ninth Corps. August 4, 1864, Ledlie was given a twenty-day leave of absence from the army, but he never returned. December 9, 1864, he was told by Grant that he could not again have a command in the Army of the Potomac, and January 23, 1865, he resigned from the army. John F. Hartranft was assigned command of Ledlie's First Division, Ninth Corps, and Benjamin C. Christ assumed command of Hartranft's First Brigade of Willcox's Third Division. August 14, 1864, Burnside left the army on a thirty-day leave, and John G. Parke, his chief of staff and senior officer of the corps, assumed command of Ninth Corps. Like Ledlie, Burnside did not return, and he resigned from the army April 15, 1865.

Hancock's Second Corps was not engaged at the

crater, and at 6:00 P.M. July 30, 1864, it moved back to the vicinity of Deserted House, where it then remained in reserve. During the night of July 30, 1864 and the morning of July 31, 1864, Ord's command of the Army of the James returned to its former positions on the line of entrenchments. That day, Turner's division of Tenth Corps was relieved from its temporary duty with Eighteenth Corps, and it returned to Bermuda Hundred.

For the organization of Grant's command at the time of the Battle of the Crater, see the following section.

Organization of the Union Forces at Petersburg and Bermuda Hundred, July 1–31, 1864.

GENERAL HEADQUARTERS
Ulysses S. Grant

ARMY OF THE POTOMAC
George G. Meade

Provost Guard, Marsena R. Patrick
Volunteer Engineer Brigade, Henry W. Benham
Battalion United States Engineers, George H. Mendell
Signal Corps, Benjamin F. Fisher
Artillery, Henry J. Hunt
  Batteries detached from Sixth Corps, William Hexamer
    4th Battery (D), Maine Light Artillery, Charles W. White
    Battery A, 1st New Jersey Light Artillery, Augustin N. Parsons
    3rd Battery, New York Light Artillery, William A. Harn
    Battery H, 1st Ohio Light Artillery, Stephen W. Dorsey
    Battery E, 1st Rhode Island Light Artillery, William B. Rhodes
    Battery E, 5th United States Artillery, John R. Brinckle

  4th New York Heavy Artillery, Thomas Allcock

  Artillery Park, Freeman McGilvery
    Company F, 15th New York Heavy Artillery, Calvin Shaffer

SECOND CORPS, Winfield S. Hancock

First Division, Francis C. Barlow, to July 29, 1864
  Nelson A. Miles
  First Brigade, Nelson A. Miles, to July 29, 1864
    James C. Lynch
  Consolidated Brigade, Clinton MacDougall, to July 3,

1864
  Levin Crandell
  Fourth Brigade, John Hastings, to July 25, 1864
    K. Oscar Broady

Second Division, John Gibbon, to July 31, 1864
  Thomas A. Smyth
  First Brigade, Francis E. Pierce
  Second Brigade, James P. McIvor, to July 14, 1864
    Mathew Murphy
  Third Brigade, Thomas A. Smyth, to July 19, 1864
    Henry Cook, to July 22, 1864
    Thomas A. Smyth, to July 31, 1864
    Samuel A. Moore

Third Division, David B. Birney, to July 23, 1864
  Gershom Mott
  First Brigade, Henry J. Madill, to July 12, 1864
    P. Regis De Trobriand
  Second Brigade, Byron R. Pierce, to July 26, 1864
    Daniel Chaplin, to July 28, 1864
    Henry J. Madill
  Third Brigade, Gershom Mott, to July 23, 1864
    Robert McAllister

Artillery Brigade, John G. Hazard

Note. The batteries of the Artillery Brigade were the same as those listed on the roster for June 1864 (above) with the following exceptions: Thomas Allcock's 3rd Battalion, 4th New York Heavy Artillery was transferred to Henry J. Hunt's artillery command, and it was replaced by Frank Seymour's Battery L, 4th New York Heavy Artillery. Also, in July 1864, Walter S. Perrin replaced G. Lyman Dwight in command of Battery A, 1st Rhode Island Light Artillery.

FIFTH CORPS, Gouverneur K. Warren

First Division, Charles Griffin, to July 21, 1864
  Joseph J. Bartlett
  First Brigade, William S. Tilton
  Second Brigade, Jacob B. Sweitzer, to July 3, 1864
    Edgar M. Gregory
  Third Brigade, Joseph J. Bartlett, to July 21, 1864
    Norval E. Welch

Second Division, Romeyn B. Ayres
  First Brigade, Joseph Hayes
  Second Brigade, Nathan T. Dushane
  Third Brigade, J. Howard Kitching

Third Division, Samuel W. Crawford
  First Brigade, Peter Lyle
  Second Brigade, Henry Baxter
    Charles Wheelock

Third Brigade, James Carle, to July 26, 1864
    William R. Hartshorne

Fourth Division, Lysander Cutler
    First Brigade, Edward S. Bragg
    Second Brigade, J. William Hofmann

Artillery Brigade, Charles S. Wainwright

Note. The batteries of the Artillery Brigade were the same as those listed on the roster for June 1864 (above), but there were the following changes in command: Charles A. Phillips commanded 5th Battery (E), Massachusetts Light Artillery; Lester I. Richardson commanded Battery D, 1st New York Light Artillery; Charles L. Anderson commanded Battery L, 1st New York Light Artillery; and Patrick Hart commanded 15th Battery, New York Light Artillery.

SIXTH CORPS, Horatio G. Wright

First Division, David A. Russell
    First Brigade, William H. Penrose
    Second Brigade, Emory Upton
    Third Brigade, Gideon Clark, to July 7, 1864
        Oliver Edwards
    Fourth Brigade, Joseph E. Hamblin, to July 6, 1864

Note 1. First Division left the Petersburg front for Washington July 10, 1864.
Note 2. Fourth Brigade was discontinued July 6, 1864, and the regiments were reassigned.

Second Division, George W. Getty
    First Brigade, Frank Wheaton
    Second Brigade, Lewis A. Grant
    Third Brigade, Daniel D. Bidwell

Note. Second Division left the Petersburg front for Washington July 10, 1864.

Third Division, James B. Ricketts
    First Brigade, William S. Truex
    Second Brigade, Benjamin F. Smith

Note. Third Division left the Petersburg front for Baltimore, Maryland July 6, 1864.

Artillery Brigade

Note. When Sixth Corps left Petersburg for Washington, the batteries of the Artillery Brigade were left with the Army of the Potomac.

NINTH CORPS, Ambrose E. Burnside

First Division, James H. Ledlie
    First Brigade, Jacob P. Gould, to July 21, 1864

        William F. Bartlett
        Joseph H. Barnes
    Second Brigade, Ebenezer W. Peirce
        Elisha G. Marshall, to July 30, 1864, captured
        Gilbert P. Robinson

Second Division, Robert B. Potter
    First Brigade, Henry Pleasants, to July 4, 1864
        Zenas R. Bliss, to July 11, 1864
        William H. P. Steere, to July 25, 1864
        Zenas R. Bliss
    Second Brigade, Simon D. Griffin

Third Division, Orlando B. Willcox
    First Brigade, John F. Hartranft
    Second Brigade, William Humphrey

Fourth Division, Edward Ferrero, to July 21, 1864
    Julius White, to July 29, 1864
    Edward Ferrero
    First Brigade, Joshua K. Sigfried
    Second Brigade, Henry G. Thomas

Artillery Brigade, J. Albert Monroe

Note. In June 1864, the artillery of Ninth Corps was assigned to the divisions of the corps, but in July it was assembled into an artillery brigade under J. Albert Monroe. The batteries remained the same as those given on the roster for June 1864, except that Benjamin F. Smiley's Mortar Battery was added to the brigade.

CAVALRY CORPS, Philip H. Sheridan

First Cavalry Division, Alfred T. A. Torbert
    First Brigade, George A. Custer
        Russell A. Alger
    Second Brigade, Thomas C. Devin
    Reserve Brigade, Wesley Merritt

Second Cavalry Division, David McM. Gregg
    First Brigade, Henry E. Davies, Jr., to July 30, 1864
        William Stedman
    Second Brigade, J. Irvin Gregg

Third Division, James H. Wilson
    First Brigade, John B. McIntosh
    Second Brigade, George H. Chapman

Horse Artillery Brigade, James M. Robertson

Note. The batteries of the Horse Artillery Brigade are the same as those given on the June 1864 roster (see above), except that Battery K, 1st United States Artillery, which had been roughly handled during the cavalry expedition to Burkeville, Virginia, was ordered to Washington July 6, 1864.

ARMY OF THE JAMES
Benjamin F. Butler

TENTH CORPS, William T. H. Brooks, to July 19, 1864
Alfred H. Terry, to July 23, 1864
David B. Birney

First Division, Alfred H. Terry, to July 19, 1864
Robert S. Foster, to July 23, 1864
Alfred H. Terry
First Brigade, Joshua B. Howell, to July 29, 1864
Francis B. Pond
Second Brigade, Joseph R. Hawley
Third Brigade, Robert S. Foster, to July 19, 1864
Harris M. Plaisted, to July 23, 1864
Robert S. Foster
Artillery Brigade, Loomis L. Langdon, to July 28, 1864
Zenas C. Warren

Note. The batteries of the Artillery Brigade were the same as those given on the roster for June 1864 (see above), but there were the following changes in command in July 1864: George P. Bliss commanded the 1st Battery, Connecticut Light Artillery; Joseph Warren commanded the 5th Battery, New Jersey Light Artillery; and Egbert W. Olcott commanded Battery M, 1st United States Artillery.

Second Division, John W. Turner
First Brigade, N. Martin Curtis
Second Brigade, Edward Eddy, Jr., to July 2, 1864
William B. Coan
Third Brigade, Louis Bell
Artillery Brigade, Frederick M. Follett

Note. The batteries of the Artillery Brigade were the same as those listed on the roster for June 1864 (see above), except Martin McDevitt's 4th Battery, Wisconsin Light Artillery, which was transferred to August V. Kautz's Cavalry Division. In July 1864, however, Joseph P. Sanger commanded Battery D, 1st United States Artillery; and Frederick M. Follett commanded Battery D, 4th United States Artillery.

Third Division, Orris S. Ferry
First Brigade, Gilman Marston
Second Brigade, James B. Armstrong
33rd Battery, New York Light Artillery, Alger M. Wheeler

4th Massachusetts Cavalry (detachment), Francis Washburn

EIGHTEENTH CORPS, William F. Smith, to July 10, 1864
John H. Martindale, to July 21, 1864
Edward O. C. Ord

First Division, George J. Stannard, to July 31, 1864, on leave
Hiram Burnham
First Brigade, Edgar M. Cullen
Aaron F. Stevens
Second Brigade, Hiram Burnham, to July 31, 1864
Edgar M. Cullen, in command July 31, 1864
Third Brigade, Guy V. Henry

Second Division, John H. Martindale, to July 10, 1864
Adelbert Ames
First Brigade, Alexander Piper, to July 24, 1864
James Stewart, Jr.
Second Brigade, Griffin A. Stedman, Jr.
Third Brigade, Adelbert Ames, to July 11, 1864
Harrison S. Fairchild

Third Division, Edward W. Hinks, to July 1, 1864
John Holman, to July 29, 1864
Joseph B. Carr
First Brigade, John H. Holman, to July 2, 1864
Jeptha Garrard
Second Brigade, Samuel A. Duncan

Artillery Brigade, Henry S. Burton, to July 24, 1864
Alexander Piper

Note. The batteries of the Artillery Brigade that were listed on the roster for June 1864 were also present with the brigade in July 1864, but in addition, four other batteries joined the brigade. These were William J. Riggs' Battery H, 3rd New York Light Artillery; George T. Anthony's 17th Battery, New York Light Artillery; Thomas G. Orwig's Battery E, 1st Pennsylvania Light Artillery; and Leonard Martin's Battery F, 5th United States Artillery.

NINETEENTH CORPS

Second Division
First Brigade, Henry W. Birge
Second Brigade, Edward L. Molineux

Note. These two brigades were a part of Detachment Nineteenth Corps, which was just arriving in Virginia from New Orleans, Department of the Gulf. They were temporarily attached to Tenth Corps July 21–31, 1864, and then they were sent on to Washington.

CAVALRY DIVISION, August V. Kautz
First Brigade, Robert M. West
Second Brigade, Samuel P. Spear

In addition to Tenth Corps, Eighteenth Corps, and the cavalry, the following organizations also belonged to the Department of Virginia and North Carolina:

Naval Brigade, Charles K. Graham

Siege Artillery, Henry L. Abbot
  1st Connecticut Heavy Artillery, Henry L. Abbot
  Companies A and H, 13th New York Heavy Artillery, William Pendrell
  Company M, 3rd Pennsylvania Heavy Artillery, Frederick Korte

OPERATIONS OF AUGUST 1864

Siege of Petersburg, August 1864. During the early part of August 1864, the Army of the Potomac and the Army of the James were relatively quiet in their positions along the lines of entrenchments at Petersburg and at Bermuda Hundred. In late July 1864, Jubal A. Early had become active in the lower Shenandoah Valley, and August 1, 1864, Alfred T. A. Torbert's First Cavalry Division of Philip H. Sheridan's Cavalry Corps, Army of the Potomac was detached and ordered to Washington, D.C. The next day, Sheridan was relieved from command of the Cavalry Corps, and also from duty with the Army of the Potomac, and was ordered to Washington. James H. Wilson's Third Cavalry Division was also ordered to Washington; with its departure, only David McM. Gregg's Second Cavalry Division, Army of the Potomac and August V. Kautz's Cavalry Division, Army of the James remained with the infantry forces near Petersburg.

August 7, 1864, Sheridan was assigned temporary command of the Middle Military Division, which was created to ensure better cooperation of the forces of the Middle Department, the Department of the Susquehanna, the Department of Washington, and the Department of West Virginia in defeating Early's command in the Shenandoah Valley.

During the first two weeks of August 1864, Gouverneur K. Warren's Fifth Corps, Ambrose E. Burnside's Ninth Corps (Burnside was relieved in command by John G. Parke August 15, 1864), and Edward O. C. Ord's Eighteenth Corps continued to occupy the line of entrenchments in front of Petersburg. Winfield S. Hancock's Second Corps remained in reserve near Deserted House until August 12, 1864. It then marched to City Point for embarkation to Deep Bottom, where it was to be joined by David B. Birney's Tenth Corps, Army of the James for a second demonstration against Richmond (see below).

In mid-August 1864, the troops on the line of entrenchments at Petersburg were in position as follows: Eighteenth Corps held the right of the line from the Appomattox River to the right of Ninth Corps. Ninth Corps occupied the center of the line, with Robert B. Potter's Second Division and Julius White's (formerly Ledlie's) First Division, in that order, to the right of the crater; Orlando B. Willcox's Third Division was on the left of Potter, with its right near the crater; and Edward Ferrero's Fourth Division was in reserve.

Fifth Corps held the remainder of the line, from the left of Ninth Corps to the Jerusalem Plank Road. Samuel W. Crawford's Third Division was on the left, near the Plank Road; Charles Griffin's First Division was on the right, next to Willcox; and Romeyn B. Ayres' Second Division was in the rear in support of the first line. Lysander Cutler's Fourth Division had been withdrawn from the corps' line August 2, 1864 and sent to picket the front from the Plank Road near the Jones house eastward to the Norfolk and Petersburg Railroad. It rejoined the corps August 14, 1864.

During the night of August 14, 1864, Fifth Corps was withdrawn from the line of entrenchments to a position in rear of the left of the line, where it remained until the morning of August 18, 1864. It then marched westward against the right of the enemy line, south of Petersburg, at Globe Tavern on the Weldon Railroad (see below). After the departure of Fifth Corps, Ninth Corps and Eighteenth Corps extended their lines to hold the entire line from the Appomattox River to the Jerusalem Plank Road. Eighteenth Corps extended its left to the crater and relieved the divisions of White and Potter, and these two divisions then marched to the left and occupied the positions previously held by the divisions of Crawford and Griffin of Fifth Corps. Potter relieved Griffin's division, and White relieved Crawford's division. The divisions of Ninth Corps were then in line between the Plank Road and the crater, in order from left to right, as follows: White, Potter, and Willcox. Ferrero's division occupied the redoubts south of the Chieves house. Two redoubts had been built on the line running south on the Plank Road. Fort Sedgwick was the northernmost of the two, and Fort Davis was about a half mile farther south. These had been completed and occupied about July 11, 1864.

August 18, 1864, Warren's Fifth Corps moved westward to Globe Tavern (or Yellow House) on the Weldon Railroad, and that day and the next was strongly attacked north of Globe Tavern (see below). Ninth Corps was then sent to support Warren. On the night of August 18, 1864, two brigades of Ord's reserves of Eighteenth Corps relieved Willcox's division, and on the morning of August 19, 1864, Gershom Mott's Third Division of Second Corps arrived from Deep Bottom and relieved White's and Potter's divisions. White, Potter, and Willcox then joined Warren that day.

After severe fighting August 18, 19, and 21, 1864, Fifth Corps, aided by Ninth Corps, firmly established a new position in the vicinity of Globe Tavern. This resulted in an extension of the Union line of entrenchments from the Jerusalem Plank Road to the Weldon Railroad. After the engagement of August 21, 1864, Willcox's division of Ninth Corps moved to the east side of the Weldon Railroad and entrenched. White's division moved up on the right of Willcox. The next day, Parke, who had assumed command of Ninth Corps August 15, 1864, began organizing a line of entrenchments from the right of Fifth Corps, at the railroad, to the left of Mott's division of Second Corps, at the Strong house, near the Jerusalem Plank Road. The divisions of Potter and White entrenched on this line.

August 25, 1864, Willcox's division marched by way of the Jerusalem Plank Road and Shay's Tavern to Reams' Station on the Weldon Railroad to support Hancock's Second Corps, which had been strongly attacked there that day (see Battle of Reams' Station, below). Also that day, Ferrero's division moved from the redoubts on the Jerusalem Plank Road and took position on the right of White's division, where it connected on its right with Mott's division, near the Jerusalem Plank Road. Also on August 25, 1864, Potter's division relieved White's division, and the latter then moved back into reserve.

Willcox returned from Reams' Station during the night of August 27, 1864 and, with White's division, relieved Ferrero's division in the trenches. Ferrero then moved back and encamped near the Gurley house. White departed on sick leave August 28,

1864, and John F. Hartranft, then commanding First Brigade, First Division, Ninth Corps, assumed command of First Division, Ninth Corps.

During this period, Fifth Corps remained along the Weldon Railroad, with Ayres' division on the right, connecting with the left of Ninth Corps, and Griffin's division on the left, near Globe Tavern. Crawford's division was pulled back from the line and, during August 23, 1864, was engaged in destroying the railroad from Globe Tavern northward toward Petersburg.

August 25, 1864, Charles Wheelock's Second Brigade of Crawford's division (formerly commanded by Richard Coulter) moved about a mile to the left of Griffin's division, east of the railroad, and entrenched near the Perkins house, facing south. The next day, Peter Lyle's First Brigade, also of Crawford's division, moved to the left and threw up works to the southeast of Globe Tavern. Fourth Division of Fifth Corps, which had been commanded by Edward S. Bragg since Cutler was wounded August 21, 1864, was broken up August 24, 1864, and the two brigades were assigned to Second Division and Third Division, Fifth Corps. For details of the reorganization, see Fifth Corps, Army of the Potomac.

By mid-August 1864, Eighteenth Corps, Army of the James had been serving in the trenches for about two months, and during that time it had been seriously reduced in numbers. August 21, 1864, Ord asked that his corps be relieved, and this request was approved. Three days later, David B. Birney's Tenth Corps was ordered to Petersburg to take the place of Eighteenth Corps in the entrenchments. When the latter was relieved, it was directed to cross to the north side of the Appomattox River and occupy the defenses at Bermuda Hundred and at Deep Bottom. The transfer was a rather slow process because it was necessarily done division by division until all of Eighteenth Corps had been relieved. Alfred H. Terry's First Division, Tenth Corps marched first, on August 24, 1864, to relieve Adelbert Ames' Second Division, Eighteenth Corps. A newly organized Third Division, Tenth Corps, under the command of William Birney, then replaced Charles J. Paine's Third Division, Eighteenth Corps. Finally, Robert S. Foster's Second Division, Tenth Corps relieved Joseph B. Carr's First Division, Eighteenth Corps. Tenth Corps then occupied the line of entrenchments at Petersburg from the right of Gershom Mott's Third Division of Second Corps to the Appomattox River. Mott had earlier relieved Potter's division of Ninth Corps in the entrenchments. Terry's division was on the left, next to Mott; William Birney's division was on the center of the line; and Foster's division was on the right, next to the river.

August 27, 1864, Nelson A. Miles' First Division and John Gibbon's Second Division of Second Corps were moved to the vicinity of the Jones house, where they were in position to support all parts of the line, and they also furnished details for the construction of works on the line.

Demonstration on the North Bank of the James River at Deep Bottom (Combats at Fussell's Mill, Gravel Hill, Bailey's Creek, Deep Run [or Creek], White's Tavern, Charles City Road, and New Market Road), Virginia, August 13–20, 1864. Early in August 1864, Grant received information that led him to believe that Robert E. Lee had detached three infantry divisions and one cavalry division to reinforce Jubal A. Early, who was at that time active in the Shenandoah Valley. Based on this information, Grant decided to make a demonstration to threaten Richmond from the north side of the James River. In this way, he hoped to prevent further detachments from Lee's army at Petersburg, and also, if possible, to cause the recall of some troops already ordered to the valley.

To accomplish this purpose, Grant sent Winfield S. Hancock, in command of his own Second Corps, David McM. Gregg's Second Cavalry Division, and the greater part of David B. Birney's Tenth Corps, Army of the James, with orders to cross to the James River at Deep Bottom and advance on the enemy lines covering Richmond. The object and nature of the expedition were the same as those of Hancock's earlier demonstration of July 26–29, 1864. See above, Operations of July 1864, Demonstration on the North Bank of the James River. The route taken by Second Corps, however, was to be different from the earlier approach. To create the impression that Second Corps was to be transferred to Washington, it was ordered to City Point, and from there it was to be sent by water up the James River to Deep Bottom.

Hancock broke camp near Deserted House

August 12, 1864 and marched to City Point. The corps then embarked on transports, and departed at 10:00 P.M. August 13, 1864 for Deep Bottom, where it arrived and disembarked the next morning. The cavalry, artillery, and trains marched to Deep Bottom by way of Point of Rocks and Bermuda Hundred.

David B. Birney's troops of Tenth Corps marched from the lines at Bermuda Hundred on the night of August 13, 1864, and arrived at Deep Bottom the next morning. Birney's command consisted of Alfred H. Terry's First Division; William B. Coan's Second Brigade and Francis A. Osborn's Third Brigade of John W. Turner's Second Division; a colored brigade, organized August 12, 1864 under William Birney; and the Artillery Brigade under Freeman McGilvery.

Hancock's plan for the demonstration was as follows: After landing at Bermuda Hundred, Mott's division was to advance on the New Market Road (or River Road) and drive the enemy back into his entrenched lines behind Bailey's Creek, and on beyond if practicable. As soon as Francis C. Barlow's First Division and John Gibbon's Second Division (the latter was commanded by Thomas A. Smyth during the temporary absence of Gibbon) were ashore, they were to move to the right of Mott's division and assault the enemy works near the Jennings house, a short distance southwest of Fussell's Mill. The mill was on the Darbytown Road, about three-fourths of a mile north of the junction of that road and the Long Bridge Road. For this movement, Smyth's division was placed temporarily under Barlow's orders. If Barlow carried the line at the Jennings house, he was to move to the left and uncover Mott's front. Mott was then to advance on the New Market Road. After Birney's command of Tenth Corps crossed the James River, it was to advance and attack the enemy position behind Four-Mile Creek (or Run) near the pontoon bridge.

At the time of Hancock's demonstration, Richard S. Ewell commanded the Confederate Department of Richmond, and Charles W. Field commanded the enemy forces on the north side of the James River. These consisted of the following: Field's division (temporarily commanded by John Gregg) of Richard H. Anderson's corps; Ambrose R. Wright's brigade (commanded by Victor J. B. Girardey), James H. Lane's brigade (commanded by James

Conner), and Samuel McGowan's brigade (commanded by Isaac F. Hunt) of Cadmus M. Wilcox's division of Ambrose P. Hill's corps; and Martin W. Gary's cavalry brigade. Later, William Mahone's division of Hill's corps and Wade Hampton's and William H. F. Lee's cavalry divisions were sent north of the James to reinforce Field.

Field's division and Wilcox's brigades occupied an advanced line that ran from Chaffin's Bluff to New Market Heights. The entrenchments extended on past Fussell's Mill to the Charles City Road, but that part of the line was covered only by patrols of Gary's cavalry brigade.

Hancock's Second Corps began disembarking at Deep Bottom early on the morning of August 14, 1864. Mott's division was ashore by 8:00 A.M., and it then advanced on the New Market Road to a place called the "Tavern and Pottery," which was a short distance east of Bailey's Creek. P. Regis De Trobriand's First Brigade then followed the skirmishers as they advanced to the enemy main line beyond the creek. When Mott found this line heavily manned, he halted his division and massed Calvin A. Craig's Second Brigade (formerly commanded by Alexander Hays) and Robert McAllister's Third Brigade on the New Market Road. A little after 5:00 P.M., Mott sent McAllister's brigade to report to Barlow, but it rejoined the division the next morning.

The first three brigades of Barlow's division had landed by daylight August 14, 1864, and the Fourth Brigade, which had been delayed en route, arrived at 9:00 A.M. Smyth's division had disembarked by 7:00 A.M. Later in the morning, these two divisions advanced on the New Market Road and the Long Bridge Road. At that time, Smyth's division was placed under Barlow's orders. It was intended that Barlow, with his two divisions, was to move directly from the point of debarkation to the Jennings house and attack with his entire force. Barlow, however, attempted to maintain contact with the other troops as he advanced, and as a result, his force was strung out along a line that was nearly a mile and a half in length. In addition, Smyth left Francis E. Pierce's Third Brigade and the artillery to protect his left as he advanced, and Barlow left Nelson A. Miles' First Brigade to hold the New Market Road and protect his left flank.

The rest of Barlow's command advanced until it encountered a line of rifle pits across the road. The 2nd New York Heavy Artillery of Miles' brigade and the Irish Brigade (formerly Second Brigade, First Division, Second Corps, but at that time a part of Levin Crandell's Consolidated Brigade of First Division) were sent forward to occupy that line, but they failed to do so. In fact they made practically no effort to capture the enemy works. Barlow then moved the former Third Brigade (then part of the Consolidated Brigade) and K. Oscar Broady's Fourth Brigade, First Division farther to the right to a hill near Fussell's Mill on the Darbytown Road. He then brought up George N. Macy's First Brigade of Smyth's division, and about 5:30 P.M. it charged against the works beyond the mill, but was repulsed. When Barlow first attacked the line on his front, it was held only by dismounted cavalry of Gary's brigade, but Field quickly came up with George T. Anderson's brigade and was able to hold the position. During the attack, Macy was injured by the fall of his horse, and Horace P. Rugg assumed command of his brigade. During the night of August 14, 1864, Barlow's division was concentrated near the junction of the Darbytown Road and the Long Bridge Road, and Smyth's division was massed in rear of the skirmish line.

On the left of Hancock's line, Birney attacked that day and captured the rifle pits and entrenchments near the Kingsland Road, but he was unable to advance farther. On the far right, Gregg's cavalry division moved up the Charles City Road to Fishers', not far from White Oak Swamp.

During the night of August 14, 1864, the greater part of Birney's command marched to Strawberry Plains and to the intersection of of the New Market Road and the Quaker Road, in rear of Second Corps. A detachment of Tenth Corps was left to hold the bridgehead at Deep Bottom, and when Robert S. Foster's Third Brigade, First Division, Tenth Corps was relieved from that duty, it rejoined Terry's First Division for an attack on the Confederate works. Birney's orders for August 15, 1864 directed him to move out and attempt to turn the left of the enemy position, but if this could not be done he was further directed to attack the line if a suitable place could be found. Gregg's cavalry was to cover the right of Birney's movement.

Accordingly, on the morning of August 15, 1864, Birney moved to the right until he had reached a point between the Darbytown (or Central) Road and the Charles City Road, and he then advanced toward the latter road. Because of the long distance that he had to march, Birney did not report that he had found the enemy line until 6:40 P.M., and by that time it was too late to attack that day.

During the movements of August 14, 1864, Mott's division of Second Corps remained on the New Market Road. The next day, Craig's brigade was detached and ordered to report to Tenth Corps, and it was then attached to Turner's Second Division, Tenth Corps. During Birney's advance August 15, 1864, Craig's brigade made a reconnaissance in force as far as the Charles City Road before returning to Turner's division that night.

During the night of August 15, 1864, Hancock prepared for an attack the next morning. He directed Gregg to move up the Charles City Road and make a strong diversion toward Richmond. Miles' brigade of Barlow's division was temporarily placed under Gregg's orders, with instructions to return to Barlow when Birney became engaged the next day. Miles was then to form on Birney's right and join in the main attack.

Gregg advanced early August 16, 1864 and drove back John R. Chambliss' cavalry beyond Deep Creek and almost to White's Tavern, about seven miles from Richmond. Chambliss was killed in the fighting that day.

At 4:40 A.M. August 16, 1864, Craig's brigade of Mott's division was ordered to report to Terry's First Division, Tenth Corps, and at 10:00 that morning, Terry advanced on the enemy works about a half mile north of Fussell's Mill. Craig's brigade and William Birney's brigade attacked on the right of Terry's division. Foster's Third Brigade of Terry's division charged against the enemy rifle pits, and it was supported on the right by Francis B. Pond's First Brigade. Joseph R. Hawley's Second Brigade was in reserve. Craig's brigade was also heavily engaged on the right, and after severe fighting, Terry succeeded in occupying a part of the enemy line.

Barlow sent Broady's brigade of his division to report to Birney and to protect his right flank. About 3:00 P.M., Smyth sent Pierce's brigade of his division to Birney, who placed it on the left of his line. It was engaged only in skirmishing during the afternoon.

Coan's Second Brigade and Osborn's Third Brigade of Turner's division of Tenth Corps were moved up to the works captured by Terry, but they were soon driven back with considerable loss. Osborn was wounded, as were his two successors, Ezra L. Walrath and Frank W. Parker, and then Robert J. Gray assumed command of Osborn's brigade. Craig, who had just returned to the army after recovering from a wound received earlier in the campaign, was killed and was succeeded in command of his brigade by John Pulford.

When Terry first attacked that day, he struck a part of the Confederate line that was held by Girardey (commanding Wright's brigade) and a North Carolina brigade on his left, drove them back for some distance in disorder, and took possession of their works. Lane's brigade (commanded by James Conner) and McGowan's brigade, both under the command of Conner, which held the enemy line farther to the left, were thus cut off. Field immediately ordered John Gregg to bring up all available troops of his, Field's, division; and then Gregg, with the help of the two broken brigades and Conner's two brigades on the left, soon recaptured the works taken earlier by Terry. Girardey was killed during the action.

During the afternoon of August 16, 1864, Mott probed from time to time at the enemy line on the New Market Road in an effort to prevent reserves from being sent to the front of Birney's line.

About 1:30 P.M. the enemy cavalry, reinforced by infantry, advanced against Gregg and Miles on the far right and forced them back to Deep Creek. At that point, Miles withdrew according to his instructions, and moved back to the right of Birney's line, where he assumed command of Broady's brigade, in addition to his own.

By that time, Grant realized that the information upon which he had based his decision to send Hancock to the north side of the James River, mainly that Lee had detached three infantry divisions to reinforce Early in the Shenandoah Valley, was erroneous, but he did not immediately order a withdrawal.

There was only skirmishing August 17, 1864. That morning, Barlow, who was sick, was sent to the hospital at City Point, and Nelson A. Miles assumed command of First Division, Second Corps. James Lynch succeeded Miles in command of First Brigade, First Division. Also that day, Coan's brigade of Turner's division relieved the detachment of Tenth Corps at Deep Bottom, and that afternoon Craig's brigade, then commanded by John Pulford, rejoined Mott's division.

On the morning of August 18, 1864, Lynch's brigade (formerly Miles' brigade) was withdrawn from the line of Tenth Corps, and at dark Broady's brigade was also withdrawn, and the entire First Division, Second Corps was deployed along the New Market Road, where it entrenched. During the late afternoon, the enemy attacked Birney's line above Fussell's Mill, and at about 5:00 P.M., Miles was sent with Lynch's and Broady's brigades to the Tenth Corps line. The enemy attack was repulsed, but Miles' brigades were not engaged, and they returned to their positions with First Division about dark.

At 8:00 P.M. August 18, 1864, Mott was ordered to return with his division to Petersburg, and upon arriving there the next morning, he relieved Julius White's First Division and Robert B. Potter's Second Division of Ninth Corps in the trenches between the Jerusalem Plank Road and the Weldon Railroad.

When Mott's division departed, Hancock shortened his line as follows: Smyth's division was on the left, and extended from Bailey's Creek, at the New Market Road, to the right along a road that ran to the Long Bridge Road; Miles' division extended from the right of Smyth's line almost to the Ruffin house, on the Long Bridge Road at a point about a mile and a half east of its intersection with the New Market Road; and Birney's Tenth Corps was on the right of Miles and occupied the high ground above the Ruffin house, and its line ran past Turners' house and Ruffins' to connect with the cavalry on the Charles City Road.

Hancock began his withdrawal from north of the James River after dark August 20, 1864. Second Corps recrossed the James and the Appomattox rivers and returned to its former camps near Deserted House, where it arrived at 6:30 P.M. August 21, 1864. August 20, 1864, First Brigade and Second Brigade of Terry's First Division, Tenth Corps returned to the entrenchments in front of Bermuda Hundred. Foster's Third Brigade relieved Coan's Second Brigade, Second Division at Deep Bottom August 21, 1864, and both Second Brigade and Third Brigade of Second Division, Tenth Corps

returned to their former camps near Hatchers'. William Birney's Colored Brigade also returned to Bermuda Hundred.

The organization of the Union troops under Hancock that demonstrated north of the James River August 13–20, 1864 was as follows:

SECOND CORPS, Winfield S. Hancock

First Division, Francis C. Barlow, to August 17, 1864, sick
  Nelson A. Miles
  First Brigade, Nelson A. Miles, to August 17, 1864
    James C. Lynch
  Consolidated Brigade, Levin C. Crandell
  Fourth Brigade, K. Oscar Broady
  Artillery
    11th Battery, New York Light Artillery, John E. Burton
    Battery K, 4th United States Artillery, John W. Roder

Note 1. Hancock was in command of all Union troops participating in the operations north of the James River.
Note 2. Barlow temporarily commanded First Division and Second Division during the advance from Deep Bottom to the line of the enemy entrenchments.

Second Division, Thomas A. Smyth
  First Brigade, Francis E. Pierce, to August 13, 1864
    George N. Macy, to August 14, 1864, disabled
    Horace P. Rugg
  Second Brigade, Mathew Murphy
  Third Brigade, Samuel A. Moore, to August 14, 1864
    Francis E. Pierce
  Artillery
    6th Battery (F), Maine Light Artillery, Edwin B. Dow
    Battery G, 1st New York Light Artillery, Nelson Ames

Note. Smyth was in temporary command of Second Division during the absence of John Gibbon, who departed on leave July 31, 1864.

Third Division, Gershom Mott
  First Brigade, P. Regis De Trobriand
  Second Brigade, Calvin A. Craig, to August 16, 1864, killed
    John Pulford
  Third Brigade, Robert McAllister
  Artillery
    Battery B, 1st New Jersey Light Artillery, A. Judson Clark
    Battery F, 1st Pennsylvania Light Artillery, R. Bruce Ricketts

Note. Craig had relieved Henry J. Madill in command of Second Brigade August 11, 1864.

TENTH CORPS, David B. Birney

First Division, Alfred H. Terry
First Brigade, Francis B. Pond, to August 16, 1864, sick
  Alvin C. Voris, to August 18, 1864
  Joshua B. Howell
Second Brigade, Joseph R. Hawley
Third Brigade, Robert S. Foster

Second Division
First Brigade, William B. Coan
Third Brigade, Louis Bell, to August 13, 1864
  Francis A. Osborn, to August 16, 1864, wounded
  Ezra L. Walrath, August 16, 1864, wounded
  Frank W. Parker, August 16, 1864, wounded
  Robert J. Gray, to August 20, 1864
  Francis A. Osborn

Note. John W. Turner, commander of Second Division, Tenth Corps, did not accompany the two brigades of his division to Deep Bottom, but remained at Bermuda Hundred in charge of the defenses there. Second Brigade and Third Brigade reported directly to Birney while north of the James River. August 19, 1864, Turner was assigned command of the troops at Deep Bottom, but he resumed command of Second Division when Hancock's command returned to Petersburg.

Colored Brigade, William Birney

Artillery Brigade, Freeman McGilvery
  1st Battery, Connecticut Light Artillery, James B. Clinton
  4th Battery, New Jersey Light Artillery, Charles R. Doane
  Battery C, 3rd Rhode Island Heavy Artillery, Martin S. James
  Batteries C and D, Redmond Tully, to August 14, 1864
    Joseph B. Sanger

SECOND CAVALRY DIVISION, ARMY OF THE POTOMAC, David Mc M. Gregg
  First Brigade, William Stedman
  Second Brigade, Michael Kerwin
  Battery A, 2nd United States Artillery, Robert Clarke

Battle of Globe Tavern (or Yellow House, Yellow Tavern, Blick's House [or Station], Weldon Railroad), Virginia, August 18–21, 1864. While Hancock was demonstrating north of the James River with his Second Corps, Army of the Potomac and Tenth Corps, Army of the James (see above),

Meade, at Grant's direction, decided to use Warren's Fifth Corps and a part of John G. Parke's Ninth Corps (Parke relieved Ambrose E. Burnside in command of Ninth Corps August 15, 1864) in an attack against what was believed to be a weakened enemy line south of Petersburg. August 14, 1864, in anticipation of this offensive movement, Grant authorized Meade to assume command of Edward O. C. Ord's Eighteenth Corps, Army of the James, in addition to his Army of the Potomac.

Meade issued orders August 14, 1864 for the withdrawal of Fifth Corps from the line of entrenchments, and during the night, it moved back and camped generally on a line from the Chieves house to Deserted House, in rear of the line of entrenchments. Ninth Corps and Eighteenth Corps extended their lines to the left to occupy the entire front from the Appomattox River to the Jerusalem Plank Road. For details, see section above, Operations of August 1864, Siege of Petersburg.

August 17, 1864, Grant directed Meade to send Warren with his Fifth Corps on an expedition to the Weldon Railroad. Meade then instructed Warren to move to the Weldon Railroad in the vicinity of the Gurley house, about two miles south of the Vaughan Road, and destroy the track as far south as possible. In addition to the destruction of the railroad, Warren was to regard his movement as a reconnaissance in force, and take advantage of any enemy weakness that he might discover, but he was not to fight under any serious disadvantage or to assault fortified positions. Samuel P. Spear's Second Brigade of August V. Kautz's Cavalry Division, Army of the James was attached to Warren's command for this operation.

Warren started promptly at 4:00 A.M. August 18, 1864, as ordered, with Charles Griffin's First Division in the lead. Griffin was followed by Romeyn B. Ayres' Second Division, Samuel W. Crawford's Third Division, and Lysander Cutler's Fourth Division, in that order. Ahead of Fifth Corps, there was only James Dearing's Confederate cavalry brigade guarding the railroad. Griffin first made contact with the enemy pickets near the Gurley house about 7:00 A.M., but he continued to advance and two hours later crossed the Weldon Railroad at Globe Tavern. Griffin then deployed William S. Tilton's First Brigade and Edgar M. Gregory's Second Brigade in line of battle to cover his position to the south and southwest. Griffin placed James Gwyn's Third Brigade in support of the other two brigades.

Ayres' division came up next and marched north along the railroad, with Joseph Hayes' First Brigade on the right of the track and Nathan T. Dushane's Second Brigade on the left. The Third Brigade of Ayres' division, formerly commanded by J. Howard Kitching, consisted at that time of only Michael Wiedrich's 15th New York Heavy Artillery (which was serving as infantry). Kitching had been ordered to Washington August 13, 1864 with his 6th New York Heavy Artillery, the other regiment of the brigade. Wiedrich, who then reported to Ayres, advanced with his regiment in support of Hayes and Dushane.

Spear's cavalry brigade was sent south to Reams' Station, where it watched the left of Warren's infantry.

Meantime, when Warren's movement toward the railroad was discovered, Beauregard sent Henry Heth, with Joseph R. Davis' and James A. Walker's brigades of his division, south from the Confederate lines to support Dearing. About a half mile north of Globe Tavern, and about a mile south of the junction of the Vaughan Road and the Halifax Road, Ayres found Heth's brigades in line of battle. Crawford's division was then ordered up on the right of Ayres to flank the enemy position, and Cutler's division was advanced in support. At 2:00 P.M., however, before these movements were completed, Heth attacked, struck the left of Ayres' division, and forced Dushane's brigade to fall back. Ayres then retired a short distance, while resisting stubbornly. About 4:00 P.M., J. William Hofmann's Second Brigade was detached from Cutler's division and sent to reinforce Ayres. Hofmann moved to the left of the railroad and relieved Dushane's brigade. Then, with Hayes' brigade of Ayres' division on the right, and also with Wiedrich's regiment, Hofmann advanced and drove the enemy from the ground that they had gained. Peter Lyle's First Brigade, which was on the left of Crawford's line, was also engaged that afternoon. Wiedrich was wounded during this attack. On the right of Ayres, Crawford's division continued to move forward, although with difficulty, until dark.

During the night of August 18, 1864, rifle pits were constructed on Ayres' front, and the troops of his command were formed on this line as follows:

Hayes' First Brigade was on the right of the railroad, facing north; 15th New York Heavy Artillery, then commanded by Louis Eiche, was on the left of Hayes, across the railroad and also facing north; Hofmann's brigade of Cutler's division continued the line on the left of the 15th New York Heavy Artillery; and Dushane's Second Brigade was on the left of the line, and it curved back until it was parallel to the railroad, facing to the west and southwest. Also that night, Meade made preparations for relieving Ninth Corps in the entrenchments so that it could be sent to support Warren.

Lee, too, was making some changes in the disposition of his troops. When he learned from Beauregard that Fifth Corps was on the Weldon Railroad, he sent back troops from north of the James River to reinforce Heth and Dearing. These consisted of William Mahone's division of Hill's corps and the cavalry divisions of William H. F. Lee and Matthew C. Butler of Wade Hampton's Cavalry Corps.

August 19, 1864, Crawford's division was up on the line of Ayres' division, and was deployed on the right of Ayres as follows: Lyle's First Brigade, on the left of Crawford's division, was next to Hayes' brigade of Ayres' division; Charles Wheelock's Second Brigade was on the center; and William R. Hartshorne's small Third Brigade of Pennsylvania Reserves was on the right. A gap of more than a mile existed between Crawford's right and the pickets of Julius White's First Division of Ninth Corps, which was near the Jerusalem Plank Road. At 4:00 P.M. August 19, 1864, Edward S. Bragg's First Brigade of Cutler's division was sent to establish a connection between the pickets of Crawford and White.

About 3:30 A.M. August 19, 1864, Orlando B. Willcox's Third Division, Ninth Corps left the Petersburg entrenchments for the Weldon Railroad, and about 7:30 A.M. reported to Warren near Globe Tavern. Willcox then bivouacked to the right of Globe Tavern, on a line parallel to the right of Crawford's division. White's division followed Willcox about 3:00 P.M. and reached the Aiken house two hours later. Robert B. Potter's Second Division followed White, and arrived on the right of the new corps' line late in the afternoon. All three divisions were placed under Warren's orders.

On August 19, 1864, Hill prepared for an attack on Warren's position. Hill moved Heth, with the brigades of Davis and Walker; Mahone, with the brigades of David A. Weisiger, Alfred H. Colquitt, and Thomas L. Clingman; and William H. F. Lee's cavalry to the intersection of the Vaughan Road and the Halifax Road, which was near the Weldon Railroad and about one mile north of Ayres' position.

At 4:15 P.M., Heth's brigades advanced and attacked on the front of Ayres' position, but they were repulsed. At about the same time, Mahone attacked on the right of Crawford's division. He broke through Bragg's picket line, and then faced to the Confederate right and moved down in rear of Crawford's line. During this attack, most of the men of Hartshorne's brigade, which were then on the skirmish line, were captured, including the brigade commander. Mahone then struck Hayes' brigade of Ayres' division from the right and rear, and captured Hayes and many of his men. The remainder of Hayes' brigade, and also Lyle's brigade of Crawford's division on its right, were forced to fall back. In this confused battle, Wheelock's brigade was subjected to fire from friend and foe alike. For a time the Federal line was in disorder, and Ayres and Crawford were forced to retire and re-form their commands.

When Mahone broke through the right of Warren's line, Willcox ordered John F. Hartranft's First Brigade of his division to move forward and support Crawford. Hartranft soon found the enemy, probably Clingman's brigade, and forced them back to Crawford's rifle pits. During this action, William Humphrey's Second Brigade of Hartranft's division arrived within supporting distance of First Brigade, and was then ordered to the left of Hartranft, toward the junction of the original lines of Ayres and Crawford. Humphrey succeeded in driving back the enemy, then recaptured the works on that part of the line and held them against repeated attacks.

White's division then came up and, conforming to Warren's orders, reported to Willcox. Hartranft's brigade, which was then on the right of Warren's line, moved to the left toward Humphrey's brigade, and it was replaced on the line by White's division. White had scarcely taken his new position on the right when he was assailed by Colquitt's brigade, but he held his ground and drove the enemy back. Heth's attacks on Ayres' front, toward the Federal left, continued until dark, but without success. Late that evening, Warren began a general advance, and by daylight August 20, 1864 had fully recovered his position of the day before, and the enemy had withdrawn from his front.

Warren expected Hill to renew his efforts to regain possession of the Weldon Railroad, and August 20, 1864, he proceeded to prepare a new line more suitable for defense. He withdrew Willcox's division from the right of the position of the day before and moved it to the vicinity of the Blick house, a short distance north of Globe Tavern, where it entrenched on a defensive line. That afternoon Warren returned Bragg's and Hofmann's brigades of Fourth Division to Cutler's command, and assigned them to a position on the left of Ayres' division. Bragg's brigade was on the right and Hofmann's brigade was on the left of a line that was roughly parallel to the Weldon Railroad, facing the Vaughan Road. Griffin's division was on the left, near Globe Tavern. Wheelock's brigade of Crawford's division moved back about a mile and threw up works at the Blick house. Lyle's brigade pulled out of the front line and entrenched on a line facing toward the northeast. Potter's and White's divisions of Ninth Corps entrenched on the right of the Weldon Railroad, facing to the north and northwest, with their right extending toward the left of Mott's position near the Jerusalem Plank Road.

About 2:00 A.M. August 21, 1864, Ayres withdrew his division about a half mile from its position of August 19, 1864 to more open ground north of Globe Tavern. About 10:00 that morning, Hill, with his own corps, a part of Hoke's division, and Lee's cavalry attacked along the north and west sides of Warren's new line, but the enemy was everywhere repulsed. Wheelock's brigade moved to support Griffin, and occupied the works near Globe Tavern. The divisions of Griffin, Cutler, and Willcox, and Lyle's brigade of Crawford's division were all engaged. Dushane was killed and Cutler was wounded during the fighting. Ayres assumed temporary command of Fourth Division, and then Bragg was ordered to replace Cutler. Samuel A. Graham succeeded Dushane in command of Second Brigade of Ayres' division.

Later in the day, Mahone again attacked Warren's line but was driven back. Johnson Hagood's brigade of Hoke's division got close to the Federal works, but most of his command was captured.

The Union cavalry was also active during the

operations along the Weldon Railroad. August 17, 1864, Spear's Second Brigade of Kautz's cavalry division, which at that time was picketing the left of the army, was ordered to join Warren. It left its position on the picket line to the east of Petersburg the next day, and reported to Warren near Globe Tavern August 19, 1864. That day it moved south and drove back the enemy pickets to within a mile of Reams' Station on the Weldon Railroad.

August 19, 1864, William Stedman's First Brigade of Gregg's cavalry division, which was then with Hancock's command north of the James River, was ordered to report to Meade for duty with Fifth Corps. Stedman marched all that night and arrived at the Gurley house, near the Weldon Railroad, about 10:00 A.M. August 20, 1864. He was then assigned to a position on the railroad, on the left of Fifth Corps. Stedman was heavily engaged that evening, but repulsed all attacks. Stedman and Spear remained on the left of the infantry during the remainder of the action.

The organization of the troops commanded by Gouverneur K. Warren during the battle on the Weldon Railroad August 18–21, 1864 was as follows:

FIFTH CORPS, Gouverneur K. Warren

First Division, Charles Griffin
    First Brigade, William S. Tilton
    Second Brigade, Edgar M. Gregory
    Third Brigade, James Gwyn

Second Division, Romeyn B. Ayres
    First Brigade, Joseph Hayes, to August 19, 1864, captured
        Frederick Winthrop
    Second Brigade, Nathan T. Dushane, to August 21, 1864, killed
        Samuel A. Graham
    Third Brigade, Michael Wiedrich

Note. Wiedrich's brigade consisted only of his 15th New York Heavy Artillery, serving as infantry.

Third Division, Samuel Crawford
    First Brigade, Peter Lyle
    Second Brigade, Richard Coulter, to August 18, 1864, sick
        Charles Wheelock
    Third Brigade, William R. Hartshorne, to August 19, 1864, captured

Note. About three-fourths of the men of Third Brigade were captured August 19, 1864, including, in addition to Hartshorne, James Carle, the next senior officer.

Fourth Division, Lysander Cutler, to August 21, 1864, wounded
    Romeyn B. Ayres, temporarily
    Edward S. Bragg, August 24, 1864
    First Brigade, Edward S. Bragg
    Second Brigade, J. William Hofmann

Note. Fourth Division was broken up August 24, 1864. First Brigade was assigned temporarily to Crawford's Third Division, and Second Brigade was assigned temporarily to Ayres' Second Division.

Artillery Brigade, Charles S. Wainwright
    3rd Battery (C), Massachusetts Light Artillery, Aaron F. Walcott
    5th Battery (E), Massachusetts Light Artillery, Joseph E. Spear
    9th Battery, Massachusetts Light Artillery, Richard S. Milton
    Battery B, 1st New York Light Artillery, Robert E. Rogers
    Battery C, 1st New York Light Artillery, Almont Barnes
    Battery D, 1st New York Light Artillery, Lester I. Richardson
    Battery H, 1st New York Light Artillery, Charles E. Mink
    Battery L, 1st New York Light Artillery, Charles L. Anderson
    15th Battery, New York Light Artillery, Patrick Hart
    Battery B, 1st Pennsylvania Light Artillery, William C. Miller
    Battery D, 5th United States Artillery, William E. Van Reed

NINTH CORPS

First Division, Julius White
    First Brigade, Joseph H. Barnes
    Second Brigade, Gilbert P. Robinson
    14th Battery, Massachusetts Light Artillery, Joseph W. B. Wright

Second Division, Robert B. Potter
    First Brigade, Zenas R. Bliss, to August 21, 1864
        John I. Curtin
    Second Brigade, Simon G. Griffin
    Artillery
        11th Battery, Massachusetts Light Artillery, Edward J. Jones
        19th Battery, New York Light Artillery, Edward W. Rogers

Third Division, Orlando B. Willcox
First Brigade, John F. Hartranft
Second Brigade, William Humphrey

Note. John G. Parke, commander of Ninth Corps, did not accompany the three divisions of his corps to the Weldon Railroad. These were temporarily placed under the command of Gouverneur K. Warren. Parke remained on the line of entrenchments with Ferrero's Fourth Division, Ninth Corps and Gershom Mott's Third Division, Second Corps, which was placed temporarily under Parke's control.

Cavalry
Second Cavalry Division, Army of the Potomac
First Brigade, William Stedman
Cavalry Division, Army of the James
Second Brigade, Samuel P. Spear

Battle of Reams' Station, Virginia, August 25, 1864. Both Grant and Lee recognized the importance of the Weldon Railroad as a supply line that connected Petersburg with the South, and as noted above, late in June 1864, it was the object of an expedition by Second Corps and Sixth Corps. These two corps, however, were unable to gain possession of the railroad. A second effort was made August 18–21, 1864 by Gouverneur K. Warren with his Fifth Corps and three divisions of Ninth Corps, and, as noted above, succeeded in establishing a firm position on the railroad in the vicinity of Globe Tavern or Yellow House. Despite this success, however, it was still possible for the enemy to bring up supplies by rail to within one day's wagon haul of Petersburg. If the railroad could be destroyed as far south as Rowanty Creek, a distance of about thirteen miles beyond Warren's left flank, the enemy would be forced to haul supplies by wagon from Stony Creek Station to Dinwiddie Court House, and from there by way of the Boydton Plank Road to Petersburg, a distance of about thirty miles. Therefore, Grant decided to send an expedition to destroy the Weldon Railroad as far as Rowanty Creek.

On the night of August 20, 1864, Hancock withdrew Francis C. Barlow's First Division (then commanded by Nelson A. Miles) and John Gibbon's Second Division from their positions north of the James River near Deep Bottom, and marched with them to their former camps near Deserted House, where they arrived at 6:30 the next morning. Mott's Third Division had already returned to Petersburg on the night of August 18, 1864, and had relieved a part of Ninth Corps in the entrenchments between the Norfolk and Petersburg Railroad and the Strong house. Hancock's men were exhausted from their night march, but at 1:00 P.M. August 21, 1864, they moved on by way of the Strong house toward the Weldon Railroad to support Warren, who was engaged there that day. That night, Miles' division camped at the Gurley house, and Gibbon's division near the Aiken house. Gregg's cavalry division watched the roads running toward the railroad from the left and to Hancock's rear.

The enemy withdrew from Warren's front August 21, 1864, and about noon the next day, Hancock sent Miles' division to Warren's left to begin work on the destruction of the railroad. That afternoon, Miles broke up about two miles of track, and by the night of August 23, 1864, he had destroyed the track as far as Reams' Station, four and a half miles south of Globe Tavern. While this work was in progress, Gregg's cavalry division and Samuel P. Spear's cavalry brigade of Kautz's cavalry division were engaged with Wade Hampton's cavalry division (commanded by Matthew C. Butler) on the roads running west toward Dinwiddie Court House.

Before dark August 23, 1864, Gibbon's division moved from the vicinity of the Aiken house toward Reams' Station, and it arrived there the next morning. It then relieved Miles' division, which occupied the entrenchments that had been constructed by Sixth Corps when it advanced to the railroad the previous June. When relieved, Miles continued the work of destruction of the railroad toward Rowanty Creek, and by nightfall had reached a point known as Malone's Crossing, approximately three miles south of Reams' Station. Spear's cavalry brigade covered the advance of the working parties, and Gregg's cavalry division held the approaches from the direction of Dinwiddie Court House and Petersburg. Gregg picketed the country to the left of Warren, and also the roads running from Reams' Station to the Jerusalem Plank Road. On the night of August 24, 1864, Miles withdrew his division to the entrenchments at Reams' Station and left Spear to hold Malone's Crossing.

When Lee was informed by Wade Hampton that Hancock was at work on the railroad, he ordered Ambrose P. Hill on August 22, 1864 to move south with an infantry force from the Petersburg entrenchments and to join the cavalry in preventing further destruction of the track. Hill took with him the brigades of James H. Lane (commanded by James Conner), Alfred M. Scales, and Samuel McGowan of Cadmus M. Wilcox's division; George T. Anderson's brigade of Charles W. Field's division; and William J. Pegram, with three batteries of artillery. In addition, Henry Heth followed Hill with the brigades of John R. Cooke and William McRae of his division, and Heth was followed later by the brigades of David A. Weisiger and John C. C. Sanders of William Mahone's division. Hampton, with Butler's cavalry division and William H. F. Lee's cavalry division (commanded by Rufus Barringer), was ordered to cooperate with Hill in an attack on Hancock's troops on the railroad. Hill left his camps near Petersburg August 24, 1864, and halted that night at Armstrong's Mill, eight miles from Petersburg. The next morning, preceded by Hampton's cavalry, he advanced to Monk's Neck Bridge, three miles from Reams' Station

Hancock was advised of Hill's movement by Army Headquarters at about 11:00 P.M. August 24, 1864, but the exact objective of this movement was not known. Hancock ordered Gibbon to move out with his division on the morning of August 25, 1864, and continue the work of destruction on the railroad, but the movement was postponed for a time until more definite information about the enemy's intentions could be obtained.

At about 8:00 that morning, Spear's cavalry began skirmishing with Hampton's troopers at Malone's Crossing, and about an hour later, Gibbon's division was sent out to support Spear. Gibbon soon discovered that the enemy cavalry was supported by infantry, and when this was reported to Hancock, he was recalled to Reams' Station. Gibbon's division was then placed in the entrenchments on the left of Miles' division. Spear's cavalry continued to oppose Hampton's advance until it reached the vicinity of Reams' Station, and then it was dismounted and placed in line on the left of Gibbon.

The western face of Hancock's entrenchments ran for about 700 yards along the west side of the Weldon Railroad. At each end of this line, the entrenchments turned back to the northeast, crossed the railroad, and ran in that direction for 800 to 1,000 yards. The two refused lines were roughly parallel to one another. The Union troops occupying these

works were in position as follows: Gibbon's division was on the left of the line, to the east of the railroad, facing to the south and southeast. Mathew Murphy's Second Brigade was on the right of the division, next to the railroad; and Thomas A. Smyth's Third Brigade was on the left. Horace P. Rugg's First Brigade had been sent to support Miles' line on the right. At the southwest angle of the works, T. Frederick Brown's Batteries A and B, 1st Rhode Island Light Artillery were in position on the right of Gibbon. J. Henry Sleeper's 10th Battery, Massachusetts Light Artillery was on the right of Brown's batteries, along the main line of works, west of the railroad.

Miles' division held the main line of entrenchments along the railroad to the right of the artillery, and also the refused part of the line east of the railroad. K. Oscar Broady's Fourth Brigade was on the left of Miles' division, next to Sleeper's battery, facing west. Levin Crandell's Consolidated Brigade was on the right of Broady, also facing west, with its right on the railroad. On the evening of August 24, 1864, Crandell was placed in charge of the picket line, and Captain Nelson Penfield was in temporary command of the brigade. (note. In one report, Major John W. Byron was given as the brigade commander.) About 1:00 P.M. August 25, 1864, Broady was assigned command of the Consolidated Brigade, in addition to his own Fourth Brigade. Rugg's brigade of Gibbon's division was placed a short distance in rear of the Consolidated Brigade. James C. Lynch's First Brigade occupied the return of the line, on the right of Consolidated Brigade. Lynch's line faced north, with its left on the railroad near the northwest angle. George K. Dauchy's 12th Battery, New York Light Artillery (formerly commanded by George F. McKnight) was in position about midway on Lynch's front. Reams' Station was a short distance in front of the junction of the Consolidated Brigade and Lynch's brigade.

When Hill arrived in front of Hancock's entrenchments, he sent McGowan's brigade to the Confederate right to join Hampton's cavalry in threatening Gibbon's line; and he moved Lane's, Scales', and Anderson's brigades to the Confederate left in preparation for an attack on the entrenchments at the northwest angle. About noon August 25, 1864, Miles' pickets on the Dinwiddie Court House road were driven in, and at 2:00 P.M., Hill's three brigades attacked on the front of Broady's brigade and the Consolidated Brigade. The enemy pushed forward almost to the Federal entrenchments, but the attack was repulsed. Hill was sick at that time, and Wilcox was in charge of the attack.

Meantime, at Meade's direction, reinforcements had been started on their way to join Hancock. At 1:30 P.M., Mott, commanding Third Division of Second Corps, sent Robert McAllister, with his own Third Brigade and a part of John Pulford's Second Brigade, down the Jerusalem Plank Road to Shay's Tavern, which was located at the junction of the Plank Road with the road to Reams' Station. McAllister arrived there at 5:00 P.M. and reported to Hancock. In addition, between 2:00 and 2:30 P.M., Meade ordered Orlando B. Willcox to march with his Third Division of Ninth Corps to the same point. Willcox arrived at Shay's Tavern about 6:00 P.M. Neither McAllister's detachment nor Willcox's division reached the battlefield.

While Meade's reinforcements were moving up, the fighting continued at Reams' Station. A second attack on Miles' line was repulsed at 3:30 P.M., and then Hill prepared for a final effort. Heth had arrived at about 3:00 P.M. with the brigades of Cooke and McRae, and also with eight guns of Pegram's artillery. Behind Heth, and still on the road, were Sanders' and Weisiger's brigades of Mahone's division. Hill was still sick, and Heth made the arrangements for the next attack.

At 5:30 P.M., after an intense artillery preparation, Heth attacked with the brigades of Lane, Cooke, and McRae, in that order from the Confederate left to right. This attack, like the two preceding attacks, was directed toward the front to Broady's brigade and the Consolidated Brigade. At the same time, Hampton's dismounted cavalry, accompanied by two regiments of McGowan's brigade, advanced against Gibbon's division. Miles' line held for a time, and then the two regiments on the right of the Consolidated Brigade gave way. At the same time, a break occurred on the right of the 125th and 126th New York regiments of the Consolidated Brigade. Rugg's brigade was ordered forward to fill the gap thus created, but the men would neither advance nor even fire at the enemy. Broady's brigade was forced to fall back, and so was Murphy's brigade on its left. The latter offered only feeble resistance. Sleeper's battery and Brown's

Battery B, 1st Rhode Island Light Artillery were captured. Miles collected a small force and recovered a part of the captured line, but was unable to hold it. Lynch formed his brigade on the left flank of the attacking brigades and continued to hold his position until dark, but he was unable to advance.

When Hampton and McGowan's regiments struck Hancock's left, from the south, that part of Murphy's brigade nearest the enemy was driven out of the works in confusion, and a short time later the rest of Gibbon's line collapsed. Gregg's cavalry, including Spear's brigade, which had been dismounted and placed in the rifle pits to the left of Gibbon's line, checked the enemy advance in that direction until dark. Gregg then fell back and formed a new line with Gibbon, a short distance in rear of the captured entrenchments.

About 6:00 P.M., Willcox was ordered to march from the Jerusalem Plank Road and join Hancock at Reams' Station, but the battle was over before it arrived. Mott's troops, under McAllister, remained at Shay's Tavern, about four miles from Reams' Station, until midnight to protect Hancock's left. Hancock withdrew from the railroad that night. Miles' division covered the retreat until he met Willcox, who had then advanced to within about a mile and a half of Reams' Station, and Willcox's division then formed the rear guard. The troops of Hancock's Second Corps marched to the vicinity of the Williams house, where they went into camp about midnight.

Willcox's division remained near Reams' Station until midnight to cover Hancock's withdrawal, and it then marched to the Gurley house, where it arrived about 7:30 the next morning. Willcox then reported to Parke, commanding Ninth Corps. Sometime after midnight, McAllister's detachment of Mott's division returned to its former positions in the entrenchments between the Strong house and the Norfolk and Petersburg Railroad.

Gregg's cavalry division took position on the Plank Road and occupied the country between the road and the left of Warren's Fifth Corps. August 26, 1864, Spear's brigade left Gregg and reported to August V. Kautz, his division commander, near Prince George Court House.

Hampton's cavalry remained at Reams' Station, but Hill's infantry returned to the entrenchments below Petersburg.

The organization of the Union forces at the Battle of Reams' Station August 25, 1864 was as follows:

SECOND CORPS, Winfield S. Hancock

First Division, Nelson A, Miles
    First Brigade, James C. Lynch
    Consolidated Brigade, Levin C. Crandell
        Nelson Penfield
    Fourth Brigade, K. Oscar Broady, wounded
        William Glenny

Note 1. In Second Corps' reports, the Consolidated Brigade was frequently referred to as Third Brigade because most of the regiments originally belonged to Third Brigade.

Note 2. During the evening of August 24, 1864, Crandell was placed in charge of the picket line, and Penfield was temporarily in command of the Consolidated Brigade. One report gave John W. Byron as the brigade commander. At 1:00 P.M. August 25, 1864, Broady was assigned command of the Consolidated Brigade, in addition to his own Fourth Brigade.

Second Division, John Gibbon
    First Brigade, Horace P. Rugg
    Second Brigade, Mathew Murphy
    Third Brigade, Thomas A. Smyth

Artillery Brigade, A. Judson Clark
    10th Battery, Massachusetts Light Artillery, Henry J. Sleeper, wounded
        Henry H. Granger
    3rd Battery (C), New Jersey Light Artillery, Christian Woerner
    12th Battery, New York Light Artillery, George K. Dauchy
    Batteries A and B, 1st Rhode Island Light Artillery, Walter S. Perrin

Note. T. Frederick Brown, commander of Batteries A and B, 1st Rhode Island Light Artillery, was assigned to special service August 23, 1864.

Second Cavalry Division, Army of the Potomac, David McM. Gregg
    First Brigade, William Stedman
    Second Brigade, Charles H. Smith

Kautz's Cavalry Division
    Second Brigade, Samuel P. Spear

OPERATIONS OF SEPTEMBER 1864

Grant's Plans for September 1864. In September 1864, the weather in Virginia improved, and new one-year regiments began to arrive from the north. Then, with cooler weather and a reinforced army, Ulysses S. Grant decided once again to take the offensive. By that time, three railroads linking Petersburg to the East and South had been rendered useless for the bringing in of supplies for Lee's army. In June 1864, the City Point Railroad and the Norfolk and Petersburg Railroad had been cut, and in August 1864, Warren's Fifth Corps had occupied the Weldon Railroad at Globe Tavern. Grant's next objective was the South Side Railroad to Lynchburg, which was used to bring supplies to Petersburg from the Shenandoah Valley and other points in the interior. To cut the South Side Railroad, Grant proposed to move troops westward, south of Petersburg, until he reached the railroad. This movement had the added advantage that it would also block the wagon road on which supplies were hauled to Petersburg from Stony Creek Station on the Weldon Railroad. In his initial plan, Grant also intended to send a force to seal the port of Wilmington, North Carolina, which was the principal point of entry through which blockade runners brought supplies to the Confederacy.

The date originally set for the advance toward the South Side Railroad was October 5, 1864, but this was later moved up to September 29, 1864 as the result of events in the Shenandoah Valley. Philip H. Sheridan's victories over Jubal A. Early's army at Opequon Creek September 19, 1864 and at Fisher's Hill September 23, 1864 caused Robert E. Lee to send Joseph B. Kershaw's infantry division and Wilfred E. Cutshaw's artillery, on the latter date, to reinforce Early; and on September 27, he also sent Thomas L. Rosser's cavalry brigade to the valley. Grant acted quickly to take advantage of the depletion of Lee's forces at Petersburg. He decided to begin his autumn offensive a week earlier than planned because he would have a better chance of success, and also because he would probably prevent further reinforcement of Early with troops from the Petersburg front.

Grant also postponed his intended operation against Wilmington, North Carolina and, largely because of the insistence of Benjamin F. Butler, decided to use the Army of the James in a secondary attack against Richmond from north of the James River. Although Grant had little confidence in Butler's ability to take Richmond, his attack north of the James would probably draw troops from the Petersburg lines to the lines east of Richmond and thus facilitate Meade's operations against the enemy supply routes south of Petersburg

Siege of Petersburg, September 1864. The siege of Petersburg was continued, without any significant events, during most of the month of September 1864. The army was engaged principally in constructing and strengthening the earthworks about the city, and this was interspersed with the daily artillery and picket fire, and also some local actions along the front.

One of the more important additions to the fortifications was a new rear line that was constructed by Second Corps and Ninth Corps to prevent an enemy attack from the south. This line extended from near Globe Tavern along the rear of the front line positions, to Blackwater Creek (or River), near Wells Station on the Norfolk and Petersburg Railroad.

A military railroad was also constructed during the early part of the month to supply the Union forces on the lines to the east and south of Petersburg. The line began at Cedar Level (or Seven-Mile Station) on the City Point Railroad, about two and a half miles behind the trenches, and it then ran in rear of, and roughly parallel to, the Union entrenchments to the Weldon Railroad at Globe Tavern. This work was completed by September 12, 1864, and depots for supplies were established as follows: Hancock's Station, at the crossing of the Jerusalem Plank Road, where Second Corps and Gregg's cavalry division were supplied; Parke's Station, near the Aiken house, about a mile east of Fort Wadsworth, which supplied Ninth Corps; and Warren's Station, near the Weldon Railroad, where Fifth Corps was supplied. In addition, Meade's Station, at the crossing of the Prince George Court House Road, was an important Union supply and hospital depot.

During September 1864, a number of the principal redoubts and earthworks along the line of entrenchments were officially designated by the names of Union officers who had lost their lives during the campaign against Petersburg. The names of these works are given below, in order from right to left, beginning on the Appomattox River:

Fort McGilvery: Near Pages' house, north of the City Point Railroad.

Fort Stedman: Near the Hare house.

Fort Morton: At the Taylor house, about three-fourths of a mile west of the Shand house.

Fort Meikel: Near the Norfolk and Petersburg Railroad.

Fort Rice: In front of Rives' Salient on the Confederate line of entrenchments.

Fort Sedgwick: An advanced work on the Jerusalem Plank Road.

Fort Davis: Southeast of Fort Sedgwick on the Jerusalem Plank Road near the Chieves house.

Fort Prescott: Near the Jones house.

Fort Alexander Hays: Just north of the Strong house.

Fort Howard: At the Chimneys, between the Strong house and the Weldon Railroad.

Fort Wadsworth: At Blicks' house on the Weldon Railroad.

Fort Dushane: At Whites' house on the Weldon Railroad.

Forts on the rear line were also officially named, and these were, in order from the Weldon Railroad to the east along the line, as follows:

Fort Davison: Near the Gurley house.

Fort McMahon: Near the Smith house.

Fort Stevenson: Near the Williams house.

Fort Blaisdell: At the Finn house on the Jeruslem Plank Road.

Fort Patrick Kelly: Near the Widow (Mrs.) Smith's house.

Fort Bross: Near Wells' Station on the Norfolk and Petersburg Railroad.

There were two significant reorganizations in the Army of the Potomac during September 1864. September 1, 1864, John G. Parke's Ninth Corps was reduced from four to three divisions. Julius White's First Division was discontinued, and the regiments were reassigned to Second Division and Third Division. Orlando B. Willcox's Third Division was redesignated as First Division; Robert B. Potter's Second Division retained its original designation; and Edward Ferrero's Fourth Division was redesignated as Third Division. For details of this reorganization, see Ninth Corps.

September 11, 1864, Gouverneur K. Warren's Fifth Corps was also reduced from four to three divisions. Lysander Cutler's Fourth Division was discontinued, and one brigade was assigned to Second Division and one brigade to Third Division. Charles Griffin was assigned command of First Division. For details of the reorganization, see Fifth Corps, Army of the the Potomac.

During most of September 1864, David B. Birney's Tenth Corps held the Petersburg entrenchments from the Appomattox River to the Norfolk and Petersburg Railroad. Gershom Mott's Third Division of Winfield S. Hancock's Second Corps was on the left of Tenth Corps, and was on the line from Fort Meikel, on the railroad, through Fort Rice, Fort Sedgwick, and Fort Davis to Fort Alexander Hays. On the night of September 24, 1864, Nelson A. Miles' First Division and John Gibbon's Second Division (then commanded by Thomas A. Smyth) of Hancock's Second Corps relieved Tenth Corps on the line of entrenchments, and Tenth Corps then moved to the rear preparatory to moving north to join Butler in his advance toward Richmond. Smyth's division occupied the left of Birney's former line, on the right of Mott, and Miles' division was on the right. Second Corps then held the line of entrenchments from the Appomattox River to Fort Alexander Hays, west of the Jerusalem Plank Road.

The above disposition of the troops on the line of entrenchments was altered somewhat by an order of September 25, 1864. Troops of Ninth Corps relieved Robert McAllister's Third Brigade of Mott's division on the line between Fort Alexander Hays and Fort Davis. One regiment and two battalions of McAllister's brigade, however, continued to garrison Fort Davis. McAllister marched to the right with the rest of his brigade, and relieved the left of Smyth's division from the Norfolk and Petersburg Railroad to Fort Morton. Smyth in turn relieved the left of Miles' division from Battery No. 13 to Fort Stedman. When these changes were completed, Miles was on the line from the Appomattox River to Fort Stedman; Smyth, from Fort Stedman to Fort Morton; and Mott, from just south of Fort Morton to, and including, Fort Davis.

During the period September 1–25, 1864, John G. Parke's Ninth Corps was on the line of entrenchments from the left of Mott's division at Fort Alexander Hays to the Weldon Railroad. Willcox's First Division was on the right, and Potter's Second Division was on the left. Ferrero's Third Division was in reserve near the Gurley house. September 25,

1864, Potter's division moved to the rear of Second Corps, near the Avery house, as a reserve. Willcox's division was also withdrawn from the line and placed in reserve to the left of the Jerusalem Plank Road. Ferrero's division moved up and occupied the entrenchments between Fort Davis and Fort Howard.

Warren's Fifth Corps remained along the Weldon Railroad from Fort Wadsworth to Fort Dushane until September 30, 1864. When Willcox's and Potter's divisions of Ninth Corps were withdrawn from the entrenchments east of the railroad, Edward S. Bragg's First Brigade of Samuel W. Crawford's Third Division, Fifth Corps was sent to the right to hold the line from Fort Wadsworth to Fort Howard.

During the early part of September 1864, August V. Kautz's Cavalry Division, Army of the James was on duty picketing the rear of the army. Robert M. West's First Brigade was between the Norfolk and Petersburg Railroad and Mount Sinai Church, which was about two miles southeast of Prince George Court House, on the Prince George Court House Road. Samuel P. Spear's Second Brigade extended West's line to the northeast. Spear's line passed by Sycamore Church, about four miles south of Coggin's Point on the James River, and extended on to Cocke's Mill, two and a half miles farther east.

On the morning of September 16, 1864, a large enemy cavalry force, commanded by Wade Hampton, broke through Spear's line at Sycamore Church and captured about 2,500 head of cattle that were grazing near Coggin's Point. Hampton withdrew about 8:00 A.M. and was pursued by Kautz's cavalry and Henry E. Davies' First Brigade of David McM. Gregg's Second Cavalry Division, Army of the Potomac. Hampton, however, succeeded in returning with the cattle to the safety of the Confederate lines. This was Hampton's so-called "Cattle Raid."

Kautz's cavalry was relieved from the picket line September 27, 1864 by Davies' brigade, and it then crossed the James River to participate in Butler's expedition against Richmond (see below).

Gregg's cavalry division was encamped in the vicinity of the Jerusalem Plank Road during most of September 1864, and it was engaged in picketing the left of the army between the Norfolk and Petersburg Railroad and the Weldon Railroad. It also conducted a number of reconnaissances, and made an unsuccessful attempt to intercept Hampton's cavalry on its return from the Cattle Raid September 16–17, 1864. September 29, 1864, Gregg left the Jerusalem Plank Road on a demonstration against the enemy positions southwest of Globe Tavern, and the next day, Fifth Corps and Ninth Corps moved west at the beginning of Grant's attempt to cut the South Side Railroad (see below).

Battle of Chaffin's Farm (Combats at Fort Harrison, Fort Gilmer, Fort Gregg, New Market Heights, and Laurel Hill), Virginia, September 29–30, 1864. When Grant decided to send Butler to attempt the capture of Richmond, the only troops of the Army of the James that were north of the James River were Charles J. Paine's garrison of the defenses at Deep Bottom, and the workers and guards at Dutch Gap. The other troops of Eighteenth Corps were at Bermuda Hundred, City Point, and posts down the James River. David B. Birney's Tenth Corps was in the trenches at Petersburg, and Kautz's cavalry was picketing the country around Prince George Court House.

Butler's first task was to concentrate his army as an effective field force. To accomplish this, Butler organized a provisional brigade of Eighteenth Corps from newly arrived one-year regiments, and assigned Joseph H. Potter to command. He then used the regiments of this brigade to replace veteran regiments that were on garrison duty at Old Court House, at posts on the James River, and in the defenses of Bermuda Hundred. The regiments thus released for more active duty were assembled at Bermuda Hundred September 27–28, 1864. Potter's men relieved the veteran regiments in the entrenchments at Bermuda Hundred during the night of September 28, 1864. As a further preparation, two regiments of United States Colored Troops from Gilman Marston's Separate Brigade on the James River, and three colored regiments from Dutch Gap rejoined Charles J. Paine's Third Division, Eighteenth Corps at Deep Bottom.

During the night of September 24, 1864, two divisions of Hancock's Second Corps had relieved Birney's Tenth Corps in the trenches at Petersburg. Birney, however, had not immediately returned to the north bank of the Appomattox River, but instead had moved back of the line of entrenchments and camped around corps headquarters at the Friend

house. Because of an apparent misunderstanding, Birney did not join Butler until between 2:00 and 3:30 A.M. September 29, 1864, the day of the Federal attack on New Market Heights.

Kautz's cavalry division was relieved from picket duty south of the James River by Gregg's cavalry, and it then moved back to Bermuda Hundred September 27, 1864.

Butler divided his army into two wings for its advance against Richmond. Edward O. C. Ord was assigned command of a Left Wing that consisted of George J. Stannard's First Division and Charles A. Heckman's Second Division of Ord's Eighteenth Corps; the Eighteenth Corps artillery under George B. Cook; and Edward W. Serrell's 1st New York Engineers. David B. Birney was assigned command of a Right Wing that consisted of Birney's Tenth Corps; Charles J. Paine's Third Division, Eighteenth Corps; and the Tenth Corps Artillery, under Richard H. Jackson.

According to Butler's plan, the Left Wing was to cross the James River at Aiken's Landing, then march up the Varina Road and drive the enemy from their entrenched camp at Chaffin's farm. From there it was to move west to the James River, destroy the bridges there, and march up the Osborne Turnpike toward Richmond. At the same time, the Right Wing was to march north from Deep Bottom, capture New Market Heights, and then advance to the northwest on the New Market Road toward Richmond. After Birney had captured New Market Heights, Kautz was to advance with the cavalry from Deep Bottom to the Darbytown Road, and then move up that road toward Richmond. The attack was to begin at 4:30 A.M. September 29, 1864.

During the night of September 28, 1864, Ord, with the divisions of Stannard and Heckman, marched from Bermuda Hundred for Aiken's Landing. A pontoon bridge was completed across the James River about 2:00 A.M. September 29, 1864, and an hour later Stannard's division began to cross. Heckman followed, and the engineers were the last to cross. Butler left about 7,000 men in the defenses at Bermuda Hundred, including Potter's Provisional Brigade, Charles K. Graham's Naval Brigade, the Pontonier Company, and the army headquarters guard.

When Butler's movement started, Paine's division of Eighteenth Corps was already on duty at

Deep Bottom, and it prepared to march with Tenth Corps the next day. Tenth Corps did not leave its camps south of the Appomattox until 3:00 P.M. September 28, 1864, and the head of the column did not arrive at Deep Bottom until 2:00 the next morning. The rest of the corps was up by 3:30 A.M., but because of the long march, the men were very tired and the corps was seriously weakened by straggling.

September 29, 1864, the Confederate defensive system east of Richmond was only weakly held. In addition, the command situation was not one to ensure a well-coordinated defense. Richard S. Ewell was in command of the Department of Richmond, which included the city and the line of defenses around it. Included in Ewell's command were Bushrod R. Johnson's former brigade, commanded by John M. Hughs; Martin W. Gary's cavalry brigade; two Virginia Reserve battalions; and one Virginia battalion. Also included in the Department of Virginia were the Richmond Forces, commanded by James L. Kemper. These consisted of Seth M. Barton's division, and also some militia and cavalry. Barton's division was composed of a Local Defense Brigade under Patrick T. Moore, and a City Brigade, commanded by Meriwether Lewis Clark. John C. Pemberton was in command of the Artillery Defenses.

On New Market Heights, outside the Department of Richmond. John Gregg commanded the two brigades of Charles W. Field's division of Richard H. Anderson's First Corps, Army of Northern Virginia. One of these brigades, Gregg's own, was commanded by Frederick S. Bass; and the other was Henry L. Benning's brigade, which was commanded by Dudley Du Bose. Ewell and Gregg operated independently of one another, and to correct this situation, First Corps headquarters was sent to Richmond, and Anderson was assigned command of the troops east of the city. Anderson, however, did not arrive at Chaffin's Bluff until 11:00 A.M. September 29, 1864, about seven hours after the fighting had started.

About 4:00 A.M. September 29, 1864, Birney's Right Wing advanced from the James River in three columns. Alfred H. Terry's First Division, Tenth Corps marched on the right along the road from Deep Bottom. When Terry reached the Kingsland Road, he deployed his division to the right along Four-Mile Creek, with Joseph C. Abbott's Second Brigade on the left, Francis B. Pond's First Brigade in the center, and Harris M. Plaisted's Third Brigade on the right.

William Birney marched with his brigade of colored troops to the left of Terry. Officially, Birney's brigade was designated as First Brigade, Third Division, Tenth Corps, but at the time of the battle, Third Division consisted only of Birney's brigade. Still farther to the left, Paine's Third Division, Eighteenth Corps advanced up the Grover House Road, and it was followed by Robert S. Foster's Second Division, Tenth Corps and Jackson's artillery.

About 5:30 A.M., Paine encountered enemy skirmishers along Four-Mile Creek, south of New Market Heights, and he deployed Samuel A. Duncan's Third Brigade, his leading brigade, in line of battle. Paine's other two brigades halted in column in rear of Duncan, near the Kingsland Road. Foster halted behind Alonzo Draper's Second Brigade of Paine's division on the Grover House Road.

The enemy forces holding the heights were, from the Confederate left to right, Gary's cavalry brigade, facing Terry's division; Bass' brigade (John Gregg's); and Wyatt M. Elliott's City of Richmond Battalion. John Guy's Virginia Reserve Battalion and Du Bose's brigade (Benning's) were on their way toward the heights.

When deployed, Duncan then launched an unsuccessful attack on New Market Heights, during which his brigade was virtually destroyed. Duncan was wounded, and John W. Ames assumed command of his brigade. Draper's brigade then attacked and, after an initial check, charged and carried the entrenchments. Terry's division advanced with Draper, and together they occupied the heights. This occurred after John Gregg had learned that Ord's divisions were marching up the Varina Road against the Confederate center, and after he, Gregg, had ordered most of the troops defending New Market Heights to Chaffin's farm to meet that threat.

Ord's Left Wing moved out from Aikens' just before daylight September 29, 1864, and, while Birney was approaching New Market Heights, it marched up the Varina Road toward the Exterior Line of Defenses of Richmond. Michael Donohoe, colonel of the 10th New Hampshire Infantry, was out in front in charge of a strong line of skirmishers.

Ord's brigades were on the road behind him, in order, from front to rear, as follows: Hiram Burnham's Second Brigade, Aaron F. Stevens' First Brigade, and Samuel H. Roberts' Third Brigade, all of Stannard's First Division; and then Edward H. Ripley's Second Brigade, James Jourdan's First Brigade, and Harrison S. Fairchild's Third Brigade of Heckman's Second Division.

As Ord approached Childreys' field, he formed Stannard's division for an attack on Fort Harrison, which was directly ahead, to the northwest, on the enemy line of works. Burnham's brigade was deployed across the Varina Road; Stevens' brigade followed in column, on the left of the road; and Roberts' brigade, also in column, advanced on the right of the road. Heckman was directed to advance with his division to the right and rear of Stannard, and then attack the Confederate left (or northern) flank of the fort. Burnham and Stannard, in person, remained behind with Ord, and Roberts, who was the senior officer with the attacking column, was in charge of the assault.

Stannard's division began its attack at 6:00 A.M., and an hour later it broke through the enemy lines and drove the defenders from the fort. Losses were heavy, and the division was temporarily much disorganized by the attack. All three brigade commanders had to be replaced. Stevens was seriously wounded early in the advance; and Roberts, who was sick at the time, collapsed shortly after entering the fort. Burnham came up from the rear and joined his brigade, and he was killed soon after entering the fort. John Raulston assumed command of Stevens' First Brigade; Michael T. Donohoe, of Burnham's Second Brigade; and Edgar M. Cullen took charge of Roberts' Third Brigade. Heckman's division was unable to join in the attack on the fort. Some of Ripley's and Jourdan's men, however, did capture Battery No. 10 and Battery No. 11, on the outer line of defenses to the northeast of the fort, and the enemy then fell back to the Intermediate Line.

After the capture of Fort Harrison, Ord, with a small group of men, and followed by Stannard with the remnants of Donohoe's and Cullen's brigades, moved down the enemy line of entrenchments toward the bridges over the James River near Chaffin's Bluff. Raulston and the stragglers of First Division remained to hold the fort. Ord and Stannard were finally halted at a work near the Osborne Turnpike (later named Fort Hoke). Ord was wounded at about that time, and Heckman, as the senior officer, assumed command of Eighteenth Corps. Heckman immediately abandoned the movement toward the enemy right, and then launched a series of uncoordinated frontal attacks against the Intermediate Line of Defenses. Ripley's brigade of Second Division attacked under a heavy fire toward Fort Gilmer and Fort Gregg, but was repulsed. Fairchild attacked from Battery No. 11, toward Fort Johnson, but he was stopped and was then driven back in disorder when struck by a flank attack. Jourdan's brigade did not advance from the Exterior Line. The attacks by Second Division ended about 11:00 A.M.

After the capture of New Market Heights, Birney, with Foster's division, pursued John Gregg's troops to the northwest along the New Market Road. By 10:00 A.M., Rufus Daggett's leading First Brigade had captured that part of the Exterior Line near Clynes' house, and had arrived near the Varina Road. Galusha Pennypacker's Second Brigade was close behind, and it was followed by Louis Bell's Third Brigade. The enemy fell back from the Exterior Line for about one and one-fourth miles to Laurel Hill Church, and formed on a new line across the New Market Road. Daggett followed and attacked, but was driven back. Then, with the help of Pennypacker and Bell, Daggett drove the enemy back to their Intermediate Line.

Foster did not follow, but turned toward Fort Gilmer, on his left and rear. He deployed along the New Market Road to the east of Laurel Hill Church, facing toward the fort, and then waited for two hours for stragglers to come up, and for the rest of David B. Birney's Right Wing to arrive. The latter finally started for the front sometime after 9:30 A.M., with Paine's division in the lead, then William Birney's Colored Brigade, and Terry's division in the rear. These troops had arrived on the Exterior Line by noon.

Birney then prepared for an attack on Fort Gilmer. Foster's division, which was already in position along the New Market Road, was to attack from the north. Pennypacker's brigade was on the right of Foster's line, Daggett's brigade was on the center, and Bell's brigade was on the left. Paine's division was to remain near Laurel Hill Church as a reserve for Foster. William Birney's brigade was deployed near the Varina Road for an attack against Fort Gilmer from the east. Plaisted's brigade of Terry's division was designated as a reserve for William Birney, and the other two brigades of Terry's division, Pond's and Abbott's, were placed at Clynes' field, near the intersection of the New Market Road and the Exterior Line.

Foster's line advanced about 1:30 P.M., but suffered heavy losses and was forced to withdraw. William Birney moved out at 2:00 P.M., after Foster's repulse, and although some of his troops reached the moat of the fort, he too was forced to fall back. Still later, Heckman sent Jourdan's First Brigade, Second Division, Eighteenth Corps against Fort Gregg, but this attack, too, was repulsed with heavy loss.

Kautz's cavalry division began crossing the James River at Deep Bottom about 6:30 A.M. September 29, 1864 and, after passing through David B. Birney's infantry at New Market Heights, marched northward to the Darbytown Road. It then turned to the left on that road and marched toward Richmond, and about 10:00 A.M. arrived in front of the fortifications, two miles from the city. After a feeble attempt to break through with Robert M. West's First Brigade, Kautz moved north to the Charles City Road to seek a better route. After several attempts to penetrate the enemy lines farther north, Kautz withdrew about midnight, and at 7:30 the next morning rejoined the army at Dr. Johnson's, near the Darbytown Road.

Shortly after 2:00 P.M. September 29, 1864, Terry, with the two brigades at Clynes' field (Pond's and Abbott's), marched to the Darbytown Road, presumably to join Kautz. At 3:00 P.M., Plaisted's brigade of Terry's division was sent to follow Terry and the other two brigades of the division. Terry arrived on the Darbytown Road about a half mile west of the Exterior Line, six hours after Kautz had moved on. Terry did not find Kautz, but remained on the Darbytown Road during the remainder of the afternoon, and then returned to Clynes' field that evening.

During the late afternoon of September 29, 1864, Foster, William Birney, and Paine fell back to defensive positions along the Exterior Line. Eighteenth Corps was also ordered to take up a defensive position.

Shortly before dark, Cullen's brigade of Stannard's division captured the earthwork near the Osborne Turnpike (later named Fort Hoke), but a short time later Heckman ordered Stannard to move back to Fort Harrison. Heckman's division was then on the left of Stannard, along the Varina Road.

There were several changes in position of the troops of Butler's army during the night of September 29, 1864 and the next morning, but as finally established, the Union line was held, from right to left, as follows: Kautz's cavalry was on the right near Dr. Johnson's, where the Darbytown Road crossed the old Exterior Line. Foster's division, William Birney's brigade, and Paine's division, in that order, occupied the Exterior Line from the New Market Road down to the right of Fort Harrison. Stannard's division was at Fort Harrison, with its left curved back to the Varina Road. There, it connected with the right of Heckman's division, which extended southward along the Varina Road. Pennypacker's brigade, which had been detached from Foster's division, covered the ground from the left of Heckman, across to Signal Hill on the James River. Grant decided not to renew the attack on September 30, 1864, and directed that the Army of the James hold its defensive position during the day.

Sometime after 5:00 A.M. September 30, 1864, Butler, who was dissatisfied with Heckman's performance of the day before, assigned Godfrey Weitzel, his chief engineer, to the command of Eighteenth Corps. Heckman resumed command of Second Division, Eighteenth Corps. Later, about 10:00 A.M., Butler issued orders that broke up the temporary wing organization of the army, and assigned each corps to the defense of a specified part of the new line. At the same time, Birney relieved Paine of the responsibility for affairs at Deep Bottom and New Market Heights, and assigned John Moore, with his 203rd Pennsylvania Regiment, to take charge of that area.

According to Butler's orders, Kautz's cavalry division was to remain on the Darbytown Road. Birney's Tenth Corps was assigned the task of guarding the right flank of the army, and it was to hold the defensive line from Clynes' field down to a point just north of Fort Harrison. Pennypacker's brigade was ordered to return from the left of the army and rejoin Tenth Corps on that line. At that time, Paine's division of Eighteenth Corps was on a part of Birney's line between the Varina Road and

Fort Harrison, and William Birney was ordered to relieve Paine. Before this could be done, however, the enemy attempted to recapture Fort Harrison, and Eighteenth Corps was ordered to occupy the line on the left of Tenth Corps. Stannard's division in Fort Harrison and Heckman's division on its left were directed to remain where they were.

When Lee learned, early on the morning of September 29, 1864, that Federal troops were north of the James River in force, he sent Charles W. Field's division of Richard H. Anderson's corps from Petersburg to reinforce Ewell and John Gregg. Then, when Lee learned of the capture of Fort Harrison, he also sent Robert Hoke's division of Pierre G. T. Beauregard's Confederate Department of North Carolina and Southern Virginia, and Hoke's division was north of the James by daylight September 30, 1864. Lee, in person, arrived near Chaffin's farm about 2:30 P.M. September 29, 1864, a short time after the Federal attack on Fort Gilmer.

During the morning of September 30, 1864, the divisions of Field and Hoke were formed for an effort to recapture Fort Harrison. Field's division was placed near Fort Johnson for an attack from the northwest, and Hoke's division was deployed west of the fort for an attack from that direction.

Fort Harrison was defended by Stannard's First Division, Eighteenth Corps. Raulston was still in command of First Brigade, but the commanders of the other two brigades had changed during the night. Cullen had taken charge of Second Brigade in place of Donohoe, who had been wounded the evening before. Stephen Moffitt followed Cullen in command of Third Brigade. These three brigades were on the division front as follows: Raulston's was on the right; Cullen's, in the center; and Moffitt's was on the left.

The enemy attack began about noon, when Field's division advanced from the northwest. This attack was quickly repulsed, and Field withdrew to the vicinity of Fort Johnson. Stannard was seriously wounded, and Cullen, as the senior officer in the fort, assumed command of First Division. Just as Hoke's division began to advance, Jourdan, whose First Brigade of Heckman's division was on the left of Stannard, came into the fort with his two New York regiments to reinforce the defenders. Jourdan was senior to Cullen, and he assumed command and took charge of the defense of the fort. This caused

other changes in command. While Cullen was briefly in command of First Division, Moffitt was in command of Second Brigade, but when Cullen resumed command of Second Brigade, Moffitt returned to Third Brigade and relieved James Brown, who had commanded temporarily during Moffitt's absence.

Only Alfred H. Colquitt's brigade and Thomas L. Clingman's brigade (then commanded by Hector M. McKethan) of Hoke's division attacked Fort Harrison that afternoon, and they were soon stopped by a devastating fire from the defenders. By 3:00 P.M. the fighting was over.

The last sizeable action of the Battle of Chaffin's Farm occurred during the afternoon of October 1, 1864, when Kautz's cavalry and Terry's First Division, Tenth Corps made a reconnaissance against the enemy works near Ropers' farm. That afternoon, Kautz, with West's First Brigade, advanced on the Darbytown Road, and Spear's Second Brigade moved out on the Charles City Road. West was followed on the Darbytown Road by Abbott's brigade, and then Pond's brigade, of Terry's division. Abbott's brigade deployed across the road and advanced to Ropers' farm. Upon approaching the enemy works there, Abbott halted his line in a ravine. Pond's brigade remained in column on the road to the rear. Terry examined the enemy works and found them manned in force, and about 5:00 P.M. that dark and rainy evening, he moved back and rejoined the corps. Kautz's cavalry, which had moved to the flanks when the infantry came up, also withdrew.

There was some activity October 2, 1864, as probes and other movements were carried out along the line, but that evening the Battle of Chaffin's Farm was definitely ended.

The organization of the troops of Benjamin F. Butler's Army of the James that were engaged at the Battle of Chaffin's Farm September 29–30, 1864 was as follows:

TENTH CORPS, David B. Birney

First Division, Alfred H. Terry
  First Brigade, Francis B. Pond
  Second Brigade, Joseph C. Abbott
  Third Brigade, Harris M. Plaisted

Second Division, Robert S. Foster

First Brigade, Rufus Daggett, to September 29, 1864, wounded

Albert M. Barney

Second Brigade, Galusha Pennypacker

Third Brigade, Louis Bell

Note. Pennypacker was slightly wounded in the attack at Fort Gilmer, and he very briefly turned over the command of the brigade to Isaiah Price. Pennypacker, however, soon resumed command.

Colored Brigade, William Birney

Artillery Brigade, Richard H. Jackson

1st Battery, Connecticut Light Artillery, James B. Clinton

4th Battery, New Jersey Light Artillery, Charles R. Doane

5th Battery, New Jersey Light Artillery, Henry H. Metcalf

Battery E, 1st Pennsylvania Light Artillery, Henry Y. Wildey

Battery C, 3rd Rhode Island Heavy Artillery, Martin S. James

Batteries C and D, 1st United States Artillery, Redmond Tully

Battery M, 1st United States Artillery, Loomis L. Langdon

Battery E, 3rd United States Artillery, John R. Myrick

Battery D, 4th United States Artillery, Frederick M. Follett

EIGHTEENTH CORPS, Edward O. C. Ord, to September 29, 1864, wounded

Charles A. Heckman, to September 30, 1864

Godfrey Weitzel

First Division, George J. Stannard, to September 30, 1864, wounded

Edgar M. Cullen, September 30, 1864, briefly

James Jourdan

First Brigade, Aaron F. Stevens, to September 29, 1864, wounded

John Raulston

Second Brigade, Hiram Burnham, to September 29, 1864, killed

Michael T. Donohoe, to late September 29, 1864, wounded

Edgar M. Cullen

Stephen Moffitt, September 30, 1864, briefly

Edgar M. Cullen

Third Brigade, Samuel H. Roberts, to September 29, 1864, sick

Edgar M. Cullen, September 29, 1864

Stephen Moffitt

James Brown

Stephen Moffitt

Second Division, Charles A. Heckman

First Brigade, James Jourdan, to September 30, 1864

George M. Guion

Second Brigade, Edward H. Ripley

Third Brigade, Harrison S. Fairchild

Note. The list of the division and brigade commanders in Second Division during the battle is not complete, and there is no definite information as to who they were. When Heckman assumed command of Eighteenth Corps September 29, 1864, Fairchild probably assumed command of the division; and either Guion, the senior officer of the division, or James L. Anderson, senior officer of Third Brigade, took charge of Fairchild's brigade.

Third Division, Charles J. Paine

First Brigade, John H. Holman

Second Brigade, Alonzo Draper, to September 30, 1864, sick

John W. Ames

Third Brigade, Samuel A. Duncan, to September 29, 1864, wounded

John W. Ames, to September 30, 1864

Augustus Boerenstein

Note. When Ames was transferred from Third Brigade to Second Brigade late on September 30, 1864, he was placed in charge of both brigades, and he continued to command them during the rest of the battle.

Temporary Brigade, David B. White

Note. The Temporary Brigade was probably organized at Bermuda Hundred October 1, 1864 from the 5th Maryland, 2nd New Hampshire, and 12th New Hampshire, and was then sent north of the James River to reinforce Butler's force already there. This brigade served as a separate unit until October 7, 1864.

Artillery Brigade, George B. Cook

Battery E, 3rd New York Light Artillery, George E. Ashby

Battery H, 3rd New York Light Artillery, William J. Riggs

Battery K, 3rd New York Light Artillery, James R. Angel

Battery M, 3rd New York Light Artillery, John H. Howell

7th Battery, New York Light Artillery, Martin V. McIntyre

16th Battery, New York Light Artillery, Richard H. Lee

17th Battery, New York Light Artillery, George T. Anthony

Battery A, 1st Pennsylvania Light Artillery, William Stitt

Battery F, 1st Rhode Island Light Artillery, Thomas Simpson

Battery B, 1st United States Artillery, Robert M. Hall

Battery L, 4th United States Artillery, Stephen L. Hubbard

Battery A, 5th United States Artillery, Israel Ludlow

Battery F, 5th United States Artillery, Alexander J. McDonald

Cavalry Division, August V. Kautz
First Brigade, Robert M. West
Second Brigade, Samuel P. Spear

Battle of Poplar Spring Church (Combats at Wyatt's Farm, Peebles' Farm, Chappell's House, Pegram's Farm, and the Vaughan Road), Virginia, September 29, 1864–October 2, 1864.

Grant's autumn offensive opened on the morning of September 29, 1864, when Butler's Army of the James attacked the eastern defenses of Richmond at Chaffin's farm and New Market Heights (see above). Grant waited for a time to observe the effects of Butler's operation on the disposition of Lee's forces south of Petersburg, and the next day he instructed Meade to begin his advance against the enemy communications west of the Weldon Railroad. The troops selected for this movement were Orlando B. Willcox's First Division (temporarily commanded by John F. Hartranft) and Robert B. Potter's Second Division of Parke's Ninth Corps, both of which were in reserve at that time; Charles Griffin's First Division and Romeyn B. Ayres' Second Division of Warren's Fifth Corps; and David McM. Gregg's Second Cavalry Division, Army of the Potomac, In addition, J. William Hofmann's Third Brigade of Samuel W. Crawford's Third Division, Fifth Corps was temporarily attached to Ayres' division. Parke was in immediate command of the two divisions of Ninth Corps and Warren of the two divisions of Fifth Corps, and both reported directly to Meade.

One of the first steps in preparation for this movement was to assemble the two divisions of Ninth Corps near the Weldon Railroad. On the morning of September 28, 1864, Potter's division moved from its reserve position in rear of the line of Hancock's Second Corps to the Gurley house, about one-half mile southeast of Globe Tavern. At 4:00 A.M. September 29, 1864, Hartranft's division (Willcox

resumed command the next day) marched west from its reserve position near the Jerusalem Plank Road and joined Potter's division at Gurleys'.

There was some preliminary activity against the enemy September 29, 1864. Early that morning, Gregg concentrated his cavalry on the Jerusalem Plank Road in preparation for a demonstration against the Confederate positions to the southwest of Globe Tavern. He then marched by way of Globe Tavern to Fort Dushane, and then down the Halifax Road to its intersection with the Lower Church Road at Wyatt's Crossing. From that point, Henry E. Davies continued on to Reams' Station with his First Brigade, and Gregg marched with Charles H. Smith's Second Brigade on the Lower Church Road toward the Vaughan Road. Against some opposition, Gregg reached the Vaughan Road, and then proceeded on westward along that road to Hatcher's Run. There he encountered Wade Hampton's cavalry, and then turned north on the Duncan Road. When he reached the vicinity of the Watkins farm, near the junction of the Harman Road, he learned that enemy infantry were ahead. He withdrew that afternoon to the Wyatt plantation, where he took up a defensive position on some high ground overlooking Arthur's Swamp. During the late afternoon, the enemy strongly attacked Gregg and drove him back to the Wyatt house. He was joined there by Edgar M. Gregory's Second Brigade of Griffin's division of Fifth Corps, which had been sent up by Warren to support the cavalry.

Meantime, Davies' brigade had arrived at Reams' Station and had then marched west on the Stage Road to a point near Monk's Neck Bridge over Rowanty Creek. He met with some resistance at that point and then returned to Reams' Station. During the night of September 29, 1864, Davies joined Gregg at the Wyatt farm and relieved Smith's brigade. Gregg, with Smith's brigade, then fell back to the vicinity of the Perkins house, near the Weldon Railroad. Gregory's brigade also left Wyatts' that night and returned to its division.

In addition to Gregg's demonstration, Henry Baxter's Second Brigade of Crawford's division was ordered out to the west of the Halifax Road on a reconnaissance to determine the enemy's strength in that direction. About 3:00 P.M. September 29, 1864, Baxter's brigade, which was garrisoning Fort Dushane, marched out on the Poplar Spring Road to the vicinity of Peebles' farm. When Baxter arrived near the farm, he found the enemy in considerable strength and, with his mission accomplished, returned to Fort Dushane about 5:00 P.M.

According to the orders for September 30, 1864, Warren was to move up the Poplar Spring Road and attempt to reach its intersection with the Squirrel Level Road. Parke was to follow Warren to Poplar Spring Church, and was then to cross Arthur's Swamp at Widow Smith's and take position on the left of Warren. Parke was then to join Warren in an advance against the enemy works on Peebles' farm. Gregg's cavalry was to take position on the left of the infantry at the E. Wilkinson farm, near the point where the Squirrel Level Road joined the Vaughan Road, about two miles south of the Poplar Spring Road. In the original orders, Meade was to begin his advance at daylight September 30, 1864, but this was subsequently delayed until 10:00 A.M. by an order from Grant.

Promptly at 10:00 A.M., Griffin's division, followed by Ayres' division, marched south on the Halifax Road to the Poplar Spring Road, and there turned west on the latter road toward Poplar Spring Church and the Peebles farm. Parke's divisions left the Gurley farm at 10:00 A.M., and a half hour later fell in behind Warren. The only enemy forces to oppose Warren's advance were the pickets of James Dearing's cavalry brigade (then commanded by Joel R. Griffin), and these fell back to Peebles' field.

Warren reached Poplar Spring Church, about 700 yards west of the Vaughan Road, at 11:00 A.M., and began preparations for an attack. He directed Ayres to turn off with his division, march north on the Vaughan Road, and then deploy across that road, facing the enemy entrenchments south of Petersburg. This movement cleared the Poplar Spring Road for the approach of Ninth Corps. Potter's division of Ninth Corps arrived at Poplar Spring Church, in rear of Griffin's division, a little after noon, and Willcox's division was close behind. John I. Curtin's First Brigade of Potter's division was formed across the road, facing west, and Simon G. Griffin's Second Brigade was placed north of the road, on the right of Curtin, facing north.

Griffin's division moved on beyond Poplar Spring Church and deployed north of the Poplar Spring Road in a ravine, just east of the Squirrel Level Road. Griffin's line faced west toward Peebles' farm, with Horatio G. Sickel's First Brigade on the left, Edgar M. Gregory's Second Brigade on the center, and James Gwyn's Third Brigade on the right, opposite the Confederate Fort Archer. Fort Archer was the principal defensive work on the enemy line at Peebles' farm, and was located just to the east of the Church Road. Joel R. Griffin and two regiments of his cavalry brigade were the only enemy troops opposing Griffin. A detachment of the 7th Confederate Cavalry under Jesse H. Sikes garrisoned the fort, and the rest of that regiment and the 8th Georgia Cavalry manned the adjoining lines on Peebles' farm.

Griffin attacked at 1:00 P.M., in a column of three brigade lines, with Gwyn's brigade in front, following the skirmishers, then Gregory's brigade, and Sickel's brigade in the rear. Thirty minutes later, Griffin's troops had captured Fort Archer and all the enemy works on Peebles' farm. Gwyn was injured near the fort when his horse fell, and Ellis Spear commanded the brigade during the rest of the day. Joseph J. Bartlett returned to the army from sick leave, and resumed command of Third Brigade the next day.

After the capture of Fort Archer, two regiments of Ellis Spear's brigade advanced northward from Fort Archer along the Confederate Squirrel Level Line, and drove the defenders as far north as Fort Cherry, which was located near the W. W. Davis house on the Squirrel Level Road. The other three regiments of Spear's brigade then came up, and the brigade held its position until relieved by Ayres' division about 4:00 P.M. Spear then rejoined the division at Peebles' farm.

Instead of crossing Arthur's Swamp to the left of Warren as originally planned, Ninth Corps simply moved up the Poplar Spring Road to take position on the line of Charles Griffin's division. Curtin's brigade turned to the north on the Squirrel Level Road, marched to the rear of Griffin's line to Robert Chappell's farm, and then established a defensive position that extended from Fort Bratton to the southwest toward Charles Griffin's position. Simon G. Griffin's brigade followed Curtin as far as Peebles' field, and then occupied the captured works west of Griffin's division, and on the northern part of the field. By that time, Willcox's division had arrived. Hartranft's Second Brigade took position on a line that extended from the left of Simon G.

Griffin's brigade toward the southeast in the direction of the Clements, house, which was just north of where present-day Route 673 joins the Squirrel Level Road from the west. Samuel Harriman's First Brigade connected with the left of Hartranft's brigade and extended back to the main stream of Arthur's Swamp, facing south. Napoleon B. McLaughlen's Third Brigade was placed in reserve near the Peebles house.

Ayres' division was ordered up to the right of Griffin's division, and Elwell S. Otis, commanding Ayres' leading First Brigade, arrived at Chappell's field between 3:00 and 3:30 P.M. Otis then relieved Curtin's brigade of Ninth Corps, and Curtin rejoined Potter's division. At that time, Ayres' other brigades were still on the road, following Otis.

While these movements were in progress, Gregg's cavalry division was advancing to the south of Ninth Corps and Fifth Corps, watching the left flank of the two corps.

At 3:00 P.M., Ninth Corps resumed its advance and moved onto Oscar Pegram's farm. It then passed the farmhouse and entered the Jones field to the north. Potter's division was in the lead, with Simon G. Griffin's brigade astride the Church Road, and Curtin's brigade on its left and rear. Willcox's division followed Potter, with Hartranft's brigade on the left rear of Curtin, and Harriman's brigade behind Hartranft, with its right at the Pegram house. McLaughlen's brigade was in column, south of the Pegram house. At this point, Parke halted his command to rearrange the troops. Simon Griffin's brigade remained in its position between the Church Road and the Pegram House Road, but Curtin's brigade was moved up to the left of Simon Griffin. Potter then remained in this position for about two hours, with the brigades of Willcox's division to his left and rear.

Earlier in the day, Charles Griffin and Parke had been opposed by only Wade Hampton's cavalry, but about 4:00 P.M., Cadmus M. Wilcox arrived in front of Parke with the brigades of James H. Lane and Samuel McGowan of his division of Ambrose P. Hill's corps. Wilcox was followed a short time later by Henry Heth, with the brigades of James J. Archer and William McRae of his division, also of Hill's corps.

Shortly after 5:00 P.M., Parke ordered Potter to attack. Simon Griffin's brigade advanced through the Jones field to a point just north of the Jones house, directly in front of Wilcox's brigades. Curtin advanced with Simon Griffin's brigade for a short time, but about halfway across the field he halted at a point well to the left and rear of Simon Griffin. At that time, Wilcox advanced and attacked Griffin's brigade in front and on both flanks, and drove it back in disorder. Then continuing his flanking attack, Wilcox broke up the entire Ninth Corps line from the Jones house to Arthur's Swamp. The two brigades of Potter's division were wrecked, and Hartranft's brigade of Willcox's division also suffered severely. Harriman's brigade of Willcox's division started forward in support, but was ordered back to the vicinity of Oscar Pegram's house. McLaughlen's brigade remained for a time south of the house.

Parke and Charles Griffin finally were able to establish a defensive line across the Pegram farm, and along this line, the enemy advance was halted that evening. Hartranft's brigade was west of the Pegram house, with its left on Arthur's Swamp; Harriman's brigade was on the right of Hartranft, with its right on the Pegram Farm Road, just north of the farmhouse; and the remnants of Potter's division were in front of the farmhouse, on the right of the road.

Griffin's division of Fifth Corps did not advance with Ninth Corps that afternoon, but it continued to hold its position at Peebles' farm. When the enemy attacked Potter's division at the Jones field, Charles Griffin was ordered at 5:30 P.M. to the Pegram field to help stop Wilcox's advance. Ellis Spear's brigade arrived just in time and deployed across the Church Road, just south of the Boswell house. Sickel's brigade then came up on the right of Spear, and Gregory's brigade on the left of Spear. McLaughlen's brigade of Willcox's division also moved up and completed the line between Gregory and Potter. There was heavy fighting for a time on this part of the field, but the Federal line held.

Hofmann's brigade did not accompany Ayres' division to Chappell's farm that day, but apparently remained at Peebles' farm. Late that afternoon, however, it was ordered to reinforce Griffin, and it arrived at the front a short time before 6:00 P.M.

During the night of September 30, 1864, Meade directed Parke, with his Ninth Corps, and Griffin, with his division of Fifth Corps, to fall back to the enemy's old Squirrel Level Line of entrenchments on the Peebles farm. They did so, but Hofmann's brigade and several regiments of pickets were left at the Pegram farm to cover the withdrawal.

On the morning of October 1, 1864, the troops of Ninth Corps and Fifth Corps were in position on the new Federal line west of the Weldon Railroad as follows: Ninth Corps was on the left, with Willcox's division on the left of the corps line, facing south and west. Willcox's line extended from Arthur's Swamp, at a point east of the Clements house, around the Clements house, and then northward to the Peebles house. Willcox's brigades were in position, from left to right, as follows: Harriman's, McLaughlen's, and Hartranft's. Potter's division was on the right of Willcox, and its line extended along the old Squirrel Level Road on the Peebles farm from Arthur's Swamp to the Church Road near Fort Archer. Potter's line faced north, with Simon Griffin's brigade on the left and Curtin's brigade on the right.

Warren's Fifth Corps held the right of the new line. Charles Griffin's division was on the left of the corps line and extended along the old Confederate trenches from, and including, Fort Archer to the Chappell farm, where it connected with Ayres' division at a point just south of Fort Bratton. Sickel's brigade was on the left, Spear's brigade (Joseph J. Bartlett assumed command October 1, 1864) was in the center, and Gregory's brigade was on the right. Ayres' division was on the right of the new line. Otis' First Brigade occupied Fort Bratton and the lines immediately to the right and left of the fort; Arthur H. Grimshaw's Third Brigade continued the line to the right, across the Chappell field, east of the Squirrel Level Road; and Samuel A. Graham's Second Brigade held the line toward the southeast, to the Northeastern Fork of Arthur's Swamp. Hofmann's brigade of Crawford's Third Division was at the Pegram farm, but it soon returned to Ayres and was placed on the right of Graham.

About 9:00 P.M. September 30, 1864, Warren had ordered Crawford to send Edward S. Bragg's First Brigade of his Third Division from its position near the Weldon Railroad to the Flowers house on the Vaughan Road. When it arrived there early on the morning of October 1, 1864, it was formed in line across the Vaughan Road. Bragg then covered the front with skirmishers from the right of Graham's line to the left of Crawford's pickets, which were out to the west of Fort Wadsworth.

It was Meade's intention to resume his advance October 1, 1864, but before he could get started, A. P. Hill launched an attack on Ayres' line at the Chappell farm. At 8:00 A.M., Heth's division advanced along the Squirrel Level Road and drove back the Federal pickets south of the W. W. Davis house to Ayres' main line of entrenchments. Earlier that morning, Cadmus M. Wilcox had formed his division for an attack north of Oscar Pegram's farm, and when he heard the firing on his left, he moved forward. He drove Hofmann's brigade and the regiments on picket at Pegram's farm back to the Federal main line in the Peebles field, and then halted to await the outcome of Heth's attack before resuming his advance. Back on Heth's front, McRae's brigade advanced at 9:00 A.M., in a pouring rain, and attacked the entrenchments that were held by Otis' and Grimshaw's brigades, but was driven back with heavy loss. Archer's brigade and Joseph R. Davis' brigades then attacked, but they too were repulsed with serious losses. When Wilcox learned of Heth's failure, he made no further attempt to advance on his part of the line. Otis was wounded during Heth's attack, and James Grindlay assumed command of his First Brigade.

On the left of Meade's army, Gregg's cavalry division was engaged in severe fighting during most of October 1, 1864. Early that morning, Gregg had brought his division to the Peebles farm, but when the engagement at Chappells' had ended, and he was no longer needed, he marched back to the Vaughan Road. He then marched down the Vaughan Road to the Wyatt Road, and there he turned eastward to McDowells', which was held by Pierce M. B. Young's brigade of Matthew C. Butler's Confederate cavalry division. Young was quickly driven from McDowells' and he then withdrew westward on the Vaughan Road to the high ground at E. Wilkinson's, just east of where the Squirrel Level Road joined the Vaughan Road. Davies' brigade of Gregg's cavalry division followed Young, but was driven back. Young was then reinforced by Butler's other brigade, commanded by John Dunovant, and together they advanced against Davies, but they were repulsed. There was continuous fighting during most of the day, but without decisive results. About 3:00 P.M., John R. Chambliss' brigade of

William H. F. Lee's Cavalry Division (Chambliss' brigade was commanded by J. Lucius Davis) joined Butler, and these three brigades, commanded by Hampton in person, again attacked Gregg's line. The action continued until almost dark, and ended with the repulse of Hampton and the death of Dunovant. Davies' brigade did most of the fighting, because most of Charles H. Smith's brigade was in the rear, guarding the line across Wyatts' plantation to the Weldon Railroad.

Despite the interruptions caused by Heth's attacks that morning, Meade was still determined to advance later in the day. He decided not to move, however, until Gershom Mott's Third Division of Winfield S. Hancock's Second Corps arrived from his position on the line of the Petersburg entrenchments. Shortly after 1:00 A.M. October 1, 1864, Mott had been ordered to withdraw his division from the trenches and join Warren and Parke. Nelson A. Miles' First Division and John Gibbon's Second Division were to extend their fronts and relieve Mott's troops. The transfer was not completed until about 8:00 A.M., and soon thereafter, Mott started for Peebles' farm. There was considerable delay in forwarding the troops by the Military Railroad to Globe Tavern, and the first units did not arrive until about 3:00 P.M. The last of the division was not up until nearly 6:00 P.M., and it was then too late to attack that evening.

About 6:45 P.M. October 1, 1864, Meade issued orders for Ninth Corps to advance the next morning. For this movement, Mott's division and Gregg's cavalry division were placed under Parke's orders. According to Meade's orders, Parke was to drive the enemy out of Pegram's field, and then to move on toward the Boydton Plank Road. Mott's division was to turn the enemy right by marching west along present-day Route 673, and then turning northward toward the Harman Road. Fifth Corps was to make reconnaissances along its front, and to be prepared to respond to any favorable situation that might develop.

Mott's division started first, shortly after 7:00 A.M. October 2, 1864. Byron R. Pierce's Second Brigade advanced in the lead along Route 673; it was followed by Robert McAllister's Third Brigade, and P. Regis De Trobriand's First Brigade brought up the rear. As the brigades advanced, McAllister's brigade moved up on the left of Pierce, and advanced along the south side of the road. Mott soon ran into the enemy pickets, who quickly withdrew to Fort McRae and the adjacent entrenchments. Fort McRae was situated just south of Route 673, where the old enemy Squirrel Level Line of entrenchments ended. At that point, Pierce's brigade came up and deployed in line of battle north of the road, in front of the old Squirrel Level Line, where it crossed the J. Wilkinson farm. To the south, McAllister arrived on the cleared ground of the J. Smith farm. There he turned north toward Route 673, and formed on the left of Pierce. Both brigades then attacked. The enemy works in this area were only lightly held, and McAllister's brigade quickly captured Fort McRae, and Pierce's brigade carried the works to the right. Mott continued on to the northwest for about a mile, and about noon arrived on the Harman Road, about three-fourths of a mile south of Mrs. Hart's house. De Trobriand then moved up on the left of McAllister to protect Mott's left flank.

Parke expected that his major opposition would be on Pegram's farm, and at 8:00 A.M. October 2, 1864, he moved in that direction. Potter's division, on the right, moved straight ahead toward Oscar Pegram's house, with Simon Griffin's brigade on the left and Curtin's brigade on the right. Willcox's division was on the left of Potter, with Harriman's brigade on the left of the division, McLaughlen's brigade in the center, and Hartranft's brigade on the right. Willcox was directed to pivot on his right and wheel toward the Pegram house. When skirmishers reported that there no enemy troops in Pegram's field, Parke halted his line in the woods at the northern border of Peebles' farm. Then, at about 9:00 A.M., he advanced toward the Pegram house. Upon arriving there, Potter formed on a line extending east from the house to the Church Road, and Willcox extended his line westward from the house to Arthur's Swamp. At that time, Mott's division was approaching on the left of Willcox.

About 9:30 A.M., Charles Griffin's division of Fifth Corps moved forward, and sometime before 11:30 A.M. it formed in line on the right of Potter. Gregory's brigade was on the right of Curtin, and Bartlett's brigade was on the right of Gregory. Sickel's brigade was held in reserve in rear of Gregory. When Parke and Griffin had completed the formation of this line, they halted to await orders. About 1:00 P.M., Parke's two divisions moved to their left, and Willcox shifted the direction of his advance from north to northwest so as to approach the enemy entrenchments that ran southwest to Mrs. Hart's. McLaughlen's brigade, which was on the center of Willcox's line, moved toward Dr. Boisseau's house. Griffin probably shifted his direction to the northwest, and moved into line with Potter, facing north. The Federal line then halted in front of the enemy entrenchments, which, in that area, ran roughly parallel to, and about a mile east of, the Boydton Plank Road.

About 3:00 P.M., while most of Mott's division skirmished with the enemy, four regiments of Pierce's brigade under George Zinn attacked along the Harman Road, but they were quickly driven back. A little later, McLaughlen's brigade moved westward from Dr. Boisseau's house and attacked, but it too was soon repulsed. These two weak attacks were the final Union effort to reach the Boydton Plank Road. During these attacks on the afternoon of October 2, 1864, only Heth's division and two cavalry brigades were on the enemy line in front of the Boydton Plank Road. McRae's brigade was across the Harman Road near Mrs. Hart's, with Rufus Barringer's cavalry brigade on the right and Joseph R. Davis' brigade on the left. Then, in order from the left of Davis' brigade were John R. Cooke's brigade, Joel R. Griffin's cavalry brigade, and James J. Archer's brigade. The left of Archer's brigade rested on the Church Road.

During the afternoon of October 2, 1864, Meade sent out orders to discontinue the offensive, and to prepare to hold the new positions gained west of the Halifax Road. A new defensive line was laid out, and that night the troops moved to occupy their assigned positions. The new front was soon strongly entrenched, and as a result of the fighting of the past few days, the siege line at Petersburg was extended westward from the Weldon Railroad to Pegram's farm.

On the morning of October 3, 1864, the troops on the new line were in position, from the Federal right to left, as follows:

Bragg's brigade of Crawford's division was at the Flowers house on the Vaughan Road.

Ayres' division held the line of defenses from the Flowers house westward to the old Confederate Squirrel Level Line, south of Fort Bratton.

Hofmann's brigade (temporarily attached to Ayres' division) was on the right of the division line, connecting with the left of Bragg's brigade; Graham's brigade was on the center of the line; and Grimshaw's brigade was on the left, with its left on the Squirrel Level Road. Two regiments of Grindlay's brigade (formerly commanded by Otis) were on the line west of the road, and the rest of the brigade was in reserve near Job Talmage's house.

From the left of Ayres' division, the line ran almost due west to Arthur's Swamp, and there it made an acute angle to the rear and ran along the east side of Arthur's Swamp. The latter part of this line faced to the southwest. Charles Griffin's division of Fifth Corps held the right of this line from the left of Ayres' division to the Pegram House Road. Gregory's brigade was on the right, next to Ayres' division; Sickel's brigade was between Gregory's brigade and the Church Road; and Bartlett's brigade was between the Church Road and the Pegram Farm Road.

Potter's division of Ninth Corps extended the line from the left of Charles Griffin's line to Arthur's Swamp. Curtin's brigade of Potter's division was on the left of Bartlett's brigade, facing north; and Potter's other brigade, under Simon Griffin, was on the left of Curtin but was at an angle to Curtin's line, and faced to the southwest toward Arthur's Swamp.

Willcox's division of Ninth Corps extended the line to the southeast along the western edge of the Pegram field to the old Squirrel Level Line, where it crossed Arthur's Swamp about 225 yards west of Fort Archer. McLaughlen's brigade was on the right of Willcox's line, Harriman's brigade was on the center, and Hartranft's brigade was on the left.

Mott's division of Second Corps was on the extreme left of the new line, along the southwestern corner of Peebles' farm. De Trobriand's brigade was on the left, across the Squirrel Level Road near the Clements house, west of Arthur's Swamp, with its left on the swamp east of the house, and its right on the swamp, north of the Clements house. McAllister's brigade was on the old Ninth Corps line, east of Arthur's Swamp, and extended from the right of De Trobriand to the vicinity of Peebles' house. This arrangement left a gap of about 400 yards between the right of McAllister and the left of Hartranft, but this interval was well covered by the fields of fire of both brigades. Pierce's brigade of Mott's division was not in line, but was placed in Peebles' field as a division reserve.

The organization of George G. Meade's troops present at the Battle of Poplar Spring Church September 29, 1864–October 2, 1864, was as follows:

SECOND CORPS

Third Division, Gershom Mott
First Brigade, P. Regis De Trobriand
Second Brigade, Byron R. Pierce
Third Brigade, Robert McAllister

Note. Mott's division joined Meade's forces west of the Weldon Railroad October 1, 1864, and was temporarily placed under Parke's control. It was engaged October 2, 1864.

FIFTH CORPS, Gouverneur K. Warren

First Division, Charles Griffin
First Brigade, Horatio G. Sickel
Second Brigade, Edgar M. Gregory
Third Brigade, James Gwyn, to September 30, 1864, disabled
Ellis Spear, September 30, 1864
Joseph J. Bartlett

Second Division, Romeyn B. Ayres
First Brigade, Elwell S. Otis, to October 1, 1864, wounded
James Grindlay
Second Brigade, Samuel A. Graham
Third Brigade, Arthur H. Grimshaw

Third Division
Third Brigade, J. William Hofmann

Note. Hofmann's brigade was temporarily attached to Ayres' Second Division during this operation.

Artillery
Battery B, 1st New York Light Artillery, Robert E. Rogers
Battery D, 1st New York Light Artillery, Lester I. Richardson
Battery H, 1st New York Light Artillery, Charles E. Mink

NINTH CORPS, John G. Parke

First Division, Orlando B. Willcox
First Brigade, Samuel Harriman

Second Brigade, John F. Hartranft
Third Brigade, Napoleon B. McLaughlen

Second Division, Robert B. Potter
First Brigade, John I. Curtin
Second Brigade, Simon G. Griffin

Artillery Brigade, J. Albert Monroe
7th Battery (G), Maine Light Artillery, Adelbert B. Twitchell
11th Battery, Massachusetts Light Artillery, Edward J. Jones
19th Battery, New York Light Artillery, Edward W. Rogers
34th Battery, New York Light Artillery, Jacob Roemer
Battery D, Pennsylvania Light Artillery, Samuel H. Rhoads

CAVALRY

Second Cavalry Division, Army of the Potomac, David McM. Gregg
First Brigade, Henry E. Davies, Jr.
Second Brigade, Charles S. Smith

Note. Robert Clarke's Battery A, 2nd United States Artillery was attached to First Brigade, and Edwin L. Garvin's Batteries H and I, 1st United States Artillery were attached to Second Brigade.

OPERATIONS OF OCTOBER 1864

Siege of Petersburg, October 1864. The lines of entrenchments held by the Army of the Potomac and the Army of the James were substantially extended as the result of Ulysses S. Grant's offensive operations of September 29, 1864–October 2, 1864 (see above). When the fighting ended October 2, 1864, Grant decided to hold the ground gained, both north of the James River and south of Petersburg, and he directed Benjamin F. Butler and George G. Meade to entrench the lines that they then occupied. When this line was completed during the month, the Federal siege line extended from the Darbytown Road, north of the James, to the vicinity of Peebles' farm, west of the Weldon Railroad. This line was located and manned as follows:

Entrenchments of the Army of the James. Butler's line north of the James River ran from Signal Hill on the river (later the site of Fort Brady) to the Varina Road, near its intersection with the Kingsland Road; then northward along the west side of the Varina Road to Fort Harrison, which was reversed and renamed Fort Burnham; and finally, along the old Confederate Exterior Line, past the Clyne house on the New Market Road to the Johnson farm on the Darbytown Road.

Godfrey Weitzel's Eighteenth Corps held the left of this line from the river to, and including, Fort Harrison. Originally, David B. White's Temporary Brigade probably picketed the the ground between Signal Hill and the Kingsland Road. Charles J. Paine's Third Division was on the right of White, and was in line in front of the Varina Road to a point just east of the Childrey house. Samuel A. Duncan's Third Brigade (then commanded by Augustus S. Boernstein) was on the left, John W. Ames' Second Brigade was in the center, and John H. Holman's First Brigade was on the right. Sometime later, White's brigade was withdrawn from the line, and Paine's division picketed the line to the river.

Charles A. Heckman's Second Division was on the right of Paine and held the entrenchments northward toward Fort Harrison. Harrison H. Fairchild's Third Brigade was on the left, Edward H. Ripley's Second Brigade was in the center, and James Jourdan's First Brigade, then temporarily commanded by George M. Guion, was on the right. First Division, Eighteenth Corps (temporarily commanded by James Jourdan) occupied Fort Harrison and the works to the immediate left of the fort. Samuel H. Roberts' Third Brigade (then commanded by Stephen Moffitt) was on the left, and connected with the right of Heckman; Edgar M. Cullen's Second Brigade was in the center; and John B. Raulston's First Brigade was on the right, and occupied Fort Harrison.

David B. Birney's Tenth Corps (commanded by Alfred H. Terry after October 10, 1864) connected on its left with Eighteenth Corps, just to the right of Fort Harrison, and occupied the old Confederate Exterior Line, northward to the Clyne farm on the New Market Road. William Birney's Colored Brigade was on the left, next to Fort Harrison. Robert S. Foster's Second Division held the line northward to a point south of the New Market Road, with Louis Bell's Third Brigade on the left, Alfred

M. Barney's First Brigade in the center, and Galusha Pennypacker's Second Brigade on the right.

Terry's First Division (commanded by Adelbert Ames after October 10, 1864) held the ground around Clynes' farm. Harris M. Plaisted's Third Brigade was on the line from the right of Foster's division to the New Market Road; Francis B. Pond's First Brigade was north of the road, opposite the junction of the Mill Road, with its right refused so that it faced north; and Joseph C. Abbott's Second Brigade was along the New Market Road to the right and rear of Pond's refused right, also facing north.

August V. Kautz's Cavalry Division extended the line to the north, beyond the Darbytown Road. Robert M. West's First Brigade was across the road at Johnson's farm, facing toward the northwest; and Samuel P. Spear's Second Brigade was near the Duke house, on the right of West's brigade and facing north. The 1st New York Mounted Rifles, an independent regiment of Kautz's command, picketed the line between the Darbytown Road and the New Market Road.

Butler's troops north of the James River remained in essentially the above position during the rest of the month, except for brief periods of activity. The first of these was October 7, 1864, when Kautz's division was driven from the Darbytown Road, and Terry's First Division, Tenth Corps went to its assistance. The second was October 13, 1864, when Terry, with Ames' First Division and William Birney's Third Division of his Tenth Corps, attempted to break up the enemy defenses on the Darbytown Road. The last was October 27–28, 1864, when most of the Army of the James marched out for a demonstration on the Darbytown Road and the Williamsburg Road. At the conclusion of each of the above operations, the troops returned to their former positions. For details of the above operations, see the following sections.

In addition to the lines north of the James River, the Army of the James also occupied the line of Defenses at Bermuda Hundred in October 1864. Prior to the start of Butler's movement to the north side of the James River September 28, 1864, these lines had been held by First Division and Second Division of Edward O. C. Ord's Eighteenth Corps. When these two divisions were withdrawn that night for the march to Aiken's Landing on the James, Ord left behind about 7,000 men to hold the defenses. These included five new one-year Pennsylvania regiments belonging to Joseph H. Potter's Provisional Brigade; the experienced 40th Massachusetts Infantry and Potter's own 12th New Hampshire Infantry; Charles K. Graham's Naval Brigade; and the artillery of the defenses, supported by the 11th Connecticut, 5th Maryland, and parts of the 9th Vermont and 13th New Hampshire. Opposing these troops, on the Confederate Howlett Line, were George E. Pickett's division of Richard H. Anderson's First Confederate Corps, and Edward L. Thomas' brigade of Cadmus M. Wilcox's division of Ambrose P. Hill's Third Corps.

October 17, 1864, Graham assumed command of all troops belonging to Butler's Department of Virginia and North Carolina that were on the lines between the James River and the Appomattox River. Graham's command was then designated as the Provisional Division, Eighteenth Corps.

Entrenchments of the Army of the Potomac. The new line that was entrenched by the Army of the Potomac during October 1864 was essentially the same as that occupied by Fifth Corps, Ninth Corps, and Gershom Mott's Third Division, Second Corps after the fighting ended around Poplar Spring Church on the night of October 2, 1864. This line extended westward from Fort Wadsworth, near the Weldon Railroad, past the Flowers house and the Chappell house to Pegram's farm; and then it curved back to the left and ran along Arthur's Swamp to Peebles' farm and the Clements house. For additional information about this part of the line, see preceding section, Operations of September 1864, Battle of Poplar Spring Church (Combats at Wyatt's Farm, Peebles' Farm, Chappell's House, Pegram's Farm, and Vaughan Road), Virginia.

A number of strong works were constructed to secure this new line south of Petersburg. These were, from right to left, as follows: Fort Keene, on the Vaughan Road near the Flowers house; Fort Tracy, between the Vaughan Road and the Squirrel Level Road; Fort Urmston, about a half mile south of the Chappell house on the Squirrel Level Road; Fort Conahey, about midway between Fort Urmston and Fort Fisher; Fort Fisher, near the Church Road, about 700 yards south of the Boswell house; Fort

Welsh, near the Pegram house; Fort Gregg, about 700 yards south of Fort Welsh; Fort Sampson, on the old Confederate line between Fort Gregg and the Clements house, on the west side of Arthur's Swamp; and Fort Cummings, about one-fourth mile southwest of the Clements house on the Squirrel Level Road. In addition to the above, Fort Wheaton (old Confederate Fort Archer) was on a second line, between Fort Urmston and Fort Gregg.

October 5, 1864, Samuel W. Crawford, commanding Third Division, Fifth Corps, was ordered to construct a rear line of entrenchments that was to extend from Fort Cummings to the Weldon Railroad. Three forts were built on this line as follows: Fort Emory, about one-fourth of a mile west of the Vaughan Road, and about the same distance south of Poplar Spring Church; Fort Seibert, just east of the Vaughan Road; and Fort Clarke, between Fort Siebert and Fort Dushane, which was on the Weldon Railroad.

There was little change in the positions of the troops on the line of entrenchments at Petersburg until October 5, 1864. The most significant of these involved the exchange of positions by Mott's division of Second Corps and Edward Ferrero's Third Division, Ninth Corps. October 5, 1864, Ferrero's division, which had been on the line from near the Weldon Railroad to Fort Alexander Hays, marched to Poplar Spring Church and rejoined Ninth Corps. It then relieved Mott's division and took position between Fort Cummings on the Squirrel Level Road and a point near Fort Dushane and the Weldon Railroad. When Mott's division was relieved, it moved back and reoccupied the position that it had vacated October 1, 1864, which extended from Fort Alexander Hays to, and including, Fort Sedgwick. John Gibbon's Second Division was on the Second Corps' line from Fort Sedgwick to, and including, Fort Morton. Nelson A. Miles' First Division, Second Corps held the rest of the line from Fort Morton to the Appomattox River.

There was also a general shift to the right by Gouverneur K. Warren's Fifth Corps. On October 3, 1864, Joseph J. Bartlett's Third Brigade of Charles Griffin's First Division, which had been on the extreme left of the corps' line, between the Pegram farm and the Church Road, was relieved by troops of John G. Parke's Ninth Corps and then moved to the right of Edgar M. Gregory's Second Brigade. Upon arriving there, it relieved Frederick Winthrop's First Brigade of Romeyn B. Ayres' Second Division, and Ayres then extended his line to the Vaughan Road, where it connected with the left of Crawford's Third Division. As noted above, on October 5, 1864, Ferrero's division was ordered out of the line of entrenchments between Crawford's division and Fort Howard when it was sent to relieve Mott, and Warren was then directed to extend his line to the right to, and including, Fort Howard. When this rearrangement was completed, Fifth Corps occupied the line from Fort Howard, on the right, to the Church Road at Fort Fisher, on the left. Crawford's division was on the right from Fort Howard to the Vaughan road at the Flowers house; Ayres' division was on the center, from the Vaughan Road to the Squirrel Level Road at Chappell's; and Griffin's division was on the left from Chappell's to Fort Fisher, on the Church Road.

Parke's Ninth Corps occupied the remainder of Meade's line from the Church Road to the Weldon Railroad at Fort Dushane. Robert B. Potter's Second Division was on the right from the Church Road to the vicinity of Arthur's Swamp; Orlando B. Willcox's First Divison was on the center, from the left of Potter to the Clements house; and Ferrero's Third Division was on the left from the Clements house to the Weldon Railroad.

On the morning of October 7, 1864, the enemy advanced north of the James against Butler's line on the Darbytown and New Market roads, and in an effort to prevent reinforcements from being sent from Petersburg to the Richmond front, Meade ordered a demonstration south of Petersburg by Fifth Corps and Ninth Corps. Crawford's division, then commanded by Henry Baxter, and Ayres' division, both of Fifth Corps, and Willcox's division of Ninth Corps advanced about a mile on their fronts, drove in the enemy pickets, and occupied some of their forward works. That evening, however, these troops returned to their former positions. For details of the operations north of the James River, see following section, Engagement at the Darbytown Road and the New Market Road (Johnson's Farm and Four-Mile Creek [or Run]), Virginia.

A further change occurred on Warren's front October 16, 1864. Griffin was directed to extend his line to the right to a point about midway between the Squirrel Level Road and the Vaughan Road; Ayres was then to hold the line from the right of Griffin to Fort Wadsworth; and Crawford's division was to continue the line to the right from Fort Wadsworth to the right of Battery No. 24.

Late in October 1864, most of the Army of the Potomac pulled out of the entrenchments and advanced October 27, 1864 in an effort to reach the South Side Railroad. This attempt failed, however, and the next day the troops resumed their former positions. For details of this movement, see below, Engagement at the Boydton Plank Road (or Hatcher's Run).

Engagement at the Darbytown Road and the New Market Road (Johnson's Farm and Four-Mile Creek [or Run]), Virginia, October 7, 1864. When the Army of the James established its new defensive line north of the James River after the Battle of Chaffin's Farm, September 29–30, 1864, Kautz's cavalry division, with two batteries, was posted at the captured Confederate trenches near Johnson's farm on the Darbytown Road to watch the right of the army.

Robert E. Lee decided to attempt to recapture that part of his old line, and on the morning of October 7, 1864 began his attack. He sent Martin W. Gary's dismounted cavalry and some infantry of Edward A. Perry's Florida Brigade to turn Kautz's right flank by the Charles City Road, while Charles W. Field made a frontal attack with the brigades of George T. Anderson, John Gregg, and John Bratton. Spear's Second Brigade on the right of Kautz's line gave way, and West's First Brigade soon followed on the Darbytown Road. The road crossed a swamp in rear of Kautz's position, and during the retreat the artillery was captured by Gary's cavalry while attempting to cross the muddy ground.

Meantime, Alfred H. Terry had been ordered to bring up his First Division, Tenth Corps and support the cavalry. Kautz retreated to the New Market Road, and there he rallied his men under the cover of the infantry. Field followed Kautz with his division, and as he approached Kautz's new position, Terry, who was just arriving, deployed his division in line of battle. He placed Plaisted's Third Brigade near Four-Mile Church, with its right on the

New Market Road; Abbott's Second Brigade on the left of Plaisted; and Pond's First Brigade on the left of Abbott.

Beginning at 9:30 A.M., Field made two determined attacks on Terry's line but was strongly repulsed each time. Robert F. Hoke's division also came up, but it failed to attack on the right of Field as ordered. Abbott's brigade suffered the heaviest casualties in the fighting.

After Field's unsuccessful attacks, the enemy abandoned their attempts to recapture their old works, and they then withdrew and began the construction of a new line. Terry followed, and reoccupied Kautz's former position, but then returned to his earlier position on the line of entrenchments.

The organization of the troops of Butler's Army of the James that were engaged on the Darbytown Road and the New Market Road October 7, 1864 was as follows:

TENTH CORPS, David B. Birney

First Division, Alfred H. Terry
    First Brigade, Francis B. Pond
    Second Brigade, Joseph C. Abbott
    Third Brigade, Harris M. Plaisted

Artillery Brigade, Richard H. Jackson
    5th Battery, New Jersey Light Artillery, Henry H. Metcalf
    Battery C, 3rd Rhode Island Light or Heavy Artillery, Martin S. James
    Batteries C and D, 1st United States Artillery, Redmond Tully
    Battery E, 3rd United States Artillery, John R. Myrick
    Battery D, 4th United States Artillery, Frederick M. Follett

Cavalry Division, August V. Kautz
    First Brigade, Robert M. West
    Second Brigade, Samuel P. Spear
    Artillery, Dorman L. Noggle
        4th Battery, Wisconsin Light Artillery, Dorman L. Noggle
        Battery B, 1st United States Artillery, Robert M. Hall

Engagement at the Darbytown Road, Virginia, October 13, 1864. October 10, 1864, Alfred H. Terry assumed command of Tenth Corps in place of David B. Birney, who was sick, and Adelbert Ames assumed command of First Division, Tenth Corps. Birney did not return to the army, but died in Philadelphia, Pennsylvania October 18, 1864.

After the defeat of Field's division on the Darbytown and New Market roads October 7, 1864 (see preceding section), the enemy constructed a new line of defenses that extended northward from Fort Gilmer to the old Exterior Line south of the Charles City Road. October 13, 1864, Terry made a limited attempt to break up this new defensive line. Starting at 4:00 A.M. that morning, Terry, with Ames' First Division and William Birney's Third Division, moved from their divisional camps to Johnson's field on the Darbytown Road. He arrived there about daybreak, and deployed his command as follows: Ames' division was on the right of the road, with Hawley's brigade on the right of the division, Plaisted's brigade in the center, and Pond's brigade on the left. William Birney's division was on the left of the road, with Alvin C. Voris' First Brigade on the right and Ulysses Doubleday's Second Brigade on the left. Kautz's cavalry division and two batteries joined Terry from Four-Mile Church, and they were sent to the right of Ames' division, where they covered the ground up to the Charles City Road.

About 6:45 A.M., Terry advanced, with sharp skirmishing, to the enemy line near the Cunningham house. He found the position there to be too strong to attack, and he extended Ames' division to the right to find a more favorable place for a breakthrough. Kautz found a part of the line that he thought was only lightly held, and about 2:30 P.M., Pond's brigade moved forward and launched a vigorous attack. Pond was repulsed with considerable loss, and Terry decided to make no further effort against the enemy works. He began to withdraw about 3:30 P.M., and by 7:00 P.M. his troops were all back in their camps.

The organization of the forces of Butler's Army of the James that were engaged at the Darbytown Road October 13, 1864 was as follows:

TENTH CORPS, Alfred H. Terry

First Division, Adelbert Ames
    First Brigade, Francis B. Pond
    Second Brigade, Joseph R. Hawley
    Third Brigade, Harris M. Plaisted

Third Division, William Birney

First Brigade, Alvin C. Voris
Second Brigade, Ulysses Doubleday

Cavalry Division, August V. Kautz
First Brigade, Robert M. West
Second Brigade, Samuel P. Spear
Third Brigade, Andrew W. Evans
Artillery, Dorman L. Noggle
    4th Battery (section), Wisconsin Light Artillery,
      Dorman L. Noggle
    Battery B, 1st United States Artillery, Robert M. Hall

Engagement at the Darbytown Road (Fair Oaks), Virginia, October 27–28, 1864. During the latter part of October 1864, Grant prepared for another attempt to reach the South Side Railroad, and as a part of this undertaking, he directed Butler to make a demonstration north of the James River with his Army of the James. Butler's plan was to demonstrate with Terry's Tenth Corps on the front of the enemy line on the Darbytown and Charles City roads and, at the same time, attempt to turn its left flank with Godfrey Weitzel's Eighteenth Corps. Kautz's Cavalry Division (temporarily commanded by Robert M. West) was to cover the flanks of Eighteenth Corps as it moved up to the right of Tenth Corps.

Terry left a sufficient force to hold the entrenchments and, with the rest of his Tenth Corps, moved out between 4:30 and 5:45 on the morning of October 27, 1864, and marched to the Darbytown Road near the Johnson house. He then deployed and advanced toward the enemy works, with Ames' First Division on the right of the road, Foster's Second Division on the left of the road, and Joseph R. Hawley's Third Division on the left of Second Division. Hawley was assigned temporary command of Third Division October 20, 1864, during the absence of William Birney. There was considerable skirmishing and firing along the line during the day, but Terry made no attack on the main line of the enemy entrenchments. About 3:00 P.M., N. Martin Curtis' First Brigade of Foster's division was ordered to push the enemy skirmishers back within their works, which he did, but with considerable loss. Tenth Corps remained in front of the enemy line until the next morning, and then returned to its camps.

For his part in Butler's demonstration on the enemy's left, Weitzel withdrew his troops of Eighteenth Corps from the entrenchments October 26, 1864 and assembled them in the Cox field, near the James River. The force that he was to take with him consisted of Gilman Marston's First Division; Edward H. Ripley's Second Brigade and Harrison S. Fairchild's Third Brigade of Charles A. Heckman's Second Division; and John H. Holman's First Brigade and Alonzo G. Draper's Second Brigade of Third Division. While at the Cox farm, Draper's brigade was temporarily attached to Second Division.

Starting at about 5:00 A.M. October 27, 1864, Eighteenth Corps marched out on the Kingsland Road to the New Market Road, with Marston's division in the lead. Heckman's division followed Marston, and Holman's brigade brought up the rear. When Weitzel reached the New Market Road, he moved up that road to a crossroad beyond Timberlake's Store, and then on that road to White's Tavern on the Charles City Road. At White's Tavern, Weitzel learned from West, whose First Cavalry Brigade had preceded him, that the cavalry held the road near the enemy works and that the latter were fully manned. Then, preceded by Spear's Second Cavalry Brigade and covered by Terry's demonstration on the left, Weitzel moved up the Charles City Road about one-half mile. He then marched by a crossroad, past Mrs. Hobson's house, across the headwaters of White Oak Swamp, and about 1:00 P.M. arrived at the old battlefield of Fair Oaks-Seven Pines, on the Williamsburg Road.

Weitzel continued on along the Williamsburg Road about a mile and a half toward Richmond, where he arrived in front of the enemy works. He found that they were only lightly held at that point and decided to attack. At the same time, he sent Holman's brigade across the York River Railroad in an attempt to turn the enemy left. Marston deployed his division on the right of the road, with Edgar M. Cullen's Second Brigade on the left, next to the road; John B. Raulston's First Brigade on the right; and Joab N. Patterson's Third Brigade in reserve. Heckman ordered Ripley, commanding Second Brigade, Second Division, and Draper, commanding Second Brigade, Third Division (the latter was under Heckman's temporary control), to form in line of battle on the left of the Williamsburg Road, and on the left of Marston's division. Heckman ordered Fairchild's Third Brigade of Second Division to take position in advance of the main line, with its right resting on the Williamsburg Road. It was to attack, in conjunction with Cullen's brigade of First Division

Weitzel attacked at 4:00 P.M., with Fairchild's brigade on the left of the road and Cullen's brigade on the right of the road. As the attack was starting, however, Hoke's Confederate division moved into the works directly ahead, and Weitzel's attack was quickly repulsed.

Meantime, Holman had crossed the railroad, as ordered, and arrived in front of the enemy works on the New Bridge Road, which were held by some of Gary's dismounted cavalry. Holman charged and captured the works, but was soon driven out. Holman was wounded, and Abial G. Chamberlain assumed command of the brigade. Chamberlain was then ordered to rejoin the main body of Weitzel's command on the Williamsburg Road. Shortly after dark October 27, 1864, Eighteenth Corps began to withdraw to the Charles City Road, where it arrived the next morning. A few hours later, it moved on toward its former camps and arrived there about 6:00 P.M.

The organization of the forces of Butler's Army of the James that were engaged at Fair Oaks and the Darbytown Road October 27–28, 1864 was as follows:

TENTH CORPS, Alfred H. Terry

First Division, Adelbert Ames
First Brigade, Alvin C. Voris
Second Brigade, Joseph C. Abbott
Third Brigade, Harris M. Plaisted

Second Division, Robert C. Foster
First Brigade, N. Martin Curtis
Second Brigade, Galusha Pennypacker
Third Brigade, Louis Bell

Third Division, Joseph R. Hawley
First Brigade, James Shaw, Jr.
Second Brigade, Ulysses Doubleday

Artillery Brigade, Richard H. Jackson
Battery C, 1st Rhode Island Heavy Artillery, Martin S. James
Battery D, 1st United States Artillery, Redmond Tully

EIGHTEENTH CORPS, Godfrey Weitzel

First Division, Gilman Marston

First Brigade, John B. Raulston
Second Brigade, Edgar M. Cullen
Third Brigade, Joab N. Patterson

Second Division, Charles A. Heckman
Second Brigade, Edward H. Ripley
Third Brigade, Harrison S. Fairchild

Third Division
First Brigade, John H. Holman, to October 27, 1864, wounded
Abial G. Chamberlain
Second Brigade, Alonzo G. Draper

Note 1. Holman was the proper commander of Third Division, but during this operation he commanded only First Brigade.

Note 2. Draper's brigade was attached to Second Division October 27, 1864.

Artillery
16th Battery, New York Light Artillery, Richard H. Lee
Battery A, 1st Pennsylvania Light Artillery, William Stitt

CAVALRY DIVISION, Robert M. West
First Brigade, George W. Lewis
Second Brigade, Samuel P. Spear
Third Brigade, Andrew W. Evans
Artillery
4th Battery, Wisconsin Light Artillery, Dorman L. Noggle
Battery B, 1st United States Artillery, Robert M. Hall

Engagement at the Boydton Plank Road (or Hatcher's Run), Virginia, October 27–28, 1864.
October 24, 1864, Grant ordered Meade to make preparations for a march early on the morning of October 27, 1864 to the South Side Railroad. After gaining possession of the road, he was to hold it and fortify a line back to the Petersburg entrenchments in the vicinity of Peebles' farm. Grant was prompted to make this movement when he received information that the enemy had extended their entrenchments below Petersburg to Hatcher's Run, at a point about two miles above the crossing of the Vaughan Road and about one mile above Armstrong's Mill. He was also informed that these works were only partially completed, and that they did not cross or extend up Hatcher's Run. He further understood that only Wade Hampton's two cavalry divisions under William H. F. Lee and Matthew C. Butler, and

James Dearing's cavalry brigade (commanded by Joel A. Griffin) were on the enemy right flank.

Meade was instructed to leave a sufficient force in the redoubts to hold the line of entrenchments, and to assemble a mobile force of 30,000–35,000 infantry and artillery, and David McM. Gregg's Second Cavalry Division. Meade was then to move with this force toward the enemy right flank in three columns as follows:

Winfield S. Hancock, with two divisions of his Second Corps, was to move by the Vaughan Road, cross Hatcher's Run, and then march west past Dabney's Mill to the Boydton Plank Road. He was then to proceed northward to Burgess' Tavern, then west on the White Oak Road to the Claiborne Road, and north on the Claiborne Road. After recrossing Hatcher's Run near the Claiborne Road Bridge, he was to continue on by a road that ran to the northeast to the South Side Railroad. Hancock was expected to strike the railroad at a point about three miles east of Sutherland's Station, and then entrench a strong position that would enable him to hold the railroad. During this march, Gregg's cavalry was to move on the left of Hancock and form a part of his command.

John G. Parke's Ninth Corps was to advance on the morning of October 27, 1864 and be in position to attack the enemy's weak entrenchments between Hatcher's Run and J. Hawk's house at dawn, or not later than 5:30 A.M. If Parke succeeded in breaking through this line, he was to follow the enemy and turn toward the right. If, on the other hand, he did not succeed, he was to remain close to the enemy works while Second Corps and Fifth Corps advanced to turn the enemy's right flank.

Gouverneur K. Warren's Fifth Corps was to move at the same time as Ninth Corps, and proceed to the vicinity of Armstrong's Mill on Hatcher's Run. Warren was then to support Parke in his attack, and if Parke broke through, Fifth Corps was to advance on the left of Ninth Corps. If, however, Parke failed in his attack, Warren was to cross Hatcher's Run and attempt to turn the enemy right by recrossing the run above the Boydton Plank Road, and, keeping on the right of Second Corps, turn up the Plank Road and clear the bridge near Burgess' Mill.

Preparations were then begun for the movement on October 27, 1864. On the night of October 24, 1864, Hancock withdrew Gershom Mott's Third Division and John Gibbon's Second Division (commanded by Thomas W. Egan during the absence of Gibbon) from the line of entrenchments, and concealed them in the rear of the lines. October 26, 1864, Hancock marched with the two divisions along the rear of the lines to the vicinity of the Weldon Railroad, where they would be ready to move on the following morning. Hancock left Nelson A. Miles' First Division to hold the works from the Appomattox River to Battery No. 24, which was about midway between the Jerusalem Plank Road and the Weldon Railroad.

Warren left Henry Baxter's Second Brigade of Samuel W. Crawford's Third Division to hold the Fifth Corps' line, and moved the rest of the corps to their camps to prepare for their march toward the Boydton Plank Road.

Parke left John I. Curtin's First Brigade of Second Division to hold the Ninth Corps' line, and held the remainder of the corps in readiness to march on the morning of October 27, 1864.

An early start by the Army of the Potomac was important because surprise was essential for the success of the expedition, and the three corps were ordered to move at 3:30 A.M. Because the morning was dark and rainy, however, the start was delayed, and all chance of surprise was lost. When Parke finally started, he moved Ninth Corps to Fort Cummings, and from there sent Orlando B. Willcox's First Division up present-day Route 673, past the Hawk house, which was near old Fort McRae. A short time later, Willcox encountered enemy skirmishers east of the Watkins house, which was near the point where Route 673 ended at the Duncan Road. Willcox then advanced to the Watkins farmhouse and extended his left to connect with Fifth Corps, which had moved up on his left. When Edward Ferrero's Third Division arrived, it moved to the right of Willcox's division and formed in front of the Wilkinson house. Robert B. Potter's Second Division deployed along the old Confederate line on a front that extended to the northeast from the Hawk house to the Federal line of entrenchments. After an inspection of the enemy works, Parke concluded that they were too strong for a successful attack, but he moved up close, and during the rest of the day and the following night, his troops entrenched their position.

Between Ninth Corps and Hatcher's Run, there were no roads leading to Warren's assigned position; and it was not until 9:00 A.M., after an advance of only four miles through difficult country, that Charles Griffin's leading First Division of Fifth Corps ran into the enemy skirmishers. Edgar M. Gregory's Second Brigade drove these back into their works, and then Gregory advanced and threw up temporary breastworks close to the enemy line. He occupied the ground between Hatcher's Run and the left of Ninth Corps, which was held by John F. Hartranft's First Brigade of Willcox's division. The Duncan Road ran north from Armstrong's Mill through Gregory's position. Horatio G. Sickel's First Brigade and Joseph J. Bartlett's Third Brigade of Griffin's division were held largely in reserve. Romeyn B. Ayres' Second Division and Samuel W. Crawford's Third Division of Fifth Corps were massed in rear of Griffin.

About 10:30 A.M., after Parke had decided that he could not break the enemy line, Warren ordered Crawford to cross Hatcher's Run with his division and move up the west side of the run to a point opposite the right of the enemy line in front of Griffin. Upon arrival there, Crawford was to recross Hatcher's Run and attack the enemy right flank, and thereby clear the way for the advance of Warren and Parke north of the run. Andrew W. Denison's Second Brigade (Maryland Brigade) was detached from Ayres' division and sent with Crawford for this attack. Warren accompanied Crawford and left Griffin in command on the north bank of Hatcher's Run with his own division and the remaining brigades of Ayres' division.

Crawford began crossing Hatcher's Run at 11:45 A.M., and once across began preparations for his advance. Edward S. Bragg's First Brigade was to lead the way, and it was formed with its right on the run; J. William Hofmann's Third Brigade was placed to cover Bragg's left; and Denison's brigade of Ayres' division was kept in reserve. Crawford started forward at 12:30 P.M., but because of extremely difficult terrain, it did not arrive opposite the enemy works until about 4:00 P.M. It was then in no condition to attack, having become much disorganized in moving through the dense woods.

Second Corps left its bivouacs in the vicinity of Fort Dushane, near the Weldon Railroad, at 3:30 on the morning of October 27, 1864, and marched down the Halifax Road to the Church Road, and then across on the latter road to the Vaughan Road. Egan's division was the first to start, and Mott's division followed. The head of Egan's division arrived at the Vaughan Road Crossing of Hatcher's Run soon after daylight, and there they found a small enemy force posted in rifle pits on the south bank. Thomas A. Smyth's Third Brigade crossed the run and captured the works, and the rest of Second Corps soon followed. Egan's division turned to the right on the first road south of the crossing and advanced to Dabney's Mill. Mott's division continued on south on the Vaughan Road for about a mile, and then marched toward Dabney's Mill by a crossroad. As soon as Mott arrived at the mill, Egan moved on toward the Boydton Plank Road, and Mott soon followed.

The road on which Hancock advanced ran roughly parallel to Hatcher's Run, and about a mile to the south of it, and when he arrived on the Boydton Plank Road near Burgess' Mill, his right was only about a mile to the northwest of the position taken by Crawford at 4:00 P.M. Because of a lack of good roads and the intervening heavy woods, however, communications were not opened between Hancock and Crawford.

At about 4:00 P.M., the enemy strongly attacked Hancock's line (see below), and Ayres' division, less Denison's brigade, was sent to its assistance. Hancock was able to repulse the attack, however, and, it then being nearly dark, Ayres' division was halted at Armstrong's Mill. Fifth Corps remained in position all night, in a heavy rain, and at daybreak the next morning, October 28, 1864, Crawford recrossed Hatcher's Run and rejoined the corps. At 7:30 that morning, Ayres, with his two brigades, was sent to report to Parke. At 11:00 A.M., Warren began to withdraw, and he then returned to his former positions in the entrenchments.

Gregg's cavalry division, which was under Hancock's orders, left the Weldon Railroad at 3:30 A.M. October 27, 1864, and marched down the Halifax Road, past Rowanty Post Office, to the crossing of Rowanty Creek below Arthur's Swamp. From there it moved to the Quaker Road, on its way to the Boydton Plank Road. Charles H. Smith's Third Brigade was in the lead, and it was followed by Michael Kerwin's Second Brigade, and then Henry E. Davies' First Brigade. Ahead of Gregg, on the road, was Wade Hampton with the cavalry divisions of William H. F. Lee and Matthew C. Butler.

Smith's brigade found a small force of the enemy in position at Rowanty Creek, but soon drove it off and continued the advance. There was no further serious opposition until the column reached the Quaker Road, where Smith found the enemy posted behind Gravelly Run. He drove them back a short distance, but when they learned that Hancock was advancing on their left, they quickly retired. Gregg then continued on toward the Boydton Plank Road.

Egan's division arrived on the Plank Road about 10:30 A.M., and Mott's division came up two hours later. Gregg's cavalry division came up a short time after Mott. About 11:30 A.M., Hancock ordered Egan's division to move up the road toward Burgess' Mill to drive back some of Hampton's dismounted cavalry that were in position across Hatcher's Run. Egan then advanced, with Horace P. Rugg's First Brigade on the left of the road, and James M. Willett's Second Brigade and Smyth's Third Brigade on the right of the road.

Hancock then started Mott's division toward the White Oak Road, on its way to the South Side Railroad. About 1:00 P.M., however, Hancock received instructions from Meade to halt his command on the Boydton Plank Road, where it then was. Mott then formed P. Regis De Trobriand's First Brigade to face the Claiborne Road Bridge over Hatcher's Run, while Egan, with Smyth's brigade, cleared the south bank of Hatcher's Run at Burgess' Mill. Egan then deployed his division across the Boydton Plank Road at its intersection with the White Oak Road. Rugg's brigade was on the left of the Boydton Plank Road, Willett's brigade was on the right of the road, and Smyth's brigade was on the right of Willett's brigade.

At about that time, Hancock received instructions from Meade to hold the position that he then occupied until the next morning, and then to retire by the same route by which he had advanced. Hancock was given the discretion, however, of returning during the night if he thought this to be advisable. It was the opinion at Army Headquarters that the slow movements of the army that day had enabled the enemy to move troops into position to oppose Han-

cock and that it was no longer possible to gain and hold the South Side Railroad. In fact, at about that time, Hampton's cavalry and Henry Heth's and William Mahone's infantry divisions were concentrating near the crossing of the Boydton Plank Road at Hatcher's Run.

About 3:00 P.M., Robert McAllister's Third Brigade of Mott's division was sent to support Egan's division. Hancock then decided to attack with Egan's reinforced division at the bridge over Hatcher's Run and drive the enemy from the high ground to the north. Enemy artillery posted there was subjecting the men of Second Corps to an annoying fire, and he wished to drive the guns away. For the attack, Egan selected Smyth's brigade, which was on the right of the Plank Road, and placed McAllister's brigade on the right and rear of Smyth.

When Egan had his division and McAllister's brigade in position across the Plank Road, the rest of Hancock's command was disposed as follows: De Trobriand's brigade of Mott's division was on the left of the Plank Road, near the intersection of the Dabney Mill Road, facing northwest toward the approaches from the upper bridge on the Claiborne Road. Kerwin's brigade of dismounted cavalry was on the left of De Trobriand, facing north. Byron R. Pierce's Second Brigade of Mott's division was supporting Richard Metcalf's section of W. Butler Beck's Batteries C and I, 5th United States Artillery, which was some distance to the east of the Plank Road on a ridge about midway between the positions of Egan and De Trobriand. Close to the right of Pierce's brigade was a dense woods, which extended back to Hatcher's Run, where Crawford's division of Fifth Corps was advancing. Pierce placed the 5th Michigan and 93rd New York regiments (subsequently reinforced by the 105th Pennsylvania) in the edge of the woods to cover his right flank. Davies' First Cavalry Brigade was back watching the Quaker Road, and Smith's Third Cavalry Brigade was on the Boydton Plank Road, south of the junction with the Quaker Road.

During the afternoon, Heth, with William McRae's brigade of his division, and Mahone, with two brigades of his division, crossed Hatcher's Run below Burgess' Mill, passed through the woods in the gap between Hancock and Crawford, and then turned to the right toward Pierce's position. At 4:00 P.M., just as Smyth's brigade was preparing to cross the bridge and attack the enemy on the high ground beyond, Heth emerged from the woods and struck the right flank of Pierce's brigade. Pierce was driven back to the Boydton Plank Road, where his troops were finally rallied, but Metcalf and his guns were captured.

The enemy then advanced across the ridge from which Pierce had been driven, and then formed in line with their right across the Plank Road, facing south, and from there opened fire on the brigades of De Trobriand and Kerwin. The latter had quickly moved back from west of the Plank Road when the firing started and had formed his brigade across the Plank Road, facing north. De Trobriand's brigade was on the right of Kerwin, just in front of the Dabney Mill Road. Kerwin and De Trobriand, with John W. Roder's Battery K, 4th United States Artillery and Beck's artillery, opened fire on Heth's troops.

When the fighting started on his right and rear, Egan promptly halted his attack on the bridge at Hatcher's Run, faced his line to the rear, and with the brigades of Willett, Smyth, and McAllister, swept down on the flank and rear of Heth's line. At the same time De Trobriand and Kerwin advanced from the opposite direction, and together they drove the enemy back into the woods.

At almost the same time that Heth attacked, 4:00 P.M., Hampton began advancing with the cavalry against Mott's skirmishers that were facing the Claiborne Road Bridge. Hampton also advanced on Gregg's cavalry on the Boydton Plank Road. The 21st Pennsylvania Cavalry on the Plank Road was soon hard pressed, and at Gregg's request, Hancock promptly sent back such cavalry regiments as were available. The other two regiments of Smith's cavalry brigade soon arrived, and they were followed by three Pennsylvania regiments of Kerwin's brigade. With this force, Gregg successfully held the road until the enemy retired at dark.

Hancock, with Meade's permission, began to withdraw his command at 10:00 that night. Mott moved out first and was followed by Egan. Egan halted his division at Dabney's Mill at daylight October 28, 1864, to cover the withdrawal of Crawford's division of Fifth Corps to the north side of Hatcher's Run, and when that movement was completed, Egan moved on after Mott. About 10:00 that morning, both divisions moved back within the line of entrenchments and returned to their old camps near the Norfolk and Petersburg Railroad.

Gregg remained on the Boydton Plank Road until 10:30 P.M. October 27, 1864, and then began to withdraw by the same route on which he had advanced that morning. Kerwin's brigade led the way, Smith's brigade followed, and Davies' brigade brought up the rear. The division arrived at the Perkins house, near the Weldon Railroad, between 7:00 and 8:00 the next morning.

The organization of Meade's forces that were engaged on the Boydton Plank Road (or Hatcher's Run) October 27–28, 1864 was as follows:

SECOND CORPS, Winfield S. Hancock

Second Division, Thomas W. Egan
First Brigade, Horace P. Rugg
Second Brigade, James M. Willett
Third Brigade, Thomas A. Smyth
Artillery
Batteries C and I, 5th United States Artillery, W. Butler Beck

Note. During Egan's attack on Heth's command during the evening of October 27, 1864, Rugg did not advance his brigade as ordered. He was tried by court-martial and was found guilty of negligence of duty and disobedience of orders, and, by an order of November 17, 1864, he was dismissed from the service. On January 26, 1865, however, the governor of New York was authorized to recommission him.

Third Division, Gershom Mott
First Brigade, P. Regis De Trobriand
Second Brigade, Byron R. Pierce
Third Brigade, Robert McAllister
Artillery
10th Battery, Massachusetts Light Artillery, Henry H. Granger
Battery K, 4th United States Artillery, John W. Roder

FIFTH CORPS, Gouverneur K. Warren

First Division, Charles Griffin
First Brigade, Horatio G. Sickel
Second Brigade, Edgar M. Gregory
Third Brigade, Joseph J. Bartlett

Second Division, Romeyn B. Ayres
First Brigade, Frederick Winthrop
Second Brigade, Andrew Denison
Third Brigade, Arthur H. Grimshaw

Third Division, Samuel W. Crawford
    First Brigade, Edward S. Bragg
    Third Brigade, J. William Hofmann

Note. Second Brigade remained in the trenches during the movement to the Boydton Plank Road.

Artillery Brigade, Charles S. Wainwright
    5th Battery (E), Massachusetts Light Artillery, Charles A. Phillips
    9th Battery, Massachusetts Light Artillery, Richard S. Milton
    Battery B, 1st New York Light Artillery, Robert E. Rogers
    Battery H, 1st New York Light Artillery, Charles E. Mink
    Battery B, 4th United States Artillery, James Stewart

NINTH CORPS, John G. Parke

First Division, Orlando B. Willcox
    First Brigade, John F. Hartranft
    Second Brigade, Byron M. Cutcheon
    Third Brigade, Napoleon B. McLaughlen

Second Division, Robert B. Potter
    First Brigade, John I. Curtin
    Second Brigade, Simon G. Griffin

Third Division, Edward Ferrero
    First Brigade, Ozora P. Stearns
    Second Brigade, Henry G. Thomas

Artillery Brigade, John C. Tidball
    19th Battery, New York Light Artillery, Edward W. Rogers
    34th Battery, New York Light Artillery, Jacob Roemer

CAVALRY

Second Cavalry Division, David McM. Gregg
    First Brigade, Henry E. Davies, Jr.
    Second Brigade, Michael Kerwin
    Third Brigade, Charles H. Smith

Note. Edwin L. Garvin's Batteries H and I, 1st United States Artillery accompanied Kerwin's brigade, and William M. Dennison's Battery A, 2nd United States Artillery accompanied Davies' brigade.

WINTER OF 1864–1865
NOVEMBER 1, 1864–MARCH 29, 1865

Siege of Petersburg, Virginia. After Grant called

off his effort to reach the South Side Railroad in late October 1864 (see above section), there were no further major offensive operations during the next few months. There were, however, several reconnaissances and expeditions during the winter, and during the entire period of the partial investment of Petersburg and Richmond, there were frequent affairs on the picket lines, especially in front of the Petersburg lines. Many of these were small local affairs, but some were more serious and involved forces of brigade or division strength. The more significant of these are described in the following sections.

The Petersburg Lines. After the troops of the Army of the Potomac had returned from their unsuccessful attempt on the South Side Railroad in late October 1864, they continued to hold the lines of entrenchments at Petersburg.

Winfield S. Hancock's Second Corps (commanded by Andrew A. Humphreys after November 26, 1864) occupied the works from the Appomattox River to Battery No. 24, which was near the Strong house. John Gibbon's Second Division (Gibbon resumed command October 29, 1864) was between the Appomattox and Fort Meikel, on the Norfolk and Petersburg Railroad; Gershom Mott's Third Division was on the line from Fort Meikel to Battery No. 24; and Nelson A. Miles' First Division was in reserve. Gouverneur K. Warren's Fifth Corps extended from the left of Second Corps to the vicinity of Fort Fisher, near the Church Road, and John G. Parke's Ninth Corps was on the line from Fort Fisher to Fort Dushane, near the Weldon Railroad.

By an order of November 28, 1864, Second Corps and Ninth Corps exchanged positions on the line of entrenchments. Miles' division of Second Corps moved from its place in reserve and relieved Orlando B. Willcox's First Division and Robert B. Potter's Second Division of Ninth Corps; and when this exchange was completed, Miles occupied the works from Fort Fisher to Fort Sampson, including both forts, and also Fort Gregg and Fort Welch. As soon as the two divisions were relieved by Miles, they marched to the right of the line and relieved the other two divisions of Second Corps. Willcox's division relieved Gibbon's division, and Potter's division relieved Mott's division. Potter connected on his left with Fifth Corps. When Mott and Gibbon were relieved, they moved to the left and, together with Miles' division, occupied the works previously held by Ninth Corps. Edward Ferrero's Third Division, Ninth Corps was transferred to the Army of the James November 26, 1864, and its place was taken on the rear line of entrenchments between Fort Cummings and Fort Siebert by six Pennsylvania Regiments of Joseph H. Potter's Provisional Brigade, Army of the James. These regiments arrived from Bermuda Hundred November 28, 1864, and were organized as a provisional brigade of Ninth Corps under John F. Hartranft. Mott's division of Second Corps then relieved Hartranft's Provisional Brigade, and November 30, 1864, Hartranft moved to the right as a reserve for Ninth Corps. Gibbon's division of Second Corps was assigned to the works on the line from Fort Siebert to a point about midway between Fort Clarke and Fort Dushane, including Fort Emory, and it connected with Mott's division on the right and with Fifth Corps on the left. The above movements were completed by November 30, 1864.

As a result of Philip H. Sheridan's successes against Jubal A. Early's Confederate army in the Shenandoah Valley in the late summer and autumn of 1864 (see Shenandoah Valley Campaign [Sheridan]), Horatio G. Wright's Sixth Corps was ordered to rejoin the Army of the Potomac at Petersburg. Upon its arrival there, it was directed to relieve Warren's Fifth Corps in the trenches. Frank Wheaton's First Division, Sixth Corps arrived at City Point December 4, 1864, and the next day relieved Samuel W. Crawford's Third Division, Fifth Corps on the right of Warren's line. Truman Seymour's Third Division, Sixth Corps arrived December 6, 1864, and that evening relieved Romeyn B. Ayres' Second Division, Fifth Corps. George W. Getty's Second Division, Sixth Corps was detained for a time in the valley, and December 6, 1864, Gibbon's division of Second Corps temporarily relieved Charles Griffin's First Division, Fifth Corps on the left of Warren's line. When Fifth Corps was relieved, Warren concentrated his divisions between the Halifax Road and the Jerusalem Plank Road in preparation for an expedition to Hicksford, Virginia. For details, see below, Warren's Expedition to Hicksford, Virginia, December 7–12, 1864.

Wright did not arrive in person from the Shenan-

doah Valley until December 12, 1864, and during his absence, Wheaton and Seymour reported to Humphreys, commanding Second Corps. Sixth Corps was finally reunited under Wright's control December 13–16, 1864, when Getty's division arrived from the valley. Getty then relieved Gibbon's division, which, as noted above, had temporarily relieved Griffin's division of Fifth Corps in the entrenchments. Gibbon's division then moved out and camped on the Vaughan Road near the Davis house, about a half mile beyond the rear line of entrenchments.

December 13, 1864, after Fifth Corps had returned from its Hicksford expedition, it encamped at a point about midway between the Halifax Road and the Jerusalem Plank Road.

There were no further significant changes on the line of entrenchments until early February 1865. Then, after Second Corps and Fifth Corps had moved up to Hatcher's Run in support of Gregg's cavalry expedition to Dinwiddie Court House, Ulysses S. Grant decided to hold the positions gained by this operation, and Meade ordered the construction of a new defensive line along the fronts of these two corps. This line extended from the left of the old works at Fort Sampson to the Vaughan Road crossing of Hatcher's Run. For details, see below, Battle of Hatcher's Run (or Dabney's Mill, Armstrong's Mill, Rowanty Creek, Vaughan Road), February 5–7, 1865.

On February 7, 1865, the corps of the army were assigned to positions on the Petersburg lines as follows: Ninth Corps from the Appomattox River to Fort Howard; Sixth Corps from Fort Howard to Fort Gregg, including both forts; and Second Corps from Fort Gregg to Armstrong's Mill. Fifth Corps was placed so as to watch the Vaughan Road crossing of Hatcher's Run, and to cover the left and rear of the new Second Corps line. The cavalry was assigned to picket the country from the left of Fifth Corps to the James River.

The above arrangement was changed somewhat during the next few days. On the morning of February 9, 1865, Getty's Second Division of Sixth Corps relieved Miles' First Division of Second Corps on the line that extended from Fort Fisher to Fort Gregg, including both forts. Miles then moved to the left and occupied the old line from Fort Gregg to Fort Sampson and the new line from Fort

Sampson to the chimneys of the Westmoreland house. Mott's division was on the line from the left of Miles' division to the right of Warren's Fifth Corps. On February 11, however, Gibbon's Second Division, Second Corps (commanded by Thomas A. Smyth since December 22, 1864, while Gibbon was on leave) was withdrawn from its position near Armstrong's Mill and was placed on the left of Humphreys' line, from the left of Mott's division to the Vaughan Road crossing of Hatcher's Run. Fifth Corps moved into camp near Hatcher's Run to watch the left and rear of Humphreys' line.

March 27, 1865, in preparation for Grant's spring offensive, Edward O. C. Ord, commanding the Army of the James, marched from his camps north of the James River with Robert S. Foster's First Division and John W. Turner's Independent Division of Twenty-Fourth Corps; William Birney's Second Division, Twenty-Fifth Corps; and Ranald S. Mackenzie's cavalry division (formerly commanded by August V. Kautz) to join the Army of the Potmac below Petersburg for the impending movement. On the night of March 28, 1865, Gibbon camped in rear of Fort Siebert, and Birney near Humphreys' Station on the Military Railroad, where they would be in position to relieve Second Corps on the line of entrenchments the next morning.

The City Point and Army Railroad (Military Railroad). On four separate occasions during the late autumn and winter, army construction crews extended the City Point and Army Railroad to provide better transportation and supply services for the army. When finally completed, the total track laid on the main line and its branches was about twenty-one and three-fourths miles, and this included numerous heavy grades and one and a fourth miles of trestlework.

November 2, 1864, work was started on an extension of the main line from Warren's headquarters at Globe Tavern toward Peebles' farm. Work was completed to the vicinity of Poplar Spring Church, with all necessary sidings, November 9, 1864. This was called the Patrick Branch, and Patrick's Station was established at the end of the line.

December 21, 1864, work was begun on another branch that ran from Hancock's Station on the main line to Fort Blaisdell on the Jerusalem Plank Road. This work was completed December 29, 1864. An extension of this branch to Crawford's headquarters near the Jerusalem Plank Road was ordered January 2, 1865, and this line, which was called the Gregg Branch, was opened January 20, 1865. The terminal station of this branch, which was two and one-half miles from Hancock's Station, was called Gregg Station.

After the Battle of Hatcher's Run, February 5–7, 1865, the Army of the Potomac held a position about five miles in advance of its former line; and to provide better communications for the troops holding the new forward line, still another extension of the railroad was ordered February 8, 1865. The route for this new line was located February 12, 1865, and construction was started the next day. The line left Warren's Station and ran down the old bed of the destroyed Weldon Railroad about two miles to a point beyond the Perkins house, and it then turned to the right and continued on to the Cummings house on the Vaughan Road. This was about one mile north of the crossing of Hatcher's Run. Work was completed February 24, 1865. The station at the Cummings house was named Humphreys' Station, and was about five miles from Warren's Station on the main line.

The Lines North of the Appomattox River. There were several changes in the organization and in the positions of the troops holding the line of entrenchments on the front of the Army of the James. Through November 1864, Eighteenth Corps continued to hold the left of the line in front of Richmond from the James River to Fort Burnham (formerly Fort Harrison), and Tenth Corps from the right of Eighteenth Corps to the New Market Road. Charles K. Graham, with his Provisional Division, Army of the James, held the line of defenses at Bermuda Hundred. During the winter, August V. Kautz's cavalry division was engaged in picketing the country on the right of the army.

During the period November 2–15, 1864, about 3,000 men of Tenth Corps and Eighteenth Corps, under the command of Joseph R. Hawley, were absent in New York, where they were sent to prevent disturbances and to protect the public property during the presidential election of that year. For additional information about Hawley's command, see Army of the James, Line of Defenses North of the James River; and also Department of the East,

January 3, 1864–June 27, 1865, November Election of November 1864 in New York.

By an order dated December 3, 1864, Tenth Corps and Eighteenth Corps were discontinued, and the troops of these two corps were assigned to the newly constituted Twenty-Fourth Corps and Twenty-Fifth Corps. Edward O. C. Ord was assigned command of Twenty-Fourth Corps, and Godfrey Weitzel of Twenty-Fifth Corps. For details of the reorganization, see Army of the James, Reorganization of the Army of the James, December 1864; and see also Twenty-Fourth Corps and Twenty-Fifth Corps, Army of the James. These two corps held the line of entrenchments east of Richmond during the rest of the winter. Twenty-Fifth Corps held the line of works near Chaffin's farm formerly held by Eighteenth Corps; and Twenty-Fourth Corps occupied the positions on the right formerly held by Tenth Corps.

There were, however, some changes in the composition of the forces holding the line during the winter. This was caused primarily by the detachment of two expeditions to North Carolina. On the evening of December 7, 1864, about 7,000 men were withdrawn from the Richmond front and embarked at Bermuda Hundred for an expedition to capture Fort Fisher at the mouth of the Cape Fear River. The object of this expedition was to close the port of Wilmington, North Carolina. Godfrey Weitzel was assigned command of the expedition, and the troops that he took with him belonged to Adelbert Ames' Second Division, Twenty-Fourth Corps and Charles J. Paine's First Division, Twenty-Fifth Corps. Benjamin F. Butler later joined the expedition and took charge of operations, but the attempt at Fort Fisher was unsuccessful, and Weitzel's command returned to its camps December 28–30, 1864. For details, see Army of the James, Butler's Expedition to Fort Fisher, North Carolina, December 7–30, 1864.

Meantime, the Army of the James had been reinforced when Thomas M. Harris arrived at City Point from the Shenandoah Valley with his First Infantry Division (formerly commanded by Joseph Thoburn) of the Army of West Virginia. During the absence of Ames' division at Fort Fisher, Harris' division was temporarily attached to Twenty-Fourth Corps.

January 2, 1865, a second expedition against Fort Fisher was organized, this time under Alfred H. Terry, and it embarked at Bermuda Landing for North Carolina January 4–5, 1865. Terry's command consisted of Ames' Second Division, Twenty-Fourth Corps; Joseph C. Abbott's Second Brigade, First Division, Twenty-Fourth Corps, which was temporarily attached to Ames' division; and Paine's Third Division, Twenty-Fifth Corps. This expedition was successful, and after the capture of Fort Fisher, Terry's command remained in North Carolina and did not return to the Army of the James. For details, see Army of the James, Terry's Expedition to Fort Fisher, January 3–17, 1865; and also Department of North Carolina, January 31, 1865–May 19, 1866, Troops in the Department of North Carolina.

There were no further major activities north of the James River until March 27, 1865. On that date Ord, commanding the Army of the James, marched with Robert S. Foster's First Division and John W. Turner's Independent Division (formerly commanded by Thomas M. Harris) of Twenty-Fourth Corps, William Birney's Second Division, Twenty-Fifth Corps, and Ranald S. Mackenzie's cavalry division (formerly commanded by August V. Kautz) to join the Army of the Potomac below Petersburg and take part in Grant's spring offensive against Lee. This left only Kautz's First Division, Twenty-Fifth Corps and Charles Devens' Third Division, Twenty-Fourth Corps, both under the command of Weitzel, to hold the line of entrenchments in front of Richmond. For additional information, see Army of the James, Reinforcements for the Army of the Potomac.

Expedition to Stony Creek Station, Virginia, December 1, 1864. December 1, 1864, David McM. Gregg led his Second Cavalry Division, Army of the Potomac on a reconnaissance to Stony Creek Station on the Weldon Railroad, which was captured by J. Irvin Gregg's Second Brigade. After destroying the station and other buildings, along with large quantities of stores and supplies, Gregg's division returned to its camps that evening.

Warren's Expedition to Hicksford, Virginia, December 7–12, 1864. On December 6, 1864, Gouverneur K. Warren, commanding Fifth Corps, Army of the Potomac, received orders to move south early the next morning on an expedition to the Weldon Railroad below Stony Creek, and to destroy it as far as Hicksford, Virginia (present-day Emporia) if possible. For this expedition, Warren took with him Charles Griffin's First Division, Romeyn B. Ayres' Second Division, and Samuel W. Crawford's Third Division of his Fifth Corps; Gershom Mott's Third Division of Second Corps, David McM. Gregg's Second Cavalry Division, and six batteries of artillery.

Warren moved out about 6:00 A.M. December 7, 1864, from a point just south of Globe Tavern, and marched past the Gurley house, the Smith house, and the Temple house to the Jerusalem Plank Road. Gregg took a road to the east of the Jerusalem Plank Road, turning out of the latter at Temples' and joining it again about a mile and a half below Warwick's Swamp. The infantry marched on the Plank Road. The cavalry covered the front, and was followed by the divisions of Crawford, Griffin, Ayres, and Mott and the wagon train, in that order. One battery accompanied each of the infantry divisions. Gregg and Crawford bivouacked at Sussex Court House that night, and the rest of the column at the Nottoway River.

The next morning, the march was resumed toward Jarrett's Station on the Weldon Railroad, with Gregg's cavalry out in front, and Crawford's division still leading the infantry. Upon reaching the railroad, the cavalry immediately began the work of destruction. The rest of Warren's command was up by sunset, and at 6:00 P.M. the three divisions of Fifth Corps moved down the track, destroying it as they advanced. The work continued by moonlight until midnight, and the road was completely wrecked from the Nottoway to a point below Jarrett's Station. Work was resumed early on the morning of December 9, 1864, while Gregg cleared the enemy out of the way to the south. Gregg also picketed the country to the north and east. He encountered some resistance at Three Creeks, and again at Belfield, but by 4:00 P.M. had driven the enemy across the Meherrin River at Hicksford. Griffin's division guarded the trains during the day.

Warren found the enemy entrenched on the south side of the Meherrin River at Hicksford and, after examining the position, concluded that it was too strong to force a crossing. It was also his opinion that a turning movement would require too much time, and so he issued orders for the expedition to begin its return the next morning. By that time, he had destroyed the railroad as far south as Belfield, a short distance north of the river, for a total distance of seventeen or eighteen miles.

After enduring a rainy night, Warren's troops began their return march on the morning of December 10, 1864, on the direct road to Sussex Court House. J. Irvin Gregg's Second Cavalry Brigade cleared the way and watched the side roads. Griffin's division, with the trains, marched after Gregg, and was followed by the divisions of Mott, Ayres, and Crawford, in that order. Henry E. Davies' First Cavalry Brigade and Charles H. Smith's Third Cavalry Brigade brought up the rear.

On December 10, 1864, a part of Robert B. Potter's Second Division, Ninth Corps and John F. Hartranft's Provisional Brigade of Ninth Corps (later organized as First Brigade, Third Division, Ninth Corps) moved out from their positions on the right of the line of entrenchments, and marched about twenty miles to the southeast to Freeman's Ford on the Nottoway River to support Warren. The head of Warren's column reached Sussex Court House at dark December 10, 1864, and the command bivouacked along the road. The next morning the column moved on to Freeman's Ford, where it was joined by Potter's force of Ninth Corps. Warren's column crossed the river before dark and camped that night near Belcher's Mill. The next day it continued on, and the troops returned to their camps. Potter's command of Ninth Corps also returned to its former positions.

Ambrose P. Hill was sent out from the entrenchments below Petersburg in an attempt to intercept Warren, but in this effort he was not successful.

The Organization of Warren's command on the expedition to Hicksford, Virginia, December 7–12, 1864, was as follows:

FIFTH CORPS, Gouverneur K. Warren

First Division, Charles Griffin
    First Brigade, Joshua L. Chamberlain
    Second Brigade, Edgar M. Gregory
    Third Brigade, Joseph J. Bartlett

Second Division, Romeyn B. Ayres
    First Brigade, Frederick Winthrop
    Second Brigade, Andrew W. Denison
    Third Brigade, James Gwyn

Third Division, Samuel W. Crawford

First Brigade, Edward S. Bragg
Second Brigade, Henry Baxter
Third Brigade, J. William Hofmann

Artillery Brigade (four batteries), Charles S. Wainwright
    5th Battery (E), Massachusetts Light Artillery, Charles A. Phillips
    Battery H, 1st New York Light Artillery, Charles E. Mink
    Battery B, 4th United States Artillery, James Stewart
    9th Battery, Massachusetts Light Artillery, Richard S. Milton

Note. Phillips' battery was with Crawford's division; Mink's battery was with Griffin's division; Stewart's battery was with Mott's division; and Milton's battery was with Ayres' division.

SECOND CORPS

Third Division, Gershom Mott
    First Brigade, P. Regis De Trobriand
    Second Brigade, Byron R. Pierce
    Third Brigade, Robert McAllister

SECOND CAVALRY DIVISION, ARMY OF THE POTOMAC, David McM. Gregg
    First Brigade, Henry E. Davies, Jr.
    Second Brigade, J. Irvin Gregg
    Third Brigade, Charles H. Smith

Reconnaissance to Hatcher's Run, December 9–10, 1864. While Warren was advancing on his expedition to Hicksford, Virginia to destroy the Weldon Railroad (see preceding section), Nelson A. Miles was ordered out on a reconnaissance toward Hatcher's Run to determine whether the enemy had detached troops to oppose this movement, and if so, what troops had been sent. At daylight December 9, 1864, Miles marched down the Vaughan Road toward Hatcher's Run, with George N. Macy's First Brigade, Clinton D. MacDougall's Third Brigade, and St. Clair A. Mulholland's Fourth Brigade of his First Division of Second Corps. Also with Miles were three regiments of cavalry under Michael Kerwin, and T. Frederick Brown's Battery B, 1st Rhode Island Light Artillery.

Miles encountered enemy pickets at the Cummings house, but pushed on toward the Vaughan Road crossing of Hatcher's Run. Upon arrival there, he found the enemy entrenched on the far side of the run. Regiments of Macy's brigade quickly crossed over and cleared the crossing. Miles also secured the ford at Armstrong's Mill and another ford on the road by the Cummings house, about a half mile below the Vaughan Road. The cavalry was then sent down the Vaughan Road to Davis' Shop, and the infantry was posted to cover the fords and the roads leading to the right.

At dark, Frank Wheaton arrived with his own First Division and Truman Seymour's Third Division of Sixth Corps. Wheaton then formed his command on the right of Miles, and extended his line along the Squirrel Level Road in the direction of the Federal line of entrenchments to keep open the Vaughan Road.

The cavalry was withdrawn from Davis' Shop at dark, and was then posted in front of the infantry on the Vaughan Road, the Duncan Road, and on the left flank of the infantry.

There was no further change in position until the afternoon of December 10, 1864, and then Miles and Wheaton returned to their camps.

Battle of Hatcher's Run (or Dabney's Mill, Armstrong's Mill, Rowanty Creek, Vaughan Road), February 5–7, 1865. During the winter of 1864–1865, Grant received information that supplies for Lee's army were being brought into Petersburg by wagon train from Hicksford, Virginia on the Weldon Railroad. The route used was said to be up the Meherrin River from Hicksford to the Boydton Plank Road, and then through Dinwiddie Court House to Petersburg. Grant decided to break up this supply line, and February 4, 1865, he informed Meade that he wanted the wagon train that was hauling the supplies destroyed. Meade assigned David McM. Gregg, with his Second Cavalry Division, to this task; and he also directed Andrew A. Humphreys, with his Second Corps, and Gouverneur K. Warrren, with his Fifth Corps, to move out and support the cavalry.

Gregg was ordered to march on the morning of February 5, 1865 by way of Reams' Station to Dinwiddie Court House, where he was to break up the supply line. Warren was ordered to march with Fifth Corps, cross Hatcher's Run below the Vaughan Road, and then take position at the J. Hargrave house. This was about a mile and a half west of the intersection of the Quaker Road and the Stage Road. The latter ran from Rowanty Creek to Dinwiddie Court House.

Humphreys was ordered to take Thomas A. Smyth's Second Division and Gershom Mott's Third Division of his Second Corps, which were then in reserve, and move to the Vaughan Road crossing of Hatcher's Run and also to Armstrong's Mill on Hatcher's Run. Humphreys was to hold those points in support of Fifth Corps, which, when in its assigned position, would be three or four miles to the southwest. Nelson A. Miles' First Division, Second Corps was to remain behind and hold the corps' line of entrenchments.

Gregg's cavalry left its camps about 3:00 A.M. February 5, 1865 and marched to Reams' Station. It then continued on down the Halifax Road to the Malone Bridge Road, then along that road to Rowanty Creek, and from there on the Military Road to Dinwiddie Court House. Gregg arrived at Dinwiddie Court House early in the day and captured a few wagons, but he found that the Boydton Plank Road was not heavily used. That evening, Gregg started back toward Malone's Bridge, where he arrived and bivouacked about 10:00 P.M.

Meantime, Warren's Fifth Corps had left its camps near the Gurley house, between the Halifax Road and the Jerusalem Plank Road, at 7:00 A.M. February 5, 1865. Romeyn B. Ayres' Second Division was in the lead, and it was followed by Charles Griffin's First Division and Samuel W. Crawford's Third Division, in that order. Three squadrons of the 6th Ohio Cavalry covered the advance of Warren's column. Ayres reached the crossing of Rowanty Creek at the W. Perkins house, near the junction of Gravelly Run and Hatcher's Run, at 10:00 A.M., and came under enemy fire. James Gwyn's Third Brigade soon forced a crossing of the creek and drove the enemy away. The rest of Warren's column was unable to cross until 4:00 P.M., when bridges were completed across the stream. Fifth Corps then moved out to the Vaughan Road, and on that road toward Dinwiddie Court House. It reached its assigned position near the intersection of the Quaker Road and the Stage Road, where it remained during the remainder of the afternoon and evening.

Humphreys, with the two divisions of his Second Corps, left his camps in front of Fort Clarke and Fort Siebert, between the Vaughan Road and the Halifax Road, and marched down the Vaughan Road. Smyth's division was in the lead, and Mott's division followed. Smyth's division arrived at the McDougall house, and from that point was sent to the right to secure the crossing of Hatcher's Run at Armstrong's Mill. Robert McAllister's Third Brigade of Mott's division was also ordered to the right to the vicinity of the Tucker house, where it was to take position on the right of Smyth. McAllister was then to cover the Vaughan Road and also a small parallel road that ran from the Squirrel Level Road to Armstrong's Mill.

About 9:30 A.M., P. Regis De Trobriand's First Brigade of Mott's division advanced on the Vaughan Road past the McDougall house, and drove a small enemy force across Hatcher's Run. It then crossed to the south side of the run and entrenched. A bridge was then built, and George W. West's Second Brigade of Mott's division also crossed and entrenched. De Trobriand's brigade was formed on the right of the road, with its left not far from the F. B. Keys house and its right on Hatcher's Run above the bridge. West established his brigade on the left of the road, with its right connecting with De Trobriand's brigade and its left on the run below the bridge.

Major Frank Hess, with the 3rd Pennsylvania Cavalry, which had reported to Humphreys, was sent forward on the Vaughan Road, and the 105th Pennsylvania Infantry of West's brigade was moved up in support.

Humphreys established his line north of Hatcher's Run as follows: Smyth's division was on the left, with his brigades in position as follows: William A. Olmsted's First Brigade was on the left of the division, near Armstrong's Mill, facing west; Mathew Murphy's Second Brigade was on the right, and it extended across the Duncan Road in front of the Armstrong house, with its right resting on a small swamp in rear of the Armstrong, Jr. house; and Francis E. Pierce's Third Brigade was held in reserve near the Armstrong house. During the afternoon, however, the regiments of Pierce's brigade were sent to help First Brigade and Second Brigade, and also to help establish a connection with McAllister's brigade of Mott's division, which had come up on the right of Smyth. McAllister arrived during the morning as directed, and at 12:30 P.M. was ordered to entrench his position. The right of

McAllister's line rested on a swamp west of and near the Squirrel Level Road, and its left extended toward the right of Smyth's division. Humphreys found that McAllister's brigade was unable to cover the ground and connect with Smyth, and at 3:30 P.M. he ordered Miles, commanding First Division, Second Corps, to send an additional brigade for that purpose. Miles sent John Ramsey's Fourth Brigade, which arrived about 4:30 P.M. and relieved McAllister's brigade. McAllister then moved to the left of Ramsey's brigade, and extended its line to the left toward the swamp upon which the right of Smyth's division rested. About 5:30 P.M., Miles sent George Von Schack's Third Brigade of Miles' division to the Tucker house to report to Ramsey, but it was not needed and returned to its camp that night.

The 3rd Pennsylvania Cavalry was ordered to open communications on the south side of Hatcher's Run between the right of De Trobriand's brigade and the left of Smyth's division.

About 3:00 P.M., the enemy opened fire on the left of Smyth's division, and at 4:30 P.M., troops belonging to John B. Gordon's and Ambrose P. Hill's corps delivered a strong attack on McAllister's brigade and the right of Smyth's division. The attack came as Ramsey was getting in position, but he was not seriously engaged. Murphy's brigade and McAllister's brigade bore the brunt of the attack, but their casualties were not heavy.

About 5:00 P.M., two regiments of West's brigade were sent to McAllister, and a short time later West followed with the rest of his brigade. West arrived in rear of McAllister's left during the fighting, and helped in repulsing the enemy attacks. West's regiments then occupied the ground between McAllister and Smyth. Altogether, Humphreys' line repulsed three separate attacks that evening. Murphy was wounded about 5:00 P.M., during the second attack, and he was succeeded in command of Second Brigade, Second Division by James P. McIvor. The fighting finally ended about 7:00 P.M., with Humphreys' line intact.

During the afternoon and late evening of February 5, 1865, additional reinforcements were sent to Second Corps. At 3:00 P.M., John F. Hartranft was ordered with his Third Division, Ninth Corps to report to Humphreys. Hartranft arrived about 8:00 P.M. and was placed on the immediate right of Second Corps, facing west. His right was in front of the Claypole house, and his left was on the swamp that covered the right of Second Corps.

At 8:00 P.M. that evening, Frank Wheaton was ordered to join Humphreys' command with his First Division, Sixth Corps. En route, while near Fort Siebert, Wheaton was ordered to deploy his division along the Squirrel Level Road on the right of Hartranft. By 11:30 P.M., Wheaton's division was in position, with Joseph E. Hamblin's Third Brigade on the left, next to Hartranft; Edward L. Campbell's First Brigade in the center; and Ranald S. Mackenzie's Second Brigade (then commanded by James Hubbard) on the right. Hubbard's line extended nearly to Fort Cummings.

About 9:00 P.M., Gregg's cavalry having withdrawn from the Boydton Plank Road, Meade ordered Warren to march back from his advanced position and join Humphreys at the Vaughan Road crossing of Hatcher's Run. Meade also ordered Gregg to move with his division from Malone's Bridge on Rowanty Creek and report to Warren, and then move with Fifth Corps to Hatcher's Run. Warren started his withdrawal about midnight, when Griffin's division started back. Ayres' division followed with the artillery, and Crawford's division brought up the rear. Gregg's cavalry division joined Warren on the Vaughan Road about 4:00 A.M. February 6, 1865, and was then directed to follow Crawford.

Between 3:00 and 4:00 A.M. February 6, 1865, Griffin relieved De Trobriand's brigade at the Vaughan Road crossing of Hatcher's Run, and the latter then moved into reserve near the Tucker house, in rear of McAllister's line. Mott's division was thus reassembled. Alfred L. Pearson's Third Brigade of Griffin's division occupied De Trobriand's old line, with its right on Hatcher's Run at Armstrong's Mill and its left just west of the Vaughan Road.

Shortly after 8:00 A.M. February 6, 1865, Warren was informed that Humphreys intended to attack if the enemy were still outside of their works. Accordingly, Fifth Corps was held in readiness to cooperate with Humphreys if necessary. A reconnaissance made by Mott and Hartranft that morning, however, revealed that the Confederate forces on their front had retired within their lines, and when Warren learned of this at 11:00 A.M., he decided to wait for further instructions.

About 1:00 P.M., Warren sent Frederick Winthrop's First Brigade of Ayres' division to hold the Vaughan Road and support Gregg's cavalry, which was then skirmishing briskly with the enemy farther south on the road.

At 12:15 P.M., Warren was ordered to make a reconnaissance to the southwest of Hatcher's Run to determine the position of enemy forces in that direction. An hour later, Crawford's division started down the Vaughan Road on its way to the Dabney's Mill Road. It was then to move forward to Dabney's Mill and locate an enemy line reported to be in the vicinity. Ayres' division was to follow Crawford, and Ayres was to take with him Winthrop's brigade of his division, which was then with Gregg on the Vaughan Road. As a part of Warren's movement, Gregg's cavalry was to advance down the Vaughan Road and drive the enemy across Gravelly Run. Gregg was also to watch the left of Crawford and Ayres as they advanced. Griffin's division was left in reserve to support either the infantry on the Dabney's Mill Road or the cavalry on the Vaughan Road. For this purpose, Griffin's division was posted at the junction of the two roads.

Meade's plans were disrupted somewhat when Gregg and Winthrop were attacked on the Vaughan Road by Jubal A. Early's division (commanded by John Pegram) of Gordon's corps. Griffin then sent Horatio G. Sickel's First Brigade of his division to aid Gregg and Winthrop. Sickel took position in support of Winthrop on the right of the road near the Keys house. The enemy attacks were repulsed, but Winthrop's brigade was unable to accompany Ayres' division to Dabney's Mill. Pearson's Third Brigade of Griffin's division was later ordered to report to Ayres in place of Winthrop.

Crawford had proceeded only a short distance on the Dabney's Mill Road when he came up to the entrenched picket line of a part of Pegram's division. The pickets were driven back by Edward S. Bragg's First Brigade, and then Crawford pushed on, with Bragg's brigade in the lead and Henry A. Morrow's Third Brigade on its left and rear. Later, Henry Baxter's Second Brigade arrived at the front and formed on the left of Morrow. Crawford soon drove

the enemy back to Dabney's Mill. The troops of Pegram's division that were holding the road at Dabney's Mill were then reinforced by Gordon's division (then commanded by Clement A. Evans), and together they attacked and drove back the left of Crawford's line. Ayres' two brigades then moved up on the left of Crawford, with Richard N. Bowerman's Second Brigade on the right, next to Crawford, and James Gwyn's Second Brigade on the left of the division. The combined Federal force then pushed forward and drove the enemy beyond Dabney's Mill.

At about that time, William Mahone's division of A. P. Hill's corps arrived and joined Pegram and Evans. The fighting then became constant and determined. At 4:15 P.M., Pearson's brigade was brought up and put in position with Ayres to help hold the left of the line, and Pearson was soon in the midst of heavy fighting.

About 2:30 P.M., Wheaton's division of Sixth Corps was ordered up to the Vaughan Road from its position of the night before to support Warren's movement. Wheaton moved down the Vaughan Road to Hatcher's Run and crossed to the south side so as to be in position to support Fifth Corps. At about the time that Pearson's brigade joined Ayres, Warren ordered at least one of Wheaton's brigades to advance; and Wheaton, with Hubbard's brigade, started in the direction of the fighting. At about the same time, the enemy attacked in great numbers, and Warren's line gave way, with the troops falling back rapidly in disorder. About 5:30 P.M., Hubbard's brigade began to encounter stragglers from Crawford's division approximately three-fourths of a mile from Hatcher's Run. Wheaton attempted to form a line, but as the fugitives from the front poured through, he was forced to fall back before Hubbard could get his brigade in position. This occurred a short time before dark. Pearson's brigade joined Wheaton and formed on the left of Hubbard. A number of officers and men also halted in their retreat and joined Wheaton. The enemy, however, did not press their attack, and the fighting ended at dark.

About 10:00 P.M., Winthrop's brigade, which had been relieved on the Vaughan Road by Sickel, arrived and relieved the skirmishers in front of Hubbard's brigade of Wheaton's division. Wheaton was then ordered to withdraw to the north side of Hatcher's Run, and Hubbard's brigade was joined there by Campbell's First Brigade and Hamblin's Third Brigade of Wheaton's division, which had been in reserve in the entrenchments to the rear. The division then recrossed Hatcher's Run and bivouacked near the Cummings house.

Warren's brigades were re-formed during the night, and Crawford's division was massed in the rear, near the Vaughan Road.

On the morning of February 7, 1865, Warren directed Crawford to relieve Winthrop's brigade, and to move out from the right near Armstrong's Mill toward Dabney's Mill and attack the enemy who had been engaged there the evening before. Crawford advanced about noon, in a heavy rain, regained most of the battlefield of the day before, and drove the enemy back into their main line of works. Shortly after noon, Hamblin's brigade of Wheaton's division crossed Hatcher's Run to support Crawford. About an hour later, Hubbard's brigade was also ordered to cross, but neither of these brigades was engaged.

About midnight, Wheaton withdrew his division from Hatcher's Run, and at 6:00 the next morning arrived at his old camps on the right of the Sixth Corps' line, on the main line of entrenchments. Crawford's division remained in position near Dabney's Mill during the night of February 7, 1865, but the next morning it withdrew to the north bank of Hatcher's Run.

The cavalry division returned to its camp February 8, 1865, and upon arriving there Gregg learned that his resignation had been accepted. Gregg was then relieved from command of Second Cavalry Division February 9, 1865, and J. Irvin Gregg assumed command the next day.

Ramsey's brigade remained near the Tucker house until February 9, 1865, and then returned to Miles' division the next day. Hartranft's division was relieved from duty with Second Corps February 10, 1865, and it then rejoined Ninth Corps.

On the morning of February 8, 1865, Meade began the preparation of a new entrenched line that was to extend from the vicinity of Fort Sampson, on the left of the old line of works, to the Vaughan Road crossing of Hatcher's Run. Meade assigned Humphreys to occupy that part of the line, and ordered Warren's Fifth Corps to occupy a position where it could defend the left and rear of Humphreys' line. For additional information, see above, Siege of Petersburg, The Petersburg Lines.

The organization of the troops commanded by George G. Meade at the Battle of Hatcher's Run February 5–7, 1865 was as follows:

SECOND CORPS

First Division
    Fourth Brigade, John Ramsey

Second Division, Thomas A. Smyth
    First Brigade, William A. Olmsted
    Second Brigade, Mathew Murphy, to February 5, 1865, mortally wounded
        James P. McIvor
    Third Brigade, Francis E. Pierce

Third Division, Gershom Mott
    First Brigade, P. Regis De Trobriand
    Second Brigade, George W. West
    Third Brigade, Robert McAllister

Artillery, John G. Hazard
    10th Battery, Massachusetts Light Artillery, J. Webb Adams
    Battery K, 4th United States Artillery, John W. Roder

FIFTH CORPS, Gouverneur K. Warren

First Division, Charles Griffin
    First Brigade, Horatio Sickel, wounded February 6, 1865
    Second Brigade, Allen L. Burr
    Third Brigade, Alfred L. Pearson

Second Division, Romeyn B. Ayres
    First Brigade, Frederick Winthrop
    Second Brigade, Richard N. Bowerman
    Third Brigade, James Gwyn

Third Division, Samuel W. Crawford
    First Brigade, Edward S. Bragg
    Second Brigade, Henry Baxter
    Third Brigade, Henry A. Morrow

Artillery, Robert H. Fitzhugh
    9th Battery, Massachusetts Light Artillery, George W. Foster
    Battery D, 1st New York Light Artillery, James B. Hazelton

Battery L, 1st New York Light Artillery, George Breck

SIXTH CORPS

First Division, Frank Wheaton
    First Brigade, Edward L. Campbell
    Second Brigade, James Hubbard
    Third Brigade, Joseph E. Hamblin

NINTH CORPS

Third Division, John F. Hartranft
    First Brigade, Charles W. Diven
    Second Brigade, Joseph A. Mathews

CAVALRY

Second Cavalry Division, David McM. Gregg
    First Brigade, Henry E. Davies, Jr., wounded February 6, 1865
    Second Brigade, J. Irvin Gregg, to February 6, 1865, wounded
        Michael Kerwin
    Third Brigade, Oliver Knowles

Note. W. Neil Dennison's Battery A, 2nd United States Artillery was with First Brigade, and Chandler P. Eakin's Batteries H and I, 1st United States Artillery of Second Brigade were detached with the Artillery Brigade of Ninth Corps.

Assault at Fort Stedman, Virginia, March 25, 1865. During the winter of 1864–1865, the Army of Northern Virginia was reduced to desperate circumstances, and Lee was forced to consider some serious options, the resolution of which would greatly affect the future of the army and of the Confederacy. Basically, Lee felt that he was left with but three alternatives: to abandon the struggle and make the best possible terms with his enemy; to withdraw from Richmond and Petersburg and march to join Joseph E. Johnston in North Carolina; or to launch an attack on the Union line of entrenchments in an attempt to break through and, at least temporarily, relieve the siege of Petersburg. The first two of these options were not regarded favorably by Jefferson Davis and the Confederate authorities, and Lee had no other choice than to order the attack.

The assault was to be made at 4:00 A.M. March 25, 1865, from Colquitt's Salient against Fort Stedman and the adjacent trenches. John B. Gordon was selected to make the attack with the divisions of James A. Walker (Early's division), Clement A.

Evans (Gordon's division), and Bryan Grimes (Rodes' division) of his corps. He was also authorized to call on the brigades of Matthew W. Ransom and William H. Wallace of Bushrod R. Johnson's division of Richard H. Anderson's corps. In addition, two brigades under James H. Lane from Cadmus M. Wilcox's division and two brigades under John R. Cooke from Henry Heth's division of A. P. Hill's corps were ordered to report to Gordon.

The right of the Union line of entrenchments, which included Fort Stedman, was held by John G. Parke's Ninth Corps. The front held by Ninth Corps extended from the Appomattox River to Fort Howard, a distance of about seven miles. Orlando B. Willcox's First Division was on the right, from the river to Fort Morton; Robert B. Potter's Second Division was on the left, between Fort Morton and Fort Howard; and John F. Hartranft's Third Division was in reserve.

Hartranft's troops were posted in the rear of Willcox and Potter, on a line about four miles long. Its right was at the Friend house, about a mile in rear of the main works; and its left was behind Fort Prescott, near the Army Railroad. Charles W. Diven's First Brigade, Third Division was on the right of the division, with the 200th Pennsylvania near the Dunn house, the 209th Pennsylvania at Meade's Station, and the 208th Pennsylvania near the Avery house. Joseph A. Mathews' Second Brigade was on the left of the division, with 205th and 207th Pennsylvania on the Army Railroad near Fort Prescott, and the 211th Pennsylvania was farther west beyond the Jerusalem Plank Road.

Willcox's division held that part of the Union line that was in front of Gordon's assembled troops. Ralph Ely's Second Brigade was on the right of the division between the Appomattox River and a point beyond Battery No. 9, which was near the City Point Railroad; Napoleon B. McLaughlen's Third Brigade, which was to bear the brunt of Gordon's attack, extended from the left of Ely's brigade to Fort Haskell, and it occupied Battery No. 10, Fort Stedman, Battery No.11, Battery No.12, and also Fort Haskell; and Samuel Harriman's First Brigade was on the left of the division from Fort Haskell to Fort Morton.

Gordon's attack began shortly after 4:00 A.M., and struck first on the breastworks to the right of Battery No. 10. The attackers quickly broke through the line, entered Battery No. 10 from the rear, and captured the battery. Immediately after this success, a second attack was launched on the rear of Fort Stedman by a large force that passed through the breach at Battery No. 10, then moved along the rear of the line, and soon gained possession of the fort. Early in the fighting, while it was still dark, Mc-Laughlen, commander of the Union forces on that part of the line, entered Fort Stedman and, not knowing that it had been captured, was taken prisoner. He was succeeded in command of Third Brigade by Gilbert P. Robinson.

The enemy troops that had first penetrated the Federal line, turned to their left and moved down the entrenchments toward Battery No. 9, which was held by men of Ely's brigade. The enemy launched an attack on the battery but were soon repulsed. Still another column passed through the line at Fort Stedman, and it too moved along the entrenchments toward Battery No. 9. It then joined the troops who had arrived earlier in a second attack on the battery, but this too was unsuccessful.

While the fighting continued on the main line, some enemy troops moved on eastward beyond Fort Stedman toward the Army Railroad.

When the enemy was established in Fort Stedman, some of their troops advanced from the fort to their right along the Union trenches toward Fort Haskell. They captured Battery No. 11 and Battery No. 12, and drove all defenders from their trenches on that part of the line. They also attacked Fort Haskell, but were repulsed after heavy fighting. By that time it was after daylight, and the main Federal line from Battery No. 9 to Fort Haskell was in possession of the enemy. These two works, however, were strongly defended, and their occupancy prevented any farther extension of the enemy gains.

At about that time, Willcox began his attempt to retake the captured positions. All Union artillery that could be brought to bear on Fort Stedman opened fire. This included the guns in the works to the right and left of Fort Stedman, from Battery No. 4 on the right to Fort Morton on the left; and also the guns of John C. Tidball's Artillery Brigade of Ninth Corps that were posted on a ridge in rear of the front line.

Very early in the day, Hartranft learned of the attack at Fort Stedman and ordered the concentration of his Third Division. He sent the 208th Pennsylvania to aid McLaughlen, and with the other two regiments of Diven's brigade, the 200th Pennsylvania and 209th Pennsylvania, which were close at hand, Hartranft advanced toward Fort Stedman. He met and drove back the enemy troops that were advancing toward the Army Railroad, but a short time later his regiments were forced to halt by a strong Confederate line. Soon after the enemy repulse in front of Fort Haskell, Hartranft's Second Brigade, under Mathews, came up and formed in line on the left of Diven's brigade. The left of Mathews' line extended toward Fort Haskell.

By that time, the enemy had been defeated on both flanks, and was under heavy artillery fire all along the line that they had captured, and when they observed Hartranft's new line on their front, they began to fall back in small groups toward their own line. At that point, George M. Randall, with his 14th New York Heavy Artillery (serving as infantry), and a part of the 100th Pennsylvania, 3rd Maryland, and 29th Massachusetts, all of McLaughlen's brigade, advanced from the vicinity of Fort Haskell along the trenches toward Fort Stedman. At about the same time, Hartranft's line advanced and soon enveloped the rear of the captured works. Diven was wounded in the attack, and was succeeded in command of the brigade by William H. H. McCall. The 17th Michigan Acting Engineers of Willcox's division, advancing on the right, also pushed forward and recaptured a part of the trenches. Gordon's men finally gave way and retired to their own lines, but many were taken prisoner.

There was some controversy over whether troops of McLaughlen's brigade or Hartranft's division recaptured Fort Stedman, but it appears that both entered the fort and the adjacent works at about the same time against only slight resistance. The Union line was restored, with all of its artillery, by 9:00 A.M.

Meade had spent the night of March 24, 1865 at City Point and was not present with the army when Gordon attacked. The wires to City Point had been cut, and Parke did not learn until 6:15 A.M. that, as senior officer on the field, he was in command of the army. Parke then ordered Horatio G. Wright to send a division of Sixth Corps to aid Ninth Corps, and he also ordered Gouverneur K. Warren to bring up two divisions of Fifth Corps. Frank Wheaton's First Division, Sixth Corps had reached a point about midway between Hancock's Station and Meade's Station on the Army Railroad when he received word that the captured Federal works had been retaken. Wheaton then returned to his former position. At about 8:30 A.M., Romeyn B. Ayres' Second Division and Samuel W. Crawford's Third Division of Fifth Corps were stopped while en route to support Ninth Corps, and they too returned to their former positions without being engaged.

There was also some sharp fighting on the Union left March 25, 1865. Andrew A. Humphreys' Second Corps and Horatio G. Wright's Sixth Corps were ordered to make strong reconnaissances toward the enemy works on their fronts, and if they were found to be only lightly held, they were to be attacked. The skirmishers of Sixth Corps advanced in front of Fort Fisher, and they found the enemy picket line strongly entrenched. Wright's skirmishers were supported by George W. Getty's Second Division, Sixth Corps and J. Warren Keifer's Second Brigade of Truman Seymour's Third Division, Sixth Corps. About 3:00 P.M., Joseph E. Hamblin's Second Brigade and Oliver Edwards' Third Brigade of Frank Wheaton's First Division, Sixth Corps were sent to support Getty. After a sharp contest, the enemy picket line near the Jones house, on the Church Road, in front of the left of Sixth Corps, was captured.

The skirmishers of Humphreys' Second Corps also advanced, and these were supported by Nelson A. Miles' First Division and Gershom Mott's Third Division of Second Corps. Miles captured the enemy picket line between the Watkins house, at the junction of present-day Route 673 with the Duncan Road and the Harman Road, and the C. Smith house on the right. Joseph J. Bartlett's Third Brigade of Charles Griffin's First Division, Fifth Corps was sent to support Humphreys, and it was engaged with Second Corps near the Watkins house that evening.

Wright and Humphreys held their captured positions until that night, but they did not attempt an attack on the enemy's main line. The troops of these two corps were withdrawn about midnight and returned to their original positions. The operations on the Federal left that day have been referred to as the Action at the Watkins House.

For details of the organization of the troops on the Federal left, see Second Corps, Fifth Corps, and Sixth Corps, Army of the Potomac.

The organization of the troops that were engaged at, and near, Fort Stedman March 25, 1865, was as follows:

NINTH CORPS, John G. Parke

First Division, Orlando B. Willcox
  First Brigade, Samuel Harriman
  Second Brigade, Ralph Ely
  Third Brigade, Napoleon B. McLaughlen, captured
    Gilbert P. Robinson

Note. First Brigade was not engaged.

Third Division, John F. Hartranft
  First Brigade, Charles W. Diven, wounded
    William H. H. McCall
  Second Brigade, Joseph A. Mathews

Artillery Brigade, John C. Tidball
  Company E, 1st Connecticut Heavy Artillery, Frank D. Bangs
  Company K, 1st Connecticut Heavy Artillery, John M. Twiss
  Company L, 1st Connecticut Heavy Artillery, Robert Lewis
  7th Battery (G), Maine Light Artillery, Adelbert B. Twitchell
  9th Battery, Massachusetts Light Artillery, Richard S. Milton
  11th Battery, Massachusetts Light Artillery, Edward J. Jones
  14th Battery, Massachusetts Light Artillery, Joseph W. B. Wright
  3rd Battery, New Jersey Light Artillery, Christian Woerner
  Battery G, 1st New York Light Artillery, Samuel A. McClellan
  Company G, 8th New York Heavy Artillery, John R. Cooper
  19th Battery, New York Light Artillery, Edward W. Rogers
  27th Battery, New York Light Artillery, John B. Eaton
  34th Battery, New York Light Artillery, Jacob Roemer
  Battery B, 1st Pennsylvania Light Artillery, William McClelland
  Battery D, Pennsylvania Light Artillery, Samuel H. Rhoads
  Batteries C and I, 5th United States Artillery, Valentine H. Stone

Note 1. 9th Battery, Massachusetts Light Artillery; 14th Battery, Massachusetts Light Artillery; and Batteries C and I, 5th United States Artillery were detached from the Artillery Reserve.

Note 2. 3rd Battery, New Jersey Light Artillery and Battery G, 1st New York Light Artillery were detached from Second Corps.

POPE'S NORTHERN VIRGINIA CAMPAIGN
JULY 30, 1862–SEPTEMBER 2, 1862

Organization of the Army of Virginia. President Lincoln believed that Thomas J. (Stonewall) Jackson's successful campaign in the Shenandoah Valley in May and June of 1862 was due in part to the lack of a unified command of the Union forces in Northern Virginia. Accordingly, on June 26, 1862, he directed that the troops of John C. Fremont's Mountain Department, Nathaniel P. Banks' Department of the Shenandoah, and Irvin McDowell's Department of the Rappahannock, including those under Samuel D. Sturgis in Washington, be consolidated into a single command to be known as the Army of Virginia, and that John Pope be assigned command.

The troops from the Mountain Department were to constitute the First Corps, Army of Virginia, under the command of Fremont; the troops of the Department of the Shenandoah were to constitute the Second Corps, under Banks; and the troops of the Department of the Rappahannock, except those in the city of Washington, were to constitute the Third Corps, under McDowell. Fremont, however, refused to serve under Pope, who was his junior in rank, and who had also served under him in the Western Department the year before. Fremont was, therefore, relieved from command of First Corps June 28, 1862, and Rufus King was assigned in his place. King refused the command, however, and Robert C. Schenck commanded the corps temporarily June 28–29, 1862, until he was relieved by Franz Sigel. Schenck was again in temporary command July 7–12, 1862, during Sigel's absence.

Pope assumed command of the Army of Virginia June 27, 1862, with headquarters in Washington. His mission was threefold: He was to cover Washington, protect the Shenandoah Valley, and move east of the Blue Ridge Mountains toward Charlottesville in an attempt to draw off Confederate troops from Robert E. Lee's forces that were then facing George B. McClellan's Army of the Potomac in front of Richmond.

The order creating the Army of Virginia was issued June 26, 1862, the day of the Battle of Mechanicsville, which was the beginning of the Seven Days' Battles on the Peninsula. On June 17, 1862, Jackson had departed with his command from the Shenandoah Valley for Richmond, and he would join Lee at Gaines' Mill June 27, 1862. With Jackson's departure, there was no significant enemy force in the area of Pope's proposed operations.

When Pope assumed command June 27, 1862, the forces composing his army were rather widely scattered and were posted as follows: Banks' corps was at Middletown in the Shenandoah Valley, with John W. Geary's Brigade guarding the Manassas Gap Railroad from Strasburg to Manassas Junction; Fremont's (later Sigel's) corps was at Strasburg, also in the Shenandoah Valley; James B. Ricketts' Second Division of McDowell's corps was at Manassas Junction; Rufus King's First Division and Abner Doubleday's Separate Brigade of McDowell's corps were at Falmouth, opposite Fredericksburg; John P. Hatch's cavalry was in the Luray Valley; and George D. Bayard's cavalry was along the Rappahannock River above Fredericksburg.

On July 10, 1862, Pope issued orders for the concentration of the army as follows: Sigel was directed to cross the Blue Ridge Mountains at Front Royal and take position at Sperryville; Banks' corps, with Geary's Brigade, was to cross the mountains at Chester Gap and move to Little Washington, a few miles east of Sperryville; and Ricketts' division was to move forward from Manassas Junction to Waterloo Bridge, where the turnpike from Warrenton to Sperryville crossed the Rappahannock River. King's division and Doubleday's Brigade were to remain at Falmouth.

The organization of the Army of Virginia, as organized in July 1862, was as follows:

ARMY OF VIRGINIA
John Pope

FIRST CORPS, Franz Sigel

First Division, Robert C. Schenck

First Brigade, Julius Stahel
Second Brigade, Nathaniel C. McLean

Note 1. First Brigade was formed from First Brigade, Louis Blenker's Division of the Mountain Department.
Note 2. Second Brigade was formed from Schenck's Brigade, Mountain Department.

Second Division, Adolph Von Steinwehr
First Brigade, John A. Koltes
Second Brigade, William R. Lloyd

Note 1. First Brigade was formed from Second Brigade, Blenker's Division, Mountain Department.
Note 2. Second Brigade was formed from unattached regiments of the Mountain Department.

Third Division, Carl Schurz
First Brigade, Henry Bohlen
Second Brigade, Wladimir Krzyzanowski

Note 1. First Brigade was organized largely from regiments of the Mountain Department.
Note 2. Second Brigade was organized from Third Brigade, Blenker's Division, Mountain Department.

Milroy's Independent Brigade, Robert H. Milroy

Note. This brigade was organized from Milroy's Brigade, Mountain Department.

Detached Brigade, A. Sanders Piatt

Note. This brigade, also known as Piatt's Brigade, was organized July 5, 1862 and posted at Winchester, Virginia. It remained there until near the end of July 1862, and then Julius White assumed command.

Cavalry Brigade, John Beardsley

SECOND CORPS, Nathaniel P. Banks

First Division, Alpheus S. Williams
First Brigade, Samuel W. Crawford
Third Brigade, George H. Gordon

Note 1. There was no Second Brigade in First Division. On May 1, 1862, Second Brigade of Williams Division, Department of the Shenandoah, commanded by George L. Hartsuff, was transferred to the Department of the Rappahannock.
Note 2. First Brigade was formed from First Brigade, First Division, Department of the Shenandoah.
Note 3. Third Brigade was formed from Third Brigade, First Division, Department of the Shenandoah.

Second Division, James Cooper, to July 11, 1862
Christopher C. Augur
First Brigade, James Cooper

Second Brigade, John P. Slough, to July 7, 1862
G. A. Scroggs
Henry Prince

Note 1. First Brigade was formed from Cooper's First Brigade, Sigel's Division, Department of the Shenandoah.
Note 2. Second Brigade was formed from Second Brigade, Sigel's Division, Department of the Shenandoah.
Note 3. Prince was ordered to report to the Army of Virginia July 1, 1862.
Note 4. Second Division was reorganized August 2, 1862. For details, see below.

Geary's Brigade, John W. Geary
Cavalry Brigade, John P. Hatch

Note. July 27, 1862, John Buford relieved Hatch and was assigned as chief of cavalry of Banks' corps. Hatch was assigned command of First Brigade, First Division of McDowell's Third Corps (formerly Augur's brigade).

THIRD CORPS, Irvin McDowell

First Division, Rufus King
First Brigade, Christopher C. Augur, to July 11, 1862
Timothy Sullivan
Second Brigade, Abner Doubleday
Third Brigade, Marsena R. Patrick
Fourth Brigade, John Gibbon

Note 1. First Division was formerly King's Third Division, Department of the Rappahannock.
Note 2. First Brigade was formed from First Brigade, Third Division, Department of the Rappahannock.
Note 3. Second Brigade was formed from Doubleday's Separate Brigade, Department of the Rappahannock August 8, 1862.
Note 4. Third Brigade was formed from Second Brigade, Third Division, Department of the Rappahannock.
Note 5. Fourth Brigade was formed from Third Brigade, Third Division, Department of the Rappahannock.

Second Division, James B. Ricketts
First Brigade, Abram Duryee
Second Brigade, Zealous B. Tower
Third Brigade, George L. Hartsuff
Fourth Brigade, Samuel S. Carroll

Note 1. First Brigade was formed from Second Brigade, Ricketts' Division (formerly Ord's Division), Department of the Rappahannock.
Note 2. Second Brigade was formed from First Brigade, Ricketts' Division (formerly Ord's Division), Department of the Rappahannock.
Note 3. Third Brigade was formed from Third Brigade, Ricketts' Division (formerly Ord's Division), Department of the Rappahannock.

Note 4. Fourth Brigade was formerly Fourth Brigade, Shields' Division, Department of the Rappahannock. It served in Sturgis' Reserve Corps during July 1862, and was assigned to Third Corps July 23, 1862. It was then ordered to report to Ricketts' division August 4, 1862.

Cavalry Brigade, George D. Bayard

Banks' corps was reorganized August 2, 1862, as follows: Erastus B. Tyler's Brigade, formerly Third Brigade of James Shields' Division, Department of the Rappahannock, and serving during July 1862 with Samuel D. Sturgis' Reserve Corps (see below) at Alexandria, arrived at Sperryville and was consolidated with John W. Geary's Brigade of Banks' corps. The combined brigades were designated as First Brigade, Second Division, Second Corps, and Geary was assigned command. Tyler was ordered to return to Alexandria and report to Sturgis to organize a new brigade. James Cooper's former First Brigade, Second Division was redesignated as Second Brigade, Second Division, and a new Third Brigade was organized from Henry Prince's Second Brigade, Second Division. George S. Greene was assigned command of this brigade. When the reorganization was completed, Second Corps was organized as follows:

SECOND CORPS, Nathaniel P. Banks

First Division, Alpheus S. Williams
    First Brigade, Samuel W. Crawford
    Second Brigade, George H. Gordon

Second Division, Christopher C. Augur
    First Brigade, John W. Geary
    Second Brigade, Henry Prince
    Third Brigade, George S. Greene

In addition to the three corps of the Army of Virginia, Pope also had under his direction Jacob D. Cox's District of the Kanawha, formerly of Fremont's Mountain Department, and Samuel D. Sturgis' command at Washington. The troops under Cox's command in the District of the Kanawha were known as the Kanawha Division, which was organized into four brigades as follows:

First Provisional Brigade, Eliakim P. Scammon
Second Provisional Brigade, Augustus Moor
Third Provisional Brigade, George Crook
Fourth Provisional Brigade, Joseph A. J. Lightburn

Cox's headquarters was at Flat Top Mountain in Western Virginia, and the troops of the Kanawha Division were posted at Charleston, Flat Top Mountain, and Meadow Bluff.

August 8, 1862, Cox was ordered to join Pope with the available troops of his division, and August 17, 1862, he turned over the command of the district to Joseph A. J. Lightburn and with the brigades of Scammon and Moor moved eastward to join the Army of Virginia. For additional information, see Mountain Department, Districts in the Mountain Department, District of the Kanawha; Army of Virginia, below; and Maryland Campaign (South Mountain and Antietam).

The Reserve Corps was originally constituted under Sturgis as an organization of the Department of the Rappahannock. When Pope assumed command of the Army of Virginia, this consisted only of a small unorganized force posted in the vicinity of Alexandria, Virginia. It was at that time in the process of organizing for field service. June 28, 1862, Erastus B. Tyler's Third Brigade and Samuel S. Carroll's Fourth Brigade, formerly of James Shields' Division, Department of the Rappahannock, were temporarily assigned to Sturgis' command. July 23, 1862, Tyler's brigade was assigned to Banks' corps and Carroll's brigade to McDowell's corps.

June 26, 1862, John Cook was assigned to duty in Sturgis' corps, and in August was given command of a brigade. A. Sanders Piatt, formerly commander of a detached brigade of Sigel's First Corps, Army of Virginia at Winchester, was ordered July 26, 1862 to report to Sturgis at Alexandria, and in August 1862 was assigned command of a new brigade. August 2, 1862, Tyler, who had taken his brigade from Sturgis' command to Banks' corps at Sperryville, was ordered to return to Alexandria and organize a new brigade.

In August 1862, Sturgis' command consisted of a division under Amiel W. Whipple, Piatt's Brigade, Cook's Brigade, and some regiments at Cloud's Mills, Tennallytown, and Fort Washington, Maryland. Piatt's Brigade was later attached to Whipple's Division. August 26, 1862, Sturgis, with Piatt's Brigade, arrived at Warrenton Junction, and the brigade was temporarily attached to Fitz John Porter's Fifth Corps, Army of the Potomac.

September 6, 1862, Sturgis was ordered to organize a division, to be known as Sturgis' Division, to consist of Piatt's Brigade and a new brigade under Tyler. This division was attached to Porter's Fifth Corps, Army of the Potomac.

There was also a brigade under Julius White at Winchester, Virginia. This brigade was formerly commanded by A. Sanders Piatt. White was assigned command July 26, 1862, and Piatt was ordered to Alexandria to report to Sturgis. September 2–3, 1862, White evacuated Winchester and moved his command to Harper's Ferry in the Middle Department.

* * * * * * * * * *

At the end of July 1862, after Pope's concentration was completed, the units of the Army of Virginia were posted as follows: Army headquarters was in Washington until July 29, 1862, at which time Pope joined the army, with headquarters in the field; Sigel's First Corps was near Sperryville; Banks' Second Corps was near Little Washington, but Samuel W. Crawford's First Brigade of Alpheus S. Williams' First Division had moved to Culpeper Court House July 14, 1862; John P. Hatch's Cavalry Brigade was operating south of Banks toward Gordonsville; Rufus King's First Division of McDowell's Third Corps was opposite Fredericksburg; James B. Ricketts' Second Division was at Waterloo, with Samuel S. Carroll's Fourth Brigade at Warrenton; and George D. Bayard's Cavalry Brigade was along the Rappahannock above Fredericksburg.

Amiel W. Whipple's Division of Samuel D. Sturgis' Reserve Corps was in the Defenses of Washington, Cook's Brigade was assigned to duty with Silas Casey in Washington August 22, 1862, and there were regiments at Tennallytown and Fort Washington. The troops of Jacob D. Cox's Kanawha Division were at Charleston, Flat Top Mountain, and Meadow Bluff in Western Virginia. Headquarters was at Flat Top Mountain.

Battle of Cedar Mountain (Slaughter's Mountain, or Cedar Run), August 9, 1862. July 11, 1862, Henry W. Halleck, then in command of the Department of the Mississippi in the West, was assigned command of the Armies of the United States as general in chief. He arrived in Washington and assumed command July 23, 1862. By this change in the command structure of the Union Army, the operations of the Army of the Potomac and the Army of Virginia were to be coordinated. A short time after Halleck arrived in Washington, McClellan was ordered to withdraw the Army of the Potomac from Harrison's Landing on the Peninsula and to transfer it to northern Virginia.

When Pope left Washington July 29, 1862 to assume command of the Army of Virginia in the field, his principal task was to prevent the concentration of Lee's forces near Richmond while McClellan was in the process of withdrawing. To accomplish this mission, Pope decided to threaten the important rail center of Gordonsville. Earlier, in mid-July 1862, Hatch had advanced with a force against the town; and King, at Fredericksburg, had sent out expeditions to destroy the Virginia Central Railroad.

On August 4, 1862, Pope ordered Ricketts to move his Second Division of McDowell's corps from Waterloo to Culpeper Court House. It arrived there two days later and joined Crawford's First Brigade of Williams' First Division of Banks' corps, which had occupied the town since July 14, 1862. Ricketts' division was increased to four brigades August 5, 1862, when Carroll's Brigade of Sturgis' Reserve Corps arrived from Alexandria and was assigned as Fourth Brigade, Second Division.

On August 7, 1862, the remainder of Banks' corps, Christopher C. Augur's Second Division and George H. Gordon's Third Brigade of Williams' First Division, was ordered forward from Little Washington to the point where the Sperryville-Culpeper Court House Turnpike crossed the Hazel River, about midway between the two towns. At that time, Sigel's corps was at Sperryville, and King's division of McDowell's corps was near Fredericksburg. John Buford's cavalry, supported by an infantry brigade of Sigel's corps, was at Madison Court House, watching the right of the army. Buford had relieved Hatch in command of the cavalry brigade July 27, 1862, and Hatch had been ordered to report to King's division to command a brigade. Bayard's Cavalry Brigade was on the left of the army, with pickets along the Rapidan River.

Meantime, on July 13, 1862, Lee had ordered Thomas J. (Stonewall) Jackson to move back from near Richmond with his own division, then under Charles S. Winder, and Richard S. Ewell's division of Jackson's corps to occupy Gordonsville; and then on July 27, 1862, he sent Ambrose P. Hill's division to join Jackson. Jackson arrived at Gordonsville July 19, 1862, and Hill began to come into the town July 29, 1862.

While at Gordonsville, Jackson was informed that Pope intended to concentrate his army at Culpeper Court House, and that at that time only a part of his forces had reached the town. Based on this intelligence, Jackson decided to move forward and attack and destroy Pope's advanced troops before the whole army could be assembled. Accordingly, on August 7, 1862, he marched with his corps from Gordonsville on the road through Orange Court House toward Culpeper Court House, which was about twenty-seven miles distant.

On August 8, 1862, Pope, aware that Jackson's advance had reached Orange Court House, decided to concentrate his army in the vicinity of Culpeper Court House in order to prevent the enemy from turning his left and interrupting his communications with King's division at Fredericksburg. That morning he ordered Banks and Sigel, with their corps, to march to Culpeper Court House. Banks moved at once with Augur's division and Gordon's brigade of Williams' division and arrived there at 11:00 that night. Sigel, however, delayed his start unnecessarily and did not reach the town until the next afternoon.

At noon August 8, 1862, Pope issued a further order to Crawford's brigade of Williams' First Division to move forward from Culpeper Court House and support Bayard's cavalry, which was then retiring before Jackson's advance from Orange Court House. Crawford marched southward on the road to Orange Court House, which, about eight miles out, crossed a small stream called Cedar Run, then passed west of Cedar Mountain (or Slaughter's Mountain), and then ran on to Robertson's Ford on the Rapidan River. Crawford joined Bayard on that road between Colvin's Tavern and Cedar Run at 4:00 P.M., and then took position on the low ground along the run. That same day, Ricketts' division of McDowell's corps was ordered out on the road taken by Crawford to a point about three miles from Culpeper Court House.

On the morning of August 9, 1862, Pope advanced Banks with Augur's division and Gordon's brigade of Williams' division to a position five miles

south of Culpeper Court House and three miles in rear of Crawford. He then sent Williams with Gordon's brigade to join Crawford on Cedar Run. Williams arrived about noon and placed Gordon's brigade on the right of Crawford's line, which was formed across, and to the right of, the road, and behind Cedar Run. Banks, with Augur's division, arrived on the field between 1:00 and 2:00 P.M., and he ordered Augur to form on the left of Williams' division, and on the left of the road. Crawford moved his brigade to the right to make room for Augur, but he remained on the left of Gordon. Augur then formed his line, with John W. Geary's First Brigade on the right of the division, next to the road; Henry Prince's Second Brigade in the center; and George S. Greene's Third Brigade on the left.

Benjamin F. Roberts, chief of cavalry on Pope's staff, accompanied Banks to the front to advise Banks as to Pope's plans. After Banks had formed his line, Roberts decided to move all the troops, except Gordon's brigade, across Cedar Run to a new position on the plateau a short distance beyond. Gordon remained behind Cedar Run in a strong position on the extreme right. The other four brigades held the same relative positions as before, with Greene's brigade, on the left toward Cedar Mountain, somewhat refused. The artillery was placed on the plateau in front of the infantry, and Bayard's cavalry skirmished with the enemy on the flanks of the infantry line.

While Banks was getting his troops in position along Cedar Run, Jackson was approaching the field on the road from Orange Court House with the divisions of Winder and Ewell. Hill's division was following at some distance to the rear. Ewell's division was on the right (the Federal left) on the road, and as it came up, Isaac R. Trimble's brigade and Harry T. Hays' brigade (then commanded by Henry Forno) diverged to the right to a position on the western slope of Cedar Mountain. Jubal A. Early's brigade moved straight ahead and formed on the right (Federal left) of the road, thus leaving a gap between the right of his brigade and the left of Forno's.

John A. Campbell's brigade of Winder's division (then commanded by Thomas S. Garnett) was on the left (Federal right) of the road, and William B. Taliaferro's brigade of the same division was on the right (Federal left) of, and nearly parallel to, the road supporting the enemy artillery. Winder's own brigade, then under Charles Ronald, was held in reserve on the road. In rear of the divisions of Winder and Ewell, Hill was coming up with the brigades of Edward L. Thomas, Lawrence O'B. Branch, James J. Archer, William D. Pender, Leroy H. Stafford, and Charles W. Field.

There was constant artillery fire from noon until about 3:00 P.M., while Jackson advanced slowly to the Federal line of battle. Banks then decided to attack, and he advanced his line to the forward edge of the plateau. According to his plan for the coming battle, Crawford was to turn the enemy left by attacking Campbell's (Garnett's) left flank while Geary and Prince moved forward against the brigades of Early and Taliaferro. The attack began at 5:30 P.M. with the advance of Geary and Prince, and then Crawford came up on Garnett's left and drove the brigade back in disorder. Crawford continued on and struck the flank of Taliaferro's brigade, which at that time was engaged on its front with Geary's brigade, and it too was forced to give way.

Taliaferro's withdrawal exposed Early's left flank, but at this juncture Thomas' brigade of Hill's division came up on the right of Early, and Ronald advanced his brigade against the exhausted troops of Crawford's brigade. Ronald was driven back, but Hill then arrived with the brigades of Archer, Branch, and Pender, and he promptly sent them in to stop the Federal advance by launching a vigorous counterattack. Crawford was forced back, and the infantry on the Federal left began to give way after Augur and Geary had been wounded and Prince captured. Banks then ordered Gordon to advance and resume the attack, but this effort was doomed to failure. Archer and Branch were in front of Gordon, and Ronald and Pender were on his right. The ensuing action was brief and deadly, and Gordon was driven back with heavy loss. Banks then withdrew his troops to their original line.

At 2:00 that afternoon, before Banks' attack, Ricketts' division had been ordered forward from north of Culpeper Court House, and it arrived on the battlefield about 7:00 P.M. It then relieved Williams' division, which had suffered heavy losses during the evening. Ricketts formed his division on the right of the road, with Samuel S. Carroll's Fourth Brigade on the left, next to the road, and Zealous B.

Tower's Second Brigade on the right. Abram Duryee's First Brigade was formed in column in rear of Carroll, and George L. Hartsuff's Third Brigade was also formed in column in rear of Tower. Ricketts' division was under fire for a time, but when its artillery began firing, the enemy withdrew, and the battle was ended. About 8:00 P.M., Robert H. Milroy's Independent Brigade of Sigel's First Corps came up, but it was not engaged.

During the night of August 11, 1862, Jackson withdrew across the Rapidan. Pope followed closely, and by the next day had established his pickets on the Rapidan River, extending on a line from Raccoon Ford to the base of the Blue Ridge Mountains.

The troops of Pope's Army of Virginia that were engaged at Cedar Mountain August 9, 1862 were as follows:

SECOND CORPS, Nathaniel P. Banks

First Division, Alpheus S. Williams
    First Brigade, Samuel W. Crawford
        5th Connecticut, George H. Chapman, captured
        10th Maine, George L. Beal
        28th New York, Dudley Donnelly, mortally wounded
        46th Pennsylvania, Joseph F. Knipe, wounded
    Third Brigade, George H. Gordon
        2nd Massachusetts, George L. Andrews
        27th Indiana, Silas Colgrove
        3rd Wisconsin, Thomas H. Ruger

Second Division, Christopher C. Augur, wounded
    Henry Prince, captured
    George S. Greene
    First Brigade, John W. Geary, wounded
        Charles Candy
        5th Ohio, John H. Patrick
        7th Ohio, William R. Creighton
        29th Ohio, William F. Stevens
        66th Ohio, Charles Candy
    Second Brigade, Henry Prince
        David De Witt
        3rd Maryland, David De Witt
        102nd New York, Joseph C. Lane
        109th Pennsylvania, Henry J. Stainrook, wounded
        111th Pennsylvania, William M. Walker
        8th and 12th United States Infantry Battalion, Thomas G. Pitcher
    Third Brigade, George S. Greene
        James A. Tait
        1st District of Columbia

78th New York

Artillery, Clermont L. Best
4th Battery (D), Maine Light Artillery, O'Neil W. Robinson
6th Battery (F), Maine Light Artillery, Freeman Mc-Gilvery
Battery K, 1st New York Light Artillery, Lorenzo Crounse
Battery L, 1st New York Light Artillery, John A. Reynolds
Battery M, 1st New York Light Artillery, George W. Cothran
Battery L, 2nd New York Light Artillery, Jacob Roemer
10th Battery, New York Light Artillery, John T. Bruen
Battery E, Pennsylvania Light Artillery, Joseph M. Knap
Battery F, 4th United States Artillery, Edward D. Muhlenberg

THIRD CORPS

Second Division, James S. Ricketts
First Brigade, Abram Duryee
Second Brigade, Zealous B. Tower
Third Brigade, George L. Hartsuff
Fourth Brigade, Samuel S. Carroll
Artillery, Davis Tillson
2nd Battery (B), Maine Light Artillery, James A. Hall
5th Battery (E), Maine Light Artillery, George F. Leppien
Battery F, 1st Pennsylvania Light Artillery, Ezra W. Matthews
Battery C, Pennsylvania Light Artillery (2nd Maryland), James Thompson
Unattached 16th Battery, Indiana Light Artillery, Charles A. Naylor

Cavalry Brigade, George D. Bayard

Reinforcements for the Army of Virginia. After the Battle of Cedar Mountain, Pope's command remained for some time along the Rapidan River. Sigel's First Corps was on the right, with its right on Robertson's River; Ricketts' division of McDowell's Third Corps was on the left; and Banks' Second Corps was in reserve near Culpeper Court House. Pope's headquarters was at Cedar Mountain.

Meantime, orders had been issued for reinforcements to join the Army of Virginia. Earlier, at the end of the Seven Days' Battles near Richmond,

troops from the Department of North Carolina and the Department of the South were ordered to Newport News, Virginia to reinforce McClellan. They were not needed, however, and July 22, 1862, they were organized into a new Ninth Corps under the command of Ambrose E. Burnside. These troops did not join the Army of the Potomac but remained at Newport News until August 1, 1862, and then Halleck ordered Burnside to embark his Ninth Corps for Aquia Creek, with instructions to take position at Fredericksburg. At the same time, he ordered McClellan to prepare for the withdrawal of the Army of the Potomac from the Peninsula as soon as possible and join the Army of Virginia.

Burnside arrived at Aquia Creek during the night of August 3, 1862, and then moved on to Fredericksburg August 4–6, 1862. Upon arrival there Ninth Corps relieved King's First Division of McDowell's corps, which then left Fredericksburg and marched toward Culpeper Court House, where it joined the rest of Pope's army on the evening of June 11, 1862.

August 12, 1862, Burnside was ordered to send all available troops of Ninth Corps to join Pope, and that same day Jesse L. Reno, with his own Second Division and Isaac I. Stevens' First Division, left Falmouth for Culpeper Court House. Reno's detachment of Ninth Corps marched up the north side of the Rappahannock River to Rappahannock Station, and then joined the Army of Virginia at Culpeper Court House August 11, 1862. Reno's command was then placed on the line of the Rapidan River on the left of McDowell. John G. Parke, with his Third Division, Ninth Corps, remained at Falmouth, and he assumed command of the post August 14, 1862, when Burnside was ordered to report to Halleck's headquarters.

In addition to the above reinforcements, troops from the Army of the Potomac were also on the way to join Pope. For details of their arrival, see the following two sections, Lee's Advance to the Rappahannock, and Jackson's Flanking March.

About mid-August 1862, the cavalry of the Army of Virginia was reorganized. Previously, it had been assigned to the three corps of the army, and did not function as a single unit. Then, on August 16, 1862, Pope directed that the cavalry of each corps be assembled as one body and placed under the command of the chief of cavalry of the corps. This still left the cavalry forces divided, with each corps having its own cavalry organization, but it was a decided improvement over the old arrangement, because it eliminated the practice of scattering the cavalry regiments within the corps organization. As noted earlier, John Buford was assigned as chief of cavalry of Banks' Second Corps July 27, 1862, relieving John P. Hatch. This order was repeated in the reorganization of August 2, 1862, and on that date George D. Bayard was ordered to assemble the cavalry force of Third Corps, and John Beardsley was ordered to assume command of the cavalry brigade of First Corps.

Lee's Advance to the Rappahannock, August 16, 1862. By August 13, 1862, Lee was convinced that McClellan was evacuating his position at Harrison's Landing on the James River, and he then sent James Longstreet's corps and James E. B. (Jeb) Stuart's cavalry to join Jackson at Gordonsville. This left only Daniel H. Hill's division confronting the Army of the Potomac at Richmond. The leading troops of Longstreet's column reached Gordonsville August 15, 1862, and Lee then arrived in person and assumed command of the combined Confederate forces there, which totaled about 55,000 men.

August 16, 1862, the Army of Northern Virginia began its advance against Pope's army, which was then concentrated north of the Rapidan River between Cedar Mountain and Clark's Mountain. Fearing a flank movement by the enemy from behind Clark's Mountain, Pope issued orders August 18, 1862 for the immediate withdrawal of his army to the north bank of the Rappahannock River. Sigel's corps, which had been on the extreme right of the army, marched to Sulfur Springs (Warrenton Springs), where it crossed the river. Reno's detachment of Ninth Corps marched from the left of the army by way of Stevensburg and crossed the Rappahannock at Barnett's Ford. Banks' corps, which at that time was under the command of Alpheus S. Williams, marched along the Orange and Alexandria Railroad from Culpeper Court House, and crossed the river at Rappahannock Station. McDowell's corps followed Banks' corps, and the cavalry of each corps served as its rear guard.

By the morning of August 20, 1862, the Army of Virginia was in position behind the Rappahannock as follows: Sigel's corps was on the right near Sulfur Springs, McDowell's corps was on the left of Sigel at Rappahannock Station, part of Banks' corps was on the left of McDowell and the rest was in reserve, and Reno's two divisions were at Kelly's Ford.

August 20–21, 1862, Lee's army followed Pope to the Rappahannock, and there Jackson's corps took position on the left of the line at Beverly Ford, and Longstreet's corps on the right at Kelly's Ford. There was some fighting at Kelly's Ford and at Beverly Ford, and then on August 22, 1862, Jackson moved upriver to Sulfur Springs. Longstreet occupied the line of the Rappahannock from Rappahannock Station to Beverly Ford or beyond.

Sigel observed Jackson's movement from across the river, and for a time marched abreast on the east bank. Henry Bohlen's First Brigade of Carl Schurz's Third Division crossed the river and attacked the rear of Jackson's column, but without success. Bohlen was mortally wounded during the fighting, and he was succeeded in command of the brigade by Alexander Schimmelfennig. Robert H. Milroy's Independent Brigade, which had the advance of Sigel's column, exchanged artillery fire with Jackson at Freeman's Ford, and the cavalry was sent across the river to reconnoiter.

Late in the afternoon of August 22, 1862, Jubal A. Early's brigade crossed to the east bank of the Rappahannock, but heavy rains prevented the rest of the division from following. Early was also unable to recross because of high water, and did not rejoin the division until 3:00 A.M. August 24, 1862.

Stuart, meantime, had advanced toward the Orange and Alexandria Railroad in Pope's rear, and on the night of August 22, 1862, in terrible weather, reached Catlett's Station, where he captured Pope's baggage train.

As noted above, troops of McClellan's Army of the Potomac on the Peninsula had been ordered to join Pope, and they were now beginning to arrive. On August 11, 1862, Truman Seymour's (formerly George McCall's) Third Division of Pennsylvania Reserves of Fitz John Porter's Fifth Corps embarked for Aquia Creek, and August 21, 1862 arrived at Fredericksburg. The division was reorganized that day under John F. Reynolds, and it immediately marched out of Falmouth on the road to Kelly's Ford on the Rappahannock. For details of the reorganization of Third Division, see Fifth Corps, Army of the Potomac. Reynolds arrived at Kelly's Ford during the evening of August 22, 1862, and the next morning marched on to Warrenton, where the division was attached to McDowell's Third Corps. In the original corps organization of the Army of the Potomac, McCall's division was assigned to McDowell's First Corps. When the army left for the Peninsula, First Corps was left behind to protect Washington, and then on April 4, 1862 it was merged into McDowell's Department of the Rappahannock. McCall's division left Fredericksburg June 10, 1862 to join McClellan's army on the Peninsula, and when it arrived there June 11–13, 1862, it was attached to Porter's Fifth Corps. The brigade was not officially transferred from McDowell's command (former First Corps), but remained as a part of the Department of the Rappahannock, on detached service. Therefore, in effect, when Reynolds' division (formerly McCall's) was attached to McDowell's corps at Warrenton, it was simply returning to its original corps.

There was little change in the position of the Army of Virginia during August 23, 1862, but that night Sigel's Corps, which was posted between Beverly Ford and Freeman's Ford, was ordered to move up the river to Sulfur Springs, and then toward Waterloo Bridge. Sigel was directed to attack any enemy force found on the east side of the river, but little was achieved by this expedition.

Additional reinforcements began to arrive from the Peninsula August 23, 1862. Samuel P. Heintzelman's Third Corps, Army of the Potomac began to disembark at Alexandria August 22, 1862, and about noon the next day Philip Kearny's Third Division joined Pope at Warrenton Junction. Heintzelman, with Joseph Hooker's Second Division, did not arrive from Alexandria until August 25, 1862.

On the morning of August 24, 1862, Buford moved with his cavalry to Waterloo. Sigel was ordered to support him, and his advance brigade under Milroy reached Waterloo late that evening. That night the Army of Virginia was in position as follows: Pope's headquarters was at Warrenton; Sigel's corps was near the Rappahannock, with the advance at Waterloo Brigde and the rear in the direction of Sulfur Springs; Banks' corps was along the river in rear of Sigel, and in contact with him; Reno's detachment of Ninth Corps was a short distance east of Sulfur Springs; Ricketts' division of

McDowell's corps was on the road from Warrenton to Waterloo Bridge; King's division of McDowell's corps was on the road between Warrenton and Sulfur Springs; Reynolds' division was at Warrenton; Kearny's division of Third Corps was at Warrenton Junction; and Buford's cavalry was on the extreme right beyond Waterloo.

Jackson's Flanking March, August 25, 1862. Meantime, after arriving on the Rappahannock River, Lee had decided to send Jackson's corps on a flanking march around the Federal right by way of Orleans, Salem (present-day Marshall), White Plains, and Thoroughfare Gap to cut Pope's rail connection with Alexandria at Manassas. On the evening of August 24, 1862, Jackson retired to Jefferson, about four miles west of Sulfur Springs, and Longstreet moved up and occupied Jackson's former position on the Rappahannock. Then, early on the morning of August 25, 1862, Jackson, with Stuart's cavalry, left Jefferson for the rear of the Army of Virginia. He marched through Amissville, crossed Hedgman's River (the name of the larger of the two streams that join at Waterloo Bridge to form the Rappahannock) at Henson's Mill, and then passed through Orleans and arrived at Salem that night. Lee, with Longstreet's corps, followed the next day.

At 8:45 A.M. August 25, 1862, Pope was informed by his signal officers of Jackson's march, but he was uncertain as to its meaning and took no immediate countermeasures. Earlier that morning, before he learned of Jackson's movement, Pope had issued orders for the formation of a new line running north and south through Warrenton, and these orders were either carried out or modified during the day. According to these orders, McDowell was to occupy the right of the line at Warrenton, and Sigel the left at Fayetteville. Banks was to move to a line extending from Bealeton to a creek near the Rappahannock, and Reno was to take position at Kelly's Ford. McDowell was already in his assigned position, but Reno, by some mistake, retired to Warrenton Junction. Banks fell back to Bealeton Station, or to a position between that place and Fayetteville, and the next day moved to Fayetteville. Sigel's orders, however, were changed. When he was about to start for Fayetteville, he received instructions to hold his position, and he then received a direct order from Pope to march to Warrenton instead of Fayetteville. Sigel reached Warrenton at 2:00 A.M. August 26, 1862.

About 9:45 P.M. August 25, 1862, Porter's Fifth Corps, Army of the Potomac joined Pope from Fredericksburg. Porter had arrived at Aquia Creek August 22, 1862, and then had been detained near Falmouth for a time to watch the lower fords of the Rappahannock. He then had marched up the Rappahannock to join Pope. George W. Morell's First Division was placed at Kelly's Ford, and George Sykes' Second Division at Bealeton Station. Thus, by late on August 25, 1862, Reno's detachment of Ninth Corps, Heintzelman's Third Corps, and Porter's Fifth Corps of the Army of the Potomac, totaling six divisions and about 23,000 men, had joined the Army of Virginia. These were the only reinforcements that Pope received until after the Second Battle of Bull Run.

During August 26, 1862, Pope appeared to be awaiting developments, and at the end of the day he had his troops in position as follows: Buford's cavalry was on the right near Waterloo; Ricketts' division was on the road between Waterloo and Warrenton, about four miles from Warrenton; King's division was on the road from Warrenton to Sulfur Springs, with one brigade near the springs; Reynolds' division was at Warrenton; Banks' corps was at Fayetteville; Sigel's corps was in camp near Warrenton; Reno's two divisions of Ninth Corps and Heintzelman's corps were near Warrenton Junction, where Pope had his headquarters; Morell's division of Porter's Fifth Corps was at Kelly's Ford; and Sykes' division of Fifth Corps was five or six miles east of Bealeton Station. That evening, Pope decided to form a new line for a battle that he believed would be fought at Warrenton. Sigel was to remain at Warrenton, and McDowell was ordered to concentrate near Sigel. Reno was directed to move at daylight the next morning from Warrenton Junction to Warrenton, and when McDowell arrived there, as ordered, he was to send Reno on to Greenwich. Porter was ordered to march through Fayetteville, where Banks then was, to the vicinity of Warrenton. Heintzelman, who was at Warrenton Junction, was ordered to send Kearny's division to Greenwich, and to retain Hooker's division near the junction.

While Pope spent the day of August 26, 1862 in a state of uncertainty, Jackson, covered on the right by Stuart's cavalry, marched steadily eastward from Salem, through White Plains, Thoroughfare Gap, Haymarket, and Gainesville, and finally, after sunset, arrived near Bristoe Station with the divisions of Taliaferro, Ambrose P. Hill, and Ewell. Jackson captured or drove off the troops guarding the station, and then proceeded to destroy the track and some trains. He sent Isaac R. Trimble with two infantry regiments and Stuart's cavalry to Manassas Junction, where he arrived after midnight and captured large quantities of stores of all kinds. Hill and Taliaferro then moved on to Manassas Junction, but Ewell's division was left for a time at Bristoe Station.

During the evening of August 26, 1862, while preparing for the concentration of the army at Warrenton, Pope learned that enemy cavalry had broken the line of the railroad near Manassas. He then ordered Heintzelman to send out a regiment to find out what had happened and to repair and hold the railroad. Early the next morning, Heintzelman's regiment reported that a strong force of the enemy was on the railroad near Bristoe Station, and Hooker's division was ordered to advance and drive it off.

Pope then decided that his position at Warrenton was no longer tenable, and he prepared orders for the movement of his entire force to a line extending from Gainesville to the crossing of Cedar Creek on the Orange and Alexandria Railroad. At 8:30 on the morning of August 27, 1862, he directed McDowell, with his own corps, Sigel's corps, and Reynolds' division, to march on the turnpike from Warrenton to Gainesville so as to arrive at the latter place that evening. McDowell at once ordered Sigel to advance a strong force from his corps to seize Buckland Mills, on Broad Run, and to follow immediately with the rest of his corps. Bayard's cavalry was to move in front of McDowell's column. Reynolds, King, and Ricketts were directed to follow McDowell. Carl Schurz's division and Robert H. Milroy's brigade of Sigel's corps reached Gainesville that evening, but Robert C. Schenck's division remained with McDowell's corps at Buckland Mills. Adolph Von Steinwehr's division remained in reserve at Buckland Bridge.

Reno's detachment of Ninth Corps, followed by Kearny's division of Heintzelman's corps, marched from Catlett's Station toward Greenwich, and both arrived there that evening. Pope ordered Porter to remain with the army trains at Warrenton Junction until Banks' corps came up from Fayetteville, and then Banks was to assume the duty of guarding the trains. Banks was to move with the army trains, and all of the railroad trains, back to Manassas as rapidly as possible.

Hooker's division, as ordered, left Warrenton Junction at 7:00 A.M. August 27, 1862 and moved eastward along the railroad. Between 2:00 and 3:00 P.M., about nine miles out, he found Ewell's division in position near Bristoe Station. Hooker attacked immediately, and there was sharp fighting until dark. Ewell was driven back across Broad Run, and later that evening rejoined Jackson at Manassas Junction.

Action at Bull Run Bridge, August 27, 1862. When Halleck at Washington learned of the capture of Manassas by the enemy, he directed that any available force be sent to Bull Run Bridge. Henry W. Slocum's First Division of William B. Franklin's Sixth Corps, Army of the Potomac had arrived from the Peninsula and had debarked at Alexandria August 24, 1862. George W. Taylor's First Brigade (the New Jersey Brigade) of this division was selected for Halleck's mission. It arrived at the railroad bridge over Bull Run (Bull Run Bridge) early on the morning of August 27, 1862, and then crossed the run and advanced toward Manassas Junction. Near Union Mills Taylor encountered four brigades of Hill's division, and was decisively beaten and driven back across the bridge. Eliakim P. Scammon arrived near the bridge at 8:00 A.M. with his First Provisional Brigade of Cox's Kanawha Division, which had just arrived from West Virginia. By this time, however, the fighting had ended, and Scammon was not engaged. Taylor was mortally wounded during the action, and Scammon assumed temporary command of the brigade. Later, Alfred T. A. Torbert relieved Scammon.

* * * * * * * * *

Pope arrived in person at Bristoe Station near the close of Hooker's action and learned that Jackson's corps and Stuart's cavalry were between him and Washington and Alexandria. Pope promptly ordered Porter to march at 1:00 A.M. from Warrenton and

be at Bristoe Station at daylight that morning. Porter postponed his departure until 3:00 A.M. and was then delayed on the road by army trains, and he did not arrive at Bristoe Station until 10:00 or 10:30 that morning. He also ordered Kearny to move from Greenwich to Bristoe Station, which was four or five miles distant, and Kearny joined Hooker there about 8:00 A.M. After Porter and Kearny had arrived, Pope had with him at Bristoe Station on the morning of August 28, 1862 the two divisions of Porter's Fifth Corps and the two divisions of Heintzelman's Third Corps, Army of the Potomac.

Meantime, the troops of the northern wing of the army on the Warrenton Turnpike had been active. At dawn August 27, 1862, Buford, with Sigel's cavalry, had set out to learn what he could of the enemy's movements. He found Confederate troops at Salem, and then forced Longstreet, who was following Jackson, to deploy and halt for a few hours at White Plains. Buford also learned that Jackson had passed through Thoroughfare Gap while moving toward Manassas Junction the day before.

At 9:00 on the evening of August 27, 1862, Pope issued orders for Reno, with his corps, and for McDowell, with his own corps and Sigel's corps, to march at dawn the next morning for Manassas Junction. Sometime before 11:30 that evening, which was before he received Pope's order of 9:00 P.M., McDowell took steps to occupy a position in front of Thoroughfare Gap. He ordered Sigel's entire corps to Haymarket and Gainesville, east of the Gap, and left Reynolds' division at Buckland Mills, with the option of operating against the flank of an enemy column passing through Thoroughfare Gap, or of marching to Haymarket, as he thought best.

Movements of August 28, 1862. McDowell received Pope's order to move on Manassas Junction about midnight August 27, 1862, and he then issued new march orders for the following morning. These orders, which were not delivered until 3:00 A.M. August 28, 1862, directed Sigel to march with his corps through Gainesville, a cluster of a few houses where the Manassas Gap Railroad crossed the Warrenton Turnpike, and then on toward Manassas Junction, with his right on the railroad. Reynolds' division was to follow Sigel to Gainesville, and was then to form en echelon on the left of Sigel; and King's division was to follow Reynolds to Gainesville, and then form en echelon on his left. In order to form on the left of Sigel, it was necessary for both Reynolds and King to pass in his rear through Gainesville and continue on beyond on the Turnpike before turning southward toward Manassas Junction. By this movement, McDowell's command would sweep the country between the Warrenton Turnpike and the Manassas Gap Railroad.

The situation at 8:00 A.M. August 28, 1862 was as follows: Sigel's corps, encumbered by his trains, had crossed to the right of the Manassas Gap Railroad and was a short distance southeast of Gainesville, between the Turnpike and the railroad. Sigel had misinterpreted his orders, and understood that he was to advance with his right on the Orange and Alexandria Railroad, which was well to the south of the Manassas Gap Railroad, his proper line of direction, and this mistake caused some delay. Reynolds' division had passed through Gainesville and was marching east on the Turnpike toward the road that branched off to the southeast toward Manassas Junction; King's division was approaching Gainesville from the west on the Turnpike, and Ricketts' division was following King; Reno's divisions were between Greenwich and Manassas Junction; Porter's corps was on the road from Warrenton to Bristoe Station; and Heintzelman's corps and Pope's headquarters were at Bristoe Station. Banks' corps, with the trains, was marching from Warrenton toward Bristoe Station, on the road along the Orange and Alexandria Railroad.

Early on the morning of August 28, 1862, Percy Wyndham's 1st New Jersey Cavalry of George D. Bayard's brigade was sent out to Thoroughfare Gap on a reconnaissance, and it reported that enemy troops were then advancing through the gap from the west. In the march order for that day, Ricketts' division was assigned to bring up the rear of McDowell's column, and was to follow on the left of King's division on the march to Manassas Junction. Instead of complying with Pope's order to march with his entire command to Manassas Junction, McDowell, on his own responsibility, detached Ricketts' division and ordered it to Thoroughfare Gap. Ricketts, who had left his bivouac near New Baltimore that morning, then marched by way of Haymarket, toward Thoroughfare Gap. He was seriously delayed on the Warrenton Turnpike by Sigel's wagon train, and did not arrive near the gap until 3:00 that afternoon. John W. Stiles' Third Brigade was leading the division, and it was supported by Abram Duryee's First Brigade and Joseph Thoburn's Fourth Brigade. Zealous B. Tower's Second Brigade was held in reserve. Duryee's brigade supported James Thompson's Battery C, Pennsylvania Artillery during the engagement. As Ricketts approached Thoroughfare Gap, he drove the enemy back up the hill and into the gap, but there they resisted all further efforts of Ricketts to advance. Ricketts' brigades, however, resolutely delayed the passage of Longstreet's troops through the gap during the rest of the day and early evening, but finally, after three enemy brigades moved through Hopewell Gap, three miles to the north, Ricketts withdrew after dark to Gainesville.

While Pope was directing the movement of the army toward Manassas Junction, Jackson withdrew during the night of August 28–29, 1862 and halted at daylight on the old battlefield of Bull Run. Hill's division was at Centerville, and Jackson, with the divisions of Taliaferro and Ewell, was in position along an unfinished railroad grade. This grade ran southwest from the vicinity of Sudley Springs to a point about one-half mile north of the Warrenton Turnpike, and a short distance east of Gainesville. The railroad was being built to give the Manassas Gap Railroad a direct connection with Alexandria without passing through Manassas Junction. At 10:00 A.M., Hill was ordered to join Jackson, and he took position on the left of the line, with his left on Bull Run at a point about a half mile southwest of Sudley Springs. Ewell's division was on the center, next to Hill, and Taliaferro's division was on the left.

Meantime, during the early part of the morning, McDowell, with the divisions of Reynolds and King, had been marching eastward on the Turnpike to their assigned positions on the left of Sigel. At 9:30 A.M., when Reynolds arrived near the junction of the road that ran off to Manassas Junction, about two or three miles beyond Gainesville, he was fired on by an enemy battery north of the Turnpike. Reynolds deployed his troops and sent out skirmishers, and after a short engagement, the enemy withdrew. Reynolds then continued on toward

Manassas Junction. The enemy troops belonged to Bradley T. Johnson's brigade (John A. Campbell's brigade) of Taliaferro's division, Jackson's Corps, which had been sent out to Groveton to watch the road from Gainesville.

King's division, following Reynolds, passed through Gainesville, and halted a short distance beyond to allow Buford's cavalry to pass on its way to Thoroughfare Gap. King then continued east on the turnpike a few miles to a country road that branched off and ran on to Manassas Junction. He turned off on this road, marched on a mile or two, and then halted in a woods sometime before noon. He remained there for several hours before he again received orders to move.

About noon August 28, 1862, when Pope arrived at Manassas Junction with Reno's corps and Kearny's division of Heintzelman's corps, he found that Jackson was no longer there, and there was no immediate information as to where he had gone. He passed the early part of the afternoon in a state of uncertainty, but he then received information that misled him as to Jackson's position. At 4:15 P.M., he wrote McDowell that the enemy was reported in force beyond Bull Run, on the Orange and Alexandria Railroad, and was also at Centerville. Pope then decided to send almost all of his army to Centerville, and proceeded to issue orders to that effect. He directed McDowell to move at once on the Warrenton Turnpike to Centerville, ten miles east of Gainesville. McDowell then ordered King, whose division was the only one of his command then with him, to return to the Warrenton Turnpike and follow it to Centerville. It was approximately 5:00 P.M., and the sun was beginning to set when King began his march northward toward the Turnpike, a few miles distant. McDowell then left for Manassas Junction to confer with Pope. He was unable to find Pope, and then became lost on his return to the Turnpike, and was unable to rejoin his command that night. Pope also ordered Reno and Heintzelmen to march to Centerville, and late that afternoon, the divisions of Reno, Stevens, Kearny, and Hooker marched through Manassas Junction toward Blackburn's Ford. He also ordered Sigel and Reynolds to Centerville, and he directed Banks to march to Kettle Run Bridge, midway between Catlett's Station and Bristoe Station, to repair the track of the Orange and Alexandria Railroad. He sent no orders to Porter or Ricketts that evening

Battle of Gainesville (or Brawner's Farm), August 28, 1862. King's division turned into the Turnpike about two and one-half miles west of Groveton, and then marched eastward along the road toward Centerville, and toward the right of Jackson's line, which was concealed in the woods along the railroad grade. John P. Hatch's First Brigade was in the lead, and it was followed, in order, by John Gibbon's Fourth Brigade, Abner Doubleday's Second Brigade, and Marsena R. Patrick's Third Brigade. King anticipated no trouble that evening; the brigades marched at rather long intervals, and Hatch's brigade was out of sight to the east when Gibbon's brigade turned on the turnpike.

The right of Jackson's line, which was held by Taliaferro's and Ewell's divisions, was just inside a woods, along a ridge called Stony Ridge (or Sudley Mountain), which ran roughly parallel to the Turnpike and approximately one-half mile north of it. A second ridge ran about midway between Jackson's line and the turnpike, and on this ridge were the farmhouse, barn, and orchard of the Brawner farm. The Brawner house was a mile east of the road where King's division turned onto the Turnpike, and a little less than a mile west of Groveton. Southeast of the Brawner house was a rectangular woods that extended along the north side of the turnpike for about 350 yards, and its northern edge was about 75 yards south of the crest of the Brawner House Ridge.

Hatch's brigade marched past the Brawner farm without discovering the enemy to the north and moved on toward Groveton. Jackson observed the passage of King's leading troops and, believing them to be in retreat toward Centerville, decided to attack. In Jackson's front line, from the Confederate right to left, were the brigades of William S. H. Baylor and William E. Starke of Taliaferro's division, and Isaac R. Trimble and Alexander R. Lawton of Ewell's division. Behind these, in supporting distance, were the remaining four brigades of the two divisions. Starke's brigade was just north of the Brawner house and orchard, and Trimble's brigade was on the left of Starke and north of the rectangular woods.

A short time before sunset, Gibbon's brigade, following Hatch, approached the Brawner farm, with the regiments in order from front to rear as follows: 6th Wisconsin; 2nd Wisconsin; 7th Wisconsin; 19th Indiana; and Battery B, 4th United States Artillery brought up the rear. Jackson's line then advanced from the woods on Stony Ridge and moved southward toward the Brawner House Ridge. Because of the intervening depression, this movement was not observed by Gibbon. Hatch, who had passed earlier, was also unaware of Jackson's presence.

Gibbon had just passed the rectangular woods when Jackson's artillery moved forward and opened fire. Battery B was brought up into the field just east of the woods and engaged Balthis' Battery, Staunton (Virginia) Artillery of Ewell's division. Gibbon directed the 2nd Wisconsin to move back through the woods and into the open field south of the Brawner house, and then move up the ridge toward the farmhouse, where Wooding's Battery, Danville (Virginia) Artillery was in action. Almost immediately 2nd Wisconsin became engaged with Starke and Baylor, and 19th Indiana was advanced to the left of 2nd Wisconsin against Baylor. The other two regiments of the brigade were also ordered up toward the ridge. The 7th Wisconsin moved to the right of 2nd Wisconsin, and 6th Wisconsin marched northward along the east side of the rectangular woods, and at the northern end it made a half wheel to the left and quickly engaged the enemy.

At this time, Gibbon's line was formed just south of the crest of the Brawner House Ridge, and it passed close to the north side of the woods and ended at the northeast corner. The 19th Indiana was on the left at the Brawner farmhouse, and then in order to the right were the 2nd Wisconsin, facing the farmyard, and 7th Wisconsin, in front of the Brawner orchard. There was a gap of several hundred yards between the right of 7th Wisconsin and the left of 6th Wisconsin, which was on the extreme right of the infantry line.

Gibbon appealed to King for help, but received no reply. Shortly after the action began, however, 56th Pennsylvania and 76th New York of Doubleday's brigade arrived and took position in the interval between the 6th and 7th Wisconsin regiments north of the woods, and they too joined in the fighting. Later, Doubleday's remaining regiment,

the 95th New York, arrived and was sent to support Battery B, on the right, but it was not engaged. For two terrible hours the fighting continued without letup and did not cease until dark. During this time, the two opposing lines were not more than seventy-five yards apart. The men fought without entrenchments or cover, and except for some slight gains and losses neither side advanced or retreated. The heaviest fighting occurred on the Federal left, in and around the farm buildings and the orchard. Losses were very heavy on both sides, especially among the officers. Both Confederate division commanders, Taliaferro and Ewell, were wounded, and Starke, commanding a brigade, was also wounded. Five Union regimental commanders were killed or wounded.

Hatch, without orders from King, turned back when he learned of Gibbon's battle, but the fighting had ended when he arrived on the field. Apparently, neither King nor Patrick did anything to aid Gibbon.

* * * * * * * * * *

During the late afternoon of August 28, 1862, Sigel, Reno, Heintzelman, and Reynolds proceeded to execute the 4:15 P.M. orders to march to Centerville. At 6:00 P.M., at the beginning of Gibbon's battle on the Warrenton Turnpike, Sigel's corps had reached Bethlehem Church, near the Manassas Gap Railroad, and about two and three-fourths miles northwest of Manassas Junction. It had then turned into the road from Sudley Springs to Manassas Junction, and was marching northward on that road. As noted earlier, Jackson believed that Pope was retreating toward Alexandria, and with that in mind, he had sent cavalry and skirmishers south on the Sudley Springs-Manassas Junction Road to harass the marching columns. They soon ran into Sigel's advance, and after some fighting they were pushed back toward the Warrenton Turnpike. Reynolds heard Sigel's guns, and also the sounds of Gibbon's battle, and he at once marched northward from the Bethlehem Church Road on the left of Sigel, and that night reached a point about a mile south of Groveton.

At 6:00 P.M. the remaining troops of Pope's army were located as follows: Kearny's division was just south of Centerville; Reno's two divisions of Ninth Corps were on the road between Blackburn's Ford and Centerville; Hooker's division was south of Bull

Run on the road to Centerville and was approaching Blackburn's Ford; Ricketts' division had withdrawn from Thoroughfare Gap and was between the gap and Gainesville; Porter's corps was at Bristoe Station; and Banks' corps was with the army trains at Kettle Run, on the Orange and Alexandria Railroad.

Movements of August 29, 1862. On the evening of August 28, 1862, Pope, at his headquarters at Blackburn's Ford, came to the conclusion that Jackson was retreating westward, and at 9:00 P.M. ordered Kearny to move at 1:00 A.M. August 29, 1862 on the Turnpike toward Warrenton in pursuit. An hour later he sent an order to Heintzelman to move Hooker to Centerville, and from there to advance his division on the Turnpike about a mile and a half west to act as a reserve to Kearny. Both divisions were directed to attack at daylight what Pope believed to be the rear of Jackson's retreating column.

After the fighting ended at the Brawner farm during the late evening of August 28, 1862, King's and Ricketts' divisions were left without orders from McDowell, who had gone to Manassas Junction to confer with Pope. King decided, despite the fact that Sigel's corps and Reynolds' division were only a short distance east of his position, to withdraw from the Turnpike at 1:00 A.M. August 29, 1862, and march by way of Gainesville to Manassas Junction. When Ricketts learned of King's intention, he retired by way of Gainesville to Bristoe Station. As a result of King's decision, both his and Ricketts' divisions were absent from the rest of the army during the greater part of August 29, 1862.

At 3:00 A.M. August 29, 1862, Pope ordered Porter to move from Bristoe Station toward Centerville as soon as it was light enough to see. He also directed Reno, whose divisions were in bivouac between Bull Run and Centerville, to move forward by crossroads to the Warrenton Turnpike, and then advance on that road in the direction of Gainesville to support Heintzelman.

At dawn August 29, 1862, Pope's troops were located as follows: Buford's cavalry brigade was at Haymarket; Porter's corps, Banks' corps, and Ricketts' division of McDowell's corps were at Bristoe Station; King's division of McDowell's corps was at Manassas Junction; Reno's corps and Heintzelman's corps were near Centerville; Reynolds' division was near Groveton; and Sigel's corps was on and near the Henry House Hill, on the old battlefield of First Bull Run.

About daylight August 29, 1862, Pope ordered Sigel, supported by Reynolds, to attack as soon as it was light and attempt to stop Jackson's supposed retreat. Porter, conforming to his orders of 3:00 A.M., had moved at once, and had passed Manassas Junction on his way to Centerville when he was informed by a staff officer that his orders had been changed. He was to return to Manassas Junction with his corps, pick up King's division, which had arrived there from Gainesville, and then march to Gainesville. This order was confirmed in writing at 9:30 A.M. after Porter had again passed Manassas Junction. King's division was attached temporarily to Porter's command because the whereabouts of McDowell and Ricketts were not known. The reason for Pope's change of plan was that, after issuing the march orders to Kearny, Heintzelman, Reno, and Porter the night before, he learned that King and Ricketts had fallen back from the Turnpike; and believing that Jackson was attempting to withdraw through Thoroughfare Gap, he decided to send Porter to help Sigel and Reynolds prevent his escape. Hooker, Kearny, and Reno needed no new orders.

From Manassas Junction, Porter marched along the Manassas Gap Railroad past Bethlehem Church, with George W. Morell's First Division in the lead. George Sykes' Second Division came next, and King's division was in the rear. About 11:30 A.M., the head of Porter's column reached a small, almost dry stream called Dawkins' Branch. There Porter observed enemy forces beyond the stream and halted his command. Daniel Butterfield's Third Brigade of Morell's division, Porter's leading brigade, deployed beyond the stream and threw out a line of skirmishers. The situation ahead was far different from that upon which Pope had based his orders for that morning. Jackson was not retreating, as Pope believed, but was still in his position along the unfinished railroad grade. Further, at about 10:30 A.M., Longstreet's leading division under John B. Hood had arrived on the field from Thoroughfare Gap, and was then forming on the left of Jackson, south of the Turnpike, and between Porter and Gainesville. Longstreet's other divisions were close behind.

It was clear to Porter at this time that Longstreet

had joined Jackson, and that he could no longer continue on the Gainesville Road until he had established a connection with Sigel and Reynolds on his right, as required by his orders. McDowell joined Porter at Dawkins' Branch, and together they examined the ground to their right and agreed that they could not march with artillery through the rough and broken country between the Manassas Gap Railroad and the Warrenton Turnpike. Faced with this situation, both generals agreed to a plan whereby McDowell would march with King's division, which was then near Bethlehem Church, up the Sudley Springs Road and form on the left of Reynolds' division. McDowell's other division, under Ricketts, was to follow later. Apparently, it was Porter's understanding that he was to act on the defensive until McDowell appeared on his right, north of the railroad. McDowell marched north at noon, but he did not succeed in putting King's division on the left of Reynolds. Meantime, Porter remained along Dawkins' Branch awaiting orders. Pope issued an order dated 4:30 P.M. August 29, 1862, directing Porter to attack the enemy right. Porter did not receive this order until 6:30 P.M. or later, and he then considered it too late to attack because of approaching darkness.

During the day Banks' corps remained at Bristoe Station guarding the trains.

Battle of Groveton (or Manassas Plains), August 29, 1862. As noted above, Pope had ordered Sigel and Reynolds to attack Jackson's corps, which he believed to be retreating on the Warrenton Turnpike, and early on the morning of August 29, 1862, they formed their troops in line of battle across the Turnpike, facing west. Reynolds' division was south of the Turnpike, with its right near Groveton. George G. Meade's First Brigade was on the right of the division, and Truman Seymour's Second Brigade and Conrad F. Jackson's Third Brigade were on the left.

Sigel formed his corps with Schenck's First Division on the left, Milroy's Independent Brigade in the center, and Schurz's Third Division on the right. Schenck marched that morning with his division to the Dogan farm, about one-half mile west of the intersection of the Turnpike with the Sudley Springs Road, and he then advanced westward on the Turnpike toward Groveton. Schenck then formed his division in line south of the road, and on the right of Reynolds, with Julius Stahel's First Brigade on the right, next to the road, and Nathaniel C. McLean's Second Brigade on the left, next to Reynolds. Milroy's brigade advanced from an elevation in front of the Stone House, near the intersection of the Turnpike and the Sudley Springs Road, and it then faced west and moved up to a position on the right of Schenck. Schurz's division crossed the Turnpike and Young's Branch, and then wheeled to the left and formed on the right of Milroy, on a line roughly parallel to the Sudley Springs Road. Wladimir Krzyzanowski's Second Brigade was on the left, next to Milroy, and Alexander Schimmelfennig's First Brigade was on the right. Adolph Von Steinwehr's Second Division, commanded by John A. Koltes, and consisting only of Koltes' First Brigade, was held in reserve.

Sigel and Reynolds advanced to the attack between 5:00 and 6:00 A.M., while the artillery shelled the woods ahead. When Reynolds arrived on the Brawner farm, Gibbon's battlefield of the evening before, he changed front to the north and advanced Meade's brigade across the Turnpike in an attempt to turn Jackson's right. Schenck's division supported this attack for a time, but then Stahel's brigade was detached and sent to aid Milroy, who was then hard pressed. With Stahel's departure, Schenck could offer little support to Reynolds, and the latter was forced to fall back some distance to a position in rear of Schenck. The fighting on this part of the line was largely with artillery and skirmishers. Meantime, on the right of the Turnpike, Milroy had advanced his brigade beyond Groveton, with Schurz's division on his right. When Milroy arrived near the rectangular woods on the Brawner farm, he diverged to the right, and Schurz inclined still farther to the right. As a result, gaps developed between Milroy and Schenck and between Milroy and Schurz. Stahel's brigade was sent to occupy the gap between Milroy and Schenck, and it remained on the left of Milroy, along Young's Branch, until 3:00 P.M., when it rejoined Schenck's division. The gap between Schurz and Milroy was closed by Schurz when he extended his line to the left. As a result of these movements, the Federal line was only thinly held, and when this was observed by the enemy, they attacked and broke through Schurz's line. Toward noon, Schurz again attacked and drove the enemy back, and Schimmelfennig succeeded in gaining possession of a part of the railroad embankment, which he held until 2:00 P.M., when the division was relieved. Sometime after noon, Koltes' brigade moved up from reserve to support Sigel's line.

Sometime before noon, Heintzelman arrived on the field with the divisions of Kearny and Hooker, and Reno came up from Centerville with his own and Stevens' division of Ninth Corps. Kearny arrived about 10:00 A.M. and was assigned to hold the right of Pope's line. Orlando M. Poe , commanding Hiram Berry's Third Brigade, was formed on the first line, on the right of Schurz, and John C. Robinson's First Brigade was placed on the right of Poe, part in line and part in reserve. David B. Birney's Second Brigade was held in reserve. The head of Hooker's division began to arrive about 11:00 A.M., and between noon and 2:00 P.M. Joseph B. Carr's Third Brigade advanced and relieved a part of Schurz's division. Between 1:00 and 2:00 P.M., at the request of Sigel, Cuvier Grover's First Brigade was sent to support Schurz.

Reno's two divisions arrived about noon, and most of the regiments were sent to support Sigel. Four regiments, however, were held in reserve behind the center of Pope's line. By this time, Sigel's troops had been maneuvering and fighting for five or six hours, and they were exhausted. Pope expected McDowell and Porter to come up on his left during the afternoon, and he allowed the men to rest. There were no heavy attacks between noon and 4:00 P.M., but there was severe skirmishing and constant artillery fire.

At 2:00 P.M. Nelson Taylor's Second Brigade of Hooker's division was ordered to relieve Carr, but as he prepared to advance, the left of Carr's brigade was driven back through Taylor's line, and the left of Second Brigade was carried away. About 4:00 P.M. Taylor and Reno relieved Carr's brigade, and it then moved back about a half mile and camped for the night. A part of Milroy's brigade also withdrew and went into camp.

During the latter part of the afternoon, Pope ordered Heintzelman to organize two simultaneous attacks by the divisions of Hooker and Kearny. Grover's brigade received the order at 3:00 P.M. and advanced against the center of Jackson's line. It succeeded in occupying a portion of the railroad embankment, and the second line beyond, but it was not supported and was finally driven back by superior numbers. Kearny, who was to have attacked at the same time as Hooker, did not advance until Grover had been forced to retire. At 5:00 P.M. Robinson's brigade attacked, gained the railroad grade, and drove back the left of Hill's line. Birney then brought up four of his regiments, and when Kearny's men advanced along the railroad bed, they almost succeeded in turning Hill's left flank. Only the 3rd Michigan of Poe's Third Brigade of Kearny's division was engaged in the attack, but most of the brigade was under artillery fire and suffered some casualties. Stevens' division of Reno's command also came up in support, but Ewell arrived with two brigades of his division and finally forced Kearny back. The fighting on the Federal right ended with darkness.

Between 5:00 and 6:00 P.M., McDowell arrived with King's division, then commanded by Hatch, because King was sick, but Ricketts' division was not yet up. Pope still believed that Jackson was retreating, and he ordered Hatch to move westward on the Turnpike toward Groveton. Hatch's brigade, then commanded by Timothy Sullivan, and Doubleday's brigade advanced in front, and they were supported by Patrick's brigade. Gibbon's brigade had been detached to support some batteries. About 6:30 P.M., Hatch struck the advance of John B. Hood's division of Longstreet's corps, and this resulted in a severe engagement. Patrick's brigade moved up and joined in the fighting, and at the same time Bayard's cavalry attacked on the left of Hatch. Reynolds also again advanced toward the enemy right and rear with Seymour's and Jackson's brigades, but he was compelled to retire under heavy artillery fire. Meade's brigade on the right continued in action on the left of Hatch until the latter withdrew at dark.

Second Battle of Bull Run (or Groveton Heights, Second Manassas), August 30, 1862. There was no fighting along Pope's front during the morning of August 30, 1862, and the corps of Sigel and Heintzelman, Reno's two divisions of Ninth Corps, and the divisions of Reynolds and Hatch of McDowell's corps remained in the positions that they had occupied the night before. Banks' corps with the trains remained at Bristoe Station.

Ricketts, with his division of McDowell's corps,

had arrived on the battlefield from Bristoe Station the evening before, and had been placed in reserve. At sunrise, he was ordered to move with two of his brigades and relieve a part of Kearny's division of Heintzelman's corps on the right. He then advanced with Abram Duryee's First Brigade and Joseph Thoburn's Fourth Brigade (formerly Samuel S. Carroll's) and took position on the left of Pope's line, west of the Sudley Springs Road. Zealous B. Tower, with his own Second Brigade and George L. Hartsuff's Third Brigade (commanded by John W. Stiles while Hartsuff was sick), was placed on the left of the other two brigades of the division.

Porter's Fifth Corps, which had been ordered the night before to march to the battlefield, arrived during the morning. Between 3:00 and 4:00 A.M. August 30, 1862, Charles W. Roberts' First Brigade and Daniel Butterfield's Third Brigade of George W. Morell's First Division left their positions on Dawkins' Branch, and marched by way of Manassas Junction and the Sudley Springs Road to the Warrenton Turnpike. Morell remained behind with Charles Griffin's Second Brigade as a rear guard, and then, because of some confusion of orders, marched with the brigade to Centerville instead of to the battlefield, and remained there the rest of the day. Samuel D. Sturgis, with A. Sanders Piatt's brigade of his Reserve Corps, which was attached to Fifth Corps, followed Griffin to Centerville, but when Piatt discovered his error he marched to the battlefield at 4:00 P.M. and joined in the battle. During the absence of Morell with Griffin, Butterfield assumed command of First Brigade and Third Brigade of First Division. Henry L. Lansing assumed temporary command of Butterfield's brigade, but he became too sick to continue, and he turned over the brigade to Henry A. Weeks. Morell did not reach the battlefield until about 5:00 P.M., after Porter's defeat, and he then resumed command of his division. Morell's brigades under Butterfield arrived on the Turnpike about 9:00 A.M. and then moved westward toward Groveton. Butterfield's brigade, under Lansing, passed through Sigel's corps and formed to the right of the Turnpike and between Sigel's position and the line of Jackson's corps along the railroad grade. Roberts' brigade followed and took position on the right of Butterfield's brigade, then commanded by Weeks.

Porter's other division, commanded by George

Sykes, arrived from near Bethlehem Church between 9:00 and 10:00 A.M. and formed in advance of the Dogan house, facing west, with its left resting on the Turnpike. Robert C. Buchanan's First Brigade of regulars was deployed on the Turnpike, on the left of Butterfield's brigade, and William Chapman's Second Brigade of regulars was placed in column in rear of Buchanan. Gouverneur K. Warren's small Third Brigade was held in reserve.

When the various movements of that morning were completed, Pope's army was in position as follows: Reynolds' division was on the left, south of the Warrenton Turnpike; Porter's Fifth Corps, Army of the Potomac was just north of the Turnpike; Sigel's First Corps, Army of Virginia was in rear of Porter, and was also north of the Turnpike; King's division of McDowell's Third Corps, Army of Virginia, then commanded by Hatch, was on the right of Porter; Reno's divisions of Ninth Corps were on the right of Hatch; and Heintzelman's Third Corps, Army of the Potomac and Ricketts' brigades of Third Corps, Army of Virginia were on the right of the army.

A reconnaissance sent out on the Union right during the morning of August 30, 1862 revealed that Jackson's troops had withdrawn from some of the positions that they had occupied the night before, and this again led Pope to believe that the enemy was retreating. He immediately began preparations for a vigorous pursuit by troops on both his right and left. He ordered Ricketts to report to Heintzelman, and directed the latter to move westward with his corps and Ricketts' division on the road from Sudley Springs to Haymarket. Pope also ordered Reynolds and Hatch to report to Porter and to support him in an attack along the Warrenton Turnpike.

Heintzelman, with Ricketts, advanced on the right as ordered, but his attack accomplished little. Kearny and Ricketts moved forward along the road, but soon encountered strong resistance that halted further progress. Hooker, with the brigades of Taylor and Carr, attacked on the left of Kearny, but apparently this was not a serious effort, and it gained no ground. Grover's brigade, which had suffered heavy losses the day before, was in the rear. Shortly after Heintzelman's attack ended, Tower, with Second Brigade and Third Brigade of Ricketts' division, was detached and sent down the Sudley Springs Road to support Pope's left.

On the Union left, about 1:00 P.M., Butterfield's two brigades advanced into a woods in front of Jackson's line, and then at 3:00 P.M. Porter was ordered to move forward and to the right against the enemy position at the cut on the grade of the unfinished railroad. The main attack was to be made over the ground of Sigel's attack of the day before, with Weeks' brigade on the left and Roberts' brigade on the right. Hatch was to advance on the right of Roberts to support the attack, and Reynolds was to move forward at the same time on the left of Weeks, south of the turnpike.

Some time was lost in establishing a connection between Roberts and Hatch, but when this was completed Porter's whole line moved forward. Butterfield's brigades almost immediately came under a devastating fire from enemy troops protected by the railroad cut, and also from Longstreet's artillery posted to the left, and they were unable to continue the advance. Hatch attacked, with his own First Brigade in front and the brigades of Patrick, Gibbon, and Doubleday following, in that order. Hatch, too, was brought to a halt by the artillery fire and the musketry of the Confederate infantry behind the railroad embankment, which was to the Union right of the cut. Hatch was wounded, and Doubleday assumed command of the division. J. William Hofmann took charge of Doubleday's brigade. At 4:00 P.M. Sykes was ordered up to support Butterfield, and he too was soon in the midst of heavy fighting. Porter's men held their ground in front of the enemy line for about a half hour, but finally, about 5:00 P.M., they were forced to withdraw. Sykes covered the retreat. Stahel's brigade of Schenck's division was ordered forward to support Porter, but the defeated troops fell back through Sigel's line and re-formed in the rear. At this point Morell arrived from Centerville and resumed command of his First Division. Weeks was wounded during the fighting, and James C. Rice assumed command of Third Brigade. When Morell relieved Butterfield in command of the division, the latter resumed command of his Third Brigade, relieving Rice.

When Porter's attack began, Reynolds advanced his skirmishers south of the Turnpike. When they arrived opposite Groveton they found the enemy in heavy force, and at 5:00 P.M. Reynolds reported this to Pope. In fact, at this time, all of Longstreet's corps was on the field and was in position to attack. Hood's division was deployed to the right and left of the Turnpike, and perpendicular to it, and it was supported by Nathan G. Evans' Independent Brigade. Cadmus M. Wilcox's division was in position to support Hood's left, and James L. Kemper's division was formed to support Hood's right. David R. Jones' division was on the Manassas Gap Railroad to the right of Kemper, and Richard H. Anderson's division, which had arrived during the morning, was in rear of Hood.

Simultaneously with Porter's defeat, Longstreet moved forward against the Federal left. The attack was made by Hood's division, and it was closely supported by Evans' brigade. Hood's line was rapidly reinforced as it advanced by Anderson's division from the rear, Kemper's and Jones' divisions from the Confederate right, and Wilcox's brigade (the other two brigades of Wilcox's division were with Jackson) from Longstreet's left. Jackson's corps, farther north, also advanced against Pope's right.

When Longstreet began his attack, most of Pope's army was north of the Turnpike, but as his line advanced, Federal troops were hurried down from the right to occupy Bald Hill and the Henry House Hill in an attempt to stop the Confederate onrush. As noted above, when Porter's attack began earlier in the afternoon, Sigel's corps was in the rear of Fifth Corps. Schenck's division was to the right of the Turnpike and in rear of the Dogan house, with McLean's Second Brigade in the first line and Stahel's First Brigade in rear of McLean. Schurz's division was in rear of Schenck as a general reserve. At 4:00 P.M. Schurz's division moved forward to a position behind Stahel's brigade, with Schimmelfennig's First Brigade on the right, Koltes' brigade of Von Steinwehr's Second Division on the left, and Krzyzanowski's Second Brigade in the rear of the interval between the other two brigades. Koltes' brigade was attached to Schurz's division August 30, 1862. A little after 4:00 P.M. McLean's brigade was sent south of the Turnpike to Bald Hill to support Reynolds' division, which was to the left of the hill. Bald Hill was an elevation about one-fourth of a mile south of the Turnpike, and about one mile west of the Henry House Hill. When Porter retreated from his attack at the railroad grade, Stahel's brigade was sent forward to support him. Koltes' brigade was also sent forward and formed to the left of Stahel. Krzyzanowski's brigade then moved forward to the left of Koltes, and it formed on a ridge on the northern slope of Bald Hill.

By that time, Longstreet's attack was well developed, and the pressure on Pope's line was mounting. Strangely, although most of the army was north of the Turnpike, Pope ordered Reynolds to move his division from the far left to the north of the Turnpike to form a line behind which Porter's defeated corps could rally. Reynolds began his withdrawal just after McLean arrived with his brigade on Bald Hill, and his departure would have left Stahel isolated on the extreme Union left, directly in the path of Hood's advance. Before the rear of Reynolds' column could leave its position, however, the enemy approached, and Conrad F. Jackson's brigade (then commanded by Robert Anderson in place of Jackson, who was ill) was forced to remain and attempt to stay the enemy advance. Reynolds, however, with the brigades of Meade and Seymour, moved to the right with much difficulty, and attempted, together with other troops, to halt Jackson's advance.

Warren's brigade of Sykes' division marched to the south of the Turnpike to occupy the gap created by Reynolds' withdrawal, and Anderson and Warren fought valiantly to hold their positions, but after a short resistance, they were driven back. McLean's brigade, which was commanded by Schenck in person, was attacked repeatedly both on the front and on the left, and Schenck was wounded while attempting to bring up reinforcements. Stahel then assumed command of First Division of Sigel's corps, and Adolphus Buschbeck took over Stahel's brigade.

At this juncture, Tower arrived from the far right with the two brigades of Ricketts' division, and they took position on Bald Hill to the right of McLean. Milroy's brigade, which had been in reserve until 4:00 P.M., was also sent to the left to reinforce the troops fighting there.

After suffering heavy losses, including the wounding of Tower, McLean's brigade of Schenck's division, Tower's two brigades of Ricketts' division, and Jackson's brigade of Reynolds' division were finally driven from Bald Hill. William H. Christian assumed command of Tower's brigade. The withdrawal of these troops

exposed the left and rear of the brigades of Koltes and Krzyzanowski to a destructive fire, and Schurz withdrew his division to the hills beyond the Stone House. Koltes was killed and George A. Muhleck assumed command of his brigade.

While the fighting around Bald Hill was in progress, Federal troops were sent south to the Henry House Hill, east of the Sudley Springs Road. McDowell, whose divisions were temporarily attached to the commands of Porter and Heintzelman, had earlier moved to the south of the Turnpike to aid in getting troops in position to protect the Federal left. He helped in placing Tower's brigades on Bald Hill, and then began preparations for the defense of the Henry House Hill, where he remained during the remainder of the action. After Porter's defeat, Sykes sent Chapman's brigade of regulars to the Henry House Hill, and upon arrival there it was sent about 600 yards to the left and front to defend the approaches to the hill from that direction, and it was soon engaged in serious fighting. Buchanan's brigade of regulars and the remnants of Warren's brigade also came up and were placed on the plateau of the Henry house and the Robinson house.

Reynolds, with the brigades of Seymour and Meade, after their various movements on the southern end of the battlefield, finally arrived on the Henry House Hill and took position to the right of the Henry house, along the Sudley Springs Road. He strongly resisted the enemy advance in that quarter for two hours until he was relieved by Buchanan's brigade. During the late afternoon, Reno's command was also sent to the Henry House Hill. Sometime after 6:00 P.M., Schimmelfennig's brigade of Schurz's division, which had been sent to support Milroy, joined Sykes and Reno, and formed on the right of Sykes. Gibbon's brigade of King's division (then commanded by Doubleday) was also sent by McDowell to the Henry House Hill. Gibbon and Schimmelfennig were among the last to leave the field, and the former remained on the Henry House Hill until two hours after dark. The defense of this position was of the utmost importance because the troops fighting there covered the retreat of Pope's army, which was then in progress. By dark, Federal forces both to the north and south of the Turnpike had been forced back about three-fourths of a mile, and the enemy had gained possession of the Sudley Springs Road. About 8:00 P.M. Pope issued orders for a general withdrawal from the field, and this was done about dark. The army crossed Bull Run at the Stone Bridge and, during the night, marched back to Centerville. Reno's command covered the retreat. Banks' corps, which during the day had remained at Bristoe Station with the trains, also marched that night to join the army at Centerville.

William B. Franklin's Sixth Corps, Army of the Potomac arrived at Centerville from Alexandria during the evening of August 30, 1862, and Edwin V. Sumner's Second Corps, Army of the Potomac was only a few miles behind. Neither corps arrived in time to take part in the Battle of Bull Run.

Battle of Chantilly (or Ox Hill), September 1, 1862. Lee's army remained on the battlefield of Bull Run during the night of August 30–31, 1862, while Pope's command retreated to a defensive position in the old works about Centerville, which they had occupied by the next morning. As his next move, Lee decided on a flanking movement around Pope's right to cut his army off from Washington, and possibly destroy it.

Shortly before noon August 31, 1862, Jackson led his corps across Bull Run at Sudley Ford and marched up what is today Loudoun County Route 659 toward the Little River Turnpike (present-day U.S. 50). Stuart's cavalry led the way, and Longstreet's corps was under orders to follow Jackson at about dark that evening. Upon arriving on the Little River Turnpike, just south of Gum Springs (present-day Arcola), Jackson turned east toward Fairfax Court House, Virginia, and that evening the head of his column reached Pleasant Valley, near the Loudoun-Fairfax county line. By dawn the next morning, the rest of his command had closed up.

While Jackson was marching toward his rear, Pope decided to concentrate his command at Germantown and again attack Lee if he should pursue. When Franklin had passed through Germantown with his Sixth Corps on his way to Centerville the day before, he had left Alfred T. A. Torbert's First Brigade, First Division to protect Pope's communications. Before midnight August 31, 1862, Pope had reason to believe that a flanking movement was in progress, and he immediately took steps to reinforce Torbert in the Germantown-Fairfax Court House area. He first ordered Edward W. Hinks, with his Third Brigade, Second Division of Edwin V.

Sumner's Second Corps, Army of the Potomac, to report to Torbert, and Hinks arrived about 7:00 A.M. September 1, 1862.

At midnight, Pope ordered McDowell to clear the road from Centerville to Fairfax Court House, and at 3:00 the next morning McDowell started Marsena R. Patrick's Third Brigade, First Division of his Third Corps, Army of Virginia to carry out this order. Patrick arrived at Fairfax Court House soon after daylight September 1, 1862. Some regiments of Darius N. Couch's First Division, Fourth Corps, Army of the Potomac had arrived near Fairfax Court House, and the rest of the division was then brought up from Alexandria, and held just east of the court house.

Before dawn September 1, 1862, Pope learned that enemy troops were on the Little River Turnpike, and he also was informed by Torbert that Stuart's cavalry was west of Germantown. By 9:00 A.M. September 1, 1862, Jackson had marched about four and a half miles southeast of Pleasant Valley on the Little River Turnpike, and had halted near 1862 Chantilly, which was near the junction of Route 645 with the Little River Turnpike. (It should be noted here that 1862 Chantilly was a little less than two miles to the southeast of present-day Chantilly, which is at the intersection of the Little River Turnpike [U.S. 50] and Route 657.) About noon, Jackson resumed his march eastward, and around 2:30 P.M. his first units arrived at Ox Hill and relieved Stuart's cavalry. Ox Hill was immediately to the southwest of the intersection of the Little River Turnpike and Route 608 (present-day Pender).

About noon, Pope ordered McDowell to march with his Third Corps, Army of Virginia from Centerville to Germantown and cover the lines of communications with Alexandria. McDowell was also instructed to assume command of the two brigades already at Germantown. Actually, however, only Hinks' brigade was still there, and it was acting under Torbert's orders. Patrick's brigade, which had completed its mission of clearing the road, had started its return to Centerville at 11:00 A.M. Shortly after noon, McDowell received Pope's order, and he directed Patrick to return to Germantown, and started Ricketts' Second Division, Third Corps, Army of Virginia for the same place. Duryee's First Brigade and Tower's Second Brigade (then under

Christian) left about noon, and Hartsuff's Third Brigade (then under Stiles) departed sometime later. Ricketts' Fourth Brigade had been detached the day before and was then on duty at Fairfax guarding stores.

At 1:00 P.M., at about the same time that McDowell was preparing to leave Centerville, Pope issued a direct order to Joseph Hooker to proceed to Germantown and assume command of the troops in the Germantown-Fairfax Court House area, and to establish strong defenses west of Germantown. This order relieved McDowell of his earlier assignment, and, accordingly, he remained near Centerville with the rest of his Third Corps, Army of Virginia. Hooker arrived at Germantown at 2:30 P.M. and found Hinks' brigade there, and a short time later Ricketts' First Brigade and Second Brigade arrived. Hooker left Hinks at Germantown, and with Ricketts' two brigades and Patrick's brigade moved west about a mile to the crest east of Difficult Run, and there formed a strong defensive line. Hooker was also joined by two regiments of Torbert's brigade and six regiments of Couch's division. Stuart, who was then advancing toward Fairfax, arrived before Hooker's position, and then, finding it too strong to attack, returned to Ox Hill, where Jackson had halted to await the arrival of Longstreet.

During the period between 2:00 and 4:00 P.M. September 1, 1862, Pope was concerned primarily with strengthening the position near Germantown. He ordered McDowell, with what remained of his corps, to march east on the Warrenton Turnpike (U.S. 29) to the headwaters of Difficult Run, and connect on the right with Hooker's line south of the Little River Turnpike. At about the same time that Pope issued the new orders to McDowell, he also directed Reno, for reasons that are not clear, to march with his two weak divisions of Ninth Corps across country from the Warrenton Turnpike to the northeast toward 1862 Chantilly. Pope also ordered Heintzelman to move east along the Warrenton Turnpike, and to keep within supporting distance of Reno. Having arranged for the above movements, Pope then started the rest of the army eastward. Sumner with his Second Corps, Army of the Potomac was directed to follow Heintzelman, and, in order, the other corps were to follow Heintzelman as follows: Sigel's First Corps, Army of Virginia; Porter's Fifth Corps, Army of the Potomac; and that

part of Franklin's Sixth Corps, Army of the Potomac that was at Centerville. Banks, with his Second Corps, Army of Virginia, and the trains of the army were to march on the Old Braddock Road to come into the Little River Turnpike east of Fairfax Court House.

Reno's Ninth Corps marched from south of Centerville at 2:00 P.M. in the following order: Stevens' First Division in the lead, then the artillery, and Edward Ferrero's Second Brigade of Reno's Second Division. James Nagle's First Brigade, Second Division followed about a half hour later. The column marched east on the Warrenton Turnpike to Willow Springs, and from there it moved northward on an old cart road to a point about 500 yards west of the Milan house, which was located about 100 yards west of Route 608, and about three-fourths of a mile south of the Little River Turnpike. Reno's leading brigade was Addison Farnsworth's Third Brigade, First Division, then commanded by David Morrison in place of Farnsworth, who had been wounded the day before.

Stevens' arrival near the Milan house was reported to Jackson, who immediately sent Ambrose P. Hill with Branch's brigade (then commanded by James H. Lane) and Field's brigade (commanded by John M. Brockenbrough) to investigate. Jackson then began to deploy the rest of his corps in preparation for battle. He established his line in a woods one-eighth to one-fourth of a mile south of the Little River Turnpike, with Hill's division on the right, Ewell's division (commanded by Alexander R. Lawton) in the center, and Jackson's division (commanded by Starke) on the left. Hill's division and most of Ewell's division were west of Route 608, and Jackson's division extended the line to the east, with its left on the Little River Turnpike.

Stevens observed Jackson's skirmishers on his front, and, probably because he was under orders to proceed to the Little River Turnpike, he prepared to attack. He advanced Morrison's brigade along the west side of Route 608 to a line south and southeast of the Reid house, which was about one-fifth of a mile west of Route 608 and a little less than a half mile south of the Little River Turnpike. Meantime, Stevens had brought up the rest of his division and formed it in three lines in a field to the southeast of the Reid house. Morrison's Third Brigade formed the first line, Benjamin C. Christ's First Brigade the

second line, and Daniel Leasure's Second Brigade (commanded by David A. Lecky) the third line. Stevens' line faced roughly to the north and northeast, toward the woods in which Jackson's command was concealed.

Reno arrived at about this time with Ferrero's Second Brigade, Second Division, but Reno, who was ill, left to Stevens the direction of the two divisions in the coming battle. Ferrero's brigade was sent into the woods east of Route 608 to cover Stevens' right flank. It was then about 4:30 P.M., and the sky was dark because of the clouds of an approaching storm when Stevens ordered his line to advance. When the leading brigade was partway across the field, between the Reid house access road and the edge of the woods to the north, Jackson's troops opened fire. Stevens' line halted, and First Brigade moved up to extend the Third Brigade line to the west, and Second Brigade also moved forward to a position behind the interval between the two front line brigades. While these movements were in progress, Nagle's First Brigade, Second Division, the last of the Ninth Corps troops, arrived on the field and was sent to the east of Route 608 to the right and rear of Ferrero's brigade.

At 5:00 P.M., the storm that had been threatening for some time broke with a torrential downpour. In spite of this, Stevens renewed the advance, and soon the two lines were engaged in deadly combat. Parts of Jackson's line gave way, but at that time Stevens was killed, and the command of the division devolved on Christ. Meantime, while Stevens was advancing, Ferrero's brigade entered the woods east of Route 608 at a point opposite the junction of the Reid house access road and Route 608; and it then advanced until a heavy enemy fire forced it to halt.

The intensity of the fighting diminished because of the storm, and also, on the Union side, because of the confusion that resulted from the death of Stevens. First Division began to fall back toward the Reid house, and it was closely followed by the enemy. Earlier, Stevens had sent back for help, and in response to this request, Kearny, whose First Division, Third Corps, Army of the Potomac was on the Warrenton Turnpike, sent forward David B. Birney's Second Brigade, and he ordered the rest of the division to prepare to follow. Birney marched up Route 608 to the vicinity of the Reid house, and there he was directed by Reno to relieve Stevens' division,

which was falling back in some confusion. Kearny, who had arrived on the field in person, was killed while attempting to establish his line of battle. Birney then assumed command of Kearny's division, and J. H. Hobart Ward took charge of Birney's brigade. At this time the battle was drawing to a close. John C. Robinson's First Brigade, First Division, Third Corps, Army of the Potomac arrived east of the Reid house, and Orlando M. Poe's Third Brigade, Second Division, Third Corps, Army of the Potomac also came up and was placed in reserve, but these two brigades were not engaged. When the fighting ended between 6:00 and 6:30 P.M., it was quite dark because of the storm.

Meantime, during Ninth Corps' battle to the north, Hooker's Second Division, Third Corps, Army of the Potomac, temporarily commanded by Cuvier Grover while Hooker was at Germantown, had been lined up along the Warrenton Turnpike between Willow Springs and the intersection of the turnpike and Route 608, but it was not ordered up to join in the battle.

After the battle, Reno's two divisions of Ninth Corps, and First Division, Third Corps, Army of the Potomac remained in the vicinity of the Reid house and the Milan house until about 2:30 A.M. September 2, 1862; and then, by Pope's order, they began to withdraw by the Warrenton Turnpike toward Fairfax Court House. Hooker's command began to withdraw from along Difficult Run at 10:00 A.M. September 2, 1862, but some regiments remained to observe the enemy until late that afternoon.

September 2, 1862, Pope, following orders, withdrew with his army to within the entrenched line in front of Washington. There the Army of Virginia and the Army of the Potomac came under the general supervision of George B. McClellan, who had been assigned command of the Defenses of Washington. September 5, 1862, the Army of Virginia and the Army of the Potomac were consolidated, and Pope was relieved from command. Then, on September 12, 1862, while McClellan's army was near Frederick, Maryland at the beginning of the Maryland Campaign, the Army of Virginia was officially discontinued, and the designations of the corps were changed as follows: First Corps, Army of Virginia was changed to Eleventh Corps, Army of the Potomac; Second Corps, Army of Virginia was changed to Twelfth Corps, Army of the

Potomac; and Third Corps, Army of Virginia was changed to First Corps, Army of the Potomac.

For further information about the troops of Pope's army, see Miscellaneous Organizations, Military District of the Defenses of Washington; and also Maryland Campaign (South Mountain and Antietam).

The organization of the Army of Virginia, the Army of the Potomac, and other cooperating forces during Pope's operations in Virginia, from the Rapidan River to the Defenses of Washington, was as follows:

ARMY OF VIRGINIA
John Pope, to September 5, 1862

FIRST CORPS, Franz Sigel

First Division, Robert C. Schenck, to August 30, 1862, wounded
Julius Stahel
First Brigade, Julius Stahel, to August 30, 1862
Adolphus Buschbeck
Second Brigade, Nathaniel C. McLean

Note. Louis Schirmer's 2nd Battery, New York Light Artillery (later commanded by Theodore Blume) was attached to First Brigade, and George B. Haskin's Battery K, 1st Ohio Light Artillery was attached to Second Brigade.

Second Division, Adolph Von Steinwehr
First Brigade, John Koltes, to August 30, 1862, killed
George A. Muhleck

Note. First Brigade was temporarily attached to Third Division August 30, 1862.

Third Division, Carl Schurz
First Brigade, Henry Bohlen, to August 22, 1862, killed
Alexander Schimmelfennig
Second Brigade, Wladimir Krzyzanowski
Unattached Artillery
Battery C, 3rd West Virginia Light Artillery, Jonathan Stahl
Battery I, 1st Ohio Light Artillery, Hubert Dilger

Note 1. First Brigade, Second Division, First Corps was temporarily attached to Third Division August 30, 1862.
Note 2. Robert B. Hampton's Battery F, Pennsylvania Light Artillery was attached to First Brigade, and Jacob Roemer's Battery L, 2nd New York Light Artillery was attached to Second Brigade.

Independent Brigade, Robert H. Milroy

Note. Aaron C. Johnson's 12th Battery, Ohio Light Artillery was attached to Milroy's brigade.

Cavalry Brigade, John Beardsley

Reserve Artillery, Frank Buell, killed
Louis Schirmer
Battery I, 1st New York Light Artillery, Michael Wiedrich
13th Battery, New York Light Artillery, Julius Dieckmann
Battery C, West Virginia Light Artillery, Wallace Hill

SECOND CORPS, Nathaniel P. Banks, to September 3, 1862
Alpheus S. Williams

First Division, Alpheus S. Williams, to September 3, 1862
Samuel W. Crawford
First Brigade, Samuel W. Crawford, to September 3, 1862
Joseph F. Knipe
Third Brigade, George H. Gordon

Cavalry Brigade, John Burford

Artillery, Clermont L. Best
4th Battery (D), Maine Light Artillery, O'Neil W. Robinson
Battery M, 1st New York Light Artillery, George W. Cothran
10th Battery, New York Light Artillery, John T. Bruen
Battery E, Pennsylvania Light Artillery, Joseph M. Knap
Battery F, 4th United States Artillery, Edward D. Muhlenberg

THIRD CORPS, Irvin McDowell, to September 7, 1862
Joseph Hooker

First Division, Rufus King, to August 29, 1862, sick
John P. Hatch, to August 30, 1862, wounded
Abner Doubleday
First Brigade, John P. Hatch, to August 29, 1862
Timothy Sullivan
Second Brigade, Abner Doubleday, to August 30, 1862
J. William Hofmann
Third Brigade, Marsena R. Patrick
Fourth Brigade, John Gibbon
Artillery, Joseph B. Campbell
1st Battery, New Hampshire Light Artillery, George A. Gerrish, captured
Frederick M. Edgell
Battery L, 1st New York Light Artillery, John A. Reynolds

Battery D, 1st Rhode Island Light Artillery, J. Albert Monroe

Battery B, 4th United States Artillery, Joseph B. Campbell

Note. McDowell was relieved from command of Third Corps at his own request.

Second Division, James B. Ricketts
First Brigade, Abram Duryee
Second Brigade, Zealous B. Tower, to August 30, 1862, wounded
William H. Christian
Third Brigade, George H. Hartsuff, to about August 24, 1862, sick
John W. Stiles
Fourth Brigade, Joseph Thoburn, to August 30, 1862, wounded
Artillery
2nd Battery (B), Maine Light Artillery, James A. Hall
5th Battery (E), Maine Light Artillery, George F. Leppien
Battery F, 1st Pennsylvania Light Artillery, Ezra W. Mathews
Battery C, Pennsylvania Light Artillery, James Thompson

Unattached Artillery
16th Battery, Indiana Light Artillery, Charles A. Naylor
Battery E, 4th United States Artillery, Joseph C. Clark, Jr.

Note 1. Samuel S. Carroll, former commander of Fourth Brigade, was wounded south of Cedar Mountain while visiting outposts after the battle, and he was succeeded by Thoburn.

Note 2. Fourth Brigade was detached August 31, 1862 and sent to Fairfax Station to guard commissary stores, and there the brigade commander reported to Edward G. Beckwith, chief commissary of the Army of Virginia.

Cavalry Brigade, George D. Bayard

Reynolds' Division, John F. Reynolds
First Brigade, George G. Meade
Second Brigade, Truman Seymour
Third Brigade, Conrad F. Jackson, to August 30, sick
Robert Anderson
Artillery, Dunbar R. Ransom
Battery A, 1st Pennsylvania Light Artillery, John G. Simpson
Battery B, 1st Pennsylvania Light Artillery, James H. Cooper
Battery G, 1st Pennsylvania Light Artillery, Mark

Kerns, mortally wounded
Frank P. Amsden
Battery C, 5th United States Artillery, Dunbar R. Ransom

Note. Reynolds' division of Fitz John Porter's Fifth Corps, Army of the Potomac arrived at Warrenton, Virginia from the Peninsula August 23, 1862, and it was temporarily attached to McDowell's Third Corps, Army of Virginia. The division was ordered to return to Fifth Corps September 4, 1862.

Reserve Corps, Samuel D. Sturgis
Piatt's Brigade, A. Sanders Piatt

Note. Piatt's Brigade was attached to Porter's Fifth Corps, Army of the Potomac, and was the only part of the Reserve Corps engaged at the Battle of Bull Run.

ARMY OF THE POTOMAC

THIRD CORPS, Samuel P. Heintzelman

First Division, Philip Kearny, to September 1, 1862, killed
David B. Birney
First Brigade, John C. Robinson
Second Brigade, David B. Birney, to September 1, 1862
J. H. Hobart Ward
Third Brigade, Orlando M. Poe
Artillery
Battery E, 1st Rhode Island Light Artillery, George E. Randolph
Battery K, 1st United States Artillery, William A. Graham

Second Division. Joseph Hooker, to September 7, 1862
Cuvier Grover
First Brigade, Cuvier Grover
Second Brigade, Nelson Taylor
Third Brigade, Joseph B. Carr
Unattached Artillery
6th Battery (F), Maine Light Artillery, Freeman McGilvery

FIFTH CORPS, Fitz John Porter

First Division, George W. Morell
First Brigade, Charles W. Roberts
Second Brigade, Charles Griffin
Third Brigade, Daniel Butterfield, to August 30, 1862
Henry Lansing, August 30, 1862, sick
Henry A. Weeks, August 30, 1862, wounded
James C. Rice, August 30, 1862
Daniel Butterfield
Artillery

3rd Battery, Massachusetts Light Artillery, Augustus P. Martin

Battery C, 1st Rhode Island Light Artillery, Richard Waterman

Battery D, 5th United States Artillery, Charles E. Hazlett

Note. Butterfield was in command of First Brigade and Third Brigade August 30, 1862, during the Battle of Bull Run, until 4:00 P.M. Morell was absent at Centerville, but returned to the battlefield at 4:00 P.M. and resumed command of the division.

Second Division, George Sykes

First Brigade (Regulars), Robert C. Buchanan

Second Brigade (Regulars), William Chapman

Third Brigade, Gouverneur K. Warren

Artillery, Stephen H. Weed

Batteries E and G, 1st United States Artillery, Alanson M. Randol

Battery I, 5th United States Artillery, Stephen Weed

Battery K, 5th United States Artillery, John R. Smead, killed

William E. Van Reed

SIXTH CORPS

Note. William B. Franklin's Sixth Corps did not arrive at Centerville until the evening of August 30, 1862, after the Battle of Bull Run. George W. Taylor's First Brigade, First Division was engaged at Bull Run Bridge August 27, 1862, while on a reconnaissance from Alexandria toward Centerville, but otherwise the corps was not engaged.

DETACHMENT NINTH CORPS
Jesse L. Reno

First Division, Isaac I. Stevens, to September 1, 1862, killed

Benjamin C. Christ, to September 8, 1862

Orlando B. Willcox

First Brigade, Benjamin C. Christ, to September 1, 1862

Frank Graves

Second Brigade, Daniel Leasure

David Lecky

Third Brigade, Addison Farnsworth, to August 30, 1862, wounded

David Morrison

Artillery

8th Battery, Massachusetts Light Artillery, Asa M. Cook

Battery E, 2nd United States Artillery, Samuel N. Benjamin

Second Division, Jesse L. Reno

First Brigade, James Nagle

Second Brigade, Edward Ferrero

Note. During the Northern Virginia Campaign, Reno was in command of First Division and Second Division. John G. Parke's Third Division remained near Fredericksburg.

KANAWHA DIVISION
Jacob D. Cox

Note. Only four regiments of the Kanawha Division were engaged during the Northern Virginia Campaign. The 11th Ohio and 12th Ohio under Eliakim P. Scammon, commander of the First Provisional Brigade of the division, were present at Bull Run Bridge August 27, 1862.

ENGAGEMENTS AT RAPPAHANNOCK STATION AND KELLY'S FORD, VIRGINIA NOVEMBER 7, 1863

At the close of the Bristoe, Virginia Campaign in October 1863 (see), the Army of the Potomac returned to the line of the Rappahannock River. President Lincoln and Henry W. Halleck then urged George G. Meade to advance and engage Robert E. Lee's Army of Northern Virginia, which at that time was in position in front of Culpeper Court House, with a bridgehead north of the Rappahannock. In response, Meade proposed to Halleck November 2, 1863 that he move with the army to Fredericksburg, and thus draw Lee from his prepared positions and engage him under more favorable circumstances. When this plan was not approved, Meade decided to force a passage of the Rappahannock and to advance toward Culpeper Court House. Before beginning this movement, Lysander Cutler's First Division and John C. Robinson's Second Division of John Newton's First Corps were ordered to move to Catlett's Station November 5, 1863, and John R. Kenly's Third Division, First Corps was assigned to guard the Orange and Alexandria Railroad from Manassas to Warrenton Junction. One brigade of Kenly's division was sent to Bristoe Station, one to Warrenton Junction, and one to guard the bridges over Cedar Run and Kettle Run. By this assignment, First Corps relieved troops of Third Corps that had been guarding the railroad, and these units then rejoined their corps.

The next day, November 6, 1863, Meade issued orders for a general movement of the army, which was to begin the following morning. The immediate objectives were the Confederate bridgehead on the north bank of the Rappahannock at Rappahannock Station, and the crossing of the river at Kelly's Ford. For this operation the army was temporarily divided into two columns or wings. The Right Column was assigned to John Sedgwick, and consisted of his Sixth Corps, temporarily under the command of Horatio G. Wright, and George Sykes' Fifth Corps. This column was to move November 7, 1863 to Rappahannock Station and capture the rifle pits and redoubts on the river near the site of the old railroad bridge. The Left Column was assigned to William H. French, and consisted of his Third Corps, temporarily commanded by David B. Birney, Gouverneur K. Warren's Second Corps, and John Newton's First Corps. This column was to march to Kelly's Ford, force a crossing of the river at that point, and then move upstream and aid Sedgwick at Rappahannock Station.

The march orders for November 7, 1863 were as follows: Sixth Corps was to march by way of Fayetteville to Rappahannock Station, and then take position with its left on the railroad and its right extending toward Beverly Ford. Fifth Corps was to march by way of Germantown to Bealeton Station, and then on to Rappahannock Station. It was then to take position of the left of Sixth Corps, with its right on the railroad. Third Corps, which was the leading corps of French's column, was to march by way of Elk Run and Morrisville to Kelly's Ford. Second Corps was to move by way of Warrenton and along the branch railroad to Bealeton, and then by way of Morrisville to Kelly's Ford. Newton was to leave Kenly's Third Division, First Corps on the railroad, and with the divisions of Cutler and Robinson follow Second Corps by way of Elk Run to Morrisville. It was to remain there, prepared to move to Kelly's Ford if needed. During the above movements John Buford's First Cavalry Division was to move on the right flank of the army. It was directed to cross the Rappahannock at the upper fords and force a passage of Hazel River at Rixeyville, and then move into position to aid Sedgwick's column. Judson Kilpatrick's Third Cavalry Division was to perform a similar service on the left flank of the army. Kilpatrick had been sent to the lower Rappahannock

November 3, 1863, to drive back some enemy cavalry that had crossed the river at Fredericksburg. He was then ordered to move back and cross the Rappahannock at Ellis' Ford and cooperate with French's column. David McM. Gregg's Second Cavalry Division was to be held in reserve to guard the trains at Bealeton and Morrisville.

Engagement at Kelly's Ford, November 7, 1863. French's column left its camps near Licking Run at 5:00 A.M. November 7, 1863 and marched toward Kelly's Ford. P. Regis De Trobriand's Third Brigade of Birney's First Division, Third Corps was in the lead and by noon had reached Mount Holly Church, a little more than a mile from the Ford. Then, while Union artillery shelled the enemy defenses across the river, De Trobriand crossed upstream at some rapids and moved down on the rear of the Confederate forces guarding the ford. These were quickly routed by a surprise attack, and by 1:30 P.M. the crossing was cleared. At 5:00 P.M., Third Corps was crossing the river and Second Corps was massed nearby.

During De Trobriand's attack, Charles H. T. Collis' First Brigade and J. H. Hobart Ward's Second Brigade, also of Birney's division, supported the artillery with rifle fire. Henry Prince's Second Division of Third Corps was formed on the right of Birney's division. Joseph B. Carr's Third Division, Third Corps did not arrive on the field until the fighting was ending. The two divisions of First Corps remained at Morrisville until the morning of November 9, 1863.

Engagement at Rappahannock Station, November 7, 1863. Sedgwick, with his Sixth Corps, temporarily under Wright, and Sykes' Fifth Corps, marched at daybreak November 7, 1863 down the Fayetteville Road toward Rappahannock Station. Gregg's cavalry, which covered the advance, encountered enemy pickets about a mile and a half from the river, but it was not until 11:00 A.M. that the infantry came up and replaced the cavalry on the skirmish line.

When Sykes arrived, he deployed his Fifth Corps on the left of the Orange and Alexandria Railroad, and then Wright's Sixth Corps came up and deployed on the right of the railroad. Sykes completed his deployment about 2:00 P.M. and formed his corps in two lines. The first line consisted of the following brigades, in order from right to left, beginning at the railroad: Joseph Hayes' First Brigade of Joseph J. Bartlett's First Division; Joshua L. Chamberlain's Third Brigade of the same division; Sidney Burbank's First Brigade of Romeyn B. Ayres' Second Division; and one brigade of Samuel W. Crawford's Third Division. The second line consisted of the remaining brigades of the three divisions.

Sykes was ordered to advance a strong line of skirmishers along the railroad embankment and attempt to reach the Rappahannock below the bridgehead. About 900 men were selected from the pickets of the three divisions of Fifth Corps, and these were placed under the command of Kenner Garrard. Garrard advanced at about 3:30 P.M. and soon reached the river. He then cleared the river bank for a distance of about 800 yards, from Norman's Ford on the left to the Confederate redoubt on the right.

Wright's Sixth Corps marched toward Rappahannock Station that morning with David A. Russell's First Division in the lead. Albion P. Howe's Second Division followed, and Henry D. Terry's Third Division brought up the rear. Upon arriving at a point about one and a half miles from the river, Wright formed the corps in two lines of battle. Russell's division was on the left, next to the railroad; Terry's division was on the right of Russell; and Howe's division was on the right of Terry.

Sixth Corps faced the Confederate defenses of the bridgehead, which consisted of two redoubts west of the railroad, with connecting rifle pits. The latter extended beyond each redoubt and circled back to the river. This line was about one mile in length. Henry T. Hays' Confederate brigade (the Louisiana Tigers) of Jubal A. Early's division, temporarily under the command of David B. Penn, occupied the works. It was later reinforced by Robert F. Hoke's brigade, then commanded by Archibald C. Godwin, also of Early's division.

When Sykes' skirmishers advanced on the left of Sixth Corps, as noted above, Sixth Corps was to advance and capture a ridge about one mile to the front. Howe's Second Division was selected to make the attack, and for this purpose Alexander Shaler's First Brigade of Terry's Third Division, and Richard Waterman's and Leonard Martin's batteries of

Charles H. Tompkins' Artillery Brigade of Sixth Corps were attached to Howe's division. Howe soon occupied the ridge, and then brought up the artillery and opened fire on the enemy works. When it appeared that the enemy intended to reinforce their troops north of the river, the rest of Sixth Corps was brought up to cover the ridge and repel a possible attack.

The Federal artillery continued to fire without significant effect, and a little before sunset an assault was ordered on the enemy works. Russell's First Division, which was in line on the slope leading up to the works, was selected to make the attack. Peter C. Ellmaker's Third Brigade was on the left near the railroad; Emory Upton's Second Brigade was on the right of Ellmaker; and Alfred T. A. Torbert's First Brigade was on the right of Upton.

The 5th Wisconsin and 6th Maine regiments of Ellmaker's brigade were detailed for the storming party, and 49th Pennsylvania and 119th Pennsylvania of the same brigade were ordered forward in close support. The attack, which was led by Russell in person, was made shortly after dark; and the 6th Maine, closely followed by the 5th Wisconsin, soon entered the earthworks. Enemy troops from a rifle pit to the right of the redoubt poured in an enfilade fire, and the 5th Maine and 121st New York of Upton's brigade were sent forward to drive them out. After desperate fighting, during which the Pennsylvania regiments were brought up to repulse an enemy counterattack, Hays' brigade fled toward the river. Godwin's brigade, however, continued fighting on the Confederate left, and Ellmaker's four regiments changed front to the right. Upton was then ordered to charge Godwin's position, which was soon surrounded, and the enemy was forced to surrender. About 1,600 men were captured, and two Confederate brigades were virtually destroyed.

Howe disposed his command so as to hold in check the enemy troops on his front, and to prevent them from opposing the storming column. Thomas H. Neill's Third Brigade, Second Division and Alexander Shaler's First Brigade, Third Division were on the front line, and Lewis A. Grant's Second Brigade, Second Division was on the second line and was not engaged. At the beginning of the action, Shaler's brigade was ordered to report to Howe, and two regiments of Henry L. Eustis' Second Brigade accompanied Shaler. Frank Wheaton's Third

Brigade and two regiments of Eustis' brigade were held in reserve, but before the fighting ended they were moved forward to the foot of the hill occupied by the artillery. They were not engaged. Torbert's brigade of First Division, Sixth Corps and the brigades of Third Division were not engaged, but they did support the artillery and were under fire.

For additional information, see Army of the Potomac, Advance across the Rappahannock, November 1863.

RICHMOND, VIRGINIA CAMPAIGN, 1864

When Ulysses S. Grant assumed command of the Armies of the United States March 9, 1864, he immediately began preparations for the spring campaigns. His basic plan was to strike hard and unremittingly at the two principal armies of the Confederacy until they were destroyed. One of his objectives was Robert E. Lee's Army of Northern Virginia, then encamped south of the Rapidan River near Orange Court House; and the other was Joseph E. Johnston's Army of Tennessee, which was in northern Georgia near Dalton. According to Grant's plans, George G. Meade's Army of the Potomac was to advance against Lee's army in Virginia; and William T. Sherman was to move against Johnston's army in Georgia with the Army of the Cumberland, the Army of the Tennessee, and the Army of the Ohio, all belonging to his Military Division of the Mississippi.

In addition to the two major campaigns, several secondary operations were to be carried out simultaneously in order to keep all Confederate forces fully occupied at the same time. Benjamin F. Butler, commander of the Army of the James, was to move to the south side of the James River and advance against Richmond from the south. Franz Sigel, commanding the Department of West Virginia, was to advance with the available troops of his department in two columns against the enemy: one column under George Crook was to move forward from the Kanawha River toward the Virginia and Tennessee Railroad; and the other, under Sigel's personal direction, was to move up the Shenandoah Valley to Staunton, and farther if possible. For details of these

operations, see Army of the James; and also Department of West Virginia, Operations of the Troops of the Department of West Virginia.

Grant also proposed a movement against Mobile, Alabama. That expedition, however, would have required the cooperation of Nathaniel P. Banks, commanding the Department of the Gulf, who at that time was absent on his Red River Expedition. When Banks' army was defeated April 8, 1864 at Mansfield (or Sabine Cross Roads), Louisiana, he was unable to take part in the proposed movement on Mobile.

Although Grant was in command of all armies of the United States that spring, he established his headquarters in the field with the Army of the Potomac, and left Henry W. Halleck, his chief of staff, in Washington in charge of the routine affairs of the office. Grant thus became in reality the commander of the Army of the Potomac, although Meade retained that title and remained in charge of the executive details of his command.

After considering various plans for the spring campaign in Virginia, Grant finally decided to advance by his left flank and then, at the proper time, turn to the right and engage Lee. The most serious objection to this plan was the nature of the country through which the army would be forced to pass. This was the so-called "Wilderness," which extended for a distance of ten or fifteen miles to the south of the Rapidan River. This region was covered by forest, usually of very dense growth, and over much of its extent there was almost impenetrable undergrowth. In addition, to further impede the movements of armies, there were numerous streams and rivulets flowing between ridges and hills, and through ravines that were difficult to cross. On the positive side, however, by advancing along the route proposed by Grant, the army could easily be supplied by sea, and by moving near the coast, it could frequently change its base of supply. In addition, the Army of the Potomac could, if successful, unite with Butler's Army of the James without giving up Fort Monroe and the surrounding country, which was of vital importance to the Union armies operating in the area.

Having considered all possibilities, on May 2, 1864, Grant issued orders for the Army of the Potomac to leave its camps around Culpeper Court House the next day and advance toward the

Rapidan. This was to be the opening move of a campaign that would result in months of almost continuous fighting, including the terrible battles of the Wilderness, Spotsylvania Court House, and Cold Harbor. In the first month of this movement alone, the army suffered about 50,000 casualties.

THE OPENING MOVEMENTS
MAY 3–4, 1864

When the orders for the Army of the Potomac to begin its advance toward the Rapidan River were received, Philip H. Sheridan's Cavalry Corps, which was to move first, was already assembled, with Alfred T. A. Torbert's First Cavalry Division and James H. Wilson's Third Cavalry Division at Stevensburg, and David McM. Gregg's Second Cavalry Division at Paoli Mills.

At 3:00 P.M. May 3, 1864, Gregg left Paoli Mills and marched to Richardsville, about two and a half miles from Ely's Ford, where he bivouacked for the night. At 2:00 A.M. May 4, 1864, Winfield S. Hancock's Second Corps left Stevensburg and followed Gregg's cavalry toward Ely's Ford. Two hours later, Henry S. Burton's Artillery Reserve followed Second Corps.

At dark May 3, 1864, Wilson's cavalry left Stevensburg and marched to Germanna Ford, where it arrived at 10:00 P.M. At midnight, Gouverneur K. Warren's Fifth Corps left Culpeper Court House and marched to Stevensburg, and from that point it followed Wilson to Germanna Ford. John Sedgwick's Sixth Corps began its march from beyond Brandy Station at 4:00 A.M. May 4, 1864, and then fell in behind Warren and followed Fifth Corps to to Germanna Ford.

Torbert's cavalry was left behind for a time to cover the upper fords of the Rapidan and to guard the rear of the army.

At daylight May 4, 1864, Gregg's cavalry resumed its advance, crossed the Rapidan at Ely's Ford, and moved on to Chancellorsville. The head of Hancock's corps arrived at the ford shortly after daylight, and it too crossed and advanced to Chancellorsville, where it arrived about 9:00 A.M. The rest of Second Corps was up by 3:00 P.M., and then the corps halted for the night. When Hancock's infantry arrived at Chancellorsville, Gregg's cavalry

division moved on south a mile or two to the Aldrich farm on the Orange Court House Plank Road (commonly called the Orange Plank Road, or simply the Plank Road).

By 6:00 A.M. May 4, 1864, Wilson's cavalry division was across the Rapidan at Germanna Ford and was moving toward the Lacy farm. It did not stop there, but continued on to Parker's Store, with pickets out to the front and on the flanks. Fifth Corps began crossing about 7:00 A.M., following the cavalry, and it marched to the southeast on the Germanna Plank Road toward Old Wilderness Tavern. When Charles Griffin's leading First Division reached the Orange Court House and Fredericksburg Turnpike (commonly called the Orange Turnpike, or simply the Turnpike) at the Tavern, it turned west on the Turnpike and then camped about a mile out in the direction of Locust Grove (Robertson's Tavern). Samuel W. Crawford's Third Division, which was following Griffin, took the Parker's Store Road, a mere lane that ran generally to the southwest along Wilderness Run to the Orange Plank Road at Parker's Store. Crawford halted for the night at the Lacy house, about one-half mile from the Turnpike. James S. Wadsworth's Fourth Division soon came up and camped opposite Crawford, on the east side of Wilderness Run. John C. Robinson's Second Division, the last of Warren's divisions to cross the Rapidan, was over by 1:00 P.M., and halted that night on the Germanna Plank Road.

Sixth Corps followed Fifth Corps across the river at Germanna Ford, and it bivouacked on the night of May 4, 1864 behind Robinson's division on the Germanna Plank Road. George W. Getty's Second Division was on Flat Run, Horatio G. Wright's First Division was a short distance to the north, and James B. Ricketts' Third Division was at Germanna Ford.

When Grant began his advance to the Rapidan, Ambrose E. Burnside's Ninth Corps was on the line of the Orange and Alexandria Railroad, with Thomas G. Stevenson's First Division and Elisha G. Marshall's Provisional Brigade at Brandy Station, and Robert B. Potter's Second Division and Orlando B. Willcox's Third Division at Bealeton. Edward Ferrero's Fourth Division had marched that morning from Manassas Junction, and by that evening it had arrived near Catlett's Station. At that time, Ninth Corps was not a part of the Army of the Potomac, but it was under Grant's direct orders, and was to remain so until May 27, 1864.

At 6:00 P.M. May 4, 1864, Grant issued orders for the army to resume its advance the next morning. Wilson's cavalry division was to move south from Parker's Store to Craig's Meeting House on the Catharpin Road; Sedgwick was to leave a division (Ricketts') at Germanna Ford to guard the crossing until Burnside arrived with Ninth Corps, and with the rest of Sixth Corps was to advance to Old Wilderness Tavern; Warren was to proceed with his Fifth Corps to Parker's Store on the Orange Plank Road and extend his right toward Sixth Corps; and Hancock's Second Corps was to march to Shady Grove Church, on the Catharpin Road, and extend his right toward Fifth Corps.

Gregg's cavalry division, which was at the Aldrich farm, was to remain in position there to cover the passage of the trains. Gregg was also to send out reconnaissances toward Spotsylvania Court House, Fredericksburg, and Hamilton's Crossing. Torbert's cavalry division, which was then approaching with the trains, was directed to cross the Rapidan and protect the right flank of the trains while they were crossing.

The activities of the various units of the Army of the Potomac on May 5, 1864, however, were to be strongly influenced by the enemy movements that were then in progress. When Grant began his advance to the Rapidan, Richard S. Ewell's Confederate Second Corps was in position south of the river, and to the west of Mine Run. Ambrose P. Hill's Third Corps was at Orange Court House, and James Longstreet's First Corps was at Gordonsville. The Federal movements on May 4, 1864 were observed from Lee's signal station on Clark's Mountain, and Lee sent Ewell's corps eastward on the Turnpike to Locust Grove, where it bivouacked for the night. He also ordered Hill's corps out on the Orange Plank Road, and it halted for the night at Mine Run, about seven miles from Wilson's position at Parker's Store. Both Confederate corps continued their advance on the morning of May 5, 1864, and they soon made contact with the Federal cavalry and Warren's Fifth Corps. Longstreet's Corps moved from Gordonsville at 4:00 P.M. May 4, 1864, and camped on the following night at Richards Shop on the Catharpin Road. It reached the battlefield near Parker's Store about dawn, May 6, 1864.

BATTLE OF THE WILDERNESS
MAY 5–6, 1864

Battle on the Turnpike, May 5, 1864. Early on the morning of May 5, 1864, the Army of the Potomac was again in motion. At daylight, Wilson left John Hammond with his 5th New York Cavalry at Parker's Store to wait until the infantry came up, and he then moved with the rest of his division to Craig's Meeting House. Charles H. Smith's 1st Maine Cavalry of J. Irvin Gregg's Second Brigade of Gregg's cavalry division started out on a reconnaissance from Piney Branch Church toward Fredericksburg and Hamilton's Crossing to verify a report that enemy cavalry were in the area. Torbert's cavalry division marched toward Chancellorsville, but it did not arrive there until midday.

At 5:00 A.M., the infantry corps began their advance. Warren's Fifth Corps started toward Parker's Store, with Crawford's division in the lead, Wadsworth's division following, and Robinson's division in the rear. Griffin's division was left behind to hold the Turnpike until Getty's division of Sixth Corps arrived from Flat Run. Getty's division began its march at 5:00 A.M. and moved on to Wilderness Tavern. Wright's division followed Getty on the Germanna Plank Road, but Ricketts' division was left at Germanna Ford. Stevenson's leading division of Burnside's Ninth Corps arrived at Germanna Ford during the morning and relieved Ricketts' division, which then moved to a position between the J. R. Spotswood house and Old Wilderness Tavern, on the Germanna Plank Road. Hancock's Second Corps left Chancellorsville at 5:00 A.M. and marched on the Furnace Road toward Shady Grove Church, and at 9:00 A.M. had reached a point about two miles beyond Todd's Tavern.

About 6:30 A.M., while the above-described movements were in progress, Joseph J. Bartlett, commanding Griffin's leading Third Brigade on the Turnpike, reported that enemy infantry were on his front. The troops that he had found were those at the head of Ewell's column, which were just arriving from Locust Grove. When Meade learned that the enemy was in force on the Turnpike, he sent out orders at 7:30 A.M. suspending the march of the army, pending further developments.

Warren's Fifth Corps, which, except Griffin's

division, was advancing on the Parker's Store Road, was ordered to take position as follows: Crawford's division was to halt at the Chewning farm; Wadsworth's division was to move to the right of the Parker's Store Road and form on the left of Griffin; and Robinson's division, which had then only reached the Lacy house, was ordered to halt there and remain in reserve.

Sedgwick's Sixth Corps halted to the right and rear of Warren, in essentially the same positions as those described above.

Hancock did not receive his orders to halt Second Corps until 9:00 A.M., and at that time his divisions were on the road as follows: John Gibbon's Second Division was about a mile out on the Catharpin Road beyond Todd's Tavern; David B. Birney's Third Division was near Todd's Tavern; Gershom Mott's Fourth Division was at the intersection of the Brock Road and the Furnace Road, near Wellford's (or Catharine's) Furnace (these names are commonly spelled Welford and Catherine); and Francis C. Barlow's First Division had not yet reached Wellford's Furnace.

Stevenson's division of Ninth Corps was at Germanna Ford, and the other divisions of the corps were approaching from north of the river.

While preparations were being made to meet the enemy on the Turnpike, a new threat was developing on the Orange Plank Road to the south. About daylight May 5, 1864, Hammond's 5th New York Cavalry of Wilson's cavalry division, which was then posted west of Parker's Store, was attacked by infantry of Henry Heth's division of Hill's corps and by 8:00 A.M. had been driven back along the Plank Road to Parker's Store. At about the same time, skirmishers sent out by Crawford from Chewnings' farm also became engaged with Heth's infantry.

When informed that enemy troops were on the Plank Road, Meade promptly made preparations to meet Hill's advance. Between 9:00 and 10:00 A.M., Thomas H. Neill's Third Brigade of Getty's Second Divison, Sixth Corps was detached from the division and sent to join Wright's division of Sixth Corps. Then Getty, with the remaining three brigades of his division, was ordered to march from Old Wilderness Tavern to the intersection of the Brock Road and the Orange Plank Road and take position in front of Hill's corps. Meade also sent an order to Hancock to march with his Second Corps

up the Brock Road from Todd's Tavern to the same crossroads, and upon arrival there to be prepared to advance with Getty's division toward Parker's Store. Hancock received this order at 11:40 A.M. and promptly started his march toward the Plank Road.

Back on the Turnpike, orders had been sent to Warren at 7:30 A.M. to attack the enemy on his front with his entire corps. Griffin's division was already on the Turnpike, but Wadsworth's division and William McCandless' First Brigade of Crawford's division experienced great difficulty in moving through the dense woods to their assigned positions, and it was nearly noon before Fifth Corps was ready to advance.

At 10:30 that morning, Wright was ordered to move up with his First Division, Sixth Corps and Neill's brigade of Getty's division to support Warren's attack. Wright was directed to advance on the Flat Run Road, which left the Germanna Plank Road at the Spotswood house and ran to the southwest about midway between Flat Run and Caton's Run, the latter of which flowed a short distance north of, and roughly parallel to, the Turnpike. The Flat Run Road joined the Turnpike about two and a half miles west of Old Wilderness Tavern. Thus, Wright's movement would bring his command in on the right of Griffin. Alexander Shaler's Fourth Brigade of Wright's division was left in the rear to guard the trains, and it did not rejoin the division until the next morning.

Before describing the Battle on the Turnpike, it will be helpful to note a feature of the area about which much of the hard fighting occurred that day. This was an old open field in the otherwise unbroken woods along the Turnpike, and it was known locally as Sanders' field (also Saunders' or Palmers' field). The Turnpike passed through this open space, which was a little less than three-fourths of a mile east of the intersection of the Turnpike with the Flat Run Road, and about one and three-fourths of a mile west of Old Wilderness Tavern.

Griffin's division and the right of Wadsworth's division had been deployed about three-fourths of a mile east of Sanders' field by about 11:30 A.M., and the men then threw up temporary breastworks along this line. Romeyn B. Ayres' First Brigade of Griffin's division was on the right, north of the Turnpike, and Joseph J. Bartlett's Third Brigade was on the left. Earlier that day, Jacob B. Sweitzer's Second Brigade had been on the left of Bartlett's brigade, but in the formation of the line of battle that morning, it was relieved by Lysander Cutler's First Brigade, which was the right brigade of Wadsworth's division. Sweitzer's brigade was then placed in reserve behind Bartlett. Roy Stone's Third Brigade of Wadsworth's division was on the left of Cutler, and on the center of Wadsworth's line, and James C. Rice's Second Brigade was on the left of Stone. Andrew W. Denison's Third Brigade of Robinson's division was sent to support Wadsworth, and it was placed in rear of the brigades of Rice and Stone. Samuel H. Leonard's First Brigade and Henry Baxter's Second Brigade of Robinson's division were held in reserve near the Lacy house.

Meantime, to the west, Ewell was also preparing for battle. Early that morning, his leading division, under Edward Johnson, had arrived on the Turnpike and had deployed in front of Griffin. John M. Jones' brigade was in the woods, along the west side of Sanders' field, and south of the Turnpike. As the other brigades of the division came up, they were formed on the left of Jones, north of the Turnpike, from the Confederate right to left as follows: George H. Steuart's, James A. Walker's (the Stonewall Brigade), and Leroy A. Stafford's. The left of Johnson's line extended northward almost to Flat Run.

Robert E. Rodes' division began to arrive a short time later, and the brigades of George Doles and Cullen A. Battle were placed to the right and rear of Jones' brigade. Junius Daniel's brigade was close behind, but Stephen D. Ramseur's brigade had been left behind on the Rapidan, and it did not rejoin the division until that night. Jubal A. Early's division was not far behind Rodes.

While Warren and Ewell were getting into position on the Turnpike, activity continued on the Plank Road to the south. Getty arrived with his Second Division, Sixth Corps at the intersection of the Brock Road and the Plank Road about 11:00 A.M., just as William W. Kirkland's brigade of Heth's division was pushing Hammond's cavalry back close to the Brock Road. Getty sent his skirmishers forward on the Plank Road, and when they met the advance of Hill's corps, about a half mile out, he deployed his division in line of battle along the Brock Road. He placed Frank Wheaton's First Brigade on the center of his line, across the Plank Road, facing west; Henry L. Eustis' Fourth Brigade on the right; and Lewis A. Grant's Second Brigade on the left. As noted above, Neill's Third Brigade had been detached, and was then serving with Wright's First Division, Sixth Corps on the Federal right. Getty felt that he was not strong enough to drive back the enemy on the Plank Road, and he proceeded to throw up breastworks and wait for Hancock's Second Corps to come up from Todd's Tavern.

Cadmus M. Wilcox's division of Hill's corps, which was following Heth on the Plank Road, was ordered to move north and attempt to form a junction with Ewell's corps. Wilcox left the brigades of Alfred M. Scales and Samuel McGowan to watch Crawford's division at Chewnings' farm, and with the brigades of James H. Lane and Edward L. Thomas, moved to the left through the woods toward Ewell's right flank.

About noon May 5, 1864, Warren had completed his deployment, and although Wright had not yet arrived on his right, he moved out of his temporary breastworks and advanced against Ewell's line. Bartlett's brigade arrived at the eastern edge of Sanders' field, some distance ahead of Ayres' brigade, which was advancing on its right, and immediately charged against Jones' brigade. Cutler's brigade, which was ahead and to the left of Bartlett, was then swinging around toward the Turnpike, and struck Jones' brigade and the left of Doles' brigade and broke through their line. In this attack, Battle's brigade, which was directly behind Jones, was so severely handled by Cutler and Bartlett that it fell back with Jones' broken brigade for a mile or more. Doles' right, however, held fast, and Daniel's brigade, moving up on Doles' left, met Stone's and Rice's brigades and soon checked the Federal advance.

Early then sent Gordon, who was arriving from Locust Grove, well to the south of the Turnpike, where he formed his brigade and charged Cutler's and Bartlett's lines, which by that time had become somewhat disordered by their attacks. Doles and Battle rallied their troops and advanced with Gordon. Jones was killed while attempting to rally his troops. Rice, Stone, and Denison were vigorously contesting Daniel's advance when they were struck by Gordon, Doles, and Battle and driven back. At about this time, Leonard's and Baxter's brigades of Robinson's division were sent out on the Turnpike to support Griffin. Bartlett's brigade was driven back in disorder to the eastern side of the old field, and then it was relieved by the brigades of Sweitzer and Leonard. Bartlett then retired to the line that he had occupied that morning. Cutler's brigade was almost surrounded and was forced to fight its way back. Sweitzer, with help from Leonard and Baxter, finally checked the enemy advance.

Meantime, Ayres' brigade, advancing on the right of the Turnpike, deployed just before it reached Sanders' field, and it then moved forward just as Bartlett and Cutler were pursuing Jones' brigade. Steuart's brigade, which had held its position in the woods west of the field during the attack, then opened fire on Ayres' brigade, and at the same time Walker and Stafford, on Steuart's left, also opened with a deadly fire.

When Griffin's line advanced, a section of George B. Winslow's Battery D, 1st New York Light Artillery, commanded by William H. Shelton and accompanied by Winslow in person, also moved out with the infantry and took position on the far side of Sanders' field. At about that time, Ayres' brigade gave way and fell back to the east side of the field. Winslow was wounded, Shelton was wounded and captured, and the guns were lost to the enemy.

When Warren's attack began, McCandless' brigade of Crawford's division was under orders to join on the left of Wadsworth's division. McCandless moved due west as directed, guided by the open fields of the Chewning farm on his left. As Wadsworth advanced, however, he swung around to his right toward the Turnpike and thus moved away from McCandless. McCandless, therefore, moved on alone and quite by accident ran into the brigades of Lane and Thomas that had come up from the Plank Road. His brigade was almost completely enveloped, but he escaped, although almost all of the 7th Pennsylvania Reserve Regiment was captured, probably by a separated regiment of Gordon's brigade.

The fighting on the Turnpike ended about 1:30 P.M., when Griffin's division retired to the breastworks that it had occupied that morning. Wadsworth's division also retired and re-formed near the Lacy house along the Parker's Store Road.

When Wadsworth withdrew, Crawford's division was left in an isolated position at the Chewning farm, and at about 2:00 P.M. it was pulled back to a position on the left of Wadsworth, about a mile southwest of the Lacy house, facing southwest toward the Chewning farm. Apparently, Joseph W. Fisher's Third Brigade of Crawford's division remained on the high ground at Chewnings' until 2:00 P.M.

The failure of Warren's attack was no doubt due, at least in part, to the failure of troops of Sedgwick's Sixth Corps to come in on the right of Fifth Corps. While Griffin was engaged on the Turnpike, Wright's command was struggling forward through one of the worst parts of the Wilderness, and it did not arrive on the right of Warren until sometime after the fighting had ended, probably between 2:00 and 3:00 P.M., or even later. Wright then deployed his division in line of battle, with Emory Upton's Second Brigade on the Turnpike, next to Griffin; Henry W. Brown's First Brigade (also called William H. Penrose's brigade) on the center of the line; and David A. Russell's Third Brigade on the right. Neill's brigade of Getty's division, which was then attached to Wright's division, was placed on the right of Russell. Shortly after Wright's arrival, the brigades of Walker and Stafford of Johnson's division advanced against the lines of Russell and Neill, but they were driven back, with the loss of Stafford, who was mortally wounded.

When Warren broke off the attack on the afternoon of May 5, 1864, Ewell extended his line to the north to check Wright's advance. He moved Harry T. Hays' brigade of Early's division to the left of Johnson's line, and later he sent John Pegram's brigade of the same division to the left of Hays. After dark that night, Gordon's brigade, also of Early's division, moved to the left of Ewell's line near Flat Run.

Shortly after Johnson's attack on Russell and Neill, Truman Seymour's Second Brigade of Ricketts' division arrived and took position on the right of Neill. William H. Morris' First Brigade of Ricketts' division moved to the rear of the junction of Fifth Corps and Sixth Corps, where it could support either corps.

About 5:00 P.M., Wright launched an attack with the brigades of Neill and Seymour and a part of Brown's (Penrose's) brigade on the line held by

Pegram and Hays. Neill was unable to make any progress and soon withdrew, but Seymour continued fighting until dark. Pegram was wounded in this attack.

The nature of the ground over which Warren attacked precluded effective use of the corps artillery, and as a result, the battle was fought essentially by the infantry alone. As noted above, one section of Winslow's Battery D, 1st New York Light Artillery was in action on the Turnpike for a time, but it was soon captured. The two remaining sections of Battery D, under the command of Lester I. Richardson, were to the rear on the Turnpike, but they were withdrawn to a position on the right of the road. Four batteries of Charles S. Wainwright's Artillery Brigade of Fifth Corps were placed on the crest of the high ground to the right of the Lacy house, where they commanded the valley below and the road to Parker's Store. These were, in order from left to right, Charles A. Phillips' Battery E, Massachusetts Light Artillery; Benjamin F. Rittenhouse's Battery D, 5th United States Artillery; Charles E. Mink's Battery H, 1st New York Light Artillery; and James H. Cooper's Battery B, 1st Pennsylvania Light Artillery. George Breck's Battery L, 1st New York Light Artillery and James Stewart's Battery B, 1st Pennsylvania Light Artillery followed Wadsworth's division when it advanced toward Parker's Store that morning, but about noon they moved back to the Lacy house. Augustus P. Martin's Battery C, Massachusetts Light Artillery was not brought up in line until the next day.

On May 5, 1864, the batteries of Charles H. Tompkins' Artillery Brigade of Sixth Corps were massed in the rear near the intersection of the Germanna Plank Road and the Turnpike. The batteries were as follows: Melville C. Kimball's 4th Battery (D), Maine Light Artillery; William H. McCartney's 1st Battery (A), Massachusetts Light Artillery; Andrew Cowan's 1st Battery, New York Light Artillery; William A. Harn's 3rd Battery, New York Light Artillery; Thomas D. Sears' 1st Battalion, 4th New York Heavy Artillery; Richard Waterman's Battery C, 1st Rhode Island Light Artillery; William B. Rhodes' Battery E, 1st Rhode Island Light Artillery; George W. Adams' Battery G, 1st Rhode Island Light Artillery; and James McKnight's Battery M, 5th United States Artillery.

Battle on the Plank Road, Afternoon of May 5, 1864. As Warren's Battle on the Turnpike was ending, preparations continued for an attack on Hill's corps on the Plank Road to the south. As noted above, Getty's division was already in position along the Brock Road awaiting the arrival of Second Corps. Hancock received Meade's order to support Getty about 11:00 A.M. May 5, 1864, and after starting his troops up the Brock Road from Todd's Tavern, he had gone on ahead and, in person, joined Getty at 1:00 P.M. As soon as Hancock arrived, he was ordered to attack with his Second Corps and Getty's division, and the latter was placed under Hancock's command.

About 2:00 P.M., David B. Birney's Third Division, Second Corps arrived near the junction of the Plank Road and the Brock Road, and deployed along the Brock Road on the left of Getty. Getty then withdrew Eustis' brigade from his line and placed it in reserve. He then moved Wheaton's brigade to the north side of the Plank Road and shifted Grant's brigade to the right until its right rested on the Plank Road on the left of Wheaton. The brigades of both Grant and Wheaton, except their skirmishers, were behind breastworks.

Gershom Mott's Fourth Division, John Gibbon's Second Division, and Francis C. Barlow's First Division, in that order, then came up and formed on the left of Birney. Barlow's division, less Paul Frank's Third Brigade, was posted on the extreme left of Hancock's line on some high, open ground west of the Brock Road. Frank's brigade was placed at the intersection of the Brock Road and the Furnace Road, which ran to the northeast toward Chancellorsville. The left of Barlow's line curved back to the east across the Brock Road near the J. Trigg and W. Stephens (Stevens) houses, about two and a fourth miles south of the junction of the Brock and Plank roads. Hancock then protected his line by throwing up breastworks.

Except for three batteries, John C. Tidball's Artillery Brigade of Second Corps was placed in line on the crest of the high, open ground on the left, where it was supported by Barlow's division. The batteries were in position from left to right as follows: J. Henry Sleeper's 10th Battery, Massachusetts Light Artillery; Nelson Ames' Battery G, 1st New York Light Artillery; William A. Arnold's Battery A, 1st Rhode Island Light Artillery; T.

Frederick Brown's Battery B, 1st Rhode Island Light Artillery; John W. Roder's Battery K, 4th United States Artillery; and James Gilliss' Batteries C and I, 5th United States Artillery. For a time Thomas Allcock's 3rd Battalion, 4th New York Heavy Artillery supported Ames' battery.

The other three batteries of the brigade were placed farther north on Hancock's line. At 2:00 P.M., Edwin B. Dow's 6th Battery (F), Maine Light Artillery and Frederick M. Edgell's 1st Battery, New Hampshire Light Artillery were placed in rear of Mott's division, but because of the dense woods they played little part in the battle that afternoon. R. Bruce Ricketts' Battery F, 1st Pennsylvania Light Artillery reported to Getty, and two sections of the battery were later engaged on the Plank Road.

At 3:30 P.M., Meade sent a peremptory order for an advance on the Plank Road. Getty's division was to make the attack, and Hancock was to support it with his entire corps, one division on the right of Getty, one on the left, and the other two in reserve. Hancock was, however, given some discretion in the placing of his troops. Accordingly, Birney was directed to send Alexander Hays' Second Brigade to the right of Getty, and Birney, commanding his own division and Mott's, was to support Getty on the left. Getty's orders were to attack without waiting for Hancock, and he began his advance before Hays' brigade reached its assigned position.

Meantime, Hill was getting Heth's division in position to attack the Federal line on its front, and it was nearly ready when Getty advanced. As Heth's division approached the Brock Road that morning, William W. Kirkland's brigade was in the lead, and next, in order, were the brigades of John R. Cooke, Henry H. Walker, and Joseph R. Davis. Cooke's brigade was on the left of the Plank Road, Walker's brigade was on the right of the road, Davis' brigade was on the left of Cooke, and Kirkland's brigade was held in reserve.

Getty moved out at about 4:15 P.M. and, after advancing about a half mile, arrived at Heth's line and immediately attacked. Wheaton's First Brigade, on the north side of the Plank Road, came up against all of Davis' brigade and the left of Cooke's brigade. Advancing south of the road, Grant's Second Brigade struck the right of Cooke's brigade and all of Walker's brigade. Hays' brigade of Birney's division finally arrived on the right of Wheaton and

attacked on the left of Davis' line. Soon there was heavy fighting all along the line. Hays was killed and was succeeded in command of Second Brigade, Third Division, Second Corps by John S. Crocker. Birney then led J. H. Hobart Ward's First Brigade of his division to the left of Getty, and Hancock ordered Mott to move forward with his two brigades and attack on the left of Ward. Robert McAllister's First Brigade was on the right of Mott's line, next to Ward, and William R. Brewster's Second Brigade (the Excelsior Brigade) was on the left. Shortly after coming under fire, Brewster's brigade gave way and retreated to the line of breastworks on the Brock Road, and McAllister's brigade followed.

As the heavy fighting continued, Federal reinforcements were hurried forward. At 4:30 P.M., Samuel S. Carroll's Third Brigade of Gibbon's Second Division was sent to support Getty on the right of the Plank Road, and about ten minutes later, Joshua T. Owen's Second Brigade of Gibbon's division was put in on both sides of the Plank Road. Gibbon was thus left with only Alexander S. Webb's First Brigade of his division, and he was assigned command of his own and Barlow's First Division.

When Mott's division moved forward, Thomas A. Smyth's Second Brigade of Barlow's First Division, Second Corps was sent to occupy a part of the position vacated by Mott, and Nelson A. Miles' First Brigade of the same division moved to the left of Smyth. Webb's brigade also helped to cover Mott's vacant line. Barlow's other two brigades were engaged late that evening. John R. Brooke's Fourth Brigade, which had brought up the rear of Hancock's column, reached the Brock Road about 5:30 P.M. and was sent to support Smyth and Miles. Paul Frank's Third Brigade was also moved up to the front.

As soon as Heth became engaged with Getty, Lee ordered Wilcox to return at once to the Plank Road with his division. Lee also personally directed Scales and McGowan, who had been watching Crawford's division near Chewnings' farm until it withdrew, to go directly to Heth's support. Wilcox, with the brigades of Lane and Thomas, quickly rejoined Hill. Thomas was then directed to advance on the left of the Plank Road, and Lane was ordered to form on the left of Thomas. When Lane arrived on the Plank Road, however, Scales' brigade, which had been on the right of Heth's line, had just collapsed, and Lane was sent to take its place on the line. Between 5:30 and 6:00 P.M., Kirkland and McGowan relieved Heth's brigades in front of Getty. The fighting continued with great severity, without decided advantage to either side, until 8:00 P.M., and then the firing ceased.

The return of Wilcox to the Plank Road was observed from Crawford's line as the brigades of Lane and Thomas crossed the Chewning farm, and Warren ordered Wadsworth with his Fourth Division and Robinson with Baxter's brigade of his Second Division to move toward Wilcox's column. It was nearly 6:00 P.M. when Wadsworth started. His progress was slow because of the dense woods, and he was finally forced to halt because of darkness. Robinson returned to his own division that night, but he left Baxter's brigade with Fourth Division. Wadsworth remained in line of battle between the Brock Road and the Widow Tapp's field and about a half mile north of the Plank Road, facing south.

Cavalry Action of May 5, 1864. Although overshadowed by the infantry battles of May 5, 1864, Sheridan's cavalry was also active during the day. After leaving Hammond's cavalry regiment at Parker's Store, Wilson marched south that morning to the Catharpin Road with his cavalry division. Upon arrival there, he placed Timothy M. Bryan's First Brigade at the intersection of the Parker's Store Road and the Catharpin Road and sent George H. Chapman's Second Brigade to Craig's Meeting House. Chapman was attacked there during the day by Thomas L. Rosser's cavalry brigade and Wade Hampton's division of James E. B. (Jeb) Stuart's cavalry, and was driven back on Bryan's brigade. Wilson then withdrew to Todd's Tavern, where he was joined by Gregg's cavalry division, which Sheridan had sent to his support. Together, Wilson and Gregg drove the enemy back to Corbin's Bridge.

Torbert's First Cavalry Division was delayed on the road by the army trains and did not reach Chancellorsville until midday. Torbert then remained there to guard the trains, and also to be in position to support Gregg.

Battle of May 6, 1864. After the fighting had ended on the evening of May 5, 1864, Grant and Meade began preparations for a renewal of the battle the next morning. Meade issued orders for his three corps to attack at 5:00 A.M. May 6, 1864, and Grant directed Burnside to have his Ninth Corps in position to cooperate at the same time. While the rest of the army was engaged May 5, 1864, three divisions of Ninth Corps had arrived near the battlefield, and Edward Ferrero's Fourth Division was not far behind. Thomas G. Stevenson's First Division crossed at Germanna Ford that morning and went into camp. Orlando B. Willcox's Third Division crossed about noon, and then moved out about two miles and relieved James B. Ricketts' Third Division of Sixth Corps, which was on the right of Sedgwick's line. Robert B. Potter's Second Division crossed at 3:00 P.M. and bivouacked at Spotswoods'. Elisha G. Marshall's Provisional Brigade of Ninth Corps crossed the river during the afternoon and took position between Stevenson and Potter.

Burnside's instructions were to march at 2:00 A.M. May 6, 1864, so as to be in position between Hancock and Warren at 5:00 A.M., and then to advance with the rest of the army. Warren and Sedgwick were to attack along, and to the north of, the Turnpike, and Hancock was to continue his attack along the Plank Road. Burnside, with the divisions of Potter and Willcox, was to advance across Wilderness Run toward Chewnings' farm, and Stevenson's division was to halt at Old Wilderness Tavern and remain there in reserve.

During the night of May 5–6, 1864, the brigades of Sixth Corps that were facing Ewell's corps north of the Turnpike were refitted in position. These were, in order from left to right, the brigades of Upton, Brown, Russell, Neill, and Seymour. Morris' brigade of Ricketts' division was shifted from its position in reserve to Fifth Corps to one in close support of Upton, near the Turnpike. Early on the morning of May 6, 1864, Alexander Shaler's Fourth Brigade of Wright's division of Sixth Corps, which had been guarding the trains, came up and was placed in reserve in rear of the center of Sixth Corps' line. That afternoon, Shaler's brigade and part of Upton's brigade were moved to the right and rear of Seymour's brigade, on the extreme right of the line.

Shortly after midnight, Griffin's division of Fifth Corps moved forward from its breastworks to the eastern edge of Sanders' field, and at 2:30 A.M. deployed in line of battle across the Turnpike. Joseph J. Bartlett's Third Brigade was on the right of the road, connecting with Sixth Corps, and Jacob B. Sweitzer's Second Brigade was on the left. Romeyn B. Ayres' First Brigade was placed in rear of Sweitzer's line. About daylight, Griffin was reinforced by about a thousand men of Ira Spaulding's 50th New York Engineers of the pontoon train. These troops were assigned to a position in the rifle pits.

Also about daylight, J. Howard Kitching's First Brigade of Henry S. Burton's Artillery Reserve arrived at the front and reported to Warren at the Lacy house. Kitching's brigade, which had been trained as infantry, consisted of his own 6th New York Heavy Artillery and Louis Schirmer's 15th New York Heavy Artillery. It formed the escort and furnished the guards for the Artillery Reserve, and was available as a reserve and as a reinforcement to the infantry corps in battle. Kitching's brigade was formed in reserve near the Lacy house, and it was joined there by Denison's brigade and Leonard's brigade of Robinson's division as a reserve for Fifth Corps. That day, Peter Lyle relieved Leonard in command of First Brigade, Second Division, Fifth Corps. While the Fifth Corps reserve was forming, Crawford's division moved to the right and took position on the left of Griffin's division. At 5:00 A.M., Burnside's divisions had not arrived at their assigned positions for the attack, and Warren sent Kitching's brigade to reinforce Wadsworth's division near the Plank Road.

Preparations were also progressing on the southern flank of the army. Hancock, who was in command of all Federal troops on that part of the field, had, in effect, created two wings by placing Birney in charge of all troops on the right of his line and Gibbon of those on the left. Birney's command consisted of his own division and Mott's division of Second Corps, Getty's division of Sixth Corps, and the brigades of Owen and Carroll of Gibbon's division of Second Corps. Gibbon's command consisted of Webb's brigade of his own division (for a short time only), Barlow's division of Second Corps, and all the corps artillery that was in position on the left.

In preparation for the attack that morning, Birney formed his troops in three lines on and near the Plank Road as follows: In the first line, Hays' brigade of Birney's division (then commanded by John S. Crocker) was on the right of the Plank Road, and

Ward's brigade of the same division was on the left of the road. McAllister's brigade of Mott's division was on the left of Ward. Getty's division was on the second line, with Wheaton's brigade astride the Plank Road, Grant's brigade on the left, and Eustis' brigade on the right. Brewster's brigade of Mott's division was also on the second line, on the left of Grant's brigade, supporting McAllister. On the third line were the brigades of Carroll and Owen, both of Gibbon's division. Carroll's brigade was on the right of the Plank Road, and Owen's brigade was on the left.

Barlow's division and most of the corps artillery (sixty-nine guns) were in position to cover the left of Hancock's position. That was the critical part of Hancock's line that day because Longstreet's corps was known to be approaching the battlefield, and it was expected to arrive on the Brock Road, or on a country road running northeast from the Catharpin Road, past Whitehall Mill and the Trigg farm, to the Brock Road. Barlow's division and the corps artillery were posted to cover these two roads. The probable positions of Barlow's brigades were, from left to right, as follows: Miles' brigade, Smyth's brigade, and Frank's brigade. Brooke's brigade was in reserve near the Cook house, at the center of Barlow's line.

Webb's brigade of Gibbon's division remained between Hancock's two wings as a general reserve. Sheridan's cavalry covered the left flank of the army and also guarded the trains at Dowdall's Tavern.

When Wadsworth's division of Fifth Corps advanced toward the Plank Road on the evening of May 5, 1864, Baxter's brigade of Robinson's division was on the right, and Stone's brigade of Wadsworth's division was on the left. Cutler's brigade of Wadsworth's division was behind Baxter, and Rice's brigade of the same division was behind Cutler. During the skirmishing that evening, Stone's brigade panicked and fled, and it was replaced by Cutler's brigade. Also, during the night Rice's brigade moved up on the right of Baxter, with its right extending toward the Widow Tapp's house. Stone's brigade was eventually halted and reformed, and was then placed in rear of the front line. Stone was disabled by the fall of his horse when his brigade broke that evening, and Edward S. Bragg was assigned command of his brigade. On the morning of May 6, 1864, Kitching's brigade of heavy artillery arrived from the Lacy house and formed on the right of Wadsworth's line in front of the Tapp field.

The first fighting of the day began a short time before 5:00 A.M., when the enemy skirmishers began firing along the fronts of both ends of the the Union line. Then promptly at 5:00 A.M., Second Corps, Fifth Corps, and Sixth Corps began their assaults. Burnside's leading division of Ninth Corps, however, did not arrive at the Lacy farm until 6:30 that morning.

On the right, along the Turnpike, the fighting did not develop into a full-scale battle, but consisted of a series of attacks by Warren and Sedgwick, all of which were repulsed. At 10:45 A.M., the commanders of Fifth Corps and Sixth Corps were instructed to suspend their attacks and throw up defensive works so that troops could be sent to aid Hancock if necessary. Skirmishers and sharpshooters, and also artillery continued to fire during most of the day.

There was, however, very heavy fighting to the south along the Plank Road. At 5:00 A.M., Birney and Wadsworth advanced toward Hill's line. It is impossible to give with certainty the positions held by the brigades of Heth and Wilcox on the morning of May 6, 1864, but as nearly as can be determined they were as follows: The brigades of Thomas, Scales, and McGowan of Wilcox's division and Davis' brigade of Heth's division (then commanded by John Marshall Stone) were on a forward line, in that order from the Confederate right to left, with Thomas and Scales south of the road and McGowan and Stone north of the road. Lane's brigade of Wilcox's division was on the Plank Road in rear of the first line, and Walker's and Kirkland's brigades of Heth's division were north of the road in rear of McGowan and Stone. These three brigades appear to have formed a second line. Cooke's brigade of Heth's division was in the rear, north of the road, and, it is interesting to note, was the only Confederate brigade to entrench its position.

On Hancock's front, McAllister, Ward, and Crocker (the latter commanding Hays' brigade) advanced toward Hill's front line, and they were followed by the brigades of Eustis, Wheaton, and Grant of Getty's division, and Brewster's brigade of Mott's division. Carroll's brigade moved up on the north side of the Plank Road, and Owen's brigade

on the south side in support of the first and second lines.

Wadsworth's division of Fifth Corps and Baxter's brigade of Robinson's division of Fifth Corps moved south from their positions of the night before, and wheeling to the right, they came in on the right of Birney's command.

As Birney's first line advanced that morning, Ward's brigade moved along the south side of the Plank Road and struck and routed Scales' brigade. Birney quickly pushed on into the gap thus created in Hill's line and drove back in disorder all of his remaining brigades except Cooke's. Cooke, with support from parts of Davis' and Kirkland's brigades, continued to resist for a time, but finally he too was forced to withdraw.

When Wadsworth advanced to join in Hancock's attack, his line moved too far south, and the brigades of Cutler and Baxter crossed to the south side of the Plank Road. This seriously interfered with Birney's assault columns by forcing many of his troops to the south side of the road, and also by blocking the advance of Getty's division, which also crossed to the south side of the road. Wadsworth finally withdrew the brigades of Cutler and Baxter to the north of the road, where he re-formed his command. He then pushed on in a column of brigades, with Cutler in the lead and Stone, Baxter, and Rice following, probably in that order.

The withdrawal of Wadsworth's two brigades from the south of the Plank Road left a gap on the right of Getty, who then shifted his division to the right and sent the brigades of Eustis and Wheaton back to the north of the road. Getty then advanced, and these two brigades became engaged with Cooke's brigade, which held for a time but finally withdrew to the Widow Tapp's.

By about 6:00 A.M., one hour after the fighting began, Wadsworth's advance was within a few hundred yards of the Tapp field, and the brigades of McAllister, Crocker, and Ward, south of the Plank Road, were within about the same distance of a prolongation of the line on the east side of the field.

Fortunately for the almost broken divisions of Heth and Wilcox, help was near at hand. James Longstreet's corps had bivouacked at Richards Shop on the Catharpin Road the previous evening, and starting at 12:30 A.M. May 6, 1864, it arrived at Parker's Store at daylight that morning. It then turned east and advanced in double column on the Plank Road toward the rear of Hill's line. Joseph B. Kershaw's division (Lafayette McLaws' division) was in the lead and was marching on the right of the road, and Charles W. Field's division was close behind, on the left of the road. The head of Kershaw's column arrived near the Widow Tapp house about sunrise. Richard H. Anderson's division of Hill's corps, which had spent the night at Verdiersville, was also approaching in rear of Longstreet's column, and it arrived on the field about 8:00 A.M. Anderson was then ordered to report to Longstreet.

Longstreet arrived at a very critical time, when the divisions of Heth and Wilcox were near collapse. He was in the process of deploying his troops when the remnants of Hill's brigades that were still fighting finally gave way and fled in confusion through his lines to the rear. Hill's disorganized troops were then re-formed under Longstreet, and when Anderson's division arrived on the field they were placed on the left of Anderson, with their line extending toward the right of Ewell's corps. Early that morning, Ewell had sent Stephen D. Ramseur's brigade of Rodes' division to the extreme right of the corps in the vicinity of Chewnings' farm. Joseph R. Davis' brigade of Heth's division (then commanded by Stone) did not accompany the rest of Hill's corps to the north of the Plank Road, but remained on the south side and fought with Kershaw during the day.

Kershaw formed his division on the Confederate right of the Plank Road, with Benjamin G. Humphreys' brigade on the left, next to the road; Kershaw's own brigade, commanded by John W. Henegan, on the right of Humphreys; and Goode Bryan's brigade on the right of Henegan, and on the right of Kershaw's line. At that time, William T. Wofford's brigade had not yet arrived. As soon as Kershaw had completed his line, he moved forward and attacked. The Federal troops on the south side of the Plank Road had, at that time, advanced with severe fighting for a mile or more through thick woods, and they had become separated and somewhat disorganized. Thus, when at about 6:20 A.M. they encountered Kershaw's fresh brigades, they were forced to halt. For some time there was a heavy exchange of fire between the two lines, but neither was able to advance. Finally, however, Kershaw's

division began to move forward, but it did so against stubborn resistance by the brigades of McAllister of Mott's division; Crocker and Ward of Birney's division; and Grant of Getty's division. In addition, Owen's brigade of Gibbon's division and Brewster's brigade of Mott's division also came up in support south of the Plank Road.

Field's division came up a short time after Kershaw, with George T. Anderson's brigade heading the column. Field was ordered to deploy on the south of the Plank Road, and he put Anderson's brigade in position there. Then, however, Field was ordered to attack the Federal right, and he moved his other brigades to the north side of the road and prepared to advance. John Gregg's brigade, which had followed Anderson's brigade to the field, was placed in line of battle just in rear of William T. Poague's Artillery Battalion of Hill's corps, which were in position along the western edge of the Tapp field. When Henry L. Benning's brigade came up it was formed in rear of Gregg, and a short time later Evander McIver Law's brigade, commanded by William F. Perry, arrived and was placed behind Benning. Micah Jenkins' brigade of the division was held in reserve. When all was ready, Field's division advanced in a column of brigades.

Gregg's brigade attacked along and across the Plank Road and struck the brigades of Eustis and Wheaton of Getty's division and Carroll's brigade of Gibbon's division as they emerged from the woods just east of the Tapp field. Gregg slowed the Federal advance, but was driven back with terrible loss. Benning's brigade, which was following Gregg, dealt the Federal line a heavy blow, but it was in turn driven back with heavy loss, including Benning, who was wounded. Dudley M. Du Bose assumed command of Benning's brigade. Perry attacked farther to the left than Gregg and Benning and struck the front and right of Cutler's brigade of Wadsworth's division. Kitching's brigade of heavy artillery, which had come up on the right of Cutler's brigade that morning, attempted to halt Perry's advance by a flank fire on his left, but Kitching was quickly driven back out of the fight by Perry's left regiment (the 15th Alabama), commanded by William C. Oates.

Oates then proceeded on and attacked Wadsworth's exposed right flank while the rest of the brigade attacked along his front. Under these combined blows, Wadsworth's line was broken and driven back in disorder. That happened sometime between 7:40 and 8:30 A.M. About half of Wadsworth's division, under Cutler, was forced to retire along the Parker's Store Road to the open ground around the Lacy house; and the rest of the division, under Wadsworth and Rice, fell back to the last line from which the enemy had been driven earlier that day. Stragglers from Baxter's brigade fell back toward the Brock Road, where about 600 men were collected by Richard Coulter and members of Hancock's staff. Baxter was wounded in the attack, and Coulter assumed command of the brigade. After the brigade was refitted and supplied with ammunition, it was sent to the left to report to Gibbon.

Meantime, while fighting was going on all along the front, especially on the Plank Road, Burnside's Ninth Corps had finally moved forward. It was to have joined in the general advance at 5:00 A.M., but it was late, and it was nearly 6:30 A.M. when Potter's leading division arrived at the Lacy house to begin its attack. Then, Potter's division, followed by Willcox's division, crossed the Lacy field and the main stream of Wilderness Run and moved into the woods beyond. Stevenson's division of Ninth Corps was left at Old Wilderness Tavern as a reserve.

Potter and Willcox moved on toward the high ground of the Chewning farm on a woods road to the right of the West Branch of Wilderness Run. Near the Jones farm, just north of Chewnings', Potter encountered enemy skirmishers and pushed them back, and then formed his division in line of battle. Simon G. Griffin's Second Brigade, which was leading the division, was placed across the road, and Zenas R. Bliss' First Brigade took position on the left of Griffin. John F. Hartranft's First Brigade, the leading brigade of Willcox's division, then came up on the left of Bliss. Benjamin C. Christ's Second Brigade of Willcox's division was held in reserve on the road. Potter was preparing to attack, but sometime after 8:00 A.M., because of affairs on the Plank Road, he was ordered to move to the left and support Hancock.

During Longstreet's attack, which began about 6:20 A.M. and then slackened about 8:40 A.M., Hancock had been making every effort to strengthen his assaulting column and to reorganize his command for a renewal of the attack. At 6:30 he ordered

Webb's brigade, which had been in reserve, to report to Birney. Webb advanced about 7:00 A.M. on the north side of the Plank Road, and he was directed by Birney to join Getty, whose division had suffered severely while holding the ground between Birney's division and Wadsworth's division. Getty was wounded during Longstreet's attack, and Frank Wheaton assumed temporary command of his three brigades. Thomas H. Neill, as senior officer, assumed command of Getty's Second Division when it was reunited on the Union right early on May 7, 1864.

At 7:00 A.M., Hancock ordered Gibbon to advance with Barlow's division and attack the right of Longstreet's line. Gibbon, however, perhaps because of concern about an enemy advance from the direction of the Trigg farm, sent only Frank's brigade. Frank advanced, against some resistance, and at about 10:30 connected with the left of McAllister's brigade of Mott's division, which at that time held the left of Birney's line.

At 8:00 A.M. Stevenson's First Division, Ninth Corps, which had been ordered up from Old Wilderness Tavern, arrived at the junction of the Brock Road and the Plank Road to reinforce Hancock. Stevenson, with Sumner Carruth's First Brigade, was sent forward to support Birney. Later, Carruth suffered from sunstroke and was relieved by J. Parker Gould. Daniel Leasure's Second Brigade was put in reserve, replacing Webb's brigade, which had moved to the front about an hour earlier.

As Webb's brigade went forward that morning, Webb was instructed to connect with Getty's division, which was in position along a line of abandoned earthworks, probably thrown up by Cooke's brigade of Hill's corps earlier in the day. It appears that Hancock intended to form the three brigades of Gibbon's division in line across the ground held by Getty, in order from left to right as follows: Owen, Carroll, and Webb. Owen and Carroll, however, had veered to the left during the advance and had passed the left of Getty's division, and when they arrived at the front they relieved the brigades of Crocker and Ward of Birney's division. Most of the men of the latter two brigades remained in close support of the front line. When Webb arrived at the front, he did not find Getty's division. Perhaps, in advancing, he passed between Grant's brigade and Wheaton's brigade without seeing them, but whatever the reason, when his brigade arrived at the front it was alone, with Wadsworth's division some distance to its right. Sometime after 8:00 A.M., Wadsworth's division of Fifth Corps was formally placed under Hancock's orders.

Carruth's brigade was probably intended to reinforce Wadsworth, but when it came up about 9:30 A.M., Webb formed a new line that included Carruth's regiments. When preparing to advance, Webb learned that Stevenson, to whose division Carruth's brigade belonged, was his senior in rank, and this created a difficulty. This was resolved when Wadsworth assumed command of both Webb's and Carruth's brigades and ordered them to attack the line held by Perry.

Mott's division, which had not been heavily engaged, was left to hold the extreme left of the line, but as noted above, Frank's brigade of Barlow's division came up about 10:30 A.M. and joined on the left of McAllister's brigade.

A little before 9:00 A.M., Hancock launched his second attack of the day with the following troops: the divisions of Wadsworth, Birney, and Mott; the brigades of Owen, Carroll, and Webb of Gibbon's division; and Carruth's brigade of Stevenson's division. There was heavy fighting for about an hour without significant result, and then the firing died away.

About 9:00 A.M., as Hancock was beginning his attack, there were indications that enemy troops were advancing on the Brock Road toward Barlow's position. This proved to be a false alarm, but at 9:10 A.M., Birney, at Hancock's direction, detached Eustis' brigade from Getty's division and ordered it to report to Gibbon to help secure the left flank. A half hour later, Hancock also sent Leasure's brigade of Stevenson's division from its position in reserve to report to Gibbon. A little later Coulter, with the remnants of Baxter's brigade, was also sent to Gibbon. Eustis' brigade remained with Gibbon for only a short time and then returned to its former position.

Meantime, Barlow had sent Brooke's brigade to reinforce Miles' brigade on the extreme left of his line, and it then was sent out on the Brock Road to find out what was happening there. At 10:00 A.M. Richard Coulter arrived on the left with Second Brigade, Second Division, Fifth Corps (formerly Baxter's) and reported to Brooke. Scouts sent out by Brooke found no enemy troops on the Brock Road,

and Brooke's brigade returned to its former position, where it arrived around noon.

Back on the Plank Road, when Longstreet was unable to make any progress against the front of Hancock's line, he decided to move against Birney's left flank. During the morning of May 6, 1864, Martin L. Smith, the chief engineer of Lee's army, joined Longstreet on the Plank Road, and while the Confederate attack was still in progress, Smith and a group of officers were sent out to make a more thorough examination of the Federal position. Smith returned about 10:00 A.M. and reported that Birney's line extended only a short distance south of the Plank Road, and that it was possible to turn the left flank of this line. Smith's party had found a practicable route for an attacking party along the bed of an unfinished railroad that was to run from Fredericksburg to Orange Court House.

Apparently, the route of this railroad was not shown on the maps of that time, but it ran eastward from a point a few hundred yards south of Parker's Store on a line that was nearly parallel to the Plank Road for a distance of about a mile, and then the Plank Road angled away to the northeast. The railroad grade, however, continued on a straight line until at a point opposite the Widow Tapp farm it was about three-fourths of a mile south of the Plank Road. About two and a half miles east of Parker's Store, and about a mile from the Brock Road, the grade made a wide curve to the southeast on a course that ran roughly parallel to the Brock Road. It then ran across the front of Barlow's line and crossed the Brock Road south of the Trigg house. Subsequently, this railroad was finished and was called the Piedmont, Fredericksburg, and Potomac Railroad.

At Longstreet's direction, G. Moxley Sorrel, his chief of staff, assembled three brigades that were to constitute the flanking column. These were George T. Anderson's brigade of Field's division, William T. Wofford's brigade of Kershaw's division, and William Mahone's brigade of Richard H. Anderson's division. For some reason, Joseph R. Davis' brigade of Heth's division (then commanded by Stone) accompanied the flanking column, but its part in the ensuing attack is difficult to determine. Sorrel accompanied the column, but Mahone, as the senior officer present, directed the movement.

Mahone moved his command to the right from the Plank Road to the unfinished railroad grade, and then marched eastward along the grade until he came to the above-mentioned curve to the southeast. At that point he was to the Federal left and rear of Birney's line. Mahone then formed his brigades along the railroad bed, with Wofford on the left, Mahone on the center, and George T. Anderson on the right. Stone's brigade was probably in reserve. At about 11:00 A.M., Mahone led his command northward through the woods toward the Plank Road. At the same time, the remaining troops of the divisions of Kershaw and Field attacked on the front of Hancock's line.

At the time of Longstreet's attack, Birney's troops were in position as follows: south of the Plank Road, and on the left of the line, was Frank's brigade of Barlow's division; next to Frank, and on his right, was McAllister's brigade of Mott's division; and between McAllister's brigade and the Plank Road were the brigades of Brewster of Mott's division, and Carroll and Owen of Gibbon's division. Birney's division was in rear of this line, and farther back and to the left was Getty's division. North of the road was Wadsworth's command, which consisted of Rice with the remaining troops of Wadsworth's division, Webb's brigade of Gibbon's division, and Carruth's brigade of Stevenson's division.

Mahone's attack first struck Frank's brigade, which was overwhelmed and driven back toward the Brock Road. McAllister then changed front to the left to meet Mahone, but he was soon under fire from the front, right, and rear and was also driven in confusion toward the Brock Road. The other brigades south of the Plank Road were in turn driven back by Mahone and by Kershaw's division, which was advancing on the south side of the Plank Road.

North of the road, Field advanced with Law's brigade, commanded by William F. Perry, Micah Jenkins' brigade of Field's division, and the divisions of Edward A. Perry and Abner M. Perrin of Richard H. Anderson's division and drove back Wadsworth's line in confusion. Wadsworth was killed in the attack, and Rice assumed command of the troops of his Fourth Division, Fifth Corps remaining on the field. J. William Hofmann assumed command of Rice's Second Brigade of the division.

Hancock attempted to form a new line along the Plank Road, but this was impossible under the cir-

cumstances, and all Federal troops along the line finally fell back to the entrenchments along the Brock Road.

Longstreet then prepared for a final assault, with Jenkins' brigade moving forward on the Plank Road and Kershaw's division advancing on his right. Field was still engaged on the Confederate left with his other brigades. Longstreet rode forward on the Plank Road, at the head of Jenkins' brigade, with Kershaw and Jenkins following a short distance behind. As this group of officers approached the Brock Road, they were fired on by troops of Mahone's flanking column, which were then near the Plank Road. Longstreet was seriously wounded and Jenkins was killed. Field then assumed command of Longstreet's corps, and John Bratton moved up to the command of Jenkins' brigade. At that point, Lee came up and postponed the intended attack until he could re-form and prepare his troops for further offensive action.

About an hour after Hancock's troops had been forced back to the Brock Road, Gibbon, at Hancock's direction, ordered Leasure to sweep northward from Barlow's position along the whole front of Hancock's line. He was to advance, keeping his right about 100 yards from the Federal breastworks on the Brock Road, and attack any Confederate forces that he might meet. Leasure did as directed and cleared the entire front of all enemy troops, who fell back without resistance. When Leasure had completed his mission, he returned to his earlier position near the right of Hancock's line.

About 2:00 P.M., John C. Robinson arrived from the Lacy house with Peter Lyle's First Brigade of his Second Division, Fifth Corps, and the 14th New York Heavy Artillery and 2nd Pennsylvania Provisional Heavy Artillery of Elisha G. Marshall's Provisional Brigade of Ninth Corps and reported to Hancock. Lyle's brigade was placed on the right of Hancock's line, and the heavy artillery regiments were formed near the Plank Road in rear of the Brock Road.

Meantime, while the fighting was going on along the Plank Road, Burnside's Ninth Corps, which had long been expected, was slowly moving forward to support Hancock. Conforming to his orders of 8:00 A.M., Burnside left Jones' field with Potter's division about 9:00 A.M. and moved through the woods to the left and rear, and then turned southward toward the Plank Road. John F. Hartranft's brigade of Willcox's division followed a short time later, but Christ's brigade was left in position on the road to picket the front toward Parker's Store. When Burnside reached a point opposite the front selected for his attack, he halted and deployed Potter's division in an open field, with Bliss' brigade on the right and Simon G. Griffin's brigade on the left. When this line was completed, Potter advanced into the woods and soon found the enemy entrenched on the opposite side of a swampy stream. It was then about 2:00 P.M. The slowness of Burnside's movement, which has never been fully explained, is shown by the fact that the three brigades of Ninth Corps required five hours, from 9:00 A.M. to 2:00 P.M., to travel the two miles from the Jones field and get ready for their attack.

When Potter came up to the enemy works, he immediately charged and struck the left of William F. Perry's (Law's) brigade and drove it back. The brigades of Edward A. Perry and Perrin of Richard H. Anderson's division then came up and, with the help of William F. Perry's brigade, soon restored the enemy line. Hartranft's brigade then arrived on the right of Potter in support of Bliss. Hartranft attacked and carried a part of the enemy works, while at the same time Potter's brigades charged the line on their front. A strong counterattack forced Potter's line to give way, and drove Hartranft's brigade back in disorder. Hartranft, however, held his position in front of the enemy works until Willcox came up in support with Christ's brigade. Christ had remained on the Parker's Store Road until mid-afternoon; his brigade then followed Burnside's column, and between 5:00 and 5:30 P.M, it arrived and took position on the left of Hartranft.

When Willcox's division was ready, it advanced to the attack and was supported by Potter. The enemy, who had advanced their line during the counterattack, were driven back into their entrenchments, and then Burnside's men broke through on the enemy left. Wofford's brigade of Kershaw's division, which had been sent up from the Plank Road, then attacked and finally restored the Confederate line. Burnside then withdrew across the swampy ground and entrenched on the far side. He did not renew the attack, but finally established connection with Hancock's command about dusk.

From about noon until 4:00 P.M., Field, under Lee's personal supervision, attempted to reorganize his troops for a final assault that evening. During the same period, Hancock worked vigorously to organize his defensive line behind the breastworks along the Brock Road in preparation for this attack. When Hancock's line was completed, it was probably held north of the Plank Road, from right to left, as follows: the two regiments of heavy artillery of Marshall's Provisional Brigade (reported to be commanded by a Colonel Morrison, but otherwise unknown); Eustis' brigade of Getty's division, Sixth Corps; Robinson, with the brigades of Lyle and Coulter of Fifth Corps; Owen's brigade of Gibbon's division of Second Corps; Wheaton's and Grant's brigades of Getty's division, both commanded by Wheaton, with their left on the Plank Road. In rear of Wheaton's line was Carroll's brigade of Gibbon's division, and in rear of Carroll was Rice's brigade (commanded by J. William Hofmann) of Wadsworth's division, which was then commanded by Rice. Leasure's brigade was also on the right, but its position is not known. It may have been on the right of Wheaton's two brigades.

A section of Edwin B. Dow's 6th Battery (F), Maine Light Artillery, under the command of William H. Rogers, was on the Plank Road at the crossing of the Brock Road. Carruth's brigade of Stevenson's division was also in position near the Plank Road, but its exact location is not known.

South of the Plank Road, also from right to left, were the following: Birney's division of Second Corps was on the left of Wheaton, with Ward's brigade on the front line and Crocker's brigade in its rear; Mott's division of Second Corps, with Brewster's brigade on the front line and McAllister's brigade on the second line; Smyth's brigade of Barlow's division of Second Corps; Webb's brigade of Gibbon's division; and then, in order, Frank's brigade, Brooke's brigade, and Miles' brigade, all of Barlow's division.

The remaining four guns of Dow's battery were in a small opening behind the left of Mott's second line, about 300 yards to the left of the Plank Road; next to them, and also to the left of the Plank Road, were six guns of Frederick M. Edgell's 1st Battery, New Hampshire Light Artillery. The remaining batteries of the Second Corps Artillery were on the left of Barlow's division, on the far left of Hancock's line.

Field finally completed the preparations for his

attack, and at 4:15 P.M. he advanced against the front of the divisions of Birney and Mott, south of the Plank Road. Rogers, Dow, and Edgell immediately opened fire with shell, case shot, and canister, and this, combined with a heavy infantry fire, brought the enemy to a halt about 100 yards in front of the Brock Road, at the slashings in front of the breastworks. Heavy firing continued for about a half hour, but there was no change in position. Then a forest fire, which had started in front of Barlow's line, spread to Mott's front and set fire to the log breastworks. Under the combined effect of the smoke and heat of the burning logs and an impetuous enemy attack, Mott's front line and Ward's brigade of Birney's division broke and fled to the rear in disorder. The enemy followed, and one brigade occupied the abandoned works. Both George T. Anderson's brigade and John Bratton's brigade (Jenkins' brigade) are reported to have been the brigade that occupied the Federal works. Which one, however, or possibly both, is apparently not definitely known. At this time of crisis, Hancock called upon Carroll's brigade, and Birney ordered Hofmann's brigade to restore the front line. Again, there is a question as to which brigade, or possibly both, drove the enemy from the break in the front line. Carroll's brigade is usually given the credit for the successful attack, but Hofmann says that his brigade reoccupied the works. In addition to Carroll and Hofmann, Gibbon also sent Brooke's brigade up from the left to aid Mott, but it arrived as the fighting was ending. At about 5:00 P.M., Lee called off the attack, and Field withdrew his command almost back to the Tapp field, where he halted for the night.

The Battle of the Wilderness, however, was not quite over. That evening, Lee made one more effort, this time against Sedgwick's Sixth Corps on the far right of the army. On the morning of May 6, 1864, Gordon discovered that Sedgwick's unprotected right flank was in the woods on his front. Gordon proposed that he attack this exposed flank with his brigade, properly supported, but he received no authorization until Lee arrived at Ewell's headquarters about 5:30 P.M. Then, late in the day, Gordon's brigade moved out. It was supported by Robert D. Johnston's brigade of Rodes' division, which had arrived that morning on the left of Ewell's line from Hanover Junction. Gordon formed his brigade on open ground near the edge of the woods

and then waited until Johnston's brigade had arrived on his left, in rear of the Sixth Corps line. About sunset, Gordon advanced and struck Shaler's brigade, which was to the right and rear of Seymour's brigade, on the extreme Federal right. Shaler's line was quickly broken and driven back, but it then ran into Johnston's line, where several hundred men were captured, including Shaler. Nelson Cross assumed command of Shaler's brigade. Gordon continued his advance and came up against the right of Seymour's brigade, which, in turn, was driven back in confusion, with the loss of some prisoners, including Seymour. Benjamin F. Smith then took command of Seymour's brigade.

While Gordon's attack was in progress, Early advanced against the front of Neill's brigade, but he made no significant progress. Meantime Morris and Upton had come up to aid Smith (Seymour), and together they held the line until darkness ended the fighting about 9:30 P.M.

During Gordon's attack, Hancock was directed to send troops to aid Sedgwick; and at 9:00 P.M., Wheaton, with his own and Eustis' brigades, was sent to rejoin the corps. The two brigades remained near Old Wilderness Tavern during the night, and took position in the line the next morning. Grant's brigade remained with Hancock until the evening of July 7, 1864. Crawford's division of Fifth Corps was also sent to Sedgwick during the evening, but it arrived after the fighting had ended.

During the night, Meade decided to draw back the entire Sixth Corps to a new position. Beginning on the right of Fifth Corps at the Turnpike, the new line ran to the northeast along a ridge between Caton's Run and Wilderness Run, crossed the Germanna Plank Road about a half mile north of its intersection with the Turnpike, and then continued on along high ground to the northeast. This line was completed at dawn May 7, 1864. Wheaton's two brigades rejoined Sixth Corps that morning, and with Neill's brigade of the division occupied the right of the new line. Neill, as the senior officer, assumed command of Second Division, Sixth Corps during the absence of Getty, who had been wounded the day before. Daniel D. Bidwell assumed command of Neill's Third Brigade. Ricketts' division held the center of the new line, and Wright's division the left.

By July 7, 1864, Stevenson's division had returned to Ninth Corps, which was then in position, facing southwest, between the left of Fifth Corps near the Parker's Store Road and the junction of the Brock Road and the Plank Road. Robinson, with the brigades of Lyle and Coulter, had returned to Fifth Corps, which then held the ground between the left of Sixth Corps and the right of Ninth Corps, facing west. Hancock's Second Corps continued to hold the line of the Brock Road, south of the Plank Road.

Cavalry Operations of May 6, 1864. At 2:00 A.M. May 6, 1864, George A. Custer, with his First Brigade of Torbert's First Cavalry Division, moved out from near Chancellorsville on the Furnace Road toward the Brock Road. His orders were to hold the intersection of the two roads. Four hours later, Thomas C. Devin was ordered to advance with his Second Brigade of Torbert's division and Edward Heaton's Batteries B and L, Second United States Artillery and take position on the right of Custer, where he would watch the left of Barlow's infantry line.

By 8:30 A.M., Custer's main line was concealed in deep woods on the east side of the Brock Road, with pickets out in a large clearing on the far side of the road. As Custer prepared to advance and attack an infantry column that had been reported on his front, his pickets were driven in by troopers of Thomas L. Rosser's brigade of Wade Hampton's cavalry division. Custer then advanced his main line, and there was a sharp but indecisive engagement. Rosser was reinforced by two regiments of Fitzhugh Lee's cavalry division, and for a time the enemy threatened Custer's communications on the Furnace Road. A section of artillery sent by David McM. Gregg from Todd's Tavern then arrived and opened fire from the high ground in rear of Custer. About this time, Devin arrived and formed on the right of Custer. Heaton's battery went into position with Gregg's section of artillery, and about 9:45 A.M., Custer's brigade and a part of Devin's brigade charged, turned Rosser's left flank, and then drove him from the field. Custer held his ground until dark and then returned to Wellford's Furnace.

Gregg's cavalry division skirmished all day with Fitzhugh Lee's cavalry at Todd's Tavern, but it was not otherwise engaged. Wesley Merritt's Reserve Brigade of Torbert's division remained near Chancellorsville guarding the trains. Early on the morning of May 6, 1864, Wilson's Third Cavalry Division moved back to Chancellorsville for food and ammunition. While it was there, John B. McIntosh arrived and assumed command of Third Brigade, Third Cavalry Division, relieving Timothy M. Bryan, Jr. McIntosh was assigned command of the brigade May 5, 1864. McIntosh then marched with his brigade to Piney Branch Church, where he remained until relieved that day by George H. Chapman's Second Brigade. McIntosh then returned to Chancellorsville.

Organization of Grant's Army during the Battle of the Wilderness, May 5–7, 1864.

ARMY OF THE POTOMAC
George G. Meade

SECOND CORPS, Winfield S. Hancock

First Division, Francis C. Barlow
    First Brigade, Nelson A. Miles
    Second Brigade, Thomas A. Smyth
    Third Brigade, Paul Frank
    Fourth Brigade, John R. Brooke

Second Division, John Gibbon
    First Brigade, Alexander S. Webb
    Second Brigade, Joshua T. Owen
    Third Brigade, Samuel S. Carroll

Third Division, David B. Birney
    First Brigade, J. H. Hobart Ward
    Second Brigade, Alexander Hays, to May 5, 1864, killed
    John S. Crocker

Fourth Division, Gershom Mott
    First Brigade, Robert McAllister
    Second Brigade, William R. Brewster

Artillery Brigade, John C. Tidball
    6th Battery (F), Maine Light Artillery, Edwin B. Dow
    10th Battery, Massachusetts Light Artillery, J. Henry Sleeper
    1st Battery, New Hampshire Light Artillery, Frederick M. Edgell
    Battery G, 1st New York Light Artillery, Nelson Ames
    3rd Battalion, 4th New York Heavy Artillery, Thomas Allcock
    Battery F, 1st Pennsylvania Light Artillery, R. Bruce Ricketts
    Battery A, 1st Rhode Island Light Artillery, William A. Arnold

Battery B, 1st Rhode Island Light Artillery, T. Frederick Brown

Battery K, 4th United States Artillery, John W. Roder

Batteries C and I, 5th United States Artillery, James Gilliss

FIFTH CORPS, Gouverneur K. Warren

First Division, Charles Griffin
First Brigade, Romeyn B. Ayres
Second Brigade, Jacob B. Sweitzer
Third Brigade, Joseph J. Bartlett

Second Division, John C. Robinson
First Brigade, Samuel H. Leonard, to May 6, 1864
Peter Lyle
Second Brigade, Henry Baxter, to May 6, 1864, wounded
Richard Coulter
Third Brigade, Andrew W. Denison

Third Division, Samuel W. Crawford
First Brigade, William McCandless
Second Brigade, Joseph W. Fisher

Fourth Division, James S. Wadsworth, to May 6, 1864, mortally wounded
James C. Rice, temporarily May 6, 1864
Lysander Cutler
First Brigade, Lysander Cutler, to May 6, 1864
William W. Robinson
Second Brigade, James C. Rice
J. William Hofmann, temporarily May 6, 1864
Third Brigade, Roy Stone, to May 6, 1864, disabled
Edward S. Bragg

Artillery Brigade, Charles S. Wainwright
Battery C, Massachusetts Light Artillery, Augustus P. Martin
Battery E, Massachusetts Light Artillery, Charles A. Phillips
Battery D, 1st New York Light Artillery, George B. Winslow
Batteries E and L, 1st New York Light Artillery, George Breck
Battery H, 1st New York Light Artillery, Charles E. Mink
2nd Battalion, 4th New York Heavy Artillery, William Arthur
Battery B, 1st Pennsylvania Light Artillery, James H. Cooper
Battery B, 4th United States Artillery, James Stewart
Battery D, 5th United States Artillery, Benjamin F. Rittenhouse

SIXTH CORPS, John Sedgwick

First Division. Horatio G. Wright
First Brigade, Henry W. Brown
Second Brigade, Emory Upton
Third Brigade, David A. Russell
Fourth Brigade, Alexander Shaler, to May 6, 1864, captured
Nelson Cross

Second Division, George W. Getty, to May 6, 1864, wounded
Frank Wheaton, temporarily May 6, 1864
Thomas H. Neill
First Brigade, Frank Wheaton
Second Brigade, Lewis A. Grant
Third Brigade, Thomas H. Neill, to May 7, 1864
Daniel D. Bidwell
Fourth Brigade, Henry L. Eustis

Third Division, James B. Ricketts
First Brigade, William H. Morris
Second Brigade, Truman Seymour, to May 6, 1864, captured
Benjamin F. Smith

Artillery Brigade, Charles H. Tompkins
4th Battery (D), Maine Light Artillery, Melville C. Kimball
1st Battery (A), Massachusetts Light Artillery, William H. McCartney
1st Battery, New York Light Artillery, Andrew Cowan
3rd Battery, New York Light Artillery, William A. Harn
1st Battalion, 4th New York Heavy Artillery, Thomas D. Sears
Battery C, 1st Rhode Island Light Artillery, Richard Waterman
Battery E, 1st Rhode Island Light Artillery, William B. Rhodes
Battery G, 1st Rhode Island Light Artillery, George W. Adams
Battery M, 5th United States Artillery, James McKnight

CAVALRY CORPS, Philip H. Sheridan

First Division, Alfred T. A. Torbert, to May 7, 1864, sick
Wesley Merritt
First Brigade, George A. Custer
Second Brigade, Thomas C. Devin
Reserve Brigade, Wesley Merritt, to May 7, 1864
Alfred Gibbs

Second Division, David McM. Gregg
First Brigade, Henry E. Davies, Jr.
Second Brigade, J. Irvin Gregg

Third Division, James H. Wilson
First Brigade, Timothy Bryan, Jr., to May 6, 1864
John B. McIntosh
Second Brigade, George H. Chapman

First Brigade, Horse Artillery, James M. Robertson
6th Battery, New York Light Artillery, Joseph W.
Martin
Batteries B and L, 2nd United States Artillery, Edward
Heaton
Battery D, 2nd United States Artillery, Edward B.
Williston
Battery M, 2nd United States Artillery, Alexander C.
M. Pennington, Jr.
Battery A, 4th United States Artillery, Rufus King, Jr.
Batteries C and E, 4th United States Artillery, Charles
L. Fitzhugh

ARTILLERY, Henry J. Hunt

Artillery Reserve, Henry S. Burton
First Brigade, J. Howard Kitching
6th New York Heavy Artillery, Edmund R. Travis
15th New York Heavy Artillery, Louis Schirmer
Second Brigade, John A. Tompkins
5th Battery (E), Maine Light Artillery, Greenleaf T.
Stevens
Battery A, 1st New Jersey Light Artillery, William
Hexamer
Battery B, 1st New Jersey Light Artillery, A. Judson
Clark
5th Battery, New York Light Artillery, Elijah D. Taft
12th Battery, New York Light Artillery, George F.
McKnight
Battery B, 1st New York Light Artillery, Albert S.
Sheldon
Third Brigade, Robert H. Fitzhugh
9th Battery, Massachusetts Light Artillery, John
Bigelow
15th Battery, New York Light Artillery, Patrick Hart
Battery C, 1st New York Light Artillery, William H.
Phillips
11th Battery, New York Light Artillery, John E.
Burton
Battery H, 1st Ohio Light Artillery, William A.
Ewing
Battery E, 5th United States Artillery, John R.
Brinckle

Horse Artillery
First Brigade, James M. Robertson

*Note. First Brigade was with the Cavalry Corps, see
above.*
Second Brigade, Dunbar R. Ransom
Batteries E and G, 1st United States Artillery, Frank
S. French
Batteries H and I, 1st United States Artillery, Alan-
son M. Randol
Battery K, 1st United States Artillery, John Egan
Battery A, 2nd United States Artillery, Robert
Clarke
Battery G, 2nd United States Artillery, William N.
Dennison
Batteries C, F, and K, 3rd United States Artillery,
James R. Kelly

NINTH CORPS
Ambrose E. Burnside

First Division, Thomas G. Stevenson
First Brigade, Sumner Carruth, to May 6, 1864,
sunstroke
J. Parker Gould
Second Brigade, Daniel Leasure
Artillery
2nd Battery (B), Maine Light Artillery, Albert F.
Thomas
14th Battery, Massachusetts Light Artillery, Joseph
W. B. Wright

Second Division, Robert B. Potter
First Brigade, Zenas R. Bliss, to May 6, 1864, sunstroke
John I. Curtin
Second Brigade, Simon G. Griffin
Artillery
11th Battery, Massachusetts Light Artillery, Edward
J. Jones
19th Battery, New York Light Artillery, Edward W.
Rogers

Third Division, Orlando B. Willcox
First Brigade, John F. Hartranft
Second Brigade, Benjamin C. Christ
Artillery
7th Battery (G), Maine Light Artillery, Adelbert B.
Twitchell
34th Battery, New York Light Artillery, Jacob
Roemer

Fourth Division, Edward Ferrero
First Brigade, Joshua K. Sigfried
Second Brigade, Henry G. Thomas
Artillery

Battery D, Pennsylvania Light Artillery, George W. Durell

3rd Battery, Vermont Light Artillery, Romeo H. Start

Note. Fourth Division was composed of regiments of United States Colored Troops. It was guarding the trains during the Battle of the Wilderness and was not engaged.

Cavalry
3rd New Jersey Cavalry, Andrew J. Morrison
22nd New York Cavalry, Samuel J. Crooks
2nd Ohio Cavalry, George A. Purington
13th Pennsylvania Cavalry, Michael Kerwin

Provisional Brigade, Elisha G. Marshall

Reserve Artillery, John Edwards, Jr.
27th Battery, New York Light Artillery, John B. Eaton
Battery D, 1st Rhode Island Light Artillery, William W. Buckley
Battery H, 1st Rhode Island Light Artillery, Crawford Allen, Jr.
Battery E, 2nd United States Artillery, James S. Dudley
Battery G, 3rd United States Artillery, Edmund Pendleton
Batteries L and M, 3rd United States Artillery, Erskine Gittings

OPERATIONS ABOUT SPOTSYLVANIA COURT HOUSE MAY 8, 1864–MAY 20, 1864

The Opening Moves. After the fighting in the Wilderness had ended May 6, 1864, Grant decided to continue his march by the left flank toward Spotsylvania Court House, where he would move into the more open country to the south. The trains started at 3:00 P.M. May 7, 1864, and the army began to move at 8:30 that night. Gouverneur K. Warren's Fifth Corps led the way on the Brock Road, but it was delayed by the cavalry for a time, and the head of the column did not arrive in the vicinity of Todd's Tavern until 3:30 A.M. May 8, 1864.

The head of John Sedgwick's Sixth Corps left Old Wilderness Tavern about 9:30 P.M. May 7, 1864 and marched to Chancellorsville, and then out on the Piney Branch Church Road toward the intersection of that road and the Brock Road. Horatio G. Wright's First Division was in the lead, and it was

followed by James B. Ricketts' Third Division. Thomas H. Neill's Second Division brought up the rear. Early the next morning, May 8, 1864, Sedgwick was ordered to leave one division at Piney Branch Church, one division at the intersection of the two roads, and the remaining division on the road between the other two.

About daybreak May 8, 1864, Ambrose E. Burnside's Ninth Corps started from Old Wilderness Tavern and marched to Chancellorsville, where it bivouacked that night. The next morning it resumed the march, following Sixth Corps, but it was then assigned to guard the trains and was halted at the Aldrich farm. This was where the Piney Branch Church Road left the Fredericksburg Plank Road, about two miles from the church. Edward Ferrero's Fourth Division was then detached to guard the trains, and it remained in this service for several weeks.

Winfield S. Hancock's Second Corps remained in position along the Brock Road until the rest of the army had moved on, and then it followed Fifth Corps toward Todd's Tavern. The start was delayed until nearly daylight because the road was occupied most of the night, and the head of the column did not reach Todd's Tavern until 9:00 A.M. Upon arriving there, Hancock relieved David McM. Gregg's Second Cavalry Division of Philip H. Sheridan's Cavalry Corps, which had been holding that point. Second Corps remained there during the day to watch the enemy movements and to guard the crossroads. Gershom Mott's Fourth Division was posted to guard the Brock Road; Francis C. Barlow's First Division was on the left of Mott; John Gibbon's Second Division covered the Catharpin Road; and David B. Birney's Third Division was held in reserve. Later, Birney moved to the left of Gibbon and took position between the Catharpin Road and the Spotsylvania Court House road.

Engagement at Alsop's Farm (Laurel Hill), May 8, 1864. When Fifth Corps arrived near Todd's Tavern early on the morning of May 8, 1864, Fitzhugh Lee's Confederate cavalry was ahead on the road contesting the Federal advance. Wesley Merritt, temporarily commanding Alfred T. A. Torbert's First Cavalry Division, was attempting to clear the way with his Reserve Brigade (commanded by Alfred Gibbs) and Thomas C. Devin's Second

Brigade of the division, but he was unable to do so. Warren then moved forward with his Fifth Corps from Todd's Tavern on the Brock Road. John C. Robinson's Second Division was in front, with Richard Coulter's Second Brigade leading the division. Some two miles out, in the direction of Spotsylvania Court House, Robinson overtook Merritt's cavalry.

About 6:00 A.M., after delaying the infantry advance for about three hours, Merritt finally got his cavalry off the road to permit the infantry to pass. Robinson then deployed his division, with Peter Lyle's First Brigade on the left and Andrew W. Denison's Third Brigade on the right, and then continued the advance against the enemy cavalry. Robinson placed Coulter's brigade in the rear of his line to protect Lyle's left flank. After advancing about a mile and a half, the troops became somewhat disordered, and Robinson then re-formed his line with Coulter's brigade on the left of the road and Lyle's and Denison's brigades on the right of the road.

Progress was slow, and it was not until about 8:30 A.M. that Robinson's division arrived on the open ground of the Alsop farm, about two and a half miles from Spotsylvania Court House. At that point the Brock Road branched, but the two branches again joined about a mile farther on. Robinson's division took the left fork, and Charles Griffin's First Division, which was following Robinson, took the right fork. Robinson's division crossed the Alsop farm and passed through a woods, and then, a short distance beyond the point where the two branches of the road rejoined, it came under a heavy fire from enemy infantry posted near the intersection of the Brock Road and the Old Court House Road.

Meantime, the enemy too had been on the march. On May 7, 1864, Richard H. Anderson was assigned command of Longstreet's corps, and that night he started with the divisions of Joseph B. Kershaw and Charles W. Field for Spotsylvania Court House. Kershaw's division, which was in the lead, arrived at the "Block House" about 7:00 A.M., and there he learned that Fitzhugh Lee was hard pressed and needed help. Kershaw immediately sent his own brigade (then commanded by John W. Henagan) and Benjamin G. Humphreys' brigade northward to support the cavalry. Kershaw also sent his two remaining brigades, commanded by William T. Wofford

and Goode Bryan, to reinforce Thomas L. Rosser's cavalry, which was threatened by James H. Wilson's Third Cavalry Division at Spotsylvania Court House.

Henagan's and Humphreys' brigades arrived near the Spindler farm and occupied some rail breastworks just as Robinson's division approached. Field's division came up a short time later and formed on the left of Kershaw's two brigades. These troops soon halted Robinson's advance and drove his division back to the shelter of some woods near the Alsop house. Robinson was severely wounded, and Coulter assumed temporary command of Second Division. James L. Bates took charge of Coulter's Second Brigade, Second Division. Denison, commanding Third Brigade, Second Division, was also wounded, and he was succeeded by Richard N. Bowerman.

Griffin's division then came up on the right of Robinson, with Joseph J. Bartlett's Third Brigade in line of battle, and Romeyn B. Ayres' First Brigade and Jacob B. Sweitzer's Second Brigade marching in column on the road. Bartlett advanced across the Alsop farm, but was soon checked by a heavy fire and driven back. The division was then formed on Ayres' brigade, which was halted at a low place in the road. Griffin then advanced to a position that he was to occupy for several days.

Lysander Cutler's Fourth Division of Fifth Corps (formerly commanded by James S. Wadsworth) came up on the right of Griffin but, being unsupported, was unable to advance. That afternoon, Samuel W. Crawford's Third Division arrived and formed on the right of Cutler. Later, before his attack that evening, Crawford moved to the left of Warren's line.

When Warren found that he was confronted by a strong enemy force, he entrenched on a line facing south, a little more than a fourth of a mile north of the intersection of the Old Court House Road and the Brock Road. His left rested on the Brock Road at the junction of the two forks mentioned above, about one mile south of the Alsop house, and his right extended to the right (west) about three-fourths of a mile.

At 1:00 P.M., George G. Meade ordered Sedgwick to move his Sixth Corps toward Spotsylvania Court House and prepare to join Warren in an attack. At 1:30 P.M., Hancock sent Gibbon's division of Second Corps from Todd's Tavern to a point in rear of Fifth Corps and Sixth Corps to support them if necessary. Sedgwick moved to join Warren as ordered, but it was late in the afternoon before his corps was in position. Wright's First Division arrived first, and William H. Penrose's First Brigade was placed on the left of Fifth Corps. The other three brigades of the division were placed on the right of Fifth Corps, in order from left to right as follows: Nelson Cross' Fourth Brigade, David A. Russell's Third Brigade, and Emory Upton's Second Brigade. Ayres' First Brigade of Griffin's division was on the right of Upton.

Penrose's brigade, reporting temporarily to Crawford, advanced against the enemy line, but after a short engagement it withdrew. About dusk, Crawford moved forward and apparently passed the Confederate right of Anderson's corps and then struck Robert E. Rodes' division of Richard S. Ewell's corps, which was just then arriving on the field. After some initial successes, Crawford was checked, and that night he withdrew to his original line. William McCandless, commanding the First Brigade of Crawford's division, was wounded after leaving Todd's Tavern and was succeeded by William C. Talley. Talley led the brigade in Crawford's attack and was captured, and Wellington H. Ent assumed command of First Brigade. Talley was recaptured the next day at Beaver Dam Station by Sheridan's cavalry, which was then on its raid toward Richmond, Virginia. For details, see below, Cavalry Operations of May 7–9, 1864, and see also Sheridan's Richmond, Virginia Raid.

Edward Johnson's division of Ewell's corps came up that evening and took position on the right of Rodes' division, and John B. Gordon's division was placed in reserve. Jubal A. Early commanded Gordon's division until he relieved Ambrose P. Hill in command of Third Corps when Hill became sick.

Engagement at Corbin's Bridge, May 8, 1864. At 11:00 A.M. May 8, 1864, Hancock ordered Nelson A. Miles to move out with his own First Brigade of Barlow's First Division and J. Irvin Gregg's Second Brigade of David McM. Gregg's Second Cavalry Division on a reconnaissance toward Corbin's Bridge, about two miles west of Todd's Tavern. Miles advanced to within a short distance of the bridge and remained there observing Wade

Hampton's cavalry across the Po River until recalled later in the day. When Miles was retiring, about 5:30 P.M., he was attacked by William Mahone's infantry division (formerly commanded by Richard H. Anderson) of Hill's corps (then commanded by Early). John R. Brooke's Fourth Brigade of Barlow's division was sent out to support Miles, and then, a short time later, all Federal troops on the Corbin's Bridge Road withdrew safely to Todd's Tavern.

Cavalry Operations of May 7–9, 1864. On May 7, 1864, George A. Custer's First Brigade and Thomas C. Devin's Second Brigade of Torbert's First Cavalry Division were near Wellford's Furnace, and Wesley Merritt's Reserve Brigade was near the Aldrich farm. During the afternoon, Torbert left for Washington because of illness, and Merritt assumed temporary command of his division. That day, Merritt marched with the Reserve Brigade to Wellford's Furnace, where Merritt assumed command of the division at 4:00 P.M., and Alfred Gibbs assumed command of the Reserve Brigade. Merritt then left Custer at the furnace and marched with the Reserve Brigade and Devin's brigade to Todd's Tavern.

Early on the morning of May 8, 1864, the Reserve Brigade, supported by Devin's brigade, advanced on the road toward Spotsylvania Court House and soon became engaged with Fitzhugh Lee's cavalry. Merritt's brigades were unable to clear the road, and about 6:00 A.M. they were relieved by Robinson's division of Warren's Fifth Corps. The cavalry brigades then moved to the rear of Fifth Corps to re-form.

On the morning of May 7, 1864, Gregg's Second Cavalry Division was at Todd's Tavern, where it was engaged with the enemy during the day. J. Irvin Gregg's Second Brigade was on the right, covering the road leading to Shady Grove Church, and Henry W. Davies' First Brigade was on the left. As noted above, on May 8, 1864, J. Irvin Gregg's brigade accompanied Miles' infantry brigade of Second Corps on a reconnaissance toward Corbin's Bridge and was engaged during the evening. That day, Gregg's cavalry division was relieved by Hancock's Second Corps.

James H. Wilson's Third Cavalry Division bivouacked at the Aldrich farm, on the Fredericksburg Plank Road, during the night of May 7, 1864, and at

5:00 the next morning it marched toward Spotsylvania Court House en route to Snell's Bridge on the Po River. Wilson reached the Fredericksburg-Spotsylvania Court House Road just north of the Ny River, and then advanced on that road, against some opposition by enemy cavalry, and occupied Spotsylvania Court House about 9:00 A.M. He remained there about two hours and was then ordered to withdraw. He moved back to the Alsop farm and bivouacked for the night.

Sheridan and Meade had disagreed for some time on the proper use of the Federal cavalry, and their differences came to a head when Sheridan was summoned to Meade's headquarters a little before noon May 8, 1864. In a confrontation there, Sheridan protested that the cavalry had been badly employed during the opening days of the campaign, and he further stated that if permitted, he could move out and defeat James E. B. (Jeb) Stuart's cavalry. When Grant was informed of Sheridan's statement, he ordered Sheridan, through Meade, to assemble his mounted force and move out against Stuart and defeat him. In accordance with this order, Merritt's (Torbert's) and Gregg's divisions marched during the evening of May 8, 1864 from the vicinity of Todd's Tavern to Silvers' plantation (or farm), which was on the Fredericksburg Plank Road, about midway between the Aldrich farm and Tabernacle Church.

At 5:00 A.M. May 9, 1864, Sheridan marched eastward with these two divisions on the Plank Road to Tabernacle Church, where he turned south on his raid toward Richmond. Also that morning, Wilson's cavalry division marched from Alsop's to the Fredericksburg Plank Road at Tabernacle Church, where it joined the other two divisions. The Cavalry Corps was absent from the Army of the Potomac until May 24, 1864, and it did not take part in any further operations around Spotsylvania Court House. For details of its activities during the period May 9–24, 1864, see Sheridan's Richmond, Virginia Raid.

Operations of May 9, 1864. Both armies spent the day of May 9, 1864 in rearranging their lines and entrenching their positions, while the skirmishers and sharpshooters were active along the front. Fifth Corps remained in about the same position that it had taken the day before, but the other corps, which had

been relatively inactive May 8, 1864, moved up to take position on both the right and left of Fifth Corps. Sedgwick's Sixth Corps, which had arrived in support of Warren the previous evening, deployed during the morning of May 9, 1864 on the left of Fifth Corps, facing east. Wright's division, which had been in line with Fifth Corps, was relieved by troops of that corps, and it then moved to the left and formed on the left of Fifth Corps. Ricketts' division moved up and took position on the left of Wright, and Neill's division (commanded by George W. Getty at the Wilderness) on the left of Ricketts, and on the left of the corps. Sedgwick's line extended northward from the left of Warren for a little more than a half mile, and it ended about the same distance due east of the Alsop house.

Hancock's Second Corps and Burnside's Ninth Corps also moved up closer to the enemy lines. On the morning of May 9, 1864, there were some indications of an enemy advance along the Catharpin Road on Birney's front. Gibbon's division was moved about a mile to the right from its advanced position toward Spotsylvania Court House to connect with Birney, and J. Howard Kitching's brigade of heavy artillery of Burton's Artillery Reserve was ordered to join Hancock. This engagement never materialized, however, and at noon May 9, 1864, Hancock moved with the divisions of Birney and Barlow down the road toward Spotsylvania Court House for about a mile, then turned to the right on a wood road, and at about 4:00 P.M. occupied the high open ground overlooking the Po River. They were joined there by Gibbon's division, which had previously been sent to the left of Hancock's line. Gibbon's division was formed to the rear of the left flank of Fifth Corps, on the left of Hancock's new line; Barlow's division was placed on the right of Gibbon; and Birney's division on the right of Barlow. Mott's division of Second Corps and the heavy artillery brigade of the Artillery Reserve were left to hold the position at Todd's Tavern. Hancock's instructions were to cross the Po River on his front, and then make a reconnaissance in force along the Shady Grove Road in an effort to turn and attack the enemy left flank if feasible.

At 6:00 P.M., after an examination of the river, Hancock ordered Birney, Barlow, and Gibbon to force a crossing to the south bank. Brooke's brigade of Barlow's division was the first to advance, and although the crossing was difficult, Brooke pushed across and drove back the enemy and gained possession of the crossroads between Glady Run and the Po. Barlow then followed with his entire division. Birney's division moved upstream from Barlow's crossing, and then forced a passage against stubborn resistance. Gibbon's division crossed below Barlow and encountered no resistance. Hancock then pressed on along the Block House Road toward the wooden bridge over the Po River. It soon became dark, and Second Corps camped for the night near the Shady Grove Church Road, to the left of the bridge.

Early on the morning of May 9, 1864, Grant directed Burnside to move with his Ninth Corps from the Aldrich farm to the Gayle house, which was located near the crossing of the Ny River by the Spotsylvania Court House-Fredericksburg Road, about a mile and a half from the court house. When Orlando B. Willcox's Third Division, which was Burnside's leading division, reached the Ny River at Gayles', Willcox seized the crossing and posted Adelbert B. Twitchell's 7th Battery (G), Maine Light Artillery and Jacob Roemer's 34th Battery, New York Light Artillery on the north bank, and then advanced Benjamin C. Christ's Second Brigade to a ridge about 300 yards from the river. When Christ was attacked, probably by a brigade of Kershaw's infantry and Rosser's dismounted cavalry, Willcox sent forward John F. Hartranft's First Brigade to support him.

About noon, Thomas G. Stevenson's First Division, Ninth Corps arrived at the Ny River, and at 3:00 P.M., Stephen N. Weld's First Brigade crossed and joined Willcox on the south side. Daniel Leasure's Second Brigade remained to guard the crossing. Robert B. Potter's Second Division advanced to the vicinity of the Alsop house that day, about one mile from the Ny, and halted there for the night.

On the evening of May 9, 1864, there was a gap of about two miles between Sixth Corps and Ninth Corps, and at 11:40 that night, Mott received orders at Todd's Tavern to move at 3:00 the next morning and take position on the left of Sixth Corps to cover this gap.

Before proceeding with a description of the enemy lines, it is necessary to note here that there were some organizational and command changes in

the Army of the Potomac May 9, 1864. During the morning, John Sedgwick was killed by a sharpshooter. At the time, he was near the entrenchments on the right of Sixth Corps, near the edge of the Alsop field where the two branches of the Brock Road rejoined (see above). This resulted in the following command changes in the corps: Horatio G. Wright, commanding First Division, was assigned command of Sixth Corps; David A. Russell, commanding Third Brigade, First Division, assumed command of Wright's division; Henry L. Eustis, commanding Fourth Brigade of Thomas H. Neill's Second Division, was assigned command of Russell's brigade; and Oliver Edwards was assigned command of Eustis' brigade. About 10:00 A.M., William H. Morris, commanding First Brigade of James B. Ricketts' Third Division, Sixth Corps, was wounded while arranging the troops on his line, and he was succeeded by John W. Schall.

When John C. Robinson was wounded May 8, 1864, he was succeeded in command of Second Division, Fifth Corps by Richard Coulter. During the evening of May 9, 1864, however, Second Division was discontinued and the brigades were reassigned as follows: Peter Lyle's First Brigade was temporarily assigned to Lysander Cutler's Fourth Division, Fifth Corps; Coulter's Second Brigade was assigned to Samuel W. Crawford's Third Division (Coulter resumed command of the brigade that evening, relieving James L. Bates); and Richard Bowerman's Third Brigade (formerly Andrew W. Denison's) was designated as an Independent Brigade, and Bowerman was ordered to report directly to Warren, the corps commander.

At noon May 9, 1864, John Ramsey, colonel of the 8th New Jersey Regiment, was assigned command of a new provisional brigade of Second Corps. This brigade was formed from five regiments of Gershom Mott's Fourth Division, Second Corps.

Now, back to the movements of Lee's army near Spotsylvania Court House. While Grant brought up his troops and prepared to resume offensive operations, the Army of Northern Virginia labored unceasingly to establish and entrench a strong defensive line in front of the court house. When this line was completed, it was located and manned by troops of Anderson's and Ewell's corps as follows: Beginning on the left, the line rested on the Po River, opposite the right of Fifth Corps, about 600 yards north of the Shady Grove Church Road Bridge. It then ran a little to the north of east for about a mile and a fourth to the junction of the Brock Road and the Block House Road. For the first 600 yards, the entrenchments were on the open ground of the J. Perry farm; and they then ran through a belt of woods, along the outer edge, across the Spindler farm to the road junction. Field's division of Anderson's corps held this part of the line. It should be noted here that the distances given for the various parts of the entrenchments are measured on a straight line, and that they were considerably longer because of their irregular courses. From the left of Field's division, the line ran to the northeast for about a half mile to the open ground of the Harrison farm, which was beyond the left flank of Fifth Corps. Kershaw's division of Longstreet's corps was on that part of the line.

The line held by Rodes' and Johnson's divisions of Ewell's corps formed a great salient, called the "Mule Shoe" by the soldiers, which extended northward from the Harrison house for about a mile and averaged about one-half mile in width. From the right of Kershaw's division the line ran north for about one-half mile to an angle, which for clarity is here called the West Angle. Rodes' division occupied this part of the line. George Doles' brigade was in position at the West Angle, with Junius Daniel's brigade on its left. Stephen D. Ramseur's brigade was between Daniel's brigade on the right and Kershaw's division on the left. Cullen A. Battle's brigade was also present, and probably was in reserve.

From the West Angle, the line ran a little north of east for about 400 yards to some high, open ground, where it turned abruptly toward the south. The angle so formed is here called the East Angle. The roughly east-west line between the two angles has sometimes been called the "salient," but in reality it was the apex of the salient. The open ground of the Landrum farm was in front of a part of the apex line. From the East Angle, the line ran somewhat to the east of south for 600–700 yards, and faced toward the east. Johnson's division occupied the entrenchments from the right of Rodes' division, near the West Angle. James A. Walker's brigade (the Stonewall Brigade) was on the left, next to Doles' brigade; Harry T. Hays, commanding his own and Leroy A. Stafford's brigades, was on the right of

Walker; John M. Jones' brigade, commanded by William Addison Witcher, held the line at the East Angle, on the right of Hays; and George H. Steuart's brigade was on the right of the division, south of the East Angle. Gordon, commanding Early's division of Ewell's corps, was in reserve near the junction of Rodes' and Kershaw's divisions. Gordon constructed a second defensive line across the salient about midway between the McCoull (also called McCool) house and the Harrison house.

On the morning of May 9, 1864, Early, commanding A. P. Hill's corps, came up from the Wilderness and took position on the right of Ewell's corps, near Spotsylvania Court House, where it covered the road from Fredericksburg. Cadmus M. Wilcox's division was placed on the left of the corps, next to Johnson's division. Henry Heth's division extended the corps line southward to Spotsylvania Court House.

On May 10, 1864, William Mahone, commanding Richard H. Anderson's division of Hill's corps, who was then up, was sent to occupy the banks of the Po River on the left of Field's division. The enemy lines were thus extended to about one mile west of the Po, on the high ground of the Graves farm, to cover the Shady Grove Church Road. Still later, the lines east of Spotsylvania Court House were extended about two miles to the south, with the extreme right on the Po River at Snell's Bridge.

Operations of May 10, 1864 (Upton's Attack). Throughout the morning of May 10, 1864, there was sharp skirmishing all along the lines, and some severe fighting occurred during the afternoon. At 10:00 A.M., Burnside was ordered to make a reconnaissance toward Spotsylvania Court House with Stevenson's division and Christ's brigade of Willcox's division, and Robert B. Potter's division was ordered to move up from Alsop's to the Gayle house in support. Elisha G. Marshall's Provisional Brigade of Ninth Corps was also moved up to Gayles'. Burnside arrived with Potter's division, and that afternoon and evening advanced with his corps south of the Ny, and by about 10:00 P.M., a part of Potter's division had reached a point within about a mile and a fourth of the court house. The troops of Ninth Corps then entrenched the line where they had halted that night. During the afternoon, Stevenson was killed by a sharpshooter, and Daniel Leasure assumed temporary command of First

Division, Ninth Corps. Gilbert P. Robinson assumed temporary command of Leasure's Second Brigade.

In an order dated 10:00 A.M. May 10, 1864, Hancock was directed to withdraw the divisions of Gibbon and Birney from the south side of the Po, and with them support Warren in an assault on the enemy works at Laurel Hill at 5:00 P.M. The position to be attacked was on the front of Warren's line near the Alsop house. Hancock was to accompany his two divisions, and during the attack he was to exercise general control of both Second Corps and Fifth Corps. Wright's Sixth Corps, with Mott's division of Second Corps on its left, was ordered to attack at the same time on the left of Warren. Gibbon's division recrossed the Po at 11:00–11:30 A.M. and formed on the right of Warren. Birney's division followed and massed in reserve in rear of Warren's line. Barlow's division was left to hold the ground south of the river.

When Lee learned that Hancock had moved south of the Po River during the evening of May 9, 1864, he directed Early to send two divisions back from Spotsylvania Court House to protect Anderson's left flank. As noted above, Mahone's division was sent to prolong Anderson's line to the west, and Early, with Heth's division, moved to the Shady Grove Church Road to check Hancock's advance. As Birney was beginning to withdraw to join Warren, his skirmishers were being driven in by Heth's skirmishers, which were advancing from the crossing of the Po at the mouth of Glady Run. As Heth continued to advance, he soon encountered the skirmishers of Barlow's division. When Meade learned that Barlow's division was thus threatened by a heavy force, he ordered Hancock to return to the south side of the river and personally supervise Barlow's withdrawal to the north bank.

At that time, Barlow had John R. Brooke's Fourth Brigade and Hiram L. Brown's Third Brigade in an advanced position south of the Shady Grove Church Road, about one mile south of the river, and with them were one section of William A. Arnold's Battery A and one section of T. Frederick Brown's Battery B of the 1st Rhode Island Light Artillery. Paul Frank, commander of the Third Brigade, had been relieved and placed under arrest that day, and Brown had succeeded him in command of the brigade. Nelson A. Miles' First Brigade and Thomas A. Smyth's Second Brigade were along the Shady

Grove Church Road, with their left near the Block House Bridge over the Po. At 2:00 P.M., Barlow recalled Brown and Brooke and formed their brigades on a wooded crest in rear of the Block House Road. As soon as these two brigades were in position, Miles and Smyth retired to some high ground on the south side of the river in front of some bridges that had been erected by Second Corps. There they deployed in line of battle and threw up breastworks to strengthen their position.

When Barlow began his withdrawal, Hancock ordered Birney to move his division to the right and occupy the heights on the north bank of the Po to cover the crossing. John C. Tidball, chief of artillery of Second Corps, left only Arnold's battery with Barlow, and placed the rest of his guns in position on the north bank to help in covering the crossing. At 2:30 P.M., Heth launched a strong attack on the line held by Brown and Brooke, but this was repulsed with severe losses. After a second attack was also thrown back, there was a lull in the fighting, and then Barlow ordered Brown and Brooke to withdraw across the river. Heth again attacked as these two brigades moved back, but they succeeded in reaching the north bank. Smyth's brigade then followed, and once across it formed in line to protect the pontoon bridge. Miles repulsed still another attack, and then he too crossed the bridge.

When all of Barlow's division had safely withdrawn, Birney's division returned to its former position on the right of Fifth Corps to take part in the attack ordered for 5:00 that afternoon. Barlow's division remained in position on the right of Birney to hold the ground that it had occupied after recrossing the river.

During the afternoon of May 10, 1864, the time for the attack, originally scheduled for 5:00 P.M., was changed. At 3:30 P.M., Meade ordered Warren to attack at once, and he also ordered Gibbon to cooperate with him with his division of Second Corps. At 3:45 P.M., Meade ordered Wright to attack with his Sixth Corps and Mott's division of Second Corps. Warren's line was formed with Cutler's division on the left, Gibbon's division in the center, and Crawford's division on the right. In Gibbon's division, Samuel S. Carroll's Third Brigade and Alexander S. Webb's First Brigade were in line, and Joshua T. Owen's Second Brigade was in reserve. Griffin's division of Fifth Corps was in reserve. Warren's line advanced through the woods, and in some places reached the enemy entrenchments, but finally it was driven back with heavy losses. James C. Rice, commanding Second Brigade of Cutler's Fourth Division, was killed, and he was succeeded by Edward B. Fowler.

After Barlow's division had completed its withdrawal from the south side of the Po River, Hancock returned to the position in front of Laurel Hill. He arrived there about 5:30 P.M., just before the end of Warren's assault, and Hancock then attacked again at 7:00 P.M. with the divisions of Gibbon and Birney and a part of Fifth Corps. This attack also ended in failure.

On the front of Wright's Sixth Corps, skirmishers found what they believed to be a vulnerable point in the enemy line. This was about a half mile south of the Spotsylvania Court House Road at the West Angle of the enemy works. On the afternoon of May 10, 1864, Wright ordered an attack, and he assigned Emory Upton to command an assaulting column. This was composed of twelve picked regiments as follows: three regiments from Upton's Second Brigade, First Division; four regiments from Eustis' Third Brigade, First Division; two regiments from Daniel D. Bidwell's Third Brigade, Second Division; and three regiments from Lewis A. Grant's Second Brigade, Second Division.

The column was formed on the open ground around the Scott (or Shelton) house, from which point a wood road led directly to the intended point of attack, about a half mile distant. The twelve regiments were formed in four lines of three regiments each, with two regiments of each line on the left of the road and one regiment on the right. The first line consisted of the regiments of Upton's brigade, with 121st New York and 96th Pennsylvania on the left of the road and 5th Maine on the right; the second line consisted of three regiments of Eustis' brigade, with 49th Pennsylvania and 6th Maine on the left and 5th Wisconsin on the right; the third line consisted of the 43rd New York and 77th New York of Bidwell's brigade on the left and the 119th Pennsylvania of Eustis' brigade on the right; and the fourth line consisted of the three regiments of Grant's brigade, with 2nd Vermont and 5th Vermont on the left and 6th Vermont on the right.

After an artillery preparation of about ten minutes by William B. Rhodes' Battery E, 1st Rhode Island Light Artillery; William H. McCartney's 1st Battery (A), Massachusetts Light Artillery; and Andrew Cowan's 1st Battery, New York Light Artillery, Upton began his attack at 6:10 P.M. Upton's column struck the enemy line just to the Federal right of the West Angle, broke through, and drove Doles' brigade back in disorder. The right of Daniel's brigade was also carried away with it. Upton then pressed on, while extending his line to the right and left, and he finally reached and captured a part of the second line of entrenchments, about a hundred yards to the rear. The enemy reacted quickly, however, and strong reinforcements soon brought the Federal advance to a halt. Battle's brigade of Rodes' division and Steuart's brigade of Johnson's division attacked on the front of Upton's line, and Gordon's division and Walker's Stonewall Brigade of Johnson's division struck on the flanks.

Meantime, at 2:00 P.M., Wright had instructed Mott, who was then under his orders, to be ready to assault the enemy works at 5:00 P.M. in support of Upton's attack. At 4:00 P.M., according to orders, Mott's division moved forward to the open ground around the Brown house, about three-fourths of a mile north of the apex of the salient in the enemy line. Mott then advanced with Robert McAllister's First Brigade in front and William R. Brewster's Second Brigade following close behind, and he soon came under a heavy artillery fire that enfiladed his lines. He was then forced to withdraw without being able to help Upton. Upton, however, held on to the captured works until night, and then, when Mott did not appear, he withdrew, under Russell's orders, under cover of darkness.

Operations of May 11, 1864. The army was relatively quiet May 11, 1864. There was the usual skirmishing along the front, but there were no serious engagements and no major troop movements. There were, however, vigorous preparations for an attack on the enemy works the next day. Little was known of the terrain or of the enemy positions immediately beyond the left of Sixth Corps, and at 9:00 A.M. Mott, whose division was near the Brown house, sent out four regiments of Brewster's brigade on a reconnaissance into this area to obtain additional information. These troops moved up close to the East Angle of the enemy entrenchments opposite the Landrum house, and they then returned to report their findings. On the basis of their information, Grant decided to launch a heavy attack on the East Angle early the next morning, May 12, 1864.

At 3:00 P.M. May 11, 1864, Meade issued the following orders: He instructed Hancock to move at dark with the divisions of Barlow, Birney, and Gibbon, and march across the rear of Fifth Corps and Sixth Corps to the vicinity of the Brown house. There they were to halt near Mott's division, which had been on the Brown farm for the past two days. Hancock was to form his command on the open ground of the Brown farm, and then advance and attack the enemy line at the East Angle at 4:00 A.M. May 12, 1864. Grant also ordered Burnside to attack with Ninth Corps on the east face of Lee's salient when Hancock attacked. Meade directed Wright to withdraw Russell's and Neill's divisions to the rear of the Sixth Corps entrenchments and hold them in readiness to move wherever they might be needed, depending on the outcome of Hancock's attack. Rickett's division was left to hold the Sixth Corps entrenchments. Meade ordered Warren to extend his line to the right so as to occupy the position vacated by Second Corps and also hold his own Fifth Corps line. Because of the increased coverage necessary, Kitching's First Brigade (Heavy Artillery) of Burton's Artillery Reserve was assigned to Warren. In addition, Richard S. Bowerman's Independent Brigade (formerly Denison's Third Brigade of Robinson's Second Division, Fifth Corps) was also placed on Warren's line. Bowerman was under Warren's direct orders.

About 10:00 P.M. May 11, 1864, Hancock moved to the left with the divisions of Barlow and Birney in darkness and a pouring rain, and a little after midnight joined Mott's division near the Brown house. Gibbon's division was in a position where it could not move without being observed by the enemy, and it did not start its march until 11:00 P.M. It then joined the other divisions of the corps about dawn May 12, 1864.

Ninth Corps was more active during May 11, 1864 than was most of the rest of the army. Burnside was ordered to withdraw his troops to the north side of the Ny River and establish a line with his right connecting with the left of Mott's division, near the Brown house, and his left on the Fredericksburg Road, near the Harris house. Burnside recrossed the Ny as ordered, and while getting his troops in posi-

tion on the left of Mott, he was ordered to return to the south side of the river and reoccupy the positions that he had held that morning. During the evening, the troops recrossed in a heavy storm, and between 9:00 and 10:00 P.M. Potter's division and Marshall's Provisional Brigade moved into the works thrown up earlier by Willcox's division. The other two divisions bivouacked nearby. While Ninth Corps was marching and countermarching, Thomas L. Crittenden arrived and assumed command of First Division. He relieved Leasure, who was in temporary command in place of Stevenson, who had been killed the day before. That night, Burnside received orders from Grant to join in a general attack by the army on the enemy works at 4:00 A.M.

There was one significant change in position by the enemy forces May 11, 1864. That morning Heth's division of Early's corps moved back from the left of the Confederate line to Spotsylvania Court House, and it then took position on the right of Wilcox's division, north of the court house, facing east.

Operations of May 12, 1864 (Hancock's Attack at the Salient). Before daylight May 12, 1864, Hancock formed his divisions for the attack on a line about 1,200 yards from the enemy works. The ground in that area was thickly wooded, except for a clearing some 400 yards wide that ran down to the Landrum house and then curved to the right directly toward the East Angle of the Confederate works. Barlow's division was formed in two lines across this clearing, with Brooke's brigade on the left and Miles' brigade on the right on the first line; and Smyth's and Brown's brigades on the second line, with Smyth's brigade in rear of Brooke and Brown's brigade in rear of Miles.

Birney's division, consisting of J. H. Hobart Ward's First Brigade and John S. Crocker's Second Brigade, was deployed in two lines on the right of Barlow. In front of Birney's division was a low marshy area, and beyond this was a thick woods of low pines When Birney had advanced about halfway to the enemy works, the left of his line moved out onto the open ground of the Landrum farm, but the right of the line continued to move forward through the woods until near the enemy entrenchments.

Mott's division, consisting of the brigades of McAllister and Brewster, deployed in rear of Birney in one line. When Gibbon's division arrived, it was placed in reserve in rear of Barlow's division, with the brigades of Owen and Carroll in the first line and Webb's brigade to their rear.

Hancock's attack was postponed because of a heavy fog until 4:35 A.M., and then Second Corps moved forward. Barlow's division advanced toward the East Angle of the salient, and it appears that it broke through the works at the angle and on that part of the line held by Steuart south of the angle. Owen's and Carroll's leading brigades of Gibbon's division hurried forward, and they entered the works with, and on the left of, Barlow's division. Webb's brigade soon came up and pushed on toward the enemy's second line. Birney's and Mott's divisions apparently broke through the line on a front that extended from a point just west of the East Angle to, and including, the West Angle, and then on southward on the west face of the salient for about 400 yards below the West Angle. McAllister's brigade of Mott's division arrived almost simultaneously with Birney's troops and crossed the enemy entrenchments with them. Brewster's brigade was close behind.

Hancock's initial attack was a complete success, and in a short time the victorious Federals were in possession of nearly a mile of the enemy works and had captured about 3,000 prisoners, including Generals Edward Johnson and George H. Steuart, and also twenty guns. Walker was wounded and the Stonewall Brigade was destroyed. Hancock's men pursued the fleeing enemy into the salient for about a half a mile, and at 5:30 A.M. reached Gordon's uncompleted line across the salient. There, after a short engagement, the Federals were stopped and then pushed back. Hiram L. Brown, commanding Third Brigade of Barlow's division, was captured, and was succeeded in command of the brigade by Clinton D. MacDougall. Alexander S. Webb, commanding First Brigade of Gibbon's division, was seriously wounded near the second line, and he was succeeded by H. Boyd McKeen, colonel of the 81st Pennsylvania Regiment of Miles' brigade of Barlow's division.

At the time of Hancock's attack, Gordon's Confederate division was in reserve, but Pegram's brigade of the division (commanded by John S. Hoffman) had been sent into the trenches near the left of Johnson's line. Clement A. Evans, then com-manding Gordon's brigade, was in front of the Mc-Coull house, and Robert D. Johnston's brigade was near the Harrison house. When Gordon heard the heavy firing at the East Angle, he sent forward Johnston's brigade, which soon encountered the right of Barlow's division and the left of Birney's division as they advanced from the captured entrenchments. Johnston's brigade was quickly broken and driven back; Johnston was wounded, and Thomas F. Toon assumed command of the brigade.

Gordon withdrew the brigades of Hoffman and Evans and formed them in line of battle near the Harrison house. He then advanced with these brigades against the left of Hancock's line and drove it back some distance toward the East Angle. At the same time, Rodes changed the front of Daniel's brigade, and then of Ramseur's brigade, from west to north; and he then moved them up through the woods east of the works against Birney and Mott, who were then moving down the west face of the salient. Ramseur was wounded and Daniel was mortally wounded in the fighting that followed.

At dawn that morning, Mahone left Ambrose R. Wright's brigade to cover the crossing of the Po River on the left of Field's line and, with his division of Early's corps (A. P. Hill's corps), moved back to the right of Lee's line, to the vicinity of Spotsylvania Court House. As soon as he arrived there, Mahone sent forward the brigades of Nathaniel H. Harris and Abner Perrin to take position on the right of Ramseur. Two hours later, Samuel McGowan's brigade of Wilcox's division was also sent to aid Ewell, and it was placed in rear of Harris and Ramseur. In the fighting that ensued, Perrin was killed and McGowan was dangerously wounded. Still later, James H. Lane's brigade of Wilcox's division and Mahone's own brigade (commanded by David Weisiger) were sent to the front. Finally, as the fighting continued, John Bratton's brigade (formerly Micah Jenkins') of Field's division and Benjamin J. Humphreys' brigade of Kershaw's division were sent to the salient to relieve some of the exhausted troops that were fighting there.

Finally, under the heavy pressure of the rein-forced Confederate line, all of Hancock's troops that had advanced into the interior of the salient had been driven out, but they continued to hold the outer face of the breastworks that they had captured that morning.

At 6:00 A.M., Meade ordered Wright to advance with the divisions of Neill and Russell of his Sixth Corps and support Hancock in his attack. Wright arrived at about the same time that the last of the troops of Second Corps retired from inside the salient. Wright was wounded as he came up, but he remained in command of his corps. It is difficult or impossible to fix the positions of the brigades of Sixth Corps during the fighting of May 12, 1864, because they were frequently moved from one point to another and were relieved when their ammunition was exhausted, or when the troops needed rest. Some of these units returned to take their place in line. Further, some brigades did not fight as units, but their regiments were separated and sent in wherever needed.

In general, Sixth Corps fought at the West Angle and along the west face of the salient. Neill's division began to arrive on the line first, and at 7:00 A.M. Edwards' brigade took position at, and to the south of, the West Angle, where it fought during the rest of the day. Grant's brigade was sent to the left of Hancock's line to relieve Barlow's division of Second Corps. Russell's division arrived in rear of Hancock's line about 9:30 A.M., and Upton's brigade was immediately sent forward to relieve a part of Mott's division. Upton was unable to reach the line of works, but he formed his brigade at an angle with them, with his left near the right of Edwards' line. Almost at once Upton opened fire on the enemy, who were attempting to regain their works. Shortly after Upton became engaged, Eustis' brigade, temporarily commanded by Joseph B. Hamblin, came up, and the regiments of the brigade were detached and used to fill the gaps at different points along the line. Penrose's brigade was sent to the extreme right, where it came under a very heavy fire and suffered severe losses. Bidwell's brigade of Neill's division was sent to support Edwards' brigade at the angle, and a part of the brigade was deployed to the right to support Upton. Bidwell then moved up into the line between Edwards and Upton, but was later relieved and sent to the left to support Second Corps.

When Russell's division became threatened, Grant's brigade was sent back from the left of Hancock's line to the West Angle, where it was engaged for about eight hours. When Frank Wheaton's First Brigade of Neill's division came

up, its regiments were used to relieve a part of Grant's brigade and a part of Hamblin's brigade. Ricketts' division followed Wright's column as soon as it could be withdrawn from the entrenchments, and at about 11:30 A.M., it arrived in rear of Neill's and Russell's divisions. At 1:00 P.M., troops of Benjamin F. Smith's Second Brigade of Ricketts' division relieved a part of Wheaton's brigade. John W. Schall's First Brigade of Ricketts' division was sent to the right, where it was engaged almost immediately and suffered severely.

At 8:00 A.M., Brooke's brigade of Barlow's division of Second Corps was sent to aid Wright, and it was used to relieve a part of Neill's division. Brooke fought on that front until his ammunition was exhausted, and he then returned to Hancock's line. Wheaton's brigade was relieved by Edward S. Bragg's Third Brigade of Cutler's Fourth Division of Fifth Corps at 3:00 P.M., and two hours later Wheaton was ordered to construct a line of rifle pits to connect Russell's division on the left with Ricketts' division on the right and form a reserve line of defense.

As the enemy troops followed the retiring Federals up the salient, they came under a very heavy fire from the Union infantry and artillery. When Hancock broke through Ewell's line that morning, he brought up a part of the Second Corps artillery to the right of the Landrum house, some 300 yards north of the captured works, and soon these guns began to fire over the heads of the infantry into the advancing lines of the enemy beyond. One section of James Gilliss' Batteries C and I, 5th United States Artillery moved up to the breastworks and opened fire at close range with canister. A section of T. Frederick Brown's Battery B, 1st Rhode Island Light Artillery also moved up to the right of the salient, and it too was effectively engaged.

The enemy pressed on, however, until they reached the inner face of the breastworks. Then began some of the most savage fighting of the war, in some places hand-to-hand, and always in a drenching rain. For a distance of nearly a mile the combatants were literally separated from one another only by piled-up logs and breastworks. This contest finally settled down to a struggle for the apex of the salient between the East Angle and the West Angle, with neither side yielding its position. The fighting was especially violent at the West Angle, which earned the name "Bloody Angle." The brigades that had suffered most severely, or had expended their ammunition, were sent to the rear to be re-formed and supplied with ammunition. Some of these brigades later returned to take their places in the line.

The fighting continued unabated all the rest of the morning and the afternoon, and it did not slacken until about dark. It did not cease then, but continued on with lesser fury until 3:00 A.M. May 13, 1864. At that time the enemy finally retired to a new line that they had constructed during the day across the base of the salient. This line was about 500 yards south of Gordon's uncompleted line, which ran across the salient about midway between the Mc-Coull house and the Harrison house. When the new line was occupied, Ewell's salient was completely eliminated.

While Hancock and Wright were engaged on the center and right center of the enemy line, Burnside and Warren attacked unsuccessfully on the enemy right and left flanks, respectively. Burnside attacked at 4:00 A.M., as ordered, by advancing Potter's Second Division, Ninth Corps against the works held by Lane's brigade of Wilcox's division. Lane's brigade was on the left of Early's line, and on the right of Johnson's division. At 5:00 A.M., Potter carried the line of works, but was soon driven back. Then, at Grant's direction, Potter and Crittenden moved their divisions forward in a series of attacks, but all were repulsed with considerable losses. At 9:15 A.M., Potter succeeded in establishing a connection with Hancock's corps on his right. Finally, Willcox's division, which had been in reserve, moved up to the left of Crittenden's division (and on the extreme left of the army) and attacked a salient held by Henry H. Walker's brigade (commanded by Robert M. Mayo) of Heth's division. Willcox advanced close to the enemy works, and was then struck by a heavy fire from Mayo's brigade and from the brigade of Edward L. Thomas on the left of Mayo, and also from Early's artillery. At the same time, Lane's brigade, supported by Weisiger's brigade, advanced against Willcox's flank and drove him back with serious losses. Burnside's only contribution to the general attack of May 12, 1864 was to contain enemy troops that might have been used to advantage against Hancock and Wright.

Meantime, on the Union right, Warren had opened that morning with all of his corps' artillery on the enemy works on his front, and had then pushed forward his skirmishers. There was no indication, however, that Anderson's line had been weakened by sending troops to oppose Hancock's assault, and Warren did not press his attack. Nevertheless, Grant believed that the enemy could not be very strong on Warren's front, and at 9:15 A.M. he ordered Warren to attack immediately. Warren made two strong attacks between 9:00 and 10:00 A.M. on a part of the line held by Field's division, but they were unsuccessful. William W. Robinson's First Brigade of Cutler's division, supported by Edward S. Bragg's Third Brigade of the same division, attacked from the front of Crawford's division, and they were accompanied by some of Crawford's men. Edward B. Fowler's Second Brigade of Cutler's division, and also Romeyn B. Ayres' First Brigade and Jacob B. Sweitzer's Second Brigade of Griffin's division joined in the attack. Joseph J. Bartlett's Third Brigade of Griffin's division was farther to the left, holding the works vacated by Second Corps, and it was not seriously engaged.

When Warren's attack failed, he was directed to send Cutler's and Griffin's division to the left to support Hancock and Wright. Cutler left behind Lyle's Brigade (formerly First Brigade of Robinson's Second Division, Fifth Corps), which was temporarily serving with his division, to hold the works on the right of Sixth Corps. In addition, Crawford's division, Kitching's brigade of heavy artillery, and Bowerman's Maryland Brigade were left to hold the Fifth Corps line. Cutler's division arrived in rear of Second Corps and Sixth Corps during the afternoon, and it soon joined Sixth Corps in the fighting. Bragg's brigade relieved Wheaton's brigade near the the West Angle, and Robinson's brigade and Fowler's brigade aided Wright in holding the captured works. Griffin's division arrived shortly after Cutler, but it does not appear to have been seriously engaged.

Operations of May 13, 1864 to May 18, 1864. May 13, 1864 was spent largely in straightening out and reorganizing the commands that had been engaged the day before. Cutler's and Griffin's divisions of Fifth Corps, which had been attached to Sixth Corps during the fighting at the salient, were sent back to the right of the line to rejoin the corps. Kitching's brigade, which had been associated with Fifth Corps since the Battle of the Wilderness, was transferred from the Artillery Reserve to Fifth Corps May 13, 1864 as an unassigned heavy artillery brigade.

Mott's Fourth Division, Second Corps had been seriously depleted by losses suffered during the campaign and by the expiration of the terms of enlistment of some troops. For this reason, the division was discontinued May 13, 1864. The brigades of the division were transferred to Birney's Third Division as follows: McAllister's First Brigade, Fourth Division became Third Brigade, Third Division; and Brewster's Second Brigade, Fourth Division became Fourth Brigade, Third Division. Mott assumed command of Third Brigade, Third Division, and McAllister resumed command of his 11th New Jersey Regiment. Brewster was assigned command of Fourth Brigade, Third Division, but William Blaisdell commanded the brigade for some time after its organization.

At daylight, May 13, 1864, when it was discovered that the enemy had retired from the salient, Gibbon was ordered to send forward a brigade to determine the new Confederate position. For this reconnaissance, Gibbon selected Owen's brigade, but he placed Carroll in command of it. Carroll advanced as ordered, and in the fighting that resulted, he was severely wounded. Theodore G. Ellis then assumed command of Carroll's brigade.

On May 13, 1864, Grant, knowing that enemy forces had been shifted toward the scene of the fighting at the salient the day before, decided on a movement to his left to attack Lee's right flank on the Fredericksburg-Spotsylvania Court House Road. He then directed that the troops be in position to attack at 4:00 A.M. the next morning, and Meade issued the necessary orders. Warren was to abandon his line of entrenchments and take the lead with his Fifth Corps in this movement, and he was to be supported by Wright's Sixth Corps. Warren was to leave his position after dark, and then march across the rear of Sixth Corps, Second Corps, and Ninth Corps to the Fredericksburg Road. Wright was to follow as soon as Warren had passed, and take position on the Massaponax Church Road. Both corps were to attack at 4:00 A.M.

Warren started at 9:00 P.M. and marched all night, through rain and mud, across fields and through woods, by way of the Scott (or Shelton)

house, the Landrum house, and the ford of the Ny River nearby; and when he finally arrived at his appointed place at 4:00 A.M., he had with him only about a thousand men. The rest were struggling along on the road behind. Wright was unable to start until 3:00 A.M., and he finally massed his corps on the Massaponax Church Road long after 4:00 A.M. An attack that morning, May 14, 1864, was not practicable, and it was called off at 9:00 A.M. The rest of the day was spent in bringing up the troops of Fifth Corps and Sixth Corps and getting them in position on the left of the army, east of Spotsylvania Court House.

Upton's brigade of Russell's division of Sixth Corps occupied a high point on the Massaponax Church Road, about a half mile south of the Ny River. A short time later, however, Upton was driven from the hill, but it was retaken by Ayres' brigade of Griffin's division of Fifth Corps. Wright then sent Russell's and Ricketts' divisions to occupy the high ground. Neill's division was placed at Andersons', on the Massaponax Church Road, to guard the left flank.

Grant received a report that the enemy had left the front of Hancock's corps during the night of May 14, 1864 and had moved toward the Federal left. To counter this movement, Hancock marched at 4:00 the next morning with the divisions of Barlow and Gibbon, and took position on the Spotsylvania Court House-Fredericksburg Road near the Ny River, in rear of Warren. Hancock left Birney's division behind to cover the right flank of Ninth Corps, and it was placed temporarily under Burnside's orders.

During the period May 15–17, 1864, Warren and Wright advanced their entrenched lines, established batteries, and opened roads for better communication. On May 18, 1864, Gibbon's division was sent several miles to the right to bring in the wounded of Second Corps and Sixth Corps, who had been lying in temporary hospitals behind the lines. This work was completed about 10:00 P.M.

At this point it is necessary to digress briefly and consider some of the administrative problems in the rear of the army. When Grant's army left Culpeper Court House May 4, 1864 on its way to the Wilderness, it abandoned the Orange and Alexandria Railroad as a line of supply and established a new base at Fredericksburg, where Edmund Schriver was assigned as military governor. It was a part of Grant's plan to open new bases that could be supplied by water as the army advanced to a line near the coast. When the army reached the vicinity of Spotsylvania Court House, its principal supply line was the Spotsylvania Court House-Fredericksburg Road. By that time, however, the problem of managing affairs in the rear areas had increased enormously. Not only was it necessary to bring forward supplies of all kinds for the army, but in addition there were many thousands of wounded to move to the rear for transfer to Washington, and also thousands of prisoners to be sent north for confinement. As an additional burden on the supply line, heavy reinforcements were soon to be sent forward from Washington. By May 16, 1864, the army had lost approximately 37,000 men, and it was imperative that these be replaced. By June 7, 1864, after the Battle of Cold Harbor, more than 48,000 reinforcements had been sent to the army from Washington. These included forty-four regiments, two provisional divisions, eight provisional brigades, and numerous detachments from the Rendezvous of Distribution.

May 10, 1864, John J. Abercrombie was ordered to Belle Plain, on an arm of the Potomac about ten miles northeast of Fredericksburg, to establish a depot for facilitating the above-described movements. Abercrombie was instructed to exercise at Belle Plain, and on the road to Fredericksburg, the authority of a post and district commander. Two days later Abercrombie assumed command of all troops at Belle Plain and Fredericksburg and all others in the vicinity. Also on May 12, 1864, Christopher C. Augur, commander of the Department of Washington and Twenty-Second Corps, was directed to abandon the railroad from Aquia Creek to Falmouth and to withdraw the troops that had been protecting it to positions on Bull Run and the Occoquan. The principal road from Belle Plain to Fredericksburg ran by White Oak Church, and at that time the road was guarded by a battalion under Nathan T. Dushane.

By May 13, 1864, the following troops had been sent to Belle Plain to guard the depot and also the prisoners that were being sent there: 1,200 men of the Veteran Reserve Corps, 600 men of the 8th Illinois Cavalry, and 700 dismounted cavalry to guard the prisoners (2,000 more men had arrived by May 17, 1864). The dismounted cavalry were placed under the command of Louis P. Di Cesnola. In addition to the above, there were 600 railroad and operating personnel, and Henry W. Benham's Engineer Brigade of 600 men to construct wharves and to repair the roads.

Before Grant left Spotsylvania May 20, 1864, he had received approximately 16,000–17,000 reinforcements from Washington, and these had arrived by way of Belle Plain and Fredericksburg. The first troops to arrive belonged to James M. Warner's 11th Vermont Regiment (1st Vermont Heavy Artillery). This regiment was assigned to Lewis A. Grant's Vermont Brigade (Second Brigade, Second Division, Sixth Corps) May 15, 1864. Warner was wounded two days later, and was succeeded in command of the regiment by Reuben C. Benton.

May 13, 1864, Henry W. Halleck ordered Augur to send to Grant's army five large heavy artillery regiments then serving as infantry in the Defenses of Washington, and he directed Robert O. Tyler to go to Belle Plain and assume command of these regiments as they arrived there. The regiments that reported to Tyler were: Daniel Chaplin's 1st Maine Heavy Artillery; Thomas R. Tannatt's 1st Massachusetts Heavy Artillery; Joseph N. G. Whistler's 2nd New York Heavy Artillery; Lewis O. Morris' 7th New York Heavy Artillery; and Peter A. Porter's 8th New York Heavy Artillery. These regiments were constituted as a temporary division under Tyler. Tyler's division joined the Army of the Potomac May 17, 1864, and it was assigned to Hancock's Second Corps as Tyler's Division of Heavy Artillery. When the division joined the corps May 18–19, 1864, it was designated as Fourth Division, Second Corps.

Also on May 17, 1864, Mathew Murphy arrived near Spotsylvania Court House with a brigade of New York regiments, commonly known as Corcoran's Legion and also as the Irish Legion. This brigade was assigned to Gibbon's division of Second Corps as Fourth Brigade, Second Division. Murphy was wounded May 18, 1864, and James P. McIvor assumed command of his brigade. For additional information about the troops sent to the Army of the Potomac, see Department of Washington, February 2, 1863–March 16, 1869.

There were also some command changes in Second Corps May 17, 1864. H. Boyd McKeen and Thomas A. Smyth reported to Gibbon to replace Carroll and Webb, who were wounded in the fighting at the Salient May 12, 1864. Gibbon assigned McKeen to the command of Webb's First Brigade, Second Division, Second Corps, and ordered Smyth to relieve Theodore G. Ellis in command of Carroll's Third Brigade, Second Division. Richard Byrnes succeeded Smyth in command of Second Brigade of Barlow's First Division, Second Corps.

Back near Spotsylvania Court House, Grant was considering new offensive operations. On May 17, 1864, he ordered Second Corps and Sixth Corps to move back during the night to the old works that they had attacked May 12, 1864, in the vicinity of the Landrum house. Then, at daylight the following morning, they were to attack the new enemy line at the base of the salient. Grant was aware that enemy troops had been drawn off to the right by the movements of Fifth Corps and Sixth Corps May 13–14, 1864, and he hoped that by a sudden attack he might find the left of Lee's line weakly held. Second Corps was to attack through the old salient, and at the same time, Sixth Corps was to attack on its right and Ninth Corps on its left. Warren was to open with his artillery, and hold his troops in readiness to take advantage of any success gained on his front.

Second Corps and Sixth Corps marched to their assigned positions on the night of May 17, 1864. Hancock had with him only the divisions of Barlow and Gibbon, because Birney's division was still with Burnside. Tyler's division of heavy artillery was formed in reserve between the Landrum house and the salient. Barlow and Gibbon attacked at 4:00 A.M. May 18, 1864, and were supported on the right by Sixth Corps, but despite the fact that the attack was pressed with great vigor, it was easily repulsed. Burnside attacked on the left of Second Corps, as directed, with the divisions of Crittenden and Potter and all the corps artillery, but he was unable to reach the enemy entrenchments. It was thus clear that the enemy line was still strongly held, and the attack was discontinued. Second Corps and Sixth Corps returned that evening to their former positions near Alexanders'.

That night, the divisions of Barlow, Gibbon, and Birney moved back to the vicinity of Anderson's Mill on the east side of the Ny River, below the left of Sixth Corps. Tyler's division of heavy artillery was left with Kitching's Heavy Artillery Brigade of Fifth Corps near the Harris house on the Spotsyl-vania Court House-Fredericksburg Road to guard the army's supply line.

Operations of May 19, 1864 (Engagement at the Harris Farm, Virginia). At 2:00 A.M. May 19, 1864, Ninth Corps moved to the left of Sixth Corps and took position on the extreme left of the army. The left of the corps was near the Po River, at the Quesenberry house, about two miles southwest of Anderson's Mill. When this movement was completed, Fifth Corps held the right of the army line, with J. Howard Kitching's Heavy Artillery Brigade of Fifth Corps and Robert O. Tyler's Fourth Division of Second Corps—which had just joined the army—to the right and rear, near the Harris house. Shortly after noon that day, Ewell moved out with his corps from his position south of the old salient on a march around the right flank of Grant's army. The purpose of this movement was to determine whether Grant was again moving the Army of the Potomac to the left, as Lee suspected.

At 3:00 P.M. Ewell crossed the Ny River, and a half hour later Ramseur's brigade, which was in the lead, struck the 4th New York Heavy Artillery of Kitching's brigade, which was in position behind a swamp, a little more than half a mile west of the Harris house. The 4th New York Heavy Artillery resisted stubbornly, while the 1st Massachusetts Heavy Artillery and the 1st Maine Heavy Artillery of Tyler's division moved up from east of the Fredericksburg-Spotsylvania Court House Road in support. Before 6:00 P.M., the 1st Massachusetts Heavy Artillery arrived near the Harris house and then took position on the ridge between the Harris house, on the left, and the Alsop house on the right. A part of 1st Maine Heavy Artillery came up and formed on the right of the 1st Massachusetts. In addition to the heavy artillery regiments, the 1st Maryland Infantry, which was on the way from Fredericksburg to Spotsylvania Court House, turned off the road and took position on the right of the 1st Maine, near the Peyton house, to which point the 4th New York had retired. That morning, Almont Barnes' Battery C, 1st New York Light Artillery had been posted near the Alsop house, where army head-quarters had been, and when Ramseur's attack began, Patrick Hart's 15th Battery, New York Light Artillery was sent to that point. Both batteries were from Charles S. Wainwright's Artillery Brigade of Fifth Corps, and were commanded during the battle by Robert H. Fitzhugh of the Artillery Reserve. They did good service in repelling the enemy attack.

Ramseur again attacked, and drove the 1st Massachusetts Heavy Artillery back to the knoll on which the Alsop house stood. Then, when his flanks were threatened, Ramseur retired about 200 yards and re-formed his command. Bryan Grimes' brigade then came up on the left of Ramseur and Cullen A. Battle's brigade on the right. Gordon, then commanding the survivors of Johnson's division, moved up on the left of Grimes.

In a flanking attack, the Federals drove Gordon's troops back in disorder, and as a consequence, Ramseur's line fell back to the place where his attack started. With the aid of Pegram's brigade (commanded by John S. Hoffman) and Wade Hampton's artillery, Ramseur was able to hold on until 9:00 P.M., and at that time Ewell withdrew across the Ny and returned to his breastworks.

When Hancock heard the sounds of the battle on the Fredericksburg Road, he sent Bowerman's Maryland Brigade of Fifth Corps to reinforce Kitching, and then at 6:00 P.M. he ordered Birney's division forward at the double quick. Hancock also went to the scene of the fighting and assumed command of all Federal troops engaged on the Harris farm. When Birney's division arrived at the Harris farm, Thomas W. Egan's First Brigade and Elijah Walker's Second Brigade went into action on the right of Tyler's division, but by that time the heaviest fighting was over. Walker had relieved John S. Crocker in command of Second Brigade of Birney's division the day before.

About dark, Crawford's division of Fifth Corps also came up to the Harris farm and was formed in support of Kitching's brigade and Bowerman's brigade on the left of the line, but it was not engaged. Russell's division of Sixth Corps was also sent up to help hold the Fredericksburg Road, and it was massed near the Harris house. It remained there during the night, and the next morning it relieved Birney's and Tyler's divisions, which then rejoined the other two divisions of Second Corps near Anderson's Mill. Crawford's division, Russell's division, and Kitching's brigade remained on the Harris farm to protect the right flank of the army.

With the engagement at the Harris farm, the fighting around Spotsylvania Court House came to an end, and the next day Grant resumed his advance by the left flank toward the North Anna River.

Organization of Grant's Army during Its Operations around Spotsylvania Court House, May 8–21, 1864.

ARMY OF THE POTOMAC
George G. Meade

SECOND CORPS, Winfield S. Hancock

First Division, Francis C. Barlow
   First Brigade, Nelson A. Miles
   Second Brigade, Thomas A. Smyth, to May 17, 1864
      Richard Byrnes
   Third Brigade, Paul Frank, to May 10, 1864
      Hiram Brown, to May 12, 1864, captured
      Clinton B. MacDougall
   Fourth Brigade, John R. Brooke

Note 1. Smyth was assigned command of Third Brigade, Second Division, Second Corps May 17, 1864.

Note 2. Frank was relieved from command of Third Brigade May 10, 1864, and was placed under arrest.

Second Division, John Gibbon
   First Brigade, Alexander S. Webb, to May 12, 1864, wounded
      H. Boyd McKeen
   Second Brigade, Joshua T. Owen
   Third Brigade, Samuel S. Carroll, to May 13, 1864, wounded
      Theodore G. Ellis, to May 17, 1864
      Thomas A. Smyth
   Fourth Brigade, Mathew Murphy, May 17–18, 1864, wounded
      James P. McIvor

Note 1. Smyth was transferred to Second Division from First Division, in which he commanded Second Brigade until May 17, 1864.

Note 2. Fourth Brigade joined the division from the Department of Washington, Twenty-Second Corps. Prior to the transfer, the brigade was known as Second Brigade, Tyler's Division, Twenty-Second Corps, but more commonly it was known as Corcoran's Legion. For more information, see Department of Washington, February 2, 1863–March 16, 1869, Troops in the Department of Washington.

Third Division, David B. Birney

First Brigade, J. H. Hobart Ward, to May 12, 1864
    Thomas W. Egan
Second Brigade, John S. Crocker, to May 18, 1864
    Elijah Walker

Note 1. Ward was relieved from command May 12, 1864 for drunkenness and misbehavior during the Battle of the Wilderness. He was arrested June 12, 1864, but was dismissed from the service July 18, 1864, without trial.

Note 2. The two brigades of Mott's Fourth Division, Second Corps (see below) were assigned to Third Division May 13, 1864 as Third Brigade and Fourth Brigade. Third Division was then organized as follows:

Third Division, David B. Birney
    First Brigade, Thomas W. Egan
    Second Brigade, John S. Crocker
    Third Brigade, Gershom Mott
    Fourth Brigade, William Blaisdell, temporarily
        William R. Brewster

Fourth Division, Gershom Mott
    First Brigade, Robert McAllister
    Second Brigade, William R. Brewster

Note 1. May 9, 1864, a provisional brigade was organized from five regiments of Mott's division, and John Ramsey was assigned command. This brigade was apparently discontinued after a few days.

Note 2. Fourth Division was discontinued May 13, 1864, and the two brigades were assigned to Third Division, Second Corps as follows: First Brigade, Fourth Division became Third Brigade, Third Division; and Second Brigade, Fourth Division became Fourth Brigade, Third Division (see Third Division, above).

Note 3. Fourth Division was reorganized May 18–19, 1864, when Robert O. Tyler, with five regiments of heavy artillery (serving as infantry), joined Second Corps from Washington. This division was known as Tyler's Division of Heavy Artillery. Two of the regiments were from Second Brigade of Joseph A. Haskin's Division, Department of Washington; two from Gustavus De Russy's Division, Department of Washington; and one from Second Separate Brigade, Middle Department, Eighth Corps.

Artillery Brigade, John C. Tidball

Note. The batteries of the artillery brigade were the same as those present at the Battle of the Wilderness (see above), except the following, which were transferred from the Artillery Reserve May 16, 1864: A. Judson Clark's Battery B, 1st New Jersey Light Artillery; John E. Burton's 11th Battery, New York Light Artillery; and George F. McKnight's 12th Battery, New York Light Artillery.

FIFTH CORPS, Gouverneur K. Warren

First Division, Charles Griffin

First Brigade, Romeyn B. Ayres
Second Brigade, Jacob B. Sweitzer
Third Brigade, Joseph J. Bartlett

Second Division, John C. Robinson, to May 8, 1864, wounded
Richard Coulter, to May 9, 1864
First Brigade, Peter Lyle, to May 9, 1864
Second Brigade, Richard Coulter, to May 8, 1864
    James L. Bates, to May 9, 1864
Third Brigade, Andrew W. Denison, to May 8, 1864, wounded
    Charles E. Phelps, May 8, 1864, wounded and captured
    Richard N. Bowerman, to May 9, 1864

Note. Second Division was temporarily disbanded May 9, 1864. First Brigade was attached to Fourth Division; Second Brigade to Third Division; and Third Brigade served as an independent brigade of Fifth Corps under the direct orders of the corps commander. This arrangement was continued until May 30, 1864, when the division was reorganized.

Third Division, Samuel W. Crawford
First Brigade, William C. McCandless, to May 8, 1864, wounded
    William C. Talley, May 8, 1864, captured
    Wellington H. Ent
    Samuel M. Jackson, to May 18, 1864
    Martin D. Hardin
Third Brigade, Joseph W. Fisher

Note. Richard Coulter resumed command of Second Brigade, Second Division May 9, 1864, when the brigade was attached to Crawford's division. Coulter was wounded May 18, 1864, and James L. Bates again assumed command of the brigade.

Fourth Division, Lysander Cutler
First Brigade, William W. Robinson
Second Brigade, James C. Rice, to May 10, 1864, killed
    Edward B. Fowler, to May 21, 1864
    J. William Hofmann
Third Brigade, Edward S. Bragg
Heavy Artillery Brigade, J. Howard Kitching

Note 1. Kitching's brigade was transferred to Fifth Corps from the Artillery Reserve May 13, 1864.

Note 2. Peter Lyle's First Brigade, Second Division, Fifth Corps was attached to Cutler's division May 9, 1864.

Artillery Brigade, Charles S. Wainwright

Note. The batteries of the Artillery Brigade were the same as those present at the Battle of the Wilderness (see above), except the following, which were transferred from the Artillery Reserve May 16, 1864: John Bigelow's 9th Battery, Massachusetts Light Artillery; Albert S. Sheldon's Battery B, 1st New York Light Artillery; William H. Phillips' Battery C, 1st New York Light Artillery; Elijah D. Taft's 5th Battery, New York Light Artillery; and Patrick Hart's 15th Battery, New York Light Artillery.

SIXTH CORPS, John Sedgwick, to May 9, 1864, killed
  Horatio G. Wright

First Division, Horatio G. Wright, to May 9, 1864
  David A. Russell
  First Brigade, Henry W. Brown
    William H. Penrose
  Second Brigade, Emory Upton
  Third Brigade, David A. Russell, to May 9, 1864
    Henry L. Eustis
  Fourth Brigade, Nelson Cross
    Joseph E. Hamblin, temporarily

Second Division, Thomas H. Neill
  First Brigade, Frank Wheaton
  Second Brigade, Lewis A. Grant
  Third Brigade, Daniel D. Bidwell
  Fourth Brigade, Henry L. Eustis, to May 9, 1864
    Oliver Edwards

Third Division, James B. Ricketts
  First Brigade, William H. Morris, to May 9, 1864, wounded
    John W. Schall, to May 14, 1864
    William S. Truex
  Second Brigade, Benjamin F. Smith

Artillery Brigade, Charles H. Tompkins

  Note. The Artillery Brigade consisted of the same batteries that were present at the Battle of the Wilderness (see above), except the following, which were transferred from the Artillery Reserve May 16, 1864: Greenleaf T. Stevens' 5th Battery (E), Maine Light Artillery; William Hexamer's Battery A, 1st New Jersey Light Artillery; William H. Ewing's Battery H, 1st Ohio Light Artillery; and John R. Brinckle's Battery E, 5th United States Artillery.

ARTILLERY, Henry J. Hunt

  Note. May 16, 1864, the batteries of Henry S. Burton's Artillery Reserve were assigned to Second Corps, Fifth Corps, and Sixth Corps (see above, artillery brigades of these corps), and Burton was assigned to Meade's staff as inspector of artillery.

Brigade, Horse Artillery, Dunbar R. Ransom
  Batteries E and G, 1st United States Artillery, Frank S. French

Batteries H and I, 1st United States Artillery, Alanson M. Randol
Battery K, 1st United States Artillery, John Egan
Battery A, 2nd United States Artillery, Robert Clarke
Battery G, 2nd United States Artillery, William Neil Dennison
Batteries C, F, and K, 3rd United States Artillery, George W. Barstow

Artillery Park, Freeman McGilvery
  2nd Battalion, 15th New York Heavy Artillery, Julius Dieckmann

UNATTACHED CAVALRY
  22nd New York Cavalry, Samuel J. Crooks

  Note. During the fighting around Spotsylvania Court House, the Cavalry Corps was absent on Sheridan's expedition toward Richmond (see Sheridan's Richmond, Virginia Raid). It departed May 9, 1864 and did not return to the army until after the battles around Spotsylvania Court House had ended. May 16, 1864, Alfred T. A. Torbert, who had undergone surgery in Washington, returned to the army and assumed command of all cavalry that had not accompanied Sheridan.

NINTH CORPS
Ambrose E. Burnside

First Division, Thomas G. Stevenson, to May 10, 1864, killed
  Daniel Leasure, to May 12, 1864
  Thomas L. Crittenden
  First Brigade, Jacob P. Gould, to May 8, 1864, sick
    Stephen M. Weld, Jr., to May 13, 1864
    James H. Ledlie
  Second Brigade, Daniel Leasure, to May 10, 1864
    Gilbert P. Robinson, to May 12, 1864
    Daniel Leasure, to May 14, 1864, sick
    Gilbert P. Robinson
  Provisional Brigade, Elisha G. Marshall

  Note. Marshall's brigade served as an unattached command of Ninth Corps until May 12, 1864, and then it was attached to First Division.

Second Division, Robert B. Potter
  First Brigade, John I. Curtin
  Second Brigade, Simon G. Griffin

Third Division, Orlando B. Willcox
  First Brigade, John F. Hartranft
  Second Brigade, Benjamin C. Christ, to May 12, 1864
    William Humphrey

Fourth Division, Edward Ferrero

First Brigade, Joshua K. Sigfried
Second Brigade, Henry G. Thomas

Note. Fourth Division, which was composed of regiments of United States Colored Troops, was on duty guarding the trains of the army and was not engaged.

Reserve Artillery, John Edwards, Jr.

Note 1. The Reserve Artillery of Ninth Corps was not engaged at Spotsylvania Court House, and it was ordered to Washington May 16, 1864.
Note 2. The divisional artillery was the same as at the Battle of the Wilderness (see above).

Cavalry
3rd New Jersey Cavalry, Andrew J. Morrison
5th New York Cavalry, John Hammond
2nd Ohio Cavalry, George A. Purington
13th Pennsylvania Cavalry, Michael Kerwin

FROM SPOTSYLVANIA COURT HOUSE TO THE NORTH ANNA RIVER MAY 21, 1864–MAY 26, 1864

May 20, 1864, the Army of the Potomac and Burnside's Ninth Corps began to move to the left from their lines at Spotsylvania Court House in the direction of Richmond. Winfield S. Hancock's Second Corps started after dark that night and, preceded by Alfred T. A. Torbert's cavalry, arrived at Guiney's Station at daybreak the next morning. It then moved on to Bowling Green, where it arrived about 10:00 A.M. About two miles farther on, at Milford Station (or Milford) on the Richmond, Fredericksburg, and Potomac Railroad, Torbert encountered a small enemy force belonging to James E. Kemper's brigade (then commanded by William R. Terry) of George E. Pickett's division, James Longstreet's corps, which had been on detached service in North Carolina. Torbert soon cleared the crossing of the Mattapony River at the Milford Bridge, and Second Corps then crossed and entrenched that afternoon a short distance west of the river. Second Corps remained in position there the rest of the day.

Gouverneur K. Warren's Fifth Corps began to withdraw from Spotsylvania Court House at 10:00 A.M. May 21, 1864, and it marched by way of Massaponax Church to Guiney's Station, where it arrived about 5:00 that evening. At that point, Warren turned south, crossed the river below the junction of the Po and Ny rivers, and then moved out a short distance on the road that ran to the southwest to Madison's Store. The store was not far from Lebanon Church, and was about a mile east of Nancy Wright's house, which was on the Telegraph Road. Warren halted for the night at the Catlett house, which was just south of the crossing at the Guiney Bridge, and at the point where the road from Mud Tavern came in from the west. Mud Tavern was located about two miles south of Stanard's Mill, on the Telegraph Road. Warren advanced J. Howard Kitching's Heavy Artillery Brigade to Madison's Store that evening.

As soon as Fifth Corps had cleared the road at Spotsylvania Court House, Ambrose E. Burnside's Ninth Corps marched to Stanard's Mill on the Po River. The Telegraph Road that ran south from Fredericksburg crossed the Po at that point and continued on toward Richmond. Burnside's orders were to cross the Po, if practicable, and then move down the Telegraph Road toward the North Anna River. Horatio G. Wright's Sixth Corps was to follow Burnside.

Robert B. Potter's Second Division, Ninth Corps marched first, and Potter immediately sent out John I. Curtin's First Brigade, with Edward J. Jones' 11th Battery, Massachusetts Light Artillery, to gain possession of the Po crossing. Potter followed with Simon G. Griffin's Second Brigade. Curtin advanced to the river, driving back the enemy pickets, and when he arrived there, he found Richard S. Ewell's corps strongly entrenched on the other side. Early that morning, Ewell had moved to the right of Lee's lines to the Po River, where he was found by Curtin. Burnside's troops skirmished for a time, but they did not attempt to force a crossing. Meantime, Thomas L. Crittenden's First Division and Orlando B. Willcox's Third Division had also started for Stanard's Mill.

Earlier that day, when Warren had abandoned his entrenchments at Spotsylvania Court House, Wright had withdrawn his Sixth Corps to a new position near the Gayle house, and there, about 6:00 P.M., his picket line was attacked by two brigades of Cadmus M. Wilcox's division that had been sent out by Early to determine whether the Federal troops had left his front. Wilcox pushed back Wright's skirmishers, and a sharp fight ensued. Burnside then sent back Willcox's division to support Wright, but the enemy did not press their attack. Willcox remained with Sixth Corps until after dark, and then resumed his march toward Stanard's Mill.

On the evening of May 21, 1864, Ambrose P. Hill, in person, arrived at Lee's headquarters and assumed command of his corps. When relieved, Early returned to Ewell's corps and resumed command of his division.

Acting under discretionary orders, Burnside changed the route of his march, and started that night for Guiney's Station. Potter left Curtin's brigade at Stanard's Mill, with orders to remain there until the rest of Ninth Corps and Sixth Corps, which was to follow, had passed, and he marched with Simon G. Griffin's brigade at the head of the column. Potter arrived at Guiney's Station at 2:00 A.M. May 22, 1864.

At 10:00 on the night of May 21, 1864, Wright withdrew his Sixth Corps from its position near the Gayle house, and followed Ninth Corps toward Guiney's Station.

Early on the morning of May 22, 1864, George G. Meade issued the march orders for the army that day. Fifth Corps was to advance from Catletts' to Harris' Store; and after Sixth Corps had halted at Guiney's Station to rest, it was to follow Fifth Corps to Madison's Store. Burnside was to resume his march from Guiney's Station at 10:00 A.M. and cross the Mattapony River at Downer's Bridge. He was then to move out on the road that ran from the bridge to Hanover Court House, and halt at Bethel (New Bethel) Church. At that point there was a crossroad running past Madison's Store to Bowling Green. Second Corps was to remain near Milford Station during the day.

Following orders, Potter, with Griffin's brigade, moved southward along the Richmond, Fredericksburg, and Potomac Railroad, and at 5:00 A.M. May 22, 1864 reached Downer's Bridge, a short distance north of Bowling Green. Potter waited there until Curtin's brigade came up from Stanard's Mill, and then crossed the river and took position about three miles west at Bethel (New Bethel) Church. Crittenden's First Division and Willcox's Third Division of Ninth Corps halted at Guiney's Station about sunrise May 22, 1864, and after resting two hours, moved on and joined Potter near Bethel Church.

At 10:00 A.M. May 22, 1864, as soon as Sixth Corps arrived from Spotsylvania Court House, Fifth Corps left Catletts' and marched by way of Madison's Store to Nancy Wright's, and then followed the Telegraph Road to Harris' Store. It bivouacked that night at Dr. Flippo's, near the Telegraph Road, on the crossroad from Chilesburg to Milford. Sixth Corps followed Fifth Corps on the Telegraph Road, but it did not join Fifth Corps until the next morning. Thus, on the night of May 22, 1864, Fifth Corps and Sixth Corps were abreast of Hancock's Second Corps, and Ninth Corps was within supporting distance. The four corps were within three or four miles of one another.

Soon after Grant began his movement toward the North Anna, Lee started the Army of Northern Virginia on the march toward Hanover Junction, which was at the intersection of the Richmond, Fredericksburg, and Potomac and the Virginia Central railroads, about two miles south of the North Anna, and twenty-two miles from Richmond. Ewell's corps started first, shortly after noon May 21, 1864, and marched to Mud Tavern, where it turned south on the Telegraph Road. Lee was with the head of Ewell's corps when it arrived at Hanover Junction at 9:30 A.M. May 22, 1864, and as his troops came up he put them in a defensive position on the south bank of the North Anna River. In front of the position that Lee had selected, there were two bridges across the North Anna. One was the railroad bridge, which crossed the river due north of Hanover Junction, and the other was Fox's Bridge, on which the Telegraph Road crossed the river. This bridge was also called Taylor's Bridge, Telegraph Bridge, and the Chesterfield Bridge. Fox's Bridge was about a half mile west of the railroad bridge.

Lee placed Ewell's corps on the right of his line, covering Hanover Junction; and when Richard H. Anderson's corps, which was following Ewell, arrived that night, it was placed on the left of Ewell, opposite the two bridges. The left of Anderson's corps extended upstream to Ox Ford, about a mile above Fox's Bridge. Hill's corps completed its withdrawal from the entrenchments at Spotsylvania Court House about 9:00 P.M. May 21, 1864 and, marching by roads to the west of, and parallel to, the Telegraph Road, reached Hewlett's Station on the

Virginia Central Railroad about noon the next day. At 7:00 A.M. May 23, 1864, Hill continued the march on a road parallel to the railroad to Anderson's Station (later called Verdon's Station), three miles west of Hanover Junction. He then bivouacked nearby.

At Hanover Junction, Lee received much-needed reinforcements for his army. May 15, 1864, John C. Breckinridge defeated a Union force commanded by Franz Sigel at New Market in the Shenandoah Valley. When Sigel retreated down the valley, Breckinridge marched to Staunton with the brigades of John Echols and Gabriel C. Wharton, and from there moved by rail to Hanover Junction May 20, 1864. Breckinridge was placed temporarily under Lee's orders, and his division was later put in line between Ewell's corps and Anderson's corps.

Pickett's division of Longstreet's corps, which had been on detached service in North Carolina and southeastern Virginia since September 1863, rejoined the Army of Northern Virginia at Hanover Junction. Montgomery D. Corse's brigade and William R. Terry's brigade (Kemper's) rejoined Anderson's corps May 22, 1864, and Seth Barton's brigade was temporarily attached to Hill's corps. Eppa Hunton's brigade rejoined later after it was relieved at Chaffin's farm below Richmond. Pickett, in person, arrived and reported to Hill May 23, 1864.

During the winter of 1863–1864, Robert F. Hoke's brigade of Early's division of Hill's corps had been detached and sent to North Carolina. This brigade, commanded by William G. Lewis, arrived from Petersburg May 22, 1864 and rejoined Early's division.

Battle of the North Anna River (Including the Combat at Jerico Mills [Jerico Bridge, or Jerico Ford]), May 23–26, 1864. On the morning of May 23, 1864, Grant's army resumed its march toward the North Anna River. Warren's Fifth Corps advanced on the right, and arrived at Mount Comfort Church on the Telegraph Road about 11:00 A.M. It then moved on to Jerico Mills, which was about three miles distant and about four miles above Fox's Bridge. Hancock's Second Corps marched on the left and reached Old Chesterfield, about four miles north of Fox's Bridge over the North Anna, at the same time that Warren passed Mount Comfort Church. Hancock then continued on, with David B.

Birney's Third Division in the lead, and during the afternoon took position about a mile north of the North Anna. Later that afternoon both Fifth Corps and Second Corps were engaged with the enemy. Burnside's Ninth Corps advanced between Fifth Corps and Second Corps to Ox Ford on the North Anna. Sixth Corps moved down the Telegraph Road and followed Fifth Corps to Jerico Mills.

When Fifth Corps reached the North Anna at Jerico Mills, Joseph J. Bartlett's Third Brigade of Charles Griffin's First Division crossed unopposed and formed on the opposite bank. Martin Van Brocklin's 50th New York Engineers then laid a pontoon bridge, and by 4:30 P.M. all of Warren's infantry was over the river. Leaving Bartlett's brigade near the crossing, Griffin advanced with Romeyn B. Ayres' First Brigade and Jacob B. Sweitzer's Second Brigade about a half to three-fourths of a mile and deployed in line of battle in front of the ford, with Sweitzer's brigade on the right and Ayres' brigade on the left. Samuel W. Crawford's Third Division then moved up and formed on the left of Griffin, with its left near the river, below the ford.

At 6:00 P.M., Lysander Cutler advanced his Fourth Division to the right of Griffin's division, with his right extending to the river above the ford. William W. Robinson's First Brigade (the Iron Brigade) was on the left of the division, next to Griffin, and Edward S. Bragg's Third Brigade was on the right. J. William Hofmann's Second Brigade was in support of the front line; and Peter Lyle's First Brigade, Second Division, Fifth Corps, which was temporarily attached to Cutler's division, was in reserve. J. Howard Kitching's Heavy Artillery Brigade was left behind to cover the bridge.

Griffin's division had just taken position when it was attacked by Cadmus M. Wilcox's division of Hill's corps. Wilcox's division consisted of the brigades of Edward L. Thomas, Samuel McGowan, James H. Lane, and Alfred M. Scales, and was deployed along the Virginia Central Railroad, with its left at Noel's Station. Griffin repulsed the attack on his front, but Wilcox also struck Robinson's brigade of Cutler's division just as it was moving up into line. This brigade quickly gave way, and it was followed by Bragg's brigade on the right. Charles H. Mink put his Battery H, 1st New York Light Artillery in position and opened fire on the advancing enemy. Robinson and Bragg re-formed their brigades in rear of the guns, and Hofmann's brigade moved up in support; together they were able to hold their position. Robinson's withdrawal uncovered the right of Griffin's position, and Bartlett's brigade was brought up to restore the line. Lyle's brigade was also moved to the rear of Griffin's line. At about that time, James L. Bates arrived with his Second Brigade, Second Division, Fifth Corps (temporarily attached to Crawford's division) and reported to Cutler. Henry Heth's division of Hill's corps came up in support of Wilcox. The fighting continued for some time, but then Hill's divisions withdrew.

The head of Sixth Corps was at Mount Carmel Church when Warren's battle began, and it moved up to Jerico Mills to support Fifth Corps. It was not needed, however, and did not cross the river until the next morning. Fifth Corps entrenched during the night and held its position south of the river.

Meantime, on the Federal left, Hancock's Second Corps had moved into position north of the North Anna River. David B. Birney's Third Division was on the right, across the Telegraph Road, and in front of Fox's Bridge. Gershom Mott's Third Brigade of the division was about a mile to the right, at Ox Ford. John Gibbon's Second Division was on the left, and it extended across the Richmond, Fredericksburg, and Potomac Railroad; and Francis C. Barlow's First Division was between the divisions of Birney and Gibbon. Robert O. Tyler's division of heavy artillery was held in reserve.

Torbert's cavalry had preceded Second Corps in its advance that day, and when Hancock arrived near the river, he learned that the enemy held a bridgehead on the north bank at Fox's Bridge. That evening, Thomas W. Egan's First Brigade and Byron R. Pierce's Second Brigade (Pierce had relieved Elijah Walker in command of the brigade that day) of Birney's division attacked just before dark and drove Kershaw's men, who held the bridgehead, across the river and seized the bridge. The following batteries of John C. Tidball's Second Corps artillery supported this attack: Edwin B. Dow's 6th Battery (F), Maine Light Artillery; William A. Arnold's Battery A, 1st Rhode Island Light Artillery; and T. Frederick Brown's Battery B, 1st Rhode Island Light Artillery. It was then too late to attempt to cross the river that evening, but the two brigades held the captured works during the night.

May 23, 1864, while Fifth Corps was advancing on the Telegraph Road on the right and Second Corps near the railroad on the left, Burnside's Ninth Corps marched between them on plantation roads toward the North Anna. Willcox's Third Division arrived at Ox Ford at sundown and relieved Mott's brigade of Second Corps, which then rejoined its division. That night, Willcox entrenched a position north of the river, and the other two divisions of the corps bivouacked to his rear.

During the night of May 23, 1864, Lee drew back his flanks and formed a new defensive position as follows: on the center and right, the line began at Ox Ford and ran along the river down to a point about a half mile above Fox's Bridge, and it then ran on to the southeast for about three miles to a point near Maurice's (Morris') Bridge, east of Hanover Junction. Beginning on the left, this line was held by Anderson's corps, Breckinridge's division, and Ewell's corps on the right. On Lee's left, the line ran southwest from Ox Ford for about a mile and a half. It crossed the Virginia Central Railroad west of Anderson's Station, and ended at Anderson's Mill on Little River, where its flank was protected by marshy ground. Hill's corps and Pickett's division held that part of the line.

The Union advance continued on May 24, 1864, but much more slowly. That morning Sixth Corps crossed the North Anna at Jerico Mills and deployed on the right of Fifth Corps. Also that morning, Crittenden's division of Ninth Corps crossed the river at Quarles' Mills, about a mile above Ox Ford, to join Crawford's Third Division of Fifth Corps for an advance along the south side of the river toward Ox Ford. The purpose of this movement was to drive the enemy from the river bank and establish a connection between Second Corps and Fifth Corps, south of the river. James H. Ledlie's First Brigade of Crittenden's division advanced to the right of Crawford's division, but it was strongly attacked by William Mahone's division of Hill's corps and driven back. Crittenden then moved back, connected with Crawford, and entrenched his line. Crittenden was then placed temporarily under Warren's orders.

On the morning of May 24, 1864, Hancock discovered that the enemy on his front had withdrawn from the south bank of the river, and at 8:00 A.M. he sent Birney's division across to occupy the abandoned works around the Fox house. Two pontoon bridges were then laid below the railroad bridge, and Gibbon's and Barlow's divisions crossed during the late morning and early afternoon. Hancock then advanced his corps and entrenched a position within 600–800 yards of the enemy line. Tyler's heavy artillery remained on the north bank to occupy the works captured the evening before.

Potter's division of Ninth Corps crossed to the south bank of the North Anna and reported to Hancock, who assigned it to a position on the right of Second Corps, between the river and the Telegraph Road. This left only Willcox's division of Ninth Corps north of the river, and it was in position at Ox Ford. From the left of Potter's line, Hancock's divisions were, in order from right to left, as follows: Birney's, Barlow's, and Gibbon's.

Late in the evening, Thomas H. Smyth's Third Brigade of Gibbon's division advanced on a reconnaissance of the enemy positions. Smyth was supported by H. Boyd McKeen's First Brigade, and later by Joshua T. Owen's Second Brigade. Smyth and McKeen soon made contact with the enemy and were engaged until dark.

A significant organizational change occurred in the army May 24, 1864. Burnside's Ninth Corps, which up to that time during the campaign had received orders directly from Grant, was assigned to the Army of the Potomac, and was placed under Meade's orders. The army then consisted of the four infantry corps and Philip H. Sheridan's Cavalry Corps. Sheridan returned that day from his Richmond raid and rejoined the army near Chesterfield. The next day, James H. Wilson's Third Cavalry Division was sent to the right of the army near Little River, and Alfred T. A. Torbert's First Cavalry Division and David McM. Gregg's Second Cavalry Division camped until May 26, 1864 in the vicinity of Pole Cat Station on the Richmond, Fredericksburg, and Potomac Railroad.

There was very little activity on the Union lines May 25, 1864. That morning, Fifth Corps, Crittenden's division of Ninth Corps, and Sixth Corps moved up to within 600–800 yards of Hill's line between Ox Ford and Little River, and as noted above, Wilson's cavalry division moved to the right of this line.

At this time, Grant also ordered another change in base to supply the army. When he departed from

the vicinity of Spotsylvania Court House, the connection with Washington and Alexandria through Fredericksburg became more difficult, and May 22, 1864, Grant ordered John J. Abercrombie to break up the installations at Belle Plain, Aquia Creek, and Fredericksburg, and establish a new base at Port Royal, Virginia, about fifteen miles below Fredericksburg on the Rappahannock River. The transfer was completed May 25, 1864, while the army was on the North Anna.

OPERATIONS ON THE PAMUNKEY RIVER MAY 27–29, 1864

By May 25, 1864, Grant realized that the army was in a difficult position. The enemy lines south of the North Anna River were in the shape of an inverted V, with the apex on the river at Ox Ford, and the positions were too strongly entrenched to be attacked with any promise of success. Because of this, Hancock's command to the east of Ox Ford was effectively separated from Warren's and Wright's corps and Crittenden's division to the west of the ford. Further, for one part of the army to support the other, it would be necessary to cross and recross the North Anna, a time-consuming operation. In view of these difficulties, Grant decided to abandon his positions on the North Anna and continue the movement of the army to the left.

At daylight May 26, 1864, David A. Russell's First Division was detached from Sixth Corps and ordered to recross the river at Jerico Mills and escort the trains to Chesterfield Station. Then, after dark that evening, the rest of the army began to withdraw to the north bank of the North Anna in preparation for marching toward the Pamunkey River in the vicinity of Hanovertown, about thirty-two miles to the southeast. The Pamunkey River was formed by the junction of the North Anna River and the South Anna River about five miles southeast of Hanover Junction.

Fifth Corps, Sixth Corps, and Crittenden's division of Ninth Corps recrossed the North Anna at Quarles' Mills, while Second Corps and Potter's division crossed at Fox's Bridge, and by 3:00 A.M. May 27, 1864, all were north of the river. Wilson's cavalry division was then brought up to guard the crossings and protect the rear of the army.

Meantime, late on May 26, 1864, Sheridan had started out with the divisions of Torbert and Gregg on the River Road, ahead of the infantry, to secure the crossings of the Pamunkey at Hanovertown. Russell's division of Sixth Corps followed the cavalry, and was under orders to make a forced march to Hanovertown. Wright followed Russell with the rest of Sixth Corps. Hancock's Second Corps began its march on the River Road, in rear of Sixth Corps, at 10:30 A.M. May 27, 1864. Fifth Corps marched at 9:00 A.M. May 27, 1864, farther to the north of the river, with orders to cross the Pamunkey at New Castle Ferry. Ninth Corps assembled at Mount Carmel Church and, during the afternoon, after Fifth Corps had cleared the road, followed Warren toward New Castle Ferry.

Sheridan occupied Hanovertown at 9:00 A.M. May 27, 1864, and then moved out to the south of the river. He soon encountered enemy cavalry and pushed them back to Crump's Creek, which flows into the Pamunkey about three and a half miles northwest of Hanovertown. Sheridan also occupied the road from Hanovertown to Atlee's Station on the Virginia Central Railroad. Russell's division of Sixth Corps, which had followed the cavalry, was also across the Pamunkey at Hanovertown by about 11:00 A.M. May 27, 1864, and it then took position to guard the crossing.

During the afternoon of May 27, 1864, the marching orders for the army were changed. Wright, with Thomas H. Neill's Second Division and James B. Ricketts' Third Division of Sixth Corps, and Hancock's Second Corps were directed to cross the Pamunkey at a point opposite Mrs. Hundley's, about one mile below the mouth of Crump's Creek. Fifth Corps and Ninth Corps were ordered to cross at Hanovertown.

There was almost constant fighting during May 27, 1864, with actions taking place at such widely scattered places as Hanover Junction, Sexton's Station, Mount Carmel Church, Dabney's Ferry, Hanovertown, Little River, Pole Cat Creek, and Salem Church.

At dawn May 27, 1864, Lee discovered that Grant's army had withdrawn from the south side of the North Anna the night before, and that he was apparently again moving to the Federal left. Lee immediately started Ewell's corps down the Richmond, Fredericksburg, and Potomac Railroad toward Ashland, and he also ordered Anderson, with his corps and Breckinridge's division, to follow Ewell. Hill's corps was to form the rear guard and, with Pickett's division, was to leave the North Anna that evening. Lee halted for the night northwest of Atlee's Station. Ewell had not been well for some time, and May 27, 1864, Jubal A. Early assumed temporary command of his corps (he was officially assigned command May 29, 1864). May 28, 1864, Stephen D. Ramseur was assigned command of Early's division, and William R. Cox assumed command of Ramseur's brigade of Robert E. Rodes' division.

May 28, 1864, Lee moved eastward from the Virginia Central Railroad and put his army in a good position on a ridge lying between the Totopotomoy River and Beaver Dam Creek. The former flows eastward, just north of Pole Green Church, and into the Pamunkey below Hanovertown. The latter is a small stream that heads in the vicinity of Bethesda Church and flows west and then south past Mechanicsville and into the Chickahominy River. Early's corps was on the right of this new line, south of the Totopotomoy, with its right near Beaver Dam Creek. It covered the road passing Pole Green Church, and also the road from Mechanicsville to Old Church. Anderson's corps, to which Pickett's division reported that day, was placed in rear of Early's line. Hill's corps was deployed on the left of Anderson, covering the point where the road from Shady Grove Church to Hanover Court House crossed the Totopotomoy. Breckinridge's division was placed between Anderson and Hill.

Engagement at Haw's Shop (Aenon, or Enon, Church), May 28, 1864. The Army of the Potomac also continued its advance May 28, 1864. That morning, Sheridan sent Gregg's cavalry division out by way of Haw's Shop, on the Mechanicsville Road, to determine the whereabouts of Lee's infantry. About three-fourths of a mile beyond Haw's Shop, Gregg found an enemy cavalry force consisting of Thomas L. Rosser's brigade of Wade Hampton's division and Williams C. Wickham's brigade of Fitzhugh Lee's division. These two brigades were then reinforced by Matthew Calbraith Butler's cavalry brigade, which had just arrived from South

Carolina. Gregg promptly attacked, and for some hours the cavalry fought, generally dismounted, in an area covered by thick woods and dense underbrush, without advantage to either side. Henry E. Davies' First Brigade attacked first, and was soon joined by J. Irvin Gregg's Second Brigade. About 2:00 P.M., George A. Custer's First Brigade of Torbert's First Cavalry Division was ordered up from Crump's Creek to support Gregg. Custer arrived on the road and formed in the center of Gregg's line, which opened to make room for his brigade. The entire Federal line then charged and drove the enemy from the area.

Sixth Corps relieved Torbert's cavalry at Crump's Creek shortly after noon, and Torbert then moved to Haw's Shop with Thomas C. Devin's Second Brigade and Wesley Merritt's Reserve Brigade. Merritt's brigade was placed on the extreme right of Gregg's line, but it was not seriously engaged. Devin's brigade was held in reserve. About dark, Gregg returned to Hanovertown, and Torbert to a point a short distance below Hanovertown.

* * * * * * * * * *

While the cavalry was engaged at Haw's Shop, the infantry was crossing the Pamunkey River. Sixth Corps had completed its crossing by shortly after noon, and it then marched to Crump's Creek, where it relieved Torbert's cavalry. Second Corps followed Sixth Corps, and when it arrived, it took position on the right of Sixth Corps. The two corps covered the road from Crump's Creek to Haw's Shop. Fifth Corps advanced from Mangohick Church and crossed the Pamunkey at Hanovertown during the late morning of May 28, 1864. It then moved out about a mile on the road to Haw's Shop and halted at Dr. Brockenbrough's, at the junction with the road running to Nelson's Ferry. The corps was then deployed, with Griffin's division on the right, Cutler's division in the center, and Crawford's division on the left. Ninth Corps reached Hanovertown between 10:00 P.M. May 28, 1864 and 1:00 A.M. May 29, 1864, and it also crossed to the south side of the river. Wilson's cavalry division, which had followed the infantry from the North Anna, remained on the north bank of the river until the morning of May 30, 1864.

OPERATIONS ON THE TOTOPOTOMOY RIVER MAY 29–30, 1864

May 29, 1864, Hancock's Second Corps and Warren's Fifth Corps moved forward to the Totopotomoy River. Second Corps advanced on the road from Haw's Shop to Atlee's Station, and Fifth Corps on the Shady Grove Road. The latter road ran from Hanovertown by way of Haw's Shop and Pole Green Church on the Totopotomoy to Shady Grove Church, and from there on to Richmond. Wright's Sixth Corps remained on the right of the army in the vicinity of Crump's Creek, with Russell's division at Hanover Court House, Neill's division about three miles from the court house, and Ricketts' division near the pontoon bridge at Widow Nelson's house. Burnside's Ninth Corps was in reserve near Haw's Shop. Sheridan, with the cavalry divisions of Torbert and Gregg, moved to the left on the Old Church Road to watch the approaches from Mechanicsville, Cold Harbor, and White House.

By the evening of May 29, 1864, Fifth Corps was on the left of Meade's line, about a mile south of the Totopotomoy, on the Shady Grove Road. Second Corps was on the center, between Fifth Corps and Sixth Corps, and was in position near the Shelton house, about a fourth of a mile north of the Totopotomoy River.

Engagement at Bethesda Church, May 30, 1864. The next day, Warren resumed the advance on the Shady Grove Road, with Griffin's division leading and the divisions of Cutler and Crawford following. Warren was stopped, however, by a swampy ravine that crossed the road, and on the far side of which was Hundley's Corner. During the day, however, Warren's skirmishers on the Old Church-Mechanicsville Road, about three-fourths of a mile south of the Shady Grove Road, were in contact with enemy troops that were beginning to threaten the left of Fifth Corps. These troops belonged to Early's corps, which that afternoon had moved to their right, across Beaver Dam Creek, to the road from Mechanicsville to Old Church, and then along that road to the vicinity of Bethesda Church. When Early left his position at Hundley's Corner at the beginning of his movement, Anderson's corps moved up to take his place.

When Warren learned of the threat to his left, he directed Crawford to send Martin D. Hardin's First Brigade of his division to Bethesda Church to secure that point, and moved Cutler up to support Griffin. Near the church, however, Hardin was attacked by Ramseur's division (mostly by Pegram's brigade, commanded by Edward Willis), which was supported by one brigade of Rodes' division, and was driven back in some confusion to the Shady Grove Road. The enemy followed, but was delayed by the Federal artillery while Crawford, with Joseph W. Fisher's Second Brigade, and Cutler's division were brought up. Cutler placed Bragg's Third Brigade and three regiments of Robinson's First Brigade between Crawford and Griffin, and formed the rest of his division in support of Crawford. Ramseur launched a strong attack on Warren's line, but when this was repulsed, the enemy withdrew.

A little after 7:00 P.M. May 30, 1864, Barlow's division of Hancock's Second Corps was ordered to attack and so relieve some of the pressure on Warren. John R. Brooke's Fourth Brigade advanced and about dark occupied the enemy's entrenched skirmish line on its front, but the attack was halted at 7:40 P.M.

* * * * * * * * * *

By an order of May 29, 1864, Second Division, Fifth Corps was reorganized under Henry S. Lockwood, and it consisted of the same brigades that formerly belonged to John C. Robinson's Second Division, Fifth Corps. These were: Peter Lyle's First Brigade, James L. Bates' Second Brigade, and the Third Brigade (Maryland Brigade), under the command of Nathan T. Dushane. The next day, Lockwood was ordered to move toward Crawford's division. Dushane's brigade advanced on the left to Bethesda Church against only slight resistance, and by 10:00 P.M. the enemy had withdrawn from that part of the field.

There were also some further changes in position of the troops of the Army of the Potomac during May 30, 1864. Ninth Corps was brought up to fill the gap between Second Corps and Fifth Corps, and during the evening it crossed the Totopotomoy River. It then took position with its right on the river near the

Whitlock house, connecting with Second Corps, and its left near the Shady Grove Road, where it connected with Fifth Corps. Wright was directed to move at daylight with his Sixth Corps to the right of Hancock's line, and attempt to strike the enemy's left flank. The heads of Crump's Creek, however, lay in the country through which Sixth Corps moved after leaving the Hanover Court House-Richmond Road, and they formed a tangled swamp that was difficult to pass. This delayed Wright's arrival on the right of Second Corps until it was too late to affect the outcome of the fighting that day. Sixth Corps then took position in the vicinity of the Overton house, near the Totopotomoy River

Sheridan, with Torbert's and Gregg's cavalry divisions, continued to cover the left of the army May 30, 1864. About 1:00 P.M., Sheridan, with Torbert's division, attacked enemy cavalry on the Matadequin Creek near Old Church and drove them back to Cold Harbor. Torbert then took position about a mile and a half from Cold Harbor. Wilson's cavalry division moved to Crump's Creek that day to cover the right flank of the army.

In addition to the engagements on Matadequin Creek and at Bethesda Church, there were also combats at Old Church, Shady Grove, and Armstrongs' farm on May 30, 1864.

The engagement at Bethesda Church was the last in which the regiments of the Pennsylvania Reserves took part. Crawford's division was composed of these regiments, and their terms of enlistment were about to expire. They were withdrawn from the front May 31, 1864, and the next day they left for Pennsylvania and muster out, under the command of Martin D. Hardin. Crawford's Third Division, Fifth Corps was thus discontinued, and Lockwood's Second Division was reorganized to take its place.

On May 30, 1864, heavy reinforcements began to join the Army of the Potomac. On May 25, 1864, Grant had ordered Benjamin F. Butler, commanding the Department of Virginia and North Carolina and the Army of the James, to send all available troops to the Army of the Potomac. Two days later, William F. Smith was assigned command of these troops, which consisted of William T. H. Brooks' First Division and John H. Martindale's Second Division of his Eighteenth Corps, Army of the James, and John W. Turner's Second Division and Adelbert

Ames' Third Division of Quincy A. Gillmore's Tenth Corps, Army of the James.

Smith's command embarked at Bermuda Hundred and City Point on the night of May 28, 1864 and the morning of May 29, 1864, then moved down the James River, and then up the York and Pamunkey rivers to White House. A brigade under Ames (formerly Samuel M. Alford's First Brigade, Second Division, Tenth Corps) was sent ahead to land at West Point and then march to White House to protect the landing of the rest of the troops. Smith's divisions began to disembark May 30, 1864, and that day Smith reorganized his command. He consolidated the Second Division and Third Division of Tenth Corps, and designated the new organization as Third Division, Eighteenth Corps.

It was organized as follows:

Third Division, Eighteenth Corps, Charles Devens, Jr.
First Brigade, William B. Barton
Second Brigade, Jeremiah C. Drake
Third Brigade, Adelbert Ames

By this reorganization, all of Smith's troops were included in Eighteenth Corps. For additional information, see Army of the James, Battle of Cold Harbor, June 1–3, 1864.

Also on May 30, 1864, reinforcements were ordered to the Army of Northern Virginia. Robert F. Hoke's division, consisting of the brigades of James G. Martin, Thomas L. Clingman, and Johnson Hagood, was detached from Pierre G. T. Beauregard's Department of North Carolina and Southern Virginia and ordered to entrain the next day for Richmond.

FROM THE TOTOPOTOMOY RIVER TO COLD HARBOR
MAY 31, 1864

On May 31, 1864, Meade's infantry resumed its advance. On the left, Warren pushed out the skirmishers of his Fifth Corps for about a mile beyond Bethesda Church, but otherwise his command was relatively quiet. On the right of Warren, Hancock resumed his effort to force a crossing of the Totopotomoy. Birney's division advanced on the right of the corps, crossed Swift Run, and then

carried the enemy's entrenched skirmish line across the Richmond Road. Gibbon and Barlow moved their divisions up close to the enemy main works, but they found them too strong to attack. On the right of Hancock, Burnside's Ninth Corps advanced under a brisk fire for about one-fourth to three-fourths of a mile and captured some detached skirmish pits. The entire corps then took position close to the enemy main line. Wright's Sixth Corps, on the right of the line, was relatively quiet during the day. May 31, 1864, Wilson's cavalry division, which was on the right of Sixth Corps, found Pierce M. B. Young's brigade of Wade Hampton's cavalry division near Hanover Court House, and after a sharp fight, took possession of the town.

By dawn May 31, 1864, the right of the Confederate line, which was held by Early's corps, had been extended beyond the Old Church Road, which ran from the Federal position at Bethesda Church to Mechanicsville, and from there on to Richmond. Early's line crossed the road about one mile west of Bethesda Church and four miles from Mechanicsville. From the road, the enemy line extended to the north and northwest for a distance of about seven and a half miles, and it ended on the Chickahominy Swamp, west of Atlee's Station. On this line, to the left of Early's corps, in order from left to right, were Anderson's corps, Breckinridge's division, and Ambrose P. Hill's corps.

May 31, 1864, Fitzhugh Lee's cavalry was beyond Early's exposed right flank, holding the crossroads at Cold Harbor. That afternoon Fitzhugh Lee reported that Sheridan's cavalry was approaching, and Clingman's infantry brigade of Hoke's division, the first brigade of the division to arrive, was ordered up from near Gaines' Mill to support the cavalry. During the afternoon, Sheridan, with Torbert's division, attacked and drove Lee's cavalry from the crossroads to a point about three-fourths of a mile beyond. Torbert then occupied the enemy position at Cold Harbor. Gregg's cavalry division, which was following Torbert, was not engaged.

About dusk, Clingman's brigade arrived to support Fitzhugh Lee's cavalry, and Sheridan, feeling that he could not maintain his position against the enemy forces assembling in front of him (the rest of Hoke's division was not far off), ordered Torbert to withdraw. A short time later, however, Sheridan received an order from Meade directing him to reoccupy Cold Harbor, and to hold it at all hazards until Wright's Sixth Corps came up in the morning. Torbert immediately returned and again took position at Cold Harbor just before daylight June 1, 1864.

Meantime, because of the strength of Lee's position behind the Totopotomoy, Grant had decided to abandon his direct approach toward Richmond, and to move instead to the left toward Cold Harbor. At 9:45 that evening, May 31, 1864, Meade ordered Wright to move that night with Sixth Corps by way of Haw's Shop and Old Church to Cold Harbor, and directed him to be there as soon after daylight the next morning as possible.

The crossroads of Cold Harbor (also called Old Cold Harbor) was to be an important point in the future operations of the Army of the Potomac. It was on the route for any further movement to the left by the army, and in addition, the roads from Bethesda Church, Old Church, and White House and from the bridges over the Chickahominy converged there. The road to White House was particularly important. On May 28, 1864, when the Army of the Potomac was arriving on the Pamunkey River, Grant ordered another change of base, this time from Port Royal to White House on the Pamunkey. The transfer was completed by June 1, 1864, and that day John J. Abercrombie arrived from Port Royal and assumed command. This, as already noted, was when the Army of the Potomac was beginning to assemble at Cold Harbor. Also, William F. Smith's Eighteenth Corps from the Army of the James was disembarking at White House, and was preparing to move from there to Cold Harbor. At 3:00 P.M. May 31, 1864, about 12,500 men of Smith's command had gone ashore and had marched toward Bassetts' house, near Old Church, where they bivouacked for the night.

From available information, Lee was almost certain that Smith's Eighteenth Corps was moving toward White House to join Grant, and that in all probability, Grant's forces would be on the march to their left to connect with Smith. Lee decided to attack before Meade's left was in position at Cold Harbor. For that purpose, late in the afternoon of May 31, 1864, Anderson's corps was withdrawn from its position between Early's corps and Breckinridge's division, and relieved the troops on the right of Early's position and extended on to the

Confederate right. To fill the gap in the line thus created, Breckinridge extended his line to the right, and Early extended his line to the left by moving Rodes' division to the west of Beaver Dam Creek. Anderson was directed to push his line out to the right until it joined Hoke's division, which was expected to be in position before daylight June 1, 1864. When finally formed, the right of Hoke's division was beyond Cold Harbor, and its left was near Beulah Church (the Woody house). Kershaw's division was on the left of Hoke, near Beulah Church, about a mile north of Cold Harbor; Pickett's division was on the left of Kershaw, and it extended toward the Walnut Grove Church Road; and Field's division was on the left of the corps line, with its left near the Mechanicsville Pike (Old Church Road).

OPERATIONS ABOUT COLD HARBOR JUNE 1–12, 1864

Early on the morning of June 1, 1864, Anderson launched his attack that Robert E. Lee had ordered the evening before. Joseph B. Kershaw was to attack with his division toward Beulah Church, and Robert F. Hoke's division, on the right, was to advance toward Cold Harbor. At 6:00 A.M., Kershaw's brigade (commanded by Lawrence M. Keitt), supported by another brigade of Kershaw's division, advanced against Alfred T. A. Torbert's cavalry division, but Keitt's brigade was driven back in disorder, and Keitt was mortally wounded. Hoke appears to have taken little or no part in this action, which was soon ended. Henry E. Davies' First Brigade of David McM. Gregg's Second Cavalry Division came up and was placed in reserve to Torbert, but it was not engaged. Torbert held his position until Horatio G. Wright's Sixth Corps began to arrive between 9:00 and 10:00 A.M. June 1, 1864, and then Philip H. Sheridan, with Torbert's and Gregg's divisions, moved off to the south toward the Chickahominy River to cover the left of the army.

Sixth Corps had arrived at Cold Harbor by 2:00 P.M., and, in preparation for an attack that afternoon, it was deployed with its right near, and in front of, Cold Harbor, and its left extending to the southeast for about a mile and a half. James B. Ricketts' Third Division was on the right, with its right near the road that ran from Old Cold Harbor to New Cold Harbor. Benjamin F. Smith's Second Brigade appears to have been on the right, and William S. Truex's First Brigade on the left. David A. Russell's First Division was on the left of Ricketts' line, with his brigades in position from right to left as follows: Emory Upton's Second Brigade, Henry L. Eustis' Third Brigade, William H. Penrose's First Brigade, and Nelson Cross' Fourth Brigade. Thomas H. Neill's Second Division was on the left of the corps' line. Lewis A. Grant's Second Brigade was next to Russell's division, and Daniel D. Bidwell's Third Brigade and Oliver Edwards' Fourth Brigade were to the rear, watching the left flank of the corps. Frank Wheaton's First Brigade was detached and was guarding the corps' trains.

The arrival of Sixth Corps was observed by the enemy, and conforming to its movements, Anderson's corps was shifted to the right. Kershaw's division closed in on the left of Hoke, and, in turn, George E. Pickett's division moved up to the left of Kershaw, and Charles W. Field's division to the left of Pickett.

It has been noted that William F. Smith's Eighteenth Corps was to join Sixth Corps at Cold Harbor, but because of an error in orders, it did not march directly to that point. During the night of May 30, 1864, and again the next morning, Smith received orders from Grant's headquarters directing him to move to New Castle Ferry on the Pamunkey River. The order should have read "Cold Harbor" instead of "New Castle Ferry." Accordingly, on the morning of June 1, 1864, Eighteenth Corps marched to New Castle Ferry, where Smith received the proper orders to move to Cold Harbor. Then, marching by way of Old Church and slowed by the trains of Sixth Corps, Eighteenth Corps arrived at Cold Harbor during the afternoon and joined Sixth Corps five or six hours later than planned.

On the morning of June 1, 1864, Smith was placed under George G. Meade's orders, and, while en route to Cold Harbor, he was directed to form on the right of Sixth Corps, along the road from Cold Harbor to Bethesda Church. Smith was also ordered to be prepared to attack with Sixth Corps that afternoon. Smith deployed his Eighteenth Corps on the right of Sixth Corps, as ordered, so as to be in position to advance with it later in the day, but he had only sufficient strength to extend his line northward to Woodys' house, near Beulah Church, about a mile north of Cold Harbor. This left a gap of about two miles between the right of Smith's corps and the left of Gouverneur K. Warren's Fifth Corps, which was then in position in front of Bethesda Church.

By 6:00 P.M., Smith's troops were in position as follows: Charles Devens' Third Division was on the right of Ricketts' division of Sixth Corps, with Jeremiah C. Drake's Second Brigade on the front line and William B. Barton's First Brigade on a second line. Adelbert Ames' Third Brigade was at White House guarding the landing. William T. H. Brooks' First Division was on the right of Devens, with Guy V. Henry's Third Brigade and 13th New Hampshire of Hiram Burnham's Second Brigade on the first line. The other three regiments of Burnham's brigade formed a second line, and Gilman Marston's First Brigade formed a third line. John H. Martindale's Second Division was on the right of the corps line, with George J. Stannard's First Brigade on the right of 13th New Hampshire; and Griffin Stedman's Second Brigade to the right and rear of Stannard, with its right refused across the Bethesda Church Road near the Woody house.

Warren's Fifth Corps was in line in front of Bethesda Church, with Henry H. Lockwood's Second Division on the left, Lysander Cutler's Fourth Division on the center, and Charles Griffin's First Division on the right. Samuel W. Crawford's Third Division was discontinued the day before when the regiments of the Pennsylvania Reserves left for home and muster out. Warren's orders were to support the attacks by Sixth Corps and Eighteenth Corps, although Fifth Corps was separated from Eighteenth Corps by a distance of about two miles.

Attack at Cold Harbor, June 1, 1864. Grant and Meade had hoped to attack in front of Cold Harbor during the morning of June 1, 1864, but preparations were not completed until 6:00 that afternoon. At that time, Sixth Corps and Eighteenth Corps moved forward toward the main line of the enemy entrenchments, which was about three-fourths of a mile distant. The space between the two lines was mostly open ground, with an entrenched enemy skirmish or picket line some 300–400 yards in front of the main line. On Wright's front, Ricketts' division, consisting of the brigades of Truex and Benjamin F. Smith, advanced along the road from Cold Harbor (Old Cold Harbor) to New Cold Harbor and, with help from Upton's brigade of Russell's division on their left, captured portions of two lines of the enemy entrenchments. Although other brigades of Sixth Corps were engaged, only Grant's brigade of Neill's division made any significant progress. Truex was wounded in the attack, and Caldwell K. Hall assumed temporary command of the brigade. John W. Schall was assigned command June 2, 1864, but he was wounded the next day, and Hall again took charge of the brigade.

Devens' division of Eighteenth Corps advanced on the right of Ricketts and captured some of the enemy's advanced works, but it failed to reach the main line. The leading brigade suffered heavy losses, including its commander, Jeremiah C. Drake, who was killed, and Zina H. Robertson assumed command of the brigade. Barton's brigade moved up in support of Drake, but it too was stopped. Brooks' division attacked on the right of Devens' division. Henry's brigade, with 13th New Hampshire and 10th New Hampshire of Burnham's brigade on its right, made the attack; and it was supported by the 8th Connecticut and 118th New York regiments of Burnham's brigade. Marston's brigade was formed in columns of division, and later moved up in support of Burnham. Henry's brigade advanced close to the enemy's main line, but could go no farther, and it entrenched its position. At dark, the 98th New York and 139th New York of Marston's brigade were sent to assist Devens, and were placed on the right of his line. Later, the 81st New York and 96th New York were formed on the right of the 98th New York, connecting on the right with Henry.

The Federal attack north of the road from Old Cold Harbor to New Cold Harbor broke through the enemy line between the left of Hoke's division and the right of Kershaw's division, but it was stopped before it had penetrated very far. Hoke's left brigade, under Thomas L. Clingman, gave way under the attack, and this movement carried with it Kershaw's right brigade, under William T. Wofford, and also the right of Goode Bryan's brigade, which was on the left of Wofford. Two regiments of Kershaw's brigade recovered the ground lost by Bryan, and John Gregg's brigade of Field's division was sent to aid Wofford. Eppa Hunton's brigade of Pickett's division reported to Hoke, and together these troops succeeded in forming a new line in rear of that part of the main line captured by the Federals.

During the night of June 1, 1864, both Sixth Corps and Eighteenth Corps entrenched on the lines that they had gained that evening.

There was also fighting on the front of Warren's Fifth Corps on June 1, 1864. That morning, Griffin's division moved to the left, from its former position on the right of the corps line, to the vicinity of Bethesda Church. There it relieved a part of Cutler's division, which then extended to the left toward the right of Smith's Eighteenth Corps. Lockwood's division was ordered to move to the left, down the road toward Cold Harbor, and join in Wright's attack if there was an opportunity to do so. Cutler was ordered to support Lockwood. Apparently because of a misunderstanding of his orders, Lockwood did not occupy the position intended by Warren, and the next day he was relieved from command of his division. Samuel W. Crawford, whose Third Division, Fifth Corps had been discontinued May 31, 1864, was assigned to succeed Lockwood. Lockwood's division was finally brought up to its proper place in the line, on the left of Cutler.

James H. Wilson's Third Cavalry Division was active on the right of the army June 1, 1864. The night before, Wilson bivouacked near Hanover Court House, where he received orders to destroy the two railroad bridges over the South Anna River. At 4:00 A.M. June 1, 1864, he sent George H. Chapman's Second Brigade to destroy the bridges, and ordered John B. McIntosh to march with his First Brigade to Ashland, on the Richmond, Fredericksburg, and Potomac Railroad, to cover Chapman's operation, and to destroy as much of the railroad as possible. McIntosh advanced to Ashland against considerable opposition, and started his work of destruction. He was then attacked by Wade Hampton with Thomas L. Rosser's brigade (according to Wilson, this was Pierce M. B. Young's brigade of Hampton's division) from the direction of Hanover Court House, and a short time later by William H. F. Lee's cavalry division from the direction of Richmond. As a result of these combined attacks, McIntosh was forced to withdraw to

Hanover Court House, with Hampton following until dark. Meantime, Chapman had completed the destruction of the bridges, and also of some track in the vicinity, and he then returned to Hanover Court House, where the division bivouacked for the night.

Movements of June 2, 1864. When Wright's Sixth Corps withdrew from the line of the Totopotomoy on the night of May 31, 1864, Winfield S. Hancock's Second Corps was left on the right of the line, with Ambrose E. Burnside's Ninth Corps on its left. About 3:30 P.M. June 1, 1864, Hancock was ordered to withdraw Second Corps after dark and march behind Ninth Corps and Fifth Corps by way of Haw's Shop, the Via house, and Gibson's Mill to Cold Harbor. Hancock started that night and arrived near Cold Harbor at 6:30 A.M. June 2, 1864. When Hancock departed, Ninth Corps was left alone on the Totopotomoy River.

After Hancock arrived at Cold Harbor, a number of changes were made in the positions of the troops occupying the Union line. Hancock was sent to the left of Sixth Corps with Francis C. Barlow's First Division and John Gibbon's Second Division, and upon arrival there, Gibbon relieved Wright's left division, commanded by Neill, and took position on the left of Russell's division of Sixth Corps. Gibbon's line extended across the road that ran from Cold Harbor by way of Barker's Mill to Dispatch Station (on the Richmond and York River Railroad). This road ran up from Dispatch Station along the foot of the high ground on the right of Lee's line until it diverged to the right toward Cold Harbor, near, and in front of, the point where the line of Gibbon's division crossed the road. Barlow's division took position on the left of Gibbon. Hancock left his other division, David B. Birney's Third Division, with Eighteenth Corps near the Woody house, but it rejoined the corps shortly after 2:00 P.M. that day, June 2, 1864.

When Gibbon relieved Neill's division, Neill moved to the right and relieved Devens' division of Eighteenth Corps, which was on the right of Ricketts' division of Sixth Corps. Devens, in turn, moved to the right of Martindale's division, on the extreme right of Eighteenth Corps.

Warren's Fifth Corps held the line to the left of Eighteenth Corps. Griffin's division was massed near Bethesda Church, and Cutler's and Crawford's divisions held the road from Bethesda Church down to Beulah Church. Cutler's division was on the right and Crawford's division on the left, next to Eighteenth Corps.

During the morning of June 2, 1864, Robert E. Lee learned that Hancock had withdrawn from his front, and he immediately sent John C. Breckinridge's division and Ambrose P. Hill with the divisions of Cadmus M. Wilcox and William Mahone of his corps to the right of the Confederate line. Upon arrival there, Breckinridge formed his command on the high ground to the right of Hoke's division, between Cold Harbor and the Chickahominy River. Hill placed Wilcox's division on the right of Breckinridge, and thus extended Lee's line to within a half mile of the Chickahominy. It is not certain, but it appears that Mahone's division was formed in support of Hoke. Fitzhugh Lee's cavalry, which had been operating on the right of Hoke, then moved across the Chickahominy and picketed down to the James River. Hunton's brigade remained in line between Hoke and Kershaw. Kershaw was supported by the brigades of George T. Anderson, Evander McIver Law, and John Gregg of Field's division. Jubal A. Early remained on the Confederate left with his own corps and Henry Heth's division of Hill's corps.

During the afternoon of June 2, 1864, Burnside's Ninth Corps moved to the left to a new line on the right and rear of Fifth Corps, so that it would be in position to support Fifth Corps if the latter was attacked, and also to protect its right flank. Robert B. Potter's Second Division and Orlando B. Willcox's Third Division had completed their withdrawal to the vicinity of Bethesda Church when Thomas L. Crittenden, whose First Division was bringing up the rear, was strongly attacked by Heth's division of Hill's corps. Shortly after Burnside began his movement to the left, Early pushed his lines forward for an attack on Meade's right flank. Robert E. Rodes' division advanced from Hundley's Corner on the Shady Grove Church Road in the direction of Bethesda Church, and John B. Gordon's division swung around to the right of Rodes. Heth's division followed Rodes for a time, and then moved up and took position on his left flank.

It was about 5:00 P.M. when Heth launched his attack on Crittenden's division, and at about the same time, Rodes' division approached the front of

Griffin's division, which was massed near Bethesda Church. Griffin then deployed his division, with Jacob B. Sweitzer's Second Brigade on the right, Joseph J. Bartlett's Third Brigade in the center, and Romeyn B. Ayres' First Brigade on the left, and advanced toward the enemy. Griffin had not gone far when he met Rodes' division and was soon engaged. Cutler, whose division was not engaged, sent J. William Hofmann's Third Brigade of his Fourth Division to support Griffin. Fighting continued until dark, and then the enemy was finally forced to fall back to the Shady Grove Church Road. When the enemy retired, Ninth Corps took position on a line on the left of Fifth Corps. It began on the left near Bethesda Church, then ran for some distance to the right parallel to the Old Church (or Mechanicsville) Road, crossed the road, and extended on to a point near the Via house, not far from the Totopotomoy River. Willcox's division was on the left of this line, and Potter's division was on the right.

Between 9:00 and 10:00 P.M. June 1, 1864, after the fighting at Cold Harbor that evening had ended, Meade issued orders for Sixth Corps and Eighteenth Corps to renew their attacks the next morning. These attacks were to begin when Second Corps, which was then on the way, arrived within supporting distance. Because of the difficulties encountered in getting the troops in position, however, the attacks ordered for the morning of June 2, 1864 were postponed until 5:00 that afternoon, and then finally they were rescheduled for 4:00 A.M. June 3, 1864.

Attack at Cold Harbor, June 3, 1864. The attack at Cold Harbor June 3, 1864 was actually two attacks. The main effort was made by Second Corps, Sixth Corps, and Eighteenth Corps on a front that extended from a point about a half mile north of the Chickahominy at Grapevine Bridge to the vicinity of the Woody house on the Cold Harbor-Bethesda Church Road. A secondary attack was made by Fifth Corps and Ninth corps, which were engaged north of Woodys', but were not directly facing the main enemy line.

The attack by Hancock, Wright, and Smith was launched at about 5:00 A.M. June 3, 1864, and in the short space of one-half to one hour, it had completely failed, with very heavy losses in killed and wounded. Hancock's corps advanced on the left of Meade's line, with Barlow's division on the left, Gibbon's division on the right, and Birney's division following in support. Barlow's division was formed in two lines, with Nelson A. Miles' First Brigade on the left and John R. Brooke's Fourth Brigade on the right of the first line; and Richard Byrnes' Second Brigade and Clinton A. MacDougall's Third Brigade in the second line. Gibbon's division was also formed in two lines, with Robert O. Tyler's Fourth Brigade and Thomas A. Smyth's Third Brigade in the first line; and H. Boyd McKeen's First Brigade and Joshua T. Owen's Second Brigade in the second line. Tyler's brigade was on the right of the first line, with McKeen's brigade in its rear; and Smyth's brigade was on the left of Tyler, with Owen's brigade behind Smyth.

Barlow's first line advanced and captured the enemy works on the road to Dispatch Station, but before the brigades of Byrnes and MacDougall came up, the first line had been driven back by troops of Hill's corps and Breckinridge's division. Barlow retired for only a short distance, however, and then took position on a slight elevation, which he held to the end of the battle. Brooke was wounded in the attack and was succeeded in command of Fourth Brigade by Orlando H. Morris. The latter was soon killed, and Lewis O. Morris assumed command of the brigade. Morris was killed the next day, and then James A. Beaver took charge of the brigade. In the Second Brigade, Byrnes was mortally wounded, and Patrick Kelly assumed command.

Gibbon's attack was even less successful than Barlow's. As Gibbon's line advanced, it was divided by a swamp that widened as it neared the enemy works. Tyler's and McKeen's brigades passed to the right of the swamp, except James P. McMahon's 164th New York Regiment of Tyler's brigade. This regiment moved up the left side of the swamp and charged over the enemy works on its front. McMahon was killed inside the enemy lines. On the right, McKeen brought up his brigade on the right of Tyler's line, and both brigades advanced toward the enemy works. Fighting was severe and losses were heavy, but the two brigades were soon forced to halt. Tyler was badly wounded in the attack, and he was succeeded by James P. McIvor. John Ramsey assumed command of the brigade June 7, 1864. McKeen was killed while bringing up his troops, and Frank A. Haskell, who succeeded McKeen, was also killed. Byron R. Pierce was assigned command of McKeen's brigade June 4, 1864.

Meantime, Smyth's brigade was advancing on the left of Tyler, with Owen's brigade following in support. When Smyth's brigade became engaged, Owen moved up on his left flank. A portion of Smyth's brigade attacked the enemy works at about the same point as the 164th New York, but failed to carry them. Owen, who had moved out of position, was unable to support Smyth as ordered, and Smyth was driven back. A portion of Gibbon's troops maintained their position near the enemy works, but they were unable to proceed farther. Charges of disobedience of orders were filed against Owen, and June 12, 1864 he was sent to Fort Monroe in arrest. He was mustered out of the United States service July 18, 1864. John Fraser assumed command of his brigade.

Wright's Sixth Corps attacked on the right of Second Corps, with Russell's division on the left, next to Second Corps, Ricketts' division in the center, and Neill's division on the right, connecting with Eighteenth Corps. Generally, Sixth Corps advanced all along the line, but it was soon stopped everywhere after only slight gains. Losses were heavy, but all divisions held on to the ground gained near the enemy works.

There is so little information available that it is impossible to determine with certainty the parts played by the brigades of Russell's division in the attack of June 3, 1864. Presumably they advanced from their positions of the night before, except Upton's brigade, which remained in its entrenchments. The other brigades of Russell's division were all strongly repulsed. On Ricketts' line, Benjamin F. Smith's brigade (temporarily commanded by John Horn) was on the right, and Truex's brigade (temporarily commanded by John W. Schall) was on the left. Horn's brigade was ordered to move forward when Neill's division, which was on his right, advanced, but for some reason, Neill's line did not advance. After some delay, Horn's right regiment finally pushed forward about 175 yards, but when Second Division still did not move, it halted. Schall's brigade did attack, and the left of Horn's brigade advanced with it, but although they captured some rifle pits, they were stopped at the enemy main line. Schall was wounded, and he was succeeded in command of the brigade by Caldwell K. Hall.

Most of the fighting of Neill's division was done by the brigades of Wheaton and Grant. Wheaton, in the first line, advanced and captured some rifle pits, but was repulsed with heavy losses at the next line. Grant's brigade followed Wheaton and supported him, but it could go no farther than Wheaton's line. Little is known about the brigades of Bidwell and Edwards, but the latter reports that he did attack.

Only the divisions of Brooks and Martindale of Smith's Eighteenth Corps joined in the general attack. In front of the right of Smith's corps was an open plain that was swept by enemy fire from the front and right, and the ground in front of the left of the line was covered by artillery fire. Near the center of the line was a small stream with marshy sides that ran toward the enemy line. On the right was a steep bank a few feet high that afforded some shelter to troops along the stream. Smith decided to deliver his main attack by advancing Martindale's division along the marshy stream. At the same time, Brooks was to advance with his division on the left of the corps, and to maintain contact with Martindale on the right and Sixth Corps on the left. Devens' division, which was on the right of the corps' line, was to protect that flank.

Brooks' division was formed on the ground held by Marston's brigade, which was on the right of Neill's division of Sixth Corps. Marston's brigade was to form the assaulting column, and Henry's brigade was formed behind Marston, and the two brigades were to advance on the left of the marshy stream. The 10th New Hampshire of Burnham's brigade was to cover the assaulting column, but the other three regiments of the brigade were to be held in reserve in the positions that they occupied that morning.

Smith's troops moved out promptly at 4:30 A.M. June 3, 1864, as ordered, and after driving in the enemy skirmishers, occupied the first line of enemy rifle pits. At that point Smith halted his brigades under a heavy fire to readjust his lines, and to wait until Sixth Corps came up on his left to protect his line from a heavy crossfire. The brigades of Marston and Henry were to the left of the stream mentioned above. In the initial attack, Marston's brigade was unable to withstand the heavy enemy fire and fell back in some confusion, but Henry moved up and occupied the enemy rifle pits and remained there during the rest of the day. At noon, after most of the fighting had ended, Burnham's brigade was moved up to the right of Sixth Corps, on the left of Brooks' line.

The brigades of Stannard and Stedman of Martindale's division were near the stream. Martindale deployed three regiments of Stedman's brigade to the right to protect that flank, and he moved Stannard's brigade to the left. Smith then directed Martindale to keep his division covered as best he could, and not to advance until Brooks resumed the attack. While waiting, Martindale heard the firing in front of Sixth Corps and, mistakenly believing it to be directed against Brooks, ordered Stannard to attack. Stannard passed through the first line of the enemy rifle pits and advanced to within fifty yards of the main line, but three successive assaults were repulsed with severe losses. Stedman's brigade also advanced and moved to the left to support Stannard, but it too was soon stopped.

Devens' division, at that time on the right of Eighteenth Corps, was disposed to protect that flank, and it did not advance with the other two divisions. Ames, with the Third Brigade of Devens' division, arrived from White House during the night of June 3, 1864, and Ames relieved Devens, who was incapacitated, in command of Third Division, Eighteenth Corps. Henry R. Guss assumed command of Ames' brigade.

Near Bethesda Church, Burnside's Ninth Corps advanced early on the morning of June 3, 1864 against the temporary line held by Heth's division of Hill's corps and Rodes' division of Early's corps. This line was to the west and northwest of Bethesda Church. Potter's division was on the right of Burnside's line, Willcox's division was on the left, and Crittenden's division was in reserve. Soon after daylight, John I. Curtin's First Brigade of Potter's division drove back the enemy skirmishers and moved up close to Early's main line. Simon G. Griffin's Second Brigade of Potter's division, which had been relieved on the extreme right of the Ninth Corps line by James H. Wilson's Third Cavalry Division, was moved up to support Curtin. Despite Potter's efforts, his division was stopped near the enemy works.

Willcox's division attacked at 6:00 A.M., and soon captured the line of the enemy rifle pits. John F. Hartranft's First Brigade, supported by Benjamin C. Christ's Second Brigade, then moved up close to the main line, but he could go no farther. Hartranft then established his brigade close to the enemy works. Crittenden's division was only slightly engaged.

Charles Griffin's division of Fifth Corps cooperated with Ninth Corps in the attack on Early's line but accomplished little. Sweitzer's brigade, which was on the left of Willcox's division, pushed forward to its left and front, and Bartlett's brigade moved forward on the left of Sweitzer, but both brigades were brought to a halt after a short advance. Ayres' brigade appears not to have taken part in this attack. Early held his position on the Shady Grove Church Road during the day, but that evening he returned to his earlier position.

The divisions of Crawford and Cutler, on the center and left of Fifth Corps, apparently did not take part in the general attack that day. At 10:30 A.M. June 3, 1864, Birney's division of Second Corps was sent from the left of Meade's line to join Warren and aid him in holding the road on the right of Eighteenth Corps, near the Woody house.

At 1:30 P.M. June 3, 1864, Meade suspended all further attacks that day and directed the corps commanders to entrench on the advanced lines that they then occupied. As early as 7:00 that morning, Grant had directed Meade to halt further offensive movements when he became certain that an assault could not succeed, and later, when he received a dispatch from Grant stating that the corps commanders did not believe that a further attack would be successful, Meade issued the 1:30 P.M. order. Fighting continued, however, throughout the afternoon, with skirmishing and limited attacks by the enemy on various parts of the line.

While the fighting on the morning of June 3, 1864 was in progress, Wilson's cavalry division, with some troops under Louis P. Di Cesnola, were in position covering the right of the army. Wilson had remained near Hanover Court House until the evening of June 2, 1864, and he had been joined there that day by a force of about 4,000 infantry and cavalry that had been brought down from Port Royal, Virginia by Di Cesnola. Only about half of that force consisted of effective troops, and the rest consisted largely of stragglers and dismounted cavalry. Elijah H. C. Cavins commanded a provisional brigade of about 600 armed men belonging to various regiments, and also some recruits. Wilson assumed command of Di Cesnola's men about 6:00 P.M. June 2, 1864, and with them and his cavalry division he marched toward Linneys' house, on the road between Bethesda Church and Old Church. The head of Wilson's column arrived at Linneys' shortly after midnight.

After establishing Di Cesnola's command on the right of Ninth Corps, Wilson moved across the Totopotomoy River about noon, June 3, 1864, and drove back Fitzhugh Lee's cavalry division from Haw's Shop. Wilson left McIntosh's brigade there and, with Chapman's brigade, marched south and attacked the rear of Heth's division, which was then facing Ninth Corps. Wilson was unable to connect with Ninth Corps, however, and he returned to Haw's Shop.

On June 4, 1864, Di Cesnola's command was broken up. The mounted cavalry was sent to the Cavalry Corps, the dismounted cavalry to the general supply trains, the 57th New York Regiment rejoined Second Corps, and Cavins' brigade was ordered to the provost marshal general for distribution.

The Army near Cold Harbor, June 4, 1864–June 12, 1864. The Army of the Potomac remained generally in the positions that it had occupied on the evening of June 3, 1864 until June 12, 1864, when it began its march toward the James River. There were some changes in position, and also some changes in the organization of the army during this period. On June 4, 1864, Burnside's Ninth Corps moved from the right of the army to a position between Fifth Corps and Eighteenth Corps, near the Woody house, where it relieved Birney's division of Second Corps. Birney then rejoined the corps and extended its left to the Chickahominy River.

On the night of June 5, 1864, Warren's Fifth Corps was withdrawn from the vicinity of Bethesda Church to the Leary house, which was south of Allen's Mill Pond and about a mile and a half northeast of Cold Harbor. This movement again left Ninth Corps on the right of the army. Willcox's division was on the left of the corps, connecting with the right of Eighteenth Corps; Potter's division was on the right of Willcox; and Crittenden's division was formed at a right angle to the right of Potter's

line, and it extended along the Matadequin Creek toward Allen's Mill.

On June 6, 1864, Fifth Corps was extensively reorganized, and the divisions were then commanded as follows: First Division, Charles Griffin; Second Division, Romeyn B. Ayres; Third Division, Samuel W. Crawford; and Fourth Division, Lysander Cutler. For details of the reorganization, see below, Organization of Grant's Army at Cold Harbor and Bethesda Church, June 1–12, 1864; and see also Fifth Corps, Army of the Potomac.

Meantime, during the advance of the army from Spotsylvania Court House to Cold Harbor, Edward Ferrero's Fourth Division, Ninth Corps had continued in its duty of guarding the trains. On May 21, 1864, the trains moved to Salem Church and then on to Bowling Green, where they arrived the next day. They were concentrated at Wright's Tavern May 24, 1864, and remained there until May 27, 1864. The trains then moved on to New Town, in King and Queen County, and the next day they continued on to Dunkirk, where they crossed the Mattapony River. May 29, 1864, they reached the Pamunkey River near Hanovertown, and June 1, 1864, they advanced south of the river to Haw's Shop. From there they were started down the Pamunkey toward White House by way of New Castle and Old Church. At that time, most of Sheridan's cavalry was on the left of the army near the Chickahominy River, and Ferrero's division crossed to the south side of the Pamunkey to picket and guard the right flank of the army. Henry G. Thomas' Second Brigade moved to Haw's Shop, and Joshua K. Sigfried's First Brigade took position on the road to Hanover Junction.

June 2, 1864, Ferrero moved back to cover the approaches to New Castle, and June 6, 1864, he concentrated his division at Old Church Tavern to cover the roads from New Castle Ferry, Hanovertown, Haw's Shop, and Bethesda Church. He remained in this position until June 12, 1864, and then moved to Tunstall's Station, near White House, to protect the trains during the movement to James River.

June 7, 1864, Griffin's and Cutler's divisions of Fifth Corps moved to the Chickahominy River and took a position that extended from the left of Hancock's corps to Dispatch Station on the Richmond and York River Railroad. Ayres' and

Crawford's divisions remained near the Leary house.

After the failure of the assaults at Cold Harbor, Grant realized that nothing could be accomplished north of the James River without excessive loss of life, and he decided as his next move to transfer the army to the south side of the James, past Lee's right flank. To aid in this movement, Grant sent Sheridan with the cavalry divisions of Torbert and Gregg toward Charlottesville on an expedition to wreck the Virginia Central Railroad. Upon completing this task, Sheridan was to move on and join David Hunter, who was expected to be at Charlottesville with a force from the Department of West Virginia. Leaving Wilson's division with Meade, Sheridan set out from New Castle Ferry June 7, and marched westward. June 11, 1864, he struck the railroad near Trevilian Station, and that day he was engaged in a battle with the cavalry divisions of Wade Hampton and Fitzhugh Lee. Sheridan encamped that night at Trevilian Station, and there he learned that Hunter was not at Charlottesville but was apparently moving toward Lynchburg. Sheridan was facing stiff opposition, and he then decided to withdraw and return to the army. He marched back by way of Spotsylvania Court House, Bowling Green, and Dunkirk to White House. Sheridan did not rejoin the army until June 28, 1864, when he reached Light House Point on the James River. For details of this expedition, see Sheridan's Trevilian Station Raid, Virginia.

On June 8, 1864, Crittenden was relieved from command of First Division, Ninth Corps at his own request, and he was succeeded the next day by James H. Ledlie. Jacob P. Gould was assigned command of Ledlie's First Brigade, First Division.

June 9, 1864, Meade ordered the construction of a strongly entrenched line in the rear of the army's position at Cold Harbor to provide a base from which to begin his withdrawal toward the James River. This new line was completed June 11, 1864, and it extended northward from Elder Swamp, just north of Barker's Mill, to Allen's Mill Pond, passing by Cold Harbor. That day, Warren moved Ayres' and Crawford's divisions from the Leary house to the Moody house, on the New Kent Court House Road, near the Richmond and York River Railroad, about four miles northeast of Bottom's Bridge on the

Chickahominy River. Thus, the four divisions of Fifth Corps were brought closer together. Also that day, Meade issued orders for the movement of the Army of the Potomac to the James River, which was to begin after dark June 12, 1864.

During this period, Lee's army was greatly reduced by the transfer of troops to the Shenandoah Valley to drive back Hunter's army of the Department of West Virginia, which was then approaching Lexington from Staunton. June 8, 1864, Breckinridge's division was withdrawn from the lines at Cold Harbor and sent by rail to Gordonsville and Charlottesville. June 11, 1864, Early's corps was moved to the rear of Hill's line, near Gaines' Mill, and the next day it was ordered to move westward to Charlottesville and the Shenandoah Valley. After arriving at Charlottesville, Early moved on to Lynchburg.

Organization of Grant's Army at Cold Harbor and Bethesda Church, June 1–12, 1864.

ARMY OF THE POTOMAC
George G. Meade

SECOND CORPS, Winfield S. Hancock

First Division, Francis C. Barlow
First Brigade, Nelson A. Miles
Second Brigade, Richard Byrnes, to June 3, 1864, wounded
Patrick Kelly
Third Brigade, Clinton B. MacDougall
Fourth Brigade, John R. Brooke, to June 3, 1864, wounded
Orlando H. Morris, June 3, 1864, killed
Lewis O. Morris, to June 4, 1864, killed
James A. Beaver

Second Division, John Gibbon
First Brigade, H. Boyd McKeen, to June 3, 1864, killed
Frank A. Haskell, June 3, 1864, killed
Byron R. Pierce, assigned June 4, 1864
Second Brigade, Joshua T. Owen, to June 12, 1864, in arrest
John Fraser
Third Brigade, Thomas A. Smyth
Fourth Brigade, Robert O. Tyler, to June 3, 1864, wounded
James P. McIvor, to June 7, 1864
John Ramsey

Third Division, David B. Birney
First Brigade, Thomas W. Egan
Second Brigade, Thomas R. Tannatt
Third Brigade, Gershom Mott
Fourth Brigade, William R. Brewster

Artillery Brigade, John C. Tidball
6th Battery (F), Maine Light Artillery, Edwin B. Dow
10th Battery, Massachusetts Light Artillery, J. Henry Sleeper
1st Battery, New Hampshire Light Artillery, Frederick M. Edgell
Battery B, 1st New Jersey Light Artillery, A. Judson Clark
Battery G, 1st New York Light Artillery, Nelson Ames
4th New York Heavy Artillery, Thomas Allcock
11th Battery, New York Light Artillery, John E. Burton
12th Battery, New York Light Artillery, George F. McKnight
Battery F, 1st Pennsylvania Light Artillery, R. Bruce Ricketts
Battery A, 1st Rhode Island Light Artillery, William A. Arnold
Battery B, 1st Rhode Island Light Artillery, T. Frederick Brown
Battery K, 4th United States Artillery, John W. Roder
Batteries C and I, 5th United States Artillery, William B. Beck

FIFTH CORPS, Gouverneur K. Warren

Note. Fifth Corps was extensively reorganized June 6, 1864, and consequently had two different organizations during this period. To avoid confusion, the organizations for the periods June 1–5, 1864 and June 6–12, 1864 are given separately.

Organization of Fifth Corps June 1–5, 1864:

First Division, Charles Griffin
First Brigade, Romeyn B. Ayres
Second Brigade, Jacob B. Sweitzer
Third Brigade, Joseph J. Bartlett

Second Division, Henry Lockwood, May 30, 1864–June 2, 1864
Samuel W. Crawford
First Brigade, Peter Lyle, from May 30, 1864
Second Brigade, James L. Bates, from May 30, 1864
Third Brigade, Nathan T. Dushane, from May 30, 1864

Note 1. Second Division was discontinued May 9, 1864, and Lyle's brigade was assigned temporarily to Fourth Division; Bates' brigade (under Richard Coulter) to Third Division; and Third Brigade (then commanded by Richard Bowerman) was assigned as an independent brigade to report directly to the corps commander.

Note 2. May 30, 1864 (ordered May 29, 1864), Second Division was reorganized from its original regiments and assigned to Henry H. Lockwood. Lockwood was relieved from command of Second Division June 2, 1864 for disobedience of orders during the attack at Cold Harbor on June 1, 1864, and was ordered to Baltimore, Maryland.

Note 3. J. Howard Kitching's Heavy Artillery Brigade was transferred to Second Division from Third Division June 2, 1864.

Third Division

Note. Third Division was discontinued May 31, 1864, when the regiments of Pennsylvania Reserves, of which the division was composed, were sent home for muster out.

Fourth Division, Lysander Cutler
First Brigade, William W. Robinson
Second Brigade, J. William Hofmann
Third Brigade, Edward S. Bragg

Artillery Brigade, Charles S. Wainwright

Note. For batteries of the brigade, see below, Organization June 6–12, 1864.

Organization of Fifth Corps June 6–12, 1864:

First Division, Charles Griffin
First Brigade, Joshua L. Chamberlain
Second Brigade, Jacob B. Sweitzer
Third Brigade, Joseph J. Bartlett

Note. First Brigade was formerly Edward S. Bragg's Third Brigade, Fourth Division.

Second Division, Romeyn B. Ayres
First Brigade, Edgar M. Gregory
Second Brigade, Nathan T. Dushane
Third Brigade, J. Howard Kitching

Note 1. First Brigade was formerly Ayres' First Brigade, First Division.

Note 2. Second Brigade was formerly Dushane's Third Brigade, Second Division.

Note 3. Kitching's Third Brigade was transferred from Third Division, Fifth Corps June 2, 1864.

Third Division, Samuel W. Crawford
First Brigade, Peter Lyle, from June 6, 1864
Second Brigade, James L. Bates, from June 6, 1864
Third Brigade, James Carle

Note 1. Third Division was reorganized June 6, 1864.

Note 2. First Brigade was formerly Lyle's First Brigade, Second Division.

Note 3. Second Brigade was formerly Bates' Second Brigade, Second Division.

Note 4. Third Brigade was organized from two new regiments, the 190th Pennsylvania (1st Veteran Reserves) and 191st Pennsylvania (2nd Pennsylvania Reserves), which were organized in the field from veterans and recruits of the Pennsylvania Reserves. These regiments were commanded by William R. Hartshorne until May 6, 1864.

Fourth Division, Lysander Cutler
  First Brigade, William W. Robinson, to June 7, 1864
    Edward S. Bragg
  Second Division, J. William Hofmann

Note. Bragg's former Third Brigade was transferred to First Division as First Brigade June 6, 1864, and Joshua L. Chamberlain was assigned command. Bragg was assigned command of Robinson's First Brigade.

Artillery Brigade, Charles S. Wainwright
  3rd Battery (C), Massachusetts Light Artillery, Aaron F. Walcott
  5th Battery (E), Massachusetts Light Artillery, Charles A. Phillips
  9th Battery, Massachusetts Light Artillery, John Bigelow
  Battery B, 1st New York Light Artillery, Albert S. Sheldon
  Battery C, 1st New York Light Artillery, Almont Barnes
  Battery D, 1st New York Light Artillery, Lester I. Richardson
  Batteries E and L, 1st New York Light Artillery, George Breck
  Battery H, 1st New York Light Artillery, Charles E. Mink
  15th Battery, New York Light Artillery, Patrick Hart
  Battery B, 1st Pennsylvania Light Artillery, James H. Cooper
  Battery B, 4th United States Artillery, James Stewart
  Battery D, 5th United States Artillery, Benjamin F. Rittenhouse

SIXTH CORPS, Horatio G. Wright

First Division, David A. Russell
  First Brigade, William H. Penrose
  Second Brigade, Emory Upton
  Third Brigade, Henry L. Eustis, to June 12, 1864
    Gideon Clark
  Fourth Brigade, Nelson Cross

Second Division, Thomas H. Neill
  First Brigade, Frank Wheaton
  Second Brigade, Lewis A. Grant
  Third Brigade, Daniel D. Bidwell
  Fourth Brigade, Oliver Edwards

Third Division, James B. Ricketts
  First Brigade, William S. Truex, to June 1, 1864, wounded
    Caldwell K. Hall, to June 2, 1864
    John W. Schall, to June 3, 1864
    Caldwell K. Hall
  Second Brigade, Benjamin F. Smith, to June 3, 1864
    John W. Horn

Note. Horn was assigned command of Second Brigade on the morning of June 3, 1864, before the attack at Cold Harbor, when Smith became incapacitated.

Artillery Brigade, Charles H. Tompkins
  4th Battery (D), Maine Light Artillery, Charles W. White
  5th Battery (E), Maine Light Artillery, Greenleaf T. Stevens
  1st Battery (A), Massachusetts Light Artillery, William H. McCartney
  Battery A, 1st New Jersey Light Artillery, William Hexamer
  1st Battery, New York Light Artillery, Andrew Cowan
  3rd Battery, New York Light Artillery, William A. Harn
  2nd Battalion, 9th New York Heavy Artillery, James W. Snyder
  Battery H, 1st Ohio Light Artillery, Stephen W. Dorsey
  Battery C, 1st Rhode Island Light Artillery, Richard Waterman
  Battery E, 1st Rhode Island Light Artillery, William B. Rhodes
  Battery G, 1st Rhode Island Light Artillery, George W. Adams
  Battery E, 5th United States Light Artillery, John R. Brinckle
  Battery M, 5th United States Artillery, James McKnight

NINTH CORPS, Ambrose E. Burnside

First Division, Thomas L. Crittenden, to June 9, 1864
  James H. Ledlie
  First Brigade, James H. Ledlie, to June 9, 1864
    Jacob P. Gould
  Second Brigade, Joseph M. Sudsburg, to June 4, 1864
    Ebenezer W. Peirce
  Third Brigade, Elisha G. Marshall
  Artillery
    2nd Battery (B), Maine Light Artillery, Albert F. Thomas
    14th Battery, Massachusetts Light Artillery, Joseph W. B. Wright

Note. Third Brigade was also called Provisional Brigade.

Second Division, Robert B. Potter
First Brigade, John I. Curtin
Second Brigade, Simon G. Griffin
Artillery
11th Battery, Massachusetts Light Artillery, Edward J. Jones
19th Battery, New York Light Artillery, Edward W. Rogers

Third Division, Orlando B. Willcox
First Brigade, John F. Hartranft
Second Brigade, Benjamin C. Christ
Artillery
7th Battery (G), Maine Light Artillery, Adelbert B. Twitchell
34th Battery, New York Light Artillery, Jacob Roemer

Fourth Division, Edward Ferrero
First Brigade, Joshua K. Sigfried
Second Brigade, Henry G. Thomas
Artillery
Battery D, Pennsylvania Light Artillery, George W. Durell
3rd Battery, Vermont Light Artillery, Romeo H. Start

Reserve Artillery, John Edwards, Jr.
27th Battery, New York Light Artillery, John B. Eaton
Battery D, 1st Rhode Island Light Artillery, William W. Buckley
Battery H, 1st Rhode Island Light Artillery, Crawford Allen, Jr.
Battery E, 2nd United States Artillery, Samuel B. McIntire

CAVALRY CORPS, Philip H. Sheridan

First Division, Alfred T. A. Torbert
First Brigade, George A. Custer
Second Brigade, Thomas C. Devin
Reserve Brigade, Wesley Merritt

Second Division, David McM. Gregg
First Brigade, Henry E. Davies, Jr.
Second Brigade, J. Irvin Gregg

Third Division, James H. Wilson
First Brigade, John B. McIntosh
Second Brigade, George H. Chapman

Horse Artillery Brigade, James M. Robertson
6th Battery, New York Light Artillery, Joseph W. Martin

Batteries B and L, 2nd United States Artillery, Edward Heaton
Battery D, 2nd United States Artillery, Edward B. Williston
Battery M, 2nd United States Artillery, Alexander C. M. Pennington, Jr.
Battery A, 4th United States Artillery, Rufus King, Jr.
Batteries C and E, 4th United States Artillery, Charles L. Fitzhugh

ARTILLERY, Henry J. Hunt

Second Brigade, Horse Artillery, Dunbar R. Ransom
Batteries E and G, 1st United States Artillery, Frank S. French
Batteries H and I, 1st United States Artillery, Alanson M. Randol
Battery K, 1st United States Artillery, John Egan
Battery A, 2nd United States Artillery, Robert Clarke
Battery G, 2nd United States Artillery, W. Neil Dennison
Batteries C, F, and K, 3rd United States Artillery, George W. Barstow

Artillery Park, Freeman McGilvery
2nd Battalion, 15th New York Heavy Artillery, Julius Dieckmann

Note. All artillery organizations with the army, except those given under this heading, are given under the corps with which they served.

EIGHTEENTH CORPS, ARMY OF THE JAMES, William F. Smith

Note. Eighteenth Corps was temporarily attached to the Army of the Potomac June 1, 1864.

First Division, William T. H. Brooks
First Brigade, Gilman Marston
Second Brigade, Hiram Burnham
Third Brigade, Guy V. Henry

Second Division, John H. Martindale
First Brigade, George J. Stannard
Second Brigade, Griffin Stedman, Jr.

Third Division, Charles Devens, Jr., to June 4, 1864, sick
Adelbert Ames
First Brigade, William B. Barton
Second Brigade, Jeremiah C. Drake, to June 1, 1864, mortally wounded
Zina H. Robinson, to June 5, 1864
Alexander Piper, to June 9, 1864, relieved
N. Martin Curtis

Third Brigade, Adelbert Ames, to June 4, 1864
  Henry R. Guss
  Louis Bell

Note. Third Division was organized temporarily May 30, 1864, and it consisted of troops previously belonging to Second Division and Third Division, Tenth Corps, Army of the James.

Artillery Brigade, Samuel S. Elder
  Battery B, 1st United States Artillery, Samuel S. Elder
  Battery L, 4th United States Artillery, John S. Hunt
  Battery A, 5th United States Artillery, Henry B. Beecher

COLD HARBOR TO THE JAMES RIVER JUNE 12–17, 1864

As soon as it was dark on the night of June 12, 1864, the Army of the Potomac began its movement from Cold Harbor to the James River. Hancock's Second Corps and Wright's Sixth Corps pulled back to the previously prepared entrenched line that extended from Allen's Mill Pond to Elder Swamp, and together they held this position until Fifth Corps had cleared the roads to the south, and until Ninth Corps and Eighteenth Corps had withdrawn from the lines at Cold Harbor. That evening, George H. Chapman's Second Brigade of James H. Wilson's Third Cavalry Division, which had been picketing the Chickahominy River since Sheridan left the army June 5, 1864 on his Trevilian Station Raid, marched to Long Bridge on the river. Wilson joined the brigade there and by midnight had succeeded in getting it across the river. Chapman then moved westward on the Long Bridge Road toward White Oak Swamp Bridge and toward the Charles City Road, the Central (or Darbytown) Road, and the New Market Road.

At 6:00 P.M. that same evening, Warren's Fifth Corps also marched toward Long Bridge. Warren, with Ayres' Second Division and Crawford's Third Division, which the day before had moved from the Leary house to the Moody house on the New Kent-Bottom's Bridge Road, advanced from the latter place, and Griffin, with his own First Division and Cutler's Fourth Division, followed Warren in sup-

port. After crossing the Chickahominy, Fifth Corps followed Wilson's cavalry to White Oak Swamp Bridge. It then took position just east of Riddell's Shop, facing west toward Richmond, with its right on White Oak Swamp. It remained in this position while the rest of the army passed by to the rear on its way to the James River.

At dark June 12, 1864, Smith's Eighteenth Corps withdrew from the lines at Cold Harbor and marched along the rear of Burnside's Ninth Corps, and on to White House, where it arrived at daylight the next morning. It then reembarked for Bermuda Hundred, and arrived at Point of Rocks on the Appomattox River during the night of June 14, 1864. That evening, Smith received orders from Grant, transmitted through Benjamin F. Butler, commander of the Army of the James, to move with his command to Petersburg the next morning.

As soon as Eighteenth corps had cleared Burnside's right flank, Ninth Corps withdrew and followed Eighteenth Corps as far as Tunstall's Station. From there, it proceeded by way of Baltimore Cross Roads and Mount Olivet Church to Jones' Bridge on the Chickahominy, about five miles below Long Bridge.

When the roads were clear, Second Corps and Sixth Corps began their withdrawal. John B. McIntosh's First Brigade of Wilson's cavalry division, which had been left to guard the right of the army, followed Second Corps and Sixth Corps, and covered the rear of the army during the night and all of the next day. Sixth Corps moved by back roads, by way of Widow Via's house, Hopkins' Mill, and the Moody house to Jones' Bridge. It crossed the Chickahominy during the evening of June 13, 1864, and marched south past Vaidens' (Vandoms') to Charles City Court House, where it arrived the next day.

Ninth Corps was delayed on the road to Jones' Bridge, and then followed Sixth Corps across the river. June 14, 1864, Ninth Corps continued on by way of Vaidens', the Clopton house, Tyler's Mill, and Charles City Court House to the vicinity of Wilcox's Landing on the James River. Second Corps moved by roads to the rear of its entrenched position, past Dispatch Station, to Long Bridge. After crossing the river there, it marched by way of Saint Mary's (or Salem) Church and Charles City

Court House to a point near Wilcox's Landing, where it arrived about 5:30 P.M. June 13, 1864.

About 8:00 P.M. June 13, 1864, after Second Corps had safely passed by in its rear, Fifth Corps began to withdraw from its position south of White Oak Swamp. During the night it marched by Saint Mary's Church to Charles City Court House, and arrived there about noon the next day.

About 11:00 P.M. June 13, 1864, Chapman's cavalry brigade retired from its positions covering the roads running out from Richmond, and followed Fifth Corps toward Charles City Court House.

When the army had safely reached the James River, Wilson's two cavalry brigades were left for a time to hold advanced positions toward White Oak Swamp and Malvern Hill, but they were withdrawn at dark June 16, 1864, in preparation for crossing the James River. They began crossing at 5:00 the next morning on a pontoon bridge that had been completed by the engineers.

The point selected for the crossing of the army was Wilcox's Landing on the north bank of the James, opposite Windmill Point. It was about three miles southwest of Charles City Court House, and was protected on the west by Herring Creek. Other embarkation points in the vicinity were also used to speed up the crossing of the troops. Most of the infantry was ferried across on transports, but a pontoon bridge was laid between Fort Powhatan and Windmill Point for the wagons and animals. The bridge was started at 4:00 P.M. June 15, 1864, and was finished seven hours later. This was accomplished despite the fact that the bridge was over 2,200 feet in length and was constructed over deep water. George H. Mendell, commander of the Engineer Battalion, and James C. Duane, chief engineer of the Army of the Potomac, began the work, but later in the afternoon, Henry W. Benham, commanding the Engineer Brigade, arrived and took charge. Most of Ninth Corps, one division of Sixth Corps, the animals and wagons, and a part of the artillery crossed on the bridge.

Second Corps was the first of the infantry to cross the James, and it began embarking on transports at Wilcox's Landing at 9:00 A.M. June 14, 1864. By early the next morning the entire corps had landed at Windmill Point. Most of Ninth Corps crossed on the bridge during the night of June 15, 1864. Fifth Corps crossed on transports from Wilcox's Landing

June 16, 1864. Sixth Corps was the last of the infantry to leave the north bank of the river. During the late evening of June 16, 1864, David A. Russell's First Division and James B. Ricketts' Third Division embarked at Wilcox's Landing, Wilson's Wharf, Hawley's Landing, and Wyanoke Wharf for Bermuda Hundred, where they arrived the next day. Thomas H. Neill's Second Division, Sixth Corps crossed on the bridge to Windmill Point during the evening of June 16, 1864.

Edward Ferrero's Fourth Division, Ninth Corps left Old Church after dark June 12, 1864 to rejoin the trains of the army at White House. The trains, then protected by Ferrero's division, moved down the south bank of the Pamunkey River to New Kent Court House, and then by way of Statesville, Cole's Ferry, and Charles City Court House to the James River. They arrived there June 16, 1864, and crossed the river on the bridge that day. Ferrero's division, which relieved Sixth Corps in guarding the crossing, followed the trains the next day. By the morning of June 17, 1864, more than 100,000 men, 5,000 wagons and ambulances, 56,000 horses and mules, and 2,800 head of cattle had crossed the river. That all of this had been done without Lee's knowledge was a remarkable achievement.

Although the army proper was then on the south bank of the James, there still remained at the depot at White House the garrison and all stores that had not yet been transferred to City Point. Sheridan, with the divisions of Torbert and Gregg, arrived at White House June 21, 1864 from his Trevilian Station Raid, and there received orders to break up the depot and escort the supply trains to Petersburg. He left the next day for the James River with 900 wagons and the garrison of the post, which was commanded by George W. Getty. Getty had relieved John J. Abercrombie June 20, 1864.

The trains, with Torbert's division and Getty's command, moved by way of Jones' Bridge to the vicinity of Wilcox's Landing, where they arrived June 24, 1864. Gregg's division moved by roads to the west to guard the exposed flank of the column. By June 25, 1864, Getty's command was on the James River opposite Fort Powhatan, and Sheridan with the trains was on Wyanoke Neck, near Douthat's Landing. The final crossings began the next day, and were completed by 11:00 A.M. June 29, 1864.

SAVANNAH CAMPAIGN (SHERMAN'S MARCH THROUGH GEORGIA) NOVEMBER 15–DECEMBER 21, 1864

Early in May 1864, William T. Sherman, commander of the Military Division of the Mississippi, advanced into Georgia from near Chattanooga with George H. Thomas' Army of the Cumberland, James B. McPherson's Army of the Tennessee, and John M. Schofield's Army of the Ohio; after a summer of marching and fighting, he occupied Atlanta September 2, 1864. John B. Hood, commander of the Confederate Army of Tennessee, withdrew southward from Atlanta and halted at Lovejoy's Station. Then, on September 18, 1864, he decided to move back and strike Sherman's line of communications and threaten Tennessee, and in this way attempt to force Sherman to withdraw from Georgia.

Sherman left Henry W. Slocum's Twentieth Corps, Army of the Cumberland to occupy Atlanta, and with the rest of his army followed Hood to Gaylesville, Alabama, near the Georgia-Alabama state line. Sherman stopped his pursuit there October 21, 1864, and then waited until October 28, 1864 before deciding on his next move. Meantime, on October 19, 1864, Sherman had proposed to Henry W. Halleck a plan for marching with his army across Georgia, from Atlanta to the sea at Savannah. This plan was approved by Ulysses S. Grant November 2, 1864.

October 26, 1864, Sherman learned that Hood had arrived at Decatur, Alabama, and he then sent Fourth Corps, Army of the Cumberland and Twenty-Third Corps, Army of the Ohio—totaling about 30,000 men—to report to George H. Thomas, commanding in Tennessee. These troops, together with those then with Thomas and those then under orders to join him in Tennessee, were deemed sufficient to hold the state and defeat Hood if he should attempt to cross the Tennessee River and move northward toward Nashville. When these arrangements were completed, Sherman began to pull back from Gaylesville.

On November 1, 1864, Peter J. Osterhaus' Fifteenth Corps and Frank P. Blair's Seventeenth Corps of the Army of the Tennessee were at Cave

Spring, about twelve miles southwest of Rome, Georgia; Jefferson C. Davis' Fourteenth Corps, Army of the Cumberland was at Rome; Judson Kilpatrick's Third Cavalry Division of the Cavalry Corps, Military Division of the Mississippi was at Marietta, Georgia; and Slocum's Twentieth Corps was at Atlanta. That day Fifteenth Corps and Seventeenth Corps left Cave Springs and marched by way of Kingston, Georgia toward Atlanta. They arrived at Smyrna Camp Ground, near Marietta, Georgia, November 5–8, 1864, and remained there in camp until November 13, 1864. Fourteenth Corps moved to Kingston November 1–2, 1864, and Sherman established his headquarters there. While there, on November 9, 1864, Sherman reorganized his army into two wings as follows:

Left Wing, Henry W. Slocum
  Fourteenth Corps, Jefferson C. Davis
  Twentieth Corps, Alpheus S. Williams

Note 1. Slocum's wing was designated as Left Wing, Army of Georgia, and later was commonly known as the Army of Georgia.
Note 2. Slocum assumed command of the Left Wing November 11, 1864, and Williams succeeded him in command of Twentieth Corps the same day.

Right Wing, Oliver O. Howard
  Fifteenth Corps, Peter J. Osterhaus
  Seventeenth Corps, Frank P. Blair, Jr.

Note. The Right Wing was also called the Army of the Tennessee.

Sherman waited until he had accumulated sufficient supplies for the march of the army through Georgia, and when the last train had left Atlanta November 13, 1864, he ordered Twentieth Corps to destroy the railroad from Atlanta to the Chattahoochee River, and Fourteenth Corps to perform a similar service from the Etowah River to Big Shanty. As a further preparation for the evacuation of Atlanta, everything of military value in the city was destroyed by detachments of the 1st Michigan Engineers and 1st Missouri Engineers, under the direction of Orlando M. Poe, chief engineer on Sherman's staff.

John M. Corse, whose Fourth Division, Fifteenth Corps had been at Rome, Georgia since September 26, 1864, destroyed all military installations there, and November 11, 1864 started toward Atlanta to rejoin the corps. Fourteenth Corps left Kingston the same day and arrived in Atlanta on the morning of November 15, 1864. November 13, 1864, Fifteenth Corps and Seventeenth Corps moved from Smyrna Camp Ground to White Hall, just south of Atlanta, on the Atlanta and West Point Railroad. Judson Kilpatrick's cavalry moved from Marietta to Atlanta November 14, 1864. The concentration of the army was thus completed, and Sherman arrived in Atlanta November 14, 1864 to begin the advance.

On the morning of November 15, 1864, Sherman's army, numbering about 60,000 officers and men, moved out of Atlanta and advanced toward Savannah on a broad front. As it advanced, it systematically destroyed railroads, factories, mills, farms, cotton gins, and storehouses, and carried off or destroyed cattle, food, forage, and other supplies. The work of destruction continued during the entire march, leaving a path of destruction fifty to sixty miles wide across the state.

Before describing the routes used by Sherman's army as it moved across the state, a brief description is given here of the courses of the larger rivers in Georgia that ran along or across the line of march. The Ocmulgee and Oconee rivers rise in northern Georgia and flow generally to the southeast in roughly parallel valleys about forty miles apart. About seventy miles southeast of Atlanta they unite to form the Altamaha River, which flows into the ocean near Darien, Georgia. The Ocmulgee rises east of Atlanta and flows to the south and southeast past Macon and Hawkinsville before joining the Oconee. The Oconee rises near Athens and flows generally southward, between Madison and Greensboro, then passes just east of Milledgeville, and on by Dublin before joining the Ocmulgee.

The Savannah River, which separates Georgia and South Carolina, flows to the southeast from a point near Hartwell, Georgia on a generally direct line to the sea below Savannah. Savannah is about fifteen miles above the mouth of the river, and Augusta is about one hundred miles above Savannah. Both cities are on the right bank of the river, in Georgia. The headwaters of the Ogeechee are about midway between Milledgeville and Augusta; the river flows to the southeast past Millen, and after passing the town, it gradually approaches the Savannah River until fifty or sixty miles from the ocean,

the two rivers flow on roughly parallel courses some fifteen to twenty miles apart.

After leaving Atlanta, the two wings of the army marched by different routes so as to threaten both Augusta and Macon. Alpheus S. Williams' Twentieth Corps of Henry W. Slocum's Left Wing marched eastward along the Georgia Railroad in the direction of Augusta until it had passed through Decatur, and it then moved by roads north of the railroad, by way of Rock Bridge and Sheffield, before returning to the railroad at Social Circle November 17, 1864. From there it continued on along the railroad for two days, through Rutledge, to Madison, seventy miles from Atlanta. During this march, Williams' troops destroyed the track for the entire distance and also the bridge over the Oconee ten or twelve miles farther on. Jefferson C. Davis' Fourteenth Corps of the Left Wing remained in Atlanta November 15, 1864, while Sherman completed the evacuation of the city and the destruction of the military facilities there, and the next day it followed Twentieth Corps toward Augusta. It marched along the railroad through Decatur, Lithonia, and Conyers, and arrived at Covington November 18, 1864. After leaving Madison, Sherman did not cross the Oconee River, but ordered the Left Wing to move to Milledgeville. With Twentieth Corps, he left the railroad and moved down the right bank of the river to the southeast, by way of Eatonton, and reached Milledgeville, about thirty miles northeast of Macon, November 22, 1864. Slocum immediately sent Nathaniel J. Jackson's First Division out to the east to secure the bridge over the Oconee River for future operations. Davis' Fourteenth Corps took an interior road from Covington, on a more direct route to the southeast, by way of Shady Dale and Eatonton, and reached Milledgeville the next day. Sherman, in person, accompanied the Left Wing to Milledgeville, and he then left to join the Right Wing near Gordon.

Oliver O. Howard's Right Wing left White Hall November 15, 1864 and advanced in two columns toward Gordon, Georgia, which was situated about twenty miles east of Macon, at the junction of the Georgia Central Railroad (Central Railroad of Georgia) and a branch line running north through Milledgeville to Eatonton. Peter J. Osterhaus' Fifteenth Corps moved down the Macon and Western Railroad through Rough and Ready to a point about five miles north of Jonesboro, and it then turned to the southeast through McDonough and Indian Springs to the crossing of the Ocmulgee River at Planter's (or Nutting's) Factory. It then crossed the river and marched to Hillsboro, where it arrived November 19, 1864. Osterhaus then took the direct road to Clinton, where William B. Hazen's Second Division arrived the next day. November 21, 1864, John E. Smith's Third Division, Fifteenth Corps took the direct road to Gordon with the trains, and Charles R. Woods' First Division and Hazen's Second Division marched on the road from Clinton to Irwinton, which crossed the Georgia Central Railroad about seven and a half miles west of Gordon. John M. Corse's Fourth Division brought up the rear with the pontoon train, the wagons of Kilpatrick's cavalry division, and 3,000 head of cattle.

Frank P. Blair's Seventeenth Corps marched by roads a little farther to the east by way of Mc-Donough, Planter's Factory, Jackson, and Monticello, and arrived in the vicinity of Hillsboro November 19, 1864. The leading division arrived at Gordon November 21, 1864, and the rest of the corps came up the next day.

Because of rains and muddy roads, the trains of the Right Wing had been moving slowly, and had become separated, and until this situation could be corrected, Howard ordered the divisions of Woods and Hazen to camp that night near the railroad, east of Macon, within supporting distance of one another. In addition, Woods was directed to make a demonstration on Macon the next morning to divert attention of the enemy from the plight of the Right Wing trains, and also to find out what enemy troops were on his front. Hazen took position on the Clinton-Irwinton Road, north of the crossroad with the Macon-Milledgeville Road; and Woods' division formed across the railroad along the Clinton-Irwinton Road, about three and a half miles southeast of Hazen's division.

November 15, 1864, Judson Kilpatrick's Third Cavalry Division, Military Division of the Mississippi left Atlanta and marched with Blair's Seventeenth Corps to Jackson, and then it moved ahead of Fifteenth Corps to Hillsboro. On November 20, 1864, the cavalry marched on the Clinton Road and on the River Road along the Ocmulgee River toward Macon, and that day it was sharply engaged with Joseph Wheeler's Confederate cavalry near the town. The next day Kilpatrick moved on and covered the roads from Macon, and that night camped north of Griswoldville, in front of Hazen's division.

At the beginning of Sherman's march, Wheeler, with 3,500 men of his cavalry corps, which had been reinforced with a brigade of William H. Jackson's cavalry division, was near Jonesboro observing the Federal forces at Atlanta. About 3,000 Georgia Militia and State Troops were in support of Wheeler at Lovejoy's Station. Howell Cobb commanded the reserve forces of Georgia, and Gustavus W. Smith was in command of the First Division of the Georgia Militia. These were the only forces in the area to oppose Sherman's advance toward Savannah. These troops fell back as Howard advanced, and they moved down the Macon and Western Railroad through Griffin and were near Macon when the Federal troops approached Gordon.

William J. Hardee was in command of the Confederate Department of South Carolina, Georgia, and Florida at that time, with headquarters at Charleston, South Carolina, but November 17, 1864, he was ordered to assume command of active operations in Georgia, and two days later he arrived at Macon. From the information then available, Hardee believed that Augusta, and not Macon, was Sherman's objective, and he ordered Gustavus W. Smith with his entire force, and a part of Cobb's troops, to move to Augusta by way of the Georgia Central Railroad. Hardee ordered Richard Taylor to take command at Macon, and he left for Savannah. As Fifteenth Corps approached Gordon November 21, 1864, it moved into the line of march of the enemy troops bound for Augusta.

Engagement at Griswoldville, Georgia, November 22, 1864. On the morning of November 22, 1864, Woods received an order from Osterhaus, commander of Fifteenth Corps, to make a demonstration toward Macon, and he selected for this purpose Charles C. Walcutt's Second Brigade, First Division. The brigade consisted of 40th Illinois, 103rd Illinois, 46th Ohio, 6th Iowa, 97th Indiana, and 100th Indiana, and also Albert F. R. Arndt's section of Battery B, 1st Michigan Light

Artillery. After advancing about a half mile along the south side of the railroad, Walcutt ran into enemy cavalry under Wheeler and drove them back two or three miles to a point beyond Griswoldville. Then, with the object of his mission accomplished, Walcutt moved back with his command to a ridge on the Duncan farm, where he threw up a line of defenses of rails and logs, and where his flanks were protected by swamps. His position was below the railroad, two miles southeast of Griswoldville, and two miles in advance of the rest of the division.

When his works were completed early that afternoon, he placed the artillery on the center of the line, and three regiments on the right and three on the left. Milo Smith's First Brigade of Woods' First Division was also in position behind barricades, on the Macon-Gordon Road, north of the railroad.

On the morning of November 22, 1864, Hardee started the Second, Third, and Fourth brigades of Georgia Militia (the First Brigade had started the day before), Beverly D. Evans' 400 men of Georgia State Line (conscription-age veterans), and Anderson's battery of artillery on the march toward Augusta. The Athens and Augusta battalions of the reserve force, under F. W. C. Cook, were already out near Griswoldville. Gustavus W. Smith was to have led this force, but he remained at Macon for a time to take care of other business, and he entrusted the command of the column to P. J. Phillips, a general of the Georgia Militia.

Shortly after 1:00 P.M., Phillips passed unopposed through Griswoldville, preceded by Cook's battalions, and he soon found Walcutt in position on the Duncan farm. Phillips deployed his force about a mile from Griswoldville, with C. D. Anderson's Militia Brigade on the left, north of the railroad; Evans' State Line troops and H. K. McKay's Militia Brigade in the center; and Cook's battalions of the Reserve Force on the right. Phillips' Militia Brigade, led by W. D. T. Mann, was in reserve.

About 2:00 or 3:00 P.M., Phillips advanced his line across an open field to a ravine, about seventy-five yards in front of Walcutt's line, and then made three assaults, each of which was repulsed with heavy losses. Walcutt was wounded, and Robert F. Catterson assumed command of his brigade. Woods, the division commander, was present during the action. During the fighting, Eli H. Murray came up with two regiments of his First Brigade of

Kilpatrick's cavalry division, and placed one regiment on each flank of Walcutt's line, but they appear not to have been engaged. About 4:00 P.M. the 12th Indiana Regiment of Milo Smith's First Brigade was sent to Catterson and was placed on the right of his line to prevent it from being turned. Fighting continued until sundown, and then Phillips withdrew to Macon. Catterson's brigade was withdrawn from the Duncan farm at dark.

Phillips then withdrew with his command, and it later moved southward by rail to Albany, then marched the sixty miles to Thomasville on the Atlantic and Gulf Railroad, and from there by rail on the Atlantic and Gulf and the Savannah, Albany, and Gulf Railroad to Savannah.

* * * * * * * * * *

After the engagement at Griswoldville, Wheeler was ordered to move to the left with his cavalry to get ahead of Sherman. He marched eastward, south of the railroad, crossed the Oconee River, and arrived at Sandersville November 26, 1864, just before Sherman's troops reached the town. He then moved on to the northeast in the direction of Augusta. Then, when all enemy troops had departed from the Federal right flank, Kilpatrick moved to Milledgeville November 24, 1864.

Slocum's Left Wing, which had reached Milledgeville November 22–23, 1864, did not remain there very long, and on November 24, 1864, it resumed the march on parallel roads north of the Georgia Central Railroad toward Sandersville. Davis' Fourteenth Corps marched on the left by way of Black Spring, and Williams' Twentieth Corps on the right marched through Hebron. Both corps arrived at Sandersville November 26, 1864, drove some enemy cavalry from the town, and then continued on toward Louisville the next day. James D. Morgan's Second Division and Absalom Baird's Third Division of Fourteenth Corps, both under Baird, marched by way of Fenn's Bridge on the Ogeechee River, about six miles north of Davisboro, to protect the left flank from enemy cavalry. Nathaniel J. Jackson's First Division and John W. Geary's Second Division of Fourteenth Corps marched to Tennille Station (Station No. 13) on the Georgia Central Railroad, and then eastward along the railroad through Davisboro to the Ogeechee River, destroying the road and bridges as they advanced. William P. Carlin's First Division, Fourteenth Corps and William T. Ward's Third Division, Twentieth Corps accompanied the respective corps' trains to Louisville on the direct road from Sandersville. Both corps camped near Louisville November 29, 1864.

November 23, 1864, Howard's Right Wing marched from the vicinity of Gordon in two columns, and two days later reached Ball's Ferry on the Oconee River, about four miles below the Georgia Central Railroad bridge. Osterhaus' Fifteenth Corps marched by way of Irwinton and Toomsboro, and Blair's Seventeenth Corps marched along the railroad. The next day both corps crossed the river and marched to the southeast by different roads on a wide front to the south of the railroad. Seventeenth Corps moved generally near the railroad, destroying the track as it advanced, and reached the Ogeechee River at a point opposite Sebastopol, or Station No. 10 (present-day Midville), on November 29, 1864. It crossed the river the next day, and then marched down the left bank, through Millen, and arrived at Scarboro (Station No. 7) December 3, 1864. It continued on and arrived before enemy rifle pits near Eden (Station No. 2) December 9, 1864. Seventeenth Corps then advanced in line of battle, and that day drove the enemy back two or three miles to Pooler (Station No. 1).

Fifteenth Corps marched from Ball's Ferry by roads to the right of Seventeenth Corps, and arrived at Irwin's Cross Roads November 27, 1864. The advance was continued the next day, with the corps marching in two columns on parallel roads through Swainsboro, Summerville, and Statesboro, and December 4–5, 1864, the left column arrived across the river from Guyton (Station No. 3), and the right column was about four miles off. December 6, 1864, the crossings of the Ogeechee were secured at Wright's and Jenks' bridges, and the next day the divisions of Woods, John E. Smith, and Corse arrived at Jenks' Bridge. Hazen's division was near King's Bridge. The next day, Fifteenth Corps crossed the Ogeechee River and advanced to the canal connecting the Ogeechee and the Savannah rivers (the Ogeechee Canal), and to the Savannah, Albany, and Gulf Railroad. On December 10, 1864, Fifteenth Corps closed in on the enemy works covering Atlanta. Osterhaus, with the right column, consisting of Corse's Fourth Division and Hazen's Second Division, marched on the King's Bridge Road; and the left column, consisting of John E. Smith's Third Division and Woods' First Division, crossed the Ogeechee at Dillon's Crossing and advanced on the towpath of the Ogeechee Canal.

Before leaving Milledgeville, Sherman ordered Kilpatrick to move northward with his cavalry, feint toward Augusta, and then attempt to burn the bridge and trestles on the Augusta and Savannah Railroad at Briar Creek, near Waynesboro, and about midway between Augusta and Millen. He was then to move on Millen and release the Federal prisoners held there. Kilpatrick crossed the Oconee and moved on the Augusta Road to the Ogeechee River, which he crossed at the shoals of Ogeechee Factory. November 25–26, 1864, he passed through Gibson and reached Sylvan Grove, where he skirmished with Wheeler's cavalry, and then struck the railroad at Waynesboro November 27, 1864. Wheeler followed closely, and, after some destruction on the railroad, Kilpatrick abandoned his effort to burn the Briar Creek Bridge. Instead he turned to the southwest from Waynesboro, and upon learning that the Federal prisoners had been removed from Millen, he rejoined the infantry of the Left Wing at Louisville November 29, 1864.

December 1, 1864, Baird's Third Division of Davis' Fourteenth Corps was sent with Kilpatrick's cavalry on a demonstration toward Waynesboro, and the other two divisions of the corps marched toward Jacksonboro (site of junction of present-day State Road 24 and U.S. 301), where they arrived December 5, 1864. Kilpatrick and the infantry advanced on the Waynesboro Road, past Thomas Station, and on December 4, 1864, two miles south of Waynesboro, Kilpatrick met Wheeler's cavalry and drove it back beyond Bear Creek. Baird's division was in close support but was not engaged. Baird and Kilpatrick then moved to Jacksonboro December 5, 1864, and Baird rejoined the two divisions of Fourteenth Corps. Fourteenth Corps then moved on to the left of the army, past Sister's Ferry, and arrived on Ebenezer Creek the next day. On December 8, 1864, the corps arrived on a line along Lochner's Creek, between Springfield and the Savannah River, and about ten miles upstream from the Savannah River crossing of the Charleston and Savannah Railroad. The next day Fourteenth Corps moved on to Cuylers' plantation.

Williams' Twentieth Corps also left Louisville December 1, 1864, and marched on a road north of, and roughly parallel to, the Georgia Central Railroad, past Birdville (also Birdsville), and the next day crossed the Augusta and Savannah Railroad near Lumpkin's Station (present-day Lumpkin), about five miles north of Millen. It then turned to the southeast, passed about five miles south of Sylvania, and arrived at Springfield December 7, 1864. From there Twentieth Corps marched east and reached Montieth Post Office on the Charleston and Savannah Railroad December 9, 1864. Sherman, with Blair's Seventeenth Corps, reached Millen December 3, 1864, and thus effectively cut railroad connections between Savannah and Augusta.

Thus, by the first week in December 1864, three corps of Sherman's army were moving down the narrowing space between the Savannah River and the Ogeechee River, while Osterhaus' Fifteenth Corps marched down the right bank of the Ogeechee in two columns, some miles apart.

Siege of Savannah, Georgia, December 10–21, 1864. In 1864, Savannah was a city of about 25,000 on the south bank of the Savannah River, and it was largely bordered on the west by suburban plantations, each with a swampy rice field in its front. These rice fields constituted a natural barrier on the northwest. These plantations were, in order southward from the Savannah River, the Williamson, Daly, Lawton, and Silk Hope plantations. Beyond these, the salt marshes of the Little Ogeechee continued the line of defenses on to the bridge of the Savannah, Albany, and Gulf Railroad. The Little Ogeechee River flows toward Ossabaw Sound between the Savannah River and the Great Ogeechee River, and it skirts the city and the adjoining plantations on the southwest. The approaches to the line of defenses were made more difficult for an attacking force because the roads into the city ran along narrow causeways.

As the Federal troops approached, Hardee's troops were on the line of defenses as follows: Gustavus W. Smith's Georgia Militia extended from the Savannah River on the right to the crossing of the Georgia Central Railroad; troops of Lafayette McLaws' Division of the Department of South Carolina. Georgia, and Florida occupied batteries at the Georgia Central Railroad and on the Louisville

Road, and his line ran on to Shaw's Dam on the Ogeechee Canal; and Ambrose R. Wright's Division was on the Confederate left, and extended from Shaw's Dam to the bridge of the Savannah, Albany, and Gulf Railroad over the Little Ogeechee River.

On December 10, 1864, Sherman's army moved forward to the enemy's defensive position in front of Savannah, and then established a siege line about the city. This line began on the left at the Savannah River, about four and a half miles above Savannah, and it extended to the southeast ten miles to Miller's Station (Station No. 1) on the Savannah, Albany, and Gulf Railroad, with troops about four miles west of Miller's Station at King's Bridge on the Great Ogeechee River.

Although there were some changes in the positions of troops on the line during the siege, especially during the first few days, it was generally occupied as follows: Williams' Twentieth Corps held the left of the line, from the Savannah River, opposite the upper end of Hutchinson's Island in the river, to the Georgia Central Railroad near its junction with the Charleston and Savannah Railroad. John W. Geary's Second Division was on the left, next to the river; Nathaniel J. Jackson's First Division was on the center; and William T. Ward's Third Division was on the right, next to the railroad. In order to strengthen the investment of Savannah, the 3rd Wisconsin Regiment of Ezra A. Carman's Second Brigade, First Division, Twentieth Corps was sent to Argyle Island in the Savannah River December 11, 1864, and it was later joined by 2nd Massachusetts of the same brigade. Then, on December 16, 1864, all of Carman's brigade crossed to the island, and from there to the South Carolina shore, where it took position at the Izard plantation.

Davis' Fourteenth Corps was on the right of Twentieth Corps, and its line extended to the southeast to the Lawton plantation, at a point about a mile beyond the Ogeechee Canal, where it connected with the left of Seventeenth Corps. Morgan's Second Division was on the left, between the Georgia Central Railroad and the canal, and Carlin's First Division was between the canal and Lawton's plantation. Baird's Third Division was to the right and rear of Carlin, along the south side of the Louisville Road.

December 9, 1864, Blair deployed Giles A.

Smith's Fourth Division of his Seventeenth Corps on the Louisville Road, and Joseph A. Mower's First Division south of the canal. On December 11, 1864, Seventeenth Corps was relieved by Fourteenth Corps, and then moved to a position on the right of Fourteenth Corps, on the Ogeechee Road (also called the Savannah Road or the Savannah and King's Bridge Road) (present-day U.S. 17). Mortimer D. Leggett's Third Division formed on the left of the road, and connected on the right with Fifteenth Corps. Giles A. Smith's Fourth Division was sent to King's Bridge on the Ogeechee River, and furnished details for building a wharf and for unloading supplies from vessels. Joseph A. Mower's First Division was also at King's Bridge until December 16, 1864, and then it moved to the Savannah, Albany, and Gulf Railroad, where it destroyed eighteen miles of track. There was no Second Division, Seventeenth Corps.

Osterhaus' Fifteenth Corps was on the right of Seventeenth Corps, and on the right of the Union line. On the night of December 11, 1864, Charles R. Woods' First Division moved to Anderson's plantation, which was situated between the canal and the Savannah, Albany, and Gulf Railroad, and about ten miles southwest of Savannah. Woods then took position on the left of the Ogeechee Road, where it connected on the right with John M. Corse's Fourth Division. Corse's division had moved as close as possible to the Savannah, Albany, and Gulf Railroad. John E. Smith's Third Division was at Miller's Station (Station No. 1) on the railroad, and was on the right of Fourth Division. William B. Hazen's Second Division was on the road two miles in rear of the front divisions, near King's Bridge, where it remained until it left for its attack on Fort McAllister December 13, 1864 (see below).

The corps of the army remained generally in the positions described above until December 21, when the Confederates evacuated Savannah.

Capture of Fort McAllister, December 13, 1864. When Sherman arrived in front of Savannah, he was in need of supplies of all kinds in order to reclothe, refit, and subsist his army. He also needed heavy artillery with which to conduct a siege of the city. A supply fleet commanded by John A. Dahlgren lay at anchor in Tybee Roads and at Port Royal Sound, but these vessels could not pass up the Great Ogeechee River to Sherman's army as long as Fort McAllister remained in enemy hands. Fort McAllister was an earthen work located at Genesis Point on the right bank of the Great Ogeechee River, ten miles east of Richmond Hill ("Cross Roads"), and it had, up to that time, successfully resisted all efforts by the navy to pass upriver beyond that point.

December 10, 1864, Sherman ordered Kilpatrick to move with his cavalry to the right, and assist Howard in opening communications with the fleet. The next day Kilpatrick made a reconnaissance south of the Ogeechee River and moved up to the vicinity of Fort McAllister. After an examination of the works, however, he decided that they were too strong to be taken by cavalry alone, and he reported this to Howard. Accordingly, on the night of December 12, 1864, Howard ordered William B. Hazen, with his Second Division of Fifteenth Corps, to cross the Ogeechee at King's Bridge, then move down the right bank of the river and assault the fort from the rear.

At dawn December 13, 1864, Hazen crossed the river, marched by way of Richmond Hill and the Bryan Neck Road, and halted at 11:00 A.M. about two miles from the fort. He then advanced his skirmishers, and about a mile from the fort they contacted the enemy pickets. Hazen then left eight regiments in reserve, and with nine regiments, three from each of the three brigades of his division, he advanced toward the fort. The advance was delayed while torpedoes were removed from the road, but the column finally arrived within 600 yards of the enemy works.

The ground to the right of the road was marshy and was cut up by deep streams that made the deployment slow and difficult, and it was not until 4:45 P.M. that the troops were ready to attack. Wells S. Jones formed the 54th Ohio, 47th Ohio, and 111th Illinois regiments of his Second Brigade on the left of the line, west of the fort and between the Ogeechee River and the road leading in to the fort. These regiments faced east. John M. Oliver's Third Brigade was formed on the right of Second Brigade, facing northeast, with its right directly south of the fort and resting on the marsh. The 70th Ohio was on the left, the 48th Illinois was in the center, and the 90th Illinois was on the left, next to the marsh. Theodore Jones formed the 6th Missouri, 13th Ohio, and 116th Illinois of his First Brigade on the right of

Third Brigade, facing west toward the fort, with its right regiment near the river.

Hazen launched his attack at 4:45 P.M. over open ground and, after fifteen minutes of violent hand-to-hand fighting, gained possession of the fort. The enemy garrison, commanded by George W. Anderson, consisted of only 230 officers and men. Wells S. Jones was wounded during the attack and was succeeded in command of Second Brigade by James S. Martin.

* * * * * * * * *

Immediately after the capture of Fort McAllister, supply vessels began moving up the Ogeechee River to King's Bridge, where a wharf and warehouses had been built by detachments of Seventeenth Corps. From there, supplies of all kinds were moved by wagons up the Ogeechee Road to the army besieging Savannah.

At 3:00 on the morning of December 21, 1864, John W. Geary, whose Second Division, Twentieth Corps was on the siege line near the Savannah River, learned that the enemy was withdrawing from his front, and he promptly advanced his division to the outskirts of Savannah. There he was met by the mayor and received the surrender of the city at 4:30 A.M. Sherman assigned Geary to the command of Savannah, and his division then moved in and occupied the city.

For details of the further operations of Sherman's Army of the Military Division of the Mississippi, see Carolinas Campaign.

The army commanded by Sherman during the period November 14, 1864–December 31, 1864 was as follows:

RIGHT WING (ARMY OF THE TENNESSEE)
Oliver O. Howard

FIFTEENTH CORPS, Peter J. Osterhaus

First Division, Charles R. Woods
First Brigade, Milo Smith
Second Brigade, Charles C. Walcutt, to November 22, 1864, wounded
Robert F. Catterson
Third Brigade, James A. Williamson

Second Division, William B. Hazen
First Brigade, Theodore Jones

Second Brigade, Wells S. Jones, to December 13, 1864, wounded
James S. Martin
Third Brigade, John M. Oliver

Note. Third Brigade had been discontinued October 19, 1863, but it was reorganized September 28, 1864.

Third Division, John E. Smith
First Brigade, Joseph B. McCown
Second Brigade, Green B. Raum

Fourth Division, John M. Corse
First Brigade, Elliott W. Rice
Second Brigade, Robert N. Adams
Third Brigade, Frederick J. Hurlbut

Artillery, Charles J. Stolbrand
Battery H, 1st Illinois Light Artillery, Francis De Gress
Battery B, 1st Michigan Light Artillery, Albert F. R. Arndt
Battery H, 1st Missouri Light Artillery, John F. Brunner
12th Battery, Wisconsin Light Artillery, William Zickerick

SEVENTEENTH CORPS, Frank P. Blair, Jr.

First Division, Joseph A. Mower
First Brigade, John W. Fuller
Second Brigade, John W. Sprague
Third Brigade, John Tillson

Third Division, Mortimer D. Leggett
First Brigade, Manning F. Force
Second Brigade, Robert K. Scott

Fourth Division, Giles A. Smith
First Brigade, Benjamin F. Potts
Third Brigade, William W. Belknap

Artillery, Allen C. Waterhouse
Battery C, 1st Michigan Light Artillery, Henry Shier
1st Battery, Minnesota Light Artillery, Henry Hurter
15th Battery, Ohio Light Artillery, George R. Caspar

LEFT WING (ARMY OF GEORGIA)
Henry W. Slocum

FOURTEENTH CORPS, Jefferson C. Davis

First Division, William P. Carlin
First Brigade, Harrison C. Hobart

Second Brigade, James H. Brigham
Third Brigade, Henry A. Hambright, to November 18, 1864, sick
David Miles

Second Division, James D. Morgan
First Brigade, Robert F. Smith
Second Brigade, John S. Pearce
Third Brigade, James W. Langley

Third Division, Absalom Baird
First Brigade, Morton C. Hunter
Second Brigade, Newell Gleason
Third Brigade, George P. Este

Artillery, Charles Houghtaling
Battery C, 1st Illinois Light Artillery, Joseph R. Channel
Battery I, 2nd Illinois Light Artillery, Alonzo W. Coe
19th Battery, Indiana Light Artillery, William P. Stackhouse
5th Battery, Wisconsin Light Artillery, Joseph McKnight

TWENTIETH CORPS, Alpheus S. Williams

First Division, Nathaniel J. Jackson
First Brigade, James L. Selfridge
Second Brigade, Ezra A. Carman
Third Brigade, James S. Robinson

Second Division, John W. Geary
First Brigade, Ario Pardee, Jr.
Second Brigade, Patrick H. Jones
Third Brigade, Henry A. Barnum

Third Division, William T. Ward
First Brigade, Franklin C. Smith
Second Brigade, Daniel Dustin
Third Brigade, Samuel Ross

Artillery, John A. Reynolds
Battery I, 1st New York Light Artillery, Charles E. Winegar
Battery M, 1st New York Light Artillery, Edward P. Newkirk
Battery C, 1st Ohio Light Artillery, Marco B. Gary, to December 12, 1864, captured
Jerome B. Stephens
Battery E, Pennsylvania Light Artillery, Thomas S. Sloan

Third Division, Cavalry Corps, Military Division of the Mississippi, Judson Kilpatrick
First Brigade, Eli H. Murray
Second Brigade, Smith D. Atkins

SHENANDOAH VALLEY CAMPAIGN (JACKSON), 1862

Occupation of Winchester and Strasburg, Virginia by Union Forces, March 12, 1862. At the beginning of the war, Harper's Ferry and the lower Shenandoah Valley were occupied by Confederate troops under Joseph E. Johnston, but when threatened by a Union army assembled at Chambersburg, Pennsylvania by Robert Patterson, commander of the Department of Pennsylvania, Johnston evacuated Harper's Ferry June 15, 1861 and withdrew to Winchester, Virginia. For details of Patterson's operations, see Department of Pennsylvania, April 27, 1861–August 24, 1861.

Confederate authorities then decided that the Baltimore and Ohio Railroad running through the area should be destroyed, and June 23, 1861, enemy forces under Thomas J. Jackson began the work of destruction. This was interrupted July 2, 1861, when Patterson's army crossed the Potomac River into Virginia, and after that the railroad remained in possession of Northern troops from Harper's Ferry to Cumberland, Maryland for nearly a month.

The Shenandoah Valley was largely abandoned by troops of both armies shortly before and after the Battle of Bull Run, which was fought July 21, 1861 (see Bull Run Campaign, Virginia [First Battle of Bull Run or Manassas]). Johnston withdrew his command from the valley just before the battle to join Pierre G. T. Beauregard's army near Manassas; and after the battle Union forces moved back into Maryland, where they remained inactive for many months guarding the line of the Potomac.

July 25, 1861, the Department of the Shenandoah, which included within its limits the Shenandoah Valley, was created under the command of Nathaniel P. Banks, but Union forces did not at once move to control the area.

During the rest of the summer the enemy resumed destruction of the railroad, but in October 1861 the Federals began repairs on the road, and this work was continued until halted by winter weather.

After the Battle of Bull Run, the Confederate Army of the Potomac under Johnston remained near Manassas until March 7–9, 1862, and then it was withdrawn behind the Rappahannock River to Culpeper Court House. On November 1, 1861, Thomas J. (Stonewall) Jackson was assigned command of the Valley District of Johnston's Confederate Department of Northern Virginia, and he then returned to Winchester, where he assumed command of the district. His command consisted of his own brigade, which was sent back from Johnston's army, William W. Loring's Division of the Confederate Army of the Northwest (or Northwestern Virginia), and Turner Ashby's cavalry. Loring's Division was at Romney, Virginia during the winter, and then in February 1862 it was broken up. Loring was sent to southwestern Virginia, and his regiments to Knoxville, Tennessee and Centerville and Fredericksburg in Virginia.

When Edwin M. Stanton became secretary of war January 20, 1862, he directed that the Baltimore and Ohio Railroad be reopened. George B. McClellan, commander of the Army of the Potomac, believed that the occupation of Winchester and Strasburg in the Shenandoah Valley would be essential for the protection of the railroad after it had been repaired, and in late February 1862, he went to Harper's Ferry to take charge of operations necessary to secure the region. Banks, with two brigades of his division of the Department of the Shenandoah, was ordered forward from Frederick, Maryland, where he had been encamped since November 1861, and February 26, 1862, he crossed the Potomac River at Harper's Ferry and occupied Charlestown, Virginia.

February 28, 1862, Frederick W. Lander, commanding a division of the Army of the Potomac near Hancock, Maryland, was ordered to Martinsburg, Virginia, where he was to join Alpheus S. Williams' Third Brigade of Banks' Division. Earlier, on January 5, 1862, Williams' brigade, then commanded by Dudley Donnelly, had been ordered to report to Lander at Hancock. In late February 1862 it was still in the Hancock area, and it too was ordered to Martinsburg by way of Williamsport. William W. Burns' and Willis A. Gorman's brigades of John Sedgwick's Division of the Army of the Potomac, which was then near Poolesville, Maryland, were ordered to Harper's Ferry to support Banks' movement.

Lander died March 2, 1862, and James Shields was assigned command of his division. Shields then joined Williams at Bunker Hill March 6, 1862, and the combined forces of Banks, Shields, and Williams moved up the valley toward Winchester. Jackson, with a smaller force, evacuated the town March 11, 1862 and moved back to Woodstock, and then on to Mount Jackson. Charles S. Hamilton's Second Brigade of Banks' Division entered Winchester the next day, March 12, 1862.

During the advance to Winchester, Banks' command was organized as follows:

Banks' Division, Nathaniel P. Banks
  First Brigade, John J. Abercrombie
  Second Brigade, Charles S. Hamilton
  Third Brigade, Alpheus S. Williams

Shields' Division, James Shields
  First Brigade, Nathan Kimball
  Second Brigade, Jeremiah C. Sullivan
  Third Brigade, Erastus B. Tyler

Geary's Independent Brigade, John W. Geary

Note. Geary's Independent Brigade was also known as Advance Brigade, Detached Brigade, or simply Geary's Brigade. At the time of the occupation of Winchester, it was operating in Loudoun County, Virginia, east of the Blue Ridge Mountains.

Banks' Division was reorganized March 14, 1862, and Williams commanded First Brigade; Abercrombie, Second Brigade; and George H. Gordon, Third Brigade. Gordon relieved Hamilton March 13, 1862, when the latter was assigned command of Third Division, Third Corps, Army of the Potomac. In the reorganization of Banks' Division, Gordon was assigned command of Third Brigade.

While at Winchester, on March 13, 1862, Banks' command was designated as Fifth Corps, Army of the Potomac. Banks did not at once assume command of the corps, but continued his advance up the valley. Shields' Division entered Strasburg March 19, 1862, and the next day Banks assumed command of Fifth Corps, and announced its organization as follows:

FIFTH CORPS, Nathaniel P. Banks

First Division, Alpheus S. Williams
  First Brigade, Dudley Donnelly
  Second Brigade, John J. Abercrombie
  Third Brigade, George H. Gordon
  Artillery
    Battery F, 4th United States Artillery, Clermont L. Best
    Battery F, Pennsylvania Light Artillery, Robert B. Hampton

Battery M, 1st New York Light Artillery, George W. Cothran

Battery E, Pennsylvania Light Artillery, Joseph M. Knap

Note. First Division was formerly Banks' Division, Army of the Potomac.

Second Division, James Shields
First Brigade, Nathan Kimball
Second Brigade, Jeremiah C. Sullivan
Third Brigade, Erastus B. Tyler
Artillery
    Battery A, 1st West Virginia Light Artillery, John Jenks
    Battery B, 1st West Virginia Light Artillery, Samuel Davey
    Battery H, 1st Ohio Light Artillery, James F. Huntington
    Battery L, 1st Ohio Light Artillery, Lucius N. Robinson
    Battery E, 4th United States Artillery, Joseph C. Clark

Cavalry, John P. Hatch (assigned March 28, 1862)

Geary's Independent Brigade, John W. Geary

Battle of Kernstown (or Winchester), Virginia, March 23, 1862. Banks' advance in the Shenandoah Valley was halted at Strasburg because of concern in Washington for the safety of the capital. At that time McClellan was moving his Army of the Potomac to the Peninsula, and to provide for the defense of Washington, he ordered Banks to move with most of his command to the vicinity of Manassas and fortify the area. He further directed Banks to leave a brigade at Strasburg, and two regiments at Winchester to cover Washington and the line of the Potomac. In compliance with this order, on March 20, 1862, Williams' division moved out of the valley and across the Blue Ridge Mountains toward Manassas, and Shields' division marched back to Winchester, to await the completion of the additional arrangements ordered by McClellan.

Meantime, Jackson, who had remained in the valley, had been instructed by Johnston to threaten Banks so as to prevent him from sending reinforcements to McClellan. Then, during the evening of March 21, 1862, Turner Ashby reported to Jackson that Federal troops were leaving Strasburg, and in accordance with his instructions to hold Federal troops in the valley, Jackson marched north at dawn March 22, 1862 with Samuel V. Fulkerson's brigade from Woodstock and Richard B. Garnett's and Jesse E. Burks' brigades from Mount Jackson. He reached Strasburg that night.

About 5:00 P.M. March 22, 1862, Ashby's cavalry, which was in front of Jackson's column, encountered Nathan Kimball's First Brigade of Shields' Second Division about one mile south of Winchester. After skirmishing for some time, the Confederate cavalry retired to Kernstown, about two miles to the south. Shields was wounded during the fighting that evening, and Kimball assumed command of the division, as well as of his own brigade.

On the morning of March 23, 1862, Kimball advanced Shields' division, and placed his own brigade on Pritchard's Hill, which was west of the Valley Pike and between that road and the Middle Road, and about three-fourths of a mile to the north and northwest of Kernstown. Jeremiah C. Sullivan's Second Brigade was formed on the left of Kimball's brigade, east of the Valley Pike, and between the pike and the Front Royal Road. It was about three-fourths of a mile northeast of Kernstown. Erastus B. Tyler's Third Brigade was held in reserve on the Valley Pike, near the junction of the pike and the Middle Road, about one and one-fourth of a mile north of Kernstown.

The advance troops of Jackson's column arrived near Kernstown about 10:00 A.M., and the main force was up by 1:00 P.M. When Jackson found Kimball's infantry in position across the road, he left Burks' brigade and Ashby's cavalry near Kernstown, and moved Fulkerson's and Garnett's brigades off to a ridge on the Confederate left for the purpose of turning the Union right. This ridge was west of the Middle Road and east of the Cedar Creek Road. The two brigades, with Fulkerson on the left and Garnett on the right, were in position between 3:00 and 4:00 P.M., and they immediately came under fire. The enemy line then advanced on both sides of the ridge. When Kimball observed Jackson's flanking movement, he advanced Tyler's brigade from its position in reserve to the right and front to the ridge west of Kernstown. It became engaged there about 4:00 P.M. Fighting soon became desperate along the stone walls in the area, and both sides brought up reinforcements. Burks' brigade was moved over to Jackson's position on the ridge, and it was formed on the right of Garnett. There was no serious fighting on the Valley Pike near Kernstown, and Kimball moved his brigade to the right, where it went into action on the left of Tyler's brigade. Eventually, during the evening, all of Sullivan's brigade, except the 39th Illinois and two guns, joined Tyler and Kimball and was engaged on the ridge.

Heavy fighting continued for about two hours, and just before nightfall Garnett's brigade, which was holding Jackson's center, began to give way, and finally Garnett ordered it to withdraw. This left the flanks of Fulkerson's and Burks' brigades exposed, and soon the entire force was driven from the ridge. Jackson then fell back to Woodstock.

The Battle of Kernstown had a number of important effects on the organization and distribution of Union forces in northern Virginia. Williams was ordered with his division to move back from Manassas and join Shields in the Shenandoah Valley; Louis Blenker's division of Second Corps, Army of the Potomac, which was then near Washington, was ordered April 1, 1862, first to the Shenandoah Valley, and then to John C. Fremont's Mountain Department, where it arrived May 4–11, 1862; Irvin McDowell's First Corps, Army of the Potomac was detached from the forces assigned to go with McClellan to the Peninsula, and April 4, 1862 it was merged into the newly created Department of the Rappahannock; and April 4, 1862, Banks' Fifth Corps, Army of the Potomac was merged into the newly created Department of the Shenandoah, and Banks was assigned command.

Jackson's Retreat up the Shenandoah Valley.

After the Battle of Kernstown, Jackson did not remain long at Woodstock, but continued on to Edenburg and Rude's Hill, where he remained until April 17, 1862. Most of Shields' and Williams' divisions followed Jackson to the vicinity of Edenburg. April 17, 1862, Jackson moved on back toward Harrisonburg, and when he reached that point he left the Valley Pike and marched to the southeast, around the southern end of the Massanutten Mountains and into the valley of Elk Run. There he went into camp near Conrad's Store, in front of Swift Run Gap in the Blue Ridge Mountains.

Banks followed slowly, with almost constant skirmishing with Ashby's cavalry, and occupied Harrisonburg April 22, 1862. While there, on May 1, 1862, Banks was ordered back to Strasburg, and four days later began his return march back down the valley.

Some changes were ordered in Banks' command while at Harrisonburg. April 30, 1862, George L. Hartsuff was assigned command of Abercrombie's Second Brigade of Williams' division, and he was ordered with this brigade to the Department of the Rappahannock. Hartsuff arrived at Warrenton Junction May 1, 1862, and reported to Irvin McDowell, commander of the department. May 1, 1862, Shields, with his Second Division, was also ordered to the Department of the Rappahannock, but his division was not relieved at New Market by Banks until May 12, 1862, and it then departed for Fredericksburg. After Shields had left the department, Banks had under his command only two brigades of Williams' division and John P. Hatch's cavalry.

Engagement at McDowell, Virginia, May 8, 1862.

While Banks was occupied with Jackson's army in the Shenandoah Valley, Federal troops in Western Virginia were becoming active. During the winter of 1861–1862, Edward Johnson's Confederate Army of the Northwest (or Army of Northwestern Virginia) occupied a position on Allegheny Mountain, a short distance west of Monterey, Virginia, covering Staunton, Virginia from a possible Union advance from the west. A Union brigade under Robert H. Milroy was at Cheat Mountain, west of Allegheny Mountain, and other Union troops were along the South Branch of the Potomac. March 11, 1862, the troops in Western Virginia were organized into the Mountain Department, and John C. Fremont was assigned command. Early in April 1862, Milroy was ordered to advance with his brigade toward Monterey, and Robert C. Schenck with a brigade was ordered to advance from Romney to Moorefield. Both brigades were then to conform as closely as possible with Banks' movements in the Shenandoah Valley.

When Johnson's position at Allegheny Mountain was threatened by Milroy's Brigade on his front, Schenck's Brigade on his right, and Banks' advance up the valley toward his rear, Johnson withdrew early in April 1862 to Shenandoah Mountain, twenty-one miles from Monterey. Then about April 20, 1862, he moved back to West View, near Buffalo Gap, about seven miles from Staunton. Milroy advanced from Cheat Mountain through Monterey, following Johnson, and on May 3, 1862 arrived within ten miles of Staunton. He found himself confronted by a superior force, however, and moved back to McDowell. Schenck's Brigade had also been advancing toward Staunton, but because of bad weather it did not arrive at Franklin until May 7, 1862.

Meantime, at Conrad's Store, Jackson learned of Fremont's movements in Western Virginia, and late in April 1862 asked for reinforcements. Richard S. Ewell's Confederate division, which had been left on the Rappahannock when Johnson withdrew his army from Manassas to Culpeper Court House April 7–9, 1862, was ordered to the Shenandoah Valley to join Jackson.

April 30, 1862, Jackson left Elk Run Valley, which was occupied by Ewell's division the next day, and moved to Port Republic. Then, on May 3, 1862, Jackson left the valley by Swift Run Gap and marched to Mechum's River Station on the Virginia Central Railroad, and from there he moved his command by rail to Staunton, where it arrived May 5–6, 1862. Jackson then marched on to West View, where he was joined by Johnson's Army of the Northwest. Together they marched westward toward McDowell.

May 7, 1862, Milroy learned of the approach of Jackson and Johnson, and he assembled the regiments of his brigade and placed them in a defensive position along the west bank of the Bull Pasture River, with his left flank across the Staunton Road, just south of McDowell. The next morning the enemy appeared on Bull Pasture Mountain, about one and three-fourths of a mile to the right and front of Milroy, who opened fire with his artillery and sent out skirmishers. At 10:00 A.M. Schenck arrived with his brigade from Franklin, and as senior officer he assumed command of both brigades.

There was occasional skirmishing and some artillery fire during the morning and early afternoon, and then at 3:00 P.M. Milroy, with Schenck's permission, made a reconnaissance to determine the strength of the enemy position. The 25th and 27th Ohio regiments crossed the Bull Pasture River and moved off to the right, and they then advanced against the left of the enemy line, which was established on Sitlington's Hill, about a mile east of the river. The enemy forces on Sitlington's Hill consisted of Z. T. Conner's and W. C. Scott's (Burks was ill) brigades of Johnson's division, and William B. Taliaferro's and John A. Campbell's brigades of Jackson's division. Charles S. Winder's brigade of Jackson's division (formerly Garnett's) had not yet arrived.

The two Ohio regiments formed, facing to the northeast, and moved up the hill. They drove the defenders beyond the crest, and then maintained their position for an hour and a half while exposed to a heavy fire. At 4:00 P.M. 32nd Ohio and 3rd West Virginia of Milroy's Brigade and 82nd Ohio of Schenck's Brigade attempted to turn the enemy right flank by advancing straight across the river, but they were unable to do so. The 12th Ohio Battery was placed on Hall's (also find Hull's) Ridge, on the extreme Federal left, to support this attack.

Fighting continued until about 8:00 P.M., and then Schenck, considering his exposed position to be untenable, withdrew with his two brigades during the night toward Franklin. Jackson followed Schenck to Franklin, but after some skirmishing about the village he withdrew toward McDowell. Fremont arrived at Franklin May 12, 1862, and sometime later Louis Blenker's Division from the Army of the Potomac joined Fremont.

United States Forces at McDowell, Robert C. Schenck
   Milroy's Brigade, Robert H. Milroy
   Schenck's Brigade, Robert C. Schenck

Note. Henry H. Hyman's Battery I, 1st Ohio Light Artillery and Aaron C. Johnson's 12th Battery, Ohio Light Artillery were attached to Milroy's Brigade, and William L. De Beck's Battery K, 1st Ohio Light Artillery was with Schenck's Brigade.

Engagements at Front Royal and Winchester, Virginia, May 23–25, 1862. On May 15, 1862, Jackson left the mountains and marched back toward the Shenandoah Valley. He arrived at Mount Solon, south of Harrisonburg, two days later, and May 20, 1862, he had reached New Market. Meantime, Ewell had marched up the South Fork of the Shenandoah River from the valley of Elk Run toward Luray. May 21, 1862, Jackson crossed the Massanutten Mountains to Luray, where he was joined by Ewell's division, and the next day the combined forces marched down the Luray Valley toward Front Royal.

Early on the afternoon of May 23, 1862, Jackson struck the Federal picket line at Front Royal, and rapidly advanced through the town. John R. Kenly was in command at Front Royal, and he had with him the 1st Maryland of Donnelly's brigade of Williams' division, two companies of the 29th Pennsylvania of Gordon's brigade of the same division, a part of the 5th New York Cavalry, some pioneers, and a part of Joseph M. Knap's 1st Pennsylvania Battery. When Jackson appeared before the town, Kenly took position on a ridge on the east side of the Winchester Pike, north of the town, and there he held the enemy in check for a time until outflanked. He then crossed both forks of the Shenandoah to a hill north of the river, but he was soon driven back to a third position near Cedarville. There he was finally overwhelmed by Confederate cavalry, and his remaining troops were scattered over the countryside.

During Kenly's engagement, Banks was at Strasburg, about twelve miles to the west and north of Front Royal, with Williams' division and Hatch's cavalry. He remained there during the day and night of May 23, 1862, uncertain as to Jackson's intentions, but the next morning, almost too late, he evacuated Strasburg and marched by way of Middletown and Newtown toward Winchester. Donnelly's brigade marched first, and at Middletown encountered enemy cavalry that had moved across from Cedarville to the Valley Pike. Donnelly drove the enemy from the town, and then continued on toward Winchester. Gordon's brigade followed Donnelly and brought up the rear. When it reached Middletown, Confederate infantry were approaching from Cedarville, and Gordon sent the 29th Pennsylvania out on the road about four miles to slow their progress. The 1st Maine Cavalry and a squadron of 1st Vermont Cavalry were then sent out to join the 29th Pennsylvania, and together they held up the enemy advance for some time during the morning. Jackson finally reached the Valley Pike at Middletown and destroyed much of the army's trains, but most of the troops of Williams' two brigades and Hatch's cavalry reached Winchester in safety late on the evening of May 24, 1862.

Upon arriving at Winchester, Banks placed his troops in a defensive position south of the town, on a broken ridge behind Abraham's (Abram's) Creek. Gordon's brigade was on the right of this line, on the west of the pike, with eight guns and a strong cavalry force in reserve. Donnelly's brigade was on the left, on the Front Royal Road, with a few squadrons of cavalry. Jackson's division was approaching this position on the Valley Pike, and Ewell's division on the Front Royal-Winchester Road.

During the night, Jackson prepared for an attack early the next morning, May 25, 1862. His plan was to use his advance guard to hold Gordon in position, and Ewell's division to engage Donnelly, and while these actions were in progress, he would move a heavy column around to Gordon's right flank and attack. Both Gordon and Donnelly repulsed the preliminary attacks on their respective fronts, but the flank attack, delivered from west of Winchester by Richard Taylor's brigade and the 2nd Virginia Regiment, was completely successful, and Gordon's brigade was forced to fall back. While passing through the streets of Winchester, all of Gordon's regiments, except the 2nd Massachusetts, lost all semblance of order, and finally fled in confusion across the fields. Donnelly was also compelled to fall back, but he did so in good order. Jackson followed Banks' shattered command for about two hours, and then gave up the pursuit.

Banks halted with what remained of his command for about two and a half hours at Martinsburg, and at sunset continued the retreat toward the Potomac. He arrived on the river across from Williamsport with 3,000 or 4,000 men, and then began to cross into Maryland. By noon May 26, 1862, his troops were all across, and were safe for the time being. Banks did not recross the Potomac and return to Winchester until June 4, 1862, after Jackson had left the lower valley. He remained there during the rest of the Valley Campaign.

Jackson followed Banks down the Shenandoah Valley after the engagement at Winchester, and by May 29, 1862 had concentrated his command at Halltown, only three miles from Harper's Ferry.

Immediately following the engagement at Winchester, some changes were made in the brigade commanders in Williams' division. Samuel W. Crawford and George S. Greene had earlier been ordered to the Department of the Shenandoah, and were with Banks during his retreat to the Potomac, but they had not been assigned to a specific command. May 27, 1862 at Williamsport, Crawford was assigned command of Donnelly's First Brigade, and Greene was assigned command of Gordon's Third Brigade. It should be remembered that Abercrombie's Second Brigade (under the command of George L. Hartsuff) had been ordered to the Department of the Rappahannock April 30, 1862.

Jackson's Withdrawal up the Shenandoah Valley. President Lincoln and Edwin M. Stanton reacted quickly to Banks' defeat at Winchester. McDowell was directed to send two divisions from the Department of the Rappahannock westward toward Strasburg, and at the same time Fremont was ordered to march with Blenker's Division and the brigades of Milroy and Schenck from Franklin, Virginia, in the Mountain Department, to Harrisonburg and join with Banks' division and McDowell's divisions in preventing the escape of Jackson up the valley. Rufus Saxton was sent with some regiments from Washington to Harper's Ferry, where he was to assume command of the troops assembling there, and to move against Jackson's rear as he withdrew up the valley. Franz Sigel was assigned command of the troops at Harper's Ferry June 1, 1862, but he did not take part in the Valley Campaign.

Shields, with the leading division from McDowell's command, arrived at Front Royal May 30, 1862, and being deceived by a demonstration of one of Jackson's brigades from Winchester, he halted east of the town. Edward O. C. Ord, with his division from the Department of the Rappahannock, joined Shields near Front Royal later in the day. Fremont, confronted by the cavalry commands of Turner Ashby and John D. Imboden, did not move to Harrisonburg as directed, but instead marched northward to Moorefield, and then turned east toward Strasburg.

May 30, 1862, Jackson learned of the movements of McDowell and Fremont, and began his withdrawal up the valley. He left Winchester the next day and passed Strasburg with his army June 1, 1862. On that day McDowell's divisions were still at Front Royal, and Fremont was at Cedar Creek, six miles west of Strasburg, facing Ashby's cavalry.

June 1, 1862, George D. Bayard's Cavalry Brigade of the Department of the Rappahannock was ordered to Strasburg to attack the enemy trains

as they moved south, but when Bayard arrived near the town he encountered Jackson's infantry passing that point, and he was unable to reach the trains.

Jackson moved back to Woodstock June 2, 1862, and then continued on through Edenburg, Mount Jackson, and New Market to Harrisonburg. At Harrisonburg he turned east toward the Blue Ridge Mountains, and on the evening of June 5, 1862, he camped along Mill Creek, two miles from Cross Keys, a collection of buildings on the creek, and seven miles from Port Republic. Ashby's cavalry served as the rear guard during the retreat.

June 2, 1862, after Jackson had passed Strasburg, Bayard reported to Fremont with his cavalry brigade, and was directed to move out in front of the main column during the pursuit. Fremont then followed Jackson up the valley, and his advance occupied Harrisonburg about noon June 6, 1862. Ashby's cavalry retired from the town about two miles to the southeast to a wooded ridge. Percy Wyndham's 1st New Jersey Cavalry followed and charged into the woods, but was thrown back with serious loss, including Wyndham, who was captured. Bayard then came up with 1st Pennsylvania Cavalry and four companies of 13th Pennsylvania Reserves (Bucktails) and a little after sundown also entered the woods. A severe engagement of a half hour followed, and then, when Gustave P. Cluseret came up in support with his brigade, the enemy retired. Ashby was killed in this action.

Meantime, on the afternoon of June 1, 1862, McDowell learned that Jackson's army was moving south from Strasburg, and he immediately sent Shields' division from Front Royal up the valley of the South Fork of the Shenandoah River toward Luray and Conrad's Store in an effort to intercept Jackson's retreat. Ord's division remained at Front Royal. Shields passed through Luray and concentrated his division at Columbia Bridge June 6, 1862. That day he received information that Jackson's army was in disorderly retreat, and because of this erroneous report he decided to push on to Port Republic as rapidly as possible. On the night of June 7, 1862, Shields' division was stretched out for more than twenty-five miles on the road through the valley of the South Fork. Samuel S. Carroll's Fourth Brigade was south of Conrad's Store, Erastus B. Tyler's Third Brigade was some miles in rear of Carroll, and Nathan Kimball's First Brigade and

Orris S. Ferry's Second Brigade were at Luray. The latter two brigades had been left because of another false report that a large enemy force was crossing the Blue Ridge at Thornton's Gap.

Jackson was aware of Shields' approach, and he left Ewell with the brigades of Isaac R. Trimble, Arnold Elzey, and George H. Steuart on Mill Creek, and moved with his division to the ridges west of Port Republic.

Engagements at Cross Keys and Port Republic, Virginia, June 8–9, 1862. Both armies were quiet June 7, 1862, but the next day they became active again. On the morning of June 8, 1862, Fremont advanced from Harrisonburg toward Cross Keys, and about 8:30 A.M. he became engaged with the enemy pickets. Ewell's division was in position on a ridge overlooking the valley through which Mill Creek flowed on a course roughly parallel to the Confederate line. Trimble's brigade was on the right; Steuart's brigade was on the left; and Elzey's brigade was in reserve near the center of the line.

At 10:00 A.M., Fremont appeared on the high ground opposite Ewell's position and opened fire with his artillery. Fremont then deployed his troops in line of battle, with Julius Stahel's First Brigade of Blenker's Division on the left, Gustave P. Cluseret's Advance Brigade in the center, and Robert H. Milroy's Brigade on the right. Henry Bohlen's Third Brigade of Blenker's Division was placed a short distance in rear of the interval between Stahel and Cluseret, and Robert C. Schenck's Brigade was formed to the right and rear of Milroy. Adolph Von Steinwehr's Second Brigade, then commanded by John A. Koltes, had not yet come up; but when it arrived, it was deployed in rear of the batteries.

Fremont decided to attack, but made only a feeble effort by advancing Stahel's brigade against Trimble's line. Fighting was determined for a time, but finally Stahel was driven back with heavy loss on Bohlen's brigade, which was moving up in support. Both brigades then fell back to the artillery line. Trimble pursued Bohlen and Stahel for a short distance, and then returned to his original position. Meantime, Blenker had arrived on the ground and had assumed command of his division. Fremont did not renew the attack, and the fighting ended at 4:00 P.M. The center and right of Fremont's line were not seriously engaged. Near the close of the action,

Richard Taylor's Brigade and a part of George S. Patton's Brigade (formerly John A. Campbell's) arrived from Port Republic to reinforce Ewell.

The organization of Fremont's command at the Battle of Cross Keys was as follows:

Blenker's Division
First Brigade, Julius Stahel
Second Brigade, John A. Koltes
Third Brigade, Henry Bohlen

Note. Frank Buell's Battery C, West Virginia Light Artillery and Louis Schirmer's 2nd Battery, New York Light Artillery were attached to First Brigade; Julius Dieckmann's 13th Battery, New York Light Artillery was attached to Second Brigade; and Michael Wiedrich's Battery I, 1st New York Light Artillery was attached to Third Brigade.

Advance Brigade, Gustave P. Cluseret

Milroy's Brigade, Robert H. Milroy

Schenck's Brigade, Robert C. Schenck

Bayard's Cavalry Brigade, George D. Bayard

Note 1. Bayard's brigade was detached from Irvin McDowell's command.
Note 2. Artillery was assigned to the above brigades as follows: Henry F. Hyman's Battery I, 1st Ohio Light Artillery and Aaron C. Johnson's 12th Battery, Ohio Light Artillery were with Milroy's Brigade (both batteries were commanded by Chatham T. Ewing); William L. De Beck's Battery K, 1st Ohio Light Artillery and Silas F. Rigby's Indiana Battery were with Schenck's Brigade; and James A. Hall's 2nd Battery (B), Maine Light Artillery was with Bayard's brigade.

Early on the morning of June 8, 1862, Carroll, commanding Fourth Brigade of Shields' division, moved forward along the South Fork of the Shenandoah with 150 cavalry and four pieces of artillery to Port Republic, which he occupied for a short time. He was soon driven out, however, by troops of Jackson's command, and he then retired on the infantry of his brigade, which had halted at the Lewis plantation, about two miles north of the village. Carroll was joined there by Tyler's brigade of Shields' division, and Tyler, as senior officer, assumed command of both brigades. Shields, with the brigades of Kimball and Ferris, remained at Columbia Bridge, opposite Fisher's Gap in the Blue Ridge Mountains.

During the evening of June 8, 1862, Jackson decided to leave a small force at Mill Creek to hold off Fremont until the next morning, and with the remainder of his army to advance against Tyler and destroy him before Fremont could arrive at Port Republic. He then planned to turn back and defeat Fremont. Accordingly, he ordered Ewell to leave Trimble's and Patton's brigades in front of Fremont, and to march very early the next morning with the remainder of his command to join Jackson near Port Republic.

Early on the morning of June 9, 1862, Tyler learned of Jackson's approach and formed his regiments in line of battle behind a small stream (Still House Run) on the Lewis plantation, between the South Fork of the Shenandoah River on the right and a spur of the Blue Ridge Mountains on the left. Tyler placed his artillery on the left, just east of Lewiston, the estate of General Lewis, and on a clearing used for making charcoal (known as the Lewiston Coaling). The artillery consisted of three guns of Joseph C. Clark's Battery E, 4th United States Artillery; three guns of James F. Huntington's Battery H; and one gun of Lucius N. Robinson's Battery L, 1st Ohio Light Artillery. Also on the left were the 84th Pennsylvania and 110th Pennsylvania of Carroll's brigade and the 66th Ohio of Tyler's brigade. The latter regiment was directly in rear of the guns. On the Federal right, which was assigned to the command of Carroll, were the 7th Indiana and 1st West Virginia of Carroll's brigade and the 29th Ohio, 7th Ohio, and 5th Ohio of Tyler's brigade.

On the morning of June 9, 1862, Jackson advanced from Port Republic with Charles S. Winder's brigade and launched a vigorous attack on Carroll's front. Winder drove back the Federal pickets, but was then forced to halt by the deadly fire of Tyler's artillery. Jackson then directed Winder to send a force to the right, through the woods, to take the Federal guns. Two regiments and a battery were sent for this purpose, but they were unsuccessful. Richard Taylor's brigade of Ewell's division then came up and was sent to the Confederate right with orders to capture or silence the Union artillery. Meantime, Winder's regiments on the left were hard pressed as the Federals advanced, and finally they were driven back in disorder. At this point, Steuart's brigade of Ewell's division, then commanded by William C. Scott since Steuart had been wounded

the day before, arrived and succeeded in halting the pursuit of Winder, but it too was was soon driven back. Taylor tried repeatedly to take the Federal batteries, and then, after being reinforced by two regiments of Scott's brigade, finally succeeded, and he then advanced with the rest of Jackson's line and forced Tyler to withdraw toward Conrad's Store. Carroll covered the retreat.

The organization of Shields' division at the time of the Battle of Port Republic was as follows:

First Division, Department of the Rappahannock, James Shields
First Brigade, Nathan Kimball
Second Brigade, Orris S. Ferry
Third Brigade, Erastus B. Tyler
Fourth Brigade, Samuel S. Carroll
Artillery, Philip Daum
    Battery H, 1st Ohio Light Artillery, James F. Huntington
    Battery L, 1st Ohio Light Artillery, Lucius N. Robinson
    Battery A, 1st West Virginia Light Artillery, John Jenks
    Battery B, 1st West Virginia Light Artillery, John V. Keeper
    Battery E, 4th United States Artillery, Joseph C. Clark

Only the brigades of Tyler and Carroll and the batteries of Huntington, Robinson, and Clark were engaged at Port Republic.

End of the Campaign. Early in June 1862, as the Shenandoah Valley Campaign was drawing to a close, Edwin M. Stanton ordered McDowell to assemble his command in preparation for a move southward toward Richmond to cooperate with McClellan, who then was threatening the city. Headquarters of the Department of the Rappahannock was moved to Manassas, and the divisions of Shields and Ricketts at Luray and Front Royal and Bayard's Cavalry Brigade with Fremont's command in the Shenandoah Valley were ordered to march eastward toward Fredericksburg.

After the Battle of Port Republic, Tyler's brigades retired to Columbia Bridge, and while there, on June 10, 1862, Shields was ordered with his division to Catlett's Station in the Department of the Rappahannock. He left for Luray the next day, and June 15, 1862, he continued on to Front Royal. Then, on

June 20, 1862, he departed for Catlett's Station. Bayard's brigade left Front Royal for Thoroughfare Gap June 17, 1862. Ord's division, which had remained near Front Royal during Shields' advance up the Luray Valley, was ordered June 8, 1862 to return to Catlett's Station, but it did not leave immediately. Duryee's Second Brigade left June 10, 1862, and Hartsuff's Third Brigade and Ricketts' First Brigade followed June 17–18, 1862.

Jackson remained in the valley until June 17, 1862, and he was then ordered to join Lee in front of Richmond.

During the Battle of Port Republic, Fremont advanced from Cross Keys toward the South Fork of the Shenandoah, but he was not engaged. He withdrew to Mount Jackson June 11–12, 1862, and then marched back by way of Woodstock June 19, 1862 and arrived at Strasburg the next day. Fremont's movement out of the mountains and into the Shenandoah Valley resulted in changes in boundaries of the Mountain Department, and also those of the departments of the Shenandoah and of the Rappahannock. Both the eastern and western boundaries of the Department of the Shenandoah were shifted eastward, and this resulted in corresponding changes in the boundaries of the other two departments. For details, see Mountain Department, Department of the Shenandoah, and Department of the Rappahannock.

The failure to destroy Jackson's army after his capture of Winchester, and his subsequent advance to the Potomac River, was at the time largely attributed to the lack of a unified command of the troops of the three departments involved. Because of this, on June 26, 1862, the Mountain Department, the Department of the Shenandoah, and the Department of the Rappahannock were merged into the Army of Virginia, which was placed under the command of John Pope. For further information, see Pope's Northern Virginia Campaign.

SHENANDOAH VALLEY CAMPAIGN (SHERIDAN) AUGUST 7–NOVEMBER 28, 1864

From the beginning of the war until the summer of 1864, the presence of Confederate troops in the Shenandoah Valley had been a source of constant concern to Northern civil and military authorities. On several occasions large numbers of Federal troops had been withheld from other important assignments to guard the Baltimore and Ohio Railroad and to prevent successful raids into Maryland and Pennsylvania. Despite these precautions, such raids had occurred, and each time the enemy had retired to the comparative safety of the upper valley, only to advance again at a later time. All efforts by Union forces to control the valley and prevent these incursions had ended in failure until the latter part of 1864.

In July 1864, a large Confederate force under Jubal A. Early invaded Maryland from the Shenandoah Valley and, marching eastward through Frederick, threatened Baltimore and Washington. Troops of Horatio G. Wright's Sixth Corps from the Army of the Potomac and a part of William H. Emory's Detachment Nineteenth Corps, which was then arriving at Fort Monroe from the Department of the Gulf, were immediately sent to Washington to aid in its defense.

When Early retired from in front of Washington July 12, 1864, Wright was placed in command of the available troops in Washington, and was sent toward the Shenandoah Valley in pursuit of Early. Wright's command consisted of his own Sixth Corps, part of Emory's Detachment Nineteenth Corps, a brigade under John R. Kenly from the Middle Department, and Charles R. Lowell's cavalry from the Department of Washington. At Purcellville, Virginia, George Crook joined Wright with his Army of the Kanawha from the Department of West Virginia. Early escaped into the Shenandoah Valley, and on July 20, 1864, Wright considered that his mission was accomplished and marched back with his command toward Washington.

After Early's success in reaching the outskirts of Washington and returning safely to the valley, Ulysses S. Grant concluded that Early's command would probably be retained there as a permanent threat to the North, and that this would prevent large numbers of troops from being sent to his army at Petersburg. Accordingly, Grant decided to concentrate a superior force against Early and destroy him if possible, and if not, drive him up the valley. Then, to prevent him from again returning to the lower valley, if at a later time Federal troops were withdrawn, he decided on drastic measures. His plan was to destroy all hay, crops, and barns, and also to destroy or bring away all horses, cows, and other livestock, and any other materials of value to the enemy, so that the valley would not thereafter support a Confederate army.

Grant also proposed that, to make these operations more effective, the several departments that were concerned with affairs in the Shenandoah Valley should be placed under a single command. These departments were the Middle Department, the Department of Washington, the Department of West Virginia, and the Department of the Susquehanna. It had been difficult to secure close cooperation among these departments, and this problem was aggravated by the distance of Grant's headquarters at City Point from the theater of operations of these departments. In fact, on July 18, 1864, Grant had expressed indirectly to Henry W. Halleck that the number of commands involved was at least one of the reasons that Early had escaped with little damage during his withdrawal from Washington, and he further stated at that time that the troops of the four departments mentioned above should be merged into a single command.

While these proposals were being considered, Early again moved down the valley and defeated Crook's army at Kernstown July 24, 1864. Wright was once more placed in command of the same troops that he had just brought to Washington on his return from the Shenandoah Valley, and was ordered to move with them into Maryland and join Crook. Wright marched westward to the Monocacy River, and after crossing he moved into the Department of West Virginia, where he came under the orders of David Hunter, commander of the department.

July 29, 1864, Hunter concentrated his command at Halltown, four miles southwest of Harper's Ferry, and the next day John McCausland's Confederate cavalry burned Chambersburg, Pennsylvania. Halleck, Grant's chief of staff, United States Army, who was also in temporary command of the troops of the Middle Department and of the departments of Washington, West Virginia, and the Susquehanna, was uncertain as to the meaning of the invasion of Maryland and Pennsylvania. As a precaution, however, he ordered Hunter to move his troops behind South Mountain and occupy the gaps so as to prevent

Early from again advancing through Maryland toward Baltimore and Washington. By August 1, 1864, Wright's Sixth Corps, a part of Detachment Nineteenth Corps, Kenly's Brigade, and Crook's army were concentrated in the vicinity of Frederick, and Lowell's cavalry was picketing the Potomac to the south. For details of the organization and operations of Wright's and Hunter's forces during the latter part of June and early July 1864, see Early's Washington Raid (and Operations in the Shenandoah Valley, Maryland, and Pennsylvania).

Following the appearance of Confederate cavalry north of the Potomac July 29, 1864, there was considerable uncertainty as to the size and composition of the enemy force in Maryland and Pennsylvania and also its intended movements. Reports received by Halleck July 30, 1864–August 1, 1864 indicated that only cavalry had crossed the river, and on August 2, 1864, Albion P. Howe, commander of the District of Harper's Ferry, Department of West Virginia, reported that Early's infantry was then falling back toward Winchester. There was then no doubt that the emergency that had prompted Halleck to concentrate the army behind South Mountain no longer existed, and the next step was to determine how best to use the troops assembled in the Frederick area.

Following Early's second advance in the Shenandoah Valley during the month, Grant moved quickly to eliminate all future threats from that direction. July 31, 1864, he ordered Philip H. Sheridan, commanding the Cavalry Corps, Army of the Potomac, to send a cavalry division from Petersburg to Washington, and the next day Alfred T. A. Torbert's First Cavalry Division began embarking at City Point. On August 4, 1864, James H. Wilson was ordered to follow with his Third Cavalry Division. Infantry reinforcements were also ordered to Washington. July 31, 1864, Henry W. Birge's First Brigade and Edward L. Molineux's Second Brigade of Cuvier Grover's Second Division, Detachment Nineteenth Corps were ordered from the Army of the James at Deep Bottom to rejoin Emory's command.

August 2, 1864, Sheridan was relieved temporarily from duty with Grant's army near Petersburg and ordered to Washington to report to Halleck for orders. At this point Sheridan's command had not been decided, but the day before, Grant had informed

Halleck that unless Hunter was in the field in person, he, Grant, wanted Sheridan to be placed in command of all troops in the field, and, as he expressed it, to follow the enemy "to the death." Sheridan reached Washington August 3, 1864, and that day Halleck suggested to Grant that a military division be created to consist of the Middle Department and the departments of Washington, West Virginia, and the Susquehanna; and he further suggested that Sheridan be assigned command of the military division as far as military operations were concerned.

On August 4, 1864, Grant left City Point to confer with Hunter, and arrived at the latter's headquarters at Monocacy Junction the following evening. After discussing troop dispositions and future operations, Grant approved of Hunter's selection of Halltown as a concentration point for his forces. Earlier, Howe had reported that enemy forces were approaching Harper's Ferry, and because of this, Hunter had already sent Emory's Detachment Nineteenth Corps to reinforce Howe on August 4, 1864. A part of Emory's command reached Harper's Ferry at 9:30 that evening, and the rest arrived the next day.

On August 5, 1864, Grant issued a series of orders in preparation for his planned campaign in the Shenandoah Valley. He directed Hunter to move the remainder of his available forces to the vicinity of Harper's Ferry, leaving in Maryland only railroad guards and garrisons for posts necessary to protect the public property. He also issued instructions for the use of these troops and informed Hunter that if Early crossed to the north bank of the Potomac in large force, he was to follow and attack him wherever he went; but if, on the other hand, only a small force crossed, Hunter was to leave sufficient force to deal with it, and move with the rest of his command and attack Early's main body. In another order of August 5, 1864, Grant instructed Halleck to send Sheridan by train the next morning to Harper's Ferry to assume command of all troops then in the field.

On the night of August 5, 1864, Crook's two infantry divisions occupied Halltown, with the left division extending to the Shenandoah River. At 9:00 the next morning, Emory, with First Division and Jacob Sharpe's Third Brigade, Second Division,

Detachment Nineteenth Corps, took position on the center of Hunter's Halltown line, and on the right of Crook. Wright's Sixth Corps came up and formed on the right of the line. George W. Getty's Second Division was on the right of the Winchester Turnpike, connecting on the left with Emory's line; James B. Ricketts' Third Division was on the right of Getty; and David A. Russell's First Division was on the right and rear of Ricketts, with its right extending almost to the Potomac, and with pickets pushed out to the river. William W. Averell's Second Cavalry Division, Department of West Virginia was absent in pursuit of McCausland, and Alfred N. Duffié's First Cavalry Division, Department of West Virginia was at Hancock, Maryland in support of Averell.

Early on the morning of August 6, 1864, Sheridan arrived at Monocacy Junction and stopped there to confer with Grant. When their meeting was finished, Grant returned to Washington and City Point, and Sheridan proceeded on to Harper's Ferry. The next day, by an order of the secretary of war, the Middle Military Division was constituted to consist of the Middle Department, the Department of Washington, the Department of West Virginia, and the Department of the Susquehanna. Sheridan formally assumed command that day at Harper's Ferry.

Meantime, during the first three days of August 1864, Early remained quietly with the main body of his army at Bunker Hill, thirteen miles north and east of Winchester. Then, on August 4, 1864, he advanced toward the Potomac and camped that night six miles beyond Martinsburg, with some of his cavalry crossing the river at Shepherdstown. The next day Robert E. Rodes' and Stephen D. Ramseur's infantry divisions crossed the Potomac at Williamsport, and John C. Breckinridge's division crossed at Shepherdstown and occupied Sharpsburg. John C. Vaughan's cavalry advanced as far as Hagerstown. It was this movement that Howe had reported earlier to Hunter, and which had caused Emory's Detachment Nineteenth Corps to be sent to Harper's Ferry August 5, 1864. On the morning of August 6, 1864, Early withdrew his whole army to Martinsburg, perhaps because of Hunter's advance to Halltown.

When Sheridan assumed command of the Middle

Military Division at Harper's Ferry August 7, 1864, his immediate forces available for field service were as follows:

SIXTH CORPS, Horatio G. Wright

First Division, David A. Russell
    First Brigade, William H. Penrose
    Second Brigade, Emory Upton
    Third Brigade, Oliver Edwards

Second Division, George W. Getty
    First Brigade, Frank Wheaton
    Second Brigade, Lewis A. Grant
    Third Brigade, Daniel D. Bidwell

Third Division, James B. Ricketts
    First Brigade, William Emerson
    Second Brigade, John F. Staunton

Artillery Brigade, Charles H. Tompkins

DETACHMENT NINETEENTH CORPS, William H. Emory

First Division, William Dwight
    First Brigade, George L. Beal
    Second Brigade, James W. McMillan
    Third Brigade, Leonard D. H. Currie

Second Division
    Third Brigade, Jacob Sharpe

ARMY OF WEST VIRGINIA, George Crook

First Infantry Division, Joseph Thoburn
    First Brigade, George D. Wells
    Second Brigade, William Ely
    Third Brigade, Jacob M. Campbell

Second Infantry Division, Isaac H. Duval
    First Brigade, Rutherford B. Hayes
    Second Brigade, Daniel D. Johnston

Crook's field force of the Department of West Virginia was formerly known as the Army of the Kanawha, and was officially designated by Sheridan August 8, 1864 as the Army of West(ern) Virginia. Additions to Crook's command of troops that had formerly belonged to Eighth Corps caused some to call it Eighth Corps, but this was not the correct designation. Eighth Corps was possibly used to avoid the longer name of Army of West Virginia, which was the official designation after August 8, 1864.

During the period August 8–17, 1864, Sheridan's army was increased in strength by the arrival of four cavalry divisions and two infantry brigades. By August 7, 1864, Torbert's First Cavalry Division had arrived in Washington from the Army of the Potomac at Petersburg, and it was then sent on to Harper's Ferry, where it was assembled by August 9, 1864. Sheridan's cavalry was then the equivalent of a full field corps, and August 8, 1864, Torbert was assigned chief of cavalry of the Middle Military Division. Torbert assumed command the next day, and Wesley Merritt assumed command of First Cavalry Division. This division was organized as follows:

First Cavalry Division, Wesley Merritt
    First Brigade, George A. Custer
    Second Brigade, Thomas C. Devin
    Third Brigade, Charles R. Lowell, Jr.
    Reserve Brigade, Alfred Gibbs

Note 1. Louis P. Di Cesnola assumed command of Second Brigade August 19, 1864, when Devin was wounded in an engagement at Front Royal. Di Cesnola remained in command until mustered out of service August 30, 1864.

Note 2. Third Brigade was organized August 9, 1864 from Lowell's Independent Brigade, and Alfred Gibbs assumed command of the Reserve Brigade August 10, 1864.

When Sheridan assumed command of the Middle Military Division August 7, 1864, Averell was absent with his Second Cavalry Division, Department of West Virginia in pursuit of McCausland's cavalry, which he defeated that day near Moorefield, West Virginia. Averell's division was organized as follows:

Second Cavalry Division, William W. Averell
    First Brigade, Thomas Gibson
    Second Brigade, William H. Powell

Note. July 29, 1864, James M. Schoonmaker, commanding First Brigade, was assigned by Sheridan to the temporary command of all reserve mounted and dismounted men of the Middle Military Division encamped in Pleasant Valley, near Harper's Ferry. He was authorized to rejoin his command when Averell arrived with the division in the Shenandoah Valley.

On August 7, 1864, Sheridan ordered Averell to concentrate his command at Hancock, Maryland, and with it join the army near Harper's Ferry as rapidly as possible. Averell arrived at Martinsburg on the evening of August 14, 1864, and was directed to remain there and await orders.

Duffie's First Cavalry Division, Department of West Virginia had been at Hancock since August 4, 1864, and it too was ordered to join Sheridan. Duffie was at Middletown August 15, 1864, at Berryville the next day, and at Charlestown August 18, 1864. The organization of Duffie's division while at Hancock was as follows:

First Cavalry Division, Alfred N. Duffie
   First Brigade, William Tibbits
   Second Brigade, Andrew J. Greenfield

Note. Greenfield relieved Jacob Higgins in command of Second Brigade July 30, 1864, and was in turn relieved by Robert F. Taylor August 15, 1864.

Meantime, on August 1, 1864, Grover had arrived in Washington from Deep Bottom with the two brigades of his Second Division, Detachment Nineteenth Corps. He remained there until August 8, 1864, and was then ordered to report to Christopher C. Augur, commander of the Department of Washington, Twenty-Second Corps, for temporary garrison duty until other troops arrived. Two days later, however, Grover was ordered to join Sheridan in the Shenandoah Valley, and he left Washington August 13, 1864. He arrived at Snicker's Gap August 17, 1864, and moved on to Berryville that night.

Wilson's Third Cavalry Division, Army of the Potomac, which had been ordered to Washington August 4, 1864, arrived at Giesboro Point August 9–10, 1864, and on the night of August 12, 1864 marched toward the Shenandoah Valley. It passed through Leesburg and Snicker's Gap, and arrived at Berryville August 16, 1864. The next day it moved on to Winchester. Wilson's division was organized as follows:

Third Cavalry Division, James H. Wilson
   First Brigade, John B. McIntosh
   Second Brigade, George H. Chapman

Shortly after assuming command of the Middle Military Division, Sheridan ordered a number of changes in the command of the Department of West Virginia. On July 8, 1864, Hunter was granted a leave of absence and left the department, and Albion P. Howe was relieved from command of the District of Harper's Ferry and ordered to report to the Department of Washington. Julius Stahel, who had recovered from a wound suffered at the Battle of Piedmont, had returned to the Department of West Virginia August 4, 1864, and when Hunter departed on leave, he assigned Stahel, as senior officer present, to the temporary command of the department. Max Weber was assigned temporary command of the District of Harper's Ferry. On August 9, however, Stahel was relieved from duty in the Department of West Virginia and was ordered to the Middle Department. Then Crook, in addition to his command of the Army of West Virginia, was assigned temporary command of the Department of West Virginia during Hunter's absence. On August 30, 1864, Hunter was relieved from duty in the Department of West Virginia, and Crook was assigned to the permanent command of the department. On August 15, 1864, John D. Stevenson was assigned command of the District of Harper's Ferry, relieving Weber.

Sheridan's First Advance up the Valley, August 10–22, 1864. On August 10, 1864, in accordance with Grant's instructions of August 5, 1864, which directed him to move up the valley and engage Early, Sheridan moved out of his lines at Halltown and marched toward Winchester. That evening he occupied a line extending from Clifton to Berryville. Wright's Sixth Corps marched through Charlestown to Clifton and formed on the right of the infantry line. Emory's Detachment Nineteenth Corps advanced along the Berryville Pike and took position on the left of Sixth Corps. On August 9, 1864, before the army moved, Kenly's Brigade, which until that time had been assigned to Detachment Nineteenth Corps, was detached and directed to remain at Halltown under Sheridan's orders. Crook's Army of West Virginia marched through Kabletown to Berryville and then formed on the left of Sheridan's line. Torbert marched with Wesley Merritt's First Cavalry Division toward Winchester. At Charlestown, Charles R. Lowell's Third Brigade left the column and marched to Summit Point, on the extreme right of the army, and the rest of the division continued on beyond Berryville to the extreme left of the army. George A. Custer's First Brigade halted on the Winchester-Millwood Pike, near Winchester; Thomas C. Devin's Second Brigade reached Chapel Run; and Alfred Gibbs' Reserve Brigade took position at White Post, east of Newtown.

The next morning, August 11, 1864, the army moved up to the line of Opequon Creek. Wright took position at the ford on the Berryville Pike; Emory at a ford three-fourths of a mile to the left of Sixth Corps; and Crook at a ford about a mile to the left of Emory. Merritt moved forward on the Millwood Pike toward Winchester, and Lowell's brigade advanced from Summit Point to the right of Sixth Corps.

In advancing to the Opequon, Sheridan had hoped to meet the enemy and defeat him in battle. Early, however, learned of Sheridan's advance August 10, 1864, while at Bunker Hill, and he marched back that night to Winchester. He did not intend to fight there because he knew that reinforcements from Robert E. Lee's army were on the road to join him, and he decided to avoid battle until they arrived. On August 11, 1864, while Sheridan was moving to the fords of the Opequon, Early retired up the valley toward Cedar Creek and Strasburg. Torbert discovered this movement and sent Merritt's division toward Newtown and Lowell's brigade through Winchester on the Valley Pike. Sheridan's infantry also followed. Sixth Corps turned to the left and marched up the right bank of Opequon Creek to the crossing of the Millwood Pike; Detachment Nineteenth Corps came up on the right, between Sixth Corps and the Front Royal Road; and the Army of West Virginia reached Nineveh (or Stony Point), about five miles east of Middletown. The next day, August 12, 1864, Early crossed Cedar Creek and occupied a strong defensive position on Fisher's Hill, two miles beyond Strasburg. Sheridan followed and halted along Cedar Creek. Crook was on the left, east of the pike; Emory was on the right of Crook, and west of the pike; and Wright was on the right of Emory. Torbert's cavalry watched the flanks of Sheridan's line.

On the morning of August 13, 1864, Sheridan ordered Sixth Corps to Strasburg, and upon arriving there, Wright's skirmishers advanced and found the enemy entrenching on Fisher's Hill. Crook and Emory remained in position on Cedar Creek. Also that morning, Sheridan received reports that a strong enemy force was moving from Culpeper Court House by way of Chester Gap toward Front Royal. This was confirmed by a dispatch received from Colonel Norton P. Chipman of the Adjutant General's Office, who arrived from Washington the next day. Because of these reports, Devin's Second Brigade of Merritt's First Cavalry Division was sent out on the evening of August 13, 1864 toward Cedarville, on the Winchester and Front Royal Pike, where he arrived the next day.

On August 14, 1864, Leonard D. H. Currie's Third Brigade, First Division, Detachment Nineteenth Corps was sent back from Cedar Creek to Winchester as an escort for a wagon train, and two days later it moved toward Harper's Ferry as an escort for the army trains. Currie's brigade arrived at Bolivar Heights August 21, 1864, and then remained there as detached in the Defenses of Harper's Ferry.

On the morning of August 15, 1864, Wright's Sixth Corps was withdrawn to the north side of Cedar Creek, and then Sheridan decided to to fall back to Halltown. On the way he would be joined by Grover's Second Division, Detachment Nineteenth Corps and Wilson's Third Cavalry Division, both of which were then approaching Berryville. That night Emory began the retreat and moved back to Winchester. Crook and Wright remained in position at Cedar Creek until 8:00 P.M. August 16, 1864, and then they too marched to Winchester, where they arrived the next morning. While this movement was in progress, Emory moved from Winchester to Berryville. During the afternoon of August 16, 1864, Sheridan established temporary headquarters at Winchester, but because he regarded the position as indefensible, he did not intend to remain there. Crook and Wright were sent on toward Clifton. When Wright, who had the rear guard, reached the Opequon on the Berryville Road, he halted to hold the crossing, but Crook marched on to Berryville.

On August 16, 1864, Merritt moved up to join Devin at Cedarville with Custer's First Brigade and Gibbs' Reserve Brigade. Custer remained at Cedarville, and Gibbs moved on to Nineveh (Stony Point). The force in front of Merritt, which was marching to join Early, consisted of Joseph B. Kershaw's infantry division of James Longstreet's corps, Army of Northern Virginia; Fitzhugh Lee's cavalry division; and Wilfred E. Cutshaw's battalion of artillery, all under the direction of Richard H. Anderson, then commanding Longstreet's corps.

During the early afternoon of August 16, 1864, the head of Anderson's column passed through Front Royal and ran into Merritt's cavalry at Cedarville. Custer's brigade was in position on the left of Merritt's line, and Devin's brigade was on the right. At 2:00 P.M. Fitzhugh Lee's cavalry advanced against Custer's brigade, which resisted stubbornly until Devin came up. The enemy then charged, but was thrown back in confusion. A brigade of Kershaw's infantry then moved to the Federal left, crossed the Shenandoah River, and pushed forward. It was met by a heavy fire from Merritt's troopers and driven back across the river. Enemy reinforcements then came up, but it was too late to achieve any successes that evening. Anderson remained south of the river and engaged only in artillery fire during the rest of the day. During the action, Merritt ordered up the Reserve Brigade, but it arrived too late to join in the fighting. Devin was wounded that afternoon, and Louis P. Di Cesnola assumed temporary command of Second Brigade, First Cavalry Division. The next day Merritt moved back to White Post. Merritt's action on August 16, 1864 has been called the Engagement at Cedarville, and also the Engagement at Guard Hill, or Front Royal.

Lowell's cavalry brigade reached Winchester during the afternoon of August 17, 1864, and he was joined there by Wilson's Third Cavalry Division, which had arrived from Washington that day. That night, Grover's Second Division, Detachment Nineteenth Corps also arrived from Washington and joined Emory, who then had under his command both First Division and Second Division, Detachment Nineteenth Corps.

Early learned of Sheridan's withdrawal from Cedar Creek at daybreak August 17, 1864, and promptly started his command and that of Anderson in pursuit. Early advanced from Fisher's Hill and Anderson from Front Royal. Sheridan left Torbert at Winchester during the afternoon of August 17, 1864 to cover the retreat of the army. Torbert's command consisted of Wilson's Third Cavalry Division,

Lowell's Third Brigade of Merritt's First Division, and William H. Penrose's First Brigade of Russell's First Division, Sixth Corps. Torbert and Penrose held the enemy cavalry in check until evening, and then they were driven out by Confederate infantry.

August 17, 1864, Sheridan's infantry occupied its former positions along the Opequon, in front of the fords, and when Wilson and Lowell fell back from Winchester that night, they took position at Summit Point. Merritt was at White Post, east of Newtown; Averell's cavalry division was at Martinsburg; and Duffie's cavalry division was at Charlestown. Thus, that evening Sheridan had all of his troops in good position in the lower Shenandoah Valley. Also that evening, Anderson's command joined Early at Winchester.

The next day, Sheridan continued his withdrawal toward Halltown, and that evening formed a line in front of Charlestown. Sixth Corps was at Welch's Spring (or Flowing Spring), about two and a half miles west of Charlestown; Detachment Nineteenth Corps was two miles south of Charlestown on the Berryville Pike; and the Army of West Virginia was at Clifton. On August 19, 1864, however, Crook moved to the left of Detachment Nineteenth Corps. Merritt moved his division to Berryville and picketed the front from Snicker's Ferry to the Opequon. Wilson's cavalry was on the right of Merritt at Point Summit, and Averell moved his division back to Shepherdstown. Sheridan maintained his position in front of Charlestown until August 21, 1864.

August 19, 1864, Early advanced to Bunker Hill, and two days later he and Anderson decided to attack. Sheridan's cavalry pickets on the Opequon were quickly driven in, and then Early with the divisions of Rodes and Ramseur advanced against Wright's Sixth Corps. There was some sharp skirmishing, and the corps suffered some losses, principally in Getty's division, but there was no major engagement. At midnight August 21, 1864, Sheridan called in Wilson's and Merritt's cavalry, and then moved his army back to the defenses at Halltown. Crook's Army of West Virginia was formed on the left of the line, next to the Shenandoah River; Emory's Detachment Nineteenth corps was on the center; and Wright's Sixth Corps was on the right, with its right on the Potomac River. Wilson's Third Cavalry Division was on the extreme left, near Halltown, picketing the front and left of the line. On

August 22, 1864, Merritt's First Cavalry Division marched to Shepherdstown, and Averell's Second Cavalry Division, which had moved to Fairplay, Maryland August 20, 1864, was picketing the Potomac River from Cherry Run to Antietam Furnace.

Early demonstrated for three days against Sheridan's line, principally on the fronts of Crook and Emory, and he then decided that the position was too strong for a successful attack. On August 25, 1864, Early proceeded to execute another plan. He left Anderson, with Kershaw's division, McCausland's cavalry, Cutshaw's artillery, and one regiment of Fitzhugh Lee's cavalry, to watch the lines at Halltown; he sent the main body of Lee's cavalry to Williamsport; and he marched northward toward Shepherdstown with the divisions of Robert E. Rodes, Stephen D. Ramseur, John B. Gordon, and Gabriel C. Wharton.

On the morning of August 25, 1864, the divisions of Merritt and Wilson, under the command of Torbert, advanced from Shepherdstown on a reconnaissance toward Leetown. They moved on separate roads to Walper's Cross Roads, where they joined and then followed the road toward Leetown. Wilson's division was on the left and Merritt's division on the right. They passed Kearneysville, on the Baltimore and Ohio Railroad, and about a half-mile beyond they encountered Early's infantry. Believing that only cavalry was on his front, Torbert ordered an attack. George H. Chapman's Second Brigade of Wilson's division was on the left of Torbert's line, and John B. McIntosh's First Brigade of Wilson's division was on the right of Chapman, next to the road. Custer's brigade was on the right of McIntosh, and Devin's brigade, then commanded by Di Cesnola, was on the right of the line. Torbert was soon in serious trouble and in danger of losing a large part of his command, but his brigades finally succeeded in withdrawing across the Potomac. That night, after Sheridan learned of the approach of Early's infantry, he sent Wilson's cavalry division to Boonsboro, Maryland to hold the gaps in South Mountain if the enemy advanced in that direction.

Early's infantry reached the vicinity of Shepherdstown August 26, 1864, and Fitzhugh Lee's cavalry, which had reached Williamsport, also moved toward Shepherdstown. This was as far north as Early was prepared to go, and he had already decided to move back to his former positions west of the Opequon. That day he moved back to Leetown, and August 27, 1864 on to Bunker Hill. On the night of August 16, 1864, Anderson moved back from the vicinity of Halltown and took position in front of Stephenson's Depot. Early's cavalry remained at Leetown and Smithfield, west of Harper's Ferry.

August 28, 1864, Sheridan again advanced his army from Halltown to a position in front of Charlestown. Merritt attacked the enemy cavalry force at Leetown and drove it back through Smithfield. Wilson, who was no longer needed at Boonsboro, marched back to Shepherdstown, and then crossed the Potomac and joined Sheridan near Charlestown. The next day Averell recrossed the Potomac and advanced to Martinsburg.

Sheridan's infantry remained near Charlestown until September 3, 1864, and then again moved to the Clifton-Berryville line. The Army of West Virginia was on the left at Berryville, Detachment Nineteenth Corps was on the center of the line, and Sixth Corps was on the right at Clifton. Torbert, with the divisions of Merritt and Wilson, was on the left at White Post, and Lowell's Reserve Brigade of Merritt's division was at Smithfield. Averell was at Martinsburg. The infantry remained relatively inactive on the Clifton-Berryville line until September 19, 1864, but the cavalry was employed every day in harassing the enemy.

During the night of September 15, 1864, Sheridan received information that Kershaw's division was moving through Winchester toward Front Royal and Chester Gap, and it was confirmed September 17–18, 1864 that Anderson, with Kershaw's division and Cutshaw's artillery, had left the valley to rejoin Lee's army at Petersburg. Fitzhugh Lee's cavalry was left behind with Early. When Sheridan was certain that Early's force had been considerably reduced, he again prepared to take the offensive.

Battle of Opequon Creek (or Winchester), Virginia, September 19, 1864. Sheridan's plan was to move his infantry, preceded by a cavalry division, along the Berryville Pike toward Winchester, and for the other two cavalry divisions to march to Stephenson's Depot, and then move to the left toward Winchester. According to Sheridan's instructions, Torbert was to march with Merritt's division from Summit Point, and after crossing the Opequon, he was to continue on to Stephenson's Depot. There he was to join Averell's division, which was to move up the pike from Darkesville. Wilson, with his cavalry division, was to cross the Opequon and advance along the Berryville Pike through a long defile west of the creek, and clear the way for Wright's Sixth Corps and Emory's Detachment Nineteenth Corps, which were to follow. When Emory reached the Opequon, he was to report to Wright for orders. Crook's Army of West Virginia was to march across country from Summit Point and take position in reserve at the Opequon crossing of the Winchester-Berryville Pike.

The important features of the country to the east and northeast of Winchester within which Sheridan's army was operating September 19, 1864 are given here in some detail because of their significance during the Battle of the Opequon. Opequon Creek, which has its origin about six miles south of Winchester, flows northward down the Shenandoah Valley and passes about four to five miles east of the town. It then continues on northward on a course roughly parallel to the Valley Pike until it empties into the Potomac River below Falling Waters. The pike from Berryville to Winchester crossed the Opequon west of Berryville, and then passed through a wooded ravine or defile, two or three miles in length, before emerging onto more or less open and rolling ground about two miles from Winchester. There were also two small tributaries of the Opequon that were of significance during the battle. Abraham's Creek crossed the Valley Pike about a mile south of Winchester, then curved around to the north, and finally ran eastward on a course roughly parallel to the Berryville Pike and three-fourths to one mile to the south of it, and emptied into the Opequon near the road crossing. Red Bud Run (or Creek) crossed the Valley Pike about one mile north of Winchester and then ran eastward, roughly parallel to and about one-half to three-fourths of a mile north of the Berryville Pike, and flowed into the Opequon about 800 yards below the mouth of Abraham's Creek. At the western end of the defile, where Sheridan formed his first line, the two creeks were about a mile and a half apart, and the Berryville Pike was approximately midway between them.

Prior to the beginning of Sheridan's advance September 19, 1864, Early's army was in position as follows: Ramseur's division and William Nelson's artillery were formed across the Berryville Pike, one mile east of Winchester and along high ground between Abraham's Creek and Red Bud Run; the divisions of Wharton, Rodes, and Gordon, with artillery, were at Stephenson's Depot; Fitzhugh Lee's cavalry division was picketing the Opequon and covering the Confederate left; and Lunsford L. Lomax's cavalry division picketed the enemy right, along the Millwood and Front Royal roads to the Shenandoah River.

At 2:00 A.M. September 19, 1864, Sheridan's army left its camps and moved, according to orders, toward Winchester. Wilson's cavalry division, with John B. McIntosh's First Brigade in the lead, advanced by the Berryville-Winchester Pike to Opequon Creek. It then crossed the creek and pushed forward, driving back the enemy skirmishers, and captured an earthwork held by some of Ramseur's infantry at the mouth of the defile. Wilson then posted his troopers to the right and left of the road to hold the position until the infantry arrived. McIntosh was wounded during the engagement, and George B. Purington assumed command of the brigade.

Wright's Sixth Corps marched across country from Clifton to the Berryville Pike, about two miles east of the Opequon, and there it encountered the head of Emory's Detachment Nineteenth Corps, which was coming up from Berryville. Emory reported to Wright, as directed, and was ordered by the latter to halt his column to allow Sixth Corps to pass. Wright, with Getty's Second Division in the lead, crossed the Opequon and marched through the defile, which had been cleared by Wilson's cavalry, and then deployed his corps on the open ground beyond. His line was about two miles from Winchester, and about one mile in front of Ramseur's position. Getty's division formed on the left, with its right resting on the Berryville Pike and its left extending to Abraham's Creek. James M. Warner's Second Brigade was on the right of Getty's line, with its right on the pike; Frank Wheaton's First Brigade was on the center; and Daniel D. Bidwell's Third Brigade was on the left, with its left near Abraham's Creek. Ricketts' Third Division crossed the Opequon about 7:00 A.M., and then moved up on the right of Getty, with its left on the Berryville Pike. William E. Emerson's First Brigade was on the left, next to the road, and J. Warren Keifer's Second Brigade was on the right. The division was in position about 9:00 A.M. Russell's First Division followed Ricketts, and was formed in support of the other two divisions of the corps. Edward L. Campbell's First Brigade was placed in rear of the left of Ricketts' division; Oliver Edwards' Third Brigade was formed on the left of the road in support of Getty's division; and Emory Upton's Second Brigade was halted on the left of the road in reserve.

When relieved by the infantry about 8:00 A.M., Wilson's cavalry moved to a position about three-fourths of a mile to the left of Getty, on the Senseney Road. It remained there until that evening, and then crossed to the Millwood Road.

When Sixth Corps had finally passed the waiting Detachment Nineteenth Corps, Emory resumed his march and followed Russell's division toward the Opequon. Cuvier Grover's Second Division was in the lead, and William Dwight's First Division was close behind. Progress through the defile was slow because the road was filled with the guns and wagons of Sixth Corps, and Emory did not arrive on the field until 11:00 A.M. Grover then formed his division in two lines on the right of Ricketts. Jacob Sharpe's Third Brigade was placed on the left of the first line, next to Ricketts, and Henry W. Birge's First Brigade was on the right of Sharpe. In the second line, David Shunk's Fourth Brigade was formed in rear of Birge, and Edward L. Molineux's Second Brigade was in rear of Sharpe. Dwight's division, of which only two brigades were present, was formed to serve as a reserve, and also to protect the right of Grover's line. George L. Beal's First Brigade was formed in rear of Shunk, and James W. McMillan's Second Brigade was formed en echelon to the left and rear of Beal's brigade. Leonard D. H. Currie's Third Brigade, it will be remembered, was detached at Harper's Ferry and was not with the division.

During the morning of September 19, 1864, Ramseur's division had been the only Confederate infantry in front of Sheridan's command as it advanced toward Winchester. Lomax, with William L. Jackson's cavalry brigade (then commanded by Henry B. Davidson) and a part of Bradley T. Johnson's cavalry brigade, was on the right of Ram-

seur watching the valley of Abraham's Creek and the Front Royal Road; and a part of Johnson's brigade occupied the space between the left of Ramseur and Red Bud Run. This arrangement, however, was soon to change. As Sheridan's troops were forming in line of battle in front of Ramseur, Gordon and Rodes marched with their divisions from Stephenson's Depot to join Ramseur in front of Winchester. Gordon's division arrived first and took position in some woods to the left of Ramseur's line, and Johnson's cavalry detachment shifted to the left, close to Red Bud Run. When Rodes came up, he moved into the space between Ramseur and Gordon.

Finally, at 11:40 A.M., Sheridan was ready, and his infantry advanced toward the strongly reinforced enemy line and was soon involved in heavy fighting. Sixth Corps moved forward on both sides of the Winchester-Berryville Pike, and forced back the troops of Ramseur's and Rodes' divisions. At the same time, Emory, with Grover's division in front, launched a strong attack on Gordon's line. On the left of Sixth Corps, Wilson's cavalry advanced on the Senseney Road and forced back Lomax's cavalry.

As Wright and Emory pushed forward, a gap of about 400–500 yards developed between them. Ricketts' division, on the right of Sixth Corps, guided on the pike, which veered off to the left, and by following it Ricketts shifted away to the south. On the other hand, Grover, whose troops were driving back Clement A. Evans' brigade (then commanded by Edmund N. Atkinson), moved straight ahead and soon lost contact with the right of Ricketts' line. Keifer, commanding the right brigade of Ricketts' division, attempted to fill the interval thus created with three regiments of his brigade. When Grover's division moved forward, Birge's brigade was on the right of the first line and Sharpe's brigade on the left, but as they advanced they became separated, and Molineux's brigade was brought up from the second line to fill the gap between them. Shunk's brigade followed Birge.

At about this time, Cullen A. Battle's brigade of Rodes' division, which had just arrived from Stephenson's Depot, charged through the woods and into the weakly defended part of the line between Sixth Corps and Detachment Nineteenth Corps. At the same time that Battle charged, an enemy battery opened fire on the Federal right, taking the brigades of Birge and Sharpe in reverse. Emory then deployed Dwight's division, which had been held in reserve, to attempt to capture or drive away this battery. Birge's brigade was soon outflanked and outnumbered, and was driven back in confusion to its original position, which was then occupied on the right by Beal's brigade of Dwight's division, and on the left by Molineux's brigade of Grover's division. Sharpe was wounded and his brigade, then commanded by Alfred Neafie, fell back a short distance, but soon rallied and held its ground.

When Grover gave way, the enemy advanced against the right of Ricketts' division, and it, in turn, was driven back in some disorder. As a result, the brigades of Warner and Wheaton, on the right of Getty's division across the pike, were forced to make a partial change in front, but they were able to hold their position.

When the front line of Sixth Corps advanced that morning, the brigades of Russell's First Division, which had been placed in support, followed in columns on the left of the Berryville Pike, and about 300 yards to the rear. The division soon came under fire, and Campbell's First Brigade and Edwards' Third Brigade deployed and advanced, with the center of First Brigade on the road, and Third Brigade to the left and front. Upton's Second Brigade moved to the right, across the road, and covered as much as possible of the interval between the right of First Brigade and the left of Detachment Nineteenth Corps. Edwards' brigade also moved across the road, and Campbell's brigade closed in on its left. When Russell's division advanced, it struck the flank of the enemy force that was driving back the Federal right and, with the aid of Greenleaf T. Stevens' 5th Battery (E), Maine Light Artillery, drove back the attackers and reestablished the Union line. At about 12:30 P.M., Russell was killed while superintending the movements of First Brigade and Third Brigade, and Upton assumed command of First Division, Sixth Corps. Joseph E. Hamblin took charge of Upton's brigade. Rodes was also killed during the Confederate attack.

The broken portions of Ricketts' line re-formed behind First Division, and then again moved forward. Meantime, Dwight's division had advanced and taken the place of Grover's division, and the latter soon rallied and moved back into line. At this point it was well past noon, and although there was

some activity along the front, there was a lull in the fighting while Sheridan prepared for a final effort to break the enemy line.

At daylight that morning, Crook's Army of West Virginia had left its camps at Summit Point and marched across country to the crossing of the Winchester-Berryville Pike at Opequon Creek, and it had remained there during the morning in reserve. At noon, shortly after Wright and Emory became engaged, Sheridan ordered Crook to move up to the battlefield, about two miles distant, and form his command on the right and rear of Detachment Nineteenth Corps to watch the right of the line. Again, as with Emory's march earlier in the day, progress was slow because of the congestion in the defile, and Crook's leading division, Joseph Thoburn's First Division, did not reach its assigned position until about 3:00 P.M. Thoburn had with him only two brigades, having left Robert S. Northcott's Second Brigade to guard the trains. He then formed his command in rear of the right flank of Emory's line, with its right flank near Red Bud Run. At Emory's request, Thoburn relieved three regiments of Beal's First Brigade of Dwight's division, and one regiment of McMillan's Second Brigade of the same division. George D. Wells' First Brigade of Thoburn's division was placed in the first line, and Thomas M. Harris' Third Brigade formed in rear of Wells. In this way Thoburn filled the space between the right of Detachment Nineteenth Corps and the swampy ground through which Red Bud Run flowed.

When Isaac H. Duval's Second Division came up, it was posted on the far side of the run, and on the right of Thoburn. Rutherford B. Hayes' First Brigade was placed in the first line, and Daniel D. Johnson's Second Brigade was formed about 60 yards to the rear, with its right extending about 100 yards beyond the right of First Brigade. The division was thus in position to swing around to the left so as to strike the Confederate left flank. The deployment of Crook's command was completed about 4:00 P.M.

While Sheridan was engaged near Winchester, Torbert's cavalry had been active during the day to the north of the town. Early on the morning of September 19, 1864, Torbert had left Summit Point with Merritt's First Cavalry Division and marched to Opequon Creek. He encountered some opposition there, but finally crossed the creek at Seivers' and Locke's fords, and marched toward Stephenson's Depot on the Charlestown Road. At the same time, Averell's Second Cavalry Division, Department of West Virginia moved south from Darkesville on the Valley Pike, through Bunker Hill, toward Stephenson's Depot.

When the order was sent that morning for the Confederate troops at Stephenson's Depot to move to Winchester, John C. Breckinridge had moved to the front with Gabriel C. Wharton's division and Floyd J. King's artillery to meet the Federal cavalry that had driven in the Confederate pickets from the Opequon on the Charlestown Road. About a mile and a half west of Opequon Creek, Merritt found Wharton's division in line across the road and was forced to halt. Meantime, Averell, who was opposed by John D. Imboden's brigade (commanded by W. D. Smith) and John McCausland's brigade (commanded by Milton J. Ferguson) of Lunsford L. Lomax's division, pressed forward to Stephenson's Depot. Upon arrival there, Averell was in rear of Wharton's division, and the latter was forced to retire and, under Breckinridge's direction, reached Winchester about 2:00 P.M. George S. Patton's Brigade was left on the road to help Fitzhugh Lee's cavalry hold back Torbert's divisions, and the other two brigades of Wharton's division were sent to Early's right. Torbert, however, continued to advance from Stephenson's Depot toward Winchester, on the Martinsburg Road, with Averell's division on the west of the road and Merritt's division on the east. The Federal cavalry reached the outskirts of Winchester, in rear of the enemy left flank, and then Wharton's two brigades, which had hurried back from the enemy right, charged Torbert's line and, with the help of Floyd J. King's artillery and some of Carter M. Braxton's guns, halted its advance.

At 4:00 P.M. Sheridan had completed his preparations for the final attack of the day, and Crook's Army of West Virginia advanced along Red Bud Run at the beginning of its flanking movement. Then, wheeling to the left, Crook charged onto the left of Gordon's division and drove it back in disorder. This was at about the same time that Torbert was engaged on the Martinsburg Road, to the left and rear of Gordon. When Crook launched his attack, Sixth Corps and Detachment Nineteenth Corps also moved forward, and under these combined attacks the whole Confederate front line gave way. Finally, Early's army was driven from its positions and through Winchester toward Strasburg. Ramseur's division covered the retreat. Sheridan's infantry did not pursue, but halted for the night near Winchester. The cavalry did move forward, but only as far as Kernstown, where it was stopped by Ramseur. Duval was wounded during the last attacks, and he was succeeded in command of Second Division, Army of West Virginia by Rutherford B. Hayes. Hiram F. Devol succeeded Hayes in command of First Brigade, Second Division. Daniel D. Johnson, commander of Second Brigade, Second Division, was also wounded, and Benjamin F. Coates assumed command of his brigade.

The organization of the Union forces commanded by Philip H. Sheridan at the Battle of the Opequon September 19, 1864 was as follows:

SIXTH CORPS, Horatio G. Wright

First Division, David A. Russell, killed
  Emory Upton, wounded
  Oliver Edwards
  First Brigade, Edward L. Campbell
  Second Brigade, Emory Upton
    Joseph E. Hamblin
  Third Brigade, Oliver Edwards
    Isaac C. Bassett

Second Division, George W. Getty
  First Brigade, Frank Wheaton
  Second Brigade, James M. Warner
  Third Brigade, Daniel D. Bidwell

Note. Amasa S. Tracy superintended a portion of the Second Brigade line.

Third Division, James B. Ricketts
  First Brigade, William Emerson
  Second Brigade, J. Warren Keifer

Artillery Brigade, Charles H. Tompkins
  5th Battery (E), Maine Light Artillery, Greenleaf T. Stevens
  1st Battery (A), Massachusetts Light Artillery, William H. McCartney
  1st Battery, New York Light Artillery, William H. Johnson, mortally wounded
    Orsamus R. Van Etten
  Battery C, 1st Rhode Island Light Artillery, Jacob H. Lamb
  Battery G, 1st Rhode Island Light Artillery, George W. Adams

Battery M, 5th United States Artillery, James Mc-Knight

DETACHMENT NINETEENTH CORPS, William H. Emory

First Division, William Dwight
First Brigade, George L. Beal
Second Brigade, James W. McMillan
Third Brigade, Leonard D. H. Currie
5th Battery, New York Light Artillery, John V. Grant

Note. Third Brigade was detached at Harper's Ferry and was not engaged.

Second Division, Cuvier Grover
First Brigade, Henry W. Birge
Second Brigade, Edward L. Molineux
Third Brigade, Jacob Sharpe, wounded
Alfred Neafie
Fourth Brigade, David Shunk
1st Battery (A), Maine Light Artillery, Albert W. Bradbury

Reserve Artillery, Elijah D. Taft
17th Battery, Indiana Light Artillery, Milton L. Miner
Battery D, 1st Rhode Island Light Artillery, Frederick Chase

ARMY OF WEST VIRGINIA, George Crook

First Division, Joseph Thoburn
First Brigade, George D. Wells
Second Brigade, Robert S. Northcott
Third Brigade, Thomas M. Harris

Note. Second Brigade was left at Opequon Creek to guard the trains, and was not present during the battle.

Second Division, Isaac H. Duval, wounded
Rutherford B. Hayes
First Brigade, Rutherford B. Hayes
Hiram F. Devol
Second Brigade, Daniel D. Johnson, wounded
Benjamin F. Coates

Artillery Brigade, Henry A. Du Pont
Battery L, 1st Ohio Light Artillery, Frank C. Gibbs
Battery D, 1st Pennsylvania Light Artillery, William Munk
Battery B, 5th United States Artillery, Henry A. Du Pont

CAVALRY, Alfred T. A. Torbert

First Division, Wesley Merritt

First Brigade, George A. Custer
Second Brigade, Thomas C. Devin
Reserve Brigade, Charles R. Lowell, Jr.

Second Division, William W. Averell
First Brigade, James M. Schoonmaker
Second Brigade, Henry Capehart
Battery L, 5th United States Artillery, Gulian V. Weir

Third Division, James H. Wilson
First Brigade, John B. McIntosh, wounded
George A. Purington
Second Brigade, George H. Chapman

Horse Artillery, La Rhett L. Livingston
6th Battery, New York Light Artillery, Joseph W. Martin
Batteries K and L, 1st United States Artillery, Franck E. Taylor
Batteries B and L, 2nd United States Artillery, Charles H. Peirce
Battery D, 2nd United States Artillery, Edward B. Williston
Battery M, 2nd United States Artillery, Carle A. Woodruff
Batteries C, F, and K, 3rd United States Artillery, Dunbar R. Ransom
Batteries C and E, 4th United States Artillery, Terrence Reilly

Note. Only Taylor's, Peirce's, and Williston's batteries were with the cavalry at the Battle of the Opequon. Martin's battery was at Sandy Hook, Maryland, and the batteries of Woodruff, Ransom, and Reilly were at Pleasant Valley, Maryland.

Battle of Fisher's Hill, Virginia, September 21–22, 1864. At daylight on the morning of September 20, 1864, Sheridan's army left Winchester in pursuit of Early. The cavalry started first, with Averell's Second Cavalry Division advancing on the Middle Road to Cedar Creek, Merritt's First Cavalry Division on the Valley Pike to Cedar Creek, and Wilson's Third Cavalry Division by way of Stephensburg to Cedarville on the Front Royal Road. Wright's Sixth Corps marched in column through the fields on the left side of the Valley Pike, and Emory's Detachment Nineteenth Corps, also in column, moved on the right of the pike. Crook's Army of West Virginia followed along the pike.

During the day, Early fell back to his former position on Fisher's Hill, beyond Strasburg, and entrenched. Merritt's cavalry found him there, and then remained in front of his works until the infantry arrived. Sheridan's infantry reached Cedar Creek during the afternoon, and Wright's Sixth Corps and Emory's Detachment Nineteenth Corps then crossed and moved into position on the heights overlooking Strasburg. Sixth Corps was on the right, north of the town, with its line on the west side of the pike. Detachment Nineteenth Corps was on the Strasburg-Front Royal Road, which was covered by troops of Emory's command. Crook, who was following Wright and Emory, halted on the east side of Cedar Creek. When Merritt was relieved by the infantry, he moved to the right of Sixth Corps. Averell's cavalry division moved across Cedar Creek and took position on the right of Merritt on the Back Road.

The line selected by Early at Fisher's Hill was naturally very strong. At that point the valley was only about four miles wide because of the Massanutten Mountains, which extended north and south as an isolated chain, about midway between North Mountain on the west and the Blue Ridge Mountains on the east. The North Fork of the Shenandoah River flowed northward along the western base of the Massanuttens to Three Top Mountain near Strasburg, and there it turned abruptly to the east, and about ten miles farther on, near Front Royal, it joined the South Fork of the Shenandoah, which flowed northward through the Luray Valley between the Blue Ridge and Massanutten mountains.

The Valley Pike ran southward from Strasburg, along the west side of the North Fork, to Staunton. About 600–700 yards to the west of the pike, and roughly parallel to it, ran the wrecked line of the Manassas Gap Railroad. Both the pike and the railroad ran through depressions in Fisher's Hill. Cedar Creek flowed southward and emptied into the North Fork just below Strasburg. Tumbling Run, a small stream, flowed eastward across the valley along the northern base of Fisher's Hill, and into the North Fork two miles above Strasburg.

Early's position on Fisher's Hill was protected on the right by the hill itself, and also by the North Fork of the Shenandoah, and the approaches to its front were made difficult by the valley of Tumbling Run and the rugged nature of the ground. In addition, immediately after he arrived, Early began the construction of a line of works that extended westward from Fisher's Hill, across the valley, to North Moun-

tain. The Confederate troops were in position on this line as follows: Wharton's division was on the enemy right, between the Valley Pike and the North Fork of the Shenandoah; Gordon's division was on the left of Wharton, between the Valley Pike and the Manassas Gap Railroad; Ramseur's former division, then commanded by John Pegram, was on the left of Gordon; Rodes' former division, then commanded by Ramseur, was on the left of Pegram; and Lomax's dismounted cavalry held the left of the line to North Mountain. Breckinridge had been sent to southwest Virginia, and was no longer with Early. On September 20, 1864, Early sent Fitzhugh Lee's cavalry, then commanded by Williams C. Wickham, and consisting of his brigade and William H. Payne's brigade, to the right to prevent Federal troops from flanking his line at Fisher's Hill by way of the Luray Valley.

Early on the morning of September 21, 1864, Emory moved his command forward, with its left at the old fort (Fort Banks) near Strasburg. Sixth Corps moved to the right and, after passing Emory's position, drove off the enemy skirmishers and formed in front of the enemy works on Fisher's Hill. Frank Wheaton's First Division (Wheaton assumed command that day, relieving Oliver Edwards) was on the left between the Valley Pike and the Manassas Gap Railroad, with Joseph E. Hamblin's Second Brigade on the left and Edward L. Campbell's First Brigade on the right. Hamblin's brigade was about a mile and a half west of Strasburg, and opposite the extreme right of Early's position. Getty's Second Division was on the center of Wright's line, with George P. Foster's Second Brigade on the left, next to the railroad; Daniel D. Bidwell's Third Brigade in the center; and James M. Warner's First Brigade on the right. Ricketts' Third Division was on the right of the line, with J. Warren Keifer's Second Brigade on the first line and William Emerson's First Brigade in support.

Shortly after this line was established, Sheridan, with Wright, observed some high ground directly in front of Second Division overlooking the enemy works beyond Tumbling Run that was a better position than the one then occupied by Sixth Corps. It was also an excellent artillery position, and afforded a good view of Early's line. About 5:00 P.M. Wright attempted to take this hill with 39th Pennsylvania of Warner's brigade and the 6th Maryland and 126th

Ohio of Keifer's brigade. This attack was unsuccessful, and at 6:00 P.M. Wright brought up the rest of Warner's brigade, and a second attempt succeeded in driving the enemy from the hill. Warner's brigade then entrenched, and Foster's brigade moved up on his right and Bidwell's brigade on his left. Wheaton's division then moved to the right to reestablish its connection with Second Division.

On the night of September 21, 1864, Emory was ordered to move forward with his command at daylight the next morning and occupy the position held until the night before by Sixth Corps. Dwight's First Division, Detachment Nineteenth Corps was directed to move to the right and front and hold this position, but instead he moved by a circuitous route to the rear and left of Sixth Corps. Henry W. Birge's and Edward L. Molineux's brigades of Grover's Second Division were close at hand, and they were brought up and placed in the position formerly occupied by Sixth Corps. Birge's brigade was on the right, and Molineux's brigade was on the left. Daniel Macauley's Third Brigade (formerly commanded by Sharpe) and David Shunk's Fourth Brigade of Grover's division were held in reserve. Finally, Dwight's division was brought up and placed between Sixth Corps on the right and Grover's division on the left. George L. Beal's First Brigade was on the left of Dwight's line, and James W. McMillan's Second Brigade was on the right. Emory's responsibility was to connect with Sixth Corps on the right, and prevent the enemy from turning Sheridan's left flank.

At 7:00 A.M. September 22, 1864, Macauley's brigade was brought up and placed on the left of Molineux, on the extreme left of the infantry line, where it occupied the space between the railroad and the North Fork of the Shenandoah. Shunk's brigade was sent to the rear of Dwight's line. At 9:30 A.M., Molineux's brigade was sent to the left to protect the line of communications with Strasburg, but when he arrived at his assigned position he found Macauley already there and engaged in throwing up defensive works. Molineux then established his brigade on a second line in rear of Macauley, and assumed command of both brigades.

Sheridan's plan for the battle that he intended to fight that afternoon was for Crook, with his Army of West Virginia, to attack and turn the enemy's left flank at North Mountain, while Sixth Corps and Detachment Nineteenth Corps engaged the enemy in front at the same time. To ensure the success of Crook's movement, it was necessary to drive back the enemy skirmishers and sharpshooters that were out to the right of Sixth Corps, and also to silence the enemy artillery on their left flank. To accomplish this, Ricketts' Third Division, Sixth Corps was sent forward at 3:00 P.M. September 22, 1864, with Keifer's brigade in front and Emerson's brigade in support. Ricketts advanced about a mile to the southwest and took position facing the enemy works, which were about one-half mile distant. Soon after Ricketts' new line was established, the other two divisions of Sixth Corps also advanced to within 700–800 yards of the enemy line, with Getty's Second Division on the left of Ricketts and Wheaton's First Division between Getty and the Manassas Gap Railroad. Averell's cavalry division moved up on the right of Ricketts.

Emory's Detachment Nineteenth Corps was also assigned a part in the coming attack. Emory was to advance his command and press the enemy so as to divert attention from Crook's attack on the enemy left. At 12:15 P.M., two regiments of Macauley's brigade and four companies of Beal's brigade charged and carried a line of rifle pits between the railroad and the Valley Pike, and about 500 yards in front of the enemy works on Fisher's Hill. This new line was entrenched and held by Beal's brigade until the general advance of the army that evening. McMillan's brigade formed in rear of Beal's line. Birge's brigade, and Shunk's brigade of Grover's division remained in rear during the day, but they too advanced that evening and joined in the pursuit of Early's defeated army.

Meantime, on the night of September 21, 1864, Crook's Army of West Virginia crossed Cedar Creek at a point about one and one-fourth mile to the north and a little west of Strasburg, and at daylight the next morning marched under cover past the right of Sixth Corps, and halted on the Back Road near the base of North Mountain. It was then near the right of Ricketts' division, and a short distance in front of the extreme left of Early's line, which was held by Lomax's dismounted cavalry. At 2:00 P.M. September 22, 1864, Sheridan ordered Crook to move up on the eastern slope of North Mountain, then south along the side of the mountain to a point beyond the left of the enemy works, and to attack on the left and rear of Lomax's line. When Crook reached the base of the mountain, he formed his command in two parallel columns, and then marched south along the eastern slope under cover of the woods until more than half the length of his columns had passed to the rear of the enemy line. This was at about 3:30 P.M. Crook then faced his command to the left, forming two parallel lines of battle as follows: Thoburn's First Division was on the left, with George D. Wells' First Brigade in the first line and Thomas M. Harris' Third Brigade in the second line; and Rutherford B. Hayes' Second Division was on the right, with Benjamin F. Coates' Second Brigade in the first line and Hiram F. Devol's First Brigade in the second line.

When Crook's lines were formed, they moved down the mountain, and then charged into the left and rear of Lomax's dismounted cavalry and drove them back in complete disorder. Ricketts' division then advanced on the left of Crook, and farther to the left the rest of Sheridan's line charged across Tumbling Run and up the slope of Fisher's Hill. After Lomax's men had fled, Ramseur and then Pegram were, in turn, routed, and a short time later the entire Confederate line broke from the trenches. Early's entire line had been carried between sundown and dark, with the capture of sixteen guns and about 1,000 prisoners, and all of his army was in full flight up the valley toward Woodstock.

Emory's troops, which had been advancing on the Valley Pike during the attack, led the pursuit, with Grover's division in the lead. Emory followed Early throughout the night, and at 3:00–4:00 A.M. September 23, 1864 halted at Woodstock. At 5:30 P.M. September 22, 1864, Devin was ordered up from Middletown to pursue Early. He reached the head of Emory's column at 10:00 P.M. and reported to Sheridan. He then moved forward through the fields on the left of the pike and the infantry until he reached Woodstock sometime after daylight. He then took over the pursuit of the enemy and followed them through Mount Jackson. Wright's Sixth Corps followed Emory during the night and halted soon after daylight beyond Woodstock. Wright commanded both Detachment Nineteenth Corps and Sixth Corps during the pursuit. Crook's Army of

West Virginia, which had advanced about five miles during the attack, halted at dark on the road to Woodstock, one to two miles beyond the line of enemy works.

The cavalry played no significant role in the day's fighting. On September 20, 1864, Torbert, at Sheridan's direction, ordered Wilson to move up the Luray Valley as far as possible with his division and determine what was happening there. The next morning, Wilson advanced and drove Wickham's command from Front Royal and up the Luray Valley. Also that day, September 21, 1864, Merritt's division, less Devin's brigade (which had been left at Middletown in rear of the army), was withdrawn from the right of Sixth Corps and from the left of Averell's division, and it then crossed the North Fork of the Shenandoah at Buckton Ford, marched through Front Royal, and camped about a mile and a half beyond. Averell's division, which had advanced from Winchester on the Middle Road the day before, moved at 5:00 A.M. to Lebanon Church. When Merritt's division was withdrawn from his left, Averell moved forward on the Middle Road and Back Road, maintaining a connection with Sixth Corps, until stopped by a strong enemy force.

September 21, 1864, Sheridan then ordered Torbert to follow the enemy up the Luray Valley with Wilson's division and the two brigades of Merritt's division, and about six miles from Front Royal he found Wickham posted in a strong position on the south side of Gooney Run. Torbert decided against a frontal attack, and at 2:00 A.M. September 22, 1864 sent Custer back to cross to the west side of the South Fork of the Shenandoah River, with orders to recross the river at McCoy's Ford, about two miles in rear of the position at Gooney Creek, and move on Wickham's rear. At 10:00 the previous night, however, Wickham had begun to withdraw and to fall back to a stronger position on the south side of Milford Creek. There he formed a new line, with his left on the South Fork of the Shenandoah River and his right on a spur of the Blue Ridge Mountains. When Torbert moved forward on the morning of September 22, 1864, he found that the enemy had withdrawn, but at 11:00 that morning he came up to Wickham's new line beyond Milford Creek. Because the creek was too deep for the men to cross and attack, and there was not sufficient room for a flank movement, Torbert decided not to attack. Then, not having learned of Sheridan's battle at Fisher's Hill, he withdrew to a point opposite McCoy's Ferry and camped for the night. On September 23, 1864, Merritt's division returned to Front Royal, but that night it returned to Milford and, after crossing Overall's Run by a ford, bivouacked until daylight September 24, 1864.

As has been noted, Devin's brigade of Merritt's division was not on the field during the battle, but it did join the pursuit that night. Early in the attack, Averell's division advanced on the right of Ricketts, and it then moved to protect Crook's rear from guerrillas, which appear to have been active during the battle. Averell did not join in the pursuit, but camped that night on the field. He was relieved from command of his division the next day, September 23, 1864, and ordered to Wheeling, West Virginia. William H. Powell assumed command of his Second Cavalry Division, Department of West Virginia.

The organization of Sheridan's command at the Battle of Fisher's Hill September 21–22, 1864 was as follows:

SIXTH CORPS, Horatio G. Wright

First Division, Oliver Edwards, to September 21, 1864
    Frank Wheaton
    First Brigade, Edward L. Campbell
    Second Brigade, Joseph E. Hamblin

Note. Oliver Edwards' Third Brigade, commanded by Isaac C. Bassett until September 21, 1864, was on duty at Winchester, where Edwards was in command of the post.

Second Division, George W. Getty
    First Brigade, Frank Wheaton, to September 21, 1864
      James M. Warner
    Second Brigade, James M. Warner, to September 21, 1864
      George P. Foster
    Third Brigade, Daniel D. Bidwell

Third Division, James B. Ricketts
    First Brigade, William Emerson
    Second Brigade, J. Warren Keifer

Artillery Brigade, Charles H. Tompkins

DETACHMENT NINETEENTH CORPS, William H. Emory

First Division, William Dwight

First Brigade, George L. Beal
Second Brigade, James W. McMillan

Second Division, Cuvier Grover
    First Brigade, Henry W. Birge
    Second Brigade, Edward L. Molineux
    Third Brigade, Alfred Neafie, to September 21, 1864
      Daniel Macauley
    Fourth Brigade, David Shunk

Note. Jacob Sharpe, former commander of Third Brigade, was wounded September 19, 1864.

Reserve Artillery, Elijah D. Taft

ARMY OF WEST VIRGINIA (EIGHTH CORPS), George Crook

First Infantry Division, Joseph Thoburn
    First Brigade, George D. Wells
    Third Brigade, Thomas M. Harris

Note. Robert S. Northcott's Second Brigade was at Winchester during the battle and was not engaged.

Second Infantry Division, Rutherford B. Hayes
    First Brigade, Hiram F. Devol
    Second Brigade, Benjamin F. Coates

Artillery Brigade, Henry A. Du Pont

CAVALRY

Second Cavalry Division, Department of West Virginia, William W. Averell
    First Brigade, James M. Schoonmaker
    Second Brigade, Henry Capehart

Alfred T. A. Torbert's other two cavalry divisions were not present on the field during the battle, but they were operating in the Luray Valley September 21–22, 1864 against the enemy cavalry. These divisions were organized as follows:

First Cavalry Division, Wesley Merritt
    First Brigade, George A. Custer
    Second Brigade, Thomas C. Devin
    Reserve Brigade, Charles R. Lowell, Jr.

Note. Devin's brigade was at Middletown during the battle, but it joined in the pursuit of Early following his defeat at Fisher's Hill.

Third Cavalry Division, James H. Wilson
    First Brigade, George A. Purington
    Second Brigade, George H. Chapman

Fisher's Hill to Cedar Creek, Virginia, September 23, 1864–October 19, 1864. On the morning of September 23, 1864, the day after the Battle of Fisher's Hill, Early continued his retreat through Mount Jackson and across the North Fork of the Shenandoah River to Rude's Hill. At daylight, Devin's cavalry brigade followed Early up the Valley Pike. About three miles south of Edenburg, Devin encountered an enemy force and drove it back to Mount Jackson. Averell, who had marched that morning from the battlefield with his Second Cavalry Division, then came up and assumed command. Devin's brigade and the two brigades of Averell's division remained in line until dark, and then retired. About 11:00 that night, Sheridan, who was displeased with Averell's performance that day and the day before, relieved him from command and assigned William H. Powell to command his division.

About 1:00 P.M. Sheridan's infantry, less Crook's Army of West Virginia, which had been left behind at Fisher's Hill to care for the wounded and to bury the dead, left Woodstock in pursuit of Early. Merritt's cavalry division marched back down the Luray Valley from Milford and halted at Cedarville. Wilson's division remained near Milford.

On the morning of September 24, 1864, Sheridan, with Sixth Corps, Detachment Nineteenth Corps, Devin's cavalry brigade, and Averell's cavalry division, then commanded by Powell, advanced through Mount Jackson toward Rude's Hill, where Early was encamped. Upon approaching the North Fork, Sheridan sent Devin's brigade across the river to move along the base of Peaked Ridge against the right of Early's position, and he directed Powell to move with his division around Early's left in the direction of Timberville. The infantry moved ahead and crossed the river on the bridge.

Sheridan's movements were observed by Early, and he retreated on south through New Market, closely followed by Wright and Emory. Sixth Corps advanced on the left of the pike, and Detachment Nineteenth Corps on the right. Devin's cavalry again took the lead. At 11:00 A.M. Powell's division moved from the pike across to the Middle Road, which ran southward through Forest Hill and Broadway to Harrisonburg. During the day Powell drove back Lomax's cavalry, and he camped that night three miles south of Broadway. About six miles beyond New Market, Early's column left the pike

and took a road that ran farther to the east, through Keezletown and Cross Keys to Port Republic. Early halted for a time at sunset, in line of battle near the junction of the Keezletown Road and the pike. Sheridan came up after dark and went into camp just out of range of the enemy line. Early then marched on about five miles and halted for the night fourteen miles north of Port Republic.

Crook's divisions, which had completed their work at Fisher's Hill, had been marching up the valley during the day, and they arrived at New Market that night. Across the Massanutten Mountains, Merritt's cavalry drove the enemy from Luray, and Wilson's division passed through the town and camped near Massanutten Gap.

Early resumed his retreat on the morning of September 25, 1864 and marched through Keezletown and Port Republic, and then he assumed a strong defensive position covering Brown's Gap. He was joined there by Lomax's cavalry, which had been driven from Mount Jackson to Harrisonburg, and also by Wickham's cavalry division, which had retreated from the Luray Valley.

The Federals continued the advance on September 25, 1864. Wright and Emory arrived in Harrisonburg at 4:00 P.M., and they remained there in camp until September 29, 1864. Crook's command was left behind at the junction of the Valley Pike and the Keezletown Road, where it camped that night. The cavalry was also active that day. Devin, who was in front of the infantry, advanced to Harrisonburg without opposition. There he learned that Early had taken the road to Keezletown, and he marched to that point, only to find that the enemy had marched toward Port Republic. Devin camped that night at Peale's Cross Roads, nearby. Powell's division arrived at Harrisonburg at noon, and two hours later moved on beyond Mount Crawford and camped on the north side of the North River. During the day, Torbert had been marching from the Luray Valley with the divisions of Merritt and Wilson, by way of Massanutten Gap and New Market, and he arrived at Harrisonburg that evening.

During the next few days only the Federal cavalry was active. Sheridan's infantry remained near Harrisonburg, and Early's army in front of Brown's Gap. There on September 26, 1864, Early was joined by Kershaw's division and Cutshaw's artillery, which had been ordered to return to the Shenandoah

Valley following Early's defeat at the Battle of the Opequon.

On September 26, 1864, Sheridan sent Torbert with Wilson's Third Cavalry Division and Lowell's Reserve Brigade of Merritt's First Cavalry Division to march by way of Staunton to Waynesboro to destroy the Virginia Central Railroad and the bridge over the South River. Merritt, with James H. Kidd's First Brigade (Custer's brigade until that morning, when he left to assume command of Second Cavalry Division, Department of West Virginia), moved to Port Republic, where he joined Devin. Merritt drove the enemy cavalry across the Middle River and into Brown's Gap, but was then checked by Confederate infantry. Powell's Second Cavalry Division marched across the valley to Middle River and Piedmont, and then to Weyer's Cave, three miles west of Brown's Gap, to cooperate with Merritt in an attempt to capture Early's trains. Powell, however, was driven back to the west side of South River, and the next day, September 27, 1864, Powell and Merritt moved to Cross Keys.

Torbert arrived in Staunton September 26, 1864, and there he captured large quantities of stores of military value. The next day he moved on to Waynesboro, and arrived there after dark. That day, September 27, 1864, Early learned that Torbert had occupied Staunton and was threatening Waynesboro, and at dawn the next morning he marched toward the latter place. Torbert spent most of September 28, 1864 destroying the railroad and the bridge at Waynesboro, but late in the afternoon Early arrived and promptly attacked. Torbert held him in check until after dark, and then fell back through Staunton to Spring Hill, a hamlet on Middle River, on the Back Road that ran from Staunton to Harrisonburg.

At Cross Keys, Custer relieved Powell in command of Second Cavalry Division September 28, 1864. When it was discovered that Early was moving in the direction of Waynesboro, Kidd's brigade of Merritt's division and James M. Schoonmaker's First Brigade of Custer's division were advanced to Port Republic. September 29, 1864, Torbert marched to Bridgewater, where he left Wilson's Third Cavalry Division and sent Lowell's Reserve Brigade to rejoin Merritt near Cross Keys. September 29, 1864, Merritt's and Custer's divisions, both under Merritt, marched across

country, covering the area from within a few miles of Waynesboro and Staunton to Mount Crawford, destroying grain, forage, and mills, and driving off cattle. Sixth Corps and Detachment Nineteenth Corps were advanced from Harrisonburg to Mount Crawford to support Merritt and Torbert. When Merritt's work was completed, he moved to Mount Crawford and camped on the left and rear of Sixth Corps and Detachment Nineteenth Corps.

September 30, 1864, Wilson was relieved from command of Third Cavalry Division, and was ordered west to report to William T. Sherman, commanding the Military Division of the Mississippi. Custer was then assigned command of Wilson's division, and Powell resumed command of Second Cavalry Division, Department of West Virginia. Custer's division remained at Bridgewater, picketing a line from Mount Crawford to the right of Bridgewater; Merritt's division was in position at Mount Crawford; and Powell's division, Wright's Sixth Corps, and Emory's Detachment Nineteenth Corps moved back to Harrisonburg. On October 1, 1864, Powell's division marched down Page Valley toward Luray, where it arrived the next day. Sheridan's army remained generally in position at Harrisonburg until October 6, 1864, with Merritt and Custer holding a line across the valley from Port Republic, along the North River, past Mount Crawford to the Back Road on the west, near Briery Branch Gap.

Early remained at Waynesboro until October 1, 1864, and he then moved across country to Mount Sidney on the Valley Pike. He took position between that place and North River, about midway between Staunton and Harrisonburg. While there he was joined by Thomas L. Rosser's cavalry brigade, which arrived from Richmond October 5, 1864. This brigade was assigned to Fitzhugh Lee's cavalry division, and Rosser was assigned command of the division (Wickham resigned).

Shortly after the Battle of Fisher's Hill, and during Sheridan's pursuit of Early's defeated army up the Shenandoah Valley, Grant and the authorities in Washington began to give serious consideration to the problem of how best to use Sheridan's army in future operations. On the day after the Battle of Fisher's Hill, Sheridan was urged to continue his advance up the valley, and September 26, 1864, the day after Sheridan reached Harrisonburg, Grant asked Sheridan to push on, if at all possible, and make a determined effort to reach Charlottesville and destroy the railroads and the James River Canal. The next day, with a movement toward Charlottesville in mind, Grant instructed Halleck to have the Orange and Alexandria Railroad opened as far as Manassas Junction, and then if Sheridan advanced toward Charlottesville, as Grant expected him to do, to repair the railroad as far as Culpeper Court House. Grant was insistent. On September 28, 1864, Halleck informed Sheridan that Grant wished him to push on toward Staunton or Charlottesville. Sheridan's cavalry had already reached Staunton and Waynesboro, but he was strongly opposed to an advance in the direction of Charlottesville for a number of important reasons, largely because of problems of supply. In addition, a further advance up the valley was largely out of the question, because the army could not depend on the arrival of supplies by way of the Shenandoah Valley beyond Harrisonburg. Having considered this problem, Sheridan proposed to Grant that he, Sheridan, end the Valley Campaign by devastating the valley so that it would not again support an enemy army, and then transferring most of the troops of his command to the Richmond-Petersburg front.

Sheridan received Grant's permission to end the campaign on October 5, 1864, and the next day his army left Harrisonburg and started down the valley toward Strasburg. The infantry moved first, and the cavalry followed in an extended line across the valley, burning crops, barns, and mills and driving off or killing cattle and horses. Early followed promptly, and his infantry reached New Market October 7, 1864. He then ordered Rosser to move forward on the Middle Road and the Back Road in pursuit of Custer, and Lomax on the Valley Pike to follow Merritt.

Sheridan's infantry passed through Woodstock, and arrived at Fisher's Hill and Strasburg October 8, 1864. That day Merritt, who was covering Sheridan's rear on the Valley Pike, reached Tom's Brook, about five miles south of Strasburg. Powell's division, which had been marching up the Luray Valley, reached Front Royal from Milford October 7, 1864, and he remained there the next day. Custer, who was moving northward on the Back Road October 8, 1864, had been hard pressed by Rosser during the day, and Merritt was sent back to support

him. Custer camped that night near Fisher's Hill, and Sheridan ordered Torbert to start at daylight the next morning, October 9, 1864, and "whip the rebel cavalry or be whipped yourself." He also ordered Custer to advance on the Back Road and Merritt to attack on the Valley Pike at the same time.

At 7:00 A.M. Custer advanced on the Back Road as ordered, with Alexander C. M. Pennington's First Brigade (commanded by George A. Purington until October 7, 1864) in the lead, and William Wells' (Chapman was wounded September 19, 1864) Second Brigade following in support. Pennington drove back the enemy pickets and came up to Rosser's main force in position beyond Tom's Brook. Custer then sent three regiments of Pennington's brigade to the right to turn Rosser's left flank, and ordered Wells to move up the road in support. Meantime, Merritt had advanced on the pike, and then extended his line toward the Back Road where Custer was engaged. He sent Kidd's First Brigade to the right toward the Back Road to strike the right flank of Rosser's line. He then ordered Lowell's Reserve Brigade to advance on the pike, cross Tom's Brook, and move to the enemy's rear. Devin's Second Brigade moved to a position midway between the pike and the Back Road, and connected on the right with Kidd and on the left with Lowell. When in position, Devin was directed to attack the enemy on his front. Lowell was soon in some trouble on the pike, and two regiments were sent to strike the left flank of the force opposing him. This attack succeeded in dividing the divisions of Rosser and Lomax, and they were forced back on both roads, and then were driven back in a complete rout to Mount Jackson, a distance of twenty miles.

After Tom's Brook, Early's infantry remained at New Market, Rosser's cavalry formed a line across the valley along Stony Creek from Edenburg to Columbia Furnace, and Lomax's cavalry was sent to Milford in the Luray Valley.

On October 10, 1864, the day after the engagement at Tom's Brook, Sheridan moved his army across Cedar Creek and occupied the high ground beyond. Emory's Detachment Nineteenth Corps was placed on the west side of the pike, and Crook's Army of West Virginia on the east side. Merritt's cavalry division covered the left flank of this line, and Custer's division the right. At this time, Sheridan received orders to retain Detachment

Nineteenth Corps in the valley, and to send Sixth Corps and a cavalry division to Grant's army at Petersburg as soon as possible. That day, October 10, 1864, Sixth Corps marched to Front Royal on its way to Washington for transfer to City Point.

Earlier, while the army was operating at some distance from Harper's Ferry, large numbers of troops were required to protect the wagon trains hauling supplies to the front from bands of guerrillas that infested the region, especially John S. Mosby's Partisan Rangers. Leonard D. H. Currie's Third Brigade, First Division, Detachment Nineteenth Corps had been detached for this duty, but it was not sufficient for the task. On September 22, 1864, the following regiments were ordered to move from the Department of Washington, by way of Harper's Ferry, to Winchester: 41st New York, 6th New York Heavy Artillery, and 9th New York Heavy Artillery of J. Howard Kitching's First Brigade of Martin D. Hardin's Division; 103rd New York and 104th Pennsylvania of William Heine's Third Brigade of Gustavus A. De Russy's Division; and 10th New York Heavy Artillery, commanded by G. De Peyster Arden, and 184th New York, both of De Russy's Division. These regiments were organized into two provisional brigades commanded by Heine and Arden, and they were used to guard trains supplying the troops at the front. When Sixth Corps moved to Front Royal, the trains, which had been parked at Winchester, were sent to join it there. The train guard consisted of 800 men of Heine's Provisional Brigade, and some other troops from Harper's Ferry.

On October 12, 1864, when Sixth Corps was ordered to Alexandria for embarkation, the provisional troops under Heine, which at that time were attached to Sixth Corps, were ordered to remain at Front Royal, where Arden with his Provisional Brigade was to join him. On October 14, 1864, Heine was ordered to report directly to Sheridan's headquarters, and shortly thereafter the two provisional brigades were organized as the Provisional Division of Sheridan's army, and Kitching was assigned command. The division was organized as follows:

Provisional Division, J. Howard Kitching
   First Brigade, William Heine
      41st New York, 103rd New York, and 104th Pennsylvania

Second Brigade, G. De Peyster Arden
   6th New York Heavy Artillery and 10th New York Heavy Artillery

While at Front Royal, on October 10, 1864, Sheridan learned that the Manassas Gap Railroad had been repaired only as far as Piedmont, and accordingly, he ordered Sixth Corps to march for Alexandria by way of Ashby's Gap. Sheridan saw no further reason for opening the railroad to Front Royal, and when he ordered Christopher C. Augur, commander of the Department of Washington, to withdraw the guards, repairs to the road practically ended. On the morning of October 13, 1864, however, Sheridan received a communication from Halleck (dated October 12, 1864), in which he transmitted Grant's request that preparations be made for operations against Charlottesville and Gordonsville. Also on October 13, 1864, Halleck informed Sheridan that Edwin M. Stanton, secretary of war, wished him to come to Washington for consultation if he could safely leave the army. Stanton and Halleck hoped to persuade Sheridan to accept their view, and also Grant's, that an operation against Charlottesville and the continued repair of the Manassas Gap Railroad were desirable. At this point, Sheridan acquiesced and countermanded the order for Sixth Corps to march to Washington.

Then Sheridan's plans were further changed by a new development. When Early learned that Sheridan was sending troops to Petersburg, he advanced from New Market and October 13, 1864 reoccupied Fisher's Hill. He then moved forward the next day through Strasburg to Hupp's Hill on a reconnaissance, and there he discovered the camp of Thoburn's division of the Army of West Virginia on Cedar Creek. Early's artillery immediately opened fire, and in response George D. Wells' First Brigade and Thomas M. Harris' Third Brigade advanced to the foot of the hill. There they formed in line of battle, with Harris' brigade on the right and Wells' brigade on the left, and then they moved up the hill. Upon reaching the crest, they were met by heavy fire, but despite this they succeeded in establishing a continuous line to the right of the road. Kershaw's division advanced to turn Thoburn's right, and Harris was forced to retire. This exposed Wells' brigade to an enfilade fire from the right, and it too was forced to retire with heavy loss, including Wells, who was killed. Thomas F. Wildes succeeded Wells in command of First Brigade. With his reconnaissance thus completed, Early withdrew to Fisher's Hill that night.

When Sheridan learned of Early's appearance at Hupp's Hill on October 14, 1864, he ordered Sixth Corps to return to the army from Millwood near the Shenandoah River, where it had arrived on the evening before. The corps arrived at Cedar Creek at noon October 14, 1864, and was placed in position on the right and rear of Detachment Nineteenth Corps, where it could support either Emory or Crook.

Grant was persistent in his desire that Sheridan move on Charlottesville, and once again, on October 15, 1864, Sheridan received a communication from Grant urging him to threaten the Virginia Central Railroad if possible. Sheridan then decided to send Torbert, with the divisions of Merritt and Powell, through Chester Gap on a raid toward the railroad. In preparation for this movement, Sheridan ordered Torbert, on the evening of October 15, 1864, to march with Merritt's division to Front Royal. Earlier, on October 11, 1864, Powell's division had moved out on an expedition from Front Royal, through Chester Gap, to Sperryville and Amissville, and it had then taken position at Flint Hill, north of Little Washington. While there, on October 15, 1864, Powell was also ordered to Front Royal to join Torbert.

Sheridan accompanied Torbert and Merritt and arrived at Front Royal October 16, 1864. There he received from Wright, who had been left in command of the army at Cedar Creek, a dispatch that included an intercepted message, purportedly from Longstreet to Early, which indicated that the former was on his way to join Early in the valley. Sheridan believed this to be a ruse, but to be safe he canceled the cavalry raid toward Charlottesville. He sent Torbert, with Merritt's division, back to Cedar Creek, where he arrived about noon that day. Merritt then resumed his position on the right and rear of Sixth Corps. Powell remained with Henry Capehart's Second Brigade at Guard Hill, on the north side of the Shenandoah River near Front Royal. Alpheus S. Moore's First Brigade, formerly commanded by Schoonmaker, moved several miles to the west to Buckton Ford on the Shenandoah, where his pickets connected with the left of Crook's command.

On October 16, 1864, Sheridan left Front Royal and went to Rectortown to confer with Augur, who had brought out from Washington a force to repair and protect the railroad. While there, Sheridan learned that Longstreet had brought no troops from Richmond, and the next morning he continued on by rail by way of Manassas Gap to Washington, where he arrived at 8:00 A.M. October 17, 1864. After conferring with Stanton and Halleck, he left Washington at noon on a special train, on the Baltimore and Ohio Railroad, for Martinsburg. He arrived there about dark, and spent the night before going on to Winchester the next day. He then stayed all night at Winchester, and when he awakened there the next morning, October 19, 1864, Early's surprise attack on Wright's army at Cedar Creek had begun.

Battle of Cedar Creek, Virginia, October 19, 1864. When Early returned to Fisher's Hill after his advance to Hupp's Hill October 13, 1864, he realized that he would be unable to remain that far down the valley because of the devastation wrought by Sheridan on his retreat from Harrisonburg. This left him with two options—to attack and defeat Sheridan's army, or to withdraw completely from the valley. He decided on the former, and his troops spent most of the night of October 17–18, 1864 in marching to their assigned positions for an attack the next morning.

At that time, the Union army was encamped on the eastern bank of Cedar Creek, just above its junction with the North Fork of the Shenandoah River. The troops were in position, partially en echelon, as follows: George Crook's Army of West Virginia (also called Eighth Corps) was near the junction of Cedar Creek and the North Fork; William H. Emory's Detachment Nineteenth Corps was to the right and rear of Crook; and Horatio G. Wright's Sixth Corps was to the right and rear of Emory.

The Army of West Virginia was on the left (east) of the Valley Pike, and was encamped in two positions. Joseph Thoburn's First Division was on the extreme left of the infantry line, entrenched on an elevated part of a high ridge overlooking Cedar Creek, and was about one mile from the left of Detachment Nineteenth Corps and three-fourths of a mile northeast of Roberts' Ford and Bowman's Mill. The line generally faced to the south and southwest, with its right near Cedar Creek. Ruther- ford B. Hayes' Second Division was in position to the rear of First Division, about one mile to the northeast on another elevation of the same ridge. It was encamped about one-fourth of a mile in rear of the left of Detachment Nineteenth Corps, and was not entrenched. It was so placed that it could readily move to support Thoburn, or face to the left to defend the pike from an enemy attack from the east. A small provisional force under J. Howard Kitching was in position on the left of Hayes.

Emory's Detachment Nineteenth Corps was on the right of Crook, and was west of the pike on a ridge or elevated plain about one-fourth mile east of Cedar Creek. It was entrenched on a line about three-fourths of a mile long, and extended from the pike on the left to Meadow Brook on the right. The line faced to the southwest toward Cedar Creek. William Dwight's First Division, then commanded by James W. McMillan, was on the right of the corps, with its right on Meadow Brook, and Cuvier Grover's Second Division was on the left, next to the pike, and across the pike from Hayes' division of Crook's command. Most of the artillery was on the left of Detachment Nineteenth Corps, where it commanded the pike. Belle Plain Mansion, which was the headquarters of Sheridan and Crook, was less than a half mile in rear of Emory's line.

Wright's Sixth Corps was on the right of Detach- ment Nineteenth Corps, and was separated from the latter by Meadow Brook. Sixth Corps was about one-half mile north of Emory's line and approximately one mile west of the Valley Pike. The corps was not entrenched, but was prepared to sup- port Crook or Emory if needed.

Wesley Merritt's First Cavalry Division was en- camped on the right of Sheridan's line, on Middle Marsh Branch, about one mile to the north of the rear of Sixth Corps. George A. Custer's Third Cavalry Division was about a mile and a half beyond Merritt to the north and west, watching the fords where the Back Road and the Mine Bank Road crossed Cedar Creek in the vicinity of Cupp's Mill. Alpheus S. Moore's First Brigade of William H. Powell's Second Cavalry Division was at Buckton Ford, where the road from Front Royal to Middletown crossed the North Fork of the Shenandoah. This was about two and one-half miles beyond the left of Crook's position near Cedar Creek. Powell, with

Henry Capehart's Second Brigade, was at Guard Hill, just north of the Shenandoah near Front Royal.

Early's plan for the battle of October 19, 1864 was to demonstrate on the Federal right with Thomas L. Rosser's cavalry, and to attack the Federal left with the divisions of Joseph B. Kershaw, John Pegram, Stephen D. Ramseur, and John B. Gordon. The latter three divisions were under the direct control of Gordon, and Clement A. Evans commanded Gordon's division while the latter was in charge of the flanking column. Gabriel C. Wharton's division and the artillery under Thomas H. Carter were to advance against the Federal center on the Valley Pike.

During the night of October 18–19, 1864, Gordon marched with his three divisions around the base of Massanutten Mountain, on the south bank of the North Fork of the Shenandoah, and before dawn October 19, 1864 arrived at McIntorff's Ford and Bowman's Ford. Early, who accompanied Kershaw's division, arrived at a point opposite Bowman's Mill on Cedar Creek, about a mile above Gordon, at 3:30 A.M. Wharton and the artillery advanced from Strasburg to Hupp's Hill. The scheduled time for the attack was 5:00 A.M. At 4:30 A.M. Kershaw crossed Cedar Creek and advanced toward Thoburn's position. At the same time, Rosser began skirmishing on the far Union right, and Gordon's divisions crossed the North Fork and marched toward the J. Cooley house, a little more than a mile and one-fourth north of Bowman's Ford. When Kershaw struck the Federal works, Thoburn's command was completely surprised and, after a brief struggle, was driven from the field and virtual- ly destroyed. An attempt was made to hold the works in front of the camp with Thomas M. Harris' Third Brigade on the right and Thomas F. Wildes' First Brigade on the right, but to no avail. Thoburn was killed in the fighting, and Harris assumed command of what was left of the division. Milton Wells took over Harris' brigade.

After this success, Kershaw immediately pushed on toward Hayes' Second Division, which, as was noted earlier, was on a height farther up the ridge. When the attack on Thoburn began, Hayes formed a line, with its right near the Valley Pike and near the left of Detachment Nineteenth Corps, and ex- tending to the northeast in front of, and nearly paral- lel to, the pike. Benjamin F. Coates' Second Brigade was on the right, and Hiram F. Devol's First Brigade was on the left. At that time, Kitching was forming two regiments of his Provisional Division near the left of Hayes' division. Hayes then closed to the right about 100 yards to connect with the left of Emory's line.

When Wright, who was in temporary command of the army while Sheridan was absent in Washington, learned of the attack on Thoburn, he turned over the command of Sixth Corps to James B. Ricketts, and hurried forward to attempt to form a line for the defense of the road back to Winchester. He was aided in this effort by Emory and Crook. Wright promptly ordered Ricketts to bring forward two divisions of Sixth Corps to the Valley Pike, and he directed Emory to form Detachment Nineteenth Corps for the defense of the pike to the right of Hayes.

Grover, whose Second Division, Detachment Nineteenth Corps was west of the pike, had been ordered to move out at 5:30 A.M. that morning on a reconnaissance toward Strasburg, with Henry W. Birge's First Brigade, Edward L. Molineux's Second Brigade, and Daniel Macauley's Third Brigade. At 5:00 A.M. the division was ready and was in position as follows: four regiments of Macauley's brigade were on the left, near the pike; Birge's brigade was on the right of Macauley; four regiments of Molineux's brigade were on the right of Birge; David Shunk's Fourth Brigade and two regiments of Molineux's brigade formed a second line. Dwight's First Division, then commanded by McMillan, was on the right of Grover, with Edwin P. Davis' First Brigade in line and McMillan's Second Brigade, then commanded by Stephen Thomas, in reserve. Currie's Third Brigade was guarding wagon trains and was not engaged in the battle. Emory's position was strong if attacked from the direction of Cedar Creek, which it faced, but it was completely commanded by the high ground on the left that was occupied by Crook's divisions.

At about 5:15 A.M., before Grover's brigades had started toward Strasburg, the firing on Thoburn's front was heard, and a short time later Emory's picket line was attacked. To strengthen the line against the attack then developing on the left and front, Grover ordered the troops of his first line to occupy the works on their immediate front, and he then drew back the 176th New York and 156th New

York, the left two regiments of Macauley's brigade, to a line nearly perpendicular to the other regiments of the brigade. He then brought up Shunk's brigade from reserve, and with it extended Macauley's line to the rear, diagonally across the pike, in the direction of Hayes' division. While these movements were in progress, the firing from the left and front became incessant, and as day dawned, the enemy appeared on the high ground to the left of Emory's position.

While Kershaw was attacking Crook near Cedar Creek, Gordon marched northward from Bowman's Ford with his three divisions. When he reached the vicinity of the J. Cooley house, he formed them in line on the left and rear of Crook and Emory, facing west. Ramseur's division was on the right, Pegram's division was in the center, and Gordon's division (under Evans) was on the left. Gordon's line moved forward, and about sunup struck Kitching's weak and untrained command. These troops broke and fled with virtually no resistance, and with the loss of Kitching, who was mortally wounded. Gordon then hit Hayes' division, which after a short stand joined Thoburn's division in flight. Crook's entire command fled in a disorganized mass northward along the pike to a point north of Middletown, and it ceased to be an effective fighting force for the next twenty-four hours. When Emory learned that the Federal left was giving way, he brought up Stephen Thomas' brigade of McMillan's division, which was then in reserve, and placed it on the left of Grover's division along the pike. Then, two regiments of Davis' brigade were left to hold the brigade line, and Davis' remaining regiments were formed in line of battle in rear of Thomas.

After driving off Kitching's troops and Hayes' division, Kershaw and Ramseur advanced on the front and flank of Thomas' brigade and, after desperate fighting, drove it back. The enemy then struck Grover's division on the right of Thomas. Shunk's brigade and Macauley's brigade were swept back, but Birge's brigade and Molineux's brigade moved to the other side of their works and continued fighting. McMillan moved the troops of his division to the right and formed a line facing the oncoming enemy, about 400 yards from the pike. There he attempted to halt the Confederate advance, but Kershaw pressed his attack, and Emory's command was finally driven off to the northwest, where it was ordered to form on the right of Sixth Corps. Macauley was wounded during the attack, and Alfred Neafie assumed command of his Third Brigade, Second Division.

Meantime, Sixth Corps was moving to get into the fight. Early that morning, the corps had been alerted, first by Rosser's firing on the right, and shortly afterward by the sounds of Crook's battle on the far left. The troops were immediately formed in front of their camps to be ready for any emergency. Frank Wheaton's First Division was on the right, with its right near Cedar Creek; James B. Ricketts' Third Division was on the left of Wheaton, with its left near Marsh Run, about a mile and a half in rear (north) of Detachment Nineteenth Corps; and George W. Getty's Second Division was in rear of Wheaton's and Ricketts' divisions. Immediately after the corps was formed, Wright turned over the command to Ricketts and went forward to direct the battle then in progress. J. Warren Keifer assumed command of Ricketts' Third Division, and William H. Ball took charge of Keifer's Second Brigade, Third Division.

At 6:00 A.M. Wheaton's First Division and Getty's Second Division moved eastward toward the Valley Pike and, upon reaching Meadow Brook, formed in line of battle, with Getty's division on the left and Wheaton's division on the right. When the line was formed, it crossed Meadow Brook and advanced toward the pike. This move was countermanded, however, when the Army of West Virginia was swept away to the north and Detachment Nineteenth Corps was driven back to the northwest. Ricketts' two divisions then recrossed Meadow Brook and formed to meet the oncoming enemy. Getty's division was placed on the left, behind Meadow Brook, facing southeast. Daniel D. Bidwell's Third Brigade was on the left; Lewis A. Grant's Second Brigade was on the center; and James M. Warner's First Brigade was on the right. Wheaton's division was on the right of Getty, to the left and rear of its former camps, and generally faced south toward the front formerly held by Detachment Nineteenth Corps. William H. Penrose's First Brigade was on the right, and Joseph E. Hamblin's Second Brigade was on the left. When this realignment was completed, Keifer's Third Division was on the right of Wheaton.

After Emory's line gave way, Keifer's division was struck on its front by Gordon's division and on its left by Kershaw's division, and it was driven back for a considerable distance to the north. At the same time, Wheaton's division was also driven back by Ramseur's division and a part of Gordon's division. Casualties were high among the officers of First Division during this engagement. Penrose, commanding First Brigade, was wounded, and was succeeded by Edward L. Campbell. A short time later, Campbell was also wounded, and Captain Baldwin Hufty, the senior officer remaining in the brigade, assumed command. Second Brigade also had three commanders during this period. Hamblin was wounded, and was succeeded by Ranald S. Mackenzie, and when Mackenzie was also wounded, Egbert Olcott assumed command of the brigade.

About 7:00 A.M., when Getty was no longer supported on his right, he withdrew his Second Division about 300 yards to a semicircular ridge, where it occupied a strong position and continued for some time to oppose Early's advance. Getty formed his line along the crest of the ridge, generally facing south, with its advanced center about one-half mile north of Belle Grove and its left about one mile due west of Middletown.

At 8:00 A.M., at about the same time that Getty occupied the ridge west of Middletown, Ricketts' and Wheaton's divisions of Sixth Corps and Emory's Detachment Nineteenth Corps halted in their movement to the rear, and took position to the right and rear of Getty. Wheaton's division was then about a half-mile to the north of Getty, with its left in rear of the right of Getty's division. Keifer's division was about a half-mile in rear of Wheaton, with its right near Middle Marsh Branch, and about a half-mile in front of the left of Detachment Nineteenth Corps. The latter was formed along Old Forge (Furnace) Road, with Grover's Second Division on the left, next to Middle Branch, and McMillan's First Division was on the right of Grover.

About 8:30 A.M. Getty's line on the ridge was attacked by the left of Gordon's division and the divisions of Kershaw, Ramseur, and Pegram, but the enemy was driven back. During the fighting, Ricketts was wounded, and Getty assumed command of Sixth Corps. Lewis A. Grant succeeded Getty in command of Second Division, and Amasa S. Tracy assumed command of Grant's Second Brigade (Vermont Brigade), Second Division. Bidwell, commanding Third Brigade, Second Division, was mortally wounded, and Winsor B. French assumed command of the brigade. Wharton's division was then brought up to join Ramseur and Pegram, and at about 9:00 A.M. the enemy again attacked Getty's position, but this attack was also repulsed. Finally, between 9:00 and 9:30 A.M., Getty, with both of his flanks exposed, moved back. He obliqued to his left to gain ground toward the pike, and then halted on a line with First Division and Third Division, which were off to his right opposite Middletown. Getty's division continued its resistance in this position until 10:00 A.M., and at that time, the entire remaining Federal line was ordered back to the north

Getty's Second Division (then commanded by Grant) established a new and final line about one mile north of Middletown at 11:00 A.M. The division was formed on the west side of the pike, facing south, and connecting with Merritt's First Cavalry Division on the left. French's Third Brigade (formerly commanded by Bidwell) was on the left, with its left on the pike; Tracy's Second Brigade (Grant's brigade) was on the center; and Warner's First Brigade was on the right. Wheaton's and Keifer's divisions and Emory's Detachment Nineteenth Corps also withdrew to the north, but they did not stop on the right of the Second Division line. Instead, the two divisions of Sixth Corps continued on, and halted for orders at 11:00 A.M. about one mile north of Second Division, and about three-fourths of a mile west of the pike. Emory ended his withdrawal a short distance to the right and rear of Wheaton and Keifer.

Meantime, Alfred T. A. Torbert's cavalry had also been active during the morning. Torbert had been alerted before daylight when Rosser advanced on the far right of the Union army, and attacked the pickets of James H. Kidd's First Brigade of Wesley Merritt's First Cavalry Division at Cupp's Ford. Charles R. Lowell's Reserve Brigade of First Cavalry Division also served for a time with Kidd's brigade, but Rosser did not press the attack. A short time after Merritt's engagement, stragglers from the front began to appear in the rear of the army, and at 8:00 A.M. Thomas C. Devin's Second Brigade of Merritt's division was ordered to the left to cover and hold the Valley Pike. While on his way to the left, Devin halted for a time a short distance west of

Middletown and attempted to prevent the fleeing infantry from passing through to the rear.

When Gordon's column marched northward that morning from Bowman's Ford, Alpheus S. Moore's First Brigade of Powell's Second Cavalry Division, which was downstream at Buckton Ford, was cut off from the army along Cedar Creek. Moore promptly marched northward, around the enemy right, and joined Devin's brigade near Middletown around 9:00 A.M. Moore formed his brigade east of the pike and just north of Middletown, and was soon engaged.

Between 9:00 and 10:00 A.M., Wright ordered Torbert to move his entire cavalry force to the left of the army, and at about 10:00 A.M., Merritt's division took position east of the pike and a short distance north of Middletown. Devin's brigade was on the right, next to the pike; Lowell's Reserve Brigade was in the center; and Kidd's First Brigade was on the left. Shortly after the division was formed, Moore was directed to report to Merritt for orders, and his brigade was placed on the left of Kidd's brigade. George A. Custer, commanding Third Cavalry Division, left William Wells with three regiments of his Second Brigade to watch the Federal right, and he marched with Alexander C. M. Pennington's First Brigade and the rest of Second Brigade to the left and took position east of the Valley Pike about three-fourths of a mile north of Middletown, and in rear of Merritt. After Merritt's division was formed, it advanced and pushed back the enemy almost to Middletown, but about noon it was withdrawn to a line to the left and front of Grant's (Getty's) division. It remained there until about 4:00 P.M. Custer's division was not engaged at this time.

At 9:00 A.M. that morning, Powell, acting under orders from Wright, fell back with Capehart's Second Brigade from Guard Hill, and marched northward on the Front Royal-Winchester Road through Nineveh (Stony Point) to a new position near Newtown, where he remained during most of the remainder of the day. Lunsford L. Lomax's cavalry followed Powell closely during his withdrawal. About 4:00 P.M., just before Sheridan's attack that evening, Moore's brigade was ordered to rejoin the division at Newtown.

It has already been noted that Sheridan had been called to Washington for a consultation. He had arrived in Winchester on his return to the army October 18, 1864, and he had remained there that night before continuing on. Early the next morning he heard firing from the direction of Cedar Creek, but he was not concerned because he believed that it was the result of Grover's reconnaissance, which had been ordered for 5:30 that morning. When the firing continued, however, he decided to go to the front, and he left Winchester at 8:30–9:00 A.M. There is some uncertainty as to the exact time that he arrived on the battlefield, but from his statements regarding the troop positions that he observed as he approached, it probably was sometime after 11:00 A.M. Other reports, however, give the time as 10:30 A.M. Sheridan stated that upon his arrival just south of Newtown, he saw Keifer's (Ricketts') and Wheaton's divisions west of the pike, and that he learned that Detachment Nineteenth Corps was a short distance to their right and rear. He also found Lewis A. Grant's (Getty's) division and the cavalry skirmishing with enemy pickets about a mile north of Middletown. At about 11:00 A.M. the above-mentioned troops occupied the positions described by Sheridan.

After examining the battlefield and making his presence known to his troops, Sheridan established his headquarters in rear of Grant's division of Sixth Corps, and ordered the other two divisions of Sixth Corps, and Detachment Nineteenth Corps, to move up and form on the right of Grant's division. He decided to take the offensive as soon as he could make the necessary preparations, and he sent Wright back to bring forward these troops. When Keifer and Wheaton arrived, Sheridan directed them to their assigned positions, and then ordered Wright to resume command of Sixth Corps, and Getty to return to the command of Second Division. The time was then about noon.

When Sixth Corps' new line was formed, it was manned as follows: Getty's Second Division was on the left, with its left on the Valley Pike; French's Third Brigade was on the left of the division, between the pike and Meadow Brook; Grant's Second Brigade was on the center; and Warner's First Brigade was on the left. Keifer's Third Division was on the right of Getty, with Ball's Second Brigade on the left and Emerson's First Brigade on the right. Wheaton's First Division was formed in two lines on the right of Keifer. The first line consisted of two

regiments and part of a third of Mackenzie's Second Brigade. Mackenzie had been wounded but remained on the field. The second line was composed of the 121st New York, and part of another regiment of Second Brigade and Baldwin Hufty's First Brigade. Egbert Olcott, lieutenant colonel of 121st New York, was given command of the second line because Hufty held only the rank of captain.

Sometime earlier, Hayes had arrived at the front with about sixty men of Crook's Army of West Virginia, and had reported to Getty, who at that time was in command of Sixth Corps. About 1:00 P.M. Hayes' small command was placed on the Sixth Corps' line between Getty and Keifer. Shortly after 3:00 P.M., Hayes was ordered to the left of the pike to join the remnants of Harris' First Division (formerly Thoburn's), Army of West Virginia.

Emory brought up his troops about 1:00 P.M., and he formed his command on the right of Sixth Corps, between Wheaton's division on the left and Middle Marsh Branch on the right. Grover's Second Division was on the left, next to Wheaton, and was formed in two lines. On the first line, Molineux's Second Brigade was on the left, and Birge's First Brigade was on the right. On the second line, Shunk's Fourth Brigade supported Molineux, and Neafie's Third Brigade (formerly commanded by Macauley) supported Birge. A short time later, Grover was wounded, and Birge assumed command of Second Division, and Thomas W. Porter took command of Birge's First Brigade. McMillan's First Division was placed on the right of Grover, on the extreme right of the infantry line. Davis' First Brigade was on the right of the division, and Thomas' Second Brigade on the left. About 2:00 P.M., Dwight resumed command of First Division, and McMillan returned to the command of his Second Brigade, First Division.

About 11:00 A.M., Custer, with Pennington's cavalry brigade of his division, was sent back to the extreme right of the army, where he reestablished connection with William Wells' regiments, which had been engaged with Rosser's cavalry. Custer aided in driving the enemy back to Cupp's Ford, and then he moved back to the left across Middle Marsh Branch and formed on the right of Detachment Nineteenth Corps.

For reasons that are not entirely clear, Early did not energetically press his attack on Sheridan's forces after Getty withdrew his Second Division, Sixth Corps from the ridge west of Middletown at about 9:30 A.M. Instead, he halted his command generally on a line along the Old Forge Road that extended westward from the Valley Pike at the northern edge of Middletown. During the forenoon, Early observed an increasing force of Federal cavalry beginning to form on his right, and on that flank he had only William H. Payne's cavalry brigade, He then moved Wharton's division to a position in front of Merritt's cavalry, just to the north of Middletown, and to the right of the pike. From about 11:00 A.M. to 1:00 P.M., Early remained inactive in front of the line that Sheridan was then forming. Early's divisions were in position as follows: Wharton's division, as already noted, was just north of Middletown, and east of the pike; Pegram's division was on the left of Wharton, between the pike and Meadow Brook; and continuing on to the left were the divisions of Ramseur, Kershaw, and Gordon, in that order. The left of Gordon's division extended to Middle Marsh Branch, and as a consequence, that part of Early's line between Gordon and Kershaw was only thinly held. Near 1:00 P.M., Early advanced his line to within about one-half mile of Sheridan's position, and Gordon made an unsuccessful attack on the front of Emory's Detachment Nineteenth Corps.

Finally, at 4:00 P.M., when all preparations were completed, Sheridan ordered his army to attack, and the entire line moved forward. Wright's Sixth Corps was on the left of the infantry line, and Emory's Detachment Nineteenth Corps was on the right. Merritt's cavalry division was on the left of Sixth Corps, and Custer's cavalry division was on the right of Emory. Crook, with as many of the troops of his Army of West Virginia as he could assemble, was formed in column in reserve, with orders to follow the other troops as they advanced. Fighting was severe and determined for a time, but finally Emory's command, under the personal direction of Sheridan, and aided by Custer's cavalry, forced Gordon's division to fall back. When these troops on the Confederate left gave way, the rest of Early's line began to crumble, and then it broke, and the troops fled in a disorderly mass across Cedar Creek, over Hupp's Hill, and through Strasburg to Fisher's Hill. During Merritt's attack on the Federal left, Lowell was mortally wounded, and Casper Crowninshield assumed command of the Reserve Brigade.

It became dark during the pursuit of Early's defeated army to Cedar Creek, and the Federal infantry halted for the night in the camps that they had occupied that morning. Custer's cavalry, however, forded Cedar Creek to the west of the pike just after dark, Merritt crossed to the east of the pike, and both divisions pursued the enemy as far as Fisher's Hill. After two hours' rest, Emory was ordered forward to Strasburg to relieve the cavalry, and to cover the removal of an immense amount of public property abandoned by the enemy.

The Union forces engaged at the Battle of Cedar Creek, Virginia October 19, 1864 were organized as follows:

SHERIDAN'S ARMY IN THE SHENANDOAH VALLEY
Horatio G. Wright
Philip H. Sheridan

SIXTH CORPS, James B. Ricketts, wounded
George W. Getty
Horatio G. Wright

First Division, Frank Wheaton
First Brigade, William H. Penrose, wounded
Edward L. Campbell, wounded
Baldwin Hufty
Second Brigade, Joseph E. Hamblin, wounded
Ranald S. Mackenzie, wounded
Egbert Olcott

Note. Oliver Edwards' Third Brigade was on duty at Winchester, and was not present at the battle.

Second Division, George W. Getty
Lewis A. Grant
George W. Getty
First Brigade, James M. Warner
Second Brigade, Lewis A. Grant
Amasa S. Tracy
Lewis A. Grant
Third Brigade, Daniel D. Bidwell, killed
Winsor B. French

Third Division, J. Warren Keifer
First Brigade, William Emerson
Second Brigade, William H. Ball

Artillery Brigade
5th Battery (E), Maine Light Artillery, Greenleaf T. Stevens

1st Battery, New York Light Artillery, Orsamus R. Van Etten

Battery C, 1st Rhode Island Light Artillery, Jacob H. Lamb

Battery G, 1st Rhode Island Light Artillery, George W. Adams

Battery M, 5th United States Artillery, James Mc-Knight

DETACHMENT NINETEENTH CORPS, William H. Emory

First Division, James W. McMillan
   William Dwight
   First Brigade, Edwin P. Davis
   Second Brigade, Stephen Thomas
   5th Battery, New York Light Artillery, Elijah D. Taft

Note. Leonard D. H. Currie's Third Brigade was guarding wagon trains, and was not engaged in the battle.

Second Division, Cuvier Grover, wounded
   Henry W. Birge
   First Brigade, Henry W. Birge
      Thomas W. Porter
   Second Brigade, Edward L. Molineux
   Third Brigade, Daniel Macauley, wounded
      Alfred Neafie
   Fourth Brigade, David Shunk
   1st Battery (A), Maine Light Artillery, John S. Snow

Reserve Artillery, Albert M. Bradbury
   17th Battery, Indiana Light Artillery, Hezekiah Hinkson
   Battery D, 1st Rhode Island Light Artillery, Frederick Chase

ARMY OF WEST VIRGINIA, George Crook

First Division, Joseph Thoburn, killed
   Thomas M. Harris
   First Brigade, Thomas F. Wildes
   Third Brigade, Thomas M. Harris
   Milton Wells

Note. William B. Curtis' Second Brigade was at Winchester and was not engaged in the battle.

Second Division, Rutherford B. Hayes
   First Brigade, Hiram F. Devol
   Second Brigade, Benjamin F. Coates

Artillery Brigade, Henry A. Du Pont
   Battery L, 1st Ohio Light Artillery, Frank C. Gibbs
   Battery D, 1st Pennsylvania Light Artillery, William Munk

Battery B, 5th United States Artillery, Henry F. Brewerton

PROVISIONAL DIVISION, J. Howard Kitching, mortally wounded
   William Heine
   First Brigade, William Heine
      Thompson D. Hart
   Second Brigade, G. De Peyster Arden

Note 1. For additional information, see Fisher's Hill to Cedar Creek, above.
Note 2. Only a detachment of First Brigade, and 2nd New York Heavy Artillery of Second Brigade were with Kitching at Cedar Creek.

CAVALRY, Alfred T. A. Torbert

First Cavalry Division, Wesley Merritt
   First Brigade, James H. Kidd
   Second Brigade, Thomas C. Devin
   Reserve Brigade, Charles R. Lowell, Jr., killed
      Casper Crowninshield

Second Cavalry Division, Department of West Virginia, William H. Powell
   First Brigade, Alpheus S. Moore
   Second Brigade, Henry Capehart

Third Cavalry Division, George A. Custer
   First Brigade, Alexander C. M. Pennington
   Second Brigade, William Wells

Horse Artillery
   Batteries B and L, 2nd United States Artillery, Charles H. Peirce
   Batteries C, F, and K, 3rd United States Artillery, Dunbar R. Ransom

Note. The name "Army of the Shenandoah" has been used as a designation for Sheridan's forces in the Shenandoah Valley, but this was not officially assigned until November 17, 1864.

End of the Campaign, October 20, 1864–November 28, 1864. The Battle of Cedar Creek virtually ended Sheridan's campaign in the Shenandoah Valley, although after the battle both armies were regrouped and for some time remained prepared for further operations. During the night of October 19, 1864, the greater part of Early's infantry halted briefly at Fisher's Hill, but at 3:00 the next morning these troops departed for New Market. Rosser's cavalry remained for a time to cover the retreat, but it too left at 10:00 A.M., and then established a line on Stony Creek, from Columbia Furnace to Edenburg. Lomax's cavalry returned to the Luray Valley.

Merritt's First Cavalry Division moved up to Fisher's Hill on the morning of October 20, 1864, and then followed Early as far as Woodstock. First Brigade and Second Brigade stopped there, but Crowninshield's Reserve Brigade pushed on beyond Edenburg. That evening the division returned to Fisher's Hill, and then on to Cedar Creek.

Sheridan's army remained in its camps at Cedar Creek until November 8, 1864, and the next day it withdrew to a position near Kernstown, where it could be supplied more readily from Harper's Ferry. Sheridan then formed a defensive line so that he would be able to detach troops to be sent to Grant at Petersburg. The camp was established at the point where Opequon Creek crossed the Winchester Pike. By an order of November 17, 1864, the camp was named Camp Russell.

Early received reports at New Market that troops had been detached from Sheridan's army, and he also learned that the Manassas Gap Railroad was being repaired, and on November 10, 1864, he once more advanced down the valley. The next day he reached Cedar Creek and found that Sheridan had moved back toward Winchester. Early moved on and took position in front of Sheridan, south of Newtown. Rosser's cavalry was on his left on the Back Road, and Lomax's cavalry was on his right, between the Valley Pike and the Front Royal Road. November 12, 1864, Torbert's cavalry advanced and engaged the enemy cavalry. Powell's Second Cavalry Division attacked Lomax near Nineveh and drove him across the Shenandoah River. Merritt's First Cavalry Division and Custer's Third Cavalry Division advanced on the Middle Road and Back Road, and after stubborn fighting drove Rosser back beyond Cedar Creek. After an examination of Sheridan's position, Early concluded that it was too strong to attack; and aware that he was beyond the reach of adequate supplies, he began to withdraw on November 12, 1864, and two days later he was back at New Market. Sheridan did not pursue.

November 21–23, 1864, in terrible weather, Torbert led Powell's and Custer's cavalry divisions on a reconnaissance up the Shenandoah Valley to Rude's Hill. He reported that Kershaw's division had left the valley for Richmond November 18, 1864, but that Early still had under his command four infantry divisions and one cavalry division. Sheridan had planned to send Sixth Corps to Petersburg, and it was then ready to go, but upon receiving Torbert's report he decided to retain it in the valley until the weather prevented any further infantry campaigning.

November 27, 1864, Rosser, with his own and Payne's brigades, crossed Great North Mountain, passed through Moorefield, and, after an all-night march, surprised and captured the garrison at New Creek, West Virginia. He took 700–800 prisoners and destroyed large quantities of commissary, ordnance, and quartermaster stores. He then sent a force to Piedmont, where it destroyed much public property, government buildings, and machine shops belonging to the railroad. Custer was sent with his cavalry division toward Moorefield on the morning of November 28, 1864 in an attempt to intercept Rosser, but returned to camp December 2, 1864, after having failed to do so. After Rosser's expedition, there were few further active military operations in the Shenandoah Valley during the winter. For additional information about Sheridan's army after the Battle of Cedar Creek, see Army of the Shenandoah (Sheridan).

SHERIDAN'S EXPEDITION FROM WINCHESTER TO PETERSBURG, VIRGINIA FEBRUARY 27–MARCH 25, 1865

By the end of December 1864, active operations in the Shenandoah Valley had virtually ceased, and most of the Confederate troops that earlier had opposed Sheridan's army in the Shenandoah Valley had been sent back to Lee's army at Petersburg. Toward the end of February 1865, Jubal A. Early, commander of the Confederate Valley District, had with him in his winter quarters at Staunton only two brigades of infantry under Gabriel C. Wharton and a few cavalrymen under Thomas L. Rosser. For information about affairs in the valley prior to this time, see Shenandoah Valley Campaign (Sheridan).

On February 8, 1865, Grant urged Sheridan to send out an expedition to destroy the Virginia

Central Railroad and the James River and Kanawha Canal, which were used to supply the Confederate troops at Petersburg and Richmond, but the exceptionally bad weather that winter prevented any such movement until late in the month. On February 27, 1865, Sheridan rode out of Winchester with 10,000 cavalrymen to break up Lee's communications as directed. He was also ordered to capture Lynchburg if practicable, and then to continue on and join William T. Sherman's army in North Carolina. As an alternative, he was authorized to return to Winchester if he considered this to be the best course. Sheridan's command consisted of Thomas C. Devin's First Cavalry Division and George A. Custer's Third Cavalry Division of the Army of the Shenandoah. These two divisions constituted an unofficial corps under the immediate command of Wesley Merritt. Marcus A. Miller's section of Companies C and E, 4th United States Artillery accompanied Devin's division, and Carle A. Woodruff's section of Company M, 2nd United States Artillery accompanied Custer's division. Alfred T. A. Torbert, chief of cavalry of the Middle Military Division, was on leave at the time of Sheridan's departure, and he was not recalled to lead the expedition. Torbert had disappointed Sheridan with his performance in the Luray Valley during the battle at Fisher's Hill and also during the raid to Gordonsville to destroy the Virginia Central Railroad, and he was therefore left behind to command the small cavalry force remaining in the Shenandoah Valley. Merritt was appointed acting chief of cavalry, and Devin assumed command of Merritt's division. Charles L. Fitzhugh succeeded Devin in command of Second Brigade, First Cavalry Division.

Engagement at Waynesboro, Virginia, March 2, 1865. Sheridan advanced up the valley past Woodstock, New Market, and Harrisonburg, and camped on the night of March 1, 1865 at Cline's Mills on Middle River, about seven miles from Staunton. When Sheridan approached, Early, whose headquarters was at Staunton, left the town with his command and marched eastward on the road to Rockfish Gap. Upon learning of Early's movement, Sheridan decided that he would not continue his march toward Lynchburg and leave an enemy force on his rear, and instead, on March 2, 1865, he sent Custer's division in pursuit of Early, with Devin's division close behind.

Custer found Early in position on a ridge south of the Virginia Central Railroad, just west of Waynesboro. Holding this line were the two infantry brigades under Wharton, Rosser's small cavalry force, and some artillery. Custer immediately sent William Wells' Second Brigade to develop the enemy position, and the latter reported that the line appeared to be strongly held. Upon learning this, Custer sent Alexander C. M. Pennington's First Brigade to the right to turn the enemy's left flank. This appeared to be feasible because the line did not extend all the way to the South Fork of the Shenandoah River (the South River). While Pennington prepared to charge, Wells' brigade demonstrated on the enemy front, and Henry Capehart's Third Brigade was held in readiness on Custer's left, near the Staunton Road.

Pennington dismounted his 2nd Ohio, 3rd New Jersey, and 1st Connecticut regiments, and moved forward through the woods into the gap between the enemy left and the river. The remainder of Pennington's brigade was held in reserve. The 2nd Ohio led the charge, and it was followed by 3rd New Jersey and 1st Connecticut. At the same time, Wells and Capehart charged the front of Early's line. Pennington's attack threw the enemy into confusion, and the 8th New York of Wells' brigade charged over the breastworks, continued on through the town, and then formed on the east side of the Shenandoah River to cut off Early's retreat. The Confederate forces were completely routed, and most of them were captured. Custer pursued the fleeing remnants through Rockfish Gap for a distance of about twelve miles and camped that night at Brookeville. Devin's division remained at Waynesboro.

* * * * * * * * *

The next morning Custer moved on to Charlottesville, where he destroyed the railroad, bridges, and stores. Devin's division joined him there March 4, 1865. Sheridan remained at Charlottesville two days while he waited for his trains to come up. These were escorted by Alfred Gibbs' Reserve Brigade (Third Brigade) of Devin's division, and they were delayed by muddy roads and did not arrive until the evening of March 5, 1865. Meantime, Sheridan's troopers destroyed the railroad toward Lynchburg and Gordonsville.

While at Charlottesville, Sheridan learned that the Confederate garrison at Lynchburg had been increased and that the fortifications had been strengthened, and he considered that it was unlikely that he could capture the town with his force. He therefore made other plans. For his next move, Sheridan separated his command into two columns, one consisting of Devin's division, and the other of Custer's division. The former, under the immediate command of Merritt, marched on March 6, 1865 to Scottsville on the James River. It then proceeded to destroy all large mills and factories, and all locks on the James River Canal from Scottsville to New Market. Custer's division marched southward along the Charlottesville and Lynchburg Railroad through North and South Gardens, and destroyed the railroad as far as Amherst Court House, sixteen miles from Lynchburg. From Amherst Court House, Custer moved across country to join Merritt's column at New Market.

At this point, east of Lynchburg, Sheridan had planned to cross the James River and march to Appomattox Court House. Heavy rains, however, had made the river unfordable, and the pontoon bridge was too short to span the swollen waters. Then, when Sheridan learned that the bridges at Duguidsville and Hardwickville had been destroyed by the enemy, he concluded that it would be impossible to join Sherman in North Carolina. He further concluded that nothing would be accomplished by returning to Winchester, and so he decided to destroy more of the Virginia Central Railroad, the James River Canal, and the Richmond, Fredericksburg, and Potomac Railroad, and then join Grant's army at Petersburg.

Starting on March 7, 1865, Fitzhugh's brigade of Devin's division was detached, and it marched east along the canal through Warminster, Hardwickville, Howardsville, Scottsville, and Columbia to a point about eight miles east of Goochland. On the way, Fitzhugh destroyed locks, cut the banks where practicable, and destroyed boats and stores, and then returned to Columbia March 11, 1865. On the morning of March 8, 1865, the remainder of Sheridan's command left New Market and moved down the canal to Columbia, where it arrived on the evening of March 10, 1865. Fitzhugh's brigade arrived the next day.

Sheridan rested a day at Columbia, and then marched northward toward the Virginia Central Railroad. Custer's division struck the railroad at Frederick's Hall Station March 12, 1865, with orders to destroy the track toward Richmond as far as Beaver Dam. Merritt, with Devin's division, moved to the railroad at Tolersville, and proceeded to destroy the track from that point to Frederick's Hall. Devin then moved along the railroad to the South Anna River and there, and also on the North Anna River, burned five bridges. He arrived at Hanover Court House March 17, 1865. Custer's division moved along the railroad, destroying the track while advancing, and on the night of March 14, 1865, it camped on the South Anna at Ground Squirrel Bridge. The next day Custer moved on to Ashland, where he received information that James Longstreet and George E. Pickett were advancing on the town. Pennington's engagement with enemy infantry that evening at Ashland supported this information.

Late on the evening of March 15, 1865, Sheridan's command crossed to the north bank of the North Anna River and bivouacked near Carmel Church. At daylight the next morning, the column started toward White House on the Pamunkey River. It marched by way of Mangohick Church, Aylett's, King William Court House, and Indiantown, and reached White House March 18–19, 1865. Sheridan rested there five days to refit and have the horses shod, and he then moved on to join Grant. He crossed the James River at Deep Bottom March 26, 1865, and joined the army at Petersburg the next day. He camped at Hancock's Station on the Army Railroad until March 29, 1865, and then marched toward Dinwiddie Court House at the beginning of Grant's final offensive at Petersburg. For further information, see Appomattox Campaign, Virginia.

The organization of Philip H. Sheridan's Army of the Shenandoah on the expedition from Winchester to Petersburg was as follows:

CAVALRY, Wesley Merritt

First Cavalry Division, Thomas C. Devin
  First Brigade, Peter Stagg

Second Brigade, Charles L. Fitzhugh
Reserve Brigade (Third Brigade), Alfred Gibbs
Companies C and E, 4th United States Artillery (one section), Marcus A. Miller

Third Cavalry Division, George A. Custer
First Brigade, Alexander C. M. Pennington
Second Brigade, William Wells
Third Brigade, Henry Capehart
Company M, 2nd United States Artillery (one section), Carle A. Woodruff

SHERIDAN'S RICHMOND, VIRGINIA RAID
MAY 9–24, 1864

On May 8, 1864, as Ulysses S. Grant's army approached Spotsylvania Court House during the Richmond, Virginia Campaign of 1864, Philip H. Sheridan was ordered to concentrate the available force of his Cavalry Corps, Army of the Potomac, and then to move out and engage the enemy cavalry under James E. B. (Jeb) Stuart. Sheridan's orders also directed him to proceed on to the James River when he was out of forage, and obtain supplies from Benjamin F. Butler's Army of the James at Bermuda Hundred.

Sheridan believed that by moving around the right of Lee's army as he advanced toward Richmond, Stuart would follow, and could be attacked with advantage somewhere to the south. Accordingly, at 5:00 A.M. May 9, 1864, the expedition started from the vicinity of the Aldrich farm, near Chancellorsville, and marched eastward on the Fredericksburg Plank Road to Tabernacle Church, and it then continued on east to the Telegraph Road. There Sheridan turned south and passed Massaponax Church and crossed the Ta River at Jarrald's Mill. Below Jarrald's Mill the Telegraph Road veered off to the east, but Sheridan took the road through Thornburg and Chilesburg to Anderson's Ford on the North Anna River. Wesley Merritt's First Cavalry Division arrived at the ford about dark and crossed to the south bank of the river, but David McM. Gregg's Second Cavalry Division and James H. Wilson's Third Cavalry Division camped that night on the north bank.

After Merritt had crossed the river, he sent George A. Custer's First Brigade on to Beaver Dam Station on the Virginia Central Railroad. There Custer destroyed buildings, track, cars, locomotives, and supplies, and also recaptured 378 Union prisoners who had been taken during the fighting at Spotsylvania Court House. These were on their way to Richmond, and included Colonel William C. Talley of the 1st Pennsylvania Reserves, who was in command of First Brigade, Third Division, Fifth Corps when captured.

Sheridan's march was observed by the enemy when the column passed Massaponax Church, and this was promptly reported to Stuart. Williams C. Wickham's brigade of Fitzhugh Lee's cavalry division, which was nearest Massaponax Church, immediately took up the pursuit. It attacked the Federal rear guard at Jarrald's Mill, and again at Mitchell's Store, where the brigade camped for the night north of Chilesburg. At this point, Stuart and Fitzhugh Lee joined Wickham with Lunsford L. Lomax's brigade of Lee's division and James B. Gordon's brigade of William H. F. Lee's division.

Early on the morning of May 10, 1864, Sheridan resumed the advance and marched toward Ground Squirrel Bridge, where the Mountain Road from Louisa Court House to Yellow Tavern crossed the South Anna River. He arrived near the bridge, and bivouacked about 3:00 A.M. May 11, 1864.

Stuart's cavalry arrived at Beaver Dam Station on the morning of May 10, 1864, just after Sheridan had left. Stuart then sent Gordon's brigade to follow the Federal column, and with Fitzhugh Lee and the brigades of Lomax and Wickham marched to Hanover Junction, and from there down the Telegraph Road to Yellow Tavern. This was an old abandoned tavern located on the Brook Turnpike to Richmond, about one-half mile south of a place called Turner's. At Turner's, the Mountain Road from the northwest joined the Telegraph Road from the north to form the Brook Turnpike, which ran on south. Stuart arrived near Yellow Tavern about 10:00 A.M. May 11, 1864, and took position to block any further Federal advance toward Richmond.

At 2:00 A.M. May 11, 1864, Sheridan sent Henry E. Davies' First Brigade of Gregg's division to Ashland Station to cut the Richmond, Fredericksburg, and Potomac Railroad, and at 7:00

A.M. he set out with the main column from Ground Squirrel Bridge on the Mountain Road toward Yellow Tavern. Merritt's division was in the lead, and Wilson's division followed. Gregg brought up the rear. Gordon's Confederate brigade followed Gregg, and was engaged during the march with J. Irvin Gregg's Second Brigade, which was serving as rear guard. When Davies' brigade had completed its work of destruction at Ashland Station, it followed the railroad south to Allen's Station (Glen Allen), where it rejoined the main column on the Mountain Road.

Engagement at Yellow Tavern, Henrico County, Virginia, May 11, 1864. Sheridan arrived at Yellow Tavern ahead of Sheridan and placed his two brigades along the east side of the Telegraph Road and the Brook Road. Lomax's brigade was on the Confederate left, with its left near Yellow Tavern and its right near the junction of the Mountain Road and the Telegraph Road with the Brook Road. Wickham's brigade was on the right of Lomax, with its right extending northward about two and a half miles to a point near Half Sink on the Chickahominy River.

From Allen's Station, Sheridan moved forward on the Mountain Road toward Yellow Tavern, with Merritt's division in front, then Wilson's division, and Gregg's division bringing up the rear. Alfred Gibbs' Reserve Brigade, Merritt's leading brigade, encountered the enemy near the junction of the Mountain Road and the Telegraph Road. Merritt then moved Thomas C. Devin's Second Brigade to the right of the Reserve Brigade, with orders to clear the Brook Road. After some sharp fighting, Devin, supported by Gibbs' brigade, swung around to the left and drove Lomax back to some high ground about a mile north of the road junction. Devin gained possession of the junction and of the Brook Road, and he then held the 17th Pennsylvania Cavalry near Yellow Tavern and sent the other two regiments of his brigade on a reconnaissance down the Brook Road to the outskirts of Richmond.

George A. Custer's First Brigade of Merritt's division then came up on the left of the Reserve Brigade, and formed in front of the junction of the Ashland Road and the Mountain Road, about one mile northwest of the junction of the latter with the Telegraph Road. George H. Chapman's Second Brigade of Wilson's division took position on the left of Custer along the Ashland Road, and John B. McIntosh's First Brigade of Wilson's division moved to the left of Chapman.

Meantime, Stuart's brigades were also occupying new positions. Lomax's brigade was formed on a line east of the Telegraph Road, facing west, with its right on the road and its left about three-fourths of a mile north and east of Yellow Tavern. Wickham formed his brigade on high ground north of Turner Run, facing almost south, with its left on the Telegraph Road near the right of Lomax, and his right extending west, almost to the Hanover Road. Wickham's line was a little more than a mile and a half north of the road junction.

After a series of probing attacks by the Federal cavalry during the early afternoon, there was a lull in the fighting until about 4:00 P.M. At that time, Custer's brigade, supported on the left by Chapman's brigade, advanced on the center and right of Stuart's line. Chapman, with his 3rd Indiana Cavalry and 8th New York Cavalry, fighting dismounted, advanced against the extreme right of the enemy line held by Wickham. At the same time, Custer, with his 5th and 6th Michigan Cavalry, commanded by Russell A. Alger, colonel of the 5th Michigan, attacked the line on his front and drove the enemy back for some distance.

Custer then decided to shift his line of attack to the right against Lomax's brigade, and capture an enemy battery that was in position on the road. Peter Stagg's 1st Michigan Cavalry was ordered to attack on the extreme enemy left, on the flank of the battery, and Alger with his two Michigan regiments was to advance against the enemy troops to their right of the battery. Addison W. Preston's 1st Vermont Cavalry of Chapman's brigade, then attached to Custer's brigade, was to advance on the left of Custer. Chapman's other two regiments were to support Custer's attack by demonstrating on the front of Wickham's brigade.

The 1st Michigan Cavalry advanced and captured the battery on the road and, with the 5th and 6th Michigan Cavalry and 1st Vermont Cavalry on the left, drove nearly the entire left and a part of the left center of the enemy line back across a ravine about one-fourth of a mile beyond the position of the battery. There the enemy rallied and halted the advance of the 1st Michigan Cavalry, and also repulsed an attack by the 7th Michigan Cavalry of Custer's brigade. Stuart was mortally wounded during the fighting, and a short time later the Confederate cavalry, then under Fitzhugh Lee, withdrew. A part of the command moved back toward Richmond, and the rest went toward Ashland.

Gregg's division remained in the rear of the divisions of Merritt and Wilson during the afternoon of May 11, 1864, holding off Gordon's Confederate brigade. J. Irvin Gregg's Second Brigade easily repulsed all enemy attacks, and protected the rear of the rest of Sheridan's command. Gordon was mortally wounded the next day at Meadow Bridge.

* * * * * * * * * *

About 11:00 P.M. on the night of May 11, 1864, Sheridan moved forward with his cavalry on the Brook Turnpike, and at daylight the next morning massed his troops on the plateau south of Meadow Bridge between the first and second lines of entrenchments north of Richmond. Sheridan sent Merritt's division to Meadow Bridge to prepare a crossing, and it was soon engaged. The bridge was finally repaired, however, and Merritt crossed against some opposition, and pursued the enemy to Gaines' Mill.

Meantime, Confederate forces advanced from the second line of works and attacked Gregg's and Wilson's divisions, but they were soon stopped and driven back. Between 3:00 and 4:00 P.M., Gregg and Wilson followed Merritt across the Chickahominy and bivouacked near Gaines' Mill. The next day, May 13, 1864, Sheridan's command continued on along the north side of the Chickahominy to Bottom's Bridge, and then on May 14, 1864, he marched by way of Malvern Hill to Haxall's Landing on the James River.

After securing supplies from the Army of the James at Bermuda Hundred, Sheridan departed May 17, 1864, and marched by way of Jones' Bridge and Baltimore Cross Roads (or Baltimore Store) to White House, on the Pamunkey River, where he arrived May 20, 1864. Then, two days later, Sheridan crossed the Pamunkey and marched through Aylett's and Dunkirk on the Mattapony River, and rejoined the Army of the Potomac near Old Chesterfield, not far from the North Anna River, on May 24, 1864.

The organization of the Cavalry Corps during Sheridan's Richmond Raid, May 9, 1864–May 24, 1864, was as follows:

CAVALRY CORPS, Philip H. Sheridan

First Cavalry Division, Wesley Merritt
  First Brigade, George A. Custer
  Second Brigade, Thomas C. Devin
  Reserve Brigade, Alfred Gibbs

Note. Merritt assumed temporary command of First Cavalry Division May 7, 1864, because of the illness of Alfred T. A. Torbert. Gibbs took charge of Merritt's Reserve Brigade.

Second Cavalry Division, David McM. Gregg
  First Brigade, Henry E. Davies, Jr.
  Second Brigade, J. Irvin Gregg

Third Cavalry Division, James H. Wilson
  First Brigade, John B. McIntosh
  Second Brigade, George H. Chapman

First Brigade, Horse Artillery, James M. Robertson
  6th Battery, New York Light Artillery, Joseph W. Martin
  Batteries B and L, 2nd United States Artillery, Edward Heaton
  Battery D, 2nd United States Artillery, Edward B. Williston
  Battery M, 2nd United States Artillery, Alexander C. M. Pennington, Jr.
  Battery A, 4th United States Artillery, Rufus King, Jr.
  Batteries C and E, 4th United States Artillery, Charles L. Fitzhugh

SHERIDAN'S TREVILIAN STATION RAID, VIRGINIA JUNE 7–28, 1864

After the costly defeat of the Army of the Potomac at the Battle of Cold Harbor, Virginia June 1–3, 1864, Ulysses S. Grant decided against any further frontal assaults. Instead, he planned to continue the movement of the army to the left, as he had done after the Wilderness, Spotsylvania Court House, the North Anna River, and the Totopotomoy River. For his next move, Grant decided to march south and cross the James River, and then continue westward along the south bank toward Petersburg. To aid in this movement, he ordered Philip H. Sheridan to move west with two divisions of his Cavalry Corps for the purpose of drawing off the enemy cavalry from the front of the Army of the Potomac, and also of destroying Robert E. Lee's communications with the Shenandoah Valley. According to Sheridan's orders, he was to proceed to Charlottesville, Virginia, where he was to join an army under David Hunter, which was then approaching that point from the north. When the work of destruction of the Virginia Central Railroad and the James River Canal had been completed, Sheridan and Hunter were to join the Army of the Potomac.

For his expedition, Sheridan took with him Alfred T. A. Torbert's First Cavalry Division and David McM. Gregg's Second Cavalry Division. He left James H. Wilson's Third Cavalry Division with Meade's Army of the Potomac, and Wilson was placed under Meade's orders. Sheridan's general plan was to march along the north side of the Pamunkey River and the North Anna River, cross the latter at Carpenter's Ford, and then strike the Virginia Central Railroad at Trevilian Station, which was about midway between Louisa Court House and Gordonsville. From Trevilian Station he intended to march by way of Gordonsville to Charlottesville.

Sheridan assembled his command at New Castle Ferry on the Pamunkey River June 6, 1864, and the next day marched to the northwest and camped that night between Aylett's and Dunkirk. On June 8, 1864, he moved on to a point two miles west of Pole Cat Station on the Richmond, Fredericksburg, and Potomac Railroad, and the next day continued on along the north bank of the North Anna, through Chilesburg and New Market to East Northeast Creek. June 10, 1864, the column marched past Twyman's Store to Carpenters' Ford on the North Anna, where it crossed to the south bank and moved out on the road to Trevilian Station. That evening, Sheridan's divisions bivouacked in the vicinity of Clayton's Store, and also at Buck Child's, about three-fourths of a mile from the store. They were then about four miles from Trevilian Station.

Lee learned of Sheridan's march a short time after he left New Castle Ferry, and June 8, 1864, he ordered Wade Hampton to take his own cavalry division and that of Fitzhugh Lee and go in pursuit. Hampton started toward Louisa Court House the next morning, and on the night of June 10, 1864 bivouacked about three miles beyond Trevilian Station on the Virginia Central Railroad. Fitzhugh Lee's division halted that night near Louisa Court House, about six miles east of Trevilian Station.

About 5:00 A.M. June 11, 1864, Torbert advanced on the road from Clayton's Store to Trevilian Station with Wesley Merritt's Reserve Brigade and Thomas C. Devin's Second Brigade. He sent George A. Custer's First Brigade out to the left to guard the roads from Louisa Court House. Sheridan held Gregg's division in the rear with the trains. Merritt's brigade, which was at the head of Torbert's column, soon became sharply engaged when it ran into Hampton's cavalry a few miles from Trevilian Station. Devin's brigade then came up and formed on Merritt's flanks, and the fighting continued for several hours as the Federal line slowly pushed forward toward the railroad.

About 6:30 A.M. Custer found a route by which he could turn Hampton's right flank. This was a wood road that ran southwest on a line roughly parallel to the Clayton Store Road, crossed the Virginia Central Railroad about two miles east of Trevilian Station, and then continued on to the southwest about a mile and a half to the Louisa Court House-Gordonsville Road. Custer's brigade followed this road, passing between Hampton's division and Fitzhugh Lee's division, and then marched west on the Gordonsville Road.

About a mile and a half south of Trevilian Station, Custer came upon Hampton's supply train and his led horses. He quickly captured about 800 horse holders and train guards and 1,500 horses, but soon his command was in serious trouble. Thomas L. Rosser's brigade of Hampton's division attacked Custer from the front, while Fitzhugh Lee's division, coming up from Louisa Court House, struck him from the rear. Custer lost much that he had just captured, but he succeeded in forming a defensive position around the station and repulsed all attacks despite heavy losses.

When Custer became engaged, Sheridan ordered Torbert to press his attack on Hampton's division with the brigades of Merritt and Devin. J. Irvin Gregg's Second Brigade of Gregg's division also came up and formed on the left of Torbert in support. Two regiments of Henry E. Davies' First Brigade of Gregg's division also engaged Fitzhugh Lee's division on the left. Torbert continued his advance until he was near the station, and finally, about 5:00 P.M., Hampton withdrew. Lee's division was also driven back, and Custer's weakened brigade, which was thus relieved, re-formed on the left and rear of Merritt's brigade. The men spent the rest of the evening burying the dead, caring for the wounded, and destroying the track.

From prisoners, Sheridan learned that Hunter was slowly moving toward Lynchburg, Virginia, and not toward Charlottesville as expected, and he also was told that Confederate forces held both Gordonsville and Charlottesville. This completely changed the situation upon which Sheridan's orders had been based, and he decided not to continue on as planned, but to return to the army by leisurely marches so as to keep Hampton's cavalry occupied while Grant crossed the James River.

During the morning and early afternoon of June 12, 1864, Federal troops continued the work of destruction on the railroad, and at 3:00 P.M. Sheridan sent Torbert's division forward to occupy the road to Mallory's Ford, where he hoped to recross the North Anna River. About two and a half miles west of Trevilian Station, near Mallory's Cross Roads, Torbert found Hampton's cavalry entrenched across the road to the ford. Torbert then formed his division for an attack, with Merritt's Reserve Brigade on the right, near the railroad, and Custer's brigade on the left near the Gordonsville Road. Devin's brigade was held in the center in position to support either of the other two brigades.

When the deployment was completed, Torbert advanced his line, but it was soon checked. He then sent Merritt's brigade to the north, across the railroad, to attack Hampton's left flank. Custer's brigade, which had been left to contain Fitzhugh Lee's cavalry, was unable to do so; and when Lee sent Williams C. Wickham's brigade of his division to aid Hampton, Merritt's brigade was not only prevented from advancing, but it was soon under heavy attack. Merritt, however, held his position with help from two regiments of Devin's brigade until the fighting ended about 10:00 P.M. Davies' brigade of Gregg's division was sent to support Torbert, but it was not engaged.

At dawn June 13, 1864, Sheridan abandoned the route to Mallory's Ford and began his return to the army, taking with him 370 prisoners, 400 wounded, and about 2,000 Negroes. He followed the road on which he had advanced from the North Anna River to Trevilian Station, recrossed the river at Carpenter's Ford, and halted for the night at Twyman's Store. From that point, Sheridan returned by a different route. On June 14, 1864, he marched to the Catharpin Road, and the next day continued on by way of Shady Grove Church and Spotsylvania Court House to the Ta River at Edge Hill Seminary. On June 16, 1864, the column marched along the north bank of the Ta River through Guiney's Station and Bowling Green to Dr. Butler's farm on the Mattapony River. From Dr. Butler's Sheridan moved along the north side of the Mattapony through Walkerton, and arrived at King and Queen Court House June 18, 1864.

When the Army of the Potomac left Cold Harbor for Petersburg, and while Sheridan was absent on his raid, Grant established a new base for the army at City Point on the James River. He also issued an order for the abandonment of the depot at White House on the Pamunkey River, and for the transfer of the stores remaining there to City Point. When Sheridan reached King and Queen Court House, he learned that the depot at White House had not yet been broken up and that much-needed supplies for his command could be obtained there. Therefore, on the morning of June 19, 1864, Sheridan sent the wounded, prisoners, and Negro followers to West Point under escort, and he then marched back to Dunkirk on the Mattapony where he could cross the river.

Meantime, Hampton's cavalry, which during Sheridan's march from Trevilian Station had kept pace on parallel roads to the south, had arrived before White House, and at that time was threatening the depot and its garrison. On June 20, 1864, Sheridan learned that John J. Abercrombie, commander of the depot, was under attack, but that the crisis appeared to be over. Sheridan bivouacked that night on the north bank of the Pamunkey River opposite Abercrombie's camp, which was still surrounded by the enemy. The next morning, Torbert's and Gregg's divisions crossed the river and forced Hampton to retire.

While at White House, Sheridan received orders to break up the depot and escort the trains to

Petersburg by way of Jones' Bridge on the Chicka-hominy River. On June 22, 1864, Sheridan started for the James River with 900 wagons carrying the stores from the abandoned depot. Torbert's division moved in front, while Gregg's division marched on a road parallel to that used by the wagon train to protect the exposed right flank. Abercrombie's troops, then commanded by George W. Getty, ac-companied the train. June 24, 1864, Gregg's division was attacked at St. Mary's Church by Hampton's cavalry, and was for a time in some difficulty, but throughout the day Gregg was able to protect the train.

Sheridan reached the James River June 25, 1864, with orders to cross at Bermuda Hundred. Beyond Charles City Court House, however, the enemy in heavy force prevented further progress, and the train moved back to Douthat's Landing, where it was ferried across the river. The cavalry followed June 27–28, 1864, and went into camp at Windmill Point. It then marched to Petersburg and rejoined the Army of the Potomac.

The organization of Sheridan's command during the raid to Trevilian Station June 7–28, 1864 was as follows:

First Cavalry Division, Alfred T. A. Torbert
  First Brigade, George A. Custer
  Second Brigade, Thomas C. Devin
  Reserve Brigade, Wesley Merritt

Second Cavalry Division, David McM. Gregg
  First Brigade, Henry E. Davies, Jr.
  Second Brigade, J. Irvin Gregg

Horse Artillery Brigade, James M. Robertson
  Batteries H and I, 1st United States Artillery, Alanson M. Randol
  Battery D, 2nd United States Artillery, Edward B. Williston
  Battery M, 2nd United States Artillery, Alexander C. M. Pennington, Jr.

James H. Wilson's Third Cavalry Division of Sheridan's Cavalry Corps remained at Cold Harbor with the Army of the Potomac, under Meade's or-ders, when Sheridan left on his raid; and it then accompanied the army on its march to Petersburg.

STONEMAN'S RAID INTO SOUTH-WESTERN VIRGINIA AND WESTERN NORTH CAROLINA MARCH 21–APRIL 25, 1865

In a communication dated January 31, 1865 (received February 6, 1865), Ulysses S. Grant directed George H. Thomas, commander of the Department of the Cumberland, to send George Stoneman's cavalry from East Tennessee on a raid into the Carolinas to aid William T. Sherman as he moved north with his army from Savannah, Georgia. Initially, Grant intended that Stoneman move south-ward into South Carolina toward Columbia to destroy railroads and military resources in the area, and also in a part of the state that was beyond the reach and control of Sherman's advancing army. Sherman was delayed in starting, however, until March 21, 1865, and by that time Sherman had captured Columbia and was approaching Goldsboro, North Carolina. This forced Stoneman to modify his plans.

Stoneman, who commanded the District of East Tennessee, Department of the Cumberland, left Knoxville, Tennessee March 21, 1865, and marched with Alvan C. Gillem's Cavalry Division, District of East Tennessee by way of Mossy Creek and Morristown, and arrived at Jonesboro, Tennessee March 26, 1865. He then moved up the Watauga River to Boone, North Carolina, and on through Watauga Gap and Wilkesboro to Jonesville, North Carolina, where he arrived April 1, 1865. Davis Tillson's Fourth Infantry Division, Department of the Cumberland did not accompany the cavalry on Stoneman's raid, but it did move forward to secure the mountain passes in its rear. The division con-centrated at Morristown March 22, 1865, and a week later reached the mouth of Roan Creek, Tennessee. From there Tillson sent out detachments, and by April 7, 1865, they had occupied and fortified Deep Gap, Watauga Gap, and Boone and Taylorsville in North Carolina. Tillson's infantry remained in these positions, covering the country from the South Branch of the Holston River to Watauga Gap, until April 20, 1865, after Lee's surrender at Appomattox Court House, and they then returned to Greenville, Tennessee.

When Stoneman reached Jonesville, he crossed the Yadkin River and marched north toward Virginia. North of Mount Airey, North Carolina he divided his command into three columns, which were to strike the Virginia and Tennessee Railroad at different points. At Hillsville, Virginia on April 3, 1865, John K. Miller, commanding Third Brigade of the cavalry division, was detached with 500 men and sent toward Wytheville, Virginia. The next day, at Jacksonville, Virginia, William Wagner with 250 men of William J. Palmer's First Brigade left for Salem, near Roanoke, Virginia. Stoneman, with the main column, continued on to Christiansburg, Virginia.

By April 6, 1865, the work of destruction on the railroad had been completed, and Stoneman marched back south through Taylorsville, Virginia to Danbury, North Carolina. He arrived there April 9, 1865, the day Lee surrendered to Grant at Appomattox Court House.

Palmer was then sent with his First Cavalry Brigade to Salem (Winston-Salem), North Carolina to destroy the factories and supplies there, and also the bridges on the Piedmont Railroad between Danville, Virginia and Greensboro, North Carolina; and on the North Carolina Railroad between Greensboro and the Yadkin River. Miller's Third Brigade and Simeon B. Brown's Second Brigade arrived at Salisbury, North Carolina April 12, 1865, and after a sharp engagement captured the town and destroyed the military supplies that had been stored there. The next day, Stoneman marched on to Statesville, North Carolina, where he was joined by Palmer's brigade.

Leaving Palmer at Statesville to watch the line of the Catawba, Stoneman marched west and arrived at Lenoir, North Carolina April 15, 1865. Two days later, Stoneman left his command, and directed Gillem to bring the division back to Tennessee. Then Gillem, with Miller's and Brown's brigades, marched to various points during the period April 18–21, 1865 in an attempt to find an undefended gap through the mountains. On April 22, 1865 at Howard's Gap in the Blue Ridge Mountains, Gillem received official notice of the armistice between the armies of William T. Sherman and Joseph E. Johnston. On April 26, 1865, the day Johnston surrendered to Sherman, Gillem arrived at Ashville, North Carolina after having marched through

Hendersonville, North Carolina. Meantime, Palmer followed with his brigade from Statesville, by way of Rutherford and Waynesville, North Carolina, and he then marched down the Little Tennessee River. On April 29, 1865, Gillem was ordered to join in the pursuit of Jefferson Davis.

During Stoneman's Raid there was frequent skirmishing, and in addition there were more serious engagements at Wytheville, Virginia April 6, 1865; Martinsville, North Carolina April 8, 1865; Salisbury, North Carolina April 12, 1865; the Catawba River near Morganton, North Carolina April 17, 1865; and near Hendersonville, North Carolina April 23, 1865.

The organization of the troops in the District of East Tennessee commanded by George Stoneman at the end of March 1865 was as follows:

Cavalry Division, Alvan C. Gillem
  First Brigade, William J. Palmer
  Second Brigade, Simeon B. Brown
  Third Brigade, John K. Miller

Fourth Infantry Division, Department of the Cumberland, Davis Tillson
  First Brigade, Chauncey G. Hawley
  Second Brigade, Horatio G. Gibson

Artillery
  21st Battery, Ohio Light Artillery, William D. Mann
  22nd Battery, Ohio Light Artillery, Harvey Burdell
  Battery L, 1st Michigan Light Artillery, Carleton Nea
  Battery M, 1st Michigan Light Artillery, Augustus H. Emery
  Battery K, 1st Illinois Light Artillery, Charles M. Judd
  Henshaw's Battery, Illinois Light Artillery, Azro C. Putnam
  Battery B, 1st Tennessee Light Artillery, William O. Beebe

WESTERN (WEST) VIRGINIA OPERATIONS MAY 26–OCTOBER 11, 1861

When the Virginia Convention passed an Ordinance of Secession April 17, 1861, Union political and military authorities were concerned about affairs in the western part of the state. There were two reasons for this: first, most of the inhabitants of the state residing west of the Allegheny Mountains were loyal to the Union, and were opposed to secession; and second, there were four important communication routes running through that region, connecting the East with the Ohio River and the western states. These were: (1) the James River and Kanawha Turnpike in the south, running from Covington, Virginia through White Sulfur Springs and Lewisburg, and then on through the Great Kanawha Valley by Gauley Bridge to Charleston, and from there to the Ohio River at Point Pleasant and Guyandotte; (2) the Parkersburg and Staunton Turnpike, which ran through the center of the state from Staunton, Virginia by way of Huttonsville, Beverly, Buckhannon, and Weston to Parkersburg; (3) the Northwestern Pike in the north, which followed the route of present-day U.S. 50 from Winchester, Virginia by way of Romney and Grafton to Parkersburg; and (4) the Baltimore and Ohio Railroad, which ran from Baltimore, Maryland through Maryland and northwestern Virginia to Wheeling, with a branch line, the Northwestern Railroad, running from Grafton to Parkersburg. Almost all of the military activities in Western Virginia, and later in West Virginia, during the Civil War were associated with these routes.

Before proceeding further with the discussion of military operations in the region, a brief explanation here will be helpful in understanding the term West Virginia as applied to what in 1861 was in fact Virginia or Western Virginia. West Virginia was not admitted to the Union as a state until June 20, 1863, but the foundations for statehood were laid at the First Wheeling Convention on May 13, 1861, for a new state to be formed from thirty-four (later increased to thirty-nine) counties of northwestern Virginia. This region was then, and thereafter, commonly called West Virginia, and the Union regiments raised there were generally designated as West Virginia regiments. It should be noted, however, that the name Western Virginia was also applied to the region, and some Union regiments were designated as Virginia regiments. To avoid confusion in this and later sections, the Western Virginia regiments are generally designated as West Virginia regiments, and Western Virginia is used instead of West Virginia in describing events that occurred prior to June 20, 1863.

Union Occupation of Western Virginia, May 26–30, 1861. Immediately after the secession of Virginia, state and Confederate authorities recognized the danger of invasion of the western part of the state by Union forces, and they promptly took steps to secure the region. April 29, 1861, John McCausland was ordered to the Kanawha Valley to recruit a force of state troops with which to occupy and hold the valley, and May 3, 1861, C. Q. Tompkins at Charleston was assigned command of all state troops that might be assembled in the Kanawha Valley. The next day George A. Porterfield was assigned command of all Virginia forces in the northwestern part of the state, and he was authorized to call out volunteers for the defense of the Baltimore and Ohio Railroad. Porterfield, who at the time was with Thomas J. Jackson's command at Harper's Ferry, arrived at Grafton May 14, 1861 and ordered all available state troops in the area to mobilize at that point.

May 3, 1861, the Union Department of the Ohio was created to consist of the states of Indiana, Illinois, and Ohio; and George B. McClellan, at that time commanding the Ohio Volunteer Militia, was assigned command. May 9, 1861, the Department of the Ohio was extended to include a part of Western Virginia. This region was bounded on the south by the Great Kanawha River, and on the east by the Greenbrier River, and from the river along a line extending northward to the southwest corner of Maryland, thence along the western state line of Maryland to the Pennsylvania state line, and then on northward to the northwest corner of McKean County in Pennsylvania. McClellan assumed command of the department May 13, 1861.

Union men in northwestern Virginia were concerned with the threat posed by the assembly of Virginia State Troops on the Baltimore and Ohio Railroad and in the Kanawha Valley, and early in May 1861, they appealed to McClellan for assistance in protecting the railroad and the loyal people of the area. McClellan hesitated for a time because he feared that sending troops into Virginia would be considered an invasion of the state, and that it might have adverse effects. Finally, however, because of the importance of the Baltimore and Ohio Railroad to the Union war effort, McClellan ordered Ohio regiments to cross the Ohio River into Western Virginia.

May 26, 1861, McClellan issued orders for Union regiments to move toward Grafton in Western Virginia. Benjamin F. Kelley, colonel of the 1st West Virginia Infantry at Wheeling, was to move with his regiment by rail toward Fairmont, twenty miles from Grafton. James Irvine, colonel of the 16th Ohio at Bellaire, Ohio, was to cross the Ohio River and follow Kelley, and support him. James B. Steedman, colonel of the 14th Ohio, was to cross the Ohio River at Marietta and occupy Parkersburg. Timothy R. Stanley, with his 18th Ohio at Athens, Ohio, was to report to Steedman at Parkersburg, and then Steedman, in command of both regiments, was to move by rail toward Grafton.

In addition to the Ohio and West Virginia regiments mentioned above, Thomas A. Morris was ordered to move from Indianapolis, Indiana to Western Virginia with an Indiana brigade composed of three-month regiments. These were: Thomas T. Crittenden's 6th Indiana; Ebenezer Dumont's 7th Indiana; William P. Benton's 8th Indiana; Robert H. Milroy's 9th Indiana; Joseph J. Reynolds' 10th Indiana; and Lewis Wallace's 11th Indiana. The 11th Indiana did not remain in Western Virginia, but was detached and sent on to Cumberland, Maryland, where it arrived June 10, 1861.

Porterfield was informed of the approach of Kelley's and Steedman's regiments, and on May 28, 1861, he retired with his command from Grafton to Philippi. Kelley with his two regiments occupied Grafton May 30, 1861, and that day Steedman with his two regiments entered Clarksburg.

Action at Philippi, Western Virginia, June 3, 1861. Morris arrived at Grafton from Indiana with a part of his command June 1, 1861, and he found that Kelley had organized an expedition to advance that night against Porterfield's force at Philippi. As senior officer, Morris assumed command of all Union troops in Western Virginia, and after a consultation with Kelley, he decided to postpone the movement until the following night. Initially, Kelley had available for his attack only six companies of his 1st West Virginia and nine companies of Milroy's 9th Indiana, but with a brigade at

Clarksburg, and other regiments coming up, Morris decided to modify Kelley's plan and advance on Philippi in two columns. One was to make a frontal attack, while the other, at the same time, moved against the enemy's right and rear. Morris ordered Kelley to move on the morning of June 2, 1861 with six companies of his 1st West Virginia, nine companies of Milroy's 9th Indiana, and six companies of Irvine's 16th Ohio on the Baltimore and Ohio Railroad to Thornton, about six miles east of Grafton. He was then to march by a circuitous route on a country road, through heavily forested country, so as to arrive on the right and rear of the enemy at Philippi at 4:00 A.M. June 3, 1861. Morris then proceeded to organize a right column under Ebenezer Dumont, who was to move by rail to Webster on the evening of June 2, 1861 with eight companies of his 7th Indiana. At Webster, Dumont was to be joined by Steedman with five companies of his 14th Ohio and two pieces of artillery, and by Thomas T. Crittenden with six companies of his 6th Indiana. Dumont was then to march toward Philippi so as to arrive before the town at 4:00 A.M. The object of Dumont's approach was to divert attention from Kelley's attack, which was to be delivered at the same time. Dumont was to assume command of all troops when the two columns joined.

Kelley's command left Grafton at 9:00 A.M. June 2, 1861, as ordered, and then it disembarked at Thornton and began its march. It was then about twenty-five miles from Philippi. During the day Dumont's right column assembled at Webster, and by 10:00 that evening it was headed south on the Prurytown-Philippi Pike. Both columns found the marching difficult that night because of stormy weather, but they arrived at their destinations without serious delay. Dumont arrived shortly before Kelley was in position to block the exit from the town, but both columns did take part in the ensuing action. The surprise was complete, and Porterfield's force was completely routed, but it managed to escape, and retreated to Beverly in Randolph County with property loss and only a few casualties.

Army of Occupation of Western Virginia. After Morris' successful operation, McClellan decided to establish a strong post at Philippi, and to strengthen the line of supply for the troops in Western Virginia.

The Baltimore and Ohio and the Northwestern railroads were open to raiding parties, and McClellan quickly assigned forty-eight companies to guard the two lines. He posted a regiment at Rowelsburg to protect the Cheat River Viaduct at that point, and also posted detachments of one or two companies at the less exposed bridges and tunnels on the lines. The principal posts on the main line west of Grafton were: a bridge two miles from Fetterman; a bridge over the Monongahela River at Benton Ferry, near Fairmont; Barnesville; between Farmington and Mannington; and between Mannington and Benwood. Along the Northwestern Railroad the posts were Webster, Bridgeport, West Union, Central, Tollgate, Ellenboro, and Petroleum. Regimental headquarters were established at Grafton, Clarksburg, and Parkersburg. Morris was charged with the defense of the Baltimore and Ohio Railroad, and his headquarters was at Grafton.

While the above arrangements were being completed, the enemy were also attempting to improve their positions in Western Virginia. June 6, 1862, Henry A. Wise was assigned command of the Virginia forces in the Kanawha Valley, and two days later Robert S. Garnett relieved Porterfield and established strong defensive positions on Laurel Hill, near Belington in Barbour County, and at Rich Mountain, near Beverly. From these points he could control the roads passing through the area.

Because of the significance of the Laurel Hill-Rich Mountain region in McClellan's Western Virginia Campaign during the early part of July 1861, a brief description is given here. The Tygart River (also Tygart's River) Valley, in which the town of Beverly is situated, lies between Cheat Mountain to the east and Rich Mountain to the west. The Staunton and Parkersburg Road divided at Beverly; the road to Parkersburg passed through a gap in Rich Mountain, and the road to Wheeling followed the Tygart River to Philippi. The ridge north of the river, where it breaks through the mountains, is known as Laurel Hill, and the Wheeling Road passed over a spur of the hill. To control the two roads by which McClellan's troops might approach from the west, Garnett sent John Pegram with a part of his force to entrench at the pass at Rich Mountain, and he established the rest of his command on Laurel Hill.

June 15, 1861, McClellan notified Morris that he was coming in person to Western Virginia with reinforcements, and within a few days the 3rd Ohio and 4th Ohio crossed the Ohio River at Bellaire and entrained for Grafton. June 21, 1861, McClellan arrived at Parkersburg with a mixed force of infantry, cavalry, and artillery, and while there he ordered William S. Rosecrans at Camp Dennison, Ohio to join him with four additional regiments. McClellan then proceeded to Grafton, but the troop trains were halted at Clarksburg, where he intended to establish a strong base. McClellan arrived at Grafton early on the morning of June 23, 1861 and assumed personal command of the troops in Western Virginia. As early as June 14, 1861, McClellan had referred to these troops as the Army of Occupation of Western Virginia.

McClellan's first concern was for the safety of the Baltimore and Ohio Railroad, and he promptly took steps to improve what he considered to be an unsatisfactory situation. He relieved Morris of the responsibility of defending the railroad, and assigned to that duty Charles W. Hill of the Ohio Militia. He was made directly responsible to McClellan, and he was instructed to hold the Cheat River line, Grafton, and the line of the railroad from that point to Wheeling. Hill was to collect his main force at Rowelsburg and to establish strong outposts at West Union and Saint George. McClellan assigned Morris to the command of the post of Philippi.

By the end of June 1861, McClellan had established his forces along the railroad, and these consisted of sixteen Ohio regiments, nine Indiana regiments, and two West Virginia regiments. About 5,000 men under Hill guarded the railroad for a distance of about 200 miles; Morris commanded a strong brigade at Philippi; and the remainder of the troops were organized into three brigades, which were forming at Clarksburg under William S. Rosecrans, Newton Schleich, and Robert L. McCook.

McClellan's Western Virginia Campaign (Engagement at Rich Mountain, July 11, 1861).

While at Grafton, McClellan received reports that an enemy force was assembling at Beverly, and he decided to move in person with his best-prepared troops and secure control of the region. His plans, which were completed by June 23, 1861, called for an advance in two columns. McClellan would lead the larger column, which was then forming at Clarksburg, to attack the Confederate position at Rich Mountain; and simultaneously Morris would move with his brigade from Philippi against Laurel Hill, which was about thirteen miles distant.

McClellan began his movement June 27, 1861 by advancing toward Buckhannon, which was twenty-four miles west of Beverly on the Parkersburg Branch of the turnpike. Rosecrans' brigade, which was in the lead, arrived at Buckhannon June 30, 1861. The brigade was organized as follows:

Rosecrans' Brigade, William S. Rosecrans
    8th Indiana, William P. Benton
    10th Indiana, Mahlon D. Manson
    19th Ohio, Samuel Beatty
    13th Indiana, Jeremiah C. Sullivan

Rosecrans remained at Buckhannon until July 2, 1861, when he was joined by the brigades of Schleich and McCook. The latter two brigades were organized as follows:

Schleich's Brigade, Newton Schleich
    3rd Ohio, Isaac H. Marrow
    15th Indiana, George D. Wagner

McCook's Brigade, Robert L. McCook
    4th Ohio, Lorin Andrews
    9th Ohio, Charles Sondershoff

Note. McCook was the colonel of 9th Ohio, which was commanded by Sondershoff, the lieutenant colonel.

The artillery with McClellan consisted of Albion P. Howe's Battery G, 4th United States Artillery; Cyrus O. Loomis' Battery A, 1st Michigan Light Artillery; James Barnett's Ohio Battery; and Philip Daum's West Virginia Battery. Oscar A. Mack's battery of United States Artillery also joined the Army of Occupation.

It should be noted that a part of the troops present in West Virginia at that time consisted of state troops that had not been mustered into the United States service, and apparently no report of these troops is found in the War Department records. Therefore it is difficult to describe exactly all units of McClellan's forces.

July 6, 1861, McCook moved forward with his brigade from Buckhannon to Middle Fork Bridge, which was about halfway to Beverly, and on the same day McClellan ordered Morris to advance with his brigade and take position about one and one-half miles in front of Garnett's camp on Laurel Hill. Morris' brigade was organized as follows:

Morris' Brigade, Thomas A. Morris
    9th Indiana, Robert H. Milroy
    7th Indiana, Ebenezer Dumont
    14th Ohio, James B. Steedman

July 9, 1861 McClellan concentrated his three brigades at Roaring Creek, about two miles in front of Pegram's position, which was at the western base of Rich Mountain. McClellan examined the ground and decided to make a frontal attack on Pegram on the morning of July 11, 1861. Morris was directed to maintain a threatening position in front of Garnett.

During the evening of July 10, 1861, McClellan changed his plan when he learned from a local man that a path ran up the mountain, south of the turnpike, and around Pegram's left flank. He assigned Rosecrans to lead an infantry column, consisting of his own brigade, with Jeremiah C. Sullivan's 13th Indiana temporarily attached, up the mountain by this path and seize the road at the Hart house on the crest.

Rosecrans required about ten hours to reach the Hart house, and there, unexpectedly, he found a force of about 350 men that Pegram had sent to the summit to guard the road. Rosecrans came out on the road during the early afternoon of July 11, 1861, and promptly attacked in a heavy rainstorm. There was sharp fighting for about two or three hours without decisive result, until a final charge by a part of the Federal line broke through the enemy position and drove the defenders from the field.

Rosecrans camped on the field that night, and at daylight found that the enemy had disappeared from the top of the mountain. He then moved down the road to the rear of Pegram's position at the base of the mountain, and found the works abandoned. During the past day and night Rosecrans had heard nothing from McClellan, who had remained in camp beyond Roaring Creek.

About half of Pegram's command escaped to Beverly during the night of July 11, 1861, and then marched southward on the Staunton Road. Pegram, with the rest of his command, surrendered to Union troops July 13, 1861, about six miles north of Beverly. Meantime, during the evening of July 11, 1861 Garnett learned of Rosecrans' victory at Rich Mountain, and at midnight he evacuated his position on Laurel Hill and marched toward Beverly. Before arriving there, however, he was erroneously informed on the morning of July 12, 1861 that the town was occupied by Union troops. He then marched back to Leedsville (Leadsville), where the Tygart River turns westward past Laurel Hill, and crossed Cheat Mountain into the Cheat River Valley in an effort to reach the Northwestern Turnpike. Garnett then followed the river northward toward Saint George and West Union, in the direction of Hill's strong outposts near the Maryland border.

At dawn July 12, 1861, Morris started in pursuit of Garnett, but he halted at Leedsville for orders and did not continue the march until the next morning. Then his advance guard, accompanied by Henry W. Benham of the engineers, came up with the Confederate column, and there was skirmishing with the rear guard for an hour or so. At 2:00 P.M. there was a sharp action at Carrick's (or Corrick's) Ford on Shaver's Fork (or "Main Fork") of Cheat River, four miles south of Parsons in Tucker County, and also at another ford about a mile farther on. Garnett was killed at the latter ford and, although his command escaped, most of the wagon train was lost. At this point, Morris discontinued his pursuit. Later, Henry R. Jackson assumed command of Garnett's troops.

Back at Rich Mountain, McClellan pursued the remnants of Pegram's command on the Staunton Road as far as Cheat River on July 13, 1861, and from there he returned to Huttonsville the next day.

Meantime, McClellan had notified Hill, commanding the Union troops on the railroad, that Garnett had abandoned his position on Laurel Hill and was retreating eastward by way of the Louisville and Saint George Pike. On July 12, 1861, McClellan directed Hill to take the field with all available troops and make an attempt to cut off Garnett's retreat by blocking the Northwestern Turnpike. At this time Irvine held the Cheat River line from Rowelsburg to Cheat River Bridge, five miles above, with his own 16th Ohio and six companies of George W. Andrews' 15th Ohio, and two companies of Kelley's 1st West Virginia. Hill, then at Grafton, received McClellan's order at 11:00 A.M. July 13, 1861. He at once informed Irvine of its contents, and then ordered the regimental com-

manders at Clarksburg, Parkersburg, Fairmont, and Wheeling to move as quickly as possible with the available troops of their respective commands toward Oakland, Maryland. Hill, in person, left Grafton on two trains with 600 men late in the afternoon of July 13, 1861, and arrived at Oakland at 10:00 P.M.

Meantime, Irvine with seven companies of the 6th Ohio had advanced to West Union during the night of July 11, 1861, and was joined there by H. G. Depuy with six companies of the 8th Ohio at 1:00 A.M. July 13, 1861. At about 6:00 A.M. July 14, 1861, Irvine learned that Garnett's column had passed Red House on the Northwestern Pike, and he immediately marched toward that point. Upon arrival there he learned that the enemy had departed at 5:00 A.M. Irvine followed, and at the North Branch Bridge he was joined by Hill. The pursuit was then abandoned, and the troops marched back to Red House and Oakland.

During the afternoon and night of July 14, 1861, the last of Hill's railroad regiments, totaling about 4,000 men, detrained at Oakland. At 2:00 P.M. the next day, Hill learned that Garnett's column had camped at Greenland, and he decided to continue the pursuit. He ordered Timothy R. Stanley, with 600 men of 18th Ohio, and Samuel H. Dunning, with 700 men of 5th Ohio, to move across the mountains from Oakland to the bridge on the Northwestern Pike at the North Branch of the Potomac. There they were to be joined by eight companies of Depuy's 8th Ohio, seven companies of Irvine's 6th Ohio, six companies of Kelley's 1st West Virginia, two guns, and the Ringgold Cavalry. This command was then to move below Greenland to cut off the enemy retreat. At the same time, Hill ordered Thomas Morton, with six companies of his 20th Ohio and two West Virginia companies, and John A. Turley, with five companies of 22nd Ohio and two guns, to proceed by rail to New Creek Station. From there they were to march south and attack the enemy at Greenland from the north. William S. Smith with 13th Ohio was to follow.

The troops under Stanley and Dunning left Oakland with Hill at 5:00 P.M., July 15, 1861, and they were joined by Irvine's troops as ordered. The combined forces then moved on and reached Groves, five miles beyond Greenland, at about 5:00 P.M. the next day. The enemy withdrew on Hill's approach and retired to Petersburg, where they arrived during the afternoon and evening of July 16, 1861.

Morton's command left Oakland at 4:00 P.M. July 15, 1861, and arrived at New Creek at 2:00 the next morning. It then marched through Ridgeville and Martin's Gap, and at the latter place learned that Greenland had been abandoned.

On the morning of July 17, 1861, McClellan ordered that the pursuit be discontinued. Depuy's troops were sent to Red House, and the rest to Oakland, where they arrived July 19, 1861.

Kanawha Valley Campaign, July 1861. When McClellan reached Buckhannon July 2, 1861, at the beginning of his Western Virginia Campaign, he received information that Henry A. Wise was present in the Great Kanawha Valley with a considerable force. McClellan then decided to move a brigade into the lower valley to hold it until he could dispose of Garnett. Jacob D. Cox, who was at that time at Camp Dennison, Ohio, was selected to lead this expedition. The only troops under Cox's immediate command were five companies of Joseph W. Frizell's 11th Ohio, but he was ordered to assume command of John W. Lowe's 12th Ohio, James V. Guthrie's 1st Kentucky, William E. Woodruff's 2nd Kentucky, a company of cavalry, and six guns. Cox was then ordered to move to Gallipolis, Ohio with his command, and there he was also to assume command of Jesse S. Norton's 21st Ohio. When his force was assembled he was to cross the Ohio River and occupy Point Pleasant, at the mouth of the Great Kanawha River. Cox was instructed to remain on the defensive until McClellan was in position to cut off Garnett's retreat from Beverly.

Cox arrived with his troops at Gallipolis July 10, 1861, but meantime his orders had been changed. The 2nd Kentucky Regiment was ordered to land at Guyandotte, on the Ohio about seventy miles below the Kanawha, and 1st Kentucky was to land at Ravenswood and proceed to Ripley, about fifty miles above the Kanawha. Further, instead of holding a defensive position, Cox was ordered to move with his command up the Kanawha Valley. The Kentucky regiments were to join him later.

July 11, 1861, Cox advanced from Point Pleasant toward Wise's principal camp, which was on a spur of Tyler Mountain. Wise also had a detachment on the south side of the Kanawha River at Scarey Creek, about twelve miles below Charleston. Half of 1st Kentucky under Lieutenant Colonel David A. Enyart joined Cox July 14, 1861, and two days later Cox arrived at the mouth of the Pocotalico River. The 2nd Kentucky arrived from Barboursville during the afternoon of July 17, 1861. Cox then decided to attack the enemy position at Scarey Creek, near present-day Nitro, West Virginia. This position was held by troops under the command of George S. Patton, grandfather of General George S. Patton of World War II. John W. Lowe, with his 12th Ohio and two companies of Jesse S. Norton's 21st Ohio, crossed the Kanawha River during the afternoon of July 17, 1861, and at 4:00 P.M. moved on the Confederate line. After some sharp fighting and some initial successes, Lowe's troops were finally driven back and were withdrawn.

Cox then took up a strong position behind the Pocotalico River, and on July 24, 1861 advanced toward the rear of Wise's position on Tyler Mountain. Wise withdrew to Charleston, and then continued on toward Gauley Bridge. When he learned of Garnett's defeat at Rich Mountain, however, he withdrew from the Kanawha Valley and reestablished his army in Greenbrier County. Cox occupied Charleston July 25, 1861, and the rest of 1st Kentucky was ordered up from Ripley to garrison the town. Cox occupied Gauley Bridge, forty miles beyond Charleston, July 29, 1861. Union forces then controlled the Kanawha Valley from the Ohio River to Gauley Bridge.

Reorganization of the Army of Occupation of Western Virginia, July 1861. July 22, 1861, McClellan was ordered to Washington to assume command of the newly created Military Division of the Potomac, and the next day William S. Rosecrans succeeded him in command of the Department of the Ohio and the Army of Occupation of Western Virginia. At that time Rosecrans held the Baltimore and Ohio Railroad through the state; the Cheat Mountain Pass, facing toward Staunton, Virginia; and also the pass at Elkwater, on the mountain summit between Huttonsville and Huntersville in Western Virginia. Rosecrans had also ordered Cox to fortify Gauley Bridge and to cover the front in all directions. Rosecrans then established a chain of posts, with one or two regiments at each, at Weston, Bulltown, Sutton, and Summersville, and this secured a line of communications between his command at Clarksburg and Gauley Bridge.

The terms of enlistment for the three-month regiments began to expire during the latter part of July 1861, and new three-year regiments began arriving to take their place. Because of this, Rosecrans issued a series of orders reorganizing the Army of Occupation of Western Virginia. July 24, 1861, Joseph J. Reynolds was assigned command of First Brigade of the army, and was ordered to Cheat Mountain to relieve Schleich, who commanded a brigade there. Schleich was directed to return to Ohio. The next day Rosecrans announced the reorganization of the three brigades of the army as follows:

First Brigade, Joseph J. Reynolds
    13th Indiana, Jeremiah C. Sullivan
    14th Indiana, Nathan Kimball
    15th Indiana, George D. Wagner
    3rd Ohio, Isaac H. Marrow
    Burdsal's Cavalry
    Cyrus Q. Loomis' Battery A, Michigan Light Artillery

Note. The depot at Beverly, consisting of 6th Ohio and detachments of 1st West Virginia and 2nd West Virginia, was attached to First Brigade.

Second Brigade (no commander given)
    7th Ohio, Erastus B. Tyler
    10th Ohio, William H. Lytle
    17th Ohio, John M. Connell
    Friedrich Schambeck's Chicago Dragoons
    Oscar A. Mack's battery of the 4th United States Artillery

Third Brigade, Robert L. McCook
    9th Ohio, Charles Sondershoff
    4th Ohio, Lorin Andrews
    Howe's Battery

As a result of the reorganization, Schleich's brigade became Reynolds' First Brigade, Army of Occupation of Western Virgina, which remained at Cheat Mountain until October 1861; Rosecrans' brigade of Volunteer Militia was broken up by the muster out of three three-month regiments and the transfer of 13th Indiana to Reynolds' First Brigade; and the designation of McCook's brigade was changed to Third Brigade, Army of Occupation of Western Virginia.

The order of July 25, 1861 also created a new brigade from Cox's command in the Kanawha Val-

ley. This was called the Brigade of the Kanawha, or more commonly the Kanawha Brigade. It was organized as follows:

Brigade of the Kanawha, Jacob D. Cox
    1st Kentucky, James V. Guthrie
    2nd Kentucky, William E. Woodruff
    11th Ohio, Charles A. DeVilliers
    12th Ohio, John W. Lowe
    19th Ohio, Samuel Beatty
    21st Ohio, Jesse S. Norton
    Portions of 18th Ohio and 22nd Ohio
    Ironton Cavalry

Note. This brigade was also to include such other regiments as might arrive in the Kanawha Valley.

In addition to the above four brigades, two military districts were also constituted in July and August 1861. July 25, 1861 the lower valley of the Tygart River and the valley of Cheat River were designated as the District of Cheat River, and Charles J. Biddle, commanding the 1st Pennsylvania at Cumberland, Maryland, was assigned command. The next day, however, Biddle was ordered with his regiment to Harper's Ferry. The District of Grafton was constituted August 3, 1861, to consist of the line of the Baltimore and Ohio Railroad from Cumberland, Maryland to Wheeling, Western Virginia, and the Northwestern Railroad from Grafton to Parkersburg. Benjamin F. Kelley was assigned command, and was ordered to relieve Hill in command of the post of Grafton and vicinity. Hill was ordered to return to Ohio.

Engagement at Carnifix Ferry, Gauley River, Virginia, September 10, 1861. There were frequent skirmishes in Western Virginia during the latter part of July and in August 1861, but there were no major engagements. There were, however, some important command changes in the Confederate forces in that part of the state during this period. July 20, 1861, William W. Loring was assigned command of the Confederate Army of the Northwest, and he assumed command at Monterey a short time later. Henry R. Jackson's command, formerly Garnett's, was at Monterey, and Wise's brigade was in the Kanawha Valley. On July 17, 1861, John B. Floyd was ordered with a brigade from southwestern Virginia to cooperate with Wise. Floyd joined Wise

August 11, 1861, and assumed command of all Virginia troops in the Kanawha Valley.

About August 1, 1861 Robert E. Lee arrived in Western Virginia in an attempt to improve the military situation in that part of the state. Lee was not specifically assigned command of the Confederate forces in Western Virginia, but his mission appears to have been to resolve differences between, and to counsel with, all of the general officers commanding troops in this region. Whatever the real nature of Lee's assignment, the result was that he did direct military operations until he returned to Richmond at the end of October 1861.

Toward the end of August 1861, under the new leadership, military activities increased. August 13, 1861, Erastus B. Tyler was ordered with his 7th Ohio from Summersville to Cross Lanes (Kessler's Cross Lanes) to cover Carnifix Ferry on the Gauley River. This position was about twenty miles above Gauley Bridge, at a point on the Gauley Bridge-Summersville Road where a road (the Sunday Road) comes in from the Lewisburg Turnpike by way of Carnifix Ferry. August 20, 1861, Wise demonstrated in front of Cox's position near Gauley Bridge, and then Floyd decided to attack Tyler's camp at Cross Lanes. Accordingly, on August 26, 1861, Floyd crossed the Gauley River at Carnifix Ferry with 200 or 300 men, and surprised and routed the 7th Ohio, which fled from the field in disorder. Floyd then fortified a strong position on high ground in front of Carnifix Ferry from which he could control Nicholas County, and cut Cox's line of communications with Clarksburg to the north.

When Rosecrans learned of Tyler's defeat, he left the Cheat Mountain region in command of Reynolds, and the Baltimore and Ohio Railroad and the line of the upper Potomac in charge of Kelley, and with the rest of his command marched from Clarksburg by way of Weston, Bulltown, Sutton, toward Summersville and Cross Lanes. At Sutton, on September 5, 1861, Rosecrans reorganized his command into three provisional brigades as follows:

First Provisional Brigade, Henry W. Benham
    10th Ohio, William H. Lytle
    12th Ohio, John W. Lowe
    13th Ohio, William S. Smith
    West's and Gilmore's cavalry
    James R. McMullin's 1st Battery, Ohio Light Artillery

Note. 10th and 13th Ohio were transferred from Second Brigade, Army of Occupation of Western Virginia, which was organized July 25, 1861; and 12th Ohio was transferred from the Kanawha Brigade.

Second Provisional Brigade, Robert L. McCook
    9th Ohio, Charles Sondershoff
    28th Ohio, Augustus Moor
    47th Ohio, Frederick Poshner
    Friedrich Schambeck's Chicago Dragoons

Note. The 9th Ohio (McCook's regiment) was transferred from Third Brigade, Army of Occupation of Western Virginia, which was organized July 25, 1861. The 18th Ohio and 47th Ohio were new regiments.

Third Provisional Brigade, Eliakim P. Scammon
    23rd Ohio,
    30th Ohio, Hugh Ewing

Note. The 23rd Ohio (Scammon's Regiment) and 30th Ohio were transferred from the Kanawha Brigade.

The effect of this reorganization on the brigades of the Army of Occupation of Western Virginia that were formed July 25, 1861 was as follows: First Brigade consisted of three-year regiments and was not changed; Second Brigade was discontinued by the muster out of 17th Ohio and the transfer of 10th Ohio and 13th Ohio to First Provisional Brigade; and Third Brigade was discontinued by the muster out of 4th Ohio and the transfer of 9th Ohio to Second Provisional Brigade.

To continue with Rosecrans' movement, he bivouacked on the night of September 9, 1861 about eight miles from Summersville, and resumed the advance at 4:15 the next morning. He reached Summersville at 8:00 A.M., and there he learned of Floyd's entrenched position in front of Carnifix Ferry. He then moved on four miles over bad roads to Cross Lanes, where he arrived about 2:00 P.M. September 10, 1861. He halted for about one-half hour for the column and trains to close up, and then advanced on the road to Carnifix Ferry toward the enemy position, which was about two and a half miles distant. Benham's First Brigade was at the head of the column, with William H. Lytle's 10th Ohio in front, and it was followed by William S. Smith's 13th Ohio, and then John W. Lowe's 12th Ohio. Robert L. McCook's Second Brigade and Eliakim P. Scammon's Third Brigade followed Benham.

As the 10th Ohio approached, the enemy opened fire and Benham ordered up his artillery. William Schneider, with two guns of 13th Ohio, took position on the road near a cornfield, about 400 yards from the enemy works, and a short time later moved about a hundred yards to the right. James R. McMullin's battery was posted farther to the right, and it was supported by the 23rd Ohio of Third Brigade and a part of 30th Ohio of the same brigade. About 3:00 P.M. the 10th Ohio was ordered forward to engage the enemy artillery, but it was soon repulsed. Lytle was wounded, and Herman J. Korff assumed command of his regiment. Korff remained close to the enemy works for about an hour, and then fell back to the cover of the cornfield, in front of Schneider's guns.

When Lytle advanced, Smith's 13th Ohio, followed by 12th Ohio, came up in rear of 10th Ohio and the artillery. Smith was then sent with his brigade to the left, down a ravine that ran parallel to the enemy works, to within 100 yards of the extreme Confederate right. Lowe with a part of his 12th Ohio moved to the right of the cornfield and deployed in front of the enemy batteries. Lowe was killed, and James D. Wallace assumed command of the four companies of the regiment. Wallace then advanced and moved to the right to within about fifty feet of the enemy works before being forced to retire.

Meantime, Smith had examined the ground on the Union left, and reported to Benham and Rosecrans that an attack by a brigade on the enemy right was practicable, and Rosecrans organized a force under Smith for this purpose. It consisted of Smith's 13th Ohio, Augustus Moor's 28th Ohio of McCook's Second Brigade, a part of Scammon's 23rd Ohio of Third Brigade, and a part of 12th Ohio under Carr B. White. Smith's command remained in position for about an hour before being ordered to attack. At the same time Korff, with 10th Ohio and the part of 12th Ohio that was under Wallace, was to attack the Confederate center and left. A storming party consisting of Charles Sondershoff's 9th Ohio of Second Brigade and six companies of Frederick Poshner's 47th Ohio of the same brigade was formed on the road in rear of Schneider's artillery. By the time Rosecrans had his troops in position to move forward, it was dusk, and progress through the thick and tangled brush was slow. It was soon dark, and both Smith and Sondershoff reported that, because of the darkness and the state of exhaustion of the men, any further advance was impossible. Accordingly, the attack was called off, and the troops remained in position that night behind the ridges in front of the enemy works.

During the night, Floyd recrossed the Gauley River and then moved back to Meadow Bluff. Wise also withdrew from in front of Gauley Bridge and joined Floyd, and the united commands then fortified a position on Sewell Mountain. This was in Fayette County, on the James River and Kanawha Turnpike.

September 13, 1861, Cox's Kanawha Brigade advanced from Gauley Bridge on the Lewisburg Road, and the next day Rosecrans sent McCook's brigade to join Cox. Cox then advanced with the two brigades to a position some distance in front of Sewell Mountain. He arrived there September 17, 1861, and established a fortified camp.

Rosecrans remained with the rest of his command at Camp Scott, near Cross Lanes, during the rest of the month, but by October 1, 1861, he had concentrated his four brigades before Sewell Mountain. His new position was about thirty-five miles from Gauley Bridge, and because of the bad weather and bad roads, it was difficult to supply his command. Therefore, on October 5, 1861, he withdrew to within three or four miles of Gauley Bridge. About October 8, 1861, Robert C. Schenck assumed command of Scammon's brigade, and he was ordered to Mountain Cove, on the Lewisburg Pike.

Meantime, on September 19, 1861, the Department of Western Virginia was created to consist of that part of Virginia lying west of the Blue Ridge Mountains. Rosecrans was assigned command, but it was not until October 11, 1861 that he assumed command at Mountain Cove. For further information about the composition and operations of the troops under Rosecrans' command, see Department of Western Virginia.

Operations at Cheat Mountain, Virginia, September 1861. During September 1861, the Cheat Mountain-Elkwater region was held by Union forces belonging to Joseph J. Reynolds' First Brigade, Army of Occupation of Western Virginia. This consisted of the following regiments: Isaac H. Marrow's 3rd Ohio, William K. Bosely's 6th Ohio, Samuel A. Gilbert's 24th Ohio, James A Jones' 25th Ohio,

Jeremiah C. Sullivan's 13th Indiana, Nathan Kimball's 14th Indiana, George D. Wagner's 15th Indiana, Milo S. Hascall's 17th Indiana, and John W. Moss' 2nd West Virginia. Kimball was in command on Cheat Mountain Summit, with 14th Indiana, 24th Ohio, and 25th Ohio. The 13th Indiana was at Cheat Mountain Pass, at the foot of the mountain, ten miles from the summit. Reynolds was at Elkwater, with 3rd Ohio, 6th Ohio, 15th Indiana, 17th Indiana, and 2nd West Virginia.

In his first major campaign since coming to Western Virginia, Robert E. Lee decided to move against Reynolds' positions in the Cheat Mountain region. On the morning of September 12, 1861, four brigades of William S. Loring's Army of the Northwest advanced up the Tygart River Valley from Valley Mountain (present-day Mace, in Pocahontas County) toward Elkwater and the rear of Cheat Mountain. Lee, with the brigades of William Gilham and Jesse S. Burks, moved up the west bank of the Tygart River toward Elkwater; Daniel S. Donelson's brigade advanced on the other side of the river so as to strike the road between Elkwater and Huttonsville, in rear of Cheat Mountain; and Samuel S. Anderson's brigade passed over the ridges to the east of Donelson's route toward the rear of Cheat Mountain. At the same time, Henry R. Jackson's command, preceded by Albert Rust's 3rd Arkansas, marched from the Greenbrier River up the Staunton and Parkersburg Pike to attack Kimball's position at Cheat Mountain Summit.

The Union pickets were driven in by the enemy advance, and Donelson succeeded in cutting the communications between Elkwater and Cheat Mountain Summit. His attacks, however, were not pressed vigorously and were easily repulsed. There was considerable marching and countermarching by the enemy troops, and on September 13, 14, and 15, 1861, they made feeble attempts against both Elkwater and Cheat Mountain Summit, but September 17, 1861, Lee withdrew his forces to Valley Mountain.

Engagement at Greenbrier River, Virginia, October 3, 1861. At midnight October 2, 1861, Reynolds left the summit of Cheat Mountain to make a reconnaissance toward the enemy position on the Greenbrier River, about twelve miles distant. His force consisted of 24th, 25th, and 32nd Ohio, and 7th, 9th, 13th, 14th, 15th, and 17th Indiana, and some cavalry and artillery. When he approached the enemy camp, Milroy's 9th Indiana drove in the pickets and deployed on the right. Kimball's 14th Indiana advanced to the front and cleared a space from which the Federal artillery opened fire. Reynolds completed a thorough examination of the ground on his front, and then marched back to Cheat Mountain, where he arrived at sundown. The enemy forces at Greenbrier River belonged to Henry R. Jackson's command, which had fallen back to the crossing of the Staunton and Parkersburg Pike after the advance to Cheat Mountain.